Medieval England

Garland Encyclopedias of the Middle Ages (Vol. 3)
Garland Reference Library of the Humanities (Vol. 907)

Medieval England

An Encyclopedia

Editors

Paul E. Szarmach

M. Teresa Tavormina

Joel T. Rosenthal

Associate Editors

Catherine E. Karkov

Peter M. Lefferts

Elizabeth Parker McLachlan

Garland Publishing, Inc.
A member of the Taylor & Francis Group
New York & London, 1998

Library of Congress Cataloging-in-Publication Data

Medieval England : an encyclopedia / edited by Paul E. Szarmach . . . [et al.].
        p.   cm. — (Garland reference library of the humanities ;
vol. 907) (Garland encyclopedias of the Middle Ages ; vol. 3.)
    Includes index.
    ISBN 0-8240-5786-4 (alk. paper)
    1. Great Britain—History—Medieval Period, 1066–1485—
Encyclopedias.   2. Great Britain—History—Anglo-Saxon period,
449–1066—Encyclopedias.   3. England—Civilization—1066–1485—
Encyclopedias.   4. England—Civilization—To 1066—Encyclopedias.
5. Middle Ages—Encyclopedias.   I. Szarmach, Paul E.   II. Series.
III. Series: Garland reference library of the humanities.   Garland
encyclopedias of the Middle Ages ; vol. 3.
DA129.M43   1998
942—dc21   97–35523
                                                   CIP

Cover art: Late twelfth-century armor. By permission of the British Library, ROY 2A XXII f220
Cover design: Lawrence Wolfson Design, New York

Printed on acid-free, 250-year-life paper
Manufactured in the United States of America

Contents

Introduction

Medieval England: An Encyclopedia is an introduction to the society and culture of England from the coming of the Anglo-Saxons in the 5th century through the accession of the Tudor dynasty (1485) and the turn of the 16th century. Its 708 entries were written by an international team of over 300 scholars from the British Isles, North America, continental Europe, Australia, New Zealand, Jordan, and Japan.

The editors have conceived of the entries as covering the fields of Old English and Middle English Language and Literature, Music and Liturgy, Art History, and History. Though the articles vary from a sentence or two to several columns, both the general reader or student and the professional scholar can turn to them—for their content and summary value as well as for their bibliographical guides to further work and reading on any given topic. In addition, by means of the *See also* annotations at the end of the entries and the general index at the end of the volume, interested readers can follow a given topic in much greater depth than is apparent from the separate entries. Thus the interdisciplinary and complementary nature of the material included in the articles, written by scholars in many disciplines and collected by the various field editors, becomes apparent and available for further exploration. The bibliographies guide the reader to the basic primary and secondary materials on a given topic and to some of the more recent scholarship. Where possible their content has been selected with an eye to accessibility for nonspecialist readers, though not to the exclusion of more advanced but essential work. Thus a higher (but not absolute) priority has been given to scholarship in English, books and journals likely to be available in university libraries, and general studies, especially those that provide good bibliographic and methodological guidance for further research. Commonly cited scholarly journals are represented by their standard abbreviations (listed in the Abbreviations section that follows).

The primary selection criterion for entry topics has been a strong relationship between the topic and the events, persons, culture, or languages of non-Celtic Great Britain. Thus most of the history and culture of Scotland and Wales has been excluded. Latin and French authors are included only when, in the editors' opinion, they have a connection to England by birth, travel, or influence (e.g., Abbo of Fleury, John of Salisbury, Marie de France, Jean Froissart). Musical, liturgical, artistic, architectural, and intellectual traditions—all of which have strong continental associations—are examined mainly as they manifested themselves in England.

A volume of this sort is the product of many hands and many schools of interpretation and scholarly expertise. The history and culture of England are too rich and complex to be summarized, even in a large reference volume, in a fashion that is both comprehensive and satisfactory to all contributors or all readers. Even to talk of "English" history and culture serves to remind us that the very words of inclusion and definition are, simultaneously, those of exclusion. While England has center stage, we are also reminded of the dense and tangled threads that tied it to the Celtic world of Wales, Scotland, and Ireland, to the French and Anglo-Norman world of the Continent, to the Viking and Scandinavian world of the North Sea, and to the general culture of medieval Christendom, which embraced theology, scientific thought, and major trends and styles in intellectual and cultural expression, all with little regard for political and geographic boundaries. Previous Garland encyclopedias on medieval Scandinavia and medieval France touched heavily on the many ties between their basic subjects and British and English history. Similarly many of the entries in this volume indicate the cultural influences that link England to the rest of Europe.

Innumerable articles in the pages that follow emphasize the peculiar tension that marks the society, political life, and culture of medieval England. In some ways England was peculiar as a result of the insularity and parochialism that seem appropriate for a kingdom located on a small island, set on the northwesterly edge of the medieval world, far from the centers of Paris, Rome, and the Mediterranean. On the other hand English history and culture are explicable only when seen as the multihued end-product of a lively and often troublesome process of diffusion, whereby a two-way exchange with the Continent—pertaining to political as well as to cultural and intellectual developments—shaped its growth. English history and life offer distinct variations on the general themes of medieval European history. The lending and borrowing of ideas, institutions, cathedral architecture, musical forms, styles of handwriting and armor, or bawdy stories in the vernacular are but a few of the topics we can trace to contacts with neighbors (be they friends or foes) who were found in any and every direction.

How to Use This Book

In British universities to this day the historiographical tradition regarding the period covered by the volume differs from the standard North American usage. In Britain the period is often divided into the Anglo-Saxon or Old English period and, after the Norman Conquest of 1066, the "medieval" period as such. In this volume we apply the term "medieval" to both the Anglo-Saxon and post-Conquest periods, though the watershed of 1066—with new institutions of government, a new relationship to France and Normandy, and a new ruling class speaking a different language—is clearly visible between and within many entries. As a reference volume, this encyclopedia does not argue consistently through its pages for any particular interpretation regarding such dilemmas as the legal or social consequences of the Norman Conquest, the vitality of vernacular literature in the 12th and 13th centuries, or the popularity of the late-medieval church, although these are certainly topics that could well interest some users of the book. Instead the editors have given contributors to the volume the freedom to cover their topics as they choose and to decide, individually and freely, how much and what direction of "spin" to give their entries. Whether King John and Richard III were good or bad kings, or good or bad men, are questions that engage both authors and students. The debates will go on for many years, and we hope that the articles included here summarize current discussions that are pertinent to their subjects, while steering readers to the means whereby they can further pursue their concerns. All entries contain elements of interpretation and intellectual partisanship, and even those that seem merely expository or narrative in presentation are necessarily and properly shaped by authorial experience, judgment, and choice.

Wherever possible we have tried to combine related entries of manageable lengths into joint articles under a single headword so that chronological or some other reasonable order could be preserved in reading about the topic. In some cases it has been possible to commission articles on related subtopics or chronological units by the same author; in other instances related articles by two authors have been combined by the editors (occasionally by the authors themselves) into joint entries. Joint entries are identified by a double byline, in which the order of the names reflects the order of the entry's separate parts. A very few entries were co-written by two authors or conflated from the work of two authors, and these are indicated by an "*" in the Contributors list. Some related entries have been left as separate articles, either because the contributors' approaches were different enough to make combination an uneasy proposition or because keeping the entries separate would make them and their references more manageable for readers. The List of Contributors identifies the entries written by each contributor.

Entries are arranged alphabetically, with the Old English character æ *(ash)* being treated as equivalent to *ae*, the Middle English character ȝ *(yogh)* coming after *g,* and the Old and Middle English characters ð *(eth)* and þ *(thorn)* treated as equivalent to *th*. Alphabetical arrangement—essential if users are to find cross-referenced articles without difficulty—means that in a number of instances chronologically related entries appear out of chronological order: "Art, Gothic" before "Art, Romanesque" and "Women in Middle English Literature" before "Women in Old English Literature," for example. Users of the book are urged to read such related entries together so as to observe the broad historical developments within the topics in question.

Medieval literary works are listed under their authors' names, where those names are known. Many medieval works are anonymous, and these have been alphabetized under their titles, normalized where possible into a modern English form (titles of Middle Scots works are left in Middle Scots, however, and titles whose sense would be significantly changed by modernization have also been left in their medieval form— e.g., *The Kingis Quair, Mum and the Sothsegger, Handlyng Synne*). Names are given in forms that the editors have judged to be readily recognizable to general readers as well as familiar to scholars. In most cases this recognizability has been achieved by following Library of Congress author and subject headings (the most notable exception being our "Becket, Thomas" instead of Thomas à Becket) and by using surnames or perceived surnames when those have achieved common usage (e.g., Bacon, Duns Scotus, Grosseteste), most commonly with figures from the 13th century or later. Individuals known primarily by their personal names followed by geographical or other cognomens (Julian of Norwich, Edmund of Abingdon, Charles of Orléans, Sedulius Scottus, Edward the Black Prince, etc.) are listed under their personal names.

Acknowledgments

Medieval England: An Encyclopedia is a project that began in 1987 when Gary Kuris approached Paul E. Szarmach about Garland's plans for a series of encyclopedias organized around the nations and cultural areas of medieval Europe. Within two years the editorial team took shape, editors contacted contributors, and the encyclopedia became, administratively, a project of the Center for Medieval and Early Renaissance Studies at SUNY-Binghamton through the Research Foundation of SUNY. As is to be expected in a project some ten years in duration, Time's fell hand had its effect. Elizabeth Parker McLachlan was unable to develop her editorial plans for Art History because of illness, and Catherine E. Karkov agreed to succeed her as editor for this field, bringing her own directions to this major area. Throughout the project Peter M. Lefferts has maintained his key and steady role as editor for entries on Music and Liturgy. When Szarmach, who was initially both general editor and Old English field editor, moved from

Binghamton to Western Michigan, progress began to slow; as a result M. Teresa Tavormina and Joel T. Rosenthal moved from service as editors for Middle English and History into roles as general editors for the later stages. Tavormina has focused on reviewing the Old English, Middle English, and Music and Liturgy fields as well as the final editing of the text itself; Rosenthal, on reviewing the History and Art History fields, coordinating illustrative material for the volume, and supervising the production phase of the project.

Many other persons and institutions have assisted with the development of the individual fields. The University of Chicago and the University of Nebraska provided assistance with the costs of photocopying and postage for the Music and Liturgy field, as have SUNY-Binghamton and Western Michigan University for Old English, SUNY-Stony Brook for History, Michigan State University for Middle English, and Miami University and Rutgers University for Art. Charlotte Newman Goldy, Timothy C. Graham, Walter Leedy, F. Donald Logan, Timothy J. McGee, Lister M. Matheson, Perette Michelli, David A.E. Pelteret, E.G. Stanley, Michael W. Twomey, and Emily Zack Tabuteau were cheerful and reliable when new or extra work was asked of them, sometimes under very short deadlines.

The History field editor is pleased to acknowledge the help of Teresa Fetzer, who helped reconstruct some texts that a Stony Brook machine devoured. Ralph A. Griffiths and Caroline Barron offered much invaluable advice when some vital entries seemed destined for the orphanage. Alan Stahl went to special pains to help with the illustrative material on coins, and George Beech, Ralph V. Turner, and Sue Sheridan Walker read proofs for colleagues no longer able to do so. Marguerite Halversen helped catch bibliographic inconsistencies at an early stage, when there was still time to learn to do things better. In Art History the generous provision of illustrative materials by George H. Brown, Sarah Brown, Carol A. Farr, Malcolm Thurlby, Walter Leedy, Elizabeth Parker, Kelley Wickham-Crowley, Thomas-Photos, and especially Jane Hawkes and Lawrence Hoey is much appreci-

ated. Many institutions, publishers, and individuals have kindly granted permission for reproduction of pictorial materials, and those permissions are recorded in detail in the captions to the illustrations.

For Middle English a large debt is owed to A.S.G. Edwards for his review of the initial versions of entries in the field. The Department of English at Michigan State provided the Middle English editor with a term of research leave early in the project, and crucial bibliographic and factual checking for the field was performed by research assistants Marguerite Halversen and Priscilla Walker and by the members of the medieval research methods seminar at Michigan State, Rebecca Arnould, Robert M. Kellerman, Sharon Kelly, Kayla Keyser, and Paul Mulligan. The advice of John A. Alford, Stephen A. Barney, Larry D. Benson, John Leyerle, E.G. Stanley, and many other colleagues over the duration of the project is gratefully acknowledged here. Special thanks are due Lister Matheson for countless editorial consultations both large and small, literary and historical, and for his much-appreciated tolerance of an enterprise that seemed destined at times to swallow up desks, floors, dining-room tables, and many other horizontal surfaces.

Contributors, whether early or late, timely or tardy, demonstrated the patience necessary for group projects, and the editors hope that the laborers of the first hour and those of the eleventh find this publication a blissful reward. The editors are also particularly grateful to Holly Holbrook, who did much of the initial inputting of entries while she pursued her graduate work in the early 1990s. The continuing support of Gary Kuris, in a real sense the *onlie begetter* of the work, made so much possible: he has been coach and cheerleader, and always a witty blend of Squire Allworthy and Thwackum. Chuck Bartelt and Marianne Lown of Garland have each given advice and support on countless occasions, and Dawn Martin has provided the project with both its index and a welcome final review of consistency and style. Humanists tend to be singles players, but *Medieval England: An Encyclopedia* has been team play from the beginning.

Contributors

†James W. Alexander
University of Georgia
Richard I

John A. Alford
Michigan State University
Bible in ME Literature
Law in ME Literature
Piers Plowman
Truth in ME Literature

C.T. Allmand
University of Liverpool
Diplomacy
Hundred Years War

Michael Altschul
Case Western Reserve University
Parliament
Treason

Mark Amsler
University of Delaware
*Literacy and Readership [ME]

Kathleen M. Ashley
University of Southern Maine
Courtesy Literature

Robert S. Babcock
Hastings College
Feudalism

Bernard S. Bachrach
University of Minnesota
Battle of Hastings
Normandy

Janet Backhouse
British Library
Lindisfarne Gospels

John H. Baker
St. Catherine's College, Cambridge
Year Books

Peter S. Baker
University of Virginia
Beowulf
Byrhtferth

Frank Barlow
University of Exeter
Edward the Confessor
William II

Priscilla Heath Barnum
Princeton, New Jersey
Dives and Pauper

Alexandra Barratt
University of Waikato
Hull, Eleanor
Moral and Religious Instruction

Christopher C. Baswell
Barnard College
Douglas, Gavin

Janet M. Bately
King's College, London
*Alfred the Great [Influence on Learning]
Anglo-Saxon Chronicle
*Literary Influences: Classical [Anglo-Saxon Period]
Orosius, Paulus

---

* joint or conflated articles

Susan Battley
State University of New York, Stony Brook
Bury St. Edmunds
Ipswich

Priscilla Bawcutt
University of Liverpool
Dunbar, William
Scottish Literature, Early

Ronald E. Baxter
Courtauld Institute of Art
Bestiaries
Medical Manuscripts and Herbals
Scientific Manuscripts, Early

Brigitte Bedos-Rezak
University of Maryland
Seals

George Beech
Western Michigan University
Angevin Empire
Gascony

Judith M. Bennett
University of North Carolina, Chapel Hill
Brewing

Michael J. Bennett
University of Tasmania
Henry VII
Wars of the Roses

C. David Benson
University of Connecticut
Henryson, Robert
*Matter of Antiquity [Troy and Thebes]

Thomas H. Bestul
University of Illinois, Chicago
Prayers

Frederick M. Biggs
University of Connecticut
Bible in OE Literature

Robert E. Bjork
Arizona State University
Cynewulf

N.F. Blake
University of Sheffield
Prose, ME

Virginia Blanton-Whetsell
Phoenix, New York
Wærferth of Worcester

Julia Boffey
Queen Mary and Westfield College
University of London
Beaufort, Margaret

Brenda M. Bolton
Queen Mary and Westfield College
University of London
Friars, Mendicant
Nuns and Nunneries

J.L. Bolton
Queen Mary and Westfield College
University of London
Mills and Sources of Power
Prices and Wages
Tunnage and Poundage

Michael R. Boudreau
University of Illinois Press
Soul and Body I and II

D'Arcy J.D. Boulton
University of Notre Dame
Dukes and Dukedoms
Earls and Earldoms
Heralds and Heraldry
Order of the Garter

Roger D. Bowers
Jesus College, Cambridge
Choirs, Choral Establishments
Organ

Ritamary Bradley
St. Ambrose University
Cloud of Unknowing
Julian of Norwich

Paul Brand
London, England
Impeachment
Lawyers
Rolls of Parliament

Mary Flowers Braswell
University of Alabama, Birmingham
Michel of Northgate
*Penitentials [Post-Conquest]
Virtues and Vices, Books of

Derek S. Brewer
Emmanuel College, Cambridge
Malory, Thomas

Anthony R. Bridbury
London School of Economics, University of London
Black Death

Richard H. Britnell
University of Durham
Food and the Food Trades

Herbert R. Broderick
Lehman College, City University of New York
Anglo-Saxon Old Testament Narrative Illustration

George Hardin Brown
Stanford University
Alcuin
Aldhelm
Bede the Venerable
Benedict of Nursia

†Marjorie Brown
Rome, New York
Sedulius

Phyllis R. Brown
Santa Clara University
Battle of Brunanburh
Deor
Dream of the Rood
Guthlac, Prose
Guthlac A and B
Seafarer
Wanderer

Sarah Brown
Royal Commission on the Historical Monuments of
 England
Stained Glass

Thomas Cable
University of Texas, Austin
Language, History of the

John Caldwell
Faculty of Music, St. Aldate's, Oxford
Discant, English
Hymns
Magnificat
Robertsbridge Codex

Robert G. Calkins
Cornell University
Great Bibles, Romanesque

James Campbell
Worcester College, Oxford
Vikings in Britain

†Miles Campbell
New Mexico State University
Æthelstan
*Armies and Military Service [Anglo-Saxon]
Dunstan of Canterbury
Wilfrid of York

D.A. Carpenter
King's College, London
Exchequer and the Pipe Rolls
Scutage
*Westminster Abbey [History]

Brendan Cassidy
University of St. Andrews
Ruthwell Cross

Jane Chance
Rice University
Literary Influences: Medieval Latin

Joanne A. Charbonneau
James Madison University
Breton Lay
Romances, ME

Martin Cherry
English Heritage, London
Architecture, Domestic

Wendy R. Childs
University of Leeds
Customs Accounts

Stephanie Christelow
Idaho State University
Eleanor of Aquitaine
Godwin, Earl of Wessex
Harold Godwinson

†Cecily Clark
Cambridge, England
Names

Linda Clark
Institute of Historical Research, University of London
Parliamentary Elections

Henry S. Cobb
House of Lords, London
Cinque Ports
Southampton
Tin Industry and Trade

Alan B. Cobban
University of Liverpool
Universities

John W. Conlee
College of William and Mary
Debate Poems
Owl and the Nightingale

Rebecca J. Coogan
Grand Valley State University
Berners, Juliana
Gaimar, Geffrei

Helen Cooper
University College, Oxford
Chaucer, Geoffrey

P.R. Coss
University of Wales, Cardiff
Baronial Reform
Battles of Lewes and Evesham
Gentry

Rosemary J. Cramp
Durham, England
Brixworth
Ecclesiastical Architecture, Early Anglo-Saxon
Kentish Churches
Wearmouth-Jarrow: Architecture

†J.E. Cross
University of Liverpool
Adrian and Ritheus; Prose
  Solomon and Saturn
Martyrology, Old English

Gareth Curtis
Manchester, England
*Mass, Polyphonic Music for [ca. 1390–ca. 1485]
Power, Leonel

Helen Damico
University of New Mexico
*Women in OE Literature [Prose]

Richard G. Davies
University of Manchester
Bishops

Sheila Delany
Simon Fraser University
Bokenham, Osbern

Lynda Dennison
North Swindon (Wilts.), England
Amesbury Psalter
Cuerden Psalter
"East Anglian School" of Illumination
Exeter Bohun Psalter
Manuscript Illumination, Gothic
Ormesby Psalter
Psalters, Gothic
Queen Mary's Psalter
Westminster Chapter House Paintings
Wilton Diptych

Anne R. DeWindt
Wayne County Community College
Manor Courts and Court Rolls

Edwin B. DeWindt
University of Detroit, Mercy
Labor Services

Regina D'Innocenzi
Basel, Switzerland
Winchester Old Minster

A.N. Doane
University of Wisconsin at Madison
Genesis A and B
*Literacy and Readership [Anglo-Saxon Period]
*Orality and Aurality [OE]

R.B. Dobson
Christ's College, Cambridge
York, City of
York, Ecclesiastical Province of

Keith R. Dockray
University of Huddersfield
Edward IV
Edward V
Richard III

Claire M. Donovan
Winchester, England
Books of Hours
Brailes, William de

Sally Dormer
London, England
Ciboria
Enamels, Gothic
Henry of Blois Plaques
Metalwork and Enamels, Romanesque

Hoyt N. Duggan
University of Virginia
Matter of Antiquity [Alexander]

Robert W. Dunning
Victoria County History, Somerset
Bristol
Chichele, Henry
Dioceses and Diocesan Structure
Parish Clergy

A.S.G. Edwards
University of Victoria
Burgh, Benedict
Lydgate, John
Shirley, John
Trevisa, John

Judith Ellis
Clark Art Institute
Apocalypses
Women and the Arts

Janet Schrunk Ericksen
Vanderbilt University
Wulf and Eadwacer

Deborah Everhart
Georgetown University
Richard the Redeless and Mum and the Sothsegger
Siege of Jerusalem

Mark Everist
University of Southampton
W1

David Fallows
University of Manchester
Carol
Morton, Robert
Songs [1380–1485]

Carol A. Farr
London, England
Manuscript Illumination, Anglo-Saxon [Early]
Stockholm Gospels
Vespasian Psalter
Wearmouth-Jarrow and the Codex Amiatinus

Susanna Fein
Kent State University
Death and Life
Truelove or Quatrefoil of Love

Peter J. Fergusson
Wellesley College
Cistercian Architecture

Rosalind P. Field
Royal Holloway College, University of London
Anglo-Norman Literature
Hue de Rotelande

Robin Fleming
Boston College
Domesday Book

Alan J. Fletcher
University College, Dublin
Mirk, John
Sermons and Homilies [ME]

Roger R. Fowler
Ottawa, Ontario
Cursor Mundi

Harold S.A. Fox
University of Leicester
Agriculture and Field Systems

Allen J. Frantzen
Loyola University, Chicago
Penitentials [Anglo-Saxon Period]

Donald K. Fry
St. Petersburg, Florida
Cædmon
Durham
Finnsburh
Hild

Melissa M. Furrow
Dalhousie University
Comic Tales

Richard Gameson
University of Kent, Canterbury
Augustine of Canterbury
Conversion of the Anglo-Saxons

Thomas J. Garbáty
University of Michigan
Ballads, English and Scottish

J.-A. George
University of Dundee
Azarias
Daniel

James L. Gillespie
Amman, Jordan
Henry V
Lancaster, Duchy of
Marches of Scotland and Wales
Modus tenendi parliamentum
Poll Tax

Warren Ginsberg
State University of New York, Albany
Froissart, Jean
Literary Influences: French
Literary Influences: Italian

Brian J. Golding
University of Southampton
Cistercians
Monasticism and the Benedictine Order

Charlotte Newman Goldy
Miami University
Anarchy
Matilda
Stephen

Anthony E. Goodman
University of Edinburgh
Lancaster, John Duke of
Richard II

Janice Gordon-Kelter
University of St. Thomas, Houston
Bacon, Roger
Books and the Book Trade
Duns Scotus, John

Timothy Graham
Western Michigan University
Æthelwold of Winchester
Elstob, Elizabeth
Nowell, Laurence

Hero Granger-Taylor
London, England
Textiles from St. Cuthbert's Tomb

Richard Firth Green
University of Western Ontario
Patronage, Literary

Diana E. Greenway
Institute of Historical Research, University of London
Cartularies
Charters
Dialogue of the Exchequer

D.C. Greetham
City University of New York
*Textual Criticism [ME]

Ralph A. Griffiths
University College of Wales, Swansea
Henry VI
Monarchy and Kingship

Christa Grössinger
University of Manchester
Misericords

DeLloyd J. Guth
University of Manitoba
Fortescue, Sir John

Cynthia Hahn
Florida State University
Matthew Paris
Saints' Lives, Illuminated

J.R. Hall
University of Mississippi
Exodus
*Textual Criticism [OE]

Thomas N. Hall
University of Illinois, Chicago
Christ I
Christ III

Mary Hamel
Mount St. Mary's College
Morte Arthure, Alliterative

Peter W. Hammond
Richard III Society, London
*Coronation [Post-Conquest]

Barbara A. Hanawalt
University of Minnesota
Children and Childhood

Kristine E. Haney
Westminster, Massachusetts
St. Albans Psalter
Winchester Psalter

Vanessa A. Harding
Birkbeck College, University of London
*Boroughs [After 1066]
Guilds and Fraternities
London

P.D.A. Harvey
University of Durham
Serfs and Villeins
Tenures

A. Jane Hawkes
University College, Cork
Art, Anglo-Saxon: Classical Influences
Coffin of St. Cuthbert
Sculpture, Anglo-Saxon
Stonework as Ecclesiastical Ornament

Michelle Head
Cambridge, Massachusetts
Lapidaries

Avril Henry
University of Exeter
Religious Allegories

J.P. Hermann
University of Alabama
*Criticism, Modern, of Medieval Literature [OE]

Andrew H. Hershey
King of Prussia, Pennsylvania
Justiciar

Kathleen M. Hewett-Smith
University of Richmond
Chaucerian Apocrypha and Imitations
Jack Upland, Friar Daw's Reply, and Upland's Rejoinder
Map, Walter
Pierce the Plowman's Creed

Michael A. Hicks
King Alfred's College, Winchester
Attainder and Forfeiture

Iain Higgins
University of British Columbia
Mandeville's Travels

Joyce Hill
University of Leeds
Æthelweard
Benedict of Aniane
Paul the Deacon
Tacitus
Waldere
Widsith

Thomas D. Hill
Cornell University
Wisdom Literature

Rodney H. Hilton
University of Birmingham
Peasant Rebellion of 1381

David A. Hinton
University of Southampton
*Archaeology [Anglo-Saxon Period]
Cemeteries and Cemetery Archaeology
*Yeavering

Lawrence Hoey
University of Wisconsin, Milwaukee
Canterbury Cathedral
Chapter Houses
Lincoln Cathedral
Parish Church Architecture
Salisbury Cathedral
Screen Facades
Vaulting
Wells Cathedral
Winchester Cathedral

Nicholas Howe
Ohio State University
Anglo-Saxon Invasions and Conquest

D.R. Howlett
Medieval Latin Dictionary
Anglo-Latin Literature to 1066
Asser

Andrew Hughes
University of Toronto
Coronation Ceremony, Music and Ritual of
Offices, New Liturgical
Thomas of Canterbury, Office for

Lois L. Huneycutt
University of Missouri at Columbia
Henry I

Roy F. Hunnisett
Public Record Office
Chancellor and Chancery
Outlawry

Eileen Jankowski
Chapman College
Barbour, John
Kingis Quair
Wace

Sharon L. Jansen
Pacific Lutheran University
Matter of Britain
Morte Arthur, Stanzaic

Helen M. Jewell
University of Liverpool
Eton College
Winchester College

David F. Johnson
Florida State University
Riddles, OE

Alexandra F. Johnston
University of Toronto
Drama, Vernacular

Michael Jones
Institute of Historical Research, University of London
Bedford, John Duke of
Peerage
Percy Family

Timothy Jones
Augustana College
Marvels of the East
Phoenix

Catherine E. Karkov
Miami University
Angel Roofs
Architecture and Architectural Sculpture, Gothic
Architecture and Architectural Sculpture, Romanesque
Art, Anglo-Saxon
Art, Gothic
Art, Viking Age
Baptismal Fonts
Bristol Harrowing of Hell Relief
Canterbury Wall Paintings
Durham Choir Screen Reliefs
Eadwine and Canterbury/Paris Psalters
Eleanor Crosses
Fuller Brooch
Hardham Wall Paintings
Hexham and Ripon
High Crosses
Iconography
Manuscript Illumination, Anglo-Saxon [Later]
Manuscript Illumination, Romanesque
Metalwork, Gothic
Repton
Salisbury Chapter House Reliefs
Sculpture, Gothic
Textiles and Embroideries, Anglo-Saxon
Tiles
Wall Painting, Romanesque
York, Anglo-Saxon Churches in
York and Ripon Minsters

Robert L. Kellogg
University of Virginia
Literary Influences: Scandinavian

Sharon Kelly
Paw Paw, Michigan
Bozon, Nicholas
Edmund of Abingdon (Edmund Rich)

Michael Kenny
National Museum of Ireland
Coins, Imagery of

Jennifer I. Kermode
University of Liverpool
Aliens and Alien Merchants
Hanseatic League
Lincoln

John L. Kirby
Streatham, London
Henry IV

Eric Klingelhofer
Mercer University
*Archaeology [After the Norman Conquest]
Deserted Villages

C.H. Knowles
University of Wales, Cardiff
Henry III
Simon de Montfort

Genevra Kornbluth
Youngstown State University
Alfred and Minster Lovell Jewels

Lucia Kornexl
Universität München
Benedictine Reform
Regularis concordia

Maryanne Kowaleski
Fordham University
Assize of Weights and Measures
Exeter
Fairs and Markets

William A. Kretzschmar, Jr.
University of Georgia
Exemplum

Margaret Wade Labarge
Ottawa, Ontario
Edward the Black Prince
Women [Post-Conquest]

Michael Lapidge
Cambridge University
Lantfred
Theodore of Tarsus

David A. Lawton
University of East Anglia
Dream Vision

Walter Leedy
Cleveland State University
Architecture, University and College
King's College, Cambridge
Westminster Abbey [Architecture]
Windsor, St. George's Chapel

Gordon Leff
University of York
Learning and Intellectual Life 1050–1200

Peter M. Lefferts
University of Nebraska, Lincoln
Agincourt Carol
Alanus, J[ohannes]
Angelus ad virginem
Caput Mass
Chapel Royal
Dunstable, John
Faburden
Godric's Songs
Harley 978
Holy Week and Easter, Music for
Lady Chapel
Lady Mass
Lai, Latin
Mass, Polyphonic Music for [ca. 900–ca. 1390]
Minstrels and Minstrelsy [Pre-Conquest]
Motet
Music: History and Theory
Notation of Polyphonic Music
Old Hall Manuscript
Planctus
Rondellus
Rota
Salve Service
Sequence
Songs [Pre-Conquest; 1066–1380]
Square
Sub arturo plebs
Sumer Canon
Trope
Winchester Songbook

Theodore Leinbaugh
University of North Carolina, Chapel Hill
Ælfric

Patrizia Lendinara
Università degli Studi di Palermo
Abbo of Fleury
Adso of Montier-en-Der
Ælfric Bata

Seth Lerer
Stanford University
Hawes, Stephen

Robert E. Lewis
Middle English Dictionary
Prick of Conscience

Carl Lindahl
University of Houston
Orality and Aurality [ME]
Popular Culture

T.H. Lloyd
University College of Wales, Swansea
Banks and Banking
Staple

Karma Lochrie
Loyola University, Chicago
Kempe, Margery

F. Donald Logan
Emmanuel College, Boston
Courts, Ecclesiastical
Excommunication

Nicola Losseff
University of York
Conductus

Graham A. Loud
University of Leeds
Knight Service and Knights' Fees
William I

Rosalind Love
St. John's College, Cambridge
Anglo-Latin Literature after 1066

Kathryn Lowe
University of Glasgow
Boniface
Penda of Mercia
Queens and Queenship

H.R. Loyn
Queen Mary and Westfield College
University of London
Hides
Thegns
Tribal Hidage

Peter J. Lucas
University College, Dublin
Capgrave, John

Douglas Mac Lean
Houston, Texas
Art, Pictish
Yeavering

Timothy J. McGee
University of Toronto
Musical Instruments

Alison K. McHardy
University of Nottingham
Pilgrimages and Pilgrims
Popular Religion
Priories, Alien

Elizabeth Parker McLachlan
Rutgers University
Canterbury Picture Leaves

J. Bard McNulty
Trinity College
Bayeux Tapestry

Pearson M. Macek
Ann Arbor, Michigan
Chichester Roundel
Painting and Wall Painting, Gothic
Westminster Retable

Tim William Machan
Marquette University
*Boethius [ME]
Translation and Paraphrase
Trevet, Nicholas

Hugh Magennis
Queen's University, Belfast
Apollonius of Tyre
Husband's Message
Judith
Ruin

William Marx
University of Wales, Lampeter
Harrowing of Hell

Mavis E. Mate
University of Oregon
Estate Management

Lister M. Matheson
Michigan State University
Brut, Prose
Caxton, William
Chronicles
Hardyng, John
Harry, "Blind"
Jacob's Well
Peter of Langtoft
Printing
Wyntoun, Andrew

Laurel Means
McMaster University
Alchemy
Astrology
Charms
Utilitarian Writings

Perette E. Michelli
St. Olaf's College
Iconography
Ivory Carving, Anglo-Saxon
Ivory Carving, Romanesque
Metalwork, Anglo-Saxon
Sculpture, Romanesque
York Virgin and Child

David Millon
Washington and Lee University
Juries and the Jury System
Statutes

Ellen Wedemeyer Moore
John Abbott College
Trade, Internal and External

Stephen R. Morillo
Wabash College
Hundreds and Hundred Rolls
Outlaws and Robin Hood
Quo Warranto Proceedings

Stephen Morrison
Université de Poitiers
Orm

Peta Motture
Victoria and Albert Museum
Gloucester Candlestick
Liturgical Combs
St. Nicholas Crosier

John H.A. Munro
University of Toronto
Cloth Manufacture and Trade

Janet L. Nelson
King's College, London
*Alfred the Great [History]
*Coronation [Anglo-Saxon]

Carol Neuman de Vegvar
Ohio Wesleyan University
Art, Anglo-Saxon: Celtic Influences
Franks Casket
Sutton Hoo

James Noble
University of New Brunswick
Geoffrey of Monmouth
Laȝamon

Daniel Nodes
Hamline University
Fathers of the Church

Katherine O'Brien O'Keeffe
University of Notre Dame
Solomon and Saturn
Wife's Lament

Patrick P. O'Neill
University of North Carolina, Chapel Hill
Literary Influences: Irish
Literary Influences: Welsh

Robin S. Oggins
State University of New York, Binghamton
Hawking and Falconry
Wardrobe

Alexandra Hennessey Olsen
University of Denver
*Women in OE Literature [Poetry]

†Kathleen M. Openshaw
University of Toronto
Benedictional of Æthelwold
Galba Psalter
Harley Psalter and the "Utrecht" Style
New Minster Charter
Psalters, Anglo-Saxon
Tiberius Psalter
"Winchester School" of Illumination

A.P.M. Orchard
Emmanuel College, Oxford
Christ and Satan
Genesis, Old Saxon
Isidore of Seville
Kentish Hymn
Letter of Alexander to Aristotle
Maxims I and II
Physiologus
Tatwine

Nicholas Orme
University of Exeter
Schools
Wainfleet, William
William of Wykeham

Michael Orr
Lawrence University
Marginalia

R.I. Page
Corpus Christi College, Cambridge
Parker, Matthew

Elizabeth C. Parker
Fordham University
Cloisters Cross

David Parsons
University of Nottingham
Runes

David A.E. Pelteret
University of Toronto
Æthelberht
Æthelred II
Cnut
Offa
Slavery and Slaves
Swein

Richard W. Pfaff
University of North Carolina, Chapel Hill
Feasts, New Liturgical
Liturgy

J.R.S. Phillips
University College, Dublin
Battles of Bannockburn and Boroughbridge
Edward II
Ordainers

L.R. Poos
Catholic University of America
Population and Demography

Michael R. Powicke
University of Toronto
*Armies and Military Service [After 1066]
Arms and Armor

Michael Prestwich
University of Durham
Edward I

Phillip Pulsiano
Villanova University
Glosses and Glossaries

Susan K. Rankin
Emmanuel College, Cambridge
Drama, Latin Liturgical
Notation of Plainsong
Winchester Organa

Daniel J. Ransom
University of Oklahoma
Harley Lyrics
Lyrics

Richard Rastall
University of Leeds
Drama, Vernacular, Role of Music in
*Minstrels and Minstrelsy [Post-Conquest]
Waits

Barbara C. Raw
University of Keele
Regularis concordia and the Arts

Carole Rawcliffe
University of East Anglia
Clare Family
Councils, Royal and Baronial
Hospitals
Households, Royal and Baronial
Medicine and Doctors

Sherry L. Reames
University of Wisconsin
*Hagiography

A. Compton Reeves
Ohio University
Great Seal
Privy Seal
Signet

Richard E. Rice
James Madison University
Science
Technology

Mary P. Richards
University of Delaware
Wulfstan of York

Gavin Richardson
Rantoul, Illinois
Judgment Day I and II

Colin F. Richmond
University of Keele
Bastard Feudalism
Family Letter Collections

Anita R. Riedinger
Southern Illinois University
Andreas
Formula

Joan Rimmer
Canterbury, England
Dance, Dance Music
Karole

Jane Roberts
King's College, London
Felix of Crowland
Vainglory

Phyllis B. Roberts
City University of New York
Grosseteste, Robert
Langton, Stephen
Libraries
William of Ockham

Elizabeth Robertson
University of Colorado
Ancrene Wisse
Katherine Group
Women in ME Literature

Christine M. Robinson
Mid Calder, West Lothian, Scotland
Speculum Vitae

Pamela R. Robinson
Institute of Romance Studies, University of London
*Paleography and Codicology [Post-Conquest]

Sally E. Roper
Llangoed, Anglesey, Gwynedd, Wales
Antiphon
Regularis concordia and the Liturgy
Votive Observance

Miri Rubin
Pembroke College, Oxford
Alms and Charity
Prostitution

Lara Ruffolo
UNITEC Institute of Technology
Auckland, New Zealand
Ars moriendi
Gerald of Wales
John of Salisbury
Marie de France
Pecock, Reginald
William of Malmesbury

Alexander R. Rumble
University of Manchester
Boroughs [Anglo-Saxon]
Burghal Hidage
Cotton, Robert, and the Cotton Library
Exeter Book
Junius Manuscript
Paleography and Codicology [Anglo-Saxon]

Timothy J. Runyan
Cleveland State University
Navy and Naval Power
Ships and Shipbuilding

Michael F. Ryan
Chester Beatty Library
Liturgical Vessels

Nick Sandon
University of Exeter
Liturgy and Church Music, History of
Processions and Processional Music
Salisbury, Use of

Michael G. Sargent
Queens College, City University of New York
Hilton, Walter
Love, Nicholas
Mystical and Devotional Writings
Rolle, Richard

Nigel E. Saul
Royal Holloway College, University of London
Appellants
Local Government

Andrew D. Saunders
Greenwich, England
Castles and Fortification

Jane E. Sayers
University College, London
Canterbury, Ecclesiastical Province of
Convocation

John Scahill
Seikei University
Friars' Miscellanies

Wendy Scase
University of Hull
Satire

V.J. Scattergood
Trinity College, Dublin
Charles of Orléans
Clanvowe, John
Davy, Adam
Scogan, Henry
Skelton, John

Helene Scheck
Rensselaer, New York
Eusebius
Theodulf of Orléans

William Schipper
Memorial University of Newfoundland
Paganism and Superstition in OE Literature

D.G. Scragg
University of Manchester
Battle of Maldon
Vercelli Book
Vercelli Homilies

†Michael M. Sheehan
Pontifical Institute of Mediaeval Studies, Toronto
Widows and Widowhood
Wills and Testaments

R.A. Shoaf
University of Florida
Criticism, Modern, of Medieval Literature [ME]

James Simpson
Girton College, Cambridge
Beast Epic and Fable
Hoccleve, Thomas
Usk, Thomas

Elizabeth S. Sklar
Wayne State University
Courtly Love

Mary E. Sokolowski
Austin, Texas
Sedulius Scottus

Diane Speed
University of Sydney
Floris and Blancheflour
Lovelich, Henry
Matter of England
Matter of France
Sir Orfeo

Robert C. Stacey
University of Washington
Jews

Pauline Stafford
University of Huddersfield
Æthelflæd
Emma
*Women [Anglo-Saxon]

Alan M. Stahl
American Numismatic Society
Coins and Coinage
Mints and Minting

E.G. Stanley
Pembroke College, Oxford
Versification

W.P. Stoneman
Houghton Library, Harvard University
Blickling Homilies

George B. Stow
La Salle University
Courts and the Court System
Palatinates

William J. Summers
Dartmouth College
Cantilena
Manuscripts of Polyphonic Music
Worcester Fragments

Heather Swanson
University of Birmingham
Leather Manufacture and Trade
Roads and the Road System
Taxes and Taxation

Paul E. Szarmach
Western Michigan University
Chrodegang of Metz
Oswald of Worcester
*Sermons and Homilies [OE]

Emily Zack Tabuteau
Michigan State University
Magna Carta
Norman Conquest
Prisons

M. Teresa Tavormina
Michigan State University
Bourchier, John
Henry of Lancaster
Prophecy Literature

Elizabeth C. Teviotdale
J. Paul Getty Museum
Santa Monica, California
Caligula Troper
Winchester Tropers

David Thomson
Cockermouth (Cumbria), England
Grammatical Treatises

J.A.F. Thomson
University of Glasgow
Chantries
Lollards
Wyclif, John

Malcolm Thurlby
York University
Durham Cathedral
Ely Cathedral
Gloucester Cathedral
Kilpeck
Malmesbury Abbey
Norwich Cathedral
Romsey Abbey
Romsey Roods
St. Albans Abbey

Jan Z. Titow
University of Nottingham
Manorialism

Robert Tittler
Concordia University
Coventry
Gloucester
Towns and Urban Life
Winchester

Joseph B. Trahern, Jr.
University of Tennessee
Caesarius of Arles

Stephanie Trigg
University of Melbourne
Winner and Waster

Ralph V. Turner
Florida State University
Bracton, Henry of
Glanville, Ranulf de
Law, Post-Conquest
Writs

Thorlac Turville-Petre
University of Nottingham
Alliterative Revival
Clerk, John
Manning, Robert
Parliament of the Three Ages
William of Palerne

Michael W. Twomey
Ithaca College
Allegory and Related Symbolism
Pearl-Poet

Juliet Vale
Oxford, England
Chivalry
Court Culture and Patronage

Deborah VanderBilt
St. John Fisher College
Hagiography

Sally N. Vaughn
University of Houston
Anselm of Canterbury
Becket, Thomas
Investiture Controversy in England
Lanfranc

†Roger Virgoe
University of East Anglia
Beaufort Family
Cade's Rebellion
Norwich

Linda E. Voigts
University of Missouri, Kansas City
Scientific and Medical Writings

Christina von Nolcken
University of Chicago
Wycliffite Texts

Sue Sheridan Walker
Northeastern Illinois University
Inquisitions Post Mortem
Marriage and Marriage Law
Mortmain
Wardship

Patricia Wallace
Florida International University
Meters of Boethius

†W.L. Warren
Queen's University, Belfast
Assize of Clarendon
Henry II
John

Scott L. Waugh
University of California, Los Angeles
Despenser Family
Edward III
Lancaster, Thomas Earl of

Winthrop Wetherbee
Cornell University
Literary Influences: Classical [ME]

Elaine E. Whitaker
University of Alabama, Birmingham
Scrope, Stephen

G.J. White
Chester College
Frankpledge
Sheriff
Shires

Hugh White
St. Catherine's College, Oxford
Nature in ME Literature
Psychology, Medieval, in ME Literature

Dana-Linn Whiteside
State University of New York, Binghamton
Chronicle Poems
Gregory of Tours

Kelley M. Wickham-Crowley
Georgetown University
Architecture, Anglo-Saxon
Barnack
Barton-on-Humber
Bradford
Earls Barton Tower
Greensted

Gernot R. Wieland
University of British Columbia
Frithegod
Literary Influences: Carolingian
Prudentius

Nigel Wilkins
Corpus Christi College, Cambridge
Puy

Benjamin Carl Withers
University of Indiana, South Bend
Art, Romanesque

Joseph S. Wittig
University of North Carolina, Chapel Hill
Boethius [Latin, OE]

Ian N. Wood
University of Leeds
Cuthbert
Heptarchy

Marjorie Curry Woods
University of Texas, Austin
Rhetoric

Linda Woolley
Victoria and Albert Museum
Opus Anglicanum

Patrick Wormald
Christ Church, Oxford
Bretwald
Feuds and Wergeld
Law, Anglo-Saxon

R.F. Yeager
University of North Carolina, Asheville
Gower, John

Charles R. Young
Duke University
Beauchamp Family
Forests, Royal
Hubert Walter
Neville Family
William Marshal

Entries, Arranged by Category

The following list contains all the entries of the *Encyclopedia,* arranged by category in order to give users a sense of the kinds of entries they can find in the pages below. A few items appear under more than one category, although the editors have sought to limit the number of such duplications to those entries that are genuinely difficult to assign to a single category.

Persons (Individuals)
Political Figures
Æthelberht
Æthelflæd
Æthelred II
Æthelstan
Alfred the Great
Bedford, John Duke of
Cnut
Edward I
Edward II
Edward III
Edward IV
Edward V
Edward the Black Prince
Edward the Confessor
Eleanor of Aquitaine
Emma
Godwin, Earl of Wessex
Harold Godwinson
Henry I
Henry II
Henry III
Henry IV
Henry V
Henry VI
Henry VII
Henry of Lancaster
Hubert Walter
John
Lancaster, John Duke of (John of Gaunt)
Lancaster, Thomas Earl of
Matilda

Offa
Penda of Mercia
Richard I
Richard II
Richard III
Simon de Montfort
Stephen
Swein
William I
William II
William Marshal

Religious Leaders
Æthelwold of Winchester
Anselm of Canterbury
Augustine of Canterbury
Becket, Thomas
Boniface
Chichele, Henry
Cuthbert
Dunstan of Canterbury
Edmund of Abingdon
Grosseteste, Robert
Hild
Lanfranc
Langton, Stephen
Oswald of Worcester
Theodore of Tarsus
Wainfleet, William
Wilfrid of York
William of Wykeham
Wulfstan of York
Wyclif, John

Kings and Queens of England

The information below is taken mainly from E.B. Fryde, D.E. Greenway, S. Porter, and I. Roy, eds., *Handbook of British Chronology,* 3d ed. (London: Royal Historical Society, 1986). Dates given for kings are for date of birth (where known), and for accession to death. For Henry VI and Edward IV the dates further reflect the "readeption" of Henry VI in 1470–1471. Dates for queens are for date of birth (where known), marriage, and death (where known).

	Birth	Reign		
Kings of Wessex				
Alfred (The Great)	849	871–899		
Edward (The Elder)		899–924		
Ælfweard		924–924		
Anglo-Saxon and Danish Kings of England				
Æthelstan		924–939		
Edmund I	921	939–946		
Eadred		946–955		
Eadwig	before 943	955–959		
Edgar I	943	957–975 (north of Thames)		
		959–975 (all England)		
Edward I	ca. 962	975–978		
Æthelred II (The Unready)	968/69?	978–1016 (dispossessed by Swein, 1013–1014)		
Swein		1013–1014		
Edmund II (Ironside)	before 993	1016–1016		
Cnut		1016–1035		
Harold I (Harefoot)	ca. 1016?	1035–1040		
Harthacnut	ca. 1018?	1035–1042		
Edward II (The Confessor)	1002/05	1042–1066		
Harold II (Godwinson)	ca. 1020	1066–1066		

Post-Conquest Kings and Queens of England

Norman Dynasty

	Birth	Reign		
William I (The Conqueror)	1027/28	1066–1087	Matilda of Flanders	m. 1050–51?, d. 1083
William II (Rufus)	1056/60	1087–1100	unmarried	
Henry I	1068	1100–1135	Edith-Matilda of Scotland	b. 1080, m. 1100, d. 1118
			Adela of Louvaine	m. 1121
Stephen	before 1100	1135–1154	Matilda of Boulogne	b. 1103, m. 1125, d. 1152

Plantagenet Dynasty — *Birth* — *Reign*

	Birth	Reign		
Plantagenet Dynasty				
Henry II	1133	1154–1189	Eleanor of Aquitaine	b. 1122, m. 1152, d. 1214
Richard I	1157	1189–1199	Berengaria of Navarre	m. 1191, d. 1230?
John	1167	1199–1216	Isabella of Gloucester	m. 1189
			Isabella of Angoulême	m. 1200, d. 1246
Henry III	1207	1216–1272	Eleanor of Provence	m. 1236, d. 1291
Edward I	1239	1272–1307	Eleanor of Castile	m. 1254, d. 1290
			Margaret of France	b. 1282?, m. 1299, d. 1318
Edward II	1284	1307–1327	Isabella of France	b. 1292, m. 1308, d. 1358
Edward III	1312	1327–1377	Philippa of Hainault	b. 1314, m. 1328, d. 1369
Richard II	1367	1377–1399	Anne of Bohemia	b. 1366, m. 1382, d. 1394
			Isabella of France	b. 1389, m. 1396, d. 1409
Lancastrian Dynasty				
Henry IV	1366	1399–1413	Mary Bohun	m 1380–81, d. 1394
			Joan of Navarre (& Brittany)	b. 1370, m. 1403, d. 1437
Henry V	1387	1413–1422	Catherine of Valois	b. 1401, m. 1420, d. 1437
Henry VI	1421	1422–1461 1470–1471	Margaret of Anjou	b. 1430, m. 1445, d. 1482
Yorkist Dynasty				
Edward IV	1442	1461–1470 1471–1483	Elizabeth Woodville	b. 1437, m. 1464, d. 1492
Edward V	1470	1483–1483	unmarried	
Richard III	1452	1483–1485	Anne Neville	m. 1472, d. 1485
Tudor Dynasty				
Henry VII	1457	1485–1509	Elizabeth of York (daughter of Edward IV)	b. 1466, m. 1486, d. 1503

Archbishops of Canterbury and York

The information below is taken mainly from E.B. Fryde, D.E. Greenway, S. Porter, and I. Roy, eds., *Handbook of British Chronology,* 3d ed. (London: Royal Historical Society, 1986). Various archbishops who were nominated but never enthroned or (in the Anglo-Saxon period) who are questionable have been omitted. In the earlier centuries some of the dates are less certain than for the later period.

Canterbury		*York*	
Augustine	597–604/9		
Laurence	604/9–619		
Mellitus	619–624	Paulinus	625–633
Justus	624–631		
Honorius	631–653	Cedda	664–669
Deusdedit	655–664	Wilfrid I	669–678
Theodore	668–690	Bosa	679–706
Berhtwald	692–731		
Tatwine	731–734	John of Beverley	706–714
Nothelm	735–739	Wilfrid II	714–732
Cuthbert	740–760	Egberht (Egbert, Ecgbert)	732–766
Bregowine	761–764	Æthelberht (Ælberht)	767–780
Jænberht	765–792	Eanbald I	780–796
Æthelheard	792–805	Eanbald II	796–808
Wulfred	805–832	Wulfsige	808–837
Ceolnoth	833–870	Wigmund	837–854
Æthelred	870–888	Wulfhere	854–900
Plegmund	890–923		
Æthelhelm	923–926	Æthelbald	900–928
Wulfhelm	926–941	Hrothweard	928–931
Oda	941–958	Wulfstan I	931–956
Ælfsige	958–959	Osketel	956–971
Byrhthelm	959	Edwald	971
Dunstan	959–988	Oswald	971–992
Æthelgar	988–990	Ealdwulf	995–1002
Sigeric	990–994		
Ælfric	995–1005		

Canterbury		York	
Ælfheah	1006–1012	Wulfstan II	1002–1023
Ælfstan	1013–1020	Ælfric	1023–1051
Æthelnoth	1020–1038	Cynesige	1051–1060
Eadsige	1038–1050	Ealdred	1061–1069
Robert of Jumièges	1051–1052		
Stigand	1052–1070		
Norman Conquest	**1066**		
Lanfranc	1070–1089		
Anselm	1093–1109	Thomas of Bayeux	1070–1100
Ralph d'Escures	1114–1122	Gerard	1100–1109
William of Corbeil	1123–1136	Thomas II	1109–1114
Theobald of Bec	1138–1161	Thurstan	1114–1140
Thomas Becket	1162–1170	William FitzHerbert	1141–1147
Richard of Dover	1173–1184	Henry Murdac	1147–1153
Baldwin	1184–1190	William FitzHerbert	1153–1154
Hubert Walter	1193–1205	Roger de Pont l'Évêque	1154–1181
		Geoffrey	1189–1212
Stephen Langton	1206–1228	Walter de Grey	1215–1255
Richard Grant	1229–1231	Sewal de Bovill	1255–1258
Edmund of Abingdon	1233–1240	Godfrey Lunham	1258–1265
Boniface of Savoy	1241–1270	Walter Giffard	1266–1279
Robert Kilwardby	1272–1278	William Wickwane	1279–1285
John Pecham	1279–1292	John le Romeys	1286–1296
Robert Winchelsey	1293–1313	Henry Newark	1296–1299
		Thomas Corbridge	1299–1304
Walter Reynolds	1313–1327	William Greenfield	1304–1315
Simon Meapham	1328–1333	William Melton	1316–1340
John Stratford	1333–1348	William Zouche	1340–1352
Thomas Bradwardine	1348–1349	John Thoresby	1352–1373
Simon Islip	1349–1366	Alexander Neville	1374–1388
Simon Langham	1366–1368	Thomas Arundel	1388–1396
William Whittlesey	1368–1374	Robert Waldby	1396–1398
Simon Sudbury	1375–1381	Richard le Scrope	1398–1405
William Courtenay	1381–1396		
Thomas Arundel	1397		
Roget Walden	1397–1399		
Thomas Arundel	1399–1414		
Henry Chichele	1414–1443	Henry Bowet	1407–1423
John Stafford	1443–1452	John Kempe	1426–1452
John Kempe	1452–1454	William Booth	1452–1464
Thomas Bourchier	1454–1486	George Neville	1465–1476
John Morton	1486–1500	Lawrence Booth	1476–1480
		Thomas Rotherham	1480–1500

Popes, 590–1503

The information below is based on William W. Kibler and Grover A. Zinn, eds., *Medieval France: An Encyclopedia* (New York: Garland, 1995), and C.R. Cheney, ed., *Handbook of Dates for Students of English History* (London: Royal Historical Society, 1978).

	Regnal Dates		*Regnal Dates*
Gregory I	590–604	Hadrian I	772–795
Sabinian	604–606	Leo III	795–816
Boniface III	607	Stephen IV (V)	816–817
Boniface IV	608–615	Paschal I	817–824
Deusdedit	615–618	Eugenius II	824–827
Boniface V	619–625	Valentine	827
Honorius I	625–638	Gregory IV	827–844
Severinus	640	[Antipope John	844]
John IV	640–642	Sergius II	844–847
Theodore I	642–649	Leo IV	847–855
Martin I	649–653	[Antipope Anastasius Bibliothecarius 855]	
Eugenius I	654–657	Benedict III	855–858
Vitalian	657–672	Nicholas I	858–867
Adeodatus	672–676	Hadrian II	867–872
Donus	676–678	John VIII	872–882
Agatho	678–681	Marinus I	882–884
Leo II	682–683	Hadrian III	884–885
Benedict II	684–685	Stephen V (VI)	885–891
John V	685–686	Formosus	891–896
Conon	686–687	Boniface VI	896
[Antipope Theodore	687]	Stephen VI (VII)	896–897
[Antipope Paschal	687]	Romanus	897
Sergius I	687–701	Theodore II	897
John VI	701–705	John IX	898–900
John VII	705–707	Benedict IV	900–903
Sisinnius	708	Leo V	903–904
Constantine I	708–715	[Antipope Christopher	903–904]
Gregory II	715–731	Sergius III	904–911
Gregory III	731–741	Anastasius III	911–913
Zacharias	741–752	Lando	913–914
Stephen (II)	752	John X	914–928
Stephen II (III)	752–757	Leo VI	928
Paul I	757–767	Stephen VII (VIII)	928–931
[Antipope Constantine II	767–768]	John XI	931–936
[Antipope Philip	768]	Leo VII	936–939
Stephen III (IV)	768–772	Stephen VIII (IX)	939–942

Marinus II	942–946	
Agapitus II	946–955	
John XII	955–963	
Leo VIII	963–965	
Benedict V	964	
John XIII	965–972	
Benedict VI	973–974	
[Antipope Boniface VII	974, 984–985]	
Benedict VII	974–983	
John XIV	983–984	
John XV	985–996	
Gregory V	996–999	
[Antipope John XVI	997–998]	
Sylvester II	999–1003	
John XVII	1003	
John XVIII	1003–1009	
Sergius IV	1009–1012	
Benedict VIII	1012–1024	
[Antipope Gregory	1012]	
John XIX	1024–1032	
Benedict IX	1032–1044, 1045, 1047–1048	
[Antipope Silvester III	1045]	
Gregory VI	1045–1046	
Clement II	1046–1047	
Damasus II	1048	
Leo IX	1049–1054	
Victor II	1055–1057	
Stephen IX (X)	1057–1058	
[Antipope Benedict X	1058–1059]	
Nicholas II	1058–1061	
[Antipope Honorius II	1061–1064]	
Alexander II	1061–1073	
Gregory VII	1073–1085	
[Antipope Clement III	1080,1084–1100]	
Victor III	1086–1087	
Urban II	1088–1099	
Paschal II	1099–1118	
[Antipope Theodoric	1100]	
[Antipope Albert	1102]	
[Antipope Silvester IV	1105–1111]	
Gelasius II	1118–1119	
[Antipope Gregory VIII	1118–1121]	
Calixtus II	1119–1124	
Honorius II	1124–1130	
[Antipope Celestine II	1124]	
Innocent II	1130–1143	
[Antipope Anacletus II	1130–1138]	
[Antipope Victor	1138]	
Celestine II	1143–1144	
Lucius II	1144–1145	
Eugenius III	1145–1153	
Anastasius IV	1153–1154	
*Hadrian IV	1154–1159	
Alexander III	1159–1181	
[Antipope Victor IV	1159–1164]	
[Antipope Paschal III	1164–1168]	

*Born in England

[Antipope Calixtus III	1168–1178]	
[Antipope Innocent III	1179–1180]	
Lucius III	1181–1185	
Urban III	1185–1187	
Gregory VIII	1187	
Clement III	1187–1191	
Celestine III	1191–1198	
Innocent III	1198–1216	
Honorius III	1216–1227	
Gregory IX	1227–1241	
Celestine IV	1241	
Innocent IV	1243–1254	
Alexander IV	1254–1261	
Urban IV	1261–1264	
Clement IV	1265–1268	
Gregory X	1271–1276	
Innocent V	1276	
Hadrian V	1276	
John XXI	1276–1277	
Nicholas III	1277–1280	
Martin IV	1281–1285	
Honorius IV	1285–1287	
Nicholas IV	1288–1292	
Celestine V	1294	
Boniface VIII	1294–1303	
Benedict XI	1303–1304	
Clement V	1305–1314	
John XXII	1316–1334	
[Antipope Nicholas	1328–1330]	
Benedict XII	1334–1342	
Clement VI	1342–1352	
Innocent VI	1352–1362	
Urban V	1362–1370	
Gregory XI	1370–1378	
Roman Line		
Urban VI	1378–1389	
Boniface IX	1389–1404	
Innocent VII	1404–1406	
Gregory XII	1406–1415	
Avignon Line		
Clement VII	1378–1394	
Benedict XIII	1394–1417	
Clement VIII	1423–1429	
Pisa Line		
Alexander V	1409–1410	
John XXIII	1410–1415	
Martin V	1417–1431	
Eugenius IV	1431–1447	
[Antipope Felix V	1439–1449]	
Nicholas V	1447–1455	
Calixtus III	1455–1458	
Pius II	1458–1464	
Paul II	1464–1471	
Sixtus IV	1471–1484	
Innocent VIII	1484–1492	
Alexander VI	1492–1503	
Pius III	1503	

Musical and Liturgical Terms

Adiastematic

See Neume

Ars Nova

A "new art," referring most narrowly to the Parisian innovations in musical notation of the first half of the 14th century, as they are so tagged in a group of treatises associated with Philippe de Vitry. More broadly, the term is used today for the music of the 14th century in contrast to that of the 13th, whose manner of notation had been correspondingly and retrospectively termed the "old art" (*ars vetus* or *ars antiqua*) by those medieval innovators.

Authentic

See Mode

Ballade

An important form of French poetry and music from the later 13th century through the 15th. It characteristically features three stanzas of poetry, each in the musical form AAB. The stanzaic structure of a ballade may consist of anywhere from seven to twelve lines. A typical eight-line stanza has the rhyme scheme ab ab bc bC, where the first four lines are sung to musical elements AA, and the continuation of four lines is sung to B. A one-line textual refrain (C) concludes each stanza. A related form popular in English song writing of the 15th century is the rhyme royal (or rime royal), whose typical seven-line stanza has the rhyme scheme ababbcc.

Bas

Bas instruments were soft instruments appropriate for playing indoors, while haut instruments were loud instruments appropriate for playing out of doors. Haut and bas minstrels specialized in playing such instruments.

Black Void (White Notation)

Modern term describing a notational innovation beginning with English sources of ca. 1400. In a rapidly increasing number of sources after that date musical scribes wrote the heads of notes as black outlines rather than as solid black figures; hence the notes look "void" or "white."

Breve

By name a relatively short note, shorter than a long but longer than a semibreve; its shape was a square. The long represented a beat in the later 12th century, but the breve replaced it in that function over the course of the next hundred years. In the 14th century the semibreve came to represent a beat, and the breve filled the modern bar or measure.

Cadence

A melodic or harmonic gesture that conveys a sense of repose or conclusion at the end of a phrase, section, or full musical composition. Different musical genres, styles, and historical periods have their own characteristic ways of making cadences and of subverting or weakening a perceived drive to a cadence.

Canon

As a liturgical term "canon" refers to the Canon of the mass, an ancient sequence of prayers, beginning "Te igitur," that is said silently by the priest as he prepares for the Communion. As a musical term "canon" may refer to a kind of imitation or to a written rule. In canonic imitation there is the exact duplication of a leading voice by a follower at a given time and pitch interval. In the sense of a rule a "canon" is a written instruction for deriving one or more unnotated voices from a notated part. It may simply explain how to generate the correct, complete melody from what has been notated incompletely or in the form of a puzzle, or it may call for one or more following voices to be generated from the given one.

Cantio

Nonliturgical, that is, secular or devotional, Latin art song, usually monophonic.

Cantus Firmus; Cantus Prius Factus

A previously existing melody that is taken as the structural basis above or around which to compose a new polyphonic composition; also called *vox principalis* or *tenor.*

Cauda

Musical term with two principal meanings. It may refer to an extended vocalization over the first or last syllable of a line of verse, stanza, or full text, as found in some 13th- and 14th-century monophonic and polyphonic conductus and motets. It may also refer to an upward or downward stem on a notehead or in a ligature. The *cauda hirundinis* ("swallow's tail") was an invention of the 14th-century English theorist Robertus Brunham that incorporated two such stems in the shape of an upright or inverted letter V.

Circle–Stem Complex

English mensural notation of the 14th century using upward and downward stems on the lozenge-shaped semibreve, dots of division to separate breve groups, and small circles to separate halves or thirds of a breve. It was used to represent a number of different time signatures and was the notation of choice for the music given to the right hand in the earliest known tablature notation for keyboard in the Robertsbridge Codex.

Clausula

Little snippet of polyphony from the late 12th or early 13th century, composed over a melisma from a musically elaborate mass chant. Its texture was mainly note-against-note counterpoint. It could be embedded in an organum or exist as an independent piece. The texting of the upper voice of the two-voice clausula gave rise to the motet.

Compass

The *ambitus,* that is, the total range of musical notes spanned by a voice part or piece.

Concordance

Another surviving source of a given word, text, or musical composition; the term is useful because it is more neutral with respect to relationships between multiply occurring appearances than words like "version," "variant," or "copy."

Constructivist

Emphasizing formalism and rigorous techniques like proportional designs, canon, imitation, or voice exchange for generating musical textures and large-scale architecture.

Contrafact

An adaptation of a vocal composition in which a new text has been substituted for the original.

Copula

In 12th- and 13th-century organum a technical term for a passage linking the sections with sustained-tone *cantus firmus* to those with a metrically organized *cantus firmus.*

Counterpoint

Polyphony; the term derives from *punctus contra punctum,* note against note, and by extension, melody against melody.

Diastematic

See Neume

Diatonic

A collection of tones epitomized by the white-note scale of the keyboard; any music confined to these tones.

Diminution

The restatement of a single musical line or polyphonic fabric in shorter values (opposite: augmentation). Such diminution is usually proportional, that is, in a fixed ratio like 2:1 or 5:3; chains of proportional diminution and augmentation, such as the series 9:6:4 or 6:4:2:3, may govern the dimensions of large compositions. In respect to musical notation diminution is the capacity of a note to take value away from an adjacent or nearby larger value.

En Mitre

Referring to organ pipes organized by size into the shape of a bishop's miter, that is, like a pyramid or the capital letter "A."

Enchiriadis Treatises

Later 9th-century music theory treatises of Frankish origin.

Estampie

An instrumental dance melody or vocal dance song; the most common form consisted of a series of melodies, each stated twice, with first and second endings shared by all strains that acted as a unifying refrain.

Ferial

A liturgical term relating to weekdays when no feast occurs (opposite: festal).

Foremass

The entrance ceremonies and service of readings that constitute the first half of the mass, to be contrasted with the sacrifice mass, the second half of the service, consisting of the offertory rites, eucharistic prayers, and communion cycle.

Gamut

In medieval music theory the lowest note of the scale, a contraction of gamma-ut. More generally the entire span of tones from bottom to top.

Guidonian Hand

In medieval music theory a diagram of the human hand with a note of the scale marked at each finger joint and tip. This was a teaching tool, named after Guido of Arezzo (fl. 1020s–1030s), that was used by the early 12th century to help memorize the scale and to aid in demonstrating the correct intervals for singers.

Haut

See Bas.

Hemiola

The flexible, dancelike grouping of six musical pulses into two beats of three pulses each or three beats of two pulses each.

Hexachord

In medieval music theory a scale segment of six notes, comprising a single fixed pattern of tones and semitones (T-T-S-T-T) and sung to the syllables Ut, Re, Mi, Fa, Sol, La.

Hocket

Either a texture within a larger musical form or an independent composition, in which a musical line is shared between two voices in rapid alternation, so that each voice part involved in the exchange consists principally of single notes separated by rests.

Imitation

Or "melodic imitation," a technique of polyphonic music involving successive, overlapping statements of a melodic contour by two or more voices.

Isorhythm

Modern term for a repeating scheme of time values in the tenor of a 14th- or 15th-century motet or mass movement. This may be restated in identical values (in the "unipartite" motet) or in proportionally diminished values, such as 2:1 or 9:6:4 (in the "bipartite" motet, "tripartite" motet, and so forth). Over the course of the 14th century the principle was extended to the other voices of the motet ("panisorhythm").

Ligature

A neume encompassing several notes, all sung to the same syllable. In mensural notation a ligature may convey information about the rhythmic values of its notes, depending on its shape and the musical context.

Macaronic

Mixing two or more languages in a single text; in particular, mixing vernacular with Latin in the English carol.

Melisma

An extended vocalization consisting of a sequence of several pitches sung to one syllable.

Mensural

Referring to measured rhythm; in *musica mensurabilis* (measured music), whether monophonic or polyphonic, each note has a fixed durational value. Mensural notation was invented in the 13th century. Mensuration is a consistent set of temporal relationships between note values, like modern meters, and can be specified in modern language as an underlying, repetitive framework or hierarchy of pulses per beat and beats per bar.

Mensuration

See Mensural

Mode

In medieval music theory "mode" refers according to context either to the church modes or to the rhythmic modes. The medieval church modes can be epitomized as a series of eight scales, two for each of the four final pitches D, E, F, and G, one (authentic) extending above the final, the other (plagal) centered on the final. The rhythmic modes were stereotypical rhythmic patterns that dominated the rhythmic language of composed church polyphony around 1200. They were notated with regularly recurring patterns of ligatures.

Monochord

A pedagogical device in medieval music theory for the demonstration of musical intervals and tunings, constructed of a single string stretched between two points with a movable bridge.

Monophony

Music composed of a single line or melody.

Morrow Mass

Not the principal mass of the day, but an additional mass celebrated just preceding the morning chapter meeting that was held some time after Prime in monasteries and collegiate churches.

Musica Mensurabilis

See Mensural

Mutation

A technical feature of medieval sightsinging when using the six solmization syllables (Ut, Re, Mi, etc.). If a melody spans more than six notes, two or more overlapping hexachords must be used to cover it. The shift from one hexachord to another is called mutation.

Neume

Any of the symbols used in the notation of plainchant. If neumes show relative pitch by vertical alignment on the page, they are heightened (intervallic, diastematic). If they do not show relative pitch, they are unheightened (adiastematic).

Offices

The sequence of liturgical services within each day, including the night hours of Vespers, Compline, Matins, and Lauds; the day hours of Prime, Terce, Sext, None; and the principal mass of the day, whose first half, the foremass, is essentially also an office. The main purposes of the offices are to recite the Psalter weekly and to read through the Bible once a year.

Ordinary

A liturgical term referring to those texts that are invariable from day to day in a given service, for example, the Ordinary of the mass. Its opposite is "Proper," referring to those texts that are used only on one particular day.

Organista

A composer or singer of organum; or, an organ player.

Organum (pl. Organa)

General term encompassing the earliest types of polyphonic music from ca. 850 to 1250. By about 1200 "organum" also came to be used in a more specific sense to designate just that kind of two-voice polyphonic texture in which a freely projected voice unfolded above a succession of sustained tones *(organum duplum, organum purum, organum per se);* two or three voices could also participate in more coordinated rhythmic and melodic counterpoint over the held tones *(organum triplum, organum quadruplum).*

Ostinato

A persistently repeated rhythmic or melodic figure.

Partsong

Vocal polyphony consisting of two or more voice parts.

Pes

Literally "foot." In English polyphony of the 13th and 14th centuries a motet voice of tenor function that was either freely composed or perhaps drawn from the realm of popular music, usually featuring chains of melodic couplets (AA BB CC DD etc.) or strict or varied ostinati. Sometimes a *cantus firmus* drawn from plainchant was also labeled a "pes" in an English source, and the repetitive two-voice accompaniment to the Sumer canon is identified as a pes.

Plagal

See Mode

Plainchant; Plainsong

The monophonic melodies of the Catholic liturgy; Gregorian chant of ca. 800 and its later medieval accretions.

Polyphony

Music composed of several simultaneously sounding lines.

Positive

A medium-sized, portable organ that was played with both hands while an assistant worked the bellows.

Precentor

A dignitary of the church ranking just below cantor; he was often the highest ranking practical musician, with authority over the choir and library.

Proper

See Ordinary

Prosa

A word carrying variable meanings, "prosa" most often identifies a musical-poetic addition to the Latin liturgy intended for performance in a location such as after the Alleluia or Gospel at mass, after the first or third Nocturne in the night office of Matins, or in processions. In some medieval manuscripts "prosa" refers to the text of a sequence or identifies what we now call a trope.

Prosula

Text added to preexisting melismatic music as a form of trope.

Rondeau

An important form of French poetry and music from the later 13th century through the 15th. It characteristically features a bipartite refrain (AB) whose music is reused for the verses in the pattern whole refrain, half verse, half refrain, whole verse, whole refrain. If lower case letters are used to represent verses set to refrain melody, then this form can be represented as ABaAabAB. Early rondeaux had two-line refrains, but in the 15th century refrains of three, four, or five lines became popular.

Score

A way of notating polyphonic music so that all the parts are arranged one above the other on separate staves and aligned so that events happening simultaneously are lined up vertically. Score notation was the standard means of notating all polyphony until the mid-13th century and remained in England the normal means of notation for all genres except the motet and its derivatives until well into the 15th century.

Semibreve

A lozenge-shaped note shorter than the breve and longer than the minim. It was used to represent the pulse in 13th-century mensural notation, and in the 14th century it was used to represent the beat.

Solfège; Solmization

A teaching tool attributed to Guido of Arezzo (fl. 1020s–1030s), by which singers learned to sing correctly the intervals of a melody using the six syllables of the hexachord—Ut, Re, Mi, Fa, Sol, La—and the Guidonian hand.

Tenor

See Cantus Firmus

Tetrachord

In medieval music theory a scale segment of four notes, comprising three possible patterns of tones and semitones (T-S-T; S-T-T; T-T-S).

Unheightened

See Neume

Versicle

A short verse or sentence; a single line of poetry or prose. In the liturgy a simple formula in the form of a brief dialogue, consisting of a versicle and response, for example, a statement by a priest and a congregational reply. In musical settings of texts "versicle" can be less ambiguous than "verse" (which could mean "line," "strophe," or "poem") in descriptions of how much text is set to a given phrase or melody. A double versicle is two lines of text, such as a poetic couplet, each set to the same melody, or by extension a repeated short melodic strain whether texted or not.

Vigiles; Vigilatores

Watchmen, usually also with musical abilities and employed as household or civic minstrels; waits.

Virelai

An important form of French poetry and music from the later 13th through the 15th centuries. It characteristically features a refrain (A) that frames three stanzas, each consisting of a couplet set to a repeating strain (bb) and a continuation with new text using the form and music of the refrain (a). Hence the overall musical form is A bba A bba A bba A.

Voice Exchange

A constructivist compositional device extensively used by English composers of the 13th and 14th centuries in conductus, motets, and chant settings of Alleluias. In one period of voice exchange two voices present melodies simultaneously over an accompaniment. Upon repetition of the accompaniment the counterpoint is exchanged between the two voices and restated. This technique is closely related to English rondellus and rota.

Architectural Terms

The Medieval Castle

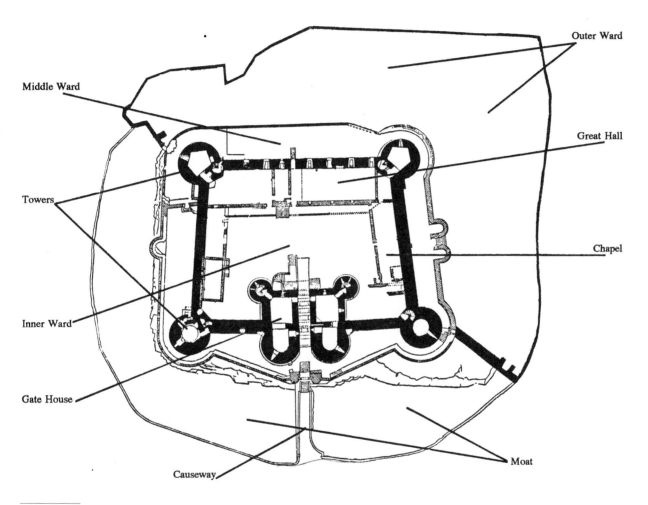

Castle Plan

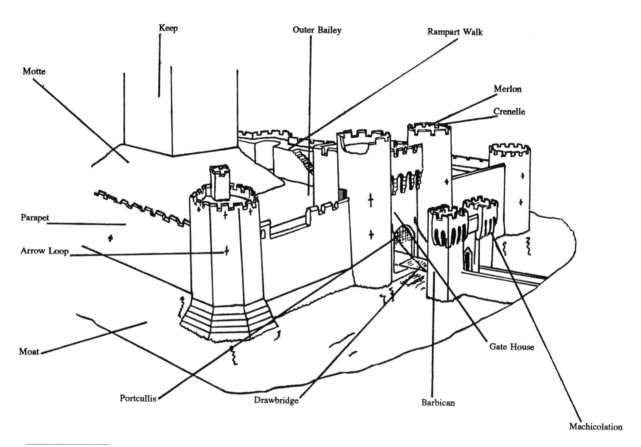

Parts of the Castle

The Medieval Church

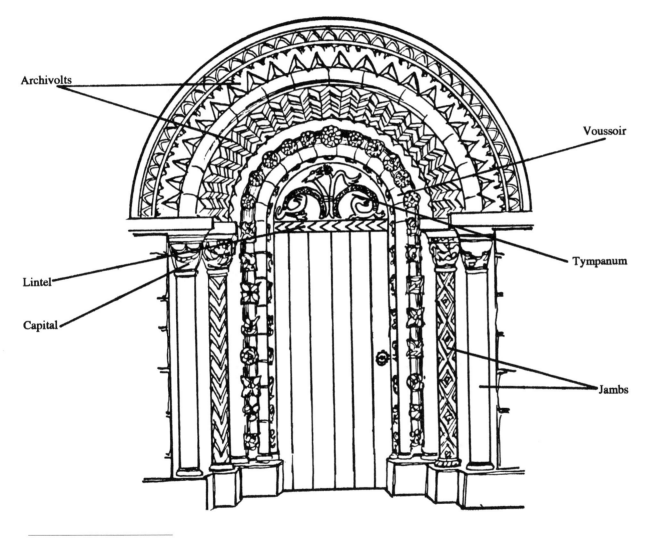

Archivolts

Voussoir

Tympanum

Lintel

Capital

Jambs

Romanesque Church Doorway

Cathedral Plan

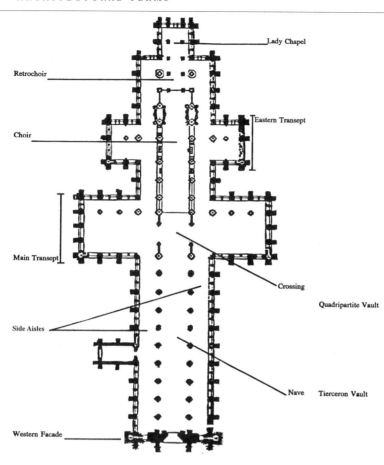

Lady Chapel

Retrochoir

Eastern Transept

Choir

Main Transept

Crossing

Side Aisles

Nave

Western Facade

Cathedral Elevation

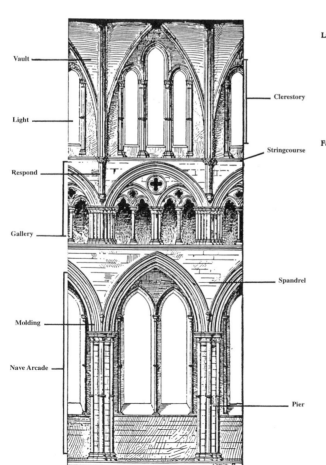

Vault

Clerestory

Light

Stringcourse

Respond

Gallery

Spandrel

Molding

Nave Arcade

Pier

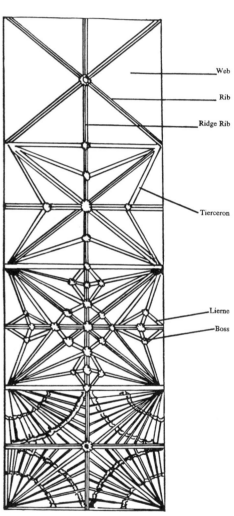

Quadripartite Vault

Web

Rib

Ridge Rib

Tierceron Vault

Tierceron

Lierne Vault

Lierne

Boss

Fan Vault

Gothic Vault Designs

Maps

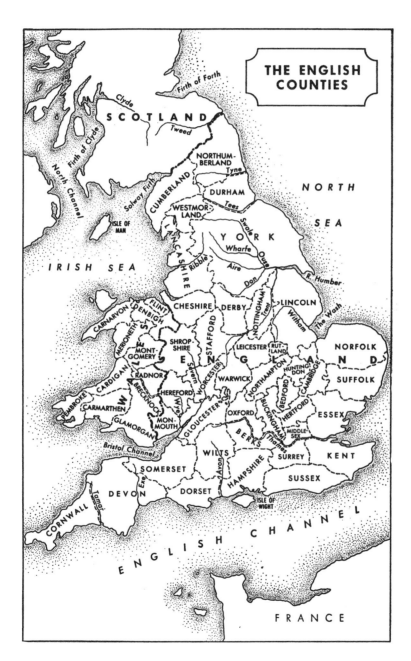

THE ENGLISH
COUNTIES

English Counties. After W.E. Lunt, History of England, *4th ed. (1956).*

Ecclesiastical England in the Middle Ages. After W.E. Lunt, History of England, 4th ed. (1956).

Anglo-Saxon England.
After W.P. Hall, R.G.
Albion, and J. Pope,
A History of England
and the Empire-
Commonwealth, 5th
ed. (1971).

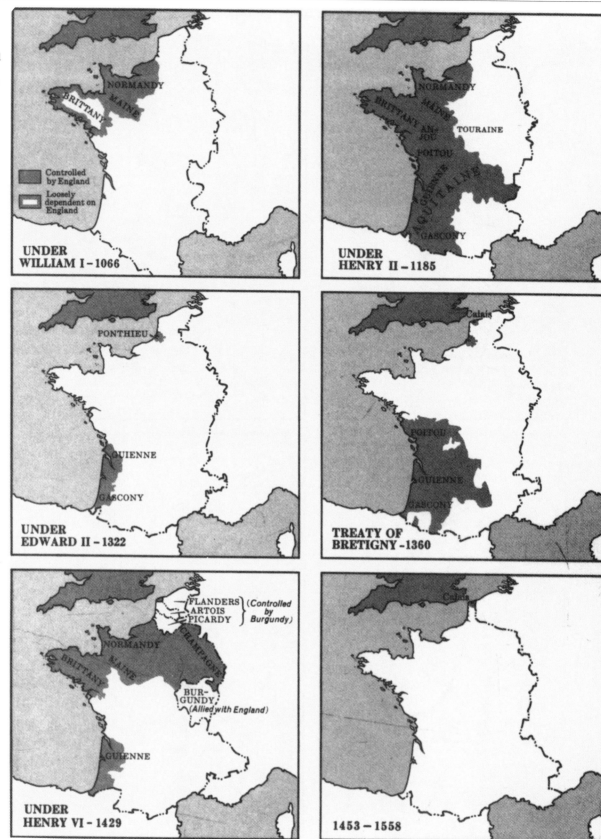

English Holdings in France, 1066–1558. After W.P. Hall, R.G. Albion, and J. Pope, A History of England and the Empire-Commonwealth, *5th ed. (1971).*

*Dominions of Henry
II. After W.E. Lunt,*
History of England,
4th ed. (1956).

DOMINIONS OF HENRY II

Ruled by Henry II directly as King

Held by Henry II as Vassal of the King of France

Held from Henry II by Vassals

Royal Domain of the King of France

Lands other than Angevin held by Vassals of the King of France

Illustrations

Abbreviations

AntJ	*Antiquaries Journal*	*IPMEP*	*Index of Printed Middle English Prose*
ANTS	Anglo-Norman Text Society	*JBAA*	*Journal of the British Archaeological Association*
Archiv	*Archiv für das Studium der neueren Sprachen und Literaturen*	*JEGP*	*Journal of English and Germanic Philology*
		JIH	*Journal of Interdisciplinary History*
ArchJ	*Archaeological Journal*	*JMH*	*Journal of Medieval History*
ASE	*Anglo-Saxon England*	*JWCI*	*Journal of the Warburg and Courtauld Institutes*
ASPR	Anglo-Saxon Poetic Records	*M&H*	*Medievalia et Humanistica*
AUMLA	*Journal of the Australasian Universities Language and Literature Association*	*MÆ*	*Medium Ævum*
		Manual	*A Manual of Writings in Middle English*
BAACT	*British Archaeological Association Conference Transactions*	ME	Middle English
		MLA	British Museum, Department of Medieval and Later Antiquities;
BAR	British Archaeological Reports		Modern Language Association
BIHR	*Bulletin of the Institute of Historical Research*	*MLQ*	*Modern Language Quarterly*
BJRL	*Bulletin of the John Rylands University Library of Manchester*	*MP*	*Modern Philology*
		MRTS	Medieval & Renaissance Texts & Studies (Binghamton; Tempe)
BL	London, British Library		
BN	Paris, Bibliothèque Nationale	*MS*	*Mediaeval Studies*
Bodl.	Oxford, Bodleian Library	n.s.	new series
CBA	Council for British Archaeology	*New CBEL*	*New Cambridge Bibliography of English Literature*
CCSL	Corpus Christianorum Series Latina	*NGD*	*New Grove Dictionary of Music and Musicians*
CEMERS	Center for Medieval and Early Renaissance Studies (Binghamton)	*NM*	*Neuphilologische Mitteilungen*
ChauR	*The Chaucer Review*	o.s.	old (or original) series
CSEL	Corpus Scriptorum Ecclesiasticorum Latinorum	OE	Old English
CUL	Cambridge, University Library	*OED*	*Oxford English Dictionary*
DNB	*Dictionary of National Biography*	*OEN*	*Old English Newsletter*
DownR	*Downside Review*	*PBA*	*Proceedings of the British Academy*
EcHR	*Economic History Review*	*PL*	*Patrologiae Latinae Cursus Completus* (ed. Migne)
EEMF	Early English Manuscripts in Facsimile	*PMLA*	*Publications of the Modern Language Association of America*
EETS	Early English Text Society		
EHR	*English Historical Review*	*PQ*	*Philological Quarterly*
EIC	*Essays in Criticism*	PRO	London, Public Record Office
ES	*English Studies*	REED	Records of Early English Drama
Greenfield and Robinson	Greenfield, Stanley B., and Fred C. Robinson, *A Bibliography of Publications on Old English Literature to the End of 1972*	repr.	reprint(ed)
		RES	*Review of English Studies*
		RPh	*Romance Philology*
HMSO	Her Majesty's Stationery Office	s.s.	supplemental (or special) series
IMEV	*Index of Middle English Verse*	*SAC*	*Studies in the Age of Chaucer*

SB	*Studies in Bibliography*	*TRHS*	*Transactions of the Royal Historical Society*
SP	*Studies in Philology*	*VCH*	*Victoria County History*
SPCK	Society for Promoting Christian Knowledge	*YLS*	*The Yearbook of Langland Studies*
STS	Scottish Text Society		

Medieval England

An Encyclopedia

Abbo of Fleury (ca. 940/45–1004)

Born at Orléans, Abbo was oblate, student, master, and from 988 abbot of Fleury (St. Benoît-sur-Loire), in a period of excellence for that monastery. In 1004 he was killed at La Réole, in Gascony. Praised by contemporaries (e.g., Fulbert of Chartres), Abbo was venerated as a martyr during the Middle Ages; Aimoin wrote his biography (*PL* 139:387–414).

Abbo was trained in the schools of Fleury, Reims, and Paris, and his production stretches over such fields as astronomy and mathematics (e.g., a commentary on the *Calculus* of Victorius of Aquitaine). An active supporter of the Cluniac reform, he opposed the power of the bishops and had a stern adversary in Arnulf of Orléans; the *Apologeticus ad Hugonem et Rodbertum* reflects this aspect of his personality. Several of his letters survive (*PL* 139). Some of his works, such as the excerpts from the Fathers, are lost and some are still unprinted. Abbo wrote a treatise on papal authority *(Excerptum de gestis romanorum pontificum),* a *Collectio canonum (Collection of Canons),* and a work on the *Syllogismi dialectici* (a treatise on logic).

Abbo spent the years 985–87 at the recently established English abbey of Ramsey, where, at the invitation of Dunstan, he wrote the *Passio sancti Eadmundi* (the source of Ælfric's *Life of Edmund*). In the *Quaestiones grammaticales* Abbo answers questions of orthography, morphology, and syntax raised by his English students. One of them, Byrhtferth, acknowledges his indebtedness to Abbo (in the *Enchiridion*) and refers to his works in Oxford, St. John's College 17. An English abbot, Wulfric, asked Abbo to turn a work (perhaps the earliest *Life of Dunstan*) into verse. He wrote acrostics and elaborate poems addressed to Otto III and the pope, one on Ramsey, and three for Dunstan.

Patrizia Lendinara

Bibliography

PRIMARY

Guerreau-Jalabert, A., ed. *Abbonis Floriacensis, Quaestiones grammaticales.* Paris: Les Belles Lettres, 1982; Van de Vyver, A., ed. *Abbonis Floriacensis opera inedita.* Bruges: De Tempel, 1966; Winterbottom, Michael, ed. *Three Lives of English Saints.* Toronto: Pontifical Institute, 1972, pp. 65–87.

SECONDARY

Evans, G.R., and A.M. Penden. "Natural Science and the Liberal Arts in Abbo of Fleury's Commentary on the *Calculus* of Victorius of Aquitaine." *Viator* 16 (1985): 109–27; Gwara, Scott. "Three Acrostic Poems by Abbo of Fleury." *Journal of Medieval Latin* 2 (1992): 203–35; Mostert, M. *The Political Theology of Abbo of Fleury.* Hilversum: Verloren, 1987; Thomson, R.B. "Further Astronomical Material of Abbo of Fleury." *MS* 50 (1988): 671–73.

See also Ælfric; Benedictine Reform; Byrhtferth; Dunstan; Grammatical Treatises; Liturgy and Church Music, History of; *Regularis concordia*

Adrian and Ritheus; Prose *Solomon and Saturn*

Two late OE lists of brief questions and answers, such as existed in other European languages, both earlier and later, with or without naming the interlocutors. These two lists, like some in medieval Latin, are formulaic in presentation ("Tell me . . .; I tell you . . .") but miscellaneous in topic, although the majority of questions demand a literal knowledge of scripture (Who first prophesied? Samuel) or of writings explaining or amplifying scripture (How long did Adam remain in paradise? Thirteen years).

Sometimes the questions have a riddling quality: What man died but was not born and was buried in his mother's womb? Adam, formed of earth (Gen. 2:7). Some items are about the physical world: the composition of the sun (burning stone), its size, where it is at night, why it is red in the evening and morning. Some are moralistic: What is best and worst? Man's word. Although the purpose of these lists was to teach, and they have some association with lists in Latin manuscripts from missionary centers in Europe, they also offer much unusual information about medieval interest and knowledge.

J.E. Cross

Bibliography

Cross, J.E., and Thomas D. Hill, eds. and trans. *The Prose Solomon and Saturn and Adrian and Ritheus.* McMaster Old English Studies and Texts 1. Toronto: University of Toronto Press, 1982 [with commentary and analogues from other European languages].

See also Riddles; *Solomon and Saturn*

Adso of Montier-en-Der (ca. 910/15–992)

Author of a highly influential 10th-century work on the Antichrist. Born of a noble family, oblate in the monastery of Luxeuil, teacher in the monastery of St. Èvre in Toul, Adso arrived at Montier-en-Der in 935, to become its abbot before 968. In 990 he was appointed abbot of St. Bénigne (Dijon); he died on a pilgrimage to the Holy Land in 992.

We know about Adso's life and works from different sources (e.g., *De diversis casibus Dervensis coenobii*). He had a good knowledge of classical literature and was a collector of rare books; a catalogue of his personal library survives. He wrote saints' lives (four of which are mentioned by his biographer) that yield proof of his commitment to the movement of spiritual renewal taking place in France. Adso's life of Frodobert has a verse preface, and two poems precede his life of Mansuetus; he was also asked by Abbo of Fleury to versify the second book of Gregory's *Dialogues,* but this and other poetic works of his do not survive.

Adso owes his renown to the *Epistola ad Gerbergam reginam de ortu et tempore Antichristi,* written between 949 and 954, at the command of Gerberga, queen of the Franks. This work exerted a significant influence on later descriptions of Doomsday and portrayals of Antichrist; it did not follow the *Revelations* of Pseudo-Methodius or the Tiburtine Sibyl, and its main sources were Bede and Haymo of Auxerre. It had immediate success and large diffusion (circulating under the names of Augustine, Alcuin, and others) and underwent several reworkings; several versions are printed by Verhelst. It was well known in England: one OE homily is the first vernacular version of Adso's work, which was also the main source of a 12th-century Latin drama, the *Ludus de Antichristo.*

Patrizia Lendinara

Bibliography

PRIMARY

Verhelst, D., ed. *De ortu et tempore Antichristi necnon et tractatus qui ab eo dependunt.* CCCM 45. Turnhout: Brepols, 1976; *PL* 137:599–686 [*Vita Frodoberti, Vita Mansueti, Vita et miracula Basoli, Vita Bercharii*].

SECONDARY

Konrad, R. *De ortu et tempore Antichristi: Antichristvorstellung und Geschichtsbild des Abtes Adso von Montier-en-Der.* Munich: Kallmünz, 1964; Verhelst, D. "La préhistoire des conceptions d'Adson concernant l'Antichrist." *Revue de théologie ancienne et moderne* 40 (1973): 52–103.

See also Abbo; Bede; Prophecy Literature; Wulfstan

Ælfric (ca. 945–ca. 1015)

Abbot of Eynsham, sometimes called "Grammaticus" ("the grammarian"), the greatest writer of English prose before the Norman Conquest and the leading scholar of his day. His contributions to the literary and religious life of 10th-century England mirror the achievements of his more illustrious predecessors from the 8th and 9th centuries, Bede and King Alfred the Great. Like Bede, whom he often consulted as a source, Ælfric produced a substantial body of homiletic and hagiographic writings. But following the example of King Alfred, Ælfric broke away from Latin, the traditional language of the church, and wrote primarily in English in order to reach a wider audience.

There seems little reason to doubt Ælfric's largely unnoticed autobiographical statement in his *Grammar* that he studied under and was ordained by Dunstan, a key figure in the Benedictine Reform who became archbishop of Canterbury in 960 and who is widely credited with restoring monastic life after its virtual demise by the middle of the 10th century ("If you were to say, 'Who taught you?' I would say 'Dunstan.' 'Who ordained you?' 'He ordained me.'"). If this statement is true, Ælfric's date of birth would almost certainly have to be placed some ten years earlier than the date of 955 given in virtually all other standard biographical references. No doubt surrounds Ælfric's later studies with another leading figure of monastic reform, Æthelwold, at the Benedictine monastery at Winchester. In 987, three years after Æthelwold's death, Ælfric obtained a position as monk and masspriest at Cernel Abbey in what is now Cerne Abbas, Dorset. Within a few years he had achieved a reputation as the preeminent literary figure of the Benedictine revival.

At Cernel Ælfric developed a remarkable and innovative "rhythmical prose" style, admirably suited for oral delivery, that resembles OE verse in its use of paired phrases linked by alliteration but differs from it in matters of tone, style, diction, and metrical constraints. Ælfric avoids, for example, the use of the kenning, *kend heiti, ókend heiti,* and other metaphoric statements commonly associated with OE heroic poetry and strives instead for "ordinary English speech" *(usitatam Anglicam sermocinationem).* Hickes praised Ælfric's prose as *purus, suavis, et regularis* ("pure, smooth, and orderly"), and W.P. Ker hailed Ælfric as "the great master of prose in all its forms." Yet his considerable skills as a prose stylist were undoubtedly of secondary importance to Ælfric, whose central and abiding literary concern (as John Pope has noted) was the instruction of the adult laity, most of whom knew no Latin, in the Christian faith.

Ælfric's seven chief works—two volumes of *Catholic Homilies* or *Sermones catholici,* two additional sets of homilies based in part on his previous writings, *De temporibus anni,* the

Grammar, and the *Lives of Saints*—form a reasonably complete educational program aimed at providing the spiritual instruction Ælfric deemed necessary for salvation. His literary canon builds upon the program of learning instituted by King Alfred a century earlier but differs from that program by virtue of its more tightly focused spiritual emphasis, its greater comprehensiveness, and its stricter accuracy in rendering Latin texts.

Ælfric reveals the impetus for his literary career by quoting in the preface to his first major work Christ's great commission to his disciples "to instruct and teach all people the things that he himself had taught them" (Matt. 28:19–20); Ælfric apparently patterned his life and writings not only upon this injunction but also upon the more dire scriptural text he cites in the same breath, namely that the Lord's servants must themselves face perdition if they fail to warn and exhort the unrighteous (Ezek. 33:8). This divine mandate lends to Ælfric's literary activities a spirit of personal mission and urgency, and this same spirit informs the inchoate program of instruction promulgated by King Alfred, which Ælfric both emulates and augments in his own writings. Ælfric borrows from King Alfred the revolutionary idea of using the vernacular to broaden the reach of instruction to "all people," which in practice meant reaching out to the uneducated majority of his countrymen who knew no Latin.

Yet Ælfric—traditional, conservative, and orthodox by temperament—proved a somewhat reluctant revolutionary. He persistently worried about the appropriateness of making Latin texts generally available to the laity, who might, for example, misconstrue scripture and believe that they might have four wives just as the patriarch Jacob did. Ælfric vowed on several occasions that he would cease from translating lest the pearls of Christ fall into disrespect, yet at the end of his career he apparently accepted the usefulness of his writings and, far from retracting them, conveniently enumerated them and in effect canonized them in the *Letter to Sigeweard.*

In addition to following Alfred's lead in translating, Ælfric turned to other sources of inspiration, such as Augustine's *De catechizandis rudibus* and *De doctrina christiana,* for more detailed guidance in establishing the range of texts and the survey of doctrine needed to fulfill the catechetical dimensions of Christ's commission to his disciples. Evangelical doctrine, therefore, forms the cornerstone of Ælfric's instructional mission, and, to that end, Ælfric composed his first major work, the *Catholic Homilies* (also known as the *Sermones catholici*), which appeared in two separate volumes, issued respectively in 989 and 992. Each set of the *Catholic Homilies* contains a series of 40 sermons arranged according to the calendar of the church year (beginning with Christmas and ending with the second Sunday in Advent) and designed for distribution among the priests of England as preaching texts for alternate years of the liturgical calendar. The texts provide instruction not only in such fundamental topics as the Creed, the Lord's Prayer, the Ten Commandments, the plan for salvation, the story of Christ, and other matters appropriate to the catechumenate, but also in more theologically advanced matters involving patristic exegesis and allied forms of allegorical and typological interpretation of scriptural texts.

Viking attacks, political tumult, the approach of the year 1000, and the disastrous reign of King Æthelred II doubtless contributed to the millenarian concerns voiced in Ælfric's preface to the first series of the *Catholic Homilies.* Yet his writings show less alarm for death at the hands of the Vikings or the coming end of the world (which, Ælfric points out, though soon, might still be distant by human measures of time) than for *gedwyld,* "error." *Gedwyld* for Ælfric meant more particularly religious error, especially the kind spread in unorthodox, apocryphal, or misleading religious writings, such as the popular *Vision of St. Paul* or works prohibited by the Gelasian Decretals, including narratives about the Virgin's birth or a certain *Passio sancti Georgii* that featured fantastic accounts of St. George's seven years of torture, the fragmentation of his body, and his several preliminary deaths and resuscitations.

The *Catholic Homilies* and later writings attempt to provide sound spiritual instruction, free from error and heresy, as weapons for the salvation of the English nation. Ælfric marshals the best patristic authorities available to him, and his corpus of writings offers an epitome of ecclesiastical thought as transmitted through the channels of Carolingian learning and the Benedictine Reform. His translations include the works of Augustine, Gregory the Great, Bede, Jerome, Smaragdus, Isidore, Ambrose, Leo the Great, Cassiodorus, Sulpicius Severus, a version of the *Vitae patrum,* Hilduin of St. Denis, Abbo of Fleury, Donatus, Priscian, a treatise on liturgy by Amalarius, and a host of other sources. Ælfric turns to his patristic authorities, particularly Augustine, Gregory, and Bede, for his exegetical homilies, which compose the great bulk of his *Catholic Homilies,* some 55 or so homilies out of 80, and he uses these and other sources for his other sermons, which include about seventeen saints' lives, expositions of the liturgy, and more thematically diverse works that encompass such general topics as creation and eschatological concerns.

Ælfric refers to the *Catholic Homilies* as a translation from Latin books, sometimes rendered literally but sometimes paraphrased to capture the sense rather than the wording of his source. Recent scholarship confirms Ælfric's enormous debt to the homiliary of Paul the Deacon, who edited and composed nearly 250 homilies at the request of Charlemagne for use throughout the Carolingian Empire. Yet those who closely scrutinize Ælfric's Latin sources now realize that he frequently consults other authorities, evaluates differences, selectively edits, conflates, and condenses to avoid tedium, amplifies to explicate an obscurity, and sometimes so deviates from his sources that his work approaches originality. As Pope has observed, the "thought is scrupulously traditional yet fully digested and feelingly his own" (1967: 150).

Nowhere is this more apparent than in Ælfric's famous *Sermon on the Sacrifice on Easter Day* (*Sermo de sacrificio in die Pascae,* item xv in *Catholic Homilies* II), the first and most controversial text ever printed in OE. Published in 1566 or 1567, Ælfric's sermon arguably marks the beginning of English studies, securing for the study of the English language an importance that had previously been accorded only to the classical languages. Printed by Archbishop Matthew Parker as ancient testimony of the continuity between the religious beliefs of the Protestant reformers and the Anglo-Saxons, particularly with regard to eucharistic teaching, Ælfric's sermon seemingly offered early evidence against the "bodely presence" of Christ in the eucharist or, as later Protestant theologians argued, against the doctrine of transubstantiation.

Although Ælfric's Easter homily raises a number of doctrinal questions, the second set of *Catholic Homilies* does not typically differ from the first by showing a keener interest in these matters of theological controversy. Ælfric instead seems to shift emphasis away from exegesis toward narrative. The second set of *Catholic Homilies,* for example, contains far more narratives of saints' lives, the Bible is more often treated as a story rather than as a text for analysis, and the narrative form itself receives sharper dramatic emphasis through Ælfric's initial and sporadic experiments with rhythmical prose.

Ælfric sustains and strengthens these narrative and stylistic impulses in his third major set of original translations, his *Lives of Saints,* which also contains 40 sermons ordered according to the church calendar, now predominantly cast in rhythmical prose. The set recounts the lives and passions of those saints honored by monks in their Latin services, but Ælfric's English translations make these lives available to a wider, presumably lay audience, including his patron, Æthelweard, who commissioned the work. Ælfric treats Old Testament saints by translating and paraphrasing sections of the book of Kings and Maccabees; he traces the passions of Roman martyrs, such as Julian, Sebastian, and George; and he honors the English saints Alban, Æthelthryth, Swithun, Oswald, and Edmund.

Even if his numerous patristic and hagiographic translations had not survived, Ælfric's reputation would have been secured for posterity solely by the survival of his brilliant biblical translations. He translated or adapted sections of Genesis, Numbers, Joshua, Judges, Kings, Esther, Judith, and Maccabees; his articulate and graceful translations of the pericopes (scriptural readings) that precede many of the *Catholic Homilies* contrast with the more awkward and mundane renderings found in the nearly contemporary West Saxon Gospels. The same ease and clarity of expression also mark Ælfric's other writings, particularly his letters and even his scientific writings, such as the *De temporibus anni,* which deals with astronomy, measures of time, the computation of Easter, and atmospheric phenomena.

Apart from his religious writings directed largely toward the educational needs of the laity, Ælfric's educational program also provided basic instructional texts for the study of Latin, presumably for future clerics, though here too the importance of the vernacular makes itself felt: Ælfric's is the first Latin grammar written in English, and his short conversation piece for boys to practice their Latin, the *Colloquy,* survives in one manuscript with a continuous interlinear English gloss. In his *Grammar* Ælfric translates and simplifies the *Excerptiones de Prisciano* (an intermediate grammar) and augments it with excerpts from Isidore's *Etymologiae,* biblical quotations, and a collection of paradigms in order to make grammar accessible to younger pupils.

In 1005 Ælfric was chosen to be the first abbot at Eynsham Monastery, about fifteen miles outside of Oxford. There he remembered his former teacher by composing a life of Æthelwold in Latin, and he also wrote a guide for his monks by abridging Æthelwold's *De consuetudine monachorum.* Other writings from this period include letters and homilies, such as *De creatore et creatura* and *De sex aetatibus mundi,* as well as reworkings of individual homilies and earlier collections of homilies. None of his works can be securely dated after about 1010, and he may have died between 1010 and 1020. The success of Ælfric's educational mission can be partially measured by the large number of surviving Anglo-Saxon manuscripts that preserve his writings; these manuscripts bear witness to the esteem of his contemporaries and to those scribes and scholars who continued to copy his writings for the next 150 years.

Theodore Leinbaugh

Bibliography

PRIMARY

Belfour, Algernon O., ed. and trans. *Twelfth-Century Homilies in MS. Bodley 343.* EETS o.s. 137. London: Kegan Paul, Trench, Trübner, 1909; Crawford, S.J., ed. *The Old English Version of the Heptateuch, Ælfric's Treatise on the Old and New Testament and His Preface to Genesis.* EETS o.s. 160. London: Oxford University Press, 1922; Godden, Malcolm, ed. *Ælfric's Catholic Homilies: The Second Series.* EETS s.s. 5. London: Oxford University Press, 1979; Pope, John C., ed. *Homilies of Ælfric: A Supplementary Collection.* EETS o.s. 259, 260. London: Oxford University Press, 1967–68; Skeat, Walter W., ed. *Ælfric's Lives of Saints.* EETS o.s. 76, 82, 94, 114. London: Trübner, 1881–1900. Repr. in 2 vols. London: Oxford University Press, 1966; Thorpe, Benjamin, ed. *The Homilies of the Anglo-Saxon Church: The First Part, Containing the Sermones Catholici, or Homilies of Ælfric, in the Original Anglo-Saxon, with an English Version.* 2 vols. London: Richard & John E. Taylor, 1844–46. Repr. New York: Johnson Reprint, 1971.

SECONDARY

Clemoes, Peter A.M. "The Chronology of Ælfric's Works." In *The Anglo-Saxons: Studies in Some Aspects of Their History and Culture Presented to Bruce Dickins,* ed. Peter A.M. Clemoes. London: Bowes & Bowes, 1959, pp. 212–47; Corrected repr. *The Chronology of Ælfric's Works. OEN Subsidia* 5. Binghamton: CEMERS, 1980; Clemoes, Peter A.M. "Ælfric." In *Continuations and Beginnings: Studies in Old English Literature,* ed. E. Stanley. London: Nelson, 1966, pp. 176–209; Cross, J.E. "Ælfric—Mainly on Memory and Creative Method in Two Catholic Homilies." *SN* 41 (1969): 135–55; Hill, Joyce. "Ælfric and Smaragdus." *ASE* 21 (1992): 203–37; Hurt, James. *Ælfric.* New York: Twayne, 1972; Law, Vivien. "Anglo-Saxon England: Ælfric's *Excerptiones de arte grammatica anglice." Histoire épistémologie langage* 9 (1987): 47–71; Leinbaugh, Theodore H. "Ælfric's *Sermo de sacrificio in die Pascae:* Anglican Polemic in the Sixteenth and Seventeenth Centuries." In *Anglo-Saxon*

Scholarship: The First Three Centuries, ed. Carl Berkhout and Milton McC. Gatch. Boston: Hall, 1982, pp. 51–68; Leinbaugh, Theodore H. "The Sources for Ælfric's Easter Sermon: The History of the Controversy and a New Source." *N&Q* n.s. 33 (1986): 294–311; Reinsma, Luke M. *Ælfric: An Annotated Bibliography.* New York: Garland, 1987 [excellent bibliographic study]; Smetana, Cyril L. "Ælfric and the Early Medieval Homiliary." *Traditio* 15 (1959): 163–204; Szarmach, Paul E. "Ælfric As Exegete: Approaches and Examples in the Study of the *Sermones catholici.*" In *Hermeneutics and Medieval Culture,* ed. Patrick J. Gallacher and Helen Damico. Albany: SUNY Press, 1989, pp. 237–47; Wilcox, Jonathan, ed. *Ælfric's Prefaces.* Durham Medieval Texts 9. Durham: Jasprint, 1994; Zettel, Patrick H. "Saints' Lives in Old English: Latin Manuscripts and Vernacular Accounts: Ælfric." *Peritia* 1 (1982): 17–37.

See also Æthelred II; Æthelwold; Alfred; Benedictine Reform; Dunstan; Fathers of the Church; Grammatical Treatises; Hagiography; Monasticism; Parker; Paul the Deacon; Scientific and Medical Writings; Sermons; Translation; Wulfstan

Ælfric Bata (fl. early 11th century)

Three colloquies or dialogues found in Oxford, St. John's College 154, are assigned, by their respective rubrics, to Ælfric Bata. From their content it is possible to infer that he was a monk and a disciple of Ælfric (possibly at Eynsham, after 1005). He taught in the school of an unidentified monastic center, perhaps at Canterbury, in the early 11th century. A certain Æ.B. is mentioned in the *Vita Dunstani* written by Osbern and in a colophon on fol. 117 of BL Cotton Tiberius A.iii.

Æ.B.'s colloquies belong to the tradition of scholastic colloquies (a teaching tool popular in the British Isles), which originally described the daily routine of a lay schoolboy. Their scheme was reworked to meet the needs of the oblates and their content reshaped to describe, albeit inconsistently, the everyday life of an English school. Though they apparently portray lively scenes of school life, these texts are actually stereotyped set pieces, full of the Graecisms and neologisms that characterize a share of Anglo-Latin literary production. Æ.B.'s third colloquy is an enlarged version of the *Colloquy* written by Ælfric: it shows several additions, stemming from Æ.B. He adds long lists of names of animals, trees, and so on drawn from Ælfric's *Glossary,* but his reworking spoils the grace and balance of the original. Another colloquy found in the Oxford manuscript might also be a work by Æ.B. The first three colloquies have occasional OE glosses, printed by Napier and Stevenson-Lindsay. The attribution of further works (e.g., the OE gloss on the *Regularis concordia*) to Æ.B. rests on no firm ground.

Patrizia Lendinara

Bibliography

PRIMARY

Napier, Arthur S., ed. *Old English Glosses, Chiefly Unpublished.* Oxford: Clarendon, 1900. Repr. Hildesheim: Olms, 1969; Stevenson, William Henry, and W.M. Lindsay, eds. *Early Scholastic Colloquies.* Oxford: Clarendon, 1929.

SECONDARY

Lapidge, Michael. "The Hermeneutic Style in Tenth Century Anglo-Latin Literature." *ASE* 4 (1975): 67–111; Lendinara, Patrizia. "Il *Colloquio* di Ælfric e il colloquio di Ælfric Bata." In *"feor ond neah."* Palermo: STASS, 1983, pp. 173–249.

See also Ælfric; Anglo-Latin Literature to 1066; Glosses; Grammatical Treatises; Schools

Æthelberht (d. 616/18)

King of Kent, he probably came to the throne in 589–93 and reigned for about 25 years. His fame rests on two acts: in 597 he accepted into his realm Augustine of Canterbury, Gregory the Great's missionary to the English, and thus permitted the reestablishment of the European church's direct links with England after these had largely been broken in the 5th century. And then, undoubtedly under the influence of Augustine and his associates, Æthelberht issued the first collection of Anglo-Saxon laws (inaccurately termed a "code"). This linked him with other Germanic rulers, who, in issuing collections of laws, placed themselves in the same tradition as the great imperial rulers of Rome, such as Theodosius and Justinian.

Unlike his continental counterparts Æthelberht issued his laws in the vernacular, not in Latin. The laws survive only in a 12th-century transcript, the so-called *Textus Roffensis,* and may have suffered omissions and amendments with the passage of time. As they stand, they lay down a scale of payments for injuries suffered by various classes of people in Kent, placing the king and the bishop at the head of the society by according them the highest level of compensation. This suggests that Æthelberht understood that an association with Christianity could enhance his own power. He was baptized and even received a letter from Pope Gregory, a copy of which Bede recorded in his *Ecclesiastical History.*

Æthelberht's power appears to have been considerable, made possible by his lengthy reign (though the regnal dates of 560 to 616 mentioned by Bede probably record his lifespan). Bede lists him as the third of the seven kings who exercised control over the kingdoms south of the Humber; his influence certainly seems to have extended to the East Saxons and East Anglia, and he came to be rivaled only by his later contemporary Rædwald of East Anglia (possibly the king associated with the Sutton Hoo ship burial).

Æthelberht's receptivity to Christianity and to the idea of issuing a collection of laws may have been encouraged by the links Kent seems to have had in the 6th century with the continental Frankish realms, evidenced by the style of archaeological artifacts that have been found in Kent. The Merovingian rulers of Gaul may even have claimed hegemony over Kent through the marriage of Æthelberht with Bertha, daughter of Charibert, king of Paris. She brought her own bishop, Liudhard, with her to the Kentish capital of Canterbury, where an old church of apparently Roman foundation dedicated (or rededicated) to St. Martin of Tours was put back into use. Though Æthelberht's son, Eadbald, initially rejected Christianity, the religion suffered only a temporary setback, as he subsequently was converted. Canterbury remains to this day the seat of the (now Anglican) primate of all England.

David A.E. Pelteret

Bibliography

PRIMARY

Attenborough, F.L., ed. and trans. *The Laws of the Earliest English Kings.* Cambridge: Cambridge University Press, 1922; Colgrave, Bertram, and R.A.B. Mynors, eds. and trans. *Bede's Ecclesiastical History of the English People.* Oxford: Clarendon, 1969, pp. 72–79, 110–15, 134–35, and 148–51.

SECONDARY

Brooks, Nicholas. "The Creation and Early Structure of the Kingdom of Kent." In *The Origins of Anglo-Saxon Kingdoms,* ed. Steven Bassett. London: Leicester University Press, 1989, pp. 55–74; Kirby, D.P. *The Earliest English Kings.* London: Unwin Hyman, 1991; Wood, Ian N. "Frankish Hegemony in England." In *The Age of Sutton Hoo: The Seventh Century in North-Western Europe,* ed. Martin O.H. Carver. Woodbridge: Boydell, 1992, pp. 235–41; Yorke, Barbara. *Kings and Kingdoms of Early Anglo-Saxon England.* London: Seaby, 1990.

See also Augustine of Canterbury; Bede; Bretwald; Conversion of the Anglo-Saxons; Law, Anglo-Saxon

Æthelflæd, Lady of the Mercians (d. 918)

Daughter of Alfred of Wessex and sister of his successor, Edward the Elder; one of the few medieval women who ruled a kingdom. Other women acted as regents for underage sons; Æthelflæd had no son, and from the death of her husband, Æthelræd, lord of the Mercians, in 911, until her own death she apparently controlled Mercia by herself. During these years she conducted the defense against Viking attacks, building fortifications in the northwest against incursions from the Irish Sea and in the northeast against English Viking settlements. She was responsible for campaigns that recovered Leicester and Derby from Viking rule, and her military power was such that the Danish settlers at York sought her as their "lord" and the Welsh kings submitted to her. Like a king she granted land by charter in her own name.

This extraordinary personal rule was a continuation of power she had possessed and exercised during her husband's lifetime; after 900 her name was already associated with his in joint grants of land. Behind her active role lies the prominence of earlier Mercian queens, growing since the 8th century. These earlier women, however, provide no direct parallel, since the political situation of the late 9th and early 10th centuries was crucial to her larger role. Her marriage sealed an important alliance between Mercia and Wessex in the face of an acute and continuing Viking threat, an alliance more nearly one of equals than indicated in the extant West Saxon sources; Mercian sensitivities were respected. Æthelflæd's situation was unique: the personification of the alliance, a partner with her brother, and heir to a Mercian tradition. On her death a section of the Mercian nobility attempted to make her daughter Ælfwyn their ruler, but Edward marched in and Wessex dominated the future of Mercia. The peculiar conjunction of tradition and circumstance that had elevated Æthelflæd was not heritable.

Pauline Stafford

Bibliography

Stafford, Pauline. "Charles the Bald, Judith and England." In *Charles the Bald,* ed. Margaret Gibson, Janet Nelson, and David Ganz. Oxford: BAR, 1981, pp. 137–51; Stafford, Pauline. "The King's Wife in Wessex 800–1066." *Past and Present* 91 (May 1981): 3–27; Stafford, Pauline. *Queens, Concubines, and Dowagers: The King's Wife in the Early Middle Ages.* Athens: University of Georgia Press; London: Batsford, 1983; Wainwright, Frederick T. "Æthelflæd, Lady of the Mercians." In *Scandinavian England: Collected Papers,* ed. H.P.R. Finberg. Chichester: Phillimore, 1975, pp. 305–24. [Stafford, "King's Wife," and Wainwright are reprinted in *New Readings on Women in Old English Literature,* ed. H. Damico and A.H. Olsen. Bloomington: Indiana University Press, 1989, pp. 56–78 and 44–55.]

See also Alfred; Heptarchy; Queens; Vikings; Women

Æthelred II (968/69?–1016; r. 978–1016)

Became king after his stepbrother, Edward, was murdered. Æthelred, who was then no more than twelve, can hardly be held responsible for the regicide. Initially the administration of the country proceeded as before; only in the 990s do Æthelred's land grants and the rise of new regional leaders suggest that he was gaining independence. But then an upsurge in Scandinavian incursion was met by a policy of buying off the attackers, a strategy that arguably may have worked for a time. Ten thousand pounds was paid out in 991 after a skirmish made memorable in the OE poem *The Battle of Maldon,* in which Ealdorman Byrhtnoth was killed.

Æthelred tried to take the initiative against the marauders, for instance, by attacking Strathclyde and the Isle of Man. On the other hand he seems to have instigated the St. Brice's Day massacre of Danes on 13 November 1002, which may well have sparked retaliatory raids by Swein of Denmark. Scandinavian attacks of increasing frequency over the next decade were met by large disbursements of silver. Internal tensions were almost inevitable, especially since unitary kingship was a relatively recent phenomenon in England. Wulfnoth Cild, the South Saxon, rebelliously harried the south coast in 1009; in 1015 Thorkell the Tall, a Danish war chief, after supporting Æthelred for a time, swung his support to Cnut. The ealdorman of Mercia, Eadric Streona ("Grasper"), vilified in the sources for his treachery, tried to maintain his family interests in the Midlands by alternately supporting Æthelred and Cnut.

Æthelred tried to shore up his power by marrying Emma, daughter of Richard II, duke of Normandy, and by marrying three of his daughters to local leaders, but by 1012 the country was in disarray. After Christmas in 1013 the king fled to Normandy; only following the death of Swein, some six weeks later, did the Anglo-Saxon leadership permit him to return as king. He lived but two more years, and even those were marred by the rebellion of his son, Edmund Ironside.

The two greatest vernacular prose stylists of the Anglo-Saxon era, Ælfric of Eynsham and Wulfstan, archbishop of York, were his contemporaries. The writings of the savant Byrhtferth and some fine Anglo-Saxon illuminated manuscripts were also products of his reign, as were the four great codices of OE poetry. The very size of the *heregeld,* the tax levied to pay the Scandinavian marauders, points to a wealthy and administratively well organized kingdom.

Paradoxically this high culture has fostered a negative assessment of the reign, largely through such works as Wulfstan's powerful sermon "To the English," outlining the evils of the day, and the Anglo-Saxon Chronicle, whose compiler had the benefit of hindsight. Post-Conquest sources sealed Æthelred's reputation, one of them giving him the punning nickname of *Unræd,* "Ill-Counsel," from which the modern English sobriquet of "Unready" derives. Only in recent years has a close examination of less emotive sources, such as his numerous charters and his coinage, permitted a more balanced appraisal of his reign.

David A.E. Pelteret

Bibliography

Hill, David, ed. *Ethelred the Unready.* BAR Brit. Ser. 59. Oxford: BAR, 1978; Keynes, Simon. *The Diplomas of King Æthelred "The Unready" 978–1016: A Study in Their Use as Evidence.* Cambridge: Cambridge University Press, 1980; Whitelock, Dorothy, ed. *English Historical Documents.* Vol. 1: *c. 500–1042.* 2d ed. London: Eyre Methuen; New York: Oxford University Press, 1979 [contains the relevant portions of the Anglo-Saxon Chronicle and "The Sermon of the Wolf to the English"].

See also Ælfric; Anglo-Saxon Chronicle; *Battle of Maldon;* Byrhtferth; Cnut; Edward the Confessor; Emma; Swein; Wulfstan

Æthelstan (d. 939; r. 924–39)

King of Wessex, Mercia, and—by the time of his death—of all England. The son, probably illegitimate, of Edward the Elder, he was an early favorite of his father and his grandfather Alfred the Great. Raised at the court of Æthelræd of Mercia and his wife, Æthelstan's aunt Æthelflæd, he may have participated with his father and Æthelflæd in the military operations that laid the foundations for the extension of West Saxon authority throughout England.

Crowned on 4 September 925, following his father's death in 924, Æthelstan's reign was devoted to gaining the submission of the independent princes of the Scandinavian north and the Celts and Britons of the western regions. Combining force, threats of force, and diplomacy, his tactics proved successful. His imperialistic policy culminated in a great victory at Brunanburh in 937, over a coalition of the kings of Scotland and Strathclyde and the Norse claimant to the Northumbrian throne, Olaf Guthfrithsson. His charters asserted, with justification, that he was "king of the English and ruler of all Britain." This theme of unifying the English kingdoms and peoples was further reflected in his assemblies. By bringing local interests and leaders together he weakened the provincialism that had previously impeded efforts toward the consolidation of the English kingdoms.

Through marriage alliances Æthelstan established contacts with a number of princes on the Continent; five of his sisters married royal figures, including Charles the Simple, king of the West Franks, and Otto, son of Henry the Fowler of the East Franks and future emperor. On at least one occasion he sent English troops to France to support the cause of Louis d'Outremer, son of the murdered Charles the Simple, who had found sanctuary in England following his father's death. Æthelstan died 27 October 939 at Gloucester. Apparently unmarried and childless, he was succeeded by his brother Edmund.

Miles Campbell

Bibliography

Stenton, F.M. *Anglo-Saxon England.* Oxford History of England 2. 3d ed. Oxford: Oxford University Press, 1971, pp. 539–57; Thorpe, Benjamin, ed. *Ancient Laws and Institutes of England.* London: Eyre & Spottiswoode, 1840; Whitelock, Dorothy. "The Dealings of the Kings of England with Northumbria in the Tenth and Eleventh Centuries." In *The Anglo-Saxons: Studies in Some Aspects of Their History and Culture Presented to Bruce Dickins,* ed. Peter Clemoes. London: Bowes & Bowes, 1959, pp. 70–88.

See also Battle of Brunanburh; Heptarchy; Vikings

Æthelweard (d. ca. 998)

Æthelweard was ealdorman of the western provinces; his charter signatures begin in 973 and end in 998, presumably not long before his death. In later years his signature heads the list as senior ealdorman. He was descended from Æthelred I, king of Wessex 865–71, and was thus a kinsman of Æthelred II (the Unready). His sister Ælfgifu was for a time the wife of King Eadwig. In common with his son Æthelmær, who founded monasteries at Cerne (987) and Eynsham (1005), he was a supporter of the Benedictine Reform and politically as well as ecclesiastically was of the same faction as Bishop Æthelwold of Winchester. William of Malmesbury believed that he founded Pershore Abbey, but this is not corroborated.

Æthelweard and Æthelmær were both patrons of the homilist Ælfric: an augmented copy of the first series of *Catholic Homilies* was prepared for Æthelweard, he commissioned Ælfric to translate parts of the Old Testament, and Ælfric's *Lives of Saints*—essentially a monastic collection—was written to meet the devotional needs of father and son; the life of Thomas was included at Æthelweard's request. Æthelweard is also famed as the author of a Latin "translation" of the Anglo-Saxon Chronicle, dedicated to his kinswoman Matilda, abbess of Essen and granddaughter of Emperor Otto I. Æthelweard's chronicle ends at 975; its source is not identical with any extant version of the Anglo-Saxon Chronicle, and it is consequently important for the history of the Chronicle, as well as for information that is not found elsewhere. It follows 10th-century Anglo-Latin fashion in being written in hermeneutic Latin, but there are features of the style that are distinctively Æthelweard's. An attempt has also been made to link Æthelweard's family with the early history of the Exeter Book, a major manuscript anthology of OE poetry.

Joyce Hill

Bibliography

PRIMARY

Campbell, A., ed. *The Chronicle of Æthelweard.* London: Nelson, 1962.

SECONDARY

Lapidge, Michael. "The Hermeneutic Style in Tenth-Century Anglo-Latin Literature." *ASE* 4 (1975): 67–111; van Houts, E. "Women and the Writing of History in the Early Middle Ages: The Case of Abbess Mathilda of Essen and Æthelweard." *Early Medieval Europe* 1 (1992): 53–68; Winterbottom, Michael. "The Style of Æthelweard." *MÆ* 36 (1967): 101–18.

See also Ælfric; Æthelred II; Æthelwold; Anglo-Latin Literature to 1066; Anglo-Saxon Chronicle; Benedictine Reform; Exeter Book

Æthelwold of Winchester (ca. 904/09–984)

Influential monastic teacher and administrator, and a principal initiator of the English Benedictine revival of the second half of the 10th century. Born at Winchester perhaps between 904 and 909, Æthelwold passed several years, probably the late 920s and much of the 930s, at the court of King Æthelstan (924–39), enjoying the royal favor that was to characterize his career. Sometime between 934 and 939, in company with Dunstan, he was ordained priest by Ælfheah, bishop of Winchester. Æthelwold subsequently studied with Dunstan at Glastonbury Abbey, where he became a monk and was later appointed *decanus* (a position of authority over other monks). Desiring to experience reformed continental Benedictine practice at first hand, Æthelwold was prevented from traveling overseas by King Eadred (946–55), who instead appointed him (ca. 954) abbot of the derelict monastery of Abingdon, which Æthelwold restored energetically: he personally participated in the building work, sustaining serious bodily injury in the process. From Abingdon he sent the monk Osgar to observe Benedictinism as practiced at Fleury, and he summoned to Abingdon monks from Corbie who provided instruction in liturgical chant. Attention to continental models continued to mark Æthelwold's later career.

In 963 Æthelwold became bishop of Winchester, an office he held until his death and in which he made a profound impact upon contemporary religious life. More severe than his fellow reformers Dunstan and Oswald, he swiftly (in 964) expelled the secular clergy resident at his cathedral and at New Minster, Winchester, and replaced them with monks. Subsequently he founded or refounded monasteries at several locations, notably Peterborough (966), Ely (970), and Thorney (972). He worked in close harmony with King Edgar (957–75), whose tutor he had been and whose royal palace stood close to Æthelwold's cathedral. At the request of Edgar and his queen, Ælfthryth, Æthelwold translated the Rule of St. Benedict into OE. He was chiefly responsible for compiling the Latin document known as the *Regularis concordia,* aimed at standardizing religious observance in the English monasteries and prompted by a council convened by King Edgar at Winchester sometime between ca. 970 and ca. 973. Æthelwold is justifiably believed to have been the author of a vernacular account of the monastic revival known as "King Edgar's Establishment of Monasteries," which he probably intended to serve as the preface to his translation of the Benedictine Rule.

Æthelwold's work at Winchester included the rebuilding of the cathedral, which was equipped with a large organ remarkable for its time. He was responsible for reform of the liturgy and may have composed offices and prayers that survive in service books of his own time and later. Under Æthelwold Winchester became a major center of manuscript production, its most sumptuous accomplishment being the Benedictional made for Æthelwold himself by the scribe Godeman. A deeply learned man, Æthelwold presided over a monastic school at Winchester whose most distinguished students included his biographers, the prolific writers Wulfstan of Winchester and Ælfric. His students' work ensured the continuation of Æthelwold's influence beyond his death on 1 August 984. He was buried in the crypt of Winchester Cathedral and translated to the choir in 996.

Timothy Graham

Bibliography

PRIMARY

Winterbottom, Michael, ed. *Three Lives of English Saints.* Toronto: Pontifical Institute, 1972 [includes the lives of Æthelwold by Wulfstan and Ælfric]; Wulfstan of Winchester. *The Life of St Æthelwold.* Ed. Michael Lapidge and Michael Winterbottom. Oxford: Clarendon, 1991.

SECONDARY

Gneuss, Helmut. "The Origin of Standard Old English and Æthelwold's School at Winchester." *ASE* 1 (1972): 63–83; Gretsch, Mechthild. "Æthelwold's Translation of the *Regula Sancti Benedicti* and Its Latin Exemplar." *ASE* 3 (1974): 125–51; Lapidge, Michael. "Three Latin Poems from Æthelwold's School at Winchester." *ASE* 1 (1972): 85–137; Lapidge, Michael. "The Hermeneutic Style in Tenth-Century Anglo-Latin Literature." *ASE* 4 (1975): 67–111, esp. 85–90; Whitelock, Dorothy. "The Authorship of the Account of King Edgar's Establishment of Monasteries." In *Philological Essays: Studies in Old and Middle English Literature in Honour of Herbert Dean Meritt,* ed. James L. Rosier. The Hague: Mouton, 1970, pp. 125–36; Yorke, Barbara, ed. *Bishop Æthelwold: His Career and Influence.* Woodbridge: Boydell, 1988.

See also Ælfric; Benedictine Reform; Benedictional of Æthelwold; Dunstan; New Minster Charter; Oswald; *Regularis concordia;* Winchester; "Winchester School"

Agincourt Carol

The best known of all English carols (also called the Agincourt Song), this composition celebrates the victory of Henry V at Agincourt in 1415 and was probably written shortly thereafter. It survives in two of the most important collections of 15th-century carols, the Trinity Roll (Cambridge, Trinity College O.3.58) and the Egerton Manuscript (BL Egerton 3307). Reference is made to the siege of Harfleur, success on the field at Agincourt, and the return to London in triumph with hostages. As is often the case, this carol mixes two languages. The *burden,* or framing refrain, is in Latin ("Deo gratias Anglia, redde pro victoria"), and the five strophes of verse are in English ("Owre Kynge went forth to Normandy," etc.). Also as in a number of other carols, there are in fact two settings of the burden. These are presumably to be sung together, one after the other, in alternation with the verses. The first begins in unison and expands to two voices while the second is for three voices throughout. The verse is for two voices, with a memorable tune in the lower part. This tune has been retexted and reharmonized for congregational singing in some modern Protestant hymnals, where it is identified as "Deo gratias."

Peter M. Lefferts

Bibliography

Greene, Richard L. *The Early English Carols.* 2d ed. Oxford: Clarendon, 1977 [text only]; Stevens, John. *Mediaeval Carols.* 2d ed. Musica Britannica 4. London: Stainer & Bell, 1958 [text and music].

See also Carol; Henry V

Agriculture and Field Systems

The wealth that made the Anglo-Saxon kingdoms so attractive to Vikings and Normans was largely derived from the fruits of a fertile countryside already well cultivated and amply exploited. Almost all types of crops to be grown by English husbandmen (farmers) during the medieval centuries were already known to the Anglo-Saxons. The importance of wheat, barley, rye, beans, and peas is reflected in a large number of OE place-names (e.g., Wheatley or Benacre); only oats are poorly represented in the toponymic record.

Similarly the range of domestic animals, though not their breeds, would have been familiar to farmers 500 years later, and indeed today; pigs, oxen for the plow, sheep whose wool earned much wealth in foreign exchange, and horses, bred by magnates perhaps more as status symbols and for warfare than for plowing. Only the large flocks of goats (with no less than 13,400 enumerated on demesne lands in southwestern England in Domesday Book) would have been unfamiliar to a later farmer transported back to the 10th or 11th century.

However, the ways in which husbandmen arranged and deployed these familiar crops and animals on the ground differed greatly from one part of England to another. The only field system studied in much detail for the Anglo-Saxon period is the Midland System, whose rhythms and institutions were to dominate innumerable communities in a broad swath across the middle of England. Here the land of each village came to be divided into either two or three large prairielike fields, each used in turn for crops and then for common grazing. If, as scholars now believe, the system was a late Saxon innovation, necessitated by the diminution of rough pasture through reclamation so plowed land had to double up with grazing, its introduction reveals an early pressure on resources.

Developments after the Norman Conquest largely took the form of adjustments to combinations of the types of crops and livestock already mentioned; changes in emphasis, not radical new departures. Did growth in population to its peak around 1300 bring improvements in land use? Certainly the cultivated area, already extensive by 1066, was pushed forward. Unlike the great frontiers for colonization found on the Continent, attractive sites for reclamation were relatively restricted. They tended to be on poorer soils, a reason for a significant increase in the growing of oats, a tolerant crop. Oats were not grown extensively in Anglo-Saxon times (unless the paleobotanical and place-name records deceive), and yet by 1300 there are many references to them, both on demesne lands and on peasants' farms. But the increasing use, on poor soils, of a crop yielding coarse fare and little food per acre can hardly be described as an improvement. It was conservative adaptation of a kind seen in other areas of husbandry.

Within the territory of the Midland field system there is no evidence of any major transformation from two to three fields, despite the increased cropped acreage such a change would have secured. The reason seems to be that two-field farmers knew that to push the land too hard would have diminished grain yields. The significant decline in goat keeping between 1066 and 1300 may be related to the need to conserve pasture and woodland, both scarce resources in some regions. Charters specifically ban goats as destructive; John Leland commented in the early 16th century on the connection between goats and the disappearance of woodland.

To say that no radical new departure in land use can be observed between 1066 and 1300 understates the vitality and local variation of agriculture and field systems. The desire for improvement is reflected, on the best-run demesne farms, in high standards of traditional husbandry. Much attention went to such details as weeding, crop choice, and the culling of sickly animals. It is difficult to believe that peasants did not strive for greater productivity within the restraints imposed by chronic shortages of capital and livestock, as they came under increasing financial pressures from landlords and the king.

Two examples of regional variation must suffice. On the poor sandy soils of the East Anglian Breckland wheat was grown hardly at all; a contemporary poem reflecting on high living at Peterborough Abbey ridicules the region as stripped of wheat by Satan. The main local grains were rye for bread, barley as a cash crop. By contrast farmers only 25 miles away on the rich coastlands of eastern Norfolk grew little rye but rather wheat, barley, oats, and legumes (beans, peas, vetches), with intensive rotations that made the region outstanding for productivity.

In a land where soil quality varies sharply over short distances, and where access to large urban markets was patchy, there were many other comparable local contrasts in the choice of crops. Presumably these differences were more strongly developed by 1300 than in the Anglo-Saxon period; increasing demands on peasants and a growing population of smallholders, forced to live off morsels of land, would have encouraged acute specialization in whatever crops the soil produced best. The same forces probably perpetuated local variations in field systems, which, outside the territory of the Midland System, we see in all their variety in 13th-century sources.

In the realm of power technology it is also difficult to discern major improvements between the Conquest and 1300. That most basic of implements, the plow, was already developed in its essentials by 1066; long before the Conquest there is a reference in the Exeter Riddles to the plow's green "flank," the moldboard to turn the sod and smother weeds. Improved harness likewise predates the Conquest. After 1066 water-powered mills spread to areas where they had been rarely mentioned in Domesday Book, and after about 1190 windmills were introduced. Neither process improved agricultural output; they reduced work, but it was a populous age when labor was not at a premium and the ultimate gains went to lords in the form of tolls on milling. The most significant change in power technology was a partial replacement of oxen by horses in carting and plowing. This permitted greater efficiency in soil preparation and in carrying but did not strike at the adverse man-land ratios that were a chronic problem.

These ratios improved during the 14th century as population dropped to produce the "very thinly inhabited" countryside that a Venetian observer marveled at in the 1490s. The most important development during the later Middle Ages was an increase in the acreage of pasture at the expense of plowland, a reverse of the earlier trend. In the lowlands of Warwickshire, for example, the proportion of land under pasture rose from 7 percent to 33 percent. People were fewer; there was less pressure to produce cereals for bread; field systems relaxed like a fist unclenched. Better standards of living meant greater demands for animal products. Some farmers seized opportunities to produce vigorously for a cash economy, encouraging the emergence of nascent farming regions geared toward specialization for markets.

Improvements associated with the demand for pasture included enclosure, particularly in such regions as southwestern England, with its flexible field systems. From small beginnings in the 13th century the trend was also toward the greater use of legumes as food for humans and beasts. These changes did not take place without social dislocation, as when the fabric of some traditional arable communities crumbled away before a falling demand for grain, and depopulation was a further consequence. Yet in ecological terms the English countryside in 1500 had a far sounder base than in 1300. Systems of cultivation were less demanding, legumes enriched the nitrogen content of the soil, there was more grassland and livestock. The stage was set for the more revolutionary changes in agriculture and farm output that took place in the post-medieval centuries.

Harold S.A. Fox

Bibliography

PRIMARY

Oschinsky, Dorothea, ed. *Walter of Henley and Other Treatises on Estate Management and Accounting.* Oxford: Clarendon, 1971 [medieval treatises for the instruction of estate managers].

SECONDARY

Agrarian History of England and Wales [the basic survey and guide to scholarly treatment of this vast subject]: Vol. I.ii, ed. H.P.R. Finberg. Cambridge: Cambridge University Press, 1972 [covers A.D. 43 to 1042]; Vol. II, ed. Herbert E. Hallam. Cambridge: Cambridge University Press, 1988 [1042–1350]; Vol. III, ed. Edward Miller. Cambridge: Cambridge University Press, 1991 [1350–1500]; Astill, Grenville, and Annie Grant, eds. *The Countryside of Medieval England.* Oxford: Blackwell, 1988; Baker, Alan R.H., and Robin A. Butlin, eds. *Studies of Field Systems in the British Isles.* Cambridge: Cambridge University Press, 1973; Dyer, Christopher. *Standards of Living in the Later Middle Ages: Social Change in England, c. 1200–1500.* Cambridge: Cambridge University Press, 1989; Gray, Howard L. *English Field Systems.* Harvard Historical Studies 22. Cambridge: Harvard University Press, 1915. Repr. London: Merlin Press, 1959 and 1969 [the pioneer work, still of value]; Miller, Edward, and John Hatcher. *Medieval England: Rural Society and Economic Change, 1086–1348.* London: Longman, 1978; Rowley, Trevor, ed. *The Origins of Open-Field Agriculture.* London: Croom Helm, 1981.

See also Domesday Book; Food; Labor Services; Manorialism; Mills; Names; Population

Alanus, J[ohannes] (d. 1373)

John Aleyn, a musician and administrator in royal service, was from 1363 to 1373 a canon of St. George's Chapel, Windsor, and from 1361 to 1373 a chaplain of the Royal Household Chapel of Edward III. The last decade of his career is well documented, and he enjoyed the frequent and lucrative patronage of Edward and Queen Philippa, holding numerous benefices. Upon his death he bequeathed a book of music to the chapel at Windsor. Though the surname is common, this individual is the strongest candidate for the J. Alanus who wrote the extraordinary musicians' motet *Sub arturo plebs* and possibly also the motet *O amicus sponsi primus*. It is likely that he is the Alanus or Magister Alanus four of whose songs are preserved in the Strassburg Manuscript. Further, it is not ruled out on the basis of musical style that he is the Aleyn (or in the second case, less probably, the W. [?] Aleyn) to whom a lively cantilena-style Gloria (no. 8) and a smooth discant setting of a Sanctus (no. 128) are attributed in the Old Hall Manuscript.

Peter M. Lefferts

Bibliography

Bent, Margaret. "Aleyn." *NGD* 1:250; Bent, Margaret, with David Howlett. *"Subtiliter alternare:* The Yoxford Motet *O amicus / Precursoris."* In *Studies in Medieval Music: Festschrift for Ernest H. Sanders,* ed. Peter M. Lefferts and Brian Seirup. *Current Musicology* 45–47 (1990): 43–84; Bowers, Roger. "Fixed Points in the Chronology of English Fourteenth-Century Polyphony." *Music and Letters* 71 (1990): 313–35; Fallows, David. "Alanus, Johannes." *NGD* 1:193–94; Wathey, Andrew. "The Peace of 1360–1369 and Anglo-French Musical Relations." *Early Music History* 9 (1990): 129–74.

See also Old Hall Manuscript; Songs; *Sub arturo plebs*

Alchemy

Alchemy can be seen as the forerunner of modern chemistry. It was developed by the Arabs from the 7th century, based on the merging of mystical, scientific, religious, and philosophical doctrines dating from the late Roman Empire. Alchemy includes speculative elements—astrology, gnosticism, the Eleusinian mystery religion, Christian heretical notions, and Hellenistic syncretism—along with its scientific orientation toward empirical and laboratory analysis. Alchemy's main object is to transmute base metal into silver or gold by freeing crude materials from "impurities," and from this primary concern it directed chemical experimentation toward and eventually beyond such goals.

Among the most important Arabic sources are alchemical treatises by Geber, Alchindus, Rhasis (al-Razi), and Avicenna. These works were transmitted to western Latin writers through the School of Toledo in the 12th century and appear in adaptations and expansions in alchemical treatises by Roger Bacon, Albertus Magnus, and others. A primary concern in these works is chemical change and the nature of materials, with a particular interest in properties of mercury that could be used in dissolving other metals. Gold- and silver-making feature as an important aspect in later writers. John of Rupescissa (fl. mid-14th century) and spurious works attributed to Ramón Lull (e.g., *Theoria*) pursue this line of inquiry.

By the late 13th century the emphasis became more focused on the notion of elixirs that induce chemical transformations. Rupescissa introduces the notion of elixir as having medical properties, a direction that was to become more important in the 16th century among such chemist-physicians as Paracelsus and Libavius. There was also an interest in the distillation of alcohol, seen as a fifth element or potent elixir, offering possibilities as an agent in causing change and transmutation.

Latin alchemical works received wide circulation in vernacular translations, paraphrases, and adaptations. Among the most popular authors was Arnald of Villanova (ca. 1240–1311), whose *Speculum philosophorum* was translated into ME as *The Mirror of Philosophy*. A work supposedly of Hermes Trismegistus, the *Dicta philosophorum,* was translated by Robert Frumitor as *The Words of the Philosophers,* and there are many other redactions of this text. John of Rupescissa's *Liber de consideracione quintae essentiae* became the *Book of Quintessence,* found in many 15th-century manuscripts, while Thomas Norton's *Ordinal of Alchemy* (ca. 1477) offers a verse compendium of many earlier alchemical works. Most of these "cookbook" manuscripts contain collections of alchemical recipes, many with marginal notations about their success or otherwise.

Because of the ambiguous and possibly heretical nature of alchemy it was never fully accepted by the church and had to be conducted as an occult and therefore a "pseudo-science." Perhaps the most poignant comment in this respect is found in a manuscript marginal note made by an English translator, possibly a Franciscan friar, of Rupescissa's *Book of Quintessence* (ca. 1485). He, being "at great unease in prison," nevertheless felt that alchemy could still be used for the "helping of man" and the "praise of God."

Laurel Means

Bibliography

PRIMARY

Geber. *The Works of Geber.* Trans. Richard Russell. London: Dent; New York: Dutton, 1928; Norton, Thomas. *Ordinal of Alchemy.* Ed. John Reidy. EETS 272. London: Oxford University Press, 1975.

SECONDARY

Braswell-Means, Laurel. "Utilitarian and Scientific Prose." In *Middle English Prose: A Critical Guide to Major Authors and Genres,* ed. A.S.G. Edwards. New Brunswick: Rutgers University Press, 1984, pp. 337–87 [a bibliographical appraisal]; Fabricius, Johannes. *Alchemy: The Medieval Alchemists and Their Royal Art.* Copenhagen: Rosenkilde & Bagger, 1976; Holmyard, E.J. *Alchemy.* Harmondsworth: Penguin, 1957; Pritchard, Alan. *Alchemy: A Bibliography of English-Language Writings.* London: Routledge & Kegan Paul, 1980; Thorndike, Lynn. *A History of Magic and Experimental Science.* 4 vols. New York: Columbia University Press, 1923–34.

See also Bacon; Learning; Science; Scientific and Medical Writings

Alcuin (ca. 730/35–804)

The foremost educational leader of the 8th century, known in Latin as Albinus and in Charlemagne's court circle often as Flaccus (after Horace). After living nearly 50 years in York, he spent some twenty years working in the Frankish kingdom as adviser and teacher of Charlemagne and his court, architect of the Carolingian political, religious, and cultural reform, poet and voluminous author of letters and treatises, rectifier of the biblical text and liturgy, and in his last years abbot of Tours.

The brief *Vita Alcuini,* anonymously composed around 829, probably at Ferrières, at the direction of Alcuin's disciple Sigulf, contains amid its reminiscences and anecdotes disappointingly few facts. Little is known of Alcuin's life at York; however, with respect to his later career on the Continent, no intellectual of the period is more amply documented. Alcuin's own letters (more than 300) and poems (more than 220), supplemented by Carolingian correspondence, chronicles, and histories, furnish us with considerable information about him. Born of noble family in Northumbria, he was educated at the cathedral school of York in its epoch as western Christendom's center of learning. His teacher and patron was Ælberht, whom Alcuin succeeded in 767 as master of the school, when Ælberht was raised to the episcopacy. Ordained as deacon, Alcuin never advanced to the priesthood and may not have taken monastic vows, even though in old age he expressed a wish to become a Benedictine monk at Fulda. Alcuin accompanied Ælberht on his travels and book-acquiring forays on the Continent, and by 778–80 he had already established a reputation among cognoscenti.

Alcuin would never have attained his subsequent renown if it were not for a momentous (though not his first) encounter with Charlemagne. In March 781, while bearing the pallium of archiepiscopal authority from Pope Hadrian I for Eanbald, Ælberht's successor to the see of York, Alcuin en route met Charlemagne at Parma. Charlemagne urgently requested him to join the Frankish court, with its prestigious group of scholars (Peter of Pisa, Paul the Deacon, Paulinus of Aquileia, soon joined by others), and to assist him in his educational and religious reforms. Alcuin forsook England to remain on the Continent for the rest of his life. He returned to England only twice, once in 786 to accompany papal legates to the synods at York and at the court of King Offa of Mercia, and once in 790–93 for a stay at York, during which time he was in correspondence with Charlemagne about the decrees of the Second Council of Nicaea (787), which the Carolingians mistakenly believed upheld the worship of images (iconolatry). However, the resulting doctrinal declarations, called the *Libri Carolini,* were made in his absence and therefore not by Alcuin. They are, judging from the script and biblical citations, probably by Theodulf.

His erudition, administrative qualities, pragmatism, and responsibility gave Alcuin immense influence with Charlemagne. In addition to his own works Alcuin more than any other in the royal entourage wrote documents, correspondence, capitularies, texts, and poems under the king's name. This is not to say that he functioned only as the king's *persona;* despite his service and extreme deference to the king Alcuin expressed himself to Charlemagne freely and sometimes reprovingly. Although he honored the king as divinely appointed defender, protector, and spreader of the church and guardian of the people's mores as well as conqueror of nations, he insisted the king was not above the law. He protested strongly against the forced baptism and tithing of the constantly resurgent Saxons and urged that the same error not be repeated among the defeated Avars, whom he chose to call Huns. In old age he excused himself from journeying to the king or accompanying him in battle or at the papal court. As abbot of St. Martin's he granted sanctuary to a condemned cleric, much to the chagrin of the culprit's bishop, Theodulf of Orléans, and of the king himself.

Traveling with Charlemagne's itinerant court until 794, when the palace of Aachen became a capital, Alcuin was the central figure of a brilliant corps of scholar-poets creating the Carolingian renaissance. This academy was responsible for mythologizing the Germanic kingdom into a new Athens, a new Rome, and a new Jerusalem. Even though Theodulf of Orléans has been judged a better poet, Alcuin's own activity as a contributor to the myth and to the body of Carolingian Latin poetry is remarkable. He composed verse epistles, inscriptions, epigrams, hymns. To his pupils he wrote lighter, more lyrical verse. The artifice of his acrostic poems addressed to Charlemagne and to the Cross demonstrates his knowledge and control of late-antique Latin prosody. His elegies are particularly notable. "O mea cella" and "The Nightingale" have been often anthologized. The elegy on the Viking destruction of Lindisfarne in 793 is one of three longer poems; the others are his metrical life of St. Willibrord and the often-cited poem *The Bishops, Kings, and Saints of York,* which contains much valuable information about the school of York, its library (probably the best in Europe), and its personalities.

As master of the court school Alcuin wrote a number of educational texts. He resurrected Cassiodorus's system of the seven liberal arts but in his treatises concentrated on the disciplines of the trivium: grammar (including a work on orthography), rhetoric, and dialectic. His *De orthographia,* his instruction in computus (calendrical reckoning), and some of his exegetical works (e.g., on John's Gospel) are revisions of Bede's works. He probably authored the little educational piece of mathematical conundrums, *Propositiones ad acuendos iuvenes.* He is responsible for spreading the *Categoriae decem,* a version of the Latin Aristotle. He compiled biblical commentaries on Genesis (questions and responses), some Psalms, the Song of Songs and Ecclesiastes, John's Gospel, Revelation, and the letters of Paul to Titus, Philemon, and Hebrews. His hagiographic works consist mainly of reediting lives of saints important to Francia: he reworked the biographies of Martin of Tours, Richarius, Vedast, and Willibrord. Alcuin also produced three moral tracts: one on the virtues and vices (a popular work), another on the nature of the soul, and the third, for the boys at St. Martin's, on confession of sins.

In the area of liturgy Alcuin made major contributions. He took charge of removing errors of transcription from scriptural and liturgical texts and bringing them into conformity with Roman usage. He assembled a *comes,* a lectionary of epistles for the mass. He produced a revision of the Hadrian (so-called Gregorian) mass book, but the supplement and its preface, long attributed to him, are probably the work of Benedict of Aniane (ca. 750–821). Alcuin composed a set of beautiful votive masses, eventually incorporated into the Roman Missal, which drew upon the Irish-English tradition of intense personal piety put to the service of public prayer. He also introduced Hiberno-English customs, such as the recitation of the Creed at mass (newly formulated with the *Filioque* clause by Paulinus of Aquileia) and the celebration of the Feast of All Saints.

The western christological doctrine called adoptionism propounded by Elipand of Toledo and Felix of Urgel, namely, that Jesus Christ in his human nature was not the natural Son of God but an adopted one, was vigorously rebutted as heretical by Charles's theologians, Paulinus and Alcuin. It was condemned at the synods of Regensburg (790), Rome (798), and Aachen (800). Although in the controversy Paulinus proved the better theologian, Alcuin participated energetically, writing three hasty apologetic treatises in response to the heresy. A more successful foray into theology is Alcuin's later tract on the Trinity, heavily indebted to Augustine's *De Trinitate* but demonstrating Alcuin's own sophisticated reasoning.

In 796 Alcuin had asked to retire as a monk at Fulda, sacred to the memory of Boniface; but Charlemagne in granting him leave made him abbot of Tours, where he remained until his death on 19 May 804. From Tours he wrote some of his most famous letters to kings, bishops, and monks in England, especially Northumbria. While lamenting the depredations of the Vikings, he exhorted his countrymen to courage and virtue. In keeping with Charlemagne's campaign to reform and publish sacred texts Alcuin resolved to correct the textual corruptions in the Vulgate Old and New Testaments, and the resultant (now lost) Bible was presented to Charlemagne in Rome on the day of his coronation as emperor, Christmas, 800. Alcuin's role in arranging for the coronation itself was like so much of his activity for the king—both behind the scene and effectual. Alcuin's leadership in creating better Latin texts led to increased care and production in Frankish scriptoria; his name is therefore associated with the creation of the Carolingian minuscule handwriting developed during the period (even though he himself continued to use insular script), and with the superb Bibles produced at Tours, which actually postdate him.

There were in the court of Charlemagne others who may have been better as grammarians or poets or diplomats or exegetes or theologians or liturgists, but Alcuin, confidant and friend of the king, not only practiced all these professions, he also taught, guided, and served as a model for each of them.

George Hardin Brown

Bibliography

PRIMARY

PL 90:667–76 and *PL* 100–01 [includes most of Alcuin's works, but in unreliable editions]; Arndt, Wilhelm, ed. *Vita Alcuini. MGH: Scriptores* 15/1 (1887): 182–97;

Daly, L.W., and W. Suchier, eds. *Altercatio Hadriani Augusti et Epicteti Philosophi.* Illinois Studies in Language and Literature 24 (1939), nos. 1 & 2; Godman, Peter, ed. and trans. *Alcuin: The Bishops, Kings, and Saints of York.* Oxford: Clarendon, 1982; Godman, Peter, ed. and trans. *Poetry of the Carolingian Renaissance.* Norman: University of Oklahoma Press, 1985, pp. 118–49; Howell, Wilbur S., ed. *The Rhetoric of Alcuin and Charlemagne.* Princeton: Princeton University Press, 1941.

SECONDARY

Bullough, Donald. "A Court of Scholars and the Revival of Learning." *The Age of Charlemagne.* London: Elek, 1965, pp. 99–128; Bullough, Donald. "Alcuin and the Kingdom of Heaven: Liturgy, Theology, and the Carolingian Age." In *Carolingian Essays,* ed. Ute-Renate Blumenthal. Washington, D.C.: Catholic University of America, 1983, pp. 1–69. Repr. in *Carolingian Renewal: Sources and Heritage.* Manchester: Manchester University Press, 1991, pp. 161–240; Duckett, Eleanor S. *Alcuin, Friend of Charlemagne.* New York: Macmillan, 1951; Ellard, Gerald. *Master Alcuin, Liturgist.* Chicago: Loyola University, 1956; Ganshof, François L. *The Carolingians and the Frankish Monarchy.* Trans. Janet Sondheimer. Ithaca: Cornell University Press, 1971, pp. 28–54; Godman, Peter. "The Anglo-Latin *Opus geminatum:* From Aldhelm to Alcuin." *MÆ* 50 (1981): 215–29; Godman, Peter. "New Athens and Renascent Rome." In *Poets and Emperors.* Oxford: Oxford University Press, 1987, pp. 38–92; Levison, Wilhelm. *England and the Continent in the Eighth Century.* Oxford: Clarendon, 1946, pp. 148–70, 314–23; Marenbon, John. *From the Circle of Alcuin to the School of Auxerre.* Cambridge: Cambridge University Press, 1981; McKitterick, Rosamond. *The Frankish Church and the Carolingian Reforms, 789–895.* London: Royal Historical Society, 1977; Meyvaert, Paul. "The Authorship of the 'Libri Carolini': Observations Prompted by a Recent Book." *Revue bénédictine* 89 (1979): 29–57; Wallach, Luitpold. *Alcuin and Charlemagne.* Ithaca: Cornell University Press, 1959; Willis, G.G. "From Bede to Alcuin." In *Further Essays in Early Roman Liturgy.* Alcuin Club 50. London: SPCK, 1968, pp. 227–42.

See also Aldhelm; Anglo-Latin Literature to 1066; Bede; Benedict of Aniane; Grammatical Treatises; Literary Influences: Carolingian; Liturgy and Church Music, History of; Paul the Deacon; Theodulf

Aldhelm (640?—709/10)

The learned founder and first major figure of Anglo-Latin letters. Aldhelm was born of noble family with royal connections in Wessex about the time of the district's conversion to Christianity. We have few details of his life. Of his education William of Malmesbury relates, without citing the source of his information, that Aldhelm received his early training from one Máelduib at the ancient Celtic foundation of Malmesbury. Later he studied under the abbot Hadrian in the renowned school of Canterbury but left after as little as two years, for health and other reasons. In one letter from Canterbury written between 670 and 673 Aldhelm lists the subjects he was then pursuing, including Roman law, 100 types of meter and poetic devices, the principles of mathematical calculation (especially fractions), and astrology (the interpretation of the zodiacal signs).

Earlier scholars hypothesized that Aldhelm learned his showy latinity from Irish tutors like Máelduib, but recent specialists have established a convincing link between Aldhelm's writings and the work of continental grammarians and poets, who gloried in the same pompous style. Aldhelm somehow acquired an astonishing command of sacred and profane literature as he developed his extraordinary skill in writing ornate Latin.

He became involved in ecclesiastical affairs, attending a synod at Hertford in 672 and becoming abbot of Malmesbury ca. 673. He was very active, traveling to Rome and to sites in southern England; he labored to establish the church in Wessex physically (he built or rebuilt several churches) and spiritually (Bede speaks of his energy and zeal). When Bishop Hæddi died in 705, the vast diocese of Wessex was split into two, with sees at Winchester and Sherborne. In 705/06 Aldhelm, well acquainted with neighboring Devon and Cornwall, was unsurprisingly chosen and consecrated bishop of the western portion, Sherborne. He presided over his bishopric for four years until his death in 709/10.

For Aldhelm Latin was not only the language of Christian culture; it was also the language of the clerical elite. He therefore fostered a hermeneutic style of the initiate, whose most striking feature is the ostentatious parade of unusual, arcane, and learned vocabulary. Both his prose and poetry exhibit florid ornament, especially alliteration and rhyme. Aldhelm's extant prose writings include a dozen letters. In epistles to his students Heahfrith and Wihtfrith he tries to convince them of the advantages of English over Irish education and demonstrates his point by outdoing the rhetorical excesses of Celtic Latin (e.g., every one of the first fifteen words of his letter to Heahfrith begins with *p*). In his letter to Geraint, king of Dumnonia (Devon), he discusses the reckoning for Easter, a much-debated topic in the 8th century among Irish and continental clerics; and in a letter to the bishop of Wessex he addresses computistical matters in addition to metrics.

His weightiest letter is the *Epistola ad Acircium*, addressed to the well-educated King Aldfrith of Northumbria (686–705). The preface of this massive tract includes the longest recorded disquisition on the allegorical significance of the number seven; the main body of the letter contains two complementary treatises on Latin metrics. To illustrate the properties of the hexameter he inserts 100 *Aenigmata*, following the example of the late Latin poet Symphosius. These *Aenigmata*, or *Riddles*, which express the mysterious nature of things, proved popular in early-medieval Europe but especially in Anglo-Saxon circles, where they were imitated in Latin (by Tatwine, archbishop of Canterbury 731–34, Eusebius, and Boniface) and OE (in the Exeter Book Riddles).

Aldhelm's longest and most notable work was a treatise on chastity, *De virginitate*, composed for Abbess Hildelith and her nuns at Barking Abbey. The topic was a favorite patristic subject, and the method of composition was also traditional, with one version in prose and another in verse, a procedure (termed *opus geminatum* or *stilus geminus*, "twinned work" or "twin style") practiced by late Latin writers like Juvencus and Caelius Sedulius and subsequently by Bede, Alcuin, and Hrabanus Maurus. But Aldhelm's texts are most unusual, for, unlike other authors whose poetic versions were much more ornate than the prose counterparts, Aldhelm's dazzling prose is if anything more obscurantist, recherché, and artificial than the poetic version, which is also highly embellished. After an elaborate introduction on the nature, value, and difficulties of virginity the prose text presents a catalogue of male virgins from the Old Testament to the Church Fathers; this is followed by a catalogue of female virgins similarly ordered, with some further considerations of Old Testament patriarchs; before ending, Aldhelm denounces showy dress worn by ecclesiastics.

The poetic twin shares the general structure of the prose version, with the sequence of male and female exemplars, but it ends quite differently, with a long allegorical confrontation between the virtues and vices. Although the poem's hexameters are metrically limited and tiresomely repetitious, his vocabulary is formidably extensive. This 2,904-line *carmen* is the first full-scale Latin poem to be composed in the British Isles; Aldhelm, who compared himself to Virgil, was aware of its significance and his achievement.

The influence of Aldhelm's writings on his contemporaries and on the following generation can be measured by their imitation of his style. His student Æthilwald produced four poems in continuous octosyllables, clearly modeled on Aldhelm's *Carmen rhythmicum*. Alcuin, whose soberer style reflects the writing of Bede, also owes something to Aldhelm. Many short Latin poems from the Anglo-Saxon period are nothing more than centos woven from Aldhelm's poetry. Aldhelm's dense prose had even more imitators. Felix of Crowland is surely indebted to him for the elaborate and verbose prose style of his *Life of St. Guthlac* (ca. 740). The great missionary Boniface and his coterie of English correspondents write Aldhelmian prose, as does Boniface's biographer, Willibald, and the biographer of Sts. Willibald and Wynnebald, the nun Hygeburg. Later Latin writings of the time of King Alfred and especially of the time of the Benedictine Reform (late 10th and early 11th centuries) likewise reveal Aldhelm's influence, diminished finally only after the Norman Conquest.

George Hardin Brown

Bibliography

PRIMARY

Ehwald, Rudolf, ed. *Aldhelmi opera omnia. MGH: Auctores antiquissimi* 15. Berlin: Weidmann, 1919; Lapidge, Michael, and Michael Herren, trans. *Aldhelm: The Prose Works.* Cambridge: Brewer, 1970; Lapidge,

Michael, and James Rosier, trans. *Aldhelm: The Poetic Works.* Cambridge: Brewer, 1985; Pitman, J.H., trans. *The Riddles of Aldhelm.* New Haven: Yale University Press, 1925. Repr. Hamden: Archon, 1970 [based on Ehwald's text of the *Aenigmata*].

SECONDARY

Browne, G.F. *St. Aldhelm.* London: SPCK, 1903; Godman, Peter. "The Anglo-Latin *Opus geminatum:* From Aldhelm to Alcuin." *MÆ* 50 (1981): 215–29; Lapidge, Michael. "The Hermeneutic Style in Tenth-Century Anglo-Latin Literature." *ASE* 4 (1975): 67–111; Lapidge, Michael. "Aldhelm's Latin Poetry and Old English Verse." *Comparative Literature* 31 (1979): 209–31; Wieland, Gernot R. "*Feminus stilus:* Studies in Anglo-Latin Hagiography." In *Insular Latin Studies,* ed. Michael W. Herren. Toronto: Pontifical Institute, 1981, pp. 113–33; Winterbottom, Michael. "Aldhelm's Prose Style and Its Origins." *ASE* 6 (1977): 39–76.

See also Alcuin; Anglo-Latin Literature to 1066; Boniface; Eusebius; Felix of Crowland; Riddles; Sedulius; Tatwine; William of Malmesbury

Alfred and Minster Lovell Jewels

These two late Saxon jewels consist of enameled upper sections, gold with filigree and granulation, and narrow tubes below. They differ in iconography, size, inscription, and the Alfred Jewel's (Oxford, Ashmolean Museum 1836, 371; fig. 1) rock-crystal covering (probably Roman, reused, determining the jewel's shape). They provide the best technical and stylistic parallels for each other, and were probably made in the same shop. They are significant for their association with Alfred the Great, their evidence of luxury metalwork production after Sutton Hoo, and their introduction of foliate motifs later common in Winchester manuscripts.

Style places both metalwork and enamel in late-9th- or early-10th-century England. The Alfred Jewel's inscription provides a narrower date: +ÆLFRED MEC HEHT GEWYRCAN (Alfred ordered me to be made). The mixed Anglian and Mercian, the royal formula *(heht gewyrcan),* the object's richness, and its find-spot (Somerset) indicate that the patron was King Alfred (871–99), confirming Asser's claim of such patronage.

The Alfred Jewel's enamel shows a half-length male figure on a stool, eyes toward the lower left. He holds two long strips, linked at the bottom center, with top elaborations. Bakka identifies these strips as flowers with distinct parts and curved stems. Others see flowered scepters. The irregular workmanship makes it possible that rigid staffs were indeed intended. Readings as a priest's rods, staffs with meat (for the Ascent of Alexander, but with parallels geographically remote and chronologically uncertain), or a looped cord binding two birds (with questionable Swedish parallels) are unconvincing.

The figure could be a saint, a king, Alfred (in unlikely portraiture), or the pope (referring to a ceremony now disputed). It is probably either Christ or the sense of sight. Al-

Fig. 1. *The Alfred Jewel (Oxford, Ashmolean Museum inv. no. 1836, 371). Courtesy of the Ashmolean Museum, Oxford.*

though unnimbed and glancing sideways, it resembles the Christ with two rods in the Book of Kells: perhaps the Wisdom of God. It could also represent Sight, as on the Fuller Brooch: a large-eyed frontal figure holding two plants (Bakka). Without the Brooch's other senses for programmatic verification, this is uncertain. The back foliate ornament and animal-head socket below are probably iconographically insignificant.

The Minster Lovell enamel shows a small cross or star within a larger Anglian cross.

The functions of the two objects are generally considered together, since both have similar narrow tubes. These must have held something, and since the Alfred Jewel's securing rivet is still in place, the lost part was probably organic. Proposed functions include pendants (with attached chain and upside down, improbable); dress pins (too heavy); and battle-standard ornaments (too small and delicate). Both could have adorned a crown, the larger in front; but different find-spots make it unlikely that they formed parts of the same object, and such Saxon crowns are unknown.

Many connect the jewels with Alfred's preface to Gregory, which specifies the attachment to each manuscript of an *aestel* worth 50 gold *mancuses*. The definition of *aestel* is unknown; linguistic evidence suggests a pointer, bookmark, or wood splinter (of the True Cross?). Most scholars define it as a pointer for following the text, and see the jewels as handgrips for such pointers. The iconography of both the Minster Lovell cross and Christ or Sight would fit this use. The Alfred Jewel's figure, however, would be held upside down; the two jewels are not equally costly, although the text gives a standard value for all *aestels;* and, most significantly, neither object shows wear from being held.

Another theory interprets the jewels as terminations of a scepter. Royal scepters were used in England by the 10th century, and perhaps in the 9th. Carolingian illustrations, which the Saxons may have imitated, show similar forms. The jewels' tubes are small but could have been attached to narrow projections like those terminating the Sutton Hoo "whetstone" and the Cologne scepter (Werner, 206). Both are fragile, but the Alfred Jewel has seen hard use, as demonstrated by a break above the animal-head socket.

The Alfred Jewel probably terminated a staff, possibly a scepter. The Minster Lovell Jewel could have been differently used (e.g., as a dress pin, since it is lighter), or similarly, though on a different object, as indicated by the different find-spots. No certain answers to questions of iconography and function can be given.

Genevra Kornbluth

Bibliography

Bakka, Egil. "The Alfred Jewel and Sight." *AntJ* 46 (1966): 277–82; Deshman, Robert. *Anglo-Saxon and Anglo-Scandinavian Art: An Annotated Bibliography.* Boston: Hali, 1984 (entries IX.11–IX.24); Hinton, David A. *A Catalogue of the Anglo-Saxon Ornamental Metalwork, 700–1100, in the Department of Antiquities, Ashmolean Museum.* Oxford: Clarendon, 1974, pp. 27–48; Kornbluth, Genevra. "The Alfred Jewel: Reuse of Roman *spolia.*" *Medieval Archaeology* 33 (1989): 32–37; Werner, Joachim. "Frankish Royal Tombs in the Cathedrals of Cologne and Saint-Denis." *Antiquity* 38 (1964): 201–16.

See also Alfred; Metalwork, Anglo-Saxon; Sutton Hoo

Alfred the Great (849–899; r. 871–99)
History

Youngest son of Æthelwulf, king of Wessex, Alfred was born at Wantage, Berkshire, in 849. This is recorded in Asser's *Life of King Alfred,* written during Alfred's lifetime and dedicated to him. In 853 Æthelwulf sent Alfred to Rome, where he received a special investiture from Pope Leo IV (844–55). Though this ritual is depicted by the Anglo-Saxon Chronicle and Asser as an anointing to kingship, in 853 Alfred had three elder brothers living. Asser also claims to have from Alfred the story of how his mother, Osburh, promised a book of "Saxon songs" to whichever son could learn it first; the winner was Alfred.

When Æthelwulf married the Carolingian princess Judith in 856, Alfred's eldest brother, Æthelbald, revolted and assumed rule of Wessex, while Æthelwulf retained Kent, Surrey, and Sussex until his own death in 858, when Æthelbald succeeded to the whole kingdom. After his death in 860 his brothers Æthelberht (860–65), then Æthelred (865–71), ruled in turn. No further partition occurred. Though Alfred was depicted by Asser as heir-apparent in the late 860s, his chances of succession were slim, since Æthelred had two sons.

In 865 a large army of Danes landed in East Anglia and in 866–67 gained control of Northumbria. In 868 Danes attacked Mercia, and Alfred joined King Burgred (his brother-in-law) in a campaign of limited success. Alfred now married Ealhswith, a Mercian noblewoman of royal descent. Asser reports that Alfred was struck down by a mysterious illness at his wedding and interprets this as divinely sent preventive medicine against pride.

In 869–70 Danes took control of East Anglia, killing King Edmund. Raids against Wessex began. When Æthelred died in 871, Alfred succeeded, excluding Æthelred's sons; their supporters were overruled. Wessex came under attack from several Danish warbands. Under 871 the Anglo-Saxon Chronicle records nine battles, most of which Alfred lost. He probably bought off attackers with tribute; his coinage became increasingly debased. In 874 Burgred departed for Rome, leaving Mercia to be partitioned between a coalition of Danish warlords and a new Mercian king, Ceolwulf. Though the written record is silent, joint coinage suggests that Alfred and Ceolwulf sometimes allied. In 876 and 877 Danes raided far into Wessex. At Wareham and Exeter Alfred pursued Danish warbands, paying tribute to induce their withdrawal. Protests from the archbishop of Canterbury imply that he extracted substantial contributions from churches, as did Carolingian contemporaries.

In January 878 a Danish force under Guthrum surprised Alfred at Chippenham, Wiltshire, and obliged him to withdraw to Athelney, Somerset, whence with his "vassals" he "harried Danes and Christians who had accepted Danish lordship" (Asser, ch. 53). In May 878 Alfred defeated Guthrum at Edington, Wiltshire. Guthrum made peace, accepting baptism and agreeing to leave Alfred's kingdom. In 879 some Danes withdrew to Mercia and then to East Anglia, while others went to Francia (the "French" or western portion of the Carolingian Empire). Victory at Edington enabled Alfred to recruit further support. It was probably now that a defector, the ealdorman of Wiltshire, was punished by loss of office and lands. Also at this time the coinage was reformed.

During the 880s, with Danes active in the Thames estuary and in Francia, Wessex was unscathed. By 883 Ceolwulf was dead and Alfred established overlordship of western Mercia, with a Mercian noble, Æthelræd, as his ealdorman. Leading Mercians joined Alfred's court; some West Saxons probably gained Mercian lands. A formal peace was made with Guthrum, leaving Alfred in control of Mercia west of Watling Street, the old Roman route that divided the southwest and the northwest. In 886 London, "restored" by

Alfred, was handed over to Æthelræd, who married Alfred's daughter Æthelflæd.

Alfred used both preexisting and new fortified settlements to organize a system of burhs covering his kingdom. A few, like Winchester, were intended as political and fiscal centers. Basically the burhs' function was military; garrisoned by mounted warriors (thegns), they could act as refuges and launchpads for counteroffensives. The followers of Alfred and his magnates (ealdormen and probably bishops) were coordinated with the *burh-thegns* (Anglo-Saxon Chronicle, 893). Alfred thus imposed heavy burdens on his nobility.

To secure cooperation Alfred wanted to retrain nobles to think of themselves as an aristocracy of service. Books purveying the service ideal and enhancing royal authority were translated into OE, and bishops were mobilized to ensure their distribution; nobles were told to learn to read and threatened, if they failed, with loss of office. Since Alfred personally participated in the translation project, it offers a unique window on the mind of a medieval king. Royal patronage attracted scholars from Mercia, Wales, and Francia and inspired the production of the Anglo-Saxon Chronicle and Asser's *Life*.

Danish attacks on Wessex resumed in 892 after their defeat in Francia. Alfred was better prepared. The Anglo-Saxon Chronicle for the years 893 to 896 is essentially a record of success, including a minor naval encounter. Alfred suffered less from Danish onslaughts than from "high mortality among his best thegns."

Alfred's law code probably belongs to this decade. It was to apply in Mercia as in Wessex. Some clauses were monuments to Alfred's talents as judge; others asserted the claims of lordship, especially royal lordship. Perhaps following Carolingian models, he imposed the death penalty for treason and probably demanded a generalized oath of fidelity. He secured acknowledgment of his overlordship from Welsh princes, weaning Anarawd of Gwynedd from alliance with the Danes at York. The marriage of Alfred's daughter Ælfthryth with Count Baldwin of Flanders signaled a new West Saxon involvement, on Alfred's terms, in Carolingian politics. Alfred sought to avert dynastic disputes by arranging for sole succession of his elder son, Edward, to his expanded kingdom, acknowledging Edward's infant son, Æthelstan, as a future king. Alfred died in October 899.

Though claims have been made for Alfred as an innovator in law, military organization, and economic planning, his essential success was political. He enhanced West Saxon royal power both practically, extending his control over part of Mercia and dealing ruthlessly with opponents, and ideologically, by publicizing Bede's construct of the unity of Englishkind and by winning aristocratic consensus. His posthumous reputation grew, helped by such legends as the 11th-century tale of how he allowed a peasant woman's cakes to burn as he mused on the fate of Wessex and the apocryphal 13th-century *Proverbs of Alfred*. It reached an apogee in his Victorian representation as father of the navy and founder of liberties and national unity. At least in proclaiming Alfred's greatness these myths have a grain of truth.

Alfred's Influence on Learning

In spite of what he described as the "various and manifold preoccupations" of his kingdom, King Alfred not only achieved considerable political success but also instigated and made a major contribution toward the revival of learning in Anglo-Saxon England. In a letter prefaced to his *Pastoral Care* he relates, not without some rhetorical exaggeration, how greatly education had declined by the time that he came to the throne, with few people able to understand Latin, the language of learning. For Alfred learning and the wisdom that could be acquired as a result of it were essential to the spiritual as well as to the economic health of his kingdom: loss of wisdom, he believed, brought with it calamity. Aware that many who did not know Latin could yet read English, he resolved to provide essential texts in the vernacular and called on his scholars to join him in translating those books that were "most necessary for all men to know."

Alfred himself produced three major works—the *Pastoral Care,* the *Consolation of Philosophy,* and the *Soliloquies*—writing mainly in prose but partly in verse; he was apparently also the translator of the first 50 prose psalms of the Paris Psalter. In addition he incorporated translation from the Bible into an important preface to his collection of laws, which set out his concepts of law and lawgiving. How far his colleagues responded to his request for translation is not known. Only one other attributable vernacular work has survived from the late 9th century, Wærferth's translation of Gregory's *Dialogues,* and Alfred's preface to this work tells us that it was commissioned for his personal use, that he "might occasionally reflect in his mind on heavenly things amid these earthly tribulations." However, he acknowledges the help of four people in his *Pastoral Care,* while the anonymous translations of Orosius's *Seven Books of History against the Pagans* and Bede's *Ecclesiastical History,* both of which were once wrongly attributed to him, probably date from this period and may also have been undertaken as part of his plan.

Alfred is sometimes described as father of English prose. His patronage and personal involvement in translation must have contributed to the acceptance of the vernacular as an appropriate medium for serious subjects. His works were still being copied in the 12th century. At the same time there seems to have been a flowering of prose literature in the last part of the 9th century. Works apparently composed in this period include not only the OE Orosius, the OE Bede, Wærferth's translation of the *Dialogues,* and Alfred's own compositions but also the first sections of the Anglo-Saxon Chronicle and the OE *Martyrology*. The Bede and the *Dialogues* follow their sources faithfully. Alfred's translations and the OE Orosius, in contrast, are rarely word-for-word. The *Pastoral Care* is essentially a paraphrase of Gregory's *Regula pastoralis* with explanations and expansions, including a metrical epilogue, based on John 7:38. Gregory was writing for those in authority in spiritual matters, advising "rulers" both how to order their own lives and how to advise the different types of people in their charge, but many of his injunctions applied to the exercise of authority in general and had come to be seen as applicable to secular rulers. In Alfred's hands it becomes virtually a treatise about power and authority.

Liberties are also taken with the text in the prose psalms: Alfred demonstrates a surprising willingness to modify scripture here and elsewhere, with explanation and comment freely inserted. So, for instance, the scribe's quill of Psalm 44:2 is "Christ, the word and tongue of God the Father"; the king's daughters of verse 10 are the souls of righteous men, while the queen is the Christian church. To all the psalms except the first are prefixed brief introductions, giving their meaning at several levels, including their significance for every human being. Indeed, what makes Alfred's writings of peculiar interest and importance is the way the king has modified and added to the substance of his (often learned) Latin originals, in order to render them intelligible to Anglo-Saxons, familiar only with a limited amount of writing in the vernacular, and, where appropriate, even to change the arguments, to bring them into line with his own thinking.

The texts in which Alfred demonstrates the most independence are the renderings of Boethius and Augustine. In the *Consolation of Philosophy* Boethius, writing in the Platonic tradition, sought to demonstrate the divine ordering of the universe without appeal to Christian revelation. Alfred, reading the work in the light of the Christian perspective of his day and as a ruler, accepting the doctrine of merit and the forgiveness of sins, rejects a number of Boethius's ideas and recasts his source. He makes substantial changes to passages involving the Platonic doctrine of Forms, the conception of a World-Soul, and a belief in the preexistence of the soul. The personifications Natura and Fortuna are removed; Lady Philosophy becomes *se heofoncund wisdom* (masc. "divine Wisdom") or *gesceadwisnes* (fem. "Discrimination, Reason"), while her interlocutor "Boethius" is frequently replaced by *Mod* ("Mind"), with the effect of making the speaker appear less of an individual and more of a representative of humanity. Many references to Boethius that are of a personal nature are removed, and attitudes reflecting the circumstances in which the original was written are softened. Boethius, the philosopher-politician, imprisoned and about to be executed by the king he had served, attacks the pursuit of wealth, position, power, and fame, all of which come under Fortune's jurisdiction and fall in abundance on the most wicked people. Alfred, the ruler, sees power and wealth as both necessary and potentially good, having been bestowed on men by God so that they may do his will. Honor and fame are not to be rejected, and it is right that a man's reputation should live after him as an encouragement and example to others. In transforming his Latin original in this way Alfred resembles the translator of Orosius, who also takes great liberties with his text and moves from an exercise in polemic, showing how evils have ever occurred in cycles, to a demonstration of God's mercy as manifested through and after Christ's birth. However, both Alfred and the Orosius translator preserve the structural divisions of their sources.

A different kind of freedom is exercised in the work known as the *Soliloquies*. A lengthy allegorical preface is followed by an adaptation of Augustine's *Soliloquies* reflecting the king's major concerns; subsequently Alfred draws on Augustine's *De videndo Deo,* the Bible, and works by Gregory the Great. The text, organized in three books, for much of its length follows Augustine in using dialogue form: the speakers are *Mod* ("Mind") and *Gesceadwisnes* ("Discrimination" or "Reason," Augustine's *Ratio*), and the subjects explored include the nature of God and of the soul, the eternal qualities of knowing, what constitutes Truth, and the many roads to Wisdom, that is, to God. Much space is devoted to the subject of the immortality of the soul, in an attempt to reply to a question asked by Augustine at the end of his *Soliloquies* but not answered there.

The interest of Alfred's works for the modern reader does not, however, lie solely in the modifications of substance that he makes to his primary sources. The perceived need for clarification has resulted in many minor additions and modifications, a need met also in the Orosius, where the Latin author's assumption of classical and historical knowledge in his audience has led the OE translator to make an extraordinary number of expansions—telling the story of Regulus, for instance, or the Rape of the Sabines, or Cato's suicide. Alfred similarly fills in a number of details, such as the fate of Busiris, and relates at some length the stories of Orpheus and Eurydice and of Ulysses and Circe. Like the translator of the Orosius he has drawn his material from an impressive range of classical and patristic sources, though whether directly or via an intermediary cannot be determined. In the case of the *Pastoral Care* we know, from Alfred's own preface, that the king had the work explained to him by the group of English, Welsh, and continental scholars he had gathered round him. The introductions to the Psalms and some of the explanations within them appear to be derived from written commentaries. Boethius's *Consolation,* according to William of Malmesbury, was explained to Alfred by Asser, though whether orally or in writing is not stated. Attempts to identify a written form of Asser's explanation have so far failed. The use of a commentary or glossed manuscripts might account for a number of the additions in Alfredian texts (as, for instance, the many identifications of biblical quotations in the *Pastoral Care*) but cannot be proven for these or indeed for the new information in the OE Orosius.

Another important and interesting group of changes reflects attempts by the king to modify the severity of some of the harsher pronouncements of his sources. So, for instance, when Gregory's *Regula pastoralis* states that all sins will be punished on Doomsday, the *Pastoral Care* refers to all sins that are unatoned for; when Gregory condemns those who abandon a good work unfinished, Alfred inserts the words "willingly and deliberately"; when Gregory quotes the statement from James 4:4 that one must not become a friend of the world, Alfred supplies the important qualification, "too immoderately." Gregory's list of sins for which God will make exception is extended to include not only sins committed out of ignorance or folly but also those committed from the instincts of the flesh or from weakness of character or from infirmity of mind or body. Similarly, in the Boethius translation, Alfred regularly reminds his reader that punishment can be avoided by repentance and constantly stresses God's mercy: God judges by the good will and not by the performance. In the Psalms the statement that God hates all who work iniquity is modified to apply only to those who do not abandon it or repent of it, and a similar qualification is added to the claim that "those who do evil shall be exterminated." In the *Soliloquies* as in the Boethius, the king refuses to agree that wealth is necessarily bad and that honor should be abandoned unless it is excessive. Perhaps the most interesting "minor" changes, however, are those that involve making potentially difficult points more accessible through simple and familiar analogues.

Alfred's love of expanded metaphor and simile manifests itself in his preface to the *Soliloquies* as well as in the body of his works. Favorite themes include flowing water and ships; others reflect the preoccupations of a ruler and the everyday concerns of his people: the ways to a king's court, for instance, or the relationship between a man and his lord, or the building of a dwelling. A Boethian simile comparing the universe to a number of spheres turning on a center, is replaced by an elaborate and carefully sustained image, explaining the relationship between various sorts and conditions of men and God in terms of a wheel set on an axle.

The chronology of Alfred's works is not known. The only vernacular text mentioned by Asser in 893 is the *Dialogues*. However, this may be because the *Life of King Alfred* was never completed. Equally inconclusive is William of Malmesbury's claim that Alfred was working on the Psalms at the time of his death: he may have drawn his conclusion from the fact that only the first 50 psalms had been translated, even though the practice of subdividing the Psalter into units of 50 seems to have been a common one. It is probable, however, that the *Pastoral Care* (circulated ca. 890–95) was the first of Alfred's translations, while verbal echoes may (less certainly) suggest that the *Soliloquies* followed the Boethius, which in its turn may have been later than the anonymous Orosius, a text possibly completed as early as 890 or 891.

Janet L. Nelson
Janet M. Bately

Bibliography

PRIMARY

Bately, Janet M., ed. *The Old English Orosius.* EETS s.s. 6. London: Oxford University Press, 1980; Bright, James W., and Robert L. Ramsay, eds. *Liber Psalmorum: The West-Saxon Psalms, Being the Prose Portion, or the "First Fifty," of the So-Called Paris Psalter.* Boston: Heath, 1907; Carnicelli, Thomas A., ed. *King Alfred's Version of St. Augustine's Soliloquies.* Cambridge: Harvard University Press, 1969; Hargrove, Henry Lee, trans. *King Alfred's Old English Version of St. Augustine's Soliloquies Turned into Modern English.* New York: Holt, 1904; Hecht, Hans, ed. *Bischof Wærferths von Worcester Übersetzung der Dialoge Gregors des Grossen.* 2 vols. Bibliothek der angelsächsischen Prosa 5. Leipzig: Wigand, 1900–07; Keynes, Simon, and Michael Lapidge, trans. *Alfred the Great: Asser's Life of King Alfred and Other Contemporary Sources.* Harmondsworth: Penguin, 1983; Kotzor, G., ed. *Das altenglische Martyrologium.* Bayerische Akademie der Wissenschaften, Phil.-Hist. Klasse 88/1–2. Munich: Bayerische Akademie der Wissenschaften, 1981; Miller, Thomas, ed. and trans. *The Old English Version of Bede's Ecclesiastical History of the English People.* EETS o.s. 95, 96, 110, 111. London: Trübner, 1890–98; Sedgefield, Walter John, ed. *King Alfred's Old English Version of Boethius De consolatione Philosophiae.* Oxford: Clarendon, 1899; Sedgefield, Walter John, trans. *King Alfred's Version of the Consolations of Boethius.* Oxford: Clarendon, 1900; Stevenson, William Henry, ed. *Asser's Life of King Alfred.* Oxford: Clarendon, 1904. Repr. Oxford: Clarendon, 1959; Sweet, Henry, ed. and trans. *King Alfred's West-Saxon Version of Gregory's "Pastoral Care."* EETS o.s. 45, 50. London: Trübner, 1871–72. Repr. with corrections by N.R. Ker. London: Oxford University Press, 1958.

HISTORY

Abels, Richard P. *Lordship and Military Obligation in Anglo-Saxon England.* Berkeley: University of California Press, 1988; Brooks, Nicholas P. "England in the Ninth Century: The Crucible of Defeat." *TRHS,* 5th ser. 29 (1979): 1–20; Campbell, James. "Asser's Life of Alfred." In *The Inheritance of Historiography, 350–900,* ed. C. Holdsworth and T.P. Wiseman. Exeter: University of Exeter, 1986, pp. 115–35; Hinton, David A. *Alfred's Kingdom: Wessex and the South, 800–1500.* London: Dent, 1977; Hodges, Richard. *The Anglo-Saxon Achievement: Archaeology and the Beginnings of English Society.* London: Duckworth, 1989; Keynes, Simon. "A Tale of Two Kings: Alfred the Great and Æthelred the Unready." *TRHS,* 5th ser. 36 (1986): 195–217; Maddicott, J.R. "Trade, Industry and the Wealth of King Alfred." *Past and Present* 123 (May 1989): 3–51; Nelson, J.L. "'A King across the Sea': Alfred in Continental Perspective." *TRHS,* 5th ser. 36 (1986): 45–68; Nelson, J.L. "Reconstructing a Royal Family: Reflections on Alfred, from Asser, Chapter 2." In *People and Places in Northern Europe, 500–1600: Essays in Honour of Peter Sawyer,* ed. Ian Wood and Niels Lund. Woodbridge: Boydell, 1990, pp. 47–66; Nelson, J.L. "The Political Ideas of Alfred of Wessex." In *Kings and Kingship in Medieval Europe.* London: King's College London, 1993, pp. 125–58; Smyth, A.P. *King Alfred the Great.* Oxford: Oxford University Press, 1995 [idiosyncratic but in parts thought-provoking study]; Sturdy, D.J. *Alfred the Great.* London: Constable, 1995; Wormald, Patrick. "The Ninth Century." In *The Anglo-Saxons,* ed. James Campbell. Oxford: Phaidon, 1982, pp. 132–59 [excellent short account, in the absence of a full-scale modern scholarly study].

ALFRED AND LEARNING

Bately, Janet. *The Literary Prose of King Alfred's Reign: Translation or Transformation?* London: King's College London, 1980. Repr. *OEN Subsidia* 10. Binghamton:

CEMERS, 1984; Frantzen, Allen J. *King Alfred.* Boston: Twayne, 1986; Liggins, Elizabeth M. "The Authorship of the Old English Orosius." *Anglia* 88 (1970): 289–322; O'Neill, Patrick. "Old English Introductions to the Prose Psalms of the Paris Psalter: Sources, Structure and Composition." *SP* 78 (1981): 20–38; Payne, F. Anne. *King Alfred and Boethius: An Analysis of the OE Version of the "Consolation of Philosophy."* Madison: University of Wisconsin Press, 1968; Potter, Simeon. *On the Relation of the Old English Bede to Werferth's Gregory and to Alfred's Translations.* Prague: Nákladem Král, 1931; Szarmach, Paul E. "The Meaning of Alfred's *Preface* to the Pastoral Care." *Mediaevalia* 6 (1982 for 1980): 57–86; Szarmach, Paul E., ed. *Studies in Earlier Old English Prose.* Albany: SUNY Press, 1986 [many relevant articles]; Whitelock, Dorothy. "The Old English Bede." *PBA* 48 (1962): 57–90. Repr. in *British Academy Papers on Anglo-Saxon England,* ed. E.G. Stanley. Oxford: Oxford University Press, 1990, pp. 227–60; Whitelock, Dorothy. "The Prose of Alfred's Reign." In *Continuations and Beginnings: Studies in Old English Literature,* ed. E.G. Stanley. London: Nelson, 1966, pp. 67–103; Wittig, Joseph S. "King Alfred's Boethius and Its Latin Sources: A Reconsideration." *ASE* 11 (1983): 157–98; Wormald, Patrick. "The Uses of Literacy in Anglo-Saxon England and Its Neighbours." *TRHS,* 5th ser. 27 (1977): 95–114.

See also Æthelflæd; Anglo-Saxon Chronicle; Asser; Bede; Boethius; Boroughs; Burghal Hidage; Fathers of the Church (Gregory); *Martyrology;* Orosius; Translation; Vikings; Wærferth

Aliens and Alien Merchants

Merchants from many nations traded relatively freely in England before national customs were systematically imposed in 1275. Attitudes toward different nationals reflected shifting patterns of commercial rivalry as well as the government's diplomatic and fiscal policy. English monarchs generally welcomed alien merchants because they paid higher customs duties than denizens and they provided valuable financial services. The Italian bankers, the Peruzzi and Bardi, were the most notable aliens active in English affairs. Besides the Italians major groups of merchants were those of the Hanse and the Low Countries; there were fewer Scandinavians, Spaniards, Portuguese, and French.

The number of aliens and their economic contributions can only be estimated. The Italians and the Hanse dominated the wool trade between 1257 and 1320, but thereafter the English handled over two-thirds of its volume. During the 14th century denizens gradually took over the bulk of the wine trade, and the Gascons who had previously controlled it retained but one-fourth or one-fifth of the activity. The Hanse concentrated on exporting cloth through east-coast ports, in close competition with merchants from the Low Countries. The Italians directed most of their trade through Southampton and London, while their banks were based mainly in London in the 14th and 15th centuries.

The *Carta mercatoria* of 1303 established a favorable framework for alien entrepreneurship, and the law merchant, evolving in the later Middle Ages, covered mercantile transactions. Some groups of aliens, such as Flemish textile workers, settled in England. All aliens were subject to and had access to English common law while in the realm. Some acquired royal letters of denization, and some became freemen of individual boroughs, where they could inherit movables but not real property.

On occasion aliens could be numerous in a particular locality; in 1304 about 480 alien traders resided in Hull. There, as in other major ports where they gathered, especially in London and Southampton, hosting regulations required each alien to lodge with a denizen during the 40 days permitted for the completion of business. Besides those from the Continent two other groups attracted attention: the Scots, traditional enemies, were particularly disliked in the north, and the Irish, subjected to special trading regulations in Bristol and Chester.

Jennifer I. Kermode

Bibliography

Beardwood, Alice. *Alien Merchants in England, 1377–1450: Their Legal and Economic Position.* Cambridge: Mediaeval Academy of America, 1931; Childs, Wendy R. *Anglo-Castilian Trade in the Later Middle Ages.* Manchester: Manchester University Press, 1978; Fryde, E.B. *Studies in Medieval Trade and Finance.* London: Hambledon, 1983 [collected papers, several dealing specifically with Italian trade and Anglo-Mediterranean cloth trade]; Lloyd, T.H. *Alien Merchants in England in the High Middle Ages.* Brighton: Harvester, 1982; Ruddock, Alwin A. *Italian Merchants and Shipping at Southampton, 1270–1600.* Southampton: University College, 1951.

See also Banks; Customs Accounts; Hanseatic League

Allegory and Related Symbolism

In this article "symbolism" is used in a broad sense, to mean "forms of signification," with allegory being considered as the most characteristic form of medieval symbolism. Color symbolism, number symbolism, and name etymology will be considered together with allegory.

"Allegory" (Lat. *allegoria,* from Gr. *allēgorein,* "otherspeaking"; also *alieniloquium*) can refer to a method of critical analysis more properly called allegoresis; to a literary image; and to a form of narrative fiction. Hence we talk about works as being read allegorically, or as containing allegorical imagery, or as being allegories. Allegory originated in the ancient Greek belief that the gods reveal themselves cryptically to the wise. When allegory is in operation, literary fiction is subordinated to an idea that is considered to be hidden by an *integumentum,* or "covering."

As a method of reading literature allegoresis seeks to discover the concept presumed hidden in the fiction. As a literary image allegory renders a concept in the form of a person or a thing. The best-known form of allegory is *personification,* in which a concept is represented by a person—e.g., Langland's Lady Meed—but the concept may also be represented by an object, as in the case of Chaucer's House of Fame.

The other chief form of allegorical imagery is *typology,* which correlates an Old Testament personage or event, called the "type," or *figura,* with a New Testament or extrabiblical personage or event, called the "antitype." David as king of the Jews foreshadows Christ as king of all humankind, and the Flood foreshadows the sacrament of baptism (see Daniélou). In various places in the Gospels Christ spoke of himself as fulfilling Old Testament prophecies, and in the Acts there are attempts at proving that the Old Testament anticipated the New, but it was Paul who polemicized these correspondences in his epistles. "Allegory" in the sense of typology is used as early as Galatians 4:22–24.

Although much allegorical interpretation can be called vertical—uncovering layered meanings within a single text—typological interpretation can be called horizontal, since it operates between texts or parts of texts. A *figura* may be distinguished from a personification in that a *figura* retains a largely literal role as a character in the narrative even as it takes on allegorical significance (see Auerbach). Whether typology was a compositional strategy in medieval literary texts is debated; however, because biblical typologies were popularized in didactic narrative (e.g., *Cursor Mundi*), sermons, the liturgy, and figural art (e.g., stained-glass windows), they were widely known, occurring in such diverse medieval English works as the Corpus Christi plays, religious lyrics, and the Prologue to Chaucer's *Prioress's Tale.*

Viewed as a literary form, "allegory" refers to a narrative whose entire reference is to something outside of itself and that contains various allegorical images, often arranged into episodic scenes serving as cues for interpretation. *Piers Plowman* and *The House of Fame* are allegories.

Allegorical Interpretation

Historically allegoresis, or reading allegorically, precedes the writing of allegorical works. Allegorical methods of reading developed primarily in connection with commentaries on classical mythology and the Bible. Greek commentaries on Homer resorted to allegoresis in order to defend his portrayal of the gods from the rationalist, demythologizing challenges of the pre-Socratics. Later the Jewish tradition exemplified by Philo (d. A.D. 50), which practiced allegoresis as a response to difficulties in the biblical text, helped advance allegoresis as a means of scriptural apology, explication, and teaching. Considering it a divinely inspired foreshadowing or "promise" of the New Testament, Christians under Greek influence read the Old Testament typologically, rather than rejecting it.

Applied to the Bible, allegoresis became a means for uncovering spiritual truths, which Augustine characterized as a process of removing the husk from a kernel of truth (*De doctrina christiana* [*On Christian Doctrine*] 3.12.18). Augustine's theory of signs, based on 2 Corinthians 3:6, "For the letter killeth, but the spirit quickeneth," insists that under the Christian dispensation signs refer to more than the things they signify—that is, they have a spiritual meaning (the "spirit") beyond their literal sense (the "letter").

In early Christianity a method of scriptural allegoresis according to four "levels" of meaning grew up. John Cassian (ca. 360–435) first formulated this fourfold system, although it is sometimes mistakenly credited to his more famous contemporary Augustine. The literal (or historical) sense referred to the ordinary sense of the text, while the three nonliteral levels expressed three distinct kinds of reference. The typological sense (in the Middle Ages called the allegorical sense) related the literal level to the life of Christ and to the church; the moral (or tropological) sense related it to moral behavior; and the anagogical sense related it to the consummation of Christian history at the end of the world, the study of which is called eschatology. The fourfold system was adapted to vernacular poetics by Dante in the "Letter to Can Grande," where he explained the *Divine Comedy* through the four levels. Important as Dante is, neither his theory nor his allegorical practice appears to have influenced medieval English authors. But if the four levels were seldom if ever applied simultaneously as a compositional strategy, there is ample evidence of allegorical imagery in OE and ME literature.

Bede (ca. 673–735), in his *De schematibus et tropis* (*On Figures of Speech*), employed the fourfold system in distinguishing factual allegory from verbal allegory and in so doing helped shape the view, echoed by Aquinas (*Summa* 1.10), that God signifies the meaning of his creation not only in the prophetic words of the Bible but also in the things signified by the words. This view licensed the allegorical "reading" of the world as a book whose significations were recorded not only in biblical commentaries but also in bestiaries, lapidaries, homilies, sermons and sermon source books, the liturgy, hymns, and encyclopedias—all rich sources of imagery for authors of sacred and secular literature (see Kaske, 1988).

The search for meaning in Creation led to allegorical interpretation even of colors, numbers, and words. Numbers can be symbolic in themselves (such as three for the Trinity) or can divide a work structurally (see Eckhardt, 1980; Reiss, 1970). The fives associated with the pentangle on Gawain's shield in *Sir Gawain and the Green Knight* present a numerical image of perfection. Colors can represent virtually anything, but color symbolism for spiritual concepts is perhaps the best-known type—e.g., white for innocence, or the Wife of Bath's notorious red hose (see Dronke). On the model of Jerome's *Liber interpretationis Hebraicorum nominum* (*The Interpretation of Hebrew Names,* ca. 400) and Isidore's great *Etymologiae* (ca. 615) words and names were analyzed etymologically for their concealed significance. The OE *Exodus* uses a name etymology from Jerome when it refers to Israel as the "right of God" (line 358b; see Robinson, Frank); Ælfric used etymologies to explicate scripture in his homilies (see Hill, 1988). In the later Middle Ages etymologies were gathered together with other allegorizations into collections called *distinctiones* ("distinctions"; see Barney, 1981), which analyzed words through their various significations. This method lies behind the various significances of bread in *Piers Plowman*, passus 13 and 14, and of the Virgin Mary in Chaucer's *Second Nun's Prologue* 29–84.

Modern criticism of medieval allegory can be said to begin with *The Allegory of Love*, C.S. Lewis's learned and engaging survey of literature influenced by the Latin tradition and by the "courtly love" tradition of the *Roman de la Rose*. In the next generation Rosemond Tuve surveyed medieval allegorical practice, showing the influence on Spenser's *Faerie Queene* of such traditional imagery as the vices and virtues and of such central texts as Guillaume de Deguileville's *Pilgrimage of the Life of Man*. D.W. Robertson, Jr., taking Augustine's *De doctrina christiana* as the key to reading medieval literature, applied the allegorical method of scriptural exegesis to secular literature in the belief that the medieval Christian context prompted secular authors to support the doctrines of the church in their writings. "Robertsonianism" or "exegesis" took any difficulty in the literal level as a cue to search for an implicit allegorical meaning that confirmed Christian doctrine. Although it was attacked for ignoring or even denying other considerations of critical analysis and for attributing the same essential interpretation to all works of medieval literature, Robertson's approach did establish that sacred and secular literature could employ the same modes of signification, and scholars now agree, largely due to the efforts of R.E. Kaske, that secular authors were familiar with ecclesiastical exegetical traditions. Kaske insisted that allegoresis must complement philological and "New Critical" analysis (Kaske, 1963), and he developed a bibliographically supported method for tracing the sources of allegorical imagery (Kaske, 1988).

Other scholars have treated medieval allegory as part of allegorical literature as a whole. Angus Fletcher saw allegory as a "symbolic mode," a general signifying process inherent in all art. Gay Clifford emphasized both the adaptability of allegory over time and such traditional features as conflict and opposition (e.g., in the quest), concreteness, and visual appeal in the representation of abstraction. Maureen Quilligan, arguing against Fletcher that allegory is a genre rather than a mode, insisted on reading allegories in light of each other in order to codify their stylistic and formal rules. However, in suggesting that language is allegory's "first focus and ultimate subject" (15) because so many allegories use puns and other wordplay, Quilligan foreshadowed deconstructionist allegoresis, which questions whether a text's various signifying strategies can lead to an unambiguous, objective (or "univocal") meaning. Deconstruction considers interpretation a "hermeneutic circle," arguing that as the reader closes in on allegorical "meaning," it is revealed as yet another sign.

It must be noted, however, that theoretical descriptions of medieval allegory do not describe the practical procedures of medieval writers of allegory but rather modern perspectives on works composed by those writers. An historical analysis of medieval allegorical practice, such as Alastair Minnis has performed for medieval ideas of authorship, is still needed.

Allegorical Literature

The paradigms of allegorical narrative in the Middle Ages are set by biblical prophecies such as the book of Revelation and by a group of works from the 5th and 6th centuries. Prudentius's *Psychomachia (The Spiritual Battle)* pitted personified virtues and vices against each other in a battle for the soul, which is figured allegorically both as the holy city Rome (via extended allusion to the *Aeneid*) and as the Heavenly Jerusalem (via extended use of biblical typology). The *Psychomachia* established personification as a central allegorical strategy. The allegorical interpretation of dreams has roots in biblical dreams such as Pharaoh's in Genesis 41 and Nebuchadnezzar's in Daniel 2 and 4, but Macrobius's *Commentary on the Dream of Scipio*, a study of dream interpretation, provided a highly influential theory for later dream-vision narratives. Also important for later allegorists is Boethius's *Consolation of Philosophy*, which introduced the theme of the allegorical dialogue between a seeker and his spiritual guide.

OLD ENGLISH

It is clear from glossed manuscripts of Prudentius, King Alfred's translation of Boethius, Ælfric's homilies and prefaces to scripture, and scriptural and hagiographical poetry, such as *Christ I* and *Andreas*, that the allegorical practice of the Anglo-Saxon period is rooted in late Roman tradition and in insular and continental biblical exegesis. *The Dream of the Rood*, in which a dreamer speaks with the Cross, is the earliest extant use in English of the dream-vision form developed by Macrobius and Boethius. *The Phoenix*, partly inspired by the nature allegories of the 2nd-century bestiary *Physiologus*, provides its own exegesis, drawing correspondences between the phoenix and the followers of Christ, who build a nest for themselves in the tree of paradise by doing good works in this life. Another image has the just as warriors of God winning eternal life in the struggle against the enemy, death, and a third has them as the plants gathered by the bird, Christ, into its nest in the tree, heaven. Similarly indebted to *Physiologus* are *The Partridge*, *The Panther*, and *The Whale*. The image of the spiritual battle, indebted to the *Psychomachia*, occurs in other, ostensibly nonallegorical OE poems, most notably in Hrothgar's "sermon" about the dangers of pride in *Beowulf*. Allegorical interpretations of *The Wanderer* and *The Seafarer* as poems about exile from the heavenly home have been advanced on the basis of suspected echoes from scriptural exegesis.

MIDDLE ENGLISH

Allegorical practice in ME literature reflects religious, classical, and "courtly love" influences. Religious allegory entered directly via works written in English or translated from French or Latin for devotional, instructional, and preaching purposes. Prudentius's personifications are not far removed from works like the 14th-century *Abbey of the Holy Ghost*, a translation of the Old French *Abbaye du Saint Esprit*, which portrays the heart as the abbey of the Holy Spirit for those who cannot enter regular religious orders; prepared by the Four Daughters of God (Peace, Mercy, Righteousness, and Truth; cf. Vulgate Ps. 84:10–11), it becomes the residence of personified virtues.

The allegory of the spiritual battle informs Robert Grosseteste's 13th-century *Chateau d'amour*, which was translated into ME several times and adapted into other works, such as the historical poem *Cursor Mundi*. At the end of the Middle Ages the spiritual battle provides the structure for the Macro plays *Castle of Perseverance*, *Wisdom*, and *Mankind*, as well as for *Everyman*. The exemplum, a pithy and frequently allegorical narrative often used in sermons, lent itself well to religious and secular literature, as in Chaucer's *Pardoner's Tale* about three rioters who meet Death.

The classical mythographical tradition (e.g., allegorizations of Ovid's *Metamorphoses*) was the second major influence on ME allegory, particularly after the 12th century, as were such classical allegorical forms as the beast fable, which lies behind Chaucer's *Nun's Priest's Tale*. The third influence, the psychological allegory of love, came to ME via the French *Roman de la Rose*, which was a conduit for the Neoplatonic personification allegories of the 12th-century School of Chartres, for the allegorical treatments of love found in the "courtly love" lyrics of Provence and northern France, and for the dream-vision and dialogue genres deriving from Macrobius and Boethius.

Dream visions, debates, and dialogues were productive forms for allegory in ME. Like the biblical book of Revelation dream visions grant a transcendent view of existence. *Summer Sunday*, for example, presents an allegory about the devastations of Fortune. Dream visions are sometimes found "embedded" in larger narratives. Arthur's two prophetic dreams in the alliterative *Morte Arthure*, based on heraldic imagery and the allegory of Fortune's wheel, pinpoint his rise and fall as he marches through the Roman Empire. Chaucer's dream visions *The Book of the Duchess*, *The House of Fame*, and *The Parliament of Fowls* (also a debate) employ embedded allegorical murals, which derive ultimately from Virgil's description of Juno's temple in *Aeneid* 1.446ff. (cf. *Knight's Tale* 1914–2088).

The debate form is a natural vehicle for allegory because the participants, insofar as they represent fixed ideologies, are personifications: reason and sensuality, soul and body, *dives* and *pauper*, and even the birds in Chaucer's *Parliament*. Dream visions, whose truth claims suit the genre's inherited interest (from Macrobius and Boethius) in social, philosophical, and moral questions, frame many ME debates. The 14th-century alliterative poems *The Parliament of the Three Ages*, *Winner and Waster*, *Mum and the Sothsegger*, and *Death and Life* are closely akin to the earlier *Owl and the Nightingale* (ca. 1200) and to other debate poems.

Debates require figures of equal status; the dialogue requires figures in the roles of teacher and student. *Pearl* presents a dialogue within a dream-vision frame: in the frame a bereaved father dreams that he finds his deceased daughter in a setting drawn from the book of Revelation; when he challenges her ranking among the saved, she instructs him on the equality of the heavenly reward and leads him to where he sees her among the 144,000 virgins in the company of the Celestial Lamb (Rev. 14), a figure for the Church Triumphant.

The dream-vision frame enclosing a debate or dialogue was the preferred allegorical strategy of Langland and Gower.

Not easily classified because of its protean shape and encyclopedic range, Langland's *Piers Plowman* (ca. 1368–ca. 1385) pursues the quest of "Long Will" through eight visions, sometimes enfolding one dream within another and often employing debates among personifications—Lady Meed, Conscience, Clergy—who represent virtually every aspect of social, moral, and religious life. Gower wrote allegorical poems in each of the three literary languages of late-14th-century England. All three (*Mirour de l'Omme*, *Vox Clamantis*, and *Confessio Amantis*, the last in English) criticize London society and the Peasants' Revolt (1381) against the background allegory of man as microcosm, depicting the ravages of the seven deadly sins upon the soul undirected by reason and suggesting that reform in the body politic begins with reform in the individual. In the *Confessio* this disordered body politic is figured by Nebuchadnezzar's dream (see Dan. 4), and the personal and social agenda of reform is accomplished by a dialogue between an aging lover and Venus's minister Genius, who guides the lover through a spiritual crisis by means of a series of stories illustrating the seven sins.

Whether the ME secular lyrics were intended to be read allegorically has been debated. However, it is clear that preachers both allegorized secular lyrics in their sermons and used them as support for allegorizations of scripture. Some religious lyrics reflect allegorical themes, as in the debates between the body and soul, in which the soul, after death, rebukes the body for its sinfulness. This theme is found as early as the OE *Soul and Body I*, but except for *As I Lay on a Winter's Night* (*Index of ME Verse* 351), in almost all cases only the soul speaks. Other ME lyrics contain condensed allegories functioning as exempla: for example, "Wen the turuf is thi tuur" (*Index of ME Verse* 4044) warns the reader,

> When the turf is your tower
> and your grave is your bower,
> your skin and your white throat
> shall prosper worms.
> Then what good will do you
> all the world's bliss?

The lyrics are a mine of such stock allegories—the grave as a house, the wheel of Fortune, the dance of death, the four daughters of God, the three living and the three dead (a *memento mori* theme)—many of which correspond to iconographic images in stained-glass windows, on church walls, and so on. The lines of such lyrics often resemble the *tituli* (or captions) that accompany visual renditions, called emblems, of the allegorical themes. Allegories also appear in occasional and political poems, as in the pageant of Nature, Grace, Fortune, Wisdom, and so on in Lydgate's coronation poem for Henry IV (*Index of ME Verse* 1398).

In general 15th-century allegorical usage continued earlier forms and practices, such as the psychological allegory, but in a conventional, imitative way. John Lydgate's *Complaint of a Lover's Life* and *Temple of Glass* follow the Chaucerian dream-vision model from *The House of Fame*, the former employing also a love allegory inspired by the *Roman de la Rose*. A dream vision leads the narrator on an allegorical pilgrimage to the Heavenly City in Lydgate's *Pilgrimage of the Life of Man*, a translation from the 14th-century French of Guillaume de Deguileville (see Wenzel, 1973). The Middle Scots poetry of the succeeding generation is often called Chaucerian for its adoption of Chaucer's "aureate" natural imagery (e.g., *Franklin's Tale* 1245–55), much of which contains embedded allegories. *The Kingis Quair*, like Lydgate's *Temple of Glass* before it, leads a dreamer through a pageant of personifications and like *Pearl* suggests a fictional autobiography. Other dream visions give a distinctly Scottish coloring to the genre (Douglas, *The Palice of Honour*, Lindsay, *The Dream*), while yet other poems follow the general late-medieval trend toward emblematizing, using allegory mainly to illustrate preexisting concepts (Dunbar, *The Thrissill and the Rois*, *The Goldyn Targe*; anon., *King Hart*). Not until Spenser did allegory once again become a means of intellectual exploration.

Michael W. Twomey

Bibliography

GENERAL STUDIES

Auerbach, Erich. "Figura." In *Scenes from the Drama of European Literature: Six Essays*, trans. Ralph Mannheim. New York: Meridian, 1959, pp. 11–76, 229–37; Barney, Stephen A. "Visible Allegory: The *Distinctiones Abel* of Peter the Chanter." In *Allegory, Myth, and Symbol*, ed. Morton W. Bloomfield. Cambridge: Harvard University Press, 1981, pp. 87–107; Beichner, Paul E. "The Allegorical Interpretation of Medieval Literature." *PMLA* 82 (1967): 33–38; Clifford, Gay. *The Transformations of Allegory*. London: Routledge & Kegan Paul, 1974; Daniélou, Jean. *From Shadows to Reality: Studies in the Biblical Typology of the Fathers*. Trans. Wulstan Hibberd. London: Burns & Oates, 1960; Dronke, Peter. "Tradition and Innovation in Medieval Western Colour-Imagery." In *Realms of Colour: Die Welt der Farben: Le monde des couleurs*, ed. Adolf Portmann and Rudolf Ritsema. Eranos Jahrbuch 41. Leiden: Brill, 1972, pp. 51–107; Eckhardt, Caroline D., ed. *Essays in the Numerical Criticism of Medieval Literature*. Lewisburg: Bucknell University Press, 1980; Fletcher, Angus. *Allegory: The Theory of a Symbolic Mode*. Ithaca: Cornell University Press, 1964; Kaske, R.E., in collaboration with Arthur Groos and Michael W. Twomey. *Medieval Christian Literary Imagery: A Guide to Interpretation*. Toronto: University of Toronto Press, 1988; Lubac, Henri de. *Exégèse médiévale: les quatres sens de l'écriture*. 2 vols in 4. Paris: Aubier, 1959–64; Quilligan, Maureen. *The Language of Allegory: Defining the Genre*. Ithaca: Cornell University Press, 1979; Reiss, Edmund. "Number Symbolism and Medieval Literature." *M&H* n.s. 1 (1970): 161–74; Robertson, D.W., Jr. *A Preface to Chaucer: Studies in Medieval Perspectives*. Princeton: Princeton University Press, 1962; Tristram, Philippa. *Figures of Life and Death in Medieval English Literature*. London: Elek, 1976; Tuve, Rosemond. *Allegorical Imagery: Some Mediaeval Books and Their Posterity*. Princeton: Princeton University Press, 1966; Wenzel, Siegfried. "The Pilgrimage of Life as a Late Medieval Genre." *MS* 35 (1973): 370–88; Williams, Arnold. "Medieval Allegory: An Operational Approach." In *Poetic Theory / Poetic Practice* (*Papers of the Midwest Modern Language Association* 1 [1969]), ed. Robert Scholes. Iowa City: Midwest MLA, 1969, pp. 77–84.

OE AND ME LITERATURE

Barney, Stephen A. *Allegories of History, Allegories of Love*. Hamden: Archon, 1979 [useful bibliographic commentary]; Barney, Stephen A. "Allegorical Visions." In *A Companion to Piers Plowman Studies*, ed. John A. Alford. Berkeley: University of California Press, 1988, pp. 117–34; DiMarco, Vincent. "Annual Bibliography." *YLS* 1– (1987–) [covers *Piers Plowman* and other didactic and allegorical alliterative poems]; Earl, James W. "Typology and Iconographic Style in Early Medieval Hagiography." *Studies in the Literary Imagination* 8 (1975): 15–46; Frank, Roberta. "Some Uses of Paronomasia in OE Scriptural Verse." *Speculum* 47 (1972): 207–26; Gradon, Pamela. "The Allegorical Picture." In *Form and Style in Early English Literature*. London: Methuen, 1971, pp. 32–92; Griffiths, Lavinia. *Personification in Piers Plowman*. Cambridge: Brewer, 1985; Hill, Joyce. "Ælfric's Use of Etymologies." *ASE* 17 (1988): 35–44; Kaske, R.E. "Chaucer and Medieval Allegory." *ELH* 30 (1963): 175–92; Robinson, Fred. "The Significance of Names in Old English Literature." *Anglia* 86 (1968): 14–58; Wimsatt, James I. *Allegory and Mirror: Tradition and Structure in Middle English Literature*. New York: Pegasus, 1970.

See also Ars moriendi; Beast Epic and Fable; Bible in ME Literature; Bible in OE Literature; Boethius; Criticism, Modern, of Medieval Literature; Debate Poems; Drama, Vernacular; Dream Vision; Exemplum; Literary Influences: French, Medieval Latin; Psychology, Medieval; Religious Allegories

Alliterative Revival

A poetic movement of the later 14th and 15th centuries, embracing a large number of poems written in various forms of the alliterative line, often unrhymed, but sometimes using rhyme as well as alliteration. At the center of the movement is a group of unrhymed alliterative poems of high literary quality and often of considerable length. Several present historical material: the life of Alexander the Great (*The Wars of Alexander, Alexander A, Alexander B*), Jewish history (*The Siege of Jerusalem*), the Troy story (*The Destruction of Troy*), and the last years of Arthur (*Morte Arthure*). There are poems based on Old Testament stories (*Cleanness* and *Patience*), romances (*William of Palerne* and *Sir Gawain and the Green Knight*), and poems presenting social, political, and ethical issues (*Winner and Waster, Piers Plowman, Richard the Redeless, Mum and the Sothsegger*), or raising questions of doctrine (*St. Erkenwald*).

What defines the works as a group is their metrical practice, but the poems also share certain characteristic attitudes of high seriousness and moral gravity, as well as a fondness for passages of grand description of scenery and violent action.

The majority of the poems are anonymous and their dates uncertain: the earliest may be *William of Palerne*, written before the death of Humphrey de Bohun in 1361, though *Winner and Waster* is thought by many to have been composed in 1352 or thereabout. The allusion by Chaucer's Parson to the revival—"I am a southren man; I kan nat geeste rum ram ruf by lettre" (*ParsProl* 42–43)—draws attention not only to the use of alliteration but also to its chief geographical location, for in Chaucer's time alliterative poetry had strong regional associations with the West Midlands, particularly the north of that area. In the 15th century the influence of alliterative verse was diffused more widely, and many of its features were adopted by poets and dramatists in the north of England and in Scotland.

The question of the origins of the Revival has been much discussed but not satisfactorily resolved. The use of alliteration as a structural principle of a verse line is an ancient Germanic form, and it is natural to assume a link with pre-Conquest verse. Features of vocabulary also recall the poetic diction of Anglo-Saxon poets. However, as far as the written record goes, the classical form of OE verse died out soon after the Conquest, to be replaced by looser forms with irregular rhythmic and alliterative patterns, making irregular use of rhyme. The most distinguished example of this is Laȝamon's *Brut*, a long chronicle of Britain composed by a priest from Areley Kings in Worcestershire in the late 12th or early 13th century. Other writers made irregular but often heavy use of alliteration in regular rhyming stanzas, and several fine examples of this are in the manuscript Harley 2253 (source of the Harley Lyrics), copied in about 1340 by a scribe from Ludlow, Shropshire, again in the Southwest Midlands.

Though Laȝamon's *Brut* and some of the Harley Lyrics show interesting similarities with the poems of the Revival in their vocabulary and verse structure, both represent a divergence from the unrhymed alliterative line, most obviously in their use of rhyme. It used to be the general view that the unrhymed alliterative line survived in oral form from the Conquest to the mid-14th century, gradually adapting to linguistic and societal changes that reshaped both meter and thematic concerns. More recently objections have been raised to this idea, in particular that the sophisticated literariness of the poems of the Revival, many of which are based on (or even closely translated from) long texts in French and Latin, can owe nothing to an oral stage of transmission. It has instead been proposed that the written tradition was maintained by monastic authors and scribes in the West Midlands, but that all manuscripts of such earlier texts have been lost.

It is undeniable that losses of early ME texts must have been enormous, and it is likely enough that texts of a literary movement that was circumscribed both regionally and socially would not have been widely circulated, and yet it is difficult to understand how all trace of such poems could have vanished entirely. An alternative hypothesis is that the movement was a new creation of 14th-century poets, developed from a variety of preexisting forms—in particular, alliterative verse in rhyming stanzas and alliterative rhythmic prose, such as some of the 13th-century saints' lives and the works of Richard Rolle (d. 1349). However, the shared metrical practices of the poets are so deep-rooted, subtle, and apparently traditional that it is difficult to see how they could have been quickly assimilated and widely adopted.

Many poems of the Revival have presumably been lost, since the majority of those that remain, such as the *Gawain* poems, *Winner and Waster*, *St. Erkenwald*, and *The Destruction of Troy*, are preserved in single copies. There are two manuscripts of parts of *The Parliament of the Three Ages* and *The Wars of Alexander*; *The Siege of Jerusalem* survives in the unusual number of eight copies and one fragment. Still more exceptional (as in many things) is *Piers Plowman*, with 52 manuscripts to its credit. Many of the manuscripts of alliterative poems are late, from the mid-15th century onward; *The Destruction of Troy* and *Alexander A* are preserved only in copies from the mid-16th century, and *Death and Life* in the 17th-century Percy Folio manuscript.

While works of Chaucer, Gower, and Lydgate are sometimes preserved in deluxe copies made for the aristocracy, manuscripts of alliterative poetry are humbler and less richly executed, suggesting ownership by a lower social class, probably including gentry and their households, as well as secular and monastic clergy. *William of Palerne* was written at the behest of Humphrey de Bohun, earl of Hereford, by a poet who names himself William, for the "ese of Englysch men," specifically "hem that knowe no Frensche," rather than for the entertainment of the patron himself. Another author for whom we have a name—but as yet no further information—is John Clerk of Whalley, Lancashire, who wrote the longest of all alliterative poems, *The Destruction of Troy*, for an unidentified knight.

Other conclusions about the nature of the authors and their audiences may tentatively be drawn from the characteristics of the poems themselves. Certainly many of the authors were highly educated and able to translate Latin and French easily and accurately, and they expected their audience to be attracted away from frivolous subjects toward a learned presentation of historical, social, and religious matters and also relied on them having an appreciation of the techniques of such arts as hawking, hunting, and siege warfare. The romantic and courtly attitude to love is notable by its absence; where love is a theme, as in *Gawain*, it features as a trap to catch the unwary rather than as a preoccupation to be indulged. A social setting that may be envisaged, but is as yet unsupported by any firm evidence, is of clerics writing for other clerics and provincial gentry. In an earlier generation this audience would have been prepared to read Anglo-Norman and Latin, but with the rise in the status of English after the mid-14th century they may have preferred writings in their mother tongue.

The concept of a sharply defined provincial audience is supported by the character of the vocabulary of alliterative poetry, which is distinctive and markedly different from that of poems by southern and eastern writers. Part of the difference is simply regional; the poets write in their own dialect using words confined to, or most common in, their own area. Such words may be found in nonalliterative northern and western texts and may survive in dialect to modern times: for example, *laik*, "play," a noun and verb of Old Norse origin, common in northern dialects even today, widespread in northern texts including alliterative poems, but quite absent from the vocabulary of Chaucer and Gower. Another set of words is mainly confined to poets of the Revival, rarely occurring even in other northwestern texts: such a word is *blonk*, "horse" (from OE), common in alliterative poems. A notable group of synonyms frequently used in alliterative poems but never by Chaucer and Gower are the words for "man, knight"; of these *gome*, *burn*, and *lede* occur occasionally in nonalliterative poems, but *freke*, *hathel*, *shalke*, *segge*, and *wyʒe* (all from OE), and *tulk* (from Old Norse), are almost entirely confined to poems of the Revival at this period. With this vocabulary the poets build up a distinctive and varied poetic diction, used to particularly vivid effect in those descriptive scenes so characteristic of the school, of sea storms, savage battles, and mountain ranges.

The metrical structure of the alliterative line is essentially straightforward and may be illustrated by lines from *Gawain*. Each line is constructed of two half-lines of two stresses; the two stresses of the first half-line alliterate with the first stress of the second half-line:

> On mony *b*ónkkes ful *b*róde ⁓ *B*rétayn he séttez.

Consonants alliterate with identical consonants, and consonant groups, such as st- or sp-, often alliterate with themselves. Any vowel may alliterate with any other vowel or with h-:

> Hit watz *É*nnias the *á*thel ⁓ and his *h*íghe kýnde.

Some first half-lines have three prominent syllables, often with alliteration on all three (though these three prominent syllables may not all be stressed):

> The *b*orʒ *b*rittened and *b*rent ⁓ to *b*rondez and askez.

Occasionally the last stress of the line joins in the alliteration:

> *M*ist *m*uged on the *m*or ⁓ *m*alt on the *m*ountez.

Other variations are found in the alliterative patterns, some of which are likely to be scribal errors. The rhythm is tightly controlled in the second half-line, so that certain patterns of regularly stressed and unstressed syllables (e.g., x/x/x or xx/xx) are avoided.

In several respects *Piers Plowman* is an uncharacteristic alliterative poem and an exception to what has been described, for Langland makes only limited use of the exclusively alliterative diction, and his line is longer and depends on a modified set of metrical practices. The explanation is that he was writing for an audience that was socially more diverse and centered on a different region, and it is significant that *Piers Plowman* survives in many more manuscripts than any other alliterative poem, few of them northern. Strongly influenced by Langland in both style and subject matter is the author of *Pierce the Plowman's Creed*.

The alliterative line was also used for poems in rhyming stanzas. The most popular arrangement was a thirteen-line stanza of eight lines rhyming abababab followed by five shorter lines of various metrical and rhyming patterns—sometimes a one-stress "bob" preceding a "wheel" of four three-stress lines. Four particularly interesting thirteen-line-stanza poems are *A Pistel of Susan* (a retelling of the biblical story of Susannah and the Elders), *The Awntyrs off Arthure* (in which Guinevere meets her dead mother's ghost), *The Three Dead Kings* (an account unique in English of the motif of the meeting of the Three Living and the Three Dead), and *The Truelove* (a poem in praise of the Virgin Mary). In *Gawain* a stanzaic arrangement is produced by combining a variable number of unrhymed lines with the "bob-and-wheel"; in *Pearl* a modified alliterative line is used in intricate twelve-line stanzas.

During the 15th century the thirteen-line stanza became popular farther north and was used in drama (e.g., *The Castle of Perseverance*) and in Scottish poems (e.g., *Rauf Coilʒear* and Holland's *Buke of the Howlat*). The unrhymed line, too, survived later in Scotland than in England, and the finest late example is Dunbar's burlesque *Tretis of the Tua Mariit Wemen and the Wedo*, from the beginning of the 16th century.

Thorlac Turville-Petre

Bibliography

PRIMARY

Turville-Petre, Thorlac, ed. *Alliterative Poetry of the Later Middle Ages: An Anthology*. London: Routledge, 1989.

SECONDARY

Duggan, Hoyt N. "The Shape of the B-Verse in Middle English Alliterative Poetry." *Speculum* 61 (1986): 564–92; Hanna, Ralph, III. "Defining Middle English Alliterative Poetry." In *The Endless Knot: Essays on Old and Middle English in Honor of Marie Borroff*, ed. M. Teresa Tavormina and R.F. Yeager. Cambridge: Brewer, 1995, pp. 43–64; Lawton, David A., ed. *Middle English Alliterative Poetry and Its Literary Background: Seven Essays*. Cambridge: Brewer, 1982; Oakden, J.P. *Alliterative Poetry in Middle English*. 2 vols. Manchester: Manchester University Press, 1930–35. Repr. as 1 vol. Hamden: Archon, 1968; Turville-Petre, Thorlac. *The Alliterative Revival*. Cambridge: Brewer, 1977.

See also Clerk; *Death and Life*; Dunbar; Harley Lyrics; Laʒamon; Matter of Antiquity; *Morte Arthure*, Alliterative; *Parliament of the Three Ages*, *Pearl*-Poet; *Pierce the Plowman's Creed*; *Piers Plowman*; *Richard the Redeless*; Rolle; Scottish Literature, Early; *Siege of Jerusalem*; *Truelove*; Versification; *William of Palerne*; *Winner and Waster*

Alms and Charity

The Gospels offered a compelling new impulse to the Judeo-Hellenistic world: love between people not bound by blood or kinship. Charity was thus a human expression of the love that bound God to humanity and was demonstrated in the sacrifice of the Son of God for their sins. The message of love that inspired the first Christians and that set itself as an antithesis to what was seen as a legalistic Jewish ethic elevated material poverty and weakness into signs of virtue and merit. Christianity inverted social hierarchies and relations to make a stranger into a brother, the poor and weak into lords of a world to come. As Christianity spread and became a mass religion, sanctioned by the Roman state and endowed with power and wealth, the tension inherent in this message became incorporated into the social structures of the Germanic peoples of western Europe and the romanized regions of southern Europe. Inasmuch as the church could maintain the force of the ideal of charity, this notion had to be harnessed to existing ideas and values.

The interpretation of charity that developed in medieval Christian society was thus dependent on context and embedded in prevailing ideas about family, social responsibility, community and cooperation, and formulations of sin, reward, penance, and punishment. From the 5th century papal legislation ordered charitable provision from bishops' incomes for the poor and for pilgrims, and throughout the early Middle Ages episcopal and then priestly office carried obligations of charity and hospitality. Charity was enjoined as an ideal for religious communities and was practiced in ritualized forms at the gates of monastic institutions. It became an idiom for human perfection, its practice a mode for spiritual improvement. Almsgiving was integrated into the routines of penance as a form of satisfaction alongside fasts and prayers. It was a normative requirement preached in the homilies of Ælfric in the 10th century as in those of Thomas Brinton, bishop of Rochester, in the 14th century.

Discussions of charity and the development of new forms of charitable practice intensified in the high Middle Ages. With the increasing definition and clarity of the notion of purgatory charity was cast as a practice carrying important spiritual returns. Almsgiving and the grateful prayers of the poor could alleviate purgatorial suffering for venial sins for which a person had not done penance before death. In the heated debates of the 12th and 13th centuries new definitions of the contours of charity and the nature of charitable obligations developed. These called not for dispossession but for the sensible allocation of "superfluous" wealth toward the needs of the "involuntary" poor, as well as to the "voluntary" religious poor. English theologians formulated ideas to be implemented and enforced by bishops and priests. Primary obligations to support kin were coupled with gentle encouragement of charitable giving to the poor at the doorstep or in the hospital (as the hospital emerged as a general charitable institution).

As borough communities developed in the 12th and 13th centuries and became preoccupied with the promotion of order, safety, and hygiene, the religious language of charity was harnessed as a framework for the organization of relief. This convergence produced hundreds of hospitals and leper houses, from around 1150 onward, mainly served by religious communities, funded by charitable bequests.

In the 13th century a new type of charitable institution developed, the academic college, providing support for poor scholars in return for prayers and commemorations. Charity was also practiced in smaller frameworks, and for the benefit of family and friends, in the familiarity of parishes or the intimacy of a religious fraternity offering mutual help. In the countryside parishes collected and allocated funds that accompanied other community provisions to help the elderly, orphans, and the needy. In the 14th and 15th centuries a greater specialization in charitable giving is evident, with the development of charitable provision in parishes, as well as the secular almshouse or hospital, such as Whittington's hospital in London, plus the numerous charities connected with craft guilds. Charity was thus experienced in medieval society as an omnipresent inducement toward participation in relief, help, and sociability, but the frequency and scope of these undertakings were left to personal discretion. It thus changed over time in its forms, intensity, and meaning.

Miri Rubin

Bibliography

Mollat, Michel. *The Poor in the Middle Ages: An Essay in Social History.* Trans. A. Goldhammer. New Haven: Yale University Press, 1986; Rosenthal, Joel T. *The Purchase of Paradise: Gift Giving and the Aristocracy, 1307–1485.* London: Routledge & Kegan Paul, 1972; Rubin, Miri. *Charity and Community in Medieval Cambridge.* Cambridge: Cambridge University Press, 1987; Thomson, John A.F. "Piety and Charity in Late Medieval London." *Journal of Ecclesiastical History* 16 (1965): 178–95.

See also Chantries; Guilds; Hospitals

Amesbury Psalter

The Amesbury Psalter (Oxford, All Souls College 6) is one of a group of five illuminated manuscripts (with another psalter, a missal, a Bible, and an Apocalypse) produced between ca. 1245 and 1255, which are important representatives of the early Gothic style in its maturity. Within ten years of their production the soft, deeply troughed drapery folds that are a feature of these works evolve into broader, more triangular fold forms under influence from France.

This psalter, "the purest gem of English medieval painting" (Holländer), has four exquisite full-page miniatures with burnished gold grounds, elaborately incised, prefacing the text. Within the psalter are large historiated initials at the ten major psalm divisions, as well as at Psalm 119 (the first of the Gradual Psalms). It has been demonstrated that the psalm initials are close iconographic copies of those in the early-13th-century Imola Psalter (Imola, Biblioteca Comunale 100), associated with Amesbury in Wiltshire, having in common biblical themes, such as Samuel anointing David (Ps. 26), the

Judgment of Solomon (Ps. 38), Doeg slaughtering Ahimelech and the priests (Ps. 51), the Temptation of Christ (Ps. 52), Jonah being cast into the whale (Ps. 68), Jacob wrestling with the angel and Jacob's dream (Ps. 80), and the Annunciation to the Shepherds (Ps. 97). The series is thus of a type that predated French influence and tended to illustrate the literal content or opening verses of the psalm (cf. Cuerden Psalter [New York, Pierpont Morgan Library M.756]).

The full-page miniatures, depicting the Annunciation, Virgin and Child (fig. 2), Crucifixion, and Christ in Majesty, relate closely to those in the Missal of Henry of Chichester (Manchester, John Rylands Library lat. 24), where some of the subjects are the same. This style, in which sincere feelings of tenderness, compassion, and devotion are expressed in the faces, is characterized by strong drapery lines and monumental figure types. The artist uses white hatching for highlights and brown tones for facial modeling. These dignified figures are, however, beginning to show signs of a graceful mannerism associated with the products of the Court School, which is seen fully developed in Queen Mary's Psalter of the early 14th century (BL Royal 2.B.vii).

There is no precise dating evidence for either the psalter or the missal, but the related Bible (BL Royal 1.B.xii) has an inscription that records that it was written by William of Hales in 1254. It is a matter of conjecture as to whether the psalter pre- or postdates the missal, although Morgan has pointed out that the draperies in the psalter show greater naturalism and refinement than do those in the missal and that they are developing toward the more softly flowing forms evident in the Paris Apocalypse (Paris, BN fr. 403) of ca. 1250–55, which he assigns to the Sarum Master. Whereas it could be argued that the greater vigor of expression and dramatic gesture in the missal might suggest that it postdates the psalter, Morgan also notes that certain pigments apparent in the psalter, but not in the missal, occur in the Bible, which is presumably of later date.

The sources of this exceptional illuminator (the "Sarum Master"), whose identity is unknown, derive ultimately from the milieu of two London-produced books: the Westminster Psalter (BL Royal 2.A.xxii) of ca. 1200 and the Glazier Psalter (New York, Pierpont Morgan Library Glazier 25) of ca. 1220. The style also bears a relationship to the wall paintings in the Chapel of the Guardian Angels at Winchester of ca. 1230 and the Chichester Roundel of ca. 1250–60. It is undoubtedly related to other monumental works of painting and sculpture, but the severe losses in the Salisbury area make a comprehensive assessment of this Master's origins impossible. The prerestoration drawings of medallions on the ceiling of Salisbury Cathedral suggest parallels with his style. In this case contemporary foreign survivals can throw much-needed light on the problem. For instance, the Amesbury Psalter miniatures have a number of unusual iconographic features for which parallels have been found in more completely preserved German wood sculpture and Norwegian panel painting, the latter under stylistic as well as iconographic influence from England. The interesting iconic representation of the *Virgo lactans* (the Virgin suckling the Child), which becomes popular in England at this time (there are instances in wall painting), is not necessarily of foreign origin and could have evolved from narrative representations of this image in earlier English illumination.

The evidence of the Sarum illuminator's *oeuvre* indisputably localizes production to the Salisbury area. The calendar of the Amesbury Psalter contains two prominent feasts of St. Melor, whose relics were at Amesbury. As to ownership, both the Virgin and Child and Christ in Majesty pages show a nun kneeling in prayer. It has recently been argued that her identification as a Benedictine nun of the order of Fontevrault, which had a convent at Amesbury, should be viewed with caution, since the calendar is not properly one of that house, and that the patron could well be a laywoman, possibly a widow.

Lynda Dennison

Bibliography

Alexander, Jonathan, and Paul Binski, eds. *Age of Chivalry: Art in Plantagenet England 1200–1400.* London: Royal Academy of Arts, 1987, cat. no. 316; Holländer, Albert. "The Sarum Illuminator and His School." *Wiltshire Archaeological and Natural History Magazine* 50 (1943): 230–62; Morgan, Nigel. *Early Gothic Manuscripts (2) 1250–1285.* A Survey of Manuscripts Illuminated in the British Isles 4:2, ed. J.J.G. Alexander. London: Harvey Miller, 1988, no. 101.

See also Chichester Roundel; Cuerden Psalter; Manuscript Illumination, Gothic; Psalters, Gothic

Anarchy

The name applied to Stephen's reign (1135–54). Though the Anarchy was actually a civil war, the idea that England lacked a central government during these years began with contemporary chroniclers and has been accepted since Tudor times.

A disputed claim to the throne started the Anarchy. After Henry I's son died in 1120, he designated his only legitimate child, Empress Matilda, widow of the Holy Roman Emperor Henry V, as his heir; the barons swore homage to her in 1126. However, in Norman history no woman had been a ruler, and Matilda was also married now to a traditional Norman enemy, Geoffrey, count of Anjou. When Henry I died (1 December 1135), many English barons were hesitant to accept her, and Henry's nephew Stephen of Blois acted quickly.

Stephen's hereditary claim was weak, but he was known to the English nobles and Henry had enriched and greatly favored him. He was acclaimed king by the people of London and Winchester and given control of the government after his brother Henry, bishop of Winchester, convinced key administrators to accept him. He was formally crowned on 22 December 1135. At first Stephen had strong support. His Charter of Liberties (1136) won over the English clergy, and by summer most of the nobles officially recognized him. Despite the lack of formal election, designation, or inheritance he appeared to be undisputed king of England.

The consensus did not last; war began in 1137. Matilda's forces held Normandy, but in England her troops, led by her family (especially her uncle, David, king of Scots, and her half-brother, Robert, earl of Gloucester), were defeated by Stephen's at the Battle of the Standard (1138). Yet this victory neither stabilized his rule nor ended the fighting. Rivalries proliferated at court, exacerbated by clerical disputes that alienated even the king's brother. Stephen's attempts to replace government personnel were often clumsy and offensive. Nobles switched sides at crucial times, sometimes repeatedly. Castles were built and land subinfeudated (vassals bestowing land upon their own vassals) without royal permission. In February 1141 Stephen was captured at the Battle of Lincoln and the empress was declared "Lady of England." In spite of heavy defections from Stephen's camp Matilda failed to keep power. A poorly handled clerical appointment made her appear an opponent to reform in the church. Londoners rebelled after she demanded financial support. Some of Stephen's former followers wanted rewards or power greater than she was willing to give. Furthermore some barons were unable to reconcile their own expectations of a woman's behavior with a king's behavior, unable to accept a woman who actually ruled.

Stephen's wife, Queen Matilda, continued the fight. After nine months Stephen resumed the crown when Robert of Gloucester was captured and their wives negotiated a hostage exchange. While Stephen gained the advantage in the field, he never recovered active noble support, relying on mercenary troops, and Matilda even remained in England until 1148. There was little progress until 1150, when Empress Matilda's son Henry (Plantagenet) assumed control of their forces. In 1153, faced with the increasing wealth and skill of Henry and the death of many of his original partisans and old enemies, Stephen accepted a negotiated peace. Emphasis was placed on the hereditary nature of the monarchy; Stephen "adopted" Henry as his "son and heir" in a public oath, passing over his own son. Royal power was reasserted as unlicensed castles were razed and all castles were to be turned over to Henry at Stephen's death. When Stephen died on 25 October 1154, Henry was in Normandy. Certain of a peaceful transfer of power, he did not come to England to assume control, as Henry II, until December.

The causes and results of the civil war are debated. The nobles' willingness to participate, much less to switch sides, may have been a feudal reaction against the centralized government of Henry I or evidence that they accepted strong rule and searched for a king stronger than Stephen. A few were merely opportunistic, the classic example being Geoffrey de Mandeville, whose double-switch was crucial to the events of 1141 and whose cruelty and pillaging were part of his normal behavior until his death, an excommunicated rebel, in 1144. Many chose sides because of the ability of the claimant, or to regain land lost under Henry I, or because a rival in a local dispute chose the other side. Disappointment in the ability or success of both claimants explains most defections. The actual extent of the Anarchy—as measured by administrative continuity or breakdown and the damage caused by military campaigns—is still a matter of debate.

Charlotte Newman Goldy

Bibliography

Callahan, Thomas. "The Impact of the Anarchy on English Monasticism, 1135–1154." *Albion* 6 (1974): 218–32; Chibnall, Marjorie. *The Empress Matilda: Queen Consort, Queen Mother and Lady of the English.* Oxford: Blackwell, 1992; Crouch, David. *The Beaumont Twins: The Roots and Branches of Power in the Twelfth Century.* Cambridge: Cambridge University Press, 1986; Davis, Henry W.C. "The Anarchy of Stephen's Reign." *EHR* 18 (1903): 630–41; Hollister, C. Warren. "Stephen's Anarchy." *Albion* 6 (1974): 233–39; King, Edmund. "The Anarchy of King Stephen's Reign." *TRHS*, 5th ser. 34 (1984): 133–53; Patterson, Robert B. "Anarchy in England, 1135–1154: The Theory of the Constitution." *Albion* 6 (1974): 189–200; Round, John Horace. *Geoffrey de Mandeville: A Study of the Anarchy.* London: Longmans, 1892. Repr. New York: Burt Franklin, n.d; White, Graeme. "Were the Midlands 'Wasted' in Stephen's Reign?" *Midland History* 10 (1985): 26–46; Yoshitake, Kenjii. "The Arrest of the Bishops in 1139 and Its Consequences." *JMH* 48 (1988): 97–114.

See also Angevin Empire; Henry I; Henry II; Investiture Controversy; Matilda; Stephen

Ancrene Wisse

An anonymous religious guide for anchoresses (ca. 1215–22). The work, first written at the request of three female recluses, was later revised for larger audiences of both men and women. English is believed to be its original language, although versions of it also exist in Latin and French. The oldest manuscript is BL Cotton Nero A.xiv, but Cambridge, Corpus Christi College (CCCC) 402, is believed to be the closest to the original. The work proliferated, yielding other versions in the 13th, 14th, and 15th centuries. Dobson localizes it to Wigmore Abbey in Herefordshire and possibly to the anchorhold of the Deerfold, where three anchoresses lived.

Tolkien has shown conclusively that the *Ancrene Wisse* is associated with five other ME religious works known as the Katherine Group; the prayers and meditations known as the Wooing Group are also closely related. The Katherine Group and the *Wisse* together are known as the AB texts, manuscript A standing for the West Midlands dialect of the *Ancrene Wisse* as it appears in CCCC 402 and B for the Katherine Group as it appears in the manuscript Bodley 34. The author of the *Wisse* is unknown, although he was most likely an Augustinian canon.

The three recluses for whom the *Wisse* was written are not named but are addressed as sisters within the work itself. In the Cotton Nero manuscript they are addressed as natural sisters and called well-born. Like other anchoresses they were committed to vows of obedience, chastity, and stability and were to live as if "dead to the world." From the work we know that these three were devout and lived comfortably in an anchorhold that consisted of bedrooms, servants' quarters, and a garden.

The title *Ancrene Wisse (Guide for Anchoresses)* appears as a rubric on fol. 1 of CCCC 402, but the work is also referred to as the *Ancrene Riwle* (*Rule for Anchoresses*). The name *Wisse* is more appropriate for the spirit of the work, for the author tells us throughout that he is concerned not with external rules but with the less definable rule of the heart. The *Wisse*'s vocabulary, syntax, and idiom have features in common with OE homiletic prose, but it also displays stylistic innovations for which it is justly praised as a masterpiece of early ME literature. It draws heavily on the works of Bernard of Clairvaux, Aelred of Rievaulx, Anselm of Canterbury, and Augustine but depends most on the Bible.

Georgianna has shown the importance of the *Wisse* as a measure and product of the 12th-century renaissance, that is, as a sophisticated psychological work concerned with the nature of the individual in society and with the recording and investigation of personal history. Grayson has shown the importance of the work's rich and complex patterns of imagery, which she describes as nonlogical, nonteleological ascending and descending spirals. Robertson argues that the work's theme, imagery, and structure, including the patterns outlined by Grayson, are shaped by the author's paternalistic and patriarchal notions of the nature of its female readers.

The *Ancrene Wisse* is divided into eight parts, two outer rules that frame the work (devotions and daily rules) and six inner rules (custody of the senses, regulation of inward feelings, temptations, confession, penance, love), all aimed at motivating and supporting the anchoress's devotion to Christ as her chosen beloved. Although union with Christ is celebrated, the work focuses more on the psychological difficulty and importance of balancing an abstract religious ideal with the demands of quotidian reality in the anchorhold. The *Wisse* conveys its message in part through its complex imagery, ranging from the chivalric topos of Christ as knightly lover to the everyday one of the sparrow outside the window. The work is one of the most sophisticated pieces of early ME devotional prose. Its blending of lyric intensity, affective piety, and homiletic purpose ultimately extended its appeal far beyond its original narrow audience.

Elizabeth Robertson

Bibliography

PRIMARY

For a full listing of editions and versions see Shepherd and Dahood below; Ackerman, Robert W., and Roger Dahood, eds. and trans. *Ancrene Riwle: Introduction and Part 1.* Binghamton: MRTS, 1984; Millett, Bella, and Jocelyn Wogan-Browne, eds. *Medieval English Prose for Women: Selections from the Katherine Group and Ancrene Wisse.* Oxford: Clarendon, 1990; Shepherd, Geoffrey, ed. *Ancrene Wisse: Parts Six and Seven.* London: Nelson, 1959 [lists other editions of English, French, and Latin versions on p. 73]; Savage, Ann, and Nicholas Watson, trans. *Anchoritic Spirituality: Ancrene Wisse and Associated Works.* New York: Paulist Press, 1991.

SECONDARY

New *CBEL* 1:498–500; *Manual* 2:458–60, 650–54; Beckwith, Sarah. "Passionate Regulation: Enclosure, Ascesis, and the Feminist Imaginary." In *Materialist Feminism*, ed. Toril Moi and Janice Radway. Special Issue of *South Atlantic Quarterly* 93 (1994): 801–24; Clark, Cecily. "Early Middle English Prose: Three Essays in Stylistics." *EIC* 18 (1968): 361–82; Dahood, Roger. "*Ancrene Wisse*, the Katherine Group, and the *Wohunge* Group." In *Middle English Prose: A Critical Guide to Major Authors and Genres*, ed. A.S.G. Edwards. New Brunswick: Rutgers University Press, 1984, pp. 1–33; Dobson, E.J. *The Origins of Ancrene Wisse.* Oxford: Clarendon, 1976; Georgianna, Linda. *The Solitary Self: Individuality in the Ancrene Wisse.* Cambridge: Harvard University Press, 1981; Grayson, Janet. *Structure and Imagery in Ancrene Wisse.* Hanover: University Press of New England, 1974; Robertson, Elizabeth. *Early English Devotional Prose and the Female Audience.* Knoxville: University of Tennessee Press, 1990; Tolkien, J.R.R. "*Ancrene Wisse* and *Hali Meiðhad.*" *Essays and Studies* 14 (1929): 104–26.

See also Katherine Group; Mystical and Devotional Writings; Nuns; Prose, ME; Women in ME Literature

Andreas

An OE narrative poem of some 1,722 lines based on an apocryphal life of St. Andrew. Probably written in the 9th century, the poem is generally believed to be a translation of a lost Latin work that was itself ultimately derived from a text similar to a 4th-century romantic Greek legend, *The Acts of Andrew and Matthew in the City of the Anthropophagi.* This work, in turn, was part of a much larger popular tradition begun at least as early as the 2nd century that imaginatively explored the fates of the apostles after Jesus commanded them to spread his teachings throughout the world (Matt. 28:19–20; Acts 1:8). The author of *Andreas* fuses this fabulous tale with the conventions of the OE Germanic-heroic poetic tradition, depicting the saint as an OE warrior who leads his loyal thegns into battle against the opposing armies of the Devil and the Anthropophagi, who are themselves fierce but unhappy hall-thegns. This merger of traditions is not always successful, but *Andreas* is nevertheless a lively and engaging testament of faith.

The poem's heroic opening praises the twelve apostles and tells of Matthew's trials among cannibals in Mermedonia (possibly Scythia), where he is blinded and imprisoned. God commands Andreas to rescue Matthew, and he sails from Achaia to Mermedonia on a ship piloted by a Helmsman and two sailors, who are Christ and angels in disguise. The stormy voyage continues for nearly 500 lines, during which Andreas recounts to the Helmsman the miracles of Christ among the unbelieving multitudes and his attempts to convert the high priests in the temple in Jerusalem. Although the Helmsman offers to put Andreas's thegns safely ashore during the storm, they protest their loyalty to Andreas in a speech that articulates the ethos of the Germanic *comitatus*, the traditional aristocratic warrior band. Andreas reassures his followers by telling of God's power to calm the raging seas. The thegns fall asleep, and the seas grow still. Having praised Christ's teachings for the whole day, Andreas, too, suddenly falls asleep, and he and his followers are borne aloft by angels and left sleeping outside the walls of Mermedonia. Upon awakening Andreas realizes the identity of the Helmsman.

The remainder of the poem concerns Andrew's confrontations with and conversion of the Mermedonians. Made invisible by God, he rescues Matthew and other prisoners. At God's command Andreas reveals himself and is taken captive by the enraged and starving enemy. For three days he suffers— tortured by day and taunted at night by the Devil. On the third day he prays to God for mercy and sees flowers bloom where his blood once flowed upon the earth. God heals Andreas, who then commands a marble pillar to flood the city, while an angel covers the fortress with flames so that none may escape. As many drown, others repent and Andreas leaves his prison, the ground becoming dry wherever he steps. He prays that the dead may be restored to life and his prayers are answered. A Christian church is built, the Mermedonians are baptized, a bishop is named. Andreas then sails once more to Achaia, while the newly converted Mermedonians sing a hymn to the glory of God.

The unique copy of *Andreas* survives in the late-10th-century Vercelli Book. Two OE prose versions are extant as well: a fragment in the late-10th-century Blickling Manuscript (Homily XIX) and a complete version in the early-11th-century manuscript Cambridge, Corpus Christi College 198. Because *Andreas* is followed in the Vercelli Book by *The Fates of the Apostles*, a short poem containing Cynewulf's runic signature, both poems were once thought to be a single work by that author. Scholars have since disproven Cynewulf's authorship of *Andreas* and have established its independence from *The Fates of the Apostles*. Other scholars, noting its many verbal and thematic similarities to *Beowulf* and other OE poems, have argued that the *Andreas*-poet was indebted to *Beowulf*.

Anita R. Riedinger

Bibliography

PRIMARY

ASPR 2:3–51; Brooks, Kenneth R., ed. *Andreas and The Fates of the Apostles*. Oxford: Clarendon, 1961; Kennedy, Charles W., trans. *Early English Christian Poetry*. New York: Oxford University Press, 1952, pp. 122–67.

SECONDARY

Allen, Michael J.B., and Daniel G. Calder, eds. and trans. *Sources and Analogues of Old English Poetry*. Cambridge: Brewer, 1976 [translation of Latin analogues]; Riedinger, Anita R. "The Formulaic Relationship between *Beowulf* and *Andreas*." In *Heroic Poetry in the Anglo-Saxon Period: Studies in Honor of Jess B. Bessinger, Jr.*, ed. Helen Damico and John Leyerle. Kalamazoo: 1993, pp. 283–312; Schaar, Claes. *Critical Studies in the Cynewulf Group*. Lund: Gleerup, 1949. Repr. New York: Haskell House, 1967.

See also Beowulf; Blickling Homilies; Cynewulf; Hagiography; Vercelli Book

Angel Roofs

Roughly contemporary with the development of the Perpendicular style in architecture was the development of the wooden "hammer-beam" truss (a horizontal timber cantilevered out from the wall to help support the roof truss). In the late 14th and 15th centuries carved angels were added to the ends of the hammer beams. While usually carved separately, there are instances in which the body of the angel is carved from the beam itself and only the wings worked separately, as in the parish church of Mildenhall, Suffolk. The roofs were particularly popular in East Anglian churches of the 15th century.

Both the hammer beam and the use of angels for decorating vaults appear early in the 14th century. In the east end of the Gloucester Cathedral choir the roof bosses above the altar are decorated with angels carrying musical instruments and the symbols of the Passion. The two seem to come together for the first time in Hugh Herland's timber roof in Westminster Hall (1394–1400). Here single rows of angels bearing shields of the king's arms project from the ends of the brackets. The roof is remarkable not only for the exquisite quality of its carvings but also for its enormous span of over 65 feet.

Hugh Herland, the king's master carpenter, enjoyed the same high status and privileges as a master mason. Both his position and the esteem in which his work was held are symptomatic of the increased demand for high-quality woodwork in England in the late Gothic period.

While angels carrying the arms of noble families do appear, angels bearing musical instruments or symbols of the Passion are more common. Musician angels in general can be understood to symbolize heavenly harmony, and their music echoes that of the congregation below. The composition of the angel roofs may often have had close ties to the liturgy and liturgical drama, as at All Saints Church, North Street, York, where the angel Gabriel faces Mary above the altar in the chancel.

By the late 15th century magnificent double-hammer-beamed roofs decorated with tiers of soaring angels were created. At March Church, Cambridgeshire (ca. 1500), two tiers of angels project from the roof beams and a third from the base of the roof posts (fig. 3). The roof of the church at Upwell, Norfolk, however, reminds us that not all was harmony, beauty, and grace. Here, beneath the outspread wings of an angel, a fuzzy-haired human is being devoured by monsters.

Catherine E. Karkov

Bibliography

Alexander, Jonathan, and Paul Binski, eds. *Age of Chivalry: Art in Plantagenet England 1200–1400*. London: Royal Academy of Arts, 1987; Coldstream, Nicola. "Architecture." In *The Cambridge Guide to the Arts in Britain*. Vol. 2: *The Middle Ages*, ed. Boris Ford. Cambridge: Cambridge University Press, 1988, pp. 42–87; Davidson, Clifford, and David E. O'Connor. *York Art: A Subject List of Extant and Lost Art Including*

Fig. 3. March Church, Cambridgeshire, nave roof. Courtesy of L. Hoey.

Items Relevant to Early Drama. Kalamazoo: Medieval Institute, 1978; Stone, Lawrence. *Sculpture in Britain: The Middle Ages.* 2d ed. Harmondsworth: Penguin, 1972.

See also Architecture and Architectural Sculpture, Gothic; Art, Gothic

Angelus ad virginem

A devotional Latin strophic song of the first half of the 13th century in five stanzas on the Annunciation of Mary. There is memorable testimony to its widespread popularity and longevity in England in a passage from the *Miller's Tale* introducing Chaucer's poor Oxford scholar "hende Nicholas," who sings *Angelus* in his lodging to the accompaniment of his psaltery:

> And al above ther lay a gay sautrie,
> On which he made a-nyghtes melodie
> So swetely that all the chambre rong;
> And *Angelus ad virginem* he song. (*MilT* 3213–16)

Most sources and references to *Angelus ad virginem* are insular (complete report in Stevens). One tuneful melody is transmitted in four English sources, twice monophonically and twice in polyphonic settings of the later 13th and mid-14th centuries; an entirely different melody survives uniquely in a 15th-century German source. *Angelus* was twice translated into English, once anonymously in the later 13th century ("Gabriel fram evene king," underlaid beneath the standard melody and Latin text in BL Arundel 248) and again in the early 15th century by John Audelay ("The angel to the vergyn said," without

music, in Bodl. Douce 302). In a reference recently discovered by Page in the anonymous 13th-century English *Speculum laicorum* Odo of Cheriton is said to attribute the authorship of *Angelus* to Philip, the chancellor of the University of Paris (ca. 1160–1236). If this is to be credited, then perhaps it was brought to England in the first half of the century by the mendicant friars. Much later in its career *Angelus* was "taken over by liturgical officialdom" (Stevens), appearing, for example, in the ordinal of St. Mary's, York, of ca. 1400 and in 16th-century missals of Cluny and Senlis as an Advent sequence for masses of the Virgin.

Peter M. Lefferts

Bibliography

PRIMARY

Dobson, Eric J., and Frank Ll. Harrison, eds. and trans. *Medieval English Songs.* London: Faber & Faber, 1979; Harrison, Frank Ll., Ernest H. Sanders, and Peter M. Lefferts, eds. *English Music for Mass and Offices (II) and Music for Other Ceremonies.* Polyphonic Music of the Fourteenth Century 17. Paris: L'Oiseau-Lyre, 1986.

SECONDARY

Page, Christopher. "*Angelus ad virginem:* A New Work by Philippe the Chancellor?" *Early Music* 11 (1983): 69–70; Stevens, John. "*Angelus ad virginem:* The History of a Medieval Song." In *Medieval Studies for J.A.W. Bennett,* ed. P.L. Heyworth. Oxford: Clarendon, 1981, pp. 297–328.

See also Hymns; Sequence; Songs

Angevin Empire

Modern historians commonly use this term for the vast collection of French and English lands ruled by descendants of the counts of Anjou in western France in the later 12th and early 13th centuries; contemporaries never called it an empire nor its ruler an emperor. During its heyday in the later 12th century it was one of the great territorial powers of Europe; its rulers, especially Henry II, were leading men of their day. Although relatively short-lived and a failure from the perspective of its attempt to unite a large part of Britain and France as a permanent territorial unit, it had lasting effects on its constituent parts, particularly England. It was a remarkable creation in that no one could have predicted its existence even a few years before it began.

Accidents of royal and princely succession played a decisive role in its origins. The Plantagenet family, the dynastic rulers of the Angevin Empire, traced its origins to late-9th-century ancestors who became viscounts, then counts of Anjou, lying mainly north of the Loire, east of Brittany. Their growing power brought them into bitter rivalry with the other major principality of the northwest, the duchy of Normandy. A dynastic marriage in 1128 brought these ruling families together and enabled the Plantagenets to succeed to the English throne in 1154. Lacking a male heir, Henry I of England arranged for the marriage of his daughter Matilda, widow of the Holy Roman Emperor Henry V, to Geoffrey, the fourteen-year-old heir of Fulk V of Anjou.

They failed to make good their claim to the English throne, but the death of Stephen's male heir in 1153 reopened the question of the English succession. By now Geoffrey was dead (1151), but his eldest son, Henry Plantagenet, born 1133, pressed his claims and gained recognition in 1153 as successor to the English throne on Stephen's death (October 1154). When Henry ascended the throne, he brought together not only the kingdom of England, his native county of Anjou with its appendages, and the duchy of Normandy, conquered by his parents in 1144, but also the huge southwestern French duchy of Aquitaine, which he had acquired by his marriage in 1152 with Eleanor, duchess and heiress of Aquitaine.

In subsequent years Henry II conquered or subjected to his authority Wales, Ireland, Scotland, and Brittany, so that, at its greatest extent, late in his life, the Angevin Empire included most of Britain and western France to the Pyrenees. He presided over the establishment and operation of a system of governmental officials and institutions that administered his far-flung lands. In England this contributed to the elaboration of common law and administrative practice. The Angevin period in England also witnessed heightened activity in education, writing (literary and historical), and the arts, especially architecture and manuscript illumination. Despite the blemish left by the murder of Thomas Becket this was a great period in the history of the English church, both secular and regular (monastic).

Since it did not collapse at once, it is difficult to assign a precise date for the end of the Angevin Empire. From its beginnings the Capetian kings of France had been its enemies,

but both Henry II and his son Richard I held them firmly in check. Their successor, Richard's brother John, failed to do so. Using a dispute with a nobleman of Poitou as a pretext, Philip II of France formally confiscated John's French fiefs and then proceeded to conquer Normandy. Though revolts of Aquitanian nobles, kindled by French success, deprived John of these lands, one modern view holds that it was the loss of La Rochelle in 1224 that marked a decisive end to Angevin rule in Aquitaine. Plantagenet kings of the 13th century continued to rule fragments of their former domains in France, but the loss of the bulk of the land gradually transformed the empire from one based primarily in France to one centered in England. At this point, it is argued, the Angevin Empire had ceased effectively to exist.

George Beech

Bibliography

Boussard, Jacques. *Le gouvernement d'Henri II Plantagenet.* Paris: Librairie d'Argenes, 1956; Gillingham, John. *The Angevin Empire.* London: Arnold, 1984; Jolliffe, John E.A. *Angevin Kingship.* 2d ed. London: A. & C. Black, 1963; Le Patourel, John. "The Plantagenet Dominions." *History* 50 (1965): 289–308; Powicke, F.M. *The Loss of Normandy, 1189–1204.* 2d ed. Manchester: Manchester University Press, 1961; Warren, W.L. *Henry II.* 1973. Rev. ed. London: Methuen, 1991.

See also Eleanor of Aquitaine; Henry II; John; Matilda; Normandy; Richard I

Anglo-Latin Literature after 1066

During the four centuries following the Norman Conquest Anglo-Latin literature continued to evolve and expand, seeming at first to blend so successfully into the landscape of European Latin literature as to be almost indistinguishable. It reemerged with a sharper profile in the 13th century and disappeared as a separate literary entity only by the middle of the 15th century, with the rise of humanism and the ascendancy of English. Much of this change was adaptation to political circumstances. The establishment of the Anglo-Angevin Empire under Henry II brought with it the height of Anglo-Latin's "europeanization" (the roots of this development go back to the 11th, possibly even late 10th, century) and its hearty participation in the 12th-century renaissance. The loss of Normandy in 1205 caused Anglo-Latin literature to become a good deal more inward-looking and insular, almost xenophobic.

Cultural shifts were just as significant. The development of popular preaching, and the ousting of French by English as the language of court and administration in the 14th century, contributed to the decline of Latin as the literary vehicle of first choice. Other influences included the early-13th-century foundation and subsequent swift spread of the mendicant orders, the Franciscans and Dominicans. With their strong emphasis on scholarship and preaching, combined with freedom of operation, they contributed to the rise of the universities in England. Notable Franciscan authors were John of Wales, Walter of Wimborne, and John Pecham. The friars in their turn became the subject of satire, as the monks had been before them.

During the same period the increased popularity of private devotion and meditation brought about a change in the focus of religious literature, away from the simple recounting of salvation history, retelling Old and New Testament stories, toward a more intensely contemplative and sentimental viewpoint: not so much scanning the long train of events in the life of man culminating in Christ crucified and risen again but gazing with heightened emotion upon the suckling infant who is at the same time the suffering Savior on the Cross of agony. This trend was prefigured in the devotional and pastoral writings of the Cistercian Aelred of Rievaulx and reached a high point in the poetry of John of Howden and Walter of Wimborne and in the contemplative works of Richard Rolle.

Another evolutionary trend was a gradual change in the circumstances of literary production. The monasteries had always been the principal centers of Anglo-Latin scholarship, and although they continued to contribute in a major way, by the early 13th century a good proportion of Anglo-Latin writers were secular clerics, holding ecclesiastical offices but decidedly in the thick of political life, like John of Salisbury (whose *Policraticus* explores the morality of politics), or attached to the royal court as justices, secretaries, or chaplains. Of the latter type was Walter Map, who satirized the royal court in his *De nugis curialium.*

A facet of England's close relationship with France was the powerful pull of the renowned teachers at Paris. Talented scholars returning to England then found a place to bring their learning to bear on the world by involvement in the swiftly developing government and amid a welter of administrative activity. Furthermore, in the later 12th century, Oxford gained preeminence, and England finally had its own Paris. Cambridge followed close behind. All these places fostered and brought forth scholars and writers of Anglo-Latin. The rediscovery and teaching of Aristotle's works at Oxford had a profound influence on thinking and writing in England. In the 14th century the grammar schools also began to provide new arenas for Latin scholarship. A mark of the general shift of balance is the fact that John Gower, the last major figure in medieval literature to write in Latin and French as well as English, may not have been in holy orders at all.

During the course of four centuries Anglo-Latin authors composed works in almost every literary genre and on a broader range of topics than ever before, as well as continuing with the fundamental activities of letter and sermon writing, biblical exegesis, and, from the 12th century onward especially, ever-widening theological, philosophical, and scientific speculation.

The second half of the 11th century saw an unprecedented burst of activity in the field of hagiography, and many Anglo-Saxon saints seem to have been commemorated in writing for the first time; Goscelin and Folcard, both of St. Bertin, were the most industrious, closely followed by Osbern and Eadmer working at Canterbury, and later Dominic of Evesham. Much hagiography survives from the period that cannot be ascribed to any named author. Once revived, hagiography never died out in Anglo-Latin; lives were written by Osbert of Clare, Jocelin of Furness, Aelred of Rievaulx, Lawrence of Durham, Senatus of Worcester, Gerald of Wales, and Matthew Paris, to name only the best known, and the cult of Thomas Becket alone generated a vast amount of material.

Hagiographic style evolved across the period. During the 12th century a formal, Rome-centric system of rigorously controlled canonization was established. Carefully authenticated dossiers were required, and this meant the production of everlonger lists of miracles, in which the names of witnesses began to be included; examples are the 102 miracles of St. Frideswide written down by Philip the Prior; the miracles of Godric of Finchale, recorded in over 250 chapters by Reginald of Coldingham; and the dossier on Gilbert of Sempringham. Verse saints' lives became popular in the 12th century: for example, Gregory of Ely's life of Æthelthryth in leonine hexameters and the anonymous lives of Katherine, Ælfheah, and Hild. Nigel Whiteacre wrote 2,345 rhymed hexameters on St. Lawrence, and a shorter poem on Paul of Thebes, and in the 13th century Henry of Avranches versified the lives of Crispin and Crispinian, Francis, Oswald, Birinus, Guthlac, Edmund, Freomund, Hugh of Lincoln, and Thomas Becket. In the 14th century, as part of a general trend toward the assembling and summarizing of knowledge, John of Tynemouth made his *Sanctilogium,* the largest surviving compilation of the lives of the saints of the British Isles, all carefully abbreviated and put in calendrical order, interspersed with brief moral tales. Similar activity is represented by two other national collections of abbreviated saints' lives, one in the British Library in London (Lansdowne 436) and one at Gotha (Forschungsbibliothek I.81).

The growth of popular preaching fostered the genre of exemplum collections, a sort of precursor to anthologies of short stories, in which were assembled any number of anecdotes, moral tales, and visions of the afterlife, from literary or oral sources, for the use of the preacher. Visions of the otherworld continued as a distinct literary genre, examples of which are Henry of Saltrey's *Purgatorium sancti Patricii* and the Vision of Thurkill.

After a long time of relative reticence writers in the 12th century began to take up the cause of England's history and national identity, just as the 11th-century hagiographers had already begun to dust off the Anglo-Saxon saints. Eadmer wrote on contemporary events; William of Malmesbury continued in the tradition of Bede as ecclesiastical historian but also concerned himself with secular events in his *Gesta regum.* Henry of Huntingdon adorned his history with short poems, mainly his own (sometimes, interestingly, attempting to reproduce the rhythms of OE verse), Geoffrey of Monmouth wrote his profoundly influential version of events in pre-Saxon Britain *(Historia regum Britanniae),* and Richard of Devises chronicled the reign of Richard I. The tradition continued into the 13th century with Matthew Paris. Local history was as much a concern as world events: William of Malmesbury wrote on Glastonbury Abbey, Matthew Paris on the abbots of St. Albans, Jocelin of Brakelond on Bury St. Edmunds, Hugh Candidus on Peterborough, and Hugh the Chanter on York.

Every kind of poetry was attempted by post-Conquest

Anglo-Latin writers. Examples of epic are Reginald of Durham's verse life of Malchus, Joseph of Exeter's *Antiocheis* and *Ylias*, Lawrence of Durham's *Hypognosticon*, and John of Garland's *De triumphis ecclesiae* on the Crusades and his *Epithalamium beatae virginis*. In the late 11th century Godfrey of Cambrai composed 238 epigrams, after the style of Martial, on historical figures. Poetry achieved a pitch of artistry and skill in the 13th century, with Michael of Cornwall and Henry of Avranches, who developed a vigorous polemic style that informed the large amount of political poetry written thereafter, much of it anonymous. Subjects included the Crusades, the capture of Richard I, the papal interdict of 1208–14, the Barons' War, the Gaveston affair. Subjects for satire were wide-ranging: monks, gluttony, and ecclesiastical abuses, then friars and crusading orders. The end of the period saw a rising tide of anticlericalism, which came hand in hand with Lollardy and the teachings of Wyclif.

Poetry throughout these years was predominantly quantitative (hexameters and elegiacs), both rhymed and unrhymed, but rhythmical, stanzaic poetry also increased greatly in popularity. About halfway through the period emphasis seemed to fall more heavily upon rhyme, which was used in increasingly complicated schemes, while unrhymed forms of the quantitative dactylic verse were abandoned until much later. Quantitative lyric meters modeled on Horace were little used except by Goscelin, Reginald of Canterbury, and Henry of Huntingdon. In this earlier period the prosimetrum was also developed, integrating prose and verse on the models of Boethius and Martianus Capella. Examples are the life of Edward the Confessor, Goscelin's life of St. Eadgyth, and Lawrence of Durham's *Consolatio de morte amici*, then somewhat later on Elias of Thriplow's *Serium senectutis* (13th century).

Grammatical and lexical aids continued to be important, and there are notable examples from all centuries: Osbern Pinnock's *Panormia*, an influential list of lexical derivatives; Alexander Neckham's *De nominibus utensilium* and *Corrogationes Promethei*, various works by John of Garland, and John Seward's writings on poetry.

As the post-Conquest period passed by, Anglo-Latin was written with more confident liberty from the constraints of classical norms. Increased day-to-day use of Latin in combination with a stress upon dialectic in the context of the universities gave rise to a certain freedom of coinage, but also a tendency toward the infiltration of vernacular words and idioms, even syntax, into written Anglo-Latin. The literature of the 13th and 14th centuries may be characterized by a liking for heavy alliteration, odd vocabulary, and a pedantic tone that to some extent reverberates with the so-called hermeneutic style affected so ostentatiously by the confident, continentalizing churchmen of the late 10th century. At the same time authors enthusiastically took up wordplay and verbal-visual trickery that went beyond established modes of rhetorical embellishment. But there seems, in a way, to have been a tug-of-war, for toward the end of our period interest in Anglo-Latin became more and more academic and analytical: literary histories (such as Thomas of Walsingham's *Prohemia*

poetarum), library catalogues, commentaries and anthologies, Anglo-Latin for Anglo-Latin's sake, rather than as a natural, casual literary vehicle. In the later 14th century there was also a distinct group of scholars, the so-called "classicizing friars," among them Nicholas Trevet and Robert Holcot, who peppered their preaching with classical allusion and "moralized" pagan tales. This was an early sign of the reawakening interest in classical antiquity, which eventually brought with it a return to the strict norms of classical Latin, heralding the era of humanism and of a different and perhaps less vital and multicolored creature, Neo-Latin.

    Rosalind Love

Bibliography

PRIMARY

Robertson, James C., and J. Brigstocke Sheppard, eds. *Materials for the History of Thomas Becket*. Rolls Series 67. 7 vols. London: Longman, 1875–85; Wright, Thomas, ed. *Political Poems and Songs Relating to English History*. Rolls Series 14. 2 vols. London: Longman, Green, Longman & Roberts, 1859–61; Wright, Thomas, ed. *The Anglo-Latin Satirical Poets and Epigrammatists of the Twelfth Century*. Rolls Series 59. 2 vols. London: Longman, 1872.

SECONDARY

Gransden, Antonia. *Historical Writing in England*. 2 vols. London: Routledge & Kegan Paul, 1974–82; Hunt, T. *Teaching and Learning Latin in Thirteenth-Century England*. 3 vols. Cambridge: Brewer, 1991; Partner, N.E. *Serious Entertainments: The Writing of History in Twelfth-Century England*. Chicago: University of Chicago Press, 1977; Raby, F.J.E. *A History of Secular Latin Poetry in the Middle Ages*. 2d ed. 2 vols. Oxford: Clarendon, 1957 [see esp. vol. 2, ch. 11]; Rigg, A.G. *A History of Anglo-Latin Literature 1066–1422*. Cambridge: Cambridge University Press, 1992; Russell, J.C. *Dictionary of Writers of Thirteenth-Century England*. *BIHR* Special Supplement 3. London: Longman, Green, 1936; Smalley, Beryl. *English Friars and Antiquity in the Early Fourteenth Century*. Oxford: Blackwell, 1960; Wright, Thomas. *Biographia Britannia Literaria*. 2 vols. London: Parker, 1842–46.

See also Anglo-Latin Literature to 1066; Chronicles; Exemplum; Friars; Geoffrey of Monmouth; Gerald of Wales; Gower; Grammatical Treatises; Hagiography; John of Salisbury; Literacy; Literary Influences: Classical, Medieval Latin; Map; Matthew Paris; Mystical and Devotional Writings; Rolle; Satire; Scientific and Medical Writings; Sermons; Trevet; William of Malmesbury; Wyclif

Anglo-Latin Literature to 1066

Evidence for transmission of Latin literary culture from classical and Christian antiquity survives in works by the Britons Pelagius, Patrick, and Faustus of Riez from the 5th century, Gildas from the 6th, and Moucan from the 7th or early 8th.

Among the Irish abroad, like Columban, and at home, like Cummianus Longus, Colmán, Augustinus Hibernicus, Laithcenn MacBaíth, Virgilius Maro Grammaticus, Aileranus Sapiens, Tirechán, Cogitosus, Muirchú Moccu Macthéni, and Adomnán, the 7th century saw a burst of creative literary activity unparalleled elsewhere in Europe. The extant Latin of all the Britons, even those like Patrick, misprised by modern scholars, is correct, polished, and brilliantly structured. References by Columban to Gildas and by Cummian to Patrick show that the British tradition had been assimilated and naturalized at the very beginning of the Irish tradition.

Anglo-Saxons might have encountered Latin literary culture upon exposure to Britons whom they dispossessed and dominated from the 5th century, to Irish missionaries from Columba's foundation at Iona after 563, or to Roman missionaries sent with Augustine by Pope Gregory the Great to Canterbury in 596. However, the earliest extant monuments of Anglo-Latin literature derive from the second half of the 7th century in direct and sustained response to the efforts of three men. Theodore of Tarsus arrived as bishop of Canterbury in 669 and Hadrian the African as abbot of Sts. Peter and Paul Canterbury in 670, accompanied by Benedict Biscop. From the school of Theodore and Hadrian emerged the earliest glossaries containing both Latin and English, glossed texts and commentaries, and original compositions. Its most illustrious pupil was Aldhelm, the first Englishman, indeed the first among all Germanic peoples, to become a Latin author. At the same time at the other end of England Benedict Biscop, enriching his foundation at St. Peter's Wearmouth and St. Paul's Jarrow with paintings and books imported from the Continent, established a library that enabled the Venerable Bede to produce in the next generation works of chronology, history, and biblical commentary unparalleled in Europe for centuries.

In a letter to Bishop Leutherius Aldhelm describes the range of his studies at Canterbury: Roman law, metrics, music, mathematics, and astronomy. Two other letters, addressed to Wihtfrith and Heahfrith, allude to their studying in Ireland, the latter affirming vigorously that the teaching of Theodore and Hadrian is superior to anything available there. In a letter addressed to King Geraint of the Dumnonians Aldhelm urges that the British church be brought into conformity with Roman traditions. The Anglo-Saxon Chronicle suggests that during Aldhelm's youth West Saxon sovereignty had advanced to the Avon and during his maturity to the Severn. As the West Saxon Regnal Table includes British names and Ine's Law Code contains provisions for British subjects, one infers that there were many opportunities for contact between British and English cultures. In the prose version of *De virginitate* Aldhelm quotes from Gildas, and at the end of the letter to Heahfrith he parodies 7th-century Hiberno-Latin heptasyllabic verse and alludes to Virgilius Maro, attesting his knowledge of both British-Latin and Irish-Latin literature. These features, like the survival of the *Orationes Moucani* in an 8th-century Mercian manuscript, help to balance Bede's testimony that the British did not share their Christian culture with the English.

Because the Irish and the English differed from the British in having no experience of the Christian Roman Empire, they wrote the first grammars of Latin adapted to the needs of those learning Latin, not as the written form of a mother tongue but as an acquired foreign language. Bede, Tatwine, Boniface, Alcuin, and several *anonymi* wrote grammars. Aldhelm, Bede, Alcuin, and Boniface also wrote tracts on meter and rhetoric, Aldhelm and Alcuin adopting the dialogue as a means of teaching both content and form. In the 10th century Ælfric employed English as a medium for teaching Latin grammar; in order to expand students' vocabulary he composed a Latin colloquy, which acquired an English gloss and served as basis for Ælfric Bata's expanded colloquy. About the same time Abbo of Fleury wrote *Quaestiones grammaticales*.

Once competence in grammar and rhetoric was attained, the literature developed quickly, with assimilation of established forms and innovation and experiment. There are poems in various classical meters (though most poets wrote dactylic hexameters and elegiac couplets) and some imitations of the heptasyllabic meter practiced by Irish poets of the 7th century. To Theodore, Aldhelm, Æthilwald, and Boniface we owe the oldest extant rhymed octosyllabic couplets. There are creditable abecedarian compositions (in which lines begin with the letters of the alphabet in order), epanaleptic poems (in which words at the beginning of a couplet are repeated at the end), and stanzaic hymns.

As the centerpiece of his prosodic treatise *De metris* and *De pedum regulis* Aldhelm composed 100 *aenigmata*, riddles or mysteries, which became the model for a collaborative effort by Tatwine, who wrote 40, and Hwætberht (*alias* Eusebius), who wrote 60. Alcuin and Boniface also wrote riddles. Some have supposed that the precedent established by Aldhelm inspired the compiler of the Exeter Book to collect 100 OE riddles.

As a preface to the *Aenigmata* Aldhelm wrote 36 hexameters that exhibit the verse *Aldhelmus cecinit millenis versibus odas* as a descending acrostic (the first letters of the lines spelling out the verse) and as a descending telestich (the last letters of the lines also spelling out the verse). The first line of the verse version of *De virginitate*, *Metrica tirones nunc promant carmina castos*, recurs as a descending acrostic and as an ascending telestich. He also devised other forms of pattern poem. Tatwine prefixed to his collection a hexameter couplet that fixes the order of poems, as the first letter of each *aenigma* from the first to the 40th spells the first line, and the last letter from the 40th to the first spells the second line. Boniface supplied the answers to his *aenigmata* in acrostics; at the end of a letter commending the study of scripture to a youth named Nithard he worked into verses at the name *Nitharde* the acrostic *Nithardus vive felix*; he prefaced his grammar with a *carmen figuratum* in which an acrostic is repeated as two diagonals of an internal diamond and a telestich is repeated as the other two diagonals around the name of Jesus Christ arranged horizontally and vertically in a cross at the center. Alcuin and his Carolingian colleagues composed pattern poems of dizzying complexity. Later in the 10th century Dunstan wrote a difficult puzzle poem, and in the 11th century an Abingdon monk devised for Abbot Sigeweard two poems about the entry of the Virgin Mary into heaven, designed to reflect the seven levels of celestial glory in a maze and to be read in two different sequences.

The texts of some prayers are so finely contrived as to merit consideration as works of art. Among the earliest are the nine *Orationes Moucani*, in which biblical words and phrases and entire verses have been arranged as centos (coherent new compositions from old elements), which survive only in a Mercian manuscript. More innovative is the rhymed and rhythmical prayer written in colored inks in the Book of Cerne, composed in perfect and comprehensive chiasmus, as the acrostic states, by *Aedeluald episcopus*, probably the successor of Bishop Eadfrith, illuminator of the Lindisfarne Gospels. More extraordinary still are the *Orationes Alchfrithi*, by an anchorite known otherwise as a correspondent of the *Hyglac presbyter et lector* celebrated in Ædiluulf's (or Æthelwulf's) *De abbatibus (On the Abbots)*, under whose name a letter survives in an Alcuinian collection.

Traditions of local and topographic occasional verse are apparent in the poems composed by Aldhelm, Alcuin, and others for inscriptions on altars, walls, and tombs. Of Bede's *Liber epigrammatum* only excerpts survive. Bede's *Ecclesiastical History* and a sense of local patriotism inspired Alcuin's *Versus de patribus regibus et sanctis Euboricensis ecclesiae (Poem on the Bishops, Kings, and Saints of York)*, which became a source for Æthelwulf's *De abbatibus*.

Bede scrupulously reproduced the texts of epistles and documents in his *Ecclesiastical History*. Others circulated in letter collections. Letters of Aldhelm survive among those of Boniface and Lul, along with those to and from Bishop Daniel of Winchester and a group of articulate and literate women. A selection of letters from the huge number written by Alcuin belonged to Archbishop Wulfstan. Among the collected letters of Lanfranc are two addressed to kings in Ireland referring to Bishop Patrick of Dublin, who had been taught with men at Worcester (to whom he addressed verses) and consecrated by Lanfranc.

The most remarkable continuity appears in hagiographic and biographic works beginning in the 8th century with the oldest *Life of Gregory the Great* by an anonymous of Whitby and a *Life of Cuthbert* by an anonymous of Lindisfarne. The latter, which quotes the *Life of Martin* by Sulpicius Severus, is in turn quoted by Eddius Stephanus or Stephen of Ripon, who wrote a partisan *Life of Wilfrid*. Shortly afterward Felix of Crowland wrote a *Life of Guthlac*, which owes much to Aldhelm and to which the OE Guthlac poems owe much. Bede rewrote an anonymous *Life of Ceolfrid* as the *Historia abbatum (History of the Abbots)*; he also rewrote the *Life of Cuthbert*, making an *opus geminatum*, or "twinned work," in both verse and prose, as Aldhelm had done previously in the prose and verse versions of *De virginitate* and as Alcuin was to do later in the prose and verse versions of his *Life of Willibrord*. In a memorial unsurpassed in the literature of the English, the *Epistola de obitu Baedae (Letter on the Death of Bede)*, the pupil Cuthbert writing about Bede quotes his master Bede writing about St. Cuthbert. The oldest biography of a layman, Asser's *Life of King Alfred*, written in 893, became a source for Byrhtferth, writing *Historia regum (History of the Kings)* in the

10th century. At Winchester Lantfred's *Life of Swithun* was versified by Wulfstan the Cantor as *Narratio metrica de sancto Swithuno*. Wulfstan's *Life of Æthelwold* was later rewritten by Ælfric. The *Life of Edmund* of East Anglia by Abbo of Fleury was followed by an account of Edmund's miracles by Herman. A group of Flemings from St. Bertin, the author of the *Encomium Emmae reginae* and Folcard and Goscelin, all composed remarkable Lives, the last being the most prolific and competent writer between Bede and William of Malmesbury.

Within this continuous tradition is the clearest evidence of inexhaustibly varied use of the most basic common source, the Vulgate. In his treatise on metrics Aldhelm commends to Aldfrith of Northumbria contemplation of the number seven in holy scripture. At the end of the *Life of Gregory* the anonymous of Whitby defends the *ordo preposterus*, "preposterous order," of narrative and the attribution of one saint's miracles to another as something learned from scripture. Cuthbert compares Bede to Paul and Christ, by putting into Bede's mouth in a single paragraph Paul's words of farewell to his converts, his last words from prison, the words of Jesus on the last day of his teaching in the Temple from Mark's Gospel, and his last words on the Cross from the Gospels of Luke and John. Asser compares King Alfred to Solomon. A generation after Asser Frithegod rewrote Stephen's prose *Life of Wilfrid* as *Breviloquium vitae beati Wilfridi*, the most difficult poem in the entire literature. To this Archbishop Oda of Canterbury prefixed a letter in equally difficult prose, dense with words borrowed from Greek and quotations from the bible and quotations from plays of Terence chiastically arranged.

Equally varied is the range of Latin styles employed throughout the Anglo-Saxon period. From the beginning Theodore and Hadrian inculcated a high arcane Late Imperial literary style in which complex syntax and recondite vocabulary produce an effect of baroque exuberance. This style, exhibited by Aldhelm, Felix, and Boniface in the 7th and 8th centuries, became even more extreme in the hands of Oda, Frithegod, Byrhtferth, and those trained in the schools influenced by the monastic reformers Æthelwold, Dunstan, and Oswald, reaching its limit in the idiolect of Æthelweard's Chronicle. In stark contrast is the limpid clarity of the prose of Bede, Cuthbert, Alcuin, and Ælfric, the latter the more remarkable as he had graduated from the school of Æthelwold, whom he venerated. Rhymed prose, appearing first in a charter of 686, became common from the 10th century. Despite education in the same centers and dependence upon the same models the styles of most Anglo-Latin authors are utterly distinct. Hardly any two are confusable.

Readers who have approached Anglo-Latin literature searching for *belles lettres* have found it conventional and correct but dull. Yet if one approaches it as a response to all the liberal arts, the effect is stunningly different. Consider the number of references to mathematics, music, and astronomy in the poetry of Aldhelm, Alcuin, and Ædiluulf, and the musical expertise of Wulfstan the Cantor, Osbern, and Goscelin. By understanding the quadrivium as arithmetic, music, geometry, and astronomy, and then bringing the ideas inculcated in these arts about the mathematical composition of heaven and earth, about the creation of the universe from harmony, about its working movements as the polyphonic music of the spheres, about chronology and computus, to literary composition, one begins to see the culture steadily and to see it whole. These literary texts are comparable with the exquisitely wrought manuscript illumination, metalwork, stone carving, architecture, and music because they are composed by the same criteria. All are conspicuous for a structural intricacy that we have nearly lost the ability even to perceive, but that, by attending to inbuilt features, we may begin to recover.

D.R. Howlett

Bibliography

Bolton, W.F. *A History of Anglo-Latin Literature 597–1066.* Vol. 1: *597–740.* Princeton: Princeton University Press, 1967; Clayton, M. "*Assumptio Mariae*: An Eleventh-Century Anglo-Latin Poem from Abingdon." *Analecta Bollandiana* 104 (1986): 419–26. Corr. in D.R. Howlett, *Pillars of Wisdom.* Dublin: Four Courts, 1997; Cross, J.E. "The Literate Anglo-Saxon—On Sources and Disseminations." *PBA* 58 (1972): 67–100; Howlett, D.R. "*Orationes Moucani*: Early Cambro-Latin Prayers." *Cambridge Medieval Celtic Studies* 24 (1992): 55–74; Howlett, D.R. "Aldhelm and Irish Learning." *Archivum Latinitatis Medii Aevi* 53 (1994): 37–75; Howlett, D.R. "The Earliest Irish Writers at Home and Abroad." *Peritia* 8 (1994): 1–17; Howlett, D.R. *Liber epistolarum sancti Patricii episcopi: The Book of Letters of Saint Patrick the Bishop.* Dublin: Four Courts, 1994; Howlett, D.R. "Two Works of Saint Columban." *Mittellateinisches Jahrbuch* 28 (1994 for 1993): 27–46; Howlett, D.R. *The Celtic Latin Tradition of Biblical Style.* Dublin: Four Courts, 1995; Howlett, D.R. "Five Experiments in Textual Reconstruction and Analysis." *Peritia* 9 (1995): 1–50; Howlett, D.R. *British Books in Biblical Style.* Dublin: Four Courts, 1996; Lapidge, Michael. *Anglo-Latin Literature 900–1066.* London: Hambledon, 1993; Lapidge, Michael. *Anglo-Latin Literature 600–899.* London: Hambledon, 1996; Lapidge, Michael, and Richard Sharpe. *A Bibliography of Celtic-Latin Literature 400–1200.* Royal Irish Academy Dictionary of Medieval Latin from Celtic Sources Ancillary Publications 1. Dublin: Royal Irish Academy, 1985; Latham, R.E., D.R. Howlett, et al. *Dictionary of Medieval Latin from British Sources.* Bibliography from Fascicules I–V. London: British Academy, 1975–96; Law, Vivien. *The Insular Latin Grammarians.* Woodbridge: Boydell, 1982; Ogilvy, J.D.A. *Books Known to the English, 597–1066.* Cambridge: Mediaeval Academy of America, 1967; Sharpe, R. *A Checklist of Latin Writers of Great Britain and Ireland before 1540. Journal of Medieval Latin Publications* 1 (1996); Stevick, R.D. *The Earliest Irish and English Bookarts: Visual and Poetic Forms before A.D. 1000.* Philadelphia: University of Pennsylvania Press, 1994.

See also Abbo; Ælfric; Ælfric Bata; Æthelweard; Alcuin; Aldhelm; Anglo-Latin Literature after 1066; Asser; Bede; Eusebius; Felix of Crowland; Frithegod; Grammatical Treatises; *Guthlac A* and *B*; Lantfred; Literacy; Prayers; Tatwine; Theodore of Tarsus

Anglo-Norman Literature

The literature written in the French vernacular of England from the Norman Conquest until the reemergence of English as a prestige vernacular in the 14th century.

The growth and influence of Anglo-Norman literature must be understood against the broader relationships between Norman and English culture, beginning in the decades before the Conquest of 1066. Edward the Confessor, son of Emma of Normandy, spent his formative years in exile in Normandy, and Norman influence on court and ecclesiastical circles in Anglo-Saxon England during his reign was strong. The influence was two-way: Norman art and sculpture show the influence of English, and English skills in such differing areas as coinage and embroidery (as in the Bayeux Tapestry) were preserved by the Conqueror. The vernacular literature of Anglo-Saxon England was well established and highly developed, with an output unequaled by any other European vernacular. In contrast Norman literature was almost nonexistent, and after the Conquest Norman writers turned to Anglo-Saxon literature, law, and cultural traditions for inspiration and information. Anglo-Saxon writing provided for the Normans a precedent for serious, high-quality literature written in the vernacular for the edification, education, and entertainment of the upper classes.

Post-Conquest England was a trilingual culture. Latin, the international language of the church and scholarship, was introduced as the language of government by the Norman kings in place of English. French became the language of the rulers and of polite society, but as a dialect that gradually differentiated from the French of the Continent. English effectively occupied third place as a literary language. Social distinctions between English-speaking and French-speaking groups are not necessarily relevant to the literary picture; within the narrow circle of the literate trilingualism or at least bilingualism would have been common. In the post-Conquest period we find that authors writing in Anglo-Norman use source material in English, Latin, and perhaps Welsh, while later writers in English draw on French or Latin material. The choice of language is dictated by the taste of public or patron or by the nature of the topic.

Nor is language yet perceived as part of national identity; patriotic, even francophobe, sentiment can be expressed in Anglo-Norman without any sense of incongruity. Material can move easily from one vernacular to another within the same manuscript (e.g., the famous BL Harley 2253) or even within the same poem. This fluidity, evident in the vast intake of Romance vocabulary into English throughout the period, means that the literary influence of Anglo-Norman is pervasive rather than distinctive.

Anglo-Norman literature develops more through its response to Latin than to English, often representing the popularization of more scholarly Latin writing. It is a literature written for the laity (or among the religious for nuns) and for those of a rank to read or commission vernacular works. For some three centuries after the Conquest this group was largely francophone or, where bilingual, preferred literature in French. Because of the aristocratic or religious nature of their public many Anglo-Norman works are attributable to named authors, writing for known patrons.

The literature of the first century after the Conquest is small in quantity but significantly ahead of developments on the Continent. From its beginning Anglo-Norman narrative literature presents the ecclesiastical and secular rulers of Anglo-Norman England with material about the lands they now ruled. This perspective is first apparent in the important work of the early-12th-century Latin historians in England and Normandy (e.g., William of Malmesbury, Henry of Huntingdon, Orderic Vitalis); it can be seen in the vernacular by shortly before 1140, in Gaimar's *Estoire* (or *Estorie*) *des Engleis*, written for a country lady and based on material from the Anglo-Saxon Chronicle and from Geoffrey of Monmouth. Gaimar produces the first history in French, using the octosyllabic couplet that was to become the medium of French courtly literature. In 1155 the Norman poet Wace completed his *Roman de Brut*, a highly influential account of British history that would be translated into English by Laȝamon, and then moved on to Norman history with the less successful *Roman de Rou* (1160–ca. 1174).

Anglo-Norman literature flourished during the reign of Henry II and Eleanor of Aquitaine, when the Angevin court had some claim to be the dominant literary center of Europe. The Angevin succession, together with the possession of Aquitaine, placed England within an empire that extended from the Welsh marches to the Pyrenees and gave access to all the cultural diversity associated with those lands. The Anglo-Norman *Tristan* of Thomas is the most striking of the new literary achievements. Sophisticated, rhetorically complex, and morally baffling, even in its fragmentary extant condition the *Tristan* towers over the history of medieval romance. Its sympathetic account of doomed and passionate adultery, and the absence of the judgmental directives commonly found in medieval writing, were evidently disturbing to some contemporary audiences. The literary reaction was largely negative, and many of the major narrative works of the following decades have been seen as "anti-*Tristans*": Chrétien's *Cligés* and the Anglo-Norman romances of *Horn*, *Protheselaus*, and *Amadas* are all concerned to substitute a positive, socially constructive view of *fin amour* to counter Thomas's subversive tragedy. But the story of Tristan and Isolde spread, to become one of the classic statements of passionate love in European literature.

It is artificial to divide this debate—or indeed the literature of the period—into insular and continental, as the Channel was no border in the Angevin cultural empire. Thomas, like Wace, Marie de France, and Chrétien, contributed to the fashionable Matter of Britain (stories about Arthur and his knights) and wrote for the immediate circle of the peripatetic and cosmopolitan royal court. The same period also saw the

development of romance written for baronial patrons and addressed to a more provincial audience, with full-scale treatments of the so-called "Matter of England" romances, partly based on genuine Anglo-Saxon or Scandinavian legend, partly fabricated. The sagalike story of Havelok first appears in Gaimar, then is slightly expanded in the courtly *Lai d'Haveloc*, and finally emerges as the longer ME *Havelok the Dane*. The Anglo-Norman *Romance of Horn* is a full-length courtly romance, written in epic laisses and one of the finest products of insular writing. Its detailed novelistic treatment of the tale is quite different in mode from the ME *King Horn* but is closer to the later *Horn Childe*. *Waldef*, a 22,000-line saga of warring kings, seems never to have been adapted into English, although the author claims, convincingly, to have used OE source material. *Boeve de Haumtone* and *Gui de Warewic* are evidently connected with the family interests of the owners of Arundel Castle and the earls of Warwick respectively, and both were translated directly into English in the early 14th century for wider audiences.

Such romances demonstrate in their plots the interests of an incoming feudal dynasty, the hero acquiring lands by marriage with an heiress, holding his own in conflict with the centralizing power of the monarchy, and borrowing the names and geography of England to establish a claim to "ancestry." To these can be added the early-14th-century *Fouke Fitzwarin*, a prose compilation of romance themes and Welsh marcher history. The original 13th-century couplet version of this work and a later ME translation, possibly in alliterative verse, are now lost; the story eventually contributes to the quintessentially English legends of Dick Whittington and Robin Hood. Exceptions to the localized, ancestral nature of Anglo-Norman romance include the *Roman de toute chevalerie* by Thomas of Kent, related to the ME *Kyng Alisaunder*, and Hue de Rotelande's *Ipomedon* and *Protheselaus*, the former of which was translated into three ME versions. The reappearance of Anglo-Norman romance in ME versions is in marked contrast to the absence of translations of Chrétien, of whose works only *Yvain* appears in an extant ME translation.

Alongside secular narrative saints' legends also developed. These legends were written for monastic and lay audiences, generally with courtly tastes and an interest in tales of those pre-Conquest saints who had shrines in the new cathedrals. The patronage of successive queens supports such 12th-century works as Benedeit's *Voyage of St. Brendan*, a colorful account of the Celtic saint's miraculous journeys, and Denis Piramus's *Life of St. Edmund*. Piramus draws on English sources in the *Life*, as do Matthew Paris's 13th-century lives of St. Alban and St. Edward the Confessor. The *Life of St. Catherine* by the nun of Barking and the later lives of Sts. Juliana and Margaret bear witness to the popularity of lives of virgin martyrs, evident also in OE and ME (e.g., *Juliene* and the Katherine Group).

Drama is well represented in the 12th century with the *Jeu* (or *Mystère*) *d'Adam* and the *Seinte Resureccion*, two liturgical plays showing a high level of literary ability and of conscious stagecraft. The *Adam* play's subtle interpretation of the Genesis story may derive from OE tradition. The nature of the surviving lyric poetry suggests that from the early 13th century the popularity of home-grown Anglo-Norman verse eclipsed that of imported troubadour lyric. It is a poetry rich in the language of chivalry, law, and courtly love and is most remarkable for its devotional verse. It mostly survives alongside the developing ME lyric, in manuscripts associated with friars, or in the trilingual anthologies like Harley 2253.

Historical writing in the vernacular continues in the late 12th and 13th centuries with the *Brut* tradition of British history and lively narrative accounts of contemporary events: Jordan Fantosme's *Chronique* on the Scottish wars of Henry II, a heroic poem on the Norman conquest of Ireland, a popular biography of Richard I. In the 14th century the tradition gives rise to Peter of Langtoft's account of the Scottish wars of Edward I, laced with the crude English songs of the campaign, and to Nicholas Trevet's *Cronicles,* written for a daughter of Edward I, which provides source material for Chaucer and Gower.

Although most of these genres of Anglo-Norman literature make their first appearance in the 12th century and some of them carry on into the 14th, it was the 13th century that saw the greatest dissemination of Anglo-Norman texts and the widest social extent of bilingualism. Anglo-Norman literature continued both to receive the patronage of queens and convents and to give expression to popular political feeling in songs and poems. Following the loss of Normandy in 1204 the 13th century also witnessed a growing sense of national identity, sharpened by resentment at incoming waves of continental courtiers and administrators.

Another important influence in this period was the new program of lay instruction initiated by the Fourth Lateran Council (1215), which was put into effect both by bishops and the new mendicant orders and led to increased emphasis on preaching, confession, and devotional works. A number of religious works come from writers more at home in Latin, writing in the vernacular to edify a lay public: Matthew Paris's lives of St. Alban and St. Edward, noted above, and the *Chateau d'Amour* of Robert Grosseteste, bishop of Lincoln, whence the allegory of the Four Daughters of God reaches Langland. Edmund of Abingdon's widely circulated treatise *Merure de Seinte Eglise (Speculum Ecclesiae)* was probably first written in French and then translated into Latin and ME; a reverse process is represented by the *Ancrene Wisse,* written in English for three sisters living as anchoresses and translated into French and Latin for wider use in nunneries.

The arrival of the Franciscans in the 1220s marked an increase in religious works in both vernaculars, including a 13th-century French sermon and an English lyric (the "Love-Rune") by Thomas of Hales and the French allegories, verse sermons, and *Contes moralisés* of the prolific early-14th-century writer Nicholas Bozon. In the mid-14th century the *Seyntz medicines* of Henry duke of Lancaster provides an early example of devotional writing by a layman. The evidence of religious writing suggests that the choice of language was often a pragmatic one and that authors would adopt the most suitable vernacular for their public. The subject matter slips easily into English when the public use of vernaculars changes,

as in Robert Manning's *Handlyng Synne,* translated from the 13th-century *Manuel des péchés.*

Bozon's and Hales's sermons are part of the more general homiletic tradition in medieval England, a tradition that can be traced back to the Anglo-Saxon period but that received significant reinforcement with the decrees of the Fourth Lateran Council. The most substantial extant sermon collection in Anglo-Norman is Robert of Gretham's *Miroir,* a 13th-century cycle of sermons on the Sunday Gospels throughout the year, translated into ME in the late 14th century. Edmund of Abingdon's *Merure de Seinte Eglise* appears to have been based in part on sermon texts, or at least partly modeled on sermon style and structure. And many sermons whose texts are now preserved in Latin, especially sermons to lay audiences, were probably originally delivered in English or French depending on the language of the particular audience addressed.

The 13th-century outpouring of hagiographical and devotional writing in Anglo-Norman shows the continuing demand for literature in this vernacular, as do the number of manuscript copies of earlier romances and the continuing production of chronicles. The relationship between the two literary vernaculars changes during the 14th century; as the audience for English grows in size and status, so the bilingual authors adapt and translate more and more material from French into English.

The problems of assessing Anglo-Norman literature are twofold: the extent to which it can be distinguished from continental French literature, and its relation to literature in English. The first problem applies to the earlier period, and it is probable that there was at first no strong sense of difference between the written forms of the various Old French dialects. Despite this fact modern scholarship is increasingly aware of the insular nature of much Anglo-Norman writing: a choice of insular material, a flirtation with English meters, a provincial interest that develops independently of continental literature. To the time of Chaucer and beyond, the royal court continued to keep up with the dominant fashions of France, but outside that circle, in the baronial halls, manor houses, and monasteries of England, the literary development of chronicle, romance, and saint's life provides a continuing tradition of vernacular provincial writing. Hence the quantity of Anglo-Norman sources for ME works—not only as sources for direct translation as with many romances but also as material used more freely by Chaucer and by Gower, the last major author to write in all three languages of medieval England.

Rosalind P. Field

Bibliography

PRIMARY

See also entries on individual Anglo-Norman authors elsewhere in this volume; Publications of the Anglo-Norman Text Society (ANTS). 1939– [the principal series of Anglo-Norman editions]; *Amadas et Ydoine.* Ed. John R. Reinhard. Paris: Champion, 1926; Aspin, Isabel S.T., ed. *Anglo-Norman Political Songs.* ANTS 11. Oxford: Blackwell, 1953; Benedeit. *The Anglo-Norman Voyage of*

St. Brendan. Ed. Ian Short and Brian Merrilees. Manchester: Manchester University Press, 1979; *Boeve de Haumtone.* Ed. Albert Stimming. Halle: Niemeyer, 1899; Clemence of Barking. *Life of St. Catherine.* Ed. William MacBain. ANTS 18. Oxford: Blackwell, 1964; *The Crusade and Death of Richard I.* Ed. R.C. Johnston. ANTS 17. Oxford: Blackwell, 1961; Denis Piramus. *La vie seint Edmund le rei.* Ed. Hilding Kjellman. Göteborg: Elanders, 1935; Fantosme, Jordan. *Jordan Fantosme's Chronicle.* Ed. R.C. Johnston. Oxford: Clarendon, 1981; *Fouke le Fitz Waryn.* Ed. E.J. Hathaway et al. ANTS 26–28. Oxford: Blackwell, 1975; *Gui de Warewic.* Ed. Alfred Ewert. 2 vols. Paris: Champion, 1932–33; Jeffrey, David L., and Brian J. Levy, eds. *The Anglo-Norman Lyric: An Anthology.* Toronto: Pontifical Institute, 1990; Matthew Paris. *La estoire de seint Aedward le rei.* Ed. Kathryn Y. Wallace. ANTS 41. London: ANTS, 1983; *Le mystère d'Adam.* Ed. Paul Studer. Manchester: Manchester University Press, 1928; *Le roman de Waldef.* Ed. A.J. Holden. Cologne-Geneva: Bodmer, 1984; *La seinte Resureccion.* Ed. Mildred K. Pope et al. ANTS 4. Oxford: Blackwell, 1943; Thomas. *The Romance of Horn.* Ed. Mildred K. Pope and T.B.W. Reid. 2 vols. ANTS 9–10, 12–13. Oxford: Blackwell, 1955–64; Thomas of Britain. *Les fragments du roman de Tristan.* Ed. Bartina H. Wind. 2d ed. Geneva: Droz, 1960; Thomas of Britain. *Tristran.* Ed. and trans. Stewart Gregory. New York: Garland, 1991; Thomas of Kent. *The Anglo-Norman Alexander (Le roman de toute chevalerie).* Ed. Brian Foster and Ian Short. 2 vols. ANTS 29–33. London: ANTS, 1976–77; Weiss, Judith, trans. *The Birth of Romance: An Anthology.* London: Dent, 1992.

SECONDARY

For further bibliography see Crane and Legge below; for Anglo-Norman drama see New *CBEL* 1:725–28; Calin, William. *The French Tradition and the Literature of Medieval England.* Toronto: University of Toronto Press, 1994; Crane, Susan. *Insular Romance: Politics, Faith, and Culture in Anglo-Norman and Middle English Literature.* Berkeley: University of California Press, 1986; Legge, Mary Dominica. *Anglo-Norman in the Cloisters: The Influence of the Orders upon Anglo-Norman Literature.* Edinburgh: University of Edinburgh Press, 1950; Legge, Mary Dominica. *Anglo-Norman Literature and Its Background.* Oxford: Clarendon, 1963; Legge, Mary Dominica. "Anglo-Norman Hagiography and the Romances." *M&H* n.s. 6 (1975): 41–49; Salter, Elizabeth. *English and International: Studies in the Literature, Art and Patronage of Medieval England.* Ed. Derek Pearsall and Nicolette Zeeman. Cambridge: Cambridge University Press, 1988; Short, Ian. "On Bilingualism in Anglo-Norman England." *RPh* 33 (1980): 467–79; Short, Ian. "Patrons and Polyglots: French Literature in Twelfth-Century England." *Anglo-Norman Studies* 14 (1992): 229–49.

See also Ancrene Wisse; Angevin Empire; *Brut,* Prose; Chronicles; Courtly Love; Friars' Miscellanies; Harley Lyrics; Katherine Group; Language; Literacy; Moral and Religious Instruction; Norman Conquest; Romances; Sermons; Songs

Anglo-Saxon Chronicle

The collections of annalistic materials known as the Anglo-Saxon Chronicle together form our most important source for the political history of the Anglo-Saxon period and are at the same time of considerable interest to paleographers, linguists, and students of medieval vernacular literature. The earliest version of the Chronicle that we can identify today was in circulation in the early 890s. However, it was subsequently considerably extended, with some versions continuing into the ME period. The so-called "first compilation" and its extensions provided source material for a number of medieval historians writing in Latin and (one) in Anglo-Norman.

Textual History

The Anglo-Saxon Chronicle has been preserved in seven manuscript copies, each with its own distinctive features. These are Cambridge, Corpus Christi College 173 ("A"), written in a series of hands dating from the late 9th or early 10th century through to the beginning of the 12th century and ending with an annal for 1070; BL Cotton Tiberius A.vi ("B"), written at the end of the 10th century and extending to 977; BL Cotton Tiberius B.i ("C"), written in the mid-11th century and extending to 1066; BL Cotton Tiberius B.iv ("D"), an imperfect copy, mostly written in the second half of the 11th century and extending to 1079, with a further single entry for 1130; Bodl. Laud. Misc. 636 ("E"), written in the 12th century and continuing to 1154; BL Cotton Domitian A.viii ("F"), a version with entries in both OE and Latin, written in the late 11th or early 12th century and breaking off in the middle of the annal for 1058 through manuscript loss; and BL Cotton Otho B.xi ("G"), an early-11th-century copy that was badly fire-damaged in 1731 but that a transcript by the 16th-century scholar Nowell shows to have continued to the year 1001.

Textual evidence suggests that G was a copy of A, made before that manuscript received its final additions and modifications, while F is essentially an abbreviated version of an ancestor of E, combined with Latin annals of Norman origin, but has a number of entries close to A. The relationships among A, B, C, D, and E are far more complicated. So, for instance, A agrees with B, C, and D in incorporating a sequence of annals from 892 to 914 and a further series beginning in the 930s and extending to 946. However, it shares only with its descendant G an important sequence from 915 to 920, as well as other entries between 931 and 1001, subsequently going its own way from that point to its final entry in 1070. Round about 1100, a group of scribes, one of whom was also the main scribe of F, erased some items and inserted others from sources including an ancestor of (D)E. B and C are so close right up to B's final entry that some scholars have taken C to be in places a direct copy of B. Yet it appears more likely that the resemblances result from the derivation of C partly from a manuscript lying also behind B and partly from a more remote common ancestor by way of at least one other copy. After B ends C joins with D and E in an extension up to at least annal 1019, subsequently continuing to agree with D but occasionally standing alone. As for D and E, these share not only extensions to the common stock (to annal 1027) but also certain modifications to it, some of which were subsequently to reach A in the form of insertions by the main scribe of F. In spite of their close agreement, however, there are also important differences between the two manuscripts even in the early sections, where D (perhaps as a result of collation and conflation) sometimes shares with B and C material that is not found in E. In A(G) and B the Chronicle is associated with a text known as the West-Saxon Regnal List and Genealogy.

The "First Compilation"
The first identifiable version of the Anglo-Saxon Chronicle is essentially a late-9th-century production, although it is obviously heavily dependent on now lost annals and records dating from earlier periods. Its *terminus post quem non* (latest possible date) is determined by the fact that material from a version of it, extending to at least annal 887 (an annal with references to events between 887 and 889), was already being used by Asser in 893). Analysis of the vocabulary suggests that in its final form it was the work of at least two compilers, the second working after 891, the first either collaborating with him or completing his work a few years earlier, that is, sometime in the late 870s or early 880s. The theory that these compilers were merely extending an older "Æthelwulf Chronicle," adding material from Bede and some "Canterbury annals," appears to be without sound foundation.

In spite of its modern title, and unlike some of its subsequent extensions, the Anglo-Saxon Chronicle in its earliest identifiable form is not in fact an attempt to chart the course of Anglo-Saxon history. Rather it concentrates on the area ruled over by the kings of the West Saxons, beginning with Cerdic at the very end of the 5th century and following the fortunes of his descendants and successors down to Æthelwulf and his sons in the second half of the 9th century (though the compilers did not hesitate to include continental and Mercian material when it was available). Not surprisingly the greatest detail is to be found from the 850s onward, when the events recorded may be assumed to have taken place within living memory. For earlier sections the compilers seem to have made use of a variety of written sources, in both OE and Latin, and apparently also oral materials, some in annalistic form, some not. Genealogies and regnal lists supplied names and dates of kings not only of the West Saxons but also of Kent, Mercia, and Northumbria; ecclesiastical records provided details of bishops and archbishops—mainly but not exclusively from the south of the country. A translation of the chronological summary in Latin that Bede appended to his *Ecclesiastical History of the English People* was also included, taking the beginning of the Chronicle back to a time before the arrival of the Anglo-Saxons in Britain, with the invasion by Julius Caesar in 60 B.C. This early material was further supplemented by a number of entries concerned with Roman and ecclesiastical history from

A.D. 1–101, probably derived from Isidore's *Chronicon*, Jerome's *De viris illustribus*, a version of the *Liber pontificalis*, and Rufinus's translation of Eusebius of Caesarea's *Ecclesiastical History*. The very layout of the Chronicle seems to owe its form to Latin models, such as Bede's chronological summary and Jerome's revision of Eusebius's *Chronicon*.

As for the earliest history of the Anglo-Saxons themselves, beginning with the arrival of Hengist and Horsa "in the reign of the emperors Martian and Valentinian," this seems to have been derived partly from Bede, but mainly from other—unidentified—sources, all presumably drawing on oral tradition. The information that these sources provided was sometimes unwittingly duplicated, sometimes given with a wording and in a form that may indicate a literary origin. In the annal for 473 we are told that the Britons fled from the English as from fire, while the encounter between Cynewulf and Cyneheard, reported briefly in annal 784 (786), anticipated in annal 755 (757) in a form that suggests paraphrase of a heroic lay, celebrates the loyalty of retainers who would rather die than follow the slayer of their lord.

Shared Continuations
After the annals for 891 and 892 the different versions of the Anglo-Saxon Chronicle generally go their own way, either separately or in pairs. An important account of the wars of Edward is found only in A(G). However, from time to time major entries are shared by several manuscripts. The first such major extension to the common core of the chronicle consists of an account of the campaigns by King Alfred against two Viking armies that invaded the south of England in the year 892, to be finally driven out in the year 896. This section, which is preserved in ABCD and G, and in modified form in F, appears to have been written as a unified entry shortly after the event. Other important distinctive units shared by two or more chronicle versions include what has been described as an "Æthelred chronicle," from 984 to 1018, which is incorporated in CDE, and the so-called Mercian Register, incorporated in BCD as annals for 902 to 924 but apparently once enjoying an independent existence. Verse entries in the 10th-century sections of ABC and (partly) D may have been composed specifically for inclusion—though it is not impossible that their first lines with the distinctive annal opening "Here" are the result of reworking of originally independent material by a compiler. Reworking is clearly responsible for the form taken by early annals in the Chronicle recension preserved in D and E. The reviser not only made use of the body of Bede's *Ecclesiastical History* to supplement material in the first compilation from Bede's chronological summary, he also inserted new material drawn from northern annals into the following section up to 806.

Authors and Centers
Only two names have been associated with the compilation or authorship of the chronicle: Alfred and Wulfstan. A passage in the style of Wulfstan appears in 959 DEF (rhythmical prose in annal 975 DE has also, less securely, been linked with him), while Plummer, following an attribution by Wil-

liam of Malmesbury, has suggested that responsibility for the original compilation and the "idea of a national Chronicle as opposed to merely local annals" are to be attributed to King Alfred, who not only directed and supervised its creation but also "may have dictated some of the later annals which describe his own wars." Certainly both the first compilation and the first continuation are biased in favor of King Alfred, the latter playing down, for instance, the role of Alfred's son Edward and his son-in-law Æthelræd of Mercia in his wars. However, both lack a number of details of a kind that Alfred and his immediate "court" circle might be expected to have been able to supply, and their concerns are often not those that might be expected of the king. Moreover the vocabulary and style of the Chronicle to 900 are markedly different from those of Alfred's translations.

Whether any of the later additions were commissioned by kings or their advisers is not known. Clearly not official records are the annals in E relating to the reign of Edward the Confessor, where the chronicler sides with the faction of Godwin and Harold against the king's French favorites, while the "Æthelred chronicle" attacks the bad policies that resulted in inaction until it was too late to avoid disaster: the Vikings were "never offered tribute in time nor fought against; but when they had done most to our injury, peace and truce were made with them" (CDE 1011).

Also uncertain is the place of origin of the different Chronicle versions. It has frequently been claimed that the first compilation was made at Winchester. As Stenton has demonstrated, however, a strong case can be made for commissioning (by a lay patron) in the southwest of England, while historical and paleographic arguments for a Winchester provenance for the oldest copy of the "first compilation" (in manuscript A) have been shown not to be firmly based. Later entries in A may indicate that the manuscript was at Winchester at least for a time before reaching the place of its final additions, Canterbury. Suggested locations for the writing of part or all of other Chronicle manuscripts are Canterbury, Abingdon, and Ramsey. Manuscript E was written at Peterborough. As for the now lost ancestor of DE, the presence of material of northern interest in both the revision of the first compilation and in subsequent sections of DE has led scholars to suggest, not implausibly, that this "northern recension" was compiled at York. A further suggestion, prompted by the absence from E of material shared by D with ABC from 893 onward—that a version of the Chronicle must have reached the north in Alfred's reign—has not found general acceptance. Indeed the work may well not have arrived there until the later part of the 10th century, when the see of York was held by archbishops of southern education.

Style

The quality of the writing in the Chronicle varies from section to section. In the first compilation the authors are restricted by lack of material relating to the early period. A number of annals consist merely of bald statements concerning the death of a king or bishop or the outcome of a battle. Where greater detail is available, there is more scope for stylistic mannerisms; however, as Cecily Clark has shown, both here and in subsequent sections, the genre of writing is that of the annal rather than that of the history, requiring the use of the plain style. A major exception is the account of the conflict between the West Saxon king Cynewulf and the brother of his deposed predecessor, Cyneheard. Here the (probable) paraphrasing of a lost heroic lay commemorating the event has resulted in extended narrative, which, exceptionally, includes a snatch of direct as well as reported speech.

Not all the annalists allowed themselves to be restricted by the demands of the plain style. A number of entries in the later part of Chronicle versions D and E are in rhythmical prose or make use of figures of rhetoric in order to direct the reader's response. "No worse deed than this for the English people was committed since they first came to England," says the annalist of the murder of King Edward at Corfe, in the entry for 979: "Men murdered him, but God honored him. In life he was an earthly king; he is now after death a heavenly saint. His earthly kinsmen would not avenge him, but his heavenly Father has greatly avenged him. The earthly slayers wished to blot out his memory on earth, but the heavenly avenger has spread abroad his memory in heaven and in earth. . . . Now we can perceive that the wisdom and contrivance of men and their plans are worthless against God's purpose." Moreover, in a section shared by A, B, and C, and partly by D, a compiler has inserted a handful of poetic annals, two with war as their subject matter, commemorating the Battle of Brunanburh and the reconquest of the Five Towns, the others recording the crowning and death of Edgar and the opening of the reign of Edward.

Middle English Extensions

Several of the versions of the Anglo-Saxon Chronicle extend beyond the Norman Conquest into the ME period. A, for instance, continues to 1070, though with little detail and—perhaps understandably—even less comment. The annal for 1066 merely reports the death of King Edward and the accession of Earl Harold, along with the length of the latter's reign (41 weeks and one day), and ends with three terse statements: "in this year William came and conquered England, and in this year Christ Church Canterbury burned, and in this year a comet appeared on the eighteenth of April." C describes in some detail events leading up to Harold's victory at Stamford Bridge but concludes abruptly at that point. D and E, in contrast, write more fully on the victory by Duke William, D seeing it as granted by God because of the sins of the people, and both continue to record events under William. Manuscript E was clearly written at Peterborough and not only covers events of local concern in the annals for the 1120s onward but has much Peterborough material interpolated into its earlier sections from 654 on.

Latin Chroniclers

The Anglo-Saxon Chronicle attracted considerable attention in the 16th and early 17th centuries, when the surviving manuscripts were annotated or transcribed by such scholars as Joscelyn, Talbot, Nowell, and William L'Isle. The first printed edition (based on G, with expansions and emendations, especially from A), was produced by Abraham Wheloc in 1643–44 as an appendix to his edition of Bede. However, it was the subject of scrutiny and use already in the medieval period by a number of writers in Latin. The first of these was Asser, who, in 893, incorporated into his life of Alfred material from a now lost manuscript resembling and probably identical with, the shared ancestor of BCDE. Nearly a century later Ealdorman Æthelweard in his *Chronicon* drew extensively on a now lost version derived from an ancestor of A, which—after certain additions and modifications had been made to it—might conceivably also have been the common ancestor of BCDE and Asser.

Interest in the Chronicle by Latin writers did not cease with the Norman Conquest: a brief series of Latin annals at the foot of a leaf of the early-12th-century manuscript Oxford, St. John's College 17, is based on the Chronicle annals for the years A.D. 1 to A.D. 99. Moreover Chronicle texts (mainly but not exclusively of the D- and E-type) were used extensively by the historians Henry of Huntingdon, "Florence of Worcester," Simeon of Durham, William of Malmesbury, Hugh Candidus, and the author of the Waverley Annals, while material derived from the Chronicle also appears in the Ramsey Computus and in the *Estoire des Engleis* by the French poet Gaimar. Finally a version to 912 was used by the compiler of the Annals of St. Neots in the early 12th century. This version was generally supposed to be derived from a chronicle text even older than the common original of the surviving vernacular versions. The variation in annal numbering on which this supposition was based, however, may merely be the result of intelligent collation and calculation by the author of the Annals of St. Neots, and his source could well be derived from the same common exemplar as the surviving Chronicle manuscripts.

Janet M. Bately

Bibliography

EDITIONS

Campbell, A., ed. *The Chronicle of Æthelweard.* London: Nelson, 1962; Classen, Ernest, and Florence E. Harmer. *An Anglo-Saxon Chronicle from British Museum, Cotton MS., Tiberius B.IV.* Manchester: Manchester University Press, 1926 [MS D]; Dumville, David N., and Simon Keynes, gen. eds. *The Anglo-Saxon Chronicle: A Collaborative Edition.* Cambridge: Brewer, 1983– [ongoing edition designed to update Thorpe: currently includes MS A, ed. Janet M. Bately (1986); MS B, ed. Simon Taylor (1983); and the Annals of St. Neots, ed. David N. Dumville and Michael Lapidge (1985)]; Lutz, Angelika, ed. *Die Version G der angelsächsischen Chronik: Rekonstruktion und Edition.* Munich: Fink, 1981; Magoun, Francis Peabody. "*Annales Domitiani Latini.*" *MS* 9 (1947): 235–95 [MS F]; Plummer, Charles, ed. *Two of the Saxon Chronicles Parallel.* 2 vols. Oxford: Clarendon, 1892–99. Repr. with revs. by Dorothy Whitelock. Oxford: Clarendon, 1952; Rositzke, Harry A., ed. *The C-Text of the Old English Chronicles.* Beiträge zur englischen Philologie 34. Bochum: Pöppinghaus, 1940. Repr. New York: Johnson Reprint, 1967; Stevenson, William Henry, ed. *Asser's Life of King Alfred.* Oxford: Clarendon, 1904. Repr. with revs. by Dorothy Whitelock. Oxford: Clarendon, 1959; Thorpe, Benjamin, ed. and trans. *The Anglo-Saxon Chronicle.* Rolls Series 23. London: Longman, Longman, Green, Longman & Roberts, 1861; Whitelock, Dorothy, ed. *English Historical Documents.* Vol. 1: *c. 500–1042.* 2d ed. London: Eyre Methuen; New York: Oxford University Press, 1979, pp. 109–25.

FACSIMILES

Dumville, David, ed. *The Anglo-Saxon Chronicle: Facsimile of Manuscript F: The Domitian Bilingual.* Cambridge: D.S. Brewer, 1995; Flower, Robin, and A. Hugh Smith, eds. *The Parker Chronicle and Laws (Corpus Christi College, Cambridge, MS. 173): A Facsimile.* EETS o.s. 208. London: Humphrey Milford, 1941; Whitelock, Dorothy, and Cecily Clark, eds. *The Peterborough Chronicle (The Bodleian Manuscript Laud Misc. 636).* EEMF 4. Copenhagen: Rosenkilde & Bagger, 1954.

SECONDARY

Barker, E.E. "The Anglo-Saxon Chronicle Used by Æthelweard." *BIHR* 40 (1967): 74–91; Bately, Janet M. "The Compilation of the Anglo-Saxon Chronicle, 60 BC to AD 890: Vocabulary as Evidence." *PBA* 64 (1978): 93–129. Repr. in *British Academy Papers on Anglo-Saxon England,* ed. E.G. Stanley. Oxford: Oxford University Press, 1990, pp. 261–97; Bately, Janet M. "Bede and the Anglo-Saxon Chronicle." In *Saints, Scholars, and Heroes,* ed. Margot H. King and Wesley M. Stevens. 2 vols. Collegeville: St. John's Abbey and University, 1979, 1:233–54; Bately, Janet M. "World History in the Anglo-Saxon Chronicle: Its Sources and Its Separateness from the Old English Orosius." *ASE* 8 (1979): 177–94; Bately, Janet M. "The Compilation of the *Anglo-Saxon Chronicle* Once More." *Leeds Studies in English,* n.s. 16 (1985): 7–26; Bately, Janet M. "Layout and the Anglo-Saxon Chronicle." *BJRL* 70 (1988): 21–43; Bately, Janet M. *The Anglo-Saxon Chronicle: Texts and Textual Relationships.* Reading Medieval Studies Monograph 3. Reading: University of Reading, 1991; Dumville, David N. "Some Aspects of Annalistic Writing at Canterbury in the Eleventh and Early Twelfth Centuries." *Peritia* 2 (1983): 23–57; Dumville, David N. "The West Saxon Genealogical Regnal List: Manuscripts and Texts." *Anglia* 104 (1986): 1–32; Hart, C. "The B-Text of the *Anglo-Saxon Chronicle.*" *JMH* 8 (1982): 241–99; Meaney, Audrey L. "St. Neots, Æthelweard and the Compilation of the *Anglo-Saxon Chronicle*: A Survey." In *Studies in Earlier Old English Prose,* ed. Paul E. Szarmach. Albany: SUNY Press, 1986, pp. 193–243; Parkes, Malcolm B. "The Palaeography of the Parker Manuscript of the *Chronicle,* Laws and Sedulius, and Historiography at Winchester in the Late Ninth and

Tenth Centuries." *ASE* 5 (1976): 149–72; Stenton, Frank M. "The South-Western Element in the Old English Chronicle." In *Essays in Medieval History Presented to T.F. Tout*, ed. A.G. Little and F.M. Powicke. Manchester: Manchester University Press, 1925, pp. 15–24.

See also Æthelweard; Alfred; Asser; *Battle of Brunanburh*; Chronicle Poems; Chronicles; Gaimar; Norman Conquest

Anglo-Saxon Invasions and Conquest

The Anglo-Saxon invasions and conquest of Britain are clearer in mythic outline than in historical fact. The surviving written sources are much later than the events and are open to interpretation. The archaeological record offers incomplete though suggestive evidence for the continental homelands and settlement patterns of the Germanic tribes that came from northwest Europe in a series of invasions that reached major proportions, probably in the 440s.

The oldest surviving references to the *adventus Saxonum*, the arrival of the Saxons (as well as the Jutes and Angles), appear in a work of a century later, Gildas's *The Ruin of Britain* (ca. 540). Gildas is not primarily concerned with historical events; he writes to exhort his fellow British Christians to spiritual reform so they might defeat the pagan invaders. The passage of a century between the first major wave of invaders and *The Ruin of Britain* indicates that the Germanic conquest followed from a protracted series of engagements rather than one decisive battle, as with the Norman Conquest of 1066.

Gildas expresses little interest in the origins or motivations of the Germanic tribes, nor does he provide anything approaching a coherent chronological account for the invasions. He depicts the invaders as a pack of cubs emerging from a barbarian lioness, that is, as uncivilized warriors from non-Latin speaking areas of Europe. While his depiction is a vivid measure of the fear felt by the soon-to-be-conquered British, it raises more questions than it answers about historical events and chronology.

The next important account of the invasions is Bede's *Ecclesiastical History of the English People* (ca. 731). Although writing almost 300 years after the fact, Bede offers the fullest surviving account of the *adventus Saxonum*. Like Gildas he presents the invasions and conquest as episodes in the spiritual history of Britain, but he writes with different cultural allegiances. To Bede the defeat of the British represents their punishment by God for failing to convert pagans to Christianity. In this account God uses the invasions of the Angles, Saxons, and Jutes to purge Britain of its sinful inhabitants so that it might be occupied by tribes that would later be converted to Christianity. Bede sets the invasions within providential history, but he does so with some chronological and geographical precision. He thus influenced not only subsequent Anglo-Saxon accounts but historians and archaeologists to the present. Research suggests that Bede's account of the invasions and settlement represents his conscious attempt to endow a complex, confusing set of events with a greater coherence than they may in fact have had.

In Book 1 of the *Ecclesiastical History* Bede sets the invasion of the Angles, Saxons, and Jutes within a sequence of events that originated in the Roman withdrawal from Britain in 410, after which the British—grown soft under Roman protection—became vulnerable to raids from such hostile tribes as the Picts and Scots. The raids became so troublesome that the British leader Vortigern (either a personal name or a term meaning "great leader") sought the services of Angles or Saxons as mercenaries. Three boatloads of mercenaries quickly repelled the northern tribes that had been harassing the British. Rather than settle for the Isle of Thanet, the agreed-upon reward, the Germanic tribesmen chose instead to attack their former masters and seize Britain because it was more fertile than their continental homeland and because its inhabitants' cowardice promised easy victory. Hearing of these developments, Bede explains, other Germanic tribes migrated to Britain and joined with those already there to form an invincible force.

These new arrivals came from the three major tribes of the Angles, Saxons, and Jutes. Modern scholars have shown that other tribes, especially Frisians and perhaps Swedes, also participated in the invasions, though Bede makes no mention of them, presumably to maintain the symmetry of his account.

Bede explains that the Jutes emigrated from their ancestral Jutland (probably in modern Denmark) and settled in Kent, parts of Wessex, and on the Isle of Wight; the Saxons emigrated from Old Saxony (between the rivers Elbe and Ems) and settled in Essex, Sussex, and Wessex; the Angles emigrated from *Angulus* (the region between the old Jutish and Saxon homelands) and settled in Anglia, Mercia, and Northumbria. These tribes were led by the brothers Hengist and Horsa. There is agreement among archaeologists that Bede's is a simplified but still accurate explanation for the complex, extended process of Anglo-Saxon settlement.

By modern standards Bede's chronology for the invasions is vague, though still far more precise than Gildas's. Bede opens the relevant chapter of the *Ecclesiastical History* (1.15) by stating that Marcian became emperor of Rome in 449. He adds that the first major wave of invasions began during his reign, which ended in 456. Elsewhere in his *History*, however, Bede dates Vortigern's invitation to the Angles and the Saxons to ca. 445 or to 446/47. In later Anglo-Saxon works the year 449 became, through a simplified reading of Bede's text, the traditional date for the invasions.

Bede's account became the dominant source for later Anglo-Saxon treatments of the ancestral invasions and settlement. The Alfredian translation of the *Ecclesiastical History* into OE retains almost the entire account of events as in Bede. The compilers of the Anglo-Saxon Chronicle drew heavily on him for their annals of mid-5th-century events. When Alcuin in the late 8th century and Wulfstan in the early 11th wrote about the incursions of the Danes, another pagan people from the north, they evoked the ancestral invasions and conquest as a warning that the Anglo-Saxons might suffer the same fate as the British. During the period the record of the Anglo-Saxon invasions and conquest became inscribed as a central historical and religious myth within the culture.

A modern account of the invasions and conquest, based more on archaeological than on documentary evidence, would be considerably less orderly than that of Bede, as well as considerably more tentative. This account would extend over a longer period of time, noting that the Saxons, along with the Scots and Picts, launched a major offensive against Roman Britain in 367, and that there were extensive settlements of Germanic tribesmen along with what came to be called the "Saxon Shore" of Britain generations before Vortigern's invitation to their compatriots. Contact between the Germanic tribes and Roman Britain began considerably earlier. Moreover the battles between the Germanic invaders and the British lasted for a longer period than Bede indicates, that is, through the last quarter of the 6th century. So, too, this modern account would admit the presence of tribes other than the Angles, Saxons, and Jutes in the invasions of the mid-5th century.

Although its conclusions must remain tentative, archaeology will eventually modify, complicate, and render less orderly the documentary record found in Gildas, Bede, and elsewhere, though it seems unlikely to alter entirely its main outlines.

Nicholas Howe

Bibliography

PRIMARY

Colgrave, Bertram, and R.A.B. Mynors, eds. and trans. *Bede's Ecclesiastical History of the English People.* Oxford: Clarendon, 1969; Gildas. *The Ruin of Britain and Other Works.* Ed. and trans. Michael Winterbottom. London: Phillimore, 1978.

SECONDARY

Arnold, C.J. *Roman Britain to Saxon Shore.* Bloomington: Indiana University Press, 1984; Howe, Nicholas. *Migration and Mythmaking in Anglo-Saxon England.* New Haven: Yale University Press, 1989; Myres, J.N.L. *The English Settlements.* Oxford: Clarendon, 1986.

See also Bede; Conversion of the Anglo-Saxons; Heptarchy; Tacitus

Anglo-Saxon Old Testament Narrative Illustration

Two extensively illustrated Old Testament manuscripts other than psalters survive from Anglo-Saxon England: the "Cædmon Manuscript" (Bodl. Junius 11) of ca. 1000 (fig. 4) and BL Cotton Claudius B.iv of ca. 1050, also known as the "Hexateuch of Ælfric." Differing in style, technique, format, and, at times, iconography, both manuscripts are similar in the large number of illustrations they contain (48 in Junius 11, 394 in Claudius B.iv), as well as the fact that these accompany Anglo-Saxon texts based on the Bible, rather than the canonical Latin text of the Bible itself.

Junius 11 consists of four poems on biblical subjects: the two-part *Genesis A* and *Genesis B; Exodus; Daniel;* and *Christ and Satan.* All are considered monuments of Anglo-Saxon poetry. Of the four texts only Genesis is illustrated, and that incompletely, although spaces for illustrations have been left throughout the remainder of Junius 11 except for the final portion, *Christ and Satan.*

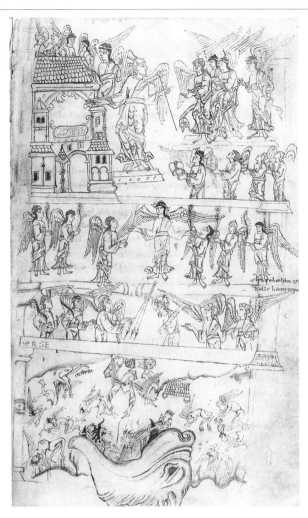

Fig. 4. Bodl. Junius 11, p. 3. Fall of the Rebel Angels. Reproduced by permission of the Bodleian Library, University of Oxford.

The resemblance of the opening lines of *Genesis A* to Cædmon's famous hymn on the Creation led to the erroneous tradition of associating the text of Junius 11 with the name of Cædmon. Similarly Claudius B.iv, a prose paraphrase of the Pentateuch and Joshua, is traditionally named after Ælfric (ca. 945–ca. 1015), abbot of Eynsham, called the "grammarian." Peter Clemoes, however, has demonstrated that the text is based only in part on a translation by Ælfric and is largely the work of a later compiler, possibly Byrhtferth of Ramsey.

Both manuscripts have traditionally been attributed to Canterbury: the Hexateuch to St. Augustine's and Junius 11 to Christ Church, though alternative provenances have been proposed for Junius 11, including Glastonbury and Malmesbury. While the Hexateuch is believed to be the work of a single artist, Junius 11 is generally thought to be the work of two 11th-century artists. Interestingly both manuscripts are unfinished projects in which the program of illustrations was never completed, this fact in the case of the Hexateuch allowing direct observation of the artist's methods. Both manuscripts also show unfortunate additions to their illustrations by later hands.

The intended use of Junius 11 is not clear, and various purposes have been suggested for it, from the devotional to the liturgical. For the Hexateuch Clemoes has suggested that the coupling of a vernacular text with illustrations was probably an educational response to the needs of laypeople, rather than something meant for a monastic audience. Whatever their intended uses, both manuscripts attest to the status of the vernacular and literary art in late Anglo-Saxon England.

The bold, simplified, full-bodied illustrations of the Hexateuch offer stark contrast to the sepia and, at times, multicolored ink outline drawings of Junius 11. The style of both manuscripts has traditionally been described as crude. Despite such negative aesthetic judgments much remains to be learned about the ultimate iconographic origins of both sets of illustrations from a more dispassionate assessment of their respective artistic styles.

A major area of scholarly disagreement concerns the nature and extent of each manuscript's indebtedness to iconographic precedents and prototypes. Numerous relationships to the iconography of an early Christian manuscript tradition similar to that of the so-called "Cotton Genesis" (BL Cotton Otho B.vi) have been indicated for both by several scholars. On the other hand, especially in the case of the Hexateuch, numerous motifs having to do with other, non-Cotton Genesis iconographic traditions, specifically that associated with the Byzantine, post-Iconoclastic Octateuchs, have been brought forward, most prominently in the work of George Henderson, as proof of a more complex iconographic origin for its illustrations. While the specific influence of the 9th-century Utrecht Psalter on certain illustrations in both Junius 11 and the Hexateuch has been demonstrated, several scholars have posited generalized Carolingian intermediaries for the illustrations as a whole of both manuscripts. It is also clear that both Junius 11 and the Hexateuch contain many similar, but not identical, extrabiblical, "apocryphal" details—some of which can be traced to the specific texts they accompany. In the case of the Hexateuch Dodwell has taken the position that its illustrations were created specifically for that particular text and have no substantial relation to any previous iconographic tradition.

Despite questions of iconographic origins there is no doubt that the illustrations of Junius 11 and the Hexateuch together represent the largest manuscript repository of Old Testament imagery before the high Middle Ages.

Herbert R. Broderick

Bibliography

PRIMARY

Dodwell, C.R., and Peter Clemoes. *The Old English Illustrated Hexateuch: British Museum Cotton Claudius B.IV.* EEMF 18. Copenhagen: Rosenkilde & Bagger, 1974; Gollancz, Israel. *The Cædmon Manuscript of Anglo-Saxon Biblical Poetry.* Oxford: Oxford University Press, 1927.

SECONDARY

Broderick, Herbert R. "Some Attitudes toward the Frame in Anglo-Saxon Manuscripts of the Tenth and Eleventh Centuries." *Artibus et Historiae* 5 (1982): 31–42; Broderick, Herbert R. "Observations on the Method of Illustration in MS Junius 11 and the Relationship of the Drawings to the Text." *Scriptorium* 37 (1983): 161–77; Deshman, Robert. *Anglo-Saxon and Anglo-Scandinavian Art: An Annotated Bibliography.* Boston: Hall, 1984; Haney, Kristine Edmondson. "Some Old Testament Pictures in the Psalter of Henry of Blois." *Gesta* 24 (1985): 33–45; Ohlgren, Thomas H. *Anglo-Saxon Textual Illustration: Photographs of Sixteen Manuscripts with Descriptions and Index.* Kalamazoo: Medieval Institute, 1992; Raw, Barbara C. "The Construction of Oxford, Bodleian Library, Junius 11." *ASE* 13 (1984): 187–208; Temple, Elżbieta. *Anglo-Saxon Manuscripts 900–1066.* A Survey of Manuscripts Illuminated in the British Isles 2, ed. J.J.G. Alexander. London: Harvey Miller, 1976; Weitzmann, Kurt, and Herbert L. Kessler. *The Cotton Genesis: British Library Codex Cotton Otho B.VI.* Princeton: Princeton University Press, 1986.

See also Ælfric; Bible in OE Literature; Byrhtferth; *Genesis A and B*; Harley Psalter; Junius Manuscript; Manuscript Illumination, Anglo-Saxon; Translation

Anselm of Canterbury (1033–1109)

The foremost theologian of his generation, best known for his pathbreaking use of reason rather than authority in philosophical arguments. His best-known work, *Proslogion*, sets out to prove the existence of God by reason alone. Also known as the ontological proof of God, Anselm's approach is admired and debated to the present for its simple, concise logic.

Anselm's *Cur Deus homo (Why God Became Man)* may well have marked an even more important break with the past. It argues the necessity for God to take human form and to save human souls, because human beings, created in God's image, were born reflecting God's goodness and thus deserve the happiness God intended; nevertheless, Christ's choice of death was entirely free. This statement reverses Augustine of Hippo's earlier belief that men are inherently sinful, opening a new age of human confidence and optimism. Anselm's more complex argument here also has been cited for its novel legal precision.

Born of an aristocratic family in Aosta, on the Burgundy-Savoy border, the young Anselm left home to study with Lanfranc at the Norman abbey of Bec, arriving before 1059. Here he may have received some legal training along with the liberal arts Lanfranc taught. When Lanfranc moved to Caen in 1060, Anselm replaced him as prior-schoolmaster. Unlike Lanfranc Anselm urged his students to become monks at Bec. During his years as prior and then abbot (1060–93) Bec was a model of efficient administration and simple devotion, and it became the wealthiest and most respected abbey in Normandy, sending its sons to rule abbeys and bishoprics throughout Normandy and England. With them spread Anselm's ideals of loving friendship for all humankind.

Anselm followed Lanfranc's footsteps to Canterbury as archbishop and primate in 1093. King William II (William Rufus), intent on exploiting the English church, opposed his efforts toward reform, with disastrous results: Anselm's exile (1097–1100). On Rufus's accidental death Henry I recalled

Anselm, resolved to cooperate in reform. But Anselm refused to pay homage to Henry and forbade the king to invest churchmen with their offices, having heard these prohibitions at the papal court. This began the great English Investiture Controversy (1100–07), a three-way struggle among king, pope, and archbishop, each seeking his own version of "right order."

Anselm suffered a second exile (1103–07), returning to England only after he had formulated the compromises among all parties and gained the "due order" he envisioned for Canterbury and England. The king and the archbishop were to rule almost as co-regents of the realm, with the pope as a distant source of law and authority; the archbishop would be primate of all Britain—including Ireland, Wales, and the Orkney Islands. A superb statesman for God, of great talent, intelligence, foresight, and integrity, Anselm was canonized through the efforts of Thomas Becket, his later successor as archbishop of Canterbury.

Sally N. Vaughn

Bibliography

PRIMARY

Eadmer. *Vita Anselmi: The Life of St. Anselm, Archbishop of Canterbury.* Ed. and trans. R.W. Southern. London: Nelson, 1962; Eadmer. *Eadmer's History of Recent Events in England.* Trans. Geoffrey Bosanquet. London: Cresset Press, 1964.

SECONDARY

Hopkins, Jasper. *A Companion to the Study of St. Anselm.* Minneapolis: University of Minnesota Press, 1972; Southern, R.W. *Saint Anselm and His Biographer: A Study of Monastic Life and Thought, 1059–1130.* Cambridge: Cambridge University Press, 1966; Vaughn, Sally N. *Anselm of Bec and Robert of Meulan: The Innocence of the Dove and the Wisdom of the Serpent.* Berkeley: University of California Press, 1987.

See also Becket; Henry I; Investiture Controversy; Lanfranc; William II

Antiphon

In most instances a short prose text sung before and after a psalm, group of psalms, or a canticle. Psalm antiphons occur in all of the offices and are the most numerous items within the repertoires of liturgical chant. Many serve to lend context to a frequently repeated psalm or canticle by direct reference to the particular feast or season to which they are assigned. The earliest antiphon texts were commonly single psalm verses, but with the growing elaboration of the liturgy texts were also taken from other parts of the Bible and from nonscriptural sources, such as biographies of the saints.

In its earliest form the antiphon was usually repeated as a refrain after each verse of the psalm it accompanied, a practice that may have originated in the Jewish synagogue. By the Middle Ages, however, the antiphon had largely lost its refrain character and usually functioned simply as a framing text. Common practice was to sing no more than the incipit of the antiphon before the psalm, so that it was heard complete only at the end.

Antiphons vary stylistically according to their function. Those allotted to ferial days are usually brief; texts are set syllabically with a restricted melodic range. Many use formulaic melodies, adapting preexistent models that were codified mostly in the latter part of the 8th century. Some of these "prototype" melodies may appear with over 50 texts in one liturgical use. Festal antiphons are more elaborate musically, commonly drawing their texts from readings used at the office or mass of the day (and in the case of antiphons for the Benedictus and Magnificat, the Gospel of the day). In performance the medieval cantor needed to ensure that the antiphon was accompanied by an appropriate psalm tone that matched in mode and had a suitable melodic ending: the medieval tonaries contain much discussion of this matter.

Antiphons also occur in the mass as the chants for the Introit, Offertory, and Communion. Originally, as in the office, each of these items incorporated a complete psalm with the antiphon serving as a refrain between verses. But as the antiphon grew more elaborate and the requirements of the liturgy changed, the psalm verses were omitted and the antiphon remained as an independent item in its own right. Remnants of this earlier refrain function are seen in the medieval Introit, which usually retains at least one integral psalm verse and *Gloria patri*, and a few Offertories and Communions.

There are other occasions in the liturgy where antiphons are prescribed without psalms—processions, votive and memorial antiphons, and the ceremonial Mandatum antiphons of Maundy Thursday among them. Like the mass chants some of these examples are not entirely divorced from psalmody since they incorporate integral psalm verses. Processions in the early church were also accompanied by antiphons with integral psalms, which continued until the procession reached its station.

Independent antiphons also form part of a group of related self-contained ceremonies each consisting of three elements—an antiphon, versicle with response, and a collect. Memorials and suffrages are the most prolific members of this family, usually occurring as appendages to Lauds and Vespers after the collect. Both are perhaps best understood as compressed offices, retaining some of the main "proper" features of the office, but omitting the psalmody. Usually they occurred when two feasts coincided, but others were simply for devotional purposes, acting as standard commemorations for a particular saint. Memorials to the Virgin and All Saints fall within this latter category.

Votive antiphons are perhaps the most familiar type of independent antiphon. Structurally the votive antiphon shared the tripartite structure of the memorial or suffrage, but it was almost invariably addressed to the Virgin, and most commonly occurred after Compline or after Compline of the Little Office of the Virgin rather than after Lauds or Vespers. Most votive antiphons were borrowed from the central liturgical repertoire (especially the Marian feasts) rather than newly composed. Others doubled as antiphons in processions in honor of the Virgin. Medieval books tend to prescribe three different types of votive antiphon. Some sources simply specify *aliqua antiphona de beata Maria*, others prescribe a specific text (most often *Salve regina*), while others give a set of seasonal alternatives. In the latter case the pattern established by the Franciscans in 1249 and taken up by the Roman Use in 1350 is the most familiar: *Alma redemptoris mater* (Advent to the Purification), *Ave regina celorum* (Lent), *Regina celi* (Eastertide), and *Salve regina* (Octave of Pentecost to Advent).

In many instances the votive antiphon served as one of the earliest vehicles for polyphony. Settings of Marian antiphons in 14th-century English sources and in the Old Hall Manuscript with no particular function may well have been used after Compline. The most substantial evidence, however, comes from the late 15th century—the collection of large-scale votive antiphons in the Eton Choirbook.

Sally E. Roper

Bibliography

Apel, Willi. *Gregorian Chant*. Bloomington: Indiana University Press, 1958; Bailey, Terence. *The Processions of Sarum and the Western Church*. Toronto: Pontifical Institute, 1971; Burstyn, Shai. "Early 15th-Century Settings of Song of Songs Antiphons." *Acta Musicologica* 49 (1977): 200–27; Canal, Jose Maria. "Salve regina misericordiae: historia y leendas en torno a esta antifona." *Temi e testi* 9 (Rome, 1963): 1, passim; Harrison, Frank Ll. "The Eton Choirbook: Its Background and Contents." *Annales musicologiques* 1 (1953): 151–75; Harrison, Frank Ll. *Music in Medieval Britain*. 2d ed. London: Routledge & Kegan Paul, 1963; Hughes, Andrew. *Medieval Manuscripts for Mass and Office: A Guide to Their Organization and Terminology*. Toronto: University of Toronto Press, 1982; Wagner, Peter. *Introduction to the Gregorian Melodies: A Handbook of Plainsong*. Trans. Agnes Orme and E.G.P. Wyatt. London: Plainsong & Mediaeval Music Society, 1901. Repr. New York: Da Capo, 1986.

See also Liturgy; Liturgy and Church Music, History of; Magnificat; Processions; Votive Observance

Apocalypses

Illuminated manuscripts of the Apocalypse (the book of Revelation and commentaries on it) might have been produced in England as early as the Anglo-Saxon period. While none survive, the style and motifs, particularly interlace, of such manuscripts as the Valenciennes Apocalypse (Valenciennes, Bibliothèque Municipale 99), made on the Continent early in the 9th century, suggest the use of insular models. A couple of 12th-century illuminated Apocalypses have come down to us: a copy of Berengaudus's Commentary (Durham, Cathedral Library A.1.10) and Bede's Commentary (Cambridge, St. John's College H.6). However, the greatest period of Apocalypse manuscript production in England was without question the third quarter of the 13th century. Beginning around 1250, a new taste for deluxe Apocalypses began to appear, most likely in part a response to current prophecies of the end

of the world. Joachim of Fiore had prophesied that the end would come in 1260, and his views were disseminated and popularized by the Franciscans.

Both the chronology and the origins of the cycles of illustrations in the English Gothic Apocalypses continue to be controversial. The first examples were probably made not much before 1250. Morgan has suggested that the English Apocalypse now in Paris (BN fr. 403) is likely to be the earliest in the series (N. Morgan, 1988). The Paris Apocalypse is in French prose; other types include those in Latin and in French and Latin. Many of all three types are glossed.

The cycle shared by the Metz and Lambeth Apocalypses (Metz, Bibliothèque Municipale Salis 38, destroyed 1944; London, Lambeth Palace 209) has been identified as the most influential. The Lambeth Apocalypse contains 78 full-color illustrations in horizontal rectangular frames above a two-columned text, with an additional 29 full-page illustrations of the life of St. John and devotional subjects. This manuscript is one of the few Apocalypses with a known patron, Countess Eleanor de Quincy, who is depicted on folio 48. The extensive series of devotional images also reflects this particular manuscript's probable function as a private devotional book. Variations on the Metz-Lambeth cycle are the basis for the images in the Cambrai (Cambrai, Bibliothèque Municipale

Fig. 5. Trinity College Apocalypse (Cambridge, Trinity College R.16.2), fol. 14v. The dragon transfers power to the beast from the sea; the beast makes war with the saints. Courtesy of the Master and Fellows of Trinity College, Cambridge.

422), Abingdon (BL Add. 42555), Gulbenkian (Lisbon, Mus. Cal. Gulbenkian, L.A. 139), and Tanner Apocalypses (Bodl. Tanner 184). The Metz-Lambeth books may have been created in London workshops (Morgan, 1988).

The most deluxe of the 13th-century Apocalypses is the enormous Trinity College Apocalypse (Cambridge, Trinity College R.16.2; fig. 5), measuring 16.9 by 12 inches. It contains 71 fully painted framed illustrations for the Apocalypse text, and an additional eleven pages with scenes of the life of St. John. Morgan has identified four different artists' hands in the miniatures. Both its text and commentary (Berengaudus) are in French, which would have appealed to a courtly patron, but primarily because of the active role of aristocratic women in several of the images, Queen Eleanor, wife of Henry III, is considered to be the most likely patron; she is one of the few laypersons who could have afforded such a sumptuous object. The influence of the Trinity College Apocalypse is still debated, but it seems to have been incorporated into some expansions of the Metz-Lambeth cycle, such as that found in the Douce Apocalypse (Bodl. Douce 180) made for Prince Edward (later Edward I) and his wife, Eleanor of Castile.

The mid-13th-century Apocalypses as a whole display a wide variation in the illustration formats, languages, and text selections, reflecting the different types of patrons for which they were made. Manuscripts like the Abingdon Apocalypse, possibly made for Giles de Bridport, bishop of Salisbury, emphasize ecclesiastical concerns; while some Apocalypses (such as London, Lambeth Palace 434 and Eton College 177) have extremely abbreviated texts and can almost be classified as picture books. By the fourth quarter of the 13th century Apocalypses had begun to fall out of fashion, and only a few illuminated examples are extant (BN fr. 9574; London, Lambeth Palace 75; Cambridge, Trinity College B.10.6; Cambridge, Fitzwilliam Museum McClean 123; Oxford, New College 65).

Apocalypses continued to be produced intermittently during the 14th century, although not in great number, and the majority feature a French text, in contrast to the Latin text of most 13th-century Apocalypses. Some new illustration formats were employed, such as the vertical rectangular shape of the miniatures in the early-14th-century Dublin Apocalypse (Dublin, Trinity College 64), which is a departure from the standard horizontal arrangement. One of the most elegant Apocalypses from the first quarter of the century is the Royal Apocalypse (BL Royal 19.B.xv), which was illuminated in part by the Queen Mary Master. Manuscripts demonstrating a clear affinity to the 13th-century Metz-Lambeth group also reappear at this time: the Canonici Apocalypse (Bodl. Canonici Bib. 62), dated ca. 1320–30, and an Apocalypse from Crowland Abbey (Cambridge, Magdalene College 5), dated ca. 1330. The 13th-century Apocalypses in general continue to influence Apocalypse illustrators throughout the 14th century; even an Apocalypse at Cambridge (Trinity College B.10.2), dated ca. 1380–1400, clearly relies on formats and compositions from the previous century.

Judith Ellis

Bibliography

Alexander, Jonathan, and Paul Binski, eds. *Age of Chivalry: Art in Plantagenet England 1200–1400.* London: Royal Academy of Arts, 1987; Brieger, Peter. *The Trinity College Apocalypse.* London: Eugrammia, 1967 [facsimile]; Morgan, Nigel. *Early Gothic Manuscripts (2) 1250–1285.* A Survey of Manuscripts Illuminated in the British Isles 4:2, ed. J.J.G. Alexander. London: Harvey Miller, 1988; Morgan, Nigel. *The Lambeth Apocalypse.* London: Harvey Miller, 1990 [facsimile]; Sandler, Lucy Freeman. *Gothic Manuscripts 1285–1385.* A Survey of Manuscripts Illuminated in the British Isles 5, ed. J.J.G. Alexander. London: Harvey Miller, 1986.

See also Manuscript Illumination, Gothic; Prophecy Literature; Women and the Arts

Apollonius of Tyre

The late OE prose romance *Apollonius of Tyre* survives in a single manuscript (Cambridge, Corpus Christi College 201 B) of the middle of the 11th century. The other contents of the manuscript are mainly sober writings of Wulfstan, with which *Apollonius of Tyre* makes a striking contrast. *Apollonius* is a translation from the Latin of a work belonging to the literary type that critics refer to as "Greek romance." As a Greek romance it is a tale of love and near-fatal misfortune, of improbable escapes and miraculous reunions, involving travel, shipwreck, pirates, and threats to feminine chastity, all leading to the obligatory happy ending. The story attracted notoriety in the Middle Ages because of the theme of incest with which it begins. It was ostensibly as an illustration of the sin of incest that the tale was included by John Gower in his *Confessio Amantis.* Other versions exist in Middle and early Modern English (as well as in other European languages), most notably in Shakespeare's *Pericles.* The OE version is a translation from a textually corrupt variant of the Latin. By comparing surviving texts of the Latin it is possible to reconstruct essential features of the immediate source used by the OE writer, but the exact Latin original has not survived.

A taste for the exotic and the marvelous is revealed in certain other OE prose writings, such as *The Wonders of the East* and the *Letter of Alexander to Aristotle,* and romance elements are apparent in some saints' lives, notably in the anonymous *Life of St. Eustace* and *Andreas. Apollonius of Tyre,* however, is a unique example of secular romance in OE. The vernacular writer shows intelligence and sensitivity in responding to the original. For the most part the OE remains close to the sense of the Latin, expressing this in smooth and fluent English prose. The writer deliberately changes some of the emphases of the original, however, tailoring the classical material to the taste of an Anglo-Saxon audience. The behavior of Apollonius himself becomes less emotional in the OE, and he acquires some of the restraint of a Germanic hero. Similarly, although the delicacy of the OE writer in treating refined sentiments and the intimacies of personal relationships has been justly admired, it has also been noted that this writer shows great reticence in matters of sex and love. The treatment of this aspect of the original is considerably toned down in the OE.

The OE text of *Apollonius of Tyre* is not complete. At least one quire appears to be missing from the manuscript, and more than a third of the story is lost. This lacuna may be purely accidental, but it is possible that it is the result of the desire of the OE writer, or of a scribe-editor, to suppress the sexual themes that are developed in the middle part of the story.

Hugh Magennis

Bibliography

Archibald, Elizabeth. *Apollonius of Tyre: Medieval and Renaissance Themes and Variations, Including the Text of the Historia Apollonii regis Tyri with an English Translation.* Cambridge: Brewer, 1991; Donner, Morton. "Prudery in Old English Fiction." *Comitatus* 3 (1972): 91–96; Goolden, Peter, ed. *The Old English Apollonius of Tyre.* London: Oxford University Press, 1958; Riedinger, Anita R. "The Englishing of Arcestrate: Woman in Apollonius of Tyre." In *New Readings on Women in Old English Literature*, ed. Helen Damico and Alexandra Hennessey Olsen. Bloomington: Indiana University Press, 1990, pp. 292–306.

See also Andreas; Gower; *Letter of Alexander; Marvels of the East;* Women in OE Literature

Appellants

The group of nobles who brought an appeal of treason against Richard II's favorites in the parliament of 1388. The origins of their action lay in the deterioration in relations between king and nobility that had occurred over the previous four years. Richard was criticized for the extravagance of his household and his favoritism toward a select group of courtiers, notably Robert de Vere, elevated to be duke of Ireland. When at Nottingham and Shrewsbury in the summer of 1387 Richard sought a clarification of his rights from the royal judges and authorized de Vere to raise a force in Cheshire, his critics realized that they would have to act quickly to defend themselves. Under the leadership of Thomas, duke of Gloucester, Richard Fitzalan, earl of Arundel, and Thomas Beauchamp, earl of Warwick, they began to muster a force, attracting further support from two junior colleagues, Henry earl of Derby, John of Gaunt's son, and Thomas Mowbray, earl of Nottingham. When news reached them that de Vere was marching south, Gloucester and Derby set off to intercept him. In a skirmish at Radcot Bridge on the Thames de Vere was defeated and Richard had no choice but to submit to his opponents' will.

The Appellants decided to prosecute the king's friends: Robert de Vere; Alexander Neville, archbishop of York; Michael de la Pole, the former chancellor; Robert Tresilian, the chief justice; and Nicholas Brembre, a former lord mayor of London. They proceeded by means of the personal action known as the appeal, probably because it could be heard before parliament. But securing verdicts to their satisfaction proved more difficult than anticipated. Brembre was found guilty only after condemnation by representatives of the London guilds. Though Tresilian, who in the meantime had been found in hiding, was dispatched more summarily, it was decided to proceed against the lesser courtiers by the more malleable process of impeachment. Simon Burley, Richard's tutor, Thomas Usk, under-sheriff of Middlesex, and three chamber knights were all tried in this way, found guilty, and executed.

The Appellants were an ill-matched group, brought together by a shared hostility to the dominant group at court. Once they had removed de Vere and cleansed what they saw as the Augean stables of the king's household, unity disappeared. By May 1389 the way was clear for Richard to gain the initiative and take the governance of the realm back into his own hands.

Nigel E. Saul

Bibliography

Hector, L.C., and Barbara F. Harvey, eds. and trans. *The Westminster Chronicle, 1381–1394.* Oxford: Clarendon, 1982.

See also Henry IV; Lancaster, John Duke of; Richard II; Usk

Archaeology
Anglo-Saxon Period

Seventeenth-century interest in the Anglo-Saxons as freeborn Englishmen, uncrushed by the Norman yoke, did not lead to an interest in their material remains or archaeology until a chronological framework for such data was established. There was no criterion for distinguishing among Romano-British, Anglo-Saxon, or Viking burial urns, for instance, even though Sir Thomas Browne wrote about such things in the 1650s. Graves excavated in Kent by the Rev. Bryan Faussett in the 18th century contained many items of jewelry, weaponry, and other objects, but these were still not universally accepted as Anglo-Saxon, even in the 1850s.

The study of archaeological objects was stimulated by the building of railways in the 1830s and 1840s, when important sites, such as the cemetery at Faversham, Kent, were disturbed. Collectors also amassed material from building sites as Victorian England expanded. Antiquarianism gave way to systematic archaeology only in the 20th century, despite a few pioneers like John M. Kemble (1807–1857). Thereafter the standard approach became that of Edward Thurlow Leeds, whose analyses of metalwork were intended to show where particular tribes of invaders came from and where they had reached by particular times, all of which was interwoven with the dates of the Anglo-Saxon Chronicle and other written sources. Only in the 1960s and 1970s did this approach come to be called in question, partly because of the realization that particular artifacts may not be uniquely distinctive of particular cultural groups and partly because the documents were being scrutinized and their apparent precision called into question.

Systematic excavation also began in the early 20th century, much of it by Leeds, a pioneer of the study of settlements, in his work at Sutton Courtenay, Berkshire (now Oxfordshire), as well as of cemeteries. Interest in the latter predominated, culminating in the excavation of the burial mounds at Sutton Hoo, Suffolk, whose great ship burial was found only in the shadow of World War II in 1939. Bomb damage diverted much archaeological interest to towns, with post-Roman histories of London and Canterbury receiving considerable attention. In the 1950s E.M. Jope took up the themes of urbanization pioneered on the Continent in his analysis of Oxford; this work was developed in the 1960s, notably at Winchester and York. At York the Vikings' role in developing town life and trade became a major research focus. Excavation in a number of towns became possible as city-center rebuilding schemes made sites available. Funding problems kept such work piecemeal, a situation that worsened in the 1980s as the central government increasingly withdrew from direct support.

Important work was done in the 1950s and early 1960s on "palace" sites, including Yeavering, Northumberland, and Cheddar, Somerset (of the 9th century onward). This work was carried forward at lesser residential complexes, such as Sulgrave, Northamptonshire, where a post-1066 castle was found to have a "thegn's" domestic buildings below it, including a stone block that proved for the first time that secular structures were not always just of wood. The economic as well as social significance of these places was shown by the iron-working complex at Ramsbury, Wiltshire; at Goltho, Lincolnshire, cloth weaving may have been on a large scale.

The late 1960s saw a resurgence of interest in rural sites as scholars began to think that an imbalance of information was being created by the urban focus. Excavations at West Stow, Suffolk, and Chalton, Hampshire, showed a higher standard of housing than previously realized and also that settlement patterns had been very fluid, with hamlets and villages in relatively short use. The 7th and 8th centuries in particular seem to have been periods when many sites were abandoned; it may have been in the 8th and 9th centuries that many places still in occupation at the Norman Conquest came into use. They are often marked by their churches, on the same site today as a thousand years ago.

In the 1980s two distinctive emphases emerged. One was the study of the economy and economic systems, the other of religion and belief systems. The former has been stimulated by urban work—not only on the origin of towns, their relationship to the rest of society, and the trade they developed but also their impact on their hinterlands, animals and crops they consumed, and specialist products made in them affecting craft activity in the countryside. Numismatists' discussions of the various classes of coin minted from the 7th century onward and their place in creating a cash rather than a barter economy have also been important.

Religion and belief systems have been explored in analyses of cemeteries: the association of different types of objects with different sexes and ages, the role of burial as an expression of group identity, the impact of Christianity in changing the places and practices of burial and attitudes to social status and relations. Other studies focus on the development of the "open field" systems and other forms of agricultural organization, on the architectural history of churches, on the composition of metal alloys and their sources, on pottery and the distributions of different wares, and on identification of "Romano-British" and Scandinavian elements in "English" culture.

After the Norman Conquest

Victorian antiquarian interest in medieval art and architecture, especially the Gothic style so favored by the readers of Sir Walter Scott, led to the first crude attempts at medieval archaeology. Upper-class investigations of abbeys and castles usually produced more destruction than detection. In the 20th century medieval archaeology took advantage of improved techniques: first, the stratigraphic controls established for the complex chronologies of classical and Near Eastern sites, and second, the precise recording of slight soil changes developed on the minimally occupied prehistoric sites of northern Europe. By the 1960s the study of medieval artifacts, led by the work of Gerald C. Dunning and John G. Hurst on diagnostic pottery, began to yield reliable dating ranges.

A standard research tool for many areas of post-Conquest studies, archaeology has greatly contributed to our knowledge of the commonplace, especially the living and working conditions of lower classes rarely mentioned in contemporary accounts. In the late 1960s the first large-scale excavation of an English town was undertaken, by Martin Biddle at Winchester. Burgage properties were found to have had surprisingly stable boundaries, while interior arrangements changed rapidly, a characteristic of the evolving neighborhoods of medieval towns. Twenty years later another Winchester site yielded a comparable picture of socioeconomic change, and in the interval similar details of urban development, as well as the activities of the middle and lower classes, were unearthed at other towns. An early-medieval craft quarter at York, later-medieval merchants' shops and homes at Southampton, and the commercial wharves of London were but some of the excavations pursuing a more focused view of urban life as well as broader trends of neighborhood use and living conditions.

The peasantry was long associated with abject serfdom and wretched poverty; the prewar excavation of Sutton Courtenay seemed to corroborate this view. Subsequent work, however, has reinterpreted those findings and brought about a new view of rural life. Important excavations at Upton in Gloucestershire, Wharram Percy in Yorkshire, and Goltho in Lincolnshire revealed regional variations in village form and composition. Fieldwork on hamlets and farmsteads, as at Hound Tor in Devon, studied alternative rural communities. The status of peasant families differed over time, as did the relationship between the peasant community and the physical presence of the two other important rural institutions, the church and the manor.

The unchanging village is an invention of recent centuries. Archaeology reveals the medieval village as a place of constant if slow evolution. Buildings within the house plots underwent generational changes in orientation, number, use, fabric, and outbuildings. The plots themselves are shown to have been created (sometimes *en bloc*), altered, merged, or abandoned. Village archaeology has aided the study of the large-scale desertion of villages in the late-medieval period, and evidence for increasingly wet and cold conditions at several sites is seen as supporting the theory of a seriously deteriorating climate in northwest Europe.

The domiciles and defenses of the elite—castles, palaces, manor houses, and urban residences—have all been studied, but one problem of special importance is the origin and development of the castle, an essential element of post-Conquest England. Excavations at Castle Neroche, Somerset, and at Hen Domen on the Welsh border, have revealed construction details of the typical Norman earth and timber "motte and bailey" castle. Stone was used when Normans adapted Roman defenses for royal castles, as at Rochester and the Tower of London, and later at Portchester. Royal castles would continue to take the lead in military architecture, as the focus of defense moved from the central or salient keep, via a massive gatehouse as at Rockingham, Northamptonshire, to the strongly towered circuit wall of the Edwardian Welsh castles, as at Conway. Excavation at the sites of baronial castles—as at Castle Acre in Norfolk, Conisborough in Yorkshire, Farnham in Surrey, and Weoley in Birmingham—records an evolution from military structure to noble residence, with the vast ruins of Kenilworth Castle testimony to John of Gaunt's power and prestige.

The spiritual side of medieval society has also attracted archaeological interest. The monastic dissolution and later Puritan actions destroyed the majority of England's larger religious structures and building complexes. Abbeys and friaries rarely survived, and few cathedrals retain their ancillary structures (chapter house, bishop's palace, and so forth). Major excavations have taken place at monastic sites like Waltham, Bordesley, and St. Albans, and at episcopal centers like Wells, Winchester, York, and the abandoned cathedral site at Old Sarum. Parish churches, such as St. Mary's at Wharram Percy, St. Mary's and St. Pancras in Winchester, St. Martin's in Lincoln, and Rivenhall church in Essex, have revealed long histories of alterations. Churches often display a post-Conquest widening of the nave to fit larger congregations and a reduction in size following the Black Death. A late increase in the amount and prominence of space devoted to mortuary use, to chantry chapels and family monuments and vaults, testifies to the greater mortality and to the rise of new families.

Archaeology has begun to contribute to other areas of medieval research. The study of early industry, especially potteries and tileries, has benefited from the analysis of products and production centers, and there has been similar work on such ubiquitous items as leather goods and stonemasonry. Excavation of watermills and windmills has contributed to the history of technology; the study of bridges and wharves sheds light on early transportation. As yet the archaeology of post-Conquest shipping in England is limited, though the discovery and raising of the Tudor warship *Mary Rose* yielded information on design and construction. Archaeological research is contributing to several newer areas of study: vernacular architecture, mainly local traditions of home and workplace construction; demographic and anthropological studies, based on the analysis of cemeteries; and environmental history, especially the exploitation of resources and the rural ecological system.

David A. Hinton
Eric Klingelhofer

Bibliography

Arnold, C.J. *An Archaeology of the Early Anglo-Saxon Kingdoms.* London: Routledge, 1988; Campbell, James, ed. *The Anglo-Saxons.* London: Phaidon, 1982; Hinton, David A. *Alfred's Kingdom: Wessex and the South, 800–1500.* London: Dent, 1977; Hinton, David A. *Archaeology, Economy and Society: England from the Fifth to the Fifteenth Century.* London: Seeby, 1990; Platt, Colin. *Medieval England: A Social History and Archaeology from the Conquest to 1600 A.D.* New York: Scribner, 1978; Rodwell, Warwick. *Medieval Finds from Excavations in London.* London: HMSO, 1987–; Rodwell, Warwick. *The Archaeology of Religious Places: Churches and Cemeteries in Britain.* Rev. ed. Philadelphia: University of Pennsylvania Press, 1989; Steane, John. *The Archaeology of Medieval England and Wales.* Beckenham: Croom Helm, 1984; Wilson, David M., ed. *The Archaeology of Anglo-Saxon England.* London: Methuen, 1976.
Archaeological journals, including *Medieval Archaeology, The Journal of the British Archaeological Association, The Archaeological Journal,* and *The Antiquaries Journal,* the journals and newsletters of the Medieval Village Research Group and the Moated Sites Research Group, and the annual journals of county historical and archaeological societies are of great value.

See also Architecture, Domestic; Castles; Cemeteries; Deserted Villages; Manorialism; Sutton Hoo

Architecture, Anglo-Saxon
Early Anglo-Saxon Architecture

As simple as a distinction between early and late architecture seems, periodization of Anglo-Saxon work forms the initial controversy when discussing architecture. Since the surviving examples are either archaeological remnants, such as groundplans or fragmentary walls, or surviving stone churches or parts of them, our theories about dates are either relative, evolutionary/typological, or based on limited historical accounts linked to surviving remains.

Harold M. and Joan Taylor's work still constitutes the most authoritative cataloguing and periodization, but ongoing archaeological discoveries coupled with rethinking made possible by their groundwork have contributed to alternative groupings. The Taylors followed the lead of early authority Baldwin Brown and grouped churches into three main divisions, A, B, and C, with A covering A.D. 600 to 800, B 800 to 950, and C 950 to 1100. Each division was then subdivided into three, designated by a subscript 1, 2, or 3. Thus C_2 meant 1000 to 1050, and the entire scheme is essentially one of chronological labels. As an alternative Fernie dates the limited number of churches he discusses by reference to the Danes: pre-Danish, post-Danish, and 1025 to the early 12th century, and more generally accepts a bipartite division of architecture with the Danish advent the central dividing point.

Gem (1986) has discussed periodization overall, and after pointing out the various inductive and deductive routes whereby dating theories have evolved, he recommends establishing cultural paradigms to develop architectural dating. As test cases he proposed two in detail, an ecclesiastical-historical paradigm with four divisions related to such aspects as conversion, consolidation, and reforms, and the second, one that assumes that cultural contacts between England and the Continent could justify a chronology of styles in continental architecture as a paradigm. Related political and economic paradigms were also suggested as yet other avenues.

For our purposes architectural forms dating from the advent of identifiable Anglo-Saxon material (6th or 7th century) up to the 9th century will be considered "Early." Work of the 9th to 12th centuries, including "Anglo-Norman" or "Overlap" material, will be discussed under Later Anglo-Saxon Architecture below.

Though the bulk of discussion about Anglo-Saxon architecture focuses on stone churches, because other forms survive only in archaeological contexts, we do have some knowledge of buildings not in stone. In particular, with the advent of Germanic peoples in Britain by the 6th century, archaeological contexts preserve evidence for rectangular sunken-floor buildings, termed *Grubenhäuser* on the Continent, as well as rectangular buildings subdivided into two or more chambers. Sunken-floor buildings, such as those found at West Stow (fig. 6) and Cowdery's Down, have been reconstructed with thatch roofing, with wooden floors at times inserted over the space dug into the soil. Other early wooden buildings demonstrate

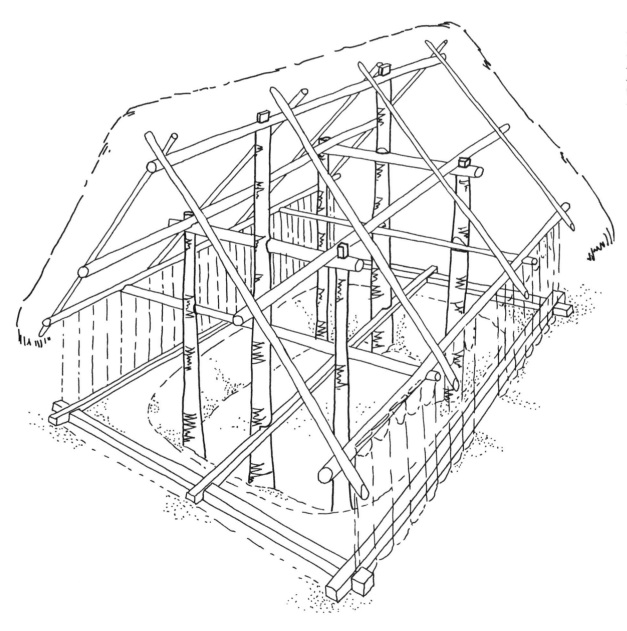

Fig. 6. Sunken-floor building, West Stow, Suffolk (SFB 49). After M. Welch, Anglo-Saxon England (1992). Courtesy of B. T. Batsford, Ltd.

a remarkably consistent form, as argued by James, Marshall, and Millett. They show a hybrid early-medieval building tradition (6th century to ca. 800) that has affinities both with native British and with Germanic forms and methods. The common attributes include the absence of sill beams, with the superstructures resting on low, substantial timber walls set deeply into the earth, and closely spaced uprights. Many were subdivided into two or more rooms on the interior, and external doors were usually paired in opposite side walls. Though some gable posts have been found as well as some freestanding ridge supports, James et al. infer in the majority of cases that the roofs had tall gables based on ridge pieces, with end-wall trenches shallower than those for side walls because they did not have to bear the roof load. A cruck form seems indicated, but it did not take the main load because the side walls did: instead "the function of the assembly was the provision of longitudinal stability rather than load transmission" (194). Such forms were not confined to secular contexts either; at Hild's monastery of Hartlepool/*Heruteu*, Cleveland, excavators found ten complete buildings of three types that conform to the early-medieval building tradition described, with the only notable difference being a single door in side walls instead of a pair.

The majority of evidence for Anglo-Saxon architecture, however, remains stone buildings in religious contexts, including monastic, episcopal, and parochial settings. Christianity already existed in Britain under the Roman occupation, but conversion began in earnest in the 7th century. Bede's comment that Benedict Biscop sent for Gallic masons to build his northern monasteries of Wearmouth and Jarrow in the Roman manner has become a commonplace, one that distinguishes the Germanic and British wooden building tradition from the Roman and continental stone style. In any case the Anglo-Saxons assimilated stone architecture but may always have been primarily adept at wooden architecture; as is often noted, their verb, *timbrian*, means "to build" in wood. Characteristics identified as diagnostically Anglo-Saxon include thick-walled, often irregularly laid out plans; tall, narrow archways with throughstones; massive side-alternate or long and short quoins; single-splayed windows; and stripwork and pilasters.

Surviving stone churches may well be a representative rather than an arbitrary sample, however, as shown by recent work of Eric Cambridge in County Durham. He demonstrated that remaining church and sculpture evidence survives in clusters and zones linked to monastic development of the area. Since the distribution of monastic churches is so markedly clustered, we can postulate that the large areas left otherwise unprovided for had timber foundations in a complementary pattern to those served by monasteries. In the areas between the zones we find several churches that served larger parishes in the later Middle Ages; this hints at possible sites for early secular minsters. If secular churches were generally timber-built, then early stone churches would have remained rare even after the monastic communities that built them disappeared. If correct, Cambridge has shown that nearly 50 percent of early stone churches still

survive in County Durham, perhaps because, while principal churches may well have suffered regular renovation, those that were small parish or dependent churches would have been rebuilt less frequently.

The larger monastic sites of the early Anglo-Saxon period have produced the most significant stone remains, though smaller churches are represented still, such as Escomb, County Durham (fig. 7), which is missing only small chambers *(porticus)* on the west and north. All churches require space for the clergy and the congregation, whether that congregation is lay or religious; thus the most basic groundplan is of a chancel and a nave, often though not necessarily divided from one another by a tall, relatively narrow chancel arch or triple arch, the latter seen especially in the south at such places as Brixworth, St. Pancras Canterbury, or Bradwell-on-Sea. Anglo-Saxon naves are generally two to three times as long as their eastern chancels, and it should be noted that such a form is identical to one commonly found in the wooden building tradition. Churches may also have small western chambers as entrance porches (Monkwearmouth) or porticus to the north and/or south opening from the chancel or nave. The east end could take the form of a rounded or square apse, and altars were originally placed not against the eastern wall but more centrally, often on the chord of the apse.

Generalizing about any one elaborated plan for early churches quickly becomes difficult, as perusal of the Taylors' volume 3 synthesis shows. Characteristic of some larger monasteries, an east-west line of churches with various dedications exists at the major foundations of Canterbury, Glastonbury, and Jarrow; Canterbury had its main church dedicated to Sts. Peter and Paul, with additional smaller buildings to Mary and Pancras, while Jarrow had its main church and a chapel to Mary that was later linked to the larger church. Many of the early sites, such as Hexham, Ripon, Monkwearmouth, and Jarrow in the north, Brixworth, Deerhurst, Cirencester, Canterbury, and Winchester in the south, were elaborate and complicated sites. Hexham, according to historical accounts, and Deerhurst, in surviving fabric, had multiple stories to the sides of the church nave, allowing for many side and upper chapels. Æthelwulf's *De abbatibus* (ca. 803–21), written by a monk in a daughter foundation of Lindisfarne, details such a church in a dream vision, so the form may have existed more widely than we can now prove. Basilican forms, such as Brixworth, may have evolved both because of imitation of things Roman and also to house increasing collections of relics, something that brought a church wealth and renown beyond its local resources. In addition to upper side chambers, raised porches at such sites as Brixworth and Monkwearmouth led to upper chambers at the west, quite possibly used as upper chapels or perhaps for resident or visiting dignitaries.

Crypts, some with ambulatories, also existed, surviving still at Brixworth, Hexham, Ripon (fig. 73: see HEXHAM AND RIPON), and Cirencester among those named above, for the veneration and display of collected relics to pilgrims. Anglo-Saxon crypts, unlike continental examples, seem to have been built for subsidiary relics, not for those of a church's dedica-

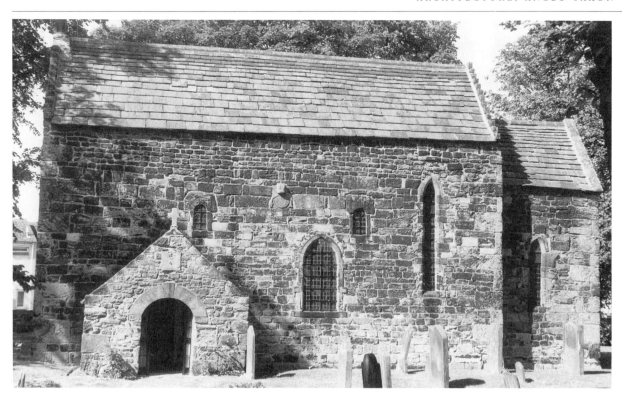

Fig. 7. Escomb, County Durham. Courtesy of A.J. Hawkes.

tory saint(s). Decoration of such churches was also elaborate, both in architectural detail and other plastic arts, which could include friezes (Hexham, Wearmouth); stained glass (Escomb, Jarrow, Repton, York); painted plaster walls and painting series hung in churches (Wearmouth and Jarrow); carved crosses, grave markers, inscriptions, stone church furniture; metal reliquaries, gospel bindings, altar frontals, lamps, and furnishings for mass (chalice, paten, etc.); and embroidery so well known it was termed Opus Anglicanum for its place of origin.

Later Anglo-Saxon Architecture

Until recently church building was seen as slowing or stopping altogether while destruction increased with the advent of the Danish invasions and settlement, but a more complex picture has begun to emerge. The Danish invasions of the 9th century produced a system of defended towns *(burhs)* whose development is attributed to Alfred; in Wessex no one was more than twenty miles, a day's march, from such a site. Nor was the destruction of churches a given: at Repton, for example, the church was incorporated into a defensive fortification by the Danish troops who wintered there, and it certainly was not destroyed. Sculptured crosses covered with depictions of Germanic and Christian myth were raised by Scandinavians at northern sites, such as Gosforth (figs. 18–19: see ART, VIKING AGE), and testify to their early impact on art and production as well.

The rise of urban centers overall was stimulated by increased international trade and the burghal system, and we can begin to trace more accurately the development of urban planning. Towns evolved their own grid systems from the 9th century on, as at Wareham, Hereford, and Winches-

ter, whose streets do not align with the earlier Roman town's grid; economic rather than military or Roman roots stimulated the growth of ports and cities, such as *Hamwih* (later Southampton), the pottery center of Norwich, and York. Excavations in the Coppergate area of York produced evidence for late-9th- and 10th-century buildings aligned with narrow ends toward the streets and long central hearths. Workshop areas were gable to gable with living quarters and probably shop space fronted on the street. Their constructions of post and wattle gave way in the mid-10th century to buildings with squared oak posts set in trenches or foundation beams, with horizontal oak planks between. We also have evidence for wooden secular halls at, for example, Cheddar in Somerset (9th–10th century); it was nearly 80 feet long, and its bowed sides sloped inward, suggesting support for an upper story. Being near Athelney, it could have served as a council hall, but no further evidence confirms its possible political source.

Alfred built little church architecture to parallel his impact on secular urban growth, though he did build a wooden church at Athelney of unusual design: posts at four corners, with an apse on all four sides forming a circular church. He is also responsible for bringing the monk Grimbald to court from Flanders, and Fernie has suggested that Edward the Elder's New Minster in Winchester, consecrated in 903, might have an immediate source in the Low Countries. Within the church of the 10th century reform movements and attention to relics helped expand and elaborate foundations, while trade and royal political power also stimulated architectural development. Extensive excavations at Winchester show the transition as the cult of St. Swithun expanded (figs. 151–52: see WINCHESTER OLD MINSTER): the church extends westward to incorporate the shrine into a larger church with many additional chambers to accommodate the traffic of pilgrims, but the city's growth architecturally was also due to its concentration of monastic, episcopal, and royal landowners in the area.

In terms of church construction the most noteworthy additions are the tower, its crossing, and increasing elaboration of the west end, called westworks after continental models, and often also the east end, by the addition of multiple chambers to house relics and accommodate new liturgies. Perhaps due to a need for increased vigilance during Danish raids, towers and bells to hang in them proliferate, and belfries become part of the diagnostic characteristics for Anglo-Saxon architecture. Forms of openings varied: round sounding holes, balusters supporting openings whose shape was reminiscent of lathe-turned (and hence carpentry-inspired) forms, monolithic headed windows with a single or double opening carved into the underside of the stone, triangular or gable-headed openings.

Recent work has documented extensive echoes of continental sites, though each major Anglo-Saxon site seems to have provided for its needs on its own terms. Monastic reform in England was part of a larger reform movement across Europe, and the reorganization of monasteries and monastic rules under the great 10th-century reformers Oswald, Dunstan, and Æthelwold expanded the links between sites because of increased uniformity of vision and continental ties. Fernie has postulated such an extensive interrelationship that he argues for using the term Romanesque for late Anglo-Saxon churches that manifest a conservative tendency he recognizes in Germany and France as they develop from the Frankish Empire, especially in the development of the westwork, the eastern tower, and the outer crypt. In the Anglo-Saxon context the development of Fernie's Romanesque is clearest in "the crossing square and the architectural decoration used to articulate the spaces and elements of the building" (1983: 112). While his definition of the term Romanesque is not widely used, Fernie's theories deserve attention not least in light of Gem's call (1986) for cultural paradigms to analyze Anglo-Saxon architecture.

But under the influence of renewed Scandinavian attacks and ensuing decreased royal support the reforms of the 10th century stagnated ca. 1000, according to Gem. He postulates a 40-year recession in English architecture, though some major sites, such as Durham, Ely, and Evesham, built what seem limited additions. Perhaps the greatest activity took place under the auspices of King Cnut and his wives, Emma and Ælfgifu, as when he built the minster church at Ashingdon to commemorate his victory of 1016 and also founded the new abbey of Bury St. Edmunds, perhaps because Edmund had been martyred by Danes in 870 and the foundation was a sound political move. But as Gem notes, Cnut was far more generous to continental foundations, replenishing treasuries of churches in England but donating to "some of the key buildings in the early development of the [European] Romanesque style" (1975: 38). While a small church in Kirkdale,

Yorkshire, could be built by a Scandinavian patron a decade before Hastings (crowned with an elaborate sundial and dedicatory inscription, not in runes but in Anglo-Saxon written in Roman letters), England's recession had put it behind continental developments, adhering to older, 10th-century traditions. By the mid-11th century, with the building of Westminster Abbey by Edward the Confessor, it began to catch up, and by 1100 it was in the vanguard of European developments. As Gem notes, however, such a position came not from indigenous roots but from continental and perhaps especially Norman roots, and with this shift the Anglo-Saxon tradition ended.

Kelley M. Wickham-Crowley

Bibliography

EARLY ANGLO-SAXON ARCHITECTURE

Butler, Lawrence A.S., and Richard K. Morris, eds. *The Anglo-Saxon Church: Papers on History, Architecture and Archaeology in Honour of Dr H.M. Taylor.* CBA Research Report 60. London: CBA, 1986; Cambridge, Eric. "The Early Church in County Durham: A Reassessment." *JBAA* 137 (1984): 65–85; Cramp, Rosemary J., and R. Daniels. "New Finds from the Anglo-Saxon Monastery at Hartlepool, Cleveland." *Antiquity* 61 (1987): 424–32; Fernie, Eric. *The Architecture of the Anglo-Saxons.* London: Batsford, 1983; Gem, Richard. "A B C: How Should We Periodize Anglo-Saxon Architecture?" In *The Anglo-Saxon Church: Papers on History, Architecture and Archaeology in Honour of Dr H.M. Taylor,* ed. Lawrence A.S. Butler and Richard K. Morris. CBA Research Report 60. London: CBA, 1986, pp. 146–55; James, Simon, Anne Marshall, and Martin Millett. "An Early Medieval Building Tradition." *ArchJ* 141 (1984): 182–215; Marshall, Anne, and Garry Marshall. "Differentiation, Change, and Continuity in Anglo-Saxon Buildings." *ArchJ* 150 (1993): 366–402 [excellent detailed survey and bibliography]; Taylor, Harold M., and Joan Taylor. *Anglo-Saxon Architecture.* 3 vols. Cambridge: Cambridge University Press, 1965–78.

LATER ANGLO-SAXON ARCHITECTURE

Gem, Richard. "A Recession in English Architecture during the Early Eleventh Century, and Its Effect on the Development of the Romanesque Style." *JBAA*, 3d ser. 38 (1975): 28–49; Morris, Richard. "Churches, Settlement, and the Beginnings of the Parochial System: c 800–1100." Chapter 5 in *The Church in British Archaeology,* ed. Richard Morris. CBA Research Report 47. London: CBA, 1983, pp. 63–76; Rollason, David. "The Shrines of Saints in Later Anglo-Saxon England: Distribution and Significance." In *The Anglo-Saxon Church: Papers on History, Architecture and Archaeology in Honour of Dr H.M. Taylor,* ed. Lawrence A.S. Butler and Richard K. Morris. CBA Research Report 60. London: CBA, 1986, pp. 32–43; Taylor, Harold M. "Tenth-Century Church

Building in England and on the Continent." In *Tenth-Century Studies: Essays in Commemoration of the Millennium of the Council of Winchester and Regularis concordia*, ed. David Parsons. London: Phillimore, 1975, pp. 141–68, 237–41.

See also Art, Anglo-Saxon; Bradford; Brixworth; Canterbury Cathedral; Earls Barton Tower; Greensted; Hexham and Ripon; Kentish Churches; Repton; Sculpture, Anglo-Saxon; Wearmouth-Jarrow: Architecture; Winchester Cathedral; Yeavering; York, Anglo-Saxon Churches in

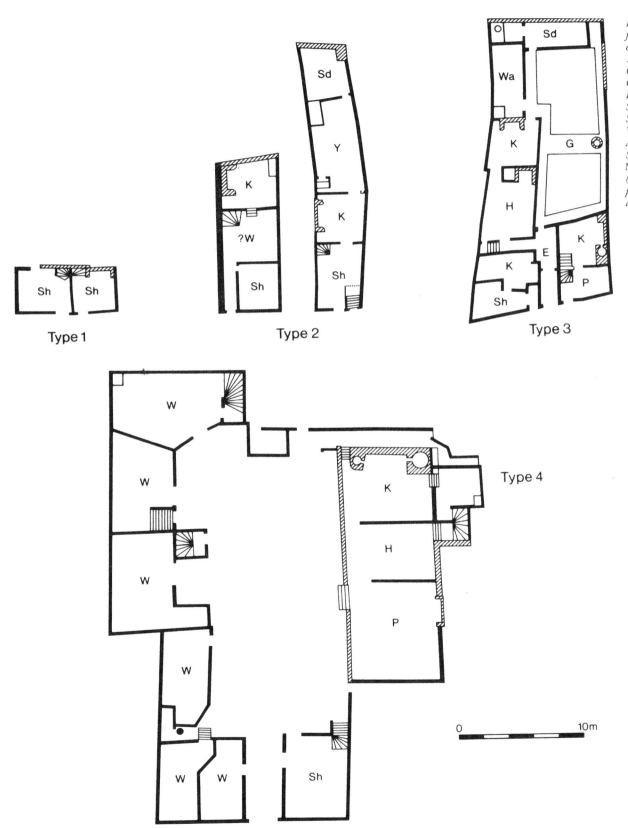

Fig. 8. House plans from London surveys of Ralph Treswell in 1612. B buttery; Ch chamber; E entry; G garden; H hall; K kitchen; P parlor; Sd shed; Sh shop; St study; W warehouse; Wa washhouse. After J. Schofield, in J. Schofield and A. Vince, Medieval Towns *(1994). Reprinted by permission of Associated University Presses.*

Architecture, Domestic

Although medieval domestic buildings have received sustained scholarly attention since the early 19th century, it was the accelerating rate of destruction of historic houses, especially after World War II, and a growing awareness of their value to historians that stimulated academic interest. From the 1950s Ronald Brunskill, Eric Mercer, J.T. Smith, and others placed the subject on a new methodological footing, and the increasingly sophisticated survey techniques pioneered by the Royal Commission on the Historical Monuments of England and the Vernacular Buildings Groups, as well as by archaeologists, have provided a mass of data still awaiting systematic analysis.

Recent work on smaller houses (as opposed to the castles and palaces of the aristocracy) cautions against a too-sharp distinction between "vernacular" and "polite" building practices. In many areas, especially in parishes with several families of similar economic but different social status, the houses of gentlemen and prosperous peasant farmers were almost indistinguishable.

The bulk of surviving houses from the later Middle Ages share a broad plan form that is remarkably consistent over the whole country (fig. 8). Typically it consists of three functional units, sometimes single rooms, sometimes subdivided. The highest-status room was the hall or principal living room, normally on the ground floor and heated by a centrally placed open hearth from which the smoke would escape through the roof, gradually blackening the timbers (an important sign in identifying a medieval house). To the end of the hall, and divided from it by a screen (to reduce drafts), was an entrance passage, set crosswise, often with opposing front and rear doorways. The other units were generally floored. Leading off the "cross passage" on the side opposite the hall was the service area, sometimes divided into a pantry and buttery. Some houses placed the principal retiring room (or solar) above the services, but in many (perhaps in most) the private room was situated at the other end of the house from the services.

Normally these three units were set end-to-end along the axis, the whole house measuring perhaps 12 to 15 feet wide by 25 to 30 feet (or more) long. Frequently, however, one of the end rooms would be placed crosswise, giving a T-plan overall; others placed both end units in this fashion, an H-plan. Cross wings afforded more commodious accommodation and were sometimes the hallmark of gentry houses. Wealthier gentlemen required additional quarters, for guests, retainers, and servants; by the 14th century these were often arranged around a courtyard with the three-unit, cross-passage range occupying one side, as was done in the colleges being built at Oxford or Cambridge.

Though such consistency of plan suggests a common derivation, it is not certain that this was the case. Some historians believe that the plan developed out of the primitive peasant "longhouse," where humans and livestock lived under the same roof, the dwelling (sometimes divided into two parts) divided from the byre or shippon (a cowhouse) by a cross passage, sometimes equipped with screens. According to archaeological evidence this house type appears to have prevailed over much of England around 1300, although by the

later Middle Ages it was restricted to smaller areas on the highland fringes of Devon and Wales. More prosperous peasants, better able to exploit the market, built specialized agricultural structures, while extending their houses to reflect the shape and plan of their predecessors, an interesting example of cultural conservatism. Poor peasants, however, probably lived in insubstantial one- or two-cell houses.

On the other hand the distinctive three-unit, cross-passage plan that had emerged by the later Middle Ages might well have been a conscious statement of status on the part of richer peasant farmers and minor gentry modeled on noble rather than longhouses: an instance of cultural diffusion downward from aristocratic precedents. In the 11th and 12th centuries the various discrete elements of a noble dwelling—a separate hall, kitchen, retainers' hall, private rooms, chapel, and other such areas—gradually coalesced; by the 13th century many of these separate buildings had become rooms, now attached to the hall range. Whatever the origins of the standard pattern it seems to have been firmly established by the 14th century.

We accept that a certain level of prosperity must be reached before a family could build a permanent house (i.e., one able to last for several generations). William G. Hoskins's seminal work (in 1953) and the debate that followed deeply influenced the study of medieval domestic building. He argued for a strong correlation between peaks of prosperity and increased building activity. Criticisms of Hoskins's dating for the "rebuilding" underlined the scale of regional variation. A number of earlier "great rebuildings" emerged; in Devon and Kent, for instance, there was a marked upswing in house building between ca. 1480 and 1530, corresponding to the increasing buoyancy of the local rural textile industries. Poorer and more remote areas, such as parts of Cornwall and the northwest, hardly reached levels of prosperity sufficient to sustain any widespread building of permanent houses, while in parts of Oxfordshire and Essex (with a proximity to the London market), the first "great rebuilding" can be placed even earlier, in the late 13th and early 14th centuries.

Numerous interrelated factors, such as soil fertility, the location of rural industries, access to markets, and tenurial patterns, all played a part in determining levels of building activity. Equally, postmedieval developments may be of great importance in shaping the distribution pattern of surviving medieval houses. A downturn in postmedieval economy could favor the retention of older houses; conversely, increasing prosperity could lead to widespread rebuilding and erase or conceal substantial houses from the earlier period. While medieval houses form a valuable source for historians, like most classes of evidence they are liable to distort the picture if used in isolation.

Rates of survival also depend on the means of construction. The 13th century saw considerable improvements in building techniques, presumably in response to increasing demands from gentry and prosperous peasants as well as nobles and ecclesiastics. Building methods show enormous regional variation and were dependent upon the local availability of materials. Only the very wealthy could afford to import bulky goods from farther afield; even so, peasant demand stimulated craftsmen, such as carpenters and smiths (to provide nails and hinges), and brought into being specialist firms of house build-ers who prepared timbers in a framing yard whence they were transported for assembly on site.

The most widely used materials were stone and timber, but where these were not easily available even gentlemen would build in mud (as in Devon). Box- or post-and-truss framing techniques (using large posts, ties, and principal trussed rafters) predominated in the lowland areas, whereas cruck framing (using pairs of heavy timbers from, or close to, ground level and meeting at or near the roof apex) was com-monest in the highland zone. In both methods survival of the materials was ensured only when the timbers ceased to be placed immediately on the ground, where they were vulner-able to damp rot, and were raised on pad stones or sill beams that rested in turn on stone. This improved method appears to have become widespread in the 13th century and helps account for the rarity of surviving houses prior to this.

Timber buildings, especially when thatched, were vulner-able to fire in nucleated settlements and towns. Closely packed town houses were often divided one from another by fire-re-sistant stone walls. However, in other respects town houses did not differ from those in rural areas as much as might be ex-pected. Many boroughs were not densely populated, and houses frequently conformed to the prevalent three-unit, cross-passage plan. Where pressures on land were higher, or boroughs were planned from the start, such houses might be aligned end-on to the street.

Toward the end of the 13th century some towns were developing highly specialized retail and service functions that resulted in variants on the normal patterns. Shops facing the street (with stalls secured by shutters) might have private accom-modation above and an open hall to the rear. Secondary struc-tures would be placed to the rear. In some cases it seems that cooking facilities were minimal; it is possible that food was cooked elsewhere, perhaps in neighboring bakeries, as is still the practice in some parts of southern Europe. Intense demand for retailing could lead to shops being provided at two levels along the street, but evidence for this survives only at Chester, and the Rows system may result from the peculiarities of the Roman urban topography rather than the extraordinary demands of the market. Normally, it seems, increased retail demand led to sub-division of tenements along the street frontages, with workshops and other ancillary buildings placed at the rear.

Martin Cherry

Bibliography

Brunskill, R.W. *Vernacular Architecture of the Lake Counties: A Field Handbook.* London: Faber, 1974; Giles, Colum. *Rural Houses of West Yorkshire, 1400–1830.* Royal Com-mission on the Historic Monuments of England. Lon-don: HMSO, 1986; Hoskins, William G. "The Rebuilding of Rural England, 1570–1640." *Past and Pres-ent* 4 (November 1953): 44–59; Mercer, Eric. *English Vernacular Houses: A Study of Traditional Farmhouses and Cottages.* London: HMSO, 1975; Pearson, S. *Rural Houses of the Lancashire Pennines, 1560–1760.* Royal Commission on Historic Monuments of England. London: HMSO, 1985; Smith, J.T. "Medieval Roofs: A Classification."

ArchJ 115 (1958): 111–49.

See also Architecture, University and College; Castles

Architecture, University and College

Oxford and Cambridge trace their origins to the 12th and 13th centuries. While students attended lectures in university buildings and in rented spaces, living arrangements were made on their own, except for those who lived in monastic houses. At first students lodged with townspeople, but soon hostels became common; these were buildings rented by groups of students and used for sleeping and eating. The university cor-poration, consisting of a group of male teachers, owned or rented facilities for meetings and ceremonies, schools for teaching, and a library.

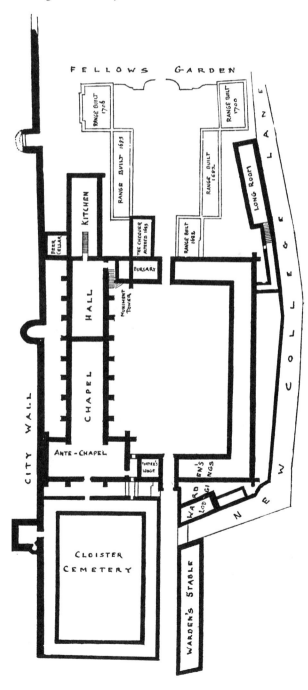

Fig. 9. Plan of New College, Oxford. After Willis and Clark (1886). Courtesy of W. Leedy.

By the late 13th century colleges began to make their appearance as permanent establishments endowed by benefactors, often for poor students, with specific regulations of discipline and study. The earliest perhaps was Merton College, Oxford, founded in 1264. While it was not planned like a monastic cloister, the buildings are arranged in an unconnected manner around a quadrangular court: a collegiate church occupies the west side, the hall stands detached on the south side with the warden's lodgings, and some other buildings stand on the east and north sides. Most commonly colleges provided lodging and meals for masters only, not undergraduates. Books were kept in their chambers in locked chests, and devotions were usually held in the local parish church.

The builders of early colleges usually built slowly and piecemeal around the perimeter of small lots, ultimately achieving the maximum building space per acreage. This practice often resulted in misshapen quadrangles, revealing that patrons had little concern for architectural regularity. As new colleges were founded and existing ones expanded, urban space—constricted because of town walls—became scarcer and thus more costly, while a desire grew for larger quadrangles and more uniform architecture.

Corpus Christi College, Oxford (built 1352–77), was perhaps the first college to be planned around a closed quadrangle with buildings all the same height. The hall, kitchen, and master's lodge were on the south and chambers with the other three sides. It had no chapel. At Cambridge the first closed quadrangle, containing all the requisite buildings, was that of Pembroke College, begun in 1346.

New College, Oxford (fig. 9), built 1379–86, set new standards for collegiate architecture. Its founder, William of Wykeham, took a personal interest in its physical layout; planned with utopian vision and quickly built, the buildings were designed by his master mason, William of Wynford. The whole ensemble was given monumental character, and, since it made provision for all college functions—chapel, hall, library, treasury, warden's lodging, sufficient chambers, cemetery, and various domestic offices—it came to serve as the model for all later large foundations at Oxford. Its buildings were arranged around an enclosed 150- by 125-foot quadrangle, entered from the west side through a tower gateway, which is employed here for the first time. The west and south sides are devoted to chambers; the east side to rooms of common use. The upper floor contains the library, the lower the bursar's rooms. The chapel and hall were built as a great unified block on the north side. A transeptal-shaped antechapel occupies the western two bays of the seven-bay chapel. This was used for disputations in civil law, canon law, and theology. This unusual T-shaped chapel plan was later used in Oxford, but not Cambridge. The butteries and kitchen are in a wing that runs eastward from the hall into a courtyard external to the quadrangle. Westward from the whole of this group a cloister cemetery was laid out with a bell tower on its side. The practice of placing chapel and hall together in a monumental block along one range of a quadrangle was adapted in the 15th century in Oxford at All Souls (begun 1437), St. John's (begun 1436), and Magdalen (begun 1473) colleges; this strategy was, however, not used in Cambridge.

The next two centuries witnessed about eighteen more colleges founded at Oxford and Cambridge, for the most part following the basic pattern laid down at New College, both in organization and quadrangular arrangement. Colleges that were founded earlier rebuilt their buildings to conform to the new arrangement.

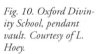

Fig. 10. Oxford Divinity School, pendant vault. Courtesy of L. Hoey.

While the precise locations of the various functions around the quadrangle are not canonical, it was common to locate the chapel on the north side, especially in Cambridge, and use the warmer, southern side for chambers. The chapel was placed on the side of the quadrangle that lay nearest to the east-west direction for religious reasons. The eastern wall of the chapel usually was left free, so a window could be placed there. The quadrangle gateway was usually placed on a street, but occasionally entry was gained through a parish churchyard. Many colleges had subsidiary or special-function quadrangles.

There are several reasons for the use of the quadrangle in English colleges. Although college "programs" were similar to monasteries—unmarried men, working and living together under a rule or body of statutes—and the disposition of buildings in courts have their analogies with monastic architecture, collegiate architecture does not directly derive from monastic architecture. A similar pattern is seen in the great houses of the 15th century, which often included a chapel among the buildings arranged around the quadrangles. Most important, the enclosed quadrangle functioned as defense against potential enemies, especially townspeople. The closing of the college with gates also gave academic authorities greater control over students, a concern that was a major factor in the growth of the collegiate system.

One of the most thought-out college programs was that for King's College, Cambridge (ca. 1446), which included, following Wykeham's precedent, a cloister cemetery. In 1448 Queens' College, Cambridge, was founded. Built around a closed quadrangle, the chapel and library are on the north side, the hall, kitchen, and butteries on the west, and chambers on the south and east. The material of construction is red brick. St. John's, Cambridge, begun 1511, is also notable for its red-brick construction.

Arising out of a national concern for the building of libraries, one of the most magnificent university buildings built was the Oxford Divinity School (1424–83), which has exceptional pendant vaulting in its lower story (fig. 10); the upper story was to house the celebrated manuscript collection of Humphrey duke of Gloucester.

In the mid-16th century a new innovation in quadrangular design appeared with the building of Gonville and Caius College in Cambridge: it was open on one side, bounded only by a wall and a monumental gate. It is this new pattern, which created the possibility of focal points and axial organization not inherent in the closed quadrangle, that was to influence collegiate design in America.

Walter Leedy

Bibliography

Colvin, Howard M. *All Souls: An Oxford College and Its Buildings.* Oxford: Oxford University Press, 1989; Great Britain, Royal Commission on Historical Monuments. *An Inventory of the Historical Monuments in the City of Oxford.* London: HMSO, 1939; Great Britain, Royal Commission on Historical Monuments. *An Inventory of the Historical Monuments in the City of Cambridge.* London: HMSO, 1959; Jacob, Ernst F. "The Building of All Souls College, 1438–1443." In *Historical Essays in Honour of James Tait*, ed. John G. Edwards. Manchester: Printed for Subscribers, 1933, pp. 121–35; Smith, Alic Halford. *New College, Oxford and Its Buildings.* London: Oxford University Press, 1952; Tibbs, Rodney. *The University and Colleges of Cambridge.* Lavenham: Dalton, 1970; Turner, Paul Venable. *Campus: An American Planning Tradition.* New York: Architectural History Foundation, 1984; Willis, Robert, and John Clark. *The Architectural History of the University of Cambridge and of the Colleges of Cambridge and Eton.* 4 vols. 1886. Repr. Cambridge: Cambridge University Press, 1988.

See also King's College, Cambridge; Learning; Universities; William of Wykeham

Architecture and Architectural Sculpture, Gothic

English Gothic architecture and architectural sculpture in many ways continue themes, styles, and trends begun in Romanesque art. In fact the transition from Romanesque to Gothic is gradual, with no clear division between the two. Architectural space gradually becomes more complex and architectural sculpture gradually becomes more naturalistic and spreads to cover more areas of the building. However, the compartmentalization that characterizes Romanesque architecture and the emphasis on surface ornament and surface effects that have characterized English art since the early Anglo-Saxon period survive in varying degrees throughout the Gothic. These survivals may be explained by the fact that English architects and artists never adopted the system or philosophy of the French style but only bits and pieces of the style, adapting them to their own tastes and traditions. Thus English Gothic architecture remains long, low, and somewhat heavy in comparison with that of France, and the relationship of sculpture to architecture is less fully articulated. In England sculpture often seems applied to, rather than an integral part of, the architectural program. It is important, however, to stress that English Gothic should not be seen as a poor cousin to French Gothic. It is a highly innovative response to international and national trends, designed to accommodate a different set of tastes, practices, and requirements.

English Gothic can be divided stylistically into four periods: 1) a Transitional period beginning ca. 1175 and lasting until the early 13th century; 2) the Early English style lasting from the early 13th century to ca. 1290; 3) the Decorated style ca. 1290–ca. 1350; 4) the Perpendicular style ca. 1350 through to the Reformation. While chronology and the defining characteristics of each of these periods have been changed and refined over the years, these basic divisions are those established by Thomas Rickman in his 1817 *An Attempt to Discriminate the Styles of English Architecture from the Conquest to the Reformation.*

Transitional Style (ca. 1175–early 13th century)

The initial spurt of building in the immediate post-Conquest period was followed by a pause in new programs and then a renewal ca. 1175, as new influences, particularly from the Ile-de-France, made their way into England. In the years 1174–75 the new style appears in the southeast in the choir of Canterbury Cathedral, in the southwest at Worcester Cathedral and Keynsham Abbey, and in the north at Ripon and Roche Abbey. The regionalism suggested by this division would remain a feature of English Gothic.

The Canterbury choir is perhaps the most famous of these early Gothic structures. Begun by the Frenchman William of Sens, it is also the most French in style, with sexpartite vaults and elegant carved foliate details. Yet even here the style is transformed by the English love of linear pattern and the retention of the English thick wall. The dark Purbeck "marble" (a type of limestone) shafts and the short responds of the vaults create a rhythmical light-and-dark pattern; along with the alternating octagonal and circular piers, they also serve to stress the horizontal layers of the structure rather than its overall architectural unity. The plan itself, with its two transepts and axial chapel, is also English. The increasing elaboration and rise in the level of the interior indicate the increasing liturgical importance of the spaces of the east end from choir to presbytery (fig. 35: see CANTERBURY CATHEDRAL) to the Trinity Chapel in which Becket's relics were displayed. Becket's martyrdom ensured the cathedral's lasting influence, although outside of southeastern England much of Gothic architecture is characterized by rejection rather than adaptation of the style introduced at Canterbury.

In the west of England linear patterns and dark-light contrasts were created through the use of complex supports in which the pier is surrounded by a thick cluster of shafts, as at Worcester (after 1175) or Wells (1180–90; fig. 146: see WELLS CATHEDRAL), rather than by the use of dark marble. The wall surfaces themselves remain relatively unadorned, stressing the massive English thick wall. At Wells the clerestory is expanded so that it is almost equal in height to the arcade, and the vault responds stop at gallery level. The result is a dissolving of the bay unit and a stress on the horizontal divisions of the elevation that may look back to such Romanesque structures as Tewkesbury or Gloucester. Statues of eight Anglo-Saxon bishops were placed on the choir screen ca. 1200, possibly as a reminder of the history of the church, certainly as part of the growing promotion of English saints and their cults, a stress on national identity and history that transcended the regional divisions of style.

In the north a strong French influence is evident at Ripon Minster (begun ca. 1170) with its spacious arcade and slender supports, yet here too the thick wall, clustered piers, and the original flat wooden roof were all in the English tradition. Churches in the north also showed a regional preference for lancet windows.

Architectural sculpture in the Transitional period is limited. Figural sculpture gradually increased in quantity and naturalism, but drapery remained stylized, conceived as patterns of folds that adorned rather than clothed the body. The figural sculptures from St. Mary's Abbey, York (ca. 1190–1200), are fine examples of this style (fig. 12: see ARCHITECTURE AND ARCHITECTURAL SCULPTURE, ROMANESQUE). Innova-

tion occurs in West Country sculpture of ca. 1220–30. At Worcester Cathedral the spandrels of the transept and Lady Chapel are carved with a variety of figures (many restored). While clearly in the tradition of the Romanesque historiated capital, the poses, dress, and interaction of these figures are more complex and naturalistic. One scene in particular shows a monk inspecting the drawing of a cross-legged architect, giving us a glimpse into the more practical side of Gothic architecture. A similar sense of individuality and character is conveyed by the figural sculpture on the choir screen and interior capitals at Wells.

Early English Style (early 13th century–ca. 1290)

The 13th century saw the development of two main versions of Early English Gothic. The first version, found mostly in south and southeastern England, can be seen at Salisbury Cathedral (1220–68) and related buildings. Salisbury (fig. 118: see SALISBURY CATHEDRAL) is unique among English cathedrals in being the only cathedral begun on a new site, and this has often been seen as the explanation for its unparalleled unity of design. The individual elements of the structure do derive from a variety of sources—the use of Purbeck marble accents in the transepts from Canterbury and Lincoln, the four-part vaulting and horizontal layering from transitional southwestern architecture such as Wells—but unity is achieved through the harmonious repetition of the Purbeck marble details and the lancet windows. The compound shafts of Wells and Worcester give way to restrained four-shaft piers in the nave, changing to eight-shaft piers in the choir, the change possibly indicating the increased liturgical importance of the choir. The low gallery level may look back to the Romanesque. The unity of interior space continues in the Lady Chapel, where slender piers and side aisles equal in height to those of the nave create an open space and diaphanous structure.

The second, and more elaborate, strand of Early English architecture is exemplified by Lincoln Cathedral (1191). Here, as at Salisbury, the English thick wall survives but is joined, particularly in St. Hugh's Choir (begun 1191), by rich polychrome effects and sculptural ornament in the Canterbury tradition. The capitals throughout are covered with stiff-leaf foliage, the piers vary in design, and the profiles of the moldings and piers are rich and complex. In St. Hugh's Choir the aisle walls are ornamented with arcading and angels emerging from thick banks of clouds. The choir is crowned by the famous Lincoln "crazy vaults." The asymmetry of these vaults and the introduction of the ridge-rib work to dissolve the compartmentalization of the bay unit, but it should be noted that the traditional longitudinal emphasis of English architecture had been working toward similar ends for quite some time. Both Lincoln and Salisbury display the rectangular choirs and flat east ends that typify the English Gothic and that have their ultimate origin in Anglo-Saxon architecture.

The 13th-century chapter house at Lincoln (fig. 38: see CHAPTER HOUSES) was as influential as the cathedral itself. It was the first of the great English chapter houses to be vaulted with a fan of ribs supported by a single slender column, like an inverted umbrella. The centralized plan of the English chapter houses distinguished them from their continental counterparts.

During the 13th century changes in the liturgy requiring an expansion of processional space led to an increasing complexity in the design of the east end of the church. Often this corresponded with the promotion of the cult of a local saint, as at Durham, where the chapel of the nine altars was constructed to house the shrine of St. Cuthbert in the 1240s.

Sculpture in the Early English period continued to spread across the interior and exterior surfaces of the church. The profusion of sculptural details applied to the interior of Lincoln Cathedral became a characteristic of English sculpture by the end of the 13th century. The marginal spaces of the church—capitals, corbels, bosses, etc.—became the locus of sculptural innovation, with narrative scenes giving way to elegant floral or foliate motifs or single inhabiting figures. The monsters and genre scenes that decorated these areas during much of the Romanesque period began to appear in yet more marginal areas, such as misericords. A fine example of an early-13th-century misericord decorated with dragons and foliage survives at Christchurch Priory, Dorset.

The period is dominated by two separate "schools," the first in the West Country centered on Wells and the second in London, with Henry III's Westminster Abbey as its major monument. By the middle of the 13th century traveling workshops comprising lay sculptors had emerged. Increasingly their names are preserved in contemporary documents.

The screen facade of Wells Cathedral (1230–50) is a prime example of West Country work (fig. 122: see SCREEN FACADES). Here architecture becomes little more than a setting for figural sculpture. The portal itself is deemphasized so that the facade becomes a great gateway under which we must pass to enter the church, the kingdom of heaven on earth, a foreshadowing of the entry of the saved into the heavenly Jerusalem. The Virgin occupies the central axis; in the tympanum over the door is the Virgin and Child, and above the portal the Coronation of the Virgin. The niches and quatrefoils are populated with statues of the resurrected, prophets, martyrs, confessors, angels, apostles, and scenes from the Old and New Testaments, capped by the large central Christ in Majesty (a modern replica). Originally the whole facade would have been brightly painted, resembling a giant altar screen, so that entry into the sacred space of the church became a literal echo of entry into the even more sacred space of the east end, and a symbolic echo of entry into paradise.

Stylistically the sculpture shows a strong French influence. The figures are monumental and elegantly dressed, with folds of drapery clearly relating to the bodies beneath. Poses are restrained and naturalistic, and faces carved with a sense of individuality free from all Romanesque distortion. The work and/or influence of the Wells workshop are evident in sculpture at Bristol, Hereford, and Salisbury and in Scandinavia.

An even greater French influence is evident at Westminster Abbey (1240s), where Henry III (and then Edward I) adopted the Rayonnant style associated with French royal patronage. Westminster Abbey (fig. 147: see WESTMINSTER ABBEY) was intended to serve as mausoleum, coronation church, and royal chapel, and Henry's architects combined elements of the three French churches that served these same functions—St. Denis, Reims, the Ste. Chapelle—in its design. The elaborate surface decoration of the interior, however, is in the English tradition; it included Purbeck marble detailing, carved arcading, corbel heads, foliage, rosettes, and painted diaper patterns. The monumental figure sculpture, which included the famous censing angels in the transept spandrels, marks the beginning of the highly influential London (or Court) School of sculptors.

Decorated Style (ca. 1290–ca. 1350)

The late Gothic Decorated style initiated a trend toward smaller, more ornamental structures. The increasing laicization of society brought church, crown, and lay culture closer together. Not surprisingly a significant amount of artistic innovation took place within parish churches and secular structures. The slender piers and large windows that first appear in mendicant (i.e., friars') churches are quickly translated into the design of parish churches (e.g., at Boston or Hull) and the chapels and chapter houses of the great cathedrals. A desire for personal display at all levels of society resulted in the multiplication of private funerary chapels, elaborate tombs, and shrines capped by ornate canopies and gables, and a proliferation of luxurious and costly reliquaries. The architecture, sculpture, and metalwork of the period exhibit a common vocabulary of style and motif, perhaps best exemplified in works associated with Edward I (1272–1307). The Eleanor crosses, erected after the death of Edward's queen and based on French prototypes, straddle the line between monumental sculpture and miniature architecture, while displaying the delicate jewellike decoration of metalwork.

The buildings erected at this time are characterized by an emphasis on decoration and artistic inventiveness at the expense of structural and architectural innovation. The architect employed in Edward's rebuilding of St. Stephen's Chapel (1292–1348) at Westminster, Michael of Canterbury, also worked on the Eleanor crosses and incorporated many aspects of their design into the new structure. While the basic plan of the chapel is based on that of the Ste. Chapelle in Paris, the elaborate tracery of the canopies of the wall arcading, the ogee arches of the window tracery, and the ogee-reticulated tracery of the east cloister (ca. 1300) all derive from the crosses. The vault of the lower chapel is among the earliest examples of a lierne vault, in which short, decorative ribs run between the diagonal ribs, and an example of the innovative tracery patterns that became one of England's greatest contributions to late Gothic style.

After St. Stephen's Chapel the key monuments of the Decorated style are Exeter (1280 to the late 14th century) and York cathedrals, the choirs of Lichfield and Wells (1320–40), the Ely octagon (1322–24), and the cloister at Norwich. The rebuilding of the east end of Wells Cathedral has been attributed to the general desire to "gain greater privacy for the liturgical choir by transferring it from the crossing to the east arm," evident throughout England in the 13th and 14th centuries (Wilson, 1990: 199). This increased desire for more private space and the proliferation of ornament within it are also part and parcel of the increasing mysticism and concentration on personal devotion that characterized the late Gothic period throughout Europe (as are the increased numbers of private chapels and monumental tombs).

The polygonal Lady Chapel at Wells is covered with an unusual domed vault decorated with a star-shaped pattern of tracery that emphasizes the chapel's centralized space. To the west of the Lady Chapel are four smaller chapels, two forming a miniature transept, and an ambulatory that makes the transition between the complex of chapels and the high east wall of the choir. The visual and spatial effects of this arrangement are complex. Looking through the arches of the east wall of the choir (originally blocked by a canopied screen), the chapels appear to be straightforward rectangular extensions of the choir; but within the ambulatory and chapels proper the thin supports and elaborate tracery patterns of the vaults and windows mold the interior into a series of distinct but interconnected spaces. The decorative tracery patterns of the chapel vaults are continued on the tunnel vault of the choir, where they echo the tracery patterns of the great east window.

Church furniture, wooden sculpture, and wooden construction became increasingly important in the first half of the 14th century. Decorative gables, ornate versions of those decorating the Eleanor crosses, covered choir screens and stalls, as on the 1308–10 choirstalls at Winchester, or the Exeter bishop's throne (1313–17). The narrative and anecdotal context of both misericords and roof bosses expanded (as at Wells), probably under the influence of manuscript illumination. In general these "marginal" images are carved with the same delicate style seen in monumental stone sculpture.

The Ely octagon, begun by the royal carpenter William Hurley after the collapse of the Anglo-Norman crossing tower in 1322, might be described as a canopied choirstall blown up to monumental proportions, as the liturgical choir and stalls were originally located directly beneath it. A technical masterpiece, it consists of an octagonal timber lantern supported by an octagonal masonry base. The lantern was originally painted to give the illusion that it too was built of stone. It functioned both as a bell tower and as a means of concealing the massive timber supports of the vaults.

On the exterior surfaces of early-14th-century churches and cathedrals the relationship between architecture and decoration was not as harmonious as it was on the interior. The screens of canopied niches filled with figural sculpture that cover the entrances of St. Mary Redcliffe, Bristol (1320), or Exeter Cathedral (1350–65) no longer follow the vertical and horizontal lines of the structure, as they did at Wells (1230–40), but conceal architectural form beneath an appliqué of surface ornament. Indeed at Exeter the sculpture dominates its architectural setting. The Exeter figures also exhibit a stiffness and crudity of carving, possibly linked to the economic and social upheavals resulting from the Hundred Years War and the Black Death (1348–49).

Perpendicular Style (ca. 1350–1525)

The Perpendicular style takes its name from the narrow arched rectangular panels created by the tracery that covers both the walls and windows of late-14th- and 15th-century structures. It first appears in the south transept and choir of Gloucester Cathedral (1351–67), where the east wall of the choir is dissolved into a curtain of glass visually united with the masonry walls by an all-over grid of tracery. The verticality of the space is heightened by the pier shafts and the responds, which descend uninterrupted from the high vault. The colors used in the great east window are restrained and the figures worked in near grisaille (almost monochrome grey), suggesting a wall of sculpture that adds to the overall unity and harmony of the choir. Carved decoration is limited to the arches of the tracery panels and the bosses and angels that decorate the elaborate lierne vault. The overall effect is restrained, almost ascetic, in comparison with the bright colors and lavish sculptural decoration of the Decorated style. It may be the result of a deliberate turn away from worldliness and ostentation in the wake of plague, war, and social upheaval.

The division of architectural surfaces into panels of tracery that begins in the choir is taken one step farther in the Gloucester cloister. The east walk of the cloister is roofed with the earliest known fan vault, a vault consisting of projecting masonry cones covered with a pattern of blind tracery ultimately derived from the rose windows of Rayonnant architecture.

The Perpendicular style rapidly became popular throughout England. The decorative restraint and increased verticality of the Gloucester choir are evident in the high narrow arcades and unbroken vertical lines of the late-14th-century naves at Winchester and Canterbury. Monumental sculptural decoration is confined to tombs and to areas immediately surrounding doorways and altars.

The two great monuments of late Perpendicular architecture are both royal structures and reflect the splendor of court culture. St. George's Chapel, Windsor (1475–1511), was built as a royal mausoleum and seat of the Order of the Garter for Edward IV. Architecturally the chapel is based on the plans of the great Perpendicular ecclesiastical structures, such as the Gloucester choir and the Canterbury nave; however, its shorter length and reduced height create an open interior that has much in common with contemporary great halls.

The last of the great Perpendicular buildings, Henry VII's Chapel at Westminster Abbey (1503–09), was also based on great church design and was intended to replace St. George's Chapel as the royal mausoleum. It too combines the traceried splendor of ecclesiastical architecture with the open space (and bay windows) of the great hall. On the exterior the sides of the building consist of alternating polygonal bay windows and masonry buttresses divided into narrow vertical panels of tracery. The turrets end in pinnacles with niches that originally held statues of apostles and prophets, and are capped by elaborately crocketed onion domes. The interior of the chapel is covered with delicate tracery and sculptural decoration, but its greatest glory is its high pendant vault, which seems to hang like a web from the great transverse arches. The illusion of weightlessness is amplified by the high profile of the tracery that causes the solid masonry to dissolve in shadow.

The figures of prophets that survive from Henry VII's Chapel are as remarkable as the architecture. Their deeply carved draperies and elaborate hats create strong patterns of light and dark akin to those of the vault. Moreover their highly individualized faces, postures, and dress create a sense of personality that foreshadows developments of the later 16th century. Taken as a whole Henry VII's Chapel and its sculpture provide a fitting swan song for the English Middle Ages.

Catherine E. Karkov

Bibliography

Alexander, Jonathan, and Paul Binski, eds. *Age of Chivalry: Art in Plantagenet England 1200–1400*. London: Royal Academy of Arts, 1987; Bony, Jean. *The English Decorated Style: Gothic Architecture Transformed 1250–1350*. Oxford: Phaidon, 1979; Colvin, Howard M., ed. *The History of the King's Works*. Vol. 2: *The Middle Ages*. London: HMSO, 1963; Harvey, J.H. *The Perpendicular Style 1330–1485*. London: Batsford, 1978; Kidson, Peter, Peter Murray, and Paul Thompson. *A History of English Architecture*. 2d ed. Harmondsworth: Penguin, 1979; Rickman, Thomas. *An Attempt to Discriminate the Styles of Architecture in England from the Conquest to the Reformation*. 7th ed. London: Parker, 1881; Stone, Lawrence. *Sculpture in Britain: The Middle Ages*. 2d ed. Harmondsworth: Penguin, 1972; Webb, Geoffrey. *Architecture in Britain: The Middle Ages*. Harmondsworth: Penguin, 1956; Wilson, Christopher. *The Gothic Cathedral: The Architecture of the Great Church 1130–1530*. London: Thames & Hudson, 1990.

See also Angel Roofs; Architecture and Architectural Sculpture, Romanesque; Art, Gothic; Canterbury Cathedral; Chapter Houses; Eleanor Crosses; King's College, Cambridge; Lady Chapel; Lincoln Cathedral; Misericords; Processions; Salisbury Cathedral; Sculpture, Gothic; Vaulting; Wells Cathedral; Westminster Abbey; Windsor, St. George's Chapel

Architecture and Architectural Sculpture, Romanesque
Architecture

The development of Romanesque architecture in England is inextricably linked to the Norman Conquest of 1066 and the church reform of the 11th and 12th centuries. Both the new political dynasty and the new religious orders demanded the construction of new buildings designed to impress through their strength, size, and beauty (not to mention the labor necessary to complete them). The massive walls, imposing towers, and enormous size of both castles and churches were the ideal symbols of king and Church Militant.

Edward the Confessor's church at Westminster Abbey (begun ca. 1050) is frequently cited as the first true Romanesque church in England. Though built before the Conquest, it was Norman rather than English in style, with towers at both west end and crossing and a spacious nave. Its scale,

however, was unprecedented in either country. It served as both the shrine for Edward's relics and as coronation church for William, an apt symbol of the merging of Anglo-Saxon and Norman traditions in the English Romanesque.

English Romanesque architecture was brought to maturity in the 1070s with the construction of St. Augustine's Abbey and the cathedral at Canterbury under Archbishop Lanfranc. Modeled on the church of St. Étienne at Caen, where Lanfranc had been abbot, Canterbury Cathedral had a typical Romanesque plan: two-towered facade, long nave with side aisles, pronounced transepts with side chapels, crossing tower, and choir and apse for use by the clergy. The elevation consisted of arcade, gallery, and clerestory levels. The repetition of the bay unit within the church served both to compartmentalize space and to create a harmony of arched forms. Lanfranc's Canterbury was clearly not a mere copy of St. Étienne. The clerestory at Canterbury does not seem to have included a wall passage (as at Caen), and Canterbury has a crypt, while Caen does not. The remains of the large Anglo-Saxon cathedral were discovered in 1993 beneath the present nave. While the excavation reports have not yet been published, the sheer size of the building may indicate that Lanfranc's Canterbury had more in common with its Anglo-Saxon predecessor than has previously been suspected.

The tradition begun at Canterbury was quickly transformed as it spread throughout England, and regional schools of architecture soon developed in the west Midlands, Lincolnshire, Hampshire, Yorkshire, and Northumbria. These schools combined the Norman plan and elevation with influences from Germany, Italy, Scandinavia, and Anglo-Saxon England.

Perhaps the most distinctive regional school was located in the west and southwest Midlands. The abbey churches of Tewkesbury (begun 1092) and Gloucester (now the Cathedral, begun 1089; fig. 68: see GLOUCESTER CATHEDRAL) are fine examples of this style. The interiors of these churches tend to break up the compartmentalization of the bay unit. At Gloucester the monumental columnar piers of the nave rise to such a height that the gallery level is reduced to a band of decorative arcading. While less graceful than the triforium of the Gothic plan, the longitudinal emphasis created by the gallery at Gloucester looks forward to the linear articulation and longitudinal emphasis of Salisbury Cathedral (fig. 118: see SALISBURY CATHEDRAL).

Monumental columnar piers are also present at Durham (begun 1093) in the north of England though here they alternate with compound piers, and their imposing bulk is softened somewhat by the enormous size of the church (modeled on Old St. Peter's) and by the geometric patterns carved into their surfaces. The interior of Durham is beautifully articulated by the sculpted details of arches, ribs, and label stops. Originally brightly painted, this interior represented a combination of early Christian forms with Romanesque style and the traditional English love of rich colors and surface patterns.

The western "galilee" at Durham, (fig. 52: see DURHAM CATHEDRAL), added in the 1170s by Bishop Hugh le Puiset, served several functions. A porch or entrance chamber in English churches, the galilee is named after Christ's journey from Galilee to Jerusalem, a journey symbolically echoed by the entry of the clergy into the church from the galilee after the Sunday procession. The Durham galilee also housed the ecclesiastical court, an altar to the Virgin, and the relics of Bede. Durham was a high point of Norman influence in the north, yet as a shrine for both the relics of Bede and St. Cuthbert (enshrined in the central apse in 1104) it was also a symbol of the Anglo-Saxon tradition.

Some of the most unusual churches were built in the north, particularly in Yorkshire and Northumbria. The Romanesque cathedral at York (begun ca. 1080 by Thomas of Bayeux) was aisleless. In the east end the presbytery (eastern portion of the chancel) was constructed as a cell separated from the surrounding shell of the outer walls by two narrow corridors. These lateral corridors may have been connected by a passage separating presbytery from apse. Relatively little remains of the structure of this east end, but it does seem to have been unusually long. Piers in the 12th-century undercroft at York are carved with decorative surface patterns similar to those found on the nave piers at Durham.

Piers carved in the Durham manner can also be seen in the nave of the Benedictine priory church at Lindisfarne (re-established ca. 1082 as a cell of Durham). Like Durham, Lindisfarne also had a stone vault, and it is likely that both churches were built by the same group of masons. Unlike Durham, Lindisfarne had an aisleless choir and a shallow transept with an apse on the east side of each arm. The most unusual feature of the church, however, was its facade, described by McAleer (1984: 614) as a "quasi-screen" facade. The west front at Lindisfarne presents us with a screen of masonry divided by stringcourses (horizontal bands forming part of the design) into four levels and flanked by projecting stair towers. At the center is a projecting porch decorated with chevron ornament and flanked by blind arcading. The porch may originally have had a gable roof and contained a small gallery. The gable that currently crowns the whole of the west front dates to the 14th century. This type of facade is an original English feature and looks forward to the full-blown screen facades of the Gothic.

One of the most impressive of all Romanesque churches is Lincoln Cathedral (fig. 82: see LINCOLN CATHEDRAL), begun by Bishop Remigius between 1070 and 1092. The plan of the church was similar to that of Canterbury, the major difference being the addition of an imposing westwork. The western facade at Lincoln is not simply a screen but a massive block designed to resemble a fortified castle. Indeed the west end of the cathedral faced the local castle just across Ermine Street.

The surface of the facade is pierced by three great triumphal arches, a feature also found in contemporary castle architecture (as well as at Tewkesbury). As was the case with Durham, this church was meant to be a statement of Norman power. The three arches of the facade beautifully sum up the amalgamation of political and religious power that the church was designed to represent. They remind the viewer of military architecture and Roman triumphal arches, but they also echo the interior space of the cathedral, specifically the three great arched openings at the entrance to the east end.

The proximity of church and castle seen at Lincoln is by no means unusual. Quite often male religious houses and castles were built in close proximity to each other, a unified statement of domination over the surrounding landscape. Until recently women's houses in Romanesque England have not received much study, perhaps because we have assumed that gender had no significance when it came to the construction and decoration of monastic buildings; however, Roberta Gilchrist (1994) has demonstrated that this is not the case. While there were exceptions, women's houses tended to be built in marginal areas, on agriculturally poor land, and were rarely built in proximity to castles—that is, they were not used to make political statements in the same way that men's houses were. Women's houses also tended to be more sparsely decorated, though some of the more important houses, such as Barking or Romsey, are significant exceptions. Although the evidence is fragmentary, scenes like the Coronation and Assumption of the Virgin in the northern tympanum of the church at Quenington, Gloucestershire (ca. 1150), suggest that women's houses might also have had their own iconography.

Sculpture

While many Anglo-Saxon churches were decorated with sculpture, it is only in the Romanesque period that architectural sculpture becomes fully integrated into the fabric of the building. Beginning around doorways, windows, and the capitals of columns in the early Romanesque period, sculptural decoration soon spread to articulate and embellish the whole of the building. However, sculpture in medieval England almost always remains surface ornament, decorating architectural forms rather than creating its own space. Unfortunately, as is the case with Anglo-Saxon sculpture, much of the material, particularly figural sculpture, was damaged or destroyed by 16th- and 17th-century iconoclasts, or disappeared during remodeling or rebuilding campaigns. As with architecture English Romanesque sculpture is eclectic, influenced by Anglo-Saxon, Scandinavian, French, German, Italian, and Byzantine art, yet combining these influences to create a new and highly expressive style.

Within the monastery the church, chapter house, and cloister received the most elaborate decoration. The walls of the 12th-century chapter house at St. Augustine's, Bristol, are decorated with interlaced blind arcades, while the ribs of both arches and vault are carved with beading and chevron ornament. Arcading also decorates the walls of the chapter house at Gloucester, a structure perhaps best known for the rich chevron ornament surrounding its doorway.

In the cloister the capitals of the arcade could receive lavish decoration. Particularly fine capitals survive from the cloisters of Glastonbury Abbey (ca. 1150), Hyde Abbey, Winchester (1125–30), and Norwich (1130). A variety of ornament was used, from foliate motifs and grotesques, as at Hyde Abbey, to figural narratives (historiated capitals), as at Norwich. The piers of the cloister could also be decorated with figural sculpture. It has been suggested that the reliefs of Sts. Peter and Paul from Ivychurch Priory, Wiltshire, might have been used in such a manner, though there is no solid evidence that this was the case.

The interior spaces of the church were frequently articulated by chevron or other types of geometric ornament applied to arches, moldings, and ribs. Label stops and corbels were enriched by human or animal heads. Durham Cathedral provides a particularly fine example of a fully articulated Romanesque interior. Sometimes, as at Durham, simple cushion or cubic capitals were used, with designs often painted onto their flat faces. Perhaps this practice helps to explain the similarity in style and iconography between many of the carved capitals and contemporary manuscripts. Capitals at both Westminster Hall and the crypt of Canterbury Cathedral, for example, have parallels in initials from Canterbury manuscripts as well as motifs found in the borders of the Bayeux Tapestry. It should also be remembered that at least some Romanesque artists were able to work in a variety of media. Master Hugo, the innovative illuminator of the Bury Bible (Cambridge, Corpus Christi College 2) was also a sculptor and a metalworker. Capitals of columns and responds, as well as label stops, could be carved with a variety of motifs from Corinthian acanthus to fabulous beasts and narrative subjects. While there is no rigid chronological development from simple cushion capital to historiated capital, it is generally true that narrative scenes became more popular and more complex over the course of the 12th century.

Exterior sculpture is concentrated around doorways, though corbel tables and stringcourses were also carved with ornament similar to that of the church interior. Grotesque human or animal heads were particularly popular on corbels, and probably had an apotropaic (evil-averting) function.

The reign of Henry I (1100–35) saw a flowering of sculpture due largely to wealthy patrons, such as Henry, his daughter Empress Matilda, and Bishop Roger of Salisbury, as well as the growing influence of Cluny. Already regional styles were beginning to emerge. The influence of the Scandinavian Ringerike and Urnes styles is evident in and around areas of Scandinavian settlement, such as Cumbria and East Anglia. Sculptors in these areas worked in a flat, highly patterned style, and were particularly fond of animal motifs, many of them derived from Scandinavian mythology, or the traditional iconography of combat (e.g., the boar tympanum of St. Nicholas, Ipswich). Dragons or serpents are frequently depicted in battle—with each other, with human beings, with St. Michael—and are probably meant to symbolize the battle between good and evil.

Royal patronage continued to play an important role in the development of Romanesque sculpture during the reign of Stephen (1135–54). The king is particularly associated with his foundation of Faversham Abbey in Kent (1148), built to house the royal mausoleum. Although only fragments have survived, the Faversham sculpture provides some of the earliest examples of the use of Purbeck marble.

Even more significant as a patron was the king's brother Henry of Blois, bishop of Winchester and abbot of Glastonbury, whose economic and aesthetic interests opened the door to a wide variety of continental influences. It was Henry who popularized the use of Tournai marble for fonts, grave slabs, and architectural details in England. Not only were objects and unworked marble imported, but the Tournai style itself had a significant, though localized, influence in England. The lush foliate ornament decorated with chevrons and beading of the capitals surviving from the cloister of Glastonbury Abbey have parallels with capitals in Tournai Cathedral. Fragments of the door jambs from Wolvesey Palace, Henry's residence at Winchester, show the influence of Abbot Suger's St. Denis. Henry's collection of classical sculpture, purchased in Rome in 1151, has also been credited with influencing the great plasticity and naturalistic forms of the centaurs decorating surviving capitals from Winchester Cathedral.

Artistic patronage and political ambition were closely linked in the mid- to late 12th century. Patronage, particularly when it involved artistic innovation, was a sign of the wealth and prominence of a community. Henry of Blois had been educated at Cluny and no doubt desired his own houses to reflect some of Cluny's style and grandeur. The similarity of the Wolvesey Palace jambs to those at St. Denis suggest that he emulated, or even saw himself in competition with, Abbot Suger. Alexander "the Magnificent," bishop of Lincoln (1123–48), emulated both Henry and Suger. Alexander rebuilt Lincoln Cathedral, adding a stone vault, sculpted decoration to the doorways, and a frieze to the western facade. Henry of Huntingdon boasted that Alexander had succeeded in turning Lincoln into "a strong church in a strong place, a beautiful church in a beautiful place: invincible to enemies as suited the times." The narrative frieze is unusual in Romanesque England, though it does have parallels on the Continent (as at Selles-sur-Cher

Fig. 11. Lincoln Cathedral, west frieze, "Sodomy" panel. Drawing by C. Karkov.

Fig. 12. Moses, St. Mary's Abbey, York. Currently in the Yorkshire Museum. Reproduced by courtesy of the Yorkshire Museum.

nography to the sculptural programs of the Romanesque pilgrimage churches, although several of the scenes, such as the "Sodomy" panel (fig. 11), are unique.

Scandinavian influence continued well into the 12th century and is particularly evident on Hereford School sculpture, as at Kilpeck (ca. 1150), though here it is merged with continental influences. The grotesque beasts decorating the doorways of such churches as St. Peter, Aulnay-de-Saintonge (ca. 1130), are assumed to have influenced the biting-beast heads on the voussoirs (the wedge-shaped pieces in an arch) at Kilpeck and other English and Irish churches, although an exact chronology is particularly difficult to establish. However, the ferocity of the English and Irish beasts and the way in which they grip the molding of the arch with prominent teeth and tongue are purely insular and can be traced back to such objects as the 8th-century Donore handle (National Museum of Ireland 1985:21 b, d, e) or the ca. 800 Book of Kells (Dublin, Trinity College A.I.6). The tiered figures of the chancel arch at Kilpeck are thought to have been influenced by similar figures at Santiago de Compostela, though the exact means of transmission remains hypothetical.

Sometime ca. 1150 carved roof bosses began to be applied to vaults. Peterborough Cathedral has some of the earliest (ca. 1150) and most interesting. The Peterborough bosses contain fantastical animals with heads and paws that bite and grip on to the ribs of the vaults—similar to the way in which the Kilpeck heads bite and grip the roll-molding.

Artistic links with the Continent expanded during the reign of Henry II (1154–89). Figural sculpture became both more popular and more three-dimensional at this time. Compare, for example, the relief of Sts. Peter and Paul (ca. 1160) from Ivychurch Priory, Wiltshire (a royal foundation), or the figural sculpture from St. Albans Abbey with the earlier Kilpeck figures. A love of rich surface pattern is still evident in the folds of the drapery and decorative details, but the figures themselves have a greater plasticity and more naturalistic sense of form and motion, and they make greater use of the effects of light and shadow.

The influence of Byzantine and Mosan (Meuse Valley) art also increased in the late 12th century. The York Virgin and Child of ca. 1155 derives from Byzantine models, while the life-sized apostles, prophets, and typological figures from St. Mary's Abbey, York (1180–85), are clearly influenced by Mosan metalwork (fig. 12). The surviving heads of the St. Mary figures show a fine sense of individuality, drapery falls in long heavy folds, and the poses display a classical weight shift. The exact position and arrangement of the York figures are unknown, but they are likely to have been arranged in tiers around the interior of the chapter house with New Testament apostles above Old Testament prophets and typological figures. Both the expanded use of large figural sculptures in an architectural setting and the increased classicism of the figures themselves point toward the naturalism and monumentality of Gothic architectural sculpture.

Catherine E. Karkov

near Blois or Modena in Italy) as well as in Anglo-Saxon England (e.g., Hexham, Wearmouth, Breedon-on-the-Hill). The Lincoln frieze depicts both Old and New Testament scenes and, while it has no exact parallels, is similar in ico-

Bibliography

Cambridge, Eric. *Lindisfarne Priory and Holy Island.* London: English Heritage, 1988; Curry, Ian. *Aspects of the Anglo-Norman Design of Durham.* Newcastle-on-Tyne: Society of Antiquaries, 1986; Gilchrist, Roberta. *Gender and Material Culture: The Archaeology of Religious Women.* London: Routledge, 1994; Heywood, Ben, ed. *Romanesque Stone Sculpture from England.* Leeds: Henry Moore Sculpture Trust, 1993; Kahn, Deborah. *Canterbury Cathedral and Its Romanesque Sculpture.* London: Harvey Miller, 1991; Kahn, Deborah. *The Romanesque Frieze and Its Spectator: The Lincoln Symposium Papers.* London: Harvey Miller, 1992; Little, Bryan. *Architecture in Norman Britain.* London: Batsford, 1985; McAleer, J. Philip. *The Romanesque Church Facade in Britain.* New York: Garland, 1984; Stone, Lawrence. *Sculpture in Britain: The Middle Ages.* 2d ed. Harmondsworth: Penguin, 1972; Zarnecki, George. *English Romanesque Sculpture 1066–1140.* London: Tiranti, 1951; Zarnecki, George. *Later English Romanesque Sculpture.* London: Tiranti, 1953; Zarnecki, George. *Studies in Romanesque Sculpture, 1979.* London: Dorian Press, 1979 [collected essays]; Zarnecki, George, Janet Holt, and Tristram Holland, eds. *English Romanesque Art 1066–1200.* London: Weidenfeld & Nicolson, 1984.

See also Canterbury Cathedral; Chapter Houses; Durham Cathedral; Gloucester Cathedral; Kilpeck; Lincoln Cathedral; Screen Facades; Sculpture, Romanesque; Westminster Abbey; York Virgin and Child

Armies and Military Service
Anglo-Saxon Armies

While many aspects of Anglo-Saxon military organization are subject to debate, it seems evident that the armies were national armies, and that normally all freemen were obliged to render some form of military service. The pre-Conquest military establishment, with roots in ancient Germanic society, pursued a path of development markedly different from that seen on the Continent, where increasingly, from the mid-8th century onward, heavy cavalrymen, the aristocratic knights of feudal society, emerged as the fundamental element in warfare.

The Anglo-Saxons instead remained committed to the infantryman. Although English warriors might ride to battle or in pursuit of the foe, they customarily dismounted and fought in the traditional shield-wall formation. The significance of this different development was reflected in the fact that prior to the Conquest English society was not based on the feudal structure, linked to knight service, as it was on much of the Continent.

Service in the *fyrd,* or national levy, together with work on bridges and borough defense, constituted the *trimoda necessitas,* the three forms of public burden imposed on all freemen and all lands by the throne. Initially the obligation of military service appears to have been calculated on the ba-sis of each hide of land—seen as the amount of land required to support one family—turning out one man when summoned. In some regions service was naval rather than military. At some undetermined point in time, perhaps to realize a better quality of service, the obligation became that of one man from several hides, possibly from five. We lack clear evidence regarding whether the five-hide system was the basis of service in all regions or if it was a model or a political and military reality. In areas not neatly "hidated," as in East Anglia or the northern Danelaw, other bases of assessment must have been utilized.

The ceorls, or free peasants, who made up the great *fyrd* are dim figures in descriptions of warfare found in the sources, a mere backdrop against which the professional warriors, the thegns (a hereditary class holding estates granted by the crown), and their semiprofessional retainers and mercenary soldiers, waged battle. Undoubtedly the average peasant was neither adequately trained nor equipped for the battlefield. It is also unclear if the ceorl's military obligations required participation in distant conflicts. While in the 9th century they normally did not fight beyond their own shire, by the 11th century this had altered, though it is likely that the full *fyrd's* primary military role remained local or regional defense.

On the other hand it is unlikely that the ceorl was a negligible factor in battle, as there is evidence that at least wealthier peasants possessed weapons and armor equal to those of less prosperous thegns. Nevertheless, the five-hide system may actually have constituted the basis of a select *fyrd,* a more efficient and better-equipped force composed of thegns, their retainers, on occasion mercenary troops, and more affluent peasants, in contrast to the general *fyrd* of all freemen.

Under any circumstances it was men of the thegn class and their retainers, or hearth men, who formed the efficient component of the military forces. Whether the obligations of thegns were, like those of the ceorls, based upon the hide system or on personal relations with their lord is open to debate.

Anglo-Saxon monarchs, as well as prominent thegns and magnates, took mercenaries into their service. Although constituting a small proportion of the military forces, they served an important role as professionals on regular service. Æthelred II (979–1016), in his struggle with the Danes, employed Scandinavian mercenaries, such as Thorkell the Tall, who entered his service in 1012 with 45 ships. Under Cnut (1016–35) the corps of royal housecarles was established. Patterned after the Jomsvikings organized by his grandfather in Denmark, it was a guild of professional warriors with its own body of laws. These men, armed with battleaxe and sword, were the backbone of the Anglo-Saxon army until their virtual annihilation at Hastings. While many housecarles were landholders, their military service was essentially that of mercenaries based upon a regular stipend and personal loyalty to the king akin to the *comitatus,* or sworn warband, of ancient Germanic society. Many thegns and aristocrats also maintained mercenary retainers, of both English and foreign origin, variously designated as hearth men, *hiredmenn,* housecarles, *lithsmen,* or *butsecarles* (the latter two terms seemingly signifying those equally proficient on land or sea).

Armies after 1066

The fiefs that William the Conqueror granted his Norman and allied followers supplied the basic structure of English armies until the 14th century. Their tenure was by knight service; each fief was assessed at a certain number of knights calculated in round numbers of five, to serve for two months at the king's summons. The total service was about 6,000 knights.

This seeming symmetry did not last long, as the lack of heirs, division of land, and dowries produced fractions as low as one-sixteenth. Church tenants often preferred to pay scutage (shield money). Sheer neglect of service was met with heavy fines. Kings responded to begrudging and partial responses to military summonses by a policy of calling up some fraction of the total service owed by their tenants in chief; mostly they summoned their nobles. These men, an hereditary feudal core, became the recruiters and leaders of a quasi-professional force.

The details of a knight's military service lay more in the realm of custom than of written law. From 1181 the basic military obligations of all freemen, including fief holders, were spelled out in royal assizes, later codified as statute (Statute of Winchester, 1285; modified by further royal writs). Even after knight service lost its military priority, the king would fine men of sufficient property who did not accept their responsibilities: fines known as distraints of knighthood.

The army was mustered by royal writs addressed to tenants in chief and to sheriffs in the counties (shires). The latter were mainly expected to raise the nonfeudal or subfeudal freemen, mostly as archers and spearmen. Small groups of more elite landholders came to oversee the raising of the forces, as a supplement to or replacement of the general service of lesser men under the supervision of the sheriffs. General military summonses, issued as commissions of array, were confined to armies called for service in the British Isles and to the lesser service of the archers and spearmen. In 1297 Edward I summoned all subjects with £40 of rent to serve in France, and he encountered resistance almost tantamount to rebellion. As late as 1346 general writs were still being issued, but not for service in France.

But it was in the great extension of the system of contract that the weaknesses of these arrays were solved. Contractual service has been traced back to the 12th century, but only in Edward I's reign was it used extensively in the raising of armies. In the conflicts of Edward II's reign both sides in the civil war raised troops in this way. It was Edward III who found the formula for raising troops, and techniques for using them, so as to stabilize his military forces at a sufficient size and level of leadership to help pave the way for the great victories in France.

Military contracts—known as indentures because the copy of each party was written on a single sheet and then separated by an indented cut—were of two principal types. Campaign indentures were usually for six months or a year. Others were for life. A campaign contract obligated the retainer to serve his lord with a given number of men-at-arms and (usually) archers for stated wages and other rewards. Usually there was a generalized commitment to serve when summoned rather than details of the muster. Wages and rewards were spelled out; for overseas war shipping was provided. As time went on, a share of ransom money among captor, retainer, and lord was defined in a "third and third of thirds" formula, so shares of ransom trickled upward. Life indentures helped back up and stabilize the fluid system of raising soldiers.

But the desired goals of victory abroad and peace at home depended much more on the person of the king than on the system. Nor should the contrast with "textbook" feudalism be exaggerated. Most of the contracting captains were already or became landlords with titles and chivalric notions. Neither did the size of armies change dramatically. Both sides at Hastings seem to have numbered about 7,000 fighting men. A single expedition or summons usually produced around 12,000 in Edward I's time and thereafter. A still larger force could be assembled, given time. The greatest English force recorded, over 30,000, was for the siege of Calais in 1346–47.

The supply of the armies was handled at first by commissioners exercising the royal right of "prise," that is, the right to levy food and materials for royal use. This too was replaced in Edward III's time by contracts with merchants. Contract was also extended to the levy of mounted archers who then operated in close cooperation with the knightly force in a mobile army that dismounted to fight and gave England her major victories.

Miles Campbell
Michael R. Powicke

Bibliography

PRIMARY

Campbell, Alistair, ed. *The Battle of Brunanburh*. London: Heinemann, 1987; Gordon, E.V., ed. *The Battle of Maldon*. 2d ed. London: Methuen, 1949. [These epic poems treat two famous battles in Anglo-Saxon history and describe armies in action.]

SECONDARY

Abels, Richard P. *Lordship and Military Obligation in Anglo-Saxon England*. Berkeley: University of California Press, 1988; Beeler, John. *Warfare in England, 1066–1189*. Ithaca: Cornell University Press, 1966; Brown, R. Allen. *The Normans and the Norman Conquest*. 2d ed. Woodbridge: Boydell, 1985; Hewitt, Herbert J. *The Organisation of War under Edward III, 1338–62*. Manchester: Manchester University Press, 1966; Hollister, C. Warren. *Anglo-Saxon Military Institutions on the Eve of the Norman Conquest*. Oxford: Clarendon, 1962; Powicke, Michael. *Military Obligation in Medieval England: A Study in Liberty and Duty*. Oxford: Clarendon, 1962; Prestwich, Michael. *The Three Edwards: War and State in England, 1272–1377*. London: Weidenfeld & Nicolson, 1980; Sanders, I.J. *Feudal Military Service in England: A Study of the Constitutional and Military Powers of the Barons in Medieval England*. London: Oxford University Press, 1956; Stenton, F.M. *The First Century of English Feudalism, 1066–1166*. 2d ed. Oxford:

Fig. 13. Bayeux Tapestry—scene from the Battle of Hastings. After A.L. Poole (1958). Reprinted by permission of Oxford University Press and by special permission of the City of Bayeux.

Clarendon, 1961; Stenton, F.M. *Anglo-Saxon England.* Oxford History of England 2. 3d ed. Oxford: Clarendon, 1971.

See also Arms and Armor; Bastard Feudalism; *Battle of Brunanburh;* Battle of Hastings; *Battle of Maldon;* Battles of Bannockburn and Boroughbridge; Battles of Lewes and Evesham; Burghal Hidage; Chivalry; Feudalism; Hides; Hundred Years War; Knight Service; Navy; Norman Conquest; Ships

Arms and Armor

Two major categories of arms predominated: those of the knightly class, which included men-at-arms (esquires or sergeants), knights, and noblemen, and those of the footmen, including mounted infantry. The depiction of the Battle of Hastings on the Bayeux Tapestry (fig. 13) shows that by the late 11th century it was usual for knights to have lance and sword, footmen to have spear or bow. The horses of the knightly class, ridden with stirrups and saddle, made possible a charge with couched lances, though it was still more usual to throw or thrust overarm. Axes, clubs, and spears were the chief weapons of the English, who fought on foot; over the years they gave way in the main to Norman weapons. The sword came to be distinctively knightly, the weapon of the final close combat and the instrument of knighting.

Evidence from art and architecture suggests that the heyday of the couched lance was between 1100 and 1300. Examples are the carved stone warriors in St. Mary's, Barfreston, an illumination in a mid-12th-century *Life of St. Edmund,* and some tiles at Little Kimble and at Chertsey Abbey (fig. 140: see TILES). In the 13th century its use is illustrated in the *La Estoire de Seint Aedward le Rei* and recounted in tales of Edward I's battles in Scotland. Thereafter it belonged to tournament, not the battlefield. The very term "lance" came to mean the unit of two men-at-arms and a servant, rather than the weapon. At the same time a less significant weapon, the dagger, was added to many knights' equipment.

The sword is even more emphatically a knightly weapon than the lance, involving the noble quality of the personal encounter. The Bayeux Tapestry shows it wielded by both cavalry and foot. Its users may well have fought with lance or spear before turning to hand-to-hand fighting. Attached to the belt, it left the hands free for other weapons until it was drawn. The ritual of knighting expressed the sword's special status, and in effigies and brasses it figures large, the hand of the knight resting on the pommel. It is also prominent in battle scenes. The shield changed, too. From being kite-shaped or round it became triangular by 1200. Thereafter, with the advent of plate armor, it became redundant in warfare but survived in its heraldic role.

The archers, already essential at Hastings, became highly skilled and mounted longbowmen, respected partners of the men-at-arms. The Welsh, so vividly described by Gerald of Wales in the 12th century, had very likely made a major contribution to this development. The longbow was about 5 feet 8 inches in length and usually of yew wood, the arrows about 3 feet. Simple to make, it required strength and skill to operate; in the 14th century kings legislated in favor of regular training.

Siege weapons developed in response to castle development. As the stone towers of the Normans evolved into the elaborate concentric fortifications of the later 13th century, engines were invented that used balances to throw bigger stones farther and harder. These were not entirely superseded by cannon, using gunpowder and iron balls, at the end of the Middle Ages. At the same time that alchemists (notably Oxford's Roger Bacon) were absorbing and developing Sino-Arabic knowledge of gunpowder, practical men invented arrow-throwing guns. It was not until the siege of Calais in 1346 that there was an extensive use of cannon firing iron balls, and the art remained too primitive to supersede balance-operated artillery for another century.

For about 250 years the "lorica" of chain mail (interlocked rings of iron) was the chief body armor. The Bayeux Tapestry shows both sides wearing it. The main distinction between the Normans and the Saxons was that the former's leg mail was full, the latter's but knee-length. This was a distinction between mounted and foot and recurs at intervals thereafter, as depicted in the Peterborough Psalter (1222). The main changes before the advent of plate armor were the addition of new pieces: for the neck ("aventail"), hands, and feet. The aventail, just possibly indicated by the "bibs" of Normans in the Tapestry, is not clearly depicted until a mid-13th-century effigy, possibly of William Marshal the Younger. Sometimes a "balaclava" of chain, often under a helmet, met this need. Around the year 1200 gloves and shoes of mail appear in statues at Hereford and wall paintings at Claverly. From then on such additions are the norm.

The biggest change in medieval armor was from chain to plate, made feasible by the development of lighter steels around 1200. The poet of the Battle of Bouvines (1214) celebrated the power of armor. But it could go too far. The chronicler of Bannockburn (1314) bemoaned the death of England's hero, the earl of Gloucester, the weight of whose armor kept him helpless after he was thrown from his horse. The rise of plate can be traced in effigies and brasses. From around 1250 they show the addition of breast plate and in rough sequence, knee, elbow, finger, shoulder, arm, and leg pieces. A high point in cover and protection is exemplified by the armor of the Black Prince (d. 1376), depicted in his effigy at Canterbury. By then the separation of effective battle armor from the monstrosities donned for ceremony and tourney had already begun.

Fig. 14. Memorial brass of Sir Hugh Hastings (d. 1347), Elsing, Norfolk. After A.L. Poole (1958). Reprinted by permission of Oxford University Press.

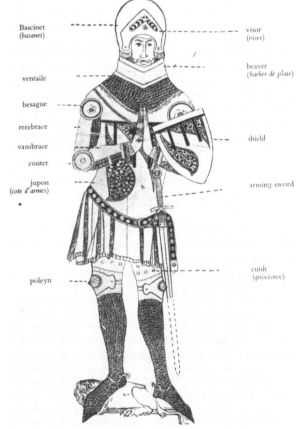

The helmet went through a parallel evolution. Initially a conical hat, usually with a nasal piece, it was replaced or at least supplemented by a variety of forms. A favorite in the 12th century was flat-topped and barrel-shaped, with full face covering, frequently of mail. Later versions had movable visors. In any case these helms, crowned with symbols of heraldry and plumes or crowns, were better suited to ceremonial use. A reversion to a simpler conical helm with some kind of face piece was much better for war.

These developments can be seen in the Bayeux Tapestry (the conical version with and without nasal), the Hereford statues (the primitive flat top with chain headware beneath), the brass of Sir Hugh Hastings at Elsing (a mid-14th-century conical helmet with hinged and pointed face piece; fig. 14), and, to take two late examples of war and tournament types, the effigy of Sir Oliver Ingham, also mid-14th-century, and the drawing of a judicial combat by John Rouse in the late 15th century. The barrel-shaped flat top survived to, or reappeared at, the end of the Middle Ages.

Footmen's armor was simpler and, where equivalent, later than that of knights. Mostly made of hard leather, there was often some minimal mail composition. The armor was capped with a plain helmet, round or conical in shape (basinet) or sallet (a metal cap). Though less protected, foot soldiers retained a flexibility of action that many knights must have envied.

Michael R. Powicke

Bibliography

Blair, Claude. *European Armour, circa 1066 to circa 1700.* London: Batsford, 1958 [best Europe-wide study, though thin on the historical evidence]; Hewitt, John. *Ancient Armour and Weapons in Europe.* 3 vols. Oxford: Henry & Parker, 1855–60; Mann, James. "Arms and Armour." In *Medieval England,* ed. Austin Lane Poole. Oxford: Clarendon, 1958, pp. 314–37; Nicolle, David C. *Arms and Armor of the Crusading Era, 1050–1350.* 2 vols. White Plains: Kraus, 1988 [good, but mostly restricted to visual materials].

See also Armies; Bayeux Tapestry; Castles; Ships

Ars moriendi (The Art of Dying)

A genre of religious instruction focusing on preparation for death. Religious treatises or parts of treatises on the "art" of dying well occur with some frequency in 14th- and 15th-century ME literature and are drawn from several distinct Latin and French sources. The earliest ME examples of the tradition occur as parts of the English translations of the *Somme le roi,* which includes a section on dying well (e.g., *The Ayenbite of Inwit, The Book of Vices and Virtues,* and Caxton's *Royal Book*). Parts of the *Horologium sapientiae* by Heinrich Suso (ca. 1296–1366) provided material for the late-14th-century *Scire mori* (*To Know How to Die*) and Thomas Hoccleve's rime royal *Ars sciendi mori* (ca. 1421–22).

Several early-15th-century ME works draw in whole or

in part on Anselm of Canterbury's *Admonitio morienti* (*Advice to the Dying*), including the prose *De visitacione infirmorum* (*On the Visitation of the Sick*), a poem of the same title by John Audelay (d. ca. 1426), and part of the anonymous *Craft of Dying*. The primary source for the *Craft of Dying*, however, is the *Tractatus* (or *Speculum*) *artis bene moriendi*, one of the major Latin works in the genre, based on Part 3 of Jean Gerson's *Opusculum tripartitum* (written in French and translated into Latin ca. 1400–10). Other ME works in the tradition include the early-15th-century *Disce mori*, in which an *ars moriendi* introduces a lengthy encyclopedia of general religious doctrine; a miscellany published by Caxton called *Ars moriendi* (1489–91); and *The Art and Craft to Know Well to Die*, Caxton's translation of a French *ars moriendi* based on the Latin *Tractatus* (1490).

The genre continued to flourish among humanist, Reformation, and Counter-Reformation writers, from Thomas Lupset (*The Way of Dying Well*, 1534) and Thomas More (*A Dialogue of Comfort*, 1534) to Jeremy Taylor (*The Rule and Exercises of Holy Dying*, 1651).

Lara Ruffolo

Bibliography

New *CBEL* 1:504–05; *Manual* 3:751, 796–97, 905, 943–44; 7:2259–61, 2263–64, 2275–76, 2360–65, 2475–79, 2482–83, 2503, 2565–68; Beaty, Nancy Lee. *The Craft of Dying: A Study in the Literary Tradition of the Ars Moriendi in England.* New Haven: Yale University Press, 1970; O'Connor, Mary Catharine. *The Art of Dying Well: The Development of the Ars Moriendi.* New York: Columbia University Press, 1942.

See also Anselm; Caxton; Hoccleve; Moral and Religious Instruction; Virtues and Vices, Books of

Art, Anglo-Saxon

Early Anglo-Saxon Art

The term "early Anglo-Saxon" describes the period ca. 600–793, roughly covering the years from the conversion to Christianity to the coming of the Vikings. This is the period that sees both the birth of English art and the birth of the English nation, although early Anglo-Saxon art is not characterized by a distinct, homogeneous style but is rather a blanket term covering a variety of changing styles and artistic and cultural influences. It has often been said that early Anglo-Saxon art is a visual expression of power and status for both institutions (the church) and individuals (nobility), but in this it is no different from art elsewhere in early-medieval Europe. If anything can be said to characterize art for the entire 200-year span, it is its surface orientation and its multivalence.

The Anglo-Saxons loved glittering, colorful, highly decorated surfaces in all media. Manuscripts, metalwork, and sculpture all display *horror vacui* (literally, a fear of empty space). The Sutton Hoo jewelry, the Lindisfarne Gospels (figs. 84–85: see LINDISFARNE GOSPELS), the Franks Casket (fig. 63: see FRANKS CASKET), and the Bewcastle Cross (fig. 74: see HIGH CROSSES) are all examples of objects on or in which a rich complexity of interlace, animal ornament, and abstract or foliate patterns cover as much of the surface as possible. Manuscripts and metalwork in particular display a love of rich and shimmering colors, the polychromy that is such a prominent part of the 8th-century "Tara-Lindisfarne" style. Metalwork also exhibits an awareness of the effects of light. The stamped gold foils embedded beneath the surfaces of the garnets on so much of the jewelry from the early period serve to reflect and refract light, to add brightness to the stones, and to break up the surface of the object. The love of surface ornament continues in English art well into the modern era.

The complexity of surface design that characterizes Anglo-Saxon art is paralleled by the complexity of its symbolism. Powerful images are layered one upon the other to produce, in effect, super symbols on both pagan and Christian objects. On the Sutton Hoo gold buckle (fig. 137: see SUTTON HOO), for example, images of aggressive creatures—serpents, birds of prey—cover the entire top surface. The buckle becomes both a symbol of warrior power and an apotropaic object designed to ward off evil and protect its wearer. The fact that the buckle may also have served as a reliquary (almost certainly pagan) would only have added to its power.

This same layering of symbolism appears in a Christian context on the cross carpet pages of such manuscripts as the Lindisfarne Gospels (BL Cotton Nero D.iv), dated ca. 698, and in the sculptural program of the 8th-century Ruthwell Cross (figs. 111–14; see RUTHWELL CROSS). In the Lindisfarne Gospels animal ornament and crosses combine with, or are embedded in, other crosses to form complex and powerful symbols that enshrine and protect the written word. On the primary faces of the Ruthwell Cross scenes of Christian doctrine are embedded within the monumental stone cross and then glossed with Latin inscriptions—adding a further level of significance to their meaning. The narrow sides of the cross are carved with Mediterranean-derived inhabited vinescroll ornament, turning the whole into a monumental tree-of-life whose meaning is further elucidated by the runic poem inscribed around these panels.

There are many different artistic and cultural influences at work in the early period, including native British art, Celtic and Irish art, and the art of Scandinavia, the Mediterranean, Byzantium, and the European continent. There is also no single center of Anglo-Saxon art but rather a variety of regions producing works in a variety of styles. In the early 7th century the south of England, particularly the kingdom of Kent, was home to an especially fine school of metalworking. Kentish metalwork includes some of the most famous pieces of Anglo-Saxon jewelry, such as the Sarre and Kingston Down brooches. The Sarre Brooch is gilt-bronze inlaid with white shell, garnets, and panels of gold filigree. The Kingston Down Brooch is gold inlaid with blue glass, white shell, garnets, and panels of zoomorphic filigree. These grand brooches, worn singly, reflect both Frankish fashion and the polychrome style of Frankish jewelry, although the Anglo-Saxon color range is more limited, characterized particularly by a love of the red and gold color combination. Kent's dominant role in trade between England and Frankish Gaul is no doubt largely responsible for the profound Frankish influence on the art of the region. Both the Sarre and Kingston Down brooches are decorated with a complex design of multiple crosses, though it is unclear whether this was meant to have any Christian significance or was simply meant as a fine ornamental design. Perhaps it was both.

Looking at manuscripts, Christian content is unequivocal. With Christianity came literacy, the written word, the book, and the need for instruction—much of it visual. One of the two great early centers of Anglo-Saxon manuscript production was the monastic complex at Canterbury in Kent. Christianity in the south of England was a Mediterranean import, and Canterbury manuscripts do show a marked Mediterranean influence, probably via such manuscripts as the 6th-century St. Augustine's Gospels (Cambridge, Corpus Christi College 286). In 8th-century Canterbury manuscripts like the Vespasian Psalter and the Stockholm Codex Aureus (BL Cotton Vespasian A.i and Stockholm, Royal Library A.135; figs. 141 and 133: see VESPASIAN PSALTER and STOCKHOLM GOSPELS), the relative three-dimensionality of the figures and the spaces they inhabit as well as the modeling of faces and forms are clearly derived from Mediterranean prototypes, though the forms themselves have become flattened and patterned, a feature particularly noticeable in the drapery. The influence of Hiberno-Saxon art is also evident in the trumpet spirals and peltae (shield-shapes) that decorate the arches around the figures, as well as in the elaborate treatment of the text. The Vespasian Psalter contains one of the earliest historiated initials (fol. 53), an insular, if not Anglo-Saxon, invention.

Both the text and miniatures of the Codex Aureus show the increasing influence of Hiberno-Saxon art, probably via Northumbrian centers, such as Lindisfarne. As in Hiberno-Saxon manuscripts the Incarnation page of the Codex Aureus has been picked out for special attention, and the text is embedded in flat panels of gold or pigment, as if it were metalwork. The book becomes, in effect, a precious relic.

A number of pages (e.g., fols. 16 and 131) display crosses surrounding discrete areas of text, the two worked in combinations of gold, silver, and colored inks, set off against a purple-stained background. Ultimately these patterns derive from the *carmina figurata* of Constantine's court poet Porfyrius, but the scribe-artist has given them a distinctly Anglo-Saxon twist. The gold and red (or purple) color combination is familiar from Kentish metalwork, but here it takes on a new meaning. The gold cross stained with purple is encountered again in both the Ruthwell poem and in the later *Dream of the Rood*, as well as on the 11th-century Brussels reliquary cross. It seems to have been a particularly powerful and long-lasting image for the Anglo-Saxons, calling up images of death and life, triumph and tragedy, and making the cross, once again, a multivalent tree-of-life. It is also interesting that while the color purple in Anglo-Saxon art certainly indicates a prestige object—as it did throughout the Middle Ages—it also seems to have had more of a sacramental symbolism than a royal one. This will change in the later period.

The lavish use of gold in southern manuscripts distinguishes them from manuscripts of the second great locus of book production, Northumbria. Today we associate these impressive works with the monasteries of Lindisfarne and Wearmouth-Jarrow, though Hartlepool, Whitby, and many of the lesser houses no doubt also produced impressive work. The northern houses were every bit as cosmopolitan as Canterbury. Their abbots and abbesses are recorded as traveling frequently to visit Rome and continental foundations. Hild planned to visit Chelles, while Benedict Biscop brought panels painted with biblical figures back to Wearmouth from Rome. Stained glass, surely an imported craft, has come from Jarrow, and the 9th-century poem *De abbatibus* records the importation of an altar from Ireland to an anonymous cell of Lindisfarne.

Lindisfarne itself was a crossroads for influences from both the Columban west and Rome. A Columban (i.e., Irish) foundation, it eventually went over to Roman practice at the Synod of Whitby (664). It seems to have been the center of production for objects in a variety of media. The complexity of the carpet pages of the Lindisfarne Gospels has already been discussed. The evangelist portraits are equally interesting, both for their combination of the native taste for patterns of line and color with ultimately Mediterranean figural models and also for their combination of Greek and Latin language. The name of each evangelist is written in Greek, while each symbol is named in Latin (e.g., *Hagios mattheus, imago hominis*).

This interesting combination of languages may be characteristic of the objects and monuments associated with Lindisfarne. It appears again on a series of commemorative "name stones" from the monastic cemetery. The name stones all display central crosses of varying design, while names are carved in the four quadrants. On at least five of the stones one name is carved in runes, the other in roman letters. In at least two cases the same name is repeated. The reasons for the practice are unclear, but it is certainly indicative of the multilingual nature of the monastery. The Ruthwell Cross has also been associated with Lindisfarne, and its combination of Anglo-Saxon runic and Roman inscriptions has already been noted.

All of these monasteries, Canterbury, Lindisfarne, and Wearmouth-Jarrow, would have been elaborately decorated with architectural sculpture and painted plaster, only traces of which now survive. Churches would also have housed precious liturgical vessels, altar cloths, and other furnishings.

Two great schools of sculpture emerged in Mercia in the 8th century, one in eastern, the other in southwestern Mercia. In the east sculpture was primarily architectural. The 8th-century architectural sculpture at Breedon-on-the-Hill in Leicestershire (figs. 134–36: see STONEWORK AS ECCLESIASTICAL ORNAMENT) is an early and prime example of the work of this school. The Breedon sculpture includes friezes of plant scroll, some densely inhabited by a throng of battling men and monstrous beasts, many of which look forward to the grotesque creatures of the later medieval period. (The same is true of such 8th-century manuscripts as the Barberini Gospels [Vatican, Biblioteca Apostolica Barberini lat. 570], itself possibly produced in Mercia.) Compared with the monumental, iconic figures of the Ruthwell or Bewcastle crosses, these Mercian creatures exhibit an agility and expression new to Anglo-Saxon sculpture. The Breedon sculptures, as much of Anglo-Saxon sculpture, were probably originally painted, and the bright colors would certainly have added to the sprightly action of the scenes. The arrangements of single and paired animals included in these scenes are also characteristic of Mercian manuscripts, such as the Barberini Gospels or the Book of Cerne (CUL Ll.I.10), as well as of metalwork. There are also examples of figural sculpture at Breedon, which, though they may be of lesser quality, display the same lively expression seen in the friezes.

In southwestern Mercia high crosses tend to take precedence over architectural sculpture. Here, too, single and paired beasts, especially beasts caught up in plant-scroll ornament, are particularly popular. In both Mercian schools this abundance of creatures may be meant to represent the fertility of life in the Christian world.

In metalwork silver begins to take precedence over gold in the Mercian period, and an interest in dark-light effects—chipcarving, niello against silver, openwork decoration—replaces the polychromy of earlier metalwork. Animal ornament remains popular, but the elaborately interlaced animals of the 7th century give way to heraldic creatures often displayed against a background of fine interlace. The late-8th-century linked pins from the River Witham (Lincolnshire) or the early-9th-century brooches from the Pentney hoard (Norfolk) are fine examples of this style.

Whether we are dealing with brooches or architectural sculpture, the art of the early Anglo-Saxon period is aristocratic, designed to enhance the power of church and state, the two more often than not working hand-in-glove. We know that women, such as Hild at Whitby or, at a later period, Æthelflæd in Mercia, had a powerful role in shaping the emerging church and nation; yet they are all but invisible in the material record. There are few references to women artists in any media, and, while we know that the Anglo-Saxons were renowned for their textiles and needlework—produced primarily by women—few examples survive. This invisibility is undoubtedly due in large part to the Christianity that ironically gave women like Hild a power base. It may also be due to the biases of chroniclers, kings, and scholars throughout the centuries.

Later Anglo-Saxon Art

The later Anglo-Saxon period covers roughly the 10th and 11th centuries. The art of this period displays a more homogeneous style than that of the early Anglo-Saxon or Viking Age periods. The influence of Scandinavia and Carolingian France is still strong but is now joined by the influence of Ottonian Germany. A significant number of elements of earlier Anglo-Saxon style do also continue and in some cases are fully developed in this later period—chief among them being the use of rich patterns of line and color, the emphasis on surface effects, and an interest in grotesque, comic, and marginal imagery. These native features are combined with foreign influences to produce an art so rich and original that the period has come to be known as the "golden age" of Anglo-Saxon art.

The 10th century ushers in a renaissance in most aspects of Anglo-Saxon life, including art. Alfred's successors gradu-

ally conquered the areas previously held by the Scandinavians, a flourishing court life appeared, and the church gained new vigor under the Benedictine Reform. The sudden burst in the amount of and variety of subjects depicted in architectural sculpture is generally linked to the decoration (or redecoration) of reformed churches. Most significant is an increased interest in the depiction of figural subjects, as evidenced by the Romsey Crucifixion scenes (fig. 110: see ROMSEY ROODS) or the Bristol Harrowing of Hell; in style and subject both have analogues in contemporary manuscripts. The patterned folds and lively poses of the figures in the Bristol relief are close to those of the figures in the Tiberius Psalter Harrowing of Hell (BL Cotton Tiberius C.vii, fol. 14) or the ivory baptism of Christ in the British Museum (MLA 1870, 8–11, 1). While the Bristol figures do not display quite the expression or energetic lines of these latter works, they do display a new sense of classicism ultimately due to continental influence.

The late Anglo-Saxon "renaissance" is most profoundly noticeable on portable objects, such as manuscripts, metalwork, and ivory carving. Some of the earliest pieces to display the new style appear in the late 9th century, the Alfred Jewel (fig. 1: see ALFRED AND MINSTER LOVELL JEWELS) and Fuller Brooch (fig. 65: see FULLER BROOCH) being prominent examples. Both objects display evidence of interest in a new, more intellectually oriented type of symbolism. To the old repertoire of apotropaic animal ornament and abstract religious symbols (cross, fish, etc.) later Anglo-Saxon artists add personification. The Fuller Brooch is decorated with personifications of the five senses surrounded by a border containing symbols of the human, animal, avian, and vegetable kingdoms. The central figure on the Fuller Brooch is a personification of Sight. The enamel figure decorating the main face of the Alfred Jewel may also represent Sight; alternatively it may represent Christ, or even Alfred. Other new iconographic types include the Beast-Mouth of Hell, the disappearing Christ, and the rough-hewn cross, all Anglo-Saxon innovations.

The new interest in the human figure is significant and undoubtedly due to continental influences brought in with the Reform, combined perhaps with a growing concern for the contemporary world of men and women. This is also the period that sees the growth of narrative (an interest in visual storytelling), "scientific" books, the beginnings of portraiture (of a very general kind), and the development of a new artistic interest in the royal court, if not a court school of art.

The two great schools of late Anglo-Saxon manuscript illumination are located at Winchester and Canterbury (although the attribution of so many manuscripts to these two centers alone has been called into question). While neither style is confined to the city for which it is named, both cities are major centers of artistic production.

The Winchester style is strongly connected to the royal court. King Edgar appears in one of the earliest Winchester manuscripts, the New Minster Charter (BL Cotton Vespasian A.viii) of ca. 966 (fig. 101: see NEW MINSTER CHARTER), while portraits of Cnut and Emma grace the New Minster Liber Vitae (BL Stowe 944) from the 1020s. The most famous manuscript of the late 10th century, the Benedictional of

Æthelwold (BL Add. 49598; fig. 26: see BENEDICTIONAL OF ÆTHELWOLD) has also been shown to contain significant royal imagery. The Winchester style is characterized by lively, expressive figures, rich pigments, color washes and color outline drawings, a profuse use of gold, and above all by its fleshy acanthus ornament, derived ultimately from Carolingian art. The style is not limited to manuscripts and can also be seen in the rich textiles commissioned for St. Cuthbert's shrine, as well as in ivory sculpture, such as the Liverpool Nativity panel (Liverpool, Merseyside County Museum Mayer Collection M 8060) or the Nativity panel in the British Museum (MLA 1974, 10–2, 1), both from the second half of the 10th century.

Movement, color, and pattern continue to develop in late Winchester- style manuscripts, such as the early-11th-century "Missal" of Robert of Jumièges (Rouen, Bibliothèque Municipale Y.6). Here lively figures are set against a background of billows and streams of color, built up from layers of multicolored lines and washes. The figures themselves are fine examples of late Anglo-Saxon draughtsmanship. Acanthus flies out from the gold trellis borders, giving the impression of a divine wind blowing across the page.

Canterbury manuscripts also have royal associations. King Edgar appears again on fol. 2v of the *Regularis concordia* (BL Cotton Tiberius A.iii) produced at Christ Church, Canterbury, in the second half of the 11th century. Indeed the role of the court in the monastic reform, as well as in the patronage and development of Anglo-Saxon art, should be borne in mind. Canterbury School manuscripts are characterized by dynamic outline drawings, some in color, some in simple black ink. Carolingian influence is clearly evident in such works as the Harley Psalter (fig. 71: see HARLEY PSALTER), a copy of the Carolingian Utrecht Psalter; however, the artists of the Harley Psalter transform the monochrome drawings of their model into brilliant color (as well as adapting many of the scenes to conform to contemporary tastes and circumstances).

Canterbury itself exhibits a profound interest in usable, instructional books, evidenced by such works as the late-10th-century copy of Aldhelm's *De virginitate* (London, Lambeth Palace Library 200); St. Dunstan's *Classbook* (Bodl. Auct. fol. 4. 32, a composite volume of 9th- through 11th-century date); or the *Psychomachia* of Prudentius (BL Cotton Cleopatra C.viii), a composite 10th- to 12th-century manuscript. Also attributed to Canterbury are the two great examples of late Anglo-Saxon vernacular manuscripts, the "Cædmon" Genesis (Bodl. Junius 11), illuminated ca. 1000, and the illustrated Hexateuch (BL Cotton Claudius B.iv), from the second quarter of the 11th century. The expanded visual narratives of these manuscripts are particularly interesting because they are not always in accord with what we read in the text. In the *Psychomachia*, for example, the text tells us that the combatants are monsters and armored warriors, but by and large we are shown images of warring women dressed in Anglo-Saxon fashion.

The verbal and visual dialogue created in these manuscripts is also found in metalwork, most notably on the Brussels Reliquary Cross (Brussels, Cathedral of St. Michael), produced in the early 11th century. The primary face of the cross has been lost, but the back is decorated with the Agnus Dei and symbols of the evangelists. A central inscription reads *Drahmal me worhte* (Drahmal made me), while a second inscription around the edges of the cross reads *Rod is min nama geo ic ricne cyning bær byfigynde blode bestemed* (Cross is my name; once, trembling and drenched with blood, I bore the mighty King). It goes on to state that Æthelmær and Æthelwold had the cross made for Christ and their brother Ælfric. The inscribed words uttered by the cross almost certainly connected the apocalyptic imagery of the rear panel with a Crucifixion on the missing front. The presence of a similar inscription on the 8th-century Ruthwell Cross indicates that the dynamic relationship between image and object (and viewer) does have precedents.

The new interest in science can be seen in such manuscripts as the *Herbal* produced at Winchester and now part of a composite 11th- to 13th-century manuscript (BL Cotton Vitellius C.iii), or the copy of *The Marvels of the East* illuminated at Canterbury in the second quarter of the 11th century and part of a collection of mainly secular scientific texts (BL Cotton Tiberius B.v). While not scientific texts in the modern sense, such works do combine genuine classical scientific studies with early-medieval stories and legends to produce a semifactual pseudo-science. The illustrations, possibly intended to lend a note of authority by making specific plants, animals, or monsters easier to recognize, are also highly entertaining, particularly in *The Marvels of the East*. The latter manuscript can, however, also be highly disturbing. Both text and illustrations tell the story of the barbarous peoples and monsters that inhabit the East, the area outside the borders of the western European civilized world. In many of the illustrations the bodies of the creatures overlap the frame of the miniature (fols. 82v, 85v, 86). Indeed the justly famous *Blemmyae* on fol. 82 stands on the lower register of the frame and grips the sides with its hands as if trapped but trying to escape. The dynamic tension this creates has been noted by many authors, but it is also threatening. These creatures cross boundaries and stand between our world and the world of the book, defying the neat ordering of the world expressed in such poems as *Maxims I*, *Maxims II*, and *The Order of the World*, or in the domesticated agricultural scenes of the calendar in the same manuscript.

Late Anglo-Saxon monsters and marginal images can, however, also be delightfully whimsical in both religious and secular contexts. The dynamic figures inhabiting the borders of the early-11th-century Bury Psalter (Vatican, Biblioteca Apostolica Reg. lat. 12) or the creatures that crawl their way across the surface of the mid-11th-century ivory pen case in the British Museum (MLA 1870, 8–11) are fine examples of both the Anglo-Saxon taste for grotesque monsters and the increasing interest in marginal space. Ultimately both have their roots in earlier Anglo-Saxon works, such as the 8th-century Barberini Gospels (Vatican, Biblioteca Apostolica Barberini lat. 570) or the carved stone friezes from Breedon-on-the-Hill, Leicestershire; however, the new energy of both creatures and compositions looks forward to the fabulous monsters of

Romanesque works like the Lincoln frieze (fig. 11: see ARCHITECTURE AND ARCHITECTURAL SCULPTURE, ROMANESQUE) or the Kilpeck doorway (fig. 76: see KILPECK).

Catherine E. Karkov

Bibliography

GENERAL

Brown, Gerard Baldwin. *The Arts in Early England*. 6 vols. London: Murray, 1903–37; Cramp, Rosemary. *Corpus of Anglo-Saxon Stone Sculpture in England*. Vol. 1: *County Durham and Northumberland*. London: Oxford University Press, 1984; Cramp, Rosemary, and Richard N. Bailey. *Corpus of Anglo-Saxon Stone Sculpture*. Vol. 2: *Cumberland, Westmorland and Lancashire North-of-the-Sands*. London: Oxford University Press, 1988; Dodwell, C.R. *Anglo-Saxon Art: A New Perspective*. Manchester: Manchester University Press, 1982; Lang, James. *Corpus of Anglo-Saxon Stone Sculpture*. Vol. 3: *York and Eastern Yorkshire*. London: Oxford University Press, 1991; Wilson, David M. *Anglo-Saxon Ornamental Metalwork, 700–1100, in the British Museum: Catalogue of Antiquities of the Later Saxon Period*. Vol. 1. London: Trustees of the British Museum, 1964; Wilson, David M. *Anglo-Saxon Art: From the Seventh Century to the Norman Conquest*. London: Thames & Hudson, 1984.

EARLY ANGLO-SAXON ART

Alexander, J.J.G. *Insular Manuscripts 6th–9th Century*. A Survey of Manuscripts Illuminated in the British Isles 1, ed. J.J.G. Alexander. London: Harvey Miller, 1978; Cather, Sharon, David Park, and Paul Williamson. *Early Medieval Wall-Painting and Painted Sculpture in England*. BAR Brit. Ser. 216. Oxford: BAR, 1990; Cramp, Rosemary. "The Artistic Influence of Lindisfarne within Northumbria." In *St. Cuthbert, His Cult and His Community to AD 1200*, ed. Gerald Bonner, David Rollason, and Clare Stancliffe. Woodbridge: Boydell, 1989, pp. 213–28; Fell, Christine with Cecilly Clark and Elizabeth Williams. *Women in Anglo-Saxon England and the Impact of 1066*. Bloomington: Indiana University Press, 1984; Henderson, George. *From Durrow to Kells: The Insular Gospel Books 650–800*. London: Thames & Hudson, 1987; Jessup, R. *Anglo-Saxon Jewellery*. London: Faber & Faber, 1950; Kendrick, T.D. *Anglo-Saxon Art to A.D. 900*. London: Methuen, 1938; Leeds, E.T. *Early Anglo-Saxon Art and Archaeology*. Oxford: Clarendon, 1936; Speake, G. *Anglo-Saxon Animal Art and Its Germanic Background*. Oxford: Clarendon, 1980; Webster, Leslie, and Janet Backhouse, eds. *The Making of England: Anglo-Saxon Art and Culture AD 600–900*. London: British Museum, 1991.

LATER ANGLO-SAXON ART

Alexander, Jonathan J.G. "The Benedictional of St. Æthelwold and Anglo-Saxon Illumination of the Reform Period." In *Tenth-Century Studies: Essays in Commemoration of the Millennium of the Council of Winchester and Regularis concordia*, ed. David Parsons. London: Phillimore, 1975, pp. 169–83, 241–45; Backhouse, Janet, Derek H. Turner, and Leslie Webster, eds. *The Golden Age of Anglo-Saxon Art 966–1066*. London: British Museum, 1984; Beckwith, John. *Ivory Carvings in Early Medieval England*. London: Harvey Miller, 1972; Broderick, Herbert R. "Some Attitudes toward the Frame in Anglo-Saxon Manuscripts of the Tenth and Eleventh Centuries." *Artibus et Historiae* 5 (1982): 31–42; Deshman, Robert. "*Christus rex et magi reges*: Kingship and Christology in Ottonian and Anglo-Saxon Art." *Frühmittelalterliche Studien* 10 (1976): 367–405; Friedman, John Block. *The Monstrous Races in Medieval Art and Thought*. Cambridge: Harvard University Press, 1981; Gameson, Richard. *The Role of Art in the Late Anglo-Saxon Church*. Oxford: Clarendon, 1995; Kendrick, T.D. *Late Saxon and Viking Art*. London: Methuen, 1949; Ohlgren, Thomas H. *Anglo-Saxon Textual Illustration: Photographs of Sixteen Manuscripts with Descriptions and Index*. Kalamazoo: Medieval Institute, 1992; Temple, Elżbieta. *Anglo-Saxon Manuscripts 900–1066*. A Survey of Manuscripts Illuminated in the British Isles 2, ed. J.J.G. Alexander. London: Harvey Miller, 1976.

See also Alfred and Minster Lovell Jewels; Anglo-Saxon Old Testament Narrative Illustration; Architecture, Anglo-Saxon; Art, Anglo-Saxon: Celtic Influences, Classical Influences; Benedictional of Æthelwold; Bestiaries; Bristol Harrowing of Hell; Fuller Brooch; Harley Psalter; High Crosses; Ivory Carving, Anglo-Saxon; Lindisfarne Gospels; Manuscript Illumination, Anglo-Saxon; Metalwork, Anglo-Saxon; Psalters, Anglo-Saxon; Romsey Roods; Ruthwell Cross; Scientific Manuscripts, Early; Sculpture, Anglo-Saxon; Stockholm Gospels; Textiles, Anglo-Saxon; "Winchester School"

Art, Anglo-Saxon: Celtic Influences

The confluence of Anglo-Saxon and Celtic artistic traditions in 7th- and 8th-century England is one of the major subthemes in the study of insular art. The recent reassessment, based on archaeological research, of the nature of the arrival of the Anglo-Saxons in England, from armed invasion to gradual settlement, has necessitated a reevaluation of the relationship between the Anglo-Saxons and their British Celtic neighbors and subjects. Further, the role of the Irish church in the conversion of the Anglo-Saxons to Christianity provided a conduit for the influence of Ireland on the developing art of early-medieval England, especially north of the Humber.

Much of the early influence from the various insular Celtic cultures on pre-Christian Anglo-Saxon art is observed in metalwork discovered as high-status Anglo-Saxon grave goods, the evidence of production for which, however, is found primarily at Celtic sites in western and northern Britain and in Ireland. David Longley's study of the distribution of type H penannular brooches and group 1 openwork escutcheons indicates a relatively long-term trade from Celtic and Pictish Scotland into eastern England. Michael Ryan has suggested that the enameled escutcheons of the largest hanging bowl found in Mound 1 at Sutton Hoo were probably made in the Irish Midlands. They could have arrived via trade, but they may also have arrived as diplomatic gifts. The influence of such objects is seen in the formation of local taste for particular ornamental techniques: *millefiori*, a popular technique in Irish Midlands enamelwork but not common in Anglian metalwork, was used in the local Sutton Hoo workshop, probably under the influence of imports like the hanging bowl, although the technique itself was most probably learned from a craftsman trained in a Celtic milieu.

Although the British Celtic and Anglo-Saxon cultures were in contact during Anglo-Saxon settlement and hegemony in England, demonstrable points of continuity in the secular realm are rare. The hanging bowls, for example, traveled from Celtic to Anglo-Saxon milieux by trade or gift, but their functions may well not have been continuous between the two cultures. In the British Celtic context they may have served as Christian liturgical vessels and/or as washbasins, as part of the civilities of secular hospitality; in pagan Anglo-Saxon graves they may have been construed as part of a banqueting assemblage for the deceased or, alternatively, used to hold cremation burials or food offerings to the dead, such as the onions and crabapples at Forddown. However, there does seem to have been some continuity in the selection of ceremonial and political centers; the Anglo-Saxon royal residence at Yeavering occupies the site of an earlier British complex.

Irish influence is clearly evident in the development of Anglo-Saxon manuscript illumination, especially in centers under the strong influence of Iona, established in 565 as a center of Irish missionary activity in Scotland and later active in the conversion of the northern Anglian kingdom of Northumbria through the establishment of Lindisfarne. The use of enlarged initials, often followed by a series of letters gradually diminishing in scale (insular diminution), is found in early manuscripts from Ireland and Irish missions on the Continent, such as Bobbio (Milan, Ambrosiana S.45.sup., Jerome, *Commentary on Isaiah*, p. 2; probably also from Bobbio, Ambrosiana D.23.sup., Orosius, *Chronicon*, fol. 2). This convention later emerges as a standard decorative technique in the products of northern English scriptoria, as in the Lindisfarne Gospels (figs. 84–85: see LINDISFARNE GOSPELS). Paleography and text recensions also demonstrate connections across the Irish sea. The documentary record indicates a considerable traffic of scholars traveling to Ireland in pursuit of higher education, with a strong emphasis on the classical tradition; Bishop Aldhelm of Sherborne's correspondent Ehfrid spent six years there, and King Aldfrith of Northumbria was also a scholar in Ireland during his predecessor Ecgfrith's reign. Despite the hostility generated by the decision of the Synod of Whitby in 664 in favor of the Roman church's calculation of the date of Easter and preferred shape of the clerical tonsure over the conflicting Irish traditions, these links continued into the 8th century. Given the mobility of manuscripts and the documented movement of clergy in both directions across the Irish Sea, there remains considerable controversy

over the origin of particular manuscripts, as, for example, the Echternach Gospels, in Irish or Anglo-Saxon centers or in their continental missionary offshoots. The generic term "insular" is often used to refer to the art of England and Ireland in the late 7th and 8th centuries so as to indicate the extent of contacts and affinities of style across the Irish Sea.

Carol Neuman de Vegvar

Bibliography

Haseloff, Günther. "Fragments of a Hanging Bowl from Bekesbourne, Kent, and Some Ornamental Problems." *Medieval Archaeology* 2 (1958): 72–103; Henry, Françoise. *Irish Art in the Early Christian Period (to 800 A.D.).* Ithaca: Cornell University Press, 1965; Longley, David. *Hanging-Bowls, Penannular Brooches, and the Anglo-Saxon Connexion.* BAR 22. Oxford: BAR, 1975; Neuman de Vegvar, Carol L. *The Northumbrian Renaissance: A Study in the Transmission of Style.* Selinsgrove: Susquehanna University Press, 1987; Nordenfalk, Carl. "Before the Book of Durrow." *Acta Archaeologica* 18 (1947): 141–74; Ryan, Michael. "The Sutton Hoo Ship-Burial and Ireland: Some Celtic Perspectives." In *Sutton Hoo: Fifty Years After*, ed. Robert T. Farrell and Carol L. Neuman de Vegvar. Oxford, Ohio: American Early Medieval Studies, 1992, pp. 83–116.

See also Art, Anglo-Saxon; Art, Pictish; High Crosses; Lindisfarne Gospels; Manuscript Illumination, Anglo-Saxon; Metalwork, Anglo-Saxon; Sculpture, Anglo-Saxon; Sutton Hoo; Yeavering

Art, Anglo-Saxon: Classical Influences

The classical influence on Anglo-Saxon art involves the Christian inheritance of Greco-Roman concepts reflected in the art of the late-antique world of Rome and Constantinople, which was introduced into England with the arrival of the Christian missions from Rome in the late 6th century. The subsequent conversion of the Anglo-Saxons resulted in a constant importation, primarily from Italy and Gaul, of classical art in the form of a variety of portable items, such as paintings, illuminated manuscripts, figured textiles, decorated glass, carved ivory and metalwork bookcovers and reliquaries, and even late-imperial coinage. These artifacts were often the genuine products of late antiquity; alternatively they could be artifacts inspired by subsequent conscious revivals of a classical inheritance, such as that which motivated Charlemagne in Carolingian France.

There is the further possibility that standing Roman structures surviving in mainland Britain also had a classicizing influence on Anglo-Saxon art. There is evidence—for example, in Bede's writings—that this material was understood by the Anglo-Saxons to be the product of the imperial world, and that it was reused by them in some of the earliest ecclesiastical contexts, as at Hexham, Northumberland. What is clear is that the classical influence, whether direct or indirect, on Anglo-Saxon art lay in both the introduction of new monument forms and in the motifs used to decorate them.

Anglo-Saxon stone sarcophagi are clear examples of a classical funerary art influencing the production of a monument form new to the Anglo-Saxons. A number of these monuments survive from the late 8th or early 9th century onward at ecclesiastical centers in Mercia (at St. Alkmund's Derby, Bakewell, and Wirksworth, in Derbyshire), and Northumbria (at Durham).

Another Anglo-Saxon monument type inspired by late antiquity is the round stone column (probably surmounted with a cross) that was produced in apparent imitation of the triumphal columns of imperial Rome. The remains of one such monument of 9th-century date survive from Reculver, Kent, and others are found at Dewsbury and Masham (Yorkshire); from a later date the 10th-century columnar shaft at Wolverhampton still stands *in situ*.

On a smaller scale classical influences also lie behind the construction of carved ivory reliquary boxes, such as the possibly late-7th-century Franks Casket (fig. 63: see FRANKS CASKET) from Northumbria, and the 8th-century Gandersheim Casket from southern England. These represent imitations of late-imperial reliquaries, such as the 4th-century Brescia Casket, whose form, in turn, was based on the large-scale sarcophagi.

It is the decoration of these and other artifacts, such as the manuscripts, that shows how widespread the influence of late-antique art was in Anglo-Saxon England. The double registers of closely packed figures on the Wirksworth sarcophagus cover, for instance, closely resemble the decoration of the early Christian Italo-Gallic sarcophagi, while the layout of the carving in registers encircling the Masham and Wolverhampton columns is reminiscent of classical triumphal columns.

The strong influence of classical art is also clear in the figural decoration of Anglo-Saxon stonework. Many of the Northumbrian crosses, such as those from Rothbury (fig. 15), Bewcastle (fig. 74: see HIGH CROSSES), and Ruthwell (figs. 111–14: see RUTHWELL CROSS), or Easby, Otley, and Collingham (in Yorkshire), are filled with clean-shaven, short-haired figures with well-modeled faces, often presented in semiprofile, wearing the classical toga and pallium. It is a figural style closely based on that which flourished in Italian art of the 5th and early 6th centuries.

This art also influenced the iconography of Anglo-Saxon carving, although overtly "classical" scenes, such as the Sack of Jerusalem and Romulus and Remus featured on the Franks Casket (and the 8th-century Larling plaque from Norfolk), are rare. More common is the influence of early Christian iconography seen in the fragmentary Ascension scene on the Reculver column, where Christ is depicted walking in profile and reaching toward heaven. This iconographic type was current in Italian art during the 4th and 5th centuries.

Such early Christian art has long been argued as having inspired the iconography of the Ruthwell and Bewcastle crosses, and its influence can also be seen on the remains of the late-8th- or early-9th-century Northumbrian cross from Rothbury. Here figures in the cross-head present attributes to Christ that were directly inspired by the symbols of power depicted on late-consular diptychs, while at the top of the

Fig. 15. Christ in Majesty, Rothbury cross shaft. Currently in the Museum of Antiquities, University of Newcastle-upon-Tyne. Courtesy of the Museum of Antiquities, University of Newcastle and the Society of Antiquaries of Newcastle upon Tyne.

cross-shaft was a scene of the Raising of Lazarus showing Martha in an exaggeratedly crouched position and Lazarus with his eyes closed; it is a scene inspired by a late-4th- or early-5th-century iconographic type from Italy. In 9th-century Mercian sculpture the same classical influences were available. On a cross-shaft at Sandbach (Cheshire) a depiction of the Nativity showing only the ox, ass, and angel adoring the Christ Child set in an ornate crib is clearly linked to an iconographic type found on 4th-century sarcophagi in Rome.

The direct influence of classical art is seen clearly in the decoration of Anglo-Saxon manuscripts, such as the late-7th-century Codex Amiatinus (Florence, Biblioteca Medicea-Laurenziana Amiatinus I; fig. 143: see WEARMOUTH-JARROW AND THE CODEX AMIATINUS) and the ca. 700 prototype of the 9th-century Antwerp Sedulius (Antwerp, Museum Plantin-Moretus M.17.4), both apparently inspired by 6th-century Italian works. The figures illustrated in these manuscripts are attired in classical garb and described in a naturalistic manner, often highlighted and treated with a sense of perspective. The classical nature of this figural style is clear when compared with that found, for instance, in the Lindisfarne Gospels (BL Cotton Nero D.iv) or the Durham Cassiodorus (Durham, Cathedral Library B.II.30), where the figural style is characterized by linear patterning with flat areas of color, and little attempt at naturalism and perspective. However, even these "insular" figures reveal the influence of late-antique art in their facial features and classical garments.

Yet it is not simply the figural style adopted in these manuscripts that reveals the influence of classical art. Much of their iconography was also inspired by late-antique types. The illustration of David the Psalmist in the mid-8th-century Vespasian Psalter (BL Cotton Vespasian A.i, fol. 30v; fig. 141: see VESPASIAN PSALTER) for instance, has its ultimate source in imperial courtly art of the late-antique world, in representations of the emperor surrounded by his courtiers. Such imperial art (probably through intermediary Carolingian imitations) also inspired the pages of gold-and-silver-inscribed purple-dyed vellum found in many of the more deluxe Anglo-Saxon manuscripts (e.g., BL Royal I.E.vi); it was also ultimately responsible for the stately portrayals of the evangelists in such manuscripts as the Stockholm Codex Aureus (Stockholm, Royal Library A.135).

Thus, while much of the earlier Christian art of Anglo-Saxon England was directly influenced by the form and decoration of late-antique artifacts imported from the Mediterranean world, some was also influenced by artifacts that were themselves the products of conscious classical revivals. The influence of such imitations on Anglo-Saxon art became more pronounced during the late 9th to 11th centuries, when much of the art, particularly that produced outside the area of the Danelaw, was inspired by the classicism of continental (Carolingian and Ottonian) intermediaries; it was these influences that gave rise to the distinctive styles of the so-called Winchester and Canterbury "schools" of the late 10th and 11th centuries.

A. Jane Hawkes

Bibliography

Dodwell, C.R. *Anglo-Saxon Art: A New Perspective.* Manchester: Manchester University Press, 1982; Greenhalgh, M. *The Survival of Roman Antiquities in the Middle Ages.* London: Duckworth, 1989; Wilson, David M. *Anglo-Saxon Art: From the Seventh Century to the Norman Conquest.* London: Thames & Hudson, 1984.

See also Art, Anglo-Saxon; Franks Casket; High Crosses; Lindisfarne Gospels; Manuscript Illumination, Anglo-Saxon; Sculpture, Anglo-Saxon; Stockholm Gospels; Vespasian Psalter; Wearmouth-Jarrow and the Codex Amiatinus; "Winchester School"

Art, Gothic

English Gothic art is often assumed to commence suddenly in 1175, when William of Sens arrived in England to begin reconstruction of the Canterbury Cathedral choir. The change from Romanesque to Gothic was in reality far more gradual and complex and occurred in different media at different times; nevertheless, the tradition is still useful in illustrating two characteristics of English Gothic art: 1) it remained first and foremost an architectural style, with innovation occurring first in architecture and subsequently spreading to the other arts; 2) it began as and remained a creative response to French developments.

The early Gothic style introduced at Canterbury was quickly modified to accord with English tastes through the addition of thick walls, linear surface patterns, strong color contrasts, and inhabited capitals, as at Wells (1180–90). The introduction of the Decorated style (ca. 1290) and Perpendicular style (ca. 1350) can also be understood as English responses to the French high Gothic and Rayonnant styles. English artists and architects, however, never adopted these French styles wholeheartedly but rather selected specific elements to include in what remained basically insular designs.

Designs or motifs used for such monuments as Westminster Abbey or the Eleanor crosses are often associated with the desire of English kings to emulate the splendor of the French court rather than with the desire of English artists to copy the styles of France.

Architecture remained important throughout the Gothic period, not only because it was the primary locus of artistic innovation, but also because it provided the setting in which all other forms of art were viewed or used. Gothic art is in many ways performative, with the church and its furnishings focused on the performance of the liturgy and the great hall with its furnishings and grounds designed for the rituals of court culture (tournaments, Round Tables, etc.). While the nature of the rituals may have differed, both church and hall were united as stages for costly and ostentatious display. Both were embellished with sculpture, painting, wall hangings, and objects of precious metal. The two were never completely separated, and from the 13th century to the end of the 15th century court culture had an enormous influence on all the arts.

The Gothic church was conceived as the kingdom of heaven on earth. In its architecture and decoration it presented a taste of what the devout Christian could expect in the heavenly Jerusalem. The cathedrals of the 13th and 14th centuries were brighter and more open than their Romanesque predecessors. Inside the nave the vertical lines of the supports, the pointed arches, and the high groin vaults moved the eye upward to heaven. The vertical emphasis was heightened in the 14th century by the addition of impressive crossing towers, as at Salisbury (ca. 1328) or Ely (1322–34), or by the addition of soaring towers to the west facade, as at Beverley, Yorkshire (1380–1420).

The architectural innovations of the Gothic style, which reduced the supporting structure of the building to its basic skeleton (a feature never as pronounced in England as it was in France), also allowed for an increase in the number and size of windows. The colors of the stained glass filling the windows transformed the sunlight of this world into multicolored jewellike light symbolic of the divine light of heaven. The scenes and figures depicted could also serve a didactic function, illustrating biblical stories and saints' lives or providing moral, religious, or even political instruction to a generally illiterate congregation. The complex compositions of the figural narratives and tracery patterns reach their climax in the great east window of Gloucester Cathedral choir (ca. 1351–67), literally a wall of glass. The delicate tracery patterns of the window here spread to cover the surfaces of the elevation and vault, suggesting a delicate metalwork reliquary.

Liturgically and visually the east end was the dramatic culmination of the Gothic church, the focus not only of the mass, but also the location of shrines, altars, relics, and the tombs of the aristocracy. In the great cathedrals the clergy was separated from the laity by a carved stone or wooden screen, between choir and nave. The screen could be elaborately embellished with gables, niches, sculpture, and painting. The shrine of St. Albans (1305–08) was a miniature architectural monument with gables, arcades, and figural sculpture, the whole made more sumptuous by the addition of paint and gilding. The liturgical vessels (figs. 87–88: see LITURGICAL VESSELS) and manuscripts used during services were not kept on permanent display but did play an important role within the mass. Their bright colors and precious materials were echoed in the vestments of the clergy.

The liturgical significance of the east end of the church was often articulated by the addition of painted or sculpted details. At St. Albans paintings on the nave supports marked the position of altars. In the angel roof of the chancel of All Saints, York (ca. 1470), the angel Gabriel and Mary were painted flanking the altar and its rood, connecting the Annunciation with the Crucifixion and providing visual punctuation for the liturgical drama. In the same church the fifteen signs of Doomsday depicted in the stained-glass windows related to the Doomsday play.

Angel roofs and choirs provided a celestial orchestra for the holy figures sculpted or painted in and around the east end of the church, as well as for the liturgical performance below. The angels carved on the roof bosses and around the high altar in the Gloucester choir accompany the celestial hierarchy of figures depicted in the east window—in descending order: stars and angels; Christ, Mary, and the apostles; abbots and bishops; shields, kings, and nobles. Christ and Mary are elegant crowned figures, king and queen of their heavenly court. The iconography reflects both the growth in the cult of the Virgin Mary and the influence of court culture and contemporary social hierarchy on art. Indeed art mirrored and helped to construct the society in which it was produced; commissioned by and for a wealthy ecclesiastical and aristocratic elite, Mary, Christ, and the saints became elegant courtly figures covered in rich robes and jewels, maintaining control over the misbehavior and ignorance of the lower classes occupying the more marginal areas of the church, such as the misericords.

Both the art produced for the secular aristocracy, as well as the aristocracy itself, looked backward for many of their images to a lost and mythologized golden age of King Arthur and his knights. At the same time, however, they looked to the contemporary French court for stylistic innovation. These two influences combined to create an art that at first glance dwells on nostalgic fantasy but that on closer inspection can be read as political propaganda advocating strength and loyalty to one's lord and country. The Chertsey Tiles (ca. 1250–70), with their scenes of battling knights (fig. 140: see TILES) and episodes from the story of Tristan and Isolde; the drawings of a king, knight, and squire added to the Westminster Psalter ca. 1250; the paintings commissioned by Henry III and Edward I for the Painted Chamber at Westminster, which included figures of the virtues and vices and good and bad kings—all centered on the theme of loyalty and virtuous kingship.

Art in a variety of media came together in the tournaments, or Round Tables, held throughout the 13th and 14th centuries. The tournament not only took place against a backdrop of castle and garden, but required theatrical sets, elaborate costumes, banners, jewels, and furnishings for the feast. Folio 202v of the Luttrell Psalter of ca. 1325–35 (BL Add. 42130) depicts Sir Geoffrey Luttrell being armed for the tournament; the theme receives a comic turn in manuscript mar-

ginalia and misericords, such as the ca. 1379 misericord with two jousting knights at Worcester Cathedral. The taste for Arthuriana and the merging of art and life culminated in Edward IV's building of St. George's Chapel at Windsor Castle (1475–1511) as the seat for the Order of the Garter, an order founded by Edward III in 1348 after his military victories in France.

While art produced by and for courtly society in the late 14th and 15th centuries stressed loyalty to king and country above all, it also manifested an increasing emphasis on personal identity, experience, and lineage. This is most clearly exemplified by the proliferation of heraldic devices in all media. Coats of arms decorated the borders of manuscripts, gables, roof bosses, and floor pavements (e.g., the shield-bearing angels in Westminster Hall), stained glass, and monumental tomb brasses (e.g., the 1375 brass of Robert of Wyvil, bishop of Salisbury, in Salisbury Cathedral). Devotion also became more personal. Funerary chapels, elaborate tombs, and memorial brasses became more common and were produced for a wider range of patrons. Books of hours, designed for private devotion and decorated with personalized imagery, also flourished. The emphasis on identity and lineage may be connected to the devastation caused by plague, war, and social unrest and to the increasing power and prominence of the wealthy professional class. The importance of middle-class patronage is evident not only in its demand for traditional aristocratic monuments, such as manuscripts and memorials, but also in its development of new forms of architecture, such as the pseudo-castle and the guildhall.

The Gothic era is also characterized by an increased presence and prominence of the artist. Records of artists' names are far more common; we know much, for example, of Matthew Paris, William de Brailes, William Ramsey, Henry Yevele, and Herman Scheerre, to name but a few. Monastic artists like Matthew Paris, and monastic scriptoria in general remained important throughout the period. However, it was the lay artist and the lay workshop that acquired real prominence.

The rise of the lay artist resulted from a complex range of historical and social factors. Prominent among them was the great increase in the number and range of works of art required in all media. The rise of the universities of Oxford and Cambridge in the 12th and 13th centuries, and the development of a middle class of merchants and other professionals in the 14th and 15th centuries, created new patrons with new requirements. Books for scholars and students had to be usable in a way that grand liturgical manuscripts did not. University buildings, commercial buildings, and the homes of the middle class demanded new architectural solutions. Artists responded to these increased demands by establishing specialized workshops in which there was a specialization of labor and industrialization of production achieved through the use of model books, exemplars, booklets, templates, and design treatises. The changes appear first in the workshops producing illuminated manuscripts, such as the ca. 1230–60 workshop of William de Brailes at Oxford, but soon spread to other media. By the late 14th century workshops of sculptors, painters, goldsmiths, masons, and architects were located throughout England, with particularly prominent workshops centered on the court in London.

The social status of artists increased accordingly. The hierarchy within the workshop reflected that of society, with an elite group of masters directing a usually anonymous group of artisans and apprentices. In fact many of the most prominent masters became members of the new moneyed elite. In the late 1330s William Ramsey, the king's chief mason, had the use of his own seal and coat of arms. Henry Yevele, architect of Westminster Palace, Westminster Abbey, and St. Paul's Cathedral from 1360 to 1400, held the rank of esquire and owned two country homes and substantial property in London. Yevele was not only an accomplished architect but also a shrewd businessman, directing workshops of both masons and sculptors as well as working as contractor and supplier of building materials.

With the increase in artistic production and the secularization of all art forms during the Gothic era it is tempting to see in the period the beginnings of a sense of art for art's sake, but this is misleading. The meaning of monuments and images continued to take prominence over visual form. Arthurian romances were lessons in virtuous behavior, the beauty and elegance of Mary and Christ symbolized their divinity, the magnificence of church and shrine were reflected in the strength of the church and the beauty of heaven. The preeminence of the message and the necessity of relaying and interpreting it correctly were driven home by the Lollards in the late 14th century. They, like St. Jerome, the Byzantine iconoclasts, and Bernard of Clairvaux before them, stressed the danger of art: beauty could seduce and corrupt as easily as it could instruct. Why, they asked, show the saints and apostles who had lived lives of poverty and suffering as though they had lived in luxury? Did not art run the risk of promoting worldly wealth and the desires of mortal men and women over the spiritual power of the image? Their views were echoed by Thomas Cromwell in 1538, and while the impact of the Lollards on art may have been limited, the impact of the Reformation was not.

Catherine E. Karkov

Bibliography

Alexander, Jonathan, and Paul Binski, eds. *Age of Chivalry: Art in Plantagenet England 1200–1400.* London: Royal Academy of Arts, 1987; Brown, R. Allen. *English Castles.* London: Batsford, 1983; Camille, Michael. *Image on the Edge: The Margins of Medieval Art and Society.* Cambridge: Harvard University Press, 1992; Morgan, Nigel. *Early Gothic Manuscripts 1190–1285.* 2 vols. A Survey of Manuscripts Illuminated in the British Isles 4, ed. J.J.G. Alexander. London: Harvey Miller, 1982–88; Sandler, Lucy Freeman. *Gothic Manuscripts 1285–1385.* A Survey of Manuscripts Illuminated in the British Isles 5, ed. J.J.G. Alexander. London: Harvey Miller, 1986; Scattergood, V.J., and James W. Sherborne, eds. *English Court Culture in the Late Middle Ages.* London: Duckworth, 1987; Scott, Kathleen L. *Later Gothic Manuscripts 1385–1490.* A Survey of Manuscripts Illuminated in the British Isles 6, ed. J.J.G. Alexander. London: Harvey Miller, 1996; Stone, Lawrence. *Sculpture in Britain: The Middle Ages.* 2d ed. Harmondsworth: Penguin, 1972; Wilson, Christopher. *The Gothic Cathedral: The Architecture of the Great Church 1130–1530.* London: Thames & Hudson, 1990.

See also Angel Roofs; Architecture and Architectural Sculpture, Gothic; Books; Books of Hours; Brailes, William de; Canterbury Cathedral; Court Culture; Eleanor Crosses; Enamels, Gothic; Manuscript Illumination, Gothic; Metalwork, Gothic; Misericords; Opus Anglicanum; Sculpture, Gothic; Stained Glass; Westminster Abbey; Windsor, St. George's Chapel

Art, Pictish

Our name for the Picts derives from *Picti*, Roman soldiers' slang for a "painted people" who may have worn tattoos at an early date. Apparent descendants of the earlier Caledonians, they lived in those areas of Scotland east of the watershed that defines the West Highlands and north of the Firth of Forth, extending into the Orkney and Shetland Islands. The meager evidence suggests that their language was a mixture of non-Indo-European and Celtic elements, in varying proportions throughout Pictland. They were unified under a single king by the late 6th century and combined their crown with that of the Scots in the mid-9th century. Their former territory is indicated by various criteria, including place-names beginning in *Pit-* and the locations of their distinctive sculptures. Although Pictish metalwork survives, their sculpture is their most important artistic legacy.

Pictish sculpture is divided into Classes I, II, and III. Class I (fig. 16) comprises rough stone slabs, set upright and incised with geometric symbols, unique to the Picts, or with

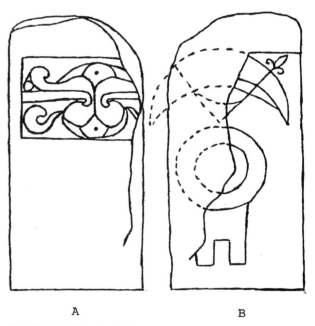

A   B

Fig. 16. Pictish Class I symbol stone, St. Peter's Church, South Ronaldsay, Orkney, (a) front, (b) back. Currently in the National Museum of Scotland, Edinburgh. After J. Romilly Allen (1903). Drawing by C. Karkov.

depictions of animals. The origins of the two most popular symbols, known as the Crescent and V-rod and Double-Disc and Z-rod, remain unknown, although among the other examples, the so-called Tuning-fork symbol may be a stylized representation of an Iron Age Celtic sword. Depictions of the sea eagle, salmon, boar, bull, wolf, stag, and snake are also found in Class I, in addition to the fantastic animal known as the Pictish Beast. The best Class I carvings feature Celtic decoration inside the geometric symbols and interior body scrolls and volutes on the animal figures, suggestive of lost predecessors in *repoussé* metalwork.

Quality is equated with originality among Pictish symbol stones, and their initial creation is therefore placed in northern Pictland, along the shores of the Moray Firth, extending northward to Orkney. Class I is broadly contemporary with the inscribed memorial stones and incised crosses found in Celtic areas of Britain and Ireland and may have shared a similar function, although its original purpose remains a source of debate. Burials, however, have occasionally been found associated with symbol stones. There is no agreement over the dating of the origins of the symbol series in stone, with proposals ranging from the 6th century to the late 7th.

The Hebridean monastery of Iona introduced the Picts to Christianity by the 7th century. But in the early 8th century the Pictish king Nechtan realigned himself with the romanizing trend in Northumbria and requested the loan of Anglo-Saxon masons from Jarrow to build a stone church "in the Roman manner." The church no longer exists, but the new Pictish knowledge of stonemasonry techniques led to the emergence of Class II Pictish sculpture: finely dressed slabs carved in relief, bearing both the cross and Pictish symbols, usually on opposite sides. Whatever Pictish symbols meant, they were compatible with Christianity. The new Class II monumental form developed in southern Pictland, near the north shore of the Firth of Tay, with examples at Glamis and Aberlemno. Conflicting views of the dating of early Class II place it either in the early 8th century, by analogy with contemporary relief cross slabs in Northumbria, or in the second half of the century.

Early Class II cross slabs are carved in low relief. Disagreement over their dates reflects the different dating schemes proposed for the higher relief of the second phase of Class II, which are aggravated by the connections between a group of stone crosses carved at Iona and contemporary sculpture in Pictland, including the southern Pictish St. Andrews Sarcophagus and the northern Pictish cross slab at Nigg. David iconography proved especially popular in Pictland, where it may have had royal associations, but it is mirrored at Iona, while rounded relief bosses, surrounded by the modeled figures of snakes, occur both on the Iona crosses and in Pictish sculpture. Opposing arguments place the related Pictish and Iona examples in a series beginning in the mid-8th century or delay its development until the early 9th. But Iona imported stone from the Scottish mainland for its later crosses, a tremendous undertaking unlikely to have been attempted after 806, when Iona suffered its most devastating Viking attack. If the higher relief of the later Pictish Class II belongs to the second

Fig. 17. Pictish Class II cross slab. St. Vigeans no. 1 (back). Courtesy of Carol A. Farr.

half of the 8th century, early Pictish cross slabs probably emerged nearer its beginning.

Despite the unification of the Picts and Scots in the mid-9th century, characteristically Pictish sculpture enjoyed local patronage for a few more generations. Major southern Pictish collections at Meigle and St. Vigeans (fig. 17) may span the whole of the 9th century, while northern cross slabs at Rosemarkie and Shandwick are among the finest examples of late Class II. The distinctive Pictish symbols were finally abandoned in the relief sculpture of Class III, at a time when the Picts were gradually subsumed within the Gaelic-speaking culture of the Scots, even though the kings of the combined peoples occasionally bore Pictish names into the 10th century. The sculptured cross, rather than the cross slab, appeared at St. Andrews and the southern Dupplin Cross combines Scottish, Pictish, and Northumbrian features, but the vigor of late Pictish sculpture is best represented in the north by the enormous Sueno's Stone, a cross slab near Forres.

Douglas Mac Lean

Bibliography

Anderson, J., and J. Romilly Allen. *The Early Christian Monuments of Scotland.* 3 vols. Edinburgh: Society of Antiquaries of Scotland, 1903; Friell, J.G.P., and W.G. Watson. *Pictish Studies: Settlement, Burial and Art in Dark Age Northern Britain.* BAR Brit. Ser. 125. Oxford: BAR, 1984; Henderson, Isabel. *The Picts.* London: Thames & Hudson, 1967; Henderson, Isabel.

"Pictish Art and the Book of Kells." In *Ireland and Early Mediaeval Europe: Studies in Memory of Kathleen Hughes*, ed. D. Whitelock et al. Cambridge: Cambridge University Press, 1982, pp. 79–105; Mac Lean, Douglas. "Snake-Bosses and Redemption at Iona and Pictland." In *The Age of Migrating Ideas: Early Medieval Art in Northern Britain and Ireland*, ed. R. Michael Spearman and John Higgitt. Edinburgh: National Museums of Scotland, 1993, pp. 245–53; Stevenson, R.B.K. "Pictish Art." In *The Problem of the Picts*, ed. F.T. Wainwright. Edinburgh: Nelson, 1955, pp. 97–128.

See also Anglo-Saxon Invasions; Art, Anglo-Saxon; Art, Anglo-Saxon: Celtic Influences; High Crosses; Sculpture, Anglo-Saxon

Art, Romanesque

The term "Romanesque" describes the cultural productions of western Europe in the 11th and 12th centuries. Seen from a modern vantage point, the characteristics that define the Romanesque—generally figures drawn or sculpted with firmly demarcated outlines, massive buildings made of square-cut stone blocks, and decorated with monumental sculpture of the same material—cross national boundaries and therefore mark the first international artistic style since the Roman Empire. Formulated in the early 19th century, the term at first referred negatively or derisively to a particular medieval practice of building "in the manner of the Romans," particularly the use of round arches. As the historical studies of this architecture and its cultural contexts developed, Romanesque art has come to be seen as driven by two simultaneous forces: the memory of a common, pan-European heritage of the Roman Empire, kept alive and motivated by medieval monastic culture; and a series of individual expressions of that memory, modified by the particular traditions and historical contexts of the various regions of Europe.

In English art the Romanesque period is roughly bracketed by the dates of ca. 1050 and ca. 1200. On one end of the temporal scale English Romanesque grows out of a mixture of Anglo-Saxon art, defined by a dynamic flow of lines and small-scale architecture, and the more severe style developed on the Continent, especially in Normandy. On the other end the Romanesque blends slowly into the refined and courtly attention to the shapes and textures of natural forms and the thin, soaring membranes of stone and stained glass that make up Gothic art and architecture. The fluid borders assigned to the Romanesque as an artistic period reflect the great losses of artwork over the last 800 years, losses that make a perfectly accurate description of influences and developments impossible. Its indeterminate chronological boundaries also mirror a growing awareness that general trends in art, such as stylistic development, result from a combination of complex forces that usually are not as readily datable as the beginning of a king's reign or the production of one particular work.

In broad and general terms English Romanesque art is dominated by the dense, regular, and imposing frame provided by the massive volumes and stocky proportions of architecture. The cathedrals and castles constructed in Romanesque England dwarf their Anglo-Saxon predecessors in number, size, and technical innovation. Following the Norman Conquest in 1066, King William and the continental abbots and bishops he appointed to English ecclesiastical positions replaced many venerable Anglo-Saxon churches, including Canterbury, Winchester, and Durham, with new and larger construction based on continental models. At the same time William and his successors built or authorized the building of stone castles, such as the Tower of London, at strategic locations. In looking toward the Continent they followed in a tradition started by King Edward the Confessor, who, in his construction of Westminster Abbey ca. 1050 (thought to be the first example of Romanesque architecture in England), seems to have borrowed from—and in turn influenced—the great abbeys of Normandy. Westminster Abbey, the Norman abbeys, and the post-Conquest churches shared a similar aesthetic: these buildings massed together long horizontal spaces of nave and transept, dominated by two vertical towers at the corners of the facade and one at the crossing. Interiors were solid and heavy. Gigantic, massive piers supported masonry walls that were divided into two, and sometimes three, distinct parts. In these early buildings side aisles were vaulted in stone, while the nave was covered by a timbered roof. Many of these projects ambitiously enclosed unprecedented amounts of space, rivaling and even surpassing the great cathedrals and abbeys on the Continent. The cathedral at Durham (figs. 52–53: see DURHAM CATHEDRAL) presents the first known Romanesque construction planned from its inception to be completely covered with stone vaults.

The architecture provided an overriding frame for decoration—generating an interest in monumental sculptural designs not seen in Europe since classical antiquity—which was concentrated around facades, doorways, and capitals. Although stone crosses and figured architectural decoration were sometimes sculpted in Anglo-Saxon England, Norman and other continental traditions provided important catalysts for English Romanesque designs, especially by inspiring the use of abstract geometric motifs, like the zig-zag chevrons applied to round arches or capitals carved with foliate motifs, human heads, or animals. The tympana—the hemispherical areas under the arched doorways in many churches—became important zones for sculpture, first for geometric patterns (Chepstow Castle, ca. 1070) and later with figural descriptions of religious scenes, such as Christ in Majesty, as at Rochester Cathedral. The arches surrounding the tympanum were often enriched with a wild menagerie of stylized vegetation, contorted animals, human heads, and "beakheads"—birdlike forms with long, dagger-shaped beaks, of which the parish churches at Kilpeck (fig. 76: see KILPECK) and Iffley preserve the outstanding examples. Unfortunately much of the sculptural decoration from the facades and interiors of churches has been lost, deliberately damaged, or blurred by weathering. Indeed one type of sculpture that we know must have existed in hundreds of examples—wooden crucifixes—is now almost completely lost.

Most of the surviving works in other media, such as metalwork, wall painting, and ivory carving, must be understood largely in terms of architecture too, as these objects would have been seen in the context of ecclesiastical ceremonies taking place within the newly constructed churches. Wall painting, much of it now destroyed or covered up by subsequent work, would have complemented and continued the sculptural programs of many churches and provided a visual reference for didactic messages aimed at the church congregation. The entire program of painting, sculpture, and architecture was directed toward the rites of worship contained within; rites that included the use of elaborately decorated patens, chalices, and ciboria constructed of precious metals, ivory, and enamels. The Gloucester Candlestick (fig. 67: see GLOUCESTER CANDLESTICK), commissioned 1107–13 and probably intended for use on or near the altar, is perhaps the most dramatic—and the only firmly datable—surviving example of the metalwork craft. Work of equal brilliance and virtuosity but intended for secular social rituals may have once existed; only a few items (drinking cups, finger rings, etc.) are known today.

In one area at least, illuminated manuscripts, we can manage to glimpse Romanesque art in a relatively unfaded, unweathered manner. In manuscripts as in buildings, paintings and drawings were organized around an architecture created by the linear flow of the text and the series of rectangular spaces created by the open book. Elaborate painted initials, another artistic idea imported from Normandy, marked the beginnings of important sections of manuscripts. These initials often combined human, animal, and hybrid (half-man/half-animal or two kinds of animals together) caught in a dense, flowing mass of vegetation. The meaning of the inhabited initials—"haunted tanglewoods" as they have been called—sometimes seems directly linked to the text that follows; other times a general meaning, linked to a monastic view of the world as a place of struggle and contention, can be attributed to the laboring figures they contain.

Although initials continued to be an important part of manuscript decoration throughout the Romanesque, English manuscripts develop a strong interest in pictorial narrative. Pictures supply the "architecture" of a story; that is, they provide narrative pillars that ground and support a reading of a text. The first extended series of narrative images that we know of, a manuscript of the *Life of St. Cuthbert* (Oxford, University College 165) from around the beginning of the 11th century, has miniatures placed alongside the text they illustrate, as a kind of visual recapitulation or extension of the story. By the second and third decades of the 11th century visual narrative becomes more independent of the text, allowed to develop a story's architecture in its own terms, as in the St. Albans Psalter (Hildesheim, St. Godehard) and the *Life of St. Edmund* (New York, Pierpont Morgan Library 736), where single scenes fill the entire space of the rectangular folio, causing the narrative to flow and ebb as the reader turns the pages of the manuscript and stops to look at a picture.

In addition to narrative, English Romanesque art by mid-century exhibits several distinctive trends. Regional schools of sculpture developed in Yorkshire and Herefordshire; the small churches at Shobdon and Kilpeck are particularly rewarding examples of how ideas and forms initiated at larger English or continental centers could be extended and transformed to fit the needs of a particular location. In a similar fashion individual artists, such as Master Hugo, who painted a Bible for the Abbey of Bury St. Edmunds (Cambridge, Corpus Christi College 2), could fuse continental, English, and Byzantine ways of painting drapery into the distinctive and dynamic patterns known as the "damp-fold." The damp-fold became an artistic convention used by carvers and metalworkers. Drapery clings to the figures modeling the curving forms of legs, thighs, and abdomens through long and graceful S-curves or tightly nested, stylized ridges.

The fact that conventions depicting drapery, such as the damp-fold style, or even ways of representing plants and plant forms were used in several kinds of media raises the question of who was responsible for their creation. Early in the Romanesque most of the work was perhaps done by the monks themselves, as similarities between foliage types from Canterbury manuscripts and some capitals from Normandy show. Later, laypeople began to be responsible for producing metalwork, carving, and painting. Some, like Master Hugo of Bury St. Edmunds, worked skillfully in different media. Others perhaps specialized in only one or two. Some of these artists could have been laypeople associated with a particular monastery or patron for a long period of time; some, like Anketyl of St. Albans, were actual members of the monastic community, while others moved from job to job. By the 1180s at least a loose association of goldsmiths existed in London, witnessing the possibilities for an artisan's independent employment.

If an artist may have become slightly less dependent on one particular church or monastery, the work produced would still have been tightly bound to the needs of an increasingly hierarchical, centralized, and interdependent English church and lay aristocracy. The small parish church at Elkstone, Gloucester (constructed ca. 1160–70), served the need of the local lord and those who worked his estates in the surrounding area. Like many local churches from the 12th century it is built of the same square-cut ashlar found in the larger, richer cathedrals. Over its south door—the principal entrance to the church—a carved tympanum depicts a theme commonly found over the doorways of the facades of monastic and cathedral churches like Rochester, Christ in Majesty, here surrounded by beakheads and grotesques similar to those at Kilpeck. All in all the church and doorway are conventional, a product of national and international trends. At Elkstone, however, on the upper right-hand corner, the artist has mistakenly replaced the angel that symbolizes Matthew with the Agnus Dei, the Lamb of God. By moving the angel to the lower right margin, the artist, consciously or unconsciously, associates the Lamb, symbolizing the earthly church, more closely with the central, in this case celestial, authority. Although the scene is derived from the written text of Revelation, the viewer does not need to be literate to understand it. Christ, frontal and unmoving, sits in judgment, his memory aided by the book in his hands, by his scroll-bearing servants, and by the symbolic presence of the church. For kings and other 12th-century lords the use and control of the book correlated to the efficient exercise of political power. Placed on the threshold of the church, the divinely inspired vision of Christ's majesty, sculpted by human hands, proclaims and reinforces the privileged bonds forged between the secular authority who would have paid for and owned the building, and the church, represented by the priest who performed in its spaces. The tympanum reminds us that the art and artifacts that have survived from the late 11th and 12th centuries must be seen not only in terms of stylistic development but as a result of and as integral to how these bonds between social actors were forged.

Benjamin Carl Withers

Bibliography

Cahn, Walter. *Romanesque Bible Illumination.* Ithaca: Cornell University Press, 1982; Camille, Michael. "Seeing and Reading: Some Visual Consequences of Medieval Literacy and Illiteracy." *Art History* 8/1 (1985): 26–49; Clanchy, M.T. *From Memory to Written Record: England 1066–1307.* 2d ed. Oxford: Blackwell, 1993; Dynes, Wayne. "Art, Language and Romanesque." *Gesta* 28/1 (1985): 3–10; Hahn, Cynthia. "*Peregrinatio et Natio:* The Illustrated Life of Edmund King and Martyr." *Gesta* 30 (1991): 119–39; Henderson, George. *Early Medieval Art.* Harmondsworth: Penguin, 1972; Kahn, Deborah. *Canterbury Cathedral and Its Romanesque Sculpture.* London: Harvey Miller, 1991; Kauffmann, C.M. "The Bury Bible (Cambridge C.C.C. Ms. 2)." *JWCI* 29 (1966): 60–81; Kauffmann, C. Michael. *Romanesque Manuscripts 1066–1190.* Survey of Manuscripts Illuminated in the British Isles 3, ed. J.J.G. Alexander. London: Harvey Miller, 1975; Macready, Sarah, and F.H. Thompson. *Art and Patronage in the English Romanesque.* London: Society of Antiquaries, 1986; Oakeshott, Walter. *The Two Winchester Bibles.* Oxford: Clarendon, 1981; Pächt, Otto, C.R. Dodwell, and Francis Wormald. *The St. Albans Psalter (Albani Psalter).* Studies of the Warburg Institute 25. London: Warburg Institute, 1960; Pächt, Otto. *The Rise of Pictorial Narrative in Twelfth-Century England.* Oxford: Clarendon, 1962; Schapiro, Meyer. *Romanesque Art.* New York: Braziller, 1977; Zarnecki, George. *English Romanesque Sculpture 1066–1140.* London: Tiranti, 1951; Zarnecki, George. *Later English Romanesque Sculpture.* London: Tiranti, 1953; Zarnecki, George, Janet Holt, and Tristram Holland, eds. *English Romanesque Art 1066–1200.* London: Weidenfeld & Nicolson, 1984.

See also Architecture and Architectural Sculpture, Romanesque; Gloucester Candlestick; Great Bibles; Kilpeck; Manuscript Illumination, Romanesque; Metalwork and Enamels, Romanesque; Parish Church Architecture; St. Albans Psalter; Sculpture, Romanesque; Wall Painting, Romanesque; Westminster Abbey; York Virgin and Child

Art, Viking Age

The Viking Age in England may be said to begin with the conquest of Anglo-Saxon York in 867 and to end with the fall of the Scandinavian kingdom of York in 954. But Scandinavian influence on Anglo-Saxon England and Anglo-Saxon art continued into the 11th century. The 10th century in particular saw a flowering of stone sculpture in the north, primarily in Yorkshire and Cumbria, the areas of Scandinavian settlement. The Vikings appear to have had relatively little impact on art in other media, except possibly in metalwork.

Four Scandinavian styles had an influence on pre-Conquest art in England: Borre, Jelling, Mammen, and Ringerike. Borre (mid-9th to late 10th century) is characterized by a ribbon-shaped gripping beast and ring-chain motif. It does not appear to be found in England in its pure form, although the ring-chain pattern seen on such monuments as the Gosforth Cross (figs. 18–19) may represent an Anglo-Scandinavian version of the style. The looping ribbon and foliate patterns of Scandinavian Borre also had a limited influence on metalwork, such as the Saffron Walden pendant (Saffron Walden

Fig. 18. Gosforth Cross, Cumbria, southeast side. Courtesy of A.J. Hawkes.

Museum), and a late-9th-century one-piece disc brooch from the River Cam (London, BM, MLA 1985, 7–2,1).

The Jelling style (late-9th to late-10th century) is the most popular of all the Scandinavian styles in England. Its characteristic motif is a double-contoured, often S-shaped ribbon animal, frequently with a curling pigtail and/or lip. Fine examples of Jelling-style beasts are found on the York Newgate cross-shaft and on a fragmentary slab from Coppergate, York. Although profoundly influential on Viking Age sculpture in England, the style had little influence on metalwork—though crude Jelling beasts decorate the early-10th-century silver niello roof-piece from a house-shaped casket in the British Museum (MLA 1954).

Mammen (ca. 960–1020) is relatively rare in England. Its characteristic motif is a double-contoured animal with lip-lappet and pigtail, often difficult to distinguish from the Jelling beast. The main difference is that Mammen beasts are fuller and heavier than their Jelling predecessors. The body of the animal may or may not be filled with pelleting. A typically Mammen beast survives on a cross-shaft from Workington, Cumbria. The style is not found in metalwork in England.

Fig. 19. Gosforth Cross, Cumbria, west side. Courtesy of A.J. Hawkes.

Ringerike is the last of the Scandinavian styles to have a significant influence on art in England. It is also noteworthy for having been developed under the influence of the Winchester style. Popular from ca. 980 to the mid-11th century, the style is typified by the addition of curling tendrils and foliate patterns to the Jelling-Mammen beast. Unlike the earlier "Viking Age" styles Ringerike was more popular in the south than in the north and is generally connected with the reign of the Danish king Cnut. The most famous example of the style to survive in sculpture is the end slab of a sarcophagus from St. Paul's, London (Museum of London). It is also seen in metalwork (e.g., the stirrup from Seagry, Wiltshire [Devizes Museum 49/1979]). It is the only one of the Scandinavian styles to be found in manuscript illumination. Ringerike designs can be seen in the architectural frames of the drawings on pp. 56 and 57 and on the blank end page of the "Cædmon" Genesis (Bodl. Junius 11), as well as in the decorative initials of a psalter in CUL Ff.1.23.

Viking Age art is characterized by more than simple stylistic considerations, particularly in the area of stone sculpture. In general Viking Age sculpture in the north was transformed from a primarily monastic to a primarily lay art. New types of monuments appear, most notably the "hogback," a memorial stone or grave marker similar in shape to Scandinavian buildings (although it is also possible that the shape of the hogback was influenced by that of Anglo-Saxon tombs and shrines). Tegullated roofs (roofs carved to look like roof-tiles) and/or roof ridges and bearlike end beasts are often carved on the stones. A variety of scenes and motifs decorate the long sides, some of purely Scandinavian nature (e.g., the Viking ship and world serpent on the Lowther [Cumbria] hogback).

The amount of Viking Age sculpture that survives in the north is somewhat surprising, as the areas from which the settlers came did not have a tradition of stone sculpture. Nevertheless, the Scandinavians were quick to adapt, decorating a typically Anglian and Christian form of monument—the free-standing stone cross—with scenes from Scandinavian mythology (Ragnarok, Sigurd, Weland the Smith); combining Christian and pagan scenes on a single monument, as at Gosforth, where the Crucifixion appears in the midst of a Scandinavian pantheon; or placing monuments with pagan scenes in Christian spaces, such as churchyards and cemeteries.

The appearance of ring-headed crosses in northern England at this time may be further proof of the Vikings' ability to assimilate. Ring-headed crosses are characteristic of Ireland and the Celtic areas of Britain, and may have been introduced to the Scandinavian settlers in England by their Irish counterparts.

Possibly under the influence of Irish metalwork Viking Age sculptors in England developed a method of laying out their designs on grids, sometimes with the aid of templates. Speaking of one of the York Minster shafts (York Minster 2), Jim Lang notes that the designs carved on the shaft are "rigidly symmetrical" and that "posture, angle, scrolls, crossings and direction of line rely upon the grid" (1986: 257). He suggests that this feature, more than any other, distinguishes Viking Age art in England and the British Isles from Viking art elsewhere.

Catherine E. Karkov

Bibliography

Backhouse, Janet, Derek H. Turner, and Leslie Webster, eds. *The Golden Age of Anglo-Saxon Art 966–1066*. London: British Museum, 1984; Bailey, Richard. *Viking Age Sculpture in Northern England*. London: Collins, 1980; Fuglesang, Signe Horn. "The Relationship between Scandinavian and English Art from the Late-Eighth to the Mid-Twelfth Century." In *Sources of Anglo-Saxon Culture*, ed. Paul E. Szarmach with Virginia D. Oggins. Kalamazoo: Medieval Institute, 1986, pp. 203–41; Hinton, David A. *A Catalogue of the Anglo-Saxon Ornamental Metalwork, 700–1100, in the Department of Antiquities, Ashmolean Museum*. Oxford: Clarendon, 1974; Lang, James. "The Distinctiveness of Viking Colonial Art." In *Sources of Anglo-Saxon Culture*, ed. Paul E. Szarmach with Virginia D. Oggins. Kalamazoo: Medieval Institute, 1986, pp. 243–60; Lang, James. *Corpus of Anglo-Saxon Stone Sculpture*. Vol. 3: *York and Eastern Yorkshire*. London: Oxford University Press, 1991; Roesdahl, Else, and David Wilson. *From Viking to Crusader: The Scandinavians in Europe 800–1200*. Rizzoli: New York, 1992; Webster, Leslie, and Janet Backhouse, eds. *The Making of England: Anglo-Saxon Art and Culture AD 600–900*. London: British Museum, 1991.

See also High Crosses; Iconography; Literary Influences: Scandinavian; Manuscript Illumination, Anglo-Saxon; Metalwork, Anglo-Saxon; Sculpture, Anglo-Saxon; Vikings

Asser (d. 909)

Biographer of Alfred the Great. Asser's *Life of King Alfred* survived into modern times only in BL Cotton Otho A.xii, dated by Wanley ca. 1000, burned in the Cotton Library fire of 23 October 1731, and now represented by a facsimile from Wise's edition of 1722 and transcripts at Corpus Christi College, Cambridge. The work was used certainly by Byrhtferth of Ramsey ca. 1000 and probably by the author of the *Encomium Emmae reginae* in the 1040s. Among other Alfredian titles in the list of books presented by Bishop Leofric to Exeter before 1072 the item *Liber Oserii* may refer to it. It was used by Florence of Worcester (d. 1118) or John (fl. 1140), whose work was used by Simeon of Durham; Simeon also incorporated Byrhtferth's work into his history. Early in the 12th century the compiler of the Annals of St. Neots drew material from Asser not found in John's work and preserved better readings than those found in the Cotton manuscript.

In his account of the year 884 Asser states that he was summoned "from the western and furthest ends of Britain to Saxony," from Dyfed in Wales to Sussex in England, to meet Alfred at Dene, where the king asked him to join his household. When Asser replied that he could not abandon the place where he had been nourished, taught, tonsured, and ordained, Alfred suggested that he spend six months with him and six in Wales. Departing on the fourth day, Asser contracted a fever in Caerwent from which he suffered for 53 weeks. After recovering he returned to Alfred with the "counsel and license of all our people," in hopes of protection for the church at St. David's from King Hemeid, who had expelled Asser's kinsman "Archbishop Nobis." Asser remained at Leonaford for eight months, reading to the king. By St. Martin's Day, 11 November 887, the king had learned to read and translate Latin. In 893 Asser wrote his biography, based upon his Latin translation of the Anglo-Saxon Chronicle and complemented with eyewitness accounts.

Asser presented Alfred as a Christian king modeled explicitly after Solomon and implicitly after Charlemagne. He adapted the genealogy found in the West Saxon regnal table from the pattern of Matthew 1:1–17 (A begat B) to a Solomonic pattern based upon the opening chapters of 1 Chronicles (the sons of A were B, C, D). Asser's stories about Alfred's character, behavior, administration, and inventions all follow the pattern of Solomon's career in Kings and Chronicles, sometimes in the very diction of the Latin Bible. Because of the alleged regnal anointing by the pope in 853 Alfred had been in 893 a king for the Solomonic span of 40 years. There is one chapter of Asser's *Life* for every year of Alfred's life, 45 in 893.

Asser implies by the structure of his narrative that the most important of Alfred's learned clerical assistants were Grimbald the Frank, John the Old Saxon, and himself. He was closely involved in the Alfredian translations of works by Orosius, Gregory the Great, and Boethius. His *Life*, together with Alfred's preface to the *Hierdeboc* (the OE translation of Gregory the Great's *Pastoral Care*), provides the clearest evidence of the origin and scope of the king's educational program.

In recognition of service Alfred made Asser abbot of Cungresbyri and Banuwille. He gave him Exeter "with the whole parish belonging to it" and later made him bishop of Sherborne. Asser's name appears among witnesses to early-10th-century charters. The Anglo-Saxon Chronicle records his death under the year 909.

D.R. Howlett

Bibliography

PRIMARY

Keynes, Simon, and Michael Lapidge, trans. *Alfred the Great: Asser's Life of King Alfred and Other Contemporary Sources*. Harmondsworth: Penguin, 1983; Stevenson, William Henry, ed. *Asser's Life of King Alfred*. Oxford: Clarendon, 1904. Repr. with article on recent work on Asser by Dorothy Whitelock. Oxford: Clarendon, 1959.

SECONDARY

Lapidge, Michael, and Richard Sharpe. *A Bibliography of Celtic-Latin Literature 400–1200*. Royal Irish Academy Dictionary of Medieval Latin from Celtic Sources, Ancillary Publications 1. Dublin: Royal Irish Academy, 1985, p. 14 (no. 30).

See also Alfred; Anglo-Latin Literature to 1066; Anglo-Saxon Chronicle; Byrhtferth; Chronicles

Assize of Clarendon

In 1166 Henry II, with the assent of his barons meeting at Clarendon, decreed procedural rules that proved to be a turning point in English criminal jurisdiction. The procedures were modified in the light of experience, and the provisions reinforced at a council of Northampton in 1176, but it was as the "Assize of Clarendon" that the key features of royal criminal justice came to be known.

The Assize (that is, this set of procedural rules) required systematic inquiries into allegations of serious crimes and the use of juries of trustworthy local men to identify suspects. Those named by the juries were to be arrested and detained pending trial. Only one of the customary forms of trial, the ordeal of water, was to be allowed to those so accused; the chattels of the guilty were forfeit to the crown. The inquiries and the arrest of suspects were not to be impeded by the holders of privileged jurisdictions. The procedures were to be monitored and the trial of the accused to be conducted before the newly instituted itinerant royal justices.

In practice the royal justices refined the procedures, "considering the probable facts and possible conjectures both for and against the accused, who must as a result be either absolved entirely or purge himself by the ordeal" (Glanville 14.1).

The importance of the Assize was threefold: first, it cut through a thicket of custom and private jurisdiction to establish a common law for the realm as a whole; second, the crown assumed direct involvement in the prosecution of serious crime; but third, an indictment by a jury was required to initiate prosecution. This "jury of presentment," besides involving the local community in law enforcement, was a major safeguard against unwarranted prosecution and has survived in the form of the "grand jury" into modern times.

W.L. Warren

Bibliography

Brand, Paul. "'Multis Vigiliis Excogitatam et Inventam': Henry II and the Creation of the English Common Law." *Haskins Society Journal* 2 (1990): 197–222; Douglas, David C., and George W. Greenaway, eds. *English Historical Documents*. Vol. 2: *1042–1189*. 2d ed. London: Eyre Methuen, 1981 [numbers 24 and 25 for the text of the Assize]; Holt, J.C. "The Assizes of Henry II: The Texts." In *The Study of Medieval Records: Essays in Honour of Kathleen Major*, ed. D.A. Bullough and R.L. Storey. Oxford: Clarendon, 1971, pp. 85–106; Hurnard, N. "The Jury of Presentment and the Assize of Clarendon." *EHR* 56 (1941): 374–410; Warren, W.L. *Henry II*. London: Eyre Methuen, 1973, pp. 281–83, 286–87.

See also Glanville; Henry II; Juries; Law, Post-Conquest

Assize of Weights and Measures

Although the Anglo-Saxon kings urged the use of just weights and measures and pointed to particular standards in their keeping, they did not copy or distribute such standards. With the growth of trade in the high Middle Ages, however, the Angevin kings began to regulate more systematically the wide variety of weights and measures employed throughout the realm. They promulgated laws, such as the Assize of Measures of 1196, which attempted to impose uniform weights and measures and to hold up certain standards, such as those of London, as models. They and their successors also had royal standards duplicated and sent out to counties and urban centers as models for local traders. The mounting legislation concerning the sale of specific commodities (like the Assize of Bread and Ale, 1266, and the various enactments for Alnage, or official measure, of cloth) included explicit provisions as to the proper weights and measures to be employed. But the frequency and repetitiveness of this legislation indicate that efforts to establish uniformity were often disregarded.

Although the king's Clerk of the Market maintained the royal standard measures and the king's commissioners could be empowered to inspect measures and punish wrongdoers, local government handled the bulk of enforcement through leet courts (the annual courts of manors and hundreds). Boroughs regularly held an assay of weights and measures to compare the measures of local traders to the town's standards. Violators were punished by fines or by being put on the pillory. Near the end of the Middle Ages certain guilds also received the right to regulate measures used in their trade. In the countryside the power of local custom dictated a wide variety of weights and measures that proved resistant to the central authority's efforts to impose uniformity.

Maryanne Kowaleski

Bibliography

Connor, R.D. *The Weights and Measures of England*. London: HMSO, 1987; Zupko, Ronald E. *British Weights and Measures: A History from Antiquity to the Seventeenth Century*. Madison: University of Wisconsin Press, 1977.

See also Boroughs; Food: Guilds; Local Government; Trade

Astrology

In its medieval definition "astrology" meant "knowledge of the stars" (Gk. *astron*, star; *logos*, knowledge), and the word was used interchangeably with "astronomy." This usage can be confusing today; when Chaucer refers to the Physician's good grounding in "astronomye" he really means astrology in its modern sense. In our usage today "astronomy" concerns "factual" data on the stars, such as size or distance from the earth, in the tradition of Ptolemy's *Almagest* (ca. A.D. 127). "Astrology," in modern usage, concerns the "laws" of influence emanating from those stars in the macrocosm, especially over human life in the microcosm it governs. Ptolemy also dealt with such influences, and his *Tetrabiblos* was the basis for all later astrological works.

According to medieval astronomical theory seven planets orbit the earth, the first being the Moon; earthly matters are called "sublunary." Next come Mercury, Venus, the Sun, Mars, Jupiter, and Saturn. Finally come the fixed stars and *primum mobile* (prime mover: moving itself, rather than controlled by forces beyond this sphere) to establish the fixed positions by which the movements of the planets are measured and the initial impetus for their orbits around the earth is given.

The fixed stars include groups that define the twelve signs of the zodiac. The planets move through these signs, with the sun entering Aries in March, followed by Taurus, Gemini, Cancer, Leo, Virgo, Libra, Scorpio, Sagittarius, Capricorn, Aquarius, and Pisces in the succeeding months. The zodiacal signs and planets have natural qualities—cold, dry, hot, moist—based upon the four elements of earth, air, fire, and water. However, their movements cause such qualities to mutate according to their relation to the earth and other planets at any given moment.

"Aspect" is the most important determinant, identifying planetary and zodiacal relationships geometrically, that is, whether two or more bodies are square to each other, opposite, or in some other arrangement. Influences are greatest when planets are in the *auge*, or highest point above the earth, least when they are moving retrograde. The ruling planets and signs are those in a particular position at a given time, the most important for horoscopes being those in the "ascendant."

A person born under the sign of Aries would have been born with Aries rising at the eastern point of intersection of the horizon and the ecliptic at the moment of nativity, on the cusp (or entrance) of the first of the twelve mundane houses. The person's physical appearance, personality, and destiny would be determined by Aries's qualities (hot, dry, mobile, and masculine), as well as by the signs and planets positioned in various aspects throughout the remaining mundane houses to determine the future regarding such matters as marriage, illness, riches, and travel. A knowledge of the data provided by astronomy and of the laws of judicial astrology make it possible to assess the advisability (or otherwise) of human activities, as well as to predict the outcome of any event, even of life itself.

Latin and vernacular astrological treatises and related works represent a high proportion of surviving medieval scientific literature, perhaps 30 percent. In addition to Albumasar's *Introductorium* and other adaptations of Ptolemy other Latin works circulated widely: Albertus Magnus used Albumasar (786–866) for his *Speculum astronomie* (ca. 1250), Michael Scot for the *Liber introductorius* (ca. 1230), and John of Eschenden for his astrological *Summa* (ca. 1348). Richard of Wallingford, abbot of St. Albans, adapted Albumasar's *Flores astrologia* for his *Exafrenon* (ca. 1318). Alhazen's *Opus astronomicum*, Alchindus's *Judicia*, and Messahalla's *De judiciis astrorum* were, like Albumasar's works, first translated from Arabic at Toledo and were instrumental in the formation and transmission of astrological theory. Such theories also incorporated aspects of Aristotelian physics and meteorology, pseudo-Aristotelian and Galenic humoral theory, and Hippocratic medicine.

Astrological theory is represented in many vernacular translations—Aschenden and Wallingford were in English by the early 15th century—and adaptations. *The Wise Book of* *Astronomy and Philosophy*, a compendium of Albumasar and others, alone circulated in at least 28 manuscripts. At the applied level prognostic works on every subject from human fate to tree grafting were enormously popular and circulated well into the 16th century, when printed almanacs began to prevail for those seeking this sort of information.

Laurel Means

Bibliography

PRIMARY

Claudius Ptolemeus. *Tetrabiblos*. Ed. F.E. Robbins. Loeb Classical Library. London: Heinemann, 1940; Richard of Wallingford. *Richard of Wallingford: An Edition of His Writings with Introductions, English Translations and Commentary*. Ed. J.D. North. 3 vols. Oxford: Clarendon, 1976.

SECONDARY

Curry, Patrick, ed. *Astrology, Science and Society: Historical Essays*. Woodbridge: Boydell, 1987; Eade, J.C. *The Forgotten Sky: A Guide to Astrology in English Literature*. Oxford: Clarendon, 1984; Kren, Claudia. *Medieval Science and Technology: A Selected, Annotated Bibliography*. New York: Garland, 1985; Means, Laurel. "Electionary, Lunary, Destinary, and Questionary: Towards Defining Categories of Middle English Prognostic Material." *SP* 89 (1992): 367–403; Means, Laurel. "'For as moche as yche man may not haue the astrolabe': Popular Middle English Variations on the Computus." *Speculum* 67 (1992): 595–623; North, J.D. *Horoscopes and History*. London: Warburg Institute, 1986; Robbins, Rossell Hope. "English Almanacks of the Fifteenth Century." *PQ* 18 (1939): 321–31.

See also Alchemy; Science; Scientific and Medical Writings; Technology; Utilitarian Writings

Attainder and Forfeiture

Treason was defined in the Statute of Treasons (1352) and extended by later statutes and legal judgments. The most shocking of crimes, it carried the most serious of penalties: the execution of the offender, in the most painful and dishonorable way possible (disemboweling, drawing, hanging, and finally quartering), and the confiscation of his possessions. Forfeiture affected not just the traitor himself but his wife and heirs. It was developed and extended into the full-blown concept of attainder in 1459. Treason, it was argued, was so heinous that it corrupted or *tainted* the blood not only of the traitor but of his descendants so that they too were unable to inherit.

In the 13th century Bracton held harsh views akin to this formulation of attainder, but for a long time lawmakers took a more lenient view. Traitors did indeed suffer forfeiture of movable goods and estates held in fee simple, and their wives lost their dowers, but property held in trust (uses) was exempt until 1388, as were the wives' own inheritances and lands held jointly with wives. In the 1320s and in 1398 Edward II and

Richard II ignored such restraints upon their vengeance, but it was not until the Wars of the Roses that acts of attainder sought to obliterate rival houses and families by the complete and permanent confiscation of estates.

This was the object of the bill of 1459 against the supporters of Richard duke of York, which declared the treasonable conduct of those listed and enacted their forfeiture. It was the model for many other bills of attainder proposed by victorious factions against their enemies, some of which, as in 1461 and 1483, proscribed hundreds of opponents. There was no need for evidence of guilt or for a trial, nor was there opportunity for a defense; parliament's acquiescence sufficed. Hence we have the employment of attainder in state trials designed to destroy those who may not have been traitors: the duke of Clarence in 1478, the earl of Warwick in 1499, the duke of Buckingham in 1521, and the countess of Salisbury in 1541.

Acts of attainder deprived those named and their heirs of lands, however held, and wives of dowers. Enormous quantities of land consequently passed to Edward IV in 1461 and Richard III in 1483, which they used to reward their supporters. Wives of traitors were allowed to retain their own inheritances or lands held jointly with their husbands, for it was normal practice to settle jointures on couples at marriage. Children could inherit property via their mothers. Thus the two dowager-countesses of Northumberland retained much of the Percy inheritance, despite the attainder of the 3rd earl in 1461, and passed it on in due course to the 4th earl.

But practice did not always accord with theory. Anxious to prevent wives from remitting money to husbands still at liberty, kings often took them and their lands in custody, perhaps consigning them to nunneries. Traitors' wives understandably found it difficult to prove their rights, to make royal favorites disgorge what they had seized, or to resist pressure to abandon their rights. The future Richard III managed to set aside the claims of Lady Hungerford, clung to the lands of the countess of Warwick, and terrified the countess of Oxford into surrendering her inheritance. Edward IV does not seem to have approved but saw no point in offending a powerful supporter (and his brother) merely to do justice to powerless old ladies.

York, Lancaster, Somerset, and Warwick are examples of peerages that were destroyed as their attainders intended. But they were the exception. Most attainders were reversed, either by specific acts of reversal or by grants under the great seal; relatively few remained in force. Of Edward IV's attainders, 64 percent were reversed before the end of his reign, and all those passed by Henry VII (1485–1509) between 1488 and 1495 were reversed by 1523.

There were several reasons for this. Successive political revolutions—1459, 1461, 1471, 1483, and 1485—revoked the attainders and restored the victims of their predecessors. Another factor was a general respect for the sanctity of inheritance and consequent distaste for permanent disinheritance. Often the heirs of traitors were less offensive and more useful than their fathers, especially when—like the 4th earl of Northumberland—they had inherited their mother's lands. When

recipients of forfeitures died or when they or their heirs lost royal favor, the king often preferred to reverse the attainder rather than maintain their grants. The death of former Yorkists fighting for Warwick against Edward IV made it much easier for him to restore erstwhile Lancastrians in 1471.

Victims were often well connected and able to exert influence at court; witness the success of the Percys and Lady Hungerford in saving more than their strict legal entitlements. Royal favorites like Edward IV's earl of Pembroke and Lord Hastings married their daughters to the heirs of attainted traitors and exerted influence to get them restored, thus providing for their daughters on the cheap. Marriage offered better security than forfeitures, which might be restored and were seen as insecure. Hence the increased willingness of recipients of forfeited property to come to terms with the attainted, to share the spoils, or to sell the lands back facilitated the reversal of attainders. Hence, too, the increasing willingness to strike a bargain in return for preventing a traitor from being attainted. This occurred even in 1461; it was commonplace by 1475. There was no need to attaint a traitor if he could be satisfactorily punished and loyal followers better-rewarded without proceeding to such extremes.

Barring a few exceptions, generally the humbler and less important traitors, attainder increasingly became a means for the king to bind traitors and adherents alike and an opportunity for politicians to peddle their influence to their own advantage. If there were winners and losers, particularly in the short term, when whole generations of families were temporarily eclipsed or promoted, attainder and forfeiture did not in practice (as used to be thought) destroy the old nobility, radically redistribute lands, or drastically enhance the financial resources of the crown.

Michael A. Hicks

Bibliography

Bellamy, John G. *The Law of Treason in England in the Later Middle Ages.* Cambridge: Cambridge University Press, 1970; Hicks, Michael A. *False, Fleeting, Perjur'd Clarence: George, Duke of Clarence, 1449–1478.* Gloucester: Sutton, 1980; Hicks, Michael A. *Richard III and His Rivals: Magnates and Their Motives in the Wars of the Roses.* London: Hambledon, 1991; Lander, J.R. "Attainder and Forfeiture, 1452–1509." In *Crown and Nobility, 1450–1509.* London: Arnold, 1976, pp. 127–58.

See also Treason; Wars of the Roses

Augustine of Canterbury (d. by 609)

First archbishop of Canterbury. Little is known about Augustine's early life beyond the fact that he was a pupil of Felix, bishop of Messana in Italy, and subsequently a monk and then prior of St. Andrew's Monastery on the Caelian Hill, Rome.

In 596 Pope Gregory I selected Augustine to lead a mission of monks to convert the English. The political climate in England was favorable for the venture, since Kent enjoyed close contact with the Christian Franks; in particular Æthelberht of

Kent, overlord of the English kings south of the Humber, had married a Frankish princess, Bertha, who practiced the faith with her own chaplain. Nevertheless, Æthelberht was initially wary of the missionaries, and he insisted on meeting them outdoors, where hostile magic could less easily harm him. Augustine and his companions met him on the Isle of Thanet, approaching (as Bede records) with a silver cross and an icon of Christ.

At first Augustine operated from the old Roman church of St. Martin, where Bertha had practiced her devotions, but by ca. 602–03 he had repaired another Roman church, which he dedicated to Christ (Christ Church, Canterbury). Nearby he began to construct a monastery (known initially as St. Peter's, subsequently as St. Augustine's), to become a necropolis for Kentish kings and archbishops. Augustine presumably founded a school at Canterbury to provide converts with the learning they needed as clerics. The books and materials he had brought were augmented by further dispatches from Rome. The impact of writing was rapidly felt in the political sphere also, for under Æthelberht the earliest written collection of Anglo-Saxon laws was produced.

Augustine is recorded as having astonishing success in winning converts; by Christmas 597, shortly after he had received episcopal consecration, 10,000 are reputed to have been baptized. Surviving correspondence reveals that he sought and received guidance from Gregory on the organization, rites, and practices of the infant church. Particularly notable is Gregory's advice that pagan temples not be destroyed but purified and rededicated to Christian service. Augustine did not manage to realize Gregory's ideals for the organization of an English church in northern and southern provinces, each with an archbishop and twelve bishops. He also failed to obtain the British (Celtic) church's recognition of his authority and their help in converting the English. Augustine's mission affected only the southeast of England, and the difficulties that beset the new church following the death of Æthelberht (in 616?) underline the extent to which the early successes had depended on the king's favor. But then Augustine did not have many years in which to work; he died somewhere between 604 and 609.

Richard Gameson

Bibliography

Attenborough, F.L., ed. and trans. *The Laws of the Earliest English Kings.* Cambridge: Cambridge University Press, 1922; Brooks, Nicholas. *The Early History of the Church of Canterbury: Christ Church from 597 to 1066.* Leicester: Leicester University Press, 1984; Chaplais, Pierre. "Who Introduced Charters into England? The Case for Augustine." In *Prisca Munimenta: Studies in Archival and Administrative History Presented to A.E.J. Hollaender,* ed. Felicity Ranger. London: University of London Press, 1973, pp. 88–107; Mayr-Harting, Henry. *The Coming of Christianity to Anglo-Saxon England.* 3d ed. University Park: Pennsylvania State University Press, 1991; Wood, Ian. "The Mission of Augustine of Canterbury to the English." *Speculum* 69 (1994): 1–17; Wormald, Francis. *The Miniatures in the Gospels of St. Augustine: Corpus Christi College, MS. 286.* Cambridge: Cambridge University Press, 1948.

See also Æthelberht; Bede; Bretwald; Conversion of the Anglo-Saxons; Fathers of the Church (Gregory); Liturgy and Church Music, History of

Azarias

An OE poem of some 191 lines, found in the Exeter Book on fols. 53–55v. Some lines of the poem have been lost through the excision of about two and one-half inches from the top of fol. 53. This loss, coupled with the fact that there are many similarities between *Azarias* and the OE poem *Daniel,* has caused certain critics to view the poem as "no more than two sections of a long poem on the theme of Daniel, which may have told the whole story on much the same lines as that in the Junius MS" (Craigie, 1924: 11). There is an obvious connection between *Azarias* and lines 279–429 of *Daniel,* especially in terms of language, though no watertight claim can be made as to the exact nature of this relationship. Both poems celebrate God and his Creation, and perhaps the best that can be said is that they may have shared a common source. Another theory is that *Azarias* is really the ending to *Guthlac B,* though this view has not gained widespread acceptance.

The composition, noted for its lyrical beauty, is in two main sections—the Song of Azarias and the Song of the Three Children uttered from the fiery furnace. The primary source for the poem is Daniel 3:24–94, though the poet does not follow the Vulgate version exactly. It has also been suggested that *Azarias* may be indebted to the Song of the Three Children as it appears in the Roman psalter.

J.-A. George

Bibliography

ASPR 3:88–94; Craigie, William. "Interpolations and Omissions in Anglo-Saxon Poetic Texts." *Philologica* 2 (1924): 5–19; Farrell, Robert T. "Some Remarks on the Exeter Book *Azarias.*" *MÆ* 41 (1972): 1–8; Farrell, Robert T., ed. *Daniel and Azarias.* London: Methuen, 1974, pp. 39–40.

See also Bible in OE Literature; *Daniel; Guthlac A and B*

B

Bacon, Roger (ca. 1213/19–1292)

Little is known of the origins of Roger Bacon, Franciscan philosopher and scientific thinker. He was born ca. 1213–19. His writings reveal his English origins: his birthplace is unknown. His family was well-off and scholarly, able to assist him in the buying of books and scientific instruments. Educated at Oxford and Paris, he received the degree of master of arts around 1240 and lectured on Aristotle's natural philosophy for many years.

Under the influence of the works of Grosseteste and Arab authors, Bacon devoted himself to the study of mathematics, and languages, including Greek and Hebrew. He also conducted observational experiments, especially in optics. He entered the Franciscan order in 1257 but found Franciscan attempts to censor his writings disturbing. He appealed to the future Pope Clement IV for assistance in the compilation of a great encyclopedia of the sciences. As a result of papal encouragement Bacon composed the *Opus maius, Opus minus,* and *Opus tertium*—works that described his proposed reform of education and society, criticized magic, suggested calendar reform, and emphasized the importance of scientific knowledge for Christianity.

For reasons not entirely clear to us his works were again condemned in 1278 by the head of his order, owing to "certain suspect novelties." It is possible that his interest in alchemy, astrology, and the teachings of Joachim of Fiore, the Italian mystical preacher, led to his condemnation. As a result Bacon may have been imprisoned for several years, although he continued to study and write. His last work, *Compendium studii theologiae* (1292), still assailed the corruption of his day.

Although many of his works were forgotten after his death, Bacon was rediscovered in the Elizabethan period as a prototype of the modern "scientist." Bacon's modernity now appears exaggerated; his experimentalism was very much in the medieval tradition, and his ultimate aim was the advancement of the new learning as a useful tool for religion. At the same time his enthusiastic support for and synthesis of the new science helped introduce it into European intellectual life.

Janice Gordon-Kelter

Bibliography

PRIMARY

Burke, Robert B., trans. *The Opus Maius of Roger Bacon.* 2 vols. Philadelphia: University of Pennsylvania Press, 1928; Lindberg, David C., ed. and trans. *Roger Bacon's Philosophy of Nature: A Critical Edition.* Oxford: Clarendon, 1983.

SECONDARY

Crowley, Theodore. *Roger Bacon: The Problem of the Soul in His Philosophical Commentaries.* Louvain: Éditions de l'Institut Supérieur de Philosophie, 1950; Easton, Stewart C. *Roger Bacon and His Search for a Universal Science.* Oxford: Blackwell, 1950.

See also Friars; Grosseteste; Science

Ballads, English and Scottish

Anonymous narrative rhymed poems, generally sung and part of the oral tradition. They were a product of the late Middle Ages, first collected by Bishop Thomas Percy (*Reliques of Ancient English Poetry,* 1765), the word "ballad" having been suggested to him by William Shenstone to separate songs of narrative action from those of "sentiment." Francis Child assembled all 305 extant ballads in his collection *The English and Scottish Popular Ballads* (1882–98), giving his name to the "Child ballads"; he also assigned the numbers to ballads in the "Child canon" by which these songs are now universally recognized.

Only eight ballads in the Child canon can be dated before 1500. They are: "Judas" (Child no. 23; 1225–75); "Inter Diabolus et Virgo" (1; ca. 1450); "Robin Hood and the Monk" (119; 1450–1500); "Saint Stephen and Herod" (22; ca. 1450); "Robin Hood and Gandeleyn" (115; ca. 1450); "Robin Hood and the Potter" (121; ca. 1500); "A Gest of Robin Hood" (117; printed by Pynson ca. 1500); and "Adam Bell" (116; printed by Wynkyn de Worde ca. 1505). Three other poems not included by Child but recognized as ballads by recent scholars also fall into this time period: "I Have a Young Sister," "The King and the Barker," and the so-called "Corpus Christi Carol."

The "medievalism" of ballads is subject to controversy. Some scholars feel that "Judas," lacking a tune, is not a true ballad. However, the story is traditional, told in compact ballad style, and written in "fourteener" couplets (iambic heptameters), which, when divided into iambic tetrameters alternating with iambic trimeters, yield the traditional ballad stanza. We also know from *Piers Plowman* that Robin Hood rhymes were extant around 1375: Sloth boasts, "I can [= know] rymes of Robyn hood and Randolf erle of Chestre" (B.5.402). Some ballads recorded after 1500 appear to have origins in medieval romances and popular tales.

Ballads present a variety of topics: a few are of religious or romance origin; more common are ballads about outlaws, fairies, revenants (the dead returning to life), and the "Border ballads" (concerning raids across the northern "Debatable Land"). Most, like "Sir Patrick Spens" (Child no. 58), "Edward" (13), and "Lord Randal" (12), are local in origin; they often concern domestic violence and are composed in semi-isolated homogeneous communities by middle-class individuals (teachers, blacksmiths, etc.). Once accepted by the folk, the songs develop in oral tradition, being recreated in different cultural settings (thus the English "Three Ravens" is optimistic and romantic, the Scottish "Twa Corbies" pessimistic and dour).

Folk aspects of ballads include refrains; conventional diction, often borrowed from romance (red roan steed, lily white hand); "incremental repetition" of statements or questions (i.e., repetition with added information); and the leaping over of unimportant elements (motivation, description, etc.) but lingering on the action. Many ballads started out as long narratives but became compressed as they evolved orally. Sometimes (e.g., "Twa Corbies") they end up close to pure lyric.

Ballads live with the folk and evolve with the singers. Those ballads that are still sung, that are alive in tradition, will treat subjects that are timeless, that appeal today. Stories of historical interest alone, which are culturally dated, like the Robin Hood songs, lose their interest and die in the oral tradition. They are no longer sung. Also the knowledge of printed versions has hindered the evolution of the songs because the singers are inhibited by what they feel is the authority of the printed word. But it is hard to define the essential quality of what appeals to the folk, which rejects much more than it accepts. The fittest, most adaptable examples of this evolutionary genre survived: certainly no stories are more set in the past than those of the romance *King Horn* (ca. 1250) and the Breton lay *Sir Orfeo* (early 14th century). Yet the former lived half a millennium in oral tradition before it surfaced again in a printed text as "Hind Horn" (Child 17) in a fragment in 1810 and a full text in 1827. The ballad "King Orfeo" (Child 19) can be traced to the medieval story and an intervening Scottish fragment of the 16th century, *King Orphius*. It was first recorded from an oral informant in 1880. Both ballads are surely alive in tradition today. "Hind Horn" was last mentioned as sung in

Nova Scotia around 1950, and "King Orfeo" in the Shetlands in 1947. Both areas are still today fertile ground for folksingers, and these two ballads have proved their ability to survive. In general, however, the medieval ballad remains embalmed in the printed words of anthologies.

Thomas J. Garbáty

Bibliography

Manual 6:1753–1808, 2019–70; Bronson, Bertrand H., ed. *The Traditional Tunes of the Child Ballads.* 4 vols. Princeton: Princeton University Press, 1959–72; Child, Francis J., ed. *The English and Scottish Popular Ballads.* 5 vols. Boston: Houghton-Mifflin, 1882–98; Dronke, Peter. "Learned Lyric and the Popular Ballad in the Early Middle Ages." *Studi medievali* (Rome) 17 (1976): 1–40; Fowler, David C. *A Literary History of the Popular Ballad.* Durham: Duke University Press, 1968; Leach, MacEdward, ed. *The Ballad Book.* New York: Harper, 1955; Percy, Thomas. *Reliques of Ancient English Poetry.* 3 vols. London: Dodsley, 1765; Vargyas, Lajos. *Researches into the Mediaeval History of Folk Ballad.* Trans. Arthur H. Whitney. Budapest: Akadémiai Kiado, 1967.

See also Carol; Matter of England; Orality; *Piers Plowman;* Popular Culture; Romances; Scottish Literature, Early; Songs; Versification

Banks and Banking

In comparison with more advanced regions of the Continent banking functions in England were primitive, and organizations that can reasonably be termed banks enjoyed but a fleeting existence. By the 12th century facilities existed for borrowing money at interest (usury), but the only practitioners were the Jews. They were expelled in 1290, though by then they had been partially superseded in this business by Italian merchants.

From an early date there must have been provision for manual exchange—the national exchange of coin in one currency for that in another. The story is obscure, but in England it may always have been, as it was later, a royal monopoly. The only other quasi-banking function was the safe-custody of treasure or valuables, sometimes deposited by the king or rich nobles in monasteries, particularly houses of the Templars. This was purely passive, the money being sealed up until called for.

The arrival of Italian merchants in the early 13th century slowly transformed the situation. The Italians were not financiers but traders, importing luxury goods and exporting cloth, wool, and tin. For most Italians trade remained the primary business, and even the few corporate societies that developed a fully fledged banking arm generally continued to trade. The first diversion was lending money to the crown, often as a favor, or even involuntarily, rather than as a strictly business proposition. The earliest loans were advanced in Rome to support the cost of English diplomacy there, but soon money was lent in England and elsewhere.

By the late 13th century, when the risk of prosecution for usury had been removed, it was safe to deal with nonroyal debtors. Many monasteries and nobles are then found to be indebted to Italian merchants, but it was still necessary to disguise payment of interest and it is seldom possible to calculate the rates charged. In this period deposit banking—where the client placed money with the banker—also appeared. Unlike the hoards that had previously been left in monasteries these deposits could be used by the bank as working capital, though the scale and precise details of the operations are a matter of dispute.

Some deposits may still have been made for reasons of security, but a person with a credit balance could draw upon it in the same way as one uses a modern checkbook account. Isabella de Forz used an account with the Riccardi to transfer money around the country for her own use; her agents in Yorkshire made payments of cash, while others took delivery in the south of England. Hugh Despenser the younger ordered his bankers to settle obligations to his creditors and instructed debtors to make payments into his account. Walter Langton, bishop of Lichfield, had interest-paying deposits with the Bellardi. There is no evidence that Despenser received interest on his accounts with the Bardi and Peruzzi, but neither did they charge him for their services.

Even more of an innovation than deposit banking, and in the long run far more significant, was the introduction of the business of international exchanges, that is, the transfer of funds from one country to another by letters of obligation. This began in the early 13th century when the papacy commissioned merchants to receive money due in England and make payment in Rome. Later the crown, nobility, and merchants turned to the Italians for similar services. Attention has focused chiefly on the outward flow of funds, but it was not a one-way business. Before the end of the 13th century English wool merchants sometimes obtained letters of obligation to repatriate profits of overseas sales.

The great era of Italian banking was the reign of Edward I. Banks were already in retreat during the reign of his son, Edward II, and largely disappeared within a few years of Edward III's succession. Crown patronage was an important factor in inspiring general public confidence, which brought success to the banks; the withdrawal of patronage was a major cause of their eclipse. Henry III had borrowed haphazardly from any merchants able and willing to lend, but Edward I elevated the Riccardi of Lucca to the status of crown banker. He assigned to them great branches of royal revenue, most notably the wool export custom. In the certainty of a regular income the company routinely met royal orders for payments. In 1294 Edward went to war with France, and when the company was not able to meet his excessive demands he closed down its English branch—an act that contributed to its international failure.

In 1299 the Frescobaldi of Florence assumed the mantle of royal banker and continued until dismissed by the Lords Ordainers in 1311. From about 1313 the Bardi of Florence moved cautiously into the breach and remained there until brought down by Edward III, soon after the outbreak of the Hundred Years War, in much the same way as his grandfather had destroyed the Riccardi. This fiasco finally put an end to the involvement of banks in government finance. It also provided a further check to the general operation of banks in England, where they had already experienced a setback after a number of failures in the early 14th century. Banking functions did not cease, but there is no evidence of deposit banking after this.

The lending of money at interest continued, and the business of foreign exchange expanded despite intermittent hostility from parliament. Legislators claimed that letters of exchange were a cause of bullion loss and tried unsuccessfully to restrict their use. Most foreign exchange probably remained in Italian hands, since its most important prerequisite was a reliable correspondent on the Continent to honor letters drawn up in England. Italians continued to have better connections than other nationalities, and banking remained an un-English affair throughout the Middle Ages.

T.H. Lloyd

Bibliography

Chiappelli, F., ed. *The Dawn of Modern Banking*. New Haven: Yale University Press, 1979; Kaeuper, Richard. *Bankers to the Crown: The Riccardi of Lucca and Edward I*. Princeton: Princeton University Press, 1973; Kaeuper, Richard. "The Frescobaldi of Florence and the English Crown." *Studies in Medieval and Renaissance History* 10 (1973): 41–95; Lloyd, T.H. *Alien Merchants in England in the High Middle Ages*. Brighton: Harvester, 1982.

See also Aliens and Alien Merchants; Exchequer; Jews; Staple

Baptismal Fonts

Baptismal fonts of stone or lead are a feature of English Romanesque art. While the Anglo-Saxons may have produced fonts of stone or wood, none has survived, although a number of Anglo-Saxon cross-shafts have been reused as fonts, the most famous example being the upside-down cross-shaft or base (dated ca. 1000) at Melbury Bubb. The Melbury Bubb font is carved with scenes from the bestiary (serpent and stag, lion breathing life into its cubs, hyena).

Fig. 20. Stone font, Eardisley Church, Herefordshire, ca. 1140. Lion. Courtesy of L. Hoey.

Fig. 21. Stone font, Eardisley Church, Herefordshire, ca. 1140. Harrowing of Hell. Courtesy of L. Hoey.

A dramatic increase in font production is evident in the third quarter of the 11th century, possibly coincident with the Norman program of church building (or rebuilding) in England. By the mid-12th century there is evidence for schools of sculptors and for production in centralized workshops. The ca. 1140 fonts at Castle Frome, Shobdon, and Eardisley in Herefordshire (figs. 20–21), Chaddesley Corbett in Worcestershire, and Stottesdon in Shropshire are associated with the work of Hereford School sculptors. The Castle Frome font is particularly fine. Its chalice-shaped bowl is carved with a combination Trinity and Baptism of Christ and symbols of the evangelists, all framed by bands of interlace at rim and stem. The base is formed of three crouching figures, possibly meant to be images of sin.

At some point in the 1160s a group of black Tournai "marble" fonts were imported into England, possibly by Henry of Blois. All seven surviving fonts have square bowls supported by a central column and four corner pillars. They appear to have been extremely popular and were soon imitated in cheaper native stone by a workshop in Norfolk (active 1160–80).

A third workshop was active in the Chiltern hills ca. 1170–90. Fonts of this school are characterized by their chalice shapes, fluted bowls, and scalloped bases carved with foliate ornament.

The last of the workshops devoted to font carving was active in the West Country (Devon and Cornwall) from ca. 1190 to ca. 1225. West Country fonts are characterized by cushion-shaped bowls supported by thick octagonal stems. The forms of the bowls are frequently decorated with single rosettes surrounded by a double-headed serpent, but the real trademark of the school is the motif of the human head (sometimes with angels' wings) that protrudes from each of the four corners of the bowl.

Many other fonts were produced by smaller or less specialized workshops, resulting in a wide variety of decorative programs ranging from simple unadorned bowls to fonts decorated with scenes from the life of Christ. The font at Bridekirk (Cumbria) includes a portrait of the sculptor Richard with chisel and mallet at work on a bit of foliate ornament. Richard also added his name in runes.

Lead fonts also became popular in the 12th century. Thirty lead fonts survive in England, sixteen of 12th-century date. Produced primarily in the two lead-mining districts, Derbyshire and the Mendips, their distribution suggests that they were most popular with parish churches in the south of England. They were produced either by casting in sections, which were then welded together, or by casting a single sheet, the ends of which could be bent round and welded together to form a cylinder onto which a circular bottom was added. Decoration was impressed into the mold.

Due to their more limited area of production as well as to the ability of the artists to reuse molds, the lead fonts are more unified in style and iconography than the stone corpus. They are decorated with three main types of decoration: foliate ornament, figures beneath arches, and alternating figures and acanthus scrolls in arcades. The latter type of decoration is characteristic of fonts produced in Gloucestershire ca. 1130–40. Four identical fonts decorated with twelve arcades containing seated figures alternating with acanthus scrolls survive at Frampton, Oxenhall, Siston, and Tidenham; two related fonts with fewer arcades also survive.

Fonts continued to be made in England to the end of the Middle Ages; never again, however, did they enjoy the prominence they achieved in the 12th century.

Catherine E. Karkov

Bibliography

Bond, Francis. *Fonts and Font Covers.* London: Frowde, 1908; Stone, Lawrence. *Sculpture in Britain: The Middle Ages.* 2d ed. Harmondsworth: Penguin, 1972; Yapp, W.B. "The Font at Melbury Bubb." *Proceedings of the Dorset Natural History & Archaeological Society* 3 (1989): 128–29; Zarnecki, George, Janet Holt, and Tristram Holland, eds. *English Romanesque Art 1066–1200.* London: Weidenfeld & Nicolson, 1984.

See also Art, Romanesque; Sculpture, Romanesque

Barbour, John (ca. 1320–1395)

Scottish poet; appointed archdeacon of Aberdeen by 1357. Barbour's verse chronicle *The Bruce* celebrates in over 13,000 lines of rhyming couplets the heroic deeds of Robert Bruce, king of the Scots from 1306 to 1329, and his follower James Douglas, including England's defeat at the Battle of Bannockburn (1314). The poem was half-completed by 1375 and apparently finished by 1378; it stands as the only near-contemporary account from the Scottish viewpoint of the events it describes. Although Barbour uses clear, well-selected facts and considerable detail in his poem, as well as excellent descriptions of adventures and combats, the historical validity of *The Bruce* has been questioned, since Barbour exaggerates several episodes, particularly inflating the number of foes Bruce faced. However, since *The Bruce* is fundamentally a patriotic epic designed to celebrate Scotland's struggle for freedom, the romantic elements—and the living picture of chivalry they provide—in fact blend well with the historical aspects of the work.

Written in the lowland Scots dialect of English, *The Bruce* survives in two manuscripts, Cambridge, St. John's College 191 (G.23), and Edinburgh, National Library of Scotland Advocates' 19.2.2.

Eileen Jankowski

Bibliography

PRIMARY

Douglas, Archibald A.H., ed. and trans. *The Bruce: An Epic Poem Written around the Year* A.D. *1375.* Glasgow: MacLellan, 1964; Skeat, Walter W., ed. *The Bruce.* 2 vols. STS 31–33. Edinburgh: Blackwood, 1894.

SECONDARY

New *CBEL* 1:466–67; *Manual* 8:2681–86, 2891–2904.

See also Battles of Bannockburn and Boroughbridge; Chivalry; Chronicles; Harry, "Blind"; Peter of Langtoft; Romances; Scottish Literature, Early

Barnack

Only the elaborate tower survives of what must have been a notable Anglo-Saxon church of Northamptonshire, though six stones at the east end of the north aisle form part of a round arch antedating the present arcade cut through the wall; the Taylors considered that the thinness of the wall favored an Anglo-Saxon date. Rodwell suggested that a possible south porch of timber once covered the entrance of the tower (167). The name Barnack may designate "warrior oak," possibly linked to a meeting or judgment place. Baldwin Brown claimed that the church was known for legal proceedings in this period.

The lower stage of the tower was a large chamber some 18 feet square internally and ca. 25 feet high, as the sills of all three windows in it are 20 feet up and the 13-foot-wide grand tower arch stands 20 feet high as well, with stripwork and notable imposts extending its size. Thus the first stage, now vaulted, occupies at least half of the total 52-foot height of the Anglo-Saxon parts of the tower, embellished internally with two openings, perhaps aumbries (recesses for sacred vessels), in the north and south walls, and a triangular-headed seat in the west wall. This seat may have been for a secular or religious person of importance, as in the legal proceedings mentioned, or it may have served a monastic context as the abbot's chair. Remains of wooden seats/benches for 40 were found on either side of the central seat in 1854–55, though their date is unknown. Arguably, then, Barnack may preserve a rare western sanctuary such as Canterbury had.

Externally the tower is covered with pilaster strips resting on corbels, dividing each side into four sections. The first stage has a south door with stripwork, upper windows on three sides, and a sundial with acanthuslike carving on the south. The south window has birds carved into the corners of the window-frame top, while the west window has a triangular-headed opening surmounted by a projecting beast's head reminiscent of Deerhurst's. Double rows of stripwork separate the two Anglo-Saxon stages. The upper stage is elaborate, with a door opening into the previously internal roof space on the

Fig. 22. Barnack, upper stage of west tower, west side. Courtesy of K.M. Wickham-Crowley.

east and the other three sides all having sculptured panels. The panels rest on plinths above the stripwork and have vines and leaves surmounted by bird carvings (fig. 22). The south panel displays a bird on top that is probably a Victorian addition, since 19th-century illustrations show the slab broken. The panels have windows to either side, except on the west, where an upper doorway perhaps once opened to a gallery. Near the top of the second stage are central belfry openings or windows. Those on the north and south have beautifully carved *transennae* (stone screens) of curving geometrical design, while the east and west have less elaborate slabs carved with four long slots, two over two, perhaps forming a cross. The final piece of sculpture from the site, found beneath the floor of the north aisle in 1931, depicts a seated haloed Christ(?) in high relief, blessing with one hand while the other rests a book or tablet on his left knee. The figure, bearded and elaborately draped, has been dated variously as late Saxon or Anglo-Norman.

Kelley M. Wickham-Crowley

Bibliography

Brown, Gerard Baldwin. *The Arts in Early England.* Vol. 2: *Anglo-Saxon Architecture.* Rev. ed. London: Murray, 1925; Fernie, Eric. *The Architecture of the Anglo-Saxons.* London: Batsford, 1983, pp. 139–41; Fisher, Ernest Arthur, "Barnack." In *The Greater Anglo-Saxon Churches: An Architectural-Historical Study.* London: Faber & Faber, 1962, pp. 190–96, pls. 83–86; Rodwell, Warwick. "Anglo-Saxon Church Building: Aspects of Design and Construction." In *The Anglo-Saxon Church: Papers on History, Architecture and Archaeology in Honour of Dr H.M. Taylor,* ed. Lawrence A.S. Butler and Richard K. Morris. CBA Research Report 60. London: CBA, 1986, pp. 156–75; Taylor, Harold M., and Joan Taylor. "Barnack." In *Anglo-Saxon Architecture.* Vol. 1. Cambridge: Cambridge University Press, 1965, pp. 43–47; Taylor, Harold M., and Joan Taylor. "Architectural Sculpture in Pre-Norman England." *JBAA,* 3d ser. 29 (1966): 4–51.

See also Architecture, Anglo-Saxon; Barton-on-Humber; Canterbury Cathedral; Earls Barton Tower

Baronial Reform (in the Reign of Henry III)

Despite the reforms that stemmed from Magna Carta relations between Henry III and his barons led to a series of political crises in the 1250s and 1260s. Questions surrounding royal executive power remained in dispute and were exacerbated when young Henry came of age.

Reform was mooted on numerous occasions between the king's assumption of personal power in 1234 and 1258, but to little effect. An armed demonstration by magnates at the parliament of April 1258 forced Henry to concede reform through a council of 24 men, twelve to be chosen by the king, twelve by the magnates. The king swore an oath to abide by their provisions, reported in the parliament at Oxford in June. Thus the reform program known as the Provisions of Oxford came into being.

Current reexamination of the 13th-century political scene argues that the movement of 1258 was born of a split within the ruling caste, the result of rivalry for influence with the king and for control of royal patronage. The prime target of what has been called a revolution within the court of Henry III was the influence of his Lusignan half-brothers and their supporters. Much of the reform was thus designed to control access to the king and to ensure that gains by the "reforming" party would not be short-lived. There was to be a council of fifteen in constant attendance upon the king; the power of the great officers of state was reaffirmed; and the office of justiciar (in effect chief judicial officer) resurrected; castles were to be placed in the hands of loyal and native castellans.

The program, however, proved to be broader than this. Wider support was essential to baronial success, so the problems and discontents of minor landowners and freehold tenants, in particular, were drawn on. Four knights were to be chosen in each county to attend the county court, hear complaints, and produce them before the justiciar when he appeared locally. Detailed reforms were contained in the Provisions of Westminster in October 1259. High on the list of items were the depredations of the sheriffs and other royal officials. Much discontent was also revealed with the behavior of baronial officials and with the rapacity of some of the magnates, particularly (though not exclusively) those of the defeated party of 1258. The reform had a further dimension; like Magna Carta (1215) the program was concerned not only to limit abuse but to sustain the essential framework of the Angevin legal and administrative system and to extend its benefits.

Despite the ultimate political failure of the reformers the activity of 1258–59 proved not to have been in vain. The attempt to control royal power died with Simon de Montfort at Evesham in 1265, but much of the detailed legislation of 1259 was reenacted in the Statute of Marlborough of 1267 and subsequently extended during Edward I's reign. Moreover the governmental procedures of enquiry, legislation, and law enforcement used so successfully by the reformers in 1258–59 were taken up and became part of the normal process of Edward I's government.

P.R. Coss

Bibliography

Carpenter, D.A. "What Happened in 1258?" In *War and Government in the Middle Ages,* ed. J.B. Gillingham and J.C. Holt. Cambridge: Boydell, 1984, pp. 106–19; Carpenter, D.A. "English Peasants in Politics, 1258–1267." *Past and Present* 136 (August 1992): 3–42; Maddicott, J.R. "Magna Carta and the Local Community 1215–1259." *Past and Present* 102 (February 1984): 25–65; Maddicott, J.R. "Edward I and the Lessons of Baronial Reform: Local Government, 1258–80." In *Thirteenth Century England* 1, ed. P.R. Coss and S.D. Lloyd. Woodbridge: Boydell, 1985, pp. 1–30; Treharne, R.F., and I.J. Sanders, eds. *Documents of the Baronial Movement of Reform and Rebellion, 1258–1267.* Oxford: Clarendon, 1973.

See also Battles of Lewes and Evesham; Edward I; Henry III; Magna Carta; Simon de Montfort

Barton-on-Humber

Late-10th-century Barton-on-Humber is important to the history of Anglo-Saxon architectural study because of its exceptionally detailed modern excavation and study, and because Thomas Rickman used it in his pioneering 1817 book to establish, by relative chronology, those features distinctive from and preceding Norman work that have survived.

He identified Anglo-Saxon remains by creating "principles of archaeological stratification in [standing] buildings" not applied to buried sites for another 50 years (Rodwell, 1990: 25).

Located in Lincolnshire, now Humberside, the original church was late Anglo-Saxon. Evidence for previous domestic occupation on the site exists from Romano-British and pagan Anglo-Saxon times. Compact gravel floors were found dating to the 5th and 6th centuries, "clearly confined by what must have been timber-framed walls of rectilinear buildings"

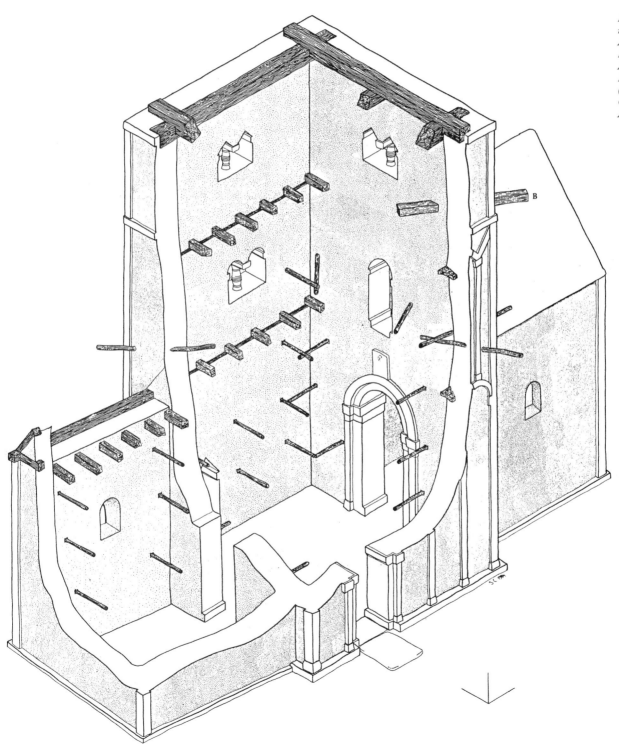

Fig. 23. Cut-away isometric drawing of the Anglo-Saxon church at Barton-on-Humber. After W. Rodwell, in Butler and Morris (1986). Courtesy of the Council for British Archaeology.

(Rodwell and Rodwell, 1982: 289). In the Middle Saxon period the ground was leveled and silt deposited over the site, while a large bank and ditch were constructed as an enclosure. No later than the 9th century a cemetery was built outside the enclosure, and the waterlogged soil has preserved a remarkable collection of wooden coffins. Some were joined with iron clenches and roves, implying a clinker-built technique such as was used in boat building. Others were made without any metal, using pegs and dowels. The Anglo-Saxon church of the late 10th century had a central tower (fig. 23) that served as nave, a western chamber that served as a baptistery, and an eastern chancel, all plastered within and without.

When the church was made redundant in 1972, it fell into disrepair but offered an unprecedented opportunity under the Rodwells' direction for "total archaeology," that is, examination of everything from the roofs and standing walls down to underground levels, while also integrating a restoration program. The tower was originally of two stages, with the lower very tall and divided into two by stripwork arcades. Rounded arcading on the north and south supports from its arches the triangular-headed arcades above it. Two upper double windows with rounded heads open on the north and south and probably provided light to the lower nave level; this implies a gallery along the walls instead of a solid floor level, to let the light pass through. The second stage, set apart by a stringcourse, has no arcading and is only distinguished by its double triangular-headed belfry windows on all sides. The original roof was most likely a spire.

The western baptistery is a rare survival, less damaged for being outside the area of later rebuildings. It is irregular in plan, though that may be due to topographic influences, as many graves predating the church also have the same orientation. Two of the windows here are remarkable for retaining oaken mid-wall slabs with holes and slots to secure some covering, while evidence survives for the other windows having been built over basketwork shapes. The font base near the southwest corner survived to identify the room, resting on a soakaway (drainage pit filled with limestone chips) whose level proved that the baptistery was a primary feature. The Rodwells suggest that a cupboard stood in the southeast corner, though it might also be the frame for a stair or ladder, and a large posthole was centrally placed in the room.

The tower contained a gallery/ringing chamber with the belfry above and served as the nave with room for about 30 standing people on its lower level. It was entered by the main south door, with an additional door in the north and doorways to the eastern and western chambers. Doors in the church were once flanked by timber doorcases, possibly ornamental and anchored in postholes. The tower's survival allowed the detailed plotting of fabric and disturbances in the fabric, yielding important information about construction methods and the role of carpentry in building. By plotting putlog holes (holes into which the ends of scaffolding timbers were inserted) and beams in the walls, Rodwell discovered how scaffolding was erected and masonry built up, determined the internal tower levels, and found the crane beam in the top tower stage that would have been used to raise heavy

materials. The chancel, though damaged because of later churches on the east, provided evidence for a screen or railing halfway across its length, to the west of which were two burials set to either side of the altar. Thus the altar backed onto the screen, leaving a smaller eastern chamber behind it that contained a single, central burial. Over the chancel arch survives a slab with an incised Anglo-Scandinavian head, probably once part of a painted Christ in Majesty.

Uncovered in the cemetery and presumed contemporary with the Anglo-Saxon building were several wells; an oven, possibly for the baking of liturgical bread (because of the lack of industrial slag or refuse), and a mortared rubble foundation half-excavated and presumed to be ca. 12 feet square (perhaps a cross base). The area has long been associated with Chad, granted 50 hides of land in ca. 669 for a monastery *Adbearw*, "At the Wood," under Wulfhere of Mercia, and several sites preserve his name. Further study is needed to integrate historical evidence with the multiple sites known to survive before a link, if any, with Barton-on-Humber is known. Rodwell considers that it may have been a cell of Peterborough Abbey. Over 1,300 graves were excavated, providing extensive study of early carpentry techniques and of burials in the later Middle Ages associated with the various rebuildings of the church to the east of the surviving two chambers. Several of these burials on the southeast of the Saxon-Norman apse were sealed by liquid clay, indicating precautions taken against disease, and two later priests' burials with chalice and paten were also discovered in the south porch of the Norman foundation. The church on the site continued to evolve after the mid-11th-century form, with three building phases in the 12th century, additional phases in each of the next three centuries, and a late Victorian addition at the east end. The two westernmost chambers of the Anglo-Saxon church survived as western annexes throughout all rebuildings.

Kelley M. Wickham-Crowley

Bibliography

Rickman, Thomas. *An Attempt to Discriminate the Styles of Architecture in England from the Conquest to the Reformation.* Seven editions in all; Rodwell recommends the 2d (London: Longman, Hurst, Rees, Orme, and Brown, 1819), 4th (London: Longman, Rees, Orme, Green & Longman, 1835), and 5th (London: Parker, 1848); Rodwell, Warwick. "Anglo-Saxon Church Building: Aspects of Design and Construction." In *The Anglo-Saxon Church: Papers on History, Architecture and Archaeology in Honour of Dr H.M. Taylor,* ed. Lawrence A.S. Butler and Richard K. Morris. CBA Research Report 60. London: CBA, 1986, pp. 156–75; Rodwell, Warwick. *The Archaeology of Religious Places: Churches and Cemeteries in Britain.* Rev. ed. Philadelphia: University of Pennsylvania Press, 1990; Rodwell, Warwick, and Kirsty Rodwell. "Barton on Humber." *Current Archaeology* 78 (1981): 108–15; Rodwell, Warwick, and Kirsty Rodwell. "St. Peter's Church, Barton-upon-Humber: Excavation and Structural Study, 1978–81." *AntJ* 62 (1982): 283–

315; Taylor, Harold M. "Old St. Peter's Church, Barton-on-Humber." *ArchJ* 131 (1974): 369–73; Taylor, Harold M., and Joan Taylor. "Barton-on-Humber." In *Anglo-Saxon Architecture*. Vol. 1. Cambridge: Cambridge University Press, 1965, pp. 52–57.

See also Barnack; Canterbury Cathedral; Earls Barton Tower

Bastard Feudalism

A phrase first used by Charles Plummer in his 1885 edition of John Fortescue's *The Governance of England,* to describe certain aspects of 15th-century English social bonds. Plummer's essay was a jejune discussion of the ills of the 15th-century English state, labeled by K.B. McFarlane as an "overrated and misleading pamphlet." Plummer's phrase has been equally overrated and misleading. Until recently the term has usurped scholarly time and energy. It is *only* a term. Moreover its underlying Victorian morality is no longer a feature in historical scholarship; later medieval English society was no worse and no better than earlier. It was, however, more complex and therefore the bonding by which people sought to hold society together more sophisticated.

In the later Middle Ages the traditional ties of feudal tenure no longer sufficed (if they ever had). Around 1300 money replaced land as the principal means by which greater men got or hoped to get lesser men to do what they wanted. This was neither more nor less efficient. It was certainly not worse in the way Plummer thought—an undermining of social and moral order. Feudalism as a tenurial structure survived, but as an outer shell.

By the mid-14th century kings were paying their armies and lords were beginning to use rent charges or cash fees to retain knights and esquires to serve in peace and war. The sociopolitical method by which English society functioned at this elite level (until the 19th century) was in place by the 15th century. The more accurate, less pejorative, but clumsier term for it is patronage-clientage. There is an additional reason for this new formulation of relationships by the second half of the 15th century (if not before); patrons and clients had no need of money to bind them together, nor of a document (the indenture of retainer) to formalize the bargain of mutual advantage. An understanding expressed in action was enough. The patron put his client in the way of the good things provided by his position in local and central affairs; the client saw to his patron's interests in those affairs.

Two exceptional and untypical retinues colored earlier thinking, those of John of Gaunt (d. 1399) and William, Lord Hastings (d. 1483). Both men were too close to the throne for too long for the number of their clients and the scale of reward to be seen as representative. The sphere of operations of all other noble and nonnoble patrons was more limited and local, the consequent gains of their clients more modest. Emphasis is now given in the scholarship to the pressure exerted on patrons by clients and the need of the former for the latter. If subjects were to be mighty they had to cultivate a following; the finesse with which they did so is what brought them success.

Colin F. Richmond

Bibliography

Coss, P.R. "Bastard Feudalism Revised." *Past and Present* 125 (November 1989): 27–64; Dunham, William H. *Lord Hastings' Indentured Retainers, 1461–1483.* New Haven: Connecticut Academy of Arts and Sciences, 1955; Hicks, Michael A. *Bastard Feudalism.* London: Longman, 1995; Holmes, George A. *The Estates of the Higher Nobility in Fourteenth Century England.* Cambridge: Cambridge University Press, 1957; Horrox, Rosemary. *Richard III: A Study of Service.* Cambridge: Cambridge University Press, 1989 [the introduction, "The Roots of Service," is an up-to-date introduction to the topic]; McFarlane, K.B. *The Nobility of Later Medieval England.* Oxford: Clarendon, 1973; McFarlane, K.B. *England in the Fifteenth Century: Collected Papers.* London: Hambledon, 1981 [a collection of major papers, especially "Parliament and Bastard Feudalism" and "Bastard Feudalism," with an important introduction by G.L. Harriss].

See also Feudalism; Knight Service; Wars of the Roses

Battle of Brunanburh, The

In four of the seven texts of the Anglo-Saxon Chronicle the sole entry for the year 937 is a 73-line poem in the style of older Anglo-Saxon poetry, *The Battle of Brunanburh.* Against the chronicle background of prose entries, many of them concerned with terrible devastation wrought by the Viking invaders both before 937 and again later, *The Battle of Brunanburh* stands out as a brilliant panegyric for King Æthelstan (924–39) and his brother Edmund (939–46). It is important both as historical document and as poem.

Independent historical sources confirm the battle's importance in the struggle to secure all of England under one overlord. The battle—whose exact site is uncertain—ended when Constantine, leader of the Scots, and Anlaf (Olaf Guthfrithsson), leader of the Norsemen, retreated, leaving five enemy kings, seven earls, and countless other nobles including Constantine's son dead on the battlefield. When Edmund died nine years later, he had fully established control by the house of Wessex over England including the north, completing the work begun by his grandfather Alfred in the 9th century.

As a poem *The Battle of Brunanburh* has received mixed reviews and has often been compared unfavorably with *The Battle of Maldon.* However, the descriptions of close combat, of the misery of defeat, of the sun's cosmic passage over the scene, and of the beasts of battle as well as the contrast between the victorious English leaders, Æthelstan and Edmund, and the utterly devastated Constantine and Anlaf qualify the poem as a great example of Anglo-Saxon literature. The poem alternates between close views of the defeated and a panoramic sweep that accentuates the balance of the two winners against the two losers and at its conclusion sets the poem firmly in a historical continuum beginning with the 5th-century conquest of Wales and England by the Angles and Saxons.

The poem's descriptive passages exemplify such Anglo-Saxon poetic devices as variation, enumeration, and antithesis. For example, in lines 5 and 6 *heowan heapolinde,* "hewed the linden-shields," varies *bordweal clufan,* "cleft the wall of shields," reversing the word order but otherwise repeating the idea. Lines 10–12a, *Hettend crungun, / Sceotta leoda and scipflotan / fæge feollan,* "The enemies perished, the people of the Scots and the sailors fell doomed," enumerate the two enemies. The description in lines 13b–17a of the sun's movement over the battlefield more elaborately employs variation of *sunne: mære tungol,* "glorious heavenly body," *Godes condel beorht,* "God's bright candle," *sio æpele gesceaft,* "that noble creation." The verb phrase *glad ofer grundas,* "glided over the ground," balances *sunne* and *mære tungol,* subjects that precede it, against *Godes condel beorht* and *sio æpele gesceaft,* which follow. The poem's dignified and measured account of the sun's motion (*op sio æpele gesceaft / sah to setle,* "until that noble creation sank to [its] setting place") enhances the sense of the battle's importance created by the larger examples of antithesis. The metaphor *sio æpele gesceaft* may also evoke a parallel between the sun and Edward's son Æthelstan, whose name means "noble stone."

The description in lines 60–65a of the beasts of battle (a traditional oral formula associating wolves and birds of prey with battlefields) employs variation and enumeration to emphasize the enjoyment of the carrion (*hræw bryttian,* 60) and contrasts sharply with the bookish final comparison of the battle to the earlier conquest of Britain. Variation emphasizes that the vanquished fled the battlefield with nothing to exult or laugh about (*hreman ne porfte,* 39, "had no need to exult"; *Gelpan ne porfte,* 44, "had no need to boast"; and *hlehhan ne porfte,* 47, "had no need to laugh") and provides an antithesis to the simple statement in line 59 that the victors returned home *wiges hremge,* "exultant in war."

Though some critics disparage *The Battle of Brunanburh* as conventional triumphalism and merely imitative of earlier verse, in fact the poem stands out in the canon of Anglo-Saxon verse as the best of the chronicle poems and probably as the best panegyric. It does draw upon earlier Anglo-Saxon poetry, but it also draws on classical rhetoric and perhaps on the Norse genre of panegyric. The result is a noble gem of a poem that celebrates with dignity and poignancy a great moment in early English history.

Phyllis R. Brown

Bibliography

PRIMARY

ASPR 6:16–20; Bradley, S.A.J., trans. *Anglo-Saxon Poetry: An Anthology of Old English Poems in Prose Translation.* London: Dent, 1982, pp. 515–18; Campbell, Alistair, ed. *The Battle of Brunanburh.* London: Heinemann, 1938; Pope, John C., ed. *Seven Old English Poems.* 2d ed. New York: Norton, 1981, pp. 5–8, 54–60.

SECONDARY

Frese, Dolores Warwick. "Poetic Prowess in *Brunanburh* and *Maldon*: Winning, Losing, and Literary Outcome." In *Modes of Interpretation in Old English Literature: Essays in Honour of Stanley B. Greenfield,* ed. Phyllis Rugg Brown, Georgia Ronan Crampton, and Fred C. Robinson. Toronto: University of Toronto Press, 1986, pp. 273–82; Lawler, Traugott. "Craft and Art." In *Literary Studies: Essays in Memory of Francis A. Drumm,* ed. John H. Dorenkamp. Wetteren, Belgium: Cultura, 1973; Lipp, Frances Randall. "Contrast and Point of View in *The Battle of Brunanburh.*" *PQ* 48 (1969): 166–77.

See also Æthelstan; Anglo-Saxon Chronicle; Armies; *Battle of Maldon;* Literary Influences: Scandinavian; Vikings

Battle of Hastings

Fought on 14 October 1066 between Harold Godwinson, king of the English, and William, duke of the Normans, who claimed the English throne. Harold commanded a force of some 8,000 fighting men, the vast majority being local levies, that is, *fyrd* troops, called up largely from the area between London and Hastings during the period beginning about 3 October. They were instructed to muster about seven miles north-northwest of Hastings, at a place now called Battle. Perhaps 1,000 or so of Harold's troops were highly trained professional fighting men, his housecarls, the personal armed followings of Harold, his brothers, and other important Anglo-Saxon magnates.

William's army comprised about 10,000 men, of whom somewhere between 2,000 and 3,000 were heavily armed horsemen. Many of William's troops were not Normans; a substantial group of mercenaries had been hired. Though he had a noteworthy contingent of archers, the Anglo-Saxons were seriously lacking in "fire power," that is, the ability to inflict damage upon the enemy's army at a distance.

Harold decisively defeated an invading Viking army around York, 190 miles from London, with great losses on both sides, only five days before learning of William's landing. He ordered the mobilization of his southern levies and rushed south with the remains of his housecarls to blockade the invaders on the Hastings peninsula and then force them to surrender or withdraw across the Channel for want of supplies, as winter made resistance impossible. On the road south, or when he reached London, Harold ordered his fleet, which was being refitted after spending the summer in the Channel to prevent the Norman crossing, to proceed to Hastings to complete the blockade.

William could not permit himself to be blockaded, and he wanted to get Harold to engage as soon as possible. In order to encourage him in this direction, and to avoid facing a fully mustered Anglo-Saxon army, William harried Sussex, where a substantial part of Harold's own estates was located.

Since Harold was not eager to engage William he took up an extremely strong defensive position on a ridge, some 2,600 feet in length, rising in spots to some 275 feet above the marshy plain. He deployed his fyrdmen in a deep phalanx with the housecarls in the front ranks to stiffen both the line and morale. William thus could have his battle, but first he would have to march his army at dawn some seven miles, establish a base below Harold, and then drive up the hill against showers of spears that would begin hitting their targets at 150 feet.

Having no choice but to fight or retreat, William had his archers loose volley after volley to "soften up" the Anglo-Saxon phalanx. Then he sent a combined force of foot and horse to attack the Anglo-Saxon lines; these held like a stone wall. A pattern of combined attacks to little or no effect was repeated into the afternoon, when William decided to try a feigned retreat with his Breton horsemen, experts in this tactic. It worked, and a portion of the right flank of the Anglo-Saxon line broke in hot pursuit of the "fleeing" Bretons. At a signal these horsemen wheeled their mounts and easily rode down the scattered foot soldiers, greatly outmatched on open ground. A second feigned retreat, now on William's right, had much the same effect. The Anglo-Saxon phalanx was much weakened as Harold's brothers and two ablest commanders were killed.

Toward dusk William's forces were gaining ground on the ridge in vigorous hand-to-hand combat when Harold was seriously wounded by an arrow, likely in the eye. With Harold's position in the center of the line overrun, the king hacked down, and the standard fallen, the Anglo-Saxon phalanx broke and a rout followed. Eudes of Boulogne and Duke William led a select force that rode down many of the fleeing enemy until exhaustion of the horses and darkness made further pursuit more dangerous than useful. Victory on the field opened the door for conquest of the kingdom.

Bernard S. Bachrach

Bibliography

Bachrach, Bernard S. "On the Origins of William the Conqueror's Horse Transports." *Technology and Culture* 26 (1985): 505–31; Bachrach, Bernard S. "Some Observations on the Military Administration of the Norman Conquest." *Anglo-Norman Studies* 7 (1985): 1–25; Brown, R. Allen. "The Battle of Hastings." *Anglo-Norman Studies* 3 (1981): 1–21.

See also Armies; Harold Goldwinson; Norman Conquest; William I

Battle of Maldon, The

OE heroic poem, of which 325 lines survive. In the summer of 991 a large fleet of Vikings (probably led by Olaf Tryggvason, king of Norway from 995 to 999/1000, and perhaps also by Swein Forkbeard, king of Denmark from 987 to 1014) raided the southeast of England, sacked Ipswich, and sailed on into the estuary of the River Blackwater to threaten Maldon. There they were opposed by Byrhtnoth, ealdorman of Essex. In the battle that followed Byrhtnoth was killed. The Vikings were left with sufficient numbers to continue to pose a military threat, for, according to the Anglo-Saxon Chronicle, they were later bought off with 10,000 pounds of silver.

At the time of his death Byrhtnoth was a senior member of the Anglo-Saxon aristocracy. He had been appointed ealdorman in 956, and for the last eight years of his life he signed second only to Ealdorman Æthelwine of East Anglia in the witness lists to royal diplomas. The violent death of so prominent a man had great social and military repercussions, and it was probably these that led Sigeric, archbishop of Canterbury, to propose buying the Vikings off. The battle was reported in many sources besides the Chronicle. Three monastic calendars note the day of Byrhtnoth's death (10 or possibly 11 August); his heroic last stand is commented upon by Byrhtferth of Ramsey in the *Life of St. Oswald,* and the battle is mentioned by many Anglo-Norman historians in the 12th century. The *Liber Eliensis (Book of Ely)* reports that Byrhtnoth's widow, Ælfflæd, gave the community at Ely, where Byrhtnoth is buried, an embroidery depicting her husband's deeds (presumably similar to the Bayeux Tapestry). In the *Liber Eliensis* there is also a more fanciful account of his dealings with the Vikings in the years leading up to his last battle. A related account, angled toward explaining why he was less generous in his will to Ramsey than he was to Ely, occurs in the Ramsey Chronicle. These stories and that on the "tapestry" are part of the legend that was wound about the memory of Byrhtnoth. It is in this context that we should view the OE heroic poem generally known as *The Battle of Maldon*.

The poem survived into the modern period in fragmentary form on three double sheets of parchment, probably used as binding leaves, which came into Sir Robert Cotton's hands at the beginning of the 17th century. He bound them into Otho A.xii, which suffered badly in the fire of 1731, when the Maldon leaves were totally lost. For our knowledge of the poem we are dependent upon an early-18th-century transcript, made probably by David Casley and now found in Bodl. Rawlinson B.203. The poem lacks both a beginning and an end, and there is now no means of dating the hand of the only surviving copy or of learning anything of the manner of its survival. Its language is for the most part uniformly late West Saxon, except that one or two spellings and some Scandinavian borrowings point to an eastern origin. It cannot be dated, but an attempt to place its composition in the reign of Cnut (1016–35), on the grounds that the term used of Byrhtnoth, *eorl,* is an anachronism, has not found general favor; rather, the tone of the piece suggests that it was intended for an audience familiar with those who died in the battle.

In the poem the story is told entirely from the English point of view. The fragment begins with Byrhtnoth deploying his troops alongside the river, across which the Vikings are evidently camped, presumably on an island. Tribute is demanded by the invaders and scornfully refused. The Vikings can attack only across a narrow causeway that is covered at high tide, and this creates a pregnant pause before the fighting starts. As the tide recedes, it becomes clear that Byrhtnoth can control the action by defending the ford, so the Vikings treacherously ask to be allowed freedom to cross and Byrhtnoth gives what the poet calls "too much land." The English form up behind a "shield wall" and battle begins. Byrhtnoth himself is engaged by one of the Vikings, whom he expertly kills, but at the moment of his triumph he suffers a severe wound, and though his squire bravely intervenes to destroy his attacker the odds are too great and Byrhtnoth falls. Some of his closest companions flee, one of them on Byrhtnoth's own horse; assuming that it is Byrhtnoth who is deserting, the company at large breaks ranks. But many remain in a doomed but noble attempt to avenge their commander, and the fragment ends with them exhorting one another to deeds of valor.

The poet adopts the heroic style of earlier OE verse. He portrays Byrhtnoth and his companions as a Germanic warlord with his *comitatus* (the traditional aristocratic warrior band), emphasizing that the battle was lost because not all the "hearth companions" maintained the loyalty owed to such a "treasure giver." At the same time the poet shows that the *comitatus* is merely a vehicle for his theme of loyalty by stressing the social, geographic, and age range of the men who died valiantly beside their leader, naming individuals from many parts of Essex but also from Mercia and Northumbria, peasant farmers alongside aristocracy, young men and old. He is not afraid to criticize his hero, condemning Byrhtnoth for allowing the Vikings across the ford but overall depicting him as an outstanding leader, a good tactician, careful of his troops, personally valiant, authoritative, generous and God-fearing. Those who die with him are characterized concisely and with skill; syntactic and verbal repetition emphasizes their common resolve. Although there are relatively few flights of fancy in its imagery, the poem is exceptionally well structured, and the selection of appropriate diction and the successful control of meter in the telling of a powerful moral tale make it one of the most dramatic and memorable short poems in the OE canon.

D.G. Scragg

Bibliography

PRIMARY

ASPR 6:7–16; Gordon, E.V., ed. *The Battle of Maldon.* With suppl. by D.G. Scragg. Manchester: Manchester University Press, 1976; Scragg, D.G., ed. *The Battle of Maldon.* Manchester: Manchester University Press, 1981.

SECONDARY

Andersen, Hans Erik. *The Battle of Maldon: The Meaning, Dating and Historicity of an Old English Poem.* Copenhagen: Department of English, University of Copenhagen, 1991; Cooper, Janet, ed. *The Battle of Maldon: Fiction and Fact.* London: Hambledon, 1993; Cross, J.E. "Oswald and Byrhtnoth: A Christian Saint and a Hero Who Is a Christian." *English Studies* 46 (1965): 93–109; Cross, J.E. "Mainly on Philology and the Interpretative Criticism of *Maldon.*" In *Old English Studies in Honour of John C. Pope,* ed. R.B. Burlin and E.B. Irving, Jr. Toronto: University of Toronto Press, 1974, pp. 235–53; Gneuss, Helmut. "*The Battle of Maldon* 89: Byrhtnoð's *ofermod* Once Again." *SP* 73 (1976): 117–37; Laborde, E.D. "The Site of *The Battle of Maldon.*" *EHR* 40 (1925): 161–73; McKinnell, J. "On the Date of *The Battle of Maldon.*" *MÆ* 44 (1975): 121–36; Rogers, H.L. "*The Battle of Maldon:* David Casley's Transcript." *N&Q* n.s. 32 (1985): 147–55; Scragg, D.G., ed. *The Battle of Maldon A.D. 991.* Oxford: Blackwell, 1991.

See also Æthelred II; *Battle of Brunanburh;* Cotton; Literary Influences: Scandinavian; Swein; Vikings

Battles of Bannockburn and Boroughbridge

The Battle of Bannockburn, fought near Stirling Castle in Scotland on 23–24 June 1314, and the Battle of Boroughbridge, fought in Yorkshire on 16 March 1322, marked turning points in the troubled reign of Edward II.

When Edward I died, the English attempt to conquer Scotland, which had been in progress since 1296, was failing. In 1306 Robert Bruce's seizure of the Scottish throne provided the Scots with energetic leadership. The English-held castles in Scotland were taken, one by one, until in 1313 Stirling Castle, strategically placed in the Lowlands, was besieged. Its constable agreed to surrender if the castle were not relieved by Midsummer's Day the following year (24 June 1314).

The challenge was taken up eagerly by Edward II, since it offered the chance of defeating the Scots in a pitched battle. Although several of his earls refused to serve, Edward II gathered an army of about 15,000 infantry (archers and spearmen) and 2,000–3,000 cavalry, with many experienced commanders. The Scottish army, which may have numbered about 7,000–10,000, included few heavy cavalry but a large number of infantrymen armed with long spears and trained to fight in circular formations ("schiltroms"). The impetuous English attack was broken up by the Scottish spearmen with heavy casualties; the English archers, who had helped win earlier battles against the Scots, never came into action, and the result was a crushing Scottish victory. Many leading English nobles were killed or captured, and Edward II had to flee for safety. Although England did not finally recognize Scottish independence until 1328, the Battle of Bannockburn humiliated England and ensured that Scotland could not be defeated. The battle also showed that cavalry forces, which had for centuries ruled the battlefields of Europe, were vulnerable to well-trained infantry prepared to stand their ground.

The Battle of Boroughbridge ended the civil war that had broken out in England in March 1321, when a group of prominent lords from the Welsh borders (the Marchers) attacked the lands of the Despensers, current royal favorites. Edward, acting with unaccustomed energy and decision, recalled the Despensers from exile, gathered an army, and early in 1322 advanced against the Marchers. Having forced the surrender or flight of most of his opponents, Edward then turned against his old enemy (and cousin), Thomas earl of Lancaster. While attempting to flee to Northumberland, Lancaster was brought to battle at Boroughbridge in Yorkshire by another royal army, advancing from the north of England and consisting mainly of "hobelers," lightly equipped cavalry used in the wars with Scotland. Lancaster was captured and executed outside his own castle of Pontefract. Though this was a major victory for Edward II, his vengeance and subsequent policies proved to be the beginning of his own downfall five years later.

J.R.S. Phillips

Bibliography

Barrow, G.W.S. *Robert Bruce and the Community of the Realm of Scotland.* 3d ed. Edinburgh: Edinburgh University Press, 1988; Maddicott, J.R. *Thomas of Lancaster, 1307–1322: A Study in the Reign of Edward II.* London: Oxford University Press, 1970; Phillips, J.R.S. *Aymer de Valence, Earl of Pembroke, 1307–1324: Baronial Politics in the Reign of Edward II.* Oxford: Clarendon, 1972; Prestwich, Michael. *The Three Edwards: War and State in England, 1272–1377.* London: Weidenfeld & Nicolson, 1980.

See also Edward I; Edward II; Edward III

Battles of Lewes and Evesham

The baronial reform movement of 1258 had resulted in the expulsion of Henry III's Lusignan half-brothers and the containing of the king. Not surprisingly the situation remained volatile, with a royalist reaction in 1261–62 and a subsequent regrouping of many of the reformers in 1263, now clearly led by the charismatic and intransigent Simon de Montfort, earl of Leicester. His decision to seek the arbitration of Louis IX of France was a major political blunder, for Louis simply gave his verdict (the Mise of Amiens, January 1264) in favor of untrammeled kingship and Henry III. The result was civil war. When the armies finally engaged, at Lewes on 14 May 1264, it was the boldness and strategy of Montfort that won the day against numerically superior forces. After ferocious fighting the king and his son Edward were in Simon's power; the Provisions of Oxford, the political platform of the earl's party, could at last be reaffirmed.

These momentous events were celebrated in verse, in the elegant *Song of Lewes,* as well as in such minor pieces as the mocking *Song against the Barons' Enemies.* However, the reformers were now in considerable difficulties, having fought against their king. The prospect of an indefinite perpetuation of Simon's power worsened the situation. The calling of burgesses from the towns as well as representatives from the counties to a parliament in January 1265 is symptomatic of the need to widen the basis of support.

With the barons from the borders in active opposition the defection of the earl of Gloucester from de Montfort's cause and Prince Edward's escape from custody were severe blows. With a second military confrontation pending Simon was effectively hemmed in west of the Severn. It was now Edward who was to prove the bold strategist. His surprise attack on the army of Simon the Younger, camped outside Kenilworth (rather than secure within the castle), effectively minimized the chances of a linkup between the two Montfortian forces upon which the old earl's success largely depended.

At Evesham, still hoping for the arrival of his son, Simon faced overwhelming odds on 4 August 1265. The result was what the Chronicle of Robert of Gloucester called "the murder of Evesham." There is a literal truth in this. After a short time of fighting Simon lay dead and his close supporters killed or captured. There followed a considerable slaughter of the fleeing footsoldiers, a feature reminiscent of Prince Edward's bloodlust against the Londoners at the Battle of Lewes. Given the military circumstances of the day there was no need for the defeated earl to die. His death was a political act. The wholesale seizure and confiscation of rebel lands considerably delayed the subsequent pacification of the realm.

The Battle of Evesham had been decisive. Although the events of the years 1258–65 were to have a profound impact upon the future government of England, the directive role of the monarchy had been secured. Meanwhile Simon de Montfort's heroic stand could not fail to have an impact upon contemporaries, just as it has captured the imagination of antiquarians and historians ever since.

P.R. Coss

Bibliography

Carpenter, D.A. *The Battles of Lewes and Evesham 1264/65.* Staffordshire: Mercia, 1987; Cox, D.C. *The Battle of Evesham: A New Account.* Evesham: The Vale of Evesham Historical Society, 1988; Kingsford, Charles L., ed. *The Song of Lewes.* Oxford: Oxford University Press, 1890; Knowles, C.H. "The Resettlement of England after the Barons' War, 1264–67." *TRHS,* 5th ser. 32 (1982): 25–41; Maddicott, J.R. "The Mise of Lewes, 1264." *EHR* 98 (1983): 588–603.

See also Baronial Reform; Edward I; Harley Lyrics; Henry III; Simon de Montfort

Bayeux Tapestry

The Bayeux Tapestry, made within the lifetime of men who fought in the Battle of Hastings, is a principal document relating to the Norman Conquest of England in 1066. In a series of pictures captioned in Latin the unknown artist recounts the rivalry of Harold Godwinson, earl of Wessex, and William, duke of Normandy, for the throne of England. The upper and lower borders of the Tapestry are filled with figures of birds and beasts, scenes from fables, and other matter. During the winter of 1982–83 the Tapestry was taken from its showcase in the former Bishop's Palace at Bayeux, photographed front and back, subjected to technical analysis, gently vacuum-cleaned, and rehung in its present quarters, the Centre Guillaume le Conquérant, near the Cathedral of Bayeux, Normandy, where it attracts ever-growing numbers of visitors.

Though called a tapestry, the work is in fact an embroidery done in colored woolen threads on a ribbon of linen about 230 feet long and 20 inches wide. It is the only large-scale example of needlework surviving from the Middle Ages. Buildings and trees help frame individual episodes, which include striking scenes of banqueting, ships at sea, fighting at Hastings (fig. 13: see ARMS AND ARMOR), royal and ducal palaces, churches, and incidents of daily life. Some 1,500 figures of men and women, horses, miscellaneous birds and beasts, ships, and buildings appear in the work. Scenes from Aesop's fables and other imagery scattered throughout the borders suggest themes appropriate to the action in the main panels.

The consistency of the design throughout strongly suggests a single designer. Though hard evidence is lacking, it is generally held that, given contemporary social conditions, the anonymous designer was almost certainly a man and the needleworkers probably both men and women.

The story in the Tapestry begins as Edward the Confessor, the reigning English monarch, sends Harold on an unspecified mission across the English Channel. The crossing ends with Harold's capture by Guy of Ponthieu. William of Normandy rescues Harold and takes him to Rouen, from which place the two men leave on a campaign in Brittany. At the successful conclusion of the campaign William rewards Harold with a suit of armor, and Harold promises that William is to succeed King Edward, who has no immediate heir, on the English throne (fig. 24). Edward dies, and Harold, breaking his oath, takes the English throne. In response William builds a fleet, crosses to England, and defeats Harold in the Battle of Hastings. Harold dies in the battle.

In part because of the Tapestry's popular appeal and because of the scarcity of surviving evidence the literature interpreting it is strikingly uneven, ranging from solid scholarship to legend and conjecture. One finds sheer guesses as to the identities of persons, birds, beasts, and actions shown in the work. Careful research like that of Helen Chefneaux's identification of eight of Aesop's fables in the borders has been followed by later attempts to expand the number of fables to as many as 40, largely on the basis of conjecture. Such efforts serve to emphasize the continuing need for well-documented, cautiously applied research.

During the 1980s scholarly consensus began to coalesce around the major issues of date, locale, and patronage. The years from the late 1060s to the mid-1090s are now widely taken to bracket the probable period during which the Tapestry was made. Broad consensus has also developed on one or more English locations, including St. Augustine's Abbey, Canterbury, as the place or places where the embroidery was done. Odo, half-brother of the Conqueror, is now widely believed to have been the patron of the work.

Discussions of the Tapestry's support of an English or a Norman point of view of the Conquest began in the late 1970s to give increasing emphasis to English elements both of design and of purpose. Debate on this issue continues. Several writers have suggested that a number of puzzling elements in the Tapestry may be attributable to English embroiderers secretly working Saxon views into its story. Bernstein gives an extended exposition of the concept of the Tapestry's hidden messages. Discussions of this topic commonly omit the possibility that there may have been, following the Conquest, various Norman as well as various Saxon views of the event—the possibility, for example, that William the Conqueror's views may have differed from those of the patron of the Tapestry, Odo, with whom the Conqueror is known to have had violent disagreements.

Behind a number of attempts to reconcile the Tapestry's account of events with accounts in various early chronicles there lies a fundamental issue: whether the Tapestry is best understood as primarily a chronicle of accurate historical information or as a work of art shaped by its own artistic needs and aims. Widespread agreement on this issue is not in sight. In any case the Tapestry cannot be taken as simply the illustrated version of any known chronicle. Vigorous efforts to bring the Tapestry's imagery into conformity with this or that written record have led to continuing debate over exactly what it is that the Tapestry itself shows.

Fig. 24. Bayeux Tapestry. Harold swears an oath before William. Reproduced by special permission of the City of Bayeux.

Among many recent studies of the Tapestry two in particular are notably helpful: David Wilson's *The Bayeux Tapestry: The Complete Tapestry in Colour* (1985) and Shirley Ann Brown's *The Bayeux Tapestry: History and Bibliography* (1988). The scale of reproduction in Wilson's book is more than half the original size (approximately 54 percent).

Brown annotates virtually every study done on the Tapestry in the past two and a half centuries. The core of her book is an annotated bibliography of more than 500 books, articles, and other material bearing on the Tapestry. For each item she gives a full bibliographical reference, a summary of content, and a list of the principal topics touched upon. Valuable appendices list ancillary material: documents, literary sources, and background readings. She gives what is probably the most complete history of the Tapestry.

J. Bard McNulty

Bibliography

Bernstein, David J. *The Mystery of the Bayeux Tapestry.* Chicago: University of Chicago Press, 1986; Brooks, Nicholas P., and Walker, H.E. "The Authority and Interpretation of the Bayeux Tapestry." *Proceedings of the Battle Conference, 1978.* Ipswich: Boydell, 1979, pp. 1–34; Brown, Shirley Ann. "The Bayeux Tapestry: History or Propaganda." In *The Anglo-Saxons: Synthesis and Achievement,* ed. J. Douglas Woods and David A.E. Pelteret. Waterloo: Wilfrid Laurier University Press, 1985, pp. 11–28; Brown, Shirley Ann. *The Bayeux Tapestry: History and Bibliography.* Woodbridge: Boydell, 1988; Cowdrey, H.E.J. "Towards an Interpretation of the Bayeux Tapestry." *Anglo-Norman Studies* 10 (1988): 49–65; Dodwell, Charles R. "The Bayeux Tapestry and the French Secular Epic." *Burlington Magazine* 108, no. 764 (1966): 549–60; Grape, Wolfgang. *The Bayeux Tapestry: Monument to a Norman Triumph.* Munich and New York: Prestel, 1994; McNulty, John Bard. *The Narrative Art of the Bayeux Tapestry Master.* New York: AMS, 1988; Stenton, F.M., ed. *The Bayeux Tapestry: A Comprehensive Survey.* 2d ed. London: Phaidon, 1965; Wilson, David M. *The Bayeux Tapestry: The Complete Tapestry in Colour.* London: Thames & Hudson, 1985.

See also Battle of Hastings; Edward the Confessor; Harold Godwinson; Norman Conquest; William I

Beast Epic and Fable

Two related yet distinct genres of European writing represented in ME. William Caxton translated and printed two books of animal stories: *The History of Reynard the Fox* (1481) and his *Aesop* (1484), taken respectively from Dutch and French. These books represent the two most important branches of animal story in medieval Europe, the Aesopic fables and the Reynardian material (also known as beast epic). The primary difference between the Aesopic collections and the Reynardian tales is a binary structure in the Aesopic material, of fable followed by morality *(moralitas),* as distinct from the continuous narrative of the beast epic. The Aesopic material also contains stories of many animals, whereas the beast epic focuses especially on the fox Reynard (sometimes on the wolf Ysengrim), and his cynical, amoral dealings in and around the court of the lion.

The Aesopic conventions are much older than the Reynardian material. The Latin collection of Phaedrus (1st century A.D.), a translation of a Greek "Aesop," represents the chief source of later fable collections, although the collection of Avianus (ca. 400?) was also a medieval school text. Phaedrus was paraphrased in a collection known as "Romulus" (ca. 350–500?), which was versified in the 12th century. This collection is behind many of the vernacular Aesops of the later Middle Ages. The Reynardian material derives ultimately from Aesop (one of its central stories, the tale of the sick lion, in which the fox tricks the wolf, appears in Aesop), but the continuous narrative characteristic of the Reynard material begins with the *Ecbasis Captivi* (mid-11th century) and is greatly developed in the *Ysengrimus* (1148–49), an important source for the earliest branches of the *Roman de Renart.*

In ME and Scots these traditions are surprisingly little represented, but what representation they do have occurs at a high level of sophistication in both Chaucer and Henryson. The beast-epic tradition first appears in a short 13th-century story, *The Fox and the Wolf;* then in an early-14th-century political poem (where the fox and wolf represent those who bribe justice); and in Chaucer's *Nun's Priest's Tale* (1396–1400), which also introduces fabular elements. The Scottish poet Henryson incorporates Reynardian material into his *Fables* (1460–80), and in the same period Caxton produces his translation, mentioned above. Aesopic material is found in Lydgate's *Isopes Fabules* (ca. 1400), Henryson's *Fables,* and Caxton. These animal stories should be distinguished from other works in which animals speak and act, like *The Owl and the Nightingale,* which draw on animal fable to some extent but owe their deepest debts to traditions of debate poetry.

The interpretive assumptions of animal fables are usually fairly simple: an uncomplicated story in abbreviated narrative style is followed by a straightforward moral or allegorical meaning. It was for this reason that fables were used as school texts. In the hands of artists like Chaucer and Henryson, however, this simplistic form becomes the occasion for the sophisticated mixing of rhetorical style and for an acute awareness of the interpretive problems raised even by simple stories. Henryson also extends the normally proverbial, "worldly wise" wisdom of fables to include more systematic philosophical perspectives, and his *Fables* must be rated as one of the finest fable collections in European literature.

James Simpson

Bibliography

PRIMARY

Bennett, J.A.W., and G.V. Smithers, eds. *The Fox and the Wolf.* In *Early Middle English Verse and Prose.* 2d corr. ed. Oxford: Clarendon, 1974, pp. 65–76; Blake, N.F., ed. *The History of Reynard the Fox, Translated from the Dutch Original by William Caxton.* EETS o.s. 263.

London: Oxford University Press, 1970; Lenaghan, R.T., ed. *Caxton's Aesop*. Cambridge: Harvard University Press, 1967; MacCracken, Henry Noble, ed. *Isopes Fabules*. In *The Minor Poems of John Lydgate*. Part 2. EETS o.s. 192. London: Humphrey Milford, 1934.

SECONDARY

Manual 3:784–87, 935–37; 4:967–76, 1138–46; 6:1857–59, 2122–23; 9:3138–51, 3473–86; Blake, N.F. "Reynard the Fox in England." In *Aspects of the Medieval Animal Epic,* ed. Edward Rombauts and Andries Welkenhuysen. Leuven: University of Leuven Press, 1975, pp. 53–65; Carnes, Pack. *Fable Scholarship: An Annotated Bibliography*. New York: Garland, 1985; Varty, Kenneth. *Reynard the Fox: A Study of the Fox in Medieval English Art*. Leicester: Leicester University Press, 1967.

See also Bestiaries; Bozon; Caxton; Chaucer; Exemplum; Henryson; Literary Influences: French, Medieval Latin; Marie de France; *Physiologus;* Satire; Schools

Beauchamp Family

From 1066, when Urse d'Abetôt fought at Hastings for William, to 1268, when William de Beauchamp became earl of Warwick, the Beauchamps were the dominant local power in Worcestershire. Later members of the family took a prominent part in the affairs of the kingdom. By the early 15th century the family had become one of the wealthiest in England.

When William de Beauchamp succeeded his maternal uncle William Malduit as earl of Warwick in 1268, he emphasized his descent from the legendary ancestor Guy of Warwick. Already a romance about Guy had become one of the most widely known of ancestral romances. William named his son Guy, and a tower added to Warwick Castle was called Guy's Tower. The badge of the earls combined the bear associated with their ancestor Urse and the ragged staff, the weapon of Guy. Earl Guy fought in Edward I's campaigns in Scotland, was one of the Ordainers in 1310, and was responsible in 1312 for the capture and execution of Piers Gaveston, Edward II's notorious favorite. The next earl, Thomas, was with the Black Prince at the battles of Crécy in 1346 and Poitiers in 1356. His son Thomas was appointed governor of young Richard II by the Good Parliament in 1377, became one of the Lords Appellant against Richard's arbitrary rule, and was later imprisoned by the king in the Tower of London (in what became known as the Beauchamp Tower).

Richard Beauchamp (1381–1439) was the most famous member of the family. Noted for feats of arms from his youth, he captured the banner of the Welsh rebel Owen Glendower in battle and later commanded half of Henry V's army in France. He held Joan of Arc prisoner during the trial that led to her execution. At his own death Richard was buried in a splendid chapel in the church at Warwick with a tomb and gilded effigy that remains one of the glories of late-medieval art.

Charles R. Young

Bibliography

Dillon, Viscount, and W.H. St. John Hope, eds. *Pageant of the Birth, Life and Death of Richard Beauchamp, Earl of Warwick, K.G., 1389–1439*. London: Longmans Green, 1914; Mason, Emma, ed. *The Beauchamp Cartulary Charters, 1100–1268*. Publications of the Pipe Roll Society n.s. 43 (1980); Mason, Emma. "Legends of the Beauchamps' Ancestors: The Use of Baronial Propaganda in Medieval England." *JMH* 10 (1984): 25–40; Ross, Charles. *The Estates and Finances of Richard Beauchamp, Earl of Warwick*. Dugdale Society, Occasional Papers 12 (1956); Rous, John. *The Rous Roll*. Intro. Charles Ross. Gloucester: Sutton, 1979.

See also Matter of England

Beaufort, Margaret (1443–1509)

Countess of Richmond and Derby; translator, literary patron, and educational benefactor. Daughter of John Beaufort and great-granddaughter of John of Gaunt, she married successively Edmund Tudor, Henry Stafford, and Thomas, Lord Stanley; in 1485 her son Henry Tudor became King Henry VII. She was famous for her learning and piety, manifested in her endowments of Oxford and Cambridge chairs of divinity and her role in the founding of Christ's College and St. John's College, Cambridge.

Lady Margaret owned books in English, French, and Latin and instigated the compilation or publication of a range of works, including ordinances for royal ceremonies; Caxton's translation of *Blanchardin and Eglantine* and his prayer collection known as *The Fifteen O's;* liturgies printed by Haghe, de Worde, and Pynson; and de Worde's editions of Hilton's *Scale of Perfection,* Watson's translation of Sebastian Brandt's *Ship of Fools,* Hatfield's translation of *The Life of St. Ursula,* and a treatise and sermon by her friend Bishop Fisher. Her own surviving translations, both first printed by Pynson, were from French versions of orthodox devotional works: a contribution to William Atkinson's rendering of *The Imitation of Christ* (1504) and *The Mirror of Gold for the Sinful Soul* (ca. 1506), attributed in its original Latin to the Carthusian monk James of Gruytroede, prior of the Charterhouse of Liège.

Julia Boffey

Bibliography

Ingram, John K., ed. *De imitatione Christi*. EETS e.s. 63. London: Kegan Paul, Trench, Trübner, 1893; Jones, Michael K., and Malcolm G. Underwood. *The King's Mother: Lady Margaret Beaufort, Countess of Richmond and Derby*. Cambridge: Cambridge University Press, 1992.

See also Beaufort Family; Henry VII; Mystical and Devotional Writings; Patronage, Literary; Printing; Translation; Women in ME Literature

Beaufort Family

The surname of the four children of John of Gaunt, duke of Lancaster, by his mistress, Katherine Swynford. They were legitimated when their parents eventually married in 1396; they and their descendants were to play an outstanding part in 15th-century politics (fig. 25). Early favors came from Richard II, but it was the accession of their half-brother, Henry IV, that brought them to prominence. Two of the brothers held earldoms, as well as high offices, while their sister, Joan, the second wife of Ralph earl of Westmorland, became through her numerous progeny the grandmother of the Yorkist kings, of Warwick the Kingmaker, and of many of the greater nobles of the time.

The outstanding member of the family was Gaunt's second son, Henry, bishop first of Lincoln and then of the wealthy see of Winchester and eventually cardinal. A man of ability and enormous wealth, he played a dominant if controversial part in English government during the minority of his great-nephew Henry VI and achieved great influence over the young king. He married his niece Joan to King James I of Scotland, and later his wealth and power assisted the careers of his nephews John and Edmund, successive dukes of Somerset (and sons of John earl and marquess of Somerset), who were active if not very successful in the French wars.

After the cardinal's death, however, the role of the Beauforts changed, as discontent grew with the rule of Henry VI and the dynastic question raised its head. In 1455 Edmund, after several years as Henry's chief minister, punctuated only by the period of Henry's insanity, was slain by York and his Neville allies at the Battle of St. Albans. His sons were to prove over the next fifteen years the most loyal and active of the Lancastrian nobility until the death of the last legitimate Beauforts at the Battle of Tewkesbury in 1471. Duke John's daughter Margaret was left as the heir of the senior line, and it was through her that her son, Henry Tudor, claimed the royal descent that allowed him to secure the throne as Henry VII in 1485. Margaret lived on into the next century, wielding much influence during her son's reign.

Roger Virgoe

Bibliography

Harriss, G.L. *Cardinal Beaufort: A Study of the Lancastrian Ascendancy and Decline.* Oxford: Clarendon, 1988 [supersedes most earlier work on Bishop Henry].

See also Beaufort, Margaret; Lancaster, John Duke of; Wars of the Roses

---

Beaufort Family Genealogy

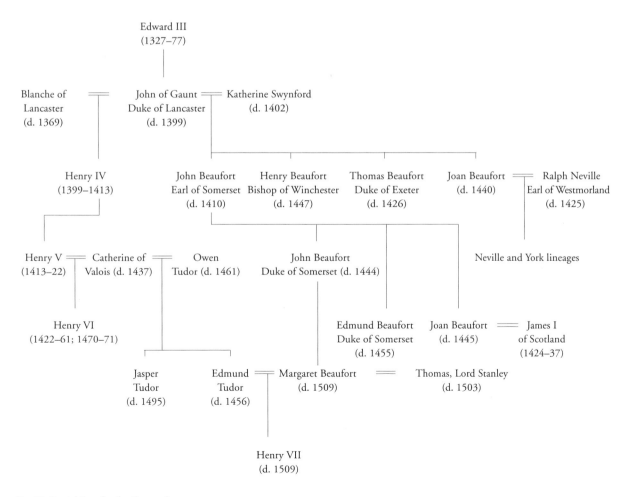

Fig. 25. Partial Beaufort family genealogy.

Becket, Thomas (1120–1170)

England's best-known saint and martyr. Archbishop Thomas was murdered in Canterbury Cathedral on 29 December 1170 by four household knights of Henry II. He subsequently became one of the greatest medieval cult figures and Canterbury one of Europe's greatest pilgrimage centers.

Thomas, son of a respectable, moderately wealthy London merchant, was educated in an Augustinian priory, a London grammar school, and Paris in its preuniversity days. From 1143 to 1145 he was apprenticed to a London banker, enjoying a wild, frivolous life; he supported the Angevin side in the civil war of Stephen's reign. Thereafter he joined the household of Archbishop Theobald of Canterbury, where his companions included John of Salisbury, Gilbert Foliot, Roger of Pont l'Évêque, John of Pagham, and John of Canterbury—scholars and future bishops who together suggested a protouniversity. He learned superb administrative skills, derived from Theobald's training at the hands of his own predecessors, Lanfranc and Anselm. Theobald supported the Angevins against Stephen and went into exile; Thomas accompanied him to Rome, learning international diplomacy. As papal legate after 1150 Theobald arranged Henry of Anjou's succession as Henry II.

When Henry acceded in 1154 at age 22, his English backers, seeking to control, counsel, and educate him, chose Thomas as the chancellor (1155–62). Becket became almost Henry's alter ego and best friend, raising the office of chancellor to new heights of power and responsibility. His magnificent lifestyle—the grandeur and ostentation befitting the king's constant companion in hunting, gaming, feasting, and joking—would haunt him later. But he counseled Henry to rule justly for the welfare of kingdom and church, and Henry obeyed. Theobald is said to have designated Thomas as his successor.

Henry chose Thomas for Canterbury, primate of the English church, on Theobald's death (1162). Immediately Thomas underwent a surprising transformation; from model courtier he became model archbishop. His lavish extravagance became lavish charity, his household of courtiers became one of scholars and learned lawyers. Days of hunting and feasting became days of study, devotion, and prayer. Scholars still cannot explain this metamorphosis.

Becket, now a fanatic reformer, clashed with Henry over royal and ecclesiastical rights. Thomas claimed his duty was to rule the church according to "law and right"—by which he may have meant the canon law just then being systematized by the papal court. Henry insisted on his duty to preserve England's "ancestral customs"—later the "precedents" of English common law—as crystallized in the Constitutions of Clarendon (1163). Thomas protested violently, fleeing into exile (1164). During the next six years both men sent secret missions to Pope Alexander III, the French king, the German emperor, and counts, abbots, bishops, and archbishops throughout Europe to gain allies. Reams of propagandistic letters flew from court to court, replete with deceptions, half-truths, and manipulations of public and private opinion. Neither man displayed statesmanlike talents in this contest,

both remaining volatile and inflexible on minor points. Thus repeated attempts to compromise failed over obscure and sometimes silly demands.

While Henry grudgingly yielded on specific issues—at last virtually acceding to Thomas's demands—he underhandedly resurrected Becket's worldly reputation as chancellor and torpedoed one settlement by refusing the Kiss of Peace. While Thomas was admired for his immovable, righteous stance, he so offended nearly everyone that he was hated almost universally in his victory. When compromise came (at Freteval, 1170), Thomas ruined it, returning to England and promptly excommunicating all Henry's supporters—including most of the bishops. This further enraged the four already-infuriated knights who took Henry's exasperated statement that none of his household were helping him against Thomas as a signal for murder.

Becket's supporters declared him a martyr. But no modern historian has yet explained satisfactorily his motivations and actions. He claimed, following his predecessor Anselm, to fight for God and Right. Indeed he succeeded in forcing Henry to submit to papal formulations of canon law and partial papal control, yet only at the near-destruction of the English church, of which Thomas was shepherd and guardian. Thus Thomas still remains a mystery, a mass of contradictions and controversies—as his companions suggested, a "sacred monster."

Sally N. Vaughn

Bibliography

Barlow, Frank. *Thomas Becket.* London: Weidenfeld & Nicolson, 1986; Knowles, David. *The Episcopal Colleagues of Archbishop Thomas Becket.* Cambridge: Cambridge University Press, 1970; Knowles, David. *Thomas Becket.* Cambridge: Cambridge University Press, 1970; Radford, Lewis B. *Thomas of London before His Consecration.* Cambridge: Cambridge University Press, 1894; Saltman, Avram. *Theobald, Archbishop of Canterbury.* London: Athlone, 1956; Smalley, Beryl. *The Becket Conflict and the Schools: A Study of Intellectuals in Politics.* Oxford: Blackwell, 1973; Wilks, Michael, ed. *The World of John of Salisbury.* Oxford: Blackwell, for the Ecclesiastical History Society, 1984.

See also Anselm; Canterbury, Ecclesiastical Province of; Henry II; Investiture Controversy; Lanfranc

Bede the Venerable (ca. 673–735)

Honored as "the Venerable" even in his own day, Bede (Baeda, Beda in earliest sources) was the foremost educator, exegete, and historian of his epoch, the Northumbrian Golden Age. Of his life Bede himself provides nearly all we know, in the short autobiographical note he appended to the last chapter of his *Ecclesiastical History of the English People,* with a list of his numerous writings. He occasionally gives a personal detail in one of his other works. Bede was born on land that a year or two later (674) was given by King Oswiu (Oswy) to Benedict Biscop to build the very monastery Bede would enter at age seven, St. Peter's, Wearmouth. In 681, two years after Bede's initiation into the community, Benedict established at nearby Jarrow the twin foundation of St. Paul's, formed as an integral part of a single monastery with St. Peter's. At some point Bede was transferred to this new foundation under the strict and learned Ceolfrith, whose place was later filled by Hwætberht. With the exception of a few short trips to Lindisfarne and York Bede spent his entire life as a monk-scholar at St. Paul's.

Ordained a deacon at the age of nineteen (six years before the usual canonical age), Bede then proceeded to the priesthood at age 30 (703). He became the "beloved father and master," as his disciple Cuthbert called him, of the thriving intellectual and spiritual center of learning. Bede taught the basic disciplines of grammar and computus: grammar, the science of the Latin language and its interpretation; computus, the science of determining time, especially the ensemble of rules by which the date of Easter is reckoned. Since the master in many early monasteries was also responsible for teaching psalmody, Bede also may have taught chant.

Bede wrote several educational treatises to complement the texts available from late antiquity. He wrote "a book on the art of meter," the *De arte metrica,* a systematic exposition of Latin versification by means of a judicious compilation of late-antique commentaries on the grammarian Donatus, demonstrated by examples from Virgil and Christian poets. The book makes evident Bede's qualities as a textbook writer: apt selection, concentration on essentials, simplicity, and precision. His own contribution to metrical history is his description in chapter 24 of isosyllabic stress rhythm, accentual meter, which eventually superseded quantitative Latin verse in medieval poetry. Bede appended to this work his *De schematibus et tropis,* "a small book on figures of speech or tropes, that is, concerning the figures and modes of speech with which the holy scriptures are adorned." Bede adds considerably to Donatus's section on the trope of allegory, with a section on symbol in deeds and in words. Bede's *De orthographia,* "a book about orthography," consists of short alphabetized entries about the meaning and correct usage or spelling of words likely to cause difficulties for a medieval Latinist.

For the basic curriculum Bede composed another little educational piece, *De natura rerum,* "a separate book on the nature of things," serving as an introduction to cosmology in 51 chapters on the earth, the heavens, stars, and planets. The text, a reworking and betterment of Isidore's *Liber rotarum* and Pseudo-Isidore's *De ordine creaturarum,* incorporates much from Pliny's *Natural History.* Near the beginning and near the end of his distinguished writing career Bede composed works on time and its calculation. The first, *De temporibus,* a radical revision of material in Isidore's *Etymologies* and Irish supplements, consists of 22 brief chapters on measurement of time, the six ages of the world, and a short chronicle of the most important events in salvation history. His recalculation of the time spans of each age according to Jerome's translation of the Hebrew Bible instead of Jerome's earlier figures from Eusebius led to a charge of heresy being leveled against Bede in Bishop Wilfrid's court at Hexham, on the grounds that he placed

Christ in the fifth instead of the sixth age—a charge he vigorously denied in a formal and ferocious letter to Plegwin, a monk of Hexham.

Bede's students found the first book on time to be too dense for easy learning, so Bede remedied this by producing a new, expanded version, *De temporum ratione.* After initial chapters on finger calculation, Greek and Roman letters symbolizing numbers, various aspects of time and historical modes of measurement he proceeds, as he did in the *De temporibus* but in much greater detail, from the smallest to the largest units of time. He includes a chapter on English months, with precious information for students of Germanic and Anglo-Saxon culture. He concludes the work with an extended discussion of the ages of the world.

Bede considered all his educational treatises, grammatical and scientific, as preparatory instruction for the study of scripture. Although Bede is known today mainly as an historian, in his own time and throughout the Middle Ages he was known primarily as an exegete. The books of the Bible he chose to interpret are of two kinds: those that were already favorites of the Fathers, such as the commentaries on Genesis and on Luke, and those that were largely ignored by earlier exegetes, such as the commentaries on Ezra and Nehemiah and on the New Testament Catholic Epistles. Both filled pedagogical needs: the former, selected and simplified for his English pupils, display Bede's talents as an adapter and synthesizer; and the latter, supplementing the Fathers, demonstrate his originality within the exegetical tradition.

Bede's usual method of commentary is the early-medieval one of phrase-by-phrase exegesis of a biblical text, from beginning to end; it is a process of rumination, fostered in the monastic tradition. Bede relies heavily on Augustine for doctrine and much of his exposition, but in interpretive spirit he favors Gregory the Great, with whom he shares a kind of spiritual affinity. Like Gregory and many of the Fathers he interprets the Bible both literally (according to the basic, obvious, surface meaning) and allegorically (according to the deeper, hidden, spiritual, symbolic meaning). Bede's exegetical practice is eclectic and literary. If appropriate, he will point out the typology (an Old Testament event as prefiguration of the New). Often he presents a twofold relationship in a text, with a single allegorical interpretation superimposed upon the literal meaning. At other times he spreads out a threefold meaning, either historical, allegorical, and moral (applying to one's own life) or historical, allegorical, and anagogic (applying to the final Judgment), or he follows the fourfold method of historical, allegorical, tropological (moral), and anagogic interpretations. Though he derived this schema from Cassian, Bede became the definitive authority in the Middle Ages for it. In addition to his biblical commentaries he compiled two biblical aids, a compendium on the places of the Holy Land, derived primarily from the itinerarium of Adomnán, and a gazetteer explaining and locating places mentioned in the Bible.

For Bede preaching was a priest's primary function and had a special, even sacramental, significance: preachers are the successors of the prophets and apostles. For the liturgical year he composed two books of 25 homilies each. In hagiography Bede revised the lives of various saints, including Felix, Athanasius, and Cuthbert; he also composed an historical martyrology, 114 brief accounts of martyrs' lives and deaths, which played an important role in the development of the Roman martyrology. Although Bede wrote "a book of hymns in various meters and rhythms" and "a book of epigrams in heroic and elegiac meter," we now possess only a few of each, about two dozen poems in all. These include a poetic tour de force in honor of St. Æthelthryth, the famous *Hymnos canamus gloriae,* and the even more famous *De die iudicii,* on Judgment Day. Although well versed in OE poetry, he may not have composed the five-line OE poem called "Bede's Death Song," which he recited on his deathbed.

Bede's fame today derives mainly from his work as an historian. His histories not only provide us with information now known only because of him; as products of his mature scholarship and long writing career they also mark momentous advances in the science of historiography. His *History of the Abbots of Wearmouth and Jarrow* first describes the life and career of the great founder of the monastery, Benedict Biscop, then incorporates and edits the anonymous life of Abbot Ceolfrith, fused with descriptions of the abbots Eosterwine and Sigefrith, and ending with Bede's coeval Hwætberht. Although he attributes no miracles to any of the five remarkable abbots, he represents them in this monastic chronicle as splendid characters. Unlike the two world chronicles he appended to his treatises on time his *Ecclesiastical History of the English People* is history in the grand and full scale, which has gained Bede the well-deserved title of "father of English history."

The first Englishman to write history with a full sense of historical responsibility and with control by his use, arrangement, and omission of materials, Bede was also the first to relate the history of England. He is the first literary authority for a structured history stretching from Roman Britain, the invasions of the Angles, Saxons, and Jutes, some events in Scotland and Ireland, to the mission of Augustine to Kent, Paulinus to Northumbria, the doings of Theodore, Chad, and Acca, the power and glory of Northumbria, and events in the recent past. Each division contains memorable events told with extraordinary but restrained artistry: Gregory the Great's apostolic love for the English, the conversion of King Edwin and his people, King Oswald and St. Aidan, Abbess Hild and the poet Cædmon.

Bede's title tells us that his work belongs to the genre and tradition of ecclesiastical history, based on biblical rather than classical concepts of time and event, presupposing a theocentric universe in which the secular is understood in terms of the sacred, tracing the progress of the church as it advances in time and geography. Furthermore it is "of the *English* people," treating the Anglo-Saxons as one nation, God's chosen, even though divided into kingdoms and privileging Northumbria in the later books. The first three books of the *History* deal primarily with the christianization of the English; the last two describe the way in which the Christian life developed among them, especially in Northumbria. The first book sweeps through 650 years, whereas each of the remaining four covers about a generation. Dedicated to Ceolwulf, king of Northumbria (729–37), the *History* emphasizes the good and bad influence of various Anglo-Saxon kings; it also stresses the influence of the clergy and their activity, offering as models John of Hexham (Beverley), Aidan, and especially Cuthbert, with whom the *History* comes to a climax in book 4.27–32. In contrast to Stephen's admiring *Life of Wilfrid,* Bede adroitly diminishes the worth and importance of Bishop Wilfrid by downplaying his role in the Northumbrian church and passing over in silence some major facts in Wilfrid's career, such as the Council of Austerfield, even while giving Wilfrid credit for gaining the victory of the Roman practice of Easter-dating and tonsure over the Irish faction under Colmán at the Synod of Whitby in 664.

The *History* is written in a soberly elegant Latin. It was translated into OE during the period of King Alfred. Over 150 manuscripts from the Middle Ages and many editions and translations of the *History* attest to its perduring importance and interest. No one was comparable to Bede as an historian until the 12th century, and his work still provides medieval English historians with endless topics for research and discussion.

Bede wrote a number of formal instructional letters, one of which has great historical importance, his late *Letter to Ecgbert,* a disciple who was to become the first archbishop of York (735) and whose brother Eadberht would become king of Northumbria (737). Whereas the *Ecclesiastical History* ends on an optimistic note of Christian progress, the letter paints a bleak picture of greed, subterfuge, and fraud. Outspoken and condemnatory of pseudo-monasteries and ecclesiastical and secular abuses, Bede details a program of reform. To meet the needs of far-flung and hard-to-reach communities, he proposes that new bishoprics be founded, based, and financed at prosperous monasteries.

Bede became an author in great demand after his death. By the 9th century the admiration for Bede was so extensive that he was considered a Father of the Church. Venerated now by Anglicans and Catholics alike, he bears the title of saint and doctor of the Catholic church.

George Hardin Brown

Bibliography

PRIMARY

The collected works of Bede *(Bedae venerabilis opera)* are being reliably edited by various hands in the Corpus Christianorum Series Latina (CCSL). Turnhout: Brepols, 1955– [vols. 118A–22 so far]; Colgrave, Bertram, ed. and trans. *Two Lives of St. Cuthbert.* Cambridge: Cambridge University Press, 1940; Colgrave, Bertram, and R.A.B. Mynors, eds. and trans. *Bede's Ecclesiastical History of the English People.* Oxford: Clarendon, 1969; Connolly, Seán, trans. *Bede: On the Temple.* Liverpool: Liverpool University Press, 1995; Holder, Arthur G., trans. *Bede: On the Tabernacle.* Liverpool: Liverpool University Press, 1994; Hurst, David, trans. *The Commentary on the Seven Catholic Epistles.* Cistercian Studies 82. Kalamazoo: Cistercian Publications, 1985; Jaager, Werner, ed. *Bedas metrische*

Vita sancti Cuthberti. Palaestra 198. Leipzig: Mayer & Müller, 1935 [verse life of Cuthbert]; Martin, Lawrence T., and David Hurst, trans. *Homilies on the Gospels.* 2 vols. Kalamazoo: Cistercian Publications, 1991; Miller, Thomas, ed. and trans. *The Old English Version of Bede's Ecclesiastical History of the English People.* EETS o.s. 95, 96, 110, 111. London: Trübner, 1890–98; Plummer, Charles, ed. *Venerabilis Baedae opera historica.* 2 vols. Oxford: Clarendon, 1896. Repr. in 1 vol. Oxford: Clarendon, 1946 [introduction and notes still valuable]; Sherley-Price, Leo, trans. *The Ecclesiastical History of the English People.* Rev. R.E. Latham. Harmondsworth: Penguin, 1968; Tanenhaus, Gussie Hecht, trans. "Bede's *De Schematibus et Tropis*—A Translation." *Quarterly Journal of Speech* 48 (1962): 237–53. Repr. in *Readings in Medieval Rhetoric,* ed. Joseph M. Miller et al. Bloomington: Indiana University Press, 1973, pp. 76–80.

SECONDARY

For recent Bedan research see "The Year's Work in Old English Studies." *Old English Newsletter,* Winter issues, and the annual bibliography in *Anglo-Saxon England;* Brown, George Hardin. *Bede the Venerable.* Boston: Twayne, 1987 [with bibliography of editions and studies until 1986]; Goffart, Walter. *The Narrators of Barbarian History (A.D. 550–800).* Ch. 4, "Bede and the Ghost of Bishop Wilfrid." Princeton: Princeton University Press, 1988, pp. 235–328 [extensive, speculative investigation of Bede's motives as an historian]; Lapidge, Michael. "Bede's Metrical *Vita S. Cuthberti.*" In *St. Cuthbert, His Cult and His Community to AD 1200,* ed. Gerald Bonner, David Rollason, and Clare Stancliffe. Woodbridge: Boydell, 1989, pp. 77–93; Lapidge, Michael, ed. *Bede and His World: The Jarrow Lectures 1958–1993.* 2 vols. Aldershot: Variorum, 1994; McCready, William D. *Miracles and the Venerable Bede.* Toronto: Pontifical Institute, 1994; Wallace-Hadrill, J.M. *Bede's Ecclesiastical History of the English People: A Historical Commentary.* Oxford: Clarendon, 1988; Webb, J.F. *The Age of Bede.* Harmondsworth: Penguin, 1983 [with translations of selected works].

See also Alfred; Allegory; Anglo-Saxon Invasions; Cædmon; Chronicles; Conversion of the Anglo-Saxons; Fathers of the Church; Grammatical Treatises; Hagiography; Scientific and Medical Writings; Translation; Wearmouth-Jarrow and the Codex Amiatinus; Wearmouth-Jarrow: Architecture

Bedford, John Duke of (1389–1435)

Third son of Henry IV; created duke of Bedford in 1414, he was a courageous soldier and gifted administrator. He served with distinction during the reign of his brother, Henry V, safeguarding the Scottish border and defeating a Franco-Genoese fleet at the Battle of the Seine (1416). After Henry's death in 1422 he became Regent of France. His determined efforts to protect the rights of Henry VI, the young heir of Henry and

Katherine of Valois, were a remarkable accomplishment upon which his fame and political reputation deservedly rest.

In the first years of regency Bedford was able to extend Henry V's conquests. His emphatic victory at Verneuil (1424), where he fought with "the strength of a lion," led to the subjugation of Maine and northern Anjou. But the advent of Joan of Arc in 1429 transformed the situation. The English were forced onto the defensive, and Bedford, conservative in religious outlook, saw Joan as a witch whose enchantments and sorcery punished the English for a lack of sound faith. The constant campaigning of Bedford's last year wore away his strength; his death in September 1435, combined with the defection of the Burgundians as allies, dealt Lancastrian France a blow from which it never recovered.

Bedford earned high praise from English and French chroniclers alike. A great landowner and possessor of rich manuscripts, vestments, and plate, he cleverly exploited the media of painting, pageantry, and poetry to promote the cause of the dual monarchy of Henry VI over England and France. His strong sense of justice, whether disciplining his troops or punishing brigands, won him universal respect. His encouragement of trade and commerce led to a revival of Normandy's economic fortunes; his willingness to employ French administrators and his use of native institutions gave his regime considerable authority.

Less of a diplomat than Henry V, Bedford sometimes allowed pride and quick temper to get the better of him. His relations with the Burgundians were not always easy, and he never fully gained the confidence of the English aristocracy. His regency nevertheless was a superb political and military accomplishment.

Michael Jones

Bibliography

Stevenson, Joseph, ed. *Letters . . . of the Wars of the English in France.* Rolls Series 22. 2 vols. in 3. London: Longmans, 1861–64; Stratford, Jenny. "The Manuscripts of John Duke of Bedford: Library and Chapel." In *England in the Fifteenth Century: Proceedings of the 1986 Harlaxton Symposium,* ed. Daniel Williams. Woodbridge: Boydell, 1987, pp. 329–50; Williams, Ethel Carleton. *My Lord of Bedford, 1389–1435.* London: Longmans, 1963 [not critical, but a useful narrative].

See also Henry V; Henry VI; Hundred Years War

Benedict of Aniane (d. 821)

Benedict (original name Witiza) of Aniane, was the son of a Visigothic count. In 780, after a period as a monk at St. Seine (Langres), he founded a reformist monastery at Aniane on his family's property in southern France. He imposed the strict observance of the Benedictine Rule, in contrast with the mixed observances common elsewhere, and when Louis the Pious succeeded Charlemagne Benedict was installed near Aachen in the specially founded monastery of Inden (consecrated 817; later known as Cornelimünster) in order to extend the reforms under royal patronage. Reforming councils were held at

Aachen in 816 and 817, and the resulting decrees were issued between 816 and 819. Their main purpose was to establish uniform observance in monasteries following the "original" text of the Benedictine Rule (the *textus purus*), but they also included supplementary customaries formalizing certain practices of daily routine that differed from or were not covered by the Rule itself.

The 10th-century reform in England was greatly influenced by these developments. The text of the Rule that was introduced was the continental *textus receptus* (received text), which had resulted from Benedict's reforms by mingling readings from the newly imposed *textus purus* with those of the previously circulating *textus interpolatus* (interpolated text). The Aachen decrees circulated widely; the reformers aimed (with royal support) for uniform observance; and they issued the *Regularis concordia* as a supplementary customary. This drew extensively on the *Memoriale qualiter*, which was one of the supplementary texts circulating with the Aachen decrees. It is doubtful whether Benedict was the author of this text, but he was responsible for its dissemination. There are five complete copies extant from Anglo-Saxon England and one part-copy, which was provided with a vernacular interlinear gloss; this glossed text is edited under the misleading title of *The Epitome of Benedict of Aniane.*

Joyce Hill

Bibliography

McKitterick, Rosamond. *The Frankish Kingdoms under the Carolingians.* London: Longman, 1983, pp. 106–24; Wallace-Hadrill, J.M. *The Frankish Church.* Oxford: Clarendon, 1983, pp. 226–303.

See also Benedict of Nursia; Benedictine Reform; Literary Influences: Carolingian; Monasticism; *Regularis concordia*

Benedict of Nursia (ca. 480–ca. 560)

A south Italian abbot and, like many other monastic leaders of his day, author of a monastic rule for his small community. By virtue of the wide adoption of that slender manual, the Benedictine Rule, Benedict became the most famous monk in the world and the patriarch of western monasticism, designated by Pope Paul VI (1963–78) "the patron of Europe." For some centuries the first and only life of Benedict was the hagiographic account by Pope Gregory the Great in the second book of his edifying *Dialogues.* Writing in 593–94, Gregory composed this melange of fact and legend at least a generation after Benedict's death; but historians accept as factual the bit of biographical data Gregory said he received from four of Benedict's disciples.

After education in Rome Benedict turned to religious life, first with a small community at Enfide and then as an anchorite near Subiaco. Attracting disciples because of his holiness, and sometimes alienating them because of his severity, Benedict eventually returned to communal religious life, organizing monasteries first in the Subiaco region and later (ca. 529) on Monte Cassino, in Campania halfway between Rome and Naples.

Benedict's real claim to fame is the rule he composed ca. 526. "This little rule for beginners" is based in part on the nearly contemporaneous *Rule of the Master,* but a comparison of the two reveals why Benedict's has been awarded the crown by history and the monastic movement. Gregory designates it well as a rule "remarkable for its discernment." The Rule is a relatively short document, consisting of a prologue, 72 brief chapters, and an epilogue. The chapters, laying down the principles of monastic life and practical directives for living it, are not logically ordered; chapters 67–72 are an appendix attached to 66.8, and the liturgical and penitential codes (8–18, 20–23) may have been inserted later. But for all its lack of order and elegant language it judiciously presents the basic principles of cenobitic life. It advocates a spirit of charity for the whole monastic family and an egalitarianism (e.g., priests have no special rank); its concern is not for the heroic achievers but for the weaker, more needful members of the group: "In drawing up its regulations, we hope to set down nothing harsh, nothing burdensome" (Prologue, 46).

During the 7th and 8th centuries the Rule was only one among many in use. In England Celtic monasticism had propagated over the north from the Irish foundation of Iona, whereas in the Midlands several foundations seemed to follow composite rules. Wilfrid was the first to introduce the Benedictine Rule in England for his Northumbrian monasteries at Ripon (ca. 661) and Hexham (674); Wilfrid also served as director of other monasteries of men and women. Benedict Biscop, founder of the joint monastery of Wearmouth (674) and Jarrow (681), whose most illustrious monk was the historian, exegete, and educator Bede, introduced a rule heavily influenced by the Benedictine but assembled from six different models. In the southwest near Winchester, Nursling, the home community of Boniface (Wynfrith), followed the Benedictine Rule.

Regular monastic life was greatly disrupted and in places disappeared during the troubled 9th century. Despite the attempts of King Alfred (871–99) to restore monastic life by founding the convent of Shaftesbury (which succeeded) and the monastery at Athelney (which did not), religious life languished. In the 10th century, under the close support of King Edgar (957–75), three dynamic monks, Dunstan (abbot of Glastonbury and later archbishop of Canterbury), the authoritarian Æthelwold (abbot of Abingdon, later bishop of Winchester), and Oswald (who became bishop of Worcester and later archbishop of York), imported the Benedictine Reform from the Continent and reinvigorated monastic life. To enforce the Benedictine Rule buttressed by effective continental and native regulations, they promulgated a code of approved practice, the *Regularis concordia* (ca. 970). The monasteries, some 40 in number with none in the north, were declared free of dependency on local nobles and became powerful supporters of the West Saxon monarchy.

Thanks to the renewed energies that resulted from the Reform, the monasteries again became centers of learning and art, providing education and culture. Æthelwold's school at Winchester developed a highly refined Latin style and produced the two finest OE prose stylists and preachers, Ælfric and Wulfstan. It was during this period that much Anglo-Latin and most extant OE texts were written, created for the most part in Benedictine scriptoria. Canterbury was especially active as a writing center, and Winchester gained particular renown for manuscript illustration, identifiable as "the Winchester School."

As the guide for traditional Benedictines (Black Monks and Nuns), augmented for Cluniacs, and reformed by the Cistercians (White Monks), the Rule of Benedict continued to dominate life in religious orders until the advent of the friars (Franciscans and Dominicans) in the 13th century. Benedictine abbeys, priories, and cells became ubiquitous throughout the realm, sometimes enormously wealthy and politically and economically powerful under forceful leaders, such as Abbot Samson of Bury St. Edmunds (ca. 1135–1212). The order also continued to foster scholars and especially historians, such as William of Malmesbury (ca. 1095–ca. 1143), and at St. Albans Roger of Wendover (d. 1236) and Matthew Paris (ca. 1199–1259).

George Hardin Brown

Bibliography

PRIMARY

Fry, Timothy, ed. and trans. *RB 1980: The Rule of St. Benedict.* Collegeville: Liturgical Press, 1981; Gregory the Great. *Life and Miracles of St. Benedict (Book Two of the Dialogues).* Trans. Odo J. Zimmermann and Benedict R. Avery. Collegeville: St. John's Abbey Press, 1949; Kornexl, Lucia, ed. *Die* Regularis Concordia *und Ihre Altenglische Interlinearversion.* Texte und Untersuchungen zur Englischen Philologie 17. Munich: Wilhelm Fink Verlag, 1993.

SECONDARY

Burton, Janet. *Monastic and Religious Orders in Britain 1000–1300.* Cambridge: Cambridge University Press, 1994; Farmer, David Hugh, ed. *Benedict's Disciples.* Leominster: Fowler Wright, 1980; Knowles, David. *The Monastic Order in England: A History of Its Development from the Times of St Dunstan to the Fourth Lateran Council, 940–1216.* 2d ed. Cambridge: Cambridge University Press, 1963; Platt, C.P.S. *The Abbeys and Priories of Medieval England.* London: Secker & Warburg, 1984; Turner, D.H., ed. *The Benedictines in Britain.* London: British Library, 1980.

See also Ælfric; Æthelwold; Anglo-Latin Literature after 1066; Anglo-Latin Literature to 1066; Bede; Benedictine Reform; Chronicles; Cistercians; Dunstan; Fathers of the Church; Friars; Liturgy and Church Music, History of; Matthew Paris; Monasticism; Oswald; *Regularis concordia;* Wilfrid; William of Malmesbury; "Winchester School"; Wulfstan

Benedictine Reform

After a period of decay this crucial reform movement led to a revival of Benedictine monasticism, culture, and learning in Anglo-Saxon England during the second half of the 10th century.

It is intimately connected with the names of three prominent ecclesiastics—Dunstan, archbishop of Canterbury (960–88), Æthelwold, bishop of Winchester (963–84), Oswald, bishop of Worcester and archbishop of York (961/71–92)—and with King Edgar (957–75), their royal patron. Political ties and clerical connections had brought the English into contact with the main branches of the continental reform initiated in the early decades of the century by Odo of Cluny and Gérard of Brogne. Dunstan's abbacy in Glastonbury (940–56) and that of his pupil and friend Æthelwold in Abingdon (ca. 954–63) can be seen as important preparatory stages on the way to a firm reestablishment of monasticism in England, but it was not until the accession of a king wholly dedicated to this cause and the promotion of its leading protagonists to key positions in the ecclesiastical hierarchy that the Reform could come to full swing.

Æthelwold apparently surpassed his fellow reformers in fervor and consistency; a good deal of what was achieved is due to his systematic endeavor and his skill in both religious affairs and worldly matters. In his own bishopric of Winchester he soon paved the way for a fundamental reorganization along monastic lines: by expelling the canons from the Old Minster with royal consent early in 964, he set the model for the typically English institution of monastic cathedrals presided over by monk-bishops; later in this year he also replaced the secular clerics in the New Minster by monks. Such new structures ensured the reform party an extended influence on Anglo-Saxon church life down to the parochial level.

By translating the Benedictine Rule into OE (ca. 970), Æthelwold made the central text of the Reform accessible to a less educated readership, including laypeople. His compilation of the *Regularis concordia*—the monastic customary that the Synod of Winchester in the early 970s agreed upon to reinforce, expound, and supplement the instructions of the Rule—marks another decisive step toward spiritual unity and uniformity in practice. To him we can also ascribe a number of primary sources that provide valuable firsthand information on the aims and progress of the Reform as seen by its chief promoters: "An Account of King Edgar's Establishment of Monasteries," originally designed to preface the OE Benedictine Rule, the "New Minster Foundation Charter," drawn up to commemorate and justify the expulsion of the canons, and the prologue as well as the charterlike epilogue to the *Regularis concordia.* In the light of monastic claims to superiority and all-pervasive change the gloomy picture of clerical decadence and widespread religious disorder, painted here and in the lives of the saintly reformers, has to be viewed with due reservations.

While the age of Bede was revered as the Golden Age of Anglo-Saxon monasticism, the close cooperation between monks and monarchy had its historic model in the Carolingian symbiosis of secular and religious power personified by Emperor Louis the Pious (814–40) and the great reforming abbot Benedict of Aniane. King Edgar's strong support for the reform movement, both nonmaterial and in the form of generous grants of land and privileges, was not merely an unselfish act of piety. His rights of interference in monastic affairs as codified in the *Regularis concordia* included a say in the election of abbots, abbesses, and monk-bishops; he and his wife Ælfthryth exercised an exclusive patronage over all Benedictine communities in England. These in turn expressed their gratitude and loyalty to the monarchy in a daily series of intercessory prayers that constituted a regular part of the divine office, thus strengthening the royal position against a powerful nobility, parts of which, after Edgar's sudden death in 975, vented their dissatisfaction at the loss of former rights of control over religious houses in the so-called "antimonastic reaction."

The reform movement had a profound effect on Anglo-Saxon culture and society. Many Benedictine abbeys were founded or restored, especially in the southern parts of England, including such important centers as Ely, Peterborough, and Ramsey. The new spirituality found its expression in an elaborate liturgy stimulating creative productivity in the arts and crafts, in church architecture and music. The increase in education and learning furthered book production, intensified the exchange of manuscripts with the Continent, and brought about a revival of Anglo-Latin literary culture. Certain groups of reformed houses associated with the three principal reformers seem to have been instrumental in the development of different styles of Anglo-Caroline script. The comprehensive reform approach favored by Æthelwold also made him exert his scholarly influence on the standardization of OE as a literary language.

Faced with increasing political instability in the wake of renewed Viking attacks, the generation following the great reformers had a rich religious and cultural heritage to preserve and a demanding didactic mission to fulfill. Both these aspects are clearly reflected in the works of Ælfric and Wulfstan, who, firmly entrenched in the reformist tradition, at the turn of the millennium led religiously inspired English prose writing to new heights.

Lucia Kornexl

Bibliography

Brooks, Nicholas, and Catherine Cubitt, eds. *St Oswald of Worcester: Life and Influence.* London: Leicester University Press, 1996; Dumville, David N. *English Caroline Script and Monastic History: Studies in Benedictinism, A.D. 950–1030.* Woodbridge: Boydell, 1993; Gneuss, Helmut. "The Origin of Standard Old English and Æthelwold's School at Winchester." *ASE* 1 (1972): 62–83; John, Eric. "The King and the Monks in the Tenth-Century Reformation." In *Orbis Britanniae and Other Studies.* Leicester: Leicester University Press, 1966, pp. 154–80; John, Eric. "The Age of Edgar." In *The Anglo-Saxons,* ed. James Campbell. Oxford: Phaidon, 1982, pp. 160–89, esp. pp. 181–89; Knowles, David. *The Monastic Order in England.* 2d ed. Cambridge: Cambridge University Press, 1963, pp. 31–82 and passim; Parsons, David, ed. *Tenth-Century Studies: Essays in Commemoration of the Millennium of the Council of Winchester and Regularis concordia.* London: Phillimore, 1975; Ramsay, Nigel, Margaret Sparks, and Tim Tatton-Brown, eds. *St Dunstan: His Life, Times and Cult.* Woodbridge: Boydell, 1992; Yorke, Barbara, ed. *Bishop Æthelwold: His Career and Influence.* Woodbridge: Boydell, 1988.

See also Ælfric; Æthelwold; Benedict of Aniane; Benedict of Nursia; Dunstan; Liturgy and Church Music, History of; Monasticism; New Minster Charter; Oswald; *Regularis concordia;* Wulfstan

Benedictional of Æthelwold

The manuscript BL Add. 49598 is the sumptuous masterwork of the "Winchester School." A poem in the manuscript tells that it was written for Bishop Æthelwold of Winchester (963–84), who ordered "many frames, well adorned and filled with various figures decorated with numerous beautiful colors and with gold." Benedictionals contain episcopal blessings for delivery during mass on important feasts. They were rarely illustrated, and Æthelwold's is the most lavish to survive, with 28 full-page miniatures (probably there were originally fifteen more), nineteen pages with decorative frames, and two historiated initials. A sophisticated script hierarchy complements the ornament.

The miniatures fall into two broad categories: prefatory pictures and pictures within the text. The prefatory sequence of framed facing pages depicts the heavenly choirs. Included now are confessors, virgins, and apostles, but six leaves are missing. Wormald suggested, by analogy with the Galba Psalter (BL Cotton Galba A.xviii), that missing leaves depicted

Fig. 26. Benedictional of Æthelwold (BL Add. 49598), fol. 90v. St. Æthelthryth. Reproduced by permission of the British Library, London.

angels, patriarchs, prophets, martyrs, and a Christ in Majesty. The pictures within the text follow the order of the liturgical year, fusing the Temporale and the Sanctorale. Excepting juxtaposed miniatures for Epiphany, each framed illustration faces a framed text page inscribed in gold with the opening words of the benediction for the feast. Illustrations of scenes from Christ's life are augmented by pictures pertaining to John the Baptist, Sts. Stephen, John the Evangelist, Benedict, and Peter, and the English Sts. Swithun and Æthelthryth (fig. 26). Miniatures of the Death and Coronation of the Virgin and of a bishop dedicating a church complete the book.

Much of the imagery is highly individualized, though probable pictorial sources have been identified for most of the miniatures. A sacramentary of the Carolingian Metz School and a Middle Byzantine lectionary likely furnished much of the narrative iconography and also influenced choice and arrangement of scenes. The Winchester artists' skills lay in their ability to synthesize disparate elements with visual references to a wide range of textual sources, producing in the process pictures of outstanding inventiveness and artistic merit.

Several themes are expressed, and the artists developed to a high degree the systematic repetition of individual motifs in successive pictures to emphasize their meaning—a technique Deshman has called "serial symbolism." The themes are united by reference to the Winchester liturgy and thought-world of the owner of the book. Indeed, in some ways, the manuscript is a manifesto for the monastic reform promulgated by Æthelwold and the king he served, King Edgar; ideologies of monasticism and rulership permeate the pictures, which were probably executed close to the date of Edgar's imperial consecration and coronation in 973.

The striking visual impact of the book stems from many factors, including an unusually varied yet subdued palette, offset with white and liberal use of gold. Most distinctive, however, are lush frames, exuberant figural style, and the symbiotic relationship between the two. Individual elements of the frames were taken from earlier continental art: rich, fleshy acanthus from the Metz School; linear, bossed frames from Franco-Saxon art. The synthesis was outstandingly creative, drawing on a deep insular love of ornamental intricacy and ambiguous relationships between frame and picture. The ambiguity was enhanced by the richly dynamic and expressive linearity of rippling "Winchester School" drapery, whose forms often echo those of the acanthus, yielding pages with dense surface patterning recalling the carpet pages of Hiberno-Saxon art.

Kathleen M. Openshaw

Bibliography

PRIMARY

Warner, George F., and Henry A. Wilson. *The Benedictional of St. Æthelwold*. London: Roxburghe Club, 1910.

SECONDARY

Alexander, Jonathan J.G. "The Benedictional of St. Æthelwold and Anglo-Saxon Illumination of the Re-form Period." In *Tenth-Century Studies: Essays in Commemoration of the Millennium of the Council of Winchester and Regularis concordia,* ed. David Parsons. London: Phillimore, 1975, pp. 169–83, 241–45; Backhouse, Janet, Derek H. Turner, and Leslie Webster, eds. *The Golden Age of Anglo-Saxon Art 966–1066*. London: British Museum, 1984, cat. no. 37; Broderick, Herbert R. "Some Attitudes toward the Frame in Anglo-Saxon Manuscripts of the Tenth and Eleventh Centuries." *Artibus et Historiae* 5 (1982): 31–42; Deshman, Robert. "*Christus rex et magi reges:* Kingship and Christology in Ottonian and Anglo-Saxon Art." *Frühmittelalterliche Studien* 10 (1976): 367–405; Deshman, Robert. "*Benedictus Monarcha et Monachus:* Early Medieval Ruler Theology and the Anglo-Saxon Reform." *Frühmittelalterliche Studien* 22 (1988): 204–40; Deshman, Robert. *The Benedictional of Æthelwold*. Princeton: Princeton University Press, 1995; Temple, Elżbieta. *Anglo-Saxon Manuscripts 900–1066*. A Survey of Manuscripts Illuminated in the British Isles 2, ed. J.J.G. Alexander. London: Harvey Miller, 1976; Wormald, Francis. *The Benedictional of St. Ethelwold*. London: Faber & Faber, 1959.

See also Æthelwold; Liturgy; Manuscript Illumination, Anglo-Saxon; "Winchester School"

Beowulf

Beowulf, by consensus the greatest literary work of the Anglo-Saxon period, tells the story of Beowulf, a hero of the Geats, a Germanic nation located probably in what is now southern Sweden. At the beginning of the 3,182-line poem Beowulf comes to the aid of Hrothgar, king of the Danes, whose magnificent hall Heorot has for twelve years been ravaged by the nocturnal man-eating monster Grendel, a descendant of the exiled Cain. Fighting without weapons, Beowulf tears off the arm of the monster, who flees to his home to die. The very next night, after the victory celebration, Grendel's vengeful mother slips into Heorot and carries off one of Hrothgar's sleeping retainers; in the morning Beowulf seeks her out in her home—a cave accessible only from the bottom of a deep lake or inlet—where he is nearly defeated, but saves himself when he finds a huge sword made by giants. With this he kills Grendel's mother and decapitates Grendel's corpse, bearing the head back to Heorot as a trophy. He returns to the Geats laden with treasure, gifts from a grateful Hrothgar, who predicts that Beowulf will become a king and warns him against greed and pride.

Much later, after Beowulf has been king of the Geats for 50 years, someone accidentally awakens a sleeping dragon by stealing a single cup from its hoard. Enraged by the loss, the night-flying dragon burns houses, strongholds, and Beowulf's own hall. The next morning Beowulf, protected by an iron shield and accompanied by the thief and eleven retainers (whom he orders to stay out of the battle), confronts the dragon. The fight goes badly until Beowulf is joined by Wiglaf, an untried retainer; together they kill the dragon, but not before it has wounded Beowulf with its venomous fangs. Before his death the old king has just enough time to admire the treasure that he has, as he says, won for his people; amid sorrowful dirges and predictions of war, his retainers bury him in a magnificent mound, and the dragon's hoard with him.

This simple tripartite storyline (organized around the three monster fights) is generously supplemented by historical and legendary material. For example, the poem describes in some detail the biblical background of Grendel's family, and after the defeat of Grendel court poets sing tales of Sigemund the dragonslayer and of the ancient feud between Finn, king of the Frisians, and Hnæf, king of the Danes. Dark allusions to future Danish troubles culminate in Beowulf's prediction, presented in some detail, of war with the Heathobards—even though Hrothgar has arranged a political marriage between his daughter Freawaru and the Heathobard king Ingeld. Even more ominously the story of the dragon fight is nearly overwhelmed by accounts of the intermittent feud between the Geats and the Swedes, which claimed the lives of two of Beowulf's royal predecessors and is certain to break out again after his death.

Beowulf is preserved in a single manuscript, BL Cotton Vitellius A.xv, written within a couple of decades of A.D. 1000. Three of the four other OE texts in the manuscript also deal prominently with monsters: they are a life of St. Christopher, an apocryphal letter from Alexander the Great to Aristotle, *The Marvels of the East,* and the poem *Judith.* The Cotton Library fire of 1731 made the edges of the leaves brittle, and on most pages the margins and some of the text have crumbled away. Modern editors have restored lost words in *Beowulf* by referring to two transcripts made in the 1780s, before the damage had become extreme. Beyond the material facts of the text's existence we know very little. Until recently it was widely believed that it was an 8th-century production, but examination of the linguistic and metrical tests used to arrive at that date has cast considerable doubt on their validity. Recent scholarship has also found that historical arguments in favor of the 8th century (e.g., that an English poet would not have written admiringly of the Scandinavians after the 790s, when the Viking wars began) can be almost precisely reversed: the Viking wars brought Scandinavian settlers, who during much of the later Anglo-Saxon period maintained friendly relations with their new neighbors. The former consensus that *Beowulf* was written in Northumbria has received less discussion, but it seems no better grounded than the older arguments as to its date. In the present state of our knowledge there is little reason to prefer an early date over a late one (dates as late as that of the manuscript have been suggested), or the north of England over the Midlands or the south.

As controversial as the question of *Beowulf*'s date and place are those of the manner of its composition and the nature of the materials that went into its making. Like most OE poems this one comes to us without an author's name, and it may well be that it never had an author, in the modern sense of a person who is responsible for the very words of a work from its beginning to its end. There is ample evidence that medieval writers often assembled works from preexisting materials, and many works—especially vernacular ones—were subject to expansion, condensation, and other kinds of revision in the course of copying from manuscript to manuscript. It is likely that, even if we had for *Beowulf* records as extensive as we have for, say, James Joyce's *Ulysses,* we would find it impossible either to identify one person who was primarily responsible for it or to distinguish clearly between its composition and the transmission of its text after composition.

In light of such considerations the long-running debate between those who see *Beowulf* as having been composed by an oral poet like those depicted in the poem and those who consider it a written composition loses much of its meaning. Almost certainly oral history and song were the ultimate sources of the poem's tales of preliterate pagan antiquity, but we now possess a written text whose immediate exemplars, at least, were probably written. We can assume neither that the originally oral tales were first written down in their present form nor that, once the written text had assumed something like its present shape, later additions and revisions were based exclusively on written materials. Speculation as to how much of the process that produced the text was oral and how much of it written has a limited prospect of success. The same considerations render less promising the question of the poem's intended audience. We know on the one hand that heroic poetry could be appreciated in the monasteries and on the other that well-to-do laypersons could own manuscripts like Cotton Vitellius A.xv; critics' views on the question of audience tend to line up conveniently with their views on questions of interpretation, such as whether we should understand Beowulf as, say, a figure of Christ or as a role model for young princes.

Beowulf, in short, is a poem unaccompanied by the external facts that we take for granted in later literature—a poem without a context more specific than that it was produced in England during a period of some three centuries. In its rich supplementary material, however, and in its commentary on the action it describes it does provide some of its own context. For example, it is minutely concerned with artifacts. Both the narrative voice and the people of whom it tells often pause to admire helmets adorned with talismanic boars, swords with serpentine patterns, newly tarred ships, and golden jewelry; sometimes the narrative stops entirely while we learn, say, the history of the sword that Wiglaf carries into battle or the future history of the necklace that Hrothgar's queen, Wealhtheow, gives to Beowulf. Such objects as these become signifiers—"words" in a sense—not only linking the action to its physical context but also offering a commentary on that action: thus the spirit and energy of Beowulf's men, newly arrived in Denmark, are conveyed by their shining and singing mail coats, and the "sermon" that Hrothgar delivers to Beowulf is given a historical and theological context by an inscription on the hilt of the giant sword describing God's destruction of the race of giants in the Flood. It is worthwhile to read *Beowulf* with a book on Anglo-Saxon archaeology close at hand; scholars have noted an especially strong resemblance between the objects described in the poem and those found in the Sutton Hoo ship burial.

Perhaps the most important contextual element that *Beowulf* supplies for itself is its thoroughly Christian point of view. Its depiction of paganism is selective (it describes funerary practices and the consultation of omens but never names the pagan gods) and rarely judgmental (it once notes with sadness that the Danes condemn themselves to damnation when, through ignorance of the true God, they make offerings to idols). Indeed this "paganism" seems for the most part to be consistent with Christianity: the poem's characters know nothing of Christ and his saints, but they speak of one God, and they believe in an afterlife where every man is judged according to his deeds. Whether the poem views them as able to achieve salvation is a matter of controversy; the only clue is an ambiguous one. When Beowulf dies, the poem says, "his soul departed from his breast to seek the judgment of the righteous"—a phrase that leaves it unclear whether he will be judged to be righteous or judged by those who are righteous.

The poem's refusal to resolve such matters as this is frustrating to some readers, but others have identified it as a major stylistic technique, not only of *Beowulf* but of much OE poetry. Where conventional modern fiction normally resolves its narrative components into a single structure from which it produces meaning, *Beowulf* juxtaposes its various components without insisting on any particular relationship among them. For example, after a poet in Hrothgar's court tells the story of the Frisian king Finn, focusing particularly on his wife, Hildeburh, who loses brother, son, and husband to a feud among men, Wealhtheow delivers a speech whose apparent purpose is to avert similar losses within the Danish royal family. Then the men go to bed and Grendel's mother arrives to avenge the loss of her son. No comparisons are drawn among these narrative elements; no cause-and-effect relationship is implied; no commentary of any kind links them. They share enough elements—all concern women who lose their sons, or may lose them—that we are tempted to look for connections, but we can just as easily leave them alone.

The same tendency can be discerned in the structure of the poem as a whole. The fights with Grendel and his mother take place in Beowulf's youth, over a two-day period; the rest of the poem describes the last day of Beowulf's life, more than 50 years later. No explicit conclusions are drawn from the relationship between these narrative elements, and some have seen the long gap between them as a flaw. The great commentator J.R.R. Tolkien, on the other hand, claimed that this bifurcated structure contributed to the meaning of the poem: *Beowulf,* he wrote, "is essentially a balance, an opposition of ends and beginnings. In its simplest terms it is a contrasted description of two moments in a great life, rising and setting; an elaboration of the ancient and intensely moving contrast between youth and age, first achievement and final death." Generations of OE scholars have found Tolkien's interpretation powerfully attractive, but other formulations are possible. It is not quite true that the events of the 50 years that separate the monster fights go undescribed; rather, tales of the wars fought by Beowulf and his predecessors on the Geatish throne are displaced into the background of the dragon fight, where they are told fully, though out of chronological order, by

Beowulf and by the messenger who announces his death to the waiting Geats. Similar tales form the backdrop of the fights with Grendel and his mother, and the story of Freawaru and Ingeld, told by Beowulf on his return home after those fights, makes the point that old strife is inevitably renewed, whatever measures men and women take to forestall it. If one sees the foreground narratives as illustrating this theme in more abstract fashion, the poem becomes not so much "an opposition of ends and beginnings" as a more seamless tale (despite the 50-year gap) of the futile attempts of men and women to contain the surging violence that continually threatens their fragile institutions. The poem gives us little or no help in choosing among these and other readings; its structure and poetic technique seem hostile to the business of interpretation.

Research into *Beowulf*'s analogues and historical background has fared better than interpretation as a literary industry. The poem connects with what modern readers think of as "history" at one point only: Gregory of Tours, in his *History of the Franks,* records that in the first quarter of the 6th century one "Chlochilaicus," king of the Danes, was killed while plundering along the Frankish coast; he is generally identified with *Beowulf*'s Geatish king Hygelac, who, the narrative voice sternly notes, got no more than what was coming to him. Another English source, the *Liber monstrorum (Book of Monsters)* agrees with *Beowulf* that "Huiglaucus" was king of the Geats, but the 13th-century Icelander Snorri Sturluson writes in *Heimskringla,* his history of the kings of Norway, that "Hugleikr" was a Swedish king who preferred staying home to making war in distant lands. The apparent discrepancies among these accounts illustrate the difficulty of working with sources based on oral history, which tends to be variable. It is often difficult to be sure whether two sources that use similar names are speaking of the same person, for as such histories are told and retold, kings sometimes change their nationalities, family members exchange names, and heroes gather new exploits to their fame.

Despite the uncertainties, there is little doubt that most of the characters mentioned in *Beowulf* are spoken of in Germanic legend, and especially in Icelandic sagas and legendary histories. The great exception is Beowulf himself, who is mentioned nowhere outside the poem. He represents, however, a type of character well attested in the Icelandic sagas. He has a close analogue in (some say he is the same person as) Boðvarr Bjarki of *Hrólfs saga kraka,* and his fights against Grendel and his mother resemble those of such characters as Þorir of *Gull-Þoris Saga,* Grettir the Strong of *Grettis saga,* and Samson the Fair of *Samsons saga fagra.* The tales in which these heroes figure resemble a type of folktale called "The Three Stolen Princesses," in which a hero first defeats a monster in a house and later rescues three princesses by pursuing to a lower world the monster that has kidnaped them; he kills the monster with a sword he finds there and later marries one of the princesses. Though Beowulf wins no princess, he resembles the heroes of "The Three Stolen Princesses" in being of great, perhaps supernatural, strength; further, these heroes are frequently the offspring of bears, and the name "Beowulf" has often been etymologized as "bee-wolf"—that is, the bear, enemy of bees.

Analogues for *Beowulf*'s dragon-fight episode are less exact, though heroes of many times and places have tested their strength against dragons. Boðvarr Bjarki fights a winged flying beast, and several Scandinavian sources tell how Sigurðr (equivalent to Siegfried in the Middle High German *Nibelungenlied* and to Siegfried's father Sigemund in *Beowulf*) killed a dragon. Beyond the presence of a dragon, a hero, and a sword, however, resemblances among these stories are slight.

In view of *Beowulf*'s many connections with folklore and Germanic legend, and the esteem in which it has been held since its first appearance in print in 1815, one might guess, and some have believed, that it was highly valued in its own time—that it was to the Anglo-Saxons as the Homeric epics were to the Greeks or Virgil's *Aeneid* to the Romans. There is, however, no evidence at all to suggest that this was the case. *Beowulf* is not mentioned, quoted, or alluded to once in extant records from Anglo-Saxon England. It has stylistic affinities with *Andreas,* the OE poetic legend of St. Andrew, but it is not clear that one influenced the other or, if there was such influence, in which direction it went. If we take numbers of surviving manuscripts as a rough guide, we must conclude that prose works like the translations of King Alfred, the sermons of Ælfric and Wulfstan, and even the OE *Herbarium* were valued more highly than any OE poem—except for a few that seem to owe their popularity primarily to being embedded in prose tracts. Among poems devotional works like *Soul and Body* and the metrical Psalms seem to have been valued more highly than heroic ones like *Beowulf, Waldere,* and *The Battle of Finnsburg.* To observe that *Beowulf* may well be enjoyed more widely now than in its own time is not at all to denigrate it but rather to remind ourselves that since taste is determined by factors that vary with time and place, we can do little more than guess at the status of the work in the culture that produced it. Like Keats's Grecian urn *Beowulf,* in its stately isolation, tempts us beyond the bounds of the knowable. And yet it is sufficient in itself, its subject being a fundamental one: the struggles of men and women to survive and to protect their social order from the mysterious foes that threaten them from without, and from the equally mysterious foes within.

Peter S. Baker

Bibliography

PRIMARY

ASPR 4:3–98; Chickering, Howell D., ed. and trans. *Beowulf: A Dual-Language Edition.* Garden City: Anchor, 1977; Greenfield, Stanley B., trans. *A Readable Beowulf.* Carbondale: Southern Illinois University Press, 1982; Kiernan, Kevin S. *Beowulf and the Beowulf Manuscript.* New Brunswick: Rutgers University Press, 1981; Klaeber, Friedrich, ed. *Beowulf and the Fight at Finnsburg.* 3d ed. Boston: Heath, 1950; Zupitza, Julius, ed. *Beowulf Reproduced in Facsimile.* 2d ed. EETS o.s. 245. London: Oxford University Press, 1959.

SECONDARY

Baker, Peter S., ed. *Beowulf: Basic Readings.* New York: Garland, 1995; Bessinger, Jess B., Jr., and Robert F. Yeager, eds. *Approaches to Teaching Beowulf.* New York: MLA, 1984; Chambers, R.W. *Beowulf: An Introduction to the Study of the Poem with a Discussion of the Stories of Offa and Finn.* 3d ed., suppl. by C.L. Wrenn. Cambridge: Cambridge University Press, 1959; Chase, Colin, ed. *The Dating of Beowulf.* Toronto: University of Toronto Press, 1981; Fulk, R.D., ed. *Interpretations of Beowulf: A Critical Anthology.* Bloomington: Indiana University Press, 1991; Garmonsway, G.N., et al. *Beowulf and Its Analogues.* London: Dent, 1968; Hasenfratz, Robert J. *Beowulf Scholarship: An Annotated Bibliography, 1979–1990.* New York: Garland, 1993; Nicholson, Lewis E., ed. *An Anthology of Beowulf Criticism.* Notre Dame: University of Notre Dame Press, 1963; Niles, John D. *Beowulf: The Poem and Its Tradition.* Cambridge: Harvard University Press, 1983; Overing, Gillian R. *Language, Sign, and Gender in Beowulf.* Carbondale: Southern Illinois University Press, 1990; Robinson, Fred C. *Beowulf and the Appositive Style.* Knoxville: University of Tennessee Press, 1985; Short, Douglas D. *Beowulf Scholarship: An Annotated Bibliography.* New York: Garland, 1980 [continued by Hasenfratz above]; Tolkien, J.R.R. "*Beowulf:* The Monsters and the Critics." *PBA* 22 (1936): 245–95 [repr. in Nicholson, pp. 51–103].

See also Andreas; Archaeology; Formula; Literary Influences: Scandinavian; Orality; Paganism; Sutton Hoo; Versification; Vikings; Women in OE Literature

Berners, Juliana (fl. ca. 1460?)

Possible author of material on hunting and hawking in *The Book of St. Albans,* which attributes its hunting section to "Dam Julyans Barnes." Biographical accounts are often highly speculative and romanticized.

The Book of St. Albans, published in 1486, contains prose hawking and heraldry treatises and a verse hunting treatise. It remained popular into the 17th century. The *Book* draws upon a rich medieval tradition of teaching the fundamentals of polite education, with particular emphasis on proper use of technical sporting terminology. Major sources include the hawking treatise called *Prince Edward's Book* (date uncertain) and two 15th-century translations of earlier French works: William Twiti's Anglo-Norman *Art of Hunting* and Gaston Phoebus's *Livre de Chasse,* translated as *The Master of Game* by Edward, duke of York (d. 1415). Like Malory's *Morte Darthur* the hunting treatise in the *Book of St. Albans* names Tristram as the originator of hunting literature.

If Berners did write parts of the *Book of St. Albans,* she has shared the fate of many medieval women writers in that questions of biography and authorship have been the focus of much related scholarship. The *Book of St. Albans* is frequently belittled as a compilation from other sources (a common feature of hawking and hunting treatises generally). But compilation was a respected form of literary production in the late Middle Ages, with examples ranging from practical treatises to collections like the *Canterbury Tales.*

Rebecca J. Coogan

Bibliography

PRIMARY

STC 3308; Hands, Rachel, intro. *English Hawking and Hunting in The Boke of St. Albans: A Partial Facsimile.* London: Oxford University Press, 1975.

SECONDARY

New *CBEL* 1:689; McDonald, John. *Quill Gordon.* Ch. 12. New York: Knopf, 1972 [reviews development of legendary biography].

See also Chivalry; Courtesy Literature; Hawking; Heralds; Printing; Prose, ME; Utilitarian Writings

Bestiaries

A wide variety of manuscripts comprising chapters drawing Christian lessons from the supposed appearance or behavior of animals were known to their medieval users as bestiaries. These books are all ultimately derived from a 2nd-century Greek text known as the *Physiologus,* or "natural philosopher," which was translated into Latin by the end of the 4th century.

Fig. 27. Bodl. Laud. misc. 247, fol. 149v. The Unicorn. Reproduced by permission of the Bodleian Library, University of Oxford.

Their variety lies in their length, ranging from fewer than 30 chapters to over 200, and in their organization.

A complete *Physiologus* contains some 37 chapters arranged according to their Christian lessons rather than zoologically. Thus the antelope that gets its horns entangled in a shrub to which it is addicted, and the fire stones that are normally inert but catch fire when two are brought together, form successive chapters of the *Physiologus* because both offer warnings against vices: intemperance and lust, respectively. Both the organization of the *Physiologus* and its orality (the simple, memorable stories, repeated phrases, and occasional use of the vocative to address an audience) suggest that it was designed as a preaching text.

What distinguishes the bestiary from a *Physiologus* are modifications of the text and chapter order. The earliest surviving Latin bestiary produced in England (Bodl. Laud misc. 247; fig. 27), probably written at Canterbury ca. 1110—30, differs from the *Physiologus* only in having short extracts from the *Etymologiae* of Isidore of Seville (ca. 560—636) appended to most of the chapters, but later recensions of the bestiary made more extensive use of Isidore's work. This had important consequences. The *Etymologiae* is an encyclopedia covering the whole of Creation and was intended to reflect this in two ways. First, it groups together those creatures made on the same day of Creation. Second, it was concerned with explaining animals' names: the eagle *(aquila),* for example, is named after the acuteness *(acumine)* of its vision. Since the animals were given their names by Adam according to their natures, these names echo the organization of the natural world as seen by the first man immediately after Creation. Bestiaries reorganized along Isidorean lines, like St. Petersburg, Saltykov-Shchedrin Q.v. V.1, often include the Genesis account of Creation in their text and have a set of Creation scenes culminating in Adam naming the animals at the beginning.

This reorganization destroys the old *Physiologus* structure, so that the work can no longer be used for preaching. Moreover Isidore's text was not designed for reading aloud like the *Physiologus:* it is too concise. These expanded bestiaries could still be used by preachers, not directly, but rather as a source book or *summa.*

At the end of the 12th century and throughout the 13th luxury bestiaries were produced with high-grade script and lavish miniatures decorated with gold and expensive pigments. The St. Petersburg Bestiary is one such, and a close copy, now New York, Pierpont Morgan Library M.81, was presented to Worksop Priory in 1187 along with other luxury books, perhaps to mark the consecration of a new church. Another luxury book, the only bestiary with evidence of secular patronage, is a mid-13th-century manuscript (now Bodley 764 in the Bodleian Library), which may have belonged to the Marcher baron Roger de Monhaut, lord of Mold.

Latin bestiaries were primarily English books of the 12th and 13th centuries, although some were produced in France and Germany as well. The religious orders, principally the Cistercians, were their main users. Examination of the sermons of Aelred of Rievaulx shows massive and regular borrowings from the bestiary. When, from the early 13th century, preachers like Stephen Langton and Odo of Cheriton began to answer the call for sermons aimed at the laity rather than a monastic audience by including exempla drawn from everyday life, the bestiary was doomed as a source book. The luxury appeal of presentation volumes extended its life to a degree, but although a few 14th- and even 15th-century bestiaries survive, the great age of bestiary production was over by the end of the 13th century.

Ronald E. Baxter

Bibliography

James, Montague Rhodes. *The Bestiary.* Oxford: Roxburghe Club, 1928; Morgan, Nigel. *Early Gothic Manuscripts (1) 1190–1250.* A Survey of Manuscripts Illuminated in the British Isles 4:1, ed. J.J.G. Alexander. London: Harvey Miller, 1982; Muratova, Xenia. *The Medieval Bestiary.* Moscow: Iskusstro, 1984; White, T.H. *The Book of Beasts.* London: Cape, 1954.

See also Allegory; Beast Epic and Fable; Exemplum; Isidore; Manuscript Illumination, Romanesque; *Marvels of the East;* Scientific Manuscripts, Early; Sermons

Bible in Middle English Literature

From the earliest days of Christianity the Bible has been seen in competition with secular literature. St. Jerome, after a period of divided loyalty, put the famous question, "What has Horace to do with the Psalter, Virgil with the Gospels, and Cicero with the Apostle [Paul]?" *(Epistle 22).* In the OE period Alcuin echoed this sentiment by asking, "What has [the Germanic hero] Ingeld to do with Christ?" *(Epistle 123).* By the later Middle Ages accommodations had been found and articulated. Still, vernacular writers of the ME period who draw heavily on scripture tend to define their work in opposition to more popular or worldly forms of literature. They may call attention explicitly to the division, like the author of *Cursor Mundi,* who complains that many people are less concerned to keep the commandments than "to here Romaunces"; or they may simply avoid mingling biblical and secular material, like Langland, who cites hundreds of biblical texts but almost no classical authors. The reverse is not true. The fabliau, whose essence is the violation of decorum, frequently drags the Bible into its comically distorted world. In Chaucer's *Merchant's Tale,* for example, lecherous January addresses his young wife in the words of the Song of Songs (2138–48), and later the pagan deities Pluto and Proserpina hurl biblical proverbs against each other.

The Bible most familiar to ME writers was Jerome's Latin translation, the Vulgate, although the older Vetus Latina still circulated. Other sources of the biblical text included commentaries, the liturgy, and writings of the early Church Fathers. Thus medieval biblical quotations that vary from the Vulgate may have come to the writer from a different textual tradition or from an intermediate source; it is unhistorical to call them "inaccurate" (especially if the standard of comparison is the Clementine edition of the Vulgate, which was not issued until 1592).

Whatever the lines of transmission, the debt of ME literature to the Bible takes primarily the following three forms.

Translation and Paraphrase

In addition to such broad retellings as *Patience* (the story of Jonah) and the Corpus Christi plays (biblical history from Creation to Doomsday), the *Manual of Writings in Middle English* lists nearly 60 biblical translations, paraphrases, and commentaries (e.g., *Genesis and Exodus, Iacob and Iosep,* Rolle's *English Psalter and Commentary,* the *Stanzaic Life of Christ,* and the Wycliffite versions of the Bible). Though generally conservative, many writers felt free to enlarge upon the implications of the biblical narrative, to update it, to fill in the gaps. The author of *Patience,* finding no explanation for Jonah's reluctance to denounce the sins of Nineveh, makes a plausible inference: the prophet is afraid that he will be arrested in Nineveh, put in prison, and tormented (73–88). The poet of "It wes upon a Shere Thorsday" tries to illumine the mental state of Judas by inventing a conversation between him and his "soster" (Sisam, *Fourteenth Century Verse and Prose:* XV.G). The cycle plays expand bare mentions of Noah's wife, Herod, and the shepherds at Christ's nativity into full-blown characters. *Iacob and Iosep* is medievalized: knights, minstrels, and moated castles are common; in Egypt Joseph "sits in hall" like a medieval king.

Borrowings

The Bible is a major source of exempla, parables, and other kinds of narrative. Gower's *Confessio Amantis* illustrates vainglory by an account of Nebuchadnezzar. *Cleanness* is constructed around three examples of impurity from the Old Testament. Chaucer's Monk warns against trusting Fortune by the "ensamples trewe and olde" of Lucifer, Adam, Samson, Nebuchadnezzar, Belshazzar, and Holofernes, as well as classical and medieval figures. The parables of Christ are at the heart of such well-known works as *Pearl* (the pearl of great price, the vineyard) and *Piers Plowman* (the good Samaritan).

In retelling biblical stories ME authors frequently transform the mode. Lydgate relates the tale of a king whose paramour, Liberality, is displaced by the hag Avarice, an allegorization of the apocryphal 1 Esdras (Vulgate 3 Esdras) 4:29–31 (*The Pilgrimage of the Life of Man* 17,360–432). Caxton's *Knight of the Tower* recasts the Redemption as a romance "Of the good knyght whiche fought ageynst the fals knyghte for the pyte of a mayde" (ch. 104). In the *Miller's Tale* the story of the Flood is turned into parody; so too in the *Summoner's Tale* are the accounts of Eliezer's oath to Abraham (Gen. 24:1–4) and Pentecost (Acts 2).

Biblical imagery is commonplace. Behind Langland's description of Lady Meed lies the Whore of Babylon (Rev. 17); behind the celestial city at the end of *Pearl* is the New Jerusalem of the Apocalypse; behind numerous examples of the gardenlike setting known as the *locus amoenus* there are the garden of Eden and the *hortus conclusus* ("garden enclosed") of Canticles.

Single verses, quoted or echoed, are the most abundant form of scriptural borrowing. Close to 2,000 examples have been identified in Chaucer's works; of the nearly 1,200 quotations spread over the three versions of *Piers Plowman* about two-thirds are biblical. Quotations are used by ME writers in a variety of ways. Most frequently they confirm a point: "Ye legistres and lawieres, if I lye witeþ Mathew: *Quodcumque vultis vt faciant vobis homines facite eis*" (*Piers Plowman* B.7.60–60a). Sometimes they are self-defining: in the morality play *Mankind* Mercy declares, "The justice of God will as I will . . . *Nolo mortem peccatoris*" (833–34); sometimes self-incriminating: Chaucer's Pardoner says, "My theme is yet, and evere was, *Radix malorum est Cupiditas*" (*PardPro* 425–26). They may furnish the refrain or *donée* (textual starting point) of a lyric poem: Isaiah 63:1, "Quis est iste, qui venit de Edom?" ("Who is this that cometh from Edom?"); Psalm 144:9, "Et miserationes eius super omnia opera eius" ("And his tender mercies are over all his works"); Canticles 2:5, "Quia amore langueo" ("Because I languish with love") (Carleton Brown, *Religious Lyrics of the XIVth Century,* 2d ed.: nos. 25, 95, 132.) When quotations used in this way are strung together, as in the *Prick of Conscience* and *Piers Plowman,* they may serve as the structural backbone of a passage. Even denser is the thicket of scriptural borrowings in the writings of Richard Rolle, about whom it could be said (as it has been of St. Bernard) that he "spoke Bible."

Adaptation of Exegetical Techniques

The body of rules and approaches that grew up around biblical hermeneutics influenced the making and the reading of vernacular literature in three important ways.

First, the dialectical use of biblical authorities is a common feature in ME literature. In *Pearl* (stanzas 9–12) the maiden recounts the parable of the vineyard (Matt. 20:1–16) to show that God will reward according to his mercy; the dreamer objects on the basis of Psalm 61:12 that God will reward according to one's deserts; the maiden responds that by this reasoning, nobody would be saved, "For non lyuyande to þe is justyfyet" (Ps. 142:2). Langland uses many of his biblical quotations in the same way. Probably the Wife of Bath is the most famous, if not the most adept, practitioner of the method.

Second, the fourfold interpretation of scripture (literal; allegorical; tropological, "pertaining to morals"; anagogical, "pertaining to the next world") inspired vernacular authors to develop multiple levels of meaning in their own compositions. Near the end of the *Canterbury Tales* the Parson explicitly directs us to think not only of the literal but also of the anagogical pilgrimage, "Of thilke parfit glorious pilgrymage / That highte Jerusalem celestial" (*ParsPro* 50–51). An important aid to multifold exegesis was the *distinctio,* that is, an array of the various meanings of a word depending on its biblical context. Thus the word *bed* is taken in Canticles 3:7 to refer to the church, in Amos 6:4 to carnal pleasure, in Job 17:13 to eternal punishment. By the 14th century the use of *distinctiones* had become so commonplace in sermons as to seem, in the words of a medieval observer, "as cheap as silver in the reign of King Solomon" (Smalley, 1983: 248).

ME writers were not isolated from the *distinctio* nor from the kind of thinking it fostered. The author of *Pearl* exploits virtually every possible sense of his title. Langland systematically describes various kinds of *bread* in passus 13 and 14 of the B text: there is the "sour loof" of *Agite penitenciam* (13.49); "payn for þe pope and provendre for his palfrey" (13.243); the literal "wafres" of Haukyn (13.263); "a pece of þe Paternoster . . . *fiat voluntas tua*" (14.49–50); the manna of the Hebrews in the wilderness (14.64); the *habundancia panis* of the Sodomites (14.77α); and, providing an anagogical focus for all these, the allusion in 14.3a to Christ's parable of the feast (Luke 14:15–24), which begins "Beatus qui manducabit panem in regno Dei."

Third, and most important, the poetic imagination was affected powerfully by the exegetical habit of reading the Old Testament as a prefiguration of the New. Christ himself encouraged the practice: "For as Jonas was in the whale's belly three days and three nights, so shall the Son of Man be in the heart of the earth three days and three nights" (Matt. 12:40). Exegetical tradition developed numerous other typologies, many of which entered the visual arts and the homiletic tradition, thereby reaching nonliterate as well as literate audiences. The Virgin Birth is foreshadowed by the burning bush; the Crucifixion by the sacrifice of Isaac; the Harrowing of Hell by Samson's carrying off the gates of Gaza. Such correspondences were elaborated by ME poets, most notably in the Corpus Christi cycles (where typology may have influenced the actual selection of stories) and in the lyrics (e.g., "Marye mayde mylde and free" [Brown, *Religious Lyrics of the XIVth Century,* 2d ed.: no. 32] and the Prioress's hymn to the Virgin in the *Canterbury Tales* [*PriorPro* 453–87]). Moreover, having learned to think in this way, poets went on to create new correspondences. The nativity of Christ, the Lamb of God, is prefigured in the *Second Shepherds' Play* by a false nativity, a stolen sheep swaddled to look like a child. The fall becomes a universal paradigm of experience, not only for humans but even (the *Nun's Priest's Tale* would have us believe) for roosters. Eventually, as illustrated by the corresponding triads in part 3 of *Sir Gawain and the Green Knight,* typological thinking frees itself entirely from its biblical matrix.

John A. Alford

Bibliography

GENERAL

Kaske, R.E. *Medieval Christian Literary Imagery: A Guide to Interpretation.* Toronto: University of Toronto Press, 1988; Lampe, G.W.H., ed. *The West from the Fathers to the Reformation.* Vol. 2 of *The Cambridge History of the Bible.* Cambridge: Cambridge University Press, 1969; Levy, Bernard S., ed. *The Bible in the Middle Ages: Its Influence on Literature and Art.* MRTS 89. Binghamton: MRTS, 1992; Smalley, Beryl. *The Study of the Bible in the Middle Ages.* 3d ed. Oxford: Blackwell, 1983.

MIDDLE ENGLISH PERIOD

Manual 2:381–407, 534–51; Besserman, Lawrence. *Chaucer and the Bible: A Critical Review of Research,*

Indexes, and Bibliography. New York: Garland, 1988; Fowler, David C. *The Bible in Middle English Literature.* Seattle: University of Washington Press, 1984; Jeffrey, David Lyle, ed. *Chaucer and Scriptural Tradition.* Ottawa: University of Ottawa Press, 1984; Robertson, D.W., Jr., and Bernard F. Huppé. *Piers Plowman and Scriptural Tradition.* Princeton: Princeton University Press, 1951.

See also Allegory; Bible in OE Literature; Criticism, Modern, of Medieval Literature; *Cursor Mundi;* Drama, Vernacular; Orm; *Pearl*-Poet; *Piers Plowman;* Rolle; Sermons; Translation; Wyclif; Wycliffite Texts

Bible in Old English Literature

As the central literary document of a Christian culture the Bible played an important role in most, if not all, of Anglo-Saxon literature. The modern English word "bible," from Greek *ta biblia* ("the books"), is not attested from the period; the *Oxford English Dictionary* cites *Cursor Mundi* as the first vernacular use, although the earliest example in Anglo-Latin is a book list from Durham Cathedral dated to 1095. A second Latin term for the Bible, "bibliotheca," appears in the writings of Aldhelm and Alcuin and occurs as *bibliođece* in vernacular writers, such as Ælfric. The common way, however, of referring to the Bible is with the term *(ge)writ,* a translation of Latin *scriptura;* the OE word is used of other writings as well.

One reason for this more general terminology is that single volumes containing the entire Bible were rare, particularly during the early period. Aside from the Codex Amiatinus (Florence, Biblioteca Medicea-Laurenziana Amiatinus 1), which was inspired by the arrival in Northumbria of Cassiodorus's Codex Grandior, a large, illustrated volume containing the Old Testament, and was written to be sent to Rome, the earliest complete Bible that survives from Anglo-Saxon England dates to the end of the 10th century (BL Royal 1.E.vii and 1.E.viii). From the 11th century are Cambridge, Trinity College B.5.2; Durham, Cathedral Library A.II.4; Lincoln, Cathedral Library 1; and San Marino, California, Huntington Library HM 62. Certainly there were others— including two made at the same time as the Amiatinus, of which only fragments remain (BL Add. 37777 and 45025)— but it was more common for parts of the Bible to circulate independently.

The manuscript evidence suggests that the most readily available books were the Psalms and the Gospels, and there are OE terms for both. OE *saltere* denotes codices containing the Psalms, often combined with other liturgical texts, such as canticles. Eighth-century manuscripts include the Vespasian Psalter (BL Cotton Vespasian A.i), the Salaberga Psalter (Berlin, Deutsche Staatsbibliothek Hamilton 553), and the Morgan Psalter (also known as the "Blickling Psalter"; New York, Pierpont Morgan Library 776). Like the Psalter the Gospels survive in many manuscripts and are referred to with OE terms, *godspel* and *Cristes boc.* Still in dispute are the origins of some early gospel books possibly produced in northern English centers under Irish influence; the important witnesses are the Book of Durrow (Dublin, Trinity College 57), the Book of Kells (Dublin, Trinity College 58), the Durham Gospels (Durham, Cathedral Library A.II.16), and the Lindisfarne Gospels (BL Cotton Nero D.iv). Also important as a witness both of the insular tradition and of a missionary text on the Continent are the Echternach Gospels (Paris, BN lat. 9389).

Not only does the semantic range of words for the Bible differ from modern usage, the text itself is not as firmly fixed during the period—particularly before the Carolingian reform—as it is today. Jerome's translation of the Bible into Latin, now referred to as the Vulgate (that is, the "commonly accepted" version), was not immediately accepted in the early church, and readings from the previous Vetus Latina (the "Old Latin" version) continued to circulate in individual manuscripts and in commentaries. The Vulgate also contains five books—Wisdom, Ecclesiasticus, 1 and 2 Maccabees, and Baruch—that Jerome did not revise and that he apparently considered apocryphal. Some other apocryphal texts were known to the Anglo-Saxons; for example, Psalm 151 is often included in psalters, and in CUL Ii.2.11 the Gospel of Nicodemus follows the four canonical Gospels in West-Saxon.

Although much remains to be learned about the circulation of particular versions of biblical books in Anglo-Saxon England, a greater number of manuscripts containing the Psalms and Gospels permits some remarks about the roles of early missionary activity and the Benedictine Reform in the dissemination of these books. In the early period the Psalms occur most often in the Roman form—traditionally considered Jerome's first revision of this book—with the manuscripts including the Vespasian, Salaberga, and Morgan psalters. This version also survives in three 10th-century psalters: the Bosworth (BL Add. 37517), the Royal (BL Royal 2.B.v), and the Junius (Bodl. Junius 27). With the Benedictine Reform manuscripts of the Gallican version—by Jerome and accepted by Alcuin for his redaction—became more prevalent; two 9th-century psalters from Reims—Cambridge, Corpus Christi College 272, and Utrecht, Universiteitsbibliotheek 32 (the Utrecht Psalter)—are among the Gallican psalters that were known in Anglo-Saxon England. By the close of the period the Gallican version is better represented than the Roman. Finally, although the manuscript evidence is much slighter, mention needs to be made of the Hebrew Psalter—Jerome's last translation of the Psalms—since it is the Irish textual family of this version that appears in the Codex Amiatinus and thus shows some evidence of Irish missionary activity in Northumbria. Also, although from the mid-12th century and thus beyond the strict limits of the Anglo-Saxon period, Eadwine's Psalter (the Canterbury Psalter; Cambridge, Trinity College R.17.1) includes the Hebrew version, along with the Roman and Gallican versions in parallel columns: the Roman is glossed in OE and the Hebrew in French. Here, as in Salisbury, Cathedral Library 180, the Hebrew version is apparently related to Alcuin's revision.

The manuscripts of the Gospels reveal more of the early missionary activity in England. Cambridge, Corpus Christi

College 286, and Bodl. Auctarium D.2.14, both written in Italy in the 6th and 7th centuries, respectively, represent the kind of mixed Italian text (so called because it contains both Vetus Latina and Vulgate readings) of the Gospels brought by the early missionaries from Rome to Canterbury. Northumbria from an early date was home to a pure Italian text of the Vulgate Gospels that is represented in the Codex Amiatinus, and the Lindisfarne Gospels, as well as in a manuscript of Stonyhurst College, Lancashire (unnumbered, on deposit at the BL), which contains the Gospel of John. Also present in northern England, due to Irish missionary activity, was the Irish family of Gospels, in which both the Vulgate and the mixed Italian type are represented: the manuscripts include the Book of Kells, the Gospels of St. Chad (Lichfield, Cathedral Library Lich 1), and the Rushworth Gospels (Bodl. Auctarium D.2.19). It has often been suggested that Alcuin turned to the English Bibles for his revision of the Gospels, although the exact links are still unclear.

In addition to manuscripts of the Bible and biblical materials used in the liturgy, the Anglo-Saxons had two other major sources for biblical lore: biblical commentaries (and homilies) and metrical paraphrases of the Bible. Commentaries by the four main Fathers of the Church, Ambrose, Augustine, Jerome, and Gregory, as well as by many others, survive in manuscripts from the period; Bede did much to perpetuate this tradition. Alcuin provides a good example of the knowledge of biblical epic. In his description of the books that Ælberht, archbishop of York, left to him he includes Caelius Sedulius, Juvencus, Alcumus Avitus, Prudentius, and Arator, all of whom he used in his *Poem on the Bishops, Kings, and Saints of York*. Most of these authors continued to be copied in the later period.

What did Anglo-Saxon vernacular writers do with this biblical material? They glossed, translated, and paraphrased it and used it for themes and images in prose and poetry. The Psalms and the Gospels deserve particular attention. The Vespasian Psalter contains a continuous vernacular gloss in a mid-9th-century hand, and there are some 9th-century glosses in the Morgan Psalter. The 9th-century gloss in the Junius Psalter may be in the same hand as the Latin, and that in the Regius Psalter from the same date as the Latin, mid-10th century. The Paris Psalter (Paris, BN lat. 8824) is noteworthy because in addition to presenting the Roman version of the Psalms in one column it contains OE translations in a second column, of which Psalms 51–150 are in verse. A metrical version of Psalm 50 also survives in BL Cotton Vespasian D.vi. With respect to the Gospels Cuthbert relates that in his final days Bede was translating John into English, but this work has never been identified. The most important early glosses are in the Lindisfarne and Rushworth Gospels and date to the 10th century. A translation was also made into West Saxon, which survives in six manuscripts. In addition to the Psalms and the Gospels a prose translation, partly by Ælfric, of the first six books—known as the Hexateuch—of the Bible survives in a number of manuscripts including one that is illustrated (BL Cotton Claudius B.iv). Ælfric provided summaries of Judges, Kings, Esther, Judith, and Maccabees as well.

Perhaps the most famous collection of OE biblical material is in the Junius Manuscript (Bodl. Junius 11), which contains versions of Genesis, Exodus, and Daniel. Earlier scholars associated these poems with Cædmon, who according to Bede used to turn "whatever he learned from holy scriptures . . . into extremely delightful and moving poetry, in English"; but this connection is no longer held. The poems differ markedly in their use of the Bible: *Genesis A,* for example, remains relatively close to the Latin, whereas *Exodus* is much freer in its retelling of events. The *Beowulf*-manuscript (BL Cotton Vitellius A.xv) contains a fragment of a poetic rendering of Judith; and *Andreas* in the Vercelli Book is based on the apocryphal acts of St. Andrew. Biblical echoes and themes have been noted in these and many other OE texts.

Frederick M. Biggs

Bibliography

GENERAL

Kaske, R.E. *Medieval Christian Literary Imagery: A Guide to Interpretation.* Toronto: University of Toronto Press, 1988; Lampe, G.W.H., ed. *The West from the Fathers to the Reformation.* Vol. 2 of *The Cambridge History of the Bible.* Cambridge: Cambridge University Press, 1969; Levy, Bernard S., ed. *The Bible in the Middle Ages: Its Influence on Literature and Art.* MRTS 89. Binghamton: MRTS, 1992; Smalley, Beryl. *The Study of the Bible in the Middle Ages.* 3d ed. Oxford: Blackwell, 1983.

OLD ENGLISH PERIOD

Biggs, Frederick M. "Apocrypha." In *The Sources of Anglo-Saxon Literary Culture: A Trial Version,* ed. Frederick M. Biggs, Thomas D. Hill, and Paul E. Szarmach. MRTS 74. Binghamton: MRTS, 1990, pp. 22–70; Doyle, Peter. "The Latin Bible in Ireland: Its Origins and Growth. In *Biblical Studies: The Medieval Irish Contribution,* ed. Martin McNamara. Dublin: Dominican Publications, 1976, pp. 30–45; Fowler, David C. *The Bible in Early English Literature.* Seattle: University of Washington Press, 1976; Gneuss, Helmut. "Liturgical Books in Anglo-Saxon England and Their Old English Terminology." In *Learning and Literature in Anglo-Saxon England: Studies Presented to Peter Clemoes on the Occasion of His Sixty-Fifth Birthday,* ed. Michael Lapidge and Helmut Gneuss. Cambridge: Cambridge University Press, 1985, pp. 91–141; McNally, Robert E. *The Bible in the Early Middle Ages.* Westminster, Md.: Newman Press, 1959; Morrell, Minnie Cate. *A Manual of Old English Biblical Materials.* Knoxville: University of Tennessee Press, 1965.

See also Ælfric; Allegory; *Azarias;* Bible in ME Literature; Cædmon; Criticism, Modern, of Medieval Literature; *Daniel;* Eadwine and Canterbury/Paris Psalters; *Exodus; Genesis,* Old Saxon; *Genesis A* and *B; Judith;* Sermons; Translation; Wearmouth-Jarrow and the Codex Amiatinus

Bishops

Bishops in the romanized Britain of the 4th century fit into the province's civil and administrative divisions and what remained of its urban base. By the 5th century the few surviving churches and their leaders, in the north and west, were associated with tribes, not territories. Augustine of Canterbury's mission from Rome in 597 aimed to establish 26 bishoprics, with fixed seats and boundaries and administrative responsibilities. This contrasted with a bishop's more personal liturgical and evangelical role in the Celtic church. Eventually the Roman model won.

Augustine's foundation of sees at London (601) and Rochester (604) was a move that fully recognized the strength of Anglo-Saxon political units and their boundaries. Theodore of Tarsus, archbishop of Canterbury (d. 690), brought the number of sees to about fifteen, aligning them with centers of population and communication, while sensibly accepting political determinants and eschewing inappropriate urban models used elsewhere in Christendom. The much-traveled St. Wilfrid (d. 709) was an exemplar for the many rumbustious, political prelates of the Middle Ages, at ease with wealth and kings, in exile when not. Bishops and kings declared each other's legitimacy and power; they needed each other. Most could reconcile sincerity and expediency; for example, the 10th-century legion of well-born saints (Dunstan, Oswald, and Æthelwold) spread reformation and Wessex dynasticism hand in hand. The late Anglo-Saxon church was neither isolated nor threadbare.

William the Conqueror replaced eight bishops with Norman monks, for political as much as moral reasons. While the two metropolitans at Canterbury and York contested each other's status and jurisdiction down to the 14th century, their fifteen English and four Welsh suffragan dioceses had settled down by the 12th century. The dioceses varied widely in wealth, size, and population. By continental standards most were both rich and large. Lincoln sprawled half the length of England; Winchester was at times the wealthiest see in western Christendom; Durham enjoyed great jurisdictions on the northern border. However, the Welsh dioceses were nearly all impoverished and fragile. Sheer size made most bishops' tasks more administrative than pastoral.

Kings always wanted to influence appointments; to remunerate servants, to ensure the loyalty of such powerful lordships, to encourage the health of church life and administration, and not infrequently to enhance a scholar or holy man. If nepotism was rife, it was not widely regarded as a sin and was probably no worse or better in effects than any other system of advancement. Royal influence was contested to crisis point by such archbishops of Canterbury as St. Anselm (d. 1109), St. Thomas Becket (d. 1170), and Robert Winchelsey (d. 1313). They won fame; more good came from tough but cooperative primates, such as Lanfranc (d. 1089), John Pecham (d. 1290), and Thomas Arundel (d. 1414). Royal yesmen imposed on the church, like Walter Reynolds (d. 1327), Henry Chichele (d. 1443), or Thomas Cranmer (d. 1556), did no one much good.

In any period the ranks of bishops included monks, scholars, magnates, and civil servants. Monks and scholars eventually faded out, partly jostled by careerist administrators, mainly because fewer such men of distinction existed. Perhaps 13th-century bishops achieved the greatest direct impact on the lives of parish clergy and people. Thereafter there was efficiency but less innovation and drive and little international or intellectual impact under generations of high-powered civil servants and lawyers. Episcopal absenteeism from dioceses can be hugely exaggerated (except in Wales).

Some men were certainly distracted by royal office, by attendance in the House of Lords, and by diplomacy, but most worked hard in their dioceses. Like many others the peerless William of Wykeham (Winchester; d. 1404) and Thomas Langley (Durham; d. 1437) served church and king with equal devotion. The episcopate never became time servers or shirkers. The Reformation of the 16th century was no fault of theirs, not even of that infamous scapegoat, the great if flawed Cardinal Thomas Wolsey (d. 1530). They coped as well as could be expected with the unparalleled and unprecedented crisis of loyalties, and with spirit, and ensured the survival of their authority into the next era.

Richard G. Davies

Bibliography

Barlow, Frank. *The English Church, 1000–1066: A History of the Later Anglo-Saxon Church.* 2d ed. London: Longman, 1979; Davies, Richard G. "The Episcopate." In *Profession, Vocation and Culture in Later Medieval England,* ed. Cecil H. Clough. Liverpool: Liverpool University Press, 1982, pp. 51–89; Knowles, Michael David. "The English Bishops, 1070–1532." In *Medieval Studies Presented to Aubrey Gwynn,* ed. J.A. Watt et al. Dublin: Lochlainn, 1961, pp. 283–96; Mayr-Harting, Henry. *The Coming of Christianity to Anglo-Saxon England.* 3d ed. University Park: Pennsylvania State University Press, 1991; Rosenthal, Joel T. *The Training of an Elite Group: English Bishops in the Fifteenth Century.* Trans. of the American Philosophical Society, new ser. 60/5. Philadelphia: American Philosophical Society, 1970.

See also Æthelwold; Aldhelm; Anselm; Asser; Augustine of Canterbury; Beaufort Family; Becket; Chichele; Cuthbert; Douglas; Dunstan; Edmund of Abingdon; Geoffrey of Monmouth; Grosseteste; Hubert Walter; Investiture Controversy; Lanfranc; Langton; Morton; Neville Family; Oswald; Pecock; Tatwine; Theodore of Tarsus; Wærferth; Wainfleet; Wilfrid; William of Wykeham; Wulfstan

Black Death

Everything about the Black Death is controversial. Nobody called it by that name in the Middle Ages; it was known simply as the pestilence. Its symptoms are well attested by contemporaries, particularly the swollen lymphatic glands in groin and armpit and the dark blotches caused by bleeding under the skin. These are certainly the symptoms of bubonic plague. But they also fit other diseases; there are good reasons for querying established beliefs about the nature of the Black Death.

Black rats are the most efficient carriers of the bacillus of bubonic plague because the fleas that live in their fur then spread it. But black rats are sedentary creatures, reluctant to migrate and repelled by the cool environment of the temperate-zone English countryside in which the pestilence raged. Bubonic plague transfers from animal to human hosts, either when the animal dies of plague and its fleas cannot find another suitable animal host or when the fleas themselves become so infected with plague that their stomachs can no longer receive the food their appetites tell them they need. In desperation they then turn to any available host, including human beings.

All this means that we must look for substantial concentrations of rats and a high mortality rate among rats before we can expect to find anything approaching an epidemic of bubonic plague in human populations. Contemporaries, however, never commented upon the size of the rat population. Nor did they speak of a profusion of dead rats. Instead they all agreed that the pestilence spread rapidly, far and wide, a thing that bubonic plague never seems to have done in more recent times.

The pestilence was first noted on the south coast in the summer of 1348. It was soon everywhere; it proved to be a formidable killer. Manorial court rolls, which recorded the deaths of servile tenants because a fine ("heriot") had to be paid on their behalf when they died, are full of heriot payments at this time. The bishops' registers, recording vacancies and fresh appointments made when rectors and vicars changed jobs or died, are full of new institutions to livings. Everyone naturally panicked. Parliament could not meet. The central law courts closed down.

Then, by 1350, it was all over. We hear no more about pestilence until 1361. This unparalleled scourge had utterly failed to make itself endemic. The economy made a complete recovery. On the land vacant tenancies were filled. More wool was exported in the 1350s than in any other decade, bar one, since records began, a sure sign that sheep were not susceptible to whatever it was that killed people. Cloth exports started their long climb. Meanwhile the political world woke up, renewed the Hundred Years War, and fought it to a glorious climax in the Treaty of Brétigny (1360).

That, however, was not the end of pestilence. It returned in 1361, again in 1368, and again in 1375. By then pestilence had become recurrent, and it is difficult to pick out years of outstanding virulence. Once it became recurrent, pestilence began to reduce the population to the point at which shortage of labor was reflected in real wages.

When the pestilence arrived in mid-century, money wages jumped. The king reacted at once. He forbade all wage earners to ask for more money than they had earned in 1346. He did not have to forbid manorial tenants to ask for improvements in their terms of tenure and service because the manorial courts, which controlled so much of their lives, were well able to discipline tenants in the interests of manorial lords. When parliament reconvened in 1351, it turned the king's ordinance into statute law and established courts specifically for the adjudication of wage law.

At first these courts had very little to do, because the prices of ordinary goods rose when wages rose and seem to have risen as fast as they did. The 1350s and 1360s were in fact decades of inflation such as the economic system had not witnessed before. If the population fell as a result of the pestilence of 1348–50, it did not fall far enough to upset the balance between wages and what wages could buy. Accordingly landlords who were asked for higher wages were content, on the whole, to pay them because prices had risen enough to absorb their extra costs.

Later things changed. Pestilence became endemic and prices fell. Both these things happened in the 1370s. And when prices fell money wages did not. This was one sign that population had fallen far enough, as a result of recurrent pestilence, to produce a surplus of land. Wherever there is a surplus of land in nonindustrialized societies, real wages rise because land surplus encourages men and women to take advantage of low rents to become tenant farmers. If anyone wants a wage laborer, in such circumstances, he can only tempt him away from farming for himself by offering him a premium for his labor, as happened in Australia, New Zealand, and Canada in the 19th century, as well as in the sugar islands of the West Indies, where cheap land created labor problems for ex-slave-owning sugar farmers who could not attract labor without offering higher wages than they thought they could afford. It was certainly what happened in late-14th-century England.

The other sign that population had fallen decisively was the disintegration of the system of demesne farming that had been a feature of the countryside for centuries. Caught between rising labor costs and falling receipts, the big demesne farmers, both lay and ecclesiastical, reacted in two ways. They began to enforce the law about wages with a will; and this, as much as anything, provoked the Peasants' Revolt of 1381. And they switched from arable farming, which required a great deal of labor, to pasture farming, which did not. Neither of these expedients solved their problems, and in the end they were forced to lease out their demesne farms when they could.

Though pestilence may have emptied the countryside, it did not make the farms that survived less productive. Indeed it probably made them more productive. Cheap land had two main consequences for farming. It enabled farmers to concentrate their efforts on the better soils and graze increasing numbers of animals; and before the age of artificial fertilizers nothing improved soil productivity more than dung. It also enabled farmers and those who worked with them and for them to live better than they had been able to do in the past. This raised farm productivity by increasing the stamina and energy with which farmwork could be done.

It is often contended that pestilence cast a pall over life in the later Middle Ages. But death had always been close, and, for many, want had made life such a lingering misery that death came as a friend. Pestilence raised mortality rates, but high mortality rates made possible higher standards of living for everyone who did not belong to the classes that had always enjoyed enough food and shelter for health. For a brief period, perhaps for less than a century, pestilence changed the meaning of the word poverty; starvation, lack of shelter, and the deficiency diseases that go with grinding poverty were banished from the common experience of life for many ordinary people, perhaps for a substantial majority of them. As time passed, the pestilence gradually lost its potency; as it did so, the population stabilized and then slowly recovered. The pace of recovery is hard to measure, but by the early 16th century real wages once more started to fall and the bulk of the population began to return to those distressing conditions of life from which the pestilence had rescued those who were not its victims.

Anthony R. Bridbury

Bibliography

Bridbury, Anthony R. "The Black Death." *EcHR*, 2d ser. 26 (1973): 577–92; Hatcher, John. *Plague, Population, and the English Economy, 1348–1530.* London: Macmillan, 1977; Hatcher, John. "England in the Aftermath of the Black Death." *Past and Present* 144 (August 1994): 3–35; Twigg, Graham. *The Black Death: A Biological Appraisal.* London: Batsford, 1984; Ziegler, Philip. *The Black Death.* London: Collins; New York: Day, 1969.

See also Manorialism; Medicine; Peasant Rebellion; Population; Prices and Wages

Blickling Homilies

The second-largest collection of anonymous vernacular homilies extant from Anglo-Saxon England, after the Vercelli Book, and one of the oldest collections of Christian sermons in a western European vernacular language. One of the homilies in the collection contains a reference that can be taken to refer to the writing of the manuscript in the year 971. The manuscript of the Blickling Homilies is now Princeton, Scheide Library 71. The homilies take their name from Blickling Hall in Norfolk, the seat of the marquess of Lothian, in whose library the manuscript remained for almost 200 years.

The origin of the codex is unknown, but studies of the vocabulary have suggested an Anglian origin. The margins of the manuscript and added folios contain records of the city of Lincoln, where it was used as an oath book. In 1724 the manuscript was given by Lincoln city officials, along with the Blickling Psalter (now New York, Pierpont Morgan Library 776), to William Pownall, who later sold both manuscripts to Richard Ellys of Nocton, Lincolnshire, an ancestor of the marquess of Lothian. The 11th marquess sold the manuscripts in 1932 to pay death duties; the Blickling Homilies were acquired by Cortlandt Field Bishop and subsequently by the Scheide family, then of Titusville, Pennsylvania, in 1938.

The manuscript is the work of two scribes and comprises eighteen homilies that mainly follow the order of the church year. Surviving signatures and the contents of the manuscript reveal that four gatherings are missing from the beginning and one from the end and possibly others from the middle of the codex. The first homily begins imperfectly but is probably for the Feast of the Annunciation. The second is for Quinquages-

ima; the third, fourth, fifth, and sixth homilies, for later Sundays in Lent. The seventh homily is for Easter. The eighth, ninth, and tenth homilies are for the three Rogation Days. Ascension Day is the occasion of the eleventh homily, and Pentecost, the twelfth. The remaining homilies represent fixed feasts in the Sanctorale (the liturgies in honor of saints): the Assumption of the Virgin Mary (15 August), the Nativity of St. John the Baptist (24 June), Sts. Peter and Paul (29 June), St. Michael (29 September), St. Martin (11 November), and St. Andrew (30 November).

The homilies are mainly not exegetical in nature; for the most part they do not explain the Gospel reading or the lives of the saints whose feasts are celebrated. Rather, they usually offer basic instruction on the fundamentals of the Christian faith, though whether for a lay or monastic audience is unclear.

W.P. Stoneman

Bibliography

PRIMARY

Morris, Richard, ed. *The Blickling Homilies.* EETS o.s. 58, 63, 73. London: Trübner, 1874–80; Willard, Rudolph, ed. *The Blickling Homilies.* EEMF 10. Copenhagen: Rosenkilde & Bagger, 1960.

SECONDARY

Gatch, Milton McC. "The Unknowable Audience of the Blickling Homilies." *ASE* 18 (1989): 99–115; Scragg, D.G. "The Corpus of Vernacular Homilies and Prose Saints' Lives before Ælfric." *ASE* 8 (1979): 223–77, no. B, at pp. 233–35; Scragg, D.G. "The Homilies of the Blickling Manuscript." In *Learning and Literature in Anglo-Saxon England,* ed. Michael Lapidge and Helmut Gneuss. Cambridge: Cambridge University Press, 1985, pp. 299–316.

See also Sermons; Vercelli Homilies

Boethius, Anicius Manlius Severinus (ca. 480–ca. 525)

Philosopher and theologian. Boethius was born into the wealthy and privileged Italian senatorial class that was the inheritor of Roman aristocracy and the forerunner of the medieval feudal lords. After his father's death, while still a boy, he was taken into the household of the Christian Quintus Aurelius Memmius Symmachus, one of the most influential and respected members of the senatorial class, a man well able to foster Boethius's education and career, of whom Boethius always wrote with affection and respect, and whose daughter Rusticiana he subsequently married.

Like his father and his patron Symmachus before him Boethius rose to the rank of consul (510), the highest honor available to a lay citizen of the empire. He reached the peak of his public career in 522, when his two sons were named consuls and he himself became "Master of the Offices" *(magister officiorum),* a powerful chief of staff to King Theodoric for the administration of the western empire. But this post was his ultimate undoing. He became somehow entangled in the political jockeying between the ailing and aging Theodoric in the West and the ambitious Justin, emperor in the East (Boethius gives his own account of this in the first book of the *Consolation*). In late 523 or early 524 he was accused of treason by Theodoric, imprisoned at Pavia, and subsequently executed, apparently after torture (ca. 525).

Although his execution by Theodoric led to his later being considered a Christian martyr, Boethius's chief importance lies in his preserving for the Latin West much of the Greek culture and learning of his age. He was not an original thinker; he was a translator, commentator, and adapter. Encouraged by the interests of his patron Symmachus, adept at Greek, and thoroughly conversant with the then prestigious Neoplatonic schools of Alexandria and Athens, he had absorbed and understood their teaching and educational programs. He composed works on mathematics, logic, and theology and wrote the *De consolatione philosophiae,* or *Consolation of Philosophy.*

Of his mathematical works the *Arithmetic (De institutione arithmetica)* and the *Music (De institutione musica)* survive more or less complete, and there are substantial traces of his translation of Euclid's *Elements.* A work on astronomy was attributed to him but has not survived. These four disciplines, which constituted what Boethius named the "quadrivium," were regarded as a fourfold bridge between the physical world of sensation and "intellectual" understanding because they trained the mind in the abstractions of number and proportion, thus preparing it for the higher study of philosophy and theology.

The Neoplatonic schools of Boethius's era combined Aristotelian logic with Platonic metaphysics and "theology" (questions of God, Providence, and evil). Boethius, clearly concerned to provide the Latin West with this logical tradition, translated Aristotle's logical works (the *Organon*) and Porphyry's *Isagoge (Introduction)* to them. He also wrote commentaries that survive on Porphyry's *Isagoge,* on Aristotle's *Categories* and *On Interpretation,* and on Cicero's *Topics,* as well as three treatises on the syllogism, one *On Division* and one *On Topical Differences.*

His theological works are five treatises, the *Opuscula sacra.* The fourth of these (named *De fide catholica* in the Middle Ages) is a survey of the whole range of beliefs concerning God and the course of salvation history; much influenced by Augustine, it offers a description of what Boethius understood to be authentic "catholic" (universal) Christianity. The other treatises use Aristotelian logic, from within the framework of Neoplatonic philosophy, in an effort to disentangle some of the terminological problems that beset discussions of how Christ can be both God and man and how the Trinity can be both one and three. Although scholars have debated whether Boethius was the author of some of these treatises, the authenticity of all five is now generally accepted.

His masterpiece, the *Consolation of Philosophy,* is his most original work and the one that achieved widest circulation. Apparently writing in prison toward the end of his life, Boethius casts the work as a dialogue between Lady Philosophy and himself. Beginning with his desperate situation, combining classical poetic tradition and Neoplatonic philosophy in

a way consonant with Christianity, Philosophy leads Boethius and the reader, in alternating "meters" and "proses" (passages of verse and prose), through the problems of Fortune, Fate, evil, and free will toward the ultimate Good.

Boethius's contemporary Cassiodorus knew of his theological writings, mentioned his mathematical works, recommended two of his logical commentaries, and used two of his logical translations. But, as often with early-medieval secular texts, evidence that Boethius's works circulated widely begins to appear only in the Carolingian renaissance (late 8th and early 9th centuries). The *Arithmetic, Music,* adaptations of his translation of Euclid, the *Opuscula sacra,* and the *Consolation of Philosophy* all became standard school texts around which medieval commentaries grew up. Of the logical works Boethius's translations of and commentaries on the more basic parts of Aristotle's *Organon* (the *Isagoge,* the *Categories,* and *On Interpretation*) were much used in the study of the "old logic." His work on Aristotle's more advanced logical subjects fell out of use, and these had to be replaced in the 12th century by fresh translations and commentaries (the "new logic").

Boethius in the Anglo-Saxon Period
The entire range of Boethius's work had at least some circulation in Anglo-Saxon England. Alcuin names Boethius as among the authors in York's library of the late 8th century. Several copies of the *Arithmetic* and *Music* written in late-10th- or early-11th-century England survive, along with a version of the Euclidean translation and a copy of the *Opuscula sacra;* surviving library catalogs of the same period mention some of the logical works (translations of or commentaries on the *Isagoge,* the *Categories,* and *On Interpretation*). But the best known of Boethius's works in England before the Norman Conquest was clearly the *Consolation.* King Alfred translated it (ca. 892) as one of those books "most necessary to know," adapting it in the process to his own christianized Germanic culture just as deftly as Boethius had originally adapted classical and Neoplatonic strains to his own Latin Christianity. And sixteen copies of Boethius's Latin text made in 10th- to 11th-century England, all but one with commentary, show that it was a standard text much read in the monastic schools.

Boethius in the Middle English Period
In the ME period Boethius was among the most influential of the late-antique authors. Several of his compositions, including the *Arithmetic* and his translations of and commentaries on Aristotle's works, were standard university texts. His *Opuscula sacra* were also well known, and so in the universities he served the causes of both philosophy and theology. His most influential work, however, remained the *Consolation of Philosophy.*

Two complete translations of the *Consolation* were written in ME. Chaucer's *Boece* (ca. 1380) is in prose and draws on Jean de Meun's Old French translation, the commentaries of Nicholas Trevet and Remigius of Auxerre, and a distinctive late-medieval version of the original Latin text known as the Vulgate version. John Walton's verse translation (1410) is based on the *Boece* and Trevet's commentary. Both translations were popular by medieval standards; there are ten extant manuscripts or fragments of the *Boece* (together with editions by Caxton and Thynne, each of which utilized a no longer extant manuscript) and over 25 of Walton's translation. Both also indicate the vital and changing nature of the *Consolation* in the ME period: Boethius's text was understood to include not simply the Latin original but also a variety of interpretive materials.

The ideas and images of the *Consolation* were influential in various ways. Thus Chaucer relied heavily on the *Consolation* in both the *Knight's Tale* and *Troilus and Criseyde*. The intellectual world of the *Knight's Tale,* as summarized by Theseus's distillation of book 2, meter 8, and book 4, prose 6, realizes the greatest potential of pre-Christian thought; and Troilus's despairing soliloquy on the futility of volition (*Tr* 4.958–1082) draws on proses 2 and 3 of book 5 of the *Consolation,* though it does not contain, significantly, the answers that Lady Philosophy provides to the sorts of questions Troilus raises. Chaucer also employed the ideas of the *Consolation* in a number of the *Canterbury Tales* and in his Boethian ballades. The larger *Consolation* tradition is reflected in a work like Robert Henryson's *Orpheus and Eurydice,* which draws on Trevet's interpretation of meter 12 of book 3.

Boethius's image of Fortune's wheel had particularly wide currency in ME. It occurs throughout Gower's *Confessio Amantis,* for instance, and is a thematic focus in both the *Kingis Quair* (where the dreamer's waking as the wheel ascends implies success in love for him) and the alliterative *Morte Arthure* (where Arthur's fall from the wheel as it descends presages his doom). This image became so pervasive in ME writings that it occurs in contexts where the connection with the *Consolation* is neither clear nor relevant; thus in William Dunbar's "Birth of Antechrist," Dame Fortune's explanation of the nature of the wheel introduces the burlesque account of one John Damian, who attempted to circumvent inevitable descent by contriving to fly.

The structure of Boethius's work—a dialogue designed to achieve consolation—was influential as well, especially in works like *Pearl* and the *Confessio Amantis,* wherein the protagonists are reconciled to their situations through the advice of supernatural characters. Given the importance of Boethius's thought in general in the Middle Ages, however, much of the *Consolation*'s influence may have come not directly or indirectly from the work itself but from other, equally influential texts that utilize Boethius's ideas—e.g., the *Divine Comedy* and the *Roman de la Rose.*

Joseph S. Wittig
Tim William Machan

Bibliography

PRIMARY

Bieler, Ludwig, ed. *Anicii Manlii Severini Boethii Philosophiae consolatio.* Corpus Christianorum Series Latina 94. Turnhout: Brepols, 1957; Bower, Calvin M., trans. *Fundamentals of Music: Anicius Manlius Severinus Boethius, Translated with Introduction and Notes.* New Haven: Yale University Press, 1989; Masi, Michael, trans. *Boethian Number Theory: A Translation of the De institutione arithmetica.* Amsterdam: Rodopi, 1983; Sedgefield, Walter J., trans. *King Alfred's Version of the Consolations of Boethius.* Oxford: Clarendon, 1900; Stewart, H.F., E.K. Rand, and S.J. Tester, eds. and trans. *The Theological Tractates with an English Translation; The Consolation of Philosophy with an English Translation.* Loeb Classical Library 74. Cambridge: Harvard University Press, 1973; Stump, Eleonore, trans. *Boethius's De topicis differentiis.* Ithaca: Cornell University Press, 1978; Stump, Eleonore, trans. *Boethius's In Ciceronis topica.* Ithaca: Cornell University Press, 1988. [For editions of Boethius's other Latin works see Chadwick (258–60) and Gibson (xxi–xxii) below. Many translations of the *Consolation* may be found, including that in the Loeb Library edition cited above.]

SECONDARY

Chadwick, Henry. *Boethius: The Consolations of Music, Logic, Theology, and Philosophy.* Oxford: Clarendon, 1981; Courcelle, Pierre. *La Consolation de Philosophie dans la tradition littéraire: antécédents et postérité de Boèce.* Paris: Études Augustiniennes, 1967; Gibson, Margaret, ed. *Boethius: His Life, Thought and Influence.* Oxford: Blackwell, 1981; Jefferson, Bernard L. *Chaucer and the Consolation of Philosophy of Boethius.* Princeton: Princeton University Press, 1917; Kaylor, Noel Harold, Jr. *The Medieval Consolation of Philosophy: An Annotated Bibliography.* New York: Garland, 1992; Means, Michael H. *The Consolatio Genre in Medieval English Literature.* Gainesville: University of Florida Press, 1972; Minnis, A.J., ed. *The Medieval Boethius: Studies in the Vernacular Translations of "De consolatione Philosophiae."* Cambridge: Brewer, 1987; Patch, Howard Rollin. *The Tradition of Boethius: A Study of His Importance in Medieval Culture.* New York: Oxford University Press, 1935.

See also Alfred; Chaucer; Debate Poems; Dream Vision; Gower; Henryson; Literary Influences: Medieval Latin; *Morte Arthure,* Alliterative; *Pearl*-Poet; Schools; Trevet

Bokenham, Osbern (1392/93–after 1463)

Augustinian friar, poet, and translator, born possibly in Norfolk. Bokenham's works include the prose *Mappula Angliae* (early 1440s), which translates part of Ranulf Higden's *Polychronicon,* and the *Legends of Holy Women* (1443–47), thirteen saints' lives in various verse forms and the first all-female hagiography in English. The legends show skill and innovation in the genre, as well as familiarity with Chaucer's works and with saints' lives by Capgrave and Lydgate. Bokenham claims (in the *Mappula*) to have translated the *Legenda aurea;* whether this translation is the extant *Gilte Legende* (1438) is debated among scholars. A translation (1445) of Claudian's *De consulatu Stilichonis* and the "Dialogue" (1456) displaying the royal descent of Richard of York have also been attributed to Bokenham.

Bokenham studied at Cambridge University; he is described as "doctor of divinity" in the manuscript of the *Leg-*

ends of Holy Women. By 1446 he had traveled to Italy at least twice and made pilgrimage to Compostela in Spain. Among his patrons for the *Legends* Bokenham praises Isabel, Lady Bourchier, sister to Richard duke of York, who in 1460 claimed the throne against Henry VI. Most of Bokenham's life was spent at Clare Priory in East Anglia, the oldest Augustinian establishment in England, where he officiated as vicar general for provincial chapter meetings in 1461 and 1463. A "master Osbern of Clare" is designated as a beneficiary in the 1463 will (probated 1467) of John Baret, an important merchant in Bury St. Edmunds; that Osbern's name was not removed before probate suggests that he survived until at least 1467.

Sheila Delany

Bibliography

PRIMARY

Barnardiston, Katherine W., ed. "Dialogue at the Grave." In *Clare Priory: Seven Centuries of a Suffolk House.* Cambridge: Heffer, 1962; Delany, Sheila, trans. *A Legend of Holy Women.* Notre Dame: University of Notre Dame Press, 1992; Serjeantson, Mary S., ed. *Legendys of Hooly Wummen.* EETS o.s. 206. London: Humphrey Milford, 1938.

SECONDARY

New *CBEL* 1:649–50; *Manual* 2:422–26, 434–35, 558–60; 3:712–14, 872; Delany, Sheila. *Impolitic Bodies: Poetry, Saints, and Society in Fifteenth-Century England.* New York: Oxford University Press, 1997.

See also Capgrave; Hagiography; Patronage, Literary; Translation; Wars of the Roses; Women in ME Literature

Boniface (ca. 675–754)

Churchman and missionary. Born as Wynfrith in Wessex, he was trained at Exeter and then at Nursling. After an unsuccessful mission in Frisia (in the Low Countries) he journeyed to Rome, where he gained a formal mandate from Pope Gregory II for his missionary endeavors and took the name of Bonifatius (719). Returning via the Rhine, he worked with Willibrord from 719 to 721 in Frisia and was consecrated bishop without episcopal seat (722) after a second visit to Rome. With the protection of Charles Martel, ruler of the Franks (d. 741), he labored in Germany (723–35), beginning with the felling of the sacred Donar Oak at Geismar. Under Pope Gregory III he was made archbishop (732).

On a final trip to Rome (737–38) the organization of a Bavarian church was planned and the country subsequently divided into four dioceses, based on existing political units. Dioceses were also established in Hesse, Thuringia, and Franconia (741). Inspired by Boniface, a series of synods, supported by Carloman and Pippin, the successors to Charles Martel, met from 742 (or 743) to restore canonical order to the Frankish church. In a synod of 745 the Franks decided to set up four provinces including one under Boniface in Cologne. However, plans were eventually abandoned, following opposition by the Frankish episcopate, and Boniface had to settle instead for the see of Mainz. In 753 he handed his duties and offices over to his disciple Lul and returned to Frisia to preach to the heathen. Killed by brigands at Dokkum on 5 June 754, he was buried at Fulda, an abbey he had founded in 744.

Boniface's greatest achievement lies in his initiation of the reform and organization of the Frankish church, without which further missionary work could not have been sustained. His correspondence supplements his biography by Willibald (written 754–68) and provides insight into his life and work.

Kathryn Lowe

Bibliography

Levison, Wilhelm. *England and the Continent in the Eighth Century.* Oxford: Clarendon, 1946; Reuter, Timothy, ed. *The Greatest Englishman: Essays on St. Boniface and the Church at Crediton.* Exeter: Paternoster Press, 1980; Talbot, C.H. *The Anglo-Saxon Missionaries in Germany.* London: Sheed & Ward, 1954 [many of the contemporary lives of the missionaries provided in translation]; Wallace-Hadrill, J.M. "A Background to St. Boniface's Mission." In *England before the Conquest: Studies in Primary Sources Presented to Dorothy Whitelock,* ed. Peter Clemoes and Kathleen Hughes. Cambridge: Cambridge University Press, 1971, pp. 35–48.

See also Conversion of the Anglo-Saxons

Books and the Book Trade

From the early Middle Ages until the 12th century the responsibility for the production and preservation of manuscripts, in England as on the Continent, fell upon the monasteries. They created scriptoria, in which monks copied and illuminated manuscripts, and libraries, in which manuscript collections were housed. Manuscripts were on parchment or vellum, materials readily available owing to the vast number of sheep, and were bound in leather. The language was almost exclusively Latin. Many manuscripts, such as the Lindisfarne Gospels, were beautifully decorated works of art. Manuscript books tended to be large, suitable for placement on a lectern so they could be read aloud to a monastic audience. Monastic book collections frequently included the scriptures, the Church Fathers, Latin classics, and secular works on history, philosophy, law, medicine, and astronomy.

Much of the monastic book trade was internal, involving the creation of manuscripts for and the exchange of books among monasteries. English monarchs often requested or purchased books from established monasteries to aid newly created ones. In addition monasteries sent men to the Continent to acquire new manuscripts for their collections. There was also a small-scale external trade through which the laity could purchase books. Books were still relatively rare and often just lumped together with other precious objects.

The expansion of schools in the 11th and 12th centuries produced a tremendous upsurge in the demand for books as texts for the new scholarly population. Books created for this audience tended to be smaller, as appropriate for private study. Manuscript production centered in urban abbeys, such as St. Frideswide and Osney in Oxford. University stationers were commissioned to arrange the copying, decorating, and binding of books for university students. They also participated in the growing secondhand book trade. Although subject to some control from the universities, they operated with fewer restrictions than counterparts at Paris. To serve the large number of customers stationers frequently resorted to the *pecia* system; sections of books were rented out for students and scholars to copy for personal use.

By the later Middle Ages the growth of a literate laity including merchants, civil servants, and gentry—women as well as men—resulted in a thriving commercial market for book production. They frequently appeared as bequests in wills or as security for loans. Books for this market were produced in the vernacular, generally in a readable business script. Until the advent of printing new manuscripts were produced on commission for a specific customer. Secondhand books were often carried by traveling peddlers or sold at the great fairs: Stourbridge near Cambridge, St. Giles near Oxford, St. Bartholomew's in London. Books were imported from the Continent as well.

The production of books in England centered in London, around St. Paul's and the Inns of Court. Producers of books were organized into guilds, as were other crafts. The most notable were the Scriveners' Company and the Stationers' Company. Stationers generally served as middlemen between the customer ordering the manuscript and the artisan who created it, although stationers might also participate in other aspects of production. Manuscript book production was highly structured, involving specialized artisans working either at home or out of small shops. The cooperation of the members of several crafts was required: parchmeners to prepare writing materials, copyists to create the text, illuminators to decorate margins and provide illustrations, bookbinders to bind the whole. Increased demand led to more efficient and less costly methods. Illustrations were often block-printed; paper, imported from France and Italy, replaced expensive parchment. Paper was the medium of choice as printing entered England.

England's first printer-publisher, William Caxton, was a native-born Englishman who learned his trade in Cologne and Bruges. Returning in 1476, he opened a movable-type print shop in Westminster. Since the Continent adequately supplied Latin and French books for the English market, he specialized in original texts and translation into English. His 100 or so printed works included romances, poetry, history, and, most notably, the *Canterbury Tales* and had a wide appeal to an expanding secular audience. He also imported books from abroad, serving as the first English retailer of printed books in a field dominated, even in England, by the French, Germans, and Dutch. Caxton's successor, Wynkyn de Worde, was actually a native of Lorraine. It was not until the mid-16th century that the English would come to dominate their own book trade.

Janice Gordon-Kelter

Bibliography

Christianson, Paul. "A Century of the Manuscript-Book Trade in Late Medieval London." *M&H* n.s. 12 (1984): 143–66; Clair, Colin. *A History of Printing in Britain*. London: Cassell, 1965; Clanchy, M.T. *From Memory to Written Record: England, 1066–1307.* 2d ed. Oxford: Blackwell, 1993; Griffiths, Jeremy, and Derek Pearsall, eds. *Book Production and Publishing in Britain, 1375–1475*. Cambridge: Cambridge University Press, 1989; Putnam, George H. *Books and Their Makers during the Middle Ages*. 2 vols. New York: Putnam, 1896–97. Repr. New York: Hillary House, 1962.

See also Caxton; Literacy; Paleography and Codicology; Printing

Books of Hours

To the well-off layperson of the later Middle Ages a book of hours (figs. 28–29) was a much-prized possession, both as a sign of wealth and as an essential guide to devotional life. The book of hours set out the pattern of the devotional day, in imitation of the daily routine of the divine office followed by the monks and clergy, praying at eight times of the day from Matins (just after midnight) to Compline (before bed): the

Fig. 28. Book of hours (BL Yates Thompson 13), fol. 139, ca. 1330–40. Opening to the beginning of Gradual Psalms: crowned woman introduced to Christ by Virgin; condemnation of the damned. Reproduced by permission of the British Library, London.

liturgical hours. This program of devotions—psalms, hymns, lessons, and prayers—as it was interpreted, chiefly for the laity, in the book of hours, was easy to follow, and the texts were chosen with a specific devotional focus.

The primary focus was always the Virgin Mary, through the hours dedicated to her honor—the essential text of the book of hours—and other devotional sequences and prayers. Often hours services were included that focused on the mysteries of the Passion, on supplication to the Holy Spirit and the Trinity, and even on hours dedicated to specific saints. The constant need for penance was satisfied by the sequence of Penitential Psalms, and the Prayer for the Dead was securely through the complex Office of the Dead and the commendations. Usually the book of hours would frame the liturgical year within a calendar of feasts, graded according to their importance both to the universal church and to local and personal cults. The pattern of devotional life, as laid out in the book of hours, followed the liturgical hours through the day but offered the devout endless scope for devotional accretions. The variety found in these books—both of formal texts and of personal prayers and devotional practices—illustrates the lively participation of the laity in the celebration of their religion.

In England the first books of hours date to the second quarter of the 13th century (earlier, in fact, than in France or

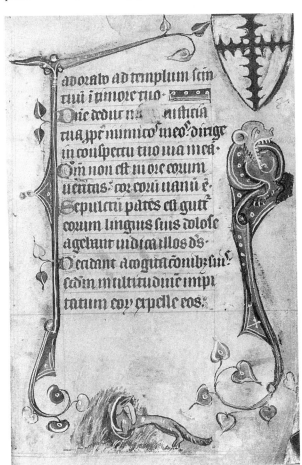

Fig. 29. Book of hours (BL Harley 6563), fol. 60, ca. 1330. Fox and hole marginalia. Reproduced by permission of the British Library, London.

Flanders), and they grew in popularity during the 14th century. In England psalters continued to be valued by the laity, as was the hybrid psalter-hours, although by the end of the 14th century in both France and Flanders books of hours had become ubiquitous. Produced in considerable numbers, both as "stock" models and adapted to the request of a patron as a "custom-made" volume, their popularity throughout Europe attests to a common devotional style; it also demonstrates the increasing literacy of the laity and their ability to pay for an expensive, if not necessarily a luxury, object. By the 15th century the English market for books of hours was supplemented by many foreign imports from the major continental workshops, the manuscripts carefully modified to accommodate the English liturgical and hagiographic traditions.

Essentially a personal possession, more than most medieval books, the book of hours could respond flexibly to the requirements of its owner. Sometimes this personal quality was present at the design stage, with scribe and illuminator working to the instruction of the patron. But often a book of hours shows the personal stamp of a new owner: coats of arms modified, prayers added, inscriptions and obits inserted. Such updating bears witness to the continuity of use across generations, and the stability of the lay devotional life until the injunctions of Edward VI ordered the end of their use and the destruction of the manuscripts.

The selection and arrangement of the decoration and illustration in the most elaborate and finely illuminated manuscripts also provided scope for the personalization of a book of hours. Right from the start books of hours were illuminated, with a program of illustration that supplemented the devotional themes of the text. The primary importance of the Virgin Mary was reflected in the constant illustration of the Virgin enthroned with the Christ Child, and the narrative series of images of his infancy, during which her role as mother was developed. These images, accompanied by prayers of praise, were interwoven to enhance the devotional impact. Similarly imagery focusing on the events of the Passion followed the passage of the liturgical day in step with Christ's sufferings, adding a meditative layer to the hours of prayer. Single images of saints, or of the Trinity or the Holy Spirit, would supplement prayer in an iconic manner—an image to lend inspiration to prayer. And very often the illustrations of the book include a portrait of the patron of the manuscript, depicted at prayer, as a constant example of the good Christian life through which these books guided their owners. Despite this the humorous strand of later medieval illumination ran riot in the pages of some books of hours (figs. 93, 94: see MARGINALIA). Usually in the freedom of the borders around the text, animals, monstrous hybrids, images from courtly romances, and sermon exempla all abound. In the *bas-de-page* spaces below the text, the sports of the lady owner of the Taymouth Hours (BL Yates Thompson 13; ca. 1340) are portrayed, together with the grisly tale of Bevis of Hampton and the many and various torments of hell.

The developing styles of English illumination are reflected in these books. The first example surviving from England—the de Brailes Hours, dating to ca. 1240 (BL Add. 49999)—

was evidently written and illuminated in Oxford (fig. 31: see BRAILES, WILLIAM DE). Fully illustrated, with narrative sequences of historiated initials for each section of the text, this follows the conventions of contemporary Oxford illumination, and it set the devotional scene for its original lady owner. The small format of this manuscript became a characteristic form for books of hours, with large clear script in a single column and historiated initials at the opening of the major texts. Exceptionally books of hours were made on a grander scale, following the characteristic tradition for psalters.

By the early years of the 15th century manuscripts made across the Channel for English use outnumbered those produced in England, both the inexpensive mass-produced imports and the elaborate works designed for the needs of a nobleman, such as John duke of Bedford, whose marriage in 1423 is commemorated in an elaborate Paris-made book of hours (BL Add. 18850), or Lord Hastings, whose Flemish-made hours (BL Add. 54782) dates to the end of the century. The heyday of the book of hours lasted well into the 16th century, by then supplemented by printed editions. Whether elaborately illuminated or not, the key to its success was the flexibility that could be offered within the constraints of a defined and regulated devotional life.

Claire M. Donovan

Bibliography

Backhouse, Janet. *The Madresfield Hours: A Fourteenth-Century Manuscript in the Library of Earl Beauchamp.* Oxford: Roxburghe Club, 1975; Backhouse, Janet. *Books of Hours.* London: British Library, 1985; Backhouse, Janet. *The Bedford Hours.* London: British Library, 1990; Delaissé, L.M.J. "The Importance of Books of Hours for the History of the Medieval Book." In *Gatherings for Dorothy E. Miner,* ed. Ursula E. McCracken, Lillian M.C. Randall, and Richard H. Randall, Jr. Baltimore: Walters Art Gallery, 1974, pp. 203–25; Donovan, Claire. "The Mise-en-page of Early Books of Hours in England." In *Medieval Book Production: Assessing the Evidence,* ed. Linda L. Brownrigg. Los Altos Hills: Anderson-Lovelace, 1990, pp. 147–61; Donovan, Claire. *The de Brailes Hours: Shaping the Book of Hours in Thirteenth-Century Oxford.* London: British Library, 1991; Harthan, John. *Books of Hours and Their Owners.* London: Thames & Hudson, 1977; Sutton, Anne F., and Livia Visser-Fuchs. *The Hours of Richard III.* Stroud: Sutton, 1990; Turner, Derek H. *The Hastings Hours: A 15th-Century Flemish Book of Hours Made for William, Lord Hastings, Now in the British Library.* London: Thames & Hudson, 1983; Wieck, Roger S. *Time Sanctified: The Book of Hours in Medieval Art and Life.* New York: Braziller, 1988 [exhibition catalogue].

See also Brailes, William de; Manuscript Illumination, Gothic; Psalters, Gothic

Boroughs

Anglo-Saxon Boroughs

Both historical and archaeological evidence shows a diversity of origin and size for settlements designated as boroughs before 1066. At all times, however, their basic role as strongholds differentiates them from other types of settlement. Some places described by the Anglo-Saxons by the OE term *burh* were in fact pre-English fortresses: Cissbury, Badbury, or Cadbury. Others were early monastic sites but presumably possessed stone buildings for protection in time of war: Malmesbury or Tetbury.

The 33 *burhs* of the Burghal Hidage included Roman towns (Winchester, Bath), Roman or Iron Age forts (Portchester, Chisbury), existing Anglo-Saxon trading or royal centers (Langport, Wilton), and new forts founded by Alfred to answer the immediate danger of the Viking threat to Wessex (Sashes, Burpham). The Alfredian *burhs* appear to have been primarily defensive in purpose, in contrast to the use of fortified sites as offensive bases by the Vikings in the Danelaw (the Five Boroughs: Derby, Leicester, Lincoln, Nottingham, and Stamford) and by Edward the Elder and Æthelflæd of Mercia in the early 10th century, in their campaigns to reconquer the Midlands (Hertford, Buckingham, Maldon, Tamworth, Warwick).

Such offensive *burhs* often became centers of royal government, their names being enshrined in their subordinate territory or shire (Hertfordshire, Derbyshire, Warwickshire). Both these offensive *burhs* and those of the Alfredian *burhs* that survived were parts of the royal demesne, under the control of a royal official or reeve. Trade and manufacturing were encouraged and they were designated as the site of mints and of officially approved markets, often described not only as *burh* but also as *port,* trading center. While tenements (*hagas:* urban dwellings) in the boroughs were often appurtenant to nearby rural estates, providing an outlet for surplus crops or raw materials, their inhabitants were subject (from at least the mid-10th century) to separate borough courts that met three times a year. The phrase *binnan burh and butan* (within the borough and without), used in royal writs, encompassed the totality of privileges, both urban and rural, granted to a beneficiary by the king.

By the 11th century the peculiarities of burghal law appear to have been propounded by "lawmen" in such boroughs as Cambridge and Stamford, while in such cities as Canterbury and Winchester, also legally classed as boroughs, associations of merchants into guilds for their mutual economic and legal support are recorded. Domesday Book shows that approximately one-tenth of the population lived in about 112 boroughs or urban settlements, varying greatly in size but sharing trading or mercantile functions to set them apart from their rural counterparts. Many of these continued as commercial and manufacturing centers in the medieval and modern periods.

Boroughs after 1066

Though "town" and "borough" are for many purposes interchangeable, in that many medieval settlements could legitimately be described as either, "borough" by the 12th century seems to have acquired a precise technical meaning; a place with a particular status whose inhabitants held their land by a distinctive free tenure, "burgage tenure." This is not the same as a town, for which Susan Reynolds offers a working definition: a permanent human settlement, many or most of whose inhabitants gain their living by a variety of nonagricultural occupations and which forms a social unit more or less distinct from the surrounding countryside.

By these definitions not all towns were boroughs, and not all boroughs really towns. It should also not be assumed that the Anglo-Saxon *burh* had the same characteristics as the later borough, though it is clear that *burhs* were places with distinctive customs and identities, and many of the more important towns of the post-Conquest period, including most of the county towns, are known to have existed in the 10th century or earlier.

In the post-Conquest period a new borough was almost always a deliberate creation by an overlord, either king or lay lord or churchman. The clearest evidence for borough status in this period is the charter conferring it; these become plentiful in the 12th and 13th centuries. Most of the earliest known boroughs, pre- and post-Conquest, had royal founders. The 13th century saw the largest number of new creations, along with the highest proportion of creations by nonroyal lords. Of the 609 known or conjectured medieval boroughs 80 percent were in existence by 1300. In the 14th century the rate of creation was falling off, as population growth slowed and then reversed; even before this there must have been a saturation factor and a number of new 13th-century boroughs failed to flourish.

Creating a borough usually involved laying out land in defined plots, centering on a street or open space; the holders of the plots became burgesses. Burgage tenure freed those who held by it from the personal and labor services attached to villein tenures and usually replaced them with a simple fixed rent. An essential feature of the borough was the holding of a market; some also had fairs. Borough status and the creation of new boroughs offered rewards to both lord and tenant. The incentive for the lord was clearly the hope that the grant of burghal status would initiate or stimulate the growth of a prosperous and profitable settlement, where the concentration of population and encouragement of market exchanges would produce a return in the form of burgage rents, tolls and market dues, and the profits of the courts that dealt with commercial disputes. Borough creation, like the building of towns, can be seen as a means of restructuring and civilizing hostile or alien society; this is an important feature of Edward I's north Welsh borough creations.

The designation "borough" covers a wide range of settlement, from the county towns and cathedral cities with populations in their thousands to places that can never have been much more than large villages. Only the more prosperous towns were counted as boroughs (paying a tenth rather than a fifteenth) for taxation purposes in the later Middle Ages, and fewer than half sent members to parliament. Boroughs were unevenly distributed across the face of the realm, with the highest concentration in the southwest and the west Midlands. Distribution was not a simple correlate of wealth, since the agriculturally prosperous and well-populated Norfolk had very few boroughs, but the greater density in southern England as a whole, compared with the north, probably does reflect real economic differences. Changes in the economic fortunes of towns and regions in the later Middle Ages and early modern period, however, have tended to locate modern concentrations of population in areas where medieval boroughs were thinly spread.

Alexander R. Rumble
Vanessa A. Harding

Bibliography

Benton, John F. *Town Origins: The Evidence from Medieval England.* Boston: Heath, 1968; Beresford, Maurice W. *New Towns of the Middle Ages: Town Plantation in England, Wales, and Gascony.* London: Lutterworth, 1967; Biddle, Martin. "Towns." In *The Archaeology of Anglo-Saxon England,* ed. David M. Wilson. London: Methuen, 1976, pp. 99–150; Darby, Henry C. *Domesday England.* Cambridge: Cambridge University Press, 1977, pp. 289–320, 364–68; Hall, R.A. "The Five Boroughs of the Danelaw: A Review of the Evidence." *ASE* 18 (1989): 150–206; Loyn, H.R. "Towns in Late Anglo-Saxon England: The Evidence and Some Possible Lines of Enquiry." In *England before the Conquest: Studies in Primary Sources Presented to Dorothy Whitelock,* ed. Peter Clemoes and Kathleen Hughes. Cambridge: Cambridge University Press, 1971, pp. 115–28; Martin, Geoffrey H. "The English Borough in the Thirteenth Century." *TRHS,* 5th ser. 13 (1963): 123–44; Reynolds, Susan. *An Introduction to the History of English Medieval Towns.* Oxford: Clarendon, 1977; Tait, James. *The Medieval English Borough.* Manchester: Manchester University Press, 1936.

See also Burghal Hidage; Fairs and Markets; Guilds; Towns

Bourchier, John, Baron Berners (ca. 1467–1533)

Tudor courtier and translator. Berners participated in diplomatic missions to France and Spain in 1514, 1518, and 1520; he was made chancellor of the exchequer in 1516 and served as deputy of Calais (1520–26, 1531–33). At his death his library contained 80 volumes, a large personal collection in his day.

Berners's extant translations were made between ca. 1514 and 1533, possibly in the following order:

- *Arthur of Little Britain* (printed ca. 1555 and ca. 1582); a chivalric prose romance notable for its fantastic elements, translated from a printed version of an early-14th-century French original.
- *Huon of Bordeaux* (printed ca. 1534? and 1601; possibly also printed between 1545 and 1561, and in 1570); a prose Charlemagne romance.
- Jean Froissart's *Chronicles* (printed 1523–25 and 1545); a 14th-century chivalric history of contemporary England, France, and other countries, translated at least partly under patronage of Henry VIII.

- *The Castle of Love* (printed 1549?, 1550, and 1560); a sentimental Spanish tale attributed to Diego de San Pedro, probably known to Berners in a French version.
- *The Golden Book of Marcus Aurelius* (printed 1535; numerous reprints); a collection of moral sayings originally compiled by Antonio de Guevara (d. 1545?) in Spanish, known to Berners in French.

In his interest in chivalric romance and history and in the content of some of his prologues Berners's work as a translator appears to have been influenced by Caxton. The latter two works, however, suggest a shift to a model more in tune with 16th-century humanist literature.

M. Teresa Tavormina

Bibliography

PRIMARY

Lee, S.L., ed. *The Boke of Duke Huon of Burdeux.* EETS e.s. 40–41. London: Trübner, 1882–87; Ker, W.P., ed. *The Chronicle of Froissart.* 6 vols. London: Nutt, 1901–03.

SECONDARY

New *CBEL* 1:678–80; Blake, N.F. "Lord Berners: A Survey." *M&H* n.s. 2 (1971): 119–32.

See also Caxton; Chronicles; Froissart; Literary Influences: French; Matter of France; Romances; Translation

Bozon, Nicholas (fl. late 13th–early 14th century)

Anglo-Norman Franciscan friar and didactic author. His works cover a wide range of verse forms and genres— allegory, poems on the Virgin, saints' lives, proverbs, and sermons—and blend practical didacticism with a lively, down-to-earth style. The *Plainte d'Amour,* Bozon's poetic masterpiece, satirizes ecclesiastical and secular corruption. His crowning literary achievement, the prose *Contes moralisés (Moralized Tales),* is a collection of 145 exempla, often followed by a moral and a supporting story on the same topic. The *Contes* grew out of the 13th- and 14th-century tradition—especially strong among the Franciscans—of compiling collections of exempla and other sermon materials for the use of preachers.

Sharon Kelly

Bibliography

PRIMARY

Smith, Lucy Toulmin, and Paul Meyer, eds. *Les contes moralisés de Nicole Bozon.* Paris: Firmin Didot, 1889.

SECONDARY

Levy, Brian J. *Nine Verse Sermons by Nicholas Bozon: The Art of an Anglo-Norman Poet and Preacher.* Oxford: Society for the Study of Mediaeval Languages and Literature, 1981.

See also Anglo-Norman Literature; Exemplum; Friars; Moral and Religious Instruction; Sermons

Bracton, Henry of (d. 1268)

Royal justice, ca. 1245–57. He entered the king's service, possibly as early as 1234 and certainly before 1239, when he was senior clerk of the court *coram rege* ("before the king"). His name derives from a Devonshire village, and he probably entered royal service through the patronage of a fellow Devon man, the great judge William Raleigh. An ecclesiastic, Bracton probably received his early education at Exeter; nothing is known of any advanced studies. He obtained church livings typical of clerics in royal government, being chancellor of Exeter Cathedral at the time of his death.

Bracton's fame comes from the tradition that he was author of the treatise *De legibus et consuetudinibus Angliae (On the Laws and Customs of England),* the most masterly work on the common law written in the Middle Ages. This authorship now appears unlikely. The latest editor of the treatise concludes that the date of writing, mostly from the 1220s or 1230s, was too early for Bracton to have written it and that it was first written by William Raleigh or under his direction, then continually revised and expanded by Bracton and others until it took its present form (ca. 1258). It suffered from the fact that it has survived only in copies with so many mistakes, omissions, and the additions of incompetent copyists and redactors that its original form can only be guessed at. This had led to scholarly speculation about the author's knowledge of Roman and canon law. Recent views depict the author as an accomplished romanist, relying on Roman legal principles to shape English law into a coherent pattern.

Ralph V. Turner

Bibliography

Maitland, Frederic W., ed. *Bracton's Note Book.* 3 vols. London: Clay, 1887. Repr. Littleton, Colo.: Rothman, 1983; Meekings, C.A.F. "Henry de Bracton, Canon of Wells." *Notes and Queries for Somerset and Dorset* 26 (1951–54): 141–43. Repr. in *Studies in 13th Century Justice and Administration.* London: Hambledon, 1981, item VII; Richardson, H.G. *Bracton: The Problem of His Text.* Selden Society, suppl. ser. 2. London: Selden Society, 1965; Thorne, Samuel E. *Henry de Bracton, 1268–1968.* Exeter: University of Exeter, 1970; Woodbine, George E., ed. *Bracton De legibus et consuetudinibus Angliae.* Rev. and trans. Samuel E. Thorne. 4 vols. New Haven: Yale University Press, 1915–42.

See also Glanville; Law, Post-Conquest

Bradford

Nothing certain links this late Anglo-Saxon (ca. 1000?) church in Wiltshire with Anglo-Saxon documentary evidence; the first statement considered to refer to the surviving church dates to the early 12th century, when William of Malmesbury described an *ecclesiola* at Bradford commonly believed built by Aldhelm (d. 709/10) and dedicated to St. Laurence. Saxon sources give two additional, relevant facts: Aldhelm remained abbot of monasteries at Malmesbury, Frome, and Bradford upon his election to the bishopric of Sherborne in 705, and in 1001 Æthelred II granted the manor of Bradford and its monastery to the nuns of Shaftesbury, as refuge from the Danes and a hiding place for the bones of Edward king and martyr.

The date of the standing fabric has remained the primary controversy since its "rediscovery" about 1857, crowded by buildings and housing the school and schoolmaster. From 1874 to 1881 restoration was supervised by J.T. Irvine, a keen and accurate observer whose careful notes and illustrations were published by Taylor (1972) and provide crucial information because of the lack of subsequent archaeological excavation. Irvine resigned in 1881, disagreeing about the destruction of the master's house on the south and the erection of buttresses; remaining restoration was done by C.S. Adye, a less reliable supervisor.

Though Gilbert has questioned whether the building is a martyrium or mausoleum, Bradford (fig. 30) is generally referred to as a church. It consists now of a chancel, a north porticus (side chamber), and a nave; originally a south porticus also existed with evidence suggesting it may have had a lower-level chamber, functioning as a crypt perhaps for Edward's remains. Though somewhat irregular in plan, the entire church rests on a plinth, and doorways survive in north and south walls of the north porticus, and to the lost south porticus, in addition to a narrow chancel arch. The existence of a west entrance is impossible to confirm, though its absence would be unusual. The exterior is ornamented on every side with pilaster strips, arcading between stringcourses, and reeded pilasters on the east gable of the nave. Levels within the church varied, with a step up to the north porticus and a step down to the chancel area. But perhaps the most famous attribute of the church is its slabs with carved angels, now high over the chancel arch. They had been found there during alterations, "imbedded"; they were later moved to the porch beside the schoolmaster's door and subsequently returned over the arch.

Discussions over the years have generated several theories about construction phases, focusing on the date of the external arcading that decorates the walls, the ashlar construction, the opening of single- to double-splayed windows, and the pilaster strips cut into the walls by the chipping away of the surface. While Mercer, Jackson, and Fletcher felt that several phases could be discerned in the building, Mercer contradicted Jackson and Fletcher's argument for rebuilding of an early church. Jackson and Fletcher refuted his arguments and reiterated their suggestion "that the church is in its groundplan and lower stages the work of Aldhelm, and that the later Anglo-Saxon features are the result of a rebuilding or refacing late in the tenth century" (1966: 71). Subsequent study of Irvine's unpublished work and personal measurement of exterior and interior elevations, however, convinced Taylor that the chapel is late Anglo-Saxon, not Aldhelm's work, and overwhelmingly of one date: "as first built, the chapel had all its present features except that the windows were probably at first single-splayed" (1973: 165) and modified before the Conquest.

Kelley M. Wickham-Crowley

Bibliography

Gilbert, Edward. "The Church of St. Laurence, Bradford-on-Avon." *Wiltshire Archaeological and Natural History Magazine* 62 (1967): 38–50; Jackson, E. Dudley C., and Eric G.M. Fletcher. "The Saxon Church at Bradford-on-Avon." *JBAA,* 3d ser. 16 (1953): 41–58; Jackson, E. Dudley C., and Eric G.M. Fletcher. "Bradford-on-Avon: A Reply to Mr. Mercer." *JBAA,* 3d ser. 29 (1966): 71–74; Mercer, Eric. "The Alleged Early Date of the Saxon Church at Bradford-on-Avon." *JBAA,* 3d ser. 29 (1966): 61–70, pls. VI–IX; Taylor, Harold M. "J.T. Irvine's Work at Bradford-on-Avon." *ArchJ* 129 (1972): 89–118; Taylor, Harold M. "The Anglo-Saxon Chapel at Bradford-on-Avon." *ArchJ* 130 (1973): 141–71; Taylor, Harold M., and Joan Taylor. "Bradford-on-Avon." In *Anglo-Saxon Architecture.* Vol. 1. Cambridge: Cambridge University Press, 1965, pp. 86–89.

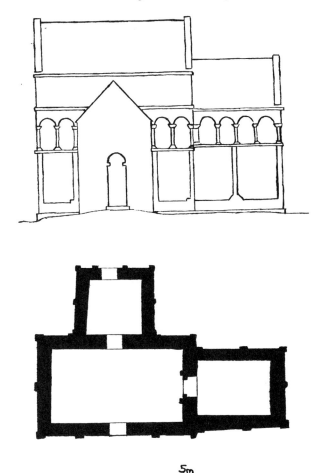

Fig. 30. Church of St. Laurence, Bradford-on-Avon. After E. Fernie, The Architecture of the Anglo-Saxons *(1983). Drawing by C. Karkov.*

See also Architecture, Anglo-Saxon; Sculpture, Anglo-Saxon

Brailes, William de (fl. 1230–60)

A 13th-century illuminator recorded in Oxford ca. 1230–60, de Brailes secured his memory—among many hundreds of unnamed illuminators—through his self-portraits, three of which survive in two manuscripts. From these, accompanied by the name *"w de brail,"* his hand and his style are established. His style is found in a considerable corpus of manuscripts, some of which were evidently produced in Oxford. Documents show that in 13th-century Oxford there was an active community of book producers living in the streets surrounding St. Mary the Virgin. Among them, ca. 1230–60, was one William de Brailes. He achieved a certain prosperity, had a wife, Celena, and probably came from Brailes in Warwickshire. His identity is near certain.

Oxford in William's time was dominated by the developing university, creating a demand for books. The variety of manuscripts illuminated by William, or by the large number of hands associated with him, would have satisfied the demands of scholars, churchmen, and laity. Characteristically his manuscripts, often pocket-sized, are illustrated with many small historiated initials, creating a visual narrative to accompany the text. Even large manuscripts or full-page images are fragmented with foliage decoration to create multiple small spaces for illustration.

Filling, even spilling over, their restricted frames, William's figures convey the narrative with emphatic gesture, dynamic poses, and firmly focused eyes (fig. 31). Although he may use established iconography, it is filtered through his imagination and retold with new immediacy. Rarely does he use elaborate settings, although the essentials are clear—a mountain for Christ's temptation, steps for the child Mary to climb to the Temple—and costume is equally important in identifying his characters, as in the case of crowned kings, mitered bishops (or high priests), round-hatted Jews, or heavy-horned devils. De Brailes's style is not one of courtly elegance. It is a "literary" one, appropriate to the books of a university town.

Claire M. Donovan

Bibliography

Cockerell, Sydney Carlyle. *The Work of W. de Brailes*. Oxford: Roxburghe Club, 1930; Donovan, Claire. *The de Brailes Hours: Shaping the Book of Hours in Thirteenth-Century Oxford*. London: British Library, 1991; Morgan, Nigel. *Early Gothic Manuscripts (1) 1190–1250*. A Survey of Manuscripts Illuminated in the British Isles 4:1, ed. J.J.G. Alexander. London: Harvey Miller, 1982, p. 14 and nos. 68–74; Pollard, G. "William de Brailes." *Bodleian Library Record* 5/4 (1955): 202–09; Swarzenski, Hanns. "Unknown Bible Pictures by W. de Brailes and Some Notes on Early English Bible Illustrations." *Journal of the Walters Art Gallery* 1 (1938): 55–69.

See also Books of Hours; Manuscript Illumination, Gothic; Psalters, Gothic; Universities

Breton Lay

The name given to eight short ME narratives, composed between 1300 and 1425. The earliest extant poems identifying themselves as Breton *lais* are those of Marie de France, who wrote in Anglo-Norman during the second half of the 12th century. Her poems, usually set in a timeless past in Brittany or Britain, center on love problems, often with supernatural elements. Marie inspired French imitators in the 13th century, some of whom shared her stylistic and thematic concerns. In the early 14th century ME poems labeling themselves "layes of Britanye" or "Brytayne layes" began to appear. Not surprisingly two of the earliest English lays, *Sir Landeval* and *Lai le Freine*, are translations of two of Marie's *lais*, and at least one other, *Sir Orfeo*, is thought to be based on a lost French *lai*. Later in the century the term "lay" became attached to tail-rhyme romances far removed from the French tradition. Even the famous alliterative romance *Sir Gawain and the Green Knight* calls itself a lay (line 30). Chaucer's *Franklin's Tale* calls itself a Breton lay (709–15), although it derives mainly from Boccaccio's *Filocolo*. Its relative narrative brevity and concern with magic provide the main connection with the lay form.

Most critics agree in assigning the generic label "Breton lay" to nine ME narratives: *Lai de Freine:* early 1300s, 340 lines (couplets), southeast or Westminster-Middlesex area; *Sir Orfeo:* early 1300s, 604 lines (couplets), southeast or Westminster-Middlesex area; *Sir Degare:* pre-1325, 1,076 lines (couplets), southwest Midlands; *Sir Launfal:* late 1300s, 1,044 lines (12-line stanzas), southeast, written by Thomas Chestre; and its earlier couplet version, *Sir Landeval:* 1300–50, 535 lines, south; *Franklin's Tale:* 1392–95, 1,624 lines (couplets), London; *Emare:* ca. 1400, 1,035 lines (12-line stanzas), northeast; *Sir*

Fig. 31. De Brailes Hours (BL Add. 49999), fol. 39. The Trial of Christ. Reproduced by permission of the British Library, London.

Gowther: ca. 1400, 757 lines (12-line stanzas), northeast Midlands; *Erle of Toulouse:* 1400–25, 1,224 lines (12-line stanzas), northeast Midlands.

As a group these narratives share certain features: brevity, quickness of pace, disregard for details, emphasis on action, focus on a single hero, strong moral coloring, a lack of rhetorical ornament, and a fairy-tale atmosphere created largely by exotic settings and supernatural persons or objects. Sir Launfal has a fairy mistress; Sir Orfeo's wife is abducted by a king from a fairy kingdom; Gowther's father is a devil; Emare wears a robe made from a dazzling cloth, which characters see as magical and dangerous; in the *Franklin's Tale* Aurelius hires a magician to make dangerous rocks seem to disappear.

Despite these fantastic surface features the stories center on real moral, social, and political issues of their times: feuds, false accusations, injustices, the exile of innocents, and the importance of keeping one's oath. Most of these stories also investigate serious problems within the family, such as the search for missing or exiled family members. Partly because of this emphasis on family relationships, the works are didactic, conventional, and stylized. Nonetheless, by blending the exotic and the familiar, all the lays provide appealing entertainment with an underlying moral message and can be favorably compared with the best popular literature of any time.

Joanne A. Charbonneau

Bibliography

PRIMARY
Rumble, Thomas C., ed. *The Breton Lays in Middle English.* Detroit: Wayne State University Press, 1965.

SECONDARY
New *CBEL* 1:435–42, 585–86; *Manual* 1:133–43, 292–97; Beston, John B. "How Much Was Known of the Breton Lai in Fourteenth-Century England?" In *The Learned and the Lewed: Studies in Chaucer and Medieval Literature,* ed. Larry D. Benson. Cambridge: Harvard University Press, 1974, pp. 319–36; Donovan, Mortimer J. *The Breton Lay: A Guide to Varieties.* Notre Dame: University of Notre Dame Press, 1969; Hume, Kathryn. "Why Chaucer Calls the *Franklin's Tale* a Breton Lai." *PQ* 51 (1972): 365–79; Rice [Charbonneau], Joanne A. *Middle English Romance: An Annotated Bibliography, 1955–1985.* New York: Garland, 1987.

See also Anglo-Norman Literature; Lai, Latin; Literary Influences: French; Marie de France; Romances; *Sir Orfeo*

Bretwald

A status that features more prominently in modern works on OE history than in sources for the Anglo-Saxon period. The word appears in only one manuscript ("A," the oldest) of one annal of the Anglo-Saxon Chronicle. This records how, in 829, King Ecgberht of Wessex conquered all of England south of the Humber and was "the eighth king who was *Bretwalda*"; the reading "Bretwalda" in this manuscript is, however, the result of a scribal correction, and it is more than likely that the "Brytenwealda" of the other manuscripts constitutes the correct text. The Chronicle then lists seven who held the title earlier: Ælle of Sussex, Ceawlin of Wessex, Æthelberht of Kent, Rædwald of East Anglia, and the Northumbrian kings Edwin, Oswald, and Oswiu.

These are the seven kings said by Bede to have held *imperium* over all the "provinces" south of the Humber. A further link between the two sources is a charter of Æthelbald of Mercia (736), entitling him "king of all provinces called by the general name South England," and then "rex Britanniae." "King of Britain" is semantically equivalent with "Brytenwealda," which more probably means "Britain-ruler" than, as has often been supposed, "wideruler."

The fact that Ælle and Ceawlin are credited with major victories over Britons suggests that a *Brytenwealda* may originally have been overall leader of combined forces from early southern kingdoms. But the very word "Britain-ruler" bespeaks hyperbole, and historians, seeking to explain the eventual emergence of a united Anglo-Saxon kingdom, may well have given it more significance than they should. They see overbearing behavior by kings as institutionalized "powers" when they could be no more than evidence of simple power. In fact some powerful kings, like Æthelbald or his successor Offa, are not in the Chronicle list, implying that perceptions of a king's rights and title held by his subjects might not be shared by his enemies. The church, with its view of one "English people" *(gens Anglorum)* and its interest in political stability, may have fostered the notion. At all events, its idea, immortalized by Bede, was an eloquent testimonial to the ideology from which one kingdom of "the English" finally emerged.

Patrick Wormald

Bibliography

Fanning, Steven. "Bede, *Imperium,* and the Bretwaldas." *Speculum* 66 (1991): 1–26; John, Eric. *Orbis Britanniae and Other Studies.* Leicester: Leicester University Press, 1966, ch. 1 [alternative views from Stenton]; Keynes, Simon. "Rædwald the Bretwalda." In *Voyage to the Other World: The Legacy of Sutton Hoo,* ed. Calvin B. Kendall and Peter S. Wells. Minneapolis: University of Minnesota Press, 1992, pp. 102–23; Stenton, F.M. *Anglo-Saxon England.* Oxford History of England 2. 3d ed. Oxford: Clarendon, 1971, chs. 2–3 and 7; Whitelock, Dorothy, ed. *English Historical Documents.* Vol. 1: *c. 500–1042.* 2d ed. London: Eyre Methuen, 1979 [translation of Chronicle (see annal for 829), most of Bede (see section II.5), Æthelbald's charter of 736 (no. 67), and other relevant charters (nos. 76–77, 79–80)]; Wormald, Patrick. "Bede, the *Bretwaldas,* and the Origins of the *Gens Anglorum.*" In *Ideal and Reality in Frankish and Anglo-Saxon Society: Studies Presented to J.M. Wallace-Hadrill,* ed. Patrick Wormald, Donald Bullough, and Roger Collins. Oxford: Blackwell, 1983, pp. 99–129.

See also Anglo-Saxon Invasions; Bede; Heptarchy

Brewing

An essential and widely practiced commercial industry. It was essential because ale, although certainly imbibed for its inebriating effects, was also a fundamental part of the medieval diet. It was widely practiced because ale was both readily made and highly perishable. Even modest peasant households possessed the utensils required to brew (pots, vats, ladles, straining cloths), and most women learned to brew as part of their domestic routine.

In many communities—both small villages and larger towns—commercial brewing was so widespread that a majority of households brewed ale for their own consumption and for sale to others. Because of its link to domestic work brewing attracted considerable female labor, and it remained an important aspect of women's work through the Middle Ages.

Technical limitations helped ensure the ubiquity of commercial brewing. The grain used for brewing, usually oats or barley, was converted into malt by careful soaking, draining, and tending. Once the malt was dried and ground, hot water was poured over it and let stand; the "wort" drawn off from this was flavored with herbs or other seasonings. Successive mixtures produced successively weaker worts and, hence, weaker ales. Although the ale produced by medieval brewers was ready to drink within hours, the brewing process itself consumed many hours and much labor. Yet medieval ale soured within a few days and transported very poorly. As a result of these constraints on production, storage, and distribution most communities had to rely upon their own brewers for ale, and most households alternated between brewing their own and buying it from others nearby.

Throughout England both local and national customs regulated the trade of brewers. Many manors levied tolls on commercial brewers; on Alciston manor, for example, brewers had to pay a "tolcester" of 2 gallons (later amended to 1½ pence) from each brewing. From at least the 12th century the Assize of Bread and Ale also regulated brewers by empowering local officials to monitor their measures, quality, and prices. The amercements, or fines, levied under the Assize eventually became a *de facto* means of licensing commercial brewers.

After the plague of 1348–49 the brewing industry began to change in two ways. First, as the market for commercial ale expanded (due primarily to urbanization and improved living standards), the brewing trade began to professionalize. In many places the once-ubiquitous business of brewing began to concentrate in the hands of a few "common brewers." In towns brewers also began belatedly to form guilds, such as that organized by London brewers in the early 15th century. As brewing professionalized, women became less prominent. Second, the process of brewing itself changed, as brewers in England began using hops to produce a new beverage, called beer to distinguish it from unhopped ale.

Introduced from the Continent in the late 14th century, beer was cheaper to produce and more easily preserved and transported. Through the 15th century beer brewing was confined to London and coastal towns and largely controlled by foreign brewers. These were the harbingers of change; after 1500 professionalization continued apace and beer production slowly won out over ale.

Judith M. Bennett

Bibliography

Bennett, Judith M. *Ale, Beer, and Brewsters in England: Women's Work in a Changing World, 1300–1600.* New York: Oxford University Press, 1996; Monckton, H.A. *A History of English Ale and Beer.* London: Bodley Head, 1966; Salter, H.E. "The Assize of Bread and Ale, 1309–1351." In *Mediaeval Archives of the University of Oxford,* ed. H.E. Salter. Vol. 2. Oxford History Society 73. Oxford, 1921, pp. 129–265.

See also Assize of Weights and Measures; Fairs and Markets; Food

Bristol

A city and port in the West Country and pioneer of cross-Atlantic trade and discovery. It lies where the Frome joins the tidal river Avon, some seven miles from the Severn estuary. The name may mean "holy place by the jetty or bridge," the second element making clear Bristol's origin as a river port, the first a place perhaps associated with the meeting of St. Augustine of Canterbury and the Celtic church leaders in 603.

The early town lay on a narrow, defensible ridge between the Frome and Avon. A mint was introduced between 1017 and 1023, and a market must therefore be assumed. By 1051 Bristol ships were trading to Ireland and within 50 years with Norway "and other overseas lands." The little town was strongly defended by 1067, and its burgesses were mentioned in Domesday Book as having some independence.

A castle was built at the east end of the same ridge in the later 11th century, probably by Bishop Geoffrey of Coutances, and its huge keep, "the flower of all the keeps of England," was the work of Robert earl of Gloucester (d. 1147). The castle was the center of Empress Matilda's resistance to Stephen and remained in significant royal use until the early 14th century.

Just outside the town an abbey (now Bristol Cathedral) was founded, ca. 1140; inside its walls were five parish churches and five gateway chapels, and the suburbs included a new borough beside St. James's Priory and the great southern suburb of Redcliffe and Temple Fee. By the end of the Middle Ages there may have been over 30 churches, chapels, and religious houses in and around the town.

The merchants, electing a mayor by 1216, developed their port by diverting the Frome and creating a complex of quays and docks. In the late 13th century Bristol was second only to London in its imports, in some years bringing in over three-quarters of a million gallons of wine. Near the great wool-producing areas of the Cotswolds and the Mendips, Bristol had two-thirds of England's trade in the 14th century, exporting cloth to France and Spain and importing wine, oil, and iron. The great church of St. Mary Redcliffe was rebuilt in the 14th and 15th centuries. In 1373 Bristol's unique character was reinforced by Edward III's charter, which made the city into a county (it had stood, almost independent already, on the borders of Somerset and Gloucester). Thereafter Bristol was ruled by two sheriffs as well as by a powerful mayor.

War with France in the 15th century compelled Bristol's merchants to look for markets elsewhere. For a century they had brought exotic goods from the Mediterranean. Iceland was their first goal in the mid-15th century, and then, in 1497, a group of Bristol's merchants financed what became John Cabot's voyage of discovery to Newfoundland. Bristolians would like to believe that Richard Ameryke, sheriff of the city in Cabot's time, gave his name to the new landfall; local myths testify to the strength of local patriotism.

An Italian visitor in the late 15th century thought that Bristol ranked with London and York as the three leading cities of England. Evidence of that prosperity still survives in stone, and much more in the city's great trading traditions. The Abbey of St. Augustine was to become, at the Reformation, the cathedral church of a newly founded diocese; the church of St. Mary Redcliffe is only one of several medieval churches to be enjoyed, including the church of the hospital of St. Mark, which uniquely belongs to the Lord Mayor of the city for the time being. The rebuilding of the city after bombing in World War II has revealed much of the medieval past, including some docks and wharves and much of the castle.

Robert W. Dunning

Bibliography

Lobel, Mary D., and E.M. Carus-Wilson. "Bristol." In *The British Atlas of Historic Towns*, gen. ed. Mary D. Lobel. Vol. 2. London: Scolar, 1975; McInnes, C.M., and W.F. Whittard. *Bristol and Its Adjoining Counties.* Bristol: British Association for the Advancement of Science, 1955.

See also Gloucester; Towns; Trade

Bristol Harrowing of Hell Relief

In 1832 twelve coffins were discovered beneath the floor of the chapter house of Bristol Cathedral (formerly St. Augustine's Abbey church). The Harrowing of Hell relief formed the lid of one of the coffins. Its size and shape suggested that this was its intended function, although it may also have been a work of architectural sculpture, possibly from a cemetery chapel. The relief is set deeply into the stone, the background scooped away, perhaps as a means of suggesting depth and motion—as if Christ emerges out of darkness—perhaps simply as a way of protecting the figural carving. The work is dated ca. 1050.

The monumental figure of Christ is shown trampling on the Devil, firmly bound within the beast-mouth of hell. With his right hand he blesses the tiny figures of Adam and Eve, who cling to the base of the cross carried in his left hand. The overall composition of the piece, the bound Devil, and the beast-mouth of hell, have led to comparisons with the Harrowing of Hell in the ca. 1060 Tiberius Psalter (BL Cotton Tiberius C.vi, fol. 14). This comparison may, however, have been overemphasized, as the differences between the two outnumber the similarities. The scene in the Tiberius Psalter includes far more

detail; five figures emerge from the mouth of hell, Adam and Eve are clothed, Christ bends and reaches down toward them, the Cross is not present, and the folds of Christ's garment are far more decorative and complex. It is possible that these differences might be explained, at least in part, by differences in media, but they should still alert us to the fact that commonality of subject matter may not always provided sufficient grounds for comparison. In any case the meaning of both scenes is likely to be the same; the Harrowing of Hell represented Christ's victory over evil, the spiritual struggle of the individual, and his or her hope for salvation.

Catherine E. Karkov

Bibliography

Dickinson, J.C. "The Origins of St. Augustine's Bristol." *Bristol & Gloucestershire Archaeological Society* 100 (1976): 109–26; Openshaw, Kathleen M. "Weapons in the Daily Battle: Images of the Conquest of Evil in the Early Medieval Psalter." *Art Bulletin* 75 (1993): 17–38; Smith, M.Q. "The Harrowing of Hell Relief in Bristol Cathedral." *Transactions of the Bristol & Gloucestershire Archaeological Society* 94 (1977): 101–06; Zarnecki, George, Janet Holt, and Tristram Holland, eds. *English Romanesque Art 1066–1200.* London: Weidenfeld & Nicolson, 1984.

See also Harrowing of Hell; Iconography; Tiberius Psalter

Brixworth

The large, impressive church at Brixworth (figs. 32–33) in Northamptonshire has excited the interest of architectural historians for many years. Its scale, externally ca. 150 feet long and 40 feet wide, together with the complexity of its plan and the excellence of its brickwork, demands comparison with continental churches. Excavations in 1981–82 established the contemporaneity of the choir, nave, northern series of porticus, and narthex, and the presumption from earlier excavations is that the southern porticus are of the same period. The structural homogeneity observed in the excavated foundations and the standing walls confirms the original plan as consisting of a western narthex, divided into five chambers, the central and largest chamber serving as a porch; a nave and chancel flanked by five chambers north and south that open onto the body of the church through tall arches with double rows of brick voussoirs (the wedged portions of an arch). The

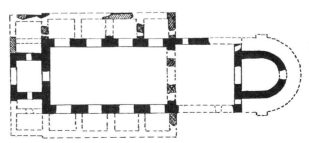

Fig. 32. All Saints, Brixworth, Northamptonshire. After E. Fernie, The Architecture of the Anglo-Saxons (1983). Drawing by C. Karkov.

50 ft

Fig. 33. Western tower, All Saints, Brixworth, Northamptonshire. Courtesy of C. Karkov.

present eastern apse is a late rebuilding but seems to reflect the early plan. Surrounding this east end is a ring crypt with burial niches in the walls. There is also a late Saxon tower with spiral staircase that was added to the west wall of the narthex.

The fact that this is a Roman site and that there is a documentary source noting a monastery at Brixworth by 675 has caused many to see this as a 7th-century church, closely copying late-antique models, but the square choir and the ring crypt are closely paralleled in Carolingian architecture, and a date in the first half of the 9th century has also been discussed. Radio carbon dates for the porticus suggest a foundation of ca. 700, and it is possible that extensive repairs and renovation occurred in the 9th or 10th centuries. These included reshaping the east end to add a ring crypt and heightening the walls (which have an offset and are thicker below the clerestory windows). At the same time the area over the porch was developed to provide an upper room with a double window looking into the church. The tower, which seems to have been built from Roman stone gathered as far away as Leicester, would have been added just before the Conquest.

Rosemary J. Cramp

Bibliography

Audouy, Michael. "Excavations at the Church of All Saints, Brixworth, Northamptonshire (1981–82)." *JBAA* 137 (1984): 1–44; Jackson, E. Dudley C., and Eric G.M. Fletcher. "Excavations at Brixworth, 1958." *JBAA*, 3d ser. 24 (1961): 1–15; Parsons, David. "Brixworth and Its Monastery Church." In *Mercian Studies*, ed. A. Dornier. Leicester: Leicester University Press, 1977, pp. 173–84; Stones, Judith. "Brixworth Church: Nineteenth- and Earlier Twentieth-Century Excavations." *JBAA* 133 (1980): 37–63; Sutherland, Diana S., and David Parsons. "The Petrological Contribution to the Survey of All Saints Church Brixworth, Northamptonshire: An Interim Account." *JBAA* 137 (1984): 45–64; Taylor, Harold M., and Joan Taylor. "Brixworth." In *Anglo-Saxon Architecture*. Vol. 1. Cambridge: Cambridge University Press, 1965, pp. 108–14.

See also Architecture, Anglo-Saxon; Ecclesiastical Architecture, Early Anglo-Saxon

Brut, Prose

A legendary and (in its later sections, continuations, and additions) historical chronicle of England. The earlier, legendary material of the *Brut* is ultimately based on Geoffrey of Monmouth's *Historia regum Britanniae* (*History of the Kings of Britain*; early 12th century). It covers the period from the settling of Britain by Brutus, the great-grandson of Aeneas, to the reign of Cadwalader. The narrative includes the stories of such kings as Leir, Coel, and especially Arthur. Subsequent material and continuations, within and without the main textual tradition, narrate the political history of England to the middle of the 15th century (in one manuscript, to 1479) and are often of great historical importance.

There is much textual variation and amalgamation with other works among individual *Brut* texts and groups of texts, and the *Manual* treats as separate works some manuscripts that the present writer considers part of the extended family of *Brut* versions and derivatives.

The *Brut* was probably the most popular secular work of late-medieval England. It survives, in whole or in part, in at least 50 Anglo-Norman manuscripts, almost 180 English manuscripts (including a few postmedieval transcripts), and about fifteen Latin manuscripts whose relationship to the Anglo-Norman and English versions is not yet fully determined. Under the title *The Chronicles of England,* or a variation thereof, the work was issued in thirteen printed editions between 1480 and 1528.

The anonymous Anglo-Norman *Brut* was probably first composed soon after 1272, at which date several of the extant manuscripts end. Two main recensions of the work survive, the Long and the Short Versions. In the course of the 14th century the text of the Anglo-Norman work received an introduction derived from a mid-13th- to early-14th-century poem, *Des Grantz Geanz,* explaining the initial settlement of "Albion" by Albine and her sisters, and various continuations, the most popular of which are designated the long and the short continuations. These continuations brought the narrative up to 1333.

Although it continued to be copied and added to in the 15th century, the Anglo-Norman *Brut* was superseded in the late 14th century by an English translation of the Long Version with the long continuation. The translator of this Common Version (as it is called) is anonymous but probably came from Herefordshire. In the 15th century the Common Version received in its turn a number of continuations (a major one ends in 1419), usually more or less adapted from the civic chronicles of London. Two principal variants of the Common Version to 1419 were also compiled: an Extended Version, which incorporates a prologue and some details taken from literary sources, and an Abbreviated Version, which is a selective cross between the Common and Extended Versions, drawing on both but also omitting large chunks of material. Many subgroups can be distinguished within these three versions of the English text. In addition there is an amorphous, heterogeneous group of Peculiar Texts and Versions, often of historical and literary importance, consisting of individual reworkings of *Brut* texts, works based on or adapted from the *Brut,* and combinations of the *Brut* with adaptations of other works. Some of these Peculiar Texts are linked with various Latin *Bruts,* whose precise relationships to the Anglo-Norman and English versions are still unclear.

In 1480 William Caxton published as the first printed history of England a Common Version *Brut* with a continuation to 1461 (probably compiled by Caxton himself) under the title *The Chronicles of England.* A second translation of the basic Anglo-Norman text was made about 1435 by John Maundevyle, rector of Burnham Thorpe in Norfolk, and his translation survives wholly or in part in only two manuscripts.

To judge from its chivalric interests and from contemporary references to ownership, the *Brut* was composed originally for the landowning gentry and the nobility. As the work developed, its appeal also spread to ecclesiastics and, especially through its English translation and eventual publication, to a middle-class and mercantile audience. As a result the prose *Brut* became a standard account of British and English history, exerting a powerful influence on national historical consciousness in medieval and postmedieval England. Tudor historians and chroniclers, such as Hall, Holinshed, and Stow, used the *Brut* as a source, and its legendary history was not generally discounted until the 17th century.

Lister M. Matheson

Bibliography

PRIMARY

Brie, Friedrich W.D., ed. *The Brut or The Chronicles of England.* 2 vols. EETS o.s. 131, 136. London: Kegan Paul, Trench, Trübner, 1906–08; Davies, John S., ed. *An English Chronicle of the Reigns of Richard II, Henry IV, Henry V, and Henry VI.* Camden Society 64. London: Camden Society, 1856; Gairdner, James, ed. *Three Fifteenth-Century Chronicles,* 1–28. Camden Society, n.s. 28. London: Camden Society, 1880.

SECONDARY

Manual 8:2629–44, 2818–36; Gransden, Antonia. *Historical Writing in England.* Vol. 2: *c. 1307 to the Early Sixteenth Century.* London: Routledge & Kegan Paul, 1982, pp. 73–77, 220–27; Kingsford, Charles Lethbridge. *English Historical Literature in the Fifteenth Century.* Oxford: Clarendon, 1913, pp. 113–39; Matheson, Lister M. "Printer and Scribe: Caxton, the *Polychronicon,* and the *Brut.*" *Speculum* 60 (1985): 593–614; Matheson, Lister M. *The Prose Brut: The Development of a Middle English Chronicle.* Tempe: MRTS, 1998; Taylor, John. *English Historical Literature in the Fourteenth Century.* Oxford: Clarendon, 1987, pp. 110–32, 274–84.

See also Anglo-Latin Literature after 1066; Anglo-Norman Literature; Books; Caxton; Chronicles; Gaimar; Geoffrey of Monmouth; Literacy; Prose, ME; Translation; Wace

Burgh, Benedict (d. 1483)

Poetic follower of John Lydgate. Burgh was educated at Oxford University and after ordination became rector of various parishes in Gloucestershire, Essex, and Suffolk from 1434 to 1460. In 1463 he was canon of Lincoln Cathedral and later held canonries and prebendaries in Colchester, Shropshire, London, and Westminster. He became chaplain to Edward IV in 1470.

One of Burgh's few original works is a brief versified fan letter to Lydgate. After Lydgate's death in 1449 Burgh completed the older poet's rendering of the *Secreta secretorum.* His other major work was also a translation, this time of the *Disticha Catonis.* He probably translated the *Distichs* in the 1430s under the patronage of Henry Bourchier, earl of Essex. Like the *Secreta* Burgh's *Distichs* seems to have been highly popular in the 15th century. There are over 30 manuscripts (and nearly 20 of the *Secreta*) and it was printed four times by Caxton.

A.S.G. Edwards

Bibliography

PRIMARY

Steele, Robert, ed. *Lydgate and Burgh's Secrees of Old Philisoffres.* EETS e.s. 66. London: Kegan Paul, Trench, Trübner, 1894.

SECONDARY

New *CBEL* 1:648; *Manual* 6:1896–99, 2152–54; Förster, Max. "Über Benedict Burghs Leben und Werke." *Archiv* 101 (1898): 29–64; Förster, Max, ed. "Die Burgsche Cato Paraphrase." *Archiv* 115 (1905): 298–323.

See also Lydgate; Translation

Burghal Hidage

At the close of the 9th century the kingdom of Wessex was seeking to defend itself against Vikings who had already overthrown the English rulers of Northumbria, Mercia, and East Anglia. Central to the defense of Wessex and the subsequent recapture of much of the Midlands was a reorganization of the army, a newly founded navy, and the use of fortified strongholds or *burhs* (boroughs). The Burghal Hidage is the name given in 1897 by F.W. Maitland to an OE list of these *burhs*. This list was composed between 914 and 919, in the reign of Edward the Elder, but represents the continuation and expansion of a defensive program begun under Edward's father, King Alfred.

It is one of the earliest administrative texts to survive from Anglo-Saxon England. Thirty-three *burhs* are named, together with the number of "hides" (a fiscal unit of land) allotted to each for its maintenance. The text survives in two variant versions (designated A and B); the A version has a section explaining how different amounts of hides were allotted to each *burh*, according to the variant circumferences of the walls and the number of men needed to repair and defend them. Thus each pole (5 ¹/₂ yards) of wall required four men, each man being supported by one hide of land, and each furlong (one-eighth of a mile: 220 yards) of wall required 160 men/hides, and so on, according to the same formula.

The Burghal Hidage was consulted by medieval lawyers and civil servants concerned with urban rights and origins. It was subsequently copied by early-modern antiquarians for its linguistic and historical value, and more recently it has been used by archaeologists as a guide to the likely extent of urban defensive remains from the reigns of Edward the Elder and Alfred. Evidence has been found of an expansion of commercial activity in southern England centered on the more attractively located *burhs*. Those named in the list are of varying sizes and antiquity, ranging from large Roman cities to small, newly constructed forts. Where existing urban areas were used, they often seem to have been given a new street layout on a regular plan.

In the text the *burhs* are listed in a clockwise circuit of central southern England and include places in the subordinate provinces of Sussex and Surrey and in the newly reconquered southern Midlands as well as in Wessex. Apart from those in the Midlands they were so distributed that none of the inhabitants of Wessex, Sussex, or Surrey would be more than 20 miles from a *burh*'s protection. They occur in the following order: *Eorpeburnan* (unidentified), Hastings, Lewes, Burpham, Chichester, Portchester, Southampton, Winchester, Wilton, Chisbury, Shaftesbury, Christchurch, Wareham, Bridport/Bredy, Exeter, Halwell, Lydford, Pilton/Barnstaple, Watchet, Axbridge, Lyng, Langport, Bath, Malmesbury, Cricklade, Oxford, Wallingford, Buckingham, Sashes, Eashing, Southwark, Worcester, Warwick. The modern layout of several of these places reflects both the line of the burghal walls and the associated Anglo-Saxon street plan.

Alexander R. Rumble

Bibliography

PRIMARY

Hill, David, and Alexander R. Rumble, eds. *The Defence of Wessex: The Burghal Hidage and Anglo-Saxon Fortifications.* Manchester: Manchester University Press, 1996 [a new edition, translation, and comprehensive discussion of the document and its context]; Keynes, Simon, and Michael Lapidge, trans. *Alfred the Great: Asser's Life of King Alfred and Other Contemporary Sources.* Harmondsworth: Penguin, 1983, pp. 193–94, 339–41.

SECONDARY

Brooks, Nicholas. "The Unidentified Forts of the Burghal Hidage." *Medieval Archaeology* 8 (1964): 74–89; Hill, David. *An Atlas of Anglo-Saxon England.* Oxford: Blackwell, 1981 [maps and diagrams illustrating the text, pp. 149–53]; Maitland, Frederic W. *Domesday Book and Beyond: Three Essays in the Early History of England.* Cambridge: Cambridge University Press, 1897, pp. 187–88, 502–06 [Maitland's views on the relationship of the hidages to those in Domesday Book and some of his identifications are no longer generally accepted].

See also Alfred; Boroughs

Bury St. Edmunds

A major town of Suffolk, known in Saxon times as Beodricsworth and later, after the martyred East Anglian king interred there in the early 10th century, as St. Edmundsbury. Cnut's reign (1016–35) saw a group of Benedictine monks installed to maintain the shrine, until then tended by secular clerics, and shortly thereafter work commenced on a stone church, the third such edifice to be erected on the site. Unfortunately the 11th- and 12th-century fabric survives only as ruins, though in layout and architecture the monastery probably resembled its Benedictine counterpart at Ely in Cambridgeshire.

Edward the Confessor favored the Abbey of St. Edmund with generous privileges and endowments, most notably the *sac* and *soc* (rights of local jurisdiction) of eight and a half hundreds of land in West Suffolk, as well as exemption from episcopal control. He also granted the abbot permission to establish a private mint at Bury. Thus the "liberty" of St. Edmund was remarkable both for its territorial size and compactness and for its independence from the bishop.

The Norman kings not only recognized their predecessors' grants to the abbey but added substantially to them. The abbot of Bury St. Edmunds was a powerful feudal lord with broad powers of regional administration, justice, and taxation. The sheriff's writ was inadmissable within the liberty of the eight and a half hundreds, men of the liberty were exempt from attendance at the shire court, and the abbot rendered his own account to the royal exchequer. As a result of royal favor, lay endowment, and outright purchase the abbey became one of the wealthiest monasteries in England, with estates as far away as Kent and Yorkshire. It was before the high altar of the Romanesque church that a group of barons swore on St. Edmund's Day, 20 November 1214, to exact a pledge from King John concerning their lawful rights; they were on the road that led to Magna Carta.

The townspeople of Bury benefited from the constant traffic of pilgrims to St. Edmund's shrine, though until the abbey's dissolution in 1539 attempts at self-government met with frustration. Riots aimed at wresting concessions from the abbot erupted in 1264, 1327, and 1381, all times of widespread political instability; however, the would-be usurpers never knew more than transient success. In the late 13th century the burgesses received permission to establish a merchant guild and to nominate aldermen, but they never enjoyed the formal corporate status and privileges (e.g., electing a mayor and returning members of parliament) associated with royal boroughs.

Town-abbey relations remained strained, with crown intervention occasionally necessary to ensure the peace. Assizes were routinely held at Bury rather than at Ipswich, the shire seat, but even the king's judges were admitted to the town only at the abbot's pleasure. Based on poll tax and lay subsidy records, the town ranked among the second dozen urban communities in terms of population (ca. 4,000) and wealth. In Anselm (abbot, 1121–48), nephew of Anselm of Canterbury, and Samson (abbot, 1182–1211) the abbey possessed two exceptional leaders. The 12th century also saw the Bury workshop at the forefront of English manuscript illumination and art production, notable extant examples being the Bury Bible (Cambridge, Corpus Christi College 2) and the Suffolk Cross (New York, Metropolitan Museum of Art).

Susan Battley

Bibliography

PRIMARY

Manuscripts of Lincoln, Bury St. Edmund's and Great Grimsby Corporation. Historical Manuscripts Commission, 14th appendix, part viii. London: HMSO, 1895.

SECONDARY

Goodwin, Albert. *The Abbey of St. Edmundsbury.* Oxford: Blackwell, 1931; Gottfried, Robert S. *Bury St. Edmunds and the Urban Crisis, 1290–1539.* Princeton: Princeton University Press, 1982; Lobel, Mary D. *The Borough of Bury St. Edmunds: A Study in the Government and Development of a Monastic Town.* Oxford: Clarendon, 1935.

See also Towns

Byrhtferth (fl. 985–1011)

Priest and monk of the Abbey of Ramsey, one of the most learned Englishmen of his time, and a student of Abbo of Fleury during Abbo's visit to England in 985–87. Byrhtferth's varied literary career appears to have begun shortly after the departure of that great scholar. His works fall into three genres: computistical, hagiographical, and historical.

Computus

Computus (OE *gerim, gerimcræft*) is the science of computation as it relates to the ecclesiastical calendar. The word can also be used of any collection of short texts on that science; these generally contained a calendar accompanied by tables and instructions for performing such tasks as finding the moon's age and calculating the dates of movable feasts.

The earliest of the datable works associated with Byrhtferth is a compilation of materials on computus. Of the three copies of this compilation all are incomplete, and two were evidently revised or augmented at later periods. The version that seems closest to Byrhtferth's is in Oxford, St. John's College 17, a large and elegant manuscript written around 1110–11 at the nearby Abbey of Thorney. This manuscript contains, among other items, several computistical works by Bede and Helperic and a computus, all accompanied by extensive marginal glosses and introduced by a Latin *Epilogus* ("preface") by Byrhtferth. Several passages in the computus and glosses date the compilation (leaving aside those items that postdate Byrhtferth) to the years 988–96. Apart from the *Epilogus* the only item in the compilation attributed to Byrhtferth is a full-page diagram (fol. 7v; fig. 121: see SCIENTIFIC MANUSCRIPTS, EARLY) illustrating the harmony of the universe, and suggesting correspondences among cosmological, numerological, and physiological aspects of the world. Though other, minor items in St. John's 17 may well be by Byrhtferth, their authorship cannot be proved; nor can it be proved beyond doubt that he was responsible for the compilation as a whole. But the date of the compilation, the presence in it of the *Epilogus* and diagram, and its close association with the *Enchiridion,* discussed below, make it likely that Byrhtferth built it up from a smaller compilation left behind at Ramsey by his teacher Abbo.

Byrhtferth's *Enchiridion* (also called his *Manual*), preserved in a single manuscript, Bodl. Ashmole 328, can be dated from internal evidence to the year 1011. Written in Latin and OE, it treats a variety of subjects; however, the largest part of it is a guide to the use of the computus. The first three of the four books of the *Enchiridion* take the student step by step through a computus evidently similar to the one in St. John's 17, introducing its tables and the calendar with explanations drawn largely from Helperic, Hrabanus Maurus, and Bede. Byrhtferth frequently digresses from the computus to touch on matters as diverse as the organization of the universe, elision of syllables in Latin verse, and rhetorical figures and diacritics. Book Four of the *Enchiridion* is a clearly presented Latin treatise on number symbolism, the fullest statement anywhere in Byrhtferth's writings of his belief that the divine order of the universe can be perceived through the study of numbers; it is also an excellent general source for the modern student interested in medieval number symbolism.

The last of Byrhtferth's works on computus is an unsigned fragment of an OE text preserved in BL Cotton Caligula A.xv, fols. 142v–143r; his authorship of the fragment is suggested by its stylistic similarity to the OE of the *Enchiridion.*

Hagiography

Two Latin saints' lives have been attributed to Byrhtferth on the basis of their stylistic affinity with the Latin of his signed works, the *Epilogus* and *Enchiridion.* These works, the *Life of St. Oswald* and the *Life of St. Ecgwine,* are preserved together in a single manuscript, BL Cotton Nero E.i, a large passional to which they were added in the last half of the 11th century. Both the original passional and the additions were written at Worcester.

The *Life of St. Oswald,* written between 996 and 1005, details the career of the bishop of Worcester and archbishop of York who, with Dunstan and Æthelwold, was one of the leaders of the Benedictine Reform of the 10th century; Byrhtferth's work is considered the most important source for his life. The *Life* is also cited as a historical source for the murder of King Edward in 978 and, more famously, for the Battle of Maldon in 991. However, the *Life* tells us little about the latter two incidents that we cannot learn from other sources, and historians have at times shown impatience with its lack of circumstantial detail—forgetting, perhaps, that hagiographers, unlike chroniclers, were interested less in events themselves than in their theological significance.

The danger of using saints' lives as historical sources is perhaps nowhere better illustrated than in Byrhtferth's *Life of St. Ecgwine*, written after the year 1000, evidently at the request of the monks of Evesham, the monastery that Ecgwine, as bishop of Worcester, had founded around the beginning of the 8th century. While Byrhtferth could draw on a wealth of documentary evidence, eyewitness report, and personal recollection in writing about St. Oswald, with Ecgwine he had no documents beyond a spurious charter and an irrelevant letter; all other evidence was filtered through some two centuries of oral tradition. It is no surprise, then, that Ecgwine emerges as an utterly conventional saint and that parallels for the incidents of his life can generally be found in the lives of other, equally conventional saints.

History

That Byrhtferth was responsible for the early sections (up to 887) of the *Historia regum (History of the Kings)* attributed to the 12th-century writer Simeon of Durham is suggested by the stylistic affinity of those sections with Byrhtferth's other works. Byrhtferth's work is diverse and might be better characterized as a "historical miscellany" than as a history. It contains the following sections: 1) legends of Kentish saints; 2) lists of Northumbrian kings; 3) material based mainly on Bede's *Historia abbatum;* 4) a chronicle covering the years 732–802; 5) a chronicle covering the years 849–87, based mainly on Asser's *Life of King Alfred.*

Like Byrhtferth's other Latin works the *Historia regum* is written in bombastic style, much loved in the 10th century, that modern critics call "hermeneutic." Like all of his works it betrays his unusual interest in computus, in numerology, and in the figural interpretation of biblical history and the material world—sometimes introducing such topics in places that seem to us inappropriate. Indeed one of the most prominent characteristics of Byrhtferth's style is his tendency to digress suddenly, for reasons that are not always apparent at first glance.

The student should be aware that some older scholars attributed to Byrhtferth an extensive set of glosses on Bede's scientific works, a life of St. Dunstan, and two works entitled *De principiis mathematicis* and *De institutione monachorum.* More recent scholarship has shown that Byrhtferth had nothing to do with the saint's life or the glosses on Bede, and it is likely that the other two works never existed.

Peter S. Baker

Bibliography

PRIMARY

Many of the older editions below are unreliable; new editions are in progress: Arnold, T., ed. *Symeonis monachi opera omnia.* Rolls Series 75. 2 vols. London: Longmans, 1882–85, 2:3–91, except for interpolations at pp. 32–38 and 47–50 [*Historia regum*]; Baker, Peter S., and Michael Lapidge, eds. *Byrhtferth's Enchiridion.* EETS s.s. 15. London: Oxford University Press, 1995; Forsey, G.F., ed. and trans. "Byrhtferth's Preface." *Speculum* 3 (1928): 505–22; Giles, J.A., ed. *Vita quorundum Anglo-Saxonum.* London: Caxton Society, 1854, pp. 349–96. Repr. New York: Burt Franklin, 1967 [*Life of St. Ecgwine*]; Raine, J., ed. *Historians of the Church of York.* Rolls Series 71. 3 vols. London: Eyre & Spottiswoode, 1879, 1:399–475 [*Life of St. Oswald*].

SECONDARY

Baker, Peter S. "The Old English Canon of Byrhtferth of Ramsey." *Speculum* 55 (1980): 22–37; Baker, Peter S. "Byrhtferth's *Enchiridion* and the Computus in Oxford, St John's College 17." *ASE* 10 (1981): 123–42; Hart, C.R. "Byrhtferth's Northumbrian Chronicle." *EHR* 97 (1982): 558–82; Lapidge, Michael. "Byrhtferth and the Vita S. Ecgwini." *MS* 41 (1979): 331–53. Repr. in *Anglo-Latin Literature, 900–1066.* London: Hambledon, 1993, pp. 293–315; Lapidge, Michael. "Byrhtferth of Ramsey and the Early Sections of the *Historia regum* Attributed to Symeon of Durham." *ASE* 10 (1981): 97–122. Repr. in *Anglo-Latin Literature, 900–1066.* London: Hambledon, 1993, pp. 317–42.

See also Abbo; Anglo-Latin Literature to 1066; Bede; Chronicles; Hagiography; Isidore; Oswald; Scientific and Medical Writings; Utilitarian Writings

C

Cade's Rebellion

Jack Cade's rebellion in the summer of 1450 was the culmination of months of discontent in parliament and throughout the realm, coinciding with the rapid loss of Normandy to the French. These months had seen the murder of Bishop Moleyns, the impeachment and killing of William duke of Suffolk, and a series of reforms forced upon Henry VI. The origins and early development of the rising are obscure, but by 5 June news of the rising had reached Leicester, where parliament was dissolved as the king and his nobles marched on London.

As in the Peasants' Rebellion in 1381 the center of the rebellion was in Kent. Its proximity to London and the Continent meant that news of high politics and of defeats in France made a direct impact, and its large number of free peasants and independent cloth workers helped produce a volatile community. Though primarily a rising of peasants and artisans, it is possible, as later alleged, that their action was encouraged by men of higher rank, perhaps associated with Richard duke of York. There will probably never be certainty about this. By 11 June a large force had fortified a camp at Blackheath, overlooking London. Its leader took the name of John Mortimer, presumably to signify a connection with the duke of York, then in Ireland, who represented the Mortimer claim to the throne. His real name appears to have been Cade and he was probably of low birth, though even hostile chroniclers admit that he was "witty and subtle" in his speech. He was clearly a natural leader.

There survive several versions of the rebels' manifestos. Their main theme is misgovernment, both central and local: "The law serveth of nought else in these days but for to do wrong. . . . [The king's] false council has lost his law, his merchandise is lost, his common people is destroyed, the sea is lost, France is lost and the king himself is so set that he may not pay for his meat and drink." Though it is clear from later indictments of rebels that there did exist radical social and religious sentiments among some Kentishmen, the manifestos do not resemble the broad social demands of 1381. Rather they

sought the return of the duke of York from Ireland, the formation of a council controlled by the great magnates, and the trial of "traitors and extortioners."

On 18 June the rebels retreated from Blackheath, unwilling to face the advance of Henry VI's army. They repulsed a pursuing force, however, and news of the rising stimulated outbreaks of violence in Essex, Wiltshire (where Bishop Ayscough of Salisbury was murdered), and elsewhere. The king's army soon disintegrated, and Henry and his court withdrew to Kenilworth in the Midlands. Thus, when Cade's forces arrived back in Southwark on 1 July, they were able to enter London unopposed. There, after a form of trial, they executed the treasurer of England, Lord Say, and several other unpopular officials. The rulers of London, fearing disorders, joined forces with troops in the Tower under Lord Scales, and on the night of 5 July there was severe fighting on London Bridge. The following day a settlement was negotiated, with general pardons for all the rebels and a promise of commissions to investigate their complaints. The rebels then dispersed. Cade's own pardon was soon nullified, and a few days later he was captured and killed in Sussex by the sheriff of Kent.

Jack Cade's rebellion completed the disintegration of the household government of Suffolk and his allies, and the return of the dukes of Somerset and York to England in the late summer brought in a new phase of Lancastrian politics, a phase dominated by magnate rivalry. Unrest continued in Kent and Sussex for several years, even though the pardons were honored and commissions were sent there to investigate complaints of extortion and misgovernment. For the next quarter of a century Kent provided a reservoir of support for opposition movements against both Lancastrians and Yorkists.

Roger Virgoe

Bibliography

PRIMARY

Calendar of the Patent Rolls, 1446–52. London: HMSO, 1910, pp. 338–74 [gives a list of pardons related to the rebellion]; Flenley, Ralph, ed. *Six Town Chronicles.*

Oxford: Clarendon, 1911 [this chronicle and those listed below offer a range of good contemporary accounts of the uprising]; Gairdner, James, ed. "William Gregory's Chronicle of London." In *The Historical Collections of a Citizen of London*. Camden Society, n.s. 17 (1876), pp. 57–239; Gairdner, James, ed. *Three Fifteenth Century Chronicles*. Camden Society, n.s. 28 (1880); Harriss, G.L., ed. *John Benet's Chronicle*. Camden Miscellany 24. Camden Society, 4th ser. 9 (1972); Harvey, I.M.W. *Jack Cade's Rebellion of 1450*. Oxford: Clarendon, 1991; Kingsford, Charles L., ed. *Chronicles of London*. Oxford: Clarendon, 1905. Repr. Dursley: Sutton, 1977.

SECONDARY

Griffiths, Ralph A. *The Reign of King Henry VI: The Exercise of Royal Authority, 1422–1461*. London: Benn, 1981, pp. 610–65; Kriehn, George. *The English Rising of 1450*. Strasburg: Heitz, 1892 [still useful, though Griffiths has the fullest account and most important analysis].

See also Henry VI; Peasant Rebellion; Wars of the Roses

Cædmon (fl. 657–80)

The first English poet with any vernacular work surviving ("Cædmon's Hymn"), who invented English religious poetry by combining secular verse techniques with Christian subject matter.

Bede tells the story in his *Ecclesiastical History* 4.24, the only source. Cædmon was a cowherd at the monastery of Abbess Hild at Whitby. One night, after leaving a feast at the monastery in order to avoid performing with the harp, he had a dream in which a man commanded him to sing. Although he demurred, the man insisted that he do so and gave him the subject matter for his song: the Creation. At this Cædmon began to sing the poem that has come to be called Cædmon's Hymn, the first recorded English poem. Upon waking Cædmon reported his dream to the steward and then to Hild and her advisers, who recited another biblical narrative to him and asked him to turn it into song as well. When he had done so, he was invited and chose to become a monk and devoted his life to composing vernacular poetry based on religious subjects.

Bede lists Cædmon's works, which included poems on Genesis and Exodus, the life of Christ, the apostles' teachings, the Last Judgment, and heaven and hell. None survive, but the list resembles the contents of Bodl. Junius 11, which has thus been called the "Cædmon Manuscript," though its contents are not now attributed to Cædmon.

Cædmon's Hymn survives in Northumbrian and West Saxon versions; the latter follows:

Nu sculon herigean heofonrices weard,
metodes meahte and his modgeþanc,
weorc wuldorfæder, swa he wundra gehwæs,
ece drihten, or onstealde.

He ærest sceop eorðan bearnum
heofon to hrofe, halig scyppend;
þa middangeard moncynnes weard,
ece drihten, æfter teode
firum foldan, frea ælmihtig.

[Now should we praise the guardian of the heavenly kingdom, the power of the Creator and the counsel of his mind, the works of the Father of glory, how he, the eternal Lord, originated every marvel. He, the holy Creator, first created the heaven, as a roof for the children of the earth; then the eternal Lord, guardian of the human race, the almighty ruler, afterward fashioned the world as a soil for men.]

Cædmon composed in the repetitious style associated with formulaic, memorized verse. The three-part poem turns on the favorite subjects of the Anglo-Saxons: praise, mind, power, time, and God, who creates the earth as a metaphorical hall ("heaven as a roof") for human beings to live in. In verse 6b the brand-new poet calls God "scyppend" (Shaper), punning on "scop" (Shaper, poet).

Some cynics dismiss the whole story as another miracle tale, but Bede, fond of miracles, never uses the term "miracle" about Cædmon. Hild's scholars saw Cædmon's accomplishment as a heavenly gift, while modern critics debate how an illiterate cowherd suddenly learned to compose sophisticated verse. Theories include overcoming stage fright, practicing secretly, and modifying formulas heard in secular verse.

Cædmon's style and subject matter dominated Anglo-Saxon verse for 400 years and probably reinforced the native tendency toward stressed meter. In that sense Cædmon, encouraged by Abbess Hild, "invented" English verse as we know it.

Donald K. Fry

Bibliography

PRIMARY

ASPR 6:105–06; Colgrave, Bertram, and R.A.B. Mynors, eds. and trans. *Bede's Ecclesiastical History of the English People*. Oxford: Clarendon, 1969, pp. 414–21.

SECONDARY

Dobbie, E.V.K. *The Manuscripts of Cædmon's Hymn and Bede's Death Song: With a Critical Text of the Epistola Cuthberti de obitu Bedae*. New York: Columbia University Press, 1937; Fritz, Donald W. "Cædmon: A Monastic Exegete." *American Benedictine Review* 25 (1974): 351–63; Fry, Donald K. "Cædmon as a Formulaic Poet." *Forum for Modern Language Studies* 10 (1974): 227–47; Fry, Donald K. "The Memory of Cædmon." In *Oral Traditional Literature: A Festschrift for Albert Bates Lord*, ed. John Miles Foley. Columbus: Slavica, 1981, pp. 282–93; Howlett, D.R. "The Theology of Cædmon's Hymn." *Leeds Studies in English*, n.s. 7 (1973–74): 1–12; Lester, G.A. "The Cædmon Story and Its Analogues." *Neophilologus* 58 (1974): 225–37; Magoun, Francis P., Jr. "Bede's Story of Cædmon: The Case History of an Anglo-Saxon Oral Singer." *Speculum* 30

(1955): 49–63; O'Keeffe, Katherine O'Brien. "Orality and the Developing Text of Cædmon's Hymn." *Speculum* 62 (1987): 1–20; Wrenn, Charles Leslie. "The Poetry of Cædmon." *PBA* 33 (1946): 277–95.

See also Bible in OE Literature; Formula; Hild; Minstrels; Orality

Caesarius of Arles (469/70–542/43)

Archbishop of Arles in southern France from 502 until his death. Caesarius presided over a number of important synods and was widely revered both for his holiness and his pastoral concern. His greatest influence on later times, and most especially in medieval England, comes through his sermons. In his day bishops had a monopoly on preaching, and Caesarius was seriously concerned that his flock could hear sermons far too seldom. He argued successfully that priests, even poorly educated ones, ought to be able to read to their parishioners sermons drawn from the Fathers of the Church, and he secured a canonical mandate that made this possible. He then produced a collection of over 200 sermons, many of which were edited, simplified, or abbreviated versions of sermons available to him from the patristic tradition.

These sermons, which convey essentially Augustinian theology in simple, clear language, appear to have answered a need at a later time when learned priests were in short supply, for Caesarius appears as a major source for a substantial number of the anonymous OE homilies as well as for the learned Ælfric. He is the source for the controlling image in the Exeter Book poem *Vainglory*, and the rhetorically powerful Last Judgment speech of Christ to the sinners in the Exeter Book poem *Christ III* is translated almost word-for-word from Caesarius.

Of the more than 30 OE texts that use Caesarius many select details that his contemporary biographers cited as reasons for the popularity of the sermons in his own day. His talent for choosing simple but striking examples clearly impressed the OE homilists, who borrowed his moving account of the rewards for offering no more than a cup of cold water or a fragment of bread, his chilling account of dry bones speaking to sinners in need of repentance, and his comparison of Lent to this world and of Easter to the next. A pastoral concern that his biographers said caused him to preach on Judgment Day in his sleep clearly contributed to the poetic speech of Christ noted above as well as to several OE sermons on the Last Judgment. And his admonitions concerning the perils of drunkenness appear in quite literal translations in a number of the English texts. His English adapters seized upon his ability to make matters memorable, but they in turn served Caesarius well, in that the most successful of their close translations of him reached a rhetorical level that was rarely exceeded in OE homilies except by Ælfric.

Joseph B. Trahern, Jr.

Bibliography

PRIMARY

Morin, Germain, ed. *Caesarii Arelatensis Sermones.* Maredsous, 1937–42. Repr. as CCSL 103–04. Turnhout: Brepols, 1953; Mueller, Mary Magdeleine, trans. *Sermons.* Fathers of the Church 31, 47, 66. Washington, D.C.: Catholic University of America Press, 1956–73.

SECONDARY

Beck, Henry G. *The Pastoral Care of Souls in South-East France during the Sixth Century.* Analecta Gregoriana 51. Rome: Gregorian University, 1950; Daly, William. "Caesarius of Arles, a Precursor of Medieval Christianity." *Traditio* 26 (1970): 1–28; Gatch, Milton McC. "Eschatology in the Anonymous Old English Homilies." *Traditio* 21 (1965): 117–65; Klingshirn, William S. *Caesarius of Arles: The Making of a Christian Community in Late Antique Gaul.* Cambridge: Cambridge University Press, 1994; Szarmach, Paul E. "Caesarius of Arles and the Vercelli Homilies." *Traditio* 26 (1970): 315–23; Trahern, J.B. "Caesarius of Arles and Old English Literature." *ASE* 5 (1976): 105–19.

See also Ælfric; *Christ III;* Sermons; *Vainglory;* Vercelli Homilies

Caligula (Cotton) Troper

A fragment of an illustrated troper of the 11th century forming the first portion of manuscript BL Cotton Caligula A.xiv and one of only three trope manuscripts surviving from Anglo-Saxon England. The troper's place of origin is unknown; Canterbury and Hereford have been suggested, neither on convincing grounds.

The manuscript contains tropes (i.e., musicotextual additions) to the Proper chants of the mass (i.e., the chants whose text and music vary from feast day to feast day, as distinct from the Ordinary chants, whose texts remain the same throughout the church year) arranged in an annual cycle. It is a troper of the anthology type, being a compilation from available trope repertoires like most French tropers rather than a prescriptive liturgical book like the famous Winchester tropers. It includes the overwhelming majority of the proper tropes represented in the Winchester trope manuscripts. It also contains a substantial number of unique tropes, but these pieces are extremely varied in style and language, and it is unlikely that they are new compositions, although some may well be English. The notation is strictly adiastematic; in contrast to most music manuscripts from Anglo-Saxon England absolutely no use is made of significative letters.

The manuscript's surviving decoration consists of one painted initial introducing the principal mass for Christmas day and eleven paintings of christological and hagiographical subject matter introducing ten feasts. The paintings are surrounded by Latin hexameter inscriptions, newly composed to accompany the pictures, which describe and comment upon the events and characters represented. The paintings are considerably varied in subject matter and format, and there is little sense of the collected illustrations as a proper picture cycle. The style and technique of the paintings are unparalleled in contemporary manuscript art, the most remarkable features of the characteristic style being the unusual palette dominated by warm colors and the use of a pair of contrasting hues to define local color. The painting technique is not consistent throughout the codex, but the modifications are not abrupt, and the paintings are most probably the work of a single artist who mastered both a fully painted style and a drawing style. The manuscript contains the earliest surviving western medieval representation of two of the subjects depicted (the Annunciation to Joachim and the Temptation of St. Martin), and the iconography of the paintings is sometimes innovative (the Ascension of Christ and St. Peter's Release from Prison). The fragment is also noteworthy for the inclusion of illustrations to common feasts (e.g., the images The Community of the Apostles and the Community of Virgins).

Elizabeth C. Teviotdale

Bibliography

Frere, Walter Howard. *The Winchester Troper: From Manuscripts of the Xth and XIth Centuries.* Henry Bradshaw Society 8. London: Harrison & Sons, 1894; Planchart, Alejandro E. *The Repertory of Tropes at Winchester.* 2 vols. Princeton: Princeton University Press, 1977; Temple, Elżbieta. *Anglo-Saxon Manuscripts 900–1066.* A Survey of Manuscripts Illuminated in the British Isles 2, ed. J.J.G. Alexander. London: Harvey Miller, 1976.

See also Liturgy and Church Music, History of; Trope; Winchester Tropers

Canterbury, Ecclesiastical Province of

Although the church of Canterbury may be said to have originated in 597, with Augustine's mission from Rome, the province itself was obviously a much later development. Whether Pope Gregory intended a diocese to be established at Canterbury or not, Augustine's conversion of Æthelberht, king of Kent, and his establishment of the first great church there gave Canterbury a definite primacy or leadership. It is unhistorical to speak of a province at this time, but the status given to Canterbury by Augustine was later seen as important in defining its archiepiscopal or metropolitan status within the church in England. His followers, Mellitus and Justus, went on to establish Christian centers or dioceses at London and Rochester, and the organization of the English church into dioceses is associated with Archbishop Theodore in the 7th century. However, it cannot really be argued that there was much structure in the English church before the 12th century.

In practice the development of the organizational framework was slow and took place after the Norman Conquest. There were three attempts in the 12th century to establish further metropolitan sees (besides Canterbury and York): by Henry of Blois at Winchester, by Gilbert Foliot at London, and by Bishop Bernard at St. David's. All were resisted, however, by a papacy increasingly concerned with organization and structure. By 1198 the territorial pattern of the English dioceses within the provinces of Canterbury and York had been settled, to remain without major alteration until the 16th century.

The English episcopal sees subject to the archbishop of Canterbury were thirteen in number: Bath and Wells, Chichester, Coventry and Lichfield, Ely, Exeter, Hereford, Lincoln, London, Norwich, Rochester, Salisbury, Winchester, and Worcester, plus the four Welsh dioceses of St. David's, St. Asaph's, Bangor, and Llandaff. These dioceses were the southern province, and they embraced England from the mouth of the Humber southward: the archbishop of Canterbury was their metropolitan. The archbishop of York, as metropolitan of the northern province, had jurisdictional rights over Durham, Carlisle, and Whithorn (although his rights in this last were seriously disputed by the Scots).

Before the 13th century and the age of archiepiscopal registers it is difficult to get a clear picture of the exercise of metropolitan rights. Afterward they may be defined as follows. First, the archbishop (as metropolitan) had the right of visiting churches in the dioceses of his province. Metropolitical visitation can be seen at its most active under Archbishop William Courtenay, who between 1384 and 1390 alone visited the dioceses and cathedrals of Exeter, Bath and Wells, Worcester, Chichester, Lincoln, and Salisbury.

Second, the archbishop could hold a convocation or council of the clergy of his province. Third, he had a provincial court, the Court of Arches, which acted as an appeals court for the province. Court records were not entered in the archiepiscopal register, and few case records survive before the Reformation. The court, however, came to have a settled venue in London, at the church of St. Mary of the Arches (or le Bow).

Fourth, the archbishop could prove wills of persons who died owning property in more than one diocese or where the goods were *notabilia* (worth more than £5). This right of the metropolitan accounts for the vast series of Prerogative Court of Canterbury wills (now in the Public Record Office, London). These include royal wills and wills of the major landowners.

Fifth, the archbishop had *sede vacante* jurisdiction, complete jurisdiction over the diocese, when any of the sees subject to him were vacant (without a bishop). His registers record the regular exercise of such jurisdiction over vacant sees. On the death of a bishop within his province the archbishop appointed a vicar or keeper of the see to perform all episcopal acts on his behalf; ordination, collation, institution, proof of wills, visitation. The registers of the keepers' transactions came to be bound into the archiepiscopal registers. Cardinal Morton's register, for example, includes miniregisters for Coventry and Lichfield (1490), Bath and Wells (1491), Winchester, Exeter (1492), Lincoln, Bath and Wells (1495), Coventry and Lichfield, Rochester (1496), Worcester (1498), and Salisbury and Norwich (1499).

Jane E. Sayers

Bibliography

Churchill, Irene J. *Canterbury Administration.* 2 vols. London: SPCK, 1933 [the classic work on the subject]; *Medieval Records of the Archbishops of Canterbury.* London: Faith Press, 1982 [lectures given in 1960 at Lambeth Palace Library by a number of leading scholars].

See also Augustine of Canterbury; Bishops; Convocation; Courts, Ecclesiastical; York, Ecclesiastical Province of

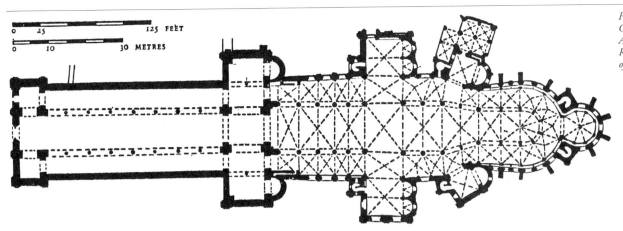

Fig. 34. Canterbury Cathedral, ca. 1200. After G. Webb (1956). Reprinted by permission of Yale University Press.

Canterbury Cathedral

Canterbury Cathedral (figs. 34–35) was, in the Middle Ages, both the seat of an archbishop, the primate of England, and the church of one of the most important monasteries in the country, whose prior might vie in importance with the archbishop when it came to architectural patronage. After 1170 Canterbury Cathedral was also the site of the most important shrine in England, that of the martyred archbishop Thomas Becket, and its architecture reflects these multiple functions and meanings. The present fabric contains work from the immediate post-Conquest period to the eve of the Reformation, and its major campaigns of construction were each extremely important in the history of English medieval architecture.

The Anglo-Saxon cathedral has only recently (1993) been discovered under the nave of the present church. While any full evaluation must await the publication of the excavations, it is clear that it was a large building, underlying almost the whole of the present nave and extending an unknown distance eastward under the crossing. This church was destroyed by fire in 1067 and was rebuilt by Archbishop Lanfranc from around 1070. The eastern arm and liturgical choir under the crossing must have been complete by 1077, and the whole building was finished by Lanfranc's death in 1089. Lanfranc had been abbot of William the Conqueror's abbey of St. Étienne at Caen before William made him archbishop of Canterbury, and the new cathedral showed a marked resemblance to the Norman abbey church. Similar are the plans with their staggered eastern chapels, transepts with tribune platforms providing access to upper transept chapels, naves of nine bays with similar dimensions, and a general similarity of elevation consisting of arcade, wood-roofed gallery, and clerestory. Canterbury, on the other hand, had a crypt while Caen did not and shows no evidence of the clerestory passage that was such an important feature at Caen. The present nave and (west) transepts preserve all the dimensions, except the vertical, of Lanfranc's church, and fragments of the 11th-century design are still visible on the transept interiors and under the aisle roofs of the present nave.

The great outburst of Anglo-Norman reconstruction that began around 1080 must have soon made the dimensions and perhaps plan of Lanfranc's church seem outmoded, and around 1096 a vast new eastern arm was put into construction. Anselm was archbishop when construction began, but the moving figure behind the new campaign was likely the prior Ernulf. In addition to providing more room for the stalls of the rapidly growing monastery the new eastern arm also made possible the better veneration of Canterbury's many relics, including those of its Anglo-Saxon saints whose sanctity had been questioned by Lanfranc but who had been rehabilitated by around 1100. The new choir replaced the

Fig. 35. Canterbury Cathedral, south elevation of presbytery from the northeast. Courtesy of L. Hoey.

en echelon apses of the first Norman church with an ambulatory opening into a square-ended axial chapel and two side chapels that originally carried towers set at an eccentric angle to the main body of the church. The new choir also included a new eastern transept and was carried on an immense crypt, the largest and most lavish ever constructed in England.

The main elevation of this work was rebuilt after the fire of 1174, and although we have the description of the Canterbury monk Gervase to aid us, certain details, particularly the precise form of the middle story, remain unclear. There was an arcade of unbroken cylindrical piers, with some sort of gallery and a clerestory above; the elevation lacked any vertical articulation except at the chord of the apse, and the whole was covered by a wood roof. William of Malmesbury's appellation of "glorious choir" has remained tied to this work, although he may have had in mind the stained glass, paintings, and furnishings more than the architecture itself. The lack of a high vault and bay-dividing shafts, as well as the use of cylindrical piers, must have given Ernulf's choir an archaic look that may have been intentional, harking back to early Christian churches in Rome. Of this grand project the crypt remains in its entirety, along with the lower parts of the outer aisle walls and eastern transepts and the chapels of St. Andrew and St. Anselm.

In 1174, four years after Becket's murder, the "glorious choir" was consumed by fire. Gervase's account makes clear that it was not completely destroyed and that the monks had hopes of rebuilding it as it had been, but the master they brought in to effect the repairs, one William of Sens, convinced them that a more complete reconstruction was advisable. Construction began in 1175 and was complete by 1185, and Gervase's account of it is the most complete such narrative we have surviving from the Middle Ages. Midway through the reconstruction William of Sens fell from the scaffolding and was unable to continue supervision of the work; his successor was another William, whom Gervase designates "the Englishman." Although the architectural work was completed in ten years, the furnishing of the choir and in particular the construction of Becket's shrine were long delayed as a result of bitter quarrels between the monks and successive archbishops in the late 12th century, followed by King John's equally bitter quarrel with the pope in the early 13th century. The new work was dedicated only in 1220.

William of Sens was forced to retain the outer walls and thus the plan of the Romanesque choir, excepting only its eastern termination. He raised these outer walls to provide the aisles the height of the Romanesque aisle and gallery combined and in the choir proper (west of the east crossing) placed a high arcade of alternating round and octagonal piers opposite them. Above this he set a gallery with grouped openings, a clerestory with an interior wall passage, and a covering of six-part rib vaults, the whole articulated liberally with dark Purbeck marble shafts. East of the east crossing, in the presbytery, the main vessel narrows as it follows the curve of the Romanesque ambulatory and the

central floor level rises in two flights of stairs toward the feretory in the Trinity Chapel. The latter, designed entirely by William the Englishman, was built beyond the limit of the Romanesque choir over a high crypt to contain the shrine of Becket. The presbytery piers are given various numbers of detached shafts to provide a visual crescendo, abetted by the narrowing and raising of the main floor level, to the shrine and its architectural surrounding, where the piers become coupled shafts of variegated colors, and the capitals themselves are carved of Purbeck marble. When combined with the stained glass, the colored inlaid floor tiles, and the glitter of the shrine itself the Trinity Chapel must have made an overwhelming impression of visual opulence. Beyond it stands the curious Corona, designed probably to contain the reliquary of Becket's scalp. The whole work might be seen as a carefully designed and theatrically effective architectural progression to enhance the relics of the martyred archbishop.

Against this view of careful planning is the obvious but difficult-to-interpret evidence of various changes in plan as the work progressed. The Trinity Chapel appears actually to have been a second thought, and the form of the originally planned eastern termination remains controversial. It is clear that these hesitations or rethinkings applied to the structural system as well. In the south choir of the gallery William of Sens employed the rare device of transverse barrel vaults, although he abandoned these in the north gallery in favor of more typical wooden roofs but with external buttressing walls that become true, if unusually low, flying buttresses in the presbytery, a system that continues in the Trinity Chapel. Given the secure dates of Canterbury, this evolving experimentation with buttressing systems is important for the history of Gothic architecture.

The Canterbury east arm is generally seen as representing the first complete appearance of a mature French Gothic style on English soil. There is no single French source for Canterbury, however, for while the three-story elevation is similar to Sens and to the putative elevation of Suger's choir at St. Denis, the detailing and detached shafts are closer to Laon and other buildings in the northeast of France. In addition the continuation of the thick-wall tradition at Canterbury is evidence that English Gothic would develop as a style with formal concerns by no means identical to those across the Channel.

The last major campaign of reconstruction began at Canterbury about 1377 with the destruction of Lanfranc's nave and the laying out of a new one, which was essentially complete by around 1405. The design, usually attributed to Henry Yevele, is associated with the royal workshops in which Yevele was active. Opportunities for such full-scale reconstructions of great churches were rare by the late 14th century, and the Canterbury nave is thus one of the most important monuments of the Perpendicular style. Although constrained by the Romanesque plan, and continuing the three-story elevation used throughout the east arm, the nave embodies all the characteristics of Perpendicular style, with its overall patterns of paneled tracery used not only in windows but also for faces of the gallery. A clarity of design is visible also in the unbroken vertical bay divisions, so different from much earlier English Gothic, and in the lierne vaults of both aisles and main vessel.

The western transepts were also remodeled in Perpendicular style in the course of the 15th century, the north to serve as a setting for the actual site of Becket's martyrdom. The last major piece of work on the medieval cathedral was the construction of a new central tower in the latter years of the same century. Projects earlier in the century for the rebuilding of the tower had not been brought to completion, and the tower as built was the design of John Wastell, one of the most important architects of late-medieval England. Until the end of its medieval history Canterbury Cathedral continued to command the services of the best designers of the day.

Lawrence Hoey

Bibliography

Bony, Jean. "French Influences on the Origins of English Gothic Architecture." *JWCI* 12 (1949): 1–15; Draper, Peter. "William of Sens and the Original Design of the Choir Termination of Canterbury Cathedral 1175–1179." *Journal of the Society of Architectural Historians* 42/3 (1983): 238–48; Fernie, Eric. "St. Anselm's Crypt." *BAACT* 5 (1982): 27–38; Gem, Richard. "The Significance of the 11th-Century Rebuilding of Christ Church and St. Augustine's." *BAACT* 5 (1982): 1–19; Hearn, M.F. "Canterbury Cathedral and the Cult of Becket." *Art Bulletin* 76 (1994): 19–52; Hoey, Lawrence. "New Studies in Canterbury Cathedral." *Avista Forum* 9/1 (1995): 6–9; Kidson, Peter. "Gervase, Becket, and William of Sens." *Speculum* 68 (1993): 969–91; Kusaba, Yoshio. "Some Observations on the Early Flying Buttresses and Choir Triforium of Canterbury Cathedral." *Gesta* 28 (1989): 175–89; Tatton-Brown, Tim. *Great Cathedrals of Britain.* London: BBC Books, 1989, pp. 75–84; Willis, Robert. *The Architectural History of Canterbury Cathedral.* London: Longman, 1845. Repr. in Robert Willis, *Architectural History of Some English Cathedrals.* 1st ser. Chicheley: Minet, 1972; Woodman, Francis. *The Architectural History of Canterbury Cathedral.* London: Routledge & Kegan Paul, 1981.

See also Architecture and Architectural Sculpture, Gothic; Architecture and Architectural Sculpture, Romanesque; Becket; Canterbury, Ecclesiastical Province of; Lanfranc

Canterbury Picture Leaves

New York, Pierpont Morgan Library M.724 (fig. 36), 521, BL Add. 37472(1), and London, Victoria and Albert Museum 661, containing over 150 Old and New Testament scenes, running from the Childhood of Moses to Pentecost, on eight large sides, are now recognized as the prefatory cycle of the Eadwine Psalter (Cambridge, Trinity College R.17.1), produced at Canterbury in the late 1150s. The cycle was designed and most of it painted by the artist who, as principal illuminator, also executed most of the psalm illustrations and painted initials in the Eadwine Psalter itself. An initial leaf with Genesis scenes, now lost, has been posited on the basis of their inclusion in the related cycle prefacing Paris, BN lat. 8846, the closely related third Canterbury copy of the Utrecht Psalter made ca. 1200.

Although the context of the Leaves' creation is monastic, the style of the principal illuminator and his assistants is a later form of that initiated at St. Albans in the 1120s, which by mid-century appears to have been appropriated also by lay professional artists working at a number of English centers. The distinctive contribution of the Leaves' designer lies in the remarkable narrative effectiveness of the pages as entire units, as well as of the individual scenes, a result achieved by lively gestures, open scrolls, and the rhythmic repetition of compositions, motifs, and colors.

While Henderson argues for a textual rather than pictorial inspiration for the cycle, many features indicate the individual scenes' dependence on earlier visual models, as well as on extrabiblical texts. Theories of an underlying early Christian prototype, based on the derivation of the Leaves' twelve-square grid layout from that of the miniature page in the 6th-century St. Augustine's Gospels (Cambridge, Corpus Christi College 286), have given way to recognition of strong Ottonian and Byzantine components, with limited Anglo-Saxon and Carolingian contributions. Though this range of sources may have been largely assimilated by mid-12th century into a general English motif pool, it reflects the rich variety of sources available to English Romanesque artists, both lay and monastic.

Elizabeth Parker McLachlan

Bibliography

Gibson, Margaret, T.A. Heslop, and Richard W. Pfaff, eds. *The Eadwine Psalter: Text, Image, and Monastic Culture in Twelfth-Century Canterbury.* London: Modern Humanities Research Association, 1992 [includes most earlier bibliography]; Gutmann, Joseph. "Josephus' *Jewish Antiquities* in Twelfth-Century Art: *Renovatio* or *Creatio?*" *Zeitschrift für Kunstgeschichte* 48 (1985): 434–41; Heimann, Adelheid. "The Last Copy of the Utrecht Psalter." In *The Year 1200: A Symposium,* ed. François Avril. New York: Metropolitan Museum of Art, 1975, pp. 313–38; Henderson, George. "'Abraham Genuit Isaac': Transitions from the Old Testament to the New Testament in the Prefatory Illustrations of Some 12th-Century Psalters." *Gesta* 26 (1987): 127–39; Kauffmann, C. Michael. *Romanesque Manuscripts 1066–1190.* A Survey of Manuscripts Illuminated in the British Isles 3, ed. J.J.G. Alexander. London: Harvey Miller, 1975.

See also Eadwine and Canterbury/Paris Psalters; Iconography; Manuscript Illumination, Romanesque

Fig. 36. The Pierpont Morgan Library, New York. M.724v. Clockwise from upper left: David offered crown of Judah, David enters Jerusalem (?), Visitation, Birth of John, Naming of John, Nativity, Tree of Jesse (with Annunciation). Reproduced by permission of the Pierpont Morgan Library, New York.

Fig. 37. St. Paul shakes the viper from his hand, Canterbury Cathedral, St. Anselm's Chapel, northeast section of apse. Courtesy of L. Hoey.

Canterbury Wall Paintings

Canterbury Cathedral appears to have displayed one of the finest cycles of wall paintings in all of England, with individual groups of frescoes dating from the 12th to the 15th century. The Romanesque paintings are the best known of the corpus due to both their excellent quality and their fine state of preservation (the result of having been covered over from the late 12th to the 19th century).

The paintings in St. Gabriel's Chapel in the crypt of the cathedral are considered the earliest of the surviving frescoes and are generally dated ca. 1155. The apse of the chapel is dominated by a monumental Christ in Majesty seated within a mandorla and flanked by four flying angels. On the south wall are scenes from the Infancy of Christ: Annunciation, Visitation, Adoration of the Magi (now lost). On the north wall are scenes from the life of St. John the Baptist: the Annunciation to Zacharias and the Naming of John the Baptist. At a slightly later date (1180s?) the vision of St. John the Evangelist with the personifications of the seven churches of Asia was added to the vaults and soffits of the outer arch. The cycle is painted in a byzantinizing style characterized by fully modeled faces, formalized expressions and gestures, damp-fold draperies, and an overall symmetry. The combination of Infancy and apocalyptic themes unites this group with the wall paintings at Hardham and other Sussex churches.

The fire of 1174 destroyed all but one of the 12th-century paintings in St. Anselm's Choir (directly above St. Gabriel's Chapel). The surviving panel, located high up in the northwest corner of the apse in St. Anselm's Chapel, shows St. Paul shaking the viper from his hand (fig. 37). The chapel was origi-

nally dedicated to SS. Peter and Paul, and this scene may originally have been balanced by an image of St. Peter on the other side of the apse. The monumental figure of St. Paul fills the whole of the panel and stands out against the brilliant blue background. The damp-fold draperies reveal a figure of massive volume, and the head is fully modeled in the byzantinizing style of the day. Both figure style and the brilliant colors of the panel have strong affinities with the style of Master Hugo and the Bury Bible (Cambridge, Corpus Christi College 2). The panel is thought to date ca. 1163, and may have been commissioned by Thomas Becket to commemorate the translation of Anselm's relics to the chapel in April of that year. It was covered over by a buttress inserted during the 13th-century rebuilding of the choir.

A third cycle of 12th-century paintings was discovered in the Infirmary Chapel in the early 20th century. The original paintings have been lost through rapid deterioration and lack of conservation, but they were recorded in drawings made by W.D. Caröe in 1911. They appear to have been similar in style to the St. Gabriel's Chapel paintings and to have consisted primarily of figural ornament in three registers.

During the 13th, 14th, and 15th centuries further wall paintings, largely figures of the saints, architectural details, or painted monuments, were added to various parts of the cathedral. Most survive as mere fragments or have vanished completely (e.g., the 13th-century cycle in the choir and Trinity Chapel). Two notable exceptions are the 14th-century painting in the chapter house, carefully restored in the late 19th century, and the late-15th-century legend of St. Eustache painted in oil in the north choir aisle.

Catherine E. Karkov

Bibliography

Caröe, W. "Wall Paintings in the Infirmary Chapel." *Archaeologia* 63 (1911–12): 51–56; Caviness, Madeline. "A Lost Cycle of Canterbury Paintings of 1220." *AntJ* 54 (1974): 66–74; Dodwell, C.R. *The Pictorial Arts of the West 800–1200.* New Haven: Yale University Press, 1993; Kahn, Deborah. "The Structural Evidence for the Dating of the St. Gabriel Chapel Wall-Paintings at Christ Church Cathedral, Canterbury." *Burlington Magazine* 126 (1984): 225–29; Nilgen, Ursula. "Thomas Becket as Patron of Arts." *Art History* 3 (1980): 357–74; Tristram, E.W. *The Paintings of Canterbury Cathedral.* Canterbury: Friends of Canterbury Cathedral, 1935; Woodman, Francis. *The Architectural History of Canterbury Cathedral.* London: Routledge & Kegan Paul, 1981.

See also Hardham Wall Paintings; Manuscript Illumination, Romanesque; Wall Painting, Romanesque

Cantilena

Medieval Latin term for song, generally applied throughout the Middle Ages to musical works composed or improvised, monophonic or polyphonic. In most cases it applies to a setting of a text, sacred or secular, but the term was also occasionally used to refer in a general way to instrumental music. It appears in medieval music-theory treatises with a variety of meanings and in a variety of contexts. For example, Johannes de Grocheio, writing in Paris in the late 13th century, uses "cantilena" as a kind of synonym for music in his definition of rondeau (rondellus): "a particular kind of *cantilena* is called rounded or a *rotundellus* by many, because it reflects back upon itself in the manner of a circle and it begins and is ended the same way." In another discussion of the same genre from the early 14th century "cantilena" seems to function as a kind of catchall term to describe chansons that appear not to belong within the confines of another medieval genre. Jacques de Liège, in book 7 of his *Speculum musice,* states that "this manner of singing (i.e., *discantus simpliciter prolatus*) has its place in ecclesiastical discants and organa measured in all their parts, in conducti, in motets, in *fugis,* in *cantilenis* or *rondellis.*" The term "cantilena" was applied to songs composed upon a *cantus firmus* as well as to free compositions. The contexts described for the performance of these songs in the theoretical literature are both secular and ecclesiastical.

The generic character of this term no doubt accounts for its attractiveness to modern music scholars, who often find themselves without adequate medieval terminology to describe the musical genres they have identified. The modern application of the label "cantilena" to specific medieval compositions began with Heinrich Besseler in 1951, when he used the term *Kantilenensatz* to describe the musical style in some of the polyphonic songs of Guillaume Dufay. This use has been expanded and clarified recently by Alejandro Planchart.

In 1963 Ernest Sanders settled upon "cantilena," from among a number of medieval Latin terms for song, to refer to some English 14th-century polyphonic compositions, specifically those works notated in two- or three-part score format with sacred or liturgical texts that were freely composed, that is, not based upon a *cantus prius factus.* This original definition has been refined in his subsequent publications to apply primarily to works with a rhymed poetic text of moderate length, usually in honor of the Virgin Mary (1980, 1986). Sanders describes this music as "treble dominated," with passages of significant length that employ parallel, complete triads configured in first inversion; that is, the chords are presented one after another with the third of the chord as the lowest sounding pitch. While there are brief examples of this type of triadic parallelism in 14th-century English works based upon a plainsong, this device was employed systematically and extensively in English polyphonic free settings and is a hallmark of their style.

Sanders's use of "cantilena" to identify these works has not met with complete acceptance. Alejandro Planchart feels that Sanders's definition is too restricted and that the term should be used to describe a number of songlike, Latin-texted polyphonic compositions, such as those by Dufay mentioned above. William Summers has noted that Sanders's application of this term to English polyphony does not rest on medieval authority. He also has shown that other medieval polyphonic repertoires that have been described as treble-dominated, such as the Petronian motet, the Ars Nova motet, or English compositions from the 14th century composed in the so-called "chanson style," are works where the composer establishes a well-defined hieratic relationship among the various parts, clearly differentiating the role of each voice in the musical fabric by one or more means, such as rhythmic activity, range, and presence or absence of text or melodic design. In English works designated as "cantilena" by Sanders all parts participate equally in the presentation of the text, move at approximately the same pace rhythmically, have comparable melodic design and ranges, and also participate fully in the continuous projection of the harmony through time. While the uppermost-sounding voice might well command some degree of attention because of its pitch level, the other voices do not play an overtly secondary role either melodically, rhythmically, or harmonically, the way supporting voices do in other demonstrably treble-dominated genres. It is perhaps more appropriate to describe this music as equal-voiced polyphonic song rather than as treble-dominated.

Recent research by Peter Lefferts has refined the definition of this English genre. The central core settings that make up this repertoire are those in honor of the Virgin with a double-versicle poetic text. The conditions for their use as substitute settings for existing liturgical categories, such as Sequence and Offertory, or as trope texts for the Ordinary and Proper of the mass, are explored and also compared with newly composed monophonic compositions that appear to have been used as substitutes for the same liturgical categories.

No English medieval commentator discussed or named this important genre. One reason for the silence of the theorists may be the fact that the genre was relatively new in the 14th century. The extremely fluid liturgical use of the cantilena, which varied from major rite to major rite and from institution to institution, may have been another cause for this silence. Today the term continues to identify this body of English compositions, which are a unique English contribution to medieval music. The application of the term "cantilena" should be extended to those monophonic compositions that closely parallel the polyphonic settings in subject matter, textual type, and liturgical function. Both groups might more accurately be designated as English Marian polyphonic or monophonic cantilenas, in recognition of the fact that their composition was strictly confined to England and that only a few examples of this genre carry texts on a topic other than the Virgin Mary. This would prevent the confusion that arises when "cantilena" is used to refer to polyphonic works from other regional Latin song traditions and also permit the appropriate cross-referencing between the monophonic and polyphonic examples in this genre.

William J. Summers

Bibliography

Harrison, Frank Ll., Ernest H. Sanders, and Peter M. Lefferts, eds. *English Music for Mass and Offices (II) and Music for Other Ceremonies.* Polyphonic Music of the Fourteenth Century 17. Paris: L'Oiseau-Lyre, 1986; Lefferts, Peter M. "Cantilena and Antiphon: Music for Marian Services in Late Medieval England." In *Studies in Medieval Music: Festschrift for Ernest H. Sanders,* ed. Peter M. Lefferts and Brian Seirup. *Current Musicology* 45–47 (1990): 247–82; Planchart, Alejandro E. "What's in a Name? Reflections on Some Works of Guillaume Du Fay." *Early Music* 16 (1988): 165–75; Sanders, Ernest H. "Cantilena." *NGD* 3:729–31; Sanders, Ernest H. "Cantilena and Discant in 14th-Century England." *Musica Disciplina* 19 (1965):7–52; Summers, William J. "The Effect of Monasticism on Fourteenth-Century English Music." *La musique et le rite sacré et profane: actes du XIIIe Congrès de la Société Internationale de Musicologie.* 2 vols. Strasbourg: Association des Publications prés les Universités de Strasbourg, 1986, 2:105–42; Summers, William J. "English Fourteenth-Century Polyphonic Music: An Inventory of the Extant Manuscript Sources." *Journal of Musicology* 8 (1990): 173–226; Summers, William J. "Fourteenth-Century English Music: A Review of Three Recent Publications." *Journal of Musicology* 8 (1990): 118–42.

See also Conductus; Hymns; Lady Mass; Salve Service; Sequence

Capgrave, John (1393–1464)

Augustinian friar of Lynn, theologian, chronicler, and biographer. One of the most learned men of his day, he wrote a number of theological commentaries in Latin, of which those on Genesis, Exodus, and Acts have survived. Capgrave is perhaps best known for his *Abbreviation of Chronicles,* a universal chronicle in English beginning with Adam and ending in 1417 and drawing much of its material from Martin of Troppau and Thomas Walsingham. He also wrote a biography of *Illustrious Henrys* in Latin and, in English, verse lives of St. Norbert and St. Katherine of Alexandria and prose lives of St. Augustine and St. Gilbert. He visited Rome in 1450 and a year later wrote a guidebook, *The Solace of Pilgrims.*

Capgrave's works constitute the classic case of autograph/holograph materials (manuscripts containing the author's handwriting) in ME and facilitate the study of 1) the language of one man writing at one time in one place and 2) how an author sought and obtained patronage. Capgrave's patrons included heads of religious houses, local dignitaries, Bishop William Gray of Ely, Humphrey duke of Gloucester, and kings Henry VI and Edward IV.

Peter J. Lucas

Bibliography

PRIMARY

Lucas, Peter J., ed. *John Capgrave's Abbreuiacion of Cronicles.* EETS o.s. 285. Oxford: Oxford University Press, 1983 [extensive bibliography, pp. xcix–cvii]; Smetana, Cyril L., ed. *The Life of St. Norbert by John Capgrave, O.E.S.A. (1393–1464).* Toronto: Pontifical Institute, 1977.

SECONDARY

New *CBEL* 1:663–65; Lucas, Peter J. "The Growth and Development of English Literary Patronage in the Later Middle Ages and Early Renaissance." *The Library,* 6th ser. 4 (1982): 219–48.

See also Hagiography; Patronage, Literary; Textual Criticism

Caput Mass

One of the most popular masses of the 15th century, surviving complete or in part in seven known English and continental sources, the *Missa Caput* is now thought to be the work of an unnamed English composer writing in the later 1430s or early 1440s. It is a cyclic mass whose five movements are unified both by a motto beginning and by the use of the same melody as structural *cantus firmus* in the tenor voice. Its name is taken from that *cantus firmus,* which is derived from a lengthy melisma on the word "caput" at the end of the responsory *Venit ad Petrum,* a plainsong sung at the Mandatum Ceremony on Holy Thursday in the medieval English Sarum rite. In each movement this melody is presented in its entirety twice, first in ternary mensuration and then in binary mensuration. Long believed to be a quintessential work by the leading continental composer of the era, Guillaume Dufay (ca. 1397–1474), the *Missa Caput* is now believed to be the "lost English Caput" hypothesized by Bukofzer. The attribution to Dufay, firmly set aside in the late 1960s and early 1970s, is still encountered in some more recent works of scholarship.

The historical significance of this masterwork is threefold. First, source evidence suggests that the *Missa Caput* took pride of place among a major group of anonymous English masses that circulated together on the Continent in the later 1440s and 1450s, including *Salve sancta parens, Quem malignus spiritus, Fuit homo,* and perhaps also *Veterem hominem.* Second, in a chain of direct emulation (and perhaps homage), the English Caput was drawn on as a model for Caput masses by two of the leading continental composers of the second half of the 15th century, Johannes Ockeghem (ca. 1410–1497) and Jacob Obrecht (ca. 1450–1505). Finally, the *Missa Caput* has a structural twin in another anonymous English mass cycle, the *Missa Veterem hominem.* There are other English mass twins as well, perhaps taking their point of departure from the *Caput / Veterem* pair, and it is believed this English practice was the stimulus for similar pairings by continental mass composers after 1450.

Peter M. Lefferts

Bibliography

PRIMARY

Planchart, Alejandro E., ed. *Missae Caput.* Collegium Musicum 5. New Haven: Yale University Department of Music, 1964.

SECONDARY

Bent, Margaret. "Trent 93 and Trent 90: Johannes Wiser at Work." In *I musicali codici trentini,* ed. Nino Pirrotta and Danilo Curti. Trent: Museo Provinciale d'Arte, 1986, pp. 84–101; Bukofzer, Manfred. "*Caput*: A Liturgico-Musical Study." In *Studies in Medieval and Renaissance Music.* New York: Norton, 1950, pp. 217–310; Planchart, Alejandro E. "Fifteenth-Century Masses: Notes on Performance and Chronology." *Studi Musicali* 10 (1981): 3–29; Strohm, Reinhard. "Quellenkritische Untersuchungen an der Missa *Caput.*" In *Quellenstudien zur Musik der Renaissance, 2: Datierung und Filiation von Musikhandschriften der Josquin-Zeit,* ed. Ludwig Finscher. Wolfenbüttler Forschungen 26. Wiesbaden: Harrassowitz, 1983, pp. 153–76; Wegman, Rob C. "An Anonymous Twin of Johannes Ockeghem's *Missa Quinti Toni* in San Pietro B80." *Tijdschrift der Vereeniging voor Nederlandsche Muziekgeschiedenis* 37 (1987): 25–48.

See also Mass, Polyphonic Music for

Carol

Though the word "carol" has a long and varied history, it is used in Middle English studies particularly as a specific term for a distinct poetic and musical form cultivated mainly during the 15th century. The complete identifiable poetic repertoire with English texts is published in Greene and amounts to almost 500 poems; a few more were excluded from that volume because of their exclusively Latin texts, though they are plainly carols of English origin and appear together with the others in the sources. Nearly all the known pre-1485 music (over 130 pieces) is published in Stevens in *Musica Britannica,* vol. 4 (1952), 2d ed., 1958. Later examples are presented alongside other material by Stevens in *Musica Britannica,* vols. 18 (1962) and 36 (1975); they are far less distinct from other music or poetry of the time and show the form losing its individuality.

Greene defined the carol as a poem "intended, or at least suitable for singing, made up of uniform stanzas and provided with a burden that begins and ends the piece and is to be repeated after each stanza." It is therefore related to the continental virelai/villancico traditions, though the carol has several distinct characteristics of its own. The refrain or burden is usually metrically distinct from the verse, which in its turn never has the repeated music for the *couplets* of the virelai and tends to lack the *tierce/vuelta* of the continental forms. Latin words, lines, or slogans are common in the poetry. The text never treats of courtly-love themes but is devotional or instructional in intent, quite often with a seasonal message for Christmas or one of the other church feasts. Most importantly there is in both text and music of most carols a popular feel, though they seem popular by destination rather than by origin and it is tempting to associate the genre with the efforts of the Franciscans. Yet a glance through the musical repertoire shows many and varied references to the virelai/villancico traditions of which it is an offshoot.

Four musical sources offer the clearest definition of the genre: the Trinity College *rotulus,* or roll (Cambridge, Trinity College O.3.58; ca. 1430), with thirteen carols in a relatively simple homophonic style; the Selden Manuscript (Bodl. Arch. Selden B.26; ca. 1440), in which some 30 carols are mixed in among liturgical material, mainly processional; the Egerton Manuscript (BL Egerton 3307; ca. 1445), with 32 carols assembled in a distinct section; and the Ritson Manuscript (BL Add. 5665; ca. 1460), containing a discrete collection of over 40 carols in a more elaborate style. The varied provenance of these sources indicates a wide dispersal of the music throughout England, and the relatively few duplications among them suggest that a newly discovered source would contain much new music. A few more fragmentary musical sources survive, and there are at least two possible English carols in continental manuscripts of the time. But the carol seems to have had virtually no international career, even though all other genres of English music in these years appear widely in the continental sources and seem to have been valued highly.

Stevens presents the music by source and in the chronological order sketched above, making it surprisingly easy to see the carol's musical and formal evolution. Various features are common to the majority of the carol music. First is the emphasis on two-voice writing, particularly for the verses, at a time when most polyphony was in three voices. Second is a tendency for the lower of those voices (the "Tenor") to carry the main melodic line, a feature found otherwise only in the rather different German song repertoire of those years. Third is the purely scribal device in the sources of laying out the music not in separate voices but in quasi-score, with the text under the bottom voice only; this is largely a function of the musical style, with all voices moving at approximately the same rate, whereas for most other music of the 15th century such a layout would result in considerable waste of space. Fourth, related to these features as well as to the likely didactic function of the carol, is a preference for clear phrases, balanced and parallel, showing an awareness of the expressive power of the dance element in sophisticated music at a time when most other polyphony favored the limpid line that avoided easy parallel structures.

On the other hand there is an enormous variety of musical style and formal devices in the music—a variety that modifies the apparent simplicity of Greene's formal definition for the poetry. It is not just that the music becomes more elaborate with the passing of the years, moving away from simple patterns to include irregularities of phrase length and bar length that are unusual for their time and deeply expressive. If the basic scheme is apparently of a three-voice burden or chorus alternating with a two-voice verse, it remains true that relatively few musical settings precisely follow that scheme. Often there are two burdens, one in two and the other in three voices, using essentially the same material. Often little snatches of three-voice music interrupt the verses, sometimes interpolating material from the burden, sometimes giving elaborated repeats of phrases from the verse.

The music is anonymous apart from the name "Childe" on *Iblessid be that lord* (Selden, fol. 28v) and "qd J.D." [John(?) Dunstable] tantalizingly at the end of the added text for *I pray you all* (Selden, fol. 5). The names "Smert" and "Trouluffe" found on many of the carols in the Ritson Manuscript can be identified with two West Country priests but do not look like ascriptions as such. All the two-voice music in one of the three known settings of *Pray for us thow prince of pes* (Stevens no. 106) appears within a Credo setting ascribed (unconvincingly) to the Burgundian court composer Binchois in a manuscript from Trent; but, pending a necessary investigation of the complicated matter of Binchois's relationship with English music, it is unlikely that he had any hand in carol composition.

There are substantial collections of carol poetry by John Audelay (ca. 1427) and James Ryman (1490s), both in manuscripts devoted to their own work. But the main body of the poetic repertoire is also anonymous and appears primarily in three scruffy little paper pocket books from the mid-15th century, all about 6 by 4 ½ inches in size: Bodl. Eng. poet. e.1 (ed. Thomas Wright, 1848); BL Sloane 2593 (ed. Thomas Wright, 1856); and Cambridge, St. John's College S.54 (ed. M.R. James and G.C. Macaulay in *The Modern Language Review* 8 [1913]: 68–87). All include a small proportion of material that is not in carol form though otherwise identical with the repertoire in its themes, tone, and language, so they cast further doubt on simple definitions of the repertoire. Any future attempt to refine our understanding of the carol must begin with these alongside the musical sources.

It is hard to believe that the genre can have existed before ca. 1415, the presumed date of the famous Agincourt Carol. Although Greene's edition uses many earlier sources, virtually all of them contain either strophic poems only later adapted as carols or the occasional piece better explained in terms of other genres, such as the virelai or the versus. There is strong source evidence for a view that sees the Trinity College *rotulus* as containing the earliest clear evidence of the carol and sees the genre—quite exceptionally—as having been "invented" at about that time.

David Fallows

Bibliography

Greene, Richard L. *The Early English Carols.* 2d ed. Oxford: Clarendon, 1977; Stevens, John, ed. *Mediaeval Carols. Musica Britannica* 4. 2d ed. London: Stainer & Bell, 1958; Stevens, John. "Carol (1–2)." *NGD* 3: 802–11.

See also Agincourt Carol; Karole; Songs

Cartularies

Registers in which are entered copies of property deeds, principally charters—hence the name "c(h)artulary." They were made, usually in the form of books, to serve as accessible compendia so landowners could refer to them without having to search among the original archives, often kept in secure conditions. Over 1,100 cartularies survive for English medieval ecclesiastical institutions, and about 180 for secular families.

Because they were created at different times to record archive material for different estates, there is considerable variation of format. Commonly charters are transcribed in full (although witness lists and routine clauses may be omitted or truncated) and arranged topographically, so charters for one particular property are grouped together. In the case of religious houses the charters relating to the foundation are often placed at the beginning of the cartulary, and there may also be special sections of papal, royal, and episcopal confirmations.

The earliest surviving cartularies date from the 11th century, and the majority are from the 13th and 14th centuries, though frequently additions were made after the original compilations had been completed. The content list of cartularies, where reference numbers to charters were given, often doubled as finding lists to the archives themselves.

Diana E. Greenway

Bibliography

Davis, Godfrey R.C. *Medieval Cartularies of Great Britain: A Short Catalogue.* London: Longmans, Green, 1958; Foulds, Trevor. "Medieval Cartularies." *Archives* 18 (1987): 3–35; Sayers, Jane E. "The Medieval Care and Custody of the Archbishop of Canterbury's Archives." *BIHR* 39 (1966): 95–107; Walker, David. "The Organization of Material in Medieval Cartularies." In *The Study of Medieval Records: Essays in Honour of Kathleen Major,* ed. D.A. Bullough and R.L. Storey. Oxford: Clarendon, 1971, pp. 132–50.

See also Charters

Castles and Fortification

The castle is a fortified residence combining administrative and judicial functions but with its military considerations as paramount. The concept goes beyond just the defended residence, which has existed for much of history. The medieval castle speaks of political power and control of land. As part of the feudal system of land tenure through military service, evolving from the disintegration of Carolingian Europe, it was a symbol and a physical representation of the fief, as well as of the social, economic, and military position of its holder.

While there is now some evidence for defended residences of Anglo-Saxon thegns in the 10th and 11th centuries, as well as fortified towns (burhs), it was 1066 that saw the introduction of the castle into England. The exception that proves the rule is a small group of documented castles in Herefordshire and one in Essex erected by Norman companions of Edward the Confessor before the Conquest. In Normandy the castle was a well-established feature of life by 1066 and was, together with the heavily armored knight, the means whereby the Norman Conquest was achieved and the way a foreign aristocracy and system of land ownership replaced that of the Anglo-Saxons.

Archaeological excavation in the last quarter-century has greatly advanced knowledge of castles. It is now unwise to take castles at the face value of their surviving structures. Most early castles, for speed and cheapness, were built of timber and earthwork, often rebuilt in stone. Earthworks were fronted or crowned with walls of timber, and towers and internal buildings were also in timber. Excavations at Hen Domen, Powys (Wales), have shown that a castle might be in use for more than 100 years without any of its elements being replaced in stone. The timber tower on the castle mound, or motte, at the royal castle at York evidently stood until 1228, when it was replaced by the masonry of Clifford's Tower in 1245.

Not all the earliest castles were timber. There were stone buildings of a palatial nature in London and East Anglia. Both the White Tower (London) and Colchester, Essex, had first-floor halls (i.e., a floor above ground level) on a grand scale and similar to the earliest known castles in northern France, Doue-le-Fontaine and Langeais. At Castle Acre, Norfolk, a masonry "country house" with a minimum of defensive enclosure was built shortly after 1066 and only later converted into a castle proper, defended by massive earthworks and enclosing walls. Elsewhere there were strong stone gatehouses of an early date, as at Exeter in Devon, Ludlow in Shropshire, and Richmond in North Yorkshire.

The two basic principles of medieval fortification were the enclosure and the tower. In the earliest English castles the most common form was the motte (a mound on a hillock) surmounted by a tower, together with an enclosure, or bailey, containing the hall and other residential and service buildings. A frequent variant was an enclosure (ringwork) without a motte but with a tower-gatehouse instead. In some instances, as at Castle Neroche in Somerset, a motte was a later addition to a ringwork.

An essential and distinguishing feature of the Anglo-Norman castle was the tower, whether on the motte or over the gate. The contemporary name for such a tower was "donjon" (Lat. dominium, "lordship"). Sometimes it is clear that the tower was constructed first and the motte thrown up around it: Abinger in Surrey and South Mimms in Hertfordshire are examples. At other times it seems to have been set upon the surface of the mound, as at Okehampton in Devon or Longtown in Herefordshire. An alternative to a tower was the shell keep; a wall around the top of the motte with buildings against its internal face, such as Launceston in Cornwall,

Totnes in Devon, and Carisbrooke, Isle of Wight.

In major castles there was a move toward concentrating the chief residential elements into a defensible tower, a development of the earlier hall tower: Norwich in Norfolk, Kenilworth in Warwickshire, and Rochester and Dover, Kent. In England these towers are termed "keeps" and could serve as defenses "of last resort" (as at the siege of Rochester Castle, 1215). Elsewhere smaller "keeps" might contain habitable rooms, though the chief buildings—the hall and chamber and guest accommodation—were usually elsewhere.

The development of castle defenses was marked by an increasingly scientific arrangement of mural towers for flanking purposes. These were originally square with a shift to circular and polygonal forms from the end of the 12th century. Later there was increasing emphasis on vertical defense. The weakest point in the defensive circuit was always the entrance, and gateways developed into well-flanked entrances between a pair of close-set towers. In the 13th and 14th centuries there was a tendency to strengthen entrances by adding barbicans (outer defenses). In the more important and chiefly royal castles concentric defenses evolved, as at the Tower of London and Dover. Elsewhere water defenses might be developed, as at Kenilworth. The apogee of the English castle in its military and defensive form, perfected in north Wales, is seen in the castles erected on the orders of Edward I and largely to the design of the Savoyard engineer Master James of St. George: Conway, Caernarvon, Harlech, and Beaumaris.

Castles dominated the medieval landscape, and they were of more than just local significance. William, as duke of Normandy, had instituted controls over the castle building of his vassals, and "licenses to crenellate" had to be obtained, in theory if not always in practice, from the crown throughout the Middle Ages. Although castles were essentially the fortified residence of an individual lord, they could become part of a royal and later national defensive policy for the coasts, harbors, and border areas, particularly with Scotland. The castle was also the means by which the baronage could demonstrate their position in society. As the recognized center of lordship the castle was a display of status and prestige; "castellated" houses were the symbol of social position long after they had lost their military function, even to the present century.

During the 14th and 15th centuries the military need for castles was much reduced. Lawlessness and aristocratic thuggery abounded, but England was not a theater of war, as were parts of France, except on the Borders, where the need for domestic protection extended a good way down the social scale. There was a move toward defensible houses that might have the title of castle, like Stokeway, Shropshire, or Nunney, Somerset, but where ostentation and domestic comfort had a far greater place than before. There was a spread of fortified manor houses, but these had ceased to be true castles. By the end of the 15th century Ralph, Lord Cromwell, would build himself a defensible tower-house at Tattershall, Lincolnshire, and at the same time the unfortified South Wingfield Manor in Derbyshire. Defensive considerations appeared to be optional.

There were other forms of fortification, involving towns.

The Normans almost invariably planted a castle inside existing *burhs.* At the same time towns were created after the Conquest, usually for economic reasons. Their defenses were often linked with those of the associated castle. The incentive to fortify towns with stone walls and towers usually came from the merchant community, as at Southampton or Norwich. When gunpowder was introduced in the 14th and 15th centuries, it is more often in town defenses, rather than in castles, that the technical improvements in military engineering are to be found.

Andrew D. Saunders

Bibliography

Barker, Philip, and Robert Higham. *Hen Domen Montgomery: A Timber Castle on the English-Welsh Border.* Vol. 1. London: Royal Archaeological Institute, 1982; Brown, R. Allen, H.M. Colvin, and A.J. Taylor, eds. *The History of the King's Works.* Vols. 1–2: *The Middle Ages.* London: HMSO, 1963; Brown, R. Allen. *English Castles.* London: Batsford, 1976; Coad, J.G., and A.D.F. Streeten. "Excavations at Castle Acre Castle, Norfolk, 1972–77: Country House and Castle of the Norman Earls of Surrey." *ArchJ* 139 (1982): 138–301; Saunders, Andrew D., intro. *Five Castle Excavations: Reports on the Institute's Research Project into the Origins of the Castle in England.* London: Royal Archaeological Institute, 1978; Saunders, Andrew D. *Fortress Britain: Artillery Fortification in the British Isles and Ireland.* Liphook: Beaufort, 1989; Turner, Hilary L. *Town Defenses in England and Wales.* London: Baker, 1970.

See also Arms and Armor; Boroughs; Burghal Hidage; Feudalism

Caxton, William (1415/24–1491/92)

Printer, publisher, translator, and merchant. Caxton was born in Kent, though probably not at Strood, which has been suggested as his birthplace. After (or perhaps toward the end of) his apprenticeship as a mercer Caxton engaged in trade between England and the Low Countries, where he may have moved in the 1440s. Eventually he was appointed Governor of the English Nation at Bruges, a major commercial town. As part of his official functions he took part in foreign trade negotiations for the English government. In 1471, presumably after resigning his office, Caxton traveled to Cologne. In the course of a stay of some eighteen months he learned the technique of printing, possibly participating in the production of an edition of Bartholomaeus Anglicus's *De proprietatibus rerum.* After returning to Bruges Caxton established a press and produced the first printed English book, *The Recuyell of the Historyes of Troye,* his own translation from the French, begun in 1469 and encouraged by Margaret, duchess of Burgundy.

In 1476 Caxton returned to England and set up his business in the precincts of Westminster Abbey (i.e., in premises belonging to and near the abbey). The first major work printed there was probably his first edition of Chaucer's *Canterbury Tales.* In the next fifteen years he published some 100 or more works. Caxton died in late 1491 or early 1492, bequeathing his business to his long-time assistant, Wynkyn de Worde.

Caxton's choice of texts to print was both a response to and an influence in shaping fashionable demand and taste. Besides two editions of the *Canterbury Tales,* one of *Troilus,* and other collections of Chaucerian verse he published Gower's *Confessio Amantis,* several works by Lydgate, and Burgh's *Cato.* In 1485 he printed Malory's *Morte Darthur,* and this edition and its reprints remained the sole witness to the *Morte* until the Winchester Manuscript was discovered in 1934. Influenced by Burgundian or French taste, he translated and published prose works in the courtly mode, including *Jason, Godefroy of Boulogne, Aesop, The Order of Chivalry, Charles the Great, Blanchardin and Eglantine,* and *Eneydos.*

Moral and religious works published by Caxton include Chaucer's *Boethius,* Mirk's *Festial,* and *The Mirror of the Blessed Life of Christ,* as well as translations by Earl Rivers *(The Cordial, The Dicts and Sayings of the Philosophers,* and *Moral Proverbs)* and by Caxton himself, such as *The Mirror of the World, The Golden Legend, The Book of the Knight of the Tower,* and *The Art of Dying.*

Caxton produced editions of the two most popular historical works of his day, Trevisa's translation of Higden's *Polychronicon* and the prose *Brut* (under the title *Chronicles of England*), both of which he brought up to date with material compiled by himself. He also published a number of practical works: *The Governal of Health,* a French-English vocabulary, statutes, devotional works, and a few Latin works on rhetoric that may have been used as university textbooks.

Of considerable importance are the prologues and epilogues to many of Caxton's publications, in which he comments on his choice and treatment of texts and on matters of style, language, and the function of literature. His own prose style is prolix and shows a predilection for elevated foreign words. As an editor he sometimes updated old-fashioned vocabulary, as in the *Polychronicon,* or revised sections of the text, as in book 5 of the *Morte Darthur* (though some scholars suggest the revisions are by Malory himself).

Caxton's translations and other publications are representative of late-medieval practices and tastes; his primary importance lies in his highly successful introduction of the revolutionary technique of printing to England.

Lister M. Matheson

Bibliography

PRIMARY

Blake, N.F. *Caxton's Own Prose.* London: Deutsch, 1973 [for a full listing of other editions through the early 1980s, see Blake's bibliography (below), pp. 15–61].

SECONDARY

New *CBEL* 1:667–74; *Manual* 3:771–807, 924–51; Blake, N.F. *Caxton and His World.* London: Deutsch, 1969; Blake, N.F. "William Caxton." In *Middle English Prose: A Critical Guide to Major Authors and Genres,* ed. A.S.G. Edwards. New Brunswick: Rutgers University Press,

1984, pp. 389–412; Blake, N.F. *William Caxton: A Bibliographical Guide.* New York: Garland, 1985; Painter, George D. *William Caxton: A Quincentenary Biography of England's First Printer.* London: Chatto & Windus, 1976.

See also Ars moriendi; Books; *Brut,* Prose; Court Culture; Literacy; Malory; Printing; Prose, ME; Translation

Cemeteries and Cemetery Archaeology

The Anglo-Saxons practiced both inhumation and cremation, many burials being accompanied by grave goods. Some of the early-5th-century urns in which incinerated bodies and objects were placed are similar to those found in the Elbe-Weser area of Germany and show where some of the migrant peoples originated. East Anglia has several cemeteries that originally must have contained more than 1,000 urns, but in the rest of England cemeteries are smaller and inhumations commoner. Sixth-century cemeteries tend to have fewer graves and fewer objects than earlier ones, but there are also more sites known. In the 7th century the custom of burying objects with the dead waned and cremation all but ceased. Some "final phase" cemeteries have graves with no more than a knife and a buckle, if that. There are also several isolated 7th-century burials in barrows—some prehistoric, some newly constructed—with richly ornamented objects and traces of elaborate ceremonial practices.

Archaeologists seek a range of information from cemeteries. Objects are informative about the wealth and contacts of the peoples who buried them. Some objects came from the Near East and Egypt, such as copper-alloy vessels usually found in what are clearly well-furnished graves. These things suggest a society in which a few had access to resources, marking them as being of high status. This trend increased during the 6th century and culminated in the 7th century with such burials as Taplow and Sutton Hoo, with objects of gold and silver, drinking vessels, textiles, musical instruments, and weapons; swords seem to have been especially prestigious. Women were more often buried with costume jewelry, beads, and such household items as keys.

Such data help us analyze the different attitudes to the sexes and their roles. While successful men seem to have been viewed as warriors rather than workers, women were expected to run the home. Occasionally skeletons are found in contorted positions; explanations of ritual slaughter or live burial are proposed but difficult to substantiate. Visualized as an entity, a cemetery suggests a relatively orderly society, the regular arrangement of the burials indicating regulation of the graveyard and careful laying-out of the bodies suggesting people with time to make seemly provision for their dead.

The human bones from cemeteries indicate an adequately nourished population, though an occasional case of rickets shows vitamin D deficiency. Average heights for women ran from 5 feet 1 inch to 5 feet 5 inches, for men another two or three inches, a range similar to European populations in the 19th century. Infant mortality was high, though difficult to estimate precisely. Those who survived childhood might expect to live until their 30s, although many young women died in childbirth and young men succumbed to accidents. A fair proportion of those who reached their mid-20s would live into their 40s and 50s. These figures are what might be expected from a society primarily concerned with agriculture and not subject to excessive food shortages or violence.

David A. Hinton

Bibliography

Rahtz, Philip, Tania Dickinson, and L. Watts, eds. *Anglo-Saxon Cemeteries, 1979.* BAR Brit. Ser. 82. Oxford: BAR, 1980; Richards, J.D. *The Significance of Form and Decoration of Anglo-Saxon Cremation Urns.* BAR Brit. Ser. 166. Oxford: BAR, 1987.

See also Archaeology; Sutton Hoo

Chancellor and Chancery

The origins of the medieval chancery are found in the scriptorium, or writing department, of the king's chapel in the Anglo-Saxon royal household. Because the king's chaplains were literate, they naturally undertook his secretarial duties, and by 1066 England had a mature secretariat that issued documents under the king's great seal and also had custody of records. It was already a chancery in all but name. Likewise the official who kept the great seal was the direct linear predecessor of the post-Conquest chancellor, although not so called. As Normandy had nothing comparable, the Conqueror took over the scriptorium and its officials. The only change he introduced was to replace OE with Latin as the language of royal writs. The title "chancellor" was first certainly applied to the head of the department early in his reign.

As the powers and range of the central government increased in the 12th century, particularly under Henry II, so the work of the chancery expanded, although it remained part of the royal household and traveled with the king. Only in the 13th century did it slowly begin to break away and become a separate institution. There were two main reasons for this development. It needed a permanent base for its ever-growing archive, which expanded rapidly after 1199, when Hubert Walter instituted the practice of keeping enrolled copies of all main documents being issued. In addition the chancery was becoming larger and its operations therefore more formal; for much of his day-to-day business the king needed an institution more flexible and closer to him, and he used first the wardrobe and then the chamber with smaller seals.

The 13th century saw the chancery at the height of its importance. Its duties as the king's secretariat were so vast that in 1244 a subdepartment, the hanaper, was created, with its own keeper to receive the fees of the great seal and to meet chancery's expenses out of them. The office of keeper (later master) of the rolls was also established. Even in the later Middle Ages the chancery remained the principal administrative department; it supplied the clerks of parliament from its staff, and all documents of any importance had still to be authenticated by the great seal. Hence the demand of the opposition, in every baronial rebellion or constitutional crisis, for control of the chancery, the great seal, and the office of chancellor.

The later Middle Ages, however, saw the chancery's judicial role overshadow its administrative functions. In common with other institutions it had built up a jurisdiction in matters arising from its own activities or concerning its officials. That was its so-called "Latin side," and in hearing such cases it acted according to the common law. During the 14th century it acquired a much more extensive equity jurisdiction, which was to expand considerably during and after the 15th century. This expanded jurisdiction arose from the chancellor's position as the most important member of the king's council and from his normally being a leading ecclesiastic with a knowledge of civil and canon law.

Petitions for the redress of grievances had for some time been addressed to the king and council. As the common-law procedures became slower, more stereotyped, and inadequate to deal with such new situations as those arising from uses (or trusts) and contracts, petitions became too numerous to be dealt with by the council. Many were therefore transferred to the chancellor, who sat in Westminster Hall, and ultimately most petitions were addressed directly to him. His equity jurisdiction was based on the relatively informal procedure of bill and answer, supplemented by interrogatory and deposition, all in the vernacular. Hence it was known as "the English side of chancery," and because of its reliance on English as its medium of argument the chancery played an important role in standardizing vernacular vocabulary and usage ("chancery standard" or "chancery English").

Chancellors were nearly all ecclesiastics. At first they had often been archdeacons or cathedral dignitaries, and they resigned as chancellor on their frequent advancement to bishoprics. Around 1200 it was normal for the chancellor to be a bishop or even an archbishop before his appointment and then to hold both offices concurrently. From Henry II's reign until 1234, and again between 1258 and 1265, the justiciar was the king's chief minister. At all other times the chancellor held that position, although he never had formal vice-regal powers. The last and greatest of the medieval chancellors was Cardinal Wolsey (1515–29). His true successor was Thomas Cromwell, a layman and the first of the powerful Tudor secretaries.

Roy F. Hunnisett

Bibliography

PRIMARY

Baildon, William P., ed. *Select Cases in Chancery, A.D. 1364 to 1471.* Selden Society 10. London: Quaritch, 1896 [contains selections from equity proceedings]; *British National Archives (Government Publications Sectional List 24).* London: HMSO, 1983 [lists the main Record Office publications of rolls and inquisitions, in transcript or calendar form]; Chaplais, Pierre. *English Royal Documents, King John–Henry VI, 1199–1461.* Oxford: Clarendon, 1971.

SECONDARY

Chrimes, Stanley B. *An Introduction to the Administrative History of Mediaeval England.* 3d ed. Oxford: Blackwell, 1966; Galbraith, Vivian H. *An Introduction to the Use of the Public Records.* Oxford: Clarendon, 1934. Corr. repr. 1952 [still the best short introduction to chancery]; Maitland, Frederic W. *Equity: A Course of Lectures.* Ed. Alfred H. Chaytor and William J. Whittaker. Rev. John Brunyate. 2d ed. Cambridge: Cambridge University Press, 1936 [on chancery as a law court]; Tout, T.F. *Chapters in the Administrative History of Mediaeval England: The Wardrobe, the Chamber and the Small Seals.* 6 vols. Manchester: Manchester University Press, 1920–33; Wilkinson, Bertie. *The Chancery under Edward III.* Manchester: Manchester University Press, 1929; Wilkinson, Bertie. "The Chancery." In *The English Government at Work, 1327–1336.* Vol. 1: *Central and Prerogative Administration,* ed. James F. Willard and William A. Morris. Cambridge: Mediaeval Academy of America, 1940, pp. 162–205.

See also Great Seal; Language; Seals; Wardrobe

Chantries

Strictly speaking a chantry was an endowed service for the souls of the founder and his relations, but the term came to include the resources attached to such endowments. The idea of providing for prayers in a permanent foundation was ancient, but it was not until the 13th century that the term *cantaria* came into general use to describe these establishments. During the later Middle Ages such foundations were a frequent form of pious endowment, particularly among the mercantile middle class, whose members wished to make spiritual provision for themselves but were not sufficiently wealthy to found a monastic house, as might be done by members of the landed class.

Chantries could be endowed in perpetuity, with landed rents, or for a term of years, by leaving a sum of money to support a priest to celebrate intercessory masses for the donor as long as funds lasted. This latter type of endowment was encouraged by the Statute of Mortmain (1279), designed to block the flow of land into the "dead hand" *(mort main)* of the church: the need to pay for a license to amortize property added to the cost of perpetual foundations.

A chantry with permanent endowments, however, could run short of funds, particularly in an age of declining rent levels, as followed the Black Death. In such cases chantries might be united, with one priest celebrating for the founders of both and arrangements being made to share the patronage. A London case of 1513 shows the right of appointment held alternately by the city authorities and the archdeacon of Colchester, while in York in 1486 agreement on the nomination was reached between two earlier patrons, the archbishop and the earl of Northumberland.

The numbers of chantries cannot be precisely estimated. In the 1530s the *Valor ecclesiasticus* records some 200 to 300 in London alone, and there were probably between 2,000 and 3,000 in the country as a whole at the time of their dissolution in the 1540s. But these were only the permanently endowed ones, and short-term chantries certainly outnumbered perpetual ones among 15th-century foundations, though one cannot say whether they lasted sufficiently long on average to be more numerous overall. Chantry priests were therefore often insecure and impoverished; a salary payable to one in Lancashire in 1485 was only 4 marks *per annum,* although a contemporary London chantry priest would probably receive 10 marks.

This explains why many chantrists undertook other tasks, particularly as elementary schoolmasters in their parishes. They also contributed to parochial life, assisting the parish priest in hearing confessions at such peak periods of the year as Easter and supplementing the liturgical life of the church—a matter of importance in view of the strong tradition of late-medieval polyphonic music. Although visitation and court records show some chantry priests to be guilty of sexual immorality, there is no reason to believe that this was general.

Henry VIII obtained statutory power in 1545 to secularize chantry property, purely on financial grounds, though only a little of it was seized before his death. Most of it passed into lay hands during Edward VI's reign (1548–53), when a Protestant regency under the duke of Somerset came to power. The new doctrines rejected the belief in purgatory, the chantries' raison d'être, and they were now dismissed as superstitious institutions.

J.A.F. Thomson

Bibliography

Kitching, Christopher J., ed. *London and Middlesex Chantry Certificates, 1548.* London Record Society 16. London: London Record Society, 1980 [a good record illustrating the resources and obligations of a particular group of chantries]; Kreider, Alan. *English Chantries: The Road to Dissolution.* Cambridge: Harvard University Press, 1979; Wood-Legh, Kathleen L. *Perpetual Chantries in Britain.* Cambridge: Cambridge University Press, 1965.

See also Mortmain; Parish Clergy; Popular Religion

Chapel Royal (Royal Household Chapel)

The household chapel of the English kings, a special group of personnel always in attendance on the ruler whose principal responsibility was to perform the divine service. The Chapel Royal is to be distinguished from two other major royal chapels of fixed abode founded by Edward III, the royal chapels of St. Stephen's at Westminster and St. George's at Windsor; its clerks and their duties are further to be distinguished from the King's Chaplains (a position emerging in the 1390s). There had always been chaplains at court who served the king, holding a variety of administrative responsibilities and functioning in a liturgical or ceremonial capacity as necessary. As a more specialized body the Chapel Royal was put on a new footing in the 13th century, in particular as documented in the 1270s during the reign of Edward I, from which time it may have begun to perform daily services. Though liturgical celebration was its day-to-day role, the most important function of the Chapel Royal was in fulfilling ceremonial needs as an emblem of kingship and of the royal presence at coronation ceremonies, crown wearings, solemn entries, anniversaries and commemorations, and other major state occasions.

The adult membership of the Chapel Royal consisted of ordained chaplains and lay clerks (the "capellani et clerici capelle domini regis"), who were joined from the early 14th century onward by a contingent of boys. Their numbers varied but were always substantial by contemporary standards; there were over 30 adults and ten boys in the mid-15th century. The Chapel Royal was the primary sphere of activity for a number of known composers, and it engaged in the performance of the most challenging polyphonic scores. Nonetheless, these activities may have preoccupied only a minority of its members; others, content to sing plainsong as demanded, became engaged in additional nonmusical activities at court, using their position simply as "one of a number of appropriate starting points for clerical careers in royal service" (Wathey: 83). Two 15th-century accounts of the composition and duties of the chapel are in the *Liber regie capelle* (1449) and the Black Book of the Household of Edward IV (ca. 1471).

Peter M. Lefferts

Bibliography

Bent, Ian. "The English Chapel Royal before 1300." *Proceedings of the Royal Musical Association* 90 (1963–64): 77–95; Bowers, Roger. "London, II, 1: Court—Chapel Royal." *NGD* 11:151–53; Wathey, Andrew. *Music in the Royal and Noble Households in Late Medieval England: Studies of Sources and Patronage.* New York: Garland, 1989.

See also Choirs; Households, Royal and Baronial; Old Hall Manuscript

Chapter Houses

The chapter house was, after the church, the most important and elaborate building of a monastic or collegiate ecclesiastical establishment. Monks would meet there daily ("in Chapter") to hear parts of the monastic rule recited, to administer or receive punishment for infractions of that rule, to remember founders and benefactors, and to make the most important decisions regarding the administration or future of their institution, including the election of abbots, bishops, or other officials or decisions concerning lawsuits or other legal matters. Chapter houses were also prestigious places of burial for abbots or others important to the monastery. The chapter house, in short, served as a kind of corporate headquarters, and its architectural form and decoration were often testimony to its institutional importance.

England is most famous for its centrally planned chapter houses, but the vast majority of chapter houses constructed

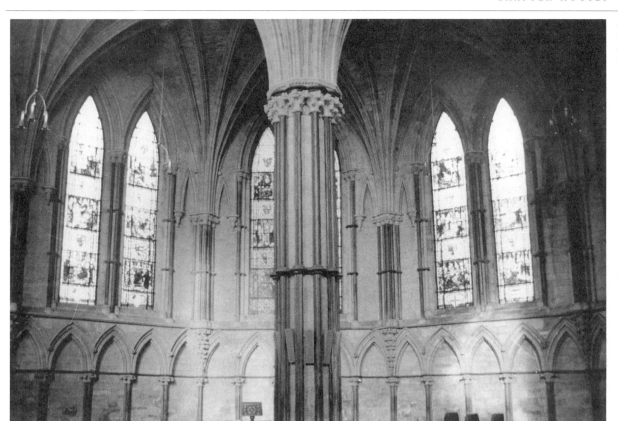

Fig. 39. Wells Cathedral Chapter House, completed ca. 1304. Courtesy of L. Hoey.

in the century after the Norman Conquest had rectangular plans, as in the surviving examples at St. Augustine's, Bristol, or at Forde Abbey in Dorset; sometimes an eastern apse sheltered the chair of the presiding officer, as at Durham Cathedral Priory or originally at St. Peter's, Gloucester. Square or rectangular plans remained popular throughout the Middle Ages in English monasteries, including most Cistercian houses, such as Fountains, Furness, Lacock, or Buildwas, to take some surviving examples. A notable Cistercian oddity was the chapter house at Rievaulx, where an aisle and ambulatory surrounded a central space and apse, perhaps the result of St. Aelred's patronage in the 1150s. Monastic chapter houses were placed off the east cloister walk, close to the south (or north, depending on the cloister placement) transept of the church, from which they were usually separated by a passageway called a slype or a sacristy of some sort. Because the height of the chapter house might interfere with the monks' access to the transept and choir from their dormitory, the former were often placed a certain distance off the east cloister walk and were preceded by a lower vestibule, as was the case at Fountains, Bristol, and most of the centrally planned chapter houses.

The earliest surviving chapter house with a central plan is that at Worcester Cathedral Priory, an originally circular building of the first quarter of the 12th century. A compelling historical reason for the adoption of this plan has yet to be found; the height of such buildings meant that they had to be placed farther from the cloister, and they probably made more awkward the performance of most of the formal rites of Chapter, which generally had an eastern orientation. Symbolic or iconographic motivations may have played a role, as they did in churches dedicated to the Holy Sepulchre, but no documents or unambiguous evidence exist to suggest just what these considerations may have been with regard to English chapter houses. Whatever the initial reason for its use at Worcester, the plan was an obvious success, and such buildings became major prestige monuments in the 13th and 14th centuries.

The next examples are the late-12th-century chapter houses at Margam and Abbey Dore, both of them geographically close enough to Worcester to be considered its progeny, although both are early Gothic in style. They also show the move toward polygonal plans; at Margam the interior is still circular as at Worcester, but the exterior is twelve-sided, while at Abbey Dore both interior and exterior were dodecagonal. The first octagonal chapter house appears to have been that at Beverley Minster, of about 1230, and it was this plan that became most common in centrally planned English chapter houses, although a ten-sided plan was used contemporaneously with Beverley at Lincoln Minster and later at Evesham, Bridlington, and Hereford.

Octagonal plans were used for the chapter houses of secular cathedrals at Lichfield (where the octagon was elongated), Salisbury, Wells, Elgin, York, and Old St. Paul's; at the quasi-cathedrals of Southwell Minster and Westminster Abbey; in the Augustinian houses of Thornton, Carlisle (also a cathedral), and Bolton; the Premonstratensian house at Cockersand; and in the collegiate foundations at Howden, Manchester, and Warwick. These buildings span the entire duration of English Gothic and attest to the great popularity of the type over time as well as across ecclesiastical institutional lines. Except for Worcester, Westminster, and Evesham, Benedictine houses are noticeably absent from this list, because most of them had built chapter houses in the 12th century when the rectangular form was prevalent and lacked the resources or ambition to rebuild their chapter houses in the later Middle Ages.

In addition to being the first octagonal chapter house the Beverley building seems also to have been the first planned for a secular church, although Lincoln is a close contender for the title. The possession of a chapter house was not the necessity for a secular church that it was for a monastery, but more a matter of prestige. Sometimes cloisters accompanied these chapter houses, as at Salisbury, Lincoln, Hereford, or Carlisle (at St. Paul's the cloister surrounded the chapter house, and at Wells chapter house and cloister were set on opposite sides of the church). Often, however, the chapter house stood alone to the north or south of the choir, connected to it by a short passage, as at York, Southwell, Elgin, or Lichfield.

English chapter houses were focuses of architectual elaboration from the first. A number of the Romanesque examples, such as Bristol, Durham, Forde, or Much Wenlock, had rib vaults, often, as in the first two examples, with geometrical decoration. Others, such as Reading or Gloucester, were covered by barrel vaults. Worcester itself was vaulted with an unusual rib vault, decorated with a dado arcade and built of polychrome masonry. Romanesque dado arcades were also built in the chapter houses at Bristol, Durham, and Glouces-

ter. Such embellishment continued into the Gothic period, with dado arcades and vaults being virtually standard features in the buildings cited above. Polygonal chapter houses were ideal venues for large traceried windows, and from Westminster Abbey in the 1250s these also became standard features. Lierne vaults of increasing complexity were made to radiate from the central pierlike umbrellas in the chapter houses at Lincoln and Wells (figs. 38–39). At York the central pier was omitted and the vault constructed of wood, while the arrangement of seat canopies there is one of the prime examples of the Decorated love of contrapuntal spatial effects. As a final example of the pride and expense of English medieval chapter houses one might cite Southwell, with its prodigious display of naturalistic foliage sculpture.

Lawrence Hoey

Bibliography

Bilson, John. "On the Discovery of Some Remains of the Chapter-House of Beverley Minster." *Archaeologia* 54 (1895): 425–32; Coldstream, Nicola. "York Chapter House." *JBAA* 35 (1972): 15–23; Fergusson, Peter, and Stuart Harrison. "The Rievaulx Abbey Chapter House." *AntJ* 74 (1994): 211–55; Stratford, Neil. "Notes on the Norman Chapter House at Worcester." *BAACT* 1 (1978): 51–70; Wickham, W.A. "Some Notes on Chapter-Houses." *Transactions of the Historical Society of Lancashire and Cheshire* 64 (1913): 143–60.

See also Architecture and Architectural Sculpture, Gothic; Architecture and Architectural Sculpture, Romanesque; Canterbury Cathedral; Cistercian Architecture; Durham Cathedral; Lincoln Cathedral; Salisbury Cathedral; Salisbury Chapter House Reliefs; Vaulting; Wells Cathedral; Westminster Abbey; Westminster Chapter House Paintings

Charles of Orléans (1394–1465)

Son of Louis duke of Orléans and nephew of the mad King Charles VI of France. In 1406 he was married to Isabella, the child-widow of Richard II, and after her death was married in 1410 to Bonne of Armagnac, daughter of the leader of the Orleanist faction in 15th-century French politics. He was captured at the Battle of Agincourt in 1415 and was not released, mainly for political reasons, until 1440.

Charles was a prolific writer in French, and during his 25-year imprisonment (spent in the country houses of various English aristocrats) he appears to have turned his attention to composition in English. The poems in BL Harley 682, some of which are rehandlings of the forms and themes of Charles's French poems, are usually accepted as his. The poems, mainly ballades, tell of two love affairs, one of which ends with the death of Lady Beauty and the other with the poet's release from prison. They are separated by a "jubilee," or celebration of love consisting of 94 roundels, though the intention was probably to have 100. The women who were the subjects of these sequences of poems, if they were based on real models, have never been satisfactorily identified.

V.J. Scattergood

Bibliography

PRIMARY

Steele, Robert, and Mabel Day, eds. *The English Poems of Charles of Orleans.* EETS o.s. 215, 220. London: Oxford University Press, 1941–46; repr. with bibliographical supplement, 1970.

SECONDARY

New *CBEL* 1:684–86; Fox, John. *The Lyric Poetry of Charles d'Orléans.* Oxford: Clarendon, 1969; Goodrich, N.L. *Charles of Orleans: A Study of Themes in His French and in His English Poetry.* Geneva: Droz, 1967; Yenal, Edith. *Charles d'Orléans: A Bibliography of Primary and Secondary Sources.* New York: AMS, 1984.

See also Henry VI; Lyrics; Songs

Charms

An ancient genre, descending from pagan oral incantations, magical in intent and ritualistic in practice. Many later written versions are extant in OE and represented in Byrhtferth's *Lacnunga,* while others are scattered in miscellaneous manuscripts: against a sudden stitch in the side (attributed to witches), against a swarm of bees, against infertile land, and so forth.

Both Latin and ME versions abound in late-medieval manuscripts, often in or accompanying medical treatises or collections of alchemical or medical prescriptions. The *Liber de diversis medicinis* (EETS o.s. 207, ed. Ogden), for example, has a Latin charm for childbirth and one in English for toothache. The most popular types are "Flume Jordan" (for stanching blood), "Saint Susan" (for healing wounds), and "Saint William" (for worms, palsy, and gout). A large number of medical-type charms are based on the magical properties of the eagle: the right eye of the eagle gives grace and friendship, the left protects against all harm. Others derive from recipes from adder's skin. Some veterinary charms propose to "Departe thys malady fro thys hors"; others are to cure diseases among cattle.

The range of topics among nonmedical charms is wide; against enemies, for getting rid of mice and rats, identifying an unknown thief, or making a woman dance naked. A large number of charms have religious significance; invoking angels while rising from bed, while it thunders, or while eating or drinking, to bring protection from evil. One might invoke Dismas, the good thief crucified with Christ, or the three Magi, as protection against thieves. Making the sign of the cross while reciting three Greek letters and the Latin names of Christ ensures a safe journey.

Laurel Means

Bibliography

ASPR 6:116–28; Braswell-Means, Laurel. "Scientific and Utilitarian Prose." In *Middle English Prose: A Critical Guide to Major Authors and Genres,* ed. A.S.G. Edwards. New Brunswick: Rutgers University Press, 1984, pp. 337–87; Grattan, J.H.G., and Charles Singer. *Anglo-Saxon Magic and Medicine.* London: Oxford University Press, 1952 [draws on *Lacnunga*]; Gray, Douglas. "Notes on Some Middle English Charms." In *Chaucer and Middle English Studies in Honour of Rossell Hope Robbins,* ed. Beryl Rowland. London: Allen & Unwin, 1974, pp. 56–71; Jolly, Karen Louise. *Popular Religion in Late Saxon England: Elf Charms in Context.* Chapel Hill: University of North Carolina Press, 1996; Sheldon, Suzanne, ed. "The Eagle: Bird of Magic and Medicine in a Middle English Translation of the *Kyranides.*" *Tulane Studies in English* 22 (1977): 1–31.

See also Alchemy; Astrology; Byrhtferth; Medicine

Charters

Documents that record gifts or grants of property or rights by one party to another. In medieval England a transaction of this sort would take place in a ceremony before witnesses, and there was no legal obligation to make a written record. But increasingly, especially from the 12th century, the parties sought to have gifts and grants written down, and for this purpose the charter was the primary form of record available. Since, however, it was at the witness ceremony that the grantor actually put the grantee in possession, a charter was usually framed in the past tense, confirming what had taken place orally, and the names of the witnesses to the gift were recorded at the end of the text.

The charter certainly existed in England by 679, the date of the earliest surviving original, but it has been argued that charters had been introduced by Augustine of Canterbury in 597, and that some of the texts for the period between 597 and the later 7th century, which survive only in later copies, may be wholly or partly genuine, that is, copied from genuine originals, since lost. About 2,000 texts survive from the period before 1066, the bulk of them issued by kings in favor of monasteries, but from the later 11th century the numbers of all charters increased and the habit of charter giving began to penetrate lower in the social scale. By the 13th century even members of the unfree peasantry might issue charters. It has been estimated that in 13th-century England as many as eight million charters may have been written for smallholders and serfs alone.

Although usually expressed in terms of gifts and grants, either in fee or in alms, charters might record other types of transactions, such as sales and leases. As the number of charters increased after 1100, so there developed a variety of forms, using largely stereotyped clauses. Royal and episcopal charters tended not to bear dating clauses until the late 12th century, and for another century lay charters were generally undated. We use internal evidence in assigning dates to undated charters, particularly the evidence of the witness clauses.

Characteristically an original charter is written on one side of single leaf of parchment, cut to fit the length of the text, and sealed with the donor's seal, which hangs on a parchment tag. Transactions in which there was an element of compromise or contract, such as agreements and leases, might be recorded in bipartite or tripartite documents. Identical copies were on a single piece of parchment, then divided along an indented line; these might be called "chirographs" or "indentures."

Only a small proportion, perhaps a third of surviving charters, now exist in the original; most are found in copies of various kinds, especially in cartularies. Historians need to test the authenticity of charters, both originals and copies of all periods, before making use of them. It was not uncommon for landowners, especially monasteries, to fabricate charter documentation to legitimize their possession of estates and rights. This was particularly frequently in the 12th century, when charters were used to defend ancient rights that had originated from gifts for which charters either had never existed or had been lost. Even when spurious such charters may be used with care by historians.

Diana E. Greenway

Bibliography

Chaplais, Pierre. "Who Introduced Charters into England? The Case for Augustine." In *Prisca Munimenta: Studies in Archival and Administrative History Presented to A.E.J. Hollaender,* ed. Felicity Ranger. London: University of London Press, 1973, pp. 88–107; Clanchy, M.T. *From Memory to Written Record: England, 1066–1307.* 2d ed. Oxford: Blackwell, 1993; Sawyer, P.H. *Anglo-Saxon Charters: An Annotated List and Bibliography.* London: Royal Historical Society, 1968; Stenton, F.M. *Transcripts of Charters Relating to the Gilbertine Houses of Sixle, Ormsby, Catley, Bullington, and Alvingham.* Horncastle: Lincoln Record Society, 1922 [a valuable introduction].

See also Cartularies; Seals

Chaucer, Geoffrey (ca. 1342–1400)

England's greatest nondramatic poet, whose superb poetry—often moving, sometimes disturbing, always immensely readable—gave a new direction to English literature.

Life

Chaucer was born into a London merchant family; by 1357 he was connected with the court, initially in the household of Elizabeth countess of Ulster, later in the service of successive kings. His wife, Philippa, was herself connected with the royal households of Elizabeth of Ulster, Queen Philippa, and Constanza of Castile, second wife of John of Gaunt; Philippa's sister, Katherine Swynford, was for many years Gaunt's mistress and eventually his third wife.

Chaucer made a number of journeys abroad on the king's business: to France on several occasions, apparently to Spain in 1366, and to Italy in 1372–73 and 1378, where he discovered the great literature of the Trecento. He held a number of senior "civil service" posts, including a controllership of customs (1374–85), the clerkship of the king's works (1389–91), and a deputy forestership in Somerset (1390s). He was a justice of the peace for Kent and represented the county in the parliament of 1386. Although there are numerous records of

payments to him in both money and kind (clothing and wine) by Edward III, Richard II, and Henry IV, and to both himself and his wife by John of Gaunt, these are always in return for work or services; there is no mention of patronage specifically for his poetry.

Linguistic and Literary Backgrounds

Chaucer's life coincided with a turning point in the history of the English language. Under Edward III the dominant language spoken and written within the royal household was French, in its Anglo-Norman form; parliamentary proceedings were conducted in the same language. By the end of the century English predominated in court and parliament, and schoolboys were translating their Latin into English instead of French. Chaucer's poetry reflects, and encouraged, the new self-confidence of the language and contributed to the standing of the London dialect. His style combines specifically English features, such as alliterating phrases, with French flexibility of sentence structure and, increasingly, a spaciousness of syntax similar to that seen in the long complex sentences found in Latin.

Chaucer was familiar with English literary forms, including alliterative verse (cf. the sea fight in the Legend of Cleopatra, *Legend of Good Women* 635–48, and the tournament in the *Knight's Tale* 2602–16) and tail rhyme (parodied in *Sir Thopas*); he probably knew Langland's work, and certainly Gower's. His earliest identifiable poetic models, however, were French. Most important was the 13th-century *Roman de la Rose* of Guillaume de Lorris and Jean de Meun, an allegorical love vision that Chaucer claims to have translated; of the three fragments of an ME translation that survive, only the first is likely to be his. It may be the earliest surviving example of his work. The *Roman* remained a key influence throughout his career, but his use of it changed significantly: his earlier poems draw most on Guillaume's account of falling in love in an idyllic courtly garden, while Jean's more cynical writing was an inspiration behind such characters as the Pardoner and the Wife of Bath. From the 1370s onward Chaucer was deeply influenced by Dante, Petrarch, and above all Boccaccio, and his poetry becomes increasingly cosmopolitan as he consciously participates in the highest western traditions of poetry. Like Dante and Boccaccio he presents himself following in the great classical line of Homer, Virgil, Ovid, Lucan, and Statius (*Troilus* 5.1792); of these Ovid was the most important to him. Other cultural traditions are represented in his work by his use of the 6th-century *Consolation of Philosophy* of Boethius, which he translated in the early 1380s, and, supremely, by his constant allusions to the Bible, the liturgy, and Christian doctrine.

Works

Chaucer's earliest known original poem, *The Book of the Duchess* (ca. 1368–72), was a response to the death of Blanche, duchess of Lancaster, first wife of John of Gaunt. It draws largely on French models and is written in a four-stress couplet form similar to French octosyllabics. Its narrator dreams of meeting a man in black who is mourning the death of his lady, named

"White": the characters bear some relationship to Chaucer, the duke, and Blanche, but Chaucer's use of the dream form enables him to transcend historical circumstance to explore the contraries of love and loss, joy and grief. Three characteristics of the poem are notable as precursors of his later work. First is his exploitation of convention in unconventional ways: most strikingly in death's invasion of the idyllic garden where the lover falls in love. Second is the sophistication of Chaucer's use of a first-person narrator. Despite his overtly muted role within the dream he is a figure for the poet; and since the dream takes place within his own mind, he is also the originator of the encomium and lament spoken by the man in black. Chaucer thus becomes the spokesman for the duke both in fact and within the structure of the poem. Third is its secular focus—a focus exceptional for elegy, but typical of the great majority of Chaucer's works: Christianity is not denied, but the field of poetic interest is this world, not the next.

Chaucer's poetry of the 1370s and early 1380s continues to use French models—the *Roman,* Guillaume de Machaut, Jean Froissart—but Ovidian and Italian influences also appear. His major works of those years, whose order of composition is uncertain, are *The Parliament of Fowls, The House of Fame,* and possibly the *Knight's Tale* under the title of "Palamon and Arcite." *The Parliament* is probably Chaucer's earliest poem in the seven-line rime royal stanza, which he would later use in the *Troilus* and the tales of pathos in the *Canterbury Tales.* It may have been written for some particular occasion, possibly to do with Richard II's future wife, Anne. It is a dream poem that analyzes the various forms that earthly love can take, as illustrated by the claustrophobic temple of Priapus, inhabited by Venus, and by the hill of Nature, God's "vicaire" or deputy, before whom all the birds from the eagle to the goose have assembled on St. Valentine's Day to choose their mates. The poem suggests a series of contraries that it in fact refuses to endorse: both temple and hill are contained within the same walled park; inscriptions over the entrance promise bliss and threaten sterility and death, but the entrance is single; the birds that are given their mates and the three eagles that endure suffering and long service in love are alike under the aegis of Nature; the broader context for the dream is Scipio's vision, from Cicero, of the great cycle of the universe, with its injunction to serve the common good, while the dream itself shows the processes of natural regeneration within a single year—processes explicitly invoked in the concluding roundel celebrating the return of summer after winter.

The House of Fame is again a dream poem, told by a narrator-dreamer named "Geffrey" and written, like *The Book of the Duchess,* in octosyllabic couplets. The subject here is the nature of poetry, specifically the problem of recording the great deeds of the past—the function of narrative poetry—when the authorities who record those deeds are fallible. The problem is epitomized in the first section by setting the *Aeneid* against Ovid's account of Dido from the *Heroides.* In the third part it arises again in the form of quarrels among the various authorities for the story of Troy and in the description of Fame herself, whose apportionment of good or bad reputation or oblivion is shown as utterly arbitrary. The dreamer ends up in the house of Rumor, where truth and lies are inextricably jumbled and where there are no authoritative histories but only "tidynges" told by shipmen and pilgrims. The poem breaks off unfinished; the occasion for its composition is unknown, but in some ways it might be seen as foreshadowing the *Canterbury Tales,* with its substitution of fallible pilgrim narrators for an authoritative poet.

Troilus and Criseyde, of the mid-1380s, tells a story regarded in the Middle Ages as historical, but Chaucer constantly stresses the impossibility of establishing truth. His main source, Boccaccio's *Filostrato,* is never mentioned (it is conceivable that he did not know who wrote it); instead he invents an authority named Lollius, to whom he appeals when he is in fact making up the story. The spare plot—of how Criseyde abandons her Trojan lover Troilus for the Greek Diomede—becomes in Chaucer's hands an elaborate work of over 8,000 lines, in poetry of an order unparalleled in earlier English, from its magnificent hymns to Love through the easy colloquialisms of conversation to the eroticism of the central book. The depth of thought in the poem results from Chaucer's setting this story from the unalterable past in counterpoint to arguments from Boethius's *Consolation* on destiny and free will and juxtaposing its theme of faithlessness against the providential ordering of the universe through "Love, that of erthe and se hath governaunce" (*Tr* 3.1744, *Consolation* 2.met.8).

The interpretations of *Troilus* over the centuries form an index to the varying responses to Chaucer: to his contemporaries it was most notable for its philosophy; the 15th and 16th centuries took it as a model of rhetorical eloquence; to the age of naturalism it was the first psychological novel; the search for values of the 1960s read it as a condemnation of inadequate secular goals; our own text-centered age stresses Chaucer's refusal to commit himself to motive, meaning, or fact. The God of the closing stanzas is the one fixed point, the unwritten author (Dante's "uncircumscript, and al maist circumscrive," *Tr* 5.1865), but the protagonists, as pagans, cannot have access to him, and the questions they raise remain unanswered.

The reason, or excuse, that Chaucer gives for writing his *Legend of Good Women,* is that his portrayal of Criseyde provoked objections; in its dream prologue (extant in two versions) he describes how the God of Love and Alcestis, model of the faithful wife, commanded him to do penance by telling the stories of good women—in practice, wronged women. Nine stories follow, mostly drawn from Ovid's *Heroides*—of Cleopatra, Thisbe, Dido, Hypsipyle and Medea, Lucretia, Ariadne, Philomela, Phyllis, and Hypermnestra; the last breaks off in mid-sentence. It has generally been assumed that Chaucer found such writing to formula restrictive; his only similar assemblage of single-subject stories forms the *Monk's Tale,* which is interrupted by the restless pilgrim audience.

The *Canterbury Tales* (ca. 1387–1400) is a story collection that achieves the maximum variety within a unifying frame. The tales are told by a group of pilgrims journeying to St. Thomas Becket's shrine at Canterbury, and both the pilgrims and their tales are selected to give a cross-section of human and literary possibility. Each pilgrim represents a different profession or social estate, on the model of the satiric social analyses offered by medieval estates literature. Chaucer's ideal figures, the Knight, Parson, and Plowman, mirror the basic tripartite division of society into those who fight, pray, and labor; the Clerk represents a fourth ideal, of those who learn and teach. The other portraits are more equivocal; Chaucer's persistent mode is superlative praise, but often aimed at the "wrong" attributes—the Friar's skill in begging, the Physician's financial success, the Prioress's social accomplishments. Women were often treated as an estate to themselves, and the one laywoman among the pilgrims, the Wife of Bath, is well capable of counterbalancing some 27 men.

The Host of the Tabard Inn, who accompanies the pilgrims as master of ceremonies, suggests that each pilgrim should tell four tales, competing with each other to tell "tales of best sentence and moost solaas"; the winning teller is to be given a dinner on their return to the Tabard. Whether or not Chaucer ever intended to write such an extensive work is unknown; he wrote only 24 tales within an incomplete framework. These stories are linked to form seven to twelve distinct fragments (the number is arguable); most editors opt for ten. There is some variation in the manuscript order of these fragments, but the most widely accepted order is that of the Ellesmere manuscript of the *Tales,* copied shortly after Chaucer's death:

I.   *General Prologue; Knight's Tale* (a high-style romance based on Boccaccio's *Teseida,* of the love of Palamon and Arcite for Emily); *Miller's Tale* and *Reeve's Tale* (rival fabliaux in which one Oxford student seduces one woman, and two Cambridge students have sex with two); the fragmentary *Cook's Tale* (of a London reveler condemned by a battery of proverbs).

II.   *Man of Law's Tale* (the trials and miraculous preservation of Custance, taken from Nicholas Trevet's *Cronicles* but treated as a pious romance).

III.   *Wife of Bath's Prologue* (a defense of marriage against the hostile clerical establishment, especially St. Jerome, in the guise of her autobiography); her *Tale* (the folktale romance of the knight who has to discover what women most desire); *Friar's Tale* (an elaboration of a preaching exemplum, of a rapacious summoner carried off by the Devil); *Summoner's Tale* (a fabliau of a scatological bequest to the friars).

IV.   *Clerk's Tale* (from Petrarch's version of Boccaccio's story of Patient Griselda); *Merchant's Tale* (a fabliau given high-style treatment, of the blind old knight January, whose sight is restored as his wife commits adultery in a pear tree).

V.   *Squire's Tale* (an unfinished romance of magic gifts and an abandoned falcon); *Franklin's Tale* (described as a Breton lay though actually adapted from Boccaccio, of a suitor who fulfills his lady's supposedly impossible condition to remove the rocks that threaten her husband).

VI.   *Physician's Tale* (Livy's story of Virginia and the unjust judge, taken from the *Roman de la Rose*); *Pardoner's Prologue* (on his methods of extorting money) and *Tale* (presented as a sample homily and including the widely disseminated tale of three rioters who find death in the form of gold).

VII.   *Shipman's Tale* (a fabliau apparently once assigned to the Wife of Bath, of an adulterous wife and a monk); *Prioress's Tale* (a miracle of the Virgin concerning a boy murdered by the Jews); two tales told by the pilgrim Chaucer that effectively write him out of the competition, *Sir Thopas* (a parody of popular romance) and the prose *Melibee* (Prudence's discourse on the need for reconciliation, translated from a French version of Albertanus of Brescia); *Monk's Tale* (the falls of great men from biblical, secular, and contemporary history); *Nun's Priest's Tale* (the beast fable of the cock and the fox).

VIII.   *Second Nun's Tale* (the life of St. Cecilia, written earlier and incorporated into the *Tales*); *Canon's Yeoman's Tale* (the autobiography of an alchemist's assistant and an account of alchemical frauds).

IX.   *Manciple's Tale* (of Phoebus and the crow, from Ovid's *Metamorphoses*).

X.   *Parson's Tale* (a prose penitential tract epitomized from Latin treatises); Chaucer's *Retractions* (which combines recording the canon of his works with revoking "worldly vanitees").

The various tales cover most possible source areas (prose and verse, classical and contemporary, English and continental, sacred and secular), five prosodic forms besides prose itself (couplets, rime royal, tail rhyme, the eight-line *Monk's Tale* stanza, and the virtuoso rhyme scheme of the *Clerk's Tale* "Envoy"), most available genres, and a wide range of rhetoric and style. Each tale also gives a distinct moral and linguistic reading of the world and humankind's goals within it, often appropriate to its teller, in a way that makes the whole work resistant to univocal interpretation.

Chaucer's shorter poems and *balades* are a mixture of serious and playful love poems, addresses to friends, patrons, and a scribe, and moral and religious pieces. Together with the Dantesque prologues to the *Prioress's Tale* and the *Second Nun's Tale,* his strongest expressions of Christian devotion are *An ABC to the Virgin* (adapted from Guillaume de Deguileville's *Pèlerinage de vie humaine*) and the *Balade de Bon Conseyl,* also called "Truth." A longer fragmentary poem, *Anelida and Arcite,* is notable for its technical experimentation. Chaucer also wrote what is possibly the first English vernacular textbook, the *Treatise on the Astrolabe;* a second, *The Equatorie of the Planetis,* may also be his. Further works were falsely attributed to him in the 15th and 16th centuries, among them some antiecclesiastical works that gave him a reputation as a proto-Protestant.

Dissemination and Influence

No manuscripts of Chaucer's works survive from his lifetime, but they were widely copied throughout the 15th century.

The *Tales* survives in some 80 manuscripts, *Troilus* in sixteen, *The Parliament* in fourteen, *Anelida* in thirteen, *The Book of the Duchess* and *The House of Fame* in three. The *Tales* was among the first books printed by Caxton, and everexpanding editions of the complete works appeared from 1483, notably Thynne's (1532), Stow's (1561), and Speght's (1598, the first to contain a glossary). Chaucerian scholarship effectively began with Tyrwhitt's edition of the *Tales* (1775–78).

Chaucer's influence made itself felt from his own lifetime. It may show in works by his contemporaries Froissart, Oton de Grandson, and Gower, though the direction of the influence is unclear. Lydgate and the "aureate" poets of the 15th century owed an explicit debt to him, usually phrased in terms of his mastery of rhetoric. Some of the major works of early Scottish literature, such as *The Kingis Quair* and Henryson's *Testament of Cresseid*, would have been impossible without him. Numerous poets, including Bokenham, Hawes, and Skelton, praised the poetic trinity of Chaucer, Gower, and Lydgate. He was the leading model for poetry throughout the 16th century, not least for Spenser, until the Elizabethan poets established their own standards of excellence. His preeminence has never been in question; he is the only ME author to have been read and praised in an unbroken tradition. There have been many adaptations and modernizations of his work, including samples by Dryden, Pope, and Wordsworth. His unique combination of accessibility and depth is indicated by his being the only poet to figure frequently both in British primary school teaching and as a key example in modern critical theory, and, in Pasolini's *Canterbury Tales*, as a box-office hit.

Helen Cooper

Bibliography

PRIMARY

Benson, Larry D., gen. ed. *The Riverside Chaucer*. 3d ed. Boston: Houghton Mifflin, 1987 [based on *The Works of Geoffrey Chaucer*, ed. F.N. Robinson]; Coghill, Nevill, trans. *Troilus and Criseyde*. Harmondsworth: Penguin, 1971; Ruggiers, Paul G., and Donald C. Baker, gen. eds. *A Variorum Edition of the Works of Geoffrey Chaucer*. Norman: University of Oklahoma Press, 1979–; Windeatt, Barry A., ed. *Troilus and Criseyde: A New Edition of "The Book of Troilus."* London: Longman, 1984; Wright, David, trans. *The Canterbury Tales*. Oxford: Oxford University Press, 1985.

SECONDARY

New *CBEL* 1:557–628; Allen, Mark, and John H. Fisher. *The Essential Chaucer: An Annotated Bibliography of Major Modern Studies*. London: Mansell, 1987 [for criticism]; *The Chaucer Bibliographies*. Toronto: University of Toronto Press, 1983– [ongoing series]; Leyerle, John, and Anne Quick. *Chaucer: A Bibliographical Introduction*. Toronto Medieval Bibliographies 10. Toronto: University of Toronto Press, 1986 [for scholarship]; *Studies in the Age of Chaucer*. 1979– [annual annotated bibliographies for 1975 on].

GENERAL CRITICISM

Boitani, Piero, and Jill Mann, eds. *The Cambridge Chaucer Companion*. Cambridge: Cambridge University Press, 1986; Burnley, David. *A Guide to Chaucer's Language*. London: Macmillan, 1983. Repr. as *The Language of Chaucer;* London: Macmillan, 1989; Crow, Martin M., and Clair C. Olson, eds. *Chaucer Life-Records*. Austin: University of Texas Press, 1966; David, Alfred. *The Strumpet Muse: Art and Morals in Chaucer's Poetry*. Bloomington: Indiana University Press, 1976; Jordan, Robert M. *Chaucer's Poetics and the Modern Reader*. Berkeley: University of California Press, 1987; Kean, P.M. *Chaucer and the Making of English Poetry*. 2 vols. London: Routledge & Kegan Paul, 1972; Mann, Jill. *Geoffrey Chaucer*. Feminist Readings. London: Harvester Wheatsheaf, 1991; Muscatine, Charles. *Chaucer and the French Tradition: A Study in Style and Meaning*. Berkeley: University of California Press, 1957; *The Oxford Guides to Chaucer:* Helen Cooper, *The Canterbury Tales;* Alastair J. Minnis, *The Shorter Poems;* Barry A. Windeatt, *Troilus and Criseyde*. Oxford: Clarendon, 1989–95; Pearsall, Derek. *The Life of Geoffrey Chaucer*. Oxford: Blackwell, 1992; Robertson, D.W., Jr. *A Preface to Chaucer: Studies in Medieval Perspectives*. Princeton: Princeton University Press, 1962; Schoeck, Richard J., and Jerome Taylor, eds. *Chaucer Criticism*. 2 vols. Notre Dame: University of Notre Dame Press, 1960 [reprints of classic essays].

SHORTER POEMS AND *TROILUS*

Wetherbee, Winthrop. *Chaucer and the Poets: An Essay on Troilus and Criseyde*. Ithaca: Cornell University Press, 1984; Windeatt, Barry A., ed. and trans. *Chaucer's Dream Poetry: Sources and Analogues*. Cambridge: Brewer, 1982.

CANTERBURY TALES

Bryan, William F., and Germaine Dempster, eds. *Sources and Analogues of Chaucer's Canterbury Tales*. Chicago: University of Chicago Press, 1941; Cooper, Helen. *The Structure of the Canterbury Tales*. London: Duckworth, 1983; Howard, Donald R. *The Idea of the Canterbury Tales*. Berkeley: University of California Press, 1976; Mann, Jill. *Chaucer and Medieval Estates Satire: The Literature of Social Classes and the General Prologue to the Canterbury Tales*. Cambridge: Cambridge University Press, 1973; Pearsall, Derek. *The Canterbury Tales*. London: Allen & Unwin, 1985.

See also Boethius; Chaucerian Apocrypha; Comic Tales; Dream Vision; Gower; Henryson; Literary Influences: Classical, French, Italian, Medieval Latin; Lydgate; Satire; Scottish Literature, Early; Women in ME Literature

Chaucerian Apocrypha and Imitations

English poetic works misattributed to Chaucer in the 15th and 16th centuries; poetry and prose associated with Chaucer by scholars in the late 18th and 19th centuries; those poems whose style imitates that of genuine Chaucerian poetry.

In the centuries following his death in 1400 Chaucer's poetic influence was widespread. Many poets paid homage to the master by imitating his style. Indeed Chaucer's rime royal stanza, dream-vision allegory, and emphasis on love were particularly appealing to such well-known poets as Gower, Lydgate, and Hoccleve, as well as to minor English Chaucerians (Ashby, Bokenham, Bradshaw, Burgh, Norton, Ripley, Usk, Walton) and to the so-called Scottish Chaucerians (Gavin Douglas, William Dunbar, Robert Henryson, James I). Because these poets followed Chaucer's style, many of their works were wrongly attributed to him and came to constitute a substantial part of the Chaucerian apocrypha.

The apocrypha consist of three spurious *Canterbury Tales* (the *Tale of Beryn,* the *Tale of Gamelyn,* and the *Plowman's Tale*), Thomas Usk's *Testament of Love,* and about 100 miscellaneous poems concerned mainly with love and courtesy. Several works once considered apocryphal—*Against Women Unconstant, Complaynt D'Amours, A Balade of Complaint, A Complaint to His Lady, Merciles Beaute, Proverbs, To Rosemounde, Womanly Noblesse,* and part of the *Romaunt of the Rose*—are now accepted as Chaucer's.

Most of the poems of the Chaucerian apocrypha may be divided into two general groups: short, mannered lyrics, such as *To My Sovereign Lady,* employing the literary conventions of courtly love, in which the poet languishes before an obdurate lady, and the "dits amoureux," more formal narratives like *La Belle Dame sans Merci* and *The Court of Love,* which depict complicated love adventures in a courtly setting. These forms, evolving from the 15th-century interest in Chaucer as the poet of love, influenced Wyatt and Surrey on the one hand and Spenser on the other.

One of the first to ascribe apocryphal works to Chaucer was John Shirley, a 15th-century English manuscript copyist and bibliophile who collected and compiled works by Chaucer, Lydgate, and others. At the beginning of two of his collections, perhaps in an effort to increase their value, Shirley attaches lists of contents, and here he attributes many minor poems, such as "The Nine Worshipfullest Ladies," to Chaucer.

Though Shirley was the main contributor to the late-15th-century development of Chaucerian apocrypha, several other manuscripts, most notably Cambridge, Trinity College R.3.19, also contain minor works that came to be linked with Chaucer's name. Some of these manuscripts were the printers' copy for the 16th-century black-letter editions of the poet's works and were later used by editors of Chaucer from the 18th century on.

In 1526 Richard Pynson added five non-Chaucerian pieces to his edition of Chaucer, including *La Belle Dame sans Merci* and *The Lamentation of Mary Magdalene.* William Thynne appended 23 apocryphal works to his 1532 edition of Chaucer, nineteen of which appear for the first time in this edition. Among them are the earliest extant text of Henryson's *Testament of Cresseid,* Lydgate's *Flower of Courtesy,* and the only surviving text of Usk's *Testament of Love.*

Finally, in his 1542 edition, Thynne added another important apocryphal item, the *Plowman's Tale,* a debate poem on ecclesiastical authority that had already been published and attributed to Chaucer by Thomas Godfray (ca. 1535).

In 1561 John Stow, a London antiquarian who had come to own many of the Shirley manuscripts, printed an edition of Chaucer that included Thynne's addenda among the genuine poems of Chaucer. Stow himself added some 23 pieces, most of them apocryphal, including *The Craft of Lovers* and *The Court of Love.* Thus by 1561 there were some 50 works in the apocrypha.

During the 16th, 17th, and 18th centuries only a few more pieces were added to what had by now become the main corpus of Chaucerian apocrypha. In 1598 Thomas Speght essentially reprinted Stow but added some well-known apocryphal poems: *The Prisoner's Complaint Against Fortune, The Flower and the Leaf, The Isle of Ladies;* in his 1602 edition Speght also included *Jack Upland,* first published and attributed to Chaucer ca. 1536. Later, in John Urry's 1721 edition of Chaucer, two further apocryphal works appeared in print, the *Tale of Beryn* (a comic tale) and the *Tale of Gamelyn* (a romance).

During the 19th century editors, including Walter W. Skeat and Frederick J. Furnivall, examined the Shirley and Stow manuscript collections and included among the apocrypha such poems as the *Plowman's Song* and the *Balade of a Reeve.* But Skeat's important edition of the apocrypha, *Chaucerian and Other Pieces* (1897), retains only 29 of the "most important" items and clearly labels them as non-Chaucerian.

Kathleen M. Hewett-Smith

Bibliography

PRIMARY

Skeat, Walter W., ed. *Chaucerian and Other Pieces: Being a Supplement to the Complete Works of Geoffrey Chaucer.* Oxford: Clarendon, 1897.

SECONDARY

New *CBEL* 1:652–63; *Manual* 4:1061–1101, 1285–1306; Brusendorff, Aage. *The Chaucer Tradition.* London: Humphrey Milford, 1925. Repr. Oxford: Oxford University Press, 1967; Green, Richard Firth. *Poets and Princepleasers: Literature and the English Court in the Late Middle Ages.* Toronto: University of Toronto Press, 1980; Peck, Russell A. *Chaucer's "Romaunt of the Rose" and "Boece," "Treatise on the Astrolabe," "Equatorie of the Planetis," Lost Works and Chaucerian Apocrypha: An Annotated Bibliography, 1900–1985.* Toronto: University of Toronto Press, 1988, pp. 243–355; Ruggiers, Paul G., ed. *Editing Chaucer: The Great Tradition.* Norman: Pilgrim Books, 1984; Skeat, Walter W. *The Chaucer Canon.* Oxford: Clarendon, 1900.

See also Caxton; Chaucer; Douglas; Dream Vision; Dunbar; Henryson; Hoccleve; *Jack Upland; Kingis Quair;* Lydgate; Satire; Scogan; Scottish Literature, Early; Shirley; Usk

Chichele, Henry (1362–1443)

Archbishop of Canterbury (1414–43), statesman, diplomat, and benefactor. Born in Higham Ferrers, Northamptonshire, he belonged to a merchant family with London connections. Educated at William of Wykeham's new colleges at Winchester and Oxford, he specialized in canon law and by 1396 was practicing in the Court of Arches in London, where he was rector of St. Stephen's, Walbrook. He became a member of the staff of Bishop Mitford of Salisbury and was rewarded by him with many benefices.

By 1404 Chichele had moved to royal service and was, in that year, appointed the king's envoy to the Roman curia. He served as Henry IV's proctor there again in 1406 and thereafter was often employed as a diplomat, four times meeting the French and once the Burgundians. In 1408 he was sent to Siena as envoy to Pope Gregory XII and while there was consecrated, on the king's nomination, as bishop of St. David's (Wales). His new status and his diplomatic skill made him an obvious choice as colleague of Bishop Hallum at the Council of Pisa in 1409.

Chichele continued as a prominent diplomat for the remainder of Henry IV's reign and on the death of Archbishop Arundel in 1414 was Henry V's choice as archbishop of Canterbury, as much for his connections with London and Oxford as for his public service. Chichele repaid the trust in his support for the king's policy in France.

Overshadowed by Cardinal Beaufort, he remained a supporter of the conciliar movement for a more representative church and was no friend of Pope Martin V. His concern for education was shown in his promotion of graduate clerks, his fund for poor scholars at Oxford, and provision of a site for St. Bernard's College there. A traditional churchman, he opposed Lollardy and established religious foundations at Higham Ferrers and Oxford, the latter the College of All Souls for graduate scholars.

Robert W. Dunning

Bibliography

Emden, Alfred B. *A Biographical Register of the University of Oxford to A.D. 1500.* Vol. 1. Oxford: Clarendon, 1957, pp. 410–12; Jacob, Ernest F., ed. *The Register of Henry Chichele, Archbishop of Canterbury, 1414–1443.* 4 vols. Oxford: Oxford University Press, 1937–47; Jacob, Ernest F. *Henry Chichele and the Ecclesiastical Politics of His Age.* Creighton Lecture in History, 1951. London: Athlone, 1952; Jacob, Ernest F. *Archbishop Henry Chichele.* London: SPCK, 1967.

See also Bishops; Canterbury, Ecclesiastical Province of; Henry V

Chichester Roundel

On the south wall of the chapel of the Bishop's Palace at Chichester a quatrefoil medallion about 32 inches in diameter encloses the image of the Virgin Mary tenderly embracing the Christ Child while two angels emerge from clouds at the sides swinging their censers. This painting, dating about 1250–60, proclaims its royal nature in both form and material. The Virgin is portrayed as the queen of heaven with all the accouterments of earthly majesty, the jeweled crown, the scepter, the eagle throne, and the royal fleur-de-lis both embroidered on her fur-lined mantle and powdering the background. Furthermore the artist used only the finest materials, gold, silver (now oxidized), and an expensive blue pigment for the background, all of which clearly set this work apart from ordinary wall paintings of the period. In style and iconography the Chichester Roundel has most frequently been compared with images of the Virgin and Child by the monastic illuminator Matthew Paris of St. Albans, who had ties to the court of King Henry III, but wall paintings recently uncovered at the Benedictine priory of Horsham St. Faith (Norfolk) are even closer in their sophistication and refinement.

Pearson M. Macek

Bibliography

Park, David. "Wall Painting." In *Age of Chivalry: Art in Plantagenet England,* ed. Jonathan Alexander and Paul Binski. London: Royal Academy of Arts, 1987, pp. 125–30.

See also Henry III; Matthew Paris; Painting, Gothic

Children and Childhood

Childhood was defined in several ways in medieval England. Common law saw it as the period from birth to twelve, when the young person became legally responsible for criminal acts. The law presumed that by twelve the culprit would have an adult understanding of the wrongfulness of his or her action. In canon law the age of marriage was twelve for girls, fourteen for boys.

Writers like Isidore of Seville and Bartholomaeus Anglicus divided childhood into two periods: *infantia* was from birth to seven, *pueritia* from seven to fourteen. Physicians were inclined to extend childhood to the late twenties, as were some of the poems on the ages of man. In more common parlance the terms "infant," "child," and "baby" covered a range of ages into the twenties.

The practical experience of childhood seems to have been marked by two major transitions, the first around age seven, the second around twelve or fourteen. The first year of life was taken up with baptism and then with the usual problems of feeding, clothing, and tending to the child. This first year was the most dangerous, with perhaps as many as 50 percent of the children succumbing to fatal illness; no evidence of widespread infanticide appears in any medieval English records. The children were swaddled during the first year and spent much of their time in a cradle near a hearth. Breastfeeding, supplemented with prechewed bread and perhaps ale, was the most common form of sustenance. Peasant and urban dwellers fed their own children, but noble women often used a wetnurse.

By the second and third years children learned to walk, play, and talk with the help of parents or nurses. During these years they also began to show an identification with the roles their parents played. Thus, among peasant children, accidental deaths indicate that young girls died imitating their mothers' daily activities, while young boys followed their fathers outside. Most of the training of children between birth and seven was the responsibility of mothers or female nurses.

By seven children had developed sufficient motor control and responsibility to move on to new activities; play began to resemble the activities of adults. Noble children might enter a period of fostering, while peasant children began to help with tasks around the house or with herding. Urban children also began to help around the house and to participate in some economic activities, such as running errands. Formal education also began at this age. Play still remained a large part of their lives but might now be directed toward supplemental economic activities, such as fishing.

By age twelve to fourteen children began to move into the adolescent phase, when they would expect to undertake more serious training for adult lives. They were old enough to become apprentices in trades and crafts, to do field work but not plowing (if peasants), to become squires (if noble). Girls learned the appropriate female counterpart activities. Peasant children tended to remain with their natal family to learn the skills of husbandry and domestic activities, while urban children moved to the house of an employer, if servants, or to a master, if apprentices. Noble boys learned the use of arms and other matters necessary for their future role at this age, and noble girls learned domestic skills. While they could also marry at these ages, child marriages were uncommon except among the nobility and for young heiresses in urban centers.

Exit from childhood into *adolescentia* could be marked by changing residence from the natal home, by service or apprenticeship, by entering training for the clergy, or by going to university. The period of adolescence was universally one of intensive training. Various changes in status marked the end of adolescence: inheritance (fourteen for heiresses, 21 for men in common law and 21 or more in customary law), marriage (perhaps late teens for women and twenties for men, depending on social class and current economic opportunities), knighting (21 was typical but could be earlier), entrance into clergy (seventeen for ordination as a subdeacon, nineteen to become a monk, and 24 to become a priest), or becoming a mastercraftsman or setting up an independent business.

Barbara A. Hanawalt

Bibliography

Hanawalt, Barbara A. *The Ties That Bound: Peasant Families in Medieval England.* New York: Oxford University Press, 1986; Hanawalt, Barbara A. *Growing Up in Medieval London: The Experience of Childhood in History.* New York: Oxford University Press, 1993; McLaughlin, Mary Martin. "Survivors and Surrogates: Children and Parents from the Ninth to the Thirteenth Centuries." In *The History of Childhood,* ed. Lloyd deMause. New York: Psychohistory Press, 1974, pp. 101–81; Orme, Nicholas. *From Childhood to Chivalry: The Education of the English Kings and Aristocracy, 1066–1530.* London: Methuen, 1984.

See also Courtesy Literature; Households, Royal and Baronial; Marriage; Schools; Wardship; Women

Chivalry

Chivalry was the culture that grew up around knights and their feats of arms. According to ecclesiastical writers there were two sides to knightly service: defense of fellow men and of the church.

From a military view, long before the advent of this concept of chivalry, the Bayeux Tapestry (late 11th century) already depicts horsemen charging with couched lances, as well as throwing their spears in traditional fashion. This new technique, and the plate armor developed in response to it, dramatically changed the character of medieval warfare.

In the late Middle Ages the knight was a powerful mobile projectile. He had to develop and perfect skills in handling the sword and lance; he also had to learn to act as part of a small team *(banniere)* under his lord, where the ability to disperse and regroup were vital. It was to promote these skills that Richard I defied a papal ban and licensed four tournament sites in England in 1194. The line between war and tournament was fine—witness the often fatal chivalric encounters in Scotland and France in the 14th century. By ca. 1400 the tournament between teams of knights had been largely superseded by the joust, often in the elaborate dramatized framework known as the *pas d'armes* (as at St. Inglevert in 1389, described by Froissart) and announced by complex and fantastic challenges.

Throughout Europe knightly consciousness was heightened by the dissemination of literature, especially Arthurian romance, inculcating the values of knightly devotion (especially to a lady), fortitude, and loyalty. This code was epitomized by such knights as Edward III's cousin Henry duke of Lancaster (d. 1361) or his own son Edward the Black Prince. Edward I and Edward III both exploited Arthurian associations and sustained their chivalric reputations by victories in the field, arbitration over individual combat, patronage of tournaments, holding baronial meetings at round tables, and jousts. Their courts were a focus for foreign knights.

From the 11th century until the fall of Acre (1291) the Crusades in the eastern Mediterranean had been an important focus for chivalric aspirations and energies. The 14th century undoubtedly witnessed a shift toward a more secular expression of the knightly ideal. In 1348 Edward III, fresh from victories in France, founded the Order of the Garter. For 24 knights of unblemished honor the Order bound individual loyalty to the service of king and infant nation-state.

War and tournament had always offered opportunities for profit and social advancement, especially welcome to the impoverished younger sons of noble families, such as William Marshal (d. 1219). In the 14th and 15th centuries profits from the Hundred Years War financed many forms of chivalric display, such as the building and furnishing of castles, collegiate churches, and chantry chapels. Heraldry was perhaps the supreme outward expression of chivalry.

Nevertheless, these men would have identified with the knight of Chaucer's *Canterbury Tales* and seen the defense of the church as an important responsibility, for they continued to crusade in northeast Europe into the 15th century. The journeys of Chaucer's Knight were roughly paralleled by or modeled on the early military exploits of the young Henry IV (as Henry Bolingbroke, earl of Derby).

Juliet Vale

Bibliography

Barber, Richard. *The Knight & Chivalry*. Harlow: Longmans, 1970; Barker, Juliet R.V. *The Tournament in England, 1100–1400*. Woodbridge: Boydell, 1986; Keen, Maurice. *Chivalry*. New Haven: Yale University Press, 1984; Tyerman, Christopher. *England and the Crusades, 1095–1588*. Chicago: University of Chicago Press, 1988; Vale, Juliet. *Edward III and Chivalry: Chivalric Society and Its Context, 1270–1350*. Woodbridge: Boydell, 1982.

See also Arms and Armor; Courtly Love; Edward III; Edward the Black Prince; Henry IV; Henry of Lancaster; Heralds; Matter of Britain; Order of the Garter

Choirs, Choral Establishments

During the Middle Ages and early Renaissance the choirs of the major ecclesiastical institutions, while constituted primarily to enact and render the plainsong of the liturgical service, provided English composers with their principal medium of performance for written polyphony. The choral forces themselves were of many diverse constitutions, origins, and natures but were united in their observance of a roughly common liturgy; and in the absence of any widespread cultivation of secular polyphony they provided the milieu for virtually all serious musical enterprise and endeavor.

Throughout western medieval Christendom the monastic ideal of the maintenance of a continuous web of worship and praise, in imitation here on earth of the hosts of heaven above, motivated religious communities of men and boys, and of women, to observe and offer within the churches built for their special use a daily liturgy that was of immense complexity, composed of three principal constituent elements: ceremony, text, and the unadorned monodic plainsong chant to which the text was sung. The monastic restoration of the second half of the 10th century added to the existing communities of secular clergy a network of major ecclesiastical centers dedicated to the full liturgical panoply of the Cluniac revival. The greatest of the monastic institutions, whether of the Benedictine or (from the 12th century) of the Augustinian or Cistercian orders, soon maintained large communities. Only in moments of crisis did the community of Christ Church, Canterbury, ever fall below 80 monks, and of Durham below 70; some 20–30 other houses maintained around or in excess of 40 members, and a fair number of the greater nunneries sustained some 20–30 or more. In monasteries and nunneries the community at worship *was* the choir, and thenceforward until the Dissolution of religious houses under Henry VIII these bodies of nonprofessional and not necessarily particularly expert bodies of men (with, until around the middle of the 12th century, oblate boys) and women observed daily the full musical rigor of the plainsong liturgy.

During the course of the 12th century the greatest of the communities of secular clergy, especially those of the cathedral churches, came to match in grandeur and resources the most prominent of the monasteries and could endeavor to emulate the elaboration of their manner of celebrating the liturgy. Originally the principal clergy of such a church were the canons, in addition to the chorister boys of the choir and in some cases some junior clerks intermediate between them. The number of canons ranged from 24 at Exeter Cathedral to 56 (later 58) at Lincoln. During the 12th century the practice of nonresidence became well established; consequently the handful of canons resident was left fully occupied merely in administration of the cathedral and its personnel and estates. To acquit them in their choir duties, therefore, all the canons appointed substitutes. Ideally these "vicars choral" were men who possessed singing voices and qualities of character sufficiently good to enable them to take the canons' places in choir and sing the services in their behalf; not always, however, was this ideal met.

In choir the vicars choral (plus the canons resident), junior choir clerks, and chorister boys were disposed by seniority in the three ranks required by the secular liturgies, as clerks respectively of the top, second, and third rows of stalls. Normally one of the vicars choral was appointed to be master of the choristers, to instruct the boys in Latin vocabulary and grammar and to coach them in the plainsong and ceremony of the liturgy. At full strength the choir of Hereford Cathedral, the smallest, consisted of 27 men and five boys; the largest were twice this size, that of Salisbury consisting of 52 men and fourteen boys, and of Wells 50 men and nine boys. Organized on lines similar to the choirs of the cathedrals were those of other collegiate churches, such as Beverley, Ripon, Southwell, Crediton, and St. Martin's le Grand in London. With 36 men and ten boys Beverley Minster more than matched the lesser cathedrals, but most in this class were on the smaller scale of, for instance, Southwell, with 20 men and eight boys. The clergy of a few of the greatest hospital foundations also observed the liturgy in a manner akin to that of the smallest collegiate churches, at least on holy days.

In essence the function of these ecclesiastical choirs remained unchanged throughout the medieval period. This was to recite and enact the text and ceremony of the liturgy—daily high mass and the office, the Lady Mass (from the 12th or 13th century onward), and the wealth of peripheral material—to its sung plainsong chant. However, the plainsong came in time to be supplemented by alternative ways of expressing the music of certain items, through the performance of polyphony, either improvised (e.g., discant) or composed. Until about the second quarter of the 13th century the performance of written polyphony may well have been cultivated only sporadically in England; thereafter it appears to have become a regular way of distinguishing certain services at the most prominent churches, most particularly the daily Lady Mass but also high mass and the greater hours on festivals.

Until the early 15th century polyphony was composed within a narrow compass of two octaves realizable by men's voices. It was performed by ensembles of not more than four solo voices—indeed there is virtually no surviving music that could not be performed by the ensemble apparently akin to two altos, one tenor, and one baritone specified for the choral staff of the small collegiate chantry of St. Mary, Epworth (Lincolnshire), at its foundation in the 1340s. The principal centers for the composition and performance of polyphony at this time appear to have been the larger monasteries. Down to ca. 1350 music apparently survives from Benedictine houses so widely distributed as Bury St. Edmunds, Peterborough, Durham, Shrewsbury, Winchcombe, Worcester, St. Albans, and Christ Church, Canterbury, and such Augustinian monasteries as Dunstable and Thurgarton. Nevertheless, it seems likely that until the second half of the 14th century there were never at any one moment more than about a couple of hundred people in England who understood the notation of polyphonic music and could compose and perform it; it remained an esoteric and exclusive art.

The late-medieval expansion in musical and choral endeavor within the English church appears to have begun in about the second quarter of the 14th century. At this time royalty and the royal aristocracy, eventually to be imitated by most of the peerage from the rank of earl upward, began so to organize their personal chapels of the household as to include, as well as priests, the clerks in minor orders and boys necessary to emulate the greatest of the secular religious communities in their manner of the daily observance of the liturgy. The Chapel Royal became an eloquent advertisement of the king's orthodoxy and of the quality of the executive musical talent available to him in the ordering of his daily devotions; from Edward III's staff of thirteen priests, four clerks and four or five boys it expanded under Henry V to a large organization of 32 priests and clerks and sixteen boys. The prestige, salaries, and fringe benefits offered by the courts of (eventually) some twenty royal and aristocratic households enabled them to attract the ablest singers. In addition, by the end of the century, the two archbishops and many if not most of the fifteen bishops likewise maintained fully staffed household chapels.

At the same time royalty, the peerage, and the episcopacy emerged as founders of a spate of new collegiate churches, created essentially to be their perpetual chantries, of which the richest were established from the start to be major choral foundations. They include, for instance, Edward III's St. George's, Windsor, and St. Stephen's, Westminster (1348), each with a choral staff of thirteen priests, four clerks, and six choristers, and Henry VI's Eton College (1440: ten, four, sixteen) and King's College, Cambridge (1441: ten, six, sixteen); the earl of Arundel's Holy Trinity Arundel (1380: thirteen, four, six), the lord la Warre's St. Mary Manchester (1421: eight, four, six) and the duke of York's St. Mary Fotheringhay (1415: twelve, four, thirteen); St. Mary's, Winchester (1392: thirteen, three, sixteen), and New College, Oxford (1392: ten, three, sixteen), founded by William of Wykeham, bishop of Winchester; and All Saints Maidstone (1395: twelve, four, eight) founded by William Courtenay, archbishop of Canterbury—to name but a few of the 30 or 40 founded by ca. 1500. It was especially in these household chapels and major chantry colleges of the secular and ecclesiastical aristocracy that the value of polyphonic music in distinguishing the services on a regular, commonly even daily, basis came to be recognized. The Old Hall Manuscript, compiled ca. 1419–20, contains a large repertoire of polyphony for high mass and/or Lady Mass on all classes of day down to the least significant and may have been written for the household chapel choir of Thomas duke of Clarence. To render such music, as the 15th century progressed, the profession of career lay singer emerged; the minor-order clerkships of the second form came increasingly to be filled by professional singers, called "lay clerks," offering specific expertise in polyphony. Nevertheless, prior to ca. 1450, few institutions allowed for more than four or six of these; solo performance was still the predominant medium for the settings of the Ordinary of the mass, motet, and votive antiphon that were the principal vehicles for polyphonic expression at this time.

Another manifestation of the zeal for enhancing the musical component of the liturgy at this time is offered by the creation at the major monastic churches of Lady Chapel choirs. At the time these consisted of just a team of boys (drawn normally from the boys of the Almonry grammar school) and a lay professional musician (commonly entitled cantor) to train them. The choir of boys attended daily in the Lady Chapel to sing the plainsong of the Ordinary of the Lady Mass; the cantor was available also to train the monks in chant and improve the standard of singing in the monks' choir. Such choirs, usually of only six or eight boys, were established at, for instance, Westminster Abbey (by ca. 1395), Winchester (1402), Ely (1404), Durham (1416), Abingdon (by 1420), Malmesbury (by 1420), and Christ Church, Canterbury (1437); by 1500 they were to be found at most of the major Benedictine and Augustinian, and some Cistercian, houses.

During the second half of the 15th century there occurred the transformation of the choral force of the major cathedral and collegiate churches from its medieval to essentially its modern form. The catalyst appears to have been the rising importance of the enhancement of the service by the regular performance of written polyphonic music, performed no longer only by adult soloists but also by the full chorus in settings with a compass of three octaves requiring the voices of boys as well as of men, normally in a five-voice disposition of treble, alto, two tenors, and bass. This provoked the transformation of the liturgical choir from an inchoate body of individual singers of plainsong (of whom only a few specialists among the men undertook to sing written part music) to a balanced choir of men and boys, trained by a recognized director to render in common enterprise the performance of settings of polyphony—especially of the Ordinary of the mass, Magnificat (at Vespers), and the votive antiphon. In the largest choirs this was fully compatible with a fall in the number of men (at Salisbury, e.g., from 50 to 30 between 1450 and 1500 and at Lincoln from around 40 to 26), creating a manageable balance with the boys. In other choirs the number of boys had to be increased to balance with the men, as at Tattershall College (from six to ten) and at Lichfield (from eight to twelve). Others were more broadly expanded simply to increase the size of the chorus; Edward IV refounded the choir of St. George's Windsor (1476–82) to stand at sixteen priests, thirteen lay clerks, and thirteen choristers, proportions that eventually became a model for many others.

Provided that a working balance for five-part music (SATTB) could be deployed, choirs did not need to be large to be effective, and so the performance of choral polyphonic music, alongside the traditional plainsong of the liturgy, was adopted at a wide variety of ecclesiastical institutions. To augment the voices of the chaplains and establish a full chorus, boys' choirs were created at such collegiate churches as Mettingham (fourteen boys) and Rushworth (seven boys), originally founded without places for choristers. Conversely men's voices had to be found to fill out the monastery Lady Chapel choirs, originally founded for boys alone. At Worcester Cathedral and Christ Church, Canterbury, competent monks were associated with the Lady Chapel boys; elsewhere, as at Glastonbury and Gloucester, a few lay clerks were taken into employment. Meanwhile, at the wealthiest of the city and urban parish churches also, professional choirs on secular collegiate models began to be recruited. These bore no resemblance to the amateur parish church choirs of today; rather they were financed normally by one or more religious fraternities of the devout and wealthy laity of the parish, who contributed to the cost of a professional organization. Notable examples of which records survive include the choirs of several of the London parish churches, such as St. Michael Cornhill and St. Mary at Hill, of the parish churches of Ludlow (Shropshire) and of Louth and Boston in Lincolnshire, St. Lawrence Reading, All Hallows Sherborne, and All Saints Bristol. The chapel personnel of some long-established hospital foundations were modernized and reorganized as professional choirs, as for instance at St. Cross Winchester (six chaplains, six clerks, six choristers), St. Katherine's London (three, seven, six), St. Antony's London (four, eight, six), and St. Mark's Bristol (four, six, ten).

The involvement of boys' voices in the performance of written polyphony from ca. 1450–60 onward was an innovation, and their training now required special skills and competence on the part of their instructor. The post of master of the choristers came to be filled by well-paid lay professional musicians, very often employed also as organ players, who filled *de facto* the role of director of the whole choir; commonly each was also a composer contributing to the stock of polyphonic music in circulation. The proliferation of choral establishments resulted in no concentration of the craft of composition in one place (e.g., at court) but rather in a healthy dispersal around the country.

By the end of the 15th century it was commonly required of not only the boys and lay clerks of choral establishments but of many of the priests and chaplains also that they be competent to contribute to the performance of polyphony, ensuring the full choral sound that ever since has been the hallmark of the English church choral tradition. Indeed, by ca. 1500, at institutions ranging from the Chapel Royal and the household chapels of the aristocracy, through monastery Lady Chapels and collegiate and parish churches possibly numbering close to 200 in all, professional choral endeavor—doubt-less of diverse quality—had come to constitute an honorable professional occupation for the large number of men and boys now appropriately employed, trained, and educated, and a vehicle making possible both the conception and the performance of a body of elaborate music—the virtuoso polyphony of such composers as John Browne, Robert Fayrfax, and Walter Lambe—of the highest quality and lasting value.

Roger D. Bowers

Bibliography

Edwards, Kathleen. *The English Secular Cathedrals in the Middle Ages.* Manchester: Manchester University Press, 1963; Harrison, Frank Ll. *Music in Medieval Britain.* 2d ed. London: Routledge & Kegan Paul, 1963; Robertson, Dora. *Sarum Close.* 2d ed. Bath: Firecrest, 1969.

See also Antiphon; Chapel Royal; Lady Chapel; Lady Mass; Liturgy and Church Music, History of; Magnificat; Old Hall Manuscript; Salve Service

Christ and Satan

The fourth and final poem in the Junius Manuscript of OE poetry. In contrast to the preceding poems, which are all concerned with Old Testament themes, *Christ and Satan* covers the whole span of biblical history and recounts a series of conflicts between Christ and Satan.

The poem can be divided into three sections. The first part (lines 1–365) consists of a series of complaints by Satan and the fallen angels, condemned to hell after their unsuccessful revolt. Unlike the two treatments of the Fall of Angels in *Genesis A* and *Genesis B* earlier in the Junius Manuscript the rebellion in *Christ and Satan* is depicted as specifically directed not against God the Father but against Christ the Son, the first of a series of conflicts in heaven, in hell, and on earth that make up the rest of the poem. The second section (lines 366–662) gives an account of the Resurrection, Ascension, and Last Judgment but focuses on Christ's Harrowing of Hell and overthrow of Satan in his own domain. The third section (lines 663–729) provides a brief but graphic account of Satan's temptation of Christ in the wilderness.

Throughout the poem emphasis is placed on the power of Christ and the powerlessness of Satan, who appears in this poem as a much more abject and pathetic figure than, for example, in *Genesis B*. A number of the motifs in the poem, such as Satan bearing Christ on his shoulders, or being condemned to measure the extent of hell with his own hands, are unparalleled and may be the innovation of a poet who, though lacking the force and vision of a Cynewulf (to whom the poem was once attributed), could still bring considerable and unorthodox sophistication to his work.

A.P.M. Orchard

Bibliography

PRIMARY

ASPR 1:135–58; Finnegan, Robert Emmett, ed. *Christ and Satan: A Critical Edition.* Waterloo: Wilfrid Laurier University Press, 1977.

SECONDARY
Harsh, Constance D. "*Christ and Satan:* The Measured Power of Christ." *NM* 90 (1989): 243–53; Keenan, Hugh T. "Satan Speaks in Sparks: *Christ and Satan* 78–79a, 161b–162b, and the *Life of St Anthony.*" *N&Q* n.s. 21 (1974): 283–84; Sleeth, Charles R. *Studies in "Christ and Satan."* Toronto: University of Toronto Press, 1982.

See also Cynewulf; *Daniel; Exodus; Genesis A* and *B; Junius Manuscript*

Christ I

The three opening poems of the Exeter Book, once believed to constitute a single work by Cynewulf on the life of Christ, are now commonly distinguished by the titles *Christ I, Christ II,* and *Christ III.* Although opinion continues to vary on whether and how the poems are structurally and thematically unified, they are usually seen as independent works and are almost certainly not the work of one author (though the attribution of *Christ II* to Cynewulf remains secure).

Christ I, also known as *Advent* or the *Advent Lyrics,* survives as a series of twelve intricate lyrics of varying length that amount to 439 lines. All save the first lyric, whose opening is lost, begin with the hortatory injunction *Eala* ("O!" or "Lo!") and address a person, place, or attribute associated with Christ in the Advent liturgy. Together the poems develop a series of themes that illustrate the movement from Advent to Christmas: Lyrics 1–10 dramatize the church's sustained anticipation of Christ's Advent, Lyric 11 brings the progression to an emotional climax in praising the Trinity for the Nativity that has now taken place, and Lyric 12 resolves the sequence by celebrating the miracle of the Virgin Birth and counseling humanity to honor God and seek his eternal reward. Lyric 7 (*Eala ioseph min,* "O my Joseph") is particularly well known as an early expression of the iconological motif of the "doubting of Mary," a revelation of Joseph's anguish and consternation over the pregnancy of his supposedly virgin bride.

The first ten of the twelve lyrics owe their themes and much of their imagery to a group of Latin antiphons that in the medieval Roman church were chanted at Vespers on the days during Advent called the Greater Ferias, from 17 December to 23 December. These antiphons, compiled over time from an early collection of seven *antiphonae maiores,* or "Great O" antiphons, and from a later group of "monastic" or "additional O" antiphons, all begin with the Latin invocative "O" and were conventionally sung once before and once after the gospel canticle known as the Magnificat (Luke 1:39–55). Of the two lyrics that do not clearly follow this pattern, one (Lyric 11) has no single widely accepted source and the other (Lyric 12) is adapted from an antiphon for Lauds on the octave of Christmas (January 1). The repertoire of antiphons available to the poet was evidently unique in that the number, order, and selection of antiphons after which the antiphons were patterned are without parallel in any extant chant books, insular or continental. Comparison with surviving collections of Latin antiphons also makes it likely that the poet originally wrote fifteen lyrics and that the first three are now lost along with the opening of Lyric 1. Because the antiphons known to the poet derive almost uniformly from Roman (rather than Gallican or insular) liturgical tradition, it is possible to speculate that the lyrics were composed well before the third quarter of the 10th century, when Roman liturgical customs in English use began to be supplanted by Frankish and Lotharingian ones in the wake of the Benedictine Reform. Together with their great lyrical power the poems' subtle reliance on biblical and patristic learning marks them as the most sophisticated examples of liturgical poetry in OE.

Thomas N. Hall

Bibliography

PRIMARY
ASPR 3:3–15; Burlin, Robert B., ed. and trans. *The Old English Advent: A Typological Commentary.* New Haven: Yale University Press, 1968; Campbell, Jackson J., ed. and trans. *The Advent Lyrics of the Exeter Book.* Princeton: Princeton University Press, 1959.

SECONDARY
Burgert, Edward. *The Dependence of Part I of Cynewulf's Christ upon the Antiphonary.* Washington, D.C.: Catholic University of America Press, 1921; Rankin, Susan. "The Liturgical Background of the OE Advent Lyrics: A Reappraisal." In *Learning and Literature in Anglo-Saxon England,* ed. Michael Lapidge and Helmut Gneuss. Cambridge: Cambridge University Press, 1985, pp. 317–40.

See also Antiphon; Cynewulf; Exeter Book; Liturgy; Liturgy and Church Music, History of; Magnificat

Christ III

The third poem of the Exeter Book, *Christ III,* once but no longer attributed to Cynewulf, is a dramatic 798-line account of Doomsday representative of a rich tradition of Anglo-Saxon penitential and eschatological literature. While the marvels it describes follow no clear sequence and are occasionally repeated, the poem's governing theme is that Judgment will take place at midnight on Mount Sion accompanied by a series of tumultuous events. Angels will blow trumpets from the four corners of the earth, the heavens will split asunder, the stars and moon will fall from the sky, the sun will turn to blood, and fire will ravage the earth as Christ appears in glory in the southeastern sky and displays his wounds. Dead bodies will rise from their graves and take on new flesh as they are reunited with their souls. The Cross will appear in the heavens, shining brilliantly through the stains of Christ's blood, and will then direct each man to come before the Lord to be judged. The thoughts, words, and deeds of each man will then be openly revealed as his flesh becomes like glass. Christ will accordingly separate the just from the unjust, casting the wicked into the depths of everlasting torment while the elect pass blissfully into the communion of angels. In a long speech that follows Christ comforts the blessed and reminds them of their good deeds while he abjures the wicked for neglecting his commandments. After a moving call for introspection and repentance in anticipation of God's judgment upon all humankind at the end of time the poem then closes with a rhapsodic description of the joys of heaven.

In addition to the biblical sources for many of these details the poem adapts its imagery and bold theology from a range of patristic texts, including Gregory the Great's *Moralia in Job* and two sermons by Caesarius of Arles, with more distant echoes of works by Ephraim Syrus and Bede. Several unusual motifs, such as the location of Judgment on Mount Sion and its occurrence at midnight, the bleeding of the trees at Christ's Passion (perhaps modeled on 4 Esdras 5:5), and the burning of the seas like wax, have close and extensive parallels only in Irish and Hiberno-Latin literature and may therefore align the poem with a distinctively insular tradition of eschatology.

Thomas N. Hall

Bibliography

PRIMARY

ASPR 3:27–49; Biggs, Frederick M. *The Sources of Christ III: A Revision of Cook's Notes.* OEN Subsidia 12. Binghamton: CEMERS, 1986; Cook, Albert S., ed. *The Christ of Cynewulf.* 2d ed. Boston: Ginn, 1909. Repr. with preface by John C. Pope. Hamden: Shoe String Press, 1964;

SECONDARY

Biggs, Frederick M. "The Fourfold Division of the Souls: The Old English *Christ III* and the Insular Homiletic Tradition." *Traditio* 45 (1989–90): 35–51; Hill, Thomas D. "Literary Tradition and Old English Poetry: The Case of *Christ I, II,* and *III.*" In *Sources of Anglo-Saxon Culture,* ed. Paul E. Szarmach, with Virginia Darrow Oggins. Studies in Medieval Culture 20. Kalamazoo: Medieval Institute, 1986, pp. 3–22.

See also Caesarius; Cynewulf; *Dream of the Rood;* Exeter Book; Fathers of the Church; Literary Influences: Irish

Chrodegang of Metz (d. 766)

Frankish clerical reformer. Born of a noble Frankish family, Chrodegang spent his early career in the Frankish court, where he was chancellor or "keeper of the seal" for Charles Martel. Later appointed bishop of Metz (742) and then archbishop (754–55), Chrodegang sought to enact reforms in several major areas, notably clerical life and liturgy, but he was also active in building campaigns, founding such important monasteries as Gorze (where he was buried in 766), Lorsch, and St. Avold. In many ways Chrodegang was a true successor to Boniface, the Apostle of Germany, and both shared a deference to Rome for practices and customs.

In Anglo-Saxon England Chrodegang's *Regula canonicorum,* or *Rule for Canons* (755), had a major impact. The original document had 34 chapters, later greatly expanded, that sought to establish a community life for clergy at a cathedral. Later versions included chapters taken from the councils of Aachen (816) and Toledo (633). Under the *Rule* cathedral clergy were not bound to poverty but lived a quasi-monastic life. Chrodegang borrowed from the Benedictine Rule but changed several things. Most obviously the bishop replaces the abbot. Chrodegang also regulates severely what Benedict saw as hospitality and, because there is no hospice at the cathedral, had to make other rules for treating the sick. The enlarged *Rule* appears in Cambridge, Corpus Christi College 191, which offers 84 chapters in Latin and OE, and partially in three other manuscripts.

Scholarship has thus far only suggested the importance of Chrodegang's *Rule* in Anglo-Saxon culture. Trahern has seen links between Chrodegang and the OE poem *Vainglory,* while recent conference activity, as yet unpublished, has explored gender adaptations of the Benedictine Rule in connection with Chrodegang. The tension between monks and clerics, as evidenced by Æthelwold's expulsion of the clerks from the Old Minster, Winchester, in 964, may have more to do with Anglo-Saxon cultural forms than hitherto understood.

Paul E. Szarmach

Bibliography

PRIMARY

Napier, Arthur S., ed. *The Old English Version of the Enlarged Rule of Chrodegang. . . .* EETS o.s. 150. London: Kegan Paul, Trench, Trübner, 1916.

SECONDARY

Saint Chrodegang: communications presentées au Colloque tenu á Metz a l'occasion de douzième centenaire de sa mort. Metz: Éditions le Lorrain, 1967; Trahern, Joseph B. "Caesarius, Chrodegang, and the Old English *Vainglory.*" In *Gesellschaft, Kultur, Literatur: Rezeption und Originalität im Wachsen einer europäischen Literatur und Geistigkeit,* ed. Karl Bosl. Stuttgart: Hiersemann, 1975, pp. 167–78.

See also Benedict of Nursia; Benedictine Reform; Boniface; *Regularis concordia*

Chronicle Poems

Poems that appear at various points in the Anglo-Saxon Chronicle and mark the close of the OE alliterative verse tradition. They can be found in four of the Chronicle manuscripts: Cambridge, Corpus Christi College 173 (the Parker Manuscript), and BL Cotton Tiberius A.vi, Cotton Tiberius B.i, and Cotton Tiberius B.iv.

Despite the difficulties of multiple authorship and manuscript variations, if viewed as a collection these poems can be seen as moving over time from a traditional to an imaginative and erratic poetic style. The deliberate use of rhyme and irregular meter in the later poems is thought to link the OE and the ME verse traditions in its variation on the ancient and conservative poetic formulas. At the same time, however, if the poems' purpose parallels that of the chronicle as a whole, they can be seen as artificially yet consciously privileging and preserving the older style for the sake of creating a national history and identity (Campbell 1938: 36–38).

The first chronicle poem is the longest, most conventional, and most famous: *The Battle of Brunanburh* (937). As opposed to the more somber *Battle of Maldon,* this is an "unrestrained song of triumph," concerned not with details of the actual battle but with making the English armies into national heroes (ASPR 6:xi). It closely follows older forms of heroic poetry in style and language. The remaining poems include *The Capture of the Five Boroughs* (942), *The Coronation of Edgar* (973), *The Death of Edgar* (975), *The Death of Alfred* (1036), *The Death of Edward* (1065), and the *Rime of William* (1086). This final poem departs greatly from OE alliterative convention by using rhyme as the dominant poetic device, and it shows the most erratic meter. A thematic movement also take place among the chronicle poetry, from celebrating English victory in the earliest poems to the reality of the oppression suffered by the English under the rule of William I.

Dana-Linn Whiteside

Bibliography

ASPR 6:16–26; Campbell, Alistair, ed. *The Battle of Brunanburh.* London: Heinemann, 1938; Dumville, David, and Simon Keynes, gen. eds. *The Anglo-Saxon Chronicle: A Collaborative Edition.* Cambridge: Brewer, 1983– [ongoing edition designed to update Thorpe]; Plummer, Charles, ed. *Two of the Saxon Chronicles Parallel.* 2 vols. Oxford: Clarendon, 1892–99; Thorpe, Benjamin, ed. and trans. *The Anglo-Saxon Chronicle.* Rolls Series 23. London: Longman, Longman, Green, Longman & Roberts, 1861.

See also Anglo-Saxon Chronicle; *Battle of Brunanburh;* Monarchy and Kingship; Norman Conquest; Versification

Chronicles

Chronicles were the major source of historical information in the Middle Ages. Their primary function was therefore utilitarian rather than aesthetic, although many of them are not devoid of literary merit. Their modern value lies partly in the historical information that they contain and partly in what they indicate regarding the historical, political, and cultural consciousness of their writers and compilers and of their medieval audience. In addition many chronicles are of linguistic interest, both inherently and as witnesses to the relative fortunes of the Latin, French, and English languages in medieval England.

Theoretically a distinction should be made between chronicles (prose or verse narratives that cover a considerable period of history) and annals (year-by-year accounts of significant events). In practice the two types frequently overlap or are combined in a single work, and no strict distinction is made in the present article. Similarly accounts covering relatively short periods of time or individual events are also considered here. It is also possible to regard narratives of ancient history (such as accounts of the siege of Troy), certain romances (such as those about Arthur), and many saints' lives

as chronicle writings, but these are not considered here.

Anglo-Saxon Period

The earliest historical work written in the Anglo-Saxon period is Gildas's mid-6th-century *De excidio et conquestu Britanniae;* its historical intent, however, is superseded by its bitter homiletic attack on contemporary British decadence. A later Celtic work, similar to Gildas in its importance as evidence for the early development of the Arthurian legend, is the *Historia Brittonum,* attributed to Nennius. Although originally written in Wales in 829/30, Nennius's *Historia* became known in England in the 10th century, and it was influential on Geoffrey of Monmouth.

Quite different in approach is Bede's *Historia ecclesiastica gentis Anglorum,* which recounts the history of England from Julius Caesar to A.D. 731, the year of the work's completion, focusing on the conversion to Christianity. Bede's meticulous, well-documented methodology is similar in many ways to that introduced by Renaissance historiography. As a major historical source Bede's work is paralleled and supplemented by the versions of the vernacular Anglo-Saxon Chronicle, which have a common ancestor in a set of annals, probably designed originally to compute the date of Easter, that were compiled in or soon after 891. Possibly at the instigation of King Alfred the Great this compilation was much copied and widely circulated, and copies subsequently received independent continuations, the latest of which, in the Peterborough version, ends in 1154. Lost versions of the Chronicle were used by Asser in his Latin biography of King Alfred, *De rebus gestis Aelfredi* (ca. 893), and by Æthelweard in his Latin *Chronicon* (late 10th century). Alfred's zeal for the advancement of learning is also reflected in the OE translations of Bede's *Historia* and of Paulus Orosius's *Historiae adversum paganos,* a universal history to A.D. 417.

Post-Conquest Latin Chronicles

After the Norman Conquest English historians writing in Latin continued to draw on Anglo-Saxon historiographical traditions. For example, taken together, the *De gestis regum Anglorum* and *De gestis pontificum Anglorum* of William of Malmesbury (both first completed ca. 1125) are reminiscent of Bede's *Historia,* while William's unfinished *Historia novella* (before 1143) is similar in its annalistic form to the Anglo-Saxon Chronicle. Similar influences are found in the *Historia Anglorum* of Henry of Huntingdon, a member of the secular clergy, which, in its latest revision (1154/55), covered the period 55 B.C. to 1154.

Monastic chronicles (with which can be considered works by other regular clergy, such as Augustinian canons), were often written by Benedictine historians or reflected their influence; they flourished from the 12th to the mid-13th century, then declined until they enjoyed a revival in the later 14th century. Such chronicles vary in historical scope, though most show a particular interest in local affairs pertaining to the history and position of the religious house in which they were produced. Notable works include John of Worcester's *Chronicon ex chronicis* (from Creation to 1140); Richard of Hexham's

De gestis Stephani et de bello standardii (1135–39); the *Gesta regum* attributed to Symeon of Durham (early 7th century to 1129) and John of Hexham's continuation thereof (1130–54); Gervase of Canterbury's *Chronica* (time of Augustine of Canterbury to 1199) and *Gesta regum* (from the legendary Brutus to 1210); Richard of Devizes's *Cronicon de tempore regis Richardi primi* (1189–92); William of Newburgh's *Historia rerum anglicarum* (1066–1198); and Ralph of Coggeshall's *Chronicon anglicanum* (1066–1224). A number of chronicles dealing in part with English history were also written and circulated in Normandy, such as Orderic Vitalis's *Historia ecclesiastica* (A.D. 1–1141) and Robert of Torigni's *Chronica* (Creation to 1186).

In the 13th century the Abbey of St. Albans became a major center of historical writing. In addition to a history of the abbey and a series of saints' lives Matthew Paris built on the work of Roger of Wendover to produce his heavily illustrated *Chronica majora* (Creation to 1259) and the derivative *Historia Anglorum,* the *Abbreviatio chronicorum,* and the *Flores historiarum.* The *Flores* later received continuations at St. Albans and elsewhere and was an influential work on subsequent histories.

Similarly influential in the 14th and 15th centuries was Ranulf Higden's *Polychronicon,* a universal history from the Creation to, in its final version by Higden, 1352. Higden's work received numerous continuations in various monastic houses and was used by such later chroniclers as John of Tynemouth, John of Brompton, and Henry Knighton and in the *Eulogium historiarum.* A *Polychronicon* continuation was also used by Thomas Walsingham, whose major historical works, the *Chronica majora* (a continuation of Matthew Paris) and *Ypodigma Neustriae,* represent a revival of the St. Albans tradition of historical writing in the late 14th and early 15th centuries. The monastic tradition, however, declined once more by the mid-15th century, due in part to the increasing popularity of vernacular histories.

Anglo-Norman Chronicles

From the mid-12th century there also developed a tradition of Anglo-Norman historical writing that, unlike the monastic chronicles, was heavily influenced in style or tone by romance literature and was at first primarily composed by members of the secular clergy. In the case of full-scale chronicles the major source for English history between Brutus and Cadwalader was Geoffrey of Monmouth's immensely popular *Historia regum Britanniae,* completed probably in 1138, which also influenced Henry of Huntingdon. Shortly before 1140 Geoffrey's *Historia* was adapted by Geffrei Gaimar to form the now-lost beginning of his verse chronicle *L'estoire des Engleis,* and it was also the source for Wace's *Roman de Brut* (ca. 1155), which supplanted the first section of Gaimar in the manuscripts. The first part of Peter of Langtoft's verse *Chronicle* is a paraphrase of Geoffrey.

Through Wace Geoffrey's *Historia* forms the basis for the early history in the Anglo-Norman prose *Brut* (first written in the reign of Edward I, though it received several continuations in the 14th century), and it was also used as a source

in other prose chronicles, such as Nicholas Trevet's *Cronicles* (Creation to early 1330s) and Sir Thomas Gray's *Scalacronica* (Brutus to 1363). The prose *Anonimalle Chronicle* (Brutus to 1381) is similar in its earlier contents to the *Brut,* which in fact is used to supply a continuation from 1307 to 1333. Romance influence and chivalric values are also present in the late-12th-century verse *Chronique de la guerre entre les Anglois et les Ecossois* by Jordan Fantosme and Ambroise's verse *Estoire de la guerre sainte,* in the early-13th-century verse *Histoire de Guillaume le Maréchal,* the late-14th-century prose *Vie du Prince Noir* by the Chandos Herald, and in the mid-14th- and early-15th-century recensions of Jean Froissart's prose *Chroniques.* In Scotland such influences are also found in John Barbour's *Bruce* and Harry's *Wallace,* both written in Middle Scots.

Middle English Chronicles

The continuations made up to the mid-12th century to the Peterborough version of the Anglo-Saxon Chronicle represent the conclusion of the vigorous OE tradition of prose chronicle writing. Later a new verse tradition of ME historical writing arose, originally modeled on French verse chronicles like those of Gaimar and Wace, resulting in the comprehensive treatments of English history found in Laȝamon's *Brut* (written ca. 1200); the A and B versions of Robert of Gloucester's *Chronicle,* the anonymous *Short Metrical Chronicle,* Robert Manning's *Chronicle* (all written ca. 1300–40); Thomas Castleford's *Chronicle* (mid-14th century); and the A and B versions of John Hardyng's *Chronicle* (mid-15th century). In Scotland Andrew Wyntoun's *Original Chronicle,* completed ca. 1420, presents a similarly full, versified account of Scottish history and its biblical and classical antecedents.

The popularity of verse chronicles, however, was small compared with that enjoyed by ME prose chronicles after their reintroduction in the late 14th century. As in the case of the verse chronicles the earliest prose chronicles were originally translations, but as linguistic confidence and nationalist pride increased many developed into independent English productions early in the 15th century. Major prose chronicles in modern editions include John Trevisa's translation of the *Polychronicon;* the first translation of the prose *Brut,* the most popular and successful of all ME secular works and one that received many continuations and adaptations in the 15th century; the various versions of the *Chronicles of London* (designed for a growing civic, lay audience); and John Capgrave's *Abbreviation of Chronicles.* Major unpublished chronicles include translations of Geoffrey of Monmouth's *Historia regum Britanniae,* of Nicholas Trevet's Anglo-Norman *Cronicles* with a continuation beginning in 1327 and breaking off in 1417 from the English prose *Brut,* and of Martin of Troppau's *Chronicon pontificum et imperatorum,* and prose paraphrases of Robert of Gloucester's *Chronicle* and Robert Manning's *Chronicle.*

Shorter ME prose chronicles focusing on specific events or periods include the *English Conquest of Ireland* (probably translated from a Latin chronicle ultimately based on the *Expugnatio hibernica* of Gerald of Wales); John Shirley's *Death of the King of Scots* (said to be translated from Latin); and the chronicle of the years 1461–74 erroneously attributed to John Warkworth, which is appended to two manuscripts of the *Brut.*

Ecclesiastical history can be represented by two ill-matched ME works. The *Book of the Foundation of St. Bartholomew's Church in London* piously relates the history of the church, with associated miracles, while a Lollard chronicle of the papacy presents a vitriolic account of the "rablement of the popes" drawn from Higden's *Polychronicon,* supplemented by Martin of Troppau's *Chronicon.*

Unlike the ideal of modern historical writings none of the above works is written from a totally detached viewpoint; the medieval chronicler does not hesitate to use history to state or draw moral judgments or to show political predilections. Even more consciously designed to influence are those short relations of recent or current events circulated as open newsletters or as propaganda pamphlets, particularly during the politically turbulent late 15th century. Official or semiofficial accounts, such as the *Chronicle of the Rebellion in Lincolnshire* (1470) and the short and long versions of the *History of the Arrival of King Edward IV* (ca. 1471), use privileged inside information and official documents. Genealogical chronicles of Edward IV, beginning with Adam, justified the legitimacy of his claim to the throne.

Some relatively short ME poems parallel in subject matter and intended audience the shorter prose texts noted above. They are common from the beginning of the 14th century, which was the heyday of the full-scale verse chronicle, until the end of the 15th century and beyond, and all are marked by some form of nationalist pride or partisanship. Most similar in general outline to the ME prose chronicles, and quite possibly derived from a *Brut* chronicle, are Lydgate's highly popular verses on the *Kings of England.* The anonymous *Battle of Halidon Hill* and John Page's *Siege of Rouen* are verse narratives that are close in style to the prose *Brut* chronicle in which they are frequently incorporated. The war poems of Laurence Minot, written over a period of twenty years (ca. 1333–52), have been linked in the surviving manuscript by short prose rubrics in the manner of the chapter headings of a prose chronicle, such as the *Brut.* The *Recovery of the Throne by Edward IV,* called "the balet [ballad] off the kynge" at the end of the text, covers much the same ground as the short Yorkist prose *History of the Arrival.*

Copies of Latin and Anglo-Norman chronicles continued to be made in the 15th century, and toward the end of the century the already widespread circulation of ME chronicles was increased by William Caxton's publication of the prose *Brut* (as the *Chronicles of England*) and of Trevisa's translation of the *Polychronicon.* Subsequent printers continued to publish these and other historical works, and the medieval chronicles remained major sources for Tudor historians, such as Edward Hall, John Stow, and Raphael Holinshed.

Lister M. Matheson

Bibliography

Manual 8 [Chronicles]; 5:1385–1536, 1631–1725 [Poems Dealing with Contemporary Conditions]; Brandt, William J. *The Shape of Medieval History: Studies in Modes of Perception.* New Haven: Yale University Press, 1966; Fletcher, Robert Huntington. *The Arthurian Material in the Chronicles, Especially Those of Great Britain and France.* 2d ed. New York: Burt Franklin, 1966; Gransden, Antonia. *Historical Writing in England.* 2 vols. London: Routledge & Kegan Paul, 1974–82 [ca. 550 to early 16th century]; Gransden, Antonia. "The Chronicles of Medieval England and Scotland." *JMH* 16 (1990): 129–50, 17 (1991): 217–43. Repr. in *Legends, Traditions and History in Medieval England.* London: Hambledon, 1992, pp. 199–238; Graves, Edgar B., ed. *A Bibliography of English History to 1485.* Oxford: Clarendon, 1975; Hanning, Robert W. *The Vision of History in Early Britain: From Gildas to Geoffrey of Monmouth.* New York: Columbia University Press, 1966; Keeler, Laura. *Geoffrey of Monmouth and the Late Latin Chroniclers 1300–1500.* University of California Publications in English 17, no. 1. Berkeley: University of California Press, 1946; Kingsford, Charles Lethbridge. *English Historical Literature in the Fifteenth Century.* Oxford: Clarendon, 1913; Matheson, Lister M. "Historical Prose." In *Middle English Prose: A Critical Guide to Major Authors and Genres,* ed. A.S.G. Edwards. New Brunswick: Rutgers University Press, 1984, pp. 209–48; Matheson, Lister M. "King Arthur and the Medieval English Chronicles." In *King Arthur through the Ages,* ed. Valerie M. Lagorio and Mildred Leake Day. 2 vols. New York: Garland, 1990, 1:248–74; Matheson, Lister M. "A Great Divide: Historical Principles in Early and Middle Scots Literature." In *Celtic Connections,* ed. David Lampe. ACTA 16. Binghamton: CEMERS, 1993 (for 1989), pp. 73–98; Matheson, Lister M. *The Prose Brut: The Development of a Middle English Chronicle.* Tempe: MRTS, 1998; Taylor, John. *English Historical Literature in the Fourteenth Century.* Oxford: Clarendon, 1987.

See also Anglo-Latin Literature after 1066; Anglo-Latin Literature to 1066; Anglo-Norman Literature; Anglo-Saxon Chronicle; *Brut,* Prose; Hagiography; Monasticism; Prose, ME; Romances; Translation

Ciboria: Morgan, Balfour, Warwick

Ciboria are vessels that held the consecrated host for distribution to those celebrating the eucharist. These three copper-gilt, forged, engraved, punched, and *champlevé* enameled ciboria, hereafter referred to as "M" (New York, Pierpont Morgan Library), "B" (London, Victoria and Albert Museum M.1–1981), and "W" (London, Victoria and Albert Museum M.159–1919; fig. 40), were all produced ca. 1150–75. M and B are in good condition, while the cover of W and the enamel on the remaining bowl have been lost.

Since the cover of W was presumably comparable with those of M and B, the three ciboria share the same form; a hemispherical bowl standing upon a splayed circular foot, with a cover of similar shape, surmounted by an ovoid handle collared with four cast leaves.

The decorative schemes of the ciboria also compare closely.

Inside each lid the Lamb of God in a roundel holds a cross-standard, with blood spilling from his chest into a chalice. Inside each bowl another roundel has Christ blessing, clasping a book and cross. The exterior of each bowl and cover is enameled with six narrative scenes set within roundels surrounded by branches of fleshy foliage blossoms. This arrangement compares well with paintings on the choir vault of the Hospital Chapel of Le Petit-Quevilly, Rouen, of the later 12th century, although the scrolling foliage is similar to that on some contemporary English sculpture and illuminated manuscripts.

New Testament christological scenes on the covers are set above their Old Testament counterparts on the bowls in a typological arrangement. Thus on B, for example, the Crucifixion is positioned above the Sacrifice of Isaac by Abraham. The varied combination of scenes emphasize different sacrificial and redemptive aspects of the eucharist. Differences in subject matter and iconography are minimal; five scenes are common to all three ciboria.

The linear, schematized figures on M and B compare closely enough to indicate that one artist executed both. The artist of W employs a distinctly more fluid style, leading some to speculate that he was of north French or Mosan (Meuse Valley) origin. Overall similarities of design and choice of subject matter and iconography, however, suggest a single workshop and a commonly available model.

Although elements of the decorative scheme and technical details relate to continental comparisons, the weight of evidence confirms that M, B, and W were produced in England. Of particular relevance are the descriptive inscriptions occupying the frame of each medallion. These are identical with a set of Latin verse inscriptions describing a now destroyed 12th-century cycle of scenes in the chapter house at Worcester. The exact relationship between the two sets of inscriptions remains open to debate, but their proximity confirms an English provenance for M, B, and W and hints at a more intimate connection; the ciboria and chapter house scenes were produced possibly by a single workshop.

Apart from attesting the skill of mid-12th-century goldsmiths, M, B, and W together provide an almost unique opportunity of examining how two artists, trained in very different traditions but working within a single workshop, interpreted commonly available sources.

Sally Dormer

Bibliography

Campbell, Marian. "'Scribe faber lima': A Crozier in Florence Reconsidered." *Burlington Magazine* 121 (1979): 364–69; Campbell, Marian. *An Introduction to Medieval Enamels.* London: Victoria and Albert Museum, 1983, pp. 26–27, 31–32; Stratford, Neil. "Three English Romanesque Enamelled Ciboria." *Burlington Magazine* 126 (1984): 204–16 [includes a full set of illustrations and inscriptions]; Williamson, Paul, ed. *The Medieval Treasury.* London: Victoria and Albert Museum, 1986, p. 130; Zarnecki, George, Janet Holt, and Tristram Holland, eds. *English Romanesque Art 1066–1200.* London: Weidenfeld & Nicolson, 1984, cat. nos. 278, 279, 280 [entries by Neil Stratford].

See also Metalwork and Enamels, Romanesque

Cinque Ports

A group of towns on the southeast coast that together supplied the king with the services of 57 ships, fully manned, for fifteen days each year. The original five "head ports" were Hastings, Romney, Hythe, Dover, and Sandwich, but more than 30 other places in Kent and Sussex, and one in Essex, became joined to the different "head ports" at various times. Chief among the affiliated "members" were the towns of Winchelsea and Rye, attached to Hastings before 1190 and later given the status of "head ports." Each member town received the right to share in the privileges of the Cinque Ports, such as freedom from most external jurisdiction and from customary taxation and tolls, in return for undertaking to discharge part of the burden of ship service.

The Cinque Ports system originated in the reign of Edward the Confessor. After the Norman Conquest ship service was increasingly important as the ports provided the Norman kings with safe transport to their French dominions. With the loss of Normandy in 1204 the Cinque Ports' fleet became vital for control of the English Channel and protection of the coastline. Although the Cinque Ports continued to perform valuable naval services in the 14th and 15th centuries, other ports overtook them as trading and naval centers, and by the end of the 16th century they were of little maritime significance. Their decline was hastened by violent storms that destroyed Romney harbor and Old Winchelsea in the late 13th century and by the eastward drift of shingle along the Channel coast, which gradually closed the old harbors of Hastings, Hythe, Dover, and Sandwich.

Deputies from each port met in the courts of the "brotherhood" and the "guestling," where common business for all the port towns was transacted, though each town ran its internal affairs. The ports remained throughout a loose confederation with no central administration, subject to the supervision from the 13th century onward of the royal warden who was also the constable of Dover.

Henry S. Cobb

Bibliography

Hull, Felix, ed. *A Calendar of the White and Black Books of the Cinque Ports, 1432–1955.* Historical Manuscripts Commission, Joint Publication 5. London: HMSO, 1966; Murray, Katherine M.E. *The Constitutional History of the Cinque Ports.* Manchester: Manchester University Press, 1935; Oppenheim, Michael. "Maritime History." In *Victoria History of the County of Sussex (VCH)*, ed. William Page. London: Constable, 1907, 2:125–67. Also in *VCH, Kent* 2:243–336, and *VCH, Sussex* 9:34–75 [these entries cover the "maritime history" of the counties].

See also Customs Accounts; Navy; Ships

Cistercian Architecture

Founded at Cîteaux in eastern France in 1098 as a reform order of Benedictine monks, the Cistercians first settled in England in 1128. The order spread rapidly, with 46 monasteries by 1154 and an eventual total of 64. For over 400 years the English abbeys played an important role in the spiritual and economic life of the country. Between 1536 and 1539 all were dissolved, and despoiled, on the orders of Henry VIII.

The greatest monasteries were in the north of England. At the four largest—Rievaulx (founded 1131), Fountains (1133; figs. 41–46), Furness (1147), and Byland (1147)—the commu-

Fig. 41. Fountains Abbey, Yorkshire, western facade of church. Courtesy of A.J. Hawkes.

Fig. 42. Fountains Abbey, Yorkshire, nave of church looking east. Courtesy of A.J. Hawkes.

nities numbered 300 to 600 at their height around 1225, with estates in excess of 100,000 acres apiece. These holdings, given over mainly to sheep farming centered on granges, were worked by lay brothers, a second category below the monks, who were otherwise part of the monastery. The order's earliest patrons were aristocratic families; only in the 13th century did the kings of England become founders, notably at Beaulieu (1204), Hailes (1246), and Vale Royal (1277). Decline in the numbers and fortunes of the Cistercians in England began in the late 13th century. By the Black Death (ca. 1350) many communities had shrunk to fewer than 30. A modest revival occurred in the 15th and early 16th centuries.

Cistercian architecture has been studied mainly in the northern abbeys, where more survives because sites were isolated and which at the Dissolution became the private properties of the king's allies and thus less open to public pillage. Scholarly study has focused largely on the churches. However, the church was only one of many buildings in a complex comprising from 60 to 90 acres overall within the surrounding wall. Significant remains of nonecclesiastical structures, both domestic and industrial, survive. Far less is known of the orchards, fishponds, and gardens that also lay within the precinct. They are known mainly through documentary accounts.

The order's earliest churches were of wood, serving the community's needs for about the first 25 years. Archaeology has recently revealed such a church at Fountains—a simple rectangular, aisleless building. For stone buildings a clear development in three stylistic phases emerges. From the period 1140–50 the churches at Rievaulx, Fountains, and Kirkstall (all in Yorkshire) are among the best examples of the order's early building. In plan they resemble Cistercian churches in Burgundy, where the movement originated, such as Fontenay

(Côte d'Or), and show a square, aisleless eastern termination, transepts with straight east walls, and aisled naves of eight to ten bays. The interior was divided into two parts: that to the east was used by the monks, that to the west by the lay brothers. In elevation the buildings were two-storied—arcade and clerestory—and timber barrel-vaulted, though the aisles had masonry barrel vaults at Rievaulx and Fountains and rib vaults at Kirkstall. Local influence appeared in architectural detailing, but the plan, simplicity of form and surface, utilization of features like barrel vaults, and the avoidance of stained glass, figurative sculpture, and high towers reflected the austerity of the order's French founders.

A second phase begins in the 1170s with the appearance of early Gothic motifs from northeast France. The most ambitious of several buildings from this phase was Byland, Yorkshire. Rivaling cathedrals at 330 feet in length, the plan showed a developed east end that preserved the traditional square-ended form but surrounded it with aisles and a range of eastern chapels. Equally French were the enriched three-story elevation with distinctive arch moldings, octofoil piers, shafts, double-walled clerestories, and an elaborate west wheel window. A timber barrel vault closed the space.

In the third phase, beginning around 1210, strong English influences dominate the order's architecture. At Fountains the monks' choir (ca. 1208–40) was moved east of the crossing and the building terminated in a sumptuous east transept with tiers of windows, marble shafting, and rib vaults. This provided for nine altars, a design later copied at Durham Cathedral (from 1242). At Rievaulx, Jervaulx, Netley, and Tintern the east end was given a seven-bay rectangular form, while at Croxden, Hailes, and Vale Royal the east end was characterized by an ambulatory with radiating chapels that

Fig. 43. Fountains Abbey, Yorkshire, choir of church, south side. Courtesy of A.J. Hawkes.

Fig. 44. Fountains Abbey, Yorkshire, cloister complex, west side. Courtesy of A.J. Hawkes.

suggests the influence of royal Westminster Abbey. Tracery appears at Netley and Tintern around 1260, again from London sources. In the assimilation of high Gothic trends from other monastic, canonic, or cathedral sources in England this phase of Cistercian architecture is interpreted as indicating a loosening of the order's sense of identity.

Much survives of buildings other than churches within the monasteries, most notably at Fountains, which is now designated a World Heritage Site. Though less elaborate than the church they are important and have been usefully studied by building type. They show the Cistercians as pioneers in planning and form, particularly in the first century of their settlement in England.

Within the claustral nucleus a number of developments altered the traditional arrangement of monastic buildings. The cloister usually lay to the south of the church, and the build-

ings on the east side provided the living quarters for the monks: chapter house, parlor, and day room, with dormitory above. Buildings on the west side met the same needs of the lay brothers. Those to the south served as refectory, kitchen, and warming room. The arrangement of both west and south sides reflected the distinctive makeup of Cistercian communities.

Outside the cloister, usually to the east of the monks' quarters, lay the abbot's residence and accommodations for distinguished visitors, and beyond these the monks' infirmary. For the latter archaeology has revealed a superb example at Fountains with its own chapel, kitchen, and two-story residence block. Dating from the 1230s, the building measured 180 feet by 78 and was fully vaulted, with a tall central space, reserved probably for great wardrobes for blankets and clothing, and lower aisles where the beds were placed against the outer walls. At other houses infirmary buildings were smaller but still impressive and

Fig. 45. Fountains Abbey, Yorkshire, cloister complex, east side. Courtesy of A.J. Hawkes.

Fig. 46. Fountains Abbey, Yorkshire, entrance to refectory from south side of cloister. Courtesy of A.J. Hawkes.

speak to new standards of care of the infirm and ill. To the east of these buildings again but still within the precinct wall lay the abbey's orchards, gardens, and fishponds.

At the west side of Cistercian abbeys were the entrance and service courts. The great gatehouse sealed the walls (the best early example is Roche from the 1180s) and controlled agricultural and industrial activity. This was grouped around the outer and inner courts and included the mill, stables, houses for oxen and cattle, the smithy, tannery, workshops, and the guest houses for the obligatory hospitality offered to strangers.

While most of the nonecclesiastical buildings date from the years of the order's greatest popularity, they remained in use until the Dissolution, despite the dramatic shrinkage of monastic populations. Some new building types, such as meat kitchens and dining areas, appear after about 1340 to satisfy relaxed dietary regulations. And by 1400 adaptations occurred in the areas occupied by the monks that satisfied needs for greater privacy and relative comfort and in the infirmary to provide a separate residence for the abbot.

Peter J. Fergusson

Bibliography

Bilson, John. "The Architecture of the Cistercians, with Special Reference to Some of Their Earlier Churches in England." *ArchJ* 66 (1909): 185–280; Coppack, G. *Fountains Abbey.* London: Batsford, 1992; Fergusson, Peter J. *Architecture of Solitude: Cistercian Abbeys in Twelfth-Century England.* Princeton: Princeton University Press, 1984; Gilyard-Beer, Roy, and G. Coppack. "Excavations at Fountains Abbey, 1976–80: The Early Development of the Monastery." *Archaeologia* 108 (1986): 147–88; Knowles, David. *The Religious Orders in England.* 3 vols. 2d ed. Cambridge: Cambridge University Press, 1979; Norton, Christopher, and David Park, eds. *Cistercian Art and Architecture in the British Isles.* Cambridge: Cambridge University Press, 1986.

See also Architecture and Architectural Sculpture, Gothic; Architecture and Architectural Sculpture, Romanesque; Art, Gothic; Cistercians

Cistercians

An order of monks, first settled in England at Waverley, Surrey, in 1128 by William Giffard, bishop of Winchester, some 30 years after Robert Harding had led the secession from Molesme that resulted in the establishment of the new order at Cîteaux (Burgundy). The order spread rapidly, and by 1152, when their General Chapter forbade further foundations, there were over 40 abbeys in England alone. Many were concentrated in the north, particularly in Yorkshire. The first Cistercian abbey there was Rievaulx, founded by Walter Espec in 1131. Its first abbot was William, a colleague and former secretary of Bernard of Clairvaux. Within a few years a number of daughter houses were founded from Rievaulx, including two, Melrose and Dundrennan, in Scotland.

Aelred, abbot of Revesby (Lincolnshire), returned to Rievaulx in 1147 to become abbot. He was the outstanding early English Cistercian and one of the great theologians and scholars of his day. Under his leadership Rievaulx expanded to become the largest Cistercian community in England, housing 140 monks by his death. A year after the foundation of Rievaulx another Cistercian abbey was founded at Fountains by reformist monks from the great Benedictine abbey of St. Mary's York. With the support of Archbishop Thurstan of York, a prominent patron of the new monasticism, and of many leading regional families Fountains soon became the wealthiest and most prestigious of the English foundations, a position it retained until the Dissolution in the 1530s, when it was the only Cistercian abbey to have an annual assessed income of more than £1,000. Like Rievaulx it was responsible for the creation of a number of daughter houses and even established a Cistercian abbey in Norway.

The Cistercian expansion was reinforced by the order's takeover in 1147 of the abbeys of the Norman congregation of Savigny. This brought some thirteen abbeys in England and Wales under Cistercian control, though the Savigniac abbeys, led by Furness, resisted the amalgamation. The first and most productive generation of growth led to new Cistercian abbeys, not only in England but also in the Celtic lands. Some, like those in Scotland, were established from English abbeys; in

Wales and Ireland there were independent foundations. In the second half of the 12th century a number of abbeys were founded in Wales through the patronage of native princes, while in Ireland the White Monks (as Cistercians were called, because of their white habits or robes) retained nationalist sympathies and had few links with their English counterparts.

There were also nunneries that followed Cistercian customs. Their precise status, particularly in the 12th century, has been questioned; the early Cistercians' attitude toward women in the religious life was at best ambivalent, at worst hostile. By the end of the 13th century, however, there were probably nearly 30 communities for women observing a version of the Cistercian rule. The influence of the English Cistercians was also felt outside their order. Cistercian practices heavily influenced the development of the order of Sempringham (or Gilbertines), and the order enjoyed close ties with other reformed monasteries and with individual hermits.

From the earliest years the Cistercian economy was founded on pastoral farming, particularly the production of wool, and though the prohibitions of their rule on the possession of manorial and spiritual revenues were soon largely ignored, the Cistercians seldom gained more than a small proportion of their income from their role as absentee landlords. Similarly, though a few late Cistercian abbeys were established in towns, such as Oxford and London, urban property was little developed, and the majority of foundations were concentrated in isolated areas.

The degree to which they "created a desert" by forcibly removing communities from their neighborhoods, as alleged by hostile critics like Walter Map or Gerald of Wales, has been debated. It is likely that Cistercians established abbeys or granges in sparsely populated areas. Granges were organized as self-contained agricultural units, supervised by lay brothers *(conversi),* though their role was increasingly taken over by peasant laborers in the later Middle Ages.

By the end of the 13th century many of the abbeys, including Fountains and Rievaulx, were in severe economic difficulties, often as a result of poor wool yields and ill-considered financial dealings with Italian merchants. Some had to be temporarily disbanded or taken into royal hands, and recovery was frequently impeded by Scottish raids in the early 14th century.

Thereafter the Cistercians suffered, as did most English monasteries, from changing economic and demographic conditions. Most gave up working the land directly and rented out their estates. Thus their way of life became scarcely distinguishable from that of the old Benedictine houses, with increasingly lavish buildings and churches and separate quarters for the abbots. By the Dissolution the numbers of Cistercian monks had fallen dramatically, and, though some abbeys resisted Henry VIII's ecclesiastical policies, by the end of 1539 all the Cistercian communities had disappeared.

Brian J. Golding

Bibliography

Burton, Janet. *Monastic and Religious Orders in Britain, 1000–1300.* Cambridge: Cambridge University Press, 1994, pp. 69–77; Donkin, R.A. *The Cistercians: Studies in the Geography of Medieval England and Wales.* Toronto: Pontifical Institute, 1978 [collected papers on settlement and the Cistercian economy]; Knowles, David. *The Religious Orders in England.* 3 vols. Cambridge: Cambridge University Press, 1948–59; Knowles, David. *The Monastic Order in England: A History of Its Development from the Time of St. Dunstan to the Fourth Lateran Council, 940–1216.* 2d ed. Cambridge: Cambridge University Press, 1963; Lekai, L.J. *The Cistercians: Ideals and Reality.* Kent: Kent State University Press, 1977; Powicke, F.M., ed. and trans. *The Life of Ailred of Rievaulx by Walter Daniel.* London: Nelson, 1950. Repr. with intro. by Marsha Dutton. Kalamazoo: Cistercian Publications, 1994 [a medieval account, giving an "inside story"]; Thompson, Sally. *Women Religious: The Founding of English Nunneries after the Norman Conquest.* Oxford: Clarendon, 1991; Wardrop, J. *Fountains Abbey and Its Benefactors: 1132–1300.* Kalamazoo: Cistercian Publications, 1982 [an exemplary study of a major house].

See also Cistercian Architecture; Friars; Monasticism; *Pierce the Plowman's Creed*

Clanvowe, John (ca. 1341–1391)

Author of *The Two Ways* and probably *The Book of Cupid.* In the 1360s and 1370s he fought in various campaigns in France led by John of Gaunt. In 1373 he entered the service of Edward III and after that king's death he continued in the household of Richard II.

In *The Two Ways* Clanvowe urges his readers to follow the narrow path to salvation by avoiding the broad way of worldliness that, on occasion, he equates with the sort of courtly lifestyle he must himself have led (lines 484–503). The chroniclers Knighton and Walsingham mention Clanvowe among the knights of Richard II's court whom they accuse of Wycliffite sympathies, and it is interesting at one point that Clanvowe applies the word "lolleris" to himself and others who believe as he does (512).

The Book of Cupid, sometimes called "The Cuckoo and the Nightingale," is a courtly St. Valentine's Day dream vision. A first-person narrator, who describes himself as "olde and unlusty" (37), overhears a debate about love between an idealistic nightingale and a cynical cuckoo. It opens by quoting the *Knight's Tale* (1785–86) and makes considerable use of devices and conventions found in several early poems by Chaucer, whom Clanvowe knew.

V.J. Scattergood

Bibliography

PRIMARY

Scattergood, V.J., ed. *The Works of Sir John Clanvowe.* Cambridge: Brewer, 1975.

SECONDARY

New *CBEL* 1:504; *Manual* 3:721–23, 883–84; 7:2314–15, 2532; Kittredge, G.L. "Chaucer and Some of His Friends." *MP* 1 (1903): 1–18; McFarlane, K.B.

Lancastrian Kings and Lollard Knights. Oxford: Clarendon, 1972, pp. 139–247.

See also Chaucer; Debate Poems; Dream Vision; Edward III; Lollards

Clare Family

The history of the Clares provides an outstanding example of how rich and powerful a dynasty could become through royal favor and strategically planned marriage alliances.

As a reward for his service in 1066 the Norman Richard FitzGilbert received 176 lordships from William the Conqueror. Many of these belonged to the honor of Clare, the Suffolk administrative center of a complex of landed estates, whence the family took its English name. The earldom of Hertford was acquired in 1138, but the most important move came with the marriage of Richard de Clare (d. 1217) to the earl of Gloucester's sole heiress. This brought the Clares a second earldom, extended their influence far into Wales and Ireland, and made them the greatest baronial landowners of their day.

They were thus equipped to play a leading role in the military and political life of the country; as the career of Gilbert, "the Red Earl" (d. 1295), shows, they were even able to defy the crown with impunity. His help made possible the defeat of Simon de Montfort in 1265; his retinue was strong enough for him to march into London against the wishes of a frightened Henry III; his demands for the restoration of those who had been disinherited in the Barons' Wars had to be met by the reluctant monarch. With a gross annual income in excess of £6,000 (about a third from Welsh lands) and huge manpower resources, he was indeed a suitable husband for Edward I's daughter Joan of Acre.

The next earl died childless at Bannockburn (1314) and brought these heady dynastic ambitions to an abrupt end. The division of his vast estates among his three sisters (one of whom founded Clare Hall, Cambridge University) effectively marked the end of the Clares as a political force, although other ambitious families, such as the Beauchamps, followed similar paths to fame and fortune.

Carole Rawcliffe

Bibliography

Altschul, Michael. *A Baronial Family in Medieval England: The Clares, 1217–1314.* Baltimore: Johns Hopkins Press, 1965; Cokayne, George E. *The Complete Peerage.* Ed. Vicary Gibbs et al. 13 vols. London: St. Catherine Press, 1910–59.

See also Battles of Bannockburn and Boroughbridge; Gloucester

Clerk, John (fl. late 14th–15th century?)

Author of the longest of all alliterative poems, *The Destruction of Troy.* He signs his name in an acrostic that reads "I[o]hannes Clerk de Whalale," i.e., "John Clerk of Whalley [Lancashire]."

Thorlac Turville-Petre

Bibliography

Turville-Petre, Thorlac. "The Author of *The Destruction of Troy.*" *MÆ* 57 (1988): 264–69.

See also Alliterative Revival; Matter of Antiquity

Cloisters Cross

The double-sided processional or altar cross in the Cloisters Collection of the Metropolitan Museum of Art in New York (fig. 47; h. 577mm, w. 362mm) is generally considered a remarkably well preserved masterpiece of English Romanesque ivory carving. Its original location and its mid-12th-century date are a matter of continuing debate, since precise documents are lacking. A proposed attribution to Bury St. Edmunds is still the one most thoroughly discussed, based principally on what is known of the intellectual and liturgical context of the abbey and its library holdings, as well as the relationship of the carving to the earlier style of Master Hugo's Bury Bible.

Nearly 100 figures and over 60 inscriptions cover the surfaces of this walrus-ivory cross, the front of which, by its lopped branches, is characterized as the Tree of Life. Old Testament prophets, for the most part, line the shaft and crossbar on the back, each figure identified and holding a scroll inscribed with a scriptural text. The central roundel on the front of the cross depicts Moses and the Brazen Serpent, surrounded by witnesses and other figures bearing Old and New Testament inscriptions. Just above it is the rare representation of the dispute of Pilate and the high priest over the wording

Fig. 47. Cloisters Cross, front (New York, The Metropolitan Museum of Art, The Cloisters Collection, [12, 63]). Courtesy of the Metropolitan Museum of Art.

of the titulus, or notice, placed on the cross (John 19:21–22). They stand on the titulus itself, which in Greek and Latin (and an indecipherable Hebrew) carries the unusual wording: "Jesus of Nazareth, King of the Confessors." Scenes of the Passion and Resurrection on the right and left terminal plaques of the cross-bar and the Ascension above are visually juxtaposed with the evangelist symbols: Luke's ox on the right, Mark's lion on the left hand terminal, and John's eagle in the top. They surround the central roundel with the Lamb, shown turning from the downcast figure of Synagogue, while an angel consoles the weeping John with a triumphant Easter message. Matthew's winged man is the subject of the missing base terminal, and presumably the Nativity was depicted on the front, just below where Adam and Eve cling to the base of the cross. Triple streams of blood on Adam's shoulder connect him to the now missing corpus once affixed to the cross; two sets of holes allowed for separate points of attachment at different periods.

Although the main elements of the format are part of a venerable, ongoing tradition, the scheme as a whole and the individual scenes vary considerably from standard models. A comparable originality informs the humanism of the tiny figures inhabiting the monumental framework of this Romanesque cross. The basic key to the complex program lies less in a direct castigation of the Jews, as has sometimes been argued, than in the function of the cross within the dramatic liturgy of Holy Week—principally Good Friday and Holy Saturday—and Easter. These associations, enriched by a choice of scriptural texts that reflects the systematic mind of a pious *litteratus* familiar with the nuances of contemporary biblical scholarship as practiced by the students of the influential Hugh of St. Victor in Paris, have only begun to be explored.

Elizabeth C. Parker

Bibliography

Parker, Elizabeth C., and Charles T. Little. *The Cloisters Cross: Its Art and Meaning*. New York: Metropolitan Museum of Art, 1994 [with complete scholarly bibliography].

See also Ivory Carving, Romanesque

Cloth Manufacture and Trade

By the end of the Middle Ages woolen cloth manufacturing had become England's leading industry, employing more labor than any other craft, consuming a large share of agricultural output in wool, and providing the country's main export. Previously England had been far more renowned as an exporter of raw wools, especially the fine, short-fibered wools from the Welsh marches, the Cotswolds, and Lincolnshire, Europe's best and an absolute requisite for high-grade luxury woolens. At the beginning of the 14th century England was exporting an average of 35,350 woolsacks (364 pounds each) a year, from about 7.5 million sheep, enough for 160,000 standard broadcloths (measuring 24 yards by 1.75 yards). Cloth exports were then unimportant, greatly exceeded by woolen imports from the Low Countries. By the late 15th

century, after a remarkable industrial transformation, England had become the leading producer of woolens in Europe, exporting an average of 51,850 broadcloths a year in the 1480s, but only 8,511 woolsacks (to make 38,300 broadcloths). Low Country merchants, who had now lost their primacy in quality textiles, compared the flood of English imports in those years to an inundation from the sea.

Many theories, none wholly satisfactory, have been advanced to explain this industrial and commercial transformation. Since the two most famous concern the technology and organization of the woolen industry, their evaluation must begin with a discussion of the manufacturing processes.

Production was generally organized by a putting-out system. Wool merchants or brokers sold raw wools to merchant-drapers or clothiers, who "put them out" to artisans to be worked into cloth. First in the chain came those who prepared the wools, cleansing them with repeated beating and washing and sorting them by staple length. The shorter, curly-fibered wools were then thoroughly greased with butter to facilitate subsequent processes, and some might be dyed blue in woad to provide the foundation for various colors in dyeing the finished cloth.

The wools so treated, dyed or undyed, were then sold to weaver-drapers, who organized the manufacturing processes. They in turn put out these wools to combers and carders, who made them suitable for spinning. Combing was the older technique for preparing all wools, while carding with wire brushes was introduced in the 12th century as a more efficient technique for disentangling and preparing short-fibered wools. The combed and carded wools were next put out to spinners to be converted into both warp and weft yarns. The weaver then claimed the yarns, paying the spinners, combers, and carders piecework wages.

As the foundation yarns for weaving, the warps (30 yards long) were wound on a roller-beam at the loom's rear and then stretched tautly onto another roller-beam at the front. The weft yarn, carried by a shuttle along grooves in the laysword, was inserted between alternating groups of warps pulled apart by heddles (loops) on pulley strings attached to foot-powered treadles. After each insertion it was beaten up into the fell of the cloth by the batten or wooden front of the laysword. Finally the weaver operated a lever to roll up the cloth and to feed out more warps from the rear beam.

This treadle-operated horizontal loom was the most important innovation in all clothmaking. From the 11th or 12th century it gradually displaced the upright "warp weighted" loom, which had produced narrow, short cloths, evidently worsted fabrics, composed of coarser, straighter-fibered yarns, with a highly visible weave, usually in a lozenge design. The diffusion of the new horizontal loom, and especially its evolution into the broadloom requiring two weavers, seems to be associated with a real revolution in textiles—the rise and ultimate supremacy of the broadcloth. A wider, longer, heavier, and generally costlier cloth, composed of fine, curly, densely packed wools, it was thoroughly felted and shorn to obliterate any trace of weave and so provide a texture comparable to some silks.

Spinning had also undergone a technological innovation, though more limited in significance, with the spinning wheel, associated with carding from the 13th century. It supplemented but did not displace the ancient method of spinning combed wool fibers by dropping a weighted, rapidly revolving spindle. The spinning wheel converted this single spindle into a horizontal axle driven by a belt attached to a hand-powered wheel, which vastly increased productivity at the expense of a yarn uneven in both strength and quality.

Thus warp yarns, necessarily tighter and stronger to withstand stress on the loom, continued to be spun from combed wools with drop spindles, while the weaker wefts came to be spun from carded wools with the new wheel. However, if traditional literature can be believed, the later medieval English industry may have been an exception in producing both yarns, warp as well as weft, from wheel-spun carded wools.

Whereas worsteds, with strong, coarse yarns, were fully manufactured when woven on the new looms, true woolens required the subsequent process of fulling. There were three objectives: to scour and cleanse the cloth; to force the weak, short, scaly fibers to interlock in a felted, strong, durable fabric; to shrink it (up to 60 percent in area), thus increasing its weight per square foot. By the traditional method a master fuller and two journeymen immersed the woven cloth in a large vat of water with soap and fuller's earth (kaolinite or hydrous aluminum silicate) and then trod upon it for three days or more. Finally the cloth was hung on a tentering frame to dry, stretched to remove wrinkles.

At this point the weaver-drapers would usually sell the cloth to merchant-clothiers, for resale or export in raw form. Or they could commission shearers and dyers to finish it: by repeated raisings or napping, with teasels, to bring up all loose fibers; by several shearings with long razor-sharp blades; and by dyeing in-the-piece, usually with a combination of woad and madder.

The crucial fulling process, which completed the manufacturing and initiated the finishing processes, had also undergone a major technological innovation: "milling," with heavy water-powered wooden trip hammers that replaced human feet. Introduced into Normandy by 1086 and England from the 12th century, water-driven fulling mills were the first and only important mechanization of cloth production before the modern Industrial Revolution. For Carus-Wilson it was a 13th-century "industrial revolution" that explained how the young industry vanquished its Flemish rivals to capture Europe's cloth markets, for "Flanders is a land of windmills rather than watermills." Fulling mills were also instrumental, in her view, in attracting the cloth industry from the lowland towns of eastern England to more advantageous rural locations in such hilly regions as the West Riding (Yorkshire), the Cotswolds, the Mendips, and Wiltshire. Such rural locations provided swiftly flowing rivers needed for fulling mills and the "freedom from the restrictions of urban guilds and high taxation."

Any thesis positing a premodern "industrial revolution" is bound to invite a reaction, and Carus-Wilson's views have fallen into disfavor. The first attack argued that the traditional urban cloth industry, unable to compete with Flemish imports in the later 13th century, had sought refuge in the countryside, not to seek out fulling mills but to reduce labor costs, chiefly by utilizing much cheaper part-time agricultural labor. In these respects rural clothmaking supposedly gained a major cost advantage over urban draperies, at home and abroad.

A more serious threat to Carus-Wilson's thesis was the discovery that water mills were used in the Low Countries during the Middle Ages; subsequently, in the 16th century, water-powered fulling mills rapidly spread into textile districts of southern Flanders and Brabant. In England water mills were even more abundant in the eastern, lowland regions, including some traditional clothmaking towns. A.R. Bridbury argues, however, that they were used for mechanical fulling only rarely, under manorial compulsion, when lords had no better use for them. He also found no important advantages for rural industry and contends that urban draperies continued to account for the larger share of late-medieval *commercial* cloth production.

In toto these arguments deny that mechanical fulling provided any decisive cost savings, though no statistics are offered. For the Low Countries and Italy, however, recent calculations indicate that fulling mills provided at least a threefold productivity gain. While traditional foot fulling accounted for about 20 percent of prefinishing production costs (at Leuven and Leiden), mechanical fulling at Florence was responsible for only 5 percent of such costs.

Rural locations, furthermore, did provide some important advantages for the English industry. First, rural fulling mills on fast-flowing upland country streams could use the relatively cheap, space-saving undershot wheel, instead of the capital-costly (though efficient) overshot wheel, with capacious millponds and millraces, required for most urban mills located downstream on slow-moving rivers. Second, clothiers could utilize the putting-out system to pass most capital costs, much lower than those in urban industry (even with a similar organization), on to the artisans, primarily agricultural workers who owned their implements and worked in their homes with family labor (the "domestic system"). Money wages were undoubtedly also far lower in rural areas; whether real labor costs, measured in productivity, were really lower is a moot question. Urban locations, on the other hand, offered the advantages of better supervision, discipline, and more skilled labor, particularly for higher-grade woolens. Thus combing, carding, and spinning were predominantly rural, while, for better-quality woolens, much of the subsequent weaving and finishing still took place in towns.

Subsequently, however, long after the establishment of this quasi-rural industrial structure, the English cloth industry gained a far more decisive advantage from the crown's late-medieval fiscal policies. From the outset of the Hundred Years War (1337–1453) the crown sharply increased the modest duties on wool exports (6s. 8d. per sack, plus variable subsidies) to often exorbitant levels, varying from 40s. to 50s. or more per sack. By the later 14th century the tax burden had risen to about 45 percent of the average wholesale wool price. Within England, however, domestic clothiers could purchase these same fine wools tax-free, while their cloth exports, first taxed in the hands of English merchants in 1347, bore a far lower rate, indeed a minimal duty of 1s. 2d., about 2 or 3 percent of current cloth-export values. Since English wools in the finer broadcloths woven in the Low Countries accounted for 60 to 70 percent of their prefinishing manufacturing costs, one can appreciate the large (if unintended) advantage that English clothiers gained from this differential in export duties.

Although English cloth exports subsequently rose strongly and wool exports fell correspondingly, the tax differential did not immediately provide the industry with that decided an advantage. First, only from the 1360s, with the formation of the Calais Staple Company as a quasi-monopolistic organization of wool sellers, was the tax incidence passed on to foreign buyers (rather than to the wool growers in lower prices). Second, wool export duties were specific, not *ad valorem;* they became truly oppressive for foreign buyers only with general deflation and the fall in wool prices during the late 14th and early 15th centuries. Major foreign buyers, in the Low Countries and Florence, responded by concentrating production in the upper luxury range, using only the finest, most expensive English wools, for which these specific duties constituted a far smaller proportion of costs.

Nevertheless, the structure of European cloth markets in the early 15th century may seem puzzling. Low Country draperies had not yet sought out alternative wools for cheaper cloths but were still thriving with luxury woolens. Indeed the concentration on luxury production with English wools explains their refusal to employ mechanical fulling—for fear of impairing quality. In Germany and central Europe Flemish woolens had regained preeminence, while the less expensive English cloths ranked a distant fourth (after Brabantine and Dutch cloths). In the Mediterranean, where costly Italian woolens were preeminent, English woolens fared even worse, despite lower prices.

A possible solution to this paradox may be found in the severe afflictions that beset the late-medieval economy, in depopulations from recurrent plagues and famines, and especially in widespread warfare, spawning periodic civil strife and social anarchy. In international trade all these adversities sharply raised marketing and transaction costs to preclude or discourage commerce in cheap textiles. They may also have produced a more highly skewed income distribution that similarly favored trade in luxury over cheaper textiles. Significantly the expansion of England's broadcloth exports mirrored the rapid fall in exports of far cheaper worsteds. Certainly English broadcloths were luxuries, when measured by the purchasing power of wages for urban craftsmen. In the late 14th century a standard broadcloth would have cost a London master mason (England's best-paid artisan at 7.5d daily) about three months' pay. Nevertheless, in both price and quality English broadcloths ranked in the lower range of luxury fabrics. It was for such a market that England's cloth exports expanded most successfully, from the 1460s.

Some reasons for that expansion lie in the rise in real incomes of Europe's middle social strata; in the reduction of the aforementioned economic afflictions by the mid-15th century; and in a general demographic and commercial expansion that helped reduce transaction costs in international trade. One powerful force for commercial expansion in this era was the central European silver-mining boom, ca. 1460–1530. South German merchants directed this new silver to markets offering the best price, chiefly the new Antwerp Fairs. There they acquired English woolens, now dyed and finished in the region, as their principal return cargo for Germany and central and eastern Europe.

At this crucial turning point another misguided adventure in English fiscal policy rendered a final, gratuitous service to the expanding English cloth trade. In 1429–30 the crown imposed the Bullion and Partition Ordinances on the Calais Staple, which had a virtual monopoly on wool exported from England to the Continent, to extort ready cash for the military garrison at Calais. In return for full control over wool sales a small clique of Staplers was required to raise wool prices and extract full payment in English coin and bullion (minted at Calais) while denying purchasers any credit. By the late 1460s, just before the crown was forced to suspend these hated ordinances, the Flemish luxury draperies had suffered a mortal blow, as indicated by the plunge in their production indices and in English wool sales (from an annual mean of 14,230 sacks in the 1420s to a mean of just 7,275 sacks in the 1460s).

Elsewhere in the Low Countries, however, the quasi-rural *nouvelles draperies* proved to be more resilient; their fortunes rose with the decay of the ultra-luxury urban draperies. Producing lesser-quality woolens, though often imitating the big urban draperies, they had been less dependent on English wools, often mixing them with others. Thus they were more receptive to a relatively new substitute: Spanish *merino* wools, whose quality had steadily improved to rival medium-grade English wools.

The final victory of the English cloth trade must be understood in the context of industrial and commercial changes abroad, especially in the Low Countries. From the late 14th century the urban draperies in Flanders and Brabant had also suffered from ruinous conflicts with the Hanseatic League, conflicts that opened up new markets for English cloths in the Baltic. By the mid-15th century, however, the Hanse and the Danes had managed to exclude English shipping from this region. The real commercial beneficiaries of expanding English cloth exports turned out to be the Dutch, who took advantage of both Anglo-Hanseatic and Flemish-Hanseatic strife to expand their own Baltic shipping, gaining dominance there by the early 16th century. That, furthermore, was a major reason why Holland's own woolen industry at Leiden survived this rapidly growing onslaught of the English cloth trade until the mid-16th century.

John H.A. Munro

Bibliography

Bridbury, Anthony R. *Medieval English Clothmaking: An Economic Survey.* London: Heinemann Educational, 1982; Carus-Wilson, E.M. "An Industrial Revolution of the Thirteenth Century." *EcHR,* 1st ser. 11 (1941):

39–60. Repr. in *Medieval Merchant Venturers*. London: Methuen, 1954, pp. 183–210; Carus-Wilson, E.M. "The Woolen Industry." In *The Cambridge Economic History of Europe*. Vol. 2: *Trade and Industry in the Middle Ages*, ed. M.M. Postan and Edward Miller. 2d ed. Cambridge: Cambridge University Press, 1987, pp. 613–90; Harte, N.B., and K.G. Ponting, eds. *Cloth and Clothing in Medieval Europe: Essays in Memory of Professor E.M. Carus-Wilson*. Pasold Studies in Textile History 2. London: Heinemann Educational, The Pasold Research Fund, 1983; Kerridge, Eric. "Wool Growing and Wool Textiles in Medieval and Early Modern Times." In *The Wool Textile Industry in Great Britain*, ed. J. Geraint Jenkins. London: Routledge & Kegan Paul, 1972, pp. 19–33; Lloyd, T.H. *The English Wool Trade in the Middle Ages*. Cambridge: Cambridge University Press, 1977; Miller, Edward. "The Fortunes of the English Textile Industry in the Thirteenth Century." *EcHR*, 2d ser. 18 (1965): 64–82; Munro, John H.A. "Wool Price Schedules and the Qualities of English Wools in the Later Middle Ages." *Textile History* 9 (1978): 118–69; Munro, John H.A. "Textile Technology" and "Textile Workers." In *Dictionary of the Middle Ages*, ed. Joseph R. Strayer. Vol. 11. New York: Scribner, 1988; Munro, John H.A. "Industrial Transformations in the North-West European Textile Trades, c. 1290–c. 1340: Economic Progress or Economic Crisis?" In *Before the Black Death: Studies in the "Crisis" of the Early Fourteenth Century*, ed. Bruce M.S. Campbell. Manchester: Manchester University Press, 1991, pp. 110–48; Munro, John H.A. *Textiles, Towns, and Trade: Essays in the Economic History of Late-Medieval England and the Low Countries*. London: Variorum, 1994; Munro, John H.A. "Anglo-Flemish Competition in the International Cloth Trade, 1340–1520." In *L'Angleterre et les pays bas bourguignonnes: relations et comparaisons, XVe–XVIe siècle*, ed. Jean-Marie Cauchies. *Publication du Centre Européen d'Études Bourguignonnes* 35 (1995): 37–60.

See also Aliens and Alien Merchants; Customs Accounts; Hanseatic League; Prices and Wages; Staple; Taxes; Trade; Tunnage and Poundage

Cloud of Unknowing, The

A treatise on prayer in the tradition of apophatic mysticism (which seeks God by going beyond images, concepts, and created attributes). The canon of its anonymous English author also includes six cognate tracts. Of these tracts *The Cloud* and *The Book of Priue Counselling* are treatises on contemplative prayer (called "the work") and are similar in content, structure, and style. *A Pistle of Preier* also deals with contemplation, drawing principally on the authority of St. Bernard. *A Pistle of Discrecioun of Stirings* is written for a disciple less advanced than the disciple addressed in *The Cloud*. The other three tracts are translations from Latin sources: *Deonise Hid Diuinite*, a translation of the *Mystical Theology* of Pseudo-Dionysius; *A Tretyse of the Stodye of Wysdome That Men Clepen Beniamyn*, an abridged paraphrase of Richard of St. Victor's *Benjamin minor*; and *A Tretis of Discrescyon of Spirites*, parts of which closely paraphrase selections from St. Bernard's *Sermones de diversis* 23 and 24.

These writings originated in the last quarter of the 14th century in the central area of the northeast Midlands. James Greenhalgh (d. 1529/30), a Carthusian, believed that Walter Hilton wrote *The Cloud*. Hodgson, along with most other scholars, discounts this theory, holding that Hilton and the *Cloud*-author were both men of learning and masters of the vernacular and knew each other's works. Clark theorizes that *The Cloud* is in part a response to Hilton's *Scale of Perfection*, book I, and that the language and theology of *The Cloud* in turn influenced book II of Hilton's treatise. Internal evidence suggests that the *Cloud*-author was a priest, probably a Carthusian, dedicated to the contemplative life, learned in patristic and monastic literature, and acquainted to some extent with the teaching of Thomas Aquinas.

At least seventeen manuscripts containing *The Cloud* and/or one or more of its related treatises are extant, including two Latin versions of *The Cloud*. Hodgson observes that the history of transmission cannot be recovered, because of the large number of random agreements and contamination caused by lateral conflation. The oldest transcription dates from the 15th century (BL Harley 674). The best known of the Latin versions is Cambridge Pembroke 221, completed in 1491 by Richard Firth of Methley, a Carthusian, and annotated by two other Carthusians.

The metaphor of "the cloud" goes back at least to the *Stromatum* of Gregory of Nyssa (ca. 335–395). While no immediate source for *The Cloud* is known, the author draws on a common tradition of contemplative spirituality. From Neoplatonism, as channeled principally through Augustine and Pseudo-Dionysius, the author derives his doctrine of dark, negative mysticism. There is a likeness, too, to the Rhineland mystics, who were generally in the same apophatic tradition and endeavored to abandon the self in the dark mystery of God in order to forget their own being. Immediate influences on the *Cloud*-author include Thomas Gallus and Hugh of Balma's *Viae Sion lugent*.

For some in the apophatic tradition divine union is a form of supraconceptual knowing and for others, a way of knowing through love; but for the *Cloud*-author, at the highest stages of ascent, mystical union takes place through love alone. *The Cloud*'s doctrine is solidly Christian and trinitarian: as Christ, the Word of God, is of the same nature as the Father but distinct from him in personality, so the mystic becomes, by grace, one nature with God while remaining distinct from the Uncreated Being in person. Nor is the work anti-intellectual or anti-institutional: the spiritual guide assumes that his disciple has previously followed the common prayer of the church and has meditated on the humanity of Christ as set forth in the Gospels. But at this stage of prayer discursive thought has lost its function and should be transcended.

The Cloud is in the form of a letter from a spiritual guide to a young man, though it is also intended for a larger audience. Its excellent prose style is marked by balance, restrained rhythms, functional alliteration, epigram, precision, and variety. The imagery is both earthy and evocative and often conjoined with faintly humorous irony. Reflecting his Dionysian sources, the author relies on paradox to suggest ineffable mysteries.

The goal of the treatise is to teach a simple prayer of longing that will pierce the "cloud of unknowing"—the privation of knowing that signifies that God can be loved but not thought or conceptualized (though the author still speaks of God in the male gender). Having entered through the door, which is Christ, and moved by special grace, the disciple must place all thoughts, images, and even the awareness of his individual being, under the "cloud of forgetting." Then by a "stirring"—an impulse of love—the disciple seeks God in the innermost spiritual center of the soul and cleaves with the will to God alone in transcendent love. This "work" is formalized in the concentrated repeating of a single word or phrase until it becomes habitual. Though the believer cannot attain identity of substance with the Uncreated, the perfect soul becomes by grace what God is by nature. They become one in loving but remain diverse in substance.

Modern readers have been quick to note that "the work" appears similar to exercises in non-Christian mysticism, especially Zen Buddhism. But in spite of similarities in language *The Cloud*'s Christian mysticism can be clearly distinguished from Zen (Johnston). Loss of self in *The Cloud* signifies that the ego-self is replaced by the true self in Christ, leading to the experience of something within loving something else. In Zen positive love is generally less conspicuous, and the practice of Zen aims at forgetting everything so that only self remains. *The Cloud,* in contrast, leads to forgetting all so that only God remains.

Ritamary Bradley

Bibliography

PRIMARY

Hodgson, Phyllis, ed. *The Cloud of Unknowing and The Book of Privy Counselling*. EETS o.s. 218. London: Humphrey Milford, 1944. Corr. repr. London: Oxford University Press, 1958; Hodgson, Phyllis, ed. *The Cloud of Unknowing and Related Treatises*. Analecta Cartusiana 3. Salzburg: Institut für Anglistik und Amerikanistik, 1982; Johnston, William, trans. *The Cloud of Unknowing and the Book of Privy Counseling*. Garden City: Doubleday, 1973; Walsh, James, trans. *The Cloud of Unknowing*. New York: Paulist Press, 1981.

SECONDARY

Manual 9:3068–73, 3425–29; Burrow, J.A. "Fantasy and Language in *The Cloud of Unknowing*." *EIC* 27 (1977): 283–98; Clark, John. "Sources and Theology in 'The Cloud of Unknowing.'" *DownR* 98 (1980): 83–109; Clark, John. "*The Cloud of Unknowing*." In *An Introduction to the Medieval Mystics of Europe,* ed. Paul E. Szarmach. Albany: SUNY Press, 1984, pp. 273–91; Johnston, William. *The Mysticism of the Cloud of Unknowing*. Foreword, Thomas Merton. 2d ed. St. Meinrad: Abbey Press, 1975; Lagorio, Valerie Marie, and Ritamary Bradley. "The *Cloud* Author." In *The 14th-Century English Mystics: A Comprehensive Annotated Bibliography*. New York: Garland, 1981, pp. 81–90; Minnis, Alastair. "*The Cloud of Unknowing* and Walter Hilton's *Scale of Perfection*." In *Middle English Prose: A Critical Guide to Major Authors and Genres,* ed. A.S.G. Edwards. New Brunswick: Rutgers University Press, 1984, pp. 61–81.

See also Hilton; Mystical and Devotional Writings; Prose, ME

Cnut (d. 1035; r. 1016–35)

Danish and English king, best known in English legend as the king whose command to the waves to stop was ignored by the incoming tide. The story, first recounted by Henry of Huntingdon in his *Historia Anglorum,* shows Cnut's posthumous fame as a man of power.

From his youth Cnut certainly understood power and wielded it ruthlessly. On the death of his father, Swein, in 1014 the Scandinavian army tried to make him king of England, but the Anglo-Saxon leadership negotiated instead for Æthelred II's return from Normandy. In Denmark Cnut's brother, Harald, had become king, so in August 1015 he again sought the throne of England, joined now by Thorkell the Tall, a former supporter of Æthelred. Cnut gained control of Wessex but failed to capture the southeast. When Æthelred died in 1016, the Londoners recognized his son, Edmund Ironside, as king, while Cnut retained his support in Wessex. After Edmund's defeat at Ashingdon in Essex he and Cnut agreed to divide the country between them.

The death of Edmund on 30 November 1016 enabled Cnut to become ruler of England. Three strategies ensured his hold on power. In July 1017 Emma, sister of Duke Richard II of Normandy and widow of Æthelred II, became his queen, thereby neutralizing any threat from Normandy, where Æthelred's two sons, Edward and Alfred, were residing. The young sons of Edmund Ironside were moved to Hungary, well beyond Cnut's grasp, unlike Edmund's brother Eadwig, who was murdered by agents of Cnut.

Cnut's second step was to eliminate several of Æthelred's supporters, most notably the duplicitous Eadric Streona; he initially depended on Thorkell the Tall and Edward the Norwegian, whom he recognized as earls of East Anglia and Northumbria, respectively. His third policy was to acknowledge the power of the church by founding monastic houses and becoming, with Emma, a lavish ecclesiastical benefactor. His generosity was doubtless assisted by the mammoth geld payment of £72,000 levied in 1017 on his new kingdom, supplemented by a further £10,500 extracted from London's citizenry.

In the first of four trips he made to Scandinavia between 1019 and 1028 Cnut obtained the throne of Denmark following his brother Harald's death. Our knowledge of his rule in the early 1020s is sketchy. In England Thorkell became an outlaw in 1021 but must have retained a substantial band of supporters, as Cnut was persuaded to accept him as his vicegerent in Denmark in 1023.

In 1027 Cnut attended the coronation of Conrad as Holy Roman Emperor in Rome, presumably in part as a diplomatic move to protect his southern Danish flank against German encroachments. The following year he conquered Norway, driving out Olaf Haraldsson and he made Ælfgifu of Northampton regent there for their young son, Swein. He had contracted a union with Ælfgifu before his marriage with Emma, and he never repudiated the English woman. In the same year Cnut received the submission of three Scottish kings, including Malcolm and (probably) Macbeth of later Shakespearean fame, possibly to ensure that the Norse settlers in northern Britain would not return to Norway to assist in rebellion against his rule there. His Norwegian conquest was nevertheless unsuccessful, and in 1035, just before his death, Ælfgifu and her son had to withdraw to Denmark.

The administrative structures in England were strong enough to continue through his reign, though few of Cnut's charters survive. Two law codes, one of them substantial and revealing the influence of Archbishop Wulfstan, were published in his name, and he issued letters to the English people in 1020 and 1027. In the latter he claims to have negotiated, during his visit to Rome, for the abolition of the tolls exacted from merchants traveling to Italy and the large sums required from archbishops for papal recognition.

In 1017 Cnut had replaced the ealdormen by four earls, though other earldoms were later created. This was to be less significant than the fact that such new men as Earl Godwin displaced the cadre of ealdormen and thegns who had formerly been tied to the Anglo-Saxon kings through a complex network of relationships. Godwin's power base in Wessex, the heartland of the English kingdom, later weakened Edward the Confessor and enabled Godwin's son, Harold, to gain the throne that he held through most of the year 1066.

Cnut did not found a lasting dynasty. After his death in 1035 Harold Harefoot, his son by Ælfgifu, eventually succeeded him in England, and in 1040 his and Emma's son, Harthacnut, became king for two years. Unlike his predecessor Æthelred II, Cnut died in time to leave his reputation intact. He gave England 20 years' respite from invasion, though he left a native dynasty fatally weakened and the country with strengthened ties to Normandy. When he died, the young William the Bastard had just inherited the Norman duchy; as "the Conqueror," William was to accomplish a far more successful *coup d'état* than Cnut and bring the Anglo-Saxon era to a close.

David A.E. Pelteret

Bibliography

PRIMARY

Arnold, Thomas, ed. *Henrici archidiaconi Huntendunensis historia Anglorum: The History of the English, by Henry of Huntingdon, from* A.D. *55 to* A.D. *1154.* Rolls Series 74. London: Longman, 1879; Greenway, Diana E. ed. and trans. *Henry, Archdeacon of Huntington: History of the English People.* Oxford: Oxford University Press, 1996; Palsson, Hermann, and Paul Edwards, trans. *Knytlinga Saga: The History of the Kings of Denmark.* Odense: City of Odense, 1986; Whitelock, Dorothy, ed. *English Historical Documents.* Vol. 1: *c. 500–1042.* 2d ed. London: Eyre Methuen, 1979 [documents 47–50 pertain to Cnut's reign].

SECONDARY

Fleming, Robin. *Kings and Lords in Conquest England.* Cambridge: Cambridge University Press, 1991; Hudson, Benjamin T. "Cnut and the Scottish Kings." *EHR* 107 (1992): 350–60; Lawson, M.K. *Cnut: The Danes in England in the Early Eleventh Century.* London: Longman, 1993; Raraty, David G.J. "Earl Godwine and Wessex: The Origins of His Power and His Political Loyalties." *History* 74 (1989): 3–19; Rumble, Alexander R., ed. *The Reign of Cnut: King of England, Denmark, and Norway.* London: Leicester University Press, 1994.

See also Æthelred II; Edward the Confessor; Emma; Godwin; Harold Godwinson; Swein; Vikings

Coffin of St. Cuthbert

Bede tells us in his *Ecclesiastical History* and *Life of St. Cuthbert* that in 698, eleven years after his death, the incorrupt body of Cuthbert, bishop of Lindisfarne, was translated to a wooden reliquary coffin, which was wrapped in linen and placed on top of a stone sarcophagus to the right of the altar in the monastic church at Lindisfarne. This reliquary coffin became the focal point of the saint's cult and continued as such even after the community left Lindisfarne (probably in 875), taking the coffin with them. It was eventually established in the church at Durham (in 995), and after being translated to a new shrine in 1104 it remained undisturbed until the 16th-century Dissolution of the monasteries under Henry VIII. At this stage the shrine was opened and the body discovered, still apparently intact; it was quickly reburied in the remains of the original wooden coffin and left untouched until a hurried investigation into the tomb was undertaken in 1827.

It was at this stage that the relics of St. Cuthbert (the gold and garnet pectoral cross, portable altar, liturgical comb, the Stonyhurst Gospel Book, textiles and liturgical vestments) were brought to light, along with the fragmentary remains of up to four wooden coffins, set one inside the other. In 1899, during a more leisurely investigation, further fragments of wood were recovered, and it was from a mass of about 6,000 pieces of wood that some 200 were eventually extracted to reconstruct the reliquary coffin originally constructed at Lindisfarne during the elevation of St. Cuthbert in 698. It was composed of six planks of oak, each lightly engraved with a number of images, and a seventh (undecorated) that formed an inner lid. The carved decoration of the

coffin (although originally swathed in linen and so not visible to those worshiping at the shrine) provides a rare example of decorated woodwork from early Anglo-Saxon England.

While what was probably the baseboard of the coffin on which the body was laid is incised with the outline of a stepped-base cross, the other five panels are covered with figural decoration. Christ in Majesty surrounded by the four evangelist symbols is depicted on the lid, with the Virgin and Child on one end panel and the archangels Michael and Gabriel on the other (fig. 48). Half-length images of five more archangels decorate one long side of the coffin, and the twelve apostles set in two ranks fill the other side. All the figures are identified by inscriptions picked out in either runes or the Latin alphabet, an eclectic epigraphic feature found elsewhere in early Northumbria on stone sculpture, coins, and the Franks Casket.

The iconography of the figures decorating the coffin reveals further the eclecticism of early Northumbrian monastic culture. The influence of the Christian Mediterranean world is seen in the figures of Christ and the apostles (which depend on Italian prototypes) and the Virgin and Child (which depend ultimately on the art of the Byzantine East), while the selection of archangels arguably demonstrates the influence of the liturgy of the Celtic church. The full-length evangelist symbols, however, with their books, halos, and wings, betray a fusion of models from the Mediterranean and Celtic worlds, which were brought together in the formation of new, insular, traditions of Christian art.

The Cuthbert Coffin thus provides valuable information about the establishment of a saint's cult in the first century of Anglo-Saxon Christianity and its continued promotion in subsequent centuries. It also demonstrates the diverse and eclectic nature of the cultural milieu of the early Northumbrian church.

A. Jane Hawkes

Bibliography

Bonner, Gerald, David Rollason, and Clare Stancliffe, eds. *St. Cuthbert, His Cult and His Community to AD 1200.* Woodbridge: Boydell, 1989; Colgrave, Bertram, ed. and trans. *Two Lives of Saint Cuthbert.* Cambridge: Cambridge University Press, 1940; Colgrave, Bertram, and R.A.B. Mynors, eds. and trans. *Bede's Ecclesiastical History of the English People.* Oxford: Clarendon, 1969; Cronyn, J.M., and C.V. Horie. *St. Cuthbert's Coffin: The History, Technology and Conservation.* Durham: Dean and Chapter, Durham Cathedral, 1985; Kitzenger, Ernst. "The Coffin Reliquary." In *The Relics of Saint Cuthbert,* ed. C.F. Battiscombe. Oxford: Oxford University Press, 1956, pp. 202–304.

See also Art, Anglo-Saxon: Celtic Influences, Classical Influences; Cuthbert; Franks Casket; Manuscript Illumination, Anglo-Saxon; Metalwork, Anglo-Saxon; Textiles from St. Cuthbert's Tomb

Coins, Imagery of

The earliest Anglo-Saxon silver coins, contemporary with the deniers of Merovingian Gaul, are known as *sceattas,* a term meaning "treasure" or "wealth." Some have Roman coins as their prototypes, some clearly show Frankish influence, and some appear to take their inspiration from Anglo-Saxon art. The larger "penny" that appeared during the second half of the 8th century became virtually the sole denomination of mid-

and late Anglo-Saxon coinage. The penny's broader flan (the blank metal disk from which a coin is made) provided more scope for design, and many of the coins are of high artistic quality. Some indeed rank as minor masterpieces of Anglo-Saxon art, as, for example, some of Offa's issues, where the royal bust shows definite attempts at portraiture. The Roman and Byzantine influence is apparent but not slavishly copied. Geometric and floral designs, decorated linear inscriptions, and coiled serpents appear as motifs, some derivative and some original. The tail-swallowing serpent on some of Offa's issues may be traced back to the conventions of Roman iconography, while at a later stage classical influence may be seen clearly on the "two emperors" type of Alfred the Great.

Carolingian influence may also be detected, in the use of a monogram-type mint signature on some reverses, adopted directly from the coins of Charlemagne (d. 814). Examples include pennies struck for Archbishop Wulfred of Canterbury (802–35) and Alfred the Great.

In the 10th century the highest level of artistic achievement was in the reign of Edward the Elder. Portraiture developed considerably from the basic and clumsy realism of Alfred the Great, and many new reverse designs appeared. Some of these, such as the Hand of Providence and floral types, may have been exceptional, but it should be noted that the commoner types were also well executed. Indeed the chief characteristics of numismatic development during Edward's reign were, in the words of one commentator, "skillful decorative treatment of design and neatness of execution." The Roman influence continued and is particularly apparent on the "burg" pennies, based directly on the city gate of Constantine's *Providentia Augusti* coins.

As the coinage developed, it became customary for each coin to carry on the obverse the name of the issuing authority and on the reverse the name of the striking moneyer. The name of the minting town, sometimes in contracted form, also appeared, particularly after the monetary reforms carried out by Edgar in 973. Even through the unsettled times of Æthelred II the standards of design and striking were maintained, and the Normans paid the ultimate compliment to the Anglo-Saxon monetary system by taking it over in its entirety.

Under the Normans periodic type changes and other controls continued but the workmanship gradually deteriorated, reaching its nadir during the anarchy of Stephen's reign, 1135–54. The "cross and crosslets" coinage of Henry II was little better and has been described as probably the ugliest of all the medieval coinages. The succeeding "Short Cross" issue spanned the reigns of Henry II, Richard I, John, and Henry III and was followed by the much improved "Long Cross" type in 1248. The cross, extending to the edge of the reverse, was intended as a safeguard against clipping.

A major monetary reform, launched under Edward I in 1279, introduced new denominations and a break with Anglo-Saxon traditions. Halfpennies and farthings were coined, and the fourpence, or groat, made its appearance. The moneyer's name disappeared, and the design—facing head on the obverse, mint name and cross on the reverse—was to remain basically unchanged until the advent of the Tudors.

The major innovation of the 14th century was the intro-duction of a stylistically novel gold coinage, under the authority of Edward III and the supervision of Florentine goldsmiths. The series consisted initially of the florin with its half and its quarter but was changed almost immediately to the noble (one third of a pound) with its half and quarter. The obverse design, showing the king standing in a ship, is thought to commemorate the naval victory over the French at Sluys in 1340. With modifications in style it continued to appear on gold coins until the 17th century.

Michael Kenny

Bibliography

Blackburn, Mark A.S., ed. *Anglo-Saxon Monetary History: Essays in Memory of Michael Dolley.* Leicester: Leicester University Press, 1986; Brooke, George C. *English Coins from the Seventh Century to the Present Day.* 3d ed. London: Methuen, 1950; Dolley, Reginald H. Michael, ed. *Anglo-Saxon Coins: Studies Presented to F.M. Stenton.* London: Methuen, 1961; Dolley, Reginald H. Michael. *Anglo-Saxon Pennies.* London: British Museum, 1964; Grierson, Philip, and Mark Blackburn. *Medieval European Coinage.* Vol. 1: *The Early Middle Ages.* Cambridge: Cambridge University Press, 1986; North, J.J. *English Hammered Coinage.* 2 vols. 3d ed. London: Spink, 1991–94.

See also Coins and Coinage

Coins and Coinage

There was a sharp discontinuity in coinage between Roman Britain and Anglo-Saxon England. No coins were minted on the island in the 5th or 6th century, and few appear to have been imported from neighboring continental regions or from Mediterranean mints. The earliest English coins were small gold coins, called *thrymsas;* these 7th-century issues, based on contemporary Frankish coins, appear to have been struck in small numbers. Coins of the early 8th century were similar in appearance but made of silver and circulated in significant numbers. These thick silver *sceattas* seldom bear legends and are often difficult to distinguish from similar coinages of Frisia or the Frankish kingdom.

In the second half of the 8th century the coinage of England again followed that of Europe; the broad style denier of Pepin, king of the Franks, became the basis of the English "penny," most notably the extensive and varied issues of the reign of Offa of Mercia. The silver penny remained virtually the only coin of the Anglo-Saxon period and the basis of English coinage throughout the Middle Ages, though its fineness and weight were frequently altered. For most of the medieval period the shilling (twelve pennies) and the pound (twenty shillings) were simply counting terms for aggregations of pennies, not actual coins.

In the 9th century pennies were issued by the kings of Mercia, Wessex, Kent, East Anglia, and Northumbria, as well as by the archbishops of Canterbury and York. The pennies of the south (except for East Anglia) were struck at three mints that changed hands frequently; the coins were uniform in appearance and con-

Table of Coins and Coin Values

12 pence (12 *d.*) = 1 shilling (1 *s.*)

20 shillings = 1 pound

  (240 silver pence = £1: The silver penny [1 *d.*] was the basic coin in actual use.)

1 farthing = ¹/₄ pence

1 halfpenny = ¹/₂ pence

  (These values might be represented by small coins or by cut pieces of a silver penny.)

1 mark = 13 *s.* 4 *d.*

¹/₂ mark = 6 *s.* 8 *d.*

  (These were values, not coins.)

1 groat = 4 *d.* (a coin struck 1351–52)

1 florin = 6 *s.* (a gold coin struck by Edward III)

1 noble = 6 *s.* 8 *d.* (a gold coin issued by Edward III)

1 angel = 6 *s.* 8 *d.* (a gold coin struck by Edward IV, 1464)

---

tent. Those of Northumbria differed in style and were of a lower silver content; they are termed *styccas*. The Viking conquerors of the north and east, who had no prior tradition of coining, initiated coinages based on those of Wessex and Mercia, including issues in the memory of King Edmund of East Anglia (killed by the Danes in 869) and in the name of kings Siefred and Cnut (who are not known from any other source).

As the Wessex kings reconquered the island, they standardized the coinage. Under Æthelstan (924–39) a regional system of minting was established with a mint in all privileged boroughs. Toward the end of his reign Edgar (957–75) expanded the number of mints to about 40. Under Æthelred II (978–1016) a system was established whereby at periodic intervals (generally every six years) the coinage was changed throughout the kingdom and all old coins called in for reminting. This system remained in operation through the reigns of Cnut (1016–35) and Edward the Confessor (1042–66).

William the Conqueror maintained the standards of the Anglo-Saxon penny and continued the system of coinage in most of its aspects; the recoinages came every three years, and regional mints were brought under stronger central control. Under Henry I the coinage was debased in weight and fineness, and standards of workmanship declined drastically. The coinages of Stephen and Matilda were even worse. In 1158 Henry II restored the weight and fineness of the penny but did not reinstall the system of periodic recoinage. In 1180 he instituted a new coin type, the "Short Cross" penny, issued in only eleven mints. This type was maintained unchanged (even in identifying the king as "Henricus") through the reigns of Richard I (d. 1199) and John (d. 1216) and through most of the reign of Henry III (d. 1272).

The type was finally changed in 1248 as a response to

1

2

3

4

clipping, and the "Long Cross" penny or "Sterling" was issued in the name of Henry and then in the name of the first three Edwards from 1279 through 1377. Though the Short Cross and Long Cross pennies were produced at a number of mints, the dies were centrally carved; the study of minute changes in details of legends and types has resulted in a chronology that allows most coins to be dated within a short range. Until 1279 pennies were cut in half or quarters to make smaller denominations; after that round halfpennies and farthings (fourths of a penny) were struck alongside pennies.

In the middle of the 13th century Florence and Genoa introduced gold coinage to Europe; England followed in 1257 with a gold penny. Issued as equivalent to twenty silver pennies, this coin was significantly undervalued and quickly disappeared from circulation. No other gold coin was issued in England for almost a century. The change from the penny type in 1279 was accompanied by the introduction of a heavy silver coin, again following continental examples. The groat of four pence was, however, slightly overvalued in relation to the coinage before it and met popular resistance; after a short time its minting was abandoned until the middle of the next century. By the death of Edward I (1307) the English coinage had returned to being based almost exclusively on silver pennies.

In 1351 the groat of four pence was reintroduced and remained a part of English currency. Gold coinage was also revived about this time, but its history was to be complex and changing. Unlike Italian issuers of gold coinage, who let the relationship of their gold to silver coins be fixed by market conditions, English kings sought to establish a fixed relationship between gold and silver issues. Changes in the gold-silver ratio on the world market led inevitably to difficulties, resulting in hoarding, the export of overvalued coins, and erratic minting in the two metals. After a false start with overvalued denominations in 1344 Edward III produced the first successful gold English coin, the "noble" (worth 80 pence), whose weight had to be adjusted twice in the decade (figs. 49–50).

Henry IV maintained the coinage system of Edward III and Richard II but lowered the weight of silver and gold coins in 1412. The new standards were maintained through the reigns of Henry V and Henry VI. A new system of relationships was introduced in 1464 under Edward IV; the gold noble retained its weight but was valued up from 80 pence to 96 pence, while the weight of the silver coinage was reduced. The noble soon gave way to a gold "ryal" worth 120 pence and an "angel" worth 80 pence. With the addition of a sovereign valued at one pound (240 pence) in 1489, this system remained unchanged until the radical coinage alterations of Henry VIII in 1526.

Alan M. Stahl

Bibliography

Blackburn, Mark A.S., ed. *Anglo-Saxon Monetary History: Essays in Memory of Michael Dolley.* Leicester: Leicester University Press, 1986; Brooke, George C. *English Coins, from the Seventh Century to the Present Day.* 3d ed. London: Methuen, 1950; Dolley, Reginald H. Michael, ed. *Anglo-Saxon Coins: Studies Presented to F.M. Stenton.* London: Methuen, 1961; Grierson, Philip, and Mark Blackburn. *Medieval European Coinage.* Vol. 1: *The Early Middle Ages.* Cambridge: Cambridge University Press, 1986 [this major study now supersedes most of the earlier literature]; Grueber, Herbert A. *Handbook of the Coins of Great Britain and Ireland in the British Museum.* 2d ed. London: Spink, 1970; North, J.J. *English Hammered Coinage.* 2 vols. 3d ed. London: Spink, 1991–94; Sutherland, C.H.V. *English Coinage, 600–1900.* London: Batsford, 1973 [best general introduction].

See also Alfred; Coins, Imagery of; Mints

Comic Tales

Few comic tales, or *bourdes,* exist in English until Chaucer, and those that do seem anomalous, genreless, within the English literary tradition. *The Fox and the Wolf* is a beast fable of the 13th century; *Dame Sirith* (also 13th century), though written with a fabliaulike plot, is more properly read as a play, like the fragmented *Interludium de clerico et puella. A Penniworth of Wit* is more moralistic than amusing. Yet on the basis of these works, Chaucer's churls' tales, and scattered strictures against dirty stories it has been argued that there was a genre of fabliaux in English comparable to the large body of French tales of the 13th and early 14th centuries and that these alleged English fabliaux have been suppressed and lost.

This argument is unlikely to be right. What did certainly exist in England before Chaucer were the above-named tales, fifteen fabliaux (twelve in Anglo-Norman and three in other French dialects but preserved in manuscripts of English provenance), and a collection of poems in Latin known as the Cambridge Songs, written in England around 1050 and including several stories on fabliau themes.

Tales on fabliau themes run across genres in the Middle Ages: such a plot can occur in a sermon exemplum, as part of a Corpus Christi play, or as one of the Cambridge Songs. But mere plot is not enough to define a genre. The French fabliaux, famously defined by Joseph Bédier as "des contes à rire en vers" ("funny stories in verse"), often involved great trickery and great stupidity and dwelt on the amusing side of sex, greed, violence, and scatology. It is this tradition of finished, clever tales that lies behind Chaucer's *Miller's, Reeve's, Friar's, Summoner's,* and *Shipman's Tales* and influences his *Merchant's Tale.* His tales in turn leave their traces in the comic tales of the 15th century.

Generic traits of these 15th-century comic tales are harder to define. If the tales have one loosely unifying trait, it is that, like the fabliaux, they variously counter the generic features of romance. One group of these tales turns upon a more or less clever trick: *The Friars of Berwick, The Lady Prioress, The Tale of the Basin, Dane Hew, Jack and His Stepdame, The Wright's Chaste Wife, How a Merchant Did His Wife Betray, Prohemy of a Marriage,* Lydgate's *Churl and the Bird,* and the Pardoner and Tapster episode in the *Tale of Beryn.* Though these English tales tend to be more moralistic than are the fabliaux, they are closely akin to them: they share the fabliau sense that ends can be achieved by plotting and doing, as opposed to the romance sense that there is a Providence that shapes our ends.

Another group of tales, like Chaucer's parodic *Tale of Sir Thopas*, displaces the rites of romance—the tourneying, feasting, hunting, wooing—into a debased context: *The Tournament of Tottenham, The Feast of Tottenham, The Hunting of the Hare, The Felon Sew,* part of *Colkelbie Sow,* and several of Dunbar's burlesque poems. A number of poems describe the chance encounter of a king incognito and a peasant, with a conflict of the systems of courtesy of court and peasantry that is not flattering to the court: *King Edward and the Shepherd, John the Reeve, The King and the Hermit, Rauf Coilʒear, The King and the Barker. Sir Corneus* (also known as *The Cokwolds' Dance*) and *The Boy and the Mantle* (a ballad in form) are set in Arthur's court and expose it to ridicule for its pervasive adultery.

The comic tales, while taking a stance that is anticourtly and unromancelike, were far from being written to engage the political sympathies of lower class audiences. The peasants depicted in the king-and-peasant poems, for example, are uncouth and laughable; the courtly rites parodied in *The Hunting of the Hare* or *The Tournament of Tottenham* are made funny precisely because the poets ignore real peasant contests and feasts, the real way peasants do battle, and depict them as awkwardly aping the nobility. As in 13th-century French fabliaux the effect of such a portrayal is double-edged: it reinforces the conviction of the impassable gulf between the nobility and peasantry that the romances quietly assume, but it also shows what aspects of romance are most idealized, most rigidly conventional, most unbending to the circumstances of everyday life and ordinary people.

Melissa M. Furrow

Bibliography

PRIMARY

Bennett, J.A.W., and G.V. Smithers, eds. *Early Middle English Verse and Prose.* 2d corr. ed. Oxford: Clarendon, 1974; Furrow, Melissa M., ed. *Ten Fifteenth-Century Comic Poems.* New York: Garland, 1985.

SECONDARY

New *CBEL* 1:455–60 (Tales), 420–21 *(Rauf Coilʒear),* 652 *(Beryn),* 687 *(Tournament and Feast),* 688 *(Wright's Chaste Wife); Manual* 9:3151–77, 3486–3501 (Middle English Comic Tales); for other tales mentioned here see *Manual* 1:96–98, 265–66 *(Rauf Coilʒear),* 4:1052–54, 1272 *(Friars of Berwick),* 6:1766–67, 1783, 1821–22, 1873, 2039, 2046, 2084–85, 2131 *(King and Barker, Boy and Mantle, Churl and Bird, Prohemy of Marriage);* Brewer, Derek. "The International Medieval Popular Comic Tale in England." In *The Popular Literature of Medieval England,* ed. Thomas J. Heffernan. Knoxville: University of Tennessee Press, 1985, pp. 131–47; Dronke, Peter. "The Rise of the Medieval Fabliau: Latin and Vernacular Evidence." *Romanische Forschungen* 85 (1973): 275–97; Furrow, Melissa M. "Middle English Fabliaux and Modern Myth." *ELH* 56 (1989): 1–18; Goodall, Peter. "An Outline History of the English Fabliau after Chaucer." *AUMLA* 57 (1982): 5–23; Lewis, Robert E. "The English Fabliau Tradition and Chaucer's 'Miller's Tale.'" *MP* 79 (1982): 241–55.

See also Anglo-Norman Literature; Beast Epic and Fable; Chaucer; Dunbar; Literary Influences: French; Popular Culture; Romances; Scottish Literature, Early

Conductus

The musical term "conductus" (pl. conductus or conducti; from Lat. *conducere:* to escort/lead together/connect) is difficult to define precisely. It does appear in medieval sources, but in rubrics that may be of only local interest. Around 1280 the English theorist known as Anonymous IV described gatherings of different types of conducti and singled out some conducti by name; reasonably or not, we have thus come to classify as conducti those pieces in the surviving gatherings that seem to match those that Anonymous IV described. Broadly speaking, the conductus is taken as a high art song—a musical setting of sacred or serious Latin rhythmic poetry in one to four voices, as cultivated throughout Europe during the late 12th and 13th centuries. The conductus often fulfilled a paraliturgical function, and on some feast days it may have been sung instead of the Benedicamus Domino in the office. Its musical-liturgical antecedents seems to have been the versus and, especially in England, the Benedicamus Domino trope.

There are two main schools of thought as to the etymology of the term. The traditional idea is that conducti were originally processional songs, designed to accompany movement inside or outside the church, and that the appellation remained for freely composed Latin art songs even though the original function had been lost. A more recent idea is that conductus refers to the performance practice of a group of singers "joining together" rather than singing *alternatim* (in alternation) as was required in the double-cursus sequence—and that the conductus was in its earliest stages a compression, or hybrid, of the hymn and sequence. This does reflect the primary meaning of the verb *conducere* more accurately and does not rule out the possibility of a processional function as well.

"Conductus" is a generic term encompassing several types. In 13th-century insular sources three main types are found: a small number of stylistically complex, purely indigenous types not found in continental sources; simple, syllabic conducti, common all over Europe and closely related to the sequence; and a large number of "Notre Dame" conducti, usually taken to have been composed at or for the Cathedral of Notre Dame in Paris (it is these of which Anonymous IV spoke). But "Notre Dame conductus" as a term has its own complications. It covers many stylistic types, and the extent to which other geographical areas contributed to the style and to the repertoire has probably been underplayed. For instance, an earlier insular style may have contributed to a greater or lesser extent to the formation of the Notre Dame conductus style.

Some of the more complex insular and Notre Dame conducti support large structures of interweaving melismas, called "caudae," whose rhythms are in one or more of the regular trochaic patterns known as the "rhythmic modes." Three-part insular conducti often contain rondelli as well as caudae. Rondelli are sections structured like a round, where each voice sings the same melody in turn. In a rondellus, though, all the parts begin and end together, and this gives the effect of the same section of music stated three times. In two insular conductus sources (Oxford, Corpus Christi College 489, and Durham University Library Bamburgh Sel. 13) passages of rondellus are even written in different-colored inks, making a relationship that is obvious to the ear more explicit to the eye. Rondellus is a technique found only in insular conducti. The other musical trait that immediately distinguishes the insular from the Notre Dame type is the frequent sonority of the interval of a third, a phenomenon contemporary English theorists themselves noted. This proliferation of thirds, an interval considered dissonant on the Continent, may in part explain why insular conducti did not find favor across the Channel; there is some evidence too of differing patterns of dissonance on strong and weak beats between the insular and continental repertoires. There is also considerable difference between the texts of the two types. Whereas Notre Dame poems are often of a moralizing or edifying nature—laments on the deaths of royalty or bishops, admonitory works railing against the corruption of the clergy, or celebrations of particular feasts using rich biblical imagery—insular texts are overwhelmingly of the votive Marian type. It has been suggested that paraliturgical conducti be distinguished from merely serious secular pieces and that the latter be designated *cantio*.

The physical layout of French sources suggests, perhaps misleadingly, that the Notre Dame conductus tradition was to a large extent homogeneous. Works of the same style tend to be grouped together. It has been more difficult to piece together a picture of how insular sources operated as they are mostly in a tattered and fragmentary state. Some insular sources do seem to have contained fascicles especially for conducti. However, in contrast to these and to French manuscripts, others group together works not only of different styles but even of different genres; for instance, insular conducti may be found next to troped chant settings or motets. This coexistence testifies to a rich mix of traditions in Britain.

The sources also indicate that conducti had a longer vogue in Britain than on the Continent; the closely related cantilena (where the melody is in the top rather than the bottom part) did not supersede the insular conductus until about 1300. In contrast continental sources seem to indicate that in France the polytextual motet had gained favor over the Notre Dame conductus by mid-century. Insular composers were evidently reluctant to give up the compositional freedom that the conductus allowed; the French motet was based on pre-existent material.

There are about twenty sources for the conductus in Britain. If the evidence of their parent volumes is to be believed, they came mostly from the larger monastic houses. Notre Dame conducti seem to appear more commonly in sources from the east of England and other areas in closer trading contact with the Continent. On the other hand insular conducti occur mainly in sources from the west and north: the Worcester fragments, two sources from Reading Abbey (Bodleian Library, Bodley 257; Oxford, Worcester College 213*), a Meaux Abbey source (Chicago, University of Chicago Library 654 App.), and a Revesby Abbey manuscript (Princeton, Princeton University Library Garrett 119). This bears out the testimony of Anonymous IV, who mentioned the singular compositional practices of what he called the "Westcuntrie." There are, however, manuscripts transmitting both types of conductus whose provenance is unknown, including Cambridge, Gonville and Caius College 820/810; Cambridge, Jesus College QB1; London, Lambeth Palace 752; Oxford, Corpus Christi College 497; Bodl. Wood 591; and Bodl. Mus.c.60. Brief mention must be made of two commonplace books, or miscellanies, that transmit a single Notre Dame conductus apiece: BL Harley 524 and 5393, and of two Bodleian manuscripts that, among other texts, preserve just the poems of 30 and 40 Notre Dame work, respectively: Add. A 44 and Rawlinson C.510.

The only more or less complete insular source is the Scottish manuscript Wolfenbüttel, Herzog-August-Bibliothek 628 (commonly known as W1), which contains about 100 pieces, representing approximately half the extant polyphonic Notre Dame repertoire plus a few local additions. Though the internal organization of this manuscript does resemble that of the other continental Notre Dame sources, the content of each fascicle is less closely focused: for instance, organal Benedicamus Domino settings and Agnus Dei tropes occur within conductus fascicles. These examples show how much there is still to be learned about the ordering of conducti relative to their function. It has been suggested that some "Notre Dame" conducti from W1 (and indeed the other major Notre Dame sources) are English because they refer to events or people in "England," including the murder of Thomas Becket, the coronation of Richard I, the death of Henry II, and the massacre of the Jews at York and London in 1189. This view is perhaps simplistic. It ignores the fact that their political subject matter would have been relevant right across the Angevin Empire. However, it does seem that in W1—as in the other major Notre Dame sources—geographical and chronological "layers" exist, though owing to copying, adding, and recopying via exemplars, these are no longer clear-cut.

It is unfortunate that the status of W1 as the only more or less complete surviving insular manuscript of polyphonic music from the 13th century has overshadowed the implications of the 50 or so fragmentary sources of insular polyphony. Although it is clear that the Notre Dame conductus was widely cultivated in Britain, the extent to which it may have dominated the English tradition is overrepresented by the evidence of W1 alone. The really exciting compositional developments of the conductus in Britain do not seem to have depended on Notre Dame.

Nicola Losseff

Bibliography

PRIMARY

Anderson, Gordon A., ed. *Notre Dame and Related Conductus: Opera omnia.* 11 vols. Henryville: Institute of Mediaeval Music, 1979–; Sanders, Ernest H., ed. *English Music of the Thirteenth and Early Fourteenth Centuries.* Polyphonic Music of the Fourteenth Century 14. Paris: L'Oiseau-Lyre, 1979.

SECONDARY

Anderson, Gordon A. "Notre Dame and Related Conductus: A Catalogue Raisonné." *Miscellanea Musicologica* 6 (1972): 153–229 and 7 (1975): 1–81; Falck, Robert. *The Notre Dame Conductus: A Study of the Repertory.* Musicological Studies 33. Henryville: Institute of Mediaeval Music, 1981; Gillingham, Bryan. "A New Etymology and Etiology for the Conductus." In *Beyond the Moon: Festschrift Luther Dittmer,* ed. Bryan Gillingham and Paul Merkley. Musicological Studies 53. Ottawa: Institute of Mediaeval Music, 1990, pp. 100–17; Losseff, Nicola. *The Best Concords: Polyphonic Music in Thirteenth-Century Britain.* New York: Garland, 1994; Stevens, John. *Words and Music in the Middle Ages: Song, Narrative, Dance and Drama, 1050–1350.* Cambridge: Cambridge University Press, 1986.

See also Cantilena; Hymns; Lai, Latin; Planctus; Rondellus; Sequence; Songs; W1; Worcester Fragments

Conversion of the Anglo-Saxons

The British Christians made no attempt to convert the Anglo-Saxon invaders; the initiative came rather from Rome and subsequently from Ireland. In 596 Pope Gregory I (590–604) dispatched the monk Augustine to England. Augustine, winning the favor of the powerful Æthelberht of Kent, and following the pope's rational guidelines, laid the foundations of the church in the southeast. The evangelization of Northumbria began with King Edwin (616–32); he married one of Æthelberht's daughters on the understanding that she could continue to practice her faith, and she was accompanied north by the Roman missionary Paulinus, who proceeded to preach to Edwin.

The case of Edwin underscores the fact that the conversion of a king was not always easily achieved. It required the combined urgings of Paulinus, the pope, and the queen to incline him toward the new religion, and even then he would only embrace it after canvassing the opinion of his council. A pagan revival followed Edwin's death. The fortunes of Christianity in the north were revived by King Oswald (634–42), whom Bede styled *Rex christianissimus,* "the very Christian king." Thankful for a miraculous victory against the forces of the British king Cadwallon, achieved under the sign of the Cross, Oswald sponsored a dynamic mission from Iona (in Scotland) led by the saintly monk-bishop Aidan.

Although marked by setbacks and vacillations (such as the relapse to paganism in Essex after a plague in 664), the conversion of the English kingdoms was achieved—at least in name—within a century. The Irish and Roman churches differed in details of observance, principally concerning the dates for the celebration of Easter, but when the Roman practices were endorsed by King Oswiu of Northumbria (642–70) at the Synod of Whitby in 664, the way was cleared for the development of a unitary church through England.

The conversion of England, as presented by Bede in his *Ecclesiastical History,* is a story of kings, and it is clear that they converted as much from political as from religious considerations. Christianity offered significant material advantages, such as written government. The missionaries stressed that the Christian king would achieve fame and prosperity in this world and in the next; the religious persuasion of an overking could be a decisive factor in defining subordinate kings' attitudes to the faith. When a king embraced the faith, his kingdom was considered Christian, though the task of instructing the populace in the official beliefs could be a difficult and lengthy one.

Material evidence, such as crosses on jewelry, reveals that Christian practices percolated into society at large during the 7th century, and by the early 8th century pagan-style burials (clothed, with grave goods, and beyond settlement boundaries) had ceased. However, church canons reveal that pagan practices continued to flourish, and Bede, writing to Bishop Egbert in 734, could complain that there were many villages not visited by preachers. By the end of the 7th century stone churches had been built in many locations, monasteries were a dynamic cultural force in society, books were being collected, and distinctive Christian artistic masterpieces, such as the Lindisfarne Gospels, were being created. What Christianity meant to the populace as a whole, however, is an open question.

Richard Gameson

Bibliography

Blair, Peter Hunter. *The World of Bede.* London: Secker & Warburg, 1970; Campbell, James. *Essays in Anglo-Saxon History.* London: Hambledon, 1986 [especially the essays "The First Century of Christianity in England" (1971) and "Observations on the Conversion of England" (1973)]; Colgrave, Bertram, and R.A.B. Mynors, eds. and trans. *Bede's Ecclesiastical History of the English People.* Oxford: Clarendon, 1969; Deanesly, Margaret. *The Pre-Conquest Church in England.* 2d ed. London: Black, 1963; Mayr-Harting, Henry. *The Coming of Christianity to Anglo-Saxon England.* 3d ed. University Park: Pennsylvania State University Press, 1991; Wormald, Patrick. *Bede and the Conversion of England: The Charter Evidence.* Jarrow Lecture, 1984. Jarrow: St. Paul's Church, 1984.

See also Æthelberht; Augustine of Canterbury; Bede; Canterbury, Ecclesiastical Province of; Cemeteries; Liturgy and Church Music, History of

Convocation

The church in England was divided into two provinces, Canterbury and York, and each had a convocation, or council, of its clergy. Convocation was summoned by a royal writ, and the usual reason for such a summons, as far as the crown was concerned, was to ask the clergy for a tax. Political reasons, both on the crown's part and on the archbishop's, might also prevail (as in 1399, when convocation was called by Archbishop Arundel to enlist clerical support for Henry IV), but once called a convocation was able to turn its attention to clerical grievances and other matters concerning the clergy.

Lists of clerical *gravamina,* or complaints, might be drawn up, complaining of financial exactions, that benefit of clergy (the right of the clergy to be tried only in church courts) was denied, that church courts were impeded in their jurisdiction by royal writs, and so on; the Convocation of Canterbury of 1421, for example, complained of the false indictment of clergy by the king's courts. So while approval of royal taxation of the clergy might be the reason for the summons, the outcome of the assembly might well be petitions and representations to the crown for redress of grievances. And once convocation had been summoned, it had legislative power to bind the clergy of the province through the issue of canons (as its legislation was called).

Though there are early roots in provincial synods, no clearly established meeting of the clergy can be seen in operation until the late 13th or early 14th century. Even after that the records are far from copious and remain so until the 1660s. For Canterbury, from the archiepiscopate of John Stratford (1333–48), however, the minutes, or *acta,* begin regularly and form a section in the archbishop's register. Canterbury registers containing good convocation data for the 14th and 15th centuries include those of archbishops Islip, Whittlesey, Courtenay, Arundel, Kempe, Bourchier, and Morton. Arundel's register has *acta* for the convocations of 1397, 1399, 1401, 1402, 1404, 1406, 1409, and 1411 and includes the articles against Wyclif and the cases against certain Lollards.

In organization convocation was divided into two houses—the upper clergy and the lower clergy. Archbishop Kempe's register includes, among the *acta* for 1453, the names of all the clergy who ought to appear in convocation: the diocesans (i.e., the bishops), the deans of the secular cathedrals and the proctors of their chapters, the priors of the monastic cathedrals and the proctors of their chapters, the archdeacons, the abbots, the priors, the heads of the collegiate institutions, and the proctors of the clergy—about 430 persons in all.

Jane E. Sayers

Bibliography

Kemp, Eric W. *Counsel and Consent.* London: SPCK, 1961, chs. 4–5; McHardy, Alison. "Clerical Taxation in Fifteenth-Century England: The Clergy as Agents of the Crown." In *The Church, Politics and Patronage in the Fifteenth Century,* ed. R.B. Dobson. Gloucester: Sutton, 1984, pp. 168–92; Powicke, F.M., and Christopher R. Cheney, eds. *Councils and Synods.* Vol. 2: *1205–1313.* Oxford: Clarendon, 1964; Storey, Robin L. "Clergy and Common Law in the Reign of Henry IV." In *Medieval Legal Records,* ed. R.F. Hunnisett and J.B. Post. London: HMSO, 1978, pp. 341–408; Weske, Dorothy B. *Convocation of the Clergy.* London: SPCK, 1937; Wilkins, David. *Concilia Magnae Britanniae et Hiberniae.* Vol. 2 (1268–1349) and Vol. 3 (1350–1545). London: Gosling, 1737.

See also Bishops; Canterbury, Ecclesiastical Province of; Parish Clergy; Taxes; York, Ecclesiastical Province of

Coronation
Anglo-Saxon

Changes in the ritual form of king making indicate institutional and ideological changes in Anglo-Saxon kingship. Pagan Anglo-Saxon kings were probably ritually inaugurated, but the earliest clear evidence dates only from the 8th century and implies ecclesiastical involvement in rituals derived from the Old Testament: Ecgfrith, son of Offa of Mercia, was "hallowed" in 787, in his father's lifetime, and Eardwulf of Northumbria was "blessed" in 796.

Ecgfrith's consecration, immediately following the visit of papal legates who invoked biblical support for the inviolability of anointed kings, owed something both to Rome and to Carolingian influence. Pope Hadrian I had consecrated Charlemagne's two young sons as subkings in 781. Links between the Northumbrian kingdom and Charlemagne's court were also close in the 790s.

In Wessex Egbert may have been consecrated in 802 on his return from exile at Charlemagne's court. A West Saxon king's consecration rite underlies the queen's *ordo* (the official order of the service) used for the Carolingian Judith when she married Æthelwulf of Wessex in 856. The first extant king's *ordo* prescribes anointing, investiture with a scepter, and the placing of a helmet on the king's head, instead of coronation. The rite ends with an acclamation and enthronement in which leading laymen participate, and the new king's enunciation of three precepts: to ensure peace, to repress crime, and to issue just judgments.

A second *ordo,* probably composed from Frankish models imported during the last decade of Alfred's reign and perhaps first used for Edward the Elder in 900, with its accompanying queen's *ordo* possibly used for Edward's wife, Ælfflaed, prescribed coronation as well as anointing. The crown became the prime royal headgear around this time. By the 11th century the liturgical representation of anointing as a spiritual coronation had helped establish the usage of "coronation" to refer to the whole inauguration rite.

In a revised version of the second *ordo,* perhaps first used for an inaugural consecration of Edgar, ca. 960, the three royal precepts, now a threefold oath, were placed at the beginning of the rite, thus becoming the precondition of the consecration. Edgar's successors, Edward and Æthelred, gave the oath in the vernacular, and a copy was laid on the altar. In a vernacular sermon Archbishop Dunstan declared, "The Christian king who keeps these engagements earns for himself worldly honor. . . . But if he violates what he promised to God, then it shall forthwith right soon grow worse among his people." There was often considerable delay between one king's death and his successor's consecration; the issue of charters in the interim suggests that a new king assumed formal authority before his coronation, once he had been accepted by leading men.

Perhaps from 839, certainly in the 10th century, the king making's normal site was Kingston-on-Thames (on the Wessex-Mercia border), and the archbishop of Canterbury officiated. Edgar's consecration at Bath in 973 was a special "imperial" occasion, followed by Edgar's ritual rowing by subordinate kings along the River Dee at Chester. It is not certain that Cnut (1017) or either of his sons was consecrated. All were ritually acknowledged by the leading men.

Edward the Confessor, proclaimed in June 1042, was consecrated on Easter Day (3 April 1043) "with great ceremony" at Winchester; this completed the legitimizing process of his royal succession. Harold was consecrated at Westminster on the day of Edward's burial there, 6 January 1066. The third *ordo,* combining its predecessor with a contemporary German rite, may have been used for Harold and for William the Conqueror in 1066 but was more likely composed later in the 11th century.

Post-Conquest
The coronation, or official crowning, was the most important ceremonial event in the life of a medieval monarch. At the coronation the monarch was recognized by his people as king and was vested with authority in a ritual process of election, consecration, and installation. The ceremony carried out today still has a recognizable relationship with the earliest recorded ceremony in western Europe, the Leofric/Egbert *ordo,* dating probably from the 9th century.

The simple original ceremony was soon replaced by the second *ordo,* dating possibly from the early 10th century and probably the one used, in a revised form, at the coronations of William I and his two sons. It was a more elaborate ceremony, consisting of a formal "election" by the people, a promise by the king, and his anointing and investiture with the ring, sword, crown, scepter, and rod (the regalia: the physical symbols of secular and spiritual rule and of the unity of the king's realm). Each presentation was accompanied by prayers and anthems, and the ceremony ended with his enthronement, followed by a mass and then a banquet.

The *ordo* contained the important elements of the services that henceforth remained relatively constant; election, the king's oath, anointing, presentation of the regalia, and enthronement. The homage of bishops and peers (a later development) came at this point in the ceremony. These elements all played their part in the symbolism of the event, reaffirming the ideal of government and consecrating the new king to his task. The ceremony started with a secular element, the "election," a relic of the old Germanic recognition of the person best fitted to be king. Then followed the oath taking, always in the vernacular, at first in French, later in English. The oath began in a threefold promise of good government,

the king promising to govern in a Christian manner. In a real sense it brought the king within the law.

The delivery of the regalia (together with the vestments) invested the monarch with the outward signs of monarchy. As the ceremony became more complex, other swords were added to the regalia, symbolizing justice. Some of the vestments were similar to those of a bishop, reinforcing popular belief in the ecclesiastical nature of an anointed king. Finally the king was anointed with oil. This consecrated him to his task and gave him a quasi-sacerdotal character as the "lord's anointed." The theories as to the effect of the anointing varied from the extreme of giving him almost priestly status to that of merely being equivalent to the sacrament of confirmation. By the end of the 15th century it was commonly believed that at least it gave the king a mixed status, a *persona mixta,* higher than that of a mere layman. This popular conception was reaffirmed by the English kings being anointed on the crown of the head, as was a bishop. From the 12th century they were anointed as well on the hands, breast, shoulders, and elbows with consecrated oil.

The coronation liturgy continued to develop after the second *ordo.* The third *ordo* was more elaborate and owed much to German influence and to the *Ordo Romanus.* This, or a version of it, was probably used in the coronation of Richard I, and just possibly at that of William I and his sons. The elaboration of *ordo* 3 is continued in the fourth and last medieval version of the rite, drawn up for the coronation of Edward II in 1308. After much revision, influenced in part by French ceremonies, this recension took its final form in the *Liber regalis,* a work associated with the name of Nicholas Litlington, abbot of Westminster (1362–88). It is the first version of the English coronation service to include detailed directions as to how the service was to be carried out. The service was lengthened considerably and prayers were added.

This fourth *ordo* itself underwent revision in the 15th century, to take account, *inter alia,* of the Holy Oil of St. Thomas (said to date from the 14th century), unaccountably omitted from the *Liber regalis.* Although we know that it was used for the coronation of Richard III, there is no evidence that this revision of the fourth *ordo* was used for the coronation of Henry VII or subsequent monarchs. The Litlington *ordo* was probably used after 1485. Certainly the Litlington version was the one translated for the coronation of James I (in 1603). In the fourth *ordo* two services for the queen were included. A service for the queen had been included in all the *ordines* except the first, but for the first time separate arrangements were made for it to be on the same day as the coronation of the king (or on another day, as was required).

Associated with the coronation liturgies are the "directories," the *Forma et modus* and the *Little Device.* These are handbooks that describe what actually happened in the service; who did what, as it were, as the *ordines* themselves were initially very plain, merely listing the prayers in order. The *Forma et modus* was a document drawn up in the 14th century, an abridged form of the fourth *ordo,* listing the prayers and the principal officers at the coronation, along with their duties. The *Little Device,* whose earliest-known version is one originally drawn up for Richard III and subsequently used for the coronations of Henry VII and Henry VIII, is a detailed plan of the ceremony, including the names of the officials taking part and which piece of regalia they carried.

These "coronation services" or supporting roles had become an increasingly important part of the ceremony. At first the disputes between claimants were settled in an *ad hoc* manner at each coronation. The first coronation at which a formal record was made of decisions between rival claimants was that of Eleanor of Provence, wife of Henry III, in 1236. In 1377, since Richard II was a minor, a formal court was set up to hear claims to services or fees, presided over by the duke of Lancaster as Lord High Steward. This court, the Court of Claims, survived, although only isolated records of its proceedings survive for the 15th-century coronations.

Janet L. Nelson
Peter W. Hammond

Bibliography

Bak, J.M., ed. *Coronations: Medieval and Early Modern Monarchic Ritual.* Berkeley: University of California Press, 1990; Garnett, G. "Coronation and Propaganda: Some Implications of the Norman Claim to the Throne of England." *TRHS,* 5th ser. 36 (1986): 91–116; Legg, Leopold G. Wickham. *English Coronation Records.* Westminster: Constable, 1901 [the most accessible edition of the *ordines;* there is still no complete edition]; Nelson, Janet L. *Politics and Ritual in Early Medieval Europe.* London: Hambledon, 1986; Sandquist, Thayron A. "The Holy Oil of St. Thomas of Canterbury." In *Essays in Mediaeval History Presented to Bertie Wilkinson,* ed. T.A. Sandquist and Michael R. Powicke. Toronto: University of Toronto Press, 1969, pp. 330–44; Schramm, Percy E. *A History of the English Coronation,* trans. L.G. Wickham Legg. Oxford: Clarendon, 1937 [best general book]; Sutton, Anne F., and Peter W. Hammond. *The Coronation of Richard III.* Gloucester: Sutton, 1983 [much general information plus a detailed look at a late-medieval ceremony].

See also Coronation Ceremony; Monarchy and Kingship

Coronation Ceremony, Music and Ritual of

Although other cities, Winchester, Bath, and Kingston-on-Thames, for example, were associated with coronations and crown-wearings, especially in the Anglo-Saxon period, after the Norman Conquest Westminster Abbey was the normal location, and the archbishop of Canterbury the normal celebrant, of the ceremony. The liturgical services associated with coronation are the consecration service itself (the *consecratio regis*) and the following mass. The former is very much like the ordination of a bishop, centered on the anointing with holy oil but also including rituals of more temporal significance.

The abbot of Westminster played a significant role in preparing and helping with the ceremonies, as did bishops from the other English sees, though the monks of the abbey probably had little active role. The special prayers and actions were the responsibility of the archbishop and his attendant clerics, and the chants would have been carried out by a special group of trained singers who later formed the nucleus of the Chapel Royal. The services are usually preserved in an *ordo consecrandi.* The *ordo* is most often found in a pontifical, a book written for the archbishop celebrant. Since he needs to know only the short passages of chant that he must sing, the choral chants must usually be sought elsewhere, in the antiphonal or gradual, for example. Rubrics about the performance of the ritual are sometimes included but are often scanty. To obtain a detailed reconstruction of the services, one must use many other sources, including nonliturgical sources like chronicles and eyewitness descriptions. Only in the later Middle Ages, from the 14th century, does one find fully noted *ordines,* with relatively complete rubrics and chants. The most famous are the *Litlington Missal* of Westminster Abbey, ca. 1383, and the *Liber regalis* of slightly later. These ordines were compiled as comprehensive reference books for use by the abbey as a result of the substantial revisions of the *ordo* that had taken place earlier in the century. Apart from the chants it is likely that other music would have been performed, although of this we know nothing. Fanfares were surely prominent, but until the 16th century none exists in writing. Polyphonic motets might have been inserted, and several from the 14th and 15th centuries have suitable texts. We have no information about this practice and must assume that such pieces would have been undertaken by the professional singers of the royal or noble chapels of the aristocracy present.

Several revisions of the *ordo,* called recensions, allow us to trace the development of the ceremony and to draw conclusions about the relative weight of its temporal, political, or liturgical elements. The earliest well-established text is the version of the second recension used for King Edgar (957–75; consecrated ca. 960?), a text greatly influenced by continental ceremonies by way of Archbishop Dunstan, and sometimes called the Dunstan *ordo.* This was revised and became known as the Edgar *ordo.* After about the year 1000 this recension was the pattern for many European coronation texts. In 1059, for example, it was made the basis for the Hungarian coronation, because of the exile of Edmund Ironside's sons in that country. The Norman Conquest brought changes, of course, and although William himself took the Anglo-Saxon oath, many of the important features of the earlier *ordo* were omitted in the third recension, used through the 13th century.

The fourth recension, essentially the last Latin version, was created for the coronation of Edward II in 1308. It admirably demonstrates the political and ecclesiastical importance of the ceremonies. Restoring features of the Anglo-Saxon *ordo* and making the ceremony more English, it was a reaction to both internal and foreign circumstances. Edward was compelled by the magnates to add to the oath that he would maintain laws chosen by his subjects. King Louis of France had been canonized in 1297: *Unxerunt Salomonem,* the chant newly composed for the anointing of Edward, seems to refer to a prominent chant for the royal English saint, Edmund, king and martyr. The papal bulls of about 1300, in which Boniface made "arrogant declarations" of his supremacy over everything, caused a "categorical assertion of the sovereign rights of the crown": Edward enters the coronation mass to a newly fashioned Introit, *Protector noster,* using a text assigned to papal entrances. Furthermore, to emphasize national authority, the recognition by the assembled people, shouted at the end of the Anglo-Saxon service and omitted by the Normans, is restored prominently at the beginning of the service, and reiterated with musical emphasis in the new chant for *Unxerunt.*

Political messages, and temporal and spiritual authority, are therefore reinforced by symbolic liturgical reminiscence and by the order, positioning, and musical emphasis of the most important elements of the service. These are the procession to Westminster; the recognition; the oaths (here the monarch swears to maintain the rights and privileges of the church and people); the anointing (making the king divine); the vesting with symbols of temporal authority (crown, sword, ring, spurs, orb, and rod of justice); the enthroning (this took place in the chair of St. Edmund placed prominently on a scaffold raised in the crossing of the abbey); and the homage (all kneel individually before the king and swear allegiance).

In the following mass, little is special. The psalms, readings, and chants naturally concentrate on regal texts. Outstanding, however, are the *laudes,* assertive and triumphant acclamations following the Gloria.

Andrew Hughes

Bibliography

Bent, Ian. "The English Chapel Royal before 1300." *Proceedings of the Royal Musical Association* 90 (1963–64): 77–95; Hughes, Andrew. "Antiphons and Acclamations: The Politics of Music in the Coronation Service of Edward II, 1308." *Journal of Musicology* 6 (1988): 149–68; Kantorowicz, Ernst H. *Laudes Regiae: A Study in Liturgical Acclamations and Mediaeval Ruler Worship.* Berkeley: University of California Press, 1946 [with an Appendix by Manfred Bukofzer, dealing with the music, pp. 188–221]; L.G. Wickham Legg, ed. *Three Coronation Orders.* Henry Bradshaw Society 19. London: Harrison & Sons, 1900; Legg, L.G. Wickham, ed. *English Coronation Records.* Westminster: Constable, 1901; Schramm, Percy E. *A History of the English Coronation,* trans. L.G. Wickham Legg. Oxford: Clarendon, 1937; Ullman, Walter, ed. *Liber regie capelle.* Henry Bradshaw Society 92. London: Henry Bradshaw Society, 1961 [with a note on the music by D.H. Turner, pp. 47–51]; Wilkinson, Bertie. *The Coronation in History.* London: Historical Association, 1953.

See also Coronation; Monarchy and Kingship; Westminster Abbey

Cotton, Robert, and the Cotton Library

The core of the Cotton Library is the collection of items made by the English scholar and courtier Sir Robert Bruce Cotton (1571–1631), to which a small amount of material was added by his son Sir Thomas (who succeeded 1631) and grandson

Sir John (succeeded 1662, d. 1702). Over four decades Sir Robert gathered together some 30,000 manuscript items (books, charters, and maps) as well as printed books, coins, monuments, and inscriptions. At first his interests lay mainly in Anglo-Saxon and early ecclesiastical material, but they later broadened to include medieval chronicles and cartularies, recent state papers, and foreign works. Items were acquired by purchase, gift, or exchange.

In 1622 Sir Robert moved his extensive library to a long, narrow room on the first floor of Cotton House within the precincts of the Palace of Westminster. By ca. 1638 the collection was arranged in twelve presses or bookcases (six having six shelves and six having five), one shelf (above the door), and one chest of drawers. Each of these fourteen subdivisions was distinguished by the name of one of twelve Roman emperors from Julius Caesar to Domitian or one of two classical females, Cleopatra and Faustina. A brass head of each of these classical figures was placed above the press or other subdivision associated with his or her name.

An item kept in one of the presses was identified by a press mark that consisted of the name of the person whose head stood above, a capital letter designating the shelf, and a roman numeral indicating the sequence of books on the shelf: e.g., Tiberius B.i. Items on the shelf designated Domitian had only the emperor's name and the roman numeral: e.g., Domitian viii. The chest of drawers (Augustus) was arranged in six parts, each given a roman numeral; some parts were complete units, but items in i (containing maps) and ii (containing charters) were identified by arabic numerals: e.g., Augustus ii.43. Volumes (over 800 by 1631) were arranged by size rather than subject, each often containing several texts distinct in origin, character, or provenance that had been bound together for Sir Robert, who added tables of contents, title pages, and frontispieces.

The location of the Cotton Library close to the Houses of Parliament at Westminster, and its owner's liberal policy of access to it, made it an important center of research for courtiers and politicians in the reign of Charles I. Sir Robert himself used it in researching matters of legal precedent for Henry Howard, earl of Northampton, the Lord Privy Seal. Fellow antiquaries, such as William Camden, Sir Henry Spelman, John Selden, and John Speed, used or borrowed manuscripts relating to genealogy, topography, and legal precedent. Eventually, however, the library was seen as too valuable a source of information for opponents of Charles I, and in 1629 Sir Robert and his librarian were arrested for possession of seditious material and the library was closed. Although soon released, Sir Robert was further punished by having only restricted access to his collections, and he died a disappointed man in 1631. Although his son Sir Thomas was allowed to reopen the library around 1633, it was never again, while it remained in the Cotton family, so well used as before.

During the English Civil War of the mid-17th century the library was evacuated to Stratton, Bedfordshire, but afterward returned to Westminster. It passed from Sir Thomas to Sir John, who on his death in 1702 bequeathed it to trustees for the benefit of the public. In 1722 it was moved to Essex

House in the Strand and in 1730 to Ashburnham House in Little Dean's Yard, Westminster. Soon after, on 23 October 1731, a catastrophic fire destroyed 114 of the library's volumes and seriously damaged a further 98. A Report of a Parliamentary Committee into the state of the library listed the damage. In 1753 the Cotton Library was made one of the foundation collections of the British Museum and is now part of the British Library.

The Cotton Library is of fundamental importance to those interested in Anglo-Saxon studies and medieval English history. A small selection of its contents must mention the Nowell Codex (including *Beowulf*), five texts of the Anglo-Saxon Chronicle (B, C, D, F, and fragments of G), two of the five earliest manuscripts of Bede's *Ecclesiastical History*, the Lindisfarne Gospels, the Vespasian Psalter, the Durham *Liber vitae*, the OE Hexateuch, as well as numerous saints' lives, cartularies, charters, later chronicles, legal texts, and ME works, such as *Sir Gawain and the Green Knight* and Laȝamon's *Brut*. The original manuscripts of Asser's *Life of King Alfred*, Æthelweard's chronicle, and *The Battle of Maldon* were destroyed in 1731, but their texts are known from early-modern transcripts. The earliest catalogue (BL Harley 6018) was begun in 1621 but is incomplete; that by Thomas Smith, published in 1696, provides a list of the collection before the 1731 fire; that by Joseph Planta, made in 1793–1802, has not yet been replaced. All these are arranged by press mark. The only printed catalogue arranged by subject is that by Samuel Hooper of 1777.

Alexander R. Rumble

Bibliography

Sharpe, Kevin. *Sir Robert Cotton 1586–1631: History and Politics in Early Modern England*. Oxford: Oxford University Press, 1979; Smith, Thomas. *Catalogue of the Manuscripts in the Cottonian Library 1696 . . . Reprinted . . . Together with Documents Relating to the Fire of 1731*, ed. Colin G.C. Tite, with translations by Godfrey E. Turton. Woodbridge: Brewer, 1984; Tite, Colin G.C. *The Manuscript Library of Sir Robert Cotton*. Panizzi Lectures 1993. London: British Library, 1994; Wright, Cyril Ernest. "The Elizabethan Society of Antiquaries and the Formation of the Cottonian Library." In *The English Library before 1700: Studies in Its History*, ed. Francis Wormald and Cyril E. Wright. London: Athlone, 1958, pp. 176–212.

See also Beowulf; Elstob; Nowell; Paleography and Codicology; Parker; *Pearl*-Poet

Councils, Royal and Baronial

It is no exaggeration to say that the whole political fabric of late-medieval royal government was built upon the concept of "counsel," whether given formally in specially summoned great councils of the realm or in the official forum of parliament, or else through more intimate exchanges between the monarch and his leading subjects, both lay and ecclesiastical.

Kings had, naturally, from the earliest times depended upon such advice, but during the reign of Henry III an identifiable *consilium regis* ("king's council") developed as a response to the need for centralization. This body gradually became more professional, although its membership remained a matter of royal discretion. As the 14th-century poet John Gower said, "Ther is nothing which mai be betre aboute a King than conseil, which is the substance of all a Kinges governance." A wise ruler instinctively understood the importance of regular consultations with a wide range of noblemen and influential commoners. Less sagacious kings were given to excessive favoritism: Edward II, Richard II, and Henry VI each came to regret the mistake of alienating men who expected, by virtue of rank or wealth, to participate in the deliberations of government.

The giving of counsel was seen as a duty incumbent upon the "sad [sober] and substantial" leaders of society. Indeed, during the 1480s, treasurers of England were actually required to take an oath promising to "councile" the king to the best of their ability; it was the senior officers of state and their more experienced associates in the royal household who constituted the backbone of the council.

Whereas great councils, with representatives from the baronial, knightly, and mercantile classes, were held intermittently to consider specific issues, such as raising of money or foreign affairs, the royal council met regularly and was composed of sworn and (almost always) salaried advisers with the dual task of formulating and implementing royal policy. The choice of personnel sometimes caused great friction between the sovereign and parliament, which, predictably, sought to avoid a council dominated by partisanship and faction.

There were times, especially during royal minorities or periods of political unrest, when the royal council had to assume *de facto* control of government; even under strong rulers like Henry V and Edward IV, who limited its independent executive authority, the volume of administrative, financial, and diplomatic business was such as to leave enormous reserves of political power in its hands. Evidence from the 15th century shows that, although in theory a large number of men could be called upon to act as councillors (105 known individuals in the reign of Edward IV), only a few put in a regular attendance at meetings.

The same considerations applied to the great magnates, whose estates were small kingdoms in themselves. As well as soliciting advice on major items of policy (marriages, important political decisions, and administrative reforms) from friends, followers, and family, nobles employed the permanent services of senior estate and household personnel (who sat *ex officio* as councillors) and a solid phalanx of lawyers, some of whom were leading members of their profession. The influential position occupied by lawyers on baronial councils (in contrast to the royal council, until the very end of the Middle Ages) was partly a result of the massive amount of litigation and general legal business in which great landowners were involved. But it is also an indication of the ever-increasing amount of work undertaken by baronial councils as tribunals for private quarrels between tenants, retainers, neighbors, and clients of great lords.

In this respect individual magnates offered a service not dissimilar to that provided by the court of chancery, whose chief merits were speed, cheapness, and relative freedom from corruption. By far the greatest proportion of conciliar activity, however, concerned the minutiae of estate administration; few items were considered too petty to escape attention. On most estates special commissions comprising a handful of senior staff and a few lawyers were set up to undertake tours of inspection so their findings and recommendations could be reported back directly to the lord. As with their royal counterpart long minorities or the absence of the magnate overseas meant that baronial councils had to assume far greater powers, a task made easier because continuity of office holding was the norm and many senior employees possessed decades of experience.

Carole Rawcliffe

Bibliography

Baldwin, James F. *The King's Council in England during the Middle Ages.* Oxford: Clarendon, 1913 [the old if general study; now outdated]; Brown, Alfred L. "The King's Councillors in Fifteenth Century England." *TRHS,* 5th ser. 19 (1969): 95–118; Lander, J.R. "The Yorkist Council and Administration." *EHR* 73 (1958): 27–46; Rawcliffe, Carole. "Baronial Councils in the Middle Ages." In *Patronage, Pedigree and Power,* ed. Charles D. Ross. Gloucester: Sutton, 1979, pp. 87–108; Rawcliffe, Carole, and S. Flower. "English Noblemen and Their Advisers: Consultation and Collaboration in the Later Middle Ages." *Journal of British Studies* 25 (1986): 157–77; Virgoe, Roger. "The Composition of the King's Council, 1437–61." *BIHR* 43 (1970): 134–60.

See also Households, Royal and Baronial; Parliament

Court Culture and Patronage

The roots of courtly patronage and the attendant development of a court culture are deep and various. Kings' courts were the centers of culture and patronage long before our earliest medieval sources; a characteristic of the Germanic war leader was the giving of gifts to his followers, and this munificence was similarly expected of the early-medieval king.

By the same token the concentration of wealth at the apex of the social pyramid led, in a hierarchical society, to clear parallels between conspicuous consumption and social standing. Throughout the Middle Ages an individual both reflected and expressed his or her position in society by such signs as clothes and the splendor and quality of material objects. Those who stood near rulers expected to be well rewarded, as they were eager to display their special status by their appearance; a reputation for generosity was among a king's assets, one for meanness a serious liability.

Though there was an inevitable concentration of artistic patronage around the king and the powerful lords who served him, the royal household was an itinerant one, and those who created and performed the arts were without a fixed abode. There was no cultural capital, at least not until the later Middle Ages, when London/Westminster became the center of this activity, as it did for so much else. Furthermore, from the coming of the Norman (and Angevins) until the second half of the 14th century, French was the language of the court and of its literary culture.

On the other hand it would be a mistake to think of English court culture as just a passive receptor of French culture. English influence, especially on literature, was strong, in theme if not necessarily in language. The story of King Arthur and his knights (the "Matter of Britain," first disseminated in substantial form by Geoffrey of Monmouth's *Historia regum Britanniae,* in the 1130s) had a huge impact on medieval writers. The English royal court under Henry II and his wife, Eleanor of Aquitaine, became a center for minstrels and writers from abroad (such as Marie de France), as well as native clerics like Walter Map, author of *De nugis curialium.*

A sharper sense of independent English identity began to develop in the 13th century, forcefully expressed in an architectural statement with the building of Westminster Abbey. Henry III planned the chapel holding the shrine of Edward the Confessor as a royal mausoleum, on the pattern of the French kings at St. Denis. Henceforward the building and furnishing of Westminster Abbey and the adjoining palace provided a focus for the royal patronage—from Henry III's magnificent tessellated pavement before the high altar, laid by Roman craftsmen, to the numerous royal funerary effigies in metal or alabaster.

The need for richly illuminated service books and embroidered sets of vestments stimulated patronage of the applied arts, and the custom of patronage, albeit on a smaller scale, was repeated in the construction or rebuilding of other royal chapels. The wall paintings at Westminster Palace demonstrate the difficulty of compartmentalizing court patronage. In the Painted Chamber Henry III and Edward I commissioned a series of paintings wherein literary material is incorporated to illustrate the qualities of kingship. Similarly Henry III had scenes from a romance of Thomas of Kent painted in Nottingham Castle. In 1333 Queen Philippa gave Edward III a cup decorated with the Nine Worthies and other heroes of epic and romance. Some 60-odd volumes of secular works can be identified in the 14th-century royal household, clearly but the tip of the iceberg.

Literature figured as prominently as the plastic arts. Wace's description of himself as *clerc lisant* ("reading clerk") at the 12th-century court applies equally to Jean Froissart, patronized by Queen Philippa (d. 1369). Their function is illustrated by a manuscript of Chaucer's *Troilus and Criseyde,* depicting the poet reading aloud to the court. Only with changes in book production from the later 14th century did volumes become more generally available and reading begin to develop as a private activity, for the middling as well as the upper classes.

The patronage of household clerics was also an important element in regional, baronial courts. Geoffrey of Monmouth belonged to the household of Robert of Gloucester; two centuries later John Trevisa made his English translations while chaplain to the Berkeleys of Gloucestershire. In the 14th century baronial courts remained an important source of patronage, especially for English alliterative poets; Humphrey de Bohun, earl of Hereford, commissioned an English version of the romance *William of Palerne* for his household, and the strongly localized alliterative masterpiece *Sir Gawain and the Green Knight* was almost certainly composed for a baronial court in the northwest. The Berkeley Crécy Window (ca. 1349) in Gloucester Cathedral has a regional setting and significance, but the comrades-in-arms depicted in the lower tier focus attention on service in the king's household, at home and abroad. Royal court and capital were steadily achieving dominance, as baronial culture came to imitate that of the king's court, and all roads led, more and more, toward the political and cultural capital of the realm.

Juliet Vale

Bibliography

Binski, Paul. *The Painted Chamber at Westminster.* London: Society of Antiquaries of London, 1986; Brown, R. Allen, H.M. Colvin, and A.J. Taylor, eds. *The History of the King's Works.* Vols. 1–2: *The Middle Ages.* London: HMSO, 1963; Legge, M. Dominica. *Anglo-Norman Literature and Its Background.* Oxford: Clarendon, 1963; Rickert, Margaret. *Painting in Britain: The Middle Ages.* 2d ed. Harmondsworth: Penguin, 1963; Scattergood, V.J., and J.W. Sherborne, eds. *English Court Culture in the Later Middle Ages.* London: Duckworth, 1983; Vale, Juliet. *Edward III and Chivalry: Chivalric Society and Its Context, 1270–1350.* Woodbridge: Boydell, 1982.

See also Froissart; Geoffrey of Monmouth; Map; Patronage, Literary; Trevisa

Courtesy Literature

Didactic literature meant to serve as a guide for secular behavior. Many works in the genre also include admonitions about religious activities like daily prayers, almsgiving, or churchgoing; proper nurture is virtuous and ultimately gains a heavenly reward. Nevertheless, the rhetoric of most courtesy literature promises that good manners and morals will lead to honor and profit in this world first.

Courtesy books may be divided into two groups: works teaching courtly etiquette, especially table manners, to young males, and works of parental instruction addressed to sons and daughters. Many of the works in English are verse imitations or translations of Latin, Anglo-Norman, and French courtesy books. Courtesy literature proliferates after the 12th century, with most English works appearing in the 15th century.

The most common type of conduct book is addressed to males learning good manners in a noble household. Sections on table manners provide an amusing, eye-opening glimpse into the world of the medieval page. He must not gnaw on bones like a hound or throw them under the table; he must not pick his nose, or his teeth and nails with his knife (Caxton's *Book of Courtesy*).

In addition to instructions about table manners books of nurture might include rules of precedence in seating or descriptions of the duties of household officials. The Sloane Manuscript *Book of Courtesy* (BL Sloane 1986) brings a great household to life in the vivid details it gives about the responsibilities of servants from the janitor and marshall of the hall to master of hounds, carver, and chandler (Furnivall, 1868: 297–327). *The Book of Nurture* by John Russell, usher to the duke of Gloucester, ranks dozens of people by social status, delineating a seating hierarchy of infinitely subtle gradations. It also includes elaborate descriptions of the meals that would be served at noble tables, with full instructions on how the servant should prepare and present each type of food (Furnivall, 1868: 115–239).

The aristocratic settings in all these courtesy books may not be accurate guides to their 15th-century readership. Manuscript evidence suggests that such literature was popular with the merchant class and town elites who were seeking manners to match their new wealth and status. Caxton prints works of both table manners and parental instruction, citing a mercer friend as patron and even supplier of a French book of manners to be translated *(The Book of Good Manners)*.

Parental instructions to children in ME include Peter Idley's (or Idle's) *Instructions to His Son* (ca. 1445–50), written in rime royal by a public official under Henry VI. Idley combined secular advice from the works of Albertanus of Brescia (on which Chaucer had also drawn in the *Tale of Melibee* and other Canterbury tales), religious instruction from Robert Manning's *Handlyng Synne,* and material from Lydgate's *Fall of Princes.* His work was popular in its time (ten manuscripts survive) and provides an interesting mirror of contemporary cultural values.

Similarly interesting are books of instruction addressed to daughters, which are generally set explicitly within a gentry or bourgeois context rather than an aristocratic one. One of the best known of these female conduct books, composed in 1371 by a French gentleman for his daughters and widely disseminated throughout Europe, was translated anonymously into ME in the mid-15th century and again by Caxton in 1484 as *The Book of the Knight of the Tower.* Through exemplary stories of good and bad female behavior it teaches young women how to earn a good name and honor rather than "blame, shame, and defame." Becoming a "good woman"—with the deliberate blurring of any distinction between morality and social reputation—is also the aim of *How the Good Wife Taught Her Daughter* (ca. 1350). The middle-class virtues of "mesure, lowenesse, and forthought" are taught with proverbial tags to each stanza (Mustanoja, 1948: 172), and the young woman is portrayed in a social setting far more diverse and unconstrained than the aristocratic household of the male etiquette books.

Kathleen M. Ashley

Bibliography

PRIMARY

D'Evelyn, Charlotte, ed. *Peter Idley's Instructions to His Son.* New York: Modern Language Association, 1935; Furnivall, Frederick J., ed. *The Babees Book.* EETS o.s.

32. London: Trübner, 1868; Furnivall, Frederick J., ed. *Caxton's Book of Curtesye*. EETS e.s. 3. London: Humphrey Milford, 1868; Mustanoja, Tauno F., ed. *How the Good Wife Taught Her Daughter*. Helsinki: Suomalaisen Kirjallisuuden Seuran, 1948; Offord, M.Y., ed. *The Book of the Knight of the Tower, Translated by William Caxton*. EETS s.s. 2. London: Oxford University Press, 1971.

SECONDARY
Manual 9:3002–06, 3376–77; Nicholls, Jonathan. *The Matter of Courtesy: Medieval Courtesy Books and the Gawain-Poet*. Woodbridge: Brewer, 1985.

See also Caxton; Children; Court Culture; Households, Royal and Baronial; Moral and Religious Instruction; Patronage, Literary; Schools; Women in ME Literature

Courtly Love

Traditional critical term for a set of conventions applied to fictive heterosexual love relationships in medieval European literary texts, particularly those produced for aristocratic audiences in 12th-century France. First appearing in the lyric poetry of the Provençal troubadours in the early 1100s, these conventions were described by Andreas Capellanus in a mock treatise, *De amore* (alternatively titled *De arte honeste amandi,* "The Art of Loving Nobly," ca. 1184–86). Modeled in part on Ovid's *Ars amatoria, De amore* serves as a handbook for would-be lovers, its contents a hodgepodge of behavioral injunctions, scripts for seduction, and *ad hoc* allegories. Because the treatise concludes with an antifeminist diatribe, some readers suspect that the entire work is ironic. Nonetheless, it has been taken by many modern scholars as the definitive medieval treatment of courtly love.

During approximately the same period courtly love gained literary currency in narrative fiction through the chivalric romances of Chrétien de Troyes. Migrating soon thereafter to Germany and elsewhere on the European continent, courtly love proved immensely popular in French elite literature; besides constituting a central motif for lyric poetry and chivalric romance, it became a prominent feature of the dream vision and other secular allegorical literature, beginning with the *Roman de la Rose* (early 13th century). Some aspects of courtly love appear in religious poetry as well, particularly in lyrics praising the Virgin.

Features of Courtly Love

In its original French manifestations courtly love is an elaborate literary game in which courtship is played out as a parody of sociocultural realities regarding male-female dominance patterns: the female love object—generally idealized and always distanced—is cast as feudal overlord, empowered to grant her favors to or (more often) withhold them from a subservient male, whose whole existence is devoted to serving his lady, his worth being enhanced by his efforts to attain her favor. Although sexual union is frequently the ulti-mate objective, sexuality is usually sublimated; the masculine partner's sufferings are foregrounded, as are his efforts to become worthy of his lady or convince her to accede to his desires. Psychic discomfort is the keynote here: love is "a certain inborn suffering" (Andreas, ed. 1941: 28), revealed by physical manifestations in the lover, such as pallor and emaciation, fueled by uncertainty and jealousy. The lover's amorous devotion to his lady is obsessive: "A true lover is constantly and without intermission possessed by the thought of his beloved" (186). Many of these precepts are enacted by Lancelot and Yvain, the protagonists of Chrétien's *Chevalier de la charrette* and *Chevalier au lion,* respectively, who endure humiliation, pain, and ethical and spiritual tests for their ladies' sakes.

Modern Views on Courtly Love

Another feature of courtly love as it is traditionally described must be treated separately here because of the special role it has played in 20th-century literary history and criticism. Andreas insisted that "love can have no place between husband and wife" (100) and that true love must therefore be adulterous in nature. For much of this century medievalists have identified adultery as one of the essential features of courtly love, due mostly to the influence of C.S. Lewis, whose *Allegory of Love* (1936) for many years served English-speaking medievalists as the definitive account of courtly love. Since the two most enduring medieval love stories, that of Lancelot and Guinevere on the one hand, and Tristan and Isolde on the other, do treat adulterous relationships, Lewis's proposition that adultery is a key feature of courtly love went largely unquestioned for nearly three decades until it was challenged in different ways by Robertson (*Preface to Chaucer,* 1962) and Donaldson ("The Myth of Courtly Love," 1970). Observing that most of the texts that Lewis addresses do not in fact involve adulterous relationships, Donaldson argued that adultery was a relatively minor theme in ME love literature up to Malory. The same might be said for much medieval French aristocratic love literature as well; it is even questionable whether adulterous love is valorized in any of the romances about Lancelot or Tristan. Thus, while one may still encounter the assertion that adultery is an essential feature of the courtly-love configuration, most modern critics no longer hold this position.

Although the specter of adultery appears to have been laid to rest, almost every other aspect of "courtly love" has been increasingly problematized in the past two decades, especially once we move away from the seminal texts discussed above. The difficulties begin with the phrase "courtly love" *(amour courtois)* itself, coined by French medievalist Gaston Paris in 1883. Some modern scholars perceive the term as an entirely modern construct rather than as an historical descriptor and advocate replacing "courtly love" with more authentic terminology, such as *fin amour, fin' amor, bon' amor,* or *amor honestus,* all of which were used by medieval writers. Other scholars suggest broadening the field of reference with more general terms, such as "noble love" or "medieval love."

Similar lack of consensus exists regarding description and definition of this literary construct. One scholar defines it in terms of structural features, such as an intense but obstructed personal relationship between a man and a woman (Calin); another proposes extending it to "any kind of elevated human love which holds center stage" (Williams, quoted in Smith and Snow, 1980: 7). A third alternative is to define it from a sociocultural standpoint, as part of a larger code of values and conduct among an aristocratic class. Thus, as Donaldson has pointed out, "The real trouble with the term . . . is that no two scholars ever seem to mean the same thing by it" (1970: 155).

The "real trouble," however, probably lies in the nature of the endeavor itself, which attempts to crowd under a single umbrella a multitude of texts produced by and for a variety of cultures (French, German, Italian, Spanish, and English for starters) in a variety of literary modes (lyric, romance, allegory), over more than three centuries. This plurality has led many scholars, most notably D.W. Robertson, Jr., to challenge the utility of courtly love as a construct and to maintain that it is merely a fiction of our own devising. Again there is no clear consensus on the issue; however, the current trend appears to be toward refinement and redefinition rather than rejection.

Courtly Love and ME Literature

At first glance ME literature appears to have reflected the general western European interest in secular love. Among the most valued texts in the traditional ME canon are the works that in some way highlight romantic or "courtly" love, including Chaucer's *Book of the Duchess, Knight's Tale,* and *Troilus and Criseyde;* Gower's *Confessio Amantis; Sir Gawain and the Green Knight;* a sizable group of lyrics; and Malory's *Morte Darthur.* Chaucer's *Legend of Good Women* should probably be included here as well. But when we turn our attention to other ME texts, it begins to look as if England's cultural climate was not altogether hospitable to the continental version of heterosexual love.

For despite the strong French influences on ME literature, and despite the fact that much 14th-century English narrative fiction was translated or directly adapted from French texts, there are notable lacunae in the production of ME translations from continental sources apposite to courtly love. There is no ME version of Andreas, for example. Ovid— even the moralized versions—had to wait until the 16th century to enter English letters outside of Chaucer and Gower. The only ME translation of the *Roman de la Rose* is the fragmentary version attributed partly to Chaucer. Although the allegorical dream vision was an established genre in ME literature, only Chaucer and Gower avail themselves prominently of the conventions of the love vision. It is in the ME romance, however, that we have the strongest indication that the subject of courtly love did not thrive in English soil. A striking instance may be found in *Yvain and Gawain* (1300–50), an adaptation of Chrétien's *Chevalier au lion* and the only one of his romances to be translated into ME. Whereas love and love-longing are strongly emphasized by Chrétien, these elements are dramatically reduced by the English redactor, who stresses chivalric conduct instead. The same pattern of curtailment and consequent reemphasis occurs in most ME romances based on French sources. This tendency to ignore or suppress matter concerning earthly love is particularly strik-ing in ME treatments of the Arthurian legend before Malory. Most ME Arthurian romances revolve around themes of kingship, national ideology, and the politics of succession. Even the stanzaic *Morte Arthur* (late 14th century), despite its inherited narrative focus on Lancelot and his relationships with Elaine of Astolat and Guinevere, focuses more on the dynastic ideal than on the love theme. In pre-Malorian English treatments of Arthurian materials Lancelot serves primarily as a chivalric model rather than as a model lover. The love of Tristan and Isolde apparently failed to capture the imagination of English audiences as well; aside from Malory's treatment, Tristan is accorded only one ME romance, *Sir Tristrem* (late 13th century), and from this single exemplar the love theme has been all but excised.

It would appear, then, that the ideological and cultural preoccupations of 14th-century English writers and readers held little space for the formalized meditation upon human love that constitutes courtly love in its continental forms. And the canonical ME texts that do explicitly address the conventions of courtly love treat their subject with varying degrees of suspicion and disapprobation. The lovesick narrator of Gower's *Confessio Amantis* learns after extensive instruction that passionate earthly love is often blind, arbitrary, an impediment to reason, and therefore to be abandoned in favor of a more spiritually grounded love of the common good. Chaucer's courtly lovers do not fare well at all. Many critics see Troilus as being sullied ethically and spiritually by his passion for Criseyde, and the conclusion to *Troilus and Criseyde* calls readers to set their hearts on the love of God. Arcite in Chaucer's *Knight's Tale* may be as close to the classical courtly lover as we meet in ME literature, even manifesting the requisite physical symptoms of lovesickness, such as pallor, "eyen holwe," and emaciation (*KnT* 1361–64); he is also one of the rare courtly lovers in all medieval literature actually to die because of love, having exchanged friendship and familial loyalty for the dubious currency of passional love. In *Sir Gawain and the Green Knight* courtly love, both as a concept and as a literary convention, is wittily pilloried as an ideological sham, conflicting with and threatening a value system that prizes courage, loyalty, chastity, and religious faith. All of these implicit critiques coalesce in Malory's *Morte Darthur.* Only in the "Book of Sir Gareth" does Malory portray earthly love as unequivocally positive. For the rest, despite its capacity for inspiring personal fidelity and sacrifice, it not only damages individual lovers but is socially disruptive as well.

The most revealing indicator of attitudes toward courtly love in medieval England may be the ME lyrics. Although the best known of these lyrics, like "The Fair Maid of Ribblesdale" or "A Wayle Whyt ase Whalles Bon," call upon some of the conventions associated with courtly love, most ME lyric poetry confirms the lack of interest in refined love inferrable from the romances and other narrative genres. In the first place religious lyrics outnumber secular lyrics by about four to one until the end of the 15th century; more important, not all ME secular lyrics are concerned with love. Only about a quarter of the Harley lyrics, for example, directly or tangentially represent the conventions of courtly love poetry. Even the Harley lyrics that draw on some of those conventions often diverge from continental models in other respects; indeed, because of the frank sensuality with which a number of these poems conclude, some critics read them as ironic or even parodic. All this suggests a general readership that had little interest in the poetic conventions of courtly love.

Manuscript evidence confirms the view that interest in French poetic models generally and courtly love poetry in particular was confined to elite audiences. Even for these audiences courtly love lyrics do not appear to have provoked any special interest *per se.* The collections in which they appear are almost all random assemblages rather than coherent anthologies, suggesting that these courtly lyrics were not perceived as a distinct genre or as having a specific literary function or value.

In sum it would appear that continental love literature is not the appropriate template for the majority of 14th- and 15th-century literary works produced for English audiences. Courtly love was evidently of little interest to the noncourtly audience; and when the conventions of courtly love were invoked, they frequently seem to have conflicted with the value systems of author and audience alike. This is not to say that ME literature is entirely loveless—one might adduce the love relationships in *Sir Orfeo, Floris and Blancheflour,* and *King Horn,* or even Chaucer's *Franklin's Tale,* as examples of representations of human love that *were* congenial to English audiences. Nor is the construct of courtly love entirely irrelevant to our understanding of ME secular texts and their audiences: absences are as eloquent as presences, and differences as useful as similarities in the process of definition. If we can discard the notion of courtly love as a yardstick for literary sophistication and hence an index of literary merit, and instead perceive it as a descriptor, a value-neutral term coined for a specific cultural phenomenon, it may yet serve to enhance our reading of medieval English literary texts.

Elizabeth S. Sklar

Bibliography

PRIMARY

Andreas Capellanus. *The Art of Courtly Love.* Trans. John Jay Parry. New York: Columbia University Press, 1941; Shapiro, Norman R., trans. *The Comedy of Eros: Medieval French Guides to the Art of Love.* Urbana: University of Illinois Press, 1971.

SECONDARY

Allen, Peter L. *The Art of Love: Amatory Fiction from Ovid to the Romance of the Rose.* Philadelphia: University of Pennsylvania Press, 1992; Barron, W.R.J. *English Medieval Romance.* New York: Longman, 1987; Boffey, Julia. *Manuscripts of English Courtly Love Lyrics in the Later Middle Ages.* Cambridge: Brewer, 1985; Calin, William. "Defense and Illustration of *Fin'Amor:* Some Polemical Comments on the Robertsonian Approach." In *The Expansion and Transformations of Courtly Literature,* ed. Nathaniel B. Smith and Joseph T. Snow. Athens: University of Georgia Press, 1980, pp. 32–48; Denomy, Alexander J. "Courtly Love and Courtliness." *Speculum* 28 (1953): 44–63; Donaldson, E.T. "The Myth of Courtly Love." In *Speaking of Chaucer.* New York: Norton, 1970, pp. 154–63; Dronke, Peter. *Medieval Latin and the Rise of European Love-Lyric.* 2d ed. 2 vols. Oxford: Clarendon, 1968; Ferrante, Joan M., and George D. Economou, eds. *In Pursuit of Perfection: Courtly Love in Medieval Literature.* Port Washington: Kennikat, 1975; Jackson, W.T.H. "The *De amore* of Andreas Capellanus and the Practice of Love at Court." *Romanic Review* 49 (1958): 243–51; Kelly, H.A. *Love and Marriage in the Age of Chaucer.* Ithaca: Cornell University Press, 1975; Lewis, C.S. *The Allegory of Love: A Study in Medieval Tradition.* London: Oxford University Press, 1936; Moore, John C. *Love in Twelfth-Century France.* Philadelphia: University of Pennsylvania Press, 1972; O'Donoghue, Bernard. *The Courtly Love Tradition: Literature in Context.* Manchester: Manchester University Press, 1982; Robertson, D.W., Jr. "The Concept of Courtly Love as an Impediment to the Understanding of Medieval Texts." In *The Meaning of Courtly Love,* ed. F.X. Newman. Albany: SUNY Press, 1968, pp. 1–18; Smith, Nathaniel B., and Joseph T. Snow, eds. *The Expansion and Transformations of Courtly Literature.* Athens: University of Georgia Press, 1980; Utley, Francis L. "Must We Abandon the Concept of Courtly Love?" *M&H* n.s. 3 (1972): 299–324.

See also Breton Lay; Charles of Orléans; Chaucer; Dream Vision; Gower; Harley Lyrics; Literary Influences: French; Lyrics; Malory; *Morte Arthur,* Stanzaic; *Pearl-*Poet; Romances; *Sir Orfeo;* Songs; Women in ME Literature

Courts, Ecclesiastical

When the courts of the church came into being as institutions, clearly distinct from secular courts, is not clear. By a decree of ca. 1072 William I separated ecclesiastical courts from the local hundred courts. Before then the situation had been murky; church and secular officials sat jointly in the hundred court, and, although bishops and archdeacons no doubt imposed ecclesiastical discipline, there probably was (in Makower's words) "no division between the judicial and administrative authorities." As highly structured judicial institutions ecclesiastical courts are found in England only after the Conquest.

A clearly defined hierarchy of church courts (frequently called "courts Christian" by common lawyers) existed, generally paralleling the church hierarchy. For all practical purposes the lowest ecclesiastical court hearing all kinds of cases was the court of the archdeacon. Each archdeacon would have a court in his archdeaconry, as would each bishop in his diocese, and each of the two archbishops in their provinces. Cases of first instance were brought to either the archdeacon's or the bishop's court. Appeals would be made to the next superior court (e.g., from the archdeacon's to the bishop's court) or from any court, *mediis intermissis* (skipping over the intermediaries), directly to the court of Rome. Appeal to Rome could be made either directly or by way of tuitorial appeal, which was in fact two appeals: an appeal of the substance to the apostolic see and an appeal for protection *(pro tuicione)* while prosecuting the appeal, to the archbishop.

The question of jurisdiction of the church courts, although at times disputed, often forcefully, can be stated clearly: the church claimed jurisdiction over ecclesiastical persons and ecclesiastical things. Thus all clerics (men who had taken tonsure) and all religious (men and women who had made religious profession for monastic or regular orders) were subject to church courts, no matter what was at issue (e.g., homicide, theft, adultery), and were consequently exempt from the jurisdiction of the secular courts. Around this issue the Becket controversy raged.

The church also claimed jurisdiction over matters ecclesiastical. Thus burning a church, stealing a chalice, or striking a cleric fell to the jurisdiction of the ecclesiastical courts. Testamentary and matrimonial cases provided a vast part of the cases heard in the church courts. Cases concerning contracts and defamation were claimed for the church courts, although the church never gained exclusive jurisdiction in these matters.

F. Donald Logan

Bibliography

Adams, Norma, and Charles Donahue, eds. *Select Cases from the Ecclesiastical Courts of the Province of Canterbury, c. 1200–1301.* Selden Society 95. London: Selden Society, 1981; Helmholz, R.H. *Marriage Litigation in Medieval England.* London: Cambridge University Press, 1974; Makower, Felix. *The Constitutional History and Constitution of the Church of England.* London: Sonnenschein, 1895; Morris, Colin. "A Consistory Court in the Middle Ages." *Journal of Ecclesiastical History* 25 (1964): 150–59; Owen, Dorothy M. "Ecclesiastical Jurisdiction 1300–1550: The Records and Their Interpretation." *Studies in Church History* 11 (1975): 190–221; Woodcock, Brian L. *Medieval Courts in the Diocese of Canterbury.* London: Oxford University Press, 1952; Wunderli, Richard M. *London Church Courts and Society on the Eve of the Reformation.* Cambridge: Medieval Academy of America, 1981.

See also Canterbury, Ecclesiastical Province of; Courts and the Court System; Dioceses; Marriage; Wills

Courts and the Court System

Courts and the court system in medieval England began with the fusion of Anglo-Norman legal concepts with those of the Anglo-Saxons, shortly after the Conquest. Across the later medieval period these concepts slowly evolved, with two main periods of change: during the common-law reforms of Henry II and during the reign of Edward I. The general direction of change was toward royal, centralized control at the expense of baronial, feudal law.

The most important court in the Anglo-Norman period was the royal court, the *curia regis*. More than merely a feudal court, it served as the court of highest appeal in the event of inadequate justice in local courts. From the nucleus of the *curia* Anglo-Norman kings gradually extended their hold over local jurisdiction by the use of several expedients. Whether backed up by the royal prerogative, the notion of the king's peace, or the concept of felony, royal justice overtook local forms until, by Henry II's time, royal-court jurisdiction enjoyed a power and popularity many times that of its earlier model.

So popular, in fact, was royal justice that demands for its services necessitated the creation of "satellite" courts to offer it in outlying districts. Thus the expansion of royal justice was implemented by a variety of officials: sheriffs, resident justices at the local level, and itinerant justices bringing royal justice to the far reaches of the realm. Also effective in spreading the influence of the *curia* were "spinoffs" from the central court. Most notable was the exchequer, which gradually assumed increased influence in matters of jurisprudence.

In addition to the *curia* and its offshoots the Anglo-Norman period witnessed the operation of justice at the local level in a series of lesser courts. Most important was the county court. Any number of cases could be heard here, ranging from criminal cases and pleas of the crown to land disputes. A distinguishing feature of this court was the greater wealth and influence of its litigants. The county court was the nexus between central and local jurisprudence; the king's itinerant justices used it to establish ties at the local level. And as the law offered by itinerant justices grew more popular, the separate power and influence of the county court gradually diminished.

Below the county court in scope of jurisdiction and the social rank of litigants was the hundred court; it too was slowly eclipsed by itinerant justices. A mosaic of feudal (private or franchisal) courts also dotted the land, controlled by feudal lords and hearing disputes among their vassals. They too fell victim to the attractiveness of royal justice, available in more and more outlying extensions of the royal court. By the same practice the borough court, reserved for disputes among burgesses, gradually gave way to the more efficient form of law offered by royal justices.

Maitland saw the reign of Henry II as "a critical moment in English legal history." Henry's government reshaped existing legal practices into a more uniform and centralized system of jurisprudence. Partly for personal and partly for political reasons, he sought to extend the influence of his justice, at the expense of local and feudal law, throughout his realm. By its end his justice was available to any freeman through the purchase of a writ. This transformation affected the courts and court system, along with legal procedure in civil and criminal cases.

Perhaps the clearest example of the expansion of royal justice is in the realm of the courts. Both their number and jurisdiction greatly increased. Three royal courts were created out of the *curia regis* to handle the growing demand. Most important was the great council. Here were heard weighty cases involving matters of royal interest, as well as disputes among the highest of the realm. Slightly below the great council in terms of influence was the small council. Matters serious enough for the king's ear, but not needing adjudication by the great barons, went to this body. Since the king often sat in on these deliberations, this court eventually became known as the court of the king's bench.

In Henry's reign the exchequer court, particularly its upper body, also began to hear pleas not necessarily connected with financial matters. Since there was little distinction between the composition of the small council and the exchequer court, Henry created yet another and smaller court. This permanent court, composed of five legal experts and resident at Westminster, was to handle the pleas of any freeman. This court had its own seal and evolved in the 13th century into the court of common pleas. Finally, in response to a demand for royal justice, Henry extended his reach into all corners of the realm by commissioning itinerant justices, each of whom could convene his own (royal) court.

Owing to the enormous popularity of the more uniform law offered by this newfangled system of courts, public and feudal courts suffered a precipitous loss of influence. County courts, now more dependent, became extensions of royal courts; here were convened the juries empaneled for civil and criminal disputes. Hundred and franchisal courts underwent an even more dramatic loss of business. And since royal courts took most cases out of local feudal lords' courts, those too were rendered all but extinct by the more rational system of the royal courts.

Of even greater importance than the changes in the courts were Henry's procedural alterations. Here again he took existing notions of legal procedure in civil and criminal cases and made them more flexible and adaptable. His principal instruments of reform were the writ and the jury. The former offered royal justice for sale; the latter had the advantage of gathering the facts of a case. A trial by jurors, ordered by a royal justice to tell the truth in a case, had the advantage over customary law—with methods of proof resting on either the oath or ordeal—of providing a more certain resolution of suits.

The advantages of the writ and jury in civil cases were quickly recognized, and over time the legal system developed a series of five royal writs (or assizes) to deal with civil disputes. Four dealt with possession: the assize utrum (1164) to determine whether land was held in alms or lay fee; novel disseisin (1166) to afford swift redress for those whose land had been unjustly seized; mort d'ancestor (1176) to settle disputed claims over inheritance in favor of the true heir; darrein presentment (1179) to facilitate settlement of disputes over church advowsons (the right to present candidates for ecclesiastical benefices). The fifth writ concerned proprietary right. By purchase of this a defendant could decline trial by combat and have a jury settlement in a royal court. In giving the defendant a choice in the mode of trial, this assize soon became enormously popular and contributed to the growing use of trial by jury.

In criminal law Henry made fewer changes. Here his desire was to improve on haphazard and uncertain Anglo-Norman methods of apprehending and trying criminals. In place of prosecutions before sheriffs or local justices he substituted trials before itinerant royal justices (in county courts) for serious crimes. The method used was the more efficient

presentment, or grand, jury, whose purpose was to indict criminals for trial.

Another major alteration was in the manner of trial. In place of trial by ordeal or compurgation the Assize of Clarendon (1166) provided that all indicted by a jury of presentment submit to trial by ordeal of water. Any who failed suffered either hanging, mutilation, or exile. As in matters of civil law Henry had extended the long arm of justice to local areas, and by developing the grand jury he made accusations of serious criminal wrongdoing both easier and more uniform.

With Edward I (1272–1307) we encounter "the great watershed in English legal history." Sometimes called "the English Justinian," after the Byzantine emperor known for codifying Roman law, he tightened and refined the well-fashioned common law, rendering it so effective and attractive that it stood almost unchanged until the modern era. All areas of common law underwent adjustment. In conceptual terms the development of the common law swung from innovations devised in the royal chancery to changes enacted in parliament. Thus was laid down the principle that all legal innovations henceforth, even if proposed by the king, would meet the approval of parliament; this was the basis of English constitutionalism. In more practical terms important changes were effected in the courts and in civil and criminal procedure.

Edward upheld changes in the courts and their jurisdiction made in the reign of Henry III. In Henry's reign Magna Carta, with one or two additions, served as the basis of statute law. According to Bracton it was then that the practice of the common law came to be based on two fundamental precepts: the writ and the concept of precedent. These notions were incorporated into Edward's reorganization of the common law, and he also made significant alterations of his own.

Essentially changes under Edward were toward separation and specialization in common law courts and procedure. The courts of King's Bench, Exchequer, and Common Pleas continued as the heart of the system, but each began to assume separate jurisdictions and functions. King's Bench heard suits related to royal interests and emerged as a court of last resort in cases of error in lower courts. Cases brought to the Exchequer dealt mainly with revenue. Common Pleas had jurisdiction over cases involving private individuals.

Above these central courts, for further review, stood the king's council (either great or small) and parliament. Below the central courts were those of itinerant justices. Whereas before Edward I it was the judicial eyre (the judges traveling on a circuit) that brought pleas into these courts, this practice died out. In its place there appeared three judicial commissions: assize (dealing with the possessory assizes of novel disseisin, mort d'ancestor, and darrein presentment), gaol delivery (which ordered the clearing out of certain jails to speed up criminal trials), and oyer and terminer (empowering royal justices to look into and bring to trial alleged felonies in local areas). Taken together these commissions ultimately brought almost all cases before the central court of Common Pleas, thus making the common law much more expedient and at the same time more desirable.

There were also changes in procedure. By the use of statute-driven legislation Edward made substantial changes in the exercise and availability of royal common law. In the Statute of Westminster (1285) he provided that all litigants desirous of a jury trial in civil cases before justices of assize could now have one locally rather than at Westminster. In criminal law the Statute of Westminster I (1275), through the use of forms of torture like *peine forte et dure,* instituted a way to force felons to accept trial by jury. Also, in the late 13th century, more and more trials occurred before petty juries, composed of some members of the presentment jury plus one or two others from other parts of the kingdom. The intention here was to separate indicting jurors from those doing justice in trials, thus marking a step toward greater impartiality.

George B. Stow

Bibliography

Baker, John H. *An Introduction to English Legal History.* 3d ed. London: Butterworths, 1990; Bellamy, John G. *Crime and Public Order in England in the Later Middle Ages.* London: Routledge & Kegan Paul, 1973; Brown, Alfred L. *The Governance of Late Medieval England, 1272–1461.* London: Arnold, 1989; Cam, Helen M. "The Law-Courts of Medieval London." In *Law-Finders and Law-Makers in Medieval England: Collected Studies in Legal and Constitutional History.* London: Merlin Press, 1962, pp. 85–94; Harding, Alan. *The Law Courts of Medieval England.* London: Allen & Unwin, 1973; Palmer, Robert C. *The County Courts of Medieval England, 1150–1350.* Princeton: Princeton University Press, 1982; Plucknett, Theodore F.T. *Legislation of Edward I.* Oxford: Clarendon, 1949; Stenton, Doris M. *English Justice between the Norman Conquest and the Great Charter, 1066–1215.* Philadelphia: American Philosophical Society, 1964; Sutherland, Donald W. *Quo Warranto Proceedings in the Reign of Edward I, 1278–1294.* Oxford: Clarendon, 1963; Sutherland, Donald W. *The Assize of Novel Disseisin.* Oxford: Clarendon, 1973; Turner, Ralph V. *The King and His Courts: The Role of John and Henry III in the Administration of Justice, 1199–1240.* Ithaca: Cornell University Press, 1968.

See also Bracton; Chancellor and Chancery; Courts, Ecclesiastical; Edward I; Exchequer; Henry II; Juries; Law, Post-Conquest; Magna Carta

Coventry

A city that originated as an Anglo-Saxon settlement on the banks of the River Sherbourne, sustained by the foundation of a nunnery by the 10th century and a Benedictine abbey in 1043. The abbey, founded by Earl Leofric and his wife, the famous Godiva, served as the focal point for local commerce and the driving force behind a fledgling wool industry. In 1088 Coventry became a possession of the earldom of Chester. When the earldom fell to a minor heir, the bishop of Chester moved his see there, laying claim to the town's northern half on the basis of what seem to be forged charters. This instigated a long battle for control between successive earls and priors, and the rivalry between the "Earl's Half" and the "Prior's Half" of the town was formally resolved only in 1355.

Through charters granted by each rival authority burgesses gained extensive rights and privileges from an early date. Powers of local self-government, already considerable in the 12th century, were extended by one of the earliest charters of incorporation in 1345. Within a generation or two Coventry was virtually autonomous, and by 1451 it gained the rare privilege of county status. During the 15th century it hosted two meetings of parliament, received several royal visits, and gained a royal mint (in 1465).

Much of Coventry's economic strength derived from its strategic location at the hub of major road links with Wales, the west Midlands, the Cotswolds, London, and the south coast. Though the Sherbourne proved an ineffective transport link, the many streams running into it provided ample water power for a successful woolen cloth industry. Especially in the "Earl's Half," or southern part of the town, cloth production as well as metal and leather working meant continued prosperity through the central Middle Ages. By the 14th century the dyers developed a strong production of blue thread, and this "Coventry blue" became the city's most distinctive product. Additional economic strength came from the cathedral and other ecclesiastical institutions, from long-distance trade, and from the affluent Warwickshire hinterland.

Coventry recovered quickly from the Black Death (1348–50) and remained prosperous for roughly a century thereafter. In 1377 it paid the fourth-highest poll tax in the kingdom, and the next decade saw considerable civic building and population growth. St. Mary's Hall, housing both the Trinity Guild and the city's court and council, symbolized the close ties between major guilds and city government. These ties were further symbolized by a rich ceremonial life, in which the guilds sponsored the annual Corpus Christi play cycle.

The latter decades of the 15th century brought increased competition and declining markets, poverty and unemployment, a flight of the wealthy from the burdens of taxation and civic office, and considerable physical decay. Coventry's deep and prolonged depression, climaxing in the 1520s and 1530s, has come to epitomize "urban crisis" at the end of the Middle Ages.

Robert Tittler

Bibliography

Gooder, Arthur, and Eileen Gooder. "Coventry before 1355: Unity or Division." *Midland History* 4 (1981): 1–38; Harris, Mary D., ed. *The Coventry Leet Book.* 2 vols. in 3 parts. EETS o.s. 134, 135, 138, 146. London: Kegan Paul, Trench, Trübner, 1907–13; Lancaster, Joan. "Coventry." In *The British Atlas of Historic Towns,* gen. ed. Mary D. Lobel. Vol. 2. London: Scolar, 1975; Phythian-Adams, Charles. *Desolation of a City: Coventry and the Urban Crisis of the Late Middle Ages.* Cambridge: Cambridge University Press, 1979; *Victoria History of the County of Warwick.* Vols. 1, 2, 8, ed. William Page, H.A. Doubleday, and W.B. Stephens. London: Constable, 1904, 1908, 1969.

See also Drama, Vernacular; Towns; Trade

Criticism, Modern, of Medieval Literature

Modern criticism of medieval literature cannot be understood fully without recognizing its roots in the intellectual habits and assumptions of earlier periods—especially those of the Enlightenment, with its Cartesian search for certainty and for abiding canons of thought and value. These roots can be clearly seen in Ernst Robert Curtius's foreword to the English translation (1953) of his *European Literature and the Latin Middle Ages* (1948), one of the most influential books in medieval studies in the 20th century:

> In order to convince, I had to use the scientific technique which is the foundation of all historical investigation: philology. For the intellectual sciences it has the same significance as mathematics has for the natural sciences. . . . I have attempted to employ it with something of the precision with which the natural sciences employ their methods. Geometry demonstrates with figures, philology with texts.

In every way but direct statement Curtius uses the "hard" sciences as the standard for demonstrating truth. Such a criterion for truthfulness is governed by its opposition to doubt: scientific knowledge is certain, predictable, its results everywhere repeatable. Knowledge of this sort fulfills the Cartesian dream of certitude, a dream that shaped criticism of medieval texts for nearly 200 years. Like his 19th-century predecessors Curtius sought to achieve "precision" and certitude with medieval texts by applying the techniques of philology, the traditional textual and historical scholarship from which modern criticism of medieval literature has sprung. Although the possibility of such certitude has been radically questioned in the 20th century, its ghost continues to haunt modern critical approaches to OE and ME literature.

Old English Literary Criticism

Modern critics of OE literature have extended 19th-century philology in several directions: philology itself, New Criticism (formal reading of rhetorical structures), exegetics (study of Christian hermeneutic contexts), and oral-formulaic theory (study of the influence of oral compositional techniques) have come to be paradigmatic forms of OE criticism. But they are paradigms currently undergoing revaluation.

Philology has traditionally focused on editing and the problems of editing: its Cartesian goal was exact scholarly elucidation of written documents. But fantastic, romanticizing elements haunt the margins—some would even say the core—of philological positivism. Editorial reconstructions of a lost original manuscript in the tradition of Karl Lachmann were based upon an imaginative vision of what Germanic poetry ought to look like. Similarly Karl Müllenhoff's 19th-century philological program of removing supposed Christian accretions from presumably pagan Anglo-Saxon works—or sifting Christian works for presumed pagan elements—relied upon imaginative reconstructive techniques and an ideology privileging primitive Germanic culture.

Although the development of OE philology into an historical criticism was founded on a positivist model, literary interpretations of early Anglo-Saxonists tended toward a sentimentalized romanticism and a belief in Germanic racial superiority. Insofar as the philological heritage still operates as a programmatic force in contemporary OE studies, it pulls in more than one direction. The philology of John Mitchell Kemble, whose studies with the brothers Grimm led him to dismiss Sharon Turner's influential survey of OE poetry as "often deficient, often mistaken," was in turn soundly rejected by Henry Sweet as "superficial," just as the idealizing editorial principles of Lachmann and Müllenhoff would be rejected by a later generation of Anglo-Saxonists.

Despite these methodological differences within philology many of the most influential editions and historical studies of Anglo-Saxon literature are grounded in the philological tradition: the monumental editions of Anglo-Saxon poetry by Friedrich Klaeber *(Beowulf)* and George Krapp and Elliott van Kirk Dobbie (the Anglo-Saxon Poetic Records) and the historical criticism of J.R.R. Tolkien, Dorothy Whitelock, Fred C. Robinson, and many others. If the approach is old, insights derived from it have often been strikingly new. And once again, in a renovation that is also a repetition, a new OE philology is asserting itself at the close of the 20th century.

The modern critical study of OE literature may be held to have begun with Tolkien's groundbreaking study of *Beowulf* (1936) and to have been greatly advanced under the impact of New Criticism in the 1950s, which led to an emphasis on the craftsmanship of OE poems. When complexity and craftsmanship became the key terms for evaluating literature, the Anglo-Saxon literary artifact reconstituted itself. Neglected poems came to be seen as skillfully crafted gems. With few exceptions, however, the strict New Criticism of OE poetry was rarely practiced. Instead Anglo-Saxonists employed close reading to demonstrate the high level of craftsmanship of OE poems, in an attempt to render them worthy of attention after the old philological perspectives of English departments shifted. When applied to OE texts, however, New Criticism seldom took up theoretical questions; it usually limited itself to demonstrating artistic skill in poems that impious modernists took to be primitive and repellent. One of the earliest book-length attempts to apply New Criticism to OE poetry was written by Neil Isaacs (1968), although the subsequent work of Stanley Greenfield (1972) proved more influential. Contemporary critics of OE poetry still tend to make New Critical assumptions about the goals of criticism: historical, exegetical, or oral-formulaic scholarship is enlisted to demonstrate a sometimes implicit, sometimes explicit, critical point—the intellectual and verbal subtlety of OE poems.

Whereas New Criticism was originally a reaction against philology's positivist historicism, with exegetics the pendulum swings back to the historical contexts of OE literature, especially those of Christian allegory, theology, and religious practice. Philology had long included an exegetical component (e.g., in the work of Friedrich Klaeber, Max Förster, and Rudolph Willard); but the old exegetical critics had few critical aspirations. Although the newer exegetics (e.g., the work of such critics as R.E. Kaske and Thomas Hill) was characterized by only a modest New Critical perspective, its influence was all the greater for such deliberate restraint. Strong exegetical/New Critical hybrids appeared in books and essays by Bernard F. Huppé, Jackson Campbell, and Daniel Calder. Although these exegetical critics put New Critical techniques to good use, OE New Critics seldom returned the favor.

Oral-formulaic theory, which challenged both exegetics and New Criticism, is a formalism like New Criticism—but it is often a philological formalism betraying a nostalgia for the primitive, evidence of the continuing influence of philology's origins. The theory is based on studies by Milman Parry, who in the 1930s argued that, like 20th-century Yugoslavian epics, Homeric poetry was composed orally with the help of traditional formulas and themes. In the 1950s Francis P. Magoun and others applied similar arguments to *Beowulf*, albeit not without controversy. Later this approach took on a broader narrative focus in type-scene analysis, and more recent modifications by John Miles Foley and Katherine O'Keeffe have paid closer attention to the influence of manuscript culture on Anglo-Saxon orality.

Whether employing oral-formulaicist, New Critical, or exegetical methodology, the critic of OE literature typically seeks to mirror the complex craftsmanship of OE texts. When exegetics and New Criticism work together they are steadfast in their fidelity to the rhetorical structures of texts. Such conceptual categories as church, heathen, Jew, saint, and devil are treated as unproblematic givens, rather than as textual processes based on a conflictual rhetoric. Scholarship and criticism based on these paradigms are oriented toward complicity with, rather than critical examination of, such textual processes. In exegetics and New Criticism—and *a fortiori* in technico-scientific philological analyses, organic literary histories, and oral-formulaic studies—the politics of text and critic is seldom broached.

Such political questions are currently being raised in the field of Anglo-Saxon prose studies. If New Criticism dichotomized "prose and poetry in genre studies which associated the former with language study and the latter with the study of literature" (Frantzen and Venegoni, 1986: 149), one outcome of the recent influence of critical theory, particularly the New Historicism, has been interest in OE prose as cultural representation.

Since the newer theoretical approaches are based upon a model of language as semiosis (a system of interactive signs) rather than mimesis (reflection of the world), critics applying structuralist and poststructuralist methods have tended to read OE texts as shaping the Anglo-Saxon world, not merely reflecting it. Recent approaches to OE literature have been made through structuralism, semiotics, speech-act theory, phenomenology, reception theory, psychoanalysis, Foucauldian archaeology, deconstruction, and feminism. Several of these critical approaches have been used to call into question the fundamental terms of traditional scholarly and critical discussion, while others offer subtle modifications of existing paradigms. Some would argue that it's all only just philology; but that term has become notoriously undecidable.

Middle English Literary Criticism

The great 19th-century editors of ME literature, like their colleagues in Anglo-Saxon studies, sought to restore primary texts, especially the works of Chaucer, to their "original" state insofar as possible. It in no way demeans the initiative and achievement of these editors to observe that much of 20th-century criticism has nonetheless had to correct their findings and judgments. Certitude in literary studies, as noted above, is an elusive ghost. These 19th-century editors and textual critics labored to construct a science of textual criticism, complete with its terms and tools—*lectio difficilior* ("the harder reading [is more likely]"), stemmata (genetic relations among manuscripts), *Überlieferungsgeschichte* ("transmission history," a term notoriously excoriated by A.E. Housman as a "longer and nobler-sounding name for 'fudge'"). Despite these efforts their labors did not produce an exact science, as Housman's lampoon testifies. But the cultural milieu of the 19th century, which exalted science, technology, and progress, and made a religion of the elimination of pseudo-fathers and the discovery of "origins" (as in the writings of Darwin, Marx, and Freud), promoted the belief that such a science was possible and indeed only a matter of time.

The quest for origins motivated not only textual criticism but also its companion "science," source study *(Quellenforschung)*, and it was to source study that some of the most talented scholars of the 19th and early 20th centuries turned—John L. Lowes, George Kittredge, Howard R. Patch, and many others too numerous to name here. Editing and source studies dominated modern ME criticism from the early 19th century to at least the years just before World War II and continues to play a significant role in the field. But already, even in the 19th century, countercurrents were stirring, especially in Germany, and these countercurrents began to find expression in literary criticism from the mid-20th-century until today.

Put most simply, even in the 19th century many doubted that criticism could be a "science" in any strict sense—*Geisteswissenschaften* (the humanities), although they are *Wissenschaften* or "sciences," are nonetheless not *Naturwissenschaften*, the physical sciences. Those who entertained such doubts found their early and arguably still most articulate spokesmen in the phenomenologists and their immediate forerunners—Dilthey, Husserl, and Husserl's student Heidegger. These philosophers first gave intelligent and intelligible voice to the doubts that criticism could be a "science." In particular Heidegger's demonstration, following Dilthey, of the "hermeneutic circle," coupled with his critique of Cartesianism, in *Sein und Zeit (Being and Time)*, provided critics with a philosophical understanding of criticism's inevitable implication in the deepest of all epistemological problems, the interference of the knower with the thing known.

At roughly the same time, in both America and Britain, practicing critics and poets, such as William Empson, John Crowe Ransom, and I.A. Richards, were arriving through practice at similar insights. These insights led to the New Criticism (see the preceding section on criticism of OE literature), arguably the most important and enduring movement in criticism in the 20th century. New Critical readers of ME literature after World War II included some of the brightest academic minds of the time—for instance, Charles Muscatine, E.T. Donaldson, and (a younger member of the group) Donald R. Howard. New Criticism did not repudiate philology or the findings of history, but neither did it seek their immutable and reproducible "scientific" truths. Focusing on the formal properties of poetry, its practitioners sought instead to read ME literature—especially Chaucer but in Donaldson's case also Langland—at levels of the original language that would be available to educated but nonspecialist readers, an agenda with clear if at the time largely unstated political motives and implications.

Unlike the New Critics the professing Christian medievalists of the mid-20th century, most notably C.S. Lewis, did seek a kind of immutable truth in poetry, with the crucial exception that these medievalists perceived ME literature as a vehicle of theological and dogmatic truth, not of "scientific" truth. Lewis and others like him (e.g., J.A.W. Bennett) used philology, textual criticism, history, and other methods to assert finally the Christian significance of ME literature. On the Cartesian graph they replaced certitude with faith.

Superficially similar to these critics are D.W. Robertson, Jr., and his followers in exegetics. Robertson's religious ideology led him to find Christian truth everywhere in ME literature, but at the same time he claimed that the discovery was the result of his "historical" method, which consists primarily in the use of biblical commentary as a source of explanatory information for ME literature. Many used such commentary and other contemporary medieval sources to explain ME literature—for instance, Judson Allen, R.E. Kaske, and V.A. Kolve—but without the relentless quest for the single truth that marks Robertson's brand of exegetics. For Robertson, in effect, his method was equivalent to "science"; and if his arguments are today condemned as "totalizing" (a common charge by cultural materialists, Marxists, and feminists), this charge in effect recognizes the pressure of the quest for certitude on critical method.

The present critical scene continues to be occupied by the fundamental Cartesian opposition between certainty and doubt. New movements still struggle around and between these poles—for example, New Historicism, represented at this moment by the work of Lee Patterson, who would ground historical criticism's "final support within experience" (1987: 48), a repetition of the Cartesian flight from the *res extensa,* or external world, into the "certitude" of the self.

Other scholars, as of this writing, are approaching ME literature through psychoanalysis (both Freudian and Lacanian), Bakhtin's notion of carnival and dialogism, feminist critiques of the politics of gender, gay studies, folklore, semiotics, anthropology, narratology, and so forth. The pluralizing of methods and approaches we have seen in the late 1980s and early 1990s may or may not promote liberation from the "oppositional thinking" of Cartesianism in criticism of ME literature, but arguably it will tend to relax the grip of positivism and the model of science on the arbitration of what is possible in criticism.

In such an event criticism of ME literature may begin to explore alternatives to the binaries certitude/doubt or experience/language and seek genuinely new modes of discourse. Feminist criticism, for example, in studying the body of woman and the inscription of literature may reorient attitudes toward the spirit/letter dichotomy ubiquitous in ME literature. Or again psychoanalytic criticism, especially that influenced by Lacan, may contribute new explanations of the fascination with body parts in late ME literature (Langland's "lyme" [penis] or the slit throat of the *Prioress's Tale* or the diseased skin of Henryson's Cresseid).

Semiotics will probably reopen the question and problem of formalism to important new scrutiny, especially in connection with revolutionary developments in computer technology (which often transpire seemingly overnight), since electronic texts make possible faster, fuller, and more accurate searches of verbal patterns that contribute to semiosis in a given text; formal analysis supported by computer technology enables new comprehension of the "subjective" element in literary interpretation, for example—showing how, say, a particular syllable "stains" a writer's work like a kind of signature. Or gender studies, by demonstrating the ways in which gender identities are "constructions" of culture with political agendas, can be expected to support refinements of deconstruction's strategy of "taking the constructions out of" cultural formations so as to examine them in terms of their complex motivations.

Work involving anthropological approaches to literature, especially folklore studies, will continue to offer fresh, often radically differing perspectives on traditional problems of literary interpretation. Analyses inspired by Bakhtin and his notion of dialogism will likely multiply in the next several years, especially in the study of Chaucer, since Chaucer's works have proven particularly receptive to categories of interpretation deriving from Bakhtinian terminology.

What seems obvious at this writing is that there is an undeniable restlessness about modern criticism of ME literature that will agitate all students for some time to come.

J.P. Hermann
R.A. Shoaf

Bibliography

GENERAL

Auerbach, Erich. *Mimesis: The Representation of Reality in Western Literature.* Trans. Willard R. Trask. Princeton: Princeton University Press, 1953; Curtius, Ernst Robert. *European Literature and the Latin Middle Ages.* Trans. Willard R. Trask. Bollingen Series 36. New York: Pantheon, 1953.

OE CRITICISM

Calder, Daniel G. *Cynewulf.* Boston: Twayne, 1981; Campbell, Jackson J. "Schematic Technique in *Judith.*" *ELH* 38 (1971): 155–72; Chambers, R.W. *Beowulf: An Introduction to the Study of the Poem with a Discussion of the Stories of Offa and Finn.* 1921. 3d ed., suppl. by C.L. Wrenn. Cambridge: Cambridge University Press, 1959; Chance, Jane. *Woman as Hero in Old English Literature.* Syracuse: Syracuse University Press,

1986; Earl, James W. "The Role of the Men's Hall in the Development of the Anglo-Saxon Superego." *Psychiatry* 46 (1983): 139–60; Faraci, Mary. "Phenomenology: Good News for Old English Studies." *Language and Style* 15 (1982): 219–24; Foley, John Miles. *The Theory of Oral Composition: History and Methodology.* Bloomington: Indiana University Press, 1988; Frantzen, Allen J. *Desire for Origins: New Language, Old English, and Teaching the Tradition.* New Brunswick: Rutgers University Press, 1990; Frantzen, Allen J., and Charles L. Venegoni. "The Desire for Origins: An Archaeology of Anglo-Saxon Studies." *Style* 20 (1986): 142–56; Greenfield, Stanley. *The Interpretation of Old English Poems.* London: Routledge & Kegan Paul, 1972; Hermann, J.P. *Allegories of War: Language and Violence in Old English Poetry.* Ann Arbor: University of Michigan Press, 1989; Hill, Thomas D. "Sapiential Structure and Figural Narrative in the Old English *Elene.*" *Traditio* 27 (1971): 159–77; Huppé, Bernard F. *The Web of Words: Structural Analyses of the Old English Poems Vainglory, The Wonder of Creation, The Dream of the Rood, and Judith.* Albany: SUNY Press, 1970; Isaacs, Neil. *Structural Principles in Old English Poetry.* Knoxville: University of Tennessee Press, 1968; Kaske, R.E. "A Poem of the Cross in the Exeter Book." *Traditio* 23 (1969): 41–71; Magoun, Francis P., Jr. "Oral-Formulaic Character of Anglo-Saxon Narrative Poetry." *Speculum* 28 (1953): 446–67; Nelson, Marie. "'Wordsige and Worcsige': Speech Acts in Three Old English Charms." *Language and Style* 17 (1984): 57–66; O'Keeffe, Katherine O'Brien. *Visible Song: Transitional Literacy in Old English Verse.* Cambridge: Cambridge University Press, 1990; Overing, Gillian. "Swords and Signs: A Semiotic Perspective on *Beowulf.*" *American Journal of Semiotics* 5 (1987): 35–57; Robinson, Fred C. *Beowulf and the Appositive Style.* Knoxville: University of Tennessee Press, 1985; Sisam, Kenneth. *Studies in the History of Old English Literature.* Oxford: Clarendon, 1953; Tolkien, J.R.R. "*Beowulf:* The Monsters and the Critics." *PBA* 22 (1936): 245–95. Repr. in *An Anthology of Beowulf Criticism,* ed. Lewis E. Nicholson. Notre Dame: University of Notre Dame Press, 1963, pp. 51–103; Whitelock, Dorothy. *The Audience of Beowulf.* Oxford: Oxford University Press, 1951.

ME CRITICISM

Aers, David. *Community, Gender, and Individual Identity: English Writing, 1360–1430.* London: Routledge, 1988; Allen, Judson B. *The Ethical Poetic of the Later Middle Ages.* Toronto: University of Toronto Press, 1982; Burrow, John A. *Ricardian Poetry: Chaucer, Gower, Langland and the Gawain-Poet.* London: Routledge & Kegan Paul, 1971; Delany, Sheila. *Writing Woman: Women Writers and Women in Literature, Medieval to Modern.* New York: Schocken, 1983; Donaldson, E. Talbot. *Speaking of Chaucer.* London: Athlone, 1970; Ferster, Judith. *Chaucer on Interpretation.* Cambridge: Cambridge University Press, 1983; Fradenburg, Louise. "Criticism, Anti-Semitism, and the Prioress' Tale." *Exemplaria* 1 (1989): 69–115; Fyler, John M. "Man, Men, and Women in Chaucer's Poetry." In *The Olde Daunce: Love, Friendship, and Desire in the Medieval World,* ed. Robert R. Edwards and Stephen Spector. Albany: SUNY Press, 1990, pp. 154–76, 276–84; Ganim, John M. *Chaucerian Theatricality.* Princeton: Princeton University Press, 1991; Gellrich, Jesse. *The Idea of the Book in the Middle Ages.* Ithaca: Cornell University Press, 1985; Howard, Donald R. *The Idea of the Canterbury Tales.* Berkeley: University of California Press, 1976; Jordan, Robert M. *Chaucer's Poetics and the Modern Reader.* Berkeley: University of California Press, 1987; Leicester, H. Marshall, Jr. "The Art of Impersonation: A General Prologue to the *Canterbury Tales.*" *PMLA* 95 (1980): 213–24; Lindahl, Carl. *Earnest Games: Folkloric Patterns in the Canterbury Tales.* Bloomington: Indiana University Press, 1987; Mann, Jill. *Geoffrey Chaucer.* Feminist Readings Series. London: Harvester Wheatsheaf, 1991; Minnis, A.J. *Medieval Theory of Authorship: Scholastic Literary Attitudes in the Later Middle Ages.* 2d ed. Aldershot: Scolar, 1988; Muscatine, Charles. *Chaucer and the French Tradition: A Study in Style and Meaning.* Berkeley: University of California Press, 1957; Patterson, Lee. *Negotiating the Past: The Historical Understanding of Medieval Literature.* Madison: University of Wisconsin Press, 1987; Robertson, D.W., Jr. *A Preface to Chaucer: Studies in Medieval Perspectives.* Princeton: Princeton University Press, 1962; Ruggiers, Paul G., ed. *Editing Chaucer: The Great Tradition.* Norman: Pilgrim Books, 1984; Shoaf, R.A. "Medieval Studies after Derrida after Heidegger." In *Sign, Sentence, Discourse: Language in Medieval Thought and Literature,* ed. Julian N. Wasserman and Lois Roney. Syracuse: Syracuse University Press, 1989, pp. 9–30; Spearing, A.C. *Medieval to Renaissance in English Poetry.* Cambridge: Cambridge University Press, 1985; Strohm, Paul. *Social Chaucer.* Cambridge: Harvard University Press, 1989; Vance, Eugene. *Mervelous Signals: Poetics and Sign Theory in the Later Middle Ages.* Lincoln: University of Nebraska Press, 1986.

See also Allegory; Bible in ME Literature; Bible in OE Literature; Hagiography; Literacy; Literary Influences; Orality; Popular Culture; Romances; Textual Criticism; Women in ME Literature; Women in OE Literature

Cuerden Psalter

The Cuerden Psalter (New York, Pierpont Morgan Library M.756) is the most lavishly illuminated of a group of manuscripts comprising mostly Bibles and psalters (there is one book of hours). The psalter has decoration in the form of roundels for the labors of the months and the signs of the zodiac (fols.

The style of the Cuerden illuminator is distinctive. The pigments are flat and shadowless (except in more monumental figures, such as the Virgin); pink and blue dominate the picture space, and these colors are carried through to the draperies. A coloristic hallmark of this artist—evident in the shading of the arches within the composite miniatures—is a mottled green, frosted with white. Prolongations, composed of both rigid and organic elements, project from the initials, some of which terminate in diagonal stems in the lower margin while others divide at a point approximately midway down the shaft and sprout horizontal elements. The *Beatus* folio, where a variety of hybrid (half-human, half-animal) forms disport themselves on these platforms, is an effective illustration of this type of decoration. The figures are markedly static, the bodies being limited to a few simple gestures; the standing figures are either upright or very slightly S-shaped, while the drapery falls vertically in linear folds or is gathered up under the arm in two or three softly painted triangular folds, a feature that also suggests French influence. The naive-looking faces are delineated skillfully with a black pen-line and remain white except for a pale-red blush mark.

The psalter was illuminated by a hand very close to that in a book of hours (BL Egerton 1151) and in the Bible of William of Devon (BL Royal 1.D.i), which gives the name to this group, the sources of which are French. Branner has shown that there are close correspondences between the style of the William of Devon painter and that of the Parisian atelier of Johannes Grusch, similarities that are especially well supported by a musical manuscript now in Florence (Biblioteca Medicea-Laurenziana Plut. 29.1). Bennett, who has added further manuscripts to the William of Devon group, in the case of the Bibles has elucidated the Parisian origin of both text and iconography.

There is a case for postulating some English influence on the group in the area of border decoration. This shows analogies with the manuscripts centered on the Salvin Hours (BL Add. 48985), the ultimate origins of which lie in the William de Brailes workshop of ca. 1230–60, both groups suggestive of an Oxford provenance. These stylistic correspondences are reinforced by the likelihood that Oxford was the center of production for the William of Devon group of manuscripts. Liturgical evidence points to a south Midlands destination for the Cuerden Psalter, since it has references to St. Fremund of Dunstable, St. Edburga of Bicester, and possibly St. Rumwold of Buckingham.

The psalter must be dated after 1262, as the Feast of St. Richard of Chichester, who was canonized in that year, appears in the calendar in the original hand. There is no internal evidence for dating the other manuscripts of the group. The Cuerden Psalter was probably produced late in the sequence of the extant works in which this illuminator can be identified, thus dating it to around 1270.

Lynda Dennison

1–6) followed by seven full-page miniatures (each divided into six compartments) comprising a New Testament cycle and depictions of various saints, some of whom defy precise identification, such as the saint who stands in a box on legs (possibly St. Rumwold). All seven miniatures are set against plain gold or colored grounds enclosed within simple architectural devices that aid in compartmentalizing the subject matter. An eighth full-page miniature on a diapered ground (fol. 10v), depicting the *Virgo lactans* with male and female donor kneeling at her feet, completes the prefatory cycle. In this representation the Virgin is unusually shown crowned as Queen of Heaven. Its devotional content is clear from the placement of the image facing the opening of the psalter text.

The text itself has a ten-part division, with initials occupying eight lines (half a text page) for Psalms 1 (fig. 51) and 109, three for Psalms 51 and 101, four for Psalms 52 and 97, and six for Psalms 26, 38, 68, and 80. All except Psalm 1, which has decoration in all the margins, have partial borders. This psalter is unusually elaborate in that every psalm and canticle (as well as the initials accompanying the litany), in addition to those already mentioned, receives decoration in the form of a three-line historiated initial, a rare feature in Gothic psalters predating those of the Bohun group, which adopt this practice. Also innovative for the date is the iconography of these psalm initials, which, like those of the major divisions, are in many cases a literal translation of some idea contained in the first few verses of the psalm, a feature pointing to influence from France.

Bibliography

Alexander, Jonathan, and Paul Binski, eds. *Age of Chivalry: Art in Plantagenet England 1200–1400.* London: Royal

Academy of Arts, 1987, cat. no. 355; Bennett, Adelaide L. "Additions to the William of Devon Group." *Art Bulletin* 54 (1972): 31–40; Branner, Robert. "The Johannes Grusch Atelier and the Continental Origins of the William of Devon Painter." *Art Bulletin* 54 (1972): 24–30; Morgan, Nigel. *Early Gothic Manuscripts (2) 1250–1285.* A Survey of Manuscripts Illuminated in the British Isles 4:2, ed. J.J.G. Alexander. London: Harvey Miller, 1988, no. 162; Watson, Bruce. "The Place of the Cuerden Psalter in English Illumination." *Gesta* 9 (1970): 34–41.

See also Amesbury Psalter; Brailes, William de; Exeter Bohun Psalter; Manuscript Illumination, Gothic; Psalters, Gothic

Cursor Mundi

A lengthy ME biblical history of the world (ca. 1300), mainly in octosyllabic couplets. The Latin title occurs in the opening rubric of several manuscripts and translates the prologue's suggestion, "Cursur o werld man aght it call, / For almast it ouer-rennes all" (267–68), "all" meaning biblical history from Creation to Doomsday.

About the author we can only make deductions from his composition. A careful study of his poem and its numerous Latin, Old French, and ME sources reveals an accurate translator, a selective borrower, someone broadly read, a competent versifier, and a writer mindful of simplification for his lay audience. The original manuscript has not survived, but the language of the oldest extant copies points to a northerner writing around 1300. The leisure (the shortest version is 24,000 lines long), extensive library (over a dozen sources have been identified), and intellectual climate essential to such an undertaking suggest his membership in a religious community.

The poem survives wholly or partially in nine manuscripts and in three different forms, none of which exactly fulfills the prologue's promise (131–222) of a chronological history of man—divided into seven ages—as well as the sorrows of Mary and the festival of her conception. The Edinburgh version alone might have had this form, but its fragmentary state (lines 18,989–24,968) precludes certainty in the matter. The second form, found in the three northern and oldest texts (the Cotton, Fairfax, and Göttingen manuscripts), adds seven works of devotion, exposition, and prayer in various combinations, sequences, and verse forms to swell the poem to over 30,000 lines. The third and shortest form occurs in the later, southern texts (the Arundel, Trinity, Laud, and BL Additional manuscripts) and ends with the seventh age, Doomsday, thereby contradicting the statement of an intention (217–20) to include Mary's sorrows and the festival of her conception. Despite these difficulties scholars agree on the poem's northern provenance and subsequent extensive southern revision (possibly late in the 14th century). Precisely how this textual transmission occurred, however, is unclear and seems likely to remain so.

The poem's popularity, by contrast, is readily explained. In the prologue the poet cites stories of such well-known figures as Alexander the Great, Julius Caesar, Brute, King Arthur,

Gawain, Charlemagne, and Tristan and Isolde, tales that are, however, "bot fantum o þis warld" (91). Although he justifies his own work on the higher moral grounds of providing biblical history in English for his unlearned countrymen, his choice of matter and narrative manner clearly indicates his concern to entertain as well. Thus he provides standard biblical highlights, such as the Creation and Fall, Noah's Flood, the Babylonian captivity, Red Sea passage, birth and death of Christ, and so on. But he also incorporates the lively debate of the Four Daughters of God (Mercy, Truth, Justice, and Peace—familiar to readers of *Piers Plowman*), an allegorical description of the Castle of Love, a moving depiction of the human anguish of the childless Joachim and Anna before Mary's conception, Mary's exemplary adolescence as a temple virgin, the aged widower Joseph's almost comic reluctance to take her as his ward and wife, and a host of other highly readable, if apocryphal, stories. These include the wonder deeds of Christ's childhood (e.g., carrying a ball of water; sowing a grain of wheat that yields a hundredfold return the same day; stretching an inaccurately cut wooden beam; and clapping his hands to bring clay pigeons to life). Similarly noncanonical and absorbing are the villainous Herod's grisly bodily afflictions and gruesome death in boiling pitch. Much of this nonscriptural matter originated in early theological polemics concerning such controversial issues as Mary's permanent virginity and Christ's dual human/divine nature. In the poem, however, this material is presented as fascinating narrative, unencumbered by obtrusive moralizing or learned commentary.

Where explanation is necessary, clarity and simplicity prevail, in keeping with the work's popular character. Hence the theological paradox of Mary's virginal conception of Christ is reduced to the simple analogy of light passing through glass; the parable of salvation (presented through the Four Daughters of God debate) employs the familiar background of law courts; and the discussion of Mary's fitness as Christ's dwelling place (the Castle of Love) makes practical use of a commonplace medieval building. Although these ideas and stories certainly did not originate with the poet, he clearly recognized their instructional value, and he gave them the kind of engaging treatment that helped establish their enduring vogue in the Middle Ages. Herein lies the poem's worth, as a storehouse of entertaining and edifying popularized material that rapidly found lasting expression in other art forms, such as drama, painting, sculpture, and stained glass.

The poem is also impressive for the variety, number, and handling of its sources, which include the Vulgate, Honorius Augustodunensis's *Elucidarium*, Herman de Valenciennes's Old French *Bible*, Comestor's *Historia scholastica*, Grosseteste's *Chateau d'amour*, Wace's *Etablissement de la Fête de la Conception*, the *Legenda aurea*, the *Gospel of Nicodemus*, *The Southern Assumption*, the *De nativitate Mariae*, the *Pseudo-Gospel of Matthew*, and the *Protevangelium of James*. The list may well be much longer, since it is often impossible to determine precise literary debts when hunting sources for widely available information. The handling of borrowed material likewise varies greatly, from careful extensive translation, to summary, to paraphrase, to continuous use of one source, to frequent change, according as the source and its style answered the poet's own notions of clear readable narrative.

Roger R. Fowler

Bibliography

PRIMARY

Horrall, Sarah M., gen ed. *The Southern Version of Cursor Mundi.* 5 vols. projected. Ottawa: University of Ottawa Press, 1978– . Vol. 1, ed. Sarah M. Horrall, 1978; vol. 2, ed. Roger R. Fowler, 1990; vol. 3, ed. Henry J. Stauffenberg, 1985; vol. 4, ed. Peter H.J. Mous, 1986; vol. 5, ed. L.M. Eldredge, forthcoming [includes notes on sources and literary traditions drawn on by *Cursor*-poet]; Morris, Richard, ed. *Cursor Mundi.* EETS o.s. 57, 59, 62, 66, 68, 99, 101. London: Kegan Paul, Trench, Trübner, 1874–93 [the northern version; critical apparatus limited and now outdated].

SECONDARY

New *CBEL* 1:500–01; *Manual* 7:2276–78, 2503–07; Mardon, Ernest G. *The Narrative Unity of the Cursor Mundi.* Glasgow: MacLellan, 1970.

See also Bible in ME Literature; Moral and Religious Instruction; Popular Culture; Religious Allegories; Translation

Customs Accounts

Kings collected money from trade through tolls and market dues from an early date, and Richard and John experimented with taxes on overseas trade. The permanent, nationwide collection of duties on such trade began in 1275. Then a wool tax was set up by Edward I with the advice of the Riccardi, a Lucchese merchant company, in order to secure the loans they made him. All merchants, English and alien, were to pay 6s. 8d. for each sack of wool or 300 woolfells, or 200 hides exported overseas.

Since this brought the king an immediate extra £8,000 a year in revenue, it is not surprising that the duties were extended. Heavy wool subsidies were introduced. Then from 1303 alien merchants paid a further 3s. 4d. for wool, fells, and hides exported, and 2s. a tun for wine imported, 1s. a cloth imported or exported, and 3d. in the pound value for all other goods imported or exported.

In 1347 duties were imposed on cloth exports at the rate of 1s. 2d. a cloth of assize (ca. 24 yards long, 2 yards wide) for English merchants, and 1s. 9d. for aliens. Better-quality cloths paid higher duties. All overseas trade was finally brought into the system with the imposition of tunnage and poundage dues, made permanent from Richard II's reign. All merchants, English and alien, paid 2s. (later 3s.) on a tun of wine, and 6d. (later 1s.) in the pound on the value of all other goods except wool, fells, hides, and, later, denizen cloth (cloth made by foreigners living in England under a special license of the king).

Duties now covered the trade of all merchants with all overseas areas, including the English dominions of Ireland, the Channel Islands, and Gascony. They did not cover coasting trade to other English ports. The duties differentiated between aliens and Englishmen; actually there were three categories of payments, since Hanseatic merchants claimed that their charter of privileges exempted them from all duties imposed after 1303. Their claim was usually accepted by the English kings, to the resentment of English merchants. Thus, for example, English merchants paid 1s. 2d. on cloth (the duty of 1347), the Hansards paid only 1s. (the duty of 1303), and other aliens paid 2s. 9d. (the duties of 1303 and 1347 together); the Hansards also refused to pay tunnage and poundage.

National duties were collected at thirteen (later fifteen) headports between Newcastle and Bristol to which merchants would bring their goods for customs clearance, but collectors might open other outports for merchants' convenience. Wales and Cheshire fell outside the system, but their ports paid local duties to the crown as landlord. When the system was fully developed, two collectors in each port kept a roll of duties paid, a controller kept a separate counter-roll to act as a check, a searcher was appointed to prevent smuggling, and supervisors of search provided further checks. The customs revenue regularly provided one-third to one-half of the royal revenue, and care was taken to see that duty was paid. There were intermittent inquiries into smuggling and corruption, high rewards for informers, and sporadic efforts to punish offenders.

The system has left various records, of which two sets are particularly useful to historians. The particular accounts are the detailed records sent from individual ports to the exchequer at the end of the year or the collectors' term of office. They list the ships in and out, with their masters, shippers, and amounts and values of cargoes. The Bristol accounts also regularly give destinations. Their survival is patchy but they are extremely valuable sources for detailed patterns of trade and for local history.

The enrolled accounts contain the final totals accepted by the royal auditors after checking the particulars. They have far fewer details but indicate the overall scale and trends of trade for all England. They survive in an almost unbroken series from 1275 to 1547, when the system changed. The reliability of the records has been questioned, but E.M. Carus-Wilson provided a good defense of their use, provided caution is exercised. Ancillary documents include the collectors' expenses, certificates of aliens' nationalities, and dockets proving payment of duty. The accounts of wine duties paid at Bordeaux also survive in some numbers for the period 1303 to 1453, when Bordeaux was lost by the English.

Local custom duties were also charged in many ports. The accounts are more difficult to use, since duties were not uniformly charged, but they did cover the coasting trade. Local accounts survive less well, but some exist for Bristol, Chester, Exeter, Great Yarmouth, Sandwich, Southampton, and Winchelsea.

Wendy R. Childs

Bibliography

Baker, Robert L. *The English Customs Service, 1307–43: A Study of Medieval Administration.* Transactions of the American Philosophical Society, n.s. 51, part 6. Philadelphia: American Philosophical Society, 1961; Carus-

Wilson, E.M. *The Overseas Trade of Bristol in the Later Middle Ages.* 2d ed. London: Merlin Press, 1967; Carus-Wilson, E.M., and Olive Coleman. *England's Export Trade, 1275–1547.* Oxford: Clarendon, 1963; Childs, Wendy R. *The Customs Accounts of Hull, 1453–1490.* Yorkshire Archaeological Society, Record Series 144. York: Printed for the Society, 1986 (for 1984); Cobb, Henry S. "Local Port Customs Accounts prior to 1550." *Journal of the Society of Archivists* 1, no. 8 (1958): 213–24; Cobb, Henry S., ed. *The Local Port Book of Southampton for 1439–40.* Southampton Record Series 5. Southampton: At the University, 1961; Cobb, Henry S., ed. *The Overseas Trade of London: Exchequer Customs Accounts 1480–1.* London Record Society 27. London: Printed for the Society, 1990; Gras, Norman S.B. *The Early English Customs System.* Cambridge: Harvard University Press, 1918; Kowaleski, Maryanne. *The Local Customs Accounts of the Port of Exeter 1266–1321.* Devon and Cornwall Record Society, n.s. 36. Exeter: Printed for the Society, 1993.

See also Aliens and Alien Merchants; Cinque Ports; Cloth; Hanseatic League; Taxes; Tunnage and Poundage

Cuthbert (ca. 635–687)

Anglo-Saxon monk and bishop. In 651 he joined the monastic community at Melrose in Scotland. Subsequently he accompanied Eata when the latter set up a monastery on estates given him by Alhfrith at Ripon, becoming guestmaster at the new foundation. When Wilfrid become bishop of Ripon, sometime before 664, Cuthbert returned to Melrose, becoming prior after the death of Boisil. Later he moved to Lindisfarne, where he was again prior, under Eata, now either abbot or bishop. In ca. 676 he retired to the island of Inner Farne to live the life of a hermit.

In 685, however, he was appointed bishop of Hexham, and although he was able to exchange sees with Eata, by now bishop of Lindisfarne, he had to leave his island retreat. He returned there late in 686 or early in 687 and died on 20 March 687. He was buried at Lindisfarne, where a cult quickly developed.

In 698 his tomb was opened and his body was found to be incorrupt; it was then translated to a new shrine. During the period of the Viking invasions his body was moved for safety, possibly to Norham on Tweed by Bishop Ecgred (830–45), to the district of Carlisle in 875, and to Chester-le-Street in 883. Finally it was transferred to Durham in 995, where it remains and where many of the saint's relics, including his coffin and pectoral cross, are preserved. The Lindisfarne Gospels, which were made for the saint's shrine, probably in association with the translation of 698, are preserved in the British Library.

Cuthbert is important as a major ascetic and a bishop. Although he was an Englishman, his style of life seems to have looked back to that of Aidan and of the Irish community on Iona. He is depicted as a saint in this mold in the anonymous *Vita Cuthberti* written ca. 698. Bede wrote a verse *Life of Cuthbert* ca. 705 (perhaps revised ca. 720), a second prose life

in ca. 720, and a final version in the *Ecclesiastical History.* These last two works depict Cuthbert as an ascetic within the model envisaged by Gregory the Great. In all probability this shift in interpretation marks a response to the *Vita Wilfridi,* composed by Stephanus shortly after 709. Certainly part of the inspiration for the promulgation of the cult of St. Cuthbert seems to have been rivalry with Wilfrid's foundations of Ripon and Hexham and with Wilfrid's episcopal style.

Ian N. Wood

Bibliography

Battiscombe, C.F. *The Relics of Saint Cuthbert.* Oxford: Oxford University Press, 1956; Bonner, Gerald, David Rollason, and Clare Stancliffe, eds. *St. Cuthbert, His Cult and His Community to AD 1200.* Woodbridge: Boydell, 1989; Colgrave, Bertram, ed. and trans. *Two Lives of Saint Cuthbert.* Cambridge: Cambridge University Press, 1940; Jaager, Werner, ed. *Bedas metrische Vita sancti Cuthberti.* Palaestra 198. Leipzig: Mayer & Müller, 1935.

See also Bede; Coffin of St. Cuthbert; Hagiography; Wilfrid

Cynewulf (fl. early 9th–late 10th century?)

One of the two named Anglo-Saxon poets (the other is Cædmon). His identity is unknown, although he wove his name into the epilogues of four poems; his dates are undetermined, although he probably did not write before 750 nor after the late 10th century; his provenance is uncertain, although dialect features of his poems indicate that he was either Mercian or Northumbrian; and his corpus has been limited in the last half-century to the four poems that bear his signature and appear in the Exeter Book *(Christ II, Juliana)* and the Vercelli Book *(The Fates of the Apostles, Elene).*

Identity and Language

Cynewulf uses runic letters to incorporate his name into his poems, spelling it CYNWULF in *The Fates of the Apostles* and *Christ II,* CYNEWULF in *Juliana* and *Elene,* and making it an integral part of his message as he asks for his audience's prayers. In three epilogues he exploits the fact that runes stand both for letters and for things or concepts such as "need" (the N rune is named *nyd,* "need, necessity") and "joy" (the W rune stands for *wynn,* "joy"). Only in *Juliana,* where he groups the letters CYN, EWU, and LF, does Cynewulf seem to use runes solely as letters. Scholars are uncertain about how to interpret the signatures just as they are about how to assess their historical significance. It has been argued that Cynewulf's signing his work merely conforms with an ancient Germanic practice of signing art objects in runes, that it reflects a vogue among contemporary Latin writers for using acrostics, and that it may signal a shift in Anglo-Saxon society from orality to literacy. It may also indicate a move away from the traditional view of both poet and poetry as communal and therefore necessarily anonymous.

Scholars in the 19th and early 20th centuries favored four candidates for being the poet: Cynewulf, bishop of

Lindisfarne in Northumbria (d. ca. 783); Cynulf, a priest of Dunwich in East Anglia (fl. 803); Cynewulf, the father of Bishop Cyneweard of Wells in Wessex (d. ca. 975); and Cenwulf or Kenulf, abbot of Peterborough in Mercia (d. 1006). Historical and linguistic evidence is far too meager to support any of these identifications. Furthermore nonliterary sources make clear that a large number of ecclesiastics named Cynewulf and theoretically capable of writing poetry lived during the period when the poet may have flourished. His identity remains a mystery.

Lacking historical data, scholars depend primarily on Cynewulf's name for determining when he may have lived. The form "Cynewulf" derives from an earlier form, "Cyniwulf." The spelling change from -i- to -e- reflects a sound change that took place because of the weak stress on the syllable in which the vowel appears, and philologists have shown that that change could have occurred as early as 750. Scholars have also found that the particular order of apostles in *The Fates of the Apostles* does not appear in comparable texts until after the early 9th century. Cynewulf was thought most probably active, therefore, around the late 8th and early 9th centuries. Recent research on a later source for *The Fates of the Apostles,* however, strongly supports the possibility that he flourished between the late 9th century and the late 10th, when the Exeter and Vercelli books were composed.

Scholars know that Cynewulf wrote in the Anglian dialect, although they still dispute whether it was Northumbrian or Mercian within that broad category. The scribes of the Exeter and Vercelli books both wrote in West Saxon, and the two imperfect leonine (internal) rhymes in *Christ II* and the four in the epilogue to *Elene* can be corrected by translating those rhymes into Anglian. Compare, for example, West Saxon *hienþu / mærþu* of *Christ II,* line 591, with Anglian *hænþu / mærþu,* or West Saxon *riht / geþeaht* of *Elene,* line 1240, with Anglian *reht / geþeht.*

Works

When Cynewulf was first discovered in 1840, one editor attributed all poems in the Exeter and Vercelli books to him. Other scholars subsequently asserted that Cynewulf wrote every OE poem that Cædmon did not and was perhaps even the final redactor of *Beowulf.* Later 19th-century scholars argued more conservatively, eventually claiming that in addition to his four signed poems Cynewulf wrote just eight others that resemble them in subject matter or style: *Guthlac A, Guthlac B, Christ I, Christ III, Physiologus* (or *The Panther, The Whale,* and *The Partridge*), and *The Phoenix* from the Exeter Book; *Andreas* and *The Dream of the Rood* from the Vercelli Book. These twelve poems constitute "the Cynewulf Group." Largely because of studies by Das, Schaar, and Diamond in the 1940s and 1950s, however, scholars now recognize only the four signed poems as Cynewulf's own. The question of the order in which Cynewulf composed his poems remains vexed, but most scholars currently feel that he wrote *Elene* last.

The Fates of the Apostles, a 122-line poem, follows *Andreas* in the Vercelli Book and was therefore once counted part of that poem; it is perhaps the least appreciated of Cynewulf's works.

Deriving from the martyrology with no single Latin source and classified primarily as a catalogue poem, it offers the barest detail about the missions and deaths of the twelve apostles. It consequently has been placed either first or last in Cynewulf's canon, the product of a clumsy novice or a feeble old man. Recent critics have treated the poem more sympathetically, arguing, for example, for a sophisticated numerical structure or for Cynewulf's establishing an implicit comparison between himself and the apostles, between their work and his, while simultaneously creating an ironic distance between himself as a fallible human being and them as transcendent followers of Christ. Notable in this poem is the unique arrangement of Cynewulf's signature: F, W, U, L, C, Y, N. The letters' dislocation and placement of the last first may reflect both the poet's sense of personal dislocation at being a sinner and personal joy in the biblical promise that the last shall be first.

Cynewulf's 426-line, meditative poem about Christ's Ascension into heaven is known as *Christ II* or *The Ascension.* It is the second of three poems in the Exeter Book about Christ. The poem's source is the final three sections of Gregory the Great's 29th homily on the Gospels, in which Gregory asks why angels did not wear white robes at the Incarnation while they did at the Ascension. Cynewulf draws mainly on that homily but mines passages of scripture as well, including the 23rd Psalm, and seems indebted to Bede's hymn on the Ascension, some patristic texts, and iconographic items. In the course of this loosely structured, reiterative poem Cynewulf describes the Ascension and human beings' and angels' reaction to it; admonishes his audience to be grateful for all God's gifts, especially salvation granted to humankind through the Ascension; likens Christ's mission on earth to the flight of a bird; praises Christ for his dignifying both angels and humankind by his actions and for granting intellectual gifts to men; thanks Christ for his six "leaps" (the Incarnation, Nativity, Crucifixion, Burial, Descent into Hell, and Ascension); encourages his audience to prepare for the Last Judgment; and concludes with a conventional but extended simile comparing human life to a sea voyage. Whereas Gregory answers the question about the angels' white robes directly, Cynewulf does not. They were appropriate at the Ascension, he implies, because Christ, angels, and human beings are all exalted through Christ's gifts and leaps.

Juliana, a 731-line poem about the early-4th-century St. Juliana of Nicomedia, vies with *The Fates of the Apostles* for being deemed Cynewulf's worst—and therefore either his first or last—work. Whatever early scholars' estimation of its quality, the poem has the distinction of being the earliest extant vernacular version of this saint's life, and recent studies show that it does have artistic merit. Cynewulf's source for the poem is probably a Latin prose life close to one contained in the *Acta sanctorum* for 16 February, in which is told the simple story of Juliana, daughter of the pagan Africanus, who promises her in marriage to the pagan prefect Heliseus. She refuses to marry Heliseus unless he converts to Christianity. He refuses, and she is imprisoned, tortured, tempted at length by a demon, and ultimately beheaded. Cynewulf polarizes the saint and her persecutors much more emphatically than does his source, and he amplifies dialogue considerably to emphasize Juliana's verbal power and spiritual resilience. Cynewulf's dislocated signature (CYN, EWU, LF), like that in *The Fates of the Apostles,* probably reflects the dislocation he feels, this time at the separation his soul must experience from his body in death.

Elene, Cynewulf's 1321-line poem about the discovery of the Cross by St. Helena, mother of Constantine, is uniformly considered his best. Its source probably closely resembles the *Acta Cyriaci* (*Acta sanctorum,* 4 May). After defeating the Goths by the sign of the Cross, which was revealed to him in a dream, Constantine is converted to Christianity and sends his mother to Jerusalem to locate the actual Cross. Elene confronts the Jews about its location through their chosen representative, Judas, who refuses to help her and whom she confines to a pit without food. Judas quickly relents and is himself converted. His prayer brings a sign indicating where the Cross lies buried, and a church, by order of Constantine, is later erected there. After being baptized, Judas becomes Cyriacus, bishop of Jerusalem, and prays for another sign to show where the nails of the Cross might be. He receives that sign, and the nails are made into a bit for Constantine's horse. The poem ends with Cynewulf's signature and a passage on the Last Judgment. The poet's major themes concern revelation and conversion (of Constantine, Judas, and Cynewulf), and he skillfully manipulates style and structure to develop those themes. The speeches in the narrative—considerable elaborations, as in *Juliana,* of their Latin source—play a crucial role in Cynewulf's affirming the Cross's transforming power.

Robert E. Bjork

Bibliography

PRIMARY

ASPR 2:51–54 [*Fates*], 66–102 [*Elene*]; 3:15–27 [*Christ II*], 113–33 [*Juliana*]; Brooks, Kenneth R., ed. *Andreas and The Fates of the Apostles.* Oxford: Clarendon, 1961; Gradon, P.O.E., ed. *Elene.* London: Methuen, 1958. Repr. Exeter: University of Exeter, 1977; Woolf, Rosemary, ed. *Juliana.* London: Methuen, 1955. Repr. Exeter: University of Exeter, 1977.

SECONDARY

Anderson, Earl R. *Cynewulf: Structure, Style, and Theme in His Poetry.* London: Associated University Presses, 1983; Bjork, Robert E. *The Old English Verse Saints' Lives: A Study in Direct Discourse and the Iconography of Style.* Toronto: University of Toronto Press, 1985 [chapters on *Elene, Juliana*]; Bjork, Robert E., ed. *Cynewulf: Basic Readings.* New York: Garland, 1996 [with reprints of Brown, Clemoes, Diamond, and Frese articles cited below]; Bridges, Margaret Enid. *Generic Contrast in Old English Hagiographical Poetry.* Copenhagen: Rosenkilde & Bagger, 1984 [chapters on *Elene, Juliana*]; Brown, George H. "The Descent-Ascent Motif in *Christ II* of Cynewulf." *JEGP* 73 (1974): 1–12; Butler, S.E. "The Cynewulf Question Revived." *NM* 83 (1982): 15–23; Calder, Daniel G. *Cynewulf.* Boston: Twayne, 1981; Clemoes, Peter. "Cynewulf's Image of the Ascension." In *England before the Conquest,* ed. Peter Clemoes and Kathleen Hughes. Cambridge: Cambridge University Press, 1971, pp. 293–304; Das, S.K. *Cynewulf and the Cynewulf Canon.* Calcutta: University of Calcutta Press, 1942; Diamond, Robert E. "The Diction of the Signed Poems of Cynewulf." *PQ* 38 (1959): 228–41; Frese, Dolores Warwick. "The Art of Cynewulf's Runic Signatures." In *Anglo-Saxon Poetry: Essays in Appreciation,* ed. Lewis E. Nicholson and Dolores Warwick Frese. Notre Dame: University of Notre Dame Press, 1975, pp. 312–34; Hermann, John P. *Allegories of War: Language and Violence in Old English Poetry.* Ann Arbor: University of Michigan Press, 1989 [chapters on *Elene, Juliana*]; Olsen, Alexandra Hennessey. *Speech, Song, and Poetic Craft: The Artistry of the Cynewulf Canon.* New York: Lang, 1984; Rice, Robert C. "The Penitential Motif in Cynewulf's *Fates of the Apostles* and in His Epilogues." *ASE* 6 (1977): 105–20; Schaar, Claes. *Critical Studies in the Cynewulf Group.* Lund: Gleerup, 1949. Repr. New York: Haskell House, 1967.

See also Exeter Book; Fathers of the Church; Hagiography; Runes; Vercelli Book; Women in OE Literature

D

Dance, Dance Music

Little is known of the dancing habits of the people who inhabited the British Isles in the second half of the first millennium A.D. Some association with the seasons in many of the earliest English texts in dance meters implies that danced rituals connected with fertility and the agricultural cycle were already long in use. Bede condemned enjoyment of the erotic arts of young professional dancing girls; on the Continent there are several burials of such performers along with their personal soundmakers. In the 12th century William Fitzstephen's description of young girls' sung dances during Easter festivities in London, though taken directly from the *Odes* of Horace, was no doubt still applicable. A 13th-century French poem on the walling of New Ross (an Anglo-Norman town in southeast Ireland) described outdoor craft processionals to pipe-and-tabor music, young people's processional karoles, and wealthy ladies' songs and recreational karoles. In the Red Book of Ossory, made in the 60-miles-distant city of Kilkenny, there are 14th-century Latin texts, in several dance meters, for some of these types. They include many examples of rondeau, a recurrence pattern not found in contemporary English karole texts.

Of figured dances for pairs the estampie seems not to have become acculturated in England. The few known notations have French associations: two polyphonically set estampies are found in the Robertsbridge Codex, and a fragment notated in Ireland in the 18th century was associated with the Hiberno-Norman Burke (de Burgh) family. Two 13th-century polyphonic notations appear to conform to the loose definition of *stantipes* given by the late-13th-century theorist Johannes de Grocheio; one has three sections *(puncta)*, the routine being repeated making six in all, and the other has seven, the last two being repetitions of the first two. Johannes approved the difficulty of execution as a deterrent to dalliance between partners. Such strictures did not operate at high social levels. After dinner at the tournament held at Windsor by Edward III in 1343 there were dances with formal embracings and kissings. There were many more men than women in great households, and women's dances (probably karoles) took place in the ladies' private chambers.

Fourteenth-century depictions of social dance are almost entirely of karole, in both linear and circular shapes, with all male, all female, or mixed participants. Many are in illustration of moralities or scenes from the Bible or romantic tales, but they are accurate on the whole, even to the open mouths of the executants in some cases. There are also some depictions of professional performers. These include acrobatic dancers, often women accompanied by a loud instrument, and the original moresque, a single dark or darkened male performer, dancing frenetically to a percussion instrument.

There is no written record of Burgundian basse-danse or the new Italian dances of the later 15th century being performed in England. But after-dinner dances, known to have been performed on occasions like the visit of Louis de Gruthuyse, Graaf van Holland, to Edward IV at Windsor in 1472, were no doubt both fashionable and known to all parties. In the early 16th century the dancings and disguisings traditional on St. Nicholas's Day, during the Christmas period and at pre-Lent Carnival and Midsummer, were elaborated into masques after the Italian fashion.

Joan Rimmer

Bibliography

PRIMARY

Harrison, Frank Ll., Ernest H. Sanders, and Peter M. Lefferts, eds. *English Music for Mass and Offices (II) and Music for Other Ceremonies.* Polyphonic Music of the Fourteenth Century 17. Paris: L'Oiseau-Lyre, 1986; McGee, Timothy J., ed. *Medieval Instrumental Dances.* Bloomington: Indiana University Press, 1989; Sanders, Ernest H., ed. *English Music of the Thirteenth and Early Fourteenth Centuries.* Polyphonic Music of the Fourteenth Century 14. Paris: L'Oiseau-Lyre, 1979.

SECONDARY

Rimmer, Joan. "An Archaeo-organological Survey of the Netherlands." *World Archaeology* 12/3 (1981): 240 [on the burials of the continental dancing girls]; Rimmer, Joan. "Dance Elements in Trouvère Repertory." *Dance Research* 3 (1985): 23–33; Rimmer, Joan. "Patronage, Style and Structure in Music Attributed to Turlough Carolan." *Early Music* 15 (1987): 164–74; Rimmer, Joan. "Carole, Rondeau and Branle in Ireland 1300–1800." *Dance Research* 7 (1989): 20–46 and 8 (1990): 27–43; Rimmer, Joan. "Medieval Instrumental Dance Music." *Music and Letters* 72/1 (1991): 61–68.

See also Karole; Robertsbridge Codex

Daniel

An OE narrative poem based loosely on the first five chapters of the Old Testament book of Daniel. Like most OE poetry *Daniel* is anonymous and undatable. At one time the poem was thought to be the work of Cædmon, but this theory has long since been disproved. Nevertheless, the manuscript in which it is found—Junius 11—is still known as the Cædmon Manuscript. *Daniel,* the third of four poems in this manuscript, is found on pages 173–212. As it stands, the poem is some 764 lines long, though such prominent critics as Israel Gollancz, Neil Ker, and Peter Lucas have viewed it as incomplete, believing that a missing leaf may have held its ending. The text itself, however, finishes at the bottom of a page, where a simple point marks what is apparently a complete sentence.

Daniel contains little of the apocalyptic and prophetic material found in the later chapters of its source. As Robert Farrell notes, "The author of the OE *Daniel* is clearly interested in the narrative portions [of the source], especially those dealing with Daniel and the Three Children in their struggles against Nabuchodonosor and his line" (1974: 30). This focus in turn bears upon another major critical debate surrounding the poem: whether or not lines 279–361, the poet's version of the Song of Azarias and introduction to the Song of the Three Children, are an interpolation. Although many questions surround the inclusion of the Song of Azarias in *Daniel,* the central problem revolves around the fact that the two Songs repeat and, in some ways, diminish one another. The OE poet, however, may simply be following his source closely here.

The central characters in *Daniel* are Nabuchodonosor, his son Baltassar, and the prophet Daniel himself. Daniel serves an important religious function in the poem (this can especially be seen if he is compared with other saintly protagonists in OE poetry, such as Elene, Andreas, and Judith). However, it is clear from his relationship with the two kings that his role is also a political one, for he is cast in the part of court counselor and adviser. Indeed it is his skill as a prophet and adviser that gains him widespread fame at the court (lines 163–67).

Throughout the poem Daniel's skill and intelligence are highlighted, and the poet makes clear that Nabuchodonosor

desires to acquire the prophet's wisdom and not, as the Vulgate source indicates, to educate him in the ways of the Chaldeans. This is just one example of the ways in which the OE *Daniel* departs from its source and helps to illustrate the fact that the poem is far from a slavish paraphrase of the Vulgate book, a view that has been held by the majority of critics for some time. Further differences, in characterization and theme, help to attest further to the originality of the Anglo-Saxon poet.

The language of the poem is predominantly West Saxon with a few examples of other dialect forms. The poem is also noted for having an unusually high percentage of hypermetric, or "long," lines.

J.-A. George

Bibliography

PRIMARY

ASPR 1:111–32; Bradley, S.A.J., trans. *Anglo-Saxon Poetry: An Anthology of Old English Poems in Prose Translation.* London: Dent, 1982, pp. 66–86; Farrell, Robert T., ed. *Daniel and Azarias.* London: Methuen, 1974, pp. 46–89.

SECONDARY

Farrell, Robert T. "A Possible Source for Old English *Daniel.*" *NM* 70 (1969): 84–90; George, J.-A. "*Daniel* 416–29: An 'Identity Crisis' Resolved?" *MÆ* 60 (1991) 73–76; Lucas, Peter J. "On the Incomplete Ending of *Daniel* and the Addition of *Christ and Satan* to MS Junius 11." *Anglia* (1979): 46–59; Overing, Gillian R. "Nebuchadnezzar's Conversion in the Old English *Daniel:* A Psychological Portrait." *Papers on Language and Literature* 20 (1984): 3–14.

See also Azarias; Bible in OE Literature; Junius Manuscript

Davy, Adam (fl. ca. 1307–08)

Author of the *Five Dreams about Edward II,* written in short couplets and preserved in Bodl. Laud Misc. 622. Davy describes himself as "þe marchal of stretford atte bowe" (113); his *Dreams,* based on traditional prophecies, erroneously predict a glorious future for Edward II just after his accession to the throne in 1307.

V.J. Scattergood

Bibliography

PRIMARY

Furnivall, Frederick J., ed. *Adam Davy's 5 Dreams about Edward II.* EETS o.s. 69. London: Trübner, 1878.

SECONDARY

New *CBEL* 1:473; *Manual* 5:1529, 1723; Phillips, J.R.S. "Edward II and the Prophets." In *England in the Fourteenth Century: Proceedings of the 1985 Harlaxton Symposium,* ed. W.M. Ormrod. Woodbridge: Boydell, 1986, pp. 189–201.

See also Dream Vision; Edward II; Prophecy Literature

Death and Life

A dream debate poem written in 458 alliterative long lines and exceptional for its command of the allegorical conventions of vision verse and for the dramatic vigor of its personified combatants, Dame Death and Lady Life. Although the date of the poem is uncertain, its assured style would seem to place it well within the mainstream of alliterative tradition late in the 14th century. The question of date remains open, however, for the poem's sole copy survives in the 17th-century Percy Folio (BL Add. 27879). Its provenance appears to be northern.

The poem allegorically enacts the theological doctrine of Life victorious at the Resurrection of Christ. The Crucifixion becomes a joust in which Death at first believes herself the winner but learns instead how she has foiled herself. Death's spear wound to Christ's side releases Life from her bower, Christ's heart, and, in a spirited retelling of the Harrowing of Hell, the two victors—Christ and Lady Life—joyously send Death to hell's hole, to abide with fiends, as they also release the Old Testament saints.

The poem opens with a narrator who finds himself enlivened by the surrounding landscape, a pleasant Maytime scene conventional in vision poems, and the poet emphasizes the narrator's personal sense of involvement with animated nature. Immediately after the spring opening the narrator dreams of Lady Life, who embodies all the formerly insensate attributes of the scenery—that is, the May scene come to life as a personification. These introductory poetic devices connect the narrator-as-everyman with the theme of Life victorious at Christ's death. The pattern of waking-sleeping-reawakening is like the pattern of human life, where living leads to dying, which leads to renewed, immortal life. The narrator's supine, deathlike dream state frees his visionary soul to experience symbolically the paradox of Christian faith, that immortal life is released only through death. Sleep "drove into his heart" (line 38) just as Death "carved through the heart" of Christ (line 347).

The prayers that frame the poem, at beginning and end, both invoke an image of the crucified Christ. The poem shows how this seeming symbol of death in fact promises life's absolute victory. This mystery informs the poem's structure (which seems modeled upon the Cross), imagery (Life's convex fullness versus Death's concave emptiness, reflected in holes filled and emptied, in bowing actions up and down, and in a landscape of hills and valleys), and linguistic sophistication (puns, alliterative sound play, flyting epithets, and subtle modulations of tone of voice).

In subject matter the poem has often been compared with *Piers Plowman* B.18 (on the Harrowing of Hell); it does not suffer from the comparison. In refashioning liturgical and scriptural elements into a poem of dramatic depth and human immediacy the poet shows himself an innovative artist of considerable power.

Susanna Fein

Bibliography

PRIMARY

Donatelli, Joseph M.P., ed. *Death and Liffe.* Cambridge: Medieval Academy of America, 1989; Hanford, James Holly, and John M. Steadman, Jr., eds. "*Death and Liffe:* An Alliterative Poem." *SP* 15 (1918): 223–94.

SECONDARY

New *CBEL* 1:546; *Manual* 5:1503–04, 1705; Fein, Susanna. "The Poetic Art of *Death and Life.*" *YLS* 2 (1988): 103–23; Reed, Thomas L., Jr. *Middle English Debate Poetry and the Aesthetics of Irresolution.* Columbia: University of Missouri Press, 1990, pp. 208–13; Tristram, Philippa. *Figures of Life and Death in Medieval English Literature.* London: Elek, 1976.

See also Alliterative Revival; Debate Poems; Dream Vision; Nature in ME Literature; *Piers Plowman;* Religious Allegories

Debate Poems

The medieval genre of debate poetry is well represented in ME and includes several poems of literary distinction. Among the most notable are the ME bird debates *The Owl and the Nightingale* and *The Cuckoo and the Nightingale,* the body-and-soul debate *As I Lay on a Winter's Night,* and the alliterative debates *Winner and Waster, The Parliament of the Three Ages,* and *Death and Life.* Considered collectively, ME debate poetry encompasses a wide variety of poems: serious didactic works, comic entertainments, satiric poems, courtly poems. Some of the ME debates have ties to the animal fable, some to medieval romance, and some to the fabliau; several ME debates are also dream visions. But despite the significant differences exhibited by the many poems belonging to the genre, central to each is a contention between emotionally aroused opponents who match wits in a series of verbal exchanges. The terms "contention poem" and "conflict dialogue" are quite apt for most of these works.

The Owl and the Nightingale is the earliest of the ME debates. It was written around 1200, shortly after debate poems first began to appear in the European vernacular literatures (Provençal and Old French in particular). Before the 12th century the debate poem had existed only in medieval Latin. The late-8th-century Latin poem *Conflictus veris et hiemis,* attributed by some scholars to Alcuin, is considered the earliest true medieval debate poem. A dispute between the personified figures of Spring and Winter is overheard by shepherds, who at the conclusion of the debate offer a judgment in favor of Spring. Debates like this one between seasons of the year, body and soul, and water and wine were common in Latin poetry, and some of these same rivalries occur in ME. Most debates involved nonhuman participants, but there are also debates with human protagonists, such as those between occupational rivals (e.g., a sailor and a farmer) and those between human debaters with contrasting beliefs (e.g., a Christian and a Jew). Depending on the nature of their disputing parties, debate poems are classified as "horizontal" debates, poems in which the disputants enjoy fairly equal status, or as "vertical" debates, in which the debating parties exist on different levels of authority or abstraction. Most of the ME debates are horizontal, but there are a few exceptions, such as the poem *Child Jesus and the Masters of the Law of the Jews,* in which the mismatched nature of the participants becomes apparent as the divine child easily confounds the learned doctors.

There are several important subcategories within ME debate poetry, most notably bird, body-and-soul, and alliterative debates. The bird debates include *The Owl and the Nightingale, The Thrush and the Nightingale, The Cuckoo and the Nightingale,* and William Dunbar's *The Merle and the Nyghtingall.* Closely related to them are *The Clerk and the Nightingale I and II* and *A Parliament of Birds* ("In May when euery herte is lyʒt"). Chaucer's *Parliament of Fowls* also bears some relation to this group. *The Owl and the Nightingale,* the first of the ME bird debates, is a sophisticated and challenging poem, commonly regarded as the greatest comic poem in English before Chaucer. The avian rivals in this poem, both of them female, are two of the most vividly drawn characters in ME literature. Their dispute touches upon a wide range of subjects and reflects the poet's familiarity with natural history, contemporary literature, and a great deal of popular lore. The *Owl and the Nightingale* is one of several ME debates in which the dispute is not finally resolved.

The Thrush and the Nightingale, which belongs to the second half of the 13th century, attempts and achieves much less than its predecessor. Here the debaters are of opposite sex and their debate focuses on the worth of women, with the male Thrush attacking women and the female Nightingale defending them. Although the Thrush appears to have the upper hand throughout most of the debate, the poem is resolved in the Nightingale's favor when she presents the Virgin Mary as the saving grace of womankind. *The Cuckoo and the Nightingale* (also called *The Book of Cupid*) is a dream vision; it was probably written late in the 14th century by Sir John Clanvowe, one of Chaucer's friends, and is an important work of the Chaucer apocrypha. The poem contains several allusions to Chaucer's work, and its wryly comic treatment of love is remarkably similar to the treatment love often receives in Chaucer's own poetry. *The Cuckoo and the Nightingale* is similar to *The Thrush and the Nightingale* in that the female Nightingale's opponent is a male bird who sharply criticizes love and lovers, but in this poem the debate is not so clearly resolved in the Nightingale's favor.

Of the ME debates between the body and the soul *As I Lay on a Winter's Night* is the most dramatic. Preserved in six manuscript texts, this popular work combines pathos and terror with verbal and situational humor. The winter's-night setting of the poem contrasts with the springtime setting found in the bird debates and some of the other ME debate poems. Although its didactic purpose is to demonstrate humanity's dire need for repentance before the arrival of death, the poem delves into the intricate relationship between body and soul, emphasizing their mutual dependence and identifying the physical and spiritual sins each may fall prey to. The poem concludes with a graphic depiction of the sinful and recalcitrant soul being dragged off to hell by demonic hellhounds, at which point the narrator awakens from his dream in a cold sweat. A late work in the ME body-and-soul tradition is the 15th-century *Disputation between the Body and the Worms,* a dream vision in which the body of a beautiful woman is confronted in the grave by a novel set of "suitors"—worms, maggots, toads, and the like. Here the thematic emphasis is on becoming reconciled to the physical realities of death rather than on becoming spiritually prepared for death.

The three alliterative debate poems in ME—*Winner and Waster, The Parliament of the Three Ages,* and *Death and Life*—are similar in length (about 450–675 lines) and structure, and each has an elaborate dream-vision framework surrounding a central debate between personified figures. *Winner and Waster,* composed probably during the 1350s or 1360s, is one of the most impressive satiric poems in ME. The author focuses on the nature of these opposing economic forces (i.e., saving vs. spending, avarice vs. prodigality) and on the social chaos that ensues when they are not held carefully in check. The speaker's disenchantment with contemporary social conditions is revealed through both overt and subtle satiric commentary. The final verses of the poem, unfortunately, are lacking from the only surviving manuscript, BL Add. 31042, one of the two ME "Thornton" manuscripts.

The Parliament of the Three Ages, probably written near the end of the 14th century, explores the spiritual dangers that stem from the pursuit of worldly pleasures and achievements. The poem also reflects the poet's familiarity with works of medieval romance and his detailed knowledge of such worldly pursuits as hunting and hawking. Especially remarkable is the lengthy opening passage detailing the activities of a solitary deer hunter. The overall design of the *Parliament,* however, is flawed by the extreme length of the sermon by Elde (Old Age), which incorporates an extended description of the Nine Worthies (the great pagan, Jewish, and Christian heroes) into its discourse on the vanity of earthly things.

In *Death and Life* the poet seeks to assuage humanity's instinctive fear of death by asserting the supremacy of eternal life and the temporary nature of death. The poem contains several vivid descriptive passages and reflects the poet's fine sense of symmetrical design. Its date is uncertain, though probably late 14th to early 15th century. Its only extant text is in the 17th-century Percy Folio.

Several of the lesser ME debates should also be mentioned. The *Debate of the Carpenter's Tools,* in which 27 personified tools participate in a dispute about the carpenter's prospects for success, given his fondness for drink. It may be a minstrel's performance piece. It is also an excellent source of information about medieval carpentry and the implements of that trade. The debate *Meed and Much Thank* depicts a lively and provocative confrontation between a sycophantic courtier and a dedicated soldier and raises fundamental questions about human motivations. In the debate poem *Nurture and Kind* (i.e., Nurture and Nature) these personified figures are concerned with which of them has the greater influence on behavior. This poem focuses on the relative importance of training versus instinct and includes an amusing anecdote involving a cat that Nurture has trained to hold a candle. The ME pastourelles, dialogue poems in which young men (often knights or clerks) attempt to seduce young women (usually of rural or village origins), also deserve mention among the many and varied ME poems belonging to the debate genre.

John W. Conlee

Bibliography

PRIMARY

Conlee, John W., ed. *Middle English Debate Poetry: A Critical Edition.* East Lansing: Colleagues, 1991; Gardner, John, trans. *The Alliterative Morte Arthure, The Owl and the Nightingale, and Five Other Middle English Poems.* Carbondale: Southern Illinois University Press, 1971 [includes *The Owl and the Nightingale, The Thrush and the Nightingale, The Debate of the Body and the Soul (As I Lay on a Winter's Night), Winner and Waster,* and *The Parliament of the Three Ages*].

SECONDARY

New *CBEL* 1:509–13, 545–48; *Manual* 3:669–745, 829–902 [includes noncontentious dialogue poetry]; 5:1500–04, 1702–05; Ackerman, Robert W. "*The Debate of the Body and the Soul* and Parochial Christianity." *Speculum* 37 (1962): 541–65; Bestul, Thomas H. *Satire and Allegory in Wynnere and Wastoure.* Lincoln: University of Nebraska Press, 1974; Fein, Susanna. "The Poetic Art of *Death and Life.*" *YLS* 2 (1988): 103–23; Hume, Kathryn. *The Owl and the Nightingale: The Poem and Its Critics.* Toronto: University of Toronto Press, 1975; Kernan, Anne. "Theme and Structure in *The Parlement of the Thre Ages.*" *NM* 75 (1974): 253–78; Peck, Russell A. "The Careful Hunter in *The Parlement of the Thre Ages.*" *ELH* 39 (1972): 333–41; Reed, Thomas L., Jr. *Middle English Debate Poetry and the Aesthetics of Irresolution.* Columbia: University of Missouri Press, 1990; Reiss, Edmund. "Conflict and Its Resolution in Medieval Dialogues." In *Arts libéraux et philosophie au Moyen Age,* Actes du Quatrième Congrès International de Philosophie Médiévale. Montreal: Institut d'Études Médiévales, 1969, pp. 863–72.

See also Alliterative Revival; Clanvowe; *Death and Life;* Dream Vision; *Owl and the Nightingale; Parliament of the Three Ages; Winner and Waster*

Deor

A 42-line poem preserved in the Exeter Book, possessing an irregular stanzaic structure marked by manuscript spacing and small capitals. *Deor* exemplifies the close association of lyric and heroic in Anglo-Saxon verse and is notable as one of two extant OE poems with a refrain. The first five stanzas (27 lines) allude tantalizingly to specific examples of adversity drawn from heroic legend. The last stanza has a natural division at line 35. Departing from the pattern of presenting examples, the first half (lines 28–34) generalizes about adversity: a passive, hopeless response to adversity is contrasted with a response acknowledging that the wise Lord distributes portions of both good fortune and bad. The second half (35–42) introduces the lyric mode by shifting from the third person to the first person and gives a final specific example purportedly drawn from the poet's own experience. Each of the six stanzas ends with the refrain, *Þæs ofereode; þisses swa mæg* ("That

passed; this can/will also"), which, with the first half of the last stanza, provides the thematic core of the poem.

Kemp Malone and other scholars who have traced the stories called to mind by the allusive names and particular details in *Deor* fill in for modern readers valuable background material from Germanic legend and history. The first story is about Weland, a famous metalsmith taken prisoner by King Niðhad, hamstrung, and forced to work for the king. *Deor* names Weland and Niðhad and stresses Weland's physical and emotional suffering during his captivity. Legend tells us Weland finally escaped after avenging himself on Niðhad, by creating works of art from the bodies of his captor's sons and raping his daughter. The second story focuses on the ravished daughter, Beadohild, whose passivity in her adversity contrasts sharply with Weland's audacity. The refrain seems to point to the outcome of the legend (not articulated in *Deor*), that the son resulting from Beadohild's pregnancy brought a turn for the better in her fortunes.

The third story recounts the sleeplessness and lamentation that Mæðhild or Geat or both suffered as a result of *sorglufu* (sorrowful love). According to two parallel legends (which, except for the possible example of *Deor,* survive only in 19th-century recordings of Scandinavian ballad) Mæðhild responds passively to adversity, her foreknowledge that a water sprite will magically draw her to her death in a river, by weeping; Geat, her husband, responds actively and artistically, playing the harp so powerfully that his music draws his wife's body out of the river. According to one version the turn for the better signified by the refrain would be the restoration of Mæðhild to her husband; in the other version it would be his recovery of her body for burial and use of her hair to restring his harp.

The fourth story is recounted most briefly, in two lines (by modern lineation), merely stating that Ðeodric had control over many people for 30 winters, with the implication that even such a long period of tyranny eventually came to an end. In the last example from legend the men ruled by Eormanric, another tyrant, sorrowfully but hopelessly wish for his overthrow. These two examples place the active ruler against the passive victim, no longer exclusively female, thus extending the implications of the refrain to loss of good fortune for the tyrant as well as an eventual passing of bad fortune for the victims.

In line 35 the speaker adopts the lyric mode of the other Anglo-Saxon elegies, shifting from the third person to the first with the line *Þæt ic bi me sylfum secgan wille* ("I want to say about myself that . . ."), transforming the poem from an impersonal commentary on adversity into a highly personal lyric. Here the speaker relates having formerly been highly valued as a *scop,* a poet-musician, but then losing his place to Heorrenda (whose reputation as a great poet of legend overshadows the fame of the lords he served). The final section invites a reader to read the refrain as having a personal application not only for the speaker in the poem—just as adversity passed for Weland, Beadohild, and Mæðhild, so it will for Deor—but also as a lesson about the condition of transience in the world. Finally the success of the poem attests to the poet's having overcome adversity and achieved immortality through his art.

Phyllis R. Brown

Bibliography

PRIMARY

ASPR 3:178–79; Crossley-Holland, Kevin, trans. "Deor." In *The Battle of Maldon and Other Old English Poems,* ed. Bruce Mitchell. New York: St. Martin, 1966, pp. 72–75; Malone, Kemp, ed. *Deor.* New York: Appleton-Century-Crofts, 1966.

SECONDARY

Bloomfield, Morton. "*Deor* Revisited." In *Modes of Interpretation in Old English Literature: Essays in Honour of Stanley B. Greenfield,* ed. Phyllis Rugg Brown, Georgia Ronan Crampton, and Fred C. Robinson. Toronto: University of Toronto Press, 1986, pp. 273–82; Condren, Edward I. "Deor's Artistic Triumph." *SP* 78 (1981): 62–76; Mandel, Jerome. "Exemplum and Refrain: The Meaning of *Deor.*" *Yearbook of English Studies* 7 (1977): 1–9.

See also Exeter Book; Literary Influences: Scandinavian; Minstrels; *Widsith*

Deserted Villages

The reduction and movement of rural population caused a widespread abandonment of villages, starting in the second quarter of the 14th century. Desertions commonly occurred in areas of less productive soils or later medieval sheep rearing. Physical remains of deserted villages are often found in pastureland, occasionally in woodland or arable; many sites were damaged or destroyed by "emparking" and landscaping for manor houses.

The village was the standard form of social and economic rural organization for much of England. Its durability is due to a long period of development in which Anglo-Saxon settlements were rarely permanent. Before the 14th century specific reasons usually exist for village desertions, such as William I's New Forest depopulations.

The widespread partial or total abandonment of late-medieval villages, however, represents a major change. Explanations are varied; three interrelated factors have been viewed as contributing. 1) Demography: the Black Death initiated and maintained an overall population loss of at least one third. 2) Agriculture: changing farming practices saw the labor-intensive cultivation (grain production) of cooperative agricultural communities shift to sheep rearing (wool production) with a smaller work force. 3) Economics: an expanding money economy caused lords to lease lands for cash rents, thus breaking up manors, and to hire labor for wages, making the village community labor force obsolete. Recent evidence suggests another factor. 4) Ecology: villages established or expanded during the population peak of the 12th and 13th centuries were abandoned because only marginal land had been available to them and its cultivation failed after several generations of depletion in an increasingly unfavorable climate.

Deserted villages have served as symbols of better times in the past, offering an idealized view of medieval society: there had once been more people, in a "traditional society," on the land. More recently, deserted villages have become an important asset for historical research, as archaeologists turn to the remains of peasant houses and lots for the unrecorded details of rural life. Results from the long-term multidisciplinary research program at Wharram Percy in Yorkshire have served to remind scholars of the prodigious power of the lord of the manor over the lives and fates of the tenants, as well as of the special permanence of the village church among less durable structures.

Eric Klingelhofer

Bibliography

Beresford, Maurice W. *Lost Villages of England.* London: Lutterworth; New York: Philosophical Library, 1954 [this book first drew serious attention to the topic]; Beresford, Maurice W., and John G. Hurst. *Deserted Medieval Villages: Studies.* London: Lutterworth, 1971 [assembles both documentary and archaeological evidence]; Beresford, Maurice W., and John G. Hurst. *Wharram Percy: Deserted Medieval Village.* London: Batsford, 1990; Village Research Group, *Newsletter* [founded in 1952; useful for keeping abreast of local scholarship].

See also Forests, Royal; Manorialism; Population and Demography

Despenser Family

Led by Hugh senior and Hugh junior, they were from a modest baronial background but rose to prominence through Edward II's patronage. The elder Hugh (b. 1261) followed a conventional career of military expeditions, local office holding, and royal counsel. For his loyalty he was named earl of Winchester in 1322.

The ascent of the younger Hugh (b. ca. 1285) was more spectacular. His career as a royal servant was unremarkable until 1318, when he was appointed or reappointed royal chamberlain. He used that position to build a large following among household and local officials. He gained enormous influence over Edward and reaped rich rewards. The territorial base gained through marriage (to one of the three Clare heiresses) proved insufficient, and he embarked on a campaign of intimidation and harassment to enlarge his holdings.

Because of the Despensers' flouting of the law and their manipulation of Edward they were driven into exile in 1321. When they returned later that year, some nobles, the "Contrariants," rebelled. The revolt failed and the rebels forfeited their lands, many of which were given to the Despensers. Over the next four years they continued to monopolize royal favor, arousing nearly universal hatred. When Isabella invaded England in 1326 and overthrew Edward II, they were quickly captured and executed.

Scott L. Waugh

Bibliography

Davies, James Conway. *The Baronial Opposition to Edward II: Its Character and Policy.* Cambridge: Cambridge University Press, 1918; Fryde, Natalie. *The Tyranny and Fall of Edward II, 1321–1326.* Cambridge: Cambridge University Press, 1979; Saul, Nigel. "The Despensers and the Downfall of Edward II." *EHR* 99 (1984): 1–33; Waugh, Scott L. "For King, Country, and Patron: The Despensers and Local Administration, 1321–1322." *Journal of British Studies* 22 (1983): 23–58.

See also Clare Family; Edward II

Dialogue of the Exchequer

A treatise, written between 1176 and 1179, as a practical introduction to the exchequer, the financial office of the English kings. The author, Richard Fitz Neal (or Nigel), was the son of Nigel, bishop of Ely, Henry I's treasurer. Richard himself was treasurer from ca. 1158 to 1196 (from 1189 to his death in 1198 he was also bishop of London).

The *Dialogue,* which bears a fulsome dedication to Henry II, was doubtless intended for apprentice exchequer clerks and is written as a conversation in simple Latin; a pupil asks questions and his master answers (a common form in textbooks of the period). The master explains that the exchequer derives its name from the checkered cloth, reminiscent of a chess board, on which counters are moved on the accounting table as on an abacus. The lower exchequer, also called the exchequer of receipt, is where money is counted and entered on rolls and tallies, and the upper exchequer is where the audit of the accounts takes place. The duties and wages of the officials of both lower and upper exchequer are detailed. The upper exchequer is the larger, and here the officers sit on four benches facing the four sides of the table. The justiciar presides, representing the king, but the treasurer is the chief official, responsible for both exchequers, and is compared by the master to the king in the game of chess.

In the battle of the exchequer, he says, the opposing chess king's place is taken by the sheriff. Each county has a sheriff, responsible for the king's revenues in the shire and summoned to the exchequer twice a year. The account is made up on the Pipe Roll at Michaelmas, when the sheriff is examined by the treasurer, regarding his "farm" of the royal receipts (the stipulated money he owes from the county's revenues), and then by the chancellor's clerk regarding the profits of justice.

Diana E. Greenway

Bibliography

Hollister, C. Warren. "The Origins of the English Treasury." *EHR* 99 (1978): 262–75; Johnson, Charles, ed. and trans. *Dialogus de Scaccario: The Course of the Exchequer, by Richard Fitz Neale.* Corr. Frank E.L. Carter and Diana E. Greenway. Oxford: Clarendon, 1983; Poole, Reginald Lane. *The Exchequer in the Twelfth Century.* Oxford: Clarendon, 1912.

See also Exchequer; Henry II; Sheriff

Dioceses and Diocesan Structure

The Christian church had been introduced into the Roman province of Britannia by the time of the martyrdom of St. Alban in 304, and the British church was represented by three bishops at the Council of Arles in 314. What area each bishop governed and in what way he governed are unknown. There may well have been some continuity, despite the pagan Saxon invasion, in western, Celtic Britain (Cornwall, Wales, and the northwest), where traditions of survival remain strong. However, only with the establishment of dioceses can an organized church be traced, beginning with the mission of Augustine to Kent in 597 and his appointment as archbishop of Canterbury in 601.

The gradual acceptance of the faith by Saxon kings led, after Æthelberht's original conversion, to the appointment of bishops at Rochester and London in 604, followed in the next 30 years by East Anglia and Dorchester. As the converted Saxons moved westward and northward, sees were founded at Worcester, Winchester, Hereford, and Lichfield. A second wave of missionary activity, from Ireland, spread into the north of England, establishing bishops at York in 626 and, in the next 50 years, at Lindisfarne, Hexham, and Ripon.

Shifting political boundaries, notably in the west of England, caused changes in the areas under the care of each bishop and alterations in titles as they moved their centers of operation (cathedrals; from Lat. *cathedra:* "throne"). From 630 East Anglia was ruled from Dunwich, for two centuries after 672 also by a second bishop from Elmham, then by one bishop based at Thetford, and only from ca. 1096 from the substantial commercial center at Norwich.

In the north the bishop of Lindisfarne was forced from his island by Viking raids and in 883 went to Chester-le-Street, changed in 995 for greater security to Durham. As the Saxon advance westward made the old see of Winchester unmanageable, a second see was founded at Sherborne ca. 705. Further advance brought the division of both and the creation ca. 909 of Ramsbury out of Winchester, and Wells and Crediton out of Sherborne.

Changes of title also resulted, both before and after the Norman Conquest, from a policy of moving sees from small, ancient sites to larger towns; the bishop of Selsey to Chichester (1070), Wells to the intellectual center of Bath (1060), Dorchester to Lincoln (1067), Crediton to Exeter (1046). Thereafter only two new bishoprics were created in the Middle Ages: Ely in 1109, Carlisle in 1133.

The laws of several Saxon kings established the status of bishops and clergy, and the names of charter witnesses suggest that bishops governed their sees with the help of clerks living in their households *(familiae).* Before the Conquest some dioceses were divided into rural deaneries, and a dean presumably acted in some sense as the bishop's deputy, as the bishop's role as Father-in-God took on judicial as well as pastoral and spiritual functions. He was becoming both corrector of his people and governor of his clergy. An increasingly complex society and expanding church activity in the 12th century forced the division or delegation of the bishop's role. Archdeacons, the eyes of the bishop, were appointed in each diocese over groups of deaneries, to bear some of the administrative and judicial burdens (the huge diocese of Lincoln had eight archdeacons, Ely one). By the end of the Middle Ages each diocese had a complex system of government that permitted every function of the bishop to be carried out by a substitute.

The absence of a diocesan bishop from his see, a common feature when he served as senior official in royal governments, in no way inhibited the work of the church in the diocese. The bishop simply appointed a suffragan bishop (Welsh or Irish bishops, or bishops with foreign titles, were usually available) to confirm children, confer holy orders, or consecrate new or defiled churches, churchyards, or holy vessels. A vicar general from among the senior clergy supervised all administrative arrangements. On the bishop's staff was usually an official principal, who presided in his name over the regular monthly consistory court, where misconduct could be corrected and canon-law cases touching matrimony or debt were heard, since the church was concerned with the consequences of breach of sacred vows.

There was also, usually, a commissary general, who held a peripatetic court dealing with probate business; the church was expected to protect the goods of orphans and widows. The rural dean remained a useful link between the bishop and his clergy, since most archdeacons were absentees (and considered as doubtful entrants into heaven: "Can an archdeacon be saved?"). They too appointed deputies, archdeacon's officials, who at least ensured that the archdeacon's fees were paid and his dues collected. The registrar of the diocese recorded the acts of the bishop and his staff, a record essential as an immediate source of information and as the main material for the historian of ecclesiastical administration.

Robert W. Dunning

Bibliography

Deanesly, Margaret. *The Pre-Conquest Church in England.* 2d ed. London: Black, 1963; Storey, Robin L. *Diocesan Administration in the Fifteenth Century.* York: St. Anthony Press, 1959; Thompson, A. Hamilton. *The English Clergy and Their Organisation in the Later Middle Ages.* Oxford: Clarendon, 1947.

See also Bishops; Canterbury, Ecclesiastical Province of; Courts, Ecclesiastical; Liturgy and Church Music, History of; York, Ecclesiastical Province of

Diplomacy

Diplomats were the king's representatives in foreign countries. The development of royal power and authority in the 13th century and the need for proper representation in relations abroad lay behind the development of the English diplomatic services from the reign of Henry III onward. Two additional factors encouraged this evolution. One was the growth of international trade, with a corresponding need to protect commercial interests. The other was the breakup of the old established links with France, with the resultant hostility that characterized relations between the two countries from the late 13th century onward. What came to be known as the Hundred Years War occurred at a time when the relations of England not only with France but with other European countries were becoming more complex, requiring a greater measure of attention from an increasingly professional body of men.

By common practice diplomats were generally treated with respect. As representatives appointed by the king and carrying powers enabling them to treat on his behalf they were usually men of rank and dignity. An embassy, especially one concerned with broad issues, might include one or more members of the greater nobility, a high churchman, such as a bishop, other clergy, knights, and merchants, all of whom enjoyed the king's personal confidence. The rank of the diplomats helped to show the importance attached to particular negotiations.

To make the diplomatic effort worthwhile and more effective those sent to treat were provided with files of the papers submitted by their predecessors on the same mission, the intention being to lend continuity of approach to relations with a particular country, continuity best achieved if the diplomats were briefed regarding those who had gone before, the arguments that had been prepared, the demands that had been put forward by both sides, and knowledge of how those with whom they had negotiated had responded.

This need for continuity of approach had already been acted upon in the reign of Henry III with the appointment, before 1268, of John of St. Denis as keeper of papal bulls and the nomination, a generation later, of the lawyer Philip Martel as keeper of the king's memoranda concerning Aquitaine. Both men were in effect archivists, whose main task was to help the members of embassies prepare themselves for their foreign missions by giving them the chance of briefing themselves by reading their predecessors' papers.

Such preparation might help an embassy pursue a consistent policy, something that might also be achieved by sending the same ambassadors more than once to the same country. Since diplomacy involved negotiations concerning trade, land, rights of various kinds, or royal marriages, it became essential for every embassy to have among its members at least one recognized expert in law, usually civil law. Thus, when proposals were made or terms agreed, the lawyers had the task of ensuring that England's rights, or those of its king, had been properly protected. Experts in law, both civil and canon, were thus in demand. When Edward II helped establish the King's Hall at Cambridge, he acted in part with the intention that the new institution should be a place where some of the crown's future servants, learned in the law, might receive their training.

To be chosen for an embassy was a clear sign of honor and royal confidence. The skills required of ambassadors were many: social, linguistic, and intellectual. However, in an age that eventually saw the beginnings of permanent embassies in Italy, opinions regarding diplomats varied. To some they were men worthy of respect; to others, glorified spies, protected by conventions that acted in their favor, men whose movements should be strictly guarded, even restricted, and most certainly observed by their hosts. As is the case today, diplomats were never free of suspicion on the part of those to whom they were accredited.

C. T. Allmand

Bibliography

Chaplais, Pierre. *English Medieval Diplomatic Practice.* 2 vols. London: HMSO, 1975–82; Chaplais, Pierre. *Essays in Medieval Diplomacy and Administration.* London: Hambledon, 1981; Cuttino, George P. *English Diplomatic Administration, 1259–1339.* 2d ed. Oxford: Clarendon, 1971; Cuttino, George P. *English Medieval Diplomacy.* Bloomington: Indiana University Press, 1985; Dickinson, Joycelyne G. *The Congress of Arras: A Study in Medieval Diplomacy.* Oxford: Clarendon, 1955; Lucas, Henry S. "The Machinery of Diplomatic Intercourse." In *The English Government at Work, 1327–1336.* Vol. 1: *Central and Prerogative Administration,* ed. James F. Willard and William A. Morris. Cambridge: Mediaeval Academy of America, 1940, pp. 300–31.

See also Hundred Years War; Monarchy and Kingship

Discant (Descant), English

A basic musical technique, *discantus* at its simplest was no more than a progression of two-part consonances. If one singer sang a preexistent melody, the other singer could improvise the added part. *Discantus* was taught in the 14th and 15th centuries, both as part of a wide-ranging course and as the subject of independent treatises. These latter are not to be seen in isolation, but they indicate a more pragmatic approach to musical education, whereby quick progress toward improvised polyphony could be made by those who needed it for professional purposes. *Discantus* was taught to boys, as well as to adults, as part of the basic training needed by all church musicians; and some of the written material is in English rather than Latin.

The 15th-century composer Leonel Power, in his short treatise (BL Lansdowne 763, fol. 105v), shows how suitable intervals may be selected against a series of schematic "plainsongs," avoiding, for example, consecutive parallel perfect consonances. He also discusses the system of "sights." Depending on his vocal range, the singer would imagine a note against one in the plainsong on the same staff and automatically transpose it to an equivalent within his vocal range. There were three sights of descant properly so-called: the quatreble, the treble, and the mean. In the quatreble sight, according to Power, the note an octave below the tenor "in sight" corresponded to a unison "in voice" and so on. An anonymous continuator, however, makes the quatreble unison "in sight" a twelfth above "in voice"; the treble unison in sight was an octave above in voice, and the mean unison in sight was a fifth above in voice. (Needless to say, the visualized intervals were not themselves necessarily consonant; for example, a "mean" singer, in order to produce a sixth, which is an imperfect consonance, had to visualize a second, which is dissonant. The advantage to those learning descant was presumably that it allowed their eyes to be glued to the staff on which the plainsong was written; with practice, fluency would be achieved and the visualizing would become unnecessary.)

The continuator also deals with the sights of counter, counter, and faburden. Sight and voice were identical for the countertenor, while for the counter the unison sight was a fifth below in voice. The faburden sight was the same as that of the counter, though the number of possible intervals was reduced to two because of the parallel fourths between the plainsong (here in the middle) and the upper voice.

Simple though these rules would have been for singers, the writers were conscious of artistic values. As the anonymous Lansdowne writer put it, "It is faire and meri singing many imperfite cordis togeder." Others, such as Richard Cutell of London (Bodleian Library, Bodley 842, fol. 48), agreed. Although a number of other such treatises exist, they do not add substantially to this doctrine. One of them (BL Add. 21455, fol. 9v) confirms that the notion of *discantus* was applicable to instruments as well as voices, but none ventures beyond the note-against-note stage, to which they sometimes also give the name "counterpoint," or *contranota.*

Yet we know from other evidence that more complex forms of multiple improvisation took place. Two related passages in 14th-century treatises describe collective improvisation in four or even five parts, the top one being highly ornamented. At that stage parallel perfect intervals were still allowed in more than two parts. Such progressions were forbidden in 15th-century (three-part) faburden, which represents a taming of wilder musical instincts; but it too gave rise to ingenious possibilities, as certain traditional detached faburdens seem to suggest. Perhaps the greatest potential for improvised *discantus* lay with the organ; but in any case the treatises of the late 14th and early 15th centuries offer a fascinating insight into the earliest formal training that budding composers in a great period will have had.

The term "English discant" (or descant) is applied in modern writings to two fundamentally different methods for the composition of written polyphony of the later 13th through the earlier 15th century. Normally both are notated in score for three voices that are differentiated by range but move in similar rhythms and sing the same text. Some of these pieces are freely composed and treble-dominated, with a counterpoint involving frequent chains of parallel imperfect consonances. Their style is sometimes referred to as "cantilena-style" because of its frequent appearance in the English cantilena repertoire. "English discant" is more appropriately reserved for the other kind of piece, composed on a *cantus firmus* (normally the middle voice of three) using the note-against-note techniques of *discantus.* The simplest of such written chant settings approach the mechanical parallelism of faburden, especially in settings of long ritual texts like the Credo and Te Deum, but more often their style is slightly elevated, exhibiting contrary motion in the counterpoint and some degree of rhythmic elaboration in the outer voices.

John Caldwell

Bibliography

PRIMARY

Bukofzer, Manfred. *Geschichte des englischen Diskants und des Fauxbourdons nach den theoretischen Quellen.* Sammlung Musikwissenschaftlicher Abhandlungen

21. Strassburg: Heitz, 1936 [Latin and English materials included]; Coussemaker, Edmond de, ed. *Scriptorum de Musica Medii Aevi.* 4 vols. Paris: Durand, 1864–76, 3:361 and 4:294 [14th-century texts describing multiple improvisation from Anon. I and the *Quatuor principalia musice* 4.2.41]; Meech, Sanford B. "Three Musical Treatises in English from a Fifteenth-Century Manuscript." *Speculum* 10 (1935): 235–69.

SECONDARY

Georgiades, Thrasybulos. *Englischen Diskanttraktate aus der ersten Hälfte des 15. Jahrhunderts: Untersuchungen zur Entwicklung der Mehrstimmigkeit im Mittelalter.* Munich: Musikwissenschaftliches Seminar der Universität München, 1937; Kenney, Sylvia. "'English Discant' and Discant in England." *Musical Quarterly* 45 (1959): 26–48; Sanders, Ernest H. "Cantilena and Discant in 14th-Century England." *Musica Disciplina* 19 (1965): 7–52; Sanders, Ernest H. "Discant, II: English Discant." *NGD* 5:492–95.

See also Cantilena; Faburden

Dives and Pauper

A long ME prose treatise on the Decalogue, or Ten Commandments, of about 200,000 words. It is a work of religious instruction in the form of a teacher-pupil dialogue between a "rich man" (Dives) and a "poor man" (Pauper)—specifically a rich layman and a poor (though highly educated) cleric. Internal evidence indicates that it was written between 1405 and 1410. Eight manuscripts of the text survive, with five text fragments, all written in various Midlands dialects of ME. The tract is anonymous, apparently deliberately so, inasmuch as its subject matter was theological in a period when opinions expressed on theological matters, especially in the vernacular, were closely scrutinized for traces of heresy or sedition.

The author has, however, left a number of clues in his text to his personality and attainments. Judged by his use of the Bible, canon law, patristic writings, and contemporaneous sources, he was a university-trained Franciscan cleric. In the spirit of his times, as well as of his profession, he placed a high value on preaching and on penitence. The drift of the dialogue suggests that one of the author's targets is not so much the ignorance or sinfulness of the rich layman but rather his leanings toward Lollard, or proto-Puritan, views on such matters as images in churches, jollity on the sabbath, or pomp in burials. On other topics, however, Dives already agrees (or is easily persuaded to agree) with Pauper: for example, that the first commandment forbids witchcraft and astrology; that the fourth commandment includes the veneration of such "fathers" as prelates, lay patrons of churches, and angels; that the seventh commandment enjoins fair prices; and that the eighth commandment, under the rubric of false witness, covers the symbolism of church vestments and the portents of the Last Judgment. The choice and treatment of these latter topics is conventional and unique only in being considerably more extended than in other Decalogue treatises of the period.

This evidence, taken together with a sermon cycle recently found by Anne Hudson to have been written by the same author (Longleat House, Wiltshire, Marquess of Bath 4), suggests a somewhat independent-minded mendicant preacher, one persuaded of the urgent need to reform certain clerical abuses but cautiously treading the line between sharp criticism and outright heresy. He is last seen (in the prologue to the Longleat sermons) taking refuge under the wing of an unnamed, powerful lay patron from those who would silence him. His story is a precursor to that of Reginald Pecock a generation or so later, with the difference that, by Pecock's time, positions had hardened. By the 1450s appeals to the lay conscience and vernacular discussion of church doctrine and practices had become prosecutable offenses.

No holograph of *Dives and Pauper* survives. The manuscripts and manuscript fragments are datable within the last three quarters of the 15th century on the basis of their handwritings. One manuscript (New Haven, Yale Beinecke 228) is dated 1465 by its scribe and said to have been written in a Lisbon monastery. The others are unsigned and undated. The manuscripts and fragments fall into two main groups. The larger, earlier group of five includes Glasgow, University Library Hunterian 270, which has been used as the base manuscript for the modern, EETS edition of the text. The smaller, derivative group includes a manuscript (Bodl. Eng.th.d.36) used as the basis of a black-letter edition of the text by the early printer Richard Pynson in 1493. Pynson's edition was reprinted in 1496 by Wynkyn de Worde and in 1536 by Thomas Berthelet, both reusing Pynson's printed text. This late pre-Reformation appearance of *Dives and Pauper* attests to a continuing interest in its subject matter as well as to its fundamental doctrinal orthodoxy.

While modern students of medieval England read *Dives and Pauper* for various reasons, a central one is the evidence it gives for the nature of Christian belief and practice at the close of the period of Chaucer and Langland. In 1401 the death penalty for heresy was enacted, and in 1407–09 further laws were instituted limiting vernacular preaching and writing on theological matters. The author of *Dives and Pauper* inveighs against these new limitations but does so anonymously. Though he chose to omit discussion of such vexed topics as the eucharist and to circumscribe his discussion of such others as baptism or the powers of the priesthood, his doctrinal caution is linked with an urgent plea for the reform of a number of ecclesiastical and pastoral practices. In this respect *Dives and Pauper* is closely related to the sermons and works of popular religious instruction of its period.

As an example of ME prose *Dives and Pauper* has been less well studied. Its style is occasionally tedious but quite often lively and pithy, and it is varied by the inclusion of poems, exempla, and anecdotes. In its exposition of the Ten Commandments it provides independent translations of passages from the Vulgate that are of interest to students of the early English Bible. Its vocabulary is copious. The first edition of the *OED* drew heavily on the Pynson and Wynkyn de Worde printings, in which words and spellings had been changed to then-current forms, for evidence of late-15th- and early-16th-century usage.

Finally *Dives and Pauper* has been used as a source of knowledge of the rites, vestments, and customs of the late-medieval English church (Rock; Aston), of folk beliefs (Thomas), and of the roots of medieval drama (Kolve).

Priscilla Heath Barnum

Bibliography

PRIMARY

STC Nos. 19212, 19213, 19214; Barnum, Priscilla Heath, ed. *Dives and Pauper.* 2 vols. EETS o.s. 275, 280. London: Oxford University Press, 1976–80 [glossary and notes forthcoming in a third volume].

SECONDARY

New *CBEL* 1:690; *Manual* 7:2287–88; 2515–16; Aston, Margaret. *England's Iconoclasts.* Vol. 1: *Laws against Images.* Oxford: Clarendon, 1988; Hudson, Anne. *The Premature Reformation: Wycliffite Texts and Lollard History.* Oxford: Clarendon, 1988; Hudson, Anne, and H.L. Spencer. "Old Author, New Work: The Sermons of MS Longleat 4." *MÆ* 53 (1984): 220–38; Kolve, V.A. *The Play Called Corpus Christi.* Stanford: Stanford University Press, 1966, pp. 131–34; Morgan, Margery M. "Pynson's Manuscript of *Dives et Pauper.*" *The Library,* 5th ser. 8 (1953): 217–28; Owst, G.R. *Preaching in Medieval England: An Introduction to Sermon Manuscripts of the Period c. 1350–1450.* Cambridge: Cambridge University Press, 1926 [draws heavily on *Dives and Pauper,* as does the following work]; Owst, G.R. *Literature and Pulpit in Medieval England.* Cambridge: Cambridge University Press, 1933; Richardson, H.G. "Dives and Pauper." *The Library,* 4th ser. 15 (1934): 31–37; Rock, Daniel. *The Church of Our Fathers.* 1849–53. Repr. (4 vols.) ed. G.W. Hart and W.H. Frere. London: Murray, 1905; Thomas, Keith V. *Religion and the Decline of Magic: Studies in Popular Beliefs in Sixteenth and Seventeenth Century England.* London: Weidenfeld & Nicolson, 1971.

See also Drama, Vernacular; Feasts, New Liturgical; Friars; Literacy; Lollards; Moral and Religious Instruction; Pecock; Penitentials; Popular Religion; Sermons; Wycliffite Texts

Domesday Book

At Christmastide, 1085, almost twenty years after William duke of Normandy had conquered England, the king "had deep discussions with his council about this country, how it was peopled and with what sorts of men." After these discussions he ordered a kingdomwide inquest to be held. According to a disapproving contemporary, "so very thoroughly did he have the kingdom investigated that there was not a single [piece of land] . . . or even (it is shameful to record but did not seem shameful to him to do), one ox or one cow or one pig that was omitted from his record; and all these records were afterward brought to him" (Anglo-Saxon Chronicle, E-Text).

The results of this inquest are recorded in Domesday Book, the first "public record" in English history and a docu-ment that resides today in London. Its entries, with relatively standardized, detailed, and quantified information for nearly every farm and village in 11th-century England south of the River Tees, constitute the most complete body of statistical, tenurial, and geographical data on medieval England. The amount of information is staggering, well illustrating William's administrative genius. We have detailed information on some 45,000 landholdings across the kingdom. The document preserves information on peasant population, agricultural productivity, tax assessment, and land values—recording thousands of mills, pastures, woodlands, ironworks, and slavewomen.

Of equal importance, Domesday records names. Generally the document tells us who held the manors and farmsteads both in January 1066—immediately before the Conquest—and in 1086, the year of the Domesday inquest. The survey also records the names of the subtenants, retainers, and allies of great Saxon and Norman lords. It notes the tenures by which Saxons and Normans held their land and on occasion preserves their legal disputes and the land transfers they made. This vast array of tenurial and manorial information is organized geographically; we can identify the great bulk of Domesday places—some 14,000 in all—and thus locate lordships, swine pastures, waste land, or areas of highest value in 11th-century England.

Domesday Book bridges the Norman Conquest, describing manorial conditions as they existed in 1066 and again in 1086. Hence it discloses the wealth, power, and political structure of two distinct cultures and societies and illuminates the revolutionary transformation in landholding that the Norman Conquest brought about. Although occasionally ambiguous, inaccurate, or incomplete, Domesday Book is singularly reliable by standards of prescientific societies. It has rightly been called "the most remarkable statistical document in the history of Europe." Indeed no land survey until the 19th century approached its comprehensiveness or detail. Used cautiously, and with the realization that its figures represent approximations rather than exact numbers, Domesday Book provides us with our best evidence for the political, economic, and social history of 11th-century England.

Robin Fleming

Bibliography

Bates, David. *A Bibliography of Domesday Book.* Woodbridge: Boydell, for the Royal Historical Society, 1986; Darby, Henry C. *Domesday England.* Cambridge: Cambridge University Press, 1977; Finn, R. Weldon. *Domesday Book: A Guide.* London: Phillimore, 1973; Galbraith, Vivian H. *Domesday Book: Its Place in Administrative History.* Oxford: Clarendon, 1974; Holt, J.C., ed. *Domesday Studies.* Woodbridge: Boydell, 1987; Maitland, Frederic W. *Domesday Book and Beyond: Three Essays in the Early History of England.* Cambridge: Cambridge University Press, 1897. Repr. with Foreword by J.C. Holt. Cambridge: Cambridge University Press, 1987; Morris, John, et al., eds. and trans. *Domesday Book: A Survey of* the Counties of England. 34 vols. Chichester: Phillimore, 1975–92 [a county-by-county text and translation, with indices for the entire Domesday Book]; Sawyer, Peter H., ed. Domesday Book: A Reassessment. London: Arnold, 1985.

See also Manorialism; Population; William I

Douglas, Gavin (ca. 1475–1522)

Scottish poet, churchman, and courtier best known for his translation of Virgil's Aeneid (Eneados, 1513). Other works include a dream vision, The Palice of Honour (1501), and possibly a brief poem on church corruption, "Conscience" (after 1513). The allegory King Hart, despite later attribution, is probably not by Douglas. The Eneados survives in several manuscripts, of which the early-16th-century Cambridge, Trinity College 1184, is the basis for the most recent scholarly edition (Coldwell); no manuscript of The Palice of Honour is extant, but it can be found in three 16th-century printed editions.

A younger son of an earl of Angus, Douglas was drawn to ambition and conflict, both at church and court. His poetic efforts were at least partly intended to attract patronage. Educated at St. Andrews and possibly Paris, he became bishop of Dunkeld in 1516, but the family fortunes declined soon afterward. Douglas ended his life in exile in England.

Douglas's literary output reflects his wide reading in Scots and English vernacular writers, continental poets, and Italian humanists. In both his major works he is deeply proud of his Scottish language yet equally aware of his ambition in introducing classical and continental forms into "rurell termes rude" (Palice 126). Indeed much of The Palice's stylistic power lies in its leaps between highly rhetorical "aureate" language and colloquial diction. The Palice shows an encyclopedic command of the conventional motifs of courtly allegory, but it also has descriptive flair and vivid, often comic, dramatic settings. Its narrative centers on the various approaches to honor, through chastity, faithful love, and especially through poetry itself. This looks forward to the Eneados, in which lay Douglas's greatest hope for honor and worldly immortality.

The ambitious task of gathering a whole prior tradition into a new language and culture also characterizes the Eneados. Douglas seeks to bring not merely the text of Virgil but also the whole medieval and Renaissance Latin tradition surrounding that text to a noble Scots vernacular readership. In addition to the justly famous Prologues to the books of the poem Douglas provides a framework of prose commentary, chapter division, and verse summaries that closely imitates the structure of Latin Virgil manuscripts and early printed editions.

The Prologues are simultaneously apologetic and boastful. They regret the "difference betwix my blunt endyte / And thy scharp sugarate sang Virgiliane" (I Pro. 28–29), and they defuse attacks on Virgil's pagan content by proposing euhemerist, astronomical, and christianizing interpretations of the gods. Yet they criticize Caxton's and Chaucer's earlier English versions of the story. Despite Douglas's modesty about his native tradition the Prologues display formal and stylistic variety as great as that which he praises in Virgil: heroic couplets, rime royal, alliterative stanzas, and other forms.

Douglas's translation itself, which replaces Virgil's hexameters with heroic couplets, is remarkably faithful to Virgil, in both spirit and detail. If Douglas rarely captures Virgil's quieter metrical nuances, he consistently succeeds with scenes of action and the more emotional speeches. He expands on Virgil at various points, sometimes adding brief explanations of Virgilian terms (usually derived from Latin glosses on the poem) and sometimes putting additional emphasis on Aeneas's political role. But even more, Douglas's expansions reflect his own readerly enthusiasms: naval technology, storms, hunts, landscapes, and battles. Here, even more than in the artificial structure of the Prologues, Virgil and his Scots translator coalesce into a single, if extended, voice.

Christopher C. Baswell

Bibliography

PRIMARY

Bawcutt, Priscilla J., ed. The Shorter Poems of Gavin Douglas. STS, 4th ser. 3. Edinburgh: Blackwood, 1967; Coldwell, David F.C., ed. Virgil's "Aeneid" Translated into Scottish Verse by Gavin Douglas, Bishop of Dunkeld. STS, 3d ser. 25, 27, 28, 30. Edinburgh: Blackwood, 1957–64.

SECONDARY

New CBEL 1:662–64; Manual 4:988–1005, 1180–1204; Bawcutt, Priscilla J. Gavin Douglas: A Critical Study. Edinburgh: Edinburgh University Press, 1976; Blyth, Charles R. "The Knychtlyke Stile": A Study of Gavin Douglas' Aeneid. New York: Garland, 1987; Scheps, Walter, and J. Anna Looney. Middle Scots Poets: A Reference Guide. Boston: Hall, 1986, pp. 195–246.

See also Dream Vision; Literary Influences: Classical; Scottish Literature, Early; Translation

Drama, Latin Liturgical

Although surviving records document a wealth of dramatic activity in medieval England, the number of extant texts of Latin liturgical dramas is surprisingly small. Even allowing for the destruction of the vast majority of liturgical books copied in medieval England, one is forced to question the degree of popularity of pure Latin drama, performed within the liturgical ritual and sung throughout, as compared with, for example, mimes and pageants, the enterprises of traveling players, and, most especially, the highly creative vernacular dramas (into which musical pieces were inserted but which were delivered mainly through speech). Nonetheless, given the vast chronological spread of the surviving Latin sources (from the last quarter of the 10th century through to the early 15th century), as well as echoes of the Latin tradition in vernacular plays, it is possible to argue for greater familiarity in England with genres of Latin drama than the extant text sources actually demonstrate.

The earliest English sources of Latin liturgical drama are all associated with Winchester in the last quarter of the 10th century and the first half of the 11th. The *Regularis concordia*, a code of monastic law ("The Monastic Agreement of the Monks and Nuns of the English Nation") issued after the Council of Winchester (ca. 973) principally under the guidance of Bishop Æthelwold, includes the text of a *Visitatio sepulchri* to be performed after the third (i.e., last) responsory of Easter Matins. Fashioned around the famous *Quem queritis* ("Whom do you seek?") dialogue, this play is strongly marked by the attempt to identify both sung texts and actions with the relevant Gospel narratives; it is thus one of the earliest examples of the *Visitatio* that explicitly depends on a high degree of representational interest. Two additional features of the *Regularis concordia* drama are significant: first, it represents the earliest record of performance of the *Quem queritis* dialogue at Easter Matins (rather than before the mass Introit, or during the procession before mass). In this transferred position Easter plays were eventually to develop much larger proportions. Second, this Winchester version brings together elements of western and eastern Frankish text traditions, presumably through English contact with a variety of continental Benedictine establishments, in particular Fleury and Ghent.

Neither source of the *Regularis concordia* has musical notation, but this can be supplied from two closely linked sources of the same period, the so-called Winchester Tropers (Cambridge, Corpus Christi College 473, and Bodleian Library, Bodley 775). The Easter drama copied in these books adds one speech to the *Regularis concordia* version, effectively dividing the drama into two episodes. The first deals with the dialogue between women and an angel at the sepulcher and the women's announcement of Christ's resurrection to the community gathered to worship; the second deals with "proof," that is, an invitation from the angel to "come and see the place where he was laid," and the women's subsequent second announcement of the Resurrection. The music notated for these speeches is that normally associated with the trope and chant texts in other liturgical contexts; here, as in most Latin liturgical dramas, texts and music tend not to be newly composed.

The only other sources of Latin liturgical drama from medieval England both come from convents and thus indicate the involvement of women in dramatic performance within churches. A 15th-century ordinal (a collection of liturgical ceremonies) of Barking Abbey (Oxford, University College 169) includes an Easter *Visitatio sepulchri* composed by Katherine of Sutton, abbess of the nunnery from 1363 to 1376. Following a particularly impressive *Elevatio* ceremony (placed, unusually, between the end of Matins and the *Visitatio*), this Easter drama shows how an energetic but judicious spirit could fashion a dramatically effective and exciting play while avoiding the frivolity and misbehavior so often cited by clerics opposed to the performance of plays.

Both this and an Easter *Visitatio sepulchri* from the convent of St. Edith's, Wilton (now preserved only in the form of a 19th-century copy of a 14th-century original: Solesmes,

Abbaye-St.-Pierre 596), indicate strong links with forms of drama practiced in French Benedictine convents, especially Origny-Ste.-Benoîte. The Barking and Wilton plays place considerable emphasis on narrative aspects of the Easter story, especially the approach of the three Marys to the tomb and Mary Magdalene's encounter with Christ in the garden. This move away from the earlier highly concentrated and brief ritual dramas centered on *Quem queritis* to longer narrative structures involving a series of tableaux accords with the European trend.

Two further sources of an Easter *Visitatio* from Dublin (Bodl. Rawlinson D.4; Dublin, Marsh's Library Z.4.2.20) probably derive from English practice; both manuscripts (processionals of the late 14th and early 15th centuries) include liturgy of the Sarum type and are copied in the same manner as English liturgical books of the period.

Of other types of Easter or Christmas liturgical dramas only traces remain: the early-15th-century Shrewsbury fragments from Lichfield Cathedral (Shrewsbury, Shrewsbury School VI) demonstrate, through their quotation of specific Latin texts, direct knowledge in England of the *Officium pastorum* and *Officium peregrinorum* traditions. Both types were first created in Normandy in the late 11th century. References in documents from Lincoln Cathedral indicate the performance there of a Magi play. There is no way of knowing whether this was performed in Latin, as part of the liturgy; it does, however, show contact in England with one of the oldest text traditions of Latin liturgical drama.

Susan K. Rankin

Bibliography

Dolan, Diane. *Le drame liturgique de Pâques en Normandie et en Angleterre au Moyen-Age.* Paris: Presses Universitaires de France, 1975; Frere, Walter Howard. *The Winchester Troper: From Manuscripts of the Xth and XIth Centuries.* Henry Bradshaw Society 8. London: Harrison & Sons, 1894; Lancashire, Ian. *Dramatic Texts and Records of Britain: A Chronological Topography to 1558.* Cambridge: Cambridge University Press, 1984; Rankin, Susan K. "A New English Source of the *Visitatio sepulchri.*" *Journal of the Plainsong and Mediaeval Music Society* 4 (1981): 1–11; Rankin, Susan K. "Liturgical Drama." *The Early Middle Ages to 1300.* New Oxford History of Music 2, ed. Richard Crocker and David Hiley. 2d ed. Oxford: Oxford University Press, 1990, pp. 310–56; Symons, Thomas, ed. and trans. *Regularis concordia anglicae nationis monachorum sanctimonialiumque: The Monastic Agreement of the Monks and Nuns of the English Nation.* London: Nelson, 1953; Young, Karl. *The Drama of the Medieval Church.* 2 vols. Oxford: Clarendon, 1933.

See also Drama, Vernacular; Drama, Vernacular, Role of Music in; Holy Week and Easter, Music for; Nuns; *Regularis concordia*; *Regularis concordia* and the Arts; Winchester Tropers

Drama, Vernacular

Vernacular plays in medieval England fall into four principal categories: three forms of religious drama (biblical plays, morality plays, and saint's plays) and the folk drama. A few dramatic texts that do not fit into these categories also survive.

Vernacular religious drama took its impetus from the educational concerns expressed by the Fourth Lateran Council of 1215 and reiterated frequently over the succeeding centuries. The council sought to educate the laity in the basic stories and doctrines of the church so that they could participate fully in the sacraments. In this way the drama has a common genesis with other didactic literature and art of the period. Unlike the Latin mimetic embellishments of the liturgy that remained in the hands of the clergy the vernacular drama from its first appearance seems to have been performed for and largely by the laity. We have no information about the authors of this drama; the plays are the work of anonymous playwrights in every part of the country.

Biblical Plays (Cycle Plays, Mystery Plays)

The most common form of vernacular drama was episodes telling the stories of the Bible. Because the majority of these plays have survived in manuscripts containing collections of plays with the episodes arranged from Creation to Judgment, it has been common critical practice since the 19th century to refer to them as cycle plays and to treat the four major collections as variants of the same form. Since the work of Prosser and Kolve it has also been a critical commonplace to call these collections Corpus Christi cycles or plays and relate the themes of the drama to the Feast of Corpus Christi. Recent scholarship, however, has demonstrated the radical differences among the four surviving major collections and has determined that only one of the collections containing the whole sweep of salvation history, the York Plays, was regularly performed at Corpus Christi. Because these biblical plays were often performed by craft guilds, they are also called mystery plays, from the ME and Old French word *mistere,* "craft, trade."

The unique manuscript of the York Plays is in the British Library (BL Add. 35290). There is also one manuscript of a single craft copy. The complete manuscript is an official "register" copy compiled for the city council in the late 1460s or 1470s. There are 48 separate episodes in the manuscript, and it is possible that at one time there were 56. The plays were produced in a cooperative annual enterprise at Corpus Christi by the corporation of the city of York and the craft guilds of the city. The first possible mention of the play is a record of the rental for the storage of a pageant wagon (possibly one of the stages) in 1376. The final performance of the play was in 1569.

The plays were performed by a mixture of professional and amateur actors, all of whom auditioned annually for the city council. Because there was no large open space within the walls of the city over which the council had jurisdiction, the producers of this play devised an unusual method of performance, playing each episode in procession from wagons that stopped to perform at designated "stations" along a predetermined route. The normal number of "stations" was twelve, but there could be as many as sixteen places offered for rent by the council. The York Plays are an exciting series of episodes of great verbal complexity that have an internal unity of theme emphasizing the teaching ministry of Christ and exhorting the audience to live a good life in this world.

The plays from Chester are preserved in five complete manuscripts, two single episodes, and one fragment. The earliest complete manuscript is dated 1591, sixteen years after the last performance of the plays in 1575. Recently discovered evidence indicates that none of the surviving texts of the Chester plays represents with complete accuracy the text as it was being performed as late as 1572. The plays were first edited for the Shakespeare Society in the 19th century. In the course of their work for the new EETS edition Lumiansky and Mills came to some radical conclusions about the nature of the preserved manuscripts, arguing that they represent a "cycle of cycles" containing every possible variant of each episode rather than presenting the text of the plays as they were performed at any one time (1983: 86). The text contains 24 separate episodes.

Although there seems to have been a Passion play performed by the Chester clergy in the 15th century, the plays as we have them could not have been written before 1521. There is evidence for only seven performances of the Chester sequence between 1546 and 1575. They were produced as in York by the city council and performed by the craft guilds with a mixture of amateur and professional players. The sequence normally ran for three days at Whitsun (the Feast of Pentecost) and was performed in procession at four stations. Unlike the situation at York, where the guilds continued to control their texts, at Chester the city council controlled the text, determining each year the content of each segment. Each guild either owned or shared in an elaborate carriage. The Chester plays are written to emphasize the miracles of God and Christ and contain many striking visual effects, sometimes built into the carriages and sometimes achieved, as in the powerful passion sequence, by arranging the actors in the familiar postures of artistic renderings of the same scenes.

The Towneley Plays are preserved in manuscript HM 1 in the Huntington Library in San Marino, California. It was the first collection of early plays to be edited, appearing in a Surtees Society volume in 1836. The manuscript, dated after 1500 (Cawley and Stevens, 1976), contains 32 episodes. Because the name "Wakefield" appears on the first folio of the Creation play and because there are some possible local allusions within some of the plays, considerable work has been done seeking to associate this collection with the town of Wakefield in the West Riding of Yorkshire. However, modern scholarship has cast serious doubt on this association and the evidence adduced to support it. Thus, although many critics have come to call this collection the "Wakefield Cycle," it seems more accurate to call it "Towneley" after the family first known to have owned the manuscript.

It seems most likely that the Towneley collection is an anthology gathering together the plays being performed in the West Riding of Yorkshire and placing them in the order of

Creation to Judgment, perhaps, as Stevens has argued, as "something like a presentation copy of the play for the safekeeping of the lord of the manor or some other eminent person" (1987: 94). Some of the episodes are clearly written for wagon performances, but others demand a "place and skaffold" configuration, using raised platforms or "skaffolds" and the ground or "place" in between, as in the Offering of the Magi and Resurrection plays. There are many anomalies among the episodes that support the idea that it does not represent a sequence that was ever performed as a unit: for example, there are two Shepherds' plays but no play on the birth of Christ, and the series is riddled with inconsistencies of character, event, and theology from one episode to another. The manuscript contains at least five plays that were borrowed from York and then altered to fit their new situation. Some of the alteration was done by the playwright considered by critics to be the most outstanding writer in the genre, the so-called Wakefield Master. The Master also wrote six separate episodes on both Old and New Testament topics, including the two Shepherds' plays, the Prima and Secunda Pastorum. The theological message of the plays associated with the Master (as well as some others in the sequence) is overwhelmingly penitential, with a deep concern for the need to die in the faith. Of all the collections this one seems most embedded in the society of 15th-century England.

The manuscript that is preserved as BL Cotton Vespasian D.viii has had three titles. It was first mistaken for the plays from Coventry and so appears in most bibliographies as the *Ludus Coventriae*. Hardin Craig called the collection the Hegge (pronounced "hedge") Cycle, after the family that owned the manuscript. Most modern scholars now refer to the collection as the N-Town Plays because the banns that appear at the beginning of the manuscript announce that a play will be performed at "N-Town." The collection was first edited by John O. Halliwell for the Shakespeare Society in 1841. The manuscript is dated after 1468 and comes from East Anglia. Modern scholars are agreed that, like the Towneley collection, this is an anthology of pageants and plays based on biblical and apocryphal material including over twenty pageants; a five-episode play on the childhood of Mary; a two-part Passion play; and a play on the Assumption of the Virgin. Some of the plays demand staging on pageant wagons, others a single fixed stage, and still others a place-and-skaffold arrangement. The collection is remarkable for its emphasis on the Virgin Mary, not only in its two separate Mary plays but also in the prominent role given to Mary in the Passion play.

The biblical sequence in Cornish, called the *Cornish Ordinalia*, survives in one medieval manuscript (Bodleian Library, Bodley 791; late 14th century) and in two postmedieval copies (Bodley 28,556–57 and National Library of Wales Peniarth 428E). The sequence covers events from the Creation to the Ascension and is organized in a different manner from the English sequences, using the legend of the True Cross as a binding thread throughout the play. The play seems to have been performed from the late 14th century to the 16th. The action, which took place in a round playing space over a three-day period, is continuous.

Episodes from what were once longer sequences also survive. Two episodes, the Nativity sequence and the Presentation of Christ in the Temple, have come down to us from what was a ten-episode play performed by the city of Coventry and its craft guilds. A 16th-century manuscript version of the Weavers' Presentation pageant remains in Coventry, but the only version of the Shearmen and Taylors' Nativity pageant now extant is that published by Thomas Sharp in 1817. From the extensive documentary evidence that survives it is possible to reconstruct the performance history of the sequence, from the late 14th century until its last performance in 1579. The play was performed from wagons in procession at Corpus Christi, but it does not seem to have had an Old Testament sequence of plays, beginning instead with the birth of Christ. The later episodes featured such allegorical characters as the Worm of Conscience and the Mother of Death, indicating that the sequence contained allegorical or morality elements as well as biblical ones.

Another city whose sequence of plays has been lost is Newcastle-upon-Tyne. Only one play survives: Noah's Ark, found in an 18th-century printed edition. The records of the city show that the sequence contained at least 25 episodes, from Creation to the Death of the Virgin. The play was played in procession on Corpus Christi Day, but the pageants were carried rather than wheeled through the city. The surviving episode contains the unusual feature of the Devil counseling Noah's wife not to enter the ark.

The city of Norwich also had a play sequence of twelve episodes from Creation to Pentecost. It was played at Corpus Christi until the first quarter of the 16th century and then at Whitsun. The Creation and Fall of Man is the only surviving episode; it exists in two fragmentary versions, first printed in 1856. The manuscript has been lost. The pageant is remarkable for its theological foreshadowing of Pentecost, achieved by the Holy Ghost's appearance at the end of the play to console Adam and Eve.

Two complete Abraham and Isaac plays, a Candlemas play, a two-part Easter play, a Cornish Creation play, and several fragments of plays on other biblical topics have also been preserved. On the analogy of the plays from Coventry, Norwich, and Newcastle these have been traditionally thought to be scattered survivals of other longer sequences of plays. However, recent research into the external evidence for playmaking in England (*Records of Early English Drama*, 1979–) is demonstrating that many towns and parishes all over the country performed single-episode plays. The surviving single plays probably represent that tradition. One important manuscript, the "Shrewsbury Fragments," represents a single actor's part in three separate episodes of the Shepherds, the Resurrection, and the Journey to Emmaus. There is also external evidence of a complete biblical sequence performed in the Yorkshire town of Beverley, although no text survives that has been identified as part of that sequence. Chronicle evidence records a complete sequence performed over several days in London at Skinners' Well in the late 14th and early 15th centuries (Lancashire, 1984: 112–13). Several towns presented biblical as well as other scenes in tableaux (using effigies) or tableaux vivants (using human actors) in their religious and civic processions.

Morality Plays

The second major genre of religious drama is the morality play, in which a central figure is tempted by forces of evil and defended by forces of good. The antagonists are sometimes demonic figures and sometimes allegorical representations of psychological characteristics, such as Sloth or Humility. Few examples of the genre survive from before 1500, but it is assumed that many of the unspecified plays mentioned in the records, particularly plays performed by the many touring troupes, were morality plays. In the 16th century this genre was popular in such school plays as the *Wit and Science* group, whose central figure is a student seeking a good education. The genre was also used for political purposes in plays that give advice to rulers, such as Skelton's *Magnificence*. Both sides of the religious debates of the 16th century used the form for propaganda purposes.

Four complete "medieval" morality plays survive in English, three in 15th-century manuscript form and one from early-16th-century printed editions. Three of these plays *(Mankind, The Castle of Perseverance,* and *Wisdom)* are preserved in Folger Library V.a.354, a collection of three separate manuscripts bound together in the early 19th century. The dialect of each of these plays places it in East Anglia, but no exact location has ever been determined. They were all once owned by the Rev. Cox Macro and so have been edited for EETS as *The Macro Plays.* An incomplete version of *Wisdom* is also found in Bodl. Digby 133.

Mankind concerns the initial fall into sin and repentance of a mankind figure who is represented as a farmer. He is caught between the moral arguments of Mercy, a clerical figure, and the attractive antics of four vice figures, Mischief and his three henchmen, Nought, Newguise, and Nowadays, aided by the demonic figure of Titivillus. The play is presumed to have been played by a traveling company of six actors with the parts of Mercy and Titivillus doubled. It contains a blatant begging passage, in which the actors go among the audience demanding money before the appearance of the devil figure. The play was written for a booth stage setting (a single stage built of planks laid on trestles or barrels and hung with curtains) that could be placed either indoors or out. Despite the bucolic setting the language is dense and academic, at times heavily laced with latinate phrases for both serious and comic effect.

The Castle of Perseverance, a much more elaborate play than *Mankind,* demands an extensive set and a large cast and seems to represent an alternative form of town drama to the biblical sequences. A unique stage plan survives in the manuscript, providing us with details of the set and some costumes. The entire life story of its central figure, Humanum Genus, is told by the play. Humanum Genus is born into an allegorical world represented by a circle of "skaffolds" representing the World, the Flesh, the Devil, Covetousness, and Heaven. The circle is dominated by the Castle of Perseverance itself standing in the center. Schematically flanked by a Good and a Bad

Angel, Humanum Genus is tempted by the seven deadly sins or vices, falls, repents, and is taken into the Castle by the seven heavenly virtues. The Castle is then besieged by the forces of evil, and in an exciting battle sequence the virtues triumph. In his old age, however, Humanum Genus succumbs to the temptation of Covetousness and dies in sin, when his soul is carried to hell. The final sequence of the play is a debate among the Four Daughters of God (Mercy, Justice, Truth, Peace; cf. Ps. 85:10–11) about whether the soul should be saved. God finally agrees to the soul's salvation. The play is written mainly in thirteen-line stanzas that seem wordy when the play is read. In performance, however, the repetitive verse carries the theme of the play to an audience seated around a large playing area. The playwrights have clearly fashioned their verse for the performance situation.

Wisdom seems to have been written to be performed in a hall setting for an upper- or middle-class lay or possibly monastic audience. The central figures are Wisdom or Christ and Anima or the soul of man. Three further characters—Mind, Will, and Understanding—represent aspects of Anima who are tempted by the Devil and fall, causing Anima to appear "in the most horrybull wyse." Exhorted to repent by Wisdom, she does so, and her former state is restored. The play is full of music and courtly dancing demanding lavish costuming, much of which is specified in the stage directions. The moral lesson is strongly carried in many speeches that come close to being short sermons.

The fourth English morality play, *Everyman,* was first published by Richard Pynson ca. 1515. It is now generally agreed that it comes from a Dutch original called *Elckerlijc* and so constitutes the one textual connection between English drama and the important morality tradition of the Low Countries. The play covers only the death of the protagonist and begins with the summoning of Everyman by Death. Everyman then searches for help and comfort as he seeks his salvation. He first appeals unsuccessfully to his family, his friends, and his material goods. None helps him, and the midpoint of the play comes with Everyman facing death alone and despairing of salvation. Then, as his physical body disintegrates, Knowledge and Good Deeds lead him to the point of confession, after which he is shriven, dies, and is received into heaven by an angel. The play is written mainly in four-stress couplets, although the playwright varied the pattern frequently for effect. It has a spare dignity without the elaborate display or bawdy humor of the native English plays and appears to have been unusually popular, with four editions from ca. 1515 to ca. 1535.

Three morality fragments have been identified. A long one from the 15th century called *The Pride of Life,* like *Everyman,* is a play about the certainty of death. The central figure, however, is a king who, despite the warnings of his wife, challenges Death to a duel and inevitably loses. Several homilies are included in the fragment that survives. An East Anglian fragment called (from the single part that survives) *Dux Moraud* dramatizes a well-known medieval story of an incestuous daughter who kills her mother, her child, and eventually her father. In the dramatization the father renounces his sin before she murders him. The fragmentary nature of the text prevents us from knowing whether the play would have ended as its narrative analogues do, with the repentance and conversion of the daughter. The final morality fragments that survive are the extracts copied by Robert Reynes of Acle (Norfolk) into his commonplace book (Bodl. Tanner 407). One is a speech of a character named Delight and the other an epilogue. These fragments are published by Davis (*Non-Cycle Plays and Fragments*).

Saint's Plays

The third genre of religious plays in the vernacular is the saint's play. Records indicate that plays based on the lives of saints were popular in England in the period. These were usually plays about the lives of the patron saints of parishes or guilds, although several on the life of Thomas Becket are recorded. Only three saint's plays survive—two English and one Cornish. *The Conversion of Paul* and *Mary Magdalene* are preserved in Bodl. Digby 133. Both are from East Anglia and are associated with Miles Blomefylde, a physician, alchemist, and book collector. Both demand elaborate and complex staging. It is possible that they also represent alternative choices for playmaking by the prosperous wool towns of the area in the 15th century.

The Conversion of Paul is based on the Acts of the Apostles and tells the story of Paul with several lively interpolations of comic devils and some spectacular stage effects. It was performed at three stations, and, unlike the practice of the English biblical plays, the audience moved from station to station in a manner similar to some continental civic plays.

The long and complex *Mary Magdalene* combines scenes based on New Testament incidents, such as the anointing of Christ's feet by Mary, the raising of Lazarus, and Christ's appearance to Mary after the Resurrection, along with apocryphal episodes from the earlier and later life of the saint. As is customary in medieval legend, Mary Magdalene is identified with Mary the sister of Martha and Lazarus. The play is in two parts. The first part has a morality structure, as Mary falls to the seduction of the World, the Flesh, and the Devil, repents, and is forgiven by Christ. It ends with the raising of Lazarus. Much of the second part is concerned with the conversion of the king of Marseilles and the death and "resurrection" of his wife in a motif considered by many to have inspired the "rebirth" of Hermione in Shakespeare's *Winter's Tale*. The play demands a large set arranged, like the N-Town Passion play, in a place-and-skaffold configuration.

The Cornish saint's play *Meriasek* dates from the early 16th century and is preserved in the Hengwrt manuscript in Peniarth. There is a circular diagram at the end of the manuscript that is presumed to indicate the mode of staging. The play does not involve the conversion of its central figure Mereadocus, bishop and confessor, but rather his healing of the sick. It also involves some spectacular stage business, including the slaying of a fiery dragon large enough to have "swallowed" several soldiers.

Only one surviving fragment of a play text has been positively identified as being from a saint's play. This is a prologue from a play on the life of Theophilus that is preserved in the library of the Dean and Chapter of Durham Cathedral.

Other Religious Drama

The one surviving text of religious drama that does not fall into the categories discussed above is the *Play of the Sacrament* (ca. 1500). The manuscript is in Trinity College, Dublin (MS 652, Art. 6), although the play is of East Anglian origin. It is identified with a village called Croxton; of the three possible Croxtons in East Anglia scholars generally favor the village near Thetford, Norfolk, close to the pilgrim route to the shrine of the Virgin in Walsingham. The play's theme, the real presence of Christ in the eucharist, makes it suitable for the Feast of Corpus Christi. The central action of the play concerns a disbelieving Jewish merchant, who, with his friends, mocks and tortures the sacrament. They are punished and then converted by the end of the play. The play contains several staging challenges, including causing the wafer of the Host to bleed and splitting apart an oven to reveal the "image" of the bleeding Christ.

There are two genres of plays for which we have records of performance but no extant texts. These are plays based on the Creed and the Lord's Prayer. The Guild of Corpus Christi in York and subsequently the city council produced a play based on the twelve articles of the Creed. The text was willed to the guild in 1446 by William Revetour. After 1495 it was substituted for the biblical sequence every ten years. The surviving records have been analyzed in an attempt to reconstruct the content of the play (Johnston, 1975). It was suppressed in 1568. The Corpus Christi play at Coventry (see above) was referred to as a "Creed Play" in 1526.

There are records of plays based on the Pater Noster at York, Lincoln, and Beverley. Early views considered that these were in some way morality plays, but more recent scholarship has suggested that they were more straightforward expositions of the articles of the prayer.

Folk Drama

Folk drama by its very ephemeral nature has until recently been hard to discuss except in terms of anthropological theory and modern revivals. However, the work being done by the Records of Early English Drama project is now documenting widespread instances of folk activities. The records are found largely in parish documents and the records of the 16th- and 17th-century ecclesiastical courts. Whatever their origins, such activities as maypoles, morris dancing, lords and ladies of the summer festivals, hocking (a courting or combat ritual), and Robin Hood plays were common, particularly in the south and west. These communal activities, most often associated with parish fundraising, took place at various times during the spring and summer. The most common date in the south was at Whitsun, in the context of a parish or church ale (a fundraising social gathering). Several towns and cities, such as York, had St. George Ridings. Mumming is less well documented. Revivals in the 18th century have as key elements in the "mumming play" the presence of St. George representing England and a death-and-resurrection sequence of varying seriousness. It is assumed that these and other local activities, such as "pace egging" (an Easter ritual), in some way represent earlier customs. Only one contemporary text for a folk drama survives from the period, *Robin Hood and the Friar*. This was appended to William Copland's *Gest of Robin Hood*, ca. 1560. The slight text is the occasion for a fight with longstaffs between Robin Hood's men and those of the Friar, amorous byplay involving Maid Marian, and a lively morris dance.

Alexandra F. Johnston

Bibliography

GENERAL

New *CBEL* 1:719–42, 1403; *Manual* 5:1315–84, 1557–1629. Important documents pertaining to medieval English drama will be found in the publications of the Records of Early English Drama (REED) project (Toronto: University of Toronto Press, 1979–) and in the *Records of Plays and Players* published by the Malone Society (London, 1907/08–). Both series are organized geographically. Facsimile editions of many medieval dramatic texts are available in the Medieval Drama Facsimile Series published by *Leeds Texts and Monographs* (Leeds, 1973–) and the Folger Facsimile Series published by the Folger Library (Washington, D.C., 1972–). Beadle, Richard, ed. *The Cambridge Companion to Medieval English Theatre*. Cambridge: Cambridge University Press, 1994; Bevington, David. *From Mankind to Marlowe*. Cambridge: Harvard University Press, 1962; Cawley, A.C., et al. *The Revels History of Drama in English*. Vol. 1: *Medieval Drama*. London: Methuen, 1983; Enders, Jody. *Rhetoric and the Origins of Medieval Drama*. Ithaca: Cornell University Press, 1992; Hardison, O.B. *Christian Rite and Christian Drama in the Middle Ages*. Baltimore: Johns Hopkins Press, 1965; Kahrl, Stanley J. *Traditions of Medieval English Drama*. London: Hutchinson, 1974; Kolve, V.A. *The Play Called Corpus Christi*. Stanford: Stanford University Press, 1966; Lancashire, Ian. *Dramatic Texts and Records of Britain: A Chronological Topography to 1558*. Toronto: University of Toronto Press; Cambridge: Cambridge University Press, 1984; Wickham, Glynne. *Early English Stages, 1300–1660*. 3 vols. London: Routledge & Kegan Paul, 1959–81.

BIBLICAL PLAYS (EDITIONS)

Beadle, Richard, ed. *The York Plays*. London: Arnold, 1982; Cawley, A.C., and Martin Stevens, eds. *The Towneley Cycle: A Facsimile of Huntington MS HM 1*. Leeds: University of Leeds School of English, 1976; Craig, Hardin, ed. *Two Coventry Corpus Christi Plays*. EETS e.s. 87. 2d ed. London: Oxford University Press, 1957; England, George, and Alfred W. Pollard, eds. *The Towneley Plays*. EETS e.s. 71. London: Humphrey Milford, 1897; Harris, Markham, trans. *The Cornish Ordinalia: A Medieval Dramatic Trilogy*. Washington, D.C.: Catholic University of America Press, 1969;

Lumiansky, Robert M., and David Mills, eds. *The Chester Mystery Cycle*. 2 vols. EETS s.s. 3, 9. London: Oxford University Press, 1974–86; Neuss, Paula, ed. and trans. *The Creacion of the World: A Critical Edition and Translation*. New York: Garland, 1983; Purvis, John S., trans. *The York Cycle of Mystery Plays*. London: SPCK, 1957; Rose, Martial, trans. *The Wakefield Mystery Plays*. Garden City: Doubleday, 1961; Spector, Stephen, ed. *The N-Town Play*. 2 vols. EETS s.s. 11–12. Oxford: Oxford University Press, 1991.

BIBLICAL PLAYS (STUDIES)

Davidson, Clifford. *From Creation to Doom: The York Cycle of Mystery Plays*. New York: AMS, 1984; Palmer, Barbara. "'Towneley Plays' or 'Wakefield Cycle' Revisited." *Comparative Drama* 22 (1988): 218–48; Stevens, Martin. *Four Middle English Mystery Cycles: Textual, Contextual, and Critical Interpretations*. Princeton: Princeton University Press, 1987; Woolf, Rosemary. *The English Mystery Plays*. London: Routledge & Kegan Paul, 1972.

MORALITY PLAYS

Cawley, A.C., ed. *Everyman*. Manchester: Manchester University Press, 1961; Eccles, Mark, ed. *The Macro Plays*. EETS o.s. 262. London: Oxford University Press, 1969.

SAINT'S PLAYS

Furnivall, Frederick J., ed. *The Digby Plays*. EETS e.s. 70. London: Kegan Paul, Trench, Trübner, 1896; Stokes, Whitley, ed. and trans. *The Life of St. Meriasek, Bishop and Confessor: A Cornish Drama*. London: Trübner, 1872.

FOLK DRAMA AND MISCELLANEOUS

Davis, Norman, ed. *Non-Cycle Plays and Fragments*. EETS s.s. 1. London: Oxford University Press, 1970; Greg, Walter W., ed. "Robin Hood." In Malone Society Collections 2:125–36. Oxford: Malone Society, 1908; Johnston, Alexandra F. "The Plays of the Religious Guilds of York: The *Creed Play* and the *Pater Noster Play*." *Speculum* 50 (1975): 55–90.

See also Allegory; Ballads; Bible in ME Literature; Drama, Latin Liturgical; Drama, Vernacular, Role of Music in; Hagiography; Holy Week and Easter, Music for; Moral and Religious Instruction; Popular Culture; Skelton

Drama, Vernacular, Role of Music in

The 12th-century Anglo-Norman *Ordo representacionis Ade (Play of Adam)* and *La seinte Resureccion (The Holy Resurrection)* apparently represent a flourishing tradition of vernacular drama in England, including a sophisticated structural use of liturgical music. For the next two and a half centuries there survive only a handful of dramatic fragments in English and French, which tell us nothing about their use of music.

From the 15th century, however, a substantial body of

biblical plays, saint plays, and moralities survives, representing a tradition that continued well into the 16th century. A biblical cycle, a separate biblical play, and a saint's play, all in Cornish, form a related strand of insular vernacular drama.

Stage directions and dialogue show that music played an important part in this drama, while civic accounts give information on the singers and minstrels who performed. The most important single use of music was to represent heaven: angels singing appropriate liturgical texts or playing *bas* (soft) instruments symbolize divine order, so that music often occurs when God intervenes in human affairs. Mortals who do God's will, such as the Virgin Mary, Simeon, and the shepherds, sing too, in overt or implied imitation of the angels. While the angels were probably sometimes accompanied by soft instruments (harps—*cithare*—are specified in the N-Town Cycle), the mortals almost certainly sang unaccompanied.

Bad characters are also identified through music. Herod's worldly pretensions are shown by the loud music of his minstrels; Mak, the sheep stealer in the Second Shepherds' Play of the Towneley Cycle, demonstrates his out-of-tuneness with God's will by singing out of tune; and Mrs. Noah's friends in the Chester play of the Flood sing a rowdy drinking song.

The forces of evil reverse heavenly musicality in a number of ways, but the actual text sung is always of prime importance. On two occasions the audience is taught a song, rather as is done in pantomimes. In the Chester Shepherds Play the most musical character, Trowle, teaches them a "merry song" (specified as "Trolly lolly lolly lo" in one manuscript) that was no doubt innocent enough: but when the vices in the morality *Mankind* do the same, an apparently innocent first line gives way to a highly indecent text to which the onlookers are committed unawares in advance, presumably to their consternation.

Music has a second set of functions, related to the dynamics of the drama. Music is often heard at the beginning or end of a play, at the entrance or exit of a character, during movement about the acting area or while time passes. While the use of these dynamic functions is not yet entirely clear, it seems certain that many of the dramatists wrote their plays with music in mind as a structural device.

Music actually notated in the play texts is rare: a single part for nine polyphonic items is in the Shrewsbury plays, the manuscript (ca. 1430) being the sole survivor of a set of three part books; two settings of each of three texts, all in two parts, are in the York Cycle manuscript (written between 1463 and 1477); the Coventry plays include the famous Lullaby and a song for the shepherds, both in three parts and probably dating from the 1530s; and the latest manuscript of the Chester Cycle (1607) has a single-line incipit for a polyphonic setting of the angels' *Gloria in excelsis,* probably dating from the middle of the 16th century. None of these pieces has a concordance, so that those in the Shrewsbury and Chester plays cannot be reconstructed: but the Coventry pieces are justly famous, while the lesser-known York music has been an important element in modern revivals of the spectacular York *Assumption of the Virgin.*

Richard Rastall

Bibliography

Dutka, JoAnna. *Music in the English Mystery Plays.* Early Drama, Art, and Music Reference Series 2. Kalamazoo: Medieval Institute, 1980; Rastall, Richard. "Music in the Cycle." In R.M. Lumiansky and David Mills, ed. *The Chester Mystery Cycle: Essays and Documents.* Chapel Hill: University of North Carolina Press, 1983, pp. 111–64; Rastall, Richard. "Vocal Range and Tessitura in Music from York Play 45." *Musical Analysis* 3 (1984): 181–99; Rastall, Richard. "Music in the Cycle Plays." In *Contexts for Early English Drama,* ed. Marianne G. Briscoe and John C. Coldewey. Bloomington: Indiana University Press, 1989, pp. 192–218; Rastall, Richard. *The Heaven Singing: Music in Early English Religious Drama.* Woodbridge: Boydell & Brewer, 1996; Stevens, John. "Medieval Drama." *NGD* 12:21–58.

See also Drama, Latin Liturgical; Drama, Vernacular; Holy Week and Easter, Music for; Musical Instruments

Dream of the Rood, The

In this 156-line, OE dream vision, after a brief introduction, the Rood (the Cross of the Crucifixion) addresses the dreamer, teaching him the significance and mystery of the Cross, Christianity's most important symbol; then the Cross instructs the dreamer to teach others what he has learned; finally the dreamer tells what the experience has meant to him. The poem survives in the Vercelli Book; interestingly fragments of the poem or of an earlier version of the poem—parts of the Cross's speech—are incised in runes on the late-7th- or early-8th-century Ruthwell Cross in Dumfriesshire, Scotland (figs. 111–14: see RUTHWELL CROSS). The Vercelli Book was compiled much later, probably in the late 10th century, but the texts are so similar that they must be closely related to one another, though the exact relationship is not clear. *The Dream of the Rood* itself may date from early in the 8th century.

Theologically the poem manages to stay within orthodox bounds during a time when the cult of the Cross was increasingly popular and several heresies were prevalent. One extreme, the Monophysite or Eutychan position, held that physical agony was impossible for Christ because he was an embodiment of the divine Word, the Logos. Another extreme, the Nestorian or Severan position, argued that the infirmities of Christ's body extended to his soul because he was human. These and other views concerning the corporeality of Christ contested with one another from at least the 5th century to the 6th, with the polemic continuing into the 8th century, despite the doctrine of redemption by incarnation specifying that Christ's divinity and humanity coexist in perfect balance. *The Dream of the Rood* is doctrinally successful in portraying the balance of Christ's divinity and humanity and is at the same time artistically successful in dramatic interaction.

The poem is shocking in a number of ways. When it first appears to the dreamer, the Cross is arrayed in glory, gilded, and gem-adorned but then rapidly alternates between being adorned with the sweat and blood of Christ's suffering and with the jewels signifying his triumph. The next shock comes when the Cross actually speaks to the dreamer; it identifies itself in a form reminiscent of Anglo-Saxon riddles, then narrates the events of the Crucifixion depicting Christ as an Anglo-Saxon hero. According to the Cross Christ bravely mounted and embraced it, forbidding it to bow down to assist its Lord or to attack its Lord's enemies.

Another striking quality of the poem is its parallel relationships that contribute to the didactic purpose. Both Christ and the Cross suffer during the Crucifixion—the Cross specifies that the nails wounded both Christ and itself and that they were both mocked in their suffering. However, the Cross is also like the dreamer who contemplates it; both see and experience Christ's agony without being able to do anything to help their Lord. At the end of the poem the Cross enjoins the dreamer to go out and teach others what he has learned from the dream vision, so the dreamer is invited to be a teacher like the Cross. Finally the reader can see that he is like the dreamer and can therefore become like the Cross, and by extension like Christ. The diction and imagery of the end of the poem contribute to this final parallel for the Anglo-Saxon reader, since Christ in majesty after the Resurrection is described in language like that of a secular lord surrounded by his thegns. The dreamer, who refers to himself as alone in this world, looks forward to sharing in the joy of the saints who surround their Lord and celebrate the victory that the Cross has so vividly described earlier in the poem.

Phyllis R. Brown

Bibliography

PRIMARY

ASPR 2:61–65; Kennedy, Charles W., trans. *An Anthology of Old English Poetry.* New York: Oxford University Press, 1960, pp. 144–48; Swanton, Michael, ed. *The Dream of the Rood.* New York: Barnes & Noble, 1970.

SECONDARY

Fleming, John. "*The Dream of the Rood* and Anglo-Saxon Monasticism." *Traditio* 22 (1966): 43–72; Irving, Edward B., Jr. "Crucifixion Witnessed, or Dramatic Interaction in *The Dream of the Rood.*" In *Modes of Interpretation in Old English Literature: Essays in Honour of Stanley B. Greenfield,* ed. Phyllis Rugg Brown, Georgia Ronan Crampton, and Fred C. Robinson. Toronto: University of Toronto Press, 1986 pp. 101–13; Woolf, Rosemary. "Doctrinal Influences on *The Dream of the Rood.*" *MÆ* 27 (1958): 137–53.

See also Allegory; Bible in OE Literature; Dream Vision; Ruthwell Cross; Vercelli Book

Dream Vision

A modern term for a shifting complex of generic features and modes gradually assembled from many disparate sources over the medieval period. It has a crucial bearing on the Christian assimilation of pagan literary texts and on the very emergence of vernacular literatures; and in the late 14th century Chaucer invents his own tradition as an English poet by sophisticated and eclectic recourse to it.

The oldest elements in the development of dream vision are mostly religious: biblical, with reference to dreams in the Old Testament (Isaiah, Daniel, Ezekiel, Numbers, and others) and, of paramount importance, the New Testament (Revelation); apocryphal as in the influential 3rd-century *Apocalypse of St. Paul;* and works in imitation of the apocalyptic mode, such as the 9th-century *Vision of Bernold,* written by Archbishop Hincmar of Reims—the subject of which is an eschatological vision of heaven and hell. In the 8th-century *Ecclesiastical History* Bede gives another such vision, that of the monk Dryhthelm.

"Vision" here is the appropriate term: no doubt is permitted concerning the truth of such dreams, and the religious mysteries they unfold are a visualization of theological concepts. Being modeled on the strong witnesses of apocalyptic works, their poet-dreamers are assigned an active role that invites critical exploration of voice. In the earliest dream vision in English, for instance, the 8th-century *Dream of the Rood,* iconography is dramatized as the Cross orders the dreamer to reveal his vision to humanity, and the dreamer speaks both as an individual who has lost his friends and as general human icon of yearning for the next world.

Already at this pre-Conquest stage the Christian dream vision has developed into a dialogue between unequals: the Cross teaches the poet-dreamer, and the element of didacticism is strong in the genre. Models were found outside formal dreams, in the *Soliloquies* of St. Augustine and particularly in the *Consolation of Philosophy* by Boethius—a text that remains vitally influential throughout the "Age of Dream Vision" (Lynch, 1988: 1), lasting from the 12th century beyond the 14th. Classical models of travel to the otherworld are also formative, especially book 6 of Virgil's *Aeneid* (itself inspired by book 10 of the *Odyssey*). Travel—to salvation or knowledge and expressed in terms of quest or pilgrimage—is therefore closely related in theme to the dream vision. This applies even in the formal absence of a dream, as demonstrated by Dante's *Divine Comedy,* in which Virgil himself is made Dante's guide and Boethian interlocutor through hell and purgatory, and a Philosophy-like Beatrice is his guide through heaven.

Another classical source, the Dream of Scipio, embedded in Cicero's *De republica,* grows in importance during the later period. Travel to the heavens leads to the bird's-eye view that induces notions both of religious salvation and of secular (often poetic) fame, and the commentary by Macrobius on this text provides the Middle Ages with a comprehensive typology of dream experiences ranging from the prophetic and oracular to the nightmarish and false. As later medieval poets investigate the ambiguities of dreams, they also bring to bear a new interest in the psychology of dreamers, dating from the 12th-century *Liber de anima* of Avicenna.

Whereas the truth value of dream visions is hardly in doubt in 12th-century Latin poetry, such as Alan of Lille's *De planctu naturae,* it becomes an issue in the vernacular dream poetry of the next century. It is 13th-century France that sees the composition of the most potent and popular medieval vernacular dream poem, the *Roman de la Rose,* begun as a courtly psychomachia by Guillaume de Lorris and extended into a kind of encyclopedic Boethian satire by Jean de Meun. Chaucer translated some or all of this poem into English. After the *Roman* dream vision is the genre of genres—of highest status and containing everything; but the term "dream vision" begins to read like an oxymoron, for the claims of vision to tell the truth are juxtaposed with the uncertainty of an ordinary dream.

The nature and possible truthfulness of dreams are an important topic for Chaucer, discussed in book 5 of *Troilus* and in the *Nun's Priest's Tale* as well as in his four dream poems. The opening of *The House of Fame,* like that of the *Roman de la Rose,* invokes Macrobius's dream categories but characteristically declines to arbitrate on their authority, drawing attention instead to the poet's rhetoric. Authority in general—poetic, philosophical, and perhaps political—is problematized in these poems, as the English writer confronts classical authors (Virgil and Ovid in *The House of Fame,* Ovid in *The Book of the Duchess,* the Dream of Scipio itself in *The Parliament of Fowls*) and attempts to construct from and in spite of them his own kind of vernacular literary tradition.

The attempt is heavily influenced by European models, Italian and particularly French. Not only does Chaucer employ a version of the highly characterized poet-dreamer-narrator persona derived from the *Roman;* he also uses recognized European subgenres such as the bird debate. In the earliest of all his dream poems, *The Book of the Duchess,* he brings into play a 14th-century French genre whose invention is ascribed to its greatest practitioner, Machaut: the courtly *dits amoureux.*

Most of the *dits amoureux* known to Chaucer, by Machaut, Froissart, Grandson, and Deschamps, do not take the form of a dream, though their poets also wrote dream poems; Chaucer, in contrast, always combines the two. The French poems focus on the position of their poets, writing for a courtly audience and in a context of courtly social practice. For Chaucer, closely connected to the English court but not quite of it, this is a valuable mine of ambivalence, worked to the full in the Prologue to *The Legend of Good Women.*

In late-14th-century English writing there are other equally major uses of dream vision that achieve different effects in a less secular vein: the rhymed alliterative poem *Pearl* presents a vision of the New Jerusalem to the eyes of a dreamer who is represented not as any kind of poet but as the father of his dream guide, the dead Pearl-maiden. In the unrhymed alliterative poem *Winner and Waster* the dream facilitates political and social commentary, and in *The Parliament of the Three Ages* the courtly and secular are pulled into the perspective of apocalypse.

Piers Plowman is the greatest of all English works seeking to come to terms with the implications of dream vision for political and social commentary, literary creation, and religious truth. The work is a sequence of one dream after another, deadlock succeeding deadlock, and the tensions of Langland's long-drawn and compendious poem are palpable. The concerns and discursive milieu are far removed from Chaucer's, but the indeterminacy of authority is a shared anxiety that for Langland includes the moral and theological.

There are also less problematic uses of dream settings, in which the dream is a variant of the *chanson d'aventure*—a way of getting a poem started—or where the authority of dream is sought for simple political propaganda, as in Adam Davy's *Five Dreams about Edward II.*

Anglo-Norman writing offers several versions of visits to the otherworld (Legge, 1963: 274) and love allegories indebted to the *Roman de la Rose;* the most elaborate of the latter is *The Dream of the Castle of Love* (Legge, 1963: 337). Late in the period Anglo-Latin provides a return to full-throated prophetic vision in Gower's *Vox Clamantis.* Gower's major English vernacular poem, by contrast, the *Confessio Amantis,* is not formally a dream at all, though—like Dante's *Divine Comedy* or even Chaucer's *Canterbury Tales*—it owes an inestimable debt to the structures and conventions of dream vision and to the *Roman de la Rose* in particular.

However, it is Chaucer's witty and erudite combination of classical traditions, European literary precedent, and courtly discourse that dictates the course of English and Scots dream poetry through the 15th century into the 16th. Some of the best examples are Scots: several by Dunbar; Henryson's Prologue to his seventh *Fable,* an interview with Aesop; Douglas's Prologue to book 13 of his *Eneados,* an interview with Mapheus Vegius (author of the source for that book, a continuation of Virgil's *Aeneid*), and his *Palice of Honour,* no less than an ambitious effort to complete the unfinished *House of Fame* by way of Boethius, Scipio's Dream, and *Troilus,* concluding with a plea for the poet's preferment.

In England the Lydgatean view of Chaucer as master rhetorician leads to such rhetorical constructs as *The Temple of Glass* or to poems like William Neville's *The Castle of Pleasure,* which allies a response to Ovid's *Metamorphoses* with an art of love and a complete educational curriculum. Even more ambitious is Stephen Hawes's *The Pastime of Pleasure,* which contains such elements and more, culminating in the narrator's account of his own death and burial—in order that Hawes might end a veritable encyclopedia of dream vision with an account of heaven and hell and his coronation by Fame.

More Chaucerian in tone are two poems by Skelton: *The Bowge of Court,* with its nightmarish court peopled by conspiratorial abstractions, and *The Garland of Laurel,* in which the dream poem finally abandons modesty and turns into a wildly admiring vision of its own poet. Even as educational, theological, and social change are about to sideline dream vision, the vernacular dreamer at last reclaims the role of seer.

David A. Lawton

Bibliography

Edwards, Robert R. *The Dream of Chaucer: Representation and Reflection in the Early Narratives.* Durham: Duke University Press, 1989; Lawton, David A. *Chaucer's Narrators.* Cambridge: Brewer, 1985; Legge, Mary Dominica. *Anglo-Norman Literature and Its Background.* Oxford: Clarendon, 1963; Lynch, Kathryn L. *The High Medieval Dream Vision: Poetry, Philosophy, and Literary Form.* Stanford: Stanford University Press,

1988; Spearing, A.C. *Medieval Dream Poetry.* Cambridge: Cambridge University Press, 1976; Wenzel, Siegfried. "The Pilgrimage of Life as a Late Medieval Genre." *MS* 35 (1973): 370–88; Windeatt, Barry A., ed. and trans. *Chaucer's Dream Poetry: Sources and Analogues.* Cambridge: Brewer, 1982.

See also Boethius; Chaucer; *Dream of the Rood;* Gower; Literary Influences: French, Medieval Latin; *Pearl*-Poet; *Piers Plowman;* Religious Allegories

Dukes and Dukedoms

In most of the kingdoms that emerged from the ruins of the western Roman Empire the Latin word *dux* ("leader") survived as the title of an important royal officer, at first military but soon omnicompetent, governing a district comparable to one or two Roman provinces. In England *dux* was used between ca. 950 and 1066 as one of several equivalents of the English titles *ealdorman* and *eorl:* a royal officer who governed a district analogous to a province. However, there was no vernacular derivative of *dux* until after the Norman Conquest, and between 1066 and 1337 it was applied only to the rulers of continental duchies.

In 1337 Edward III erected the lands, or *honor,* of the earldom of Cornwall into a duchy for his eldest son, Edward the Black Prince, already earl of Chester. This dukedom was entailed to descend automatically to the eldest sons of the king's successors, as it has to this day. Edward's elevation of his son to the still higher dignity of Prince of Wales (1343) cleared the way for the creation of a second duchy, and in 1351 Edward made his cousin Henry of Grosmont duke of Lancaster.

In both cases the ducal estate was scattered across several counties, quite distinct from the county named in the title. In 1362 Edward bestowed the then-vacant duchy of Lancaster on his son John of Gaunt, who had married Henry's heiress, and Edward simultaneously created a third ducal dignity, Clarence, for his son Lionel. In this case, and in all subsequent ones in England, the ducal dignity was not attached to a specific baronial estate; it was a dignity without any specific territorial jurisdiction, conveying high rank and honorific privilege but no guaranteed income or landed estate.

No further dukedoms were created until 1385, when Richard II made his father's two youngest brothers the dukes of York and Gloucester. In 1386 he created a sixth dukedom (of Ireland), for his favorite Robert de Vere, earl of Oxford, whom in 1385 he had made marquess of Dublin—the first dignity of that rank in his domain. This was the first duke not a member of the royal house. In 1397 (after Vere had been stripped of his new dignity) Richard conferred five new dukedoms: those of Hereford, Aumale, Surrey, Exeter, and Norfolk (the last three being given to men not of the royal house).

Henry IV and Henry V kept the title within the ranks of royal blood, and on the latter's death in 1422 there were six dukes. Henry VI (through his uncle, the regent Gloucester) revived the dukedom of Norfolk for John Mowbray but made no further dukes until 1443. The Exeter dukedom was then revived, and new ones of Somerset, Buckingham, Warwick, and Suffolk were created. No new dukedoms would be created until 1525. Forfeitures and death without male heirs kept the number low, and when Edward IV (duke of York) came to the throne in 1461, there were only three. He created eight more, but thereafter there were never more than eight dukes at any single time.

Altogether the sixteen dukedoms bestowed before the death of Henry VIII (1547) were held by some 51 men, of whom 26 were of the Plantagenet royal family, eight of the Tudors. Most dukedoms were conferred with an entailment to heirs male of the body of the grantee, though some of the earliest were for life only. Even when formally heritable, ducal status was always precarious; of the sixteen dukedoms created only six (Cornwall, Lancaster, York, Buckingham, Norfolk, and Suffolk) passed even once before 1547 to the immediate heir of the original grantee; none passed to more than two heirs in unbroken succession.

Dukes were elevated by a charter or letters patent and invested, at first through the simple girding of a sword (as were earls), but from 1362 with the addition of a cap of estate and coronet comparable to that first used to create a prince in 1343.

D'Arcy J.D. Boulton

Bibliography

Cokayne, George E. *The Complete Peerage.* Ed. Vicary Gibbs et al. 13 vols. London: St. Catherine Press, 1910–59; Fryde, E.B., et al., eds. *Handbook of British Chronology.* 3d ed. London: Royal Historical Society, 1986; Powell, J. Enoch, and Keith Wallis. *The House of Lords in the Middle Ages: A History of the English House of Lords to 1540.* London: Weidenfeld & Nicolson, 1968.

See also Earls; Monarchy and Kingship; Peerage

Dunbar, William (ca. 1460–ca. 1513)

The most brilliant of the late-medieval Scottish poets. Dunbar graduated from St. Andrews University in 1479. For the next twenty years biographical evidence is lacking, but he may have been abroad; in 1500–01 he was in England. The most fully documented period in Dunbar's life is from 1500 to 1513; he then received a generous "pensioun," or annual salary, as a "servitour" in the household of James IV. Yet the details of Dunbar's court career remain mysterious. This is one reason why it is difficult to establish the chronology of the 80 or so poems attributed to him. Although a chaplain, Dunbar never obtained high office in the church. Several poems voice hopes for a benefice, yet there is no evidence that he obtained even the humble "kirk scant coverit with hadder [heather]" mentioned in one of them. It is likely that Dunbar had some role in the royal secretariat, perhaps as a scribe or envoy. He is last mentioned on 14 May 1513, but there is a gap in the records following the Battle of Flodden (September 1513), in which James IV died; Dunbar possibly survived into James V's reign, but there is no evidence that he did so.

The court provided Dunbar not only with a livelihood but also with his primary audience and much of his subject matter. Many of his poems are located "heir at hame" in Scotland; he writes of actual people, sometimes explicitly, sometimes obliquely, through the medium of dream, fable, and fantasy. He celebrates some of the great festive occasions in James IV's reign—*The Thrissill and the Rois* treats of the king's marriage to Margaret Tudor in 1503, and another poem describes the queen's visit to Aberdeen in 1511. He employs two favorite courtly modes, eulogy and elegy: greeting the distinguished knight Bernard Stewart in one piece and lamenting his death in another. But Dunbar also writes, more informally, about trivial events—what he sees, in his own words, "Daylie in court befoir myn e [eye]." He devises comic squibs about fellow servitors, including fools and alchemists. Many poems were written, in the first instance, for a small group of people—king, queen, and courtiers, several of whom were, like Dunbar, both "clerkis" and poets. These poems are playful and recreative, intimate in tone and often colloquial.

Scholars have sought, with little success, to establish Dunbar's indebtedness to earlier writers. It is often easier to indicate the genres to which his poems belong than to pinpoint sources. Yet "Timor Mortis Conturbat Me" reveals keen interest in other Scottish poets, from the 14th century to his own time; and he was also familiar with alliterative works, such as Richard Holland's *Buke of the Howlat*. Dunbar seems aware of the Gaelic literary tradition but humorously dissociates himself from it in *The Flyting of Dunbar and Kennedy*. Ignoring the political boundaries between England and Scotland, Dunbar embraces their shared language and poetic traditions. At the close of *The Goldyn Targe* he speaks of "oure Inglisch," and pays homage to the high style of poetry associated with Chaucer and Lydgate; he himself writes in this tradition effectively.

Yet Dunbar was also familiar with less sophisticated literary forms—drinking songs, bawdy love poems, and the ballads he mentions in "Schir Thomas Norny." Casual, throwaway remarks in this and other poems provide our chief clues both to Dunbar's literary tastes and his view of himself as a poet. He calls himself a "makar" and his poetry "making." Such terms lay stress on the poet as craftsman and the poem as artifact; most critics see Dunbar in this light, praising him less for the originality of his ideas than for his verbal "energy" and metrical virtuosity.

Dunbar's finest poems almost all contain some strain of comedy. His range of tone is wide: occasionally flippant and bantering but more often sardonic and derisive. He does not merely mock deviants and outsiders, traditional comic butts like the friars, or those low in the social hierarchy; he makes fun of himself and can be disrespectful to the king. Dunbar delights in exploiting areas of social tension, between Lowlanders and Highlanders, clerics and laypeople, or men and women. Certain modes seem particularly congenial. He is a master of invective and grotesque portraiture and also excels at parody and burlesque. Several poems are mock-chivalric, and two, "The Dregy" and "The Testament of Andro Kennedy," draw upon the tradition of medieval Latin parody. Dunbar is a witty poet, but his wit is contextual, displayed less in neat epigrams than in topical allusions, puns, and a pervasive irony, particularly evident in his ambitious poem the *Tretis of the Tua Mariit Wemen and the Wedo*. A cluster of dream poems displays a strikingly black "eldritch" comedy.

Dunbar also wrote fine hymnlike religious poems and other wholly serious verse, some of which is didactic in a manner uncongenial to modern readers; yet such pieces were popular with contemporaries. Their style is plain, and their tone impersonal and hortatory. Many could have been written by any competent poet of the time; indeed several attributed to Dunbar in one manuscript are elsewhere assigned to another poet or anonymous. This uncertainty as to authorship is symptomatic of their extreme conventionality. Yet some of Dunbar's moral poems, which undoubtedly spring from this same tradition, have far greater individuality. Two of the finest, "Timor Mortis Conturbat Me" and "In to thir Dirk and Drublie Dayis" (by later editors called "The Lament for the Makaris" and "Meditatioun in Wyntir"), give poignant expression to ancient commonplaces about death and mutability.

Dunbar's poems are so varied that critics find it difficult to form a coherent image of their protean author. Some seek to reconcile the disparate elements in his poetry through an underlying "morality"; others stress rather the generic nature of his poems. The exact degree of self-expression in Dunbar remains difficult to assess but seems to fluctuate. The "I"-figure of some poems is largely a narrative persona, and in others a spokesman for orthodox morality; but in some, particularly the petitionary poems, we hear an intimate and private-sounding voice.

Priscilla Bawcutt

Bibliography

PRIMARY

Bawcutt, Priscilla, ed. *William Dunbar: Selected Poems*. London: Longman, 1996; Kinsley, James, ed. *The Poems of William Dunbar*. Oxford: Clarendon, 1979.

SECONDARY

New *CBEL* 1:660–62; *Manual* 4:1005–60, 1204–84; Bawcutt, Priscilla. "Aspects of Dunbar's Imagery." In *Chaucer and Middle English Studies,* ed. Beryl Rowland. London: Allen & Unwin, 1974, pp. 190–200; Bawcutt, Priscilla. "William Dunbar and Gavin Douglas." In *The History of Scottish Literature*. Vol. 1, ed. R.D.S. Jack. Aberdeen: Aberdeen University Press, 1988, pp. 73–89; Bawcutt, Priscilla. *Dunbar the Makar*. Oxford: Clarendon, 1992; Baxter, J.W. *William Dunbar: A Biographical Study*. Edinburgh: Oliver & Boyd, 1952; Fox, Denton. "Dunbar's *The Golden Targe*." *ELH* 26 (1959): 311–34; Morgan, Edwin. "Dunbar and the Language of Poetry." *EIC* 2 (1952): 138–58; Reiss, Edmund. *William Dunbar*. Boston: Twayne, 1979; Ross, Ian. *William Dunbar*. Leiden: Brill, 1981; Roth, Elizabeth. "Criticism and Taste: Readings of Dunbar's *Tretis*." *Scottish Literary Journal* Supplement 15 (1981): 57–90; Scheps, Walter, and J. Anna Looney. *Middle Scots Poets: A Reference Guide*. Boston: Hall, 1986, pp. 119–94.

See also Alliterative Revival; Chaucer; Chaucerian Apocrypha; Douglas; Henryson; Satire; Scottish Literature, Early; Women in ME Literature

Duns Scotus, John (ca. 1266–1308)

Franciscan philosopher and theologian of Scottish origin; probably born in the village of Duns, county Berwick. Duns Scotus entered the Franciscan order and was ordained priest in 1291. He studied and lectured at Oxford and Paris, where he developed his philosophical and theological ideas. Caught up in the political difficulties between Pope Boniface VIII and Philip IV of France, propapal Duns Scotus was forced by royal anger to interrupt his studies and leave Paris. Returning in 1304, he received the degree of master in theology, occupied the Franciscan chair at the University of Paris, and distinguished himself by his ardent support of the doctrine of the Immaculate Conception of the Virgin Mary. His last year was spent lecturing in Cologne; his life ended there in 1308.

Owing to his sudden death, his works were completed by his students; it is difficult to separate the spurious from the authentic. The most important source for his ideas is the *Opus Oxoniense (Ordinatio),* a commentary on Peter Lombard's *Sentences.* Other important works include the *Reportata Parisiensia,* a second commentary on the *Sentences; De primo principio,* which reveals Duns Scotus's mystical side; and several commentaries on the work of Aristotle.

Duns Scotus attempted to develop a critical synthesis of the major philosophical schools of his day, the Augustinian and the Thomist-Aristotelian. He developed a complex proof for the existence of God, stressed the primacy of will over intellect, and argued that human reason can attain truth without divine illumination. He stressed the importance of the individual essence, *haecceitas,* which makes each being unique. Fearful of oversimplification, Duns Scotus expressed his ideas through a carefully defined and redefined system of argumentation. The convolutions of his thought inspired later humanists to derive the insulting term "dunce" from his name; his complex intricacies earned him the 14th-century designation "doctor subtilis."

Janice Gordon-Kelter

Bibliography

PRIMARY

Alluntis, Felix, and Allan Wolter, eds. and trans. *God and Creatures: The Quodlibetal Questions.* Princeton: Princeton University Press, 1975; Balic, Carlo, ed. *Opera Omnia.* Vatican City: Typis Polyglottis Vaticanis, 1950– [in preparation, a critical edition of Duns Scotus's complete works]; Wolter, Allan, ed. and trans. *Philosophical Writings: A Selection.* Edinburgh: Nelson, 1962.

SECONDARY

Bettoni, Efrem. *Duns Scotus: The Basic Principles of His Philosophy.* Washington, D.C.: Catholic University of America Press, 1961.

See also Learning; Universities

Dunstable, John (ca. 1395–1453)

Composer, mathematician, and astronomer. He is the author of over 70 surviving works, including music for masses, offices, Marian devotions, isorhythmic motets, and secular songs. Dunstable (or Dunstaple) stands at the head of an influential group of English composers whose music, beginning in the later 1420s and 1430s, circulated on the Continent, where it had an immense stylistic impact. Fifteenth-century musical commentators recognized Dunstable's importance, and he held a high posthumous reputation for many subsequent generations.

Of Dunstable's biography we know little. The paucity of documentation seems to be due to a career that kept him out of the records of the court, and there is no evidence of a direct association with any cathedral or monastic establishment or the Chapel Royal. He seems to have begun composing around 1415, but he is not represented in the first layer of the Old Hall Manuscript, which was copied by 1421. A few long-known pieces of evidence, along with important recent archival discoveries, suggest that Dunstable was in service to John duke of Bedford before 1427; moved into the household of the duke's stepmother, the dowager Queen Joan, from 1427 until her death in 1437; and at that point entered the *familia* (household) of her stepson and John's brother, Humphrey duke of Gloucester. Dunstable's relationship with Gloucester is described as that of "serviteur et familier domestique," an appellation that probably can be extended to his previous relationships with John and Joan, suggesting a high-ranking role in administrative service while not, significantly, a member of the household chapel. Though Dunstable's music is preserved mainly in continental sources, it now appears that his personal presence in France was limited and intermittent. Thus he is not likely to be the central agent in the transmission of English music across the Channel that he was once thought to be.

The scale and nature of the rewards Dunstable received from his patrons indicate the high regard they held for him. He enjoyed lavish gifts, landed income at a high level, and a large annuity from Queen Joan; and he held a lordship, estates, and fiefs in Normandy under the patronage of Gloucester in the years 1437–41. In England Dunstable owned property in Cambridgeshire, Essex, and London. Documents style him esquire or armiger, suggesting he was a wealthy landholder of an order of society just below the knightly class. In London he held rents in the parish of St. Stephen Walbroke, in which church he was buried, outlived by his wife and other descendants. The church and his monument do not survive, but his epitaph there was recorded. A second epitaph, by John of Wheathampstead, abbot of St. Albans, is also known. Dunstable's further ties to St. Albans include two motets, one on St. Alban (the text is possibly by Wheathampstead) and another on St. Germanus. The composer's link to the abbey undoubtedly came through two of his employers, Queen Joan and Gloucester, who were among its principal aristocratic benefactors (Gloucester was buried there).

Dunstable's music is the preeminent exemplification of the influential "nouvelle practique" that one continental observer of around 1440 called "la contenance Angloise." Chief features of this style include the predominance of triple meter in flowing rhythms of quarter notes and eighth notes with gentle syncopations and hemiola, smooth triadic melodies with distinctive cadential turns of phrase, and a uniformly consonant harmonic-contrapuntal language rich with the warm sound of imperfect consonances—thirds, sixths, and tenths.

Dunstable's eleven isorhythmic motets are among the last in an English and continental tradition stretching back to the middle of the 14th century. Polytextual, based on plainsong tenors, and written for three or four voices, they are almost all variations upon a "classical" pattern with tripartite proportional diminution. Sustaining a particularly English tradition, their texts are all sacred, with six dedicated to saints (John the Baptist, Catherine, Alban, Germanus, Michael, Anne), three to the Virgin Mary, and two for Whitsunday. Their origins are likely to have been ceremonial rather than strictly liturgical. From the testimony of a chronicler it appears that Dunstable's motet on John the Baptist, *Preco preheminencie / Precursor premittitur* with tenor *Inter natos* (perhaps one of his earliest compositions), was sung before Henry V and Emperor Sigismund in Canterbury Cathedral on 21 August 1416 to celebrate victory at the siege of Harfleur and the Battle of the Seine.

For settings of liturgical texts outside the mass Ordinary Dunstable principally draws upon processional and office antiphons for Mary, constructing compositions of roughly the same dimensions as an isorhythmic motet or mass movement that are destined for performance at Marian devotions. These pieces are nearly all for three voices, occasionally reducing to two, with a songlike top part over a supporting tenor and contratenor; some are based on chant but the majority are freely composed. Though neither polytextual nor isorhythmic, they were apparently regarded as a species of motet by some continental scribes, and they are called motets by many modern authorities. It has been shown recently that careful mathematical planning governs their proportions.

Most of Dunstable's compositions for the Ordinary of the mass (Kyrie, Gloria, Credo, Sanctus, Agnus) are single isolated movements; all but three of these pieces are freely composed, without reference to plainsong. In the 1420s and 1430s, however, Dunstable and his English contemporaries, including Leonel Power and John Benet, pioneered the musical integration of a complete five-movement mass cycle, achieving unification by using the same "alien" *cantus firmus* as the tenor in all movements. These early English cyclic tenor masses were based on sacred plainsongs (antiphons and responds); Dunstable's cycles include *Jesu Christi fili Dei*, *Da gaudiorum premia*, *Rex seculorum* (also ascribed to Leonel), and a *Missa "sine nomine"* (also ascribed to Leonel and Benet). It may be the case that a number of anonymous cycles of the 1440s are also of Dunstable's authorship. Continental composers, such as Guillaume Dufay, began to imitate these English cycles around 1450.

Few secular songs survive by members of Dunstable's generation. Sources credit him with just three, two of which are plausibly attributed elsewhere to a younger contemporary, John Bedingham, leaving only a French-texted rondeau, *Puisque m'amour*, to represent the courtly side of his output.

However, Dunstable's lifetime saw the great flowering of the polyphonic carol, and amid this anonymous repertoire are likely to be works by the great English master.

Peter M. Lefferts

Bibliography

PRIMARY

Bukofzer, Manfred, ed. *John Dunstable: Complete Works.* 2d rev. ed., prepared by Margaret Bent, Ian Bent, and Brian Trowell. Musica Britannica 8. London: Stainer & Bell, 1970.

SECONDARY

Bent, Margaret. *Dunstaple.* London: Oxford University Press, 1981; Bent, Margaret. "Dunstable." *NGD* 5:720–25; Stell, Judith, and Andrew Wathey. "New Light on the Biography of John Dunstable?" *Music and Letters* 62 (1981): 60–63; Trowell, Brian. "Proportion in the Music of Dunstable." *Proceedings of the Royal Musical Association* 105 (1978–79): 100–41; Wathey, Andrew. "Dunstable in France." *Music and Letters* 67 (1986): 1–36.

See also Carol; Power, Leonel; Mass, Polyphonic Music for; Motet; Songs

Dunstan of Canterbury (ca. 910–988)

Monk and archbishop of Canterbury. The son of a Somerset noble, he was educated at Glastonbury Abbey, probably by Irish monks. Related to the royal line with several kinsmen who held episcopal sees, in his youth he was often at the court of King Æthelstan. The enmity of other young nobles, however, led to his expulsion. He stayed for a period with his uncle Ælfheah, bishop of Winchester, under whose influence and in the wake of a serious illness he committed himself to the monastic life. Retiring to a hermitage near Glastonbury, he studied scriptures and served as a scribe, illuminator, composer, and metalworker.

Recalled to court by Æthelstan's brother and successor Edmund (939–46), he became one of his counselors, only to be again banished. Soon afterward Edmund, nearly killed in a riding accident, concluded that he had wronged Dunstan; he named him abbot of Glastonbury and promised to endow that institution as a regular monastery. Under Dunstan's guidance a monastery was built with an organized community of monks adhering to the Benedictine Rule. Its foundation is seen as marking a long-enduring revival of English monasticism after several generations of decay.

Under Edmund's successor Eadred (946–55) Dunstan and his monastery were the recipients of even greater favors, but his fortunes waned with the accession of Eadwig (955–59). In 956, having angered an influential woman at court, he was forced into exile in Flanders. Restored by Edgar (957–75), he became the king's chief adviser and treasurer. Named bishop of Worcester (957) and London (959), in 960 he became archbishop of Canterbury. On Edgar's death he supported the royal claim of Edward the Martyr and, after Edward's murder in 979, the claim of

Æthelred II. Dunstan's final years were spent at Canterbury, devoted to prayer, study, and teaching. He died on 19 May 988, the "patron and father of the monks of medieval England."

Miles Campbell

Bibliography

Knowles, David. *The Monastic Order in England: A History of Its Development from the Times of St. Dunstan to the Fourth Lateran Council, 940–1216.* 2d ed. Cambridge: Cambridge University Press, 1963; Robinson, Joseph Armitage. *The Times of Saint Dunstan.* Oxford: Clarendon, 1923; Stubbs, William, ed. *Memorials of Saint Dunstan, Archbishop of Canterbury.* Rolls Series 63. London: Longman, 1874; Symons, Thomas. "The English Monastic Reform of the Tenth Century." *DownR* 60 (1942): 1–22, 196–222, 268–79.

See also Æthelwold; Benedictine Reform; Monasticism

Durham

The latest known OE poem, surviving in three versions: CUL Ff.i.27, page 202; Hickes's *Thesaurus* (1705) 1.178–9, from BL Cotton Vitellius D.xx, fol. 20v, lost in the 1731 fire; and Stanford University Libraries Misc 010, pages 1a–d, a 17th-century transcription by Franciscus Junius from an unknown manuscript. The 21-line poem, dated ca. 1104–09, praises three aspects of the city of Durham in northeast England. Lines 1–8 describe the beautiful landscape, with the River Wear and bountiful fishing and hunting. Lines 9–17 list famous people buried in the cathedral: Cuthbert, King Oswald (only his head), Bishop Aidan, kings Eadberht and Eadfrith, Bishop Æthelwold, the "breoma bocera" (famous scholar) Bede, and Bishop Boisil. Lines 18–21 mention the countless relics housed there and the miracles they perform. Scholars assign the poem to the *encomium urbis* (praise of a city) subgenre.

Donald K. Fry

Bibliography

PRIMARY

ASPR 6:27, 151–53 [edits Cambridge with Hickes variants]; Fry, Donald K. "A Newly Discovered Version of the Old English Poem 'Durham.'" In *Old English and New: Studies in Language and Linguistics in Honor of Frederic G. Cassidy,* ed. Joan H. Hall, Nick Doane, and Dick Ringler. New York: Garland, 1992, pp. 83–96; Hamer, Richard, trans. *A Choice of Anglo-Saxon Verse.* London: Faber & Faber, 1970, pp. 32–33.

SECONDARY

Howlett, D.R. "Two Old English Encomia." *English Studies* 57 (1976): 289–93; Kendall, Calvin B. "Let Us Now Praise a Famous City: Wordplay in the OE *Durham* and the Cult of St. Cuthbert." *JEGP* 87 (1988): 507–21; Robinson, Fred C. "The Royal Epithet *Engle leo* in the Old English *Durham* Poem." *MÆ* 37 (1968): 249–52.

See also Bede; Cotton; Durham Cathedral

Durham Cathedral

Commenced in 1093 by Bishop William of St. Calais, Durham Cathedral (figs. 52–53) stands with the castle on a peninsula high above the River Wear as a proud symbol of Norman achievement. The eastern arm was finished for the translation of St. Cuthbert in 1104, and by 1133 the church was completed, with the exception of the superstructure of the twin western towers. These towers were probably finished by Bishop Hugh le Puiset (1153–95), who also added the galilee, or entrance chamber, at the west end. After 1242 the presbytery high vault was rebuilt and the Romanesque apses were replaced with the Chapel of the Altars.

The rib vaults throughout the church and the pointed transverse arches in the nave high vault have often led to the classification of Durham Cathedral as a proto-Gothic structure, and in this regard the quadrant arches in the nave galleries have even been construed as embryonic flying buttresses. However, the quadrant arches were erected in connection with a transverse gabled roof in each bay, the outlines of which are still visible on the north-wall exterior. The rib vaults and the pointed arches are better understood in the context of English architecture around 1100.

Durham Cathedral was conceived in rivalry with the other great churches in Europe. The aim of the patron seems to have been to create the finest church in Christendom. Its huge scale vies, for example, with St. Albans (1077) and Winchester (1079) and recalls the great early Christian basilicas of Rome. The association between Durham and Rome is specific. The overall length of the church is taken from Old St. Peter's, and the incised spirals on the columnar piers of the presbytery and transepts are iconographically related to the Solomonic columns around St. Peter's shrine. The "furniture" of St. Peter's shrine was thereby integrated into the architectural setting for St. Cuthbert.

The analogy may be taken further, for the quadripartite ribs of the Durham vaults suggest an association with the open ribs of the canopy above St. Peter's shrine. Also, if the staircases that flanked the apse of Old St. Peter's were carried up as towers, they explain the towers above the aisle apses, and flanking the main apse, at Durham. Eastern towers may also relate to the imperial cathedral of Speyer and possibly to Winchester and St. Albans. These two English buildings were important for Durham. At St. Albans the four-bay presbytery had a high groin vault, a precursor of the high rib vault at Durham, while the St. Albans transept-angle turrets presage those at Durham. Winchester also had a four-bay presbytery, albeit unvaulted, but, like Durham, with alternating compound and columnar piers in the main arcade as part of a full three-story elevation. Furthermore the aisles at Winchester are enriched with a round-headed dado arcade and stepped shafted responds for the groin vaults.

Durham matched or surpassed these features: linear groins evolved into molded ribs, plain dado arcades became molded and intersected, and plain main arcade and gallery arches metamorphosed into bold plastic forms. The intersecting arcades may reflect Anglo-Saxon or even Islamic sources, while the elaborate arch moldings isolated at the crossing of

St. Étienne at Caen are applied throughout Durham. Similarly the exterior dado arcade on the apse at St. Nicholas at Caen becomes ubiquitous at Durham. The commodious width of the Durham staircases is paralleled in castles, a military association that suggests that the cathedral was conceived as the fortified heavenly counterpart to the secular castle.

The high vaults in the presbytery and north transept were completed as intended but a change in plan introduced a wood roof in the south transept. This was removed and the present vault was constructed at the same time as the plan for a wood roof in the nave was changed to a high vault.

The first campaign stopped with the completion of two bays of the main arcade and one bay of the gallery on both sides of the nave. In the second campaign (ca. 1115) chevron ornament is introduced, and pointed transverse arches are used in the nave high vault. These facilitate level crowns in the vaults without the stilting necessary with round-headed transverse arches. The north and south doorway are unusual in that their inner faces are richly carved. The exterior of the north doorway was heavily reworked in 1778; its original two-story form is best reflected in the north-transept portal of Kelso Abbey (Roxboroughshire).

Durham Cathedral had an immediate influence on British architecture, from Waltham Abbey in the south to Kirkwall Cathedral on Orkney. It also set the standard for elaborate linear articulation that was to remain an essential feature throughout English medieval architecture.

Malcolm Thurlby

Bibliography

Bilson, John. "Durham Cathedral: A Chronology of Its Vaults." *ArchJ* 79 (1922): 101–60; Jackson, Michael J., ed. *Engineering a Cathedral.* London: Telford, 1992 [articles by Eric Fernie and Malcolm Thurlby]; Thurlby, Malcolm. "The Building of the Cathedral: The Romanesque and Early Gothic Fabric." In *Durham Cathedral: A Celebration,* ed. Douglas Pocock. Durham: City of Durham Trust, 1993, pp. 15–35; Thurlby, Malcolm.

Fig. 52. Durham Cathedral, galilee chapel. Courtesy of George Hardin Brown.

"The Roles of the Patron and the Master Mason in the First Design of the Romanesque Cathedral of Durham." In *Anglo-Norman Durham,* ed. David Rollason. Woodbridge: Boydell, 1994, pp. 161–84.

See also Architecture and Architectural Sculpture, Romanesque; St. Albans Abbey; Winchester Cathedral

Durham Choir Screen Reliefs

Two sandstone panels, each with two scenes from the life of Christ carved in deep relief (ca. 1155), were discovered reused as building material at Durham Cathedral. Two of the scenes show episodes from the Transfiguration, the other two show Christ's appearance to Mary Magdalene and Christ's appearance to the two Marys. The faces of all the figures have been destroyed. In his 1934 volume, *English Romanesque Architecture after the Conquest,* Clapham identified the reliefs as part of the original screen separating the choir from the nave. The screen is described in the 1593 *Rites of Durham* as having been decorated with gilded reliefs showing the Passion of Christ, and images of the twelve apostles, sixteen kings, and sixteen bishops, all surmounted by a crucifix. It seems to have been created before ca. 1155 by sculptors in the employ of Hugh le Puiset, the last of the bishops to be included in its decoration.

Fig. 53. Durham Cathedral, plan of Romanesque church. After G. Webb (1956). Reprinted by permission of Yale University Press.

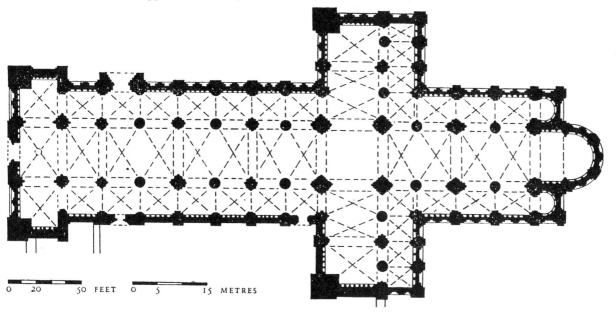

O   20   50 FEET   O   5   15 METRES

The two sets of scenes are treated differently. The Transfiguration is set against a plain background, while stylized trees punctuate the backgrounds of Christ's appearance to the Marys. Additional details, such as the damp-fold drapery with beaded hems and borders and the differing treatment of Christ's halo (cruciform in the scenes of Christ's appearance, plain in the scenes of the Transfiguration), suggest the work of two different artists. Both artists, however, were capable of depicting the forms of the bodies and their movement beneath the clinging draperies, as well as a lively sense of narrative through the expressive gestures and poses of the figures.

Catherine E. Karkov

Bibliography

Stone, Lawrence. *Sculpture in Britain: The Middle Ages.* 2d ed. Harmondsworth: Penguin, 1972; Zarnecki, George, Janet Holt, and Tristram Holland, eds. *English Romanesque Art 1066–1200.* London: Weidenfeld & Nicolson, 1984, cat. no. 154.

See also Architecture and Architectural Sculpture, Romanesque; Durham Cathedral; Sculpture, Romanesque

E

Eadwine and Canterbury/Paris Psalters

The Eadwine Psalter (Cambridge, Trinity College R.17.1; fig. 54) and Canterbury/Paris Psalter (Paris, BN lat. 8846; fig. 55) were produced in Canterbury in the 1150s and 1180s, respectively. Along with the Harley Psalter (BL Harley 603; fig. 71: see HARLEY PSALTER) of ca. 1000, they are descendants of the Utrecht Psalter (Utrecht, Rijksuniversiteit 32) of 816–35. The relationship among the three English manuscripts is problematic, as each shows iconographic innovations, indicating that they are not mere slavish copies, and each exhibits similarities to and differences from the others. While the Harley Psalter is thought to have been made directly from Utrecht, the Eadwine and Paris psalters are considered by many to be copies of a lost intermediary manuscript, itself copied directly from Utrecht. It has recently been suggested, however, that Eadwine may actually have been one of the sources for Paris (Gibson et al., 1992: 26).

The Eadwine Psalter stands out among the Utrecht family of manuscripts both for the completeness of its illustrated cycle and for its scholarly assemblage of texts: the *Hebraicum, Romanum,* and *Gallicanum* run in three neat columns throughout the manuscript, accompanied by interlinear glosses in Anglo-Norman, Anglo-Saxon, and Latin, respectively. The decoration consists of 166 tinted outline drawings, over 500 fully painted initials highlighted with gold and silver, and minor initials in gold and silver. Originally the psalter was preceded by a series of pages with fully painted narrative scenes from the Old and New Testaments (over 130 individual subjects). This set of introductory pages, possibly an innovation of the Eadwine artists, is now divided between New York (Pierpont Morgan Library Morgan 724, 521) and London (BL Add. 37472[1]; Victoria and Albert Museum 661). Its purpose may have been to illustrate the failure of the Old Law and the promise of the New (Gibson et al., 1992: 42). Around 1170 a portrait of the scribe Eadwine (fol. 283v), a plan of Christ Church, Canterbury, with the waterworks installed by Prior Wibert (fol. 284v–285), and a fragmentary second plan (fol. 286) were added to the manuscript.

The portrait of Eadwine is executed in an elegant calligraphic derivative of the damp-fold style, and accompanied by a gloss in the form of a dialogue between scribe and letter that perfectly exemplifies the textuality of the community in and for which the manuscript was produced. It reads in part:

> The prince of scribes am I: neither my praises nor my fame shall ever die; shout out, oh my letter who I may be.
>
> By its fame your script proclaims you, Eadwine, whom the painted figure represents, alive through the ages, whose genius the beauty of this book demonstrates. . . .

While the manuscript shows the hands of a group of scribes

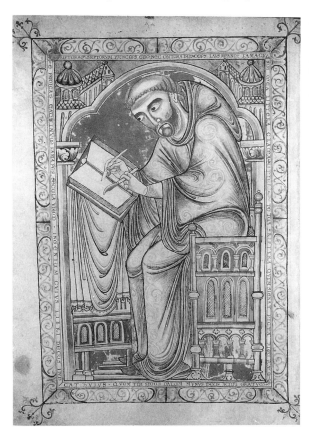

Fig. 54. Eadwine Psalter (Cambridge, Trinity College R.17.1), fol. 283v. Portrait of the scribe Eadwine. Courtesy of the Master and Fellows of Trinity College, Cambridge.

*Fig. 55. Canterbury/
Paris Psalter (Paris,
BN lat. 8846), fol.
21. Psalm 12. ©
Bibliothèque Nationale
de France Paris, used
by permission.*

paciamur circumda acicum al
ticudinem tua filios hominum
in terra iacencium & corpora fer
ua & corda pacifica. P.

monachi qd diuia in seruicio di fatigan.ia segnes
efficium. qd segnicione necco subsequit suggestio.
deinde delectacio.in illa diabolica suggestione in
confensu. De quibz ia gaudec mimis.ibs in pma

parte habitut in secunda agit iste psalmus de
istoz omniu sigillati penitentia quacione ad
deum.ut inde peccacores liberentur.

and artists (one primary master, four secondary artists), Eadwine is thought to have been responsible for overseeing its production.

The Paris Psalter is the last and most lavish of the English descendants of Utrecht. It is complete only to verse 6 of
Psalm 96. The manuscript opens with eight pages, each divided into twelve square compartments (eighteen medallions
on fol. 4) with 46 Old Testament and 39 New Testament
narrative scenes. There are miniatures illustrating each of the
psalms, and the first verse of each psalm is decorated with an
elaborate initial. The textual arrangement of Paris is close to
that of Eadwine: the *Hebraicum, Romanum,* and *Gallicanum*
run parallel to each other throughout, accompanied by interlinear glosses in French, Anglo-Saxon (a partial gloss), and
Latin. The miniatures are in a fine byzantinizing style with
deep rich colors and dark outlines. They differ most markedly
from Eadwine in that they are fully painted and set against
highly polished gold backgrounds. The number of figures
within the scenes has been reduced, and the figures themselves
show a new monumentality, refinement of pose and gesture,
and strong sense of modeling. They also inhabit larger, more
detailed architectural settings. Graceful unfurled scrolls for
text inscriptions replace the more informal arrangement of inscription and image that characterizes Eadwine. Two artists
whose styles are quite similar completed fols. 5v–70, 75–78v,
84, and 88v–92; the rest of the manuscript was decorated in
the 14th century by a Catalan artist.

Catherine E. Karkov

Bibliography

Dodwell, C.R. *The Canterbury School of Illumination 1066–
1200.* Cambridge: Cambridge University Press, 1954;
Gibson, Margaret, T.A. Heslop, and Richard W. Pfaff,
eds. *The Eadwine Psalter: Text, Image, and Monastic Cul-
ture in Twelfth-Century Canterbury.* London: Modern
Humanities Research Association, 1992; Heimann,
Adelheid. "The Last Copy of the Utrecht Psalter." In
The Year 1200: A Symposium, ed. François Avril. New
York: Metropolitan Museum of Art, 1975, pp. 313–38;
Kauffmann, C. Michael. *Romanesque Manuscripts
1066–1190.* A Survey of Manuscripts Illuminated in
the British Isles 3, ed. J.J.G. Alexander. London: Harvey
Miller, 1975, cat. no. 68; Morgan, Nigel. *Early Gothic
Manuscripts (1) 1190–1250.* A Survey of Manuscripts
Illuminated in the British Isles 4:1, ed. J.J.G. Alexander.
London: Harvey Miller, 1982, cat. no. 1.

See also Bible in OE Literature; Canterbury Picture Leaves;
Harley Psalter; Manuscript Illumination, Romanesque

Earls and Earldoms

The oldest of the nobiliary dignities in England, associated since
about 1290 mainly with the parliamentary peerage. In its earliest
form it was associated with the government of a shire (from the
mid-8th century). The history of the title falls into four periods.

1. Ca. 750–1016: The dignitary was designated in the
   vernacular as *ealdormann* or *aldormann* ("man standing
   in the place of a chief").
2. Ca. 1016–66: After the Danish conquest *eorl* replaced
   ealdormann. The Danish cognate *jarl* (whence "earl")
   had a comparable meaning and presumably seemed
   more familiar to Cnut in designating his highest-
   ranking lieutenants.

3. 1066–ca. 1400: Anglo-Norman usage leaned toward *comes,* and the dignity and jurisdiction of the dignity carried the dual sense of "countship" and "county."

4. 1400 to present: When the court returned to English usage, "earl" replaced the French *counte* (though an earl's wife is still styled a "countess").

The earliest ealdormen seem to have been created by the kings of Wessex on the model of the Frankish counts and were appointed to govern single districts or "shires." They governed the shire in the king's name, commanded the *fyrd* (or militia), and presided, with the local bishop, over the shire court. For this each ealdorman received one-third of the profits of justice, called the "third penny." Though ealdormen were usually of leading families, they seem to have held office at the king's pleasure and before the 11th century probably did not acquire hereditary rights to office or to land in their shire.

Between 925 and the Norman Conquest larger blocks of territory—often contiguous shires—were placed under the jurisdiction of individual ealdormen, or earls, and in the 11th century the four major earls governed blocks of territory corresponding roughly to the old Anglo-Saxon kingdoms: Wessex, Mercia, East Anglia, and Northumbria. After Cnut's conquest the dignity of *eorl* became the prerogative of a few great patrilineages, and they furnished the high nobles with whom Edward the Confessor was confronted.

Under William I the dignity of earl (effectively renamed "count," just as the shire was renamed "county") was transformed from a regular appointive office into a feudal, and therefore hereditary, position. The model for this was Normandy, and the earls (or counts) were mostly placed in control of key border regions, while sheriffs were responsible for the more central counties. The lands given to the earl or count were apt to be scattered within the territory under his nominal rule. Though the *honor,* or barony, of the earldom might be partible among a count's heirs, the dignity was indivisible, and, in the failure of a male heir, the king's choice for its descent among co-heirs or the consort of an heiress determined the future of the dignity.

From the time of William II most earls or counts were devoid of public authority or a function within the county. The number of such men was greatly increased in the Anarchy, as both sides sought to win the support of the great barons, and when Henry II came to the throne there were 23 earls in England. Thereafter the numbers were kept strictly in check, and between 1227 and 1307 five of the eight men promoted afresh to this rank were kings' sons.

As parliament became a regular institution in the 14th century, the earls emerged as major barons in what became the House of Lords (though eventually, as new dignities were created and bestowed, they stood below princes, dukes, and marquesses). Edward II created six new earldoms, Edward III seventeen (with six coming on a single day in 1337), Richard II fifteen. When Edward IV came to the throne (1461), there were 24 earls. Six Lancastrians were then deprived of their titles, but new Yorkist creations brought the number back into the low twenties, where it remained until the accession of Henry VII.

From the reign of Stephen counts or earls were elevated by charter or letters patent and were invested in a public ceremony that always included girding them with the sword—whence the expression "belted earl."

D'Arcy J.D. Boulton

Bibliography

Crouch, David. *The Image of Aristocracy in Britain, 1000–1300.* London: Routledge, 1992; Ellis, G. *Earldoms in Fee: A Study in Peerage Law and History.* London: St. Catherine Press, 1963; Powell, J. Enoch, and Keith Wallis. *The House of Lords in the Middle Ages: A History of the English House of Lords to 1540.* London: Weidenfeld & Nicolson, 1968.

See also Dukes; Parliament; Peerage

Earls Barton Tower

This massive 24-foot-square late Anglo-Saxon, 950–1050 tower (fig. 56), on high ground near a mound and ditch above the River Nene in Northamptonshire, once formed the nave of a church. Vertical pilaster strips with round- and gable-

Fig. 56. Earls Barton, Northamptonshire, tower from the southwest. Courtesy of A.J. Hawkes.

headed arcading cover the structure, prompting debate over the extent to which carpentry influenced masonry here. Considered one of the most interesting survivals of late Anglo-Saxon architecture, Earls Barton graced a British stamp in 1972.

In 1979–80 a small excavation established from cemetery evidence that several churches probably preceded the 60-foot tower. The tower also postdated the mound and ditch to its northwest, suggesting that it could perhaps have functioned as part of a legal or defensive construction, thus having both secular and religious functions. The scarcity of openings on the north protects the tower should anyone take the mound.

Rising from a plinth and divided by stringcourses, the four stages of the tower decrease in size toward the belfry. The tall first stage has a double, round-headed window on the south just below the stringcourse, with transennae (stone screens) cut by crosses; crosses are carved into the basket arches over each opening, and there is also a cross within a circle on a slab to the west. Such elaboration emphasizes the use of the lowest level as a nave; the effect of light shining through the transennae crosses would have been striking, given how elevated the tower is in the landscape. On the west a large doorway with arcading incised on the imposts may once have had a wooden porch or roof, as the pilaster strips stop with corbels just above the doorway. A blocked opening similar to that on the south appears above a Norman window.

The next two stages have pilasters, round and gabled arcading, and doorways resting on the stringcourses. The external upper doorways could have been used for such purposes as relic display and preaching to crowds too large for the church or perhaps to groups assembled on the mound. The belfry has gabled arcading, with five round-headed openings on all sides, separated by stone slabs with balusters at their outer faces. The east face differs slightly and has two circular holes cut over the northernmost openings.

Older accounts of the tower described it as showing a combination of ambition and incompetence, as several pilasters fit badly and destroy a regular pattern, and the north face is one foot off square. Pilaster strips remain a debated architectural technique, claimed at various times as Roman, German, and English, argued for as decorative or functional, and considered of uncertain origin. Their resemblance to timber framing prompts debate on the relevance of carpentry to the function and origin of the pilasters and arcading, but Taylor noted that "almost without exception" churches with tall pilaster strips have walls of fairly small rubble; the pilasters bind deeply into the wall for anchoring. Rodwell's recent work on carpentry joints, however, argues that pieces were prefabricated at Earls Barton according to carpentry methods, then incorrectly assembled: "The design of its prototype was wholly for timber, where prefabricated framing would be brought onto site ready for erection" (174). The presumption would be that here carpenters were pressed into service for an impressive project to which their skills were not wholly suited. Taylor noted 24 churches with pilaster work in the Midlands and southwest.

Kelley M. Wickham-Crowley

Bibliography

Audouy, Michael. "Excavations at All Saints Church, Earls Barton, Northamptonshire 1979/80: SP852638." *Northamptonshire Archaeology* 16 (1981): 73–86; Hewett, Cecil A. "Anglo-Saxon Carpentry." *ASE* 7 (1978): 205–29; Rodwell, Warwick. "Anglo-Saxon Church Building: Aspects of Design and Construction." In *The Anglo-Saxon Church: Papers on History, Architecture and Archaeology in Honour of Dr H.M. Taylor,* ed. Lawrence A.S. Butler and Richard K. Morris. CBA Research Report 60. London: CBA, 1986, pp. 156–75; Taylor, Harold M. "The Origin, Purpose and Date of Pilaster-Strips in Anglo-Saxon Architecture." *North Staffordshire Journal of Field Studies* 10 (1970): 21–48; Taylor, Harold M., and Joan Taylor. "Earls Barton." In *Anglo-Saxon Architecture*. Vol. 1. Cambridge: Cambridge University Press, 1965, pp. 222–26, figs. 457, 458.

See also Architecture, Anglo-Saxon; Ecclesiastical Architecture, Early Anglo-Saxon

"East Anglian School" of Illumination

The term "East Anglian School" was first used by Sir Sydney Cockerell in 1907 to describe certain manuscripts produced in England in approximately the first third of the 14th century. The books he placed in this category had to meet certain criteria of script and decoration. Most, but by no means all, were connected by provenance or destination to the geographical region of East Anglia (Norfolk, Suffolk, Essex, and parts of Lincolnshire). Cockerell grouped some eighteen manuscripts under this heading, at least five of which (the Rutland, Alfonso, and Isabella psalters, a Petrus Comestor, and the Grey-Fitzpayn Hours) are now considered inappropriate for this classification. (Shelf marks for manuscripts discussed here and below appear at the end of the entry in the order in which they are discussed.)

In his chapter entitled "The East Anglian School" (1928) Millar included twelve of the books listed by Cockerell (the Gorleston, Barlow, Howard, Ormesby, Ramsey, Douai, St. Omer, and Luttrell psalters, the Peterborough Psalter in Brussels, the Stowe Breviary, the Tiptoft Missal, and the Emmanuel *Moralia in Job*) and added a further three (the Bromholm and All Souls psalters and the second, later portion, of the De Lisle Psalter—the last no longer considered to be an East Anglian product). For both Cockerell and Millar manuscripts of this "school" are broadly linked by an "extraordinary richness and vigour of decoration" (Millar). The borders, often large in scale and bold in execution, are the principal vehicles of decoration; they contain a wealth of plant forms, interspersed with a variety of grotesques (also called hybrids or drolleries), as well as heraldic shields.

It is the manuscripts listed in Millar's chapter comprising the Queen Mary and Tickhill Psalter groups, some of which he sees as having a bearing on the East Anglian books, that may have prompted Rickert (1954 and 1965) to include them erroneously under the heading "East Anglian School."

Millar acknowledged the enigmatic position occupied by one such manuscript, the Peterborough Psalter and Bestiary, which has a Peterborough destination but contains illumination in the Queen Mary style.

With Rickert's contribution the term "East Anglian" was rapidly becoming a convenient label for any richly illuminated manuscript produced in England in the first 40 years of the 14th century. As further manuscripts have come to light, it has long been realized that the "East Anglian School" is too simplistic a term and requires redefinition. An important step in that direction took place in 1972 with an exhibition held at Norwich. Here Morgan validated East Anglia as a major region of artistic production between about 1300 and 1340, with the ecclesiastical centers at Peterborough (for manuscripts associated with the Peterborough Psalter in Brussels) and Norwich (for manuscripts associated with the Gorleston and Ormesby psalters) as likely locations for this activity, but with the proviso that the artists were probably laymen who traveled around the region or who worked in purely secular shops, thus reinforcing Cockerell's view (1907). Included in this exhibition, however, were certain books in the Queen Mary style that are East Anglian in neither provenance nor decoration, having been produced in London: these are the *Somme le roi,* the Chertsey Breviary, and Bodl. Douce 79.

A recent discussion of the East Anglian question is that by Sandler (1986). Under the heading "East Anglian Groups" she outlines six subsections: the Fenland, Ormesby, Gorleston, Stowe, Barlow, and Italianate groups. She discards some court style and other manuscripts from Cockerell's list, retaining twelve of his original eighteen, while adding a further ten. One, the Fenland group (principally the Peterborough Psalter in Brussels, the Ramsey Psalter, and the Gough leaves), comprises perhaps the earliest manuscripts that can be deemed East Anglian by virtue of Sandler's geographical definition (Norfolk, Suffolk, parts of Cambridgeshire, the Isle of Ely, and the Northamptonshire Fenlands). It is this group that raises the question of the origins of the style that may lie ultimately in certain London-produced manuscripts of the late 13th century.

It was Wormald's contention (1949) that the sources of the East Anglian style lay at the court, and the apparently earliest hands in the psalter in Brussels relate stylistically and formally to the opening hand of the Alfonso Psalter. The strong monastic associations of the Peterborough Psalter group's works pose the question of whether the illuminators were based in the Peterborough area or were itinerant, traveling perhaps from a base in Norwich, London, or possibly Cambridge: there is not sufficient evidence to postulate a center with certainty. The period of activity of this group is approximately 1300 to 1325.

Since her 1974 study Sandler has chronologically separated the stylistically related Barlow Psalter and two Apocalypses from the other products of the Peterborough group, seeing them as a subgroup of the 1320s, but Bennett (1982) has put forward convincing evidence for a date before 1321 for the Barlow Psalter. This in turn suggests a more cohesive group whose period of production spans 25 years from

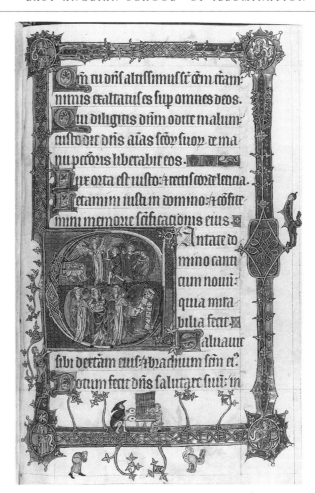

Fig. 57. The Gorleston Psalter (BL Add. 49622), fol. 126. Psalm 97. Reproduced by permission of the British Library, London.

ca. 1300 to 1325 without the break of approximately ten years as proposed by Sandler.

With the group of manuscripts stylistically related to the principal hand in the famous Ormesby Psalter (fig. 102: see ORMESBY PSALTER) there is firmer evidence as to workshop location, with strong Norwich associations pointing to an origin in that city and a period of production spanning ca. 1310 to 1320. Produced at about the same time are the manuscripts associated with the Gorleston Psalter (fig. 57), principally the Howard Psalter, the Longleat Breviary, and the Harnhulle Psalter-Hours; it is less easy to determine where these artists were working. Owing to the Howard Psalter artist's association with an illuminator of the Queen Mary group (the Subsidiary Queen Mary Artist), and the links of both with East Anglian patrons, there may be a case for postulating that these two illuminators were engaged in itinerant work in the region, possibly with a base at one of the centers outlined above (it is now accepted that London was the location for the central Queen Mary activity). Sandler separates the Stowe group, comprising the Escorial and Schloss Herdringen psalters and the Tiptoft Missal (fig. 92: see MANUSCRIPT ILLUMINATION, GOTHIC), from the Gorleston group, presumably on grounds of dating (the 1320s). There appears, however, to be a direct stylistic development from one group to the other, the Stowe Breviary seeming to be a late work by one of the Gorleston Psalter artists. The East Anglian location of this workshop is as yet uncertain, but it may again raise the question of peripatetic workshop practices. The manuscripts of this group are conspicuous for their lack of the marginal grotesques normally associated with the products of the region.

A further distinctive style is associated with innovative italianate techniques and compositions, as found in the Douai Psalter and related works (the additions in the Gorleston and Ormesby Psalters, the Castle Acre Psalter, and the 14th-century portion of the St. Omer Psalter). The traditional dating for this material, based on the historical notes in the Douai Psalter, is ca. 1322–25/30, but more recently an argument for ca. 1330 at the earliest has been forwarded. This material was probably produced in Norwich ca. 1330–40. Within this group Sandler places certain other manuscripts that show italianisms but that seem to constitute further subgroups—the one associated with the enigmatic Luttrell Psalter, another with Bodl. Douce 131 and related manuscripts (principally the Brescia Psalter, the Psalter of Simon de Montacute, the Astor Psalter-Hours, and the first campaign in the Vienna Bohun Psalter). It is with this group that Cambridge emerges as a likely center of artistic activity from ca. 1340 until (and possibly just beyond) the Black Death of 1348–49. Moreover strands of circumstantial evidence link the Fitzwarin Psalter Artist to this area toward the end of his career (ca. 1348/49). A probable focusing of activity in the 1340s on this center, which was badly affected by the plague, may account for the extermination of a number of illuminators. The main Bohun workshop, which established itself at Pleshey Castle in Essex ca. 1350–55, in a sense perpetuated the East Anglian tradition until London reestablished itself as an important center in the early 1370s.

A redefinition of the term "East Anglian School" in no way diminishes the importance of this region as a focus of manuscript production during the first half of the 14th century. A single school it clearly was not, however. With few exceptions it is still not possible to locate the precise areas of this artistic activity, a question that will be exceedingly difficult to resolve until more is discovered about the working methods of these illuminators, whether from existing documents or from further close analysis of the manuscripts themselves.

Lynda Dennison

Bibliography

Bennett, Adelaide L. Review of L.F. Sandler, *The Peterborough Psalter in Brussels. Art Bulletin* 64 (1982): 502–08; Cockerell, Sydney Carlyle. *The Gorleston Psalter: A Manuscript of the Beginning of the Fourteenth Century in the Library of C.W. Dyson Perrins.* London: Chiswick Press, 1907; Dennison, Lynda. "'The Fitzwarin Psalter and Its Allies': A Reappraisal." In *England in the Fourteenth Century: Proceedings of the 1985 Harlaxton Symposium,* ed. W.M. Ormrod. Woodbridge: Boydell, 1986, pp. 42–66; Dennison, Lynda. "Some Unlocated Leaves from an English 14th-Century Book of Hours, Now in Paris." In *England in the Fourteenth Century: Proceedings of the 1991 Harlaxton Symposium,* ed.

Nicholas Rogers. Stamford: Watkins, 1993, pp. 15–33; Dennison, Lynda. "Monastic or Secular? The Artist of the Ramsey Psalter Now at Holkham Hall, Norfolk." In *Monasteries and Society in Medieval England,* ed. B. Thompson. Stamford: Watkins, 1998, pp. 323–63; Lasko, Peter, and Nigel J. Morgan, eds. *Medieval Art in East Anglia 1300–1520.* London: Thames & Hudson, 1974, pp. 7–28; Millar, Eric George. *English Illuminated Manuscripts of the XIVth and XVth Centuries.* Paris: van Oest, 1928; Rickert, Margaret. *Painting in Britain: The Middle Ages.* 2d ed. Harmondsworth: Penguin, 1965, pp. 122–45; Sandler, Lucy Freeman. *The Peterborough Psalter in Brussels and Other Fenland Manuscripts.* London: Harvey Miller, 1974; Sandler, Lucy Freeman. *Gothic Manuscripts 1285–1385.* A Survey of Manuscripts Illuminated in the British Isles 5, ed. J.J.G. Alexander. London: Harvey Miller, 1986, esp. pp. 27–30; Wormald, Francis. "Paintings in Westminster Abbey and Contemporary Paintings." *PBA* 35 (1949): 161–76. Repr. in *Francis Wormald: Collected Writings,* ed. Jonathan J.G. Alexander, T. Julian Brown, and Joan Gibbs. Vol. 2. London: Harvey Miller, 1988, pp. 75–87.

Appendix of Manuscripts

Rutland Psalter (BL Add. 62925); Alfonso Psalter (BL Add. 24686); Isabella Psalter (Munich, Bayerische Staatsbibliothek gall. 16); Petrus Comestor (BL Royal 3.D.vi); Grey-Fitzpayn Hours (Cambridge, Fitzwilliam Mus. 242); Gorleston Psalter (BL Add. 49622); Barlow Psalter (Bodl. Barlow 22); Howard Psalter (BL Arundel 83, pt. 1); Ormesby Psalter (Bodl. Douce 366); Ramsey Psalter (St. Paul in Lavantthal, Stiftsbibliothek XXV/2, 19, and New York, Pierpont Morgan Library M.302); Douai Psalter (Douai, Bibliothèque Municipale 171); St. Omer Psalter (BL Yates Thompson 14 [Add. 39810]); Luttrell Psalter (BL Add. 42130); Peterborough Psalter (Brussels, Bibliothèque Royale 9961–62); Stowe Breviary (BL Stowe 12); Tiptoft Missal (New York, Pierpont Morgan Library M.107); Emmanuel *Moralia in Job* (Cambridge, Emmanuel College 112); Bromholm Psalter (Bodl. Ashmole 1523); All Souls Psalter (Oxford, All Souls College 7); De Lisle Psalter (BL Arundel 83, pt. 2); Peterborough Psalter and Bestiary (Cambridge, Corpus Christi College 53); *La somme le roi* (Cambridge, St. John's College S.30 [256]); Chertsey Breviary (Bodl. Lat. liturg. d.42, e.6, e.37, e.39); Gough leaves (Bodl. Gough liturg. 8 and Rawlinson lit. e.1*); Crowland Apocalypse (Cambridge, Magdalene College 5); Canonici Apocalypse (Bodl. Canonici Bibl. lat. 62); Longleat Breviary (Longleat House, Wiltshire, Marquess of Bath 10); Harnhulle Psalter-Hours (Downside Abbey 26533); Escorial Psalter (El Escorial, Biblioteca del Escorial Q.II.6); Schloss Herdringen Psalter (Schloss Herdringen, Fürstenbergische Bibliothek 8); Castle Acre Psalter (New Haven, Yale Beinecke 417); Brescia Psalter (Brescia, Biblioteca Queriniana A.V.17); Psalter of

Simon de Montacute (Cambridge, St. John's College D.30 [103**]); Astor Psalter-Hours (formerly Astor family, Ginge Manor, Oxfordshire and Bodl. Deposit A.1, sold at Sotheby's on 21 June 1988, present whereabouts unknown); Vienna Psalter (Vienna, Österreichische Nationalbibliothek 1826*); Fitzwarin Psalter (Paris, BN lat. 765).

See also Exeter Bohun Psalter; Manuscript Illumination, Gothic; Ormesby Psalter; Psalters, Gothic; Queen Mary's Psalter

Ecclesiastical Architecture, Early Anglo-Saxon

The chronological framework for "early" Anglo-Saxon architecture is not very secure. Brown, Taylor, and Cherry would see it as ca. A.D. 600–800, with an "obscure," intermediate period ca. A.D. 800–975, when the "late" period begins. Others, like Fernie, extend "early" to the period of the Viking invasions and settlements in the last quarter of the 9th century, when "late" begins.

Modern excavations of churches and other buildings have revealed how many pre-Conquest phases of development a building can have and how difficult they are to date. Architectural historians are still a long way from the definition of national and regional styles and are only just beginning to appreciate the complexities of timber architecture, with which both secular and many church buildings were constructed; the following discussion will therefore be confined to stone, which effectively means ecclesiastical, architecture.

Distinctive Anglo-Saxon architectural styles were first recognized in relation to late Saxon features. This is not surprising, since if there is one characteristic of early Anglo-Saxon architecture it is its variety, reflecting no doubt the individual enterprise of churchmen and other patrons.

The traditionally distinctive styles of Kent and Northumbria are considered separately. In scale most 7th- to 8th-century buildings are small, rarely more than 85 feet long, and 18 feet wide, although on monastic sites there are often several churches on the same axis. Scale increased and plans became more complex after ca. 800, but most early types continue throughout. These are single-celled or double-celled, usually with a rectangular east end, as at Jarrow (fig. 145: see WEARMOUTH-JARROW: ARCHITECTURE), Glastonbury, or Winchester (figs. 151–52: see WINCHESTER OLD MINSTER), but with apsidal east ends where there is strong Roman influence, as at Lincoln (St. Paul's), in the Kentish group, or, later, at Brixworth (figs. 32–33: see BRIXWORTH) or Wing. Most styles have north and south or west adjuncts (porticus), and, although the main entrance seems to be through the western door, additional north and south doors are common.

More elaborate plans, in which the nave is flanked by a row of side chambers (as at Brixworth) or even by a true aisle (as at Lydd), occur but are rare. So far the only centrally planned building to set beside the documentary references is the crypt chapel of Repton. There is, however, evidence in the shape of upper doorways and beam settings that there could have been upper stories as well as western galleries and two-storied porches. High towers are a feature of late Saxon architecture, but it seems probable that low crossing towers could have developed by the 9th century.

Fabrics differ according to regionally available materials, but openings are cut straight through walls, and windows are single splayed. Little evidence survives for columns and capitals even of the crudest types, such as are commonplace on the Continent, although the royal mausoleum of the Saxon kings at Repton is an exception, and there are uncontexted capitals from Canterbury that could be ca. 800. Openings were normally supported on imposts that could be rectangular, champfered, or stepped and were usually decorated with simple moldings, although some, such as Hexham, Jarrow, Repton, or Winchester could be elaborate. In areas where good stone was available most buildings were decorated with carved ornament in the form of friezes and wall panels, as in the early Northumbrian buildings, such as Hexham, Wearmouth, and Jarrow, but most elaborately in late-8th- to early-9th-century buildings, such as Breedon (figs. 134–36: see STONEWORK AS ECCLESIASTICAL ORNAMENT) or Fletton. In addition there are decorated door openings, such as Ledsham, Yorkshire, or Britford, Wiltshire.

Rosemary J. Cramp

Bibliography

Brown, Gerard Baldwin. *The Arts in Early England.* Vol. 2: *Anglo-Saxon Architecture.* Rev. ed. London: Murray, 1925; Butler, Lawrence A.S., and Richard K. Morris. *The Anglo-Saxon Church: Papers on History, Architecture and Archaeology in Honour of Dr H.M. Taylor.* CBA Research Report 60. London: CBA, 1986; Cherry, Bridget. "Ecclesiastical Architecture." In *The Archaeology of Anglo-Saxon England,* ed. David M. Wilson. London: Methuen, 1976; Fernie, Eric. *The Architecture of the Anglo-Saxons.* London: Batsford, 1983; Taylor, Harold M. *Anglo-Saxon Architecture.* Vol. 3. Cambridge: Cambridge University Press, 1978; Taylor, Harold M., and Joan Taylor. *Anglo-Saxon Architecture.* Vols. 1–2. Cambridge: Cambridge University Press, 1965.

See also Architecture, Anglo-Saxon; Brixworth; Hexham and Ripon; Kentish Churches; Repton; Sculpture, Anglo-Saxon; Stonework as Ecclesiastical Ornament; Wearmouth-Jarrow: Architecture; Winchester Old Minster; York, Anglo-Saxon Churches in

Edmund of Abingdon, or Edmund Rich (ca. 1170–1240)

Scholar and theologian, who taught at Oxford. Shortly after his election as archbishop of Canterbury (1233) he helped arbitrate a dispute between Henry III and a rebellious faction of barons, thereby averting civil war. His episcopate was fraught with conflict, and in 1240 he left England and died abroad. He was canonized 16 December 1246.

Edmund's best-known work is his *Speculum ecclesiae,* a treatise on the spiritual life that significantly influenced later devotional writings in England. It was probably first written in French for a religious community and later translated into

Latin and ME; the famous ME lyric "Nou goth sonne vnder wod" appears in over 40 ME, French, and Latin manuscripts of the *Speculum,* as part of a meditation on Christ's passion.

Sharon Kelly

Bibliography

PRIMARY

Horstmann, Carl, ed. "The Mirror of St. Edmund." In *Yorkshire Writers.* 2 vols. New York: Macmillan, 1895, 1:219–61.

SECONDARY

Lawrence, C.H. *St. Edmund of Abingdon: A Study in Hagiography and History.* Oxford: Clarendon, 1960.

See also Bishops; Henry III; Moral and Religious Instruction; Mystical and Devotional Writings; Universities: Oxford and Cambridge

Edward I (1239–1307; r. 1272–1307)

Usually rated as one of the great kings of medieval England. His reign witnessed military triumphs against the Welsh and considerable successes against Scotland, apparently conquered by 1304. A magnificent chain of castles in north Wales is testament to the confidence of the age, and a succession of statutes bears witness to Edward's efforts to reform the legal system. In constitutional terms this reign was of fundamental importance in the development of parliament. Yet there are shadows in this picture. The later years of the reign lacked the constructive qualities of the earlier. War imposed an increasing strain upon political society and the economy. Law and order were not maintained with the expected vigor.

Edward is not an easy character to assess. Son of Henry III, he served a hard apprenticeship in his youth, displaying energy and ambition, with a reputation for false dealing in the civil wars of the early 1260s. He went on St. Louis's crusade in 1270 and was the only one of the leaders who did not abandon the expedition. He went on to the Holy Land, where he achieved little but greatly improved his public image.

On his return to England in 1274 major reforms were instituted. A massive inquiry that yielded the Hundred Rolls demonstrated that the king was committed to at least some of the concepts that had inspired the baronial reform movement of 1258. Yet there was no single principle providing consistency to the new statutes. Individual measures were devised to deal with particular problems; some favored the magnates, some their tenants, and some the merchants. A concerted campaign of *quo warranto* inquiries ("by what warrant") into baronial rights over jurisdiction lacked proper direction from above and became bogged down in technicalities, until a compromise was eventually worked out in 1290. The extent to which Edward was himself responsible for the legal measures is hard to assess; it seems probable that he left the details of drafting to his experts. In his personal conduct he was certainly not above manipulating the law in a cynical fashion. His desire to acquire sufficient lands with which to endow his children led him into some highly suspect dealing, such as defrauding the rightful heir to the Forz inheritance.

Edward was jealous of his own rights and privileges, and insensitive to those of others. He took an exalted view of his feudal rights of suzerainty in Wales and Scotland, and in both cases this led him into war. An autocratic determination to enforce his interpretation of his rights drove both Welsh and Scots to take up arms against him. Failure to reward his allies, such as the Welsh prince Dafydd and the Scottish magnate Robert Bruce, led to serious rebellions. He met his match, however, in Philip IV of France, and in 1294 English diplomacy suffered a serious reverse when the king's brother, Edmund of Lancaster, was duped into handing over the duchy of Gascony to the French without receiving adequate guarantees that it would be returned.

Edward's successes in war were not achieved by any brilliant strokes of generalship. Rather, efficient administration mustered the resources of the realm, in terms of men, money, and materials, on an unprecedented scale. This had severe political consequences; successive years of heavy taxation, after 1294, led to the major political crisis in 1297. The determination of Archbishop Winchelsey to follow the papal line, set out in the bull *Clericis laicos,* of not paying taxes to the lay power, added to the problems. Though civil war threatened, Edward persisted in his plans for a campaign in the Low Countries, for which he did not have an adequate army. He was fortunate in that the French king failed to appreciate the weakness of the English position, while a defeat in Scotland at Stirling Bridge brought the English baronage back to a sense of patriotic duty. The political crisis was settled with the issue of the *Confirmatio cartarum* (Confirmation of the Charters).

Edward's reign was important for the evolution of parliament. The hearing of petitions and determination of cases have been stressed by some historians, but parliament was also the occasion for the discussion of great affairs of state. Representatives of shire and borough, and of lower clergy, attended only a minority of parliaments, but the concept that they should come with full power *(plena potestas)* to consent on behalf of their communities was established. How far the king considered himself bound by such ideas as "What touches all should be approved by all" *(quod omnes tangit)* is open to doubt; that phrase was used only once in a parliamentary summons and is likely to have been inserted by a clerk, not the king himself. Examination of the limited nature of royal patronage does not suggest that Edward was a man who believed in the subtle arts of political management; his style was brusque, autocratic, and effective.

Edward was a conventionally religious man who founded the Abbey of Vale Royal in fulfillment of a vow taken when he thought he was about to be shipwrecked. The work on the abbey, however, was abruptly terminated in 1290. His piety did not lead him into any subservience to the church. He faced considerable difficulties from archbishops Pecham and Winchelsey, two of the few able to stand up to the masterful king. He was clearly fond of his first queen, Eleanor of Castile, in whose honor he had a fine series of commemorative crosses built. He also seems to have been fond of his daughters, but his relationship with his heir, the unsatisfactory Edward II, was a stormy one.

The final years of the reign were difficult. There were financial problems, with a debt increasing to about £200,000. Public order was poorly maintained as a result of the government's singleminded concentration on war. English forces proved incapable of dealing with the Scots under Robert Bruce. The legacy Edward left his son was an impossible one.

Michael Prestwich

Bibliography

Gransden, Antonia. *Historical Writing in England.* Vol. 1: *c. 550 to c. 1307.* London: Routledge & Kegan Paul, 1974, pp. 439–86 [on the contemporary chronicles]; Parsons, John Carmi. *Eleanor of Castile: Queen and Society in Thirteenth-Century England.* New York: St. Martins, 1995; Powicke, F.M. *The Thirteenth Century, 1216–1307.* 2d ed. Oxford: Clarendon, 1962 [this study, originally published in 1953, dominated thinking on the period for many years]; Prestwich, Michael. *Edward I.* London: Methuen, 1988 [the most recent full study]; Rothwell, Harry, ed. *English Historical Documents.* Vol. 3: *1189–1327.* London: Eyre & Spottiswoode, 1975 [translated texts].

See also Baronial Reform; Courts and the Court System; Edward II; Eleanor Crosses; Henry III; Hundreds; Parliament; Quo Warranto Proceedings; Simon de Montfort

Edward II (1284–1327; r. 1307–27)

Fourth but only surviving son of Edward I and Eleanor of Castile; born at Carnarvon (modern Caernarvon) in north Wales in April 1284. The tradition that Edward was presented to the recently conquered Welsh as a prince born in their own land and knowing no English may be unsupported, but there is little doubt that Edward I wished his latest child to be born in Wales to strengthen the allegiance of the Welsh to his crown. In any event Wales was a thread that ran through the career of Edward of Carnarvon; he became Prince of Wales in 1301, he fled there in a vain search for safety in 1326, and it was from Wales that one of the conspiracies to release him from captivity arose in 1327.

Edward's early career was shaped by the conflicts of his father's reign. He was in nominal charge of England as regent during the crisis of 1297–98, while his father was in Flanders fighting the French; he was present at the siege of the Scottish castle of Caerlaverock in 1300 and held his first independent military command in Scotland in 1301. While he achieved nothing spectacular on any of these occasions, he was following the practical education of a young prince, destined to become king, and left a generally good initial impression.

Edward's personal relations with his father deteriorated in Edward I's last years. No son could have matched the energy and determination of Edward I or have avoided arousing the old king's ferocious temper, made worse by the ills of old age and the sense of failure in Scotland. But it was also becoming apparent that the younger Edward lacked seriousness and application; his reliance on favorites was likely to cause severe political problems when he succeeded his father.

The earliest and most controversial of the favorites was the young Gascon knight Piers Gaveston. It is ironic that his membership in the household of the future king, which he had joined by the end of 1300, was occasioned by Edward I himself, impressed by Gaveston in the Flemish campaign of 1297 and thinking him a suitable model for his son. Although it is usually considered that a sexual relationship developed between Edward II and Gaveston, this is far from certain. Both men also married and produced children, with in Edward's case at least one illegitimate offspring as well.

Trouble swiftly followed Edward's accession in July 1307. The financial and administrative confusion left by Edward I led to demands for reform of royal government; baronial resentment at the promotion of Gaveston to the royal earldom of Cornwall ensured that the demands would be combined with personal enmity. The reform program of the Ordainers, the nobles who banded together in 1310–11, presenting ordinances in which they summarized their demands, and the exile of Gaveston that followed did not solve these problems. After Gaveston was murdered in 1312 by the king's opponents, the earls of Warwick and Lancaster, Edward was consumed by a desire for vengeance, finally achieved in 1322.

In the meantime England went through a prolonged crisis. In June 1314 Edward II's attempt to renew the war in Scotland failed; a humiliating defeat at Bannockburn was followed by destructive Scottish raids on the north and a Scottish invasion of Ireland. Military defeat led to further political tension, as Warwick and Lancaster attempted to enforce the Ordinances.

Bad weather, famine, and disease in 1315 and 1316 spread general misery throughout the realm. A political settlement between Edward and Lancaster in 1318, after long and tortuous negotiations, was disrupted by the rise of another royal favorite, Hugh Despenser the Younger. The civil war that had threatened since 1312 finally broke out in 1321 and ended in March 1322, with Edward's victory at Boroughbridge, the execution of Lancaster and other opponents, and the annulment of the Ordinances.

Edward's ruthlessness in victory and the power exercised by Despenser led swiftly to the final disasters of the reign. In September 1326 Edward's estranged wife, the French princess Isabella, invaded England with her lover, Roger Mortimer of Wigmore. In January 1327 Edward II was deposed and his son Edward III crowned in his place. Edward II was imprisoned in Berkeley Castle near Bristol, and in September 1327 it was announced that he had died. Although the terrifying description of Edward's death recorded by some of the chroniclers cannot be confirmed, it is likely that he was murdered, probably on the orders of Mortimer.

Ironically the king who had been a failure in life was regarded by some as a martyr; his tomb at Gloucester Abbey became a place of pilgrimage and alleged miracles. Nonetheless, for a few years, rumors circulated that he had escaped from Berkeley. The most circumstantial of these claimed that he had wandered through Europe before settling in Italy as a hermit. In 1385 Edward's great-grandson Richard II began a long but unsuccessful attempt to have Edward canonized.

Edward II's personal failings accounted for many of the problems of his reign. But it is also certain that he inherited many problems, financial, political, and military. Under the circumstances it is doubtful if Edward II could have succeeded, even if he had possessed all the talents and energy of his redoubtable father.

J.R.S. Phillips

Bibliography

Fryde, Natalie. *The Tyranny and Fall of Edward II, 1321–1326.* Cambridge: Cambridge University Press, 1979; Haines, Roy M. *The Church and Politics in Fourteenth-Century England: The Career of Adam Orleton, c. 1275–1345.* Cambridge: Cambridge University Press, 1978; Hamilton, J.S. *Piers Gaveston, Earl of Cornwall, 1307–1312: Politics and Patronage in the Reign of Edward II.* Detroit: Wayne State University Press, 1988; Maddicott, J.R. *Thomas of Lancaster, 1307–1322: A Study in the Reign of Edward II.* London: Oxford University Press, 1970; Phillips, J.R.S. *Aymer de Valence, Earl of Pembroke, 1307–1324: Baronial Politics in the Reign of Edward II.* Oxford: Clarendon, 1972; Phillips, J.R.S. "Edward II and the Prophets." In *England in the Fourteenth Century: Proceedings of the 1985 Harlaxton Symposium,* ed. W.M. Ormrod. Woodbridge: Boydell, 1986, pp. 189–201; Phillips, J.R.S. "Edward II." *New Dictionary of National Biography.* Oxford: Clarendon, forthcoming; Prestwich, Michael. *The Three Edwards: War and State in England, 1272–1377.* London: Weidenfeld & Nicolson, 1980.

See also Battles of Bannockburn and Boroughbridge; Davy; Despenser Family; Edward I; Edward III; Ordainers

Edward III (1312–1377; r. 1327–77)

Edward achieved stunning military success against Scotland and France while maintaining domestic harmony for most of the 50 years he ruled. His early years were overshadowed by the political storms that had engulfed Edward II. When he was sent to France in 1325 to do homage for Gascony, he joined his mother, Isabella, who engineered Edward II's overthrow the following year. The young Edward was crowned on 25 January 1327, only fourteen years old, after parliament had deposed his father. A year later he married Philippa of Hainault, whose father had contributed heavily to Isabella's invasion.

Edward was tightly controlled by his mother and her lover, Roger Mortimer, sparking new conflict. Henry of Lancaster led an abortive rebellion in 1329, and Edward's uncle the earl of Kent was summarily executed in 1330 for plotting against them. Finally Edward and a group of young courtiers seized Mortimer in October 1330. He was tried in parliament and executed. Isabella received a generous estate, where she lived until her death in 1358.

Edward then turned his attention to Scotland. After covertly aiding Edward Balliol, a claimant to the Scottish throne, and the "Disinherited" (Balliol's followers) in their attempt to recover power he marched northward in 1333, defeated the Scots at Halidon Hill on 19 July, and captured Berwick. It was the first English victory in years, but it did not subdue the Scots. Subsequent campaigns likewise failed to deliver a decisive blow.

France also demanded Edward's attention. The last Capetian king, Charles IV, had died in 1328 without descendants, and his cousin Philip of Valois had taken the throne. Edward had a claim through his mother, Charles's sister, even though he had twice performed homage for Gascony. When Philip moved to seize Gascony as well as aid the Scots, Edward won parliamentary approval in 1337 to pursue his claim. The enterprise was a disaster. He spent lavishly but achieved little. Despite a victory over the French fleet at Sluys on 24 June, by the end of 1340 he was broke and forced to conclude an ignominious truce.

This fiasco precipitated a political crisis in 1341. Unjustly blaming his officials for the failure, Edward stormed back to England, fired them, and launched an investigation into their misconduct. His anger focused in particular on his chancellor, the archbishop of Canterbury, John Stratford. In reality the wartime demands had been excessive. A restive population spurred Commons to demand reforms. Edward was forced to concede a statute limiting his power, though he overturned it later in the year.

The disputed inheritance of Brittany in 1342 gave Edward an opportunity to return to campaigning, and when the truce with France expired in 1345 he was ready for war. Armies under the earls of Lancaster and Northampton were successful in Gascony and Brittany. The greatest victory came in 1346, when Edward defeated the much larger French army at Crécy on 24 August. Then, on 17 October, the English defeated the Scots and captured King David at the Battle of Neville's Cross. The following year Calais fell to Edward.

Despite these brilliant victories Scottish resistance continued and the French refused to accede to Edward's demands, especially after Philip died in 1350 and John II (1350–64) came to the throne. Though Edward's prestige had risen tremendously, throughout the 1340s Commons still complained about taxation and purveyance. The complaints did not provoke conflict, but Edward had to negotiate carefully. Furthermore the Black Death struck in 1348–49, causing widespread death and havoc.

The war with France resumed in 1355, when Edward dispatched two armies under his son Edward the Black Prince and his cousin Henry of Lancaster. They were smaller than earlier ones but more destructive. The campaigns, called *chevauchées,* were intended to disrupt the enemy, rather than engage in set battle. The French army under King John, however, on 19 September managed to catch the Black Prince at Poitiers, where the English again prevailed over superior forces and even took John prisoner. Despite the triumph the French refused to give in to Edward's demands. He led another army to France in 1359 with the aim of being crowned at Reims, but the mission failed. In 1360 he concluded the Treaty of Brétigny, which gave him some of the territory and authority he sought.

Despite these disappointments Edward was at the peak of his career. His fame spread throughout Europe, and he was popular at home. Through his military triumphs, his participation in tournaments, and his founding of the Order of the Garter in 1346–47 he had become a chivalric hero. During the 1350s and 1360s revenues from customs and the ransoms of David of Scotland and John of France allowed him to reduce the level of direct taxation, producing greater harmony with parliament. His family was large and illustrious.

The end of his reign was less glorious. Queen Philippa's death in 1369 seems to have affected him deeply, though he took a mistress, Alice Perrers. When war resumed with France in 1369, the English position disintegrated. Edward's son John of Gaunt, who took over leadership, was less capable than his ailing elder brother, the Black Prince, and expeditions in 1369 and 1373 produced little. England was forced to give ground. Moreover discontent at home increased as high taxation resumed. Plague struck again in 1360–61 and 1374. The court was dominated by a small group of courtiers around the grasping Alice, enriching themselves at public expense. In the Good Parliament of 1376 Commons impeached the courtiers and called for sweeping reforms. Edward, who did not participate, was forced to grant its demands. He died less than a year later, on 21 June 1377, and was succeeded by his grandson Richard II, whose father, the Black Prince, had died in 1376.

Edward's character is difficult to reconstruct, because chroniclers tended to treat him heroically without offering personal insights. He clearly inspired great *esprit de corps* among the nobility and soldiers. He loved display and indulged in tournaments, ceremonies, and pageants. He was also quick-tempered and tended to blame others for his misfortunes. He was conventionally pious, making pilgrimages to holy sites in England before and after campaigns and giving to the church; he also distrusted clergymen and for the first time appointed laymen as chancellor and treasurer in 1341 and 1371. Finally, despite their immediate glory, his victories in France did not bring lasting success nor were they universally popular in England, where peasants and townsfolk had to shoulder the burden of paying for war.

Scott L. Waugh

Bibliography

Allmand, C.T. *The Hundred Years War: England and France at War, c. 1300–c. 1450.* Cambridge: Cambridge University Press, 1988; Given-Wilson, Chris. *The English Nobility in the Late Middle Ages: The Fourteenth-Century Political Community.* London: Routledge & Kegan Paul, 1987; McKisack, May. *The Fourteenth Century, 1307–1399.* Oxford History of England 5. Oxford: Clarendon, 1959; Ormrod, W.M. *The Reign of Edward III: Crown and Political Society in England, 1327–1377.* New Haven: Yale University Press, 1990; Prestwich, Michael. *The Three Edwards: War and State in England, 1272–1377.* London: Weidenfeld & Nicolson, 1980; Tout, T.F. *Chapters in the Administrative History of Mediaeval England: The Wardrobe, the Chamber and the Small Seals.* Vol. 3. Manchester: Manchester University Press, 1928; Waugh, Scott L. *England in the Reign of Edward III.* Cambridge: Cambridge University Press, 1991.

See also Chivalry; Edward II; Edward the Black Prince; Froissart; Hundred Years War; Lancaster, John Duke of; Order of the Garter; Richard II

Edward IV (1442–1483; r. 1461–70, 1471–83)

Contemporaries and near-contemporaries found Edward a man of contradictions; historians since have brought in contrasting—even conflicting—verdicts. The influential Burgundian commentator Philippe de Commynes, who met him at least twice, portrayed Edward as a handsome and courageous prince but an indolent and pleasure-loving king, preferring mistresses to ministers and with little taste for the arduous day-to-day business of government.

The second continuator of the Crowland Chronicle probably knew Edward well and found much to admire in his administration; yet he was puzzled that a man generally thought "in his day to have indulged too intemperately his own passions and desire for luxury" should have been so successful. Similarly the Italian Dominic Mancini, in London in 1482/83, found his character and behavior paradoxical: a man of "gentle nature and cheerful aspect" and "easy of access," who lent a "willing ear" to complaints of injustice, yet "licentious in the extreme" and notably avaricious.

Historical verdicts on Edward IV have ranged widely indeed. Early Tudor writers certainly believed he had been a judicious and popular king whose political achievements were as noteworthy as his sexual stamina and athleticism. "Much given to bodily lust," declared Polydore Vergil, but sufficiently "diligent in his affairs" to bequeath "a most wealthy realm abounding in all things." Whatever his moral failing, echoed Sir Thomas More, in Edward's later years "this realm was in quiet and prosperous estate." Yet the Victorian Bishop Stubbs concluded that Edward was "a man vicious beyond any king . . . since the days of King John, and more cruel and bloodthirsty than any king [England] had ever known." By contrast Stubbs's contemporary J.R. Green believed that the king's "indolence and gaiety" were "mere veils beneath which [he] shrouded a profound political ability."

More recently J.R. Lander has viewed Edward as "a strong man who began to restore order and even, possibly, financial stability." Charles Ross has concluded that Edward, though intelligent, good-natured, courageous, and fully committed, too often lacked foresight and consistency and bequeathed a potentially disastrous political legacy to his young son.

The eldest son of Richard duke of York, Edward earl of March spent his teenage years in the shadow of the Wars of the Roses, as his father mounted an increasingly determined and violent challenge to the inept Henry VI and his notoriously partisan regime. After a victory at St. Albans in February 1461 Edward entered London, and the kingdom was willing to accept him as king (formal accession 4 March 1461). Once king, Edward IV was a startling contrast to his predecessor: presiding over a magnificent court, firmly controlling his council, personally appearing in parliament, progressing regularly around his realm, and taking responsibility for policy making from the very beginning.

Militarily Edward's victories at Mortimer's Cross and

Towton in 1461 were crucial in establishing him on the throne. The defeat of the Lincolnshire rebellion in 1470 owed much to the king's energy and speed of action, and the campaign of March to May 1471 was a triumph. And yet he was strangely inactive in countering Lancastrian resistance in the early 1460s, and his sluggish response to rebellion in 1469 resulted in the debacle at Edgecote and his own short-lived imprisonment by Warwick the Kingmaker.

Politically the pattern is similar. Edward's shrewd generosity to men like William, Lord Hastings, paid off spectacularly, while John Tiptoft, earl of Worcester, proved a disaster. The king's marriage to Elizabeth Wydeville, an ambitious Lancastrian widow with two children, was politically inept (however much he may have loved her). His pro-Burgundian foreign policy, entailing as it did the alienation of Warwick, eventually culminated in the short-lived Readeption of Henry VI (the phrase used to refer to Henry's brief return to the throne, under Warwick's control, from October 1470 to April 1471).

Edward's real achievements, such as they were, came after his restoration in 1471. Then he made real progress in reestablishing royal authority, largely through the medium of his household. He tackled the problem of royal insolvency with some success (as the well-informed Crowland chronicler emphasized), and the years of civil war seemed at last to be over. Yet the king's growing high-handedness (as in the trial and execution of his brother Clarence in 1477/78) and avarice brought charges of despotism, and his foreign policy left England isolated and apparently on the brink of a new continental war. Edward's failure to resolve factionalism certainly helped create the opportunity for Richard of Gloucester's usurpation following Edward's sudden death in April 1483.

Keith R. Dockray

Bibliography

PRIMARY

Commynes, Philippe de. *Memoirs: The Reign of Louis XI, 1461–83.* Trans. Michael Jones. Harmondsworth: Penguin, 1972 [a Burgundian writer, often ill-informed and inaccurate]; Pronay, Nicholas, and John Cox, eds. *The Crowland Chronicle Continuations, 1459–1486.* London: Sutton, for the Richard III and Yorkist History Trust, 1986; Thomas, A.H., and Isabel D. Thornley, eds. *The Great Chronicle of London.* Gloucester: Sutton, 1983.

SECONDARY

Lander, J.R. "Edward IV: The Modern Legend and a Revision." *History* 41 (1956): 38–52. Repr. in *Crown and Nobility, 1450–1509.* London: Arnold, 1976, pp. 159–70 [first major postwar reassessment]; Ross, Charles. *Edward IV.* London: Eyre Methuen, 1974 [most recent and best scholarly biography]; Scofield, Cora L. *The Life and Reign of Edward the Fourth: King of England and France and Lord of Ireland.* 2 vols. London: Longmans, Green, 1923 [most detailed account of the reign].

See also Edward V; Henry VI; Richard III; Wars of the Roses

Edward V (1470–1483)

Elder son of Edward IV. There has been endless speculation about Edward's birth: whether or not he was illegitimate, as Richard III alleged at his usurpation. There is still more regarding his death: when, by whose orders, or even whether he and his younger brother, Richard of York, were murdered in the Tower of London. Even during the few weeks he nominally occupied the throne he can only be glimpsed fleetingly.

Born in the sanctuary of Westminster Abbey on 2 November 1470 (where his mother, Queen Elizabeth Wydeville, had fled on the eve of the Readeption, or restoration to the throne, of Henry VI, October 1470 to April 1471), he spent most of his life at Ludlow in the Welsh march, a Wydeville-dominated environment. In 1473 the queen's brother Anthony, Lord Rivers, was appointed "governor and ruler" of the prince. John Alcock, bishop of Rochester, became his tutor and took charge of his household, and elaborate ordinances for his daily life and education were drawn up. Every waking moment was to be occupied, seemingly, whether in Christian devotions, listening to "such noble stories as it behoveth a prince to understand," or undertaking suitable "disports and exercises." By 1483, according to the antiquary John Rous, "brought up virtuously by virtuous men," he was already "remarkably gifted and well advanced in learning for his years."

Arguably, once his father, Edward IV, died on 9 April 1483 and Richard of Gloucester set his sights on the throne, Edward V's days were numbered. Within four weeks the young king had been firmly secured by his uncle, his companions arrested. The rest of his life was spent in the Tower, where his brother joined him on 16 July, and, although they may have been seen "shooting and playing in the garden" there for a time, they soon vanished.

"I have seen many men burst into tears and lamentations when mention was made" of the newly bastardized and deposed Edward V, recollected Dominic Mancini in 1483, "and already there was a suspicion that he had been done away with." The balance of likelihood is that Edward and his brother did indeed meet a violent end before the rebellion in October 1483 and that responsibility for their deaths lay with their uncle, Richard III.

Keith R. Dockray

Bibliography

Armstrong, C.A.J., ed. and trans. *Dominic Mancini: The Usurpation of Richard III.* 2d ed. Oxford: Clarendon, 1969; Dockray, Keith. *Richard III: A Reader in History.* Gloucester: Sutton, 1988, pp. 89–96 [key documents and commentary on Edward V's fate]; Orme, Nicholas. "The Education of Edward V." *BIHR* 57 (1984): 119–30.

See also Edward IV; Richard III

Edward the Black Prince (1330–1376)

Eldest son of Edward III and Queen Philippa of Hainault, earl of Cornwall and Chester, Prince of Wales, and legendary exemplar of 14th-century chivalry and knighthood. His military reputation rests on his major share in great victories of the Hundred Years War. As a youth he fought at Crécy (1346). Appointed king's lieutenant in the duchy of Aquitaine in 1355, he successfully led the Anglo-Gascon troops at Poitiers (1356), capturing the French king. His final success was at Najéra (1367), where he led a large Anglo-Gascon army across the Pyrenees to defeat the combined French and Spanish forces, again taking valuable prisoners.

These victories brought the prince personal glory and valuable ransoms and loot, as did the raiding expeditions he initiated from Aquitaine; they achieved no permanent advantage for England. His peacetime passion for tournaments and rich spectacles enhanced his chivalric prestige among his contemporaries. When in 1362 Edward was named prince of an Aquitaine now greatly extended by English conquests, he had the difficult task of incorporating the new territories into the old duchy. He proved incompetent both as ruler and statesman.

His delayed marriage, at age 30 to Joan of Kent, a widow famed for her beauty, appears to have been happy but provided neither diplomatic nor political advantages for the crown. Easily outmaneuvered politically by Charles V of France, Edward indulged in expensive dreams of Spanish conquest while the French recovered their losses in Aquitaine. In 1371 he returned to England a sick man. He died in 1376, leaving his nine-year-old son Richard as heir to the throne. Pious, extravagant, brave, but ultimately ineffective, the Black Prince's fame rests on his reputation as the ideal representative of 14th-century chivalry. His traditional sobriquet is a reference to the black suit of armor in which he fought.

Margaret Wade Labarge

Bibliography

PRIMARY

Froissart, Jean. *Chronicles.* Trans. Geoffrey Brereton. Harmondsworth: Penguin, 1978 [a handy edition, with references to more elaborate translations and editions]; Pope, Mildred K., and Eleanor C. Lodge, eds. and trans. *Life of the Black Prince by the Herald of Sir John Chandos.* Oxford: Clarendon, 1910. Repr. New York: AMS, 1974 [this and Froissart are the best primary sources].

SECONDARY

Barber, Richard. *Edward, Prince of Wales and Aquitaine: A Biography of the Black Prince.* London: Lane, 1978 [most recent full biography]; Hewitt, Herbert J. *The Black Prince's Expedition of 1355–1357.* Manchester: Manchester University Press, 1958 [good on military activities].

See also Chivalry; Edward III; Hundred Years War; Richard II

Edward the Confessor (1002/05–1066; r. 1042–66)

Edward owes his title of Confessor to his canonization in 1161 by Pope Alexander III at the request of Henry II and the church and at the instigation of the monks of Westminster Abbey, where he was buried. Although the historical figure and the image of the Confessor have little in common, the title serves to distinguish him from such Anglo-Saxon kings as Edward the Elder and Edward the Martyr.

Edward was born at Islip, near Oxford, between 1002 and 1005, the seventh son of Æthelred II, "the Unready," and the first from his second marriage, to Emma, sister of Duke Richard II of Normandy, an alliance designed to protect the king from Viking attacks. Edward's "miraculous" acquisition of the throne in 1042, after 24 years of obscure exile in Normandy and its environs (1017–41), was made possible by the deaths of the Danish usurpers Cnut and his sons, Harold Harefoot and Harthacnut, and of most other potential pretenders, his younger brother, Alfred, and his six senior half-brothers, represented only by Edmund Ironside's son, Edward "the Exile," in Hungary.

But to gain and hold the throne Edward had to accept the protection of Godwin, earl of Wessex, marry Godwin's daughter, Edith (Eadgyth), and raise his sons to earldoms. Edward found it hard to break free. Because of Cnut's division of the kingdom into great provincial earldoms and the erosion of the royal demesne Edward could provide only small estates for his French followers. Although he had more scope in the church and appointed some interesting continentals to bishoprics, his best hope of independence lay in the suspicion of Godwin felt by the other great earls, the English Leofric of Mercia and the Danish Siward of Northumbria.

Like his father, Æthelred II, Edward has an undeserved reputation as a weak king. Healthy, a keen hunter and soldier, a great survivor, and—although occasionally rash and ill advised—determined not to go on his travels again, he warded off his external enemies by warlike gestures and shrewd diplomacy. He exploited his childlessness—explained by later legend as due to an unconsummated marriage—as a diplomatic asset, making empty promises of the succession to Earl Godwin's nephew, King Swein of Denmark, in the 1040s; his cousin-once-removed William duke of Normandy, at the end of the decade; his half-nephew, Edward the Exile, in 1054–57. He may also have aroused the hopes of other relatives of his parents and wife.

In 1051, under the influence of Robert of Jumièges, a Norman abbot whom he made bishop of London and then archbishop of Canterbury, Edward fell foul of his father-in-law and provoked a showdown. Godwin's half-hearted rebellion collapsed when earls Leofric and Siward supported the king; the rebel and his sons were outlawed and fled abroad. In the following year, however, they returned by force and, as Leofric and Siward, alienated by Edward's willfulness, now stood aloof, secured their restoration. This time it was Robert of Jumièges and other Frenchmen who fled.

After Godwin's death in 1053 Edward and the Godwinsons reached a *modus vivendi,* and a period of prosperity set in. According to the *Vita Aedwardi regis,* an early account of the reign, the dominance of Godwin's children made England great. Harold, earl of Wessex after 1053, ruled the south; Tostig, after 1055 earl of Northumbria, ruled the north; Queen Edith ruled the court. The Welsh and the Scots were dominated, good laws prevailed, and the king and queen refounded monasteries as their mausoleums. But in 1065 some of Tostig's vassals rebelled against his harsh rule, Harold would not save his brother from exile, and Edward's mortification was such that he suffered a fatal stroke.

He died on 5 January 1066, just after the dedication of his new church at Westminster (pictured on the Bayeux Tapestry). His achievement was to have held his unstable kingdom together for 24 years and bequeath it intact to his brother-in-law Harold. No wonder that in the following centuries the "Laws of King Edward" became the symbol of a Golden Age.

Frank Barlow

Bibliography

PRIMARY

Barlow, Frank, ed. and trans. *The Life of King Edward Who Rests at Westminster* [*Vita Aedwardi regis*]. 2d ed. Oxford: Clarendon, 1992; Whitelock, Dorothy, ed., with David C. Douglas and Susie I. Tucker. *The Anglo-Saxon Chronicle: A Revised Translation.* London: Eyre & Spottiswoode, 1961.

SECONDARY

Barlow, Frank. *Edward the Confessor.* Berkeley: University of California Press, 1970 [the only modern biography]; Loyn, H.R. *Anglo-Saxon England and the Norman Conquest.* London: Longmans, 1962.

See also Æthelred II; Bayeux Tapestry; Emma; Godwin; Harold; Norman Conquest; William I

Eleanor Crosses

Twelve sculpted stone crosses were erected by Edward I between 1291 and 1295 to mark the resting places of the funeral procession of his wife, Eleanor of Castile (d. 1290), from Hardby in Lincolnshire, where she died, to Westminster, where she was buried. Crosses were erected at Lincoln, Grantham, Stamford, Geddington, Hardingstone, Stony Stratford, Woburn, Dunstable, St. Albans, Waltham, Cheapside, and Charing; only the crosses at Geddington, Hardingstone (Northamptonshire), and Waltham (Essex) survive. The crosses are generally considered to signal the beginning of the Decorated style of English Gothic.

A record of payments for the Eleanor crosses survives (London, PRO E.101/353/1), which provides a detailed account of the artists involved in the monuments' production. Richard of Stow was responsible for the cross at Lincoln; Michael of Canterbury carved the Cheapside cross, for which he received £300; Richard of Crundale made the cross at Charing; five of the crosses (Hardingstone, Dunstable, St. Albans, Stony Stratford, and Woburn) were the work of John of Battle.

The Hardingstone cross is one of the most luxurious. The base is octagonal in form and divided into three tiers; the lowest tier is decorated with blind arcades articulated by seaweed foliage and enclosing open books and the arms of Ponthieu, Castile, Leon, and England, the arches separated by

pinnacles; the middle tier consists of four open cusped ogee arches decorated with blind tracery and foliage and housing statues of the queen; the top story is decorated with blind arches capped by foliate pinnacles. The three statues of Eleanor by William of Ireland show an awareness of continental developments. The queen is idealized with a delicate head and long flowing hair. Her body appears somewhat short and fat, due in part to the voluminous and decorative folds of her drapery.

The Geddington cross is delicate in appearance, employing many of the motifs popular in contemporary metalwork. The lower tiers are decorated with diaper pattern and shields; the gabled arches (blind on the lower tier, open on the middle tier) are capped with foliate finials. The emphasis is on straight vertical lines. The statues of the queen are in a much simpler and less refined style than William of Ireland's, suggesting the work of provincial craftsmen.

The Waltham cross is identical in plan to that at Hardingstone, but the decoration is quite different. The lowest tier is covered with elaborate blind tracery and niches housing shields; the middle tier consists of graduated buttresses capped with foliate finials and houses three statues of the queen by Alexander of Abingdon (also the sculptor of the Charing statues). Alexander's statues are the most refined and elegant of the group. Again Eleanor is idealized with a graceful face and long flowing hair; her slim body is carved in a slightly swaying pose, one hand delicately holding the strings of her cloak.

The Eleanor crosses were erected out of Edward's love for his dead queen but also out of emulation of the French court; they appear to have been inspired by a series of similar crosses erected for St. Louis by Philip III in 1271. They are also part of a much larger series of monuments memorializing Eleanor, including her tomb at Westminster; a shrine encasing her heart in London Blackfriars, which consisted of a golden angel set on a cenotaph decorated with weepers; a tomb for her bowels in the Lincoln Lady Chapel decorated with metal weepers and a gilt-bronze effigy of the queen; and chantries at Hardby, Lincoln, Peterborough, and London Blackfriars.

Catherine E. Karkov

Bibliography

Alexander, Jonathan, and Paul Binski, eds. *Age of Chivalry: Art in Plantagenet England 1200–1400.* London: Royal Academy of Arts, 1987, cat. nos. 368–76; Evans, Joan. *English Art 1307–1461.* Oxford: Clarendon, 1949; Parsons, David, ed. *Eleanor of Castile, 1290–1990: Essays to Commemorate the 700th Anniversary of Her Death.* Stamford: Watkins, 1991; Stone, Lawrence. *Sculpture in Britain: The Middle Ages.* 2d ed. Harmondsworth: Penguin, 1972.

See also Architecture and Architectural Sculpture, Gothic; Art, Gothic; Chantries; Edward I; Iconography; Metalwork, Gothic; Sculpture, Gothic

Eleanor of Aquitaine (ca. 1122–1204)

The duchy of Aquitaine was the largest, most populous region of France in the 12th and 13th centuries. Its proximity to the Mediterranean and its cultural and commercial contacts with the Greek and Byzantine worlds attracted wealth and immigrants. It was openly coveted by French kings, who, in the 13th century, would rely on the pretext of eradicating heresy to invade it. Earlier, in the 10th and 11th centuries, it had been controlled, for the most part with generosity and flexibility, by dukes whose creativity and precocity are legendary. William III founded the Abbey of Cluny in 910; William IX offered his irreverent troubadour poems to the courts of Europe.

In 1137 the only child of William X, Eleanor, who possessed the spirited character of her forebears, inherited the duchy and was immediately married to the French king, Louis VII. Later, after befriending Geoffrey, count of Anjou, she became wife to his son, the future Henry II of England. The marriage not only transferred the richness of Aquitaine from the French to the English monarchy, where it remained until 1214, but it united two formerly competing provinces.

Thus it might be supposed that Eleanor was a key individual in the government of the Angevin Empire, but the evidence for her influence is slight. Narrative sources deal mainly with the kings, and she appears fleetingly in them. Few charters are extant from Poitou, which Eleanor governed in the 1160s and 1180s. In other areas of the Angevin Empire, where more charters survive, she attested infrequently—a reflection, perhaps, of the time spent early on bearing children and her long interval of imprisonment.

Eleanor supported Henry II's early endeavors to expand and control Angevin lands and, later, her sons' revolts against their father to obtain portions of those lands; her independent policies are difficult to trace. Her cultural influence may have been pervasive, however. The movement of her court from southern to northern France and England helped convey the ideals of courtly love to the European nobility. Romantic themes found full literary expression at the court of her daughter, Marie countess of Champagne, who sponsored the work of Chrétien de Troyes, and in her son Richard the Lionheart, whose love songs were sung throughout France.

Thus Eleanor is often viewed as a mirror of her husbands' and sons' achievements. It is perhaps more instructive to view her condition as fairly typical of women of the upper nobility in the high Middle Ages. Despite her talent and strength of character her key roles involved bearing children and the transfer of land. Married at fifteen, she lost her first child when he was three years old, and she bore her last, John, in what was likely to have been a difficult pregnancy, at 44. Her willful nature embarrassed Louis VII, incurred the censure of his clerical friends, and may have brought about their divorce after fifteen years of marriage (1137–52), although there is some suggestion that Eleanor herself engineered the split.

She protested the infidelity of her second husband, Henry, whom she married at 30 (when he was only 19) and to whom she would be wife for 37 years (1152–89). This audacity, together with her power over her children and her influence in Aquitaine and at the English and Angevin courts, resulted in imprisonment at Winchester for sixteen years (1173–89, when Henry died). After regaining her freedom she acted as regent for both Richard and John, realizing her potential only in widowhood.

Eleanor's acts involved a reversal of Henry's oppression—amnesty for those awaiting judicial trial and a relaxing of obligations imposed on abbeys—as well as patronage. She protected Richard's interests against the ambitions of France's Philip Augustus and Prince John. Then, when Richard died in 1199, Eleanor undertook goodwill visits on John's behalf. Toward the end of her life, dispirited and worn, she took up residence at the Angevin abbey of Fontevrault, where she is buried.

Stephanie Christelow

Bibliography

Duby, Georges. *Medieval Marriage: Two Models from Twelfth-Century France.* Trans. Elborg Forster. Baltimore: Johns Hopkins University Press, 1978; Kelly, Amy. *Eleanor of Aquitaine and the Four Kings.* Cambridge: Harvard University Press, 1950; Warren, W.L. *Henry II.* Rev. ed. London: Methuen, 1991.

See also Angevin Empire; Anglo-Norman Literature; Courtly Love; Henry II; John; Queens; Richard I

Elstob, Elizabeth (1683–1756)

Anglo-Saxonist and advocate of women's education. Born in Newcastle-upon-Tyne, Elstob lost her father when she was five and her mother, who instilled in her the love of learning, three years later. She then passed into the guardianship of her uncle the Rev. Charles Elstob, prebendary of Canterbury, who refused to allow her to continue her study of Latin on the grounds that "one Tongue is enough for a Woman" (as Elizabeth later explained), although eventually he permitted her to study French.

In 1691 Elstob's brother William (1673–1715) entered Queen's College, Oxford—the preeminent center for Anglo-Saxon studies in the late 17th and early 18th centuries—and in 1696 was elected Fellow of University College, whose master, Arthur Charlett, promoted Anglo-Saxon studies and encouraged the great Anglo-Saxon paleographer Humfrey Wanley (1672–1726). It was William's transcription, made in 1698, of the OE version of Orosius's *History against the Pagans* that fired his sister's interest in the language. When in 1702 William moved to London as rector of St. Swithun's, Elizabeth joined him there and was able to pursue unhindered her zest for scholarly work. Her first publication, a translation of the *Discours de la gloire* by Madeleine de Scudéry (1607–1701), appeared in 1708 and was followed a year later by her edition and English translation of Ælfric's homily on Pope Gregory the Great, which she entitled *An English-Saxon Homily on the Birth-Day of St. Gregory.* By now she was well known to the circle of Anglo-Saxonists and enjoyed the support of George Hickes (1642–1715), the foremost English scholar of the northern European languages and a proponent of female education.

Elstob's final publication, *The Rudiments of Grammar for the English-Saxon Tongue* (1715), drew upon Hickes's own monumental study of OE grammar in his *Linguarum veterum septentrionalium thesaurus* of 1703–05. Elstob also made an unpublished transcription of the Textus Roffensis, a Rochester Cathedral manuscript containing Anglo-Saxon laws, and planned a complete edition of Ælfric's homilies. The greater part of her manuscript for this edition, described by Hickes as "the most correct that I ever saw or read," survives as BL Lansdowne 370–74 and Egerton 838. Although 36 pages of proofs were issued by the Oxford press, the edition never appeared, for, following the death of both Hickes and her brother William in 1715, Elstob's fortunes declined dramatically. Within a few years, burdened by debt, she left London, entrusting her books and papers to a neighbor who emigrated to the West Indies soon after; Elstob never recovered her belongings.

Elstob herself disappeared from view for several years, and she never revived her scholarly career. By 1735, when she began a fruitful correspondence with the antiquary George Ballard (1706–1755), she was teaching in an elementary school at Evesham, Worcestershire. Dogged by ill-health for the rest of her life, in 1739 she was appointed governess to the children of Margaret, duchess of Portland (daughter of Edward Harley, second earl of Oxford), a post that she retained until her death. Her correspondence with Ballard and others, while attesting to her happiness in overseeing the education of her charges, reveals also an abiding regret at her isolation from the scholarly world.

Elstob's achievement in the period of her life that she devoted to OE studies was notable. On her own analysis she was "the first Woman that has Studied that Language since it was spoke." Her *English-Saxon Homily* provided, for the first time, a full edition of one of Ælfric's homilies accompanied by both footnotes and an English translation. Elstob's lengthy introduction to the book—which, along with the long list of subscribers at the end, prompted the Oxford antiquary Thomas Hearne (1678–1735) to dismiss the work, unjustly, as "this Farrago of Vanity"—incorporated a feminized vision of English history that stressed the role of Bertha, queen of Kent, in the conversion of the Anglo-Saxons by St. Augustine and furnished a list of illustrious English women down to Queen Anne herself, to whom the book was dedicated. The initial that begins Elstob's English translation of the homily includes her own portrait.

The *Rudiments of Grammar,* conceived after a young woman had expressed to her a wish to learn OE, was intended by Elstob to enable other women to attain "the Pleasure I myself had reaped from the Knowledge I have gained from this Original of our Mother Tongue." By writing the book in English rather than Latin Elstob made it accessible to women and was able to demonstrate the kinship between OE and the English of her own day. In the *Apology for the Study of Northern Antiquities* with which she prefaced the work, she vigorously defended OE against the attacks of, among others, Jonathan Swift (1667–1745), who had branded the language as barbarous. It is to be lamented that Elstob's scholarly career was abruptly curtailed by circumstance. She herself, in her letters and in the brief autobiographical memoir that she wrote for Ballard in 1638 (Bodl. Ballard 43, fols. 59v–60r), showed a keen awareness of the many disappointments of her life. Nonetheless, her published work, admired by her contemporary Anglo-Saxonists, stands as a landmark in the history of OE studies.

Timothy Graham

Bibliography

PRIMARY

Elstob, Elizabeth, ed. *An English-Saxon Homily on the Birth-Day of St. Gregory: Anciently Used in the English-Saxon Church.* London: Bowyer, 1709; Elstob, Elizabeth. *The Rudiments of Grammar for the English-Saxon Tongue, First Given in English, with an Apology for the Study of Northern Antiquities.* London: W. Bowyer, 1715.

SECONDARY

Ashdown, Margaret. "Elizabeth Elstob, the Learned Saxonist." *Modern Language Review* 20 (1925): 125–46; Berkhout, Carl T., and Milton McC. Gatch, eds. *Anglo-Saxon Scholarship: The First Three Centuries.* Boston: Hall, 1982 [see Sarah H. Collins, "The Elstobs and the End of the Saxon Revival," pp. 107–18, and Shaun F.D. Hughes, "The Anglo-Saxon Grammars of George Hickes and Elizabeth Elstob," pp. 119–47]; Green, Mary Elizabeth. "Elizabeth Elstob: 'The Saxon Nymph' (1683–1756)." In *Female Scholars: A Tradition of Learned Women before 1800,* ed. J.R. Brink. Montreal: Eden Press, 1980, pp. 137–60; Robinson, Fred C. "Eight Letters from Elizabeth Elstob." In *The Endless Knot: Essays on Old and Middle English in Honor of Marie Borroff,* ed. M. Teresa Tavormina and R.F. Yeager. Cambridge: Brewer, 1995, pp. 241–52; Sutherland, Kathryn. "Editing for a New Century: Elizabeth Elstob's Anglo-Saxon Manifesto and Ælfric's St. Gregory Homily." In *The Editing of Old English: Papers from the 1990 Manchester Conference,* ed. D.G. Scragg and Paul E. Szarmach. Cambridge: Brewer, 1994, pp. 213–37.

See also Ælfric; Cotton; Nowell; Parker; Queens

Ely Cathedral

The Benedictine abbey church of Ely (fig. 58) was commenced about 1081 by Abbot Simeon, brother of Walkelin, bishop of Winchester. The eastern arm and probably the transepts and eastern bays of the nave were finished for the 1106 translation of St. Etheldreda. Cathedral status was granted in 1109. The presbytery was built between 1234 and 1251, and the choir was rebuilt after the fall of the tower in 1322, at which time the crossing was expanded into the magnificent Octagon.

Of the four-bay Romanesque presbytery the responds of the triumphal arch are extant. The stilted apse was soon squared off. The aisles terminated in flat east walls. At the apse chord the galleries and clerestories were probably linked with spiral staircases, as at Peterborough Cathedral. The Romanesque transepts and nave are well preserved. As at Winchester the transepts have eastern and western aisles, and were built with cross-aisles. The latter were replaced (ca. 1150) by the present walkways. The thirteen-bay nave terminated in an aisleless western transept (of which only the southern arm is preserved) with double-story apsidal chapels to the east, a single tower, and a galilee porch, the latter built by Bishop Eustace (1197–1215). The great length of the church recalls the largest early Christian basilicas in Rome and conforms to the post-Conquest trend established at St. Albans (1077) and Winchester (1079) for churches with the relics of important local saints. The three-story elevation with equally proportioned main arcade and subdivided gallery arches, and a clerestory with wall passage, evolves from Winchester and belongs to the type established at St. Étienne at Caen. The transept main arcades have plain two-order arches carried on volute capitals except in the west arcade of the north transept, where scalloped capitals are introduced. Compound and columnar piers are used but not in a straightforward alternation; in the north transept the middle pier of both arcades is columnar, while in the south transept the column is the third from the crossing—a strange arrangement given that it originally carried the arch of the terminal aisle.

This variety in pier design continues with more complex forms in the second campaign of construction in the transept galleries, in which cushion capitals are used exclusively and the arches have three orders and roll moldings. In the main arcades of the nave, major compound piers alternate with minor piers of columnar plan that, like the major piers, have dosserets (additional stone blocks between their capitals and the arch spandrels) and half-shafts on the back and front to uniformly accommodate the transverse arches of the aisle vaults and the vertical articulation to the top of the wall. The minor piers in the nave galleries also have shafts to east and west to carry subarches. The aisles are groin-vaulted throughout and in the nave, on the model of Norwich Cathedral, have round-headed dado arcades below chevron stringcourses. The influence of the Norwich crossing tower is evident in the lavish interior articulation of the southwest transept, on which work was completed by Bishop Riddel (1173–89).

The Monks' and Prior's doorways are richly carved, the latter with Christ in Majesty in the tympanum. Certain forms suggest Italian connections, while the figure style conforms to late Anglo-Saxon traditions. The luxuriant foliage forms also appear in the possibly contemporary vault paintings in the south nave aisle.

Malcolm Thurlby

Bibliography

Fernie, Eric. "Observations on the Norman Plan of Ely Cathedral." In *Medieval Art and Architecture at Ely Cathedral. BAACT* for 1976. London: British Archaeological Association, 1979, pp. 1–7; McAleer, J. Philip. "A Note about the Transept Cross Aisles of Ely Cathedral." *Proceedings of the Cambridge Antiquarian Society* 81 (1992): 51–70; McAleer, J. Philip. "Some Observations about the Romanesque Choir of Ely Cathedral." *Journal of the Society of Architectural Historians* 53 (1994): 80–94;

Fig. 58. Ely Cathedral, nave interior. Courtesy RCHME, copyright Batsford.

Stewart, D.J. *On the Architectural History of Ely Cathedral.* London: van Voorst, 1868.

See also Architecture and Architectural Sculpture, Romanesque; Norwich Cathedral; St. Albans Abbey; Sculpture, Romanesque; Winchester Cathedral

Emma (ca. 985–1052)

Danish attacks, conquest, and the resulting complexity of succession to the English throne in the 11th century were the context of the power and role of Emma, queen of England. Daughter of the duke of Normandy, she was married to Æthelred II in 1002 as part of an alliance against Danish attacks. In 1017 Cnut took her as wife in his quest for legitimacy and security. Emma had sons by both husbands: Edward the Confessor and Alfred by Æthelred, Harthacnut by Cnut.

Emma's role in Æthelred's reign mirrored that of 10th-century queens, important at court but rarely dominant during the husband's lifetime. As Cnut's wife she was prominent. Cnut's insecurity and his prolonged absences in Denmark gave her an increasing role in patronage and at court; she may have acted as regent. On his death Emma attempted to ensure the rule of one of her sons against Cnut's son Harold Harefoot, born to Ælfgifu of Northampton. She seized the treasure at Winchester, but her initiative was thwarted, since Harthacnut lingered in Denmark and Edward and Alfred attracted little support from the English nobility. Harold gained ground and Emma was exiled. Harold's death in 1040 allowed her to return with Harthacnut; in 1041 they brought Edward into association as the probable heir.

After Edward's accession in 1042 Emma's power waned. She had little influence over an adult son, who had been exiled for 25 years. She spent her last decade in religious obscurity in Winchester.

Emma was an active political woman at a time when complex and turbulent English politics proved a graveyard for many reputations. She answered the accusations touching her shifting loyalties and family alliances by commissioning the fascinating *Encomium Emmae,* written in the 1040s by an anonymous monk of St. Bertin or St. Omer in Flanders. That work, like her career, shows her fortunes bound to those of husband and sons and the lack of an independent basis of action for even the most powerful and able woman.

Pauline Stafford

Bibliography

Campbell, Alistair, ed. *Encomium Emmae reginae.* Camden Society, 3d ser. 72 (1949); Campbell, Miles W. "The *Encomium Emmae reginae:* Personal Panegyric or Political Propaganda?" *Annuale mediaevale* 19 (1979): 27–45; John, Eric. "The *Encomium Emmae reginae:* A Riddle and a Solution." *BJRL* 63 (1980): 58–94; Stafford, Pauline. "The King's Wife in Wessex 800–1066." *Past and Present* 91 (May 1981): 3–27; Stafford, Pauline. *Queens, Concubines, and Dowagers: The King's Wife in the Early Middle Ages.* Athens: University of Georgia Press, 1983; Stafford, Pauline. *Emma and Edith: Queens and Queenship in Eleventh-Century England.* Oxford: Blackwell, 1997.

See also Æthelred II; Cnut; Edward the Confessor; Queens; Women; Women in OE Literature

Enamels, Gothic

Among the handful of surviving English Gothic metalwork objects only a fraction demonstrate the skill of the enameler. Enameled ecclesiastical items suffered the same intentional destruction as other types of metalwork during the Dissolution of the monasteries in the 16th century, while secular pieces frequently fell prey to changes in late-medieval taste. In addition the fragility and high intrinsic value of Gothic enamels made their survival even more hazardous. Many of the rare enameled survivals have lost much, or all, of their original enamel: an example is the silver-gilt Bermondsey Dish (London, Bermondsey parish church, on loan to the Victoria and Albert Museum), ca. 1325. The central medallion, showing a woman handing a helm to a kneeling knight, retains only minute traces of translucent enamel. The silver-gilt Swinburne Pyx (London, Victoria and Albert Museum M.15–1950), 1310–25, originally covered with enamel, is now virtually uncolored: only vestiges of enamel occupy some areas of engraving.

Evidence suggests that by the mid-13th century the majority of English goldsmiths were laymen, working in large towns like London and York for both ecclesiastical and lay patrons. For some goldsmiths enameling was an integral part of their metalworking skills, but amid the increasing specialization of the Gothic period many worked exclusively as enamelers: in 1292 a Richard, "esmailleur de Londres," is recorded as working in Paris. Ordinances of the goldsmiths' guilds furnish further evidence of specialization and demonstrate the links established among types of goldsmith. The 1370 Ordinances of the London Goldsmiths place enamelers and seal engravers in one category, since their work involved many of the same skills. Close connections are also apparent between some enamelers and manuscript painters. For example, the designs on the

Fig. 59. Valence Casket (London, Victoria and Albert Museum 4–1865). Reproduced by permission of the Board of Trustees of the Victoria and Albert Museum, London.

Swinburne Pyx and in two contemporary East Anglian manuscripts (CUL Dd.4.17 and Cambridge, Corpus Christi College 53), are clearly derived from a common source.

Extant pieces adequately demonstrate the competence of English Gothic enamelers, but their work was largely influenced by technical developments occurring in France and Italy. Some Englishmen, such as Richard the Enameler, traveled abroad to gain expertise; others learned at first hand from continental goldsmiths working in England or from the quantities of enameled objects imported from metalworking centers like Limoges in southwest France. Thus objects like the Valence Casket (London, Victoria and Albert Museum 4–1865; fig. 59), ca. 1300, are difficult to localize. The heraldic decoration on this jewel or trinket box confirms its production for either Aymer de Valence (d. 1324) or his father, William (d. 1296), both of them English noblemen. The *champlevé* technique and form, however, relate most closely to Limoges work. The casket may be English and much influenced by Limoges models or the handiwork of a Limoges goldsmith working in either France or England. Evidence that numerous Limoges objects were produced specifically for the English market is demonstrated by 40 or more surviving *châsses*, or reliquary caskets, dating from the late 12th and 13th centuries; they depict the martyrdom of St. Thomas Becket, archbishop of Canterbury (d. 1170), and were designed to contain his relics.

Champlevé enamel, which was preferred to the exclusion of virtually any other technique during the 12th century (the Romanesque period), became less popular during the Gothic period. Sturdy, base-metal objects decorated with bold armorial designs, such as the Valence Casket and numerous small shield-shaped ornaments for horse trappings, demonstrate that *champlevé* did not die out completely. It was largely eclipsed, however, by a new technique developed in France or Italy in the late 13th century. The earliest extant piece of *basse taille*, or translucent enamel, is on a chalice in the treasury of San Francesco, Assisi, made and signed by Guccio di Mannaia for Pope Nicholas IV (1288–92). The emergence of this technique, which is successful only on gold or silver and thus tends to be executed on a relatively small scale, coincided advantageously with a greater availability of precious metals and higher levels of wealth among the nobility and middle classes in western Europe. In addition it was ideally suited to the fluid naturalism of Gothic style, enabling the goldsmith to dispense with rigid metal divisions between adjacent fields of enamel that had dominated opaque *champlevé* work. Instead the gold or silver plaque was engraved or chased in low relief with a design, and then coated entirely with an extremely thin layer of translucent enamel. The transparency of the enamel enhanced the skill of the engraving beneath, casting areas of deep relief into shadow and highlighting areas of low relief.

The majority of extant English *basse taille* enamels are executed on silver, but occasional gold pieces survive, such as the Campion Hall Triptych (Oxford, Campion Hall, on loan to the Victoria and Albert Museum), ca. 1350. Objects decorated with *rouge cler*, a translucent red enamel, are an exception to this general rule, as, for technical reasons, *rouge cler* was used only on gold. A number of similar silver-gilt triptychs and diptychs, designed as devotional aids for wealthy lay individuals, survive from the 14th century (e.g., London, Victoria and

Albert Museum M.544–1910, 217–1874, and M.545–1910). *Basse taille* provided the perfect technique for illustrating them on a miniature scale with popular scenes from the Life of the Virgin, the Passion, and saints' lives.

English *basse taille* enamels displaying purely secular subject matter are much rarer. A pendant case of the mid-14th century (London, Victoria and Albert Museum 218–1874) depicts scenes from a romance, possibly that of Sir Enyas and the *wodewose,* or wildman. The two paneled silver bands at the bell of the 12th-century Savernake Horn (London, British Museum MLA 1975, 4–1, 1), 1325–50, show a king, a bishop, and a forester surrounded by hunting dogs, forest animals, a unicorn, and a lion. The reserved, silver-gilt figures are set against grounds of translucent enamel. The silver-gilt, bell-shaped King John Cup (Borough Council of King's Lynn and West Norfolk), ca. 1340, also shows hunting and hawking scenes reserved against enameled grounds on the panels decorating its cover, cup, and foot (the present enamel is not original). This is the earliest surviving English medieval secular cup, and, although the exact nature of its royal connections is obscure, it represents an extremely lavish commission.

Technical advances made in the second half of the 14th century in Paris produced a new enameling technique, *email en ronde bosse,* or encrusted enamel. This involved covering gold or silver figures or objects engraved in high relief, or cast in the round, with a skin of opaque enamel. Superficial roughening of the metal's surface ensured that the enamel adhered firmly to it. Only two extant pieces can be tentatively identified as of English workmanship. The Dunstable Swan Jewel (London, British Museum MLA 1966, 7–3, I; fig. 60), ca. 1400, a small gold swan enameled in white *email en ronde bosse,* was designed as a livery badge, worn to denote its owner's allegiance. The reliquary of the Order of Sainte Esprit (Paris, Musée du Louvre), ca. 1410, decorated with encrusted enamel figures, was made for Joan of Navarre, Henry IV's second wife. This provenance, together with the presence of St. Edmund, king of the East Angles, makes it almost certainly English, perhaps London work.

Rare survivals like these back up the frequent descriptions in inventories of equally elaborate royal and noble commissions and testify to the enameling skills of English Gothic goldsmiths.

Sally Dormer

Bibliography

Alexander, Jonathan, and Paul Binski. *Age of Chivalry: Art in Plantagenet England 1200–1400.* London: Royal Academy of Arts, 1987 [exhibition catalogue]; Campbell, Marian. *An Introduction to Medieval Enamels.* London: Victoria and Albert Museum, 1983; Campbell, Marian. "Gold, Silver and Precious Stones." In *English Medieval Industries,* ed. J. Blair and N. Ramsey. London: Hambledon, 1991, pp. 107–66; Chamot, Mary. *English Mediaeval Enamels.* London: University College, 1930; Cherry, John. *Medieval Craftsmen: Goldsmiths.* London: British Museum, 1992; Gauthier, M.M. *Émaux du moyen âge occidental.* Fribourg: Office du Livre, 1972; Lightbown, R.W. *Secular Goldsmiths' Work in Medieval France: A History.* London: Society of Antiquaries of London, 1978 [provides details of contemporary continental goldsmiths' work].

See also Art, Gothic; "East Anglian School"; Liturgical Vessels; Manuscript Illumination, Gothic; Metalwork and Enamels, Romanesque

Estate Management

Lords expected their estates to provide both revenues and food for their household. In the 11th and early 12th centuries most lords, therefore, leased their estates (or manors) for a combination of goods (payments in kind) and money. The lessee would provide fixed sums of grain (e.g., 80 quarters of wheat, 120 quarters of barley, and 20 quarters of oats), a specified number of pigs, cheeses, and goods like honey or eels, plus a small cash sum. The system was inherently flexible, with the rent or "farm" varying from manor to manor and from year to year as the needs of the lord changed.

But there were serious problems with this system. Any extra profits, in years of good harvests, for example, would go into the hands of the lessee, not those of the lord. Some lessees did not pay rent on time, others wasted the property, cutting down trees and failing to manure the land. To combat this problem some monastic estates appointed monks as farmers or lessees. But this led to problems of a different nature, as the monk-farmer, living away from the monastery, acquired secular habits. When inflation hit around the turn of the 13th century, lords' expenses increased while incomes remained fixed. Gradually, one by one, in the course of the 13th century both lay and ecclesiastical lords gave up leasing their estates in favor of direct management.

The success of direct management depended heavily on the competence of local officials (serjeants or reeves), who actually ran the estates, and the effectiveness of centralized supervision. The serjeant (usually a free man) or the reeve (usually a villein) was responsible for seeing that fields were plowed, sown, and then weeded, meadows mowed, buildings, carts, and other implements kept in good repair, and grain harvested and stored. In addition he was responsible for the livestock—from doves and geese to sheep, cows, and oxen—and expected to record the number that had died, been consumed or sold, or remained at the end of each year. His accounts were carefully scrutinized by the lord's auditors, who might refuse to accept any item, insisting, for example, that the serjeant had paid too high a wage or, conversely, had accepted too low a price for any sales.

But although the serjeant was in charge of the day-to-day running of the estate, major policy decisions were made by the lord or his steward. It was this central figure who decided whether the grain or stock produced on a manor should be sent to feed the household, whether it should be sold, or whether part of it should be sold and part saved for the household. Furthermore changes in the normal agricultural pattern—the introduction of such new crops as beans or the introduction of dairy cattle—would be initiated at the central level.

Agricultural policies differed from place to place. Along the coast in southern and eastern England (Sussex, Kent,

Norfolk) grain was usually sown at a high rate of seed per acre; four bushels for wheat, five for barley, and six to eight for oats. Such dense sowing helped smother the weeds and led to higher yields per acre, even though the yields per seed often remained low. In addition many lords in these areas sowed legumes—peas, beans, or vetch—on land that would otherwise have lain fallow. These crops not only added nitrogen to the soil but provided forage for animals, so it was possible to keep larger flocks and herds. Lords took advantage of the high wool prices and the expansion of the overseas wool trade to increase the sheep flocks. Many of them also began to keep dairy cattle and either sold the cheese or leased the cows to a cheeseman.

Consequently in these areas direct demesne farming remained profitable right up to the 1370s. In contrast, in other parts of the country, few or no legumes were used and grain was sown at low seeding rates; one and a half to two bushels for wheat and two and a half to three for oats and barley, leading to low yields per acre. Faced with the need to feed an expanding population, the area under cultivation increased; marginal land and former pasture came under the plow. But without adequate pasture or supplementary forage, it was impossible to keep large flocks and herds. In some places the number of animals dwindled and with them the supply of manure. As a result the productivity of some land diminished. In parts of the Midlands and northern England, by the 1320s, lords were forced to cut back the area under cultivation and were facing a reduction in revenues.

In the mid-14th century a series of crises shook people's faith in the advisability of direct management. Heavy rains in 1315 and 1316 destroyed much of the wheat, leading to an acute shortage of grain. In many places sheep died of disease. In 1319–21 cattle disease attacked all parts of the country, often wiping out cow and ox herds. Lords had either to restock or switch to using horses for plowing. The start of the Hundred Years War brought further problems, including disruption of the wool trade. At the same time the country faced a serious deflation.

Although some lords coped with these crises by exploiting nonagricultural sources of revenue, especially the sale of timber, others abandoned direct management in favor of leasing. The sharp drop in population after the Black Death added a new set of problems. Wages rose, despite the attempt of the Statute of Labourers to keep them down. Villeins often refused to carry out customary labor services, and lords had no option but to commute them into a money payment.

Uncertain what policy to pursue, lords leased out some of their manors and kept others in hand. But at the end of the 14th century, when deflation set in, leasing once more became the normal practice. Lords, however, still had to provision their households. Thus knightly families frequently kept at least one manor in hand to serve as a home farm. On the great ecclesiastical estates, rents, although expressed in money, were in practice often paid in kind. A lessee, for example, might be charged an annual rent of £10 but would meet his obligations by supplying grain or stock to the household. By the 15th century the system of estate management had thus come full circle.

Mavis E. Mate

Bibliography

Dyer, Christopher. *Lords and Peasants in a Changing Society: The Estates of the Bishopric of Worcester, 860–1540.* Cambridge: Cambridge University Press, 1981; Harvey, Barbara. *Westminster Abbey and Its Estates in the Middle Ages.* Oxford: Clarendon, 1977; Lomas, R.S. "The Priory of Durham and Its Demesnes in the Fourteenth and Fifteenth Centuries." *EcHR,* 2d ser. 31 (1978): 339–53; Mate, Mavis. "The Farming Out of Manors: A New Look at the Evidence from Canterbury Cathedral Priory." *JMH* 9 (1983): 331–43 [on the return to leasing]; Miller, Edward. "England in the Twelfth and Thirteenth Centuries—An Economic Contrast?" *EcHR,* 2d ser. 24 (1971): 1–14; Miller, Edward. "The Farming of Manors and Direct Management." *EcHR,* 2d ser. 26 (1973): 138–40 [both of Miller's essays explore the rationale behind leasing policies]; Saul, Nigel. *Scenes from Provincial Life: Knightly Families in Sussex, 1280–1400.* Oxford: Clarendon, 1986 [with Harvey, Dyer, and Lomas, excellent case studies of specific groups of estates].

See also Agriculture; Black Death; Labor Services; Manorialism; Prices and Wages

Eton College

The college of Our Lady at Eton (Buckinghamshire) was founded by Henry VI in 1440. For twenty years it received royal patronage and papal and episcopal favors; when Henry was overthrown in 1461 its fortunes declined and it only narrowly escaped disbanding and annexation to St. George's, Windsor. Largely through the tenacity of the fourth provost, Westbury, it survived, though on a reduced scale, weathering the political upheavals of late-15th-century England and the religious upheaval of the Reformation.

Eton's 1440 foundation charter provided for a provost, ten fellows, four clerks, six choristers, a schoolmaster, 25 poor and indigent scholars, and 25 poor and infirm men. A secular college incorporating a school and almshouse, Eton was soon linked with Henry's Cambridge foundation, King's College, on the model of Wykeham's foundations of Winchester College and New College, Oxford.

William Wainfleet, master at Winchester, was appointed Eton's first schoolmaster, becoming provost by 1443. Revised statutes of Henry VI brought the educational element into greater prominence, providing for 70 scholars, ten fellows, ten chaplains, ten clerks, and sixteen choristers, but only thirteen almsmen. An usher was added to assist the master, fee-paying boarders were admitted, and free Latin grammar schooling was to be offered to an indefinite number of boys from anywhere in England. The scholarships were allocated on conditions similar to those at Winchester.

Henry VI forbade rival establishments within ten miles of Eton. The original schoolroom is still intact, but the earliest solid information about the school's organization and routine is found in the *Consuetudinarium* of 1560. Eton and Winchester, originally designed as feeder schools for their related university colleges, were excepted, along with Oxford and Cambridge, from secularizing legislation under Henry VIII and Edward VI, as places where "yowth and good wyttes be educated and noryshed in vertue and larning."

Helen M. Jewell

Bibliography

Chandler, Richard. *The Life of William Waynflete, Bishop of Winchester.* London: White & Cochran, 1811; Hussey, Christopher. *Eton College.* 4th ed. London: Country Life, 1952; Lyte, Henry Churchill Maxwell. *History of Eton College, 1440–1910.* 4th ed. London: Macmillan, 1911.

See also Henry VI; Schools; Wainfleet; Winchester

Eusebius (fl. 8th century)

An 8th-century Anglo-Saxon cleric and poet, Eusebius was the author of one of the collections of Latin *enigmata,* or riddles. His identity is uncertain. He has traditionally been associated with Hwætberht, abbot of Wearmouth-Jarrow and friend of Bede, based on Bede's statement that Hwætberht was also known as Eusebius. Michael Lapidge, however, following Neil Wright, believes Eusebius to be a Southumbrian, otherwise unknown, based on the metrical and stylistic characteristics of the riddles, which emulate more closely the work of Aldhelm and Tatwine than that of Bede. That he finishes a collection of riddles written by Tatwine, archbishop of Canterbury, supports the theory.

Eusebius supplements Tatwine's collection of 40 *enigmata* with 60 of his own, bringing the total number up to 100, following the models of Symphosius and Aldhelm. It is generally agreed that Eusebius's riddles, however, do not match the high style and intellect of Aldhelm, Tatwine, or Symphosius. He is ultimately unable to sustain the theological framework with which he begins and toward the end simply copies his sources.

While Eusebius could not rise to the model set by his predecessors, it may be that he did not share their vision. Aldhelm and Tatwine focus heavily on metrics. Moreover their collections contain several riddles dealing with articles of Christian worship, but only one or two pertaining to writing. In contrast not one of Eusebius's riddles refers to the mass, but many show a great interest in language. For Eusebius, perhaps a scribe writing within a closed monastic community, reading and writing provided the strongest link between divine and human. His collection contains eleven riddles related to the art of writing, language, and letters, with solutions that include speech, the letters of the alphabet, and writing implements. In addition, following Isidore of Seville, his nature riddles are concerned largely with how things are named. Perhaps the modern reader, expecting another Aldhelm or Tatwine, too hastily judges Eusebius's work against standards that do not obtain.

Helene Scheck

Bibliography

PRIMARY

Glorie, F., ed., and Erika von Erhardt-Siebold, trans. *Aenigmata Evsebii.* In *Tatvini Opera Omnia; Variae*
Collectiones Aenigmatvm Merovingicae Aetatis, ed. Maria De Marco and F. Glorie. CCSL 133. Turnhout: Brepols, 1968, pp. 211–71.

SECONDARY

Bolton, W.F. *A History of Anglo-Latin Literature 597–1066.* Vol. 1: *597–740.* Princeton: Princeton University Press, 1967; Lapidge, Michael. "The Anglo-Latin Background." In *A New Critical History of Old English Literature,* ed. Stanley B. Greenfield and Daniel G. Calder. New York: New York University Press, 1986, pp. 5–37; Lendinara, Patrizia. "The World of Anglo-Saxon Learning." In *The Cambridge Companion to Old English Literature,* ed. Malcolm Godden and Michael Lapidge. Cambridge: Cambridge University Press, 1991.

See also Aldhelm; Anglo-Latin Literature to 1066; Bede; Riddles; Tatwine

Exchequer and the Pipe Rolls

The exchequer was the greatest of the central offices of English government. Its function was to exact and disburse the revenue due to the king and to audit annually the accounts of the sheriffs and other bailiffs responsible for collection. These accounts were recorded on the pipe rolls.

The first certain reference to the exchequer comes around 1110. Before 1154 only one pipe roll survives, the roll for the accounts heard in the Michaelmas (29 September) term, 1130. From 1154 on there is an almost continuous annual series until their abolition in 1834. The pipe rolls and other exchequer records, together with the *Dialogue of the Exchequer,* reveal in detail how the exchequer worked. It usually sat at Westminster and was divided into two departments, the lower exchequer, or exchequer of receipt, where the money was received, and the upper exchequer, where the audits took place.

The chief officials were called the "barons." The president, down to 1234, was the chief justiciar, and thereafter, the justiciarship having been abolished, the first place was taken by the treasurer of the exchequer. From the 13th century the exchequer's seal, authenticating the letters sent to summon the sheriffs and other debtors to settle their accounts, was kept by the chancellor of the exchequer. Twice a year, before Easter and Michaelmas, the exchequer prepared and sent to the sheriffs "the summonses," the lists of debts they were to collect and pay into the lower exchequer on the day after the close of Easter and on the day after Michaelmas.

In practice, by the 13th century, the bulk of the money was not received immediately on these days but came in gradually. The lower exchequer remained open for the receipt of cash through most of the year. This money was recorded on receipt rolls, of which there were two for each financial year, one beginning at Easter, the other at Michaelmas. As proof that the sheriff had indeed paid the money demanded, the exchequer gave him a tally stick, normally one for each individual debt. This was a stick with the amount of money paid in written along its left- and righthand side and then cut down the middle in a jagged line. The sheriff kept one half, the exchequer the other.

Every Michaelmas the sheriffs were summoned to account at the upper exchequer for all debts they had been ordered to pay since the audit of the previous financial year. By the 13th century hearing these accounts occupied the exchequer from Michaelmas through to the following summer. Each sheriff was taken in turn. He would sit with the barons of the exchequer around a table covered by a checkered cloth; from this cloth, resembling a chessboard *(scaccarium),* the exchequer derived its name. Separate columns were marked for pence, shillings, pounds, and twenties, hundreds, and thousands of pounds.

The amount outstanding from each debt was set out in counters. The sheriff proved how much he had paid in by producing his half of the tally stick to match with the half kept by the exchequer. Alternatively the sheriff could show, by producing a warrant in the form of a writ, that he had spent a given sum on the king's orders. The amount of the debt discharged in either of these ways was likewise set up in counters and the process of subtraction became easy to follow.

The exchequer recorded the accounts thus heard on annual pipe rolls, each dated by the regnal year. The pipe roll that records the accounts heard between Michaelmas 1221 and 21 June 1222 is thus called the roll for the fifth year of King Henry III. The pipe roll was made up of a number of *rotuli* (sixteen in the roll for the fifth year of Henry III), each of which consisted of two membranes of sheepskin sewn together, the total length (in the 13th century) being around 5 feet and the width some 14 inches. These *rotuli* were sewn together at the top and rolled up to resemble a "pipe" (French), hence the name pipe roll. The Pipe Roll Society (founded 1884) has to date published all the rolls down to the fifth year of Henry III.

Alongside the pipe rolls the exchequer kept memoranda rolls, one begun at Michaelmas, one at Easter. These recorded, among other things, letters sent to and despatched by the exchequer, decisions of the barons, and pronouncements made at the exchequer by the king. The legal cases heard by the exchequer, which from the 13th century chiefly concerned disputes over debts, were recorded on the plea rolls of the exchequer.

The exchequer was also involved in disbursing the king's money. That paid into the lower exchequer was usually stored in a treasury over which the treasurer and chamberlains of the exchequer had control. The king was constantly sending letters (writs of *liberate*) that ordered these officials to pay out money for a wide variety of purposes. The sums disbursed were recorded on issue rolls, of which, again, one was begun at Easter, another at Michaelmas.

The origins of the exchequer are obscure. The first certain reference is from around 1110, but before that the kings must have had some means of auditing the money owed them. To what extent those means were less elaborate and sophisticated than the system revealed by the pipe roll of 1130 is hard to say. *The Dialogue of the Exchequer* preserves a memory of a central office of audit before the development of the exchequer cloth; it states that the words "at the exchequer" had once been "at the tallies."

In the 12th century the exchequer had been the only central office of government and had frequently combined its financial functions with those of a court, hearing a wide variety of judicial pleas. This ceased in the 1190s, when a separate judicial court, the Bench, was established at Westminster. The exchequer's financial work, meanwhile, became rapidly more burdensome and time-consuming. This was partly because the revenue with which it dealt was expanding; partly because that revenue came increasingly from numerous small individual debts rather than from limited numbers of large sums derived from land.

The rolls of the exchequer multiplied in size until they became almost impossibly cumbersome. Efforts at reform were made in 1270 and in the 1320s, when "desperate" debts and other redundant items were removed from the pipe rolls. If, however, the exchequer was sometimes bypassed—with revenue being paid directly into the king's wardrobe or chamber—it remained the chief financial institution of English government for the rest of the Middle Ages and beyond.

D.A. Carpenter

Bibliography

The Pipe Rolls have been edited and published under the auspices of the Pipe Roll Society since 1884; Galbraith, Vivian H. *An Introduction to the Use of the Public Records.* Oxford: Clarendon, 1934. Corr. repr. 1952; Johnson, Charles, ed. and trans. *Dialogus de Scaccario: The Course of the Exchequer, by Richard Fitz Neale.* Corr. Frank E.L. Carter and Diana E. Greenway. Oxford: Clarendon, 1983 [this modern edition of *The Dialogue of the Exchequer* offers a solid introduction to the topic]; Poole, Reginald Lane. *The Exchequer in the Twelfth Century.* Oxford: Clarendon, 1912; Steel, Anthony B. *The Receipt of the Exchequer, 1377–1485.* Cambridge: Cambridge University Press, 1954.

See also Courts and the Court System; *Dialogue of the Exchequer;* Justiciar; Sheriff; Taxes; Wardrobe

Excommunication

The severing of a Christian from the Christian community stands at the heart of excommunication. Other communities in medieval Europe exercised similar penalties; the imperial ban in Germany and outlawry in England were parallel procedures. For the church excommunication constituted the separation of an erring member from the communion of the faithful, the ultimate ecclesiastical penalty. The essential offence for which excommunication was imposed was contumacy—a hardening of the heart—against the very authority of the church. Although specific crimes (e.g., the laying of violent hands on a cleric) provoked this penalty, it was the contumacy inherent in such a crime that justified this sentence.

The classical canonists from the late 12th century distinguished minor and major excommunication. The former could scarcely be called excommunication; it could be imposed and removed by a parish priest, and its consequences were the same as those for mortal sin (i.e., a separation from the eucharistic body of Christ). Major excommunication, whether imposed by law *(a iure)* or by an individual churchman *(ab homine)*, and whether incurred *ipso facto* by the commission of a certain crime or by a judgment made after the fact of the crime, had the same effects: exclusion from Christian communion.

The excommunicate lost all religious rights; he suffered exclusion from entry into a church, from the social company of the faithful (even, in some instances, from his own family), from pleading in courts (secular as well as ecclesiastical), from holding an ecclesiastical benefice, and, in general, from all legitimate ecclesiastical acts. The penalty pursued him even after death by excluding his body from Christian burial. Excommunication, in effect, amounted to almost complete social ostracism.

The ceremony of excommunication by bell, book, and candle, although found in books of rituals, was seldom used. A study of over 16,000 excommunications in England reveals not one instance of the formal ceremony of anathema. Commonly the excommunicating official (e.g., an abbot, bishop, ecclesiastical judge) would simply say, "I excommunicate you" *(excommunico te)*. Of course appeals were allowed and had the effect, in practice, of suspending sentences for a year. Intended as a medicinal penalty—to cure the offender—excommunication could be removed by the promise of obedience and penance. The Great Curse (a list of excommunicable offenses) was read four times a year in every parish church, and excommunicates were denounced from local pulpits.

Examples of the excommunication of kings (John in 1209) and of bishops (Robert Grosseteste of Lincoln in 1253) should not obscure the fact that in England, as elsewhere in Christendom, excommunication was routinely imposed on ordinary people. The study of English excommunicates shows that it was imposed, apparently without favor, on peasants and parsons, gentlemen and abbots, shoemakers and weavers, physicians and grocers; in fact on a representative cross-section of contemporary society.

If the medicine of excommunication failed to heal the criminal, the church could and frequently did invoke the aid of the secular arm to promote repentance. From the early 13th century a procedure existed whereby obdurate excommunicates, unabsolved for more than 40 days, were subject to arrest and imprisonment by the secular authority until absolved.

The Henrician Reformation changed neither the use of excommunication nor its consequences. The penalty and even the invocation of the secular arm continued throughout the 16th century and, in a diminishing degree, in later centuries.

F. Donald Logan

Bibliography

Hill, Rosalind M.T. "Public Penance: Some Problems of a Thirteenth Century Bishop." *History* 36 (1951): 213–26; Hill, Rosalind M.T. "The Theory and Practice of Excommunication in Medieval England." *History* 42

(1957): 1–11; Logan, F. Donald. *Excommunication and the Secular Arm in Medieval England.* Toronto: Pontifical Institute, 1968; Vodola, Elisabeth. *Excommunication in the Middle Ages.* Berkeley: University of California Press, 1986 [doctrinal analysis and references to many cases].

See also Courts, Ecclesiastical

Exemplum

A rhetorical and literary form. According to John of Garland (fl. 13th century) an exemplum is a statement or deed from some authoritative (*autentica*, also meaning "trustworthy" or "real") person worthy of imitation. The medieval term "exemplum" (plur. exempla) is not the same as "example" in the modern sense but had a broader application, whether used of evidence in argument or of a narrative and its attendant interpretation.

Aristotle described examples in rhetorical use as a kind of inductive reasoning (*Rhetoric* 2.20); they supplement maxims and logical argument (enthymemes) as evidence or can stand as arguments themselves. He divided examples into the historical and the invented and further distinguished two sorts of invented example, the illustrative parallel and the fiction. These ideas were transmitted through Roman rhetoricians to the Middle Ages, when the exemplum attained the status of a recognized literary form in itself in addition to its rhetorical function. Within a rhetorical context, such as a sermon, a notable statement or brief narrative could be adduced as evidence in support of an argument; such uses might not include any comment other than a tag like "as _____ said" or "for example." In other cases, especially when an argument was made from the exemplum, the author would take pains to interpret the statement or narrative according to his intention, thus yielding a two-part structure, statement/narrative plus interpretation.

Sources for the narratives in exempla were various—almost any work of human or natural history would serve, as could the imagination of the author, or very often an existing exemplum—and are now difficult to trace. The church preferred biblical and historical exemplary narratives and authoritative statements of Church Fathers; illustrative parallels (hypothetical actions of unnamed or typical characters or general conditions of life, such as the physical environment or the behavior of animals) were also frequent. Fictional exemplary narratives were subject to condemnation but were still used, especially beast fables. Modes of interpretation ranged from simple paraphrase to elaborate allegorical moralizations.

As a literary form exempla most often appear in collections and show the two-part, self-interpreting structure. Especially in the 13th and 14th centuries exempla were drawn from sermons and many other sources and compiled into collections of materials for preaching (such as John Bromyard's *Summa praedicantium* or the *Contes moralisés* of Nicholas Bozon), encyclopedic collections (such as the *Alphabetum narrationum* or *Speculum exemplorum*), and topical collections (such as collections of beast fables, the *Gesta Romanorum*, or even the *Ovide moralisé*). Such collections were usually composed in Latin and later translated into the vernacular; English translations often date from the 15th century (Caxton printed several).

Removed from rhetorical context and presented more for their own sake, exempla could be structurally manipulated. Authors could expand the interpretations, as in the figural expositions common in the *Gesta Romanorum*. Alternatively narratives could become longer and more complex, more attuned to literary ends, at the expense of the interpretive commentary: Chaucer's *Nun's Priest's Tale* has only a few lines of interpretation at the end of a 600-line narrative. Imbalances between the two parts of exemplum structure can make it difficult to decide whether a given medieval text ought to be called an exemplum or instead be relegated to religious commentary or to some other literary category.

William A. Kretzschmar, Jr.

Bibliography

PRIMARY

Crane, Thomas F., ed. and trans. *The Exempla or Illustrative Stories from the Sermones Vulgares of Jacques de Vitry.* Publications of the Folk-Lore Society 26. London: Nutt, 1890; Herrtage, Sidney J.H., ed. *The Early English Versions of the Gesta Romanorum.* EETS e.s. 33. London: Humphrey Milford, 1879.

SECONDARY

Allen, Judson B. *The Friar As Critic: Literary Attitudes in the Later Middle Ages.* Nashville: Vanderbilt University Press, 1971 [on allegorical moralizations]; Bremond, Claude, et al. *L' "Exemplum."* Turnhout: Brepols, 1982; Scanlon, Larry. *Narrative, Authority and Power: The Medieval Exemplum and the Chaucerian Tradition.* Cambridge: Cambridge University Press, 1993; Tubach, Frederic C. *Index Exemplorum: A Handbook of Medieval Religious Tales.* FF Communications 204. Helsinki: Suomalainen Tiedakatemia, 1969.

See also Anglo-Latin Literature after 1066; Beast Epic and Fable; Bozon; Caxton; Literary Influences: Classical, Medieval Latin; Moral and Religious Instruction; *Physiologus;* Rhetoric; Sermons; Translation

Exeter

The Romans built a legionary fortress at Exeter, ca. A.D. 55–60, on a hill overlooking the lowest bridging point of the Exe River. The fortress soon became a town, called *Isca Dumnoniorum,* the capital of the Dumnonii, the native inhabitants of Devon and Cornwall.

In the 7th century a Saxon minster was founded; St. Boniface is known to have been educated at its monastery. By the end of the 9th century, when Alfred established a mint at Exeter, the city had become Wessex's major seaport and an important fortified *burh.* Trade with France and Ireland, as well as the central role it must have played as an exporter of tin mined on Dartmoor, was the basis of the city's 10th- and 11th-century prosperity. An indication of Exeter's growing status was the transfer of the episcopal see, from Crediton to Exeter, in 1050. Another mark of status was its privilege of paying geld (tribute or tax) only when London, York, and Winchester did so. By 1068 Domesday Book records some 399 houses in Exeter; some 2,500 people lived in the town.

Orderic Vitalis described Exeter as a "wealthy and ancient city, strongly fortified" in his account of William the Conqueror's siege of the city in 1068. Although the town walls resisted efforts to undermine them, the city eventually surrendered and William solidified his victory by building a royal castle on the highest point within the town, demolishing 48 houses in the process. William of Malmesbury described Norman Exeter as "magnificent and wealthy, abounding in every kind of merchandise." This assessment was echoed in the city's substantial contributions to 12th- and early-13th-century royal aids (taxes collected on special occasions, such as the marriage of the king's eldest daughter) and tallages (arbitrary taxes levied on towns); Exeter ranked about sixth among English cities. But its fortunes declined in the 13th century, as it lost its prominence as a tin exporter and eastern towns and ports took a more dominant role in the cloth industry and export trade.

By 1334 Exeter ranked only 24th among English towns, according to the lay subsidy returns. In 1377, following the severe plagues of 1349 and 1361, the population of Exeter, including its western suburb of Exe Island, was about 3,000, placing it behind 21 other towns in size.

Throughout the 14th and early 15th centuries Exeter was noteworthy primarily as the regional capital of the southwestern peninsula, the seat of a bishopric that encompassed Devon and Cornwall, an administrative center for the king's itinerant justices, and the region's chief market town and seaport. In the mid- to late 15th century, however, Exeter's fortunes rose once again, as the city was able to draw upon its expanding local and regional cloth industries, becoming one of the top exporters of cloth at the close of the Middle Ages and ranking as one of the richest towns in the early-modern period.

Maryanne Kowaleski

Bibliography

Allen, John, Christopher Henderson, and Robert Higham. "Saxon Exeter." In *Anglo-Saxon Towns in Southern England,* ed. Jeremy Haslam. Chichester: Phillimore, 1984, pp. 385–414; Kowaleski, Maryanne. *Local Markets and Regional Trade in Medieval Exeter.* Cambridge: Cambridge University Press, 1995; Wilkinson, Bertie. *The Mediaeval Council of Exeter.* Manchester: Manchester University Press, 1931.

See also Bristol; Cloth; Gloucester; Tin; Towns

Exeter Bohun Psalter

Oxford, Exeter College 47, is one of a group of manuscripts commissioned by the Bohun family. The text of the Psalms is preceded by a calendar and followed by canticles, litany, *memoriae* to various saints, and, finally, Gospel sequences. Every page, whether or not it has a psalm initial, receives border decoration on all four margins of the text. This 127-folio volume has unfortunately been severely mutilated. Only the major frontispieces to Psalms 51 and 52, which occur on adjacent pages, survive (figs. 61–62). In all, the illustrations to 34 psalms are lacking.

A remarkable feature of this psalter (shared with the Bohun Psalter in Vienna [Vienna, Österreichische Nationalbibliothek 1826*] and the Bohun Psalter-Hours in the British Library [Egerton 3277]) is that every psalm receives historiation (cf. Cuerden Psalter). The frontispieces to the psalms and canticles form a connected iconographic series, unrelated to the text, which unfolds in an uninterrupted sequence of Old Testament narrative starting at the Creation and ending arbitrarily at the end of chapter 32 of the book of Numbers, at the point where Moses arrives at the River Jordan. It is possible to reconstruct the subject matter of the missing psalm pages by reference to the Bohun Psalter-Hours in Oxford (Bodl. Auct. D.4.4), but there the cycle is contained in miniatures and historiated initials at the principal psalm and hours divisions only. From the end of the canticles the iconography changes: the *memoriae* are illustrated by representations of the respective saints and the sequences of the Gospels likewise. Slender gold bars surround all pages of the text and at focal points develop cusped formations to accommo-

date a variety of foliage, flower, animal, and hybrid forms.

This psalter is more complex than it first appears. Whereas the text (except the calendar) indicates that it was prepared in one campaign, stylistic and codicological evidence suggests that there were three separate programs of illumination, a factor that has an important bearing on the dating and ownership of the book, executed over a period of some 40 years. The work of five illuminators can be identified. One artist, contemporary with the writing of the text, illuminated all the one-line verse initials and line-fillers, as well as some of the borders in a single gathering. An additional artist, working at the same time, painted the historiated initials and remaining borders constituting the first campaign (fols. 20–77v). His style relates closely to that of the final work in the Vienna Psalter, undertaken sometime between 1350/55 and 1360. In both portions the figures are small and there is a tendency to make the heads overlarge for the bodies; the eyes are composed of narrow slits with black dots for the irises, and the majority of younger men have tiny moustaches with wispy beards.

This same artist, at a later stage in his career, returned to the Exeter Psalter but completed only folios 9–19v. This phase of the illuminator's development, which is characterized by

Fig. 61. Exeter Bohun Psalter (Oxford, Exeter College 47), fol. 33v. Psalm 51. Reproduced by permission of the Rector and Fellows of Exeter College, Oxford.

Fig. 62. Exeter Bohun Psalter (Oxford, Exeter College 47), fol. 34. Psalm 52. Reproduced by permission of the Rector and Fellows of Exeter College, Oxford.

greater naturalism and softer modeling, relates stylistically to his work in Auct. D.4.4, a further Bohun Psalter (Cambridge, Fitzwilliam Museum 38–1950), the two Bohun manuscripts in Copenhagen (Royal Library Thott. 517.4° and Thott. 547.4°), and another in the collection of Graf von Schönborn in Pommersfelden (2934), works variously datable to between ca. 1370 and 1380, in which he continued to collaborate with the artist with whom he shared the first campaign in the Exeter Psalter.

The final seven gatherings (fols. 3–8 and 78–126v), in which three contemporary artists are discernible, were illuminated by a workshop employing different methods, the principal hand of which used the acanthus leaf, not utilized by the earlier illuminators, and monumental figures dressed in classical clinging draperies, clearly inspired by Italian forms. This artist also participated in Hatfield House, Hertfordshire CP 290, while his assistants in Exeter 47 are found working in two books of a London provenance, *Omne bonum* (BL Royal 6.E.vi and 6.E.vii) and a copy of William of Nottingham's Commentary on the Gospels (Bodl. Laud Misc. 165). These manuscripts, and other London-produced works to which they relate, suggest that by the date of the final campaign in Exeter 47 (ca. 1390–1400) the Bohun family were commissioning their books from the capital.

Documentary evidence survives that indicates that up until ca. 1385 the Bohuns had their own resident illuminators based at their castle at Pleshey, Essex, chief of whom was one John de Tye. This illuminator, whose origins are clearly English, though showing some Italian influence, participated in both first and second Exeter campaigns. His only collaborator in the psalter, and in the Bohun manuscripts produced between ca. 1350/55 and 1385, is of Flemish origin.

As to ownership the Exeter Psalter appears to have been worked on for three successive generations of the Bohun family, starting with Humphrey de Bohun (the name Humphrey occurs in the *memoriae*), the sixth earl. The project was probably halted by his death in 1361. It was continued for another member of the Bohun family between ca. 1380 and 1385, with the manuscript still at Pleshey. Some time in the last decade of the 14th century, when Eleanor de Bohun and her husband, Thomas of Woodstock, were involved in ordering other books from London-based illuminators, the psalter was completed, either for them or as a gift, by artists who were clearly pursuing a more commercial form of workshop practice that heralded developments of the early 15th century.

Lynda Dennison

Bibliography

Alexander, Jonathan, and Paul Binski, eds. *Age of Chivalry: Art in Plantagenet England 1200–1400.* London: Royal Academy of Arts, 1987, cat. no. 687; Dennison, Lynda. "Oxford, Exeter College MS 47: The Importance of Stylistic and Codicological Analysis in Its Dating and Localization." In *Medieval Book Production: Assessing the Evidence,* ed. Linda L. Brownrigg. Los Altos Hills: Anderson-Lovelace, 1990, pp. 41–59; James, Montague Rhodes, and Eric G. Millar. *The Bohun Manuscripts.* Oxford: Roxburghe Club, 1936; Sandler, Lucy Freeman. *Gothic Manuscripts 1285–1385.* A Survey of Manuscripts Illuminated in the British Isles 5, ed. J.J.G. Alexander. London: Harvey Miller, 1986, cat. no. 56.

See also Court Culture; Cuerden Psalter; "East Anglian School"; Manuscript Illumination, Gothic; Psalters, Gothic

Exeter Book

The Exeter Book (Exeter Cathedral Library 3501, fols. 8–130) is a codex of OE poetry containing 123 folios (each ca. 12.2–12.5 by 8.6–8.9 inches). A preliminary quire (probably added in the 15th century but previously belonging to the manuscript of the West Saxon Gospels now CUL Ii.2.11) contains documentary material as well as a list of the books given to his cathedral at Exeter by Bishop Leofric in 1072, in which the Exeter Book itself is probably identifiable as "i great English book about all things, composed in verse." The poetic contents may be divided into three "booklets" or self-contained textual units. The first contains long religious poems *(Christ I–III, Guthlac A, B).* The second contains elegies, category poems, allegorical and shorter religious poems *(Azarias, The Phoenix, Juliana, The Wanderer, The Gifts of Men, Precepts, The Seafarer, Vainglory, Widsith, The Fortunes of Men, Maxims I, The Order of the World, The Riming Poem, The Panther, The Whale,* and *The Partridge,* lines 1–2a). The third contains riddles, elegies, and short religious poems *(Homiletic Fragment III = The Partridge* lines 3–16, *Soul and Body II, Deor, Wulf and Eadwacer,* Riddles 1–59, *The Wife's Lament, Judgment Day I, Resignation A, B, The Descent into Hell, Almsgiving, Pharaoh, The Lord's Prayer I, Homiletic Fragment II,* Riddle 30b and Riddle 60, *The Husband's Message, The Ruin,* and Riddles 61–95). The manuscript contains texts of all the known OE elegies. One text *(Soul and Body II)* also appears in the Vercelli Book.

The poetic codex consisted of at least seventeen quires (the first sixteen of them, at least, consisting of eight folios) copied by a single scribe in the 10th century (ca. 950–70?), perhaps at Exeter itself, in a well-formed Anglo-Saxon Square Minuscule script. The same hand occurs in two Latin manuscripts: London, Lambeth Palace 149, fols. 1–138 (Bede, *Expositio super Apocalypsin,* and Augustine, *De adulterinis coniugiis)* and Bodleian Library, Bodley 319 (Isidore, *De fide catholica).* Both, like the Exeter Book, were also probably given (or confirmed) to his cathedral by Bishop Leofric. Lambeth 149 has a partly erased inscription on fol. 138v recording its previous gift in 1018 by an Ealdorman Æthelweard to an unidentified religious house dedicated to the Virgin Mary.

Paleographical features (such as the distribution of certain letter forms and ligatures), as well as differences in the quality and preparation of the leaves, suggest that the three textual booklets represent three separate stints of scribal production. The present first booklet (fols. 8–52v) may have been the last to be written, the second (fols. 53–97v) first, and the third (fols. 98–130v) second. The poems *Christ I–III* and *Guthlac A, B* may have been arranged in these sequences for the first time in their particular booklet, causing the scribe to modify parts of the texts to help the arrangement. Individual pages are written in 21 to 23 long lines, without illumination but with some use of embellished initials, capital script, and diminuendo at the beginning of items. Punctuation in ink is sparse, but some extra marks have been added in drypoint. Drypoint drawings of figures and patterns occur in some margins. The end of items is usually marked by a combination of punctuation marks, sometimes by Latin *Amen* or *Finit* and/or by the leaving of blank lines. Runic letters are found in the signatures of the poet Cynewulf and indicating the solution to some riddles (e.g., in Riddle 36, the H-rune stands for *Homo*); cryptic writing also occurs where consonants are placed instead of vowels.

A number of leaves (e.g., after fols. 37, 69, 73, 97, 105, 111), with consequent loss of text, were already missing in the late 16th century, when the volume was first foliated (being refoliated by 1705). Other leaves are damaged: for example, fols. 117–130 contain holes made by burning, fol. 8 has both been cut by a knife and stained by the base of a pot of liquid. Some of the damaged leaves have deteriorated further since 1832, when a facsimile transcript was made for the British Museum by Richard Chambers (BL Add. 9067); this was used by John Mitchell Kemble while preparing his second edition of *Beowulf* (1835–37) and possibly for the first edition (1833). The Exeter Book was consulted in the 16th century by the antiquaries John Joscelyn (for Matthew Parker's *A Testimonie of Antiquitie*, 1566) and Laurence Nowell; the latter added an interlinear English gloss to seven lines of *Christ I* on fol. 9, and four lines on fol. 10. The manuscript was studied by George Hickes and Humfrey Wanley before 1705 and by Nikolai Frederik Severin Grundtvig in 1830.

Some poems from the Exeter Book were published with Latin and modern English translations by John Josias Conybeare in 1814 (*Archaeologia* 17) but the first comprehensive edition was by Benjamin Thorpe (*Codex Exoniensis*, London, 1842). Bindings are known to have been added in the 15th century and ca. 1700; the latter was removed in 1932 for the making of the photographic facsimile and was replaced by the present binding.

Alexander R. Rumble

Bibliography

PRIMARY

ASPR 3; Chambers, R.W., Max Förster, and Robin Flower, eds. *The Exeter Book of Old English Poetry.* London: Lund, Humphries, 1933; Muir, Bernard, ed. *The Exeter Book Anthology of Old English Poetry: An Edition of Exeter Dean and Chapter MS 3501.* Exeter: University of Exeter Press, 1994.

SECONDARY

Conner, Patrick W. *Anglo-Saxon Exeter: A Tenth-Century Cultural History.* Woodbridge: Boydell, 1993 [detailed study of the physical features, content, and background of the manuscript].

See also Nowell; Parker; Vercelli Book

Exodus

A 590-line narrative poem preserved in Bodl. Junius 11 (copied ca. 1000–35), a volume devoted to OE biblical verse. Like other poems in Junius 11 *Exodus* has suffered textual loss from imperfect scribal transmission and from the direct removal of manuscript leaves; as originally composed, the poem probably had 690–740 lines. Scholars have differed widely on the date of the poem's composition, the estimates ranging from the late 7th century to the second half of the 10th. Although a majority of scholars over the years have favored an 8th-century date, today there seems little consensus. In large part the uncertainty reflects the debate over the dating of *Beowulf,* with which *Exodus* shows affinities in meter, diction, formula, and the use of digressions.

In important ways, however, the poem is much different from *Beowulf. Exodus* is remarkable for its convoluted syntax, daring imagery, narrative obscurity, intense compression of meaning, and large number of words not elsewhere attested. Some scholars (e.g., Hill) believe the poet was influenced by Latin hermeneutic literature; others (e.g., Frank) suggest the influence of Old Norse skaldic verse. Another possibility is that the poet, perhaps influenced by both kinds of literature, took to an extreme tendencies inherent in OE verse itself.

Exodus is not a paraphrase but a free re-creation of the biblical account. Employing Anglo-Saxon heroic diction, the poet tells the story of the Israelites' release from Egyptian bondage, their journey to and crossing of the Red Sea, and the destruction of the pursuing Egyptians in the water. The poet's main source was the book of Exodus, especially chapters 13 and 14; but he shows familiarity with other biblical books, most notably Genesis (which he may have known in a version combining Vulgate and Old Latin readings). Apart from the Bible the poet's sources are uncertain. Scholars have pointed out nonscriptural parallels between *Exodus* and two other narrative accounts of the exodus: Josephus's *Jewish Antiquities,* book 2, and Avitus's *De transitu maris rubri.* Other scholars, however, have dismissed the parallels as inconclusive, and the attribution in either case remains controversial.

Also controversial are the nature and the extent of the poet's reliance on Christian Latin exegesis, particularly the symbolic reading of scripture prominent in most commentaries. That the poet was concerned with the symbolic dimension is clear: unlike other OE biblical poets he expressly refers to the desirability of unlocking scripture with *gastes cægon,* "keys of the spirit," then characterizes life on earth as a period of exile from which the Lord will one day lead the faithful to heaven (lines 523–48). Accordingly, several scholars have sought to explain the poem's ambiguities and "*unrealistic* collocations" (Cross and Tucker) by reference to Christian symbolism. Yet others have rejected this approach as often unwarranted, arguing that *Exodus* should be read primarily on the literal or historical level. All scholars would agree, however, that no single approach can solve all the problems of interpretation. If the poet, in pondering and celebrating the early history of Israel, aimed to compose a challenging poem, he succeeded almost too well.

J.R. Hall

Bibliography

PRIMARY

ASPR 1:91–107; Lucas, Peter J., ed. *Exodus.* London: Methuen, 1977; Tolkien, J.R.R., ed. and trans. *The Old English Exodus.* Ed. Joan Turville-Petre. Oxford: Clarendon, 1981.

SECONDARY

Cross, J.E., and Susie I. Tucker. "Allegorical Tradition and the Old English *Exodus.*" *Neophilologus* 44 (1960): 122–27; Earl, James W. "Christian Traditions in the Old English *Exodus.*" *NM* 71 (1970): 541–70; Frank, Roberta. "What Kind of Poetry Is *Exodus?*" In *Germania: Comparative Studies in the Old Germanic Languages and Literatures,* ed. Daniel G. Calder and T. Craig Christy. Woodbridge: Brewer, 1988, pp. 191–205; Hall, J.R. "Old English *Exodus* and the Sea of Contradiction." *Mediaevalia* 9 (1986 for 1983): 25–44; Hill, Thomas D. "The *virga* of Moses and the Old English *Exodus.*" In *Old English Literature in Context: Ten Essays,* ed. John D. Niles. Cambridge: Brewer, 1980, pp. 57–65, 165–67; Irving, Edward B., Jr. "*Exodus* Retraced." In *Old English Studies in Honour of John C. Pope,* ed. Robert B. Burlin and Edward B. Irving, Jr. Toronto: University of Toronto Press, 1974, pp. 203–23.

See also Beowulf; Bible in OE Literature; Junius Manuscript

F

Faburden

A distinctive English musical technique in which a simple form of three-voice polyphony is created by the addition of two extemporized voices to a preexistent plainsong. The term may also refer to the whole complex of voices, or simply to the faburden proper, the lowest voice, from which the technique takes its name. In this technique the plainsong voice, or mean (because musically it is in the middle), is doubled at the fourth above by the treble. The bass part, or faburden, proceeds mainly at the third below the chant, singing a fifth beneath at the beginning and end, and at the ends of words. Harmonically speaking, the result is a chain of parallel 6/3 sonorities, bounded and inflected by 8/5 sonorities. Continental "fauxbourdon" derives philologically and in terms of sonorous ideal (though not in the details of practice) from English faburden.

The technique of faburden seems to have been codified early in the first quarter of the 15th century, though its roots go back about two centuries in both oral tradition and in a repertoire of unpretentious three-voice written polyphony for the liturgy. It is particularly associated with the performance of lengthy processional and antiphonal choral chants, such as hymns, litanies, processional psalms, the Te Deum, and the Magnificat. Though a single faburdener could invent a new faburden for each performance, in practice (especially if several voices were to sing the line) a version would come to be fixed in a choir's repertoire. For reference purposes these traditional faburdens were copied into collections of monophonic bass parts, and they were also added into chant manuscripts as dots, strokes, or plainsong symbols directly on the same staves as the plainsong. Faburdens were also potentially squares; that is, some were incorporated as a *cantus prius factus* (preexistent melody used as a structural basis) into more elaborately composed polyphony of the later 15th and 16th centuries, said then to be "on the faburden."

Faburden was taught to boys and singing men as one of the fundamental skills that singers of the liturgy had to have. It is described in a number of 15th- and 16th-century treatises in English (rather than Latin) so as to be particularly accessible to this audience.
Peter M. Lefferts

Bibliography

Trowell, Brian. "Faburden," "Fauxbourdon." *NGD* 6:350–54, 433–38; Trowell, Brian. "Faburden—New Sources, New Evidence: A Preliminary Survey." In *Modern Musical Scholarship,* ed. Edward Olleson. London: Stocksfield, 1978, pp. 28–78.

See also Discant; Holy Week and Easter, Music for; Magnificat; Music: History and Theory; Processions; Square

Fairs and Markets

Fairs and markets provided structure and organization for most commercial activity by furnishing traders with secure surroundings, access to a steady stream of customers, quick justice under law merchant (the common law adapted for on-the-spot settlement of commercial disputes) when problems arose, and facilities and services for storage, transport, and display.

The owners of fairs and markets, who by the early 13th century were required to obtain a royal charter to start a fair or market, profited from rents on stalls, tolls from buyers and sellers, and fines arising from the jurisdiction of market courts. Well over 3,000 market charters were granted to lay and ecclesiastical lords during the 13th century in response to rising local demand fueled by population growth and an expanding economy. This pace slowed considerably in the 14th century; few fairs and markets were founded after the Black Death (1348–49), and some disappeared altogether as population stagnated, private trade increased, and certain urban markets grew more dominant at the expense of fairs and village markets.

Fairs and markets differed primarily in timing. Fairs were annual events, normally held for about three days around the feast of a locally prominent saint. Most fairs took place in towns and attracted buyers and sellers from the surrounding region. Some were international in scope, concentrating largely on wholesale trade. Those at Stamford, St. Ives, Boston, and Winchester were particularly important, lasting up to four weeks and drawing merchants from throughout northern Europe.

The heyday of international fairs was from the late 12th through the early 13th century, when England's wool and cloth were in demand throughout Europe. By the end of the 13th century, however, these great fairs were in decline, as foreign merchants, as well as many English merchants who traveled long distances, ceased to attend. Various factors were responsible for this decline: changes in the cloth industry that dispersed the production and marketing of cloth; wars with Flanders and France that disrupted trade; alterations in the customs and staple systems that allowed traders to bypass fairs; the growing pull of London commerce.

Unlike fairs markets were held on a weekly basis and attracted primarily local residents who concentrated on retail trade and the supply of foodstuffs and household items. The larger towns held markets three days a week (six in the case of London); most places possessed a once-weekly market. Urban marketplaces were held in large open spaces where visiting peasants and petty retailers could display goods on payment of a small fee. Many cities also built market halls to protect traders from bad weather and to provide separate facilities for specialty items like cloth, hides, and furs. Bordering the marketplace were shops, stalls, and warehouses, rented out to local merchants and artisans. In contrast village marketplaces often occupied only a small widening in the main street where a few peasants, traveling chapmen, and some local residents might gather for a half-day once a week to conduct trade in basic foodstuffs and small wares.

Maryanne Kowaleski

Bibliography

Britnell, Richard H. "The Proliferation of Markets in England, 1200–1349." *EcHR,* 2d ser. 34 (1981): 209–21; Moore, Ellen Wedemeyer. *The Fairs of Medieval England: An Introductory Study.* Toronto: Pontifical Institute, 1985; Unwin, Tim. "Rural Marketing in Medieval Nottinghamshire." *Journal of Historical Geography* 7 (1981): 231–51.

See also Assize of Weights and Measures; Food; Roads

Family Letter Collections

There are four major collections of letters and papers of English families. In order of size and therefore of importance that of the Paston family of Paston and Oxnead, Norfolk, comes first by a wide margin. Well over 1,000 letters and other documents survive for the 15th century alone. They cover the family's rise from lowly farming origins to their acceptance into the county elite after the Battle of Bosworth (1485).

The fortunes of the Pastons were established by judge William Paston's hugely successful legal career; he purchased many properties in Norfolk, mainly in the northeast of the county where Paston lies; Oxnead was one of these estates, Gresham another. Many of the deals William made were decidedly shady. His eldest son, John, succeeded him in 1444. William had procured for John in the 1430s a bride, Margaret Mautby, who was of an impeccable Norfolk family and heiress to nine East Anglian manors. John was the epitome of an English gentleman: mean and grasping. Typically he overreached himself. His attempt to obtain the estates of his patron and employer, Sir John Fastolf of Caister, Norfolk, on Fastolf's death in 1459 failed dismally, and he died (possibly in jail in London) in 1466, fatally eroded by uncompromising greed.

The bulk of the collection of letters concerns this affair of Fastolf's will. John was usually in London, Margaret in Norfolk. After her husband's death she did not remarry but lived at her family home at Mautby; her two sons, John II and John III, were more often in London and Calais than Norfolk. Letters passed between mother and sons regularly until Margaret's death in 1484. Thereafter they tail off; John II had died a bachelor in 1479, his brother, now head of the family, in 1504. Though the letters are an unparalleled source for 15th-century English history, their great number and some serious problems of interpretation (many of them are long, and individual letters often touch on a wide variety of topics) mean that they have not been as thoroughly mined as their importance would call for.

The second collection, that of the Stonor family of Stonor, Oxfordshire, has been even more neglected. Although a study of the Stonors of the 15th century would be an easier undertaking than that of the Pastons, it has not been attempted. This is curious. There are no more than 350 published letters and associated papers, superbly edited by C.L. Kingsford. There is also a wealth of unpublished but readily accessible estate material. Moreover the Stonor menfolk were of a less self-serving and acquisitive temperament than the Pastons. This is probably because they had been accepted members of the "open" society of the mid-Thames valley since judge John Stonor had established the family there in the first half of the 14th century.

Sir William Stonor (d. 1494) is the last of the three generations that the collection covers. He is an attractive character whose Yorkist allegiance led him into rebellion against Richard III in October 1483. His first wife, Elizabeth Ryche, was also an engaging and lively person. The widow of a mercer, she brought London ways to rural Stonor. The Stonors are invaluable for suggesting another perspective on English upper-class life to that offered by the Pastons: harmony rather than discord.

The third collection returns us to disharmony, but in the case of the Plumptons of the West Riding of Yorkshire it is self-inflicted. A Letter Book and a Coucher Book survive from the early 17th century, where in the first case letters, and in the second charters, deeds, and "official" correspondence from the 15th and early 16th centuries were transcribed. There are over 250 letters: 180 of them are addressed to Sir Robert Plumpton in the period 1480–1520. Sir Robert, the legitimized heir-male, spent much of his adult life fending off the claims of the heirs-general, his two stepnieces, and their influential and predatory supporters. It is a stirring and highly instructive story. In addition the collection provides a unique source for northern history in the 30 years either side of 1500.

The fourth collection is that of the Cely family. The Celys were Londoners, active in the wool trade. There are almost 250 published letters of the 1470s and 1480s, plus a large archive of business papers. It is from the letters and the commercial documents of this family that most of our knowledge of the workings of the trade in English wool is derived.

Colin F. Richmond

Bibliography

PRIMARY

Carpenter, Christine, ed. *Kingsford's The Stonor Letters and Papers, 1290–1483.* Cambridge: Cambridge University Press, 1996; Davis, Norman, ed. *The Paston Letters and Papers of the Fifteenth Century.* 2 vols. Oxford: Clarendon, 1971–76; Gairdner, James, ed. *The Paston Letters, A.D. 1422–1503.* 6 vols. London: Chatto & Windus, 1904 [both editions are necessary: Gairdner arranges the letters chronologically, while Davis separates those from the Pastons (Vol. 1) and those to them (Vol. 2) in a fashion not always helpful to readers and historians. But he does print many letters in full and generally reedits and corrects much of Gairdner's earlier work]; Hanham, Alison, ed. *The Cely Letters, 1472–1488: An English Merchant Family of the Fifteenth Century.* EETS o.s. 273. London: Oxford University Press, 1975; Kirby, Joan, ed. The Plumpton Letters and Papers. Camden Society, 5th ser., 8 (1996); Moore, Stuart A., ed. *Letters and Papers of John Shillingford, Mayor of Exeter, 1447–50.* Camden Society, n.s. 2 (1871) [a lesser collection but of some interest].

SECONDARY

Bennett, Henry S. *The Pastons and Their England.* 2d ed. Cambridge: Cambridge University Press, 1932; Dockray, Keith. "The Troubles of the Yorkshire Plumptons." *History Today* 27 (1977): 459–66; Du Boulay, F.R.H. *An Age of Ambition: English Society in the Late Middle Ages.* London: Nelson, 1970; Hanham, Alison. *The Celys and Their World: An English Merchant Family of the Fifteenth Century.* Cambridge: Cambridge University Press, 1985; Power, Eileen. "Thomas Betson, A Merchant of the Staple in the Fifteenth Century." In *Medieval People.* London: Methuen, 1924. Repr. New York: Barnes & Noble, 1963, pp. 120–51; Richmond, Colin. *The Paston Family in the Fifteenth Century: The First Phase.* Cambridge: Cambridge University Press, 1990; Taylor, John. "The Plumpton Letters, 1416–1552." *Northern History* 10 (1975): 72–87.

See also Gentry; Prose, ME

Fathers of the Church (Western)

A term applied to influential Christian writers of the first several centuries after Christ, many of whom also held important positions within the church hierarchy. Through both their written work and their activity within the church they have played a major role in shaping Christianity as it developed from the time of Christ and the apostles. Church Fathers are also referred to as Doctors of the Church and as patristic writers, and study of their work is known as patristics. Patristic writing typically includes theological treatises, biblical commentaries, sermons, letters, apologetic treatises (explanations and justifications of Christianity), polemics against heretical or non-Christian positions, saints' lives, and other work.

In the western, or Latin, church (the branch of Christianity that looked to Rome rather than the Greek-speaking Byzantine church for leadership) the most important patristic writers are usually identified as Ambrose of Milan, Augustine of Hippo, Pope Gregory the Great, and Jerome. Augustine and Gregory are generally seen as the most significant, especially for England, followed by Jerome and Ambrose, but they will be presented in chronological order in the following article.

Ambrose of Milan (ca. 339–397)

Bishop of Milan from 374 to 397. Through his writings many patristic traditions were fostered and communicated to the Middle Ages and affected many aspects of medieval religious, artistic, and social life. Ambrose could read Greek and was a vehicle for the transmission of eastern thought to the West, notably the teachings of Origen and the Alexandrian school, and Basil and the Cappadocian Fathers. Ambrose's reading of scripture was characterized by allegorical interpretation after the manner of many eastern exegetes. Ambrose was also remembered as a powerful supporter of ecclesiastical authority and as the man who converted and baptized Augustine of Hippo in 387.

Some of Ambrose's writings were available early in Anglo-Saxon England; others arrived a century or more after the Roman mission of 597. Ambrose's *Commentary on Luke* was used by the author of the *Anonymous Life of Cuthbert,* which is one of the earliest surviving English writings. Bede (7th–8th century) and his contemporaries admired Ambrose's learning and piety and used his works as resources and points of departure for their own projects. The English bishop Acca of Hexham encouraged Bede to undertake a commentary on Luke, a difficult work that "had been taken up earlier by that most learned and most holy priest Ambrose." Bede, desiring to "follow the footsteps of the Fathers," acknowledges Ambrose frequently, drawing on Ambrose's exegetical homilies for his own and on the *Hexaemeron* (a commentary on the six days of Creation) as a source of information for his treatise *De natura rerum.* According to Cuthbert, Bede's friend and fellow scholar, Bede on his deathbed often quoted Ambrose's saying, "I have not lived so that I am ashamed to live among you, and I do not fear to die for God is gracious." Ambrose is also included in the prose *De virginitate* among the Church Fathers selected by Aldhelm as exemplars of chaste life, and Aldhelm may have drawn on Ambrose's treatises on virginity for this work. Ambrose's Latin hymns and several hymns attributed to him were quoted and used in Anglo-Saxon England.

Although the degree of patristic influence on vernacular poetry has long been debated, Ambrose's teachings appear to have been communicated to the English through this medium. The cosmological configuration in Cædmon's Hymn, for example, has been traced through Bede to the first section of Ambrose's *Hexaemeron,* and the second part of the Exeter Book's *The Phoenix* contains an allegory of the Resurrection that was probably based on the *Hexaemeron* 5.23. Similarly the end of the Cynewulfian poem *Elene,* suggesting the Judgment Day, appears to be based on Ambrose.

Jerome (347–419/20)

Greek and Hebrew scholar, translator of the Bible, exegete, and polemicist. Born in Dalmatia, Jerome studied under the grammarian Donatus in Rome. From 372 on he lived in the East, except for a short second visit to Rome (382–85). In the East he learned Greek and Hebrew, was ordained a priest, founded a monastery in Bethlehem, and devoted his life to asceticism and study of the Bible. His writings were points of reference on biblical topics, but they affected a wide range of intellectual pursuits in the Middle Ages. His Latin Vulgate translation of the Bible became the standard in medieval Europe, and he composed many other influential translations, treatises, commentaries, homilies, saints' lives, polemics, letters, and continuations of Greek reference works. His *Liber de situ et nominibus locorum Hebraicorum (On the Site and Names of Hebrew Places)* is a translation and continuation of Eusebius's *Onomasticon.* He also continued Eusebius's *Chronicle* and helped set a literary precedent for the Middle Ages to relate contemporary events to Christian ideas of the scope of eternity.

Although Christian Britain was for Jerome "a world apart" (*Epistle* 46.10), his writings were instrumental in the reconversion of the island after the Anglo-Saxon invasions. In addition to the Vulgate several of his works had a distinctive presence in Anglo-Saxon England. His correspondence with Pope Damasus was among the writings that Augustine of Canterbury brought with him to England. Aldhelm's prose treatise *De virginitate* reveals the influence of a large number of early Christian writings, including Jerome's *Life of [the Monk] Malchus.* Aldhelm, Bede, and Alcuin made much use of the linguistic, geographical, and scientific information contained in Jerome's treatises, particularly those on the meaning and interpretation of Hebrew names. They also used many of Jerome's letters and commentaries on the minor prophets. Although on the whole Bede cites Augustine more than any other patristic author, in his commentaries *In Marcum* and *In Lucam* he cites Jerome from a variety of sources far more frequently than he does even Augustine. Bede drew on Jerome's *Chronicle* for his *De temporum ratione (On the Reckoning of Time)* and mentions and quotes from Jerome in his commentary on the Acts of the Apostles.

An incident described in a passage from Jerome's *Life of St. Paul [the Hermit]* is the only nonbiblical subject depicted on the principal panels of the Ruthwell Cross. Jerome's influ-ence is also noticeable in OE vernacular literature. The English homilist Ælfric cites Jerome in his *Lives of the Saints* (a third series of homilies), and his other homilies are modeled on those of Jerome and other patristic authors. The Alfredian version of St. Augustine's *Soliloquies* is supplemented by passages from Jerome's commentary on Luke.

Augustine of Hippo (354–430)

Bishop of Hippo from 396 on; probably the most influential Christian writer after St. Paul, not only for the Middle Ages but also for the Protestant Reformation. Augustine was born of a pagan father and a Christian mother in Tagaste, North Africa. He studied at Madaura and Carthage and later taught in Tagaste, Carthage, and Rome. He became professor of rhetoric in Milan and was baptized there by St. Ambrose in 387. The following year he returned to North Africa. For four years he lived a semimonastic life but in 391 was ordained a priest and in 396 consecrated bishop of Hippo. Augustine's numerous writings reflect a powerful intellect and deep emotional insight. He debated the Manicheans, a sect to which he had once belonged, and later, having gained a reputation as a leading theologian and polemicist, he refuted the Donatists and Pelagians. His most important theological work is the *De Trinitate (On the Trinity).* Of major importance are the *Confessions,* a deeply personal reflection on divine glory and human weakness; *The City of God,* a grand-scale Christian "apology" presented as a reflection on history and divine Providence; and the *De doctrina christiana (On Christian Doctrine),* a treatise on the proper way to understand scripture. He also wrote scriptural commentaries, sermons, and letters. The direct impact of these writings on the Latin West was enhanced by the indirect influence of numerous intermediaries who propounded Augustinian ideas. In this group are included Eucherius of Lyon, Boethius, Caesarius of Arles, Prosper of Aquitaine, and Cassiodorus.

Augustine's theology and his theories of human nature were in the forefront of medieval English consciousness, and his teachings had a pervasive influence on Anglo-Saxon culture. Many of his works were known firsthand. *The City of God* is known to have been of major significance, although relatively few English manuscripts have survived. Other popular works were the *De Trinitate,* the *Enarrationes in Psalmos* and other exegetical commentaries, and numerous sermons. Among influential English writers Bede in particular was on intimate terms with Augustine's works. His knowledge of Augustine includes at least eighteen works and surpasses his familiarity with Ambrose, Gregory, or Jerome. He employed Augustine's commentaries and homilies for his own writings in these genres. He quotes Augustine in his correspondence, as in the letter to Helmwaldum, which includes a lengthy passage from *De Trinitate.* Bede admits that he derived much of the substance of his *Catholic Letters* from the homilies of Augustine, particularly the *Tractatus X in Joannis epistolam.* The *Chronica minora* (chapters 17–22 of *De temporibus*) contains strong echoes of Augustine's *De Trinitate.* Bede's *Martyrologium,* verse *Life of Cuthbert,* and *De natura rerum,* as well as the verse *Death Song* sometimes attributed to him all show profound influence by Augustine. Bede claimed that his *Retractatio* was modeled after Augustine's.

Augustine's thought penetrated Anglo-Latin literature in a secondary manner as well. Alcuin based his discourse on the Trinity, *De anima ratione,* on Augustine's *De Trinitate.* Alcuin reflects Augustine's theology of the Trinity in his letters and in other places where he presents trinitarian analogues (like thought, word, deed). Augustine's teachings were also strongly represented in the curriculum of the monastic schools. Besides transmitting Augustinian exegesis and theology English churchmen like Bede and those who followed him were instrumental in communicating Augustinian perspectives into the general culture, including his literary theory and penchant for allegory. Aldhelm, for example, communicated Augustinian poetic theory to the English through such works as his Latin riddle *Lorica,* "iron breastplate," which was probably intended as a spiritual symbol. This poem was early translated into English. Alcuin, in his *De rhetorica,* echoes Augustine's distinction (from *De doctrina*) between "use" and "enjoyment" of literature, wherein literary art is considered something not so much to be enjoyed in itself as to be used as a means of enjoying God.

Scholars have long recognized the pervasive influence of Augustinian thought on OE vernacular literature. Augustine's *Soliloquies* were translated into English, possibly by Alfred. Some doubt exists that Alfred himself translated this work (neither Asser's *Life of King Alfred* nor the Anglo-Saxon Chronicle lists it among Alfred's writings), but internal evidence satisfies most scholars that the work is Alfred's own. In any case the OE *Soliloquies* provides strong testimony to the strength of patristic, and especially Augustinian, influence on Alfred. The OE version includes passages from other works of Augustine, Gregory, and Jerome. Book 3, for example, is based on Augustine's *De videndo Deo* (*Epistle* 147) and is supplemented by passages from Gregory's *Moralia in Job,* the *Dialogues,* and Jerome's *Commentary on Luke.* Ælfric names Augustine as a major source for his *Catholic Homilies.* The *Lives of Saints* (a third series of homilies by Ælfric) cites Augustine frequently, and the trinitarian interpretation of the first chapters of Genesis in Ælfric's *Heptateuch* shows Augustinian influence.

OE poetry also reflects the efforts of writers to take extra pains to point out exegetical commonplaces derived from Augustine. The understanding of time and space that guides Cædmon's Hymn, for example, has been traced to Augustine's discussion of this subject in book 9 of the *Confessions.* The OE *Wanderer* has been interpreted as a meditative poem in the strict tradition of meditative exercises begun by St. Augustine. The poem speaks of the three powers of mind as Augustine does in *De Trinitate.* Similarly some scholars see Augustine's influence on the theological implications of *Genesis B,* an Old Saxon poem that was translated into OE. This poem may have been intended to show that covert evil can defeat the most wary of men if they lack grace. *Christ III* has been considered "a tissue of poeticized material from Gregory, Augustine, Caesarius of Arles, and others."

As with Anglo-Latin literature the Augustinian literary aesthetic is also communicated in OE poetry. Examples of the application of the principles of *De doctrina christiana* can be found in the *Advent Lyrics* of the Exeter Book.

Gregory the Great (ca. 540–604)

Prefect of Rome, born of a wealthy family and the first monk to become pope (590). Gregory was the motivating force behind the reconversion of Britain after the Anglo-Saxon invasions. His efforts to strengthen the presence of Christianity in western Europe and to spread monastic culture included Augustine of Canterbury's mission to the Anglo-Saxons, which arrived in southern England in 597. The well-known pun on the tribal name *Angli* as *angeli* (Angles/angels), referred to as a legend in Bede's *Ecclesiastical History* 2.1, suggests his fondness for that nation. Not only had he encountered Anglo-Saxons in Rome, he became convinced that the English "were eager for conversion" (*Epistle* 6.49). Some of the correspondence between Augustine of Canterbury and Gregory is extant and provides an insight into Gregory's missionary policy, which was wisely tolerant. This is evidenced by his instructions to the missionaries, as reported in the *Ecclesiastical History* 1.30, to transform rather than destroy English shrines and customs.

Gregory never visited England, although he did travel to Constantinople in 578 as representative of his papal predecessor, Pelagius II. While in Constantinople he began his famous commentary on the book of Job, the *Moralia* or *Expositio in Job.* After his return to Rome in 585 he lived as a monk but was elected pope in 590. His writings include extensive treatment of scripture in sermons and commentaries that are characterized by allegorical interpretation. His *Dialogues* and the *Regula pastoralis* are especially important. A copy of the *Regula* may have made its way to England with the mission of Augustine, and the *Moralia* and *Dialogues* were available early. Gregory's homilies also had considerable influence on English homilists from Bede on. Gregory's writings in fact provided one of the principal ways in which patristic ecclesiology and exegesis were incorporated into Anglo-Saxon culture.

Gregory, a model saint for the Anglo-Saxons, is mentioned and quoted frequently. Anglo-Latin literature from the earliest times contains testimony to the reverence the English had for him. The earliest life of Gregory is the *Vita antiquissima sancti Gregorii,* based on Gregory's own *Dialogues.* The *Vita* is preserved in a single manuscript now at St. Gall. Its author was probably a monk of Whitby in northern England. In addition to the Saxon life, as that version is commonly known, another important life of Gregory is found in book 2 of the *Ecclesiastical History,* which disagrees in some details from the *Vita antiquissima.* Bede was profoundly influenced by Gregory's character and universal vision of the church. The account of his life occupies more space in the *Ecclesiastical History* than does that of any English king. *Ecclesiastical History* 2.1 even presents a verse epitaph to Gregory. Bede knew several of Gregory's writings firsthand and identifies Gregory as the source of individual quotations. He recommended the *Regula* to Ecgbert of York and quotes from it in the *Ecclesiastical History.* He also includes a tribute to Gregory in book 6 of the commentary *In Cantica canticorum* (*On the Song of Songs*).

Felix of Crowland's *Life of St. Guthlac* (ca. 740–50), particularly the account of the author's visit to the saint, is inspired by Gregory's *Dialogues*. In addition the apocalypses or visions of Fursey the Irish hermit, preserved in an anonymous version and in the *Ecclesiastical History* 3.19, and of Dryhthelm (*Ecclesiastical History* 5.12) owe their origin largely to the *Dialogues*. Aldhelm was also deeply influenced by Gregory's writings. He drew on them extensively, for example, for his treatises on virginity. Alcuin shared with Bede a deep reverence for the *Regula* and recommended it to Eanbald of York for frequent reading by preachers and pastors.

Gregory's writings also have a prominent place in the vernacular tradition. The corrected version of the *Regula pastoralis* was one of the first works to be translated from the Latin into OE by King Alfred, presumably with help. In the preface to this translation the king treats of numerous themes touching on the search for wisdom and the state of learning in England. In a second verse preface the king includes a passage in alliterative verse containing a tribute to Gregory as "Christ's warrior, the pope of Rome." The West Saxon translation of the *Dialogues* by Bishop Wærferth of Worcester owed its inspiration directly to Alfred, and passages from the *Moralia* supplement the OE version of the *Soliloquies* of Augustine of Hippo. Vernacular homilies also show Gregory's influence. English hagiographical literature in particular owes much to him. Ælfric devoted part of his second series of sermons to the foundation of the English church under Gregory. Ælfric's *Lives of Saints,* a third series of homilies composed by the most popular Anglo-Saxon homilist, is more indebted to Gregory than to any other author.

Just as English clerics who knew the pope's exegetical writings imparted his teachings to their audience in their homilies, poets often drew on Gregorian exegetical traditions. The poem known as *Christ II,* contained in the Exeter Book, has as its principal source the conclusion of Gregory's homily on the Ascension (Hom. 29). Similarly *The Gifts of Men,* also in the Exeter Book, appears to have this same Ascension homily as an indirect source.

Daniel Nodes

Bibliography

PRIMARY

Latin editions of many Church Fathers (not just Ambrose, Augustine, Gregory, and Jerome) may be found in the Patrologia Latina (usually abbreviated PL; contains older and often less reliable editions), the Corpus Scriptorum Ecclesiasticorum Latinorum (CSEL), the Corpus Christianorum, Series Latina (CCSL and sometimes simply CCL or CC), the French series Sources Chrétiennes (SC), and in some cases in editions of particular works. English translations may be found in such series as The Ante-Nicene Fathers, A Select Library of the Nicene and Post-Nicene Fathers of the Christian Church, Ancient Christian Writers: The Works of the Fathers in Translation, The Fathers of the Church: A New Translation, the Loeb Classical Library (for several Greek and Latin Fathers), and in individual translations like those selected here.

Albertson, Clinton, ed. and trans. *Anglo-Saxon Saints and Heroes.* New York: Fordham University Press, 1967; Augustine. *Concerning the City of God against the Pagans.* Trans. Henry Bettenson. Harmondsworth: Penguin, 1972; Augustine. *Confessions.* Trans. R.S. Pine-Coffin. Harmondsworth: Penguin, 1961; Carlson, Ingvar, ed. *The Pastoral Care.* 2 vols. Stockholm: Almqvist & Wiksell, 1975–78; Carnicelli, Thomas A., ed. *King Alfred's Version of St. Augustine's Soliloquies.* Cambridge: Harvard University Press, 1969; Colgrave, Bertram, ed. and trans. *The Earliest Life of Gregory the Great by an Anonymous Monk of Whitby.* Lawrence: University Press of Kansas, 1968; Hecht, Hans, ed. *Bischof Wærferths von Worcester Übersetzung der Dialoge Gregors des Grossen.* 2 vols. Bibliothek der angelsächsischen Prosa 5. Leipzig: Wigand, 1900–07. Repr. Darmstadt: Wissenschaftliche Buchsgesellschaft, 1965; Jerome. *Saint Jerome's Hebrew Questions on Genesis.* Trans. C.T.R. Hayward. Oxford: Clarendon, 1995; Sweet, Henry, ed. and trans. *King Alfred's West-Saxon Version of Gregory's Pastoral Care.* EETS o.s. 45, 50. London: Trübner, 1871–72. Repr. with corrections by N.R. Ker. London: Oxford University Press, 1958.

SECONDARY

Bloomfield, Morton W. "Patristics and Old English Literature: Notes on Some Poems." *Comparative Literature* 14 (1962): 36–43; Bolton, W.F. *A History of Anglo-Latin Literature 597–1066.* Vol. 1: *597–740.* Princeton: Princeton University Press, 1967; Brown, Peter. *Augustine of Hippo: A Biography.* Berkeley: University of California Press, 1967; Campbell, J.M. "Patristic Studies and the Literature of Medieval England." *Speculum* 7 (1933): 465–78; Cross, J.E. "*Ubi Sunt* Passages in Old English—Sources and Relationships." *Vetenskaps-societeten i Lund Årsbok* (1956): 25–44; Cross, J.E. "The Literate Anglo-Saxon—On Sources and Disseminations." *PBA* 58 (1972): 67–100; Dubs, Kathleen E. "*Genesis B:* A Study in Grace." *American Benedictine Review* 33 (1982): 47–64; Eckenrode, T.R. "The Venerable Bede and the Pastoral Affirmation of the Christian Message in Anglo-Saxon England." *DownR* 99 (1981): 258–78; Frantzen, Allen J. *King Alfred.* Boston: Twayne, 1986; Greenfield, Stanley B., and Daniel G. Calder. *A New Critical History of Old English Literature.* New York: New York University Press, 1986; Hall, Thomas N. "A Gregorian Model for Eve's *Biter Drync* in *Guthlac B.*" *RES* 44 (1993): 157–76; Huppé, Bernard F. *Doctrine and Poetry: Augustine's Influence on Old English Poetry.* New York: SUNY Press, 1959; Laistner, M.L.W. *The Intellectual Heritage of the Early Middle Ages: Selected Essays,* ed. Chester G. Starr. Ithaca: Cornell University Press, 1957; Meyvaert, Paul. *Bede and Gregory the Great.* Newcastle-upon-Tyne: Bualls, 1946; Meyvaert, Paul. *Benedict, Gregory, Bede and Others.* London: Variorum

Reprints, 1977; O'Donnell, James J. *Augustine*. Boston: Twayne, 1985; Ogilvy, J.D.A. *Books Known to the English, 597–1066*. Cambridge: Mediaeval Academy of America, 1967; Seltzer, John L. "The Wanderer and the Meditative Tradition." *SP* 80 (1983): 227–37; Straw, Carole. *Gregory the Great: Perfection in Imperfection*. Berkeley: University of California Press, 1988; Thundy, Zacharias P. *Covenant in Anglo-Saxon Thought: The Influence of the Bible, Church Fathers, and Germanic Tradition on Anglo-Saxon Laws, History, and the Poems The Battle of Maldon and Guthlac*. Madras: Macmillan, 1972.

See also Ælfric; Alcuin; Aldhelm; Alfred; Anglo-Latin Literature to 1066; Augustine of Canterbury; Bede; Bible in OE Literature; Cædmon; Conversion of the Anglo-Saxons; Criticism, Modern, of Medieval Literature; Felix of Crowland; Orosius; Paul the Deacon; Sermons; Translation; Wærferth

Feasts, New Liturgical

The idea of new liturgical feasts presupposes a generally accepted calendar of observances. Though there was never in medieval England a single uniformly followed liturgical calendar, from roughly the beginning of the 13th century awareness of new feasts as an identifiable phenomenon becomes widespread.

Such feasts are of two kinds, of individuals and of occasions or more abstract devotions. Notable among those of individuals are the feasts of Thomas Becket (29 December), almost universally observed following his canonization in 1173, and of three English bishops canonized in the 13th century: Edmund Rich of Abingdon, archbishop of Canterbury (16 November; d. 1240); Richard Wych, bishop of Chichester (3 April; d. 1253); and Thomas Cantilupe, bishop of Hereford (2 October; d. 1282). The 14th century was less productive of new feasts of this kind (Anne, mother of the Virgin Mary, at 26 July is an important exception, though observed sporadically earlier), and the 15th is marked by the retrospective popularity of several figures from the Anglo-Saxon or British past—notably David of Wales (1 March), Chad of Lichfield (2 March), John of Beverley (7 May), Frideswide of Oxford (19 October), Winefride of Holywell (3 November)—as well as of Osmund (4 December), the first Norman bishop of Salisbury (Old Sarum). Only the first and last among these were officially canonized.

Not all of these saints' feasts were observed in all English churches, despite various enactments by the Convocations of Canterbury or York or by individual diocesan synods; in places where they were observed, a translation feast was also sometimes celebrated, marking the moving of a saint's body to a new burial site or shrine. Of course many other new figures can also be found introduced into one calendar or another.

The same lack of uniformity is evident in the introduction of feasts commemorating occasions or devotions. The most widespread, as well as earliest, is that of Corpus Christi, found in many English service books from the early 14th century on. In the later Middle Ages three new feasts come to be regarded as specially important, sometimes to the extent of having the liturgical forms developed for them produced in pamphlets called simply *nova festa*. These are the Transfiguration (6 August), which has a very long history but comes to be generally observed only from 1457, following a papal decree of thanksgiving for a notable defeat of the Turks; the Visitation (of the Virgin Mary to Elizabeth; 2 July), which arose in the context of efforts to end the late-14th-century Great Schism; and the Name of Jesus or Holy Name (7 August), which emerges from being a popular private devotion to widespread liturgical celebration only by the early 16th century.

Other new feasts starting to gain popularity toward the end of the Middle Ages include the Five Wounds (which, however, never had a date attached), the Crown of Thorns (occasionally found on 4 May), the Compassion of the Virgin (no date at all widely observed), and her Presentation (21 November), which actually goes back to an 11th-century feast called the Oblation of the Virgin but gained new popularity in the late 14th century.

Because complete liturgical uniformity comes into being only with the Reformation and Counter-Reformation (abetted by the technology of printing), caution is necessary in dealing with new feasts in the Middle Ages. No blanket statement can be made about the spread of any particular feast until the widest possible range of evidence for its actual observance has been examined.

Richard W. Pfaff

Bibliography

Farmer, David Hugh. *The Oxford Dictionary of Saints*. 3d ed. Oxford: Oxford University Press, 1992; Hughes, Jonathan. "New Cults of Saints in the Diocese of York." Ch. 6 in *Pastors and Visionaries: Religion and Secular Life in Late Medieval Yorkshire*. Woodbridge: Boydell, 1988, pp. 298–346; Pfaff, Richard W. *New Liturgical Feasts in Later Medieval England*. Oxford: Clarendon, 1970.

See also Edmund of Abingdon; Offices, New Liturgical; Votive Observance; Thomas of Canterbury, Office for

Felix of Crowland (fl. ca. 740–50)

Author of the Latin *Life of St. Guthlac (Vita sancti Guthlaci)*, the only piece of historical writing to have come down from early Mercia. By the time of Guthlac's birth (ca. 674) Æthelred was already king. Guthlac's ancestry is traced back through Mercian genealogy to Icel, five generations before Penda, and his name to a family famed in legend, the Guthlacingas. His parents, Penwalh (or Penwald) and Tette, are otherwise unknown.

After a successful career as a leader on the western borders of Mercia Guthlac suddenly turned to religious life at the age of 24, first at Repton Abbey under the direction of Abbess Ælfthryth and later in the empty fens. Like the desert Fathers he counseled many, drawn to Crowland by his reputation; Æthelbald, future king of Mercia, often visited him there. Felix's *Life* is also the source of our knowledge of

Guthlac's sister Pege, a hermit who lived in Peakirk, Northamptonshire. The Anglo-Saxon Chronicle gives Guthlac's death as occurring in 714, a date consistent with Felix's account.

Felix wrote up Guthlac's life in the 740s for King Ælfwald of East Anglia. There is, however, no need to assume that Felix was East Anglian, given that Ælfwald's predecessor's daughter was abbess of Repton during Guthlac's later years at Crowland. A particularly fine section of the *Life* tells of Guthlac's arrival at Crowland on St. Bartholomew's Day; his temptation to despair, from which he is saved by the appearance and teaching of Bartholomew; and his deliverance at the gates of hell through Bartholomew's intervention.

The *Life* is a polished piece of writing, indebted to well-established hagiographical conventions, especially in the deathbed scene, where it is similar to Evagrius's life of Anthony and Bede's life of Cuthbert. Stylistically Felix also owes much to Aldhelm. Nothing is known of Felix beyond his own identification of himself as someone in orders. There is no evidence to support the traditional assumption that he was a monk of Crowland and none indeed for organized monastic life at Crowland before Thurketyl's abbey in the 970s.

Jane Roberts

Bibliography

PRIMARY

Colgrave, Bertram, ed. and trans. *Felix's Life of Saint Guthlac*. Cambridge: Cambridge University Press, 1956; Jones, Charles Williams. *Saints' Lives and Chronicles in Early England*. Ithaca: Cornell University Press, 1947 [Includes *Life of St. Guthlac*].

SECONDARY

Kurtz, B.J. "From St. Anthony to St. Guthlac." *University of California Publications in Modern Philology* 12 (1926): 103–46; Roberts, Jane. "An Inventory of Early Guthlac Materials." *MS* 32 (1970): 193–233.

See also Guthlac A and B; Guthlac, Prose; Hagiography

Feudalism

There are two definitions of feudalism, and historians do not agree which is to be preferred. One, generally favored by continental historians, encompasses nearly every medieval society from the 9th to the 12th century by identifying as feudal characteristics a subject peasantry, the supremacy of a class of specialized warriors, and ties of obedience that bind man to man, intertwined with other forms of associations, such as family and state.

Historians of England have tended to favor a narrower definition, focusing on military tenure and exactly defined contractual relationships, with one noble owing military service to another. In this relationship a noble, the "lord," grants the hereditary use of a piece of land, the "fief," to another noble, the "vassal." In return the vassal pledges particular military obligations to his lord. This agreement had the binding power of a contract, and to ensure that both parties honored their obligations a system of private courts was created. Discussions of English feudalism, then, emphasize vassalage, fiefs, service in arms owed the lord, and private administration of justice.

Few debates in English history have been as heated or as long-running as that over the introduction of this kind of feudalism into England. Historians once accepted Anglo-Saxon England as a "prefeudal" society. Military obligation arose, it was believed, not from a contract centered on land tenure but from the almost primordial Germanic duty of free men to defend their country in the *fyrd,* the free nation in arms. Because military obligation in Anglo-Saxon England was pretenurial feudalism was introduced during the Conquest by the Normans, whose military organization was based on tenurial relationships.

Such a view had its origins in the Victorian idea of Anglo-Saxon England as a peasant commonwealth with a constitutional kingship. This view of the kingdom and of its military organization does not hold up well today. The Anglo-Saxon military organization included many tenurial and contractual characteristics now identified as "feudal." The origins of Anglo-Saxon military obligation were not based on tenurial contracts, however, but on lordship; a warrior took an oath to be his lord's man. The king could—and usually did—reward his warriors with a gift of land, but this land, Bede's "loanland," was held at the king's pleasure and did not automatically pass to the warrior's heir.

Bookland tenure and the Viking invasions changed the conditions under which the king granted land. Bookland, introduced by churchmen in the 7th century, was given by royal charter in perpetuity. Loanland could be given to a warrior for his life and then to another after the first's death. Bookland did not have that "reusable" quality, so it became necessary to create obligations associated with bookland that were as permanent and hereditary as the tenure itself. The Mercian kings imposed bridge work, fortress work, and *fyrd* attendance on the possession of bookland.

The Viking invasions of the 9th and 10th centuries caused the West Saxon kings to redefine these terms, so that "fortress work" included the maintenance and defense of a system of boroughs and "*fyrd* attendance" was participation in a standing army. By the reign of Edward the Confessor (1042–66) the amount of service owed by one who held bookland was directly related to the value of his bookland in hidage (a tax paid on each hide of land, originally in service but later in money). Concurrent with the development of this system, however, was the continuation of obligation through personal oaths and ties between the magnates, who held bookland from the king, and the lesser warriors, who served them.

The military organization of pre-Conquest Normandy was based less on tenurial relationships than was once thought. The Norman Conquest did dramatically change the tenurial—and thus the feudal—relationship between king and subject in England. The very process of conquest provided both the opportunity and the need for sharply defined military relationships among the conquering Normans. William had won for himself an entire kingdom, and he could organize it in any way he saw fit, but he needed to defend it immediately against threats from without and within.

William distributed the lands of the kingdom to the new Norman nobility in return for what became fixed military services defined in written surveys. By the end of his reign the nobility was organized in a strict feudal hierarchy. All land was held of the king, either directly or by subinfeudation (vassals bestowing fiefs upon their own vassals) from one of the great magnates who held vast territories of the king. All English nobles thus owed the king military service and were ultimately subject to decisions made in feudal courts.

These conditions developed over the course of William's reign and may have become exactly defined only by the reign of Henry I, but they would be the theoretical basis for the exercise of royal power throughout the medieval period. Henry II was able to introduce and enforce his royal system of justice by insisting on his rights as feudal overlord. Feudal dues became an important source of royal wealth. The knight's fee, a fief from which the service of a single knight was due, became the basic unit of feudal organization. The holder of that fief was obliged to send one knight to serve the king or to send scutage, an amount of money that would enable the king to hire a mercenary knight. Yearly knight service could be commuted by a yearly payment of scutage. Feudal surveys, such as the *Cartae baronum,* doubled as tax surveys, and through feudal dues the English crown became wealthy.

The feudal relationship between the king and his nobles limited both parties. When a king overstepped his limitations, his vassals were no longer obligated to him. Such was the case with John, who manipulated his position as feudal overlord so excessively and with such greed that his barons rebelled and forced him to reaffirm limitations on royal power by accepting Magna Carta. The conflicts resulting in Magna Carta were symptomatic of the growing complexity of society. The invention of "private" property, expensive overseas wars, and an increasingly unstable political situation all served to change the way the feudal relationship worked. The best-known and most destructive change was the advent of bastard feudalism, the reliance upon paid retainers rather than upon tenure and the service based in landholding.

Robert S. Babcock

Bibliography

Abels, Richard P. *Lordship and Military Obligation in Anglo-Saxon England.* Berkeley: University of California Press, 1988; Barlow, Frank. *The Feudal Kingdom of England, 1042–1216.* 4th ed. London: Longman, 1988; Clanchy, M.T. *England and Its Rulers, 1066–1272.* Totowa: Barnes & Noble, 1983 [compare with Barlow for the varieties of interpretation]; Hollister, C. Warren. *Anglo-Saxon Military Institutions on the Eve of the Norman Conquest.* Oxford: Clarendon, 1962 [on the extent to which pre-Conquest England can be seen as a feudal kingdom]; John, Eric. *Land Tenure in Early England: A Discussion of Some Problems.* Leicester: Leicester University Press, 1960 [on Anglo-Saxon land tenure]; Stenton, F.M. *The First Century of English Feudalism, 1066–1166.* 2d ed. Oxford: Clarendon, 1961 [still valuable and intellectually demanding on the introduction of feudalism into England].

See also Armies; Bastard Feudalism; Knight Service; Magna Carta; Norman Conquest; Tenures

Feuds and Wergeld

Traditional legal history saw bloodfeud as an "interminable antiphony of violence." Modern scholars have learned from anthropologists that the mechanisms of feud not only contribute to social peace but provide the only realistic chance of peace in a society whose government lacks the means or will to enforce it.

The basic mechanisms are two: death or injury can be compensated by mutually acceptable payments in cash or kind; injuries borne by individuals may be avenged by any one of their recognized associates or any recognized associate of the individual responsible. The prospect of revenge is a disincentive for would-be offenders and an incentive for their associates and those of their victim to seek peace through compensation. The same cast of mind applies to theft; revenge is taken at once on thieves caught *in flagrante,* while theft detected by formal process is amended by restoring the stolen goods or their value, perhaps multiplied.

The Anglo-Saxon bloodfeud confronts historians in three main areas. First, early law codes record the *wergeld* ("man money"), the blood price of free men or different classes of aristocrat. These were 100 and 300 shillings in the code of Æthelberht of Kent (before 616), and 200, 600, and 1,200 shillings in Ine's Wessex code (ca. 690). The codes of Æthelberht and Alfred also give lists of a wide variety of bodily injuries, with the sum due for each. The point of these, as of wergelds, was as alternatives to application of the "eye for an eye" principle. Vengeance is taken by a victim's, or against an offender's kindred (i.e., a more or less "extended" family of collaterals). These are also payees or payers of compensation, though Ine likewise specifies sums due to lords. It is envisaged that pursuit of revenge or compensation is exclusively the business of victim or associates. In the realm of theft the king is more involved, to the extent of forbidding revenge for those caught red-handed, while convicted thieves must not only make restitution to owners but pay a fine to the king.

A second illustrative area is "heroic" literature, where vendetta is prominent, both actually and figuratively (as when Beowulf's fight with Grendel and his mother is seen as a feud). An important feature of literary feuds is their focus on divided loyalties; between lord and kin, or women torn between husband and father. Presumably these crises attract poetic attention because they are atypical. Nevertheless, conflicts with this sort of mixed feeling are exactly those spotlighted by anthropologists concerned with the paradox of peace in the bloodfeud.

The third category of evidence is (or ought to be) tales of historical as opposed to literary feuds. One of these is the story of Cynewulf and Cyneheard in the Anglo-Saxon

Chronicle for 757 (with classic kin-lord dilemma). After the year 900 or so such tales are hard to find. Almost the only example is a Northumbrian feud of the 11th century, recently reinterpreted as a struggle for political power in the north. This ties up with the important point that Edmund's code (ca. 945) took major steps to disrupt the feud mechanism, notably by limiting the liabilities of kin. In late Anglo-Saxon laws *bot* ("compensation") is usually owed to God or king, and wergeld is paid not as blood money by offender to offended kin but as the price of life by criminals to an outraged crown. "Vengeance is mine," said 10th-century kings.

Patrick Wormald

Bibliography

PRIMARY

Whitelock, Dorothy, ed. *English Historical Documents.* Vol. 1: *c. 500–1042.* 2d ed. London: Eyre Methuen, 1979 [contains Edmund's code on the feud, and relevant excerpts from the Anglo-Saxon Chronicle].

SECONDARY

Gluckman, Max. *Custom and Conflict in Africa.* Oxford: Blackwell, 1955 [the classic anthropological exposition]; Kapelle, William E. *The Norman Conquest of the North: The Region and Its Transformation, 1000–1135.* Chapel Hill: University of North Carolina Press, 1979 [ch. 1 treats the Northumbrian feud]; Wallace-Hadrill, J.M. "The Bloodfeud of the Franks." In *The Long-Haired Kings.* London: Methuen, 1962, pp. 121–47; White, Stephen D. "Kinship and Lordship in Early Medieval England." *Viator* 20 (1989): 1–18; Whitelock, Dorothy, ed. *The Audience of Beowulf.* Oxford: Clarendon, 1951 [ch. 1 is useful]; Wormald, Jennifer. "Bloodfeud, Kindred and Government in Early Modern Scotland." *Past and Present* 87 (May 1980): 54–97; Wormald, Patrick. "Giving God and King Their Due: Conflict and Its Regulation in the Early English State." *Settimane di Studio del Centro Italiano di Studi sull'alto Medioevo* 44 (1997), forthcoming.

See also Beowulf; Finnsburh Law, Anglo-Saxon

Finnsburh

The "Finnsburh Episode" comprises *Beowulf* 1063–1160a, and the "Finnsburh Fragment" survives as a 48-line poem edited in Hickes's *Thesaurus* 1:192–93. Hickes says he found the fragment, since lost, on a single leaf in a "Semi-Saxon" homily collection in Lambeth Palace Library. Only two Lambeth manuscripts fit his description: MS 489 of the 11th century and MS 487 of the 13th century. Neither codex contains the "fragment," probably a loose leaf or part of the binding.

The two texts tell different parts of the same story, something like this: With 60 retainers the Danish prince Hnæf visits Finnsburh, the fortress of his sister Hildeburh, queen of the Frisian king Finn. For reasons not stated the Frisians attack the Danes in a hall at dawn. The "Fragment" begins when a Danish watchman reports a light to Hnæf, who correctly identifies it as the flashing of Frisian armor. He awakens his troops, and the Danes rush to arm themselves and defend the doors at each end of the hall. Outside a Frisian named Garulf urges his colleague Guthere not to risk his life against the Danes, but Guthere shouts a challenge to the defenders. From inside the Dane Sigeferth taunts the two Frisians outside. The battle begins, and ironically Garulf falls first. The fight continues with Frisian casualties only. Here the "Fragment" ends.

The "Episode" begins with Queen Hildeburh awakening to a battle in progress, which rages for five days before any Danes die. The Frisians kill Hnæf and an unstated number of Danes. Finn has insufficient forces to overcome the Danes, who cannot escape from the hall. The Danes offer terms to the Frisians. Finn and the new Danish commander, Hengest, swear an oath, and either pledge money is exchanged or Hnæf's wergeld is paid, or both. Hildeburh presides over the cremation of the slain, including her son and her brother Hnæf. The Frisians return to their homes. Hengest considers sailing back to Denmark but chooses to remain at Finnsburh with his retainers for a tense winter. Spring tames the winter seas, and Hengest yearns to leave. But first he intends to avenge Hnæf. In a Danish council Hengest accepts a sword from Hunlafing, whose uncles Guthlaf and Oslaf encourage the Danes by reciting all their woes since the original voyage to Frisia. The Danes attack the Frisians, kill Finn, loot Finnsburh, and return Hildeburh to Denmark.

The events of the story happen in the late 4th or early 5th centuries, and Hengest may be the Hengist who invaded Britain ca. 429–49 (Bede, *Ecclesiastical History* 1.15). Both texts appear in traditional late West Saxon language, but date and location remain uncertain.

Scholars generally regard the "Fragment" as a "heroic lay," a short poem characterized by fast narration, tight description, and terse dialogue, such as *Waldere.* The *Beowulf*-poet calls the "Episode" a *gidd* (1065b, 1160a) and a *leod* (1159b), both meaning "song." Both texts have epic characteristics, for example, high-ranking warriors struggling heroically over tribal or national fortunes in elevated diction and aristocratic imagery. But the term "epic" invites misleading comparisons with classical epic. Both texts resemble a page or two detached from a larger poem rather than a freestanding lay.

The two texts differ stylistically, although both feature fast action. The "Fragment" brims with dramatic speeches and closely observed, stark detail. The *Beowulf*-poet tells the "Episode" densely and allusively, full of thought and emotion, brooding on revenge and inescapable violence.

Donald K. Fry

Bibliography

PRIMARY

ASPR 4:33–36 ["Episode"], 6:3–4 ["Fragment"]; Fry, Donald K., ed. *Finnsburh Fragment and Episode.* London: Methuen, 1974; Hickes, George. *Linguarum Veterum Septentrionalium Thesaurus.* 2 vols. Oxford, 1705, 1:192–93; Klaeber, Friedrich, ed. *Beowulf and the Fight at Finnsburg.* 3d ed. Boston: Heath, 1950.

SECONDARY

Brodeur, A.G. "The Climax of the Finn Episode." *University of California Publications in English* 3 (1943): 285–361; Brodeur, A.G. "Design and Motive in the Finn Episode." *Essays & Studies, University of California Publications in English* 14 (1943): 1–42; Chambers, R.W. *Beowulf: An Introduction to the Study of the Poem with a Discussion of the Stories of Offa and Finn.* 3d ed., suppl. by C.L. Wrenn. Cambridge: Cambridge University Press, 1959; Fry, Donald K. *Beowulf and the Fight at Finnsburh: A Bibliography.* Charlottesville: University Press of Virginia, 1969; Moore, Bruce. "The Relevance of the Finnsburh Episode." *JEGP* 75 (1976): 317–29.

See also Anglo-Saxon Invasions; *Beowulf;* Feuds and Wergeld; Women in OE Literature

Floris and Blancheflour

An anonymous narrative poem composed in the east Midlands ca. 1250–1300, apparently in octosyllabic couplets. It may be the earliest extant English romance, if this place does not fall to *King Horn. Floris* survives in four manuscripts: BL Cotton Vitellius D.3, from before 1300, but largely burned in 1731; CUL Gg. 4.27.2, ca. 1300; the Auchinleck Manuscript (Edinburgh, National Library of Scotland Advocates' 19.2.1), ca. 1330–40; and Trentham (BL Egerton 2862), ca. 1400. The beginning of the poem has been lost, but its general content can be deduced from the French work on which the English is based; the extant text of the rest runs to 1,311 lines in Taylor's edition.

Two versions of the story are represented in extant French texts; these have been distinguished as the "aristocratic" (and earlier) version and the "popular." In company with versions in various Germanic languages the English poem belongs to the "aristocratic" tradition. It opens when Floris and Blancheflour are small children, but it must once have explained that Blancheflour's mother is a Christian prisoner of the pagan king of Spain and that she and the queen have given birth to their children on the same day. Floris and Blancheflour share their schooling, and by the time they are twelve they have come to love each other so intensely that the king decides to separate them.

Blancheflour is sold to Babylonian merchants, and Floris is told she has died; but when they see how he pines for her, Floris's parents allow him to go after her. He traces her to the Emir's "tower of maidens" in Babylon, where she is to become the Emir's next wife. On the advice of a friend he bribes the porter to smuggle him into the tower in a basket of flowers. He and Blancheflour are reunited, but two days later they are discovered in bed by the Emir's chamberlain and sentenced to death. As each lover tries to save the other, however, the Emir is so impressed by their mutual devotion that he spares them, knights Floris, and allows them to marry. He himself marries Blancheflour's confidante, Clarice, and is apparently converted. When Floris's father dies, the couple return to Spain, where Floris and, implicitly, his kingdom become Christian.

The story may have had a Byzantine origin. The love element bears some resemblance to that of French idyllic romance, thought to derive ultimately from certain Greek works; and the tricks by which the hero achieves his goal recall Greek New Comedy. Both these aspects of the story imply a degree of amorality at the individual level, set paradoxically against a concern with religious propriety at the national level.

The English poem is only one-third the length of the French text. The emphasis is less on the descriptive and more on the dramatic, and less interest is shown in love and religion than in wit and ingenuity.

Diane Speed

Bibliography

PRIMARY

De Vries, Franciscus C., ed. *Floris and Blauncheflur: A Middle English Romance.* Gröningen: Drukkerij V.R.B., 1966; Taylor, Albert B., ed. *Floris and Blancheflour: A Middle-English Romance.* Oxford: Clarendon, 1927.

SECONDARY

New *CBEL* 1:451–52; *Manual* 1:144–46, 299–301; Barnes, Geraldine. "Cunning and Ingenuity in the Middle English *Floris and Blauncheflur.*" *MÆ* 53 (1984): 10–25; Rice, Joanne A. *Middle English Romance: An Annotated Bibliography, 1955–1985.* New York: Garland, 1987, pp. 255–58.

See also Literary Influences: Classical, French; Romances

Food and the Food Trades

Accounts of wealthy medieval households show the consumption of all sorts of exotic fare. Some spices traveled halfway across the world before being purchased in London or at one of the greater fairs, and many of the delicate meats consumed at great banquets were expensive regional specialties. But from the broad perspective of England's food supplies these luxuries were side issues, even for large households.

The food trades chiefly involved cereals (for bread, gruel, and ale), cheese, fish, eggs, poultry, and meat. Fruit, vegetables, and milk were not regularly traded but made a useful contribution to the diet of families who could produce their own. In all parts of England there was some food from the wild, but such resources could not be relied on in densely settled areas.

Regional patterns of cereal cropping had implications for eating habits. In most villages bread had to be made from what was grown and traded nearby. The best indicators of local diet are wages and mill rents paid in grain, recorded in manorial accounts. Wheat was the preferred bread grain, and always the most expensive, but much bread was made from mixtures of wheat and rye or wheat and barley. Barley was a staple in Norfolk, England's most densely populated shire. Sometimes the cheapest bread flour contained peasmeal and beanmeal. Oats, unsuitable for bread, were used for gruel and in brewing. Though chiefly used as animal feed, they were important for the diet of the northwest and some upland areas.

During the period for which we have documentary evidence dietary patterns and the composition of the food trades varied with changes in real income. Between 1200 and the Black Death (1348–49) the majority of the population was overwhelmingly dependent on cereals. Protein deficiency may have been widespread. After the Black Death, as standards of living rose, the consumption of wheaten bread and barley ale grew at the expense of inferior cereals; the average consumption of meat rose dramatically.

Even at the peak of urban growth, around 1300, probably over half of all English households grew most of their own food and depended on the market only for small quantities of salt, meat, and cheese. Throughout the period, too, much trade between neighbors bypassed formal markets, and this was mostly within the law. But population growth and increasing economic specialization encouraged the proliferation of weekly markets. One of the reasons for this was the concentration of landless consumers in small communities.

Domesday Book's list of 153 boroughs and markets is an imperfect guide to formal marketing in the 11th century; different groups of Domesday commissioners performed their task differently, and the concept of a market was still imprecise. There must already have been more marketlike institutions, particularly in the eastern counties. After 1086 the number of formal markets increased to the point where by 1300 few households were more than a few miles from one. The highest densities were in East Anglia. During the 14th century severe losses of population contributed to the contraction or discontinuation of many smaller markets.

Village markets and small towns could be supplied with most of their needs from within a ten-mile radius. But where communications by water were available trade over longer distances was common, and from at least the mid-13th century the largest towns depended on water-borne supplies from 100 miles away or more. Londoners bought grain from the Thames Valley and fertile areas of the east coast. Bristol's supplies of grain came by river from far up the Severn. The fatstock (livestock) trade of large towns covered considerable distances overland, and fish were brought from far-off fishing grounds.

Many towns had markets for grain and fish on the waterfront, where wholesalers could buy in bulk and where townsmen were given special provision for supplying their own households. Such, for example, were Queenhithe and Billingsgate in London. Bristol had similar quays on the Severn, York on the Ouse, and Norwich on the Wensum. The largest towns had a separate wholesale fatstock market, like London's Smithfield. These wholesale markets supplied the central urban grain, fish, and meat markets, which handled only retail trade. Most town markets were held more than once a week.

From the late 12th century the importance of the food trades for urban welfare resulted in the multiplication of regulations, some of dubious benefit to the communities they were supposed to protect. The Assize of Weights and Measures (1194) and Magna Carta regulated measures in the grain trade. By 1202 assizes of bread and ale were enforced to tie the price of ale and the size of the farthing loaf to the market price of grain. These regulations were enforced by local authorities on behalf of the crown, though in time they came to be valued more as a source of income from fines than for their original purpose. In the 13th century local by-laws governing the food trades multiplied, chiefly to protect burgesses at the expense of nonburgesses. In the 14th century the food trades were further hampered by poorly drafted laws against the monopolizing of produce by "forestallers," who bought in advance to drive up prices, and against uncontrolled levels of profit in selling.

The food trades have a particular sociological interest because of the prominence of women in some branches. Butchery, milling, and baking were male occupations, but brewing and the retailing of ale were predominantly women's work. Langland's Rose the regrator ("retail trader") and Skelton's Elynour Rummynge are informative portraits of medieval alewives, despite their pejorative presentation. Women were also prominent in the retailing of fish, poultry, and eggs, as is clear from the lists of those reported for forestalling in urban court records.

Richard H. Britnell

Bibliography

Biddick, Kathleen. "Missing Links: Taxable Wealth, Markets and Stratification among Medieval English Peasants." *JIH* 18 (1987): 277–98; Britnell, Richard H. "The Proliferation of Markets in England, 1200–1349." *EcHR,* 2d ser. 34 (1981): 209–21 [one of a number of studies cited here on the marketing of produce]; Britnell, Richard H. "*Forstall,* Forestalling and the Statute of Forestallers." *EHR* 102 (1987): 89–102; Campbell, Bruce M.S., and James A. Galloway, Derek Keene, and Margaret Murphy. *A Medieval Capital and Its Grain Supply: Agrarian Production and Distribution in the London Region c. 1300.* Historical Geography Research Series 30. London: Historical Geography Research Series, 1993; Dyer, Christopher. "The Consumer and the Market in the Later Middle Ages." *EcHR,* 2d ser. 42 (1989): 305–27; Dyer, Christopher. *Standards of Living in the Later Middle Ages: Social Change in England, c. 1200–1500.* Cambridge: Cambridge University Press, 1989; Farmer, David L. "Two Wiltshire Manors and Their Markets." *Agricultural History Review* 37 (1989): 1–11; Hanawalt, Barbara A., ed. *Women and Work in Preindustrial Europe.* Bloomington: Indiana University Press, 1986 [essays by Judith M. Bennett and Maryanne Kowaleski are especially helpful]; Hilton, Rodney H. "Women Traders in Medieval England." In *Class Conflict and the Crisis of Feudalism: Essays in Medieval Social History.* 2d ed. London: Verso, 1990, pp. 132–42; Kowaleski, Maryanne. *Local Markets and Regional Trade in Medieval Exeter.* Cambridge: Cambridge University Press, 1995.

See also Agriculture; Assize of Weights and Measures; Black Death; Brewing; Fairs and Markets; *Piers Plowman;* Population; Roads; Skelton

Forests, Royal

Areas established by the king with special laws to protect the "beasts of the forest" and their habitat for the king's hunting. The beasts were the red, fallow, and roe deer and the wild boar (until the roe was removed from the list in 1339). The Normans brought the notion of the royal forest to England and established the New Forest as an early example of the concept.

Under Henry II the royal forests reached their greatest extent, and they continued to include an estimated one-fourth of the realm in the 13th century. Efforts by the barons to restrict them resulted in specific chapters in Magna Carta in 1215, a separate Forest Charter in 1217, and later confirmations of both charters. However, massive disafforestation occurred only in 1327. Enforcement of forest law then deteriorated, and a mere shell of the medieval royal forest existed when described by John Manwood in one of the first books on the subject, *A Treatise and Discourse of the Laws of the Forest* (1598).

Hunting was prohibited in a royal forest; so also was the cutting of trees, bringing land into cultivation, pasturing farm animals, and other activities related to the use of forest products. Income from fines for violations and user fees were a significant factor in royal income by the later 12th century. For barons who had manors within the royal forest and the villagers who lived there the restrictions meant a heavy burden. Enforcement was carried out by means of a hierarchy of forest courts and officials. When the Anglo-Saxon Chronicle stated that William the Conqueror "loved the stags as if he were their father," it expressed the hatred of a forest law that valued a deer more than the life of a man, and the harsh reality of that law provided the background for a fictional Robin Hood transmitted to future generations through popular ballads.

Charles R. Young

Bibliography

Bazeley, Margaret Ley. "The Extent of the English Forest in the Thirteenth Century." *TRHS,* 4th ser. 4 (1921): 140–72; Neilson, Nellie. "The Forests." In *The English Government at Work, 1327–1336.* Vol. 1: *Central and Prerogative Administration,* ed. James F. Willard and William A. Morris. Cambridge: Mediaeval Academy of America, 1940, pp. 394–467; Young, Charles R. *The Royal Forests of Medieval England.* Philadelphia: University of Pennsylvania Press, 1979.

See also Magna Carta; Outlaws; William I

Formula

A type of poetic phrase first used by oral poets as one of several aids to rapid composition before an audience. For example, if an OE oral poet wished to praise a leader, he need only call to mind a formula like *þæt wæs god cyning!* ("That was a good king!") or *sinces brytta* ("giver of treasure"). Such phrases were available to the poet for a broad spectrum of ideas, sometimes repeated verbatim, sometimes not. Formulas could be varied to suit their prosodic, thematic, or narrative contexts, as well as the artistic impulse of the poet.

Specifically a formula is a member of a set of verses in which one word, usually stressed, is constant and at least one stressed word may be varied, usually synonymously, to suit the alliterative or narrative context. For example, the following phrases are found a total of thirteen times in five different poems: *sinces brytta* ("giver of treasure"), *goldes bryttan* ("giver of gold"), and *beaga bryttan* ("giver of rings"). All three verses are the same formula: all express the same general concept, "giver of wealth," and all serve the same purpose, to denote an ideal king or chieftain. In this instance the poets probably recalled the pattern *[wealth] brytta* (or *bryttan,* when the accusative case was required) and then varied the synonyms for "wealth" to accord with their alliterative needs. That is, if an "s" alliterator governed the line, the poet chose *sinces;* if he needed a "b" alliterator, he chose *beaga;* and so forth.

Formulas usually share the same poetic meter and are usually one verse, or half-line, in length (though not all half-lines of OE poetry are formulas). Further they are often part of larger formulaic systems that provided patterns for the creation of new metrical phrases: *X brytta,* for example, is a systemic pattern that lies behind not only *[wealth] brytta,* but also *lifes brytta* ("giver of life"), a formula denoting God; and *morþres, hearmes,* or *synna brytta* ("giver of crimes," "of harm," or "of sins"), a formula denoting the Devil. The verses *[wealth] brytta, [life] brytta,* and *[evil] brytta* represent three different formulas, all members of the system *X brytta.* Although formulas derive originally from oral poetry, they were used extensively by poets writing in our earliest literary tradition.

Anita R. Riedinger

Bibliography

Fry, Donald K. "Old English Formulas and Systems." *ES* 48 (1967): 193–204; Niles, John. *Beowulf: The Poem and Its Tradition.* Cambridge: Harvard University Press, 1983; Riedinger, Anita R. "The Old English Formula in Context." *Speculum* (1985): 294–317.

See also Minstrels; Orality; Versification

Fortescue, Sir John (ca. 1390–1479)

The most prolific and widely quoted man of law of 15th-century England, Fortescue supported Lancastrian interests so passionately that he earned a traitor's attainder and exile into France for ten years after the Yorkist victory at Towton (1461). The exile sharpened his perspective for comparative Anglo-French law and, after his last Lancastrian battle, at Tewkesbury (1471), for a more mellowed view toward Edward IV's dynastic claims. A royal councillor for at least four years in the 1470s in the Star Chamber, Sir John died, according to Devonshire legend, at age 90.

Fortescue began legal training at Lincoln's Inn before 1420 and served as member of eight parliaments from Devon,

1421–36. Active as a justice of peace since 1418 and on dozens of commissions of *oyer et terminer,* he obtained Henry VI's appointment as king's serjeant in 1441 and as chief justice of King's Bench in 1442. Before 1461 he was the most important working judge in England, scattering his name across miles of parchment plea rolls, patent rolls, and diverse other public and private records, including the Paston Letters.

Eleven essays survive in his name, another five have been attributed to him, and five more are known but lost. Of these 21, at least eleven are pamphlets promoting the Lancastrian succession; seven others are minor didactic essays. The final three are major works of political jurisprudence and goldmines for readers and writers of late-medieval constitutional law. *De natura legis naturae (On the Nature of the Law of Nature)* distinguishes law from justice, divine from natural, and then examines at length why women cannot rule. Fortescue partially recanted this strong antifeminist tract, to make personal peace with the Yorkists, but John Knox picked up the argument a century later against the Tudor queens, in his tract *Against the Monstrous Regiment of Women* (1558).

De laudibus legum Anglie (In Praise of the Laws of England) compares absolute and limited monarchy, at the expense of France, extolling the English balance of natural, customary, and statute laws as a superior system for civil and criminal justice. Like his distinguished fellow judge Sir Thomas Littleton (1415–1481) Fortescue emphasizes legal theory over formalism. This treatise ends with the first detailed description of English legal education and judicial practice.

His final tract, *De dominio regale et politico (On Regal and Political Lordship)* continues Fortescue's thoughts on the theme of absolute versus limited monarchy, borrowed from Thomas Aquinas. Fortescue's writings may lack originality of ideas, but they offer vital information for pre-Reformation law and government, as well as sound models for the lawyer's style of political advocacy.

DeLloyd J. Guth

Bibliography

PRIMARY
Chrimes, Stanley B., ed. and trans. *Sir John Fortescue: De laudibus legum Anglie.* Cambridge: Cambridge University Press, 1942; Fortescue, Thomas (Lord Clermont). *The Works of Sir John Fortescue.* 2 vols. London: Printed for Private Distribution, 1869.

SECONDARY
Plummer, Charles, ed. and trans. *The Governance of England.* Oxford: Clarendon, 1885.

See also Law, Post-Conquest; Law in ME Literature; Wars of the Roses; Year Books

Frankpledge

The frankpledge system, a form of corporate responsibility for bringing offenders to trial, was a key element in local law enforcement in southern, midland, and eastern England in the 12th and 13th centuries. Its origins lay in two late Saxon institutions, the tithing (a unit for the pursuit of criminals) and suretyship (a pledge of appearance in court). By the early 12th century the concepts had fused, possibly as a result of peacekeeping reforms by William I. The tithing not only had a police function but was also the "frankpledge," or collective security for its members.

South of the Thames the number in a tithing only approximated to ten; tithing and township were commonly identical. All males over twelve, except clergy, vagrants, the disabled, and families and household retainers of lords, were required to be in a tithing. Wealthier freeholders were exempt in practice; it was mostly unfree peasants who were in frankpledge by the 13th century. If a man accused of crime did not appear in court, his tithing would be amerced (fined) for his absence. If he had no tithing, and should have had one, the whole township would be amerced.

Sheriffs held a "view of frankpledge" to check the composition of tithings and take customary payments at special twice-yearly sessions of the hundred courts (the "sheriff's tourn"). After the Assize of Clarendon in 1166 these became important occasions for searching out criminals, and the chief pledges (the heads of each tithing) were among those required to present (formally report) offenders. This was also the practice when the right to view of frankpledge was acquired by a feudal lord or a borough. Although the system decayed in the late 13th and 14th centuries, as new peacekeeping measures were devised and sheriffs ceased to check tithing lists, view of frankpledge remained a valuable franchise and a useful means to maintain local discipline. Accordingly it continued as a feature of the "court leet," or local court, held in many manors through the 15th century and beyond.

G.J. White

Bibliography

Crowley, Douglas. "The Later History of Frankpledge." *BIHR* 48 (1975): 1–15; Morris, William A. *The Frankpledge System.* New York: Longmans, Green, 1910 [this classic is still important]; Warren, W.L. *The Governance of Norman and Angevin England, 1086–1272.* London: Arnold, 1987 [chs. 2 and 7 are especially useful].

See also Courts and the Court System; Hundreds; Local Government; Tenures

Franks Casket

This whalebone casket (London, British Museum MLA 1867, 1–20.1; approx. 9 inches long by 5 inches high by 7.5 inches wide) was probably made in 8th-century Northumbria. The front, back, left side, and central panel of the lid were discovered in the mid-19th century in Auzon near Brioude (Haute Loire), France, and passed into the collection of Sir Augustus Franks, who gave them to the British Museum in 1867. The right side of the casket was found in the same house in Auzon and passed through the Carrand Collection in Lyon to the Bargello Museum in Florence. In 1890 Sven Söderberg of Copenhagen noted the relationship of the Bargello panel to those in the British Museum.

The casket (fig. 63) is joined by tenons in the panels extending into mortises in corner uprights, secured by wooden pegs. The lid was originally seated into a rebate around the top of the box body and lifted by a central knob or handle once attached to the center of the surviving lid fragment.

The front panel shows two scenes, separated by a short strip of guilloche (interlace design). At the right is an Adoration of the Magi, labeled "mægi" in runes. At the left is the Revenge of Weland the Smith. The runic inscription around the perimeter of both scenes reads, "Whalebone. The flood cast the fish up on the life mountain. The mighty one was sad when he was cast up."

The surviving lid fragment shows an enclosure defended against a warband by an archer, labeled "Ægili." A woman seated behind the archer extends an arrow toward him. The archer has been tentatively linked with Weland's brother Egil, but the scene does not correspond to any event in the extant literary sources.

The left side panel shows the suckling and discovery of Romulus and Remus, with the unusual addition of a second wolf, and with four hunters kneeling, suggesting a reference to twin cults (Becker). The runic inscription reads, "Romulus and Remus, two brothers. The she-wolf raised them in the area of Rome."

The back of the casket shows the conquest of Jerusalem by Titus, with the inscription, "Here fight Titus and the Jews.

Here flee the inhabitants of Jerusalem," the first line in runes, the second in Latin letters. The scene is depicted in two registers around a central building. In the upper register, Roman soldiers enter at left, while civilians flee at right. Below at left a scene of judgment, labeled "dom," is balanced by a group of captives, labeled "gisl," "a hostage," at right.

The interpretation of the scene on the Bargello panel is controversial. At left a warrior confronts a monster. At center a horse confronts a chalice- and rod-bearing woman above a tomb(?). At right two cloaked flanking figures seize a third between them. The inscription, using variant runes, reads, "Herhoes sits on the hill of injury. She works misery, as Erta commanded her. They created grief, sorrow, and anguish of heart."

The fusion of Christian and pagan motifs demonstrates the cultural diversity and richness of the Northumbrian renaissance.

Carol Neuman de Vegvar

Bibliography

Becker, Alfred. *Franks Casket: Zu den Bildern und Inschriften des Runenkästchens von Auzon.* Sprache und Literatur: Regensburger Arbeiten zur Anglistik und Amerikanistik 5. Regensburg: Carl, 1973; Frank, Roberta. Review of A. Becker, *Franks Casket. Speculum* 52 (1977): 120–22; Osborn, Marijane. "The Lid as

Conclusion of the Syncretic Theme of the Franks Casket." In *Old English Runes and Their Continental Background,* ed. Alfred Bammesberger. Heidelberg: Winter, 1991, pp. 249–68; Vandersall, Amy L. "The Date and Provenance of the Franks Casket." *Gesta* 11 (1972): 9–26; Webster, Leslie. "Stylistic Aspects of the Franks Casket." In *The Vikings,* ed. Robert T. Farrell. London: Phillimore, 1982, pp. 20–31; Werner, Martin. *Insular Art: An Annotated Bibliography.* Boston: Hall, 1984, entries F.12.12–22.

See also Art, Anglo-Saxon; Ivory Carving, Anglo-Saxon; Runes

Friars, Mendicant

Friars are members of religious orders that combine a noncloistered religious life with economic dependency on alms originally gained by begging (mendicancy). The Friars Preachers, or Dominicans, were founded by Dominic of Caleruega (ca. 1172–1221), and the Friars Minor, or Franciscans, were founded by Francis of Assisi (1181/82–1226). They aimed to reintroduce the apostolic life of the New Testament into the growing towns of the early 13th century. The friars' involvement with the people of these urban communities, while more immediate than that of monks (who were ordinarily expected to remain inside their monasteries), became something of an economic threat to the secular clergy (clergy not in religious orders, who served most parish churches). With the mendicant ideals of evangelical poverty, charitable love, and preaching while wandering across the land the friars deliberately made themselves dependent on alms freely given for their sustenance, as the first apostles were when sent out by Christ in pairs (Matt. 10:7–10). The Dominicans were ordained priests, dedicated to the salvation of souls through preaching and teaching. On the other hand Francis and his first companions were laymen whose message was the imitation of Christ himself, as revealed in the practice of poverty, mendicancy, and mission. By the end of the 13th century the Franciscans were also mostly ordained and had begun to take on a priestly role.

In 1217 Dominicans and Franciscans alike dispersed throughout Christendom, and within five years the first missions reached England. On 5 August 1221 thirteen Dominicans, or Black Friars, led by Gilbert de Presnay and including several Englishmen, landed at Dover and went directly to Oxford, there to undertake a thorough preparation for the later stages of their mission. Dominic himself and the second general chapter of the order confirmed the instruction to restrict the initial settlement to Oxford.

Contemporary evidence for the Franciscan mission comes from the chronicle of Thomas of Eccleston, ca. 1258–59. Nine Franciscans, or Grey Friars, arrived in England on 10 September 1224, led by Agnellus of Pisa and assisted by three Englishmen, Richard of Ingworth, Richard of Devon, and William of Esseby. In contrast to the Dominicans the Franciscans separated immediately and made three important urban settlements within six weeks at Canterbury, London, and Oxford, followed rapidly by a fourth in Northampton.

Between 1225 and 1230 a further twelve foundations were made. Numbers so increased in individual houses that 40 Franciscan friars were counted in Oxford by 1233, 80 in London by 1243, and 60 in Canterbury by 1289. By 1300 some 59 Franciscan foundations out of a final total of 63 were in existence.

The earliest Franciscan settlements were simple, consisting of a small tenement with no open space for extra building. At first the corporate poverty enjoined by Francis was rigidly observed, but later a third party or "spiritual friend," often an urban community, such as Cambridge or Northampton, was legally able to hold property for use without possession by the Franciscans. Although vowed to individual poverty, the Dominicans were never bound to corporate poverty. They could own their priories and hold landed property on which their houses stood. They were also able to accept revenues from ecclesiastical sources, thus ensuring a considerable element of stability as they expanded. Both orders attracted gifts of property, legacies, and benefactions. Henry III provided gifts of timber from his forests, while his successors down to Richard II proved equally generous as patrons.

Such rapid popularity revealed the need for controlled organization. Both orders established provinces in England. The English Dominican province, which became the largest in the order, had to be divided into four visitations for disciplinary purposes: London, York, Oxford, and Cambridge. Each new foundation had to be approved by the general chapter on the recommendation of the provincial chapter, while a constitutional requirement laid down that each priory should have its own theologically trained priest. By 1250 there were already 24 foundations; by 1300 some 48 of the final total of 57 English Dominican houses were in existence. The Dominicans, however, never quite managed to outstrip the Franciscans numerically. Thomas of Eccleston estimated that by 1255 there were 1,242 Franciscans in England, averaging about 25 per house. The Franciscan general chapter divided the English province into custodies, each with its own *custos,* centered on London, Oxford, Bristol, Cambridge, Worcester, York, Newcastle, and Salisbury. It is interesting that the two orders found no problem in working together (fig. 64).

Dominicans and Franciscans alike made academic training a precondition for the office of preaching to the laity. Both were noted for remarkable intellectual achievement. With the exodus of masters from Paris in 1229 the universities of Oxford and Cambridge grew in importance, built up by the mendicants as centers of excellence and helped by the orders' efficient network of schools and libraries. The significant difference between the two orders was revealed in their attitude to the apostolic model of preaching and teaching. The Dominicans, while stressing individual poverty, concentrated on the need to preach what they had learned in their studies. Every Dominican priory was a house of studies with a resident doctor of theology. The Franciscans, traveling in pairs, stressed the moral conversion of their audience by the example of apostolic poverty and simplicity. Their itinerant preaching, supported as it was by their

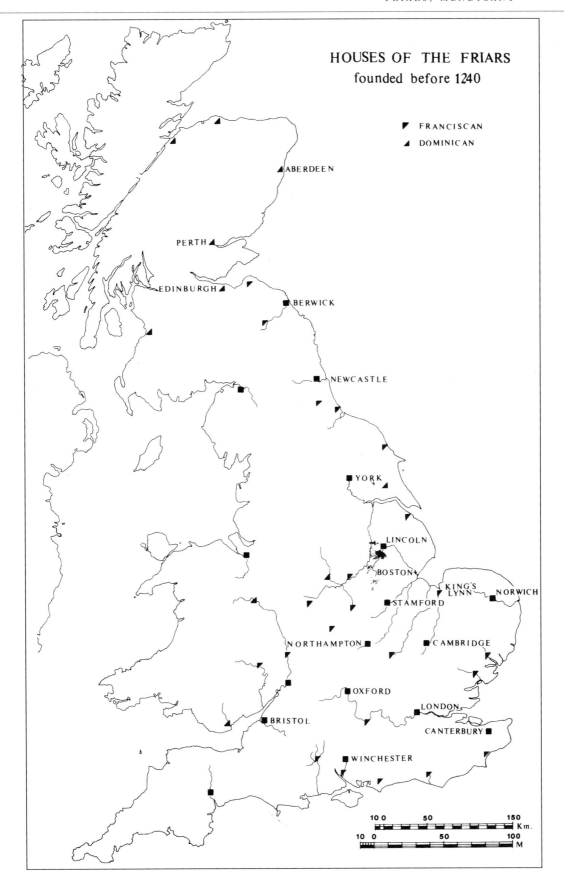

HOUSES OF THE FRIARS
founded before 1240

▼ FRANCISCAN
◢ DOMINICAN

ABERDEEN

PERTH

EDINBURGH

BERWICK

NEWCASTLE

YORK

LINCOLN

BOSTON

KING'S
LYNN

NORWICH

STAMFORD

NORTHAMPTON

CAMBRIDGE

OXFORD

LONDON

BRISTOL

CANTERBURY

WINCHESTER

10 0   50   150
                              Km.

10 0   50   100
                              M

Fig. 64. Friaries founded before 1240. After L.A.S. Butler (1984), in J. Scho-field and R. Leech, Urban Archaeology in Britain (1987). Reprinted with permission of the Council for British Archaeology.

pocket-sized books and material aids, received strong support and encouragement from John Pecham (ca. 1220–1292), the first Franciscan to become archbishop of Canterbury (1279–1292). He reinforced this support by legislation in the English synods of the late 13th century, particularly with respect to the hearing of confessions in Lent.

Both orders attracted the most talented scholars of their day. The Englishman and Paris doctor Haymo of Faversham, appointed as provincial minister of the Franciscans in 1239 to unite mendicant zeal and austerity with the selflessness and intellectual discipline of the universities, was elevated as minister general of the whole order within a year. Robert Grosseteste (1175–1253), patron of both orders of friars and the first lecturer (1229–30) to the Franciscans of Oxford, was not himself a mendicant but was immensely important in fostering Franciscan learning. The Franciscans' Oxford house of studies became a center of excellence in theology for the province, and its great library was build up by Adam March and then by Grosseteste. The reputation of such men as Alexander of Hales, Roger Bacon, Duns Scotus, and William of Ockham attracted Franciscans from all parts of Christendom.

The Dominicans' academic reputation was enhanced by the reception into the order of the Paris master John of St. Giles in 1230 and by the work of the regent master Robert Bacon, his pupil Richard Fishacre, and Simon de Bovill, chancellor of Oxford. Robert Kilwardby, noted scholar, former provincial minister (1260), and the first Dominican archbishop of Canterbury (1272–78), helped the London Dominicans to procure a new site at Baynard's Castle near the Tower.

The mendicants' use of the liturgy also revealed differences between them. The Franciscans in particular, because of their itinerant preaching and consequent instability, needed to say the offices wherever they happened to be. They were responsible for the introduction of the portable breviary, a single collection in one volume of all the necessary elements for the recitation of the offices previously distributed throughout several anthologies. The Dominicans, on the other hand, retained the pattern of normal liturgical prayer but from the beginning allowed dispensations for the purposes of study and preaching.

Mendicant architecture was to develop its own distinctive style to accommodate the growing congregations attracted to the friars. In their churches choirstalls were often placed in the chancel to leave the nave entirely free. Slender pillars, windows of great proportions, and an ample floor area created the illusion of unlimited space and light. Unique to English Dominican churches was the oblong "walking place" between the supporting walls of tower and belfry, which served as an entrance to the church from the great cloister and the street. Franciscan buildings often surpassed in size those of the Dominicans; the vast new Greyfriars' Church in London measured 300 feet by 83 feet.

In the later Middle Ages the progress of both orders followed the path laid down by their predecessors. Despite virulent polemics and satire against the friars by some monks, secular clergy, and vernacular authors, recruitment remained buoyant, and some 1,500 friars continued to receive gifts and benefactions in money and kind. The reformed Franciscans, known as Observants, so popular on the Continent, aroused little interest in England. By 1507 only six Observant houses had been founded, and these were the first to suffer during the Protestant Reformation, in the visitation of 1534. In 1538 Richard Ingworth, bishop of Dover and previously provincial prior of the Dominicans, was instructed to visit all friaries, as part of Henry VIII's and Thomas Cromwell's policy of harassment. Within a year the mendicant orders had almost entirely withdrawn from England.

Brenda M. Bolton

Bibliography

PRIMARY

Thomas of Eccleston. *The Coming of the Franciscans.* Trans. Leo Sherley-Price. London: Mowbray, 1964.

SECONDARY

Bourdillon, A.F.C. *The Order of Minoresses in England.* Manchester: Manchester University Press, 1926; Brooke, Rosalind B. *The Coming of the Friars.* London: Allen & Unwin, 1975; Douie, Decima L. *Archbishop Pecham.* Oxford: Clarendon, 1952; Hinnebusch, William A. *The Early English Friars Preacher.* Rome: Istituto Storica Domenicano, 1951; Little, A.G. *The Grey Friars in Oxford.* Oxford: Clarendon, 1892; Moorman, John R.H. *A History of the Franciscan Order from Its Origins to the Year 1517.* Oxford: Clarendon, 1968; Norton, Christopher, David Park, and Paul Binski, eds. *Dominican Painting in East Anglia.* Bury St. Edmunds: Boydell, 1987; O'Carroll, Maura. "The Educational Organisation of the Dominicans in England and Wales, 1221–1348: A Multi-Disciplinary Approach." *Archivum Fratrum Praedicatorum* 50 (1980): 23–62; Smalley, Beryl. *English Friars and Antiquity in the Early Fourteenth Century.* Oxford: Blackwell, 1960.

See also Architecture and Architectural Sculpture, Gothic; Bacon; Duns Scotus; Friars' Miscellanies; Grosseteste; Learning; Liturgy and Church Music, History of; Monasticism; Mystical and Devotional Writings; Painting, Gothic; Popular Religion; Satire; Sermons; Universities; William of Ockham

Friars' Miscellanies

A designation that has been applied to a number of manuscripts (up to eight) containing much of the extant English verse from the later 12th and the 13th centuries. They have been grouped together because they contain lyrics in English and labeled "friars' miscellanies" because of a belief that early ME lyrics were composed and circulated principally by friars.

These manuscripts are best seen as a sample of the ways in which English literary traditions were preserved and developed for a variety of functions and audiences between the mid-13th and mid-14th centuries. The compilers made significant use of longer poems from around the late 12th century, such as the *Proverbs of Alfred, Poema morale,* Laȝamon's *Brut,* and *The Owl and the Nightingale,* and there are continuities with pre-Conquest literature. New developments associated with the Fourth Lateran Council (1215) and the popular preaching of the friars are certainly present. But English lyrics are not the major constituent of any of these compilations, and they all combine English verse with substantial proportions of French or Latin or both. For example, Cambridge, Trinity College B.14.39 is predominantly homiletic, Bodl. Digby 2 scholarly, BL Harley 913 Latin and clerical; BL Egerton 613 is designed at least partly for devout women. The remainder—BL Cotton Caligula A.ix, Bodl. Digby 86, Oxford, Jesus College 29, and Harley 2253—contain a greater element of the vernacular, secular, and literary.

This grouping has been encouraged by the manuscripts' sharing of some items and their closeness in date and provenance—they range from the 1250s to the 1330s, and are all from the southwest Midlands, except Digby 2 (probably Oxford) and Harley 913 (Ireland). This does indeed suggest a particular local strength of English as a written language *vis-à-vis* French.

However, only for those two outsiders is there strong evidence of origins among the friars. (For "friars" one can generally read "Franciscans": as Frankis has shown, the evidence linking such miscellanies with the Dominicans or other mendicant orders is weak.) The occurrence of texts with mendicant associations, and an element of vernacular preaching, some of it popular in tone, is hardly decisive; recent scholarship has emphasized the possibilities of compilation by Augustinian or Premonstratensian canons and of lay readership and ownership. Securely attributed comparable manuscripts are few, and as a result our knowledge of the kinds of collections that mendicant and other institutions might have made and used is incomplete. Nevertheless, Harley 2253 was recognized even by those who first grouped it with these manuscripts as not originating with the friars.

These manuscripts do show sporadic signs of homiletic use and homiletic sources. They were also drawn upon in 14th-century preaching handbooks and exemplum collections (including some works certainly by friars), such as Bromyard's *Summa praedicantium,* the *Fasciculus morum,* and John Grimestone's *Commonplace Book.* However, the later collections contrast strikingly with the miscellanies in their consistent homiletic character, Latin framework, systematic organization, and restriction of English mainly to illustrative verses.

John Scahill

Bibliography

PRIMARY

Reichl, Karl, ed. *Religiöse Dichtung im englischen Hochmittelalter.* Munich: Fink, 1973 [critical edition of Cambridge, Trinity College B.14.39; extensive bibliography].

SECONDARY

Frankis, John. "The Social Context of Vernacular Writing in Thirteenth Century England." In *Thirteenth Century England,* ed. Peter R. Coss and Simon D. Lloyd. Vol. 1. Woodbridge: Boydell, 1986, pp. 175–84; Jeffrey, David L. *The Early English Lyric and Franciscan Spirituality.* Lincoln: University of Nebraska Press, 1975; Pearsall, Derek. *Old English and Middle English Poetry.* London: Routledge & Kegan Paul, 1977, pp. 94–102; Robbins, Rossell Hope. "The Authors of the Middle English Religious Lyrics." *JEGP* 39 (1940): 230–38.

See also Bozon; Friars; Harley Lyrics; Laȝamon; Lyrics; *Owl and the Nightingale;* Popular Culture; Sermons

Frithegod (fl. ca. 950)

Poet and scholar, whose authorship of the *Breuiloquium uitae Wilfredi* is the only ascertainable fact in his life. Opinions differ about his nationality; traditionally he has been considered an Anglo-Saxon, but recently the theory has been put forward that he was a Frank. Whether he wrote any works other than the *Breuiloquium* is an open question. The octosyllabic poem "Ciues caelestis patriae," a *Vita Audoeni,* a work beginning with the words *De peccatrice in euangelio,* and the so-called *caritas-lieder* (charity songs) are all said to have been composed by him, but none can certainly be proven to be his work.

As the only work definitely attributed to Frithegod, the *Breuiloquium* must stand at the center of any investigation about him. Stylistically it is characterized by the use of Greek words, some of them obscure. The appearance of the same stylistic feature in "Ciues caelestis patriae" and the *caritas-lieder* suggests that Frithegod composed these poems as well. Since Anglo-Saxons of the mid-10th century generally did not possess the knowledge of Greek exhibited in the *Breuiloquium,* Frithegod was traditionally thought to have been influenced by the Irish, but the most recent theory declares him to be a foreigner from Francia.

The *Breuiloquium* also provides an indication of the time at which Frithegod flourished. In the epilogue it is dedicated to Archbishop Oda, who died in 958; Canterbury received the relics of St. Wilfrid in 948, so that the poem must have been written between 948 and 958. Frithegod's connection with Oda in turn allows the following conjectures: Oda had been in France in 936, and it may well have been on this occasion that Oda invited Frithegod to come to England. Oda also acquired some relics of St. Audoenus for Canterbury, which could have given the impulse for the composition of the *Vita sancti Audoeni* (none of the surviving lives of St. Audoenus can with certainty be attributed to Frithegod). Finally no traces of Frithegod can be found in England after Oda's death, which would suggest that he returned to his native land once he was deprived of a patron in England.

Gernot R. Wieland

Bibliography

PRIMARY

Campbell, Alistair, ed. *Frithegodi Monachi Breuiloquium uitae beati Wilfredi et Wulfstani Cantoris Narratio metrica de sancto Swithuno.* Zurich: Thesaurus Mundi, 1950, pp. 1–62.

SECONDARY

Kitson, Peter. "Lapidary Traditions in Anglo-Saxon England: Part II, Bede's *Explanatio Apocalypsis* and Related Works." *ASE* 12 (1983): 109–23 [on Frithegod's authorship of "Ciues caelestis patriae" and an edition of the poem]; Lapidge, Michael. "A Frankish Scholar in Tenth-Century England: Frithegod of Canterbury/Fredegaud of Brioude." *ASE* 17 (1988): 45–65.

See also Anglo-Latin Literature to 1066; Hagiography; Wilfrid

Froissart, Jean (1337?–1410?)

French poet and historian. Born at Valenciennes, he became a cleric, initially serving the counts of Hainault. In 1361 he came to England as a clerk to Queen Philippa and stayed until her death in 1369. He returned to Valenciennes, received ecclesiastical appointments, and continued to write for other patrons.

Froissart wrote courtly lyrics, allegorical verse narratives, prose chronicles, and the long verse romance *Méliador,* his major poem. Some of his shorter narratives influenced Chaucer. Froissart was most renowned in England for his massive *Chroniques de France, d'Engleterre, et des pais voisons (Chronicles of France, England, and Neighboring Countries),* which are notable for their emphasis on chivalric virtues in descriptions of the wars with France, and their disparagement of the lower classes in descriptions of popular uprisings.

Warren Ginsberg

Bibliography

PRIMARY

Jolliffe, John, trans. *Jean Froissart: Chronicles.* New York: Modern Library, 1968; Scheler, Auguste, ed. *Oeuvres de Froissart: Poésies.* 3 vols. 1870–72. Repr. Geneva: Slatkine, 1977.

SECONDARY

Palmer, J.J.N., ed. *Froissart, Historian.* Woodbridge: Boydell, 1981.

See also Chaucer; Chronicles; Edward III; Literary Influences: French

Fuller Brooch

A silver disc brooch inlaid with niello, the unprovenanced Fuller Brooch (fig. 65) is one of the masterpieces of late-9th-century metalwork. The brooch takes its name from the 20th-century collector Capt. A.W.F. Fuller. Although the original pin mechanism has been lost, the excellent condition of the brooch itself suggests that it has never been buried (Wilson, 1984: 9). The brooch measures about 4.5 inches in diameter and is divided into three primary zones of decoration: a central lozenge or cruciform shape, four lentoid panels, and an openwork outer border.

The iconographic program is made up of personifications of the four senses in the central medallion and symbols of the different realms of the natural world in the roundels of the border. At the center of both the brooch and its program of decoration is the large, iconic figure of Sight holding foliate branches, scepters, or cornucopias and dressed in the pallium (a band worn over the shoulders and down the chest, symbolizing episcopal authority). Surrounding Sight are personifications of Smell, hands behind his back, sniffing a plant (upper right); Touch, clasping his hands together (lower right); Hearing, in a dancing posture, one hand cupped to his ear (lower left); and Taste, his right hand in his mouth (upper left). The border is divided into four equal arcs, each containing roundels with the image of a man, quadruped, bird, and foliate design. Together these images represent both the world in which human beings live and the means by which they experience that world.

The central image of Sight is very close to, and has often been compared with, the figure of Sight or Wisdom on the Alfred Jewel, also of late-9th-century date (fig. 1: see ALFRED AND MINSTER LOVELL JEWELS). The intellectual nature of the brooch's symbolism, the emphasis on divine creation (in the border), and the gaining of wisdom (through the senses, primarily sight) are in full accord with the educational reforms of the Alfredian era.

Catherine E. Karkov

Bibliography

Webster, Leslie, and Janet Backhouse, eds. *The Making of England: Anglo-Saxon Art and Culture* AD *600–900.* London: British Museum, 1991, cat. no. 257; Wilson, David M. *Anglo-Saxon Ornamental Metalwork, 700–1100, in the British Museum: Catalogue of Antiquities of the Later Saxon Period.* Vol. 1. London: Trustees of the British Museum, 1964; Wilson, David M. *Anglo-Saxon Art: From the Seventh Century to the Norman Conquest.* London: Thames & Hudson, 1984.

See also Alfred and Minster Lovell Jewels; Art, Anglo-Saxon; Metalwork, Anglo-Saxon

G

Gaimar, Geffrei (fl. ca. 1140)

Anglo-Norman chronicler; composed a history of England for Custance Fitz Gilbert around 1140, probably in Hampshire and Lincolnshire.

The extant text, *L'estoire des Engleis,* is only a portion of the complete work as described in Gaimar's epilogue. Written in octosyllabic couplets, it survives in four manuscripts and treats the period between 495 and 1100. Up until the reign of Edgar the text is largely a translation of the Anglo-Saxon Chronicle; thereafter Gaimar uses a variety of sources. The *Estoire* is of particular interest for its interpolated narratives, such as the story of Havelok the Dane, Gaimar's version of which is the earliest known.

Rebecca J. Coogan

Bibliography

Bell, Alexander, ed. *L'estoire des Engleis.* ANTS 14–16. Oxford: Blackwell, 1960.

See also Anglo-Norman Literature; *Brut,* Prose; Chronicles; Geoffrey of Monmouth; Matter of England; Patronage, Literary; Wace

Galba Psalter

BL Cotton Galba A.xviii is a small, luxurious Carolingian psalter traditionally, though probably erroneously, associated with King Æthelstan. English additions, made at Winchester in three phases in the early 10th century, include computus tables, a metrical calendar designed for private devotional use and illustrated with zodiac signs and figures of saints, prayers, a litany in Greek, and a series of full-page christological miniatures on inserted leaves. Only three remain in the book: one (the Nativity) is detached and housed in the Bodleian Library (Rawlinson B.484, fol. 85), and one has been lost.

When complete, the picture cycle marked the threefold psalter division and important points in the prefatory text. It comprised a Nativity at Psalm 1, probably a Crucifixion at Psalm 51, an Ascension at Psalm 101, and two scenes of Christ

the Judge set within the prefatory texts. This first surviving unified Christ cycle decorating a psalter was probably inspired by insular emphasis on christological interpretations of the Psalms and by texts equating the Psalter with the whole of salvation history. The placement of the images at the major divisions of the Psalter text adapted insular tradition and in turn influenced succeeding artists.

For the Nativity and Ascension pictures the artists utilized Byzantine iconography, and post-Iconoclastic Byzantine art also influenced their figural style. The two complex scenes of Christ the Judge surrounded by heavenly choirs (fig. 66)

Fig. 66. Galba Psalter. (BL Cotton Galba A. xviii), fol. 2v. Christ in Majesty with Prophets and Apostles. Reproduced by permission of the British Library, London.

are deeply rooted in insular art, fusing earlier insular Last Judgment iconography with typologically related Old Testament, ecclesiological, and sacrificial concepts. The first is the psalter's frontispiece, while the second prefaces a devotional prayer complementing its imagery. Subsequent prayers reflect the litanic quality of the miniature.

The display of the instruments of the Passion in the first and of Christ's wounded side in the second precociously points forward to Romanesque Last Judgment iconography. The two pictures influenced the decoration of several later Winchester manuscripts, such as the Benedictional of Æthelwold (BL Add. 49969; fig. 26: see BENEDICTIONAL OF ÆTHELWOLD), the Grimbald Gospels (BL Add. 34890), and the Tiberius Psalter (BL Cotton Tiberius C.vi; fig. 139: see TIBERIUS PSALTER).

Kathleen M. Openshaw

Bibliography

Alexander, Jonathan J.G. "The Benedictional of St. Æthelwold and Anglo-Saxon Illumination of the Reform Period." In *Tenth-Century Studies: Essays in Commemoration of the Millennium of the Council of Winchester and Regularis concordia,* ed. David Parsons. London: Phillimore, 1975, pp. 169–83, 241–45; Backhouse, Janet, Derek H. Turner, and Leslie Webster, eds. *The Golden Age of Anglo-Saxon Art 966–1066.* London: British Museum, 1984, cat. no. 4; Deshman, Robert. "Anglo-Saxon Art after Alfred." *Art Bulletin* 56 (1974): 176–200; Deshman, Robert. "The Imagery of the Living *Ecclesia* and the English Monastic Reform." In *Sources of Anglo-Saxon Culture,* ed. Paul E. Szarmach. Kalamazoo: Medieval Institute, 1986, pp. 261–82; Keynes, Simon. "King Æthelstan's Books." In *Learning and Literature in Anglo-Saxon England: Studies Presented to Peter Clemoes,* ed. Michael Lapidge and Helmut Gneuss. Cambridge: Cambridge University Press, 1985, pp. 143–201; McLachlan, Elizabeth. "The Æthelstan Psalter and the Gallican Connection." *Proceedings of the Third Annual Canadian Conference of Medieval Art Historians* (1982): 21–27; Openshaw, Kathleen M. "The Symbolic Illustration of the Psalter: An Insular Tradition." *Arte medievale* 2, ser. 6 (1992): 41–60; Temple, Elzbieta. *Anglo-Saxon Manuscripts 900–1066.* A Survey of Manuscripts Illuminated in the British Isles 2, ed. J.J.G. Alexander. London: Harvey Miller, 1976.

See also Æthelstan; Benedictional of Æthelwold; Psalters, Anglo-Saxon; "Winchester School"

Gascony

The southwestern French province of Gascony did not correspond to a natural geographical region but was an historical creation of the early Middle Ages, comprising a number of counties (principally Armagnac, Bigorre, Comminges, Rezensac, Lomagne, Albret, Marsamme, and Béarn), extending from the Garonne River in the north to the Pyrenees in the south and Languedoc (Toulouse) in the east. It separated from Aquitaine to become an independent duchy in the 9th century, with its capital at Bordeaux. In the mid-11th century the dukes of Aquitaine added it to their great duchy, with their capital at Poitiers.

In 1152 the comital family of Anjou acquired Gascony through the marriage of Henry Plantagenet with Eleanor, heiress of Aquitaine-Gascony, and when Henry ascended the English throne in 1154 the province became part of the vast Angevin Empire. During the reign of John the Capetian kings of France, aided by local nobles restive under English rule, began attacking the Angevin domains with the goal of expelling the English from their kingdom. The English, however, maintained their control of Gascony even when losing almost all the rest of Aquitaine by the mid-13th century. From the later 13th century the dispute was aggravated by the English claim to Gascony as a sovereign state, independent of the French crown, whereas the French kings insisted on recognition of the province held as their fief.

The Hundred Years War inaugurated a new and what proved to be the final phase in the struggle for Gascony, in the process inflicting great suffering on the Gascon population. After notable successes in the war's early phases, when they regained much of the larger duchy of Aquitaine, the English steadily lost ground in the 15th century, and the surrender of Bordeaux in 1453 brought their control of Gascony to an end.

During their more than two centuries of rule the English developed a system of local and centralized administration in Gascony, a system that served them well but imposed a heavy financial burden on the monarchy. One of the strongest links between England and Gascony in the 14th and 15th centuries was the wine trade that sent prodigious quantities of Gascon wine to England through the port of Bordeaux.

George Beech

Bibliography

James, Margery K. *Studies in the Medieval Wine Trade.* Ed. Elspeth M. Veale. Oxford: Clarendon, 1971; Labarge, Margaret Wade. *Gascony, England's First Colony, 1204–1453.* London: Hamilton, 1980; Lodge, Eleanor C. *Gascony under English Rule.* London: Methuen, 1926; Vale, Malcolm G.A. *English Gascony, 1399–1453.* London: Oxford University Press, 1970.

See also Angevin Empire; Eleanor of Aquitaine; Henry II; Hundred Years War

Genesis, Old Saxon

Five passages from an Old Saxon poem on Genesis were copied alongside much extraneous material into a manuscript that contains a series of Latin computistical texts and a calendar. The manuscript, Vatican pal. lat. 1447, also contains a brief extract from the Old Saxon *Heliand,* a lengthy poem on the life of Christ. The surviving portions of the Old Saxon *Genesis* describe a speech by Adam to Eve after he has eaten the apple (lines 1–26a); part of the story of Cain and Abel (27–80); the plight of Adam, Eve, Seth, and Enoch after the Fall

(81–150); Abraham's plea for Sodom (151–250); and its destruction (251–337). In each case the Old Saxon poem expands the biblical account dramatically, with recourse to other scriptural sources as well as to popular apocryphal and apocalyptic traditions.

The opening section of the poem corresponds perfectly to lines 791–815a of the OE poem *Genesis,* and the discovery of the Old Saxon *Genesis* by Zangemeister in 1894 confirmed the brilliant suggestion of the young Sievers in 1875 that lines 235–851 of the OE *Genesis,* which he designated *Genesis B,* drew on an Old Saxon original. In particular Sievers pointed out that *Genesis B* includes a number of Old Saxon words and employs a looser meter than the rest of the poem, now known as *Genesis A,* that contains it. More recently Raw has indicated that not only has the text of *Genesis B* been drawn wholesale from the Old Saxon *Genesis,* but the illustrations in the Junius manuscript have themselves a similar provenance. Such evidence suggests the extent of our loss: the surviving portions of the Old Saxon *Genesis* represent but a tiny fragment of a substantial and lavishly illustrated original.

A.P.M. Orchard

Bibliography

PRIMARY

Doane, A.N., ed. *The Saxon Genesis.* Madison: University of Wisconsin Press, 1991.

SECONDARY

Doane, A.N. "Towards a Poetics of Old Saxon: Intertextuality and the Sodom Episodes in *Heliand* and *Genesis.*" In *Medieval German Literature,* ed. Albrecht Classen. Göppinger Arbeiten zur Germanistik 507. Göppingen: Kümmerle, 1989, pp. 1–19; Raw, Barbara C. "The Probable Derivation of Most of the Illustrations in Junius 11 from an Old Saxon Genesis." *ASE* 5 (1976): 133–48.

See also Anglo-Saxon Old Testament Narrative Illustration; Bible in OE Literature; Cædmon; *Genesis A* and *B;* Literary Influences: Carolingian; Translation

Genesis A and B

The first text in the illustrated codex of OE poetry Junius 11, written ca. 1025, perhaps at Canterbury, and preserved in the Bodleian Library, Oxford. Its 2,936 long alliterative lines form a more-or-less continuous paraphrase of the first half of the biblical book of Genesis, with a few omissions and losses. It was long attributed to Cædmon—hence its older title, "The Cædmonian Genesis"—but the actual origins and date of most of this text are unknown. In 1875, on the basis of vocabulary, syntax, and meter, E. Sievers convincingly postulated that lines 235–851 were translated from an Old Saxon (continental Saxon) original. He named the "Saxon" part *Genesis B* and the rest *Genesis A.* His general hypothesis was dramatically proved by the discovery in 1894 of three fragments of the Old Saxon version in a Vatican manuscript.

The first of these fragments corresponds almost word-for-word to Genesis 791–815a.

Genesis A is a relatively faithful paraphrase, following verse by verse a mixed text of the Latin Bible literally enough that in dozens of places readings from the Old Latin version of the Bible stand out against the Vulgate background. It also adds material that brings the paraphrase into the style and meter of OE poetry and minimally explains the meaning of biblical material. So, for example, "et appeareat arida . . . et vocavit Deus aridam terram" ("'and let the dry land appear.'. . . And God called the dry land Earth"; Gen. 1:9–10) is rendered "geseah þa lifes weard / drige stowe, dugoða hyrde, / wide æteowde þa se wuldorcyning / eorðe nemde" ("life's Guardian, the protector of men, saw the dry place, the king of glory revealed it afar, named it Earth"; lines 163b–66a). Close as it is to the Latin, this rendering supplies both the alliteration and variation of poetic style and a rationale for "appeareat" at a time before there was anybody to perceive the dry land. Numerous elaborations beyond the biblical text, almost always explaining or expanding the literal meaning, depend ultimately on patristic commentary. For example, Adam's shamefaced remark that he now bears on himself the symbol ("tacen") of his sin (885–86) goes back to Augustine's remark that the outer sign of original sin was the "new motion of the flesh" (*City of God* 16.17). Similarly, the poet's explanation that Noe's raven, "se feond," did not return to the ark because it stayed to feed on floating carrion (1446) goes back to the rabbis and was canonized by Augustine (*Quaestiones in Heptateuchum* 33.5).

Repetitions of material are avoided fairly consistently, leading to many omissions; for example, about half the original verses are omitted from the Flood narrative. Overall the poet omits about 150 verses while representing about 350. The intent seems to be to preserve the continuous gist, not narratively interesting moments, for quite prosaic material is retained, such as the details of the genealogies. There are about 300 additions of material that go beyond mere poetic expansions, though few that are obviously legendary or apocryphal. The two most obvious additions illustrate their nature: the lengthy proem in lines 1–111 provides an "hexameral" (i.e., "six days of Creation") opening that establishes a theme of praise based on the Preface to the Canon of the mass, and describes the creation and fall of angels, the reason for the creation of humankind, and the creation through the Logos, all standard topics in Christian Genesis commentaries; the expansion of Genesis 14:1–16 (1960–2101) is a Germanic battle epic in miniature that has only the haziest motivation in the text.

Though *Genesis A* has often been condemned as dull and unpoetic, it is in fact a learned and carefully crafted poem, marked by a masterly traditional style while showing a taste for figuration, wordplay, and the deliberately complex obscurity of expression sometimes called "hisperic" (see, e.g., 985ff.). It sometimes rises to expressive heights, as in the episodes depicting the doubting of Sara and the sacrifice of Isaac. As a sustained effort to fully represent a biblical text in both its literal and interpretive dimensions there is nothing to compare with it in English until *Cursor Mundi.*

Genesis B depicts the Fall of Angels and the Fall of Man; its interpolation into *Genesis A,* just at the place where the Fall should be, implies that it is making up for text lost from a previous copy of A. The Saxon original was composed ca. 840–50, probably for the court of Louis the Pious (d. 842) or his son Louis the German. The poem was in England by ca. 900, probably in its complete Saxon form and in an illustrated codex, perhaps as part of an ensemble including the Old Saxon biblical epic, the *Heliand,* a retelling of the Gospel story (see Raw). Old Saxon and West Saxon are closely related dialects and were probably mutually intelligible in the 10th century. The mixture of early and late West Saxon forms in *Genesis B* and the inconsistencies of vocabulary (such as the three different treatments of Old Saxon *thwingan*) and syntax suggest it was transliterated gradually in successive copies rather than systematically translated.

Often called the Anglo-Saxon *Paradise Lost, Genesis B* is one of the finest poems in OE, with its straightforward narrative style, striking drama, psychological detail, and theological coherence. It is unlike any other OE poem in the originality of its plot and its intellectual density (see Burchmore). In these features as well as in its vocabulary and its long "Saxon" metrical lines it betrays its Carolingian origins. A free retelling of the two Falls, in the spirit of the apocryphal Adam books, the poem emphasizes good and bad will and obedience. Satan is given speeches that mock him by showing how blind he is to the gifts (grace) he has received and how he futilely struggles against God's plan. The demon approaches Adam first and only then tempts Eve. Eve is seduced by a promise, which she interprets as "angelic," of gifts that will give her power and authority over Adam. The weakness of humankind and the grace of God are emphasized by a conclusion that shows not God's condemnation of Adam and Eve but their ritual repentance and recommitment to obedience. The whole poem, which is studded with explicit comments by the narrator, is a tropological warning to the audience about disobedience against ecclesiastical discipline and secular order.

A.N. Doane

Bibliography

PRIMARY

ASPR 1:3–87; Doane, A.N., ed. *Genesis A: A New Edition.* Madison: University of Wisconsin Press, 1978; Doane, A.N., ed. *The Saxon Genesis.* Madison: University of Wisconsin Press, 1991; Gollancz, Israel, ed. *The Cædmon Manuscript of Anglo-Saxon Biblical Poetry, Junius XI in the Bodleian Library.* Oxford: Oxford University Press, 1927 [facsimile].

SECONDARY

Burchmore, Susan. "Traditional Exegesis and the Question of Guilt in the Old English *Genesis B.*" *Traditio* 41 (1985): 117–44; Raw, Barbara C. "The Probable Derivation of Most of the Illustrations in Junius 11 from an Old Saxon Genesis." *ASE* 5 (1976): 133–48; Remley, Paul. "The Latin Textual Basis of Genesis A." *ASE* 17 (1988): 163–89; Schwab, Ute. "Ansätze zu einer Interpretation der As. Genesisdichtung." *Annali. Sezione germanica.* Naples: Istituto Universitario Orientale. Vols. 17 (1974): 111–86, 18 (1975): 7–88, 19 (1976): 7–52, 20 (1977): 7–79.

See also Anglo-Saxon Old Testament Narrative Illustration; Bible in OE Literature; Cædmon; *Cursor Mundi;* Fathers of the Church (Augustine); *Genesis,* Old Saxon; Junius Manuscript; Literary Influences: Carolingian; Translation

Gentry

Although "gentry" began as a synonym for gentility and hence for the nobility as a whole, it has come to be used by historians to refer essentially to the lesser nobility as a subdivided landed class below the aristocracy.

Three basic gradations evolved: the knights, the esquires, and the mere gentlemen. The thinning of knightly ranks during the 13th century and their transformation into a territorial elite facilitated a system of social gradation that eventually become more clearly delineated. The esquires emerged as a definite second rank among the country gentry during the early to mid-14th century. The hard core of these came, beyond doubt, from a secondary thinning of the knightly class, from collaterals of the knightly families, and to some degree from the strata immediately below them. It was from these strata, too, that the third gradation, the gentleman, was ultimately born and brought to maturity by the Statute of Additions of 1413.

While the essence of the gentry was that of a landed elite with a shared and primarily military ethos, it came to include others with a claim to gentility (upwardly mobile professionals, for example, and scions of the established gentry) who were not necessarily so endowed. Some historians would prefer to replace the medieval terminology with such divisions as parish gentry, county gentry, or upper gentry. In many of their activities as landlords, and in their way of life, the upper gentry in particular were not readily distinguishable, except in terms of degree, from the aristocracy, although the development of the parliamentary peerage during the 14th century tended to make the distinction more discernible. Among the debates that exercise historians of the gentry was their degree of dependence upon the aristocracy, the extent to which they were organized upon a territorial (essentially a county) basis, and their role in economic change.

Arguably, "gentry" has tended to be used too loosely; a full definition would need to comprehend a number of vital factors, including the following: 1) a territorial elite, based essentially on ancient land ownership but reinforced by upward mobility; 2) a degree of separation from the great landowners, while sharing with them a developed notion of gentility and a specific elite mentality, the latter drawing its force from a military ethos and even more from its trappings; 3) a system of fairly well defined social gradations; 4) a degree of devolved judicial authority, exercised collectively through commissions of the peace; 5) local office holding under the crown and a system of parliamentary representation that served to some degree at least both to enhance the sense of community and to bind this community to the central government.

This combination of characteristics crystallized during the course of the 14th century to produce a distinctive social formation. It might be better to restrict the term "gentry" to this period onward.

P.R. Coss

Bibliography

Given-Wilson, Chris. *The English Nobility in the Late Middle Ages: The Fourteenth-Century Political Community.* London: Routledge & Kegan Paul, 1987; Mingay, G.E. *The Gentry: The Rise and Fall of a Ruling Class.* London: Longman, 1976; Morgan, D.A.L. "The Individual Style of the English Gentleman." In *Gentry and Lesser Nobility in Late Medieval Europe,* ed. Michael Jones. Gloucester: Sutton, 1986, pp. 15–35; Saul, Nigel. *Knights and Esquires: The Gloucestershire Gentry in the Fourteenth Century.* Oxford: Clarendon, 1981; Scammell, Jean. "The Formation of the English Social Structure: Freedom, Knights, and Gentry, 1066–1300." *Speculum* 68 (1993): 591–618.

See also Chivalry; Local Government

Geoffrey of Monmouth (ca. 1100–1155)

Author of the highly influential *Historia regum Britanniae (History of the Kings of Britain).* Probably born in Wales and possibly of Breton descent, Geoffrey lived in Oxford from 1129 to 1151, presumably as a secular canon at the College of St. George, where he was engaged in teaching. By 1151 or 1152 he had been elected bishop of St. Asaph in northeast Wales, although there is no evidence to suggest that he ever visited his Welsh see.

Geoffrey's first book, the *Prophetiae Merlini,* or *Prophecies of Merlin* (ca. 1135), purports to be a series of prophecies delivered by Merlin to the 5th-century king Vortigern and translated from British verse into Latin. The prophecies are retrospective, anticipatory, or apocalyptic: that is, some allude to events before Geoffrey's time; others to events that in 1135 seemed relatively imminent (e.g., the Norman conquest of Ireland); and still others to events that might be anticipated at the end of the world. Although the *Prophecies* stems mainly from Geoffrey's vivid imagination, parts of it betray a debt to native prophetic traditions and to such written sources as Lucan's *Pharsalia* and the Bible. Having circulated independently in a manuscript or manuscripts no longer extant, the prophecies were ultimately incorporated into the enormously popular *History of the Kings of Britain,* a Latin work that was probably completed in 1138 and survives in over 200 manuscripts.

Geoffrey claims that he translated his history of the Britons from the time of Brutus to the reign of Cadwalader from an ancient book in the Breton (or Welsh) tongue. That which Geoffrey did not simply invent for the purposes of his history, however, seems to be derived from not one but several sources.

Much of his account of the founding of the British nation, for example, derives from Virgil and from Nennius's *Historia Brittonum.* The history of Britain from its founding by Brutus to the reigns of Uther Pendragon and Arthur would seem to derive largely from Welsh genealogies and legends. Geoffrey concludes his history with an account of the Saxon conquest that owes much to these same sources and to accounts of the conquest found in Gildas and Bede.

The impact of the *History of the Kings of Britain* on later literature has been considerable, for to this work we owe not only the vernacular *Bruts* of Wace, Laȝamon, and several Welsh poets but also some of the works of such distinguished writers as Chrétien de Troyes, Malory, Spenser, Tennyson, Morris, Twain, Swinburne, and E.A. Robinson. Much less influential was Geoffrey's last work, the *Vita Merlini,* or *Life of Merlin* (ca. 1150), a Latin poem recounting the story of Merlin's going mad after a battle and retreating to the forest of Calidon. He is visited there by his sister Ganieda, the learned bard Taliesin, and the latter's friend Maeldinus. Merlin eventually regains his sanity, whereupon he and his three visitors decide to end their days in the forest, engaging themselves in the pursuit of esoteric knowledge.

Because the central character of the *Life* is not the Merlin Ambrosius of the *History* but the Celtic Merlin Calidonius (or Silvester), Geoffrey's tale of Merlin is thought to have originated in the Welsh prophetic and poetic traditions. Sources for the work, which contains numerous contemporary political allusions and extensive passages of learned or prophetic discourse, include Bede, Isidore of Seville, and material from Geoffrey's own *Prophecies of Merlin.*

James Noble

Bibliography

PRIMARY

Thorpe, Lewis, trans. *The History of the Kings of Britain.* Harmondsworth: Penguin, 1966; Clarke, Basil, ed. and trans. *Life of Merlin: Vita Merlini.* Cardiff: University of Wales Press, 1973.

SECONDARY

New *CBEL* 1:393–96, 478; *Manual* 1:41–42, 231–32; 46, 234–35; Curley, Michael J. *Geoffrey of Monmouth.* New York: Twayne, 1994; Leckie, R. William, Jr. *The Passage of Dominion: Geoffrey of Monmouth and the Periodization of Insular History in the Twelfth Century.* Toronto: University of Toronto Press, 1981; Parry, John J., and Robert A. Caldwell. "Geoffrey of Monmouth." In *Arthurian Literature in the Middle Ages: A Collaborative History,* ed. Roger Sherman Loomis. Oxford: Clarendon, 1959, pp. 72–93; Reiss, Edmund, et al. *Arthurian Legend and Literature: An Annotated Bibliography.* Vol. 1. New York: Garland, 1984, pp. 66–68; Tatlock, John S.P. *The Legendary History of Britain: Geoffrey of Monmouth's "Historia Regum Britanniae" and Its Early Vernacular Versions.* Berkeley: University of California Press, 1950.

See also Anglo-Latin Literature after 1066; Bede; Chronicles; Laȝamon; Literary Influences: Welsh; Matter of Britain; Prophecy Literature; Wace

Gerald of Wales (Giraldus Cambrensis, Gerald de Barri; ca. 1146–ca. 1223)

Archdeacon of Brecon, in the diocese of St. David's, Wales; historical and geographical writer. His writings include an autobiography, the lives of several Welsh and English saints, historical and geographical works about Ireland and Wales, and works on priestly responsibilities and ecclesiastical controversies. A disappointed candidate for the bishopric of St. David's, Gerald was an acute but often biased observer of contemporary secular and ecclesiastical politics; his works are interesting both for the opinions they express and their eyewitness observations. One of his works, the *Conquest of Ireland,* was translated into ME in the 15th century. Recently Gerald's writings have been studied to determine the combination and conflict of national and regional affiliations in late-12th-century England.

Lara Ruffolo

Bibliography

PRIMARY

For editions to 1982 see Bartlett; Loomis, Richard M., ed. and trans. *The Life of St. Hugh of Avalon, Bishop of Lincoln 1186–1200.* New York: Garland, 1985; Thorpe, Lewis, trans. *The Journey through Wales and the Description of Wales.* Harmondsworth: Penguin, 1978.

SECONDARY

New *CBEL* 1:771–72; Bartlett, Robert. *Gerald of Wales, 1146–1223.* Oxford: Clarendon, 1982 [bibliography, pp. 226–36].

See also Anglo-Latin Literature after 1066; Bishops; Map; Marches

Glanville (Glanvill), Ranulf de (ca. 1120/30–1190)

Henry II's chief justiciar (chief judicial official and virtually the royal lieutenant), 1180–89, typical of the "new men" rising from knightly families to wealth and power in the king's service. Glanville's father, a Suffolk subtenant, left him but little land; marriage to a neighboring lord's daughter brought him more property. He began his career as sheriff of Yorkshire (1163), fell from royal favor in 1170, and regained favor with his dramatic capture of the Scottish king William the Lion during the 1173–74 rebellion by Henry II's sons.

Glanville became chief justiciar following Richard de Lucy's retirement from the office in 1179. He took responsibility for implementing Henry II's legal reforms, heading frequent circuits of itinerant justices around the kingdom and earning a reputation for learning and law. The law as administered during Glanville's justiciarship is recorded in the *Treatise on the Laws and Customs of England,* written ca. 1187–89, often called *Glanville* and long attributed to him. In fact he is unlikely to have authored the book, although he may have sponsored its writing by some lesser royal justice. Glanville retired or was dismissed from office on Richard I's accession, and he accompanied the king on his crusade, dying at Acre in 1190. He left no sons, but like other new men in the king's service he had brought other relatives into government, most notably his nephew Hubert Walter.

Ralph V. Turner

Bibliography

Hall, G.D.G., ed. *The Treatise on the Laws and Customs of the Realm of England, Commonly Called Glanvill.* 2d ed. Oxford: Oxford University Press, 1993; Mortimer, Richard. "The Family of Rannulf de Glanville." *BIHR* 54 (1981): 1–16; Turner, Ralph V. *The English Judiciary in the Age of Glanvill and Bracton, c. 1176–1239.* Cambridge: Cambridge University Press, 1985; West, Francis. *The Justiciarship in England, 1066–1232.* Cambridge: Cambridge University Press, 1966.

See also Hubert Walter; Justiciar; Law, Post-Conquest; Lawyers

Glosses and Glossaries

Glosses are explanations, usually brief, of difficult words or expressions in a text, typically written in the margins or between the lines of text; glossaries are collections of glosses, drawn together for easier reference. Of the nearly 1,000 extant manuscripts written or owned in Anglo-Saxon England, roughly one-quarter contain OE glosses or Latin-OE glossaries. The number of manuscripts containing Latin glosses or Latin-Latin glossaries has not been reckoned but can be assumed to be significant. Often glossaries combine Latin-OE and Latin-Latin glosses. Glosses can be divided into a number of categories: 1) lexical glosses, which generally provide synonyms; 2) commentary glosses, a category that subsumes within it encyclopedic, etymological, and interpretive glosses; and 3) grammatical glosses, often used to clarify grammatical relationships or provide alternative forms.

To these categories may be added syntactical or "construe," glosses in which dots, flanking signs, "paving letters" (interlinear letters serving as syntactic notation), and various other forms of notation are used to clarify syntax. Less within the scope of glosses and glossaries, but noteworthy nonetheless, are "glosses" indicating stress in prosody and typically taking the form of acute accents (Wieland, 1984). These are not to be confused with tonic accents indicating syllabic stress. Glosses may be written in ink or recorded as scratched glosses, where a drypoint stylus is used to scratch the gloss into the vellum. This practice is commonly found among interlinear glosses but also occurs in glossaries (e.g., BL Arundel 60, fols. 8v–11r, margins).

Among glossed texts can be distinguished those that bear a continuous gloss and those containing occasional or sporadic glosses. Scattered or occasional glosses are ubiquitous and are not confined to any particular category of texts. Over 30 manuscripts contain Latin texts that are accompanied by a continuous interlinear OE gloss. The bulk of these manuscripts are liturgical or paraliturgical, of which the psalters (with canticles) constitute the largest group, with eleven psalters carrying a complete continuous gloss, one a continuous gloss for selected psalms, two containing sporadic glosses, and two glossed binding strips.

The psalms of the Lambeth Psalter (Lambeth Palace Library 427) are useful in illustrating the variety of different methods of glossing. The gloss, for the most part, is word-for-word, with synonyms often supplied, for example, *in terris* : *on eorðan uel landum* (Ps. 48:12). Grammatical glosses typically take the form of the insertion of "o" to indicate the vocative case, as in *deus* : *o god* (Ps. 50:15). Lexical and interpretive glosses, the latter drawn mainly from the commentaries on the Psalms by Cassiodorus, Augustine, and Pseudo-Jerome, occur throughout: *in inferno* : *on helle id est in tartaro* (Ps. 6:6), *syon* : *sceawere id est sanctam ecclesiam* (Ps. 2:6). The psalter also includes a variety of elliptical compound glosses: *nequita* : *man uel niðscipe* (Ps. 8:10), where the first word is completed by the second element of the second word (i.e., *manscipe uel niðscipe*). Analogously we find *blodgita uel geotende* (i.e., *blodgita uel blodgeotende;* Ps. 5:7). Syntactical glosses, usually taking the form of an inserted *est* : *is* (or other forms of *sum* : *beon*) occur commonly. The psalter also makes use throughout of subscript dots, flanking signs, and the like to indicate "syntactical glossing." The continuous gloss to the Benedictine Rule in BL Cotton Tiberius A.iii offers a system based on the use of letters of the alphabet to indicate word order, a practice found elsewhere in the corpus.

Roughly 65 glossaries containing OE are extant, the most important of which are the Corpus, Épinal, Erfurt, Leiden, Werden, Cleopatra, Otho, and Harley glossaries (Ker, *Catalogue,* 1957: items 36, 114, 143, 184, 240, App. 10, 18, 39). Glossaries offer a number of systems of arrangement, such as *a* order (alphabetized by first letter) or *ab* order (alphabetized by first two letters), or they may be arranged as class glossaries under specific headings, for example, *De avibus, De piscibus, De metallis,* which may also include "batches" of glosses, the sources of which can often be traced to particular works, such as Isidore of Seville's *Etymologies* or the Bible. A combination of ordering systems is usually the norm. Glossaries may be written in columns or in long lines, or a combination of both. They may offer pairs of lexical items (i.e., lemma and gloss; e.g., *anxius* : *sorgendi*), multiple synonyms (e.g., *Effectus id est factus, operatio, portatus,* etc.), or extended definitions (e.g., *Corporeum est quicquid constat ex corpore*). While nearly all of the Latin-OE glossary entries have been printed, the publication of Latin-Latin glossaries and Latin-Latin glosses entered alongside Latin-OE glosses remains a desideratum in the field of glossography, despite the early work of Goetz, Lindsay, and Du Cange.

Phillip Pulsiano

Bibliography

Du Cange, Charles du Fresne. *Glossarium Mediae et Infimae Latinitatis.* Ed. Leopold Favre. 10 vols. Paris: Librarie des Sciences et des Arts, 1937–38; Goetz, G., ed. *Corpus Glossariorum Latinorum.* 7 vols. Leipzig: Teubner, 1888–1923; Ker, N.R. *Catalogue of Manuscripts Containing Anglo-Saxon.* Oxford: Clarendon, 1957; Lindsay, W.M., et al., eds. *Glossaria Latina.* 5 vols. Paris: Les Belles Lettres, 1926–31; Meritt, Herbert Dean. *The Old English Prudentius Glosses at Boulogne-sur-Mer.* Stanford: Stanford University Press, 1959; Meritt, Herbert Dean. *Some of the Hardest Glosses in Old English.* Stanford: Stanford University Press, 1968; Napier, Arthur S., ed. *Old English Glosses, Chiefly Unpublished.* Oxford: Clarendon, 1900. Repr. Hildesheim: Olms, 1969; Oliphant, Robert T. *The Harley Latin–Old English Glossary.* The Hague: Mouton, 1966; Pheifer, J.D., ed. *Old English Glosses in the Épinal-Erfurt Glossary.* Oxford: Clarendon, 1974; Wieland, Gernot R. "Latin Lemma—Latin Gloss: The Stepchild of Glossologists." *Mittellateinisches Jahrbuch* 19 (1984): 91–99; Wright, Thomas, and Richard Paul Wülcker, eds. *Anglo-Saxon and Old English Vocabularies.* 2 vols. London: Trübner, 1884.

See also Ælfric Bata; Benedict of Nursia; Grammatical Treatises; Paleography and Codicology; Psalters

Gloucester

Its proximity to Wales and the Midlands, its network of fine roads, and its position on the upper Severn gave this city a natural commercial and strategic importance throughout the Middle Ages. Though there is little firm evidence of its continual occupation between the departure of the Romans in the 5th century and the Norman Conquest, Bede described it as "one of the noblest cities in the kingdom [of Mercia]." By the Conquest it had become the preeminent city of the west Midlands, favored by kings and nobles alike.

In economic terms pre-Conquest Gloucester served as a commercial center for the entire west Midlands. It had a royal mint, supplied goods and services to its two monasteries (St. Peter's and St. Oswald's), and manufactured iron implements from ore in the forest of Dean. William I considered it a royal city, with Winchester and Westminster, ensuring its continued growth and importance. Extrapolations from Domesday Book suggest a population of some 3,000 in the late 11th century. The addition of a castle and expansion of both religious houses sustained its position. By the early 12th century, with an economy based on trade, services, manufacture of cloth and iron, a rich fishery on the Severn, and a Jewish community to provide financial services, Gloucester can be reckoned as one of the ten wealthiest cities in the kingdom.

The national population decline of the early 14th century, caused by climatic change, poor harvests, and especially the Black Death, hit Gloucester hard, though it recovered relatively quickly. Over the longer span its position relative to other centers, as measured by assessed taxes (in 1334), taxpaying population (in 1377), and subsidy paid to the crown (in 1523–27), remained remarkably steady, moving in rank only from sixteenth to fifteenth to seventeenth, respectively.

Yet by the mid-15th century, along with many other towns, Gloucester entered a period of prolonged decline. We read of pestilence, corporate impoverishment, and decayed houses (300 dwellings alone were cited as decayed in 1487–88). Though this may be attributed to factors that applied to many towns at that time, Gloucester suffered an additional wound when, with the pacification of Wales, it lost much of its strategic importance; its castle was razed in 1489, royal visits became infrequent, and even the abbeys went into decline.

Politically Gloucester enjoyed the status of a royal borough from the Conquest, but the crown shared its lordship with several others. Its first important charter, from Henry II, granted the right of fee farm (the annual fee due to the king) and freedom from toll. Despite an abortive attempt to form a commune in the 1160s the Guild Merchant (the ruling oligarchy of powerful merchants) retained sufficient local power to erect a guildhall in 1192 and to gain a full charter of liberties in 1200 for those parts of the town held of the crown. Shortly thereafter Gloucester became the county town, hosting the annual courts and in 1278 even a parliament. The apotheosis of Gloucester's medieval political development came with its acquisition of county status in 1483 and its incorporation in 1541.

Robert Tittler

Bibliography

PRIMARY

Douglas, Audrey, and Peter Greenfield, eds. *Records of Early English Drama: Cumberland, Westmorland and Gloucestershire.* Toronto: University of Toronto Press, 1986; Stevenson, William H., ed. *Calendar of the Records of the Corporation of Gloucester.* Gloucester: Bellows, 1893.

SECONDARY

Lobel, Mary D., and J. Tann. "Gloucester." In *The British Atlas of Historic Towns,* gen. ed. Mary D. Lobel. Vol. 1. London: Lovell Johns, 1969.

See also Bristol; Exeter; Gloucester Cathedral; Towns

Gloucester Candlestick

This candlestick (London, Victoria and Albert Museum M.7649–1861) consists of three separate sections of cast and gilded copper alloy: a triangular base with dragon feet and a lower knop; the shaft, decorated with foliage inhabited by beasts and human figures, with the four evangelists' symbols on a central knop; and a drip pan supported by dragons. There are three Latin inscriptions, translated as: "The gentle devotion of Abbot Peter and his flock gave me to the Church of St. Peter at Gloucester"; "This flood of light, this work of virtue, bright with holy doctrine, instructs us, so that man shall not be benighted by vice"; and (of later date) "Thomas of Poché gave this object to the Church of Le Mans when the sun renewed the year."

This exquisite candlestick (fig. 67) is a rare example of a dated medieval object, the first inscription indicating that it was commissioned by Peter, abbot of Gloucester (1107–13). It is also one of the earliest altar candlesticks to survive, close in design to 11th-century Ottonian examples, particularly those made ca. 1000 for Bishop Bernward of Hildesheim.

The decoration of the candlestick is stylistically close to English manuscript illumination of the 11th and 12th centuries. However, although it is accepted as having been made in England (perhaps Canterbury), the evidence is inconclusive regarding the center of production. The secular decoration has been interpreted, in relation to the second inscription, as illustrating the struggle between good and evil. The date of the third inscription is disputed but is possibly from the second quarter of the 12th century.

Peta Evelyn

Fig. 67. Gloucester Candlestick (London, Victoria and Albert Museum 7649–1861). Reproduced by permission of the Board of Trustees of the Victoria and Albert Museum, London.

Bibliography

Borg, Alan. "The Gloucester Candlestick." In *Medieval Art and Architecture at Gloucester and Tewkesbury. BAACT* for 1981. London: British Archaeological Association, 1985, pp. 85–92 and pls. XIV, XV; Zarnecki, George, Janet Holt, and Tristram Holland, eds. *English Romanesque Art 1066–1200*. London: Weidenfeld & Nicolson, 1984 [exhibition catalogue; provides bibliography to 1981].

See also Art, Romanesque; Liturgical Vessels; Metalwork and Enamels, Romanesque

Gloucester Cathedral

The Benedictine abbey church (now cathedral) of St. Peter at Gloucester (fig. 68) is a fine example of the West Country School of Romanesque architecture that developed independently from works like Winchester Cathedral, inspired by St. Étienne at Caen. It was commenced by Abbot Serlo in 1089, was built as far as the nave by 1100, and was probably completed ca. 1130. The original fabric is considerably remodeled: the nave vault dates from 1242; the south nave aisle was rebuilt after its Norman predecessor threatened collapse in 1318, and, starting in 1331, the transepts and presbytery were remodeled with lierne vaults and large clerestory windows, while a tracery veneer was hung in front of the Romanesque arcades and galleries.

The apse of the three-bay Romanesque presbytery was destroyed in the Perpendicular rebuilding, but traces of arch springers on the apse-chord piers and the excavation of the two eastern piers provide evidence for a three-sided apse like the extant example at Tewkesbury Abbey. Sainte Croix at Loudun (Vienne), ca. 1060, provides a model for this motif and for the ambulatory with polygonal chapels and the large columnar piers. Two-story radiating and transept chapels, and the groin-vaulted crypt that extends under the entire presbytery, follow Worcester Cathedral (1084–89).

Settlement in the crypt soon necessitated the reinforcement of its main arcades, aisle responds, and vaults, the latter involving a rare structural use of diagonal ribs. The presbytery aisles are groin-vaulted and have plain transverse arches, carried on cushion capitals atop half-shafts that are flanked by continuous quadrant moldings of the wall arches. This alternation of continuous and noncontinuous orders remained a favorite of West Country masons into the 13th century. The quadrant vaults in the presbytery galleries were probably intended to abut the thrust of a high vault, but the form of this vault and the Romanesque elevation above the galleries are problematical. The apse probably had a four-part rib vault, while the straight bays may have had a barrel vault over a two-story elevation, a one-story version of which exists at Ewenny Priory, a daughter house of Gloucester. Alternatively there may have been a three-story elevation and a groin vault, as in the presbytery of Hereford Cathedral. The three-story aisleless transepts were wood-roofed, and the ground story of their chapels has complex groin vaults.

The nave elevation contrasts with the equally proportioned main arcade and gallery in the presbytery. It has a tall

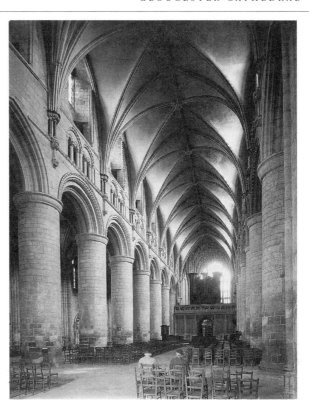

Fig. 68. Gloucester Cathedral, nave interior. RCHME, © Crown copyright.

main arcade with columnar piers, a triforium, and (remodeled) clerestory with wall passage. Similar contrasts between presbytery and nave elevations occur locally at Tewkesbury and Pershore abbeys and Hereford Cathedral. The north nave aisle preserves its Romanesque rib vault with monumental five-shaft responds. The rich articulation of the nave with twin soffit rolls to the main arcade and a wealth of chevron ornament set at right angles to the wall contrasts with the plain presbytery. Evidence remains for a Romanesque high rib vault carried on grouped shafts on the triforium sill like those above the columnar piers of the presbytery at Durham Cathedral.

Of the Romanesque monastic buildings the barrel-vaulted eastern and western slypes remain. There is a barrel-vaulted room above the western slype and the richly arcaded chapter house, which is vaulted with a pointed barrel.

Malcolm Thurlby

Bibliography

Thurlby, Malcolm. "The Elevations of the Romanesque Abbey Churches of St Mary at Tewkesbury and St Peter at Gloucester." *Medieval Art and Architecture at Gloucester and Tewkesbury. BAACT* for 1981. London: British Archaeological Association, 1985, pp. 36–51; Wilson, Christopher. "About Serlo's Church at Gloucester 1089–1100: Its Place in Romanesque Architecture." *Medieval Art and Architecture at Gloucester and Tewkesbury. BAACT* for 1981. London: British Archaeological Association, 1985, pp. 52–83.

See also Architecture and Architectural Sculpture, Romanesque; Gloucester

Godric's Songs

Three monophonic religious songs of the mid-12th century ("Sainte marie viergene," "Kirieleison: Crist and sainte marie," and "Sainte Nicholas Godes druth") that are the earliest English-language lyrics to survive with their melodies; found in a number of manuscript sources, including three with music, they are also known as Godric's Hymns. Their composer, St. Godric (ca. 1070/80–1170), wrote them some time after he retired to a hermitage at Finchale, north of Durham, following a career as a merchant trader and ship's captain. Godric's life as a hermit was one of ascetic hardship, punctuated by visions in which the songs were taught to him; he later sang them to his future biographers. In respect to style the settings are reflective of certain contemporaneous Latin hymns in rhyme, meter, and melody.

Peter M. Lefferts

Bibliography

Dobson, Eric J., and Frank Ll. Harrison, eds. and trans. *Medieval English Songs.* London: Faber & Faber, 1979; Trowell, Brian. "Godric." *NGD* 7:486–87; Zupitza, Julius. "Cantus beati Godrici." *Englische Studien* 11 (1887): 401–32.

See also Hymns; Songs

Godwin, Earl of Wessex (d. 1053)

An Anglo-Saxon favorite of King Cnut (1016–35), who gave him the earldom of Wessex and his sister-in-law, Gytha, in marriage. Godwin was a proponent of Anglo-Danish interests after Cnut's death and may have been indirectly involved in the murder of Æthelred II's son Alfred, a main competitor with Cnut's son Harold for the English throne. Edward the Confessor, Æthelred's son, whose claim to the throne was made good in 1042, adopted a conciliatory approach toward Godwin and heaped favors on his family. The king married Edith, Godwin's daughter, in 1045, and he entrusted Godwin's sons with the regional authority of earls.

Godwin seems to have dominated the events of Edward's reign, and he strongly influenced domestic and foreign policies. Some see the source of Godwin's power in the tremendous landed resources of his family; altogether "the Godwins" held over 6,300 plowlands with an annual income of £5,159. The Confessor's landed wealth paled by comparison; 5,100 plowlands, worth £3,605 a year. Furthermore the Godwins' estates were located in militarily sensitive areas, since, as earls, they were responsible for regional defense. Hence they enjoyed easy access to important roads, like fossway, Ermine Street, and Icknield Way, and controlled key defensible sites. One can hardly study Godwin without his children, for the Godwins supported their father's endeavors to the extent of joining him in revolt against the king in 1052.

Initially Edward seems to have needed Godwin, but Godwin's earlier opposition to the Anglo-Saxon royal dynasty created a niggling suspicion of disloyalty. Edward's distrust eventually manifested itself as he turned from the Godwins to Norman friends. By 1046 Edith was no longer witnessing Edward's charters, and Godwin's authority—roughly that of a 12th-century vice-regent—was supplanted by that of Robert of Jumièges, Norman archbishop of Canterbury. Relations, already strained, were not helped by Swein Godwinson's revolt in 1045. In 1046 Godwin and his family protested Edward's favoring of Normans; Edward retaliated with a threat of force. Three years later the king, acting on information that Godwin was plotting his death, went so far as to exile the Godwins and to commit Edith to a nunnery at Wilton or Wherewell.

Godwin's spectacular rise to power might be explained by his ambition and his ability; he was noticed by Cnut and proved indispensable. Cnut was a forceful man who could be surrounded by strong personalities, but Edward was overshadowed both in influence and landed wealth. The events of 1051 might be understood in this light. Moreover, if Edward and Edith had had children, Godwin's position, as grandfather to the heir, would have been much more secure. But they did not, for reasons about which we can only speculate, and Godwin's position deteriorated so much that within a decade of Edward's accession (in 1042) Normans at court formed an anti-Godwin faction. Edward was probably uncomfortable with Godwin's avowed Danish sympathies and feared a coup of sorts. But the king misjudged Godwin's tenacity and the extent of his support.

Godwin clearly had too much to lose to accept dispossession. In 1052 he launched attacks on England from Flanders (where Count Baldwin was an ally) and from Ireland, where Harold Godwinson had collected an army. Godwin seems to have had a huge following at home, and he used this to apply pressure on Edward. Godwin was able to face his accusers at court and to clear himself.

Then, the Anglo-Saxon Chronicle explains, "Godwin was given his earldom unconditionally, and as fully and completely as he had ever held it, and all his sons all that they had held before, and his wife and daughter as fully and completely as they had held it before." But Godwin did not enjoy his victory for long; he died in 1053, succeeded as earl of Wessex by his son Harold.

Stephanie Christelow

Bibliography

PRIMARY

Barlow, Frank, ed. and trans. *The Life of King Edward Who Rests at Westminster [Vita Aedwardi regis].* 2d ed. Oxford: Clarendon, 1992; Whitelock, Dorothy, ed., with David C. Douglas and Susie I. Tucker. *The Anglo-Saxon Chronicle: A Revised Translation.* London: Eyre & Spottiswoode, 1961.

SECONDARY

Barlow, Frank. *Edward the Confessor.* Berkeley: University of California Press, 1970; Fleming, Robin. "Domesday Estates of the King and the Godwines: A Study in Late Saxon Politics." *Speculum* 58 (1983): 987–1007.

See also Cnut; Edward the Confessor; Emma; Harold Godwinson

Gower, John (1330?–1408)

Poet and friend of Chaucer. Gower was probably born of a Kentish family during the third decade of the 14th century. He may have attended the Inns of Court, perhaps with Chaucer, acquiring legal training possibly put to use in land dealings recorded of a "John Gower" in the Close Rolls ca. 1365–74. We have better evidence that Gower the poet owned lands in Norfolk, Suffolk, and Kent by 1382 and that he was familiar enough with the Lancastrian house to be awarded a collar of silver "SS" links upon the ascension of Henry IV in 1399.

In his later years Gower took an interest in the monastery of St. Mary Overeys in Southwark, apparently restoring several of its buildings with his own and friends' money. Sometime after 1377 he took his residence there, probably as a lay brother, for he did not join the order. On 23 January 1398 Gower received a license from the see of Winchester to marry one Agnes Groundolf (probably his nurse) at his house on the priory grounds. Gower's will, dated 15 August 1408, divides substantial property among several religious houses and his wife. It gives no evidence of an earlier marriage or of children. An elaborate tomb, surmounted by a near-life-sized effigy wearing the "SS" collar, representations of his three major works, and protective angels, rests in the north aisle of St. Saviour's Church, Southwark.

A prolific and versatile writer, Gower composed nearly 80,000 lines of poetry in French, Latin, and English. Although the chronology of individual works remains imprecise, it is generally thought that his earliest compositions were in Anglo-Norman and that his English poems were the product of the last two decades of his life. He continued to write in Latin and French until the end, however, making him a truly trilingual poet—an achievement unique among English literary figures.

French Works

Of the French poems the earliest and longest is commonly known by the title *Mirour de l'Omme.* (Alternative names are *Speculum Hominis* or *Speculum Meditantis,* but these are used infrequently.) The *Mirour* exists in one manuscript only, copied by a single hand: CUL Add. 3035, presently containing 28,603 lines, but missing at least a dozen leaves. It seems likely that the complete poem consisted of approximately 31,000 lines. The *Mirour* is written in twelve-line stanzas of octosyllabic verse, rhyming aab aab bba bba.

The subject of the *Mirour de l'Omme* is the complete moral life of man. To describe this Gower created a poem in three parts, unequal in length but seemingly equivalent in import. The first section—about two-thirds of the work—presents a complex but familiar allegory: the begetting of Death by the Devil on Sin, his own daughter; the subsequent coupling of Sin and Death to produce seven "daughters," the deadly sins or Vices; the marriage of the World to the seven Vices, as a strategy to beget helpers to seduce Man; their mutual assault on Man; the prayer of Conscience and Reason to God for assistance; the divinely arranged marriage of the seven Virtues to Reason, and the description of their daughters; the oppositional pairing of the Virtues and their offspring against the Vices and their offspring. The second section considers how the battle of good and evil is going in the world. The Three Estates—clergy, knights or lords, and peasants—are subdivided and examined, from pope to parish priest, emperor to laborer; all are found thoroughly corrupt and incapable of reforming themselves without merciful grace. The poem concludes with a third section describing the source of this extraordinary succor—the Virgin Mary, whose life, joys, and sorrows are related in some detail. The final lines of the *Mirour* as we have them are the poet's prayer to the Virgin for mercy and a list of her names and titles, cut short by the missing manuscript leaves.

Gower's remaining French poetry consists of two sequences of ballades, one generally known as the *Cinkante Balades,* the other as the *Traitié pour Essampler les Amantz Marietz,* or simply the *Traitié.* Although an early date was once assumed for the *Cinkante Balades* and a late one for the *Traitié,* in fact no firm evidence exists to establish when, or in what context or order, Gower composed these poems. Theories connecting the former sequence with a still-flourishing merchant *puy* (a bourgeois literary and social organization) in London, or the latter with Gower's marriage (whatever might be true of individual ballades), are without firm foundation. The *Cinkante Balades (Fifty Ballades),* despite the title found in its unique manuscript, actually contains 54 poems, each in seven- or eight-line stanzas and almost all with standard four-line envois (short closing stanzas). The poems trace the correspondence of two lovers during an affair, with both a male and female voice represented. The collection is overtly critical of amoral dalliance and seems created to offer alternative images of love and love poetry compatible with Christian marriage.

The eighteen ballades known as the *Traitié* repeat the same firm directives concerning the unique propriety of lawful affection and (by extension) poetics. These poems, each consisting of three seven-line stanzas without envoi, exist in ten manuscripts, never alone. On eight occasions they follow Gower's major English work, the *Confessio Amantis,* and would seem, if the French prose introduction and the Latin prose sidenotes are authorial, to have been intended as a sort of a coda or conclusion to the *Confessio.* Because the *Traitié* ends with a Latin poem in which Gower speaks of his own impending marriage, the sequence has sometimes been considered a late work, possibly composed in 1398, though some of its ballades may have actually been written earlier, without relation to the marriage.

Latin Works

Gower's independent extant Latin poetry amounts to somewhat fewer than 13,000 lines, mostly in unrhymed elegiac couplets. By far his most significant Latin poem is the *Vox Clamantis,* the title of which derives from the "vox clamantis in deserto" ("a voice of one crying in the desert") of John 1:23. Spanning 10,265 lines, it is known in ten manuscripts, of which four are contemporary with the author and probably show signs of personal revision. Although dating is uncertain, the *Vox* seems motivated by the social unrest resulting in the Peasants' Revolt of 1381.

The *Vox* resembles classical models in form, being arranged in seven books. This structural neoclassicism is supported by Gower's incorporation of many lines borrowed intact from Roman authors, primarily Ovid, and such medieval authorities as Alexander Neckham (in particular his *De vita monachorum*) and Peter Riga (author of the *Aurora,* a versified Bible).

The contents of the *Vox* may be summarized briefly as follows. Book 1 ("Visio") relates a horrific dream of the author, who witnesses the destruction of "New Troy" by anthropomorphic animals. In fear for his life the dreamer flees, first on foot and then by ship; after storms and attacks by monsters the ship eventually regains port, on the island of "Brute," from which the journey began. The dream is usually read as a thinly disguised allegory of major figures and events in the Peasants' Revolt. Book 2 describes human misery, condemns Fortune and her misperceived power, and concludes by reaffirming the Christian view of the order of things and urging its readers to hold fast to their Christian faith.

In the next three books the degeneracies of the Three Estates are enumerated (somewhat in the manner of the *Mirour*), beginning with the clergy (books 3 and 4), then treating the knights and peasants (5). Book 6 addresses the failures of the "ministers of law"; it concludes with extensive advice to the king, as chief guardian of the nation and its legal tradition. Finally, in book 7, the statue of Nebuchadnezzar's dream from the second chapter of Daniel (one of Gower's favorite metaphors) is used to focus discussion on the sinfulness of man and his precarious mortal circumstances. The *Vox* ends with a pointed (and poignant) appeal to the English to follow the advice of the dream and make their country a place of peace and decency.

Of next importance after the *Vox* is the *Cronica Tripertita,* written in leonine hexameters (hexameter lines with internal rhyme). It treats the failed government of Richard II, brought down by treachery and weakness, and celebrates the new order to come under his successor, Henry IV. Besides these two longer poems Gower's Latin poetry includes about twenty short pieces on political, moral, and personal themes, and the Latin verses interposed throughout the *Confessio Amantis.*

English Works

Gower's ME verse consists of two poems, the *Confessio Amantis,* his best-known and most admired work, and "To King Henry IV, In Praise of Peace." Comprising some 33,000 lines, the *Confessio* was frequently copied (over 40 manuscripts survive) and later was among the earliest books printed in England, with blackletter editions by Caxton (1483) and Berthelette (1532 and 1554). The text exists in a variety of versions, the exact relationship of which is presently under fresh study. The best manuscript of the poem seems to be Bodl. Fairfax 3, on which the best scholarly edition (Macaulay's) is based.

With the *Confessio* Gower helps establish his native language as a medium for poetry while displaying extraordinary erudition and reaching new levels of fiction making and characterization in English poetry. The poem consists of a pro-

logue and eight books, all in tetrameter couplets except for some twelve rime royal stanzas in book 8 and occasional Latin verses highlighting the themes of the poem. The framing fiction is, as the title indicates, the confession of a lover ("Amans") to Genius, the priest of Venus. Each of the books is concerned with one of the seven cardinal sins and its branches, except book 7, which rehearses the education given Prince Alexander by Aristotle. In the process of the lover's confession Amans and Genius grow as characters, becoming multidimensional by the end; in addition many stories are told, primarily by Genius, who uses them to illustrate his moral points to Amans.

While the sources of the *Confessio Amantis* are understandably too numerous to list completely, its broad outline suggests major debts to the *Roman de la Rose,* manuals of the penitential tradition, such as the *Somme le roi,* Lucretius's *De rerum natura,* and Boethius's *Consolation of Philosophy.* To these may be added a thorough acquaintance with the works of Ovid, Statius, the *Aeneid,* the *Ovide moralisé,* the *Legenda aurea,* and Brunetto Latini's *Trésor.*

The *Confessio Amantis* opens with a prologue in which the author attributes the anarchy of his times to corrupt leadership and division within society. Central to the opening is Nebuchadnezzar's dream from the book of Daniel (2:31–45), concerning the giant statue of gold, silver, brass, steel, and clay, symbolizing the decline of civilization. The prologue concludes with a prayer that a new Arion (a legendary harper of classical mythology) might be found to bring back the golden age of peace and harmony with his musicianship. Book 1 sets the frame for the poem itself. The poet, lovesick and seeking solace, goes one May morning into the woods. He prays to Cupid and Venus, the king and queen of love, who then appear to him; Cupid pierces his heart with a fiery dart, and Venus commands him to confess his sins to Genius, the priest of love. Genius presents his method: he will question Amans concerning his sins, after the manner of a confessor; but since he is a priest only of love, he will speak of sin only as it affects love. The remainder of book 1 is devoted to describing several "branches" of Pride (Hypocrisy, Disobedience, Presumption, Boasting, and Vain Glory), each made memorable by one or more illustrative stories, or exempla, of varied length and complexity. The last section of book 1 offers a description of Humility, Pride's opposing virtue, and an exemplum of humble behavior.

This pattern—the subdivision of a sin into its branches, the use of exempla to illustrate these branch sins, and (usually) the presentation and illustration of a major opposing virtue—recurs in books 2 through 6, which cover Envy, Wrath, Sloth, Avarice, and Gluttony. Book 3 also includes a digression in which Amans inquires about the morality of war, a question of great importance to Gower. Book 7, on the education of Alexander, devotes most of its space to a *speculum principum,* or "mirror for princes," in which five "points of policy" (Truth, Largesse, Justice, Pity, and Chastity) are identified as the central elements of good kingship. Again exempla of varying length illustrate the points under discussion. Book 8 turns to Lechery, the remaining cardinal sin, focusing almost entirely on a single branch sin, Incest. For most of the book Genius tells the tale of Apollonius of Tyre, which illustrates not merely the commission and avoidance of incest and lechery but also the other six sins and their opposing virtues. Book 8 thus simultaneously explores the worst kind of lechery and effectively recapitulates the themes of the first seven books.

Following his confession Amans again meets the Queen of Love and identifies himself at last as "John Gower." Surprisingly Venus now holds up a mirror so that the lover can see that he is old, and unfit for the kind of dalliance he pursues. She also removes the fiery dart from Amans's heart, releasing him from his passion. Finally Genius absolves Amans and Venus gives the cured lover a set of beads and the admonition to "pray for the peace." In the poem's closing lines we are returned to the universal themes of the prologue, including the evils of division and the hope for good kingship and loving harmony in society.

"To King Henry IV, In Praise of Peace" is Gower's only other extant English poem. Containing 55 rime royal stanzas, it occurs in one manuscript version (BL Add. 59495, the Trentham Manuscript) and was printed by Thynne in his 1532 edition of Chaucer's *Works*. As in the *Confessio* Gower's pacifistic concern for an end to domestic and international strife receives a prominent place.

Although Gower has been slighted by modern critical opinion (usually, indeed, dismissed as "moral Gower," as Chaucer calls him, albeit with no denigrating intent, at the conclusion of *Troilus*), recent scholarship is returning his work to its earlier prominence. Clearly Chaucer's most significant poetic confidant, Gower appears to have influenced his friend at least in the tales they tell in common, notably those of "Constance" *(MLT),* "Florent" *(WBT),* "Phebus and Cornide" *(MancT),* and "Tereus" ("Philomela" in *LGW*). For "Constance" and the *Man of Law's Tale* it is thought that the two friends exchanged drafts of their work, with Gower's assumed to be the earlier version.

Gower's reputation remained high during the 15th century, his name appearing in paeans by Lydgate, Hoccleve, Henryson, Dunbar, and others as a cofounder, with Chaucer, of the national poetic language. In the 16th and 17th centuries his work was praised and plundered by Spenser, Milton, and Shakespeare (whose *Pericles* adapts the "Apollonius of Tyre" story and brings "Ancient Gower" onto the stage as chorus). A moralist and scholar, Gower is often lauded for the spare, no-nonsense approach he takes to narration—a quality especially visible in the *Confessio Amantis*—and he is increasingly perceived as an independent literary theorist with strong views as to the role poetry might play in making a just, peaceful society.

R.F. Yeager

Bibliography

PRIMARY

Echard, Siân, and Claire Fanger, trans. *The Latin Verses in the Confessio Amantis: An Annotated Translation.* East Lansing: Colleagues, 1991; Macaulay, G.C., ed. *The Complete Works of John Gower.* 4 vols. Oxford: Clarendon, 1899–1902. Vols. 2 and 3 repr. as *The English Works of John Gower,* EETS e.s. 81–82. London: Kegan Paul, Trench, Trübner, 1900–01; Peck, Russell A., ed. *Confessio Amantis.* New York: Holt, Rinehart & Winston, 1968; Stockton, Eric W., trans. *The Major Latin Works of John Gower.* Seattle: University of Washington Press, 1962; Wilson, William B., trans. *John Gower's Mirour de l'Omme.* East Lansing: Colleagues, 1992.

SECONDARY

New *CBEL* 1:553–56, 804; *Manual* 7:2195–2210, 2399–2418; Beidler, Peter G., ed. *John Gower's Literary Transformations in the Confessio Amantis: Original Articles and Translations.* Washington, D.C.: University Press of America, 1982; Bennett, J.A.W. "Gower's 'Honeste Love.'" In *Patterns of Love and Courtesy: Essays in Memory of C.S. Lewis,* ed. John Lawlor. London: Arnold, 1966, pp. 107–21; Burrow, John A. *Ricardian Poetry: Chaucer, Gower, Langland and the Gawain-Poet.* London: Routledge & Kegan Paul, 1971; Burrow, John A. "The Poet As Petitioner." *SAC* 3 (1981): 61–75; Fisher, John H. *John Gower: Moral Philosopher and Friend of Chaucer.* New York: New York University Press, 1964; Middleton, Anne. "The Idea of Public Poetry in the Reign of Richard II." *Speculum* 53 (1978): 94–114; Minnis, Alastair J. "The Influence of Academic Prologues on the Prologues and Literary Attitudes of Late Medieval English Writers." *MS* 43 (1981): 342–83; Minnis, Alastair J., ed. *Gower's Confessio Amantis: Responses and Reassessments.* Cambridge: Brewer, 1983; Nicholson, Peter. *An Annotated Index to the Commentary on Gower's Confessio Amantis.* MRTS 62. Binghamton: MRTS, 1989; Olsson, Kurt. "Natural Law and John Gower's *Confessio Amantis.*" *M&H* n.s. 11 (1982): 229–61; Pearsall, Derek. "Gower's Narrative Art." *PMLA* 81 (1966): 475–84; Peck, Russell A. *Kingship and Common Profit in Gower's Confessio Amantis.* Carbondale: Southern Illinois University Press, 1978; Pickles, J.D., and J.L. Dawson, eds. *A Concordance to John Gower's Confessio Amantis.* Cambridge: Brewer, 1987; Scanlon, Larry. *Narrative, Authority and Power: The Medieval Exemplum and the Chaucerian Tradition.* Cambridge: Cambridge University Press, 1993; Schueler, Donald G. "Gower's Characterization of Genius in the *Confessio Amantis.*" *MLQ* 33 (1972): 240–56; Simpson, James. *Sciences and the Self in Medieval Poetry: Alan of Lille's Anticlaudianus and John Gower's Confessio Amantis.* Cambridge: Cambridge University Press, 1995; Strohm, Paul. "Form and Social Statement in *Confessio Amantis* and *The Canterbury Tales.*" *SAC* 1 (1979): 17–40; Wickert, Maria. *Studies in John Gower.* Trans. Robert J. Meindl. Washington, D.C.: University Press of America, 1981 [only book-length study of *Vox Clamantis*]; Yeager, R.F. *John Gower Materials: A Bibliography through 1979.* New York: Garland, 1981; Yeager, R.F. "*Pax Poetica:* On the Pacifism of Chaucer and Gower." *SAC* 9 (1987): 97–121; Yeager, R.F., ed. *John Gower: Recent Readings.* Kalamazoo: Medieval Institute, 1989; Yeager, R.F. *John Gower's Poetic: The Search for a New Arion.* Cambridge: Brewer, 1990.

See also Anglo-Latin Literature after 1066; Anglo-Norman Literature; Chaucer; Literary Influences: Medieval Latin; Penitentials; *Puy;* Religious Allegories; Satire

Grammatical Treatises

These treatises have their roots in late-classical grammars, especially in Donatus's *Ars minor* (4th century) and Priscian's *Institutiones* (ca. 500). These and other classical treatises were transmitted to the Middle Ages through the Christian monastic tradition and were probably brought to Britain by missionaries from Ireland during the 6th century. Alongside the classical texts stood christianized variations, such as the *Ars Asporii,* and practical teaching aids, like the *Declinationes nominum.* The *Anonymus ad Cuimnanum, Ars ambrosiana,* and the work of Malsachanus and perhaps Virgilius Maro Grammaticus are also attributable to 7th- and 8th-century Ireland or Irish centers on the Continent. The treatises are surrounded (as in all periods) by marginal and interlinear grammatical annotation to reading texts and isolated notes and comments: even by Donatus's time Latin was a book language.

This bookishness also shows itself in some texts, like the *Hisperica famina,* as an almost whimsical inventiveness in vocabulary and style; a still more complex invention characterizes the writing of the Anglo-Saxon scholar Aldhelm (d. 709/10), who may have learned his grammar from an Irishman named Máelduib as well as the Roman missionaries Theodore and Hadrian. Among the first Anglo-Saxons to write grammatical treatises as such was Bede (d. 735), a monk at the Northumbrian foundation of Wearmouth-Jarrow. His treatises on orthography, meter, and schemes and tropes (figures of speech) represent a pragmatic application of grammar to the needs of monastic life.

Bede's southern English contemporaries Archbishop Tatwine (d. 734) and the missionary Boniface (d. 754) also saw the production of grammars as part of their clerical duties. Their grammars are different in style, the one traditional, the other novel and highly wrought, but both have the functional aim of opening up the full meaning of scripture and the services of the church. They re-present, concisely and systematically, the facts of a contemporary ecclesiastical Latin that had changed sufficiently from its classical forms to warrant such new work.

With Boniface the cultural initiative passes to the Continent, although the Englishman Alcuin (d. 804) played an important part in establishing a newly uniform latinity and higher standard of literacy throughout Charlemagne's empire, "in order that those who aim to please God by living correctly should in addition not fail to please him by speaking correctly" (mandate of Charlemagne to Baugulf, abbot of Fulda, ca. 795).

In the late 9th century King Alfred made a conscious attempt to follow Charlemagne by sponsoring a similar revival in England. Observing that "there were very few who could understand their [Latin] services in English, let alone translate a letter into English from Latin," he sought to have "the works that are most necessary to know" translated into the vernacular. Alfred's educational program did not include the production of any grammatical texts, but some 100 years later it found its fulfillment in Ælfric's *Grammar,* the first grammar of Latin to be written in English and the earliest known in any vernacular. Ælfric's work is marked by careful English neologisms for Latin grammatical terms and the occasional recognition of differences between the two languages: "words are often of one gender in Latin and another in English: we say *hic liber* [masculine] in Latin but *þeos boc* [feminine] in English."

The Norman Conquest left Ælfric's grammar as an isolated flowering of the vernacular, not to be emulated for three centuries. The mainstream of development continued on the Continent, with a move in the late 11th century toward commentary on Priscian. Such writers as Anselm of Laon and Manegold of Lautenbach (Chartres?), followed by William of Conches and Petrus Helias, absorbed the rediscovered writings of Aristotle and established linguistic science as the foundation of the new university curriculum. "Why?" not "What?" became the primary focus of study.

The rise of Oxford University in the 13th century brought these texts to England but also saw the growth of a particularly English scientific approach to grammar, to which Robert Grosseteste, Robert Kilwardby, and Roger Bacon bear witness. Articulatory phonetics, performative and contextual semantics, and phoneme theory give a surprisingly modern ring to their work. It was, however, a group of Danes in Paris who developed the most fascinating treatment of syntax and semantics in the speculative grammar of the last years of the 13th century. Using lexeme and feature analysis and a many-layered approach to meaning, they attempted to develop a universal theory of semantic structure.

Thomas of Erfurt's *Grammatica speculativa,* which shows this tradition in a fully developed form, was in use at Oxford University in the 14th century. The native grammars of this period show occasional signs of his influence but are in general both more traditional and more pragmatic in intent. This was also the case in Italy, so that such works as John of Genoa's *Catholicon* (1286) circulate in England together with the works of Richard of Hambury, Adam Nidyard (or Shidyard), Thomas of Hanney, and John of Cornwall. John of Cornwall is also noteworthy as the first grammar master to teach Latin grammar in English rather than French, beginning sometime after the outbreak of plague in 1349.

Alongside the growth of theoretical grammar came new pedagogic treatises in verse, including Alexander of Villedieu's *Doctrinale,* Eberhardt of Béthune's *Graecismus,* and the works of the Englishman John of Garland, all of which circulated widely throughout Europe. Garland also produced works on vocabulary, and his *Dictionarius* may be the first to have borne that name.

Increasingly, however, in the late 14th and 15th centuries, the *Summa* or *Speculum* offering a compendious treatment of grammar gave way to a plethora of short, specific treatises. These circulated in the increasing number of local grammar schools and were often adapted by local masters. The availability of paper meant that masters and pupils alike could compile their own selection of grammatical texts. Out of this fluid situation grew the first clearly stated ideas of curriculum and graded texts, the most elementary of which were written in the various European vernaculars, including ME.

In England these developments and some of these vernacular treatises are associated with the teaching of John Leylond (or Leland; d. 1428) in the schools attached to Oxford University; such schools and teaching made it possible for a would-be schoolmaster to acquire a bachelor of grammar degree, much as a teaching certificate would be acquired today. It was in this environment that the standard textbook grammars of the modern period began to develop, most of them still visibly grounded in Donatus and Priscian. At the elementary level, if not the theoretical, grammar teaching shows remarkable continuity from its roots in the 4th century right through to the present day.

David Thomson

Bibliography

PRIMARY

Thomson, David, ed. *An Edition of the Middle English Grammatical Texts.* New York: Garland, 1984.

SECONDARY

Bursill-Hall, G.L. *Speculative Grammars of the Middle Ages: The Doctrine of Partes Orationis of the Modistae.* The Hague: Mouton, 1971; Bursill-Hall, G.L. *A Census of Medieval Latin Grammatical Manuscripts.* Grammatica speculativa 4. Stuttgart–Bad Canstatt: Frommann-Holzboog, 1981; Covington, Michael A. *Syntactic Theory in the High Middle Ages: Modistic Models of Sentence Structure.* Cambridge: Cambridge University Press, 1984; Hunt, R.W. *The History of Grammar in the Middle Ages: Collected Papers.* Ed. G.L. Bursill-Hall. Amsterdam: Benjamins, 1980; Law, Vivien. *The Insular Latin Grammarians.* Woodbridge: Boydell, 1982; Robins, R.H. *A Short History of Linguistics.* 2d ed. London: Longmans, 1979, chs. 3–4; Thomson, David. *A Descriptive Catalogue of Middle English Grammatical Texts.* New York: Garland, 1979.

See also Ælfric; Alfred; Bacon; Bede; Grosseteste; Language; Schools; Translation; Universities; Utilitarian Writings

Great Bibles, Romanesque

Illuminated Bibles of large format, often in two or more volumes, came into vogue in England in the 12th century, paralleling a similar development on the Continent. Some of these, such as that written and illuminated at Bury St. Edmunds ca. 1135 by Master Hugo (Cambridge, Corpus Christi College 2), served as lectern Bibles, to be read during meals in the refectory. Eight major examples were extensively decorated, either with ornamental capital letters, or historiated initials containing biblical scenes, or miniatures, or a combination of any of these.

Various pictorial sources have been proposed for the illustrations. In general, because of the prevalence of copiously illustrated early Octateuchs (the first eight books of the Old Testament, Genesis to Ruth) in the Byzantine East, scholars have traced compositional and iconographical groupings in English 12th-century Bibles to manuscripts from this area. In addition the Byzantine practice of introducing the books of the prophets with portraits of their authors was also emulated in the English Bibles, although this tradition may have been transmitted by continental intermediaries. For other books of the Old Testament, however—Kings, Esther, Judith, and Maccabees, as well as the less frequently illustrated sapiential books of Proverbs, Ecclesiastes, the Song of Songs, Wisdom, and Ecclesiasticus—the pictorial sources seem to be primarily western, from manuscripts originating in the Meuse Valley and Burgundy.

Although some patterns in the placement of decoration were becoming standardized, considerable variety was exercised in the presentation of the illustrations as well as in the selection of individual scenes. The simplest pattern of decoration was to provide decorative or historiated initials before each of the books, perhaps with smaller decorative initials before their prologues. A variation of this system is found in the earliest illuminated English Bible of ca. 1100, now divided between the libraries of Lincoln Cathedral (A.I.2) and Trinity College, Cambridge (B.5.2), where 86 foliate and thirteen figurative initials introduce the books and many of their prologues. The Dover Bible (Cambridge, Corpus Christi College 3–4) reveals the same pattern and similar uniformity of decoration, with, however, an increased richness of imagery in its 38 historiated initials in contrast to nineteen decorative ones, mostly in the second half of the manuscript.

This arrangement of decoration also serves as the basis for the spectacular Winchester Bible (Winchester, Cathedral Library), begun perhaps around 1150 and continued to about 1180 by several different artists, probably at the Cathedral Priory of St. Swithun. Here 51, perhaps as many as 58, historiated initials introduce almost every book, as opposed to only sixteen decorated ones for lesser divisions. To this arrangement were added, however, miniatures as frontispieces to Judith and to 1 Maccabees and, perhaps intended to be inserted but never used, two miniatures to the book of Samuel on a single leaf (now New York, Pierpont Morgan Library M.619). This dramatic pictorial emphasis upon these three books *vis-à-vis* the relative uniformity in the consistent use of historiated initials to introduce the books in the rest of the manuscript has not yet been adequately explained.

In two other lavishly illustrated 12th-century Bibles, however, the distribution of miniatures and decorations is more irregular, raising the possibility of a programmatic pictorial emphasis. The first of these, the Bury St. Edmunds Bible cited above (CCCC 2), originally contained twelve miniatures

Samuel, 3 and 4 Kings) that may well have emphasized the virtues of just kingship, though, since these illustrations are missing, this possible theme can only be conjectural. Also given considerable weight are the books of the prophets: the four major prophets, Isaiah, Jeremiah, Ezekiel, and Daniel were each introduced by a frontispiece (that for Jeremiah is now missing), while most of the remaining prophetical books are introduced by historiated initials. The book of Daniel, however, is given an especially strong decorative emphasis, with a frontispiece, four historiated initials, and one decorative one. These emphases may reflect the antipagan and antiheretical tenor of contemporary sermons and paraliturgical dramas, as well as the visionary and proclamatory iconography of Romanesque portals.

For some books the choice of iconography is fairly uniform—as in the representation of the Creation for Genesis or portraits of prophets for the minor prophets, but a surprising variety is evident in the choice of scenes for the other books. Thus, while stylistic and compositional sources for individual illustrations in these Bibles have been frequently discussed, the question of the relative weight and pictorial emphasis on some books and not on others, and of the selection of a particular iconographic program that might reflect the specific circumstances of a given monastery or patron, is still open to investigation.

Robert G. Calkins

Bibliography

Cahn, Walter. *Romanesque Bibles*. Ithaca: Cornell University Press, 1982, pp. 259–62; Calkins, Robert. "Additional Lacunae in the Lambeth Bible." *Gesta* 30 (1989): 127–29; Calkins, Robert. "Pictorial Emphases in Early Biblical Manuscripts." In *The Bible in the Middle Ages: Its Influence on Literature and Art,* ed. Bernard S. Levy. MRTS 89. Binghamton: MRTS, 1992, pp. 79–102; Dodwell, C.R. *The Great Lambeth Bible*. London: Faber & Faber, 1959; Kauffmann, C. Michael. *Romanesque Manuscripts 1066–1190*. A Survey of Manuscripts Illuminated in the British Isles 3, ed. J.J.G. Alexander. London: Harvey Miller, 1975 [see esp. pp. 32–41 and nos. 13, 45, 56, 59, 69, 70, 82, 83, 84, 91, 98, 103]; Oakeshott, Walter. *The Artists of the Winchester Bible*. London: Faber & Faber, 1945; Oakeshott, Walter. *The Two Winchester Bibles*. Oxford: Clarendon, 1981; Wormald, Francis. "Bible Illustration in Medieval Manuscripts." In *The Cambridge History of the Bible*. Vol. 2: *The West from the Fathers to the Reformation,* ed. G.W.H. Lampe. Cambridge: Cambridge University Press, 1969, pp. 309–37.

See also Manuscript Illumination, Romanesque

(only six have survived), three historiated initials, and 39 elaborate decorated letters. The first seven books, perhaps reflecting a tradition of illustrated Pentateuchs, would have been introduced by miniatures. In addition miniatures prefaced 1 Samuel, Isaiah, Jeremiah, Ezekiel, and Job, while historiated initials of Isaiah, Amos, and Micah open the texts of their appropriate books. This concentration of images, in contrast with the usual openings of decorative letters, appears to place a pictorial emphasis on the early historical books, and on the linking of the Law and the prophecies through the illustration of the birth of Samuel, the last of the great judges and first of the prophets, and on the four major prophets.

An even more elaborate, but selective and focused, program of illumination is found in the Lambeth Bible (London, Lambeth Palace Library 3 and Maidstone Museum 70), believed by some scholars to have been illuminated at St. Augustine's, Canterbury, ca. 1140–50 (fig. 69), although this attribution has been questioned. Originally it may have contained fourteen introductory miniatures (only six survive), 24 historiated initials, and only nineteen decorative ones. Of the Pentateuch only Genesis and Numbers have frontispieces, both with unusual representations of scenes that emphasize the unity of Old and New Testaments and foretell Christ's redemptive sacrifice (Genesis frontispiece) and the promulgation of the Law (Numbers frontispiece). Miniatures for Ruth and Joshua (only that for Ruth survives) place an emphasis on Old Testament heroes and heroines. In addition there may have been an unprecedented concentration of frontispiece miniatures for Judges and the four books of Kings (1 and 2

Great Seal

Also known as the seal of majesty, royal seal, or *sigillum regis,* it bestowed authenticity to the documents to which it was attached. The use of seals had been common in antiquity, but the practice had died out in the early-medieval period. It is possible that royal letters in England were being authenticated by seals in the late 9th century, but the earliest surviving example is from the reign of Edward the Confessor (1042–66).

Though kings of Germany and France were using single-faced seals attached to the face of documents in the 11th century, the seal of Edward the Confessor was double-faced and attached, pendent, to a tongue of parchment cut from the margin of the document. The precedents for a double-faced seal could have been the seals employed by the papacy or the Byzantine court.

The existence of the royal seal, together with the need to maintain its security and use it responsibly, led to the development of a royal secretariat. This occurred before the Norman Conquest, but the titles of the primary officer in the secretariat, the chancellor, and of his office, the chancery, may not have been used until after the Confessor's reign. The royal secretariat was an aspect of the royal household; clerics formed its staff, since writing skills were essentially a monopoly of the clergy. When a description of the royal household, the *Constitutio domus regis,* was composed in the reign of Henry I (1100–35), it shows the chancellor as preeminent among household officers, responsible for the royal seal, supervisor of secretarial work, and head of the royal chapel. The chancellor and chancery remained within the royal household through the 12th century and beyond, while the scope of secretarial work expanded as royal government extended its activities and as respect for authentic written records increased.

With the reign of King John (1199–1216) came a significant innovation in chancery procedure. The chancery either began to enroll copies of the three main types of documents issued under the great seal, or at least the survival of the copies began at this time. The copies were entered onto membranes of parchment sewn end to end and rolled up for storage.

The most formal sorts of documents, charters, were entered on the Charter Rolls; letters sent to individuals, folded up and closed by seal, were entered upon the Close Rolls; letters of a more public nature, issued open with the seal attached, were entered on the Patent Rolls. The survival of these records of central government, from the time of John onward, constitute a major source for historical research. Nor were these the only sets of records preserved in the early 13th century. For convenience the chancery clerks also found it helpful to make collections of outgoing documents along geographical lines, such as the Norman Rolls, Gascon Rolls, Welsh Rolls, Scotch Rolls, or French Rolls, or along topical lines, such as the letters close (i.e., letters closed by seal) sent to the royal exchequer directing that payments be made: the Liberate Rolls.

The enrollment of the three main series of chancery instruments, together with the numerous other types of rolls, meant that eventually chancery collected a rich and voluminous archive. Pressure built for the chancery to separate from the royal household and to establish a fixed location not only because of the difficulty of the staff and archive moving with the king but also for the convenience of those who wished recourse to its official instruments and who found it difficult to track down the king as he traveled.

In the first half of the 14th century the chancery came increasingly to be headquartered at Westminster. By this time there were other seals (particularly the privy seal) whereby the king communicated his wishes to chancery for issuing letters under the great seal; compared with these smaller seals, the royal seal could now be viewed as the great seal. Even with the chancery located at Westminster, instruments issued under the great seal continued to be the mechanism for implementing the majority of major administrative decisions, and the chancellor continued to be a principal administrative official whose political importance was enhanced by his prominent place on the king's council.

A. Compton Reeves

Bibliography

Chrimes, Stanley B. *An Introduction to the Administrative History of Mediaeval England.* 3d ed. Oxford: Blackwell, 1966; Clanchy, M.T. *From Memory to Written Record: England, 1066–1307.* 2d ed. Oxford: Blackwell, 1993; Fryde, E.B., et al., eds. *Handbook of British Chronology.* 3d ed. London: Royal Historical Society, 1986; Lyte, Henry Churchill Maxwell. *Historical Notes on the Use of the Great Seal of England.* London: HMSO, 1926; Tout, T.F. *Chapters in the Administrative History of Mediaeval England: The Wardrobe, the Chamber and the Small Seals.* 6 vols. Manchester: Manchester University Press, 1920–33.

See also Chancellor and Chancery; Privy Seal; Seals

Greensted

First noted in 1789 by S. Lethieullier, Greensted, Essex, preserves the only surviving Anglo-Saxon wooden church (ca. 28.9 feet by 16.7 feet; built between mid-9th and early 11th century?). Hewett and Christie both mention that a modern guide to the church dates it to 845, reckoned from tree rings of the logs that compose the walls (no documentation given). A 13th-century history records St. Edmund's body resting near Ongar on the journey from London to Bury in 1013, but no contemporary records confirm this and the church is not specified. While carbon-14 dating would be desirable, the logs were impregnated with insecticide in the 1950s and again around 1965, and so contaminated.

Only the nave of the wooden church survives (fig. 70), much mutilated by extensive rebuilding in 1848, when the walls were replaced on a new oak sill set atop a brick plinth.

Fig. 70. The Anglo-Saxon church at Greensted. After Lethieullier's drawing of 1748, published in Christie, Olsen, and Taylor (1979). Drawing by C. Karkov.

The walls consist of small, split oak logs without bark, set up so that the rounded side faces out. The logs are cut flat on the sides and grooved to accept tongues that fit the planks tightly together and weatherproof the wall. Each plank has a tenon fitting into the wall plate and sill and on the exterior an elliptical beveling cut from the top to form a decorative variation. The exterior shows traces of tar, while the interior was at one time plastered and perhaps painted. Greensted has two unique construction aspects: a west gable wall of posts extending straight up to the roof with no tie-beam and unusual corner posts, of a single log from which a quadrant has been taken on the inside to form an angle.

In 1960 a limited excavation within the chancel yielded an early, narrower chamber with walls set directly into the ground without a sill, and a later chancel replacing it, with a wooden sill that "may therefore be assumed to have been of the same general type as the existing nave" (Christie et al., 110). The transition from post holes to timber sills was an important change in Scandinavian architecture, and Scandinavian examples (e.g., Hemse on Gotland) remain the closest analogues.

Kelley M. Wickham-Crowley

Bibliography

Christie, Håkon, Olaf Olsen, and H.M. Taylor. "The Wooden Church of St. Andrew at Greensted, Essex." *AntJ* 59 (1979): 92–112, pls. XXVI–XXXI; Hewett, Cecil A. "Anglo-Saxon Carpentry." *ASE* 7 (1978): 205–29; Rodwell, Warwick. "Anglo-Saxon Church Building: Aspects of Design and Construction." In *The Anglo-Saxon Church: Papers on History, Architecture and Archaeology in Honour of Dr. H.M. Taylor*, ed. Lawrence A.S. Butler and Richard K. Morris. CBA Research Report 60. London: CBA, 1986, pp. 156–75; Taylor, Harold M., and Joan Taylor. "Greensted." In *Anglo-Saxon Architecture*. Vol. 1. Cambridge: Cambridge University Press, 1965, pp. 262–64.

See also Architecture, Anglo-Saxon; Earls Barton Tower

Gregory of Tours (ca. 538–594)

Frankish historian and bishop of Tours. Considered the "father of French history," Gregory was probably born in Auvergne, in the diocese of Clermont, to an ancient Gallo-Roman family. In 573 he was appointed by the Frankish king Sigibert I to the bishopric of Tours, where he remained to his death. His *Decem libri historiarum (Ten Books of History)*, which has been erroneously known as the *Liber historia Francorum (History of the Franks)*, is the only contemporary source for much of the history of Gaul in the 6th century. This work is regarded as a principal model for Bede's *Ecclesiastical History of the English People*, especially in its focus on one people only and its conclusion.

Like his English successor, Bede, Gregory used as the model for his own history ecclesiastical histories like that of Eusebius of Caesarea. There is evidence that he was influenced by Virgil and by Sallust's *Catiline*, as well as by the Christian writers Sulpicius Severus, Prudentius, Sidonius Apollinaris, and Fortunatus. As with other medieval histories Gregory's *History* relies on hearsay and legend for many of its historical facts. Gregory is concerned with religious orthodoxy, presenting a narrative of kings and saints instead of an historical record of events. His writing style is at times direct and realistic and at times full of literary convention. The anecdotal style of Gregory's miracle stories influenced many later writers, and his methods of storytelling for historiographical and hagiographical genres helped to define the traditions themselves. His Latin is colloquial and difficult for the modern reader. Celtic and Germanic vocabulary additions are common, as well as the sometimes extremely erratic grammar usage.

Of additional relevance to OE studies is Gregory's mention of the death of the historical Hygelac (*History* 3.3), also noted in *Beowulf*.

Dana-Linn Whiteside

Bibliography

PRIMARY

Dalton, O.M., trans. *The History of the Franks, by Gregory of Tours*. 2 vols. Oxford: Clarendon, 1927; Thorpe, Lewis, trans. *Gregory of Tours: The History of the Franks*. Harmondsworth: Penguin, 1974.

SECONDARY

Wallace-Hadrill, J.M. *The Long-Haired Kings and Other Studies in Frankish History*. London: Methuen, 1962, pp. 49–70.

See also Bede; *Beowulf*; Chronicles; Hagiography

Grosseteste, Robert (ca. 1170–1253)

The great English scholar and bishop of Lincoln (1235–53). Born in Suffolk of humble parentage, he probably spent his early years as clerk in the episcopal households at Lincoln and Hereford. While his education in Oxford or Paris is a matter of conjecture, he was master of theology in Oxford by the early 1220s and was subsequently elected chancellor of the university. In 1229–30 he was the first Oxford lecturer to the newly arrived Franciscans.

As a scholar Grosseteste was among the early-13th-century theologians who contributed to the development of the western scientific tradition. A scientific observer of causes and predictor of consequences, he urged the use of experiments in natural sciences. In his methodology he began with individual cases and worked to formulate general rules. His study of optics, for example, led him to ascribe to light a central role in the production and constitution of the physical world.

Grosseteste's works, written in Latin, French, and English, included scientific, philosophical, theological, and pastoral treatises. His theological works included the *Hexaemeron* (1230s) and numerous biblical commentaries and sermons. He wrote important commentaries on Aristotle's *Posterior Analytics* and *Physics* and translated the *Nicomachean Ethics* from Greek into Latin. His scientific interests were reflected in books on astronomy, comets, the tides, mathematics, and the rainbow.

As a bishop with a strong sense of pastoral responsibilities Grosseteste was an important figure in the reform movement in the 13th-century church; his devotional treatises were influential and widely read. While he supported the doctrine of papal plenitude of power, he clashed with the papacy over the growing practice of papal provisions (direct papal appointment of ecclesiastical personnel) and attacked corrupt papal politics at Rome in 1250.

Robert Grosseteste died on 9 October 1253. His books and notes were bequeathed to the Franciscan library at Oxford, ensuring his continuing scholarly influence on later generations of Oxford scholars.

Phyllis B. Roberts

Bibliography

Callus, Daniel A., ed. *Robert Grosseteste: Scholar and Bishop.* Oxford: Clarendon, 1955; Crombie, A.C. *Robert Grosseteste and the Origins of Experimental Science, 1100–1700.* Oxford: Clarendon, 1953; Southern, R.W. *Robert Grosseteste: The Growth of an English Mind in Medieval Europe.* Oxford: Clarendon, 1986.

See also Bacon; Friars; Learning; Moral and Religious Instruction; Mystical and Devotional Writings; Science; Universities

Guilds and Fraternities

Medieval guilds and fraternities—the nomenclature is of little significance—were essentially voluntary associations of individuals for a social, religious, political, or economic purpose. None of these purposes was primary or common to all such associations; what was common was the sense of commitment, sometimes by a sworn oath, often by a financial contribution, to a shared objective. Some borrowed the language of the family, with members calling each other brother and sister; most had some kind of shared festivity.

The functions that by the later Middle Ages made religious fraternities and craft guilds appear as distinct kinds of organizations had evolved slowly, or had been added at particular moments, modifying the original form and purpose, but they still had many features in common. Guilds and fraternities for all purposes proliferated in towns, in whose populous and changing environment the need for association and mutual support was perhaps more keenly felt, though they were not confined to urban societies.

There was nothing essentially subversive in the idea of a guild, and in Anglo-Saxon England guilds were formed for peacekeeping purposes. Later merchant guilds in provincial towns and craft associations of London came to play a significant role in government and the ordering of society. But there was room for suspicion that such associations might, because of their sworn confederacy, offer opportunities or cover for seditious or heretical activities; hence the inquiry into guilds and fraternities in 1388–89.

Simple religious fraternities were formed, principally by lay persons, to ensure the performance of particular services or devotions. They might center on a parish church or, more rarely, a cathedral. Membership was usually circumscribed by locality.

Often, especially in the later Middle Ages, when they are better recorded, they appear as communal chantries or burial clubs, securing for their members the essentials of Christian burial and prayers after death. Some raised subscriptions to support members in distress, but relatively few acquired significant real property and most seem to have had a modest scale of operations.

Associations of craftsmen and traders formed in many towns, not always distinguishable from religious fraternities, especially given the tendency for craftsmen to live near one another where locality helped to define membership. There is no need to assume that an association existed for every recorded occupation, nor that if there were an association of craftsmen of a particular kind they necessarily acted together for economic ends.

The pressures that drove craftsmen and traders to form guilds included neighborliness and the need for mutual moral support, and a religious fraternity lay at the heart of many such associations. But if a fraternity existed it could well become the instrument through which, at a subsequent date, economic or political ends were pursued. Economic pressures—the challenge of interlopers, for example, or the need to secure supplies of raw materials from monopolist distributors—often brought fellow craftsmen together, and the social and religious aspects of association came later, strengthening their bonds.

The craft associations began to diverge from the voluntary origins of the guild when they obtained monopolies of manufacture or retail trade or control over access to citizenship. The development of formal apprenticeship systems also contributed. The control of a guild or craft association over a field of economic activity was never complete, and there was much jockeying for advantage. By the later Middle Ages most large towns had fairly complete systems of guilds to which citizens belonged and through which much economic and political activity was organized.

The London craft guilds, for a brief period (1376–84), were the constituencies from which the Common Council was elected. Later they sent representatives to the assembly that elected the mayor. In some provincial towns the crafts became instruments of control in the hands of town government, wherein lay the power to authorize and amend ordinances covering the practice of the craft. Craft guilds also, typically, made an important contribution to the cost and organization of civic display, whether in the form of plays and pageants, the Corpus Christi processions of many provincial cities, or of royal entries and mayoral shows, as in London.

Craft associations were most numerous and diverse in London, with over 1,200 in the early 15th century. Here they developed more complex constitutions, with the wardens or masters (common to most kinds of guild or fraternity) augmented by other officers. Some larger and wealthier associations had a two-tier membership, with liverymen and others, sometimes called bachelors or "the young men." Forty-seven companies had a livery division in 1501–02; of the 784 men more than 600 came from the eleven leading companies whose interests were primarily mercantile.

The larger companies acquired, through donations and bequests, a considerable amount of real property, and with the rental income and members' subscriptions they built halls for meetings and celebrations and maintained a lavish communal life. They devoted money to charitable and pious purposes, especially chantries and commemorations for deceased members. Some guilds obtained royal charters, confirming their holdings and their control of a particular activity, though these did not always prove a secure defense. The modest resources of the smaller companies of artisans kept their communal activities confined to a small scale, and they always remained more concerned with regulation of their specific craft.

Vanessa A. Harding

Bibliography

Barron, Caroline M. "The Parish Fraternities in Medieval London." In *The Church in Pre-Reformation Society: Essays in Honour of F.R.H. Du Boulay,* ed. Caroline M. Barron and Christopher Harper-Bill. Woodbridge: Boydell, 1985, pp. 13–37; McRee, Ben R. "Religious Gilds and Civic Order: The Case of Norwich in the Late Middle Ages." *Speculum* 67 (1992): 69–97; Reynolds, Susan. *Kingdoms and Communities in Western Europe, 900–1300.* Oxford: Clarendon, 1984; Swanson, Heather. "The Illusion of Economic Structure: Craft Guilds in Late Medieval English Towns." *Past and Present* 121 (November 1988): 29–48; Thrupp, Sylvia. "The Gilds." In *The Cambridge Economic History of Europe,* ed. M.M. Postan, E.E. Rich, and Edward Miller. Cambridge: Cambridge University Press, 1963, vol. 3:230–80; Unwin, George. *The Gilds and Companies of London.* 4th ed. New York: Barnes & Noble, 1964; Westlake, Herbert F. *The Parish Gilds of Medieval England.* London: SPCK, 1919.

See also Chantries; Popular Religion; *Puy;* Towns

Guthlac, Prose

An anonymous prose translation of Felix of Crowland's *Vita sancti Guthlaci* (*Life of St. Guthlac;* 740s), surviving in BL Cotton Vespasian D.xxi, fols. 18–40v. Five chapters of Felix's *Vita* (28–32) also survive as Homily 23 in the Vercelli Book.

Though not a homily in the usual sense of the term, the Vercelli Homily focuses the reader's interest on three closely related temptation scenes. The scenes build climactically from Guthlac's first temptation, when he is pierced with the arrows of despair, to his most famous temptation, when he is carried by evil spirits to the mouth of hell to see the pain and suffering of damnation. In each scene Guthlac demonstrates the superior power invested in his weapons, the Psalms. In the first and third temptations his patron saint, Bartholomew, arrives to strengthen him after he has vanquished his enemies. All three scenes illustrate Guthlac's ability to see the real weakness of evil spirits and their advice (in the second temptation, to fast excessively) as long as he remains loyal to God.

The prose *Guthlac* found in the Vespasian manuscript includes most of the details of the Latin *Vita* and therefore is considerably longer than the Vercelli Homily (though shorter than the *Vita*). The Vespasian translator—or an earlier

translator who provides the exemplar for the Vespasian text—is adept at converting Felix's difficult Latin into readable Anglo-Saxon prose. Many short chapters in the Latin *Vita* are compressed into longer, unified sections. The Vespasian *Guthlac* includes some of the figurative language of the Latin *Vita* but reduces the quantity of it.

The Vespasian text, like the Vercelli Homily, emphasizes the saint's ability to distinguish between the power of devils, which once recognized is really no power at all, and the power of God. Then, when sickness overtakes Guthlac in chapter 20, even though its symptoms are very like the torments of the evil spirits described earlier in the work, he immediately acknowledges God's will that he should die. His acceptance of God's will undermines the power of the evil spirits who had resided where Guthlac established his hermitage. Although the translator, following Felix, alludes frequently to other saints and holy men whose lives parallel Guthlac's—St. Martin, St. Paul, St. Benedict of Nursia, Benedict Biscop, to name a few—there is remarkably little reference to Christ himself or to the Crucifixion or Resurrection. Indeed Guthlac's weapons of the faith are most often Old Testament psalms. The major exception to this reticence is the emphasis in chapter 20 (as in Felix's chapter 50) on the facts that Guthlac's illness began the Wednesday before Easter, that he died on the Wednesday after Easter, and that his death, like Christ's, was accompanied by an earthquake.

Phyllis R. Brown

Bibliography

PRIMARY

Scragg, D.G., ed. *The Vercelli Homilies and Related Texts.* EETS o.s. 300. Oxford: Oxford University Press, 1992, pp. 381–94; Swanton, Michael, ed. and trans. *Anglo-Saxon Prose.* London: Dent, 1975, pp. 39–62.

SECONDARY

Bolton, W.F. "The Manuscript Source of the Old English Prose Life of St. Guthlac." *Archiv* 197 (1961): 301–03; Colgrave, Bertram, ed. and trans. *Felix's Life of Saint Guthlac.* Cambridge: Cambridge University Press, 1956; Roberts, Jane. "The Old English Prose Translation of Felix's *Vita sancti Guthlaci.*" In *Studies in Earlier Old English Prose,* ed. Paul E. Szarmach. Albany: SUNY Press, 1986, pp. 363–79; Szarmach, Paul E. "The Vercelli Homilies: Style and Structure." In *The Old English Homily and Its Backgrounds,* ed. Paul E. Szarmach and Bernard F. Huppé. Albany: SUNY Press, 1978, pp. 241–67.

See also Felix of Crowland; *Guthlac A* and *B;* Hagiography

Guthlac A and B

OE poetic lives of the Mercian saint Guthlac (ca. 674–714), found in the Exeter Book. Despite the manuscript's large capitals and spacing at the beginnings of *Guthlac A* and *Guthlac B* early editors considered the beginning of *Guthlac A* to be part of *Christ III* and treated the remainder of *Guthlac A* and

B as one continuous poem. In this century stylistic and metrical analyses have corroborated the paleographic evidence of two separate poems with different authors. Early scholarship and criticism of *Guthlac A* and *B* focused on possible authorship, sources, and literary parallels; since the 1960s *Guthlac A* and *Guthlac B* have attracted more attention as poems in their own right, though they remain relatively neglected.

Both poems are lives of saints and thus edifying and religious. *Guthlac A,* which draws on writings of the Church Fathers and oral tradition, emphasizes conflicts between good and evil personified in the encounters between Guthlac and various evil spirits. *Guthlac B* depends on Felix of Crowland's *Vita sancti Guthlaci* (740s) as a primary source but collapses the account of the saint's life into a few lines and focuses on the saint's death, the material presented in Felix's chapter 50. Both *Guthlac A* and *B* draw upon Anglo-Saxon secular poetic tradition (themes of exile, territorial disputes, the relationship between a thegn and his lord, and the ways of achieving heroic stature) in the expression of their Christian, didactic messages.

In *Guthlac A* the setting of the hermitage, emphasized in descriptive and symbolic passages (e.g., "the secret spot stood in God's mind"), and the saint's winning of a location that had been firmly in the hands of evil spirits both relate to the theme of Guthlac as God's warrior and contribute to a larger symbolic meaning. The action of *Guthlac A*—building the hermitage, turning back the verbal and physical onslaught of the evil spirits, and overcoming the temptations offered, especially when he is shown the moral laxity of monks of his day and when he is physically carried to the mouth of hell—is intricately tied to the larger didactic purpose of illustrating that this world is a fallen place, vastly inferior to the salvation offered by Christianity.

Guthlac B emphasizes setting less and recounts little physical action; it is largely discourse between the saint and his servant Beccel after Guthlac has firmly established himself in his hermitage. After a prologue describing Adam and Eve's sin, which brought death into the world, the poem briefly recounts Guthlac's good deeds, which—empowered by God's grace—have allowed him to understand death as a release from suffering as well as a punishment for sins. The dialogue establishes an antithesis between Guthlac's spiritual maturity and understanding of the Christian view of death and Beccel's worldly sorrow at the prospect of his master's death. As the poem progresses, however, the questions the servant asks help the poem's audience understand the difficult lessons about death, especially that a Christian must die in order to have eternal life. Particularly attractive in *Guthlac B* are the figurative elements, many of which relate the themes of death and of life as exile. In a passage reminiscent of *Beowulf* death is personified as a thief who unlocks life's treasure and steals it away.

Guthlac A and *B* may not meet 20th-century standards of unity and coherence, perhaps partly because at least a folio of *Guthlac A* and the ending of *Guthlac B* are missing from the manuscript. Both poems, however, establish in their opening lines themes and images and proceed to develop them in ways that allow us to see the poems as part of larger traditions—both hagiographical and poetic—while at the same time making their own individual contributions.

Phyllis R. Brown

Bibliography

PRIMARY

ASPR 3:49–88; Bradley, S.A.J., trans. *Anglo-Saxon Poetry: An Anthology of Old English Poems in Prose Translation.* London: Dent, 1982, pp. 248–83; Roberts, Jane, ed. *The Guthlac Poems of the Exeter Book.* Oxford: Clarendon, 1979.

SECONDARY

Calder, Daniel G. "Theme and Strategy in *Guthlac B*." *Papers on Language and Literature* 8 (1972): 227–42; Calder, Daniel G. "*Guthlac A* and *B*: Some Discriminations." In *Anglo-Saxon Poetry: Essays in Appreciation,* ed. Lewis E. Nicholson and Dolores Warwick Frese. Notre Dame: Notre Dame University Press, 1975, pp. 65–80; Lipp, Frances Randall. "*Guthlac A:* An Interpretation." *MS* 33 (1971): 46–62; Mussetter, Sally. "Type as Prophet in the Old English *Guthlac B*." *Viator* 14 (1983): 41–58; Reichardt, Paul F. "*Guthlac A* and the Landscape of Spiritual Perfection." *Neophilologus* 58 (1974): 331–38; Rosier, James. "Death and Transfiguration: *Guthlac B*." In *Philological Essays: Studies in Old and Middle English Language and Literature in Honour of Herbert Dean Meritt,* ed. James Rosier. The Hague: Mouton, 1970, pp. 82–92.

See also Felix of Crowland; *Guthlac,* Prose; Hagiography

Hagiography

Edifying literature that recounts the lives, deaths, or posthumous miracles of holy men and women; also known as saints' lives or saints' legends. Most hagiographical works bear little resemblance to sober, factual biographies—and logically so, since most hagiographers are preachers and publicists, not disinterested historians. Their central task is to glorify the memory of particular saints, generally for such practical purposes as strengthening the morale of the saint's community, driving home some point of doctrine or morality, winning new adherents to the saint's way of life, and drawing pilgrims to the saint's shrine.

Although similar stories have been told about the heroes of other religions, hagiography is associated above all with Catholic Christianity from late antiquity to the end of the Middle Ages. During this long period hagiographical works seem to have been popular in all sectors of Christian society, finding receptive audiences among the clergy and laity, upper classes and peasantry, learned and illiterate alike.

Definition and Interpretations

Despite its popularity and importance in medieval culture, hagiography has been treated as a marginal genre in modern times because it lacks many of the qualities that modern readers have learned to value. Even by medieval standards the legends represent an exceptionally conventionalized and conservative kind of literature. For more than a millennium, in fact, western European hagiography was shaped by the influence of a few key sources: the lives of Christ and Mary as found in a combination of canonical and apocryphal gospels; the biblical accounts of the persecuted faithful, from the early prophets to Stephen and Paul; and three seminal biographies of early Christian confessors, saints who did not undergo literal martyrdom—Athanasius's *Life of Anthony,* Sulpicius Severus's *Life of Martin of Tours,* and the *Life of Benedict* in Gregory the Great's *Dialogues.*

Vernacular retellings of legends were more open to variety and change than the Latin versions; but hagiographers in general seem to have taken for granted that the best way of proving the blessedness of new saints was to show how closely their experiences replicated those of their earliest and most eminent predecessors. Thus one finds the same conventions—and frequently even the same words—used in legend after legend. Like the seven Maccabean brothers in the Vulgate Bible (2 Maccabees 7) most martyrs in medieval legends eloquently defy their persecutors and endure incredible tortures before they die. Like the desert fathers of the early church most confessors (saints who are not martyred) in these legends renounce the world, withdraw into solitude to engage the Devil in single combat, miraculously provide for the physical needs of their followers, manifest the gift of prophecy by seeing things hidden from ordinary human sight, and make edifying speeches as they die.

The favorite motifs in medieval legends tend to portray the saints in exaggerated or idealized terms, not realistic ones. One can of course find legends that contain even more fantastic material than is typical of the genre—such as the hagiographic romance about St. George, who kills a dragon, rescues a princess, and survives every imaginable torture before he is martyred. But medieval hagiography in general asks the reader to accept two premises that are unrealistic by 20th-century standards: that the saints' experience is pervaded by manifestations of the supernatural—miracles, visions, encounters with the Devil, visits from angels—and that the saints' characters are fundamentally simple and fixed. Instead of giving us rounded, recognizable portraits of human beings who gradually grow into saints the majority of the legends suggest that from the moment of their conversion, or earlier still, the saints are distinguished from ordinary mortals by their heroic virtue, their apparent immunity to self-doubt, and the supernatural signs that surround them. In some of the favorite medieval legends there is not even a turning point, because the saint's holiness is manifest from infancy on; in others the saint affirms late in life that he or she has never even been seriously tempted to sin. This predilection for idealized, one-dimensional saints does not deprive the legends of dramatic conflict, since the saints' virtue can still be tested against devils, human persecutors, and other opponents; but it tends to reduce the conflicts to simple black-and-white terms and to heighten the apparent wickedness and perversity of the saints' opponents.

Given the gap between such conventions and their own expectations, modern scholars have not ordinarily devoted much serious attention to medieval hagiography. Even Hippolyte Delehaye, who was perhaps the world's preeminent authority on the old legends in the early 20th century, regretfully dismissed the majority of them as a kind of childish folklore that had substituted itself for authentic, valuable historical documents. In the past few decades, however, students of medieval culture have begun to rediscover the potential usefulness and interest of this large body of literature. Applying narrative theory to early hagiography, for example, Alison G. Elliott treats the genre as a serious variety of folklore, or myth, analyzing the structural patterns that underlie it and the functions served by its conventions. Elliott develops an important distinction suggested in 1975 by Charles Altman: whereas the typical structure of a martyr's *passio* sets good in diametrical opposition to evil, the typical structure of a confessor's *vita* "presents a gradational view of the universe, in which *good* is opposed to *better* and *worse*" (Elliott, 1987: 17). To the former Altman and Elliott relate medieval epic; to the latter, romance.

Recent historical studies have begun to illuminate other facets of hagiography by studying legends in relation to their cultural and historical contexts. Peter Brown has explored the psychological and social needs that were met by the cult of the saints in late antiquity, in the process revealing unexpected depths of meaning in certain conventional features of the legends. André Vauchez and Richard Kieckhefer, among others, have done similarly far-reaching studies for the late Middle Ages, showing how the new spiritual movements and emphases of these centuries were reflected in the veneration of new kinds of saints. Caroline Bynum has focused on particular motifs, studying large samples of hagiography and other religious writings to determine the significance of such phenomena as the burgeoning of feminine images of sanctity in the 12th and 13th centuries and the prominent imagery of food and feeding in the lives and writings of late-medieval women saints. Focusing on the patterns of emphasis in a single hagiographical collection, the *Legenda aurea*, Sherry Reames has shown how the influential hagiographer Jacobus de Voragine reshaped existing legends in the 13th century, adapting the old stories to a new audience and new polemical purposes.

Although the studies just mentioned deal primarily with the Latin tradition, they are obviously relevant to understanding vernacular legends as well. For one thing they demonstrate that even Latin hagiography is less monolithic than it looks. Despite the continuing use of the same conventions, there are often significant differences between legends, or between successive retellings of the same legend, which a knowledgeable reader can recognize. Such comparisons readily offer themselves in English vernacular hagiography, since nearly all the legends in both OE and ME are directly dependent on Latin sources.

OE Saints' Lives

An impressive amount of hagiographical literature in the vernacular has survived from Anglo-Saxon England. The earliest saints' legends in England were written in Latin by the mid-8th century, and vernacular legends began appearing by the 9th. The bulk of surviving OE hagiography is in prose, due largely to the enormous contribution of Ælfric, who wrote in the late 10th to early 11th century. Ælfric's two homiletic collections, extensively copied, include more than twenty saints' lives, ranging from New Testament figures like Stephen to the English Cuthbert. Ælfric also wrote a third collection, the *Lives of Saints,* containing some 26 saints' lives as well as other materials. These *Lives* were intended for the private reading of monks and included saints especially honored in monastic circles. Also in prose are earlier works like the Mercian 9th-century *Life of St. Chad,* a translation of Felix's *Life of St. Guthlac,* and the OE Martyrology, again from Mercia, which gives short narratives about the saints in the order of the liturgical calendar, including about twenty English saints. Additional vernacular prose hagiography occurs in the translations of Bede's *Ecclesiastical History* and Gregory's *Dialogues* that were produced by Alfred's circle of scholars and in anonymous collections like the Blickling Homilies and the Vercelli Book, which together include some half-dozen saints' lives among their homilies.

Early hagiographical poetry in OE appears to date from approximately the same time and place as the earliest prose—9th-century Mercia—suggesting that Mercia was an early center of interest in the vernacular production of saints' legends. There are five or six extant poetic legends and several other poems that exhibit the influence of this tradition. Two of the poems, *Juliana* and *The Fates of the Apostles,* were written by Cynewulf, whose name we know due to his habit of ending his poems with riddling passages containing his signature in runes. *Juliana* deals with the Byzantine virgin who died during the Diocletian persecution, and *The Fates* is a shorter poem outlining the martyrdoms of the twelve apostles. The other saints' lives in poetry are *Andreas,* an extended narrative of the apostle Andrew's conversion of the cannibalistic Mermedonians, and *Guthlac A* and *B,* two poems about the Mercian saint of that name (d. 714). The poems *Judith* and *Elene* (the latter also composed by Cynewulf and sometimes called a saint's life) are not saints' lives in the strictest sense; however, both show the influence of hagiography in their characterizations.

In contrast to the bulk of OE prose hagiography OE hagiographical poetry often transforms its Latin sources radically (in the case of *Guthlac B,* differences are so thoroughgoing that its dependence on a Latin source is questionable). One important feature of the transformation, seen especially in the Cynewulf poems, *Andreas,* and *Guthlac A,* is the "heroicizing" of the narrative. Thanks in large part to the influence of the traditional poetic diction these legends are transformed into fit traditional subjects of OE poetry. Martyrs become warriors of God, such hagiographical conventions as spiritual combat with the Devil are expressed in terms of martial strength, companions become the Germanic *comitatus,* or warrior band, and so on. Admittedly, there are other influences that facilitate this process—for example, the martial imagery in the Pauline epistles. But we can assume that the strongest influence is the oral traditional style because such heroicizing occurs only rarely in OE prose; in fact it is confined almost entirely to Ælfric's *Lives of Saints,* which use a rhythmical prose style with some similarities to OE poetry. The employment of traditional poetic diction and concepts in hagiography was not simply mechanical and could, for example, create subtle rhetorical effects through the ironic use of those conventions.

Two other characteristics clearly distinguish the OE poetic legends from the Latin versions behind them. The use of typology and iconography typical of medieval hagiography is especially prominent in these poems. For example, *Andreas* frequently makes use of exaggerated plot devices and patterns of imagery in order to emphasize the iconography of baptism and eucharist. Thus the Mermedonians are punished for their sinfulness by both a great flood and a huge conflagration, and the shoulder-high waters issue from a single rock. Secondly, although OE prose legends generally deal with the entire narrative as found in their Latin sources, several of the poems—for instance, *Andreas* and *Guthlac A* and *B*—concentrate on a limited number of events from the life of the saint. *Juliana* and *The Fates of the Apostles* also pass over early parts of the saints' lives, but this is more typical of the subgenres to which they belong—the *passio* and the martyrology, respectively.

ME Saints' Lives

For a time after the Norman Conquest most vernacular hagiography written in England was in French. But Ælfric's accounts of the saints continued to be copied until the second half of the 12th century, showing that there was a continuing audience for English-language hagiography. From the late 13th century on striking proof of the genre's popularity is provided by the textual history of two monumental ME collections. The earlier of these, the *South English Legendary,* consists of versified legends and other material for church festivals and was apparently written for oral delivery to unlettered members of the laity. The wide circulation of the *Legendary* is attested by its survival in more than 60 manuscripts (counting fragments), ranging in date from about 1300 to 1500, and by the diversity of those manuscripts in both dialect and contents. The fullest ones contain over 90 saints' legends. The other great monument of ME hagiography is Caxton's *Golden Legend,* a massive prose compilation that contains some 250 legends, most of them adapted from Jean de Vignay's French translation of the *Legenda aurea.* Caxton's version, evidently designed for private reading by prosperous and well-educated laypeople, was a bestseller from its first publication in 1483 until well into the 1520s.

As these first two examples suggest, it is difficult to generalize about ME hagiography, because it was written for diverse audiences and includes a wide range of literary forms, purposes, and levels of sophistication. At one extreme are unvarnished popularizations that emphasize colorful, dramatic storytelling, sacrificing the layers of symbolic meaning in the Latin versions for an engaging narrative and some simple lessons about faith and conduct. Works in this category include a number of individual saints' legends retold in the style of popular verse romances, which were sometimes copied into the same manuscript anthologies with those romances, and most chapters of the *South English Legendary.*

At the opposite extreme one finds some ME legends composed for an elite readership and displaying considerable literary ambition. The most obvious examples come from the 15th century: Bokenham's *Legends of Holy Women,* comprising thirteen lives of female saints, written in a variety of metrical forms and dedicated to various patrons; Capgrave's courtly-epic version of the life of Katherine of Alexandria and his lives of Augustine, Gilbert, and Norbert; and Lydgate's nine hagiographical poems, most of which are still more elaborate and rhetorical. Also quite ambitious, though in a different way, are the three early ME legends in the Katherine Group (ca. 1190–1220)—skillfully elaborated accounts in vivid alliterative prose of the virgin martyrs Juliana, Margaret, and Katherine. And even the greatest of the late-14th-century poets sometimes turned their hands to hagiography. Chaucer translated at least one genuine saint's legend, the account of St. Cecilia assigned to the Second Nun in the *Canterbury Tales,* and expertly imitated the genre on a number of other occasions—most obviously in the *Prioress's Tale, Man of Law's Tale, Clerk's Tale,* and *Legend of Good Women.* Gower retold one famous legend, Pope Sylvester's conversion of Constantine, in the *Confessio Amantis.* A contemporary master of the alliterative tradition, thought by some to be the same poet who wrote *Sir Gawain* and *Pearl,* produced the anonymous poem *St. Erkenwald.*

Most typical of the period, however, are utilitarian-looking collections of ME legends. There are, for example, two manuscripts of the *Northern Homily Cycle,* both copied around 1400, that add to the cycle's usual contents a series of some 30 legends written in short couplets. The exact sources of these legends have yet to be identified. The other collections in this category all depend to a large extent on Jacobus de Voragine's *Legenda aurea,* but no two of them are alike. John Mirk's *Festial* (ca. 1400), a prose compilation that remained popular enough to warrant nearly twenty early printed editions, includes some 30 brief accounts of saints among its homilies and narratives for church festivals; Mirk's book was evidently designed to help parish priests prepare their sermons. Roughly contemporary with Mirk are two verse translations of parts of the *Legenda aurea,* each surviving in just one manuscript: the *Scottish Legendary,* which consists of a prologue and 50 legends selected and rearranged by the translator, who calls himself a retired "mynistere of haly kirke," and the so-called Vernon *Golden Legend,* a selection of nine legends, including some unusually long and interesting ones, found in a famous manuscript probably owned originally by a community of nuns or monks. Finally, nearly half a century before Caxton's full-scale adaptation of the *Legenda aurea,* an anonymous English translator produced a prose version, usually called the *1438 Golden Legend* or *Gilte Legende,* that contains up to 178 legends and survives in at least seven reasonably complete manuscripts and some fragments. Most of this collection has still not been published, and one can only speculate about the particular readership and purposes for which it was written.

Much remains to be learned about the huge corpus of ME legends, but recent developments in scholarship have given a new impetus to the study of such works, both as examples of popular literature and as documents in cultural and religious history. One important development is the discovery that hagiography—and especially vernacular hagiography, with its diversity of intended audiences—provides a wealth of evidence on issues of gender, class, language, and ideology in medieval culture (well illustrated by the essays recently edited by Blumenfeld-Kosinski and Szell). Even more important is the development of interdisciplinary methodologies that can do justice to the richness and complexity of the evidence; some of the best examples to date are found in Ashley and Sheingorn's collection of articles on the symbolic functions of St. Anne.

Sherry L. Reames
Deborah VanderBilt

Bibliography

New *CBEL* 1:237–39, 277–78, 287–88, 317–21, 326 (OE); 523–33 (ME); *Manual* 2:410–57, 553–649 [collections and individual saints' lives]; 9:3177–3258, 3501–51 [Miracles of the Virgin]; Anderson, Earl R. *Cynewulf: Structure, Style, and Theme in His Poetry.* Rutherford: Associated University Presses, 1983; Ashley, Kathleen, and Pamela Sheingorn, eds. *Interpreting Cultural Symbols: Saint Anne in Late Medieval Society.* Athens: University of Georgia Press, 1990; Bjork, Robert E. *The Old English Verse Saints' Lives: A Study in Direct Discourse and the Iconography of Style.* Toronto: University of Toronto Press, 1985; Blumenfeld-Kosinski, Renate, and Timea Szell, eds. *Images of Sainthood in Medieval Europe.* Ithaca: Cornell University Press, 1991; Brown, Peter. *The Cult of the Saints: Its Rise and Function in Latin Christianity.* Chicago: University of Chicago Press, 1981; Bynum, Caroline Walker. *Holy Feast and Holy Fast: The Religious Significance of Food to Medieval Women.* Berkeley: University of California Press, 1987; Delehaye, Hippolyte. *The Legends of the Saints.* Trans. Donald Attwater. New York: Fordham University Press, 1962; Elliott, Alison Goddard. *Roads to Paradise: Reading the Lives of the Early Saints.* Hanover: University Press of New England, 1987; Görlach, Manfred. *The Textual Tradition of the South English Legendary.* Leeds Texts and Monographs n.s. 6. Leeds: University of Leeds School of English, 1974; Jones, Charles W. *Saints' Lives and Chronicles in Early England.* Ithaca: Cornell University Press, 1947; Kieckhefer, Richard. *Unquiet Souls: Fourteenth-Century Saints and Their Religious Milieu.* Chicago: University of Chicago Press, 1984; *Medievalia et Humanistica,* n.s. 6 (1975) [special issue on medieval hagiography and romance; see esp. Charles F. Altman, "Two Types of Opposition and the Structure of Latin Saints' Lives" (1–11); Thomas J. Heffernan, "An Analysis of the Narrative Motifs in the Legend of St. Eustace" (63–89); Derek Pearsall, "John Capgrave's Life of St. Katharine and Popular Romance Style" (121–37)]; Philippart, Guy, ed. *Hagiographies: histoire internationale de la littérature hagiographique, latine et vernaculaire, des origines à 1550.* Turnhout: Brepols, 1994– [see esp. J.E. Cross, "English Vernacular Saints' Lives before 1000 A.D." (2:413–27); E.G. Whatley, "Late Old English Hagiography, ca. 950–1150" (2:429–99)]; Reames, Sherry L. *The Legenda Aurea: A Reexamination of Its Paradoxical History.* Madison: University of Wisconsin Press, 1985; Vauchez, André. *La sainteté en occident aux derniers siècles du Moyen Age d'après les procès de canonisation et les documents hagiographiques.* Bibliothèque des Écoles Françaises d'Athènes et de Rome, fasc. 241. Rome: École Française de Rome, 1981.

See also Ælfric; *Andreas;* Anglo-Norman Literature; Bokenham; Capgrave; Cynewulf; Feasts, New Liturgical; *Guthlac A and B; Guthlac,* Prose; *Judith;* Katherine Group; Lydgate; *Martyrology,* Old English; Mirk; Offices, New Liturgical; Saints' Lives, Illuminated; Vercelli Homilies

Hanseatic League

The league began with the founding at Lübeck in the mid-12th century of a loose association of about 180 German towns to protect their commercial interests. Within a century German merchants dominated Baltic and North Sea trade, and in the 14th century they expanded their investment into France, Portugal, Spain, and southern Italy. The Hanse made loans to English kings, and when the privileges granted in exchange for customs duties by the 1303 *Carta mercatoria* were withdrawn from other aliens by Edward II, the Hanse retained theirs and received further advantages in 1347 from Edward III.

The internal organization was intended to maintain control over Hanse merchants in every country. However, political differences persisted between the northern Prussians and the southern Wendish towns, despite united diplomacy. Four main communities, in London, Bruges, Bergen, and Novgorod, were subordinate to the Hanse Diet and were responsible for secondary settlements. Thus the London Steelyard, an autonomous enclave established by 1320, controlled Hanse merchants in Newcastle, York, Hull, Boston, Lynn, Yarmouth, and Ipswich. They made up the largest group of alien merchants; their imports and exports of cloth fluctuated, running between 7 and 24 percent of England's trade.

There was an inherent imbalance in Hanseatic trade. Although Flemish, Dutch, and English cloth comprised their major import, plus ale and beer, and later salt, these did not balance the valuable raw materials the Hanse exported west: Norwegian fish, Swedish and Hungarian minerals, Russian furs and wax, Prussian grain and timber, Rhenish wine from Cologne. Hostile relations with most of its European trading partners from the 1350s transformed the Hanse into a major political power, now based in only 55 to 80 towns.

Attempts by English merchants to penetrate the Baltic in the 1360s and 1370s were frustrated by the Hanse refusal to reciprocate trading privileges and led to major conflict with England. Until the Peace of 1474 embargoes, piracy, and open war were particularly damaging for the east-coast ports, notably Boston, where Hanse cloth exports had been concentrated. The league survived until 1630, though signs of contraction were apparent a century earlier.

Jennifer I. Kermode

Bibliography

Carus-Wilson, E.M., and Olive Coleman. *England's Export Trade, 1275–1547.* Oxford: Clarendon, 1963 [a digest of the Enrolled Customs Accounts in the Public Record Office]; Dollinger, Philippe. *The German Hansa.* Trans. D.S. Ault and S.H. Steinberg. London: Macmillan, 1970; Lloyd, T.H. *Alien Merchants in England in the High Middle Ages.* Brighton: Harvester, 1982; Lloyd, T.H. *England and the German Hanse, 1157–1622: A Study in Their Trade and Commercial Diplomacy.* Cambridge: Cambridge University Press, 1991; Postan, M.M. "The Economic and Political Relations of England and the Hanse from 1400 to 1475." In *Studies in English Trade in the Fifteenth Century,* ed. Eileen Power and M.M. Postan. London: Routledge, 1933, pp. 91–153.

See also Aliens and Alien Merchants; Cloth; Customs Accounts

Hardham Wall Paintings

One of the most complete cycles of English Romanesque wall paintings survives in St. Botolph's Church, Hardham, West Sussex. Dated to the early 12th century, the cycle consists of approximately 40 scenes arranged in two tiers in both the nave and chancel of the church. The painting is done in true fresco technique (on wet plaster) with details added in secco (on dry plaster).

The iconographic program begins and ends on the west wall of the nave with the Last Judgment. The walls of the nave are painted with scenes from the Infancy of Christ (Annunciation to Baptism) and from the life of the warrior St. George and two of the twelve labors of the months. The Adoration of the Lamb is placed centrally over the west wall of the chancel arch. The east side of the chancel arch displays the Temptation of Adam and Eve and their labors. The Temptation is painted as an imitation tapestry hung from a rod, the only one of the Hardham scenes to be painted in this fashion. The north and south walls of the chancel show figures of the apostles and elders of the Apocalypse above scenes of Christ's Passion, the latter having an obvious liturgical significance. The program originally culminated in a monumental Christ in Majesty flanked by cherubim and seraphim on the east wall of the chancel. Together the scenes framed the celebration of the mass with images of judgment, sacrifice, and the body of Christ, serving as a warning for the congregation, as well as a visual manifestation of the body and blood of Christ before them. The scenes of St. George might have summoned up visions of the First Crusade, while his dragon was paralleled by the dragon from whom Eve takes the apple in the Hardham Temptation, signifying that danger and spiritual battle threatened both at home and abroad.

The Hardham paintings are finely executed, with elongated figures, expressive gestures, and bright colors. The iconography has some unusual features: the dragon tapestry and dragon format of the Temptation, Eve shown milking a cow, instead of spinning, as her labor. The source of the paintings is problematic. A number of scholars have felt that, while Romanesque in date, the paintings are a continuation of the Anglo-Saxon tradition, linking them specifically with such late Anglo-Saxon manuscripts as the "Cædmon" Genesis (Bodl. Junius 11), as well as with the decoration of 12th-century Danish churches at Ørreslev, Fjenneslev, and Jørlunde. Audrey Baker identifies a Cluniac influence filtered through Lewes Priory, David Park sees a clear Ottonian influence, while C.R. Dodwell believes the paintings to be fully Norman in style, with parallels in manuscripts produced at Jumièges and St. Ouen. Given the increasingly international nature of society in the 12th century, we should not be surprised that an artist working in Anglo-Norman England might combine elements of Anglo-Saxon, Norman, and Ottonian styles in the creation of a highly original composition.

The Hardham paintings have also been linked both stylistically and iconographically with paintings in four other nearby churches: Clayton, Plumpton, Coombes, and Westmeston. The group as a whole has been labeled the "Lewes Group," as the paintings in all five churches are thought to be derived from (or sponsored by) Lewes Priory. While there are certainly comparisons to be made among the cycles, the validity of the label has been called into question. Each cycle is unique in its own way, none contains the unusual elements found at Hardham, and, perhaps most important, only fragments of wall paintings are known from Lewes Priory.

Catherine E. Karkov

Bibliography

Baker, Audrey. "Lewes Priory and the Early Group of Wall Paintings in Sussex." *Walpole Society* 31 (1942–43): 1–44; Cather, Sharon, David Park, and Paul Williamson. *Early Medieval Wall Painting and Painted Sculpture in England.* BAR Brit. Ser. 216. Oxford: BAR, 1990; Dodwell, C.R. *The Pictorial Arts of the West 800–1200.* New Haven: Yale University Press, 1993; Grabar, André. *Romanesque Painting.* New York: Skira, 1958; Park, David. "The 'Lewes Group' of Wall Paintings in Sussex." *Anglo-Norman Studies* 6 (1984): 201–37; Tristram, E.W. *English Medieval Wall Painting.* Vol. 1: *The Twelfth Century.* Oxford: Oxford University Press, 1944.

See also Canterbury Cathedral; Iconography; Wall Painting, Romanesque

Hardyng, John (1378–ca. 1465)

Author of a chronicle of Britain and England from their settlement to the mid-15th century; after military service at Agincourt and in the Scottish marches he was appointed constable of Warkworth Castle in Yorkshire and later Kyme Castle in Lincolnshire. His *Chronicle* is found in two versions. The first, extant in one manuscript, was presented to Henry VI in 1457. The shorter revised version was presented to Edward IV in 1464; it survives in twelve manuscripts and four fragments.

The *Chronicle,* which was known to Malory and Spenser, incorporates material on the Grail story and is of historical value for the reign of Henry VI. It is also interesting for its political agendas concerning English rule of Scotland and the Lancastrian and Yorkist claims to the English throne.

Lister M. Matheson

Bibliography

PRIMARY

Ellis, Henry, ed. *The Chronicle of Iohn Hardyng . . . Together with the Continuation by Richard Grafton.* London, 1812. Repr. New York: AMS, 1974.

SECONDARY

Manual 8:2644–47, 2836–45.

See also Chronicles; Matter of Britain; Wars of the Roses

Harley Lyrics

The ME lyrics found in BL Harley 2253, a compilation made partly in the late 13th century and partly in the 1330s. The earlier portion of the manuscript contains religious narratives in Anglo-Norman; the later portion (fols. 49–140) is a collection of religious and secular works, in prose and verse, written in Latin, Anglo-Norman, or English, including saints' lives, fabliaux, proverbs, debate poems, dream lore, *King Horn,* and a travel guide to Jerusalem. Harley 2253 is famous, however, for its preservation (between fols. 55 and 128) of 49 short poems in English, among which are nine historical-satirical poems, nineteen religious and sixteen secular lyrics, and five miscellaneous pieces. Of these poems 31 are unique to this manuscript, which is our most important witness for the history of the early, and especially the secular, English lyric.

The manuscript was made in the west Midlands near the borders of Herefordshire, Shropshire, and Wales; its later part was copied by a scribe working in or near Ludlow, Shropshire, whose hand is found in other literary and documentary manuscripts of the early 14th century. Some of its poems were composed locally, as indicated by references to place-names—Ribblesdale, the River Wye, and Wirral—and by their metrical and stylistic affinities with Welsh poetry. It contains other materials that are clearly of local interest. Some lyrics, however, are evidently by poets who lived elsewhere—"bituene Lyncolne ant Lyndeseye, Norhamptoun and Lounde"; philological data show that various lyrics were composed in various dialects, and a few appear in manuscripts produced in other parts of England.

The lyrics are usually dated as late-13th- or early-14th-century. More precisely datable are the political poems, which presumably were composed fairly soon after the events they describe: the battles of Lewes (1264), Courtrai (1302), and possibly Bannockburn (1314); the execution of Sir Simon Fraser (1306); and the death of Edward I (1307). Less certain are the dates of the *Complaint of the Husbandman* (ca. 1300?) and the satires against fashion, the consistory courts, and the retinues of noble households. It is noteworthy that the historical and satirical poems, though strident in tone, show a sophistication in meter and in style that compares well with the more polished performances of the lyrics.

Harley 2253 contains many fine religious lyrics, notably "Erthe toc of erthe," but its chief glory is its unprecedented collection of secular lyrics. The artistry of these indicates that they must have had forebears in English—though none survives. There are analogues of sorts in the Anglo-Norman tradition, which blends French modes of poetry with native English traditions. Striking in the Harley lyrics is the tendency to combine features of different genres or styles to create unusual effects—courtly matter and popular refrain, love allegory and lyric lament, pastourelle and formal description, amorous praise and ribald suggestion, personal reference in what is ordinarily an impersonal mode of writing. Because so few early ME lyrics survive, one cannot know how representative the Harley poems are, but as literary documents they are extraordinary.

Daniel J. Ransom

Bibliography

PRIMARY

Brook, G.L., ed. *The Harley Lyrics.* 4th ed. Manchester: Manchester University Press, 1968; Ker, N.R., intro. *British Museum MS Harley 2253.* EETS o.s. 255. London: Oxford University Press, 1965 [facsimile]; Robbins, Rossell Hope, ed. *Historical Poems of the XIVth and XVth Centuries.* New York: Columbia University Press, 1959.

SECONDARY

Matonis, A.T.E. "The Harley Lyrics: English and Welsh Convergence." *MP* 86 (1988): 1–21; Pearsall, Derek. *Old English and Middle English Poetry.* London: Routledge & Kegan Paul, 1977, pp. 120–32; Ransom, Daniel J. *Poets at Play: Irony and Parody in the Harley Lyrics.* Norman: Pilgrim Books, 1985; Schmolke-Hasselmann, Beate. "Middle English Lyrics and French Tradition—Some Missing Links." In *The Spirit of the Court,* ed. Glyn S. Burgess et al. Woodbridge: Brewer, 1985, pp. 298–320.

See also Alliterative Revival; Anglo-Norman Literature; Battles of Bannockburn and Boroughbridge; Battles of Lewes and Evesham; Courtly Love; Debate Poems; Lyrics; Matter of England; Popular Culture; Satire

Harley 978

A well-known manuscript from Reading Abbey (BL Harley 978), compiled sometime in the period 1245–65, probably at the behest of a single individual. Its contents are eclectic and reflective of wide intellectual interests and sources, suggesting a university connection. Famous principally because it contains the canon "Sumer is icumen in," Harley 978 also possesses the unique text of the "Song of Lewes" *(Calamo velociter),* the best English collection of goliardic verse, the largest surviving collection of the fables and lais of Marie de France, an index to the extensive contents of an otherwise lost book of polyphony, and other items. In addition to the Sumer canon the musical contents of the manuscript's first large section include ten lengthy monophonic Latin songs of the sequence or lai type, one three-voice motet, three two-voice textless (instrumental?) pieces, and two pages of elementary music-instruction material.

Peter M. Lefferts

Bibliography

Hohler, Christopher. "Reflections on Some Manuscripts Containing 13th-Century Polyphony." *Journal of the Plainsong and Mediaeval Music Society* 1 (1978): 2–38; Kingsford, Charles Lethbridge, ed. *The Song of Lewes.* Oxford: Oxford University Press, 1890; Sanders, Ernest H., ed. *English Music of the Thirteenth and Early Fourteenth Century.* Polyphonic Music of the Fourteenth Century 14. Paris: L'Oiseau-Lyre, 1979; Stevens, John. *Words and Music in the Middle Ages: Song, Narrative, Dance and Drama, 1050–1350.* Cambridge: Cambridge University Press, 1986.

See also Breton Lay; Conductus; Hymns; Marie de France; Motet; Sequence; Simon de Montfort; Songs; Sumer Canon

Harley Psalter and the "Utrecht" Style

BL Harley 603 is the first of three English medieval copies of the Carolingian masterpiece of illusionistic drawing, the Utrecht Psalter (Utrecht, Rijksuniversiteit 32). Each psalm in the Carolingian book is headed by a sepia drawing with literal illustrations of psalm verses set into rolling landscapes reminiscent of antique art. The Harley Psalter (fig. 71), produced at Canterbury during the first half of the 11th century, was conceived as a copy of this manuscript, though the Roman Psalter text was substituted for the Carolingian manuscript's Gallican text and a more legible minuscule for the rustic capitals of the original. Only 111 drawings were ever completed, twelve of them in the 12th century. The precise chronology of the extended production process remains unclear, and as many as six different artists worked on the Anglo-Saxon phases of the decoration. Specific circumstances of patronage and function are also uncertain. The archbishop

Fig. 71. Harley Psalter (BL Harley 603), fol. 1. Psalms 1 and 2. Reproduced by permission of the British Library, London.

depicted at the feet of Christ in the historiated *Beatus* initial may well have commissioned the psalter, perhaps for King Cnut (1016–35) or Emma, his queen.

Harley 603 is famous for faithful copies of the Carolingian imagery, rendered in the nonnaturalistic and often kaleidoscopic colored line much favored by late Anglo-Saxon artists. Less well known are the pictures that adapt and transform the Utrecht scenes, often in response to contemporary political and religious considerations, some diverging completely from the imagery of the Utrecht Psalter. In addition to the innovative psalm illustrations and the *Beatus* initial a unique painted miniature of the Trinity was added to preface the book.

Both the style and the imagery of the Utrecht Psalter exerted continuing influence on medieval English art. The early pictures of the Harley Psalter exemplify the expressive and dynamic Anglo-Saxon drawing technique labeled by Wormald the "Utrecht" style (1952). Figures are executed with short, sharp strokes; heads push forward and draperies flutter. Wormald considered the art of Reims a major contributing factor in the development of this stylistic phase, which peaked in the early 11th century but was evident well before the millennium. As Deshman has emphasized (1977), the native insular predilection for flickering line and nervous dynamism, seen already in the Leofric Missal (Bodleian Library, Bodley 579) and the Æthelwold Benedictional (BL Add. 49969; fig. 26: see BENEDICTIONAL OF ÆTHELWOLD), must have predisposed English artists to their avid response to the Utrecht manuscript. The Crucifixion of the Ramsey Psalter (BL Harley 2904) and an Aratus manuscript of the late 10th century (BL Harley 2506) are fine examples of developed "Utrecht" style, which is further evident in early-11th-century drawings of the New Minster Liber Vitae (BL Stowe 944). Artists of the Ælfwine Prayerbook (BL Cotton Titus D.xxvi and D.xxvii), working in the same style, were among the many Anglo-Saxons who also adapted some of the Carolingian psalter's iconographic formulas.

Kathleen M. Openshaw

Bibliography

Backhouse, Janet, Derek H. Turner, and Leslie Webster, eds. *The Golden Age of Anglo-Saxon Art 966–1066.* London: British Museum, 1984; Deshman, Robert. "The Leofric Missal and Tenth-Century English Art." *ASE* 6 (1977): 145–73; Deshman, Robert. *The Benedictional of Æthelwold.* Princeton: Princeton University Press, 1995; Dufrenne, Suzy. "Les copies anglaises du Psautier d'Utrecht." *Scriptorium* 18 (1964): 185–97; Gameson, Richard. "The Anglo-Saxon Artists of the Harley 603 Psalter." *JBAA* 143 (1990): 29–48; Kidd, J.A. "The Quinity of Winchester Reconsidered." *Studies in Iconography* 7–8 (1981–82): 21–33; Ohlgren, Thomas H. *Anglo-Saxon Textual Illustration: Photographs of Sixteen Manuscripts with Descriptions and Index.* Kalamazoo: Medieval Institute, 1992; Openshaw, Kathleen M. "Weapons in the Daily Battle: Images of the Conquest of Evil in the Early Medieval Psalter." *Art Bulletin* 75 (1993): 17–38; Temple, Elzbieta. *Anglo-Saxon Manuscripts 900–1066.*

A Survey of Manuscripts Illuminated in the British Isles 2, ed. J.J.G. Alexander. London: Harvey Miller, 1976; Tselos, Dmitri. "English Manuscript Illustration and the Utrecht Psalter." *Art Bulletin* 41 (1959): 137–49; Wormald, Francis. *English Drawings of the Tenth and Eleventh Centuries.* London: Faber & Faber, 1952.

See also Psalters, Anglo-Saxon; "Winchester School"

Harold Godwinson (ca. 1020–1066)

On 14 October 1066 Harold Godwinson, the last Saxon king of England, lay dead on the field of Battle, near Hastings in Kent. The hopes of his family to create a royal dynasty were dashed, the fortunes and lives of his supporters wasted in what may have been as audacious a bid for royal power as that of William the Conqueror.

Harold had been opposed by several contenders for the throne after the death of Edward the Confessor in January 1066 and had defeated them all, including his brother Tostig and Tostig's ally, King Harald of Norway, at the Battle of Stamford Bridge in late September 1066. The decision to undertake a forced march from Stamford, near York, to Hastings, where William waited with his continental army, is often seen as a move made in desperation; it is likely that Harold was confident of victory or, at the very least, of a temporary repulse of William.

William's success has dominated the history of late Anglo-Saxon times. It is often forgotten that Harold, formerly earl of Wessex, had been king for nearly a year. The short duration of his reign means that little was written about it, or about Harold's character, by the historians of the day. William of Poitiers, who wrote his *Gesta Guillelmi ducis Normannorum et regis Anglorum* in the 1070s, describes Harold as brave, ambitious, and clever, but an unwise dispenser of patronage. The English author of the *Vita Aedwardi regis* is more enthusiastic; Harold "was a true friend of his race and country, he wielded his father's powers even more actively, and walked in his ways, that is, in patience and mercy, and with kindness to men of good will." It is not entirely surprising that legends of Harold's survival after Hastings circulated for some years after the battle.

Harold was 27 when he inherited the earldom of Wessex on Godwin's death in 1053. Harold and his brothers Leofwine, Gyrth, and Tostig controlled, as earls, all of southern England, including East Anglia and even a part of Northumbria. Harold and Tostig were successful in England's defense against Welsh and Scottish forces, and both won Edward's gratitude. But it was to Harold that the dying king commended his wife (Harold's sister Edith) and kingdom in January 1066.

Harold had held a special position at court, referred to as Edward's governor by the *Vita Aedwardi regis,* and in 1064 or 1065 royal ambassador to Normandy. This visit, at which Harold presumably promised to support William's claim to the English throne, is recorded mainly in pro-Norman sources; the story is difficult to reconcile with the silence of Anglo-Saxon writers on the subject. The *Vita Aedwardi* hints of the visit, but the Anglo-Saxon Chronicle does not refer to it. Harold clearly believed, at Stamford Bridge and Hastings, that he was defending England from its enemies, not that he was asserting a doubtful claim.

It is possible that the Confessor may have fed the hopes of several contenders with hints of a future bequest. Such a ploy would have been useful in preventing invasions from Scandinavia and France during his lifetime. As a prominent royal adviser, Harold may have been cognizant of the double dealing and thus unlikely to take seriously foreign claims to the throne.

It is impossible to know what kind of king Harold would have made or what tone he would have established had he repelled the Normans. The combination of lands inherited from Edward and his own earldom made him extraordinarily powerful, and the successful exploitation of these resources gave him the means to finance important projects. His founding of a college of canons at Waltham suggests that patronage of religious houses would have been one aspect of his policies. His efforts to extend English influence in Wales would no doubt have continued after 1066, and he might have built his own retinue of loyal, powerful nobles.

Stephanie Christelow

Bibliography.

PRIMARY

Barlow, Frank, ed. and trans. *The Life of King Edward Who Rests at Westminster* [*Vita Aedwardi Regis*]. 2d ed. Oxford: Clarendon, 1992.

SECONDARY

Barlow, Frank. *Edward the Confessor*. Berkeley: University of California Press, 1970; Williams, Ann. "Land and Power in the Eleventh Century: The Estates of Harold Godwineson." *Anglo-Norman Studies* 3 (1981): 171–87, 230–34.

See also Edward the Confessor; Godwin; Norman Conquest; William I

Harrowing of Hell

The "plundering" or "harrying" (ME *herien*, "to pillage, plunder") of hell by Christ, after his death, of the souls of the righteous held by Satan. The principal source for the medieval legend is the Latin account of Christ's descent into hell appended to a translation of the Greek *Acta Pilati* (dated variously from 425 to 600) to form the text known as the *Gospel of Nicodemus*. Extracts from the *Gospel's* account of the harrowing are found in encyclopedic texts, such as the *Legenda aurea* of Jacobus de Voragine and the *Speculum historiale* of Vincent de Beauvais, as well as the Pseudo-Augustinian Homily 160, *De Pascha* ("On Easter").

The *Gospel of Nicodemus* consists of three main episodes: the trial of Christ before Pilate and the Crucifixion; the imprisonment of Joseph of Arimathea by the Jews and his miraculous release on Holy Saturday by Christ; and the eyewitness account of the harrowing given by the two sons of Simeon after Christ's resurrection. The harrowing appears in ME in a variety of forms and genres. There are works in both verse and prose that closely follow the whole *Gospel*. In other works a translation of the *Gospel's* harrowing is linked to an episode from another source, as in the verse *Harrowing of Hell and Destruction of Jerusalem* and the prose *Complaint of Our Lady and Gospel of Nicodemus*. Treatments more independent of the *Gospel of Nicodemus* are found in dramatic and quasi-dramatic forms that exploit the potential of the physical and verbal conflict between Christ and the devils: for example, the Harrowing of Hell cycle plays, the *Devils' Parliament* (a verse sermon), *Piers Plowman* B.18/C.20, and *Death and Life*.

The harrowing is used for three major themes in ME literature. First, the imprisonment and release of Joseph of Arimathea and the account of Christ's descent by the sons of Simeon, Karinus and Leucius, are testimony of the Resurrection. Second, the legend is typological in that it is designed to show the fulfillment of prophecies. The account of the harrowing in the *Gospel of Nicodemus* dramatizes this through speeches of Christ and the prophets in hell, and ME texts, principally the drama, tend to amplify this part of the episode. A third theme is the Redemption, a topic that involves a number of related issues, all with their roots in the *Gospel*. Most obviously the harrowing shows Christ's defeat of the Devil. The *Ludus Coventriae* (N-Town plays) and the *Devils' Parliament* develop the idea of the deception of the devils, who realize only at the harrowing that Christ is not just man but divine. In the York and Towneley plays, the ME *Harrowing of Hell*, the *Devils' Parliament*, and *Piers Plowman* the harrowing becomes the forum for a debate between Christ and the devils on the justice of freeing the souls in hell. The treatment of the harrowing in ME thus becomes a mirror of changing doctrine on the Redemption.

William Marx

Bibliography

PRIMARY

Hennecke, Edgar, trans. *New Testament Apocrypha*. Ed. Wilhelm Schneemelcher. Trans. from the German by R. McL. Wilson. 1:444–84. London: SCM Press, 1963; Hulme, William Henry, ed. *The Middle English Harrowing of Hell and Gospel of Nicodemus*. EETS e.s. 100. London: Kegan Paul, Trench, Trübner, 1907; Kim, H.C., ed. *The Gospel of Nicodemus: Gesta Salvatoris*. Toronto: Pontifical Institute, 1973; Marx, William, ed. *The Devils' Parliament and the Harrowing of Hell and Destruction of Jerusalem*. Heidelberg: Winter, 1993; Marx, William, and Jeanne F. Drennan, eds. *The Middle English Prose Complaint of Our Lady and Gospel of Nicodemus*. Heidelberg: Winter, 1987.

SECONDARY

Manual 2:448–50, 640–42; MacCulloch, J.A. *The Harrowing of Hell: A Comparative Study of an Early Christian Doctrine*. Edinburgh: Clark, 1930.

See also Cursor Mundi; Death and Life; Drama, Vernacular; *Piers Plowman*

Harry (or Hary), "Blind" (fl. ca. 1476–78)

The author of *The Wallace,* a vehemently anti-English, often fictitious account of the Scottish hero William Wallace's struggle against the English between 1293 and 1306. The first Scottish work to employ the pentameter couplet, *The Wallace* survives in a single manuscript (National Library of Scotland Advocates' 19.2.2), copied in 1488, which also contains a text of Barbour's *Bruce.* Harry's poem was first printed ca. 1509, though only fragments of that edition remain. *The Wallace* is indebted to a multitude of chronicle, romance, and courtly writers; it was one of the earliest (and later most popular) works printed in Scotland. The poet's traditional epithet "blind" can be traced back to the 1490s; however, Harry's vivid and accurate use of visual detail has led most modern scholars to believe that he was in fact not blind from birth.

Lister M. Matheson

Bibliography

PRIMARY

McDiarmid, Matthew P., ed. *Hary's Wallace.* STS 4th ser. 4, 5. Edinburgh: STS, 1968–69.

SECONDARY

New *CBEL* 1:657; *Manual* 8:2692–99, 2915–24.

See also Barbour; Chronicles; Scottish Literature, Early

Hawes, Stephen (ca. 1470–ca. 1529)

Early Tudor humanist and courtier, best known today for his long allegorical poem *The Pastime of Pleasure* (1505/06; pub. 1509). Chronicling the education and adventures of its hero, Graund Amour, the *Pastime* bridges the worlds of medieval visionary allegory and early Renaissance courtier poetics. Throughout the *Pastime,* as well as in other works *(The Example of Virtue, Conversion of Swearers, A Joyful Meditation,* and *The Comfort of Lovers),* Hawes develops his theories of poetry as a form of prophecy and his attitudes toward aureate (that is, highly latinate) diction as a way of purifying the language of vernacular verse.

Most modern readers know Hawes as a follower of Lydgate and Chaucer, as a source for Spenser's courtly allegories, and as a witness to the practices of early humanist rhetoric. His poetry has long been considered an example of what C.S. Lewis called the "Drab Age" of English letters. But Hawes is now receiving new attention from scholars of the history of printing, court culture, and the complex shift from "Medieval" to "Renaissance" in poetry and criticism. One of England's first poets to write exclusively for print, Hawes often reflects on the power of books to confer literary fame, and he develops metaphors of impression and understanding drawn from the technologies of movable type.

Seth Lerer

Bibliography

PRIMARY

Gluck, Florence W., and Alice B. Morgan, eds. *Stephen Hawes: The Minor Poems.* EETS o.s. 271. London: Oxford University Press, 1974; Mead, William Edward, ed. *The Pastime of Pleasure.* EETS o.s. 173. London: Humphrey Milford, 1928.

SECONDARY

New *CBEL* 1:650–51, 1114–15; *Manual* 4:1091–1100, 1305–06; Edwards, A.S.G. *Stephen Hawes.* Boston: Twayne, 1983 [bibliography, pp. 119–25].

See also Chaucerian Apocrypha; Court Culture; Dream Vision; Printing

Hawking and Falconry

The two forms of hunting with different kinds of raptorial birds. Falcons have pointed wings and long narrow tails; they typically hunt by diving ("stooping") at their prey at high speed from a considerable height, killing on impact, and so are best suited for open country. Hawks have shorter, rounded wings and wider tails for greater maneuverability; they can be flown in brush or wooded areas. They fly down their prey with a burst of speed and kill with their talons.

Among both falcons and hawks the female is generally larger and stronger than the male and is therefore used more in hunting, since she can bring down larger and more active prey. Hawks (the generic term) used in medieval falconry (the word included the flying of hawks) were the gerfalcon, peregrine, lanner, merlin, goshawk, sparrowhawk, and (more rarely) the saker and hobby. Although hawks and falcons were flown at a variety of prey, crane, heron, and duck were the most prized.

The training of hawks was time-consuming. The birds had to become accustomed to handling and were trained to return to an aural or visual cue. Falcons were taught to fly to a lure, hawks to return to the fist. Falcons selected to hunt crane or heron (large birds that falcons do not naturally attack) had to be taught to hunt those birds. Once a hawk had been trained, she had to be flown regularly to keep her in condition.

To practice falconry, then, meant having leisure to devote to one's birds or money to hire someone to do so. The most prized birds were expensive, costing up to half a knight's yearly income. Falconry was thus from an early date associated with the upper levels of society. Not only was it extremely popular, but owning and flying hawks was a status symbol and handling them part of an upper-class education, for women as well as for men.

In England the recorded history of falconry begins with St. Boniface, who in the 8th century noted in a letter to Æthelbald of Mercia that he had sent a hawk and two falcons. From then on a growing number of references to falconry appears in royal records, literature, and art. By the late 10th century well-to-do laypeople and some clergy practiced hawking, and from the mid-11th century on all the kings are recorded as flying hawks.

Domesday Book names hawkers for Edward the Confessor and William I. Both Henry II and Thomas Becket were skilled falconers, and Richard I had falcons sent to him while he was in captivity. Perhaps the greatest English royal falconer was Edward I, who built a splendid royal mews at Charing

Cross, spent close to £900 on falconry in one year, and in some years paid more than 100 men for service connected with the sport.

Robin S. Oggins

Bibliography

Frederick II. *The Art of Falconry.* Ed. and trans. Casey A. Wood and F. Marjorie Fyfe. Stanford: Stanford University Press, 1943; Hands, Rachel. *English Hawking and Hunting in The Boke of St. Albans: A Facsimile Edition.* London: Oxford University Press, 1975; Oggins, Robin S. "Falconry in Anglo-Saxon England." *Mediaevalia* 7 (1981): 173–208.

See also Berners, Juliana

Henry I (1067/68–1135; r. 1100–35)

Youngest son of William the Conqueror and Matilda of Flanders, he was left rich but landless on William's death in 1087. He used part of his inheritance to purchase the Cotentin and Avranchin from his eldest brother, the perpetually penniless Robert Curthose, duke of Normandy. In 1091 he lost these provinces to the combined military forces of his brothers Robert and William Rufus, king of England, but he later came to terms with Rufus. In 1096 Robert pawned Normandy to William and set off upon crusade. As Robert was returning in 1100, William was killed in a hunting accident and Henry seized the throne. Because of the timing of the death Henry has been suspected of being in a murder plot, but the evidence supports the view that Rufus was accidentally shot.

Upon his accession Henry issued a coronation charter, denouncing the abuses of his brother's reign and agreeing to rule England by the laws of Edward the Confessor. He set about filling some of the vacant bishoprics and recalled Anselm, archbishop of Canterbury, from continental exile. He then married the Scottish princess Matilda, who carried the blood of the line of Alfred the Great. The marriage produced two children, Matilda (b. 1102) and William (b. 1103). Matilda was betrothed to the German emperor Henry V and left England in 1110.

The first years of Henry's reign were spent consolidating his rule and fighting against Robert Curthose, who invaded in 1101 to claim the throne. In the Treaty of Alton Robert renounced his claim to the throne in return for an annual pension. However, he continued to be troublesome, and because he could not keep peace in the duchy of Normandy Henry was asked to intervene. In July 1106 Henry launched an invasion that culminated in the pitched battle at Tinchebrai on 28 September. Robert was captured and remained in captivity until he died in 1134. Even then Henry could not be secure in his possession of Normandy, because Robert's son, William Clito, also had a claim to the duchy, and Henry had to put down several revolts.

A major challenge to Henry came in 1111, when Louis VI of France joined with the counts of Anjou and Flanders. Henry emerged the victor by negotiating a separate peace with the count of Anjou; Louis was forced to recognize English overlordship in Maine and Brittany. Hostilities resumed in 1116, when some Norman barons joined a rebellion in favor of Clito. When the count of Flanders was killed in 1118, Henry again used his diplomatic skills, marrying his son William to the daughter of the Angevin count. At this point Louis complained to the pope about Henry's action, but Calixtus II remained friendly to both sides and Normandy was at peace by 1120.

Tragedy struck in 1120, with the death of Henry's only legitimate son, William, drowned when his ship struck a rock in the Channel. With this death the succession was thrown into doubt. Henry's queen had died in 1118, and after William's death Henry quickly married Adeliza (or Alice) of Louvain in 1121. But as time passed, it became clear that they were not going to produce children, and Henry was forced to make plans for a successor.

The years 1123–24 were marked by Norman insurrection. When Henry V of Germany died in 1125, Henry recalled his daughter and began to concentrate on making her a viable candidate for the throne. After obtaining a promise from his barons to support Matilda, Henry married her to Geoffrey of Anjou. This marriage was not popular with the barons, and Matilda herself did not command their loyalty. After Henry's death in 1135 the throne was seized by his nephew Stephen of Blois. After years of civil war Matilda renounced her own claim, and Stephen agreed to recognize her eldest son, Henry, as his heir.

Henry I's reign occurred during the European investiture controversy, in which the reform papacy struggled with secular powers for control of the bishoprics. In England this crisis came to a head when Archbishop Anselm refused to do homage to Henry for his fiefs and to consecrate bishops whom Henry had already invested with the ring and staff, the symbols of episcopal office. When the pope refused to condone the English customs concerning lay investiture of clerics, Anselm returned to the Continent. A compromise, giving the church the right to invest the ring and staff but permitting the king to take oaths of homage from the prelates, was effected in 1106.

In addition to unprecedented peace and prosperity Henry I's reign also saw the development of important institutions of government. One of his accomplishments was the reform of the *curia regis* (king's court). He organized royal offices and instituted regular payments to his officials. This eliminated the need to plunder the countryside as they moved about with the itinerant king. Henry also systematized the treasury, and his reign saw the development of the exchequer's twice-yearly meetings for collecting the taxes due the king. These sessions were recorded onto the "pipe rolls." One pipe roll (from 1130) survives for Henry's reign, and its completeness and sophistication argue that it is one of a series of such documents. It is a rich source, showing among other things that many legal reforms once credited to Henry II were operative by the reign of his grandfather.

Although some historians have characterized Henry's rule over England and Normandy as harsh, others have shown that contemporaries considered the reign to be successful; it provided England with 33 years of peace and prosperity. Even in Normandy, which traditionally suffered from a fractious barony, Henry's peace was seriously broken only twice after 1106. His accomplishments in war and diplomacy, law, and administration combine to show him as one of England's most able and effective rulers.

Lois L. Honeycutt

Bibliography

Green, Judith A. *The Government of England under Henry I.* Cambridge: Cambridge University Press, 1986; Hollister, C. Warren. *Monarchy, Magnates, and Institutions in the Anglo-Norman World.* London: Hambledon, 1986 [valuable collected papers, mainly on political and administrative topics]; Hollister, C. Warren. "Courtly Culture and Courtly Style in the Anglo-Norman World." *Albion* 20 (1988): 1–17; Mooers, Stephanie I. "A Reevaluation of Royal Justice under Henry I of England." *American Historical Review* 93 (1988): 340–58; Newman, Charlotte A. *The Anglo-Norman Nobility in the Reign of Henry I: The Second Generation.* Philadelphia: University of Pennsylvania Press, 1988.

See also Anarchy; Exchequer; Investiture Controversy; Matilda; Stephen; William I; William II

Henry II (1133–1189; r. 1154–89)

The eldest son of Count Geoffrey of Anjou and Matilda of England (heiress of Henry I), born 5 March 1133. He became duke of Normandy in 1150 and count of Anjou in 1151. In May 1152 he married Eleanor, duchess of Aquitaine and disowned wife of Louis VII of France. On the death of Stephen he became king of England, at age 21, and was crowned on 19 December 1154. His children included Henry (d. 1183), Matilda, Richard the Lionheart, Geoffrey, duke of Brittany, Eleanor, Joan, and John, as well as the illegitimate Geoffrey archbishop of York and William Longsword, earl of Salisbury. He died on 6 July 1189.

Tireless, well educated, and dismissive of conventional wisdom, Henry was also a man of seemingly contradictory qualities: willful but calculating, obstinate but open-minded, volatile but purposeful, both magnanimous and vindictive, jealous of his rights but indifferent to pomp and personal dignity. He was an enigma to contemporaries and has elicited varying judgments from historians. Few students have denied that he exercised a major influence on the course of western European history.

The wide dominions under his direct rule, covering more than half of France as well as England, may have seemed largely ungovernable, but Henry's achievement was to oblige all over whom he claimed jurisdiction to respect his authority and to overcome resistance swiftly and decisively. It was achieved largely by a daring use of mercenary forces skilled in siege techniques, thus devaluing the castle as the traditional base of defense. His dominance aroused not only the resentment of the greater barons but also the apprehensions of his neighbors.

The most publicized but by no means the only example of Henry challenging special interest groups was his conflict with the church. Though not opposed in principle to the church extending and refining its jurisdiction, Henry insisted that it should neither encroach on the crown's jurisdiction nor threaten crown interests. His tactic for ensuring smooth relations by installing an ally, his chancellor and friend Thomas Becket, as archbishop of Canterbury, backfired when Becket, showing a dedication to the church's power and independence that surprised many who had been lukewarm about his nomination, vigorously defended his own authority.

Henry tried to settle the issue by fiat, by issuing his Constitutions of Clarendon (1166), based largely but selectively on customary practice. His demand for an unprecedented oath of observance from the bishops united them in resistance. It did not, however, unite them in support of Becket; some believed him to be mistakenly provocative and tactically inept. Henry's not unreasonable stance was undermined by his vindictive harrying of the archbishop, and it culminated, after a purported reconciliation, in intemperate words that prompted some members of the royal household to murder Becket in December 1170. Henry was obliged to retreat publicly. Eventually he salvaged much of what he had originally sought, though in a less provocative form. There are parallels to this in other aspects of his career.

All who resented his dominance sought to profit from the setback to his reputation in the wake of Becket's martyrdom. In 1173–74 Louis VII of France organized a coalition of Henry's opponents, both internal and external, in a determined attempt to unseat him by insurrection and invasion. Henry, sustained by the loyalty of his servants and by popular support, survived triumphantly. He exacted no revenge, save upon his headstrong wife, who remained in close confinement for the rest of his life, for having conspired with her former husband Louis to replace Henry with their malleable eldest son, the young king Henry. His victory persuaded most barons that their future lay in cooperating with the king to secure his patronage instead of striving for autonomy.

Whether Henry intended the formation of an "Angevin Empire" is debatable. His initial aggressiveness suggested expansionist aims, but there are clear signs that he came to detest the wasteful futility of warfare and limited his objectives to internal order. His intervention in Ireland (1171) seems to have been a reluctant response to the need to control Anglo-Norman adventurers. He was content to secure amicable relations with the Irish, as with the Welsh and the Scots. He intended to partition his dominions among his sons; it was his successors who sought to consolidate a unitary control that collapsed before a resurgent French monarchy. Henry's rule had, however, demonstrated how to make authority respected and how to harness it to effective government.

In the kingdom of England there was, in Henry's reign, a transformation in the processes of government and in the methods of administering justice. It rested essentially on three linked developments. First, the decision to rest responsibility for bringing criminal prosecutions not on official prosecutors but on local communities through "juries of presentment" (the origins of the grand jury). Second, the supervision of the operations of local government by investigative teams of justices, who carried royal government into the shires, empowered but also limited by the terms of a carefully framed commission. Third, the offer of the new and much swifter methods of righting civil wrongs by means of common-form writs that set in motion standardized procedures and rested decisions on questions of fact put to juries under the supervision of royal justices who could put the power of the crown behind enforcement.

The flood of business that ensued prompted the development of central courts of justice and a quest for more rational and sophisticated methods in all aspects of administration. In essence Henry and his advisers had found a solution to the age-old problem of how to deploy royal authority effectively without putting too much discretionary power into the hands of subordinates. A less welcome consequence was the enhanced power of the crown to discriminate against individuals who were out of favor. A necessary corrective to overweening royal government was eventually to be found in Magna Carta, but it is significant that there was no attempt in the Great Charter to reverse the trends that Henry II had fostered, that the closer integration of central and local government was accepted and the development of the common law welcomed.

W.L. Warren

Bibliography

Gillingham, John. *The Angevin Empire.* London: Arnold, 1984; Turner, Ralph V. "The Problem of Survival for the Angevin 'Empire': Henry II's and His Sons' Visions versus Late Twelfth-Century Realities." *American Historical Review* 100 (1995): 78–96; Warren, W.L. *The Governance of Norman and Angevin England, 1086–1272.* London: Arnold, 1987 [differs in interpretation from Gillingham's study]; Warren, W.L. *Henry II.* Rev. ed. London: Methuen, 1991.

See also Angevin Empire; Becket; Eleanor of Aquitaine; John; Juries; Law, Post-Conquest; Matilda; Richard I

Henry III (1207–1272; r. 1216–72)

Born 1 October 1207, the eldest son of King John by his second wife, Isabella of Angoulême. His accession (28 October 1216) inaugurated the first royal minority in England since the Conquest.

Few English kings have begun their reign under less auspicious circumstances: much of the country was in the hands of rebels who supported the claim of Louis, son of Philip II of France. The strenuous aid of the papal legate Guala, to whom Henry did homage as the pope's representative, for his kingdom, helped save the situation and ensure that the king remained ever conscious of his debt to the papacy.

For its part the regency council, headed by William Marshal, earl of Pembroke (d. 1219), reissued Magna Carta and settled the civil war by expelling the invaders and granting an amnesty, including restoration of all confiscated lands. In the 1220s the leading role was played by the able and am-

bitious Hubert de Burgh, who had been made justiciar by John. With his dismissal in 1232 a new group of administrators gathered around Henry, headed by Peter des Roches and his nephew Peter des Rivaux.

Henry came of age in stages between 1223 and 1227, but he did not finally emerge from the control of ministers inherited from his father until 1234. Although mercurial and sharp-tongued, he was an amiable, accessible, and devout man who took the cross on three occasions (1216, 1250, and 1271), though he never actually went on crusade. He was a notable patron of the arts who lavishly embellished his royal residences and rebuilt and enlarged Westminster Abbey, destined as the burialplace of himself and many of his successors, in honor of his patron saint, Edward the Confessor. He married Eleanor of Provence in 1236; their children included Edward (later Edward I), Margaret, Beatrice, and Edmund "Crouchback," earl of Lancaster.

Although he tried, by a series of marriages, to associate the barons with his family and court, and claimed that the maintenance of internal peace was his greatest achievement, his relations with the barons were never free from suspicion and hostility.

The humiliating failure of his campaign in France in 1242, in pursuit of his ambition to regain the territories lost by his father, demonstrated his military ineptitude. He was too indulgent to his closest supporters, notably the Savoyard relatives of Eleanor of Provence, whom he married on 20 January 1236; the impecunious Simon de Montfort, who married his sister in 1238; and his Lusignan half-brothers, the children of his mother's second marriage. The Lusignans, who came to England in 1247, presumed on their relationship to abuse royal authority and behave as though they were above the law. His unrealistic ambitions for his family, which led him in 1254 to accept the papal offer of the kingdom of Sicily for his second son, Edmund, plunged him deeply into debt.

In the various crises of Henry's middle years the magnates rejected his lofty notions of kingship and demanded that they be consulted on questions of policy and the appointment of great officers of state. In 1258 their leading members, including his brother-in-law Simon de Montfort, expelled the Lusignans and, in an unprecedented restriction on the crown's rights and powers, imposed a baronial council on Henry in the Provisions of Oxford. Acting in his name, they reorganized local government, widely regarded as oppressive and corrupt, reformed the law (the Provisions of Westminster), and settled outstanding differences with France by the Treaty of Paris in 1259, by which the king surrendered his claim to most of the French territories.

Before long, however, Henry began scheming to escape the intolerable controls. In 1261 the pope absolved him of his oath to the Provisions; Simon de Montfort, his most implacable opponent, went into exile; Henry was king again in fact as well as name. Success was short-lived. He needlessly antagonized some magnates; in 1263, as disorder spread, Simon returned to lead the insurgents. Later that year Henry and Simon agreed to submit to the arbitration of Louis IX of France. Louis declared in favor of Henry and condemned the

Provisions of Oxford in the Mise of Amiens, 23 January 1264; civil war broke out.

Although it started auspiciously for Henry, with the capture of Northampton, he was defeated at Lewes, 4 May 1264, and forced to surrender. From May 1264 until August 1265 Henry was kept in confinement and Simon was the effective ruler of England. Henry was forced to accept a new system of government, concentrating power in Simon's hands.

This scheme was intended to remain in force throughout Henry's last years and into the reign of his son Edward. But it offered no basis for peace, though Simon sought to strengthen his position by summoning representatives of the towns and counties to the parliament of January 1265. In May 1265 Edward, who had been a hostage for his father's good behavior, escaped and defeated and killed Simon at the Battle of Evesham, 4 August 1265.

All Simon's acts since Lewes were now annulled, his supporters deprived of their lands. But the rebels were impossible to subdue. Eventually, with the help of the papal legate, a settlement was devised in the Dictum of Kenilworth, 31 October 1266, by which the Montfortians were punished according to their degree of complicity in the rebellion. The bitter and devastating war with the "Disinherited" ended in 1267, the year that the Provisions of Westminster were reissued, in revised form, as the Statute of Marlborough.

The last years of Henry's reign were dominated by preparations for the crusade, led by Edward, which set out for the Holy Land in 1270. Henry died on 16 November 1272, but his widow, Eleanor, lived until 25 June 1291.

C.H. Knowles

Bibliography

Carpenter, D.A. *The Minority of Henry III*. London: Methuen, 1990; Carpenter, D.A. *The Reign of Henry III*. London: Hambledon, 1996; Powicke, F.M. *King Henry III and the Lord Edward: The Community of the Realm in the Thirteenth Century*. 2 vols. Oxford: Clarendon, 1947 [fullest survey of the reign]; Stacey, Robert C. *Politics, Policy and Finance under Henry III, 1216–1245*. Oxford: Clarendon, 1987; Treharne, R.F. *The Baronial Plan of Reform, 1258–1263*. 1932. Repr. with additional material. Manchester: Manchester University Press, 1971; Treharne, R.F., and I.J. Sanders, eds. *Documents of the Baronial Movement of Reform and Rebellion, 1258–1267*. Oxford: Clarendon, 1973 [key documents of the crises].

See also Baronial Reform; Battles of Lewes and Evesham; Edward I; John; Simon de Montfort; Westminster Abbey; William Marshal

Henry IV (1366–1413; r. 1399–1413)

The only legitimate son of John of Gaunt, duke of Lancaster, a younger son of Edward III. Henry was born at Bolingbroke, Lincolnshire, probably in April 1366. Although a king's grandson, he could never have had any real expectations of becoming king and received no training for kingship.

He played a political role as one of the appellant lords who opposed Richard II and accused, or "appealed," his close advisers of treason in the Merciless Parliament of 1388, but much of his early life was devoted to jousting, fighting in Prussia, and journeying to the Holy Land. Early in 1381, when only fourteen, he was married to Mary de Bohun, a joint heiress to the earldoms of Essex and Hereford, then aged about eleven. Their eldest son, the future Henry V, was born in 1387, and Mary died in 1394, leaving four sons and two daughters.

When Richard II banished him for life and confiscated the vast estates (1398), most of which he had inherited from his father, Henry had only two real choices: to remain in exile for life or to return and lead a rebellion. Joined by Archbishop Arundel of Canterbury, also exiled by Richard, and with a few other followers, he landed at Ravenspur, Yorkshire, in July 1399. Tenants of his Lancaster manors hastened to join him; his army grew rapidly, owing its main strength to the support of the Percys: Henry earl of Northumberland, Thomas earl of Worcester (Northumberland's brother, formerly steward of Richard's household), and Hotspur, Northumberland's renowned warrior son.

England was overrun without a fight. Richard was captured and induced to abdicate by the guile of Arundel and Northumberland. The oath that Henry swore at Doncaster—that he had come to claim his own inhe itance, not the crown—was conveniently forgotten. On 30 September 1399 in the parliament at Westminster, without specifying the exact nature of his title, Henry claimed the throne. Twelve days later he was crowned king. Holding the crown was to prove more difficult than winning it.

Among the nobility and gentry Henry found little support, and he was afraid to offend them by asking his parliaments for the taxes he needed. In the early part of the reign the great officers of state, the chancellor and treasurer and other counselors, were drawn from the humbler ranks of clerks and squires. Lack of money and financial inexperience were his greatest handicaps. Lavish grants from the royal revenues were made in the hope of winning friends and loyal support; they only added to the problem. Plots to depose Henry and restore Richard helped ensure the latter's death but did not end opposition to the new king.

Moreover in 1403 he married, as his second wife, Joan of Navarre, widowed duchess of Brittany, whom he may have met while in exile. A foreign queen, generously endowed with estates and a household that was, like Henry's, regarded by the Commons as extravagant, provided a further target for critics. Though earlier rebellions had been easily suppressed, the Welsh rising led by Owen Glendower proved a serious harassment for most of the reign. The Percys, entrusted to defend the northern border and to govern north Wales, defeated the Scots at Homildon Hill in 1402 but soon became discontented with the role Henry permitted them and with the payments he was able to afford them.

The Percys' first rebellion was defeated at Shrewsbury in 1403, owing to Henry's swift reaction. Hotspur was killed in battle and his uncle Worcester captured and beheaded, but the old earl of Northumberland lived to rebel again and finally to menace Henry from exile in Scotland. With his parliaments Henry had a constant struggle to secure money and to prevent them taking control of his council, from which his humbler friends were slowly excluded. After the Long Parliament of 1406 Arundel, his ablest counselor, became chancellor and controlled the government for several years but had to face new rivals: the emerging Beaufort family, the children of Gaunt's mistress and then wife, Katherine Swynford, and thus the king's half-brothers.

Meanwhile Henry had been stricken with the mysterious illness that disfigured, disabled, and eventually killed him. After several years of campaigning in Wales the king's eldest son, Henry, succeeded in defeating the rebels and now joined the Beauforts to control the council. Thomas Beaufort replaced Arundel as chancellor. At some point the Beauforts tried to force Henry to abdicate in favor of the prince, but as the plot failed evidence is almost entirely lacking. After some disputes, mainly over the question of war with France, a formal reconciliation between father and son was effected, and Henry the usurper was able to leave his son an undisputed succession when he died in 1413.

John L. Kirby

Bibliography

Brown, Alfred L. "The Commons and the Council in the Reign of Henry IV." *EHR* 79 (1964): 125–56; Davies, Richard G. "Thomas Arundel as Archbishop of Canterbury, 1396–1414." *Journal of Ecclesiastical History* 19 (1973): 9–21; Harriss, G.L. *Cardinal Beaufort: A Study of the Lancastrian Ascendancy and Decline.* Oxford: Clarendon, 1988 [especially valuable for the later part of the reign]; Kirby, John L. *Henry IV of England.* London: Constable, 1970 [modern and concise compared with Wylie]; McNiven, Peter. "Prince Henry and the English Political Crisis of 1412." *History* 65 (1980): 1–16; McNiven, Peter. *Heresy and Politics in the Reign of Henry IV: The Burning of John Badby.* Woodbridge: Boydell, 1987 [a broader study than the title suggests]; Wylie, James H. *History of England under Henry the Fourth.* 4 vols. London: Longmans Green, 1884–98 [still valuable, though mostly an uncritical collection of facts].

See also Appellants; Beaufort Family; Henry V; Lancaster, John Duke of; Lollards; Percy Family; Richard II

Henry V (1387–1422; r. 1413–22)

The popular and Shakespearean hero-king *par excellence*, although liberal historians have been less impressed with his militarism and religious intolerance. Born in 1387 to the future Henry IV and Mary de Bohun, he was too young to be involved in the political intrigues of Richard II's reign. Richard took him to Ireland in 1399 and knighted him during this expedition, which opened England to the invasion and usurpation of Henry IV. Henry V would later rebury Richard among the kings at Westminster Abbey.

Young Henry was made Prince of Wales; from 1400 to 1408 he earned his spurs combating the Welsh revolt of Owen Glendower and the Percys. The prince played a major role at the Battle of Shrewsbury in 1403. During his father's illness (1410–11) Henry and his supporters dominated the royal council, but Henry IV feared his ambition and differed with the prince over which faction to support as France fell into turmoil. The king removed his son from the council. The final two years of Henry IV's reign were a period of tension and frustration for the Prince, which may explain the later stories of his dissipated lifestyle.

Henry succeeded on 20 March 1413. He was faced with both religious and political plots that threatened the tranquility of his realm. His erstwhile friend Sir John Oldcastle, perhaps the model for Shakespeare's Falstaff, led a Lollard conspiracy in 1414 to kill the king and seize London. The conspiracy was discovered and put down, but Oldcastle remained at large until 1417, when he was taken and executed. The king remained a vigorous persecutor of Lollards. Henry, self-righteously pious, supported the efforts of the Council of Constance to end the Great Schism of the papacy, and he was a supporter of elaborate public liturgy. The king joined public worship and private devotion in his monastic foundations, a form of piety long out of fashion with monarchs. The palace at Sheen was to be restored, almost in anticipation of the Escorial (in Spain, by Charles V), with a Carthusian house and a house of Brigettine nuns.

On the political front Henry V was faced in 1415 with a plot led by the earl of Cambridge, Lord Scrope, and Sir Thomas Grey to eliminate the Lancastrian dynasty and declare the earl of March as the legitimate heir of Richard II. March revealed the plot to the king as Henry was preparing to invade France. The leaders were executed, and Henry, his domestic enemies all in flight, was free to pursue foreign ambitions.

Ignoring his questionable title to the English throne and sure of his right, Henry V revived Edward III's claim to the French crown, and it is with his French conquests that Henry is forever identified. France was torn by strife between the aristocratic factions of Armagnacs and Burgundians under the mentally ill Charles VI. Henry led a plundering expedition to Normandy in August 1415. The English captured Harfleur and then marched toward Calais. On 15 October they were overtaken by a vastly superior French army at Agincourt. Henry proved an inspirational leader who skillfully deployed his archers to win a stunning victory that encouraged English ambition and a desire for French wealth and ransoms.

Henry returned to Normandy with a second expedition in 1417, bent now upon a genuine conquest. When the Armagnacs murdered the duke of Burgundy in 1419, the new duke, Philip the Good, allied with Henry. Careful diplomacy and continued military pressure forced Charles VI to agree to the Treaty of Troyes, 21 May 1420. Under its terms Charles disinherited his son (the future Charles VII) in favor of Henry V, who became regent of France and married Charles's daughter, Catherine of Valois.

France south of the Loire remained defiant and unconquered. With the vital support of his Burgundian allies Henry pursued his conquests against the disinherited dauphin and his Armagnac allies. During the course of the campaign Henry contracted dysentery; he died at Bois de Vincennes on 31 August 1422, not yet 35 years of age. Charles VI outlived him by two months. Under the terms of the Treaty of Troyes the crowns of England and France passed to Henry V's infant son, Henry VI, who grew up to be an incompetent and hopeless weakling.

Henry V's dream of a French conquest was lost by 1453, and he has been condemned by historians for squandering England's resources in an unattainable quest for foreign glory. Yet to contemporaries he was an heroic figure. A cunning propagandist and diplomat, a skillful and ruthless general, and—as historians are discovering—a just and careful administrator, he can be faulted for dying inopportunely.

James L. Gillespie

Bibliography

Allmand, C.T. *Henry V.* Berkeley: University of California Press, 1992; Harriss, G.L., ed. *Henry V: The Practice of Kingship.* Oxford: Oxford University Press, 1985; Kingsford, Charles L., ed. *The First English Life of King Henry the Fifth.* Oxford: Clarendon, 1911; Labarge, Margaret Wade. *Henry V: The Cautious Conqueror.* London: Secker & Warburg, 1975; McFarlane, K.B. *Lancastrian Kings and Lollard Knights.* Oxford: Clarendon, 1972 [for the view of Henry as the "greatest man that ever ruled England"]; Taylor, Frank, and John S. Roskell, eds. and trans. *Gesta Henrici Quinti: The Deeds of Henry the Fifth.* Oxford: Clarendon, 1975; Wylie, James H., and W.T. Waugh. *The Reign of Henry the Fifth.* 3 vols. Cambridge: Cambridge University Press, 1914–29.

See also Chichele; Henry IV; Henry VI; Hundred Years War; Lollards

Henry VI (1421–1471; r. 1422–61, 1470–71)

The third and last Lancastrian was a remarkable king but far from a great one. Born at Windsor on 6 December 1421, the son of Henry V and Catherine of Valois, daughter of Charles VI of France, he was the youngest monarch ever to ascend the English throne (1 September 1422); his minority was accordingly the longest.

His peaceful accession is a tribute to the stability won by Henry IV and Henry V after the Lancastrian revolution in 1399. Henry VI is also the only English king to have been crowned king of France (Paris, December 1431), thereby reaping the fruits of Henry V's campaigns and shouldering unique obligations of government and conquest. At age 31 he became one of the few English kings to suffer mental collapse, which fatally impaired his ability to govern. By 1450 his cousin Richard duke of York had already challenged his capacity to rule; he eventually (by 1460) challenged Henry's right to reign, and Henry was deposed by Richard's son, Edward (crowned as Edward IV), on 4 March 1461.

Unlike Edward II and Richard II he escaped death and thus was a rallying point for Edward IV's opponents, to the extent that Henry was restored to his throne in October 1470—the first king since the Norman Conquest to have two reigns. In 1471, when Edward returned and crushed his opponents with a new ruthlessness, Henry was put to death in the Tower of London on Edward's order (21 May). But the manner of his death made him a political martyr, and when his nephew Henry Tudor seized the crown in 1485, as Henry VII, Tudor propagandists exploited Henry VI's reputation as a martyred innocent, unjustly deposed by the usurping Yorkists, a myth designed to further Tudor claims to the throne. Henry VII sought to have him canonized, and only Henry VIII's break with Rome brought the process to a halt. Today the Henry VI Society keeps alive Henry's memory as a deeply wronged monarch.

The tragedy of Henry VI is matched by his disastrous rule. Shakespeare's portrayal of him, not as the central figure of his reign but as the passive victim of forces beyond his control, is not completely fictional. Generally acceptable arrangements were made for the government of England and English France after Henry V died. The baby king was put in the charge of relatives and respected soldiers, with Queen Catherine standing at his side until ca. 1431. He was bright and healthy, but tensions between his uncles—especially Henry V's brothers, John duke of Bedford (d. 1435) and Humphrey duke of Gloucester (d. 1447), and his great-uncle Henry Beaufort, cardinal-bishop of Winchester (d. 1447)—were disruptive for the realm and unsettling for Henry. These divisions were reflected in attitudes to the growing military crisis in France, precipitated by Joan of Arc's victories (1428–30), and they were not removed by Henry's coronation in Paris (December 1431).

The king was carefully educated in "good manners, letters, languages, courtesy, and nurture"; he had an instructive library and an interest in history, religion, and education (reflected, for example, in his fascination with King Alfred). The most notable result was the founding of Eton College and King's College, Cambridge. But successful kingship demanded more than sound education and moral precept. As he emerged from his minority (ca. 1436), he seemed naive, trusting, and without a warrior's instincts. He governed increasingly by faction, based in his household, and he sought an end to the French war in which his father and the nobles made their reputations and fortunes. While Cardinal Beaufort and William de la Pole, earl of Suffolk, were his mentors, others, like the duke of Gloucester, were alienated.

The war and the "dual monarchy" of England and Lancastrian France stretched England's resources, and Henry tried radical ways to arrange peace, including releasing Charles, duke of Orléans (captured at Agincourt, 1415), marrying Margaret of Anjou (1445), and surrendering Maine. These were unpopular policies, and his commitment to Edmund Beaufort as chief adviser, after he had surrendered Normandy (1450), was resented by nobles, parliament, and soldiers.

The events of 1450—when Suffolk was murdered, the southeast rebelled under Jack Cade, and the duke of York returned menacingly from Ireland—were a severe crisis. Henry's mental collapse (August 1453) caused confusion in government and worsened relations between the court and York; the country was brought to the brink of civil war.

At St. Albans (May 1455) Henry was wounded in a confrontation with York, and thereafter Queen Margaret controlled both king and government. In July 1460 Henry was captured at Northampton by York's allies, the earls of Salisbury and Warwick, and forced to accept York as his heir. But when Warwick was himself defeated at St. Albans (February 1461), Henry was reunited with his queen and their only son, Edward, and fled to the north.

Captured in the north in 1465, he was imprisoned until Edward IV's own difficulties allowed Henry's ineffectual restoration (the "readeption" of October 1470). Nemesis came when his son was killed and his queen captured by Edward at Tewkesbury (May 1471); the pathetic monarch was killed shortly afterward. As a king Henry VI was incompetent rather than malevolent; though with laudable intentions and qualities admirable in a private person, he lacked the practical and political abilities to be a successful ruler.

Ralph A. Griffiths

Bibliography

Allmand, C.T. *Lancastrian Normandy, 1415–1450: The History of a Medieval Occupation.* Oxford: Clarendon, 1983 [for the French wars of the day]; Griffiths, Ralph A. *The Reign of King Henry VI: The Exercise of Royal Authority, 1422–1461.* London: Benn, 1981 [major modern study of the reign]; Harriss, G.L. *Cardinal Beaufort: A Study of the Lancastrian Ascendancy and Decline.* Oxford: Clarendon, 1988; Johnson, P.A. *Duke Richard of York, 1411–1460.* Oxford: Clarendon, 1988 [this and Harriss's are the authoritative biographical and political studies]; Vickers, Kenneth H. *Humphrey, Duke of Gloucester.* London: Constable, 1907; Wolffe, Bertram P. *Henry VI.* London: Eyre Methuen, 1981.

See also Beaufort Family; Bedford, John Duke of; Cade's Rebellion; Charles of Orléans; Edward IV; Eton; Henry V; Henry VII; Wars of the Roses

Henry VII (1457–1509; r. 1485–1509)

Henry had two links with the house of Lancaster. His father, Edmund Tudor, was the son of a Welsh squire and Catherine of Valois, Henry V's widow. His mother, Margaret Beaufort, was a descendant of John of Gaunt.

Finding favor at the court of Henry VI, the Tudors sought refuge in Brittany after the return of Edward IV in 1471. Styling himself earl of Richmond, Henry cannot have seemed a serious threat to the Yorkist monarchy, but his prospects were transformed in 1483 when in rebellion against Richard III he forged an alliance between Lancastrian diehards and men loyal to Edward IV's children. In 1485 this coalition was successful, overthrowing Richard at Bosworth Field (22 August), establishing Henry VII on the throne, and securing the union of the Roses through his marriage to Elizabeth of York, Edward IV's daughter.

The establishment of the Tudor dynasty was Henry VII's main achievement. For the first few years his regime was precarious, but with the birth of Prince Arthur (1486) and the defeat of the Lambert Simnel rising (1487) it could be seen to be putting down roots. The king, however, had cause to be anxious until the end. The Yorkist imposter Perkin Warbeck proved troublesome until his capture and execution in 1499, and the death of Henry's heir in 1502 was a tragic blow. All depended on his second son, the future Henry VIII, who succeeded him peaceably in 1509.

Henry VII was an astute ruler, well schooled by his exile. His rule was characterized by caution and calculation and by a reliance on a select circle of peers, bishops, and knights, many of whom he had learned to trust as fellow exiles. His government was far from novel in terms of personnel and policies; continuities with Edward IV's reign are striking. In essence his rule amounted to a reinvigoration of personal monarchy through the council, household, and chamber. In his strengthening of the crown and disciplining of the nobility he was favored by circumstances. The civil wars and difficult times under Richard III had weakened the aristocracy, giving the crown new scope for a broader power base in the political nation.

Henry is often remembered as a parsimonious accountant-king. In his early years he was not ungenerous, and lavish spending on pageantry and building projects indicates that he knew the importance of princely munificence. He also knew that money was power, and he used every means to strengthen the crown financially. Throughout his reign he imposed fines on recalcitrant subjects, and in his last years few great subjects were not ensnared in bonds for good behavior. In the last decade of his reign he was generally felt to be miserly and rapacious; his death in 1509 was a relief to many of his subjects.

Henry VII's reign was a time of economic and cultural revival in northwest Europe, and under him England shared in this general vitality. He took a prominent part in the emerging concept of Europe as a group of nation-states, led by the more visible "new monarchs," and was responsible for some striking diplomatic and trading initiatives, the most celebrated being the Treaty of Medina del Campo (1489) with Spain and his sponsorship of the Atlantic voyages of the Cabot brothers. England was ever more open to European cultural influence, Italian as well as French and Netherlandish. Henry invited the Italian humanist Polydore Vergil to write the *Historia anglica,* the best account of his reign. The Florentine artist Pietro Torrigiano executed the fine effigy under which he came to rest in his own chapel in Westminster Abbey.

Michael J. Bennett

Bibliography

Chrimes, Stanley B. *Henry VII.* London: Eyre Methuen, 1972; Grant, A. *Henry VII: The Importance of His Reign in English History.* London: Methuen, 1985.

See also Beaufort Family; Edward IV; Richard III; Wars of the Roses

Henry of Blois Plaques

The Henry of Blois Plaques (London, British Museum MLA.52, 3–27,1), made before 1171, are two semicircular, concave, copper-alloy plaques (diameter 7.01, 7.05 inches), forged, engraved, gilded, and enameled in the *champlevé* technique (fig. 72). One shows two bust-length angels, one holding a chalice, emerging from clouds and swinging censers. The inscription around the curved edge reads:

> The aforementioned slave shapes gifts pleasing to God. May the angel take the giver to heaven after his gifts, but not just yet, lest England groan for it, since on him it depends for peace and war. (Stratford 1983)

The other has a kneeling, bearded, and tonsured figure holding a crosier and proffering a rectangular object. An inscription identifies the donor as Bishop Henry. The border inscription reads:

> Art comes before gold and gems, the author before everything. Henry, alive in bronze, gives gifts to God. Henry, whose fame commends him to men, whose character commends him to the heavens, a man equal in mind to the Muses and in eloquence higher than Marcus (that is Cicero). (Stratford 1983)

Once believed to be English, the plaques are now accepted on the strength of stylistic and technical comparisons with mid-12th-century continental manuscripts and enamels as Mosan workmanship (that is, originally from the Meuse Valley), possibly produced in England. Made for Henry of Blois between 1129, when he became bishop of Winchester, and his death in 1171, they originally belonged with a group of now lost plaques. Thus the two surviving inscriptions should not be read continuously. Traditionally Henry was thought to be clasping the shrine of St. Swithun. No document, however, specifically mentions his enrichment of this Winchester shrine, making it more likely that he offers an altar, which could have been commissioned by Henry for any English house. The two surviving plaques were perhaps attached to such an altar or possibly occupied the top and bottom terminals of an associated altar cross. They bear testimony to the close links between a prestigious English patron and a Mosan goldsmith during the mid-12th century.

Sally Dormer

Bibliography

Haney, Kristine Edmondsen. "Some Mosan Sources for the Henry of Blois Enamels." *Burlington Magazine* 34 (1982): 220–30; Stratford, Neil. "The 'Henry of Blois Plaques' in the British Museum." *British Archaeological*

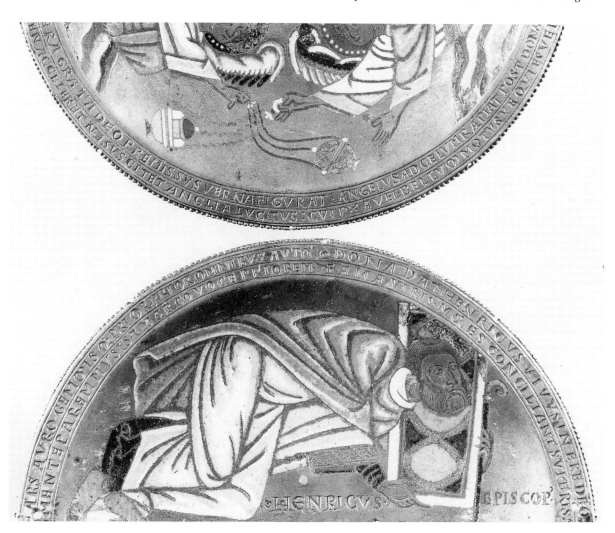

Fig. 72. Henry of Blois Plaques (London, British Museum MLA 52, 3–27,1). Courtesy of the Trustees of the British Museum, London.

Association Conference 6 (1980): 28–37; Stratford, Neil. *Medieval Enamels: Masterpieces from the Keir Collection.* London: British Museum, 1983; Stratford, Neil. *Catalogue of Medieval Enamels in the British Museum.* Vol. 2: *Northern Romanesque Enamels.* London: British Museum, 1993, cat. nos. 1–2; Zarnecki, George, Janet Holt, and Tristram Holland, eds. *English Romanesque Art 1066–1200.* London: Weidenfeld & Nicolson, 1984, pp. 261–62 [cat. no. 277a–b, by Neil Stratford].

See also Metalwork and Enamels, Romanesque

Henry of Lancaster (ca. 1310–1361)

Son of Henry earl of Lancaster; second cousin and trusted adviser of Edward III; created duke of Lancaster in 1351. Henry was renowned throughout Europe for his military prowess, diplomatic skill, chivalry, and piety. His extensive estates descended through his younger daughter, Blanche, to her husband, John of Gaunt.

In 1354 Henry wrote a religious allegory, the *Livre de seyntz medicines,* which survives in two manuscripts and a fragment. Noteworthy for its lay authorship and relative originality, the book offers frequent glimpses into contemporary aristocratic life, from war and hunting to flirtation, feasting, and popular medicine.

M. Teresa Tavormina

Bibliography

Arnould, E.J., ed. *Le livre de seyntz medicines.* ANTS 2. Oxford: Blackwell, 1940; Fowler, Kenneth. *The King's Lieutenant: Henry of Grosmont, First Duke of Lancaster 1310–1361.* London: Elek, 1969.

See also Anglo-Norman Literature; Chivalry; Diplomacy; Dukes; Edward III; Lancaster, Duchy of; Lancaster, John Duke of; Literacy; Medicine; Religious Allegories; Virtues and Vices, Books of

Henryson, Robert (ca. 1425/35–1505)

Scottish poet. Although Robert Henryson was perhaps the greatest poet writing in English during the 15th century (his dialect was Middle Scots), little is known about his life. The only sure information is Dunbar's brief reference in "Timor Mortis Conturbat Me," amid mention of other dead Scots writers, to a "Maister Robert Henrisoun" of Dunfermline. The name is a common one, but a Master Robert Henryson, who may be the poet, is listed at the University of Glasgow in 1462 and as a witness to three deeds in Dunfermline during 1477–78. Many early manuscripts and prints refer to him as schoolmaster at Dunfermline, an important royal and monastic town. In unpublished notes to his 17th-century Latin translation of Henryson's *Testament* (and Chaucer's *Troilus*) Sir Francis Kynaston tells a humorous if dubious anecdote about the poet's death, though he also perceptively notes his wit, learning, and literary skill. It seems likely that Henryson was born about 1425, though some would say a decade later; from Dunbar's poem we know he must have been dead by 1505.

Perhaps a notary as well as a schoolmaster, Henryson does not seem to have held ecclesiastical office.

The three major works in the canon—the *Fables, Testament of Cresseid,* and *Orpheus and Eurydice*—are undoubtedly by Henryson, though we have no sure idea of their dates or order of composition. Some of the dozen or so short poems usually attributed to him are more doubtful. The textual tradition of Henryson's poetry is almost as uncertain as his biography. Most of the works are found in witnesses that date from at least 75 years after the presumed time of his death. Moreover the printed editions of his works (many of which have been lost or exist only in unique copies) are generally more authoritative than the surviving manuscripts, which were often copied from prints. Henryson's influence on later Scots literature was not great, and he was so obscure to English readers that his *Testament* was included in editions of Chaucer throughout the 16th century as the conclusion to *Troilus and Criseyde.* Its true authorship was not recognized in print until Urry's edition of Chaucer in 1721.

As is also true for Dunbar, Henryson's short poems are written in various genres and meters, which he handles with skill. They range from "Sum Practysis of Medecyne," an extravagant, and often gross, rhymed alliterative burlesque of quack prescriptions (supporting the belief of some that Henryson had studied medicine), to the devout lyricism of "The Annunciation." Most of the short poems deal with serious Christian themes, especially the uncertainties of this world. "The Ressoning betuix Aige and Yowth" and "The Ressoning betuix Deth and Man" are vigorous *memento mori* debates about the inevitable passing of earthly joy, which is also the subject of three powerful meditations: "The Praise of Age," "The Thre Deid Pollis," and "The Abbey Walk." A more humorous treatment of temporality is found in the superb and original *pastourelle* "Robene and Makyne," in which a shepherd returns a maiden's love too late. "The Bludy Serk" and "The Garmont of Gud Ladeis" are chivalric moral allegories in ballad stanzas, more vividly told than their probable sources. The metrically complex "Ane Prayer for the Pest" is a more topical poem whose sense of human powerlessness before the divine is also found in the poet's longer works. Like "Sum Practysis of Medecyne" "Against Hasty Credence" is fierce social satire (against flatterers) that may derive from Lydgate. Another secular satire, "The Want of Wyse Men," is probably not by Henryson.

The least well regarded of Henryson's major works is *Orpheus and Eurydice,* a 414-line narrative in rime royal (with Orpheus's complaint in ten-line stanzas) followed by a 218-line *moralitas,* or moral, in heroic couplets. The poem tells the familiar story of how Orpheus's beloved wife, Eurydice, fleeing the attempted rape by Aristaeus, was bitten by a serpent and taken to Hades, where she was finally discovered by her grief-stricken husband. By his harp playing Orpheus made the infernal gods promise that she could leave with him, on condition that he not look back. Moved by affection, he did so look on the return journey and so lost her forever. The *moralitas* identifies Orpheus as the intellectual part of the soul, Eurydice as the affectionate part, and Aristaeus as virtue.

The narrative in *Orpheus and Eurydice* is based on Boethius's *Consolation of Philosophy* (book 3, meter 12), whereas the *moralitas* and some of the narrative details are based on Nicholas Trevet's commentary on the *Consolation,* itself derived from the commentary of William of Conches. The poem reveals Henryson's interest in human limitation, his poetic skill (especially in Orpheus's complaint), and perhaps even his allegorical audacity (as in his not unprecedented identification of the rapist with virtue). Very different from the ME romance *Sir Orfeo,* Henryson's poem is a learned, rhetorically sophisticated allegory that is also a defense of poetry. Like Boethius Henryson allows no explicitly Christian reference in this deeply Christian work.

The *Testament of Cresseid,* 79 rime royal stanzas plus Cresseid's complaint in seven nine-line stanzas, is Henryson's acknowledged masterpiece. On a cold night in Lent the poet reads Chaucer's account of Cresseid before turning to another book about her wretched end. Having become a prostitute after her rejection by Diomede, Cresseid is then punished with leprosy by the planetary gods for her blasphemy in blaming her misfortune on Venus and Cupid. As she is begging one day with other lepers, Cresseid encounters Troilus. Though neither recognizes the other, Troilus gives her alms in memory of his lost love. After learning the identity of her benefactor Cresseid praises Troilus, blames only herself for what happened, makes her final testament, and dies.

Although the *Testament* is strikingly original, it obviously draws on *Troilus and Criseyde,* as well as on other Chaucerian poems. The formal descriptions of the planetary gods are based on traditional information, though the specific influence of Chaucer, Lydgate, Boccaccio, and the mythography of Pseudo-Albricus has been claimed. The relationship of the *Testament* to the somewhat similar story in the *Spektakle of Luf* (1492) is unclear. The poem reveals a detailed knowledge of medicine (in the account of Cresseid's leprosy), law, and meteorology. Henryson brilliantly adapts a number of literary topoi to his own purposes, including a seasonal opening, citation of a famous source, trial scene, complaint, and testament.

In part because its tone and structure are so deliberately different the *Testament* is the worthiest successor to *Troilus and Criseyde.* Henryson not only understands but is also able to reproduce such diverse Chaucerian achievements as consistent but developing characterization, a believable pagan setting, deliberately obtuse narration, and rime royal (in contrast to the metrical ineptness of the English Chaucerians). Henryson is also virtually alone with Chaucer in his sympathy for Cresseid. Although some modern critics judge the *Testament* to be pessimistic or unforgiving, Henryson's Cresseid, for all her physical suffering, grows throughout the poem until, though still a pagan, she fully accepts responsibility for her own actions. Because the *Testament* was printed as the conclusion to *Troilus* beginning with Thynne's 1532 edition of Chaucer, most English Renaissance portraits of Cresseid (including Shakespeare's) depend as much on Henryson as on Chaucer.

Henryson's most complex work is the *Fables,* which consists of a prologue and thirteen beast fables, each with a narrative followed by a *moralitas,* for a total of 2,975 lines, mostly in rime royal stanzas. Beast fables in the Middle Ages were not only elementary school texts but also an important literary genre. The source for Henryson's prologue and seven of the fables is the popular 12th-century Latin *Romulus* collection now attributed to Walter the Englishman. Henryson also drew on Chaucer's *Nun's Priest's Tale* for "The Cock and the Fox" and, directly or indirectly, on Petrus Alfonsi for "The Fox, the Wolf, and the Husbandman." For some of the other tales he may have used other Latin fable collections, some version of the *Roman de Renart,* Lydgate's fables, Caxton's *Reynard* and *Aesop,* and the French Isopets, though specific borrowings are much debated.

Older critics saw the *Fables* as examples of social realism or rustic humor, but, without denying the political seriousness of these works or their insight into Scottish life, critics have increasingly appreciated their strictly literary achievement in recent years. The order of the fables seems carefully designed, and the wit of "The Cock and the Fox" at moments surpasses even its Chaucerian model. The prologue is a sophisticated discussion of the complex relationship between story and lesson, which is then demonstrated in the fables themselves. Henryson's moralities are not dull or dutiful but have an intricate, often ironic, connection with the preceding narratives and constantly challenge the reader. The pessimism with which the natural world is portrayed in the fables is less a questioning of divine justice than a passionate statement of our need for God's mercy. Henryson the man remains a mysterious figure, but his poetry, which is still too often treated as primarily regional, is the most substantial work in English verse between Chaucer and Spenser.

C. David Benson

Bibliography

PRIMARY

Bawcutt, P., and Felicity Riddy, eds. *Selected Poems of Henryson and Dunbar.* Edinburgh: Scottish Academic Press, 1992; Fox, Denton, ed. *The Poems of Robert Henryson.* Oxford: Clarendon, 1981.

SECONDARY

New *CBEL* 1:658–60; *Manual* 4:965–88, 1137–80; Gray, Douglas. *Robert Henryson.* Leiden: Brill, 1979; Gros Louis, Kenneth R.R. "Robert Henryson's *Orpheus and Eurydice* and the Orpheus Traditions of the Middle Ages." *Speculum* 41 (1966): 643–55; Jamieson, I.W.A. "The Minor Poems of Robert Henryson." *Studies in Scottish Literature* 9 (1971): 125–47; Kindrick, Robert. *Robert Henryson.* Boston: Twayne, 1979; Scheps, Walter, and J. Anna Looney. *Middle Scots Poets: A Reference Guide.* Boston: Hall, 1986, pp. 53–117; Spearing, A.C. "The *Testament of Cresseid* and the 'High Concise Style.'" *Speculum* 37 (1962): 208–25. Repr. in *Criticism and Medieval Poetry.* 2d ed. New York: Barnes & Noble, 1972, pp. 157–92; Yeager, R.F., ed. *Fifteenth-Century Studies: Recent Essays.* Hamden: Archon, 1984, pp. 65–92, 215–35, 275–81 [bibliographic and interpretive essays on Henryson].

See also Beast Epic and Fable; Boethius; Chaucer; Douglas; Dunbar; Exemplum; Scottish Literature, Early

Heptarchy

The word is used in Anglo-Saxon history to refer to the seven kingdoms of Kent, Sussex, Essex, East Anglia, Wessex, Mercia, and Northumbria. The period in which these seven kingdoms were the basis of political organization is between the 6th and the 9th century. "Heptarchy" was already in use before the Scandinavian settlement of the 11th century, but it was given more general currency by such 16th-century writers as William Camden. Essentially it reflects the information provided by Bede for the kingdoms of the 7th and early 8th centuries. Popular in the writings of 19th-century historians, it has now fallen out of favor.

The term is misleading; it tends to imply that all seven kingdoms were comparable in structure, development, and importance. In fact the differences among them are immense, and it has recently been suggested on the grounds of political importance that it would be better to characterize the period before ca. 800 as that of a Pentarchy: Northumbria, Mercia, East Anglia, Kent, and Wessex; and from the mid-9th century, a Tetrarchy, omitting Kent on account of its absorption by Wessex.

Certainly after the end of the 7th century neither Sussex nor Essex was a force to be reckoned with. Sussex, of some importance in origin legends recorded by Bede and the Anglo-Saxon Chronicle, was treated by Offa of Mercia as a subkingdom, ruled by *duces* and never to regain its independence. Similarly, Essex lost power to the Mercians in the 8th century; in the early 9th it was subordinate to Wessex. There is mention of an East Saxon king after 825, but it is unclear whether the kingdom survived until the Viking conquest of East Anglia.

The kingdoms of the Heptarchy were therefore never equal in importance, although at one moment or another each exercised some dominance over its neighbors. The chief evidence for this is again in Bede, in his famous list of seven kings who exerted authority over the other regions south of the Humber. The kings are Ælle of Sussex, Cælin of Wessex, Æthelberht of Kent, Rædwald of East Anglia, and Edwin, Oswald, and Oswiu of Northumbria. In addition Mercian dominance can be detected in Bede's narrative and more explicitly in the 8th-century charters of Æthelbald and Offa. A 7th-century charter also reveals a brief period of East Saxon overlordship in Kent, during the reign of Sigehere in the 680s.

The question of overlordship draws attention to another aspect of the political structure of the pre-Viking period obscured by the term "Heptarchy." Although the exercise of authority over neighboring kingdoms was an important element, each kingdom was also an overlordship, made up of individual regions, or *provinciae,* some of them apparently ruled by kings or subkings but subordinate to central authority or authorities.

These subkingdoms could be powerful in their own right and not much less significant than the smaller kingdoms of the Heptarchy. The most important subkingdoms are Deira and Bernicia, the two districts that together made up Northumbria. In the late 6th and early 7th centuries both had their own royal dynasties, in competition for overall control of a combined Northumbrian kingdom. Later there were occasions when each province had its own king, one usually being subordinate to the other. In addition, by the end of the 7th century, Northumbria included at least two British kingdoms, Elmet and Rheged.

Mercia was also made up of a number of provinces, some of which, like that of the Hwicce, had royal dynasties. The provincial structure of Mercia is seen in the Tribal Hidage, which lists at least some of the subordinate units. Wessex also included provinces, and Bede and Stephanus describe the takeover of Jutish kingdoms in Hampshire and the Isle of Wight, the last being an identifiable unit in the Tribal Hidage. In East Anglia, Essex, and Kent references to joint-kingship apparently provide further indications of the existence of separate provinces within the individual kingdoms.

The term "Heptarchy" therefore does not do justice to the complexity of the structure of pre-Viking England, nor does it allow for the considerable changes between the establishment of the Anglo-Saxons and the settlement of the Vikings. It implies that the seven kingdoms described by Bede were all created at roughly the same period (late 5th or 6th century) and that thereafter they constituted the backbone of English political geography.

In fact the origins of the kingdoms are obscure. Genealogies and regnal lists suggest that the ruling dynasties were established during the 6th century, but the origin legends of the Anglo-Saxon kingdoms, as preserved in such sources as the Anglo-Saxon Chronicle, need to be treated with the utmost care. Moreover it is clear from Bede that the process of state formation was still under way in the 7th century.

This is most apparent with Wessex. Not only does Bede describe the conquest of the Isle of Wight and the Jutish territories on the mainland, but he also states that the West Saxons had once been called the *Geuisse,* and he refers to them by this term in his account of the period before 688. Thus the kingdom of the West Saxons was being defined as such only in the late 7th century. Similar problems of nomenclature can be seen in references to the Northumbrians and the *Humbrenses,* suggesting that the kingdoms were still developing through the 7th century.

Thus, although at a superficial level "Heptarchy" is a convenient shorthand to describe the political situation revealed in Bede's *Ecclesiastical History,* where seven kingdoms seem to emerge as being of importance, the term is misleading. It fossilizes a depiction that may have been relatively accurate when Bede wrote but does an injustice to the gradual evolution of the political structure of the 7th and 8th centuries and to the complex pattern of subkingdoms and overlordships that formed the basis of that structure.

Ian N. Wood

Bibliography

Bassett, Steven, ed. *The Origins of Anglo-Saxon Kingdoms.* Leicester: Leicester University Press, 1989 [covers most of the kingdoms]; Howe, Nicholas. *Migration and Mythmaking in Anglo-Saxon England.* New Haven: Yale University Press, 1989; Kirby, D.P. *The Earliest English Kings.* London: Unwin Hyman, 1991; Stenton, F.M. *Anglo-Saxon England.* Oxford History of England 2. 3d ed. Oxford: Clarendon, 1971 [the kingdoms of the Heptarchy described here, as in all other major accounts of Anglo-Saxon England]; Yorke, Barbara. *Kings and Kingdoms of Early Anglo-Saxon England.* London: Seaby, 1990.

See also Æthelberht; Anglo-Saxon Invasions; Bede; Bretwald; Offa; Penda; Tribal Hidage

Heralds and Heraldry

The term "herald" was applied by 1170, in France, to men who specialized in matters associated with tournaments. Heralds were at first associated with minstrels and may be seen as an offshoot of that profession.

From at least 1272, and probably from as far back as 1194, English heralds were sent forth with some regularity to proclaim tournaments at royal and baronial courts, both in England and on the Continent. They would return with the replies of those challenged and then accompany their master to the place appointed. At the tournament they would announce the combatants as they entered the field.

From the heralds' need to recognize knights in the contests developed a special interest in the cognizances, or "arms," whose use (on shields, pennons, and banners) became general among knights between 1160 and 1220. By 1275 some English heralds were keeping books or rolls of arms to assist them in remembering the hundreds of distinct but often similar arms they encountered.

Thus "heraldry" came to be used more narrowly to designate the arcane "science" related to the design, description, analysis, and recognition of shields or coats of arms. This knowledge was gradually extended to the crest borne atop the helmet, to headgear of dignity (crowns, coronets, etc.), to badges worn by servants (ca. 1360), and to insignia of the Order of the Garter and other knightly orders.

By 1276 England was divided at the Trent into two territories, or "marches of arms," each with a king of arms. Within his march each king oversaw matters touching tournaments, armorial bearings, and chivalry. Apprentice heralds were called "pursuivants of arms," and by Edward III's time kings of arms, heralds, and pursuivants bore special styles of appointment: Norroy King of Arms (north of the Trent), Clarenceux King of Arms (south of the Trent), Windsor Herald, Hastings Pursuivant, etc.

From the 1330s heralds were entrusted with weighty diplomatic duties, though formal jurisdiction regarding duties and functions was loosely defined into the 15th century. Henry V created the office of Garter King of Arms, with precedence over the provincial kings. The kings of arms had the authority to visit the counties to determine who therein had the right to use armorial bearings and to record those arms that were legitimately borne. This ended the custom of assuming arms as men chose.

Within a few decades the officers of arms came to exercise the significant right to devise and grant armorial bearings, both to individuals and corporations—a right rarely seen outside England. On 2 March 1484 the principal members of the "office of arms" became incorporated as the College of Arms, with a building at Coldharbour in the City of London. Though Richard III's letter patent to create the college was revoked after his fall, the college was reconstituted and reendowed in 1555.

D'Arcy J.D. Boulton

Bibliography

Dennys, R. *Heraldry and the Heralds.* London: Cape, 1982; Wagner, Anthony Richard. *Heralds and Heraldry in the Middle Ages.* 2d ed. Oxford: Oxford University Press, 1956; Wagner, Anthony Richard. *The Heralds of England: A History of the Office and College of Arms.* London: HMSO, 1967; Woodcock, T., and J.M. Robinson. *The Oxford Guide to Heraldry.* Oxford: Oxford University Press, 1988.

See also Arms and Armor; Chivalry; Diplomacy; Minstrels

Hexham and Ripon

The Anglo-Saxon churches of St. Andrew's, Hexham, and St. Peter's, Ripon, are linked by the figure of St. Wilfrid. Wilfrid became abbot of Ripon in 660, bishop of Hexham 686–91 and again from 702 to his death in 709, and was named bishop of York in 669. It was while he was bishop of York that he built the churches at Hexham and Ripon. All that remains of the Wilfridian fabric of both churches are their crypts (fig. 73). There is also a small pre-Conquest apsidal chapel, possibly a mausoleum, east of St. Andrew's at Hexham.

Hexham was a typically Anglo-Saxon monastic site housing at least two churches, St. Mary's and St. Andrew's. A church dedicated to St. Peter may also have been located nearby, although the evidence for its existence is circumstantial (Cambridge and Williams, 1995). The church of St. Andrew was described by Wilfrid's contemporary biographer, Eddius, as multistoried. In the 12th century Richard of Hexham wrote that the church was divided into three stories and that it was possible to walk around the interior on more than one level, suggesting an elevation consisting of nave, gallery, and clerestory. The present church dates mainly from the 12th and 13th centuries; the nave is modern (1908), although evidence of a late-medieval nave has been uncovered (Cambridge, 1979, 1980).

The crypt at Hexham was constructed of reused Roman stone and originally plastered and painted. The main chamber is approximately 14 feet by 18 feet and covered with a barrel vault. There are three niches with cavities for oil lamps sunk into the walls. The relics housed within the main chamber would have been viewed through a grille from the smaller

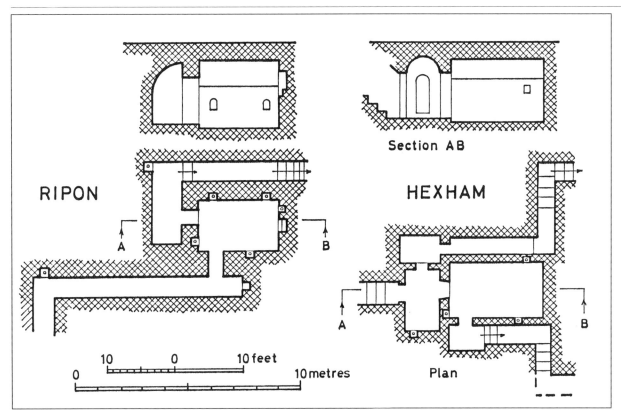

Fig. 73. The Anglo-Saxon crypts at Hexham and Ripon. After H.M. Taylor (1978), vol. 3. Reprinted with the permission of Cambridge University Press.

antechamber, which was approximately 9 feet by 5 feet. There are two approaches to the antechamber, the first via a long passage that leads from the exterior of the building down and along the north wall of the crypt and the second via a staircase that descends from the nave. While it is possible to enter and exit from both directions, it is most likely that movement was from the exterior, through the dark northern passage, into the light of the crypt, and on into the church. The symbolism of this movement from darkness into light would have appropriately mirrored the spiritual passage of the pilgrim. A third staircase to the south of the crypt was probably for use by the clergy but may also have provided an alternative exit for those not wishing to disturb proceedings in the church above.

The crypt at Ripon is similar in design to that at Hexham, though not quite so complex. The main chamber measures 11 feet 6 inches by 7 feet 6 inches and is covered by a barrel vault; the antechamber measures 12 feet 6 inches by 4 feet 6 inches and is covered by a quadrant vault. As at Hexham the main chamber contains recessed niches for oil lamps but also a large niche in the east wall probably for relics. At Ripon there are only two passages, one passing along the north wall of the crypt and leading into the antechamber, the second leading directly into the main chamber from the south. It is possible that one was for use by the clergy, the other for the congregation, but it is more likely that one was an entrance and the other an exit, as attempts to move back and forth through a single passage would have led to congestion. The more neatly worked out system of entrance and exit at Hexham may indicate that it represented a slightly later improvement of the Ripon plan.

The design of both crypts is unusual and has no exact parallels. Wilfrid traveled extensively on the Continent, but the crypts do not copy continental crypt designs. They may, however, be an eclectic and original combination of specific elements borrowed from traditional plans.

Catherine E. Karkov

Bibliography

Bailey, Richard N. "The Anglo-Saxon Church at Hexham." *Archaeologia Aeliana,* 5th ser. 4 (1976): 47–67; Bailey, Richard N. "St. Wilfrid, Ripon and Hexham." In *Studies in Insular Art and Archaeology,* ed. Robert T. Farrell and Catherine E. Karkov. Oxford, Ohio: American Early Medieval Studies, 1991, pp. 3–25; Cambridge, Eric. "C.C. Hodges and the Nave of Hexham Abbey." *Archaeologia Aeliana,* 5th ser. 7, 8 (1979, 1980): 158–68, 172–73; Cambridge, Eric, and Alan Williams. "Hexham Abbey: A Review of Recent Work and Its Implications." *Archaeologia Aeliana,* 5th ser. 23 (1995): 51–138; Fernie, Eric. *The Architecture of the Anglo-Saxons.* London: Batsford, 1983; Taylor, Harold M. *Anglo-Saxon Architecture.* Vol. 3. Cambridge: Cambridge University Press, 1978; Taylor, Harold M., and Joan Taylor. "Hexham" and "Ripon." In *Anglo-Saxon Architecture.* Cambridge: Cambridge University Press, 1965, 1:297–312 and 2:516–18.

See also Architecture, Anglo-Saxon; Ecclesiastical Architecture, Early Anglo-Saxon; Stonework as Ecclesiastical Ornament; Wilfrid; York and Ripon Minsters

Hides

The basic unit behind the term "hide" was the area of land sufficient to meet the needs of a single *familia,* or household. The Tribal Hidage (7th century, with 8th-century revisions), a tax levied on regions defined mainly in terms of old tribal units, assessed most of England south of the Humber in terms of hidage; 7,000 hides was regarded as appropriate for a substantial people, such as the Hwicce in the Severn Valley or the East Saxons, 300 or 600 hides for many small groups, especially in the Fenlands. Three hundred hides was later regarded as a reasonable endowment for a bishopric.

In early Anglo-Saxon times the term was not connected with exact measurements of area. Bede used the phrase "terra unius familiae" (later translated as "hide") freely. Drawing information presumably from a lost tribute list of a Northumbrian king, he described the Isle of Man as containing 300 such units, Anglesey 960. The two islands are of roughly the same size, but the fertility of Anglesey may account for the discrepancy. Bede's estimates rarely coincide with the Tribal Hidage, though both sources attribute 7,000 hides to the South Saxons.

The term "hide" was adapted for use in tribute collection and taxation and remained the basic unit for such activity for much of England throughout the Anglo-Saxon period. Kent was an exception; there the tax unit was the "sulung" (plowland) or double hide, divided into four "yokes." In much of the Danelaw the term "carucate" (again, plowland) took the place of the hide, and was normally divided, in Scandinavian fashion, into eight bovates. But for the Midlands, East Anglia, and most of the south the normal assessment units at the time of Domesday Book were the hide and its subdivision, the virgate or quarter-hide.

The hide was naturally closely associated with the amount of arable under the plow. For the eastern shires certainly, and probably for much of England, 120 acres was regarded as the proper arable constituent of a hide, with a virgate of 30 acres as the normal holding of a free peasant operating in an open-field system. In parts of Wessex there is evidence of a small hide of 40 acres. Land varied in quality. Hides and virgates and their cognates were primarily part of the sophisticated system of taxation in late Anglo-Saxon England, when the normal imposition of general tax was levied at the rate of two shillings per hide.

H.R. Loyn

Bibliography

Blair, Peter Hunter. *An Introduction to Anglo-Saxon England.* 2d ed. Cambridge: Cambridge University Press, 1977; Loyn, H.R. *Anglo-Saxon England and the Norman Conquest.* 2d ed. London: Longmans, 1991; Williams, Ann, ed. *Domesday Book: Studies.* London: Alecto Historical Editions, 1987.

See also Agriculture; Local Government; Manorialism; Tribal Hidage

High Crosses

The high cross, or freestanding stone cross, is a monument type characteristic of the Anglo-Saxon period. The function of the high cross was primarily either commemorative or didactic, though crosses could also be used for the more mundane purposes of marking boundaries or consecrating ecclesiastical sites. Frequently the function of a particular cross is revealed by its inscription. The didactic function of the Ruthwell (Dumfriesshire) Cross (figs. 111–14: see RUTHWELL CROSS) is emphasized by its inscriptions, all of which deal with biblical events and many of which relate to contemporary liturgical texts; while the memorial function of the Urswick 1 (Lancashire) Cross is indicated by its inscription: "Tunwini erected this cross in memory of his *bæurnæ* (son or lord) Torhtred. Pray for his soul." Often, whatever its specific function, the cross itself is conceived as a tree of life, with the use of ornament (e.g., the vinescroll at Hexham in Northumberland or the flowering cross at Kirkby Wharfe in Yorkshire North Riding) or inscriptions (the runic poem at Ruthwell or the personal names included between panels of foliate ornament at Bewcastle) underscoring this symbolism.

The origins and development of the high cross are subjects of controversy. Some scholars see it as developing in Ireland or western Scotland and spreading into England, while others see it as originating in the Anglo-Saxon areas and spreading west. There is also no consensus on whether the stone crosses evolved from cross-slabs carved in shallow relief

Fig. 74. Bewcastle Cross, west face. John the Baptist with the Agnus Dei, Christ over the beasts, runic inscription, nobleman with bird. Courtesy of George Hardin Brown.

or from freestanding wooden crosses, though the latter has become the more widely accepted scenario.

The form of the cross-shaft may be either angular or round, while the form of the cross-head may take a great variety of shapes. Carved ornament also varies greatly. Some crosses received no ornament at all; others were decorated with elaborate patterns of interlace (Irton 1, Cumbria), vinescroll (Hexham), or animal ornament (York, Minster 2). The more elaborate crosses, such as the 8th-century Ruthwell and Bewcastle (Cumberland) crosses (fig. 74) or the 10th-century Gosforth (Cumberland) Cross (figs. 18–19: see ART, VIKING AGE), display complex iconographic programs whose exact meanings are still the topic of debate.

Styles and motifs vary chronologically and regionally. In the 8th century a classicizing early Christian influence is evident in Northumbrian vinescroll ornament; stylistically in the deeply carved monumental figures of Ruthwell or Bewcastle; and iconographically in the complex program of biblical motifs on such crosses as Ruthwell. Little Carolingian influence can be detected on the Anglo-Saxon crosses, although the classicizing style of the Reculver fragments and a number of the motifs on the Wolverhampton Pillar have been cited as having late-antique or Carolingian parallels. For the most part Carolingian influence on stone sculpture was indirect, via the 10th-century Winchester style of manuscript illumination. Scandinavian influence, on the other hand, is widespread and enduring. Scandinavian styles and motifs become prominent in the late 9th century, particularly in the north of England, and remain popular through to the Norman Conquest. The Viking period also sees a marked change from ecclesiastical to secular patronage.

The complexity of regional styles of sculpture during the Anglo-Saxon period is only now beginning to be appreciated, thanks to the work of the *Corpus of Anglo-Saxon Stone Sculpture*. This project promises to shed much-needed light not only on the origins of freestanding stone sculpture in Anglo-Saxon England but also on the development of forms, styles, and iconography throughout the Anglo-Saxon period.

Catherine E. Karkov

Bibliography

Collingwood, W.G. *Northumbrian Crosses of the Pre-Norman Age*. London: Faber & Gwyer, 1927. Repr. Lampeter: Llanarch Enterprises, 1989; Cramp, Rosemary. *Corpus of Anglo-Saxon Stone Sculpture in England*. Vol. 1: *County Durham and Northumberland*. London: Oxford University Press, 1984; Cramp, Rosemary, and Richard N. Bailey. *Corpus of Anglo-Saxon Stone Sculpture*. Vol. 2: *Cumberland, Westmorland and Lancashire North-of-the-Sands*. London: Oxford University Press, 1988; Lang, James. *Corpus of Anglo-Saxon Stone Sculpture*. Vol. 3: *York and Eastern Yorkshire*. London: Oxford University Press, 1991; Wilson, David M. *Anglo-Saxon Art: From the Seventh Century to the Norman Conquest*. London: Thames & Hudson, 1984; comprehensive bibliographies for individual monuments can be found in the relevant *Corpus* volumes.

See also Art, Anglo-Saxon; Art, Viking; Ruthwell Cross

Hild (ca. 614–680)

Hild (or Hilda) lived a dual life: 33 years as a princess, then 33 years as an abbess and teacher. Bede's *Ecclesiastical History* tells most of what we know about her. She was born ca. 614, posthumously and in exile, to Princess Breguswith and Hereric, a nephew of King Edwin (616–33). As a child she shared exile in East Anglia at the court of King Rædwald with her great-uncle Edwin. After Edwin regained his kingdom in 617, Hild returned with him to Northumbria. She may have observed his famous council in 627, after which she received baptism with him and 12,000 of his subjects on 12 April after religious instruction from Bishop Paulinus (*Ecclesiastical History* 2.13–14). When Edwin died in 633, Hild returned to exile in East Anglia with her mother, Breguswith, and her sister, Hereswith, who later married King Æthelhere there. In 647 Hild, probably a widow, became a nun and the following year founded the nunnery at Wear. In 649 she became abbess of Hartlepool and in 657 abbess of the double monastery at Whitby (OE *Streoneshealch*).

In 664 she hosted the Synod of Whitby, where King Oswiu of Northumbria decided that the English church would follow Roman practice rather than Irish (*Ecclesiastical History* 3.25). Her side lost, and she observed Roman rules thereafter. During her reign at Whitby she promoted the training of missionaries and scholars. Five of her students became bishops: Ætla, of Dorchester; Bosa, of Deira and York; John, of Hexham and York; Oftfor, of Worcester; and Wilfrid II, of York. Hearing Cædmon sing his inspired Hymn, she recruited him into religious life and sponsored his career as a composer of religious verse, probably used for conversion and strengthening faith (*Ecclesiastical History* 4.24).

Hild suffered a long illness beginning in 674, dying on 17 November 680. One of the nuns of her monastery, Ælfflæd, King Oswiu's daughter, succeeded her as abbess, ruling with her mother, Eanflæd. Several nuns saw visions of Hild's death and ascent into heaven (*Ecclesiastical History* 4.23). Her remains were translated to Glastonbury in the 10th century.

Donald K. Fry

Bibliography

Colgrave, Bertram, and R.A.B. Mynors, eds. and trans. *Bede's Ecclesiastical History of the English People*. Oxford: Clarendon, 1969, pp. 404–21 and passim; Cross, J.E. "A Lost Life of Hilda of Whitby: The Evidence of the *Old English Martyrology*." *Acta* 5 (1979): 21–43; Fell, Christine E. "Hild, Abbess of Streoneshalch." In *Hagiography and Medieval Literature: A Symposium,* ed. Hans Bekker-Nielsen et al. Odense: Odense University Press, 1981, pp. 76–99; Hession, Ætheldreda. "St Hilda and St Etheldreda." In *Benedict's Disciples,* ed. D.H. Farmer. Leominster: Fowler Wright, 1980, pp. 70–85.

See also Bede; Cædmon; Conversion of the Anglo-Saxons; Monasticism; Nuns; Women in OE Literature

Hilton, Walter (d. 1396)

Mystical writer; a hermit probably until the mid-1380s, then an Augustinian canon at Thurgarton in Nottinghamshire. Probably to be identified with the bachelor of civil law recorded in Lincoln and Ely in the early 1370s; *inceptor* in canon law in the early 1380s. If he was an M.A. before proceeding to the study of law (which is not necessary), he would have been born in the early 1340s.

The chronology of Hilton's works is uncertain. Clark and Taylor have suggested that the Latin tract *De imagine peccati* was Hilton's earliest extant work, written soon after 1381–82. The letter *De utilitate et prerogativis religionis* (or *Epistola aurea*), written to encourage Adam Horsley in his decision to lay down civil office and enter the Carthusian order, was probably written shortly before 1387. The idea of the perversion of the human soul from an image of the divine Trinity into an image of sin is important particularly in the first of these pieces and in the first book of Hilton's most important work, the English *Scale of Perfection;* there are also similarities between *Scale* I and the *De utilitate* and his English letter *On the Mixed Life* that suggest that all four of these works were written in the mid-1380s. Hilton probably wrote his *De adoracione imaginum,* an anti-Wycliffite defense of the use of images (painting, sculpture, etc.) in worship, in the late 1380s.

The dating of Hilton's other writings is even less certain. These works include the English translations of *Eight Chapters on Perfection* by Lluis de Font, an Aragonese Franciscan contemporary of Hilton's at Cambridge, and the Pseudo-Bonaventuran *Stimulus amoris (The Pricking of Love* or *Goad of Love);* commentaries on the texts "Qui Habitat" (Ps. 90:1) and "Bonum Est" (Ps. 91:1); and *On Angels' Song,* a work on the dangers of seeking physical expression of mystical experience. The attribution to Hilton of a further English commentary on the "Benedictus" is unsure. Three other Latin treatises survive: the *Epistola de leccione, intencione, oracione, meditacione et aliis,* the *Epistola ad quemdam seculo renunciare volentem,* and *Quantum ad futura* (also known as "Firmissima crede"). Finally we should note that the second book of Hilton's *Scale of Perfection* probably marks the culmination of his thought and experience.

Because the two books of *The Scale of Perfection* were written as many as ten years apart, their relationship to each other has been a major focus of the discussion of Hilton's works. Prospective editors of the *Scale* have noted the presence of a long expository passage on the devotion to the name of Jesus (and two other similar passages) apparently added to the text of *Scale* I after it was already in circulation, as well as a number of smaller additions and rewordings, many of which appear to focus on devotion to the person of Christ, rather than the Trinity or the Godhead itself. All of these christocentric additions and alterations were added in the margins and on inserted scraps of paper in BL Harley 6579, on which all modern editions of the *Scale* to date have been based. Despite this widespread editorial practice the current consensus of scholars and textual critics is that the "Holy Name" passage and the passages similar to it were probably added by Hilton himself, whereas the "christocentric" additions were made by later scribes. The forthcoming EETS edition of the *Scale* will therefore base *Scale* I on a manuscript whose text predates both the "Holy Name" and the "christocentric" additions, as well as the writing of *Scale* II. The importance of this textual decision is that it renders invalid a good deal of earlier discussion of the "christocentricity" of Hilton's mysticism.

Probably the most important idea in Hilton's works is that of the human soul as an image of the divine Trinity, perverted into an image of sin: an idea that originates in Augustine's *De Trinitate* and is expanded upon by the Victorines and the early Franciscan writers. According to this trinitarian psychology the soul comprises the faculties of Memory (or Mind, as it was usually translated into ME), corresponding to the Father; Understanding (or Reason), corresponding to the Son; and Will, corresponding to the Holy Spirit. Through original sin, however, the soul has been perverted into the image of the seven deadly sins. Because the recently enclosed anchoress for whom Hilton wrote *Scale* I could not read and meditate on the Latin text of scripture, Hilton proposes for her an exercise of introspection aimed at discovering and extirpating each of these sins in herself.

Hilton's contemplative exercises for his anchoress correspondent go significantly beyond the meditation on the Passion of Christ that was normally enjoined upon women at that time, though he does briefly discuss such Passion meditations, immediately before proposing his more introspective exercises. This same concern with providing alternative modes of contemplation for nonmonastic or nonclerical audiences also informs his letter *On the Mixed Life,* whose opening sections echo those of *Scale* I. In this innovative treatise Hilton proposes a life of both action and contemplation to a man whose worldly activities and responsibilities do not allow him to retire from the world as a monk or hermit but who feels the same stirrings of devotion that they do.

In *Scale* II Hilton covers much of the same ground as in *Scale* I, with greater psychological and theological precision. Clark has suggested that at one point, at least, his intention was to express more carefully an idea for which he had been criticized (anonymously) in *The Cloud of Unknowing. Scale* II describes particularly the progress from "reformation in faith" to "reformation in faith and feeling" (i.e., the point where one actually feels as true what one had previously known only by faith), culminating with the allegory of the journey to the heavenly Jerusalem and a discussion of contemplative prayer and the special gifts of God.

Hilton's works were influential in the century immediately preceding the Reformation, surviving in numerous manuscripts, transmitted in Latin to continental Europe, and printed several times at the end of the 15th century and the beginning of the 16th.

Michael G. Sargent

Bibliography

PRIMARY

There is no critical edition of *The Scale of Perfection,* but an
    EETS edition is in preparation; Clark, John P.H., and
    Rosemary Dorward, trans. *The Scale of Perfection.* New

York: Paulist Press, 1991; Clark, J.P.H., and Cheryl Taylor, eds. *Walter Hilton's Latin Writings*. Salzburg: Institut für Anglistik und Amerikanistik, 1987; Jones, Dorothy, ed. *Minor Works of Walter Hilton*. London: Burns, Oates, & Washbourne, 1929 [modernized text]; Kane, Harold, ed. *The Prickynge of Love*. Salzburg: Institut für Anglistik und Amerikanistik, 1983; Ogilvie-Thomson, S.J., ed. *Walter Hilton's Mixed Life*. Salzburg: Institut für Anglistik und Amerikanistik, 1986; Wallner, Björn, ed. *An Exposition of "Qui Habitat" and "Bonum Est" in English*. Lund: Gleerup, 1954.

SECONDARY

Manual 9:3074–82, 3430–38; Clark, J.P.H. "Walter Hilton in Defense of the Religious Life and of the Veneration of Images." *DownR* 102 (1985): 1–25 [the latest in an important series of studies of Hilton's works]; Milosh, Joseph E. *The Scale of Perfection and the English Mystical Tradition*. Madison: University of Wisconsin Press, 1966; Minnis, Alastair. "The *Cloud of Unknowing* and Walter Hilton's *Scale of Perfection*." In *Middle English Prose: A Critical Guide to Major Authors and Genres,* ed. A.S.G. Edwards. New Brunswick: Rutgers University Press, 1984, pp. 61–81; Sargent, Michael G. "Walter Hilton's *Scale of Perfection:* The London Manuscript Group Reconsidered." *MÆ* 52 (1983): 189–216.

See also Anglo-Latin Literature after 1066; Bible in ME Literature; *Cloud of Unknowing;* Mystical and Devotional Writings; Prose, ME; Psychology, Medieval; Rolle

Hoccleve, Thomas (ca. 1366–1426)

Poet, scribe, and minor bureaucrat; author of *The Letter of Cupid* (1402), *La Male Regle* (1405–06), *The Regement of Princes* (1411), a compilation in verse and prose now known as the *Series* (including the *Complaint,* the *Dialogue with a Friend,* and *Learn to Die;* 1419–21), and many shorter religious and political poems.

Hoccleve's biography looms large in any account of him as a poet, since his supposedly autobiographical passages constitute the main attraction for modern readers, treating as they do Hoccleve's poverty and mental breakdown in an often subtly comic or moving manner. At the same time caution must be exercised in accepting these passages as historical. What is certain is that from 1387 Hoccleve was a clerk at the office of the privy seal in London, where he remained for the rest of his working life. The last payment to him is made in 1426, where he is described as "lately" a clerk of the privy seal. In his *Complaint* he describes the result of a mental breakdown he had five years earlier; his payment for 1416 was paid to him through friends. Most of his poetry is addressed to powerful patrons, often in the explicit hope of reward.

The Letter of Cupid, a translation of Christine de Pizan's *Epistre au dieu d'amours,* praises the virtues of women. It survives in ten manuscripts, two of which are autographs (Dur-

ham University Cosin V.ii.13 and Huntington HM 744). *La Male Regle,* written in the form of a confession for a misspent youth, is really a well-shaped begging poem; it is found in Huntington HM 111, another autograph, which contains many other short occasional and religious pieces by Hoccleve. Hoccleve's largest work, *The Regement of Princes,* is in the "mirror for princes" genre and is largely indebted to Latin works in the genre; 45 manuscripts contain the text, of which BL Arundel 38 and Harley 4866 are the most authoritative. The complete *Series* appears in five manuscripts, of which Durham University Cosin V.iii.9 is an autograph, except for the *Complaint.*

Hoccleve claims Chaucer as his master and friend (e.g., *Regement* 2077–2107, 4982–98). From Chaucer Hoccleve certainly learns much, in particular, perhaps, the presentation of the author's own persona in his work as a self-deprecating and naive character. But in Hoccleve's case this topos dominates the poetry (see especially *La Male Regle,* the Prologue to the *Regement,* and the *Series*), and discussion of it has dominated recent critical studies. Some critics take Hoccleve's self-presentation as purely conventional, whereas others have tried to define the ways in which Hoccleve draws on conventional topoi to negotiate his way out of the crises of poverty and mental instability.

James Simpson

Bibliography

PRIMARY

Furnivall, Frederick J., ed. *Hoccleve's Regement of Princes and Fourteen Minor Poems.* EETS e.s. 72. London: Humphrey Milford, 1897; Furnivall, Frederick J., and Israel Gollancz, eds. *Hoccleve's Works: The Minor Poems.* Rev. Jerome Mitchell and A.I. Doyle. 2 vols. in 1. EETS e.s. 61, 73. London: Oxford University Press, 1970.

SECONDARY

New *CBEL* 1:646–47; *Manual* 3:746–56, 903–08; Burrow, J.A. "Hoccleve's *Series:* Experience and Books." In *Fifteenth-Century Studies: Recent Essays,* ed. R.F. Yeager. Hamden: Archon, 1984, pp. 259–73; Burrow, J.A. *Thomas Hoccleve.* Aldershot: Variorum, 1994; Greetham, D.C. "Self-Referential Artifacts: Hoccleve's Persona As a Literary Device." *MP* 86 (1989): 242–51; Mitchell, Jerome. "Hoccleve Studies, 1965–81." In *Fifteenth-Century Studies: Recent Essays,* ed. R.F. Yeager. Hamden: Archon, 1984, pp. 49–63.

See also Ars moriendi; Chaucer; Privy Seal

Holy Week and Easter, Music for

The later medieval church celebrated Holy Week and Easter with many unique liturgical forms and ceremonies, often of an intrinsically dramatic character. These included major processions on Palm Sunday, Maundy Thursday, Holy Saturday, and Easter Sunday; the singing of the passions during mass as the New Testament Gospel on Palm Sunday (St. Matthew Passion), Wednesday (St. Luke Passion), and Good Friday (St.

John Passion); and in many locales in northern France and England, the performance of two Latin liturgical dramas—the *Visitatio sepulchri,* performed at the end of Matins on Easter Sunday morning, and the *Officium peregrinorum,* performed at Vespers that same evening or on the Monday or Tuesday following. Music is a less significant if still salient component of the extraliturgical, primarily spoken vernacular dramas and cycles of Eastertide and Corpus Christi.

Before the 15th century only a few of these occasions attracted written polyphony in England. There are motets on the Passion of Christ, the Resurrection, and on Mary Magdalene at the tomb, but their performance contexts are uncertain. There are also polyphonic settings of the refrain hymn *Gloria laus et honor* for the Palm Sunday procession, the *Alleluia pascha nostrum* for Easter mass, and the verses of two antiphons sung in processions to the Cross on Easter and subsequent weekdays *(Crucifixum in carne* from *Sedit angelus* and *Dicant nunc Iudei* from *Christus resurgens).* In the 15th century, however, the written repertoire was expanded into a significant corpus of liturgically rooted, functional polyphony for the processions and passions. This was music distinct in its sources and patterns of transmission from the elaborate English polyphonic mass cycles, motets, and antiphons that circulated so widely at home and on the Continent in the same time period. Several of its sources, including Shrewsbury School, Manuscript VI (ca. 1430, from Lichfield Cathedral), and BL Egerton 3307 (ca. 1440, perhaps from St. George's, Windsor), are relatively comprehensive in coverage and arranged in clear liturgical order.

The 15th-century music for Holy Week and Easter consists of unpretentious settings, mostly for two or three solo voices, some based on chant but most freely composed; it is highly probable that a tradition of simple, improvised settings lies behind these only slightly more sophisticated pieces and continued alongside them well into the 16th century. The music for processions includes settings of processional hymns, antiphons, psalms, and litanies. In the passions, a more extended form mixing chant and partsong, polyphony was applied to all direct speech apart from the words of Christ, thus including the words of the crowd *(turba)* and other individual characters. The narrative passages of the Evangelist and the words of Christ remained in plainsong following traditional "Passion tones." Performance of the passions had from an early time taken an essentially dramatic approach, indicated by *litterae significativae,* or letter symbols, that distinguished roles in the biblical text and prescribed qualities of performance for the reader. In missals of the English Use of Salisbury these letters were *m (media vox)* for the Evangelist, *b (bassa vox)* for Christ, and *a (alta vox)* for the rest. The English passions, setting only the *a* words polyphonically, are the earliest in a lengthy and distinguished European musical tradition.

Peter M. Lefferts

Bibliography

PRIMARY

Charles, Sydney Robinson, ed. *The Music of the Pepys MS 1236.* Corpus Mensurabilis Musicae 40. Rome: American Institute of Musicology, 1967; Hughes, Andrew, ed. *Fifteenth-Century Liturgical Music.* Vol. 1: *Antiphons and Music for Holy Week and Easter.* Early English Church Music 8. London: Stainer & Bell, 1967; McPeek, Gwynn S., ed. *The British Museum Manuscript Egerton 3307.* London: Oxford University Press, 1963.

SECONDARY

Allenson, Stephen. "The Inverness Fragments: Music from a Pre-Reformation Scottish Parish Church and School." *Music and Letters* 70 (1989): 1–45; Bukofzer, Manfred F. "Holy-Week Music and Carols at Meaux Abbey." In *Studies in Medieval and Renaissance Music.* New York: Norton, 1950, pp. 113–75; Fischer, Kurt von, and Werner Braun. "Passion." *NGD* 14:276–86; Harrison, Frank Ll. "Music for the Sarum Rite: MS 1236 in the Pepys Library, Magdalene College, Cambridge." *Annales musicologiques* 6 (1958–63): 99–144; Rankin, Susan K. "Shrewsbury School, Manuscript VI: A Medieval Part-Book?" *Proceedings of the Royal Musical Association* 102 (1975–76): 129–44.

See also Drama, Latin Liturgical; Drama, Vernacular, Role of Music in; Hymns; Processions

Hospitals

Medieval English hospitals differed completely from their modern counterparts; besides being small (usually with a mere handful of inmates, rarely able to accommodate 100 beds), they were almost always religious institutions, either part of a monastery or run by secular clergy on behalf of pious lay people.

Their function was also different; rather than caring for anyone who was ill, they catered only to those who could not afford medical treatment (customarily administered at home, even in extreme cases), as well as offering shelter for the deserving homeless, the aged poor, and travelers. Many hospitals refused to admit pregnant women, but a few in larger cities provided refuge for those who had "gone amiss," equipping their unfortunate offspring with a rudimentary education. Special hospitals (to a number over 350 during the high Middle Ages) were set up for the isolation of lepers, and others took custody of dangerous lunatics; the aim was to detain rather than to cure.

Well over 750 almshouses were founded in England before 1547, part of a growing fashion for the performance of good works to speed the donor's soul through purgatory and to ensure his or her lasting fame on earth. Londoners like Richard Whittington (d. 1424) and such noblemen as William de la Pole, duke of Suffolk (d. 1450), led the van in this respect; less impressive foundations were endowed by guilds and fraternities to care for brethren who had fallen on hard times. English hospitals offered little in the way of professional medical care, concentrating mainly on cleanliness, tranquility, and a nourishing diet. There can, however, be little doubt that some monks could prepare complex remedies and were in many ways as skilled as trained physicians.

The health of the soul was placed well above that of the body, with the result that all but the feeblest patients were obliged to participate in an incessant round of prayer and meditation. Since many hospitals were housed in the naves of churches, in sight of the high altar, the common requirement that prayers should be said daily for the soul of the founder was easily enforced. The practice of using the wardenship of a hospital as an ecclesiastical preferment encouraged abuses and financial problems; the later Middle Ages saw the creation of royal commissions to investigate incompetent or dishonest administration. Church authorities also were concerned about the possibility of sexual misconduct when nuns were employed in menial nursing tasks.

But money was always the major problem. All institutions relied heavily upon charitable donations and bequests in kind as in cash. Despite these shortcomings medieval hospitals provided a welcome haven for those "poore, sykke, blinde, aged and impotent persones" who, after the Dissolution of the monasteries in the 16th century, found themselves destitute and without succor.

Carole Rawcliffe

Bibliography

Clay, Rotha M. *The Mediaeval Hospitals of England.* London: Methuen, 1909. Repr. New York: Barnes & Noble, 1969; Grandshaw, Lindsay, and Roy Porter, eds. *The Hospital in History.* London: Wellcome Institute, 1989; Knowles, David, and R. Neville Hadcock. *Medieval Religious Houses: England and Wales.* New ed. London: Longman, 1971; Orme, Nicholas, and Margaret Webster. *The English Hospital 1070–1570.* New Haven: Yale University Press, 1995; Rawcliffe, Carole. "The Hospitals of Medieval London." *Medical History* 28 (1984): 1–24; Talbot, C.H. *Medicine in Medieval England.* London: Oldbourne, 1967.

See also Chantries; Guilds; Medicine

Households, Royal and Baronial

From the outset Anglo-Saxon kings surrounded themselves with permanent entourages that developed gradually into the sophisticated establishments known to us from 7th-century sources. As well as undertaking essentially domestic tasks, the household staff (in particular those of the bedchamber and wardrobe) acted in the financial and political sphere, since, being constantly about the monarch's person, they were available to perform his wishes. Throughout the Middle Ages the household was both a public and a private extension of his person, and it is often impossible to separate the dual functions, especially under strong rulers like Edward I or Henry V.

Contemporaries certainly made attempts to differentiate between ministers of state and offices of the household; it was taken for granted that government by the monarch would be personal, effected through his intimates. The only question was the cost and relative efficiency of such a system and occasionally the king's capacity as a judge of men. The *Constitutio domus regis* provides a valuable and early insight into the royal household in the reign of Henry I, by which time a further subdivision into departments headed by the chancellor, treasurer, chamberlain, stewards, and butler had occurred.

Over the next century the treasury, exchequer, and chancery were split off, to work separately at Westminster, but the chamber (with the privy seal) still perambulated with the king, meeting routine expenses and urgent fiscal needs. It was in response to growing demands for money that the wardrobe, hitherto a storehouse for the monarch's goods, began to demonstrate the flexibility and potential for expansion characteristic of each component of the household. By the late 13th century it was playing a leading role in the government, notably on overseas campaigns, when it functioned much as a modern war office.

A set of household ordinances from 1279 shows the wardrobe not only as "the brain and hand of the court" but as a highly complex financial and administrative machine. This system worked when the king was assertive and able (although Edward I left a great burden of debt), but Edward II's reliance upon unsuitable and unpopular favorites led the baronial opposition to demand a purge of the household and the implementation of further ordinances (1318 to 1326), designed to impose accountability.

It was partly as a result of these reforms, concentrating on the wardrobe, that Edward II began to exploit the chamber as a potential organ of government. This trend was continued by Edward III, whose costly foreign wars provided an impetus for further developments along similar lines. Parliament voiced strong opinions about the composition of the royal household, either because of corruption and incompetence (as during the dotage of Edward III) or in response to the emergence of a powerful and politically unacceptable "court party" (as in the reign of Richard II).

Richard's decision to defy his critics by augmenting the military element of his entourage and employing an inner ring of royal knights to enforce his absolutist policies led to his deposition. Henry V deployed experienced soldiers in the household, so he might pursue war with France; this was hailed as evidence of *his* strategic skills.

The character of the monarch thus remained a vital factor in determining the strengths and weaknesses of the household, not least as far as finance was concerned. The feeble and unworldly Henry VI hopelessly overspent the budget of £10,000 a year assigned him in 1440; by 1449 household expenses had reached the staggering total of £24,000 a year and were still rising, despite parliament's insistence on economies. Part of the problem was the sheer size of Henry's establishment, increasing from 360 people (well above the level maintained by Henry V, and about that supported by Edward III and Edward IV) in 1437, to 420 ten years later.

Shrewder and more businesslike, Edward IV initiated improvements—set out in the Black Book (1472) and Household Ordinances (1478)—with the intention of rationalizing expenditure. He kept his outlay well below £12,000 a year, while giving the impression of splendor and majesty.

Baronial households likewise served to advertise the wealth and magnificence of the aristocracy, who regarded investment in lavish entertainment, hospitality, and spectacle as money well spent. Indeed the crown was always aware of an element of competition from this quarter, which explains why savage cuts were never seriously attempted at court. Justice Fortescue's famous maxim that "subgettes woll rather goo with a lord that is riche and may pay their wages and espenses then with thair Kynge that hath noght in his purse" illustrates the importance of ostentatious display to demonstrate political and financial power and attract support.

During the 15th century Humphrey, duke of Buckingham (d. 1460), spent £2,200 (or half his net income) on his household; George, duke of Clarence (d. 1478), set aside about twice this sum on an establishment of 299 staff, whose annual food consumption came to 365 tuns of ale, 2,700 sheep, and 650 quarters of wheat.

Like the royal model, baronial households were divided into separate departments, headed by a treasurer who controlled overall expenditure and presented annual accounts. These were compiled from books kept by the clerks or yeomen responsible for the kitchen, pantry, chamber, stables, kennels, and other offices, and the level of supervision was high. Right up to the close of the Middle Ages, when a more sedentary lifestyle became fashionable, noblemen pursued a peripatetic existence, traveling with great baggage trains from one castle and manor house to another, with a smaller "riding" household in constant attendance. This enabled them to keep an eye on their far-flung estates and eased the problem of purveyance; the lord could move elsewhere once the reserves of an area had been exhausted.

Carole Rawcliffe

Bibliography

Chrimes, Stanley B. *An Introduction to the Administrative History of Mediaeval England.* 3d ed. Oxford: Blackwell, 1966; Denholm-Young, Noel. *Seignorial Administration in England.* London: Oxford University Press, 1937; Mertes, Kate. *The English Noble Household, 1250–1600.* Oxford: Blackwell, 1988; Myers, A.R. *The Household of Edward IV: The Black Book and the Ordinance of 1478.* Manchester: Manchester University Press, 1959; Ross, Charles D. "The Household Accounts of Elizabeth Berkeley, Countess of Warwick, 1420–21." *Transactions of the Bristol and Gloucestershire Archaeological Society* 79 (1951): 81–105; Tout, T.F. *Chapters in the Administrative History of Mediaeval England: The Wardrobe, the Chamber and the Small Seals.* 6 vols. Manchester: Manchester University Press, 1920–33.

See also Chancellor and Chancery; Chapel Royal; Exchequer; Great Seal; Privy Seal; Wardrobe

Hubert Walter (d. 1205)

Archbishop of Canterbury and a leading royal official during the reigns of Richard I and John, who combined the administration of church and state. Trained in the household of his uncle Ranulf de Glanville, the justiciar, Hubert served as a baron of the exchequer and rose from dean of York to bishop of Salisbury before joining Richard I on the Third Crusade. On the death of Archbishop Baldwin of Canterbury Hubert became the principal clerical leader on the crusade and close adviser to the king.

Though captured while returning from the crusade, King Richard was able to send letters to England successfully urging the election of Hubert to the vacant see of Canterbury in 1193. Two years later the pope extended the archbishop's authority by naming him papal legate for England.

From 1193 to 1198 Hubert was justiciar and headed the government in Richard's absence. His extensive instructions for the judicial eyre (judges traveling on a circuit) of 1194 provide the basis for his administrative reputation. Through these detailed administrative and judicial instructions he was responsible for establishing the office of coroner, and he also began the practice of keeping a third copy on file when land disputes were settled by a final concord.

Archbishop Hubert was persuaded to support John as successor to Richard, in 1199, and he helped prepare John's acceptance by the barons. Under John he became chancellor. As chancellor he is credited with beginning the practice of enrolling copies of charters and letters issued from chancery.

Hubert's sarcophagus can be seen in Canterbury Cathedral, and various objects removed in 1890 are on display in the cathedral museum.

Charles R. Young

Bibliography

Cheney, Christopher R. *Hubert Walter.* London: Nelson, 1967 [concentrates on the religious side of the career]; Young, Charles R. *Hubert Walter, Lord of Canterbury and Lord of England.* Durham: Duke University Press, 1968 [covers secular career as well].

See also Bishops; Chancellor and Chancery; Glanville; John; Richard I

Hue de Rotelande, or Rhuddlan (fl. 1174–91)

Anglo-Norman poet; author of two long courtly romances, *Ipomedon* and its sequel, *Protheselaus*. He lived at Credenhill, near Hereford, and wrote for Gilbert Fitz-Baderon, lord of Monmouth. References in his work suggest his friendship with Walter Map. His romances, set in Norman Sicily and Calabria, are constructed from conventional romance plot elements; they are, however, remarkable for their rhetorical and psychological sophistication and their humorous burlesque of a genre only recently established in French courtly poetry. *Ipomedon* was adapted into three ME versions.

Rosalind P. Field

Bibliography

PRIMARY

Holden, A.J., ed. *Ipomedon.* Paris: Klincksieck, 1979; Holden, A.J., ed. *Protheselaus.* ANTS 47–49. London: ANTS, 1991–93.

SECONDARY

Calin, William. *The French Tradition and the Literature of Medieval England.* Toronto: University of Toronto Press, 1994; Hanning, Robert W. *The Individual in Twelfth-Century Romance.* New Haven: Yale University Press, 1977.

See also Anglo-Norman Literature; Map; Romances

Hull, Eleanor (ca. 1394–1460)

Translator from the French of a commentary on the seven Penitential Psalms and a collection of prayers and meditations, both extant in CUL Kk.1.6, and the latter also in University of Illinois MS 80.

Daughter of Sir John Malet of Enmore, Somersetshire, Eleanor married Sir John Hull ca. 1410 and bore one son, Edward (d. 1453). She served Queen Joan of Navarre, Henry IV's second wife, and was associated with the Benedictine Abbey of St. Albans. Widowed before 1421, she often stayed at Sopwell, a priory of Benedictine nuns, and never remarried. Later she retired to the Benedictine priory at Cannington, near Enmore, where she died.

Eleanor's meditations are composed in a common style of affective piety; in contrast her commentary on the Penitential Psalms, which draws heavily on Augustine and Peter Lombard, is learned and latinate. Her prose is competent by the standards of ME translation: generally she controls her long sentences, probably modeled on the "style clergial" of her French original; there are no obvious gross mistranslations; her vocabulary is not excessively Gallic; and she skillfully works in the Latin quotations that are an integral part of the commentary. It is the work of an honest craftswoman carrying out a task for which she had few models, except perhaps Rolle's *English Psalter.*

Alexandra Barratt

Bibliography

PRIMARY

Barratt, Alexandra, ed. *The Seven Psalms: A Commentary on the Penitential Psalms Translated from French into English by Dame Eleanor Hull.* EETS o.s. 307. Oxford: Oxford University Press, 1995.

SECONDARY

Manual 2:389, 541; 9:3115–16, 3460; Barratt, Alexandra. "Dame Eleanor Hull: A Fifteenth-Century Translator." In *The Medieval Translator: The Theory and Practice of Translation in the Middle Ages,* ed. Roger Ellis. Cambridge: Brewer, 1989, pp. 87–101.

See also Bible in ME Literature; Literacy; Mystical and Devotional Writings; Prose, ME; Rolle; Translation; Women in ME Literature

Hundred Years War

The historical context of the Hundred Years War (a term first used, in its French form, about 1860 and popularized in English by J.R. Green in his *Short History of the English People* [1874]) is the broadly contemporary development of French and English nationhood, expressed in territorial expansion, in the English case through war in Wales, Scotland, and France from the 1270s to the 1450s. In England it was also the result of a growing sense of national consciousness and pride, shown in the perceived obligation to defend territorial interests in France when the kings of France tried to bring them under their control by emphasizing their dying sense of feudal superiority over the kings of England.

In the early 14th century western Europe was at a crossroads. The conflicting attitudes of French and English kings ("feudal" on the one hand, "national" on the other) toward the future of lands in France, ruled by successive kings of England, were at the roots of a war that was to witness England's disengagement from her historic links with territories now passing under the effective rule of the crown of France.

The sequence of events leading up to the war may be regarded as having begun in 1259, when Henry III renounced his claim to former English lands in return for a new feudal relationship in Aquitaine. A series of acts of confiscation by the French crown soured relations in the coming years. On the death in 1328 of the last Valois king, Charles IV, Edward III claimed the French crown through his mother, Isabella, Charles's sister. The claim was rejected. Soldier that he was, Edward could not tolerate such an action. War, he hoped, would settle both this problem and the uneasy status of Aquitaine. By 1340 the two kingdoms were at war.

While some of the war's battles are well known, there were few formal encounters between opposing armies in the years to come. English practice was to launch *chevauchées,* or raids, into France's heartlands from a number of points on the coast, such raids being carried out by armies ranging from 5,000 to 13,000 fighting men. It was on one such expedition, led by Edward III and Edward the Black Prince in 1346 that, after a campaign of looting and pillaging, the English army was caught at Crécy, in northern France, and secured victory by using its archers to the best effect. Ten years later, the Black Death having in the meantime taken its toll of the population, the Black Prince met and defeated a French army near Poitiers and took the French king, John II, prisoner.

Two great defeats, the capture of the king, and social troubles at home made France seal a treaty that was territorially favorable to England, at Brétigny in 1360. While the main issues were not settled, direct confrontation between England and France was to be avoided for a decade, although in 1367 the Black Prince won a major victory at Nájera, in northern Spain, in a war closely connected to the main conflict.

In 1369 the war began again. In the next quarter of a century English fortunes declined considerably and the French gradually regained lands ceded in 1360. With the death of the Black Prince (1376) and Edward III (1377), and with Richard II on the throne, a king more inclined to peace, negotiations began. In 1396 a 28-year truce was arranged.

Little more than half that time had elapsed when Henry V, convinced of the justice of his claims, invaded in 1415 and won the historic victory at Agincourt. Finding that the French would not meet his demands, he returned in 1417, but with a different aim; this was now to be a war not of raids but of conquest and settlement by Englishmen. By 1419 he had won Normandy by following a policy of besieging castles and fortified towns, a form of war in which the king made good use of cannon, the latest weapon now available. With the help of John and Philip, successive dukes of Burgundy, Henry imposed upon the French in 1420 the Treaty of Troyes, by whose terms he was to succeed to the crown of France when the king, Charles VI, came to die. But Henry V died first; he could only pass on to his son, Henry VI, the right that he himself had never enjoyed.

After his death the English fought for more than a generation to increase and defend his conquests. They began well, with the important victory won against a Franco-Scottish army at Verneuil in 1424. By 1429, however, with the appearance of Joan of Arc and her triumph at Orléans, the high point of English success had passed. In 1435 the French persuaded Philip of Burgundy to abandon his alliance with the English. Without it their military task, supported by diminishing financial resources and declining support at home, became increasingly difficult. On the other hand the French saw that military reorganization could win what they wanted: the expulsion, by force of arms, of the English. In 1449–50 a campaign achieved the recovery of Normandy; in 1453, after initial setbacks, the same was achieved in Aquitaine. The Hundred Years War was over.

Much of the historical significance of the war lies in the impact it had upon the societies involved in it. That it touched both England and France profoundly cannot be doubted. War had to be paid for, and new fiscal measures influenced everybody, directly or otherwise. Armies had to be raised, organized, led, and paid; the institutional developments required to meet these demands were to be influential, then and later. The period also witnessed new concepts of how war might be fought, new developments in strategy, and, in particular, new weapons to make those strategies effective. The growing appreciation of the importance of war at sea was one such development with a future before it. The need to communicate and negotiate with the enemy led to developments in methods of diplomacy.

Finally the war made the English people more conscious of their history and individual character, by helping to set them aside from the French, who, although their neighbors, were also their enemies. During the period, and largely owing to the war, English nationalism and self-awareness took a great step forward.

C.T. Allmand

Bibliography

Allmand, C.T. *The Hundred Years War: England and France at War, c. 1300–c. 1450.* Cambridge: Cambridge University Press, 1988; Fowler, Kenneth. *The Age of Plantagenet and Valois: The Struggle for Supremacy, 1328–1498.* London: Elek, 1967; Fowler, Kenneth, ed. *The Hundred Years War.* London: Macmillan, 1971; Perroy, Edouard. *The Hundred Years War.* London: Eyre & Spottiswoode, 1951; Sumption, Jonathan. *The Hundred Years War.* Vol. 1: *Trial by Battle.* London: Faber & Faber, 1990.

See also Edward III; Edward the Black Prince; Gascony; Henry V

Hundreds and Hundred Rolls

The hundred, known as the "wapentake" in the Danelaw, was the primary subdivision of the shire for purposes of local government. Theoretically the hundred encompassed 100 hides of land, whence the name. But in fact the size of hundreds varied widely. The chief officer for a hundred was the hundred bailiff. At the heart of the hundred's function was the hundred court, which met every four weeks to hear local pleas and conduct local business.

The origins of the hundreds are much disputed. Possibly they date from the military and administrative reforms set in motion by Alfred the Great; certainly by the 11th century they formed an active and popular part of the system of local government. Hundreds and their courts came in two forms: royally held and privately held. Private hundreds differed in their degree of private control. In some the lord of the hundred merely shared the revenue of the court with the king, while in others he appointed the bailiff, kept court revenues, and had extensive legal powers within the hundred. But whether royally or privately held, the business of the hundred court was always the king's business. Private hundreds meant private executive power, not private jurisdiction.

Hundreds and their courts were retained by William I and his successors. The role of the hundred in local administration was multifaceted. It served as a unit for taxation, justice, police work, legal procedure, and military defense. The Normans and Angevins made particular use of the hundred jury as a tool for gathering information. Royal inquests posed questions to the juries of hundreds; responses were recorded on rolls for future reference. Few of these have survived, but one large group did, and these have come to be known as the Hundred Rolls.

The Hundred Rolls were the product of the great royal inquest of 1274. Edward I sent out commissioners to present questions to juries in all the hundreds in England. The questions fell into two groups: those about the usurpation of royal rights by magnates and those about the conduct of officials running the king's government. The answers were the basis for much of the reform legislation Edward introduced, starting with the first Statute of Winchester.

Printed in two large volumes by the Record Office in 1818, the Hundred Rolls are an invaluable resource for the history of local government in the 13th century. In particular they show the hundred as a vital connection between local population and the king, a channel of communication between central government and its constituents. The selection of representatives and jurors of the hundred for the shire court, as well as the habit of bringing local problems to the king's attention, prepared rural England for the development of an effective parliament.

Stephen R. Morillo

Bibliography

Cam, Helen M. *Studies in the Hundred Rolls: Some Aspects of Thirteenth Century Administration.* Oxford: Clarendon, 1921; Cam, Helen M. *Liberties and Communities in Medieval England.* Cambridge: Cambridge University Press, 1944; Cam, Helen M. *Law-Finders and Law-Makers in Medieval England: Collected Studies in Legal and Constitutional History.* London: Merlin Press, 1962.

See also Edward I; Juries; Local Government

Husband's Message, The

A short OE poem near the end of the Exeter Book. Because of its mode of expression and its concern with the themes of separation and loss of former happiness the 54-line *Husband's Message* is usually referred to as one of the OE "elegies." The term "elegy," however, can hardly be regarded as satisfactory for this poem, in which past troubles are presented as having been overcome and the future is looked forward to with tentative hope. The speaker of *The Husband's Message* has been sent over the sea to convey to a woman the message that the man with whom she made vows of love in the past has surmounted the woes that afflicted him and now wishes her to join him again so that the two of them may live together as lord and lady.

Although the essential meaning of the poem comes across clearly, several fundamental questions of interpretation present themselves. The first concerns the nature of the speaker who conveys the message. Most commentators have taken the speaker to be a human messenger sent by the lord to speak to the woman on his behalf. Some critics, however, offer a less naturalistic reading of the poem and suggest that there is no human speaker at all but that *The Husband's Message* represents a poetic expansion of a message carved on a piece of wood; the "speaker" of the poem is the piece of wood itself. Similar personifications are found throughout the Riddles of the Exeter Book. Related to the question of the speaker is that of the dimensions of the poem. Immediately before the 54 lines of *The Husband's Message* comes a passage of verse that scholars have traditionally interpreted as a riddle (Riddle 60), spoken by a "reed." But some commentators insist that this passage is in fact the beginning of *The Husband's Message* and that in it the speaker introduces itself as a piece of wood.

The final interpretive problem of *The Husband's Message* is that of the passage of runes in the closing sentence of the poem. This cryptic passage has been deciphered in several ways, most notably as the terms of an oath that the man swears to the woman and as his secret instructions concerning the journey she must make to find him. The difficulties of the runes and the other uncertainties in *The Husband's*

Message continue to exercise critics but do not detract from the poem's appeal. *The Husband's Message* is remarkable for the restraint and formality with which its heartfelt message is expressed. The underlying emotion is sublimated by the intervening figure of the messenger but remains evident nonetheless.

Hugh Magennis

Bibliography

PRIMARY

ASPR 3:225–27; Klinck, Anne L., ed. *The Old English Elegies: A Critical Edition and Genre Study.* Montreal: McGill-Queen's University Press, 1992, pp. 58–60, 100–02, 199–208; Leslie, Roy F., ed. *Three Old English Elegies.* Rev. ed. Exeter: University of Exeter, 1988, pp. 49–50, 59–66.

SECONDARY

Elliott, Ralph W.V. "The Runes in *The Husband's Message.*" *JEGP* 54 (1955): 1–8; Pope, John C. "Paleography and Poetry: Some Solved and Unsolved Problems of the Exeter Book." In *Mediaeval Scribes, Manuscripts and Libraries: Essays Presented to N.R. Ker*, ed. Malcolm B. Parkes and Andrew G. Watson. London: Scolar, 1978, pp. 25–65; Renoir, Alain. "The Least Elegiac of the Elegies: A Contextual Glance at *The Husband's Message.*" *Studia Neophilologica* 53 (1981): 69–76.

See also Exeter Book; Riddles; Runes

Hymns

The hymn was originally a popular form of Christian devotion, and in some respects it maintained this character throughout the Middle Ages. The medieval hymn in England was almost invariably in Latin, in uniform stanzas, and set to a unison chant repeated for every stanza. It was practically always used in the offices, whether said or sung (the Office of the Dead, and those of the period from Maundy Thursday to the Saturday of Easter week being the only significant exceptions), and in some form or other it was available as an aid to various other devotions.

The majority of the hymns used in medieval England were the common property of the western church: their texts were by such figures as Ambrose of Milan, Prudentius, Hilary of Poitiers, Venantius Fortunatus, and their contemporaries and successors. Their chants, too, enjoyed a European circulation, though in their English form (and especially in manuscripts of the Use of Salisbury) they often differed in detail from the continental versions. Irishmen like Columba and Columbanus and Englishmen like Bede contributed to early Latin hymnody, but few of their hymns entered the standard repertoire, and they were probably sung to existing chants.

Latin hymns are usually straightforward in versification, whether quantitative or accentual. Each melodic repetition normally requires a textual unit having the same number of syllables, so that even where the scansion is by quantity the isosyllabic principle is usually observed. The tunes themselves vary from syllabic (one syllable to each note), quasi-recitational formulas to elaborate melodies in which some syllables at least carry several notes. The original rhythm of such melodies is open to doubt, but in the later Middle Ages each note was probably given a roughly equal duration.

The standard English office hymn thus differed in no significant way from its continental counterpart. There was more scope for individuality in the composition of less formal devotional hymnody, of which a large quantity circulated in medieval England. Some of this was similar in form to the sequence. Sequences, when provided with a text *(prosa),* were sometimes referred to as hymns (the traditional title of Notker's collection is *Liber hymnorum);* at first their texts were neither metrical nor uniformly stanzaic, but as time went on they began to settle into a pattern of trochaic six-line stanzas with the rhyme scheme aabccb, each pair of half-stanzas or versicles being musically identical. A great deal of devotional hymnody, much of it apparently meant for the evening devotion sung daily at the conclusion of Compline, is based on this pattern.

Processions were another context for hymns. Fortunatus's poem *Tempora florigero rutilant distincta sereno,* written in elegiac couplets, was dismembered to make an Easter processional, using the couplet beginning "Salve festa dies" as a refrain; and in the Use of Salisbury it was imitated for use on a number of other feasts, such as Ascension and Pentecost. An extract from another poem in the same meter, Theodulf of Orléans's *Gloria, laus et honor,* was also converted into a refrain song and sung at the Palm Sunday procession. These hymns were unusual in not being strictly isosyllabic, so that the melody for the stanzas had to be adapted to fit the variable length of each couplet. Other hymns used processionally were Fortunatus's *Pange lingua* on Good Friday, using the stanza "Crux fidelis" as a refrain, and Prudentius's *Inventor rutili* on Holy Saturday.

The standard hymn and sequence meters, or "rhythms," were imitated in a considerable body of religious poetry, not all of which was intended to be sung. But an interesting case of devotional hymnody is provided by *Dulcis Jesu memoria,* formerly attributed to St. Bernard but now usually regarded as the work of an English Cistercian monk who wrote in the late 12th century. This is in iambic rhythm, with 42 four-line stanzas, and it provided several hymns for the Breviary. But its music was not originally strophic: each stanza had a separate melody, though certain phrases were carried over from one stanza to another. It carried the title *Iubilus rhythmicus de nomine Iesu,* implying a relationship with the sequence—i.e., as a replacement for the final jubilus (melisma) of the Alleluia at mass—a relationship that is borne out by the style of the music.

Vernacular religious poetry was also influenced by the sequence and hymn, and some such poems survive with music. These are mostly imitations of the *Stabat mater* or are devotions on the Passion of Christ, using the trochaic sequence stanza. "Stand wel moder under rode" has music in two manuscripts, while "Iesu cristes milde moder" exists in a two-part setting. "Gabriel from evene-king," for the Annunciation, is a paraphrase of *Angelus ad virginem,* while "Edi beo thu, hevene quene," in praise of Mary, is again given a two-part setting. Yet another body of hymnic material is to be found in the repertoire of conductus and versified trope.

Latin liturgical hymns were frequently set polyphonically from the 14th century onward, usually with the plainchant melody or its faburden as a basis. A common procedure was for the polyphony to alternate with plainsong, usually so that the first and other odd-numbered verses were sung in plainsong and the others in polyphony. Tallis and Sheppard are among those who treated the hymn in this way in the period immediately prior to the Reformation. The organ was also used to alternate with plainsong, in which case it was usually allotted the odd-numbered verses, the words of which were therefore not heard at all.

The melodies of hymns are given in noted breviaries, in manuscript hymnals (usually attached to psalters), and, for the Salisbury hymns, in printed editions from 1518 on. There are no English sources for the melodies of the office hymns before the 13th century, though there are earlier continental sources for many of them, while textual sources, some with OE glosses, go back to the Anglo-Saxon period. Processional hymns are given in manuscript processionals from the 14th to the 16th century and in 16th-century printed processionals; those for Palm Sunday and Holy Week, and sometimes the others as well, are also given in graduals from the 13th century at least.

John Caldwell

Bibliography

PRIMARY

Bernard, J.H., and R. Atkinson, eds. *The Irish Liber hymnorum.* Henry Bradshaw Society 13–14. London: Harrison & Sons, 1898; Dreves, Guido M., Clemens Blume, and Henry M. Bannister, eds. *Analecta Hymnica Medii Aevi.* 55 vols. Leipzig: Reisland, 1886–1922. *Register,* ed. Max Lütolf. 3 vols. Bern: Francke, 1978; Hesbert, Rene-Jean, ed. *Le tropaire-prosaire de Dublin.* Monumenta musicae sacrae 4. Rouen: Imprimerie Rouennaise, 1966 [facsimile]; *Hymnarium Sarisburiense . . . pars prima.* London, 1851; Plainsong and Mediaeval Music Society. *Plainsong Hymn Melodies and Sequences.* London: Printed for the Society, 1896; Stäblein, Bruno, ed. *Die mittelalterliche Hymnenmelodien des Abendlandes.* Kassel: Bärenreiter, 1956; Warren, Frederick E., ed. *The Antiphonary of Bangor.* Henry Bradshaw Society 4, 10. London: Harrison & Sons, 1893–95; Wilmart, André, ed. *Le "Jubilus" dit de Saint Bernard.* Rome: Edizioni di Storia e Letteratura, 1944.

SECONDARY

Bailey, Terence. *The Processions of Sarum and the Western Church.* Toronto: Pontifical Institute, 1971; Chevalier, Ulysse. *Repertorium Hymnologicum.* 6 vols. Louvain: Lefever, Polleunis & Centerick, Société des Bollandistes, 1892–1921; Gneuss, Helmut. *Hymnar und Hymnen in englischen Mittelalter.* Tübingen: Niemeyer, 1968; Gneuss, Helmut. "Latin Hymns in Medieval England: Future Research." In *Chaucer and Middle English Studies in Honour of Rossell Hope Robbins,* ed. Beryl Rowland. London: Allen & Unwin, 1974, pp. 407–24; Julian, John. *A Dictionary of Hymnology.* 2d ed. London: Murray, 1907. Repr. New York: Dover, 1957; Mearns, James. *Early Latin Hymnaries: An Index of Hymns in Hymnaries before 1100.* Cambridge: Cambridge University Press, 1913. Repr. Hildesheim: Olms, 1970; Milfull, Inge B. *The Hymns of the Anglo-Saxon Church: A Study and Edition of the "Durham Hymnal."* Cambridge: Cambridge University Press, 1996. Stäblein, Bruno. "Hymnus B: Der lateinische Hymnus." *Die Musik in Geschichte und Gegenwart* 6 (1957): 993–1018; Walpole, Arthur S. *Early Latin Hymns.* Cambridge: Cambridge University Press, 1922. Repr. Hildesheim: Olms, 1966.

See also Angelus ad virginem; Cantilena; Conductus; Faburden; Holy Week and Easter, Music for; Processions; Sequence; Songs

I

Iconography

There is a growing belief that the spirals, interlaced birds and beasts, and foliate elements of early insular art may have conveyed specific ideas. Wamers has shown that on European artifacts decorated in a predominantly insular style, interlaced animals appear on arms, armor, and horse trappings, while religious objects always include foliage. The inhabited vinescroll on many churches and crosses (e.g., the Ruthwell Cross; fig. 114: see RUTHWELL CROSS) was taken over from Mediterranean traditions, and it, too, may have been symbolic, not merely decorative, possibly representing Christ as the true vine. Stevenson has identified miniature crosses incorporated in insular patterns; and the Chi symbol may have been used in a similar way. If true, the cross-carpet pages of insular Gospel books may be considered iconographic as well as formal innovations (fig. 84: see LINDISFARNE GOSPELS).

Early Christian art was also known. Sixth-century Italian painted books had arrived in England by the 7th century: the St. Augustine Gospels (Cambridge, Corpus Christi College 286) were at Canterbury and still survive; and Northumbria acquired books from Cassiodorus's monastery, the Vivarium, in Italy, including an illustrated Bible pandect, the Codex Grandior, and a nine-volume Bible, the *Novem codices.* Roman icons were brought to Northumbria at the same time. In the following centuries two distinct traditions that may owe their origins to these sources spread from Canterbury and Northumbria.

Among the earliest figurative subjects were evangelist portraits. In the Northumbrian Lindisfarne Gospels of ca. 700 (BL Cotton Nero D.iv) they appear to be based on an early Christian tradition of seated figures against an undefined ground, as might have appeared in the Gospel volume of the *Novem codices,* but they are also enriched with elements from other sources. St. John's frontal stance, reminiscent of a Majesty, and his *Hodegetria* ("showing the way") gesture of pointing out the way to salvation (both possibly derived from icons) may emphasize his revelatory nature. St. Matthew's witness has been compared with the peeping scribe in the *Registrum Gregori* (983). If valid,

this, too, could refer to revelation. The leaping symbols, which appear in other northern manuscripts, such as the Lichfield and Echternach gospels (Lichfield, Cathedral Treasury; Paris, BN lat. 9389), and on the Cuthbert coffin are best paralleled in the Majesty of the Codex Amiatinus (Florence, Biblioteca Medicea-Laurenziana Amiatinus 1), which is based on an early Christian model, possibly the Codex Grandior itself.

In the southern Stockholm Codex Aureus (Stockholm, Royal Library A.135) evangelists are seated under architectural canopies, and in the lunettes half-length symbols have books tucked under their arms. All this echoes the St. Augustine Gospels.

Other images flourished briefly. The Cuthbert coffin has a Virgin and Child (fig. 48: see COFFIN OF ST. CUTHBERT) that blends two early Christian iconographies in the Child's sideways stance with his mother's hand on his shoulder (an *Eleousa,* or "mercy," gesture) and the Virgin's flat-handed gesture toward the Child (as in the *Hodegetria*). The Durham Gospel fragment A.II.17 has an early Christian Crucifixion to which seraphs are added. Both these iconographies proved more popular in Irish circles and quickly vanished from Anglo-Saxon art.

After the mid-9th century Scandinavian mythological imagery appears on stonework, such as the "hogback" grave markers and the Gosforth Cross (figs. 18–19: see ART, VIKING AGE), juxtaposed thematically with Christian imagery. A new sense of thematic (or allegorical) concepts also develops, exemplified by the five senses on the Fuller Brooch (fig. 65: see FULLER BROOCH) and the sense of Sight (?) on the Alfred Jewel (fig. 1: see ALFRED AND MINSTER LOVELL JEWELS).

Under Æthelstan (924–39) strong contacts with Europe led to the presence at Winchester of Louis, the exiled Carolingian prince, and monks from St. Bertin settling at Bath (944) and Winchester (966). An influx of Carolingian manuscripts is likely, since the Winchester style that flourished immediately afterward reproduces features from the Franco-Saxon, Metz, and Reims schools and continental images are introduced. Continental Crucifixion iconography appears in several psalters, the soldiers Stephaton and Longinus replaced by the Virgin and St. John, and the colobium, or tunic, by a loincloth.

By the end of the century copies of the Utrecht Psalter were being made, and the sudden popularity of narrative art may be attributable to its influence. The Three Marys at the Sepulcher in the Benedictional of St. Æthelwold (BL Add. 49598) and the Missal of Robert of Jumièges (Rouen, Bibliothèque Municipale Y.6) reproduce the winged angel and swinging censer of that scene in the Utrecht Psalter, two features that differentiate it from the older early Christian iconography. In the Cotton calendars (BL Cotton Julius A.vi; Tiberius B.v) images for the labors of the months are reminiscent of pastoral scenes in the Utrecht Psalter. Once assimilated, narrative art appears in new contexts such as the "Cædmon" Genesis and the New Minster Liber Vitae.

At the same time northern ideas resurfaced. The evangelists in the late-Winchester style Grimbald Gospels (BL Add. 34890) recall those of the Lindisfarne Gospels with their leaping symbols and single-draped curtains, no longer confined to St. Matthew; and the witness figure reappears in the Copenhagen Gospels (Copenhagen, Royal Library G.K.S. 10,2), one of whose scribes had earlier worked on the Missal of Robert of Jumièges.

Anglo-Saxon iconography shares many features with Irish and Scandinavian work. Most notable is the will to superimpose and juxtapose known images to create a rich and subtle artistic language different in concept from the most literal continental art. Where each image in the Utrecht Psalter is complete and independent, those on the Gosforth Cross, or in the "Cædmon" Genesis depend on each other for their meanings to become clear; they create a visual narrative that can be read in conjunction with or independent of the text.

Many of the iconographic innovations of the Anglo-Saxons remained popular long after the Conquest. The "disappearing Christ" Ascension and the beast-mouth of hell, for example, continue to appear in both manuscripts and sculpture (e.g., the 12th-century Winchester Psalter [BL Cotton Nero C.iv; fig. 153: see WINCHESTER PSALTER] and the Lincoln Cathedral frieze from ca. 1140). Indeed the mouth of hell was popular throughout Europe in the Romanesque period, possibly due to its obvious iconographic connection with the sins of gluttony and sodomy (Camille, 1993).

The 11th and 12th centuries are also characterized by the competing iconographies of English and Norman nationalism. The fortified castles and cathedrals that began to appear shortly after the Conquest, with their two-towered facades and strong mural emphasis, were symbols of Norman imperialism. The indigenous clergy may have countered these images with a revival of particularly important, or politically useful, national saints. The cult of St. Cuthbert at Durham, for example, was particularly strong, but his image changed from the peaceful man associated with the Lindisfarne Gospels to an unhappy, irritable, and misogynistic saint who was not to be crossed. His illustrated life (BL Add. 39943; ca. 1200) shows him resting uneasily within his tomb.

The events depicted in *The Life and Miracles of Edmund*

King and Martyr (New York, Pierpont Morgan Library M.736; ca. 1130) may have been chosen specifically for their political content. Edmund is shown saving the monastery of Bury St. Edmunds from thieves and Danes and exercising just leadership at all times; the scenes may have been meant as a warning against contemporary infringements on the abbey's rights.

Romanesque artists were also inventive in their own right, developing a number of alternative iconographies for traditional scenes. Details included in the 12th-century wall paintings in the churches at Hardham and Coombes, for example, are quite unusual. At Hardham Eve milking a cow replaces the usual image of Eve spinning, while at Coombes Joseph appears as part of the Annunciation.

Artists in the Gothic era continued to combine elements of unique, or traditionally English, iconography with new stylistic developments. On a general level the English response to the development of the Gothic style in France was to adopt selected images and other elements of French art and to work them into traditional interests and programs. The English Gothic cathedral, like its French counterpart, was meant to represent the kingdom of heaven on earth, focused largely on the figure of Mary; however, English Gothic artists and architects illustrated this concept through screenlike sculpted facades (which included numerous historical figures) and Lady Chapels rather than through monumental sculpture and a proliferation of rose windows. The flat east end of English Gothic cathedrals was also a structural, and perhaps iconographic, link with the Anglo-Saxon tradition.

Historical references are evident throughout Gothic art in England. The tournaments and Round Tables that were so much a part of court life were designed to invoke the legendary golden age of King Arthur, while the display of coats of arms, banners, and other "hereditary devices" provided visual chronicles of personal and family history. The arms of Ponthieu, Castile, Leon, and England that decorated the Eleanor crosses (ca. 1291), or those of England, Clare, and Poitou on the 1271/72 pavement of the old refectory at Cleeve Abbey (Somerset), are public displays of family titles, alliances, and power (in both cases royal).

The interest in personal history and identity that the display of such images suggests was not limited to the aristocracy. The 14th century in particular witnessed an increase in the power of wealthy professionals, especially merchants, and a corresponding increase in their visibility in art. Lacking, in most cases, the heraldic devices of the nobility, this group displayed their individuality through symbols of their profession (e.g., the funerary brass of the late-14th-century merchant and his wife in the Church of Sts. Peter and Paul, Northleach, Gloucestershire, on which the merchant stands on the symbol of his profession, a woolsack).

The increased display of images of personal identity of all types should be linked to the rise of a new type of image: the portrait. Images of important rulers and clerics had certainly been present in art for centuries, but it is only in the late Gothic era that likenesses, such as that of Richard II on the 1394–95 panel in Westminster, begin to appear.

Perette E. Michelli
Catherine E. Karkov

Bibliography

Alexander, J.J.G. *Insular Manuscripts 6th–9th Century.* A Survey of Manuscripts Illuminated in the British Isles 1, ed. J.J.G. Alexander. London: Harvey Miller, 1978; Alexander, Jonathan, and Paul Binski, eds. *Age of Chivalry: Art in Plantagenet England 1200–1400.* London: Royal Academy of Arts, 1987; Bruce-Mitford, Rupert L.S. *The Art of the Codex Amiatinus.* Jarrow Lecture, 1967. Jarrow: St. Paul's Church, 1967. Repr. *JBAA,* 3d ser. 32 (1969): 1–25; Camille, Michael. "Mouths and Meanings: Towards an Anti-Iconography of Medieval Art." In *Iconography at the Crossroads,* ed. Brendan Cassidy. Princeton: Index of Christian Art, 1993, pp. 43–57; Carver, Martin O.H. *The Age of Sutton Hoo.* Woodbridge: Boydell, 1992; Hahn, Cynthia. "*Peregrinatio et Natio:* The Illustrated Life of Edmund King and Martyr." *Gesta* 30 (1991): 119–39; Henderson, George. *Early Medieval* Style and Civilization Series. Rev. ed. Harmondsworth: Penguin, 1977. Repr. Toronto: University of Toronto Press, 1993; Kendrick, T.D., et al. *Evangeliorum Quattuor Codex Lindisfarnensis.* 2 vols. Lausanne: Urs Graf, 1956 [facsimile] and 1960 [commentary]; Stevenson, Robert. "Aspects of Ambiguity in Crosses and Interlace." *Ulster Journal of Archaeology* 44–45 (1981): 1–27; Temple, Elzbieta. *Anglo-Saxon Manuscripts 900–1066.* A Survey of Manuscripts Illuminated in the British Isles 2, ed. J.J.G. Alexander. London: Harvey Miller, 1976; Wamers, Egon. "Insular Art in Carolingian Europe: The Reception of Old Ideas in a New Empire." In *The Age of Migrating Ideas: Early Medieval Art in Northern Britain and Ireland,* ed. R. Michael Spearman and John Higgitt. Edinburgh: National Museums of Scotland, 1993, pp. 35–44.

See also Allegory; Architecture and Architectural Sculpture, Gothic; Architecture and Architectural Sculpture, Romanesque; Art, Anglo-Saxon: Celtic Influences, Classical Influences; Art, Gothic; Art, Romanesque; Coffin of St. Cuthbert; Eleanor Crosses; Hardham Wall Paintings; Harley Psalter; Lindisfarne Gospels; Manuscript Illumination, Anglo-Saxon; Metalwork, Gothic; Ruthwell Cross; Saints' Lives, Illuminated; Wall Painting, Romanesque

Impeachment

When impeachment was revived in the early 17th century, it was understood to have a precise meaning: a special form of criminal trial in which the House of Commons presented articles of impeachment against the accused and appointed managers to prosecute these charges and present evidence to support them before the House of Lords. The Lords gave final judgment, acting as judge and jury. The procedure was normally used to try the king's ministers for misconduct while in office.

Impeachments in parliament following much this kind of procedure are found in the Middle Ages. The first took place in the "Good Parliament" of 1376; impeachment was used against Lords Latimer and Nevill, the king's chamberlain and the steward of his household, and against Edward III's mistress Alice Perrers and a group of London merchants (Richard Lyons, William Elys, John Pecche, and Adam Bury). In 1386 it was used—against the wishes of Richard II—to try his chancellor, Michael de la Pole, earl of Suffolk. In 1387 Richard obtained a legal opinion from some of the judges holding that impeachment could not be brought against his ministers without his consent; in 1388 the judges who had given that opinion, along with other royal intimates, were impeached against the king's will at the "Merciless Parliament." It was used once more in 1397 at Richard II's own instigation to secure the condemnation of Archbishop Arundel, Sir Thomas Mortimer, and John, Lord Cobham.

No further attempt was made to use the procedure until 1450, when the Commons tried to impeach William de la Pole, duke of Suffolk, for high treason. Suffolk placed himself in the king's hands, and, to avoid the impeachment proceeding, Henry VI sentenced him to banishment. The procedure then lay dormant until its revival in 1621.

A number of variants on this procedure are also called impeachments in contemporary sources, such as a criminal trial before the Lords on the initiative of a single royal servant acting on the king's instructions. Examples are the 1383 prosecution of the bishop of Norwich, where impeachment was through the chancellor, and the 1397 prosecution of Thomas Haxey, through the steward of England, John of Gaunt. William of Wykeham's trial before the king's council in 1376 is also described as an impeachment.

Paul Brand

Bibliography

Collas, John P., ed. *Year Books of Edward II.* Vol. 25: *12 Edward II.* Selden Society 81. London: Quaritch, 1964, pp. lxvi–lxx [looks at etymology of "impeach" and development of its specialist senses]; Lambrick, Gabrielle. "The Impeachment of the Abbot of Abingdon in 1358." *EHR* 82 (1967): 250–76 [challenges Plucknett's thesis; not wholly convincing]; Plucknett, Theodore F.T. "The Origin of Impeachment." *TRHS,* 4th ser. 24 (1942): 47–71; Plucknett, Theodore F.T. "The Impeachment of 1376." *TRHS,* 5th ser. 1 (1951): 153–64; Plucknett, Theodore F.T. "State Trials under Richard II." *TRHS,* 5th ser. 2 (1952): 159–71; Plucknett, Theodore F.T. "Impeachment and Attainder." *TRHS,* 5th ser. 3 (1953): 145–58.

See also Attainder

Inquisitions Post Mortem

In the strict sense of the term this was an administrative jury summoned by a royal official, the escheator, to make an inquisition after the death of a tenant-in-chief of the crown (a vassal who held a fief directly from the king). The jury was to determine what lands were held by the deceased on the day of death, of whom the lands were held and by what service, and the name and age of the next heir.

The purpose of the inquiry was to secure to the king his feudal perquisites—wardship, marriage, and relief—as well as to seize any lands now escheating, or reverting to the king as feudal lord, through lack of a legitimate heir or by forfeiture. The return by the jury often gives information about the widow's dower and evidence of the resettling of the fee to create a joint tenancy for husband and wife to remove portions of the estate from nonfiduciary wardship, should the heir be a minor.

The inquisition was set in motion by the writ, *diem clausit extremum,* which directed the king's officials to ascertain the lands held directly from the king when a tenant-in-chief died, or "closed his (her) final day." The earliest extant examples are from the 39th year of Henry III's reign (1254–55). Zeal to secure all possible revenue for the crown meant that the jury reported on many deceased persons who, it was discovered, held nothing directly from the king. Therefore the records are a rich source for information on feudal land and socage land (land held by a specific service, in contrast to the more arbitrary holding by knight service) as well as tenants-in-chief.

In the Public Record Office the inquisitions are combined with a broader set of related records dealing with hereditary descent of land, assignment of dower, lands of lunatics, and proofs of age. The process of proving age was a picturesque one; persons wishing to establish that they had reached their majority requested the verdict of a jury. This jury contained persons of widely varying social class, from a bishop who had baptized the child of a prominent feudatory to manorial workers or household servants who remembered the birth or baptism. The charm of these returns is in the link between folk memory and an event in the life of a juror who married at the time, broke a leg, came home from war, or had a relative enter a monastery at the crucial time, and who *therefore* remembered that the heir must now be 21 or more years old.

Some potential jurors, probably as an aid to future memory, had been given a gift in celebration of the birth, or entertained at a baptismal party, or saw the event written in a church service book or a chronicle. One juror named Hugh the Carpenter concluded his testimony that the heir had reached majority by asserting that his "memory" was perfect. The age of jurors was always given. The jurors were never cross-examined and few inquests had their findings rejected or even questioned on the ground of misinformation. Some returns have an evident flaw that goes unchallenged.

The feudal guardian was invited to the inquest, and he or she either sent a representative to say that there was no objection or was noted as warned to come but did not appear. Occasionally guardians agreed that the heir or heiress was of age but claimed that the ward still owed the guardian for the right to marry freely. The defects in some details and the formulaic character of the "proofs" should not obscure the fact that proof represented the sense of the neighborhood that the heir was of age.

Sue Sheridan Walker

Bibliography

Calendar of Inquisitions Post Mortem. 18 vols. London: HMSO, 1904– [introduction by H.C. Maxwell Lyte, in vol. 1, is a guide to the documents, now running to the early 15th century]; Hunnisett, R.F. "The Reliability of Inquisitions as Historical Evidence." In *The Study of Medieval Records: Essays in Honour of Kathleen Major,* ed. D.A. Bullough and R.L. Storey. Oxford: Clarendon, 1971, pp. 206–35; Walker, Sue Sheridan. "Proof of Age of Feudal Heirs in Medieval England." *MS* 35 (1973): 306–32.

See also Feudalism; Juries

Investiture Controversy in England

The great controversy between secular and ecclesiastical authority over the appointment of clerics to office. In England the controversy ran from 1100 to 1107; it began when Henry I ascended the throne and recalled from exile Anselm, archbishop of Canterbury and primate of the English church. Henry requested the traditional homage from his archbishop, but Anselm, having heard the pope ban churchmen from homage to laymen, and laymen from investing churchmen, refused. Homage, a reciprocal oath binding vassal to lord, was the foundation of Henry's political and military power and authority; to lose it meant losing customary rights and legal, practical control over churchmen and their fiefs (which constituted a large part of his realm).

Losing investiture—the granting of ring and staff as symbols of ecclesiastical office—diminished royal power to choose and appoint ecclesiastical rulers. Popes, however, viewed these practices as diminishing the church's liberty to appoint its own men and to bind their loyalties to Rome, not to kings; they sought to establish papal control over the ecclesiastical hierarchy.

These issues had surfaced in the time of William II (William Rufus). Anselm had struggled continuously with Rufus to combat his control of the English church and its income. The king refused Anselm permission to correspond with, appeal to, or visit popes, or to hold reform councils in England. Anselm had gone into exile in 1097. But Henry agreed to cooperate, until Anselm refused him the traditional homage, previously paid to Rufus. At first archbishop and king sent joint missions to persuade Pope Paschal to rescind the homage ban for England. When this failed, Anselm obediently took Paschal's side, entering exile in 1103. Then began an intricate ballet of propagandistic justification from all sides, threats and counterthreats, rumors, and political manipulations. Henry claimed his customary rights and sought to conquer Normandy as the "Savior of the Norman Churches"; Anselm suffered as the wronged victim of an ill-advised king; Paschal floundered about.

As Henry swept through Normandy in 1105, Anselm moved quickly, threatening Henry's excommunication. Henry's allies began to desert and his sister Adela, countess of Blois, arranged a meeting. King and archbishop agreed to compromise; Henry would retain homage but abandon investiture. Paschal approved, but Anselm agreed to return to England (thus visibly ratifying Henry's piety) only when the pope implemented Anselm's political philosophy; king and archbishop would be co-rulers of church and state.

Now, finally, Henry could conquer Normandy. From Paschal Anselm won ratification of his primacy and independence from direct papal control. Anselm, through intelligent statesmanship, emerged the victor. Immediately Henry, with Anselm's approval, appointed new pastors to the English and Norman churches. They saw the pope as a distant source of law. The compromise set the pattern for the later papal settlement with the Holy Roman Emperor Henry V (Henry I's son-in-law) in the German investiture controversy (Concordat of Worms, 1122). Although the investiture conflict in England was formally resolved by 1107, feeling about the choice and investiture of clerics would run high well into the middle of the 12th century.

Sally N. Vaughn

Bibliography

Barlow, Frank. *The English Church, 1066–1154: A History of the Anglo-Norman Church*. London: Longman, 1979; Brooke, Zachary N. *The English Church and the Papacy, from the Conquest to the Reign of John*. Cambridge: Cambridge University Press, 1931; Cantor, Norman. *Church, Kingship, and Lay Investiture in England, 1089–1135*. Princeton: Princeton University Press, 1969; Vaughn, Sally N. *Anselm of Bec and Robert of Meulan: The Innocence of the Dove and the Wisdom of the Serpent*. Berkeley: University of California Press, 1987.

See also Anselm; Canterbury, Ecclesiastical Province of; Henry I; William II

Ipswich

Situated at the mouth of the Orwell River in southeast Suffolk, an Anglo-Saxon *burh* complete with royal mint in Edgar's time (957–75). In 991 the Viking Olaf ravaged the town before vanquishing the Saxon host at the Battle of Maldon. By 1016 Ipswich was part of the Danelaw ruled by Cnut.

At the time of the Conquest the half-hundred of Ipswich, which included the town and immediate environs, was a prosperous settlement of 538 burgesses and a dozen churches. Some catastrophe clearly befell the town thereafter, for Domesday Book records that only 110 burgesses were able to pay dues to the king in 1086; more than 300 homes lay in waste. It remains unclear whether the town suffered from Norman reprisals, a late Danish raid, or other factors.

A century later, however, Ipswich was a thriving community, its merchants engaged in commerce throughout northern Europe, particularly with the Low Countries. As the port of the Orwell, the one easily navigable river in Suffolk, it served as a regional entrepot and transshipping point. In the early phases of the Hundred Years War Ipswich enjoyed strategic importance as the base for naval operations. The fleet that vanquished the French armada at Sluys (1340) set sail from the Orwell.

In 1200 King John granted the burgesses a charter of incorporation whereby they could elect officers, hear crown pleas, and organize a guild merchant (an oligarchy of powerful merchants that was tantamount to the town's government). Over the centuries the town's governors were to have these privileges reconfirmed and expanded, culminating in Henry VI's grant of admiralty jurisdiction in 1446. Knights of the shire for Suffolk were traditionally elected at Ipswich, and the town remained the administrative center for county matters even after crown assizes were removed to Bury St. Edmunds in the 14th century.

Just prior to the Black Death the town ranked fourteenth in the kingdom, based on its lay subsidy assessment. In the 15th and 16th centuries Ipswich merchants were active in the burgeoning cloth industry of rural Suffolk, and the profits of that trade renewed much of the town fabric. The 1523–24 lay subsidy returns revealed the town to be among the ten wealthiest in England.

Ipswich custom allowed a boy to declare his majority at fourteen if he could prove his ability to count and measure, whereas males usually were not considered to be of full age until they reached 21. Another singular tradition mandated that burgage property be distributed equally among all male heirs at the father's death, not just to the eldest son. The shrine of Our Lady of Grace was a popular pilgrimage site until the agents of Thomas Cromwell, earl of Essex, absconded with the golden image in 1535.

Susan Battley

Bibliography

Bacon, Nathaniel. *The Annalls of Ipswiche, 1664*. Ed. William H. Richardson. Ipswich: Cowell, 1884; Cross, Robert L. *Justice in Ipswich, 1200–1968*. Ipswich: Ipswich Corporation, 1968; Redstone, Vincent. *Ipswich Borough Records*. Ipswich: East Anglia Daily Times, 1926–39.

See also Bury St. Edmunds; Towns

Isidore of Seville (ca. 560–636)

The encyclopedic works of Archbishop Isidore of Seville proved of enduring interest and importance to English writers throughout the medieval period. His most celebrated work, the *Etymologies (Etymologiae)*, composed in twenty books, argues that the nature of every thing can be derived etymologically from its name. Although many of the etymologies appear fanciful or fantastic, the treatise was hugely influential from the earliest period and was scoured for information by such authors as Aldhelm and Eusebius.

An earlier work, *On the Nature of Things (De natura rerum)*, describes such subjects as the elements, planetary motion, and the nature of eclipses and made Isidore, along with Pliny, one of the most influential authors on questions of natural history in the early Middle Ages. The work was used heavily by Bede, for example, in the composition of his own important scientific treatises. A further work by Isidore, the *Differences (Differentiae)*, demonstrates his characteristic approach. The *Differences* is carefully divided into two parts, the first of which is alphabetical and discusses the difference between pairs of Latin words (e.g., *religio*, "religion," and *fides*, "faith"), while the second part considers the differences between contrasting concepts, such as the grace of God and the will of man, or the lives of action and contemplation. It is the clarity and care of Isidore's exposition here and in his other works that made his books so attractive to later medieval audiences.

Much of the rest of Isidore's prolific writings concern topics of ecclesiastical administration and biblical exegesis, and a wide range of his works were preserved in a large number of English manuscripts, some dating from the earliest period. Special mention might be made of his *Synonyma* (*PL* 83: 827–68), an introduction to Christian spirituality, parts of which were translated into the vernacular, and which appears to have been the ultimate source for several passages in OE, both in prose homilies and in verse, including part of *The Seafarer*.

A.P.M. Orchard

Bibliography

PRIMARY

Fontaine, Jacques, ed. *Isidore de Séville: Traité de la nature.* Bordeaux: Féret & Fils, 1950; Lindsay, W.M., ed. *Hispalensis episcopi etymologiarum sive originum libri XX.* 2 vols. Oxford: Oxford University Press, 1911.

SECONDARY

Brehaut, Ernest. *An Encyclopedist of the Dark Ages: Isidore of Seville.* New York: Columbia University Press, 1912; Fontaine, Jacques. *Isidore de Séville et la culture classique dans l'Espagne wisigothique.* 3 vols. Paris: Études Augustiniennes, 1959–83.

See also Aldhelm; Bede; Eusebius; Scientific and Medical Writings; *Seafarer*

Ivory Carving, Anglo-Saxon

The study of Anglo-Saxon ivories is problematic. Most have no provenance, and scholars cannot agree on dates and attributions. They have never been set in any kind of continuous context.

Elephant ivory was used by the whole Mediterranean Christian world from the 4th to the 6th century, at which point it disappeared. It is not clear where the Mediterranean world acquired its ivory, but it is known that "vast fleets" of Roman merchant ships regularly traded with India for luxury goods, completing the circuit within a year. But with the collapse of the Roman Empire and the rise of the new Muslim Empire in the 7th and 8th centuries, international trade was drastically reduced. The Muslims were also traders, but they limited themselves to expensive land transport and thus were not in a position to supply ivory. The loss seems to have been keenly felt in Europe.

No more decorated elephant ivory survives from European contexts before the 9th century, but Anglo-Saxon and Scandinavian artisans made enterprising use of whalebone instead. Perhaps the earliest example is a writing tablet from Blythborough, Suffolk (London, British Museum MLA 1903, 3–15, 1), decorated with an interlace design similar to 8th-century work. But the finest example must be the little Gandersheim Casket (Braunschweig, Herzog Anton-Ulrich Museum MA58), decorated all over with neatly carved panels of two-footed, winged beasts enmeshed in interlace formed from their own tails. These creatures, called "Anglian beasts," also appear on 8th-century Northumbrian crosses like the ones at Ruthwell and Rothbury. As on the crosses the design on the casket is carved in a rounded profile against a flat ground. In fact it is thought to be derived from the inhabited vinescroll motif of the same crosses, representing the design in its final, most abstract phase. A small plaque from Larling, Norfolk, has a similar Anglian beast and also an image of Romulus and Remus (Norwich, Castle Museum 184.970).

Whalebone was obviously a good substitute for ivory (the Gandersheim Casket has a warm color and a pleasing waxy gleam), and in the absence of ivory it must have been used extensively; objects like the Gandersheim Casket do not get produced in isolation. But few whalebone artifacts survive. Perhaps it was easily broken, as most surviving whalebone objects have large pieces broken off.

In the 9th century ivory became available again in Europe. It was widely used by continental craftsmen but not by Anglo-Saxons. It is not entirely clear why this happened. This was the time at which Charlemagne established his huge, wealthy, and stable empire; Constantinople recovered from Muslim attacks and resumed trading with India and the Far East; and Venice became a powerful sea-trading state that Charlemagne attempted to conquer. It all came together neatly: luxury goods arrived in Constantinople, Venetian traders transported them to Europe, and Charlemagne controlled the European markets. Venetian traders also encouraged the Muslims to export goods from deeper in Africa, and thus may have opened an additional source of ivory.

Some of this new ivory apparently reached St. Omer in Flanders, where it was carved in styles derived from Charlemagne's court scriptorium (also called the Ada School). Its own scriptorium produced a style known as "Franco-Saxon." This was the only place in Europe where three trade routes met, and in the 11th century it was also the starting point for English pilgrims to Spain. The wealth of artifacts pouring into St. Omer is unimaginable.

In the 10th and 11th centuries the Anglo-Saxon kings had their capital at Winchester. In 944 Grimbald of St. Bertin founded a daughter house at Bath, transferring to the New Minster at Winchester in 966. This is important because St. Bertin was a neighbor and daughter house of St. Omer. Contacts between the New Minster and St. Bertin were evidently frequent, with good Roman roads between Winchester, London, and Canterbury, and with St. Omer and St. Bertin just across the Channel.

It seems that Grimbald brought with him several Carolingian manuscripts and ivories that were also formative in creating the new "Winchester" style of painting. At the same time "ivories" in the same style began to appear. In fact Europe was still monopolizing the ivory supplies, and Anglo-Saxon craftsmen found a new substitute: morse (walrus tusk), which seems to have been more durable than whalebone.

Grimbald's possessions apparently included a Majesty in a mandorla that may well be the pierced ivory plaque once on an early-10th-century Franco-Saxon Gospel book from Marchiennes, near St. Bertin (New York, Pierpont Morgan

Library M.319A), and an ivory Crucifixion scene (Brussels, private collection) that was copied exactly into the Sherborne Pontifical (Paris, BN lat. 943). The scene shows Christ wearing a loincloth tied with a distinctive and genuinely tieable knot, flanked by a grieving Virgin and St. John the Evangelist, with a pair of flying angels and the hand of God above. These two sources spawned a series of carvings from both Winchester and St. Bertin, including two Majesties, a grieving Virgin and St. John (St. Omer, Musée Sandelin 2822), a Corpus now mounted on a filigreed cross-reliquary (London, Victoria and Albert Museum 7943–1862), a host of Crucifixion plaques that were produced well into the 11th century, and the Heribert Tau (Cologne, Cathedral Treasury). The common features of these objects clearly go back to the two specific original sources mentioned above, and these sources were almost certainly kept at Grimbald's New Minster, because all the elements reappear, composed into new pictures, in the New Minster Charter (BL Cotton Vespasian A.viii) and the Liber Vitae, also from New Minster (BL Stowe 944).

The Majesty figure also appears in several manuscripts, including one written by Odbert of St. Bertin but illustrated by an Anglo-Saxon artist and another that Odbert illustrated himself. Other images are also duplicated at Winchester and St. Bertin. A small ivory Nativity (Liverpool, Merseyside County Museum Mayer Collection M 8060) reproduces the scene from the Benedictional of Æthelwold (BL Add. 49598) and from the Boulogne Gospels (Boulogne, Bibliothèque Municipale 11), which were written at St. Bertin and painted by an Anglo-Saxon artist; and an ivory Baptism of Christ (London, British Museum MLA 1974, 10–2,1) reproduces the figure from the Second Coming in the Benedictional of Æthelwold.

The connections between St. Bertin and the New Minster seem undeniable. But there were also connections between the New Minster and Canterbury. These are seen most clearly in manuscript work, where Edui Bassan of Christ Church, Canterbury, betrays intimate knowledge of the New Minster motifs in his "Grimbald Gospels" of perhaps ca. 1020 (BL Add. 34890). These Gospels contain a copy of the original letter in which Grimbald of St. Bertin was recommended to the Anglo-Saxon king. Lavishly illustrated, they duplicate the New Minster images of the Majesty, the flying angels, and also the enthroned Virgin and Child from a lobed ivory plaque in the Winchester style (Oxford, Ashmolean Museum 1978.332). Edui or his pupil apparently also produced the Missal of Robert of Jumièges by ca. 1023 (Rouen, Bibliothèque Municipale Y.6), where more New Minster imagery appears in the Nativity and in the Deposition scene, which is adapted from the original Crucifixion and the Baptism plaque. New Minster imagery now becomes common in manuscripts attributed to Canterbury.

Associated with those manuscripts is a series of plaques that are not morse but real ivory. Goldschmidt thought they were a provincial subgroup of the Carolingian Reims School, but Beckwith identified them as Anglo-Saxon. Unfortunately he attributed them to the 8th, 9th, and 10th centuries, which

is not possible. Reims is where the Utrecht Psalter (Utrecht, Rijksuniversiteit 32) was produced: dating to ca. 830, it is lavishly illustrated with energetic, funny little sketches, and it was at Canterbury being copied in the 1020s and 1030s, where it changed the whole character of Anglo-Saxon drawing. But it had originally stimulated a series of matching ivory plaques from Reims, the best of which are still on the covers of the Prayerbook and Psalter of Charles the Bald, and it probably had similar plaques on its own covers. These Reims School ivories appear to have stimulated a new style of carving at Canterbury.

Beckwith identified eight plaques (Beckwith nos. 5, 6, 7, 9, 21, 22, 23, 24) as being Anglo-Saxon productions, not provincial Carolingian works. Some of the plaques have older carvings on their backs that have been cut down. The Transfiguration panel has a Last Judgment on its back that shows a cross-legged dancing angel waking the dead and the damned being consumed by the Jaws of Hell (London, Victoria and Albert Museum 253–1867). Cross-legged figures became common in the early 11th century, and Beckwith showed that they were known in a Prudentius manuscript from Christ Church, Canterbury. But the Jaws of Hell motif was a specifically Anglo-Saxon invention, first seen in the Tiberius Psalter from Winchester in the 1020s (BL Cotton Tiberius C.vi) and then in the New Minster Liber Vitae of ca. 1031. So the primary carving on this panel cannot be earlier than the 11th century and must be Anglo-Saxon. The Transfiguration on the front may look Carolingian, but it cannot be earlier than the 11th-century carving on the back, and this must also be true of the complementary Ascension panel (London, Victoria and Albert Museum 254–1867).

The Traditio Legis and Enthroned Virgin panels (two halves of a book cover; Paris, BN lat. 323) have acanthus frames very like those on the Transfiguration and Ascension. All four panels show strong influence from the Utrecht Psalter or Reims School ivories, as seen in the gently bulging, flexible bodies, the splayed hand gestures, the style and placing of the ground and clouds, and especially the central apostle of the Transfiguration, who is very like the Nathan on the cover of the Psalter of Charles the Bald. This distinctive figure reappeared as the Psalmist on the cover of the prayerbook of Charles the Bald by the same craftsman.

Anglo-Saxon craftsmen used motifs from other sources, too. The Traditio Legis seems rather Ottonian, with its flat relief and its figure-of-eight–shaped mandorla. The mandorla is made of layered acanthus leaves, as in the dedication panel from the Magdeburg antependium (front panel of an altar). This was donated by Otto I, and it features the enormous, rimmed halos also seen in the Transfiguration, Ascension, Traditio Legis, and Enthroned Madonna. Another significant source may be an ivory or manuscript from New Minster, as Peter and Paul in the Traditio Legis panel seem to be based on the New Minster flying angels. This combination of influences echoes the influences on the manuscripts attributed to Canterbury. So perhaps the ivories were also made at Canterbury.

But more ivories belong to this group. In the Braunschweig Museum is an ivory casket in the same style. Its lid is decorated with New Minster flying angels, and on the side is a Baptism incredibly like the one in the Benedictional of Æthelwold. Beckwith's list included two panels with an extraordinary image of Christ baptized in a tub (London, Victoria and Albert Museum 257–1867; Paris, Musée de Cluny). This image reappears in another plaque now in Florence and is currently believed to belong to the "later Metz" group. The plaque is carved in the same style as the casket, with an identical acanthus frame, and has an identical figure rushing forward with a towel. None of this material has been recognized before, but Canterbury now emerges with a character of its own and appears to have monopolized the supply of elephant ivory.

In summary England's peripheral position forced it to use whalebone and morse before it gained temporary access to ivory in the 11th century. In the 8th century the style mimicked contemporary stone crosses; but Carolingian ivory workers mimicked the work of manuscript illumination instead, and the strong European influence at Winchester and Canterbury evidently encouraged Anglo-Saxon carvers to do the same.

In this context it is difficult to know what to make of three objects. The whalebone Franks Casket (London, British Museum MLA 1867, 1–20.1; fig. 63: see FRANKS CASKET) is usually accepted as 8th-century Northumbrian; although there is no comparative material, it has clear Scandinavian content, and runes continued to be used well into the 11th century. In fact an 11th-century date has also been argued for the casket, and this might fit the context better. The ivory Genoels-Elderen Diptych (Brussels, Musées Royaux d'Art et d'Histoire 1474) was identified as Anglo-Saxon by Beckwith, but most scholars now see it as European. And an enormous whalebone Adoration plaque has been attributed to Anglo-Norman England and to Spain (London, Victoria and Albert Museum 142–1866).

Perette E. Michelli

Bibliography

Backhouse, Janet, Derek H. Turner, and Leslie Webster, eds. *The Golden Age of Anglo-Saxon Art 966–1066.* London: British Museum, 1984; Beckwith, John. *Ivory Carvings in Early Medieval England.* London: Harvey Miller, 1972; Curtis, P.D. *Cross-Cultural Trade in World History.* Cambridge: Cambridge University Press, 1984; Dodwell, C.R. *Painting in Europe 800–1200.* Harmondsworth: Penguin, 1971; Gibson, Margaret. *The Liverpool Ivories: Late Antique and Medieval Ivories and Bone Carvings in the Liverpool Museum and the Walker Art Gallery.* London: HMSO, 1994; Goldschmidt, Adolph. *Die Elfenbeinskulpturen aus der Zeit der karolingischen und sächsischen Kaiser VIII–XI. Jahrhundert.* Vol. 1. Berlin: Deutscher Verlag für Kunstwissenschaft, 1914; Lasko, Peter. *Ars Sacra 800–1200.* 2d ed. New Haven: Yale University Press, 1994; Swarzenski, Hanns. *Monuments of Romanesque Art: The Art of Church Treasures in North-Western Europe.* 2d ed. London: Faber & Faber, 1974; Vandersall, Amy L. "The Date and Provenance of the Franks Casket." *Gesta* 11 (1972): 9–26; Webster, Leslie, and Janet Backhouse, eds. *The Making of England: Anglo-Saxon Art and Culture AD 600–900.* London: British Museum, 1991; Wilson, David M. *Anglo-Saxon Art: From the Seventh Century to the Norman Conquest.* London: Thames & Hudson, 1984; Zarnecki, George, Janet Holt, and Tristram Holland, eds. *English Romanesque Art 1066–1200.* London: Weidenfeld & Nicolson, 1984.

See also Art, Anglo-Saxon; Benedictional of Æthelwold; Franks Casket; Harley Psalter; Ivory Carving, Romanesque; New Minster Charter; Runes; Ruthwell Cross; Tiberius Psalter; "Winchester School"

Ivory Carving, Romanesque

Although they survive in large quantities, most English ivories lack inscription and provenance and have become detached from their original objects, so they can be dated or classified only through stylistic analysis. This is subjective at best, but it is more than usually difficult in this case because of the wide range of techniques, details, and artistic habits found on each object. Few pieces seem to be by the same hand, or even from the same workshop, and scholars disagree dramatically about every aspect of the field.

But there are some generally accepted conclusions about English Romanesque ivories. Most of them are morse ivory (walrus tusk), which became common during the 11th and 12th centuries, while in Europe elephant tusk continued to be used. The two media have different aesthetic properties. Morse is a fine-grained white substance that takes a sharp edge and lends itself to tiny detail; elephant tusk looks more like cream swirled with melted butter and seems to be softer or at least more easily worn. Both can darken with age. The properties of these materials cause noticeable differences between the kinds of work practiced on the Continent and in England during the Romanesque period.

Much European Romanesque ivory was carved in the Low Countries and continues a 600- to 700-year-long tradition stretching back through the Carolingians to early Christian times. These are narrative panels showing biblical scenes on a flat undetailed background and surrounded with a classicizing acanthus frame. Some English Romanesque ivory joins this tradition, but the more interesting material exploits the working qualities of morse and differs markedly from European work. It is smaller in scale, rich with exquisite detail, and experimental in type and concept.

These properties are especially suited to work in the style of the Canterbury School, which can also be identified in contemporary stonework and manuscripts. The style is typified by fibrous foliage, raised beads in borders and foliage, pierced beads, chevrons, and figures with some sort of dampfold drapery. The style can be seen beginning in an early- or mid-11th-century tau cross from the royal Norman Abbey of Jumièges (Rouen, Musée Départmental des Antiquités). This

Fig. 75. Tau Crosier with Christ Pantocrator (London, Victoria and Albert Museum 371–1871). Reproduced by permission of the Board of Trustees of the Victoria and Albert Museum, London.

gave rise to a series of similar English taus, whose rich foliage is highly evocative of the older royal Winchester style. One of these is an early- to mid-12th-century tau from Battle Abbey. Battle Abbey was founded by the first Norman king of England, William I, so in ivory, as in other media, the Romanesque Canterbury style seems to be a royal Norman response to an existing royal Anglo-Saxon style.

Most of the ivories in this style are of the highest quality, and one of the most exquisite is a tau cross from Liège Cathedral (London, Victoria and Albert Museum 371–1871; fig. 75) that has been dated variously from ca. 1100 to ca. 1150 and later. In type and style it belongs to the Jumièges–Battle Abbey tradition. An interesting feature of this tau and others like it is its ambiguity. It contains a Virgin and Child on one side and a Pantocrator on the other, and in the volutes are St. Michael and human figures fighting monsters that develop out of the foliate arms of the volute. The veins in the leaves and the hairs on the monsters' necks are individually sculpted. But, exquisite as it is, what does it mean?

An earlier example from this group is the John of Beverley Crosier (private collection on deposit in the British Museum), dated mid- to late-11th-century. John of Beverley was bishop of Hexham 687–706 and archbishop of York from 706 to 714(?). He died in 721 and was canonized in 1037; this crosier may have been made for, or as a result of, that canonization. Like the taus discussed above the crosier has a foliate volute framing figurative scenes. Scholars cannot agree on the interpretation of these scenes. Bede, writing in the 8th century, likened some of the miracles of John of Beverley to those of Sts. Peter and John the Evangelist, and this may be the clue. On one side the central figure grasps the chin of a seated man with thick hair. This closely follows the story of how John of Beverley cured a skin-diseased mute whose speech and hair returned instantly. The incident was witnessed by the deacon Berethun, who can be seen in the background. But that figure bears a large key and may also represent St. Peter, while the other two figures could be Christ curing a leper or a dumb youth. On the other side Sts. Peter and John the Evangelist cure a lame man (Acts 3:5), but one of the saints holds a long-armed cross, so the scene could instead be a Harrowing of

Hell, or it could illustrate several other miracles by John of Beverley in which he healed people without touching them. The cryptic inscription could refer to any of these events, and one is forced to wonder if the ambiguity is deliberate.

A second group of ivories, while associated with this royal Canterbury School, do not seem to belong directly to it, having more unusual compositions and greater affinities with metalwork. One is the unique St. Nicholas Crosier (London, Victoria and Albert Museum 218–1865; fig. 116: see ST. NICHOLAS CROSIER), whose interpretation has long been debated. This object has a curious "Art Deco" quality to it, in that the ivory of the volute appears to split and burst and curl into foliage. In one place it grows a tendril that becomes the crib of the Nativity.

Consider also the equally unique Cloisters Cross (New York, Metropolitan Museum, Cloister Collection 63.12; fig. 47: see CLOISTERS CROSS). Like the St. Nicholas Crosier it swarms with tiny, exquisite figures, and its interpretation is also still being debated. Similar in style and quality is a tiny statuette of the Flight into Egypt (New York, Metropolitan Museum Dodge Fund 940.B100 [40.62]). Both objects eschew decorative tricks like beading, zigzag patterns, or repeating drapery patterns and make their impact through the sheer technical genius of their craftsmen.

An interesting feature of the Cloisters Cross is its apparent affinity with the best imperial metalwork. In design and decorative structure it is very like several crosses by the European craftsman Roger of Helmarshausen, who worked in imperial circles on the Continent. The Liège Tau, discussed above, may also have imperial connections, in that it could well have been made in a royal English center, such as Winchester or Canterbury, at precisely the time when imperial enamelwork, possibly by Godefroide of Huy, was acquired by Henry of Blois, bishop of Winchester and brother of King Stephen. Liège itself is an imperial center near Godefroide's native Huy, and it is tempting to wonder if there was some sort of exchange.

All the ivories discussed above are innovative in design and concept, exquisite in detail and finish, and often minute in scale. This is what makes them different from European work, and the whole approach may have been stimulated by the unique qualities of the new morse medium. They appear to have been prized in imperial and royal circles in England and abroad and to have been personal property rather than official paraphernalia or general decoration; none could be adequately appreciated from a distance, as the European narrative plaques might have been, and it is possible that there was some kind of elite connoisseurs' market for this material.

A third, coherent group of ivories, although of lesser quality, is associated with the mid-12th-century Lewis Chessmen (now in the British Museum) and with work in Scandinavia. This group is clearly discussed and illustrated by Michael Taylor. It may have been practiced on both sides of the North Sea: in addition to Scandinavian elements (such as the "berserker" pawns biting their shields and several Urnes-style motifs) this group shares several foliate motifs with the royal Canterbury group discussed above and many of its innovative and ambiguous tendencies, too. It might be remembered, for example, that chess was an exotic new introduction to England at this date, and no other chess sets are remotely like the Lewis figures.

The Canterbury group may not be the only one to parallel developments in stone. A portable altar from Norwich and two plaques in the Bargello Museum, Florence, may parallel the style of contemporary architectural friezes (e.g., the frieze on the west facade of Lincoln Cathedral), while a bizarre Deposition plaque may relate to the group of sculpture schools around Hereford with their mixture of Irish and Scandinavian elements and their smattering of motifs garnered from the pilgrim routes to Santiago. But these examples are rare, and no useful discussion can be made here.

In the final analysis it is difficult to establish clearly distinguished schools of ivory working and even harder to define dates or interpretations. It is easier to point to the undeniable qualities of the work: its organic, "Art Deco–like" qualities, its possibly deliberate ambiguities, its attention to detail, its fine finish, its generally small scale, and its experimental, innovative nature. In all these respects English Romanesque ivory differs markedly from contemporary European work, and it may have commanded highly prestigious and specialized markets.

Perette E. Michelli

Bibliography

Beckwith, John. *Ivory Carvings in Early Medieval England.* London: Harvey Miller, 1972; Bede. *A History of the English Church and People.* Trans. Leo Sherley-Price. Harmondsworth: Penguin, 1988, pp. 271–79; Gibson, Margaret. *The Liverpool Ivories: Late Antique and Medieval Ivories and Bone Carvings in the Liverpool Museum and the Walker Art Gallery.* London: HMSO, 1994; Parker, Elizabeth C., and Charles T. Little. *The Cloisters Cross: Its Art and Meaning.* London: Harvey Miller, 1993; Taylor, Michael. *The Lewis Chessmen.* London: British Museum, 1978; Zarnecki, George, Janet Holt, and Tristram Holland, eds. *English Romanesque Art 1066–1200.* London: Weidenfeld & Nicolson, 1984.

See also Art, Romanesque; Cloisters Cross; Henry of Blois Plaques; Ivory Carving, Anglo-Saxon; Manuscript Illumination, Romanesque; Sculpture, Romanesque; "Winchester School"

J

Jack Upland, Friar Daw's Reply, and Upland's Rejoinder

Three related works exemplifying the English vernacular tradition of attacking (and defending) the friars. Written between ca. 1390 and ca. 1450 in the Midlands dialect, they are explicitly Wycliffite or anti-Wycliffite in sentiment. Because they are concerned primarily with detailed exposition of mendicant practices, church doctrine, and canon law, these works are generally considered more polemical than poetic.

Jack Upland, an item-by-item prose critique of the behavior of the friars, was composed by an anonymous Wycliffite. The author's persona, an unlettered but truth-telling countryman, may be partly indebted to William Langland's Piers Plowman. The piece survives in two manuscripts and, with a misattribution to Chaucer, in three early printed editions.

Friar Daw's Reply is a contemporary response to *Jack Upland,* written in rough alliterative verse by an author who adopts the persona of an unlearned friar ("Daw Topias"); he is named John Walsingham in the scribal *explicit* at the end of the poem. It survives in a unique copy, Bodl. Digby 41, together with *Upland's Rejoinder.* In this educated and strident retort the poet defends the friars from the attacks made in *Jack Upland* and in the course of the poem insists that Lollards should be burned as heretics.

Upland's Rejoinder, a scathing response to "Friar Daw," also in rough alliterative verse, is written in the margins of *Friar Daw's Reply.* The *Rejoinder* displays a variety of coarse, personally directed attacks against the Friar, as well as a significant degree of Latin learning. Its author is unknown.

Kathleen M. Hewett-Smith

Bibliography

PRIMARY

Heyworth, Peter L., ed. *Jack Upland, Friar Daw's Reply and Upland's Rejoinder.* London: Oxford University Press, 1968.

SECONDARY

New *CBEL* 1:546, 687–88; *Manual* 5:1449–51, 1678–79; Hudson, Anne. "'No newe thyng': The Printing of Medieval Texts in the Early Reformation Period." In *Middle English Studies Presented to Norman Davis in Honour of His Seventieth Birthday,* ed. Douglas Gray and Eric G. Stanley. Oxford: Clarendon, 1983, pp. 153–74.

See also Alliterative Revival; Chaucerian Apocrypha; Friars; Lollards; *Pierce the Plowman's Creed; Piers Plowman;* Popular Religion; Satire; Wycliffite Texts

Jacob's Well

An early-15th-century sermon collection in ME prose. The work survives in a single manuscript (Salisbury Cathedral 103) written ca. 1450. It is one of many vernacular manuals intended to assist priests in their pastoral duty of religious instruction. In *Jacob's Well* internal emphases and references suggest an unsophisticated rural audience. The clerical author is anonymous.

The collection is divided into 95 chapters, each comprising a sermon of approximately 30 minutes' speaking length. The sermons seem to have been intended for daily oral delivery—in the first chapter the author says that the succeeding chapters will take 94 days, and in the final chapter he notes that the preceding chapters will have taken two whole months and more.

The modern title of the work derives from "fons Jacob" in the heading to the first chapter, a reference to the well on whose curb Christ rested while journeying to Samaria and where he talked with the Samaritan woman (John 4:6–26). The collection is structured around an elaborate allegory of the human body as a shallow pit that must be made into a deep well. Through its five entrances, the senses, the pit allows the ingress of the streams of the Great Curse (the automatic excommunication imposed for certain sins, the particulars of which were read in churches four times a year). Beneath these waters is a deep ooze, the seven deadly sins, which must be removed using various implements of contrition, confession, and satisfaction. The watergates of the senses must be stopped up and the pit deepened with the spade of cleanness until the seven springs of grace, the gifts of the Holy Ghost, are found. The bottom of the well must be leveled with equity; corbels (projecting stone supports) representing the articles of faith must be laid. The mortar consists of sand (memory of sin), water (tears), and lime (burning love of Christ). By the plumb-line of truth the well is built of this mortar and of stones (the works of faith). To ascend to heaven the soul must use the ladder of charity. To draw the water of grace from the well one must use a windlass (the mind), a rope (belief, a threefold intertwining of faith, hope, and charity), and a bucket (spiritual desire for all goodness). Thus may one drink one's fill of the sweet water of grace and, ultimately, the sweet wine of joy.

The allegory is worked out in punctilious detail, foot by foot, inch by inch, rung by rung, using colloquial language, down-to-earth similes and metaphors, and vivid references to everyday life. Much of the doctrinal substance of the work is based on the *Speculum Vitae* and the sermons are enlivened by numerous narrative exempla that the author took from the Latin *Alphabetum narrationum*.

Lister M. Matheson

Bibliography

PRIMARY

Brandeis, Arthur, ed. *Jacob's Well: An English Treatise on the Cleansing of Man's Conscience*. Part 1. EETS o.s. 115. London: Kegan Paul, Trench, Trübner, 1900 [the first 50 sermons].

SECONDARY

Manual 7:2262, 2481–82; Gregg, Joan Y. "The Exempla of *Jacob's Well:* A Study in the Transmission of Medieval Sermon Stories." *Traditio* 33 (1977): 359–80; Owst, G.R. *Literature and Pulpit in Medieval England.* 2d ed. Oxford: Blackwell, 1961 [numerous references to *Jacob's Well,* including quotations of unedited part].

See also Excommunication; Exemplum; Moral and Religious Instruction; Orality; Popular Culture; Prose, ME; Religious Allegories; Sermons; *Speculum Vitae*

Jews

Jews first arrived in England in the decades after the Norman Conquest. These first settlers, from Rouen in Normandy, probably came to London at the command of the king, perhaps to strengthen mercantile links between the two cities. The community flourished, and by the 1140s the Jewish population had spread to several provincial towns, a process that may have begun even before 1100. But despite its increasing financial importance, intellectually and culturally, English Jewry remained closely linked to the community of Rouen until the conquest of Normandy by Philip II (Philip Augustus) of France in 1204.

Throughout the reigns of William II (William Rufus) and Henry I the Jews of London remained closely tied to the royal court. Rufus prevented massacres in England of the sort that devastated the Rouen community in 1096, during preparations for the First Crusade, and Henry I issued a formal charter of liberties, asserting direct royal jurisdiction over all Jews in England and guaranteeing their right to travel freely, avoid local tolls, and hold land. Stephen tried to continue this policy, but the Anarchy witnessed a distancing of the Jewish communities from the court; Jews sought locally a protection the king could no longer provide. By the end of his reign (1154) Jewish settlements were established at Oxford, Norwich, Winchester, Cambridge, and a number of smaller towns, including several under seigneurial rather than royal jurisdiction. It may also have been in Stephen's reign that moneylending replaced trade as the primary economic support of the community.

Henry II's reign brought renewed stability and newly expanded cultural and intellectual contacts with the Jews of Spain, Provence, Italy, Germany, and northern France. Jewish and Christian lenders competed on more or less equal terms to supply the liquid capital required by the expanding economy. Some extraordinary Jewish fortunes were made through moneylending, including that of Aaron of Lincoln (d. 1186), the wealthiest Englishman of his day.

Henry II protected these financiers in the traditional way, borrowing from them in his early years, then shifting to direct taxation, particularly during his last decade. But storm-clouds were building. In the years after 1144 the first known charges of ritual murder—i.e., that Jews crucified Christian children—circulated around Norwich. Further charges were reported in Gloucester in 1168 and in Bury in 1181. Thomas Becket's supporters complained publicly that the king treated Jews better than he did the Christian clergy, and the 1180s saw the first attempts by local lords to expel Jewish communities from their territories.

With the coronation of Richard I (1189) the stormclouds broke. An attack on the Jews of London was followed within six months by massacres in Norwich, Lynn, and York, where virtually the entire Jewish population was murdered by a mob or committed suicide. Enthusiasm for the Third Crusade and the resentments of local knights indebted to Jewish lenders contributed to the outrages at York; the rioters carefully burned all records of Jewish debts they could lay hands on. These events helped prompt a reorganization of the king's administration of Jewish debts and brought renewed orders to royal officials to protect "the king's Jews" from attack. But the motives for royal concern were largely financial. Under Richard, John, and Henry III taxation of the Jews became a more and more important royal resource, with ultimately disastrous consequences for the prosperity of English Jewry.

Between 1210 and 1217 heavy taxation combined with civil war to reduce the Jewish population. Thereafter, however, the pressure eased; by 1240 the Jews had recovered both their prosperity and their numbers. Altogether there may have been around 5,000 Jews in mid-13th-century England, and between 1240 and 1260 they paid close to £70,000 in royal taxes. This ruinous taxation fell mostly on their wealthiest leaders and permanently reduced their financial value to the crown.

It also exacerbated tensions between the Jews and the Christian majority. To pay their taxes Jewish lenders were often forced to sell their bonds at a discount to Christian lenders, who would then foreclose on the mortgaged estates, acquiring them at a fraction of true value. Henry III's courtiers were active in this traffic, which became one of the many complaints voiced against his government in 1258. Simon de Montfort's followers were particularly anti-Jewish and perpetrated several massacres in 1263 and 1264.

The English Jews never recovered from this combination of taxation and attack. Restrictive legislation between 1269 and 1275 made it illegal for Jews to hold feudal property and eventually forbade their lending money. By this date, however, few other occupations were open. Some lending probably continued, therefore, even after its prohibition in 1275, but under subterfuges that make it difficult to trace. Pressure to convert had emanated from the royal court since the 1230s, when Henry III founded a special house in London to support such converts. This pressure mounted under Edward I, though with little success. Royal taxation also continued, but its receipts were paltry in comparison to the years between 1240 and 1260. The Jewish community was never a significant financial resource for the monarchy under Edward I, particularly in comparison with the receipts from parliamentary taxation.

Jews were a frequent target of crusade-inspired legislation, and in 1288 Edward, in connection with his oath to go again on crusade, expelled the Jews from Gascony. The expulsion of the English community in 1290 was also associated with this planned crusade, but its immediate cause was a bargain the king struck in parliament between April and July 1290. When Edward returned from Gascony in 1289, after three years abroad, he faced large debts and a rising chorus of complaint. To secure a tax he agreed to a number of reforms.

The final concession he made was to expel all the Jews from England; it was specifically in gratitude for this that his subjects granted him a tax of more than £100,000. And so the expulsion was announced. Jews were permitted to take their liquid wealth; their debts and real estate were confiscated by the crown. Their departure was completed by 1 November 1290. Several vessels were lost in rough seas, and at least one group of Jews was deliberately drowned by the sailors transporting them. The survivors traveled first to France, and some probably remained there despite the French order to expel them. Others traveled to Italy, Savoy, Germany, Spain, and the Holy Land.

No organized Jewish community was permitted to settle in England again until the 1650s, when Oliver Cromwell readmitted the Jews as part of his spiritual preparations for the end of the world.

Robert C. Stacey

Bibliography

Jacobs, Joseph, trans. *The Jews of Angevin England.* London: Nutt, 1893 [useful collection of translated extracts from original documents]; Richardson, H.G. *The English Jewry under Angevin Kings.* London: Methuen, 1960 [sophisticated treatment of the topic]; Roth, Cecil. *A History of the Jews in England.* 3d ed. Oxford: Clarendon, 1964 [the standard treatment]; Stacey, Robert C. "Recent Work on Medieval English Jewish History." *Jewish History* 2 (1987): 61–72 [also covers the principal primary sources].

See also Banks; Edward I

John (1167–1216; r. 1199–1216)

Born on December 24, 1167, he was the youngest of the four sons of Henry II and Eleanor of Aquitaine to reach manhood. His father intended him to be the ruler of an autonomous kingdom of Ireland (and from 1185 he bore the title Lord of Ireland), but with the deaths of his elder brothers he aspired to wider ambitions. After the death of the childless Richard (1199) he became king of England, duke of Normandy, duke of Aquitaine, and count of Anjou, and he prevailed against the claims of his nephew Arthur of Brittany, son of his brother Geoffrey.

It was a difficult inheritance. The financial burdens of Richard's reign had been extraordinarily heavy, for his crusade and ransom, and for the defense of the continental dominions against persistent attacks and subversion by Philip II (Philip Augustus) of France. The revenues of England, vital for survival, were devalued by inflation. The balance of advantage in resources and influence had tipped decisively in favor of the French crown. Normandy was war-weary, weakened, and demoralized; when Philip renewed his attack in 1204, the will to resist suddenly collapsed and John retired to England without putting up a fight.

John never reconciled himself to the loss of Normandy. His efforts to accumulate a war chest were remarkably successful, but achieved by a relentless and ruthless exploitation of royal rights over subjects that exposed the arbitrary nature of many of his royal powers and called their legitimacy into question. His barons, seeking to rebuild family fortunes after the loss of their Norman estates, had to bid expensively for royal favors granted, or withheld, capriciously.

Disaffection was for a time deflected by John's resistance to Pope Innocent III, who set aside a royal nominee for the archbishopric of Canterbury and instead appointed Stephen Langton, whom the king rejected. John's stand was generally supported by the laity, who patiently endured an interdict for six years. John confidently disregarded a sentence of excommunication while his coffers were augmented by the appropriated revenues of the clergy. That the English clergy should be so completely at his mercy was, however, a chilling demonstration of royal power to override established rights, and there was a growing feeling among some of the barons that their own safety and their families' fortunes depended on getting rid of him.

Faced by incipient rebellions and an invasion fleet mustered by Philip of France, John could not ignore the ultimate papal weapon, a sentence of deposition. He accepted the pope's terms for lifting the sanctions and in addition offered his kingdoms of England and Ireland as fiefs of the papacy, in effect putting them under the protection of the Holy See.

John's carefully nurtured grand strategy for the defeat of the French king collapsed when his allies, the count of Flanders and his nephew Emperor Otto IV of Germany, were decisively defeated by Philip at the Battle of Bouvines, May 1214. Open rebellion erupted in England. At a moment when neither side could be sure of winning, an attempt at a negotiated peace produced Magna Carta (June 1215), by which the crown's claims to executive privilege were brought within the bounds of agreed law. As a peace formula it failed, and John had it annulled by the pope. He was winning the civil war when he died (October 1216). Loyalists reissued Magna Carta to rally support for his infant son, Henry III.

While curtailing the possibility of tyranny Magna Carta also recognized the advantages of efficient royal government, which John had done much to foster. He understood administration and did much in a short reign to refine and rationalize it. He created a precedent (in the Thirteenth of 1207) for a proper taxation system. He created the navy that thwarted Philip's projected invasion. He failed, however, at the crucial arts of government in the management of men and what was currently recognized as "good lordship."

John has been portrayed as a monster of depravity. This is a fanciful elaboration of a distorting half-truth. He was no more domineering than his father and brother, and hardly more morally reprehensible, but he lacked their redeeming qualities. He was crafty and vindictive and instead of charismatic leadership could offer only dogged determination. Failing to inspire loyalty, he tried to dominate by menace and—constantly fearing disloyalty—he fed his fears by a corrosive suspicion. He is a classic case of a ruler undone not merely by adverse circumstances but by defects of personality.

W.L. Warren

Bibliography

Hollister, C. Warren. "King John and the Historians." *Journal of British Studies* 1 (1961): 1–29; Holt, J.C. *The Northerners: A Study in the Reign of King John.* London: Oxford University Press, 1961; Holt, J.C. *Magna Carta and Medieval Government.* London: Hambledon, 1985 [collected papers; especially valuable are "King John," first published in 1963, and "The End of the Anglo-Norman Realm," from 1975]; Turner, Ralph V. *King John.* New York: Longman, 1994; Warren, W.L. *King John.* 2d ed. London: Eyre Methuen, 1978; Warren, W.L. "Painter's King John Forty Years On." *Haskins Society Journal* 1 (1989): 1–9.

See also Angevin Empire; Eleanor of Aquitaine; Henry II; Henry III; Langton; Magna Carta; Richard I

John of Salisbury (ca. 1115–1180)

Scholar, diplomat, friend of Thomas Becket, and bishop of Chartres, renowned chiefly for his *Policraticus,* a treatise on contemporary *mores* and political philosophy, and his *Metalogicon,* a defense of the trivium (grammar, logic, rhetoric) and commentary on Aristotle's recently rediscovered *Organon;* both works were completed and dedicated to Becket in 1159. His letters, a number of which are to Becket, are valued for both their historical content and their style. He also wrote a memoir of the papal court *(Historia pontificalis),* lives of Becket and Anselm of Canterbury, and two more obscure pieces of philosophic poetry, the *Entheticus maior* and *Entheticus minor.*

Lara Ruffolo

Bibliography

PRIMARY

Laarhoven, Jan van, ed. and trans. *Entheticus maior and minor.* 3 vols. Leiden: Brill, 1957 [extensive bibliography, 3:447–68]; Nederman, Cary J., ed. and trans. *Policraticus: Of the Frivolities of Courtiers and the Footprints of Philosophers.* Cambridge: Cambridge University Press, 1990.

SECONDARY

New *CBEL* 1:762–63.

See also Anselm; Becket; Learning; Universities

Judgment Day I and II

Judgment Day I is an anonymous OE poem of 119 lines from the Exeter Book. Its date and source are unknown, though it was most probably composed ca. 800 and loosely based on 2 Peter 3:6ff. While undoubtedly an eschatological work, *Judgment Day I* may also be considered a wisdom poem with Doomsday as its theme.

The poem opens with "That shall happen," abruptly establishing Doomsday's inevitability. The poet follows with details of earth's destruction and an aftermath of desolation. Set against these descriptions are exempla of three kinds of men. The "grim-thinking" man will seek hell on Doomsday, damned for his material concerns. Another sinful soul is likened to a feaster, who thinks little beyond the banquet before him. Yet the man who is mindful of his sinful nature will rise to heaven on Doomsday. The poet closes by imploring the audience to repeat the poem's principal message: one must "think well" now in order to share the glories of heaven.

Judgment Day II is a 306-line anonymous translation of Bede's *Versus de die iudicii* found in a single manuscript, Cambridge, Corpus Christi College 201. It was probably composed in the late 10th century, possibly in conjunction with the Benedictine Reform. Its provenance is unknown, though arguments have been made for Worcester, York, and Canterbury. A prose rendering of *Judgment Day II* comprises much of the homily known as "Wulfstan XXIX."

The poem opens with a description of a forest grove in which a speaker chastises himself for his iniquity, employing the discourse of soul-body dialogues. Interwoven into this confession are vivid descriptions of what Doomsday will hold for all humanity, "each according to his deeds." The poet depicts hell, with its torments of extreme heat and cold, while portraying a heaven devoid of worldly afflictions. Yet these details are not mere displays of poetic virtuosity; Graham D. Caie counts *Judgment Day II* among "devotional exercises that act as an incentive to penance."

Gavin Richardson

Bibliography

PRIMARY

ASPR 3:212–15 [*Judgment Day I*], 6:58–67 [*Judgment Day II*]: Kennedy, Charles W., trans. *Early English Christian Poetry.* New York: Oxford University Press, 1952, pp. 259–67 [*Judgment Day II*].

SECONDARY

Caie, Graham D. *The Judgment Day Theme in Old English Poetry.* Copenhagen: Nova, 1976; Richards, Mary P. "Prosaic Poetry: Late Old English Poetic Composition." In *Old English and New: Studies in Language and Linguistics in Honor of Frederic G. Cassidy,* ed. Joan Hall et al. New York: Garland, 1992, pp. 63–75.

See also Bede; Exeter Book; Sermons; *Soul and Body;* Wisdom Literature

Judith

An incomplete OE biblical poem, surviving in BL Cotton Vitellius A.xv, coming immediately after *Beowulf.* Although *Judith* was copied by the same scribe who wrote the text of *Beowulf* from line 1939b to the end of the poem, the parts of the manuscript containing the two poems were originally separate, as is indicated by the battered condition of the last page of *Beowulf* (originally an outside leaf) and by the textual deficiency at the beginning of *Judith.* The damage to this manuscript caused by the Cotton fire of 1731 affected the text of *Judith* in places. In modern editions of the poem manuscript readings are supplemented by reference to the edition of Edward Thwaites (1698).

In its present state *Judith* begins with the last word of a metrical line and consists of 348 lines and this single word. The text is complete to the end of the poem. There has been considerable debate as to how much of the beginning is missing. It has been argued both that the poem is substantially complete with only a few lines lacking and that about three-quarters of the original composition (some 1,000 lines) may be missing. The latter view is more widely accepted and is supported by the "fitt" division of *Judith* in the manuscript. The text of the poem begins near the end of a fitt (IX) and continues through fitts X to XII, with something over 100 lines in each fitt. The view that a large part of *Judith* has been lost is borne out by comparison of the OE text with its source, the book of Judith. The OE covers about a quarter of the book of Judith, concentrating particularly on chapters 12–15. It should be noted, however, that the poet's treatment of the source is not uniform: in particular most of the final chapter (16) is omitted, although the ending of the OE is complete.

The *Judith*-poet shows great assurance in adapting biblical material to the structures of vernacular poetry. Working probably in the 10th century, this poet re-creates the original in strikingly Germanic terms, exploiting the ideals of the heroic tradition to express approval for Judith and the Bethulians and condemnation of the unheroic Assyrians and their contemptible chieftain Holofernes. The OE poet even introduces a battle, complete with beasts of battle, to give solidity to the presentation of the retreat of the Assyrians. The poet's treatment of the source, however, is also consistent with traditions of exegesis of the book of Judith current in the early Middle Ages. The approach is not narrowly allegorical and contrasts strongly with that of Ælfric in his "Homily on the Book of Judith," but the themes of the Bethulians as the people of God and of Judith herself as a figure of the people of God in a hostile world (as developed most systematically in the 9th-century commentary of Hrabanus Maurus) are sensitively explored.

Hugh Magennis

Bibliography

PRIMARY

ASPR 4:99–109; Timmer, B.J., ed. *Judith.* Rev. ed. Exeter: University of Exeter Press, 1978.

SECONDARY

Belanoff, Patricia A. "*Judith:* Sacred and Secular Heroine." In *Heroic Poetry in the Anglo-Saxon Period: Studies in Honor of Jess B. Bessinger, Jr.,* ed. Helen Damico and John Leyerle. Kalamazoo: Medieval Institute, 1993, pp. 247–64; Chamberlain, David. "*Judith:* A Fragmentary and Political Poem." In *Anglo-Saxon Poetry: Essays in Appreciation for John C. McGalliard,* ed. Lewis E. Nicholson and Dolores Warwick Frese. Notre Dame: University of Notre Dame Press, 1975, pp. 135–59; Heinemann, F.J. "*Judith:* A Mock-Heroic Approach-to-Battle Type-Scene." *NM* 71 (1970): 83–96; Magennis, Hugh. "Contrasting Narrative Emphases in the Old English Poem *Judith* and Ælfric's Paraphrase of the Book of Judith." *NM* 96 (1995): 61–66; Pringle, Ian. "*Judith:* The Homily and the Poem." *Traditio* 31 (1975): 83–97.

See also Ælfric; Bible in OE Literature; Cotton; Hagiography; Women in OE Literature

Julian of Norwich (1342/43–after 1416)

Mystical writer and the first known woman author in English literature. Her book of *Showings,* or *Revelations of Divine Love,* ranks with the best medieval English prose and is a primary text in the literature of mysticism. It is extant in a short version, probably written first, and in an extended form, completed 20 years later.

Biographical information about Julian is sparse. It is limited to facts in her own text, mention in a few wills, and a passage in the *Book of Margery Kempe.* Julian's birthplace is unknown. The dialect in the oldest extant copy of her book shows northern features, leading to the conjecture that she may have come from Yorkshire. Sometime between 1413 and 1416 Margery Kempe visited Julian and received counsel from her. As late as 1416 Julian was living in Norwich in Norfolk as an anchoress, enclosed in a cell attached to the Church of St. Julian. She may have received the name Julian upon her entrance into the anchorhold.

On 8 May (or possibly 13 May) 1373, at the age of 30 and a half, she fell seriously ill, most likely while still at home.

She then recalled having prayed in her youth for a bodily sickness, to prepare her for death, and for the wounds of true contrition, natural compassion, and resolute longing for God. Surrounded by her mother and friends, and attended by a priest, she believed, with them, that she was about to die. Suddenly, however, while she was looking at a crucifix, her health returned. Then followed a series of fifteen visions, mostly of the crucified Christ. These were interrupted by attacks from the Devil, and then confirmed in a sixteenth and final showing. This experience gives the content to the short version of her book, in which she explains that the visions were threefold in character—visual, intellectual, and spiritual or intuitive. The long version of the text is enriched with 20 years of theological reflection, pastoral counseling, and spiritual growth. Her teachings are oriented to the instruction of other believers, her "even-Christians."

The shorter version of Julian's book is extant in one manuscript copy—the 15th-century Amherst Manuscript (BL Add. 37790). The longer text is complete in three manuscripts: the Paris Manuscript (BN Fonds angl. 40), copied around 1650; and two Sloane manuscripts (Sloane 1—BL Sloane 2499, early 17th century; Sloane 2—BL Sloane 3705, an 18th-century modernization of Sloane l). Excerpts from the longer version exist in Westminster Treasury 4 (W), written in the early 16th century; and in a 17th-century manuscript from Upholland Northern Institute (formerly St. Joseph's College). The Upholland manuscript was written by English Benedictine nuns, living at Cambrai, after the Dissolution of the monasteries. The earliest printed edition (1670) is by Serenus Cressy, an English Benedictine, chaplain for the Paris house of the nuns.

T.S. Eliot, in the *Four Quartets,* familiarized the literary world with Julian's key phrase, "All shall be well," and with some of her mystical symbolism. Thomas Merton cited her as "one of the greatest English theologians" (1967). An observance at Norwich (1973) commemorated the sixth centenary of her showings. Since then Julian has become the focus of extensive study by literary scholars and theologians and has a growing following as a spiritual guide.

Textual critics disagree on the choice of a preferred copy text for a Julian edition. Colledge and Walsh (1978) opted for Paris, favoring its more conventionally correct rhetorical structures. Marion Glasscoe selected Sloane 1 for a student edition (2d ed. 1986). Glasscoe notes the pitfalls of following, in disputed readings, either Sloane 1 or Paris, or creating an eclectic text; nonetheless, she finds special qualities to recommend reliance on Sloane 1, which, she says, often reflects "a greater sense of theology as a live issue at the heart of human creativity" (1989: 119) thereby coming closer to Julian's central concern.

Theological approaches diverge widely. A plethora of devotional books have been based on a surface reading of the *Revelations,* stressing Julian's optimism and oversimplifying her doctrine of love. Her terms "substance" and "sensuality" are often misunderstood. A misreading, sometimes abetted by inaccurate translations, assumes that by "substance" Julian means the human soul and by "sensuality" the body or the five senses. Substance designates, rather, "the truth of our being,

body and soul: the way we are meant to be, as whole persons" (Pelphrey, 1982: 90): "Where the blessed soul of Christ is, there is the substance of all souls that will be saved by Christ. . . . Our soul is made to be God's dwelling place, and the dwelling place of the soul is God. . . . It is a high understanding inwardly to see and to know that God our creator dwells in our soul; and a higher understanding it is inwardly to see and to know that our soul which is created dwells in God's substance, of which substance, through God, we are what we are" (Long Text, ch. 54).

Usually "sensuality" refers to that human existence which becomes God's in the Incarnation: it is the "place" of the city of God, the glory of the Trinity abiding in collective humanity. Human beings are called to be helpers or partners in the unfolding of what humanity is meant to become—a city fit for God to reign and find rest in. These difficult concepts are carefully explored by Pelphrey, who succinctly summarizes Julian's teaching about divine love: "The reflection of divine love into humanity is . . . seen to take place in three ways: in the creation of humanity (our capacity for God); in the maturing or 'increasing' of humanity (to which she also refers as our 'remaking' in Christ); and in the perfecting or fulfilling of human beings through the indwelling Christ" (1982: 90).

Julian presents this theology principally through the parable of the Lord and the Servant: "This story conveys Julian's insights about the first Adam, the cosmic Christ, the Trinity, and the unity of all who are to be saved. The one great reality in the parable is the person of Christ, in whom are mysterious compenetrations of other realities—the Adam of Genesis; the total Adam (all humanity); Christ as the second Adam (and in one sense the first Adam, since to his eternal image all things were made); and Christ, meaning all humanity to be saved. The basic parable weaves into other metaphors: for example, the sinful Adam fell in misery to the earth, but likewise the divine Adam falls on the earth—into human nature in Mary's womb—and makes the garden of the earth spring forth with food and drink for which the Father thirsts and longs, in his unending love for the treasure which was hidden in the earth" (Bradley, 1984: 209). The Trinity is revealed in Christ. God is active as "maker, preserver, and lover," an insight Julian experienced when she saw creation in the likeness of a hazelnut. Since God is the ground of the soul, the desire for God is natural, and sin (all that is not good) is unnatural. Prayer unites the soul to God, the foundation from which the prayer arises. In the depths or core of the believer, the being of God intersects with the being of the creature and is the root of a "godly will" that always inclines toward the good. Nonetheless, humanity continues to sin, for evil was permitted to arise contrary to goodness, which will triumph in the end in the form of a good greater than what would otherwise have been. How "all things shall be well," as Christ promised Julian, will remain hidden until a great deed is accomplished on the Last Day (Long Text, ch. 32).

Literary and linguistic critics contribute to the explication of this mystical core. Reynolds explores the key images of Christ as courteous and "homely," in its medieval sense. Courtesy signifies that Christ possesses without limit the largesse and fidelity attributed to the medieval knight. Courtesy fuses with "homeliness," the familiar manner used at home, among equals, and implies nearness, so that "we are clothed and enclosed in the goodness of God" (Long Text, ch. 6). In his familiar aspect Christ is mother, an image rooted in scripture and in biblical exegesis but developed with originality by Julian. As the archetypal mother Christ bears his children not to pain and dying but to joy and endless living. His Passion is a birthing, which entailed the sharpest throes that ever were, and was undertaken to satisfy his love. The maternal image further signifies that humanity dwells in Christ, as in a mother's womb, and is also fed, nurtured, chastised, and tenderly cared for, as a child. The sensual nature of humanity (that which is born into time) is in the second person, Jesus Christ, and is knit—as in fabric making—to its ground in God. This motherhood metaphor has attracted the attention of feminist criticism, adding to Julian's popularity today. The overall lesson of the revelations is love in three meanings: uncreated love, or God; created love—the human soul in God; and a love that is bestowed as virtue, enabling believers to love God, themselves, and all creation, especially their "even-Christians."

Ritamary Bradley

Bibliography

PRIMARY

Colledge, Edmund, and James Walsh, eds. *A Book of Showings to the Anchoress Julian of Norwich.* 2 vols. Toronto: Pontifical Institute, 1978; Colledge, Edmund, and James Walsh, trans. *Showings.* New York: Paulist Press, 1978; del Mastro, M.L., trans. *Revelation of Divine Love in Sixteen Showings.* Liguori, Mo.: Triumph Books, 1994; Glasscoe, Marion, ed. *A Revelation of Love.* 2d ed. Exeter: University of Exeter, 1986.

SECONDARY

New *CBEL* 1:522–24; *Manual* 9:3082–84, 3438–44; Bradley, Ritamary. "Julian of Norwich: Writer and Mystic." In *An Introduction to the Medieval Mystics of Europe,* ed. Paul E. Szarmach. Albany: SUNY Press, 1984, pp. 195–216; Bradley, Ritamary. *Julian's Way: A Practical Commentary on Julian of Norwich.* London: HarperCollins, 1992; Glasscoe, Marion. "Visions and Revisions: A Further Look at the Manuscripts of Julian of Norwich." *SB* 42 (1989): 103–20; Lagorio, Valerie Marie, and Ritamary Bradley. "Julian of Norwich." In *The 14th-Century English Mystics: A Comprehensive Annotated Bibliography.* New York: Garland, 1981, pp. 105–26; Llewelyn, Robert, ed. *Julian: Woman of Our Day.* Mystic: Twenty-Third Publications, 1987; Molinari, Paolo. *Julian of Norwich: The Teaching of a 14th Century English Mystic.* London: Longmans, Green, 1958; Nuth, Joan. *Wisdom's Daughter.* New York: Crossroad, 1991; Pelphrey, Brant. *Love Was His Meaning: The Theology and Mysticism of Julian of Norwich.* Salzburg: Institut für Anglistik und Amerikanistik, 1982; Reynolds, Anna Maria. "'Courtesy' and 'Homeliness' in the Revelations of Julian of Norwich." *14th-Century English Mystics Newsletter (Mystics Quarterly)* 5/2 (1979): 12–20; von Nolcken, Christina. "Julian of Norwich." In *Middle English Prose: A Critical Guide to Major Genres and Authors,* ed. A.S.G. Edwards. New Brunswick: Rutgers University Press, 1984, pp. 97–108.

See also Ancrene Wisse; Katherine Group; Kempe; Mystical and Devotional Writings; Norwich; Nuns; Prose, ME; Religious Allegories; Women in ME Literature

Junius Manuscript

Bodl. Junius 11, a partially illustrated codex of OE biblical poetry, consisting of two textual booklets. Book I (pp. 1–212) contains *Genesis A, Genesis B, Exodus,* and *Daniel,* metrical paraphrases of much of Genesis, Exodus 13–14, and Daniel 1–5; Book II (pp. 213–29) contains the religious poem *Christ and Satan,* linking the Old and New Testaments. The Anglo-Saxonist Francis Junius (Du Jon) the Younger acquired the manuscript ca. 1651 from James Ussher, archbishop of Armagh, and published an edition of its contents at Amsterdam in 1655 (*Cædmonis Monachi Paraphrasis Poetica Genesios ac præcipuarum Sacræ paginæ Historiarum, abhinc annos MLXX*). Influence of the poems on John Milton's *Paradise Lost* (written 1650–63) has been suggested but not proven. Because of the subject matter of the poems Junius ascribed their authorship to Cædmon, the 7th-century Anglo-Saxon poet referred to by Bede, and consequently the codex became known as the "Cædmon Manuscript." The Bodleian Library acquired it in 1678, after Junius's death. Before its acquisition by Junius Sir Simonds D'Ewes (1602–1650) may have had it on loan from Ussher, when William Somner made a transcript from it.

Pages 1–229 were paginated by Junius: page 230 is blank. Leaves measure ca. 12.7 by 7.7 inches and are arranged in seventeen quires, mostly once consisting of eight folios, but with several leaves now lost. Book I was written in Anglo-Saxon Square Minuscule by a single scribe ca. 1000; Book II was written by three different scribes in rounder hands ca. 1000–25. The manuscript was corrected by another scribe who altered spellings from Anglian to late West Saxon orthography. The writing in Book I is well spaced in a fairly narrow column of 26 lines, that in Book II is cramped into a wider column of 27 lines.

Forty-eight outline drawings in Book I, illustrating the Genesis poems, were executed by two artists, the second using colored inks (red, green, black, brown); seventeen are full- or nearly full-page; some have OE captions added. There are many blank spaces left for illustrations that were never completed. A few drypoint drawings also occur. The first artist also added zoomorphic and floreate initials at the beginning of sections of text in the first part of Book I; plainer initials, sometimes paneled, on pp. 75, 83–136, and 156–209 were executed by the scribe. The second artist also illustrated Cambridge, Corpus Christi College 23, fols. 1–40 (Prudentius, *Psychomachia*), which was given to Malmesbury Abbey ca. 1033–44. A third artist added drawings on pp. 31 and 96 in the later 12th century.

The use of a combination of leather thongs and cord for the five bands of the present binding may date it in part to before ca. 1050. The bound codex was probably at one time chained. A design for the cover and spine of a binding (but probably not for this manuscript) may be preserved on p. 225. There is a 14th-century title *Genesis in anglico* (p. ii); M.R. James suggested the manuscript was the *Genesis anglice depicta* listed in the early-14th-century catalogue of Christ Church Canterbury, but this is not proven.

Alexander R. Rumble

Bibliography

PRIMARY

ASPR 1; Gollancz, Israel, ed. *The Cædmon Manuscript of Anglo-Saxon Biblical Poetry: Junius XI in the Bodleian Library*. Oxford: Oxford University Press, 1927 [facsimile].

SECONDARY

Broderick, Herbert R. "Observations on the Method of Illustration in MS Junius 11 and the Relationship of the Drawings to the Text." *Scriptorium* 37 (1983): 161–77; Lucas, Peter J. "On the Incomplete Ending of *Daniel* and the Addition of *Christ and Satan* to MS Junius 11." *Anglia* 97 (1979): 46–59 [relationship between books I and II]; Temple, Elzbieta. *Anglo-Saxon Manuscripts 900–1066*. A Survey of Manuscripts Illuminated in the British Isles 2, ed. J.J.G. Alexander. London: Harvey Miller, 1976, no. 58 [argues for Christ Church Canterbury as the probable place of origin].

See also Bede; Cædmon; *Christ and Satan; Daniel; Exodus; Genesis A* and *B*

Juries and the Jury System

Trial by jury is a method for resolving legal disputes that relies on a group of laypeople to provide answers to particular questions. As this procedure developed, such a group was referred to as a "jury" *(jurata),* reflecting its duty to answer under oath; its answer, required to be truthful, was the "verdict" *(veredictum)*. Trial by jury, though not universally available, was characteristic of a great deal of civil and criminal litigation in the Middle Ages.

Long before actual trial by jury became the norm, Anglo-Norman monarchs used panels of sworn laypersons to identify suspected criminals. This was but an instance of the more general reliance upon the citizenry to provide information for a variety of legal, administrative, or fiscal purposes, a practice with both Scandinavian and Carolingian roots. The most noteworthy example of this practice is the massive collection of landholding information in Domesday Book. Where jurors were used to identify suspected criminals, trial of guilt or innocence was originally by means of an ordeal, typically the ordeal of water. Only with the papal abolition of clerical participation in ordeals in 1215 did a jury verdict become the typical procedure for resolving questions of criminal culpability.

By 1215 jury trial had already been used in civil cases with some frequency. During the later 12th century Henry II had made it available to decide certain land disputes. These juries were referred to either as petty assizes or grand assizes, depending on the nature of the plaintiff's claim. From these beginnings trial by jury in civil cases was made more widely available. During the 13th century new forms of action relating to real property claims were developed, as were writs of trespass, remedies for wrongs to person or property. Trial by jury was the standard mode of proof in all these cases. Not all civil claims were triable by jury, however. Most notably defendants in the contractual actions of debt and covenant were allowed to wage their law (swear an oath supported by eleven "oath helpers") to avoid liability.

Medieval legal theory conceived of the juror as, in effect, a witness to the facts to be tried, possessing knowledge obtained before trial. Thus sheriffs were required to impanel jurors from the locality nearest the place where the facts in question occurred. Unlike a modern jury knowledge of the parties or the facts was not a ground for disqualification, although bias or interest was. While some research suggests that jurors had largely ceased to be "self-informing" before 1400, Sir John Fortescue, in the mid-15th century, still referred to them as witnesses. In any event the notion that jury verdicts should be based entirely on evidence presented in open court is a modern one, a principle that did not emerge until the 18th century.

While early jury trials in civil cases were often conducted in the royal courts at Westminster, in the 14th century procedures were established so that most civil jury trials could take place in the county in which the operative facts occurred; from around 1220 the vast majority of jury trials in criminal cases were held in the counties. In civil cases the central courts continued to keep track of pleadings and other procedural matters in voluminous detail; there is little direct evidence of what went on at trials.

What little we know suggests a process a good deal more informal than anything we would recognize today. The idea that rules of evidence should limit the parties' freedom during trial does not appear to have been important. Nor is there any reason to believe that trial judges attempted to exercise firm control over process or outcome. The jurors, after hearing the evidence and perhaps the legal arguments from the parties, were charged simply to decide "according to conscience."

In criminal cases there is reason to believe that jurors often concocted verdicts to impede the harsh penalties of the law. Thus, for example, recent scholarship has demonstrated that jurors often gave fictitious accounts of homicides to justify self-defense verdicts where that defense would not have been available if an accurate factual account had been given. In such cases jurors in effect nullified the common law to the extent it was inconsistent with societal notions of culpability.

While an analogous nullification phenomenon may have been at work in civil cases, it has yet to be documented. However, no procedural device existed by which judges could review a jury verdict after the fact and reverse it as inconsistent with common law. The action of attaint, whereby a second jury was called upon to state whether an earlier jury had made a "false oath," seems to have been limited to cases of corrupt or bad-faith verdicts. Thus common-law procedure lacked a mechanism for ensuring that verdicts would be according to substantive common-law rules. Accordingly it is possible that jurors in civil cases enjoyed considerable discretion to apply communal notions of justice, even where inconsistent with common law.

David Millon

Bibliography

Arnold, Morris S. "Law and Fact in the Medieval Jury Trial: Out of Sight, Out of Mind." *American Journal of Legal History* 18 (1974): 267–80 [especially on the absence of controls over the discretion of juries in civil cases]; Baker, John H. *An Introduction to English Legal History.* 3d ed. London: Butterworths, 1990; Green, Thomas A. *Verdict according to Conscience: Perspectives on the English Criminal Trial Jury, 1200–1800.* Chicago: University of Chicago Press, 1985 [chs. 2 and 3 are important on the question of whether juries adjusted verdicts to fit conscience and local social interest]; Groot, Roger D. "The Jury of Presentment before 1215." *American Journal of Legal History* 26 (1982): 1–24; Groot, Roger D. "The Jury in Private Criminal Prosecutions before 1215." *American Journal of Legal History* 27 (1982): 113–42; Groot, Roger D. "The Early-Thirteenth-Century Criminal Jury." In *Twelve Good Men and True: The Criminal Trial Jury in England, 1200–1800,* ed. J.S. Cockburn and T.A. Green. Princeton: Princeton University Press, 1988, ch. 1 [Groot's essays deal with the shift from ordeal to jury trial in criminal cases]; Millon, David. "Positivism in the Historiography of the Common Law." *Wisconsin Law Review,* 1989, pp. 669–714; Turner, Ralph V. "The Origins of the Medieval English Jury." *Journal of British Studies* 7 (1968): 1–10.

See also Courts and the Court System; Inquisitions Post Mortem; Law, Post-Conquest

Justiciar

The king's justiciar was the official authorized to act on the king's behalf. The need for such a deputy emerged from the nature of the medieval English monarchy and the lands it governed. The king was at the center of administration, his personal rule of paramount importance to the daily affairs of the realm. The realm, from the Norman Conquest onward, often comprised various lands of which England was but one. To govern each of these areas effectively the king was required to travel; yet in his absence matters in England necessitated his presence.

To alleviate this problem the king came to place a great reliance in administrative matters on his kinsmen and close associates. Soon after the Conquest Odo, William's half-brother, deputized for him during his journey to Normandy. Henry I continued this practice and drew his deputy, Roger of Salisbury, from the ranks of the professional administrators. Roger's duties included handling matters of justice, such as presiding over the exchequer. Furthermore Roger issued writs in his own name; contemporaries described him as "second to the king." The term "justiciar," however, was not yet associated with Roger or his office.

The title came into being during Henry II's reign, although the duties of this *justitiarius* were much the same as under Roger. The main distinction was that justiciars in Henry II's time, such as Richard de Luci and later Ranulf Glanville, handled a far greater volume of business. The loss of Normandy in John's reign curtailed the need for a deputy to the king, as he now spent most of his time in England. However, the justiciar, until his dismissal in 1234, did play a significant role in governing during the minority of Henry III and subsequently during the baronial movements of 1258–65. Nonetheless, after regaining control from the barons, Henry III felt that such an office was too high and exercised a control too independent of the king; he allowed the justiciarship to lapse.

Andrew H. Hershey

Bibliography

Bates, David. "The Origins of the Justiciarship." *Anglo-Norman Studies* 4 (1982): 1–12; Carpenter, D.A. *The Minority of Henry III.* London: Methuen, 1990; Green, Judith A. *The Government of England under Henry I.* Cambridge: Cambridge University Press, 1986; Knowles, C.H. "The Justiciarship in England, 1258–1265." In *British Government and Administration: Studies Presented to S.B. Chrimes,* ed. H. Hearder and H.R. Loyn. Cardiff: University of Wales Press, 1974, pp. 16–26; West, Francis. *The Justiciarship in England, 1066–1232.* Cambridge: Cambridge University Press, 1966.

See also Angevin Empire; Glanville; Hubert Walter; Monarchy and Kingship

K

Karole

The karole (Eng.) or *carole* (Fr.) was a genre of communally performed dance used in much of western Europe between the 12th and 16th centuries. It was executed to music sung by the participants, who were linked by hand, little finger, or sometimes by kerchiefs or sticks, into a single line. This could follow any track established by the karole leader or join into a closed circle that moved clockwise. Every step unit started with the left foot.

Modules of text, of tune, and of step units in specific dance meters were assembled in various combinations and in various recurrence patterns of unchanging text sung by all and changing text (open to improvisation) sung by the leader. Recurrence patterns included burden-and-stanza, stanza-and-refrain, rondeau, virelai, and some more complex than these. Surviving texts, most of which are literate creations, range from the simple and repetitive to the complex and virtuosic. The three components of text, tune, and dance were combined to greatly different effect for different subjects, which included the seasonal calendar, Christian doctrine, narratives, personal love and complaints, satire, and topical comment. Occasions of use included agricultural rituals, Christian holidays, and private after-dinner recreation. The exhilarating, even cathartic, potential of the karole was greatly feared by the Christian church, and numerous pious and doctrinally orthodox karole texts are evidence of attempts to harness it to blameless use. Some pious stanzaic texts whose stanzas consist of two units in different dance meters may have been made after secular or impious models, but with both the improvisatory possibility and the leader-and-group relationship eliminated.

The term "carol" is now used indiscriminately for karole and for contemporary and later songs (generally associated with Christmas) whose texts have no structural dance component.

Joan Rimmer

Bibliography

Page, Christopher. *Voices and Instruments of the Middle Ages: Instrumental Practice and Songs in France 1100–1300.* Berkeley: University of California Press, 1986; Page, Christopher. *The Owl and the Nightingale: Musical Life and Ideas in France 1100–1300.* Berkeley: University of California Press, 1989; Stevens, John. "Carole." *NGD* 3:814–15; Stevens, John. *Words and Music in the Middle Ages: Song, Narrative, Dance and Drama, 1050–1350.* Cambridge: Cambridge University Press, 1986.

See also Carol; Dance; Songs

Katherine Group

Five ME religious prose works, written ca. 1190–1230 and found together in the Bodleian Library manuscript Bodley 34, although also occurring in other manuscripts, individually or in partial groups with other texts, such as the *Ancrene Wisse.* The Group includes the *Life of St. Katherine,* the *Life of St. Margaret,* and the *Life of St. Juliana;* a religious allegory about the protection of the soul, *Sawles Warde (The Guardianship of the Soul);* and a treatise on virginity, *Hali Meiðhad (Holy Virginity).* Its earliest manuscript witness, Bodley 34, is written in the same west Midlands dialect as the *Ancrene Wisse* (named the "AB dialect" by Tolkien).

According to Dobson the Katherine Group and the *Ancrene Wisse* can be localized in Herefordshire and possibly more precisely to the anchorhold of the Deerfold associated with Wigmore Abbey. The *Ancrene Wisse* is known to have been written for female recluses. Whether the five texts of the Katherine Group were intended for the same or a similar audience is unknown, although the *Ancrene Wisse* specifically recommends one of them, the *Life of St. Margaret.* In addition source study indicates that the English works were composed with female readers in mind.

Although the six texts of the AB dialect are closely related, there is little reason to assume they were written by the same author. The survival of such a consistent group of works written by different authors but all devoted to the exposition of a distinctive and predominantly feminine spirituality raises questions of the training and concerns of the authors as well as about the role the female audience played in the inspiration of such material.

The three saints' lives provide models of female saints successful in their conquest of temptation. Although the three lives have much in common with their Latin sources, the English versions highlight specifically feminine concerns, such as feminine weakness and dependence, the female contemplative's presumed fear of isolation, the disadvantages of the uneducated woman in the face of temptation, the Devil's interest in women and his presence even in the most domestic of settings, and the dangers of the sexual temptation of the female saint. These feminine aspects of temptation are resolved in all three lives by the female protagonist's dependent, romantic relationship with her betrothed, Christ, a concretization of the *sponsa christi* ("bride of Christ") motif that is characteristic of both the Katherine Group and the *Ancrene Wisse.*

Sawles Warde, once thought to derive from Hugh of St. Victor's *De anima,* is now believed to be a translation of a Latin sermon attributed to Anselm of Canterbury, "De custodia interioris hominis"; both the Latin and English works are allegorical explications of Matthew 24:43–51. The English work, however, significantly develops the drama of the household, one of whose members is an unruly female character, Will. Furthermore it has been altered to emphasize the needs and concerns of the female reader. In keeping with the developments of the 12th-century renaissance the work provides a psychologically sophisticated exploration of the fluctuations of the human heart in its pursuit of abstract goals.

Of the five works in the Katherine Group *Hali Meiðhad* most fully develops the assumption that lies behind them all— that Christ is the best husband for the female recluse. By exploring the nature of marriage, childbirth, and the care of a home in contrast to the more secure and rewarding life as a contemplative betrothed to God, the work shows the female recluse how to transform all her earthly desires into desire for Christ. Most startling is the assumption that women transfer rather than transcend the desires of the flesh, an assumption that can be shown to underlie many texts written for women in the religious life.

Along with the *Ancrene Wisse* the works in the Katherine Group constitute an important step in the stylistic development of early ME prose. But their style is not as narrowly dependent on that of OE religious prose as was once thought; rather it is indebted to both the native English and continental Latin tradition, and the stylistic sophistication of the works is due in large part to their fusion of the two traditions (Millett and Wogan-Browne, 1990: xiii–xiv, xxxiv–xxxviii). Like the *Wisse* the Katherine Group is also noteworthy for being among the earliest ME writing composed for a specifically female audience.

Elizabeth Robertson

Bibliography

PRIMARY

For editions see Dahood and other bibliographies below; Millett, Bella, and Jocelyn Wogan-Browne, eds. and trans. *Medieval English Prose for Women: Selections from the Katherine Group and Ancrene Wisse.* Oxford: Clarendon, 1990; Wilson, R.M., ed. *Sawles Warde.* Kendal: Wilson, 1938.

SECONDARY

New *CBEL* 1:523–26; *Manual* 2:597–98 (Juliana), 599–600 (Katherine), 606–07 (Margaret); 9:3089–94, 3447–51 (*Sawles Warde* and *Hali Meiðhad*); Dahood, Roger. "*Ancrene Wisse,* the Katherine Group, and the *Wohunge* Group." In *Middle English Prose: A Critical Guide to Major Authors and Genres,* ed. A.S.G. Edwards. New Brunswick: Rutgers University Press, 1984, pp. 1–33; Dobson, E.J. *The Origins of Ancrene Wisse.* Oxford: Clarendon, 1976; Robertson, Elizabeth. *Early English Devotional Prose and the Female Audience.* Knoxville: University of Tennessee Press, 1990; Tolkien, J.R.R. "*Ancrene Wisse* and *Hali Meiðhad.*" *Essays and Studies* 14 (1929): 104–26.

See also Ancrene Wisse; Hagiography; Mystical and Devotional Writings; Nuns; Prose, ME; Psychology, Medieval; Women in ME Literature

Kempe, Margery (ca. 1373–after 1438)

Controversial mystic and author of the first extant autobiography in English. *The Book of Margery Kempe* is both a mystical treatise consisting of the author's visions and conversations with Christ and a narrative of her life, including her conversion, pilgrimages, and arguments with church authorities. Kempe, who was illiterate, dictated her autobiography to two different scribes. The original manuscript has been lost, but a 15th-century copy was discovered in 1934.

Born in the East Anglian town of King's Lynn ca. 1373, Margery was the daughter of John Brunham, mayor of the town. At the age of twenty she married John Kempe. After the difficult birth of their first child Kempe suffered a breakdown. This experience, followed by business failures in brewing and milling, led eventually to her mystical conversion. Her first ordeal as a mystic was to convince her husband to be celibate, but only after twenty years of marriage and fourteen children did he agree, on the condition that she pay off all his debts. With the consent of her husband and the church Kempe was finally free to pursue her vocation as a mystic.

The "way to high perfection," however, was fraught with difficulties. Kempe encountered hostility from people who doubted her holiness and questioned her orthodoxy. She traveled around England seeking support and verification of her visions from many holy people, including the anchoress Julian of Norwich. Nevertheless, she continued to arouse suspicion and persecution for her behavior, including her bold speech and her "boisterous weeping." She was arrested as a Lollard, threatened with burning at the stake by her English detractors, and deserted by her fellow pilgrims on her travels abroad. Kempe's weeping in particular inspired her contemporaries to revile her and modern readers to label her "hysterical."

Kempe's travels took her to the Holy Land, Italy, Santiago de Compostela, and finally, near the end of her life, to Danzig,

Prussia. The *Book* ends with her return to King's Lynn, where she still inspires both hostility and marvel as a woman in her sixties.

The *Book of Margery Kempe* departs from the medieval saint's life and mystical treatise. Unlike the saint's life, which is biographical, Kempe's book is autobiographical. As author and narrator of her own life Kempe develops some hagiographic conventions, such as the themes of her suffering, patience, and charity, while ignoring others. Her book is also unusual as a mystical treatise. Kempe's visions and revelations are grounded in everyday, autobiographical details, including her struggles for acceptance, her fears for her own safety, and her travels.

Kempe's work is divided into two sections, or books. The first book ends with the death of her scribe. Kempe spent four years trying to convince the second scribe to recopy and finish her book. He hesitated because of her notoriety and the illegibility of the first scribe's writing but finally agreed. The 15th-century manuscript that survives may be a copy of the original dictated by Kempe to the second scribe. This copy belonged to Mount Grace, a Carthusian monastery in Yorkshire, but was later lost. William Butler-Bowdon discovered it in 1934 in his family library, and Hope Emily Allen identified it as *The Book of Margery Kempe.* (It is now BL Add. 61823.) Until 1934 only brief extracts of Kempe's book had been known; these extracts, printed by Wynkyn de Worde (ca. 1501) and Henry Pepwell (1521), misleadingly omit Kempe's autobiographical passages, and one incorrectly labels her a "devout anchoress."

As a mystical treatise Kempe's *Book* is often compared with the work of her contemporary Julian of Norwich. Kempe's mysticism, like Julian's, belongs to the tradition called affective piety, characterized by personal devotion to Christ's humanity, particularly in the Nativity and Passion. The emotions, or affections, play a crucial role in this devotion. By identifying with the suffering humanity of Christ the mystic is transported through her emotions to spiritual love.

Kempe's life and mysticism, however, differ considerably from Julian's. Her boisterous weeping, her insistent identification with Christ, her self-preoccupation, and her refusal to live the more orthodox life of a nun or recluse distinguish her from Julian of Norwich. Critics in her own time as well as today fault her for the excessive emotionalism and literalness of her visions. Yet Kempe's mysticism was not unique. She found models for it in the lives and mystical works of other female mystics, such as Marie d'Oignies, Birgitta (Bridget) of Sweden, and Elizabeth of Hungary, and in the writings of the English mystic Richard Rolle.

The core of the controversy about Margery Kempe is her version of imitating Christ. Although the practice of imitating Christ's suffering was common in medieval spirituality, Kempe is preoccupied with this suffering. Her meditations on the Passion elicit this suffering and her roaring draws attention to it, disrupting sermons and disturbing the people around her. In addition Kempe's use of erotic language to describe mystical union—words like ravishment, dalliance, and even homeliness—is boldly literal. She translates the mystical concept of marriage to Christ into an alarmingly worldly one, as Christ instructs Kempe to take him to bed with her as her husband (ch. 36). Although Rolle before her had used sensual imagery to describe mystical union, Kempe's usage startles with its emphasis on the literal rather than the figurative or symbolic.

Kempe's book poses problems for literary analysis as well. Her narrative is not strictly chronological, and with its digressions and repetitions it seems unconstructed. How much Kempe's scribes contributed to the shape of the narrative is a further problem facing literary analysis. Finally Kempe's illiteracy makes the question of influence an interesting one. She exhibits some knowledge of both Latin and vernacular religious texts in spite of her inability to read or write.

Like her book Margery Kempe is an interesting and problematic subject. As a woman charting her own "way to high perfection" she challenged the religious, social, and gender expectations of her time. Her book offers valuable insight into the struggles of an extraordinary medieval woman who refused to conform to those expectations in her pursuit of a "singular grace."

Karma Lochrie

Bibliography

PRIMARY

Butler-Bowdon, William, ed. and trans. *The Book of Margery Kempe.* New York: Devin-Adair, 1944; Meech, Sanford Brown, and Hope Emily Allen, eds. *The Book of Margery Kempe.* EETS o.s. 212. London: Oxford University Press, 1940; Windeatt, B.A., trans. *The Book of Margery Kempe.* New York: Penguin, 1985.

SECONDARY

New *CBEL* 1:524; *Manual* 9:3084–86, 3444–45; Atkinson, Clarissa W. *Mystic and Pilgrim: The Book and the World of Margery Kempe.* Ithaca: Cornell University Press, 1983; Beckwith, Sarah. "A Very Material Mysticism: The Medieval Mysticism of Margery Kempe." In *Medieval Literature: Criticism, Ideology & History,* ed. David Aers. New York: St. Martin, 1986, pp. 34–57; Fries, Maureen. "Margery Kempe." In *An Introduction to the Medieval Mystics of Europe,* ed. Paul E. Szarmach. Albany: SUNY Press, 1984, pp. 217–35; Goodman, Anthony E. "The Piety of John Brunham's Daughter, of Lynn." In *Medieval Women,* ed. Derek Baker. Oxford: Blackwell, 1978, pp. 347–58; Hirsh, John C. "Margery Kempe." In *Middle English Prose: A Critical Guide to Major Authors and Genres,* ed. A.S.G. Edwards. New Brunswick: Rutgers University Press, 1984, pp. 109–19; Lochrie, Karma. *Margery Kempe and Translations of the Flesh.* Philadelphia: University of Pennsylvania Press, 1991; McEntire, Sandra J., ed. *Margery Kempe: A Book of Essays.* New York: Garland, 1992.

See also Ancrene Wisse; Julian of Norwich; Katherine Group; Mystical and Devotional Writings; Prose, ME; Rolle; Women in ME Literature

Kentish Churches

The earliest churches of Kent have long been identified as a distinct group, which, because of their Mediterranean appearance and use of traditional Roman materials, are usually associated with the Augustinian mission, and dated between 597 and 669. Kent is the only area of Anglo-Saxon England where it is recorded that Roman churches were still standing and adaptable at the time of the mission, and the churches of Stone-by-Faversham, St. Martin, Canterbury, and St. Pancras, Canterbury, can claim some Roman fabric.

The churches that constitute this group in Kent are Sts. Peter and Paul, St. Mary, St. Pancras, and St. Martin at Canterbury; St. Andrew at Rochester; St. Mary at Lyminge; St. Mary at Reculver. The naves are short—about one and a half times the width, which ranges from 28 feet to 22.5 feet. All, where reconstructible, have rounded eastern apses, nearly as wide as the nave. These can be stilted and are sometimes divided from the nave by triple columns or piers. There are entrances in the northern, southern, and western walls, while each doorway and each corner is marked by a pair of buttresses. In several churches there are side porticus, or chambers, that may have had a variety of functions, such as sacristy or funerary chapel. The Church of Sts. Peter and Paul, Canterbury, had a burial porticus for the royal family on the south and for the early archbishops of Canterbury on the north.

This church, as befits a mission center, also possessed a narthex in its earliest phases. Excavations have revealed how the core of the 7th-century church survived the many later Anglo-Saxon developments of the west and east ends.

The fabric of these buildings is a mixture of Roman brick and flint, and the floors were of brick-faced concrete. The triple-arched columns at Reculver were decorated with restrained cable and stepped patterns, and from Canterbury some loose capitals of possibly 8th- to 9th-century date have survived, but on the whole there is much less sculptural decoration than in the Northumbrian churches. The inspiration for the plan and arrangement of these churches probably derives from Italy.

Rosemary J. Cramp

Bibliography

Clapham, Arthur W. *Romanesque Architecture before the Conquest.* Oxford: Clarendon, 1930, pp. 16–33; Fernie, Eric. *The Architecture of the Anglo-Saxons.* London: Batsford, 1983, pp. 32–46; Fletcher, Eric. "Early Kentish Churches." *Medieval Archaeology* 9 (1965): 16–31; Saunders, Andrew D. "Excavations at the Church of St. Augustine's Abbey, Canterbury, 1955–58." *Medieval Archaeology* 22 (1978): 25–63; Taylor, Harold M., and Joan Taylor. "Canterbury." In *Anglo-Saxon Architecture.* Vol. 1. Cambridge: Cambridge University Press, 1965, pp. 134–48.

See also Architecture, Anglo-Saxon; Sculpture, Anglo-Saxon

Kentish Hymn

An elaborate, 43-line celebration of the Trinity, based on a loose combined rendering of the Te Deum and Gloria, liturgical hymns that are both represented elsewhere in OE. The poem begins with a brief exhortation to Christian people to love and praise God (lines 1–6), while the rest of the *Hymn* consists of a lengthy address in praise of God, begging for his mercy. A similar blend of the Te Deum and the Gloria (along with some psalms) has been observed in the Antiphonary of Bangor, compiled in Ireland toward the end of the 7th century, but neither hymn appears to have been common in liturgical use in England before the 10th century.

The *Hymn* is found in BL Cotton Vespasian D.vi alongside a long poetic paraphrase of Psalm 50 in the same mixture of West Saxon and Kentish dialect; the manuscript also contains a number of interlinear Kentish glosses. The Kentish verse rendering of Psalm 50 appears to have been composed by a poet different from the author of the *Hymn*, but both poems were probably inspired as part of the 10th-century Benedictine Reform.

A.P.M. Orchard

Bibliography

PRIMARY
ASPR 6:87–88.

SECONDARY
Shepherd, Geoffrey. "The Sources of the OE *Kentish Hymn.*" *Modern Language Notes* 67 (1952): 395–97.

See also Benedictine Reform; Liturgy and Church Music, History of; Prayers

Kilpeck

Kilpeck Church in Herefordshire was given to St. Peter's Abbey (now Cathedral), Gloucester, in 1134. Located immediately to the east of the castle, it has one of the richest displays of sculpture on a small church in England and is the best surviving example of the so-called Hereford (or Herefordshire) School. The three-cell plan has a stilted apsidal sanctuary, square presbytery, and rectangular nave. Architecturally it depends on local sources: the rib-vaulted apse with short barrel-vaulted forebay comes from the south-transept chapel at Tewkesbury, the pilaster responds with quadrant shafts in the apse recall Hereford Cathedral presbytery, while Gloucester Cathedral provides the continuous quadrant molding of the east window and the right-angled chevron on the south doorway and the chancel arch. These churches also inspire some of the figurative and foliage sculpture at Kilpeck: ribbed draperies and some corbel heads relate to capitals in the west bays of the north nave triforium at Tewkesbury, while the grotesque heads on the south doorway (fig. 76) recall one at the apex of the westernmost arch of the nave arcade at Gloucester. The Tree of Life tympanum is allied to the local Dymock School, modified with foliage details from the crossing capitals at Hereford Cathedral. Hereford is also the source for the beaded medallions on the south doorway and the egg-shaped heads and bulbous eyes of the jamb figures of the chancel arch. The latter detail also appears locally on the bronze door knocker at Dormington. The form of the chancel-arch figures relates to Hereford Cathedral MS. P.4.iii, while their super-

Fig. 76. Kilpeck, Herefordshire, detail of south doorway. RCHME, © Crown copyright.

posed arrangement may derive from the south-transept portals at Santiago de Compostela. The dragons' heads projecting from the west wall and the intertwined decoration of the jambs of the south doorway speak of a Viking tradition.

Sculpture related to Kilpeck is found at Shobdon, Leominster, Castle Frome, Eardisley, and Rowlestone and, outside the county, at Billesley (Warwickshire), Ruardean (Gloucestershire), Stottesden (Worcestershire), and Llanbadarn Fawr (Powys).

Malcolm Thurlby

Bibliography

Thurlby, Malcolm. "A Note on the Romanesque Sculpture at Hereford Cathedral and the Herefordshire School of Sculpture." *Burlington Magazine* 126 (1984): 233–34; Zarnecki, George. *Later English Romanesque Sculpture.* London: Tiranti, 1953; Zarnecki, George, Janet Holt, and Tristram Holland, eds. *English Romanesque Art 1066–1200.* London: Weidenfeld & Nicolson, 1984.

See also Architecture and Architectural Sculpture, Romanesque; Sculpture, Romanesque

Kingis Quair, The (The King's Book)

The earliest Scottish love vision (ca. 1424?), describing the poet's courtship of a highborn lady; the poem survives uniquely in Bodl. Arch. Selden B.24.

The authorship question has not been fully resolved. Norton-Smith, the most recent editor, accepts the evidence of a scribal colophon attributing the work to James I of Scotland (1394–1437) as well as the correspondence between James's historical situation and the events in the poem. Other critics consider the work's failure to receive acknowledgment and praise from contemporaries the most serious evidence against James's authorship. The language of the poem indicates Scottish origin, heavily influenced stylistically by Chaucer and, to a lesser extent, Lydgate.

The poem is 1,379 lines long and written in rime royal. In its opening stanzas the sleepless poet turns to Boethius's *Consolation of Philosophy* and muses on Fortune's instability; after hearing the Matins bell he begins to tell of events that have befallen him. Clearly echoing Palamon in Chaucer's *Knight's Tale,* the poet had seen a lady from the window of a tower in which he was imprisoned and prayed to Venus for help in winning the lady. That night he fell asleep and dreamed of being carried up in a heavenly journey to visit Venus and Minerva; the goddesses warn him that love must be grounded in reason and virtue, then send him back to earth to implore Fortune's help in his courtship. Fortune lifts him high on her wheel and wishes him well, then tweaks his ear to awaken him. A white dove carrying a hopeful message confirms Fortune's apparent promise of comfort, and the poem ends on a note of joy and thanks.

The Kingis Quair mixes realistic and imaginative elements as the poet fulfills his stated intention to write "sum newe thing" (89). Events follow sequentially, interrupted only by the "flashback" narration of the dream vision. The poet moves from despair and uncertainty after his youthful capture at sea to a Boethian acceptance of divine governance over Fortune's wheel. The details of capture and imprisonment may reflect James's real situation as a prisoner in England for eighteen years (1406–24), at the end of which time his marriage to Lady Joan Beaufort took place. Conventional poetic devices with a rich literary ancestry raise the poem above mere narration: an ascent through the spheres, meetings with divine or semidivine instructresses, descriptions of an ideal landscape and its population of "diuerse kynd[s]" of plant and animal species, and so on.

The Kingis Quair does not concern itself primarily with formal philosophical or metaphysical issues but rather with representing the dreamer's psychological state as he contemplates the vagaries of love and fate. The poet's unqualified pleasure in recounting his experience marks a stylistic departure from Chaucer's narratorial stance, in spite of the many Chaucerian influences evident throughout the work. In both style and content *The Kingis Quair* remains one of the finest examples of 15th-century dream poetry.

Eileen Jankowski

Bibliography

PRIMARY

Norton-Smith, John, ed. *The Kingis Quair.* Oxford: Clarendon, 1971.

SECONDARY

New *CBEL* 1:655–56; *Manual* 4:961–65, 1123–37;
    MacQueen, John. "Tradition and the Interpretation of
    The Kingis Quair." *RES* n.s. 12 (1961): 117–31;
    Quinn, William. "Memory and the Matrix of Unity in
    The Kingis Quair." *ChauR* 15 (1981): 332–55.

See also Beaufort Family; Boethius; Chaucer; Chaucerian
Apocrypha; Dream Vision; Scottish Literature, Early

King's College, Cambridge

Founded by King Henry VI in 1441, the college was foreseen
as modest in size, and a three-storied college building—the
first of that height in Cambridge—was begun on a restricted
site. Soon Henry was prompted to provide an extravagant
endowment and to enlarge the college to 70 scholars; its mission, almost exclusively to train theologians, set it apart from
other Cambridge colleges. A bold new site, fronting on the
town's major commercial and religious street, was put together
contiguous to the original location, and the area was cleared
of existing structures.

Henry VI gave written instructions for a series of integrated college buildings around a large, 238- by 230-foot
closed quadrangle with a chapel occupying its entire north
side. A cloister cemetery with a tall bell tower between the
chapel and the river was envisioned. Although the east side of
the quadrangle was started, only the chapel was actually completed. The present open quadrangle, roughly the same size
and in the same position as originally planned, was completed
in the 18th and 19th centuries, leaving the chapel isolated with
its famous vista from the river unimpeded.

King's College Chapel (figs. 77–79), one of the most extraordinary buildings from the late Gothic period, was begun
in the late 1440s under the direction of master mason Reginald

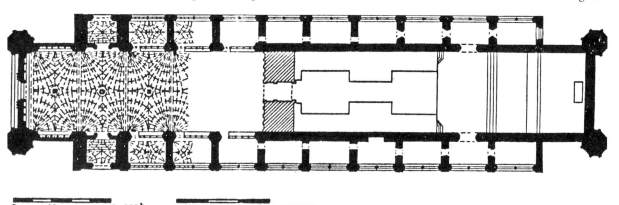

Fig. 77. King's College, Cambridge, chapel. After G. Webb (1956). Reprinted by permission of Yale University Press.

Fig. 78. King's College, Cambridge, chapel exterior, south side. Courtesy of L. Hoey.

Fig. 79. King's College, Cambridge, chapel interior. After anonymous 19th-century lithograph. Courtesy of W. Leedy.

Ely, who is given credit for the architectural details and essential elements of its elevation; the stylistic features evolved out of earlier work in England, especially East Anglia. From the exterior the 288-foot-long chapel with towers at its four corners appears to have one interior space with a row of lower side chapels—to provide privacy for religious contemplation—located between the buttresses; however, the interior is actually divided by a low screen into an antechapel, serving as an educational space and anticipatory in visual expression, and the chapel proper, which imparts a sense of enclosure that resolves the spatial tensions.

Construction was slowed by 1461, when Henry VI was deposed. The foundations for the whole structure were laid, but less than half the building was actually built.

Work speeded up again ca. 1476 under the direction of John Wolryche and carried on under Simon Clerk from 1477 until 1485, when Richard III was slain at Bosworth. By then the walls of five eastern bays were complete with their outer roof. Work continued in a desultory way until 1506, when Henry VII (d. 1509) started to fund construction on a grand scale and later left instructions in his will that the chapel be completed. The design for the antechapel, the great fan vault over the entire chapel, towers, and battlements were finalized and built by 1515 by John Wastell. The stained-glass windows, rood screen, and choirstalls were finished by 1538. Work carried out after 1515 was funded largely by Henry VIII.

Over time the concept for the chapel changed from an act of piety and religious conviction—Henry VI had wanted

"no curious entail or busy moldings"—to one of dynastic propaganda and artistic splendor under Henry VII. The iconographic program for completion of the chapel included extraordinary large-scale heraldic sculpture and elaborate fan vaulting with heraldic bosses that were intended to influence public opinion through art by proclaiming the efficacy of the new Tudor dynasty. The idea was to reinforce the notion that Henry VII was the legitimate holder of the throne, a claim made through his "uncle of most blessid memory," Henry VI.

Walter Leedy

Bibliography

Clark, John W., and Montague R. James. *The Will of King Henry the Sixth.* Cambridge: Cambridge University Press, 1896; Great Britain, Royal Commission on Historical Monuments. *An Inventory of the Historical Monuments in the City of Cambridge.* London: HMSO, 1959; Leedy, Walter. *Fan Vaulting: A Study of Form, Technology, and Meaning.* London: Arts & Architecture Press, 1980; Leedy, Walter. "King's College, Cambridge: Observations on Its Context and Foundations." In *Medieval Architecture and Its Intellectual Context: Studies in Honour of Peter Kidson,* ed. Paul Crossley and Eric Fernie. London: Hambledon, 1990, pp. 209–17; Willis, Robert, and John Clark. *The Architectural History of the University of Cambridge and of the Colleges of Cambridge and Eton.* Vol. 1. 1886. Repr. Cambridge: Cambridge University Press, 1988; Woodman, Francis. *The Architectural History of King's College Chapel and Its Place in the Development of Late Gothic Architecture in England and France.* London: Routledge & Kegan Paul, 1986.

See also Architecture, University and College; Architecture and Architectural Sculpture, Gothic; Henry VI; Henry VII; Vaulting

Knight Service and Knights' Fees

The Norman Conquest introduced knight service into England. William's chief followers accepted their land as a fief (Lat. *feodum*) from the king in return for military service, and in turn provided that service by granting out some of their land as fiefs to knights *(milites)* in return for service. Similar obligations were imposed on the lands held by churches.

The usual term of such service in England was 40 days a year. Yet arguably the difference from before 1066 was of degree, not of kind. Military obligations in Anglo-Saxon England had ultimately rested on possession of land. What the Conquest did was to replace a relatively uniform system of military obligation, based on one man serving for every five hides worth of land, with a series of arbitrary arrangements between the king and his tenants-in-chief (nobles who held fiefs directly from the king). The king came to agreement with an individual landholder on the number of knights with whom he would serve when military service was levied.

These quotas were established in the time of William I, although lordships were often confiscated, and regranted piecemeal, or split up when heirs failed or daughters inherited, and fresh units emerged, with new quotas of knight service. From the time of Henry I these usually reflected the number of knights actually enfeoffed on the land in question. Our analysis of such matters must be to some extent conjectural; the earliest list of the quotas comes in the *cartae baronum* of 1166, Henry II's attempt to record what obligations tenants-in-chief owed and how many knights they had in fact enfeoffed on their lands.

If arrangements between the king and his great nobles followed soon after the Conquest, those between the nobles and their knights who actually performed the service owed the king crystallized slowly. To begin with, most service was probably performed by knights who lived in the lord's household, maintained directly without being granted land. By the time of Domesday Book (1086) many lords had granted out portions of their land in return for service, but most of the early grants were life tenures only; only under Henry I did grants of hereditary fiefs become the norm.

There is evidence that under the first two Norman kings the number of knights owed by the subtenants may have fluctuated. One of the earliest surviving charters of enfeoffment, from the Abbey of Bury St. Edmunds in the reign of William I, grants a fief for the service of either three or four knights. The bishop of Worcester and his subtenants were still disputing how much service the latter owed the bishop in 1095.

Furthermore, while the Norman system of military obligation had been designed to provide military service for the crown, from early on elements of that service were commuted for money payments with which professional knights were hired. Tenants-in-chief might hire knights when the king required actual service, or the king might demand money (*scutagium*: scutage—"shield money") and hire troops, particularly for service in Normandy. Alternatively, after the 40 days of unpaid service were up some or all of those serving unpaid might continue to serve, now for pay.

The first use of the term "scutage" is in 1102, but this is probably after the actual appearance of the levy. Abbot Suger of St. Denis described William II (William Rufus) as "a great merchant and paymaster of knights." This financial element meant that what became important was not so much the knight himself but the unit of obligation, the knight's fief or fee. This was what had been granted for the maintenance of the individual knight; there was no fixed value, nor was the fee necessarily a coherent economic unit, though scutage was usually levied at 30 shillings per fee, irrespective of the value of individual fees.

Other factors encouraged this development. Lords expected other obligations beyond military service. Castle guard was one, but more important in this context was the aid, a financial levy either by consent or as of right on certain specified occasions. Magna Carta limited these to two: knighting of the lord's eldest son and the marriage of his eldest daughter. Those holding directly of the king would, in addition, have to contribute an aid to help ransom him if he were captured.

On most lordships many subtenants owed the service of less than a full knight. On the Clare lands in Kent and East Anglia, in 1166, 23 of 66 subtenants owed less than one knight's service, and others had quotas with a fractional element. The "service" for such fractional fees was almost inevitably in terms of money, whether or not the king might want actual knights from the lords.

By the late 12th century the knight's fee had clearly become the key to the military system, since even where service was raised it no longer bore any exact correspondence to the number of knights theoretically enfeoffed. In 1198 Richard I levied knight service for the defense of Normandy. He asked not for the service of all the fees owed but for one-tenth of this amount, to be, however, for a year rather than 40 days. General inflation, particularly the increased cost of military equipment and wages (where paid), meant that a single knight's fee no longer sufficed to support a knight. By the early years of Henry III the crown recognized this and formally divorced the obligation for actual service from the number of knights' fees on which scutage or aids were paid. The earldom of Cornwall, given to Henry's brother in 1231, was assessed at 215 knights' fees for scutage, though the actual service was but five knights.

By now many landowners who would once have been knights were unable or unwilling to face the financial burdens of knight service and were no longer being knighted. And such was the maze of subtenancies and fractional fees (created not least by divisions among coheiresses in default of a male heir), as well as of men holding fiefs from more than one lord, that scutage was difficult to collect and failed to yield the sum it theoretically should have.

By the time of Edward I the old system of military obligation was anachronistic. He tried to reform and revive the concept of unpaid service by imposing the obligation on all freeholders with land worth over a certain amount; in 1297 he attempted to levy overseas service on those owning land worth over £20 a year. Such measures proved ineffective and unpopular. Though the king still might resort to the traditional "feudal" levy, this no longer raised sufficient troops, and magnates were sometimes asked to bring as many extra men as they could, often at their own expense, but with the hope of reward from the profits and conquests of the campaign.

However, more and more men served for money. Nobles were given indentures (contracts) in which they agreed to raise a set number of men—not necessarily knights—in return for money for wages and expenses. Such contractual service began on a large scale with Edward I's wars in Wales and Scotland and was to be the norm for the 14th century.

The last two occasions on which knight service on the old assessment basis was raised were in 1327 and 1385, in both cases for campaigns against Scotland. Whether the final levy in 1385 was intended as a serious military effort or as an excuse to raise scutage to provide help to a nearly bankrupt government has been much debated. Certainly the limited period of unpaid service was a major disadvantage, and the traditional levy was, by the 14th century, outdated. So, too, was scutage; the few thousand pounds it could raise were a drop in the ocean given the spiraling costs of warfare; the crown had to look to other and more effective methods of raising money.

Graham A. Loud

Bibliography

Gillingham, John. "The Introduction of Knight Service into England." *Anglo-Norman Studies* 4 (1982): 53–64, 181–87 [for recent views of this controversial topic]; Harvey, Sally. "The Knight and the Knight's Fee in England." *Past and Present* 49 (November 1970): 3–43; Holt, J.C. "The Introduction of Knight Service in England." *Anglo-Norman Studies* 6 (1984): 89–106; Keefe, Thomas K. *Feudal Assessments and the Political Community under Henry II and His Sons.* Berkeley: University of California Press, 1983; Lewis, Norman B. "The Feudal Summons of 1385." *EHR* 100 (1985): 729–46 [with a comment by J.J.N. Palmer]; Powicke, Michael. *Military Obligation in Medieval England: A Study in Liberty and Duty.* Oxford: Clarendon, 1962 [esp. chs. 4, 6, and 9]; Prestwich, John O. "War and Finance in the Anglo-Norman State." *TRHS*, 5th ser. 4 (1954): 19–43; Prestwich, Michael. *War, Politics and Finance under Edward I.* London: Faber; Totowa: Rowman & Littlefield, 1972; Stenton, F.M. *The First Century of English Feudalism, 1066–1166.* 2d ed. Oxford: Clarendon, 1961 [the classic work, esp. chs. 4–5; now to be read in light of J.O. Prestwich's comments].

See also Armies; Bastard Feudalism; Feudalism; Scutage; William I

L

Labor Services

The holding of land obligated tenants to perform specific services. These services varied with the types of tenurial relationship common at the time. Thus tenants of knights' fees rendered military service to their lords. Tenants in grand serjeanty performed exalted personal services, while those in petty serjeanty rendered more menial ones. Tenants in socage—freeholders—frequently made annual payments or nominal payments in kind, such as a pound of pepper or a rose. However, the bulk of the rural population consisted of the dependent or unfree peasantry (villeins, serfs, or naifs), and their landholding required the rendering to their lords of both customary rents, in money or kind, and labor, or work services.

Work services comprised a broad range of activities, clearly affected by the varieties of the rural economy throughout England. But whether in open field, woodland, or fen, the services embraced the many kinds of agricultural labor. The works were usually designated "week work," meaning services to be rendered each week, usually in terms of a specific number of days per week. The obligation to plow the lord's demesne, at least once a week, was ubiquitous in the fields of the Midlands and of east and southeast England.

Other commonly encountered duties included reaping, binding, threshing, hay making, winnowing, mowing, digging, hedge planting, pruning, scouring of ditches, carting services, and repairs to farm buildings and fences. Detailed lists of such services are readily found in manorial extents (surveys of manorial resources, including anticipated revenues and services), especially those of the 13th century, when many English landlords—and probably peasants as well—were determined to have local agricultural customs set down in writing.

The works described in careful detail in the 13th-century extents are comprehensive in their coverage of rural labor, so much so that it is difficult to take seriously the not uncommon medieval charge that servile tenure was characterized by an "uncertainty" of services. At first glance, indeed, the work obligations appear to have been relentless in their frequency.

However, many of the works—often described as constituting the obligation for one day—could have been performed in half a day's time or less.

In addition the degree to which the actual work services were in fact exacted was affected by local economic need, personal health, individual willingness to work, and religious duty. Works could be commuted into money payments. Instead of rendering labor services personally—or through substitutes—peasants were sometimes excused all or some of the services for their monetary equivalent. This was especially common in the 12th century and again from the latter half of the 14th century to the 16th.

Illness also canceled work services. Entries in the annual account rolls of manors often record the number of works excused specific individuals because of illness. Conversely court rolls frequently contain notices of people refusing to work and being amerced (fined), a reminder that "absenteeism," for whatever reasons, is not just a modern industrial problem.

Religious feasts, or holy days, canceled work services by effectively prohibiting all servile work. Sundays and the universal celebrations of Christianity were such times; so were the more local saints' feast days. The number of such feast days varied from region to region, of course, but it was not unusual for anywhere from a dozen to forty days a year to be removed from the work calendar of this world of a six-day working week.

As arduous as work services were, their descriptions in manorial extents suggest that they were not necessarily the results of arbitrary decrees by ruthless landlords. Some degree of peasant cooperation was required not only for the system to function but even to exist at all. This is reflected in the degree to which work obligations have their own internal limitation. For example, the number of work "days" each week is usually restricted, often to three or four. In such works as digging the length, breadth, and depth of trenches are frequently noted; the amount of grain to be threshed is set down; in carting services the distances to be traveled are specified, and it is sometimes made clear whose animal or cart is to be used.

Even at the harvest season, when the maximum amount of work was often demanded, with the peasant bringing his whole family and additional labor to the fields, it was not uncommon to find lords being obligated to provide meals.

Work services as a condition of servile tenure existed throughout the medieval period. Their origins are obscure, with both Germanic and late Roman antecedents having been proposed. But whatever and wherever the beginnings, the system was at its peak in the 13th century, when population pressures created a time of high farming by landlords who, eager to derive maximum profit from favorable market conditions, exacted work services from the peasantry more vigorously than in either the 12th or 14th and 15th centuries, when commutation was more common than in the 13th. By the 16th century villein or customary tenure had been transformed into copyhold tenure, which made tenure fairly secure by basing it on set terms or rents, and although documents still spoke of the duty to render "all accustomed services owed," the English countryside had become a world dominated by the payment of rent.

Edwin B. DeWindt

Bibliography

Bennett, Henry S. *Life on the English Manor: A Study of Peasant Conditions, 1150–1400.* Cambridge: Cambridge University Press, 1937; Hilton, Rodney H. *A Medieval Society: The West Midlands at the End of the Thirteenth Century.* London: Weidenfeld & Nicolson, 1966; Lennard, Reginald. *Rural England, 1086–1135: A Study of Social and Agrarian Conditions.* Oxford: Clarendon, 1959; Postan, M.M. *The Medieval Economy and Society: An Economic History of Britain in the Middle Ages.* London: Weidenfeld & Nicolson, 1972; Postan, M.M. *Essays on Medieval Agriculture and General Problems of the Medieval Economy.* Cambridge: Cambridge University Press, 1973; Titow, Jan Z. *English Rural Society, 1200–1350.* London: Allen & Unwin, 1969; Vinogradoff, Paul. *Villeinage in England.* Oxford: Clarendon, 1892.

See also Agriculture; Manorialism; Population; Prices and Wages; Serfs and Villeins

Lady Chapel

A distinctive formal feature of English Gothic church architecture; provision of a Lady Chapel was a central objective of the campaigns of choir remodeling and eastern extension that altered the floorplans of most English cathedrals and abbey churches from the later 12th through the 14th century. The Lady Chapel, a large hall church of roughly the same dimensions as the choir itself, was most frequently located in a rectangular space thrusting eastward from the east end of the choir. In churches laid out like Salisbury this was a low, projecting space emerging from the main mass of the building by only a few bays, as at Salisbury itself, or almost entirely freestanding, as at Gloucester or Westminster. High projecting Lady Chapels sustained the roofline of the main building, as

at Bristol or Worcester. A second popular location for the Lady Chapel was in the place of honor immediately beneath the east window in churches with an aisled rectangle plan and flush east end, as at York. There are a number of common exceptions to these schemes of eastern axial placement, the most significant being north of the choir in a location east of the north transept, as at Ely.

The rapid proliferation of Lady Chapels in England is tangible expression of the intensification of devotion to the Virgin Mary in later medieval England and the pressure to house new Marian liturgies (in particular the daily morning Lady Mass and evening Salve service) in appropriate spaces. An element of popular demand for access to worship services may have also played a role (an issue that needs more scholarly exploration); certainly in abbeys and cathedrals the chapel became an important place of worship for pilgrims and the local laity, especially devout women, and a center of guild and confraternity activities. Archival data establishes the endowing of choirs (including boys) and the presence of organs in the Lady Chapel from an early date, and by the 15th century in many places the master of the Lady Chapel's music became the highest-ranking practicing musician in ecclesiastical service. A considerable portion of the medieval English repertoire of polyphonic mass music and Marian antiphons was composed for performance in the Lady Chapel.

Peter M. Lefferts

Bibliography

Draper, Peter. "Architecture and Liturgy." In *Age of Chivalry: Art in Plantagenet England 1200–1400,* ed. Jonathan Alexander and Paul Binski. London: Royal Academy of Arts, 1987, pp. 83–91; Draper, Peter. "'Seeing that it was Done in all the Noble Churches in England.'" In *Medieval Architecture and Its Intellectual Context: Studies in Honour of Peter Kidson,* ed. Eric Fernie and Paul Crossley. London: Hambledon, 1990, pp. 137–42; Harvey, John H. *Cathedrals of England and Wales.* 2d ed. New York: Batsford, 1974.

See also Architecture and Architectural Sculpture, Gothic; Lady Mass; Mass, Polyphonic Music for; Salve Service; Votive Observance

Lady Mass

A daily votive mass to the Virgin Mary, usually celebrated as a morning mass around the time of Prime. Daily Lady Mass is to be distinguished from the celebration of a weekly votive mass for Mary on Saturday as part of the Marian Commemoration, normally substituting for the principal mass that day. The latter is an older custom widespread in England by the 12th century that had its roots in the Carolingian era. Adoption of Lady Mass began in major English establishments in the mid-12th century and was nearly universal by the early 13th, when Abbot William Trumpington of St. Albans (1214–35) ordained that the abbey celebrate a Lady Mass daily "seeing that it was done in all the noble churches in England." Like the earlier introduction of the Feast of the Conception of the Virgin in the 1120s and the later adoption of the evening Salve service, the emergence of the Lady Mass testifies to a particularly intense devotional fervor for the Virgin Mary in England. It seems additionally to reflect a growing popular demand by the lay public (including women) for greater access to worship services, a pressure also addressed by the building of Lady Chapels to house votive Marian services (the daily morning Lady Mass and evening Salve service).

Lady Mass was a solemn, sung mass rather than a low, spoken mass. Surviving liturgies show it to have been observed with a great deal of flexibility in the choice of liturgical forms, including substitutions and interpolations that involved polyphonic music. Lady Mass, indeed, was the principal focal point for new liturgical composition and polyphonic music making in England from ca. 1200 to 1400, and most surviving English mass music of these years appears to have been intended for it. Endowed choral positions (including boys) and organs are documented in Lady Chapels from an early date, and these would principally have been employed in the performance of Lady Mass.

Peter M. Lefferts

Bibliography

Harrison, Frank Ll. *Music in Medieval Britain.* 2d ed. London: Routledge & Kegan Paul, 1963; Lefferts, Peter M. "Cantilena and Antiphon: Music for Marian Services in Late Medieval England." In *Studies in Medieval Music: Festschrift for Ernest H. Sanders,* ed. Peter M. Lefferts and Brian Seirup. *Current Musicology* 45–47 (1990): 247–82.

See also Cantilena; Choirs; Lady Chapel; Liturgy and Church Music, History of; Mass, Polyphonic Music for; Salve Service; Votive Observance; W1

Laȝamon or Layamon (fl. ca. 1200–25?)

Author of the *Brut,* a major poem of the early ME period that contains, among other items of interest, the first account in English of the Arthurian legend. Laȝamon identifies himself in the opening lines of his poem as a priest residing in Ernleȝe (Areley Kings, Worcestershire). Having resolved to write a history of England, he says, he consulted as source material Bede's *Ecclesiastical History,* a Latin book written by Sts. Albin and Augustine, and Wace's *Roman de Brut.* In fact Laȝamon appears to have made little use of Bede's history (tentatively identified by scholars as the OE translation of Bede) or the untitled Latin text (identified still more tentatively as a book containing selections by Albin and Augustine of Canterbury, the Latin text of Bede, or a mere fiction invented by the poet to display his erudition). Thus, with some significant modifications and additions, Laȝamon's poem is essentially an English paraphrase of Wace's *Brut* rendered into alliterative long lines, some 16,000 in number. Because of an allusion in the opening lines of the poem to Eleanor, "who was Henry's queen," it is generally accepted that the *Brut* was written some time after the death of Henry

II in 1189 and possibly even after the death of Eleanor herself in 1204; but scholarly opinion relating to the precise date of composition ranges from the late 12th century to the second half of the 13th.

The *Brut* survives in two manuscripts dating from 1250–1350. Although both are thought to derive from a common archetype, BL Cotton Caligula A.ix is commonly held to be closer to its exemplar—and hence to Laȝamon's original text—than is BL Cotton Otho C.xiii. The latter is considered an inferior text because its scribe apparently attempted to modernize his original by eliminating many of the rhetorical embellishments intended to give it what has been called an "antique colouring" (Stanley). These embellishments include lengthy repetitions of detail and incident and archaisms of the type that survive in and characterize the Caligula text—that is, the many coinages and poetic compounds with a distinctly Anglo-Saxon ring about them and the marked preference for words of Anglo-Saxon origin (many of which have been replaced in the Otho text by French loanwords).

In subject matter and method Laȝamon imitates Wace so as to be able to afford his readers a history of the Britons from the time of Brutus, great-grandson of Aeneas, to the ascendancy of the Saxons over the Britons during the reign of Cadwalader in the 7th century. Laȝamon's additions to and modifications of his Anglo-Norman source have much to tell us, however, about his purpose in adapting Wace's poem into English: as scholars have been quick to notice, Laȝamon's numerous accounts of feasts, sea voyages, and battles, many of which have no counterparts in Wace's poem, evoke the ethos of OE poetic accounts of such events and seem to have been intended to do so. Similarly Wace's interest in love, courtesy, and the ideals of chivalry is not one that Laȝamon shares: indeed, in his adaptation of many of the events described in Wace's poem, we find Laȝamon attempting to recreate the ethos of the heroic, as opposed to the chivalric, world. His Arthur, for example, is not a Norman king presiding over a chivalric court as in Wace, but a Saxon chieftain as disposed to committing acts of brutality and violence as to rewarding his faithful retainers, after a battle, with rings, garments, and horses. As in the meadhalls of OE poetry, there are *scops* in Arthur's court and *dream* (joy) when a victory is being celebrated; by the same token here and elsewhere in the poem there prevails, as in OE verse, an overwhelming sense of the role played by Fate in the human lives, but especially in the lives of those destined to enter the field of battle.

Further evidence of Laȝamon's familiarity with and desire to imitate the verse of OE poets can be discerned in his use of formulas, not simply as tags and line fillers but also to advance his narrative in a manner in keeping with the formulaic practices of OE poetry. Not surprisingly, perhaps, the *Brut* is most noticeably formulaic in passages that have no counterpart in Wace and in which Laȝamon seems to have been particularly eager to recreate the ethos of the past, such as his accounts of feasts, sea voyages, and battles. Equally indicative of Laȝamon's admiration for the verse of the OE poets is his use of certain rhetorical tropes and patterns found in their poetry. With an unmistakable sense of what he is about Laȝamon employs, with varying degrees of frequency, the kenning, the descriptive epithet, the simile, litotes, variation, chiasmus, and more complex structural repetitions, such as the envelope pattern, repetition parallels, and balance parallels.

Laȝamon's unmistakable nostalgia for the pre-Conquest period is reflected not only in the poem's style and content but also in its verse form. He patterns his verse, like his language and themes, after that of the OE poets. Laȝamon's basic metrical unit is the alliterative long line consisting of two two-stress hemistichs linked by alliteration, rhyme, or both. His use of rhyme as well as alliteration, of a longer line (to accommodate the hypotactic constructions of ME), and of some metrical patterns that do not conform to the metrical patterns of OE verse suggest that Laȝamon was working within a much more flexible prosody than that governing the composition of OE poetry; however, his verse should not be relegated, as some of his critics have suggested, to the ranks of "popular" poetry. Rather it is an evolutionary form of the "classical" alliterative verse of the English Middle Ages.

James Noble

Bibliography

PRIMARY

Brook, G.L., and R.F. Leslie, eds. *Laȝamon: Brut.* 2 vols. EETS o.s. 250, 277. London: Oxford University Press, 1963–78; Bzdyl, Donald G., trans. *Layamon's Brut: A History of the Britons.* Binghamton: MRTS, 1989.

SECONDARY

New *CBEL* 1:460–63; Le Saux, Françoise H.M. *Laȝamon's Brut: The Poem and Its Sources.* Cambridge: Brewer, 1989; Le Saux, Françoise H.M. *The Text and Tradition of Laȝamon's Brut.* Cambridge: Brewer, 1994; Reiss, Edmund, et al. *Arthurian Legend and Literature: An Annotated Bibliography.* Vol. 1. New York: Garland, 1984, pp. 79–80; Stanley, E.G. "Layamon's Antiquarian Sentiments." *MÆ* 38 (1969): 23–37.

See also Alliterative Revival; Geoffrey of Monmouth; Matter of Britain; Versification; Wace

Lai, Latin

One of the most expansive and impressive genres of medieval lyric poetry and nonliturgical musical composition, cultivated primarily from the 12th to the 14th century. In formal terms the Latin lai is essentially a secular sequence, constructed on the principle of progressive repetition wherein each formal unit is normally stated twice, creating a chain of double versicles, or musically paired lines of text. Unlike the sequence, however, it may also feature triple and quadruple versicles, repetition of musical phrases within the individual versicle, and the return of earlier musical material. The Latin lai is to be distinguished from the narrative lai and Arthurian lai in French (which were also evidently sung in their original performance contexts), but not from the independent lyrical lai

in French, with which it shares its form, distinctive melodic idiom, and important contrafact relationships (the crafting of new texts for existing melodies). The later Latin sequence and planctus are also closely related stylistically and formally. Among examples in insular sources *Samson dux fortissime* and *Omnis caro peccaverat* (the *Song of the Flood*) are the most ambitious. Important English sources of the Latin lai with music include the Later Cambridge Songs (CUL Ff.i.17), BL Harley 978, and BL Arundel 248; sources without music include the Bekyngton Anthology (Bodl. Add. A.44), BL Arundel 384, and Bodl. Rawlinson C.510.

Peter M. Lefferts

Bibliography

Fallows, David. "Lai." *NGD* 10:364–76; Stevens, John. *Words and Music in the Middle Ages: Song, Narrative, Dance and Drama, 1050–1350.* Cambridge: Cambridge University Press, 1986.

See also Conductus; Harley 978; Hymns; Planctus; Sequence; Songs

Lancaster, Duchy of

The duchy of Lancaster was the greatest and richest landed estate of late-medieval England. It expanded into a collection of manors, castles, and jurisdictions in nearly every county of England and Wales. It had its origins in the Norman honor of Lancaster, erected into an earldom and joined with the earldom of Leicester by Henry III for his younger son, Edmund Crouchback.

Edmund's son Thomas married the heiress to the earldom of Lincoln, Alice de Lacy. He suffered forfeiture and death as the leader of the opposition to Edward II, but his nephew Henry of Grosmont proved a loyal servant of Edward III and was restored to the earldom in 1345. In 1351 the earldom was elevated to a duchy, and Duke Henry was given palatine (i.e., semiregal) powers in the county of Lancaster. Henry's heiress, Blanche, married Edward III's fourth son, John of Gaunt, who succeeded his father-in-law as duke in 1362.

John was the greatest lord in England in the final years of Edward III's reign and throughout the reign of his nephew Richard II. He created a strong retinue based upon the duchy, and he developed its administrative cohesion and independence. John attempted to add to the family's wealth through the marriage of his heir, Henry Bolingbroke, to the Bohun co-heiress Mary. Henry, however, became involved in the Appellant opposition to Richard II (1388); he was exiled in 1398. When Gaunt died in 1399, the threat posed by the duchy's wealth and power led Richard II to confiscate it. Henry returned to England as the champion of property rights. At his landing he claimed only the duchy, though he proceeded to depose Richard and assume the crown.

Henry IV protected the duchy by an act of parliament, providing it would remain the private possession of his family. It thus continued to enjoy its own administration. The attainder of Henry VI gave the duchy to the Yorkists, and Edward IV, by act of parliament, joined the County Palatine to the duchy and made them estates tied to the crown. The palatine court was abolished in 1873. The chancellor of the duchy still serves as a minister without portfolio. The sovereign, when traveling in a private capacity, still does so as the duke or duchess of Lancaster.

James L. Gillespie

Bibliography

Fowler, Kenneth. *The King's Lieutenant: Henry of Grosmont, First Duke of Lancaster, 1310–1361.* London: Elek, 1969; Goodman, Anthony. *John of Gaunt: The Exercise of Princely Power in Fourteenth-Century Europe.* New York: St. Martin, 1992; Smith, Sydney Armitage. *John of Gaunt.* London: Constable, 1904; Somerville, Robert. *History of the Duchy of Lancaster.* 2 vols. London: Chancellor and Council of the Duchy of Lancaster, 1953–70.

See also Dukes; Henry of Lancaster; Lancaster, John Duke of; Lancaster, Thomas Earl of; Palatinates; Wars of the Roses

Lancaster, John Duke of (John of Gaunt; 1340–1399)

The fourth son of Edward III and Philippa of Hainault; earl of Richmond (1342–72), duke of Lancaster in 1362 after receiving the largest English inheritance in right of his wife Blanche (d. 1368).

From 1366 to 1374 Gaunt deployed Lancastrian resources as a retinue captain and royal lieutenant, first to support his elder brother the Black Prince's intervention in Castile (1367) and from 1369 as a mainstay of his father's shrinking power in France. In 1372 he assumed the titular kingship of Castile after marriage to Constanza (d. 1394), daughter and heir of the deposed Pedro I. In 1376–77 Gaunt's defense of his enfeebled father's government, undermined in the Good Parliament of 1376, and his maladroit attacks on the privileges of London and the church (in the course of which he was a patron to John Wyclif) brought him widespread unpopularity.

From 1377 to 1385 he cooperated with fellow nobles in council and parliament, and at conferences and on campaign, in defending his nephew Richard II's authority, though failing to cement good relations with Richard and the envious court favorites who emerged in the 1380s. From 1386 to 1389 he withdrew abroad, first pursuing (1386–87) and then compromising (Treaty of Bayonne, 1388) his Castilian claim, and then acting as royal lieutenant in Aquitaine (1388–89). In 1390 a chastened and friendlier Richard created Gaunt duke of Aquitaine for life, probably with the idea that he and his heirs would hold the duchy as part of the peace settlement he tried to negotiate with the French crown over the next few years.

Gaunt's support, backed by his huge permanent retinue, was again a stabilizing force in Richard's rule. The duke was dependent on royal favor to uphold his authority against Gascon opposition and to advance his Beaufort children (by Katherine Swynford, whom he married in 1396, facilitating

their legitimation). A strong believer in royal prerogative, Gaunt continued to support Richard, despite the suspicious death of his brother, Thomas duke of Gloucester (1397), and the exile of his son Henry of Bolingbroke (1398). Gaunt died at Leicester on 3 February 1399 and was buried in St. Paul's Cathedral, London.

His lasting achievement was the acquisition in heredity of semiregal (palatine) powers in the county of Lancaster for his successors. His memory was to be honored as the forebear of ruling houses in 15th-century England, Portugal, Castile, and Aragon, and—through the Beauforts—of the Tudor dynasty. Chaucer's *Book of the Duchess* is an elegy on Gaunt's first wife, Blanche, perhaps written for him. An impression of the magnificence of his household can be gained from the ruins of the domestic apartments he built at Kenilworth Castle, Warwickshire.

Anthony E. Goodman

Bibliography

Goodman, Anthony. "John of Gaunt." In *England in the Fourteenth Century: Proceedings of the 1985 Harlaxton Symposium,* ed. W.M. Ormrod. Woodbridge: Boydell, 1986, pp. 67–87; Goodman, Anthony. *John of Gaunt: The Exercise of Princely Power in Fourteenth-Century Europe.* New York: St. Martin, 1992; Lopes, Fernão. *The English in Portugal, 1367–87.* Ed. and trans. D.W. Lomax and R.J. Oakley. Westminster: Aris & Phillips, 1988; Palmer, J.J.N. "The Anglo-French Peace Negotiations, 1390–96." *TRHS,* 5th ser. 16 (1966): 81–94; Palmer, J., and B. Powell, eds. *The Treaty of Bayonne (1388).* Exeter Hispanic Texts 47. Exeter: University of Exeter, 1988; Russell, P.E. *The English Intervention in Spain and Portugal in the Time of Edward III and Richard II.* Oxford: Clarendon, 1955; Walker, Simon. *The Lancastrian Affinity, 1361–1389.* Oxford: Clarendon, 1990.

See also Beaufort Family; Edward III; Edward the Black Prince; Henry IV; Hundred Years War; Lancaster, Duchy of; Richard II

Lancaster, Thomas Earl of (ca. 1278–1322)

The most powerful nobleman of his time and determined opponent of Edward II. Through inheritance and marriage he controlled five earldoms: Lancaster, Leicester, Lincoln, Salisbury, and Derby. Their enormous wealth enabled him to amass the largest private retinue in the kingdom.

As Edward II's cousin Thomas was a natural ally of the new king in 1307. Yet he soon changed course. In 1311 he helped draft the Ordinances and in 1312 shared responsibility for Piers Gaveston's execution. Thereafter he steadfastly championed the Ordinances. Between 1314 and 1318, after the rout at Bannockburn, Edward needed Thomas's retinue to fight the Scots in the north, giving Thomas the opportunity to implement reforms.

Unfortunately Thomas himself sapped the effort. Instead of applying himself to government he held aloof. He was not widely liked or trusted by his peers. Some thought that his insistence on reform cloaked an urge to seize power. He was prone to feuding and could be violent, arrogant, self-righteous, and grasping. Even his wife, Alice de Lacy, deserted him.

After 1318 Edward outmaneuvered Thomas and ousted him from government. When the Marchers rebelled in 1321, Thomas joined in, but their forces were defeated at Boroughbridge. Thomas was captured and summarily executed on 22 March 1322. His stance as a staunch defender of the popular Ordinances probably accounts for his posthumous reputation. Almost immediately after his death it was said that miracles were performed at the sites of his execution and burial, and common people called for his canonization.

Scott L. Waugh

Bibliography

Denholm-Young, Noel, ed. and trans. *The Life of Edward the Second.* London: Nelson, 1957 [best available contemporary source]; Maddicott, J.R. *Thomas of Lancaster, 1307–1322: A Study in the Reign of Edward II.* London: Oxford University Press, 1970 [magisterial modern treatment].

See also Battles of Bannockburn and Boroughbridge; Despenser Family; Edward II; Ordainers

Lanfranc (ca. 1010–1089)

An Italian, from Pavia, of legal background, Lanfranc arrived in Normandy ca. 1042. After briefly teaching in Avranches he entered the newly founded Abbey of Bec and became its first prior-schoolmaster, accepting lay and ecclesiastical students from throughout Europe to study the liberal arts at Normandy's foremost school. One contemporary remarked that there was no learning in Normandy before Lanfranc's light shone throughout the land.

Lanfranc's scholarly reputation brought him into contact with the earliest of the reform popes, Leo IX, and with subsequent papal reformers throughout his career. In his most famous work, *Liber de corpore et sanguine Domini* (*On the Body and Blood of the Lord,* 1059), written at papal request, he stated the papal case against Berengar of Tours's denial of the transformation of bread and wine into the body and blood of Christ, for which Berengar was declared a heretic. Lanfranc remained in close contact with his own student Pope Alexander II, who granted Duke William of Normandy the papal banner to conquer England in 1066.

By the 1050s Lanfranc may have been William's closest adviser. His biographer reports that William "set him on a watchtower" over all the churches of Normandy and England. In 1060 he became the first abbot of the ducal monastery, St. Étienne at Caen, built by William, perhaps at Lanfranc's arrangement, to reconcile papal protests against William's marriage to Matilda of Flanders (who concurrently built the nunnery of Holy Trinity in Caen).

Declining election in 1067 as archbishop of Rouen, in 1070 Lanfranc accepted the archbishopric of Canterbury and became primate of England at William's request and Pope Alexander's order. He became William's collaborator in re-

forming the church, investigating and systematizing its traditions, and bringing monks from Bec and Caen to rule English abbeys and sees.

Lanfranc joined with William to obstruct the radical Pope Gregory VII's effort to subject England and William to papal lordship. He sometimes served as regent in the king's absence, once quashing a serious baronial rebellion. His involvement in the Domesday Survey (1086) seems clear. Lanfranc successfully controlled the Conqueror's son and successor, William II (William Rufus), until he died in 1089; thereafter Rufus despoiled the church, attempting to reverse many of the Conqueror's and Lanfranc's policies. But his reforms, reinstituted by his student Anselm, set a pattern for the English church to the present day.

Sally N. Vaughn

Bibliography

Barlow, Frank. *The English Church, 1066–1154: A History of the Anglo-Norman Church.* London: Longman, 1979; Gibson, Margaret. *Lanfranc of Bec.* Oxford: Clarendon, 1978; Vaughn, Sally N. *The Abbey of Bec and the Anglo-Norman State, 1034–1136.* Woodbridge: Boydell, 1981.

See also Anselm; Investiture Controversy; William I; William II

Langton, Stephen (ca. 1155–1228)

A notable biblical scholar, theologian, preacher, and archbishop of Canterbury. Born in Lincolnshire, Langton went ca. 1170 to study in Paris, where he became master of theology. In a lengthy and productive career he wrote the *Questiones theologice* (lectures on theological and moral problems), commentaries on scripture, and numerous sermons. The modern system of chapter-division for the Bible is also attributed to him.

In 1206 Langton was made a cardinal-priest by his former Paris friend Lothar of Segni, Pope Innocent III. Immediately thereafter Langton became involved in the events associated with the disputed election to the see of Canterbury following the death of Hubert Walter in 1205. Innocent voided the elections of the two candidates supported by the monks of Christ Church Canterbury and by King John and pressed instead for the election of Langton, whom he consecrated on 17 June 1207. John's refusal to accept Langton as archbishop led to six tumultuous years during which England was placed under interdict and the king excommunicated. Returning to England in 1213, Langton mediated the struggle between the barons and the king that led to the drafting of Magna Carta. It is likely that he was responsible for those provisions of the Charter guaranteeing the liberties of the church.

Langton attended the Fourth Lateran Council in Rome in 1215. Despite his suspension by the pope for his failure to enforce papal censures against the barons opposing John he supported the broad program of church reform initiated by Rome. From 1218, when he returned to England, until his death in 1228 Langton was a loyal supporter of the young

Henry III. As archbishop of Canterbury he was an able administrator and defender of the interests of the English church. Langton's efforts to raise the standard of the English episcopate paved the way for such reformers as Grosseteste and Pecham and for a wide participation by bishops in the life of medieval England.

Phyllis B. Roberts

Bibliography

Lacombe, George, and Arthur M. Landgraf. "The *Questiones* of Cardinal Stephen Langton." *New Scholasticism* 3 (1929): 1–18, 113–58, and 4 (1930): 1–22, 97–164; Lacombe, George, et al. "Studies on the Commentaries of Stephen Langton." *Archives d'histoire doctrinale et littéraire du Moyen Age* 5 (1930); Powicke, F.M. *Stephen Langton.* Oxford: Clarendon, 1928; Quinto, Riccardo. *"Doctor Nominatissimus": Stefano Langton (†1228) e la tradizione delle sue opere.* Münster: Aschendorff, 1994; Roberts, Phyllis B. *Studies in the Sermons of Stephen Langton.* Toronto: Pontifical Institute, 1968; Roberts, Phyllis B., ed. *Selected Sermons of Stephen Langton.* Toronto: Pontifical Institute, 1980.

See also Bishops; Grosseteste; Hubert Walter; John; Magna Carta; Sermons

Language, History of the

Old English

When the last of the Roman legions withdrew from Britain in the early 5th century, the inhabitants of the parts of the island that had been under Roman rule for four centuries were left to defend themselves. These Celtic Britons, who had come to depend on Roman arms for protection, found themselves vulnerable to attack from the Picts and the Scots in the north, as well as from seafaring raiders along the southeastern coast. According to Bede in the year 449 Vortigern, one of the Celtic leaders, asked for help from a Germanic tribe on the Continent, who responded to the call but then turned on their Celtic hosts. Traditionally this date has been taken as the beginning of the migration to Britain of Angles, Saxons, and Jutes, although there is a growing body of archaeological evidence for a Germanic population in Britain during the 4th century. With the arrival of these Germanic peoples, who spoke related dialects, the English language can be said to have begun (the name "English" itself being derived from the name for the Angles).

Anglo-Saxon, or Old English (OE), is a West Germanic language, most closely akin genealogically to Dutch and Frisian. It has dialectal divisions that probably reflected differences already present in the continental homes of the invaders as well as some features that developed in England after the settlement. Of the four OE dialects West Saxon is the one in which the most extensive collection of texts is preserved. Kentish was spoken in the southeast; Mercian, in the Midlands between the Thames and the Humber; and Northum-

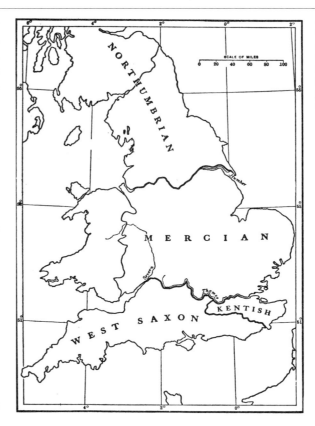

Fig. 80. Dialects of Old English. After A.C. Baugh and T. Cable, A History of the English Language *(1993). Reprinted by permission of Prentice Hall.*

brian, north of the Humber (fig. 80). Except for place-names, including especially names of rivers, OE shows little influence from the Celtic language of the population who had been in the British Isles for perhaps a thousand years. As more of the Germanic settlers arrived, the Celts were driven to the western and northern parts of the island and to Ireland.

Although little affected by the Celtic language that it displaced, OE did incorporate considerable vocabulary from two other foreign sources, Latin and the Scandinavian languages. Beginning in 597 with the arrival of Augustine, the conversion of Britain to Roman Christianity introduced words into OE to describe the new religion and the new religious and cultural concepts. (Augustine's mission was actually a reintroduction of Christianity, because Irish monks had been preaching the gospel in the north since the founding of Iona by Columba in 563. However, 597 marks the beginning of a systematic attempt on the part of Rome to convert the inhabitants.) From the earliest period of Christian influence come words that survive in only slightly altered form into Modern English: *abbot, angel, bishop, candle, deacon, disciple, hymn, martyr, mass, noon, nun, palm, pope, priest, rule, shrine, temple,* and many others. From the Benedictine Reform of the latter half of the 10th century come additional borrowings, many of which, as before, have to do with religious matters: *apostle, cell, cloister, creed, demon, dirge, font, idol, prophet, sabbath, synagogue.*

Scandinavian attacks upon England during a period of nearly 300 years left their mark on the history and language of the Anglo-Saxons. Between 787 and 1042 there were at least three waves of invasions and subsiding activity. Alfred the Great's victory over the Danes in 878 resulted in the Treaty of Wedmore, by which the Danes withdrew from Alfred's territory and remained east of a line running from Chester to London. This territory was subject to Danish law and hence became known as the Danelaw. The chief effects of contact with Old Norse, the ancestor of the modern Scandinavian languages, can be seen in the borrowings of individual words, some of them forming new semantic distinctions with their English cognates; for example, *skirt, scale, scab,* and *loan* developed from Old Norse borrowings, while native English *shirt, shale, shab(by),* and *lend* continued to be used with shifts in meanings.

Loanwords from Latin and Old Norse appear above in their Modern English spelling. For some of these words the OE pronunciation would not be far from that of present-day English. King Alfred's West Saxon pronunciation of *arcebiscop* 'archbishop,' for example, would probably be understandable now, a fact concealed by superficial conventions of spelling. The sequence *sc* represented the *sh* sound, and the letter *c* by itself represented either the *ch* sound in *arch* or the [k] sound now spelled sometimes with *c (cat),* sometimes with *k (king,* OE *cyning).* Other spelling differences that cause a page of OE to look strange are equally superficial. The "a-e digraph" [æ], known as "ash" in OE, is the short vowel in the word "ash" itself, pronounced in OE as in Modern English, but spelled *æsc.* The two symbols þ (thorn) and ð (eth) were the equivalent of Modern English *th-;* like *th-* either symbol could represent either the voiceless *th-* (as in *thin*) or the voiced *th-* (as in *then*). With a few such rules of thumb many OE words are immediately recognizable and pronounceable: *bæþ* 'bath,' *scip* 'ship,' *fisc* 'fish,' *bæc* 'back,' and so on.

However, just as spelling conventions of different periods can conceal similarities, so can they conceal differences. All the OE words cited above have a short vowel. The long vowels that survived into ME were affected by the 15th-century Great Vowel Shift, which caused the phonology, or sound system, of Modern English to be strikingly different from that of OE, ME, and indeed other modern European languages, such as French, Spanish, Italian, and German. Thus, in reading both *Beowulf* and Chaucer, it is important to know that *rīde* 'ride' has approximately the vowel of Modern English *reed; mē* "me" that of *may;* and so on.

Foreign influence on vocabulary by way of loanwords is easier to identify than influence on morphology (inflectional forms) and syntactic structure. The inflectional system of OE was reduced from that of Indo-European but still quite full in comparison with that of Modern English. Endings on words were used extensively to show grammatical and semantic relationships. For example, although the noun was no longer inflected for the locative, ablative, and vocative cases, as in Indo-European, it did have forms for the nominative, genitive, dative, and accusative (as well as sometimes the instrumental). Nouns also had grammatical gender (masculine, feminine, and neuter), and declensions were further determined by the vowel or the consonant that preceded the case ending at a prehistoric stage of the language. The definite article agreed with the noun in gender, num-

ber, and case. The adjective, which in present-day English is inflected only in the comparative and superlative, had in OE even more grammatical categories than the noun that it modified. It agreed with the noun in gender, number, and case; it had the positive, comparative, and superlative degrees; and it was inflected differently depending on whether a definite article or possessive pronoun preceded the adjective (the "weak" form) or no such determiner occurred (the "strong" form).

With all these grammatical distinctions available in the noun phrase alone, any one phrase will illustrate only a minority of the possible categories. Consider the OE equivalent of "that good king" (where N, G, D, and A represent the nominative, genitive, dative, and accusative cases, respectively):

SINGULAR	PLURAL
N. sē gōd-a cyning	N. ðā gōd-an cyning-as
G. ðæs gōd-an cyning-es	G. ðāra gōd-ena cyning-a
D. ðæm gōd-an cyning-e	D. ðæm gōd-um cyning-um
A. ðone gōd-an cyning	A. ðā gōd-an cyning-as

To give an adequate illustration of noun-phrase inflections it would be necessary to show similar paradigms for a feminine noun (e.g. *wund,* "wound"), a neuter noun (*scēap* "sheep"), a consonant-stem noun (*oxa* "ox"), and several minor noun declensions (such as the "mutated plurals" of *fōt, fēt* "foot, feet") and to repeat all of these examples in a phrase that did not have a demonstrative or possessive pronoun and thus would follow the strong pattern.

The personal pronoun had the categories of gender, number, and case that the noun had, and in addition it was inflected for the dual number, meaning "we two" and "you two." Despite the loss of the dual number the pronoun of present-day English retains the earlier inflections more fully than any other part of speech:

SINGULAR				
N. ic (I)	þū (you)	hēo (he)	hē (she)	hit (it)
G. mīn	þīn	his	hiere	his
D. mē	þē	him	hiere	him
A. mē	þē	hine	hīe	hit

DUAL		PLURAL		
N. wit (we two)	git (you two)	N. wē (we)	gē (you)	hīe (they)
G. uncer	incer	G. ūre	ēower	hiera
D. unc	inc	D. ūs	ēow	him
A. unc	inc	A. ūs	ēow	hīe

The verb in OE showed distinctions of person, number, and mood that are almost completely lost in Modern English, as well as distinctions of tense that are retained. OE also had many more "strong" verbs (called "irregular" in grammars of Modern English), which formed their past tense and past participle by a vowel change: for example, *sing, sang, sung.* The personal endings may be illustrated by the strong verb *drīfan:*

INDICATIVE	SUBJUNCTIVE	INDICATIVE	SUBJUNCTIVE
Present	*Present*	*Past*	*Past*
ic drīf-e	ic drīf-e	ic drāf	ic drif-e
þū drīf-st (-est)	þū drīf-e	þū drif-e	þū drif-e
hē drīf-ð (-eð)	hē drīf-e	hē drāf	hē drif-e
wē drīf-að	wē drīf-en	wē drif-on	wē drif-en
gē drīf-að	gē drīf-en	gē drif-on	gē drif-en
hīe drīf-að	hīe drīf-en	hīe drif-on	hīe drif-en

It is often remarked that the highly inflected grammar of OE—its *synthetic* quality—allowed a freer word order than that of Modern English, an *analytic* language. If such relationships as Subject, Object, and Indirect Object can be shown by endings on words, then it would stand to reason that a relatively fixed word order, like SVO (subject, verb, object) in Modern English, would not be necessary in OE. As useful as this generalization is for the overall history of the language, it is sometimes taken as implying too much. OE syntax did indeed allow patterns that do not occur in Modern English, but it would be wrong to say that OE syntax was "free." Recent studies have revealed increasingly subtle rules governing patterns that occurred and, significantly, patterns that did not occur.

For example, a word like *þā* could be either an adverb ("then") or a subordinating conjunction ("when"). *Þā* thus introduces different syntactic structures in its role as two different parts of speech, although one cannot always be certain which reading was intended; for example, modern texts punctuate *þā* as an adverb in *Beowulf* 1274, *Þā hē hēan gewāt,* "then he wretched departed," but as a conjunction in 512, *þā git on sund rēon,* "when you two on sea swam." To read either of these clauses with the other part of speech would change meaning and style, with implications for the relative degrees of parataxis and hypotaxis in a text. For clauses with *þā* over which modern readers disagree, ongoing studies in OE syntax are revealing hitherto unnoticed regularities. In this pattern as in others (negation, question, conjunction, etc.) the apparent freedom of OE syntax has less to do with its rich inflectional system than with our incomplete understanding of the syntax.

Middle English

The Middle English (ME) period illustrates both the influence upon language by the forces of history and culture and also the lack of precise fit between linguistic periods and historical periods. Traditional dates for ME (e.g., 1150–1500) can vary by a century, depending on the criteria used. The most important external event, not only for ME but for English history generally, was the Norman Conquest in 1066. Yet some of the changes in phonology and grammar that set ME apart from OE were already in progress, and the full impact of French loanwords entering English would be greatest two centuries later.

When Edward the Confessor died childless in January 1066, Harold, the son of Godwin, Edward's principal adviser, was elected king. His election was challenged, however, by William, the duke of Normandy and a second cousin to the late king, who saw that the only way to gain the English throne was by force. After elaborate preparations William landed in England in September and the next month, near Hastings, defeated Harold's army in one of the great battles of history. Harold died on the battlefield, and William was crowned king of England on Christmas Day, 1066.

With William's victory came the introduction of a new nobility into England. For the next 200 years French was the language of everyday affairs among the upper classes. English continued to be spoken by the mass of the population, many of whom knew no French. In its unofficial status, and without a standard variety to serve as a conservative influence, the English language underwent momentous changes and increased dialectal diversity. These changes occurred in all aspects of the language—its phonology, morphology, syntax, and lexicon. They were so extensive in each component that it is difficult to say which is the most significant; in any event the changes in phonology and grammar reinforced each other.

In considering phonological change it is natural to think first of developments in the stressed, root vowels of words, and indeed, between OE and ME, there were half a dozen to a dozen important changes in stressed vowels, depending on the dialects: the vowel [æ] in *sæt* "sat" was backed to [ɑ] in ME (only to return to [æ] in Modern English); the long and short high front vowels [ü] in *synn* "sin" and *hȳdan* "hide" were unrounded; the West Saxon diphthongs *ea* and *eo* were "smoothed" to monophthongs, and so on. However, the most sweeping phonological change between OE and ME occurred in unstressed syllables, where full vowels were reduced to the mid-central vowel [ə], known as "schwa," pronounced "uh." In OE the qualitative distinctions among unstressed vowels spelled *e, a, u* were necessary to keep inflectional endings separate. When these were reduced to schwa, the grammatical distinctions were no longer conveyed. A separate change of final *-m* to *-n,* and then the dropping of all inflectional *-n*'s, contributed to the leveling of inflections; for example, the dative plural ending *-um,* the weak ending *-an,* and the dative singular ending *-e* all became [ə], spelled *-e.*

The effect of these changes on the inflections of the nouns, adjectives, and verbs, and the further simplification that was brought about by the operation of analogy (e.g., *shine/shone* becoming *shine/shined*), changed English from a highly inflected, or synthetic, language to an extremely analytic one. A noun phrase like *the good king,* for example, was declined almost as in present-day English, with the *-s* ending in the genitive singular and in the plural, but otherwise no inflections of the noun, and no inflections of agreement for any categories of gender, number, and case for the article or the adjective. (The apostrophe for the genitive was an 18th-century innovation, based on a misunderstanding of the history of the language.) The only inflections of the adjective that occurred in the 14th century but not today were for the plural and for the weak form, when the adjective followed an adjective or possessive pronoun, as in *the goode king.* Even these remnants were disappearing, as evidenced by the omission of the inflectional *-e* for metrical purposes in Chaucer's poetry.

The personal pronoun lost fewer categories than other parts of speech because of a greater need for separate forms for the different genders and cases. The dual number disappeared, and dative and accusative cases were combined. For the third person plural *(they, their, them)* *th-* forms were adopted from Scandinavian to replace the *h-* forms of OE. This replacement occurred earliest in the north of England and more slowly in the south. Chaucer's usual forms were a mixture of the two sources: *thei, here, hem.*

Among the verbs the leveling of inflections followed the general tendency, although as we shall see in the discussion of ME dialects, certain distinctions of person and number that have since been lost were still used in ME and into the Renaissance. The principal change is the marked decrease of strong verbs. Nearly a third of the strong verbs in OE died out early in the ME period, and many of the rest reformed their past tense and past participles with *-ed* rather than with a vowel change. Thus, *sing-sang-sung* has remained strong into Modern English, but more than 40 strong verbs from OE, such as *help-helped-helped* (originally *helpan-healp/hulpon-holpen*), followed the pull of analogy. New verbs that were formed from nouns and adjectives or borrowed from other languages were regularly conjugated as weak.

The changing syntax of English, as the language moved from the highly synthetic stage of late OE to the increasingly analytic stage of early ME, can be seen in a document like the Peterborough Chronicle. Written in installments between 1070 and 1154, this text of the Anglo-Saxon Chronicle spans an important transitional period. Although we have seen that OE word order cannot be called free, it regularly employed certain patterns of subject and verb that became increasingly rare in the later ME period. In addition to the Modern English order SV, OE had VS and, in subordinate clauses, S . . . V (with the finite verb in final position). All of these patterns are still possible even in the last years of the Peterborough

Chronicle. Thus the word order looked much like that of OE at a time when the inflectional system looked much like that of Modern English. By the time Chaucer was writing, two centuries later, the pattern S . . . V was no longer normal English syntax, and VS was used mainly in questions.

While the loss of inflections and the consequent simplification of English grammar were only indirectly due to the use of French in England, French influence upon the vocabulary is much more direct and observable. The full-scale borrowing of French vocabulary occurred especially toward the end of the ME period, when upper-class French speakers were learning English. To cite such examples as *government, empire, liberty, religion, confession, faith, judge, jury, fashion, dress, coat, beef, bacon, salad, peach, poet, geometry, grammar, marriage, sound,* and *vision* is simply to point toward whole areas of everyday life where hundreds of additional French borrowings into ME now seem indispensably a part of English.

Reading Chaucer's poetry is easier for speakers of Modern English than reading many other ME texts composed about the same time—for example, *Sir Gawain and the Green Knight* from the northwest Midlands or Barbour's *Bruce* from the north. The reason is that Chaucer's English was the London variety of the East Midland dialect, one of five traditionally identified dialects of ME (along with West Midland, Northern, Southern, and Kentish; fig. 81). For reasons having to do with the external history of English—the economic, political, cultural, and social settings of the language—it was the London dialect that became the basis of the international standard variety of modern times. If a city in the west Midlands had been the center of government and commerce instead of London, then standard English today would no doubt have many more of the features that are found in the alliterative poems of that region, and those texts, such as *Gawain* and *Piers Plowman*, would be easier to read now. Still, as the following lines from *Gawain* show, there were features of dialects beyond London that eventually became standard, displacing the London forms. The first four and the last four lines of a 30-line stanza are given below. The opening lines, in the alliterative long-line meter, show Gawain in bed in the morning; the last four lines, which are in the rhyming meter of the "wheel" that ends each stanza, describe the unexpected visitor to his bedroom.

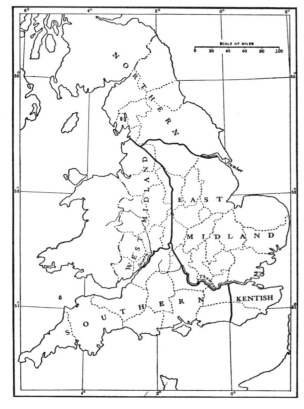

Fig. 81. Dialects of Middle English. *After A.C. Baugh and T. Cable,* A History of the English Language *(1993). Reprinted by permission of Prentice Hall.*

Þus laykez þis lorde by lynde-wodez euez,   1178
   plays   woods'   edge
And Gawayn þe god mon in gay bed lygez,
                   fair   lies
Lurkkez quyl we daylyȝt lemed on þe wowes,
Lies snug while   shone   walls
Vnder couertour ful clere, cortyned aboute. . . .
      coverlet   bright curtained

Wyth chynne and cheke ful swete,   1204
Boþe quit and red in blande,
     white   mingled together
Ful lufly con ho lete
   amiably did she speak
Wyth lyppez smal laȝande.
   lips   slender laughing

Characteristic of the West Midland dialect are the rounded vowel in *mon* "man"; the pronoun *ho* for "she"; and the present participle ending *-ande* in *laȝande* "laughing" instead of *-ing*. In all of these features Chaucer's London dialect has the form that continued into Modern English. However, for the third person present indicative, Gawain has the modern form in *laykez* "plays" and *lygez* "lies," whereas Chaucer has the *-eth* ending. These lines from the *Miller's Tale* illustrate some of the differences between the two dialects:

He syngeth, brokkynge as a nyghtyngale;   3377
    trilling
He sente hire pyment,   meeth, and spiced ale,
    spiced wine,   mead
And wafres, pipyng hoot out of the gleede;
    cakes   fire
And, for she was of towne, he profred meede.
                city-bred   offered   money
For som folk wol ben wonnen for richesse,
                won   by
And somme for strokes, and somme for gentillesse.
        by force   by gentleness
Somtyme, to shewe his lightnesse and maistrye,
            agility   skill
He pleyeth Herodes   upon a scaffold hye.   3384
    the part of Herod   stage   high

The feminine pronoun is now *she,* and the present participle has the modern ending, spelled *-yng(e),* in *brokkynge* and *pipyng.* The older ending *-eth* for the third person present indicative occurs in *syngeth* and *pleyeth,* which are spelled with the *th* letters of modern orthography instead of the thorn, *þ,* of the *Gawain* text. Thus a comparison of the excerpts from *Gawain* and from the *Canterbury Tales* reveals the sources of several significant grammatical categories in Modern English. Through such comparisons philologists have gained a fairly full picture of the language throughout the ME period and of ME sources of sounds, inflections, and syntactic structures in English of the present day.

Thomas Cable

Bibliography

GENERAL

New *CBEL* 1:59–76, 117–22, 143–54, 163–70; Baugh, Albert C., and Thomas Cable. *A History of the English Language.* 4th ed. Englewood Cliffs: Prentice Hall, 1993; *The Cambridge History of the English Language.* Vol. 1: *The Beginnings to 1066,* ed. Richard M. Hogg, and Vol. 2: *1066–1476,* ed. N.F. Blake. Cambridge: Cambridge University Press, 1992; Luick, Karl. *Historische Grammatik der englischen Sprache.* 2 vols. Stuttgart: Tauchnitz, 1914–40; Moore, Samuel. *Historical Outlines of English Sounds and Inflections.* Rev. Albert H. Marckwardt. Ann Arbor: Wahr, 1951; Tajima, Matsuji. *Old and Middle English Language Studies: A Classified Bibliography, 1923–1985.* Amsterdam: Benjamins, 1988.

OLD ENGLISH

Bosworth, J. *An Anglo-Saxon Dictionary.* Ed. T. Northcote Toller. Oxford: Oxford University Press, 1898. With Supplement by T. Northcote Toller. Oxford: Oxford University Press, 1921; Cameron, Angus, et al. *Old English Word Studies: A Preliminary Author and Word Index.* Toronto: University of Toronto Press, 1983; Campbell, Alistair. *Old English Grammar.* Rev. ed. Oxford: Clarendon, 1962; Cassidy, F.G., and Richard N. Ringler. *Bright's Old English Grammar and Reader.* 3d ed. New York: Holt, Rinehart & Winston, 1971; Colman, Fran. *Evidence for Old English: Material and Theoretical Bases for Reconstruction.* Edinburgh Studies in the English Language 2. Edinburgh: Donald, 1992; Davis, Norman. *Sweet's Anglo-Saxon Primer.* 9th ed. Oxford: Clarendon, 1953. Repr. with corrections. Oxford: Clarendon, 1955, 1970; Fulk, R.D. *A History of Old English Meter.* Philadelphia: University of Pennsylvania Press, 1992; Hall, J.R. Clark. *A Concise Anglo-Saxon Dictionary.* 4th ed., with supplement by H.D. Meritt. Cambridge: Cambridge University Press, 1969. Repr. Toronto: University of Toronto Press, 1984; Hogg, Richard. *A Grammar of Old English.* Vol. 1: *Phonology.* Oxford: Blackwell, 1992; Mitchell, Bruce. *Old English Syntax.* 2 vols. Oxford: Clarendon, 1985; Mitchell, Bruce. *A Critical Bibliography of Old English Syntax to the End of 1984.* Oxford: Blackwell, 1990; Mitchell, Bruce, and Fred C. Robinson. *A Guide to Old English.* 5th ed. Oxford: Blackwell, 1992; Quirk, Randolph, and C.L. Wrenn. *An Old English Grammar.* 2d ed. London: Methuen, 1973.

MIDDLE ENGLISH

Brunner, Karl. *An Outline of Middle English Grammar.* Trans. Grahame Johnston. Cambridge: Harvard University Press, 1963; Burnley, J. David. *A Guide to Chaucer's Language.* Norman: University of Oklahoma Press, 1983. Repr. as *The Language of Chaucer.* London: Macmillan, 1989; Burrow, J.A., and Thorlac Turville-Petre. *A Book of Middle English.* 2d ed. Oxford: Blackwell, 1996; Davis, Norman, et al. *A Chaucer Glossary.* Oxford: Clarendon, 1979; Jordan, Richard. *Handbook of Middle English Grammar: Phonology.* Trans. and rev. Eugene J. Crook. The Hague: Mouton, 1974; Kökeritz, Helge. *A Guide to Chaucer's Pronunciation.* Rev. ed. New York: Holt, Rinehart & Winston, 1962. Repr. Toronto: University of Toronto Press, 1978; McIntosh, Angus, et al. *A Linguistic Atlas of Late Mediaeval English.* 4 vols. Aberdeen: Aberdeen University Press, 1986; *Middle English Dictionary.* Ed. Hans Kurath et al. Ann Arbor: University of Michigan Press, 1952–; Mossé, Fernand. *A Handbook of Middle English.* Trans. James A. Walker. Baltimore: Johns Hopkins University Press, 1952; Mustanoja, Tauno F. *A Middle English Syntax.* Vol. 1: *Parts of Speech.* Mémoires de la Société Néophilologique de Helsinki 23. Helsinki: Société Néophilologique, 1960; Oakden,

J.P. *Alliterative Poetry in Middle English*. 2 vols. Manchester: Manchester University Press, 1930–35. Repr. 2 vols. in 1. Hamden: Archon, 1968; Sandved, Arthur O. *Introduction to Chaucerian English*. Cambridge: Brewer, 1985; Smithers, G.V. "Early Middle English." In *Early Middle English Verse and Prose*. Ed. J.A.W. Bennett and G.V. Smithers. Oxford: Clarendon, 1966, pp. xviii–lviii.

See also Alliterative Revival; Anglo-Norman Literature; Anglo-Saxon Invasions; Grammatical Treatises; Literary Influences; French, Scandinavian; Norman Conquest; Versification

Lantfred (fl. ca. 970–80)

A Frankish monk, perhaps from Fleury, who spent a number of years during the 970s at the Old Minster, Winchester, perhaps at the invitation of Bishop Æthelwold (963–84). Lantfred is known principally from a corpus of Latin writings, of which the most important is the prose *Translatio et miracula sancti Swithuni,* composed ca. 975 to commemorate and publicize the translation of the relics of St. Swithun (an obscure 9th-century Winchester bishop) to a shrine within the Old Minster on 15 July 971, as well as the many miracles that took place at the shrine.

Lantfred's *Translatio* is the first Anglo-Latin work to commemorate the "translation" of a saint (i.e., the relocation and reconsecration of a saint's relics), a form of veneration that became increasingly popular in subsequent centuries. The work is stylistically ambitious, being written throughout in rhyming prose and displaying a large number of learned-sounding Greek words. Lantfred was an eyewitness to many of the miracles he describes, and his work gives important firsthand reports of many features of Anglo-Saxon life.

The cult of St. Swithun became widely established in England, partly as a result of Lantfred's *Translatio,* and the work itself was subsequently rendered into hexameters by Wulfstan of Winchester, probably in the early 990s. Some other Latin works may be attributed to Lantfred on stylistic grounds, including two satirical poems on the procedures of a Winchester classroom, a longer poem on the role of divine Providence in human life, and a letter apparently written after Lantfred's return to Fleury requesting the return of books that he had left behind in England.

Michael Lapidge

Bibliography

PRIMARY

Lapidge, Michael. *The Cult of St Swithun*. Oxford: Oxford University Press, forthcoming [includes new edition of the *Translatio*]; Stubbs, W., ed. *Memorials of St Dunstan*. Rolls Series 63. London: Longman, 1874, pp. 376–77 [Lantfred's letter concerning the books].

SECONDARY

Lapidge, Michael. *Anglo-Latin Literature 900–1066*. London: Hambledon, 1993, pp. 124–25 [on Lantfred's prose style], 225–77 [for the poems].

See also Æthelwold; Anglo-Latin Literature to 1066; Hagiography; Winchester Old Minster

Lapidaries

Treatises on the properties and uses of precious stones and gems, commonly compiled in the ancient period and popular in the Middle Ages as well. The standard sources of information on gems for the Middle Ages included Pliny's *Natural History* (book 37) and two later sources drawn from it, Solinus's *Collectanea rerum memorabilium (Notes on Memorable Things)* and Isidore of Seville's *Etymologies* (book 16). Pliny and Solinus record the physical properties of stones but demonstrate their skepticism about the few magical properties that they record; Isidore includes medicinal properties.

Apart from these sources early-medieval lapidaries followed two traditions: the Christian tradition that focused on biblical exegesis and the secular tradition that focused on magical and medicinal properties of stones. Examples of the Christian tradition occur in biblical commentaries, which center on three lists of jewels: the twelve jewels of the high priest's breastplate (Exod. 28:17–20); the nine ornaments of the king of Tyre (Ezek. 28:13); and the twelve foundations of the holy city (the New Jerusalem; Rev. 21:19-20).

The earliest–known Christian lapidary, Epiphanius's *De duodecim lapidibus* (*On the Twelve Stones;* A.D. 394) describes the stones, including medicinal uses, and interprets them figuratively in terms of the Old Testament tribes of Israel. Bede's commentary on Revelation (*Explanatio Apocalypsis*), which contains a detailed description of the jewels that form the foundations of the holy city, includes Epiphanius as a source. Aldhelm, Alcuin, and Boniface also made use of the Christian lapidary tradition. The OE Lapidary (mid-11th century), the oldest known lapidary in a vernacular language, derives its material from Latin glossaries on the stones in the book of Revelation.

As a source of the secular tradition the Latin medical lapidary ascribed to Damigeron (1st century A.D.) features magical properties ascribed to each stone. In the well-known *Liber lapidum seu de gemmis* (*Book of Stones or Gems;* ca. 1067–81) Bishop Marbode of Rennes appears to have used Damigeron's lapidary as his primary source for the stones' magical properties. The *Liber lapidum,* a lapidary poem of 740 Latin hexameters that includes some 60 stones, survives in 160 manuscripts as well as translations into vernacular languages. Marbode's lapidary poem was widely cited as an authority in the 13th century and formed the basis of most late-medieval lapidaries both Latin and vernacular.

In the latter half of the 12th century and later the influence of eastern lapidaries led to the production of lapidaries detailing the magical properties of gems engraved with sacred or symbolic characters, often astrological in nature. The earliest known English references to magical engraved gems occur in a medical lapidary extant in Bodl. Digby 13 (12th century), a manuscript that also contains Marbode's treatise and Isidore's *De gemmis.*

From the 13th century on lapidaries began to demonstrate an increased reliance on observation, as well as an increased interest in the medicinal properties of precious stones and their relationship to other aspects of the observed universe. So while Arnoldus Saxo (13th century) and other later lapidary writers (including Albertus Magnus, the leading figure of natural science of the 13th century) repeated some of the fabulous material from Marbode, they also cited other sources and increasingly attempted to concentrate on the physical properties of stones.

Michelle Head

Bibliography

PRIMARY

Evans, Joan, and Mary S. Sergeantson, eds. *English Medieval Lapidaries.* EETS o.s. 190. Oxford: Oxford University Press, 1933; Riddle, John M., ed. *Marbode of Rennes' (1035–1123) De lapidibus, Considered as a Medical Treatise.* Trans. C.W. King. Sudhoffs Archiv 20. Wiesbaden: Steiner, 1977; Studer, Paul, and Joan Evans, eds. *Anglo-Norman Lapidaries.* Paris: Champion, 1924.

SECONDARY

Evans, Joan. *Magical Jewels of the Middle Ages and the Renaissance, Particularly in England.* Oxford: Clarendon, 1922; Garrett, Robert Max. *Precious Stones in Old English Literature.* Leipzig: Deichert, 1909; Kitson, Peter. "Lapidary Traditions in Anglo-Saxon England." *ASE* 7 (1978): 9–60, 12 (1983): 73–123.

See also Bede; Bestiaries; Bible in OE Literature; Isidore; *Pearl*-Poet; *Physiologus;* Science; Scientific and Medical Writings; Utilitarian Writings

Law, Anglo-Saxon

Early English law is documented in three main ways. First there is a substantial series of law codes, issued by kings or, less often, by some "unofficial" authority. These are unique among the early-medieval Germanic codes in that they are couched in the vernacular. They are also alone insofar as the four 7th-century codes, broadly similar to the legislation of Merovingian Gaul, are followed by a long sequence of royal edicts by most kings from Alfred to Cnut, quite like Carolingian capitularies but with no real 10th- and 11th-century parallels west of the Byzantine Empire.

In addition there are retrospective statements of "traditional" law and custom in post-Conquest sources, from Domesday Book through the late 12th century, the most important of which is the "unofficial" *Leges Henrici primi* (ca. 1115). Finally the corpus of about 1,500 charters, comprising outright grants of property or privilege along with leases and wills, provides evidence for property law, barely mentioned by the codes. It is possible to isolate from these and the various narrative sources about 180 cases of law in action, covering "criminal" as well as "civil" justice.

Despite this wealth of material, and Liebermann's huge and heroic edition and glossary of the codes, pre-Conquest law has not drawn the attention from historians that its interest and importance warrant. The general view is that law reveals the "archaism" of the Anglo-Saxon polity. But there is ample evidence for dynamic and creative change.

The early codes have their context in the mechanisms of feud and wergeld. Redress of injury to person or property was left to the victim or his or her associates. The king's part was to speak for those with no associates, like traders without local kin; to penalize abuse of feuding procedure, like avenging a thief legitimately slain because caught in the act; and to underwrite social peace generally, hence taking fines from thieves convicted by process rather than caught red-handed, who were otherwise liable only for restoring the stolen goods.

Courts in the earlier period were either local moots, where royal officials might preside, or the royal court itself. Documents of the 8th and 9th centuries bestow rights to take fines. Early charters are otherwise "church law"; they grant land in perpetuity and with free disposition, so permitting church endowment. Such advantages were also sought by laypeople, who founded what Bede saw as pseudo-monasteries to pass royal donations on to the heirs of their choice, normally their children.

Each of these areas saw major changes from 900 to 1066. There was, first, a deliberate development of an idea of crime against society as a whole. Free subjects at the age of twelve took an oath not only to be loyal but also to abstain from serious crime and to report crimes by neighbors. Charters and archaeology, as well as legislation, show that thieves, even if not caught in the act, forfeited their goods and were executed and buried in unconsecrated ground. The common-law notion of "felony"—that is, of major crime as breach of faith and punished as such—is Anglo-Saxon in origin.

After 900 a hierarchy of courts was created, with the local moot reorganized as the hundred ("wapentake" in the Danelaw), and courts of the borough or shire interposed between it and the royal court proper. Recorded lawsuits came about as often to the shire as to the king himself. Shire and borough courts certainly had royal appointees (bishop, ealdorman, and the reeve, developing eventually into the shire-reeve or sheriff) as presidents; their possible role is revealed by regular complaints of pressure and corruption. "Private" justice remained a reality at local levels, in some hundreds, but shires were never "privatized" as in feudal Europe. There are almost no records of hearings in lord's courts before 1066.

Lastly "bookland" (land held by charter) was now the expectation of laity, though many also held land on lease from major ecclesiastical and secular lords. Bookland could be alienated and distributed by wills; lawsuits tend to focus on the legitimacy of alienations that litigants claimed to be hereditary and therefore inalienable from the kin. Bookland was "freehold," as feudal tenure was not. But it could be granted only by kings, and grants remained conditional on performance of obligations, notably military service. Suits over bookland must be heard in the king's court. Close links between kingship and bookland are shown by the way that will makers invoke royal support for their bequests.

Thus in many ways Anglo-Saxon law resembles the "common law" supposedly founded by Henry II. It seems likely that England's unique legal system owes much to the vigorous institutions inherited by the Normans and Angevins from their Anglo-Saxon predecessors.

Patrick Wormald

Bibliography

PRIMARY

Attenborough, F.L., ed. and trans. *The Laws of the Earliest English Kings.* Cambridge: Cambridge University Press, 1922; Liebermann, Felix. *Die Gesetze der Angelsachsen.* 3 vols. Halle: Niemeyer, 1903–16 [still the basic edition; vol. 2 is glossary, vol. 3 commentary]; Robertson, Agnes J. *The Laws of the Kings of England from Edmund to Henry I.* Cambridge: Cambridge University Press, 1925; Robertson, Agnes J. *Anglo-Saxon Charters.* 2d ed. Cambridge: Cambridge University Press, 1956 [vernacular documents]; Whitelock, Dorothy, ed. and trans. *Anglo-Saxon Wills.* Cambridge: Cambridge University Press, 1930 [a full selection]; Whitelock, Dorothy, ed. *English Historical Documents.* Vol. 1: *c. 500–1042.* 2d ed. London: Eyre Methuen; New York: Oxford University Press, 1979 [most codes and many charters, in translation, with Bede's "Letter to Egbert" on pseudo-monasteries].

SECONDARY

Cam, Helen M. *Law-Finders and Law-Makers in Medieval England: Collected Studies in Legal and Constitutional History.* London: Merlin Press, 1962 [chs. 1 and 3]; Goebel, Julius. *Felony and Misdemeanor: A Study in the History of Criminal Law.* 2d ed. Ed. Edward Peters. Philadelphia: University of Pennsylvania Press, 1976 [chs. 1 and 6 deal with the criminal law]; John, Eric. *Land Tenure in Early England: A Discussion of Some Problems.* Leicester: Leicester University Press, 1960; Pollock, Frederick, and Frederic W. Maitland. *The History of English Law before the Time of Edward I.* 2d ed. 2 vols. Ed. S.F.C. Milsom. London: Cambridge University Press, 1968 [see ch. 2 for a traditional view of OE law]; Wormald, Patrick. "Charters, Law and the Settlement of Disputes in Anglo-Saxon England." In *The Settlement of Disputes in Early Medieval Europe,* ed. Wendy Davies and Paul Fouracre. Cambridge: Cambridge University Press, 1986, pp. 149–68; Wormald, Patrick. "'*Inter Cetera Bona Genti Suae*': Law-Making and Peace-Keeping in the Earliest English Kingdoms." *Settimane di Studio del Centro Italiano di Studi sull'alto Medioevo* 42 (1995): 963–96; Wormald, Patrick. "Lordship and Justice in the Early English Kingdom: Oswaldslow Revisited." In *Property and Power in the Early Middle Ages,* ed. Wendy Davies and Paul Fouracre. Cambridge: Cambridge University Press, 1995, pp. 114–36.

See also Alfred; Charters; Feuds and Wergeld; Hundreds; Wills

Law, Post-Conquest

England in the high Middle Ages developed a pattern of law largely independent of continental Roman and canon law that still sets the Anglo-American legal system apart.

As in other early medieval kingdoms the early Anglo-Saxon kingdoms' laws consisted of unwritten custom, characterized by family or community responsibility for prosecution of criminals and by methods of proof that seemed reasonable in their own social context, strange though they may seem both to modern eyes and to the lawyers of post-Conquest kings. Even though periodic attempts would be made to write down England's laws, they would never be codified in the manner of Roman or canon law. Eventually a multiplicity of courts arose; besides the king's court there were traditional popular courts, lords' private courts, and the church's jurisdiction.

Growth of lordship meant that lords set up courts to give justice to their peasant farmers, taking responsibility from the family and village community. Some notion of royal supervision of justice survived, however, along with Roman and Carolingian precepts of royal authority. Serious crimes became "pleas of the crown," which the king and his sheriffs were responsible for punishing. The "king's peace," his special protection for members of his household, could be extended to privileged persons or groups beyond the royal entourage, and it eventually would cover the entire kingdom.

The Norman Conquest brought great change in English law, even though William I promised to maintain the laws of his Anglo-Saxon predecessors. The triumph of dependent forms of land tenure or feudalism brought a revolution in land law, weakening the idea of property or land ownership. Basic features of the land law evolved later in the Anglo-Norman period, as knights holding uncertain tenures gradually acquired something approaching hereditary right. Feudal landholding also strengthened lords' control over their nonfree peasant farmers through private courts, and it led to new feudal courts for disputes concerning free knightly tenants. Feudal courts defined the lord-tenant relationship with little supervision by the king or his court.

Still another category of courts appeared after 1066, when William I sanctioned the creation of separate ecclesiastical courts; their jurisdiction over spiritual matters included marriages and testamentary bequests. The Conqueror and his sons were concerned to punish serious crimes—felonies—and the concepts of "pleas of the crown" and "king's peace" expanded. A result was a need for itinerant justices to circulate about the counties, taking some judicial work off the sheriffs' shoulders.

Henry II wrought a revolution in English law, moving the kingdom closer to a common law, a single law for all free subjects, enforceable in the royal courts and overriding old local and feudal customs. Henry launched a two-pronged attack. One aspect was a royal campaign for suppression of crime; the problem could no longer be left to the victim's initiative. The king commanded that local juries of presentment accuse suspects to be tried by ordeal before itinerant justices. The second aspect was supervision of the lords' feudal courts to protect tenants from arbitrary seizure of land. The king sought to ensure that the feudal courts functioned in accord with "due process of law" by imposing the royal court's supervision over magnates' courts.

Henry II and his advisers devised several instruments to achieve these ends. Royal writs became readily available to litigants, enabling purchasers to transfer suits from county courts or from their lords' courts to the king's court, where they expected an impartial hearing. Juries, an information-gathering instrument or institution used by the Frankish kings, were transformed into means of settling disputes; groups of neighbors gave evidence collectively about disputed landholdings—the possessory assizes—or brought accusations against those suspected of committing crimes in their community—juries of presentment, forerunners of the grand jury. Henry I's practice of sending itinerant justices on circuits to hear cases, taking royal justice to the people, was revived. By the end of the 12th century royal justices were also sitting regularly at Westminster.

Henry II's innovations set the basic shape of English law until modern times, although change continued. By the early 13th century use of the jury expanded, as it replaced the ordeal as the means of proof in criminal cases. Also in the 13th and 14th centuries the action of trespass appeared, providing remedies for torts, that is, wrongs not criminal in intent but nonetheless resulting in damages to the victim. Henry II's efforts to make the feudal courts work effectively had the long-term effect of reducing their role, for more and more disputes between lords and tenants moved into the royal courts. The result was that lords steadily lost control over their tenants and derived little benefit from their lordship.

This loss of lordly privilege affected the king, greatest feudal lord of all. Edward I, at the end of the 13th century, resolved to remedy this; he sponsored a series of statutes reforming England's land law. His statutes aimed mainly at protecting lords' rights to the few feudal privileges they still enjoyed, the "feudal incidents," financial windfalls chiefly when a tenant died without heir or with minor heirs.

It was too late, however. The balance of power had shifted from lords to their knightly tenants, and the tenants were claiming the right to alienate their land freely, with almost full proprietary rights over tenures. Royal judges, mainly from tenant families, sympathized with tenant interests. They sanctioned subterfuges, such as uses and trusts, devised by tenants to prevent land from falling under the lords' control, escaping the feudal incidents.

English common law, originally concerned chiefly with felonies and with rights to feudal tenures, expanded its scope to accommodate a growing number of commercial cases, such as contracts and debts. Also the decline of the church courts brought into the common law courts some cases formerly heard by ecclesiastical judges. Another late-medieval trend was growth of conciliar courts, branches of the king's council that would attain greater prominence in the Tudor period. These courts were not bound by the increasingly rigid rules that hampered the common law courts, and they were influenced by the Roman tradition of placing safety of the state ahead of individual rights. One conciliar court, chancery, has special significance. The chancellor, responsible for issuing the writs

originating common law pleas, began to hear disputes for which no available writ offered a remedy. The result was growth of an alternative to the traditional royal courts, a court of equity capable of greater flexibility than the common law courts.

Ralph V. Turner

Bibliography

PRIMARY

Evans, Michael, and R. Ian Jack, eds. *Sources of English Legal and Constitutional History.* Sydney: Butterworths, 1984; Hall, G.D.G., ed. *The Treatise on the Laws and Customs of the Realm of England, Commonly Called Glanvill.* 2d ed. Oxford: Oxford University Press, 1993; Robertson, Agnes J. *The Laws of the Kings of England from Edmund to Henry I.* Cambridge: Cambridge University Press, 1925; *Statutes of the Realm.* London: Eyre & Strahan, 1810–28. Repr. London: Dawsons, 1963 [editorial work not up to current standards, but the only extensive collection of the statutes]; van Caenegem, R.C., ed. *Royal Writs in England from the Conquest to Glanvill.* Selden Society 77. London: Quaritch, 1959; van Caenegem, R.C., ed. *English Lawsuits from William I to Richard I.* Selden Society 106, 107. London: Selden Society, 1990–91; Woodbine, George E., ed. *Bracton De legibus et consuetudinibus Angliae.* Rev. and trans. Samuel E. Thorne. 4 vols. New Haven: Yale University Press, 1915–42.

SECONDARY

Baker, John H. *An Introduction to English Legal History.* 3d ed. London: Butterworths, 1990; Bean, J.M.W. *The Decline of English Feudalism, 1215–1540.* Manchester: Manchester University Press, 1968; Harding, Alan. *The Law Courts of Medieval England.* London: Allen & Unwin, 1973; Helmholz, R.H. *Canon Law and English Common Law.* Selden Society Lecture for 1982. London: Selden Society, 1983; Milsom, S.F.C. *The Legal Framework of English Feudalism.* Cambridge: Cambridge University Press, 1976; Milsom, S.F.C. *Historical Foundations of the Common Law.* 2d ed. London: Butterworths, 1981; Palmer, Robert C. "The Feudal Framework of English Law." *Michigan Law Review* 79 (1981): 1130–64 [essential for grasping Milsom's views]; Pollock, Frederick, and Frederic W. Maitland. *The History of English Law before the Time of Edward I.* 2d ed. 2 vols. Ed. S.F.C. Milsom. London: Cambridge University Press, 1968; Simpson, A.W.B. *A History of the Land Law.* 2d ed. of *An Introduction to the History of the Land Law* (1961). Oxford: Clarendon, 1986; Stenton, Doris M. *English Justice between the Norman Conquest and the Great Charter, 1066–1215.* Philadelphia: American Philosophical Society, 1964; van Caenegem, R.C. *The Birth of the English Common Law.* 2d ed. Cambridge: Cambridge University Press, 1988.

See also Assize of Clarendon; Bracton; Chancellor and Chancery; Charters; Courts, Ecclesiastical; Courts and the Court System; Edward I; Fortescue; Henry II; Hundreds; Juries; Law in ME Literature; Lawyers; Marriage; Mortmain; Outlawry; Quo Warranto Proceedings; Statutes; Tenures; Wardship; Wills

Law in Middle English Literature

Law is one of the great themes of ME literature. The focus is usually on one or more of the following areas:

Legal Procedure

Virtually every genre of ME literature contains trial scenes. Outstanding examples from romance are *Launfal, Gamelyn, Havelok the Dane,* and *Bevis of Hampton;* from drama, *Mankind, Wisdom,* and all four of the major Corpus Christi cycles; from beast fable, Henryson's "Taill of the Sheip and the Doige" and Caxton's *Reynard the Fox;* from lyric, "London Lickpenny," "The Power of the Purse," "Quia Amore Langueo" (allusions); from vision and allegory, *Pearl, Piers Plowman, The Assembly of Ladies;* from the short narrative poem, the tales given by Chaucer to the Man of Law, the Physician, and the Second Nun. Much of the writing is directed against contemporary abuses of the law. The primary targets are corruption of the judicial system (e.g., *Gamelyn,* Langland's account of the trial of Lady Meed) and the widespread use of law by the powerful to oppress the poor and weak (e.g., the *Second Shepherds' Play,* the trial of Wrong in *Piers Plowman*).

Legal Terminology

The ME poetic vocabulary is rife with terms, often highly technical, taken from the sphere of law. One of the earliest instances is the 13th-century debate poem *The Owl and the Nightingale.* The most impressive instance is *Piers Plowman,* which contains over 700 words and phrases with legal significance, more than 100 of which are the first recorded examples in English. Because the language of law was rich in metaphorical possibilities, most of its words having taken on specialized meanings while retaining broader meanings in ordinary usage, it lent itself to poetic exploitation. The form and terminology of legal documents proved especially popular—for example, Usk's *Testament of Love,* the *Charters of Christ,* and the deeds, wills, and letters patent in *Piers Plowman.*

Legal Philosophy

The literary use of legal procedure and terminology often exists within the larger framework of theories about justice, the nature of law, and the relations among its various kinds. Gower's *Confessio Amantis* and Chaucer's *Parliament of Fowls* take as their philosophical basis the doctrine of natural law. The conflict of justice and mercy in *Mankind* and *The Castle of Perseverance,* as well as the rival claims of the Old and New Laws in *St. Erkenwald, Piers,* and the cycle plays, has been seen by many critics to reflect the historical tension between the common law and the late-14th-century rise of equity law (a system of justice not bound by strict common-law rules).

Several factors contributed to the marriage of law and literature in the Middle Ages. Many writers had themselves received a legal education, the practical alternative to a university degree, or held some administrative position in government. Noteworthy instances include Chaucer, Gower, Usk, Hoccleve, Henryson, and almost certainly the author of *Piers Plowman.* If one's theme was religious, it was virtually impossible to avoid the use of legal terms and concepts. Penitential doctrine relies heavily on the language of the law; and the story of salvation itself (the breaking of God's law, the consequent punishment on earth and in the "penitentiary" of purgatory, the chance for pardon, the Last Judgment) is legal to the core. It is not surprising that the heaviest concentration of legal diction in Chaucer is to be found in the *Parson's Tale.*

The cosmic view of law that prevailed during the period offered the broadest possible context for the metaphorical development of legal themes. As expounded by Thomas Aquinas, this view derives the validity of positive or legislated law from the principles of natural law, which in turn derive from the divine or eternal law of God. No matter how great the multiplicity of laws, therefore, their ultimate authority is always the same. In essence all law is one law. This perspective guaranteed the propriety of such terms as *felon* (perpetrator of a serious crime), *seisin* (possession of real property), and *escheat* (reversion of property to one's lord for lack of heirs or in punishment for a crime) in poetic treatments of sin and salvation.

When the conditions that supported the union of law and literature faded in importance—a postmedieval development—so did the union itself. Its persuasive appeal was much diminished by the spread of general education, the rise of secular literature, and the growth of legal positivism, which rejects the idea that all law is one law—indeed, even the idea that divine and natural law are worthy of the name.

John A. Alford

Bibliography

Alford, John A. *Piers Plowman: A Glossary of Legal Diction.* Cambridge: Brewer, 1988; Alford, John A., and Dennis P. Seniff. *Literature and Law in the Middle Ages: A Bibliography of Scholarship.* New York: Garland, 1984; Hornsby, Joseph Allen. *Chaucer and the Law.* Norman: Pilgrim Books, 1988; Stokes, Myra. *Justice and Mercy in Piers Plowman: A Reading of the B Text Visio.* London: Croom Helm, 1984.

See also Charters; Courts, Ecclesiastical; Courts and the Court System; Juries; Law, Post-Conquest; Lawyers; Marriage; Nature in ME Literature; Truth in ME Literature; Writs

Lawyers

By 1300 there were professional lawyers practicing in almost all courts above the level of the purely local manorial court. The church courts were the province of canon lawyers. They consisted of a small elite of university-trained advocates, whose practice was largely confined to the consistory courts of each diocese, the provincial courts of Canterbury and York, and the courts held by papal judges delegate, and a much larger group of proctors, of whom few had studied canon law at university and who represented their clients in these and other courts.

The lay courts were the province of the common lawyers. Their elite were the serjeants of the Common Bench, specialist advocates in the main central court for civil litigation, normally holding its sessions at Westminster. The Year Books report the arguments these men advanced for their clients in Westminster Hall and the judges' reactions to the arguments. The same small group of around 30 men also represented clients in the other main royal courts: King's Bench, the Eyres, and the Assizes. Separate groups of serjeants, also specialist advocates, were to be found in the county courts and in the courts of the City of London and other major cities, but their numbers were much smaller.

Each of the royal courts also had its own professional attorneys; lawyers whose functions were to appear in court in place of their client, sue process on their behalf, and engage and brief serjeants when a case came up for hearing. The largest group of professional attorneys was to be found in the Common Bench: over 200 of them by 1300. Professional attorneys were also to be found in city courts but perhaps not in county or other local courts. The common lawyers were not university-trained, but there is evidence that well before 1300 formal instruction in common law was being given at an elementary and a more advanced level. Among the attorneys of the Common Bench was to be found a group of "apprentices" (learners) whom the court encouraged to attend the hearing of litigation so that they might master the skills of the serjeant.

There had been professional canon lawyers in England for well over a century by 1300, and canon law had been studied in English universities for as long a period. Prior to the emergence of the two universities men are known to have gone to the Continent (especially to Bologna) to study canon law. By 1200 professional lawyers were beginning to emerge in the common-law courts. Their emergence was made possible by changes in the conduct of litigation and in the rules relating to the appointment, by litigants, of legal representatives. By the mid-13th century there was a group of serjeants specializing in advocacy in the Common Bench at Westminster and a separate group in the London city courts. There was also a small group of professional attorneys in the Common Bench.

The years between 1356 and 1367 saw a drastic and permanent reduction in the size of the elite of Common Bench serjeants, down to little more than one-third of its size in 1300. Either then, or shortly afterward, the crown came to control admission to this elite.

The first royal judge to be appointed from the ranks of serjeants of the Common Bench was Richard of Boyland, appointed a justice in eyre in 1279: by the reign of Edward II serjeants supplied a majority of the judges of Common Bench and King's Bench. By 1330 permanent appointments to the higher judiciary were made only from their ranks. The serjeants had a monopoly of advocacy only in the Common Bench; during the 14th century a group of senior apprentices came to play a significant role in providing specialist advocacy for litigants in other royal courts.

By the mid-14th century senior and junior apprentices were living together in the Inns of Court. Three of the four inns (the Middle and Inner Temples, and Gray's Inn) were in existence by 1388, Lincoln's Inn by 1422. The Inns of Court also provided educational facilities; so, too, at a more basic level, did a number of inns of chancery.

Paul Brand

Bibliography

Baker, John H. *The Order of Serjeants at Law.* Selden Society, Suppl. Ser. 5. London: Selden Society, 1984; Baker, John H. *The Legal Profession and the Common Law: Historical Essays.* London: Hambledon, 1986 [collected papers; several are relevant to the establishment of the legal profession]; Brand, Paul. "Courtroom and Schoolroom: The Education of Lawyers in England prior to 1400." *Historical Research* 60 (1987): 147–65; Brand, Paul. *The Origins of the English Legal Profession.* Oxford: Blackwell, 1992.

See also Courts, Ecclesiastical; Courts and the Court System; Juries; Law, Post-Conquest; Schools; Year Books

Learning and Intellectual Life (1050–1200)

The period between approximately 1050 and 1200 has come to be identified intellectually and culturally as the "Renaissance of the Twelfth Century." Even though it does not exclusively correspond to a single century, it signifies a distinct phase in an intellectual movement that represented a new attitude to the universe in virtually every respect. That attitude can be briefly described as the rediscovered belief in the value of the created order and in the efficacy of secondary, created causes. From having been largely discounted or ignored in an inimical world between the 5th and the 10th centuries, where God was treated primarily as the avenging God of the Old Testament aspect, to be feared and placated, the world in the 11th century gradually came to be seen as a more amenable place, with God increasingly depicted as man's friend as well as judge, through the person of his Son.

The new sense of the humanity of Christ was one of the salient changes in the religious outlook of the Middle Ages. It extended from the spirituality particularly associated with Cistercian monasteries in the early 12th century to new apostolic groups like the Arnoldists and Waldensians, new monastic orders like the Cistercians and Premonstratensians, and in the 13th century the Dominican and Franciscan friars. It carried a renewed emphasis upon man as having been made in God's image, developed by Augustine in his doctrine of the Trinity. Hence an individual, in coming to know himself—another of the imperatives of 11th- and 12th-century religious experience—came to recognize his affinity with Christ as God-man, which, among the apostolic groups, entailed living as Christ had lived in this world, without possessions or powers other than those of spiritual ministration.

Human beings accordingly received a new dignity, even if, religiously, that dignity was most fully manifested in submitting to Christ and emulating his life of renunciation and humility. It gave a new interior character to religion, expressed in the new sacramental emphasis in the 12th century upon private penance and atonement as an internal spiritual state, in contrast to their public forms, and upon the quality of religious life as the true test of Christian discipleship.

At the same time, but not always among the same people, there was a corresponding recognition of the dignity and worth of the natural world as being just as much God's creation as the work of divine reason in which man participated. The world thereby became a more intelligible place; the order and regularity of the heavens and the earth were visible expressions of God's causality. Until the middle of the 12th century this new cosmological awareness of nature and the universe as subject to a rational order arose from a new reading of the predominantly Platonic and Neoplatonic sources, known in the West since the 5th century (apart from recently acquired Arabic medical knowledge) from translations made probably at the Benedictine Abbey of Monte Cassino in southern Italy.

The new outlook therefore began indigenously, as did the new religious awareness. It was only in the middle and second half of the 12th century that this outlook was reinforced and, in the case of cosmology and knowledge of nature, largely transformed by the influx of a large body of translated Arabic and Greek science, mathematics, and philosophy. By the early 13th century this new knowledge included the greater part of Aristotle's writings, now the background to an intellectual life focused on the universities, the new centers of learning.

Even before the translations, however, in the first half of the 12th century, the educational setting for most learning was changing from the monasteries, which had been the intellectual centers from the 6th to the 11th century, to the new cathedral schools, accompanied by the emergence of professional teachers, such as Peter Abelard (d. 1142), who traveled from one center to another, attracting a following of students. It was in the cathedral schools, especially around Paris and northeastern France, that the new systematic study of the Bible, theology, and nature occurred, freed from the monastic demands of liturgy and corporate life.

This secular milieu of the cathedral school, based upon a town and directed toward the world, rather than within the cloister, was lacking in pre-Conquest England, where cathedrals had mostly been monastic communities. They had therefore missed the new intellectual developments that had begun in the 11th century, largely insulated as they were from the revival of monasticism and canon law as part of the movement for religious reform on the Continent. Those came with the Normans. The association of Lanfranc and Anselm with the Norman Abbey of Bec, the outstanding Benedictine monastery north of the Alps in the later 11th century, brought to England two of the foremost religious and intellectual figures of the age.

Probably as a direct consequence of Lanfranc's presence there was a school for grammar and music at Canterbury in 1087; by the early 12th century new schools were coming into existence in such towns as Winchester, Oxford, and Lincoln,

to be followed by those in the other main centers during the rest of the 12th century. Apart from Oxford, however, they did not attain more than local standing, and Oxford's important time as a university was to be in the succeeding centuries.

Intellectually, as well as religiously, despite the spread of the new monastic orders, especially the Cistercians from the 1120s, England remained on the periphery. The intellectual traffic was mostly one-way, from England to the Continent, above all to the major cathedral schools: Reims, Chartres, Tours, and Paris, among others. That need and attraction for the other side of the English Channel engendered a tradition of travel long before the 18th-century Grand Tour; in the 12th century it led English scholars to Spain, in the wake of the reconquest from the Muslims, and put them in the forefront of the discovery and transmission of Arabic and Greek scientific and medical texts, previously unknown in the West.

These different circumstances, distinguishing intellectual life in England from that on the Continent, gave English activity a particular stamp, accentuated by a political tradition of two centuries of comparatively strong late Anglo-Saxon government. We can point to three main characteristics as their product. The widespread practice of historical writing was part of a monastic culture going back to Bede, reinforced by the Anglo-Saxon Chronicle: a unique vernacular record of a country's history, which continued until the 1130s. Monastic writers of history remained dominant in the 12th century, varying from the very good, like William of Malmesbury, Orderic Vitalis (who wrote in Normandy), and William of Newburgh, to Geoffrey of Monmouth, hardly to be taken seriously by the later 12th century. Furthermore secular clerics, such as Roger of Hoveden and Ralph of Diceto, were also writing history.

The second characteristic was the association of English scholars with the renewed study of natural phenomena and their involvement in the discovery and transmission of Arabic astronomy, mathematics, and medicine as well as engaging in their own investigations and composition of treatises. Their independent activities, for the most part not associated with any school, testify to the late development of institutional successors to the monasteries in the first half of the 12th century. By an odd chance a number of these naturalists were from the West Country, foremost among them Adelard of Bath. Others included Daniel of Morley, Robert of Chester, Robert of Ketton, Roger of Hereford, and Alfred Sareshel. They were the precursors of an Oxford scientific tradition that extended through the Middle Ages.

Finally there were the works on law and government, like those by Glanville and the *Dialogue of the Exchequer,* drawn from experience of the one state in northern Europe that, at the time, had an established system of law and central and local organs of government. They were complemented by John of Salisbury's *Policraticus,* affirming the legitimacy of secular government as natural to man, and not—according to the hitherto prevailing Augustinian doctrine—the result of sin. In forming his view John was confirming from his own involvement in government the Stoic belief, learned from Cicero and Seneca, that man was naturally a civic and social being who should live in human association. Sixty years after the *Policraticus* the barons, in Magna Carta, expressed in a nontheoretical way their belief in the legitimacy of rights within a political community, a belief never to be lost.

Gordon Leff

Bibliography.

PRIMARY

Anselm of Bec. *Basic Writings.* Trans. S.N. Deane. 2d ed. La Salle: Open Court, 1962; Hyman, A., and J.J. Walsh. *Philosophy in the Middle Ages.* New York: Harper & Row, 1967; John of Salisbury. *Policraticus.* Trans. J. Dickinson (books 1–3, parts of 7–8, as *The Statesman's Book of John of Salisbury*). New York: Knopf, 1927; McKeon, Richard P. *Selections from Medieval Philosophers.* 2 vols. New York: Scribner, 1929; Wippel, J.F., and A.B. Wolter. *Medieval Philosophy from St. Augustine to Nicholas of Cusa.* New York: Free Press, 1969.

SECONDARY

Benson, Robert, and Giles Constable, eds. *Renaissance and Renewal in the Twelfth Century.* Oxford: Clarendon, 1982; Dronke, Peter, ed. *A History of Twelfth-Century Western Philosophy.* Cambridge: Cambridge University Press, 1988; Ferguson, Chris D. *Europe in Transition: A Select, Annotated Bibliography of the Twelfth-Century Renaissance.* New York: Garland, 1989; Gilson, Étienne. *History of Christian Philosophy in the Middle Ages.* London: Sheed & Ward, 1955; Haskins, Charles H. *The Renaissance of the Twelfth Century.* Cambridge: Harvard University Press, 1927; Haskins, Charles H. *Studies in the History of Mediaeval Science.* 2d ed. Cambridge: Harvard University Press, 1927; Morris, Colin. *The Discovery of the Individual, 1050–1200.* London: SPCK, 1972; Southern, R.W. *Medieval Humanism and Other Studies.* Oxford: Blackwell, 1970.

See also Anselm; Bacon; Chronicles; *Dialogue of the Exchequer;* Glanville; Grosseteste; Investiture Controversy; John of Salisbury; Lanfranc; Libraries; Monasticism; Science; Scientific and Medical Writings; Universities

Leather Manufacture and Trade

Leather was an essential commodity in the Middle Ages, used for clothing, containers, saddlery, armor, and, in the form of parchment, for books and record documents. There was also an extensive internal and overseas trade in hides. It was not a commodity from which huge profits could be made, but because of its ubiquitous use it was of fundamental importance in the economy. Though there were village tanneries, the manufacture of leather and leather goods was from early on concentrated in towns. The number of artisans involved in the industry and the importance of the trade in hides are reflected in the formation of urban craft associations of leatherworkers in the 12th century. In small towns the richest leatherworkers retained a position of importance in the social hierarchy throughout the Middle Ages.

There were two main divisions in the leather industry: cow- and oxhides were tanned; sheep-, goat-, and calfskins were tawed, as were furs. In both cases the process was designed to drive moisture out of the skin and to replace it with a preservative.

Tanning was a lengthy process; skins were scraped and cleaned and then soaked in a series of liquids usually made with oak bark (from which was derived tannin). The enormous quantities of water used meant that tanners were frequently sited by rivers. The completed process, which should have taken a number of months, left a stiff product, red leather, which then had to be curried with tallow, oil, or other lubricants to render it supple. The tanned and curried leather was bought by shoemakers, girdlers, armorers, saddlers, and bookbinders for manufacture.

If tanners manufactured leather goods, there was a danger that they would use badly tanned and substandard leather. Therefore, within towns, strenuous efforts were made to separate the occupations of shoemaker and tanner and at times to distinguish the craft of currier as well. Such efforts were not always successful, and the confusing terminology of the leather industry reflects this overlapping of interests. Tanners tended to be the most successful of these groups; they controlled the supply of raw materials. Shoemakers, in contrast, were one of the most numerous groups of artisans but were generally badly paid and of low repute.

Tawing preserved leather without the use of tannin. It embraced a wide variety of techniques, many involving the application of oil or alum to hides, and it could be a simple process, more economical of space than was tanning. Sheep-, goat-, and calfskins were usually treated with alum, rubbed in to give a stiff white leather (giving rise to the term "whittawer," or "white-tawer," for craftsmen engaged in this activity). This was then worked over to render it supple and treated with emollients, such as oil or eggs. Tawed skins could be very fine; they were used for the expensive Cordovan leather from which the name "cordwainer," for shoemaker, derives. However, most shoes were made of the more durable tanned leather; tawed leather, being more flexible and elastic, was generally used for gloves, points (laces), bags, and purses.

A specialized branch of the craft was greytawing, the tawing of furs, generally restricted to major cities. A related occupation was parchment making, where the leather was stretched and thinly shaved and deprived of as much grease as possible. Tawing and the making of goods from tawed leather were far less subject to national and local regulation than the manufacture and use of tanned leather. Industries, like glovemaking, that used tawed leather employed a great many women, often as piece workers, and outside London there was no real attempt to demarcate manufacture among different craft groups.

The sale of leather benefited those who marketed it, as opposed to those who worked it. There was an extensive but unquantifiable internal trade in hides and red leather. Much came to the market on the hoof, and in the later Middle Ages urban butchers increasingly profited from the sale of hides as a byproduct. Hides and red leather were also brought to town by country merchants and tanners. Hides were exported from Ireland to England and from England to the Continent. Although less important than the internal trade, this overseas trade can be more readily traced through the customs accounts after the erratic local system of tolls was welded into a national customs system in the time of Edward I.

Heather Swanson

Bibliography

Kowaleski, Maryanne. "Town and Country in Late Medieval England: The Examples of the Hide and Leather Trade." In *Work in Towns, 850–1850,* ed. Penelope Corfield and Derek Keene. London: Leicester University Press, 1990; Power, Eileen, and M.M. Postan. *Studies in English Trade in the Fifteenth Century.* London: Routledge, 1933; Singer, Charles, et al., eds. *A History of Technology.* Vol. 2: *The Mediterranean Civilizations and the Middle Ages, c. 700 B.C. to c. 1500 A.D.* Oxford: Clarendon, 1956; Swanson, Heather. *Medieval Artisans: An Urban Class in Late Medieval England.* Oxford: Blackwell, 1989; Theophilus. *On Divers Arts.* Ed. and trans. John G. Hawthorne and Cyril Stanley Smith. Chicago: University of Chicago Press, 1963; Veale, Elspeth M. *The English Fur Trade in the Later Middle Ages.* Oxford: Clarendon, 1966.

See also Customs Accounts; Guilds; Towns; Trade

Letter of Alexander to Aristotle

The earliest vernacular version of the immensely popular Latin *Epistola Alexandri ad Aristotelem,* of which later medieval translations exist in Middle Irish, Old Icelandic, French (twice), ME, and German. The two English translations are unconnected and the OE version in particular demonstrates considerable divergence from its source. The Latin *Epistola* purports to be the text of a letter sent by Alexander the Great to his former teacher, Aristotle, describing the natural wonders he has seen in the course of his campaigns in India. The account of the curiosities to be found in India, such as men with the heads of dogs *(cynocephali),* proved hugely influential, and spawned a great number of related medieval treatises on marvels and monsters. The OE translation is found in the same manuscript as *Beowulf,* together with two further works, the *Life of St. Christopher* and *The Marvels of the East,* which both deal with monsters, including *cynocephali.*

The OE translator of the *Letter,* however, appears to be aware of a parallel tradition, exemplified by Orosius, whose *History against the Pagans* (early 5th century), which was translated into OE, interpreted Alexander himself as morally monstrous, a figure of overweening pride. The OE *Letter* subtly alters and edits its source to point up Alexander's arrogance in a way unparalleled in any other vernacular rendering.

Three closely related English manuscripts of the Latin *Epistola* survive, including one from the Anglo-Saxon period, which together provide a witness to a particular variant form of the text that is identical to that translated into ME. The absolute and slavish literalness of the ME version, however,

only serves to point up the originality of the OE translator, who appears to have been working within a quite different tradition.

A.P.M. Orchard

Bibliography

PRIMARY

Davidson, D., and A.P. Campbell, trans. "The *Letter of Alexander the Great to Aristotle:* The Old English Version Turned into Modern English." *Humanities Association Bulletin* 23 (1972): 3–16; Hahn, Thomas. "The Middle English *Letter of Alexander to Aristotle.*" *MS* 41 (1979): 106–60; Rypins, Stanley, ed. *Three Old English Prose Texts in MS. Cotton Vitellius A.xv.* EETS o.s. 161. London: Humphrey Milford, 1924.

SECONDARY

Butturff, Douglas R. "Style as a Clue to Meaning: A Note on the Old English Translation of the *Epistola Alexandri ad Aristotelem.*" *English Language Notes* 8 (1970–71): 81–86; Cary, George A. *The Medieval Alexander.* Ed. D.J.A. Ross. Cambridge: Cambridge University Press, 1956.

See also Beowulf; Marvels of the East; Matter of Antiquity; Orosius; Scientific Manuscripts, Early

Libraries

The libraries of medieval England shared in the preservation of the culture of Latin Christendom and contributed to the growth of literacy. The early libraries were monastic and rural. Benedictine houses preserved the tradition of books and regular reading and provided that each monk receive one book and be given a year in which to read it.

By the 12th century houses of the new monastic orders maintained the practice of copying manuscript books in their scriptoria and housed libraries according to guidelines established by Cassiodorus (d. ca. 583) and Isidore of Seville (ca. 560–636), authors of basic rules for the transcription and copying of manuscripts and the care of books. The places for book storage in monasteries varied and often became designated as the library: *arca, archiva* (arc, or chest); the *scrinium* (a stack attached to a desk); or *armarium* (book press).

By the 12th century, however, the "library" was usually a separate book room or building. Changes in terminology came to reflect a growing specialization in institutional development: *libraria* generally denoted libraries that lent books (derived from *liber,* meaning either a single book or a collection of books); *biblioteca* (from the Greek *bibliotheke,* a book case or chest) came to designate a nonlending research depository.

We can learn about the contents of medieval libraries first by studying extant catalogues, inventories, or shelf-lists that show what books were available in particular libraries at particular times. Some of the earliest English library lists date from the 12th century and include those of Christ Church, Canterbury (ca. 1170), Durham, Lincoln, Bury, Reading, and

Rochester (1202). A second way of determining the books of a given library is to identify the provenance of as many surviving books as possible, taking note of handwriting, illumination of manuscripts, notes on ownership and transfer, press marks, and the survival of medieval bindings.

An excellent example of the "reconstruction" of a medieval collection is the 12th-century library of the Benedictine house at Bury St. Edmunds. Developed by gift, purchase, and copies made in its scriptorium (especially under Abbot Anselm, 1121–48), the main categories of books included Bibles and commentaries, liturgical books, the texts of the major Church Fathers (especially Augustine, Ambrose, Jerome, and Gregory the Great), Latin classics (e.g., Virgil, Pliny, Plautus, Terence, Cicero, Seneca), histories, 12th-century scholastic textbooks (e.g., Peter Lombard's *Sentences*), works on canon law, standard authors like Boethius, Cassiodorus, and Isidore, books of sermons, grammar, rhetoric, and "modern" Latin literature, such as the poems of Walter of Châtillon. The expansion of library holdings is evident by the latter half of the 13th century, when a Franciscan author compiled the *Registrum Anglie de libris doctorum et auctorum,* a "union catalogue" of the principal books in the libraries of 183 English religious houses.

The friars were also largely responsible for additional innovations. The Dominican Humbert de Romans (ca. 1260) set down the principal duties of librarians and librarianship and recognized the need for extensive reference libraries. Libraries by the 13th century included more reference tools: encyclopedias, abstracts in florilegia (volumes composed of extracts), and dictionaries and lexicons whose use was facilitated by such new technologies as alphabetization. Books in common use for reference, such as Bibles, papal decretals, sermons, and chronicles, were kept in a chained reference section *(libri catenati).* Books used less frequently and duplicate copies were available for circulation.

Books were costly and valuable commodities. Paper was scarcely known in England before 1307; most books were of parchment. The finest was vellum or calfskin; somewhat less expensive was sheepskin. Parchment, ink, binding materials, and, not least, the scribe's time contributed to the high cost. It has been estimated that labor and materials for a Bible could equal more than 1,500 hours of work and vellum from a dozen animals.

By the 12th and 13th centuries there was a remarkable growth in the book trade and the manufacture of smaller books. Book fairs were held at Paris, Oxford, and London. Libraries acquired books as gifts, often as duplicates from mother abbeys. Books were also routed on a circuit and copied in scriptoria. Rome lent books to Canterbury, for example, and Canterbury made books available to diocesan sees. There were also donations by patrons and bequests in wills. Oxford's late-medieval library reflected the important bequest of Humphrey, duke of Gloucester (in 1439). Royal patronage also facilitated the growth of libraries and bishops frequently endowed episcopal and chapter libraries.

The newer libraries of the high Middle Ages were urban, reflecting the growth of schools and universities. Cathedral libraries served the needs of their schools and the developing universities. York, Durham, and Canterbury housed the most famous cathedral libraries, and many college libraries at Oxford and Cambridge retain substantial numbers of their medieval books. Although the size of medieval libraries is difficult to estimate, about 4,200 manuscript codices attest some 500 library collections by the 16th century. These were the libraries of medieval England in all their diversity: libraries of monastic and religious houses, of cathedral and collegiate churches, and of universities and colleges.

Phyllis B. Roberts

Bibliography

Clanchy, M.T. *From Memory to Written Record: England, 1066–1307.* 2d ed. Oxford: Blackwell, 1993; Ker, N.R., ed. *Medieval Libraries of Great Britain: A List of Surviving Books.* 2d ed. London: Royal Historical Society, 1964; Ker, N.R., ed. *Medieval Manuscripts in British Libraries.* 4 vols. Oxford: Clarendon, 1969–92; Kristeller, Paul O. *Latin Manuscript Books before 1600: A List of the Printed Catalogues and Unpublished Inventories of Extant Collections.* 3d ed. New York: Fordham University Press, 1964; Ogilvy, J.D.A. *Books Known to the English, 597–1066.* Cambridge: Mediaeval Academy of America, 1967; Thomson, Rodney M. "The Library of Bury St. Edmunds Abbey in the Eleventh and Twelfth Centuries." *Speculum* 47 (1972): 617–45; Watson, Andrew, ed. *Medieval Libraries of Great Britain: A List of Surviving Books, Supplement.* London: Royal Historical Society, 1987; Wormald, Francis, and Cyril E. Wright, eds. *The English Library before 1700: Studies in Its History.* London: Athlone, 1958.

See also Books; Learning; Literacy; Monasticism; Schools; Universities

Lincoln

In 1086 Lincoln had 970 inhabited houses and was worth £100 in annual revenues to the king. With its rebuilt minster and castle it commanded the junction to two Roman roads, the Foss and Ermine ways, in addition to having access to the North Sea at Boston via the River Witham and to the Midlands via the Fossdyke (the dike or ditch running on each side of the Fossway, the old Roman road from Axminster to Lincoln) and the River Trent. Strategic battles were fought there in 1141, 1216–17, and 1266.

Links with the Continent, especially Norway, drew Lincoln into international trade, and Henry II granted it a monopoly of trade throughout Lincolnshire. By 1202–04 it ranked as fourth-wealthiest town in England. By 1130 Lincoln was held at farm: the city paid a fixed sum to the king—£140 in the 1150s, increased to £180 in 1156—in lieu of taxes. It had the largest and wealthiest Jewry, outside London, by 1194. The weavers bought their own charter in 1130, and Lincoln cloth was traded internationally. Autonomy emerged slowly from the guild merchant; there were two bailiffs by 1154, an alderman of the guild merchant from ca. 1189, transformed into mayor by 1217, a council of 24 (possibly by 1206, definitely by 1219), four coroners from 1200, and its own common seal by 1220–30. Two burgesses were sent to the 1264 parliament and regularly thereafter.

Lincoln's large Jewish population had a synagogue by the marketplace and brought wealth and skill but also tension. In 1191 citizens were fined for assaulting Jews, and in 1255 the Jews were accused of the ritual murder of Little St. Hugh. In 1265 24 citizens were named to protect Lincoln's Jews. In other respects Lincoln society was the typical urban mixture of craftsmen, merchants, minor gentlemen, cathedral clergy, Gilbertine monks from St. Katherine's Priory, and friars from the five main orders. The city also supported three hospitals.

Lincoln had three weekly markets and St. Botolph's annual fair, confirmed in 1327. It was the region's center for wool and grain. In 1334 and 1377 Lincoln was England's fifth-wealthiest town, though recession was apparent by the early 14th century. The weavers' guild was impoverished, and although in 1326 Lincoln became a "home staple," or port through which wool was required to be traded, it could not afford to maintain its vital waterways. The Black Death killed possibly 60 percent of the inhabitants, and by 1365 the city was in decay. In 1369 the home staple was moved to Boston and some Lincoln merchants followed.

While other towns prospered in the late 14th century, Lincoln declined. Its tax-paying population had fallen to 3,569 by 1377 (from an early-14th-century population between 5,000 and 10,000). In 1378 three bailiffs were appointed to share the burden of the fee farm, the annual tax sum owed the king, and four were so charged in 1401. By the 1390s the citizens could not maintain all their 38 to 46 parish churches, and disturbances between oligarchy and commonalty flared at election times. Routine constitutional squabbling over the liberty of the dean and chapter, and that of the constable of the castle, intensified; in 1390 the mayor and councillors attacked market stalls within the cathedral close.

Lincoln's plea of poverty, for a reduced fee farm in 1409, elicited unusual sympathy. Henry IV granted it county status, with its own quarter sessions, plus enhanced economic opportunities, through the granting of more judicial responsibilities and a second annual fair. However, by 1428 there were three uninhabited parishes and seventeen drastically depopulated ones. In 1434 and 1436 Lincoln was remitted half of its taxes; nine complete tax exemptions were granted between 1437 and 1472.

Decline was attributed in 1447 to "continual pestilence and the withdrawal of merchants." A handful of merchants of the Staple were active in the 1460s, but Lincoln had been overtaken by Boston and Hull. Attempts to revitalize the city by adding adjacent rural townships in 1464 and 1484 were in vain. By the subsidy of 1524–25 Lincoln had fallen to eighteenth in urban ranking, its inhabited area having shrunk to virtually a single street. The union of parishes in 1549 left only nine functioning.

Jennifer I. Kermode

Bibliography

Foster, Charles W., ed. *Lincoln Wills Registered in the District Probate Registry at Lincoln.* Vol. 1: *1271–1526.* Lincoln Record Society 5. Lincoln: Record Society, 1914; Hill, J.W.F. *Medieval Lincoln.* Cambridge: Cambridge University Press, 1948; *Historical Manuscripts Commission.* 12th Report, Appendix ix (Dean and Chapter and Bishops' Records), and 14th Report, Appendix viii (Corporation Records). London: HMSO, 1891–1895; Page, William, ed. *Victoria History of the County of Lincoln.* Vol 2. London: Constable, 1906.

See also Coventry; Jews; Lincoln Cathedral; Staple; Towns

Lincoln Cathedral

Lincoln was the seat of a huge diocese stretching from the Thames to the Humber. The Anglo-Saxon cathedral had been at Dorchester-on-Thames, but the see was moved to Lincoln about 1072 as a result of the Norman preference for linking cathedrals with important towns or cities. The new building was begun by Bishop Remigius in the 1070s and may have been close to completion when Remigius died in 1092. The Romanesque cathedral had a three-bay eastern arm with solid side walls that may indicate a high vault. The echelon plan of the cathedral—whereby the nave and side aisles end in semicircular apses—is similar to others in the first generation of Anglo-Norman architecture, such as Canterbury Cathedral and St. Albans Abbey, although the rectangular chapels opening off the east sides of the transepts are less easy to parallel.

The most unusual feature of Remigius's cathedral was its western end, which seems to have taken the form of a fully defensible castle keep. This structure was two bays deep and projected beyond the line of the nave aisle walls to both north and south. Three great arches form a facade reminiscent of Roman triumphal arches or city gates; they have parallels in contemporary castle architecture as well. Items like machicolations and garderobes testify to the seriousness of defensive intent on the part of the builders. The uncertainty of Norman control in the north may have inspired this extraordinary combination of church and donjon, but the only time it was likely used as the latter was in 1141, during the civil war between King Stephen and Empress Matilda. The cathedral may well have been burned as a result of this military action, and the repairs and alterations undertaken by Bishop Alexander in the mid-1140s transformed the Romanesque church. Alexander added elaborately sculpted portals and a sculpted frieze to the west facade, as well as two richly decorated west towers. He seems also to have vaulted the nave, presumably with a rib vault.

In 1185 the cathedral was damaged by what the chroniclers call an earthquake, perhaps the collapse of a vault. The rebuilding that followed, beginning in 1192, resulted eventually in the complete replacement of the Romanesque church, with the exception of part of the west block and towers. The original eastern termination of this early Gothic structure has itself been rebuilt, but excavations have shown it to have had an unusual polygonal plan. The new project also included eastern transepts with eastern chapels on the model of Canterbury

Cathedral, and a new choir known today as St. Hugh's after the bishop of the time of its construction. All this is the work of one of the most innovative and excessive master masons in the history of Gothic architecture. The style of the work, including the three-story elevation (fig. 82) and the use of detached Purbeck marble shafting, is derived from Canterbury but is interpreted in a more extravagant way. The piers and responds have complexly molded cores and varying numbers of detached shafts, the arch moldings are deeply undercut and embellished with dogtooth, and the upper stories are also richly articulated with shafts, dogtooth, and punched-foil figures. In the east transepts there are pier cores covered with vertical crockets, and in the choir aisles a high dado with one blind arcade superimposed on another forms a striking pattern of spatial and visual syncopation.

The most famous part of St. Hugh's Choir is its high vault, because of its asymmetrical design. There is a ridge rib here for the first time in English Gothic, plus the extra diagonal ribs known as tiercerons. These latter, with the regular diagonal ribs, meet on the ridge at two distinct junctures instead of the usual one. Three ribs meet at each boss, two from one side and one from the other, and it is these alternating three-toed patterns that give the vault its unique asymmetry. This design may be the result of the master's attempt to combine the six-part vaults set over each bay of the eastern transepts with the triple clerestory windows deemed more advisable in

Fig. 82. Lincoln Cathedral, south nave elevation from east. Courtesy of L. Hoey.

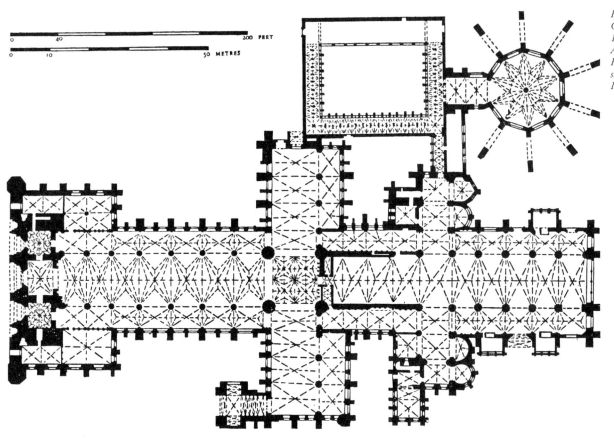

Fig. 83. Lincoln Cathedral, plan of 13th-century church. After G. Webb (1956). Reprinted by permission of Yale University Press.

the main choir; the multiple bosses may also continue the pattern established in the vaulting of the lost eastern apse. Although the asymmetry of the vault had no future in English Gothic, the introduction of tiercerons and ridge ribs was to be influential.

Work continued westward with the reconstruction of the western transepts, probably in the second decade of the 13th century. By the 1220s the nave was underway and by the 1230s, the west front. In 1237/39 the new central tower collapsed and the main crossing piers and adjacent areas of choir and transepts had to be replaced, hastily, as it would appear from the crudity of some of the work. The design of the western parts follows in general the lines of St. Hugh's Choir; the most important difference is the greater bay length in the nave,

Fig. 85. Lindisfarne Gospels (BL Cotton Nere D. iv.), fol. 27. Opening to Matthew. Reproduced by permission of the British Library, London.

which gives an unimpeded oblique view of the lateral spaces of the aisles, and the nave vault, where the tiercerons of the choir are arranged symmetrically along the ridge to form a heavily textured pattern that would provide the inspiration for the majority of English high vaults over the next several decades. The new west front incorporated the Norman west block, but extended it upward and outward to form a huge

screen of blind arcading below the western towers.

In 1256 attention turned again to the east end of the cathedral, where the polygonal apse was removed and a new presbytery was built as a more appropriate setting for the shrine of St. Hugh. This work, known today as the Angel Choir, was complete by 1280, and continues the three-story elevation of the earlier work to which it was joined. It is still richer in its use of sculptural and coloristic effects than the nave, and incorporates the window tracery first introduced at Westminster Abbey. While the tracery patterns themselves are by no means visually dominant in the designs of the aisle or main wall elevations, they are used to overwhelming effect in the flat east wall, where a huge eight-light geometrical window fills almost the entire facade. This happy marriage of traceried window with terminal wall would dominate English church architecture for the rest of the Middle Ages.

Lincoln remains an essentially 13th-century building (fig. 83); the only notable work of the later Middle Ages was the heightening of the central and western towers and the replacement of windows in the south transept and west faces.

Lawrence Hoey

Bibliography

Bilson, John. "The Plan of the First Cathedral Church of Lincoln." *Archaeologia* 62 (1911): 543–64; Frankl, Paul. "The 'Crazy Vaults' of Lincoln Cathedral." *Art Bulletin* 35 (1953): 96–107; Gem, Richard. "Lincoln Minster: Ecclesia Pulchra, Ecclesia Fortis." *BAACT* 8 (1986): 9–28; Kidson, Peter. "St. Hugh's Choir." *BAACT* 8 (1986): 29–42; Kidson, Peter. "Architectural History." In *A History of Lincoln Minster,* ed. Dorothy Owen. Cambridge: Cambridge University Press, 1994, pp. 14–46; Pevsner, Nikolaus, and Priscilla Metcalf. *The Cathedrals of England: Midland, Eastern and Northern England.* New York: Viking, 1985, pp. 196–230; Stocker, David. "The Mystery of the Shrines of St. Hugh." In *St. Hugh of Lincoln,* ed. Henry Mayr-Harting. Oxford: Clarendon, 1987, pp. 89–124.

See also Architecture and Architectural Sculpture, Gothic; Architecture and Architectural Sculpture, Romanesque; Canterbury Cathedral; Lincoln

Lindisfarne Gospels

One of the first and greatest masterpieces of European book painting, the manuscript BL Cotton Nero D.iv is of supreme importance both as an individual work of art and, because it is relatively securely dated and localized, as a touchstone for the study of all other works of art of its period. A colophon added in the 10th century, presumably drawing upon oral tradition, tells us that the manuscript was written by Eadfrith, who became bishop of Lindisfarne in 698; that the original binding was supplied by Ethelwald, who succeeded him in 721; and that it was ornamented on the outside with precious metals and gems by Billfrith, an anchorite. Modern study has revealed that Eadfrith the scribe was also responsible for the design and execution of the illumination.

Complete apart from its binding, which was presumably lost at the Reformation, the manuscript contains the four Gospels, each of which is introduced by a miniature of its evangelist, a cross-carpet page, and a major initial (figs. 84–85). Lesser decorated initials occur among the preliminaries to each Gospel. The Gospels are preceded by St. Jerome's letter to Pope Damasus, also introduced by a page of decoration and an initial page, and by sixteen pages of Eusebian canon tables enclosed in decorated arcades.

The intricate ornament of the book combines motifs that may be compared with metalwork and jewelry, such as pieces from the Sutton Hoo treasure, with complicated patterns composed of birds and beasts, some of which appear directly inspired by nature. The evangelist miniatures, though clearly the work of an insular hand, are adapted from Mediterranean models, possibly from southern Italy. All the painting is carried out in an unusually large and varied range of pigments from animal, vegetable, and mineral sources.

The Latin gospel text is a remarkably pure version of St. Jerome's Vulgate, probably also of Italian origin and perhaps copied from an exemplar provided by the library of Wearmouth-Jarrow, some 50 miles south of Lindisfarne, where books imported from Italy were available. The script in which it is written is a magnificent insular majuscule, developed in early Christian Ireland and transmitted to Northumbria via Iona and the Irish missionaries.

According to the added colophon the manuscript was created for God and for St. Cuthbert, a bishop of Lindisfarne who died in 687. His relics were raised to the altar in 698, and preparations for this event seem to have begun soon after his death, for his saintliness had been recognized even in his lifetime. It is likely that the book was made to honor this translation of his relics. The manuscript certainly cannot be later than 721, the year of Eadfrith's death. Both Eadfrith and Ethelwald had been monks of the community in Cuthbert's time and were personally acquainted with the saint.

In the late 9th century, after a succession of Viking raids upon their monastery, the Lindisfarne community left their island home, taking with them St. Cuthbert's relics and other treasures, including the Gospels. After seven years of wandering they settled for a century at Chester-le-Street in County Durham. There the colophon was added by a priest named Aldred, identifiable as a member of the community about the middle of the 10th century. He also added an interlinear word-for-word translation of the text into OE, and this is now one of the two earliest surviving translations of the Gospels into any form of the English language.

Janet Backhouse

Bibliography

Alexander, J.J.G. *Insular Manuscripts 6th–9th Century.* A Survey of Manuscripts Illuminated in the British Isles 1, ed. J.J.G. Alexander. London: Harvey Miller, 1978; Backhouse, Janet. *The Lindisfarne Gospels.* Oxford: Phaidon, 1981; Kendrick, T.D., et al. *Evangeliorum Quattuor Codex Lindisfarnensis.* 2 vols. Lausanne: Urs Graf, 1956 [facsimile] and 1960 [commentary]; Millar, Eric G. *The Lindisfarne Gospels.* London: Oxford University Press, 1923.

See also Art, Anglo-Saxon: Celtic Influences; Bible in OE Literature; Coffin of St. Cuthbert; Cuthbert; Manuscript Illumination, Anglo-Saxon; Sutton Hoo; Textiles from St. Cuthbert's Tomb; Translation; Wearmouth-Jarrow and the Codex Amiatinus

Literacy and Readership
Anglo-Saxon Period

In Anglo-Saxon England, as in all of early-medieval Europe, the vast majority of people lived traditional lives without the use of writing or reading. "Literacy" was a category of Latin, a language controlled by the clergy. Thus, in this period, reading and, even more so, writing pertained to a group of specialists whose services tended to be at the disposal of lay elites. The clergy themselves were mostly bicultural, and the uses of literacy were not confined to those who could actually read and write, so that the contact of the technically "illiterate" with literate culture was more than merely casual or conflictive. From the earliest times after the Conversion Anglo-Saxon kings accorded Latin culture high prestige and found use for Latin and its "chaplains" as instruments of power conceived along traditional lines. In fact, from the 7th century, a court literacy, however shallow, was often part and parcel of Anglo-Saxon kingship.

Yet traditional oral forms for the retention and transmission of power remained preeminent: writing recorded the "deeds" and legal decisions of the magnates; it did not supplant spoken forms for many centuries, though writing came into more systematic use as the period progressed. The secular nobility, while deferring to the wisdom available though a secondary association with literate practices, did not easily relinquish the positive benefits of preliterate traditions. It may well be, as Busse argues, that by the 10th century the authority of clerically controlled books became strong enough to conflict with the authority of the warrior class. The deeply socialized traditional formations of the secular nobility, embedded in oral culture, depended on personal contact and were thus fundamentally threatened by the universalistic and impersonal forces of literacy. If it is true, as Susan Kelly has recently argued, that "at the end of this [Anglo-Saxon] period . . . written documentation had an important place in secular society and was used in ways which could imply a degree of literacy among certain sections of the laity" (1990: 36), it was true only insofar as the lay ruling class had been "clericalized" in its interests and behavior (e.g., began to depend on written records of property transfers, formally promulgated codes of law, etc.). It is interesting to note, for example, that Alfred's secular law code begins with a summary of Mosaic law and modifications thereto derived from the Acts of the Apostles.

In most of Europe the hegemony of Latin writing delayed the emergence of vernacular writing until the high Middle Ages, but in England, alongside one of the richest traditions of Latin writing in Europe, sporadic experiments in vernacular writing began at an early stage and increased considerably in quantity and interest from Alfred the Great's time (d. 899). It is doubtful, however, that there ever was a continuous or widely disseminated tradition of OE writing. Furthermore the existence of isolated vernacular monuments does not in itself attest to widespread vernacular literacy. Social literacy is a statistical concept, and there are no statistics, only anecdotes about literate laypersons, most of whom were probably unusual. Though many laypeople could indeed read (and occasionally write), these cases are known to us because they are remarkable exceptions to the rule of lay illiteracy. Beyond this, as can be demonstrated from the practices of scribes and the features of poetic manuscripts, literacy itself may have involved methods quite different from the modern method of the silent, speedy scanning of clear and regular textual patterns; Anglo-Saxon scribes (who give the most immediate evidence of the skills of reading) seem to have struggled through the irregular textuality of manuscripts using oralization, guesswork, and traditional memory to arrive at the general gists of texts.

The basically clerical nature of extant OE literature is attested by the fact that it parallels in its genres and contents the Christian and pan-European concerns of contemporary Latin writing. The bulk of OE writings are adaptations or translations of Latin works. These works imply "illiterate" audiences of sufficient importance or wealth that clerics who knew Latin were willing to make such books for them and that these audiences had become sufficiently convinced of the importance of Latin learning to get it by hearing books read in the mother-tongue or by mastering vernacular reading as a substitute for latinity. Clerical works in OE also imply that much of the clergy was monolingual and hence technically "illiterate." They do not of necessity imply that the bulk of the intended audience could read them for themselves; many of these works must have been meant for reading aloud to monastic audiences.

Much of the prose is modeled in its vocabulary and syntax on Latin. Even the poetry, the most seemingly oralistic OE writing, is with few exceptions assimilated to the subject matter and genres of Latin writing. On the other hand traditional oral style affected writing and the particular shape vernacular literacy took in England, so that by the early 11th century English had become a powerful, fluent, and autonomous medium of communication in the writings of Ælfric and Wulfstan.

While Latin remained the model of literacy in the vernacular, the appearance of vernacular writing seems to have sparked the idea that reading could become a widely disseminated skill. The preface to the English translation of Gregory the Great's *Pastoral Care,* part of the famous "educational program" of King Alfred (who himself remained illiterate until middle age and was no doubt in his policies continuing a royal tradition of using literacy for purposes of prestige and control), presents the most explicit evidence we have. Alfred laments the decay of learning "south of the Humber" and the almost total absence, even among the clergy, of those who could translate or understand Latin. For this reason he is undertaking to translate those books most needful for all men to know, which might be read in English even if Latin learning was at a low ebb. He projects that all the sons of "free men" (sons of the political elite, in effect) could be taught to read and write English as long as conditions allowed and that some could be further trained up into Latin learning as preparation for clerical office. Clearly, for Alfred, learning in English is a second-best but an undertaking necessary for the functioning of the realm and the salvation of souls. At the same time he gives the impression that such widespread literacy in the vernacular would be something unprecedented.

It is doubtful that Alfred's ambitious program was realized or that systematically organized schools for laypeople ever existed. In the succeeding century the Benedictine Reform generated many English texts, but these seem to have been more often for use within the cloister than outside it. Yet Ælfric (d. ca. 1015) had lay patrons, one of whom, Æthelweard, was the composer of a translation of the Anglo-Saxon Chronicle into Latin. But we can see how Ælfric's attitude to the lay user of books and the clerical differs by his comments on the book of Judith to the different audiences. To Ealdorman Sigeweard he teaches a particularistic oral-traditional message: through the fortitude of Judith you learn how "you should protect your country with weapons against an invading army." To an audience of nuns he interprets the same figure in terms of universalistic allegory: Judith is Christ's church keeping itself pure by cutting off the "head of the Devil," and on the moral level she is a figure of virginity.

Both Bishop Æthelwold (d. 984) and Ælfric apologized for their use of English and attributed its necessity to the loss of learning. Nevertheless, the so-called school of Æthelwold fostered a standard grapholect, or form of written language, based on West Saxon; this grapholect was used with remarkable uniformity throughout the land for several decades. Such uniformity implies systematic training in *English* writing, while the concomitant increase in intelligibility between dialects would have at least made reading easier. England was not to have a comparable written standard again until the early Elizabethans.

Middle English Period

After the year 1200 or so the clerical control of literacy in England was challenged by increasingly diverse types of lay readers and by a widening circulation of texts in society. Although universal literacy was never a goal, those who read, wrote, and used texts included more aristocrats, more people from the commercial and lower classes, and more women. It is estimated that by 1400 at least 30 percent of the English population, including most of the nobles and gentry, were able to read and often write in English and perhaps French or Latin. During this same period the wills of aristocrats, gentry, merchants, and tradespeople regularly list the Bibles, devotional books, histories, and grammar texts they bequeath to others. The evidence of literacy claims and book ownership indicates that by the 14th century minimal literacy skills were being taken for granted among the upper and middle classes.

After the Norman Conquest English literate culture was shaped by the mixture of Latin, French, and English languages. Versions of Anglo-Norman French became the language of power and prestige, the imposed public discourse of the subjected Anglo-Saxons and the ruling Normans. Latin remained the dominant bookish language for learning and theology, despite a strong tradition of OE intellectual writing. English continued to be the spoken language of the villages. English law bridged the gap between learned and lay communities. In 1258, for example, the barons' proclamation ("Provisions of Oxford") was sent to sheriffs in Latin, French, and English to be read aloud publicly in whichever language the audience would understand. By the 13th century members of the upper class were expected to be at least functionally bilingual in French and English, with perhaps a small reading knowledge of Latin. However, by the late 14th century English had emerged not only as the spoken language of the majority of people but also as the written language of many official records, and of the courtly poetry of Chaucer and the alliterative poetry of Langland.

Until the 13th century the term *literatus* was applied to anyone "able to read and write Latin" (or sometimes French), usually the male clergy. By definition everyone else was *illiteratus*, regardless of whether they could read and write English. The English terms *lered* ("learned") and *lewed* ("unlearned") were comparable to the Latin *literatus* and *illiteratus*. Traditionally *clericus* meant the male clergy and was therefore associated with those able to read and write Latin. But in the 14th century *literatus* and *lered* could mean someone able to read English, while *clericus* often referred to any man able to read and write Latin. *Clerk* could mean a member of the clergy, a student, a university-educated layman, a scholar, or a male writer.

A number of factors led to the increased use of writing and books in later medieval England. First, schooling was becoming more accessible to the laity, enabling children of the gentry, tradespeople, and even peasants to acquire basic literacy in French or English. Not only monasteries and cathedrals but also convents, parishes, towns, and guilds sponsored grammar schools, despite economic and political uncertainties and sometimes scarce resources. Young boys were taught Latin literacy and grammar, but most used their skills to master vernacular literacy. Aristocratic boys were usually entrusted to tutors who used the same textbooks and models of literate discourse as the grammar masters. Girls, more educated than we have commonly thought, were most often taught privately to read and less often to write in English or French. After the Conquest literacy training in nunneries was usually in French, but by the 14th century English literacy was common in women's schooling.

Second, changes in book formats made texts more accessible and easier to handle. Calls for a more educated clergy (such as those of the Fourth Lateran Council of 1215) and the creation of the preaching orders of friars encouraged the copying of devotional books in smaller, "pocket" versions, more portable than the lavish vellum texts copied for cathedrals and wealthy patrons. Aids to reading that began in university texts—tables of contents, chapter headings, indices, and line numbers—spread to devotional and secular books for lay readers. Collections of romances, sermons, and documents were compiled on cheaper and lighter parchment and written in a more readable "business" script.

Third, these changes in book format and the laicization of literacy affected people's reading habits. Throughout the Middle Ages reading normally meant reading aloud, whether publicly, in small private groups, or individually. *Lector* meant "reader" and especially "one who reads a text aloud." The written text was usually a prompt to vocalize the book, even to oneself; many works describe their imagined audiences as "all who read or hear read" or "read and listen to" the narrative or treatise. In literate households families shared religious books together after the evening meal, as the father and children took turns reading aloud from the Bible or a devotional text.

But scholasticism and the academic study of texts, together with the growing urban book trade and a wider readership, helped foster silent, private reading and the individual practice of mulling over a text. Books of hours, saints' lives, and other devotional texts were composed for individual, private, and perhaps silent readers. In *The Parliament of Fowls* Chaucer's narrator describes himself unexceptionally as reading privately in his own bed. But some cultural authorities associated books in English for lay readers with heresy and skepticism and with a dangerous kind of freedom. The avid book collector Richard de Bury (d. 1345) lamented the growing number of lay and especially women readers as a sign of social disorder brought on by the decline of the clergy's control over literacy.

Whether they read themselves or were read to, later medieval lay readers had greater access than their ancestors to traditionally clerical writings through English translations of the Bible, commentaries, sermons, psalters, and penitentials. Anticlericalism and the preachings of Wyclif's followers supported the translation of the Bible into English for lay readers. In addition there circulated among both religious and lay readers the writings of such mystics as Richard Rolle, originally in English or translated into English, as well as translations of saints' lives. Fueled by the spirit of lay piety, prayer books and other devotional books were translated and copied into the vernacular for lay readers, especially gentry and upper-middle-class men and women.

The increasing importance of documents in English legal, economic, and political life also fostered the laicization of literacy. After 1200 many men and some women wrote and signed their wills in English in their own hands; deeds and account records were recorded in family or personal papers. The great collections of family letters (Pastons, Celys, Stonors) date from the late 15th century. A noble or bourgeois household might own not only a Bible but also anthologies of courtly narratives and religious tales (such as the Auchinleck Manuscript) and a domestic book containing family records, advice on conduct and how to run the household, recipes, remedies, herbal lore, and other practical information previously maintained in oral culture.

The lives and writings of medieval English women reveal the complexities of later medieval literacies. Both Julian of Norwich (1342/43–after 1416) and Margery Kempe (ca. 1373–after 1438) describe themselves as "unlettered," but they also dictate long works on their spiritual experiences to scribes. Julian's *Book of Showings* resonates deeply with the biblical and Latin religious writings she heard read or perhaps read herself. Kempe, a brewer and daughter of the mayor of Lynn, participated actively in vernacular culture by having her priests read devotional works to her. Margaret Paston (d. 1484), a member of the landed gentry in Norfolk, composed numerous letters in English to her husband and family concerning both private and public matters; most she dictated to clerks, but a few she inscribed in her own hand. These women were active in English literary culture, were read to by clerks or priests, and used texts as part of their devotional or pragmatic literacy.

By the 15th century private and vernacular reading was widely practiced along with reading aloud in groups among both religious and lay people. English had emerged as the language of both official and familiar writing and reading. From the king's council to the town council to the household late-medieval England was increasingly familiar with and dependent on written texts.

A.N. Doane
Mark Amsler

Bibliography

ANGLO-SAXON PERIOD

Busse, Wilhelm G. "Boceras: Written and Oral Traditions in the Late Tenth Century." In *Mündlichkeit und Schriftlichkeit im englischen Mittelalter,* ed. Willi Erzgräber and Sabine Volk. ScriptOralia 5. Tübingen: Narr, 1988, pp. 27–37; Gneuss, Helmut. "The Origin of Standard Old English and Æthelwold's School at Winchester." *ASE* 1 (1972): 63–83; Grundmann, H. "Litteratus-illiteratus." *Archiv für Kulturgeschichte* 40 (1958): 1–65; McKitterick, Rosamond, ed. *The Uses of Literacy in Early Mediaeval Europe.* Cambridge: Cambridge University Press, 1990 [see esp. Susan Kelly, "Anglo-Saxon Lay Society and the Written Word," pp. 36–62, and Simon Keynes, "Royal Government and the Written Word in Late Anglo-Saxon England," pp. 226–57]; O'Keeffe, Katherine O'Brien. *Visible Song: Transitional Literacy in Old English Verse.* Cambridge: Cambridge University Press, 1990; Wormald, C.P. "The Uses of Literacy in Anglo-Saxon England and Its Neighbours." *TRHS,* 5th ser. 27 (1977): 95–114.

MIDDLE ENGLISH PERIOD

Alexander, J.J.G., and M.T. Gibson, eds. *Medieval Learning and Literature: Essays Presented to Richard William Hunt.* Oxford: Clarendon, 1976 [see esp. William Abel Pantin, "Instructions for a Devout and Literate Layman," pp. 398–422, and Malcolm B. Parkes, "The Influence of the Concepts of *Ordinatio* and *Compilatio* on the Development of the Book," pp. 115–41]; Aston, Margaret. *Lollards and Reformers: Images and Literacy in Late Medieval Religion.* London: Hambledon, 1984; Bell, Susan Groag. "Medieval Women Book Owners: Arbiters of Lay Piety and Ambassadors of Culture." In *Women and Power in the Middle Ages,* ed. Mary Erler and Maryanne Kowaleski. Athens: University of Georgia Press, 1988, pp. 149–87; Clanchy, Michael T. *From Memory to Written Record: England, 1066–1307.* 2d ed. Oxford: Blackwell, 1993; Coleman, Janet. *Medieval Readers and Writers, 1350–1400.* London: Hutchinson, 1981;

Davies, W.J. Frank. *Teaching Reading in Early England.* New York: Barnes & Noble, 1974; Goody, Jack. *The Logic of Writing and the Organization of Society.* Cambridge: Cambridge University Press, 1986; Justice, Steven. *Writing and Rebellion: England in 1381.* Berkeley: University of California Press, 1994; Lerer, Seth. *Chaucer and His Readers: Imagining the Author in Late-Medieval England.* Princeton: Princeton University Press, 1993; Lochrie, Karma. *Margery Kempe and Translations of the Flesh.* Philadelphia: University of Pennsylvania Press, 1991; Ong, Walter J. *Orality and Literacy: The Technologizing of the Word.* London: Methuen, 1982; Saenger, Paul. "Silent Reading: Its Impact on Late Medieval Script and Society." *Viator* 12 (1982): 367–414; Stock, Brian. *The Implications of Literacy: Written Language and Models of Interpretation in the Eleventh and Twelfth Centuries.* Princeton: Princeton University Press, 1983; Strohm, Paul. *Social Chaucer.* Cambridge: Harvard University Press, 1989.

See also Ælfric; Æthelwold; Alfred; Bible in ME Literature; Bible in OE Literature; Books; Books of Hours; Chancellor and Chancery; Courtesy Literature; Family Letter Collections; Grammatical Treatises; Language; Learning; Libraries; Moral and Religious Instruction; Mystical and Devotional Writings; Orality; Patronage, Literary; Runes; Translation; Utilitarian Writings; Women; Women in ME Literature; Women in OE Literature; Wulfstan; Wycliffite Texts

Literary Influences: Carolingian

The beginning and the end of the Carolingian dynasty are easily determined: Pepin the Short established the dynasty in 751 by deposing the Merovingian king Childeric III; the Carolingians were replaced by a different royal house in 911 in Germany, and in 987 in France. The dates for Carolingian culture, however, can be less clearly defined: it takes its beginning and is most vital under Charlemagne (king of the Franks from 768; emperor of the West 800–14), continues during the 9th century, and then wanes in the beginning of the 10th.

Carolingian culture grew out of Charlemagne's desire to establish a learned clergy with uniform practices throughout his realm. Books were therefore at the center of his cultural program. Whatever their content, books had to be copied, and copied accurately; if existing texts were not accurate, they had to be corrected, or correct texts had to be established with reference to texts that were accurate. As far as possible gaps had to be filled. Correct texts and texts considered necessary for the education of the clergy were ordered from abroad, primarily from Rome. The early center for much of this activity was Charlemagne's court at Aachen; there he gathered not only the learned men of his own realm, such as Angilbert of St. Riquier, but also from abroad: Peter of Pisa, Paul the Deacon, and Paulinus of Aquileia from Italy; Theodulf of Orléans from Spain or southern Gaul; Josephus Scotus from Ireland; Alcuin of York from England. While still at the court these men not only corrected deficient texts but also became authors in their own right, their poetry being characterized by a con-scious imitation of classical forms. Later these scholars dispersed throughout the realm and established centers of learning at whatever abbey or bishopric they received from Charlemagne (e.g., Alcuin at the Abbey of Tours).

Carolingian culture must have had a certain influence on Anglo-Saxon England during the period in which Alcuin was still alive. His letters contain evidence of "presents" sent to England; these are sometimes identified as metalwork, clothes, and other valuable items, but presumably they also included books (*Epistles* 102, 103, 104). He dedicates and sends his *Interrogationes de libro Geneseos (Questions on the Book of Genesis)* to one Sigwulf, whose name suggests that he was an Anglo-Saxon (*Epistle* 80). His letters also speak of one of his students whom he sent back to England to teach there (*Epistle* 64). His *vita* relates that he received many English visitors at Tours. It is hardly conceivable that these visitors did not bring word back to England about Carolingian culture and that they did not take books back as well. Nonetheless, because of the scarcity of extant books that can be clearly shown to have been taken from France to England in the early 9th century, and in the absence of any Anglo-Latin writers of that period whose work could be scrutinized for echoes of Carolingian writers, any statement about Carolingian influence on England during the early 9th century has to remain speculative.

While learning declined in Anglo-Saxon England during the 9th century, partly no doubt because of continuous Viking raids from about 850 onward, the impetus Charlemagne had given to Carolingian culture retained its momentum and produced such scholars and poets as Abbo of St. Germain (d. ca. 921), Ado of Vienne (d. 875), Adrevald of Fleury (fl. ca. 850), Amalarius of Metz (d. ca. 850), Benedict of Aniane (d. 821), Florus Diaconus (d. ca. 860), Freculphus of Lisieux (d. 852), Halitgar of Cambrai (d. 831), Helperic of Auxerre (fl. mid-9th century), Hrabanus Maurus (d. 856), Hugbald of St. Amand (d. 930), Milo of St. Amand (d. 872), Paschasius Radbertus (d. 860), Remigius of Auxerre (d. 908), and Smaragdus of St. Mihiel (fl. in the second and third decades of the 9th century). Whether any of these authors immediately influenced England during the 9th century is almost impossible to ascertain because of the scarcity of English manuscripts during this period and because of the apparent absence of English authors writing at this time.

Learning was revived in England in the last decade of the 9th century under Alfred the Great, and this revival drew heavily on the expertise in Francia. Alfred was directly connected to the Carolingian court through his stepmother, Judith. Two of Alfred's advisers came from the Continent, Grimbald from the Flemish monastery St. Bertin's and John the Old Saxon presumably from a monastery in eastern Francia (possibly Corvey). Specific traces of their activities can no longer be ascertained, but there can be no doubt that they were influential. Alfred himself, in the prose preface to his translation of Gregory's *Pastoral Care* mentions that he translated the work "as I learned it from . . . Grimbald my mass-priest and from John my mass-priest." Alfred's biographer, the Welshman Asser, is also influenced by Carolingian culture: he echoes Einhard's *Vita Caroli,* mentions recent events of Frankish history, and even uses some

Latin words considered to be specifically Frankish. The inclusion of events of Frankish history in the Anglo-Saxon Chronicle, which was started during Alfred's reign, also attests to Carolingian influence on England. The exact sources for Alfred's and his circle's translations have not been completely determined, but without doubt both texts and commentaries produced in Carolingian Francia were among them.

Carolingian culture exerted its greatest influence on England in the period when the Carolingian dynasty was replaced by other royal houses in Germany and France. The Benedictine Reform in England (beginning ca. 940) itself was an importation from the Continent; two of its leading men, St. Dunstan and St. Oswald, had spent some time in continental monasteries and must have come in contact with Carolingian culture there. The Reform brought with it the need for manuscripts that seems to have been filled at least partly by scribes in Francia. Of the manuscripts owned in Anglo-Saxon England more than 70 were written in Francia in the 9th and 10th centuries and brought over to England; some of these manuscripts may have arrived in England as early as the late 9th century (i.e., under Alfred the Great), but the bulk came to England in the course of the 10th century.

The content of these manuscripts is the best indication for the areas of major Carolingian influence on England: they include biblical, liturgical, patristic, hagiographic, administrative, and didactic works. Eleven manuscripts, for instance, contain the Gospels, another four the Psalms; the bulk of the manuscripts (nearly twenty) contain patristic works, such as Caesarius of Arles's *Expositio in Apocalypsin,* Augustine's *Soliloquies,* or Gregory's *Dialogues* and his *Moralia in Job.* Among the continental manuscripts is a surprisingly large number containing works by Anglo-Saxon authors (not including the four manuscripts with works by Alcuin that, since he produced most of them on the Continent, by necessity had to come from Francia to England): ten manuscripts contain such works as Aldhelm's *Aenigmata* (BL Royal 15.A.xvi) and his *Carmen de virginitate* (Oxford, Oriel College 34; Bodley 849), *De templo Salomonis* (Cambridge, Pembroke College 81), *In Evangelium Lucae* (Cambridge, Pembroke College 83; Oxford, Bodley 218), and *De temporum ratione* (BL Cotton Vespasian B.vi; Royal 15.B.xix; Salisbury, Cathedral Library 158). Five manuscripts contain works by Carolingian authors: the *De ecclesiasticis officiis* by Amalarius of Metz; the *Expositio super Sedulium* and *In Martianum Capellam* by Remigius of Auxerre; and the *In epistolas Pauli, In Judith,* and *In Hester* by Hrabanus Maurus.

Manuscripts imported from Francia thus do not primarily bring the works of Carolingian authors to England but rather restock English libraries with works essential for the school and church. That works by Anglo-Saxon authors were reimported from Francia indicates how depleted English libraries were; some works by Anglo-Saxon authors, such as Bede's *De templo Salomonis, In canticum Habacum,* and *In regum librum,* all found in Cambridge, Pembroke College 81, are extant in England only in manuscripts imported from Francia.

The Anglo-Saxons were familiar with more Carolingian authors than is indicated above; many of them appear not in manuscripts imported from Francia but in manuscripts copied in Anglo-Saxon England and, one might add as an additional Carolingian influence on England, increasingly copied in the Caroline script from the middle of the 10th century onward. Authors whose works are preserved in manuscripts written by the Anglo-Saxons (not including manuscripts written in the second half of the 11th century, since these may already be Norman imports) are Abbo of St. Germain, Adrevald of Fleury, Amalarius of Metz, Hrabanus Maurus, Hugbald of St. Amand, Milo of St. Amand, Paschasius Radbertus, Remigius of Auxerre, Smaragdus of St. Mihiel, and Theodulf of Orléans.

The preservation of these works in Anglo-Saxon manuscripts suggests that many more manuscripts than are extant had been imported from the Continent and were either destroyed, lost, or returned after they had been copied. What is true here specifically of manuscripts containing Carolingian authors is also true generally of other authors. Two of the ten extant Anglo-Saxon *Psychomachia* manuscripts, for instance, come from Francia, but they do not contain the textual variants, the glosses, or the illustrations found in the other eight, so that several manuscripts must be presumed lost or returned to the Continent after they had been copied.

Anglo-Saxon interest in matters Carolingian also appears in the OE glosses to Abbo of St. Germain's *Bella Parisiacae urbis,* to Amalarius's *Liber officialis,* to Benedict of Aniane's *Memoriale,* and to Milo's *De sobrietate,* and even more so in the translations of parts of Amalarius's *De regula canonicorum,* Halitgar's *Penitential,* and Theodulf's *Capitula.* One might add here both the OE glosses to and translation of Chrodegang's *Rule,* even though Chrodegang is strictly speaking a pre-Carolingian author (d. 766); nonetheless, there can be no doubt that his work was transmitted to England via Carolingian Francia.

The Latin works written by the Carolingians clearly influenced the Anglo-Saxons most strongly, but this influence also extends to the vernacular. BL Cotton Caligula A.vii, written in the 10th century in England, contains the Old Saxon version of the *Heliand,* a poem composed about 830 possibly at Fulda in eastern Francia; the OE poem known as *Genesis B,* as Sievers had originally postulated and as a fragment from the Vatican library later confirmed, is a translation from an Old Saxon poem composed around the same time as the *Heliand.* The Carolingians in the 10th century thus returned to the Anglo-Saxons a type of poetry with which Anglo-Saxon missionaries probably first acquainted them in the 8th.

The Norman Conquest, though ending the Anglo-Saxon period, brought with it one last extensive influx of Carolingian works into England. Among the manuscripts produced at Salisbury immediately after the Conquest, for instance, are some containing Freculphus's *Chronicon,* Paschasius Radbertus's *De corpore et sanguine domini,* Amalarius's *De ecclesiasticis officiis,* and Helpericus's *De computo;* the Durham scriptorium of the same period produced manuscripts with Paul the Deacon's *Homiliary* and Hrabanus Maurus's *In Matthaeum.* The exemplars for these works had in all probability been brought over to England by the new Norman masters.

Gernot R. Wieland

Bibliography

Bately, J. "Grimbald of St. Bertin's." *MÆ* 35 (1966): 1–10; Bestul, T.H. "Continental Sources of Anglo-Saxon Devotional Writing." In *Sources of Anglo-Saxon Culture,* ed. Paul E. Szarmach, with Virginia Darrow Oggins. Studies in Medieval Culture 20. Kalamazoo: Medieval Institute, 1986, pp. 103–26; Gneuss, Helmut. "A Preliminary List of Manuscripts Written or Owned in England up to 1100." *ASE* 9 (1981): 1–60; Napier, Arthur S., ed. *The Old English Version of the Enlarged Rule of Chrodegang . . .; An Old English Version of the Capitula of Theodulf . . .; An Interlinear Old English Rendering of the Epitome of Benedict of Aniane.* EETS o.s. 150. London: Kegan Paul, Trench, Trübner, 1916; Parsons, David, ed. *Tenth-Century Studies: Essays in Commemoration of the Millennium of the Council of Winchester and Regularis concordia.* London: Phillimore, 1975 [see esp. D.A. Bullough, "The Continental Background of the Reform," pp. 20–36; Christopher Hohler, "Some Service Books of the Later Saxon Church," pp. 60–83]; Sweet, Henry, ed. *King Alfred's West-Saxon Version of Gregory's Pastoral Care.* EETS o.s. 45, 50. London: Trübner, 1871–72. Repr. with corrections by N.R. Ker. London: Oxford University Press, 1958; Wieland, Gernot R. "The Anglo-Saxon Manuscripts of Prudentius's *Psychomachia.*" *ASE* 16 (1987): 213–31.

See also Abbo; Alcuin; Anglo-Latin Literature to 1066; Asser; Benedict of Aniane; Benedictine Reform; *Genesis,* Old Saxon; *Genesis A* and *B;* Paul the Deacon; Penitentials; Prudentius; *Regularis concordia;* Theodulf

Literary Influences: Classical
Anglo-Saxon Period

If we were dependent solely on the evidence of surviving manuscript copies from the Anglo-Saxon period for our knowledge of the extent to which classical texts were available and being read in the England of that time, then the list of texts that we would be able to compile would be small indeed. From the period before ca. 900 we would be able to cite only Pliny, Cicero *(Aratea),* Pompeius Trogus (via Justinus's *Epitome),* and commentaries on Virgil by Servius, though the scholar Alcuin's description of the library at York refers to works not merely by these three (assuming that in giving the name "Pompeius" Alcuin is referring to the Pompeius Trogus *Epitome),* but also by Virgil himself, Statius, Lucan, and a number of grammarians including Aelius Donatus.

Moving on to the late 9th and the 10th centuries, we would be able to confirm the presence of texts of Statius *(Thebaid),* Virgil, and the grammarian Aelius Donatus, and to add to our list poetical works by Ovid *(Ars amatoria),* Juvenal, and Persius *(Satirae).* Assignable to the first part of the 11th century are manuscripts of Hyginus's *Poeticon astronomicon,* medical texts by Pseudo-Apuleius, Pseudo-Dioscorides, and Sextus Placitus, and possibly also the *Collectanea*

of Solinus and Vegetius's *Epitome rei militaris,* though the two last-named manuscript copies may not have been written until after the Norman Conquest. Considered late-11th-century and thus certainly post-Conquest are copies of Avianus *(Fabulae),* Cicero *(De officiis),* Seneca *(De clementia),* Statius *(Achilleis),* and Vitruvius *(De architectura).*

These are all Latin texts. Of the Greek texts available in England before the Conquest we know almost nothing—though it seems likely that a substantial portion, if not all, of them would have been the work of the Greek Church Fathers. However, although there was clearly a far greater readership for Christian Latin writings than for pagan ones (Bede likens Christians who made use of pagan writings to Israelites going to the blacksmith of the Philistines to sharpen their iron tools), the classical knowledge of at least some Anglo-Saxons seems in fact to have been substantial. Surviving Latin and vernacular works demonstrate familiarity with a range of major poets and prose writers, though sometimes at second hand, through such authors as Isidore, Macrobius, Martianus Capella, Orosius, Servius, Jerome, and Augustine and in particular through illustrative quotations in the writings of Latin grammarians, both classical and postclassical. (Alcuin is excluded from the discussion of Anglo-Saxon Latin writers below, since almost all his writing and possibly much of his reading of classical texts was done on the Continent, though including Alcuin would allow the addition of Valerius Maximus, Aulus Gellius, and Tacitus to the list.) So of Bede's citations or echoes of Cato, Cicero, Donatus, Eutropius, Horace, Julius Africanus, Livy, Lucan, Lucilius, Lucretius, Martial, Ovid, Plato, Plautus, Pliny, Pompeius (Festus), Propertius, Sallust, Solinus, Suetonius, Terence, Varro, Vegetius, and even the much-quoted Virgil, the great majority can be shown to be based on materials available to him through secondary sources, and in most cases there is insufficient evidence to suggest any first-hand knowledge of any of the works from which they are ultimately derived. Indeed it is only from Eutropius, Pliny, Vegetius, and Solinus that material is used in such a way that direct knowledge seems unquestionable.

Some acquaintance with classical poets is also shown by minor Anglo-Saxon writers in Latin, with, for instance, an anonymous 10th-century poet of the time of Æthelstan echoing Horace, and with Ovid and Virgil quoted or echoed in the 7th and 8th centuries by Tatwine, Boniface, Lul, and Æthelwold (though material from Horace and Martial in the works of Eddi, Milret, and Boniface is probably derived at second hand, while Boniface and Tatwine are heavily indebted to the grammarians).

The 7th-century scholar and poet Aldhelm, in contrast, seems to have had firsthand knowledge of Virgil, whom he cites freely in his work on meter and who also influenced his diction in his poem *De virginitate.* Other of the quotations with which his work is liberally sprinkled are from Ovid *(Metamorphoses),* Juvenal, Lucan *(Pharsalia),* Cicero *(In Catiline* and *In Verrem),* Claudian (both *Consulatus iii Honorii* and *Epithalamium Laurenti*), Persius, Pliny, Seneca *(Agamemnon),* Servius, Solinus, Suetonius, Terence *(Phormio* and *Adelphaei),* and Aelius Donatus *(Vita Virgili).* Aldhelm is also greatly indebted to the grammarians of the imperial period and their successors—Audax, Donatus, Pompeius, Phocas, Victorinus, Sergius, and Priscian—and it is from their works rather than from the originals that he appears to have derived material from Lucretius, Cicero, Sallust, and Ennius (though his knowledge of Julius Africanus has come to him via Jerome).

Despite the fact that some quotations from classical authors found in Latin writings of the Anglo-Saxon period seem to have been taken from secondary sources all the above identifications can be made with reasonable confidence, on the grounds of verbal identity. Far more difficult to pin down are the precise sources of classical material in vernacular texts, where sense-for-sense, not word-for-word, renderings are the norm. And in the case of writers like Ælfric and Byrhtferth (a user of both Latin and OE in his *Enchiridion*) this material can generally be shown to have reached them via grammarians, commentary writers, and encyclopedists, such as Donatus, Macrobius, Priscian, and Isidore, or via their own countrymen Aldhelm and Bede. Medical texts owe much to Latin compilations, among which Pseudo-Apuleius, Pseudo-Dioscorides, and Sextus Placitus figure prominently.

However, even here the list of classical texts from which material has been drawn is impressive—not the least because it is derived almost exclusively from the work of two writers: King Alfred and his anonymous contemporary the translator of Orosius's *History against the Pagans,* writers who have made substantial alterations and additions to their primary sources, 5th-century Latin works that themselves have drawn more or less heavily on classical texts.

In Alfred's Boethius some of this additional material can be traced to a version of the *Liber de viris illustribus,* possibly also Tacitus *(Annals),* Macrobius *(In somnium Scipionis),* Pliny (perhaps via Solinus) and Valerius Maximus, with mythological material from Virgil *(Aeneid* and *Georgics),* Servius on Virgil, and Ovid *(Metamorphoses).* In the case of the OE Orosius, details of military stratagems are derived from Livy, Valerius Maximus, Sallust, and Frontinus, and certain incidents in the life of Alexander the Great from Quintus Curtius. Also used is Pliny. Other possible sources include Velleius Paterculus, Eutropius, Florus, Festus, Solinus, Suetonius, and the *Liber de viris illustribus.* However, the style of translation is such that it is often not possible to determine which of a range of possible sources has in any given case been used—or indeed whether some of the material might have come from a lost commentary on the primary source, or even (as can be demonstrated with respect to a quotation from Ennius) from material interpolated in that primary source. So, for instance, information about Theseus at Marathon may have been derived from either Pomponius Mela or the postclassical Lactantius Placidus *(Commentary on the Thebaid of Statius),* a handful of details concerning the Rape of the Sabines from Ovid's *Fasti,* either direct or via scholia (learned annotations) on Juvenal or on Lucan, information about the Amazons and about Nectanebus from Julius Valerius directly or via Jordanes or Servius (for the Amazons) and Fulgentius or Lucan scholia (for Nectanebus), while knowledge of Regulus's oath could come from a wide range of sources including Livy, the *Liber*

de viris illustribus, Silius Italicus, Eutropius, and Augustine. Whatever the route, however, it is clear from those contexts, vernacular and Latin, that a range of material from classical sources was available and classical texts were being read in Anglo-Saxon England throughout the period after the Conversion and up to the Norman Conquest.

Middle English Period

The ME contribution to the classical tradition begins and nearly ends with Chaucer and Gower. From the 12th century, when the court of Henry II became a center of Latin culture, through the 14th, when "classicizing friars" at Oxford and Cambridge incorporated ancient mythology and moral philosophy into their sermons and commentaries, a tradition of classical learning was maintained. But early ME writing, though many of its practitioners certainly had some classical education, adapts itself to the cultural horizons of its audience and shows no sign of the influence of ancient literature. *The Owl and the Nightingale* (ca. 1200) deploys an ultimately classical rhetoric but is devoid of classical reference. Parallels, but no clear connection, have been discovered between the similes of Laȝamon's *Brut* (ca. 1200–25?) and those of the *Aeneid.* If the wolf and ram who swim side by side in the Flood narrative of *Cursor Mundi* 1785–86 (ca. 1300) recall the flood in Ovid's *Metamorphoses* 1.304, the allusion remains a solitary flowering.

Even poems on classical themes have nonclassical models. *Kyng Alisaunder* (early 14th century) echoes the learned Latin *Alexandreis* of Walter of Châtillon (ca. 1175), but its principal source is the Anglo-Norman *Roman de toute chevalerie* (late 12th century). The composer of *Sir Orfeo* (early 14th century) must have known Boethius's lyric on Orpheus and Eurydice, and his treatment of Orfeo's music probably borrows from Latin commentary on Boethius's *Consolation,* but his artistry consists largely in his transmutation of the story into the terms of Celtic mythology. To Langland's *Piers Plowman* ancient culture contributes only scraps from the *Distichs* of Cato, a standard primer text, and a single echo of Juvenal (B.14.304; cf. Juvenal, *Satire* 10.22). Even the cultivated poet of *Pearl* and *Sir Gawain and the Green Knight* gives no clear evidence of borrowing from ancient sources, though traces of early Virgil commentary have been detected in the "historical" opening of *Sir Gawain,* and some of that poem's reflections on the uncertainty of human life have been traced, perhaps via an intermediary source, to Seneca.

In this sparse setting the achievement of Chaucer and Gower is all the more impressive. Both addressed an educated audience and saw themselves as writing in the tradition of the ancient *auctores,* taking their cue from the French poets Jean de Meun and Guillaume de Machaut and in Chaucer's case Boccaccio and Dante. Chaucer was one of the most learned English laymen of his day. His considerable knowledge of ancient philosophy is difficult to trace to particular sources beyond the omnipresent Boethius, but he knew thoroughly the major classical Latin poets and the commentary traditions associated with them. He was also steeped in medieval vernacular poetry, French and Italian, and his poems depend on an interplay between the classical and the medieval courtly tradition. Thus *The House of Fame* (ca. 1380?) incorporates into a Virgilian account of Aeneas and Dido a feminine perspective, derived from Ovid's *Heroides,* that reflects the medieval tradition of adapting classical themes to the mode of romance. *Troilus and Criseyde* and the *Knight's Tale* infuse the love stories of Boccaccio's classicizing *Filostrato* and *Teseida* with a darker view of human experience that evokes Virgil and Statius. Virtually every classical reference in Chaucer requires recourse to an ancient text for its full interpretation, and this is true also for Gower, whose learning, if more conventional, is hardly less wide-ranging, and whose *Confessio Amantis* (1390) shows a deep appreciation of Ovid. Together the two poets created an English poetry capable of claiming a place in the European classical tradition.

Most 15th-century poetry shows little interest in this aspect of Chaucer and Gower. Despite the example of Chaucer's *Troilus* the *Laud Troy Book* and *The Destruction of Troy* (both ca. 1400) ignore classical poetry (the Laud poem includes a vague citation of Statius's *Achilleid,* a common school text). Their model is the Latin "Trojan History" of Guido delle Colonne (1287), itself a reworking of the *Roman de Troie* of Benoît de Sainte-Maure (ca. 1165) and ultimately of the late-antique writers "Dares Phrygius" and "Dictys Cretensis," who claim to present pre-Homeric, warrior's-eye accounts of the Trojan War, truer than those of Homer, Virgil, and Ovid. John Lydgate's *Troy Book* (1412–20) likewise follows Guido, though Lydgate also emulates Chaucer's *Troilus,* drawing covertly on Ovid for classicizing detail. His *Siege of Thebes* (ca. 1420–21) is based on the French *Roman de Thebes* rather than on Statius, but cites Seneca's *Oedipus* and Martianus Capella.

Lydgate's appreciation of things classical grew over the course of his long career. Though the *Troy Book* follows Guido in repudiating the authority of ancient poetry and vehemently condemns the pagan pantheon (4.6948–90), *The Fall of Princes* (1431–38), based on Boccaccio, displays an appreciative interest in ancient religion and includes extended praise of Ovid and Virgil (4.64–98). Lydgate expands several stories with Ovidian material and incorporates Ovid's tale of Canace and Machareus.

The Fall of Princes also commends the devotion to "bookis of antiquite" of Lydgate's patron, Duke Humphrey of Gloucester (1.395–98), the best known of a number of bibliophiles whose support for classical studies provided an avenue for the entry of Italian humanism into England. His commissioning of Latin translations of the *Republic* of Plato and Aristotle's *Politics* attests a renewal of interest in ancient thought, as do the several vernacular versions of the compendium known as *The Dicts and Sayings of the Philosophers* and Caxton's publication of a version of Cicero's *De amicitia (On Friendship),* though the latter, like all Caxton's "classics," is based on an earlier medieval vernacularization. But poetry after Lydgate remains unresponsive to these developments until the end of the century, when the Scottish poet Gavin Douglas produces a translation of the *Aeneid* (1513) that has been called truer to Virgil than Dryden's. In John Skelton, a university man versed in the rudiments of Greek as well as in

a full-fledged humanist Latin, we encounter a poet who, though wary of the extremes to which the humanist devotion to classical style might lead in both pedagogy and literary practice, takes the cultural ideals of humanism largely for granted and glories in the title of Poet Laureate conferred on him by both Oxford and Cambridge. Both Douglas and Skelton were acutely conscious of working in the tradition of Chaucer, and their work confirms his importance to the growth of an English classical tradition.

Janet M. Bately
Winthrop Wetherbee

Bibliography

ANGLO-SAXON PERIOD

Bately, Janet M. "The Classical Additions to the Old English Orosius." In *England before the Conquest,* ed. Peter Clemoes and Kathleen Hughes. Cambridge: Cambridge University Press, 1971, pp. 237–51; Bately, Janet M. "Evidence for Knowledge of Latin Literature in Old English." In *Sources of Anglo-Saxon Culture,* ed. Paul E. Szarmach, with Virginia Darrow Oggins. Studies in Medieval Culture 20. Kalamazoo: Medieval Institute, 1986, pp. 35–51; Bately, Janet M. "'Those Books That Are Most Necessary for All Men to Know': The Classics and Late Ninth-Century England—A Reappraisal." In *The Classics in the Middle Ages,* ed. A.S. Bernardo and S. Levin. MRTS 69. Binghamton: MRTS, 1990, pp. 45–78; Bolton, Diane K. "The Study of the *Consolation of Philosophy* in Anglo-Saxon England." *Archives d'histoire doctrinale et littéraire du Moyen Age* 44 (1978 for 1977): 33–78; Brown, T. Julian. "An Historical Introduction to the Use of Classical Latin Authors in the British Isles from the Fifth to the Eleventh Century." *Settimane* (Spoleto) 22 (1975): 239–99. Repr. in *A Palaeographer's View,* ed. Janet M. Bately et al. London: Harvey Miller, 1993, pp. 141–77; Cameron, M.L. "The Sources of Medical Knowledge in Anglo-Saxon England." *ASE* 11 (1983): 135–55; Gneuss, Helmut. "A Preliminary List of Manuscripts Written or Owned in England up to 1100." *ASE* 9 (1981): 1–60; Hunter Blair, Peter. "From Bede to Alcuin." In *Famulus Christi,* ed. Gerald Bonner. London: SPCK, 1986, pp. 75–97; Irvine, Martin. "Bede the Grammarian and the Scope of Grammatical Studies in 8th c Northumbria." *ASE* 15 (1986): 15–44; Laistner, M.L.W. "The Library of the Venerable Bede." In *Bede: His Life, Times and Writings,* ed. A. Hamilton Thompson. Oxford: Clarendon, 1935. Repr. New York: Russell & Russell, 1966, pp. 237–66; Lapidge, Michael. "Surviving Booklists from Anglo-Saxon England." In *Learning and Literature in Anglo-Saxon England,* ed. Michael Lapidge and Helmut Gneuss. Cambridge: Cambridge University Press, 1985, pp. 33–89; Law, Vivien. "The Study of Latin Grammar in Eighth-Century Southumbria." *ASE* 12 (1983): 43–71; Ogilvy, J.D.A. *Books Known to the English.* Cambridge: Mediaeval Academy of

America, 1967; Wittig, Joseph S. "King Alfred's Boethius and Its Latin Sources: A Reconsideration." *ASE* 11 (1983): 157–98.

MIDDLE ENGLISH PERIOD
Benson, C. David. *The History of Troy in Middle English Literature.* Woodbridge: Brewer, 1980; Bolgar, R.R. *The Classical Heritage and Its Beneficiaries.* Cambridge: Cambridge University Press, 1954; Fleming, John V. *Classical Imitation and Interpretation in Chaucer's Troilus.* Lincoln: University of Nebraska Press, 1992; Minnis, A.J. *Chaucer and Pagan Antiquity.* Cambridge: Brewer, 1982; Weiss, Roberto. *Humanism in England in the Fifteenth Century.* 2d ed. Oxford: Blackwell, 1957.

See also Ælfric; Alcuin; Aldhelm; Anglo-Latin Literature after 1066; Anglo-Latin Literature to 1066; Boethius; Caxton; Chaucer; Douglas; Gower; Grammatical Treatises; Literary Influences: Medieval Latin; Lydgate; Matter of Antiquity; Orosius; Scientific and Medical Writings; Schools; Skelton; Tacitus

Literary Influences: French

The influence of French on ME literature is immense; it affected not only the kinds of writing that have survived but also the language they were written in. With the Norman Conquest (1066) and for at least the next two centuries French was the language of the nobility in England. During this time English continued to be spoken by the common people, but it seems that by the 13th century many in the middle class were comfortable with French as well. Inevitably French forms began to modify English pronunciation, vocabulary, and grammar.

Almost at once, however, linguistic and political pressure also began to alter the Norman French originally spoken in England. By the turn of the 13th century we hear of English children sent to France to rid them of their barbarous native French. After 1204, when England lost Normandy, the English nobility became increasingly insular: no one could hold lands in both countries after 1244. All these conditions favored the increasing use of English not only as a spoken but as a literary language; a large number of French words began to enter English at this time. By the second half of the 13th century most of the aristocracy spoke English; by the start of the 14th century it was the everyday language of almost everyone in England.

Yet French remained the official language of the court, parliament, law courts, public records, and town councils well into the 14th century, and in some cases beyond; it was also the international language of diplomacy, commerce, chivalry, and culture throughout the Middle Ages. Almost all the literature in ME that survives (an important qualification) reflects the influence of French models, either by simply translating them or by reacting to them.

Until 1350 ME writings were local and domestic; they were generally either religious and instructional or romances, songs, or chronicles meant to entertain. A large proportion of both kinds of extant texts have sources or analogues in French. The *Ancrene Wisse* (ca. 1215–22), for example, an early devotional treatise, exists in French and English versions so similar that it is difficult to tell which was written first. The English version, which is now considered to be the original, is distinguished by the personality of its author; nevertheless, like most vernacular sermons and homiletic tracts addressed to English gentry, it was probably modeled on French and Latin exemplars. The debate poem *The Owl and the Nightingale* (ca. 1200) also shows the influence of French models not only in its form—it is the first English poem in French octosyllabic couplets—but also in its irony and witty rhetoric, which owe much to French debate poems. Even Laȝamon's *Brut* (ca. 1200–25?), despite its seemingly deliberate intention to continue the alliterative tradition of OE poetry and to avoid using French words, still draws on Wace's French translation of Geoffrey of Monmouth.

As for romances, even the earliest (several of which deal with events before the Conquest) are in French stanzaic and metrical forms and probably were adapted from Anglo-Norman originals. Similarly histories in English, such as Robert Manning's *Chronicle,* or *Story of England* (1338), take French chronicles as their models.

After 1350 the impulse to rely on French models continued unabated but began to jockey with an emerging awareness that the native tongue could support independent, sophisticated literature as well. Little survives that shows there was national pride in English as a language, and England still lacked a significant written literary tradition it could call its own. Anglo-Norman texts continued to be written in England throughout the 14th century; literature virtually meant French literature. But England had gone to war against France in 1337; the skirmishes and battles of the Hundred Years War would continue intermittently until 1453. To rouse national feeling Edward III claimed that the French wanted to invade England and destroy the English language (allegations already made by Edward I for similarly political purposes). The climate of the times thus licensed the ongoing translation of French models but also warranted their transformation into something that began to express English sensibilities in the native language.

At one end of this spectrum between translation and transformation are such texts as *Mandeville's Travels* (ca. 1357), which was written in French, copied into Anglo-French, and then translated into several English versions. At the other end stand the poems of the alliterative revival: a number of them in fact have French sources but are quite English in form and feeling. A figure like Gower occupies a middle position: he wrote in French (and Latin) as well as in English; his *Mirour de l'Omme* (ca. 1378?) returns the penitential tradition to the language from which most earlier English texts were translated. But the one author who best captures the impulses of his age, who embraced French literature as his own yet also established English as an independent literary language, is Chaucer.

Chaucer probably began his poetic career as translator of the *Roman de la Rose;* he may also have composed songs in

French. His early poems (notably *The Book of the Duchess*) were heavily indebted to works by Machaut, Deschamps, Froissart, and other French poets, but by the time he wrote *The Parliament of Fowls* (ca. 1380?) Chaucer had produced a work that not only relied on French as well as Italian and Latin models but was also peculiarly English in its assumption of the audience's knowledge of the workings of parliament. The Prologue to *The Legend of Good Women* (ca. 1386?) again is French in its inspiration but new in its form: it may be the first narrative in English in decasyllabic couplets. Most of the 24 *Canterbury Tales* (ca. 1386–1400) are in some way associated with French literature; each of them, however, is narrated by a character who for all his or her ties to traditional French and Latin estates satire is discernibly English.

Chaucer's genius makes him exceptional in many respects, but his making of works that could rival French sophistication yet seem distinctly English does correspond to the temper of the times. Those who followed Chaucer in the 15th century praised him chiefly for ennobling the English language; not surprisingly, however, writers like Hoccleve and Lydgate continued to depend heavily on French models. Hoccleve's poems were in English, but French and Latin were still the languages in which he composed official documents. Lydgate's *Fall of Princes* (ca. 1431–39) is typical in that it translates a French translation of Boccaccio's *De casibus virorum illustrium*. Caxton's nostalgia for chivalry and courtliness led him to translate French romances (e.g., *Blanchardin and Eglantine* and *The Recuyell of the Histories of Troy*) and conduct books (e.g., *The Book of the Knight of the Tower*); John Bourchier, Lord Berners (ca. 1467–1533) continued the tradition into the 16th century with his translations of Froissart and *Arthur of Little Britain* (ca. 1514–25?). But it is really with Malory's *Morte Darthur* (ca. 1469–70), that we find for the last time in ME the amalgam of French sources and English sensibilities that characterizes the influence of one continental pedigree in England in its most complex form.

Warren Ginsberg

Bibliography

Baugh, Albert C. *A Literary History of England: The Middle Ages.* 2d ed. New York: Appleton-Century-Crofts, 1967; Bossuat, Robert, and Jacques Monfrin. *Manuel bibliographique de la littérature française du Moyen Age.* Melun: Librairie d'Argences, 1951–61; Braddy, Haldeen. "The French Influence on Chaucer." In *Companion to Chaucer Studies,* ed. Beryl Rowland. Rev. ed. New York: Oxford University Press, 1979, pp. 143–59; Burrow, J.A. *Medieval Writers and Their Work: Middle English Literature and Its Background: 1100–1500.* Oxford: Oxford University Press, 1982; Crépin, André. "Chaucer and the French." In *Medieval and Pseudo-Medieval Literature,* ed. Piero Boitani and Anna Torti. Tübingen: Narr; Cambridge: Brewer, 1984, pp. 55–78; Fisher, John. "Chaucer and the French Influence." In *New Perspectives in Chaucer Criticism,* ed. Donald M. Rose. Norman: Pilgrim Books, 1981, pp. 177–91; Legge, Mary Dominica. *Anglo-Norman Literature and Its Background.* Oxford: Clarendon, 1963; Muscatine, Charles. *Chaucer and the French Tradition: A Study in Style and Meaning.* Berkeley: University of California Press, 1957; Salter, Elizabeth. *Fourteenth-Century English Poetry: Contexts and Readings.* Oxford: Clarendon, 1983; Short, Ian. "On Bilingualism in Anglo-Norman England." *RPh* 33 (1980): 467–79 [good bibliographical notes].

See also Ancrene Wisse; Anglo-Norman Literature; Chaucer; Gower; Hoccleve; Hundred Years War; Language; Laʒamon; Lydgate; Malory; *Mandeville's Travels; Owl and the Nightingale*

Literary Influences: Irish

The favorable circumstances of Ireland's geographical proximity, its well-documented historical and cultural connections with England, and its flourishing native literature (both vernacular and Latin) invite investigation of Irish influence on medieval English literature. So far the results have been inconclusive. An earlier approach that tended to attribute to Irish sources anything in OE literature judged exuberant, bizarre, or esoteric (and without alternative explanation) was followed by skepticism about Ireland's cultural achievements abroad and an emphasis on the shared Latin-Christian ("insular") culture of the two areas.

Old English

The stage for Irish influence was set by the mid-7th century with Irish missionaries acting as the primary agents of Christianity and literacy in Northumbria and the west Midlands. Probably dating from the early 8th century are a Latin commentary on the Psalms, of Irish origin and with Old Irish glosses, written by a Northumbrian, Edilbericht; and the "Penitential" associated with Theodore of Canterbury, which incorporated matter from "a little [penitential] book of the Irish." Slightly later Bede drew on Irish computistica (works on calendar calculations), hagiography, and biblical exegesis. Although composed in Latin, these works provide a paradigm for the investigation of Irish influence on OE: the borrowing is usually anonymous or unacknowledged; it is censored by the authority of an English ecclesiastic; it is monastic in provenance; and it is effected through Latin rather than the vernacular. The possibility that the large corpus of Old and Middle Irish literature (ca. 600–1200) was directly accessible to the Anglo-Saxons seems remote. The scarcity of Old Irish loanwords in OE suggests a limited exchange between the two languages, as does the use of garbled Irish words in OE charms, implying efficacy through obscurity.

While in theory Irish influences might operate at any time, in practice certain periods and places were more conducive to such influence than others. Northumbria in the 7th and early 8th centuries would have provided an especially favorable environment, first with the presence of Irish missionaries (635–64), then with the migration of Northumbrian students to Ireland (ca. 650), and finally with the well-documented ties of King Aldfrith (685–705) with Ireland, both directly and via the monastic community of Iona. Another likely conduit would have been monasteries in Ireland with strong Anglo-Saxon representation, notable Rath Melsigi (mentioned by Bede but only recently identified) in the southeast of Ireland, and Mag-nEo ("Mayo of the Saxons") in the west. The latter, founded ca. 670 by Northumbrian monks who had left with Bishop Colmán after the Synod of Whitby (664), still maintained contacts with Northumbria into the late 8th century.

Alfred's Wessex offers another link with Ireland, as attested by Asser, his biographer, and the Anglo-Saxon Chronicle, both of which mention Irishmen at Alfred's court. The OE prose translation of the first 50 psalms (now generally accepted as Alfred's) relies heavily on Hiberno-Latin exegesis. Also documented, through the survival of two Irish Gospel books, are connections between Ireland and the court of Æthelstan. Finally, throughout most of the OE period, the presence of Irish people in England must be reckoned with. Some were teachers, such as Máelduib at Malmesbury (ca. 670) or Colcu at York (ca. 790); others were pilgrims on their way to the Continent who stopped off at the monasteries of Worcester, Glastonbury, Winchester, and Canterbury.

For ease of reference the numerous claims for Irish influence on OE literature are categorized (and selectively exemplified) as follows.

1. IDEAS

    It is argued that Irish missionaries in Northumbria imparted to their converts their own enthusiasm for the vernacular as a medium of religious expression and thereby encouraged literacy in OE; that Irish theological interest in the possibility of salvation for non-Christians finds literary expression in *Beowulf* (through the concept of the natural good); that the Irish concept of exile for the sake of Christ underlies the meaning of *The Seafarer*.

2. LITERARY GENRES

    Claims are made for Old Irish religious lyrics as literary models for Cædmon's Hymn and the OE elegies; for the Irish *lorica,* a litanic prayer to ward off evil, as a model for certain OE poems, such as *Solomon* and *Saturn I.*

3. WORKS, SECULAR AND ECCLESIASTICAL

    These have been proposed as sources for a considerable corpus of OE poetry and prose, such as Cynewulf's *Fates of the Apostles,* certain OE homilies, and Ælfric's version of *De duodecim abusiuis saeculi.* Purportedly the Old Irish saga *Táin Bó Fraích* was a primary source of *Beowulf.*

4. MOTIFS

    Attributed to Irish sources are the concept of seven heavens, the three "victories" of the wind, the number of years Adam lived, and the story of the Flood carved on Grendel's sword and the watchman motif in *Beowulf.*

By the nature of the evidence that they require, claims 1 and 2 do not admit of ready proof, though where they shed significant interpretive light on an OE work (as with *The Sea-*

farer) they gain credibility. The prospects for claim 3 are better, since textual comparison is possible (though weakened by the exclusion of direct verbal correspondences), and when evidence exists that the putative Irish source was independently known in Anglo-Saxon England, as with *De duodecim abusiuis saeculi,* near certainty can be achieved. Claim 4 now attracts the most scholarly attention, especially with the recent identification of a large corpus of Hiberno-Latin biblical exegesis, which is being examined (perhaps too closely) as a potential source for unexplained motifs in OE religious literature. To be convincing such identifications must on the English side reveal peculiarities that can be explained only by reference to an originally Irish context.

Middle English

For this period evidence is meager. The demise of the Anglo-Saxon monasteries after the Norman Conquest also meant the loss of intellectual compatibility with Irish learning that had been so conducive to borrowing. Furthermore Norman rule encouraged the revival of claims by Canterbury and Winchester for control over the Irish church and, with the conquest of Ireland (1169), hostile stereotypes about "the wild Irish," circumstances that made receptivity to Irish cultural influence unlikely. In any case Ireland no longer produced any influential Latin scholarship as it had in the earlier period.

Significantly, in the ME period, Ireland is presented not as a venerable center of learning but as a land of marvels and an entry to the otherworld. Stories on this theme that fascinated English audiences include *The Voyage of Brendan,* Sir Owain's otherworld experiences at St. Patrick's Purgatory, and *The Vision of Tundale.* Claims for immediate Irish sources for another genre of the marvelous, the Arthurian romance, specifically for *Sir Gawain and the Green Knight* and the *Wife of Bath's Tale,* have not been substantiated; most likely the "Celtic" elements in such works have been mediated through French sources. In the ME hagiographical collections Irish saints with accompanying Irish motifs and background occasionally appear, but derived from Anglo-Latin originals. A genuine ME witness to Gaelic-Irish influence is the so-called "Kildare poems," a collection of ME poems emanating from the Anglo-Irish colony in Ireland of the early 14th century.

Ideally claims for Irish influence on medieval English literature should be located within a plausible historical context of time and place, one that also reconciles textual history on both sides. But given the huge gaps in current knowledge of both literary cultures, these criteria will probably remain an ideal to be attempted rather than achieved.

Patrick P. O'Neill

Bibliography

OLD ENGLISH

Carney, James. *Studies in Irish Literature and History.*
    Dublin: Dublin Institute for Advanced Studies, 1955, ch. 3; Donahue, Charles. "*Beowulf,* Ireland and the Natural Good." *Traditio* 7 (1951): 263–77; Henry, P.L. *The Early English and Celtic Lyric.* London: Allen & Unwin, 1966; Whitelock, Dorothy. "The Interpre-

tation of *The Seafarer.*" In *The Early Cultures of North-West Europe,* ed. C. Fox and Bruce Dickins. Cambridge: Cambridge University Press, 1950, pp. 259–72; Wright, Charles D. "Hiberno-Latin and Irish-Influenced Biblical Commentaries, Florilegia, and Homily Collections." In *Sources of Anglo-Saxon Literary Culture: A Trial Version,* ed. Frederick M. Biggs, Thomas D. Hill, and Paul E. Szarmach. MRTS 74. Binghamton: MRTS, 1990, pp. 87–123; Wright, Charles D. "The Three 'Victories' of the Wind: A Hibernicism in the *Hisperica Famina, Collectanea Bedae,* and the Old English Prose *Solomon and Saturn Pater Noster Dialogue.*" *Ériu* 41 (1990): 13–25; Wright, Charles D. *The Irish Tradition in Old English Literature.* Cambridge: Cambridge University Press, 1993.

MIDDLE ENGLISH

Bliss, Alan, and Joseph Long. "Literature in Norman French and English to 1534." In *A New History of Ireland.* Vol. 2: *Medieval Ireland 1169–1534,* ed. Art Cosgrove. Oxford: Clarendon, 1987, pp. 708–36; McIntosh, Angus, and M.L. Samuels. "Prolegomena to a Study of Mediaeval Anglo-Irish." *MÆ* 37 (1968): 1–11 [on ME written in Ireland].

See also Grammatical Treatises; Lyrics; Penitentials; *Seafarer*

Literary Influences: Italian

To speak of the influence of Italian literature on ME prose and poetry is to speak of Chaucer. Although the setting of some early ME religious lyrics to popular tunes followed the practice of Italian friars, and although the alliterative *Morte Arthure* mentions the "vernage [sweet white wine] of Venyce," Chaucer was the only English poet who knew vernacular works of Dante, Petrarch, and Boccaccio well. The fourteenth eclogue from Boccaccio's *Bucolicum carmen,* "Olympia," has been suggested as a source of *Pearl.* Hoccleve made use of Giles of Rome's *De regimine principum* in *The Regement of Princes* (1411), and John Tiptoft, earl of Worcester (1427–1470), translated Buonaccorso's *Dialogus de vera nobilitate* (printed as *The Dialogue of True Nobility* by Caxton in 1481). But all these sources are Latin works; even Lydgate, who knew of Dante and Petrarch, knew them indirectly through the works of Chaucer and Boccaccio, and the Boccaccian works that Lydgate translated (with the help of French intermediaries) were Latin encyclopedias, not vernacular fictions.

Chaucer owes his unique knowledge to the good fortune of having visited Italy at least twice. Even before his sojourns an educated Englishman could have learned a good deal about Italy's people and history; a Londoner with ties to the court might well have heard about a text like Dante's *Divine Comedy.* England maintained economic, political, and intellectual contact with Italy throughout the Middle Ages. Merchants from northern Italy had traded with England since the 12th century; by the 14th a sizable number, mostly from Florence and Lucca, were active in the City of London (over 300 names

have been noted in records from 1360 to 1390). During this time Genoese merchants were continuously present in Southampton. At the royal court there were numerous opportunities to meet Italian diplomats and soldiers. Churchmen and pilgrims had long traveled to both lands; after 1305 many English visited the papal court at Avignon, where Italian thought and culture were discussed.

Despite these ties, however, judging from the silence of other English poets, Italian literature's influence in England was at most subterranean. Even if, as seems likely, Chaucer had learned some Italian before he journeyed to Italy, until he actually had been in Genoa and Florence in 1372–73 and in Milan in 1378, and had acquired copies of Italian texts there, he was probably no more than curious about works he had heard of only in passing.

The literature Chaucer found in Italy deeply affected his poetry. But determining influence remains problematical, not least because we cannot tell how many more works by Dante, Petrarch, and Boccaccio Chaucer read than his fiction gives direct evidence of. Was Italian influence limited only to formal innovations—the decasyllabic line and perhaps the rime royal stanza—or did it inform the new subject matter and techniques of representation Chaucer would adopt in his own poetry? For beyond the interest in fame and pagan antiquity that all three Italian poets show, beyond Dante's way of making perceptible the philosophically abstract or spiritually transcendent, beyond Petrarch's lyric self-absorption and Boccaccio's attempt to marry courtly themes with popular traditions, each poet had a profoundly different idea of what poetry itself was. Did reading works insistently concerned with their own status as literature change Chaucer's own attitude toward poetry?

Chaucer's knowledge of the *dolce stil novo* ("sweet new style"; *Purgatorio* 24.57), for example, and its erudite exploration of the psychology of love comes from Dante. The texts Chaucer knew, however, criticize the kind of poetry Dante wrote in the *Vita nuova,* the hallmark text of the *dolce stil novo* but one that Chaucer never alludes to. The *Convivio* severely qualifies the earlier poetry's philosophical pretensions, while in the *Comedy* Dante rejects all poetry that is not in a real sense written by God. When Dante's subject is poetry itself, his concrete, dramatic presentation of abstract processes or doctrine is inextricably part of a revisionary polemic that definitely would have interested Chaucer. But if Chaucer did not know the *Vita nuova,* how much of it did he implicitly understand?

Determining the effect of Boccaccio and Petrarch on Chaucer's conception of poetry is equally difficult, not only because both differ radically from Dante but also because Chaucer may have gained his impression of Petrarch's poetics only through Boccaccio's works. Direct evidence suggests that Chaucer knew just one sonnet from the *Canzoniere* (*Troilus* 1.400–20); from that alone he could not have gained any idea of the scope of Petrarch's obsessive desire to constitute reality entirely from within his lyric sequence rather than from without. Moreover Petrarch's fixation on Laura as poetic object leads naturally to Boccaccio's view that literature is essentially amoral, be it pornographic or theological. Boccaccio's position is adduced most often from the *Decameron,* which Chaucer probably did not know directly, but it is also articulated in early works Chaucer did use, such as the *Filostrato* and *Teseida.* Does Chaucer's perception that literature mediates between experience and meaning, between science and opinion, ultimately reflect his grappling with Dante's insistence that literature should become a transparency through which God may be seen, and Boccaccio's divorce of literature from its traditional rhetorical function of judging the rightness of actions? One cannot be sure; it nonetheless seems likely that, beyond the possibilities for representation it opened to him, Italian literature's greatest influence on Chaucer was its continuing meditation about poetry itself.

Warren Ginsberg

Bibliography

PRIMARY

Havely, Nicholas, ed. and trans. *Chaucer's Boccaccio: Sources of Troilus and the Knight's and Franklin's Tales.* Woodbridge: Brewer, 1980.

SECONDARY

Anderson, David. *Before the Knight's Tale: Imitation of Classical Epic in Boccaccio's Teseida.* Philadelphia: University of Pennsylvania Press, 1988; Boitani, Piero, ed. *Chaucer and the Italian Trecento.* Cambridge: Cambridge University Press, 1983 [good essays on cultural background]; Ginsberg, Warren. *The Cast of Character: The Representation of Personality in Ancient and Medieval Literature.* Toronto: University of Toronto Press, 1983; Ruggiers, Paul. "The Italian Influence on Chaucer." In *Companion to Chaucer Studies,* ed. Beryl Rowland. Rev. ed. New York: Oxford University Press, 1979, pp. 160–84; Schless, Howard. *Chaucer and Dante: A Revaluation.* Norman: Pilgrim Books, 1984; Shoaf, R.A. *Dante, Chaucer, and the Currency of the Word: Money, Images, and Reference in Late Medieval Poetry.* Norman: Pilgrim Books, 1983; Wallace, David. *Chaucer and the Early Writings of Boccaccio.* Woodbridge: Brewer, 1985.

See also Chaucer; Hoccleve; Lydgate; *Pearl*-Poet

Literary Influences: Medieval Latin

The medieval Latin learned tradition powerfully shaped both the form and the substance of ME literature. From works of medieval Latin literature (themselves modeled on classical forms) by Boethius, Martianus Capella, Claudian, Prudentius, Fulgentius, "Theodulus" *(Ecloga Theoduli),* and in the 12th century by Alan of Lille and Bernardus Silvestris, writers in the vernacular borrowed literary forms (*satura,* debate, dialogue, consolation, apocalypse, vision, complaint); narrative structures (the psychological battle, the cosmological journey); and characters (allegorical personifications, such as Philosophy, Fortune, Wisdom, Nature, Reason, Genius). From Latin school commentaries on the classical authors Virgil, Cicero, Statius, Lucan, and Ovid and the medieval authors Boethius,

Martianus, and "Theodulus," medieval poets learned allegorical moralizations for the myths of classical gods and heroes featured in their poetic fictions (e.g., Venus, Apollo, Jupiter, Orpheus, Hercules).

Most ME writers studied Latin grammar at school, where drill and memorization grounded literacy in a few important texts. Throughout the Middle Ages Latin was the universal language of learning and carried with it a literary tradition on which vernacular poets regularly drew. Some of the most seminal mythological Latin works were contained in the 9th-century anthology known as the *Liber Catonianus* (later developing into a collection called the *Auctores octo*), from which Chaucer, Lydgate, Gower, and other ME poets may have learned their Latin grammar. The *Liber Catonianus* included the Latin *Iliad* (omitted by the 13th century, when the collection had become part of the grammar curriculum), the *Ecloga Theoduli,* Cato's *Distichs,* Avianus's *Fables,* the *Elegies* of Maximianus, Statius's *Achilleid,* and Claudian's *De raptu Proserpinae.*

Probably the most influential source for the transmission of medieval Latin literary theory and fabulous narrative was Macrobius's 5th-century commentary on Cicero's *Somnium Scipionis,* a work that imitated Plato's Vision of Er in its discussion of the afterlife of the soul. Macrobius established two paradigms that would be adopted by later writers—a classification of true and false dreams (1.3.1–11) and a definition of fabulous or fictional narrative as double-leveled (1.2.9–18). Of the truthful dreams the influential enigmatic dream *(somnium)*—which veils its truths with strange shapes—served as the model for what would become the vernacular literary dream vision. In addition Macrobius's Neoplatonic definition of mythological narrative as double-leveled provided the foundation for much medieval fiction: the philosopher, and later the poet, could use stories of the gods to veil truths about the soul from the eyes of base men—the veil, in short, of allegory.

The philosophical origins of the medieval use of allegory to compose fiction and of mythological imagery as a basis for characterization thus strongly emphasized matters noetic (pertaining to the mind or soul). "Allegory," or "other-speaking," suggests a nonliteral mode of understanding and discourse, as do the experiences of the soul released by the dreaming body. For this reason many medieval Latin fictions centered on dramas of the soul, as in Prudentius's 5th-century *Psychomachia (The Spiritual Battle),* an allegorical epic describing the war between the vices and virtues. Other allegories present different conflicts within the soul, such as those between Philosophy (linked with Virtue) and poetry (linked with Fortune) in Boethius's *Consolation of Philosophy.* Martianus Capella's *Marriage of Philology and Mercury* traces the soul's "journey" to wisdom, seen in Philology's (Learning's) ascent through the spheres to marry Mercury (Eloquence), with the personified liberal arts as handmaidens.

Both Martianus and Boethius promote a classical form known as *prosimetrum* (intermingled prose and meter) or *satura* ("mixed style"; literally a "stew"), blending philosophy and fiction as well as prose and poetry. This mixed style, which resulted partly from the diminished value given to poetry and fiction in the Platonic tradition, would be imitated in a number of 12th-century medieval Latin works, including Bernardus Silvestris's *Cosmographia* and Alan of Lille's *De planctu Naturae.*

The Neoplatonic devaluation of the fleshly and earthly also affected the manner in which sacred and secular Latin texts were read, so that the literal meaning was understood as equivalent to the carnal level and the more figurative meaning equivalent to the spiritual level. In addition the devaluation of poetic fiction also encouraged the development of polyvalence in poetic texts, with the "carnal" letter of the text veiling its spiritual significations. This concept of polyvalent meaning combines with the notion of the soul drama in one of the most common forms of fabulous narrative in the Middle Ages: the allegorical vision with two or more speakers engaged in conversation, often in a way that can be interpreted as signifying an interior struggle, mental or psychological.

These narratives take several shapes, from the Platonic dialogue between an instructor and pupil (as transmitted by Cicero and Lucian); the debate or *disputatio* (derived from the pastoral eclogue and bolstered by the *Ecloga Theoduli* and later Peter Abelard's scholastic *Sic et non*); and the multivoiced "parliament" or "assembly." These discursive forms dominated learned Latin works of the 12th and 13th centuries and allowed for a wide variety of subject matter—for example, Bernardus's *Cosmographia* (a cosmological epic journey describing the creation of the first human soul and body); Alan of Lille's *De planctu Naturae* (a complaint on human sexual and spiritual degeneration) and *Anticlaudianus* (an epic describing a celestial journey and a battle of virtues and vices); and Jean de Hanville's *Architrenius* (a satiric complaint on the lust and vanity of the world that offers the journeying "Arch-Weeper" the prospect of marriage to Moderation).

This same philosophical concept and discursive method affected later ME narratives that depicted the authorial persona as ignorant, despairing, or grieving, like "Boethius" or "Alanus"—"Chaucer," "John Gower," "Will Langland." Both the Latin and vernacular personas required magisterial instruction or divine consolation in the dialogic vision, whether from Latin authorities like Philosophy or Virgil or from Chaucer's learned Eagle, the priest Genius, or various psychological faculties (Reason, Imaginatyf, Anima). Although many ME poems continued the genre of the dialogic allegorical vision—*Pearl,* Chaucer's dream visions, the *Confessio Amantis, Piers Plowman, The Parliament of the Three Ages, The Kingis Quair, The Assembly of Gods*—others retained the scholastic flavor of the debate, as in *The Owl and the Nightingale, The Debate between the Body and Soul,* and *Winner and Waster.*

The Stoic tradition also influenced medieval Latin literary practice, thereby affecting vernacular literature as well. Greek Stoic philosophers had defended Homer by offering allegorical moralizations of the gods in his works; this classical practice was encouraged by medieval Latin scholars like Alan of Lille and the French satiric poet Jean de Meun in his continuation of the *Roman de la Rose.* Informing both imagery and characterization, allegorized conceptions of the classical gods strongly shaped the mythological fictions of ME poets, especially Chaucer, Gower, Lydgate, Henryson, and Dunbar.

On a more particular level various medieval Latin works and forms provided source material for individual vernacular works. The Goliards, with their bawdy and satiric songs, contributed to a larger tradition of Latin satire and complaint that continued in the vernacular; the themes and imagery of Latin hymns are often reflected in vernacular religious lyrics; the Latin liturgy plays an important role in the development of medieval drama. The medieval Troy story was derived from early Latin accounts by "Dares Phrygius" and "Dictys Cretensis," elaborated by Joseph of Exeter's epic *Frigii Daretis Ylias.* These accounts, and their later French and Italian reflexes, linked Troy and Britain through Brutus, the eponymous founder of Britain and descendant of Aeneas; they thus appealed to writers of both Arthurian and Trojan narratives (e.g., *Sir Gawain and the Green Knight, Troilus and Criseyde*). Collections of saints' legends like the *Legenda aurea* inspired Chaucer's ironic *Legend of Good Women,* whose heroines were drawn from classical or mythological rather than hagiographical sources.

Other long Latin works that influenced ME literature to some extent include manuals of rhetoric like Geoffrey of Vinsauf's *Poetria nova;* encyclopedias of science like the *Secreta secretorum;* political, philosophical, and pedagogical works like John of Salisbury's *Policraticus* or *Metalogicon;* travel books like Gerald of Wales's *Journey to Wales;* and Andreas Capellanus's codification of courtly love, *De arte honeste amandi,* a reworking of Ovid's *Ars amatoria.*

Jane Chance

Bibliography

Benson, Larry D., gen. ed. *The Riverside Chaucer.* 3d ed. Boston: Houghton Mifflin, 1987, pp. 781–90 [a convenient list of editions and translations of many influential medieval Latin literary works]; Chance, Jane. *Medieval Mythography: From Roman North Africa to the School of Chartres,* A.D. *433–1177.* Gainesville: University of Florida Press, 1994; Chance, Jane. *The Mythographic Chaucer: The Fabulation of Sexual Politics.* Minneapolis: University of Minnesota Press, 1995; Curtius, Ernst Robert. *European Literature and the Latin Middle Ages.* Trans. Willard R. Trask. Bollingen Series 36. New York: Pantheon, 1953; Dronke, Peter. *Medieval Latin and the Rise of European Love-Lyric.* 2d ed. 2 vols. Oxford: Clarendon, 1968; Dronke, Peter, and Jill Mann. "Chaucer and the Medieval Latin Poets." In *Writers and Their Background: Geoffrey Chaucer,* ed. Derek Brewer. London: Bell, 1974, pp. 154–83; Lewis, C.S. *The Allegory of Love: A Study in Medieval Tradition.* London: Oxford University Press, 1936 [see esp. pp. 44–111]; Lewis, C.S. *The Discarded Image: An Introduction to Medieval and Renaissance Literature.* Cambridge: Cambridge University Press, 1964 [see esp. pp. 45–91]; Lynch, Kathryn L. *The High Medieval Dream Vision: Poetry, Philosophy, and*

Literary Form. Stanford: Stanford University Press, 1988; Raby, F.J.E. *A History of Secular Latin Poetry in the Middle Ages.* 2 vols. Oxford: Clarendon, 1934; Simpson, James. *Sciences and the Self in Medieval Poetry: Alan of Lille's "Anticlaudianus" and John Gower's "Confessio Amantis."* Cambridge: Cambridge University Press, 1995.

See also Allegory; Anglo-Latin Literature after 1066; Bible in ME Literature; Boethius; Chronicles; Courtly Love; Debate Poems; Drama, Latin Liturgical; Dream Vision; Hagiography; Literary Influences: Classical; Liturgy; Lyrics; Matter of Antiquity; Rhetoric; Satire; Songs; Translation

Literary Influences: Scandinavian

When toward the end of the 1st century the English people first appear in the pages of history as Tacitus's *Anglii* (*Germania* 40), they are a small nation living at the base of the Jutland peninsula near the present-day city of Schleswig in northern Germany. Tacitus does not name the Danes, and it is not clear how they are to be distinguished at that time from the Anglii. If they were a separate people on the islands to the north and east of the Angles, the two cultures were closely related. Bede, our chief authority on the Germanic invasions of Britain (*Ecclesiastical History* 1.15–16), does not mention any Scandinavian peoples as participants in this conquest. It is likely, however, that some of them were in fact present. On the Continent cultural relations between the ancestors of the English and the Danish had been continuous from the time of Tacitus, and representatives of the two peoples probably served together as auxiliaries in the Roman armies in Britain during the 2nd and 3rd centuries.

The Scandinavian element in medieval English literature is nowhere more pervasive than in the epic poem *Beowulf,* whose characters and events are located entirely in Denmark and Sweden. At many points the legendary-historical details of the poem accord with traditions that have been preserved in other, albeit later, Scandinavian works, inviting our inquiry into the source of Scandinavian material in a work of English literature—material, especially, that is in some cases so allusive as to suggest the English audience's deep familiarity with it.

In the search for sources of literary influence on Anglo-Saxon England from Norway and Denmark the most likely candidates are not only the Vikings, who began raiding in England and settling there in large numbers from the 9th century onward. Literary and historical material from Scandinavia must have come to England with the first Germanic conquerors in the 5th century. Additional elements continued to derive from Scandinavians living in England, from the Viking settlements through the later Danish rule of England by Cnut (1016–35), Harold Harefoot (1035–40), and Harthacnut (1035–42), until the time that such identifiably Scandinavian families in England as those of Thurkill of Arden and Colswein of Lincoln fell from power in the 12th century (Stenton: 618). Both before and after their migration to Britain in the 5th century the English shared with the other Germanic nations not only their languages but also a common body of myth, legend, and oral poetic forms.

Memories of these legendary stories of the Germanic peoples were preserved not only in *Beowulf* but also in the poems *Deor* (mentioning Goths and Baltic tribes), *Widsith* (a catalogue of heroic peoples), *Waldere* (a Burgundian story), *The Fight at Finnsburg* (Frisians along the North Sea coast), *The Rune Poem* (gods and mythic heroes), and here and there in the short poems of the Exeter Book. These works are the oldest written form in which this orally disseminated Germanic material can be found, and it is remarkable that none of the heroic allusions in Anglo-Saxon poetry are to the English themselves.

The process by which oral-formulaic poetry was converted into written texts in England is not well understood, nor even the date at which the surviving texts may originally have been composed in writing. We know that in Scandinavia (mainly in Iceland) these texts did not begin taking written form until the late 12th and early 13th centuries. The English manuscript texts, on the other hand, are considerably older, dating from the 10th or early 11th centuries, antedating the Icelandic manuscripts by at least two centuries. We are unable to speak in the ordinary way, therefore, of the influence of Scandinavian literature on English. Except for some runic inscriptions we have no evidence that a Scandinavian language was ever written in medieval England—or, before the 12th century, in Scandinavia itself. In whatever way the English poets may have worked, they were not influenced by written literary versions of Scandinavian story. The similarities between Anglo-Saxon heroic poems and the earliest written narratives of Denmark and Norway, in such matters as place-names, family histories, historical events, and other legendary, mythic, and poetic material, are best understood not as the influence of one work on another but rather as parallels and analogues, evidence of the survival of cognate traditions from a common Germanic ancestor.

Friedrich Klaeber's edition of *Beowulf* (3d ed., 1950) lists the principal Scandinavian parallels and analogues of the poem. They are also the works that might be cited to illustrate more general similarities between medieval English and Scandinavian literature in tone and ethical values. The most notable of them are the following:

Saxo Grammaticus, *Gesta Danorum (History of the Danes),* written ca. 1190–1210. This Latin work parallels much of the history of the Danes, Geats, Heathobards, Goths, and Swedes in *Beowulf.* It is especially interesting for its story of the Anglian king Offa, the only "Englishman" in *Beowulf.*

Several works by Snorri Sturluson (1178–1241), Iceland's greatest writer. The collection of histories of the kings of Norway called *Heimskringla* begins with *Ynglinga saga,* a mythical account of the origins of the Swedish royal family with the richest concentration of parallels to *Beowulf* (e.g., Scyld, Froda, Ohthere, Eadgils, Ongentheow). Snorri's *Saga of St. Olaf* in the same collection quotes two stanzas of *Bjarkamál,* a poem also known to Saxo but otherwise lost, on Bjarki, the figure answering to Beowulf in the Danish legends. In Snorri's *Edda* there are a number of *Beowulf* parallels, in both the *Gylfaginning* section (e.g., Heremod) and the *Skáldskaparmál* (Scyld, Hrothulf, Healfdene, Froda).

Skjöldunga saga, a late-12th-century legendary history of the Danish royal family, similar in kind to Snorri's *Ynglinga saga* on the mythical Swedish kings but surviving only in an abstract made by the Icelandic scholar Arngrímur Jónsson in 1596. It contains an earlier version of the material in Saxo and in the next item.

The *Poetic Edda,* a 13th-century Icelandic collection of short mythic and legendary lays, about half of which are devoted to the Völsungs (Sigemund and Fitela in *Beowulf*). One poem, *Hyndluljóð,* refers to more than half a dozen of the heroes mentioned in *Beowulf,* and Hrothgar's brother Halga is probably the hero Helgi in *Helgakviða Hundingsbana I* and *II. Völsunga saga,* a legendary saga written in Iceland ca. 1270, closely parallels several of the poems in the *Poetic Edda* on the Völsungs.

Hrólfs saga kraka, a legendary saga written in Iceland ca. 1400, telling the story of the Scyldings (Skjöldungar) after Hrothulf (Hrólfr) has succeeded Hrothgar (Hróarr) at Heorot (Leire). The Beowulf figure, Boðvarr Bjarki, appears in Hrólfr's court, a generation later than he had appeared in *Beowulf.* Based on this saga and on *Skjöldunga saga* is *Bjarkarímur,* an Icelandic narrative poem from the 15th century.

Þiðreks saga af Bern, a 14th-century compendium of legendary history probably compiled in Norway. Among many parallels are to be found the stories of Hama and Eormanric.

Grettis saga, an early-14th-century Icelandic family saga in which the story motifs rather than the history are analogs of *Beowulf.* Grettir wrestles with a Grendel-like monster in an abandoned hall and also has an underwater encounter similar to Beowulf's.

The older view that *Beowulf* must have been composed as early as the 7th or 8th century because an English poet could not have been attracted to these ancient Scandinavian subjects during the period of the Viking raids (9th to 11th centuries) oversimplified the nature of relationships between English and Scandinavians, especially the nobility. For example, the Parker Manuscript of the Anglo-Saxon Chronicle for the year 991, after noting the presence of Olaf Tryggvason (the future king of Norway) at the Battle of Maldon and the death there of Ealdorman Byrhtnoth, states that "afterward peace was made with them [the Vikings] and the king [Æthelred II] stood sponsor to him [Olaf] afterward at his confirmation." By the time of the Domesday survey (1086) every region of England (even in the south and west) had families with Scandinavian names. The political and ethnic distinction between Scandinavians and Englishmen tended to disappear entirely in the presence of the French-speaking Normans. There is no reason for doubting that Scandinavian families in England were loyal subjects of the English kings in the 10th and 11th centuries, as English families were of Scandinavian kings.

The political assimilation of English and Scandinavians in this period was matched by an Anglo-Norse cultural style. Some evidence suggests that poets writing in English during this late Anglo-Saxon period were familiar with the language and conventions of Norse skaldic poetry. A type of Anglo-Saxon narrative, represented by *The Battle of Maldon* and by passages in both prose and verse in the Anglo-Saxon Chronicle, differed in subject matter from the old "pan-Germanic" material of *Beowulf, Deor,* and *Widsith* by concerning itself with more recent and exclusively English events, many of which occurred in an Anglo-Scandinavian context. On this basis it may be thought of as "saga" narrative in contrast to the "epic" material of *Beowulf.* At one time a good deal of saga narrative apparently existed in English prose texts that were eventually lost. The early-12th-century *Gesta Herewardi saxonis,* for example, claims to be in part a translation of a now lost English work by Leofric, a follower of Hereward, the English hero who opposed the Normans in and around Ely. It has much in common with later Scandinavian outlaw stories. Traditional oral poetry also seems to have passed without written intermediary directly into 11th- and 12th-century Anglo-Latin historical prose. William of Malmesbury, Henry of Huntingdon, and other writers cite as their authority the songs *(cantilenae)* about Anglo-Saxon kings and heroes that were still current when they wrote.

Late Anglo-Saxon history was interesting and eventful, involving energetic and ambitious leaders, and it is not surprising that it appealed to authors writing in Latin after the Norman Conquest. Like the older epic material these stories also have their parallels and analogs in later Scandinavian literature. The Icelandic *Kormáks saga* (ca. 1250) mentions the founding of Scarborough and Flamborough in general agreement with an English tradition recorded by Robert Manning of Brunne, who gives the names of the founders as Scarthe (Skarði) and Flayn (Fleinn) in a story he claims to have derived from now lost English works by Thomas Kendal and "Master Edmond" (*Chronicle* 2.514). The Icelandic *Egils saga* (ca. 1240) includes a detailed and plausible account of Æthelstan's victory over a combined force of Scots and Norwegian Vikings in a battle answering to *The Battle of Brunanburh* in the Anglo-Saxon Chronicle (937). Foster-father of King Harald Fairhair's son Hákon, Æthelstan was a figure of interest to writers of Norwegian history.

Events involving Scandinavians in England that were only briefly mentioned in the Chronicle sometimes received much more extended treatment in Anglo-Latin literature. The leaders of the Danish invasion of Northumbria in 866 are in Anglo-Latin sources called Inwære (Ívarr) and Hubba (Ubba) and are also credited with the martyrdom in 870 of King Edmund of East Anglia, an event familiar to English readers in Ælfric's translation of Abbo of Fleury's *Passio sancti Eadmundi.* Some parts of the story were probably borrowed from Danish oral traditions. And all of the traditions associated with Inwære and Hubba, together with their father, Ragnarr Loðbrók, are an amalgam of history and fantasy. The fullest written account of the killing of King Edmund is in Roger of Wendover's *Flores historiarum* (1235), where the two Vikings kill the king in the mistaken belief that he was responsible for the death of their father, the mysterious Danish Viking Lothbroc, a guest in Edmund's court. In a later, rich Scandinavian tradition Lothbroc was identified with the Reginheri (Ragnarr) who is said by contemporary Frankish histories to have sacked Paris in 845. Neither Reginheri nor the figure who combines Reginheri with Lothbroc, Ragnarr Loðbrók, found for the first time in the *Íslendingabók* of Ari Þorgilsson (ca. 1130), appears anywhere in surviving English tradition, although in Saxo Grammaticus and the Icelandic *Ragnars saga loðbrókar* (ca. 1300) Ragnarr Loðbrók is said to have been killed in a pit full of snakes in Northumbria by King Ælla, in retribution for which his sons mounted the attack mentioned by the Anglo-Saxon Chronicle in 866.

An historical personage of some importance, Siward Digri ("the Strong"), earl of Northumbria and Huntingdon, who defeated the Scottish king Macbeth in 1054, appears in both the Anglo-Saxon Chronicle and in legendary sagas whose events parallel the Ragnarr Loðbrók tradition (he receives from the god Oðinn a banner depicting a raven, through which the outcome of battle can be foretold), *Hrólfs saga kraka* (his father is the son of a bear), and *Völsunga saga* (he kills a dragon or drives it away from the Orkneys). The main textual witnesses of Siward's saga are two redactions of a Latin history of the earls of Huntingdon written in Croyland. Like the stories of Loðbrók and his sons, the Siward story reflects an Anglo-Scandinavian literary culture capable of producing legendary sagas generically similar to the *fornaldasögur* (sagas of antiquity) of 14th-century Iceland.

A soberer work of history, deriving from the political and military events of Anglo-Scandinavian England, is the *Encomium Emmae reginae*, written in the 1040s. Resembling a 13th-century Icelandic kings' saga, it is an account of the career of Cnut (Knútr), the great Danish king of England, which was written in praise of his wife, Emma, the daughter of Richard duke of Normandy. Emma became queen of England in 1002, first as the wife of Æthelred II (978–1016) and then of Cnut (1016–35). Two of her sons also became kings of England, Harthacnut (1035–42) and Edward the Confessor (1042–66).

After the Norman Conquest Anglo-Scandinavian traditions were preserved in French verse narratives as well as in Latin prose. The earliest of these was Geffrei Gaimar's *Estoire des Engleis* from shortly before 1140. The original work does not survive intact, the first part having been replaced by Wace's *Roman de Brut*. What remains is essentially a paraphrase of a lost version of the Anglo-Saxon Chronicle with interpolated legends and folklore, much of it from the areas of Danish and Norwegian settlement in the north of England. Gaimar's *Estoire* begins with a version of the story of Haveloc, a legendary king of Lindsey, who in an independent version is the hero of the ME metrical romance *Havelok the Dane* (ca. 1280). Two other versions of this story, one an Anglo-Norman *lai* and the other an episode in the *Chronicle* of Robert Manning of Brunne, also seem to have been independently derived from a common tradition, which attracted allusions to historical people and places. Havelok's name, for example, has been thought to derive from Irish *Abloc*, a form of Norse *Óláfr*, and to refer to the famous Viking Olaf Cuarán (Sigtryggsson), king of Dublin. Much

of the story takes place in Denmark and in Grimsby and Lincoln and is told in a language rich with Scandinavian loanwords.

Well into the ME period the effect on English literature of Scandinavian language, culture, law, and royal reign in England continued to be a matter of parallels and analogues, sometimes remarkably close ones, rather than of outright borrowing. Still largely a matter of oral tradition, such written records as we have of folk customs and beliefs, ballads, outlaw stories, fragmentary epic survivals, and historical narratives based on 11th-century Anglo-Danish historical figures in the Anglo-Saxon Chronicle give ample evidence of a strong continuing Scandinavian presence in English life and literary imagination.

Robert L. Kellogg

Bibliography

PRIMARY

Colgrave, Bertram, and R.A.B. Mynors, eds. and trans. *Bede's Ecclesiastical History of the English People.* Oxford: Clarendon, 1969; Garmonsway, G.N., trans. *Anglo-Saxon Chronicle.* London: Dent, 1953; Garmonsway, G.N., Jacqueline Simpson, and Hilda Ellis Davidson. *Beowulf and Its Analogues.* London: Dent, 1968; Manning, Robert. *The Story of England,* ed. F.J. Furnivall. 2 vols. Rolls Series 87. London: Eyre & Spottiswoode, 1887.

SECONDARY

Chambers, R.W. *Beowulf: An Introduction to the Study of the Poem with a Discussion of the Stories of Offa and Finn.* 1921. 3d ed., suppl. by C.L. Wrenn. Cambridge: Cambridge University Press, 1959; Frank, Roberta. "Did Anglo-Saxon Audiences Have a Skaldic Tooth?" In *Anglo-Scandinavian England,* ed. John Niles and Mark Amodio. Special Issue, *Scandinavian Studies* 59.3 (Summer 1987): 338–55; Hunter Blair, Peter. *An Introduction to Anglo-Saxon England.* Cambridge: Cambridge University Press, 1956; Lawson, M.K. *Cnut: The Danes in England in the Early Eleventh Century.* London: Longman, 1993; Loyn, H.R. *Anglo-Saxon England and the Norman Conquest.* New York: St. Martin, 1962; Partridge, A.C. *A Companion to Old and Middle English Studies.* London: Deutsch, 1982; Smyth, Alfred P. *Scandinavian Kings in the British Isles, 850–880.* Oxford: Oxford University Press, 1977; Stenton, F.M. *Anglo-Saxon England.* Oxford History of England 2. 2d ed. Oxford: Clarendon, 1947; Wilson, R.M. *The Lost Literature of Medieval England.* London: Methuen, 1952; Wilson, R.M. *Early Middle English Literature.* 3d ed. London: Methuen, 1968; Wright, C.E. *The Cultivation of Saga in Anglo-Saxon England.* Edinburgh: Oliver & Boyd, 1939.

See also Anglo-Saxon Invasions; *Beowulf;* Cnut; Emma; Gaimar; Language; Manning; Matter of England; Names; Swein; Tacitus; Vikings

Literary Influences: Welsh

Despite geographical contiguity and a formidable literary tradition Welsh influence on medieval English literature is slight and tenuous. In this respect Ireland, the other major Celtic-speaking culture of the British Isles, provides a telling contrast. Whereas the Irish played a major role in the conversion of the Anglo-Saxons and consequently were well positioned to influence them, the Welsh church refused to work with those whom they regarded as the pagan usurpers of Britain. Nor did relations much improve after the Conversion, judging by the unfavorable references to the Welsh and Britons in the earliest Anglo-Latin hagiography (early 8th century), in Aldhelm, and in Bede. Welsh intransigence about the dating of Easter and related ecclesiastical matters undoubtedly explains much of this hostility. So does intermittent warfare between Wales and Mercia, which continued into the early 10th century. Nor did Wales during this period produce the vigorous learning that made Ireland well known abroad.

Old English

Given this background of cultural isolation and political hostility, it is not surprising that evidence of Welsh culture in Anglo-Saxon England does not emerge for two centuries. In the last quarter of the 9th century a political alliance between Wessex and southern Wales brought Asser, a Welsh monk from St. David's, and Welsh intellectual influence to King Alfred's court. But although Asser played a formative role in Alfred's plan of educational reform and wrote the king's biography in Latin, nothing Welsh has yet been detected in the OE translations associated with these reforms. In the 10th century there is some evidence (e.g., from St. Dunstan's *Classbook*) that the monastery at Glastonbury served as a conduit of Welsh (Latin) influence in Wessex.

In the absence of concrete textual evidence claims made for Welsh influence depend heavily on the theory of an oral substratum of British culture surviving in Anglo-Saxon England and influencing its literature. For example, noting the British origins of Cædmon's name, some scholars have sought to explain his Hymn and poetic gifts by reference to this substratum. Others, arguing for striking similarities in atmosphere, tone, and motifs between the OE elegies and the Welsh poetic cycles of Llywarch Hen and Heledd (9th or 10th century), have proposed that the OE poems are ultimately of "Celtic inspiration." But to raise such claims above the level of mere analogue and literary parallel would require more information about the origins, development, and date of both Welsh and OE poetry than is currently available and probably ever achievable. Symptomatic of the problem of tracing Welsh influence is the studied vagueness of the term often used to describe it: "Celtic" may mean (depending on the needs of the argument) British, Welsh, Irish, or a putative ancestor of all three.

Middle English

During this period evidence for Welsh influence is equally hard to come by. Ironically Wales and the Matter of Wales (preeminently the legend of Arthur) were profoundly influential, but only through the agency of foreign literatures. The process began with Geoffrey of Monmouth's *Historia regum Britanniae (History of the Kings of Britain)*, which aroused in England "romantic curiosity" about Wales as a repository of Arthurian lore. However, when England subsequently developed its own Arthurian literature, the sources and models were French not Welsh. Walter Map's *De nugis curialium (Courtiers' Trifles)* and Gerald of Wales's Latin writings also helped to bring Wales to the attention of English audiences; at least one of Gerald's works was translated into ME. Another possible witness to Welsh influences is the Harley Lyrics (in BL Harley 2253), a collection of ME poems copied in Herefordshire, near the Welsh border, ca. 1330. The collection certainly contains a few Welsh words and possibly a poem modeled on a Welsh folksong; that it may also reflect the influence of Welsh and Irish metrics has recently been argued.

Patrick P. O'Neill

Bibliography

Chadwick, Nora K. "The Celtic Background of Early Anglo-Saxon England." In *Celt and Saxon: Studies in the Early British Border,* ed. Kenneth Jackson et al. Cambridge: Cambridge University Press, 1963, pp. 323–52; Henry, P.L. *The Early English and Celtic Lyric.* London: Allen & Unwin, 1966; Matonis, A.T.E. "An Investigation of Celtic Influence on MS. Harley 2253." *MP* 70 (1972): 91–108.

See also Anglo-Saxon Invasions; Asser; Cædmon; Geoffrey of Monmouth; Gerald of Wales; Harley Lyrics; Map; Marches; Matter of Britain; *Pearl*-Poet

Liturgical Combs

It is unclear when combs were first used for liturgical purposes, but the earliest documentary evidence is provided toward the end of the 13th century. Bishops and priests were instructed to comb their hair before (and sometimes during) the celebration of mass, this practical action also symbolizing the ordering and tidying of the mind. But perhaps the most important occasion was that prescribed by the pontifical of the Roman curia during the consecration of a bishop, following his anointment.

The earliest surviving "liturgical" comb of English origin was found in the tomb of St. Cuthbert at Durham in 1827. Peter Lasko convincingly argues that it is a genuine relic of the saint (ca. A.D. 650–87)

Three highly decorated, double-sided ivory combs of the type traditionally associated with liturgical use can be dated by stylistic comparison with other media, particularly manuscripts. The pierced, foliate decoration of the British Museum comb (MLA 56.2–23, 29) is paralleled in the initials of late-11th-century Canterbury manuscripts (Zarnecki et al., 1984: cat. no. 184). The other combs in London (Victoria and Albert Museum A.27–1977; fig. 86) and Verdun (Museé de la Princerie) are unusual in their elaborate

and crowded narrative decoration, depicting scenes from the Infancy (London comb only) and Passion of Christ. The similarity between the stiff figure style and crowded composition of these combs and the illuminations of the St. Albans Psalter suggests that they were produced in that workshop, about 1120–30 (Lasko, 1972: 235; Zarnecki et al., 1984: cat. nos. 197, 198).

Inventories and texts indicate a large number of combs (some no doubt imported) that have been lost, particularly in the 13th and 14th centuries.

Peta Evelyn

Bibliography

Lasko, Peter. "The Comb of St. Cuthbert." In *The Relics of Saint Cuthbert,* ed. C.F. Battiscombe. Oxford: Oxford University Press, 1956; Lasko, Peter. *Ars Sacra 800–1200.* 2d ed. New Haven: Yale University Press, 1994; Longhurst, Margaret H. *English Ivories.* London: Putnam, 1926; Zarnecki, George, Janet Holt, and Tristram Holland, eds. *English Romanesque Art 1066–1200.* London: Weidenfeld & Nicolson, 1984 [exhibition catalogue, with additional bibliography to 1982 for individual comb entries].

See also Coffin of St. Cuthbert; Eadwine and Canterbury/Paris Psalters; Ivory Carving, Anglo-Saxon; Ivory Carving, Romanesque; St. Albans Psalter

Liturgical Vessels
Pre-Conquest

Relatively little is known about eucharistic vessels in pre-Conquest England. Only two chalices survive, while the abundant literary references tend to be either laconic or perhaps formulaic. A few speak of vessels of precious metals and of jeweled or engraved chalices and patens, and during the 8th and 9th centuries the popes received rich gifts of vessels of Anglo-Saxon workmanship of distinctive style that were recorded in the *Liber pontificalis*. A large Anglo-Saxon chalice and its paten, presented by a royal benefactor, were preserved at Monte Cassino in early-medieval times. In addition to vessels made at home imports of altar vessels are attested: a chalice of onyx mounted on a stem in the form of a golden lion was found in the tomb of St. Cuthbert, and a Greek paten was presented to Chester-le-Street by King Æthelstan.

The appearance of the sumptuous altar vessels can only be guessed at. Recently it has been suggested that the well-known poem of Aldhelm referring to a jeweled vessel in a West Country monastery might refer to a vessel similar to the two great Irish eucharistic chalices of Ardagh and Derrynaflan. These Irish examples carry appliqué glass and filigree decoration, unlike contemporary European vessels, such as the lost chalice of Chelles, thought to have been from the atelier of St. Eligius (Wilson, 1992: 8–9).

The typological evidence of the two chalices from this period that do survive, one from a hoard of metalwork found at Trewhiddle (near St. Austell in Cornwall) and the other

from a grave at Hexham Abbey in Yorkshire, suggests that some Anglo-Saxon chalices may have been in a distinctively insular rather than a continental tradition. The Trewhiddle Chalice is a composite piece made of three principal components: a domed foot with rim flange, a stem and knop in one piece of double-hourglass shape, and a broad cup gilt internally; all three components are riveted together. Incised decoration occurs on the outer surface, and there may at one time have been an applied rim, rivet holes for which occur just below the lip. It is 4.96 inches high and 4.57 inches in diameter at the rim. It was found in 1774 in a hoard of Anglo-Saxon ornaments and coins together with a Celtic brooch and a scourge of knitted wire. The coins provide a date of deposition of about 868. A closely similar chalice was recently found at Lough Kinale in Ireland (Ryan, 1990: 292) together with a matching paten. The Hexham Chalice is made of bronze-gilt. It stands 2.56 inches high and is 2.44 inches in diameter. There is no independent dating evidence for the piece, but

Elbern suggested that it might be 11th-century. The Hexham Chalice has the same tripartite structure as the Trewhiddle Chalice, with the addition of a beaded collar at the bowl-stem junction. A diminutive example, it was clearly intended for use in traveling or for deposition in a grave. The two surviving Anglo-Saxon chalices, in their use of a composite structure, having a large domed foot with rim flange, and in their rather squat proportions, seem to derive from a tradition in common with the Irish communion cups of the period.

Two other chalices have been regarded as having Anglo-Saxon connections—the Tassilo Chalice preserved at Kremsmünster in Austria and the so-called Lebuinus Chalice from Deventer now in Utrecht. The former is considered to have strong Anglo-Saxon influence in its animal and vinescroll decoration as well as its figurative iconography. The latter is traditionally associated with the Anglo-Saxon saint Leofwin but the chalice, made of carved ivory, is clearly a product of the Palace School at Aachen of about 800. Neither chalice shows any Anglo-Saxon or insular typological traits.

Of the other vessels necessary for the altar little is known. Situlae, or buckets for holy water, are mentioned in texts, but how these might be distinguished from secular examples is unknown. No paten survives, and while some of the imported silver plates from Sutton Hoo Mound I seem to have clear Christian overtones, as do the two spoons from the grave, the context would appear to rule out their liturgical function. Here we may have examples of religious motifs applied to secular objects for devotional or protective purposes. Whether they were understood as such by those who used them in 7th-century England is moot. The silver and bronze Ormside Bowl (fig. 97: see METALWORK, ANGLO-SAXON) may well have had a liturgical function (for the ablutions before the eucharist), but this is speculation. Despite frequent references to them, no ewer has been preserved. It has recently been suggested by Wamers that the distinctive Anglo-Saxon vessels, such as the Fejø Cup, may have been pyxes, but this too is speculative. There can be little doubt that Anglo-Saxon churchmen and pious laity endowed their churches with rich and imposing altar vessels and that these were highly regarded abroad—but the surviving material does not reflect the wealth that once existed.

Post-Conquest

Despite the destruction of most of the plate of the medieval English church at the Dissolution of the monasteries in 1537, enough pieces—grave chalices, chance finds of concealed objects, and a few that survived the attentions of Henry VIII's commissioners—have come down to us to enable the main lines of development to be sketched. Documentary evidence, such as inventories, and, from the earlier 14th century onward, statutes and records of the Company of Goldsmiths of London, fill in the details of the picture. Significant workshops existed in the Benedictine abbeys of Ely—where goldsmithing was hereditary in a single family from the mid-12th century to the early-14th—and St. Albans, and in London, where commissions from the provinces were executed. Hallmarking of silver was introduced in the early-14th century, but less than a third of sur-

viving medieval altar plate is marked, and a much higher proportion of this marked plate was manufactured in the late-15th and early-16th centuries than earlier. The use of base metals for liturgical vessels was actively campaigned against by prelates up to the end of the 13th century, but it is likely that only impoverished churches lacked a silver chalice. In wealthy churches especially fine plate was reserved for important feast days; plainer vessels were designed for everyday use.

The typological development of English chalices in the period between the Norman Conquest and the Reformation seems clear. The earliest example to survive is that from the grave of Hubert Walter (archbishop of Canterbury 1193–1205). This small chalice has a shallow bowl, and a broad funnel-shaped stem ending in a round foot. The stem has decorative lobes with engraved scrollwork and foliage. The knop is gadrooned (i.e., fluted or notched). Simple chalices with similar hemispherical or sub-hemispherical bowls, funnel-shaped stem, and round foot, with round, polygonal, writhen, or lobed knops, seem to have been in vogue up to the late 13th century—a small example in Lincoln Cathedral was found in the tomb of Bishop Richard de Gravesend (1258–79) but there is some question that the chalice may have been old at the time of deposition. The silver-gilt Dolgelly Chalice, found with its paten on a hillside, is the most sumptuous of the type to survive—its elaborate lobed knop and stem and fine ornament testify to the skill of the craftsman, Nicholas of Hereford, whose name is recorded in an inscription on it. Similar chalices have been found at Børsa and Dragsmark, both in modern Sweden but in medieval times in a part of Norway where English influence was strong.

By the early-14th century a deeper, flared cup replaced the earlier shallow vessels and the practice of engraving on, or adding an appliqué crucifix, to the foot appears about this time—an early example was found in the grave of William de Melton, archbishop of York (d. 1340). In the mid-14th century the round foot gives way to a form, hexagonal with incurved sides, that seems to be a response to the liturgical practice of laying the chalice on its side on the paten after mass. The earliest example may be that found with a paten during the early-19th century at Hamstall Ridware, Staffordshire. It has a shallow bowl, twisted knop, and faceted stem that continues the form of the foot.

Later pre-Reformation chalices are essentially variations on this theme, with slight modifications to the form of the bowl and, in some surviving examples, the freer use of figurative ornament and of decoration generally. In the late-15th century, for example, cast ornament was added to the points of the foot, and in the 16th century the sexfoil foot appears. The practice of forming the stem to continue the sides of the foot is in part replaced by the fashion for a domed foot. The later pre-Reformation chalices show a tendency toward more straight-sided cups.

Patens in this period fall into two types—those with a single central round depression or those with a double depression of which the inner one is multifoil. Both types seem to have been current from the beginning of the period. Patens, unlike chalices, carried figurative and other iconographical

motifs from the outset. The paten from Hubert Walter's tomb has a single round depression with an Agnus Dei in the center and around it an invocation "Agnus dei qui tollit peccata mundi miserere nobis"; a rim inscription refers to a popular contemporary commentary on the symbolism of the altar, paten, chalice, and communion veil. The paten found with the Dolgelly Chalice has a sexfoil depression with an engraved Christ in Majesty in the center and evangelist symbols in the spandrels. The Manus Dei (Hand of God) and Agnus Dei were popular motifs for engraving on patens. Also popular were quotations from the Psalms, usually the opening lines, perhaps, as Oman believed, derived from breviary responses. *Fistulae* or *calami,* tubes of metal used for the partaking of communion wine, are attested in a number of records from the 11th and 13th centuries, but none survives. A small number of cruets for eucharistic wine and water have survived— a 14th-century example from White Castle, Gwent, is in the National Museum of Wales in Cardiff, and another from Ashby de la Zouche Castle is in the Victoria and Albert Museum, London. Both are of pewter. Undoubtedly the finest surviving ecclesiastical plate from medieval England are the censer and incense boat (figs. 87–88) found about 1850 by fisherman in Whittlesey Mere, Cambridgeshire, not far from Ramsey Abbey. The silver-gilt censer's lower half takes the form of a hemispherical bowl on a round-footed pedestal; the upper half is in the shape of a six-sided tower with traceried windows. The incense boat is parcel-gilt silver and follows the usual form for vessels of this type. Ram's-head finials are taken to be an allusion to Ramsey Abbey. The pieces are probably mid-14th-century in date.

Michael F. Ryan

Bibliography

Alexander, Jonathan, and Paul Binski. *Age of Chivalry: Art in Plantagenet England 1200–1400.* London: Royal Academy of Arts, 1987; Bailey, Richard N. "The Anglo-Saxon Metalwork from Hexham." In *Saint Wilfrid at Hexham,* ed. D.P. Kirby. Newcastle-on-Tyne: Oriel Press, 1974, pp. 141–67; Battiscombe, C.F. "Historical Introduction." In *The Relics of Saint Cuthbert,* ed. C.F. Battiscombe. Oxford: Oxford University Press, 1956, pp. 1–114; Dodwell, C.R. *Anglo-Saxon Art: A New Perspective.* Manchester: Manchester University Press, 1982; Oman, Charles C. *English Church Plate 597–1830.* London: Oxford University Press, 1957; Ryan, Michael. "The Formal Relationships of Insular Early Medieval Eucharistic Chalices." *Proceedings of the Royal Irish Academy* 90 C (1990): 281–356; Wamers, Egon. "Insular Art in Carolingian Europe: The Reception of Old Ideas in a New Empire." In *The Age of Migrating Ideas: Early Medieval Art in Northern Britain and Ireland,* ed. R. Michael Spearman and John Higgitt. Edinburgh: National Museums of Scotland, 1993, pp. 35–44; Webster, Leslie, and Janet Backhouse, eds. *The Making of England: Anglo-Saxon Art and Culture AD 600–900.* London: British Museum, 1991; Wilson, David M. "Sutton Hoo: Pro and Con." In *Sutton Hoo: Fifty Years After,* ed. Robert T. Farrell and Carol L. Neuman de Vegvar. Oxford, Ohio: American Early Medieval Studies, 1992, pp. 5–12; Wilson, David M., and C.E. Blunt. "The Trewhiddle Hoard." *Archaeologia* 98 (1961): 75–122.

See also Coffin of St. Cuthbert; Metalwork, Anglo-Saxon; Metalwork, Gothic; Metalwork and Enamels, Romanesque

Liturgy

An attempt to provide an adequate account of this subject would have to take as its purview the range of liturgical worship at, eventually, seventeen cathedrals, hundreds of religious houses, and upward of 10,000 parish churches, over a period of centuries—in a few cases (e.g., Canterbury Cathedral) more than 900 years. Instead this article aims to supply basic facts about the principal types of services and the books used for them and will be limited largely to the period from ca. 1100 on.

The services of Christian worship conducted in medieval England fall into three main categories. The mass (eucharist) was the central sacramental service, celebrated with great frequency—in many places daily, and in some great establishments several times a day. By the 12th century the principal book needed for the celebration of the mass was the *missal,* which contained not only the words said or sung by the celebrant but also (usually) the texts of the two scriptural lessons and of the four chants: elements that, along with the celebrant's three or four variable prayers *(orationes,* earlier contained in the celebrant's distinctive book, the *sacramentary)* were specific to each liturgical day or occasion. This made for quite a large book in itself, but where the mass was celebrated with music and special solemnity there could also be used separate codices containing the Epistles and Gospels *(epistolarium* and *evangeliarum* or *evangelistarum)* and the music as well as text of the chants *(graduale* or *antiphonale missarum).* The basic structure of the mass and the majority of the texts—especially the central prayer of consecration, the *Canon*—were uniform throughout not only England but also most of western Christendom in the high and late Middle Ages. This mass form, fundamentally Roman, was subject to local variations: often of ceremony, sometimes of texts, and to a considerable degree of the saints whose days were celebrated liturgically. Where such variations come to form an extensive and discrete whole, they are often called *uses,* or sometimes *rites.* In England the principal uses were those of Sarum (Salisbury), York, and Hereford, and manuscript and early printed missals of all three survive.

The regular nonsacramental service goes by various names, of which *divine office* and *daily office* are the commonest, and it consisted of prayers said or sung at specified times of day and night. These *hours* of prayer were officially eight in number: in the standard medieval terminology Matins (in the early Middle Ages called Nocturns or Vigils), Lauds *(laudes matutinae,* earlier called Matins), Prime, Terce, Sext, None, Vespers, and Compline. In theory all clerics of the order of subdeacon, deacon, or priest (including bishop) were obliged to say these services daily, and in monastic or multiclergy establishments they tended to be sung. When sung, these services would require a large chunk of the day and many books: psalter, capitulary, Bible, legendary, homiliary, and a collection of office chants and texts *(antiphonale* or *antiphonarium)* are the principal ones in question. For private or nonchoral recitation of the daily office the basic elements of each of these books could be abstracted and arranged into a compendium called the *breviary* or sometimes *portiforium.* This again tends to be a large book, especially a "choir breviary," which will often contain some chant notation. To become genuinely portable the breviary needs to be split up, the commonest division being that of *pars hiemalis* (the winter half) and *pars aestivalis* (summer half) of the year. As with missals, breviaries and other books for the daily office are classified according to the use to which they belong, but with an important additional distinction: the daily office in monastic contexts had a somewhat different structure, especially for Matins, so that a monastic breviary has to be distinguished from a secular breviary (of whatever use) in a way not necessary for missals.

The third basic category of services is that performed only when occasion requires and therefore termed *occasional offices.* Most of these occasions are sacramental—baptism, penance, marriage, and unction—but other liturgical rites, like blessings of various sorts and the often elaborate services surrounding the burial of the dead, fall under this heading also. The priest's book that contains these occasional services is called the *manual* or sometimes, confusingly, the *ritual.* By contrast the *pontifical* gathers up the services peculiar to a bishop: ordination, confirmation, consecrations of churches, even coronations of monarchs (just in case), and various blessings. As might be expected, it is often a splendid book. The blessings, especially those pronounced at mass by the bishop on solemn occasions, are sometimes detached into a separate volume called a *benedictional;* these become rare after the 11th century.

Instructions as to how the services are to be conducted and how the various items are to be selected and ordered are contained not only in the rubrics of service books themselves but also in separate volumes: *ordinal* and *customary (consuetudinary)* are the commonest of these, while the *processional* includes both instructions and texts for the numerous processions common in medieval worship, especially the Sarum Rite. (The *book of hours,* or *horae,* is used in private devotion, not liturgical worship.)

The regular services—mass and the office—were performed day by day and week by week throughout a liturgical year that was always a complex combination of a temporal cycle (based ultimately on Easter, and thence Sunday by Sunday throughout the year, with different liturgical structures added by Advent and Christmastide) and a sanctoral cycle (based on fixed dates for a large number of saints' days and other set occasions like Dedication feasts or the Sarum Feast of Relics). The temporal cycle, reflected in the *proprium temporum* section in service books for mass and office, was largely set by, at the latest, the beginning of the 11th century. The two most important later elements are Trinity Sunday (the octave day of Pentecost, itself 50 days after Easter) and, from the late 13th century on, Corpus Christi, the following Thursday. But the sanctoral cycle, treated in the *proprium sanctorum* and *commune sanctorum* sections, was in a continual state of flux, with a variety of additions making the calendars of all the secular uses and of the principal religious orders densely crowded by the end of the Middle Ages.

Richard W. Pfaff

Bibliography

Editions of the liturgical books discussed above are listed in the first four of the following items; Harper, John. *The Forms and Orders of Western Liturgy from the Tenth to the Eighteenth Century: A Historical Introduction and Guide for Students and Musicians.* Oxford: Clarendon, 1991; Hughes, Andrew. *Medieval Manuscripts for Mass and Office: A Guide to Their Organization and Terminology.* Toronto: University of Toronto Press, 1982; Pfaff, Richard W. *New Liturgical Feasts in Later Medieval England.* Oxford: Clarendon,

1970; Pfaff, Richard W. *Medieval Latin Liturgy: A Select Bibliography.* Toronto Medieval Bibliographies 9. Toronto: University of Toronto Press, 1982; Vogel, Cyrille. *Medieval Liturgy: An Introduction to the Sources.* Rev. and trans. William G. Storey and Niels K. Rasmussen. Washington, D.C.: Pastoral Press, 1986; Wordsworth, Christopher, and Henry Littlehales. *The Old Service Books of the English Church.* London: Methuen, 1904.

See also Books of Hours; Choirs; Drama, Latin Liturgical; Feasts, New Liturgical; Holy Week and Easter, Music for; Liturgy and Church Music, History of; Mass, Polyphonic Music for; Monasticism; Offices, New Liturgical; Processions; *Regularis concordia;* Salisbury, Use of; Votive Observance

Liturgy and Church Music, History of
Romano-British

The early history of Christianity in the British Isles is obscure. Its dissemination was probably due largely to the Roman conquest and colonization of lowland Britain that began in the mid-1st century. Romanization was, however, apparently not the only means whereby Christianity reached Britain. Writing ca. 200, Tertullian mentioned the reception of the faith in regions of Britain independent of Rome, by which he presumably meant the western mainland from Cornwall to north Wales (and perhaps parts of Ireland as well). Christianity would have reached these regions by way of the ancient trade routes of Celtic Europe. The Christianity of both Roman and Celtic Britain can hardly have avoided being heavily influenced by that of Gaul—the beginning of an important element in British church history that continued to operate throughout the Middle Ages—but there may also have been both direct and indirect influence from the Mediterranean and the East. The Roman withdrawal in the early 5th century apparently had relatively little immediate impact on the British church. However, the Anglo-Saxon invasions, which began in the mid-5th century, seem to have had a disastrous effect; wherever the pagan invaders settled, which eventually came to mean most of the area previously under Roman occupation, virtually all signs of organized Christianity disappeared.

Information about liturgical practices in Britain in these early centuries is meager. At first Romano-British and Celtic Christians probably worshiped in much the same way, observing the customs generally current in western Europe. These would have included a weekly communion service with prayers and scriptural readings preceding the eucharist itself, individual or communal prayer at the beginning and ending of the day (and perhaps at other times as well), and a considerable element of improvisation in the structure, content, and conduct of worship. In the 4th century, when Rome first tolerated and then adopted Christianity, worship in Britain is likely to have become more public and ceremonious and less improvisatory, as it certainly did on the Continent. Of the music sung in these services, which presumably included sing-ing just as continental services did, nothing definite is known. The western church did not begin to notate its plainchant until the 9th century, and it took a further two centuries for the notation to become melodically precise. It seems likely, however, that liturgical melodies may have been disseminated orally, as they indubitably were in later centuries. If this did happen, British congregations may have shared in the earliest traditions of western chant.

By the early 5th century the churches of western Europe had come to share a heritage of customs and material forming a core around which local traditions subsequently grew. Yet after the 5th century the practices of the Roman church increasingly diverged from those of other churches, mainly because—either through conservatism or due to deteriorating communications—Roman innovations were not generally adopted elsewhere. Only in the 8th and 9th centuries did Rome succeed in imposing its renovated customs on most of the western church, and even then some areas proved resistant and others were successful in retaining at least part of their own patrimony. Vestiges of the earlier common heritage survive in the family of liturgies commonly known as Gallican, which includes that of Merovingian Gaul itself, the Mozarabic Rite of Visigothic Spain, and the Milanese or Ambrosian Rite of northern Italy. Traditional Gallican liturgical practice differed from reformed Roman in many respects. In the mass, for example, there might be several prolix Collects rather than a single succinct one, the congregation was addressed more frequently, a prayer separated the Sanctus from the Words of Institution, and there was a complicated ritual for the Fraction. Except for the Milanese Rite little now remains of these Gallican liturgies apart from their texts, because their supplanting by the reformed Roman Rite came too early for their own music to have been fully notated. Such Gallican chants as have survived tend to be either far more ornate than their Roman counterparts, or much simpler.

Anglo-Saxon

Whether or not the famous meeting between the future Pope Gregory the Great (590–604) and Anglo-Saxon children in the slave markets of Rome ever took place—and there seems no good reason to reject the story—the decision to evangelize a heathen race was typical of a pope who considered it his duty to nourish and increase the flock that his predecessors had tended. Although Gregory planned the conversion of the Anglo-Saxons with care and good sense, he cannot have known much about the situation in Britain. In particular he seems not to have realized the extent to which the church had survived in Celtic Britain or have been aware that a few priests from Gaul were already working among the Anglo-Saxons. In fact the first Roman mission, headed by St. Augustine of Canterbury, encountered Gaulish priests as soon as it arrived in Kent in 597, and it came into contact with Celtic Christianity shortly afterward. The complex problem of reconciling the differences between the Roman and non-Roman traditions took well over a century to solve.

The conversion of the Anglo-Saxon kingdoms was accomplished largely by the mid-7th century. It now became possible to confront the increasingly urgent question of relations between the Anglo-Saxon and Celtic churches. The issues were complicated, involving understandable political tensions and such religious issues as the differences between Roman and indigenous liturgical customs and methods of computing the date of Easter. A meeting between representatives of the two traditions held at Whitby, Yorkshire, in 664 opted to follow Roman customs, and these were henceforth observed throughout Anglo-Saxon England, although parts of Celtic Britain and Ireland took up to 100 years to accept them. The Synod of Whitby ushered in a century and a half of stability for the English church. Now firmly established, it was able to cultivate learning and the arts and develop its structure and institutions.

The end of this period of prosperity came in 835, when pagan Scandinavian raiders began regularly to attack England. No part of the country was safe from them, for they sailed up the rivers and raided inland on stolen horses. In 850–51 they began to winter in England, and their piracy turned to settlement. By 878 they had conquered all of the Anglo-Saxon kingdoms except for a small area of the southern kingdom of Wessex, where King Alfred (871–99) led a stubborn resistance. In 878 Alfred resoundingly defeated the invaders at Edington, Wiltshire; the treaty that followed partitioned the country between the two races, the newcomers keeping the north and Midlands and their leaders accepting baptism. The English military revival begun under Alfred continued for nearly a century under his successors. During the reign of Æthelred II (978–1016), however, the situation deteriorated again, to the extent that a Danish dynasty ruled England from 1016 until the Saxon line resumed with Edward the Confessor in 1042.

The half-century after 835 was catastrophic for the English church, not so much for the widespread looting and destruction of property so bitterly lamented by contemporaries as for the chronic disruption of ecclesiastical life. Monasticism suffered particularly severely and may be said to have come to a temporary end. Although the secular church seems generally to have maintained at least a semblance of continuity, in some parts of the country it, too, disappeared virtually without trace. Even in those religious communities that did survive the troubles of the times can hardly have failed to lower standards. Resuscitating the church was important to Alfred and his successors, who seem in this to have sought to emulate Carolingian monarchs, such as Charlemagne and Louis the Pious. The leaders of the English church in the later 10th century—Dunstan, archbishop of Canterbury (d. 988), Oswald, archbishop of York (d. 992), and Æthelwold, bishop of Winchester (d. 984)—concentrated on reviving monasticism. They were helped by the existence of a powerful movement for monastic revival in contemporary France, led by the reformed Benedictine Abbey of Cluny in Burgundy, founded in 910. The Benedictine Abbey of Fleury or St. Benoît-sur-Loire near Orléans, itself reformed by Cluny ca. 930, was especially influential in England, supplying monks to repopulate English monasteries and training English novices for the same purpose. The most important document of the reform movement in England was the *Regularis concordia anglicae*

nationis monachorum sanctimonialumque. As its title—literally "The Harmonization of Rule of the Monks and Nuns of the English Nation"—implies, this was a set of precepts and regulations designed to ensure sound and uniform observance in religious houses. Issued by royal mandate ca. 970, it gives valuable information on contemporary liturgical practices and their background.

Anglo-Saxon churches seem to have been adequately and sometimes generously provided with service books and theological works. The earliest of these must have been manuscripts from Gaul or Italy brought in by missionaries. Some of the books that St. Augustine brought with him to England were apparently still kept behind the high altar of his abbey church in Canterbury until the Reformation; they had gained the status of relics. English churchmen traveling abroad also brought books home with them, although not all can have been as enthusiastic about this as Benedict Biscop (ca. 628–689), who equipped his monasteries at Wearmouth and Jarrow with magnificent libraries collected during no fewer than six visits to Rome. English scriptoria had begun to produce Bibles and service books by the later 7th century, and presumably the production of such articles tended to increase, except during the Danish raids. Throughout the Anglo-Saxon period, however, liturgical books continued to be imported. This involved a large element of chance and must have led to considerable liturgical variation according to the provenance of the imported books. The Lindisfarne Gospels were evidently copied from a Gospel book emanating from Naples; a Capuan mass book seems to have been circulating in northern England around 700; and the main part of the Leofric Missal is a 10th-century mass book from northeastern France.

Our knowledge of Anglo-Saxon liturgy is limited by several factors. Few sources remain from the early period, while the later ones can hardly be said to be numerous. Most of the surviving manuscripts contain only the material needed by the priest (the prayers and prefaces of mass, blessings, exorcisms, and so on), not the entire material needed for a service. The few manuscripts that include any of the choral items either give the texts alone, omitting musical notation altogether, or use early types of notation that cannot now be read with certainty. In the absence of musical notation, which was devised only in the 9th century and remained ambiguous for another 200 years, plainchant melodies could be disseminated only by skilled musicians who could memorize them and teach them to other singers. There are several contemporary references to such singers: James the Deacon, a missionary in Northumbria in the 630s, is referred to as an expert singer; Putta, bishop of Rochester, is said to have taught chant after he retired in 676; in 678 Benedict Biscop brought John the arch-chanter from Rome to Northumbria to teach his monks Roman chant; much later a request from Æthelwold led the abbot of Corbie to send a party of monks to teach chant to their English brethren.

While Bede's statement that Gregorian (i.e., Roman) chant was introduced into and disseminated through England by Roman missionaries appears to be substantially correct and applicable also to liturgy in general, there must have been considerable diversity of practice and a sizable presence of non-Roman elements, caused by the survival of indigenous traditions and the adoption of newer Gallican customs. Anglo-Saxon liturgies seem to have had many Gallican characteristics, and some Gallican ceremonies (such as the anointing of the monarch during the coronation, the blessing of the paschal candle and the new fire, and the *Exultet*) survived in England until the Reformation. The overall shape of an early Anglo-Saxon mass would have been familiar to a modern traditionalist, although there were many divergences in detail. One of the main differences was that those liturgical items that were later reduced to a single psalm verse—the Introit, Gradual, Offertory, and Communion—still consisted of complete psalms, or as many verses of a psalm as were required to cover the necessary action, with an antiphon or responsory repeated after every verse. The Introit might be followed by a litany rather than a Kyrie; the latter, which was introduced by Pope Gregory as a substitute for the litany, took some time to catch on. Instead of a single concise Collect there might be two or three more rambling ones, as in the Gallican rites. Although the Epistle and Gospel were probably recited in Latin, there may sometimes have been a homily in the vernacular. Before the 9th century there would be no Sequence, for the form had yet to be invented, and no Credo, which became part of the Frankish mass only in 798 and was not taken up at Rome until 1014. The Preface leading into the Sanctus might change its text almost from day to day, again as in the Gallican rites. Even the Canon—the most sacrosanct and unchanging part of the mass—might contain variations in phrasing. The Agnus Dei did not become part of the mass until the early 8th century.

Our main sources for later Anglo-Saxon liturgy include the *Regularis concordia,* the Leofric Missal and a number of other roughly contemporary mass books, and several benedictionals containing collections of episcopal blessings. The *Regularis concordia* describes the daily monastic routine in winter and summer and gives detailed liturgical instructions for certain important feast days. The daily schedule includes many features familiar from later liturgies: Nocturns (Matins) preceded by the *trina oratio* ("triple prayer"), Lauds followed by antiphons of the Holy Cross and the Virgin and saints honored in the church, Matins of All Saints and Lauds of the Dead in a side chapel, Prime at dawn, private reading until Terce, the morrow mass followed by Chapter, the conventual mass followed by Sext and None, the midday meal, Vespers, Collation, and Compline. Some ceremonies are set out in especial detail: the Purification, the imposition of ashes, the procession to the mother church on Palm Sunday, the Maundy and blessing of the new fire on Holy Thursday (the latter repeated on the two following days), the veneration of the Cross and the reproaches on Good Friday, and the placing of the Cross in the Easter sepulcher on Saturday. The Easter Day liturgy is climactic, the discovery of the Lord's resurrection being reenacted at the Easter sepulcher (now emptied of its cross) by the brethren in an early example of liturgical drama. Other interesting details include references to peals of bells, a ban on shaving during the first three weeks of Lent, instruc-

tions for the monk on duty in the cloister, and mention of the *tabula*—a wooden sounding board struck to summon the brethren, still used in Orthodox monasteries.

Given to Exeter Cathedral by Bishop Leofric (1050–72), the missal bearing his name consists of a 10th-century sacramentary from Lorraine (where Leofric was brought up), to which have been added a later Anglo-Saxon ecclesiastical calendar and a large amount of miscellaneous liturgical and historical material. Even though it gives incomplete information about the services of Leofric's day (its liturgical contents are limited to the items that the bishop himself would have recited when celebrating mass and carrying out other priestly and episcopal duties), the book displays many non-Roman characteristics. One of the most striking is the great number of proper prefaces; nearly every mass has its own preface, and there are about 300 altogether. Some of the prefaces and prayers show typical Gallican verbosity, where Rome prefers concision. The missal also contains numerous episcopal blessings to be given in mass after the Fraction (the breaking of the consecrated host): a feature of English, Gallican, and Mozarabic liturgies that entered post-Conquest English rites but was never taken up by Rome. There are several exorcisms, some of them lengthy, countering a hair-raising range of eventualities, including bodily diseases, witchcraft, necromancy, attacks by monsters, and diabolic possession. On a more mundane level several turns of phrase indicate that communion was given in both kinds (bread and wine).

A unique monument of late Anglo-Saxon liturgy is the musical source known as the Winchester Troper, dating from the late 10th century. A troper contains tropes, which are expansions of existing plainchant items (such as the Introit and Gloria) through the addition of extra words, extra music, or both. Most tropes are monophonic, like the chants into which they fit. The practice of troping seems to have started somewhere around the lower Rhine about 800, as a means of adding to the liturgy without destroying existing liturgical structures. Troping quickly became popular in the Frankish Empire, where it flourished until about 1150, but it was never adopted by the Roman church; the existence of troping in England is yet another indication of the close ties between the English and Frankish churches. In addition to troped Introits, Kyries, and Glorias the Winchester Troper contains untroped items for the mass (Kyries, Glorias, Graduals, Alleluias, Tracts, and Sequences) and the divine office (invitatories, antiphons, and responsories). Sometimes described as a collection of two-part polyphonic music, it is more precisely a collection of melodies designed to create two-part polyphony when sung simultaneously with the plainchant melodies to which the texts were usually performed; presumably the chants themselves would have been sung from memory or read from another book. Luckily the plainchant melodies have survived in a slightly later manuscript, a troped gradual also from Winchester. However, the notation of both of these sources fails to indicate accurately the intervals of the melodies, so a completely accurate transcription cannot be guaranteed. While English musicologists are understandably proud of the Winchester Troper—the earliest known source of functional polyphony surviving from anywhere—it must be admitted that the music that it contains strongly resembles polyphony in slightly later northern French sources. It is at least possible that, like so many features of the late Anglo-Saxon church, the Winchester music was imported.

Post-Conquest

The Norman Conquest of England in 1066 brought the kingdom fully into the European mainstream, ensuring that it did not drift into isolation. In particular it forged close, multifarious, and enduring links between England and France. In peace and in war many Englishmen had business in France; whether their interests were diplomatic, military, ecclesiastical, or commercial, they could hardly remain impervious to the most sophisticated and influential culture of late-medieval Europe.

William and his successors thoroughly reorganized the English dioceses. Several cathedral churches were transferred to more populous or otherwise more convenient sites, two new dioceses were created, and the peculiar Anglo-Saxon practice of making cathedral churches monastic was retained and extended. Although reliable figures are hard to establish, the parochial system seems to have expanded considerably in the two centuries after 1066. Relatively few new parish churches were founded, but chapels were built in large parishes for the convenience of people who lived a long way from the existing church, and some existing chapels were apparently elevated into parish churches. By 1300 there may have been about 9,500 parish churches in England. In addition to new construction a great deal of rebuilding was carried out, particularly during the second half of the 12th century, evidence of which can still be seen in many churches.

Monastic life expanded greatly in post-Conquest England, as it did throughout western Europe. The total number of English monasteries rose from some 60 in 1066 to around 700 in the early 13th century, reached a maximum of about 1,000 in the mid-14th century, and settled at approximately 900 after the Black Death. The monastic population increased from some 1,100 at the Conquest to a peak of about 18,000 immediately before the Black Death, falling back to around 12,000 in 1500. In 1066 the Benedictine Rule was observed in all English monasteries. Although Benedictine houses continued to be founded, much of the increased vitality of monastic life was due to the advent of new orders of monks observing reformed versions of the Benedictine Rule: the Cluniacs and (especially) the Cistercians. Also important were Augustinian, or Austin, canons, secular priests observing a communal regime loosely based on a rule written by Augustine of Hippo (d. 430). By the early 13th century the impetus of monastic expansion was almost spent, and the initiative passed to the new orders of mendicant friars, particularly the Dominicans and the Franciscans, who reached England in 1221 and 1224, respectively. Two other orders, the Carmelite and Austin friars, arrived a little later.

The foundation of parish churches and monasteries almost ceased after about 1350. The main growth areas of the church in the 14th and 15th centuries were chantries and colleges, which were founded mainly by royalty, the nobility,

prelates, the greater gentry, and civic fraternities and guilds. A chantry was a foundation employing one or more priests to say masses in perpetuity for the souls of the patron and his nominees. Chantries varied greatly in size and wealth, from tiny chapels served by individual priests in parish churches to grand chapels served by groups of clerics in larger churches, and from extremely modest independent structures to imposing complexes of specially designed buildings. Colleges housing communities of nonmonastic religious had been a prominent feature of the Anglo-Saxon church, but they had declined during the post-Conquest period and some had even been converted into monasteries. Between the mid-14th century and the Reformation they enjoyed a revival, their numbers doubling from about 75 in 1200 to about 150 in 1500. Late-medieval colleges had various functions. Many were chantries, but most of these had additional responsibilities, usually in education or other charitable work. The importance attached to maintaining high standards of professionalism in worship is evident in the careful provision made by many colleges for selecting musically skilled choirmen and training choristers; the remarkable musical achievement of late-medieval England was due in no small part to the contribution of these colleges.

During the later Middle Ages the leaders of society tended to make increasingly elaborate provision for religious worship within their own households. It had long been customary for a magnate to employ a domestic chaplain or two to conduct his services and assist with his administration. During the 14th and 15th centuries the numbers of chaplains employed in the greater households tended to increase, and they were often supplemented by singing men (often known as clerks of the chapel) and boy choristers, whose participation enhanced the ceremonial and musical impact of the liturgy. As so often, royalty set the example. Edward III set up sizable chapels within the royal palaces of Westminster and Windsor, and he may also have reorganized the royal household chapel, the body of religious attached to the royal household itself, which was certainly augmented by the Lancastrian kings. Although on one level these developments merely reflect the contemporary reliance on ostentation as a means of enhancing prestige, sometimes at least they may have been prompted by genuine personal piety. They may also have had a political purpose: an explicit rejection of the unadorned worship advocated by Wyclif and his followers.

The Norman prelates who took control of the English church after the Conquest seem generally to have replaced Anglo-Saxon liturgical customs and plainchant with the usages and chant of their own country. Although the scarcity of contemporary documents, particularly service books, obscures many details of this process, the broad pattern is clear: English monastic liturgies were revised following the examples of Cluny and the great abbeys of Normandy, such as Bec, Fécamp, and Jumièges, while the secular cathedrals and their dependent diocesan churches adopted liturgies modeled on those of Norman cathedrals, such as Bayeux, Évreux, and Rouen. These innovations must often have been repugnant to the English clergy, and they were sometimes physically resisted: in 1083 Abbot Turstin's attempt to introduce the customs of Fécamp to Glastonbury provoked violence in the abbey choir itself.

The liturgical changes imposed on the secular cathedrals went hand-in-hand with thorough constitutional revision, defining the composition of the cathedral chapters and the duties and rights of their members and sometimes describing details of the daily nonliturgical routine. Before 1200 most of the nine secular cathedrals (Chichester, Exeter, Hereford, Lichfield, Lincoln, London, Salisbury, Wells, and York) had already received new constitutions, which were subsequently brought up to date from time to time. The constitutional and liturgical traditions that made a religious community's formal conduct distinctive were known as its "use." Essentially only secular cathedrals and the religious orders had their own uses. Such uses were by no means confined to England: those of the religious orders were international, while virtually every cathedral in western Christendom could claim to have had its own use at one time or another, even though this might subsequently have been superseded by the more influential use of another institution. The use of a secular cathedral was followed as far as was practicable, and perhaps with minor variants reflecting local circumstances, by the secular churches of the diocese, while monastic and friary churches observed the use of their particular order, again possibly with small local variations.

One of the secular English uses, that of Salisbury, or Sarum, gradually became preeminent. Salisbury's influence was at first mainly constitutional, later liturgical. Together with Lincoln and York Old Sarum had been in the vanguard of constitutional reform, issuing new statutes as early as the 1090s. During the 12th and 13th centuries several cathedrals, including Lincoln itself, Chichester, Lichfield, and Wells, incorporated some of Salisbury's constitutional provisions in their own statutes. During the 14th and 15th centuries it was the turn of Salisbury's liturgy to be disseminated. The liturgical changes made at Exeter by Bishop Grandisson (1327–69) were heavily influenced by Salisbury, as were those made at Hereford apparently by Bishop Trillek (1344–60). In 1391 Exeter adopted the Salisbury liturgy virtually entire, retaining only a few local customs; London did the same in 1414, as did Lichfield during the time of Bishop Heyworth (1420–47). Chichester, Lincoln, and Wells seem also to have accepted the Salisbury Use, although Lincoln may have retained some individual features. The secular use most resistant to Sarum influence was that of York, which remained independent until extinguished by the Reformation. Hereford nominally kept its independence until 1542, but it already contained numerous Salisbury elements. The Use of Salisbury was also observed in chantries, colleges, and private chapels, by Augustinian houses, and in those English dioceses with monastic cathedrals employing liturgies that would have been inappropriate in secular churches. It also spread to dioceses in Wales, Scotland, and Ireland, and—exceptionally—even farther afield to Braga in Portugal.

The liturgical changes that followed the Conquest chiefly entailed the substitution of Norman customs and material where these differed from those of the Anglo-Saxon church.

Thus, for example, the nonstandard masses for major feasts, the masses for minor English saints, the alternative Collects, and the multitudinous proper prefaces that occur in Anglo-Saxon missals are almost entirely absent from post-Conquest missals. An 11th-century missal from Canterbury (Cambridge, Corpus Christi College 270) shows interesting evidence of revision, in that most of the extra proper prefaces that it originally contained have been subsequently erased. The break with past practice was, however, far from complete. The Anglo-Saxon and Norman liturgies did, of course, have a great deal of material in common, which there was no need to change; some pre-Conquest liturgical items and practices seem to have been adopted by the Normans (but the scarcity of contemporary service books, particularly notated ones, makes these adoptions difficult to trace); and by no means every Anglo-Saxon saint disappeared from the calendar. Some ancient Gallican ceremonies, such as the blessing of the paschal candle and the new fire, presumably survived because the Normans were familiar with them in their own country.

After a short initial period of hostility (typified by Lanfranc's refusal to recognize the credentials of even so revered a figure as St. Dunstan) the Normans softened their attitude to Anglo-Saxon saints, whose feasts appear in some quantity in later medieval calendars and service books, even though they are generally given fairly low gradings. Salisbury, for instance, included about 25 such feasts, four of which were 15th-century additions. Some of the figures thus commemorated (such as Cuthbert, Edmund the Martyr, and Oswald) were of major stature, but others (such as Cuthburga and Kenelm) were less significant, and their survival is something of a mystery. As was common throughout Europe, individual dioceses and institutions might keep the anniversary of a local saint, as London commemorated St. Erkenwald and the monks of Much Wenlock remembered St. Milburga. The Normans and Angevins introduced and promoted some of their own saints, such as St. Romanus of Rouen and St. Julian of Le Mans. Other feasts were added from time to time, following either the canonization of a new saint (e.g., Thomas of Canterbury in 1173 and Hugh of Lincoln in 1220) or an official injunction relating to an existing one. Such injunctions might be international (as with the Visitation, extended to the whole church by Pope Urban VI), national (as with St. Anne, prescribed for England in 1382), provincial (as with St. Winefride, enjoined for the ecclesiastical province of Canterbury in 1398), or diocesan (as with the upgrading of St. Gabriel for Exeter in 1278). Despite the presence of sizable amounts of local material English liturgical calendars continued to have as their core the major feasts observed throughout western Christendom: those of Christ and his mother, the disciples and apostles, the doctors of the church, and the saints of the Roman martyrology.

In all essential aspects later medieval English liturgies resembled those performed wherever the Roman usage prevailed. Mass and the services of the divine office had the same basic structure that they had everywhere; mass included the full and unvaried Roman Canon; the standard Collects, Secrets, and Postcommunions (and in many cases the standard plainchant propers) were used on most of the major feasts; the proper prefaces numbered no more than the nine sanctioned by the Roman church; and much if not most of the plainchant repertoire was truly international. Most of the points on which English uses differed both from continental uses and from each other—such as the grading of feasts, detailed points of ceremonial, the conduct of processions and special ceremonies, the choice of proper chants and readings for particular festivals, the repertoires of hymns, sequences, and ordinary chants, and the versions of individual chant melodies—were traditional and unexceptionable points of variance among uses. Rather than give an extensive list of such mundane divergencies it will be more illuminating to examine some individual features of English liturgical practice.

By the early 12th century troping was going out of fashion, and tropes largely disappeared from continental service books after about 1200. The English uses, however, seem to have retained an above-average number of tropes, although many were discarded. Those that survived were mainly tropes of the Ordinary of the mass. In the uses of Salisbury, York, and Hereford these came to be limited to a handful of Kyrie tropes or *prosulae,* such as *Deus creator* and *Rex genitor* (each use having its own selection), a single Gloria trope *Spiritus et alme orphanorum,* a single Sanctus trope *Benedictus Mariae filius,* and a troped Prophecy sung in dialogue on Christmas Eve. Vestiges of much earlier troping techniques also survived in a few instances in which what had originally been tropes of responsories became independent items called proses, which had the poetic form of the sequence; the proses *O mater nostra* (for St. Katherine) and *Sospitati dedit aegros* (for St. Nicholas) are cases in point. Other now irrecoverable secular uses may have been more liberal in their use of tropes; a late-13th-century inventory from St. Paul's, London, mentions service books containing troped Epistles and at least one troped Agnus Dei. Some English monasteries apparently continued to employ tropes in considerable variety and quantity at least until the early 14th century.

Although processions formed a part of religious ceremonial throughout Christendom, they seem to have been particularly elaborate and impressive in England. They occurred regularly on Sundays and major feast days before high mass and after Vespers, also on some other days, such as Rogation Days, and for special purposes, such as the reception of a visiting dignitary. The members of the institution were arranged in a precise order, the details of which varied with the importance of the occasion. Processions were normally headed by a group of functionaries: virgers bearing wands, boys with holy water, processional crosses, tapers, and censers, a subdeacon and deacon carrying precious copies of the Gospels, the officiating cleric and any singers with prominent solo roles; the rest of the community followed, two by two, in ascending order of seniority, and the bishop, abbot, or other chief dignitary and his attendants brought up the rear. Like its disposition the route of the procession varied according to the occasion. Lesser processions began in the choir, circuited the interior of the church, and returned to the choir; greater processions were extended to take in the cloisters and other parts of the site. On exceptional days, such as Palm Sunday, the procession might travel to a neighboring church or even subdivide and reunite. During a procession antiphons and responsories were sung, and halts or stations were made at predetermined points, where special prayers might be said.

In addition to mass and the canonical hours three types of additional devotion were widely performed in later medieval England: commemorations, memorials, and votive antiphons. Commemorations were complete offices of eight hours—Matins, Lauds, Prime, Terce, Sext, None, Vespers, and Compline—said in honor of a particular saint, usually the Virgin. They had originated as a monastic devotion to the Virgin in the 10th century, were taken up by secular institutions during the 11th and 12th, and began to be adopted by private individuals in the late 13th. The hours of the Virgin form the main content of the books of hours that constitute one of the most beautiful legacies of the later Middle Ages. In the English secular uses the office of the Virgin customarily replaced the ordinary daily office on Saturdays, and the daily offices of one or two other days were often replaced by a second commemoration, normally of the patron saint of the church (e.g., St. Chad at Lichfield and St. Andrew at Wells, but St. Thomas of Canterbury at Salisbury, where the Virgin herself was the patron saint). Memorials were compact services consisting of an antiphon, versicle, response, and collect, in honor of saints or appropriate to particular seasons, occasions, or causes. They were said after Lauds and Vespers, and several might be said in succession. The votive antiphon was originally an antiphon sung by itself, usually as a post-Compline devotion before the altar or image of a saint; the most popular texts in England included *Salve regina, Ave regina caelorum, Benedicta es caelorum regina,* and *Regina caeli laetare.* By the 14th century this devotion often expanded to take the shape of a full memorial with a versicle, response, and prayer following the antiphon. In this format it was frequently utilized by the founders of chantries, who typically required an antiphon to be sung and prayers said daily after Compline on behalf of themselves and their nominees. From modest beginnings in the 14th century the polyphonic votive antiphon became one of the grandest musical forms of late-medieval England, as the settings in the Eton Choirbook amply testify.

The cult of the Virgin flourished exceedingly in late-medieval England, as the magnificent Lady Chapels of many churches demonstrate. In addition to commemorations, memorials, and votive antiphons votive masses were regularly said in her honor, at first mainly on Saturdays but from the 13th century onward usually every day. The Lady Mass, as the votive mass of the Virgin is usually known, had a different set of propers for the various seasons of the year, and the Kyrie, Alleluia, and Sequence might change from day to day. A great deal of late-medieval English polyphony was apparently intended for the Lady Mass, presumably to emphasize the honor in which she was held and to make the best use of the small group of skilled singers who commonly performed this mass. The fact that in some uses it was permissible to replace the Sequence of the Lady Mass with another musical item may also have stimulated composers to provide polyphonic substitutes.

Perhaps the most distinctive feature of later medieval English services was the large amount of polyphonic music that they might incorporate. The practice of singing parts of a service in polyphony instead of plainchant had probably been current in various parts of western Europe, including England, at least as early as the end of the 9th century. Sacred polyphony from 11th- and 12th-century France and England already shows considerable sophistication, and the achievements of Parisian church composers in the later 12th century have deservedly become famous. Much of this early sacred polyphony was liturgical: it set texts that formed an integral part of the liturgy. During the later 13th century, however, the attention of French composers shifted away from sacred to ceremonial and secular music, and they produced relatively little sacred polyphony for the next century and a half. English composers, on the other hand, continued to concentrate on sacred polyphony, either setting liturgical texts or creating pieces that could be added to or substituted for liturgical items. This activity is reflected in the provisions made by some uses (such as that of Exeter) for the singing of polyphony during services and also in frequent documentary references to the skills in reading and improvising polyphonic music required of ecclesiastical singers. The music in the Worcester Fragments and the Old Hall Manuscript bears impressive witness to the expertise of both composers and singers in the service of the late-medieval English church.

Nick Sandon

Bibliography

ROMANO-BRITISH AND ANGLO-SAXON

Deanesly, Margaret. *The Pre-Conquest Church in England.* 2d ed. London: Black, 1963; Gatch, Milton McC. "The Office in Late Anglo-Saxon Monasticism." In *Learning and Literature in Anglo-Saxon England,* ed. Michael Lapidge and Helmut Gneuss. Cambridge: Cambridge University Press, 1985, pp. 341–62; Gneuss, Helmut. "A Preliminary List of Manuscripts Written or Owned in England up to 1100." *ASE* 9 (1981): 1–60; Gneuss, Helmut. "Liturgical Books in Anglo-Saxon England and Their Old English Terminology." In *Learning and Literature in Anglo-Saxon England,* ed. Michael Lapidge and Helmut Gneuss. Cambridge: Cambridge University Press, 1985, pp. 91–141; Hohler, Christopher. "Some Service Books of the Later Saxon Church." In *Tenth-Century Studies: Essays in Commemoration of the Millennium of the Council of Winchester and Regularis concordia,* ed. David Parsons. London: Phillimore, 1975, pp. 60–83; Mayr-Harting, Henry. *The Coming of Christianity to Anglo-Saxon England.* London: Batsford, 1972; Planchart, Alejandro E. *The Repertory of Tropes at Winchester.* 2 vols. Princeton: Princeton University Press, 1977; Rankin, Susan. "From Memory to Written Record: Musical Notations in Manuscripts from Exeter." *ASE* 13 (1984): 97–112.

POST-CONQUEST

Dickinson, John Compton. *Monastic Life in Medieval England.* London: Black, 1961; Dickinson, John Compton. *The Later Middle Ages from the Norman Conquest to the Eve of the Reformation.* London: Black, 1979; Harper, John. *The Forms and Orders of Western Liturgy from the Tenth to the Eighteenth Century: A Historical Introduction and Guide for Students and Musicians.* Oxford: Clarendon, 1991; Harrison, Frank Ll. *Music in Medieval Britain.* 2d ed. London: Routledge & Kegan Paul, 1963; Hiley, David. "Thurston of Caen and Plainchant at Glastonbury: Musicological Reflections on the Norman Conquest." *Proceedings of the British Academy* 72 (1986) 57–90; Knowles, David. *The Monastic Order in England: A History of Its Development from the Times of St. Dunstan to the Fourth Lateran Council, 940–1216.* 2d ed. Cambridge: Cambridge University Press, 1963; Pfaff, Richard W. *Medieval Latin Liturgy: A Select Bibliography.* Toronto Medieval Bibliographies 9. Toronto: University of Toronto Press, 1982.

See also Augustine of Canterbury; Benedictional of Æthelwold; Caligula Troper; Canterbury, Ecclesiastical Province of; Choirs; Conversion of the Anglo-Saxons; Dioceses; Feasts, New Liturgical; Friars; Lady Mass; Liturgy; Monasticism; Notation of Plainsong; Notation of Polyphonic Music; Offices, New Liturgical; Prayers; Processions; *Regularis concordia;* Salisbury, Use of; Trope; Votive Observance; Winchester Organa; Winchester Tropers; York, Ecclesiastical Province of

Local Government

English local government in the Middle Ages was a system of "self-government at the king's command." Its essence lay in the reconciliation of the often divergent rhythms of local and national life.

Before the 10th century local communities had been almost entirely self-governing. Kings lacked the means to deal directly with their subjects, except at the highest level; those farther down were left, almost by default, to manage their own affairs. Order was maintained by a system of social control drawing on the complementary resources of kinship and lordship, and justice was dispensed by the owners—usually the lords—of the local courts. Beyond the performance of these tasks there was little that needed to be done.

What led to the development of a more formal structure of government was the strain placed on the body politic by the Viking onslaught of the 9th and 10th centuries. As the king's need for money and manpower became more acute, it became necessary to create a structure for the exaction of dues. This was satisfied in the 900s by the creation of some 30 or so shires, each under the direction of an official called the sheriff (shire-reeve). Those in Wessex were often based on preexisting folk groupings, as Somerset was on that of the "Somersaeten." Those in the south and east were based on former kingdoms, such as Essex and Kent, now absorbed into Wessex, while those in the Midlands had no apparent ancestry at all: just arbitrary creations of administrative convenience, organized around important royal towns or *burhs* in the wake of Wessex's advance into Mercia.

At this time units of administration beneath the shire were also called into being. Known in the Midlands and south as hundreds and in the Danelaw as wapentakes, these, too, varied greatly in size and origin. Some of the larger ones may, like the Midland shires, have been arbitrary creations, but others probably had a lengthy prehistory as units for the collection of tribute or taxation in the age of the Mercian supremacy.

The lives of both hundred and shire were patterned by the regular holding of courts. Hundred courts were convened every three weeks in some prominent open-air spot and attended by suitors who owed their attendance or suit as a service from land. Before the Conquest considerable judicial activity took place at these sessions; from the 12th century their judicial competence became concentrated in the twice-yearly frankpledge sessions, or "tourns," at which the sheriff inspected the tithing groups and heard reports of offenses that would later be dealt with by the justices.

Meetings of the shire court had originally been held less frequently—often no more than twice yearly—but by the 13th century they were generally held monthly. As in the hundreds attendance was required of those whose lands were burdened with the duty of attending. In their presence a variety of business was transacted, at first mainly judicial but later increasingly administrative and political. The judicial work was sharply reduced after 1215, when pleas of the crown were reserved to the judiciary. Thereafter, though the court retained a residual importance as the forum in which outlawries were promulgated, it was in other areas that its importance was to lie—in the election of representatives to parliament and the drafting of parliamentary petitions.

The presiding official at the shire court was the sheriff, who by the 12th century was the principal local agent of royal government. He collected the royal farms, called out the posse, enforced the king's peace, and executed the ever-increasing number of writs issued in the king's name. This formidable concentration of power inevitably raised problems of control that had to be addressed if the king was to maintain his authority. A solution was found in two ways: first by subjecting the sheriff to a measure of central supervision and second by transferring some of his duties to other officials.

Supervision was exercised in two areas, financial and judicial. From the reign of Henry I the sheriff was required to account twice yearly at the exchequer for the issues of his bailiwick—thus preventing him from creaming off money that should have gone to the king. In addition, from the reign of Henry I, he was subjected to searching inquiries by the itinerant eyre justices, dispatched on periodic visitations of the shires with a brief to stamp out crime and eliminate corruption. The transfer of some of his duties to new officials began a generation or two later, in the reign of Richard I. Responsibility for keeping the pleas of the crown and for holding inquests on sudden deaths by accident was assigned in 1194 to the coroners, of whom there were to be four in each county, three knights and a clerk.

In 1232 separate arrangements were made for the collection of feudal revenues. Two escheators were appointed in each county to account for the wardships and escheats (feudal windfalls) that fell in during minorities and in default of heirs, respectively. And finally, in the late 13th century, separate arrangements were made for the keeping of the peace. The keepers were appointed in each shire with the duty of reporting breaches of the peace in their bailiwicks. When in the next century they also acquired the power of determining (i.e., trying) cases and were thereby transformed into the justices of the peace, they were well on the way to replacing the sheriff as chief agent of royal government in the localities.

The justices of the peace and the coroners are the best known of the new officials of the late Middle Ages. But there were others, such as the commissioners of array, who raised soldiers in time of war, and the commissioners of sewers, who inspected and made arrangements for the clearing of ditches. These men were all drawn from the ranks of the local gentry and, with the exception of the justices of the peace (and members of parliament), received no pay. To compensate themselves for inconvenience, and to make a small profit on the side, they inevitably succumbed to the temptations of corruption. But by the later 13th century, as exchequer supervision intensified, there was probably less profit in office holding. Its main attraction lay in the power that it gave the officeholder over his neighbors.

The system of local government developed in the late Middle Ages was one of the most sophisticated of its time. Local and national interests were reconciled with a degree of success rarely attained elsewhere. Only in the privileged enclaves known as franchises was kingly authority seriously compromised. Here the devolution of government to an important local lord obviously blunted its impact. Writs that the sheriff would otherwise have executed were now executed by the lord's bailiffs; fugitives whom he would have arrested were arrested instead by the lord's constables. Given the extent of devolution involved, it might be supposed that power exercised by the king was substantially reduced. In fact this was far from being the case. The privileges of franchises were stated, by the king's justices, to involve responsibilities as well as immunities, and continued enjoyment of them depended on their effective exercise. If a bailiff failed to execute a writ delivered by the sheriff, the sheriff was commanded to disregard the exemption and enter the franchise. Privilege, as Helen Cam has shown, was insensibly being turned into obligation, exemption into burden. Under the vigorous direction of the Angevin kings franchises were integrated into a national system of local government, producing a structure at once uniform and devolved and characterized by the enforcement of common standards of behavior.

Nigel E. Saul

Bibliography

Cam, Helen M. *The Hundred and the Hundred Rolls.* London: Methuen, 1930 [for a description of the system in its prime]; Cam, Helen M. "The Evolution of the

Medieval English Franchise." In *Law-Finders and Law-Makers in Medieval England: Collected Studies in Legal and Constitutional History.* London: Merlin Press, 1962, pp. 22–43; Jewell, Helen M. *English Local Administration in the Middle Ages.* Newton Abbot: David & Charles, 1972; Loyn, H.R. *The Governance of Anglo-Saxon England 500–1087.* London: Arnold, 1984.

See also Boroughs; Courts and the Court System; Exchequer; Frankpledge; Gentry; Hundreds; Parliamentary Elections; Sheriff; Shires; Towns

Lollards

The most famous and original English heretical movement between the conversion of the Anglo-Saxons and the Reformation of the 16th century. Traditionally the Lollards are seen as the followers of the English philosopher and theologian John Wyclif (ca. 1330–1384), spreading his teachings and surviving as a heretical sect between the late 14th century and the Reformation. There is a substratum of truth in this, but recent work has shown that the movement was more complex, comprising both a short-lived academic wing, which survived for a time in Oxford, and a popular, largely lay division, which looked for inspiration to Wyclif in some matters and derived other characteristics from more widespread and not necessarily heretical evangelical piety.

Indeed some of the early uses of the term "Lollard," generally taken to denote a mumbler of prayers, may not even have had the connotations of heretic. Many of the later Lollards were not academically trained, and it is hardly surprising that they were unable to appreciate the theological subtlety of Wyclif's thought. When they did derive inspiration from his teaching, it was generally in a simplified form.

Wyclif's influence on academic Lollardy must be understood as characteristic scholastic loyalty to a distinguished master. When he first fell foul of the church, he still had support from leading university figures who did not necessarily share his theological opinions but who resented the jurisdictional interference of the archbishop of Canterbury. As his teachings became increasingly unorthodox, however, the university fell into line with the establishment; several of his earlier followers (most notably Philip Repingdon and Nicholas Hereford) made their peace with the authorities and pursued successful careers within the church.

Although his theological ideas were proscribed, there were still men in the arts faculty who were interested in his philosophical writings and who copied them into manuscripts without giving any attribution of authorship. These academic Lollards were also responsible for producing the English versions of the Bible and a heretical sermon cycle, and in the first decade of the 15th century there was a sufficient resurgence of heresy at Oxford for Archbishop Arundel to purge the university. This was successful; by the mid-15th century Lollardy had ceased to be an academic movement, as its last survivors died or were executed.

The survival of academic Lollardy outside the university was assisted by support from influential laymen, some of whom presented heretical priests to benefices of which they had the patronage. This protection gave opportunities to copy Lollard manuscripts and provided a defense against enquiring bishops. These patrons may not necessarily have shared all the views of their protégés, nor of the latter's inspiration, Wyclif, since their actions, including support for pilgrimages and crusades, runs counter to the expressed views of some Lollard theorists. In some cases the "Lollard Knights" may have been inspired by evangelical piety, in others perhaps by a desire to seize ecclesiastical property.

Church authorities, however, were only too prepared to regard as heretics those who sought church disendowment, even though their theological views cannot be ascertained. Some, most notably Sir John Oldcastle, an experienced knight and soldier and a close friend of Henry V, undoubtedly held unorthodox beliefs. As early as 1410 he was associated with the academic Lollard Richard Wyche, writing to one of the lay supporters of the Bohemian reformer Jan Hus on the same day as Wyche himself wrote to Hus. When Arundel prosecuted Oldcastle for heresy in 1413, he did not deny his beliefs and was condemned to death. He escaped and raised a rebellion in 1414, but though he drew support from a wide variety of areas his followers were few in number and easily overcome. Futile though the revolt was, it created considerable alarm among the secular authorities, fully echoed in the day's chronicles.

Although the death penalty for heresy had been enacted in 1401, only two men went to the stake in Henry IV's reign. However, after Oldcastle's fiasco persecution was intensified. Most lay supporters were warned off by the association of Lollardy with treason, and no later leader commanded loyalty similar to Oldcastle's. Persecution eased off after the suppression of his rising and depended on the activity of individual bishops. This was seldom totally effective; in only one area, East Anglia, did a substantial Lollard community disappear entirely after episcopal proceedings, those of Bishop Alnwick in 1428–30. Elsewhere the recurrence of trials at different periods demonstrates the survival of Lollard groups in Bristol, Coventry, the Chilterns, south Kent, and London. Channels of communication existed between different groups, and itinerant evangelists helped circulate the vernacular scriptures, the staple literature of the movement.

Most Lollards were lay, though one Berkshire parish priest was executed in 1508, and a parish priest of unchallenged orthodoxy was on friendly terms with men later condemned for heresy in Coventry. Socially most were drawn from the artisan class, although there was mercantile support in the towns and in southern Buckinghamshire patronage from the lesser landed class.

It is sometimes hard to identify the genuine Lollards; the boundaries between heresy and orthodoxy were indistinct, and the question was complicated by an anticlericalism often devoid of doctrinal deviation. Indeed the procedure of investigation employed by church authorities—interrogation on a series of doctrinal articles—may have imposed a spurious precision upon the confused ideas of some suspects. Bishops, however, do appear to have been more concerned with ascertaining the truth than with obtaining convictions at any price, as shown by the experiences of Margery Kempe, questioned and acquitted several times.

There were variations of belief among Lollard communities, and sometimes even within them, perhaps depending on the views of individual teachers, as in Norfolk in 1428–30. The possession of vernacular scripture texts is good proof of genuine heresy, and recurring beliefs include a denial of transubstantiation and hostility to pilgrimages and to the veneration of images. The Lollards were also strongly antipapal but had no monopoly in this. They differed, however, from much contemporary continental heresy in that traces of millenarian teaching are few.

Their skill in self-concealment makes it hard to estimate their numbers, and one should guard against overstressing their importance. In the century after Oldcastle's revolt the number of executions probably was below 100, that of abjurations below 1,000. Only in a few areas, notably south Buckinghamshire, were they more than a small, uninfluential minority in society. Nevertheless, the church's concern with suppressing them, however intermittently, suggests that they must be seen as a movement, not just as a series of isolated dissidents.

J.A.F. Thomson

Bibliography

Aston, Margaret. *Lollards and Reformers: Images and Literacy in Late Medieval Religion.* London: Hambledon, 1984 [a collection of valuable papers]; Hudson, Anne, ed. *Selections from English Wycliffite Writings.* Cambridge: Cambridge University Press, 1978 [the most accessible body of printed source materials]; Hudson, Anne, and Pamela Gradon, eds. *English Wycliffite Sermons.* 5 vols. Oxford: Clarendon, 1983–96; Hudson, Anne, and Pamela Gradon, eds. *The Premature Reformation: Wycliffite Texts and Lollard History.* Oxford: Clarendon, 1988 [fullest work on the "movement"]; McFarlane, K.B. *John Wycliffe and the Beginnings of English Nonconformity.* London: English Universities Press, 1952; McFarlane, K.B. *Lancastrian Kings and Lollard Knights.* Oxford: Clarendon, 1972 [essential studies in modern Lollard historiography]; McSheffrey, Shannon. *Gender and Heresy: Women and Men in Lollard Communities, 1420–1530.* Philadelphia: University of Pennsylvania Press, 1995; Plumb, Derek. "Social and Economic Spread of Rural Lollardy: A Reappraisal." *Studies in Church History* 23 (1986): 111–29 [the value of a prosopographical approach]; Thomson, John A.F. *The Later Lollards, 1414–1520.* London: Oxford University Press, 1965 [describes the Lollard groups in various regions]; Thomson, John A.F. "Orthodox Religion and the Origins of Lollardy." *History* 74 (1989): 39–55 [contemporary spiritual attitudes that helped heresy to take root].

See also Bishops; Clanvowe; Kempe; Popular Religion; Translation; Universities; Wyclif; Wycliffite Texts

London

London (Londinium) had been a major urban center in Roman Britain. However, its decline in population and economic importance began even before the withdrawal of the Roman legions in the late 4th or early 5th century. All the evidence we have suggests that town life collapsed in London after the early 5th century. No longer a colonial capital, bolstered by networks of trade and authority, Londinium appears to have become depopulated and decayed within a relatively short period. Some small settlement may have survived, but its characteristics and function are unknown; the monumental remains of the Roman city must have ensured that the site's identity was not lost.

By the end of the 6th century, when new patterns of kingdoms and hegemonies were starting to stabilize, London was within the kingdom of Essex. Though Augustine's mission had intended to establish a metropolitan see in the old Roman capital, political realities determined its location in Christian Kent, at Canterbury.

Literary evidence for a 7th-century trading center in "London" may refer to the settlement of which archaeologists have found traces, situated to the west of the city walls. Occupation layers and small finds of the mid-Saxon period in the area of the Strand and Aldwych contrast with the featureless layers of dark earth that overlie the Roman settlement, within the walls, and the grey silt sealing the elaborate Roman quayside structures. If there was habitation within the walls at this date, as the 7th-century founding of the cathedral suggests, it can only have been on a limited scale. London was prosperous enough to attract Mercian interest in the 8th and early 9th centuries and was occupied by the Danish invaders in 871–72.

After recapturing London in 886 Alfred improved its defenses, refurbishing the walls and granting plots of land, probably because of its position only a few miles from the Danelaw frontier along the River Lea. The grid pattern of the medieval streets was probably initiated at this time. Later events in the Anglo-Danish struggle confirm that London was a strategic and valuable center; in the 10th and 11th centuries churches were founded, governing institutions—aldermen, wards, and assemblies—took shape, and foreign trade continued.

The Norman conquerors built the Tower and two smaller castles within the walls, and confirmed Westminster, the burial place of Edward the Confessor, as an important royal center. Over the next two centuries the city's wealth and importance to the crown were increased by the immigration of Jews and the concentration of minting activity. Trade with France expanded, foreign merchants came to the city. Gradually London, with Westminster, became the focus of much royal activity, ceremonial as well as governmental. The treasury was moved from Winchester to London in the 13th century, and chancery, the exchequer, and the king's courts settled at Westminster. Increasingly the crown turned to the London market, rather than to fairs, for wine, luxuries, and other imports. By 1200 the city was populous and prosperous, with over 100 parish churches and many great stone houses (fig. 89a).

Fig. 89a. London in the 12th century. After W. Page (1923). Reprinted with permission of Constable & Co.

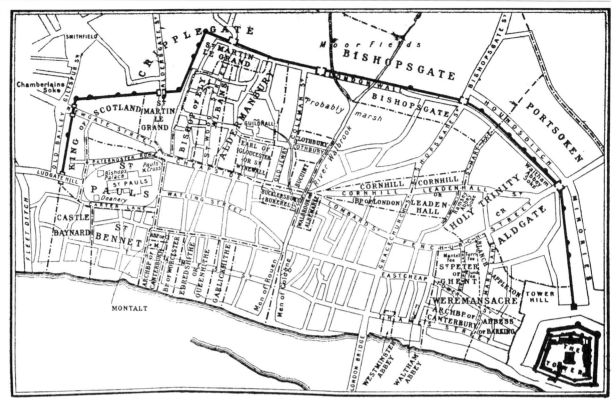

In the 12th century the Londoners achieved the right to appoint their own sheriffs and communal responsibility for payment of the fee farm, the fixed annual rent paid the king by the city's officials in lieu of other rents and dues—the price of self-government. Eventually they were able to form a sworn commune with a leader or mayor in the 1190s, confirmed by charter in 1215. Government in the 13th century was dominated by the interests of 24 long-serving aldermen, drawn from a mercantile and landowning elite, often with court connections.

Craftsmen and artisans were sometimes restless under this rule, anxious to secure political rights, and keenly supportive of Simon de Montfort and the baronial party against Henry III. Continuing internal conflict, and the importance of asserting control over his largest city, led Edward I to impose direct rule through a royal warden (1285–99). This period also provided the opportunity for the revision of administrative and peacekeeping practices, and the issue of a detailed regulatory code. Edward II's charter of 1319 confirmed the constitution of mayor and aldermen but also gave considerable power—through control of the entry to citizenship—to the associations of craftsmen.

A complex legal and administrative system emerged, starting with the pre-Conquest court of husting, the main citizen assembly where matters of general civic import were discussed and publicized. By 1300 this was a court of law, dealing principally with matters concerning real property, inheritance, and tenure, whereas the newer mayor's court heard cases of debt and contract, and the sheriffs' court dealt with minor assaults and trespass. The mayor and aldermen together formed the principal administrative council. Larger assemblies of citizens met to elect the mayor and approve taxation, and the 14th century saw the formalization of the Common Council, made up of men elected by the wards.

At the lower level the city was administered through the local meetings, or wardmotes, presided over by an alderman. London's population had continued to grow, probably largely through immigration, as the city's function as a great regional and national marketplace developed; by 1300 it may have exceeded 80,000, most of whom must have lived in the tightly packed area within the walls. The jurisdiction of the mayor and aldermen covered the walled city and the immediate suburb but not the vills of Westminster and Southwark.

The Black Death and subsequent plagues had an enormous impact on the population, cutting it by almost half. In the Poll Tax of 1377, 23,414 persons were assessed in the city, giving a total population for London, Westminster, and Southwark, at the most generous estimate, of 45,000–50,000. Rapid change in living conditions and expectations led to unrest among ordinary Londoners, while at the same time the city's rulers were divided. Foreign wars and changes in patterns of trade, complicated by the crown's exploitation of staple policies and foreign sources of finance, led to divergences of political and economic interests among the mercantile rulers and opened the way for factional struggles.

London merchants were seen as propping up the decadent regime of Edward III and backing Richard II's assertion of independence, so that London affairs were at the forefront in the conflicts of the Good Parliament of 1376, the Peasants' Revolt (which paralyzed the city for several days in June 1381), and the crisis of the Lords Appellant. For a brief period (1376–84) the dominance of the merchant groups in London government was challenged, with elections to the Common Council being made by the crafts, and aldermen allowed to hold office for one year only.

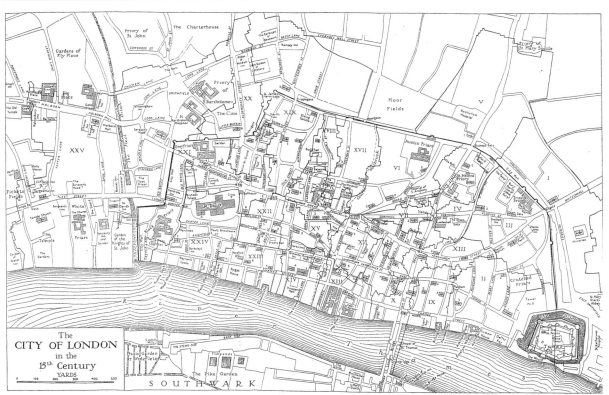

Fig. 89b. London in the 15th century. After C.L. Kingsford, Prejudice and Promise in XVth Century England *(1925). Reprinted by permission of Frank Cass, Ltd.*

By the end of the century the previous situation had been restored, although London government did perhaps become more broadly based in the 15th century with the growth in size and importance of the Common Council. In the deposition of Richard II and the Wars of the Roses London's support proved crucial to the successful seizure of power, but the city's leaders played a conservative part, tending to support the party in control (to which they might be committed in loans and financial support) until the scales were already tipping to the other side.

In the 14th and 15th centuries Westminster developed into a sizable settlement, focusing on the abbey and royal palace. Service industries for travelers and temporary residents were especially important, and the retail of luxury goods developed. The houses of nobles and ecclesiastics along the Strand linked Westminster with the growing legal quarter to the west of the city. By contrast Southwark, now partly under the city's jurisdiction, was characterized by industrial production and by alien settlement, as to a lesser extent were the suburbs to the east and north (fig. 89b).

Though the city had a diminished and probably static population in the 15th century, its economy, based on overseas trade, remained relatively buoyant. The cloth export trade came to focus on London at the expense of other ports, helped by the growth of Antwerp as a major European market, and London merchants, especially members of the Mercers' Company, dominated the Merchant Adventurers' organization. By 1500 about 70 percent of England's cloth exports and 45 percent of its wool were passing through the port of London. It is estimated that London's share of the national taxable wealth increased from 2 percent in 1334 to nearly 9 percent in 1515.

Mercantile wealth enriched the appearance and public life of the city. In the early 15th century Richard Whittington endowed a college of priests and founded an almshouse; other successful merchants made generous benefactions to their parish churches or to their guilds or companies. Some individuals built splendid residences like Crosby Hall. The city engaged in several public building programs, most notably the enlargement of Guildhall (1411–ca. 1430) and the new granary at Leadenhall in the 1440s. The pomp and status of the mayoralty increased, and London saw a succession of magnificent royal entries and processions for which no expense was spared.

Vanessa A. Harding

Bibliography

PRIMARY

Keene, Derek, and Vanessa Harding. *A Survey of Documentary Sources for Property Holding in London before the Great Fire.* London Record Society 22. London: London Record Society, 1985; Riley, Henry T., trans. *Liber Albus: The White Book of the City of London.* London: Griffin, 1861; Sharpe, Reginald R., ed. *Calendar of Wills Proved and Enrolled in the Court of Husting, London,* A.D. *1258*–A.D. *1688.* 2 vols. London: Francis, 1889–90; Sharpe, Reginald R., ed. *Calendar of Letter-books . . . of the City of London.* 11 vols. *Letter-book A: ca.* A.D. *1275–1298* to *Letter-book L: Temp. Edward IV–Henry VII.* London: Francis, 1899–1912; Thomas, A.H., ed. *Calendar of Early Mayor's Court Rolls . . . 1298–1307.* Cambridge: Cambridge University Press, 1924; Thomas, A.H., and Philip E. Jones, eds. *Calendar of Plea and Memoranda Rolls . . . of the City of London.* 6 vols. Cambridge: Cambridge University Press, 1926–61 [covers the years 1323–1482].

SECONDARY

Barron, Caroline M. *Revolt in London, 11th–15th June, 1381.* London: Museum of London, 1981; Bird, Ruth. *The Turbulent London of Richard II.* London: Longmans Green, 1949; Brooke, Christopher N.L., and Gillian Keir. *London, 800–1215: The Shaping of a City.* London: Secker & Warburg, 1975; Nightingale, Pamela. "Capitalists, Crafts, and Constitutional Change in Late Fourteenth-Century London." *Past and Present* 124 (August 1989): 3–35; Rosser, Gervase. *Medieval Westminster, 1200–1540.* Oxford: Clarendon, 1989; Thrupp, Sylvia L. *The Merchant Class of Medieval London, 1300–1500.* Ann Arbor: University of Michigan Press, 1948; Williams, Gwyn A. *Medieval London: From Commune to Capital.* London: Athlone, 1963.

See also Guilds; Towns

Love, Nicholas (d. 1423/24)

Prior of Mount Grace Charterhouse in Yorkshire; author of *The Mirror of the Blessed Life of Jesus Christ.* Love's *Mirror* is a translation and adaptation of the Pseudo-Bonaventuran *Meditationes vitae Christi* (early 14th century), an influential Franciscan collection of meditations on the life of Christ. Little is known of Love's own life aside from his appointment as rector of Mount Grace and promotion to prior in 1410. Testamentary evidence confirms that he was still prior in 1415 but suggests that he may have been replaced by 1417.

According to a "Memorandum" in most manuscripts of the *Mirror* Love submitted his work to Archbishop Thomas Arundel for approbation around 1410, obeying the Lambeth Constitutions of 1409. Arundel licensed the translation and encouraged its publication "for the edification of the faithful and the confutation of heretics or Lollards." Love's alterations to the text—particularly his addition of a treatise on the eucharist—were often specifically anti-Wycliffite in aim.

The *Mirror* became an important piece in the ecclesiastical rearguard in the century preceding the Reformation. It survives in 49 complete manuscripts and fourteen fragments, extracts, or composite texts and was printed nine times between 1484 and 1530. Thomas More invoked it in arguing against the Lutheran Bible translator William Tyndale.

Michael G. Sargent

Bibliography

PRIMARY

Sargent, Michael G., ed. *The Mirror of the Blessed Life of Jesus Christ.* New York: Garland, 1993.

SECONDARY

Manual 9:3103–06, 3454–56; Doyle, A.I. "Reflections on Some Manuscripts of Nicholas Love's *Myrrour of the Blessed Lyf of Jesu Christ.*" *Leeds Studies in English* n.s. 14 (1983): 82–93; Salter, Elizabeth. *Nicholas Love's "Myrrour of the Blessed Lyf of Jesu Christ.*" Salzburg: Institut für Anglistik und Amerikanistik, 1974; Sargent, Michael G. "Versions of the Life of Christ: Nicholas Love's *Mirror* and Related Works." *Poetica* 42 (1995, for 1994): 39–70.

See also Lollards; Mystical and Devotional Writings; Prose, ME; Wyclif; Wycliffite Texts

Lovelich, Henry (fl. ca. 1425?)

London businessman and author of two Arthurian poems: *The History of the Holy Grail,* the fullest English version of the early part of the Grail story, from Joseph of Arimathea to Lancelot's grandfather; and *Merlin,* a presentation of Merlin as Grail prophet. These poems are translations from the French prose of the first two branches of the Vulgate Cycle, the *Estoire del Saint Graal* and the *Merlin,* in couplets of often lengthy four-stress lines. They are the sole contents of the unique manuscript, Cambridge, Corpus Christi College 80, which may have been executed at Lovelich's direction. Folios containing the first fifth of the *History* are missing at the beginning, leaving 23,788 lines. *Merlin* consists of 27,852 lines, equivalent to about half the French account: the manuscript may be incomplete, or Lovelich may not have written more. He evidently translated the works at the urging of Sir Henry Barton, a fellow member of the London Company of Skinners and twice Lord Mayor, in his own mature years and some time before Barton's death in 1434. Although the writing is pedestrian, the undertaking provides an interesting comment on middle-class tastes and concerns of the time.

Diane Speed

Bibliography

PRIMARY

Furnivall, Frederick J., ed. *The History of the Holy Grail.* EETS e.s. 20, 24, 28, 30. Intro. Dorothy Kempe. EETS e.s. 95. London: Trübner; Kegan Paul, Trench, Trübner; Humphrey Milford; 1874–1905. Repr. in 2 vols. Millwood: Kraus, 1973; Kock, Ernst A., ed. *Merlin.* EETS e.s. 93, 112, o.s. 185. London: Humphrey Milford, 1904–32.

SECONDARY

New *CBEL* 1:398, 414; *Manual* 1:49, 74–75, 236, 252–53; Rice, Joanne A. *Middle English Romance: An Annotated Bibliography, 1955–1985.* New York: Garland, 1987, pp. 293, 333–34.

See also Literacy; Literary Influences: French, Welsh; Matter of Britain; Romances; Translation

Lydgate, John (ca. 1370–1449)

The most prolific versifier of the 15th century. Lydgate was probably born in the village of Lydgate in Suffolk and apparently educated at the Benedictine monastery at Bury St. Edmunds, at which he was professed at the age of fifteen. He later studied at Oxford, probably at Gloucester Hall. He was ordained priest in the Benedictine order in 1397. In 1406 Prince Henry supported his return to study at Oxford. It was possibly while at Oxford that he wrote his translation of Aesop's *Fables*. His subsequent career suggests that he enjoyed Henry V's patronage. In 1423, after Henry's death, Lydgate became prior of Hatfield Broadoak in Essex. But from 1426 to 1429 he was in Paris as part of the entourage of John duke of Bedford, regent of France. By 1433 he had returned to Bury. Most of his later works seem to have been written there. He received a royal annuity in 1439 and died ten years later.

Lydgate's earliest major work was probably his *Troy Book*, a translation of Guido delle Colonne's *Historia destruccionis Troiae* (30,117 lines in couplets), which was begun at the behest of Henry V in 1412 and completed in 1420. Its composition appears to have been interrupted by the writing of *The Life of Our Lady*, ca. 1415–16 (5,932 lines, mostly in rime royal stanzas), written, he says, at Henry's "excitacioun." *The Siege of Thebes*, a history of the Theban legend, apparently based on a French source, was probably composed ca. 1420–21, as a continuation of Chaucer's *Canterbury Tales*. While in France in the late 1420s Lydgate probably wrote his translation of Deguileville's *Pilgrimage of the Life of Man* (24,832 lines in couplets) for Thomas Montacute, earl of Salisbury. Some of his shorter poems, including the *Danse Machabre*, also date from this time.

After his return to England in 1429 Lydgate wrote a number of celebratory verses for Henry VI's coronation. His *Lives of Sts. Edmund and Fremund* (3,508 lines in rime royal) was presented to the king in the 1430s, probably after the king's visit to Bury St. Edmunds in 1433–34. For the king's brother, Humphrey, duke of Gloucester, Lydgate wrote his longest work, *The Fall of Princes* (36,365 lines in rime royal), between ca. 1431 and 1438. It is a rendering of Laurent de Premierfait's French prose translation of Boccaccio's *De casibus virorum illustrium*. His last major works seem to have been his *Lives of Sts. Albon and Amphibel* (4,724 lines in rime royal), commissioned in 1439 by John Whethamstede, abbot of St. Albans, and a rime royal translation of the Pseudo-Aristotelian *Secreta secretorum*, left incomplete on his death and finished by Benedict Burgh. Other substantial poems attributed to Lydgate include a lengthy allegory, *Reason and Sensuality* (7,042 lines in couplets), and many shorter poems of doubtful canonicity.

In addition to these long poems there are numerous shorter ones on a variety of subjects. These include a popular dream vision, *The Temple of Glass,* and short verse narratives, such as his *Debate of the Horse Sheep and Goose* and *The Churl and the Bird,* several mummings, and a number of devotional lyrics. But the variety of Lydgate's poetic output resists concise summary: it ranges from his translation of Aesop to a treatise for laundresses and a dietary (instructions on healthy diet

and behavior). By the most capacious estimates it runs to about 150,000 lines of verse. His sole prose work, *The Serpent of Division,* is a brief history of Rome.

This range of subject matter is reflected in the range of his patrons, which extended from royalty and nobility through a broad spectrum of English society, both religious and lay, male and female, individual and institutional. He was at the call of those who wished him to entertain, instruct, admonish, and propagandize on their behalf.

Lydgate stands crucially between Chaucer and the later evolution of English poetry. He wrote in the generation immediately after Chaucer's death and acknowledges Chaucer as his "master" in frequent lavish tributes. A number of his works are self-consciously conceived within a tradition of Chaucer's works that is reflected in imitation at conceptual, stylistic, and verbal levels. Thus his *Troy Book* sets itself in relation to the subject matter of *Troilus and Criseyde; The Siege of Thebes* contains an imitation of the beginning of the General Prologue and extensive verbal borrowings from the *Knight's Tale; The Complaint of the Black Knight* and *The Temple of Glass* imitate Chaucer's dream visions, *The Book of the Duchess* and *The House of Fame,* respectively. Lydgate was to play an important role in the creation and dissemination of the Chaucer tradition, particularly through his own popularizing of Chaucerian style and subjects.

Lydgate's Chaucerian imitation is related to the most distinctive tendency in his art, its rhetorical amplification. His instinct was to elaborate his materials, often on a massive scale. The most striking—or notorious—example of this tendency is the opening sentence of his *Siege of Thebes,* which imitates the opening sentence of Chaucer's General Prologue. Lydgate's sentence extends Chaucer's from eighteen to 65 lines. Indeed much of Lydgate's amplification comes from a natural tendency nurtured by a careful reading of Chaucer, through which poetic hints of his "master" could be vastly expanded. Thus, out of suggestions in Chaucer's language, he created a distinctive aureate diction, a Latin-derived, polysyllabic language that often characterizes his "high style," particularly in his religious verse. At its least successful, in conjunction with elaboration of allusion and syntax, it could lead to the obscurity that has earned him the condemnation of many modern critics.

Lydgate's meter systematizes Chaucer's versification through a regular use of five types of iambic pentameter line. One particularly striking feature of this systematization is the frequent use of the "headless" line (one that lacks an initial stressed syllable). Lydgate's own development of Chaucer's metrics was the "broken-backed" line, in which stressed syllables clash across the caesura.

It was probably through his amplification and systematization of Chaucer's art that Lydgate gained his considerable reputation in the 15th and 16th centuries. Allusions in that period acclaim him as part of a great triumvirate of ME poets, together with Chaucer and Gower. And in simple quantitative terms, in numbers of surviving manuscripts, Lydgate was the most popular of all ME poets. His *Fall of Princes* survives in complete or selected forms in over 80 manuscripts, his *Life of Our Lady* in nearly 50, *The Siege of Thebes* in 30. Among Lydgate's shorter poems both his *Verses on the Kings of England* and his *Dietary* exist in over 50 copies. In addition many of his works were issued by the early printers, Caxton, Pynson, and de Worde, often more than once.

This massive dissemination of Lydgate's works during the later Middle Ages led to his wide-ranging influence on later writers and forms. *The Fall of Princes* shaped literary conceptions of tragedy in the early Renaissance. His mummings are important texts in the evolution of English drama. And the works of (among others) Dunbar, Henryson, Douglas, Hawes, and Skelton, as well as many lesser figures, show the influence of his work in their writings, an influence that extended into the 17th century.

A.S.G. Edwards

Bibliography

PRIMARY

Bergen, Henry, ed. *Lydgate's Troy Book.* 4 vols. EETS e.s. 97, 103, 106, 126. London: Humphrey Milford, 1906–35; Bergen, Henry, ed. *Lydgate's Fall of Princes.* 4 vols. EETS e.s. 121–24. London: Humphrey Milford, 1924–27; Erdmann, Axel, and Eilert Ekwall, eds. *Lydgate's Siege of Thebes.* 2 vols. EETS e.s. 108, 125. London: Kegan Paul, Trench, Trübner, 1911–30; Furnivall, Frederick J., and Katherine B. Locock, eds. *The Pilgrimage of the Life of Man.* 3 vols. EETS e.s. 77, 83, 92. London: Kegan Paul, Trench, Trübner, 1899–1904; Lauritis, Joseph A., R.A. Klinefelter, and V.F. Gallagher, eds. *A Critical Edition of John Lydgate's Life of Our Lady.* Pittsburgh: Duquesne University, 1961; MacCracken, Henry Noble, ed. *The Minor Poems of John Lydgate.* 2 vols. EETS e.s. 107, o.s. 192. London: Kegan Paul, Trench, Trübner, 1911; Humphrey Milford, 1934; Norton-Smith, John, ed. *John Lydgate: Poems.* Oxford: Clarendon, 1966; Reinecke, George F., ed. *Saint Albon and Saint Amphibalus.* New York: Garland, 1985; Steele, Robert, ed. *Lydgate and Burgh's Secrees of Old Philisoffres.* EETS e.s. 66. London: Kegan Paul, Trench, Trübner, 1894.

SECONDARY

New *CBEL* 1:639–46, 740; *Manual* 6:1809–1920, 2071–2175; Edwards, A.S.G. "Lydgate Scholarship: Progress and Prospects." In *Fifteenth Century Studies: Recent Essays,* ed. Robert F. Yeager. Hamden: Archon, 1984, pp. 29–47; Pearsall, Derek. *John Lydgate.* London: Routledge & Kegan Paul, 1970; Schirmer, Walter F. *John Lydgate: A Study in the Culture of the XVth Century.* Trans. Ann E. Keep. Berkeley: University of California Press, 1961.

See also Beast Epic and Fable; Burgh; Chaucer; Chaucerian Apocrypha; Henry V; Henry VI; Literary Influences: Italian; Matter of Antiquity

Lyrics

ME lyric by the broadest definition includes any short poem written in English between 1150 and the early part of the 16th century. Apart from a few songs by St. Godric (d. 1170) only tantalizing hints of a popular lyric tradition survive from the 12th century. The earliest of the fragmentary remains, "Merie sungen the muneches binnen [monks in] Ely," is attributed (dubiously) to King Cnut in Thomas of Ely's 12th-century *Historia Eliensis.* A mere handful of lyrics comes down from the period before 1250; perhaps about 100 extant lyrics were composed during the remainder of the 13th century. A much larger number of lyrics survive from the 14th century, and hundreds from the 15th, many of which are carols. Omitted from the present discussion are ballads (not to be confused with ballades), debate poems, and satires, which are treated separately in this book. The short poems outside of these groups may be classified roughly on the basis of content. The broadest division separates secular from religious lyrics, and though even this division is not absolute, the following anatomy will proceed as though it were.

The vast majority of extant lyrics, including the earliest, are religious. Predominant themes are the Passion of Christ, the joys of the Virgin Mary (particularly the Annunciation, Nativity, and Assumption), and death. Whether one describes these poems as meditative, hortatory, didactic, or monitory, and whether one traces their roots to the liturgy, to hymns, to sermons, or to biblical commentary, they clearly express an affective piety, one that appeals to the heart rather than to the head. Impetus for this kind of expression was given a boost with the advent of the friars (particularly Franciscans), who were in England by 1224. These self-styled minstrels of God (*joculatores Dei*) sought to arouse religious feeling in the laity by depicting the humanity of Jesus and Mary and the pathos of the human condition generally.

The Commonplace Book of Friar John Grimestone (fl. 1372) offers examples of such treatment, but perhaps its best illustration is found in a justly famous 13th-century poem:

> Nou goth sonne vnder wod,—
> me reweth, marie, thi faire Rode.
> Nou goth sonne vnder tre,—
> me reweth, marie, thi sone and the.

The poet imagines not the king and queen of heaven but a mother and son. Mary is not preternaturally beautiful but simply a woman of fair complexion ("Rode"). The poet expresses not awe but pity. The crucifixion of Christ is presented not as an event of profound theological import but as an instance of the vulnerability to which all human beings are liable, the onset of death.

This poem, one of the best of its kind, epitomizes the affective piety that characterizes many a religious lyric. It also exemplifies features of lyric style. Brevity and simplicity of utterance are keys to the poetic power of many medieval lyrics; long lyrics tend to be discursive and less forceful. Repetition, such as one sometimes finds in ballads, is also used to focus attention and thus to concentrate the emotional effect.

The imagery and the diction are plain; the poet creates a scene, not a narrative, though there is a hint of action or passage of time in the setting of the sun. Finally one should observe that the poem appeals not only to the heart but also to the mind. Its verbal wit—wordplay on *sonne* (sun/son) and on *wod, tre,* and possibly *Rode* (cross)—infuses the literal imagery with theological content.

Many lyrics address their subject—Jesus, Mary, the Cross—as in prayer: in these the reader or listener identifies with the lyric voice or speaker. In some poems the audience does not "speak" but is spoken to ("Man, thus on rode I hyng for the"). The effect of intimacy is the same; the audience is part of a drama, one side of a conversation. The dramatic potential is more fully actualized in poems in which the audience does not participate but is a witness, as in lullabies sung by Mary to the infant Jesus or in laments addressed by her to the crucified Christ. These sometimes take the form of dialogues—Jesus, for example, will respond to Mary; in most instances the humanity of the speakers is emphasized and the affective piety arises from sympathy.

Other religious poems attenuate the dramatic effect, generally seeking to edify rather than arouse emotion. The first-person speaker of such poems is scarcely evident and in a few instances disappears altogether. This disappearance is a natural extension of the characteristic anonymity of the poetic "I." Composers of medieval English lyrics tended not to stamp their work with personal impression; they cultivated rather a universal voice. Even when a poet can be identified—William Herebert, John Grimestone, Michael Kildare, Thomas of Hales (all friars), William of Shoreham, even Richard Rolle—a distinctive poetic voice does not emerge. From the late 14th century on authorial personalities and identifiable poetic styles begin to appear, in the work of such authors as Chaucer, Hoccleve, Lydgate, Dunbar, Henryson, and Skelton; also John Audelay and Walter Kennedy. But other authorial "identifications"—Jacob Ryman, H. Bowesper, John Hawghton, Reginald Pecock, Richard de Caistre, John Halsham, R. Stokys, Richard Spaldyng (in an acrostic)—attach to poems that remain stylistically "anonymous," utterly like the unclaimed lyrics of the medieval English tradition.

Nevertheless, late ME religious lyrics manifest a self-conscious literary style previously not much seen. The simple meters and diction of earlier verse persist, but a nearly unprecedented imitation of secular lyrics introduces more complicated metrical schemes (e.g., rime royal) and the new "aureate" diction ("O Radiant luminar of light eterminable"), abstract latinisms to gild the rhetoric of elevated matter. Borrowings from the secular lyric include such motifs as the exchange of hearts and description of female beauty (the Virgin Mary's), the narrative framework of the *chanson d'aventure* ("Bi a wode as I gon ryde"), and even the rhetorical frame of a letter ("Goe, lytyll byll"). In a few poems the rhetoric is so thoroughly taken over that the religious theme virtually disappears (cf. "Trewloue trewe, on you I truste").

The ambiguity of reference that makes problematical the distinction of religious from secular verse appears quite early. In "Myrie it is while sumer ilast" (13th century) the speaker's winter and long night of woe may be literal or figurative: reference to harsh weather, to love languor, to the evanescence of life, or to spiritually necessary mortification of the flesh. In "Foweles in the frith" the natural world is a foil for one who walks in sorrow "for beste of bon and blod." But celebrations of life in the world are also to be found. The best-known and earliest surviving example is "Sumer is icumen in," one of the few English *reverdies,* or joyous descriptions of earth in springtime. Related to such a theme is, of course, the theme of love.

Unfortunately few secular lyrics on any theme survive from the 13th century. In addition to the three poems mentioned above one may count a love plaint ("Theh thet hi can wittes fule-wis" ["Though I know much that is full wise"]); two paradoxical definitions of love ("Loue is a selkud wodenesse [strange madness]" and "Loue is sofft, loue is swet"); the folkloric "Say me, viit in the brom" ["Tell me, creature in the broom-shrub"]; and a *chanson d'aventure* ("Nou sprinkes the sprai" ["Now the branch leafs out"]); and perhaps a few of the Harley Lyrics. Otherwise only fragments of secular lyrics remain, mostly in sermons where they are quoted to illustrate a point. From the 12th century we hear the refrain "Swete lemman dhin are" ("Sweet lover, [grant] your mercy"); the gnomic lines "euer is the eie to the wude leie [drawn] / therinne is thet ich luuie [the one I love]"; and a snatch of a popular song, "Atte wrastlinge mi lemman i ches [chose], / and atte ston-kasting i him for-les [lost]." From the 13th century comes "He [*read* I ne] may cume to mi lef [beloved] bute by the watere." In addition to some of the Harley Lyrics a few bits and pieces survive from the first half of the 14th century, notably "Brid one brere" (possibly from the 13th century) and the Rawlinson lyrics, "Ich am of Irlaunde," "Of euerykune tre," "Al nist [night] by the rose, rose," "Maiden in the mor lay," and "D[ronken] dronken."

Because the evidence is so fragmentary, much of the early history of the ME secular lyric must be conjectured. How much of it is popular in origin? How much is literary? There can be no doubt that a popular tradition existed; it occasions the clerical diatribes that preserve some of the early fragments. And probability suggests that some English poets were influenced by the clerical, goliardic, and courtly traditions of verse. A debate poem of the 13th century, "The Thrush and the Nightingale," shows evidence of all three influences: it has learned allusions to Adam, Samson, Alexander, and Constantine; it offers spirited antifeminist satire; it adduces romance (Sir Gawain) and the love ethic of courtly poetry—*driwerie, hendinese, curteisie.* Similar evidence appears in a religious lyric, Friar Thomas of Hales's "Love Ron," written for a young woman to whom Christ is portrayed as a noble lover, a "soth lefmon."

Of particular interest is the relationship of the English love lyrics to continental models. The paucity of amorous verse—only the Harley Lyrics provide a substantial body of evidence—makes analysis difficult. But Anglo-Norman culture in 13th- and early-14th-century England clearly must have introduced to English poets the forms, motifs, and concepts of French *chansons d'amours.* It is even possible that the more complicated meters of the Harley poems owe a debt to

Provençal troubadours, some of whom accompanied Eleanor of Aquitaine to England in the 12th century. Until more evidence comes to light, one can only speculate.

The early lyric tradition in England culminates in the Harley Lyrics (late 13th to early 14th century). The remainder of the 14th century produced few extant secular lyrics apart from those composed by Chaucer, who imitated contemporary French models, not the earlier styles that may have influenced previous writers. Following Machaut, Graunson, and Deschamps, Chaucer wrote in the metrical structures of the ballade, the rondel, and the virelai (his virelais do not survive), each originally, like the carol, a dance song. Among these *formes fixes* are "complaints" (rueful statements about the exigencies of love), poems praising his lady, philosophical lyrics, verse epistles, and an ABC to the Virgin Mary. The artificiality of the courtly pieces is offset by the wit and humor of the Envoys to Bukton and Scogan, the chiding of Adam Scriveyn, the *jeu d'esprit* "To Rosemounde," and the parodic "Merciles Beaute" and "Complaint of Chaucer to His Purse."

Chaucer's lyrics, of which many probably do not survive, are the foundation for the secular lyrics of the 15th century that pretend to some refinement. Noteworthy among these are poems associated with Charles of Orléans. But the courtly tradition degenerates after Chaucer, the verse becoming exceedingly artificial, sometimes serving merely as a vehicle for music. It is significant that the first Chaucer epigone, Thomas Hoccleve, wrote no courtly lyrics, only eight begging poems and three parodic rondeaux to Lady Money. The parodies recall Chaucer's "Complaint to His Purse"; the begging poems, like Chaucer's, introduce personal references that give the "universal" voice typical of medieval lyric a different pitch, that of an individual, historical personage. Lydgate, another follower of Chaucer, wrote nearly 80 secular "lyrics," including eight love lyrics, eight antifeminist satires, a begging poem, and numerous occasional, practical, and moralistic poems. The writing is competent, not as florid as that of Lydgate's aureate religious lyrics, and it occasionally shows some sensitivity and wit. But in this verse Chaucer's seed can scarcely be said to have flourished.

Perhaps because more verse survives from the 15th century, it preserves a variety not seen among earlier extant lyrics: mnemonic poems, charms, gnomic verse, epitaphs, poems about money, occasional verse, punctuation poems. The more engaging lyric poetry in the 15th century tends to be "popular" in tone: drinking and feasting songs, holly-and-ivy poems, minstrels' verse; vulgar treatments of love, marriage, and sex, with double entendres. The vitality of the popular voice is eventually grafted onto the stock of learning, especially by the so-called Scottish Chaucerians writing at the end of the century. Only then does one find a truly inventive energy invigorating the conventions of late-medieval secular lyrics. Especially notable is Henryson's "Robene and Makyne," a pastourelle with an ironic *carpe diem* theme, precursor to Dunbar's parodic portrayal of rustic lovers ("In secret place"); also Henryson's burlesque "Sum Practysis of Medecyne," which anticipates the spirited vulgarity of language in Dunbar's raucous poems. Dunbar's verbal brilliance, however, coruscates in the high style as well as the low. Whereas Henryson opts for clarity and economy of expression, Dunbar takes the heavy gilt of Lydgate's most ornate language and makes it sparkle.

The Englishman Skelton, Dunbar's contemporary, seems also to have been drawn to more popular, less refined modes of writing. Initially working the vein of Lydgate's aureation, in due course he gave it up for a rollicking style now known as Skeltonics. The poems in this idiosyncratic style, however, had little influence on subsequent verse. The songs and lyrics of the Tudor tradition, virtually untouched by Skelton or the Scots, grew from the conventional, impersonal verse of the 15th century. It was soon cultivated in the Petrarchan manner by Wyatt and Surrey, and with the advent of the Italian influence the ME lyric may be said to have come to an end.

Daniel J. Ransom

Bibliography

PRIMARY

Brown, Carleton, ed. *English Lyrics of the XIIIth Century.* Oxford: Clarendon, 1932; Brown, Carleton, ed. *Religious Lyrics of the XVth Century.* Oxford: Clarendon, 1939; Brown, Carleton, ed. *Religious Lyrics of the XIVth Century.* 2d ed. Rev. G.V. Smithers. Oxford: Clarendon, 1952; Davies, Reginald Thorne, ed. *Medieval English Lyrics: A Critical Anthology.* London: Faber & Faber, 1963 [with glosses and useful notes]; Dobson, Eric J., and Frank Ll. Harrison, eds. and trans. *Medieval English Songs.* London: Faber & Faber, 1979 [elaborate edition of 33 lyrics composed before 1400 and preserved with music; provides copious annotation and music in modern notation]; Gray, Douglas, ed. *A Selection of Religious Lyrics.* Oxford: Clarendon, 1975; Luria, Maxwell S., and Richard L. Hoffman, eds. *Middle English Lyrics.* New York: Norton, 1974. Repr. with corrections, 1986 [with glosses, basic bibliography up to 1972, and selections of representative criticism]; Robbins, Rossell Hope, ed. *Secular Lyrics of the XIVth and XVth Centuries.* 2d ed. Oxford: Clarendon, 1955; Stone, Brian, trans. *Medieval English Verse.* Harmondsworth: Penguin, 1964; Wenzel, Siegfried. *Verses in Sermons: Fasciculus Morum and Its Middle English Poems.* Cambridge: Medieval Academy of America, 1978.

SECONDARY

New *CBEL* 1:697–712; Boffey, Julia. *Manuscripts of English Courtly Love Lyrics in the Later Middle Ages.* Cambridge: Brewer, 1985; Brown, Carleton, and Hope Robbins Rossell. *The Index of Middle English Verse.* New York: Columbia University Press, 1943. With Robbins, Rossell Hope, and John L. Cutler. *Supplement to the Index of Middle English Verse.* Lexington: University of Kentucky Press, 1965; Diehl, Patrick S. *The Medieval European Religious Lyric: An Ars Poetica.* Berkeley: University of California Press, 1985 [with a useful, lightly annotated bibliography for ME religious lyrics on pp. 245–47]; Dronke, Peter. *The Medieval Lyric.* 2d ed. London: Hutchinson, 1978; Gray, Douglas. *Themes and Images in the Medieval English Religious Lyric.* London: Routledge & Kegan Paul, 1972; Pearsall, Derek. *Old English and Middle English Poetry.* London: Routledge & Kegan Paul, 1977; Preston, Michael J. *A Concordance to the Middle English Shorter Poem.* 2 vols. Leeds: Maney, 1975; Wenzel, Siegfried. *Preachers, Poets, and the Early English Lyric.* Princeton: Princeton University Press, 1986; Woolf, Rosemary. *The English Religious Lyric in the Middle Ages.* Oxford: Clarendon, 1968.

See also Ballads; Carol; Charles of Orléans; Chaucer; Chaucerian Apocrypha; Dunbar; Friars' Miscellanies; Godric's Songs; Harley Lyrics; Karole; Literary Influences: French; Minstrels; Popular Culture; Rolle; Satire; Scottish Literature, Early; Skelton; Songs; Sumer Canon

M

Magna Carta (The Great Charter)

Issued by King John in June 1215 at Runnymede, in Surrey. In form the document is a royal charter, in Latin, granting privileges to "all the free men of our realm": in fact it consists of concessions that the king made in hope of ending the baronial rebellion that had broken out against him in the autumn of 1214.

The Charter may be modeled in part on the coronation charter of Henry I. It was based largely on several lists of demands prepared by the king's baronial opponents in the spring of 1215, though the Charter is often less radical than these antecedent drafts. The final version's relatively moderate tone has been credited by various scholars to several factors: the need of both sides to compromise to achieve an agreement; the influence and drafting habits of the royal scribes probably responsible for its actual wording; and the mediation of Archbishop Stephen Langton and, perhaps, William Marshal, earl of Pembroke, who was soon to be regent for John's son, Henry III.

The motives of the drafters of the document have been interpreted very differently. At one extreme they are seen as foresighted and altruistic, desiring to establish liberty for all persons in England. At the other they are viewed as reactionary and selfish, attempting to roll back the tide of expanding royal power and restore good old days when the barons dominated government and law.

The history of the Charter is complicated. In July 1215 John requested that the pope quash it. Innocent III replied by issuing a papal bull, dated 24 August, in which Magna Carta is annulled on the grounds that the king had been coerced into sealing it. Civil war was already brewing, again, over questions of the interpretation and enforcement of the Charter and grew worse after the papal bull became known about the end of September. After John's death in 1216, in an attempt to calm the situation, the regents for the young Henry III hastily reissued the Charter, shorn of many clauses either relevant only to the situation of 1215 or offensive to the royalist position.

In 1217 the same authorities carefully edited the Charter and reissued it again. The last reissue of Magna Carta, with relatively few changes, was made in 1225 by Henry III, now an adult, "spontaneously and of his own good will," in return for the grant of a tax. In 1217 the clauses of the charter of 1215 concerning the forest law (clauses 44, 47–48) were expanded into a separate document, the Charter of the Forest. The name "Magna Carta," the "Great Charter," developed in the 13th century because the document so called is the longer of the two charters which, from 1217 on, have shared a common history.

Because Magna Carta was never again reissued, the text of 1225 remained the legally valid version; but both charters were confirmed, without changes in wording, over 50 times between 1237 and the early 15th century, sometimes in moments of political tension. The most significant confirmation occurred in 1297, when, in the "Confirmation of the Charters," Edward I recognized Magna Carta and the Charter of the Forest as statutes.

After the first quarter of the 15th century the charters lost their role in political disputes; knowledge of them was preserved primarily in the context of legal cases, until, in the early 17th century, the parliamentary opponents of the Stuart monarchs revived Magna Carta as a symbol of the rights of Englishmen, which they saw themselves defending against royal attacks. The American colonists took Magna Carta as a touchstone of rights from these parliamentarians, especially Sir Edward Coke. The constitution of each state in the United States incorporates portions of Magna Carta in some form, and several provisions of the federal constitution derive directly or indirectly from it. In Great Britain the movement for law reform of the 19th and 20th centuries has resulted in the repeal of all but four clauses; only clauses (cl.) 1, 39, 40, and the general saving clause added in 1217, are still in force.

Given its genesis, the 1215 version can be read as an indictment of the conduct of royal government by John and, to some extent, of Henry II and Richard I. It can be presumed—and confirmed by comparison with the extant earlier drafts—that most of what John promised were concessions to the demands of his opponents; they therefore indicate what the barons did not like about the way the king had been running the country.

Two of these clauses have nonetheless been important throughout English and American history: clauses 39 and 40. In clause 40 the king promises not to sell, deny, or delay justice. In clause 39 he promises not to punish, in various specified ways, any free man "except by the lawful judgement of his peers or by the law of the land." Despite a great deal of dispute about the exact meaning of those phrases in and after 1215 there is a clear line of development, recorded in 14th-century statutes, from "law of the land" to "due process of law." The interpretation of "judgement of peers" as "trial by jury" is a more modern phenomenon, primarily of the 17th century. These two clauses, which together express a timeless ideal of impartial justice, are primarily responsible for the reputation of Magna Carta as the foundation of liberties for citizens of countries deriving their political and legal traditions from medieval England.

Most of the clauses, however, are more specific to their 13th-century context. A good many are concerned primarily with abolishing detested practices by which John had tried to coerce or frighten the barons into obedience; the taking of hostages and charters (cl. 49, 58–59) and use of mercenaries as soldiers and royal officials (cl. 50–51). These all disappear from the document by the 1216 reissue. Others, most of which remain in the reissues, impose limits on the king's demands for various services from his feudal tenants: the amounts chargeable for reliefs are set (cl. 2); the exercise of the feudal incidents of wardship and marriage is regulated (cl. 3–6, 37); widows' rights are protected (cl. 7–8); consent is required for scutages—money paid to the king in lieu of providing knights for battle—and all feudal aids except for specific types (cl. 12, 14); increased and additional services are forbidden (cl. 16, 23, 29, 43); baronial custody of vacant baronial abbeys is confirmed (cl. 46). Clauses 15 and 60 require that the barons grant their own vassals the feudal concessions that the king has granted them.

Another sizable group of clauses, most of which, again, remain in the reissues, regulate the conduct of royal government: methods used to collect debts due the king (cl. 9–11, 26–27), royal profits from administrative districts (cl. 25), and purveyance, the acquisition of foodstuffs for the king's household (cl. 28, 30–31). Still others concern royal justice: the enforcement of clause 39 (cl. 52–53, 56–57), the qualifications of royal justices and other officials (cl. 45), aspects of the holding of royal courts (cl. 17–19, 24), unsupported accusations by royal administrators (cl. 38) and by women (cl. 54), the means of assessing judicial fines (cl. 20–22, 55), and royal rights over the lands of felons (cl. 32).

Praecipe, a writ that, the Charter alleges, might cause a "free man" to "lose his court," is abolished (cl. 34), but the "writ of life and limb," which enabled a person accused of felony to avoid trial by battle under certain circumstances, is to be available without charge (cl. 36). In addition the first clause confirms the liberties of the church, referring to concessions John had already made in 1214; several clauses make grants whose principal beneficiaries were merchants (cl. 13, 33, 41–42) or their customers (cl. 35).

The last three clauses (61–63) provide a general enforcement mechanism, pardon royal subjects for opposition to the king, and formally enact all that precedes. Of these clause 61 holds the greatest interest, for in it the drafters of the charter confront the problem of how to force the king to adhere to the document. The solution is that he grants the barons the right to choose 25 of their number to constitute a committee that operates by majority rule when all its members cannot agree. The committee is to oversee royal adherence to the document, to hear complaints of noncompliance by the king and his officials, to remonstrate with the king about such failures, and, if necessary, to "distrain and distress us [the king] in every way they can, namely by seizing castles, lands and possessions, and in such other ways as they can, saving our person and those of our queen and our children, until, in their judgement, amends have been made." Although this is not quite a license to wage war on the king, such disputes over the meaning and enforcement of the charter were exactly what led, in the months after its issuance, to the recurrence of armed struggle between the king and his opponents among the barons.

Emily Zack Tabuteau

Bibliography

Holt, J.C. *Magna Carta and Medieval Government.* London: Hambledon, 1985 [collected essays]; Holt, J.C. *Magna Carta.* 2d ed. Cambridge: Cambridge University Press, 1992 [the translations used here are from this scholarly treatment and edition; see appendix 6]; Howard, A.E. Dick. *The Road from Runnymede: Magna Carta and Constitutionalism in America.* Charlottesville: University Press of Virginia, 1968; McKechnie, William S. *Magna Carta: A Commentary on the Great Charter of King John.* 2d ed. Glasgow: Maclehose, 1914. Repr. New York: Burt Franklin, 1958; Pallister, Anne. *Magna Carta: The Heritage of Liberty.* Oxford: Clarendon, 1971; Swindler, William F. *Magna Carta: Legend and Legacy.* Indianapolis: Bobbs-Merrill, 1965; Thompson, Faith. *The First Century of Magna Carta: Why It Persisted as a Document.* Minneapolis: University of Minnesota Press, 1925. Repr. New York: Russell & Russell, 1967; Thompson, Faith. *Magna Carta: Its Role in the Making of the English Constitution, 1300–1629.* Minneapolis: University of Minnesota Press, 1948.

See also Charters; Edward I; Henry III; John; Knight Service; Scutage; Wardship; William Marshal

Magnificat

The Magnificat, or Song of the Blessed Virgin Mary (Luke 1:46–55), was invariably sung or said at the office of Vespers, preceded and followed by the appointed antiphon. In the Salisbury Rite, as in most others, it was chanted to a more ornate version of the appropriate psalm tone, this and its ending being determined by the accompanying antiphon. The intonation was included in every verse, not just the first as in normal psalmody.

From the 14th century we find polyphonic settings of the Magnificat; English settings are the earliest known. It could also be sung in faburden, a form of three-part polyphony based on the chant and so simple that it could be improvised. The lowest part of such improvised polyphony (the faburden proper) could also be detached and used as the basis of more elaborate polyphonic settings, and this was indeed the usual method in the later Middle Ages in England. In at least one case, however, the so-called faburden is derived from the lowest voice of a notated 14th-century mensural setting, so that it is in fact, by definition, a "square." Magnificat faburdens in general seem to inhabit the border between the derivatives of improvised and simple written polyphony.

The polyphonic Magnificat was widely cultivated in the 15th and early 16th centuries by such composers as Dunstable, Fayrfax, Ludford, Taverner, and Cornysh. It was usually, though not invariably, a setting of the even-numbered verses of the canticle and made use of the faburden of the chant. The procedure in such cases was not that of a *cantus firmus* but rather was motivic in technique. In these circumstances the identification of the tone on which the Magnificat is ultimately based (and to which the alternate verses must be sung) has occasionally proved difficult. But Taverner's three settings are all directly built on the tone itself; and there is a faburden setting for organ of the odd-numbered verses (minus the intonation to the first verse) bearing the quaint title "The viij tune in c faut"—that is, it is derived from tone 8 transposed down a 5th.

John Caldwell

Bibliography

Harrison, Frank Ll. *Music in Medieval Britain.* 2d ed. London: Routledge & Kegan Paul, 1963; Steiner, Ruth, Winfried Kirsch, and Roger Bullivant. "Magnificat." *NGD* 11:495–500.

See also Discant; Faburden; Square

Malmesbury Abbey

Of the Romanesque Benedictine abbey church of Malmesbury, in Wiltshire (fig. 90), which was probably commenced by Abbot Peter Moraunt (1140–58), the nave survives as the parish church albeit with the west front and three western bays only partially preserved. The west wall of the south transept remains to the top of the triforium, and the northeast crossing pier is extant with adjacent

Fig. 90. Malmesbury Abbey, nave interior. Courtesy RCHME, copyright Batsford.

stumps of the north transept and the north side of the presbytery with its aisle. High rib vaults covered the presbytery and transepts, but the nave was originally wood-roofed, as evidenced by the continuation of the triple wall shafts to the top of the wall above the early-14th-century lierne vault. Rib vaults were used in the presbytery aisles and are still extant in the nave aisles and south porch. The elevation comprises a pointed main arcade on columnar piers, a round-headed false gallery, and a (remodeled) clerestory with wall passage.

Numerous motifs, including the pointed arches, beaded medallions around the clerestory windows, and arched corbels beneath the presbytery gallery stringcourse, may be associated with Burgundy and possibly serve as a visual reminder of Peter Moraunt's earlier career as a monk at Cluny and prior of La Charité-sur-Loire. However, the detailing speaks of a West Country training for the master mason: the pointed arches on columnar piers were earlier used at Exeter Cathedral (after 1114), and beaded medallions appeared at Hereford Cathedral (after 1107–15) and on the triumphal arch and presbytery south windows at Llandaff Cathedral (after 1120). The rich articulation of the main arcade and gallery arches evolves from the nave of Gloucester Cathedral (fig. 68: see GLOUCESTER CATHEDRAL; witness the twin soffit rolls and the label masks of the main arcade and the 90-degree chevron in the gallery. The triple shafts above the main-arcade capitals recall those in the dado arcade of Evesham Abbey gatehouse, while the dragon's-head label stops appear in pre-Conquest Deerhurst Priory.

The magnificent south porch is probably inspired by southwestern French models like Moissac, even though there seems to be no parallel either iconographically or stylistically with work in that region. Christ in Majesty, flanked by flying angels, occupies the small tympanum of the south doorway. The tympana of the side walls of the porch are carved on a large scale with apostles, while on the entrance arch to the porch five orders are enriched with stylized foliage patterns, and three medallions occupied with virtues and vices from the *Psychomachia,* and with Old and New Testament scenes. Iconographically the sources are Anglo-Saxon, while stylistically the figures belong with those inspired by Bishop Roger's work at Old Sarum, such as the Christ above the north doorway at Lullington (Somerset).

The richly arcaded west front of Malmesbury stands at the beginning of the tradition of the screen facade in English architecture, as at Wells (fig. 122: see Screen Facades) and Salisbury cathedrals. Details of the Malmesbury facade, like the alternation of continuous and noncontinuous orders of the west doorway, and continuous orders in blind arches, are also influential in the local West Country School of Gothic architecture.

Malcolm Thurlby

Bibliography

Brakspear, H. "Malmesbury Abbey." *Archaeologia* 64 (1913): 399–436; Brakspear, H. "A West Country School of Masons." *Archaeologia* 81 (1931): 1–18; Wilson, Christopher. "The Sources of the Late Twelfth-Century Work at Worcester Cathedral." *Medieval Art and Architecture at Worcester Cathedral.* *BAACT* for 1975. London: British Archaeological Association, 1978, pp. 80–90.

See also Architecture and Architectural Sculpture, Romanesque; Gloucester Cathedral; Screen Facades; Sculpture, Romanesque

Malory, Thomas (1414/18–1471)

One of the latest and most effective of the many medieval writers about King Arthur and his knights of the Round Table. In his book traditionally called *Le Morte Darthur (The Death of Arthur)* Malory gathers together the results of centuries of storytelling, mainly by medieval French authors. He synthesizes the narratives into one massive, varied book of the life, acts, and death of Arthur and his company. The wealth of incident, rich implications, and laconic style make his the only version of the huge number of medieval Arthurian tales in European languages that continues to be read directly and simply for pleasure by the modern reader. The main characters—King Arthur himself; Sir Lancelot, his best knight, but also lover of his queen, Guinevere; his sister's son the violent Sir Gawain; his incestuously begotten son and nephew Sir Mordred, who kills him; Merlin the magician—are at the center of a set of tales of wonders, bravery, love, joy, and tragedy. But Malory tells romance as history—the history of England said to be in the 5th century, but actually represented in terms of the feelings, strivings, ideals, betrayals, even the armor and the geography (e.g., Camelot is identified with Winchester) of Malory's own troubled 15th-century England. Malory's achievement is the source of many of the retellings of Arthurian story so common today in the United States and Britain.

Life

Identification of the Sir Thomas Malory who names himself as author of *Le Morte Darthur* has been controversial, but thanks to the work of P.J.C. Field and others it seems once more to be probable that he was the Sir Thomas Malory of Newbold Revel in Warwickshire. He was the son of a country gentleman, inherited his lands in 1433 or 1434, was knighted, and perhaps served as a soldier in France. In 1445 he became a member of parliament—a sign of gentry status, not of democratic election. He also became embroiled in the factional disturbances of the times and was on numerous occasions in the next ten years accused of such violent crimes as ambush, rape, extortion, cattle stealing, theft of money, and prison breaking. He underwent a series of imprisonments and despite his escapes spent much time in jail. Some of the accusations, perhaps some of the violence, may have been politically motivated, for Malory supported various noblemen (including Warwick the "Kingmaker") who contended for power during the Wars of the Roses, following now one king, the Lancastrian Henry VI, and now another, the Yorkist Edward IV.

After a period of freedom Malory spent the years 1468–70 in prison, where he wrote *Le Morte Darthur.* The book is full of violent adventure and concludes in civil war and Arthur's death. But it is also deeply concerned with the high ideals of chivalry, with honor, loyalty, and goodness. It may seem that the book's inherent nobility contrasts strangely with the apparent criminality of the author. But perhaps Malory saw himself in imagination as a modern Sir Lancelot fighting for and asserting his own and his lord's rights against other "false recreant knights," as he might have called them.

Text

Two versions of *Le Morte Darthur* survive, neither originating immediately from Malory's hand. One is the edition printed by Caxton in 1485, reprinted 1498, 1529, 1557, circa 1578, again (somewhat changed) in 1634, then not again till 1816. In the later 19th century began the modern series of editions based on Caxton, including that notoriously illustrated by Aubrey Beardsley (1893–94). But in 1934 a manuscript of *Le Morte Darthur* now in the British Library (Add. 59678) was discovered in Winchester College; it was first edited in 1947 by Eugène Vinaver.

The Winchester manuscript contains a text slightly different from Caxton's, including fuller versions of eight addresses by Malory to the reader, varying in length from a few sentences to the paragraph at the end of the whole book. They come at the end of substantial sections and are known as *explicits* (*explicit*, "it is finished"). From these *explicits* Vinaver deduced that, instead of one book, Malory wrote eight entirely separate romances. Their apparent separateness is enhanced in his edition by such typographical devices as capitals at the end of the sections for which there is no manuscript justification. Vinaver's edition is thus confusingly entitled *The Works of Sir Thomas Malory.* Virtually all scholars and critics now reject this concept of totally separate works but do accept the episodic nature of the work even within the eight main sections and the existence of a number of inevitable inconsistencies both between and within the main sections.

The Winchester manuscript is separated from Malory's own writing by at least one intermediate copy and lacks a few leaves at beginning and end. Although Caxton had the Winchester manuscript in his shop for a period of time, his own edition differs from it significantly. He edited the text by cutting it into 21 books comprising 507 chapters, adding a fine Prologue and chapter headings, reducing some of the *explicits,* shortening (to its advantage) the episode of the Roman War by almost half, and making some other minor verbal changes. By comparing the two versions we can reconstruct Malory's authentic text, which is now most nearly approached by Vinaver's edition.

The language of the Winchester manuscript and Caxton's edition is mainly standard mid-15th-century London English, with occasional northernisms. Being prose, it is easily modernized; the original, though old-fashioned and containing a few unfamiliar words, offers no difficulty apart from idiosyncratic spelling. As a narrative the story is engrossing, but it is not at all like a modern novel, and to read it as such is to court disappointment and misunderstanding.

Summary

Malory plunges straight into his story, telling of the begetting of Arthur by Uther Pendragon, king of all England, on the beautiful widow (as she has just unwittingly become) of the duke of Cornwall, Uther being magically transformed by Merlin into the duke's likeness so as to enter her bedroom. The laconic matter-of-fact style, concentrating on essentials, contrasts piquantly with the drama of passionate feeling and the magic. This contrast, much developed, is part of Malory's unending fascination. As his great story progresses, he makes less use of magic, though it is always an element of mystery in the background, suggesting a dimension beyond the material world and becoming prominent again near the end, with the return of Excalibur to the lake and the queens who carry off the dying Arthur.

We learn of Arthur's fostering, his acceptance as king by the miracle that he alone can draw a sword from a stone, and the gradual establishment of his power over dissident barons and neighboring kings. Merlin's magic helps. Arthur lusts after King Lot of Orkney's wife, Morgause, mother of Gawain and other heroic knights and, unknown to him, his own half-sister. On her he begets Mordred, who will ultimately be his death. Arthur loves and marries Guinevere, though Merlin warns him that she and Lancelot will love each other. She brings with her the Round Table, which henceforth will denote the elite company of knights in Arthur's court.

This first section thus sets the scene and establishes Arthur's supremacy, though with its account of wars it is a little less typical of Malory's mature style, which concentrates more on individual adventures. Malory is attempting to summarize his complex sources of French prose romance, turning them into a kind of history, and minor inconsistencies inevitably arise. This section also contains the tragic tale of the brothers Balin and Balan; with its concentration on individuals, its fated accidents, nobility of temper, deceit, dissension, and tragedy it is as stark and moving a story as any Icelandic saga.

But there are also stories of mystery, magic, adventure, betrayal, and mishap that end in triumph. Arthur gains the magic sword Excalibur from the Lady of the Lake. The noble concept of the High Order of Knighthood is affirmed, reinforced as it is by the oath, sworn by knights of the Round Table at the annual feast of Pentecost, never to do wrong, always to honor ladies, and so on.

Malory's *explicit* to the first main section refers to himself as a "knight-prisoner" and appears to suggest that he may not be able to continue to write. But the opening words of the second section echo this *explicit* so clearly as to make continuity certain. This next section is based mainly on a 14th-century English alliterative poem, the *Morte Arthure,* which makes Malory's own style more alliterative. It tells how Arthur rejects the obligation to pay tribute to the emperor of Rome and how he wages successful war right into Italy. Here Lancelot makes his first appearance as a brave young warrior.

The third main section moves into the area Malory has made his own for ever—the feats of individual knights wandering in search of adventure in strange forests and castles. The hero of this book is Lancelot himself, Malory's favorite knight, killing wicked knights, rescuing ladies, resisting seduction. He is rumored to be the lover of Queen Guinevere, which he denies, and Malory does not describe their love. It is a relatively short section, delightfully varied and vividly interesting in event, created from a cunning selection of incidents widely spaced in Malory's voluminous source, the French prose *Lancelot.*

Having now established both Arthur with his Round Table and Lancelot, the supreme example of chivalry, Malory turns in his fourth section to the story of another knight, significant to the whole history, exemplary in himself, and an adornment to the Round Table—Sir Gareth of Orkney, brother to Sir Gawain. The source is unknown. The story is based on the familiar general pattern of the Fair Unknown, who is a young hero, handsome, brave, and clever but unrecognized. He achieves success by defeating foes older and more experienced than he, winning his beloved, and establishing his identity and his place in society. This has been termed a version of the "family drama," common in fairy tale and romance. It also illustrates the Malorian themes of bravery, noble bearing, and courtesy.

There follows the long section, over a third of the whole work, centered on the story of Tristram and Isolde, with so many other knights and adventures intermingled that it is impossible to summarize adequately. The ancient tragedy of Tristram's and Isolde's obsessive mutual infatuation had already been diluted by Malory's French sources, and at the end of Malory's version the lovers retire to adulterous bliss in Lancelot's castle of Joyous Gard. Tristram is here an adventurous knight similar and almost equal to Lancelot. He has a jesting companion, Sir Dinadan, who brings commonsensical skepticism to the craziness of knight-errantry but is a good knight of his hands for all that. King Mark, husband of Isolde, is portrayed as a treacherous villain. Only incidentally, in a later section, is Mark's murder of Tristram noted. This Tristram section, full of adventures, disguises, unexpected meetings, unexplained departures, and arbitrary battles, has all the mystery and excitement of romance. It is the part of Malory's work least like the world of plausible appearances of the novel.

A digression toward the end of the Tristram section tells how Lancelot was tricked into begetting Sir Galahad upon Elaine, daughter of Sir Pelles. This leads naturally to the sixth section, in which Sir Galahad, now a pure virginal young knight, comes to King Arthur's court. Miraculous events initiate the Quest of the Holy Grail. The Grail, according to Malory, is the dish from which Christ ate with the apostles on Easter, brought to England by Joseph of Arimathea and endowed with properties both holy and magical. Hermits exhort the knights in their quest, visions and allegories abound, though Malory greatly abbreviates the religious didacticism of his French source. Only Galahad, Percival, and Bors succeed in seeing the Grail; Galahad and Percival both die, passing beyond human ken, and Bors is the only successful Grail knight to return to Camelot. Lancelot is granted only a partial vision of the Grail. He is flawed by his love of Guinevere, but Malory changes the monastic spirit of the original, so that Lancelot remains in a sense the hero. Despite all the changes many beautiful and magical scenes remain, as in the appearance of the ship with Percival's sister.

The last two sections of *Le Morte Darthur,* the seventh and eighth, may be considered as one, for they tell of the supreme glory of the Round Table and its tragic end in a series of closely connected episodes. Malory's art is here at its greatest. He blends French and English sources, but what he makes, fleshed out with his own invention, is entirely his own and one of the great achievements of English literature. The core of the story is the continuing love between Lancelot and Guinevere, and the determination of some malcontents to trap them, so that King Arthur has to condemn them. Lancelot has to rescue the queen three times, and on one occasion he accidentally kills Sir Gareth, his beloved friend, whom he had himself knighted. This joins Gareth's brother Gawain to Lancelot's enemies, and eventually Arthur is forced by Gawain to declare war on Lancelot.

During Arthur's absence at the war Mordred claims the throne and attempts to marry Guinevere. Ultimately, after Gawain has repented of his vengeful feud against Lancelot and died from wounds, Mordred confronts Arthur in battle. The bastard son and noble father kill each other in the desolation of the corpse-strewn battlefield. Arthur dies slowly by a "water-side." Excalibur is thrown into a lake and a hand mysteriously grasps it. Queens come in a boat to take Arthur to Avalon. It is an unforgettably eerie scene, rich in the ancient potent symbolism of the separation, dissolution, and healing power of death. Guinevere enters a nunnery; after a final interview with her Lancelot withdraws to a hermitage, and they die without meeting again.

No mere summary can convey the power, beauty, and pathos of these two sections. Much of the action is conveyed through brilliant terse dialogue, occasionally with a touch of grim or sarcastic humor. There is a wealth of incident in such episodes as Lancelot's rescues of Guinevere, or in the beautiful account of the Fair Maid of Ascolat (later spelled Astolat), who dies for love of Lancelot, or the moving story of Lancelot's healing of Sir Urry. The best knight in the world weeps in humility as he performs the miraculous cure, yet he is the one who causes the destruction of Arthur's Round Table.

Malory's imaginative world is narrow. It is composed only of Arthur, of good or bad knights, and a few desirable or treacherous ladies who, with two or three exceptions, are hardly more than ciphers. No ordinary concerns of life appear. Simple themes are illustrated by simple actions, performed by characters with few traits and virtually no inner life. Yet Malory's earnest concentration on fundamental issues of loyalty, love, and combat, guided by a complex system of honor, is intensely alive. The encounters, friendly or hostile, the wanderings, the seemingly arbitrary events combined with the sense of destiny, the comradeship and the betrayals, create a profound symbol of life that we can easily relate to. Malory's prose creates a sense of the man as in his essence he would be: no mere "narrator" but writing directly to us in the colloquial yet dignified manner of a brave and courteous country gentleman, on a subject that deeply matters to him, the history of Arthur, of England, of all of us.

Derek S. Brewer

Bibliography

PRIMARY

Brewer, Derek Stanley, ed. *The Morte Darthur, Parts Seven and Eight.* London: Arnold, 1968 [modernized text]; Cowen, Janet, ed. *Le Morte D'Arthur.* 2 vols. Harmondsworth: Penguin, 1969 [Caxton's edition in modernized spelling]; *Le Morte D'Arthur Printed by William Caxton 1485.* London: Scolar, 1976 [facsimile]; Spisak, James W., ed. *Caxton's Malory.* 2 vols. Berkeley: University of California Press, 1983; Vinaver, Eugène, ed. *The Works of Sir Thomas Malory.* 3d ed. Rev. P.J.C. Field. 3 vols. Oxford: Clarendon, 1990; *The Winchester Malory.* EETS s.s. 4. London: Oxford University Press, 1976 [facsimile].

SECONDARY

New *CBEL* 1:674–78; *Manual* 3:757–71, 909–24;
Archibald, Elizabeth, and A.S.G. Edwards, eds. *A
Companion to Malory*. Cambridge: Brewer, 1996;
Bennett, J.A.W., ed. *Essays on Malory*. Oxford:
Clarendon, 1963; Benson, Larry D. *Malory's Morte
Darthur*. Cambridge: Harvard University Press, 1976;
Brewer, Derek Stanley. *Symbolic Stories: Traditional
Narratives of the Family Drama in English Literature*.
Cambridge: Brewer, 1980 [on the story of Sir Gareth];
Field, P.J.C. *The Life and Times of Sir Thomas Malory*.
Cambridge: Brewer, 1993; Gaines, Barry. *Sir Thomas
Malory: An Anecdotal Bibliography of Editions 1485–
1985*. New York: AMS, 1990; Ihle, Sandra Ness.
*Malory's Grail Quest: Invention and Adaptation in Me-
dieval Prose Romance*. Madison: University of Wiscon-
sin Press, 1983; Kato, Tomomi, ed. *A Concordance to
the Works of Sir Thomas Malory*. Tokyo: University of
Tokyo Press, 1974; Kennedy, Beverly. *Knighthood in
the Morte Darthur*. Cambridge: Brewer, 1985; Knight,
Stephen. *Arthurian Literature and Society*. London:
Macmillan, 1983; Lambert, Mark. *Malory: Style and
Vision in Le Morte Darthur*. New Haven: Yale Univer-
sity Press, 1975; Life, Page West. *Sir Thomas Malory
and the Morte Darthur: A Survey of Scholarship and
Annotated Bibliography*. Charlottesville: University
Press of Virginia, 1980; McCarthy, Terence. *An Intro-
duction to Malory*. Cambridge: Brewer, 1993; Parins,
Marylyn Jackson, ed. *Malory: The Critical Heritage*.
London: Routledge, 1988; Riddy, Felicity. *Sir Thomas
Malory*. Leiden: Brill, 1987; Sandved, Arthur O. *Stud-
ies in the Language of Caxton's Malory and That of the
Winchester Manuscript*. Oslo: Norwegian Universities
Press, 1968; Spisak, James W., ed. *Studies in Malory*.
Kalamazoo: Medieval Institute, 1985; Takamiya,
Toshiyuki, and Derek S. Brewer, eds. *Aspects of Malory*.
Cambridge: Brewer, 1981. Repr. with updated bibli-
ography, 1986; Whitaker, Muriel. *Arthur's Kingdom of
Adventure: The World of Malory's Morte Darthur*. Cam-
bridge: Brewer, 1984.

See also Caxton; Chivalry; Literary Influences: French; Matter of Britain; *Morte Arthur,* Stanzaic; *Morte Arthure,* Alliterative; Prose, ME; Romances; Wars of the Roses

Mandeville's Travels

A 14th-century account of the Near and the Far East. The English versions of the work, like those in eight other languages,
are translations, the original having been written in French,
probably around 1357, possibly on the Continent, by an unknown author. There is little specifically English or even
French about the book, which is as heterogeneous as the world
it describes, being at once a guide for genuine and vicarious
pilgrims to Jerusalem and the Holy Land, a piece of crusading propaganda, a satire on the moral and political failings of
Latin Christendom, an ethnogeography and natural history
of northern Africa and Asia, an extended argument that natu-

ral law has given all peoples some knowledge of God, and a
collection of tales and "diversities."

Still *Mandeville's Travels* has at least one important connection with England: its claim to be the work of a certain
John Mandeville, knight, born at St. Albans near London,
who traveled the world for 34 years (1322–56) before returning home to write about "some part of the things that are
there." This claim found ready acceptance for five centuries,
and the book came to occupy "a special place in English literature" (Bennett, 1954: 9). Only in the 19th century did
scholars show both that the *Mandeville* author was not "the
father of English prose" and that he may not have traveled at
all. Following the common medieval practice of rewriting
other works, he compiled his imaginative "memoirs" from
numerous sources, among them William of Boldensele's pilgrimage itinerary (1336) and Odoric of Pordenone's account
of the Far East (1330).

The compilation was so popular with European audiences that roughly 300 manuscripts have survived. Nor did
its popularity wane with the invention of printing, the first
editions appearing as early as the 1480s. Unraveling the complicated textual tradition has proved difficult, however. Scholars have shown that the French original gave rise to two independent scribal traditions, one continental, the other insular
or "English." The latter is represented by some 80 manuscripts, dating from 1390 on, all of which are considered descendants of an Anglo-French version of the original: 3 Irish,
13 Latin, 21 or 22 French, and 44 English. The English manuscripts represent at least six separate versions of the *Travels,*
including an abridgment, a metrical adaptation, and a stanzaic fragment.

Most numerous of these is the Defective version, so called
because of a large gap in the text. Found in over 30 manuscripts and frequently printed from 1496 on, this version was
the only English text available until 1725, when the unique
Cotton version appeared (BL Cotton Titus C.xvi). In 1889
another unique manuscript was published, the Egerton version (BL Egerton 1982). Only the Cotton and the Egerton
versions offer full texts, Cotton being closer to the Anglo-
French source but less assured than Egerton. Partly because of
its closeness to a French source, and partly because the Egerton
version was not readily available until 1953, the Cotton text
has become the most commonly cited English version. Hanna's arguments for the Defective version as "the English *Mandeville*" have some merit, but it is worth remembering that
there is no consensus on "what a Mandeville text should be"
(Hanna, 1984: 123).

Mandeville's Travels opens with a prologue that sounds
like a call for a crusade, but the book is far more than crusading propaganda. Intended for those who want to "hear speak
of the Holy Land" and of the "many diverse lands . . . [and]
diverse folk . . . of diverse customs and laws," the book considers the Near East in considerable detail (Cotton text, chs.
1–15) before turning to other lands, mainly in Asia (chs. 16–
34). A useful visual analog to its world may be found in the
encyclopedic medieval world maps, such as the Hereford and
Ebstorf *mappaemundi* or the *Catalan Atlas*. The book is mostly

organized as a descriptive itinerary ("and from there one goes to . . ."), using its roughly linear geographical tour as an opportunity for presenting information and telling an occasional tale. Subjects touched on include pilgrimage and travel routes, sites and relics in the Holy Land, different religious and social practices, languages and alphabets, geography, the Sultan of Egypt, the Great Khan, Prester John, curious flora and fauna, and monstrous races.

We hear little of "Sir John's" own experiences as a traveler, yet one gets a distinct sense of his personality: faithful yet skeptical, pious yet curious, humble yet brazen, genial and humane yet mercenary (he claims to have fought for the Sultan of Egypt against the Bedouin and for the Great Khan against the King of Manzi). So striking is this almost Chaucerian narrator that many readers have been tempted to see him as a portrait of the author, though the matter is uncertain at best.

As a literary work *Mandeville's Travels* offers little out of the ordinary. A few internal cross-references show that it was constructed with some thought to the whole, but its form is largely a matter of convenience. This is also true of its paratactic prose style, which nevertheless has a certain charm and even a compelling directness. For most modern readers the book's interest will lie in its curious content, not its style, and they will read the text as a "romance of travel" (Bennett, 1954: 39–53).

This may well have always been the case, but with one important difference where early readers are concerned: for them romance and history were not necessarily as distinct as we assume them to be, and Sir John's "romance" could easily have been read as true. In some Latin and French manuscripts, for example, it appears alongside Marco Polo's *Travels,* each presumably confirming the truth of the other. Also there are few adaptations like the Metrical version, which treats the *Travels* largely as a collection of stories and diversities. The surviving versions suggest that those texts offering more than entertainment were also more popular. Although it often appears alone in manuscripts, the *Travels* is sometimes found alongside other texts: *Piers Plowman* five times, the *Prick of Conscience,* and various religious texts in prose and verse. Here, one suspects, the book was being read for its concern with the state of Christendom, for its information about Christian history, and perhaps even as a devotional text. Nor was the book's early audience restricted to those who wanted entertainment, history, or piety. Cosmographers and explorers like Richard Hakluyt and Martin Frobisher turned to it for information; for them it was "a *summa* of travel lore" (Howard, 1971: 2). There is nothing else in ME quite like it, even among other geographical and travel writings.

Iain Higgins

Bibliography

PRIMARY

Letts, Malcolm, ed. and trans. *Mandeville's Travels: Texts and Translations.* 2 vols. Hakluyt Society 2d ser. 101–02. London: Hakluyt Society, 1953 [contains the Egerton version (modernized), the earliest known text (French), and an English abridgment]; Moseley, Charles W.R.D., trans. *The Travels of Sir John Mandeville.* Harmondsworth: Penguin, 1983 [Egerton version; useful introduction]; Seymour, Michael C., ed. *Mandeville's Travels.* Oxford: Clarendon, 1967 [Cotton version; modernized text published 1968 for Oxford World's Classics series]; Seymour, Michael C., ed. *The Metrical Version of Mandeville's Travels.* EETS o.s. 269. London: Oxford University Press, 1973; Warner, George F., ed. *The Buke of John Maundeuill.* Roxburghe Club. Westminster: Nichols, 1889 [Egerton version; hard to obtain, but contains the best annotations and an Anglo-French text].

SECONDARY

New *CBEL* 1:467–74, 2141; *Manual* 7:2235–54, 2449–66; Bennett, Josephine Waters. *The Rediscovery of Sir John Mandeville.* New York: Modern Language Association, 1954; Hanna, Ralph, III. "Mandeville." In *Middle English Prose: A Critical Guide to Major Authors and Genres,* ed. A.S.G. Edwards. New Brunswick: Rutgers University Press, 1984, pp. 121–32; Higgins, Iain. *Writing East: The Fourteenth-Century "Travels" of Sir John Mandeville.* Philadelphia: University of Pennsylvania Press, forthcoming; Howard, Donald R. "The World of Mandeville's Travels." *Yearbook of English Studies* 1 (1971): 1–17.

See also Anglo-Norman Literature; *Marvels of the East;* Matter of Antiquity; *Piers Plowman;* Pilgrimages; Prose, ME; Scientific and Medical Writings; Scientific Manuscripts, Early; Textual Criticism; Translation

Manning, Robert (fl. 1303–38)

Author of two long ME poems, *Handlyng Synne* and the *Chronicle,* or *Story of England.* Most of the facts about his life come from his own information in these works, especially in the prologues. He was a canon of the Gilbertine order, which had its main strength in Lincolnshire. He writes that he is "of Brunne," that is, Bourne in south Lincolnshire. Around 1300 he was at Cambridge, where he met Robert Bruce; perhaps he was a student there at the Gilbertine house of St. Edmund's Hall. He began *Handlyng Synne* in 1303 while at Sempringham, the mother house of the Gilbertines, a few miles north of Bourne. An independent record of 1327 notes him as a chaplain in Lincoln. It was apparently at Sixhills Priory, northwest of Lincoln, that he completed his *Chronicle* in 1338.

Handlyng Synne (Manning's title means "Treating of Sin") is based on an Anglo-Norman treatise, the *Manuel des péchés,* attributed to one William of Waddington. Almost 13,000 lines long, it is an aid to confession, directed at "lewde men" (i.e., the laity), giving basic and practical guidance on church teaching, and structured around the Ten Commandments, the seven deadly sins, the sin of sacrilege, the seven sacraments, and the twelve rules and graces of confession. Manning writes in a straightforward style in four-stress couplets for those who like to listen to "talys and rymys," so as to draw them away from foolish stories to spend their time more profitably. To this end the consequences of sinfulness are illustrated by a series of embedded tales, so that the structure of the work is akin to that of Gower's *Confessio Amantis.* Manning adds a number of local stories to his Anglo-Norman source, such as those of the sacrilegious Norfolk knight who was reproved by a villager for allowing his cattle to graze in the churchyard, and the Lincolnshire executors who took the testator's money for themselves.

The point of the work is to show how "we handel synne every day," and so for Manning sin is no abstract concept but a matter of everyday behavior. Sloth is the rich man who, unconcerned with Matins and other such "giblets" (extras), spends a leisurely Sunday sleeping late and playing chess. Pride is the desire to be called "lorde or syre," "madame or lady"; it is the man's delight in "ryche beddyng, yn hors, yn harneys," and the woman's delight in saffron wimples, covering yellow skin with yellow cloth—"yelugh under yelugh they hyde." The message constantly repeated throughout *Handlyng Synne* is that sin is ever present and must be confessed to a priest. Salvation is possible only through the good offices of the church, which in response must be supported by the laity with bequests and payment for masses for the dead.

Handlyng Synne is preserved in whole or in part in nine manuscripts, of which the most complete are the three closely related texts in Bodleian Library, Bodley 415; Washington, D.C., Folger Library V.b.236; and BL Harley 1701, all from the earlier 15th century, as well as the later CUL Ii.4.9 and Yale University Osborn a.2.

The *Chronicle* falls into two parts, both based on works by Anglo-Norman writers. The first part, beginning with the flight of Aeneas from Troy and the settlement of Britain by his descendant Brutus, and ending with the reign of Cadwalader, is legendary, derived principally from the 12th-century *Roman de Brut* by Wace, with additional material from Bede, Geoffrey of Monmouth, and other sources. It consists of nearly 17,000 lines in four-stress couplets. The second part, which takes the account up to the death of Edward I in 1307, relies mainly on the Anglo-Norman *Chronicle* of Peter of Langtoft, with additional material from such historians as Aelred of Rievaulx and Henry of Huntingdon, the "romaunce" of Richard the Lionheart (probably in French), and some information Manning has collected from oral sources. This part contains over 8,300 lines in alexandrine couplets (six-stress lines), varied with occasional tail-rhyme stanzas and four-stress couplets.

The tone of Manning's *Chronicle* is nationalistic. Following Langtoft, Manning venomously denounces the Scots for their wars with Edward I and in virulent tail-rhyme stanzas exults in their defeat. He glories in the crusading exploits of King Richard and portrays Arthur's court as the summit of European civilization, while complaining that English readers have to go to French books for accounts of Arthur's adventures. He is particularly interested in local events and, know-ing the English romance of *Havelok,* is puzzled because no authoritative historian has given an account of this Lincolnshire hero.

The *Chronicle* was written at the behest of Robert of Malton, probably a Gilbertine from Malton Abbey in Yorkshire. One of the motives for the commission was presumably an attempt to mobilize sentiment against the Scots, since the Gilbertines together with the Lincolnshire population as a whole were financially heavily involved in the Scottish wars of the 1330s. Also expressed in the *Chronicle* is the bitter resentment felt by the English people at the serfdom imposed by their lords. Manning traces this back to the coming of the Normans, thereby aligning the Gilbertines with the local population with whom they lived in mutual dependence.

The *Chronicle* survives in two manuscripts, a somewhat abbreviated text of the later 14th century in Inner Temple Library Petyt 511, vol. 7, and a slightly revised, mid-15th-century version in Lambeth Palace Library 131. Both manuscripts are from Lincolnshire. A short fragment is also preserved in Bodl. Rawlinson D.913.

The *Meditations on the Supper of Our Lord,* a poem preserved together with *Handlyng Synne* in three manuscripts, used to be ascribed to Manning, but there is nothing to support this attribution.

Thorlac Turville-Petre

Bibliography

PRIMARY

Furnivall, Frederick J., ed. *The Story of England by Robert Manning of Brunne.* 2 vols. Rolls Series 87. London: Eyre & Spottiswoode, 1887 [*Chronicle,* part 1]; Furnivall, Frederick J., ed. *Robert of Brunne's "Handlyng Synne."* EETS o.s. 119, 123. London: Kegan Paul, Trench, Trübner, 1901–03; Hearne, Thomas, ed. *Peter Langtoft's Chronicle.* 2 vols. Oxford, 1725. Repr. London: Bagster, 1810 [*Chronicle,* part 2]; Sullens, Idelle, ed. *Robert Mannyng of Brunne: Handlyng Synne.* MRTS 14. Binghamton: MRTS, 1983; Sullens, Idelle, ed. *Robert Mannyng of Brunne: The Chronicle.* MRTS 153. Binghamton: MRTS, 1996.

SECONDARY

New *CBEL* 1:465–66 (*Chronicle*), 503–04 (*Handlyng Synne*); *Manual* 5:1400–03, 1648–49, 8:2625–28, 2811–18 (*Chronicle*); 7:2255–57, 2470–74 (*Handlyng Synne*); Crosby, Ruth. "Robert Mannyng of Brunne: A New Biography." *PMLA* 57 (1942): 15–28; Robertson, D.W., Jr. "The Cultural Tradition of *Handlyng Synne.*" *Speculum* 22 (1947): 162–85; Summerfield, Thea. *The Matter of Kings' Lives: The Design of Past and Present in the Early Fourteenth-Century Verse Chronicles by Pierre de Langtoft and Robert Mannyng.* Amsterdam: Rodopi, forthcoming; Turville-Petre, Thorlac. "Politics and Poetry in the Early Fourteenth Century: The Case of Robert Manning's *Chronicle.*" *RES* n.s. 39 (1988): 1–28.

See also Anglo-Norman Literature; Chronicles; Geoffrey of Monmouth; Gower; Moral and Religious Instruction; Penitentials; Peter of Langtoft

Manor Courts and Court Rolls

Manor courts, also called leet courts and customary courts, performed a variety of functions, including many associated today with such disparate institutions as small-claims courts, licensing agencies, "neighborhood watch" programs, and town-council meetings. Presided over by the landlord's steward, these courts were held in some villages every three to four weeks; elsewhere they met but once or twice a year.

As tenants who tilled the soil and raised livestock the peasants used manor courts to regulate their communal systems of agriculture. The court jurors, usually twelve in number, were local village residents. Their responsibility was to present their neighbors for such infractions as breaking fences or hedges, allowing livestock to wander onto sown fields, leaving refuse in public roadways, or polluting village streams.

The village jurors were also called upon to identify tenants who defaulted in obligations to the lord of the manor. For example, if peasants refused to perform required work services on the landlord's demesne or transferred property without first surrendering their land into the lord's hands in court, a fine could be collected. The offenders identified by the jurors were fined, and the proceeds were collected and turned over to the landlord. The manor courts thus provided an institution that could be used by both peasant tenants and landlord to protect their respective interests.

The manor court provided a public record of contracts among local peasants and enforced them through jurors' presentments. For example, village property transfers, debt contracts, employment and family maintenance arrangements, whereby a parent surrendered property to a grown child in exchange for food and shelter, could all be included in the court's written rolls.

Jurors also enforced communal norms by fining individuals for a variety of offenses, varying from village to village and decade to decade. Sometimes the playing of games, such as tennis or cards, was prohibited. At times pre-marital sex was discouraged through the imposition of leyrwite fines (penalties for fornication, usually levied on unmarried women). Sometimes drunkenness, assault, and the theft of items under the value of twelve pence could result in a fine. Felonies were tried before royal judges and did not lie within manorial jurisdiction.

When the jurisdiction of the manor court included the view of frankpledge, the court enforced the obligations all adult men owed their monarch to associate themselves in a tithing group of at least ten members, responsible for each other's good behavior. The court might also be responsible for enforcing other royal regulations, such as the assizes of bread, ale, or victuals, which established standards of price and quality for goods sold in the village.

Finally the manor court organized the election of individuals to serve in a wide variety of official capacities associated with local government. Haywards, constables, ale tasters, and jurors, among others, were chosen, appointed, and sometimes fined for dereliction of duty.

Records of manorial court proceedings were written on strips of parchment or paper, then sewn together at the top edge and rolled up for convenient storage. Court clerks used a heavily abbreviated and formulaic Latin style until the 16th century, when English began to be used for some entries. The earliest surviving manor-court rolls date from the early 13th century, and many communities continued to record proceedings from their local courts until the early 20th century.

Manor-court records often reveal a consistent but flexible pattern in their order of business, as reminiscent of the minutes of a town meeting as of a judicial proceeding. For example, most of the entries in a series of Huntingdonshire manor rolls from the late 14th century were arranged in the following sequence. First came the list of jurors' names, followed by a notation of the *capitagium* fine arising from the view of frankpledge, paid by those who chose not to attend the view. Next followed the names of those fined for failure to appear in court for other business, and then those presented by the ale tasters for violating the assize of ale. After the brewing fines came the list of fines collected from guilty parties in debt disputes, and then the jury presentments for assault, breaking the assizes of bread, for various agricultural trespasses, or for disputes over the raising of the hue and cry (the need to respond to the outcry with which felons were to be pursued). Frequently land transfers among the tenants were also recorded here. Finally entries recorded the election and swearing in of such officials as the ale tasters and constables.

Manor court rolls are of particular interest to historians for information about the social, economic, and demographic history of local peasant communities.

Anne R. DeWindt

Bibliography

Ault, Warren O. *Private Jurisdiction in England.* New Haven: Yale University Press, 1923; Ault, Warren O. *The Self-Directing Activities of Village Communities in Medieval England.* Boston: Boston University Press, 1952; DeWindt, Edwin B. *The Court Rolls of Ramsey, Hepmangrove and Bury, 1268 to 1600.* Toronto: Pontifical Institute, 1990; Harvey, P.D.A. *Manorial Records of Cuxham, Oxfordshire, circa 1200–1359.* London: HMSO, 1976; Homans, George C. *English Villagers of the Thirteenth Century.* Cambridge: Harvard University Press, 1941; Jewell, Helen M. *The Court Rolls of the Manor of Wakefield from September, 1348 to September, 1350.* Leeds: Yorkshire Archaeological Society, 1981; Raftis, J.A. *Tenure and Mobility: Studies in the Social History of the Mediaeval English Village.* Toronto: Pontifical Institute, 1964; Walker, Sue Sheridan. *The Court Rolls of the Manor of Wakefield from October, 1331 to September, 1333.* Leeds: Yorkshire Archaeological Society, 1983.

See also Courts and the Court System; Frankpledge; Labor Services; Manorialism; Serfs and Villeins

Manorialism (Manorial System)

The name historians give to the way in which medieval land-lords exploited their estates and controlled rural communities. At the center of the system was the manor, the lowest unit of estate administration and local jurisdiction.

Although the institution itself goes back beyond 1066, the term "manor" appears to have been introduced by the Normans. Although two rather fragmentary pieces of earlier documentary evidence exist, the Domesday Book (1086) and a handful of 12th-century surveys of great estates are the first documents allowing more than a superficial view of the structure of manorial estates. However, it is only with the survival of large numbers of manorial account rolls and court rolls in the 13th century that the operation of the system and the activities of the landlords can be studied on a year-to-year basis and in depth.

Essentially a manor was a landed estate that provided its owner with his livelihood and at the same time conferred upon him jurisdiction over the population residing within its boundaries. It is this element of lordship that turned a landed estate into a manor; for an estate to be a manor it had to be held as a manor. The weakness of some definitions (as that of Kosminskii) is that they do not explicitly include lordship among the criteria employed.

Initially manors tended to be similar in type; in time considerable divergences from the early model—usually referred to as the "classical" manor—developed. In its classical form the manor always involved certain key elements. The land of the manor, apart from the uncultivated reserves, consisted of two parts: land directly cultivated for the landlord—his demesne, or home farm—and land in the hands of the tenants, held on a variety of tenures and for a variety of customary services and obligations.

Although persons of high social standing occasionally held land of somebody else's manor, the vast majority of the manorial population consisted of the dependent peasantry. Tenurially speaking, tenants were classified as free or servile, according to whether they held by "free" service or "base" service. Some holdings were always regarded as free land, but it seems that from the 12th century onward customary holdings, held for cash rents only, also came to be regarded as "free."

The main hallmark of servile (villein) holdings was their liability to heavy labor services on the demesne, particularly week work, which could be as heavy as five days a week throughout the year. Villein holdings were also subject to a payment known as "heriot," usually consisting of the best beast, on the death of the tenant. The obligation to pay heriot came in time to be regarded a standard criterion of tenure in villeinage. In terms of personal status the population of the manor was also classified as free *(liberi)* or servile *(nativi, villani),* the latter condition being regarded as an inheritable trait.

The lord of the manor exercised jurisdiction over all those residing within the confines of his manor, though the extent of authority was greater over persons of servile status or tenure than over persons of free status or tenure. In regions of dispersed settlement, or predominantly pastoral character,

manorial control could be almost purely nominal; in areas of dense settlement, where manors often coincided with villages, it was real and direct.

What the landlord could or could not legitimately do; what was due to him, or from him to the population of the manor; what were the rights of the various categories of the manorial population—these were determined by the "custom of the manor." At first this was unwritten, but with the appearance in the 12th century of manorial surveys, and in the 13th century of manorial court rolls, it was often committed to parchment, at least in some of its aspects. Undoubtedly some landlords did resort to arbitrary action in violation of what was right and proper according to the custom of the manor, though how frequent or widespread such arbitrary action was is a matter of controversy.

The manor was not an immutable, ossified institution. The theoretical structure of the system may have remained the same, but within that framework the way in which the landlords chose to exploit their estates changed with changing economic circumstances.

Two fundamental aspects of manorialism were particularly subject to change; the extent of demesne cultivation and, correspondingly, the extent to which labor services were exacted. When demesnes expanded, labor services tended to be more fully exacted; when demesnes contracted, labor services tended to be commuted into cash payments. Labor services also tended to be commuted when the tenantry was in the position to resist such demands, as was the case after the depopulation caused by the Black Death of 1348–49 and the periodic outbreaks of the plague in the latter 14th century and throughout the 15th.

Looking at the broad sweep between 1086 and the end of the Middle Ages, we see a high degree of conformity in the way in which the landlords of the great estates—they are the ones we know most about—exploited their estates. The usual practice in the 11th and the 12th centuries was to opt for a fixed income by leasing the manors—"farming out" is the technical term—to a lessee *(firmarius)* for a fixed rent. With rising population and, from the late 12th century, rapidly rising prices of agricultural products the landlords took back their manors and not only resumed direct cultivation of demesnes but in most cases expanded them by reclaiming land from the wastes. This period of "high farming" ended for the most part in the late 13th and early 14th centuries.

Considerable contraction of arable cultivation occurred on some estates, such as those of the bishop of Winchester, and there is evidence to suggest that this may have been the result of overcultivation and soil exhaustion, though not all historians accept such an explanation. The concomitant of this development (though other factors also played a part) was the progressive disappearance of labor services by way of commutation. The arrival of the plague in 1348–49 and its recurrences well into the 15th century brought difficult times for landlords, who suffered from vacant tenancies, lost rents, labor shortages, high costs, and, from about 1380 onward, low prices for their produce.

The cumulative effect of these difficulties led in the second half of the 14th century to a widespread and general contraction of manorial demesnes, followed—as early as the 1360s on some estates, much later on others—by the total withdrawal by the great landlords from direct involvement in arable cultivations. By about 1470 the demesnes of virtually all the great estates we can analyze were once again in the hands of the *firmarii*. When this happened, such labor services as had managed to survive were finally disposed of.

Some historians see the "disintegration" of the manorial system in these developments, but the word is misleading. Though two important elements of "classical" manorialism, the demesne and the labor service, did indeed disappear, the framework of manorial organization, the exploitation of remaining manorial resources, and, above all, manorial jurisdiction continued well beyond the traditional limits of the Middle Ages.

Jan Z. Titow

Bibliography

Aston, Trevor H. "The Origins of the Manor in England." *TRHS,* 5th ser. 8 (1958): 59–83; Bennett, Henry S. *Life on the English Manor: A Study of Peasant Conditions, 1150–1500.* Cambridge: Cambridge University Press, 1937; Hilton, Rodney H. "The Content and Sources of Agrarian History before 1500." *Agricultural History Review* 3 (1955): 3–19; Kosminskii, E.A. *Studies in the Agrarian History of England in the Thirteenth Century.* Oxford: Blackwell, 1956; Lennard, Reginald. *Rural England, 1086–1135: A Study of Social and Agrarian Conditions.* Oxford: Clarendon, 1959; Palmer, J.J.N. "The Domesday Manor." In *Domesday Studies,* ed. J.C. Holt. Woodbridge: Boydell, 1987, pp. 139–53; Postan, M.M. *The Medieval Economy and Society: An Economic History of Britain in the Middle Ages.* London: Weidenfeld & Nicolson, 1972; Titow, Jan Z. *English Rural Society, 1200–1350.* London: Allen & Unwin, 1969 [introduction and discussion, and transcripts of manorial documents].

See also Agriculture; Black Death; Labor Services; Prices and Wages; Tenures

Manuscript Illumination, Anglo-Saxon
Early Period

Books and reading came to the Anglo-Saxons as part of the Mediterranean culture of Christianity. But although Anglo-Saxon manuscript art began as an import, it continuously merged foreign and native, participating in the formation of a medieval culture.

Christianity was brought to the Anglo-Saxons during the late-6th and 7th centuries from two sources: Ireland and Italy. Irish Christianity, preserving practices outdated in Italy, had been implanted into a tribal society from sub-Roman Britain. The Irish introduced an archaic tradition of book production rooted in provincial Britain's semiprofessional industry. Late-6th-century Rome sent theology and liturgy formed in an urban context under centralized ecclesiastical authority. Medi-

terranean book production had increased in sophistication, serving a large, wealthy audience literate in Latin and versed in Greco-Roman culture. The Irish converted Northumbria; the Roman mission converted the southern Anglo-Saxon kingdoms, or Southumbria, centering at Canterbury.

In the later 7th and 8th centuries two developments affected manuscript art. Mediterranean influence intensified with the arrival in 669 of Theodore of Tarsus, the new Greek-speaking archbishop of Canterbury, and Hadrian, an African who became abbot of St. Augustine's. Theodore's efforts for reform and education, along with those of such enthusiasts as Benedict Biscop and Wilfrid of York, ensured increasingly lavish book production. Mercian domination from the mid-8th century through the early-9th instigated another wave of foreign connections. Southumbrian ecclesiastics reacted to Mercian exploitation by developing ties with the Continent in an effort to minimize secular interference. Frequent contact between Charlemagne and Offa is evidence of their mutual interest. The resulting flow of Carolingian, Mediterranean, and eastern influences via Southumbria decisively changed the style of Anglo-Saxon art. The early Anglo-Saxon period ends in the mid-9th century after Mercian hegemony had loosened, concurrent with the rise of Wessex and arrival of the Viking armies.

Decoration of surviving manuscripts produced by the early Anglo-Saxons presents an art style sometimes called the "insular" or "Hiberno-Saxon" style. In 7th-century Northumbrian scriptoria late-antique manuscript art was transformed by fusion with Celtic and Anglo-Saxon traditions, the latter known today mainly from prestige metalwork objects, such as those found at Sutton Hoo. Scriptoria may have existed at all major monastic sites, but just two Northumbrian luxury manuscripts, the Lindisfarne Gospels (BL Cotton Nero D.iv; figs. 84–85: see Lindisfarne Gospels) and the Codex Amiatinus (Florence, Biblioteca Medicea-Laurenziana Amiatinus 1; fig. 143: see Wearmouth-Jarrow and the Codex Amiatinus), can be linked solidly to their places of production, at Lindisfarne and Wearmouth-Jarrow. Two variations of Northumbrian monastic culture developed at these centers: at Lindisfarne a synthesis of Celtic, Anglo-Saxon, and Mediterranean; at Wearmouth-Jarrow a romanizing culture imitating Mediterranean forms. Inclusion of the books of Durrow (Dublin, Trinity College 57) and Kells (Dublin, Trinity College 58) as Northumbrian is not universally accepted, but such attribution attests to Northumbria's close cultural relationship to Ireland in the 7th and 8th centuries.

Italianate elements surface commonly in Northumbrian manuscripts. Only one surviving luxuriously decorated Northumbrian manuscript (Durham, Cathedral Library A.II.10) likely predates the Synod of Whitby (664) and the advent of Theodore and Hadrian. On the other hand Mediterranean influence cannot have been the only stimulus underlying the achievement of Northumbrian book art, because even the most opulent 7th-century Italian manuscript decoration does not approach its richness and variety. The period's major source, Bede, is informative on neither the contribution of the Celtic churches nor the use of native art traditions in the new Christian context. Many questions remain to be answered by paleography and archaeology.

Southumbrian manuscripts in the early period reflect continued close interaction with the Continent. Figural style resembles late-antique styles and 6th- and 7th-century north Italian and early Byzantine examples. Fragments of a 6th-century illustrated Gospel book of Italian origin, the "Gospels of St. Augustine" (Cambridge, Corpus Christi College 286), offer concrete evidence of the Mediterranean artistic sources. Known to have arrived in England by the 8th century, the manuscript is traditionally associated with Augustine of Canterbury, who headed Pope Gregory's mission in 597. Treatments of the codex page, exemplified in the Stockholm Gospels (Stockholm, Royal Library A.135; fig. 133: see STOCKHOLM GOSPELS), duplicate Mediterranean luxury manuscript decoration, and much of the nonfigural decoration imitates Mediterranean forms, such as vinescrolls and illusionistic border patterns. Animal ornament in the manuscripts appears to parallel developments in Anglo-Saxon metalwork decoration. Trumpet spirals and pelta (shield-shaped) forms appear within separate parallel areas in borders of decorated pages or within the letters of the text, as seen in the Vespasian Psalter (BL Cotton Vespasian A.i; fig. 141: see VESPASIAN PSALTER), the major early example. The Vespasian Psalter and the Leningrad Bede (Leningrad, Public Library Cod.Q.v.18) provide examples of another probable native development, the historiated initial.

Manuscript art produced during the period of Mercian domination is characterized by vinelike interlace and fanciful animal forms remaining separate from interlace. Contours are looser, more softly curving than those of earlier insular decoration. Human figures, such as the evangelist portraits in the Barberini Gospels (Rome, Biblioteca Apostolica Barberini Lat. 570), display Italo-Byzantine influence in their naturalism. Capital letters with foliate and beast-head terminals are set within panels, as in the Tiberius Bede (BL Cotton Tiberius C.ii).

Earlier scholarship assumed that Canterbury produced nearly all these stylistically related manuscripts, calling them the "Canterbury group." The term is now outdated, the importance of other centers, such as Lichfield, York, and Worcester, having been recognized. They are alternatively called the "Tiberius group," after the Tiberius Bede. Their impressive style of textual presentation may represent a response to needs arising from contending, often litigious interests of Mercian overlords, local potentates, and ecclesiastics. It lent prestige to various texts, including charters, gospels, and devotional works such as the Book of Cerne (CUL Ll.I.10). The recent suggestion of a Mercian "writing area" defined by geography and unified cultural production as apart from political or ecclesiastical structures takes into account the multiple centers and interests that shaped this rich style.

Later Period

Late Anglo-Saxon manuscripts are generally considered to be those manuscripts produced between the late-9th century and the Norman Conquest of 1066. Manuscripts produced within this period are characterized by an innovative style and iconography that display an awareness of both continental developments and native traditions; a propagandistic as well as a didactic purpose; and a new bond to king and court. Because of the Scandinavian presence in the north it is largely a southern phenomenon, centered primarily on Canterbury and the monasteries associated with Winchester and the court.

King Alfred (871–99) succeeded in defending the kingdom of Wessex against the Scandinavian invaders and ensured a period of peace during which artistic and intellectual endeavors could flourish. The revival of book production at this time is traditionally linked to Alfred's import of scholars from throughout the British Isles and the Continent, as well as to his personal patronage and interest in learning, exemplified by his translation of Latin texts, including Gregory's *Pastoral Care*.

Stylistic innovation first becomes apparent in the marginal areas of the page: the decorated initials. Lush foliate patterns and naturalistic animal and human forms are added to the patterns of color and interlace that characterize 8th- and early-9th-century southern manuscripts. The dragons', birds', and dogs' heads sprouting or interspersed with foliate ornament drawn in brown ink in the ca. 900 copy of Aldhelm's *De virginitate* (BL Royal 5.F.iii) are excellent examples of this early style. During the first half of the 10th century initials strike a beautiful balance between continental naturalism and native Anglo-Saxon concerns with dynamic movement and elegant surface patterns, as in the Junius Psalter (Bodl. Junius 27) produced at Winchester ca. 925–50. Francis Wormald divided late Anglo-Saxon initials into two types: Type I, letters formed by whole creatures; Type II, letters containing only the heads of animals. Wormald's basic division is still in use today.

Continental influence is also evident in the expanded use of full-page miniatures and the new monumental style of the figures they contain, as in the set of full-page miniatures added to the Galba Psalter (BL Cotton Galba A.xviii and Bodl. Rawlinson B.484, fol. 85) in the second quarter of the 10th century (fig. 66: see GALBA PSALTER). The manuscript is frequently linked with King Æthelstan, whose cosmopolitan court rivaled that of Charlemagne. Æthelstan appears on fol. 1 of a ca. 937 copy of Bede's lives of St. Cuthbert (Cambridge, Corpus Christi College 183) presenting the manuscript to the saint. This is the earliest surviving manuscript portrait of an Anglo-Saxon ruler. Its presentation of the king as equal in status to, and in direct communication with, the saint is an effective form of royal propaganda that would be adopted by later artists and patrons to glorify the kings and bishops associated with the monastic reform.

The first of the two great styles of late Anglo-Saxon illumination, the "Winchester style," developed in the second half of the 10th century. The name is misleading, as the style was by no means limited to Winchester. Its development can be linked to the introduction of the monastic reform by Dunstan at Glastonbury (940) and Æthelwold at Abingdon (954) and to royal support of the reform and its agenda. The New Minster Charter (BL Cotton Vespasian A.viii) produced at Winchester ca. 966 is the first great Winchester School manuscript. The frontispiece (fol. 2v) shows King Edgar between

Mary and Peter offering the charter to Christ (fig. 101: see NEW MINSTER CHARTER). The combination of royal and religious imagery and Edgar's stature within the miniature are typical of manuscripts associated with the reform.

The solidity of the figures, linear patterns of the drapery, lush acanthus trellis border, rich colors, and lavish use of gold are all characteristic of Winchester-style manuscripts. The figure style, acanthus leaves, and striped backgrounds of the most lavish of these manuscripts (e.g., the Benedictional of Æthelwold [BL Add. 49598]) are derived from Carolingian art but are reinterpreted with an emphasis on movement, linear pattern, and shimmering surfaces that is wholly Anglo-Saxon.

The second major style of late Anglo-Saxon illumination is sometimes referred to as the "Utrecht style," due to the profound influence of the Utrecht Psalter and other Carolingian Reims-style manuscripts on its development. It, too, is frequently linked with a particular locale—Canterbury—though it was popular throughout the south. The style is characterized by an elegant outline drawing technique with expressive figures, fluttering draperies, and shimmering colors; it is exemplified by the drawings in the ca. 1000 Harley Psalter (BL Harley 603; fig. 71: see HARLEY PSALTER).

During the first half of the 11th century the Winchester and Utrecht styles were merged to produce a new style that combined the linear patterns and softer forms of "Utrecht" with the color washes, expressive brush strokes, and lavish borders of "Winchester." A fine example of this style is the figure of Christ Triumphant on fol. 40 of a psalter of ca. 1036 (Bodl. Douce 296).

A great variety of manuscripts were illuminated in late Anglo-Saxon England. Gospel books, psalters, and books for use within the church were the most numerous types of manuscripts produced and the most likely to receive lavish decoration; however, Old Testament narratives and "scientific manuscripts" (herbals, *Marvels of the East*) also appear.

The period is also characterized by an iconographic inventiveness. The "disappearing" Christ Ascension, "horned" Moses, and beast-mouth of hell are among the late Anglo-Saxon creations. Even manuscripts that are direct copies of other manuscripts show a remarkable inventiveness and originality. The Harley Psalter, for example, the first surviving copy of the Utrecht Psalter made in England, introduces both stylistic and iconographic changes (e.g., the use of color and the addition of the tree-of-life cross) that are not derived from its model.

Late Anglo-Saxon manuscripts are characterized by a new and dynamic relationship between illustration and text. In the Bury Psalter (Rome, Vatican, Biblioteca Apostolica Reg. lat. 12) of ca. 1025–50 individual episodes or images from the Psalms are picked out for special emphasis and enacted by figures who tumble, climb, and battle with each other around and across the margins of the page. In such manuscripts as the ca. 1000 "Cædmon" Genesis (Bodl. Junius 11) or the four late-10th- or 11th-century copies of Prudentius's *Psychomachia* produced in England, the artists departed in places from the textual description, causing us to stop and consider the relationship between text and drawing and indicating clearly that late Anglo-Saxon miniatures are by no means simple illustrations of the words they accompany.

Carol A. Farr
Catherine E. Karkov

Bibliography

EARLY PERIOD

Alexander, J.J.G. *Insular Manuscripts 6th–9th Century.* A Survey of Manuscripts Illuminated in the British Isles 1, ed. J.J.G. Alexander. London: Harvey Miller, 1978; Bischoff, Bernhard. *Latin Paleography: Antiquity and the Middle Ages.* Trans. Dáibhí Ó Cróinín and David Ganz. Cambridge: Cambridge University Press, 1990; Boyle, Leonard. *Medieval Latin Paleography: A Bibliographical Introduction.* Toronto Medieval Bibliography 8. Toronto: University of Toronto Press, 1984; Brown, Michelle P. *Anglo-Saxon Manuscripts.* London: British Library, 1991; Dodwell, C.R. *Anglo-Saxon Art: A New Perspective.* Manchester: Manchester University Press, 1982; Farr, Carol A. "Liturgical Influences on the Decoration of the Book of Kells." In *Studies in Insular Art and Archaeology,* ed. Catherine Karkov and Robert T. Farrell. Oxford, Ohio: American Early Medieval Studies, 1991, pp. 127–41; Henderson, George. *From Durrow to Kells: The Insular Gospel Books 650–800.* London: Thames & Hudson, 1987; McGurk, Patrick. "The Gospel Book in Celtic Lands before A.D. 850: Contents and Arrangement." In *Irland und die Christenheit,* ed. P. Ní Chatháin and M. Richter. Europa Zentrums Tübingen Kulturwissenschaftliche Reihe. Stuttgart: Klett-Cotta, 1987, pp. 166–89; Netzer, Nancy. *The Trier Gospels (Trier Domschatz 61).* Cambridge Studies in Paleography and Codicology. Cambridge: Cambridge University Press, 1991; Nordenfalk, Carl. *Celtic and Anglo-Saxon Painting: Book Illumination in the British Isles 600–800.* New York: Braziller, 1977; O'Mahony, Felicity, ed. *The Book of Kells: Proceedings of a Conference at Trinity College, Dublin, 6–9 September 1992.* Aldershot: Scolar, 1994; Spearman, R. Michael, and John Higgitt, eds. *The Age of Migrating Ideas: Early Medieval Art in Northern Britain and Ireland.* Edinburgh: National Museums of Scotland, 1993; Verey, Christopher D., et al., eds. *The Durham Gospels, Together with Fragments of a Gospel Book in Uncial: Durham, Cathedral Library, MS A.II.17.* EEMF 20. Copenhagen: Rosenkilde & Bagger, 1980; Webster, Leslie, and Janet Backhouse, eds. *The Making of England: Anglo-Saxon Art and Culture A.D. 600–900.* London: British Museum, 1991.

LATER PERIOD

Alexander, Jonathan J.G. "The Benedictional of St. Æthelwold and Anglo-Saxon Illumination of the Reform Period." In *Tenth-Century Studies: Essays in Commemoration of the Millennium of the Council of Winchester and Regularis concordia,* ed. David Parsons. London: Phillimore, 1975, pp. 169–83, 241–45;

Brown, Michelle P. *Anglo-Saxon Manuscripts.* London: British Library, 1991; Deshman, Robert. "Anglo-Saxon Art after Alfred." *Art Bulletin* 56 (1974): 176–200; Deshman, Robert. *The Benedictional of St. Æthelwold.* Princeton: Princeton University Press, 1995; Dodwell, C.R., and Peter Clemoes. *The Old English Illustrated Hexateuch: British Museum Cotton Claudius B.IV.* EEMF 18. Copenhagen: Rosenkilde & Bagger, 1974; Gameson, Richard. *The Role of Art in the Late Anglo-Saxon Church.* Oxford: Clarendon, 1995; Ohlgren, Thomas H. *Anglo-Saxon Textual Illustration: Photographs of Sixteen Manuscripts with Descriptions and Index.* Kalamazoo: Medieval Institute, 1992; Raw, Barbara C. *Anglo-Saxon Crucifixion Iconography and the Art of the Monastic Revival.* Cambridge: Cambridge University Press, 1990; Temple, Elzbieta. *Anglo-Saxon Manuscripts 900–1066.* A Survey of Manuscripts Illuminated in the British Isles 2, ed. J.J.G. Alexander. London: Harvey Miller, 1976; Wormald, Francis. *English Drawings of the Tenth and Eleventh Centuries.* London: Faber & Faber, 1952.

See also Anglo-Saxon Old Testament Narrative Illustration; Art, Anglo-Saxon; Art, Anglo-Saxon: Celtic Influences, Classical Influences; Benedictional of Æthelwold; Galba Psalter; Harley Psalter; Lindisfarne Gospels; Metalwork, Anglo-Saxon; New Minster Charter; Psalters, Anglo-Saxon; Stockholm Gospels; Sutton Hoo; Tiberius Psalter; Vespasian Psalter; Wearmouth-Jarrow and the Codex Amiatinus; "Winchester School"

Manuscript Illumination, Gothic

The sources of the Gothic style in English painting lie in the "transitional" period from ca. 1180 to 1220, during which there was a revival of classical forms, disseminated via Byzantine sources. This signaled a move away from the stylized decorativeness of Romanesque art toward greater naturalism. Solid, monumental figures replaced angular forms and linear schematic draperies. These humanizing tendencies have their origin in the more progressive painters of the Winchester Bible and are fully exemplified in the miniatures that preface the text in the Westminster Psalter, especially that of the Christ in Majesty. (Shelf marks for manuscripts discussed here and below appear at the end of the entry in the order in which they are discussed.)

This change in style was accompanied by a corresponding shift in patronage from the monastic to the aristocratic and an increased interest in didactic narrative illustration. The luxury psalter became the book for private devotion, and the bestiary and illustrated saints' lives became popular texts. Bede's life of St. Cuthbert, a "transitional" work, shows increased psychological communication between the figures, compared with some of the earlier biblical narratives. The monumental qualities of the Westminster Psalter and the Glossed Gospels in Trinity College, Cambridge, soon give way to softer, more elongated forms. This greater delicacy is apparent in the Creation scenes prefacing the Ashmole and Aberdeen bestiaries. Coupled with this greater elegance certain mannerisms, such as the jutting necks and exaggerated gestures, herald the arrival of the early Gothic style, which by ca. 1220 is fully evident in the prefatory miniatures in the two Peterborough psalters (Fitzwilliam Museum and Society of Antiquaries).

Skill in the tinted-drawing tradition is exquisitely expressed in the Guthlac Roll of ca. 1210, which shows some of the delicacy of the Ashmole Bestiary, though with less exaggerated gestures and elongation of form. The Glazier Psalter, produced in London around 1220, is a direct descendant of the monumental tendencies of the Westminster Psalter, although comparison of the Christ in Majesty figures in both manuscripts underlines the changes that have occurred in the 20 to 30 years that separate them. The figure is more attenuated, and the draperies, though still defining the form beneath, are more linear and decorative.

A less delicate, more solid rendition of form leading from the Westminster Psalter is apparent in a group of manuscripts produced in Oxford between ca. 1200 and 1220, such as the Munich and Arundel psalters of ca. 1200–10, BL Royal 1.D.x and the Iona Psalter of ca. 1210, and the Huntingfield Psalter of ca. 1210–20. The rise in importance of Oxford as an artistic center may in part be explained by the rise of the university in that city. Although these books lack the mannerisms of the London-produced Glazier Psalter, the elongation of form evident in the Christ in Majesty of Royal 1.D.x is a stylistic mediator between the earlier Westminster and later Glazier Psalter's representation of the subject.

By 1250 the Oxford tradition is well established in the works of William de Brailes and his circle, who were operating in Catte Street, Oxford, between ca. 1230 and 1260. They bring to a climax the greater use of narrative engendered by the earlier miniature cycles prefacing psalters, while at the same time demonstrating a new interest in border decoration. These exclusively liturgical works, which include the earliest extant English book of hours (BL Add. 49999; fig. 31: see BRAILES, WILLIAM DE), lead via the Salvin Hours and related works to the William of Devon group, again localizable to Oxford ca. 1260–70.

The de Brailes style is characterized by mostly small-scale figures, reduced for narrative expediency, pale faces, and calligraphically rendered features. There is some schematization of the draperies and a tendency to divide the picture space into compartments to accommodate the extensive narrative. The border decoration is confined mostly to dragon forms that extend from the initials and terminate in blocky foliage elements. In the William of Devon manuscripts the border has developed into distinctive horizontal, vertical, and diagonal platforms; the latter provide anchorage for a wide variety of birds, animals, and hybrids. The William of Devon group, which specialized in Bible illustration, shows strong northern French influence. By 1280 Oxford seems to have ceased as a center of manuscript production, with a possible shift toward London.

Narrative as a principal source of artistic expression is paramount in the lives of the saints and chronicles illustrated by the St. Albans monk Matthew Paris in the 1240s and 1250s

(fig. 95: see MATTHEW PARIS). Out of the monumental works of ca. 1200 Paris devised a precise and economical method of tinted line drawing of considerable directness. Certain examples, such as the heads in the chronicle in Corpus Christi College, Cambridge, and the Virgin and Child in the British Library chronicle, have an exquisite beauty and strong devotional quality. In his smaller-scale illustrations his technique is less formal and more lively. Paris was a highly competent imitator of the "court" school of Apocalypse illustration developed under the influence of the so-called Sarum Master. The Sarum Master brought the early Gothic phase to its full maturation in a group of manuscripts probably produced at Salisbury ca. 1250–60. His is an elegant, monumental style that follows a path of development leading from the Westminster Psalter, via the Glazier Psalter. It is more elongated, angular, and emotionally expressive than that of Matthew Paris; the draperies have fluttering edges and a tendency toward trough folds.

These stylistic characteristics are reflected in the earliest Apocalypses, such as Paris, BN fr. 403, which may be by the Sarum Master's hand. The popularity of the Apocalypse (approximately twenty extant examples were produced between ca. 1250 and 1275) was in part engendered by Joachim of Fiore's belief that the end of the world was imminent. Stylistically these picture books are of particular value in documenting the development away from the early Gothic style to a more fully developed form of Gothic, where the soft troughed forms of the Paris, Metz, and Tanner Apocalypses of 1250–55 develop into broader, more angular forms under influence from Parisian art. This style is fully expressed in the Lambeth (fig. 154: see WOMEN AND THE ARTS), Gulbenkian, and Abingdon Apocalypses of ca. 1260–70. The Douce Apocalypse (fig. 91) shows a mature assimilation of these forms, devoid of the mannered interpretation of the broad-fold style of the Lambeth Apocalypse. It has been convincingly argued that these works were produced mostly by lay illuminators in London, Salisbury, and Oxford rather than in the "School of St. Albans" under Matthew Paris. It is some of these London works that most closely approximate the concept of a court school of illumination. A pivotal manuscript in the formation of this style is the life of St. Edward the Confessor in Cambridge University Library, produced in Westminster ca. 1255–60.

By ca. 1285 the angularity of the broad-fold drapery style had softened, and in London-produced works, such as the Windmill Psalter, Petrus Comestor, and the early material in the Alfonso Psalter (made for Edward I's son), the figures show greater solidity and modeling of the draperies. These courtly works have much in common with those of the Parisian miniaturist Master Honoré and point forward to the 14th century.

This style is reflected in the earliest hands of the Peterborough Psalter, begun around 1300, as well as in the Isabella Psalter and the Tickhill Psalter (fig. 106: see PSALTERS, GOTHIC) of 1300–10. The Tickhill group may have been produced in the York diocese, while the Peterborough Psalter and related

works were probably produced in a Fenlands monastery. Comparatively restrained borders, in which the grotesque element is minimized and naturalistic representations of animal, bird, and plant life are emphasized, characterize these manuscripts. It is this more reserved approach that separates illumination of ca. 1285–1310 from the more robust, typically East Anglian border decoration that is a distinctive feature of manuscripts produced in the Norwich region, such as the Gorleston Psalter (fig. 57: see "EAST ANGLIAN SCHOOL") of ca. 1310–20 and the main hand of the Ormesby Psalter (fig. 102: see ORMESBY PSALTER). The latter is also important in showing the first clear wave of Italian influence.

One of the artists of the Gorleston Psalter, who also illuminated the Howard Psalter, appears to have been itinerant in the East Anglian region, executing portions of such manuscripts as the Harnhulle Psalter-Hours. This important manuscript links the Howard artist's style to a close imitator of the Queen Mary's Psalter artist, who executed commissions in East Anglia as well as London.

Whereas the main Ormesby illuminator seems to have worked mainly in a monastic milieu, the Gorleston and Howard artists produced work for lay patrons. The approximately ten manuscripts of the central Queen Mary group, produced in London between ca. 1310 and 1333, testify to monastic and aristocratic, as well as scholarly, patronage. The final work in this series, a book of statutes now in Norwich Castle Museum, was illuminated by the Queen Mary Artist's only collaborator, the Ancient 6 Master, in 1333. It is stylistically related to the later italiate work in the Ormesby Psalter, a style also found in the Douai Psalter, the Gorleston Psalter Crucifixion page, and the St. Omer Psalter. This style of painting, with vigorous highlighting in white pigment and rather pointed figures, is now considered to date from between ca. 1330 and 1340, and not to the 1320s as previously argued.

London may have provided the arena for the origin and dissemination of the style associated with the prolific group of artists who produced the Milemete Treatise in Christ Church, Oxford, and the Pseudo-Aristotle in the British Library intended for presentation to Edward III by Walter de Milemete, the king's clerk, in 1326 or 1327. These artists have been identified in manuscripts with destinations other than London, such as a book of hours (Bodl. Douce 231) of the diocese of Lincoln, a number of liturgical books from East Anglia (the Tiptoft Missal [fig. 92], the Stowe Breviary, and the All Souls Psalter), and several historical volumes with Oxford and Cambridge connections; this raises the possibility that further "Milemete" workshops existed in these locations.

In the 1330s and 1340s, with the growing conformity to the Use of Sarum, localizing centers of artistic activity becomes more conjectural, with the result that "local" features are minimized. A group of manuscripts that fall into this vexed category are the Taymouth Hours, BL Egerton 2781, and the Vatican Hours, all three of which may have been produced in Oxford or Cambridge, or perhaps testify to a final blossoming of London as an artistic center in the 1330s and 1340s (before its apparent demise and revival as a major center in the 1370s).

The artist of the Fitzwarin Psalter may have begun his career in Oxford but, like a number of other illuminators, seems to have gravitated to Cambridge in the 1340s. The style of the Fitzwarin Psalter, in which there are mannerisms of pose and drapery, relates directly to that in the Dublin and Walters hours. More firmly localizable to Cambridge is the illuminator responsible for a Cambridge University Charter, the Brescia Psalter (which has an Ely diocese calendar), and the first campaign in the Vienna Bohun Psalter, curtailed by the Black Death of 1348–49.

The Black Death disrupted artistic activity, and few illuminators working before 1350 are identifiable in manuscripts produced after that date. This almost total collapse is supported by a unique situation that arose in the 1350s. Documentary and stylistic evidence indicate that the Bohun family, who had previously patronized the Cambridge illuminators, set up their own workshop under the Austin Friar John de Tye in Pleshey Castle, Essex. This artist worked in a style that had evolved from East Anglian illumination of the first half of the 14th century, employing a rich repertoire of border forms on to which he grafted certain italiate features, most notably the oval faces with narrow, slanting eyes. His only collaborator, although anonymous, can be identified in Flemish manuscripts of the 1340s. His figure style is less plastic and his borders distinctly rectilinear. The two illuminators collaborated from the mid-1350s to the early 1380s, producing the highest-quality work in England in this period. Codicologically and stylistically the Bohun manuscripts are complex, and reliance on these methods of analysis is paramount when internal evidence for dating is lacking. There are breaks in campaign in three of the major psalters (those in Vienna, the British Library, and Exeter College, Oxford), which are essential to consider when determining the initial, or eventual, owner of each manuscript, because in some cases a single book was worked on for successive generations of the same family.

The final campaign in the Exeter Bohun Psalter (figs. 61–62: see EXETER BOHUN PSALTER) suggests that by the late 1380s the two Bohun illuminators had died and the family was forced to use a London workshop to complete the psalter in the 1390s—the city having risen again in importance for illumination in the 1370s. The three artists in question, whose methods suggest a more commercial form of workshop practice, also worked in *Omne bonum* and the William of Nottingham Commentary on the Gospels, both written by a London scribe, James le Palmer. With the exception of one of these artists, whose fine style can be seen in a religious miscellany now in Hatfield House, their work is not of the highest quality.

At this time the Bohun family employed one of the illuminators (Rickert's Hand C) of the Carmelite Missal of the early 1400s. This artist, also responsible for the Edinburgh Psalter-Hours, employed a distinctive type of border decoration, characterized by slender gold bars, ornamented with an array of leaf and flower sprays, with interlace and gold berry forms. These borders, first seen in the Lytlington Missal and related manuscripts of the 1380s, and have an origin in three London-produced charters for Bristol of 1373. They became standard for the large body of manuscripts executed in London in the last quarter of the 14th century. The Belknap artist, one of the artists of the Lytlington Missal, made for Westminster Abbey in 1384, had a sizable *oeuvre* spanning three decades. His influence, and that of the Edinburgh Bohun Hand, extended into the first decade of the 15th century, even after the more innovative border and figure styles of the Carmelite Missal had been introduced from the Continent. Hand A in the missal probably came to England from the Low Countries. His style, characterized by elaborate perspectival settings reminiscent of Broederlam's Dijon altarpiece of ca. 1390, realistic facial types, and softly modeled draperies, was to be the most influential of the foreign trends current in England ca. 1400–10.

English painting at this time entered the so-called International Gothic phase. A style close to that of Hand A in the Carmelite Missal is seen in the full-page miniature of the Annunciation in the Beaufort Hours, signed by Herman Scheerre, a Netherlandish artist who also worked in the Chichele Breviary, the Bedford Psalter-Hours, and other manuscripts ranging in date from ca. 1403/04 to ca. 1430.

A second illuminator in the Bedford book, whose style also relates closely to that of Hand A, was "Johannes," whose signature is found on one of the miniatures in a Marco Polo manuscript on which he worked with assistants. The Hours of "Elizabeth the Quene" is possibly his latest and finest work. In the work of Johannes and the artist who illuminated the only miniature in a *Troilus and Criseyde* manuscript the International Gothic style is fully absorbed by English illuminators.

Another illuminator working in the first quarter of the 15th century was John Siferwas, a Dominican friar, who painted a fine missal for the Benedictine Abbey of Sherborne sometime before 1406. The borders of this manuscript are full of naturalistic depictions of plants, animals, and birds reminiscent of the English countryside, but the figure style betrays German or Bohemian contacts. It is possible that he trained in London in the 1390s (his style holds much in common with *Liber regalis,* Hand B of the Carmelite Missal, and the Apocalypse paintings in the Westminster Chapter House) before settling in the West Country, where he carried out his commissions. The Pepysian sketchbook in Magdalene College, Cambridge, a rare survival from the Gothic period, has work in a related style.

The International style prevailed until the demise of the Scheerre and Johannes workshops in the 1430s, after which London declined as a center for high-quality illumination, though echoes of Scheerre's style continue in an inventive provincial school based at Bury St. Edmunds in the 1430s and 1440s. Manuscripts of this school are distinguished by the use of different pigments and a softer modeling of the border decoration, as in Cambridge, Fitzwilliam Museum 3–1979.

In London remnants of the International style are evident in one of the hands of the Warwick Hours. The other hand in this book has been identified as William Abell, active ca. 1440–65, who also painted some of the miniatures in the Beaufort Hours and the Abingdon Missal, which has a fine Crucifixion. His style is a conscious reaction against the International Gothic. It is linear, has abstract conventions, and denies perspective, but in its robust individuality it is also a reassertion of indigenous English qualities that had been suppressed for well over a quarter of a century. Abell's works, which connect him with the City of London, consist of illustrated charters, statutes, heraldic manuscripts, and some literary works.

With few exceptions it can be concluded that after 1430 English illumination fell into an irrevocable decline. Foreign books, notably from Flanders, made for the English market became increasingly popular, and English illuminators were not sufficiently innovative or enterprising to compete. These books, commercially produced in large numbers, catered to the needs of a growing clientele, a situation dramatically contrasting with that which had prevailed in England in the early Gothic period.

Lynda Dennison

Bibliography

Alexander, Jonathan, and Paul Binski, eds. *Age of Chivalry: Art in Plantagenet England 1200–1400.* London: Royal Academy of Arts, 1987; Dennison, Lynda. "'The Fitzwarin Psalter and Its Allies': A Reappraisal." In *England in the Fourteenth Century: Proceedings of the 1985 Harlaxton Symposium,* ed. W.M. Ormrod. Woodbridge: Boydell, 1986, pp. 42–66; Dennison, Lynda. "Oxford, Exeter College MS 47: The Importance of Stylistic and Codicological Analysis in Its Dating and Localization." In *Medieval Book Production: Assessing the Evidence,* ed. Linda L. Brownrigg. Los Altos Hills: Anderson-Lovelace, 1990, pp. 41–59; Marks, Richard, and Nigel Morgan. *The Golden Age of English Manuscript Painting 1200–1500.* London: Chatto & Windus, 1981; Morgan, Nigel. *Early Gothic Manuscripts 1190–1285.* 2 vols. A Survey of Manuscripts Illuminated in the British Isles 4, ed. J.J.G. Alexander. London: Harvey Miller, 1982–88; Rickert, Margaret. *Painting in Britain: The Middle Ages.* 2d ed. Harmondsworth: Penguin, 1965; Rogers, Nicholas J. "Fitzwilliam Museum MS 3–1979: A Bury St. Edmunds Book of Hours and the Origins of the Bury Style." In *England in the Fifteenth Century: Proceedings of the 1986 Harlaxton Symposium,* ed. Daniel Williams. Woodbridge: Boydell, 1987, pp. 229–43; Sandler, Lucy Freeman. *Gothic Manuscripts 1285–1385.* A Survey of Manuscripts Illuminated in the British Isles 5, ed. J.J.G. Alexander. London: Harvey Miller, 1986; Scott, Kathleen L. *Later Gothic Manuscripts 1385–1490.* A Survey of Manuscripts Illuminated in the British Isles 6, ed. J.J.G. Alexander. London: Harvey Miller, 1996.

APPENDIX

Westminster Psalter (BL Royal 2.A.xxii); Bede, *Life of St. Cuthbert* (BL Yates Thompson 26 [Add. 39943]); Glossed Gospels (Cambridge, Trinity College B.5.3); Ashmole Bestiary (Bodl. Ashmole 1511); Aberdeen Bestiary (Aberdeen, University Library 24); Peterborough Psalters (Cambridge, Fitzwilliam Museum 12, and London, Society of Antiquaries 59); Guthlac Roll (BL Harley Y.6); Glazier Psalter (New York, Pierpont Morgan Library Glazier 25); Munich Psalter (Munich, Bayerische Staatsbibliothek Clm.835); Arundel Psalter (BL Arundel 157); Iona Psalter (Edinburgh, National Library of Scotland 10000); Huntingfield Psalter (New York, Pierpont Morgan Library 43); Salvin Hours (BL Add. 48985); *Chronica maiora,* parts I, II (Cambridge, Corpus Christi College 26 and 16); *Chronica maiora,* part III

(BL Royal 14.C.vii); Metz Apocalypse (Metz, Bibliothèque Municipale Salis 38); Tanner Apocalypse (Bodl. Tanner 184); Lambeth Apocalypse (London, Lambeth Palace Library 209); Gulbenkian Apocalypse (Lisbon, Museu Calouste Gulbenkian L.A. 139); Abingdon Apocalypse (BL Add. 42555); Douce Apocalypse (Bodl. Douce 180); *Life of Edward the Confessor* (CUL Ee.3.59); Windmill Psalter (New York, Pierpont Morgan Library M.102); Petrus Comestor (BL Royal 13.D.vi); Alfonso Psalter (BL Add. 24686); Peterborough Psalter (Brussels, Bibliothèque Royale 9961–62); Isabella Psalter (Munich, Staatsbibliothek gall. 16); Tickhill Psalter (New York, Public Library Spencer 26); Gorleston Psalter (BL Add. 49622); Ormesby Psalter (Bodl. Douce 366); Howard Psalter (BL Arundel 83, part I); Harnhulle Psalter-Hours (Downside Abbey, Somerset 26533); Queen Mary's Psalter (BL Royal 2.B.vii); Statutes (Norwich, Castle Museum 158–926/4d); Douai Psalter (Douai, Bibliothèque Municipale 171); St. Omer Psalter (BL Yates Thompson 14 [Add. 39810]); Milemete Treatise (Oxford, Christ Church 92); Pseudo-Aristotle (BL Add. 47680); Tiptoft Missal (New York, Pierpont Morgan Library M.107); Stowe Breviary (BL Stowe 12); All Souls Psalter (Oxford, All Souls College 7); Taymouth Hours (BL Yates Thompson 13); Vatican Hours (Rome, Biblioteca Apostolica Vaticana Pal. lat. 537); Fitzwarin Psalter (Paris, BN lat. 765); Dublin Hours (Dublin, Trinity College 94 [F.5.21]); Walters Hours (Baltimore, Walters Art Gallery W.105); Charter (CUL Luard *33a); Brescia Psalter (Brescia, Biblioteca Queriniana A.V.17); Bohun Psalter (Vienna, Österreichische Nationalbibliothek Cod. 1826*); Bohun Psalter-Hours (BL Egerton 3277); Bohun Psalter (Oxford, Exeter College 47); *Omne bonum* (BL Royal 6.E.vi, 6.E.vii); William of Nottingham, *Commentary on the Gospels* (Bodl. Laud Misc. 165); Religious miscellany (Hatfield House, Herts., Marquess of Salisbury, CP.290); Carmelite Missal (BL Add. 29704–05); Edinburgh Psalter-Hours (Edinburgh, National Library of Scotland Advocates' 18.6.5); Lytlington Missal (London, Westminster Abbey 37); Charter (Bristol, Record Office, Charter of 8 August 1373); Charter (Bristol, Record Office, Charter of 30 October 1373); Charter (Bristol, Record Office, Charter of 20 December 1373); Beaufort Hours (BL Royal 2.A.xviii); Chichele Breviary (London, Lambeth Palace Library 69); Bedford Psalter-Hours (BL Add. 42131); Marco Polo (Bodleian Library, Bodley 264); Hours of Elizabeth the Quene (BL Add. 50001); *Troilus and Criseyde* (Cambridge, Corpus Christi College 61); Sherborne Missal (on loan to the British Library [loan MS.82] from the Trustees of the will of the 9th duke of Northumberland of Alnwick Castle); *Liber regalis* (London, Westminster Abbey 38); Pepysian sketchbook (Cambridge, Magdalene College, Pepysian Li-

brary 1916); Warwick Psalter-Hours (New York, Pierpont Morgan Library M.893); Abingdon Missal (Bodl. Digby 227 and Oxford, Trinity College 75).

See also Amesbury Psalter; Cuerden Psalter; "East Anglian School"; Exeter Bohun Psalter; Marginalia; Ormesby Psalter; Psalters, Gothic; Queen Mary's Psalter; Westminster Chapter House Paintings; Wilton Diptych

Manuscript Illumination, Romanesque

The Romanesque period (ca. 1066–1190) witnessed a growth in both the number and variety of manuscripts produced as well as an apparent growth in literacy and an increased awareness of the presence of scribes, artists, and readers within manuscripts, in the form of signatures, colophons, "self-portraits," donor portraits, and new page layouts designed for usability and the needs of the learned reader.

The period did not begin with a sudden change of style or even a change in the number or types of books produced. Manuscripts produced in the years immediately following the Conquest show a hardening of the dynamic Anglo-Saxon line and a solidifying of Anglo-Saxon forms, but the native taste for outline drawing and elegant surface patterns survived, as did a number of Anglo-Saxon iconographic innovations, such as the disappearing Christ and the beast-mouth of hell. This is due in part to the cosmopolitan nature of late Anglo-Saxon illumination, which incorporated Carolingian, Ottonian, and Byzantine influences, and in part to the dependence of 11th-century Norman illumination on Anglo-Saxon styles. In fact, until the 1120s, the Canterbury scriptoria, so active in the production of pre-Conquest manuscripts, continued to be among the most active.

The change to a new Romanesque style began in the 12th century with the introduction of stronger, brighter colors and darker, heavier outlines. This was accompanied by the development of a new approach to depicting the human body, characterized by expressive poses, gestures, and faces, while stylized draperies were used to reveal the form of the body itself. The St. Albans Psalter (Hildesheim, St. Godehard) of 1120–35, and the Bury Bible (Cambridge, Corpus Christi College 2) illuminated ca. 1135, are both masterpieces of the new style, though they differ significantly in detail.

The St. Albans Psalter is remarkable for the number and quality of its full-page illustrations and historiated initials (211), as well as for its association with the recluse Christina of Markyate, for whom it was probably revised between 1120 and 1135. The artists of the St. Albans Psalter worked in a style influenced by Ottonian and northern French illumination. Figures are monumental and elongated, with expressive faces and straight profiles. The stylized draperies serve to reveal form through alternating areas of flat clinging fabric and gathered folds; a device that looks forward to the damp-fold style of the Bury Bible. Backgrounds consist of abstract areas of solid color and abbreviated architectural or landscape motifs.

The most skilled and influential of the St. Albans Psalter artists was the St. Alexis Master, named for a page illustrating scenes from the life of St. Alexis that was added when the psalter was revised. His figures are among the most lively and expressive, and it is his mastery of drapery and depiction of the human form that may have been most influential in the development of the damp-fold style. The Alexis Master is associated with four other manuscripts, and while his identity remains unknown, it is likely that he may have been a lay artist.

The damp-fold style was fully developed by another probable lay artist, Master Hugo, in the Bury Bible. Here the drapery clings to the body, as if wet at stomach, thigh, knee, and shin. The development of the style in this manuscript is attributed to the influence of Byzantine art (other Byzantine elements include dark, naturalistic faces with stern expressions and the use of linear patterns of light and dark for highlighting and shading). However, what begins in Byzantine art as an attempt at classical naturalism is transformed by Master Hugo and his successors into a stylistic device that both articulates form and satisfies the native taste for dynamic surface patterns. The damp-fold style was influential and remained popular until ca. 1170.

In the Winchester Psalter of ca. 1145–55 (BL Cotton Nero C.iv; fig. 153: see WINCHESTER PSALTER) the decorative potential of the damp-fold style is clear. In this manuscript, rather than revealing naturalistic form, the damp-fold drapery dissolves figures into animated linear patterns. The poses and expressions of the figures are also exaggerated, making this one of the most expressive of all English Romanesque manuscripts. The Winchester Psalter artists also borrowed heavily from the Anglo-Saxon tradition: the expanded introductory cycle of miniatures, the grotesque faces of many of the figures, the dynamic relationship between the spaces within and without the frame, such iconographic details as the beast-mouth of hell, and portions of the text all have their origins in Anglo-Saxon manuscript illumination (e.g., Bodl. Junius 11 and BL Cotton Tiberius C.vi).

The two miniatures on fols. 29 and 30, the death of the Virgin and the Virgin as queen of heaven, are in a startlingly different byzantinizing style characterized by monumental classicizing figures and full color. Their presence may be due to direct Byzantine influence or perhaps indirect Byzantine influence via Ottonian art.

Around 1170 a new style of illumination developed that was heavily influenced by the art of Paris and northern France. Due to its popularity in both France and England it became known as the "Channel style." Large and complex historiated or inhabited initials became smaller and consequently simpler; foliage became thinner; burnished-gold backgrounds and decorative patterns of white lines began to dominate. Darker and more naturalistic faces and more fully modeled forms also attest to a renewal of Byzantine influence. The Copenhagen Psalter (Copenhagen, Royal Library, Thott. 1432), created in northern England ca. 1170, is a fine example of this style. The change in style was accompanied by a change in format: books became smaller with smaller writing, while glosses were expanded so that they ran parallel to the text and were frequently introduced by their own decorative initial.

Romanesque manuscript illumination is not simply a matter of stylistic development; it is also the product of a new type of artist creating books for an expanded audience. The 12th century saw the rise of the lay artist working in monastic employ (e.g., Master Hugo and the Alexis Master). Moreover manuscripts were produced not just within monastic scriptoria but also within cathedral scriptoria and, probably, lay workshops. Certainly by the end of the century lay artists had come to dominate artistic production, and by the early-13th century they were incorporated into the guild system (although the earliest surviving evidence for a separate illuminator's guild dates from 1389).

The manuscripts produced were largely learned, usable books, frequently with glossed texts and often with glosses in more than one language (e.g., the Eadwine Psalter). In many manuscripts miniatures and historiated initials may be understood as forming an additional visual gloss or narrative rather than simply illustrating the verbal text (e.g., the St. Albans Psalter). Artists probably used pattern books and copied other manuscripts. Copying, however, was generally done with an eye to invention (as with the various copies of the Utrecht Psalter) rather than as slavish imitation.

The most extensively illustrated type of manuscript was the Psalter. In the most lavish psalters the prefatory cycles of Old and New Testament miniatures developed by the Anglo-Saxons were expanded, while each psalm was accompanied by a miniature or historiated initial. During the 12th century specific subjects came to be associated with the major liturgical divisions of the Psalter (Pss. 1, 26, 38, 51, 52, 68, 80, 97, 101, 109); the author portrait of David, for example, became the standard illustration for Psalm 1. Great Bibles and saints' lives formed the next-most-significant group of extensively illustrated manuscripts. Scientific and medical manuscripts, bestiaries, chronicles, the writings of the Church Fathers, and the works of classical authors were also illustrated. In manuscripts of all types initials provided one of the major fields for innovative and imaginative illustrations. Romanesque initials, particularly those of the second quarter of the 12th century, are full of comic or grotesque scenes and clambering humans, animals, and hybrids that frequently look forward to the marginalia of English Gothic manuscripts.

Books were illuminated for a variety of patrons and purposes. Though it is safe to say that most manuscripts continued to be produced for liturgical or scholarly use within the confines of church and monastery, manuscripts may also have been produced for lay patrons. It is likely that some of the many psalters, particularly those including glosses or additions in the vernacular, may have been made for private patrons.

This was also a period in which a number of great libraries were built up and their contents catalogued. Complete or partial 12th-century catalogues survive from Abingdon (partial), Burton-on-Trent Abbey, Christ Church, Canterbury (partial), Durham Cathedral, Lincoln Cathedral, Peterborough Abbey, Reading Abbey, Rochester Cathedral, Waltham (partial), Whitby Abbey, and Worcester (partial). The catalogue of Reading Abbey records nearly 300 volumes, including four Bibles of two or three volumes each; a series of separate glossed books of the Bible (all but seven books of the

Bible are mentioned); eighteen volumes of the writings of St. Augustine; works by Seneca, Virgil, Horace, and Juvenal; saints' lives; a two-volume breviary in a cloister chapel; four breviaries divided between the guest house, infirmary, and abbot's house; three volumes for reading at meals; three missals in the church, two in precious covers, and one for early morning service; seventeen small missals for use by the monks; fifteen graduals; six full processionals and seven smaller processionals; seven antiphonaries; three psalters for use by the novices; four psalters secured by chains in the church and infirmary; a variety of lectionaries, tropers, collectars, and other liturgical texts. While not all of these manuscripts would have been illuminated, the catalogue does give a glimpse into the variety, function, and distribution of books within the Romanesque monastery.

Catherine E. Karkov

Bibliography

Alexander, Jonathan J.G. *Medieval Illuminators and Their Methods of Work*. New Haven: Yale University Press, 1992; Cahn, Walter. *Romanesque Bible Illumination*. Ithaca: Cornell University Press, 1992; de Hamel, Christopher. *A History of Illuminated Manuscripts*. Boston: Godine, 1986; Dodwell, C.R. *The Canterbury School of Illumination 1066–1200*. Cambridge: Cambridge University Press, 1954; Dodwell, C.R. *The Pictorial Arts of the West 800–1200*. New Haven: Yale University Press, 1993; Kauffmann, C. Michael. *Romanesque Manuscripts 1066–1190*. A Survey of Manuscripts Illuminated in the British Isles 3, ed. J.J.G. Alexander. London: Harvey Miller, 1975; Ker, N.R. *Medieval Libraries of Great Britain: A List of Surviving Books*. London: Royal Historical Society, 1964; Zarnecki, George, Janet Holt, and Tristram Holland, eds. *English Romanesque Art 1066–1200*. London: Weidenfeld & Nicolson, 1984.

See also Apocalypses; Art, Romanesque; Bestiaries; Eadwine and Canterbury/Paris Psalters; Great Bibles; Libraries; Manuscript Illumination, Anglo-Saxon; Manuscript Illumination, Gothic; St. Albans Psalter; Saints' Lives, Illuminated; Scientific Manuscripts, Early; Winchester Psalter; Women and the Arts

Manuscripts of Polyphonic Music

The manuscript sources that transmit medieval English polyphonic music are fragmentary, with but three well-known exceptions, the Winchester Troper, W1, and the Old Hall Manuscript. Even these sources are incomplete. There are about 15 incomplete manuscripts from the 11th and 12th centuries, 65 fragments of the 13th, over 85 fragments of the 14th, and a similar number of insular sources of the 15th. They contain a polyphonic repertoire in excess of 700 individual works. Considerable evidence suggests that many large books of polyphony were produced in medieval England, with their number dramatically increasing during the 13th and 14th centuries, a circumstance that roughly parallels the survival pattern on the Continent.

In respect to size 173 polyphonic compositions in two parts are given in the late-10th-century manuscript known as the Winchester Troper. They carry texts from the foremass, both Ordinary and Proper, and for the divine office, invitatories and responsories in particular. At least one 13th-century music book, dismembered at Worcester Cathedral, contained more than 138 folios. One other sizable manuscript may have suffered the same fate at Worcester. A large codex from the same century (Cambridge, Corpus Christi College 8) had page numbers that reached to 558, and it is estimated that it originally contained over 200 works. For one large collection of 13th-century polyphony from Reading Abbey only a table of contents with titles has survived, in BL Harley 978. This index records 164 polyphonic compositions, including 37 Alleluias, 38 conducti, and 81 motets. At least five large-scale motet collections can be identified from English 14th-century fragments, among them Oxford, New College 362, with 90 folios originally, and Cambridge, Corpus Christi College 65, originally with 100 folios. The manuscripts Lincoln Cathedral Library 52, BL Add. 24198, and Bodleian Library, Bodley 652, were all alphabetically arranged motet collections whose contents may have reached to almost 100 pieces.

Other sources are difficult to classify and do not fall into the tidy compartments that have generally been applied to continental manuscript sources. Some appear to have been modest collections of liturgical polyphony jotted on previously used parchment, such as the *rotulus,* or roll, from the Public Record Office (E/149/7/23) or similar sized collections notated in a manuscript originally intended for this purpose, such as Norwich, Norfolk County Record Office, Flitcham 299. Other collections contain a mixture of motets and devotional compositions, such as New York, Pierpont Morgan Library M.978. The majority of sources appears never to have been part of a large music book and may well have been working copies of compositions destined either for personal use by a particular singer-composer or as working exemplars for works destined for inclusion in a more formal book. In a number of cases polyphonic compositions were added into music books originally devoted to plainsong, as is the case with CUL Add. 710.

Shaping some coherent picture of the actual number and makeup of the original sources is difficult, given this blizzard of fragments, especially from the 13th and 14th centuries. Many of them are badly damaged, and some even are palimpsest. Most never preserve enough information about the original parent source to make reconstruction even hypothetically possible. Equally troubling is the chronic lack of information from the fragments themselves that would provide information about the location of their production. In the 14th century no fragment exceeds fourteen folios, and almost none of them could be described as having been originally part of a sumptuous presentation volume intended for royal or noble use, though important anthology collections were produced in scriptoria of considerable sophistication.

An example of this kind of manuscript is the late-13th-century collection of conducti, originally from Bury St. Edmunds, now preserved in Cambridge, Jesus College QB1. Here all of the hallmarks of a fine scriptorium are in evidence, such as the finely produced parchment, highly elaborate and finely decorated initials, and sophisticated musical notation. Some of the fragments also appear to have been working copies of a small, discrete mixed corpus notated on *rotuli* and/or parchment gatherings already once used, such as Berkeley Castle Select Roll 55. Musical sources like this were considered eminently discardable from the very beginning and survive to our time because of their value as carriers of important legal or economic information. More often, though, fragments survive simply because of the value assigned to their parchment, a product that could be readily used by the medieval bookbinder.

A significant proportion of the fragments has been recovered from bindings produced in the 15th century. The main contents of these manuscripts are virtually always unrelated to the music. The best-known example in this regard is a group of 62 leaves, most of which were recovered from bindings fabricated in the late 14th or early 15th century for manuscripts belonging to the Worcester Cathedral Library (the "Worcester fragments"). Other examples are known from Bury St. Edmunds, Norwich, Durham, Ely, Canterbury, and St. Albans. This apparent concentration of musical sources in the greater monastic houses may suggest that the music was composed there or, equally reasonably, that these large and sometimes wealthy institutions collected large libraries and undertook regular rebinding of their manuscripts, a process that required a constant supply of reusable parchment. Even though little direct evidence has been amassed concerning the production of these many music manuscripts, it is certainly appropriate to conclude that England had an active tradition of polyphonic composition and manuscript production from the 10th century right through to the end of the Middle Ages. The breadth, diversity, and beauty of this large body of polyphonic music are only now becoming known to the greater musical public through recent recordings, facsimiles, and performing editions.

William J. Summers

Bibliography

PRIMARY

Dittmer, Luther, ed. *Worcester Add. 68; Westminster Abbey 33327; Madrid, Bibl. Nac. 192.* Brooklyn: Institute of Mediaeval Music, 1959 [facsimile]; Dittmer, Luther, ed. *Oxford, Latin Liturgical D 20; London, Add. MS. 25031; Chicago, MS. 654 App.* Brooklyn: Institute of Mediaeval Music, 1960 [facsimile]; Harrison, Frank Ll., and Roger Wibberley, eds., *Manuscripts of Fourteenth-Century English Polyphony: A Selection of Facsimiles.* London: Stainer & Bell, 1981; Hughes, Anselm, ed. *Worcester Mediaeval Harmony of the Thirteenth and Fourteenth Centuries.* Burnham: Plainsong & Mediaeval Music Society, 1928. Repr. Hildesheim: Olms, 1971 [partial ed. and facsimile]; Stainer, John, et al., eds. *Early Bodleian Music: Sacred and Secular Songs . . . in the Bodleian Library.* 3 vols. London:

Novello, 1901–13. Repr. Farnborough: Gregg, 1967 [facsimile]; Summers, William J., ed. *English Fourteenth-Century Polyphony: Facsimile Edition of Sources Notated in Score.* Tutzing: Schneider, 1983; Summers, William J., and Peter M. Lefferts. *English Thirteenth-Century Polyphonic Music: A Facsimile Edition of the Manuscript Sources.* London: British Academy, forthcoming; Wooldridge, Harry E., and Humphrey V. Hughes, eds. *Early English Harmony from the 10th to the 15th Century.* 2 vols. London: Quaritch, 1897; Plainsong & Mediaeval Music Society, 1913. Repr. New York: AMS, 1976.

SECONDARY

Baltzer, Rebecca. "Notre Dame Manuscripts and Their Owners: Lost and Found." *Journal of Musicology* 5 (1987): 380–99; Wathey, Andrew. "Lost Books of Polyphony in England: A List to 1500." *Research Chronicle* 21 (1988): 1–19; Wathey, Andrew. "The Production of Books of Liturgical Polyphony." In *Book Production and Publishing in Britain 1375–1475,* ed. Jeremy Griffiths and Derek Pearsall. Cambridge: Cambridge University Press, 1989.

CATALOGUES

Census-Catalogue of Manuscript Sources of Polyphonic Music, 1400–1550. 5 vols. Renaissance Manuscript Studies 1. Neuhausen-Stuttgart: Hänssler, 1979–88; *Repertoire international des sources musicales.* Ser. B, vol. 4, parts 1–4. Munich-Duisberg: Henle, 1966–72; Supplement 1: *The British Isles, 1100–1400.* Munich: Henle, 1993. Frere, Walter Howard. *Bibliotheca Musico-liturgica: A Descriptive Handlist of the Musical and Latin-Liturgical MSS of the Middle Ages Preserved in the Libraries of Great Britain and Ireland.* 2 vols. London: Quaritch, 1901–32; Ker, N.R. *Medieval Libraries of Great Britain.* 2d ed. London: Royal Historical Society, 1964. *Supplement.* London: Royal Historical Society, 1987; Ker, N.R. *Medieval Manuscripts in British Libraries.* 4 vols. Oxford: Clarendon, 1969–90.

See also Harley 978; Old Hall Manuscript; W1; Winchester Songbook; Winchester Tropers; Worcester Fragments

Map, Walter (ca. 1130/35–1209/10)

Secular clerk who served Gilbert Foliot, bishop of London and Hereford, and King Henry II; appointed archdeacon of Oxford in 1196 or 1197.

Until the 19th century Map was considered the author of much of the best late-12th-century secular Latin verse and of a cycle of French romances. Modern scholars contend, however, that all Map's certainly authentic work is contained in his *De nugis curialium (Courtiers' Trifles)*, a collection of witty, satiric tales and exempla, noteworthy for its vivid humor and erudite allusions to biblical, classical, and scholastic sources.

Kathleen M. Hewett-Smith

Bibliography

PRIMARY

James, Montague Rhodes, ed. and trans. *De nugis curialium: Courtiers' Trifles.* Rev. C.N.L. Brooke and R.A.B. Mynors. Oxford: Clarendon, 1983.

SECONDARY

New *CBEL* 1:783.

See also Anglo-Latin Literature after 1066; Court Culture; Dioceses; Exemplum; Geoffrey of Monmouth; Henry II; Satire; Universities

Marches of Scotland and Wales

The areas of the kingdom that bordered on Scotland and Wales required a concentration of military and juridical power in the hands of local magnates who could meet the threats of raid and invasion. These regions thus developed a special character and quasi-independence until their assimilation in Tudor times.

Scotland

The Scottish march had been the special purview of the Northumbrian earls under the house of Wessex. After the Norman Conquest the bishop of Durham assumed special military responsibilities, and the palatinate (semiregal) lordship of Durham became England's northern bastion. Edward I's Scottish campaigns and the Hundred Years War exacerbated the problem of the borders. Under Richard II a warden of the east march, centered on Berwick, and a warden of the west march, centered on Carlisle, were regularly appointed. Military power and generous exchequer subsidies caused these offices to be coveted by the two great rival northern families, the Nevilles and the Percys, and the inability of the crown to pay the subsidies was a source of grievance that fueled rebellion. As late as 1569 Lord Hunsdon could write that men of the north knew no other prince but a Percy or a Neville. The power of the wardens was weakened by Richard III, who had a personal interest in the region, and by the Tudor Council in the North, which replaced the wardens.

Wales

The Norman barons created a series of marcher lordships along the Welsh border and in south Wales to contain the Welsh and serve as bases for further conquest. The lords marcher enjoyed considerable independence, and a mixture of Welsh custom and English law known as the "custom of the march" grew up in these lordships. A group of marcher lords led by Richard de Clare brought the English presence to Ireland in Henry II's time. Edward I's conquest of Wales did not end the marcher lordships. In the 14th and 15th centuries they fell into the hands of the great magnate families. The Despensers and the Mortimers were rival marcher lords in Edward II's reign. The tendency of the marches toward criminal disorder and civil strife continued in the Wars of the Roses. Edward IV attempted to check the problem in 1471 by the creation of a Council of the Marches of Wales, at Ludlow. By the Act of Union of 1536 some 135 marcher lordships were absorbed into the administrative structure of the kingdom.

James L. Gillespie

Bibliography

Bartlett, R., and Angus MacKay, eds. *Medieval Frontier Societies.* Oxford: Clarendon, 1989; Chrimes, Stanley B., Charles D. Ross, and Ralph A. Griffiths, eds. *Fifteenth-Century England, 1399–1509: Studies in Politics and Society.* Manchester: Manchester University Press, 1972 [the chapters by Robin L. Storey and by Griffiths, along with the Bartlett and MacKay volume, are the best general surveys]; Pugh, T.B., ed. *The Marcher Lordships of South Wales, 1415–1536.* Cardiff: University of Wales Press, 1963; Reeves, A.C. *The Marcher Lords.* Llandybie: Davies, 1983; Storey, Robin L. "The Wardens of the Marches of England towards Scotland, 1377–1489." *EHR* 72 (1957): 593–615.

See also Despenser Family; Palatinates; Percy Family

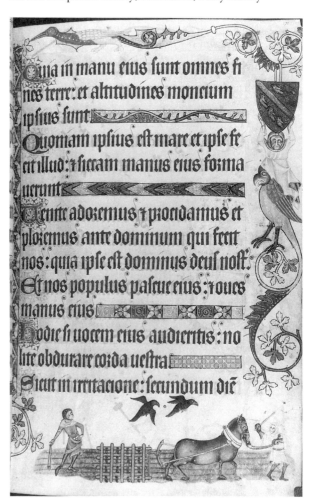

Fig. 93. Luttrell Psalter (BL Add. 42130), fol. 171, ca. 1335–40. Harrowing. Reproduced by permission of the British Library, London.

Marginalia

"Marginalia" refers to the small animated scenes of humans, animals, and grotesques (imaginary hybrid monsters) that enliven the margins of Gothic manuscripts. Also known as drolleries, these scenes depict a wide range of subject matter that ranges from the sacred to the profane and from the mundane to the fantastic. Major categories of English marginalia include (1) scenes from daily life, such as domestic activities, peasant labor, sports and entertainment, and chivalric pursuits (fig. 93); (2) scenes of humans, animals, and grotesques parodying real-life situations often with a "world turned upside-down" theme (fig. 94); (3) religious subjects drawn from the Old and New Testaments, saints' lives, the miracles of the Virgin, and contemporary religious practice; (4) scenes based on fables, popular legends, proverbs, and moralized anecdotes from sermons; (5) subjects taken from the bestiary; and (6) nonnarrative motifs, such as single grotesques, naturalistically rendered birds and animals, and heraldic devices.

Although Gothic marginalia can appear anywhere in the border, the *bas-de-page* (lower margin) held a privileged position. Cycles of iconographically related scenes were commonly placed in the *bas-de-page* of adjacent leaves in order to present continuous narrative sequences or thematic groupings of religious and secular subjects.

First appearing in fully developed form in the Rutland Psalter (BL Add. 62925) of ca. 1260, marginalia became widespread in English manuscript illumination toward the end of the 13th century. Distinguished by its variety and inventiveness, English marginalia achieved a peak of popularity during the 14th century and became one of the hallmarks of the East Anglian School and the manuscripts made for the Bohun family. A similar taste for marginal ornament also manifested itself at this time in misericord carvings and architectural detailing. By the end of the 14th century the popularity of marginalia had declined, and during the early 15th century it ceased to be a major element in English illumination. Although individual figures, animals, and other motifs continued to be included in manuscript borders for much of the century, the lively and imaginative vignettes that characterize 13th- and 14th-century marginalia no longer appeared.

Gothic marginalia occurs predominantly in religious texts, such as psalters and books of hours, while being largely absent from most secular books. Its purpose has proved difficult to ascertain. Although in some cases the marginalia illustrates the text or expands on other illustrations in the book, frequently no clear relationship can be established between the marginalia and the book as a whole. Marginalia is generally thought to have been intended to amuse or divert the reader but may have also served as a mnemonic device to assist in memorizing the accompanying text. Particularly problematical are the exuberantly humorous, bawdy, or obscene compositions that sometimes fill the margins of devotional or liturgical texts. Revealing a freedom of artistic expression rarely encountered in other art forms, they provide a dramatic contrast to the religious content of the text. The juxtaposition of opposites may have been deliberately intended to provoke the reader's attention and to affirm the authority of the text through the marginalization

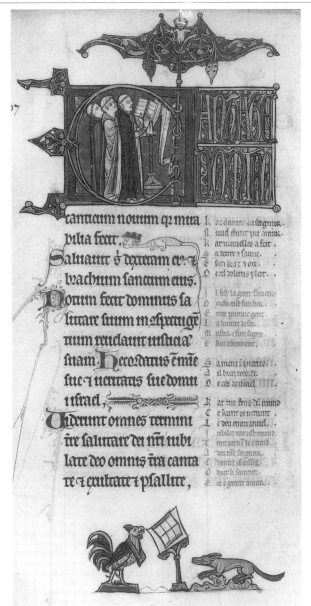

Fig. 94. Oscott Psalter (BL Add. 50000), fol. 146v, ca. 1270. Cock preaching to a fox. Reproduced by permission of the British Library, London.

of pictorial elements opposed to it.

Michael Orr

Bibliography

Baltrusaitis, Jurgen. *Reveils et prodiges: le gothique fantastique.* Paris: Colin, 1960; Camille, Michael. *Image on the Edge: The Margins of Medieval Art and Society.* Cambridge: Harvard University Press, 1992; Carruthers, Mary. *The Book of Memory: A Study of Memory in Medieval Culture.* Cambridge: Cambridge University Press, 1990; Janson, Horst. *Apes and Ape Lore in the Middle Ages and Renaissance.* London: Warburg Institute, 1952; Morgan, Nigel. *Early Gothic Manuscripts (2) 1250–1285.* A Survey of Manuscripts Illuminated in the British Isles 4:2, ed. J.J.G. Alexander. London: Harvey Miller, 1988; Randall, Lilian. "*Exempla* as a Source of Gothic Marginal Illumination." *Art Bulletin* 39 (1957): 97–107; Randall,

Lilian. *Images in the Margins of Gothic Manuscripts.* Berkeley: University of California Press, 1966; Sandler, Lucy Freeman. *Gothic Manuscripts 1285–1385.* A Survey of Manuscripts Illuminated in the British Isles 5, ed. J.J.G. Alexander. London: Harvey Miller, 1986.

See also Books of Hours; "East Anglian School"; Manuscript Illumination, Gothic; Psalters, Gothic

Marie de France (fl. ca. 1160–1215)

The first known woman writer of vernacular narrative poetry in western Europe. Connected to the English court of Henry II and Eleanor of Aquitaine, where French was spoken, she wrote her three extant works in French. She translated *St. Patrick's Purgatory* and her Aesopic *Fables* from Latin and English sources, respectively, but there is no known literary source for her best-known work, the *Lais,* twelve short romances treating problems of love and morality, sometimes with supernatural elements. Two of her *Lais (Lanval* and *Le Fresne)* were translated into ME.

Lara Ruffolo

Bibliography

PRIMARY

Burgess, Glyn S., and Keith Busby, trans. *The Lais of Marie de France.* London: Penguin, 1986 [bibliography, pp. 129–31]; Spiegel, Harriet, ed. and trans. *Fables.* Toronto: University of Toronto Press, 1987.

SECONDARY

Mickel, Emanuel J., Jr. *Marie de France.* New York: Twayne, 1974.

See also Anglo-Norman Literature; Beast Epic and Fable; Breton Lay; Courtly Love; Harley 978; Literary Influences: French; Romances; Women in ME Literature

Marriage and Marriage Law

In the Middle Ages marriage came to be both a sacrament and a contract with important civil consequences. In Anglo-Saxon times marriage was viewed primarily as a private affair, though some kings intervened to issue laws assuring women a free choice of a spouse and regulating the law about adultery. Only gradually was the law of marriage brought under the rule of the church, and the exclusive jurisdiction of canon law was not established until the mid-12th century.

Making a marriage both valid and licit involved several considerations; both parties must be of age (twelve for females, fourteen for males), not too closely related by ties of consanguinity or affinity, not bound by vows of celibacy, nor forced to consent. While a valid marriage could be made in private (clandestinely), a licit marriage required the observance of the forms prescribed by the church, including calling of banns. Canonists in the 12th and 13th centuries debated about the essential nature of a valid marriage. Vicarius, an English civil-law writer, treated it as parallel to Roman law of purchase.

However, the consent theories of Gratian, Peter Lombard, and Pope Alexander III (1159–81) prevailed, especially in the papal formulation.

Marriages were of two basic types. Present consent *(sponsalia de praesenti)*—"I take you as wife/husband"—created the bond of marriage. Future consent *(sponsalia de futuro)*—"I promise to take you as wife/husband"—if followed by carnal consummation, made a valid marriage. The complex rules of the church, the tradition of clandestine marriage, and the reluctance of people to accept that marriage was not a private matter brought many cases before the ecclesiastical courts.

The most common matrimonial cause was the suit to enforce a marriage contract. Some "divorces"—essentially annulments—were granted. There were also judicial separations; in both these cases property settlements were made and child support, if necessary, was mandated by the church court. The English law of marriage was the medieval canon law. It survived the Reformation, to be altered by Lord Hardwicke's marriage law in the 18th century.

Because marriage had important consequences for the land law, common-law courts often adjourned cases until a request for proof of a marriage was answered by the church courts. This cooperation between ecclesiastical and secular jurisdictions is graphically depicted by a mitered hat, such as bishops wear, drawn upon the margin of a royal court plea roll. Because illegitimacy was a bar to the inheritance of feudal property, many suits in common-law courts turned on proof from the canon-law court of the legitimacy of an heir.

A valid marriage was a requirement for receipt of dower, the widow's right to one-third or one-half her late husband's property. If defendants in common-law courts sought to deny a widow her dower on the ground that she had not been married to the man of whom she claimed dower, a request went from the royal court to the church court to certify the marriage. One advantage of suing in royal court was that it could seek such certification from the ecclesiastical court. A few persons tried to get out of providing dower by alleging that there had been a divorce; the same procedure was followed. The report from the church court as to the marriage was decisive.

Church courts had spiritual jurisdiction to punish men and women who committed adultery. Canon-law courts may not always have lived up to their ideal of making adultery an equal offense for both sexes, and in so far as it touched the law of real property, adultery was overwhelmingly the offense of a married woman. A statute of 13 Edward I (1284–85) barred an adulterous woman from the enjoyment of common-law dower unless she had been freely forgiven by her husband. In such cases, however, the ecclesiastical courts were not consulted. Instead recourse was made to the knowledgeable neighbors on the common-law jury. A widow suing for dower in 1301 was met with the defendant's claim that she was an adulteress who had left his ancestor to live with her lover. The widow argued that her husband, two days before his death, had forgiven her. The lover, present in the court, supported her claim of reconciliation, as did the jury; she got her dower.

The free consent required to make marriage valid in the eyes of the church had temporal consequences; it contributed to limiting the influence of families and feudal lords on the choice of partners. Families naturally had a profound interest in marriage; prominent families might betroth very young children, even though the marriage could be repudiated by either spouse upon reaching the age of consent. The settlements of land made at marriage show the freedom feudatories had to resettle estates to provide for children not apt to inherit under primogeniture.

The interest of the feudal lord came to be equivalent to the payment of a fine or forfeiture for refusal to marry at his behest: twice the value of the marriage for a self-determined marriage while still a ward. Widespread feudal disobedience over marriage demonstrates the willingness to pay for such free choice. A ward, of course, was the heir and could use his inheritance to pay for forfeiture of marriage. One ward, sued for forfeiture of marriage, succeeded in shifting the burden of the fine for his marriage onto his mother and stepfather. He said that, by alternating "threats" and "flattering speech," they had forced him into a marriage against both his own wishes and those of his feudal lord. We do not know if the young man later tried to get out of the marriage in the church courts, but the verdict of the common-law jury in 1280 determined that the fine for his marriage came from his mother and stepfather.

Widows in the king's gift were subject to control over their remarriage, but Magna Carta (cl. 8) allowed them the freedom *not* to marry again. The granting of dower came to be coupled with a promise not to marry without royal license. Some widows paid a fine in advance to be allowed to marry as they wished; some took a chance on a husband offered by the crown, knowing that they had the right to refuse; many widows flouted the law to marry without license and paid the fine, later, when it might be paid by the new husband. Dower lands could be seized by the king until the fine was paid, but the land was not lost permanently.

Lesser lords were eager to claim wardships and marriage of minor heirs, but they do not seem to have been able to collect from tenants' widows when they remarried. Manorial lords collected a marriage fine, *merchet,* when daughters of servile tenants married, especially to freemen or peasants from other manors. Even though there was no official registration of marriages until the 19th century, public, private, and canonical documents contain a wealth of information about the important matter of marriage.

Sue Sheridan Walker

Bibliography

Brundage, James A. *Law, Sex, and Christian Society in Medieval Europe.* Chicago: University of Chicago Press, 1987; Donahue, Charles, Jr. "The Canon Law on the Formation of Marriage and Social Practice in the Later Middle Ages." *Journal of Family History* 8 (1983): 144–58; Helmholz, R.H. *Marriage Litigation in Medieval England.* London: Cambridge University Press, 1974; Palmer, Robert C. "Contexts of Marriage in Medieval England: Evidence from the King's Court circa 1300." *Speculum* 59 (1984): 42–67; Searle, Eleanor. "Seigneurial Control of Women's Marriage: The Antecedents and Function of Merchet in England." *Past and Present* 82 (February 1979): 3–43; Sheehan, Michael M. "Choice of Marriage Partner in the Middle Ages: Development and Mode of Application of a Theory of Marriage." *Studies in Medieval and Renaissance History,* n.s. 1 (1978): 3–33; Walker, Sue Sheridan. "Feudal Constraint and Free Consent in the Making of Marriages in Medieval England: Widows in the King's Gift." In *Canadian Historical Association Papers 1979,* ed. Terry Cook. Ottawa: Canadian Historical Association, n.d., pp. 97–110; Walker, Sue Sheridan. "Free Consent and the Marriage of Feudal Wards in Medieval England." *JMH* 8 (1982): 123–34.

See also Children; Wardship; Widows; Women

Martyrology, Old English

The term "martyrology" was often used of "calendars," or lists of names of saints (not only martyrs) recorded against their feast days. Bede added brief notes on each saint to produce the first "historical" or "narrative" martyrology. The OE *Martyrology* is such a "narrative" martyrology, originally created to include saints' days for the whole liturgical year but now extant in five fragmentary OE texts, some of considerable extent, and one 16th-century transcript of a partial entry for St. Patrick (17 March). Two manuscripts are of the late 9th century (BL Add. 23 211 and 40 165A), the others later (BL Cotton Julius A.x, ca. 1000, and Cambridge, Corpus Christi College 41 and 196, both 11th-century). Altogether the manuscripts present entries (or "notices") for nearly the entire year, apart from a large loss for most of February, beginning probably on 26 January, and smaller losses from 14–16 March inclusive and from 22–24 December inclusive. About 200 saints, or groups of saints, have "narrative notices," some running to about a modern printed page in length. There are also nineteen notices on such general feasts as Christmas and Ascension Day and nineteen calendar entries of names only.

This martyrology, the earliest in vernacular prose in Europe, is also one of the earliest narrative prose texts in English, if not the earliest. Only one of the later manuscripts updates the information, and only for one item, so the texts represent a record of festivals celebrated in the composer's house sometime in the 9th century. Some scholars have suggested that it was written in Mercia, which is not unlikely; others have thought that it was a translation of a martyrology in Latin. Evidence is not conclusive for either opinion.

Relevant sections of martyrologies were read aloud at the monastic chapter office (a daily meeting of monks in a monastery) to recall the commemoration of saints for the following day and sometimes for sick brothers in the infirmary, but hints in this martyrology suggest that it was intended for private reading. Its learned composer created the sections in a variety of ways, following no rigid formula of presentation and taking information from a number of other books as well as from saints' legends. The writer was a fluent latinist in a period when knowledge of Latin was reputedly in decay and a good précis writer with an eye to retain an image and an ear for a snatch of dialogue. Unlike some continental Latin martyrologists of the 9th century he did not merely copy Bede's words and then add a little more but chose his own material to present a sequence of notices, which, although functional in purpose, is fascinatingly readable.

J. E. Cross

Bibliography

PRIMARY

Herzfeld, G., ed. and trans. *An Old English Martyrology.* EETS o.s. 116. London: Kegan Paul, Trench, Trübner, 1900 [text not always accurate]; Kotzor, G., ed. *Das altenglische Martyrologium.* Bayerische Akademie der Wissenschaften, Phil.-Hist. Klasse 88/1–2. Munich: Bayerische Akademie der Wissenschaften, 1981 [better text].

SECONDARY

Cross, J.E. "On the Library of the Old English Martyrologist." In *Learning and Literature in Anglo-Saxon England: Studies Presented to Peter Clemoes,* ed. Michael Lapidge and Helmut Gneuss. Cambridge: Cambridge University Press, 1985, pp. 227–49.

See also Bede; Hagiography; Liturgy and Church Music, History of; Monasticism

Marvels of the East, The

The Marvels, or *Wonders, of the East,* an account of fantastic oriental creatures, is an Anglo-Saxon contribution to the *mirabilia* genre, literature in which a traveler in foreign lands describes exotic sights in a letter home. In this case the creatures are mostly gigantic and anthropomorphic: *blemmyae* (headless people with eyes and a mouth in their chests), *cynocephali* (dog-headed people), *panotii* (people with ears large enough to cover their bodies), women thirteen feet tall with boar tusks and ox tails. Such monsters are ultimately drawn from Pliny and the Alexander legends, but the immediate source appears to be the Latin Letter of Farasmanes to Hadrian. The form may derive from a Greek original, since the *mirabilia* resemble Greek *periploi,* guidebooks for sailors and merchants. In *The Marvels,* however, little narrative context remains and only a few scholars have found literary merit in the work (e.g., Campbell, who approaches it from the perspective of the grotesque).

The Marvels survives in three early English manuscripts: as an Anglo-Saxon text in the *Beowulf* codex, BL Cotton Vitellius A.xv; as parallel Anglo-Saxon and Latin versions in Cotton Tiberius B.v; and as a Latin text in Bodleian Library, Bodley 614. All three manuscripts are illustrated, the Tiberius most elaborately, with 38 miniatures.

Of the three English manuscripts the Bodley and Tiberius are more closely related to each other than to the Vitellius: the Bodley and Tiberius manuscripts also contain maps, astronomical pictures, and other cosmographical items, while the compiler of the Vitellius manuscript may have been chiefly interested in monsters. Nevertheless, all three may derive from a common Anglo-Latin source.

Timothy Jones

Bibliography

PRIMARY

Malone, Kemp, ed. *The Nowell Codex.* EEMF 12. Copenhagen: Rosenkilde & Bagger, 1963 [Cotton Vitellius A.xv]; McGurk, P., et al., eds. *An Eleventh-Century Anglo-Saxon Illustrated Miscellany.* EEMF 21. Copenhagen: Rosenkilde & Bagger, 1983 [Cotton Tiberius B.v]; Rypins, Stanley, ed. *Three Old English Prose Texts in MS. Cotton Vitellius A xv.* EETS o.s. 161. London: Humphrey Milford, 1924.

SECONDARY

Campbell, Mary. *The Witness and the Other World: Exotic European Travel Writing 400–1600.* Ithaca: Cornell University Press, 1988; Friedman, John Block. *The Monstrous Races in Medieval Art and Thought.* Cambridge: Harvard University Press, 1981.

See also Letter of Alexander; Mandeville's Travels; Manuscript Illumination, Anglo-Saxon; Scientific Manuscripts, Early

Mass, Polyphonic Music for
ca. 900–ca. 1390

The clergy of France, Normandy, and the British Isles held in common a number of important outlets for musical creativity within the medieval liturgy, including the composition of new chants, the amplification of plainsongs with tropes, and the adornment of plainsongs with polyphony. The composition and performance of polyphony, though geographically widespread, was a specialized skill—the province of a few trained musicians principally working in the choirs of the greater Benedictine abbeys and cathedrals. Its practice was from the 9th to the 12th century mainly unwritten, relying on improvisation and memory in an oral tradition stabilized by only a few notated models. Its style ranged from the addition of a sober note-against-note counterpoint whose contour ran mainly parallel to that of the chant being decorated, to the florid, melismatic ornamentation by one or more solo singers of the slowly sung notes of a chant. The 12th and 13th centuries saw a shift toward notation and fixity in ecclesiastical polyphony that brought, as an important consequence of musical literacy and a new reliance on the written note, a more rapid evolution of style and turnover of repertoire and an increased number of centers of performance.

From the 10th to the 13th century the repertoire of polyphony for mass and offices was primarily festal and Proper, that is, comprehensive in its coverage of major holidays and setting liturgical texts specific to the occasion. It was widely disseminated by a latinate clerical culture sharing common musical and educational roots, so it was to a fairly large degree uniform among the institutions in which it was cultivated, though subject to local additions and modifications. The only musical sources from the British Isles to survive more or less complete from this broad timespan, the Winchester tropers (late 10th century) and W1 (early 13th century), conveniently frame and characterize it. The Winchester organa (polyphonic settings of plainsongs) consist of a yearly cycle for the Old Minster of Alleluias and Tracts for the Temporale and Sanctorale (including the Common of Saints), plus shorter series of Introits and Sequences, Kyries and Glorias, office responsories, and other items. An artistic product of the Benedictine Reform, the Winchester tradition reflects at several removes the practices of northern France, especially at Fleury and Corbie. W1 contains a version of the late-12th-century Parisian *Magnus liber*, a yearly cycle of organa for Propers of the mass (Graduals and Alleluias) and offices (Vespers and Matins responsories) originally composed for Notre Dame, as well as local additions for the Augustinian Priory of St. Andrews, Scotland, for which the manuscript was copied in the 1230s.

The long tradition of composing cycles of polyphonic Propers for the mass and offices lost impetus in France in the 13th century with the canonization of the *Magnus liber*. Outside of versions of this collection there is virtually no evidence for any attention to mass Propers by French composers in this period. In 13th- and 14th-century England, however, composers continue to cultivate Proper cycles of an indigenous genre, the troped-chant setting of Alleluias.

A new wave of composition for the mass that began in the later 12th and early 13th centuries involves the provision of chant and polyphony for daily Lady Mass—a new votive service performed outside of choir with its own special complement of performers and a distinctive (lay) audience. Most significant in the light of the later history of polyphonic mass music is the new emphasis here on setting the fixed texts of the Ordinary of the mass (Kyrie, Gloria, Credo, Sanctus, Agnus, and Ite/Deo gratias, either with or without additional Latin trope texts) in addition to some Propers. Kyrie, Sanctus, Agnus, and Ite/Deo gratias were sung daily, with the addition of the Gloria on Saturdays and feasts and the Credo only on high feasts—a frequency of performance reflected directly in the proportional numbers of surviving settings. Marian Propers were also set polyphonically, including troped-chant Alleluias (and there are isolated settings of Marian Introits, Gradual verses, and Tracts), but most novel is the English enrichment and diversification of the repertoire of Marian Sequences and Offertories.

Widespread continental adoption of the practice of setting mass Ordinaries (the invariable texts of the mass) lags significantly behind the English. Aside from some 13th-century activity on the Iberian peninsula, only isolated settings precede two northern French landmarks, the anonymously compiled mass for Tournai Cathedral of 1349 and a mass for Reims Cathedral by Guillaume de Machaut of the early 1360s. Both of these significantly parallel English practice in that they were intended for Marian devotional masses outside of choir and include settings of all six mass Ordinary texts.

In most locales the standard musical fare at daily Lady Mass would have been plainchant, and where polyphony was heard it would have been mainly in the form of one or two extemporized voices added to a plainchant. Written polyphony did not at first reach much higher in artistic ambition. Insular composers worked in a narrow stylistic range, principally writing note-against-note (discant) settings of troped and untroped chants in two or three voices notated in score; composing free settings of the liturgical texts in three voices, also notated in score; or constructing motetlike troped chant settings notated in parts with additional tropic texts. These simple ferial settings were also compiled into weekly, biweekly, or seasonal cycles by genre (seven Kyries, fourteen Sequences, etc.), a tradition whose first witness in a book of polyphony is the eleventh fascicle of W1. Though the early-13th-century repertoire contained settings of troped Sanctus and Agnus, a distinctive feature of the English mass repertoire enduring into the 14th century is settings of Latin-texted Kyries (including an extraordinary setting for St. Cuthbert, the *Kyrie Cuthberte*) and Gloria tropes—troped chant settings of the Gloria trope *Regnum tuum solidum* with its prosulae *O rex glorie, Salve virgo virginum,* and *Decus virginum,* and the Marian Gloria trope *Spiritus et alme.* Belying the generally unpretentious character of these works is a masterly setting of *Spiritus et alme* for four voices probably composed by R. de Burgate, abbot of Reading, 1268–90 (Sanders, 1979: no. App. 15).

A significant development of the later 14th century was the establishment of personal household choirs by the great secular and ecclesiastical magnates, following the earlier lead of French and English monarchs. This movement provided new places, new occasions, and new forces for the performance of mass music and introduced a new emphasis on festal polyphony for mass as part of ostentatious display in court culture. One consequence is an increase in frequency of Gloria and Credo settings. More fundamentally we see composers elevating their ambitions in respect to the impressiveness of mass music, leading to a new artfulness and complexity through the adoption of motet style, accompanied-song style, and canonic intricacies. The Old Hall Manuscript (ca. 1420) shows a systematic division in its mass music between more functional ferial settings in score, some of which may date back to the third quarter of the 14th century, and more elaborate display works and festal settings in parts.

ca. 1390–ca. 1485

Late-14th- and early-15th-century England witnessed a rise to prominence of secular institutions like the royal and other household chapels and a new wave of choral foundations. With these came a trend toward more elaborate and often ostentatious music, designed to demonstrate the excellence of a given establishment as much as to adorn the liturgy. Increasingly pride of place was given to music composed for the Ordinary of the mass, and about 400 to 500 separate movements survive, the majority from the first half of the 15th century. Of these some are self-standing and some grouped into pairs (Gloria-Credo or Sanctus–Agnus Dei); later full cycles predominate, these often with a preceding Kyrie, which might or might not include prosulae.

In tracing the development of Ordinary settings from the end of the 14th to the late 15th century it is convenient to divide the period into five phases, the exact limits of which need, on current knowledge, to be treated with caution: 1) ca. 1390–ca. 1415, representing the main body of the Old Hall Manuscript; 2) the second and third decades of the 15th century, including the later Old Hall works; 3) a period of far-reaching stylistic change, which occurred largely in the 1430s and perhaps the early 1440s; 4) a time of stabilization from the early 1440s to around the early 1460s; 5) a more problematic phase—probably beginning in the early to middle 1460s—from which little mass music remains.

Most of the surviving repertoire from the early years of the 15th century is preserved in the Old Hall Manuscript, which includes music by Bittering, Cooke, Excetre, Oliver, Power, Pycard, Queldryk, Tyes, and a number of other named composers, some of whom are known to have had associations with the Chapel Royal or one of the ducal chapels; also represented is one Roy Henry, possibly Henry V. The majority of pieces are individual settings of the Gloria, Credo, Sanctus, and Agnus Dei, though there are also a few Deo gratias substitutes. Only a handful of Kyries survive from this period, possibly because that section of Old Hall has been lost rather than because they never existed in the first place.

The range of styles is remarkable, from simple block-chord settings with plainchant in the middle voice (so-called English discant) to highly florid pieces that must have required virtuoso singers. The idiom of the more elaborate settings matches most closely that of late-14th-century French music: lively rhythms driving short melodic phrases and a racy use of dissonance arising from the collision of independently moving voices. It is clear that ingenuity of artifice was highly valued, with many pieces using abstract structural techniques like isorhythm and canon, and some communicated through the most abstruse notational devices. A few settings, mainly of the Gloria and Credo, are paired by use of similar voice ranges, parallel structures, and so on.

A relative simplification of style occurs in the more composerly works of the later Old Hall repertoire, with a trend toward more florid melodic lines and longer phrases and away from self-consciously learned techniques. Apart from Cooke and Power composers featured here include Damett and Sturgeon, both members of the Chapel Royal.

To some extent English composers continued to produce individual and paired movements throughout the 15th century; however, around 1430—the exact date is uncertain—composers like Dunstable, Power, and Benet extended the idea of pairing into the compilation of full cycles. Not only were these unified through established practices like parallel structuring, often they also made common use of a plainsong *cantus firmus,* the choice of which was probably determined by the event for which the work was composed. It is the cyclic mass, and in particular the *cantus firmus* or tenor mass, that seems to have become the most highly regarded genre of the period and that superseded the isorhythmic motet as the chief vehicle for the celebration of great festive occasions.

With the rise of the new genre came also a radical change in musical taste, the new manner favoring smoother melodic lines, fluid rather than bouncy rhythms, and a more controlled use of dissonance. These, together with a closer attention to the interaction of voice parts, generated a completely new style that soon took over in England and, somewhat later, on the Continent.

In fact, in the absence of major insular manuscripts, most English music of the post–Old Hall period survives only in continental sources—often anonymously—and such sources were plainly crucial in the wider dissemination of the new style. They are, however, not without their problems: most notably copyists frequently suppressed the Kyries of English cycles, perhaps because the prosulae rendered them unsuitable outside Sarum usage.

A younger generation of composers including Frye, Bedingham, and Plummer—also, perhaps, the composer of the anonymous Caput Mass—dominated English music of the mid-15th century. Though masses for three voices (the most common layout for the early cycles) continued to be written, a richer effect was increasingly sought by the addition of a fourth part; indeed fragments of five-voice *cantus firmus* masses survive, too, probably from the late 1450s or 1460s. Historically, though, it was the four-part *cantus firmus* mass that was adopted and developed by continental composers as the genre for their most prestigious sacred music.

Little remains from the period after about 1460–85, the greatest loss being that we have practically no mass music by the masters of the Eton Choirbook. This gap arises partly from the dearth of English sources and an evident collapse of interest in English music on the Continent; however, it may also reflect greater competition from other genres, especially the Marian antiphon. Be that as it may, inventories show evidence of lost volumes from the last quarter of the 15th century that contained masses in five, six, and even seven parts; this ambitious-sounding repertoire naturally looks forward to the 16th-century six-part festal mass. What little has survived shows considerable variety and ranges from the simple, so-called "playnsong" style of Turges's mass in the Ritson Manuscript to the florid manner of some of the York masses.

Clearly, in the more austere 15th-century settings, adornment of the liturgy is limited enough. In the discant pieces, for example, musical structures are determined entirely by the chants of which they are the straightforward harmonizations, and these in turn are shaped by the words involved. With the greater elaboration of more complex music, however, composers rarely used the chants proper to the texts they were setting; instead, as we have already seen, a variety of abstract technical preoccupations took them far beyond the bare presentation of the liturgy. Indeed, even after such procedures as isorhythm and canon had fallen out of fashion, it long remained normal to compose within preordained formal schemes, these often being strict and largely independent of the structure of a given text. Most obviously such schemes involved the use of approximately parallel structures for the constituent movements of pairs or cyclic masses. However, in single movements, pairs, and cycles alike it was also common for musical structure to be governed by a system of numerical proportions. Sometimes, too, such proportions seem to have involved numerological symbolism, as has been found in the work of John Dunstable.

Not only could the structure of a text be secondary to musical consideration, the florid nature of many melodic lines suggests that propriety did not require clarity of word setting either. Indeed many settings of the Credo (sometimes also of the Gloria) even involved the singing of different portions of the text at the same time, perhaps following the precedent set by isorhythmic motets. This procedure, known as telescoping, was later replaced by the setting of abbreviated versions of the texts, in the case of the Credo usually omitting the Holy Spirit articles.

It does not appear that polyphonic mass Propers were cultivated to the same extent as Ordinaries, and what survives suggests that they did not require the same elaboration of style. However, there survive a number of short, mainly unpretentious items, including Communions and a complete set of Alleluias for Lady Mass, Alleluias for other feasts, and settings of the Benedicamus and the Laudes Deo (the troped lesson for midnight mass of Christmas). Of particular interest is a group of pieces to be performed at the masses of Holy Week and Easter that are preserved in BL Egerton 3307, which also contains the only surviving polyphonic Missa Brevis of the period.

Peter M. Lefferts
Gareth Curtis

Bibliography

CA. 900–CA. 1390

Harrison, Frank Ll. *Music in Medieval Britain.* 2d ed. London: Routledge & Kegan Paul, 1963; Harrison, Frank Ll., Ernest H. Sanders, and Peter M. Lefferts, eds. *English Music for Mass and Offices.* 2 vols. Polyphonic Music of the Fourteenth Century 16–17. Paris: L'Oiseau-Lyre, 1983–86; Holschneider, Andreas. *Die Organa von Winchester: Studien zum ältesten Repertoire polyphoner Musik.* Hildesheim: Olms, 1968; Lütolf, Max. *Die mehrstimmigen Ordinarium Missae-Sätze vom ausgehenden 11. bis zur Wende des 13. zum 14 Jahrhundert.* 2 vols. Bern: Haupt, 1970; Planchart, Alejandro E. *The Repertory of Tropes at Winchester.* 2 vols. Princeton: Princeton University Press, 1977; Roesner, Edward, ed. *Thirteenth-Century Polyphony for the Missa de Beata Virgine: Fascicle XI of Wolfenbüttel, MS 628.* Madison: A-R Editions, forthcoming; Sanders, Ernest H., ed. *English Music of the Thirteenth and Early Fourteenth Centuries.* Polyphonic Music of the Fourteenth Century 14. Paris: L'Oiseau-Lyre, 1979.

CA. 1390–CA. 1485

Benham, Hugh. *Latin Church Music in England 1460–1575.* London: Barrie & Jenkins, 1977; Bent, Margaret, ed. *Fifteenth-Century Liturgical Music.* Vol. 2: *Four Anonymous Masses.* Early English Church Music 22. London: Stainer & Bell, 1979; Bukofzer, Manfred. *Studies in Medieval and Renaissance Music.* New York: Norton, 1950; Charles, Sydney Robinson, ed. *The Music of the Pepys MS 1236.* Corpus Mensurabilis Musicae 40. Rome: American Institute of Musicology, 1967; Curtis, Gareth. "Stylistic Layers in the English Mass Repertory, c. 1400–1450." *Proceedings of the Royal Musical Association* 109 (1982–83): 23–28; Curtis, Gareth, ed. *Fifteenth-Century Liturgical Music.* Vol. 3: *The Brussels Masses.* Early English Church Music 34. London: Stainer & Bell, 1989; Curtis, Gareth, and Andrew Wathey. "Fifteenth-Century English Liturgical Music: A List of the Surviving Repertory." *Research Chronicle of the Royal Musical Association* 27 (1994): 1–69; Hughes, Andrew, ed. *Fifteenth-Century Liturgical Music.* Vol. 1: *Antiphons and Music for Holy Week and Easter.* Early English Church Music 8. London: Stainer & Bell, 1967; Hughes, Andrew, and Margaret Bent, eds. *The Old Hall Manuscript.* 3 vols. in 4. Corpus Mensurabilis Musicae 46. Rome: American Institute of Musicology, 1969–73.

See also Caput Mass; Discant; Dunstable; Holy Week and Easter, Music for; Lady Mass; Old Hall Manuscript; Power, Leonel; Trope; W1; Winchester Organa; Winchester Tropers

Matilda (ca. 1102–1167)

The eldest child of Henry I and Matilda of Scotland. Nothing is known of Matilda's life prior to her betrothal at age seven to Henry V, Holy Roman Emperor. She left for the Empire during Lent 1110, having just turned eight, and remained there for the next sixteen years, the last years of the Investiture Controversy. She was crowned queen upon her arrival in Mainz (25 July 1110) but was sent to Trier to be educated and did not begin her public life until January 1114, when she and Henry were married in Worms. Though she used the title empress until her death, its legitimacy is questionable because it was bestowed by an antipope (Rome, July 1117). The role of empress was more defined than that of contemporary English queens. She served as a formal intercessor and performed ceremonial duties, but she probably did not make decisions even when she was nominally in charge of Tuscany. Her success as empress is underscored by the memory of her in a German chronicle as "the good Matilda." When she became a childless widow in 1125, Matilda was called back to England. Her only legitimate sibling, William, had died (1120), and her father's second wife, Adeliza, still had no children, so the 23-year-old empress arrived in England in 1126 to be placed in an unprecedented position as a female heir to the royal throne. In January 1127 the Christmas court swore allegiance (though not homage) to her as heir.

Matilda's second marriage, in 1128, was to Geoffrey Plantagenet (1113–1151), count of Anjou from 1129. The union was intended to guarantee a peaceful border between Normandy and Anjou, but within a year the couple was estranged and lived apart until 1131. At a great council in that year the decision was made that Matilda should return to her husband, most likely with the hope that she would produce a male heir. Only then did many swear or renew their oaths of fealty. She subsequently gave birth to three sons, Henry (the future Henry II) in 1133, Geoffrey in 1134, and William in 1136. Though she spent most of these years in Normandy with her father, she was involved in a border dispute with him when Henry I died on 1 December 1135.

The empress claimed both England and the duchy of Normandy as the designated heir but was challenged by her cousin Stephen of Blois. Stephen had hurried from his wife's territory of Boulogne to Winchester, where his brother was bishop, and quickly took control of the treasury, gained support of nobles and clergy, and was crowned on 22 December 1135. Civil war began in 1137 in both England and Normandy. Contemporary comment on the war between the two claimants to the throne and the behavior of some nobles who more than once switched allegiance has led this period to be mislabeled "the Anarchy." Matilda's supporters were defeated in England in 1138 (Battle of the Standard), while Matilda and Geoffrey quickly established themselves in Normandy, although it took five years to secure it. By 1139 the empress's forces, led by two of her half-brothers, Robert of Gloucester and Reginald of Dunstanville, and her uncle David, king of Scots, invaded England, posing a serious military challenge to Stephen, who was simultaneously alienating supporters. In February 1141 her forces defeated and captured Stephen at the Battle of Lincoln. In the following month Henry of Blois, as papal legate, publicly received her as "Lady of England and Normandy" (alternately termed "Lady of the English"), and the royal crown and treasure were handed over to her. It is unclear if the unusual title was meant to be temporary until her coronation as queen or to indicate that she ruled only until her son came of age. She arranged for a formal coronation and a seal was struck, but Londoners barred her entry into the city and eventually attacked, forcing her back to Oxford. Meanwhile her handling of a clerical appointment and her reluctance to reward defectors from Stephen's side caused her support to wane. Her forces were routed at Winchester later in 1141 and Robert of Gloucester was captured. When a prisoner exchange released both Robert and Stephen, it was clear to many supporters that the empress would never be crowned. She remained in England, holding a few castles, until 1148, when she returned to Normandy and dropped the title "Lady of the English." By the time of her departure Matilda's fourteen-year-old son Henry had already attempted an invasion of England (ca. 1147), and he took over the fight for the throne. Matilda resided mainly in Rouen and appears to have counseled Henry. In 1153 Stephen accepted a negotiated peace, designating Henry as his heir. Following his 1154 coronation Henry II confirmed many of the grants Matilda had made, giving some permanence to her year as "Lady of the English." The Empress continued to rule Normandy jointly with Henry or in his name and continued to advise him until her death on 10 September 1167. She was buried at Bec-Helⁱouin, where she also willed her jewels, many of which were imperial.

Contemporary chroniclers of the Anarchy, supporters of both Stephen and Matilda, criticized her manner, usually characterizing her as haughty or as a virago, lacking feminine qualities. After her death legends grew along these lines. Even in the 20th century most historians of the Anarchy have accepted these judgments and at most credited her with being a conduit of legitimacy from her father to her son. In spite of her unique life, and of being the only female claimant to the medieval English throne, no full-scale scholarly biography was published until 1992. Recent study of her charters, the chronicle accounts, and both the imperial and English phases of her life has led to a reassessment. Her recent biographer characterizes her as a careful and judicious ruler, who ruled Normandy and what she held in England in no way differently from her father or son, although her mistakes in 1141 were crucially ill-timed. Ultimately it was the expectations of a 12th-century nobility and clergy about the character of kings and women that prevented them from accepting a queen who acted as independently as a king.

Charlotte Newman Goldy

Bibliography

Chibnall, Marjorie. *The Empress Matilda: Queen Consort, Queen Mother and Lady of the English.* Oxford: Blackwell, 1992 [the most comprehensive and recent biography, including complete bibliographic information on primary and secondary sources]; Cronne, H.A., and R.H.C. Davis, eds. *Regesta Regum Anglo-Normannorum, 1066–1154.* Vol. 3: *Regesta Regis Stephani ac Matildis Imperatricis ac Gaufridi et Henrici Ducum Normannorum, 1135–1154.* Oxford: Clarendon, 1968 [Matilda's charters in a scholarly edition]; Potter, K.R., ed. and trans. *William of Malmesbury: Historia Novella.* London: Nelson, 1955 [major source for the Anarchy years; pro-Matilda bias].

See also Anarchy; Henry I; Henry II; Investiture Controversy; Queens; Stephen; Women

Matter of Antiquity (or Rome)

The classical stories drawn upon by medieval historians and romance writers, including stories of Thebes (especially the events surrounding Oedipus and his kin), Troy (including the subsequent history of Aeneas and Rome), and Alexander the Great.

Troy and Thebes

The story of Troy is the West's most persistent secular narrative. Classical Trojan episodes are common in ME literature (e.g., in Chaucer's *House of Fame* and Gower's *Confessio Amantis*). In addition to these fictional treatments the Middle Ages possessed what it believed to be the true history of the Trojan War, based on the supposed eyewitness journals of two fictitious authors, "Dares the Phrygian" and "Dictys of Crete." Trojan history was of interest in Britain because the island was said to have been colonized by and named for Brutus, a descendant of Aeneas, the Trojan prince and founder of Rome. The Brutus tradition is evoked at the beginning of *Sir Gawain and the Green Knight,* and the "history" of the Trojan War forms the background to Chaucer's *Troilus and Criseyde.*

The crude Latin narratives of Dares (6th century A.D.?) and Dictys (4th century A.D.) were transformed by Benoît de Sainte-Maure into a lavish French poem, the *Roman de Troie* (ca. 1165). These materials, along with additions from the Latin prose *Excidium Troiae* and classical sources, lie behind the earliest full Troy narrative in ME, the anonymous *Siege of Troy* (ca. 1300–25), a vigorous northwest Midlands romance in about 1,000 rhymed couplets.

The principal poems about the Trojan War in ME derive directly from Guido delle Colonne's *Historia destructionis Troiae* (1287), a sober, learned reworking of Benoît in Latin prose that became the standard medieval history of Troy. Three complete English translations of Guido, which all take pains to preserve its presumed factual truth, were produced within a few years of one another, perhaps in response to the popularity of Chaucer's *Troilus*. The most faithful is the northern *Destruction of Troy* (ca. 1400?), apparently by John Clerk of Whalley, whose skillful alliterative verse often overcomes Guido's intractable material. The anonymous *Laud Troy Book* (ca. 1400) is an energetic romance in four-stress couplets that glories in war and its chivalric heroes, especially Hector. The most ambitious and popular ME translation of Guido is John Lydgate's *Troy Book* (1412–20), whose learned and rhetorical additions extend the story to over 30,000 lines.

The brief *Prose Siege of Troy* (1425–50) is based on Lydgate (with some knowledge of Chaucer), and two anonymous 15th-century *Scottish Troy Fragments* were used to fill gaps in Scottish manuscripts of Lydgate's *Troy Book*. Caxton's long prose *Recuyell of the Historyes of Troye*, the first book printed in English (Bruges, ca. 1474), is a translation of the mid-15th-century *Receuil des histoires de Troyes*, much of whose strictly Trojan information derives from Guido's *Historia*.

The main events of the story of Thebes are set a generation or two before the Trojan War, and as a narrative subject Thebes was no less popular than Troy in classical and medieval continental literature. But the complete retelling of the story in ME (as opposed to the use of episodes by such writers as Gower and Chaucer, especially in *Troilus* and the *Knight's Tale*) had to await John Lydgate's *Siege of Thebes* (1420–22), which presents itself as a continuation of the *Canterbury Tales*. Perhaps because of its relative brevity (4,716 lines in rhymed couplets) it is Lydgate's finest narrative. A brief *Prose Siege of Thebes* derived from Lydgate was produced in the 15th century.

Alexander

In England, as throughout Europe, the legendary history of Alexander the Great was "so commune / That every wight that hath discrecioun / Hath herd somwhat or al of his fortune" (Chaucer, *MkT* 2631–33). Over 80 versions in more than twenty languages are known. However, the legend failed to engage the imaginations of English writers after the 15th century. The Alexander story lacked a Malory or, more to the point, a Caxton to print the best ME works on the subject—*Kyng Alisaunder* and *The Wars of Alexander*. Consequently the Alexander romance, once as popular as the Arthurian, had lost its English audience by 1500.

The Alexander romance in Britain is derivative, though often superior to its sources. Its major texts issue via translation or adaptation from Latin or French works, derived themselves at some remove from the Pseudo-Callisthenes, a mediocre 3rd-century Greek prose romance, the source for dozens of versions in every European language. The British tradition reflects material adapted either from the 4th-century *Res gestae Alexandri magni* of Julius Valerius or from two different redactions of the *Historia de preliis Alexandri magni*, both elaborations of the mid-10th-century *Nativitas et victoria Alexandri magni*, translated from the Greek by the archpriest Leo of Naples. Thus *Kyng Alisaunder* (early 14th century) and the *Cassamus* fragment (15th century) are derived from Julius Valerius, by way of Thomas of Kent's 12th-century *Roman de toute chevalerie* and Jacques de Longuyon's *Voeux du paon* (ca. 1312), respectively. The *Historia de preliis* inspired the mid-14th- to mid-15th-century alliterative poems *Alisaunder, Alexander and Dindimus,* and *The Wars of Alexander*, as well as the *Thornton Prose Alexander* (1400–50). The 15th-century Scottish poems *The Buik of Alexander* and Sir Gilbert Hay's *Buik of King Alexander the Conquerour* adapt the *Fuerre de Gadres*, by a certain Eustache, and the *Voeux du paon*.

Anecdotal accounts of Alexander's life in collections like the *Gesta Romanorum* present Alexander as a *de casibus* tragic figure (a protagonist who falls from prosperity into woe) and as a negative exemplum of excessive pride. The longer narratives celebrate his magnanimity, generosity, and courage, inverting the moralizing comment on the ambition that propelled him to conquer the known world. The massive 15th-century Scottish poems, reflecting closer connections with French culture, are less historical and more concerned with courtly manners and love.

Kyng Alisaunder and *The Wars of Alexander*, though derived from different traditions, include similar elements: Anectanabus's seduction of Alexander's mother, Alexander's birth and childhood exploits, Philip's death, Alexander's challenge to Persian authority, his conquest of Egypt, Rome, the other Greek city states, the siege of Tyre, Darius's defeat and death, and Alexander's coronation as emperor of Persia. The first half of the common narrative line, up to the Persian conquest, though not free from fantastic elements like Anectanabus's appearance as a flying dragon or the man-eating horse Bucephalus, clearly exploits historical fact. More episodic, the second half details Alexander's conquest of Porus's Indian empire; exotic encounters with the Amazons, Gymnosophists, Brahmans, and apelike men; a visit to the Earthly Paradise and the Trees of the Sun and Moon; and the courtship of Candace, queen of Ethiopia. Although *The Wars of Alexander* breaks off before Alexander's death, *Kyng Alisaunder* continues to the end of his life and concludes with moralizations on his death by poisoning after his return to Babylon.

C. David Benson
Hoyt N. Duggan

Bibliography

PRIMARY

Duggan, Hoyt N., and Thorlac Turville-Petre, eds. *The Wars of Alexander*. EETS s.s. 10. Oxford: Oxford University Press, 1989; Hay, Sir Gilbert. *The Buik of King Alexander the Conquerour.* 3 vols. projected. Ed. John Cartwright. STS 4th ser., 16, 18. Edinburgh: Scottish Text Society, 1986–; Panton, George A., and David Donaldson, eds. *The "Gest Hystoriale" of the Destruction of Troy: An Alliterative Romance Translated from Guido de Colonna's "Hystoria Troiana."* EETS o.s. 39, 56. London: Trübner, 1869–74; Smithers, G. V., ed. *Kyng Alisaunder.* EETS o.s. 227, 237. London: Oxford University Press, 1952–57; Wülfing, J. Ernst, ed. *Laud Troy Book.* EETS o.s. 121, 122. London: Kegan Paul, 1902–03.

SECONDARY

New *CBEL* 1:421–28; *Manual* 1:104–19, 268–77; 3:776–78, 930–31; 6:1901–04, 1913–17, 2155–58, 2168–73; Benson, C. David. *The History of Troy in Middle English Literature.* Woodbridge: Brewer, 1980; Cary, George A. *The Medieval Alexander.* Ed. D.J.A. Ross. Cambridge: Cambridge University Press, 1956; Ross, D.J.A. *Alexander Historiatus: A Guide to Medieval Illustrated Alexander Literature.* 2d ed. Frankfurt am Main: Athenäum, 1988; Spearing, A.C. "Lydgate's Canterbury Tale: *The Siege of Thebes* and Fifteenth-Century Chaucerianism." In *Fifteenth-Century Studies: Recent Essays,* ed. Robert F. Yeager. Hamden: Archon, 1984, pp. 333–64.

See also Alliterative Revival; Caxton; Chaucer; Chronicles; Clerk; *Letter of Alexander;* Literary Influences: Classical; Lydgate; Romances; Scottish Literature, Early; Translation

Matter of Britain

The name given to the great body of medieval romance devoted to stories of King Arthur and his knights. The term derives from the 12th-century French poet Jean Bodel's classification of the subjects, or "matters," of romance: "Ne sont que .iij. matieres à nul home antandant / De France, et de Bretaigne, et de Rome la grant" ("There are but three matters that anyone knows—those of France, of Britain, and of Rome the great"; *Chanson des Saxons* 6–7). To Bodel's three divisions modern critics have added a fourth, romances devoted to the Matter of England. More than all the stories about French, classical, and English heroes, however, those about the British Arthur provided the most popular subject for romance during the Middle Ages.

Considerable scholarly energy has been devoted to finding the source of the stories that were to form the Matter of Britain. The figure of Arthur himself seems to derive from both history and myth. The historical Arthur is generally agreed to have been a late-5th- to early-6th-century British commander who fought against the Saxons. Such a figure is mentioned by the 6th-century historian Gildas, with a more specific reference to Arthur following in Nennius's *Historia Brittonum* (ca. 800). During the same period stories of Arthur also grew in Welsh legend and poetry. When Geoffrey of Monmouth combined historical "fact" with such Celtic fancy

in his *Historia regum Britanniae* (ca. 1138), the resulting mixture proved explosive.

Attempts to explain the transmission of Arthurian stories to the Continent, their widespread popularity there, the rise of the romance form, and the eventual reintroduction of the "Matter of Britain" into the country of its origin have raised difficult questions for critics, and their varied answers to these questions occupy many articles and books. For complicated and sometimes disputed reasons ME Arthurian romances do not appear until the last half of the 13th century, but the numerous works composed during the 14th and 15th centuries are impressive in their number and variety.

In his essay in *Arthurian Literature in the Middle Ages* Ackerman calculates that about one-fourth of all surviving ME romances treat episodes belonging to the Matter of Britain. The *Manual* groups them by subject: "The Whole Life of Arthur," "Merlin and the Youth of Arthur," "Launcelot and the Last Years of Arthur," "Gawain," "Perceval," "The Holy Grail," "Tristram," and "Arthur of Little Britain." The whole cycle of Arthurian stories is thus covered in English, for the Matter of Britain had expanded to include the life and career of Merlin, the begetting and birth of Arthur, the youthful career of King Arthur, the relationship of Lancelot and Guinevere, the history of the Holy Grail, and the final disasters that resulted in King Arthur's death. ME romances are also devoted to the knights who came to be associated with Arthur's court, such as Perceval, Tristan, and, most popular, Gawain.

ME romances on these Arthurian subjects appear in rhyme, in alliterative lines, and in prose. Those in rhyme employ varied schemes, including couplets, six-, eight-, even eleven-line stanzas, and tail rhyme stanzas of several sorts. The romances in alliterative lines are products of the 14th-century Alliterative Revival. Only one effort before Malory, a version of the Merlin story, is in prose. Notable works treating the Matter of Britain include Laȝamon's *Brut,* the stanzaic *Morte Arthur,* the alliterative *Morte Arthure, Sir Gawain and the Green Knight,* Thomas Chestre's tail rhyme *Sir Launfal,* Geoffrey Chaucer's *Wife of Bath's Tale,* and Sir Thomas Malory's *Morte Darthur.*

Critics differ in their assessments of the quality of ME romances treating the Matter of Britain. Complicating their evaluations are questions about the relationship of these relatively late works to their sources. With few exceptions, notably the alliterative *Morte Arthure, Sir Gawain and the Green Knight,* and the works of Chaucer and Malory, ME versions of Arthurian stories have suffered (not always justly) by such comparisons, often dismissed as inept translations or hack reworkings of French originals. Questions about authorship also remain, as do uncertainties about the audience for which such stories were intended and the circumstances of their composition.

Despite stylistic defects these ME works demonstrate a love both of storytelling and of stories of action, heroes, and adventure. Considerable effort will no doubt be made to try to provide answers for the critical questions that remain, but the ME Arthurian romances remain widely popular, perhaps in spite of scholars and scholarly opinion.

Sharon L. Jansen

Bibliography

New *CBEL* 1:389–416; *Manual* 1:38–79, 224–56; Lacy, Norris J., et al., eds. *The New Arthurian Encyclopedia.* New York: Garland, 1991; Loomis, Roger Sherman, ed. *Arthurian Literature in the Middle Ages: A Collaborative History.* Oxford: Clarendon, 1959.

See also Breton Lay; Geoffrey of Monmouth; Laȝamon; Lovelich; Malory; *Morte Arthur,* Stanzaic; *Morte Arthure,* Alliterative; *Pearl*-Poet; Romances

Matter of England

The subject of a number of romances and related works, mostly anonymous, celebrating legendary heroes of England.

Horn is first celebrated in the Anglo-Norman *Romance of Horn* by Thomas (ca. 1170). *King Horn,* from the London area (ca. 1270–80 or perhaps a bit earlier), may be the earliest extant English romance, if this place does not fall to *Floris and Blancheflour.* Driven from Suddene by Saracens who have killed his father the king, Horn overcomes various obstacles to marry Rimenhild of Westernesse and regain Suddene (the identity of which remains uncertain). *King Horn* survives in three manuscripts: CUL Gg. 4.27.2, Bodl. Laud Misc. 108, and BL Harley 2253. Other English accounts are *Horn Child,* an incomplete, early-14th-century northern romance in the Auchinleck Manuscript (Edinburgh, National Library of Scotland Advocates' 19.2.1); several 19th-century versions of a ballad, *Hind Horn;* and the prose *King Ponthus,* probably from the London area (ca. 1400–50), found in both manuscript form and early-16th-century prints and translated from the French *Ponthus* attributed to Geoffrey IV de La Tour Landry.

Havelok's story is first recounted in the Anglo-Norman *Estoire des Engleis* by Gaimar (ca. 1135–40), then in the Anglo-French *Lai d'Haveloc* (ca. 1200). The English poem *Havelok,* from Lincolnshire (ca. 1280–1300), survives in Bodl. Laud Misc. 108 and fragments. Havelok, heir to Denmark, is saved from a treacherous death and taken to England by the fisherman Grim, founder of Grimsby. Later, as a laborer in Lincoln, Havelok is forcibly married to Goldeboru, heir to England. Eventually they defeat their respective persecutors and regain both Denmark and England, Havelok taking the place of Goldeboru's father as the ideal king of England. Subsequent references to Havelok in chronicles, together with local traditions in Lincoln and Grimsby, further indicate his prominence in that community's self-awareness.

A 12th-century Anglo-Norman account of Bevis of Hampton was probably the archetype of the romances in continental French, English, and other European languages, as well as the extant 13th-century Anglo-Norman *Boeve de Haumtone.* The English *Bevis of Hampton,* from the Southampton area (ca. 1300), first appears in the Auchinleck Manuscript. As a result of treachery Bevis, heir to the earldom of Southampton, arrives in Armenia, whose Saracen princess, Josian, falls in love with him. She gives him a warhorse called Arundel, and after many adventures he regains Southampton, marries the now baptized Josian, and builds Arundel Castle, his deeds glorifying both places, as local traditions attest. After further adventures the two die in saintly fashion, leaving Bevis's old protector as earl, one son as king of Armenia, and the other as heir to the English king Edgar. The poem is also found in six other manuscripts of the 14th and 15th centuries and in 16th-century printed editions.

The 13th-century Anglo-Norman *Gui de Warewic* lies behind all other accounts of Guy of Warwick, legendary ancestor of the Beauchamps. An English *Guy of Warwick* was probably produced ca. 1300 in Warwickshire, but extant texts vary in detail and provenance. The earliest, in the Auchinleck Manuscript, defective at beginning and end, runs to 12,000 lines. Guy of Wallingford loves Felice, daughter of the earl of Warwick, and after proving himself in adventures abroad returns to marry her. He then departs on a pilgrimage to atone for his life of fighting. After saving King Athelstan and England by defeating the African giant Colbrond, champion of the Danes, he goes to Warwick, where both he and Felice have a pious end. In the last part of the story, separately headed *Reinbrun* in this text, their son of this name is stolen away but eventually returns. *Guy* is also found in four other manuscripts of the 14th and 15th centuries and in 16th-century printed editions. The story of Guy was disseminated abroad less widely than that of Bevis, but in England it appeared in numerous adaptations down to the 19th century, including Lydgate's *Guy of Warwick,* the northern romance *Guy and Colbrond* (ca. 1500?), and historical writings. Chaucer alludes to Guy, Bevis, and Horn in *Sir Thopas.*

Three other extant romances may also be placed under this heading: the incomplete *Richard Coer de Lyon,* from the London area (early 14th century), a romanticized account of the crusading king, found in the Auchinleck and six other manuscripts and two 16th-century printed editions; *Gamelyn,* from the east Midlands (ca. 1350–70), the story of an outlaw hero reinstated, found in 25 manuscripts of the *Canterbury Tales;* and *Athelston,* found in a single east Midlands manuscript (later 14th century), a fiction about the 10th-century king Æthelstan, *trouthe* and justice, and the infant St. Edmund of East Anglia.

The hero Wade survives as little more than a name, and the stories of Waldef and Hereward survive only in Anglo-Norman and Latin accounts, respectively.

Diane Speed

Bibliography

PRIMARY

For additional editions and criticism of works mentioned in this article and published before 1985 see bibliographies below; Allen, Rosamund, ed. *King Horn.* New York: Garland, 1984; Mills, Maldwyn, ed. *Horn Childe and Maiden Rimnild.* Heidelberg: Winter, 1988; Smithers, G.V. *Havelok.* Oxford: Clarendon, 1987; Speed, Diane, ed. *Havelok.* In *Medieval English Romances.* 2 pts. 4th ed. Durham: Durham University Press, 1993.

SECONDARY

New *CBEL* 1:429–35; *Manual* 1:17–34, 158–60, 206–23, 315–18; Allen, Rosamund. "The Date and Provenance of *King Horn:* Some Interim Reassessments." In *Medieval English Studies Presented to George Kane,* ed. Edward Donald Kennedy et al. Cambridge: Brewer, 1988, pp. 99–125; Rice, Joanne A. *Middle English Romance: An Annotated Bibliography, 1955–1985.* New York: Garland, 1987; Richmond, Velma B. *The Legend of Guy of Warwick.* New York: Garland, 1996.

See also Anglo-Norman Literature; Ballads; Beauchamp Family; Chaucerian Apocrypha; Chronicles; Gaimar; Literary Influences: French; Manning; Monarchy and Kingship; Outlaws; Romances; Truth in ME Literature

Matter of France

The subject of several romances, mostly anonymous, based on the Charlemagne cycle of *chansons de geste,* including stories of Charlemagne, Roland, and other heroes, both French and Saracen.

The earliest extant works come from the east Midlands, where the most concentrated copying and adapting of the French materials themselves was undertaken in the Anglo-Norman period. These early-14th-century English poems include the incomplete *Otuel a Knight* and *Roland and Vernagu;* the second of these was evidently once the first part of a longer poem whose second part, *Otuel and Roland,* survives in a late-15th-century copy. Also in the *Otuel (Otinel)* group, but from the north, ca. 1400, are *Duke Roland and Sir Otuel of Spain* and *The Siege of Melayne,* which precedes *Duke Roland* in their common manuscript and probably constitutes a prelude to it.

Another group is focused on Ferumbras (Fierabras), like Otuel a converted Saracen: *Firumbras,* from the east Midlands, and *Sir Ferumbras,* from the southwest, both late-14th-century and incomplete; *The Sowdon of Babylon,* from the east Midlands, ca. 1400; and Caxton's prose translation *Charles the Great* (Westminster, 1485). The remaining works are the incomplete *Song of Roland,* from the east Midlands, ca. 1400; the Scottish *Taill of Rauf Coilȝear,* ca. 1450–1500, the best of the poems though the least related to the Matter; Caxton's prose translation *The Four Sons of Aymon* (London, 1489–91); and Lord Berners's prose translation *The Book of Duke Huon of Bordeaux* (London, ca. 1534).

Despite the evident appeal of its lively action and piety the transported Matter of France seems not to have achieved the popularity of the matters of either Britain or England, but it undoubtedly had an important influence on the development of both.

Diane Speed

Bibliography

PRIMARY

For additional editions and criticism of works mentioned in this article and published before 1985 see the bibliographies below; Speed, Diane, ed. *Rauf Coilȝear.* In *Medieval English Romances.* 2 pts. 4th ed. Durham: Durham University Press, 1993.

SECONDARY

New *CBEL* 1:415–22; *Manual* 1:80–100, 256–66; Rice, Joanne A. *Middle English Romance: An Annotated Bibliography, 1955–1985.* New York: Garland, 1987.

See also Anglo-Norman Literature; Caxton; Literary Influences: French; Matter of Britain; Matter of England; Prose, ME; Romances; Scottish Literature, Early

Matthew Paris (ca. 1199–1259)

A monk at St. Albans from 1217 until his death in 1259, Matthew inherited the duties of historian from his predecessor in that capacity, Roger of Wendover, and continued work on Roger's *Chronica majora,* to some extent rewriting but primarily extending and illustrating the text (Cambridge, Corpus Christi College 26 and 16, and BL Royal 14.C.vii, fols. 157–218). He also produced other Latin historical texts generally associated with the Chronicles *(Historia Anglorum,* BL Royal 14.C.vii, fols. 1–156; *Liber additamentorum,* BL Cotton Nero D.i; *Abbreviatio chronicorum,* BL Cotton Claudius D.vi) among others, and four saints' lives in Anglo-Norman.

The great bulk of Matthew's illustrative work in the historical texts may be characterized as *signa,* abbreviated symbols that help readers find their way in the text and signal important events. In addition Matthew included itineraries, maps, illustrated genealogies, and the oldest preserved record of heraldic arms. Narrative illustrations are added to the histories but tend to take a minor part and assume a telegraphic, hurried, yet also vividly dramatic aspect. A few full-page iconic illustrations (the Virgin and Child, the Veronica head of Christ) appended to the Chronicles are the only miniatures that could be considered polished works of art.

It is in his illustrated saints' lives that Matthew fully explores the possibilities of narrative and, in the *Vie de seint Auban* in Dublin (Trinity College 177; fig. 95), produces his most artistically complex work. The Dublin manuscript has been dated in the 1240s as Matthew's first attempt to illustrate the life of a saint and contains Latin versions of the lives, liturgical offices, and charters in addition to Matthew's Anglo-Norman text. The romance text is illustrated by framed miniatures across the top of the three-column page, and these continue above the Latin texts, after the romance text has ended, to detail the foundation of the monastery through the efforts of King Offa. Matthew worked in an accomplished but late version of the "Style 1200." His illustrations for the Dublin manuscript are done in line with some touches of color, primarily green, but also vermilion, blue, and ocher. Notes at the bottom of the pages in Matthew's hand give evidence that the iconography of the miniatures was carefully planned.

It would seem that similar planning would explain Matthew's involvement in the illustration of two other manuscripts of lives of saints. The *Life of St. Thomas of Canterbury* in Anglo-Norman (BL Loan 88) and the *Estoire de seint Aedward le rei* (CUL Ee.3.59) are executed in a different style from the Dublin manuscript but retain many of the features associated with Matthew, even compositions and the drawing of such details as ships and horses. All three manuscripts show an involvement with contemporary political concerns and were intended for an aristocratic audience: the life of Edward is dedicated to Queen Eleanor, and notes on the flyleaf of the Dublin manuscript detail its loan and that of other manuscripts of the lives of saints to aristocratic ladies.

Although Matthew made important innovations in format and narrative in illustrated lives of the saints that in turn influenced the illustration of Apocalypses and other English manuscripts, in general his work must be characterized as eccentric and isolated. He apparently worked apart from the scriptorium at St. Albans and produced his manuscripts as virtually a one-man effort, even writing his own fair copy. If he did plan the London and Cambridge manuscripts, he probably sent them off to London or Westminster for execution.

Matthew received a special commission as historian from Henry III and harbored many courtly prejudices, yet he lived in a monastery away from court and voiced some remarkably strong antiroyal opinions. Similarly he was a religious man who had little patience with the papacy. The unique form and visual content of his Chronicles, which he surely counted as his greatest achievement, had no successor and, as a recent scholar has lamented, have been little studied.

Cynthia Hahn

Bibliography

PRIMARY

Lowe, W.R.L., and E.F. Jacob, eds. *Illustrations to the Life of St. Alban.* Intro. M.R. James. Oxford: Clarendon, 1924; Paris, Matthew. *Chronica majora.* Ed. Henry R. Luard. 7 vols. Rolls Series. London: Longman, 1872–83; Paris, Matthew. *La estoire de seint Aedward le rei.* Ed. Montague Rhodes James. Oxford: Roxburghe Club, 1920 [facsimile].

SECONDARY

Backhouse, Janet, and Christopher de Hamel. *The Becket Leaves.* London: British Library, 1988; Hahn, Cynthia. "Absent No Longer: The Saint and the Sign in Late Medieval Pictorial Hagiography." In *Hagiographie und Kunst,* ed. G. Kerscher. Berlin: Dietrich Reimer, 1993, pp. 152–75; Lewis, Suzanne. *The Art of Matthew Paris in the Chronica majora.* Berkeley: University of California Press, 1987 [extensive bibliography and analysis of Chronicle illustrations]; Morgan, Nigel. *Early Gothic Manuscripts 1190–1285.* 2 vols. A Survey of Manuscripts Illuminated in the British Isles 4, ed. J.J.G. Alexander. London: Harvey Miller, 1982–88; Vaughan, Richard. *Matthew Paris.* Cambridge: Cambridge University Press, 1958.

See also Chronicles; Manuscript Illumination, Gothic; Saints' Lives, Illuminated

Fig. 95. Vie de Seint Auban *(Dublin, Trinity College 177), fol. 45. Martyrdom of Amphibalus. Reproduced by permission of the Board of Trinity College Dublin.*

Maxims I and II

The most extensive examples in OE of a genre of wisdom literature consisting entirely of a series of proverbs or maxims. The genre can be found elsewhere in the medieval period in Norse, Irish, and Welsh and can be traced back to comparable classical and biblical collections. Such gnomic verse in OE is generally based on factual observation of what is (OE *bið*) or ethical observation of what ought to be (OE *sceal*), although the distinction between these categories is not always clear. Gnomic sentiments, found widely in OE verse, are particularly apparent in such poems as *Beowulf* and *The Wanderer.*

Maxims I is found in the Exeter Book and is divided in the manuscript into three sections, perhaps recalling the fact that, for Anglo-Saxons like Bede, the biblical wisdom books of Proverbs and Psalms were also considered tripartite structures. The opening section of *Maxims I* (lines 1–70) begins with a dialogue suggesting the kind of wisdom contest found elsewhere in OE (e.g., in *Solomon and Saturn*) and in Norse. The second section (71–137) begins with a series of maxims concerning phenomena, such as frost, fire, and ice, before considering the human world, including a famous passage on the joy of the Frisian wife welcoming her husband home from the sea. The section concludes with an explicit comparison of Woden, who created idols, and the true God, who created the world. The third section (137–204) contains reflection on the wandering life of the exile, the comfort of song, the dangers of human violence, and the need to be courageous in the face of adversity.

Unlike *Maxims I,* which is found in a purely poetic manuscript, *Maxims II* occurs in BL Cotton Tiberius B.i, a compendium that seems devoted to factual and historical matter, including the OE translation of Orosius's world history and a version of the Anglo-Saxon Chronicle. *Maxims II,* although shorter than *Maxims I,* seems to share a similar tripartite structure. The first section (lines 1–13) consists almost exclusively of factual maxims concerning what is (*bið*), the second section (14–57a) of sentiments considering what ought to be *(sceal),* while the third (57b–66) is not couched in gnomic terms at all. The opening words of each section seem structurally significant, as we move from king, to young prince, to God; from what is circumscribed by nature, to what is circumscribed by custom, to what cannot be circumscribed. Syntactic patterning underlines this larger structure, suggesting that *Maxims II* is a skillfully constructed work. It can be argued that each maxim is implicitly linked to its neighbor and that, far from being a haphazard list of commonplaces, *Maxims II* (like *Maxims I*) has a coherent organic structure.

A.P.M. Orchard

Bibliography

PRIMARY

ASPR 3:156–63 (*Maxims I*), 6:55–57 (*Maxims II*); Shippey, T.A., ed. and trans. *Poems of Wisdom and Learning in Old English.* Cambridge: Brewer, 1976, pp. 12–20, 64–79.

SECONDARY

Barley, N.F. "Structure in the Cotton Gnomes." *NM* 78 (1977): 244–49; Bollard, J.K. "The Cotton Maxims." *Neophilologus* 57 (1973): 179–87; Nelson, Marie. "'Is' and 'Ought' in the Exeter Book Maxims." *Southern Folklore Quarterly* 45 (1984 for 1981): 109–21; Williams, Blanche Colton. *Gnomic Poetry in Anglo-Saxon.* New York: Columbia University Press, 1914.

See also Adrian and Ritheus; Beowulf; Solomon and Saturn; Wanderer; Wisdom Literature

Medical Manuscripts and Herbals

A selection of medical books was to be found in every medieval monastic library of any size, and it is possible with the help of library catalogues to reconstruct medieval medical practices. Diagnosis was by reading the pulse, examining the color of the patient's urine, and astrology, which is why astrological texts are sometimes found bound with more conventional medical treatises, as in Durham, Hunter 100, written at Durham ca. 1100–20. Medications were prepared from herbs or occasionally from animal or mineral extracts. Cautery with hot irons was used for sterilizing wounds but also in a manner similar to modern acupuncture. Diseases attributed to the blood were invariably treated by bloodletting with knives or leeches: in fact bloodletting was generally thought beneficial, even for the healthy, and monks were bled annually on days chosen as propitious by astrological means. Surgery was employed for wounds and the like, and for insanity, which was treated by trepanning the skull if medicines made with peonies failed to work. Manuscripts survive dealing with orthopedics, obstetrics, and dentistry.

Most of these texts were originally either classical treatises lost to the West but surviving in Arabic translations or themselves Arabic works. Many of the works attributed to Galen (ca. A.D. 130–200) and Hippocrates (ca. 460–ca. 377 B.C.), for example, were translated by Constantinus Africanus (ca. 1015–1087) into Latin alongside texts by Arab scholars. To these must be added later Greek texts, like Theophilus on urine and Philaretus on the pulse, both 7th-century compositions. Salerno, the oldest of the universities, was the center of western medicine until the 12th century, and physicians based there began to produce original texts as early as the 11th. The most celebrated of these was Roger of Salerno (fl. ca. 1170), whose *Summa de cirurgia* became a standard work. It is found in an Anglo-Norman French translation in Cambridge, Trinity College O.1.20, produced in England ca. 1230–40 and illustrated with more than 50 marginal drawings (fig. 96).

Few medical texts were regularly illustrated. Herbals were used to identify plants and gave the diseases for which they were indicated. Accurate drawings would seem to be essential for herbals, but in general illustrations were simply copied from one manuscript to another without consulting nature. Bodleian Library, Bodley 130, produced at Bury St. Edmunds ca. 1100, is an exception, and its lifelike drawings are accom-

Fig. 96. Summa de cirurgia *of Roger of Salerno (Cambridge, Trinity College O.1.20), fol. 242v. Head operation with scalpel and forceps. Courtesy of the Master and Fellows of Trinity College, Cambridge.*

panied by extracts from the two most popular medieval herbal texts, attributed to Dioscorides, a physician of the 1st century A.D., and Apuleius Barbarus, of whom nothing is known. Bodley 130 also includes the treatise on the medicinal properties of animals attributed to Sextus Placitus, a combination also found in the early-11th-century treatise BL Cotton Vitellius C.iii.

BL Sloane 2839 of ca. 1100 and Hunter 100 both contain cautery drawings, showing where the hot iron is to be applied to treat various diseases. The former manuscript is illustrated with diagrammatic nudes; the latter with semiclad figures, sometimes in architectural settings; but in both cases the cautery points are as clearly marked as the stars on an astronomical constellation.

Ronald E. Baxter

Bibliography

Blunt, Wilfrid, and Sandra Raphael. *The Illustrated Herbal.* New York: Thames & Hudson, 1979; Herrlinger, Robert. *History of Medical Illustration from Antiquity to A.D. 1600.* London: Pitman Medical, 1970; MacKinney, Loren. *Medical Illustrations in Medieval MSS.* Wellcome Historical Medical Library, n.s. 5. London: Wellcome Library, 1965.

See also Medicine; Science; Scientific and Medical Writings; Scientific Manuscripts, Early; Universities

Medicine and Doctors

Medieval medical theory was based on the writings of the Greek physician Galen (ca. A.D. 130–200), whose works constituted an established body of thought from which most other ideas were derived. The bulk of his output, or at least that attributed to him, came to the West in the 12th century and exercised an enormous influence for the next three or four centuries. His belief that health depended upon the equilibrium of the four "qualities" (hot, cold, dry, and moist) and that an imbalance in the bodily juices or humors (blood, phlegm, yellow bile, and black bile) could cause disease formed the bedrock of medical teaching in the universities, where study was almost entirely textual, without any real opportunity for examination of the human body, either alive or dead.

An edict of the Lateran Council of 1215, decreeing that persons in holy orders were henceforth debarred from the practice of surgery (i.e., of shedding blood), intensified the already academic nature of medicine, since almost all physicians at this date were clerics. Even such an apparently practical skill as urology (diagnosis through the analysis of urine samples) was initially learned from books; although it was not without importance once a physician began to practice, clinical observation took second place to astrological prediction.

Through the influence of Arab medicine, contemporaries not only believed that each house of the zodiac controlled a particular part of the body (Pisces, e.g., ruled the feet) but were also convinced that the likely outcome of disease or injury could be forecast by a careful study of the planets. Extremely elaborate prognostic charts and devices were employed to decide how the sick might best be treated (or, indeed, if it was worth treating them at all), and some doctors favored a similar method for establishing either the virginity or pregnancy of their female patients.

The main staples of surgical treatment were bloodletting (performed by a surgeon or a barber surgeon) and the administration of ferocious purges, both intended to restore a balance between the humors but often fatal in their effects. But in other respects, notably the emphasis placed upon moderation in diet and the use of herbal remedies, some benefit may have accrued to the patient.

Whereas physicians were held to rank between canon lawyers and practitioners of civil law, surgeons occupied a fairly low place in the social order. The medieval maxim that "physic is to surgery what geometry is to carpentry," reflects a scale of values that saw surgeons as superior craftsmen rather than professional persons. Yet although English surgeons and barber surgeons formed themselves into craft guilds and rarely enjoyed the privilege of a university education, they did at least reap the benefits of a more pragmatic training.

Some surgeons, such as the celebrated John Arderne (fl. ca. 1370), who devised his own surgical instruments and perfected new operating techniques, scored remarkable successes in an age without anesthetics, antiseptics, or blood transfusion. The services of both physicians and surgeons were, however, expensive and thus unavailable to the majority of the population. For this reason doctors were often the victims of satire that ridiculed their "special love of gold" and indifference to human suffering, while most ordinary people had to rely upon wise women, herbalists, and folk medicine. In many cases cures were undertaken in the home by women, whose wifely duties included nursing the sick and making up their own remedies.

Carole Rawcliffe

Bibliography

Beck, Richard Theodore. *The Cutting Edge: Early History of the Surgeons of London.* London: Lund Humphries, 1974; Jones, Peter Murray. *Medieval Medical Miniatures.* London: British Library, 1984; Kealey, Edward. *Medieval Medicus: A Social History of Anglo-Norman Medicine.* Baltimore: Johns Hopkins University Press, 1981; Rawcliffe, Carole. *Medicine and Society in Later Medieval England.* Stroud: Sutton, 1995; Rubin, Stanley. *Medieval English Medicine.* Newton Abbot: David & Charles, 1974; Siraisi, Nancy. *Medieval and Early Renaissance Medicine: An Introduction to Knowledge and Practice.* Chicago: University of Chicago Press, 1990; Talbot, C.H., and E.A. Hammond. *The Medical Practitioners in Medieval England: A Biographical Register.* London: Wellcome Institute, 1965.

See also Astrology; Charms; Hospitals; Medical Manuscripts; Science; Scientific and Medical Writings

Fig. 97. The Ormside Bowl (York, Yorkshire Museum 1990–35). Reproduced courtesy of the Yorkshire Museum.

Metalwork, Anglo-Saxon

Metalwork in the Anglo-Saxon period reflects the traditions of several cultural groups: the Angles, Saxons, and Jutes who invaded England in the 5th century as well as the resident Celtic Britons, who were driven into Cornwall, Wales, and Cumbria by the invaders.

Saxon metalwork is red and gold, owing to the lavish use of garnets, sliced and cut into complex shapes, and densely applied beaded gold filigree. Many examples come from the Jutish or Saxon kingdom of Kent, including the early-7th-century disc brooch from Kingston Down (National Museums and Galleries Merseyside, Liverpool Museum M6226). Disc brooches were a common Anglo-Saxon type, their decoration organized around five bosses with an obvious cruciform design between or through them. The complex, purely geometric design of the Kingston Down Brooch is typical of the refined 7th-century Kentish work, with panels of finely beaded filigree set in a mosaic of garnet and blue glass, the effect further brightened by the gold-foil fields whose facets glitter through the translucent red garnets.

Anglian metalwork typically shows interlaced animals executed in a faceted casting technique called "chipcarving," or *kerbschnitt* work. These are derived from the Scandinavian animal style known as "Style II" and are found on the early-7th-century great gold buckle from the Sutton Hoo ship burial in East Anglia, an early Anglian kingdom (London, British Museum MLA 1939, 10–10,1). But the Angles and Saxons were already fusing their identities, as can be seen on the shoulder clasps from the same burial, whose Style II animals are executed in the Saxon technique of mosaic garnets and gold filigree. Included in the mosaic is *millefiori* glass, a technique that may have been learned from the Romans.

The burial also contained hanging bowls with *champlevé* enameled escutcheons showing geometric interconnecting spiral designs in reserved metal against a red ground. These seem to have been highly prized objects commissioned or imported from British craftsmen, and many examples have been found in Anglo-Saxon contexts and in Scandinavia.

This was the range of peoples and metalworking styles that existed when St. Augustine brought Christianity to Kent in 597. Soon afterward Christianity was also brought to the Anglo-Saxon kingdom of Northumbria, coming this time from Ireland and bringing with it an increased Celtic influence on art. With Christianity came a new demand for books, and it seems to have been this demand that caused these diverse arts to become fused in the "Hiberno-Saxon" or "Insular" style that first appeared in books like the Book of Durrow (Dublin, Trinity College A.4.5[57]), before passing quickly back to metalwork. The problem with this style is that the elements are so completely fused that there is no agreement as to where the style originated, and it is equally well represented in England and Ireland. Some of the finest examples of the style in metalwork are in fact Irish, such as the Tara Brooch and the Ardagh Chalice, where all the techniques and motifs come together in a harmonious and exciting way.

But Christian Northumbria was also concerned to imitate Mediterranean ideas. This can be seen in the Codex Amiatinus (Florence, Biblioteca Medicea-Laurenziana Amiatinus 1) and the Ruthwell and Bewcastle crosses, each with their naturalistic figurative decoration and complex plant trails mixed with native interlaced patterns. The same trend appears in metalwork in the fragmentary portable altar from St. Cuthbert's Coffin (Dean and Chapter, Durham Cathedral). This object is of hammered silver (also called embossed, or *repoussé,* work), a technique introduced from Mediterranean areas. Here foliate designs of ultimately Mediterranean origin surround a cross filled with interlacing, whose faceted recesses recall the older technique of chipcarving where the pattern originated. Romanizing *repoussé* work continued into the 8th century with the Ormside Bowl (York, Yorkshire Museum 1990-35; fig. 97) and the Rupertus Cross (Bischofshofen parish church, Salzburg Diocesan Museum), on which the animals acquire a fabulous whimsical nature.

Meanwhile the original Hiberno-Saxon style was dying out. A late example is the 8th-century Coppergate Helmet (York, Castle Museum YORCM CA665), whose nose guard has a chipcarved pattern of interlaced beasts like those in the Lindisfarne Gospels (BL Cotton Nero D.iv). But chipcarving now begins to lose its crispness. The metalwork on the Gandersheim Casket (Braunschweig, Herzog Anton-Ulrich Museum MA58) is interlaced, but the designs are simplified and the recesses no longer faceted. And on the Witham pins (London, British Museum MLA 1856, 11–11,4) several weakly faceted recesses are touched up with a punch, and others are rounded. The Lindisfarne Gospel–like beasts have been replaced by the short-snouted, winged, two-legged beasts also seen on the Gandersheim Casket, where they are likewise enmeshed in a net of interlace.

During the 7th to 8th centuries, mundane metalwork was also produced, and scholarly attention increasingly focuses on minor dress pins. These cheap, utilitarian objects are less useful chronological indicators than might have been hoped, since they are inherently archaic in nature and slow to reflect new artistic trends. But they do reflect an unofficial hierarchy of decoration. Thus most decoration consists of scratchy engraving, punching, and occasionally thin silvering or gilding. A relatively fine example is a gilt and engraved pin from Brandon in Suffolk (East Anglia), decorated with beasts like those on the Witham pins (Brandon Remembrance Playing Field Committee SAV BRD 018 8679). None of these techniques appears on more prestigious artifacts during this period.

Then, suddenly, Anglo-Saxon production seems to stop in all media. This has been attributed to the Scandinavians who arrived as marauding Vikings at the end of the 8th century and then settled in farms and cities as more or less obstreperous neighbors during the 9th and 10th centuries. These were artistically active people who supplied all their own needs for brooches, pendants, straptags, sword chapes, and horse trappings, as well as stone gravemarkers; and they decorated it all in their native styles.

The Scandinavians settled in the Midlands and East Anglia, and from these areas comes a series of silver disc brooches, similar in kind to 7th-century Anglo-Saxon examples, such as the Kingston Down Brooch. A hoard of six disc brooches from Pentney in East Anglia (London, British Museum MLA 1980, 10–8, 1–6) is currently dated to the first third of the 9th century. The brooches are decorated with smooth metal bosses linked by beaded borders containing individual or paired animals with stippled bodies, the designs picked out with inlaid niello or emphasized by complex openwork. These brooches are usually seen as native Anglo-Saxon productions, but this seems unlikely for several reasons. Disc brooches had not apparently been used in England for 200 years, so these new silver ones are unlikely to be directly derived from the original gold-and-garnet Anglo-Saxon version. But Scandinavia's own continuing tradition of brooch production included disc brooches from the 9th century. Scandinavian disc brooches tend to be decorated with thick twisted wire and heavy granulation, but other Scandinavian brooch types had smooth metal bosses linked with beaded or patterned borders containing animals with stippled bodies; and niello and complex openwork are both common in Scandinavian metalwork. For all these reasons it seems likely that the bossed silver disc brooches of the 9th and 10th centuries are not local Anglo-Saxon productions but a new introduction from Scandinavia. Perhaps this is most clearly seen in the Strickland Brooch (London, British Museum MLA 1949, 7–2,1), whose decoration includes beast heads closely related to the Scandinavian Borre style.

The evidence seems to suggest that the native Anglo-Saxon tradition did not survive the Vikings, although the Vikings themselves continued to produce the kind of work they were accustomed to have around them at home. Alfred the Great (871–99) reported that by his time England's treasures had been destroyed and the country was in a state of ignorance and degradation. His biographer, Asser, adds that Alfred rectified this by seeking out foreign scholars and craftsmen for his court. The Alfred Jewel (Oxford, Ashmolean Museum 1836, 371; fig. 1: see ALFRED AND MINSTER LOVELL JEWELS) is thought to have been made for him. It is arranged around a beast head that looks Anglo-Saxon, but its heavy granulation, openwork, and engraving are all Scandinavian

techniques, not hitherto known on prestigious metalwork in England. So it is possible that this is an attempt by a foreign (in this case, Scandinavian) craftsman to evoke or recreate a lost Anglo-Saxon tradition in metalwork.

The Fuller Brooch (fig. 65; London, British Museum MLA 1952, 4–4,1) may be another instance. This large niello and silver disc brooch is made with the techniques used for the contemporary disc brooches discussed above, but its iconography of the five senses is unique. In fact the figure of Sight is similar to the figure on the Alfred Jewel. So here again foreign techniques are apparently being used to suggest or create a contemporary Anglo-Saxon idiom. While not all scholars agree on this point, it should be noted that the combination of Anglo-Saxon and Scandinavian features in late-9th- to 11th-century metalwork finds a literary parallel in *Beowulf,* a poem that combines Anglo-Saxon and Scandinavian traditions and that was produced for the same aristocratic audience as the metalwork discussed here.

During Alfred's reign the niello-and-silver technique spread into Anglo-Saxon areas, as seen in the hoards from Trewhiddle in Alfred's kingdom of Wessex (London, British Museum MLA 1880, 4–10, 1–12, 14, 19; coin dated ca. 872–75) and Beeston Tor in Mercia (London, British Museum MLA 1925, 1–14, 1–6; coin dated ca. 874), and two inlaid silver plaques from an early-10th-century house-shaped shrine (London, British Museum MLA 1954) whose Scandinavian style is unmistakable, although it too often is attributed to Anglo-Saxon craftsmen.

The process of renewal may have continued under Æthelstan (924–39) in a series of knobbly looking cast straptags, censers, and a spouted jug. The jug (London, British Museum MLA AF 3175) shows beasts whose nearest relatives are on the 8th-century Ormside Bowl, and the straptags show inhabited plant trails reminiscent of those on Northumbrian stone crosses. Again it seems possible that new techniques were being used to evoke or recreate a lost native tradition.

In 1016 the Scandinavian Cnut took the crown and was succeeded by his sons, Harold Harefoot and Harthacnut, and stepson, Edward the Confessor. At this date contemporary foreign documents comment on the excellence of "Anglo-Saxon" metalwork. These are sometimes cited to prove that high-quality native Anglo-Saxon metalwork continued to be produced, despite the fact that craftsmen worked for rulers who lived significant portions of their lives outside of Anglo-Saxon England. If true, the courageous spirit of these craftsmen who heroically preserved their Anglo-Saxon integrity in the face of foreign imperialism must be admired. Sadly no work survives, so it is worth reconsidering what those documents actually meant. Since Scandinavians had been living in England for 200 years by this time and intermarrying with the indigenous Anglo-Saxons, they probably identified themselves with their adopted country, rather as today's descendants of immigrants from all over the world consider themselves citizens of their adopted countries.

What did "Anglo-Saxon" metalwork look like in the 11th century? It can be argued that no native traditions survived at all, and it looked thoroughly Scandinavian. A large disc brooch from Sutton, Isle of Ely in East Anglia (London, British Museum MLA 1951, 11–1,1), is of flat silver with the design picked out in niello. It is executed in a mixture of Scandinavian Mammen and Ringerike styles, with large beasts bordered by rudimentary acanthus foliage. The runic inscription on the back shows that it belonged to an Anglo-Saxon woman, which may support the idea that there was no longer much distinction between Anglo-Saxon and Scandinavian.

There are also mounts in the Ringerike style, and a superb openwork disc brooch from Pitney in Somerset (Wessex/Mercia), which is cast in a good imitation of the Scandinavian Urnes style (London, British Museum MLA 1979, 11–1,1). This sinuous and graceful style consists of entwined beasts, snakes, and noded tendrils. The streamlined animals have profile eyes with the point forward, giving them the unnerving effect of looking backward. "Anglo-Saxon" versions are often embellished with beading, as on the Pitney Brooch and many other 11th-century mounts and plaques.

Other surviving metalwork consists of sheet silver with engraved designs picked out in gold and niello. The style used here owes nothing to earlier traditions of metalwork but has come from the 10th-century Winchester style of manuscript illumination, which continued to be practiced into the 11th century. Examples include the portable altar in the Cluny Museum (CL II.459) and the Drahmal Cross (Brussels, Cathedral of St. Michael). There is not a beast or a plant trail anywhere on them. Instead alert human figures with fluttering, wind-blown draperies and excited gestures are engraved in a lively calligraphic style. In terms of iconography the combination of inscription and imagery on the Drahmal Cross is related to earlier Anglo-Saxon sculpture, such as the Ruthwell Cross (figs. 111–14: see RUTHWELL CROSS) or the Durham Cathedral cross-heads.

In the final analysis Anglo-Saxon metalwork is an elusive phenomenon, and perhaps in the strictest sense it can be found only between the 7th and 8th centuries. Thereafter it seems to have been an eclectic construct, increasingly incorporating foreign elements until the native features vanish altogether.

Perette E. Michelli

Bibliography

Backhouse, Janet, Derek H. Turner, and Leslie Webster, eds. *The Golden Age of Anglo-Saxon Art 966–1066.* London: British Museum, 1984; Dodwell, C.R. *Anglo-Saxon Art: A New Perspective.* Manchester: Manchester University Press, 1982; Keynes, Simon, and Michael Lapidge, trans. *Alfred the Great: Asser's Life of King Alfred and Other Contemporary Sources.* Harmondsworth: Penguin, 1983; Webster, Leslie, and Janet Backhouse, eds. *The Making of England: Anglo-Saxon Art and Culture AD 600–900.* London: British Museum, 1991; Wilson, David M. *Anglo-Saxon Art: From the Seventh Century to the Norman Conquest.* London: Thames & Hudson, 1984.

See also Alfred and Minster Lovell Jewels; Art, Viking; *Beowulf;* Fuller Brooch; Lindisfarne Gospels; Metalwork, Gothic; Metalwork and Enamels, Romanesque; Ruthwell Cross; Sutton Hoo; Wearmouth-Jarrow and the Codex Amiatinus; "Winchester School"

Metalwork, Gothic

Although we have numerous descriptions of English Gothic metalwork, and references to the metalworkers themselves from a variety of sources, relatively few actual works have survived. The Dissolution of the monasteries decimated the treasuries of the English church, while loss, reuse of metal, and the ravages of time have all contributed to losses in the secular realm. Nevertheless, fine metalworking was a prestige art, and England was renowned for its metalworkers, particularly for its goldsmiths.

In Anglo-Saxon times abbots and bishops were frequently also goldsmiths, and one of the most famous of these early artists, St. Dunstan (ca. 910–988), became the patron saint of the Company of Goldsmiths on its foundation in 1327. Fines against unlicensed goldsmiths indicate that they must have been organized into a powerful guild by the relatively early date of 1180. Quality control seems to have remained a concern in theory, if not in practice. Beginning in 1238 the City of London appointed six wardens from among the goldsmiths to ensure that silver was of sterling quality or better. In 1300 the hallmark, in the form of a leopard's head, was introduced.

The majority of Gothic metalworkers were lay persons; many, however, were employed by the church, an arrangement that offered economic security for the smith and a secure supply of skilled craftsmen for the church or monastery—in fact many of these artists' names are preserved in the monastic chronicles. In the mid-13th century Matthew Paris (himself an artist) recorded the employment of three artists, Master Walter of Colchester, his brother, and his nephew, at St. Albans. Walter is recorded as having made an altar frontal and two book covers for the church, as well as collaborating with Master Elias of Dereham on a shrine for the translation of Becket's remains. None of these items has survived.

Between the 13th and 15th centuries metalworking moved out of the monasteries and into the cities, primarily London, although quality workshops existed in other cities as well. The move did nothing to lower the status of the craft, as a number of London's mayors were also practicing goldsmiths.

The Ordinances of the Company of Goldsmiths reveal that in the period 1327–94 apprenticeship lasted ten years; in 1394 this was lowered to seven years. During apprenticeship workers were required to master a variety of skills, including figure drawing, modeling, design, carving, gem setting, enameling, forging, casting, and niello work. The fact that the metalworker had to be familiar with many of the techniques, and consequently styles, of illuminators and sculptors is likely to account at least in part for the similarities, particularly in figure style, among the media. While metalworkers were most renowned for their prestige items—church plate, jewelry, regalia—they also manufactured more mundane items, such as buckles, cups, and pendants for horse trappings. Molds and designs were frequently handed down from one metalworker to another; consequently the forms produced were not on the whole unusual, and the general trend throughout the period was toward traditionalism rather than innovation. For example, the ca. 1260 silver-gilt scepter of Richard of Cornwall (Aachen, Domschatz G51) is surmounted by a cast and chased dove, a scepter type that goes back at least as far as Edward the Confessor (1042–66). However, the picture may be partially skewed by the limited amount of material that survives; documentary sources do reveal that some unusual pieces were produced, such as the gold and jeweled peacocks made for Henry III in the 13th century.

Surviving evidence does indicate a change in the late-14th and 15th centuries, possibly due to the ravages of war and plague. Beginning in the second half of the 14th century all manner of metalwork from jewelry to funerary brasses became more intricate and luxurious. The change brought both prosperity and increasing specialization to English metalworkers.

Prestige items were made for the church, the court, and the increasingly powerful merchant class. Few fragments of the elaborate shrines, processional crosses, and liturgical vessels that we know to have been created have survived. A series of funerary chalices and patens from the graves of 13th- and 14th-century bishops does reflect the form if not the grandeur of the more elaborate altar vessels. The finest surviving liturgical vessels are the Ramsey Abbey censer and incense boat of ca. 1325 and ca. 1350 (London, Victoria and Albert Museum M.268–1923, M.269–1923; figs. 87–88: see LITURGICAL VESSELS). The Book of Llandaf Christ in Majesty, made ca. 1250–65 (Aberystwyth, National Library of Wales 17110 E), may originally have been part of a retable or a large house-shaped shrine. The figure is hollow cast, engraved, and gilded, and its size (6.73 inches high) and quality would make it appropriate to either type of monument. The gentle facial expression and thick V-fold drapery are also seen in contemporary manuscripts, such as the Amesbury Psalter (Oxford, All Souls College 6; fig. 2: see AMESBURY PSALTER).

The ca. 1367 Wykeham Crosier (Oxford, New College) is a fine example of the late-14th-century trend toward ornate luxury objects (fig. 98). The crosier is silver-gilt with enamel panels and cast figures. The central architectural knop is supported by angels and decorated with figures of Christ, the Virgin, and apostles; below the feet of the angels a second architectural canopy contains figures of Christ, the Virgin, and male and female saints. The crosier head is decorated with enamel plaques containing angels playing musical instruments. A winged angel supports the crook, within which a bearded man kneels before the Annunciation. It is unclear how many of the figures are original, as the crosier has been heavily reworked. The style of the architectural knop is close to that of the Eleanor crosses erected by Edward I for his dead queen.

Fig. 98. Wykeham Crosier (Oxford, New College). Reproduced by permission of the Warden and Fellow, New College, Oxford, and Thomas-Photos, Oxford.

Tin and lead, major English resources and exports, were used to make a variety of inexpensive or utilitarian items. One of the most interesting groups of such items is the series of ampullae and badges produced as cheap souvenirs for pilgrims

in the 13th and 14th centuries (fig. 99). The majority of these objects were made for pilgrims to Canterbury, although they were also produced for other sites such as Bury St. Edmunds and St. Albans. The Canterbury souvenirs are decorated with scenes from the life and miracles of St. Thomas and often include inscriptions referring to his miraculous ability to heal. As with the more prestigious items, both ampullae and badges became more intricate in the late-14th century.

Regalia and such unusual items as Henry III's jeweled peacocks were produced specifically for the court. Again little survives, with a few significant exceptions like the King John Cup (Borough Council of King's Lynn and West Norfolk) of ca. 1340 and a girdle of ca. 1350–1400 (Oxford, New College). The basic shape of the King John Cup, with its flaring foot, knop, and cup, is similar, though not identical, to that of contemporary chalices. Its decoration, however, is purely secular, consisting of enameled panels depicting elegantly dressed lords and ladies, some hawking or hunting, in addition to dogs, rabbits, and a fox. In both subject matter and style these scenes are close to those of contemporary manuscripts. Another standard courtly scene, a lady placing a helm on the head of a kneeling knight, decorates the center of the ca. 1335–45 Bermondsey Dish (St. Mary Magdalen, Bermondsey). The dish is silver, parcel-gilt with traces of enamel, and fragile; it may have been made purely as a display piece.

The New College, Oxford, Girdle, like Wykeham's Crosier, is a reflection of the luxurious tastes of the late 14th century. The girdle consists of alternating panels of green and white paste, crystals surrounded by pearls, and enamel panels decorated with monkeys, rabbits, and deer, all set in silver-gilt. The animals of the enamel panels are similar to those that appear in the margins of contemporary manuscripts and suggest that the girdle was a secular piece. There

is no indication of whether it was designed for a man or a woman.

The silver, parcel-gilt Studley Bowl of ca. 1400 (London, Victoria and Albert Museum M.I–1914) is a fine and unusual piece. Both bowl and rim are decorated with a cross, followed by the alphabet and a set of common abbreviations. The decoration reflects the design of contemporary primers, and the bowl may have been intended for use by an aristocratic child.

Such items as silver plate, jewelry, seals, and memorial brasses were designed for the church, court, and the wealthy merchant classes. Memorial brasses in particular provide useful images of the structure of Gothic society, and England preserves more such brasses than any other European country.

Monumental memorial brasses have their origins in Mosan art (from the Meuse Valley), but during the second half of the 13th century English metalworkers developed the practice of inlaying sheets of brass, more properly called latten (an alloy of copper and tin), into marble. This method required less metal and thus opened the market up to a wider segment of society. The process began with the inlay of simple inscriptions (this was also the least expensive form of memorial); sometimes latten crosses were added (slightly more expensive); and finally monumental figure effigies were included (the most costly form of this type of tomb slab). The earliest surviving fragment of a monumental figure brass comes from the ca. 1287 tomb of Thomas de Cantilupe at Hereford Cathedral.

As with other forms of metalwork the London workshops formed the center of the industry, although workshops did flourish in other cities as well. The workshop of Adam of Corfe, established in London ca. 1300–10, manufactured a range of brasses in standard forms. The output of this workshop spans most of the 14th century.

Brasses of the 14th century fall into three stylistic phases: 1) ca. 1300–30: pristine design with static figures and clear, bold engraving; 2) ca. 1330–70: figural poses become more dynamic, engraving more refined, and architectural details, such as canopies, are added; 3) ca. 1370–1400: high-quality brasses worked to standard forms, but lacking the inventiveness of phase 2. The change around the mid-century to more ornate brasses should be understood as part of the trend toward increased luxury seen in all the arts at that time. Interestingly this phase also sees the introduction of symbols of family or personal history and lineage to the brasses, perhaps in response to the decimation of families by plague and war. A fine example of this type of brass is the 1375 brass of Robert of Wyvil, bishop of Salisbury (in Salisbury Cathedral). Wyvil appears within Sherborne Castle surrounded by shields and (originally) the four symbols of the evangelists. Rabbits appear in the abbreviated landscape before the castle, and Robert (Richard?) Shawell stands in the gateway. The brass refers to Wyvil's recovery of Sherborne Castle and Bere Chase (the landscape with rabbits) for Salisbury with the help of his champion Shawell. The brass also includes an inscription explaining the imagery.

The brasses of an unidentified late-14th-century merchant and his wife in the church of SS. Peter and Paul, Northleach, Gloucestershire, are fine examples of the standard late-

14th-century slabs produced in London. The merchant stands on a woolsack, symbol of his profession, while his wife stands with a lapdog, symbol of her loyalty to him, at her feet.

Seals, like brasses, varied in size, form, and complexity according to the wealth and social status of their user. An enormous corpus of seals survives, and some of the most interesting items are the seals of the merchant class. Two fine examples are the copper-alloy matrix decorated with a squirrel (London, Society of Antiquaries) and the gold-handled intaglio gem engraved with a woman's face in profile (London, British Museum MLA 81, 3–12,1), both of ca. 1300. The British Museum seal is inscribed CLAUSA SECRETA TEGO ("I conceal secrets"; the Society of Antiquaries seal is inscribed I CRAKE NUTIS SWETE. Both imply that the enclosed letters are hidden secrets, probably love letters, certainly personal correspondence. The intaglio was certainly the seal of a woman; the squirrel matrix may have been as well, though this is less certain. In contemporary manuscripts (e.g., Bodl. Douce 366, fol. 131 [the Ormesby Psalter]) the squirrel appears as a typically female pet. It may also have had a bawdy meaning as a symbol of the female genitalia. If that is its meaning here, the play on the idea of the hidden sweet, the letter, and the female body would be apt. Whatever its meaning it is a wonderful example of the humor and inventiveness that characterize so much of English Gothic art.

Catherine E. Karkov

Bibliography

Alexander, Jonathan, and Paul Binski, eds. *Age of Chivalry: Art in Plantagenet England 1200–1400.* London: Royal Academy of Arts, 1987; Bertram, Jerome, ed. *Monumental Brasses as Art and History.* Stroud: Sutton, 1996; Camille, Michael. *Image on the Edge: The Margins of Medieval Art and Society.* Cambridge: Harvard University Press, 1992; Campbell, Marian. "Gold, Silver and Precious Stones." In *English Medieval Industries,* ed. J. Blair and N. Ramsey. London: Hambledon, 1991, pp. 107–66; Cherry, John. *Medieval Craftsmen: Goldsmiths.* London: British Museum, 1992; Coales, J., ed. *The Earliest English Brasses: Patronage, Style and Workshops 1270–1350.* London: Monumental Brass Society, 1987; Henderson, G. "Romance and Politics in Some Medieval English Seals." *Art History* 1 (1978): 26–42; Heslop, T.A. "The Visual Arts and Crafts." In *The Cambridge Guide to the Arts in Britain.* Vol. 2: *The Middle Ages,* ed. Boris Ford. Cambridge: Cambridge University Press, 1988, pp. 154–99; Hinton, David A. *Medieval Jewellery from the Eleventh to the Fifteenth Century.* Aylesbury: Shire Publications, 1982; Lightbown, R.W. *Mediaeval European Jewellery, with a Catalogue of the Collection in the Victoria and Albert Museum.* London: Victoria and Albert Museum, 1992; Norris, Malcolm. *Monumental Brasses: The Craft.* London: Faber & Faber, 1978; Norris, Malcolm. *Monumental Brasses: The Memorials.* 2 vols. London: Phillips & Page, 1978; Oman, Charles C. *English Church Plate 597–1830.* London: Oxford University Press, 1957; Reddaway, Thomas. *The Early History of the Goldsmiths' Company 1327–1509.* London: Arnold, 1975.

See also Amesbury Psalter; Architecture and Architectural Sculpture, Gothic; Art, Gothic; Eleanor Crosses; Enamels, Gothic; Liturgical Vessels; Matthew Paris; Metalwork, Anglo-Saxon; Metalwork and Enamels, Romanesque; Ormesby Psalter; Sculpture, Gothic

Metalwork and Enamels, Romanesque

The relatively small number of extant Romanesque metal objects constitutes only a tiny proportion of those originally produced by English metalworkers in the late-11th century and throughout the 12th. Both secular and ecclesiastical metalwork was frequently melted down and the raw materials reused during the Middle Ages. While changing fashions encouraged the refashioning or recycling of numerous secular objects, ecclesiastical pieces were sometimes destroyed for more pressing needs. The monks of Reading Abbey, Berkshire, for example, settled their accounts with Richard I by removing gold leaf from a reliquary housing the hand of St. James. The most catastrophic destruction of ecclesiastical metalwork occurred in the 16th and 17th centuries. The English Reformation and Revolution ensured that no Romanesque church treasury remained intact. The shrine of St. Cuthbert in Durham Cathedral alone yielded 1,578 ounces of precious metals when Henry VIII's commissioners dismantled it in 1537–38. Inventories of the 12th century testify to the abundance of metal objects produced during the period and reveal how great the losses have been.

Patrons of English Romanesque metalworkers fall into two main categories: secular and ecclesiastical. Late-11th- and 12th-century western Europe witnessed greater stability and hence prosperity than had been enjoyed since the disintegration of the Roman Empire. In this climate kings and nobles commissioned jewelry and domestic plate, while the church, increasing in authority and prestige, embarked on a large-scale rebuilding program. Numerous churches were erected, the majority of them monastic, prompting the production of a wide variety of metal furnishings, ranging from monumental doors and baptismal fonts to small liturgical vessels, such as reliquaries, chalices, and ciboria. Consecrated objects like these were frequently decorated with biblical scenes, Christian symbols, or typological schemes. They tend to have been carefully preserved and thus survive in greater numbers than their secular counterparts.

Continental metalworkers, based in established centers of their trade along the valleys of the Meuse and Rhine, dominated the production of metal objects during the Romanesque period, but extant pieces eloquently display the skill of their English counterparts. Various types of metalworker existed: those referred to as *aurifaber* were goldsmiths, working predominantly with precious metals, copper alloys, enamel, and gems. Others, such as smiths, worked solely with base metals. It is often difficult to establish the social status of goldsmiths during this period. Documentary evidence suggests that royal and noble patrons tended to employ secular craftsmen, whereas monastic patrons commissioned both lay and monastic metalworkers. Thus, in the mid-12th century, the abbot of St. Albans Abbey instructed the monk Anketyl to begin a shrine for the remains of St. Alban, aided by Salaman of Ely, a lay assistant. Later in the 12th century the abbot of the same house employed two prestigious lay goldsmiths to embellish the shrine further: John of St. Albans and Master Baldwin. A lay goldsmith had complete freedom of movement compared with his monastic counterpart, and by the late 12th century such metalworkers were beginning to organize guilds to protect the rights and privileges of themselves and their customers.

The only surviving early-12th-century technical treatise on, among other things, the craft of metalworking, *De diversis artibus (On the Diverse Arts),* was composed by the German monk "Theophilus." Its principles and procedures, however, are essentially compatible with those practiced contemporaneously in England. The text confirms that many goldsmiths worked with materials other than metal. Just as Theophilus was conversant with fashioning metal, carving ivory, making stained glass, and painting on walls and in manuscripts, Master Hugo, working for the Abbey of Bury St. Edmunds, Suffolk, in the 1120s and 30s, cast a pair of bronze doors and possibly a bell, as well as carving a rood and illuminating the Bury Bible (Cambridge, Corpus Christi College 2). Such an interdisciplinary approach satisfactorily explains the intimate

Fig. 100. The "Masters Plaque" (London, Victoria and Albert Museum M.209– 1925). Last Judgment. Reproduced by permission of the Trustees of the Victoria and Albert Museum, London.

stylistic relations between metal objects and other media during the Romanesque period.

The Norman Conquest did not trigger instantaneous change. English goldsmiths continued to work in the Anglo-Saxon, "Winchester School" tradition well into the 12th century. The Gloucester Candlestick (London, Victoria and Albert Museum M.7649–1861; fig. 67: see GLOUCESTER CANDLESTICK), the only firmly dated piece of Romanesque English metalwork, was made between 1107 and 1113 for Abbot Peter and his monks at Gloucester. Its intricate design of intertwined foliage stems, human figures, fantastical grotesques, and dragons reflects the frenetic energy of the "Winchester School," although the figures have become a little stiffer and more monumental. The work of this exceptional goldsmith imitates the initials in contemporary manuscripts from Christ Church, Canterbury, betraying the candlestick's likely provenance.

By mid-century the general tendency to pattern draperies in the "damp-fold" style and elongate monumental figures into mannered poses is evident in goldsmiths' work. The Masters Plaque (London, Victoria and Albert Museum M.209—1925; fig. 100), ca. 1150–60, once part of a larger object, shows the Last Judgment, with Christ Triumphant flanked by two angels surveying the torments of hell below. The draperies cling tightly to the vigorous figures' shoulders, thighs, and calves in tear-shaped panels. Manuscript parallels to this style abound, as in the Lambeth Bible (London, Lambeth Palace Library 3), ca. 1150.

The softer, more fluid style that evolved toward the end of the 12th century in English painting and sculpture is also evident in metalwork. The expressive figures personifying the liberal arts on the copper-gilt and *champlevé* enamel casket (London, Victoria and Albert Museum M.7955—1862), ca. 1180–1200, are clothed in equally graceful draperies.

The techniques practiced by English Romanesque goldsmiths compare exactly with those discussed in Theophilus's treatise. The majority of objects were either cast or hammered, that is, forged. Monumental pieces, such as the great bronze sanctuary knocker (Durham, Dean and Chapter) from Durham Cathedral, ca. 1180, or lead baptismal fonts, such as that in St. James's Church, Lancaut, Gloucestershire, ca. 1130–40, were cast in molds of hollowed clay or carved stone. The ancient lost-wax, or *cire-perdu,* method was reserved for more intricate three-dimensional work demanding expert precision, for example, the Gloucester Candlestick or elaborate "architectural" censers (London, British Museum MLA 1919 II–II, 1; ca. 1150–75).

Other pieces, particularly such vessels as chalices and ciboria, were hammered or forged and then enriched with engraving, chasing, *repoussé,* or filigree work. The silver-gilt, mid-12th-century chalice and paten (Canterbury, Dean and Chapter) from the coffin of Archbishop Hubert Walter was forged and engraved. The silver-gilt ciborium, ca. 1200, of St. Maurice d'Agaune (Sion, Switzerland, Treasury of the Abbey of St. Maurice d'Agaune) was also forged and then embellished with *repoussé* scenes set within medallions.

On a more monumental scale iron was forged or wrought

to produce decorative hinges and grilles. The south door at All Saints Church in Staplehurst, Kent, retains the remnants of such work dating from the 12th and 13th centuries, with designs including a boat, four fish, a dragon, and other decorative elements. A 12th-century grille, erected to protect the shrine of St. Swithun, still stands in Winchester Cathedral.

Various techniques were employed to decorate objects. Both base metal and silver were frequently gilded, either partially (parcel-gilt) or completely, to lend an impression of luxury. Such treatment was particularly common during the 12th century when stocks of gold in western Europe were low. Niello, a black metal alloy made from melting silver, copper, and lead together with sulfur, was often rubbed into designs engraved on silver, as seen on the Masters Plaque and the St. Maurice d'Agaune Flask (Sion, Switzerland, Treasury of the Abbey of St. Maurice d'Agaune), ca. 1130–40.

Written sources also speak of goldsmiths' work set with cabochon polished precious and semiprecious gems, pastes, pearls, or antique cameos or intaglios (deemed appropriate despite their pagan subject matter). Both precious stones and antique gems were commonly believed to possess amuletic properties. Only a limited number of such objects survive from England, and many of these are pieces of jewelry. A 12th-century gold ring, set with an antique (Greco-Egyptian) intaglio engraved with *Chenoubis,* a lion-headed serpent-god surrounded by a sunburst and an identifying inscription (Canterbury, Dean and Chapter), was found in Archbishop Hubert Walter's tomb. Matthew Paris (d. 1259), the monk-chronicler of St. Albans Abbey, includes a short treatise on the rings and gems of the house in his *Liber additamentorum* (BL Cotton Nero D.i, fols. 146v–147). He illustrates and describes, among others, a pontifical ring with a central sapphire surrounded by pearls and garnets, given by Henry of Blois, bishop of Winchester (1129–71). The Lark Hill Hoard (London, Trustees of the British Museum), discovered at Lark Hill near Worcester in 1853 and datable to the 1170s from associated coin evidence, contains examples of secular rings set with crystals, amethysts, and pastes to simulate precious gems.

But the technique perhaps most utilized by the Romanesque goldsmith to embellish his work was enameling: the fusing of powdered, colored glass onto a metal base at high temperatures. Although the enamel itself was intrinsically inexpensive, the vibrant colors of the glass gave objects a spectacular appearance and ensured that they were highly prized. Enameling also facilitated the inclusion of colorful, clear narrative cycles and decorative schemes on small objects.

It is certain that enameled objects were produced in England during the Anglo-Saxon period, but it seems likely that the technique most widely used during the 12th century, *champlevé,* was reimported into England from Mosan and Rhenish metalworking centers and from even farther afield in southwest France and northern Spain during the second quarter of the 12th century. *Champlevé,* the technique whereby a design is gouged out of a relatively thick metal base plate, usually pure copper, to a depth of .05 to .3 inches, provided an ideal way of compensating for the dearth of gold in 12th-century western Europe and producing enamels that visually emulated the Byzantine technique of *cloisonné* enamel on gold. The grounds of the gouged fields were keyed or roughened, to ensure that the enamel adhered to the metal. The fields were then filled with powdered glass colored by the addition of various metallic oxides. When fired to temperatures of 1650°F, the enamel fused into areas of solid, jewellike color that were polished to lie flush with the surface of the reserved metal, which was often gilded. In the majority of instances reserved figures were set against enameled grounds (following Rhenish practice), although this was not always the case.

A wide variety of high-quality liturgical and secular objects, produced between ca. 1160 and 1200, were decorated using this technique, although few survive. They include some complete pieces: caskets, such as the Boston Casket (Boston, Museum of Fine Arts 52, 1381, Helen and Alice Colburn Fund), ca. 1170, decorated with fantastical beasts and "blossom" foliage, and crosier-heads, such as the Whithorn Crosier (Edinburgh, National Museum of Scotland), ca. 1180–90. In addition a number of enameled plaques removed from their original settings survive. The most famous of these comprises seven plaques depicting scenes from the lives of Sts. Peter and Paul housed in five collections (Dijon, Musée des Beaux-Arts, Collection Trimolet nos. 1249 and 1250; Nuremberg, Germanisches Nationalmuseum KG.609; New York, Metropolitan Museum of Art 17.190.445; Lyon, Musée des Beaux Arts Objet d'Art D.79; London, Victoria and Albert Museum M.223–1874 and M.312–1926), ca. 1170–80. Their dimensions and style suggest that they belong together, and each rectangular copper plate has four corner pinholes indicating that they were originally attached to a now lost wooden core, perhaps of a large altarpiece or reliquary *châsse.* The figures and background elements are engraved on the reserved gilt metal, set against grounds enameled in purple, dark blue, turquoise, and dark green. They compare convincingly with contemporary English manuscripts.

Many of the extant English Romanesque enamels demonstrate clearly the debt English goldsmiths owed their continental contemporaries. Such links are not unexpected, since England's political relations with European metalworking centers were particularly close during the 12th century. Limoges, for example, an important center of enamel production in 12th- and 13th-century France, was ruled by the English after Henry II married Eleanor of Aquitaine in 1152. Farther east Henry's family was allied with Duke Henry the Lion of Lower Saxony. It is difficult to prove conclusively that such diplomatic connections influenced metalworkers. Links established through trade provide more concrete evidence. By the late-11th century there were both German and Netherlandish colonies in London, and merchants from Cologne had established a guildhall there by the mid-12th century.

These connections, coupled with the portable and, hence, peripatetic nature of many metalwork objects, inevitably makes the localization of some pieces problematic. Some stylistic and technical evidence points to English patrons commissioning continental goldsmiths. The Henry of Blois Plaques (London, British Museum MLA 52, 3–27, 1; fig. 72:

see HENRY OF BLOIS PLAQUES), before 1171, were in all likelihood made for Henry of Blois, bishop of Winchester, by a Mosan goldsmith, although whether they were produced on the Continent or in England is impossible to establish. The reliquary casket showing scenes of the martyrdom and burial of St. Thomas Becket (New York, Metropolitan Museum of Art 17.190.520, gift of J. Pierpont Morgan, 1971), ca. 1173–80, presents a similar problem. Its purpose and subject matter indicate that it was intended for the English market, but the figure style is distinctively Rhenish. The Morgan, Balfour (fig. 40: see CIBORIA), and Warwick ciboria (New York, Pierpont Morgan Library; London, Victoria and Albert Museum M.159—1919 and M.1—1981), ca. 1150–75, provide more conclusive proof of a Mosan goldsmith working in an English workshop alongside English goldsmiths. Together with more technical evidence such examples demonstrate the intimate connections linking English metalworkers and their continental counterparts during the Romanesque period. Both they and their products need to be viewed within a European context.

Sally Dormer

Bibliography

Campbell, Marian. *An Introduction to Medieval Enamels.* London: Victoria and Albert Museum, 1983; Campbell, Marian. "Gold, Silver and Precious Stones." In *English Medieval Industries,* ed. J. Blair and N. Ramsay. London: Hambledon, 1991, pp. 107–66; Cherry, John. *Medieval Craftsmen: Goldsmiths.* London: British Museum, 1992; Gauthier, M.M. *Émaux du Moyen Age Occidental.* Fribourg: Office du Livre, 1972; Lasko, Peter. *Ars Sacra 800–1200.* 2d ed. New Haven: Yale University Press, 1994 [sets English metalwork into its continental context]; Stratford, Neil. *Catalogue of Medieval Enamels in the British Museum.* Vol. 2: *Northern Romanesque Enamels.* London: British Museum, 1993; Theophilus. *De diversis artibus.* Ed. and trans. C.R. Dodwell. London: Nelson, 1961 [the best Latin text available with parallel English translation]; Zarnecki, George, Janet Holt, and Tristram Holland, eds. *English Romanesque Art 1066–1200.* London: Weidenfeld & Nicolson, 1984, pp. 232–97.

See also Art, Romanesque; Baptismal Fonts; Ciboria; Enamels, Gothic; Gloucester Candlestick; Great Bibles; Henry of Blois Plaques; Liturgical Vessels; Manuscript Illumination, Romanesque; Matthew Paris; Metalwork, Anglo-Saxon; Metalwork, Gothic; "Winchester School"

Meters of Boethius

A series of poems based on the OE version of Boethius's *Consolation of Philosophy.* These poems, which correspond somewhat to the *metra* (verse sections) of the original Latin, survive in one manuscript, BL Cotton Otho A.vi, and Junius's modern transcription. Likely composed shortly after the completion of the OE Boethius, the *Meters* probably date to the late 9th century and certainly before 970, the approximate date of the manuscript.

In the manuscript, which also contains the OE translation of the *Consolation,* the *Meters* immediately follow the prose passages that they paraphrase; only modern editors gather them together to publish them as a separate text. Although the most recent edition (ed. Griffiths) felicitously presents the *Meters* alongside the matching prose passages drawn from the OE *Consolation* (Bodleian Library, Bodley 180), Krapp's 1932 edition (in ASPR 5), taken with the corresponding prose of the Cottonian manuscript, remains the best representation of the OE verses.

Censuring the *Meters* as inferior poetry that merely adds poetical tags to the prose version, some scholars have wanted to distance them from Alfred, the only English king to enjoy the epithet "the Great." The *Meters* have been criticized for their conspicuous lack of originality; even the most striking departure from the prose version—likening the universe to an egg—apparently stems from a Latin source. Lack of originality does not, however, signal a lack of ingenuity. The composer of these verses, whether Alfred or not, managed to turn prose into the different language of OE poetry and effectively fulfill the requirements of meter, alliteration, and poetic diction, while remaining faithful to a difficult and sometimes intractable philosophical treatise.

Patricia Wallace

Bibliography

PRIMARY

ASPR 5:153–203; Griffiths, Bill, ed. *Alfred's Metres of Boethius.* Middlesex: Anglo-Saxon Books, 1991; Sedgefield, Walter John, ed. *King Alfred's Old English Version of Boethius De consolatione Philosophiae.* Oxford: Clarendon, 1899.

SECONDARY

Metcalf, Allan A. *Poetic Diction in the Old English "Meters of Boethius."* The Hague: Mouton, 1973; Monnin, Pierre-Eric. "Poetic Improvements in the Old English *Metres of Boethius.*" ES 60 (1979): 346–60.

See also Alfred; Boethius; Translation

Michel of Northgate (fl. 1340)

Copyist and presumed author of *The Ayenbite of Inwit (The Remorse of Conscience),* a didactic religious work translated in 1340 into Kentish dialect from Friar Laurent's *Somme le roi* (ca. 1280); written mainly in prose, it survives in an autograph manuscript (BL Arundel 57). After entering the priesthood in 1296 Dan (i.e., "Master") Michel became a Benedictine monk of St. Augustine's, Canterbury. His scholarly bent is reflected in the 24 religious and scientific manuscripts he donated to the monastery library. Three of these manuscripts have been identified, containing primarily astronomical and arithmetical writings; Dan Michel appears to have copied most of one manuscript and a large part of another, and annotated the third.

Mary Flowers Braswell

Bibliography

PRIMARY

Gradon, Pamela, ed. *Dan Michel's "Ayenbite of Inwit."* 2 vols. EETS o.s. 23 (rev. ed. of Richard Morris's text, 1866) and 278. Oxford: Oxford University Press, 1965–79 [for bibliography see 2:108–11].

SECONDARY

New *CBEL* 1:502; *Manual* 7:2258–59, 2475–77.

See also Moral and Religious Instruction; Translation; Virtues and Vices, Books of

Mills and Sources of Power

The use of water- or wind-driven mills to grind corn (grain) was one of the major technological innovations of the medieval period, since machinery was being used to increase the productivity of manpower. Bread grains could be ground into flour by hand querns, in the home, but where a manorial milling monopoly existed this home grinding often created conflicts between lords and tenants; it was also a time-consuming process. Manorial or privately owned mills were quicker and produced better flour.

It was the water mill, with either a horizontally or, more usually, a vertically mounted wheel driven by a stream passing over or under it, and with its power being transferred to the mill's stones and hoists by a series of cogs and barrel gears, that was most common in England. It was found in Roman Britain, and, if the technology disappeared in the Dark Ages, it was soon found again. There are charter references to water mills from the late 8th century.

From then to the Norman Conquest water mills were built in substantial numbers, no less than 6,082 being mentioned in the Domesday survey (1086). They represent a considerable capital investment, in the machinery, mill race, ponds, and sluices to maintain an even flow of water in flood and drought, and then in maintenance and repairs to gears and bearings and the dressing or recutting of the pattern of grooves in the grinding stones.

Not surprisingly, both before and particularly after the Conquest, it was mostly manorial lords who undertook that investment, notably in the 12th and 13th centuries, when a growing population meant more corn to be ground and more income to be drawn from multure—the fee paid by manorial tenants when they milled—and from rents for mills in cash and kind.

As Domesday shows, there were areas, particularly in eastern England, where, compared with the population, the number of water mills was small. Corn still had to be ground; revenues were there for the taking, but a new source of power was needed. So the wind was harnessed, by means of sails that drove the millstones on a lower rather than an upper floor. These sails had to be kept into the wind and the whole structure held upright, so it was mounted on a single massive post, braced by tie beams with the foundations buried in the soil, and the mill turned into the wind by means of a tail pole. Initial building costs were not high, but maintenance was, since a gale could topple the mill.

These post mills were found first in eastern England, where the technology seems to have developed locally, in the 1180s and 1190s. The main building period was in the mid-13th century, when profits outweighed costs. By 1300 there were at least 10,000 to 12,000 water and wind mills in England, though these numbers could not be sustained as the population and demand for grain fell. Private mills, where family labor bore some of the increased wage costs, were less severely affected, but it seems likely that the total number of mills was halved by the end of the 14th century.

Though the use of water and wind power to grind corn was a technological advance, some historians have taken the argument farther and argued that water power could be used for other purposes and that this led to an industrial revolution in the 13th century. It is difficult to sustain this argument. Water power was widely used in only one industry other than the milling of corn, clothmaking, where a water mill drove triphammers to pound newly woven cloth, immersed in troughs containing a mixture of water and fullers' earth to cleanse and felt it. These fulling mills reduced labor costs, which, as the theory runs, proved attractive to urban manufacturers and led to a relocation of the industry from town to countryside, where the mills were located on swift streams.

Fulling mills were expensive to build, offered lords far less return than corn mills, had insubstantial cost savings compared with those to be had from the use of cheaper country labor for spinning and weaving, and the greatest concentration of mills was to be found in south Wales, never a major cloth-producing region. Therefore the argument for an industrial revolution will not stand scrutiny. The area where water power might have increased productivity substantially was in iron and steel manufacture, to work bellows to produce a fiercer blast for the furnace, making smelting simpler and more efficient. But, again, the capital investment does not appear to have been forthcoming, and there was no industrial revolution based on water power.

J.L. Bolton

Bibliography

Holt, Richard. *The Mills of Medieval England.* Oxford: Blackwell, 1988 [the standard work on wind and water mills, with a comprehensive bibliography, pp. 182–93; excellent discussion of the question of an industrial revolution].

See also Cloth; Technology

Minstrels and Minstrelsy
Pre-Conquest

In the OE period considerable literary evidence refers to professional musical performers and performances. The principal bardic figures are the *scop* and *gleoman,* both of whom are singers of *gesta* (i.e., heroic, epic verse) whose musical activities are sometimes associated with harp music. Though in some literary contexts these names may be broadly emblematic of musical activity, a distinction can be drawn between them, although the differentiation of roles may have greater historical validity for the 7th century than for the 10th, by which time in practice their functions may have been indistinguishable.

The scop was a serious and respected member of the community, a maker and performer of poetry attached to the court of the ruling king or chief. His function was to perform on the field of battle and on ceremonial occasions that possessed strong ritual connotations, singing incitements to battle, eulogies of the ruler and his ancestors, and elegies for departed members of the community. The normal public performance of such heroic, epic narrative poetry was musical, but precisely in what manner—whether recited, chanted, or fully sung—we simply do not know (though modern theories and controversies abound). The gleoman was of a lower class, an itinerant professional entertainer who was paid for individual performances. The term is generic, encompassing not only singing but harping and piping, juggling, clowning, acting, and dancing. He would sing his convivial songs (and heroic narratives as well) simply to entertain on the street or indoors by the fire in halls and taverns.

The harp (OE *hearpe*) was the quintessential string instrument of the Anglo-Saxons. Its remains have been found in the burial at Sutton Hoo and at other 7th- and 8th-century grave sites, clearly demonstrating the esteem it carried among high levels of society. But its popularity was widespread; it was played by amateurs from cowherds to kings, and accounts of St. Dunstan refer to his reputation as a harper. The term *hearpe* might be used generically to encompass other string instruments (such as the fiddle-type rebec and the lute-type crwth), just as the verb *hearpian* could be used to encompass all indoor music making. When more specific in applicability, *hearpe* referred in the 7th and 8th centuries to a quadrangular kind of lyre (such as that found at Sutton Hoo), while from the 9th century on it more probably indicated a kind of pillar harp. Both apparently were strung with gut or horsehair and tuned diatonically. The harp was used for solo instrumental playing as well as to accompany the voice. The degree to which it may have been used for vocal accompaniment, the song repertoires so accompanied (especially epic narrative), and the rhythmic-melodic accompanimental style that would have been used are open questions subject to much modern speculation.

Post-Conquest

After the Norman Conquest there is increasing information about the king's minstrels and, eventually, those of other nobles. William I's minstrel-herald, Taillefer, encouraged the Norman army at Hastings by juggling with his sword and singing the song of Roland, but he was killed in the battle. A successor—Berdic, the king's "joculator"—is named in Domesday Book (1086). The singer of heroic epics was perhaps the usual type of minstrel in the Norman period: what relation this apparently oral tradition bore to that of written courtly song is arguable. It will, however, be remembered that Richard I (1189–99) was himself a trouvère and presumably encouraged the courtly art of song.

Throughout the later Middle Ages the king's harper was usually one of his closest servants, but the king's household included other minstrels of various kinds. Toward the end of his reign Edward I (1272–1307) apparently employed four trumpeters, a nakerer, a taborer, eight harpers, and at least three other *bas* (soft instrument) minstrels. In addition his household included three or four *vigiles* and other servants capable of making minstrelsy. These numbers are conservative, and they do not take account of the households of the queen, the Prince of Wales, and the king's younger sons, all of which included minstrels. Edward I and later kings also increased the available minstrelsy by employing visiting minstrels on an *ad hoc* basis, sometimes for days, sometimes for months.

The word "minstrel" in these circumstances clearly had two distinct meanings. Those whose names appeared in the household lists as "the king's minstrels" *(ministralli regis)* were basically singers and instrumentalists whose main function was that of entertainment or the music associated with ceremonial: their occasional use for diplomacy, espionage, or the carrying of letters was dependent on the social freedom demanded by their minstrelsy. On the other hand those capable of making minstrelsy included several whose primary function was something else—the waferers, *vigiles,* and sometimes such employees as grooms of the chamber or huntsmen who had a talent for minstrelsy. "Minstrelsy" is itself difficult to define in these circumstances, although it seems likely to have been an entertainment that was primarily or at least substantially musical.

The king's payments for such entertainment were large. In the latter part of his reign Edward I spent an average of £25 per year on casual gifts for minstrelsy. Special occasions might raise the annual sum by £40 or more, as Princess Elizabeth's wedding did in 25 Edward I (1296–97); and the 34th year of his reign (1305–06) cost him a total of £224 14s. 8d., of which £170 10s. 8d. was spent on minstrelsy at the Pentecost feast (when the Prince of Wales was knighted) and the weddings of two favorite nobles. Later monarchs generally tried to lower the level of expenditure on minstrelsy, but without notable success. These expenses, in any case, were additional to the daily payments made to minstrels at court. Most royal minstrels, as squires of the household, took 7 ½d. per day, while the *vigiles* and junior minstrels took 4 ½d. Minstrels were not required at court throughout the year, although a nucleus was always needed: so although some minstrels spent as much as 160 to 200 days in court, most were in residence for fewer than 100 days in the year.

When not in court the royal minstrels could live at home and work as necessary. A single minstrel could earn 3s. 4d. from a town or noble, while 6s. 8d. was a normal gift to a group of royal minstrels. The gifts made to the minstrels of other nobles were smaller but also substantial, and until the late 15th century (by which time many places had their own bands of waits) towns tended to be generous to local minstrels as well.

Less is known about the minstrels working in towns and villages than of those wearing a nobleman's livery. The secular celebrations connected with such events as weddings and mayoral elections always gave work to local minstrels. But the full-time professionals, at least, also needed to travel, and a patronal festival at a large abbey, such as Durham, or a major festival celebrated in a city like York, attracted minstrels year after year. Often the records show that the same minstrels returned.

The maintainance of law and order required some control to be exercised over this itinerant minstrel population, which always included a criminal element. A system of licensing, undertaken at fair times, when the largest number of minstrels would be present, was operating by the beginning of the 13th century. Evidence exists for minstrel courts at Chester, Newcastle-under-Lyme, Tutbury, and Beverley. These controls were probably implemented by the kings of heralds and minstrels, at least until the late 14th century. Thereafter the herald kings seem not to have been minstrels as well, and the minstrel courts generally became disorganized. In the late 15th century the minstrel courts began to take on the appearance, and apparently the functions also, of guilds: it is in the latter form that the Chester and Tutbury controls survived beyond the 15th century and the Beverley court was revived in the mid-16th.

Most minstrelsy was by a single entertainer: it is clear that harpers and others were able to provide acceptable entertainment alone. Harpers were probably often *gestours,* singers of epic stories, while the fiddle, too, could be used to accompany a song. Song titles known to us are "The Song of Colbrond" (presumably part of the story of Guy of Warwick), "Queen Emma Delivered from the Plowshares," "The Seven Martyred Sleepers," and "Greysteil." It is impossible to know what relation these bear to the surviving texts.

Minstrels also performed in consort: one plucked and one bowed stringed instrument, a pair of fiddles, two trumpets (with or without nakers), and two or three shawms with a trumpet are all known as apparently standard combinations. Again, as the repertoire was transmitted aurally, it is difficult to show any relationship between their music and the surviving notated sources. That minstrelsy was a rich and varied facet of life in medieval England, however, the documentary and iconographic sources leave us in no doubt.

Peter M. Lefferts
Richard Rastall

Bibliography

PRE-CONQUEST

Opland, Jeff. *Anglo-Saxon Oral Poetry: A Study of the Traditions.* New Haven: Yale University Press, 1980; Page, Christopher. "Music." *The Cambridge Guide to the Arts in Britain.* Vol. 1: *Prehistoric, Roman, and Early Medieval,* ed. Boris Ford. Cambridge: Cambridge University Press, 1988, pp. 247–53, 294–95 [includes bibliography]; Stevens, John. "The Old English Period." In *Words and Music in the Middle Ages: Song, Narrative, Dance and Drama 1050–1350.* Cambridge: Cambridge University Press, 1986, pp. 204–12 [with further literature cited].

POST-CONQUEST

Bullock-Davies, Constance. *Menestrellorum Multitudo: Minstrels at a Royal Feast.* Cardiff: University of Wales Press, 1978; Bullock-Davies, Constance. *A Register of Royal and Baronial Domestic Minstrels, 1272–1327.* Woodbridge: Boydell, 1986; Chambers, Edmund K. *The Mediaeval Stage.* 2 vols. Oxford: Clarendon, 1903; Hays, Rosalind Conklin, Richard Rastall, and Andrew Taylor. *Minstrels and Minstrelsy in England, 1272–1560,* forthcoming; Rastall, Richard. "The Minstrels of the English Royal Households, 25 Edward I–1 Henry VIII: An Inventory." *Royal Musical Association Research Chronicle* 4 (1967): 1–41; Rastall, Richard. "Minstrelsy, Church and Clergy in Medieval England." *Proceedings of the Royal Musical Association* 97 (1971): 83–98; Rastall, Richard. "Some English Consort-Groupings of the Late Middle Ages." *Music and Letters* 55 (1974): 179–202; Rastall, Richard. "The Minstrel Court in Medieval England." *Proceedings of the Leeds Literary and Philosophical Society, Literary and Historical Section* 18 (1982): 96–105; Southworth, John. *The English Medieval Minstrel.* Woodbridge: Boydell, 1989.

See also Heralds; Musical Instruments; Orality and Aurality; Patronage, Literary; *Puy;* Songs; Waits

Mints and Minting

Minting in England was always in the control of its kings. This is different from the situation in France and the German-Italian Empire, where the coinage of the monarch was in competition with that of a variety of secular lords, ecclesiastics, and urban communes. Though the English king always maintained the power to set the standards and appearance of the coinage, the actual minting was often dispersed and put under the administration of officials with varying degrees of control and profit.

Little is known about the organization of English minting before the 8th century; many of the early coinages cannot be assigned to specific kingdoms. In the late 8th and 9th centuries four mints appear to have operated more or less continuously; Canterbury, London, Rochester (after about 810), and at an unknown site in East Anglia. These mints produced coins in the names of Kentish, Mercian, West Saxon, and East Anglian kings, as well as for some bishops (an exception to the general royal control). A mint at York served the Northumbrian kings and, after some interruption, the Viking rulers. A large number of moneyers are named on the coins of this era, many of whom served successive kings of different dynasties at a given mint.

Additional mints appear to have been opened in the late 9th and early 10th centuries, though seldom identified on the coins. In his decree of Grateley Æthelstan of Wessex (924–39) specified that certain mints in his realm (Canterbury, Rochester, London, Winchester, Lewes, Southampton, Wareham, Exeter, and Shaftesbury) were to have more than one moneyer each, while all other boroughs would have one; a total of 35 mints are identified on his coins. By the turn of the millennium as many as 75 mints were in operation, and a system of periodic design changes and recoinages was in place. Dies were distributed from central engraving workshops, and standards and types were uniform throughout the kingdom.

The system of borough mints and centralized die cutting and control was maintained after the Conquest, as was the practice of periodic recoinages. Under the Norman kings, however, the coinage declined in standards of content and appearance, and the number of mints decreased. The civil war in Stephen's reign undermined the unity of English minting, with the appearance, for the only time in English history, of baronial issues. In his monetary reform of 1158 Henry II issued coins from 30 mints. By the time of his 1180 recoinage only eleven mints were in operation. After this date the coinage was unchanged for seven decades; recoinage was ordered only for pieces that had lost weight through wear or clipping. Though the great recoinage of 1248–50 involved about twenty mints, by the end of the reign of Edward I (1307) most minting was done in London.

As the coining became concentrated in London, and the mint moved from the City to the Tower, an administrative system developed that would last well into the modern period. The actual running of the mint was in the hands of a master, often of continental origin, who contracted to mint coins of prescribed standards at a stated rate of profit. As he was responsible for the entire coinage of the kingdom, mint masters' names were no longer put on the coins. The actual production was done by workers who specialized in one of four operations (melters, sizers, blanchers, and strikers) and who were paid according to the amount of bullion processed. The size of the productive staff varied with the quantity of coinage produced.

The king controlled the minting through various officials whom he paid directly. Chief among these were the warden and the keeper of the exchange, sometimes the same individual. At some periods merchants could bring plate and foreign coins directly to the mint; at other times they had to deal through the keeper of the exchange. The quality of the coinage was overseen by the "trial of the pyx." One penny out of each £10 produced was deposited in a special box (the pyx), whose contents were assayed four times a year in the presence of the barons of the exchequer and compared with standards of fineness and weight. Secret ("privy") marks in the form of special letter forms and punctuation allowed the identification of the mint master under whom a given coin was issued.

The proliferation of denominations and the inception of minting in gold in the middle of the 14th century brought little change to the operation of the mint; usually only gold or silver was coined at a given time. A major change was the operation of the English mint at Calais, which between 1347 and 1452 rivaled and often exceeded the production of the Tower mint. The most striking aspect of English minting in the later Middle Ages is the marked decline in the amount of metal (both silver and gold) coined after about 1362, which can be interpreted as a result of an English trade deficit and as part of the overall contraction of the European supply of bullion.

Alan M. Stahl

Bibliography

Challis, C.E., ed. *A New History of the Royal Mint.* Cambridge: Cambridge University Press, 1992; Craig, John. *The Mint: A History of the London Mint from A.D. 287 to 1948.* Cambridge: Cambridge University Press, 1953 [the classic work; largely superseded by Challis]; Johnson, Charles, ed. and trans. *The De moneta of Nicholas Oresme and English Mint Documents.* London: Nelson, 1956 [important sources]; Smart, Veronica. *Cumulative Index of Volumes 1–20 of the Sylloge of Coins of the British Isles.* Sylloge of Coins of the British Isles 28. London: Oxford University Press, for the British Academy, 1981 [with a comprehensive listing of mint and minters' names and activities].

See also Coins, Imagery of; Coins and Coinage

Mirk, John (fl. ca. 1382–ca. 1414?)

Augustinian canon of Lilleshall Abbey in Shropshire; best known for his *Festial* (ca. 1382–90), a collection of ME Temporale and Sanctorale sermons much indebted to Jacobus de Voragine's *Legenda aurea* (ca. 1263–67). The *Festial* gave 15th-century England what probably became its most influential sermon cycle. Mirk wrote two other extant works: his ME verse *Instructions for Parish Priests,* a practical guide to conducting the liturgy and teaching the laity, and his Latin *Manuale sacerdotis* (ca. 1414?), a more reflective work aimed at promoting in parish priests the right attitude to their vocation.

The dates of Mirk's birth and death are unknown, and his works are the sole source of information on him. However, their thrust makes it clear that he was closely in touch with the ethos of his order and its pastoral involvement at the grass roots of society (the Augustinian canons, unusual among religious, often exercised cure of souls). By the time he wrote the *Manuale* he had been elected prior of his community. His *Festial* is stoutly orthodox, sometimes sensational, stocked full with exempla to delight and instruct the "lewed folk"; it offers a good example of one type of preaching to which many late-medieval men and women were exposed.

Alan J. Fletcher

Bibliography

PRIMARY

Erbe, Theodore, ed. *Mirk's Festial.* EETS e.s. 96. London: Kegan Paul, Trench, Trübner, 1905; Kristensson, Gillis, ed. *Instructions for Parish Priests.* Lund: Gleerup, 1974.

SECONDARY

New *CBEL* 1:488, 497, 687, 692; *Manual* 7:2369–71, 2575–76 [*Instructions*]; Fletcher, Alan J. "John Mirk and the Lollards." *MÆ* 56 (1987): 217–24.

See also Exemplum; Moral and Religious Instruction; Sermons

Misericords

The misericord is a hinged choirstall seat that, when tipped up, gives support to the clergy, who according to the Rule of St. Benedict were required to stand during the divine offices, consisting of the eight canonical hours.

The term "misericord" is first mentioned in the 11th-century *Constitutiones* of Hirsau (Germany), and the earliest misericords with carvings on their undersides are from the 13th century (e.g., Exeter Cathedral, ca. 1250). Although situated in the sacred choir, the subject matter on misericords is predominantly secular and at times obscene; their position low down and underneath human bottoms allowing for license, comparable to the marginal spaces in manuscripts. Proverbs, games, fables, romances, daily life, the "labors of the months," professions, and a vast repertoire of hybrid and mythological creatures, as well as real animals and plants, are illustrated. Most popular are scenes of the devious fox and of woman as virago, while scenes based on the scriptures are few (e.g., in Worcester Cathedral). However, the apparently humorous stories often have moral implications, inspired by sermons, and the animals are frequently derived from bestiaries that ascribed moral meanings to them. In the 13th century the motifs were simple, and the foliage was of trefoil or cinquefoil pattern (e.g., Salisbury Cathedral); this gradually changed to a naturalistic type in the early 14th century (seen in Winchester Cathedral), and is found fully developed in Wells Cathedral, ca. 1330–40. The motifs developed parallel to contemporary stone carvings and manuscript illuminations in style and iconography and by the beginning of the 14th century came to be closely related to marginal drolleries in manuscripts. The Renaissance style came to fruition in the misericords of King's College Chapel, Cambridge (1533–38).

In England, unlike other countries, misericords have subsidiary carvings, called supporters, emanating from either side of the seat ledge. The subject matter is thus able to spill over into the supporters, which resulted in an expansion of the narrative, as in agricultural scenes in Lincoln Cathedral misericords.

Misericords were carved under the direction of a master carver, and there is evidence of William Bromflet and his assistants working on the Ripon Minster choirstalls 1489–94, but generally carvers are not recorded. Similarities in style and iconography among sets of misericords point to the movement of carvers and the use of common models, as demonstrated by the connections between the misericords of Lincoln Cathedral (1370s), Chester Cathedral (1380s), and Nantwich Parish Church (1390s), or those of Manchester Cathedral (ca. 1506) and Beverley Minster (1520–24). At the end of the 15th and the beginning of the 16th centuries in particular Flemish carvers are found working abroad, as at St. George's Chapel at Windsor Castle and Westminster Abbey, London. The dissemination of patterns in the 14th and much of the 15th centuries was through sketchbooks and manuscripts; prints were available from the second half of the 15th century. The carvers of Ripon Cathedral first made use of German engravings. They were followed by the carvers of Henry VII's Chapel in Westminster Abbey, who copied Albrecht Dürer, Israhel van Meckenem, and the Master bxg.

Christa Grössinger

Bibliography

Bond, Francis. *Wood Carvings in English Churches.* Vol. 1: *Misericords.* London: Oxford University Press, 1910; Grössinger, Christa. *The World Upside-Down: English Misericords.* London: Harvey Miller, 1996; Laird, Marshall. *English Misericords.* London: Murray, 1986; Remnant, G.L. *A Catalogue of Misericords in Great Britain.* Oxford: Clarendon, 1969 [includes an essay on their iconography by M.D. Anderson]; Tracy, Charles. *English Gothic Choir-Stalls 1200–1400.* Woodbridge: Boydell, 1987; Tracy, Charles. *English Gothic Choir-Stalls 1400–1540.* Woodbridge: Boydell, 1990.

See also King's College, Cambridge; Lincoln Cathedral; Marginalia; Wells Cathedral; Westminster Abbey; Winchester Cathedral

Modus tenendi parliamentum

The only surviving medieval treatise on the organization and operation of parliament. Its purpose, date of composition, and provenance have all provoked scholarly debate. The text is composed of some 26 short Latin chapters, detailing the anonymous author's conception of an ideal parliament, set in the time of Edward the Confessor, rather than his analysis of contemporary parliamentary realities. The significance of the treatise is centered on the importance of the representative character of parliament. Chapter 23 asserts that in granting money to the crown representatives of the communities are more important than the lords; it declares that there can be no parliament without such representatives. The *Modus* became controversial in Tudor-Stuart times, as it was used to support the ancient and independent privileges of parliamentary representatives and the myth of the Norman Yoke— that is, the idea that primitive Anglo-Saxon freedom and free society had been crushed by the Normans at the time of William I. A copy of the *Modus* is found in the *Lords Journal* of 1510.

The tract appears to have been written during the politically troubled 1320s, which would link its representative sentiments to the Statute of York (1322). Although it may have had a political purpose, it served as a guide for lawyers in defining the ideal parliament. Two major versions of the text survive. One is found in collections of common and statute law used by common lawyers; the second is in collections used by civil lawyers involved with the courts of chivalry. There is a French version, derived from a compilation of the two Latin texts. A version was also prepared in Ireland with features peculiar to the Irish parliament. It has been argued that the Irish version is the original and that the English versions date to the political troubles of Richard II's reign. This is, however, a minority view. A fragment of a Scottish version of the *Modus* also survives.

James L. Gillespie

Bibliography

Clarke, Maude V. *Medieval Representation and Consent.* London: Longmans, Green, 1936. Repr. New York:

Russell & Russell, 1964 [stimulating but controversial views]; Galbraith, Vivian H. "The Modus tenendi parliamentum." *JWCI* 16 (1953): 81–99; Pronay, Nicholas, and John Taylor, eds. *Parliamentary Texts of the Latter Middle Ages*. Oxford: Clarendon, 1980 [the English and Irish texts, with translations]; Taylor, John. *English Historical Literature in the Fourteenth Century*. Oxford: Clarendon, 1987 [best analysis of textual problems].

See also Parliament

Monarchy and Kingship

As a form of government and social organization, monarchy emerged in the provinces of Britannia after the withdrawal of the Roman legions ca. 410. In the following millennium its character in what became England significantly changed, but at no time was monarchy abandoned. To begin with there were many monarchies, ruled by *reges* (kings) practicing kingship in territories called kingdoms.

Only in the early 10th century did a monarchy, based on Wessex (and to some extent Mercia) successfully claim the allegiance of all the English. This monarchy owed much to foreigners: to Roman ideas of government as well as Celtic antecedents; to early Germanic settlers—Angles, Saxons, Jutes, and Franks—as well as Danes and Norsemen (from the late 9th century); to Normans and Angevins (in the 11th and 12th centuries); to Carolingian practice, and, above all, to Christian influences following Augustine's mission (597).

The monarchy's place in society gradually broadened to become the bedrock of political and social life and the embodiment of statehood and—well before the end of the Middle Ages—the nation. It enjoyed practical authority of government and administration, and it legitimized a social hierarchy at whose pinnacle it stood. Using the metaphor of the body, John of Salisbury (d. 1180) said, "The place of the head in the body of the Commonwealth is filled by the prince, who is subject only to God and to those who exercise His office and represent Him on earth, even as in the human body the head is quickened and governed by the soul." In the next three centuries Englishmen were inclined to place monarchs even higher, with God alone as their superior.

From an early date the powers of monarchy were matched with duties: to defend, administer, and judge. Some monarchs were incompetent or foolish, others were tyrannical, and many were unpopular; critics and opponents, even rebels, abounded. What is remarkable is that the institution of monarchy nevertheless became more sophisticated and developed its own ideology, so that it survived the reigns of unsatisfactory kings.

Right to the end of the Middle Ages kings were sometimes removed violently (six times between 1399 and 1485: Richard II, Henry VI, Edward IV, Henry VI, Edward V, and Richard III), though the justifications became increasingly contrived and tortuous. From time to time the monarchy was assailed by political, social, and religious forces; its economic resources and the ambitions of its kings within the British Isles and in western Europe taxed its capacity. By 1500 all these factors had molded a monarchy that transcended the person of the king, controlled a compact and centralized kingdom with extensive dominions beyond its frontiers, and could withstand depositions, minorities, and dynastic disputes.

Three major phases in the development of the medieval monarchy may be identified. But for the Vikings and their defeat of every English kingdom save Wessex, a unitary kingdom might not have emerged in England, at least not in the 10th century. Edgar (d. 975) called himself *Albionis Imperator Augustus* (Augustus: Emperor of England), and the kingdom's strength was such that it kept its identity when absorbed into the Baltic "empire" of Cnut (d. 1035) and conquered by William of Normandy in 1066. In each case the conqueror acquired a richer and better organized dominion and a more sophisticated monarchy than his own.

Close reciprocal relations with the church were symbolized by ceremonies of anointing and consecration, and the ritual of Edgar's coronation (973) is still at the heart of the ceremony. Christian kingship enhanced regal authority, promoted monarchical stability, and highlighted the concept of "royal blood" (with implications for hereditary succession). The struggle against the Vikings also elaborated systems of military service, taxation and coinage, administration via *burhs* and hundreds, and royal lawgiving. And these developments underline the importance of nobles and a settled capital, which, until the 12th century, was Winchester.

When England was part of larger continental "empires" (1066–1216), its monarchy shifted inevitably into a new phase, emphasizing the powers and status of kings and the kingly office but also demonstrating the need for cooperation with subjects (especially nobles). Relations with the church remained valuable, but reform movements produced conflict and under John (in 1213) the submission of England to the papacy in fiefdom. Adapting Anglo-Saxon law and administration to Danish and French rule was not easy, but it enhanced royal authority and kings' capacity to exploit their kingdom.

The ideology of monarchy developed further, combining coronation with charters of liberties that expressed the prerogatives and duties of monarch and subject. But to record is to invite complaint, and it required Magna Carta (1215) to attempt to bring John to heel. By the 13th century the monarchy was no longer the Wessex monarchy writ large. The overseas commitments of its kings made English government more settled; the capital moved to Westminster, and a noble-dominated society geared for royal war was buttressed by tighter economic, social, and financial arrangements based on obligation and service. The civil wars of Stephen's reign showed the dangers of dynastic dispute; but when John died (1216), Henry III could succeed him at the age of nine, the first minor since the Norman Conquest.

In its third phase, from the mid-13th century on, the monarchy was able, despite its paradoxes, to embark on unprecedented conquests in the British Isles and France, creating dominions organized from England. Henceforth the monarchy was thoroughly English, its kings regarding their

English realm as their first priority and as an independent, sovereign "empire." Even certain papal claims were rejected, but without forfeiting the essential Christian quality of monarchy. The mystical character of kingship received new emphasis: "Not all the water in the rough rude sea / Can wash the balm off from an anointed king," as Shakespeare plausibly made Richard II say.

At the same time the king's subjects required sensitive handling, especially when parliament emerged as a forum for criticism in the mid-13th century, and kings waged lengthy and expensive wars (from Edward I on). Significant limitations were imposed, tempering the authoritarianism of the 11th and 12th centuries. Moreover, although the convention of hereditary succession (it was not a principle) was usually upheld, noble ambition, fears, or exasperation could set it aside, and more kings were deposed in the 15th century than at any other time. Yet no one attacked monarchy itself or proposed an alternative to hereditary succession.

By 1500 there was a delicate balance between hereditary monarchy in the male line and political pragmatism; between the king as an earthly officer and a semipriest; between his prerogatives and majesty, and customary limitations on his power. Several kings struck the wrong balance and suffered for it, but the monarchy remained inviolable.

Ralph A. Griffiths

Bibliography

Brown, Alfred L. *The Governance of Late Medieval England, 1272–1461*. London: Arnold, 1989 [covers institutions of government, including monarchy]; Cannon, John, and Ralph A. Griffiths. *The Oxford Illustrated History of the British Monarchy*. Oxford: Oxford University Press, 1988 [the only general account of medieval monarchy]; Chrimes, Stanley B. *English Constitutional Ideas in the Fifteenth Century*. Cambridge: Cambridge University Press, 1936; Loyn, H.R. *The Governance of Anglo-Saxon England 500–1087*. London: Arnold, 1984; Reynolds, Susan. *Kingdoms and Communities in Western Europe, 900–1300*. Oxford: Clarendon, 1984 [English developments placed in a European context]; Scattergood, V. J., and J.W. Sherborne, eds. *English Court Culture in the Later Middle Ages*. London: Duckworth, 1983 [aspects of the court and royal cultural involvement]; Warren, W.L. *The Governance of Norman and Angevin England, 1086–1272*. London: Arnold, 1987.

See also Anarchy; Angevin Empire; Coronation; Coronation Ceremony; Heptarchy; Magna Carta; Parliament; Queens; Wars of the Roses

Monasticism and the Benedictine Order

St. Benedict of Nursia codified his monastic Rule around the middle of the 6th century. Though this came to be regarded as the premier monastic *ordo* (rule for community life) of the Middle Ages, it was for long in competition with others, such as those of Benedict's contemporary Caesarius of Arles, and

with those from the alternative, Celtic tradition that flourished along the Atlantic seaboard and in France and Germany for some centuries. Benedict's Rule was itself derivative, owing much to ascetic customs and regulations for cenobitic communities (that is, for those living together in a common life) in the late Roman Empire.

The earliest surviving manuscript of the Rule is from ca. 750 and was for use in a monastery in Anglo-Saxon England. However, the earliest monasteries established in post-Roman Britain—the first being St. Augustine's, Canterbury, founded ca. 598 by the mission sent by Pope Gregory—were not strictly speaking Benedictine, though their way of life was broadly similar. The monasteries of northern England associated with Aidan and other charismatic founders represented Celtic, not Italian, monasticism. Until the latter part of the 7th century monasticism in England was distinguished by heterogeneity and eclecticism. The most important monastic figure in England, Benedict Biscop, who founded Wearmouth and Jarrow (where Bede was a monk), though heavily influenced by Benedictine customs, built a rule that borrowed from many traditions. Of more significance for the coming primacy of Benedict's Rule were the activities of Wilfrid in the north and the Italian Hadrian, abbot of St. Augustine's, Canterbury.

The late 7th and 8th centuries witnessed the rapid growth of monastic foundations, both large and small, and increasingly subject to the Benedictine Rule. Many were founded by royal families or great lords, endowed with vast estates that were the basis of their economic prosperity until the Dissolution in the 1530s. Of particular importance were three groups of foundations: in the west Midlands, a group including Worcester, Evesham, and Pershore, owing much to the patronage of the Mercian kings, especially Offa; in East Anglia, where Peterborough, Ely, and Crowland were the largest foundations; and the monasteries of the kingdom of Wessex, including the Old Minster at Winchester and Glastonbury. This period also saw the foundation of the two greatest medieval Benedictine houses, Westminster and St. Albans.

This golden age was dramatically interrupted by the Viking invasions that began in ca. 787 and lasted for over a century. Monasteries represented rich and easy plunder. By the beginning of Alfred's reign (871) the monasteries of the north and east had been destroyed or abandoned, and conditions were little better in the south and west. Monastic life and learning had been devastated, both by the Vikings and by lay lords to whom the monks had turned for protection. Lay control of monasteries may have had a longer and more harmful effect than the raids. Many houses were now colonized by secular clerics, and it has been suggested that only St. Augustine's, Canterbury, continued unbroken Benedictine observance during this period.

Recovery began under the kings of Wessex, notably Alfred, Edward the Elder, and Æthelstan. The Wessex dynasty was responsible for the refoundation of many monasteries, as well as the establishment of new ones, including the New Minster, Winchester. They also founded a group of Benedictine nunneries. Communities of religious women had not been unknown, often being organized as double houses for women and men, under the overall control of an abbess. The most notable of these was Hild of Whitby in the 7th century, but these were mostly in areas of Celtic influence. The new nunneries, such as Romsey and Shaftesbury, were wealthy and exclusively aristocratic, often ruled by a female representative of the royal house.

By the mid-10th century a monastic group, led by the moderate Dunstan, archbishop of Canterbury, the more radical Æthelwold, bishop of Winchester, and Oswald, bishop of Worcester, with the active support of King Edgar, began a far-reaching reform of English Benedictinism designed to give the monasteries greater freedom from secular control and to reassert ascetic values. This reflected trends in continental Europe, where the Abbey of Cluny in Burgundy, founded in 909, stressed independence from both lay and episcopal control, and a group of abbeys in Lorraine, led by Gorze, looked for reform along the lines promoted by Benedict of Aniane early in the 9th century, in which a sympathetic lay power could take an active part. Cluny was to become the most influential expression of Benedictine monasticism for the next 200 years, while the reforms of Gorze provided a model for English reform culminating in 970 with the *Regularis concordia,* an attempt to impose uniformity of observance in all English Benedictine communities.

The 10th-century reform led to the refoundation of a number of dormant monasteries, like Glastonbury and Abingdon, as well as the foundation of new ones, such as Ramsey. On the death of Edgar (975) an antimonastic reaction set in and some gains were lost. The state of monasticism between Edgar's death and the Conquest has been much debated. It has been seen as "decadent" and "backward" in comparison with other parts of western Europe, isolated from new trends in monastic observance emanating from Cluny and elsewhere. The return of political instability at the end of the 10th century affected some of the monasteries. Nevertheless, such monasteries as Winchester or Sherborne were important centers of artistic and literary production, bishops were generally recruited from monastic communities, and important houses, such as Bury St. Edmunds, were founded.

The Conquest changed the direction of English monasticism. Since ca. 1000 the dukes of Normandy and their leading magnates had founded a number of Benedictine abbeys in the duchy. The presence of the Cluniac William of Volpiano, at the invitation of Duke Richard II, had a beneficial effect on monasticism, and such houses as Fécamp, Mont St. Michel, and Jumièges became leading reformed houses. Anglo-Norman magnates often granted these monasteries extensive estates in England, the sites of daughter houses (known as "alien priories"), dependent upon the Norman house and often colonized by Norman monks. Despite logistic and disciplinary problems many of these survived until the Dissolution, though during the wars with France some were seized by the crown and granted to other abbeys or to endow new educational establishments, such as Winchester or Eton colleges. Others achieved independent status.

A few new abbeys were founded in post-Conquest England. The most famous was Battle, established by William I on the spot where Harold had been killed in 1066. Other important new abbeys were Shrewsbury and Chester, founded by the end of the 12th century. The first Cluniac priory was founded in England, due to the patronage of William of Warenne, at Lewes, Sussex; others quickly followed. The Normans also affected the long-established Anglo-Saxon abbeys. Two successive archbishops of Canterbury, Lanfranc and Anselm, had been monks of Bec in Normandy, and under their influence many English abbeys were organized and reformed in accordance with Norman practices. Lanfranc issued "Constitutions" for Christ Church, Canterbury, copied and imitated elsewhere, and Norman abbots were appointed in place of Anglo-Saxons.

Undoubtedly the most significant Benedictine development at the time was the monastic colonization of the north, resulting in the refoundation of Whitby Abbey and the creation of St. Mary's Abbey at York and the monastic community at Durham Cathedral. This movement, patronized by local magnates as well as by the archbishop of York and bishop of Durham, foreshadowed the great expansion of the "new orders" in the following generation.

The emergence of reformed Benedictine communities, notably the Cistercians, as a reaction to the perceived laxity and affluence of many older Benedictine houses as well as of the Augustinian and other orders, which represent a return to older "apostolic" and eremitical ideals, ensured new and powerful competition during the first half of the 12th century. Comparatively few new Benedictine abbeys were founded; they had ceased to be fashionable and were expensive to endow at a time of pressure on economic resources, particularly land. Nevertheless, great Benedictine abbeys, such as St. Albans, long continued as centers of artistic and scholarly activity; their buildings were in the forefront of architectural innovation and splendor, and (particularly in the south) they dominated local economies.

New threats to their preeminence came from various quarters during the 13th century. The emergence of the universities ended their virtual monopoly of academic studies. The friars proved successful rivals, both for the benefactions of the faithful and as patrons of learning. It was increasingly rare for bishops to be recruited from the Black Monks (the Benedictines), and their influence in ecclesiastical politics waned. Virtually no new Benedictine abbeys were founded after ca. 1200, except for collegiate foundations in Oxford and Cambridge.

The later Middle Ages was a period of slow decline. The falling away in monastic and spiritual fervor of the Black Monks has probably been exaggerated, particularly by polemicists. Many of the larger abbeys were able to survive the harsh economic climate that affected great landholders after the Black Death with relatively little pain. But the overwhelming impression of the Benedictine abbeys in the years before the Dissolution of the 1530s is of small communities in difficulties that in extreme cases led to their dissolution; however, the greater abbeys—with their large quota of paying long-term guests and lay servants, their abbots of high social status with a place in parliament and usually now living apart from their community in sumptuous lodgings, and the monks themselves—remained well fed and affluent, centuries removed from their roots in Anglo-Saxon England.

Brian Golding

Bibliography

Baskerville, Geoffrey. *English Monks and the Suppression of the Monasteries.* New Haven: Yale University Press, 1937; Binns, Alison. *Dedications of Monastic Houses in England and Wales, 1066–1216.* Woodbridge: Boydell, 1989; Burton, Janet E. *Monastic and Religious Orders in Britain, 1000–1300.* Cambridge: Cambridge University Press, 1994; Constable, Giles. *Medieval Monasticism: A Select Bibliography.* Toronto Medieval Bibliographies 6. Toronto: University of Toronto Press, 1976; Harvey, Barbara. *Living and Dying in England, 1100–1540: The Monastic Experience.* Oxford: Clarendon, 1993; Knowles, David. *The Monastic Order in England: A History of Its Development from the Times of St. Dunstan to the Fourth Lateran Council, 940–1216.* 2d ed. Cambridge: Cambridge University Press, 1963; Knowles, David, C.N.L. Brooke, and Vera C.M. London. *Heads of Religious Houses in England.* Cambridge: Cambridge University Press, 1972; Powicke, F. M., ed. and trans. *The Life of Ailred of Rievaulx by Walter Daniel.* London: Nelson, 1950 [lively and informed inside view of monastic life].

See also Benedict of Aniane; Benedict of Nursia; Benedictine Reform; Cistercians; Conversion of the Anglo-Saxons; Dunstan; Friars; Lanfranc; Liturgy and Church Music, History of; Nuns; Priories, Alien; *Regularis concordia*

Moral and Religious Instruction

An astonishing variety of ME texts could be classified as works of moral and religious instruction, for the genre must be one of the most comprehensive in the language. Its audience was equally wide-ranging—male and female, clerical and lay, learned and unlearned, young and old. The literary status of the texts also varies: most are translations, usually from French or Latin; many are compilations of passages recycled from other, longer texts; some have no obvious immediate source. But none is "original" in any modern sense: in the Middle Ages it was impossible to write an original treatise about sin.

All later medieval works of religious instruction owe their origin, directly or indirectly, to the same stimulus: the Fourth Lateran Council of 1215, which decreed that at least once a year Christians of both sexes should confess to, and receive communion from, their parish priest. The council thereby stimulated—consciously or not—the first program of mass education that the West, and possibly the world, had ever seen. In response to this decree, *Omnis utriusque sexus,* a large number of treatises was produced all over Europe, at first in Latin for a clerical audience, but very quickly in the vernaculars (in England both Anglo-Norman and ME) for the laity, women religious, and the less educated parish clergy.

Subsequent episcopal decrees in England, culminating in the Lambeth Statutes of 1281, laid down a basic catechetical program that varied in fullness and detail but always included a knowledge (in the vernacular) of the Lord's Prayer and Apostles' Creed, an understanding of the sacrament of penance (confession), and of the seven deadly sins. The treatises composed in response to these requirements are either comprehensive, attempting to cover all the catechetical topics (e.g., *Memoriale credencium* [*IPMEP* 448]), or more selective, concentrating on a single topic such as the Ten Commandments (e.g., *Dives and Pauper* [*IPMEP* 156]), the five senses or wits (e.g., *Tractatus de quinque sensibus,* derived from *Ancrene Wisse* [*IPMEP* 507]), or the seven deadly sins (e.g., Richard Lavynham's *Little Treatise* [*IPMEP* 789]).

Most use a straightforward didactic mode of exposition and argument, often with such mnemonic devices as short verses or numbered lists. Some use an allegorical fiction as a framework (e.g., *The Abbey of the Holy Ghost* [*IPMEP* 39], *The Pilgrimage of the Life of the Manhood* [*IPMEP* 781]—both translations of Anglo-Norman or Old French texts—and *The Desert of Religion* [*IMEV* 672]). Most of the earlier texts are written in verse, which until the 15th century was the dominant medium for practical instruction, probably because it was easier to remember than prose: for example, Robert Manning's early-14th-century *Handlyng Synne* (*IMEV* 778), a translation of the late-13th-century Anglo-Norman poem *Manuel des péchés;* William of Nassington's immensely popular *Speculum Vitae* (*IMEV* 245), derived like many others from Friar Laurent's *Somme le roi,* a French prose text compiled ca. 1280 for Philip III of France; and *An ABC of Devotion* (*IMEV* 664) found in the register of Godstow Nunnery.

Some texts were composed for specific audiences: *A Book to a Mother* (*IPMEP* 767) was written by a priest for his widowed mother; the mid-15th-century *Disce mori,* which in spite of a title meaning "Learn to Die" covers all the standard topics of instruction, was written for Dame Alice, a woman in religious orders. *The Pater Noster of Richard Hermit* (*IPMEP* 150), a long exposition of the Lord's Prayer, and *The Cleansing of Man's Soul,* a comprehensive treatment of the sacrament of penance, were both written for nuns. Peter Idley's mid-15th-century instructions to his son (*IMEV* 1540), books 2 and 3 of which rework *Handlyng Synne,* is a text written for children. *Ignorancia sacerdotum,* which derives from *Disce mori,* and the ME translation of the mainly Latin compilation *Speculum christiani* (*IPMEP* 6) were both written for priests.

The varied transformations of a single source can briefly be demonstrated by the manifestations of the *Somme le roi* in ME: there are ten surviving translations, of which the best known are Michel of Northgate's *Ayenbite of Inwit* (*IPMEP* 55), completed in 1340; the late-14th-century *Book of Vices and Virtues* (*IPMEP* 668); and *The Ryal Book* (*IPMEP* 824), dated 1484. But there are many other texts, such as the *Speculum Vitae, A Mirror to Lewed Men and Women* (*IPMEP* 209), *Jacob's Well* (*IPMEP* 817), and Caxton's *Doctrinal of Sapience* (*IPMEP* 748), that also use it.

It may be thought that such texts make unrewarding reading. Far from it: they contain much information about medieval mentalities, especially attitudes toward sexuality, analyses of deviance, and so on. In addition their influence on better-known, more "literary" ME texts is immense. It is arguable that *Ancrene Wisse,* for instance, is nothing but an elaboration, adapted for a specific audience, of the standard catechetical topics (Barratt, 1987: 16); much of *Piers Plowman* is incomprehensible without the background of these texts. Even if the *Canterbury Tales* is not in fact structured on the seven deadly sins, as was once argued, Chaucer himself produced in the *Parson's Tale* (*IPMEP* 529) a typical work of religious instruction, based ultimately on two Latin compilations although its direct source seems to have been French. In the *Melibee* (*IPMEP* 18) he introduces a lengthy work of moral instruction by invoking the catechetical topic of the five senses. But the influence can be even more far-reaching: a full appreciation of the dilemma of the hero in *Sir Gawain and the Green Knight,* or of Sir Lancelot in Malory's *Morte Darthur,* is available only to an audience whose moral sensibilities have been finely honed by the subtle analysis of human behavior, the so-called casuistry, inculcated by the best examples of the genre.

Alexandra Barratt

Bibliography

PRIMARY

Brown, Carleton, and Rossell Hope Robbins. *The Index of Middle English Verse.* New York: Columbia University Press, 1943. With Robbins, Rossell Hope, and John L. Cutler. *Supplement to the Index of Middle English Verse.* Lexington: University of Kentucky Press, 1965 [*IMEV*]; Lewis, Robert E., et al. *Index of Printed Middle English Prose.* New York: Garland, 1985 [*IPMEP*].

SECONDARY

New *CBEL* 1:496–506; *Manual* 7:2255–2372, 2375–78, 2470–2577, 2581–82; 9:3006–48, 3258–68, 3377–3404, 3551–59; Barratt, Alexandra. "Works of Religious Instruction." In *Middle English Prose: A Critical Guide to Major Authors and Genres,* ed. A.S.G. Edwards. New Brunswick: Rutgers University Press, 1984, pp. 413–32; Barratt, Alexandra. "The Five Wits and Their Structural Significance in Part II of *Ancrene Wisse.*" *MÆ* 56 (1987): 12–24; Bloomfield, Morton W., et al., eds. *Incipits of Latin Works on the Virtues and Vices, 1100–1500 A.D.* Cambridge: Medieval Academy of America, 1979; Gillespie, Vincent. "*Doctrina* and *Predicacio:* The Design and Function of Some Pastoral Manuals." *Leeds Studies in English* n.s. 11 (1980): 36–50 [stresses the educational function of this genre and distinguishes it from preaching]; Jolliffe, Peter S. *A Check-List of Middle English Prose Writings of Spiritual Guidance.* Toronto: Pontifical Institute, 1974.

See also Ancrene Wisse; Ars moriendi; Dives and Pauper; Edmund of Abingdon; *Jacob's Well;* Manning; Penitentials; *Prick of Conscience; Speculum Vitae;* Virtues and Vices, Books of

Morte Arthur, Stanzaic

A verse romance of the mid- to late 14th century, narrating in rapid succession a series of accidents, conflicts, and betrayals leading inexorably to the death of King Arthur and the destruction of his kingdom.

Questions about date and authorship remain, complicated by the circumstances of the poem's transmission. Critics generally agree that the unknown 14th-century poet composed the original in a north Midlands dialect, but the work has been preserved in a single 15th-century text made by two scribes, each writing in different dialects, their copy incorporated into the 16th-century commonplace book of a London mercer, John Colyns (BL Harley 2252, fols. 86–133). This unique text is incomplete: some 3,969 lines survive, but an entire leaf of the manuscript is missing and occasional irregularities in the stanza lengths may indicate still other lost lines.

Because of the tight narrative structuring such losses are not critical to following the romance's story of the final catastrophes that envelop Arthur's kingdom. The poem focuses on Lancelot's love for Arthur's queen, here called Gaynor, and on the tragic consequences of the couple's divided loyalties. The action begins in a court already poisoned by suspicion. The lovers' efforts to allay these suspicions result in disaster: the Maid of Ascolot's hopeless love for Lancelot, Gaynor's unreasoning jealousy, the queen's condemnation for murder, her rescue by Lancelot, the lovers' betrayal, Lancelot's unwitting murder of Gawain's brothers, Gawain's implacable quest for vengeance, and Mordred's treachery. Arthur grimly faces the battles he knows will end both his kingdom and his life. Receiving his death wound, he returns Excalibur to the sea and departs for Avalon. The poem concludes with the lovers' final parting and eventual death.

The stanzaic *Morte Arthur* has long been compared with the roughly contemporary and justly praised alliterative *Morte Arthure,* but it has suffered from the comparison. Recent critical evaluation has aimed at restoring its reputation. Although clearly aimed at a less sophisticated audience than that intended for the alliterative *Morte,* the episodes have been carefully adapted by the poet, resulting in a tightly constructed and thematically coherent narrative. The quiet and detached narrative voice contributes to the poem's swift pace and its almost elegiac tone. The occasional dismissal of the poem's "minstrel" style ignores the poet's choice of a demanding eight-line stanza (unique among ME romances) rhyming abababab, each stanza thus requiring two sets of four rhyme words. The poet incorporates long passages of dialogue into the quickly moving narrative. Alliteration and stanza linking also contribute to the poem's stylistic complexity.

Critical attention has emphasized the poem's place in the development of the Arthurian romance. The stanzaic *Morte Arthur* has as its source the French prose *Mort Artu,* but the English poet has skillfully reshaped the interlaced episodes of this source. More important, the 14th-century poem is perhaps most valued because it was used by Thomas Malory as a source for "The Book of Sir Launcelot and Queen Guinevere" and "The Most Piteous Tale of the Morte Arthur Saunz Guerdon."

Sharon L. Jansen

Bibliography

PRIMARY

Benson, Larry D., ed. *King Arthur's Death: The Middle English Stanzaic Morte Arthur and Alliterative Morte Arthure.* Indianapolis: Bobbs-Merrill, 1974; Bruce, J. Douglas, ed. *Le Morte Arthur.* EETS e.s. 88. London: Kegan Paul, Trench, Trübner, 1903; Kahn, Sharon. *The Stanzaic Morte: A Verse Translation of Le Morte Arthur.* Lanham: University Press of America, 1986.

SECONDARY

New *CBEL* 1:400; *Manual* 1:51–53, 237–38; Jansen [Jaech], Sharon L. "The Parting of Lancelot and Gaynor: The Effect of Repetition in the Stanzaic *Morte Arthur.*" *Interpretations* 15 (1984): 59–69; Knopp, Sherron. "Artistic Design in the Stanzaic *Morte Arthur.*" *ELH* 45 (1978): 563–82; Wertime, Richard A. "The Theme and Structure of the Stanzaic *Morte Arthur.*" *PMLA* 87 (1972): 1075–82.

See also Malory; Matter of Britain; *Morte Arthure,* Alliterative; Romances

Morte Arthure, Alliterative

One of the great works of the Alliterative Revival, written ca. 1400. It recounts in 4,346 lines King Arthur's triumph over the Roman emperor Lucius Iberius and near-coronation as emperor himself before his own rule collapses by treachery. Like many Arthurian romances it opens with a feast that is disrupted by a challenger, a senator from Rome come to call Arthur and the Round Table to account for their conquests of Roman lands. In the campaign that follows not only are great victories won in pitched battle, ambush, and siege but there are also single combats, one between Arthur and a cannibalistic giant, another between Sir Gawain and a Greek knight-errant. At the height of his success, expecting within a week to be crowned emperor by the pope, Arthur has a dream of Fortune's wheel and the Nine Worthies that warns him of impending disaster; the next day he learns that in his absence from Britain his nephew Mordred has usurped both his throne and his wife. Returning hurriedly, Arthur's army manages to defeat the rebels in battle but Arthur himself and most of his Round Table are slain. The narrative ends with a majestic but somber funeral.

Though the poem survives in a unique source, the well-known Thornton Manuscript from Yorkshire (Lincoln Cathedral Library 91), its influence can be seen in later romance, particularly in Sir Thomas Malory's "Tale of Arthur and Lucius" (Caxton's book 5). It was composed in a northeast Midlands dialect by an unknown author, whose inferrable traits include wide experience of the world; reading in English, French, Latin, and perhaps Italian; and familiarity with the language of law, diplomacy, and bureaucracy, with military and naval theory and practice, and with travel routes abroad, court ceremonial, and fashionable cookery.

The poem is a romance only in the widest sense of the word, as a work about knights and chivalry with some elements of quest-romance structure. At the same time it partakes of enough of the characteristics of *chanson de geste,* in its central focus on war, conquest, and doomed heroism, to be called an epic; it also has characteristics of medieval tragedy, particularly the use of Fortune's wheel as a pivotal image. The problem of genre is partly a result of the poet's choice of source materials; primary sources are the Arthurian chronicles of Geoffrey of Monmouth, Wace, Laȝamon, and Manning, but to these he added structures, ideas, images, and language from a variety of romances and other texts, including the Old French *Mort Artu* and the English alliterative *Siege of Jerusalem* and *Parliament of the Three Ages.*

Genre is less problematic than interpretation. Some have argued that Arthur should be seen as a great hero who falls simply by the action of Fortune's wheel and treachery from the man he trusts most; others would judge him as a conqueror corrupted by success and pride, whose actions become evil and result in evil for himself and his nation as for others. The poet's view of war seems ambivalent: on the one hand battle descriptions are full of the sharply observed detail, knowledgeable commentary, and partisan enthusiasm of a participant; on the other hand few medieval works express sharper criticism of the warrior athirst for personal honor without regard to military and political objectives or of the destructive effects of war on the bystander. A further complication is the poem's apparent commentary on its times; the contemporary issues of war, leadership, neglectful rule and usurpation, religious schism and failed crusade, all seem reflected in this work of the 15th century's turn.

The *Morte Arthure's* author shared with other alliterative poets a highly rhetorical style and the impulse to recreate sources and traditional materials with fresh and vivid language and concrete details, particularly in passages of description and dialogue. The poem's style has some unusual features as well, most notably the repeated grouping of two to ten lines by the use of a single alliterating sound. This habit provides the framework for a good deal of experimentation with unconventional alliterative patterns and for the maximum exploitation of formulaic techniques. It also offers wide scope for the poet's fondness for wordplay and makes full use of his extraordinary lexical resources. For this poet, with technical terms from a number of fields and many unusual or even unique borrowings from French and Old Norse, was one of the most innovative users of the English language before Shakespeare.

Mary Hamel

Bibliography

PRIMARY

Hamel, Mary, ed. *Morte Arthure: A Critical Edition.* New York: Garland, 1984; Krishna, Valerie, ed. *The Alliterative Morte Arthure: A Critical Edition.* New York: Burt Franklin, 1976; Krishna, Valerie, trans. *The Alliterative Morte Arthure: A New Verse Translation.* Lanham: University Press of America, 1983; Stone, Brian, trans. *King Arthur's Death.* London: Penguin, 1988.

SECONDARY

New *CBEL* 1:396–97; *Manual* 1:44–46, 233–34; Foley, Michael. "The Alliterative *Morte Arthure:* An Annotated Bibliography, 1950–1975." *ChauR* 14 (1979): 166–87; Göller, Karl Heinz, ed. *The Alliterative Morte Arthure: A Reassessment of the Poem.* Cambridge: Brewer, 1981; Matthews, William. *The Tragedy of Arthur: A Study of the Alliterative "Morte Arthure."* Berkeley: University of California Press, 1960; Patterson, Lee. *Negotiating the Past: The Historical Understanding of Medieval Literature.* Madison: University of Wisconsin Press, 1987, pp. 197–230; Spearing, A.C. *Readings in Medieval Poetry.* Cambridge: Cambridge University Press, 1987, pp. 148–65.

See also Alliterative Revival; Boethius; Chivalry; Chronicles; Geoffrey of Monmouth; Hundred Years War; La3amon; Malory; Manning; Matter of Britain; Romances; Wace

Mortmain (Dead Hand)

On the death of a vassal feudal lands yielded valuable incidents (financial perquisites): wardship (the holding of a minor heir's property), marriage (the control of his or her marriage), and relief (the fee paid to recover the fief upon coming of age). But if the land were vested in a "dead hand"—a corporation, such as the church, that never married or died—these fiscal perquisites could never be collected.

Most grants to the church were in free alms (*frankalmoigne*); the only service required in return was prayer. Because the usual service from and value of the fee were diminished or jeopardized, there was a move to restrict alienations made in mortmain. Such restraints, first mentioned in the early 13th century, were among the complaints of the barons against Henry III, embodied in the Provisions of Westminster of 1259 (chapter 14).

The famous 1279 Statute of Mortmain, which bears the title "Of Religious Men" *(De viris religiosis),* claimed that despite ordinances the clergy had been entering fees without the license and will of the chief lord. They had been appropriating and buying land as well as receiving it as a gift. The statute forbade such amortizing of land under pain of forfeiture. The forfeited land would go to the lord of the fee. If the lesser lords neglected the matter, the forfeiture went to the crown. Further regulations and reinforcement came in the 1285 statute of Westminster II and the 1290 statute *Quia emptores.*

None of these pronouncements mentioned exemption from the penalty for amortization by means of a crown license. And yet licenses to give land in mortmain began in 1280. In 1291–92 a statute offered a royal writ to launch an inquisition to determine the loss to the king or other lord if land be given to the church. While a statute of 1297 discussed fines for licenses, Magna Carta of 1297, cl. 36, repeated the ban on fraudulent gifts in mortmain.

Mortmain was important to feudal lords for two reasons: they were troubled about the erosion of their earthly seigniories and also worried about restraint upon their ability to make gifts to the church to "purchase paradise." The crown had similar concerns, as well as the intermittent desire to contain the power of the church, placate the nobility, control alienation, and raise revenue by selling licenses. Mortmain is also of interest to historians: it illustrates the important issues regarding the alienability of feudal tenures and the power of the crown *vis-à-vis* lesser lords. It has been seen as the beginning of the attempt to control the church. The licenses granted by Edward I suggest not merely a revenue-raising device but an early example of the royal ability to grant exemption from the operation of a statute (a point recognized by the 17th-century parliamentary patriot Sir Edward Coke).

The granting of licenses can be connected to increased need for money in wartime; the licenses with reasons for amortizing are crucial indicators of the spiritual or philanthropic concerns of the donors. No land was to be amortized without an inquisition *ad quod damnum* ("to what damage"), conducted by the minor royal official known as the "escheator," to determine who would lose if the lands were so granted.

Because the process involved in securing a license from the king was often extended, and the time between fixing the cost of the license and payment considerable, it became customary to employ a device whereby the land was granted, without fraud, to lay nominees. However, it became common to allow the arrangement to stand indefinitely without a license. While the statute of 1391 forbade this, the practice formed an important stage in the development of the law of trusts. The motivation behind the statutes concerning mortmain and the royal enterprise as to the selling of exemption by license are still being debated by historians.

Sue Sheridan Walker

Bibliography

Brand, Paul. "Control of Mortmain Alienation in England." In *Legal Records and the Historian,* ed. J.H. Baker. London: Royal Historical Society, 1978, pp. 29–40; Milsom, S.F.C. *Historical Foundations of the Common Law.* 2d ed. London: Butterworths, 1981; Raban, Sandra. *Mortmain Legislation and the English Church, 1279–1500.* Cambridge: Cambridge University Press, 1982; Rosenthal, Joel T. *The Purchase of Paradise: Gift Giving and the Aristocracy, 1307–1485.* London: Routledge & Kegan Paul, 1972; Rothwell, Harry, ed. *English Historical Documents.* Vol. 3: *1189–1327.* London: Eyre & Spottiswoode, 1975 [item 53 contains a good English translation of the 1279 statute; item 119 is a 1280 license for alienation in mortmain].

See also Alms; Chantries; Wills

Morton, Robert (1430?–1497?)

Composer documented as a "chappellain angloix" at the Burgundian court chapel choir from 1457 to June 1475, though until 1471 he occupied the relatively humble position of "clerc" within that institution. He was certainly a priest by 1460; and he was still alive in March 1479, when he resigned the parish of Goutswaard Koorndijk in the diocese of Utrecht.

There seems a good case for identifying him with the Robert Morton who had studied at Oxford, later becoming master of the rolls (January 1479) and bishop of Worcester (1486–97), under the patronage of his brother, Cardinal John Morton. His Burgundian career coincides with the years when the family was in political difficulties; his disappearance from the continental records just precedes the real political career of Bishop Robert Morton, and it coincides with a diplomatic visit to Burgundy by the newly reestablished John Morton.

Twelve songs are ascribed to Morton. Four are of contested authorship. But the other eight, all setting French rondeau texts, include two of the most widely copied and quoted songs of their generation: *Le souvenir de vous me tue* (fourteen sources) and *N'aray je jamais mieulx que j'ay* (fifteen sources). His *Il sera pour vous combatu,* built over the famous *L'homme armé* tune and perhaps one of the earliest known settings of it, pokes fun at a colleague in the Burgundian choir, Simon Le Breton, possibly on the occasion of his retirement in 1464. The anonymous rondeau *La plus grant chiere que jamais* describes a visit to Cambrai by Morton and another famous song composer, Hayne van Ghizeghem.

Morton's music appears in none of the few surviving English song sources, but it is in continental manuscripts copied as far afield as Florence, Naples, the Loire Valley, and Poland. The theorist Tinctoris praised Morton as one of the most famous composers of his day.

David Fallows

Bibliography

PRIMARY

Atlas, Allan, ed. *Robert Morton: The Collected Works.* Masters and Monuments of the Renaissance 2. New York: Broude, 1981.

SECONDARY

Emden, Alfred B. *A Biographical Register of the University of Oxford to A.D. 1500.* 3 vols. Oxford: Clarendon, 1957; Fallows, David. "Morton, Robert." *NGD* 12:596–97.

See also Songs

Motet

The most significant and intensely cultivated genre of polyphonic music in England and France during the 13th and early 14th centuries (the name is perpetuated in music composed in an evolving tradition down to the present day). The motet at its inception was a Parisian development of the years just after 1200, the product of a fruitful collaboration between Perotin, precentor of the Cathedral of Notre Dame, and Philip, chancellor of the University of Paris. The early motet, in which text was added to the upper voice or voices of a discant clausula, was the only long-lived outcome of experiments that involved writing texts for other progressive, melismatic polyphony as well, including the caudae of conductus and the melismas of organum. English contributions to the earliest layers of the 13th-century motet repertoire may be unrecoverable, but by ca. 1240–50 a distinct corpus emerges

in insular sources that is markedly different in many respects from French approaches. From that time down to the end of the medieval period the newly composed French and English motet repertoires are of comparable size, and their traditions richly cross-fertilize.

The medieval motet is a short part song for a small group of soloists, singing one to a line. It is most frequently composed for two rhythmically and melodically independent upper voices over a slower moving, melismatic, and rhythmically patterned bottom voice, the tenor. Characteristic of the motet is polytextuality, wherein each of the upper voices has its own text. In performance the motet projects a polyphony not only of melodies but also of lyrics, and composers exploit a hierarchical organization both of musical lines and of texts, playing with sound and sense.

The first motets had sacred Latin words, but in the Parisian tradition these were supplanted by French secular texts around 1225, which were in turn supplanted by secular Latin lyrics of a political or celebratory nature after about 1310 (with the exception of the motets of Machaut, which mainly set courtly French love poetry). Outside of Paris, and especially in England, however, motets retained both their religious orientation and the Latin language.

With their dense thicket of lyrics and their sophisticated, ingenious musical designs motets were not for the common folk but rather for cultivated men and those who seek intricacy in art, as we are told directly by Johannes de Grocheio, writing in Paris around 1300. The French motet became a kind of refined chamber music for aristocrats, bureaucrats, clergy, and university students, before taking on in the 14th century a more public (propagandistic or ceremonial) role. In England, on the other hand, the motet remained principally a sacred genre—its performance context, presumably, was in one of those places in the late-medieval liturgy that was most flexible, especially as an interpolation after the Sanctus or a substitution for the Ite missa est at mass, or as a Deo gratias substitute in the offices. Only in a handful of the largest and wealthiest monastic or secular choral establishments would the performance of motets have been regularly undertaken, and then only by a small number of talented individuals—the "precentor et qui cum eo erunt" ("the precentor and those who will be with him") or "certe organiste" ("certain singers of polyphony") as the ordinals say, or the "thre or foure proude & lecherous lorellis" out of a choir of 40 or 50 as described with some hostility by Wyclif. Motets might be copied from time to time onto flyleaves or into private commonplace books, but they were usually collected into large, well-ordered manuscripts. In striking contrast to the well-preserved sources of French motets no integral, large-scale motet codex survives from England before ca. 1500, though scattered remains of earlier books turn up with some frequency.

English motet production falls into three periods distinguished by the forms of notation and musical construction employed: ca. 1240–90, ca. 1290–1360, and ca. 1360–1450. From the first period around 100 pieces survive, mostly fragmentary; in addition there are textual incipits for 81, mostly otherwise unknown, in the surviving index to a lost book of polyphony (BL Harley 978, fols. 160v–161). They are notated in separate parts (thus to be distinguished from the layout in score that was otherwise prevalent in England) and mostly written in English mensural notation. Fewer than half are built upon a tenor *cantus firmus* consisting of two or more statements of a segment of plainchant, on the French model. The greater number are constructed over a *pes,* a voice of tenor function that is either freely composed or perhaps drawn from the popular sphere, often featuring strict or varied *ostinati.* Pes motets are further distinguished according to whether the pes consists of multiple statements of one short idea (up to nine, eleven, or even thirteen times) or a chain of differing ideas (usually between three and six) repeated in pairs, and whether tenor repetition engenders voice exchange between the upper parts. While most early insular motets are polytextual, a significant minority set a single text, or alternate in the presentation of two texts. This repertoire, in particular the freely composed voice-exchange motets, has melodic, rhythmic, harmonic, textural, and structural affinities with contemporaneous English repertoires of conductus and rondellus in score notation. These in turn are influenced by the motet: late-13th-century examples are sometimes polytextual, or written in parts. The troped chant setting also adopted many features of the motet at the end of the century.

From the second period perhaps 125 motets survive. Abandoning English mensural notation, their notation at first follows the continental fashions of Franco of Cologne and Petrus de Cruce, but by the second or third decade of the 14th century composers turned to new English notations. A striking feature of the motets of the era 1290–1360 is their restriction to a small number of well-defined formal types employing strict and varied voice exchange, strophic repetition with variation, refrains, and various kinds of recondite numerical disposition of phrase and section lengths, especially involving isoperiodicity (equal but staggered phrases in all voices) and rhythmic patterning in the upper voices. Large-scale collections of these motets apparently provided compositions for all major feasts of the church year (Sanctorale and Temporale, Proper and Common). One remarkable specimen composed before 1326 that survives only as an extended fragment, *Rota versatilis* (on St. Katherine of Alexandria), has five lengthy sections of voice exchange that stand in the relative proportions of 12:8:4:9:6. Known only from a 15th-century book index is a treatise on the construction of this piece, entitled *Modus componendi rotam versatilem.*

At least 70 English pieces survive from the period of the final flowering of the medieval motet, ca. 1360–1450. These later works adopt French Ars Nova notation and abandon English structural approaches for the kinds of isorhythmic designs in three and four voices developed by Philippe de Vitry and Guillaume de Machaut, leading eventually to the classic tripartite isorhythmic motets with proportional diminution by John Dunstable, John Benet, and their contemporaries. Among a handful of exceptions are insular motet types in Ars Nova notation and hybrids with individualistic, insular responses to French influence in details of counterpoint and structure. (There are also many unique variations on isorhythmic design in the motet-style mass movements of the Fountains fragments and the Old Hall Manuscript.) Our view of the main line of development of the English and "Anglo-French" motet in the second half of the 14th century is undergoing major revision at present with the discovery of an English source for the motet *Sub arturo plebs vallata* and the dating of this piece to the early 1370s shortly before the death of its composer, Johannes Alanus (John Aleyn). The remarkable technical virtuosity and ingenuity of *Sub arturo* and related English works, some of which were discovered only in the 1980s, and the revelation of strong ties between English and continental traditions of "musicians' motets" (including *Sub arturo,* the anonymous *Musicorum collegio,* and an insular version of *Apollinis eclipsatur*), imply direct contact and a spirit of friendly competition across the Channel.

Aside from the "musicians' motets" and a few secular pieces imported from the Continent the English motet repertoire of the 14th and 15th centuries remained sacred in its orientation, now with an almost exclusive focus on Mary and the saints. Apparently no longer written in sufficient numbers to provide motets for all major feasts, the motet seems to have come to play a more occasional, perhaps ceremonial, role. For instance, it has been suggested that motets on St. George and Mary by Damett, Cooke, and Sturgeon in the Old Hall Manuscript (nos. 111, 112, 113) might have been performed at the reception of Henry V in London after the English victory at Agincourt. And John Dunstable's motets on St. Alban and St. Germanus form part of his demonstrable links to the Benedictine Abbey of St. Albans. One exceptional late example, the anonymous *O potores exquisiti* (from BL Egerton 3307), sets the text of an old goliardic drinking song.

Following the precedent of some 15th-century continental manuscripts, modern scholars also refer to English polyphonic settings of cantilenas and antiphons from the 1420s and beyond as motets.

Peter M. Lefferts

Bibliography

PRIMARY

Everist, Mark, ed. *Five Anglo-Norman Motets.* Newton Abbot: Antico Edition, 1986; Harrison, Frank Ll., ed. *Motets of English Provenance.* Polyphonic Music of the Fourteenth Century 15. Paris: L'Oiseau-Lyre, 1980; Harrison, Frank Ll., Ernest H. Sanders, and Peter M. Lefferts, eds. *English Music for Mass and Offices.* 2 vols. Polyphonic Music of the Fourteenth Century 16–17. Paris: L'Oiseau-Lyre, 1983–86; Sanders, Ernest H., ed. *English Music of the Thirteenth and Early Fourteenth Centuries.* Polyphonic Music of the Fourteenth Century 14. Paris: L'Oiseau-Lyre, 1979.

SECONDARY

Bent, Margaret. "Rota versatilis: Towards a Reconstruction." In *Source Materials and the Interpretation of Music: A Memorial Volume to Thurston Dart,* ed. Ian Bent. London: Stainer & Bell, 1981, pp. 65–98; Bent, Margaret, with David Howlett. "*Subtiliter alternare*: The

Yoxford Motet *O amicus / Precursoris.*" In *Studies in Medieval Music: Festschrift for Ernest H. Sanders,* ed. Peter M. Lefferts and Brian Seirup. *Current Musicology* 45–47 (1990): 43–84; Lefferts, Peter M. *The Motet in England in the Fourteenth Century.* Ann Arbor: UMI Research Press, 1986; Sanders, Ernest H. "The Medieval Motet." In *Gattungen der Musik in Einzeldarstellungen: Gedenkschrift Leo Schrade,* ed. Wulf Arlt et al. Munich: Francke, 1973, pp. 497–573.

See also Alanus; Notation of Polyphonic Music; *Sub arturo plebs*

Music: History and Theory
History

Writing the history of music in medieval England is a difficult undertaking, as it would be for any cultural or geographic region in an era so distant from us in time, so alien in its customs and modes of thought, and so fragmented and incomplete in its evidentiary record. The practice of music poses particular problems in that it took place mostly in a notationless culture, and its instruments were fragile, circumstances drastically curtailing the number and kinds of artifacts that could survive. In this field the historian who wishes to depict the panoramic landscape—or, better, soundscape—of musical activity must have a full grasp of the information provided us by the few extant musical scores, the iconography of music, and literary references; an ethnologist's knowledge of the nonmedieval and nonwestern cultures that might be appropriately compared with that of ancient Britain; and the boldness of imagination to unite these into a descriptive anthropology of the full range of musical activity that might once have been practiced there. (This is admittedly idealistic; no modern account is so ambitious in its diachronic or synchronic sweep.) Histories of medieval English music have been further handicapped by the unjust prejudice that England is (or was prior to the late 19th century) "the land without music" and by the preoccupation of musicologists over the last 150 years with the musical achievements of medieval France. It has only been with a spate of new scholarship after the Second World War that the significant dimensions, the vigor, and the creativity of medieval English musical life have begun to emerge with full clarity.

One point of entry into music is linguistic, for those who sang, spoke, and wrote in Anglo-Saxon or Middle English, French or Anglo-Norman, and Latin formed distinct if sometimes overlapping music cultures in Britain with their own histories, genres, and dynamics of change. Each of these cultures will be briefly taken up in turn below.

With respect to the English language no songs survive with accompanying musical notation prior to Godric's sacred songs of the mid-12th century. Thus we do not know the tune of Cædmon's Hymn or have the formulas to which the oral predecessors to narrative poetry like *Beowulf* were intoned. At least some of the more elite sung texts were preserved in literary form; what was sung for dancing, or in the tavern, or out in the fields is entirely lost. Indeed music of the lower levels of English-speaking society remains virtually inaccessible to

the historian throughout the remainder of the Middle Ages. But there are always reminders of its presence. For instance, William FitzStephen, Thomas Becket's clerk, chronicles how when Becket was in France in the late 1150s on royal business as chancellor of the English king, his household would process into French towns on their route with 250 footmen in the vanguard, "singing English songs as was the English custom." Gerald of Wales reports around 1200 that a kind of folk polyphony was sung by the Welsh and by the English of Northumberland and says the southern English people generally did not perform this way, implying that their music was mainly monophonic. Later two surviving motets of ca. 1300 use tenors based on English songs, and a number of the Latin hymns of the Red Book of Ossory, written ca. 1320–60 by the English Franciscan Richard Ledrede, bishop of Ossory, are evidently sacred contrafacts of secular songs, some of which are identified by a vernacular English textual tag indicating the more familiar words by which the tune and rhythm would be known. Though the reinvigoration of English as a literary language began in the later 12th and 13th centuries, it never became an important vehicle for the motet or for aristocratic songs of courtly love, and though the narrative romance and ballad were sung, no medieval melodies are extant. Just one known sacred motet and one conductus fragment set English texts, and the few English lyrics surviving with melodies before ca. 1400 have pious, devotional subject matter. The polyphonic repertoire of the Winchester Songbook, and English part songs and carols of the 15th century, even when clearly in a popular vein ("Tappster, drinker, fille another ale"), were the entertainment music of an educated, mainly clerical elite. An outstanding research question concerns the degree to which the distinctive melodic, rhythmic, harmonic-contrapuntal, and formal features of insular church music, both monophonic and polyphonic, may bear the influence of local folk or popular idioms of English speakers. It may be, for instance, that the unique and artful "Sumer is icumen in" has its roots in the kind of part song described by Gerald of Wales.

The contribution of French speakers in the realm of vernacular music is equally difficult to trace. From the time of the Conquest the Normans introduced their own traditions of secular music making, culminating in the brilliant court culture of Henry II and Eleanor of Aquitaine. While not nearly as much lyric repertoire survives from the courts of the later Plantagenets, trouvères and minstrels enjoyed the patronage of the aristocracy well into the 15th century. As on the Continent the vogue for courtly song began to be seen among the middle classes; in the late 13th century the traders of the London Guildhall established a *puy,* a literary-musical social organization, one of whose songs still survives on a leaf in the Public Record Office (E 163/22/1/2). A handful of motets and conducti set Anglo-Norman texts, mainly sacred in content, while a few motet tenors draw on a coarser range of popular lyrics. The court remained francophile throughout the 14th century, as exemplified by the men of letters, artists, and musicians in the circle of Edward III's queen, Philippa of Hainault, and it is not surprising to read in Chaucer's *Parliament of Fowls* (ca. 1382) that when birds sang a "roundel" (i.e., rondeau), "the note, I trowe, maked was in Fraunce" (lines 673–92). But in the later 14th and 15th centuries there were native composers who set not only English lyrics but also original French texts in the fixed forms of virelai, rondeau, and ballade. Again questions about musical interchange and cross-influence here are easy to frame but hard to answer.

The culture whose music we know best is that of the church and of the educated clerics, whether in ecclesiastical or government service, whose *lingua franca* was Latin. The principal music of this culture, day in and day out, was liturgical chant. The nature and extent of development of the chant are hard to assess in Roman and early Anglo-Saxon Britain, but we can be sure the primary influences were the tradition of Rome itself and the Gallican and Hiberno-Celtic chant dialects. Regular religious life was virtually extinguished by the 9th-century Viking invasions. Its restoration in the later 9th and 10th centuries, driven by the powerful force of Benedictine monasticism, implanted the hybrid Franco-Roman dialect known as Gregorian chant, especially as it was sung at northern French houses, such as Fleury, Corbie, and St. Denis. After 1066 Norman influences, especially reflecting the practices of Cluny and Bec, had a powerful effect upon pre-Conquest chant traditions. Within the Gregorian musical tradition, which the later medieval British church shared with most of western Christendom, there was much scope for small-scale divergences in liturgy, ceremonial, chant selection, and melodic dialect; if these deviations became pronounced enough, one might come to recognize a distinctive local "use." The most famous and influential of these to develop in medieval England was the Use of Salisbury (or Sarum). A corollary to the development of the chant concerns the choral establishments constituted to sing it, first in monasteries and then in communities of secular clergy. Their expansion and transformation up through the 15th century established an English church-choir tradition that is still admired and functioning today.

Never static, the 9th-century nucleus of liturgy and Gregorian chant grew steadily by a process of accretion that was halted in England only by the turmoil of the 16th century. Englishmen contributed amply to the development of new liturgical feasts, new offices, votive observances, commemorations, and processions; in addition to the composition of texts and music for these new services, new plainchants also included individual antiphons, conducti, sequences, offertories, and hymns, and a wealth of tropes and prosulae. A few examples will serve to indicate this activity; the subject is relatively underexplored, and only recently has it become the subject of intense scholarly interest.

In the Anglo-Saxon period, for instance, St. Dunstan (ca. 910–988) reputedly composed the melody for the Kyrie *Rex splendens;* and Winchester became a center of the cultivation of plainchant tropes and polyphony. (Like some other 10th-century monastic churches the Old Minster also possessed a famous organ.) A rich repertoire of hymns, sequences, and full offices for Anglo-Saxon saints continued to be augmented even after the Norman Conquest. A later work, and probably the most influential office ever written in England, the Office for Thomas of Canterbury by Abbot Benedict of Peterborough (ca. 1180), was rapidly and widely disseminated across all of Europe. Archbishop Stephen Langton's popular Pentecost sequence, *Veni sancti spiritus,* achieved equally universal distribution. Of more local fame, although equally indicative of the continued composition of plainchant down to the end of the Middle Ages, are the offices, commemorations, and individual antiphons, hymns, and sequences for later English saints and near-saints, including such likely and unlikely candidates as Osmund, Simon de Montfort, Thomas of Hereford, and Thomas of Lancaster.

From the 9th century on the liturgy was also augmented regularly by polyphonic organa and, beginning ca. 1200, by a rich and distinctive body of Latin-texted sacred motets and polyphony for the mass and office that decisively parts company from continental practices. This insular music made a significant impact on the Continent in the 15th century, when it was influential in a decisive shift in genres and compositional approaches that is taken by historians to mark the beginning of the Renaissance in music.

Outside of the choir churchmen, clerks, and scholars were not averse to turning their musical talents and fluency in Latin to the ends of edification and entertainment. Their nonliturgical Latin song is known by numerous and diverse names—carmen, versus, ritmus, conductus, cantio, cantilena, modus, planctus, hymn, sequence, carol—and encompasses lyric poetry of a wide range of subjects. Most songs survive, stripped of their melodies, in text anthologies and florilegia, but for some there are musical settings; these vary tremendously in style, form, and aesthetic intent. The Older Cambridge Songbook of the mid-11th century, and the Younger Cambridge Songbook of the late 12th or early 13th century, with its affinities to the famous *Carmina burana,* are but two of the better-known secular collections. To this worldly repertoire we may add mention of such devotional songs as the widespread *Dulcis Jesu memoria* and *Angelus ad virginem,* the pious songs of Ledrede's Red Book of Ossory, and the Latin and macaronic (i.e., multilingual) carols of the late 14th and 15th centuries.

Dance music and instrumental music were ubiquitous and should loom large in any properly balanced social history of music, though a dearth of sounding music survives for them. The harp, the fiddle, the pipe-and-tabor, the organ, and many other kinds of instruments are attested by archaeological finds, medieval pictorial images, sculpture in wood and stone, and written accounts. Documentation for dance, especially for the communal karole, is also plentiful, and it is even possible to deduce certain information about choreography and dance meters from iconography and the accentual lyrics of vocal dance songs. The slender remains of medieval English instrumental dance music (atypical by definition, since they are notated) include a monophonic dance with a polyphonic coda in Bodl. Douce 138; three textless, two-voice compositions in BL Harley 978; and keyboard intabulations of estampies in the Robertsbridge Codex (BL Add. 28550). All are from the 13th and 14th centuries and exhibit a marked metricism in rhythmic language within highly repetitive forms. The Robertsbridge Codex also has intabulations of two continental Latin motets and a Latin-texted English cantilena. The role of instruments in the accompaniment of solo song is an area of active modern speculation and experimentation by scholars and performers.

Theory

Medieval musical theory encompasses the wide variety of topics addressed by medieval writers on music, including both more abstract theoretical subject matter (*musica theorica* or *speculativa*) and practical topics (*musica practica*), ranging from discussions of the origins and definitions of music, the etymology of the word "music" and the names of notes, intervals, and scales, to rhythmics and metrics, the construction and tuning of organ pipes, and the composition of chants and motets. Speculative music theory was a mathematical, ultimately Pythagorean discipline through which music earned its place in the medieval quadrivium next to arithmetic, geometry, and astronomy. It concerned itself with the tonal system, intervals, scales, tuning, and species of consonance and dissonance. At its heart was the arithmetic theory of proportions of intervals and their demonstration by the division of the monochord. Practical music theory in the West originated in the 9th century and was concerned with topics of direct application to the learning, singing, and composing of ecclesiastical chant. Its topics included psalm tones and liturgical modes, modal assignment, tonal behaviors in chant, and techniques for sightsinging that involved the gamut, hexachords, mutation, and the Guidonian hand. With the rise of polyphony practical theory turned its attention to discant and counterpoint and to *musica mensurabilis,* including discussions of systems of rhythmic notation and the genres of mensural (mainly polyphonic) music.

In the earlier Middle Ages the two strands of music theory were regarded as distinct, with more regard accorded the learned *musicus,* who had mastered *musica theorica,* than the workaday *cantor,* whose field was *musica practica.* In the later Middle Ages these two theoretical traditions were linked as complementary parts of a single field in which the major treatises combined both with varied emphasis; quadrivial music education in the schools and at university came to possess a practical as well as a theoretical component, just as arithmetic had its practical side in abacus and computus. Variety in topic and emphasis speaks to the nature of the audience for music theory. Much of it was destined for the instruction of boys (*juvenes, pueruli, adolescentes*) in the rudiments of music, while some represents the elite discourse between *musici.* The Englishman Johannes Hanboys says that he writes (ca. 1370) for *compositores et cantores* ("composers and singers"), most likely meaning working professionals. Latin was the language for music theory until the 14th century, when vernacular treatises begin to appear in English, French, and Italian.

No contributions by Englishmen played a central role in the international development of medieval music theory, but there was a notably vigorous local tradition of dissemination and innovation. Much traditional material about music dating back to late classical antiquity circulated in copies or abstracts of treatises from the early Christian era, preeminently the *De institutione musica* of Boethius (ca. 500) and also such works as Augustine's *De musica* and the encyclopedias of Cassiodorus and Isidore. Later continental treatises of the 9th through the 11th centuries enjoyed similarly wide distribution and influence in England, including the Enchiriadis treatises and works by Aurelian, (Pseudo)-Odo, Guido, and Berno. Also particularly well represented in English sources are the late-13th-century tradition of Franco of Cologne and the Parisian Ars Nova treatises of Jehan de Murs (Johannes de Muris) from the first half of the 14th century.

The individuals who copied, compiled, or on occasion authored theoretical treatises were mainly monastic cantors and precentors, the officials responsible for the monastic library and education as well as musical performance. A thin yet unbroken line of such theorist-precentor-cantors known to us by name can be traced from the 10th to the 16th century. In the Anglo-Saxon and early Norman periods the great monastic cathedrals at Winchester and Canterbury were centers of musical creation and scholarship. William of Malmesbury attributes to Wulfstan the cantor of Winchester (fl. ca. 980–1010) an opus *De tonorum armonia* that has not survived. Osbern of Canterbury (fl. ca. 1070–89), monk and precentor at Christ Church during the tenure of Archbishop Lanfranc and, like Wulfstan, an important author of accounts of the lives and miracles of English saints, wrote two surviving music treatises, *De vocum consonantiis* and *De re musica.* The tradition of musical learning at Canterbury can be extended into the mid-12th century through the figure of Theinred, a monk and precentor of the Benedictine priory at Dover, which was a dependency of Christ Church, Canterbury. Theinred is probably the learned and respected monk, a grammarian and phonetician, who is mentioned by John of Salisbury in his *Metalogicon* of 1159, which was written at Canterbury while John was in the *familia* of Archbishop Theobald. Theinred's surviving theory treatise, *De legitimis ordinibus pentachordorum et tetrachordorum,* is addressed to Aluredus of Canterbury, and its final line ("Explicit informacio juvenum") indicates it to have been intended for the youths being educated in the cathedral's care.

The English theorist known to modern musicology as Anonymous IV (fl. ca. 1275) is our chief informant about Parisian and English practices of the late 12th and earlier 13th centuries in his *De mensuris et discantu;* he may have been a monk (and perhaps precentor) of the great abbey at Bury St. Edmunds. A direct contemporary is W. de Wycombe, a monk of Reading who is known to have worked as a scribe for four years in the later 1270s or 1280s at Leominster Priory, where he rose to the position of precentor. Wycombe has left a list of the materials he copied at Leominster, including music and music theory, and he is probably to be identified as the author of a cycle of 37 polyphonic Alleluia settings, some of which are preserved among the late-13th-century repertoire. Contemporary with these Benedictines, but enjoying a different career, was the English priest Amerus, who served as a clerk in the *familia* of the Italian Cardinal Ottobuono in Rome, where he may also have been a member of the papal Schola

Cantorum and teacher of the young singers there. In 1271, while in Italy, Amerus compiled a music treatise, the *Practica artis musicae,* intended for the education of boys, which circulated both on the Continent and in England.

With the rise of the universities and secular choral establishments in England new career paths for theorists and new venues for the teaching and writing of theory started to emerge. The Benedictine tradition began to intersect with that of the universities in the figure of Walter Odington (fl. 1298–1316), a monk of Evesham who was an important scholar at Oxford in the early 14th century. Odington wrote complete treatises on each of the subjects of the quadrivium, including music (the *Summa de speculatione musicae*); his other works include a popular alchemical treatise. Many later 14th-century English music treatises are heavily indebted to Odington's and are charged with the language and patterns of argument of the schools. One of the most substantial, the anonymous *Quatuor principalia,* is also particularly indebted to the Frenchmen Jehan de Murs and Philippe de Vitry in its fourth section, on *musica mensurabilis.* This treatise exists in two versions; multiple copies of the longer still survive, including one made in 1351 at Oxford by the Franciscan friar John of Tewkesbury (who may indeed be its author), which he returned to the Franciscans at Oxford in 1388. Late in the 14th century Thomas Walsingham (d. ca. 1422), the great historical chronicler who was precentor and *scripturarius* (chief scribe) at St. Albans, wrote a treatise on notation, the *Regulae de musica mensurabili;* Richard Cutell, a minor canon at St. Paul's, London, in the 1390s, has left us a vernacular treatise on counterpoint; and a Frater G. de Anglia copied Latin music treatises at Pavia in 1391.

From the 15th century the major figure is John Hothby (ca. 1410–1487), a peripatetic English Carmelite monk, composer, and prolific music theorist, who enjoyed a career in Florence in the 1450s and 1460s, followed by employment at the Cathedral of St. Martin in Lucca from the endowment of its polyphonic choir in 1467 until his recall to England by Henry VII in 1486. His numerous treatises appear in both continental and English manuscripts. The composer Leonel Power's surviving treatise is a plain vernacular teaching manual aimed at the education of boys in simple improvised counterpoint; it probably dates from his years as master of the Lady Chapel choir at Canterbury Cathedral (1439–45). Other theorists known to us by name were principally compilers. John Wylde, precentor (or perhaps preceptor) of the Abbey of the Holy Cross at Waltham, made an important collection of treatises, now BL Lansdowne 763 (ca. 1450). John Tucke, bachelor of arts and fellow of New College, Oxford, compiled and edited around 1500 the manuscript now BL Add. 10366. And a copy of Tucke's manuscript, now London, Lambeth Palace 466, was completed in 1526 by William Chelle, precentor of Hereford Cathedral, who had taken his B.A. at Oxford in 1524.

Some distinctive English contributions and specific references to local practice deserve brief notice here. In the realm of *musica speculativa,* for example, Theinred of Dover's theory of species is a novel theoretical justification of chromatically altered tones. An unorthodox Guidonian Greater Perfect System that amalgamates modern musical systems with those of antiquity is advocated by Roger Caperon in his *Commentum super cantum* (a work most likely of the 13th century but possibly from the 15th), which attracted the attention of the later 15th-century Spanish theorist Ramos da Pareia. A greater tolerance of the third and sixth as consonances than is countenanced by mainstream theory can be discerned in the works of Theinred, Anonymous IV, and Walter Odington; it is also a point made about the English in the *Musica* (1357) of the Dutch priest and music theorist Johannes Boen (d. 1367), who had attended Oxford around the middle of the century.

Concerning musical notation the *Regule* (1326) of Robertus de Handlo and the *Summa* of Johannes Hanboys (ca. 1370) together provide a detailed picture of the evolution from the Ars Antiqua to the Ars Nova both in England and on the Continent, with information on distinctive insular notational practices and the contributions of other English authorities, including Robertus de Brunham, Robertus Trowell, and W. de Doncastre. Hanboys may have worked within the circle of an elite company of musicians named in the motet *Sub arturo plebs* who served Edward III and the Black Prince in the middle years of the century. Insular treatises of the late 14th and 15th centuries in Latin and Middle English discuss distinctive local techniques for improvised counterpoint—discant and faburden—according to the doctrine of "sights"; this kind of counterpoint is also the subject of passages in the *De preceptis artis musicae* of the later 15th-century Italian theorist Guillelmus Monachus headed "Ad habendum . . . cognitionem modi Anglicorum" and "Incipiunt regulae contrapuncti anglicorum." As a last tantalizing example of *musica practica* we can cite a 15th-century index to the manuscript BL Royal 12.C.vi that lists a now lost treatise, *De modo componendi rotam versatilem,* which evidently described the means of construction of the extraordinary early-14th-century English voice-exchange motet *Rota versatilis,* a work that itself survives only in fragments.

Writings on music were not solely the provenance of professional musicians. Music was a topic of discussion in other related disciplines and sciences, as in the works of Robert Grosseteste, Roger Bacon, and Robert Kilwardby. It is surveyed, too, by the encyclopedist Bartholomaeus Anglicus.

Peter M. Lefferts

Bibliography

There is need for a comprehensive monograph on medieval English music; the standard work, Harrison's *Music in Medieval Britain,* is by now out of date, due in no small part to later specialized research by Harrison himself. No current textbook surveying the music of the Middle Ages deals adequately with the topic. The best available treatment at length is by Caldwell (1991), who devotes over 200 pages to the period before 1450, with many music examples and an emphasis on musical style; for reliable shorter, chapter-length surveys for the general reader see Lefferts (1990) and the essays by Sandon and Page (1988).

HISTORY
Caldwell, John. *The Oxford History of English Music*. Vol. 1:
    From the Beginnings to c. 1715. Oxford: Clarendon,
    1991; Harrison, Frank Ll. *Music in Medieval Britain*.
    2d ed. London: Routledge & Kegan Paul, 1963;
    Hughes, Andrew. "The British Isles." In *Medieval Mu-
    sic: The Sixth Liberal Art*. Toronto Medieval Bibliogra-
    phies 4. Rev. ed. Toronto: University of Toronto Press,
    1980; Lefferts, Peter M. "Medieval England, 950–
    1450." In *Music and Society*. Vol. 1: *Antiquity and the
    Middle Ages: From Ancient Greece to the Fifteenth Cen-
    tury*, ed. James McKinnon. Englewood Cliffs: Prentice
    Hall, 1990, pp. 170–96; Page, Christopher. "Music."
    In *The Cambridge Guide to the Arts in Britain*. Vol. 1:
    Prehistoric, Roman, and Early Medieval, ed. Boris Ford.
    Cambridge: Cambridge University Press, 1988, pp.
    247–53, 294–95 [includes bibliography]; Remnant,
    Mary. *Early English Bowed Instruments from Anglo-
    Saxon to Tudor Times*. Oxford: Clarendon, 1987;
    Sanders, Ernest H. "England: From the Beginnings to
    c. 1540." In *Music from the Middle Ages to the Renais-
    sance*, ed. Frederick W. Sternfeld. New York: Praeger,
    1973, pp. 255–313; Sandon, Nick, and Christopher
    Page. "Music." In *The Cambridge Guide to the Arts in
    Britain*. Vol. 2: *The Middle Ages*, ed. Boris Ford. Cam-
    bridge: Cambridge University Press, 1988, pp. 215–
    50, 279–81 [includes bibliography and discography].

THEORY
For the treatises and contributions of most English theorists
    see entries in the *New Grove Dictionary of Music and
    Musicians* (1980); Hughes, Andrew. "The British Isles."
    In *Medieval Music: The Sixth Liberal Art*. Toronto Medi-
    eval Bibliographies 4. Rev. ed. Toronto: University of
    Toronto Press, 1980; Moyer, Ann E. *Musica Scientia*.
    Ithaca: Cornell University Press, 1992; Palisca, Claude.
    "Theory, theorists." *NGD* 18:741–62.

See also Antiphon; Choirs; Dance; Discant; Faburden; Hymns;
Liturgy; Liturgy and Church Music, History of; Manuscripts
of Polyphonic Music; Mass, Polyphonic Music for; Minstrels;
Motet; Musical Instruments; Notation of Plainsong; Notation
of Polyphonic Music; Sarum, Use of; Sequence; Songs; Square;
Sub arturo plebs; Trope

Musical Instruments

Literary and iconographic evidence testifies to the use of
musical instruments for a wide variety of functions both public and private during the Middle Ages. They accompanied the
telling of tales and the recitation of poetry; announced important people and events; provided music for singing, dancing,
and dining, enlivening large banquets and small gatherings;
added pomp to official ceremonies; accompanied armies into
battle; and served during sacred church services and private
devotion.

It is not possible to discuss musical instruments in medieval England as essentially different from those used on the
Continent during the same period; most of them were in use
broadly throughout Europe. But the various geographical
areas did differ somewhat in their preference for certain instruments, and there are several variants that can be identified as
particular to the British Isles. The number of different shapes,
sizes, and sound colors of musical instruments during the
Middle Ages was large—the result of the combination of
numerous cultural influences from all over the known world
and a lack of interest in standardizing many of the types of
instruments. Indeed, although certain of the ceremonial instruments do show signs of uniformity, paintings and sculptures from the period provide ample evidence that instrument
makers delighted in the variety of designs for the minor—and
sometimes major—features of the bowed and plucked instruments.

In order to discuss instruments here it is useful to refer
to them in terms of "families"—plucked strings, woodwinds,
etc.—even though that type of classification is from a later
period. People of the Middle Ages thought of the instruments
as belonging to two basic groups according to volume: *haut*
and *bas,* or, as Chaucer referred to them, "loude and soft
minstralcye." Those instruments with loud or shrill sound,
haut, were considered separate from those whose sound was
soft, *bas,* and it was in these groups that they were played.
Various combinations were possible within each group, but at
no point would the instruments of one of these groups perform in the company of the other. In general the loud instruments were those used out of doors, with the military, or for
those festive occasions where loud sounds added to the excitement, such as weddings, tournaments, or large feasts. In this
group were the trumpets (both folded and straight), drums
called nakers (a pair of small kettledrums that usually hung
from the waist) and tabors (large field drums), bagpipes (often called cornemuse), cymbals, and the double-reed instruments known as shawms or shalmyes (predecessor of the
modern oboe). The soft instruments were those that would
generally accompany songs—a large variety of bowed and
plucked instruments, the softer-sounding woodwinds, key-
boards, and the voice itself.

The loud instruments were played individually on some
occasions, but they are more often found in groups. Trumpets
and shawms were often played in pairs, but groups of four or
six were not unusual, and on some extraordinary ceremonial
occasions the chroniclers record dozens. They were found
grouped in ensembles of similar instruments or mixed together.
Chaucer describes one such gathering in *The House of Fame:*

> Many thousand tymes twelve,
> That maden lowde mynstralcies
> In cornemuse and shalemyes,
> And many other maner pipe.   1216–19

A similar group, including drums, accompanies a battle scene
in the *Knight's Tale:*

> Pypes, trompes, nakers, clariounes,
> That in the bataille blowen blody sounes.   2511–12

Another reference to the same instruments is found in a ballad about defeat of the Scots at Halidon Hill in 1333:

This was don with merrie sowne
With pipis, trompes and tabers thereto
And loude clarionis thei blew also.

And at the vigil in the abbey church of Westminster preceding the feast for the knighting of Edward of Carnarvon, Prince of Wales, on 22 May 1306, the monks were unable to hear the singing of the Jubilatio from one side of the choir to the other because of the sound outside caused by trumpets and people shouting.

The scenes quoted above depict the loud instruments performing a function that we would not consider actually "musical"; it would be better described as noise making (even though the ballad describes it as a "merry sound"). But this was definitely one of the functions of these musical instruments during the Middle Ages, and one that they still perform to some extent. Their use in the military included signals by individual trumpets and drums to coordinate movements of the soldiers during battle and large group performance for the purpose of rallying and inspiring the troops to charge the enemy and at the same time as an attempt to frighten their opponents. But these same instruments had far more potential than simply making noise—the shawms and bagpipes could play the entire musical scale, and the trumpets and drums were capable of sophisticated fanfares and musical sounds when not being used in this manner. We know of the shawms and bagpipes as commonly used as instruments for dance music and to provide general musical background on festive occasions, including civic celebrations and private weddings. On these occasions they were played either alone or in ensembles of two or three.

The 10th-century mention of "reodpipere" in the supplement to Ælfric's *Saxon Vocabulary* is the earliest literary reference we have to instruments that employ a reed, although it is not clear whether this refers to a shawm or a bagpipe—or to both. Manuscript illuminations depict both instruments in northern Europe by the late 9th century and document their continued use from that time. Throughout Europe both instruments kept their associations with festive music making and military functions during the late Middle Ages. Bagpipes were particularly popular in the British Isles, especially their use in large numbers with the military.

Shawms and trumpets also served as signal instruments in civic situations. They were played by watchmen from the towers and at the gates of towns and castles and were known as "waits." By the 15th century this duty had been expanded to include nocturnal street patrols and became exclusively the duty of shawm players; the instrument they played was so closely identified with this function in England that often it was referred to as a "wait pipe." The signaling cannot be thought of as musical, but the duties of these players eventually included the performance of music on social and formal occasions, and so at some point the positions were filled by people with musical ability. Sometime in the late 15th

century a trombone was added to the waits ensemble, and by the middle of the 16th century in England (several decades earlier on the Continent) the civic waits are known to have performed both publicly and privately for dancing and other types of entertainment, eventually adding to their abilities the performance on a number of the soft instruments and even singing.

As the duties of waits became more and more the responsibility of shawm players in the late Middle Ages, the trumpeters' role became that of serving as symbols of civic authority, announcing the comings and goings of rulers when they acted in an official capacity. The trumpets were adorned with banners that displayed the emblem of their employers, and the repertoire was a set of sophisticated fanfarelike calls. As late as the 16th century the two groups of instruments, shawms and trumpets, were still combined for special ceremonial occasions, such as the one recorded for the visit of Cardinal Wolsey to St. Paul's in 1527, where "the Lord Cardinall began Te Deum the which was solemnlie songen with the King's trumpetts and shalmes as well Inglish men as Venetians."

The soft instruments served for all other occasions. The most popular of these, especially in the British Isles, were the instruments of the harp family that were the favorite instrument of the nobles and minstrels. At the 1306 knighting of the Prince of Wales, for example, among the hundreds of minstrels recorded as present, players of the harp-type instruments outnumber all others. St. Dunstan (ca. 910–988) is referred to as a harper, and in *Apollonius of Tyre,* from the mid-11th century, a woman accompanies her voice with a harp: "Then she sent out and ordered her harp to be fetched; and as soon as she began to harp she mingled the harp's sound and her pleasing voice together."

The importance of the harp in the early Middle Ages and its place as a treasured possession are attested to by the fact that the remains of instruments of this family have been found in several graves from the 7th and 8th centuries, including that at Sutton Hoo. The 7th-century poem *Widsith* describes a singer of heroic songs as singing to the harp: "Thonne wit Scilling sciran reorde / for uncrum sigedryhtne song ahofan, / hlude bi hearpan hleothor swinsade" ("When Scilling and I with clear voice raised the song before our victorious lord—loud to the harp the song made music.") And *Beowulf* also records a harp in a scene that includes singing and storytelling: "There was singing and merriment. An aged Scylding of great experience told tales of long ago. At times one bold in battle drew sweetness from the harp, the joywood; at times one wrought a measure true and sad; at times the large-hearted king told a wondrous story in fitting fashion."

In all of the above quotes the word "harp" is used, but contemporary reference is also found to "lyre" as interchangeable. Both instruments were performed in the same manner, plucked with fingers, but distinction is made in the later centuries between the two instruments according to shape (lyres are rectangular, meaning that all the strings are the same length; harps are triangular, allowing for strings of different lengths), and number of strings (lyres have five to eight; early harps have the same number but grow to 24 or 25 by the end of the 14th century). In the earlier centuries, however, literary references do not always make a distinction (e.g., describing someone who "harpes with his lyre"), and in literature and iconographic representations they would appear to serve identical functions: accompaniment to singing and reciting, and music for dancing. In Ireland, Scotland, and Wales the harp/lyre was also often referred to as a "cruit" (crot, crwth) or "rote" (hrotta, rotta, rotte), words that sometimes were applied indiscriminately to all bowed and plucked instruments. Chaucer says of the Friar:

> Wel koude he synge and pleyen on a rote;. . .
> And in his harpyng, whan that he hadde songe,
> His eyen twynkled in his heed aryght
> As doon the sterres in the frosty nyght   GP 236, 266–68

In common use in the British Isles beginning sometime after the 10th century were instruments plucked with a quill or plectrum that were called gittern, mandore, citole, lute— all versions of fretted plucked instruments having different shapes, string material (wire or gut), and resonance chambers but serving the same function as those of the harp family— song accompaniment and dance. All of them are found in a variety of secular situations, although the gittern is more frequently associated with ribald singing in taverns or barbershops.

From approximately the same time we know of the psaltery and dulcimer, instruments resembling a modern zither and descending from the Arabic *q'nun,* with strings (eight to 24) stretched across a soundbox and either plucked with fingers or plectrum (psaltery) or hammered with wooden sticks (dulcimer). The best-known reference to the psaltery is Chaucer's poor scholar Nicholas, who employed it for private devotion:

> And al above ther lay a gay sautrie,
> On which he made a-nyghtes melodie
> So swetely that all the chambre rong;
> And Angelus ad virginem he song.   MilT 3213–16

The bowed strings include large and small instruments with flat or rounded sides, flat or rounded backs, with and without fingerboard and frets, and having from three to five strings, variously named crowd (Welsh *crwth*), rebec (rubebe, ribible), and fiddle. The earliest known references are from the 11th century, and several versions are depicted in the 14th-century nave carvings in Beverley Minster, Yorkshire (along with many of the other instruments named above and below). In Chaucer's *Miller's Tale*, Absolon, the parish clerk, plays both rebec and gittern, one while dancing, the other when visiting alehouses:

> In twenty manere koude he trippe and daunce
> After the scole of Oxenforde tho,
> And with his legges casten to and fro,
> And pleyen songes on a smal rubible;

> Therto he song som tyme a loud quynyble;
> And as wel koude he pleye on a giterne.
> In al the toun nas brewhous ne taverne
> That he ne visited with his solas.   3328–35

By the late 15th century the viol family, a set of treble, tenor, and bass bowed instruments with frets and six strings, was introduced into the British Isles, and during the 16th century the viol became a favorite instrument for ensemble performance. It was one of the favorite instruments of Henry VIII, and beginning in his reign there developed a large and sophisticated repertoire of music for viol consorts (sets of three to six instruments) written by English composers.

Soft wind instruments included the recorder, often referred to as a flute, known in the British Isles from as early as the 12th century. It is frequently associated with dance music in literature and iconography but was adaptable to all types of secular music and is often depicted with a variety of other soft instruments. During the Middle Ages only instruments of approximately the alto range are found, but during the late 15th century both larger and smaller sizes were developed. The transverse flute is also seen in early paintings, occasionally with the military, but it does not seem to have been as popular as the recorder for music making until the 16th century. A one-handed pipe, played along with a small tabor, is also found from the same period. This is almost always found in association with dance music and usually in solo performance.

Organs are known in England from as early as the 10th century in conjunction with the church. According to the description by the monk Wulstan (d. 963), Bishop Elphege of Winchester built an enormous organ that had 400 pipes and needed 70 blowers and two players. Until the end of the 14th century the principal purpose of organs was to supply loud sound at the appropriate places in church services; their use after that time in conjunction with singing was to alternate with the choir, not accompaniment, a function that organs did not assume until the late 15th century. According to the Chronicle of St. Albans, during the 1396 reception of Abbot John Moote the Te Deum was solemnly sung by the community with "the organ alternating." A small portable instrument (called a portative organ), playable by a single person who would finger the keys with one hand and pump a small bellows with the other, is known from as early as the 14th century. It served for both private devotion and for secular music and is often depicted in the company of other soft instruments as part of a small ensemble of three or four performers, usually including a singer.

A keyboard instrument called the echiquier, which may have employed the clavichord mechanism of striking the strings, or the harpsichord device of plucking strings, is known in English records from as early as the late 14th century, although the reference is not clear. Clavichords and harpsichords grew in popularity in England especially during the 16th century. Because of its extremely soft sound the clavichord was useful only for solo performance, but the harpsichord was popular as a solo or ensemble instrument and became one of the principal instruments both for private and public music making. Various shapes of the harpsichord (triangular or rectangular) were referred to as virginal or spinet.

The popularity of many of the musical instruments changed during the late Middle Ages as the general taste for music changed more and more in the direction of polyphonic music (music in several parts). Certain of the instruments were best suited for monophonic performance (melody only), and those lost popularity with the musically educated population and were relegated more or less to music of the lower classes (e.g., the bagpipe and certain members of the plucked and bowed string families that were not adaptable for polyphonic performance). Other instruments were modified to fit the requirements of the new repertoire (e.g., lute, harp), and new sets and sizes of instruments with larger ranges were developed (e.g., the viol, violin, and lute families). Instruments that could play multiple lines, such as organ, harpsichord, and lute became the most useful of all for the upper classes, who were captivated by composed polyphony to the near exclusion of most of the earlier type of repertoire and the instruments that traditionally played it.

Timothy J. McGee

Bibliography

Bullock-Davies, Constance. *Menestrellorum Multitudo: Minstrels at a Royal Feast.* Cardiff: University of Wales Press, 1978; Galpin, Francis W. *Old English Instruments of Music.* 4th ed. Rev. Thurston Dart. London: Methuen, 1965; Godwin, Joscelyn. "'Main divers acors': Some Instrument Collections of the Ars Nova Period." *Early Music* 5 (1977): 148–59; Harrison, Frank Ll. *Music in Medieval Britain.* 2d ed. London: Routledge & Kegan Paul, 1963; McGee, Timothy J. *Medieval and Renaissance Music: A Performer's Guide.* Toronto: University of Toronto Press, 1985, ch. 4; Montagu, Jeremy. *The World of Medieval and Renaissance Musical Instruments.* Newton Abbot: David & Charles, 1976; Rastall, Richard. "The Minstrels of the English Royal Households, 25 Edward I–1 Henry VIII: An Inventory." *Royal Musical Association Research Chronicle* 4 (1967): 1–41; Wilkins, Nigel E. *Music in the Age of Chaucer.* Cambridge: Brewer, 1979.

See also Coronation Ceremony; Dance; Drama, Vernacular, Role of Music in; Karole; Minstrels; Organ; Processions; Waits

Mystical and Devotional Writings, Middle English

The terms "mysticism," "contemplation," and "devotion" are difficult to distinguish, in part for theological and in part for social and cultural reasons. Within the Christian tradition all three terms refer to a set of exercises and phenomena that are fundamentally related in that they all derive from a single act of the individual human will to conform itself as fully as possible to the divine—an act of will that, whatever its resultant gifts (visions, revelations, sensual warmth, etc.), derives from a single special grace of God. In the following discussion,

however, we will distinguish between mysticism, as the exercise and experience of conformity with the Godhead directly, and devotion, as the exercise and experience of conformity with the will of God as manifested in the humanity of Christ or in the lives of the saints. The term "contemplation" will refer to the activity by which one seeks to attain this conformity, rather than the experience itself; this activity may be either mystical or devotional in its immediate end.

To understand the kinds of mystical and devotional writing found in ME it is important to set that writing within the contemplative tradition of western medieval Christianity. In that tradition a number of modes or genres of contemplative literature can be distinguished, varying according to their method or focus. The first of these is the monastic mode of contemplation, based on the verbal association of scriptural texts. A second mode, employed most prominently by Anselm of Canterbury (1033–1109) and his followers, may be characterized as "Isidorean" or rhetorical. The third major mode, usually characterized as "Franciscan," employs the powers of the imagination to recreate the events of the life of Christ and the saints. A fourth mode or genre, deriving in some ways from the third, consists of visions and revelations of Jesus, Mary, and the saints. Works in this genre were often, although not exclusively, written by women, as were two related genres: collections of the lives of contemporary holy women and didactic visions centered on a female personification of Love, or *Minne* (the last three genres were all more common on the Continent than in England). A seventh contemplative genre comprises works of introspective meditation; and an eighth, works in the negative, "Dionysian" school of mysticism.

The most important form of contemplation in the early Middle Ages was the tradition of "rumination" on the text of the Bible, a tradition that developed within Benedictine monasticism. The sources of this tradition lie both in the patristic tradition of commentary on scripture and in the liturgical chanting of the biblical text enjoined by the Benedictine Rule upon the monastic communities as "the work of God" (*opus Dei*). This gave rise to the exercise of "reading, meditation, and prayer" that dominates monastic contemplative literature. As Jean Leclercq has pointed out, the fact that reading was normally a physical or communal activity in the Middle Ages (reading was normally done aloud, or at least subvocalized, but almost never in total silence) meant that the common description of meditative reading as the "rumination" or "chewing" of scripture was more literally grounded than we often realize. Further, the constant reinforcement of the verbal memory of the scriptural text by liturgical practice and rumination resulted in the mental association of texts clustered around similar key words and phrases. It is from this tradition that the practice of commenting on the "four senses" of scripture (literal, historical, allegorical, and anagogical) derived.

Although it occurs relatively late in the medieval monastic tradition, the best-known and most striking example of this contemplative exercise may be found in the *Sermons on the Song of Songs* by Bernard of Clairvaux (1090/91–1153). There are no true examples of this form of contemplation in English literature in the Middle Ages, although what is often termed "biblical *imitatio*" in the Latin works of Richard Rolle (d. 1349) derives at least in part from it. The primary reason for this lack is that monastic contemplation depended on the words of the Vulgate Bible, so that many verbal associations that seem appropriate in Latin simply do not work in the vernacular. In fact one argument against the translation of the Bible into the vernacular is that it would render this entire tradition of scriptural contemplation and commentary invalid.

A second important tradition in contemplative writing in the early and high Middle Ages is that which we have here termed "Isidorean." The definition comes from a passage of the *Parisiana poetria* of John of Garland (ca. 1195–ca. 1272), where he defines the "four curial styles" of prose writing. According to John the "Isidorean style" features balanced clauses with similar, usually rhyming, endings; they appear to have equal numbers of syllables, although they may not in fact. The effect is a nearly chantlike cadence of repetitive short clauses. The *Soliloquies* of Augustine of Hippo (354–430) are, as John notes, the primary example of this form of contemplative writing in the western European tradition; Augustine also employs the style in the *Confessions.* Isidore of Seville (ca. 560–636) used this style in his *Synonyma* (whence John of Garland derived its name); but its most influential practitioner was Anselm of Canterbury. Through the Latin meditations of Anselm and those associated with his name, the Isidorean tradition of meditative writing was introduced to England. The early-13th-century English *Wooing of Our Lord* and its cognate tracts are written in this style, as is the later *Talking of the Love of God,* which derives in part from two of the tracts of the "Wooing Group." In his introduction the author-compiler of the *Talking* quotes (without acknowledgment) from Anselm's letter sending a copy of his meditations to Countess Matilda, thus suggesting his awareness of the source of his own type of meditational writing. Richard Rolle's tendency to rhetorical repetition and alliteration (particularly in his Latin work, the *Melos amoris*) may also derive in part from this tradition, but his use of it is idiosyncratic.

The third contemplative mode, in which the subject imagines himself or herself actually present at the great events of the life of Christ, also grew up within the monastic setting. In his *Sermons on the Song of Songs* Bernard of Clairvaux describes such contemplation as the "carnal" love of the humanity of Christ: a kind of love that is lower than the "spiritual" love of his divinity or of the Godhead itself. For Bernard and other monastic writers this mode of contemplation is enjoined upon "carnal-minded" men, and upon novices who were only recently converted from the world. Women religious were usually considered the spiritual equivalent of such "carnal-minded" men, or of novices—and meditation on the life of Christ was the usual exercise prescribed in treatises written for the spiritual guidance of women. A particularly important example in England was the 12th-century Aelred of Rievaulx's *Rule of Life for a Recluse,* which was twice translated into ME, and drawn upon by the author of the *Ancrene Wisse* (ca. 1215–22). Aelred's *Rule,* originally written for his sister, describes three kinds of meditation: on things past, things present, and things to come. The "meditation on things past" incorporates

a set of imaginative exercises based on the events of the Gospel story.

This form of meditation became particularly prominent in the later Middle Ages because of its adoption by Francis of Assisi (1182?–1226) and his followers. The imaginative, verbal, and representational recreation of the scene of Christ's birth in Bethlehem or of his Passion and death (as in the Christmas crèche or Francis's vision of the crucified Christ when he received the stigmata) figures prominently in Francis's personal spirituality, as well as in the sermons and treatises by or attributed to him and his followers. The two most important works in this tradition, both anonymous although commonly attributed to St. Bonaventure (1221–1274), were the 13th-century *Stimulus amoris* and the early-14th-century *Meditationes vitae Christi.* Both of these works were translated into ME: the former as *The Pricking of Love,* attributed to Walter Hilton (d. 1396); the latter as Nicholas Love's *Mirror of the Blessed Life of Jesus Christ* (ca. 1410). The primary impetus of Franciscan spirituality in England in the Middle Ages seems, however, not to have been in the translation of the major Franciscan texts into English (in which the order itself appears to have played virtually no role) but in the incorporation of the Franciscan form of meditation into the English lyric. It is unclear whether the prominence of affective lyrics representing the birth and the passion of Jesus was due entirely to the influence of the Franciscan order. It may also have resulted from the confluence of Franciscan spirituality and native English devotional traditions or be at least partly derived from the importance of Franciscan-style meditations in the experiences and widely circulated writings of Richard Rolle.

The highest point of the Franciscan type of contemplation is reached when the subject, no longer consciously focusing the imagination on the Gospel story, is granted the spiritual vision of Christ, Mary, or the saints and angels. Descriptions of this type of visionary experience had existed before the Franciscan movement (as in the revelations of the 12th-century seer Hildegard of Bingen); but they become particularly prominent among women in the 13th and 14th centuries. In these writings, too, the latent eroticism of the allegorized Song of Songs, interpreted as the description of the contemplative's union with God (see Bernard's sermons), often transforms itself into the marriage of Christ and his bride. These collections of revelations were often not written by the subjects themselves but dictated (often in the vernacular) to religious sisters or spiritual advisers who wrote them down and translated them into Latin.

Many of these revelations are intensely personal documents; many are devoted to filling in details of the lives of Jesus and Mary that the Gospels had not mentioned; and many, equally, were of great public importance, both politically and culturally. By invoking the authority of their visions Catherine of Siena (1347–1380) and Birgitta (Bridget) of Sweden (1303–1373), in particular, played an important role in returning the papacy to Rome from Avignon in the late 14th century. Both Birgitta's *Revelations* and Catherine's *Dialogue* were translated into ME: the latter as the *Orchard of Sion,* made for the nuns of the only English house of the order founded by Birgitta. A similar collection of revelations translated into English in the early 15th century was the *Book of Ghostly Grace* of Mechtild of Hackeborn. Two original ME works were also written in this genre: the late-14th-century *Revelations* of Julian of Norwich and *The Book of Margery Kempe* (ca. 1438).

The collections of revelations of late-medieval women visionaries were often at least semiautobiographical in nature (as with Julian and Margery) or included biographical sections written by others. On the Continent lives of visionary nuns and women saints were also collected in this period: *The Book of Margery Kempe* may in fact more closely resemble this genre, although its length is more like that of the greater collections of revelations. Three lives of 13th-century Rhineland mystics (Elizabeth of Spalbeek, Christina Mirabilis, and Mary of Oignies), together with a life of Catherine of Siena by her contemporary Stephen of Siena, were also translated together into ME. These two genres of visionary literature (revelations and lives) do not seem to have been prominent in England, since none survives in more than a single medieval manuscript, although Julian of Norwich's *Revelations* is found in a few postmedieval manuscripts and Margery Kempe's *Book* appears in an early printed extract.

A related genre of medieval visionary literature comprises the works of what is called "Love-" or "*Minne*-mysticism," often written by beguines (members of irregular communities of women, as opposed to the traditional women's religious orders). The primary works in this tradition were the letters and poems of Hadewijch of Brabant (fl. second quarter of the 13th century), the *Mirouer des simples âmes (Mirror of Simple Souls)* of Marguerite Porete (d. 1310), and the revelations of Mechtild of Magdeburg (ca. 1212–1282?). The devotion of these writers is focused on Love itself, conceived as a feminine personification. There seems to have been almost no interest in this kind of mysticism in England: Marguerite's *Mirouer* was the only work of this genre translated into ME, and even it circulated only in a single translation, with explanatory additions to defuse its "dangerous" teachings, apparently only among the theologically sophisticated 15th-century Carthusians.

Two final genres of contemplative literature in the Middle Ages were primarily didactic in aim—advising readers who were dedicated to the life of devotion or mystical growth rather than recording the experiences of the authors. The first of these emphasizes moral and psychological introspection and is related to the "meditation on things present" in Aelred's *Rule;* like that *Rule* works in this tradition tended to be written for nuns or women recluses. Because of this audience most of the works in this genre were written in the vernacular rather than Latin. The most important continental writers of this tradition were the 13th- and 14th-century mystics Meister Eckhart, Johannes Tauler, and Heinrich Suso (all German Dominicans) and Jan van Ruusbroec: Suso's *Horologium* and Ruusbroec's *Geestelijke Bruilocht* were extracted in the ME *Seven Points of True Love and Everlasting Wisdom* and *The Chastising of God's Children;* Ruusbroec's *Van den blinckenden Steen* was translated as *The Treatise of Perfection of the Sons of*

God. The most important ME works in this genre are those of Walter Hilton.

The second specifically didactic genre of contemplative writings in the Middle Ages comprises the tradition of the Pseudo-Dionysius. We do not know the actual identity of the writer (presumably a late-4th- or 5th-century Syrian) who identified himself as the "Dionysius the Areopagite" of Acts 17:22–34, but the tracts that bear his name are the *locus classicus* of the "negative way" of mysticism in the western tradition. This form of mysticism began from the observation of the ultimate unknowability of God and proceeded by denying the use of the human imagination or intellect in contemplation. The will alone could find unity with God, in love. Among the most important works in this genre were those of the anonymous late-14th-century English author of *The Cloud of Unknowing,* also known for his translations of the *Mystica theologia (Deonise Hid Diuinite)* of the Pseudo-Dionysius and the *Benjamin minor* of Richard of St. Victor (d. 1173), among other works.

Except for a few of Rolle's Latin and English works, Hilton's English works, and the ME translations of Pseudo-Bonaventure, Suso, and (to a lesser extent) Ruusbroec mystical literature does not seem to have achieved any real popularity in late-medieval England. Rolle does appear to have significantly influenced the course of both religious and popular devotion in the 14th and 15th centuries. The relative popularity of Hilton, of the Pseudo-Bonaventuran *Stimulus amoris* and Nicholas Love's *Mirror,* and of the extracted versions of Suso and Ruusbroec seems rather to have been the result of 15th-century London burghers adopting works originally written for more religious, contemplative audiences as appropriate for their own devotional life. Few English mystical or devotional writers had any influence outside of England: a number of Rolle's Latin writings circulated on the Continent; Hilton's *Scale of Perfection* survives in a contemporary Latin translation in a few late-medieval manuscripts belonging to continental Carthusian houses; the *Cloud* was twice translated into Latin (once by an English Carthusian) but appears to have been unknown on the Continent. But this is the norm for vernacular writing: besides Hilton's *Scale* the only piece of ME literature that we know reached the Continent is John Gower's *Confessio Amantis,* which survives in a single copy of a Spanish translation.

Michael G. Sargent

Bibliography

PRIMARY

For works and authors with their own entries in this volume see the bibliographies under those entries; Aelred of Rievaulx. *De institutione inclusarum: Two English Versions.* Ed. John Ayto and Alexandra Barratt. EETS o.s. 287. London: Oxford University Press, 1984; Birgitta of Sweden. *The Revelations of St. Birgitta.* Ed. William Patterson Cumming. EETS o.s. 178. London: Humphrey Milford, 1929; Birgitta of Sweden. *The Liber celestis of St. Bridget of Sweden.* Ed. Roger Ellis. EETS o.s. 291. Oxford: Oxford University Press, 1987;

Catherine of Siena. *The Orcherd of Syon.* Ed. Phyllis Hodgson and Gabriel M. Liegey. EETS o.s. 258. London: Oxford University Press, 1966; Horstmann, Karl, ed. "Prosalegenden: Die Legenden des MS. Douce 114." *Anglia* 8 (1885): 102–96 [lives of Elizabeth of Spalbeek, Christina Mirabilis, Mary of Oignies, and Catherine of Siena]; Mechtild of Hackeborn. *The Booke of Gostlye Grace.* Ed. Theresa A. Halligan. Toronto: Pontifical Institute, 1979; Porete, Marguerite. "*The Mirror of Simple Souls:* A Middle English Translation." Ed. Marilyn Doiron. *Archivio italiano per la storia della pietà* 5 (1968): 243–382; Suso, Henry. "*Orologium Sapientiae,* or *The Seven Poyntes of Trewe Wisdom.*" Ed. Karl Horstmann. *Anglia* 10 (1888): 323–89; *A Talkyng of þe Love of God.* Ed. Cecilia M. Westra. The Hague: Nijhoff, 1950; [van Ruusbroec, Jan]. *The Chastising of God's Children and the Treatise of Perfection of the Sons of God.* Ed. Joyce Bazire and Eric Colledge. Oxford: Blackwell, 1957; *þe Wohunge of Ure Lauerd.* Ed. W. Meredith Thompson. EETS o.s. 241. London: Oxford University Press, 1958.

SECONDARY

Manual 9:3049–3137, 3405–71; Edwards, A.S.G., ed. *Middle English Prose: A Critical Guide to Major Authors and Genres.* New Brunswick: Rutgers University Press, 1984, pp. 1–119, 147–75 [chapters on *Ancrene Wisse* and the Katherine and *Wohunge* groups, Rolle, the *Cloud*-author and Hilton, Love, Julian of Norwich, Margery Kempe, and minor devotional writings]; Knowles, David. *The English Mystical Tradition.* London: Burns & Oates, 1961; Knowlton, Mary Arthur. *The Influence of Richard Rolle and of Julian of Norwich on the Middle English Lyrics.* The Hague: Mouton, 1973; Leclercq, Jean. *The Love of Learning and the Desire for God.* Trans. Catharine Misrahi. New York: Fordham University Press, 1961; Robertson, Elizabeth. *Early English Devotional Prose and the Female Audience.* Knoxville: University of Tennessee Press, 1990; Szarmach, Paul E. *An Introduction to the Medieval Mystics of Europe.* Albany: SUNY Press, 1984; Walsh, James, ed. *Pre-Reformation English Spirituality.* New York: Fordham University Press, 1965.

See also Ancrene Wisse; Anselm; *Ars moriendi;* Books of Hours; *Cloud of Unknowing;* Fathers of the Church (Augustine); Hagiography; Hilton; Julian of Norwich; Katherine Group; Kempe; Love; Lyrics; Moral and Religious Instruction; Popular Religion; Prose, ME; Rolle; Women in ME Literature

Names

Personal Names

The OE personal-name system not only lacked familial surnames but involved a baptismal-name stock virtually unrelated to the modern English one.

As among all Germanic people each individual bore a single distinctive name, or "idionym." Idionyms were formed chiefly by the paired permutation of conventional elements or "themes," carrying "heroic" meanings; gender was marked by specialization of second-element or "deuterothemes" (e.g., masc. *Æthelwulf, Leofgar;* fem. *Leofgifu, Wulfflæd*). Family connection might be underlined by theme repetition (e.g., Wulfstan, son of Æthelstan and Wulfgifu). Alternative styles included "monothematic" names based on single themes, "short forms" based on simplified stems, and descriptive forms or "original nicknames."

From the 870s a further name stock was introduced by the Vikings in the north and east. This stock, although related to the OE one, differed not only through operation of the standard sound changes but also through the favoring of different themes (e.g., *Ketil-/-ketill*) and of nickname formation. Soon many families were using OE and Anglo-Scandinavian (AS) forms side by side. A few Continental West Germanic (CWG) names were also adopted, fruits of ecclesiastical and mercantile contacts. Yet, despite so ample a name vocabulary, by the late 11th century much repetition had set in with disproportionate reliance on a few items.

Within a generation of the Norman Conquest baptismal names characteristic of the continental settlers were appearing among the native English. Within 200 years these had all but ousted the older names, constituting a stock almost that of modern English. This consisted mainly of CWG forms, etymologically similar to OE ones, in addition to names taken from biblical characters and saints, both sorts often being adopted in gallicized forms (e.g., *Aubri* < CWG *Alberic* = OE *Ælfric; Maud* < Old French *Mahaut* < CWG *Mahthildis; Adam, Isabel* = *Elizabeth*). Again, as on the Continent, certain items became disproportionately favored, notably *John* and

William. Variety was maintained by recourse to diminutives, some native, some from French or Flemish.

The crucial change taking place during the Middle English (ME) period was the development of familial surnames. In OE usage an idionym was occasionally supplemented by a descriptive phrase or "by-name," usually postposed, but only when distinction was needed between individuals identically named. Such by-names fall into four categories: familial ("son of X," "widow of X"), local ("from Winchester," "beside the well"), occupational ("the dairymaid," "the smith"), and characteristic ("the red-haired," "the stammerer").

As certain baptismal names became disproportionately favored, so by-naming spread. In promoting its use administrative needs were backed by the example of the immigrant nobility, most of whom had from the start sported by-names. Although first used mainly for identifying individuals, by-names soon passed from father to heir and thus, by degrees, evolved into set hereditary family names. Although this process was under way in the 12th century, it was completed, throughout the country, only in the 17th century.

Medieval by-names therefore survive as modern surnames. Furthermore, except for a few items (e.g., *Edith, Edward*) retaining currency as baptismal names, the only guise in which OE and AS idionyms are preserved is as originally patronymic or matronymic surnames (e.g., *Arkell* < AS *Arnke[ti]ll; Gunnell* < AS fem. *Gunnild; Wooldridge* < OE *Wulfric;* and so on).

Place-Names

The history of English place-naming begins with the Germanic settlement of southern Britain, ca. 450. Names and name elements that the settlers took over from the partly romanized Britons referred to Roman cities (e.g., *Winchester* < OE *Wintanceaster* < Romano-British *Venta [Belgarum]*); others to rivers and other natural features (e.g., *Avon* < British *auon,* "river," *Creech* < *cruc,* "hill"). Such names and name elements were integrated into the newcomers' own system.

OE place-names normally began as descriptive or possessory noun-phrases based upon current terms, usually with cognates in the other Germanic languages to denote types either of settlement or of topographical feature ("generics"). Those denoting settlement types ("habitative generics") were based on roots variously meaning "abode" (e.g., *ham,* cf. German *Heim*), "enclosure" (e.g., *tun,* cf. OE *tynan,* "to fence"), "defensible place" (e.g., *burg,* dative *byrig,* cf. OE *beorgan,* "to protect"), or "site" (e.g., *stede, stoc, stow,* cf. OE *standan* and German *stehen*).

A generic of either sort might stand alone (e.g., *Bury* < OE dative *byrig* and *Leigh* < OE *leah,* "woodland clearing"); but more often it was prefixed by a "specific," either an adjective, another substantive in an adjectival role, or the genitive of a personal or tribal name.

A tribal name (or "*–ingas* form") sometimes stood alone (e.g., *Hastings* < *Hastingas, Reading* < OE dative plural *Readingum*). The reason why a modern form sometimes, as shown, derives from an OE dative is that in context a place-name was usually governed by a preposition, such as OE *æt, in/on,* or *to.* Because of tendencies to treat toponymics as virtually a branch of archaeology, that is, a source of clues to prehistoric settlement, much recent research has focused upon possible chronological stratification of the various modes of formation.

The Scandinavians who from the 870s settled north and east of Watling Street partly modified local place-name patterns to fit their own related but distinctive usages, forming many fresh names on their characteristic habitative generic, *-by.* In some districts Scandinavian speech habits were dominant enough to affect the phonological development of such OE names as the colonists adopted. Intensities of Scandinavian settlement and usage vary, apparently according to durations of Scandinavian hegemony in the areas concerned. They run from slight, in the southeast Midlands, to overwhelming, in parts of Lincolnshire and Yorkshire.

"Major" English place-names (i.e., ones referring to chief landscape features or to settlements of at least village size) were mostly fixed well before being recorded in Domesday Book (1086) and have since undergone only phonological change. The impact of the Norman Conquest upon English toponymy was limited; French coinages were rare, being mostly names for castles and manor houses; few OE names were supplanted. For major names, the main innovations of the ME period, involved the sporadic use of so-called "(manorial) affixes" for distinguishing between neighboring places of like names (e.g., *Halicon Bumpstead* beside *Steeple Bumpstead, Deeping St. James* beside *Market Deeping,* and so on). More significant was the growth of "minor names," that is, field names and street names, whose proliferation reflects the increasing size and complexity of rural as well as urban settlements.

Cecily Clark

Bibliography

GENERAL

Clark, Cecily. "Onomastics." In *The Cambridge History of the English Language.* I: *The Beginnings to 1066,* ed. R.M. Hogg. Cambridge: Cambridge University Press, 1992, pp. 452–89; Clark, Cecily. "Onomastics." In *The Cambridge History of the English Language.* II: *1066–1476,* ed. Norman Blake. Cambridge: Cambridge University Press, 1992, pp. 542–606.

PERSONAL NAMES

Nomina is a scholarly journal devoted to new and current work on names. For family naming the English Surnames Series, under the auspices of the Department of English Local History, University of Leicester, will be a valuable guide. Clark, Cecily. "English Personal Names ca. 650–1300: Some Prosopographical Bearings." *Medieval Prosopography* 8/1 (1988): 31–60; Ekwall, Eilert. *Early London Personal Names.* Lund: Gleerup, 1947; Fellows-Jensen, Gillian. *Scandinavian Personal Names in Lincolnshire and Yorkshire.* Copenhagen: Akademisk Forlag, 1968; Reaney, P.H. *The Origin of English Surnames.* London: Routledge & Kegan Paul, 1967 [not always reliable but a good starting point for baptismal and family names]; Reaney, P.H. *Dictionary of British Surnames.* 3d ed. London: Routledge, 1991 [a starting point]; von Feilitzen, Olof. *The Pre-Conquest Personal Names of Domesday Book.* Uppsala: Almqvist & Wiksells, 1937.

PLACE-NAMES

The volumes published for the English Place-Name Society are the best guides to the names of the counties. Cameron, Kenneth. *English Place-Names.* Rev. ed. London: Batsford, 1988; Ekwall, Eilert. *Concise Oxford Dictionary of English Place-Names.* 4th ed. Oxford: Clarendon, 1960 [basic but now a bit outdated]; Field, John. *English Field-Names: A Dictionary.* Newton Abbot: David & Charles, 1972 [general treatment]; Gelling, Margaret, et al. *The Names of Towns and Cities in Britain.* London: Batsford, 1970 [this book, and that of Cameron, recommended as starting point]; Rivet, A.L.F., and Colin Smith. *The Place-Names of Roman Britain.* London: Batsford, 1979 [the standard treatment].

See also Language; Towns

Nature *(Kynde)* in Middle English Literature

Certain ME works give considerable prominence to the idea of the natural; personifications of Nature or Kynde are frequent, but less emphatic invocation of nature, *kynde,* and cognate terms is also widespread, with many writers using naturalness as a moral norm.

Testimony to the goodness of the natural could be found in such influential writers as Augustine and Boethius and in medieval theories of natural law. The law of nature is frequently understood as the law of reason, by which human beings have a natural knowledge of the moral law. It came to be identified with the moral stipulations of the Old (Mosaic) Law and the Gospel, taken to require love of God and neighbor. However, the law of nature was also seen as the law of animal impulse, an idea that renders the natural morally problematic and affects some ME literature.

In *Piers Plowman* Langland makes extensive use of the idea of the natural. He finds *kynde wit,* or natural understanding, a powerful force for good, but he also displays its inadequacies in relation to Christian revelation and God's grace. (Many writers oppose God's graceful provision to what is available in the natural course of things.) Langland believes that the natural can urge toward sin in the sexual sphere. But he exploits the relationship between the natural and Christian love (implicit by Langland's time in the semantic range of *kynde* and its derivatives, regardless of other factors) to make naturalness a prime moral desideratum. To be unnatural is to sin against the Holy Ghost (*Piers Plowman* B.17.198–298). It would also seem to be against the nature of God the Father, who, in his aspect as Creator of the world and of such natural processes as generation, disease, and death, is actually designated Kynde (B.9.25–29, 20.80–108).

Usually, however, vernacular writers follow the tradition established by 12th-century Latin authors and represent Nature as a female power subordinate to God, responsible for the processes, particularly the generative processes, of the mutable sublunary world. In *The Parliament of Fowls* Chaucer presents such a Nature, offering her initially as a benign figure who orders the world harmoniously. She stands at the center of an apparently positive vision of sexual love. But the female eagle's refusal to mate stimulates doubts as to whether Nature does order sexual love satisfactorily. She tellingly concedes that she is not Reason and may in fact be closer to Venus, in whose temple love is imaged as distressful and decadent. A divided literary inheritance may help produce Chaucer's figure: in *The Complaint of Nature* Alan of Lille aligns Reason and Nature; in Jean de Meun's continuation of the *Roman de la Rose* we find a Nature so concerned to see procreation take place that she aligns herself with a Venus of whose ethos Reason disapproves.

Consciousness of a distance between Nature and Reason is evident in Gower's *Confessio Amantis.* Nature presides over impulse, and *kynde* is frequently used to designate the nonrational, animal side of man. Though Nature and *kynde* can sponsor right moral action, man's natural sexuality can urge him forcefully toward wrong action. The natural sexual urge should be restrained by Reason, but it is not clear that Nature's anarchic power in the sexual sphere can in the regular course of things be finally subdued.

The uncomfortable power of *kynde* in the amatory sphere is registered in Chaucer's *Troilus and Criseyde.* Against suggestions in the text that the law of *kynde* operates benignly, by constraining Troilus to love, stands Criseyde's betrayal of Troilus and the narrator's repudiation of earthly love and recommendation of love of Christ at the poem's close. Chaucer also probes the idea of nature in *The Book of the Duchess* and the *Physician's Tale,* and in spite of the former's association of Nature with the virtue of moderation and the latter's affirmation of Nature's superlative creative ability (both traditional features of Nature) the possibility that Nature's influence over human life may not be entirely satisfactory is raised in each.

After the 14th century the Nature figure is more frequently found in comfortable association with Reason as a force for good and less often subjected to questioning or criticism on moral grounds (see *Reason and Sensuality,* perhaps by Lydgate, and Medwall's *Nature*). But *The Assembly of the Gods,* which has Nature in "her carnall myght" (line 1381) aligned against Reason, shows that consciousness of a different kind of Nature remains, even if the moral ambivalence of the idea is only occasionally exploited in post-14th-century medieval literature (see, e.g., Dunbar's *The Merle and the Nyghtingall*).

Hugh White

Bibliography

PRIMARY

Alan of Lille. *The Plaint of Nature.* Trans. James J. Sheridan. Toronto: University of Toronto Press, 1980; *The Assembly of the Gods.* Ed. Oscar L. Triggs. EETS e.s. 69. London: Kegan Paul, Trench, Trübner, 1896; Guillaume de Lorris and Jean de Meun. *The Romance of the Rose.* Trans. Charles Dahlberg. 3d ed. Princeton: Princeton University Press, 1995; Lydgate, John (?). *Reson and Sensuallyte.* Ed. Ernst Sieper. EETS e.s. 84, 89. London: Kegan Paul, Trench, Trübner, 1901–03; Medwall, Henry. *Nature.* In *Quellen des Weltlichen Dramas in England vor Shakespeare,* ed. Alois Brandl. Strassburg: Trübner, 1898, pp. 73–158.

SECONDARY

Bennett, J.A.W. *The Parlement of Foules: An Interpretation.* Oxford: Clarendon, 1957; Economou, George D. *The Goddess Natura in Medieval Literature.* Cambridge: Harvard University Press, 1972; Olsson, Kurt. "Natural Law and John Gower's *Confessio Amantis.*" *M&H* n.s. 11 (1982): 229–61; White, Hugh. *Nature and Salvation in Piers Plowman.* Cambridge: Brewer, 1988; White, Hugh. "Chaucer Compromising Nature." *RES* n.s. 40 (1989): 157–78.

See also Boethius; Chaucer; Gower; Law in ME Literature; Literary Influences: French, Medieval Latin; Lydgate; Moral and Religious Instruction; *Piers Plowman;* Psychology, Medieval

Navy and Naval Power

English history owes much to the influence of geography. As an island Britain was isolated from the affairs of Europe until the seas were readily bridged by vessels capable of crossing the English Channel and North Sea. These waters present great hazards, illustrated best by the numerous vessels wrecked there. The first efforts to control the seas around Britain were to build vessels that could withstand their winds and waves. Only later would conflict between warring sides at sea be a concern.

The early Celtic settlers came in early craft of which we have little record: oared vessels without mast or sail. The Romans introduced naval power to Britain and frequent travel to the Continent, following their invasions of 55 B.C. and A.D. 43. For four centuries they moved men and material to and from Britain, establishing their power on sea as well as on land.

However, they faced opposition from Germanic peoples along the northwest coast of Europe who raided sporadically. A defensive system of lookouts and warning signals was developed, directed by the Count of the Saxon Shore.

Following Roman withdrawal in the early 5th century, the Angles and Saxons overran Britain, wresting it from the Celtic Britons. They maintained regular communication with their homelands across the North Sea, using large oared ships to cross the open waters. They may have used sailing ships. Trade goods came to Britain from Gaul, Italy, Spain, Scandinavia, and beyond, while tin, gold, and other commodities were exported. A trade developed that contributed to the prosperity of Anglo-Saxon England. Unfortunately this made the Anglo-Saxons a target of the Vikings, who began their attacks in the late 8th century. Although most of the conflicts were waged on land, it was the unique ability of the Viking longships to cross the North Sea and—with their shallow drafts—to sail up rivers to such cities as York that ensured their success. The Anglo-Saxons countered with a navy of their own, first organized by Alfred the Great. He almost lost Britain to the Danes, but through surprising victories on land and at sea the Danes were defeated.

The Anglo-Saxon era ended in 1066, with the successful amphibious attacks of the Normans. Sailing in single-masted Viking-style ships large enough to carry horses, the Normans won a great victory at Hastings. As Norman occupation followed, the Channel became a highway for the transport of men and equipment. The Anglo-Norman rulers expanded their control in Britain to Wales and Scotland. Under Henry II this rule expanded to Ireland and on the Continent included his family lands of Normandy, Anjou, Maine, and the lands of Queen Eleanor of Aquitaine. The northern seas were dominated by this Angevin Empire. But no great standing royal navy was developed, perhaps because after the Viking era they feared no maritime rivals. They depended upon the Cinque Ports (Hastings, Romney, Hythe, Dover, and Sandwich) to supply ships when needed in return for special favors.

Richard I organized a large fleet from England and the Continent to sail to the eastern Mediterranean on the Third Crusade. His fleets won victories over the Muslims. Throughout the 13th century Anglo-French conflict led to intermittent war at sea. John and Henry III built galleys to pursue the war against France in a vain effort to recover Normandy and hold their other territories. The French response was to accelerate privateering (raids by private vessels, supported by the crown) and to build an arsenal to construct galleys at Rouen.

Edward I responded with his own program of shipbuilding in the 1290s. He reorganized the naval establishment, ashore and on the sea, and instituted the formal office of admiral. But the number of ships built by medieval kings was always relatively small, and most ships were impressed from the local seaports. In 1297, for example, Edward raised a fleet of 305 ships, mainly from merchant shipping, and about 5,800 sailors. The fleet enabled him to complete his conquest of Wales and Scotland, as well as to resist the French. He carried over 9,000 troops into France in the 1290s. Of course

medieval knights required horses, which had to be transported in ships as well.

Hostilities between France and England erupted in the Hundred Years War (1337–1453), which immediately involved English naval forces. A French fleet raided the south coast of England and preyed on English shipping. The French, aided by Genoese and Castilian mariners, assembled an invasion fleet at Sluys. Edward III took the initiative and boldly sailed his own fleet to Sluys, where he defeated the combined forces in 1340. In 1347 he raised an armada of some 738 ships and 15,000 seamen to transport 2,000 soldiers to besiege Calais. Aided by his son Edward, the Black Prince, he fought again at sea off Winchelsea in 1350 in an engagement known as the *Espagnols sur Mer,* where he won a victory over the Castilians. Records indicate that Edward built about 50 vessels between 1340 and 1360. Most of them were large sailing vessels, cogs, rather than oared galleys. He suffered a loss in 1372 off La Rochelle when the Castilians destroyed an English fleet. At Edward's death in 1377 many of the royal ships were sold off to pay his debts. Attempts to assemble and maintain any sort of royal naval force languished.

After initial successes in the Hundred Years War the English suffered defeat and domestic upheaval. But the need for a naval force was revived in the early 15th century, again because of Anglo-French hostility. Henry V opened a new initiative in the Hundred Years War and took the war to the Continent. He rebuilt the English fleet, which remained a force at sea for the next two decades. His expeditionary forces won a victory at Agincourt in 1415, and later his fleet enabled him to capture King James I of Scotland at sea and end that monarch's attempts to ally with the French.

Piracy and privateering diminished under the influence of Henry's fleet, and English ships could safely sail the northern seas and into the Mediterranean. English merchant ships began to call regularly at Portugal, Sicily, Norway, and Denmark. The major trade routes of wool and cloth to and from Flanders, and the delivery of wine from Bordeaux to England, flourished because of the protection afforded by the navy. However, the war again turned against the English after the 1430s. French victories forced their withdrawal from Bordeaux in 1453. After 116 years of fighting the English retained only the port city of Calais, because it could be supplied by sea. Furthermore the Hanseatic League restricted English trade into its waters, and there was no longer a navy capable of protecting merchant shipping. Under Henry VI the fleet was once again disbanded and the king's ships sold.

Medieval English kings were never systematic in their efforts to build and maintain a royal navy. While some such efforts were calculated attempts to prepare for aggressive warfare, most were sporadic responses to emergencies prompted by threats from abroad. Navies were expensive to build and to maintain, and in an age of chivalry most fighting was done by mounted knights, not mariners aboard ships.

Some, however, did recognize the value of a standing navy. The anonymous author of *The Libel of English Policy,* a pronaval treatise written in 1437, advised his countrymen to control the seas around Britain and espoused a kind of mercantilism as an answer to economic and maritime troubles. But little was done to remedy things until after 1485, when Henry VII began a program of shipbuilding that set England upon a new maritime course that would bring her future greatness.

Timothy J. Runyan

Bibliography

Brooks, F.W. *The English Naval Forces, 1199–1272.* London: Brown, 1932; Lewis, Archibald R., and Timothy J. Runyan. *European Naval and Maritime History, 300–1500.* Bloomington: Indiana University Press, 1985; Richmond, Colin F. "English Naval Power in the Fourteenth Century." *History* 52 (February 1967): 1–15; Richmond, Colin F. "The War at Sea." In *The Hundred Years War,* ed. K. Fowler. London: Macmillan, 1971, pp. 96–121; Runyan, Timothy J. "Ships and Fleets in Anglo-French Warfare, 1337–1360." *American Neptune* 46/2 (Spring 1986): 91–99; Runyan, Timothy J. "The Organization of Royal Fleets in Medieval England." In *Ships, Seafaring, and Society: Essays in Maritime History,* ed. Timothy J. Runyan. Detroit: Wayne State University Press, 1987, pp. 37–52; Sherborne, J.W. "The Battle of La Rochelle and the War at Sea, 1372–1375." *BIHR* 42 (1969): 17–29.

See also Cinque Ports; Hanseatic League; Ships

Neville Family

The ancestor of the Nevilles was duly rewarded after 1066 with lands in Lincolnshire. However, Alan de Neville, who became chief justice of royal forests and led the first general inspection of forest boundaries and royal rights (the general forest eyre of 1166), was the first of the family to emerge from obscurity. In the next generation Hugh de Neville became chief justice of the forests under John and is listed in the preamble to Magna Carta as one of John's supporters. Through marriage he became founder of the Essex branch of the family. His cousin Geoffrey was royal chamberlain, and other Nevilles were sheriffs, justices, and other lesser officials. In the next reign Ralph de Neville, known by that name in spite of his illegitimacy, became chancellor and bishop of Chichester and helped several of his kinsmen to positions. The house he built in London gave its name to Chancery Lane.

Lands attained through marriages provided the foundation for northern branches of the family in Yorkshire and Durham, where castles held by the Nevilles were located: Raby, Middleham, Sheriff Hutton, and Brancepeth. In the 14th century Nevilles helped Edward I and Edward II fight against the Scots. As wardens of the marches the Nevilles and the Percys ruled northern England by the later 14th century. In 1397 Richard II created Richard Neville earl of Westmorland. However, Alexander Neville, archbishop of York, was forced to leave England when Richard was deposed.

The most famous member of the family was Richard Neville, earl of Warwick in 1449, after his marriage to Anne Beauchamp. Later writers dubbed him "Warwick the Kingmaker" for his role in supporting the Lancastrian Henry VI, then his Yorkist rival Edward IV, and finally switching back to Henry VI. He was aided by his brother George, archbishop of York and royal chancellor, his brother John, earl of Northumberland, and other Nevilles. As leader of the Lancastrian cause he was defeated and killed at the Battle of Barnet in 1471.

Charles R. Young

Bibliography

Cokayne, George E. *The Complete Peerage.* Ed. Vicary Gibbs et al. 13 vols. London: St. Catherine Press, 1910–59; Kendall, Paul Murray. *Warwick the Kingmaker.* New York: Norton, 1957; Young, Charles R. *The Making of the Neville Family in England 1166–1400.* Woodbridge: Boydell & Brewer, 1996.

See also Beauchamp Family; Marches; Percy Family

New Minster Charter

The New Minster Charter (BL Cotton Vespasian A.viii) is a slender codex produced at Winchester after 964. Drafted by Bishop Æthelwold in the opening stages of the monastic reform, shortly after the New Minster had been forcibly converted to a reformed Benedictine community, the charter confirms the new regime. Beyond this the polemical text sets forth King Edgar's plan for his own spiritual renewal as a model for that of his flock. These intentions are set within broader contexts of salvation history and eschatological hopes. The charter was witnessed by the royal family and Dunstan and Æthelwold.

Fig. 101. New Minster Charter (BL Vespasian A.viii), fol. 2v. King Edgar offers the charter to Christ. Reproduced by permission of the British Library, London.

Written entirely in gold, the codex contains a frontispiece miniature that is the first known charter illustration (fig. 101). Flanked by the New Minster's patron saints, the Virgin Mary and St. Peter, King Edgar proffers the charter to Christ, enthroned above him in a mandorla carried by angels. The miniature draws on insular traditions for intercessory imagery and adapts it to the specific circumstances of the charter by placing the king between the two chief insular intercessors. Mary bears the cross making possible man's salvation, and the palm branch of victory for those who are saved, while Peter bears the key to the kingdom of heaven. These attributes convey visually the king's hopes, expressed verbally in the charter he presents to Christ. The miniature is often cited as the earliest surviving example of developed "Winchester School" painting. The frame of parallel golden bars supports an acanthus "tree" whose segmented sections and blossom terminals recall those of the earlier St. Cuthbert Maniple from Winchester. The stocky figures of the Virgin and Peter echo earlier Winchester figures in the Galba Psalter (fig. 66: see GALBA PSALTER), and their arrangement on the page, touching the frame, forms a patterned trellis against the vellum, hearkening back ultimately to the pre-Carolingian art of the Lindisfarne Gospel evangelist portraits. However, the drapery of all the figures is dynamic and energized, with flaring trumpet folds and curvilinear patterns characteristic of "Winchester School" art of the later 10th century.

Kathleen M. Openshaw

Bibliography

Backhouse, Janet, Derek H. Turner, and Leslie Webster, eds. *The Golden Age of Anglo-Saxon Art 966–1066.* London: British Museum, 1984, cat. no. 26; Deshman, Robert. "*Benedictus Monarcha et Monachus:* Early Medieval Ruler Theology and the Anglo-Saxon Reform." *Frühmittelalterliche Studien* 22 (1988): 204–240; Deshman, Robert. *The Benedictional of Æthelwold.* Princeton: Princeton University Press, 1995; Temple, Elżbieta. *Anglo-Saxon Manuscripts 900–1066.* A Survey of Manuscripts Illuminated in the British Isles 2, ed. J.J.G. Alexander. London: Harvey Miller, 1976; Wilson, David M. *Anglo-Saxon Art: From the Seventh Century to the Norman Conquest.* London: Thames & Hudson, 1984; Wormald, Francis. "Late Anglo-Saxon Art: Some Questions and Suggestions." In *Studies in Western Art: Acts of the 20th International Congress on the History of Art,* ed. Millard Meiss. Vol. 1: *Romanesque and Gothic.* Princeton: Princeton University Press, 1963, pp. 19–26. Repr. in *Francis Wormald: Collected Writings,* ed. Jonathan J.G. Alexander, T. Julian Brown, and Joan Gibbs. Vol. 1. London: Harvey Miller, 1984, pp. 105–10.

See also Æthelwold; Benedictine Reform; Dunstan; Galba Psalter; Lindisfarne Gospels; Monasticism; Textiles from St. Cuthbert's Tomb; "Winchester School"

Norman Conquest

King Edward the Confessor died in January 1066, leaving the throne of England to his brother-in-law, Harold Godwinson; but Edward's cousin William, duke of the French province of Normandy, also claimed the throne. After elaborate preparations William invaded England in late September. His army met Harold's at the Battle of Hastings on 14 October, and Harold's death in the battle gave victory to William, who was crowned king of England in Westminster Abbey on Christmas Day and has since been known as William the Conqueror (William I).

The grounds on which each contender claimed the throne as Edward's successor were problematic, for neither was a member by blood of the Anglo-Saxon royal family, which had previously been the all-important criterion for kingship. Harold's sister Edith (Eadgyth) was Edward's wife, and William's great-aunt Emma, daughter of Duke Richard I of Normandy, was Edward's mother. A third claimant, Harald Hardrada, king of Norway, asserted a right to the English throne in 1066 on the basis of an alleged treaty between his predecessor Magnus and the Danish king of England, Harthacnut, whereby the survivor of the two was to succeed to the other's kingdom.

The most mysterious aspect of the events of 1066 is why the obvious heir to the throne was overlooked: this was Edgar Atheling, grandson of Edward's elder half-brother Edmund Ironside, who had briefly succeeded his and Edward's father, Æthelred the Unready, as king in 1016. Edgar Atheling was only in his middle teens in 1066, but earlier Anglo-Saxon kings had inherited the throne at comparable ages. Perhaps the weakness of personality that later characterized Edgar was already evident and induced Edward to overlook his great-nephew.

Norman propagandists later claimed that Edward had promised William the throne as early as the early 1050s, because of their relationship and in gratitude for the protection that Normandy had afforded him during the rule of the Danish kings between 1016 and 1042. One version of the Anglo-Saxon Chronicle says that William visited England in 1051, at which time, according to the Norman account of events, the promise was made to him in person. The Normans also interpreted the expedition that Harold Godwinson made to the Continent in about 1064 as a mission on which Edward had sent Harold to confirm the promise. They said that, while he was with William in Normandy, Harold had taken an oath to support William's succession in England.

Whether Edward ever made a promise to William or not he clearly thought at later times of other possible heirs. In the mid-1050s, for example, he recalled his nephew Edward Atheling (son of Edmund Ironside and father of Edgar Atheling), from Hungary, and this Edward might well have been designated heir had he not died in 1057, shortly after his arrival in England. Moreover there is no doubt that on his deathbed Edward the Confessor did name Harold Godwinson to succeed him, and such a designation was valid in current English practice. Even the Norman sources do not deny the designation. If they address the issue directly, they accuse Harold of perjury for breaking his oath to support William's right to the crown, rather than of usurpation of the throne.

In short William had no real right to the throne. The rich kingdom of England simply presented an attractive prize, and a fortunate but coincidental vacuum of power in France left William without serious worries about the security of Normandy if he and most of the military force of the duchy departed on an extended foreign adventure.

The expedition was nonetheless risky and might well have turned out disastrously had not events played out in ways that favored William. He was ready to attempt the crossing of the Channel by the middle of August, but unfavorable winds kept the fleet from sailing for six weeks, during which the most he could do was to sail north along the French coast to St. Valéry-sur-Somme, from which the crossing to England was shorter than it was from farther south. Although this delay irked William, it worked to his advantage in two ways. First, Harold had called out the defensive peasant army of the southern shires to guard the coasts and prevent a successful Norman landing, but the logistics of supplying this large force and the peasants' need to harvest their crops caused him to disband this force on 8 September and to retire with his bodyguard of crack troops to London. Second, by the time of William's crossing, Harold had been drawn away to the north of England by Harald Hardrada's attempt to take England for himself, in which he was aided by Harold Godwinson's disloyal brother Tostig. Armies led by Harald Hardrada and Tostig joined in the north of England in mid-September and defeated the local defensive forces at Fulford on 20 September. On hearing of Hardrada's arrival Harold marched north, arriving so quickly that he was able to meet the enemy in battle at Stamford Bridge near York on 25 September and score a great victory. Both Hardrada and Tostig were killed in the battle, and the northern threat was ended.

Therefore, when William finally was able to cross the Channel on the night of 27–28 September, he landed at Pevensey unopposed even by a containing force, with his principal rival far to the north. He was able to disembark his forces at leisure, establish a sizable beachhead centered on Hastings, arrange the provisioning of his army, and begin ravaging the countryside, perhaps with the intent of drawing Harold into battle. Harold moved south in response, stopping for only a few days at London.

Harold reached Hastings during the night of 13–14 October, and news of his arrival enabled William to attack in the morning before the Anglo-Saxon troops were ready. Despite William's surprise attack and the exhaustion of Harold's elite troops, the outcome of the battle was by no means a foregone conclusion until Harold was killed on the field. After his death, however, the battle turned into a rout. Despite subsequent rebellions and attacks by two kings of Denmark, Swein Estrithson and Cnut IV, who claimed the kingdom as heirs of Cnut the Great, England remained Norman from that day forward.

Of all the great events that have shaped the course of human history the Norman Conquest of England ranks as one of the least inevitable. Nonetheless, its effects were profound. Because the Conquest was not followed by a mass immigration of Normans, its direct effects were primarily on matters with which the upper classes of medieval society were most concerned: government, law, and culture. Probably no more than several thousand French warriors acquired land in England as a result of the Conquest, but they replaced the Anglo-Saxon nobility almost completely. These Frenchmen were primarily Normans; because William had recruited his invasion force as widely as he could, the new lords also included significant numbers of men from Brittany and Flanders and a scattering from farther afield. Most were already endowed with land in their homelands, which they did not give up when they acquired land in England. Hence, for a number of generations, the post-Conquest English ruling class remained French in its orientation, as did the royal family. As a result England became much more thoroughly involved, diplomatically and militarily, in continental affairs than it had been before 1066, including an ongoing war between Normandy and the kingdom of France: a war that can be seen as lasting, with interruptions and modifications, down to the defeat of Napoleon in 1815.

The English upper class remained primarily French-speaking and French in culture for several centuries after 1066, with significant effects on literature, architecture, art, and the language itself. English acquired both a simpler structure than most modern languages and a second, romance-based terminology that makes its vocabulary larger and more nuanced than that of most other languages. The new French lords of England also introduced feudal tenure, with which they were familiar in their continental homes; this method of holding land in return for military and other honorable services profoundly affected the development of the English common law and of English constitutional ideas and practices. They built many castles. As Norman settlers in England began to move into Wales, Scotland, and eventually Ireland, they carried many of these governmental, legal, and cultural developments with them.

By the end of the reign of William the Conqueror not only the cream of lay society but also the leaders of the church were continental, primarily French, in origin. William secured a papal deposition of the last Anglo-Saxon archbishop of Canterbury in 1070 and replaced him with Lanfranc, an Italian who had long been a prominent cleric in Normandy. After 1080 only one Anglo-Saxon prelate was left, Wulfstan, bishop of Worcester (d. 1095). Anglo-Saxon abbots and abbesses, when they died, were normally replaced by relatives or protégés of French lords; lesser church dignities were also rapidly monopolized by the conquerors. As a result the English church was brought, not always easily, into closer conformity with continental norms than it had known before 1066.

Some hundreds of French townsmen came to England in the wake of the Conquest, settling in the larger boroughs, often in their own enclaves; but they supplemented rather than replaced the native English burgesses. Their presence and connections meant that England became more involved in trade with the Continent. It also acquired its first population of Jews, who formed part of this bourgeois migration. No peasant is known to have migrated from the Continent to England as a result of the Conquest, however; the effects on the peasantry were thus less immediate, less direct, and probably less dramatic than the effects on the other elements of the population.

It is true that large numbers of northern peasants were killed or greatly harmed by the harrying of the north; and peasants in various parts of the country were burdened by the imposition on them of a code of rules, the forest law, whose purpose was to protect the "great game," the deer and boar whose hunting the Norman kings reserved to themselves. Nonetheless, most of the post-Conquest developments in the social, economic, and legal status of the peasants appear to be continuations of trends that began before the Conquest, including the disappearance of slavery and the generalization of serfdom.

Emily Zack Tabuteau

Bibliography

Brown, R. Allen. *The Normans and the Norman Conquest.* 2d ed. Woodbridge: Boydell, 1985; Chibnall, Marjorie. *Anglo-Norman England, 1066–1166.* Oxford: Oxford University Press, 1986; Davis, R.H.C. "The Norman Conquest." *History* 51 (1966): 279–86; Fleming, Robin. *Kings and Lords in Conquest England.* Cambridge: Cambridge University Press, 1991; Kapelle, William E. *The Norman Conquest of the North: The Region and Its Transformation, 1000–1135.* Chapel Hill: University of North Carolina Press, 1979; Körner, Sten. *The Battle of Hastings, England, and Europe, 1035–1066.* Lund: Gleerup, 1964; Whitelock, Dorothy, et al., *The Norman Conquest: Its Setting and Impact.* London: Eyre & Spottiswoode, 1966.

See also Anglo-Norman Literature; Battle of Hastings; Bayeux Tapestry; Castles; Domesday Book; Edward the Confessor; Feudalism; Forests; Godwinson; Harold; Knight Service; Lanfranc; Normandy; William I

Normandy

The counties of Normandy pertaining to the archbishopric of Rouen extend over approximately the same region that previously had comprised the Roman province of *Lugdunensis secunda.* Authority to rule these counties as an agent of the king of *Francia occidentalis* was delegated in 911 by Charles the Simple to a Viking chief named Rollo, through a treaty made at St. Clair-sur-Epte.

During the next century and a half Rollo's descendants, who made their capital at Rouen and often worked closely with the archbishops—conversion to Christianity having been a requirement in 911—struggled to assert authority over the rest of Normandy. In this lengthy but largely successful process the counts of Rouen gradually emerged as dukes of the Normans.

Administratively and culturally Rollo's descendants and their Viking followers were rapidly assimilated into the Romanic world of post-Carolingian Francia. Their Scandinavian language was replaced by an early form of French. Christianity gradually took hold after the initial conversion, probably

more formal than spiritual, and Carolingian administrative practices dominated the region. By the second generation even the Norman duke had to learn Norse as a second language; assimilation had come so far by the second half of the 11th century that the duke had no fleet. However, until ca. 1025, the Norman rulers maintained Rouen as an open city for Viking raiders and benefited greatly in an economic sense by providing necessities at high prices to the pirates.

The importance of Normandy in English history dates from well before William's victory at Hastings and the conquest of 1066 that made England part of a trans-Channel Norman Empire. Yet the momentous events of 1066 and the subsequent rule of England by Normans far overshadowed the past and raises serious questions concerning Norman influence on the development of English institutions. Among the most controversial of these matters are the introduction of "feudalism," a putative revolution in the military, massive changes in the Anglo-Saxon church, the nature and development of economic connections between England and the Continent, and intellectual developments.

These questions remain controversial after generations of scholarship. What is emerging today is a consensus that late Anglo-Saxon England, like contemporary Normandy, was a Carolingian-type state that itself owed much to later Roman institutions. The putative Germanic character of both Anglo-Saxon England and the Carolingian Empire are being vigorously downplayed, despite the linguistic realities of the former, as is the Nordic (Germanic) character of the Normans. In addition "feudalism," however defined, is also being regarded as an unhelpful way of characterizing the system of Norman aristocratic tenures and military organization in the pre-1066 period. The peculiarities of the Anglo-Saxon church, once highlighted by scholars, now receive less attention than the church's adaptation of the continental norms.

In short Anglo-Saxon England and Normandy are seen as more similar to each other and to the successor states of the Carolingian Empire that had once been a part of the Roman Empire, and thus the peculiar impact of the Norman Conquest upon England is being given less attention than was once the case.

The Norman Empire, created by Duke William through the unification of his continental holdings with England, did not, in its first phase, outlive the Conqueror. William established his eldest son, Robert Curthose, as duke, in keeping with arrangements made even before the conquest of England, while William Rufus, his second son, was made king of England. The idea of the empire, still exemplified by a Norman aristocracy that also held extensive lands in England, was alive and a source of inspiration to both sons to strive, throughout their respective careers, to reestablish the unity created by their father. However, it was not until William II was succeeded by his younger brother, Henry, as king of England that the empire was recreated, with the military defeat and life imprisonment of Duke Robert.

When Henry I died (1135), a civil war, known as the Anarchy, broke out between the claimants to the throne, Henry's daughter, Matilda, and his nephew Stephen. Peace came when Matilda's oldest son, Henry Plantagenet, was accepted by all parties as king of England, Henry II, in 1154. During the war Henry's father, Geoffrey of Anjou, had conquered Normandy; it thus became part of the Angevin Empire as one of Henry II's possessions. Henry's administrative and legal reforms affected Normandy, as other parts of the Angevin Empire; in 1171 he carried out an inquest into knights' fees and in 1174 issued what amounted to major legislation on criminal matters in Normandy, much as he was doing in England.

Although Normandy benefited in economic matters from being part of the Angevin Empire, a subject still in need of basic research, the duchy's primary political role was as the front line of the Angevin kings' aggressive policy toward the Capetian kings of France. Under Henry's successors, Richard and especially John, the Norman military establishment became one of the most effective fighting forces on the Continent. However, the weak military leadership of John saw the fall of Château Gaillard and the loss of Normandy in 1204. The disasters of this year led directly to the collapse of the Angevin Empire and the dissolution of the direct bonds between England and Normandy.

Bernard S. Bachrach

Bibliography

Bates, David. *Normandy before 1066.* London: Longman, 1982; Hallam, Elizabeth. *Capetian France: 987–1328.* London: Longman, 1980 [gives additional perspective on both the Norman and Angevin empires]; Le Patourel, John. *The Norman Empire.* Oxford: Clarendon, 1976; Searle, Eleanor. *Predatory Kinship and the Creation of Norman Power, 840–1066.* Berkeley: University of California Press, 1988 [reacts against the growing consensus outlined in this entry].

See also Anarchy; Feudalism; Henry I; Henry II; Knight Service; Matilda; Norman Conquest; Stephen; William I; William II

Norwich

In spite of much recent excavation the early history of Norwich remains obscure. It seems to have developed from a group of settlements at what may have been an ancient junction of river and land routes at the confluence of the rivers Wensum and Yare. By the 10th century it had its own mint, and Domesday Book shows that in 1086 it was one of the largest boroughs in England, with a population between 5,000 and 10,000.

The Conquest brought great changes, both in the destruction of houses to make way for the castle and in the development to the west of the "French Borough," absorbed during the following century. In the 1090s the building of the great monastic cathedral brought a new element to the topography of the city. The county of Norwich was administered from the castle, the diocese of Norwich from the cathedral; thus the city was the regional capital, though its importance lay primarily in its commercial and industrial role. With its good communications by river and road it was the market for the agricultural products of the rich and populous farming region of east Norfolk and also, by the 14th century, for the large amounts of worsted cloth produced in the villages and small towns of eastern Norfolk, as well as in Norwich itself.

Norwich was also a major manufacturing town, with particularly flourishing cloth, leather, iron, and building industries. More than 100 trades and crafts were represented among the Norwich freemen of the 14th century. On the eve of the Black Death it was one of the half-dozen richest towns in England; its population may have reached 20,000, and its buildings occupied an increasing part of the walled area, though open spaces continued to be an important part of its topography. It possessed some 60 parish churches, four friaries, and other religious colleges and hospitals, as well as the great cathedral priory, whose privileges frequently caused conflict with the city. Like similar towns Norwich had received royal charters granting wide power of self-government, and it returned members, usually its own leading citizens, to all parliaments.

The Black Death struck Norwich hard; though its population was probably more than halved, the continued prosperity of many inhabitants is shown not only by the great civic buildings of the 15th century but also by the extensive rebuilding of parish churches and friaries and probably by a substantial renewal of housing. Its leading citizens were wealthy and ambitious enough to purchase major new charters from the crown, giving Norwich county status, with its own mayor and sheriffs. The early 15th century saw dissension among the citizens, and the charters were twice temporarily revoked, but the 1450s saw a new era of internal stability, with control increasingly in the hands of an elite group of richer merchants. A disastrous fire and some decline in the worsted industry did not prevent Norwich from still being among the six wealthiest English towns on the eve of the Reformation.

Roger Virgoe

Bibliography

Blomefield, Francis. *An Essay towards a Topographical History of the County of Norfolk.* 2d ed. 11 volumes. London: Printed for W. Miller, 1805–10 [volumes 3 and 4 remain the fullest compilation of material on Norwich]; Campbell, James. "Norwich." In *The British Atlas of Historic Towns,* gen. ed. Mary D. Lobel. Vol. 2. London: Scolar, 1975 [maps and a discussion of the topography]; Carter, Alan. "The Anglo-Saxon Origins of Norwich." *ASE* 7 (1978): 175–204 [summary of recent archaeological finds]; Green, Barbara, and Rachel M.R. Young. *Norwich: The Growth of a City.* Norwich: Norwich Museums Services, 1981 [best short history]; Hudson, William, and John C. Tingey. *The Records of the City of Norwich.* 2 vols. Norwich: Jarrold, 1906–10 [prints many important documents].

See also Bury St. Edmunds; Ipswich; Norwich Cathedral; Towns

Norwich Cathedral

After the Conquest the see of East Anglia was moved from North Elmham to Thetford and then, in 1094, to Norwich. Bishop Herbert de Losinga (1096–1119) built the cathedral as far as the altar of the Holy Cross—the fifth bay of the nave. It was completed by Bishop Eborard (1121–45).

The vast length of the church conforms to the post-Conquest revival of the great early Christian basilicas of Rome, as at Winchester (1079). Norwich has a fourteen-bay nave and a four-bay presbytery with the best-preserved Romanesque apse-ambulatory scheme in England. The two-cell, angled radiating chapels may follow French examples like Mehun-sur-Yèvre (ca. 1050) near Bourges, although the Norwich chapels are different in having two stories. The aisles have round-headed dado arcades and groin vaults throughout. The transepts are aisleless with two-story chapels to the east and superposed wall passages with large windows on the terminal and west walls that presage the early Gothic of northern France. In the nave, and formerly in the presbytery, the three-story elevation of main arcade, gallery, and clerestory with wall passage derives from St. Étienne at Caen.

Rich articulation was used from the first: all arches are molded, and paired or single half-shafts create strong bay divisions at major and minor piers, respectively. The major piers of the nave arcade and all the gallery piers have the inner order carried on triple parallel shafts, a possible adaptation of the Anglo-Saxon crossing at Great Paxton (Huntingdonshire). The third and fifth piers in the nave have incised spiral decoration as in the presbytery and transepts at Durham Cathedral. They mark the altar of the Holy Cross. The crossing tower is patterned with a regularized version of Anglo-Saxon stripwork (cf. Earls Barton, Northamptonshire).

Norwich Cathedral profoundly influenced architecture in East Anglia, as in the monastic churches at Binham, Wymondham, Castle Acre, and Peterborough (now cathedral), the castle at Castle Rising, and numerous parish churches, including Great Dunham and Attleborough (Norfolk).

Malcolm Thurlby

Bibliography

Fernie, Eric. *An Architectural History of Norwich Cathedral.* Oxford: Clarendon, 1993; Hoey, Lawrence. "Pier Form and Vertical Wall Articulation in English Romanesque Architecture." *Journal of the Society of Architectural Historians* 48 (1989): 258–83.

See also Architecture and Architectural Sculpture, Romanesque; Earls Barton Tower; Norwich

Notation of Plainsong

The history of insular musical notation before 980 is obscure; we are confronted not only by a lack of examples of notated music but also by an almost total lack of insular service books, so that it is difficult to tell whether such books might have been prepared for musical notation or not. A type of musical notation recognized as insular appears in more than 100 manuscript sources of the late 10th and the 11th centuries;

many of these sources may be linked with such major ecclesiastical centers as Worcester, Exeter, Sherborne, Canterbury, Durham, and Winchester. While it is possible that knowledge of musical notation reached England from France during the 9th century, it was apparently not until after the mid-10th century, when the Benedictine revival occasioned numerous contacts between England and the Continent, that music writing became established in England. Several insular manuscripts of the 10th century have contemporary notation, and they show the use at this period of two neumatic systems. One system—closely related to northern and central French notations, particularly those of Corbie and Fleury—was to set the pattern for the great majority of 11th-century insular notations (late-10th-century examples include Rouen, Bibliothèque Municipale 368, 369); the other type, related to notations of Breton provenance, appears mainly confined to sources originating in southwest England (e.g., the Sherborne Pontifical, now Paris, BN lat. 943). The breadth of notational detail in one of the Winchester tropers (Cambridge, Corpus Christi College 473) indicates that the practice of notating music was well established, at least at Winchester, by the year 1000.

During the second half of the 11th century, in such houses as those at Canterbury, Norman neume forms (i.e., symbols used in notating plainchant) began to infiltrate and sometimes to dominate insular notations (as in the Canterbury Gradual: Durham, University Library Cosin V.V.6). Some examples of the insular and Norman notations of this period betray attempts to infuse the essentially adiastematic (unheighted) notation with more exact pitch characteristics. And by the last years of the century notation on a stave had arrived (e.g., in BL Harley 3908, from Canterbury). In some centers, such as Worcester, however, the old adiastematic insular neumes continued to be used right up to the end of the 11th century.

Insular neumes (of the French rather than the Breton type) are characterized by parallel ascending and descending strokes on a vertical or almost vertical axis; their perpendicularity is quite distinctive when compared with French forms, which tend to lean more to the right. The range of insular neume forms is large, including many cursive and liquescent variations, as well as one neume used specifically in the notation of polyphony. Insular notators also commonly used significative letters to indicate details of intervallic structure or length of a note. Few insular sources show precise diastemacy before the beginning of the 12th century; on the other hand few are purely adiastematic. Many examples of insular music script are, like the text script with which they appear, highly calligraphic (e.g., the Winchester Troper [Bodleian Library, Bodley 775] and the Caligula [Cotton] Troper [BL Cotton Caligula A.xiv]).

Susan K. Rankin

Bibliography

Corbin, Solange. "Englische Neumen." In *Die Neumen.* Cologne: Volk, 1977, pp. 131–40; Hartzell, K. Drew. "A St. Albans Miscellany in New York." *Mittellateinisches Jahrbuch* 10 (1975): 20–61; Hartzell, K. Drew. "An

Unknown English Benedictine Gradual of the Eleventh Century." *ASE* 4 (1975): 131–44; Hartzell, K. Drew. "The Early Provenance of the Harkness Gospels." *Bulletin of Research in the Humanities* 84 (1981): 85–97; Rankin, Susan. "Musical Notations in Manuscripts from Exeter." *ASE* 13 (1984): 97–112; Rankin, Susan. "Neumatic Notations in Anglo-Saxon England." In *Musicologie médiévale: notations et séquences,* ed. Michel Huglo. Paris: Champion, 1987, pp. 129–44.

See also Caligula Troper; Liturgy and Church Music, History of; Notation of Polyphonic Music; Winchester Tropers

Notation of Polyphonic Music

From the late-10th-century neumes of the Winchester organa to the early 13th-century square notation of W1, insular polyphonic music used for its notation virtually unmodified the graphic forms developed in the context of liturgical monophony. Earlier dialects of plainchant neumes can help to localize manuscripts, but the turn to square notation in the 12th century has a leveling and universalizing effect that presents difficulties for the analysis of the date and provenance of later sources of polyphony. For example, in regard to the 35 Latin songs in the well-known "Later Cambridge Songbook" (CUL Ff.i.17 [1]), thirteen of which are polyphonic, there is still no consensus about whether they were copied in the late 12th or early 13th century and whether in England or on the Continent. Slightly later text and music hands (again—French or simply French-trained?) narrow the date but are similarly unhelpful about establishing a place of manufacture for W1, whose flourished initials, however, point to an insular provenance (perhaps even at the Augustinian cathedral priory of St. Andrews, Scotland, for which the book was undoubtedly commissioned).

In the first half of the 13th century, as a corollary to the emergence of distinctive insular musical genres and rhythmic-harmonic language, English musicians began to develop their own notational dialects for polyphony. The most important of these, referred to as English mensural notation, uses a lozenge rather than a square to represent the breve, on which the beat falls. English mensural notation was used to indicate varieties of the first, second, and third rhythmic modes and also binary mensuration. It most characteristically employed paired breves that are to be read unequally in trochaic rhythm (two beats–one beat). By the turn of the 14th century it was supplanted by French notation, with its square breve and lozenge-shaped semibreve, following the influential Parisian precepts of Franco of Cologne (*Ars cantus mensurabilis,* ca. 1280) and Petrus de Cruce. Some English compositions of this era follow an anti-Franconian tradition in respect to the subdivision of the breve by two identical but mensurally unequal semibreves, in which the first of the pair, rather than the second, is the longer of the two.

The next period of notational invention was in the second and third decades of the 14th century, when, in developments paralleled in France by the work of Jehan de Murs (Johannes de Muris) and Philippe de Vitry, and in Italy by

Marchetto da Padua, English musicians explored new rhythmic idioms and invented new notational systems. The most individualistic of these were the circle-stem complex of mensurations and English ternary breve-semibreve notation. Important innovators whom we know by name include Robertus de Handlo, Johannes de Garlandia, W. de Doncastre, Frater Robertus de Brunham, Robertus Trowell, and Johannes Hanboys. By the last quarter of the century, however, the English had fully assimilated French Ars Nova practices, retaining only a few idiosyncrasies from their own "new art," including certain rest shapes and the use of the *cauda hirundinis* (literally "swallow-tail," describing the appearance of the note) to indicate alteration. An innovation of around 1400 that was to have universal significance was the use in some sources of black void (i.e., a black outline around a white interior) instead of solid black notation, a change that swept the rest of northern Europe from about 1420, with the start of the great influx of English mass music onto the Continent in the second and third quarters of the 15th century. Further peculiarities of English notation and custom with which continental scribes of this era had to contend, and which in turn influenced continental composers and scribal practices, involved mainly the tempo and proportional relationships of note values when certain mensurations were performed simultaneously or successively.

A phenomenon of the second half of the 15th century was the emergence of simplified notations, paralleling the shift from soloistic ensembles to larger choral forces for the performance of sacred polyphony. Heavily represented in these choirs were singers inexperienced in the complexities of mensural notation, because their responsibilities had not previously extended beyond plainsong. Simplified notations addressing this problem were of two basic types. In one each pitch symbol has the same value, denoting one beat; the notation may be confined to a single rhythmic figure, such as a long or a breve or a simple vertical stroke (hence "stroke notation"), or use various rhythmic figures or contemporary plainsong notation without mensural differentiation. In the other type there were two symbols, denoting two values, one twice as long as the other; the shorter was a black breve, while the longer was a black breve with two descending tails (a "strene note," hence "strene notation"). Use of these simplified notations declined sharply after 1500, as generations of English choristers grew up who were familiar with mensural music.

Peter M. Lefferts

Bibliography

NOTATION BEFORE 1400

Bent, Margaret. "A Preliminary Assessment of the Independence of English Trecento Notations." In *L'Ars nova italiana del Trecento IV (1975),* ed. Agostino Ziino. Certaldo: Centro di Studi sull'Ars Nova Italiana del Trecento, 1978, pp. 65-82; Lefferts, Peter M. *The Motet in England in the Fourteenth Century.* Ann Arbor: UMI Research Press, 1986; Sanders, Ernest H. "Duple Rhythm and Alternate Third

Mode in the 13th Century." *Journal of the American Musicological Society* 15 (1962): 249–91; Wibberley, Roger. "Notation in the Thirteenth and Fourteenth Centuries." In *Manuscripts of Fourteenth-Century English Polyphony: A Selection of Facsimiles,* ed. Frank Ll. Harrison and Roger Wibberley. Early English Church Music 26. London: Stainer & Bell, 1981, pp. xix–xxviii.

SIMPLIFIED POLYPHONIC NOTATIONS

Benham, Hugh. "'Stroke' and 'Strene' Notation in Fifteenth- and Sixteenth-Century Equal-Note Cantus Firmi." *Plainsong and Medieval Music* 2 (1993): 153–67; Bent, Margaret. "New and Little-Known Fragments of English Medieval Polyphony." *Journal of the American Musicological Society* 21 (1968): 137–56; Bent, Margaret, and Roger Bowers. "The Saxilby Fragment." *Early Music History* 1 (1981): 1–27; Bowers, Roger, and Andrew Wathey. "New Sources of English Fourteenth- and Fifteenth-Century Polyphony." *Early Music History* 3 (1983): 123–73; Hughes, Andrew. "The Choir in Fifteenth-Century English Music: Non-Mensural Polyphony." In *Essays in Honor of Dragan Plamenac,* ed. Gustave Reese and Robert J. Snow. Pittsburgh: University of Pittsburgh Press, 1969, pp. 127–37; Sandon, Nick. "Mary, Meditations, Monks and Music: Poetry, Prose, Processions and Plagues in a Durham Cathedral Manuscript." *Early Music* 10 (1982): 43–55.

See also Notation of Plainsong

Nowell, Laurence (d. 1569 or soon after)

Antiquary, linguist, and cartographer who continued the Tudor recovery of the heritage of medieval England begun by John Bale (1495–1563), John Leland (ca. 1506–1552), and Robert Talbot (ca. 1505–1558). For long confused by scholars with his namesake and cousin the dean of Lichfield (d. 1576), Nowell was the son of Alexander and Grace Nowell of Whalley, Lancashire; his date of birth is unknown. Having spent much of the 1550s in France and Italy, studying in Paris and acting as tutor to young Englishmen abroad, by 1562 Nowell had joined the household of Queen Elizabeth's secretary of state Sir William Cecil (1520–1598), where he acted as tutor to Cecil's ward the young earl of Oxford. Nowell accomplished his most productive antiquarian work during the ensuing five years. In 1567 he departed for the Continent to pursue his studies, leaving his books and papers in the hands of his friend the lawyer and antiquary William Lambarde (1536–1601). He died in unknown circumstances some time after reaching Leipzig in August 1569.

Although Nowell published nothing, he energetically transcribed numerous sources for the history of medieval Britain, including the Anglo-Saxon Chronicle, the OE translation of Bede's *Ecclesiastical History,* the *Historia minor* of Matthew Paris, the *Polychronicon* of Ranulf Higden, Gerald of Wales's *Description of Wales* and *Itinerary through Wales,* and materials for the history of Ireland. Among his surviving transcriptions are BL Add. 43703–43710, Cotton Domitian A.xviii, and Cotton Vespasian A.v. These transcriptions, which were studied and copied by his contemporaries, reveal that Nowell often excerpted from his sources those specific passages that related to British topography. In his concern with historical topography Nowell advanced the work begun by Leland and prepared the way for the great county histories of England, of which Lambarde's *Perambulation of Kent* (1576) was the first. The same concern characterizes Nowell's maps. Those in Cotton Domitian A.xviii represent the different regions of England, with place-names entered in OE. Another (BL Add. 62540, fol. 3v) whimsically includes a self-portrait in which Nowell despondently holds his empty purse within view of his patron Cecil.

Nowell is now esteemed chiefly for his contribution to the recovery of the OE language. Here his work encompassed not only transcriptions—including copies of the Anglo-Saxon laws used by Lambarde for his edition of 1568, the *Archaionomia*—but also an OE dictionary of some 6,000 entries finally published in 1952. Independent from yet associated with the Anglo-Saxon studies of the circle of Archbishop Matthew Parker (1504–1575), Nowell alone among his contemporaries showed an interest in OE poetic texts: he was the owner of the *Beowulf* manuscript (Cotton Vitellius A.xv, fols. 94–209) and annotated the Exeter Book of OE poetry (Exeter Cathedral Library 3501). In his OE studies as in his wider antiquarian work he broke new ground and laid the foundations for future achievements.

Timothy Graham

Bibliography

PRIMARY

Marckwardt, Albert H., ed. *Laurence Nowell's "Vocabularium Saxonicum."* Ann Arbor: University of Michigan Press, 1952.

SECONDARY

Berkhout, Carl T. "The Pedigree of Laurence Nowell the Antiquary." *English Language Notes* 23/2 (1985): 15–26; Black, Pamela M. "Some New Light on the Career of Laurence Nowell the Antiquary." *Antiquaries Journal* 62 (1982): 116–23; Buckalew, Ronald E. "Nowell, Lambarde, and Leland: The Significance of Laurence Nowell's Transcript of Ælfric's *Grammar and Glossary.*" In *Anglo-Saxon Scholarship: The First Three Centuries,* ed. Carl T. Berkhout and Milton McC. Gatch. Boston: Hall, 1982, pp. 19–50; Flower, Robin. "Laurence Nowell and the Discovery of England in Tudor Times." *PBA* 21 (1935): 47–73. Repr. in *British Academy Papers on Anglo-Saxon England,* ed. E.G. Stanley. Oxford: Oxford University Press, 1990, pp. 1–27.

See also Bede; *Beowulf;* Chronicles; Cotton; Exeter Book; Gerald of Wales; Matthew Paris; Parker

Nuns and Nunneries

Although the life of the nun demanded a particular form of religious dedication, women of all ages became nuns for a variety of reasons. Most wanted to follow the traditional dedication of "bride of Christ," whether out of a sense of vocation or an aversion to marriage. Many young girls were placed in nunneries by their families as a gift to the church on their behalf. Other patrons found places for their female relatives, particularly those born outside wedlock. Widows, not all of them old but seeking to escape remarriage, came to the nunnery to find comfort and succor. Some women found the male-dominated society of their time irksome and wished to seek some form of independence through joining the practice of the religious life and finding Christ's "easy yoke" more bearable.

Male influence, however, could not be totally removed from the convent. Men still had essential roles, whether as the local bishop or as the chaplain who administered the eucharist, dispensed pastoral care, heard confessions, and buried the dead. Not all the women who wished to become nuns were able to do so; the lack of a place to which to go was often a major obstacle. In addition women needed private resources to support themselves in an environment where self-sufficiency was not really possible. With fees or dowries being payable upon entry in a convent, nuns came generally from those social groups that could afford to pay.

Formal houses for women came into existence in Europe in the early 6th century. In Gaul and the Iberian Peninsula the institution of the double monastery enabled the necessary ministrations of the clergy to be more easily performed. In such houses women lived with men, but in strictly separated communities within the same enclosure, directed by one head—usually the abbess—and using a common church for the liturgical offices. With the christianization of the Anglo-Saxon kingdoms the example of the double monastery was introduced from Gaul by nuns who had trained at Chelles and Jouarre.

English double monasteries reached their zenith in the 7th and 8th centuries, under a series of outstanding abbesses of royal or aristocratic blood. The most celebrated was Hild (614–680), related to the royal lines of both Northumbria and East Anglia. Born a heathen, she had been brought to the faith in 627 by Paulinus, Rome's first missionary to Northumbria. Aidan, bishop of Lindisfarne, in 649 appointed her abbess of Hartlepool, where Hild developed her own interpretation of the monastic life, based on the *Regula mixta* as practiced by Benedict Biscop (ca. 628–689) at the nearby male community of Wearmouth-Jarrow. The double community at Whitby that she founded in 657 followed the example of the primitive church; its members held everything in common and led the simple life. Archaeological excavations at Whitby have revealed a group of small cells "for praying and reading," while loom weights found in the same area suggest that the nuns also engaged in spinning and weaving.

The outstanding reputation of Hild's communities at Hartlepool and Whitby made them places of serious Christian monastic life and of education at a period when monasteries were beginning to play a major intellectual role in the newly literate society. Standards of female literacy in the double houses were remarkable. Aldhelm of Malmesbury's prose work *De virginitate,* addressed to Abbess Hildelith and her community at Barking, took for granted that the nuns could both read and appreciate the style of his complex Latin. The strength and enthusiasm of Anglo-Saxon nuns played a remarkable role in the intellectual renaissance of the early 8th century. They excelled in the production of books for personal study and for the training of others, especially relating to the education and conversion of the heathen. The degree of freedom and independence that these English nuns enjoyed, the influence they were able to exert, and the confidence they inspired in those they counseled and advised is a tribute to the strength of the monastic tradition in which they were trained.

The early double communities dwindled and disappeared, suddenly, as at Whitby, burned in 867 by the Danes, or else more slowly, reflecting a society in which the male element was becoming dominant. Alfred, realizing the need, founded a nunnery at Shaftesbury and placed his daughter Æthelgifu there as abbess. Other houses came under royal protection, showing that even noble women had need of protection to enable them to overcome the apparent decline in esteem for the female version of the religious life. Indeed the attitude seems to have prevailed that the prayers of women were somehow less effective than those of men, and it seems certain that nunneries were not founded in sufficient numbers to satisfy the growing demand for places within their cloisters. At the Conquest, therefore, only nine fully organized nunneries remained in England; six were concentrated in Wessex.

After the Conquest the picture changes, with strong social pressures to create more opportunities for women. Although by 1100 the number of nunneries had only doubled, by 1250 more than 130 new female foundations had come into existence, some 24 being founded in Yorkshire alone between ca. 1125 and ca. 1200. While charter and other written evidence for the growth of English nunneries at this early period is fragmentary, it is clear that there was a sudden influx of women demanding to enter the religious life. In England this demand took various distinct routes: the grouping of religious women around a recluse, forming the nucleus of a convent; the incorporation of nunneries into existing or new orders; and a return to the institution of the double monastery. One early-13th-century source, the *Mappa mundi,* attempted a stark classification of the religious life of nuns according to the color of their habits.

Several nunneries in post-Conquest England grew out of the close association between a recluse and her followers. This movement toward the more community-based, or cenobitic, lifestyle is no more clearly described than at St. Albans in the *Life of Christina of Markyate* (ca. 1140), though other small groups of female recluses formed the nuclei of the convents of Crabhouse in Norfolk, Kilburn in Middlesex, and Cheshunt and Flamstead in Hertfordshire.

Most nunneries founded after the Conquest were poor. The poverty of many of these impelled the abbesses to receive more inmates than they could afford, and with this poverty came a downgrading in their educational status. It was often made worse in that the nuns had difficulty in finding educated men to advise them. The prioress of Ankerwyke despaired of understanding an official mandate she had received and returned it, complaining that she did not understand it herself, and neither was there any man of skill who could show her what to do.

The 12th century brought complex relationships with the new male orders. Several English nunneries claimed to have links with the new order of Cîteaux, despite strong resistance from the General Chapter that lasted until 1213. Women seem to have been attracted as much by Cistercian austerity and fervor as by the valuable exemptions and privileges, not just from tithes but also from episcopal control, enjoyed by the male houses. Two convents with the status of abbey, Marham in Norfolk, founded in 1249, and Tarrant in Dorset, mentioned as Cistercian in 1233, were formally incorporated into the order. But of the numerous other aspirants many merely imitated Cistercian customs without any official recognition.

One group of nuns was able both to imitate the Cistercians and to return to the model of the old double monastery. The community of Sempringham was founded in 1131 by Gilbert, a Lincolnshire priest, to care for and teach seven local girls. These "handmaidens of God" were enclosed by the bishop of Lincoln in cells against the wall of the parish church. There they were segregated from the world, consecrated to virginity, and reserved for their bridegroom, Christ. At first, as with anchoresses, all necessities of life were passed through the windows of the cells by female lay servants. Later these took the habit as lay sisters, while lay brothers were added on Cistercian lines.

With the foundation of a second house at Haverholme in 1139 Gilbert was forced to address the problem of regulating a community of women that also contained men. In 1147 he went to Cîteaux to seek admittance for his nuns to the Cistercian order. Although this request was refused, the rule of life he drew up had the support of St. Bernard himself. Gilbert founded an order with a clear constitutional framework that provided men, both canons and lay brothers, to care for the needs of nuns, plus an organization to link the houses and provide for their mutual support. That he did this so successfully is shown by the 1,500 cloistered nuns in England by 1200, and by many small foundations, localized in Lincolnshire and Yorkshire.

Another later successful foundation for women was made in the name of Birgitta (Bridget) of Sweden (1303–1373), whose Order of the Holy Savior was better known in England as the Brigettines. In the 15th century the order spread from the mother house at Vadstena in Sweden and drew royal support. Henry V's foundation at Syon soon became one of the richest and most respected nunneries in England. The special devotion of the nuns to the wounds of Christ, their observance of the canonical hours, and their meditation and reception of vernacular sermons by the brothers added to the order's considerable and well-deserved reputation.

By 1450 there were about 140 female communities in England, containing just over 2,000 nuns. Most of the houses were small and impoverished, in contrast with the many well-endowed male houses. Two-thirds of all nunneries had gross incomes of less than £100 a year, while the income of one-third fell even below £50 a year. The low incomes were matched by their small size. After 1350 only nine houses are known to have had communities of more than 30 nuns. The small scale of endowments reflected the religious and social aspirations of the local founders. They aspired to the status of patron and sought perpetual prayers for themselves and their families; the desire to fund a nunnery may, on many occasions, have outstripped their ability to make an adequate endowment.

While convents gained small bequests, dowries, and annuities, the greater part of their revenue was derived from lands, rents, and sales of produce. Rents from distant properties were hard to collect and might run well in arrears. Even as landholders engaged in economic activities, convents were supervised and overseen by men. The local bishop, at his visitation for their spiritual welfare, also inspected their lands. Little was to change, and by the Dissolution the two largest and wealthiest houses were Shaftesbury in Dorset, with 57 nuns, and Syon, near London, with 52. At the other end of the scale were the Yorkshire houses of Marrick and Nunburnholme with twenty and six nuns, respectively, and incomes of £100 and £10.

Brenda M. Bolton

Bibliography

Berman, Constance H. "Men's Houses, Women's Houses: The Relationship between the Sexes in Twelfth-Century Monasticism." In *Medieval Studies at Minnesota* 2: *The Medieval Monastery,* ed. Andrew MacLeish. St. Cloud: North Star Press, 1988, pp. 42–53; Burton, Janet E. *The Yorkshire Nunneries in the Twelfth and Thirteenth Centuries.* Borthwick Paper 56. York: Borthwick Institute, 1979; Golding, Brian. "Hermits, Monks, and Women in Twelfth-Century France and England: The Experience of Obazine and Sempringham." *Monastic Studies* 1 (1990): 127–45; Hicks, M. "The English Minoresses and Their Early Benefactors, 1281–1367." *Monastic Studies* 2 (1991): 158–70; Holdsworth, Christopher J. "Christina of Markyate." In *Medieval Women,* ed. Derek Baker. Oxford: Blackwell, 1978, pp. 185–204; Knowles, David, and R. Neville Hadcock. *Medieval Religious Houses: England and Wales.* New ed. London: Longman, 1971; Mayer, M.A. "Women and the Tenth-Century English Monastic Reform." *Revue Bénédictine* 87 (1977): 34–61; Millinger, Susan. "Humility and Power: Anglo-Saxon Nuns in Anglo-Norman Hagiography." In *Medieval Religious Women.* Vol. 1: *Distant Echoes,* ed. John A. Nichols and Lillian Thomas Shank. Cistercian Studies Series 71. Kalamazoo: Cistercian Publications, 1984, pp. 115–29; Mountain, J. "Nunnery Finances in the Early Fifteenth Century." *Monastic Studies* 2 (1991): 263–72; Nicholson, Joan. "*Feminae gloriosae:* Women in the Age of Bede." In *Me-*

dieval Women, ed. Derek Baker. Oxford: Blackwell, 1978, pp. 15–29; Power, Eileen. *Medieval English Nunneries c. 1275 to 1535.* Cambridge: Cambridge University Press, 1922; Thompson, Sally. "Why English Nunneries Had No History: A Study of the Problems of the English Nunneries Founded after the Conquest." In *Medieval Religious Women.* Vol. 1: *Distant Echoes,* ed. John A. Nichols and Lillian Thomas Shank. Cistercian Studies Series 71. Kalamazoo: Cistercian Publications, 1984, pp. 131–49; Thompson, Sally. *Women Religious: The Founding of English Nunneries after the Norman Conquest.* Oxford: Clarendon, 1991; Tillotson, J.H. *Marrick Priory: A Nunnery in Late Medieval Yorkshire.* Borthwick Paper 75. York: Borthwick Institute, 1989; Warren, Ann K. *Anchorites and Their Patrons in Medieval England.* Berkeley: University of California Press, 1985.

See also Cistercians; Monasticism; Women

Offa (r. 757–96)

King of Mercia in 757, after ousting another claimant. By the time of his death on 28 July 796 Offa also held sway over Sussex, Kent, and East Anglia. His daughters married rulers of Wessex and Northumbria, thus extending his sphere of influence. He clashed with the Welsh, which probably led him to construct the dike that bears his name. Running along much of the nearly 150 miles of the Welsh frontier, from the Severn estuary to a few miles south of the Dee estuary, Offa's Dyke is the longest earthwork in Britain. It could have been planned in one season and completed in the next; if this was indeed so, it is testimony to the organizational and coercive power that made him the leading English ruler of his day.

Offa utilized the church to enhance his power. He persuaded Pope Hadrian to sanction the creation of a new archdiocese at Lichfield in 787, only a few miles from his palace at Tamworth, thus effectively neutralizing the hostile archbishop of Canterbury. Probably imitating Charlemagne, he had his son, Ecgfrith, consecrated as his successor in 787, the first royal anointing in English history.

Offa seems to have had extensive trade contacts with the Carolingian realm, which in turn appears to have made monetary reform possible. His silver penny, influenced by a Carolingian model, was the basis of the English coinage until the reign of Henry III. He appreciated the coin's potential for symbolism; many bear his name and a finely wrought effigy, and some even carry the likeness of his wife, Cynethryth, a practice drawn either from Byzantine Italy or even late-imperial Rome.

The poems *Beowulf* and *Widsith,* a tribute list known as "The Tribal Hidage"—even the origin of a system of burghal defense later associated with Alfred the Great of Wessex—have been associated with Offa. Much more research will be needed, however, before a balanced assessment of the cultural and social contributions of his reign can be made.

Though his achievements did not long survive him, he was regarded as a great figure in the Middle Ages. Alfred claimed to have adopted and modified his laws; a sword reputed to be his was still treasured two centuries after his death; a 14th-century *Life* was composed by the monks of St. Albans, who revered him as their founder. An imitator rather than an innovator; his image of greatness derived from his longevity, ruthlessness, and astute ability to exploit the imagery of rulership. Apart from the dike little evidence of his power survives; the Mercian archives are lost, as is his burial place. His palace at Tamworth probably lies under the parish churchyard and so cannot be excavated.

David A.E. Pelteret

Bibliography

Blunt, Christopher E. "The Coinage of Offa." In *Anglo-Saxon Coins: Studies Presented to F.M. Stenton on the Occasion of His 80th Birthday,* ed. R.H.M. Dolley. London: Methuen, 1961, pp. 39–62; Brooks, Nicholas. "The Development of Military Obligations in Eighth- and Ninth-Century England." In *England before the Conquest: Studies in Primary Sources Presented to Dorothy Whitelock,* ed. Peter Clemoes and Kathleen Hughes. Cambridge: Cambridge University Press, 1971, pp. 69–84; Hart, Cyril. "The Kingdom of Mercia." In *Mercian Studies,* ed. Ann Dornier. Leicester: Leicester University Press, 1977, pp. 43–61; Keynes, Simon. "Changing Faces: Offa, King of Mercia." *History Today* 40/11 (November 1990): 14–19; Levison, Wilhelm. *England and the Continent in the Eighth Century.* Oxford: Clarendon, 1946; Noble, Frank. *Offa's Dyke Reviewed.* Ed. Margaret Gelling. BAR Brit. Ser. 114. Oxford: BAR, 1983; Stenton, F.M. "The Supremacy of the Mercian Kings." In *Preparatory to Anglo-Saxon England,* ed. Doris M. Stenton. Oxford: Clarendon, 1970, pp. 48–66; Wormald, Patrick. "The Age of Offa and Alcuin." In *The Anglo-Saxons,* ed. James Campbell. Oxford: Phaidon, 1982, pp. 101–31; Wormald, Patrick. "In Search of King Offa's 'Law-Code.'" In *People and Places in Northern Europe 500–1600: Essays in Honour of Peter Hayes Sawyer,* ed. Ian Wood and Niels Lund. Woodbridge: Boydell, 1991, pp. 25–45.

See also Heptarchy

Offices, New Liturgical

When established for universal use, proper offices for such feasts as Trinity Sunday and Corpus Christi were added to English rites, as they were elsewhere. Also, as in most countries of western Europe, new national saints and feasts were added to the calendar prolifically. Many were provided with complete proper texts and chants for Matins, Lauds, Vespers, and, less often, for the other hours. Proper hymns were sometimes included. The composition of new or adapted texts and chants for the antiphons, responsories, and verses were thus one of the chief occupations of ecclesiastical poets and composers. Normally the poet and composer was the same individual, probably the precentor. Because the new texts centered on a biographical narrative of the saint, his deeds, and miracles, they were called *historiae.*

The Norman Conquest had a major impact on the style of English composition, as it did on the suppression of Anglo-Saxon saints and introduction of new ones. One of the earliest offices known in England, in honor of St. Cuthbert, was written early in the 10th century for the court chapel of Æthelstan or his father, Edward the Elder, probably by a clerk from the Low Countries. Surviving the Conquest, it was adapted for monastic use between 1083 and 1150. Although the *vita* of St. Birinus, the missionary to the West Saxons, was reworked in the 13th century, no evidence confirms the continued liturgical use of his office. St. Alphege was venerated later, although only fragments of an office survive. An elaborate vigil and feast day office for Edmund, king and martyr, written about 987, was expanded by a Norman cleric, and remained in use. The office for St. Alban, written about 1000, survived: John Dunstable wrote a 15th-century isorhythmic motet based on one of its chants, and its texts are found in later breviaries. Most of its chants are lost. Of other Anglo-Saxon offices little is known, and there is not even a comprehensive catalogue.

Although the texts appear to be prose, like most of the standard repertoire, and the chants are on the surface indistinguishable from the general style of plainsong, it is clear that both words and music were often structured in some way. In certain items regular poetry occurs: the antiphons for Cuthbert have monosyllabic rhymes in eight-syllable lines, but the responsories are essentially rhymed prose. For Birinus the surviving responsories and some of the antiphons are in rhymed prose, and other antiphons are in leonine (rhyming) hexameters.

As well as techniques that seem to foreshadow the use of full rhyme and regularly accented lines there occur other literary devices not usually found in the standard repertoire. Among these are rhymed prose, regularly accented lines without rhyme, prose with deliberate and extensive use of the literary cursus, and classical meters. Some of these literary structures seem to be reinforced by musical means. Even when presented in a notation that is not directly transcribable, it is sometimes possible to ascertain the musical modes of the chants. Within each service the antiphons may be arranged in modal order from 1 to 8 followed by a return to 1, and the responsories in a separate similar order. Hymns, if they are proper at all, do not form a part of this modal sequence.

A full study of these early offices needs to be undertaken. No doubt the techniques used in them continued even after the fully rhymed office was usual. But because many manuscripts have been lost, it is rarely possible to know whether an office in, say, a 13th-century manuscript faithfully reflects an Anglo-Saxon version. A noted breviary of about 1300, for example, has offices for Æthelwold and for Kyneburga and Kyneswitha (local to East Anglia): most of the texts are loosely structured. No earlier chants are known, so we cannot know what changes may have taken place. The same is true of the office for St. Ethelbert in the Hereford noted breviary of the 1250s.

An extensive monastic office for St. Oswin, unfortunately incomplete, exists in a 12th-century source. It uses irregularly structured texts and chants. The last known composition of offices in the earlier non- or semistructured style is in the late 12th century. Ralph Niger, born about 1140, wrote a treatise on the four major Marian feasts, including the corresponding offices, about which he says "I sought out [composed?] new chant for the antiphons and responsories." Although neither rhyme nor classical meter occurs, signs of other kinds of structure are present.

From the 12th century and later new offices were mostly strictly rhymed and regularly poetic, conforming to a general change in European liturgical poetry. Of these later "rhymed" compositions few are known or have been investigated, and only recently has a catalogue been published. Many of their texts were printed, without chant, about a century ago in Dreves and Blume's *Analecta hymnica.* In this later repertoire every sung item of the office (as opposed to intoned items) is normally rhymed and completely regular in accent and number of syllables. Typical of the poetic forms are the goliardic meter (lines of seven and six syllables) and the Victorine sequence form (lines of eight and seven syllables). The verses of responsories are occasionally in prose or classical meters. The chants of this repertoire seem to use the modal system and modal order of chants rather rigidly as a prescriptive device for composition, so that the modal character of each item is usually clear: cadences or subcadences at each line or rhyme strengthen the modal clarity. Occasionally the range is extended so that both authentic and plagal versions of the mode are combined. Responsory verses, usually sung to an elaborate tone in the standard repertoire, are now provided with an elaborate melody. The melodic style of the chants is less restrained than that of the standard repertoire. Occasionally overt word painting is present: for example, in the late-11th-century office of St. Mildred of Thanet, the phrase *stella radians,* "shining star," is set in the highest register an octave above the final; in the mid-15th-century office of the last English saint canonized in the Middle Ages, St. Osmund, the word *scandere,* "to climb," occurs with a melisma on *scan-* that rises stepwise through nine scale degrees and falls similarly to its starting point. The latter office is noteworthy also because of its prominent use of classical meters.

Perhaps the earliest completely regular rhymed office in England is that of St. Thomas of Canterbury (Thomas Becket). It is surely the most important. Written before 1193 by Abbot Benedict of Peterborough, it was quickly made into a form suitable for secular use in the newly emerged Sarum liturgy that became the standard for much of the British Isles. Of high literary and musical quality, it spread across the whole of Europe and even nowadays exists in several hundred known manuscript sources. Both in Europe and England dozens, perhaps scores, of later offices were modeled on it, using its poetic forms and adapting its chants. Here, other than the important office for David of Wales, those for the translation of Thomas himself, Chadd, and Edmund Rich (Edmund of Abingdon), a later archbishop of Canterbury, are relevant. Several other offices for Thomas also exist, some in English sources.

Franciscan and Dominican offices were not greatly important, if the surviving sources are any guide. John Pecham, another archbishop of Canterbury (1279–92), imitated the office of St. Francis in his composition for Trinity Sunday; perhaps about 1389 John Horneby is said to have written an office for the Visitation of the Blessed Virgin, with strong Franciscan connections; about 1381 Thomas Stubbs modeled his office for St. Anne on that of Dominic. The sole Augustinian office, although not modeled on a known exemplar, is for John of Bridlington, canonized in 1401: the first responsory of Matins served as the tenor for a cyclic mass later in the century. Unique offices survive to St. Helen the empress (finder of the Cross) and to Gilbert of Sempringham. Most of the metropolitan centers of England produced offices: honoring William (archbishop of York), Wulstan, Richard, and Thomas (bishops of Worcester, Chichester, and Hereford, respectively); Edmund Lacy, bishop of Hereford, wrote one in honor of the archangel Raphael. The office for Osmund (bishop of Salisbury) was the last. Many of these survive with their chants.

Of numerous other national saints, some of considerable importance, there remain only isolated prayers or sung texts, sometimes poetic. Frequently these appear in the books of hours of the 15th century and later. These texts may have been written as commemorations of the saints, to be incorporated into offices of higher liturgical priority, and thus all that ever existed; or they may be survivors of complete offices now lost. The list is long: Aldhelm, Alphege, Augustine of Canterbury, Dunstan, Edward the Confessor, Ethelburga, Etheldred, Frideswide, Guthlac, Hugh of Lincoln, John of Beverley, Oswald, Swithun, Wilfrid, Willibrord, Winefride, Withburga.

Intriguing are poetic offices (or parts of offices) for saints who were never canonized and in some cases were never likely to be: examples are Simon de Montfort (earl of Leicester, d. 1265) and the mystic Richard Rolle of Hampole (d. 1349). Such offices, which cannot have been authorized for use, may have been written to promote a canonization that never occurred.

Closely related to these English offices and often dependent on the same liturgical use are those of saints from Scotland, Wales, and Ireland, such as Kentigern, Kenneth, David, Patrick, Brigid, and Finian.

Also worth mentioning are three elaborate prose (or semistructured) offices, all monastic. The Cluniac monastery of St. John the Evangelist at Pontefract, Yorkshire, celebrated a special office for the Relics, and for St. John at the Latin Gate, the latter known also in continental sources. Also otherwise associated with sources in Switzerland is the office of St. James in a manuscript thought to be from Reading Abbey, which had a relic of the saint. In a possibly 15th-century manuscript for Ely Priory are found a number of unusual offices. Several are in honor of the Virgin, with partly rhymed items in a single nocturn, a special invitatory, and rhymed Te Deum. Similar is another office and mass said to be entitled *de sancta sophia* (or *de eterna sapiencia*, "holy/eternal wisdom") in "the old books."

No doubt chants and texts were often borrowed and adapted within this repertoire of offices, but the web of relations has yet to be charted. The antiphon *Ave rex gentis* in various forms, with its chant, runs like a thread from Edmund, king and martyr, and Alban (10th century), to Ethelbert and Oswin (12th century), Edmund Rich of Abingdon (13th century), and a polyphonic motet of the 14th century.

Andrew Hughes

Bibliography

Flahiff, G.B. "Ralph Niger." *MS* 2 (1940): 104–26; Hartzell, K. Drew. "A St. Albans Miscellany in New York." *Mittellateinisches Jahrbuch* 10 (1975): 20–61; Hohler, Christopher. "The Durham Services in Honour of St. Cuthbert." In *The Relics of Saint Cuthbert*, ed. C.F. Battiscombe. Oxford: Oxford University Press, 1956, pp. 155–91; Hughes, Andrew. "Modal Order and Disorder in the Rhymed Office." *Musica Disciplina* 37 (1983): 29–52; Hughes, Andrew. "Research Report: Late Medieval Rhymed Offices." *Journal of the Plainsong and Mediaeval Music Society* 8 (1985): 33–49; Hughes, Andrew. "Chants in the Rhymed Office of St Thomas of Canterbury." *Early Music* 16 (1988): 185–202; Hughes, Andrew. "British Rhymed Offices: A Catalogue and Commentary." In *Music in the Medieval English Liturgy: Plainsong and Mediaeval Music Society Centennial Essays,* ed. Susan K. Rankin and David Hiley. Oxford: Clarendon, 1993, pp. 239–84; Hughes, Andrew. *Late Medieval Liturgical Offices: Resources for Electronic Research.* Subsidia Mediaevalia 23 (Texts) and 24 (Sources and Chants). Toronto: Pontifical Institute, 1994–96; Thomson, Rodney M. "The Music for the Office of St. Edmund King and Martyr." *Music and Letters* 65 (1984): 189–93; Wagner, Peter. "Zur mittelalterlichen Offiziumskomposition." *Kirchenmusikalisches Jahrbuch* 21 (1908): 13–32.

See also Edmund of Abingdon; Feasts, New Liturgical; Liturgy; Liturgy and Church Music, History of; Thomas of Canterbury, Office for; Votive Observance

Old Hall Manuscript

An early-15th-century manuscript of music for mass, one of only three relatively complete collections of English polyphony to survive from before ca. 1500, the other two being the organa of the Winchester Troper from ca. 980 and the eleventh fascicle of W1 from ca. 1240. Its contents represent the first body of English music to which names can be attached, and well over half the pieces are by named English composers. The Old Hall Manuscript (named for its home from 1893 to 1973 at St. Edmund's College at Old Hall Green near Ware, Hertfordshire) was purchased by the British Library in 1973 and is now BL Add. 57950. According to a scenario established recently by Bowers it was principally compiled ca. 1419–20 for the household chapel of Thomas duke of Clarence. Upon Clarence's death in 1421 the preparation of the manuscript was interrupted and it passed into the hands of the Royal Household Chapel of his elder brother, King Henry V, whose musicians made additions to it. Its whereabouts between the later 15th and early 19th centuries are difficult to trace with certainty.

The Old Hall Manuscript is a large book in vertical format (16.4 by 10.9 inches). It was originally planned for a minimum of 121 folios (of which 98 survive) and later had at least sixteen additional leaves inserted (of which fourteen survive). Thus the present 112 folios, containing 147 musical items, represent the torso of a volume that has lost more than a quarter of its original leaves, a loss whose dimensions would be amplified if, as is likely, the manuscript once began with a gathering of Kyries, of which there is now no trace. The manuscript has been further mutilated by the removal, in the 19th century, of the more ornate initial capital letters, along with some surrounding music.

The contents of this book fall into two distinct layers. The first layer, mainly copied by a single scribe, represents music compiled for Thomas duke of Clarence, probably under the supervision of Leonel Power, who was his chapel's leading musician. What was intended was evidently a large anthology of pieces from the half-century or more spanning ca. 1370 to 1421, though most of its repertoire, on stylistic and biographical grounds, appears to date from ca. 1390 to 1410. This layer was subject to rigorous organizational principles. On the broadest level pieces were grouped according to liturgical category for use at mass: (Kyrie), Gloria, antiphons and cantilenas (to be used as Sequence and Offertory substitutes), Credo, Sanctus, Agnus, and motets (by their placement and texts, evidently Deo gratias substitutes). The Gloria, Credo, Sanctus, and Agnus gatherings were further subdivided so that the simpler settings notated in score precede the more complex settings notated in separate parts. As a further mark of planning there are two pieces, one beginning the section of Sanctus settings in score, the other heading up the section of Gloria settings in parts, that are ascribed to Roy Henry, who is most probably to be identified with Henry V.

In making the second-layer additions later scribes followed the organization of the first layer, adding works on blank staves or tipping in new leaves as necessary. The one exception to this behavior is a group of three second-layer motets inserted between the Sanctus and Agnus sections. These motets seem to be intended as Sanctus sequels rather than as Deo gratias substitutes and may originally have been written for the triumphal entry of Henry V into London after the victory at Agincourt in 1415. As a rule the repertoire of the second layer dates from the 1410s and early 1420s; its copyists may have included those among the composers represented who were members of Henry's Royal Household Chapel, thus preserving rare medieval authorial holographs. A younger companion volume ("H6") from the same environment, modeled on Old Hall and overlapping in contents but mainly preserving the repertoire of the Royal Household Chapel at a slightly later date (during the infancy of Henry VI, in the mid- to late 1420s), survives today only in scattered fragments.

The physical division of the music of Old Hall into score or part notation reflects a division of musical style and function as well. The sonorous, chordal, three-voice pieces in score, some freely composed and some enveloping a plainchant in two outer parts, represent a conventional, functional, and not overly elaborate music for daily (ferial) mass. The compositions in parts are more diverse in approach, employing strict or free isorhythm, strict canon or pseudo-canon (i.e., written out), or some form of treble-dominated texture under less overtly constructivist control. Less conventional, they are more "artificial," representing a higher and more ostentatious register of musical discourse appropriate to feast days and public ceremonies.

Peter M. Lefferts

Bibliography

PRIMARY

Hughes, Andrew, and Margaret Bent, eds. *The Old Hall Manuscript.* 3 vols. in 4. Corpus Mensurabilis Musicae 46. Rome: American Institute of Musicology, 1969–73.

SECONDARY

Bent, Margaret. "The Old Hall Manuscript." *Early Music* 2 (1974): 2–14; Bent, Margaret. "The Progeny of Old Hall: More Leaves from a Royal English Choirbook." In *Gordon Athol Anderson (1929–1981) in Memoriam,* ed. Luther Dittmer. 2 vols. Henryville: Institute of Mediaeval Music, 1984, 1:1–54; Bent, Margaret. "Old Hall MS." *NGD* 13:526–29; Bowers, Roger. "Some Observations on the Life and Career of Lionel Power." *Proceedings of the Royal Musical Association* 102 (1975–76): 103–27; Hughes, Andrew. "The Old Hall Manuscript: A Reappraisal." *Musica Disciplina* 21 (1967): 97–129; Hughes, Andrew, and Margaret Bent. "The Old Hall Manuscript: An Inventory." *Musica Disciplina* 21 (1967): 130–47.

See also Discant; Mass, Polyphonic Music for; Motet; Power, Leonel; W1; Winchester Tropers

Opus Anglicanum

English medieval embroidery in silk and gold (silver-gilt) thread, designated as Opus Anglicanum ("English work") in contemporary documents, carried English art and design to every country in western Europe.

Superb embroideries, a few of which survive, were already being produced in the Anglo-Saxon period. Some 9th-century fragments preserved at Maeseyck in Belgium have designs of arches and circles containing animals and interlace. An early-10th-century stole and maniple at Durham Cathedral in England have a design of superb quality in silk on a gold background, derived from late-classical textiles with standing figures, one above the other. Different from these in style and scale is the massive 11th-century narrative hanging of the Norman invasion of England embroidered in wool on linen, known as the Bayeux Tapestry.

In contrast to the lively style of these earlier embroideries those of the Romanesque and early Gothic periods are more severe, with figures and ornaments stiffly drawn. The embroidery is worked mainly in gold in underside couching (in which the thread is laid on the surface of the material and fixed at intervals by means of a linen thread on the back of the material) on silk backgrounds, with foliate ornament, animals, or human figures within rectangles, circles, or rounded arches. A maniple and two amice apparels of about 1140–70 associated with the great English saint Thomas of Canterbury have foliate crosses within a lattice of interlaced circles (Sens Cathedral and Erdington Abbey, Birmingham). Some early-13th-century fragments of bishop's buskins have foliate scrolls containing figures of kings (London, British Museum and Victoria and Albert Museum). A more graceful development of this style is found in the Clare Chasuble (Victoria and Albert Museum), made for a member of the royal family in about the 1270s, in which coiling stems enclose lions and griffins and a band of quatrefoils contains angularly drawn sacred subjects. The development toward Gothic grace and naturalism was a feature of 13th-century embroidery, with details worked in natural colors in silk threads and the gold parts worked with chevron patterns instead of the bricklike patterns of the preceding century.

The international reputation of English embroidery grew at this time, and the flow of embroidery increased as popes and other potentates began to collect. The famous Vatican Inventory of 1295 includes over 100 embroideries designated as Opus Anglicanum.

A richer, more flexible style developed in the later-13th to early-14th century, now exemplified in three copies: one with a design based on the Tree of Jesse (Victoria and Albert Museum), and two others in the Vatican and Switzerland (Bern, Abegg-Stiftung). These have elegant draped figures within scrolling or geometric compartments on gold or red backgrounds.

During the first half of the 14th century, coinciding with the Decorated style in English Gothic architecture and so-called East Anglian manuscripts, English embroidery reached its finest quality. This is exemplified by a panel from a cope (Victoria and Albert Museum) that shows Christ in Majesty and is similar in date, style, and large scale to the Melk Chasuble with a Crucifixion scene (from a monastery at Melk, now in Vienna, Österreichisches Museum für Kunst). The elegantly posed figures in embroideries of this period, with wavy hair and costumes with convoluted folds, are identical with those depicted by court painters, who must also have supplied the embroidery designs. The finest embroideries, regarded as the equal of paintings or goldsmiths' work, were immensely costly.

The lively storytelling seen in some pieces, such as the scenes from the life of the Virgin on an incomplete set of alb apparels of 1320–40 (Victoria and Albert Museum), was another element contributed by painters.

The design scheme of copes changed in the 14th century from that with sacred scenes in quatrefoils, represented by the Syon Cope (1300–20) and Steeple Aston Cope (1310–40), both in the Victoria and Albert Museum, to an arrangement following the curved contours of the cope with scenes in rows of concentric arcades. This more pleasing style is represented by a cope in Bologna (1315–35) and another in Pienza Cathedral (1315–35), the latter one of the finest surviving examples of Opus Anglicanum.

Velvet became a popular background material at this time, providing an excellent foil for the silk and gold embroidery. Examples include the Butler-Bowdon Cope (1330–50) in the Victoria and Albert Museum, the closely related Chichester-Constable Chasuble (New York, Metropolitan Museum) and a cope (1340–70) now in Vich in Spain.

A trend toward a more severe style related to that of Perpendicular architecture is represented by the design of the Lateran Cope of 1340–60 (Rome) and a cope orphrey of 1340–60 (Stockholm, State Historical Museum), where gold backgrounds with rectilinear patterns replace the rich curvilinear patterns of the early-14th century.

From the mid-14th century onward English embroidery workshops were still prolific, but the embroideries produced were not of the luxurious quality of the preceding period. Economic and social factors depressed all the arts in England, including embroidery, and the workshops had to meet increasing competition from imports of Italian patterned silks. In response techniques and designs were simplified. Underside couching was replaced by surface couching and narrative scenes were replaced with single or paired saints beneath architectural canopies. Large pieces, such as copes and altar frontals, were decorated with applied motifs powdered over the surface.

Most surviving medieval English embroidery is ecclesiastical work, preserved in the relatively safe environment of the church, although contemporary documents indicate that numerous secular embroideries were produced as well. A few secular pieces, mostly heraldic, survive, including fragments of a royal horse trapper (1330–40), embroidered with the leopards of England (Paris, Cluny Museum), and the 14th-century Black Prince's heraldic surcoat (made before 1376) at Canterbury Cathedral.

All known surviving embroideries were made by professional workshops, with the exception of one band from an altar frontlet (1290–1340) that has the name of the nun who embroidered it on the back (Victoria and Albert Museum). Workshops were situated in the City of London, where the capital necessary for the costly materials required was most readily available. Although the craft required little apparatus, the silks and velvets used for the ground materials and the silk and metal threads for the embroidery all had to be imported, mainly from Italy and Asia.

Embroiderers, both men and women, underwent a rigorous seven-year period of apprenticeship, the gold embroiderers being the most highly skilled and sought-after. Popes Alexander IV (1254–61) and Urban IV (1261–64) had a gold embroiderer, Gregory of London, attached to the papal household. The authorities dealt directly with the workshops or via merchants. Adam of Basing, a wealthy merchant, sold silk cloths and embroideries to King Henry III between 1238 and 1260, but the king also commissioned several embroideries directly from Mabel of Bury St. Edmunds between 1239 and 1244.

The long tradition of religious embroidery in England was abruptly halted by the Reformation, after which embroideries with sacred subjects were no longer required. Much embroidery was destroyed at that time, but sufficient numbers survive, although often altered or worn, to give a glimpse of the riches of an art that was much prized.

Linda Woolley

Bibliography

Christie, A.G.I. *English Medieval Embroidery*. Oxford: Clarendon, 1938; King, Donald. *Opus Anglicanum*. London: Arts Council & Victoria and Albert Museum, 1963 [exhibition catalogue]; King, Donald, and Santina Levey. *The Victoria and Albert Museum's Textile Collection: Embroidery in Britain from 1200–1750*. London: Victoria and Albert Museum, 1993.

See also Architecture and Architectural Sculpture, Gothic; Art, Gothic; Art, Romanesque; Bayeux Tapestry; "East Anglian School"; Manuscript Illumination, Gothic; Painting, Gothic; Saints' Lives, Illuminated; Textiles, Anglo-Saxon; Textiles from St. Cuthbert's Tomb

Orality and Aurality
Old English

"Orality" refers to the type of discourse produced by a culture depending significantly on immediate subject-to-subject vocality for the transmission of information, ritual, traditions, entertainments, and instruction. Though writing was produced with increasing frequency as the Anglo-Saxon period progressed, writing in the OE vernacular, rather than being conceived of as an autonomous medium for the origination of textual discourse, as in modern societies, was used to a large extent as an auxiliary to the voice and as a cue for memory, recording oral events (poems, medicinal recipes and spells, legal transactions and decisions).

Anglo-Saxon society, at least after the period of the Conversion (600–700), cannot, however, be thought of as a "pri-

mary" oral culture, since writing increasingly shaped discourse (and everything we know of Anglo-Saxon "oral discourse" derives from written sources). Yet orality also continued to influence texts. Even when a text was a new composition—rather than the record of an oral or memorial event—oral habits of vocabulary, organization, and thinking often shaped the form and message. The OE poetic style, with its dependence on a relatively small inventory of syntactic and metrical frames, repetition and variation of stock vocabulary, additive style, and arrangement into simple oppositions of scenes and characters, clearly derives from a traditional oral style and continues even in the work of poets, such as Cynewulf, who, fairly certainly, composed by writing.

Oral features, mixed with imitation of Latin style, are the rule in OE prose as well. OE texts tend to be, like oral utterances, context-dependent—that is, they are not designed to be self-explanatory to a reader after the occasion that gave rise to the utterance is absent, which is why so much of OE literature is not only anonymous but without date and provenance, and often obscure as to its intellectual connections and intentions. "Oral style" continued to manifest itself in written work not just because of nostalgia or conservative stylistic habits but because "oral thinking" was deeply ingrained (autonomous textuality being a concomitant of a deeply literate and long-established written tradition) and because almost all OE texts, even when literate in their origins (e.g., the sermons of Wulfstan and Ælfric), were nevertheless intended for oral delivery to audiences not necessarily literate themselves.

The issue of orality in Anglo-Saxon literature has for many years been centered on "oral-formulaic theory," an offshoot of Homeric studies. In the 1930s Milman Parry, aiming to establish beyond doubt the orality of Homeric poetry (see the discussion in Lord), found an analogue in the demonstrably oral epics of contemporary Yugoslavia. He posited that this poetry was composed by use of traditional *formulas* and *themes*. He defined the formula as "a group of words which is regularly employed under the same metrical conditions to express a given essential idea" and a theme as "the groups of ideas regularly used in telling a tale in the formulaic style." The Homeric poems were inferred to be oral and extemporaneous (i.e., not memorized from a fixed text) because of stylistic features (formulas and themes) analogous to those in the Yugoslav songs. A key concept was "formulaic density"; a song showing a high proportion of formulas was thereby concluded to be oral.

In 1953 Magoun somewhat mechanically carried this method over into OE studies, finding that the presence of formulas in *Beowulf* was dense enough that it could be deemed an orally composed poem. Magoun's article set off a storm of debate that has never quite subsided. Benson demonstrated that many OE poems translated from or heavily influenced by Latin were just as formulaic as *Beowulf*. He argued for a mixture of oral and written poems in the poetic canon. Meanwhile Fry modified the concept of "formula" to fit the particular literary and linguistic conditions of OE, as opposed to those of Homeric Greek or present-day Serbo-Croatian. The latter use syllabic meters formed around syntactically related word units, while OE meter depends on alliteration and stress distributed over a line of indeterminate syllable length. Fry redefined the OE formula as a "group of half-lines, usually loosely related metrically and semantically, which are related in form by the identical relative placement of two elements, one a variable word or element of a compound usually supplying the alliteration, and the other a constant word or element of a compound, with approximately the same distribution of non-stressed elements" (Fry, 1967: 203).

More recently Foley has shown the flexibility and productiveness of the formula as a "multi-form" depending on a deep "rhythmic sub-strate" that cannot be explained by its individual surface appearances. He has pointed out that one tradition cannot explain the features of another simply by analogy. During the heyday of New Criticism oral-formulaic theory caused much anxiety because it seemed to some that poetry composed by the recollection of preexisting expressions, apparently without individualized forethought and according to entirely traditional ideas and methods, could not possibly be creative or aesthetically significant. The response among such critics was often simply to reject the theory. Others (notably Creed and Renoir) attempted to use features of the oral-formulaic theory to show how poems so composed could be original and distinguished while still remaining within the parameters of oral style. Lately work has begun to stress the increasingly symbiotic relation of orality and writing throughout the period, with related methods of memorial retention, recollection, and production and influencing one another as to subject matter, form, and style (see O'Keeffe, Doane, Carruthers).

Middle English

The terms "orality" and "aurality" designate the spoken performance of texts, the former usually indicating a degree of extemporaneous composition at the time of performance and the latter designating spoken performances aided by written texts. Orality and aurality were inescapable phenomena in the Middle Ages, assuming a variety of forms in all social and occupational ranks. To a degree almost unimaginable in the 20th-century West the arts of the spoken word pervaded medieval education and entertainment.

To begin to assess the ways in which orality affected medieval culture it is necessary to consider some important differences between written and oral expression. Unlike writing oral communication is fluid. Although verbatim memorization occurred in some medieval traditions, oral artists generally recreated their stories at each telling, tailoring each performance to fit the mood and composition of a live audience. Written speech, however, is fixed and portable. It can be shared with strangers who have never met its creator. Written style is standardized and objectified to aid communications in the absence of its author.

In oral performance the audience stands face to face with the performer, exerting an immediate and powerful influence, editing the teller as they listen. If listeners reject a speaker's communication, it is unlikely to survive. Thus the spoken word becomes both a matter of personalized art and community consensus, while written speech, though standardized, allows unpopular individual opinions to outlast the context in which they were formed. The growth of literacy marked the replacement of a number of smaller, oral communities by larger, impersonal societies.

The relationship between spoken and written expression—never simple—grew increasingly complex in late-medieval England. One may assume with some security that most OE poetry was never written down and that much of what does survive was conceived by literate authors to be performed before largely illiterate audiences. In the ME period, however, literacy was nearly universal among those authors whose work survives and greatly expanded among their audiences. Yet live oral performance continued in force—now increasingly as an option rather than a necessity.

Orality was essential to education. Rhetoric students learned not only how to compose verse but also how to deliver it. Even the most delicate arts of philosophy and logic were understood as outgrowths of spoken communication. Though Anselm of Canterbury and other philosophers of the 11th and later centuries associated orality with illiteracy (Stock, 1988: 335), oral dialogues and disputations—in which teacher and student arrive at important insights through question and answer as well as spoken argument—continued to flourish in educational settings throughout the Middle Ages.

As important as oral arts were to literate society, they were all the more crucial to the illiterate, who required oral instruction. Although documentation is scant, we assume that customary oral education took place in situations of shared labor, in households at night, and in special meeting places, such as the mill in the country and the marketplace in the city.

Literate and oral worlds met everywhere. One of the most important crossroads was the pulpit; many preaching manuals include advice to learned preachers on techniques of addressing popular audiences. British oral tradition is rife with folktales that grew out of the great repertoire of sermon exempla shaped in a continuous dialogue between priest and peasant (Owst, ch. 4).

Nor were books completely inaccessible to the illiterate, since the writing and reading of books often involved orality and aurality. For example, *The Book of Margery Kempe* was composed and dictated by an illiterate. This first English autobiography demonstrates that even verbally skillful persons of relatively high social standing (Kempe's father was a mayor of Lynn) could lack reading and writing skills but nonetheless have access to the content of books read aloud to them and to the recording of their ideas by scribes. Kempe's style is influenced by pulpit diction—for example, she continually refers to herself in the third person as "this creature," a standard epithet in homilies.

In the realm of entertainment the preference for live, spoken arts lasted well beyond the age of the oral poet (who composed his work while performing it). Minstrels worked with written and memorized texts before live audiences in a variety of settings, from royal halls to crowded streets. We know of minstrels' activities largely through the disparaging words of clerics like the 14th-century writer John Bromyard, who characterizes them as unholy beggars and chastises those who reward them with money.

In addition to paid specialists amateurs regularly performed oral arts. Squires and pages in noble households were expected to master the arts of singing and versification. Merchant-class artists engaged in oral pastimes imitating courtly entertainments. Thirteenth-century London was the site of a *puy,* a social club of merchants convened to hold song competitions. The composer of the best entry had his creation crowned a "royal song." The *puy's* songs were in French, but by the 15th century English had become the language of literary supper clubs that met in merchant households to exchange poems.

The oral folktale was popular among all groups but became increasingly associated with the tastes of the lower classes. According to Robert Manning (fl. 1303–38) commoners craved to hear tales at games, on holidays, over ale. Though we do not know the form these stories took, they were clearly plentiful. It is from this great pool of oral narrative that many of the tales in collections like Manning's *Handlyng Synne,* Chaucer's *Canterbury Tales,* and the *Gesta Romanorum* ultimately derive, even when they have been mediated at least in part by other written texts.

> *A. N. Doane*
> *Carl Lindahl*

Bibliography

OLD ENGLISH

Benson, Larry D. "The Literary Character of Anglo-Saxon Formulaic Poetry." *PMLA* 81 (1966): 334–41; Carruthers, Mary J. *The Book of Memory: A Study of Memory in Medieval Culture.* Cambridge: Cambridge University Press, 1990; Creed, Robert P. "The Making of an Anglo-Saxon Poem." *ELH* 26 (1959): 445–54; Doane, A.N. "Oral Texts, Intertexts, and Intratexts: Editing Old English." In *Influence and Intertextuality in Literary History,* ed. Jay Clayton and Eric Rothstein. Madison: University of Wisconsin Press, 1991, pp. 75–113; Foley, John Miles. *Immanent Art: From Structure to Meaning in Oral Epic.* Bloomington: Indiana University Press, 1991; Fry, Donald K., Jr. "Old English Formulas and Systems." *English Studies* 48 (1967): 193–204; Lord, Albert Bates. *The Singer of Tales.* Cambridge: Harvard University Press, 1960; Magoun, Francis P., Jr. "Oral-Formulaic Character of Anglo-Saxon Narrative Poetry." *Speculum* 28 (1953): 446–67; O'Keeffe, Katherine O'Brien. *Visible Song: Transitional Literacy in Old English Verse.* Cambridge: Cambridge University Press, 1990; Ong, Walter J. *Orality and Literacy: The Technologizing of the Word.* London: Methuen, 1982; Opland, Jeff. *Anglo-Saxon Oral Poetry: A Study of the Traditions.* New Haven: Yale University Press, 1980; Renoir, Alain. *A Key to Old Poems: The Oral-Formulaic Approach to the Interpretation of the West-Germanic Verse.* University Park: Pennsylvania State University Press, 1988.

MIDDLE ENGLISH

Baugh, A.C. "The Middle English Romance: Some Questions of Creation, Presentation, and Preservation." *Speculum* 42 (1967): 1–31; Bäuml, Franz H. "Varieties and Consequences of Medieval Literacy and Illiteracy." *Speculum* 55 (1980): 237–65; Bowden, Betsy. *Chaucer Aloud: The Varieties of Textual Interpretation.* Philadelphia: University of Pennsylvania Press, 1987; Crosby, Ruth. "Oral Delivery in the Middle Ages." *Speculum* 11 (1936) 88–110; Lindahl, Carl. *Earnest Games: Folkloric Patterns in the Canterbury Tales.* Bloomington: Indiana University Press, 1987; Owst, G.R. *Literature and Pulpit in Medieval England.* 2d ed. Oxford: Blackwell, 1961; Southworth, John. *The English Medieval Minstrel.* Woodbridge: Boydell, 1989; Stock, Brian. *The Implications of Literacy: Written Language and Models of Interpretation in the Eleventh and Twelfth Centuries.* Princeton: Princeton University Press, 1983; Utley, Francis Lee. "Some Implications of Chaucer's Folktales." *Laographia* 22 (1965): 580–99; Zumthor, Paul. "The Text and the Voice." *New Literary History* 16 (1984): 67–92.

See also Drama, Vernacular; Exemplum; Literacy; Minstrels; Popular Culture; *Puy;* Rhetoric; Schools; Sermons; Songs; Universities

Ordainers

In March 1310, following a petition from his leading subjects, Edward II consented to the election of a commission of twenty earls, barons, and bishops—the "Ordainers"—to draw up proposals or ordinances for the reform of government. Many of their grievances, such as the purchase of food supplies for royal uses (prises), and the preference given in repaying royal debts owed to Italian merchants, had first arisen in the closing years of Edward I under pressure of war and royal financial constraints.

But a new feature was the hostility of the Ordainers to the favorites who had gained influence over the king, in particular to Piers Gaveston, to whom Edward II had granted the royal earldom of Cornwall. The Ordainers' work was completed in October 1311, when a document containing 41 ordinances was issued with royal approval. These ranged from prohibitions on the king's departure from England, on the raising of new forms of taxation, on the making of grants of land, and on the appointment of the leading members of the administration and household without baronial approval, to demands that certain individuals, most notably Gaveston, held to have been "evil counselors" of the king, should be removed from court.

The enforcement of the Ordinances was hampered by Edward's wish to retain Gaveston's company. After Gaveston's execution in June 1312 and the return of some of the former Ordainers to the king's side, Edward was more determined than ever to annul the Ordinances. This finally took place in May 1322, after Edward had defeated and executed his chief opponent, Thomas of Lancaster, at the Battle of Boroughbridge.

> *J.R.S. Phillips*

Bibliography

Phillips, J.R.S. *Aymer de Valence, Earl of Pembroke, 1307–1324: Baronial Politics in the Reign of Edward II.* Oxford: Clarendon, 1972; Prestwich, Michael. *The Three Edwards: War and State in England, 1272–1377.* London: Weidenfeld & Nicolson, 1980; Prestwich, Michael. "The Ordinances of 1311 and the Politics of the Early Fourteenth Century." In *Politics and Crisis in Fourteenth-Century England,* ed. J. Taylor and W. Childs. Gloucester: Sutton, 1990, pp. 1–18.

See also Battles of Bannockburn and Boroughbridge; Despenser Family; Edward II; Lancaster, Thomas Earl of

Order of the Garter

The society of lay knights founded by Edward III in 1348–49; it was the second monarchical order in Latin Christendom (after the Castilian Order of the Band) and the model for most of the later foundations.

Edward first proposed to restore the legendary Company of the Round Table, as he proclaimed at a tournament of 1344. The new Round Table was to have had 300 knights. When he returned from the victorious Crécy campaign in 1347, he founded a more exclusive society dedicated to St. George, the patron of knighthood. Its device was a blue garter, in the form of a belt buckled in a circle (probably representing the belt of knighthood), bearing the motto *Hony soyt ke mal y pense* ("Shamed be he who thinks ill of it").

Actually established in stages in 1348/49, the order was a confraternity with three distinct colleges. The first and principal one had 26 knights, inducted as "companions," including the king as hereditary "sovereign" or president; the second college was of a similar number of secular priests, thirteen as "canons" and thirteen as "vicars" for the canons. The third college was to be composed of "poor veteran knights," appointed to serve as vicars for the companions when the latter were absent from the order's chapel at Windsor. The priests and veteran knights were united in the College of St. George at Windsor, and they were to offer daily prayers and masses for their companions' souls. By 1365 the order had a magnificent new hall in Windsor Castle, and between 1475 and 1485 a new and much larger chapel was also built, west of the previous one. Both have been in continuous use ever since.

The companions undertook obligations of loyalty to their sovereign, and also certain fraternal obligations: to refrain from bearing arms against each other (except in the war of their sovereign lord or their own just quarrel) and to have a large number of masses sung for those who had recently died. They met regularly as a body once a year, either on St. George's Day (23 April) or on the second Sunday after Easter. They had, on those occasions, common prayers and a formal banquet. New companions were formally installed during the course of the mass of the feast day.

Edward seems to have founded the order to increase his own prestige and that of his house and kingdom by promoting the image of himself as an heroic king in the tradition of Arthur, surrounded by a company of knights selected for noble birth and chivalrous deeds. Knights from outside England were elected, eventually including foreign princes and kings. The order was also, perhaps, a perpetual memorial to the king's great victory at Crécy and to the knights who fought with him there. It still exists, with newly elected knights installed in the royal chapel at Windsor.

D'Arcy J.D. Boulton

Bibliography

Ashmole, Elias. *The Institution, Laws, and Ceremonies of the Most Noble Order of the Garter.* London, 1672. Repr. Baltimore: Genealogical Publishing, 1971; Beltz, G.F. *Memorials of the Most Noble Order of the Garter.* London: Pickering, 1841; Boulton, D'Arcy J.D. *The Knights of the Crown: The Monarchical Orders of Knighthood in Later Medieval Europe, 1325–1520.* Woodbridge: Boydell, 1987.

See also Chivalry; Edward III; Heralds; Matter of Britain; Windsor, St. George's Chapel

Organ

As an appurtenance of Christian worship, the organ was introduced into England soon after 957, part of the general importation of Cluniac ceremonial principles that vitalized the restoration of Benedictine monastic observance under Archbishop Dunstan and King Edgar. As a striking novelty the presence of such a machine had been noted before A.D. 1000 at the abbeys of Malmesbury, Ramsey, Abingdon, and Winchester Old Minster. The original organ at Winchester, dating from before 984, was enlarged ca. 990, and it seems that the instrument was built on principles similar to those expressed by a slightly later continental writer, the monk Theophilus. The typical organ of the period was modest, both in overall size and technical complexity; the Winchester organ was somewhat larger, having two operators, each managing his own octave (diatonic, plus B-flat). They worked not a keyboard but crude sets of perforated sliders that permitted air from the windchest (supplied by pairs of leather bellows pumped by assistants) to sound the bronze or copper pipes, arranged in one or two inseparable ranks. Such other Benedictine monasteries as Ely Cathedral (ca. 1165), Christ Church, Canterbury (1174), Bury St. Edmunds (1182), and Rochester Cathedral (1192) are known to have possessed organs before the end of the 12th century. Thereafter references to the occurrence of organs in Benedictine and Augustinian monastery churches become commonplace and begin to occur also at the greater secular churches, such as York (1236), Exeter (1280), Wells (1310), and Lincoln (1310).

The quality of the 10th-century organ most striking to contemporaries was its ability to make noise that was penetrating and loud, and as late as 1235 the organ of St. Albans Abbey could still be nicknamed "The Mules." Indeed the organ of the early and high Middle Ages was not created to be in any way a musical instrument. It was installed as a generator of loud and joyful but fairly random noise, to be sounded on festivals and other occasions of importance just to lend grandeur to the ceremonies, in much the same manner as peals and clashes of tower bells. Such recorded occasions included patronal feasts, the reception of distinguished guests, and the presentation of abbots-elect. For purposes like these the normal location for the machine was an elevated position in the body of the church, not necessarily close to the liturgical choir. For instance, in 1174 the organ of Christ Church, Canterbury, stood some 28 feet above floor level, on a tribune gallery in the southwest transept, and as late as 1332 it was located on a timber gallery outside the choir—as was also the case at Wells in 1310 and Ely in 1329.

During the second half of the 13th century the finger-pressure sprung keyboard was developed, making possible the exercise of some delicacy of control over the sounds emitted by the organ. Thus was rendered possible its evolution from a mere noise machine of limited refinement into a genuine instrument of music making. In England this transition was probably in course by around the second quarter of the 14th century. By 1337 the Exeter Cathedral Ordinal admitted the sound of the organ even to the liturgical service on occasions substituting for the final versicle and response at Matins and Vespers, and following the Sanctus at high mass.

Pictorial evidence from ca. 1100 onward is helpful in portraying the construction and nature of the instrument and the manner and chronology of its development. Essentially all church organs down to the early 15th century were positives (medium-sized, portable organs) of various degrees of elaboration, played by one individual and pumped simultaneously by another. The instrument was still of modest size and of not more than two ranks and apparently did not exceed two octaves in compass (see, e.g., the simplified depiction in the Peterborough Psalter of ca. 1320). Unfortunately little is known about the actual use of the organ at this time. No doubt its long-established functions continued alongside newer ones more musical in nature. There is no evidence whatever to suggest that up to ca. 1500 the church organ in England ever made music *simultaneously* with voices. Rather it seems that it was used principally to enhance the ceremonial impact of certain major items of the plainsong liturgy, through interspersing interludes improvised upon the proper melody between the verses or sections of items sung in the choral monody of plainsong as, for instance, during the singing of Te Deum in 1396 at the reception of the abbot-elect of St. Albans.

Reflecting its closer association with the music of the liturgy, the principal church organ from ca. 1350 onward was commonly located in immediate proximity to the liturgical choir of the church. It comes to be referred to as *magna organa,* the "great organ," to distinguish it from a second, smaller, instrument that is found widely from ca. 1390 onward and was set up in the Lady Chapel for participation in the performance of the daily votive mass of the Virgin Mary. In England the commonest location for the great organ was the pulpitum, the open loft on top of the choir screen. By the end of the 14th century the use of the organ—equipped by now with a fully chromatic keyboard—was sufficiently routine for its playing to be deputed to particular individuals among the musical staff; to some extent, that is, a distinct and particular skill of church organ playing was coming to be recognized.

During the 15th century the instrument steadily expanded in both physical size and technical sophistication; the number of organs also increased, since from ca. 1430 onward organs began to be installed in many of the wealthier parish churches of the cities, country towns, and even some villages. However, at least by comparison with contemporary Dutch and German instruments, the English organ appears to have remained relatively small, of a single manual, unequipped with pedals, and until the late 15th century enjoying no written repertoire. Nevertheless, the diversity of the sums of money expended on new instruments suggests that organs could be built in a variety of sizes, and while the smaller sums were doubtless for positives of the long-established design, the largest works and expenses involved—as at St. Albans ca. 1425–28, at Lincoln in 1473, and at Lichfield in 1482—were probably for case organs after the continental fashion. This design was of a substantial instrument in which the pipework was enclosed in an imposing timber case; the front of this was primarily an open frame in which the visible pipes were arranged not in scalar but in decorative order—most frequently, *en mitre,* or in an A-shaped arrangement. The common English placement was upon the choir screen. Two early-16th-century organ contracts specify keyboard compasses of 27 "white" notes, and contemporary documents speak of instruments of up to five to seven ranks, separable by stops, played from a single manual without pedals. However, in the absence of surviving pipework it is impossible even to guess at the character of sound that was cultivated.

As the physical size and complexity of the organ increased, the esteem for its player also rose, and the 1453 statutes of King's College, Cambridge, and Eton College are the earliest to make provision among the chapel staff for a specific player of the organ; thereafter instances of the creation of this office rapidly become commonplace. The most usual direction was that the organ in choir be played on Sundays and major feasts and the smaller Lady Chapel organ daily in association with Lady Mass. Some 15th-century inventories of books for service use include volumes described as "for the organs"; these are always plainsong service books, most commonly antiphoners, with a few graduals. Inventories of late-15th-century written music now lost also mention composed music, written for insertion into, or alternation within, such items as hymns and canticles, and the Alleluia, Sequence, Kyrie, Sanctus, and Agnus from the mass. Apparently the role of the organ at this period was still mainly to lend distinction to the service on principal days by alternating with the choir, or substituting for it, by means of passages of improvised or written elaboration upon the plainsong proper at that particular point.

Roger D. Bowers

Bibliography

Bowles, Edmund. "A Preliminary Check-List of Fifteenth-Century Representations of Organs in Paintings and Manuscript Illuminations." *Organ Yearbook* 13 (1982): 5–30; Harrison, Frank Ll. *Music in Medieval Britain.* 2d ed. London: Routledge & Kegan Paul, 1963, pp. 202–18;

McKinnon, James W. "The Tenth-Century Organ at Winchester." *Organ Yearbook* 5 (1974): 4–19; Marshall, Kimberly. *Iconographical Evidence for the Late-Medieval Organ in French, Flemish and English Manuscripts,* forthcoming; Perrot, Jean. *The Organ from Its Invention in the Hellenistic Period to the End of the Thirteenth Century.* Trans. Norma Deane. London: Oxford University Press, 1971, chs. 12–15; Williams, Peter. *A New History of the Organ.* Bloomington: Indiana University Press, 1980, pp. 34–70.

See also Benedictine Reform; Lady Chapel; Lady Mass; Magnificat; Mass, Polyphonic Music for; Musical Instruments; Robertsbridge Codex

Orm (fl. ca. 1170)

Augustinian canon and author of a series of exegetical homilies in verse, which he named *Ormulum* and which expound the life of Christ on the basis of a harmonization, or synthesis, of the Gospel accounts. It was probably written ca. 1160–80, somewhere in the Peterborough-Stamford area, and was conceived of as an aid to preachers. It is a key document for understanding linguistic and cultural developments in 12th-century England.

The work, now a fragment, is preserved in one manuscript, Bodl. Junius 1, the author's holograph. The homilies are preceded by a paraphrase of the pericope (the scriptural reading being explicated) and occasionally end with a short prayer. The exegesis is traditional and nonscholastic; although the precise identity of his sources is unknown, Orm probably worked from a glossed gospel of a type exemplified by the *Glossa ordinaria* and related commentaries of the 11th and early 12th centuries.

His language has a strong Old Norse element and displays innovative uniformity in spelling and vocabulary, in an attempt to remedy contemporary linguistic confusion and establish a literary standard. Although the verse form, the *septenarius* (a line of seven poetic feet), is of Latin origin, his homiletic rhetoric clearly derives partly from native models, inviting comparison with late OE homilies.

Stephen Morrison

Bibliography

PRIMARY

Holt, Robert, ed. *The Ormulum, with the Notes and Glossary of Dr. R.M. White.* 2 vols. Oxford: Clarendon, 1878.

SECONDARY

New *CBEL* 1:485–86; Morrison, Stephen. "Orm's English Sources." *Archiv* 221 (1984): 54–64; Parkes, Malcolm B. "On the Presumed Date and Possible Origin of the Manuscript of the '*Orrmulum*': Oxford, Bodleian Library, MS Junius 1." In *Five Hundred Years of Words and Sounds: A Festschrift for Eric Dobson,* ed. Eric G. Stanley and Douglas Gray. Cambridge: Brewer, 1983, pp. 115–27.

See also Bible in ME Literature; Language; Literary Influences: Scandinavian; Sermons; Translation; Versification

Ormesby Psalter

The Ormesby Psalter (Bodl. Douce 366; fig. 102), one of the most enigmatic and sumptuously decorated of all 14th-century manuscripts, takes its name from Robert Ormesby, whose gift of the book to the Benedictine Priory of Norwich, where he was a monk, is recorded in an inscription on fol. 1v. Cockerell gives a detailed account of the book's structure and iconographic contents. There were three or four separate campaigns spanning some 50 years (ca. 1280–1330), depending on the dating limits accepted, and the work of at least eight illuminators can be identified. The entire text of the psalter, with the exception of the added calendar and litany of Norwich Cathedral Priory, was prepared in the 13th century (probably ca. 1280), when most likely only one (fols. 10–21) of the seventeen original gatherings was fully illuminated in a style bearing many similarities to the William of Devon group of manuscripts (e.g., the Cuerden Psalter [New York, Pierpont Morgan Library M.756]) or those related to the Huth Psalter (BL Add. 38116). This style is characterized by linear faces, simple figure forms, and dragon motifs that extend from the initials and terminate in rectilinear and cusped foliage elements, some of which provide platforms for hybrids. There is also some unfinished work of this date in the form of outline drawing and gilding.

It is not known for whom the psalter was initiated or, indeed, for whom it was continued at some time between ca. 1310 and ca. 1320, when all the borders and historiated initials at the ten major divisions, except those for Psalm 1 and possibly Psalm 26, were executed by an artist of the highest order. Progressive tendencies in the rendering of the human figure, in which there is attention to anatomical structure, coupled with innovative iconographic motifs, such as the classical trumpeter (fol. 147) and the nude male riding on the back of a lion (fol. 147v), suggest an early instance of Italian influence. These forms may have derived from illuminated Bolognese civil and canon law books circulating in England at the time. The margins on these folios are filled with borders of considerable richness and exuberance, comprising a wealth of naturalistic foliate and flower forms, a variety of hybrids, and narrative genre elements. This unique artist illuminated, single-handed, three other extant works (the Bromholm Psalter, Bodl. Ashmole 1523; a *Moralia in Job,* Cambridge, Emmanuel College 112; and an Apocalypse, Dublin, Trinity College 64 [K.4.31]), but none contains internal evidence for dating.

The artist who illuminated the historiated initial and border at Psalm 26 of the psalter was also responsible for painting the Beatus leaf from another psalter (with the exception of the kneeling monk and bishop who cover the original text) now inserted at the beginning of the Ormesby Psalter's text of the Psalms; it thus forms a splendid frontispiece to the volume. The initial B encloses a kneeling female and male in heraldic dress of the Bardolf and Foliot families. The rest of the frontispiece consists of an elaborate Jesse Tree, one of the most splendid of surviving examples. Whether this portion (including Psalm 26) dates to before or after the

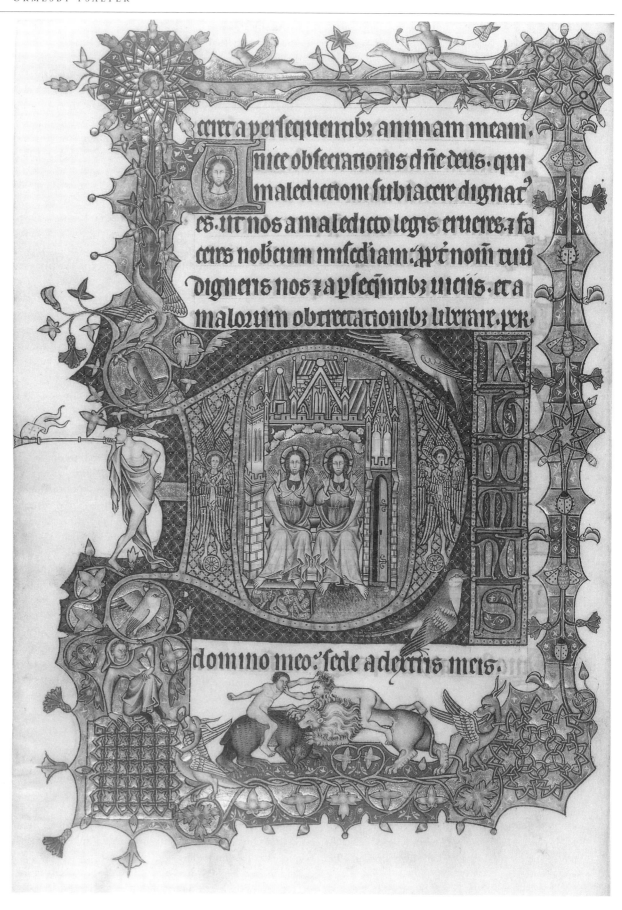

Fig. 102. Ormesby Psalter (Bodl. Douce 366), fol. 147v. Psalm 109: Dixit Dominus *with Father and Son. Reproduced by permission of the Bodleian Library, University of Oxford.*

ca. 1310–20 campaign will be difficult to establish, but the fact that no evidence has been found of a marriage between these families at the date in question may explain why the psalter was again laid aside.

This artist, although thought by Cockerell to postdate the main illuminator, has a more linear style mostly untouched by italianisms. However, the artist who painted the half-page miniature of the harping David at Psalm 1 (fol. 10) and the inset of the monk and bishop on the Jesse frontispiece (fol. 9v) develops the italianate approaches of the main illuminator, but with a vastly different outcome, resulting from the influence of Italian panel painting rather than illumination. This style, often described as Ducciesque, constitutes an important advance toward naturalism. It displays novel technical experimentation, greater corporeality of the human figure, and three-dimensionality in spatial modeling, features well illustrated by the Beatus miniature. Particularly characteristic of this artist is his idiosyncratic use of large amounts of thick white pigment.

This illuminator, who works in the same style as the now damaged Douai Psalter (Douai, Bibliothèque Municipale 171) and the added Crucifixion of the Gorleston Psalter (BL Add. 49622), may also have illuminated the 14th-century portion of the St. Omer Psalter (BL Yates Thompson 14 [Add. 39810]). The dating of this, the final campaign in the Ormesby Psalter, is traditionally based on the supposed dating of between 1322 and 1325 of the related Douai Psalter. Further research, however, may confirm a date in the 1330s for this style, a dating that would make greater sense in the light of developments of the 1340s. If this were the case, then the bishop to whom Robert Ormesby is presenting his psalter would be William de Ayermin, bishop between 1325 and 1336, and not Bishop Salmon. At the time Robert made his gift, the calendar of Norwich Cathedral Priory (fols. 2–7) and a further litany, with collects (fols. 209v–213), also of the priory, were prepared, and the book was finally bound.

This fine example of "East Anglian" illumination is still in its original binding with a chemise of heavy sheepskin. There is little doubt that the 14th-century illumination of the psalter was produced in a workshop somewhere in East Anglia, possibly in Norwich itself. A number of manuscripts to which the various Ormesby artists relate have strong Norwich associations. A precise dating for the various campaigns, however, must await further research.

Lynda Dennison

Bibliography

Alexander, Jonathan, and Paul Binski, eds. *Age of Chivalry: Art in Plantagenet England 1200–1400*. London: Royal Academy of Arts, 1987, cat. no. 573; Cockerell, Sydney Carlyle, and Montague Rhodes James. *Two East Anglian Psalters in the Bodleian Library, Oxford*. Oxford: Roxburghe Club, 1926; Lasko, Peter, and Nigel J. Morgan, eds. *Medieval Art in East Anglia 1300–1520*. London: Thames & Hudson, 1974, cat. no. 21; Sandler, Lucy Freeman. *Gothic Manuscripts 1285–1385*. A Survey of Manuscripts Illuminated in the British Isles 5, ed. J.J.G. Alexander. London: Harvey Miller, 1986, cat. no. 43.

See also Cuerden Psalter; "East Anglian School"; Manuscript Illumination, Gothic; Psalters, Gothic

Orosius, Paulus (fl. early 5th century)

Christian priest, apologist, and historian, who became the pupil of Augustine of Hippo in 414. In 415 he went to Palestine, bearing a letter from Augustine to Jerome, whom he joined in his struggle against the Pelagian heresy. After a synod in Jerusalem, where he confronted Pelagius and was himself accused of holding not entirely orthodox opinions, he composed the *Liber apologeticus contra Pelagianos* to clear himself. An earlier work demonstrating his concern for orthodoxy was his *Commonitorium de errore Priscillianistarum et Origenistarum*—a text that prompted Augustine's treatise *Ad Orosium contra Priscillianistas et Origenistas*.

Orosius is best known for the *Historiarum adversum paganos libri septem (Seven Books of History against the Pagans)*, undertaken at the request of Augustine and intended to provide a context for the latter's *City of God* by providing a history of the whole world up to 414. After a brief survey of the geography of the world Orosius presents the fortunes of the four great empires: Babylon, Macedon, Carthage, and Rome. Seeing the *pax Romana* as foreordained by God for Christ's coming, he argued that the whole of history had been leading to the universal empire of Rome, God being the one ruler of all ages, kingdoms, and places. In reply to allegations that the troubles of his time were the result of the abandonment of the pagan gods, he also used history to demonstrate that calamities had always occurred in cycles. Among his many sources were the Bible and a range of both pagan and patristic authors, from Livy, Caesar, Suetonius, Justinus, and Eutropius to Tertullian and Jerome's revision of Eusebius's *Chronicon*.

The *History against the Pagans* achieved great popularity in the Middle Ages, surviving in over 250 manuscript copies and attracting both commentators and translators. Translations include an OE translation possibly undertaken under the sponsorship of King Alfred the Great in the late 9th century, containing additional material based on contemporary reports. The first printed edition of the Latin text was published in Augsburg in 1471.

Janet M. Bately

Bibliography

PRIMARY

Bately, Janet M., ed. *The Old English Orosius*. EETS s.s. 6. London: Oxford University Press, 1980; Deferrari, Roy J., trans. *Paulus Orosius: The Seven Books of History against the Pagans*. The Fathers of the Church 50. Washington, D.C.: Catholic University of America Press, 1964; Zangemeister, C., ed. *Historiarum adversum paganos libri septem*. CSEL 5. Vienna: Gerold, 1882.

SECONDARY
Bately, Janet M. "King Alfred and the Old English Translation of Orosius." *Anglia* 88 (1970): 433–60.

See also Alfred; Chronicles; Fathers of the Church; Translation

Oswald of Worcester (d. 992)

Bishop of Worcester (961–92), archbishop of York (971–92), and one of the three leading figures in the Benedictine Reform of the late 10th century, along with Dunstan of Canterbury and Æthelwold of Winchester. The youngest of the three and by many scholarly accounts the most moderate, Oswald established Worcester with its related monastic foundations as a powerful cultural force that continued in influence beyond the Norman Conquest. Oswald's Ramsey, for example, became a model house and Byrhtferth its most famous writer. Byrhtferth's life of Oswald, while depicting Oswald as an icon of Benedictine monasticism, also notes Oswald's wealth, his large retinue, and his gout.

Paul E. Szarmach

Bibliography

Brooks, Nicholas, and Catherine Cubitt, eds. *St Oswald of Worcester: Life and Influence.* London: Leicester University Press, 1996 [fifteen essays providing a strong basis for future study].

See also Æthelwold; Benedictine Reform; Byrhtferth; Dunstan

Outlawry

Known in early Anglo-Saxon customary law, although how it evolved is unclear. For nearly 200 years after the Conquest only men accused of felonies—the more serious crimes—could be outlawed, but in the 13th century outlawry was extended to those accused of trespass committed with force and later to defendants in an increasing number of civil actions, such as debt.

When appeals (formal private accusations) of felony were made in the county court, the process of "exigent," which preceded outlawry, began at the second sitting of the court. If the accused did not appear when felonies were prosecuted publicly before the king's justices, the exigent was initiated on their orders. In all other cases it needed a writ to the sheriff of the county. The procedure was unvarying; the accused had to be "exacted," or called to surrender to the king's peace, at four successive sittings of the (normally monthly) county court, or at five if sureties were found at the fourth for his appearance at the fifth. If, as was usual, he still did not appear, he was then outlawed. Exactions and outlawries were invalid if proclaimed in the absence of the county coroners, who had to record them.

Strictly outlaws "bore the wolf's head" and could be captured or, if they resisted, slain with impunity. In practice summary execution, even of criminals, was rare and became virtually unknown after 1300. It never applied to those outlawed in civil actions, in which outlawry was merely the culmination of long and complex series of attempts to get defendants to stand trial. Such outlaws, who became numerous, were far removed from the violent but romantic outlaws of legend. Nevertheless, they were outside the protection of the law, had no legal rights, and should have forfeited their possessions. Therefore most—sooner or later—purchased a pardon or had their outlawry revoked on a technicality. Children under twelve and women could not be outlawed; women, however, could be exacted and "waived," which had the same effect as outlawry.

Roy F. Hunnisett

Bibliography

Gross, Charles, ed. *Select Cases from the Coroners' Rolls, A.D. 1265–1413.* Selden Society 9. London: Quaritch, 1896 for 1895 [other Selden Society volumes also contain transcriptions and translations of records of outlawry]; Hunnisett, R.F. *The Medieval Coroner.* Cambridge: Cambridge University Press, 1961; Keen, Maurice. *The Outlaws of Medieval Legend.* Rev. ed. London: Routledge & Kegan Paul, 1987.

See also Juries; Law, Post-Conquest; Outlaws

Outlaws and Robin Hood

"Outlaw" in medieval England had a technical meaning: a person put outside the protection of the laws of the realm. It was in one way the ultimate penalty for crime. The outlaw was a "nonperson"; his property was subject to invasion, his person open to murder without punishment. Yet the sentence of outlawry also reveals the limited reach and effectiveness of medieval law enforcement. It was the sentence passed on criminals who escaped arrest and could not be brought to trial. Either they had disappeared into areas beyond royal control, such as the forests, or they commanded an armed band and local sympathy, making forcible arrest impractical, or both.

The sympathy some criminals enjoyed points out the other weakness of medieval justice. It was open to corruption, to domination by king's favorites or powerful nobles, and was therefore often less than just. The histories of outlaws are tales of bought justices and stacked juries. At the least this was a common perception of the problem and contributed to the literary popularity of the outlaw figure in romance, epic, and ballad.

Certainly the most enduringly popular of outlaw heroes is Robin Hood. While earlier heroes of story and song, such as Hereward the Wake and Fulk FitzWarin, had recognizable historical careers, the original Robin Hood is much harder to pin down. And whereas Hereward and Fulk were celebrated in French and Latin romances, the earliest Robin is known through English ballads, though elements of the romances clearly influenced the Robin Hood tales.

Whether there was an original Robin Hood or not, the type was real enough. The most plausible hypotheses about Robin's career place his activities sometime in the 13th century, probably in the vicinity of Barnesdale in south Yorkshire. The legend grew and spread from there, gaining elaboration in the 14th century. His stomping grounds soon included Sherwood Forest, south of Barnesdale. The Sheriff of Nottingham became the traditional enemy, and Little John, Will Scarlett, and Much the Miller's Son joined the merry men early on. Friar Tuck and Maid Marian seem not to enter the tales until well into the 15th century. Robin was from the first a great archer. He lived by poaching the king's deer and by ambushing travelers, especially monks and the sheriff's men.

Initially popular among the yeoman retainers of great feudal households (the early Robin is "a good yeoman"), the minstrels' ballads adapted to the changing social and geographical range of their audience. With the writing down and then printing of the tales in the 15th century the outlaw entered into several centuries of literary metamorphosis. He emerged as the romantic woodsman of 19th-century imagination who stole from the rich and gave to the poor. It is doubtful whether the original outlaw would recognize his socially progressive descendant.

Stephen R. Morillo

Bibliography

Dobson, R.B., and J. Taylor, eds. *Rymes of Robin Hood: An Introduction to the English Outlaw.* Rev. ed. Gloucester: Sutton, 1989; Holt, J.C. *Robin Hood.* London: Thames & Hudson, 1982.

See also Ballads; Forests; Matter of England; Outlawry

Owl and the Nightingale, The

One of several ME debate poems of literary distinction. It is also one of the masterworks of early ME literature and probably the greatest comic poem in English before Chaucer. Composed in the south of England around 1200, perhaps by a provincial cleric named Nicholas of Guildford, *The Owl and the Nightingale* is the earliest of the ME debate poems, created shortly after the first vernacular debates began to appear in Provençal and Old French during the 12th century. *The Owl and the Nightingale* reflects many of the conventions that had developed within Latin debate poetry, but it is superior to most of the earlier Latin debates; and although *The Owl and the Nightingale* was composed in English rather than French, it appears to be closely tied to the Anglo-Norman culture of late-12th-century England. Its metrical form is the octosyllabic couplet, a meter used in many contemporary French narrative poems, and it contains allusions to such 12th-century Anglo-Norman works as the *Lais* and *Fables* of Marie de France.

The Owl and the Nightingale is told by a first-person narrator who offers an ear-witness account of a confrontation between two highly contentious birds. The narrator sets the scene, introduces the avian rivals, and provides transitions between their lengthy speeches. He also comments on the inner feelings and thoughts of the birds, but his neutral presence never obtrudes upon the birds' colorful, colloquial exchanges, which occupy the greater part of the poem's nearly 1,800 verses. The birds' exchanges appear to be freewheeling and spontaneous, but they are actually carefully structured. Their debate consists of a preliminary skirmish (lines 29–176) and a "debate proper" that begins about line 215 and continues to about line 1634, where it breaks down. The preliminary skirmish, which consists mostly of insults and threats, is initiated by the Nightingale's disparaging remarks about the Owl's physical appearance and singing ability. The "debate proper" follows the birds' agreement to adopt more formal debating procedures and to submit their views to the judgment of Nicholas of Guildford, a human figure who is praised by both birds. Throughout the remainder of their debate they take turns being on the offensive and the defensive, perhaps somewhat in imitation of legal or ecclesiastical proceedings.

No single issue dominates the birds' attention, and they move through a variety of concerns, sometimes returning to an earlier issue after other matters have intervened. Of particular importance to them are their assessments of the quality and the value of their songs, and related to this are their claims of service to humankind. Their arguments are characterized by quick-wittedness and ingenuity but also by inconsistency and faulty logic. Their most arresting comments concern the sexual behavior of women. When the Nightingale speaks in defense of single women who have committed fornication, the Owl in turn justifies the adultery of married women. These comments, which reflect the birds' mutual sympathies for women (both of the birds, it should be noted, are female), may also reflect the medieval poet's concern for the well-being of women. In any event, when the birds' debate finally collapses into disorder and violence is again threatened, the Wren intervenes, cautions them about breaking the king's peace, and reminds them of their agreement to accept the judgment of Nicholas of Guildford. The poem ends without being resolved; the birds fly off in search of Nicholas, and the narrator states, "Ne can ich eu na more telle" ("I can't tell you anything more").

The author of *The Owl and the Nightingale* exhibits many talents, including a flair for writing colloquial dialogue, the ability to create vivid and psychologically plausible characters, skill at handling a complex structure, and a sophisticated sense of comedy. The identity of this talented poet, however, remains uncertain. Perhaps the author was the "Master Nicholas of Guildford" whose virtuous character is twice described in the poem (lines 191–214 and 1746–80), but attempts to identify a minor churchman of this name have been inconclusive. Because the poem expresses chagrin at Nicholas's neglect by his ecclesiastical superiors, it is also possible that the author was one of Nicholas's sympathizers or a close friend. However, if the poem was meant to serve as a plea for Nicholas's preferment, as some critics believe, one wonders whether the poem's harsh criticisms of Nicholas's superiors would be likely to further that purpose. The poet's attitude toward Nicholas may have an ironic edge, and the birds' praise of Nicholas may be intentionally hyperbolic. Yet the evaluation of Nicholas offered by the wise little Wren near the end of the poem seems sincere and reinforces our perception of Nicholas as a man of humanity and discretion.

The Owl and the Nightingale has generated a substantial body of scholarship. In addition to considerations of its date and authorship much has been written about the possible symbolic and allegorical meanings of the two birds, about the poem's possible relationships to particular historical contexts, and about the poet's use of sophisticated rhetorical strategies. There is not a great deal of consensus on these matters, but most critics do agree that the two birds represent contrasting attitudes toward living. Whereas previously there was interest in determining which bird was the likely victor, most recent critics favor the view that neither bird emerges as a clear winner and that the poet's satiric commentary on human nature and human behavior involves both birds fairly equally.

The text of *The Owl and the Nightingale* is preserved in only two manuscripts, BL Cotton Caligula A.ix and Oxford, Jesus College 29, both of which were probably compiled during the second half of the 13th century. These two versions of the poem may have derived independently from a common source. Because the version in the Jesus manuscript contains many scribal emendations, most editors of *The Owl and the Nightingale* have based their editions upon the version preserved in the Cotton manuscript.

John W. Conlee

Bibliography

PRIMARY

Gardner, John, trans. *The Alliterative Morte Arthure, The Owl and the Nightingale, and Five Other Middle English Poems.* Carbondale: Southern Illinois University Press, 1971; Stanley, Eric G., ed. *The Owl and the Nightingale.* London: Nelson, 1960; Stone, Brian, trans. *The Owl and the Nightingale, Cleanness, St. Erkenwald.* 2d ed. London: Penguin, 1988.

SECONDARY

New *CBEL* 1:509–11; *Manual* 3:716–20, 874–82; Conlee, John W. "*The Owl and the Nightingale* and Latin Debate Tradition." *The Comparatist* 4 (1980): 57–67; Eadie, J. "The Authorship of *The Owl and the Nightingale*: A Reappraisal." *ES* 67 (1986): 471–77 [suggests female authorship]; Hume, Kathryn. *The Owl and the Nightingale: The Poem and Its Critics.* Toronto: University of Toronto Press, 1975; Murphy, James J. "Rhetoric and Dialectic in *The Owl and the Nightingale.*" In *Medieval Eloquence: Studies in the Theory and Practice of Medieval Rhetoric,* ed. James J. Murphy. Berkeley: University of California Press, 1978, pp. 198–230.

See also Anglo-Norman Literature; Debate Poems; Marie de France

P

Paganism and Superstition in Old English Literature

Both "paganism" (from Lat. *paganus,* "rural") and "superstition" (from Lat. *superstitio,* a word whose semantic derivation has been disputed since Cicero) are value-laden terms. The former, semantically similar to OE *hæpennisse* and *hæpendom* (cognate with German *Heidentum*), implies that these beliefs are connected with the unsophisticated countryside and rustic culture, while the latter has a connotation similar to that of the German *Aberglaube,* indicating a set of religious beliefs and practices at variance with, but often tolerated by, orthodox religion (Harmening, 1979). The use of "non-Christian" and "pre-Christian" changes the semantics again, as those terms imply customs that are either outside of, or earlier than, established Christian orthodoxy and hence suggest a pejorative connotation. Indeed all such terms, when used of Anglo-Saxon beliefs and practices, are biased in favor of Christianity; moreover the Anglo-Saxon church itself took the view that Christianity was the superior religion. Since it is the Anglo-Saxon church that has enabled the survival of most source material for the investigation of "pagan" and "superstitious" beliefs and practices in pre-Conquest England, it comes as no surprise to find the negative bias associated with these terms reflected in the sources as well.

The sources for our knowledge of Anglo-Saxon pagan beliefs and superstitious practices are sparse. For the period prior to the coming of Christianity with Augustine we are limited to archaeological evidence (often subject to widely divergent interpretations; cf. Hills, 1979) and the reports of outside observers (e.g., Tacitus in his *Germania,* a notoriously jaundiced source; or Venantius Fortunatus writing about Gaul in the 6th century, his views strongly colored by his opinion that the Germanic peoples were barbarians); or even Snorri Sturluson's descriptions of the ancient gods, sometimes used as evidence for the religious practices of an earlier age. In any event what Tacitus, Fortunatus, and Snorri have to say about practices among the Germanic tribes of the 1st or the 6th century or later does not shed much light on beliefs and practices in England.

For the period after 600 we have some additional sources; Bede and Aldhelm are remarkably taciturn about non-Christian beliefs, though they must have had some notion of both the extent and nature of these beliefs. The earliest Anglo-Saxon laws contain condemnations of pagan beliefs, but in general the laws are laconic, and it requires considerable effort on the part of historians and comparative folklorists to tease any kind of "reality" out of them (see especially Liebermann's voluminous commentaries). The same is true of the penitential handbooks, noteworthy in part for their association, rightly or wrongly, with some famous churchmen (Archbishop Theodore of Tarsus, Egbert of York, even Bede, though the ascription of a penitential to him is probably in error).

The proliferation of penances for various kinds of beliefs contrary to orthodox teachings may indicate that some of these beliefs persisted long after the complete conversion of the English to Christianity. Many of these practices can be explained through reference to Celtic practices, some of which have been more extensively described than English ones. They may not be specifically Anglo-Saxon at all but may have been carried over from continental sources or been common to the entire Germanic world, as seems clear from the fact that the same proscriptions also appear in continental handbooks of penance (e.g., that of Burckhard of Worms). We also have a description in the Legatine Report to Pope Hadrian (742), but the best-known sources are no doubt Wulfstan's *Sermo Lupi ad Anglos* and Ælfric's homilies *De diis gentium (On the Gods of the Nations)* and *De auguria (On Divination)*. Taken together these form but a small corpus of evidence for pagan beliefs and superstitious practices in pre-Conquest England.

The evidence can be supplemented from several sources. Bede's famous story of the sparrow (*Ecclesiastical History* 2.13) may throw some light on a non-Christian worldview in the Northumbria of his day, though it must be used cautiously, since we have only Bede's word for the historicity of this story. The reproving words of the *Beowulf*-poet about the Danes reverting to their ancient beliefs are perhaps the best-known statement on this topic, though his attitude is strictly in line with the orthodox teachings expressed by writers from Theodore to Ælfric. Yet little can be said with certainty about the beliefs and practices of the English during this time, other than to point to some of them: divination with birds, horses, sneezing, dogs (Ælfric lists these in the *De auguria*), stars, thunder, meteors, comets, dreams, and the moon; pin-sticking magic (recorded in a charter of 895); holy wells (their pre-Christian origins obscured by the syncretism of the Anglo-Saxon church); and medical charms. And the laws contain a variety of punishments for witches and sorcerers, though just how they practiced their *scincræft* is not specified.

The heroic ethos, expressed as an ideal in *Beowulf* and *Maldon,* and adapted to Christianity in *The Dream of the Rood* (early on, it would seem, from the lines carved on the Ruthwell Cross), clearly predates Christianity, though like religious beliefs it may have been as often attended to in the breach as in the observance. The same is true of the traditional methods of composing poetry, both in its preferred themes and imagery (e.g., the notion of *wyrd*) and in its versification, whose formal metrical properties were at the same time complex and full of scope for the talented poet. The skills required for a poet (ascribed to divine inspiration by Bede in the story of Cædmon) and the knowledge of stories about pagan heroes (demonstrated in the many "digressions" in *Beowulf* or Aldhelm's complaint about the monks of Sherborne singing secular songs about pagan heroes) are a clear legacy of "pagan" and pre-Christian England. This legacy not only survived in the secular poetry but was also adapted by Christian poets for the composition of religious poetry.

William Schipper

Bibliography

The following list is only a small sampling of work in the area; for additional bibliography see Bonser (1963 below), Greenfield and Robinson (esp. pp. 43–46), and the annual listings in *ASE;* Bonser, Wilfrid. *The Medical Background of Anglo-Saxon England.* London: Wellcome Museum for the History of Medicine, 1963; Cameron, M.L. "Anglo-Saxon Medicine and Magic." *ASE* 17 (1988): 191–215; Davidson, H.R. Ellis. *Myths and Symbols in Pagan Europe.* Manchester: Manchester University Press, 1988; Flint, Valerie J. *The Rise of Magic in Early Medieval Europe.* Princeton: Princeton University Press, 1991; Förster, Max. "Beiträge zur mittelalterlichen Volkskunde. I–II, IV–IX. *Archiv* 120 (1908): 43–52, 296–305; 125 (1910): 39–70; 128 (1912): 55–71, 285–308; 129 (1912): 16–49; 134 (1916): 264–93; Frantzen, Allen J. *The Literature of Penance in Anglo-Saxon England.* New Brunswick: Rutgers University Press, 1983; Harmening, Dieter. *Superstitio: Überlieferungs- und theoriegeschichtliche Untersuchungen zur kirchlich-theologischen Aberglaubensliteratur des Mittelalters.* Berlin: Schmidt, 1979; Hills, Catherine. "The Archaeology of Anglo-Saxon England in the Pagan Period: A Review." *ASE* 8 (1979): 297–330; Hutton, Ronald. *The Pagan Religions of the Ancient British Isles.*

Oxford: Blackwell, 1991; Liebermann, Felix. *Die Gesetze der Angelsachsen.* Tübingen: Niemeyer, 1905–16; Magoun, Francis P., Jr. "On Some Survivals of Pagan Beliefs in Anglo-Saxon England." *Harvard Theological Review* 40 (1947): 33–46; Stanley, E.G. *The Search for Anglo-Saxon Paganism.* Cambridge: Brewer, 1975; Wilson, David R. *Anglo-Saxon Paganism.* New York: Routledge, 1992.

See also Ælfric; Anglo-Saxon Invasions; *Battle of Maldon; Beowulf;* Conversion of the Anglo-Saxons; Literary Influences: Scandinavian; Penitentials; Tacitus; Vikings; *Waldere; Widsith;* Wulfstan

Painting and Wall Painting, Gothic

English Gothic painting, long neglected because so little survives, is a field rich in isolated works of high quality, often innovative in both subject and technique. Substantial documentation of lost works supplements this lean material. The fact that the two finest panel paintings, the Westminster Retable (a panel designed to be placed behind an altar) and the Wilton Diptych (fig. 149: see WILTON DIPTYCH), equal and perhaps surpass anything produced on the Continent at the time underscores the importance of this field. But the paucity of examples necessarily limits the available avenues of study.

The study of panel painting begins with the Westminster Retable, a unique survival from the 13th century in either England or France. East Anglian altarpieces of the 14th century share its general shape and material (oak) and its textured brilliance: the Thornham Parva Retable, the Cluny Panel, the Norwich Retable, and isolated panels from several Passion retables now in the Fitzwilliam and Ipswich Museums, and the panels from St. Michael-at-Plea in Norwich Cathedral. Numerous stylistic parallels are to be found in other media, especially manuscript illumination and Opus Anglicanum.

The Thornham Parva Retable (Suffolk) and the panel with scenes from the life of the Virgin (Paris, Cluny Museum), long recognized as coming from the same workshop because of the stamps used in their raised backgrounds, have recently been shown to have adorned the same altar as retable and frontal, probably the altar of the Dominican Thetford Priory in Norfolk, founded in 1335. At the center of the retable Christ on the Cross is flanked by the Virgin Mary and St. John the Evangelist, while to either side are saints identifiable by their attributes: Dominic, Katherine of Alexandria, John the Baptist, Edmund, Margaret, and Peter Martyr. The Cluny Panel's design is more unusual, featuring Marian narratives in cusped medallions reminiscent of contemporary manuscript illumination. The Nativity, the Death of the Virgin, the Adoration of the Magi, and the Education of the Virgin were probably supplemented by an Annunciation at the far left, thus making the center the Death of the Virgin, a subject thematically aligned with the Crucifixion on the retable above.

As a less expensive alternative to panel painting wall paintings sometimes served as altarpieces. Examples include the paintings along the piers on the north side of the nave at St. Albans, in the chapel of St. Faith in Westminster Abbey, and at Brent Eleigh (Suffolk).

The Newport Chest (Essex) functioned as a portable altar with the open lid serving as the altarpiece showing the Crucifixion flanked by the Virgin Mary, St. John the Evangelist, St. Peter, and St. Paul (repeating the central grouping of the Thornham Parva Retable). Other painted chests include that given by Sir William de Lillebonne (d. 1334) to Winchester Cathedral and the chest of Richard of Bury, bishop of Durham 1334–45 (Glasgow, Burrell Collection).

Paintings often embellished furniture. The Coronation Chair in Westminster Abbey should be the most significant example, but its paintings, including the image of a seated king on the back, barely survive. Better preserved are the paintings on the sedilia, the seats for clergy, in Westminster Abbey (early 14th century). On the altar side, images of standing kings fill the first and third bays, but only the lower vestments of the figure in between escaped defacement, while nothing survives of the fourth figure—the board itself is a replacement. On the back, figures were paired: the Virgin with the angel of the Annunciation and St. Edward the Confessor presumably with the Pilgrim, a subject also depicted on an isolated 14th-century panel at Forthampton Court.

Choirstalls were sometimes painted on the back. The important cycle of types and antitypes at Peterborough has been lost, but at Gloucester Cathedral some of the stalls retain small, charming paintings of Reynard the Fox. Later painted stalls include those at St. George's Chapel, Windsor, and at Carlisle.

Tombs often had paintings, sometimes on the stone base, as, for example, the tomb of Eleanor of Castile (Westminster Abbey, ca. 1291), or, especially later, on a wooden tester over the effigy, such as the tester of the tomb of the Black Prince (Canterbury Cathedral, ca. 1376) and that over the tomb of Richard II and Anne of Bohemia (Westminster Abbey, ca. 1394). More surprising was the discovery of a life-sized effigy of Archbishop Walter de Gray hidden on the inside of his coffin lid and painted in the finest materials, including lapis lazuli and gold leaf (York Minster, ca. 1255).

Two panel portraits of Richard II, the large portrait of the enthroned king in Westminster Abbey and the small, private Wilton Diptych (London, National Gallery), supplement his effigy likeness. These are much higher quality works than the genealogy series that became fashionable in the 15th and 16th centuries.

Gothic walls were usually painted, whether the building was ecclesiastical or domestic. Simple masonry and drapery patterns were popular, as were geometric, floral, or heraldic motifs, but complex, figured compositions were also created. Nearly complete cycles survive in the Chapel of the Holy Sepulcher at Winchester Cathedral (compare Sigena Chapter House in Aragon), Longthorpe Tower near Peterborough, several parish churches, such as the Church of St. Mary at Chalgrove, the Last Judgment and Apocalypse in the Chapter House at Westminster Abbey, and the extraordinary Miracles of the Virgin covering the side walls of Eton College Chapel.

The most famous royal cycle, the Painted Chamber at Westminster Palace, was destroyed by fire in 1834 but is reasonably well documented. Copies record the scene of the coronation of St. Edward located over the king's bed, the Old Testament scenes on the walls, and the virtues and vices along the windows. Fragments from a major cycle in St. Stephen's Chapel at Westminster (British Museum) supplement the copies and documents for that royal project. However, for the beautiful, damaged wall paintings in Byward Tower, the main gatehouse of the Tower of London, no documents confirm their proposed dating to the reign of Richard II.

Ceilings were another important field for paintings, as is clear from the nave at Peterborough (repainted in the 18th and 19th centuries). For the heavenly vault in the Chapel of the Guardian Angels at Winchester gilded wooden stars and rosettes enriched the painted medallions of angels. The chapter house at York Minster had large figures painted on the oak webbing of the vault similar to those that survive on the stone vaults of the Norwich Antereliquary chapel.

However, full cycles, whether walls or ceilings, rarely survive; more often mere fragments must remind us of the visual richness now lost. We lack the context for the three heads at Windsor, the Chichester Roundel, the Wheel of Fortune in Rochester Cathedral, and the images of St. Christopher and the Incredulity of Thomas in the south transept of Westminster Abbey. Some fragments in lesser-known locations are of impressive quality, such as those at Horsham St. Faith (Norfolk, ca. 1250).

Painted wooden screens survive in some quantity from the 15th century, especially in the parish churches of East Anglia and the West Country. The screens at Barton Turf (Norfolk), Ranworth (Norfolk), and Southwold (Suffolk) are especially fine.

Finally the Hereford Mappa Mundi defies categorization. Painted by Richard de Bello of Halingham and Lafford ca. 1277–89, this large map on vellum attached to an oak panel shows Jerusalem at the center of a round earth.

From this survey the incredible richness of Gothic design is clear, yet the paintings should not be considered in isolation but rather in the context of the architecture, sculpture, stained glass, embroidered vestments, manuscripts, metalwork, hangings, tapestries, and tiled floors that they were created to complement and compliment.

Pearson M. Macek

Bibliography

Alexander, Jonathan, and Paul Binski, eds. *Age of Chivalry: Art in Plantagenet England 1200–1400.* London: Royal Academy of Arts, 1987; Binski, Paul. *Painters.* London: British Museum, 1991; Norton, Christopher, David Park, and Paul Binski. *Dominican Painting in East Anglia: The Thornham Parva Retable and the Musée de Cluny Frontal.* Woodbridge: Boydell, 1987.

See also Canterbury Wall Paintings; Chichester Roundel; "East Anglian School"; Iconography; Manuscript Illumination, Gothic; Matthew Paris; Opus Anglicanum; Wall Painting, Romanesque; Westminster Abbey; Westminster Chapter House Paintings; Westminster Retable; Wilton Diptych; Windsor, St. George's Chapel

Palatinates

The term "palatinate" designates select regions ruled by feudal magnates who owed allegiance to the king. Palatinates had Frankish origins; in Merovingian and Carolingian France the *comes palatinus* or *comes palatii* was an important court official who carried out legal and judicial duties on behalf of the ruler. After the collapse of Carolingian central authority the *comes palatii* emerged as a semiautonomous local ruler; by the 11th century his power diminished as the central government resumed its power. In 12th-century Germany, however, counts palatine had extended local power, best exemplified by the count palatine of the Rhine.

William I introduced the concept of palatinates to England; Orderic Vitalis refers to Odo of Bayeux as "consul palatinus." From that point until the 13th century its development remains obscure. Palatinates, whether called "liberties" or "franchises," were at first without a clear legal definition. Nevertheless, they were understood for what they were; areas of considerable distance from the seat of government, in which royal powers were enjoyed by powerful—but not independent—local lords. By 1300 the three greatest palatinates were Chester, Durham, and Lancaster. With the exception of Lancaster power in these regions included the power to raise armies, levy taxes, and exercise justice.

The counties palatine of Chester and Durham had separate histories. Cheshire was created an earldom by William I in 1071 as a northern buffer state against Mercian rebellions. In 1237 Henry III attached it to the crown. After that date (specifically in 1293, when a *quo warranto* proceeding—an investigation into legal rights to specific powers—uses "palatine" in referring to Chester), it had the advantage of palatine privileges: earls of Chester presided over county courts; royal writs "did not run"; taxes levied by parliament did not apply; feudal military levies exempted Cheshire men. Cheshire was taken under direct crown control in 1377, and Richard II, who recruited his infamous Cheshire bodyguard there, accorded it special status by raising it to the rank of a principality (in 1397). Richard's deposition in 1399 returned Chester to its palatine status, but its privileges remained through the 15th century.

Even before the 1293 *quo warranto* proceedings acknowledged its select status, Durham enjoyed palatine privileges. Based ultimately on the ancient immunity of St. Cuthbert, successive bishops of Durham were granted charters of liberty from post-Conquest kings. Like Cheshire the liberty of Durham had most of the benefits of palatine status, including a county charter of liberties issued in 1303. Indeed Durham enjoyed even wider franchisal rights than Cheshire, as it could claim ecclesiastical immunities atop lay liberties. These extensive rights, however, were not exhaustive. Henry II made it clear that royal justice would obtain in "the land of the blessed Cuthbert," and from time to time the bishopric's autonomy was curtailed by royal seizures of some of its lands.

George B. Stow

Bibliography

Alexander, James W. "New Evidence on the Palatinate of Chester." *EHR* 85 (1970): 715–29; Barraclough, Geoffrey. *The Earldom and County Palatine of Chester.* Oxford: Blackwell, 1953; Lapsley, Gaillard. *The County Palatine of Durham.* New York: Longmans, Green, 1900; Painter, Sidney. *Studies in the History of the English Feudal Barony.* Baltimore: Johns Hopkins Press, 1943; Scammell, Jean. "The Origin and Limitations of the Liberty of Durham." *EHR* 81 (1966): 449–73; Somerville, Robert. *History of the Duchy of Lancaster.* Vol. 1: *1265–1603.* London: Chancellor and Council of the Duchy of Lancaster, 1953.

See also Lancaster, Duchy of; Marches

Paleography and Codicology
Anglo-Saxon

Although the earliest Anglo-Saxons were familiar with writing in runes and some of them may have been aware of the use of other forms of writing from contact with romanized peoples, it was not until their conversion to Christianity that they themselves became literate in the Latin alphabet. Christian missionaries, from Ireland to the north and west of England and from Rome to the east and south, brought both a new religion and an emphasis on the written word. Although most of these writings were in Latin and ecclesiastical in nature, certain texts, such as the Anglo-Saxon laws, were written down in the vernacular from the earliest days of the Conversion, requiring some adaptation of the sound values of some letters in the Latin alphabet to suit OE.

Latin texts written in 7th- and 8th-century England were usually written in local interpretations of the formal book-scripts used in late Roman ecclesiastical manuscripts. The earliest Anglo-Saxon Gospel books, Bibles, and diplomas were written in majuscule or semimajuscule scripts (Uncials or Half-uncials). The latter are found in books produced in churches associated with the Irish mission and the former in those with closer links to Rome. From the 8th century books and documents were increasingly written in minuscule scripts, those characterized by the use of ascenders and descenders. The earliest varieties are described as forms of "Insular Minuscule"—that is, of a type produced within the British Isles but not specific to any one of the constituent regions. In "Phase I" of this period, before ca. 700, the minuscule script is cursive and has many ligatures (links between neighboring letters); in "Phase II," from ca. 700 to the first half of the 9th century, the script exists in a hierarchy of grades of formality (hybrid, set, cursive, and current) that could be adapted to a variety of texts.

By the late 9th century it is possible to distinguish an English style (Pointed Anglo-Saxon Minuscule) distinct from Irish or Welsh types of script; this script still allows a number of ligatures (particularly that of high *e* with a following letter) and the "underslung" form of *l*, and has a pointed top to *a*. This was succeeded during the 10th century by Square Anglo-

Saxon Minuscule, a reformed script originating in southern England, in which ligatures and the "underslung" *l* were generally avoided, and in which the module of *a, n, o,* and *u* is square. Although this script continued in use at some writing centers for both Latin and English texts for most of the century, in those monasteries that were reconstituted by the mid-10th-century Benedictine Reform it was usually retained only for English; in Latin texts its place was taken by Caroline Minuscule. In bilingual texts both scripts were used, one for each language, and in these one can most plainly see the contrasting forms of the letters *a, d, f, g, h, r,* and *s.*

Caroline Minuscule was a script that had been developed ca. 800 at the court of Charlemagne and had soon spread widely on the Continent but had not hitherto been generally used in England. Its greater legibility as compared with earlier scripts was helped by the scarcity of ligatures and the reduced number of letters having descenders, there being none on *f, r,* or high *s.* In England two varieties may be discerned—Style I in manuscripts written at monasteries associated with Bishop Æthelwold, such as the Old and New Minsters, Winchester, and Abingdon Abbey; Style II in those, such as Canterbury and Glastonbury, associated with Archbishop Dunstan. By the mid-11th century the size of letters in English Caroline Minuscule is generally larger than in the contemporary Norman variety. There is also a difference in the treatment of feet on minims, the short vertical strokes used in such letters as *i, n, m,* and *u;* scribes trained in England tended to make the feet horizontal, while those trained in Normandy formed them at an angle of 45 degrees.

The script used for vernacular texts developed from Square to Round Anglo-Saxon Minuscule in the early 11th century. In this, as in the preceding Insular, Pointed Anglo-Saxon, and Square Anglo-Saxon Minuscule scripts, when OE texts are written there occur the letters ash *(æ),* thorn *(þ),* eth *(ð),* and wynn *(ƿ),* the 7-shaped abbreviation for *and,* the abbreviation for *þæt,* but few other abbreviations.

A study of script can sometimes provide evidence for the origin of a particular manuscript or at least lead to the identification of a group of manuscripts or documents written by the same scribe. Where one of these can be precisely dated from its content, such dating can then give an approximate date to the others. Codicology, the study of the physical features of a manuscript book, may also give significant information relative to its precise origin but usually reveals facts only about its later history. Differences in the character of the parchment (usually calf- or sheepskin) on which the text was written may indicate that it was imported from the Continent rather than produced in Britain—early insular types being thicker and more suedelike and having less contrast between hair and flesh sides. Similarly the method of pricking the parchment sheets to guide the page rulings in each quire of a book (the gatherings of leaves folded and sewn together within a book) may reflect the book's early insular origin. In Britain before ca. 900 such quires were pricked after folding rather than before and therefore show pricks in both margins of each page rather than in only the outer one.

Different styles of decoration, the range of colored inks used in a book, the number and arrangement of sheets used to make its quires, and the manner in which quires are marked for the binder, as well as the nature of any original binding itself, may each relate to a particular place or region of production and should be carefully recorded. Additional features, such as glosses, marginalia, flyleaves, later bindings, marks of ownership or sale, and library marks, can also tell of the later use and location of a manuscript before it reached its present home. All such external features of manuscripts are relevant to our knowledge of the original patronage, the intended audience, and the continued use of early-medieval texts into the modern period.

Post-Conquest

After the Norman Conquest scribes did not suddenly cease copying OE texts. The Anglo-Saxon Chronicle was still being kept at Peterborough in the mid-12th century, while copies of Ælfric's *Catholic Homilies,* saints' lives, the West Saxon Gospels, and Bede's Death Song were being made elsewhere in the late 12th or early 13th centuries. However, by 1220, it is clear from errors of transcription that scribes had difficulty comprehending the language they were copying, and this inspired a monk at Worcester to provide glosses (usually in Latin but occasionally in early ME) to 23 Anglo-Saxon manuscripts (Ker, 1985: 67–69).

Copies of OE texts were only a small fraction of the total output of book production in 12th-century England. As the century progressed, the demand for books grew rapidly. Cathedral and monastic libraries were anxious to build up their holdings and sought in particular to acquire the works of the Fathers of the Church (Ambrose, Augustine, Gregory, Jerome). Students at the emerging universities required copies of their set texts and commentaries on them. In the 13th century the new orders of friars needed books. Laypeople who read for profit and pleasure also began to desire books (Parkes, 1991).

The increasing demand for books could not be met by monastic scriptoria. Even for a monastery's own needs it soon became necessary to employ outside scribes to help in the task of copying: according to the late-12th-century chronicler of Abingdon Abbot Faricius (1100–17) employed six *scriptores* to copy patristic manuscripts, while the copying of service books was reserved for the monks (the *claustrales*). At Cirencester, ca. 1150, Ralph Pulleham, *scriptor,* was hired to assist canon Alexander produce a copy of Bede. Professional scribes who were paid for copying supplied the new markets created by the secularization of learning and advances in lay literacy. By the mid-13th century a book trade thrived in the university towns, where both new and secondhand copies of texts could be bought by scholars (Parkes, 1991), while in London the trade was firmly established near St. Paul's Cathedral by the end of the 14th century (Christianson, 1989).

Although one speaks of the "book trade," this does not necessarily mean that scribes were paid to work in an organized bookshop on a regular footing. John Lutton of Oxford, who copied two manuscripts of Higden's *Polychronicon,* one for Hyde Abbey, Winchester, and the other for Bath Priory, is recorded in 1410 both as a scribe and a brewer (Doyle, 1990: 18). In London the poet Thomas Hoccleve, clerk of the privy-seal office, was one of five early-15th-century scribes who worked independently to produce a manuscript of Gower's *Confessio Amantis* (Cambridge, Trinity College R.3.2); he must have been "moonlighting" to eke out his income. The mid-14th-century scribe of the Harley Lyrics (BL Harley 2253), the Anglo-Norman romance *Fouke Fitzwarin* (BL Royal 12.C.xii), and of at least 40 documents conveying property for burgesses, craftsmen, clerics, and widows in the Ludlow area may have been the parish clerk.

Scribes like those of the Trinity Gower were probably employed by an entrepreneur who undertook financial responsibility for arranging the copying of a work and who accepted commissions from the book-buying public (Doyle and Parkes, 1978). Hoccleve's co-workers included one scribe who, since he also copied six other copies of the *Confessio Amantis,* two copies of the *Canterbury Tales,* a copy of *Piers Plowman,* and part of Trevisa's *De proprietatibus rerum,* seems to have been a full-time specialist in vernacular book production. A second scribe copied both the Hengwrt and Ellesmere manuscripts of the *Canterbury Tales* (National Library of Wales Peniarth 392; San Marino, Huntington Library 29 C 9). On the other hand scribes could also be hired directly by a patron, as was William Ebesham by Sir John Paston to copy a "Grete Boke" of chivalry (BL Lansdowne 285).

Ebesham's bill for the "Grete Boke" gives some idea of the costs incurred in producing a relatively plain manuscript in the late 15th century. For copying and rubricating (adding headings and other features in red ink) he charged Sir John 63*s.* 8*d.* Earlier accounts itemizing the costs of parchment, copying, decoration, and binding are noted on the flyleaves of books given by William Dyngley, bursar, to Peterhouse, Cambridge (MSS 88, 110, 114, 142, 154, 193). Little was spent on rubricating (only 6*d.* to 12*d.* a volume) as opposed to copying these books for the library (from 16*d.* to 20*d.* a quire). By contrast a two-volume missal commissioned in 1382–84 by Nicholas Lytlington, abbot of Westminster, containing over 50 historiated initials and miniatures, had cost £4 for copying but £22 3*d.* for illumination. Because of such costs relatively few ME books had pictures: only six copies of the *Canterbury Tales* were illustrated (Parkes and Beadle, 1980: 3:58 n.72), including the Ellesmere Manuscript, which has portraits of each pilgrim who tells a story. The copy of *Troilus and Criseyde* found in Cambridge, Corpus Christi College 61, was intended to be illustrated with about 90 pictures, but only the frontispiece was executed (Parkes and Salter, 1978).

Some people copied their own books, thereby saving money: Robert Thornton, a frugal Yorkshire gentleman, copied two large compilations of religious texts, medical tracts, and romances (Lincoln Cathedral 91; BL Add. 31042), and sixteen-year-old Thomas Spirleng shared with his father, Geoffrey (a burgess of Norwich), the copying of the *Canterbury Tales* (Glasgow University Library Hunterian U.1.1).

Books were written in one of three basic kinds of script depending on the type of book: 1) *Textura,* also called Gothic Bookhand or Textualis (Brown, 1990: 80–89), an elaborate, angular "display" script used especially for psalters, liturgical books, and books of hours. A smaller version with drastically modified letter forms was used for academic books. 2) *Anglicana,* a cursive script introduced into books toward the end of the 13th century, which was more familiar to readers who were accustomed to read documents (Parkes, 1979: xiv–xvi and pls. 1–3). Cheap books of vernacular prose and verse were produced in this script throughout the 14th and 15th centuries. A more calligraphic variety of the script, *Anglicana Formata,* was used in more expensive manuscripts containing works like the *Canterbury Tales* and *Confessio Amantis* (the Ellesmere and Hengwrt manuscripts and the Trinity Gower). A third variety was *Bastard Anglicana* (Parkes, 1979: pls. 7–8), used in deluxe books. This was a mixture of the cursive hand of documents and the Textura script of the most expensive books or between a "base" and a "noble" hand, hence described as "Bastard." 3) *Secretary,* a cursive script imported from France at the end of the 14th century (Parkes, 1979: pls. 11–13); it rapidly became popular, completely superseding Anglicana by the 16th century. The upmarket variety of this script, *Bastard Secretary,* developed from a mixture of Secretary and Textura (Parkes, 1979: pls. 14–15). Throughout the 15th century, however, books were often produced by scribes unconcerned with calligraphy who wrote mixed hands with letter forms appropriate to Anglicana and Secretary appearing together in their individual repertoires.

In most surviving manuscripts text was copied across quire boundaries, the quire being a gathering of conjoint leaves (often eight) secured one within the other by sewing through the middle of the center bifolium. Many manuscripts, however, consist of separate groups of quires where one group or "booklet" originated as an independent unit from another group and included self-contained text. Collecting a number of such booklets together was the cheapest and easiest way to build up a private library.

Because many medieval books contain "libraries" of texts rather than a single item it is often possible to discern from the tastes reflected in the choice of contents the class of reader for whom a particular manuscript was intended. The mid-14th-century Auchinleck Manuscript (Edinburgh, National Library of Scotland Advocates' 19.2.1) is a compilation of ME religious and secular texts, perhaps produced for a wealthy London merchant who wished to emulate the lettered chivalry in his choice of reading. Like the French books of romances that the latter would have been reading the Auchinleck Manuscript contains illustrated copies of "household romances" *(Guy of Warwick, Bevis of Hampton)* and histories *(Richard Coer de Lyon).* The massive Vernon Manuscript (Bodl. Eng. poet. a.1) contains almost every item of religious and devotional prose and verse available at the time it was produced (ca. 1400), perhaps for a community of women (Doyle, 1987). The title "sowlehele" at the head of its table of contents emphasizes its function as a spiritual encyclopedia. A plain unillustrated volume containing texts from the Primer, saints' lives, and popular and pious romances (CUL Ff.2.38) seems intended for the edification of a devout bourgeois family of the late 15th century. The ownership of a volume (when it can be established) can provide even more specific information about the reception of a work. Thus, from the number of anthologies of courtly verse owned by 15th-century knightly families, it clearly was fashionable among them to read Chaucer's and Lydgate's minor verse (Bodley 638 facsimile, p. xxxv).

Alexander R. Rumble
Pamela R. Robinson

Bibliography

PRIMARY
Scripts
Brown, Michelle P. *A Guide to Western Historical Scripts from Antiquity to 1600.* London: British Library, 1990; Parkes, Malcolm B. *English Cursive Book Hands 1250–1500.* Oxford: Clarendon, 1969. Repr. with minor revs. London: Scolar, 1979.

Manuscript Facsimiles
Facsimiles of whole Anglo-Saxon manuscripts in the series Early English Manuscripts in Facsimile. Copenhagen: Rosenkilde & Bagger, 1951–; *The Auchinleck Manuscript.* London: Scolar, 1977; *British Museum MS Harley 2253.* Ed. N.R. Ker. EETS o.s. 255. London: Oxford University Press, 1965; *Cambridge University Library MS Ff.2.38.* London: Scolar, 1979; *The Canterbury Tales: A Facsimile and Transcription of the Hengwrt Manuscript.* Intro. Donald C. Baker, A. Ian Doyle, and Malcolm B. Parkes. Norman: Pilgrim Books, 1979; *The Ellesmere Manuscript.* Intro. Ralph Hanna III. Woodbridge: Brewer, 1989; *A Facsimile of Cambridge University Library MS Gg.4.27.* Intro. Malcolm B. Parkes and Richard Beadle. 3 vols. Norman: Pilgrim Books, 1979–80; *The Facsimile Series of the Works of Geoffrey Chaucer.* 6 vols. Gen. ed. Paul G. Ruggiers. Norman: Pilgrim Books, 1979–87 [includes Tanner 346, Bodley 638, St. John's Cambridge L.1, Pierpont Morgan M.817, Trinity College Cambridge R.3.19, and Pepys 2006]; *The Thornton Manuscript.* London: Scolar, 1975; *Troilus and Criseyde: A Facsimile of Corpus Christi College Cambridge MS 61.* Ed. Malcolm B. Parkes and Elizabeth Salter. Cambridge: Brewer, 1978; *The Vernon Manuscript.* Ed. A. Ian Doyle. Cambridge: Brewer, 1987.

SECONDARY
Anglo-Saxon
Bishop, Terence Alan Martyn. *English Caroline Minuscule.* Oxford: Clarendon, 1971; Brown, Michelle P. *Anglo-Saxon Manuscripts.* London: British Library, 1991; Dumville, David N. "English Square Minuscule Script: The Background and Earliest Stages." *ASE* 16 (1987): 147–79; Dumville, David N. "English Square Minuscule Script: The Mid-Century Phases." *ASE* 23 (1994): 133–64; Ker, N.R. *Catalogue of Manuscripts Containing Anglo-Saxon.* Oxford: Clarendon, 1957

[see esp. the Introduction]; Richards, Mary P., ed. *Anglo-Saxon Manuscripts: Basic Readings.* New York: Garland, 1994.

Middle English
New *CBEL* 1:218–19; Christianson, C. Paul. "A Community of Book Artisans in Chaucer's London." *Viator* 20 (1989): 209–18; Doyle, A. Ian. "The English Provincial Book Trade before Printing." In *Six Centuries of the Provincial Book Trade in Britain,* ed. Peter Isaac. Winchester: St. Paul's Bibliographies, 1990, pp. 13–29; Doyle, A. Ian, and Malcolm B. Parkes. "The Production of Copies of the *Canterbury Tales* and the *Confessio Amantis* in the Early Fifteenth Century." In *Medieval Scribes, Manuscripts and Libraries: Essays Presented to N.R. Ker,* ed. Malcolm B. Parkes and Andrew G. Watson. London: Scolar, 1978, pp. 163–210; Griffiths, Jeremy, and Derek Pearsall, eds. *Book Production and Publishing in Britain 1375–1475.* Cambridge: Cambridge University Press, 1989; Ker, N.R. *Books, Collectors and Libraries: Studies in the Medieval Heritage.* Ed. Andrew G. Watson. London: Hambledon, 1985; Parkes, Malcolm B. *Scribes, Scripts and Readers: Studies in the Communication, Presentation and Dissemination of Medieval Texts.* London: Hambledon, 1991.

See also Books; Chaucer; Friars; Harley Lyrics; Hoccleve; Literacy; Manuscripts of Polyphonic Music; Notation of Plainsong; Notation of Polyphonic Music; Patronage, Literary; Textual Criticism; Universities; Wycliffite Texts

Parish Church Architecture
The division of England into parishes was a long and complex process, beginning in the later Anglo-Saxon period and continuing into the 12th century. In the Anglo-Saxon period churches with multiple clergy, known as minsters, were the mother churches of areas much larger than the later medieval parishes. The foundation of other churches in the minster's *peruchia,* whether by local thegns, larger monasteries, or even by the clergy of the minster itself, led to the breakdown of the minsters' authority and their eventual relegation to parish-church status themselves, although they sometimes retained special privileges in an area, a higher status often reflected in their post-Conquest architecture, particularly in their possession of cruciform plans.

There appears to have been a "great rebuilding" or building of small local churches, whatever their precise status, in stone during the century ca. 1050–1150. The vast majority of these buildings appear to have been simple structures of two parts, the larger a general assembly area for the congregation—the nave—and the other, at the east, a sanctuary for the altar. The latter space might be apsidal but was more commonly square, though usually narrower than the western compartment. The arch separating the two areas might be decorated with carved capitals or rudimentary arch moldings, and the same might be true of the doorway(s) into the nave, which was

generally placed on the north or south side rather than in the west wall. Botolphs in Sussex or Kempley in Gloucestershire might serve as examples of these simple churches.

Simple parish churches of this sort continued to be built throughout the 12th century, but after 1100 and especially after ca. 1120 more elaborate buildings began to appear, generally at sites owned by prominent patrons, lay or ecclesiastical. These buildings might retain the simple two-cell plan but add elaborate ornamentation (Steetley in Derbyshire or Barfeston in Kent), or they might expand the plan by adding new cells or a tower (Peterchurch in Herefordshire or Castle Rising in Norfolk). Rib-vaulted chancels became popular in certain regions, particularly in the west (Elkstone in Gloucestershire or the two parish churches of Devizes in Wiltshire), and the grandest parish churches, particularly those in prosperous towns, might sport nave aisles, although these are usually mid-12th-century or later (St. Margaret-at-Cliffs or New Romsey in Kent, Steyning in Sussex, Lambourn and Faringdon in Berkshire, or Melbourne in Derbyshire).

While rare in the Romanesque period, aisles were among the most common additions in the early Gothic, particularly to naves but also to chancels, often in the form of chapels. The reasons for these additions may have to do with increasing population or simply with increasing prosperity that brought a desire for larger buildings on the part of patrons or parishioners. Nave aisles were often added piecemeal, north and south separately, or in even smaller increments, so that pier and arch forms may differ widely in opposing aisles, or even

in the same arcade (St. Nicholas-at-Wade in Kent or St. Mary in Barton-on-Humber). These aisles were covered with steeply sloping wood roofs and low outer walls that were almost always replaced by flatter roofs and higher-windowed walls in the later Middle Ages. Clerestories were sometimes but by no means always built with Early English arcades (Eastry in Kent or Bottesford in Lincolnshire).

Chancels were also often enlarged in the 13th century, those in the southern part of the country during the first half and those in the Midlands more frequently in the second. The increasing emphasis on the separation of the clergy from the laity in the 13th century may help account for this rash of chancel construction, but it is not clear who financed these works, and it may as likely have been the congregation as the patron or clergy. The strict division of responsibility for nave and chancel upkeep between parishioners and patron, respectively, becomes clear only in the 14th century. These enlargements of the east arm were almost always rectangular in plan, with a flat facade lit by lancets or later by a large traceried window. Before the advent of traceried windows in mid-century, masons embellished their chancels with dado arcades (Cheriton in Kent or Burgh-next-Aylsham in Norfolk), windows set in shafted arcades (Cherry Hinton in Cambridgeshire or Bamburgh in Northumberland), and occasionally (but rarely in relation to the total of rebuilt chancels) vaults (Stoke d'Abernon in Surrey, Crondall in Hampshire, or Bishop Cannings in Wiltshire).

Tracery transformed the appearance of parish churches, especially in those areas of the Midlands or West Country prosperous from the wool trade in the 14th century and later. Windows of geometrical or curvilinear Decorated tracery are particularly spectacular in Lincolnshire, in such town churches as Grantham or Sleaford or even in such village churches as Navenby or Ewerby. Chartham in Kent and Patrington in Yorkshire (fig. 103) provide further examples of churches with exceptional Decorated window tracery.

Patrington is a cruciform building and this plan was frequent in more ambitious parish churches (Ashbourne or Wirksworth in Derbyshire are other examples), although, like the addition of aisles in the 13th century, transept arms were often of different dates. In the 14th and 15th centuries the endowment of chantries and chapels led to an increasing complexity in the plans of prosperous churches. Buildings like Cirencester parish church might end up with a bewildering number of aisles, chapels, porches, or annexes by the time the Reformation put a stop to most parish church building. The piecemeal character already apparent in many buildings by the 13th century was much more marked by the 16th.

After about 1330 Perpendicular tracery replaced Decorated, and indeed Perpendicular windows often literally replaced earlier lancets or Norman openings. Churches entirely or largely rebuilt in this period show a great spaciousness, with thin high piers, elegant wood ceilings, and huge, gridded windows. Examples might include Northleach or Chipping Camden in the Cotswolds, Lavenham in Suffolk, or Newark in Nottinghamshire. Large clerestories of almost continuous windows are also a feature of Perpendicular naves, as again at Lavenham, or at Gedney in Lincolnshire.

Towers were also a focus of attention for the parish-church builders of all periods, but especially from the 13th century on, with sharp stone spires the rule in the limestone belt, as at Ketton in Rutland or Grantham in Lincolnshire, while flat-roofed towers were common elsewhere, as at Tenterden in Kent or in many Perpendicular towers in Somerset. Parish-church towers could attain vertiginous height, as in the famous Boston stump or the more elegant spire of near 300 feet at Louth. By the end of the Middle Ages one might argue that more architectural energy was being invested in parish churches than any other type of building.

Lawrence Hoey

Bibliography

Blair, John, ed. *Minsters and Parish Churches: The Local Church in Transition, 950–1220.* Oxford University Committee for Archaeology, Monograph no. 17 (1988); Hoey, Lawrence. "Pier Alternation in Early English Gothic Architecture." *JBAA* 139 (1986): 45–67; Hoey, Lawrence. "Stone Vaults in English Parish Churches in the Early Gothic and Decorated Periods." *JBAA* 147 (1994): 36–51; Morris, Richard. *The Church in the Landscape.* London: Dent, 1989; Platt, Colin. *The Parish Churches of Medieval England.* London: Secker & Warburg, 1981; Rodwell, Warwick. *Church Archaeology.* 2d ed. London: Batsford, 1989.

See also Chantries; Parish Clergy; Popular Religion

Parish Clergy

From the time of Augustine of Canterbury in the early 7th century priests, deacons, and clergy in minor orders had a privileged place in society, first established by the laws of Æthelberht (d. 616/18). He who stole the property of a bishop should pay elevenfold, of a priest ninefold, of a deacon sixfold, of a lesser cleric threefold. Priests acting as witnesses to charters in the Saxon period testify to their place in political society, and the surviving number of Norman baptismal fonts as well as complete Norman churches are clear signs that the parochial system was established through most of England and Wales, though Domesday Book mentions few clergy.

Sparsely settled countryside in the north might produce a parish like Halifax, seventeen miles by eleven; in contrast Winchester in the 12th century had at least 36 parishes, Lincoln and Norwich 46 each, and London just over 100.

The Saxon kings planted clergy on royal lands to convert their people, and Saxon landowners built churches on their estates for themselves and their tenants and appointed and supported priests to care for their souls. The Gregorian reforms of the 11th century sought to remove churches from lay control and, by enforcing celibacy, put an end to hereditary priests. The lord retained the right to choose his priest, but the right of the bishop to approve and to regulate the priests' behavior was clearly established. Lords still retained control of the endowment of each church; an unforeseen consequence of the reform was that by the mid-12th century a quarter of all parish churches had passed to monastic ownership, endowments being diverted from the original support of the priest.

Thus, to reflect the complex realities of the "ownership" of parish churches, the parish priest became either a rector, a vicar, or a parochial chaplain, depending on legal status and the agreed share of income he enjoyed.

The rector held a parish that either remained (probably because of its poor income) independent of outside interference or that paid all but a small proportion of its income as a pension to a monastic house, cathedral, or other religious body. A vicar, a legal substitute, was a parish priest permanently endowed with part of the ancient income—usually the small tithes of hay and lesser crops but not wheat—while the greater share was paid to the monastery or other owner, legally the rector or parson and also the patron with the right to appoint the vicar. A third possibility was to appoint a priest, a vicar or parochial chaplain, with no such endowment, on occasion not even subject to approval by the bishop.

By the 13th century bishops had established reasonable control over parochial clergy of every status but needed to reinforce it by statutes against concubines and excessive drink. The huge losses of clergy at the Black Death suggest that many took their pastoral duties seriously, though laymen and bishops alike still took advantage of church funds by appointing beneficed clergy to work as administrators while they drew incomes from the parish, as the crown employed bishops in offices of state at little cost to itself.

In addition the income from a parochial living might be used to support an aspiring cleric at university. Pluralism (holding more than one benefice at a time) and absenteeism were common, and perhaps a majority of parishes were actually staffed by unbeneficed chaplains living on a pittance and often also serving chantries and teaching for additional income.

By the early 16th century bishops had succeeded in raising clerical standards; many were university graduates, and candidates for ordination were rejected for illiteracy. Visitation records suggest that most were carrying out their pastoral and liturgical duties, though celibacy was increasingly irksome and inflation a serious problem. The post-Reformation clergy were fewer in number but better educated.

Robert W. Dunning

Bibliography

Bowker, Margaret. *The Secular Clergy of the Diocese of Lincoln, 1495–1520.* Cambridge: Cambridge University Press, 1968; Heath, Peter. *English Parish Clergy on the Eve of the Reformation.* London: Routledge & Kegan Paul, 1969; Moorman, John R.H. *Church Life in England in the Thirteenth Century.* Cambridge: Cambridge University Press, 1945; Pantin, William A. *The English Church in the Fourteenth Century.* Cambridge: Cambridge University Press, 1955. Repr. Toronto: University of Toronto Press, 1980; Tanner, Norman P. *The Church in Late Medieval Norwich, 1370–1532.* Toronto: Pontifical Institute, 1984; Thompson, A. Hamilton. *The English Clergy and Their Organisation in the Later Middle Ages.* Oxford: Clarendon, 1947.

See also Chantries; Dioceses; Popular Religion

Parker, Matthew (1504–1575)

Cleric, reformer, administrator, and bibliophile; born in Norwich and educated at Corpus Christi College, Cambridge, where he became a fellow in 1527. A supporter of Henry VIII's reformation of the English church, he developed close contacts with the court, becoming Queen Anne Boleyn's chaplain. He was elected master of his college in 1544 and later became dean of Lincoln. Parker served twice as the university's vice-chancellor, an office that linked him more closely to central government.

In 1553 Mary's accession to the throne threatened exponents of the reformed church. Parker went into retirement, living in some distress during Mary's reign. When Elizabeth succeeded in 1558, he made clear he wished to resume his mastership, but Elizabeth required him to accept the archbishopric of Canterbury, which he occupied until his death. He had responsibility for overseeing the foundation of the Church of England in its modern sense, defining its doctrine and discipline, and setting it on its middle way between Roman Catholicism and the more extreme continental Reformation. The Church of England was, he believed, no new creation; it was the natural successor to the church introduced by Augustine at the end of the 6th century, though purges of later Romish corruptions had become necessary.

Parker set about collecting historical documents that cast light on the history, writing, and practice of the Anglo-Saxon and medieval churches and so laid the basis of a superb collection of medieval codices, which, supported by a library of printed books, he left in the care of his old college. They include such splendid manuscripts as the Augustine Gospels, a 6th-century Italian Gospel book supposedly brought by Augustine himself, the Dover and Bury Bibles, magnificently illustrated Romanesque display works, and two illustrated volumes of Matthew Paris's *Chronica majora*.

Archbishop Parker is the most important figure in the 16th-century revival of interest in early English studies. He collected around him a group of scholars, secretaries, and craftsmen who discovered, investigated, and preserved the early records of England and its church.

R.I. Page

Bibliography

Brook, V.J.K. *A Life of Archbishop Parker*. Oxford: Oxford University Press, 1962; Greg, W.W. "Books and Bookmen in the Correspondence of Archbishop Parker." *The Library*, 4th ser. 16 (1935–36): 243–79; Page, R.I. *Matthew Parker and His Books*. Kalamazoo: Medieval Institute, 1993; Wright, C.E. "The Dispersal of the Monastic Libraries and the Beginnings of Anglo-Saxon Studies. Matthew Parker and His Circle: A Preliminary Study." *Transactions of the Cambridge Bibliographical Society* 1 (1949–53): 208–37.

See also Ælfric; Cotton; Elstob; Nowell

Parliament

The history of the English parliament is rooted in conditions common to the states of medieval Europe: the need for money to finance the costs and objectives of government, especially war, and the concomitant need for political consultation with those social groups directly involved in or affected by government action. Parliamentary institutions and representative assemblies were hardly unique to England; most parts of Europe saw their development and maturation simultaneously with, or even before, England's. However, the English parliament developed a structure, composition, and range of functions that enabled it to outlast, in terms of real power, its continental counterparts.

This continuity formed the ultimate basis of the modern British tradition of parliamentary sovereignty. It is nonetheless essential to emphasize that medieval English parliaments were creations of, and creatures of, royal power, devised and designed by kings as special instruments to extend and formalize their authority and to make the implementation of their political agenda and public policies more efficient and effective.

The composition and functions of parliament took definite shape during the reigns of Edward I (1272–1307) and Edward II (1307–27). In effect Edward I invented parliamentary assemblies as royalist and consensual vehicles to support and help pay for his wars and to facilitate the tasks of government. Each assembly was separate and ad hoc; strictly speaking, one must always refer to "parliaments," for it is inaccurate to use the term "Parliament" as if it were a single, continuous, or autonomous institution. Magnates (earls and other great tenants-in-chief) and prelates (archbishops, bishops, and most abbots) were summoned individually; they represented themselves. Lesser aristocracy and borough elites elected two of their number from each shire and each town to speak for, and to bind, those communities—hence the so-called "knights of the shire" and the borough representatives. The sizes of these groups fluctuated. In the mid- to late 14th century, there were usually 50 to 60 lay peers, 21 English and Welsh bishops (including the two archbishops), over 25 abbots and priors (down from about 50 to 56 in the early 14th century), 72 knights of the shire, and two men each from about 70 to 100 towns and boroughs. These are the numbers summoned; many never attended. Lesser clergy were rarely represented (through diocesan proctors); the "Model Parliament" of 1295, which included them, was exceptional, and clerical representation in parliaments ceased altogether after that.

Continental assemblies generally developed a tripartite structure: upper (and some lower) clergy; upper and lower aristocracy; merchants and urban officials. English parliaments, by contrast, were bipartite and wholly lay in character, because prelates were summoned essentially as landlords: upper aristocracy and upper clergy (magnates, prelates) on the one hand, lower aristocracy and borough elites on the other. Under Edward II this structure became formally bicameral: magnates (with an increasingly fixed list of "peers" who automatically qualified for individual summons, regardless of title) and prelates together as the House of Lords, knights of the shire and borough representatives together as the House of Commons.

Not every assembly, however, had or was required to have all these groups present. There were meetings of magnates only, of borough representatives only, and (more commonly) of varying combinations. Every assembly did contain the king, his chief advisory officials, and justices; it is they who determined the agenda, and thus the composition of each particular parliamentary meeting. Parliaments were flexible in composition and multicompetent in function. They might handle petitions, unusual or difficult cases or sensitive political trials, notarize statutes, and, above all, serve as sounding boards for political propaganda and assent to taxation for wars. Edward I and Edward II had recourse to parliaments on a nearly annual basis. Their utility and prominence made them *functionally* essential but not yet *constitutionally* essential as an agency of central government and the welfare of the kingdom.

From the mid-14th century parliaments moved from definite (albeit flexible) to definitive shape. Beginning with Edward III (1327–77), parliamentary taxation was fixed on personal (movable) property at the rates of one-fifteenth (6 $^2/_3$ percent) on rural and one-tenth (10 percent) on urban property. Only in the 17th century was this system of source and rates replaced by a modernized real-property, or real-estate, system and in the 20th century by the income tax.

In 1340, hard pressed for ready cash for his invasion of France, Edward agreed to allow customs duties to come under parliamentary control. The customs and personal-property taxes now formed the overwhelming bulk of a vastly increased royal revenue; but these sources were subject to parliamentary vote, negotiated largely on an ad hoc, noncontinuous basis, often obtained only with strings attached—a process encapsulated in the phrase "redress of grievance preceding supply."

Of equal importance, the presence of all consultative and participatory constituencies—magnates, prelates, knights of the shire, and borough representatives, grouped into the two houses of Lords and Commons—was now deemed essential to the legal composition and functioning of parliaments. In addition they took on a specifically legislative cast. By Edward III's time statutes were passed by, no longer merely announced at, parliamentary sessions. Following the convenient fiction that the entire community was represented by the Commons, statutory legislation began in the form of a "commune petition" to the king as the source of law and enforcer of justice. Naturally royal officials drafted most statutes, but there were occasions where one or both houses initiated bills or, more frequently, made substantial changes in those presented to them. The legislative scope of parliamentary statutes extended into important areas of social and economic concern, common law, and the church.

When this legislative function is seen in conjunction with the taxation powers and the corporate consciousness of the two houses (singly and jointly) is taken into account, parliament had indeed come of age as a self-conscious and often proactive institution.

Finally, in the late Middle Ages, parliaments became the arena for spectacular and dangerous forays into factional power politics. The power to impeach and the recourse to acts of attainder for treason were frequent features of national politics. Most dramatic of all was parliament as the setting for solemnizing changes in the kingship itself: the "voluntary abdication" of Edward II in 1327, of Richard II in 1399 and the 1460 treaty whereby the Lancastrian Henry VI "voluntarily" recognized Richard duke of York as his rightful heir. The great lords clearly felt it expedient or even necessary to legitimate their actions in a parliamentary context. Parliament was the single, central agency for the bulk of governmental revenues and for statutory legislation. By the 14th century it was the favored vehicle to initiate or to ratify the recourse to violence in high politics.

All this, however, did not make England a "parliamentary monarchy." Legally speaking, parliaments existed only at the king's pleasure; he was entitled to govern without them, if he could manage financially. By the simple expedient of abandoning the Hundred Years War Edward IV and Henry VII needed far less parliamentary taxation—and so summoned far fewer parliaments. Even when relying heavily on them, moreover, kings worth their salt could manipulate or dominate them, for example by using the speaker of the Commons to control debate on bills.

In the enunciation of political theory, as later articulated by the Tudor monarchs, parliaments existed to bring information to the royal notice and to vote a simple "yea" or "nay," with a minimum of discussion, on requests for taxation or other business brought before them. The model envisioned was of a conflict-free passive instrument of royal governance, designed to facilitate the realization of the shared interests of the king and of the upper classes that parliaments represented. Medieval kings would certainly have recognized and applauded that model.

Michael Altschul

Bibliography

Edwards, John Goronwy. *The Second Century of the English Parliament*. Oxford: Clarendon, 1979 [illuminating account of how members met, voted, and acted, mainly in the 14th and 15th centuries]; Harriss, G.L. *King, Parliament, and Public Finance in Medieval England to 1369*. Oxford: Clarendon, 1975 [financial and public-policy aspects of parliamentary growth]; Myers, A.R. *Parliaments and Estates in Europe to 1789*. London: Thames & Hudson, 1975 [puts the English institution into a wider context]; Roskell, John S. "Perspective in English Parliamentary History." In *Historical Studies of the English Parliament,* ed. E.B. Fryde and Edward Miller. Vol. 2: *1399–1603*. Cambridge: Cambridge University Press, 1970, pp. 296–323 [valuable survey of main theories about origins and nature of parliament]; Sayles, G.O. *The King's Parliament of England*. New York: Norton, 1974 [background and origins, with emphasis on royalist perspective; heavy weight given to judicial role and function of parliament];

Thompson, Faith. *A Short History of Parliament,
1295–1642.* Minneapolis: University of Minnesota
Press, 1953 [old but still the only full-scale survey].

See also Attainder; Customs Accounts; Edward I; Impeachment; *Modus tenendi parliamentum;* Parliamentary Elections;
Peerage; Rolls of Parliament; Taxes

Parliament of the Three Ages, The

An unrhymed alliterative poem of 665 lines preserved in the
Thornton Manuscript, BL Add. 31042 (ca. 1425–50), where
it is followed by *Winner and Waster,* and (lacking the first 225
lines) in BL Add. 33994 (late 15th century). Both the authorship and date are unknown, though stylistic features and details of dress suggest a date around 1400.

Like *Winner and Waster* the poem is a debate set within
a dream. In the prologue, the most attractive part of the poem,
the narrator vividly describes how he went poaching early one
May morning. He shot a fine hart, dismembered it, and hid
it from the forester. Waiting for the cover of night, he fell
asleep and dreamed of three men, Youth, Middle Elde, and
Elde (Old Age), each defending the merits of his perspective
on life. Youth, elegantly dressed, describes the service he does
for his mistress, his sport of hawking, and his devotion to the
courtly activities of chess, reading romances, and dancing.
Middle Elde describes his money-making enterprises and
scorns the extravagance of Youth's life. Elde calls both his
companions fools, telling them that all such worldly occupations are valueless. He recounts at considerable length the lives
of the Nine Worthies: the pagans Hector, Alexander, and
Caesar; the Jews Joshua, David, and Judas Maccabeus; and the
Christians Arthur, Godfrey de Bouillon, and Charlemagne.
All these great lives have come to nothing. Elde then mentions
the famous wise men and the lovers, all now dead, and advises
his companions to learn from this that all is vanity. The
dreamer is woken by the sound of a horn and returns home
from the beautiful wood.

Elde's arguments are not disputed, but neither are they
final, for the reader is left with vivid impressions of the beauty
of the May morning, the excitement of hawking, and indeed
the grand achievements of the Worthies. The sun is setting as
the narrator goes home, the horn (is it Death's horn?) has
sounded, but the experiences of the day have been absorbing
and cannot be dismissed.

The principal source for the account of the Worthies is
a passage in a French poem of ca. 1312, Jacques de Longuyon's
Voeux du paon, lines 7484–579, supplemented by the English
poet's surprisingly inaccurate memory. The accounts of Hector, Alexander, Arthur, and Charlemagne are much fuller than
in the *Voeux.* The lively and detailed descriptions of the dismembering of the deer and the practices of hawking may be
indebted to contemporary manuals on hunting and hawking.
The structure of the dream-vision debate and some of Middle
Elde's arguments are reminiscent of *Winner and Waster,* and
there are further structural and thematic parallels with *Death
and Life,* but no certain influence can be demonstrated. There
are also some verbal parallels with the descriptions of the

Worthies in the alliterative *Morte Arthure.* In diction and style
the poem is to be associated with other unrhymed alliterative
poems of the northwest Midlands, but there is no secure evidence of original dialect.

Thorlac Turville-Petre

Bibliography

PRIMARY

Offord, M.Y., ed. *The Parlement of the Thre Ages.* EETS o.s.
246. London: Oxford University Press, 1959; Turville-Petre, Thorlac, ed. *Alliterative Poetry of the Later
Middle Ages: An Anthology.* London: Routledge, 1989.

SECONDARY

New *CBEL* 1:547; *Manual* 5:1501–03, 1703–05; Kernan,
Anne. "Theme and Structure in *The Parlement of the
Thre Ages.*" *NM* 75 (1974): 253–78; Rowland, Beryl.
"The Three Ages of *The Parlement of the Three Ages.*"
ChauR 9 (1975): 342–52; Turville-Petre, Thorlac.
"The Ages of Man in *The Parlement of the Thre Ages.*"
MÆ 46 (1977): 66–76; Waldron, Ronald A. "The
Prologue to *The Parlement of the Thre Ages.*" *NM* 73
(1972): 786–94.

See also Alliterative Revival; *Death and Life;* Debate Poems;
Dream Vision; Literary Influences: French; *Morte Arthure,
Alliterative; Winner and Waster*

Parliamentary Elections

From the late 13th century elections were regularly held in
response to writs of summons issued by royal command from
chancery to the sheriffs. The sheriff in turn sent precepts to
certain cities and boroughs within his bailiwick, directing the
authorities to submit the names of their chosen representatives.
Each sheriff duly returned the writ to chancery, endorsed with
a statement noting that elections had been held and listing the
successful candidates.

As many as 36 shires and 99 cities and boroughs were
represented in the Commons before 1485 (each sending two
members, save for London, with four), although not all of
them made returns to every parliament; the House rarely had
its full complement of 272. In the shires elections were held
at a full session of the county court, but since sheriffs sometimes returned themselves, without bothering to observe the
formalities, an ordinance of 1372 barred anyone who occupied a shrievalty from the Commons. In the "Good Parliament" of 1376 the House asked that shire knights might
henceforth be chosen by "the better gentlemen" of the counties; electoral legislation passed in the following century was
directed toward this end, intending to secure free elections and
prevent malpractice.

A statute of 1406 provided that advance notice of parliaments should be given, that elections should be held
openly, and that the returns should bear the names and seals
of the more important persons present. In practice only a few
individuals were actually listed, although "many others" were

often recorded as in attendance. When these new-style returns (known as indentures) *do* contain an unusually large number of names, the elections were probably contested. Legislation of 1413 ordered that shire knights should live in the counties they represented and that electors should be resident there, too.

Disputed elections to the parliaments of 1427 and 1429, when a number of fraudulent returns were made by sheriffs, led to a statute of 1430, determining the county franchise until 1832. In future the electorate was to consist only of those who swore on oath that they enjoyed an annual landed income of 40 shillings; sheriffs were threatened with a year's imprisonment, as well as a stringent fine of £100, should they tamper with the results. An act of 1445 brought the elections of borough representatives within the scope of this legislation and greatly increased the penalties. But despite their growing severity the statutes did not prove effective.

One of the grounds for Richard II's deposition in 1399 had been his blatant interference in parliamentary elections; the Yorkists used a similar pretext for declaring the parliament of 1459 illegal. As seats in the Commons became more sought after, magnates tried to manipulate the electoral procedure to favor their own men, even resorting to violence. In East Anglia they had to employ more sophisticated methods, although the gentry still maintained a staunch sense of independence. The Derbyshire elections of 1433 became a confrontation between two gangs of armed men when Sir Richard Vernon challenged Lord Grey of Codnor's candidates. To rebut Lord Tiptoft's authority in Cambridgeshire, in 1439, Sir James Ormond displayed his retainers about the county for three weeks, "charging [the commons] to gyf the voyces atte the eleccion . . . to suche men as they wold have, managyng them yef they did the contrary to be bete and sleyn." When some 2,000 people, "fulle of malesse," turned up at Cambridge Castle on election day, the sheriff refused to proceed for fear of "man slaughter." Nevertheless, Ormond's rabble went ahead, even though most, being outsiders or local laborers, were ineligible to vote.

In cities and boroughs practice at elections depended more on local custom. A few towns and cities (eleven by 1463) ranked as incorporated shires, but only Bristol stuck rigidly to the statute of 1430 by restricting the franchise to 40-shilling freeholders. The four London members of parliament were chosen by an unusually large electorate of 150 or so in the court of common council. Elsewhere elections took place in borough courts, meeting in local guildhalls, and the results were sent to the sheriff for transmission to chancery. Generally the franchise was restricted to freemen of the borough, though in some places a narrower property qualification obtained.

The electorate often reflected the oligarchical nature of medieval urban life, a select body of burgesses acting as the self-imposed delegates of the rest. Only the *potentiores* (powerful men) of Bishop's Lynn were allowed to nominate the twelve jurors who made the choice for the entire community, although Shrewsbury was evidently more democratic. Over 100 burgesses witnessed the indenture of 1478, and when this was disputed a second document bearing an additional 69 names was produced. Here, as elsewhere, the election was made in the first instance by acclamation, the freemen selecting their candidates "with a hoole voyce."

Linda Clark

Bibliography

Edwards, John Goronwy. "The Huntingdonshire Parliamentary Election of 1450." In *Essays in Medieval History Presented to Bertie Wilkinson,* ed. T.A. Sandquist and M.R. Powicke. Toronto: University of Toronto Press, 1969, pp. 383–95; Houghton, K.N. "Theory and Practice in Borough Elections to Parliament during the Later Fifteenth Century." *BIHR* 29 (1966): 130–42; McFarlane, K.B. "Parliament and Bastard Feudalism." *TRHS,* 4th ser. 26 (1944): 56–65; McKisack, May. *The Parliamentary Representation of the English Boroughs during the Middle Ages.* London: Oxford University Press, 1932; Roskell, John S. *The Commons in the Parliament of 1422.* Manchester: Manchester University Press, 1954; Virgoe, Roger. "Three Suffolk Parliamentary Elections of the Mid-Fifteenth Century." *BIHR* 39 (1966): 185–96; Virgoe, Roger. "An Election Dispute of 1483." *Historical Research* 60 (1987): 24–44.

See also Local Government; Parliament

Patronage, Literary

In a period before widespread literacy, printing and copyright laws had combined to offer authors a chance to earn their living by their pen alone, private patronage—that is, a system under which a person of wealth and position supports an artist in return for the honor bestowed by a laudatory dedication—would seem to have provided the only real opportunity for authors to enjoy any degree of security. Yet, perhaps because such a system depends upon the author's being held in high esteem, the Middle Ages seem to have known little of the kind of patronage practiced in imperial Rome by Augustus and Maecenas. Scholars were certainly drawn to the courts of the great (as Alcuin of York was drawn to Charlemagne's in the late 8th century), but they seem seldom to have been afforded the opportunity for a life of undisturbed study. The 12th-century court of Henry II of England was comparatively enlightened, yet Walter Map describes how he had to write his *De nugis curialium* "raptim" (by snatches) and even goes on to complain that "the Muses are fugitives from all courts" (*De nugis* 4.2). Broadly speaking, we may distinguish three phases in the changing relationship of author and patron in the Middle Ages: the age of the bard (the Anglo-Saxon *scop*), the period of the minstrel, and the rise of the vernacular author.

Of the first of these Girvan has written that "the patron had no important part in encouraging vernacular writing" (1951: 90). There seem to be two reasons for this. To be a *scop* in anything like a professional sense would have forced a storyteller working within an oral tradition to keep on the move if he were not to exhaust his repertoire. If he did not, like

Waldere, peddle his wares from court to court, he risked being, like Deor, supplanted by a rival. Second, the *scop*'s art was not one that set him apart from his social betters. In the *Skaldskaparmal* section of the *Prose Edda* the Icelander Snorri Sturluson (d. 1241) implies that mastery of skaldic verse was an accomplishment worthy of a thegn (*Prose Edda* 2.65); the man who tells the tale of Sigmund in *Beowulf* is not a professional poet but one of Hrothgar's retainers, a "guma gilphlæden" ("proud warrior"); and Taillefer, who Wace tells us recited the *Song of Roland* before the Battle of Hastings (1066), was also a warrior and leader of the Norman vanguard. Only the author who can lay claim to an exclusive skill is likely to be able to reap the full benefit of a system of patronage.

In this respect the lot of the *scop*'s successor, the minstrel of the high Middle Ages, was happier. Though still primarily oral entertainers who were forced by economic circumstances to lead a peripatetic existence, minstrels at least enjoyed the status of professionals with a particular and marketable talent. At the highest level (as with Chrétien de Troyes at the court of Marie de Champagne) they may even have enjoyed the fruits of patronage in something like its classical sense, but lower down the scale they could at least aspire to knowledge of an art not shared by their superiors. The emergence of corporations and *confréries* of minstrels in northern France (often attended by visitors from other countries, including England) attests to this sense of professionalism. Nevertheless, the position of minstrels, whether reciting their own work or that of others, was far from that of the true recipient of patronage—much closer to that of the journeyman, paid for performing a service. That service might indeed be commissioned: laudatory biographies like the 13th-century *Histoire de Guillaume le Maréchal* or the 14th-century *Vie du Prince Noir* by the Chandos Herald were minstrel work (at this period there was no great distinction between the roles of heralds and minstrels); minstrels also composed versified history and political propaganda (e.g., Laurence Minot's poems on Edward III's French and Scottish wars). Even here, however, their masters remained primarily consumers buying a product, not (as the true patron must be) investors involved in literary speculation. By the end of the 14th century the status of the minstrel, never high, had declined even further, and in the households of great magnates the term had come to designate a professional musician rather than a literary practitioner; late-medieval romances attributed to the work of minstrels are often uncourtly in tone, and even when we can identify a minstrel-author he is likely to remain (like the Thomas Chestre who composed *Sir Launfal*) little more than a name.

The authors of the late Middle Ages differed from the minstrels who preceded them in a number of important ways. They have names and social status and their biographies can often be reconstructed in some detail. They wrote not only for oral performance but also for private readers. Many of them enjoyed the security of regular employment in the households of kings and princes (e.g., the king's esquire Chaucer and the royal tutors Scogan and Skelton); some of them were asked to employ their skills for political ends (see Lydgate's *Title and Pedigree of Henry VI* or Skelton's *Douty Duke of Albany*). Unlike their minstrel predecessors, however, the new court poets could no longer boast of possessing an exclusive skill. Literature had become a fashionable pursuit of the aristocracy, and princes, though no doubt happy to discover poetic talent among their servants, seem rarely to have been willing to support them for this talent alone; literature in the late Middle Ages became, as Samuel Moore puts it, not a vocation but an avocation (1913: 369). The origins of the new fashion can be detected as early as the Sicilian court of Frederick II (d. 1250), but by the end of the 14th century it had spread, by way of the court of Robert of Anjou (d. 1343) in Naples, to most of the courts of northern Europe. Though authors abound in the households of late-medieval English kings and noblemen from Richard II's reign onward, few, it appears, were employed primarily for their literary abilities; typically the new men of letters were members of a secular civil service, employed, like Chaucer, in bureaucratic posts that can hardly be regarded as sinecures. Even at the sophisticated 15th-century court of the dukes of Burgundy the offices held by authors seem to have had nothing in common with their literary calling; as the administrative historian T.F. Tout remarks, "Mediaeval conditions made literature an impossible profession" (1929: 381). The French author Christine de Pizan (ca. 1364–ca. 1431) appears to have been unique among courtly authors, outside Italy at least, in being able to make her living largely by her pen. Only with the Renaissance, and a growing recognition of the importance of literature in fostering princely reputations, do we find anything approaching a system of patronage as it is classically understood.

It remains surprisingly difficult to document even the limited encouragement that late-medieval English courts offered practicing poets. Account books, at least the kind that might record casual payments for literary performance, have not survived, and the more formalized records are generally uninformative: Chaucer was a busy civil servant whose name appears frequently in exchequer and wardrobe accounts, yet not a single record gives any indication that he was a poet or suggests that he was officially rewarded for practicing his craft. Far more promising is the evidence of book ownership. We should be wary of automatically assuming that because a nobleman or woman owned a copy of a vernacular work they would have been happy to reward its author (presentation copies were not always encouraged or read, and inherited libraries might be maintained simply because of the value attached to books as expensive artifacts); nevertheless, the purchasing and commissioning of books offer the best evidence we have of active encouragement of literature on the part of royal or aristocratic patrons. Continuing research into the early ownership of surviving manuscripts and on the library catalogues and book lists of individual collectors seems the most promising avenue for future discoveries about the literary tastes and private patronage of the late Middle Ages. In the current state of our knowledge comparative claims for the literary sophistication of one patron against another (Richard II, say, against Edward IV) seem premature.

It has been claimed that the end of the Middle Ages witnessed the rise of a "new reading public" among the merchant class, but the influence of such a public on the production of literary works has probably been exaggerated. The prestige of great courts was by no means on the wane, and it seems unlikely that a middle-class public would have developed tastes essentially different from those of its social superiors. The author's best hope of reward still lay with those who had the greatest power and wealth, and though families like the Pastons might purchase the products of commercial scriptoria, it would be a long time before their literary interests would provide any tangible benefits for the authors themselves. Even the introduction of the printing press had little immediate effect on the unsatisfactory system of private patronage that had developed in the late Middle Ages, and William Caxton was drawn to wealthy patrons and protectors as surely as his predecessors had been.

Richard Firth Green

Bibliography

Bloomfield, Morton W., and Charles W. Dunn. *The Role of the Poet in Early Societies.* Cambridge: Brewer, 1989; Boffey, Julia. *Manuscripts of English Courtly Love Lyrics in the Later Middle Ages.* Cambridge: Brewer, 1985; Girvan, Ritchie. "The Medieval Poet and His Public." *English Studies Today.* Vol. 1, ed. C.L. Wrenn and G. Bullough. London: Oxford University Press, 1951, pp. 85–97; Green, Richard Firth. *Poets and Princepleasers: Literature and the English Court in the Late Middle Ages.* Toronto: University of Toronto Press, 1980; Holzknecht, Karl J. *Literary Patronage in the Middle Ages.* Philadelphia, 1923 [classic general survey]; Lucas, Peter J. "The Growth and Development of English Literary Patronage in the Later Middle Ages and Early Renaissance." *The Library,* 6th ser. 4 (1982): 219–48 [excellent study with extensive bibliography]; Mathew, Gervase. *The Court of Richard II.* London: Murray, 1968; Moore, Samuel. "General Aspects of Literary Patronage in the Middle Ages." *The Library,* 3d ser. 4 (1913): 369–92; Scattergood, V. J., and J.W. Sherborne, eds. *English Court Culture in the Later Middle Ages.* London: Duckworth, 1983; Southworth, John. *The English Medieval Minstrel.* Woodbridge: Boydell, 1989; Tout, T.F. "Literature and Learning in the English Civil Service in the Fourteenth Century." *Speculum* 4 (1929): 365–89.

See also Bokenham; Books; Capgrave; Caxton; Chaucer; Court Culture; Literacy; Lydgate; Minstrels; Shirley; Skelton

Paul the Deacon (ca. 720–799)

Paul the Deacon, from Friuli (Lombardy), was educated in Pavia and entered the monastery of Monte Cassino in 774. Following the Friuli insurrection in 776 against Charlemagne's annexation of Lombardy Paul went to Francia to obtain the release of his brother, who had been taken prisoner; he expected the visit to be brief but remained for several years,

caught up in the early stages of the Carolingian renaissance. He returned to Monte Cassino by 787.

Paul was a historian of stature: he wrote an abbreviated world history, a history of the Romans, a history of the bishops of Metz, and a six-book history of the Lombards. He also wrote a major commentary on the Benedictine Rule and, at Charlemagne's direction, compiled a Latin homiliary (based on Italian models) that was intended to be the authoritative, standard collection for use at the night office (the prayers and readings used by monks in the night hours of the divine office).

This homiliary was introduced into England at the time of the 10th-century Benedictine Reform, along with others from the Carolingian period, but surviving manuscripts indicate that it was Paul's homiliary that was preeminent. It was liturgically organized and was mainly an anthology of whole patristic homilies that provided exegesis of the Gospel pericope, or reading for the day. From the outset many of the feast days had several expositions, but subsequent users added to these, so that it has been necessary for modern scholars to reconstruct the original. The manuscripts from Anglo-Saxon England are augmented versions, and it was an augmented text that was used by the vernacular homilist Ælfric. In the preface to the *Catholic Homilies* Ælfric names Augustine, Jerome, Bede, and Gregory as his major authorities, but it has been shown that his immediate source for much of this material was Paul's homiliary, where Ælfric would have found that the patristic authorities were specified.

Joyce Hill

Bibliography

Goffart, Walter. *The Narrators of Barbarian History* (A.D. *550–800).* Princeton: Princeton University Press, 1988, pp. 329–431; Smetana, Cyril L. "Ælfric and the Early Medieval Homiliary." *Traditio* 15 (1959): 163–204; Smetana, Cyril L. "Paul the Deacon's Patristic Anthology." In *The Old English Homily and Its Backgrounds,* ed. Paul E. Szarmach and Bernard F. Huppé. Albany: SUNY Press, 1978, pp. 75–99.

See also Ælfric; Bede; Benedictine Reform; Fathers of the Church; Literary Influences: Carolingian; Sermons

Pearl-Poet

The designation given to an anonymous late-14th-century poet who is generally assumed to have written the poems *Pearl, Cleanness, Patience,* and *Sir Gawain and the Green Knight,* all found in BL Cotton Nero A.x. Untitled in the manuscript, the first three of the poems are known by their first words, and the fourth by its general subject. Because *Gawain* is the best known of the four poems, the poet is also referred to as the *Gawain*-poet.

The poems are regarded as the highest achievement of the 14th-century Alliterative Revival. *Cleanness* (1,812 lines) and *Patience* (531 lines) both employ only the classic long alliterative line: four heavy stresses, a caesura between the second and third stresses, and alliteration of the first three stressed words. Marks in the manuscript are thought to divide these two poems into four-line stanzas. In *Gawain* (2,530 lines) the poet employs stanzas of varying lengths: the main body of each stanza is written in long alliterative lines and concludes with a "bob" and "wheel" (terms coined in the 19th century)—a one-stress line (bob), usually otiose, leading into a rhyming quatrain of three-stress lines (wheel), the whole five-line group having the rhyme scheme ababa. *Pearl's* demanding verse form uses alliteration, rhyme, and concatenation (linking stanzas by beginning with the previous stanza's last word). Most lines have four stresses, though the poet usually alliterates no more than two stresses per line. The 101 twelve-line stanzas, each rhyming ababababbcbc, are in twenty groups of five—each with its own concatenating word—except for group XV, which has six stanzas, yielding a total of 1,212 lines. *Pearl, Patience,* and *Gawain* end by echoing their opening lines.

There is no external evidence of the author's identity; nevertheless, it does seem more likely that one person wrote all four poems than that two or more such remarkable talents arose at the same time and place. Arguments for common authorship of the four poems compare vocabulary, phraseology, stylistic features, versification, imagery, and themes shared by two or more of the poems. Attempts to identify the author on the basis of the names "J. Macy," written on fol. 62v, and "Hugo de," written on fol. 91, have been inconclusive. The Macy (or Mascy or Massey) theory, which has been supported by arguments for a numerological code, an acrostic signature, and puns on *mascellez* in stanza group XIII of *Pearl,* is currently frustrated by the number of possible candidates, for there were many Macys/Mascys/Masseys in the geographical area of the manuscript and at least five who might have signed themselves "J. Macy."

The Cotton Nero manuscript offers little help in resolving the authorship question. It was copied in one hand, in places written over, which has been dated variously between the late 14th century and the early 15th, a dating supported by the clothing styles depicted in the manuscript's twelve crude illustrations, which were executed by someone who is as unknown as the author and scribe. These illustrations—four for *Pearl,* two for *Cleanness,* two for *Patience,* and four for *Gawain*—do not always represent the text accurately. On the basis of its language the manuscript originated in the northwest Midlands, probably in southeast Cheshire or northeast Staffordshire.

Assuming one author, critics have often taken *Patience* and *Cleanness* to be works of the author's youth, whereas *Pearl* and *Gawain,* whose poetic artistry and handling of the material more readily impress modern sensibility, are regarded as works of his maturity. The fact that *Cleanness* borrows from *Mandeville's Travels,* written in French ca. 1357, establishes a *terminus post quem* (earliest possible date) of the 1360s or 70s for that poem, depending on how soon the poet encountered the *Travels.* The date of the manuscript itself establishes a *terminus ante quem* (latest possible date) of the late 14th to early 15th century. The author's knowledge of the Bible and biblical commentary, the arts of preaching, and popular theology suggests that he was a cleric. His familiarity with chivalry and court life, such secular texts as the *Romance of the Rose,* and

the legends of Troy and of Arthur does not argue against this supposition; but if he was indeed a cleric, he had strong worldly interests and sensibilities, and if he was a layman, he was unusually learned. The poems themselves cannot resolve this question, since none of the narrators' self-references need be taken as autobiographical. *Pearl,* for example, might have been written for rather than by a bereaved father.

A fifth poem, *St. Erkenwald,* also of the late 14th century, has often been attributed to the *Pearl*-poet. Its 352 lines relate the otherwise unrecorded story of how the saint, a 7th-century bishop of London, recalls to life and baptizes a pagan judge whose miraculously uncorrupted body is uncovered during church excavations. *Erkenwald* is in a different manuscript—BL Harley 2250, scribally dated 1477—and it is in a different hand and dialect from Cotton Nero A.x. Though this may indicate only that a different scribe copied the poem, other evidence argues against common authorship. *Erkenwald's* subject matter connects it with London rather than the northwest Midlands, and its vocabulary, phraseology, and style have little in common with the *Pearl* poems.

Pearl, for which Boccaccio's *Olympia* is at least an analogue, combines elegy, allegory, homily, debate, and dream vision. Set within the frame of a medieval dream vision, it takes place on an August day when the narrator, searching in a garden at the spot where he has lost a most precious pearl, falls asleep and dreams that he is in a jeweled landscape by a stream, beyond which stands his daughter in white apparel studded with pearls. Elegy quickly yields to debate when the narrator and the maiden argue his right to mourn and her right to be a queen of heaven, child preaching to father via the parable of the workers in the vineyard (Matt. 20). The maiden obtains for the narrator the privilege of seeing the heavenly Jerusalem (cf. Rev. 21–22), in the streets of which is a procession led by the Lamb. Seeing the maiden among the 144,000 virgins (cf. Rev. 14:1–5), the narrator attempts to cross the stream and join her, but he awakens, once again in the garden. Though he wishes to return to his vision, he reflects that only submission to God's will could lead him to more of God's mysteries, and his concluding stanza, which returns to the present, speaks of his contentment with this consolation.

The pearl image unifies the poem's experience: the pearl is first a jewel, then a daughter, then the perfected heavenly state itself. But like Dante, whose *Purgatorio* 28–33 may have inspired him, the poet of *Pearl* presents this experience from the twin perspectives of a narrator undergoing a spiritual struggle and a redeemed maiden secure in divine certainty. And, like Dante, he preserves the drama and passion of the narrator's struggle even though it is already over. In this psychologically and symbolically rich work the poet shows a sure and unaffected grasp of medieval theology, lapidary lore, courtesy literature, and even styles of clothing. *Pearl* thus ranks with Milton's *Lycidas* as one of the language's most learned, as well as enduring, poems about loss.

Cleanness affirms the power of spiritual purity to help human beings gain the beatific vision; it accomplishes its goal mainly by recounting incidents from biblical history in which God punished spiritual impurity. The poem's theme is the sixth Beatitude from the Sermon on the Mount ("Blessed are the clean of heart," Matt. 5:8). After illustrating the punishment awaiting the unclean through a retelling of Christ's parable of the Wedding Feast (Matt. 22:1–14; Luke 14:16–24) the poet develops three main examples of God's angry punishment of sinners: the Flood (Gen. 6:1–9:7), the destruction of Sodom (Gen. 19:1–19:28), and Belshazzar's feast (Dan. 5). These are set off by other biblical stories that are instances of lesser punishments, of cleanness, and of repentance. The falls of Adam and Lucifer introduce the Flood; the story of Abraham receiving God in Mambre (Gen. 18) introduces the destruction of Sodom; Nebuchadnezzar's capture of Jerusalem (4 Kings 24:18–25:17; AV 2 Kings 24:18–25:17) introduces the story of Belshazzar, which is interrupted part-way through by the story of Nebuchadnezzar's madness and repentance (Dan. 4:32–37, 5:21).

Despite its obvious debt to the Bible and commentary *Cleanness* remains an original work throughout. The poet's combination and handling of biblical episodes around the theme of the sixth Beatitude has no known source. The poem also contains startling juxtapositions and adopts unexpected points of view. Some of the author's most striking touches are in the linking passage between the first two and the third of these groups of major and minor examples, a Nativity scene that leads into an excursus on how penance washes the soul clean like a pearl washed in wine (lines 1065–1148). Where we expect moral dryness, *Cleanness* does not deliver it: the poet praises marital sexuality, and a scene describing the torment of the doomed sinners as the Flood waters overtake them contains genuine pathos.

Since *Patience* stays close to one biblical source, it is sometimes considered the earliest of the four poems in the manuscript. The story follows the Old Testament book of Jonah so closely that every verse is rendered, but the poet expands with originality and imagination. In some places the Vulgate is translated directly into ME; in others it is modified with material from other sources, such as Tertullian's *Liber de patientia*. Throughout the poem the author improvises on his original; for example, Jonah floats into the whale's mouth "like a mote going through a church door" (268). The poet retells the story with an eye toward the psychological motives of God as well as of Jonah. This humanized God, like that in *Cleanness,* resembles the figure of God in medieval drama, but such an idea of God is virtually unknown in 14th-century theological literature.

The narrative's frame poses as autobiography. Hearing the eight Beatitudes in the Sermon on the Mount one day in mass, the poet ponders the relationship between the first, poverty, and the last, patience, applying them to his own life. To illustrate the dangers he would incur without patience he retells the story of Jonah, who is here an example of impatience because he could not endure (cf. Lat. *patior,* "suffer, endure") the hardship imposed on him by his call to preach to the Ninevites. In medieval handbooks on sin and penance patience was the virtue opposed to sloth, which Jonah demonstrates at various points. But even as the story shows Jonah's impatience, querulousness, and selfishness, it emphasizes

God's constant mercy in response to human behavior. God explains to Jonah in the poem's conclusion that his mercy is the love he feels for creatures whom he has nurtured and thus does not wish to harm. Despite the narrator's faith in the ultimate benignness of tests like Jonah's—and, presumably, his own—his refrain is the hardship that must be borne, not the rewards of patience, for these must be deferred until the time in heaven promised by the Beatitudes.

Sir Gawain and the Green Knight has captivated readers since its recovery in the 19th century and has even been adapted (freely) into a feature film. In it Arthur's court is challenged by a green knight, the agent of Morgan le Fay (Fr. Morgain la fée), who arrives at the New Year's feast with an axe and a twig of holly. Accepting the challenge, Gawain cuts off the knight's head, only to see him pick it up and depart uttering a reminder that now Gawain must endure a return stroke in a year. Later, searching for the Green Knight, Gawain is put up at the castle of Bertilak de Hautdesert, who involves "the fine father of manners" in an exchange of daily winnings that turns out to be a test of Gawain's ability to withstand his host's wife's daily sexual advances. Gawain secretly accepts and keeps the wife's purportedly magic girdle in the hope that it will protect him from death when he meets the Green Knight, whose "green chapel" turns out to be in the neighborhood of Bertilak's castle. Meeting the Green Knight, Gawain flinches at the first axe blow but then endures a second, feigned blow and a third, barely deflected stroke, which wounds him slightly. After the three blows the Green Knight reveals that he is Bertilak. Gawain, feeling shame over his behavior, determines to wear the green girdle as an emblem of his fault, and returns to Arthur's court, where his report is received with indulgence and everyone puts on a green baldric, apparently in solidarity.

The simplicity, wonder, and charm of *Gawain* conceal imaginative depths still actively explored by readers of the poem. It is a romance in which the conventions, such as the Yuletide feast at Arthur's court, the challenge, the arming of the knight, the quest, and the return of the hero, are all recreated in terms that impress readers as both symbolic and realistic. Its symmetrical plot presents a series of vignettes of varied purpose but whose underlying interest is in the inner experience of life as Gawain, often seen as an everyman, lives it. Gawain's world, represented by the Yuletide feast interrupted by the Green Knight (himself a complex symbol of nature and natural processes), remains courtly and ritualistic, but Gawain's understanding of his relationship to it changes. Gawain is tested twice unexpectedly: first by the beheading game and then by the bedroom temptations, which turn out to be the test behind the beheading. In the course of the testing Gawain is made aware of his own aloneness and vulnerability; he seizes on the green girdle as protection against an afterlife that he obviously fears, but in the end he is isolated by the discovery of his sinfulness and mortality. Neither a saint nor the ladykiller of other romances (a reputation of which he is reminded at Bertilak's court), he is an original creation without precedent in Arthurian literature.

Since the late 1800s *Gawain* has been the object of studies of its language, meter, authorship, provenance, and sources and analogues in legend. Throughout the 20th century critics have recognized the poem's moral thrust, examining Gawain against the heroic, social, and religious ethos of the poem, often through the symbols of the pentangle and the green girdle. Recently critics have discussed—among other matters—the role of games in the story and the playfulness of the narration; the many dualities and appearances that, like the double identity of the Green Knight/Bertilak, produce the poem's ambiguities; the intricate networks of imagery; intertextual relations with French Arthurian romances; and even the poet's application of specialized fields of study, such as law.

Michael W. Twomey

Bibliography

PRIMARY

Anderson, J. J., ed. *Patience.* Manchester: Manchester University Press, 1969; Anderson, J. J., ed. *Cleanness.* Manchester: Manchester University Press, 1977; Andrew, Malcolm, and Ronald Waldron, eds. *The Poems of the Pearl Manuscript.* 2d ed. London: Arnold, 1982; Gordon, E. V., ed. *Pearl.* Oxford: Clarendon, 1953; Tolkien, J.R.R., and E.V. Gordon, ed. *Sir Gawain and the Green Knight.* 2d ed. Rev. Norman Davis. Oxford: Clarendon, 1967; Vantuono, William, ed. and trans. *The Pearl-Poems: An Omnibus Edition.* 2 vols. New York: Garland, 1984; Williams, Margaret, trans. *The Pearl-Poet: His Complete Works.* New York: Random House, 1967.

SECONDARY

General

New *CBEL* 1:401–06, 547–54; *Manual* 1:53–57, 238–43; 2:339–53, 503–16; Andrew, Malcolm. *The Gawain-Poet: An Annotated Bibliography 1839–1977.* New York: Garland, 1979; Blanch, Robert J., ed. *Sir Gawain and Pearl: Critical Essays.* Bloomington: Indiana University Press, 1966; Blanch, Robert J. *Sir Gawain and the Green Knight: A Reference Guide.* Troy: Whitston, 1983; Kottler, Barnet, and Alan M. Markman. *A Concordance to Five Middle English Poems: Cleanness, St. Erkenwald, Sir Gawain and the Green Knight, Patience, Pearl.* Pittsburgh: University of Pittsburgh Press, 1966; Nicholls, Jonathan. *The Matter of Courtesy: Medieval Courtesy Books and the Gawain-Poet.* Woodbridge: Brewer, 1985; Stainsby, Meg. *Sir Gawain and the Green Knight: An Annotated Bibliography 1978–1989.* New York: Garland, 1992; Wilson, Edward. *The Gawain-Poet.* Leiden: Brill, 1976.

Pearl

Bishop, Ian. *Pearl in Its Setting: A Critical Study of the Structure and Meaning of the Middle English Poem.* Oxford: Blackwell, 1968; Conley, John, ed. *The Middle English Pearl: Critical Essays.* Notre Dame: University of Notre Dame Press, 1970; Kean, P.M. *The Pearl: An Interpretation.* London: Routledge & Kegan Paul, 1967.

Cleanness

Morse, Charlotte C. *The Pattern of Judgment in the Queste and Cleanness.* Columbia: University of Missouri Press, 1978.

Sir Gawain

Benson, Larry D. *Art and Tradition in Sir Gawain and the Green Knight.* New Brunswick: Rutgers University Press, 1965; Brewer, Charlotte, ed. *Sir Gawain and the Green Knight: Sources and Analogues.* Cambridge: Brewer, 1992; Burrow, J.A. *A Reading of Sir Gawain and the Green Knight.* London: Routledge & Kegan Paul, 1965; Howard, Donald R., and Christian Zacher, eds. *Critical Studies of Sir Gawain and the Green Knight.* Notre Dame: University of Notre Dame Press, 1968; Putter, Ad. *Sir Gawain and the Green Knight and French Arthurian Romance.* Oxford: Clarendon, 1995; Twomey, Michael W. "Morgain la Fée in *Sir Gawain and the Green Knight:* From Troy to Camelot." In *Text and Intertext in Medieval Arthurian Literature: Arthurian Yearbook 5,* ed. Norris J. Lacy. New York: Garland, 1996, pp. 91–115.

See also Alliterative Revival; Bible in ME Literature; Debate Poems; Dream Vision; Law in ME Literature; Literary Influences: French, Italian; Nature in ME Literature; Religious Allegories; Romances; Sermons; Truth in ME Literature

Peasant Rebellion of 1381

The rebellion began as a reaction to the collection of the poll tax, toward the end of May 1381, mainly in Essex, Kent, and East Anglia. Its high point was reached when the rebels, under their leader, Wat Tyler, presented their program of demands to Richard II at Smithfield in London on 15 June. Tyler was killed by William Walworth, mayor of London, as he stood before the king, and his dismayed followers were dispersed. Sporadic rebellions, as far away from the original focus of the movement as Worcester and Chester, continued into July, but the crown and nobility had suppressed the main centers of rebellion by the end of June.

It was not an unpredictable outburst. It could be regarded as the culmination of a series of localized peasant rebellions going back to the late 12th century. Nor was it unexpected at the time. Fears had been expressed in parliament in 1377 of a repeat of the French Jacquerie of 1358, for the 14th century was an epoch of widespread discontent and rebellion throughout Europe of which the English land-owning ruling class could not but be aware. Many of the demands expressed in previous village protests were repeated in 1381, especially the demand for freedom for all.

The rebellion was by no means a protest of the poverty-stricken against the rich and powerful. It was more a reaction against attempts to deny social aspirations that were encouraged by the economic conditions of postplague England. The population decline resulted in a surplus of available land and a shortage of wage labor. The long-term trends were toward a fall in rents and services from tenants to landlords and a rise in daily wages. But there occurred what has been called a "feudal reaction" by the government and by the landowners, whose interests were represented by parliament—the so-called Commons as well as the Lords.

The Statute of Labourers, confirming in 1351 the Ordinance of 1349, gave justices of the peace (nominated from the nobility and gentry) power to punish anyone demanding wages above the level of 1346. This was a response to the great mobility of the work force in the period after the Black Death. Punishment was harshly and systematically imposed. At the same time landowners reacted to the shortage of tenants and the consequent fall in their rent income. In the long term they had to offer favorable terms to would-be tenants, but in the 1350s, 1360s, and 1370s they attempted to increase rents and to raise the monetary cost of such servile dues as marriage fines and death duties, as well as exacting high entry fines from tenants.

Pressures on peasants, artisans, and wage workers were exacerbated by the imposition of heavy taxation from 1371 onward, after a period of freedom from state taxation since 1358. In 1371 a new parish tax was levied that bore heavily on small parishes with many poor inhabitants, especially in the southeast. This was followed by a series of lay subsidies. These were taxes originally based on a proportion (such as a fifteenth or a tenth) of the value of the movable goods of better-off villagers. After 1334 it was levied as a lump sum, due from each village, and liable, therefore, to inequitable distribution. Six and a half of these subsidies were levied between 1373 and 1380, in addition to the poll taxes of 1377, 1379, and 1380–81. These were essentially regressive. That of 1380–81, involving a charge of one shilling a head from all persons of fifteen years and over, was particularly heavy. Advice that the rich should help the poor had little impact, especially in the heavily populated southeastern counties.

Although referred to as a peasants' rebellion, the rising of 1381 had a social composition that included village and urban artisans as well as the lesser people of London. The majority were indeed peasants, reflecting their proportion of the whole population. Many of the leaders were well-to-do peasants, often manorial officials. It was a rising of the bulk of the population, below the gentry, nobility, and wealthy church institutions.

Very interesting is the identification with the rebels of many members of the lesser clergy, of whom John Ball is the best known. This could be due in part to the sympathies of the parish clergy for the grievances of their parishioners. But we must also take into account the medieval tradition of Christian egalitarianism, often but not always associated with heretical movements. There is no indication that John Ball or the other rebel priests held heretical views, unless the old saying used by Ball in sermons ("When Adam delved and Eve span, who was then the gentleman?") can be considered heretical.

The program put forward by the rebels is deduced mainly from the reports of hostile chroniclers. Nevertheless, there is a consistency, both in the contemporary evidence and with

that of earlier movements. There was a combination of immediate and far-reaching demands, the latter suggesting the influence of Christian egalitarian ideology. Immediate demands included a proposal that wage workers be free to engage in employment on the basis of a written contract with employers; another that private fisheries and game preserves be open to all, another that land rent be reduced to 4d. per acre.

The far-reaching demands, if utopian, are interesting in that they imply a rejection of the much-preached social theory of the three orders. According to this theory those who pray, those who fight, and those who work (clergy, nobility, and peasants) should all remain in their place. The rebels proposed not only the abolition of serfdom but also the end of lordship, except for that of the king; the abolition of the church hierarchy, except for one bishop; the confiscation of church property and its redistribution among the people; a guarantee of reasonable subsistence to the parish clergy; and the abolition of monasteries, except for two houses of religion. The proposals concerning law are obscure, but it is clear that the abolition of the existing legal system and of all lawyers was proposed, to be replaced by a law enforced by the local communities (the "Law of Winchester").

The defeat of the rebels, the utopian character of their demands, and the fact that the events of 1381 hardly seemed to alter the post–Black Death trend in rents and wages have encouraged a view of the revolt as an irrelevant episode in English history. This is mistaken. Just as the "feudal reaction" was partly responsible for the rebellion, the rebellion put an end to any further "feudal reaction." Wages continued to rise. There is good explicit evidence from manorial records that lords were afraid to put up rents or demand unpopular customary services. Landlord self-assertion on these issues effectively began again only in the changed economic and social conditions of the late 15th century.

Rodney H. Hilton

Bibliography

Aston, Margaret. "Corpus Christi and Corpus Regni: Heresy and the Peasants' Rebellion." *Past and Present* 143 (May 1994): 3–47; Dobson, R. B., ed. *The Peasants' Revolt of 1381*. 2d ed. London: Macmillan, 1983 [a collection of original sources in translation]; Hilton, Rodney H. "Peasant Movements in England before 1381." *EcHR,* 2d ser. 2 (1949): 117–36. Repr. in *Essays in Economic History,* ed. E.M. Carus-Wilson. Vol. 2. London: Arnold, 1966, pp. 73–90; Hilton, Rodney H. *Bond Men Made Free: Medieval Peasant Movements and the English Rising of 1381.* London: Temple Smith, 1973 [deals with other European revolts as well as that of 1381]; Hilton, Rodney H. *The Decline of Serfdom in Medieval England.* 2d ed. London: Macmillan, 1983; Hilton, Rodney H., and Trevor Aston, eds. *The English Rising of 1381.* Cambridge: Cambridge University Press, 1984 [a collection of articles on various aspects of the rising]; Oman, Charles. *The Great Revolt of 1381.* New edition, ed. E.B. Fryde. Oxford: Clarendon, 1969 [reprint of old study, but still important for details, especially concerning taxation].

See also Black Death; Cade's Rebellion; Labor Services; Poll Tax; Serfs and Villeins; Taxes; Tenures

Pecock, Reginald (early 1390s–ca. 1460)

Theologian, religious educator, and bishop tried for and convicted of heresy. Pecock was a fellow of Oriel College, Oxford (ca. 1414–24); rector of St. Michael's, Gloucester (1424–31); rector of St. Michael Royal (also called St. Michael in Riola) and master of Whittington College (1431–44); bishop of St. Asaph (1444–50); and bishop of Chichester (1450–58). He was unusual in that he tried to bring the Lollards out of error by means of logical persuasion in vernacular treatises, especially in his *Repressor of Over Much Blaming of the Clergy.* Ironically the legal ground for his trial may have been an ecclesiastical statute originally designed to suppress Lollardy, not only because he wrote in English but also because he stressed the authority of reason, and particularly of syllogistic logic, over that of the church doctors, of the scriptures, and sometimes of the church itself.

Pecock's position on these issues was not as extreme as his accusers asserted, but enough evidence was found in his works (many of which, he pointed out, had circulated without his approval) to convict him of heresy in 1457. Upon conviction he was offered the choice of recanting or being burned at the stake. He publicly abjured and handed over fourteen of his books, which were consigned to flames. Although he was reinstated in his bishopric for one more year, his enemies were soon able to remove him from office and have him placed under restrictive house arrest at Thorney Abbey in 1459. Not long after, perhaps within a year or so, he died there.

Pecock wrote or planned to write some 30 to 50 books in Latin and English, but only a few have survived. We know of at least some of those that perished by their mention in the surviving works, which in probable chronological order are these: *The Rule of Christian Religion* (ca. 1443); *The Donet* (ca. 1443–49); *The Poor Men's Mirror* (an extract of part 1 of *The Donet*); the "Abbreviatio Reginaldi Pecok" (ca. 1447); *The Folewer to the Donet* (ca. 1453–54); *The Repressor of Over Much Blaming of the Clergy* (written ca. 1449, published ca. 1455); and *The Book of Faith* (ca. 1456).

Pecock's extant English treatises are notable for their prose style, which is strongly shaped by the attempt to render theological and philosophical concepts in a relatively nonlatinate English, leading to frequent neologisms (e.g., *un-away-fallable; folewer* for "sequel"; *eendal* and *meenal* for "pertaining to ends" and "pertaining to means"). His language is often abstract and syntactically complex, especially in his expositions of logical arguments. He thoroughly reorganized the standard religious instructional topics (vices and virtues, sacraments, articles of faith, etc.) into a nontraditional arrangement of 31 virtues. Not surprisingly, given the destruction of many of his books and the dense, complex style of those few that survived, Pecock's works had little influence on later writers. Nonetheless, they remain worthy of study for what they reveal about the capacities of late ME prose as a medium for philosophical discourse and the degree to which 15th-century English religious instruction could—

and could not—diverge from institutionally approved form and content.

Lara Ruffolo

Bibliography

PRIMARY

Babington, Churchill, ed. *The Repressor of Over Much Blaming of the Clergy.* 2 vols. Rolls Series. London: Longman, Green, Longman, & Roberts, 1860; Greet, William Cabell, ed. *The Reule of Crysten Religioun.* EETS o.s. 171. London: Humphrey Milford, 1927; Hitchcock, Elsie Vaughan, ed. *The Donet* and *The Folewer to the Donet.* EETS o.s. 156, 164. London: Humphrey Milford, 1921–24; Morison, John L., ed. *The Book of Faith.* Glasgow: Maclehose, 1909.

SECONDARY

New *CBEL* 1:665–66, 805; Brockwell, Charles W., Jr. "Answering the 'Known Men': Bishop Reginald Pecock and Mr. Richard Hooker." *Church History* 49 (1980): 133–46; Patrouch, Joseph F., Jr. *Reginald Pecock.* New York: Twayne, 1970.

See also Bishops; Lollards; Moral and Religious Instruction; Prose, ME; Translation; Virtues and Vices, Books of; Wyclif; Wycliffite Texts

Peerage

A common description of the native aristocracy, a social group that went through a profound period of evolution and redefinition in the later Middle Ages. Whereas in 1300 only earls were separated from the rest of the nobility, by the end of the 15th century the peerage consisted of a hierarchy of five ranks: in descending order, dukes, marquesses, earls, viscounts, and barons. Within each rank was an order of precedence, claimed and quarreled over.

In part this trend represented an enlargement of royal patronage; the crown rewarded service by promotion within the peerage. But in a broader sense it reflected a growth in ideas of social standing and awareness. Such a sense of definition was revealed by a 14th-century statute decreeing that only temporal lords—in contrast to mere knights—could give livery (badges and uniforms) to their servants. The technical distinction between the ranks of the peerage and the gentry was a personal summons to parliament or royal patent of creation. A broader popular recognition of this division can be found in a letter of the 1450s from Thomas, Lord Scales, distinguishing between the "good lordship" (i.e., patronage from a lord) of one such as himself and the "good mastership" of his correspondent, Sir John Fastolf, rich and influential though Fastolf was.

The preeminence of the aristocracy rested first and foremost on landed wealth. Within the peerage incomes were delineated as appropriate for certain ranks: 2,000 marks a year for a duke, 1,000 marks for an earl. A peer whose estates were deemed insufficient could be demoted from his rank (as happened to George duke of Bedford in 1478). Noblemen regarded their inheritance as a sacred trust. William, Lord Berkeley, fell under the opprobrium of future generations of his family for willfully surrendering his estates at the end of the 15th century.

Interference by the crown with the laws of inheritance (as happened in 1397–99) almost guaranteed a political crisis. Noble rebels frequently sought the sympathy of the broader community by claiming they had been wrongfully deprived of their inheritance. The search to protect the integrity of estates encompassed such legal devices as entails (arrangements that limited the course of inheritance) and enfeoffments to use (enfeoffments to one person for the benefit and "use" of another) in reaction to the threat of extinction in the male line or the problem of dowagers.

Yet, by the late Middle Ages, the position of the peerage rested on a combination of wealth and political service. Income alone did not confirm social status. In the 14th and 15th centuries rich and influential knights, such as Sir Robert Knollys and Sir John Fastolf, were better off than many of the poorer barons. Title was seen as commensurate with leadership, as John Russell, bishop of Lincoln, commented in 1483: "The politic rule of every region well ordained standeth in the nobles." Henry VI wrote Lord Egremont in 1453, reminding him that he had been promoted "to the worship and estate of a baron" for the "keeping of the rest and peace of our land." Similar responsibility was expected in times of war. Outstanding military service in Wales, Scotland, and France earned the Montagues their promotion to the earldom of Salisbury in the 14th century. In the reign of Henry V William Montague was the outstanding English war captain.

The development of the concept of the peerage as natural leaders of society found concrete expression in the evolution of the House of Lords. Since the frequent parliaments of the 1320s and 1330s the right of summons included bishops, abbots, and secular lords; a corporate identity as the high court of parliament quickly developed. The result was a forum for regular involvement in the everyday business of government. A journal of the House of Lords in 1461 shows peers listening to the reading of bills, referring to committees, and consulting with king and Commons. The rate of attendance varied; in the 15th century some two-thirds of the secular lords might participate. The enhanced prestige of the body can be seen in precedence disputes over seating and the pride with which a peer like John, Lord Scrope, left his parliament robe to his son in 1451.

Through the late-medieval period the peerage had become a broader and more defined group. Creation of peers by royal patent and charter and promotions within the peerage became deliberate aspects of crown policy. Sometimes these were controversial, as with Richard II's notorious "duketti" ("little dukes," in derision) in 1397. More often they reflected the demands of an increasingly aware and socially hierarchical society.

Michael Jones

Bibliography

Given-Wilson, Chris. *The English Nobility in the Late Middle Ages: The Fourteenth-Century Political Community.* London: Routledge & Kegan Paul, 1987 [general treatment, mostly drawing on 14th-century examples]; McFarlane, K.B. *The Nobility of Later Medieval England.* Oxford: Clarendon, 1973 [classic introduction]; Powell, J. Enoch, and Keith Wallis. *The House of Lords in the Middle Ages: A History of the English House of Lords to 1540.* London: Weidenfeld & Nicolson, 1968 [information on individuals summoned and precedence]; Rosenthal, Joel T. *Nobles and the Noble Life.* London: Allen & Unwin, 1976 [includes a variety of pertinent documents in translation].

See also Dukes; Earls; Parliament

Penda of Mercia (r. 633–55)

Penda first appears in the Anglo-Saxon Chronicle for the entry of 628, when he came to terms with the West Saxons at Cirencester after battle. The agreement doubtless involved Mercian annexation of land along the lower Severn that later became the subkingdom of the Hwicce. At this stage Penda's exact status is unclear, but he was certainly king of Mercia by 633, when, in alliance with the Christian Cadwallon of Gwynedd, he ravaged Deira and slew Edwin, king of Northumbria, at Hatfield Chase.

In 642 Penda killed Oswald of Bernicia at Maserfeld (identified with Oswestry). In 645 he drove the West Saxon king Cenwealh into exile following the latter's repudiation of Penda's sister. Penda was killed by Oswiu of Northumbria near Leeds, 15 November 655. Although sources recounting the episode differ significantly, it seems that Oswiu had earlier been forced to offer Penda treasure for peace following his invasion of Bernicia.

Although pagan, Penda permitted his son Paeda to introduce Christianity into the subkingdom of the Middle Angles (653). Penda greatly extended Mercian power, establishing a series of principalities across the Midlands. After his death Mercia became Christian, and Oswiu was overlord of Mercia for three years until Penda's son Wulfhere reestablished control in southern England.

Kathryn Lowe

Bibliography

Davies, Wendy. "Annals and the Origin of Mercia." In *Mercian Studies,* ed. Ann Dornier. Leicester: Leicester University Press, 1977, pp. 17–29; Prestwich, John O. "King Æthelhere and the Battle of Winwaed." *EHR* 83 (1968): 89–95.

See also Bretwald; Heptarchy; Offa

Penitentials

Catalogues listing sins and the penances assigned to them by the priest in confession. Penitentials are often called "handbooks of penance," but most penitentials survive in manuscript form as parts of larger codices rather than as small, self-contained booklets. A few handbook-sized manuscripts do, however, exist, and presumably they were common in the Middle Ages. Penitentials always include lists of sins and penances (these lists are sometimes called "tariffs") and often contain prefatory material telling the priest how to interrogate penitents, determine their spiritual disposition and sincerity in repenting, and weigh the seriousness of their sins. In the later Middle Ages penance required only confession, with its attendant embarrassment, and prayer; during the Anglo-Saxon period private confession was followed by the performance of various penitential acts assigned by the priest according to the catalogue of penances in the penitential.

Penitentials appear to have originated in Ireland, where they were written in both Latin and Old Irish, and to have reached England through the work of Irish missionaries. By the late 7th century the handbook had become an important pastoral text in England. Theodore of Canterbury was the first non-Irish authority to issue a penitential (ca. 690); early handbooks attributed to 8th-century English ecclesiastics (including Egbert of York and the Venerable Bede) show that the form was quickly assimilated into the disciplinary literature of the English church. During the 9th century penitentials of Irish origin were the subject of prolonged controversy on the Continent, but disputes about the orthodoxy of private penance and the literature that regulated it do not appear in English records.

Anglo-Saxon Period

England was second only to Ireland in developing a vernacular literature of penance built around the private penitential system. This literature included—in addition to the penitentials—confessional prayers, liturgies, and other forms, such as homilies, laws, and clerical letters, that quote the penitentials or share textual sources with them. The Anglo-Saxons organized comprehensive collections that included penitentials, ceremonies for public penance, and confessional prayers, and they made excerpts from these sources for devotional reading and instruction (e.g., Ælfric's collections at the end of CUL Gg.3.28).

Penitentials in Anglo-Saxon England were written in both Latin and the vernacular (the Latin texts being more numerous) and took various forms; those with elaborate prefatory apparatus circulated alongside those that merely listed tariffs for sins. Only three vernacular texts, all anonymous but closely related to older Latin handbooks, are known (see editions by Fowler, Frantzen, Raith, and Spindler below), and they are confined to a small number of important 11th-century manuscripts. The vernacular penitentials list penances identical to those found in 8th-century texts, a fact that cannot be overlooked when the social significance of these texts is discussed. It is expected that penitential tariffs would have been revised as the handbooks passed from region to region and century to century. But the tariffs found in the surviving documents show little change, thus complicating assumptions about how closely penitential practice reflects local customs and daily life in the Middle Ages.

The major holy seasons of the church year—Advent, Lent, and Pentecost—were those in which penance was performed. Three forms were practiced: private penance, public penance, and voluntary acts of pious devotion. Public penance, which in the early church could be undertaken only once, was required for the gravest sins; for example, fratricide or the murder of a cleric carried the penance of exile. Private penance, which could be repeated, entailed a wide range of penances. The most frequent was fasting, for periods ranging from a few days to several years. For theft and crimes involving personal injury restitution was necessary before absolution could be given, a requirement that suggests the importance of ecclesiastical penance in maintaining social order. The interaction of penance and secular law is apparent as early as the laws of King Alfred (d. 899) and continues in the laws Archbishop Wulfstan (d. 1023) wrote for King Cnut (d. 1035).

Penitentials should be studied in the context of both devotional and disciplinary traditions, for the practice of penance regulated by the penitentials was only part of the large place of confession in medieval spiritual life. In Anglo-Saxon England confession was made in three ways: private acknowledgment of sins to the priest; public acknowledgment of sins before the bishop; and devotional exercise in which the sinner confessed in prayer to a ritualized list of sins that probably had little correspondence to his or her spiritual conduct. Of these three forms private confession to the priest eventually became the norm, but the body of evidence attesting to the tradition is too vague and incomplete to permit our characterizing any one of these modes as dominant in Anglo-Saxon confessional practice. The traditional 19th-century model of regular confession to the priest cannot be traced to the Anglo-Saxon period; nor can a postmedieval stereotype of penance as a form of social control be automatically applied to Anglo-Saxon sources. The educational function of confession and penance is rarely recognized, and the relationship of these practices to historical problems of literacy—the use of written texts in a society whose literature and legal system were primarily oral—remains unexplored.

Post-Conquest Period

Penitentials after the Conquest form an amorphous lot, varying in audience, language, and structure. They are often found nestled among the folios of larger compendia of religious instruction. Some include long sections concerning excommunication, canon law, or marriage; others deal with the Creed, the Lord's Prayer, the articles of faith, methods of celebrating mass, or contrition. All contain material on the seven deadly sins and their branches, and they often alert confessors as to the specific responses they might hear from sinners and the penances they are to assign. Priests were expected to use this information to guide their penitents and to coax the more recalcitrant ones into responding in more detail. Although most penitential manuals were written in Latin for priests, they also gave rise to vernacular writings aimed at less-educated audiences, including some clergy, but mainly the laity and nuns.

Relatively few penitential handbooks, Latin or vernacular, have been edited. For the ME period these include the

Liber poenitentialis of Bartholomew, bishop of Exeter (ca. 1150–70); the *Liber poenitentialis* of Robert of Flamborough (ca. 1208–15); and the *Summa confessorum* of Thomas of Chobham (completed by ca. 1216). Stimulated by the reforms of the Fourth Lateran Council (1215), which mandated annual confession to one's parish priest for all Christians, many 13th-century English bishops included instructions for hearing confessions in diocesan statutes, along with other spiritual information to be imparted to the laity in their own language (English or French). This educational program led to vernacular works like the *Manuel des péchés* (ca. 1250–75), translated into ME by Robert Manning as *Handlyng Synne* (1303–17); the anonymous *Cleansing of Man's Soul* (late 14th century), addressed to nuns and lay readers; Chaucer's *Parson's Tale*; and John Mirk's *Instructions for Parish Priests* and the anonymous *Speculum Christiani,* pastoral manuals addressed to priests (late 14th to early 15th century).

Because laity as well as clergy were required to confess, everyone could be expected to know the general content and structure of penitential manuals. It is not surprising, therefore, that authors like Langland, the *Pearl*-poet, Gower, and Chaucer employed penitential motifs in their works, clearly anticipating audiences capable of discerning them. Thanks to the Fourth Lateran Council, the sinner had come to be a common literary figure, knowledgeable about his or her actions, motives, and degree of guilt. Common, too, in later medieval literature is the use of a questioning lay figure functioning as priest; of contrition, confession, and satisfaction in building storylines; and of "confessional words"—*absolve, confess, grope* ("to examine someone's conscience"), *guilt, intent, repent, shame*—in secular contexts, forcing the reader to recall the psychological and spiritual experience of penance. The influence of penitential manuals can be seen in genres as diverse as devotional treatises and the literature of courtly love where one lover laments his or her transgressions against the other.

Allen J. Frantzen
Mary Flowers Braswell

Bibliography

PRIMARY
Old English
Fowler, Roger. "A Late OE Handbook for the Use of a Confessor." *Anglia* 83 (1965): 1–34; Frantzen, Allen J., ed. *An Electronic Edition of the Corpus of Anglo-Saxon Penitentials,* forthcoming; McNeill, John T., and Helena M. Gamer, trans. *Medieval Handbooks of Penance.* New York: Columbia University Press, 1938. Repr. New York: Columbia University Press, 1990; Raith, J. *Die altenglische Version des Halitgar'schen Bussbuches (sog. Pönitentiale Pseudo-Ecgberti).* Bibliothek der angelsächsischen Prosa 13. Hamburg: Grand, 1933. Repr. with new introduction. Darmstadt: Wissenschaftliche Buchgesellschaft, 1964; Spindler, R., ed. *Das altenglische Bussbuch (sog. Confessionale Pseudo-Egberti).* Leipzig: Tauchnitz, 1934.

Middle English
Robert of Flamborough. *Liber poenitentialis.* Ed. J.J. Francis Firth. Toronto: Pontifical Institute, 1971; Thomas de Chobham. *Summa confessorum.* Ed. F. Broomfield. Louvain: Nauwelaerts, 1968.

SECONDARY
Old English
Frantzen, Allen J. *The Literature of Penance in Anglo-Saxon England.* New Brunswick: Rutgers University Press, 1983; Frantzen, Allen J. "The Tradition of Penitentials in Anglo-Saxon England." *ASE* 11 (1983): 23–56; Oakley, Thomas P. *English Penitential Discipline and Anglo-Saxon Law in Their Joint Influence.* New York: Columbia University Press, 1923; Oakley, Thomas P. "The Cooperation of Medieval Penance and Secular Law." *Speculum* 7 (1932): 515–24; Payer, Pierre J. *Sex and the Penitentials: The Development of a Sexual Code 550–1150.* Toronto: University of Toronto Press, 1984; Vogel, Cyrille. *Les "Libri Paenitentiales."* Typologie des Sources du Moyen Age Occidental 27. Turnhout: Brepols, 1978. Corr. and rev. Allen J. Frantzen. Turnhout: Brepols, 1985.

Middle English
Manual 7:2255–2372, 2467–2577; Braswell, Mary Flowers. *The Medieval Sinner: Characterization and Confession in the Literature of the English Middle Ages.* London: Associated University Presses, 1983; Jolliffe, Peter S. *A Check-List of Middle English Prose Writings of Spiritual Guidance.* Toronto: Pontifical Institute, 1974; McNally, John J. "The Penitential and Courtly Traditions in Gower's *Confessio Amantis.*" *Studies in Medieval Culture* 1 (1964): 74–94; Patterson, Lee W. "The 'Parson's Tale' and the Quitting of the *Canterbury Tales.*" *Traditio* 34 (1978): 331–80; Pfander, Homer G. "Some Medieval Manuals of Religious Instruction in England and Observations on Chaucer's *Parson's Tale.*" *JEGP* 35 (1936): 243–58.

See also Ars moriendi; Bishops; Edmund of Abingdon; Grosseteste; Manning; Mirk; Moral and Religious Instruction; Popular Religion; Theodore of Tarsus; Virtues and Vices, Books of; Wulfstan

Percy Family

The Percys were originally a Yorkshire baronial family. Their position was transformed in the 14th century when they became a major aristocratic house, dominating the north. While remaining a force in the later medieval period, their power underwent a decline in the 15th century and their broader political influence was sporadic.

The Percys' rise began in the reign of Edward I, when service on the great expedition of 1296 was rewarded with grants of confiscated Scottish estates. In 1310 they purchased Alnwick in Northumberland. Deliberately establishing a role in border politics, they acquired another residence at Warkworth in the 1330s. But a more dramatic territorial expansion occurred in the last 30 years of the 14th century. Purchase of the marriage of the Strathbogie heiresses brought in the baronies of Mitford and Tynedale. In 1376 Gilbert Umfraville was persuaded to make over half his inheritance (including the barony of Prudhoe on the Tyne). On his death in 1382 Henry Percy married Gilbert's widow, Maud, heiress to the barony of Cockermouth in Cumberland.

Percy, elevated to earl of Northumberland in 1377, now had a superb power base in the north; in Northumberland itself his family owned no less than four castles, five baronies, and 70 manors. Growth in territorial power coincided with an increasing involvement in the defense of the border; by the 1390s the office of warden of the march toward Scotland was monopolized by the Percys.

The rewards for the help given to Henry IV in 1399 marked the zenith of the family's importance. But inevitably neither the family's subsequent influence on the new king nor their tangible rewards came up to their expectations, and a rift soon developed between the Percys and the king. Their unsuccessful revolts of 1403 and 1406 led to attainder and forfeiture. The crown increasingly lent its support to the rising Neville family of Raby. By the 1440s the income of the Nevilles' northern lands outstripped that of the Percys. A violent rivalry between the two families led to an armed clash at Stamford (1454) and caused the Percys to enter the Wars of the Roses on the Lancastrian side. Military defeat further curtailed their role. Although the Percy heir was restored as earl in 1469 and managed to retain some influence in Northumberland, the mantle of leadership of northern society passed first to Richard Neville, earl of Warwick, and then to Richard duke of Gloucester.

In the Tudor period ballads romanticized a Percy hegemony in the late Middle Ages. Northern society was clannish by nature, and such families as the Yorkshire Plumptons had a record of service to the Percys over four generations. The restoration of Henry Percy in 1469 was certainly a popular measure. Yet the much-quoted adage, "The north knoweth no Prince but a Percy," disguises the waning influence of the family in the 15th century.

Michael Jones

Bibliography

Bean, J.M.W. *The Estates of the Percy Family, 1416–1537.* London: Oxford University Press, 1958 [surveys lands and revenues, telling of the long decline]; Hicks, M.A. "Dynastic Change and Northern Society: The Career of the Fourth Earl of Northumberland, 1470–89." *Northern History* 14 (1978): 78–107; Tuck, Anthony. "The Emergence of a Northern Nobility, 1250–1400." *Northern History* 22 (1986): 1–17; Weiss, Michael. "A Power in the North? The Percies in the Fifteenth Century." *Historical Journal* 19 (1976): 501–09 [questions the idea of their "vice-regal" power].

See also Marches; Neville Family; Wars of the Roses

Peter of Langtoft, or Pierre de Langtoft (fl. 1271–1307)

Augustinian canon of Bridlington, Yorkshire, and author of a lengthy Anglo-Norman verse chronicle of England, completed in the early 14th century. The fullest manuscripts of his *Chronicle* extend from Brutus, the legendary founder of Britain, to the death of Edward I in 1307. One manuscript states that the work was written at the request of a certain "Scaffeld," perhaps John of Sheffield, sheriff of Northumberland and a partisan of Anthony Bek, bishop of Durham (1283–1311).

The first section, from Brutus to Cadwalader, paraphrases Geoffrey of Monmouth; thereafter Langtoft draws on well-known Latin prose chronicles, romances, saints' lives, official documents, and personal knowledge for his material. The narrative of Edward I's reign is valuable for its account of Anglo-Scottish relations, though it is virulently anti-Scottish. Langtoft's *Chronicle* was a major source for the second part of Robert Manning's English *Chronicle*.

Lister M. Matheson

Bibliography

PRIMARY

Wright, Thomas, ed. *The Chronicle of Pierre de Langtoft.* 2 vols. Rolls Series 47. London: Longmans, Green, Reader, & Dyer, 1866–68.

SECONDARY

Manual 5:1400–03, 1648–49 [on ME political songs incorporated by Langtoft]; Gransden, Antonia. *Historical Writing in England.* Vol. 1: *c. 550 to c. 1307.* London: Routledge & Kegan Paul, 1974, pp. 476–86; Summerfield, Thea. *The Matter of Kings' Lives: The Design of Past and Present in the Early Fourteenth-Century Verse Chronicles by Pierre de Langtoft and Robert Mannyng.* Amsterdam: Rodopi, forthcoming.

See also Anglo-Norman Literature; Chronicles; Geoffrey of Monmouth; Manning

Phoenix, The

The OE *Phoenix* survives in the Exeter Book miscellany of Anglo-Saxon poetry. Like many OE Christian poems it was once attributed to Cynewulf, but since it lacks a runic signature this idea is now generally discounted, although the possibility of influence is accepted. The text appears to be complete and has been edited and translated often. A shorter version of the phoenix myth survives in two OE homilies.

The first 380 lines of *The Phoenix* are a paraphrase of the Latin *De ave phoenice* of Lactantius, from which the pagan elements have been removed. The remainder is a homiletic elaboration of the myth based partly on Ambrose's *Hexaemeron* 5.79–82 and partly on Job 29:18, perhaps following the explication of this passage in a commentary attributed to Philip the Presbyter. The poem concludes with eleven macaronic lines combining OE and Latin.

Though some critics prefer a less rigid reading, most criticism of the poem has centered on its allegorical dimension, with Cross finding a complete allegory on four levels: in addition to the literal narrative of the marvelous bird, allegorically the phoenix is a type of Christ; morally it represents the good Christian, especially the soldier of God; and anagogically it prefigures the soul in heaven. Bugge notes a monastic sentiment in the emphasis on the bird's virginity and ascetic life. In contrast to the christological reading Heffernan's anthropological approach to the phoenix myth finds feminine and specifically Marian imagery at work as well.

Timothy Jones

Bibliography

PRIMARY

ASPR 3:94–113; Blake, Norman F., ed. *The Phoenix.* Rev. ed. Exeter: Exeter University Press, 1990; Gordon, R.K., trans. *Anglo-Saxon Poetry.* Rev. ed. London: Dent, 1954, pp. 239–51 [prose]; Kennedy, Charles W., trans. *Early English Christian Poetry.* New York: Oxford University Press, 1952, pp. 231–48 [verse].

SECONDARY

Broek, R. van den. *The Myth of the Phoenix.* Trans. I. Seeger. Leiden: Brill, 1972 [on European traditions of the phoenix myth]; Bugge, John. "The Virgin Phoenix." *MS* 38 (1976): 332–50; Cross, James E. "The Conception of the Old English *Phoenix.*" In *Old English Poetry,* ed. Robert Creed. Providence: Brown University Press, 1967; Heffernan, Carol Falvo. *The Phoenix at the Fountain: Images of Women and Eternity in Lactantius's "Carmen de Ave Phoenice" and the Old English "Phoenix."* Newark: University of Delaware Press, 1988.

See also Allegory; Beast Epic and Fable; Bestiaries; Fathers of the Church (Ambrose); Literary Influences: Medieval Latin; *Physiologus;* Translation

Physiologus

The *Physiologus,* or bestiary, genre can be traced back to classical times, but as transmitted to the Middle Ages the collection came to be associated more with Christian allegory than with scientific natural history. All or part of the Latin *Physiologus* was translated into numerous vernaculars; the OE verse rendering, found in the Exeter Book, describes three creatures usually identified as Panther, Whale, and Partridge. The identity of the third creature is particularly uncertain, since the poem breaks off after a single line describing the bird, resuming after the presumed loss of a single leaf to conclude with fifteen lines of allegorical interpretation. The word *Finit* at the end of "The Partridge" signals the close of a descriptive and allegorical cycle that has considered creatures of earth, sea, and sky (representing earth, hell, and heaven).

The Panther (or perhaps Leopard) is described as a gentle beast of many colors, who arises from a three-day sleep with such fragrant breath that all are drawn to him and who is hostile to none except the dragon; a lengthy allegorical interpretation identifies the Panther with Christ. By contrast the Whale (originally a turtle in the Latin tradition), interpreted as Satan, draws little fish to their death by his sweet breath and deceives weary sailors, who mistake his body for an island and are drowned.

The OE *Physiologus* continues an allegorical tradition in Anglo-Saxon poetry that goes back to Aldhelm's Latin *Aenigmata* and finds its finest and most complex expression in the OE *Phoenix,* also contained in the Exeter Book. The *Phoenix,* though immediately drawn from a Latin poem by Lactantius, itself ultimately derives from the same *Physiologus* tradition. The OE *Physiologus,* moreover, was but the first of a long series of translations of the work, which proved of enduring importance and influence throughout the medieval period.

A.P.M. Orchard

Bibliography

PRIMARY

ASPR 3:169–74; Curley, Michael J., ed. and trans. *Physiologus.* Austin: University of Texas Press, 1979; Squires, Ann. *The Old English Physiologus.* Durham: Durham Medieval Texts, 1988.

SECONDARY

Campbell, Thomas P. "Thematic Unity in the Old English *Physiologus.*" *Archiv* 215 (1978): 73–79; Diekstra, F.N.M. "The *Physiologus,* the Bestiaries and Medieval Animal Lore." *Neophilologus* 69 (1985): 142–55; Marchand, James W. "The *Partridge?* An Old English Multiquote." *Neophilologus* 75 (1991): 603–11.

See also Aldhelm; Allegory; Bestiaries; Exeter Book; *Phoenix;* Riddles; Scientific and Medical Writings; Scientific Manuscripts, Early

Pierce the Plowman's Creed

An important work in the English vernacular tradition of antimendicant satire, surviving in three manuscripts and two early printed editions. Written ca. 1394 in the southwest Midlands dialect by an anonymous author, this poem is the first and some would say the best imitation of William Langland's *Piers Plowman.* Indeed, from the time of its composition until well into the 16th century, *Pierce the Plowman's Creed* and many other imitations of *Piers* were popular, particularly as documents of discontent with and attack upon the clergy and church authority.

Pierce the Plowman's Creed consists of 855 alliterative long lines and contains savage antimendicant satire and biting social and political commentary. The poem begins with the narrator's statement that he knows his Our Father and Hail Mary but is ignorant of the Creed. In a scene echoing Will's encounter with the Minorite (Franciscan) friars before the third Dream in *Piers Plowman* the narrator sets out in search of the person who will best be able to teach him his creed. He meets in turn a Franciscan, a Dominican, an Augustinian, and a Carmelite friar, each of whom discourses at length upon the degenerate practices of one of the other orders. About half-way through the poem the narrator encounters the suffering family of a poor plowman, Pierce, who sharply criticizes the worldliness of all friars and teaches the narrator his creed. Much of the poem's effectiveness and artistic merit springs from its richly detailed descriptions of buildings, people, activities, and emotions.

   Kathleen M. Hewett-Smith

Bibliography

PRIMARY

Barr, Helen, ed. *The Piers Plowman Tradition.* London: Dent, 1993 [edition of *Pierce the Plowman's Creed* and related works]; Skeat, Walter W., ed. *Pierce the Ploughman's Crede.* EETS o.s. 30. London: Trübner, 1867.

SECONDARY

New *CBEL* 1:544–45; *Manual* 5:1447, 1676–77; Lampe, David. "The Satiric Strategy of *Peres the Ploughman's Crede.*" In *The Alliterative Tradition in the Fourteenth Century,* ed. Bernard S. Levy and Paul E. Szarmach. Kent: Kent State University Press, 1981, pp. 69–80; von Nolcken, Christina. "*Piers Plowman,* the Wycliffites, and *Pierce the Plowman's Creed.*" YLS 2 (1988): 71–102.

See also Alliterative Revival; Alms; Friars; *Jack Upland;* Lollards; *Piers Plowman;* Popular Religion; Satire

Piers Plowman

An allegorical dream vision (ca. 1368–85) in alliterative verse, concerned with contemporary social and religious problems. The content of *Piers Plowman* is best summarized as a dilation on the proverb quoted near the beginning, "When all treasures are tried, truth is the best." In a series of dreams Will the narrator describes society's pilgrimage to Truth, and then his own personal quest (through the stages of Do-well, Do-better, and Do-best). Of the many 14th-century poems on the same or similar subjects *Piers Plowman* is the longest and most complex. Since the late 19th century scholars have recognized three distinct versions: the A text, consisting of a prologue and twelve sections called passus (about 2,560 lines); the B text, a revision and continuation consisting of a prologue and twenty passus (about 7,300 lines); and the C text, a further and apparently unfinished revision consisting of a prologue and 22 passus (about 7,340 lines). The name of the author is uncertain. It is conventional to call him William Langland, on the basis of a note in an early manuscript of the C text, but other external evidence is lacking. Internal support includes a possible anagram in B.15.152, where the dreamer says, "I haue lyued in londe . . . my name is longe wille."

Textual Tradition

There are 52 manuscripts, a black-letter edition of 1550 (by Robert Crowley) that represents a 53rd, and three fragments of other manuscripts. Since no two are alike, the original number of manuscripts must have been considerably higher. From internal evidence the A text has been dated 1368–74, the B text 1377–81, and the C text 1381–85. Recently A.G. Rigg and Charlotte Brewer proposed that MS Bodley 851 represents a fourth version, which they call the Z text, earlier than any of the other three; opinion on the matter remains divided.

   The complexity of the manuscript tradition and particularly the existence of three distinct versions led early-20th-century critics to propose multiple authorship. J.M. Manly argued for as many as five authors in a reference work that ensured wide circulation of his theory, the *Cambridge History of English Literature* (1908). Most critics now assume single authorship. The controversy is examined in George Kane's *Piers Plowman: The Evidence for Authorship* (1965).

   Skeat's editions of the three versions, standard for a century, have been superseded by the Athlone editions under the general editorship of George Kane. Skeat's method was to present the best manuscript of each version with a minimum of editorial intervention; Kane's procedure was to identify obvious errors, based on the knowledge of "scribal tendencies," and then to emend accordingly. Not all scholars have accepted the Athlone editions as definitive; as Kane himself concedes in his introduction to the A version, "The authority of a text of this kind must vary from line to line" (165). Nevertheless, the Athlone editions are generally regarded as the standard tools of *Piers* scholarship, not because their readings are infallible but because their full display of variant readings allows other scholars to weigh the manuscript evidence for themselves. The classroom editions by Schmidt and Pearsall also deserve mention, especially for their helpful notes. There is a good verse translation of the B text by E. Talbot Donaldson.

Language and Versification

Although the surviving manuscripts were produced in many different parts of the country, certain dialectal features common to them all suggest that the author's holographs were written in the dialect of southwest Worcestershire. This conclusion agrees with the narrator's statement that he had his visions "on maluerne hilles" (A.Prol.5). The poem also contains a fair number of recent French loanwords (a higher proportion, in fact, than Chaucer's works), as well as several hundred Latin quotations, many of which are joined macaronically with the English (e.g., "*Qui loquitur turpiloquium* is luciferes hyne"—"He who speaks filth is Lucifer's servant").

   The poem is in alliterative verse. The basic pattern is aa/ax. That is, there are four stressed syllables per line; and the alliteration of both stresses in the a-verse is picked up in the first stress of the b-verse (e.g., "I seiʒ a tóur on a tóft / tríeliche ymáked"). Lines with fewer than three alliterating syllables (ax/ax, aa/xx, etc.) are not uncommon but may be defective; lines with more than three sometimes occur in moments of importance or high formality, as in the opening line, "In a sómer séson whan sófte was þe sónne." Like many other alliterative poems *Piers* is full of formulaic half-lines, for example, "so me god helpe"; these appear almost always as b-verses.

Summary

The following summary is based on the B version, the one most often studied and quoted. The poem begins like many other dream visions of the period. The narrator relates that on a May morning, as he lay by a stream on the Malvern Hills, he fell asleep and had a "merueillous" dream (actually the first of eight dreams). In it he sees "a fair feeld ful of folk" between two castles, a "tour," or keep, on a hill and a "dongeon," or donjon, in the valley below. Many of the folk are conscientiously going about their work; others are idle or seeking an easy way to get ahead.

What does the scene mean? A lady clothed in linen (a conventional guide figure, later identified as Holy Church) descends from the hill castle and explains it all to the dreamer. The "tour on þe toft," she says, is the home of Truth, the father of faith and loyalty (God); the "dongeon in þe dale" is the home of Wrong, the father of falsehood and treachery (the Devil); the folk on the field are divided into those who serve Truth and those who serve Wrong. Holy Church explains that "truth is the best," for it is the way to salvation itself. Those who "werche wel . . . shal wende to heuene," but those who "werchen with wrong" shall follow him to hell.

This opposition provides the basic framework of the poem in all three versions. The scheme is starkly simple. The poet adds complexity, however, by showing in one episode after another that the will is not always inclined to follow truth and, even when it is, that the intellect is not always able to show the way.

In the first episode the opposition of truth and wrong is restated and dramatized in terms of a rivalry between Lady Holy Church and Lady Meed. Holy Church complains that Meed (wealth, reward) undermines loyalty *(leaute)* and the rule of law. Looking to his left, the dreamer sees a richly arrayed woman, surrounded by a crowd of greedy sycophants, about to be married to False. Theology is alarmed by the prospect of such a match: "God graunted to gyue Mede to truþe" (2.120). The case is brought before the king. The trial that follows is an exercise in the casuistry of conscience. Meed's defense rests on a recital of her positive actions—the giving of wages, gifts, alms, benefices, and so forth. Conscience, backed up by Reason, counters that there are two kinds of meed, one "measureless" (bribery, usury, excessive fees) and the other "measurable" (honest wages, payment for merchandise). Lady Meed represents the former. The king, convinced that Meed "muche truþe letteþ [hinders]," rules against her and invites Reason and Conscience to continue as his counselors. Here the first vision ends.

In the next vision, stirred by Reason's sermon to seek "Seynt Truþe," the folk confess their sins and set out on a pilgrimage to the shrine of Truth. Their guide is Piers the Plowman. He is the very incarnation of the virtue they seek. "I do," he says, "what truþe hoteþ [commands]." He promises to lead them to truth if they will help him plow his half-acre. However, it gradually becomes apparent that in "working well" under the direction of Piers, the folk are in fact already on their way to truth. For truth is not a geographical destination but a form of conduct. Truth himself acknowl-

edges as much by sending to Piers's helpers a pardon. It reads, "Et qui bona egerunt ibunt in vitam eternam; Qui vero mala in ignem eternum"—"And those who do well will go into eternal life; those who do evil, into eternal fire." This, of course, is precisely what Holy Church said earlier; and yet one of her own priests, having offered to construe the Latin, is unable to understand it as a pardon. His ignorance or blindness is another measure of how far the church has departed from its ideals. In righteous anger Piers tears the document in half and vows to be less solicitous about material things and more given to a life of prayers and penitence.

Piers's resolve marks an important shift in the poem's argument. From the emphasis on truth in the first two visions as a social obligation, manifested primarily in obedience and good works, Langland descends in the third to an examination of its source in the heart. No longer is the dreamer a spectator only; "Will" is now the center of the action. Concerned about his own salvation, he begins his personal quest for truth. What does it mean to "do well"? He consults Thought, who, true to his own analytical nature, divides the concept into three parts: Do-well, Do-better, and Do-best. Will's desire to know more about these takes him from Thought to other personifications of the intellectual life: Wit (native intelligence), Study (application), Clergy (learning), Scripture (books), Imaginatif (prudential judgment). The further Will proceeds, however, the more confused he becomes. The promise of *qui bona egerunt*, "do well and be saved," is not so simple as it looked at first. Frustrated, Will becomes increasingly impatient with his teachers, until, in a dream within the dream (11.5–406), he rebukes Reason itself. This absurdity shames him into the realization that his own disposition is the main problem. The fault lies not with Reason but with Will. He has been committed to the search intellectually but not affectively. He has looked everywhere except the one place where Piers Plowman directed the pilgrims to look—"in þyn herte" (5.606).

To express the unity of Do-well, Do-better, and Do-best—and its basis in the will—Langland often has recourse to the corresponding triad of "words, works, and will" and, more profoundly, to the Trinity itself. Like the three persons of the Trinity the three stages of truth are distinct but inseparable. Each component contains something of the others. Apart from Do-best it is impossible truly to Do-well or Do-better.

This insight is dramatized in the fourth vision (passus 13–14) by two of the poet's most memorable creations. First the dreamer encounters a gluttonous friar, who is full of words about "do well" but has no works to match them. Then he meets Haukyn the Active Man, whose words and works are in apparent harmony. Here, it seems, is the embodiment of "do well"—until Conscience observes that his coat is stained with sins of every kind. Haukyn confesses that hardly a day passes that he does not foul it "þoru3 werk or þoru3 word or wille of myn herte" (14.14–15). The vision ends with Haukyn sobbing, "So hard it is . . . to lyue and to do synne."

The recognition that words and works alone are inadequate to truth leads to a concentration on will in the fifth vision. The dreamer's guide, appropriately, is the soul itself, Anima, who exhorts him to charity. The dreamer asks for further instruction: "I haue lyued in londe . . . my name is longe wille, / And fond I neuere ful charite" (15.152–53). Charity cannot be known, says Anima, "Neiþer þoruȝ wordes ne werkes, but þoruȝ wil oone" (15.210). There follows a long treatise on the nature of charity, culminating in a description of the tree of charity. The *arbor caritatis,* a conventional image, summarizes in visual form the teachings of Anima. Its root is mercy, its trunk pity, its leaves "lele wordes," its fruit charity. This image gives way to Christ's parable of the good Samaritan, the chief biblical exemplar of charity. The parable is allegorized. The man who fell among thieves and was left for dead is mankind; the priest who passes him by is Faith (Abraham), and the Levite who does the same is Hope (Moses); the good Samaritan who saves the man is Charity (Christ).

The supreme act of Charity, Christ's sacrifice on the Cross, is dramatized in the sixth vision. The dream begins on Palm Sunday. Jesus enters Jerusalem like a knight on his way to a tournament; he is wearing the armor of Piers the Plowman, that is, *humana natura.* The battle is joined on the Cross itself. Christ triumphs (in his death defeating Death), descends into hell, and, after a debate with the Devil over who has legal rights to mankind, leads forth his own. Through the Redemption the prophecy of Psalm 84:11 is fulfilled: "Mercy and truth have met each other; justice and peace have kissed" (18.421a). The sound of Easter bells awakens the dreamer, who, with his wife, Kit, and daughter, Calote, goes to church to celebrate the Resurrection.

At this climactic moment the poet might have ended his work, and many readers have wished that he had. But the Resurrection is not the end of mankind's struggle to do well; rather it is the triumph that makes possible his own. In the last two visions, therefore, Langland returns to the field of folk to show the unfinished work of the church. Christ gives to Piers (St. Peter, the pope) the power to forgive sins. The Holy Spirit at Pentecost distributes to the folk the gifts of grace with which to withstand sin; and to Piers, the four seeds of the cardinal virtues and the four oxen of the Gospels with which "to till truth." To store the harvest of truth Piers builds a barn, Unity, "holy chirche on englissh" (19.238).

The action at the end of the poem is clearly a reprise of the pilgrimage to truth on Piers's half-acre. But this time the threat is more insidious. In contrast to the easily identified wasters on the half-acre the forces of Antichrist occupy the highest offices of church and state, and having the appearance of truth they undermine the system from within. The friars are the worst. One "Sire *Penetrans domos*" (2 Tim. 3:6), acting as spiritual physician to those in Unity, lets sinners get by with token penance, "a litel siluer." The sacrament of confession, upon which salvation depends, is compromised. Equally alarming is the helplessness of Conscience; misled by the guile of the friars and others, the moral faculty has lost its bearings. The poem ends as Conscience sets out to "seken Piers we Plowman." The cycle established earlier—the pilgrimage to truth, the search for Do-well—must be repeated yet again, this time by the very guide who had once so confidently led Will. The final lesson of the poem is that in such treacherous times and circumstances the will's hard-earned desire to "do well" is, tragically, not enough.

Versions

So far as narrative sequence is concerned, the above summary of the B version is more or less faithful to the corresponding portions of A and C as well. In other respects, however, the three versions differ greatly. B and C are nearly three times the length of A; they are also more introspective, apocalyptic, and theologically speculative. Between B and C there are also significant differences. C is generally regarded as poetically inferior to B, even by its greatest champion, E. Talbot Donaldson. Its chief aim seems to be clarity. It omits the puzzling tearing of the pardon and numerous other passages that threaten to distract or confuse. On the other hand it also adds much that is new and interesting, such as the grammatical metaphor at 3.333–406a and the important autobiographical passage at 5.1–108. In general the C revision is looser, more prosaic, and shows (in Donaldson's words) "a mounting ascendancy of idea over form" (1949: 42).

Criticism

The history of *Piers Plowman* criticism has been one of growing respect for the poet's craft, learning, and architectural sense. Early interest focused on the *visio* (as the first two dreams are called in several manuscripts), largely because of its satire, "realism," and topical allusions. It is hardly surprising that from this limited perspective the poem was valued chiefly as an historical document. The occupations of the folk on the field, the corruption of Lady Meed, the breakdown of feudal authority on the half-acre—such things were taken to be an accurate reflection of the times. There was less admiration for the much longer and more abstract *vita* (as the rest of the poem is often called).

The features that distanced many readers (especially from the *vita*)—the allegory, the theology, the heavy use of Latin quotations—were the very features that attracted a new critical approach in the mid-20th century. Robertson and Huppé, reasserting a view expressed earlier by Dunning, argued that the poem could be interpreted only in the context of patristic exegesis, that is, the scriptural tradition developed by the writings of the Church Fathers (e.g., Ambrose, Augustine, Jerome, Gregory). Subsequent critics refined the approach. Controversial though it was, exegetical criticism forced a sweeping reevaluation of the poem. The result was a more serious, more positive regard for the poet's art and learning (and, just as important, an increase in the tools available for literary research in the period).

Stimulated in part by the discoveries of exegetical criticism, other critics have sought to define more precisely the poet's intellectual milieu. Bloomfield sees the poem as the expression of a peculiarly monastic outlook and philosophy. Coleman argues that the poet's system of thought reflects mainly "the influence of Oxford and Cambridge thinkers whom we shall designate as the fourteenth century *moderni*"

(1981: 17). Scase examines the principal issues of the poem in the light of contemporary (as distinguished from "traditional") anticlerical writings. Other scholars have made important connections between the poem and grammar, law, antifriar polemic, and both modern and medieval economic and political theory.

Though widely divergent, and often in opposition to one another, such recent approaches have made possible new and complex readings of the poem. The assumption that the author was a careful and sophisticated thinker has proved far more productive than the earlier assumption that he was not.

John A. Alford

Bibliography

PRIMARY

Donaldson, E. Talbot, trans. *Piers Plowman: An Alliterative Verse Translation*. Ed. Elizabeth D. Kirk and Judith H. Anderson. New York: Norton, 1990; Goodridge, J.F., trans. *Piers the Ploughman*. Rev. ed. Harmondsworth: Penguin, 1966 [prose]; Kane, George, ed. *Piers Plowman: The A Version*. 1960. Rev. ed. London: Athlone, 1988 [the "Athlone Edition" comprises this volume, the next, and the one by Russell and Kane]; Kane, George, and E. Talbot Donaldson, eds. *Piers Plowman: The B Version*. 1975. Rev. ed. London: Athlone, 1988; Pearsall, Derek, ed. *Piers Plowman: An Edition of the C-text*. London: Arnold, 1978; Russell, George, and George Kane, eds. *Piers Plowman: The C Version*. London: Athlone, 1997; Schmidt, A.V.C., ed. *The Vision of Piers Plowman: A Critical Edition of the B-Text*. 1978. New ed. London: Dent, 1987; Skeat, Walter W., ed. *The Vision of William concerning Piers the Plowman in Three Parallel Texts*. 2 vols. 1886. Repr. with new bibliography. Oxford: Oxford University Press, 1954.

SECONDARY

New *CBEL* 1:533–44; *Manual* 7:2211–34, 2419–48; Alford, John A., ed. *A Companion to Piers Plowman*. Berkeley: University of California Press, 1988; Bloomfield, Morton W. *Piers Plowman as a Fourteenth-Century Apocalypse*. New Brunswick: Rutgers University Press, 1962; Coleman, Janet. *Piers Plowman and the Moderni*. Rome: Edizioni di Storia e Letteratura, 1981; Donaldson, E. Talbot. *Piers Plowman: The C-Text and Its Poet*. New Haven: Yale University Press, 1949; Dunning, T.P. *Piers Plowman: An Interpretation of the A Text*. 2d ed. Rev. and ed. T.P. Dolan. Oxford: Clarendon, 1980; Frank, Robert Worth, Jr. *Piers Plowman and the Scheme of Salvation: An Interpretation of Dowel, Dobet, and Dobest*. New Haven: Yale University Press, 1957; Pearsall, Derek. *An Annotated Critical Bibliography of Langland*. London: Harvester Wheatsheaf, 1990; Robertson, D. W., Jr., and Bernard F. Huppé. *Piers Plowman and Scriptural Tradition*. Princeton: Princeton University Press, 1951; Scase, Wendy. *Piers Plowman and the New Anticlericalism*. Cambridge: Cambridge University Press, 1989; Simpson, James. *Piers Plowman:*

An Introduction to the B-Text. London: Longman, 1990; *The Yearbook of Langland Studies*. East Lansing: Colleagues, 1987– [contains an annual bibliography of work on *Piers Plowman*].

See also Allegory; Alliterative Revival; Dream Vision; Law in ME Literature; Nature in ME Literature; *Parliament of the Three Ages; Pierce the Plowman's Creed; Richard the Redeless*; Truth in ME Literature; *Winner and Waster*

Pilgrimages and Pilgrims

Pilgrimage is a journey to a place of particular holiness: the burial place of a saint, location of a relic, or site associated with miraculous events. Pilgrims sought that the holy one associated with the place would intercede with God on their behalf. Pilgrims were privileged travelers; recognizable by staff, badge, and scrip (a small bag or satchel), they were exempt from tolls, were to be treated respectfully, and—especially at journey's end—could expect a hostel to provide free lodging.

Englishmen made pilgrimages to Jerusalem, Rome, or Compostela in Spain, but within England there were a number of notable shrines. That of St. Thomas the Martyr (Thomas Becket, killed in 1170, canonized 1171) in Canterbury Cathedral was the most celebrated, its fame ensured long before Chaucer's *Canterbury Tales*. It attracted pilgrims of every class including royalty, both English and foreign. Pilgrims from Winchester or London took well-defined routes, whose courses are still known; that from London by way of Rochester was well organized, with changes of horses available to hire. At popular shrines pilgrims could buy metal badges proving that they had made the journey; at Canterbury these took the shape of St. Thomas or were small flasks filled with holy water.

The shrine of Our Lady of Walsingham was next in importance, within England. About 1130 a widow, Richelde, was instructed by the Virgin to build a replica of the Holy Family's house at Nazareth; the house was used as a chapel. Later it was adorned with a jeweled statue of Mary and furnished with a reliquary believed to contain some of her miraculous milk. From the mid-13th century the fame of Walsingham grew steadily and by the late 15th century probably surpassed that of Canterbury. Other centers of enduring fame and national significance included the shrine of St. Cuthbert at Durham, the Holy Well of St. Winefride in north Wales, the Holy Rood at Bromholm (Norfolk), the shrine of the martyr Alban at St. Albans Abbey (Hertfordshire), and Glastonbury (Somerset), with the holy thorn tree and a church believed to have been founded by Joseph of Arimathea.

There were numerous places of pilgrimage whose importance was almost entirely local. Swings of fashion brought them into prominence for a time. Thus the tombs of St. William of Norwich (d. 1144) and Little St. Hugh of Lincoln (d. 1255) were visited for a time because the boys, who died violently, were popularly believed to have been ritually murdered by local Jews. Later the tombs of such political "martyrs" as Simon de Montfort, Thomas of Lancaster, and Edward II attracted pilgrims, though no official claim for their sanctity was ever made.

Though fashions for particular shrines fluctuated, enthusiasm for pilgrimages in general remained undiminished, despite criticisms by John Wyclif and the Lollards. Pilgrims made offerings at the shrines they visited, and these resulted in great wealth for the monasteries and churches in which they were located. Canterbury Cathedral was rebuilt with the offerings at St. Thomas's tomb, while the monks of Gloucester undertook extensive reconstruction of the abbey church with the offerings made at Edward II's tomb. Shrines of saints were lavishly decorated with gold, silver, and gems; Thomas Becket's was outstanding for its opulence. All these were destroyed at the Reformation.

Alison K. McHardy

Bibliography

Farmer, David Hugh. *The Oxford Dictionary of Saints.* 3d ed. Oxford: Oxford University Press, 1992; Hall, D.J. *English Medieval Pilgrimage.* London: Routledge & Kegan Paul, 1965; Jusserand, J.J. *English Wayfaring Life in the Middle Ages.* 4th ed. New York: Barnes & Noble, 1950; Ward, Benedicta. *Miracles and the Medieval Mind.* Rev. ed. Aldershot: Wildwood, 1987.

See also Becket; Chaucer; Clanvowe; Cuthbert; *Piers Plowman;* Popular Religion

Planctus

A lament, most usually upon the death of an important person or the destruction of a city; other types include the planctus on a biblical or classical figure (e.g., David's lament over Saul and Jonathan) and the dramatic or semidramatic Lament of the Virgin at the Cross. As a type of funeral verse the planctus (plur. planctus) was superseded by the elegy in the early 15th century. There are planctus in Latin and all the major medieval European vernaculars. To a large degree the planctus were intended for music in their original performance contexts, and melodies survive for a surprising number. The term denotes no particular metrical or musical shape, though the planctus is often constructed as a chain of repeating versicles, like the lai or sequence. The Latin planctus, sequence, and lai also frequently share a common melodic idiom.

Almost two dozen Latin planctus refer to English figures, with a roughly similar total in the various vernaculars—English, French, or Provençal. For instance, *Anglia planctus itera* memorializes Henry II (d. 1189); Gaucelm Faidit's *Fortz cauza es* laments Richard the Lionheart (d. 1199); *Seignurs, oiez pur dieu le grant* honors Edward I (d. 1307); and *A dere God what may this be* responds to the loss of Edward III (d. 1377). Among a number of laments of the Virgin in English, *Stond wel moder ounder rode* is the most widely distributed. One internationally popular Marian lament in Latin, Geoffrey of St. Victor's *Planctus ante nescia,* provided the melody for the Middle English "Prisoner's Prayer," *Ar ne kuthe,* which survives along with an alternative French text, *Eyns ne soy,* in London, Guildhall, Records Office, Liber de Antiquis Legibus, fols. 160v–161v. There are a number of insular examples of the related genre of Latin lai, of which *Samson dux fortissime* and *Omnis caro peccaverat* (the *Song of the Flood*) are the most ambitious.

Peter M. Lefferts

Bibliography

Dobson, Eric J., and Frank Ll. Harrison, eds. and trans. *Medieval English Songs.* London: Faber & Faber, 1979; Stevens, John. "Planctus." *NGD* 14:847–48; Stevens, John. *Words and Music in the Middle Ages: Song, Narrative, Dance and Drama, 1050–1350.* Cambridge: Cambridge University Press, 1986; Yearley, Janthia. "A Bibliography of Planctus in Latin, Provençal, French, German, English, Italian, Catalan, and Galician-Portuguese from the Time of Bede to the Early Fifteenth Century." *Journal of the Plainsong and Mediaeval Music Society* 4 (1981): 12–52.

See also Conductus; Hymns; Lai, Latin; Sequence; Songs

Poll Tax

By the late 14th century the traditional subsidies levied on personal wealth had become fixed in yield and thus unable to supply the increasing needs of the exchequer. The last parliament of Edward III attempted to augment revenue in 1377 through the introduction of a poll tax, levied on individuals rather than property. The 1377 tax was set at a rate of one groat (4*d.*) from all persons over fourteen (except beggars); the palatinates of Chester and Durham were excluded. The tax raised about £20,000, and the returns have provided historians with data for estimates of regional and national population.

A second poll tax was granted in 1379 for persons over sixteen. A graduated scale of assessment, ranging from a groat for the poor to ten marks (£6 13*s.* 4*d.*) for the dukes of Lancaster and Brittany and the two archbishops, was employed to make the tax more equitable and increase the yield. The results were disappointing—only £27,000 was collected—due to increased evasion of the tax.

In November 1380 parliament was summoned to cramped quarters at Northampton to deal in expeditious fashion with a mounting financial crisis. The result was the third and most famous poll tax. It was decided that the needed funds would require a trebling of the basic rate—a shilling a head on all persons over fifteen. The rich were encouraged to help the poor, but there was no graduated scale. Further, even this pious hope was vitiated by the provision that no man and wife were to pay more than twenty shillings. The tax met widescale evasion; fully one-third the number on the rolls in 1377 had disappeared from the 1381 rolls. Commissions of revision were sent to sixteen counties to counter such evasion. These attempts at collection were a key ingredient in the explosive mixture that produced the Peasant Rebellion of 1381, which began in Essex and Kent.

James L. Gillespie

Bibliography

Beresford, Maurice W. *The Lay Subsidies: The Poll Taxes of 1377, 1379, and 1381.* Canterbury: Phillimore, 1963; Graves, Edgar. *A Bibliography of English History to 1485.* Oxford: Clarendon, 1975 [in this comprehensive bibliography the index entries for "poll tax" are a good introduction]; Kowaleski, Maryanne. "Poll Tax, England." In *Dictionary of the Middle Ages,* ed. Joseph R. Strayer. Vol. 10. New York: Scribner, 1988; Russell, Josiah C. *British Medieval Population.* Albuquerque: University of New Mexico Press, 1948 [on the poll tax as a source for historical demography].

See also Peasant Rebellion; Population; Taxes

Popular (or Folk) Culture

A term used to designate the lifestyles, beliefs, value systems, and artistic creations of those groups set apart from the elite by poverty, illiteracy, and lack of power. Most medievalists include among these nonelite groups the rural peasantry, poorer urban artisans, and traveling tradespeople. Because these classes had little access to writing and scant representation in the ruling institutions of church, court, and government, there is great ignorance and great debate concerning the nature of medieval popular culture. Attempting to rediscover this elusive society, scholars have long relied on literary descriptions, though recent scholarship often turns to other sources in hopes of finding less (or at least differently) slanted evidence.

The least contestable evidence of medieval popular culture consists of archaeological excavations and such official records as manorial rolls and coroners' reports. These sources lead social historians like M.M. Postan and Barbara Hanawalt to conclude that peasants' material life and daily practices changed little from century to century. This relative stasis, labeled the *longue durée* ("long term") by French historians of the *Annales* school, has been used to justify resorting to the relatively rich writings of the 15th, 16th, and 17th centuries to help explain the culture of earlier, more sparsely documented times. However, the seeming continuities in technology and material culture do not of themselves guarantee that popular stories, beliefs, and values remained the same for centuries. Researchers must still turn to the more ambiguous evidence of medieval literature. To assess this literature it is necessary to distinguish at least two viewpoints, the outsiders' and the insiders'.

Outsiders' views, sparse in the early Middle Ages, grow more numerous with passing centuries. During the Anglo-Saxon period a few works (e.g., Ælfric's *Colloquy*) described the practices of farmers, fishers, and other ordinary workers. Although descriptions of popular culture grew much more common in the later Middle Ages, they generally reflect a negative bias. One important genre, the estates satire, catalogues various occupations and contrasts their ideal behavior with their actual practices. Typical is John Gower's 14th-century Latin work *Vox Clamantis,* a diatribe accusing peasants of undermining society by abandoning their duties. Only a few works, like *Piers Plowman,* show peasants "working very hard planting and sowing," only to "win what wastrels destroy with gluttony" (B.Prol.21–22).

Because elite authors so often condemn the lower classes, it is not surprising that some medievalists view popular culture as a counterculture, defining itself principally in terms of its opposition to the ruling class. In the *Canterbury Tales* Chaucer divides his pilgrims into *gentils* and *cherles*. The "perfect, *gentil*" Knight tells a refined romance of courtly love and noble battles, but the *cherlish* Miller responds with an earthy comic tale mocking courtly conventions. The *Canterbury Tales,* like a number of other ME works, stresses class conflict.

Some medievalists distinguish popular culture not by its opposition to, but by its dependence on elite culture: in their opinion popular culture is not creative in its own right but simply borrows, producing poor imitations of refined art. The idea that culture moves only from the top down is labeled by the German term *gesunkenes Kulturgut*. Among adherents of this view was the Celticist R.S. Loomis, who maintained that the Arthurian romances could never have been created in "the fancies of plowmen, goose girls, blacksmiths, midwives, or yokels of any kind." According to the perspective of *gesunkenes Kulturgut* a work like *The Tournament of Tottenham* represents peasants' pitiful attempts to imitate noble culture. In this mock romance the peasant contestants use flails instead of swords as they fight for the favor of a bailiff's daughter, rather than the noble heroines of elite poems.

Most medievalists now reject the more extreme forms of the two arguments just described. Because no known culture exists merely to oppose or merely to imitate another, evidence of a distinct popular culture, with its own *insiders' view,* will emerge from certain texts. Among the richest sources of popular culture are religious narratives and romances. An excellent gauge of popular taste is the literature aimed at the lower classes from the pulpits. Striving to keep their parishioners' attention, preachers (often of nonelite origins themselves) drew upon well-known, well-liked stories, including fables and folktales, converting these to exempla—tales told to underline moral precepts. Robert Manning's *Handlyng Synne* presents many exempla, including one in which a witch's spells make a bag move about by itself, sucking milk from cows. She displays her arts for a bishop, who attempts to imitate her but fails. The witch explains that the bishop's magic won't work because he does not believe the spell; he then commands her not to believe it either. This story illustrates a folk belief that can still be found in the 20th century. The author is himself a practitioner of popular culture, for his story grants witches magical powers that the official church denied. In Manning's story, as in popular culture, pre-Christian magical belief and official church doctrine intermingle freely.

Another important popular genre is romance. Although some claim a courtly origin for romance, others see it as evolving from oral folktales. More important than their origins—impossible to trace—is the fact that many romances are told from or directed toward the point of view of popular culture. Some stories combine elite and popular perspectives; *Havelok,* for example, creates heroes of both a king and his fisherman friend. Other romance plots exist in both elite and popular treatments, and comparing the two may reveal much about the popular view. Gower's *Tale of Florent,* written for a courtly audience, shares a plot with a less refined tale, *The Wedding of Sir Gawain and Dame Ragnall.* Gower's hero is an emperor's nephew incapable of wrong action, who disenchants a princess by granting her the upper hand in love. In contrast the hero of the anonymous *Gawain and Ragnall* is a good servant (Gawain) who acts heroically to help his king (Arthur) save face. Arthur has seized lands from a knight and broken vows of silence, but Gawain intercedes to save Arthur's life. Gawain is ultimately rewarded more generously by a hag (who is transformed into a beautiful woman) than by the king he has faithfully served. These slight changes in plot and great differences in perspective owe much to the different class allegiances of the two authors and their audiences.

As the Middle Ages drew to a close, the romance became progressively the property of popular culture. From Caxton's printing of Malory's *Morte Darthur* (1485) onward book and chapbook publication reached ever broader audiences, as such tales as *Guy of Warwick* and *Bevis of Hampton* were retold in prose form into the 19th century. Oral folktales based on romance themes also thrived, and their descendants have been collected in Scotland late in the 20th century.

Carl Lindahl

Bibliography

Gurevich, Aron. *Medieval Popular Culture: Problems of Belief and Perception.* Trans. János M. Bak and Paul A. Hollingsworth. Cambridge: Cambridge University Press, 1988; Hanawalt, Barbara A. *The Ties That Bound: Peasant Families in Medieval England.* New York: Oxford University Press, 1986; Heffernan, Thomas J., ed. *The Popular Literature of Medieval England.* Knoxville: University of Tennessee Press, 1985; Kaplan, Stephen L., ed. *Understanding Popular Culture: Europe from the Middle Ages to the Nineteenth Century.* Berlin: Mouton, 1984; Le Goff, Jacques. *Time, Work, and Culture in the Middle Ages.* Trans. Arthur Goldhammer. Chicago: University of Chicago Press, 1980; Lindahl, Carl. *Earnest Games: Folkloric Patterns in the Canterbury Tales.* Bloomington: Indiana University Press, 1987; Lindahl, Carl. "The Oral Undertones of Late Medieval Romance." In *Oral Tradition in the Middle Ages,* ed. W.F.H. Nicolaisen. Binghamton: CEMERS, 1992; Loomis, Roger Sherman. "Arthurian Tradition and Folklore." *Folklore* 69 (1958): 1–25; Mann, Jill. *Chaucer and Medieval Estates Satire: The Literature of Social Classes and the General Prologue to the Canterbury Tales.* Cambridge: Cambridge University Press, 1973; Owst, G.R. *Literature and Pulpit in Medieval England.* 2d ed. Oxford: Blackwell, 1961; Postan, M.M. *Medieval Economy and Society: An Economic History of Britain in the Middle Ages.* London: Pelican, 1972; Rosenberg, Bruce A. "Folklore Methodology and Medieval Literature." *Journal of the Folklore Institute* 13 (1976): 311–25.

See also Ballads; Breton Lay; Exemplum; Manning; Matter of England; Outlaws; Peasant Rebellion; *Piers Plowman;* Popular Religion; Romances; Satire

Popular Religion

During the Middle Ages the character of popular religion underwent many changes, but it can be most easily and completely seen during the years after 1300. Popular religion centered on parishes, of which there were some 8,600 in England and Wales. The ministrations of the parochial clergy were highly prized, and in large parishes, with a number of hamlets remote from the parish church, dependent chapelries were sometimes brought into existence when funds permitted.

The parochial clergy provided a succession of liturgical services. During the day the priest said the divine office and mass at least once a week, though not more than once a day. From 1215 the laity were bound to make confession and take communion once a year, though in the later Middle Ages there was increasing demand to receive communion more frequently. Perhaps the respectable norm was to attend church on Sundays, feast days, and special occasions and to go oftener when opportunity offered.

The feasts of the liturgical year provided memory milestones and coincided with the agricultural calendar. It is sometimes said that the Middle Ages were fundamentally pagan, Christianity a mere veneer, and that Christianity harnessed and utilized ancient festivals that marked the passing seasons and the annual round of farming tasks. Thus Christmas satisfied a need for cheerfulness in midwinter, while Easter marked the return of spring. The calendar year began with the Annunciation of the Blessed Virgin Mary, "Lady Day," on 25 March, but the liturgical year began with Advent (approximately 1–24 December). To commemorations of the life of Christ—Christmas (25 December), Epiphany (6 January), Lent and Easter (late winter and early spring), Whitsun (early summer)—were added a number of saints' feasts that were similarly easy to remember and that also marked the passing of the months and seasons: St. Hilary (13 January), the Nativity of St. John the Baptist (24 June), St. Michael or Michaelmas (29 September), All Saints (1 November).

Within this general framework liturgy and religious observance were subject to local variations. In England there were five liturgical uses (rites): those of Hereford, York, Lincoln, Bangor, and Sarum (Salisbury), but in the course of the 14th and 15th centuries the Sarum Use gained in popularity over the others. Ironically England became liturgically united on the eve of the Reformation. Some saints' cults were also localized, yet the number of saints' days celebrated was probably similar all over the country, with some 50 a year being observed. In the absence of vacations these holy days were the only respites from work generally allowed. Feast days were often literally the occasion for festivities and sometimes for community celebrations: "church ales" to raise parish funds.

At every critical point in an individual's life the parish church provided rituals that marked the occasion and enabled families and communities to express emotion. Babies were baptized into the church and given godparents, whose relationship to the child was regarded by the church as equal to the blood tie. The sacrament of confirmation, in theory universal, is rarely mentioned in contemporary sources, but weddings were conducted in church porches. Parish clergy heard the confession of, and gave absolution to, the dying. Above all they performed funerals that were important religious, emotional, social, even economic occasions, used by families to express wealth and status and to give charity to the poor, as well as to benefit the deceased's soul. Wills show a preoccupation with the form the funeral was to take, the numbers to be present, and the hospitality to be given. Subsequent services a month later (the "month-mind") and a year later (the "obit," or "year's-mind") were intended to commemorate the dead and to generate prayers for the good of his or her soul.

Life expectancy was low, sudden death common, and the pains of hell and purgatory a constant preoccupation. From the 13th century on concern for the soul after death and efforts to speed its passage through purgatory formed the most notable features of popular religion. Almost every member of the propertied classes made some provision for masses to be said for the good of the soul after death, the number depending on the individual's wealth. Those rich enough—nobility, gentry, and successful merchants—could found a perpetual chantry, an endowment that supported one or more chaplains to say masses for the founder's soul forever. The largest chantries were colleges with substantial buildings, and some had a secondary object of providing education. Many founders of perpetual chantries built chapels, which survive, on to their parish church. Chantries offered a way for the living and the dead to collaborate and should not be viewed as morbid.

Many individuals were able to contribute to the maintenance of a chaplain and to participate in church rituals of enhanced splendor through membership in a guild. Many, perhaps the majority of, parishes had a guild, and some had a number of them. Guilds raised money to support clergy and musicians who arranged feast-day services and ensured that members' funerals were impressive, organized social events; they contributed to a sense of community. Some guilds mounted biblical and morality plays, and perhaps through guilds parishioners organized the repair and rebuilding of church naves, which were their responsibility.

Devotion to the saints was strong and found its expression in the veneration and adornment of their statues and in pilgrimages to their shrines. Religious and secular good works were not separated, so that giving money to dower poor girls, repairing roads, and maintaining bridges were as much religious acts as making donations to parish churches or religious houses.

At the same time as money and effort were put into making parish services more impressive, interest in private devotion was growing. Gentry families sought the privilege of choosing their own confessor and hearing mass in private chapels, while the pious sought the advice of recluses rather than of parish priests. As lay literacy became commoner, it became fashionable to follow the liturgy in a book of hours, and when printed books became widespread around 1500, the book of hours (the Little Office of the Virgin Mary) became a bestseller.

Alison K. McHardy

Bibliography

Burgess, Clive. "'For the Increase of Divine Service': Chantries in the Parish in Late Medieval Bristol." *Journal of Ecclesiastical History* 36 (1985): 46–65; Burgess, Clive. "'By Quick and by Dead': Wills and Pious Provision in Later Medieval Bristol." *EHR* 102 (1987): 837–58; McHardy, Alison K. "Some Late-Medieval Eton College Wills." *Journal of Ecclesiastical History* 28 (1977): 387–95; Meade, Dorothy M. *The Medieval Church in England.* London: Churchman, 1988; Moorman, John R.H. *Church Life in England in the Thirteenth Century.* Cambridge: Cambridge University Press, 1945; Wood-Legh, Kathleen L. *Perpetual Chantries in Britain.* Cambridge: Cambridge University Press, 1965.

See also Alms; Books of Hours; Chantries; Guilds; Lady Mass; Liturgy; Moral and Religious Instruction; Parish Clergy; Penitentials; Pilgrimages; Popular Culture; Sermons; Wills

Population and Demography

During the generation after World War II historians, influenced by the newer social sciences, turned increasing attention to demography as a critical factor influencing the economies of preindustrial societies. In the case of medieval England M.M. Postan, professor of economic history at Cambridge 1938–65, was the most influential exponent of a demographically based interpretation of economic and social history. In a series of articles he depicted an agrarian economy whose long-term rhythms reflected aggregate growth and decline in the English population.

Briefly stated, Postan's argument was that English population expanded by a factor of two or three from the time of Domesday Book (1086) to some point around the turn of the 13th and 14th centuries. The results of demographic growth included a great expansion of the area of land under cultivation, eventual impoverishment and land hunger for the poorest peasants (manifested particularly in the famine years 1315–17), and ultimately a contraction of population due to famine and disease that the Black Death (1348–49) only hastened. The century and a half after that was essentially a prolonged economic contraction, the consequence of an English population probably no more than half its size at its high-medieval peak.

It is noteworthy that little of this early theorizing about medieval English demographic history rested upon a base of directly demographic data. Its major underlying premise was a particular relationship between population and such economic indices as prices, rents, and wages. Having postulated this relationship, one then (following this logic) inspects the abundant available series of economic indices as if they were surrogates for population trends.

Perhaps unfortunately theories like Postan's (and that of Emmanuel Le Roy Ladurie for France) have attracted the label "Malthusian"—even if such a label is erroneous in relation to what Malthus really argued—chiefly because they envisage preindustrial population growth as tending to outrun food

English Population, 1086–1600, in millions

HIGH/LOW ESTIMATES (1086–1520) AND PARISH-REGISTER-BASED DATA (1541–1600)

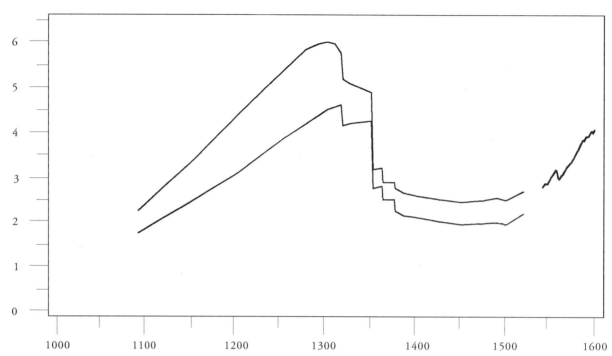

Fig. 104. English population, 1086–1600, in millions. Based on data in J. Hatcher (1977), and E.A. Wrigley and R.S. Schofield (1989). Prepared by L.R. Poos.

supplies and to bring the inevitable repercussion of a population crash after every boom. Theories like Postan's tend to regard demographic change as an "exogenous" variable, that is, something "outside" the economy and society and capable of controlling them rather than being controlled by them. And so critics of such theories (especially Marxist critics) charge that demographically based models of economic and social change are deterministic and mechanical and ignore relationships of political and social power, a charge Postan himself vehemently denied.

It may be useful to sum up the present state of knowledge about medieval English population under two broad headings: generally accepted empirical observations about important demographic variables, and ongoing debates about the mutual relationships between population processes and the economic environment in which they took place. The broad outlines of aggregate change in the English national population are generally agreed upon, even if debate remains concerning its precise chronology and geography; they are much as Postan asserted. There was sustained growth over the first three centuries of the millennium, a deceleration or even reversal of trend between 1300 and 1348 (including mortality of as much as 10 percent during the harvest failure of the second decade of that century), the abrupt collapse of the Black Death and lesser subsequent plague epidemics, and the prolonged demographic depression lasting at least until the latter decades of the 15th century (fig. 104).

When we come to estimates of the absolute population, we have some definite guidelines, despite the temptation to join in what one historian called "the popular sport of guessing at the population of England over the broad sweep of almost half a millennium." Domesday Book, arguably the most remarkable statistical record in European history, recorded about 275,000 persons in 1086. But this document, concerned mostly with property, enumerated people mainly as an adjunct to land, so that historians have variously argued for English population totals at the time as ranging from 1.75 to 2.25 million.

Three centuries later the returns of the first poll tax (1377) included 1,355,201 taxpayers, supposedly equal to all male and female laypersons aged fourteen years and older except for the most needy. Here too, historians have engaged in lengthy arguments over degrees of tax evasion and the percentage to be allocated to the under-fourteens and the clergy, and corresponding estimates of national population have ranged between 2.5 and 3 million. Projecting backward from this figure, on the assumption that the Black Death and other 14th-century epidemics had reduced English population by 40 to 50 percent in the preceding three-quarters of a century, would suggest a population of 4.5 to 6 million for the country at large around 1300. Other evidence buttressing this general picture of overall change includes changes over time in field systems and settlement patterns and in distributions of peasant land-holding sizes.

More recently historical demographers have used the excellent English parish registers of baptisms, marriages, and burials that began in 1538 to reconstruct by computer the national population from thenceforth. The results of this research indicate that during the 1540s and 1550s England possessed between 2.8 and 3.1 million people and that at that point demographic growth regularly approached or exceeded 1 percent per annum. In short, by the midpoint of the Tudor century, England was already well into another phase of expanding population after the late-medieval depression.

In broad terms these relatively fixed points of estimation fit comfortably within the overall scheme of change laid out earlier. And whatever their shortcomings for absolute totals, all these sources concur in showing that the population of England was unevenly distributed spatially throughout the period: the lowland, arable south and east of the country were considerably more densely populated than the upland, pastoral north and west.

It has proven much more difficult to derive empirically based estimates of the more detailed demographic factors that contributed to aggregate growth or decline, such as mortality rates or life expectancies, fertility patterns and ages at marriage, migration, or the size and composition of household units. Regular censuslike data or serial records of birth, marriage, and death from medieval England are virtually nonexistent or at best survive from such specialized, particular, or local contexts that they are difficult to project onto the bulk of ordinary English men's and women's experiences. It is necessary to emphasize that most of these matters continue to be the subject of debate.

Historians interested in mortality have attempted to use records of such things as the deaths of tenants-in-chief of the crown, or of peasants in manorial records, or of admissions of monks to abbeys and their subsequent deaths, to calculate life expectancy at birth (e_0) in a way comparable with other times and places. The results produced to date have implied an e_0 as low as the range from about 25 to 30 years for the period after the Black Death, when plague had established its presence in England, or in other words as much as ten years lower than in the England of Elizabeth. But since these records deal with the experiences of adults (whereas infant and child mortality may exert a disproportionately strong effect upon e_0) it is difficult to know how much weight to place upon them.

Traditional fascination with the Black Death and bubonic plague, and the presumption of theorists like Postan that mortality necessarily played the major role in adjusting demographic growth, have been giving way in recent years to a new appreciation that fertility, and the nuptiality that was its chief determinant, were at least as important in the demographic equation of premodern England. Parish-register data have shown that after the mid-16th century English men and women married late in life (in their mid-twenties, typically) and that a substantial minority never married at all. Fertility was therefore much lower than its theoretical maximum, and changes in marriage age and incidence raised or lowered fertility enough to set national population rising or falling.

There has been considerable discussion concerning how far this was true of medieval England. Studies of 14th-century poll taxes, wills, and manorial records have yielded a mixed picture, some data implying a late-marrying regime, other data being less clearcut. At the present state of knowledge one should perhaps conclude simply that mortality is unlikely to have accounted for all of the aggregate population movements sketched out here and that the historical demography of medieval England, properly construed, overlaps considerably into areas of family history, popular culture, and economic history.

L.R. Poos

Bibliography

Bailey, Mark. "Demographic Decline in Late Medieval England: Some Thoughts on Recent Research." *EcHR* 49 (1996): 1–19; Campbell, Bruce M.S., ed. *Before the Black Death: Studies in the "Crisis" of the Early Fourteenth Century*. Manchester: Manchester University Press, 1991; Harvey, Barbara. *Living and Dying in England 1100–1540: The Monastic Experience*. Oxford: Oxford University Press, 1993; Hatcher, John. *Plague, Population, and the English Economy, 1348–1530*. London: Macmillan, 1977; Poos, L.R. *A Rural Society after the Black Death: Essex 1350–1525*. Cambridge: Cambridge University Press, 1991; Smith, R.M. "Human Resources." In *The Countryside of Medieval England*, ed. Grenville Astill and Annie Grant. Oxford: Blackwell, 1988, pp. 188–212; Wrigley, E.A., and R.S. Schofield. *The Population History of England 1541–1871: A Reconstruction*. 2d ed. Cambridge: Cambridge University Press, 1989.

See also Black Death; Domesday Book; Prices and Wages

Power, Leonel (ca. 1375/85–1445)

Composer and music theorist, one of the most prolific and influential in the first half of the 15th century. The first reference to Leonel occurs in 1418 in the records of the household chapel of Thomas duke of Clarence, where he was probably employed as a specialist musician rather than as a cleric. Since his name is given second in the accounts, he may have been one of its most senior members, recruited perhaps as early as 1411–13. After Clarence's death in 1421 Leonel's movements become uncertain, though he may have worked in one of the other English ducal chapels. In 1423 he became a member of the confraternity of the priory at Christ Church, Canterbury, but there is no evidence that this involved any professional duties. That he spent his last years in Canterbury is confirmed by a legal document of 1438 and by records suggesting that from 1439 until his death he acted as master of the Lady Chapel choir of the cathedral.

Most of Leonel's substantial surviving output (over 40 pieces, not counting those with conflicting attributions) is either for the Ordinary of the mass or for Marian services; secular music and isorhythmic motets are lacking. This narrow range of genres is, however, counterbalanced by an unusually wide variety of styles, much wider than that shown by his younger contemporary Dunstable, and his music accurately reflects the important technical changes that occurred during his long career.

Leonel's earliest surviving music comes mainly from the Old Hall Manuscript and bears the hallmark of a skilled and inventive composer fully conversant with the techniques available at the beginning of the 15th century; clearly he was proficient at all levels of elaboration, from austere discant through florid melodic writing to ingenious use of isorhythm. He seems, however, to have taken a particular delight in rhythmic intricacies expressed through notational tricks that are esoteric even by the standards of Old Hall. Some of Leonel's music seems to be contrived around numerical relationships; in this respect he is typical of composers of his time, though his usage is notably less involved than that of Dunstable.

About this time he and others began to group mass movements in pairs, an idea that eventually led to the establishment of the cyclic mass. Only one such cycle survives with an undisputed attribution to Leonel (built on the plainsong *Alma redemptoris mater*), but two more carry conflicting ascriptions. In this and later music he inclined toward the melodically, rhythmically, and harmonically smoother style cultivated from the 1430s onward; and what appear to be his last Marian antiphons are as forward-looking as anything of the period. Most of these more modern-sounding works are preserved only in continental sources, and doubtless there is further music by Leonel among the many anonymous pieces in the earlier Trent Codices and other mid-century continental manuscripts.

Leonel's short treatise in the vernacular "for hem that wilbe syngers or makers or techers" provides a lucid explanation of improvised counterpoint, especially as it involves boys' voices.

Gareth Curtis

Bibliography

PRIMARY

Hamm, Charles, ed. *Leonel Power: Complete Works.* Corpus Mensurabilis Musicae 50. Rome: American Institute of Musicology, 1969; Hughes, Andrew, and Margaret Bent, eds. *The Old Hall Manuscript.* 3 vols. in 4. Corpus Mensurabilis Musicae 46. Rome: American Institute of Musicology, 1969–73; Meech, Sanford B. "Three Musical Treatises in English from a Fifteenth-Century Manuscript." *Speculum* 10 (1935): 235–69.

SECONDARY

Bent, Margaret. "Power, Leonel." *NGD* 15:174–79; Bowers, Roger D. "Some Observations on the Life and Career of Lionel Power." *Proceedings of the Royal Musical Association* 102 (1975–76): 103–27.

See also Dunstable; Mass, Polyphonic Music for; Old Hall Manuscript

Prayers

A notable product of Anglo-Saxon literary culture and spiritual life is an extensive body of private prayers, found in manuscripts from both early and late in the period. The prayers are written in Latin prose, but in the 11th century some of them were translated into or glossed in OE. The prayers are termed "private" in order to distinguish them from prayers used in the liturgy, the public ceremonies and worship of the church. The private prayers, it is assumed, were used in personal devotions and as the basis of private meditation, predominantly if not exclusively in a monastic setting.

In monasteries, besides being read in solitude, these prayers may have been recited aloud communally at times set aside for public reading, or they may have been memorized and recited by monks (perhaps orally in a low voice) at times provided for individual prayer. The late Anglo-Saxon monastic consuetudinary (a manual of customary religious practices) known as the *Regularis concordia* prescribes the recitation of prayers by individual monks as part of the daily routine in preparation for corporate worship in the divine office. It is important to recognize that the dividing line between public worship and private devotion was almost certainly not so distinct as it became later. Private prayers were often based on the collects and prayers that formed the liturgy, and during the divine office described in the *Regularis concordia* intervals were allowed for individual prayer.

The private prayers of Anglo-Saxon England are found in separate anthologies or in collections of prayers in other kinds of manuscripts, chiefly psalters. There are four prayer anthologies from early Anglo-Saxon England, dating from about 750 to 825. These anthologies might include, in addition to the private prayers, litanies, creeds, hymns, psalms, and extracts from the Gospels. The prayers come from a variety of sources, including the liturgy, hagiography, and the writings of Augustine, Sedulius, Isidore of Seville, and possibly Bede. Many of the prayers are attributed to Augustine, Gregory, or Jerome, often without foundation in fact. The prayers are usually addressed to the Trinity, Christ, and God the Father; less frequently, to the Virgin, angels, and saints. One type of prayer found in the early collections is the *lorica,* or prayer for protection from spiritual and bodily enemies, which is Irish in origin.

Later Anglo-Saxon collections of prayers, most of which date from the 11th century, are usually found in psalters, where they typically follow the Canticles. This is appropriate, since the Psalms had been used as a basis for private prayer from the beginnings of Christianity. The later collections incorporate many prayers from earlier collections as well as adding new prayers that had been written on the Continent in the time of Charlemagne and his successors.

The prayers of both early and late collections are diverse in character, varying considerably in length and tone. Some are closely adapted from brief liturgical prayers and retain the austerity and formality of the Roman liturgy. Others are more lengthy, effusive, and personal, obviously not suited for the requirements of public worship. But even the most extensive of these prayers should probably not be regarded as expressions of personal feelings and the interior life of their authors. In certain of the prayers one may find what seems to be an emotional effusiveness, but on the whole they are much more restrained than the private prayers of the high and later Middle Ages. There is nothing here, for example, to match the intense emotion, agonized self-examination, or lively remorse that characterizes the devotional prayers of Anselm of Canterbury and the devotional writing of his followers in the late 11th and 12th centuries.

The cultural setting of the prayers is important. The early English anthologies do not appear to rest on continental models but are commonly thought to reveal the strong influence of Irish and Celtic spirituality. The cultivation of private prayer can be seen as an aspect of a particularly Irish attention to the individual soul, also manifested in the early Irish development of private confession and penance. At the same time the prayer books show the influence of Roman service books and the continental ecclesiastical culture that was brought to England beginning with the arrival of the Roman mission in 597. It is assumed that the audience for the English anthologies was primarily monastic and male. Yet one of the anthologies, the fragmentary Harley Prayer Book (BL Harley 7653), may have been a book of private devotions for a woman, and an early prayer from an Oxford manuscript is also likely to have been written by or for a woman (Bodl. Selden supra 30). One of the early anthologies (the Book of Nunnaminster) may have been owned by Ealhswith, wife of Alfred the Great. These examples are interesting in relation to the complex matter of the status of female monasticism in Anglo-Saxon England and the vexed issue of women's literacy in the earlier Middle Ages.

The English anthologies should also be viewed in conjunction with continental developments associated with the renewal of the church in the age of Charlemagne. Alcuin of York was a leader of the reform movement who wrote devotional manuals incorporating private prayers. Perhaps under his inspiration the private prayer book became an established feature of reformed Carolingian spirituality, both lay and monastic. The influence of this renewed Carolingian spirituality is especially visible in the later English collections of prayers, which are best regarded as a product of the revival of monasticism in 10th- and 11th-century England known as the Benedictine Reform, itself strongly inspired by the Carolingian example.

Private prayers may have influenced OE literary composition, at least in a general way. An OE poem known as *A Prayer* is best understood within the broader context of Latin devotional prayer, and a poem of the Exeter Book, *Resignation,* also seems to owe something to this tradition. Certain passages in the biblical narrative poems *Judith, Christ II, Daniel, Azarias,* and the hagiographical *Guthlac A* may have been influenced by the private prayers, specifically the Celtic *lorica* tradition. Ælfric quite certainly was familiar with prayers of this type and may have incorporated some of their phraseology and structure into his *Lives of Saints* and *Catholic Homilies.*

Thomas H. Bestul

Bibliography

PRIMARY

Günzel, Beate, ed. *Ælfwine's Prayerbook.* Henry Bradshaw Society 108. Woodbridge: Boydell, 1993; Kuypers, A. B., ed. *The Prayer Book of Aedeluald the Bishop, Commonly Called the Book of Cerne.* Cambridge: Cambridge University Press, 1902; Muir, Bernard, ed. *A Pre-Conquest English Prayer-Book.* Henry Bradshaw Society 103. Woodbridge: Brewer, 1988; Symons, Thomas, Sigrid Spath, et al., eds. *Regularis concordia anglicae nationis.* Rev. ed. *Corpus Consuetudinarum Monasticarum* 7/3 (Consuetudinum Saeculi X/XI/XII Monumenta Non-Cluniacensia), ed. Kassius Hallinger. Siegburg: Schmitt, 1984; Wilmart, André, ed. *Precum Libelli Quattuor Aevi Karolini.* Rome: Ephemerides Liturgicae, 1940.

SECONDARY

Bestul, Thomas H. "Continental Sources of Anglo-Saxon Devotional Writing." In *Sources of Anglo-Saxon Culture,* ed. Paul E. Szarmach. Kalamazoo: Medieval Institute 1986, pp. 103–26; Hill, Thomas D. "Invocation of the Trinity and the Tradition of the *Lorica* in Old English Poetry." *Speculum* 56 (1981): 259–67; Hughes, Kathleen. "Some Aspects of Irish Influence on Early English Private Prayer." *Studia Celtica* 5 (1970): 48–61; Wilmart, André. *Auteurs spirituels et textes dévots du Moyen Age latin.* Paris: Bloud & Guy, 1932. Repr. Paris: Études Augustiniennes, 1971.

See also Alcuin; Benedictine Reform; Literary Influences: Irish; Liturgy and Church Music, History of; Monasticism; Penitentials; Regularis concordia; Women in OE Literature

Prices and Wages

Without statistics for either gross national or domestic product, or per capita incomes or production, it is difficult to measure the performance of the medieval economy or to chart possible rising and falling standards of living for the mass of the population.

The use of price and wage tables can provide a partial answer to the problem. Provided the value of money remained reasonably constant and there were no significant improvements in farming techniques, then a sustained upward movement in prices (especially for cereals; bread was literally the staff of life) might indicate a rising population, beginning to push the limits of subsistence. This would also be reflected in rising rents, entry fines, and income from land, as lords sought to exploit estates to produce for the market. A surplus of labor would be reflected in falling wage rates, and the purchasing power of wages would fall as price inflation began to be felt. Standards of living would fall, and if the population continued to expand there might well be widespread rural impoverishment and the beginnings of Malthusian checks.

On the other hand a cataclysmic decline in population, subsequent to the advent of endemic plague in 1348, would result in falling prices and rents, as land went out of use, and in rising wages, as labor became scarcer. The precise point at which prices moved downward and wages upward would indicate when the plague finally began to cause major economic changes and long-term population decline set in. That might be catastrophic for the land-holding or rentier class, but the standard of living of the mass of the population, who now had sufficient land to feed their families and wages with substantially improved purchasing power, might well rise.

This can be described as the "demographic" interpretation of the economy, with prices and wages being, in the absence of other reliable information, a main indicator of rising and falling population and standards of living. Medieval people were keenly aware of the significance of price levels and wage rates. Towns regularly attempted to control both, while the first comprehensive wage-price regulation came with the Ordinance and Statute of Labourers in 1349–51.

But the use of tables in which the movement of prices and wages is expressed in terms of a base year or decade, according to value in grams of silver or given annually or decennially in sterling, really begins in the 19th century, with the gathering of data by J. Thorold Rogers, a member of parliament, whose extensive studies *Six Centuries of Work and Wages* and *A History of Agriculture and Prices in England* remain invaluable. Rogers was followed by Sir William Beveridge, with articles on Winchester and Westminster wages, by Phelps Brown on the purchasing power of building workers' wages, and by D.L. Farmer and J.Z. Titow on the agricultural economy.

Care must be taken in the use of such tables. Year-on-year prices often show rapid fluctuations due to good or bad harvests, and, where the base cost of a basket of consumables—wheat, cheese, meat, or cloth—has been constructed to show subsequent changes in the purchasing power of wages, allowance must be made for alterations in the composition of the basket. Less wheat and more meat might be bought when standards of living were rising, the reverse when they fell. Evidence drawn from great estates, mainly in the south, might not be applicable to the whole country, especially pastoral areas where livestock prices need consideration. Large towns like London exercised a "pull" on the surrounding region, and large-scale imports of grain from, say, the Baltic region could have alleviated high prices in time of dearth. But despite these drawbacks price and wage movements provide one of the important keys to monitoring the performance of the agrarian economy.

What do they show? Little before 1180, since the evidence is sparse. Between 1180 and 1220 there was rapid inflation, especially in grain prices, which then stagnated in the mid-13th century (although at the higher levels of previous decades) but rose again in the last decades of that century and the first decades of the 14th, reaching a peak in the famine years 1315–25. Livestock prices show roughly the same trends, while at the same time wages were low or static and fell in real terms. In the two decades before the Black Death prices and wages moved slowly downward, but then came a few years of wild fluctuation, followed by a decade when prices and wages again moved together. Only in the mid-1370s did they part company. Prices fell and stayed low; wages rose and in both monetary and real terms remained high for the rest of the Middle Ages.

This story argues for an expanding population, reaching the limits of subsistence by the end of the 13th century, a point of crisis in the early 14th century, and the lowering of the population by perhaps as much as a half after the mid-1370s. It also corresponds to the period of vigorous demesne exploitation and production for the market by the great landlords, with a heavy burden upon the peasantry in the 13th century and the return to a rentier economy, and a general rise in the standards of living in the later Middle Ages.

This is a cogent explanation of change in the economy, but the argument depends on the value of money remaining constant. In the last 30 years this assumption has been challenged. It was not a matter of frequent debasements causing price fluctuations, for English currency was renowned throughout Europe for its quality. There was frequent recoinage, needed to maintain, not to alter, the fineness of the coins. If, however, too few or too many coins were issued, it could, theoretically, have deflationary or inflationary consequences. Similarly changes in the value of the bullion content of the coins could alter their purchasing power.

Silver and gold moved freely around Europe. A shortage in silver, due to a fall in mining output or to the metal being drawn to an area where it was in demand, would push up its value and that of fine coins. When gold coins were struck widely in western Europe (from the mid-13th century onward, but in England chiefly from the reign of Edward III), bimetallic flows emerged. Gold was highly valued in the west, silver in the Muslim world. The exchange of metals created a shortage of silver, the metal most widely in circulation, increasing the value and the intrinsic worth of coins struck from it, and so depressing prices. Silver might also have flowed into England as a result of favorable trade balances from the export of wool and cloth, creating a glut; it could also be shipped abroad to pay for military campaigns or alliances, causing monetary deflation.

Numismatists and monetary historians argue that these factors must be taken into account when discussing prices and wage levels and the performance of the economy in general: the "boom" of the 13th century, the depression of the 15th. The inflation of 1180–1220, with high prices from agriculture to stimulate the change to demesne farming by great landlords, was caused by an influx of silver from wool exports. Edward I's recoinage of 1279 led to lower prices, due to the limited number of fine coins issued; that of 1304–09, at a time when there was a glut of silver (again from wool exports), to higher prices, as too many coins came into circulation. In the late 1330s and early 1340s payments abroad in the opening stages of the Hundred Years War had deflationary consequences, while the European silver famine of the 15th century meant lower prices and economic depression. At critical points, then, price and wage levels are explicable in monetary rather than demographic terms, an argument with considerable implications for economic historians.

But such interpretations have not found universal acceptance. The correlation of grain-price fluctuations with monetary changes in the 13th and early 14th centuries "strains credulity," according to A.R. Bridbury, and can be achieved only by ignoring similar fluctuations with different causes at other times. It is also unlikely that all the profits of the wool trade between 1180 and 1220 would have been brought back as silver. Some must have been spent on imports, and large amounts of coin were shipped abroad to pay for the Angevin wars.

Foreign wars may also have caused the deflation of the 1330s and 1340s, though no convincing monetary explanation has been given for the way in which prices and wages moved divergently in the 15th century. Had this been the result of a silver famine, they should have moved together. They did not; the best explanation is a fall in the population.

Prices and wages obviously did respond to changes in the money supply but more to increases or decreases in the numbers of people, and they remain one of the best ways of charting those fluctuations and more general changes in the medieval economy.

J.L. Bolton

Bibliography

Bolton, J.L. *The Medieval English Economy, 1150–1500.* London: Dent, 1980 [contains full bibliographies on prices, wages, money, and bullion]; Bolton, J.L. "Inflation, Economics and Politics in Thirteenth-Century England." In *Thirteenth-Century England IV: Proceedings of the Newcastle upon Tyne Conference 1991,* ed. P.R. Coss and S.D. Lloyd. Woodbridge: Boydell, 1992, pp. 1–14; Bridbury, Anthony R. "Thirteenth-Century Prices and the Money Supply." *Agricultural History Review* 33 (1985): 1–21; Farmer, D.L. "Prices and Wages." In *The Agrarian History of England and Wales.* Vol. 2: *1042–1350,* ed. H.E. Hallam. Cambridge: Cambridge University Press, 1988, pp. 716–817; Farmer, D.L. "Prices and Wages." In *The Agrarian History of England and Wales.* Vol. 3: *1350–1500,* ed. E. Miller. Cambridge: Cambridge University Press, 1991, pp. 431–525; Mayhew, N.J. "Money and Prices in England, from Henry II to Edward III." *Agricultural History Review* 35 (1987): 121–32; Spufford, Peter. *Money and Its Use in Medieval Europe.* Cambridge: Cambridge University Press, 1988 [bibliographies, pp. 423–42, are relevant to England].

See also Black Death; Mints; Peasant Rebellion; Population

Prick of Conscience, The

A long verse compilation (over 9,600 lines in rhyming couplets), primarily eschatological, treating the wretchedness of man's condition, the world, death, purgatory, Judgment Day, the pains of hell, and the joys of heaven. The author has not been identified, but the poem was probably composed in the north of England toward the mid-14th century.

The poem is divided into a prologue, seven books, and a brief conclusion or epilogue. The prologue is concerned primarily with the importance of knowing oneself and one's condition as the prerequisite for knowing God, living a good life, and coming to a good end. Book 1 is about the wretchedness of man at his birth, during the course of his life, and at his death; the concerns of this book are standard ones from the *contemptus mundi* ("contempt of the world") tradition. Book 2 treats the world and the conditions thereof; it begins by distinguishing among the kinds of worlds and then describes at length the transitory and untrustworthy nature of the earthly and human varieties of the lower visible world. Book 3 is about death and the four reasons why it is to be feared. Book 4 treats purgatory, its location and varieties, the seven pains encountered there, who goes there and for what kinds of sins, and how those in purgatory may have their pains alleviated and shortened.

Book 5 begins by describing in detail the fifteen signs that precede the Last Judgment, ending with the fire that will consume the world, and then goes on to the events of Judgment Day itself, when Christ will separate the good from the evil. Book 6 describes the pains of hell, first the fourteen specific ones and then the principal one, the endless yearning for the sight of God; it ends with a discussion of the behavior of those condemned to hell. Book 7 is on the location, nature, and joys of heaven, with special attention to the seven kinds of joys that belong to the body and the seven kinds that belong to the soul, the greatest of which is the sight of God and the Trinity. In his conclusion the author explains that he chose to call his work *The Prick of Conscience* because if a man will read and understand the matters in it, his conscience will be made sensitive, his heart will be stirred to fear and meekness and a yearning for the bliss of heaven, and he will thus mend his evil ways.

The *Prick of Conscience* is based on many sources, as the author himself says in his conclusion; a partial list of those quoted (arranged in order of appearance) attests to his wide learning: Pseudo-Bernard's *Meditations,* Pope Innocent III's *De miseria humanae conditionis,* the *De proprietatibus rerum* of Bartholomaeus Anglicus, the *Compendium theologicae veritatis* of Hugh Ripelin of Strasbourg, Augustine's *City of God,* the *Distichs* of Cato, the second *Meditation* of Anselm of Canterbury, Isidore of Seville's *Sententiae,* the French version of Robert Grosseteste's *De poenis purgatorii,* Jerome's *Regula monachorum,* the *Sententiae* of Peter of Poitiers, and the *Elucidarium* of Honorius of Autun—not to mention the Bible, which is quoted more than any other single work.

The poem itself exists in three versions: an original or main version; a southern recension; and an abbreviated version entitled *Speculum huius vitae.* The main version (in 98 manuscripts) originated in the north of England, probably Yorkshire, and has a preponderance of manuscripts from that area and the north Midlands, but it extended also into the west Midlands and East Anglia and even occasionally into the southeast and the southwest. The southern recension (in nineteen manuscripts) is shorter than the main version and represents a thorough revision; it originated somewhere in the south, perhaps the Thames Valley, and its distribution is more restricted than that of the main version. The *Speculum Huius Vitae* (in two manuscripts) is a heavily revised and abbreviated version of the main version; its manner is admonitional, whereas the original is primarily didactic.

To judge from the number of extant manuscripts of the three versions *The Prick of Conscience* was the most popular English poem of the Middle Ages and was surpassed in English only by the two versions of the Wycliffite prose translation of the Bible and the prose *Brut.* This indication of popularity is supported by other signs: 80 percent of the counties of England can claim at least one copy of the poem, and some have two or more; extracts circulated separately (twelve in eight manuscripts); the poem was quoted in a number of other ME poems (*Stimulus conscienciae minor, Desert of Religion, Of the Flood of the World, Wheel of Fortune*) as well as in a stained-glass window at All Saints Church, York; it was translated into

Latin prose in the 14th century (six manuscripts exist); and it appears in wills and book lists.

For a long time the poem was thought to have been written by Richard Rolle, to whom it is attributed in five manuscripts, but his authorship was persuasively rejected by Hope Emily Allen. Three manuscripts attribute the poem to Robert Grosseteste, but he lived too early to have been the author; a 20th-century suggestion is William of Nassington, the author of the *Speculum vitae,* but there is as yet no proof for this. In genre *The Prick of Conscience* is unlike any other extant ME work in verse or prose, though it has some similarities to and has been compared with the *Speculum vitae;* its primary function was probably as a compendium of knowledge from which a parish priest could instruct his flock or draw material for his sermons. Its wide circulation in the 14th and 15th centuries indicates that it achieved its purpose.

Robert E. Lewis

Bibliography

PRIMARY

Morris, Richard, ed. *The Pricke of Conscience (Stimulus Conscientiae): A Northumbrian Poem by Richard Rolle de Hampole.* Berlin: Asher, 1863. Repr. New York: AMS, 1973.

SECONDARY

New *CBEL* 1:503; *Manual* 7:2268–70, 2486–92; Allen, Hope Emily. "The Authorship of the *Prick of Conscience.*" In *Studies in English and Comparative Literature.* Radcliffe College Monographs 15. Boston: Ginn, 1910, pp. 115–70; Allen, Hope Emily. *Writings Ascribed to Richard Rolle, Hermit of Hampole, and Materials for His Biography.* New York: Heath, 1927, pp. 372–97; Britton, Derek. "Unnoticed Fragments of the *Prick of Conscience.*" *NM* 80 (1979): 327–34 [textual relations of northern manuscripts; reiterates attribution to William of Nassington]; Lewis, Robert E., and Angus McIntosh. *A Descriptive Guide to the Manuscripts of the Prick of Conscience.* Medium Ævum Monographs n.s. 12. Oxford: Society for the Study of Mediaeval Languages and Literature, 1982.

See also Bible in ME Literature; Grosseteste; Moral and Religious Instruction; Rolle; *Speculum vitae*

Printing

Printing from movable type was a major technological advance of the late Middle Ages, although its full cultural impact and implications belong to the 16th and succeeding centuries.

The western invention of printing is attributed to Johannes Gutenberg, a goldsmith, who solved the problems of designing a printing press, preparing a suitable ink, and, most importantly, casting multiple identical metal types. The first major work to appear by the new process was Gutenberg's 42-line Bible, printed in the German town of Mainz between 1450 and 1455. The first dated printed book was the Mainz Psalter of 1457. In the next two decades printing spread rapidly throughout Germany, Italy, France, the Low Countries, Poland, and Spain, almost exclusively through German printers, attracted by potential patronage and university markets. By the end of the 15th century presses were established in most of the countries of Europe (though Scotland continued to rely on French printers until 1508).

In 1476 printing was introduced into England by William Caxton. Caxton, a merchant who had lived in the Low Countries in 1471–72, had learned the printing business in Cologne, where he may have participated with Johannes Veldener in the publication of an edition of Bartholomaeus Anglicus's *De proprietatibus rerum.* Returning to Bruges, and perhaps having recruited Wynkyn de Worde as his assistant, Caxton established a press and printed two English books, *The Recuyell of the Historyes of Troye* (late 1473/early 1474) and *The Game of Chess* (1474), and four French editions. In 1476 he moved his press to England, to the precincts of (i.e., premises belonging to) Westminster Abbey.

Until his death in late 1491 or early 1492 Caxton remained the dominant publisher in England, producing around 100 editions, including a number of reprints. Most of these works were in English and they included many translations by Caxton himself and some by aristocratic writers. He catered primarily to an upper-class and wealthy merchant clientele, as his choice of texts reflects. He published courtly poets (Chaucer, Lydgate, Gower), chivalric romances (Malory's *Morte Darthur),* popular historical works *(Chronicles of England, Polychronicon),* a popular encyclopedia (*Mirror of the World*), moral and social handbooks, and popular religious works (*Golden Legend,* Mirk's *Festial*).

A press was established at Oxford around 1478 by Theoderic Rood of Cologne, issuing as its first book the *Expositio symboli (Exposition of the Creed)* of Rufinus, bearing the erroneous date 1468 in the colophon. The Oxford press remained active for about eight years, producing works that suggest incipient interest in humanism at the university. Similarly the first books produced at the St. Albans press, begun in 1479 or 1480, were school or university textbooks in Latin. These were followed by two English books, a version of the *Chronicles of England* and *The Boke of St. Albans* (1486), published by the "Schoolmaster-Printer."

In 1480 printing was brought to London by John Lettou, who soon formed a short-lived partnership with William de Machlinia, specializing in law books for a legal and mercantile market. Machlinia continued to print until at least 1486, expanding his list to include theological works, a plague treatise, schoolbooks, and an edition of the *Chronicles of England* (1486).

Richard Pynson began printing in London ca. 1490 and produced about 550 items before his death in 1530. The printing of legal material remained the financial base of his business, but he also printed many popular literary works, including a fine edition of the *Canterbury Tales,* works by Lydgate, *Dives and Pauper, Guy of Warwick,* and *Mandeville's Travels.* He also issued the plays of Terence, schoolbooks, grammars, and other scholarly and theological works. The missal that he printed in 1500 at the expense of Cardinal Morton is arguably the finest English book of the 15th century. In 1508 or 1509 he succeeded William Faques as royal printer, issuing government documents and in 1521 publishing Henry VIII's *Assertio septem sacramentorum (Defense of the Seven Sacraments),* an anti-Lutheran treatise that circulated widely in Europe during the years before Henry's own break with Rome (1534).

Contemporary with Pynson was Wynkyn de Worde, who inherited Caxton's business in Westminster in 1491 or 1492. He moved to London in 1500, motivated probably by a conscious commercial decision to appeal to a wider, noncourtly market. Many of de Worde's publications were popular in literary nature, but he also catered to clerical patrons and an ecclesiastical market. When Julyan Notary also moved his business to London, soon after de Worde, the capital became the undisputed center of printing and publishing in England.

Wynkyn de Worde's output was enormous—some 810 items by his death in 1535. The financial basis of his business was the schoolbook trade of grammars by traditional and modern writers, such as Donatus, Colet, Erasmus, and Whittinton. De Worde's publishing debt to Caxton was large: he printed Caxton's translation of the *Vitae patrum* about 1495 and reprinted many Caxton translations and editions (as well as works originally printed by Pynson and the Schoolmaster-Printer). He published previously unprinted works by Chaucer and Lydgate and a number of English prose works, including Hilton's *Scale of Perfection,* excerpts from *The Book of Margery Kempe,* and Trevisa's translation of *De proprietatibus rerum.*

With the notable exception of Caxton, printing in England was primarily in the hands of foreign-born printers, and books were also printed abroad for sale in England by stationers, many of whom were foreigners. Most of these books were Latin liturgical works, but in 1492 and 1493 Gerard de Leew published four English books at Antwerp, three of which were reprints of Caxton editions. An Act of Parliament of 1484, repealed only in 1534, allowed free access to the English market and unimpeded residence to alien printers and stationers. The result was to cripple printing in England temporarily; with the exception of Caxton's almost all first-generation English presses closed ca. 1486.

The impact of printing in England was not immediately apparent. Manuscripts and printed books supplemented one another, and dealers in one were often traders in the other also. Printing ultimately allowed a widespread dissemination of literature and knowledge, especially humanist knowledge, through multiple, essentially identical copies; it had a major effect in increasing literacy and education and in altering the relationship between author and audience. In Europe it encouraged the growth of the Reformation through translations of the scriptures and the production of propagandist tracts. The effects of printing on the English language were to support the rise of a written standard based on Chancery English, the standardized language of central government.

Lister M. Matheson

Bibliography

New *CBEL* 1:941–1006; Bennett, Henry S. *English Books and Readers, 1475–1557.* Cambridge: Cambridge University Press, 1952; Blake, N.F. "Wynkyn de Worde: The Early Years" and "Wynkyn de Worde: The Later Years." *Gutenberg Jahrbuch* (1971): 62–69 and (1972): 128–38; Blake, N.F. *Caxton: England's First Publisher.* London: Osprey, 1976; Bühler, Curt F. *The Fifteenth-Century Book: The Scribes, the Printers, the Decorators.* Philadelphia: University of Pennsylvania Press, 1960; Duff, E. Gordon. *The Printers, Stationers and Bookbinders of Westminster and London from 1476 to 1535.* Cambridge: Cambridge University Press, 1906. Repr. New York: Arno, 1977; Eisenstein, Elizabeth L. *The Printing Press as an Agent of Change: Communications and Cultural Transformations in Early-Modern Europe.* 2 vols. Cambridge: Cambridge University Press, 1979. Abr. and repr. as 1 vol., 1983; Febvre, Lucien, and Henri-Jean Martin. *The Coming of the Book: The Impact of Printing 1450–1800.* Trans. David Gerard. London: NLB, 1976; Heilbronner, Walter L. *Printing and the Book in Fifteenth-Century England: A Bibliographical Survey.* Charlottesville: Bibliographical Society, 1967; Hellinga, Lotte. *Caxton in Focus: The Beginning of Printing in England.* London: British Library, 1982.

See also Books; Caxton; Court Culture; Literacy; London; Schools; Translation; Universities; Westminster Abbey

Priories, Alien

A term used to describe small religious houses dependent on overseas abbeys. Founded mainly in England (with some examples in Ireland and Scotland) by Anglo-Norman families as thank offerings for the Norman Conquest and subsequent colonization, most were dependent on Norman abbeys, though abbeys elsewhere in northern France also benefited. The English dependencies of French Cluniac houses are also commonly included in this group. The foreign abbeys with the greatest number of English daughter houses were Bec-Hellouin, Fécamp, Marmoutier, St. Étienne at Caen, St. Nicholas at Angers (all Benedictine), and Fontevrault (Cluniac). These and other abbeys held not only priories but manors and rights of ecclesiastical patronage.

All the alien priories were small, with at best a handful of monks; it is not clear that they were ever particularly profitable to the French abbeys, the extensive lands of Bec perhaps excepted. Anglo-French warfare in the later Middle Ages resulted first in the coining of the term "alien priory" (in 1295) and then in the seizure of these houses into the king's hand, from Edward I's reign onward. The excuse for this was that these outposts of France were a security risk, and alien priories attracted unfavorable attention in parliament during periods of unsuccessful warfare, as in 1378.

Through the 14th century, however, the crown was often content to allow the French priors to administer their houses on payment of an annual "farm" (a rent) to the exchequer, though it always reserved their ecclesiastical patronage to itself. The annual sums to be paid by the priories' administrators ("farmers") to the exchequer were unrealistically high, and recruitment of new monks from France was prohibited. So from the later 14th century the larger houses applied for denization to become English houses, while many of the smaller ones were sold by their mother abbeys to Englishmen, who used them as endowments for new foundations of their own. Among the new foundations that benefited most were Winchester College; New College, Oxford; Eton College; King's College, Cambridge; and St. George's College, Windsor.

Alison K. McHardy

Bibliography

McHardy, Alison K. "The Alien Priories and the Expulsion of Aliens from England in 1378." *Studies in Church History* 12 (1975): 133–42; McHardy, Alison K. "The Effects of War on the Church: The Case of the Alien Priories in the Fourteenth Century." In *England and Her Neighbours 1066–1453: Essays in Honour of Pierre Chaplais,* ed. Michael Jones and Malcolm Vale. London: Hambledon, 1989, pp. 277–95; Matthew, Donald. *Norman Monasteries and Their English Possessions.* Oxford: Oxford University Press, 1962; Morgan, Marjorie. *The English Lands of the Abbey of Bec.* Oxford: Oxford University Press, 1946.

See also Eton; Hundred Years War; Monasticism; Schools; Universities

Prisons

Also called "gaols" (pronounced "jails"), prisons did not play as large a role in criminal justice in medieval times as now; other devices were more often used. To ensure appearance at trial sureties and bonds were employed, and to punish, judicial authorities resorted to execution, mutilation, and amercements (fines).

Nonetheless, examples of imprisonment for both purposes occur in Anglo-Saxon times; their continuous history can be traced from the 12th century on, and from the late 13th century, statutes multiply the occasions for penal imprisonment. Sentences were usually either for brief periods, typically a year, or for life. Incarceration was also used coercively, to compel performance of some act, especially payment of debt. From 1275 on, moreover, deliberately uncomfortable imprisonment—typically on bread and water (bread one day, water the next), and often including "pressing," that is, crushing under heavy objects—was used to coerce accused felons to agree to be tried by juries. This practice was known as *prison forte et dure,* later as *peine forte et dure.*

Physically a prison might be a separate, usually wooden building in a castle yard. More often it was a room in a larger building, often a castle. Gaol breaks were neither difficult nor uncommon. From 1166 on the sheriff of each county was required to maintain a prison for crown prisoners, but many other authorities had prisons: bishops, monasteries, private

lordships, boroughs, and lesser governmental units. Conditions of prisoners varied with the reasons for imprisonment and their wealth. At least for poorer prisoners gaols were crowded, dirty, frigid in winter, hot in summer. Disease, especially the lethal "gaol fever" (probably typhus), was endemic. Food, clothing, and other necessities usually had to be provided by the prisoners themselves, though charitable contributions sometimes aided the very poor; sheriffs and other gaolers were notoriously corrupt in exploiting their control of living conditions for purposes of extortion.

Emily Zack Tabuteau

Bibliography

Bellamy, John G. *Crime and Public Order in England in the Later Middle Ages.* London: Routledge & Kegan Paul, 1973 [esp. ch. 6]; Harding, Christopher, et al. *Imprisonment in England and Wales: A Concise History.* London: Croom Helm, 1985 [part I incorporates recent scholarship]; Morris, Norval, and David J. Rothman, eds. *The Oxford History of the Prison: The Practice of Punishment in Western Society.* Oxford: Oxford University Press, 1995; Pugh, Ralph B. *Imprisonment in Medieval England.* Cambridge: Cambridge University Press, 1968 [the fundamental work on the subject].

See also Juries; Law, Post-Conquest; Outlawry

Privy Seal

By the reign of John, if not earlier, the king had a small or privy seal available for the authentication of documents in addition to the royal (or great) seal in the custody of the chancellor. The privy seal was normally in the custody of officers of the king's chamber, a branch of the royal household, and so would be ever available to the king for administrative purposes. Thus there evolved a secretariat in the chamber, in addition to the more general household secretariat of the chancery, led by the chancellor. The privy seal, a single-faced seal bearing a shield of the royal arms, could be used for independent chamber administration or to communicate with the chancery to set in motion actions under the great seal.

During the minority of Henry III there was not, by lack of necessity, any privy seal; from 1230 a privy seal reappeared and its use continued to develop. In the 1230s the privy seal was established as the seal of the wardrobe, for a time the most important administrative department of the household, functioning as its financial and accounting department. The privy seal did not come to have major administrative significance, however, because the great seal was still sufficiently attached to the household to be available for the king's needs. At the same time the existence of the privy seal facilitated the slow separation of the great seal and chancery from the household to permanent headquarters at Westminster.

The Household Ordinance of 12 November 1279 notes that the chief officer of the wardrobe was the keeper, and next after him the controller, whose duties included keeping the privy seal, which caused him to function as private secretary to the king. The controller of the wardrobe was the only administrator keeping a royal seal and not under the chancellor's authority.

The place of the privy seal in royal administration was considerably enhanced in the reign of Edward I. He used the privy seal with increasing frequency to move the chancery and exchequer to action, as well as for correspondence of personal, diplomatic, or other sorts. The active employment of the privy seal to give expression to the royal will continued into the reign of Edward II. Its heavy use may explain why, in the Household Ordinance of York of 1318, custody of the privy seal is no longer the responsibility of the controller of the wardrobe but of a distinct individual, the clerk or keeper of the privy seal. A staff to handle the business of the privy seal had thus become a separate department in the wardrobe.

As the functions of the privy seal achieved a greater degree of formalism and tradition, an office of privy seal was gradually defined and set on the path toward evolving out of the household to permanent headquarters, as had been the case with the exchequer and chancery. Coincidental with this was the development of other authentic instruments to respond immediately to the king's will: the secret seal, the signet seal, and the royal sign-manual (the king's signature or initials). By 1360 the privy seal had separated from the household, and in the reign of Richard II it was solidly established at Westminster as a department of state, along with—though without the prestige of—the chancery and the exchequer. In separating from the household the seal did not lose administrative significance. The instruments it authenticated continued to be central to the initiation of administrative processes, and the keeper of the seal, both as head of his department and member of the king's council, was one of the most eminent officers of state in the late-medieval period. The privy seal was also used to give administrative action to decisions of the king's council, which did not obtain its own seal until 1556.

It was never the practice of the office of privy seal to enroll copies of outgoing letters, and thus the privy seal did not develop a substantial archive, as did the chancery. In the 15th century, however, the privy-seal clerk Thomas Hoccleve compiled a formulary of the types of documents commonly issued under the privy seal (BL Add. 24062).

A. Compton Reeves

Bibliography

Brown, A.L. "The Privy Seal Clerks in the Early Fifteenth Century." In *The Study of Medieval Records: Essays in Honour of Kathleen Major,* ed. D.A. Bullough and R.L. Storey. Oxford: Clarendon, 1971, pp. 260–81; Chrimes, Stanley B. *An Introduction to the Administrative History of Mediaeval England.* 3d ed. Oxford: Blackwell, 1966; Lyte, Henry Churchill Maxwell. *Historical Notes on the Use of the Great Seal of England.* London: HMSO, 1926; Tout, T.F. *Chapters in the Administrative History of Mediaeval England: The Wardrobe, the Chamber and the Small Seals.* 6 vols. Manchester: Manchester University Press, 1920–33.

See also Chancellor and Chancery; Great Seal; Hoccleve; Households, Royal and Baronial; Seals; Signet

Processions and Processional Music

Here "procession" implies a group with a particular membership and disposition, moving in a prescribed manner from one place to another, either within a larger ceremony or as an independent one. The concepts of hierarchy, minute regulation, and calculated display so characteristic of medieval thinking are implicit in this phenomenon. Medieval processions commonly served to enhance the solemnity of secular and sacred occasions; processional elements also touched medieval life in other ways, for instance in courtly conduct and culture. Resonances of processions are particularly evident in liturgical and vernacular drama. This article describes processions within the liturgy.

Although liturgical processions reached their greatest complexity only in the later Middle Ages, processions more or less formal in character had figured in Christian worship since time immemorial. The adoption of Christianity as the official religion of the Roman Empire encouraged the development of public ceremonial, and processions were increasingly utilized to show the prestige and dignity of the church. The liturgical processions of medieval England, like the liturgies to which they belonged, superimposed layers of local variation and innovation on a Romano-Frankish base; essentially similar to their continental counterparts, they nevertheless had many individual features.

Processions occurred on particular days in several liturgical contexts: before high mass, after Vespers, on certain special days, such as Palm Sunday, and for particular causes, such as the reception of a dignitary. The participants were usually disposed roughly as follows: virger, aquifer, crucifer(s), taperers, thurifer(s), subdeacon, deacon, officiating priest, choir members in pairs in ascending order of dignity, and finally the head of the establishment. Typically they wore silken copes over their other vestments. Minor processions also took place within services, for example during mass immediately before the Gospel.

Processions followed set routes, usually starting from the choir, moving through the church (and possibly other parts of the complex as well), making a halt or station before the Rood and ending in choir or wherever the next liturgical event was to occur. On Palm Sunday and other special days the procession was often longer and more elaborate, perhaps going outside the church, subdividing, making several stations, or visiting a neighboring church. During processions ritual actions, such as the sprinkling of altars, might be performed.

Ecclesiastical buildings were customarily designed with reference to the processions that would have to take place within them. This would, for instance, affect the width of aisles and doorways. Subsequent structural alterations could have interesting consequences, as when a church was extended over the ground where outdoor processions had been accustomed to pass. In such cases, if the proximity of the site boundary prevented the processional path being moved, a passage for the procession might be constructed below the new building. Examples of a north-south passage beneath the nave of a church survive at St. Peter, Mancroft, and St. Gregory, Norwich; and the church at Dedham, Essex, has a similar passage through the base of the tower at the west end. Conversely standard processional routes might have to be altered if the layout of a site was exceptional. At Canterbury Cathedral, for example, the unusual location of the cloister to the north of the church means that the usual sequence of left and right turns in processions would have had to be reversed.

The basic processional material consisted of responsories and antiphons existing elsewhere in the liturgy. If antiphons were sung during the outward progress, responsories were sung during the return, and vice versa. The return to the choir was often carried out to the singing of one of the popular Marian antiphons, such as *Ave regina caelorum* and *Alma redemptoris mater*. Prayers were said or sermons given at stations, and most processions ended with a versicle, response, and prayer. On some major festivals a prosa was sung, and on penitential occasions litanies were chanted. The survival of faburdens—melodies that formed the basis of simple improvised harmony—for many processional texts presumably reflects the practicalities of singing in procession. While the solemnity of a procession might encourage the singing of something more special than plainchant, the difficulties of walking while reading would discourage reliance upon notation. Improvised polyphony was an obvious and attractive solution. A large number of the faburden melodies that have come down to us are in fact associated with processional texts, for example the prosa *Salve festa dies*.

Until about 1300 the rubrics and chant for processions were normally included in the service books for office and mass. Thereafter this increasingly bulky and complicated material was usually given its own book, the processional. Contemporary inventories often listed much larger numbers of processionals than of other service books, emphasizing that a processional was essentially for individual use. Many processionals survive from English secular and monastic foundations; some seem to have been copied by amateurs, perhaps implying that choir members might be expected to provide copies for themselves. The Salisbury processional was printed several times, suggesting a constant and appreciable demand.

Nick Sandon

Bibliography

Bailey, Terence. *The Processions of Sarum and the Western Church.* Toronto: Pontifical Institute, 1971; Davison, Nigel. "So Which Way Round Did They Go? The Palm Sunday Procession at Salisbury." *Music and Letters* 61 (1980): 1–14; Huglo, Michel. "Processional." *NGD* 15:278–81; *Processionale ad Usum Sarum: Facsimile Edition of Richard Pynson's Printed Salisbury Processional of 1502.* Clifden, Co. Kilkenny: Boethius Press, 1980; Wordsworth, Christopher, ed. *Ceremonies and Processions of the Cathedral Church of Salisbury.* Cambridge: Cambridge University Press, 1901.

See also Antiphon; Faburden; Holy Week and Easter, Music for; Hymn; Salisbury, Use of

Prophecy Literature

Medieval prophecy literature in Britain was written in Latin, French, Welsh, and English; its concerns were sometimes primarily political, sometimes religious, and sometimes a mixture of both. Prophecies generally contained a certain amount of historical fact (usually presented as having been prophesied before the event) followed by predictions of the future; such predictions were often aimed, especially in secular prophecies, at shaping public opinion and interpretations of past and present events as well as influencing future events. The content of prophecy literature tends to be deliberately obscured or coded by the use of initials, anagrams, wordplay, symbols (animals, plants, astronomical objects), and other metaphoric devices requiring special knowledge to decipher. These codes frequently received various readings depending on when and by whom they were interpreted, and prophetic works were regularly modified to fit new political situations and actual events. Prophecies were taken sufficiently seriously by their audiences that they were occasionally prohibited by law or used as evidence of subversive activities; on the other hand some of them were respected enough to receive substantial explanatory commentaries.

In the political realm the most influential examples of the genre were the so-called "Galfridian" or Merlin prophecies, which originated in Geoffrey of Monmouth's *Prophetiae Merlini* (*Prophecies of Merlin;* found as book 7 of the *History of the Kings of Britain* and as a separate work), and characteristically used animal symbols for political figures. Related to the Galfridian type are versions of the "Six Kings" prophecy, which purports to predict the careers of the English kings after King John. In Wales secular prophetic literature usually emphasized the eventual regaining of control over Britain by the Welsh and was invoked in support of the political aspirations of such leaders as Owen Glendower and Henry Tudor.

A small but influential tradition is represented by a set of Latin and English prophecies attributed to Thomas Becket, and in some cases associated with a vial of sacred oil supposedly given to him by the Virgin Mary for the crowning of the "true" kings of England. Also significant are the prophecies on Scottish and northern English political history attributed to Thomas of Erceldoune, or Thomas the Rhymer, a 13th-century Scotsman later said to have gained prophetic insight by spending several years in fairyland, and prophecies on 14th-century English, French, and Scottish events, usually attributed to the Augustinian prior John of Bridlington (d. 1379).

Important religious prophecies in the Middle Ages included eschatological predictions concerning the end of the world and the coming of Antichrist, deriving from the Bible and from such early Christian works as the Sibylline prophecies of the late 4th century, the late-7th-century *Revelations* of Pseudo-Methodius, and the 10th-century *Libellus de Antichristo* of Adso of Montier-en-Der. Another major strand of religious prophecy, concerned with salvation history and the future of the church, originated in the work of the 12th-century abbot Joachim of Fiore. Joachim's followers developed his ideas into extreme forms that led to major politico-religious controversy over the next three centuries, especially on the Continent and often in connection with conflicts surrounding the mendicant orders. Though not solely eschatological in its origins, Joachimite prophecy lent itself well to conflation with older eschatological traditions, as well as to the secular political ends of some of Joachim's followers.

The vernacular literature of medieval England reflected these prophetic traditions both directly and indirectly. Prophecies of Merlin, Erceldoune, Bridlington, Becket, and others can be found in ME and sometimes in Anglo-Norman, as well as in Latin. Authors like William Langland, John Gower, or the writer of *Richard the Redeless* and *Mum and the Sothsegger* use Galfridian symbolism in their commentaries on political events of their own times, mainly in an interpretive rather than a prophetic mode; Adam Davy's *Five Dreams* combines political and religious prophecies about Edward II. The direct influence of Joachimite prophecy on English vernacular literature is relatively minor, but it contributes obliquely to the eschatological imagery of much antimendicant satire. In contrast predictions about Antichrist and the end of the world appear in a wide range of works, from *The Fifteen Signs before Doomsday* and the Chester *Coming of Antichrist* play to allegories like *Piers Plowman* and such didactic works as *Cursor Mundi* and *The Prick of Conscience*.

M. Teresa Tavormina

Bibliography

PRIMARY

Murray, J.A.H., ed. *The Romance and Prophecies of Thomas of Erceldoune.* EETS o.s. 61. London: Trübner, 1875; Thorpe, Lewis, trans. *Geoffrey of Monmouth: The History of the Kings of Britain.* Harmondsworth: Penguin, 1966, pp. 170–85 [prophecies of Merlin].

SECONDARY

Manual 5:1516–36, 1714–25; Allan, Alison. "Yorkist Propaganda: Pedigree, Prophecy and the 'British History' in the Reign of Edward IV." In *Patronage, Pedigree and Power in Later Medieval England,* ed. Charles Ross. London: Sutton, 1979, pp. 171–92; Emmerson, Richard Kenneth. *Antichrist in the Middle Ages: A Study of Medieval Apocalypticism, Art, and Literature.* Seattle: University of Washington Press, 1981; Heist, William A. *The Fifteen Signs before Doomsday.* East Lansing: Michigan State College Press, 1952; Kerby-Fulton, Kathryn. *Reformist Apocalypticism and Piers Plowman.* Cambridge: Cambridge University Press, 1990; Reeves, Marjorie. *The Influence of Prophecy in the Later Middle Ages: A Study in Joachimism.* Oxford: Clarendon, 1969; Taylor, Rupert. *The Political Prophecy in England.* New York: Columbia University Press, 1911.

See also Adso; *Cursor Mundi;* Davy; Friars; Geoffrey of Monmouth; Gower; *Piers Plowman; Prick of Conscience; Richard the Redeless;* Satire

Prose, Middle English

When William the Conqueror invaded England in 1066, there was a flourishing prose tradition in OE, principally in historical and didactic writing. In the former category the major work was the Anglo-Saxon Chronicle, initiated by Alfred and carried on at various monastic houses. In the latter category are sermons and saints' lives, of which Ælfric had been the foremost composer. It is hardly surprising that after the Norman Conquest it was historical and didactic writing that continued to flourish in English.

Historiography

The Anglo-Saxon Chronicle was continued in the version known today as the Peterborough Chronicle. Found in a 12th-century manuscript from Peterborough, this chronicle extends a copy of the Anglo-Saxon Chronicle with entries up to 1154, a continuation that lasted almost 100 years after the Conquest. This continuation consists of several parts, of which the First Continuation, written in blocks from 1122 to 1131, and the Final Continuation (1131–54) were certainly written at Peterborough. Although the Peterborough Chronicle usually keeps the annalistic approach of the Anglo-Saxon Chronicle, some entries for a given year stretch forward or backward in time to present small narratives not unlike the Cynewulf and Cyneheard narrative of the earlier Chronicle.

The Peterborough Chronicle is a major historical source for its period, even though that period also witnessed the rise of the great Anglo-Latin historical tradition, including such writers as Henry of Huntingdon and Orderic Vitalis. But it has the great advantage over them of being written more or less contemporaneously with the events it describes. Equally important, the Peterborough Chronicle provides the earliest example of the East Midland dialect in ME and illustrates how the language was changing from OE to ME.

After 1154 historical writing in English became principally latinate until the 14th century, when Trevisa translated Higden's *Polychronicon* and an anonymous translator produced his version of the Anglo-Norman *Brut.* These two texts provided the springboard for historical writing in English in the 15th century, writing that often took the form of continuations to the ME prose *Brut,* though new historical texts, such as Capgrave's *Chronicle* and various London chronicles, were also written. However, no English history in the later Middle Ages has the same historical and literary value as the Peterborough Chronicle; this is partly because the later ones all had Latin competitors and partly because, having arisen as translations, they rarely achieved the effective narrative style found in the Peterborough Chronicle.

Homilies and Saints' Lives

There was continuity also in the homiletic tradition from OE to ME. Many of Ælfric's works were copied up to the 12th century; the 12th-century homilies in Bodleian Library, Bodley 343, may be copies of OE homilies no longer extant or they may have been composed in the 12th century in imitation of the Anglo-Saxon tradition. Many of them are written in the West Saxon literary language found in the pre-Conquest period or at least an approximation of it. In the OE period there had also been a strong literary tradition in the Kentish dialect, and some early ME sermons continue that tradition, particularly the collections of sermons known as the Cotton Vespasian Homilies and the Trinity Homilies. These collections also probably date from the 12th century. It is, however, principally in the west Midlands that the Anglo-Saxon homiletic tradition survives most strongly, and this may be due to the long episcopacy (1062–95) of Wulfstan of Worcester and to the distance of places like Worcester from the main areas of French influence. After Wulfstan's death his biography was written in English by Coleman, a monk of Worcester, but this text has not survived. Its composition testifies to the strength and continuity of the native tradition in the west. A particularly important collection, the Lambeth Homilies of the late 12th century, represents a late flowering of the OE tradition before the influence of French begins to be felt, though many of the sermons have little literary value.

After the 12th century the homiletic tradition continues with the texts associated with *Ancrene Wisse,* although most sermons and saints' lives from this time were written in Latin and French and were only gradually translated into English. Increasingly sermons were gathered into collections, often linked with the festivals of the church. Such collections were not stable, in that writers would add sermons or saints' lives that had local relevance or importance and they could omit others. In their English form they could be in verse or prose. The two major prose collections of the latter ME period were the *Festial* by John Mirk and the ME translations of the *Legenda aurea.* Mirk was an Augustinian canon of Lilleshall (Shropshire) writing in the late 14th and early 15th centuries, whose *Festial* is a collection of sermons for all the feasts of the church's calendar. Intended for the edification of the clergy, they had an educative and populist aim and provided the parish priest with ready-to-use sermons. The collection was immensely popular: it was constantly copied and adapted, and it was the first English sermon collection to be printed.

The *Legenda aurea* (or *Golden Legend*) was a collection of sermons in Latin written ca. 1263–67 by Jacobus de Voragine, a Dominican friar and archbishop of Genoa (1292–98). This work was a legendary, a collection of saints' lives, which also became popular and was translated into most European languages. Two English translations were made in the 15th century, and the second (by Caxton) was printed. Mirk's *Festial* and Caxton's *Golden Legend* may stand as prose examples of the sermons and saints' lives current in the later ME period. Direct, dramatic, and with a good story line, they were both popular and influential.

Devotional and Mystical Writing

Although the influence of Latin and French grew in the 13th century, the needs of educating the illiterate and barely literate encouraged the writing of books in English. The reforms of the Fourth Lateran Council (1215) spurred this development, as did the growth of religious houses for women, who often required devotional material in English. This latter need became linked with the west Midlands homiletic tradition to produce

the texts associated with the *Ancrene Wisse,* which in their turn promoted the growth of a more mystical approach to Christianity. *Ancrene Wisse* is a guide for anchoresses written in the early 13th century, though in later copies the audience undergoes some change. It is characterized by a sensitive and humane approach to the life that the anchoresses will follow. The associated texts include legends of three female saints (Katherine, Margaret, and Juliana), a treatise on virginity (*Hali Meiðhad*), and a didactic prose homily (*Sawles Warde*). Most of these texts are based on Latin sources. Linked to them is the so-called Wooing Group, a series of texts that are more like lyrical prayers of an affective nature than like homilies. They illustrate the growth of mysticism in England and the influence of St. Bernard's devotion to the Passion of Christ and to the Virgin Mary.

It is likely that such texts were intended for a restricted audience, as were the mystical works written in the 14th and 15th centuries. These works were often written to direct the spiritual life of a disciple, whether male or female, or to provide a rule for a community. The growth of more strictly enclosed orders like the Carthusians and of specialized orders like the Brigettines facilitated the production and dissemination of works of this type. Richard Rolle (d. 1349) wrote many works of a devotional nature in which the sweetness of Christ and his name are dominant. Written in the northern dialect, his works are rhetorical and emotional in their impact. Although offering advice to his disciples, Rolle describes his own spiritual experiences.

Most subsequent English mystical writers were more discreet in their approach than Rolle. Walter Hilton and the author of *The Cloud of Unknowing* composed treatises to guide their disciples, but their advice is cautious and restrained, and the language in which they write is measured and thoughtful. The *Revelations* of Julian of Norwich are different again, for they describe a series of revelations she experienced in 1373, which she passed on for the benefit of her fellow Christians. The one mystic to go against this trend toward greater discretion is Margery Kempe, the daughter of the mayor of King's Lynn, whose mysticism has often been considered hysterical (though recent criticism suggests alternative characterizations of her spirituality). *The Book of Margery Kempe* describes her mystical and social progression, sometimes in a passionate language. A proper examination of her spirituality remains to be made. Although didactic and sermon literature continued to be written at this time, the glory of later ME prose is undoubtedly the writings of the mystics. They achieve a balance between content and expression, between instruction and affective description, that other texts could not emulate.

Other Prose Works

Although in Anglo-Saxon England some parts of scripture had been glossed and translated, there was no translation of the whole Bible. A project to undertake a translation of the Bible was launched at the end of the 14th century and is linked with the name of the Oxford scholar John Wyclif (d. 1384). Wyclif wrote and inspired many sermons and treatises attacking clerical and papal abuses, works eventually condemned as heretical. The translation of the Bible also fell under archiepiscopal interdict, because it was associated with the Lollards and their campaign against the clergy. However, the translation was completed in two versions that survive today. The English writings attributed to Wyclif were aimed at less educated people (though one should not think of this audience as uneducated), and their style is relatively simple and direct. Wyclif's intent was to teach and to persuade, and the Lollards (also called Wycliffites) continued to produce works with similar goals well into the 15th century. Although the precise attribution of extant prose writings said to be by Wyclif remains problematical, the influence of these writings on English style and the English language should not be underestimated despite the fact that many have been lost and all were proscribed.

Although there had been a few romancelike works in OE, such as *Apollonius of Tyre,* they ceased entirely in early ME. When romances were reintroduced in the 13th century, they were first written in verse; only gradually did prose versions arise. Sometimes these were translated from the ME verse forms, sometimes they were translated directly from French originals, and finally some were written directly in English prose. The most famous example is Malory's *Morte Darthur,* most of which is translated from French although one episode is a prose version of the alliterative *Morte Arthure.* Most other ME prose romances share with the *Morte Darthur* a date in the second half of the 15th century, as well as great length. There can be little doubt that this prose genre was popularized by Caxton, England's first printer and publisher. He translated many romances from French and printed them. They must have circulated widely and helped to drive the poetic versions out of circulation. Although the critical literature on Malory is extensive, little has been written about the other prose romances. Many of them are courtly in nature, though it may well be that we should extend the genre to include more popular works like *Reynard the Fox* from the beast-epic tradition and *Mandeville's Travels,* a fictional travel book that has many romance features. It is certainly possible to see in these works the seeds of the future novel.

It should not be forgotten that particularly in the later ME period works of scientific or technical interest were also written. Latin was confined to a certain class, and as English became more established as a literary language, it began to be used to meet a growing demand for informational works. Chaucer himself wrote a treatise on the astrolabe and may have written *The Equatorie of the Planetis.* Recipes, charms, prognostications, cookery books, medical works, books of etiquette, and other treatises were all produced. Even theology could be written in English, as the writings of Bishop Pecock reveal, although there was always the inherent danger that such works might be declared heretical. More academic works, such as Sir John Fortescue's writings on law and political theory, are more characteristic of the end of our period.

In ME studies prose tends to attract less attention than poetry. Compared with Latin and even French, the output was not great; but it was uninterrupted and it continued to grow in quantity. By the end of the ME period prose works in English were common enough and set fair to increase their share of what was written.

N.F. Blake

Bibliography

PRIMARY

Bennett, J.A.W., and G.V. Smithers, eds. *Early Middle English Verse and Prose.* 2d corr. ed. Oxford: Clarendon, 1974; Blake, N.F., ed. *Middle English Religious Prose.* London: Arnold, 1972; Gray, Douglas, ed. *The Oxford Book of Late Medieval Verse and Prose.* Oxford: Clarendon, 1985.

SECONDARY

Edwards, A.S.G., ed. *Middle English Prose: A Critical Guide to Major Authors and Genres.* New Brunswick: Rutgers University Press, 1984 [the most important research tool for ME prose; survey chapters with full bibliographies]; Gordon, Ian. *The Movement of English Prose.* London: Longmans, 1966; Krapp, George Philip. *The Rise of English Literary Prose.* London: Oxford University Press, 1915; Lewis, Robert E., et al. *Index of Printed Middle English Prose.* New York: Garland, 1985.

See also Chronicles; Hagiography; Moral and Religious Instruction; Mystical and Devotional Writings; Scientific and Medical Writings; Sermons; Translation; Utilitarian Writings; Wycliffite Texts

Prostitution

Evidence relating to prostitution in the Middle Ages derives from religious, medical, and legal sources, of which much survives from the 13th century and later. Whereas medieval theologians unanimously rejected prostitution on moral grounds, they nonetheless recognized that prostitutes provided vital sexual services.

The prostitute's sin was the sin of lust *(luxuria),* but inasmuch as she turned herself into a "common woman" she protected other, "honest" women. Were it not for prostitutes, the clergy, scholars, young artisans, and widowers might menace, seduce, and even rape other men's wives, sisters, and daughters. The attitude followed the idea expressed by Augustine: "If you expel prostitutes from society, prostitution will spread everywhere . . . the prostitutes in towns are like sewers in a palace."

Since medical and theological lore saw women as lustful by nature, prostitution, an expression of excessive sensuousness in a woman, was a manifestation of a feminine quality; her feigning of love and desire was only an extreme form of what was presented in misogynistic literature as the wily and deceitful behavior of all women. Thus a deep ambivalence surrounded the discussion, as well as the treatment, of prostitutes. She was at once sinner, wage earner, neighbor, figure of fun at fairs and carnivals, and source of constant revenue for tenement landlords and town treasurers; she was also vulnerable. Following the scriptural example, prostitutes were sometimes offered the road of penance, and a path to reintegration into "respectable" society, with the aid of philanthropic bodies, such as the charitable "Magdalene" houses.

The ambivalence engendered in the religious sphere, stemming from deep anxieties about sexuality, was carried over into the legal discussion of prostitution. Treatment of such issues as a prostitute's property rights raised a variety of legal opinions but produced by the late 12th century consensus regarding her right to enjoy her earnings, the just reward for her work. Some canon lawyers even regarded the alms given to the church from a prostitute's earnings to be acceptable.

Town authorities attempted to regulate the transaction between prostitute and client, and between prostitute and brothel keeper, to ensure that neither side was defrauded or forced to participate against his or her will. The 15th-century statutes of Sandwich stipulated the price brothel keepers could charge prostitutes for ale, and in Southwark fines were ordained for overzealous seizures of prospective clients off the street. Although regulated similarly to other urban trades, prostitution condemned a woman in many ways to a social "death"; she could neither sue nor attest in a court, nor in some cases inherit property. Legislation attempted to protect the prostitute against violence and rape.

Thus in villages and towns alike, under seigneurial gaze or the control of town fathers, attempts were made to regulate prostitution, to keep it away from respectable quarters, to limit soliciting in the streets, and to protect both clients and prostitutes. Some cities, like London, had a "red light" district; others had regulated brothels, like the baths of Southwark.

Regulation also produced a steady flow of income to urban and seigneurial coffers, from frequent fining of prostitutes and of brothel keepers, a practice tantamount to taxation or licensing for prostitution and procuring. There is evidence from 15th-century York to suggest that in periods of economic stagnation and contraction in the labor market, more single women may have been forced into prostitution. Prostitutes were part of the life of every community, albeit in a marginal position, and changes in their status, earning capacity, and security reflect general patterns in the social and cultural trends that affected the life and work of women in general.

Miri Rubin

Bibliography

Brundage, James A. "Prostitution in Medieval Canon Law." *Signs* 1 (1976): 825–45; Bullough, Vern L. "The Prostitute in the Middle Ages." *Studies in Medieval Culture* 10 (1977): 9–17; Karras, Ruth Mazo. *Common Women: Prostitution and Sexuality in Medieval England.* Oxford: Oxford University Press, 1996; Rossiaud, Jacques. *Medieval Prostitution.* Trans. L.G. Cochrane. Oxford: Blackwell, 1988.

See also Towns; Women

Prudentius (348–ca. 410)

Latin poet from Spain. After a career in the civil service, Prudentius began writing poetry; he is the author of *Cathemerinon* (a collection of hymns for daily use), *Apotheosis* (an argument for the divinity of Christ directed at the pagans and certain heretics), *Hamartigenia* (a discussion of the origin of evil and sin in this world), *Psychomachia* (an allegory portray-

ing the fight of the seven vices against the seven virtues), *Contra Symmachum* (an attack against Symmachus's efforts to revive the Roman pagan religion), *Peristephanon* (a series of poems in praise of various martyrs), and *Dittochaeon* (a series of short poems pairing events of the Old Testament with events of the New Testament).

All of his works were available to the Anglo-Saxons, as the extant manuscripts as well as echoes and quotations in Aldhelm, Bede, and Alcuin show. Though the extant manuscripts contain Latin glosses for all but the *Apotheosis* and the *Dittochaeon,* there can be little doubt that the work the Anglo-Saxons studied most intensively was the *Psychomachia,* since it is extant in ten manuscripts, seven of which are heavily glossed in Latin. Four *Psychomachia* texts are illustrated, indicating a more than usual interest in that particular text.

Prudentius's works were influential on the Latin poems produced by the Anglo-Saxons; his influence on the OE works, however, is less certain, since there are no verbal parallels. Nonetheless, passages in *Christ II, Juliana, The Phoenix,* and the poetic *Solomon and Saturn* leave no doubt that OE poets were familiar with psychomachia allegory, though it has not been decided yet whether Prudentius's *Psychomachia* is the ultimate source for the images used in the OE poems.

Gernot R. Wieland

Bibliography

PRIMARY

Thomson, H. J., ed. and trans. *Prudentius.* 2 vols. Loeb Classical Library. Cambridge: Harvard University Press, 1949–53.

SECONDARY

Hermann, John P. "Some Varieties of Psychomachia in Old English." *American Benedictine Review* 34 (1983): 74–86, 188–222; Irvine, Martin. "Cynewulf's Use of Psychomachia Allegory: The Latin Sources of Some 'Interpolated' Passages." In *Allegory, Myth and Symbol,* ed. Morton W. Bloomfield. Cambridge: Harvard University Press, 1981, pp. 39–62; Wieland, Gernot R. "Aldhelm's *De octo vitiis principalibus* and Prudentius' *Psychomachia.*" *MÆ* 55 (1986): 85–92.

See also Allegory; Anglo-Latin Literature to 1066; Literary Influences: Medieval Latin; Virtues and Vices, Books of

Psalters, Anglo-Saxon

The biblical book of Psalms, commonly known as the Psalter, was one of the most frequently illustrated books of the Middle Ages, its poetic text inspiring many pictorial approaches. Psalters from Anglo-Saxon England preserve examples of many of these types, providing the most generous and coherent body of psalter illustration to survive from the early Middle Ages. Within it we can trace indigenous traditions, adaptations of continental and Byzantine traditions, and new syntheses. The manuscripts are also frequently witnesses to the much admired originality of the Anglo-Saxon monastic artists who produced them.

The Irish world furnished a tradition for symbolic and typological picture programs expressing overall perceptions of the Psalter and used to articulate the major functional divisions of the book. This tradition was first adapted in Anglo-Saxon England when full-page miniatures were inserted in the Carolingian Galba Psalter (BL Cotton Galba A.xviii; fig. 66: see GALBA PSALTER) at the threefold psalter division and important points in the prefatory texts: its continuing influence can be seen in several 11th-century manuscripts. In the Winchcombe Psalter (CUL Ff.1.23) four miniatures mark the psalms of the threefold division, 1, 51, and 101, plus the most important psalm of the liturgical psalter division, Psalm 109. Similar articulation occurs in the Tiberius Psalter (BL Cotton Tiberius C.vi) and the Werden Psalter (Berlin, Preuss. Kulturbes., theol. lat. fol. 258), a mid-11th-century German manuscript that reflects in part an Anglo-Saxon psalter. Demonstrating the intermingling of illustrative traditions, the latter three psalters also incorporate within their picture programs adaptations of a continental European tradition of psalter frontispieces based on the common psalter preface *Origo psalmorum* and portraying David as the regal psalmist surrounded by the co-psalmists named in the text.

Drawing on indigenous ornamental traditions, the early-10th-century Junius Psalter (Bodl. Junius 27) is decorated at every psalm with twining initials of foliage and snapping beasts. Similar initials are found in the mutilated Salisbury Psalter (Salisbury, Cathedral Library 150). The Junius Psalter also has a single historiated initial depicting David fighting the lion (fig. 105), one of the few such initials preserved in Anglo-Saxon psalters. BL Arundel 155 contains an initial with David fighting Goliath, and the Crowland Psalter (Bodl. Douce 296) one with St. Michael fighting a dragon: not until the Romanesque St. Albans Psalter (Hildesheim, St. Godehard) do we find a full cycle of historiated initials in an English psalter, though the evidence of the Werden Psalter initials and those of the earlier insular Vespasian Psalter (BL Cotton Vespasian A.i) suggests that this is an accident of survival.

Of continental psalter traditions adapted in Anglo-Saxon England perhaps the most pervasive is that of the Carolingian Utrecht Psalter, which was in England in the Middle Ages. Many of the drawings accompanying each psalm of this 9th-century masterwork were meticulously copied in the 11th-century BL Harley 603 Psalter (fig. 71: see HARLEY PSALTER), the only concession to Anglo-Saxon taste being the substitution of colored inks for the brown of the exemplar. However, several artists worked on the Harley Psalter over many decades, and some were extraordinarily creative, abandoning the Carolingian iconography or incorporating imagery from other pictorial traditions, besides references to contemporary thought. In addition it seems possible that beyond the Utrecht manuscript itself Anglo-Saxon artists knew a psalter with interlinear illustrations from the Utrecht Psalter tradition (Harris, 1963). Reflections are found in the few interlinear illustrations of Paris, BN lat. 8824 (a psalter manuscript that also once contained miniatures at its major divisions); and in the Bury St. Edmunds Psalter (Vatican, Biblioteca Apostolica Reg. lat. 12). The latter, probably executed at Canterbury about 1050, has an extensive cycle

Fig. 105. Junius Psalter (Bodl. Junius 27), fol. 118, Psalm 109: David and the Lion. Reproduced by permission of the Bodleian Library, University of Oxford.

of dynamic marginal drawings of superb quality, in which Anglo-Saxon erudition, inventiveness, and artistic skill are developed to a high degree.

Anglo-Saxon synthesis of Franco-Saxon letter forms and "Winchester School" ornament yielded the great letter B introducing Psalm 1 in the late-10th-century Ramsey Psalter (BL Harley 2904); succeeding psalters influenced by this *Beatus* initial include BL Arundel 155, Stowe 2, and the Tiberius Psalter, with the tradition enduring through the Romanesque period. The Harley 2904 Psalter also contains a full-page Crucifixion drawing of extraordinary pathos. The earliest surviving example of the tinted line drawing that became a prominent medium in late Anglo-Saxon manuscripts, this picture is innovative iconographically and is in addition just one pictorial manifestation of a pronounced insular emphasis on christological interpretations of the Psalter. The programs of the Winchcombe, Galba, Werden, and Tiberius psalters all reflect this emphasis.

Several approaches to illustration of the Psalter were combined in the late Anglo-Saxon Tiberius Psalter (fig. 139: see TIBERIUS PSALTER), yielding in the process a new kind of psalter illustration: this psalter is known as the first to contain a prefatory picture cycle of Old and New Testament miniatures. Typologically related David and Christ picture sequences, fusing Byzantine and insular traditions, are framed by images of the Creation and Christ the Judge, and the extensive picture cycle expresses themes appropriate for the psalter's use in the private devotions of a monastic owner: coincidentally it inaugurated one of the major later medieval systems of psalter decoration.

Kathleen M. Openshaw

Bibliography

Backhouse, Janet. "The Making of the Harley Psalter." *British Library Journal* 10 (1984): 97–113; Dufrenne, Suzy. "Les copies anglaises du Psautier d'Utrecht." *Scriptorium* 18 (1964): 185–97; Gameson, Richard. "The Anglo-Saxon Artists of the Harley 603 Psalter." *JBAA* 143 (1990): 29–48; Gneuss, Helmut. "Liturgical Books in Anglo-Saxon England and Their Old English Terminology." In *Learning and Literature in Anglo-Saxon England: Studies Presented to Peter Clemoes,* ed. Michael Lapidge and Helmut Gneuss. Cambridge: Cambridge University Press, 1985, pp. 91–141; Harris, Robert M. "The Marginal Drawings of the Bury St. Edmund's Psalter." Ph.D. diss., Princeton Univ., Univ. Micro-films, 1960; Harris, Robert M. "An Illustration of an Anglo-Saxon Psalter in Paris." *JWCI* 26 (1963): 255–63; Heimann, Adelheid. "Three Illustrations from the Bury St. Edmunds Psalter and Their Prototypes." *JWCI* 29 (1966): 39–59; McLachlan, Elizabeth. "The Athelstan Psalter and the Gallican Connection." *Proceedings of the Third Annual Canadian Conference of Medieval Art Historians* (1982): 21–27; Ohlgren, Thomas H. "The Battle between Christ and Satan in the Tiberius Psalter." *JWCI* 52 (1989): 14–33; Ohlgren, Thomas H. *Anglo-Saxon Textual Illustration: Photographs of Sixteen Manuscripts with Descriptions and Index.* Kalamazoo: Medieval Institute, 1992; Openshaw, Kathleen M. "The Symbolic Illustration of the Psalter: An Insular Tradition." *Arte Medievale* 2, ser. 6 (1992): 41–60; Openshaw, Kathleen M. "Weapons in the Daily Battle: Images of the Conquest of Evil in the Early Medieval Psalter." *Art Bulletin* 75 (1993): 17–38; Temple, Elżbieta. *Anglo-Saxon Manuscripts 900–1066.* A Survey of Manuscripts Illuminated in the British Isles 2, ed. J.J.G. Alexander. London: Harvey Miller, 1976; Wormald, Francis. "An English Eleventh-Century Psalter with Pictures." *Walpole Society* 38 (1960–62): 1–13. Repr. in *Francis Wormald: Collected Writings,* ed. Jonathan J.G. Alexander, T. Julian Brown, and Joan Gibbs. Vol. 1. London: Harvey Miller, 1984, pp. 123–37.

See also Galba Psalter; Harley Psalter; Psalters, Gothic; St. Albans Psalter; Tiberius Psalter; "Winchester School"

Psalters, Gothic

From the early Gothic period (ca. 1210–20) until the mid- to late 14th century, when it began to be superseded by the book of hours, the Psalter remained the most popular devotional text to receive lavish and extensive illustration. Although it has been suggested that the Psalter's popularity was due in part to a more literate society, with few exceptions only eminent ecclesiastics, religious communities, or members of the aristocracy were able to commission a richly ornamented psalter text during the greater part of the period.

As an office book, either for private devotions or for use in the church, a psalter was divided into sections corresponding to the canonical hours. Psalms 1, 26, 38, 52, 68, 80 (the first psalm said at Matins each day of the week), and 109 (the first psalm of Sunday Vespers) are distinguished by having larger and more elaborate initials, historiated with scenes derived from the psalm itself or more commonly, in English psalters, from Old Testament iconography. Psalms 51 and 101 are often also historiated, a throwback to an earlier tradition in which the Psalter was divided into three principal parts; but these initials are normally smaller in scale than those for the other main psalm divisions.

The Psalter usually contains additional material, such as a calendar, litany, canticles, the office of the dead, and further prayers. The tendency to illustrate the opening words of each major psalm in literal form (e.g., *Dominus illuminatio mea,* the opening words of Psalm 26, having King David supplicating before God and pointing to his eye) is a convention derived from France and one that became increasingly standard in English psalters from the late 13th century onward. Up until the onset of French influence, around 1270, English psalter illustration mostly had subjects distinct from contemporary French manuscripts, such as the Anointing of David at Psalm 26 (see Amesbury Psalter [Oxford, All Souls College 6]).

The English Gothic psalter does not lend itself to generalizations; there is considerable variability throughout the period, with regard to both iconography and decoration. A number of examples—predominantly those of the early 13th century— have a set of miniatures prefacing the psalter text and interspersed among the psalms, a notable example being the Munich Psalter of ca. 1200–10, which has 46 full-page miniatures before the text and further picture sections after Psalms 51, 100, 108, and 150, illustrating scenes from the Old and New Testaments. This approach can be largely contrasted with the procedure followed from the mid-13th century of reducing the length of the cycle (Queen Mary's Psalter is an obvious exception, having an extensive set of prefatory miniatures), and the initials then become more of a focus for the iconography. The Cuerden Psalter of ca. 1270 retains a prefatory cycle of miniatures, though diminished in number to eight, and the Peterborough Psalter in Brussels of ca. 1300–10 is unusual among 14th-century examples in having full-page miniatures interspersed at various points within the psalter text, as in the Munich Psalter. (Shelf marks for the psalters discussed here and below appear at the end of the entry in the order in which they are discussed.)

From the mid-13th century a further important development occurs, first evident in the group of manuscripts associated with the de Brailes workshop (as in the Oxford, New College Psalter of ca. 1240–60), in which the foliate elements comprising the letter forms of the historiated initials erupt and extend into the margins, a tendency that is developed in the William of Devon group of manuscripts (as in the Cuerden Psalter; fig. 51: see CUERDEN PSALTER), where the rectilinear border elements provide platforms for a variety of birds and hybrids (also referred to as grotesques or drolleries). The Rutland Psalter of ca. 1260 is probably the earliest 13th-century manuscript to contain hybrids. From around 1270 marginal decoration becomes a significant element in the ornamentation of the page, reaching a height of development in the products of the "East Anglian School" of approximately the first third of the 14th century (as in the Gorleston, Howard, Ormesby, and Luttrell psalters; figs. 57, 102, and 93: see "East Anglian School," Ormesby Psalter, and Marginalia).

Although the marginal decoration is almost invariably extraneous to the text—as in the Ormesby Psalter, which is rich in animal and plant motifs as well as grotesques—there is a notable exception in the St. Omer Psalter of ca. 1340, produced toward the end of the Psalter's period of outstanding popularity. Here subject matter (an Old and New Testament cycle) is contained within the foliage roundels of the borders. These are in turn further ornamented with charming quotations from rural life. Another variation is provided by the way in which the marginal themes are handled in the Luttrell Psalter, also of ca. 1340, comprising *bas-de-page* (lower-margin) scenes of New Testament subjects and scenes from rural life, while the other margins testify to an extraordinary repertoire of grotesques unequaled in their inventiveness. In the Tickhill Psalter (fig. 106), where the initials are enlarged, a sequential narrative extends from the initials into the lower margins; and an elaborate series of *bas-de-page* scenes can be found in Queen Mary's Psalter (fig. 107: see Queen Mary's Psalter). During the last great flowering of the Psalter three psalters commissioned by the Bohun family (now in the Nationalbibliothek in Vienna, the British Library, and Exeter College, Oxford) are exceptional in that every initial, not only those singled out for special decoration at the major psalm divisions, becomes a vehicle for the narrative, underscoring the variety of approach characteristic of English psalter illumination. Standardization in format and iconographic content does not establish itself in England until the end of the 14th century and into the 15th, by which date the most popular service book is no longer the psalter but the book of hours.

In the late 14th century the psalter as a richly decorated text is almost always found as one element of a psalter-hours, as in two Bohun books, BL Egerton 3277 (ca. 1385) and Edinburgh, National Library of Scotland Advocates' 18.6.5 (ca. 1390). An example from the 15th century is the Bedford Psalter-Hours of after 1415. The decline in psalter production in the 15th century cannot be attributed solely to the rise in popularity of the book of hours but may also be due to the number already in circulation from the earlier Gothic period.

While for the 13th century it has been observed that certain groups of artists seem to have specialized in psalter illustration (the Munich, Lansdowne, and Glazier groups), it is not possible to draw such clear-cut conclusions for the 14th century, except that, judging from extant examples, psalters were the most popular books produced by the majority of workshops, the Walter de Milemete group forming a major exception. In the 13th century there appear to have been two main methods of working, the more common being that of a single illuminator who was concerned with all aspects of a book's decoration, and the other—evident in the Sarum and William of Devon groups—that of a division of labor between the major and minor aspects of the decoration. There are instances of both methods in the 14th century, as well as the practice adopted in the case of the central Queen Mary and principal Bohun workshops, in which two artists operate in partnership, dividing the labor on a more democratic basis.

The 13th century was dominated by two principal stylistic phases—the one, early Gothic, evolving away from the classicizing trend of ca. 1200, manifested in the Munich Psalter group, in which there is emphasis on linear drapery patterns and troughed folds. This first phase culminated in the elegant, monumental figure types of the Sarum Master, as epitomized in the Amesbury Psalter (fig. 2: see Amesbury Psalter). Also evolving from the style of the Munich/Huntingfield Psalter group, though following a different path of development, is that of the William de Brailes workshop, where the emphasis is on more abbreviated figure forms in order to accommodate strong narrative elements. The other main trend in 13th-century illumination was dominated by French influence, resulting in a strong linear style, where chalky white faces are etched with calligraphic flourishes for the features and the draperies are rendered in flat areas of color with sparse black lines for the folds, as in the Cuerden Psalter. For the period of the 14th century when the Psalter was still the most popular devotional text, two main stylistic trends again dominate—the "East Anglian style" and the Parisian-influenced Queen Mary's Psalter and Tickhill Psalter styles. After ca. 1330 Parisian influence gives way to influences from Flanders and Italy that become fully integrated with the indigenous English style, as in the Bohun Psalters.

It has been concluded that in the 13th century most workshops producing psalters seem to have operated for relatively local consumption. Of the few artistic centers that can be established with any certainty Oxford was important for most of the 13th century, and there is tentative evidence to suggest that it remained so through the 1320s and 1330s.

A similar pattern is suggested for London in the same period, with a decline in the 1330s. When London revived again in the later 14th century the Psalter was well on its decline in popularity. There is evidence for York and Norwich as centers that produced psalters in the early 14th century, in the case of Norwich until the 1330s. The years around 1335–40 suggest that there was a migration from these other centers (notably Norwich, Oxford, and London) to Cambridge, but a workshop there appears to have been comparatively short-lived, its artistic activity curtailed by the Black Death of 1348–49. The Bohun family were the first major patrons of psalter production after the Black Death until ca. 1380, by which time London had revived. As a result of the breakdown of secular workshops the Bohuns established a center at Pleshey in Essex, but their illuminators produced books solely for the family.

The dating of manuscripts remains tentative throughout this period, for very few have a firm date. Inevitably much dating depends upon the interpretation of stylistic developments.

Lynda Dennison

Bibliography

Dennison, Lynda. "'The Fitzwarin Psalter and Its Allies': A Reappraisal." In *England in the Fourteenth Century: Proceedings of the 1985 Harlaxton Symposium,* ed. W.M. Ormrod. Woodbridge: Boydell, 1986, pp. 42–66; Morgan, Nigel. *Early Gothic Manuscripts 1190–1285.* 2 vols. A Survey of Manuscripts Illuminated in the British Isles 4, ed. J.J.G. Alexander. London: Harvey Miller, 1982–88; Sandler, Lucy Freeman. *Gothic Manuscripts 1285–1385.* A Survey of Manuscripts Illuminated in the British Isles 5, ed. J.J.G. Alexander. London: Harvey Miller, 1986.

APPENDIX

Munich Psalter (Munich, Bayerische Staatsbibliothek Clm.835); Queen Mary's Psalter (BL Royal 2.B.vii); Cuerden Psalter (New York, Pierpont Morgan Library M.756); Peterborough Psalter (Brussels, Bibliothèque Royale 9961–62); Oxford Psalter (Oxford, New College 322); Rutland Psalter (BL Add. 62925); Gorleston Psalter (BL Add. 49622); Howard Psalter (BL Arundel 83, pt. 1); Ormesby Psalter (Bodl. Douce 366); Luttrell Psalter (BL Add. 42130); St. Omer Psalter (BL Yates Thompson 14 [Add. 39810]); Tickhill Psalter (New York, Public Library Spencer 26); Vienna Psalter (Vienna, Österreichische Nationalbibliothek 1826*); British Library Bohun Psalter-Hours (BL Egerton 3277); Exeter College Bohun Psalter (Oxford, Exeter College 47); Bedford Psalter-Hours (BL Add. 42131).

See also Amesbury Psalter; Brailes, William de; Cuerden Psalter; "East Anglian School"; Exeter Bohun Psalter; Manuscript Illumination, Gothic; Marginalia; Ormesby Psalter; Psalters, Anglo-Saxon; Queen Mary's Psalter

Psychology, Medieval, in Middle English Literature

ME writers employ a variety of psychological schemes developed in antiquity and the Middle Ages. The richness of the intellectual inheritance, the eclecticism (and possibly incomplete understanding) with which different systems are used by vernacular writers, and the terminological instability in the varied translations of Latin technical vocabulary permit here only a very general mapping of a complex area.

ME psychological writing is conditioned by a theological understanding of man's nature and destiny, according to which man is essentially a soul, created in God's image and striving, in the pursuit of virtue, to be united with him. Psychological terms are frequently invoked to explain moral conflict within man. The theme of interior conflict can be traced back to Plato, as can the dualism of matter and spirit in terms of which ME authors generally envisage it (certain biblical remarks are influential here also). The soul is often regarded as having its inclinations toward God thwarted by the body (e.g., Gower's *Confessio Amantis* 7.490–520). But the frequent opposition between reason and sensuality (as in the poem *Reason and Sensuality,* perhaps by Lydgate) sees the soul itself as an arena of conflict between the higher part of human nature that knows the moral truth and aspires heavenward and the part interested solely in the material world, a realm that is available to the senses and stimulates nonrational impulses. The reason/sensuality categorization has similarities to the Aristotelian distinction between three kinds of soul: the vegetative, possessed by plants and giving life pure and simple; the sensitive, through which animals have life and prerational sensationary capacities; and the rational, possessed by human beings, who have not only life and sensation but also the ability to reason abstractly and recognize moral imperatives. (On this scheme, and generally, see Trevisa's translation of Bartholomaeus Anglicus's *De proprietatibus rerum.*)

ME writers sometimes oppose reason (or "wit," though this is not always an equivalent of reason) to will. Will is often associated with bodily impulses and seen as tending to lead man morally astray, if it is not controlled by reason (cf. *Sawles Warde*). However, will can also specify the power of free choice, which does not in itself have any tendency toward evil. Virtue may be said to occur when a person wills what reason perceives to be good. The possession of reason and free will distinguishes human beings from the animals. This highest, specifically human, part of the person was influentially analyzed as an image of the Trinity by St. Augustine. The morality play *Wisdom* (among many other works) reflects Augustine's thought in offering a tripartite scheme of the soul as mind (Augustine's *memoria,* the soul in its most fundamental aspect, which corresponds to the Father), understanding (*intelligentia,* corresponding to the Son), and will (*voluntas,* corresponding to the Holy Spirit).

The author of *The Cloud of Unknowing,* following Richard of St. Victor, sees mind, reason, and will as the primary powers of the soul. The secondary powers, unlike the primary, have to do with the material world and are identified as imagination (cognitive) and sensuality (affective), conceived as often ill-disciplined servants of reason and will, respectively (chs. 62–66). Medieval writers generally understand the imagination as retaining sense images and passing them on to reason. Some writers also have it manipulating sense images fictively. In *Piers Plowman* B.11–12 the imaginative power reviews the earthly creation, finds there pointers to God's love, and stimulates the narrator to contemplate his approaching end.

Reason is often regarded as the highest power of the soul, but to the sequence sense-imagination-reason some thinkers add a further term or terms designating the soul's capacity for mental activity more exalted than reason's. Boethius's influential *Consolation of Philosophy* (5.pr.4) speaks of intelligence going beyond the sense-perceptible universe and apprehending the forms of things as they exist in the mind of God.

Work on Aristotle's *On the Soul* made available to later ME writers complex schemes for understanding postsensationary, prerational (animal-like) processes. (Aristotelian thinking took the soul to possess distinct faculties, as against Augustinian views, which saw the soul's powers as names given to a single entity as it performed various operations: Langland and Trevisa both use a set of such names derived from Isidore of Seville's *Etymologies*.) In Pecock's *Donet* the postsensationary faculties or "inward bodily wittis" (elsewhere "inwits") are 1) common wit, which synthesizes impressions received from the various senses; 2) imagination, which retains those impressions; 3) fantasy, which combines them into imaginary structures; 4) estimation, which is responsible for instinctive awarenesses not dependent on sense impressions; and 5) mind, which retains what the others provide.

Hugh White

Bibliography

PRIMARY

Dickins, Bruce, ed. *The Conflict of Wit and Will.* Kendal: Wilson, 1937; Lydgate, John (?). *Reson and Sensuallyte.* Ed. Ernst Sieper. EETS e.s. 84, 89. London: Kegan Paul, Trench, Trübner, 1901–03; *Wisdom.* In *The Macro Plays,* ed. Mark Eccles. EETS o.s. 262. London: Oxford University Press, 1969.

SECONDARY

Ackerman, Robert W. "*The Debate of the Body and the Soul* and Parochial Christianity." *Speculum* 37 (1962): 541–65; Bundy, Murray W. *The Theory of Imagination in Classical and Medieval Thought.* Urbana: University of Illinois, 1927; Gilson, Étienne. *The Christian Philosophy of St. Augustine.* Trans. L.E.M. Lynch. London: Gollancz, 1961; Grube, G.M.A. *Plato's Thought.* Rev. ed. London: Athlone, 1980; Harvey, E. Ruth. *The Inward Wits: Psychological Theory in the Middle Ages and the Renaissance.* London: Warburg Institute, 1975; Kretzmann, Norman, et al., eds. *The Cambridge History of Later Medieval Philosophy.* Part 8. Cambridge: Cambridge University Press, 1982, pp. 593–654; Lewis, C.S. *The Discarded Image: An Introduction to Medieval and Renaissance Literature.* Cambridge: Cambridge University Press, 1964; Minnis, Alastair J. "Langland's Ymaginatif and Late-Medieval Theories of Imagination." *Comparative Criticism* 3 (1981): 71–103.

See also Boethius; *Cloud of Unknowing;* Debate Poems; Drama, Vernacular; Hilton; Katherine Group; Moral and Religious Instruction; Mystical and Devotional Writings; Nature in ME Literature; *Piers Plowman*

Puy

The word traditionally used for poetic and musical guilds in northern France and Flanders in the Middle Ages. Normally these guilds had religious origins and affiliations but fostered secular song, often in contests, and drama also. There were important *puys* in Arras, Amiens, Lille, Valenciennes, Abbeville, Douai, Cambrai, and Rouen. In England at the close of the 13th century the London *puy,* a guild of French merchants dedicated to God, the Virgin, and All Saints, is of particular interest, not least because of the survival of its informative Statutes, written in Anglo-Norman French. At the main feast of the year competing "roials chaunsouns" were performed. There was great insistance on the need for musical competence on the part of the judges, and no *chant royal* could win if it lacked "the sweetness of a melody to be sung." The winning composer was elected Prince for the following year and awarded a crown. His arms were to be mounted in the banqueting hall and beneath was to be suspended a fair copy "clearly and well written, without mistake" of the winning song. No singer might begin at the annual contest unless he saw the previous year's winning entry duly displayed. A principal purpose of the guild's activities was to "nourish and encourage good companionship, pleasant pastime and enjoyment between people . . . and to forget one's cares." In a different category are minstrels' guilds, such as those in Paris, London, Chester, Tutbury, and Beverley, which are, rather, professional trade unions.

Nigel Wilkins

Bibliography

Chambers, Edmund K. *The Mediaeval Stage.* 2 vols. Oxford: Clarendon, 1903, 2:258–62; Riley, Henry Thomas, ed. *Munimenta Gildhallae Londoniensis.* Vol. 2: *Liber Custumarum.* Rolls Series 12. London: Longman, Green, Longman, and Roberts, 1859–62; Roessler, M. "Der Londoner Pui." *Zeitschrift für romanische Philologie* 41 (1921): 111–16; Sutton, A. "Merchants, Music and Social Harmony: The London Puy and Its French and London Contexts, circa 1300." *London Journal* 17 (1992): 1–17; Wilkins, Nigel. "Poetry and Music at Court: England and France in the Late Middle Ages." In *English Court Culture in the Later Middle Ages,* ed. V.J. Scattergood and J.W. Sherborn. London: Duckworth, 1983, pp. 185–86; Wilkins, Nigel. *The Lyric Art of Medieval France.* Fulbourne, Cambs.: New Press, 1989, pp. 9–35.

See also Anglo-Norman Literature; Gower; Guilds; Minstrels; Popular Culture; Songs

Queen Mary's Psalter

Queen Mary's Psalter (BL Royal 2.B.vii; fig. 107), an early-14th-century manuscript of 319 folios that once belonged to Queen Mary I (1553–58), contains an extraordinary wealth of decoration, chiefly in the form of elaborate picture cycles. The Psalter text is preceded by a series of 223 Old Testament scenes (fols. 1v–66v), mostly arranged two to a page. These give an account of the Bible narrative from the fall of Lucifer and the Creation to the death of Solomon. The compositions are set against plain vellum grounds and executed with great delicacy in a pen-and-wash technique. Beneath each miniature is an explanatory rubric in Anglo-Norman. The Tree of Jesse (fol. 67v) and three composite miniatures (fols. 68–69v), illustrating the genealogy of Christ and prophets and apostles, arranged typologically, are the first of a large number of miniatures in fuller color.

These subjects provide an effective link between the preceding Old Testament cycle and the New Testament narrative that follows. Between these (on fols. 71v–83) is the calendar, in which each month is spread over two facing pages: the left page is topped with an oblong miniature representing the labor of the month, while the right page has a miniature of the same type incorporating the corresponding sign of the zodiac within an actual scene (e.g., at April, for Taurus, men herd bulls and at July, for Cancer, fishermen heave a large crab into a boat).

The Psalter itself (fols. 85–280) is illustrated with scenes from the life of Christ. Within the ten-part division of the text the cycle is unusually detailed, having not only a historiated initial but also a miniature at the beginning and end of each section. The majority of miniatures and initials have grounds of colored diaper or of plain, pounced, or hatched burnished gold, the larger scenes being enclosed within Gothic architectural canopies. With the exception of the Crucifixion scene on fol. 256v the format of the illuminations then changes to accommodate a cycle of fourteen composite miniatures, set within simpler frames and each divided into four compartments. These miniatures, which are dispersed throughout the remaining psalms up to the opening of the first of the canticles

Fig. 107. Queen Mary's Psalter (BL Royal 2.B.vii), fol. 168v. Psalm 68: Marriage feast at Cana, Jonah and the whale. Reproduced by permission of the British Library, London.

(fols. 234–281), illustrate the Northern Passion, a verse narrative covering the events from the conspiracy of the Jews up to the soldiers' report of the Resurrection. The canticles are mostly illustrated with historiated initials. The unusually lavish litany (fols. 302v–318) is decorated with sixteen rectangular miniatures opening with the Last Judgment, but consisting mainly of standing figures of saints.

The decorative and iconographic richness of this fine psalter is further enhanced by an extensive cycle of *bas-de-page* (lower-margin) scenes, 464 in all, which begin on the second page of the psalms (fol. 85v) and continue to the end of the book. They are in the same tinted drawing technique as the prefatory Old Testament cycle and comprise a variety of subjects. The first series, depicting such scenes as a hedgehog gathering apples and the correct method for slaying a unicorn, relates to the bestiary. From fol. 130 this gives way to conflicts between knights and monsters, followed by scenes of secular life, such as hunting, feasting, and playing draughts, after which the tone becomes more serious with 36 miracles of the Virgin (fols. 204–232). The final cycle, that of the lives and passions of the saints, forms a particularly fitting accompaniment to the litany, where these scenes are married both to the miniature cycle above and to the text.

The Psalter is illuminated in a courtly style. Many of the figures are S-shaped, having restrained yet expressive head and arm gestures. The draperies fall in soft, straight folds or elegantly sweeping curves, the faces are pear-shaped, and the facial features are drawn with extreme delicacy. This manuscript, which is of considerable importance for the development of English painting in the early 14th century, can be assigned to a single anonymous hand (the Queen Mary Artist). The so-called Psalter of Richard of Canterbury (New York, Pierpont Morgan Library Glazier 53) was also illuminated entirely by him. This master worked in collaboration with another illuminator (the Ancient 6 Master) throughout a career that spanned some fifteen to twenty years (ca. 1310–25). His hand also appears in Bodl. Douce 79, but since this was probably once joined to Paris, BN fr. 13342 (a tract on the mass), in which the Ancient 6 Master also participated, it must be classed as a collaborative work. These two illuminators, who worked with no other artists, collaborated in two other extant manuscripts, and there are others linked to this workshop, illuminated by the Ancient 6 Master alone. The Queen Mary Artist has been erroneously assigned the first sixteen folios of an Apocalypse (BL Royal 19.B.xv), but this portion is by a clever copyist.

Queen Mary's Psalter is devoid of internal evidence for dating and provenance. However, as a result of a close study of the related manuscripts, a date between 1310 and 1320 has been proposed. For the Queen Mary books that contain evidence for localization London emerges as the most likely center of production, a provenance further reinforced by the stylistically and iconographically derivative *Liber Horn* of 1311 or 1312 and the *Liber custumarum* of 1321, both now in the Corporation of London Records Office and indisputably linked to London. The Queen Mary Artist and the Ancient 6 Master constitute a presumably London-based central workshop, while a further close imitator of their style (the Subsidiary Queen Mary Artist), who produced portions of a psalter and bestiary (Cambridge, Corpus Christi College 53), the Alice de Reydon Hours (CUL Dd.4.17), and other works, seems to have been operating mostly in East Anglia.

Both the iconographic and stylistic sources of Queen Mary's Psalter have yet to be fully explained, but the iconography appears largely to have an origin in literary material, while the often cited Parisian qualities of the style are readily explained by the political connections existing between the French and English courts at that time. Although it may never be possible to be more precise about its origin, or to determine the original owner, Queen Mary's Psalter stands as a unique product of English "court" art of the early 14th century.

Lynda Dennison

Bibliography

Dennison, Lynda. "An Illuminator of the Queen Mary Psalter Group: The Ancient 6 Master." *AntJ* 66 (1986): 287–314; Dennison, Lynda. "'Liber Horn,' 'Liber Custumarum' and Other Manuscripts of the Queen Mary Psalter Workshops." In *Medieval Art, Architecture and Archaeology in London,* ed. Lindy Grant. *BAACT* for 1984. London: British Archaeological Association, 1990, pp. 118–34, pls. XXVI–XXXIX; Dennison, Lynda. "The Apocalypse, British Library, Royal MS. 19 B.XV: A Reassessment of Its Artistic Context in Early Fourteenth-Century English Manuscript Illumination." *British Library Journal* 20 (1994): 35–54; Sandler, Lucy Freeman. *Gothic Manuscripts 1285–1385*. A Survey of Manuscripts Illuminated in the British Isles 5, ed. J.J.G. Alexander. London: Harvey Miller, 1986, cat. no. 56; Warner, George. *Queen Mary's Psalter: Miniatures and Drawings by an English Artist of the 14th Century Reproduced from Royal MS. 2.B.VII in the British Museum.* London: British Museum, 1912.

See also "East Anglian School"; Manuscript Illumination, Gothic; Marginalia; Psalters, Gothic

Queens and Queenship

Royal wives were not automatically designated "queens" *(reginae)* in the pre-Conquest period. Asser explains how West Saxon royal wives lost the title following the disgrace of Eadburh after the death of her husband, King Beorhtric, in 802. Their low status seems reflected by charter evidence; while 9th-century Mercian queens are regular witnesses to royal diplomas, West Saxon royal wives are noticeably absent. Gradually the situation changes. From the mid-10th century royal wives and mothers were designated "queens." The practice of their consecration, developed earlier on the Continent, seems to have been adopted in Wessex in 973, when Ælfthryth, third wife of King Edgar I, was anointed.

Royal wives were generally chosen from great noble clans, and the subsequent support of her powerful family for her husband, the king, often proved crucial in the survival of a dynasty. Circumstances of conversion and female monasticism opened up opportunities for royal women all over Europe. Noble women had rights of possession and free disposal of land and were often generous supporters and allies of the church.

During the ecclesiastical reform of the 10th century divorce became increasingly problematic, thus strengthening the royal wife's position. In pre-Conquest England primogeniture had not been established, and queens often wielded greater power as widows and mothers than as wives. Although some queens are mentioned in the earlier period—Seaxburh, believed to have ruled Wessex for a year after her husband Cenwealh's death in 762, or Æthelburh, Ine's queen, who demolished Taunton in 722—detailed evidence does not emerge until the 10th century.

Æthelflæd (d. 918) took over as virtually independent ruler of Mercia following her husband Æthelræd's death in 911. Described in the Mercian Register as *Myrcna hlæfdige*, the exact equivalent of *Myrcna hlaford* (the title by which Æthelræd had been known), she built and defended a line of fortresses against the Vikings and Welsh, making possible her brother Edward's (899–925) reconquest of the Danish Midlands and the subsequent unification of England under the West Saxon royal house.

Edward's wife, Eadgifu (d. 966/67), a great patron of the monastic revival, used her position at court to influence her sons in favor of the ecclesiastical reformers. Much of her extensive landed possessions were given to reformers and religious communities. Her influence is shown by her frequent appearance in witness lists of royal diplomas, where she signs after the king but before all other witnesses, including the archbishops and athelings (princes), a position she retained after her elder son's marriage. Dominant during the reigns of Æthelstan and her two sons, Edmund and Eadred, she and Dunstan were pushed aside in Eadwig's reign (955–59) in his attempt to break the power of the reform group. Backing the claims of Edgar, her younger grandson, she fell from power. Her lands were confiscated, to be restored to her on the succession of Edgar after Eadwig's death.

The events of 1035–37 exemplify the risks of intervention in succession disputes. Following Cnut's death in 1035, Emma chose to support the claims of Harthacnut, the king of Denmark and her son by Cnut, rather than either of her sons by Æthelred II, hoping to gain support from the Anglo-Danish aristocracy. However, Harold Harefoot, Cnut's son by his mistress Ælfgifu, had many supporters, and he was appointed to act as regent until Harthacnut's delayed arrival from Denmark. In 1036 Harold was in a sufficiently strong position to seize the royal treasure and regalia from Emma, and in the following year—actively helped by his mother—was proclaimed the *de jure* king of England. Emma's former ally Godwin switched support to Harold; Emma was exiled. After Harold's death (1040) Emma and Harthacnut returned to England. But when Æthelred and Emma's son Edward the Confessor succeeded Harthacnut, Emma was deprived of her treasures for failing to support his claims.

The queen's power was gradually eclipsed in the later Middle Ages by the implementation of primogeniture. Queens were no longer considered the automatic choice as regent to a minor. In order to preserve family property, their rights to inherit and freely to dispose of property were curtailed, further reducing their influence. Few post-Conquest queens exercised real power. An exception is the remarkable Eleanor of Aquitaine (d. 1204), wife of Louis VII of France and then of Henry II. As queen of England she frequently served as regent and promoted her sons' interest at Henry's expense. After her active participation in her eldest son's rebellion (1173), she was kept under watch until Henry's death. While her son Richard was in captivity during the Crusades, his mother virtually ruled England, successfully thwarting John's ambitions.

Until Edward IV married Elizabeth Wydeville in 1464, all the queens after Eleanor of Aquitaine were from abroad, and the story of the king's marriage belongs more to the realm of diplomatic history than to that of social or domestic affairs. However, the queens sometimes played a prominent role. Isabella of France was instrumental in the deposition of her husband, Edward II, in 1327, and Margaret of Anjou led the Lancastrian cause after Henry VI's inability to govern became apparent in the 1450s. The queens had no formal or designated role in government; they were just expected to bear children and offer their counsel in private. Nevertheless, they were figures with their own households and estates. They often engaged in philanthropic activity with the church, educational institutions, and the nameless sick poor as their beneficiaries.

Kathryn Lowe

Bibliography

Campbell, Miles W. "Queen Emma and Ælfgifu of Northampton, Canute the Great's Women." *Medieval Scandinavia* 4 (1971): 66–70; Frey, Linda, Marsha Frey, and Joanne Schneider, eds. *Women in Western European History: A Select Chronological, Geographical and Topical Bibliography from Antiquity to the French Revolution.* Brighton: Harvester, 1982; John, Eric. "The *Encomium Emmae reginae:* A Riddle and a Solution." *BJRL* 63 (1980): 58–94; Kelly, Amy. *Eleanor of Aquitaine and the Four Kings.* Cambridge: Harvard University Press, 1950; Kibler, William W., ed. *Eleanor of Aquitaine: Patron and Politician.* Austin: University of Texas Press, 1976; Parsons, John Carmi, ed. *Medieval Queenship.* London: St. Martin, 1993 [see esp. the articles by John Parsons, Pauline Stafford, and Armin Wolf]; Wainwright, Frederick T. "Æthelflæd, Lady of the Mercians." In *Scandinavian England: Collected Papers,* ed. H.P.R. Finberg. Chichester: Phillimore, 1975, pp. 305–24.

See also Æthelflæd; Eleanor of Aquitaine; Emma; Matilda; Monarchy and Kingship; Women

Quo Warranto Proceedings

The administrative and legislative reforms undertaken by Edward I on his return from crusade included investigation not only into maladministration but into fundamental questions of who held what liberties (privileges ranging from hunting rights to holding courts) and by what warrant *(quo warranto)* those liberties were held. Edward issued the Statute of Gloucester in 1278, authorizing the itinerant justices in eyre to enquire by writs of quo warranto into all privately held liberties in the realm. His purpose was to establish the principle that all liberties belonged to the king, held privately only by royal authorization. He did not plan to take all private liberties into royal hands. In fact liberties found to be held without proper warrant were almost always granted back on payment of a healthy fine.

Proof of right to a liberty was demonstrated either by a charter from the king or by long use and possession. Defining the latter caused trouble and prolonged litigation. In 1290 the Statute of *Quo Warranto* defined long use as continuous possession back to the accession of Richard I (1189), a date accepted as the limit of legal memory for other purposes.

Edward's success in the quo warranto proceedings was mixed. Though the principle that all liberties were royal ones came to be accepted, the process of enquiry and the overtones of extortion aroused resentment. In practice writs quo warranto were gradually abandoned by the crown as a means of controlling private liberties because a judgment in favor of the defendant secured the liberty permanently from crown control. Other means were developed to further the crown's authority and the trend away from private and personal government toward public and bureaucratic government.

Stephen R. Morillo

Bibliography

Cam, Helen M. *Liberties and Communities in Medieval England.* Cambridge: Cambridge University Press, 1944; Plucknett, Theodore F.T. *Legislation of Edward I.* Oxford: Clarendon, 1949; Powicke, F.M. *The Thirteenth Century, 1216–1307.* 2d ed. Oxford: Clarendon, 1962.

See also Edward I; Mortmain

R

Regularis concordia

The key document of the Benedictine Reform in England, resulting from a national council of bishops, abbots, and abbesses held in Winchester in the early 970s. As indicated by its programmatic title—*Regularis concordia anglicae nationis monachorum sanctimonialiumque (The Monastic Agreement of the Monks and Nuns of the English Nation)*—it was meant to establish a uniform observance for monks and nuns throughout the country on the basis of the Rule of St. Benedict. The heterogeneous compilation contains relatively few traces of individual authorship; those discernible point to Æthelwold rather than Dunstan, to whom the work was formerly attributed. It has come down to us in two loosely related copies, both probably produced at Christ Church, Canterbury, about the middle of the 11th century: BL Cotton Tiberius A.iii, fols. 3r–27v, a complete version, augmented by an OE interlinear gloss and a thematic frontispiece, and BL Cotton Faustina B.iii, fols. 159r–198r, a reproduction of the Latin text, lacking the epilogue, and with its final leaf cut off and bound with BL Tiberius A.iii (now fol. 177) in the Cottonian library. There are also two fragmentary OE prose translations, an adaptation in Latin by Ælfric—known as the "Letter to the Monks of Eynsham"—and a number of more or less faithful verbal echoes in other liturgical documents.

The main body of the *Regularis concordia* is subdivided into twelve chapters that contain regulations on liturgical practice throughout the year and instructions on monastic life in general. These largely accord with reformed monasticism on the Continent, especially with the customs of Fleury, but there are also a number of genuinely English traits. One of the outstanding features of the *Regularis concordia* is its inclusion in the Easter office of the *Quem quaeritis* trope that marks the beginnings of liturgical drama in medieval England.

In form as well as in content the prologue and the epilogue stand out against the customary proper; written in the "hermeneutic style" as practiced by Æthelwold, these parts reveal the political dimensions of the reform, attesting to a mutually profitable alliance of the royal house, represented by King Edgar (957–75) and Queen Ælfthryth, and the monastic reform party, at the expense of the nobility losing its rights to exert lay dominion over monasteries.

There is only scant information as regards the long-term impact of the *Regularis concordia* on monastic life in England. The two surviving copies attest to a prolonged interest in the document, though in drawing up his post-Conquest constitutions for the Christ Church monks Archbishop Lanfranc showed a characteristic disregard of what once constituted the unifying bond among all Anglo-Saxon monastic communities.

Lucia Kornexl

Bibliography

PRIMARY

Kornexl, Lucia, ed. *Die Regularis Concordia und ihre altenglische Interlinearversion*. Munich: Fink, 1993; Kornexl, Lucia. "The *Regularis concordia* and Its Old English Gloss." *ASE* 24 (1995): 95–130; Symons, Thomas, ed. and trans. *Regularis concordia anglicae nationis monachorum sanctimonialiumque: The Monastic Agreement of the Monks and Nuns of the English Nation*. London: Nelson, 1953; Symons, Thomas, Sigrid Spath et al., eds. *Regularis concordia anglicae nationis*. Rev. ed. *Corpus Consuetudinum Monasticarum* 7/3 (Consuetudinum Saeculi X/XI/XII Monumenta Non-Cluniacensia), ed. Kassius Hallinger. Siegburg: Schmitt, 1984, pp. 61–147 [with extensive liturgical notes].

SECONDARY

Hill, Joyce. "The *Regularis concordia* and Its Latin and Old English Reflexes." *Revue bénédictine* 101 (1991): 299–315; Parsons, David, ed. *Tenth-Century Studies: Essays in Commemoration of the Millennium of the Council of Winchester and Regularis concordia*. London: Phillimore, 1975.

See also Ælfric; Æthelwold; Benedict of Nursia; Benedictine Reform; Drama, Latin Liturgical; Dunstan; Lanfranc; Literary Influences: Carolingian; Liturgy and Church Music, History of; Monasticism; Nuns; *Regularis concordia* and the Arts; *Regularis concordia* and the Liturgy

Regularis concordia and the Arts

The *Regularis concordia,* the document that describes the common rule of life accepted ca. 970 by the English monastic houses, says nothing specifically about the arts. The Benedictine order had always cultivated the arts, however, and art played an important part in Anglo-Saxon monastic life. The monastic church was the place where Christ's incarnation, death, and resurrection were made present through the liturgy, and its design and decoration had to reflect that fact. The paintings in liturgical manuscripts did not simply recall the historical events being commemorated; they showed the significance of those events, leading those who saw them away from the temporal to the eternal. This much is common to all monastic art.

The leaders of the 10th-century monastic revival added three things to their Benedictine inheritance: royal patronage, uniformity of observance, and a sense of unity with the reformed monastic houses on the Continent. The close links between English monasteries and the royal family, seen particularly in the prayers for the royal family enjoined upon the monks, are reflected in the numerous crowned crucifixes and other crowned figures of Christ from late Anglo-Saxon England, as well as in the appearance of royal insignia in paintings of the Adoration of the Magi and the Baptism of Christ in such manuscripts as the Benedictional of Æthelwold. The emphasis on uniformity, together with the controlling influence of the three founders of the English monastic revival (Dunstan, Æthelwold, and Oswald), meant that monastic houses were grouped in families with common tastes and ideas. Monks moved from one monastery to another, books were written in one monastery for presentation to another, and together with the books went a transfer of style and iconography. Contacts with continental monastic houses resulted in a form of manuscript decoration that was closely dependent on Carolingian art. The liturgical provisions of the *Regularis concordia,* and the forms of piety associated with it, affected the layout of churches and their decoration. Space was needed for processions, for the Good Friday veneration of the Cross, and for the dramatization of the *Quem quaeritis* trope on Easter Sunday. Towers and crypts were built for the display of relics, and side chapels were provided for private prayer.

Barbara C. Raw

Bibliography

PRIMARY
Deshman, Robert. *The Benedictional of Æthelwold.* Princeton: Princeton University Press, 1995; Symons, Thomas, ed. and trans. *Regularis concordia anglicae nationis monachorum sanctimonialiumque: The Monastic Agreement of the Monks and Nuns of the English Nation.* London: Nelson, 1953.

SECONDARY
Dodwell, C.R. *Anglo-Saxon Art: A New Perspective.* Manchester: Manchester University Press, 1982; Raw, Barbara C. *Anglo-Saxon Crucifixion Iconography and the Art of the Monastic Revival.* Cambridge: Cambridge University Press, 1990; Verdon, Timothy G., ed. *Monasticism and the Arts.* Syracuse: Syracuse University Press, 1984.

See also Benedictine Reform; Cloisters Cross; Drama, Latin Liturgical; Iconography; Liturgy; Literary Influences: Carolingian; Monasticism; *Regularis concordia; Regularis concordia* and the Liturgy; "Winchester School"

Regularis concordia and the Liturgy

The earliest surviving English monastic customary, containing extensive information on contemporary liturgical, monastic, and social customs. It is also one of the most significant documents of the 10th-century revival of monasticism in England. It was compiled ca. 970 by a council of bishops, abbots, and abbesses in an attempt to establish a nationally uniform pattern of monastic lifestyle. Edgar, king of all England from 959 to 975, presided over the council at Winchester, at this period the seat of the royal household, the site of three Benedictine foundations, and the major center of book production and illumination in England. *Regularis concordia* has never been conclusively attributed to a single author, but the central role of the reformer St. Æthelwold (d. 984) in the compilation of the document is unquestionable. It survives in two sources, both likely to have been copied at Christ Church, Canterbury (a house influenced by Winchester), in the late 10th century and the mid-11th century, respectively, and it also forms the basis of a customary compiled by Ælfric "the Grammarian" (ca. 945–ca. 1015) for the new Benedictine community at Eynsham in Oxfordshire (founded 1005).

Regularis concordia takes the Rule of St. Benedict (ca. 526) as the authoritative model for the monastic life, while acknowledging that the Rule in itself is not adequate as a means of securing the desired level of conformity of practice. To this end the Winchester council summoned representatives from Fleury and Ghent, two of the major centers of reformed European monasticism, to discuss different interpretations of the Rule. Consequently there are several strands of influence within the document. Thomas Symons's extensive research has identified customs borrowed from the legislation of Benedict of Aniane (d. 821) and the late-8th-century customary *Memoriale qualiter,* in addition to more recent practices drawn from the Cluniac and Lotharingian uses (represented by Fleury and Ghent, respectively).

There is also substantial evidence of uniquely English customs. The close relationship between king and monks (underlined by the physical proximity of monasteries and royal palace at Winchester) is referred to several times in the document, but it is most overtly reflected in the daily custom of offering psalms and collects for the royal family after each of the hours (except Prime) and after high mass. The morrow mass was also offered for the king on certain occasions, and the king had the right to participate in abbatial elections. Other customs that do not feature in contemporary continental customaries include a recommendation for daily reception of the eucharist, the pealing of bells during Christmas week, and the prescription of a room with a fire during winter.

Regularis concordia consists of a prologue outlining the history of the monastic revival and the Council of Winchester, followed by twelve chapters dealing with the daily monastic routine. These cover the observance of feasts, matters of discipline, reception of guests, and rites for the sick and the dead. Numerous appended liturgical ceremonies are described, including the votive offices of the dead and of All Saints, several groups of specially chosen psalms recited before and after offices, and a series of three independent antiphons addressed to the Cross, the Virgin Mary, and the patron saint, respectively, which followed Lauds and Vespers outside Advent. There is also a particularly full description of the ceremonies of Holy Week. The details for the performance of the dramatic liturgical dialogue *Visitatio sepulchri* on Easter Day are especially important, for they clarify the context of the same ceremony which is included in the famous Winchester Tropers and found in many contemporary continental manuscripts. *Regularis concordia* does not supply complete texts for the *Visitatio,* but it describes precisely the manner in which the ceremony was performed and specifies its liturgical place, between the third (and last) respond and the Te Deum at Matins on Easter Day.

Sally E. Roper

Bibliography

PRIMARY

Nocent, Hadrianus [Adrien], et al., eds. *Aelfrici abbatis epistula ad monachos Egneshamnenses directa.* Rev. ed. *Corpus Consuetudinum Monasticarum 7/3* (Consuetudinum Saeculi X/XI/XII Monumenta Non-Cluniacensia), ed. Kassius Hallinger. Siegburg: Schmitt, 1984, pp. 149–85; Symons, Thomas, ed. and trans. *Regularis concordia anglicae nationis monachorum sanctimonialiumque: The Monastic Agreement of the Monks and Nuns of the English Nation.* London: Nelson, 1953; Symons, Thomas, Sigrid Spath, et al., eds. *Regularis concordia anglicae nationis.* Rev. ed. *Corpus Consuetudinum Monasticarum 7/3* ed. Kassius Hallinger. Siegburg: Schmitt, 1984, pp. 61–147.

SECONDARY

Dales, Douglas. *Dunstan: Saint and Statesman.* Cambridge: Lutterworth, 1988, pp. 81–86; Knowles, David. *The Monastic Order in England: A History of Its Development from the Times of St. Dunstan to the Fourth Lateran Council, 940–1216.* 2d ed. Cambridge: Cambridge University Press, 1963; Parsons, David, ed. *Tenth-Century Studies: Essays in Commemoration of the Millennium of the Council of Winchester and Regularis concordia.* London: Phillimore, 1975; Symons, Thomas. "The *Regularis concordia.*" DownR 40 (1922): 15–30; Symons, Thomas. "The *Regularis concordia* and the Council of Winchester." DownR 80 (1962): 140–56; Yorke, Barbara, ed. *Bishop Æthelwold: His Career and Influence.* Woodbridge: Boydell, 1988.

See also Æthelwold; Benedictine Reform; Drama, Latin Liturgical; Dunstan; Liturgy and Church Music, History of; *Regularis concordia; Regularis concordia* and The Arts; Winchester Tropers

Religious Allegories

Extremely varied in form and complexity, ME religious allegories elude simple summary. At one end of the spectrum we find static allegories devised to assist recall of basic truths. These include allegorical buildings (e.g., *The Abbey of the Holy Ghost* or *The Castle of Love,* based on Robert Grosseteste's *Chateau d'amour*); charters (the several versions of *The Charter of Christ*); clothing and armor, often with reference to Ephesians 6 (*A Treatise of Ghostly Battle*); landscapes, trees, and other plants (*The Desert of Religion, The Truelove,* and various trees of virtues and vices). Allegorical ships, ladders, oceans, beds, wells, and so on can also be found.

These static allegorical devices need not be mechanical or simplistic. Among the most moving is the versified *Long Charter of Christ* (mid- to late 14th century). Speaking in words from the Good Friday liturgy, the crucified Christ offers a charter granting joy in return for love; his skin is the parchment, his wounds are words made by the pen of the scourge, and so on. Legacies of the eucharist and the sacrament of penance complete the linking of love and suffering. The emotion of the recalled Passion is intensified by being set in and contrasted with the liturgical and legal formulas. In static allegory spiritual relationships may also be suggested: the granary of Meditation in the prose *Abbey of the Holy Ghost* is above the cellar of Devotion because it is more important; Pity distributes not only wheat from the granary and wine from the cellar but also the product of meditation and devotion, the oil of Comfort. The unrelated prose *Charter of the Abbey of the Holy Ghost* links the Abbey's inhabitants to the implications of the Fall and to Christ's life. It also modulates its style subtly and effectively. For example, the charter itself is full of conditionals expressing God's regret for its coming invalidation: this neatly suggests divine timelessness, pity preceding the action that will deserve it. The Fall is presented in a variety of modes ranging from the charter's formality to the uncontrolled outburst of Adam's confession.

Less static and thus more capable of suggesting process and change are allegories of the life journey, often represented as a pilgrimage. Noteworthy examples are the ME versions of the first two parts of Guillaume de Deguileville's important poetic trilogy: the *Pèlerinage de la vie humaine* and *Pèlerinage de l'âme.* The anonymous prose *Pilgrimage of the Life of the Manhood,* translating the first recension (1330–31) of the *Vie,* allegorizes the interdependence of the sacraments and includes a rare allegorical mass imaginatively interwoven with holy orders and penance. The diffuse second recension was translated into verse by Lydgate. The prose *Pilgrimage of the Soul* modifies the *Ame* for a lay audience, demonstrating man's need of Christ through the soul's experience after death. (Part 3, the *Pèlerinage de Jhesucrist,* has no ME version.)

More than one of the allegorical devices described here may appear in any given allegorical work, as with the *Charter of the Abbey* above, or the allegory of the green tree and the dry tree embedded in the *Pilgrimage of the Soul.* Another device common to many religious allegories is personification allegory, frequently used to represent virtues and vices and often able to suggest spiritual relationships and interactions more fully than is possible with inanimate allegorical entities alone. Of particular interest are the allegorical narratives of the Four Daughters of God (Truth, Justice, Mercy, and Peace, drawn ultimately from Ps. 84:11 AV), who debate such issues as the Incarnation, Grace, or the release of souls from Limbo and are eventually reconciled. The device is widespread, appearing in *The Castle of Love, The Charter of the Abbey, Piers Plowman, Cursor Mundi,* and elsewhere. Personification allegory, the life journey, and allegorical buildings can also be found in the morality plays, such as *Everyman, Mankind,* and *The Castle of Perseverance.*

Religious allegories in ME generally echo accepted values and doctrine. Nonetheless, the greatest of them resist easy classification or analysis, because they are more concerned with exploring spiritual relationships and process than with mere statement. The subtlest in ideas and most varied in allegorical modes is *Piers Plowman,* which, like *Pearl,* concerns spiritual transformation; both poems show how language itself—with its figurative, allegorical capacities—reveals to man his spiritual purpose.

Avril Henry

Bibliography

PRIMARY

Editions of most ME religious allegories may be found in the *Manual* as cited below; works not listed there include Henry, Avril, ed. *The Pilgrimage of the Lyfe of the Manhode.* 2 vols. EETS o.s. 288, 292. London: Oxford University Press, 1985–88; McGerr, Rosemarie P., ed. *The Pilgrimage of the Soul.* New York: Garland, 1990.

SECONDARY

For theories of allegory see article on ALLEGORY above; *Manual* 7:2331–49, 2540–55; Clifford, Gay. *The Transformations of Allegory.* London: Routledge & Kegan Paul, 1974; Cornelius, Roberta Douglas. *The Figurative Castle: A Study in the Mediaeval Allegory of the Edifice.* Bryn Mawr: Bryn Mawr College, 1930; Hagen, Susan. *Allegorical Remembrance: A Study of the "Pilgrimage of the Life of Man" As a Medieval Treatise on Seeing and Remembering.* Athens: University of Georgia Press, 1990; Henry, Avril. "The Pilgrimage of the Lyfe of the Manhode: The Structure of Book 1" and "The Large Design, with Special Reference to Books 2–4." *NM* 87 (1986): 128–41, 229–36; Katzenellenbogen, Adolf. *Allegories of the Virtues and Vices in Mediaeval Art from Early Christian Times to the Thirteenth Century.*

Trans. Alan J.P. Crick. London: Warburg, 1939. Repr. Toronto: University of Toronto Press, 1989; Quilligan, Maureen. *The Language of Allegory: Defining the Genre.* Ithaca: Cornell University Press, 1979; Traver, Hope. *The Four Daughters of God.* Philadelphia: Winston, 1907; Tuve, Rosamond. *Allegorical Imagery: Some Mediaeval Books and Their Posterity.* Princeton: Princeton University Press, 1966; Wailes, Stephen L. *Medieval Allegories of Jesus's Parables.* Berkeley: University of California Press, 1987; Wenzel, Siegfried. "The Pilgrimage of Life As a Late Medieval Genre." *MS* 35 (1973): 370–88.

See also Allegory; *Death and Life;* Drama, Vernacular; Dream Visions; Grosseteste; Henry of Lancaster; *Jacob's Well;* Lydgate; Moral and Religious Instruction; Mystical and Devotional Writings; *Pearl-*Poet; *Piers Plowman; Prudentius; Truelove;* Virtues and Vices, Books of

Repton

The Church of St. Wystan, Repton (Derbyshire), was originally part of a double monastery (a community of both men and women under the rule of an abbess) founded in the 7th century. There were several phases of construction at the site

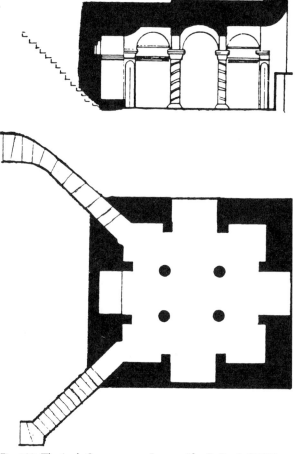

Fig. 108. The Anglo-Saxon crypt at Repton. After E. Fernie (1983). Drawing by C. Karkov.

during the pre-Conquest period. The Anglo-Saxon monastery was succeeded by a Norman priory, and the nave and west end of the church were rebuilt in the later medieval period.

All that remains of the pre-Conquest fabric (fig. 108) are the square-ended chancel, the crypt beneath it, the two eastern angles of a central crossing that separated chancel and nave, fragments of the north transept, and a monolithic window head. The church as reconstructed had a central tower with north and south porticus. The crossing tower was wider than the chancel and northern and southern arms, a characteristically Anglo-Saxon feature of ecclesiastical architecture. Sections of stringcourses and moldings are preserved on the eastern walls of the central crossing, and a stringcourse and pilaster strips decorate the exterior of the east end.

Excavations at Repton have uncovered fragments of window glass and imported glass vessels that suggest the presence of a 7th- or 8th-century church predating the present crypt. The earliest feature surviving at the site is the crypt, originally an independent mausoleum, partially below ground, that was eventually incorporated into the fabric of the church. The crypt is a single room, approximately 15 feet square divided into nine vaulted bays by transverse arches set on four monolithic columns. The columns are carved with ornamental spirals possibly in imitation of those that covered the shrine of St. Peter in Rome. At the center of all four walls are deep recesses (possibly later insertions) that originally housed tombs, shrines, or important relics. The corners of the niches are articulated by square pilasters.

There is evidence for three or four Anglo-Saxon building campaigns within the present fabric. The lower part of the crypt walls, constructed of long, brownish, well-dressed stones, is all that remains of the first phase of construction. Just above this level is a second phase characterized by more roughly hewn stones and massive quoins at the corner angles. The third phase begins just beneath the level of the later medieval windows and is marked by a change to smaller rectangular stones of a light grey color. Pilaster strips decorate the exterior of the building at this level. The four spiral columns and pilaster responds that support the vaults belong to the third phase. Lastly the diagonal staircases that originally entered the crypt from the north and south porticus were added.

The dates of these phases are controversial. Taylor dates phase 1 to the 7th and 8th centuries, suggesting that the mausoleum was built to house the remains of King Æthelbald of Mercia (d. 757); phase 2, 8th to 9th century; phase 3, associated with King Wiglaf (827–40); and phase 4, with the death of Wystan in 849. Fernie suggests that Wiglaf built the mausoleum and dates phase 1 to 827–40 and phases 2, 3, and 4 to 850–1035, probably 920–1020, on the basis of parallels both within England and on the Continent.

The Vikings spent the winter of 873/74 at Repton. The church was incorporated into their fortifications, and a cemetery, possibly centered on a royal burial, was sited to the west of the church.

Catherine E. Karkov

Bibliography

Biddle, Martin. "Archaeology, Architecture and the Cult of Saints." In *The Anglo-Saxon Church: Papers on History, Architecture and Archaeology in Honour of Dr H.M. Taylor,* ed. Lawrence A.S. Butler and Richard K. Morris. CBA Research Report 60. London: CBA, 1986, pp. 1–31; Biddle, Martin, and Birthe Kjølbye Biddle. "Repton and the Vikings." *Antiquity* 66 (1992): 36–41; Fernie, Eric. *The Architecture of the Anglo-Saxons.* London: Batsford, 1983; Taylor, Harold M. "Repton Reconsidered." In *England before the Conquest,* ed. Peter Clemoes and Kathleen Hughes. Cambridge: Cambridge University Press, 1971, pp. 391–408; Taylor, Harold M., and Joan Taylor. "Repton." In *Anglo-Saxon Architecture.* Vol. 2. Cambridge: Cambridge University Press, 1965, pp. 510–16.

See also Architecture, Anglo-Saxon; Ecclesiastical Architecture, Early Anglo-Saxon

Rhetoric

In contrast to the modern, postromantic tradition's emphasis on the expressive aspect of language, rhetoric examines the effect of language on an audience. Rhetoric was the dominant theory of discourse in the premodern West; its structures, terminology, and character shaped the way that those who thought about language expressed their thoughts. Originally rhetoric was concerned with the persuasiveness of an argument presented in a public forum. But almost from the beginning of the ancient Greeks' systematic study and teaching of rhetoric they recognized its importance to understanding the effectiveness of written as well as oral texts.

Classical rhetoric, with its emphasis on adult male political and judicial decision making, is often considered to be the most fundamental type of rhetoric (Kennedy). But during the Middle Ages the pedagogical aspect of rhetoric—its use as a tool to teach literacy, particularly the ability to read, write, and analyze Latin texts—was more important. One of the most illuminating descriptions of medieval rhetorical pedagogy is John of Salisbury's description of the methods of a famous teacher, Bernard of Chartres. Bernard gave close readings of the Latin authors, including explanations of grammatical rules and rhetorical techniques, which he dispensed "gradually, in a manner commensurate with [the students'] powers of assimilation"; he assigned daily exercises in memorization, recitation, and imitation that were tailored to the strengths and weaknesses of individual students; he gave evening instruction that included explanations of the "poets and orators who were to serve as models for the boys in their introductory exercises in imitating prose and poetry"; and he demanded daily compositions in poetry and prose that were then presented in informal competitions (*Metalogicon* 1.24).

The analytical terminology used during the Middle Ages to talk about rhetorical discourse derives from Roman treatises that taught one how to compose and present oral arguments. The traditional division of rhetoric into five parts (invention of material, arrangement, style, memory, and delivery) and the definitions of these parts (also called the canons, aspects, or topics of rhetoric) reflect the origin of rhetoric in the composition of speeches. A classical rhetorical treatise that was influential during the later Middle Ages and much of the Renaissance reads, "Invention is the devising of matter, true or plausible, that would make the case convincing. Arrangement is the ordering and distribution of the matter, making clear the place to which each thing is to be assigned. Style is the adaptation of suitable words and sentences to the matter devised. Memory is the firm retention in the mind of the matter, words, and arrangement. Delivery is the graceful regulation of voice, countenance, and gesture" (*Rhetorica ad Herennium* 1.3).

The *Rhetorica ad Herennium,* from which these definitions are quoted, was attributed to Cicero during the Middle Ages and early Renaissance. From the 9th century on it was a supplement to another Roman treatise also popular during the Middle Ages, one by the young Cicero that concentrates on the first part of rhetoric: *De inventione.* For most of the Middle Ages these texts, although originally written to teach the rhetoric of Roman courts of law, were used as textbooks for all kinds of language study.

Aristotle's *Rhetoric,* a text much admired today but almost unknown in the ancient world, was known but not widely read during the later Middle Ages. Yet the translation of Aristotle's work on memory into Latin in the 13th century may have helped to codify treatments of the fourth part of rhetoric and reintroduce it into scholastic rhetoric in medieval Europe, especially medieval England (Carruthers). Taught in the medieval universities, scholastic rhetoric examined systematically the relationship between rhetoric and dialectic (Fredborg), a question already raised in the *De differentiis topicis* of Boethius (ca. 480–ca. 525), a work that remained influential throughout the Middle Ages. In medieval schools, however, as we see in John of Salisbury's description, the teaching of rhetoric overlapped with the teaching of grammar and the analysis of specific Latin texts.

The great rhetorical narrative poems of the 12th century, such as the *Cosmographia* of Bernardus Silvestris and the *Anticlaudianus* and *Complaint of Nature* of Alan of Lille, helped to inspire a new group of rhetorical treatises, the arts of poetry, or *artes poetriae.* The rhetorical principles of these treatises were based on classical rhetorical manuals; unlike the manuals, however, and like Horace's *Ars poetica* (another of their classical sources), the *artes poetriae* emphasized the composition of verse. The most famous of these and the one most widely read during the later Middle Ages was the *Poetria nova* of Geoffrey of Vinsauf, written about 1200–15.

While the *Poetria nova* specifically treats poetic composition, and while this work and excerpts from it were so well known in England that a vernacular writer like Chaucer could paraphrase (*Troilus* 1.1065–69) and parody (*NPT* 3337–51) it, the work was used to teach prose composition as well. Arts of poetry by other Englishmen, such as John of Garland and Gervase of Melkley, also included sections devoted to prose composition. Treatises on letter writing according to rhetorical principles (*artes dictaminis*) became popular about the same time as the arts of poetry, but in England the *artes poetriae* seem

to have been at least as popular as the *artes dictaminis* for teaching all kinds of composition (Camargo, 1988).

Medieval rhetorical techniques taught in the *Poetria nova* and emphasized in commentaries on it include textual amplification and abbreviation; the use of proverbs and exempla to begin a work and focus the attention of the audience; and the division of figurative language into "difficult ornament," or metaphoric transference, and "easy ornament," or the construction of sentences in such a way as to create deliberate patterns in the words themselves or in the arrangement of the content of short passages.

The arts of poetry are meant to be comprehensive treatises, but to modern readers they seem to emphasize the third part of rhetoric, style, especially the figurative aspects of language. In fact separate lists of definitions and examples of the tropes and figures of speech were popular throughout the Middle Ages. Most of the medieval arts of poetry draw on earlier lists and definitions of tropes and figures, like those in book 4 of the *Rhetorica ad Herennium,* although the authors of the medieval treatises tinkered with the lists and usually inserted or made up their own examples.

The examples of rhetorical tropes and figures in the arts of poetry, as well as in earlier, shorter treatises like Bede's *De schematibus et tropis* (*On Figures of Speech,* ca. 700), were as likely to be drawn from Christian as from classical stories and traditions. The association of rhetoric with paganism that centuries earlier inspired Augustine of Hippo to write a book on using rhetoric for specifically Christian purposes seems not to have been the source of so much concern or fear for most later medieval teachers of rhetoric, although the potential harm of pagan texts continued to be debated in other circles.

However, Augustine's treatise on a christianized rhetoric, *On Christian Doctrine (De doctrina christiana),* did give rise to a distinct rhetorical tradition of its own. This tradition has been called "counterrhetorical" (Camargo, 1983) because of Augustine's rejection of precepts (4.3.4) and his emphasis on clarity and directness (4.8.22) rather than sophistication of composition and style. But it paved the way for the development of the medieval arts of preaching (*artes praedicandi*) as well as the later medieval controversy about circumscribed access to and uses made of the text of the Bible, most notable in England in the Wycliffite movement.

The practical interest in preaching caused by the challenge to the church of the powerful heresies and the Crusades of the 12th and 13th centuries led to a change in the function of sermons in medieval religious life and the need for texts and aids to help in their composition. The arts of preaching were influenced by scholastic methods of textual analysis, both in the use of biblical quotations as a focus for thematic development and amplification and in an emphasis on division into parts. Collections of sermons were as influential as preceptive manuals in the teaching of the composition of sermons, and these collections indicate that the intended audience influenced the choice of compositional structure and method of development.

Because many medieval rhetorical manuscripts still remain unedited and even unread by modern scholars, there are many questions about medieval rhetoric, especially rhetoric in England, that are only just now beginning to be answered: What texts were used in which medieval schools and universities? Were those who were excluded from institutionalized education during the Middle Ages also affected by the rhetorical tradition inherited from the classical world? How did knowledge of rhetorical treatises that were not part of the pedagogical system spread? What was the result of rhetorical teaching on writers in the vernacular? Much more work must be done before we can answer those questions fully.

Marjorie Curry Woods

Bibliography

PRIMARY

Augustine of Hippo. *On Christian Doctrine.* Trans. D.W. Robertson, Jr. New York: Liberal Arts Press, 1958; Cicero. *De inventione, De optimo genere oratorum, Topica.* Ed. and trans. H.M. Hubbell. Cambridge: Harvard University Press, 1949; John of Salisbury. *Metalogicon: A Twelfth-Century Defense of the Verbal and Logical Arts of the Trivium.* Trans. Daniel D. McGarry. Berkeley: University of California Press, 1955; Murphy, James J., ed. and trans. *Three Medieval Rhetorical Arts.* Berkeley: University of California Press, 1971 [an art of letter writing, an art of poetry, and an art of preaching]; Pseudo-Cicero. *Ad C. Herennium de Ratione Dicendi (Rhetorica ad Herennium).* Ed. and trans. Harry Caplan. Cambridge: Harvard University Press, 1954; Woods, Marjorie Curry, ed. and trans. *An Early Commentary on the Poetria nova of Geoffrey of Vinsauf.* New York: Garland, 1985.

SECONDARY

New *CBEL* 1:345–46 (Bede), 762–63 (John of Salisbury), 771 (Geoffrey of Vinsauf, Gervase of Melkley), 773–74 (John of Garland); Camargo, Martin. "Rhetoric." In *The Seven Liberal Arts in the Middle Ages,* ed. David L. Wagner. Bloomington: Indiana University Press, 1983, pp. 96–124 [a good starting place]; Camargo, Martin. "Toward a Comprehensive Art of Written Discourse: Geoffrey of Vinsauf and the *Ars dictaminis.*" *Rhetorica* 6 (1988): 167–94; Carruthers, Mary J. *The Book of Memory: A Study of Memory in Medieval Culture.* Cambridge: Cambridge University Press, 1990; Fredborg, Karin Margareta. "The Scholastic Teaching of Rhetoric in the Middle Ages." *Cahiers de l'Institut du Moyen-Age Grec et Latin* 55 (1987): 85–105; Kelly, Douglas. *The Arts of Poetry and Prose.* Typologie des Sources du Moyen Age Occidental, fasc. 59. Turnhout: Brepols, 1991; Kennedy, George A. *Classical Rhetoric and Its Christian and Secular Tradition from Ancient to Modern Times.* Chapel Hill: University of North Carolina Press, 1980; Murphy, James J. *Rhetoric in the Middle Ages: A History of Rhetorical Theory from Saint Augustine to the Renaissance.* Berke-ley: University of California Press, 1974; Murphy, James J. *Medieval Rhetoric: A Select Bibliography.* Toronto Medieval Bibliographies 3. 2d ed. Toronto: University of Toronto Press, 1989 [extensive and comprehensive]; Murphy, James J., and Martin Camargo. "The Middle Ages." In *The Present State of Scholarship in Historical and Contemporary Rhetoric,* ed. Winifred Bryan Horner. Rev. ed. Columbia: University of Missouri Press, 1990, pp. 45–83 [useful and accessible].

See also Bede; Boethius; Chaucer; Exemplum; Fathers of the Church (Augustine); Grammatical Treatises; John of Salisbury; Literary Influences: Classical, Medieval Latin; Schools; Sermons; Universities; Wycliffite Texts

Richard I (1157–1199; r. 1189–99)

Son of Henry II and Eleanor of Aquitaine. Richard the Lionheart was already duke of Aquitaine in right of his mother and heir-apparent to the English throne upon the death of his elder brother, Henry "the Young King," in 1183. His nickname, "the Lionheart" (Fr. "Coeur de Lion"), can be traced back to Gerald of Wales (d. ca. 1223), who compared the king to a lion, and can already be found circulating in a 13th-century romance of Richard's life.

Just as his late brother would have been a disastrous king, Richard could have been a great one had he spent his reign in England rather than on crusade and in the Angevin lands across the Channel. Although a man of knightly prowess, a writer of courtly poetry, patron of culture, cunning politician, and diplomat, Richard exhibited qualities regarded today as repulsive. Even by contemporary standards he could be less than humane, vengeful and beastly; however, he was the ideal martial king and a masterful leader of men. A recent study (by Gillingham) has refuted the view that Richard was homosexual. His reign is most conveniently examined by looking at his role in Angevin politics on the Continent, at his conduct of the Third Crusade, and at the governance of England during his nine-and-a-half-year absence.

Filial piety was not a characteristic of Richard's personality. Henry II sought to maintain the territorial integrity of his lands in France, fighting a doomed struggle against Louis VII (1137–80) and Philip II (1180–1223), a struggle that, under Richard's youngest brother, John, would result in the loss of all English holdings north of the Loire. Richard, desiring effective control of his inheritance, revolted against his father in 1173–74 and again in 1188–89, both times in alliance with the king of France. The warfare was not only patricidal, but fratricidal as well—as John and his brother Geoffrey of Brittany fought against both Henry II and Richard.

Although the conflict was not resolved before the death of Henry, after his return from crusade the fighting decisively favored the Lionheart. The promising course of the wars ended with Richard's death, while fighting a contumacious vassal in Aquitaine: an engagement waged over political issues, not over treasure trove (as some romantic versions of the story have it). Perhaps the greatest tragedy of Richard's early death was not the coming frustration of English ambitions on the Continent but the opportunity denied him to demonstrate his potential greatness as king of England.

Richard was best known in his own day as a crusader, as he is in literature, owing to the once great popularity of Walter Scott's *The Talisman.* For European affairs the most important development of the Crusade was the Treaty of Messina, sealed in 1191. Philip II (Philip Augustus) of France granted territorial boons to Richard, but by this agreement Richard recognized Philip's suzerainty over the Angevin lands on the Continent. Shortly after the two kings arrived in the Holy Land, Philip, a reluctant crusader, fell conveniently ill and returned home, motivated largely by his hope of taking advantage of Richard's absence so as to meddle in the English lordships in France. Richard conducted himself brilliantly as soldier and general and entered into Scott's legend as a revered and worthy opponent and respected friend of Saladin.

After helping to settle the political problems of the Latin kingdom of Jerusalem Richard left for England in October 1192. However, nature and politics interrupted the journey; a victim of shipwreck, he then fell into the hands of the duke of Austria, who delivered him to Henry, the Holy Roman Emperor. Henry, with the active support of Philip of France, kept the Lionheart in captivity until April 1194, when he was released after paying a king's ransom.

Richard had made careful plans for the governance of England during his absence; his kingdom, of course, had been accustomed to an absent king ever since the Norman conquest, owing to the royal policy of ruling personally over their French lands as over their English ones. Richard had a smoothly functioning machinery of government, guided such by able and experienced administrators as William Longchamp, Hubert Walter, and Geoffrey Fitz Peter. Every source of revenue was efficiently exploited, though at Richard's death the treasury was empty—unremitting warfare being the most expensive activity in which a government engages.

Despite the continuing plots of Prince John the country remained loyal to its king and his ministers. In Richard's absence there was less initiation of new institutions than refinement in administration; the great inquest of 1194 checked up on the enforcement of royal judicial, feudal, and financial rights. The role of what would become known as the gentry expanded in the administration of justice; while the end was not foreseen by Richard's ministers, the ultimate result of this enlargement of nonnobles' participation in government gave those of less than noble birth a sense that the government was theirs as well as the king's.

Until recent decades historians have tended to deprecate Richard, as they have Henry V. And yet the popular opinion of his own day is worth something. Wars were not viewed from a modern perspective, nor were their aims to be construed in terms of the goals of modern war. Richard was highly regarded by his contemporaries; perhaps they knew better than we what it meant to be a chivalric hero.

James W. Alexander

Bibliography

Appleby, John. *England without Richard, 1189–1199.* Ithaca: Cornell University Press, 1965; Bridge, Antony. *Richard the Lionheart.* London: Grafton, 1989; Gillingham, John. *Richard the Lionheart.* 2d ed. London: Weidenfeld & Nicolson, 1989 [the "select bibliography" and the chapter notes provide a full bibliography]; Gillingham, John. *Richard Coeur de Lion: Kingship, Chivalry and War in the Twelfth Century.* London: Hambledon, 1994; Landon, Lionel. *The Itinerary of King Richard I.* Pipe Roll Society 51. London: Pipe Roll Society, 1935; Nelson, Janet L., ed. *Richard Coeur de Lion in History and Myth.* London: King's College London, 1992; Painter, Sidney. "The Third Crusade: Richard Lionhearted and Philip Augustus." In *A History of the Crusades,* gen. ed. Kenneth M. Setton. 2d ed. Vol. 2: *The Later Crusades, 1189–1311,* ed. Robert Lee Wolff and Harry W. Hazard. Madison: University of Wisconsin Press, 1969, pp. 45–86.

See also Angevin Empire; Eleanor of Aquitaine; Henry II; Hubert Walter; John; Matter of England; William Marshal

Richard II (1367–1399; r. 1377–99)

Born at Bordeaux on 6 January 1367, the second son of Edward the Black Prince, Prince of Wales (d. 1376). After Richard succeeded his grandfather Edward III in 1377, government in his minority was conducted jointly by his three uncles (especially the eldest, John of Gaunt), the earls, and leading officials of his grandfather and father.

Richard displayed courage and leadership during the Peasant Rebellion of 1381 and in the next few years was encouraged by bosom companions and some officials to assert his will over patronage and policies. His prestige was enhanced by his childless marriage in 1382 to Anne of Bohemia (d. 1394), daughter of the late Emperor Charles IV, and by his first major expedition to Scotland (1385). But parliaments were concerned about royal finances, and there was growing disquiet, expressed by some magnates, over failures to check the French in war and over royal indulgence of court intrigues against Gaunt. In 1386 Richard, freed from Gaunt's shadow by the latter's expedition to Castile, alienated public opinion by the evasion of financial restraints and the failure to prevent the buildup of an invasion threat from a French armada in Flanders.

In the autumn parliament of 1386 the Commons, abetted by the king's uncle Thomas of Woodstock, duke of Gloucester, and Thomas Arundel, bishop of Ely, secured the dismissal from the chancellorship and the impeachment of a royal favorite, Michael de la Pole, earl of Suffolk. A commission was appointed with wide powers to monitor administration for a year. Determined to evade its control, Richard toured the realm in 1387, seeking support. He prompted the judges to define recent political initiatives as treasonable encroachments on royal prerogative; he aroused suspicions of a sellout to the French by seeking a conference with King Charles VI.

In November Gloucester and the earls of Arundel and Warwick rose in arms and launched an Appeal of Treason against five of the king's supporters. Richard conceded that the appeal would be heard in parliament.

The "Appellants" were joined by Gaunt's son Henry Bolingbroke and by Thomas Mowbray, earl of Nottingham. Richard's close friend Robert de Vere, duke of Ireland, raised an army at his instigation, only to be defeated by the Appellants at Radcot Bridge (in Oxfordshire). In parliament in 1388 the appellees were found guilty; the two in custody, the Londoner Nicholas Brembre and Chief Justice Robert Tresilian, were executed. The Commons impeached other judges and four household officers; the latter (notably Sir Simon Burley, who had tutored the king) were executed.

The Appellants soon lost common purpose and support. The schemes of Gloucester and Arundel for an invasion of France failed, and in August, at Otterburn in Northumberland, the English suffered the worst defeat by the Scots since Bannockburn (1314). In May 1389 Richard declared himself of age and took control of government; in the early 1390s his moderate exercise of authority was underpinned by the returned Gaunt, principal negotiator in attempts to make a final peace with the French.

Richard boosted his authority by suspending the liberties of London (1391–92) and leading an expedition to Ireland (1394–95); London citizens and Irish chieftains alike submitted to his mercy. Continuous truces with the French since 1389 culminated in 1396 in a truce for 28 years; Richard married Charles VI's daughter Isabella.

But the moves in the 1390s toward an Anglo-French rapprochement provoked widespread disquiet; the earl of Arundel was a leading critic, and from 1395 Gloucester emerged as one. In July 1397 Richard arrested Gloucester, Arundel, and Warwick; young nobles made an Appeal of Treason against them for their acts in 1386–88, and they were found guilty in the September parliament. It was announced then that Gloucester had died in custody; Arundel was executed, Warwick sentenced to life imprisonment. The condemnations of 1388 were reversed, and Richard rewarded his noble partisans, such as his half-brother John Holland, earl of Huntingdon, with exalted peerage titles and the forfeited estates of the traitors.

In 1397 Richard had a more solid base of noble support than in 1387 and could call on the many knights and esquires he had retained in recent years, as well as his bodyguard of Cheshire archers. But the general alarm caused by his policies was augmented by the exclusion from the general pardon of January 1398, of those who had ridden against him. Supporters of the Appellants in 1387–88 now had to seek the royal mercy and pay fines. Richard's daring restructuring of magnate power was threatened when, in this session, Bolingbroke accused Thomas Mowbray, his fellow Appellant of 1387–88 and 1397, of treason. In September Richard intervened when the parties were about to settle their quarrel by judicial duel and sentenced Mowbray to exile, for life and Bolingbroke for ten years. On the death of Bolingbroke's father, Gaunt, in February 1399 Richard made his banishment perpetual and confiscated the Lancastrian inheritance.

In June, soon after Richard had gone on expedition to Ireland to salvage his 1395 settlement, Bolingbroke sailed with a small company from France and landed in Yorkshire. He was soon joined by Lancastrian retainers and northern lords, including the earls of Northumberland and Westmorland, disgruntled by Richard's interference in their sphere of influence. Bolingbroke advanced through the Midlands to seize Bristol; Richard's uncle and regent, Edmund duke of York, along with other supporters, was unable to rally effective opposition. From Bristol Bolingbroke moved up through the Welsh marches to capture Chester, the main bastion of Ricardian sentiment.

In Ireland Richard failed to appreciate the urgent need to rally support in person in north Wales and Cheshire; he landed too late in south Wales, moving north to Conway after his forces had disintegrated. The mediating earl of Northumberland betrayed Richard into Bolingbroke's hands; he was conveyed as a prisoner from Flint to the Tower of London. There he was apparently forced to abdicate, and in September a version of this agreement was submitted to the parliament summoned in his name. His requests for a public hearing were refused; the estates accepted the charges made against him in parliament as ground for deposition and acknowledged Bolingbroke's claim to the throne.

The deposed Richard was moved to other prisons, eventually to Pontefract in Yorkshire, where he died (or was killed) after the rising in January 1400 by some of his former favorites—Huntingdon, Huntingdon's nephew Thomas Holland, earl of Kent, John Montague, earl of Salisbury, and Thomas, Lord Despenser. It was easily suppressed. In February Richard's body was brought from his prison for public view in London and buried obscurely in the Dominican friary at Langley, Hertfordshire. In 1416 Henry V moved it to the splendid tomb Richard had prepared for himself in Westminster Abbey.

Richard was 6 feet tall, well built, handsome, and light-haired. Willful, devious, vindictive, sharp-tempered but not bloodthirsty, he was capable of showing affection and inspiring loyalty. He wanted his majesty to awe his subjects but could exert the common touch. He shared the conventional tastes of the higher nobility: hunting, the tournament (mainly as a spectator), courtly poetry. Not notably pious, in maturity he shared with Charles VI an enthusiasm for peace among Christians, an end to the Great Schism of the papacy, and a crusade against the Turks.

His real passion was to stabilize the personal authority of kingship, raising respect for its holy nature by trying to procure the canonization of Edward II and adopting the supposed heraldic arms of Edward the Confessor. His regal ideals and some of the ways in which he tried to project them can be seen in his portrait in Westminster Abbey, in the Wilton Diptych (National Gallery, London), and in his rebuilding of Westminster Hall. Denunciations of his rule are to be found in the poem *Richard the Redeless* and in John Gower's *Tripartite Chronicle*.

Anthony E. Goodman

Bibliography

PRIMARY

Creton, Jean. *A Metrical History of the Deposition of Richard II.* Ed. J. Webb. *Archaeologia* 20 (1824): 295–423; Given-Wilson, Chris, ed. and trans. *Chronicles of the Revolution, 1397–1400: The Reign of Richard II.* Manchester: Manchester University Press, 1993; Hector, L.C., and Barbara F. Harvey, eds. and trans. *The Westminster Chronicle, 1381–1394.* Oxford: Clarendon, 1982; de Mézières, Philippe de. *Letter to Richard II.* Trans. G.W. Coopland. Liverpool: Liverpool University Press, 1975.

SECONDARY

Aston, Margaret. *Thomas Arundel: A Study of Church Life in the Reign of Richard II.* Oxford: Clarendon, 1967; Barron, Caroline M. "The Tyranny of Richard II." *BIHR* 41 (1968): 1–18; Clarke, Maude V. *Fourteenth Century Studies.* Oxford: Clarendon, 1937; Du Boulay, F.R.H., and Caroline M. Barron, eds. *The Reign of Richard II: Essays in Honour of May McKisack.* London: University of London, Athlone, 1971; Gillespie, James L. "Richard II's Archers of the Crown." *Journal of British Studies* 18 (1979): 14–29; Given-Wilson, Chris. *The Royal Household and the King's Affinity: Service, Politics and Finance in England, 1360–1413.* New Haven: Yale University Press, 1986; Goodman, Anthony. *The Loyal Conspiracy: The Lords Appellant under Richard II.* London: Routledge & Kegan Paul, 1971; Harvey, John H. "The Wilton Diptych—A Reexamination." *Archaeologia* 98 (1961): 1–28; Mathew, Gervase. *The Court of Richard II.* London: Murray, 1968; Palmer, J.J.N. *England, France and Christendom, 1377–99.* London: Routledge & Kegan Paul, 1972; Saul, Nigel. *Richard II.* New Haven and London: Yale University Press, 1997; Scattergood, V. J., and J.W. Sherborne, eds. *English Court Culture in the Later Middle Ages.* London: Duckworth, 1983; Tuck, Anthony. *Richard II and the English Nobility.* London: Arnold, 1973.

See also Appellants; Edward the Black Prince; Gower; Henry IV; Impeachment; Lancaster, John Duke of; Monarchy and Kingship; *Richard the Redeless;* Westminster Abbey; Wilton Diptych

Richard III (1452–1485; r. 1483–85)

No medieval English king has generated more controversy and emotion, not least as a result of Shakespeare's portrayal of him as the personification of evil. Shakespeare, moreover, clearly reflected images already well formed in early Tudor times. Polydore Vergil, for instance, considered Richard a man who "thought of nothing but tyranny and cruelty"; Sir Thomas More derided him as an ambitious and ruthless monstrosity "who spared no man's death whose life withstood his purpose." Even the king's contemporaries were frequently critical. Dominic Mancini, writing within a few months of his seizure of the throne in June 1483, remarked forcefully on his "ambition and lust for power," and the well-informed Crowland chronicler was scathing on the tyrannical northern-dominated regime that, he believed, Richard established in the south.

Yet the last Yorkist king has always had his admirers as well as critics. Thomas Langton, bishop of St. David's, declared in August 1483 that "he contents the people wherever he goes better than ever did any prince," and the York Civic Records reported "great heaviness" in the city when news arrived of his fate ("piteously slain and murdered") on Bosworth Field in 1485. Modern historians, too, have brought in notably contrasting verdicts, ranging from Charles Ross's conclusion that no one familiar with "the careers of King Louis XI of France, in Richard's own time, or Henry VIII of England . . . would wish to cast any special slur on Richard, still less to select him as the exemplar of a tyrant" to Desmond Seward's hostile biography of this "peculiarly grim young English precursor of Machiavelli's Prince."

The youngest son of Richard of York, Richard duke of Gloucester proved notably loyal to his brother Edward IV during the crisis of 1469–71 and in the 1470s showed himself as reliable and trustworthy as any of the king's servants (and was rewarded accordingly). His rule of the north during these years was singularly successful; he built a powerful affinity there. Mancini admitted that he "acquired the favour of the people." No one will ever know for certain whether he set his sights on the throne as soon as he heard of Edward IV's sudden death on 9 April 1483, or if, at first, he merely intended to obtain control of his nephew Edward V so as to prevent the Wydevilles—the family of young Edward's mother—from securing power. What is clear is that the series of preemptive strikes by which he outmaneuvered the queen's family, seized Edward V, eliminated William, Lord Hastings, and rendered the Yorkist establishment impotent, enabled him to become king in his own right before the end of June 1483. The probable murder of his nephews in the Tower of London was the inevitable culmination of this ruthless pursuit of power.

Richard III may have been convinced that he was indeed serving the interest of the nation; such, through the ages, has been the politician's justification for arbitrary action. The critical turning point in his fortunes probably was the rebellion of the duke of Buckingham (hitherto his closest and most spectacularly rewarded supporter) in October 1483. Edward IV's men, who for the most part had accepted Richard's protectorate and even acquiesced in his usurpation, now deserted him in droves in the south and west. Even more ominously the exiled Henry Tudor, earl of Richmond, emerged at the same time as a potentially serious rival. The king responded vigorously to these threats; the rebellion was put down. In its aftermath, however, given the extent of southern defection and the numbers who now fled the country, he was forced more and more into dependence on his own affinity. This meant, in particular, men from the north. Their advancement in the royal household and appointments to office, not only in southern and western counties but in the Midlands, is amply documented.

Since he reigned for so short a time, it is difficult either to judge Richard's potential and qualities as a ruler or to draw meaningful conclusions about his government. The 15th-century antiquary John Rous, later one of his harshest critics, recorded that he ruled his subjects "full commendably, punishing offenders of his laws, especially extortioners and oppressors of his commons," and won the "love of all his subjects rich and poor." His only parliament—perhaps with his personal encouragement—passed measures clearly benefiting the people; and his establishment of the Council of the North in July 1484 was both popular and enduring.

Though he did make considerable efforts to widen the basis of his support, with the threat of Henry Tudor looming ever larger, his reliance on his own affinity, largely from the north, remained paramount. When he at last faced his rival on the battlefield of Bosworth on 22 August 1485, he was backed largely by the same men who had brought him to power; many, though by no means all, probably fought for him with vigor. However, his own death (in the midst of the action and, according to the Crowland continuator, striving to the end "like a spirited and most courageous prince") made the accession of Henry VII inevitable.

Keith R. Dockray

Bibliography

PRIMARY

Armstrong, C.A.J., ed. and trans. *Dominic Mancini: The Usurpation of Richard III.* 2d ed. Oxford: Clarendon, 1969; Pronay, Nicholas, and John Cox, eds. *The Crowland Chronicle Continuations, 1459–1486.* London: Sutton, for the Richard III and Yorkist History Trust, 1986.

SECONDARY

Dockray, Keith. *Richard III: A Reader in History.* Gloucester: Sutton, 1988 [commentary plus a selection of documents]; Hicks, Michael. *Richard III: The Man behind the Myth.* London: Collins & Brown, 1991; Horrox, Rosemary. *Richard III: A Study of Service.* Cambridge: Cambridge University Press, 1989 [scholarly treatment of politics and government]; Markham, Clements R. *Richard III: His Life and Character, Reviewed in the Light of Recent Research.* London: Smith, Elder, 1906 [very sympathetic]; Pollard, A.J. *Richard III and the Princes in the Tower.* Stroud: Sutton, 1991; Ross, Charles. *Richard III.* London: Eyre Methuen, 1981 [major modern scholarly treatment]; Seward, Desmond. *Richard III: England's Black Legend.* London: Country Life, 1983 [the case against].

See also Bastard Feudalism; Edward IV; Edward V; Henry VI; Henry VII; Wars of the Roses

Richard the Redeless and Mum and the Sothsegger

Two related fragments of alliterative verse (1399–1400; 1403–06) concerning King Richard II of England and his successor, Henry IV. The two fragments were once considered to be parts of one longer poem (sometimes referred to together as *Mum and the Sothsegger*), but recent scholarship has shown that they are probably separate works, perhaps by the same poet. Both are written in alliterative long lines, and only one manuscript of each survives (*Richard*, CUL Ll.4.14; *Mum*, BL Add. 41666). *Richard* is 857 lines long, broken off at the end; *Mum* is 1,751 lines long, with material missing before the point where the manuscript begins. The author or authors of the fragments are unknown, but the original dialect of both fragments was probably Southwest Midland.

Richard the Redeless can be dated between August 1399, when Richard was taken prisoner, and February 1400, when he died. The fragment is divided into a prologue and four sections called passus. In the prologue the poet hears news of Henry's invasion of England, and he uses the occasion to write a poem of advice to King Richard. Passus 1 criticizes Richard's favorites; passus 2 and 3 denounce his retainers, the White Harts, who attacked the duke of Gloucester, the earl of Warwick, and the earl of Arundel and his son, allegorized as the Swan, the Bear, and the Horse and the Colt. Passus 4 criticizes Richard's extravagances and the corruption of the parliament of 1397.

Mum and the Sothsegger can be dated after the execution of certain friars for treason in 1402; other events in the fragment suggest that it was completed by 1406. At the beginning of the fragment the poet is discussing King Henry's household and asserts that a truthteller ("sothsegger") is needed in the court. Unfortunately no one dares to fill this post, and instead all follow the example of Mum, who profits by remaining silent. Troubled, the poet searches for answers in the university, the friary, the abbey, the monastery, and the cathedral. He finds that Mum is master everywhere. Wearied, the poet falls asleep and in a dream vision he encounters a gardener keeping bees who tells him that all evil has its source in Mum. The gardener advises the poet to follow the truthteller, who resides in the heart of man, and to write his poem and send it to the king. Upon waking the poet does so.

Both fragments reflect the poet's (or poets') awareness of political theories similar to those of William of Ockham and Marsilius of Padua, who emphasized the rights of the governed as a limit on royal power. Verbal similarities between *Mum* and *Piers Plowman* suggest that the poet was familiar with Langland's work. *Mandeville's Travels* and the *De proprietatibus rerum* of Bartholomaeus Anglicus are direct sources for passages in *Mum*.

Deborah Everhart

Bibliography

PRIMARY

Barr, Helen, ed. *The Piers Plowman Tradition.* London: Dent, 1993 [edition of *Richard, Mum,* and related poems]; Day, Mabel, and Robert Steele, eds. *Mum and the Sothsegger.* EETS o.s. 199. London: Humphrey Milford, 1936.

SECONDARY

New *CBEL* 1:545; *Manual* 5:1504–06, 1705–07; Barr, Helen. "The Relationship of *Richard the Redeless* and *Mum and the Sothsegger:* Some New Evidence." *YLS* 4

(1990): 105–33; Ferguson, Arthur B. "The Problem of Counsel in *Mum and the Sothsegger.*" *Studies in the Renaissance* 2 (1955): 67–83; Mohl, Ruth. "Theories of Monarchy in *Mum and the Sothsegger.*" *PMLA* 59 (1944): 26–44; Scattergood, V.J. *Politics and Poetry in the Fifteenth Century.* London: Blandford, 1971.

See also Alliterative Revival; Henry IV; *Mandeville's Travels; Piers Plowman;* Richard II; Satire; William of Ockham

Riddles, Old English

The composition of riddles, both popular and literary, is a virtually universal cultural phenomenon. Whereas in the Western "literary" tradition of discourse, riddles have today lost any significant status, they appear to have formed a serious genre in the early Middle Ages, particularly in Anglo-Saxon England. The Exeter Book collection of nearly 100 OE riddles (including one Latin riddle) stands witness to this, as do the several extensive collections of Latin riddles, or *aenigmata,* written by Anglo-Saxon authors chiefly in the 7th and 8th centuries. The vernacular riddles show especially close affinities with that ubiquitous metaphoric form of Germanic literature the kenning, a feature that lies at the core of much Anglo-Saxon poetry as well.

Of primary importance for the development of the genre of Latin literary *aenigmata* is the collection of Symphosius, dated to the 4th or 5th century. His 100 *Aenigmata* consist of three hexameter lines each and form the earliest complete collection extant; they also seem to have had some influence on subsequent Anglo-Latin riddles of the Anglo-Saxon period. This influence is most clearly evident in the 100 riddles written by Aldhelm, abbot of Malmesbury and first archbishop of Sherborne (640?–709/10). Aldhelm explicitly acknowledges his debt to Symphosius in his *Letter to Acircius,* in which the *aenigmata* are intended to serve as illustrations of the metrical theory expounded in other parts of this letter, *De metris (On Meter)* and *De pedum regulis (On the Rules of Poetic Feet).* But whereas Symphosius's riddles lack religious orientation, Aldhelm imbues many of his with a Christian character.

Indebted to Aldhelm's *aenigmata* in subject matter and theme are the 40 riddles (nearly one-third of which deal with theological subjects) written by his younger contemporary Tatwine, archbishop of Canterbury (d. 734). This "incomplete" collection was supplemented by the Anglo-Latin writer Eusebius, also believed to be Hwætberht, friend of Bede and abbot of Wearmouth-Jarrow (ca. 680–ca. 744/47), who sought to expand the collection to 100 riddles by adding 60 of his own. Also among the known Anglo-Latin riddlers is Boniface, missionary to Germany, who wrote 20 *aenigmata* on the Christian virtues and vices.

The single most important and certainly finest collection of riddles of the period from a literary point of view is that found in the OE Exeter Book. While the manuscript can be dated to the late 10th century, scholars have reached no consensus on the date of composition of the riddles themselves. Attempts to date them by linguistic means have been largely unsatisfactory, and nothing is known of their authorship. The theory current in the late 19th century that Cynewulf penned them all is no longer accepted. The relationship of the Latin riddling tradition to the Exeter Book riddles has long been a matter of debate. Beyond the close translations of two of Aldhelm's enigmas (nos. 33 and 40) only three of the OE riddles show an undeniable debt in terms of subject matter, content, and form (nos. 47, 85, and 86 correspond to riddles by Symphosius). In other cases any resemblance between the Latin and the OE may be due as much to their common subjects, themes, and motifs as to any direct derivation.

In comparison with the Latin collections the Exeter Book riddles are a heterogeneous compilation, exhibiting greater diversity in their subject matter, length, and form, a fact that many feel supports the notion that the collection was compiled from disparate sources rather than composed by one author. Unlike their Latin counterparts no solutions appear in the manuscript (with the exception of five cryptographic riddles, whose solutions are coded and concealed in runes), and as a consequence much of OE riddle scholarship has devoted itself to debating their solutions.

In addition to the Exeter Book collection the 9th- to 10th-century poetic dialogue *Solomon and Saturn II* contains riddling questions, many of which resemble the Exeter Book riddles in form and style. That such riddling dialogues were popular among the Anglo-Saxons is suggested by the survival of a number of them, in both Anglo-Latin and the vernacular. To the latter belong the prose *Solomon and Saturn* and *Adrian and Ritheus,* to the former Alcuin's *Disputatio Pippini cum Albino,* the Pseudo-Bede riddles of the so-called *Flores* collection, and the *Jocaseria* in CUL Gg.v.35. A lone prose riddle in OE survives in the Vitellius Psalter (BL Cotton Vitellius E.xviii).

But the apparent taste among the Anglo-Saxons for lyric riddling is attested elsewhere in the corpus of vernacular literature as well. Other works notable for their riddlelike qualities include the OE *Rune Poem* and *The Ruin,* and it has often been remarked that such gnomic verses as *Maxims I* and *II* come close to being a frame for riddles. Furthermore, in *Christ I* and *II,* while dealing with two baffling mysteries in his subject matter (the Trinity in *Christ I* 216–24; the absence of angels dressed in white garments at Christ's birth in *Christ II* 440–41), the poets use language that is strongly and appropriately reminiscent of OE riddling diction. The opening of the Cross's speech in *The Dream of the Rood* also shows affinities with the riddles, and the poem's dominant rhetorical mode—prosopopoeia (speech attributed to an object)—is shared by about half of the OE riddles in the Exeter Book. In fact Aldhelm draws an explicit connection between riddling and prosopopoeia and the appropriateness of both for composing poetry on scriptural themes. This connection has in turn led to the belief that Aldhelm's *Letter to Acircius*—which contains both his 100 *aenigmata* and the discussion of prosopopoeia—may have had an influence on the composition of *The Dream of the Rood.*

David F. Johnson

Bibliography

PRIMARY

ASPR 3:180–210, 224–25, 229–43; Crossley-Holland, Kevin, trans. *The Exeter Book Riddles.* Rev. ed. London: Penguin, 1993; Muir, Bernard, ed. *The Exeter Anthology of Old English Poetry: An Edition of Exeter Dean and Chapter MS 3501.* Exeter: University of Exeter Press, 1994; Tupper, Frederick, ed. *The Riddles of the Exeter Book.* Boston: Ginn, 1910 [an older but still valuable edition and study]; Williamson, Craig, ed. *The Old English Riddles of the Exeter Book.* Chapel Hill: University of North Carolina Press, 1977; Williamson, Craig, trans. *A Feast of Creatures: Anglo-Saxon Riddle-Songs.* Philadelphia: University of Pennsylvania Press, 1982.

SECONDARY

Fry, Donald K. "Exeter Book Riddle Solutions." *OEN* 15/1 (Fall 1981): 22–33 [summary of proposed solutions to 1980]; Orton, Paul. "The Technique of Object-Personification in *The Dream of the Rood* and a Comparison with the Old English Riddles." *Leeds Studies in English* n.s. 11 (1980): 1–18; Rowe, Elizabeth Ashman. "Irony in the Old English and Old Norse Interrogative Situation." *Neophilologus* 73 (1989): 477–79; Sorrell, Paul. "Oaks, Ship Riddles, and the Old English *Rune Poem.*" *ASE* 19 (1990): 103–16; Stewart, Ann Harleman. "Kenning and Riddle in Old English." *Papers on Language and Literature* 15 (1979): 115–36.

See also Adrian and Ritheus; Aldhelm; Anglo-Latin Literature to 1066; *Dream of the Rood;* Eusebius; Exeter Book; *Husband's Message; Maxims;* Runes; *Solomon and Saturn;* Tatwine; Wisdom Literature

Roads and the Road System

Ancient tracks formed the basis of a local network of roads in the early Middle Ages; continued use was also made of major Roman roads. However, a proper system of roads developed only with the centralization of government in the two centuries after the Conquest, as traffic became focused on London. A fully established system, with main roads radiating out from London, was established by the mid-14th century and is shown on the Gough Map (Bodl. Gough Gen. Top. 16; ca. 1360); there was no fundamental change in this network before 1600.

From Anglo-Saxon times roads of special importance were under the protection of the king. The definition of the "king's highway" was extended to include all routes between markets and to ports; additionally the crown assumed the right to regulate the maintenance of private as well as public highways—and highways also included bridges and causeways. In the country main roads were wide enough for two wagons. Roads were not surfaced and were maintained largely by the passage of feet; flooding was the main hazard, and maintenance usually meant clearing drainage ditches. The responsi-

bility for this, with that for building and repairing bridges and causeways, was deemed to lie with the owner of the land through which the highway ran.

Maintenance was a complex and contentious issue, especially with regard to building bridges, which were expensive. Grants of pontage were made by the crown to help defray these expenses. Many new bridges and causeways were in fact built, a testimony to the growth in traffic and the increased significance of the road system. In urban areas town councils assumed responsibility for the maintenance of roads, and the main urban streets were often paved. The council was assisted by grants of pontage and pavage; properties were also donated by townspeople so their rents would form a fund for bridge maintenance. Pious donations were responsible for the upkeep of many routes, particularly those leading from the town to important local markets.

Traffic on the roads was heavy. By preference people traveled by land, not by water. The Norman and Angevin kings were constantly on the move, summer and winter; with them went a vast baggage train. Subsequently the centralization of government in London and the extension of royal power increased the travel of royal servants and justices. War brought the movement of troops and arms, and that of royal purveyors, collecting forced levies of food. War against the Scots entailed moving the government machine to York with wagonloads of legal and administrative records. Ordinary people took to the road on pilgrimage, to seek justice, to buy and sell. Traders carried valuable commodities, such as cloth, by pack horse. Although bulky goods were transported by water where feasible, many went by cart. This was the commonest means of transport to market; one of the duties of a peasant was to cart goods for his lord.

Heather Swanson

Bibliography

Flower, C.T., ed. *Public Works in Mediaeval Law.* Selden Society 32, 40. London: Quaritch, 1915–23; Stenton, Doris M. "Communications." In *Medieval England,* ed. Austin Lane Poole. New ed. Oxford: Clarendon, 1958, pp. 196–208; Stenton, F.M. "The Road System of Medieval England." *EcHR,* 1st ser. 7 (1936): 1–21; Willard, James F. "Inland Transport in the Fifteenth Century." *Speculum* 1 (1926): 361–74.

See also Fairs and Markets; Pilgrimages; Trade

Robertsbridge Codex

This is the name usually given to the oldest piece of notated keyboard music in existence, though it is in fact not a codex but a music fragment used in the binding of an old register of Robertsbridge Abbey in East Sussex (BL Add. 28550, fols. 43 and 44). It contains the fragmentary conclusion of an *estampie* or similar dance form, two complete *estampies,* two arrangements of motets from the *Roman de Fauvel* (1316), and an incomplete arrangement of an English sacred cantilena. The date, formerly believed to be ca. 1325, is more plausibly put at ca. 1360.

The fragment is certainly English in origin (the repeat structure of the *estampies* is clarified by the word "return"), but most of the music in it is not English. The *estampies,* not so called in the manuscript, are related in style to the Italian 14th-century *istampita;* the two motets are French, and only the last piece, "Flos vernalis," is of undoubted English origin. The notation throughout is italianate in character, and its manifest archaisms are what prompted the earlier of the dates mentioned above. But no native Italian manuscript of Ars Nova polyphony can be shown to predate 1350, and as the notation is used to clarify the originally ambiguous semibreve groupings of the French works, a date in the second half of the 14th century seems more likely. This is confirmed by the fact that the overall compass required (*c–e*) is fully chromatic from *f* upward, something again that is otherwise unknown prior to the later part of the century.

The music is conceived idiomatically for a keyboard instrument, being based on an elaborately ornamented top part accompanied by left-hand chords interspersed with melodic progressions. In the *estampies* there are also passages of hocket between the hands.

Its original purpose is not known for certain, but the manuscript may have been associated with the court of the captive King John II of France, who was a prisoner of Edward III from 1357 to 1360. In 1360 Edward gave John an *echiquier,* a generic name for a stringed keyboard instrument; the Robertsbridge fragment perhaps offers us a glimpse of the repertoire for which it was destined, or of one of the king's court organists.

John Caldwell

Bibliography

PRIMARY

Apel, Willi, ed. *Keyboard Music of the Fourteenth and Fifteenth Centuries.* Corpus of Early Keyboard Music 1. N.p.: American Institute of Musicology, 1963.

SECONDARY

Apel, Willi. *The Notation of Polyphonic Music 900–1600.* 4th ed. Cambridge: Mediaeval Academy of America, 1953; Caldwell, John. *English Keyboard Music before the Nineteenth Century.* Oxford: Blackwell, 1973; Harrison, Frank Ll. "Plainsong into Polyphony: Repertories and Structures *c.* 1270–*c.* 1420." In *Music in the Medieval English Liturgy: Plainsong and Mediaeval Music Society Centennial Essays,* ed. Susan K. Rankin and David Hiley. Oxford: Clarendon, 1993, pp. 303–54; Parrish, Carl. *The Notation of Medieval Music.* New York: Norton, 1957; Roesner, Edward H. Introduction. *Philippe de Vitry: Complete Works.* Monaco: L'Oiseau-Lyre, 1984, pp. v–vi.

See also Cantilena; Dance; Motet; Notation of Polyphonic Music; Organ

Rolle, Richard, of Hampole (d. 1349)

Hermit and mystical writer. Little is known of Rolle's life, although some facts can be gleaned from the readings of the liturgical office prepared for the possibility of his canonization, and some conjectures can be made based on his writings. According to the office he came from Thornton, near Pickering, in the diocese of York, and was sent to Oxford with the support of Thomas Neville, archdeacon of Durham. He left the university at nineteen, however, and returned home, where he retired to the forest to live as a hermit. Shortly thereafter he was taken in by John de Dalton, a local squire, and given an eremitic lodging within Dalton's household. This proved inadequate, and he removed to some other place— apparently against Dalton's will. Rolle seems also at this time to have been tempted to take a lover (possibly a real person was involved, or perhaps only a diabolical apparition) but resisted the temptation by invoking the precious blood of Jesus.

Rolle's writings contain a number of passages referring to criticism, particularly for irregularity in changing his place of hermitage. However, no record survives indicating either his formal enclosure as a hermit or formal proceedings against him. Records of his education and possible ordination are similarly lacking. We do not know when he took up residence at Hampole, Yorkshire, nor in what relation he stood to the Cistercian convent there, in whose cemetery (later church) he was buried.

Although we have only the vaguest knowledge of his worldly life, Rolle has left us some clear indications of the progress of his spiritual development. In the *Incendium amoris* he describes the reception of the gifts of "heat, sweetness, and song" that are characteristic of his spirituality. The first gift he received was that of actual physical heat warming his breast. At first, he says, he thought that what he felt was some form of temptation; but he came to recognize it as corresponding to a second gift, of sweetness in prayers. Finally, while at prayer in chapel one day, he heard "as it were a ringing of singers of psalms, or rather, of songs." Time and again Rolle writes of this threefold gift of heat, sweetness, and song *(calor, dulcor, canor).*

Works

Rolle's works can be divided into three classes: scriptural commentaries, original mystical treatises, and lyrical and poetic compositions.

The most important scriptural commentaries are the Latin and English commentaries on the Psalter; Rolle also composed Latin commentaries on the first few verses of the Song of Songs, the first six chapters of the book of Revelation, and the Lamentations of Jeremiah. Five other treatises (including, particularly, the *Judica me Deus*) also derive their name and form from their commentary on particular scriptural verses. Another four commentaries are based on biblical texts used in the liturgy or on ecclesiastical texts. All of these lesser commentaries are in Latin. Although the commentaries are based for the most part on earlier works in the same genre (the Psalter commentaries, for example, derive largely from the "literal" explication in Peter Lombard's *Commentarium*), they also develop a number of themes characteristic of Rolle's interests and teaching, such as devotion to the name of Jesus, and the experience of heat, sweetness, and song. These works probably derive from the period of Rolle's spiritual maturity.

The most important works in Rolle's canon are his three great Latin treatises and his four Latin and English epistolary tracts. The first treatise, *De amore Dei contra amatores mundi,* compares the eternal joys of the lover of God with the passing pleasures of this world. In each of its seven chapters Rolle describes a different aspect of worldly love and shows how the lovers of this world, though they seem happier, will be betrayed in the end into eternal sorrow. The second major treatise, the *Incendium amoris,* deals more specifically than any of Rolle's other writings with his experience of spiritual heat, sweetness, and song and is more autobiographical as well. Although focused on these themes, the *Incendium* also treats discursively a number of theological topics—yet it always returns to Rolle's own spiritual experience and to the idea that God's contemplative gifts to those who love him alone far outweigh the worldly satisfaction of merely intellectual pursuits. The *Incendium* was translated into ME, along with the *Emendatio vitae,* by the Carmelite Richard Misyn. The third of Rolle's Latin treatises, the *Melos amoris,* is in some ways the most difficult of his works to describe: highly alliterative in style and allusive in form, it appears to represent and attempt to reproduce in writing the transformation of contemplative prayer into heavenly song that he describes as the culmination of his spiritual experience. The probable aim of the *Melos* is not so much persuasion as mystagogy—the re-creation in the reader's mind of the author's spiritual experience, which by grace the reader may also attain. The style of the *Melos* has led many to regard it as an immature work; but Arnould, its editor, has pointed out that it more probably manifests the latest stage of his spirituality.

Rolle's most important epistolary tract, and by far his most popular work, is the *Emendatio vitae.* This letter and the parallel English *Form of Living* are addressed in some manuscripts to two of Rolle's disciples—William (Stopes?) in the former case, Margaret Kirkby in the latter—and are probably the last things he wrote. Of particular importance in both is the treatment of the "three stages of love": insuperable, inseparable, and singular. The treatises also exhort Rolle's audience to an immediate rejection of the world's blandishments and conversion to God in the eremitic life. The *Form of Living* was translated into Latin, and the *Emendatio vitae* into English by Richard Misyn and no fewer than six other, independent translators. The themes of the stages of the love of God and the necessity of total conversion to him also occur in Rolle's two other English epistolary tracts, the *Commandment* and the *Ego dormio.* Rolle included a number of lyrics in the *Ego dormio* and the *Form of Living;* a further collection of eight to ten lyrics is attributed to him in two manuscripts. He also wrote the *Canticum amoris,* a Latin hymn of praise to the Virgin Mary.

Rolle's reputation, like that of many influential medieval writers, was so great that many works not written by him came to be associated with his name. Hope Emily Allen's *Writings Ascribed to Richard Rolle* has proven decisive in establishing his canon, although her conclusions regarding chronology and biographical references must still be viewed with some skepticism.

Teaching and Influence
The most distinctive feature of Richard Rolle's spirituality is the experience of the graces of heat, sweetness, and song that follows upon the total conversion from the world to God. He is not always consistent in the hierarchical and chronological ordering of these graces, however; nor despite important similarities, is their description entirely consistent with that of the three degrees of love—insuperable, inseparable, and singular—found in the later epistles. These three degrees apparently derive from Richard of St. Victor's *Quattuor gradus violentae charitatis,* minus the fourth (insatiable) degree.

For Rolle the rejection of the false pleasures of this world and a complete conversion to God are the *sine qua non* of the contemplative life, which he believes is most fully lived in the eremitic life. He considered the religious vocation to be comparatively worldly and grouped members of religious orders together with other lovers of this world.

The experience of heavenly song, with that of sensible heat and sweetness in prayer, is particularly characteristic of Rolle's spirituality and that of his followers. Certain sections of *The Cloud of Unknowing* and of Walter Hilton's *Scale of Perfection* and *Of Angels' Song* caution against using words like "heat," "sweetness," or "song" too literally in describing spiritual experience, a fact that suggests that this form of affective mysticism was popular in the later 14th century. These negative comments, together with more positive presentations of this kind of affective mysticism by Thomas Basset, Richard Methley, and John Norton, can be taken as evidence for an informal "school" of Richard Rolle.

Rolle achieved his greatest degree of popular influence with the spread of the devotion (particularly in lyric poetry) to the Passion of Christ and to the Holy Name of Jesus. According to Knowlton the cult of the Holy Name does not seem to have been prominent in England, despite imitations of the "Dulcis Jesu Memoria" and devotional pieces in the tradition of Anselm of Canterbury's *Meditations,* until after the time of Rolle. A number of late-14th- and 15th-century ME lyrics reflect not merely these devotional themes but also the phrasing of Rolle's devotional poems and descriptions of his own spiritual experiences. Rolle was not merely the first of the 14th-century English mystics; he also had the greatest influence on popular piety before the Reformation.

Michael G. Sargent

Bibliography
PRIMARY
Allen, Hope Emily, ed. *English Writings of Richard Rolle, Hermit of Hampole.* Oxford: Clarendon, 1931; Allen, Rosamund S., trans. *The English Writings.* New York: Paulist Press, 1988; Arnould, E.J.F., ed. *The Melos Amoris of Richard Rolle of Hampole.* Oxford: Blackwell, 1957; Deanesly, Margaret, ed. *The Incendium amoris of Richard Rolle of Hampole.* Manchester: Manchester

University Press, 1915; del Mastro, M.L., trans. *The Fire of Love and the Mending of Life.* New York: Doubleday, 1981; Harvey, Ralph, ed. *The Fire of Love and the Mending of Life, or The Rule of Living of Richard Rolle.* EETS o.s. 106. Oxford: Kegan Paul, Trench, Trübner, 1896; Ogilvie-Thomson, Sarah J., ed. *Richard Rolle: Prose and Verse.* EETS o.s. 293. Oxford: Oxford University Press, 1988; Theiner, Paul F., ed. *The Contra amatores mundi of Richard Rolle of Hampole.* Berkeley: University of California Press, 1968.

SECONDARY

Manual 9:3051–68, 3411–25; Alford, John A. "Richard Rolle and Related Works." In *Middle English Prose: A Critical Guide to Major Authors and Genres,* ed. A.S.G. Edwards. New Brunswick: Rutgers University Press, 1984, pp. 35–60; Allen, Hope Emily. *Writings Ascribed to Richard Rolle, Hermit of Hampole, and Materials for His Biography.* New York: Heath, 1927; Clark, J.P.H. "Richard Rolle: A Theological Re-Assessment." *DownR* 101 (1983): 108–39; Clark, J.P.H. "Richard Rolle as a Biblical Commentator." *DownR* 104 (1986): 165–213; Knowlton, Mary Arthur. *The Influence of Richard Rolle and of Julian of Norwich on the Middle English Lyrics.* The Hague: Mouton, 1973; Watson, Nicholas. "Richard Rolle as Elitist and as Popularist: The Case of *Judica me.*" In *De Cella in Seculum: Religious and Secular Life and Devotion in Late Medieval England,* ed. Michael G. Sargent. Cambridge: Brewer, 1989, pp. 123–43; Watson, Nicholas. *Richard Rolle and the Invention of Authority.* Cambridge: Cambridge University Press, 1991.

See also Anglo-Latin Literature after 1066; Bible in ME Literature; *Cloud of Unknowing;* Hilton; Lyrics; Mystical and Devotional Writings; Popular Religion; Prose, ME

Rolls of Parliament

From the very beginning some kind of memorandum must have been kept of business transacted at meetings of parliament. However, the earliest surviving records of such business come only from the early years of Edward I. These are brief and clearly not intended to form any kind of permanent record. Matters of major import were enrolled elsewhere among the records of chancery, exchequer, and the common-law courts.

A decision was apparently taken in 1290 to keep a much fuller permanent record of business done at meetings of parliament. Initially this took the form not of a single comprehensive roll of parliament but of a number of separate rolls recording the different types of business transacted. The first known clerk of the parliament, responsible for drawing up the rolls between 1290 and 1314, was Gilbert of Rothbury, who was not a chancery clerk. His successor was; it soon became established practice to appoint senior chancery clerks to this post, as they combined occasional parliamentary responsibilities with their continuing duties in chancery.

Prior to 1327 it appears to have been the practice to make at least two copies of the main rolls, one of which passed into the custody of the exchequer, the other remaining in the custody of the clerk of parliament or passing to the king's wardrobe. Thereafter only a single copy appears to have been made, and it was retained among the records of chancery. It was also early in Edward III's reign that we first find a single roll of parliament, recording most of the important business done at parliamentary sessions. However, the legislation enacted there continued to be recorded separately on the statute roll until 1483.

The rolls of parliament are not a full record of everything said and done at parliament but only a formal summary of some of the important business done by parliament as a whole. The rolls provide no record of what was said in the two houses when they were meeting separately; they do record the common petitions and the grants of taxation, the outcome of the Commons sessions.

Paul Brand

Bibliography

Maitland, Frederic W. *Memoranda de Parliamento.* Rolls Series 98. London: HMSO, 1893; Richardson, H.G., and G.O. Sayles. *Rotuli Parliamentorum Anglie Hactenu Inediti, mcclxxix–mccclxxiii.* Camden Society, 3d ser. 51 (1935); Richardson, H.G., and G.O. Sayles. *The English Parliament in the Middle Ages.* London: Hambledon, 1981 [the collected papers of Richardson and Sayles are the best modern discussion of the rolls]; Topham, John, and Philip Morant, ed. *Rotuli Parliamentorum.* London, 1783 [remains the major edition, despite its age; a new edition and translation is currently planned under the general editorship of Chris Given-Wilson].

See also Parliament

Romances, Middle English

A loose designation for a group of over 110 narrative works composed between 1225 and 1550. Depending on whether different versions or fragments are counted, and excluding tales by Chaucer and Gower, there are about 90 verse romances and about twenty in prose.

Unlike modern romances, which are primarily love stories, ME romances may best be characterized as a type of adventure story, often with no love interest whatsoever. Some romances focus on the activities of a militant Christian champion (such as *Bevis of Hampton, Guy of Warwick,* or *Richard Coer de Lyon*), while others are variations of the Constance story with attention focused on a long-suffering female protagonist (such as the heroines in *Emare, Octavian, Sir Eglamour of Artois, Sir Torrent of Portyngale,* and *Sir Triamour*).

If these narratives are unlike modern romances, they are also unlike their medieval counterparts in France and Germany. Most romances in England were written after the great flowering of romance during the 12th century, best exemplified by the French writer Chrétien de Troyes and the German

Wolfram von Eschenbach. Only eight of the extant ME romances are thought to date from before 1300: *King Horn* (ca. 1225), *Floris and Blancheflour* (ca. 1250), *Arthour and Merlin* (ca. 1250–1300), *Havelok* (ca. 1280–1300), and *Sir Tristrem, Amis and Amiloun, Guy of Warwick,* and *Bevis of Hampton* (all near the end of the 13th century). Four of these early works deal with native English heroes or typically English concerns, and only two of them with Arthurian legend. The remaining ME romances were written in the 14th and 15th centuries, with the prose romances all composed after 1400 (mostly ca. 1450 or later). Generally speaking, then, the stories of heroes from the courts of Arthur or Charlemagne and those from classical legend did not concern ME writers until the 14th century. Thus the initial impetus for ME romance did not spring primarily from the chivalric or courtly-love traditions associated with continental Arthurian romance. Out of the whole corpus of ME romances only twenty to 25 are based on Arthurian knights or the Matter of Britain.

When compared with French courtly romances the ME works have often been considered debased, incompetent, and unsophisticated. Frequently the adjective "minstrel" or "kitchen" has been applied to ME romances, so as to distinguish them from their French aristocratic counterparts. Even Chaucer, in *Sir Thopas,* parodies some of the worst features of the genre by referring to its "drasty speche" and "rym dogerel." Most, however, are not as trivial or superficial as Chaucer's criticism might indicate.

The comparison with French romance is inevitable, not only because the French works are anterior but also because many of the ME romances have Anglo-Norman or French originals. Yet it is wrong to assume that ME writers intended to write French romances in English. Clearly they retained many motifs and elements found in courtly French romance: aristocratic or courtly settings, knights with idealized codes of chivalry, and the quest pattern as a structuring principle. Nonetheless, the English product is often nothing like the French original. The bookishness, rhetorical ornamentation, elaborate descriptions of courtly life, and internal debates and monologues that characterize French and German romance generally are not features of the English romance. The commonest meter in ME romance is the tail-rhyme stanza, not the octosyllabic couplet of the French romances. The social, economic, political, and literary conditions in England were dramatically different from those that gave rise to the romance in France. These differences cannot be overestimated. For ME romance the most striking characteristics are its frequent bourgeois and baronial orientations and its strongly moral, didactic flavor.

ME romance constitutes an especially problematic genre, even among medieval genres, which are notoriously difficult to define satisfactorily in terms familiar to modern readers. Texts within the generic boundaries of ME romance range from histories with clear moralizing tendencies to adventure stories with connections to folktales and ballads. Often these works seem to have little in common to distinguish them as "romances," and only twenty verse romances actually use that label in describing themselves. Instead of using the term "romance" most refer to themselves as "boke," "geste," "story," "tale," or "vita." Even the word "romance," which originally meant only that the work was written in French rather than Latin, did not appear in titles of collections of these verse works until the early 1800s, with the editions of Joseph Ritson and George Ellis. Since then these narratives have retained this not altogether satisfactory generic label. The works themselves span several centuries, from the early-13th-century *King Horn* to the mid-16th-century *Carle off Carlile*; they treat heroes as disparate as Charlemagne, Joseph of Arimathea, and Havelok the Dane; they vary in length from 370 lines to over 700 pages in modern editions; and the verse romances employ different metrical forms, from the four-stress rhymed couplet and tail-rhyme stanza to the alliterative long line. Nonetheless, as diverse and dissimilar as they are, these narratives cluster along a spectrum that can be distinguished from other recognizable literary forms, such as saints' lives, sermons, epics, or ballads.

Types of Romance

Since the romances are an unwieldy group as a whole, many scholars have tried to find productive ways of classifying smaller sets of texts within the genre. One of the earliest attempts was that of George Ellis in 1805. Following the lead of the 12th-century writer Jean Bodel, who divided medieval French romances into the Matter of France (heroes indigenous to France, such as Roland and Charlemagne), the Matter of Britain (Arthurian knights), and the Matter of Rome (heroes taken from classical legend and history), Ellis added the Matter of England to account for stories about native English heroes not found in French romances. Although this classification has the advantage of being based on a medieval perception of the genre, it tends to bring together texts that vary widely in style, form, audience, and purpose and whose only similarity may lie in a broadly defined common subject matter. Furthermore these four "matters" include only some 65 of the 110-plus ME romances.

Despite its problematic nature classification by subject matter has remained popular into the 20th century. Anna Hunt Billings's *Guide to Middle English Metrical Romance* (1901) deals specifically with 37 verse romances under three general headings much like those of Ellis: English and Germanic Legends, Charlemagne Legends, and Arthurian Legends. The *Manual of Writings in Middle English* (1967) classifies the romances as English Legends, Arthurian Legends, and Charlemagne Legends; Legends of Godfrey of Bouillon, Alexander, Troy, and Thebes; Eustace-Constance Legends; Breton Lays; and Miscellaneous Romances. A different extension of the matter categories appears in Laura Hibbard Loomis's *Mediaeval Romance in England* (1924), a study of 39 texts not covered by Bodel's *matières,* grouped under three broad headings: romances of trial and faith, romances of legendary English heroes, and romances of love and adventure. Loomis's divisions, while useful in identifying common thematic concerns among texts, are more important in their suggestion of the generic range of ME romance, from exemplary tale to popular ballad.

This view of ME romances focuses on the texts' general purposes, broadly conceived, from edification and education to entertainment. The largest group of romances, between a quarter and a half of the extant texts, are stories that educate their audience or inform them about historical or semi-historical events and figures, such as the sieges of Troy and Thebes, Alexander, Arthur, Charlemagne, and Godfrey of Bouillon (or Boulogne). Most offer history as a moral exemplum (e.g., *Alexander B,* the stanzaic *Morte Arthur,* and Lydgate's *Siege of Thebes* and *Troy Book*) or celebrate the militant Christian spirit that infused many of the French *chansons de geste.* All the works classified as the Matter of France fall into this grouping: *Sir Ferumbras* as well as all the Otuel and Roland stories. The remaining pseudo-histories also translate or adapt historical or legendary material for an audience that would otherwise not have access to it.

ME writers often modified their sources with the specific purpose of showing patterns of behavior for the reader's edification. Lydgate's *Siege of Thebes* and *Troy Book* are good examples of this moral intention. Even the stanzaic *Morte Arthur,* which might be expected to represent chivalric romance at its pinnacle, emphasizes instead the moral implications of the tragic outcome of Lancelot's involvement with Guinevere. It ends not with the tragic death of Arthur but with the subsequent religious lives of Guinevere and Lancelot: she as a nun until her death and burial at Glastonbury Abbey and Lancelot as a hermit-priest until a revelation through visions of his salvation and his own death. Such an ending softens the tragic fall of the Round Table by shifting the work from a chivalric to a moral context, in which actions are judged not by a secular code but by a religious one in which repentance and salvation are possible.

Other works, romantic histories, embellish primarily historical accounts with more affective motifs and conventions from chivalric, courtly, and epic traditions, including descriptions of battles, the *enfances* (childhoods) of the heroes, the joys of feasting and music, and heroic laments for a hero's death. The best example of this type of narrative is the Laud *Troy Book,* based on Guido delle Colonne's *Historia destructionis Troiae;* it omits or expands elements from its source in order to romanticize history and create a romance about Hector. Although the ME author called his work a romance—the only account of Troy or Thebes to do so—the work remains a history overlaid with techniques and conventions of romance. The alliterative *Morte Arthure* also reflects this interplay of history, epic, and romance, with its heroic tone and structure and moral complexity. The author, however, successfully reshapes chronicle tradition to reflect 14th-century views on chivalry, kingship, and tragedy in his poem. Even many of the courtly or chivalric romances discussed below set their action against a background considered to be historical, as in *Sir Gawain and the Green Knight* or *The Earl of Toulouse.* Most of the works associated with the traditional "matters" are of this historical or semihistorical type.

The next-largest group of romances comprises didactic, pious tales with similarities to hagiography. Hanspeter Schelp discusses about twenty ME works as "Exemplary Romance," Dieter Mehl labels nine as "Homiletic Romances," and Diana Childress identifies thirteen as "Secular Legend." Regardless

of the nomenclature or number of works classified it is clear that certain ME romances revolve around a set of overtly moral and religious messages that determine the structure and presentation of their stories. Although these works may contain some motifs from secular romance, they consistently point to the religious significance of their stories: in conversions (*Amoryus and Cleopes* and *King of Tars*), in spiritual regeneration and repentance (*Roberd of Cisyle, Sir Gowther,* and *Bone Florence of Rome*), or in heavenly aid to the innocent (*Chevalere Assigne* and *Bone Florence of Rome*). Seven works (variants of the Constance and Griselda stories) emphasize the innocence and self-sacrificing nature of a female character, as well as her humility, piety, and patience. These include *Octavian, Sir Eglamour of Artois, Sir Torrent of Portyngale, Sir Triamour, Emare* (sometimes called a Breton lay), *Le Bone Florence of Rome,* and *Chevalere Assigne.* They usually involve a mother's unmerited suffering and exile, her son's childhood, the reunification of the family, and the punishment or repentance of wrongdoers. Other works tied closely to these include *Sir Isumbras, Roberd of Cisyle,* and *King of Tars.*

Despite their basic similarity of subject matter these pious tales employ a variety of plot structures, often emphasizing different themes. Some, such as *Sir Isumbras, Sir Amadace,* and *Amis and Amiloun,* follow a test-reward pattern; others, like *Athelston,* follow a sin-repentance structure. *Sir Isumbras* demonstrates the Job-like patience of its protagonist, who loses and regains his wealth, wife, and children. *Amis and Amiloun* and *Athelston* focus on the testing of sworn brotherhood and male friendships. The exemplary, didactic nature of these works is also suggested by their manuscript placement. In the Auchinleck Manuscript (National Library of Scotland Advocates' 19.2.1), one of the most important collections of ME romance, *King of Tars* is preceded by a saint's legend and followed by eight religious or homiletic pieces, *Amis and Amiloun,* five religious pieces, and then *Sir Degare.* The Vernon Manuscript (Bodl. Eng. poet. a.1), often considered a purely religious manuscript, contains *King of Tars, Joseph of Arimathie,* and *Roberd of Cisyle.* Two other homiletic or didactic collections—the Thornton Manuscript (Lincoln Cathedral 91) and CUL Ff.2.38—contain thirteen versions of these ME pious romances.

The moral implications of a story are such a dominant force in ME romance that four works attempt to transform chivalric romances into stories with serious religious meaning. *Bevis of Hampton* is the most successful, with its hero fighting heathens, falling in love with and converting the Saracen Josian, reestablishing justice, and finally retiring to Mombrant, where he dies a holy death with his converted wife. *Guy of Warwick* is less successful in presenting a lover-knight and religious exemplar because the change in Guy is handled mechanically and has little effect on his behavior. Both *Guy of Warwick* and the *Romauns of Partenay* deal with the religious choices of chivalric knights whose virtues shift from martial deeds to piety and repentance. A fourth work, *Richard Coer de Lyon,* is markedly different in tone and glorifies a brutally militant Christian spirit.

At least some of the ME romances fulfill the expected criteria of continental romance: a chivalric ethic and courtly knights, quests, an interest in questions of honor and love, and some element of mystery or supernatural or magic. The best example is *Sir Gawain and the Green Knight,* which has also been viewed as an antiromance because of the ways its author undercuts the elements of the genre. For example, he twists the typical mysterious challenger into a Green Knight, who combines elements of the Wild Man and the Green Man traditions; he also converts the beheading, the typical convention for breaking an enchantment, into a challenge at the story's beginning. Other English romances—*Generides, Ipomadon A, Partonope of Blois, Sir Degrevant, Squire of Low Degree,* and *William of Palerne*—are more conventional, especially in their interest in love. *Ipomadon A* fairly closely follows its source, Hue de Rotelande's 12th-century *Ipomedon,* which may be seen as a psychological study of the woman as tormented lover. In subordinating action to contemplation and introspection the author delights in describing the changes that love creates in the characters' perception of their world.

William of Palerne is the only other ME romance (excluding Chaucer's *Troilus*) at all like *Ipomadon A* in its exploration of the painful and disruptive energy unleashed by love and passion. Instead of marrying a Greek prince Melior runs away with her lover, William. Disguised at first in bearskins, they encounter many hardships in their exile, which never breaks their devotion and idyllic love. This poem successfully combines a picture of its protagonist as courtly lover, valiant knight, and ideal ruler—a portrait more complete than any other in ME romance. *Sir Degrevant* pushes the limits of romance into realism by employing romance conventions (the love of an enemy's daughter, the secret meetings aided by faithful squire and maid, the treacherous steward, the three-day joust) but placing them firmly in a realistic feudal situation of a knight summoned home from the Crusades to defend his land from a neighboring earl.

At the far end of the scale of works considered romance are those resembling minstrel tales, marked by a style that is both popular and simple. They often contain jingling or easy rhymes to aid oral delivery, almost-meaningless tags to fill out metrical lines, and a straightforward, unembellished method of narration. When a French source exists, it is sharply diminished. Some of these—*Gamelyn, Havelok, King Horn*—carry a political and moral message. The works usually considered Breton lays fall into this group as well: these include *Earl of Toulous, Emare, Lai le Freine, Sir Degare, Sir Orfeo, Sir Gowther,* and *Sir Launfal.* Several chivalric tales move even farther from a learned style toward a balladlike presentation, using such techniques as parallelism, repetition, brevity, and narrative speed and pacing. *Eger and Grime, Carle off Carlile,* and *Grene Knight* all demonstrate their closeness to popular ballad in their diction, verbal patterning, and structural parallels.

Dissemination

The range and diversity of tales that fall within the boundaries of ME romance suggest the wide appeal and popularity of the genre. They were not confined to an aristocratic or courtier class, nor do they belong exclusively to the bourgeoisie or common people. The popular appeal of certain romances is attested by the number of manuscripts in which these works appear. There are five or more manuscripts of *Guy of Warwick, Sir Degare, Partonope of Blois, Libeaus Desconus, Siege of Jerusalem,* and *Arthour and Merlin;* ten or more manuscripts, fragments, or prints of *Titus and Vespasian, Bevis of Hampton, Sir Isumbras, Roberd of Cisyle, Sir Eglamour of Artois, Richard Coer de Lyon,* and *Gamelyn.* The striking popularity of these romances is particularly noteworthy given the fact that about two-thirds of the romances are known from a single manuscript or solely from printed editions. Our knowledge of the historically based romances is based on especially slender evidence, since most of the romances in the great cycles concerning Thebes, Troy, Alexander, Charlemagne, and Roland and Otuel exist in only one surviving version. Many of the best-known or most highly prized ME romances likewise occur in only one extant version: *Sir Gawain and the Green Knight,* the alliterative *Morte Arthure,* the stanzaic *Morte Arthur, Havelok, Athelston, William of Palerne, Chevalere Assigne,* and *Sir Perceval of Galles.* Given the accidents of transmission and the survival rate of medieval manuscripts, our view of the genre is necessarily partial and must often remain speculative. There is no way of knowing how much was lost or how well what survives today represents the romance tradition as it existed in medieval England.

Joanne A. Charbonneau

Bibliography

New *CBEL* 1:383–454; *Manual* 1; Baugh, Albert C. "Convention and Individuality in the Middle English Romance." In *Medieval Literature and Folklore Studies: Essays in Honor of Francis Lee Utley,* ed. Jerome Mandel and Bruce A. Rosenberg. New Brunswick: Rutgers University Press, 1970, pp. 123–46; Beer, Gillian. *The Romance.* London: Methuen, 1970; Benson, C. David. *The History of Troy in Middle English Literature.* Woodbridge: Brewer, 1980; Billings, Anna Hunt. *A Guide to the Middle English Metrical Romances.* New York: Holt, 1901; Boitani, Piero. *English Medieval Narrative in the Thirteenth and Fourteenth Centuries.* Trans. Joan Krakover Hall. Cambridge: Cambridge University Press, 1982; Bordman, Gerald. *Motif-Index of the English Metrical Romances.* FF (Folklore Forum) Communications 190. Helsinki: Suomalainen Tiedeakatemia, 1963; Brewer, Derek Stanley. *Symbolic Stories: Traditional Narratives of the Family Drama in English Literature.* Cambridge: Brewer, 1980; Brewer, Derek. *English Gothic Literature.* New York: Schocken, 1983; Childress, Diana T. "Between Romance and Legend: 'Secular Hagiography' in Middle English Literature." *PQ* 57 (1978): 311–22; Crane, Susan. *Insular Romance: Politics, Faith, and Culture in Anglo-Norman and Middle English Literature.* Berkeley: University of California Press, 1986; Everett, Dorothy. *Essays on Middle English Literature.* Ed. Patricia Kean. Oxford: Clarendon, 1955; Finlayson, John. "Definitions of Middle English Romance." *ChauR* 15 (1980): 44–62, 168–81; Fowler, David C. *A Literary History of the*

Popular Ballad. Durham: Duke University Press, 1968; Ganim, John M. *Style and Consciousness in Middle English Narrative.* Princeton: Princeton University Press, 1983; Gradon, Pamela. *Form and Style in Early English Literature.* London: Methuen, 1971; Hibbard [Loomis], Laura A. *Mediaeval Romance in England: A Study of the Sources and Analogues of the Non-Cyclic Metrical Romances.* 2d ed. New York: Burt Franklin, 1960; Mehl, Dieter. *The Middle English Romances of the Thirteenth and Fourteenth Centuries.* London: Routledge & Kegan Paul, 1968; Quinn, William Anthony, and Audley S. Hall. *Jongleur: A Modified Theory of Oral Improvisation and Its Effects on the Performance and Transmission of Middle English Romance.* Washington, D.C.: University Press of America, 1982; Ramsey, Lee C. *Chivalric Romances: Popular Literature in Medieval England.* Bloomington: Indiana University Press, 1983; Rice [Charbonneau], Joanne A. *Middle English Romance: An Annotated Bibliography, 1955–1985.* New York: Garland, 1987 [editions and criticism]; Richmond, Velma Bourgeois. *The Popularity of Middle English Romance.* Bowling Green: Bowling Green University Popular Press, 1975; Salter, Elizabeth. *Fourteenth-Century English Poetry: Contexts and Readings.* Oxford: Clarendon, 1983; Schelp, Hanspeter. *Exemplarische Romanzen im Mittelenglischen.* Palaestra 246. Göttingen: Vandenhoeck & Ruprecht, 1967; Speirs, John. *Medieval English Poetry: The Non-Chaucerian Tradition.* London: Faber & Faber, 1957; Stevens, John. *Medieval Romance: Themes and Approaches.* New York: Norton, 1973; Wittig, Susan. *Stylistic and Narrative Structures in the Middle English Romances.* Austin: University of Texas Press, 1978.

See also Anglo-Norman Literature; Ballads; Breton Lay; Chivalry; Chronicles; Courtly Love; Literary Influences: French; Matter of Antiquity; Matter of Britain; Matter of England; Matter of France; Minstrels; Popular Culture

Romsey Abbey

The starting date of Romanesque Romsey (fig. 109) is not documented. Comparison of the sculptured capitals with those in Canterbury Cathedral crypt and elsewhere, and of the architectural details with the post-1107 fall-of-the-tower work at Winchester, suggests that construction commenced ca. 1110–20. Building advanced as far as the first bay of the nave by ca. 1150, after which time work slowed dramatically until the nave was completed ca. 1230. During this long building program the proportions of the elevation continue unchanged, while the articulation, pier form, capitals, and moldings reflect current fashions.

Romsey preserves the earliest extant example of a square ambulatory, a feature later used extensively in English architecture as at Byland Abbey and Salisbury and Exeter Cathedrals. The three-story elevation with main arcade, gallery, and clerestory with wall passage, and the crossing tower with wall passage and lantern windows, belong to the family of St. Étienne at Caen as transmitted through Winchester Cathedral. As at Winchester, the main spans at Romsey are wood-roofed while the aisles are rib-vaulted, as in the post-1107 work at Winchester. Whether ribs were initially intended at Romsey is a moot point; they are not consistently articulated from the ground, but uniformity is seldom deemed essential or even desirable in English architecture.

In the bays connecting the transepts with the nave aisles and galleries the giant order is introduced. The outer shaft of the pier rises through two stories to support the inner enclosing order of the gallery arch, in contrast to the separate main arcade and gallery piers in the presbytery and the east side of the transepts. The giant order is continued throughout the nave but with an interesting variation in the first nave pier. It is cylindrical rather than compound and may well have been a liturgical marker for the nave altar.

Malcolm Thurlby

Bibliography

Fernie, Eric. "The Use of Varied Nave Supports in Romanesque and Early Gothic Churches." *Gesta* 23 (1984): 107–17; Hearn, M.F. "A Note on the Chronology of Romsey Abbey." *JBAA,* 3d ser. 32 (1969): 30–37; Hearn, M.F. "Romsey Abbey: A Progenitor of the English National Tradition in Architecture." *Gesta* 14 (1975): 27–40.

See also Architecture and Architectural Sculpture, Romanesque; Canterbury Cathedral; Romsey Roods; Sculpture, Romanesque; Winchester Cathedral

Romsey Roods

Two Anglo-Saxon roods (carved depictions of the Crucifixion) reset in the Romanesque fabric of Romsey Abbey. One (29 inches high by 17.5 inches wide) serves as a reredos, or high screen behind an altar, in the eastern apse of the south presbytery aisle; the other (max. height 88.5 inches; max. width 70.5 inches) is found on the exterior west wall of the south transept (fig. 110). The small rood, which has poorly preserved surface detail, is carved in shallow relief with a living, upright Christ on a cross with T-shaped terminals. Beneath the arms of the cross Mary stands to his right and, below her, Stephaton bears the sponge. To his left is John and, below, Longinus with the spear. There is a demifigure of an angel above each cross arm, and plant ornament flanks the stem of the cross. The iconography and animated poses of the attendant figures depend on Metz School ivories of the 9th and 10th centuries (A. Goldschmidt, *Die Elfenbeinskulpturen aus der Zeit der karolingischen und sächsischen Kaiser VIII–XI. Jahrhundert,* Vol. 1 [Berlin, 1914], nos. 78, 85, 86, 88, 89, 115). The T-shaped terminals to the cross are paralleled in Anglo-Saxon manuscripts, as in the Arenberg Gospels (Temple, cat. no. 56).

The monumental rood, which is carved in deep relief from three pieces of stone, is the best-preserved example of what may have been a common Anglo-Saxon type. Other instances in the Winchester diocese, albeit poorly preserved, are

above the south doorway of Breamore (Hampshire), and on the former west wall of the pre-Conquest church at Headborne Worthy (Hampshire). The bearded Romsey Christ holds his head erect in triumph over death. His feet rest on a sloping *suppedaneum* (foot support). The Manus Dei (Hand of God) appears from a stylized cloud above his head, as at Headborne Worthy. This feature and the *suppedaneum* are common in Anglo-Saxon art (Temple, cat. nos. 35, 56, 77, 82, 103). The clinging drapery of the loincloth has been compared with the frieze on the Romanesque facade of Lincoln Cathedral, but the flying angels above the chancel arch at St. Laurence, Bradford-on-Avon (Wiltshire), provide an appropriate pre-Conquest analogue. Originally the Bradford-on-Avon angels may have flanked a large-scale rood, and it is possible that the monumental rood at Romsey occupied a similar position.

The Anglo-Saxon nunnery at Romsey was reformed or re-founded in 967, possibly under the reforming influence of Æthelwold, bishop of Winchester (963–84). It was patronized by King Edgar, who had his infant son, Edmund, buried there in 971. This royal association is relevant on two counts. First, it helps explain the similarity to monumental Ottonian roods; the example at Ringelheim (Hanover) is especially close. Second, in keeping with Æthelwold's ideas of kingship, it suggests that the flat top, and the drill hole to the side, of Christ's head in the large rood indicate that the Christ figure wore a metal crown.

Malcolm Thurlby

Fig. 110. Romsey Abbey, monumental rood on west wall of south transept. Courtesy RCHME, copyright Hampshire Field Club.

Bibliography

Coatsworth, Elizabeth. "Late Pre-Conquest Sculptures with the Crucifixion South of the Humber." In *Bishop Æthelwold: His Career and Influence,* ed. Barbara Yorke. Woodbridge: Boydell, 1988, pp. 161–93; Temple, Elzbieta. *Anglo-Saxon Manuscripts 900–1066.* A Survey of Manuscripts Illuminated in the British Isles 2, ed. J.J.G. Alexander. London: Harvey Miller, 1976; Tweddle, Dominic, Martin Biddle, and Birthe Kjølbye-Biddle. *Corpus of Anglo-Saxon Stone Sculpture.* Vol. 4: *South-East England.* London: Oxford University Press, 1995.

See also Architecture and Architectural Sculpture, Romanesque; Art, Anglo-Saxon; Romsey Abbey; Sculpture, Anglo-Saxon

Rondellus

Literally either "a small circular object" or, in poetry, "a rondeau." Music historians use the term to identify a distinctive technique in the 13th-century English polyphonic repertoire in which all voices begin together, presenting musical material that is then permuted or exchanged between voices in subsequent periods until all voices have sung all parts. One unit of rondellus in three voices could be represented as

$$
\begin{array}{ccc}
a & b & c \\
c & a & b \\
b & c & a
\end{array}
$$

Insular techniques of rota and voice exchange, cultivated in the same era, are related but not identical (and it is the rota that most closely approximates a modern "round").

The term "rondellus" is attested in this sense only in music theorist Walter Odington's *Summa de speculatione musicae* (ca. 1300), with one example, *Ave mater domini.* Rondellus techniques occur in conducti and motets ("conductus-rondellus" and "rondellus-motet"), troped settings of Alleluias, and independent rondelli, mostly in three voices. For a complete listing see Lefferts (1986: 31); the publishable pieces are edited by Sanders (1979).

Peter M. Lefferts

Bibliography

PRIMARY

Sanders, Ernest H., ed. *English Music of the Thirteenth and Early Fourteenth Centuries.* Polyphonic Music of the Fourteenth Century 14. Paris: L'Oiseau-Lyre, 1979.

SECONDARY

Lefferts, Peter M. *The Motet in England in the Fourteenth Century.* Ann Arbor: UMI Research Press, 1986; Odington, Walter. *Summa de speculatione musicae.* Ed. Frederick Hammond. Corpus Scriptorum de Musica 14. Rome: American Institute of Musicology, 1970; Sanders, Ernest H. "Rondellus." *NGD* 16:170–72.

See also Conductus; Motet; Rota; Songs

Rota

Literally "wheel." Music historians use the term to identify the rare, distinctive technique of round canon at the unison as it occurs in the 13th-century English polyphonic repertoire. Insular techniques of rondellus and voice exchange, cultivated in the same era, are related but not identical. *Munda Maria* is the only known unaccompanied rota, while the well-known Sumer Canon places a rota above a two-voice ostinato accompaniment (both are edited, among other places, in Sanders, 1979). The fragmentary *Salve Symon Montisfortis* may also have been an accompanied rota.

The term "rota" is attested in this sense only in the elaborate set of performance instructions that survives for the Sumer Canon. In the text of a large-scale English voice-exchange motet of the early 14th century, *Rota versatilis,* the word specifically denotes the Katherine wheel while also clearly alluding to the musical means of construction, which is in this case noncanonic.

Peter M. Lefferts

Bibliography

PRIMARY

Sanders, Ernest H., ed. *English Music of the Thirteenth and Early Fourteenth Centuries.* Polyphonic Music of the Fourteenth Century 14. Paris: L'Oiseau-Lyre, 1979.

SECONDARY

Bent, Margaret. "Rota versatilis: Towards a Reconstruction." In *Source Materials and the Interpretation of Music: A Memorial Volume to Thurston Dart,* ed. Ian Bent. London: Stainer & Bell, 1981, pp. 65–98; Cooper, Barry. "A Thirteenth-Century Canon Reconstructed." *Music Review* 42 (1981): 85–90; Lefferts, Peter M. "Two English Motets on Simon de Montfort." *Early Music History* 1 (1981): 203–25; Sanders, Ernest H. "Rota." *NGD* 16:255.

See also Rondellus; Sumer Canon

Ruin, The

One of the so-called elegies of the Exeter Book. Like the other elegies *The Ruin* presents a contrast between past and present, but in this poem the contrast takes the form of an impersonal contemplation rather than, as in other elegies, arising from the speaker's own experience. The speaker of the poem observes the remains of what he refers to as "the work of giants," the ruins of a great city of the past.

A Latin analogue to *The Ruin* is a 6th-century poem by Venantius Fortunatus, *De excidio Thoringae,* but closer parallels are to be found in the vernacular tradition. The conventional theme of the ruined hall appears in *The Wanderer* and *Beowulf.* A similar theme is reflected in early Welsh poetry. The version in *The Ruin* is remarkable for the specific detail of its depiction of the ruined city, this detail being evidently the result of observation as well as of conventional description. The poet pays particular attention to the baths of the city, which are described with admiration and fascination. The emphasis on the baths, indeed, has encouraged some scholars to identify the place described as the Roman city of Bath, although the evidence for such an identification is hardly conclusive.

The Ruin presents a contemplation on the relentlessness of time. Some critics suggest that the poet implies a powerful condemnation of the worldliness of the people who once heedlessly enjoyed the splendor of a Babylon-like city. The poem is entirely lacking in homiletic castigation, however, and its evocation of the life of the inhabitants of this city is not unsympathetic. The people are presented in Germanic terms, as proud warriors experiencing the bright joys of the hall and living a life of wealth and success. Their lives and dwelling places are overcome by *wyrd* (fate), as their splendor is destroyed. The object of the poem's preoccupation is the effect of time rather than the wickedness of the people who lived in glory in the past. The poet adopts an attitude of observation rather than renunciation.

The damage to the closing pages of the Exeter Book, caused, it seems, by a burning fragment of wood, has rendered the text of *The Ruin* deficient in two places, affecting thirteen of the poem's 49 lines. The second of these lacunae represents a particularly unfortunate loss, since it impairs much of the description of the baths with which the text ends.

Hugh Magennis

Bibliography

PRIMARY

ASPR 3:227–29; Klinck, Anne L., ed. *The Old English Elegies: A Critical Edition and Genre Study.* Montreal: McGill-Queen's University Press, 1992, pp. 61–63, 103–05, 208–19; Leslie, Roy F., ed. *Three Old English Elegies.* Rev. ed. Exeter: University of Exeter, 1988, pp. 51–52, 67–76.

SECONDARY

Calder, Daniel G. "Perspective and Movement in *The Ruin.*" *NM* 72 (1971): 442–45; Doubleday, James F. "*The Ruin:* Structure and Theme." *JEGP* 71 (1972): 369–81; Renoir, Alain. "The Old English *Ruin*: Contrastive Structure and Affective Impact." In *The Old English Elegies: New Essays in Criticism and Research,* ed. Martin Green. Rutherford: Fairleigh Dickinson University Press, 1983, pp. 148–73.

See also Exeter Book; *Wanderer*

Runes

By the 5th century A.D. the use of runes, the Germanic adaptation of the Roman (or a related) alphabet, is attested across Europe from Scandinavia to the Black Sea. A knowledge of the script was certainly shared by some of the earliest Anglo-Saxon settlers: about twenty inscriptions dating from the 5th to the 7th century have been discovered, mostly in the south and east of England. During this period, in response to a series of sound changes that shaped the OE language, the values of some old runes were altered and several new symbols were invented, giving the Anglo-Saxon script an appearance distinct from that of its neighbors (though Frisia shared some of the developments). In Scandinavia the runic alphabet is termed the *futhark,* a modern coinage derived from the values of the opening runes of the traditional sequence; the alterations in England produce instead the *futhorc.*

Like most Anglo-Saxon artifacts of the period almost all the early runic inscriptions come from burial contexts; they are found on cremation urns and on a range of objects—such as sword fittings, brooches, and domestic vessels—buried as grave goods. None of these early texts is longer than three words, and many are obscure. Among the identifiable sequences there are some echoes of "charm words" known from contemporary runic inscriptions in Scandinavia, and there are several personal names. Since inscriptions on perishable material, such as wood, have not survived, it is difficult to comment with authority on the extent of early Anglo-Saxon literacy or the uses to which it may have been put. It might be noted only that, so far, the earliest texts provide no evidence of a commercial or overtly religious function for runic writing. Instead they reveal a taste for the prosaic: the ankle bone of a roe deer, found in a 5th-century cremation urn, is apparently labeled "roe deer's"; and a 7th-century brooch, damaged and mended (none too expertly) in antiquity, proclaims "Luda repaired the brooch."

A more obviously practical application appears in the 7th century, when runes are used on some of the earliest Anglo-Saxon gold coinage. From the end of that century until the 9th, coin legends in Kent, East Anglia, and Northumbria are cut sometimes in Roman, sometimes in runic, and sometimes in a mixture of the scripts. Other types of inscription reinforce the impression that during this period, in parts of the east and north of England, the two scripts tended to be used with little distinction of purpose. A series of memorial stones from the religious houses of the northeast coast simply record the names of the deceased in either Roman or runic; another series, bearing versions of a short vernacular prayer in loosely alliterative verse, is evidenced across Northumbria in both scripts.

All of these memorial stones are explicitly Christian in content or context, and this holds true of the great majority of 8th- and 9th-century runic inscriptions. Some pieces, such as a pair of silver tweezers bearing just a personal name, and a gold finger ring recording owner and maker in a mixture of scripts, indicate their owner's faith only by the symbol of a cross. Others, like a casket found in Normandy but probably made in northern Mercia or Northumbria and a bone comb recovered from a midden near the monastery at Whitby, carry short prayers. Most strikingly some of the figures incised on the wooden coffin of St. Cuthbert, historically datable to the translation of his body by the Lindisfarne community in 698, are labeled in runic script. Unusual in having no apparent religious content are three rings bearing versions of the same nonsense text, which is related to sequences found in Anglo-Saxon manuscripts that may ultimately derive from meaningful Irish charms.

The longest Anglo-Saxon runic inscriptions are found on a pair of monuments that are both typical of, and far exceed, the rest of the corpus. Like other inscribed pieces the Franks Casket and Ruthwell Cross are Christian and use both scripts; but, in contrast to the usual short and prosaic texts, their extensive inscriptions are also among the most significant early Anglo-Saxon literary and linguistic records. Both are probably in Northumbrian dialects of the first half of the 8th century.

Runes also appear in manuscripts, though it is evident that, whereas they were considered an acceptable alternative to Roman in inscriptions, in books they were not used as a primary script. Often they are listed, either in futhorc order or rearranged into alphabetical order. Such lists are particularly common in manuscripts written on the Continent from the end of the 8th century onward, and it is probable that they reflect the runic knowledge of Anglo-Saxon scholars and missionaries who traveled south during the 8th century. (The Anglo-Saxon pilgrims who carved their names in runes at sites in Italy might be compared.) More ambitious than these simple lists is the *Rune Poem,* which recounts gnomic lore attaching to the names by which the runes were known (*lagu,* "water," for *l, dæg,* "day," for *d,* etc.). These rune names were exploited in various ways. Some scribes occasionally drew the runic symbols as shorthand ideographs for their names; the poet Cynewulf "signed" four compositions by working the names of the runes that spelled his name into his text.

The Anglo-Saxons' attitude to runes no doubt changed over time and probably varied also according to region. It has sometimes been suggested that runes carried connotations of paganism into the Christian period, but the evidence of the inscriptions suggests the contrary. Christine Fell has shown also that the word *rūn* itself, for most of the OE period, means "thought" or "truth" rather than "secret" or "mystery," as it has generally been glossed. Toward the end of the period, however, there may have been a change. Few Anglo-Saxon runic inscriptions are dated later than ca. 900, and over the following centuries runes probably came to be considered unusual or archaic. A scatter of inscriptions across the country attests to the arrival of the Vikings with their own distinctive version of the script. The Vikings were certainly reviled as heathen invaders, and it is perhaps against that background that Ælfric's explicit association of runes and *drycræft,* "sorcery," around the beginning of the 11th century, should be set.

David Parsons

Bibliography

PRIMARY

Halsall, Maureen, ed. *The Old English Rune Poem: A Critical Edition.* McMaster Old English Studies and Texts 2. Toronto: University of Toronto Press, 1981.

SECONDARY

Bammesberger, Alfred, ed. *Old English Runes and Their Continental Background.* Heidelberg: Winter, 1991 [see esp. Mark Blackburn, "A Survey of Anglo-Saxon and Frisian Coins with Runic Inscriptions," pp. 137–89; Christine E. Fell, "Runes and Semantics," pp. 195–229]; Derolez, René. *Runica Manuscripta: The English Tradition.* Bruges: De Tempel, 1954; Elliott, Ralph W.V. *Runes:*

An Introduction. 2d ed. Manchester: Manchester University Press, 1989; Hines, John. "The Runic Inscriptions of Early Anglo-Saxon England." In *Britain 400–600: Language and History,* ed. Alfred Bammesberger and Alfred Wollmann. Heidelberg: Winter, 1990, pp. 437–55; Page, R.I. "Anglo-Saxon Runes and Magic." *JBAA,* 3d ser. 27 (1964): 14–31; Page, R.I. *An Introduction to English Runes.* London: Methuen, 1973.

See also Archaeology; Cemeteries; Coffin of St. Cuthbert; Coins and Coinage; Cynewulf; Franks Casket; *Husband's Message;* Literacy; Ruthwell Cross

Ruthwell Cross

The Ruthwell Cross (figs. 111–14) stands today in the church in the village of Ruthwell (Dumfriesshire), near the Scottish border with England. Struck down by Presbyterian iconoclasts in 1642, it lay for a while embedded in the church floor before being abandoned to the churchyard. This mistreatment has left it scarred and incomplete. In 1887 it was declared a national monument and reinstalled within the church. And there it remains, rising to 17 feet 4 inches in height, from a well set into the apse behind the altar.

Together with the comparable cross at Bewcastle it is undoubtedly the most important sculptural survival from

Fig. 111. Ruthwell Cross, Dumfriesshire. Courtesy of A.J. Hawkes.

Fig. 112. Ruthwell Cross, Dumfriesshire. Detail of Christ and Mary Magdalene. Courtesy of A.J. Hawkes.

Fig. 113. Ruthwell Cross, Dumfriesshire. Detail of Christ being adored by beasts. Courtesy of A.J. Hawkes.

Anglo-Saxon Britain and arguably from early-medieval Europe. Constructed of two blocks of local sandstone, it is ornamented on all four sides with carved images and inscriptions in both Latin letters and Anglo-Saxon runes. On the principal faces are figures and scenes drawn mainly from the life of Christ. On what was probably the front (original west face) of the cross are the Crucifixion, the Flight into Egypt, SS. Paul and Anthony meeting in the desert, Christ being adored by beasts, and St. John the Baptist. In the cross head, of which only two of the original arms remain, are small reliefs of the evangelist Matthew with his symbol, and at the top the evangelist John with his eagle. On the reverse (original east face) at the bottom is a panel now completely obliterated. Above is the Annunciation, the miracle of the man born blind, Mary Magdalene wiping Christ's feet with her hair, and two women embracing, possibly the Virgin Mary and Elizabeth at the Visitation or Martha and Mary. In the cross head is a kneeling archer stretching taut his bow and taking aim with an arrow, and at the top an eagle perched on a branch. Around the panels are

Latin inscriptions, mostly drawn from passages in the Bible, identifying the scenes.

The sides of the cross are ornamented with plant scroll inhabited by animals and birds. The runic inscription in the frame around the scrollwork is related to the Anglo-Saxon poem *The Dream of the Rood* (preserved in a 10th-century manuscript), though the exact nature of the relationship between the two texts is problematic. In both poems the Cross tells of its experiences on that first Good Friday when it supported the dying body of Christ.

Although the Ruthwell Cross has attracted an extensive body of scholarship, many controversial questions remain. The date is still in dispute, with opinion being divided between the late 7th century and the middle of the 8th. The sudden appearance in Britain of carving of this quality, unique in Europe at the time, has been associated with the import of foreign masons by Benedict Biscop and Wilfrid of York in the 670s to build their churches at Wearmouth and Hexham. Suggestions as to the origins of the foreign influence apparent in the style of the

Fig. 114. Ruthwell Cross, Dumfriesshire. Detail of vinescroll. Courtesy of A.J. Hawkes.

Fig. 114. Ruthwell Cross, Dumfriesshire. Detail of vinescroll. Courtesy of A.J. Hawkes.

figure sculpture and ornament have ranged from Gaul to Italy to Syria and Coptic Egypt. The elaborate iconographic program has likewise inspired numerous interpretations; even the identity of some of the scenes is not agreed upon. A consensus has been reached, however, that the broad message of the figure sculpture reflects the eremitic ideals of the early Northumbrian church. Although the Ruthwell Cross is only one of a series of Northumbrian crosses, it is the finest and most complete of the group and of pivotal importance to the understanding of Anglo-Saxon art.

Brendan Cassidy

Bibliography

Brown, Gerard Baldwin. *The Arts in Early England.* Vol. 5: *The Ruthwell and Bewcastle Crosses, the Gospels of Lindisfarne, and Other Christian Monuments of Northumbria.* London: Murray, 1921; Cassidy, Brendan, ed. *The Ruthwell Cross.* Index of Christian Art, Occasional Papers 1. Princeton: Index of Christian Art; Dept. of Art and Archaeology, 1992; Saxl, Fritz. "The Ruthwell Cross." *JWCI* 6 (1943): 1–19; Schapiro, Meyer. "The Religious Meaning of the Ruthwell Cross." *Art Bulletin* 26 (1944): 232–45. Repr. in M. Schapiro. *Late Antique, Early Christian and Medieval Art: Selected Papers.* Vol. 3. New York: Braziller, 1979, pp. 177–86.

See also Art, Anglo-Saxon; High Crosses

S

St. Albans Abbey

The Benedictine abbey church of St. Albans (fig. 115) was commenced by Abbot Paul of Caen (1077–88). It was the first post-Conquest church to be conceived on the vast scale of 4th-century imperial Christian basilicas in Rome. The setting for the shrine of St. Alban was thereby associated with St. Peter's, Rome, while the monumentality of the new church stood as a powerful symbol of Norman administration. Solid walls separated the four-bay presbytery from its five-bay aisles. The east end probably terminated in three apses, with those to the aisles enclosed in flat east walls. Of the groin-vaulted presbytery aisles there remain the two western bays on the south and the westernmost on the north. The painted decoration of these groin vaults is 13th-century, but traces of similar work underneath suggest that the ribbons on the groins and the false ashlar webbing reflect Romanesque precedent. The presbytery originally had a high groin vault, while the transepts and nave were wood-roofed. The aisleless transepts, formerly with two apsidal chapels to the east, have a three-story elevation with superposed triforium and clerestory passages. In the nave the second story takes the form of a low gallery. The crossing lantern tower, with superposed wall passages, recalls St. Étienne at Caen, but the upper external passage may derive from imperial Germany.

Built of reused Roman brick from Verulamium and flint rubble, Romanesque St. Albans is often dismissed as a plain, even crude building. However, in the crossing and nave it uses three-order arches, and in the transepts and nave stringcourses balance the vertical thrust of the pilasters. These elements stand at the beginning of the tradition of rich articulation in English Romanesque churches. The nave arcades preserve a great variety of Romanesque painted patterns, while the fifth and sixth piers of the north arcade break from the straightforward compound type to signify the area of the nave altar.

Malcolm Thurlby

Bibliography

Buckler, John C., and Charles A. Buckler. *A History of the Architecture of the Abbey Church of St. Alban*. London: Longman, Brown, Green, & Longmans, 1847; Van Zanten, David T. "The Romanesque Church of St. Albans." *Gesta* 4 (1965): 23–27.

See also Architecture and Architectural Sculpture, Romanesque; Durham Cathedral

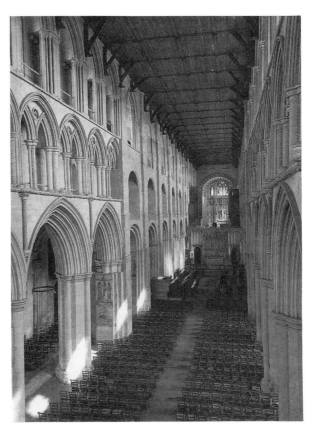

Fig. 115. St. Albans Abbey, nave interior. RCHME, © Crown copyright.

St. Albans Psalter

The St. Albans or Albani Psalter (Hildesheim, St. Godehard) ranks as one of the most important English Romanesque illuminated manuscripts because of its extensive miniature cycle. The psalter text is preceded by calendar illustrations, 40 full-page framed scenes drawn mainly from the New Testament, and five tinted drawings from the life of St. Alexis and the Emmaus story. There are two full-page miniatures depicting the martyrdom of St. Alban and David with his musicians at the end of the manuscript. In addition 211 historiated initials accompany the psalms.

The manuscript's provenance and date have been established on the basis of entries in the calendar, several of which may suggest that it was made for the anchoress Christina of Markyate, a disciple of Roger, who had been for a time a monk at St. Albans and later lived the life of a hermit in the vicinity. Since Roger died before 1124 and the entry for his death was made after the calendar was completed, an approximate date before 1130 has been assigned to the manuscript.

This dating makes the St. Albans Psalter the first extant English manuscript with a cycle of full-page painted miniatures since the 10th century. The style and iconography of both miniatures and historiated initials differ substantially from Anglo-Saxon works, making them the earliest surviving representatives of a new pictorial tradition in the Romanesque period. The figure style is characterized by elongated figures shown in profile and clothed in clinging draperies overspun by a fine cobweb of white highlights. Pächt viewed the style as a new development in English art introduced by the main artist, whom he called the Alexis Master, and identified the major source of this artist's inspiration as Italo-Byzantine art. Swarzenski and Kauffmann questioned this interpretation by pointing to elements of the style in manuscripts produced in England or under English influence in the first quarter of the 12th century.

A similar debate exists concerning the iconographical sources for the miniatures. Pächt indicated that the Alexis Master drew directly upon a wide range of sources, including Anglo-Saxon, Ottonian, and, to a greater extent, Italo-Byzantine models in creating this cycle. Others have expressed doubt about the originality of the cycle as a whole and have also questioned which sources shaped it. Kauffmann, drawing attention to similarities between the St. Albans cycle and two other 12th-century New Testament cycles, suggested a common archetype for the group, thereby removing the Alexis Master from a major role in the creative process. Swarzenski questioned the originality of particular iconographical details, citing precedents in earlier continental manuscripts, and stressed the importance of Ottonian art as the major influence on the New Testament cycle.

The tinted drawings are grouped together with the earliest extant Anglo-Norman French version of the *Vie de saint Alexis*. Pächt argued that the inclusion of this particular text and the specific scenes chosen for illustration had a special relevance for Christina, thereby underlining the private, individualized nature of these miniatures.

Some of the 211 historiated initials, such as those of David as Psalmist and Christ Trampling the Beasts, follow well-established models used in liturgical psalters. However, the majority echo commentaries on the psalms, principally that of St. Augustine. While some compositional similarities exist elsewhere, Dodwell viewed the initials as fairly original creations that emphasize monastic values. Stylistic parallels exist in Norman and Flemish manuscripts.

Kristine E. Haney

Bibliography

Haney, Kristine E. "The St. Albans Psalter: A Reconsideration." *JWCI* 58 (1995): 1–28; Kauffmann, C. Michael. *Romanesque Manuscripts 1066–1190*. A Survey of Manuscripts Illuminated in the British Isles 3, ed. J.J.G. Alexander. London: Harvey Miller, 1975; Pächt, Otto, C.R. Dodwell, and Francis Wormald. *The St. Albans Psalter (Albani Psalter)*. Studies of the Warburg Institute 25. London: Warburg Institute, 1960; Swarzenski, Hanns. Review of *The St. Albans Psalter*. *Kunstchronik* 16 (1963): 77–85; Thomson, Rodney. *Manuscripts from St. Albans Abbey 1066–1235*. Woodbridge: Brewer, 1982.

See also Manuscript Illumination, Romanesque; St. Albans Abbey; Women and the Arts

St. Nicholas Crosier

This ivory crosier, or bishop's staff of office (London, Victoria and Albert Museum inv. no. 218–1865; fig. 116), shows scenes from the life of Christ (the Nativity and the Agnus Dei supported by an angel on the volute and the Annunciation to the Shepherds on the stem), and three scenes from the life of St. Nicholas: his birth, his refusal of milk from his mother's breast on fast days, and his gift of dowries to the daughters of an impoverished nobleman of Myra to prevent their being sent into prostitution.

Originally interpreted as representing the infancy and passion of Christ, the crosier has been attributed variously to Germany, France, and England, and to dates in both the 11th and 12th centuries. However, Dale identified the iconography by comparison with the stained glass at Chartres, dating the ivory to about 1175.

The importance of St. Nicholas (established by the 6th century) grew considerably following the translation of his body from Myra to Bari in 1087. The inclusion of scenes from his legend suggests that the crosier was commissioned for a church dedicated to the saint or for a bishop of that name.

Although stylistic comparisons have been made with stained glass and sculpture at Canterbury (1174–80), and with the Portail Royal at Chartres, the most convincing parallel for the distinctive figure style is offered by the Winchester Bible (Swarzenski, figs. 310–14) and thus supports a date of about 1150. The crosier is generally accepted as English, although Gaborit-Chopin relates it to reliefs at St. Aubin d'Angers executed for Abbot Robert de la Tour Landry (1127–54), suggesting Angers as a possible place of origin.

The beautiful carving is unusual in its lack of purely decorative motifs and in its details, such as the apparent emergence

Fig. 116. St. Nicholas Crosier (London, Victoria and Albert Museum 218–1865). Reproduced by permission of the Board of Trustees of the Victoria and Albert Museum, London.

of St. Nicholas's father from the ivory itself. The use of elephant ivory was also still rare in England at this date.

Peta Evelyn

Bibliography

Dale, William S.A. "An English Crosier of the Transitional Period." *Art Bulletin* 38 (1956): 137–41; Gaborit-Chopin, Danielle. *Ivoires du Moyen Age*. Fribourg: Office du Livre, 1978; Sauerländer, Willibald. "'The Year 1200': A Centennial Exhibition at the Metropolitan Museum of Art, February 12–May 10, 1970." *Art Bulletin* 53 (1971): 506–16 [exhibition review]; Swarzenski, Hanns. *Monuments of Romanesque Art: The Art of Church Treasures in North-Western Europe*. 2d ed. London: Faber & Faber, 1974; Zarnecki, George, Janet Holt, and Tristram Holland, eds. *English Romanesque Art 1066–1200*. London: Weidenfeld & Nicolson, 1984, cat. no. 213.

See also Great Bibles; Ivory Carving, Romanesque; Liturgical Vessels

Saints' Lives, Illuminated

Libelli are small books containing various types of cult material concerning one saint (or occasionally two), usually produced by and for the monastery of which the saint is patron. England was late in producing an independent illustrated *libellus* of a saint's life, presumably because of the disruptions of the Conquest, but succeeded by the end of the Middle Ages in producing perhaps the most interesting and beautiful group of such books.

The first English example is the tiny manuscript of Bede's *Life of Cuthbert* (Oxford, University College 165; fig. 117), supplemented with translation and miracle accounts, made at Durham and dated variously between 1100 and 1120. It has been connected with Norman monastic appropriation of the Anglo-Saxon cult of Cuthbert previously sponsored by canons at Durham and Lindisfarne. In particular a translation of Cuthbert's holy, incorrupt body to a new shrine took place in 1104. However, the tiny size and intimate quality of the manuscript argue against its use in public ceremony, and Baker has suggested that it was produced for a private patron. The 55 charming multicolor line drawings, each in the space of a few square inches of text column preceding its chapter, advance a lively narrative. Special emphasis is placed on Cuthbert's monastic life and his asceticism but also on his public life.

A second copy of the *Life of Cuthbert* (BL Yates Thompson 26), produced at Durham ca. 1200, provides a striking contrast to the Oxford manuscript. Although also quite small, it is a lavish manuscript with 45 remaining miniatures framed and painted in full color and gold. Again the miniatures precede the chapters of Bede's *Life* and added miracles. Although occasionally miniatures on both pages of an opening allow narrative to move across space, in general the lively quality of the earlier Cuthbert illustrations has been transformed into a more monumental, almost iconic vision. Scholars have argued

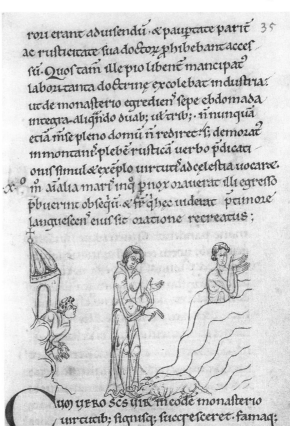

Fig. 117. Life of Cuthbert *(Oxford, University College 165), p. 35. Cuthbert prays through the night in the sea; otters dry his feet. Reproduced by permission of the Master and Fellows of University College, Oxford.*

that the copies of Cuthbert's life in manuscripts and other media all spring from the same family tree.

The illustrated *Life* of Edmund, king of East Anglia and martyr, now in the Pierpont Morgan Library (M.736), contains 32 full-page, full-color miniatures preceded by a few preliminary texts and followed by miracles, the *Life* by Abbo of Fleury, and an office decorated with historiated initials. While the text is in a Bury St. Edmunds hand, the miniatures are closely allied to if not actually by the hand of the Alexis Master of the St. Albans Psalter and may be dated ca. 1120–30. The manuscript may represent a special project intended to enhance the prestige of Bury's patron saint, commissioned by Abbot Anselm from a visiting artist. To that end the miniatures focus on themes of pilgrimage, kingship, and the proper exercise of power, as well as on the saint's ability after his death to defend his monastery by miraculous intervention.

The Guthlac Roll (BL Harley Roll Y.6), produced for the monastery of Crowland ca. 1220, is a beautiful if late example of line drawings in the "Style 1200." Although loosely based on the *Life* of the ascetic saint by Felix, the roll is exclusively pictorial, with only a few short *tituli,* or captions. It has been suggested that the series of eighteen contingent roundels on the Roll was intended as a model for stained glass or for some object, such as an enamel shrine. However, the finished quality of the drawing also allows the recent suggestion that the roll was intended for display in the monastic church on the occasion of the saint's feast. The last roundel represents donors making gifts at the altar and has been associated with forged charters and land disputes in which the monastery was involved at the time.

Between ca. 1230 and 1259 Matthew Paris produced at least one illustrated *libellus* himself, that of the patron of his monastery, St. Alban (Dublin, Trinity College 177; fig. 95: see MATTHEW PARIS), and probably wrote the Anglo-Norman text and provided sketches for two others, those of St. Thomas of Canterbury (BL Loan 88) and St. Edward the Confessor (CUL Ee.3.59). These manuscripts show an innovative narrative approach. Matthew works in framed rectangular miniatures running across the top of the page, above two or three columns of text. Often both miniatures in an opening work together to create an active, complex visual narrative that complements and even extends the written text. Matthew uses line drawings enhanced with color in a style more common earlier in the century, allied to the "Style 1200." The Dublin manuscript contains notations about the lending of Matthew's manuscripts of saints' lives to ladies, clearly defining his intended audience as the aristocracy, an audience reflected in his concern for chivalric and courtly values.

Cynthia Hahn

Bibliography

Abou-el-Haj, Barbara. "Bury St. Edmunds Abbey between 1070 and 1124: A History of Property, Privilege, and Monastic Art Production." *Art History* 7 (1983): 1–29; Baker, M. "Medieval Illustrations of Bede's 'Life of St. Cuthbert.'" With an appendix by D.H. Farmer. *JWCI* 41 (1978): 16–49; Hahn, Cynthia. "*Peregrinatio et Natio:* The Illustrated Life of Edmund King and Martyr." *Gesta* 30 (1991): 119–39; Kauffmann, C. Michael. *Romanesque Manuscripts 1066–1190.* A Survey of Manuscripts Illuminated in the British Isles 3, ed. J.J.G. Alexander. London: Harvey Miller, 1975; Kelly, Kimberly. "Forgery, Invention and Propaganda: Factors behind the Production of the Guthlac Roll (British Museum Harley Roll Y.6)." *Athanor* 8 (1989): 1–14; Lewis, Suzanne. *The Art of Matthew Paris in the Chronica majora.* Berkeley: University of California Press, 1987; Morgan, Nigel. *Early Gothic Manuscripts 1190–1285.* 2 vols. A Survey of Manuscripts Illuminated in the British Isles 4, ed. J.J.G. Alexander. London: Harvey Miller, 1982–88; Wormald, Francis. "Some Illustrated Manuscripts of the Lives of the Saints." *BJRL* 35 (1952): 248–68.

See also Manuscript Illumination, Gothic; Manuscript Illumination, Romanesque; Matthew Paris

Salisbury (Sarum), Use of

The liturgical customs of Salisbury Cathedral in the southern English county of Wiltshire. The form "Sarum," current since the Middle Ages, is a misreading of an abbreviation for Salisbury's Latin name, *Sarisburia.* Formed mainly between the late 11th and mid-14th centuries and described in great detail in contemporary documents, this use became increasingly influential in Britain between the early 13th century and the Reformation, and it was even observed abroad.

In modern times, particularly between about 1850 and 1920, there has been a major revival of interest in the Use of Salisbury. This was largely prompted and sustained by controversy between High and Low factions within the Church of England, by the reemergence of the Roman Catholic church as a potent force in English religious life, and by the deep vein of nostalgia running through Victorian culture. Although the tendency of English scholars to concentrate heavily on the Use of Salisbury at the expense of other English and continental uses has produced an exaggerated impression of its uniqueness and quality, the integrity and sophistication of the use and its immense importance in the context of English liturgy are undeniable.

A use is a body of regulation and custom ordering the corporate activity of an ecclesiastical foundation or group of foundations, such as a cathedral church and its diocesan churches, or a religious order, such as the Cistercians or Franciscans. Such uses were common in late-medieval Europe, particularly at diocesan and metropolitan levels, and many were recorded in writing. Although some medieval uses made provision for various constitutional and administrative matters, most concentrated on the liturgy: the content of the services (the rite), their conduct (the ceremonial), and the liturgical responsibilities of the institution's members. Since in most medieval services any text intended to be audible was sung rather than spoken, there was an intimate connection between the rite and its associated music. Thus the musical repertoire particular to an institution can arguably be regarded as part of its use. This repertoire would normally consist entirely of plainchant, although some uses envisaged the performance of polyphony and even prescribed specific polyphonic items.

In the later Middle Ages, because of the wide dissemination of Roman liturgy and plainchant in revised and augmented Carolingian versions, most of western Christendom shared a common liturgical tradition. This embraced the main elements of the liturgical calendar, the basic structure of mass and the divine office, the nature of the chief liturgical forms and the methods of performing them, and the central repertoire of plainchant. There nevertheless remained scope for local divergence and variation. In view of the impracticability of establishing and maintaining complete and widespread uniformity this was probably inevitable; it was also desirable and perhaps even encouraged, because it allowed churches to respond to local conditions and requirements, thereby enhancing a community's sense of identification with the liturgy. Divergence commonly involved the observance of local saints' days, changes in the detailed structure of services, differences in methods of performance, and the use of variant or nonstandard plainchant melodies. Deviation attained the status of a use when it became sufficiently extensive and systematic to be recognized in its own right.

The diocese of Salisbury came into being in 1075, when William the Conqueror made his new town of Salisbury (located on the site now called Old Sarum) the administrative center of what had previously been the diocese of Sherborne; the latter had been founded about 705, some 70 years after St. Birinus's successful evangelization of the Saxon kingdom of Wessex. With a few minor anomalies Salisbury diocese encompassed the counties of Dorset, Wiltshire, and Berkshire. When the see fell vacant in 1078, William secured the appointment of Osmund, a fellow Norman who was currently his chancellor. At Salisbury Osmund introduced constitutional and administrative reforms probably based on the example of Norman cathedrals, such as Bayeux, Évreux, and Rouen. Like several Saxon cathedral churches Sherborne/Salisbury had been a Benedictine monastery, but by 1089 Osmund had replaced the monks with resident secular canons, perhaps because the site available was too cramped for conventual buildings. In 1091 he provided a constitution for the new body in the form of documents known as the *Charta Osmundi* and the *Institutio Osmundi*. None of this was revolutionary; reform had been taking place in the post-Conquest English church since the appointment of Lanfranc to Canterbury in 1070, and already in 1090 Thomas of Bayeux and Remigius of Fécamp had created similar legislation for their cathedral churches of York and Lincoln. Osmund's surviving ordinances for Salisbury are only peripherally concerned with liturgy, and there is no proof that he made innovations in liturgy and chant to match his constitutional reforms. It does, however, seem likely that he did, because the change from a monastic community to a secular chapter would itself have had liturgical implications. Lack of evidence on this crucial issue means that the sources from which the Salisbury liturgy and its chant were assembled remain obscure; Rouen seems a likely source of influence.

The bleak site of Old Sarum proved unsuitable for settlement, and in 1218 the town was moved about a mile south to what is now Salisbury, where a new cathedral was built between 1220 and 1266. The dominant personality in the cathedral at this time was Richard Poore, dean from 1197 to 1215 and bishop from 1217 to 1228. Poore seems to have been another efficient administrator, and the earliest surviving detailed account of the cathedral's customs apparently dates from his time. It is contained in two principal documents, an ordinal and a consuetudinary; the former is essentially a service book listing the items to be performed in each service and describing the method of performance, while the latter is basically an administrative handbook defining the liturgical and some other duties of the cathedral's personnel. The ordinal and consuetudinary together formed the basis for most subsequent documents describing the use. Again there was nothing novel about these developments; Lichfield already had an ordinal and consuetudinary in the time of Hugh de Nonant, bishop from 1188 to 1198. Our ignorance of liturgical usage at Salisbury between Osmund's reconstitution and the move to New Sarum makes it impossible to assess how far Poore was recording established liturgical practice and how far he was describing recent innovations. Nor is it clear whether he inherited any substantial documentary tradition; the phrases from the *Charta Osmundi* and the *Institutio Osmundi* incorporated into the consuetudinary dealt with constitutional rather than liturgical matters.

In addition to the ordinal and consuetudinary Salisbury had the full range of service books common in the later Middle Ages: missal, breviary, gradual, antiphoner, processional, manual, pontifical, tonal, and so on. In the earlier 14th century a new book called the customary was introduced; apparently intended for parish churches, it was derived from the consuetudinary, omitting most of the constitutional material and concentrating more on the divine office than on mass or the processions. It seems to have largely supplanted the consuetudinary, often being copied as a supplement to the ordinal. The rubrics of the missal, breviary, and other service books were drawn mainly from the ordinal, the consuetudinary, or the customary. Like most other liturgies that of Salisbury was in a constant state of development, adopting new feasts, altering the grading of existing feasts, and making various other changes, particularly in ceremonial. The liturgical books were altered from time to time in response to these developments. Initially the alterations were made piecemeal, but eventually the ordinal particularly became so unwieldy and confusing that a thorough revision was necessary. This revision, carried out in the mid-14th century, resulted in what became known as the "New Ordinal." The preeminence of Salisbury Use is attested by the fact that in the late 14th century the Wycliffites singled it out for attack on account of its elaborateness.

During the 15th century Salisbury's reputation for liturgical propriety declined, probably partly because the ever increasing complexity of the liturgy made it difficult for anybody to understand all its workings and partly because the canons of the cathedral genuinely lacked interest or expertise in such matters. In the middle of the century Clement Maydestone, a member of the Brigettine community of Syon, wrote three tracts on aspects of the use. The *Directorium sacerdotum* (ca. 1440) clarified some of the ordinal's complicated provisions for reading the Old Testament histories, singing responsories, and observing commemorations. The *Defensorium directorii* (ca. 1448) sought to justify the *Directorium* by exposing discrepancies between the ordinal and current faulty interpretations of its regulations. *Crede michi* (ca. 1452) listed and criticized answers recently given by the canons of Salisbury to certain questions on liturgy and added numerous other comments. It should be noted that such criticisms were directed not at the use itself but at contemporary errors in observing it. The advent of printed service books in the later 15th century seems to have stimulated efforts to restore the purity of the use; the *Directorium sacerdotum* was printed several times in a revision by the Cambridge scholar William Clerke, and the rubrics of the breviary were recast for the 1509 edition. Salisbury service books were printed remarkably often from about 1475 onward, mainly in Paris but also in Rouen, Venice, London, and elsewhere. Before the abolition of the use there were more than 40 printings of the breviary and even more of the missal. Salisbury chant books were also printed, notably the processional (about 25 times between 1502 and 1554), the gradual (1527, 1528, and 1532), and the monumental edition of the antiphoner (1519–20).

The splendor and elaboration of Salisbury's liturgy and the comprehensiveness and order of its regulations impressed contemporaries and invited imitation. The use's success in southern England also reflects a lack of competition, in particular the unsuitability of Canterbury's monastic liturgy to serve as a model for secular institutions. Salisbury's early influence seems to have been primarily constitutional, gradually but surely being overtaken by its liturgical influence. From the 12th century onward many dioceses, including Lincoln, Lichfield, Moray, Glasgow, Chichester, Dublin, Wells, Exeter, and London, imported elements of Salisbury Use, while the Austin canons, academic colleges, and royal and aristocratic household chapels also observed it. It is easier to list the dioceses that remained aloof; foremost among these were York and to a lesser extent Hereford, which preserved distinctive constitutions and liturgies until the Reformation. The Use of Salisbury was even carried abroad—for instance, wherever English royal and aristocratic household chapels happened to be functioning and to Braga in Portugal when Philippa, daughter of John of Gaunt, married John I in 1385. The adoption of the use throughout the southern (Canterbury) province of the English church in 1542 must have seemed a natural and inevitable recognition of Salisbury's liturgical primacy. A few years later, however, came the Protestant vernacular liturgy embodied in the prayerbooks of 1549 and 1552; the former was closely based on Salisbury Use, but the latter was considerably more independent of it. The Use of Salisbury itself was reintroduced during the Marian revival of 1553–58, but the Elizabethan religious settlement finally abolished it. Vestiges still remain in the Book of Common Prayer, for example some of the Collects and many of the Epistles and Gospels.

Comparison of the three major nonmonastic uses of medieval England, those of Salisbury, York, and Hereford, reveals frequent but mainly minor discrepancies. The text of an item on a certain day may vary; for example, in mass on Saturday in the third week of Advent Salisbury, York, and Hereford have the Secrets *Super has hostias, Sacrificiis praesentibus,* and *Ecclesiae tuae,* respectively. Among plainchant items the Sequences often differ; in the dawn mass of Christmas Salisbury has *Sonent regi,* York *Laetabundus exultet,* and Hereford *Caeleste organum.* The series of Alleluia verses for the Sundays between Trinity and Advent are also different, as on the sixth Sunday after Trinity, when Salisbury's *Eripe me* contrasts with York's *In te domine* and Hereford's *Omnes gentes.* Similar discrepancies occur within the divine office, so that (for instance) in Salisbury Use the verse to the eighth responsory *Intuemini* at Matins on the fourth Sunday of Advent is *Et dominabitur,* whereas in York and Hereford it is *Precursor pro nobis.* There are also variations in spoken items and ceremonial, such as the procedure for the giving of the Pax (Kiss of Peace) within the Canon of the mass: in Salisbury Use the prayer *Domine sancte pater* precedes the Pax, whereas in the York and Hereford uses it follows it; the ceremony concerning the articles on the altar differs; and the celebrant gives the Pax with different words. As one might expect, some of Salisbury's plainchant melodies contain characteristic variants.

The Use of Salisbury makes little or no mention of polyphony; the customary prescribes the singing of the *Benedicamus* "dupliciter" on a few special days, but the intended meaning could conceivably be "by two people" rather than "in two voices." However, some other English uses (such as that of Exeter) make less ambiguous and more extensive provision for polyphony both within the regular liturgy and in extraliturgical acts of devotion. Many surviving polyphonic compositions show evidence of having been intended for such usage, and there are also numerous references to polyphony being improvised in these contexts by using such techniques as discant and faburden. Often polyphony replaced the normal plainchant performance of a liturgical form, such as a hymn, a Lady-Mass Alleluia, or an item from the Ordinary of the mass; in such cases the original plainchant melody was commonly incorporated into the polyphonic setting as a *cantus firmus.* Polyphonic settings of additional nonliturgical texts could also be inserted into services (e.g., after the Sanctus of the mass) or substituted for certain liturgical items such as the *Benedicamus* at the end of Matins and Lauds. In the 15th century it became common to sing a polyphonic votive antiphon with a versicle, response, and prayer as an independent act of devotion after Vespers or Compline. Sources of polyphony apparently closely connected with the Salisbury liturgy include the Old Hall Manuscript (BL Add. 57950, probably from the household chapel of Henry V's brother Thomas of Clarence) and the Pepys Manuscript (Cambridge, Magdalene College Pepys 1236, possibly from the Almonry Chapel of Canterbury Cathedral). Although during the later Middle Ages polyphony was presumably cultivated at Salisbury just as at other secular cathedrals, the earliest surviving music by a composer associated with the cathedral appears to be the mass *Libera nos* and some smaller pieces by Thomas Knyght, instructor of the choristers between about 1529 and 1549.

Nick Sandon

Bibliography

Berry, Mary. "Sarum Rite, Music of the." *NGD* 16:512–13; Dickinson, Francis, ed. *Missale ad Usum Insignis et Praeclare Ecclesiae Sarum.* Burntisland: Parker, 1861–83. Repr. Farnborough: Gregg, 1969; Frere, Walter Howard, ed. *Antiphonale Sarisburiense.* 6 vols. London: Plainsong & Mediaeval Music Society, 1901–25. Repr. Farnborough: Gregg, 1966 [facsimile]; Frere, Walter Howard, ed. *Graduale Sarisburiense.* London: Quaritch, 1891–94. Repr. Farnborough: Gregg, 1966 [facsimile]; Frere, Walter Howard, ed. *The Use of Sarum.* Vol. 1: *The Sarum Customs As Set Forth in the Consuetudinary and Customary.* Vol. 2: *The Ordinal and Tonal.* Cambridge: Cambridge University Press, 1898–1901. Repr. Westmead: Gregg, 1969; Pfaff, Richard W. *Medieval Latin Liturgy: A Select Bibliography.* Toronto Medieval Bibliographies 9. Toronto: Toronto University Press, 1982; Sandon, Nick, ed. *The Use of Salisbury.* 4 vols. to date. Vol. 1: *The Ordinary of the Mass.* Vol. 2: *Mass Propers from Advent to Septuagesima.* Vol. 3: *Mass Propers from Septuagesima to Palm Sunday.* Vol. 4: *The Masses and Ceremonies of Holy Week.* Newton Abbot: Antico Editions, 1984–96.

See also Liturgy; Liturgy and Church Music, History of; Old Hall Manuscript; Salisbury Cathedral

Salisbury Cathedral

Salisbury Cathedral (figs. 118–19) is the most historically and stylistically homogeneous of English medieval cathedrals, being almost entirely the result of a single extended campaign of construction from 1220 to 1266. This uniformity is partly the result of the wealth of chapter and bishop that allowed such a prodigious and continuous outlay of funds and partly the result of building on a virgin site devoid of any previous church. The Romanesque cathedral of Sarum was located some two miles north, on a site within a castle bailey that had proved too cramped to allow the expansion deemed commensurate with the prestige of a 13th-century bishop. The new site allowed patron and architect the unwonted luxury of any design they could afford.

The design they chose has sometimes been taken to represent the quintessential Early English cathedral, but the individuality of all English early Gothic cathedrals makes the search for quintessence a misguided one. Salisbury has the horizontal expansiveness characteristic of much English medieval architecture, both in its plan, with two sets of transepts and a long nave and choir, and in its elevation, with vault shafts rising only from the gallery spandrels so as not to interfere with the longitudinal flow of arcade and gallery, a flow aided by the judicious use of Purbeck marble shafting, particularly in the complex clustered piers of the middle story. Arch

moldings are complex in profile as in any Early English building, and there are six different pier designs, all except one with detached Purbeck shafts set around coursed cores of various shapes.

While these features give Salisbury a visual opulence when set against the designs of contemporary French cathedrals, Salisbury is usually compared with its English contemporary at Lincoln, where decorative forms are used with much greater abandon than at Salisbury. In particular Salisbury lacks the fanciful rib patterns of Lincoln, being covered entirely with four-part vaults, and the rich foliage sculpture and dado arcades of the northern building. Some have seen the relative austerity of the Salisbury design as a conscious rebuke or at least repudiation of the exuberance of Lincoln, perhaps connected with the liturgical reforms of Bishop Richard Poore (1217–28), who began the project. Whether the work in progress at Lincoln would have weighed so heavily on the minds of southern ecclesiastics may be open to question; more interesting is the continuity with the old church of Sarum that Poore and his chapter seem to have been interested in preserving.

There is some evidence that the new building was related to the old in its dimensions, and it seems clear that the eastern projecting Trinity Chapel at the former was a modern version of the eastern chapel of Bishop Roger's east arm at Old Sarum. The elegant Trinity Chapel, a miniature hall church with slender Purbeck piers, may have been designed as a shrine for Osmund, the first important post-Conquest bishop of the see, whose canonization the chapter sought. In the event

Fig. 118. Salisbury Cathedral, nave interior, north elevation. Courtesy of L. Hoey.

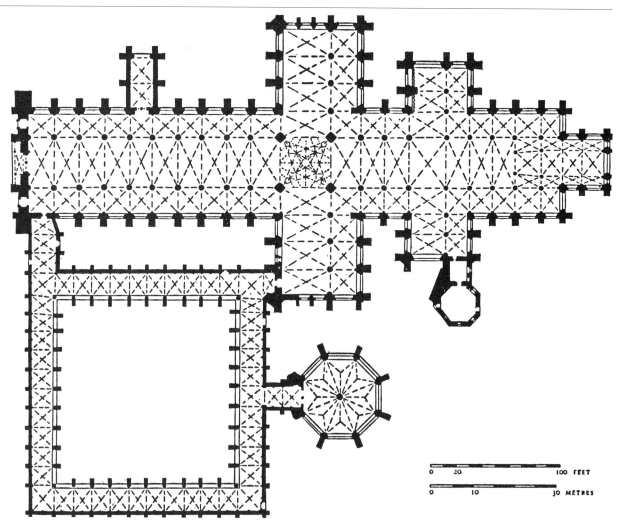

Osmund was not made a saint until 1457, after which his shrine did indeed stand in the Trinity Chapel. If this was its original intent, the inspiration would have been the Trinity Chapel at Canterbury, where Thomas Becket was enshrined.

The exterior of Salisbury is extremely regular in its serried rows of double lancets at aisle level and triple lancets at clerestory level. Flying buttresses were absent from the 13th-century scheme, although there are hidden buttresses under the gallery roofs, derived from Wells. Coming also from Wells was the idea of a screen facade with small portals but covered with gabled statue niches.

The most striking exterior feature of Salisbury is its central tower and 400-foot spire. This addition, begun probably in the last decade of the 13th century (its dating is controversial), has dimensions that may well have been determined according to the proportional schemes of the original building. As spectacular as its stone skin is the 13th-century wooden interior scaffolding used to construct the tower and left inside afterward as a kind of brace.

Lawrence Hoey

Bibliography

Blum, Pamela. "The Sequence of the Building Campaigns at Salisbury." *Art Bulletin* 73 (1991): 6–38; Cocke, Thomas, and Peter Kidson. *Salisbury Cathedral: Perspectives on the Architectural History.* London: Royal Commission on the Historical Monuments of England, 1993; Tatton-Brown, Tim. "Building the Tower and Spire of Salisbury Cathedral." *Antiquity* 65 (1991): 74–96; Willis, Robert. "Minutes of Lecture on the Architecture of Salisbury Cathedral Delivered by . . . Robert Willis . . . July 26, 1849." In Robert Willis, *Architectural History of Some English Cathedrals.* 2d ser. Chicheley: Minet, 1973.

See also Architecture and Architectural Sculpture, Gothic; Salisbury, Use of; Screen Facades; Wells Cathedral

Salisbury Chapter House Reliefs

Carved ca. 1280, these Old Testament scenes are set in the spandrels of the wall arcade on the interior of the chapter house (fig. 120). The narrative begins and ends with the figure of Christ presiding over the entrance on the west wall. It includes 60 separate scenes: Creation, Creation of the Firmament (west wall, right of entrance); Creation of Plants to Adam and Eve Hiding (northwest wall); the Expulsion to Noah's Vineyard (north wall); Drunkenness of Noah to Sacrifice of Isaac (northeast wall); Jacob Blessed by Isaac to Meeting of Jacob and Esau (east wall); Joseph's Dream to Joseph Accused by Potiphar's Wife (southeast wall); Joseph Imprisoned to the Cup in Benjamin's Sack (south wall); Moses Striking the Rock

Fig. 120. Salisbury Chapter House Reliefs. The Fall. Courtesy of C. Karkov.

and Receiving the Tablets of the Law (southwest wall). The final scene and the central figure of Christ over the doorway set the business of the cathedral chapter that was conducted within the room firmly within the context of Old and New Testament law.

The scenes, carved in relatively deep relief, were originally richly painted. All are set in a stylized landscape consisting of wavy groundlines, decorative patterned trees, and formulaic architecture. Some of the figures are executed in a classicizing style with graceful bodies and gestures and thin clinging draperies. Others are carved in an expressive style characterized by animated poses and lively gestures. It has been suggested that stylistically the reliefs are closer to contemporary painting (e.g., the scenes of the months on the ceiling of the Salisbury choir) than they are to contemporary sculpture (Stone, 1972: 132).

Perhaps the most remarkable aspect of the reliefs is the clarity with which their narrative content is expressed. There is much drama, but scenes are readily identified and the flow of the narrative is easily followed.

The heads of all the figures were destroyed in the 17th century, when a parliamentary committee sat in the chapter house. They were replaced in the 1860s during John Birnie Phillip's somewhat heavy-handed campaign of restoration.

Catherine E. Karkov

Bibliography

Cook, G.H. *Portrait of Salisbury.* New York: Chanticleer Press, 1949; Crook, J.M. *William Burges and the High Victorian Dream.* London: Murray, 1981; Stone, Lawrence. *Sculpture in Britain: The Middle Ages.* 2d ed. Harmondsworth: Penguin, 1972.

See also Chapter Houses; Salisbury Cathedral

Salve Service

An evening votive observance in honor of the Virgin Mary, sung after Compline and taking the form of a memorial consisting of an antiphon, versicle, and collect. Its name is derived from one of the most popular and frequently performed Marian votive antiphons, *Salve regina.* This short service, new in England in the mid-13th century, was performed either in choir or at another location in the church, such as in the Lady Chapel or at a statue or side altar. In the later 14th and 15th centuries the Salve was specifically included in the customs of many new secular choral foundations, and it grew to occupy a position of ritual and ceremonial importance in the life of these institutions. The chief musical ornament of the service was the antiphon, increasingly set in elaborate polyphony. From the mid-14th century to the mid-16th the polyphonic Marian antiphon was one of the most numerous and significant genres of English composition.

Peter M. Lefferts

Bibliography

Harrison, Frank Ll. *Music in Medieval Britain.* 2d ed. London: Routledge & Kegan Paul, 1963; Lefferts, Peter M. "Cantilena and Antiphon: Music for Marian Services in Late Medieval England." In *Studies in Medieval Music: Festschrift for Ernest H. Sanders,* ed. Peter M. Lefferts and Brian Seirup. *Current Musicology* 45–47 (1990): 247–82.

See also Antiphon; Cantilena; Choirs; Lady Chapel; Lady Mass; Liturgy and Church Music, History of; Votive Observance

Satire

The satire of classical Rome was widely known in the Middle Ages through the inclusion of Horace, Juvenal, Persius, and other satirical authors in the school curriculum. Many medieval writers drew on, commented on, and cited classical satire in their own works. Medieval literary theorists treated satire as part of the rhetoric of praise and blame, praising classical satire for its reproof of human vice. In the classical period satire was thought of as a genre characterized by medley and variety, and therefore appropriately termed *satura,* "fullness" or "mixed stew." These and other speculative etymologies for *satura*—sometimes spelled *satira* or *satyra* in postclassical writings—were known in the Middle Ages. It used to be widely believed among literary historians that in the Middle Ages satire was thought of as a mode rather than a genre until self-conscious imitation of the classical genre began in the Renaissance. However, recent research into the reception of classical satire in the Middle Ages has shown that medieval commentators developed from their reading of classical satirists a full theory of the genre, in which satire was seen as forthright, unadorned verse that aims to reform vice and spares no one from censure, not even the poet.

In some modern bibliographies and critical works satire has been coupled with complaint, creating a loose category of writings on the condition of the world. Greater awareness of medieval literary theory has recently led to an appreciation that "complaint" is a term better reserved for the medieval planctus, a genre distinguished from satire by its aim of evoking pity for the speaker, not reform in society.

Medieval satiric theory was but one of a number of potential influences on ME satire. The favorite targets of the ME satirist were often the same as those of satirists writing in other vernaculars and in Latin. Studies of some of the main medieval satirical themes—the evils of women and marriage, the luxury of the monasteries, the ignorance of the parish clergy, the hypocrisies of the friars, corruption in court and church, the professional dereliction of lawyers and doctors, the general failings of all estates of society—have revealed close links between ME satire and earlier and contemporary satire in other languages, especially Latin and French.

In the second half of the 12th century England saw a flowering of satirical writing in Latin. One of the most important poems from this period is the *Speculum stultorum* (1179–80) by Nigel Longchamps or Wireker. The poem is a general satire *(satira communis)*, a review of society as a whole. Following the adventures of Burnellus the ass, the poet exposes the follies of ecclesiastics, religious orders, and university clerics. Chaucer evidently knew the work, for he refers to the poem of "Daun Burnel the Asse" in the *Nun's Priest's Tale*. John Gower exploited the general satire in all of his major works and drew on Nigel's poem in his Latin satire on the evils of the times, the *Vox Clamantis*. Another 12th-century writer who acquired a name as a satirist was Walter Map. Map was the author of one of the best-known antifeminist satires of the Middle Ages, the *Dissuasio Valerii ad Ruffinum philosophum ne uxorem ducat* (before ca. 1181). The *Dissuasio* is a Latin prose epistle in which Valerius attempts to dissuade Ruffinus from marriage by cataloguing examples of its snares and disasters. The treatise circulated widely in England and provided some of the antifeminist satire adapted by Chaucer for the *Wife of Bath's Prologue*. Map incorporated the epistle into a longer prose satire on the court and the religious orders, *De nugis curialium* or *Courtiers' Trifles* (ca. 1181–92).

It is thought that Map's *De nugis* hardly circulated at all during the Middle Ages. Map's medieval reputation as a satirist rested largely on scurrilous goliardic verses that were attributed to him by scribes but that he almost certainly did not write. The term "goliardic" is often used of satirical poetry or prose issuing from a clerical milieu, usually in Latin, mostly on antifeminist or anticlerical subjects and characterized by delight in parody, burlesque, and wordplay. Such works are often associated with a burlesque of the clerical order that imagines a "Bishop Golias" and associated dissolute clerics, the Goliards. Among the best-known examples are the *Apocalypsis Goliae episcopi,* a parody of the book of Revelation that exposes the corruption of the clergy, and *Golias de conjuge non ducenda,* an antimarriage satire that was translated into ME. Gower's *Vox Clamantis* shows the influence of goliardic techniques, and although much of the wordplay was untranslatable from Latin to English, traces of goliardic traditions have been detected in *Piers Plowman* and other ME satire.

Some satire was composed in Anglo-Norman on political, anticlerical, and antifeminist subjects, Gower's *Mirour de l'Omme* (ca. 1376–79) being one of the latest and most notable examples. However, the *Roman de la Rose,* written on the Continent in the mid-13th century, was perhaps the most influential French satirical work for ME writers. The poem was well known in England, and parts of it were translated into English. Chaucer drew on the figure of Faus Semblant (False-Seeming) for his friars and the Pardoner and on the Vieille (Old Woman) for the Wife of Bath. Another important continental satire was the cycle of narratives dealing with Reynard the fox. Versions of this beast-epic satire of court and church appeared in several vernaculars. There was no ME version of the full epic until 1481, when William Caxton printed the *History of Reynard the Fox,* but images and episodes from the narrative cycle appeared earlier in English art and to a lesser extent in English literature (most notably in Chaucer *Nun's Priest's Tale* and Henryson's *Fables*).

Alongside these literary influences on ME satirists there are thought to have been satirical traditions of a popular, subliterary, and even oral kind. Because of their nature less evidence for these traditions has survived, and their impact on ME satirists is more difficult to estimate. Scurrilous popular songs were composed for and against despised social groups, and named individuals were attacked in invectives. The "flyting" was a verbal contest in which opponents poured torrents of extravagant abuse at one another. The Scots poet William Dunbar included flyting and invective in his rich repertoire of satire.

Popular sermons were another occasion for satire. Some commentators have considered the pulpit a more important source of inspiration for ME poets than satirical works in Latin or French. A favorite subject for preachers' satire was the failings of the clergy. Orthodox and heterodox preachers alike castigated the failings of the clergy in sermons to the laity.

From the first half of the 14th century English was increasingly used for satire on political subjects and topical grievances, such as the government of the realm, war, taxation, miscarriages of justice, and the oppression of the poor by their masters. Notable early-14th-century examples are the *Complaint of the Husbandman* (ca. 1300–40), on the oppression of the rural poor, and *The Simonie,* a topical review of society in three versions, the earliest dating from 1322 to 1326/30. *Winner and Waster,* from mid-century (1352–70?), is a debate on the relative merits of getting and spending wealth that includes much satire, especially on the friars, merchant classes, and extravagant aristocracy. Few authors of this kind of verse have been identified, and it may be best thought of as generically anonymous. In the 15th century, however, this anonymous clerical tradition changes somewhat, with the appearance of satirical and political verse by identified authors, such as Thomas Hoccleve and John Lydgate.

The later 14th century produced the most important ME satirical poets: Geoffrey Chaucer and William Langland. Chaucer's General Prologue to the *Canterbury Tales* satirizes a wide range of social classes. The Prologue owes much to traditional "estates satire," but Chaucer transcends tradition by questioning the possibility of moral certainty. Chaucer's *Wife of Bath's Prologue* draws on classical and medieval antifeminist traditions in a similarly innovative way.

Langland's *Piers Plowman* satirizes many of the estates and classes of society and includes various political and topical allusions, with an emphasis on anticlerical satire. Many critics have seen Langland's satire as conventional and derivative, but recent study of the poem's anticlerical satire in the light of the contemporary historical context has shown how satirical tradition could be given new meanings in new circumstances.

Chaucer and Langland influenced satire to the close of the Middle Ages and beyond. Chaucer's reputation as an anticlerical satirist led 16th- and 17th-century editors to attribute to him the virulently antimendicant *Jack Upland* and the anticlerical *Plowman's Tale,* works from the early 15th or possibly late 14th century. Langland's achievements were imitated and developed, notably in *Richard the Redeless* (1399–1400), and the probably distinct work *Mum and the Sothsegger* (ca. 1403–06), both satires on the government of the realm, and the antimendicant *Pierce the Plowman's Creed* (ca. 1394). In the 16th century the figure of the plowman was associated with the Protestant reformers' ideals.

Wendy Scase

Bibliography

PRIMARY

Map, Walter. *De nugis curialium: Courtiers' Trifles.* Ed. and trans. Montague Rhodes James, rev. C.N.L. Brooke and R.A.B. Mynors. Oxford: Clarendon, 1983; Robbins, Rossell Hope, ed. *Historical Poems of the XIVth and XVth Centuries.* New York: Columbia University Press, 1959; Wright, Thomas, ed. *The Political Songs of England.* Camden Society o.s. 6. London: Nichols, 1839; Wright, Thomas, ed. *The Latin Poems Commonly Attributed to Walter Mapes.* Camden Society o.s. 16. London: Nichols, 1841; Wright, Thomas, ed. *Political Poems and Songs Relating to English History.* Rolls Series 14. 2 vols. London: Longman, Green, Longman, & Roberts, 1859–61; Wright, Thomas, ed. *The Anglo-Latin Satirical Poets and Epigrammatists of the Twelfth Century.* Rolls Series 59. 2 vols. London: Longman, 1872.

SECONDARY

Manual 5:1385–1536, 1631–1725; Gray, Douglas. "Rough Music: Some Early Invectives and Flytings." In *English Satire and the Satiric Tradition,* ed. Claude Rawson. Oxford: Blackwell, 1984, pp. 21–43; Maddicott, J.R. "Poems of Social Protest in Fourteenth-Century England." In *England in the Fourteenth Century: Proceedings of the 1985 Harlaxton Symposium,* ed. W.M. Ormrod. Woodbridge: Boydell, 1986, pp. 130–44; Mann, Jill. *Chaucer and Medieval Estates Satire: The Literature of Social Classes and the General Prologue to the Canterbury Tales.* Cambridge: Cambridge University Press, 1973; Miller, Paul. "John Gower, Satiric Poet." In *Gower's Confessio Amantis: Responses and Reassessments,* ed. A.J. Minnis. Cambridge: Brewer, 1983, pp. 79–105; Owst, G.R. *Literature and Pulpit in Medieval England.* 2d ed. Oxford: Blackwell, 1961; Peter, John. *Complaint and Satire in Early English Literature.* Oxford: Clarendon, 1956; Scase, Wendy. *Piers Plowman and the New Anticlericalism.* Cambridge: Cambridge University Press, 1989; Scattergood, V.J. *Politics and Poetry in the Fifteenth Century.* London: Blandford, 1971; Szittya, Penn R. *The Antifraternal Tradition in Medieval Literature.* Princeton: Princeton University Press, 1986; Utley, Francis Lee. *The Crooked Rib: An Analytical Index to the Argument about Women . . . to . . . 1568.* Columbus: Ohio State University Press, 1944; Yunck, John A. *The Lineage of Lady Meed: The Development of Mediaeval Venality Satire.* Notre Dame: University of Notre Dame Press, 1963.

See also Beast Epic and Fable; Chaucer; Dunbar; Gower; *Jack Upland;* Map; *Pierce the Plowman's Creed; Piers Plowman; Richard the Redeless; Winner and Waster;* Wycliffite Texts

Schools

Everyone was educated in medieval England, in the sense of acquiring social education and training for work. This usually began at home with one's parents, but as children grew older they were frequently sent away to live and learn in other people's houses. Aristocratic boys and girls were placed in noble or royal households as pages and attendants, and nonaristocratic children were dispatched to work on farms or in domestic service or, in the case of boys and a few girls from moderately wealthy families, to be apprenticed to craftsmen or merchants. These practices can be traced down to the Renaissance and beyond.

Education in the narrower sense of literary education dates from the conversion to Christianity in the 7th century. The church recruited clergy, first monks and later secular clergy living in the world, and required them to be literate in order to pray and study. The language of the church was Latin, and as Latin was so different from English it needed to be formally learned in schools. Some found the language too difficult and, having studied the alphabet, used it merely to read and write in English. Secular literature and some documents were written in this way. From the Anglo-Saxon period onward we find both elementary teaching of the Latin alphabet, preparatory to the reading of English (or, after the Norman Conquest, French), and more advanced teaching of Latin ("grammar," as it was called), leading to a full knowledge of the language. Grammar was taught in the best schools and had the greatest prestige, but elementary teaching and learning were very common.

The earliest schools were in monasteries and other religious houses. At first monks were admitted in boyhood as well as in adulthood, and in 749 the Synod of Clofeshoh laid down that such children should study in schools. The teachers were adult monks. In the 12th century the admission of children as monks was abolished; monastic schools accordingly became confined to older novices, aged seventeen or more. There continued to be boys in monasteries, however, helping as servers and choristers, in addition to noblemen's sons, sent to live with the abbot as in a great lay household. These other boys were taught separately from the monks by a nonmonastic chaplain or schoolmaster, and many Englishmen received their education in this way down to the Reformation. Some became monks, but others left the cloister and followed careers in the world as parish clergy or laymen.

From about the 8th century religious houses were supplemented by parish churches, served by secular clergy whose duties included the teaching of basic prayers, beliefs, and practices to the laity. Around 1005–08 the "Canons of Edgar" directed the clergy to teach boys to assist them in services, and by the 11th and 12th centuries examples occur of them giving instruction in reading and grammar. The chronicler Orderic Vitalis was taught by a cleric at Shrewsbury, and John of Salisbury at Old Sarum. Such teaching was never universal, but a few parish clergy kept schools to supplement their income and many more taught single pupils to assist them. This was a widespread source of education throughout the Middle Ages.

Self-contained schools, taught by professional schoolmasters, first appear in records in the late 11th century. They occur in cathedral cities, county towns, and the larger ports and by the 13th century were spreading to smaller places. The masters were secular priests, clerks in minor orders, or laymen (sometimes married), working for fees and giving instruction in reading, song (i.e., plainsong such as the clergy used), and Latin grammar. In the 12th century some cathedral cities (notably Exeter, Hereford, Lincoln, London, Salisbury, and York) had masters teaching the liberal arts, canon and civil law, or theology; by the 13th century these studies became chiefly concentrated at the new universities. Lectures in theology and canon law, however, continued to be provided by some monasteries and friaries for their own members and by some cathedrals for the local parish clergy.

The early town schools might be discontinuous; masters came and left. This problem was met in many places by the intervention of a patron (bishop, monastery, lay lord, or, later, the town council) who assumed responsibility for appointing the master and often gave him a monopoly of local teaching to ensure a reasonable livelihood. As time went on, benefactors (both clergy and laity) provided buildings, books, and scholarships to help the schools, and in the late 14th century endowments began to be given to provide the master with a salary to teach without fees. Early examples of such schools were Wykeham's wealthy college at Winchester (1382) and Lady Katherine Berkeley's small-town grammar school at Wotton-under-Edge in Gloucestershire (1384). Over 80 other towns and villages acquired free schools by the 1530s.

Girls did not attend most of the schools described here. Nunneries were fewer than monasteries, and they trained their own members. Noble girls learned to read at home from parents or visiting clergy or in nunneries. Schools for girls are first mentioned in London and Boston in the 15th century, taught by men or women and catering to the daughters of wealthier townspeople, sometimes taking in small boys as well. With some notable exceptions girls tended to be schooled in English or French rather than Latin and in reading rather than writing; their education was general and informal rather than specialized and formal. A few women nevertheless learned enough to become authors, especially in the 12th and 15th centuries.

Teachers of Latin, in both monasteries and town schools, were inventive in helping pupils master the language. The Anglo-Saxons and Celts were the first in Europe to devise grammars for non-Latin speakers, and Ælfric of Eynsham (ca. 945–1020) wrote a Latin grammar in English as well as a Latin *Colloquy* about everyday life to capture his students' interest. The grammar-school curriculum included the study of grammar and vocabulary, using texts in verse or in question-and-answer forms that were easy to remember. Pupils practiced writing sentences and formal letters *(dictamen)*, while disputations and speeches developed oral skills. Poetry was studied and written, and logic and philosophy were sometimes learned, especially in monastic schools. Arithmetic, law, and commercial subjects, however, appear to have been taught by specialized private tutors or by employers, rather than in schools.

The later Middle Ages saw renewed activity in the writing of grammars by such men as John Cornwall (fl. 1344–49) and John Leland (fl. 1415–28), both in Oxford, which had the most influential schools of the day. Cornwall compiled the first Latin grammar since Ælfric to include an element of English, and Leland improved on this by writing a series of short, clear Latin grammars entirely in English, used until well into the Renaissance. Other 15th-century authors produced the first Latin-English and English-Latin dictionaries for schools, and collections of sentences *(vulgaria)* were written for pupils to translate, paralleling Ælfric's work by dealing with news, jokes, scraps of rhyme and folklore, and descriptions of the everyday world. Late-medieval grammar was in a flourishing condition when the arrival of humanist studies from abroad brought about further changes in the early Tudor period.

Nicholas Orme

Bibliography

Courtenay, William J. *Schools and Scholars in Fourteenth-Century England.* Princeton: Princeton University Press, 1987; Moran, Jo Ann Hoeppner. *The Growth of English Schooling, 1340–1548: Learning, Literacy, and Laicization in Pre-Reformation York Diocese.* Princeton: Princeton University Press, 1985; Orme, Nicholas. *English Schools in the Middle Ages.* London: Methuen, 1973; Orme, Nicholas. *Education in the West of England.* Exeter: University of Exeter Press, 1976; Orme, Nicholas. *From*

Childhood to Chivalry: The Education of the English Kings and Aristocracy, 1066–1530. London: Methuen, 1984; Orme, Nicholas. *Education and Society in Medieval and Renaissance England.* London: Hambledon, 1989 [collected papers on medieval education]; Orme, Nicholas. "The Culture of Children in Medieval England." *Past and Present* 148 (August 1995): 48–88.

See also Ælfric; Children; Grammatical Treatises; Learning; Universities; Wainfleet; William of Wykeham

Science

Prior to the 12th century scientific knowledge in western Europe was largely that derived from Greek writings available through the Latin encyclopedists. There were compilations from Greek sources, such as Pliny the Elder's *Natural History*; translations, such as those by Boethius (d. ca. 525) of parts of Aristotle's *Organon,* and of Porphyry's (d. 304) *Introduction to Aristotle's Categories*; commentaries, such as that of Chalcidius (fl. early 4th century A.D.) on Plato's *Timaeus;* and more or less original writings inspired by Greek learning, such as Martianus Capella's (d. 439) *On the Marriage of Philology and Mercury.*

Bede (d. 735) was one of the greatest Latin encyclopedists. Although his encyclopedic *On the Nature of Things (De natura rerum)* is based largely on Pliny, he presents the classical theories of astronomy, meteorology, and geography within the context of Christian theology. Bede was among the first to use the birth of Christ as the reference for dating, and his two treatises *On the Division of Time (De temporibus)* and *On the Reckoning of Time (De temporum ratione)* examine problems of calendars and chronology and contain information on astronomy, the annual determination of Easter, and the tides.

Because Boethius never completed his intended translation of all of Aristotle into Latin, the bulk of Aristotelian philosophy remained unknown in the West until its discovery, near the end of the 11th century, in Arabic translations in the great Muslim libraries of Spain and Sicily. Not only were Aristotle and other Greek philosophers translated into Latin for the first time in the 12th and 13th centuries, but so were more than a thousand years' accumulation of critical commentaries, a corpus of Neoplatonic thought, and more recent Arabic and Jewish scholarship.

One of the first and foremost of the early translators from England was Adelard of Bath (fl. 1116–42), who traveled extensively in search of Arabic learning. His Latin translations of the astronomical tables of the Arab mathematician al-Khwarizmi (fl. 813–33) and Euclid's *Elements* introduced trigonometry to the West. His summary and interpretation of the learning that he found in Arab texts, the *Quaestiones naturales,* discussed astronomy and astrology, meteorology, and the nature of humans, animals, and plants. Other writings attributed to him include treatises on the abacus, the astrolabe, and falconry, as well as a revision of an earlier alchemical work.

A countryman of Adelard, Robert of Chester (fl. ca. 1150), helped introduce alchemy and algebra, previously unknown, to the Latin West through translations of *On the Composition of Alchemy* and al-Khwarizmi's *Algebra.* Other translators from England included Roger of Hereford (fl. 1170–1200) and Daniel of Morley (fl. 1180–90), both of whom translated astronomical works, as well as Alfred of Sareshel (fl. 1180–1220), who translated several works of Aristotle, including the *Physics,* and some alchemical works of the Persian philosopher Avicenna (980–1037). The translations, commentaries, and original writings of such English scholars show a distinct inclination toward the description of nature, rather than pure philosophy, and thus helped establish Oxford University as a medieval center for the study of the physical universe.

Translations from Greek and Arabic into Latin continued into the 13th century; an increasing number were made directly from Greek, offering improved versions of some previous translations from Arabic. At the same time this new-found knowledge was being assimilated by scholars and reconciled with Christian theology. This synthesis was due largely to the Englishman Alexander of Hales (d. 1245), the German Albertus Magnus (d. 1280), and the Italian Thomas Aquinas (d. 1274). While Alexander is the least familiar of the three today, he was actually the first to undertake a systematic interpretation of Aristotle—his *Metaphysics, Physics,* and other scientific writings—within the framework of Christian thought.

Of the many commentaries and popularizations written in the 12th century the textbooks by John of Sacrobosco (or Holywood) (d. 1244 or 1256?) on astronomy and mathematics were widely read and remained popular well into the Renaissance. His handbook on astronomy, *On the Sphere,* was the first European exposition of Ptolemy's *Almagest* and contributed to the acceptance of the Ptolemaic system over the less accurate system of Aristotle. John's *Common Algorism* was influential in the eventual adoption of Arabic numerals, which reached the West from India through the Arabs.

This 13th-century synthesis, which institutionalized Aristotelian thought within the church, effectively prevented progress in most sciences beyond the works of the officially sanctioned Greek philosophers. Physics and astronomy were notable exceptions; some of the first medieval advances in these fields came from Robert Grosseteste (d. 1253), the greatest English intellectual force of his time. He wrote some of the first and most influential European commentaries on Aristotle's *Posterior Analytics* and *Physics,* as well as treatises on calendars, calendar reform, astronomy, and cosmology. He held that the stars consist of the same elements and are subject to the same laws as the earth.

Grosseteste's own cosmology, derived from both Ptolemy and Aristotle, is noteworthy for the central role it assigns to light, identified with the light of God. As a proponent of the "light metaphysics" he believed that an understanding of the nature of light would help reveal the mystery of God to man, and he is best known for his theoretical and experimental work on optics. He was one of the first to recognize and promote the importance of observation and experiment, coupled with logical and mathematical analysis in the study of nature.

Among the followers of Grosseteste, Roger Bacon (d. ca. 1292) is the best known, though his enduring fame seems to rest more on his elaboration of Grosseteste's ideas than on his own work. He was already an outstanding scholar in theology and philosophy before turning to natural philosophy and mathematics at Oxford. His career, however, was a curious one. While claiming to have spent more than £2,000 of his own money on books, instruments, and experiments during a twenty-year period, he made no substantial contribution to any science. Bacon was a fervent believer in alchemy, magic, and astronomy, beliefs that caused him continuous trouble with the church. After his death his scholarly writings were quickly forgotten, but his legendary fame as an alchemist and necromancer persisted for centuries.

Bacon was successful in spreading ideas about the importance of experiment and mathematical analysis, and by the beginning of the 14th century there were vigorous debates over the proper role for induction in the study of nature. Two of Grosseteste's philosophical heirs, John Duns Scotus (ca. 1266–1308) and William of Ockham (ca. 1285–1347), were prominent participants in these debates. Duns Scotus advocated the need to distinguish between empirical generalizations, as indications of *how* natural events occur, and causal laws, as indications of *why* they occur.

Ockham argued for the necessity of induction from the observation of particular instances, as the only knowledge possible, rather than deduction from supposed universals handed down by authority. His ideas formed the basis for the school of thought known as nominalism, though today he is remembered mainly for the principle of analytical parsimony known as "Ockham's razor," which states that assumptions should be kept to a minimum needed. In addition to his philosophical treatises he wrote commentaries on Aristotle, including the *Physics;* his unfinished *Natural Philosophy* contains a novel treatment of place, time, and motion.

These are the same concepts at the heart of the work carried out in the second quarter of the 14th century by the so-called *calculatores,* the calculators, of Merton College, Oxford. Thomas Bradwardine (ca. 1290–1349), John Dumbleton (fl. 1330–1350), Richard Swineshead (fl. 1340–1355), and William Heytesbury (d. ca. 1372), the most famous of the *calculatores,* are credited with at least four significant contributions to the science of mechanics, including the mean-speed theorem. That theorem asserts that "a body moving with a uniformly accelerated motion covers the same distance in a given time as if it were to move for the same duration with a uniform speed equal to its mean (or average) speed" (Lindberg, 1992: 300). Of the various proofs of the theorem in the Middle Ages that of the Paris philosopher Nicole Oresme (ca. 1320–1382) was one of the best known and provided the basis for Galileo's treatment of freely falling bodies.

Galileo's use of results from the medieval natural philosophers shows that science persisted and in some cases even flourished during the Middle Ages. Just as the great plays of Shakespeare emerged out of a long—and now largely unknown—tradition of medieval drama, the Scientific Revolution arose from an even longer tradition of medieval thought and study on natural phenomena.

Richard E. Rice

Bibliography

Crombie, A.C. *Augustine to Galileo.* 2d ed. 2 vols. Cambridge: Harvard University Press, 1961; Dales, Richard C., ed. *The Scientific Achievement of the Middle Ages.* Philadelphia: University of Pennsylvania Press, 1973; *Dictionary of Scientific Biography.* Gen. ed. Charles C. Gillispie. 16 vols. New York: Scribner, 1970–80 [full biographies of most figures]; Duhem, Pierre. *Medieval Cosmology: Theories of Infinity, Place, Time, Void, and the Plurality of Worlds.* Ed. and trans. Roger Ariew. Chicago: University of Chicago Press, 1985; Grant, Edward. *Physical Science in the Middle Ages.* New York: Wiley, 1971; Grant, Edward, ed. *A Source Book in Medieval Science.* Cambridge: Harvard University Press, 1974; *Isis Current Bibliography of the History of Science and Its Cultural Influences* [produced annually for *Isis,* the major journal devoted to the history of science]; Kren, Claudia. *Medieval Science and Technology: A Selected, Annotated Bibliography.* New York: Garland, 1985; Lindberg, David C., ed. *Science in the Middle Ages.* Chicago: University of Chicago Press, 1978; Lindberg, David C. *The Beginnings of Western Science: The European Scientific Tradition in Philosophical, Religious, and Institutional Context, 600 B.C. to A.D. 1450.* Chicago: University of Chicago Press, 1992; Maier, Anneliese. *On the Threshold of Exact Science: Selected Writings of Anneliese Maier on Late Medieval Natural Philosophy.* Ed. and trans. Steven D. Sargent. Philadelphia: University of Pennsylvania Press, 1982; Thorndike, Lynn. *A History of Magic and Experimental Science.* 4 vols. New York: Columbia University Press, 1923–34.

See also Alchemy; Astrology; Bacon; Bede; Duns Scotus; Grosseteste; Learning; Medical Manuscripts; Scientific and Medical Writings; Scientific Manuscripts, Early; Technology; Universities; Utilitarian Writings; William of Ockham

Scientific and Medical Writings

Treatises on science and medicine from medieval England survive in considerable numbers in several languages: in Latin and OE until the Norman Conquest; in Latin and Anglo-Norman until the second half of the 14th century; and in Latin and, increasingly, ME from the second half of the 14th century to 1500. Such writings, particularly those in Latin, must be understood as part of the larger European tradition of scientific and medical texts (see Thorndike, *History,* 1923–34; Siraisi, 1990; and, for specific authors, the *Dictionary of Scientific Biography*). The earliest medieval Latin texts were monastic, but monastic learning was joined by cathedral schools in the 12th century and by university study from the late 12th century until the end of the Middle Ages; Latin texts are catalogued by Thorndike and Kibre. In addition a great many texts written in vernacular languages, often outside traditional institutions, survive from both the early- and late-medieval periods. Upward of 8,000 OE and ME scientific and medical texts are extant (Voigts and Kurtz).

Surviving scientific texts from the Anglo-Saxon period have largely to do with the reckoning of time. Bede (672/73–735) wrote two important Latin treatises to address the need for ascertaining the liturgical year, *De temporibus* (703) and *De temporum ratione* (725). These texts determine calendrical usages still applicable, such as the modern dating system based on the Christian era (A.D.). Bede treated other subjects with originality as well; for example, *De temporum ratione* formulates a law of tidal action. He also compiled *De natura rerum* (703), an encyclopedia drawing heavily on Pliny's *Natural History*.

Bede's first treatise on time was the major source of the *Enchiridion* (or *Manual*) compiled in 1011 by the monk Byrhtferth of Ramsey; it was written in a mixture of Latin and OE. Likewise at the beginning of the 11th century the abbot Ælfric drew on all three of Bede's scientific works for his OE *De temporibus anni*. A number of short OE texts dealing with calendrical questions were also composed in Anglo-Saxon England. Another OE scientific text was the early-11th-century *Lapidary*, deriving from earlier Latin works.

The largest body of vernacular writing from the pre-Conquest period was medical. In addition to glossed recipes, charms, and a few short texts scattered through a number of manuscripts five major OE medical works survive. The five include four remedy books—*Leechbook* I and II, the *Lacnunga*, and the Greek-titled *Peri Didaxeon*—and a large compendium (surviving in four copies) comprising the *Herbal* of Pseudo-Apuleius, an herbal wrongly attributed to Dioscorides, and two late Roman texts on medicines derived from animals. The manuscripts for all these medical treatises were copied in the last two centuries of the Anglo-Saxon period, but the texts seem to incorporate earlier material. Both Latin and OE medical texts from the Anglo-Saxon period are practical rather than theoretical and derive mostly from Roman medicine, although a recent focus of study has been the Greek sources behind some texts.

After the Norman Conquest vernacular English scientific and medical texts were eclipsed by those written in Latin and Anglo-Norman; except for medical recipes almost nothing written in English survives from post-Conquest England until after 1350. Latin texts on the calendar (computus) continued to be produced, and a number of important Latin treatises were written in the 12th century by Englishmen who traveled on the Continent. For example, Alexander Neckham (1157–1217) compiled an encyclopedia titled *De naturis rerum* (ca. 1195); its first two books (of five) deal with natural history.

Other 12th-century English travelers to the Continent played a major role in the introduction of Arabic science—and Greek science via Arabic texts—to the West. These include Adelard of Bath (fl. 1116–42; *Quaestiones naturales*); Daniel of Morley (fl. 1180–90; *Liber de naturis inferiorum et superiorum*), and Alfred of Sareshel or Shareshull (fl. 1180–1220; *De motu cordis*). Daniel, Alfred, and Roger of Hereford (fl. 1170–1200; *Computus; Theorica planetarum*) are associated with the important 12th-century center of scientific study at the cathedral school of Hereford.

The writings of these Hereford masters influenced the study of science at Oxford, particularly the writings of Robert Grosseteste. From the 13th century most Latin scientific writing in England appears to have emanated from the universities, especially Oxford, where texts deriving from the continental reception of Arabic learning were known. A number of important 13th-century Latin texts were written by three Oxford Franciscans, Bishop Robert Grosseteste (ca. 1170–1253), Roger Bacon (ca. 1213/19–ca. 1292), and Archbishop John Pecham (or Peckham, ca. 1230–1292); all are known for their writings on optics and astronomy.

Grosseteste's scientific writings, composed between 1220 and 1235, include his *De iride* and *De sphera*, which advanced the study of refraction and cosmology, and his *De lineis, angulis, et figuris*, which deals with the application of mathematics to the natural sciences. Roger Bacon's most important scientific treatise is the *Opus maius*; part 4 deals with the importance of mathematics, and part 5 (titled *De perspectiva*, a work that circulated independently) advances Grosseteste's optics in its treatment of lenses. Bacon's arguments for calendrical reform were also ahead of his time. His treatise on aging *(De retardatione accidentium senectutis)* circulated widely in late-medieval England, in both Latin and English translation. In later centuries a number of Latin and ME texts, especially alchemical treatises, were wrongly attributed to Bacon because of his reputation as an alchemist. Although John Pecham's writings are less innovative, his *Perspectiva communis* has been called the most popular medieval text on optics.

A great deal of scientific and medical lore was also compiled by another 13th-century Franciscan, Bartholomaeus Anglicus (fl. 1230–50), in an encyclopedia titled *De proprietatibus rerum*. This compendium was probably the most popular encyclopedia of the Middle Ages; it was translated into ME by John Trevisa in the late 14th century, and Trevisa's translation—in its printed form—was still in use 350 years after the work was originally composed, by Shakespeare and his contemporaries. Another 13th-century scientific writer of considerable influence was John of Holywood, better known as Sacrobosco (d. 1244 or 1256?), probably first educated at Oxford. His major writings, however, on mathematics *(De algorismo)*, on calendrical reform *(De computo*, a work that suggested the Gregorian calendar reform of 1582, which was adopted in England in 1752), and on cosmology and astronomy *(De sphera)*, were written in Paris. *De sphera*, arguably the most popular astronomical treatise of medieval Europe, became the first printed book on astronomy (1472) and continued to be used as a textbook into the 17th century.

In the late 12th and 13th centuries three Englishmen were responsible for important Latin medical treatises written on the Continent. Ricardus Anglicus's *Micrologus* (late 12th century) was a compendium of medical knowledge at Salerno and Montpellier, two major medical centers of Europe; Henry of Winchester (early 13th century; *De naturalibus et medicinalibus*) was a Montpellier master. The most influential of these medical writers was Gilbertus Anglicus (fl. ca. 1230), whose *Compendium medicinae*, a practical compilation incorporating scholastic methods, circulated in Latin and later in English translation.

Vernacular medical texts in 13th-century England were written almost exclusively in Anglo-Norman. Anglo-Norman recipe books from the 13th century were joined by Anglo-Norman translations of surgeries and more theoretical texts in the 14th.

In the 14th century Latin medical texts by Englishmen were written in England rather than on the Continent, as had previously been the case. John of Gaddesden compiled his *Rosa anglica* in the first half of the 14th century, and Simon de Bredon (d. ca. 1368) composed a lengthy, incomplete medical treatise called the *Trifolium* (in addition to mathematical and astronomical writings). Both Gaddesden and Bredon were associated with Merton College at Oxford. By the end of the 14th century Latin medical and surgical treatises were also being written outside the university. The *Breviarium Bartholomaei* of John of Mirfield was compiled in London. The surgeon John Arderne of Newark was apparently not university-educated, although he was well read in treatises by university teachers of surgery on the Continent. Arderne was the author of a number of texts written after 1370, the best known of which deals with the surgical treatment of anal fistula. His works were soon translated into English.

In the Latin scientific tradition of 14th-century England the Oxford-educated abbot of St. Albans, Richard of Wallingford (ca. 1292–1336), wrote a number of texts on mathematics, time, astronomy, astrology, and astronomical instruments. His *Quadripartitum* has been called the first medieval treatise on trigonometry. His texts on instruments dealt with his own inventions, the most famous of which *(Tractatus Albionis)* was the "albion" (a pun on "all-by-one"), an equatorium—a device for calculating planetary positions—with ancillary instruments. At least two of his texts, his *Exafrenon* and his *Declarationes,* circulated in English.

Another genre of 14th-century scientific writing was the *kalendarium,* incorporating astronomical information in text and tables. The tables of planetary positions derive from the so-called Alfonsine Tables (associated with Alfonso X of Castile) and enable an astronomer to compute positions of celestial objects for any point in time, calculation that is essential to astrology as well as astronomy. Best known among 14th- and 15th-century Englishmen responsible for *kalendaria* were William Rede, John Somer, Nicholas of Lynn, John Holbrook, and John Somerset.

From the standpoint of modern science perhaps the most important scientific writings produced in 14th-century England were those of the mid-century writers on what we now call physics, especially mechanics—the so-called *calculatores* associated with Merton College at Oxford. Treatises by Thomas Bradwardine (ca. 1290–1349), Richard Swineshead (fl. 1340–55), and William Heytesbury (d. ca. 1372) articulate mathematical laws on motion, velocity, and resistance. These concerns with what we now call laws of physics were largely the outgrowth of the philosophical analysis of problems in logic, some of them known as "sophisms," puzzling propositions to be resolved by logical rules and sometimes by mathematical calculation. A typical text is the *Regulae solvendi sophismata (Rules for Solving Sophisms)* of William Heytesbury.

Bradwardine's *Geometria speculativa* also addresses the relationships between mathematics and philosophy.

The 15th century is often seen as a period of stagnation in Latin scientific and medical writing produced in England, but a considerable amount of Latin alchemical writing, much of it falsely attributed to Roger Bacon and the 13th- to 14th-century Catalan philosopher Ramón Lull (including texts actually translated in England from Catalan into Latin), was produced in the later Middle Ages.

In contrast to the declining production of Latin treatises in the late 14th and 15th centuries there was in this period a remarkable surge of interest in translating scientific and medical treatises into ME and in composing texts in the vernacular. The best known of such 14th-century efforts are two texts on astronomy and astronomical instruments, the *Treatise on the Astrolabe* by Chaucer and *The Equatorie of the Planetis,* perhaps also by Chaucer. Another 14th-century figure, the Dominican friar Henry Daniel, translated (and apparently compiled) both a lengthy treatise on uroscopy, which contains much other information on such topics as physiology and astronomy, and a text on herbal medicine. The late 14th century also saw the translation of the encyclopedia of Bartholomaeus Anglicus by John Trevisa and of the Latin writings of the surgeon John Arderne, as well as the composition in the 1390s of what appears to be an original English-language surgery treatise by an anonymous London surgeon.

The translation—and to a lesser degree composition—of scientific and medical writings in English continued unabated in the 15th century. However, only a few of these texts are available in modern editions: Trevisa's translation of Bartholomaeus's encyclopedia, some remedy books, two versions of one of the several gynecological texts of the period, the compendium of Gilbertus Anglicus, and surgery texts by a number of authors (Arderne, Lanfranc, two versions of Guy de Chauliac, and a text wrongly attributed to Thomas Morstede). The rest must still be consulted in manuscript.

Other unedited and unstudied ME texts include translations of other continental surgery treatises, a number of plague treatises, and translations of medical writings of Galen, Hunayn ibn Ishaq, Constantinus Africanus, Roger Bacon, Benvenutus Grassus, Petrus Hispanus, Arnald of Villanova, and Bernard of Gordon. ME translations and translations-with-commentary of scientific texts by Haly Abenragel, Abraham ibn Ezra, Roger Bacon, and Regiomontanus also survive, as do the ME verse alchemy of Thomas Norton (fl. 1477), alchemical writings ascribed to George Ripley (1470s), and many anonymous ME alchemical treatises. The study of these writings, singly and collectively, remains a desideratum.

Linda E. Voigts

Bibliography

GENERAL

Dictionary of Scientific Biography. Gen. ed. Charles C. Gillispie. 16 vols. New York: Scribner, 1970–80; Jones, Peter Murray. "Medical Books before the Invention of Printing." In *Thornton's Medical Books, Libraries and Collectors,* ed. Alain Besson. 3d rev. ed. Aldershot:

Gower, 1990, pp. 1–29; Lindberg, David C. *The Beginnings of Western Science: The European Scientific Tradition in Philosophical, Religious, and Institutional Context, 600 B.C. to A.D. 1450.* Chicago: University of Chicago Press, 1992; Siraisi, Nancy. *Medieval and Early Renaissance Medicine: An Introduction to Theory and Practice.* Chicago: University of Chicago Press, 1990; Talbot, C.H. *Medicine in Medieval England.* London: Oldbourne, 1967; Thorndike, Lynn. *A History of Magic and Experimental Science.* 4 vols. New York: Columbia University Press, 1923–34; Voigts, Linda. "Medical Prose." In *Middle English Prose: A Critical Guide to Major Authors and Genres,* ed. A.S.G. Edwards. New Brunswick: Rutgers University Press, 1984, pp. 315–35; Voigts, Linda. "Scientific and Medical Books." In *Book Production and Publishing in Britain 1375–1475,* ed. Jeremy Griffiths and Derek Pearsall. Cambridge: Cambridge University Press, 1989, pp. 345–402.

CATALOGUES OF MANUSCRIPT WORKS

Thorndike, Lynn, and Pearl Kibre. *A Catalogue of Incipits of Mediaeval Scientific Writings in Latin.* 2d ed. Cambridge: Mediaeval Academy of America, 1963; Voigts, Linda, and Patricia Deery Kurtz. *A Catalogue of Incipits of Medieval Scientific and Medical Writings in Old and Middle English.* Database, forthcoming on CD-ROM.

PRIMARY

Baker, Peter S., and Michael Lapidge, eds. *Byrhtferth's Enchiridion.* EETS s.s. 15. London: Oxford University Press, 1995; Eisner, Sigmund, ed. *The Kalendarium of Nicholas of Lynn.* Athens: University of Georgia Press, 1980; Getz, Faye Marie, ed. *Healing and Society in Medieval England.* Madison: University of Wisconsin Press, 1991 [Gilbertus Anglicus]; Lindberg, David C., ed. and trans. *John Pecham and the Science of Optics: "Perspectiva communis."* Madison: University of Wisconsin Press, 1970; Matheson, Lister M., ed. *Popular and Practical Science of Medieval England.* East Lansing: Colleagues Press, 1994; North, J.D., ed. and trans. *Richard of Wallingford: An Edition of His Writings.* 3 vols. Oxford: Clarendon, 1976; Ogden, Margaret S., ed. *The Liber de Diversis Medicinis in the Thornton Manuscript.* EETS o.s. 207. London: Oxford University Press, 1938; Ogden, Margaret S., ed. *The Cyrurgie of Guy de Chauliac.* EETS o.s. 265. London: Oxford University Press, 1971; Reidy, John A., ed. *Thomas Norton's Ordinal of Alchemy.* EETS o.s. 272. London: Oxford University Press, 1975; Rowland, Beryl, ed. *Medieval Woman's Guide to Health: The First English Gynecological Handbook.* Kent: Kent State University Press, 1981; Seymour, M.C., gen. ed. *On the Properties of Things: John Trevisa's Translation of Bartholomaeus Anglicus De proprietatibus rerum.* 3 vols. Oxford: Clarendon, 1975–88.

SECONDARY

Burnett, Charles, ed. *Adelard of Bath: An English Scientist and Arabist of the Early 13th Century.* London: Warburg Institute, 1989; Cameron, M.L. *Anglo-Saxon Medicine.* Cambridge: Cambridge University Press, 1993; Carey, Hilary M. *Courting Disaster: Astrology at the English Court and University in the Later Middle Ages.* New York: St. Martin, 1992; Green, Monica. "Obstetrical and Gynecological Texts in Middle English." *SAC* 14 (1992): 53–88; Hunt, Tony. *Popular Medicine in Thirteenth-Century England.* Cambridge: Brewer, 1990; North, J.D. "The Alfonsine Tables in England." In *Prismata,* ed. Y. Maeyama and W.G. Saltzer. Wiesbaden: Steiner, 1987, pp. 269–301; North, J.D. *Chaucer's Universe.* Oxford: Clarendon, 1988; Rawcliffe, Carole. *Medicine and Society in Later Medieval England.* Stroud: Sutton, 1995; Sylla, Edith. "The Oxford Calculators." In *The Cambridge History of Later Medieval Philosophy.* Cambridge: Cambridge University Press, 1982, pp. 540–63; Voigts, Linda. "Anglo-Saxon Plant Remedies and the Anglo-Saxons." *Isis* 70 (1979): 250–68; Voigts, Linda. "The Character of the *Carecter:* Ambiguous Sigils in Scientific and Medical Texts." In *Latin and Vernacular,* ed. A.J. Minnis. Cambridge: Brewer, 1989, pp. 91–109.

See also Ælfric; Alchemy; Assize of Weights and Measures; Astrology; Bacon; Byrhtferth; Charms; Grosseteste; Hawking; Medicine; Prose, ME; Science; Technology; Trevisa; Utilitarian Writings

Scientific Manuscripts, Early

Most medieval libraries possessed little scientific material beyond a few treatises on the subjects of the quadrivium: Boethius for arithmetic and music; Euclid for geometry; and Ptolemy's *Almagest* for astronomy. These might be supplemented by an anonymous Algorismus, or elementary arithmetic book, a computus to reckon astronomical time, and treatises on the astronomical instruments, such as the sphere and astrolabe. Anything beyond this depended on whether there was someone in authority who was involved in the subject, and the illustrated manuscripts here discussed gain much of their interest for just that reason.

In 986 Dunstan invited Abbo of Fleury to teach at Ramsey. Abbo stayed for only two years, but this contact with Fleury brought about the introduction to England of two separate bodies of learning that made Ramsey the dominant center of monastic science in the early period. The first was Cicero's translation of the astronomical poem by the 3rd-century B.C. Stoic Aratus, usually called the *Aratea.* The ultimate source of the English manuscripts of the *Aratea* was the 9th-century Fleury Book (BL Harley 647), which contains a page written in an English hand datable to around the time of Abbo's visit. As a poem the *Aratea* has its merits, but it is short on astronomical information. It therefore attracted a scholarly gloss to make it more informative, and in Harley 647 the poem is written below the drawings of constellations while the

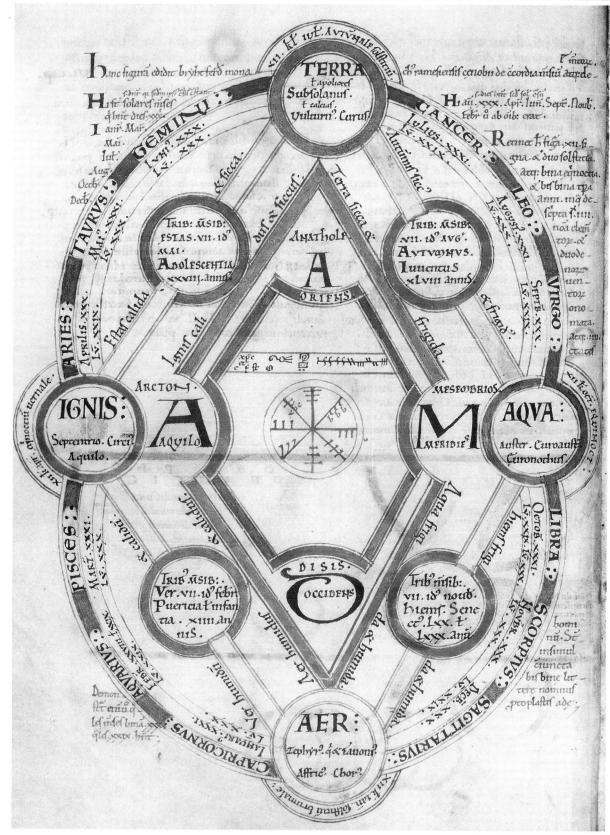

Fig. 121. Byrhtferth's diagram of the harmony of the "physical and physiological fours" (Oxford, St. John's College 17), fol. 7v. Reproduced by permission of the President and Fellows of St. John's College, Oxford.

gloss is written inside their bodies. This scheme was not universally adopted in England, but it is found in BL Cotton Tiberius C.i, a Peterborough manuscript datable to ca. 1122.

As well as the *Aratea* Tiberius C.i contains a series of computistical and cosmological diagrams with accompanying text traceable directly to Abbo himself. Byrhtferth, Abbo's pupil, made copious notes, and although the original of these does not survive, a copy made around 1110–11 (Oxford, St. John's College 17), richly illustrated with diagrams (fig. 121), reveals that Abbo's teaching was based largely on Bede's *De natura rerum,* Isidore's *Etymologies,* and Abbo's own writings. The diagrams show in graphic form a network of microcosmic and macrocosmic relationships between humankind and the cosmos. BL Harley 1506, written at Fleury in the late 10th century, contains a similar combination of Abbo's teaching and the *Aratea,* with illustrations by an Anglo-Saxon artist.

The last of the English astronomical manuscripts in this tradition, before the massive penetration of Arabic science into Europe, are Bodleian Library, Bodley 614 (ca. 1120–40), and Digby 83 (perhaps a decade or two later); and indeed the latter shows some effect of this in its use of Arabic names for the planets.

The microcosmic cosmology taught by Abbo provided a theoretical connection between astrology and medicine that was to make the two disciplines inseparable. Durham, Hunter 100, a Durham manuscript of ca. 1100–20, combines cosmological works and the *Aratea* with various medical texts, including remedies and cautery illustrations.

The Marvels of the East is a 4th-century account of the fabulous peoples encountered on an imaginary journey to India: people with dogs' heads *(Cynocephali),* with horses' hooves *(Hippopodes),* with faces in their chests *(Lemniae).* Its earliest appearance in its complete and illustrated form is in Anglo-Saxon manuscripts of ca. 1000: BL Cotton Vitellius A.xv (which also contains *Beowulf*), with an Anglo-Saxon text, and BL Cotton Tiberius B.v, in Latin. In the latter, and in Bodley 614, the *Marvels* is found in combination with the astronomical and cosmological treatises discussed above, but it also found its way into bestiaries like Westminster Abbey 22.

Ronald E. Baxter

Bibliography

Friedman, John Block. *The Monstrous Races in Medieval Art and Thought.* Cambridge: Harvard University Press, 1981; James, Montague Rhodes. *Marvels of the East.* Oxford: Roxburghe Club, 1929; Kauffmann, C. Michael. *Romanesque Manuscripts 1066–1190.* A Survey of Manuscripts Illuminated in the British Isles 3, ed. J.J.G. Alexander. London: Harvey Miller, 1975, cat. nos. 37 (Tiberius C.i), 38 (Bodley 614), and 74 (Digby 83); Saxl, Fritz. "Illuminated Science Manuscripts in England." In Fritz Saxl, *Lectures.* Vol. 1. London: Warburg Institute, 1957, pp. 96–110.

See also Abbo; Astrology; Bestiaries; Byrhtferth; Dunstan; Manuscript Illumination, Anglo-Saxon; Manuscript Illumination, Romanesque; Medical Manuscripts; Science; Scientific and Medical Writings

Scogan, Henry (1361?–1407)

An esquire in Richard II's household and later tutor to the sons of Henry IV. In his *Moral Balade* Scogan urges the princes to cultivate virtue; to help substantiate his point he quotes the whole of Chaucer's *Gentilesse* in his own poem. Chaucer's *Envoy to Scogan* is probably addressed to this man.

V. J. Scattergood

Bibliography

PRIMARY

Skeat, Walter W., ed. "A Moral Balade." In *The Complete Works of Geoffrey Chaucer.* Supplement (vol. 7). Oxford: Clarendon, 1897, pp. 237–44.

SECONDARY

Lenaghan, R.T. "Chaucer's Circle of Gentlemen and Clerks." *ChauR* 18 (1983): 155–60.

See also Chaucer; Chaucerian Apocrypha

Scottish Literature, Early

The greatest poets of late-medieval Scotland—Robert Henryson, William Dunbar, and Gavin Douglas—did not flourish in a cultural vacuum. There existed from the 14th century onward a lively tradition of vernacular poetry, not wholly separate from that of England yet highly distinctive. (Early Scottish prose is less sophisticated, and its character is largely didactic or theological. Literature in Gaelic does not fall within the scope of this volume.)

Our picture of this literature, however, is inevitably distorted, since much has been lost. Dunbar, in "Timor Mortis Conturbat Me" (by later editors called "The Lament for the Makaris"), names 21 poets "of this cuntre"; some of these are still well known, but of others not a scrap of verse remains. Few love songs or religious lyrics survive from medieval Scotland; the cataclysm of the Reformation swept away much frivolous secular verse as well as overtly "papistical" works. The Reformers were likewise responsible for the destruction of most medieval Scottish drama, leaving Sir David Lindsay's powerful morality play, *Ane Satyre of the Thrie Estaitis,* strangely isolated. Nonetheless, much excellent and varied poetry has been preserved, particularly in the great 16th-century manuscript anthologies associated with the names of John Asloan, George Bannatyne, and Sir Richard Maitland.

Scotland was a small, impoverished country on the northern fringe of Europe, but it was not culturally isolated nor were its writers parochial. For political reasons Scotland was particularly receptive to the influence of France, its "Auld Ally." Many works were free translations from Latin and French: some of these were fairly short, such as the formal lament for the young Scottish princess Margaret (d. 1445), briefly married to the dauphin, later Louis XI of France; others were compositions on a larger scale, such as *The Buik of Alexander* (ca. 1438) and the prose writings of Sir Gilbert Hay. Latin, in Scotland as elsewhere, was not only the language of the church but the medium of education—the essential means of acquiring knowledge of law, theology, history, rhetoric, and ancient poetry. By the end of the 15th century there was also a growing interest among

Scottish scholars in the new humanistic ideas emanating from Italy; one fruit of this was the *Eneados,* Douglas's celebrated translation of Virgil's *Aeneid* (1513).

But England, despite being nicknamed "the Auld Enemy," was Scotland's closest neighbor. It is clear that English books of many kinds—manuscripts at first and printed editions later on—circulated in Scotland. Dunbar referred casually to the story of *Bevis of Hampton,* and Douglas denounced Caxton, in spirited terms, for mangling Virgil in Caxton's *Eneydos* (1490). The first books to be printed in Scotland (ca. 1508) included the English romance *Eglamour* and Lydgate's *Complaint of the Black Knight.* Glowing tributes to Chaucer, Gower, and Lydgate were voiced by Scottish poets from the early 15th century onward; the influence upon them of Chaucer and the courtly verse associated with his name, although sometimes denied, is incontrovertible. They, no less than their English contemporaries, regarded Chaucer as the master of a type of poem then the dominant literary form—the dream allegory—and as the model for a new, subtle, and sophisticated mode of writing.

Chaucer's practice also popularized the seven-line stanza known as rime royal, introduced to Scotland in *The Kingis Quair* (1424?). This, the finest medieval Scottish love poem, is clearly indebted to *Troilus and Criseyde* and also to works by Lydgate. Later Scottish poets, though in no way servile imitators, also learned much from Chaucer and delighted to acknowledge this. Henryson's *Testament of Cresseid,* Dunbar's *Thrissill and the Rois,* and Douglas's *Palice of Honour* often echo Chaucerian phrases, themes, and motifs yet are highly original poems.

But there was great diversity of theme and subject. Medieval Scots were interested in history, particularly that of their own country. This taste was supplied not only by Latin chronicles but also by such vernacular poems as John Barbour's *Bruce* (ca. 1375), which celebrated Robert Bruce (1274–1329), the hero of the War of Independence; Andrew Wyntoun's *Orygynale Cronykil* (ca. 1420); and Harry's popular and influential *The Wallace* (1470s). Scotland also shared the European taste for stories about Troy, Alexander the Great, Charlemagne, and King Arthur. Most of the important medieval literary kinds and genres were known, though they sometimes reached Scotland belatedly: fabliaux and romances, saints' lives and other religious verse, and dream poems of widely different types. The beast fable, practiced superbly by Henryson, was ingeniously combined with many other topics in Richard Holland's *Buke of the Howlat* (ca. 1448). The didactic tradition of the *speculum principum,* or "mirror for princes," was remarkably popular in the late 15th century; it figures in works as various as Henryson's *Fables,* Dunbar's *Thrissill and the Rois,* and the anonymous *Thre Preistis of Peblis* (1490?). One minor literary form, the testament, enjoyed a vogue among Scottish poets; the poet of *King Hart* (formerly attributed to Douglas), Henryson, Dunbar, and Lindsay all put it to varied use.

A striking feature of Scottish poetry in the 15th and early 16th centuries was a rich tradition of descriptive poetry: this includes the formal "erbere," or walled garden, of *The Kingis Quair,* the wintry opening of Henryson's *Testament of Cresseid,* and the glittering dawn scene in Dunbar's *Goldyn Targe* and culminates in the grand panoramic landscapes of the "Nature" Prologues to Douglas's *Eneados.* Scottish poets also excelled at storytelling; this is particularly true of Barbour and Henryson but is also evident in the alliterative *Rauf Coilʒear,* the fabliau-type *Friars of Berwick,* and the many short comic tales in the Bannatyne Manuscript. This manuscript also contains a distinctive group of short pieces—including *Kynd Kittok, The Gyre Carling, King Berdok,* and *Colkelbie Sow*—that blend comedy with the supernatural. They have much in common with Dunbar's comic fantasies, and it is clear that he shared the same imaginative heritage as these poets.

Another strength of Scottish poets was their metrical competence; they were not afflicted by the clumsiness that characterized much contemporary English verse. Certain forms, notably the octosyllabic couplet and rime royal, were popular, as in England, but some poets—Dunbar in particular—seemed to enjoy experimenting with stanzas of varied shape and length. There was an impressive tradition of alliterative poetry; it reached Scotland late, flourishing toward the end of the 15th century, at a time when it was becoming moribund in England. Most Scottish poets favored the combination of alliteration with an elaborate thirteen-line stanza; the unrhymed form occurs only in Dunbar's *Tua Mariit Wemen and the Wedo.* Alliterative verse was employed for straight narrative—as in the Arthurian romance *Golagros and Gawane*—but was increasingly restricted to comic and satiric purposes, as is evident in Henryson's "Sum Practysis of Medecyne" or Douglas's Eighth Prologue.

Much Scottish verse, as so often in the medieval period, was anonymous. Even when the names of poets survive, we possess little information about their lives and careers. Many were "clerks," or educated men, with university degrees and often held some kind of office in the church: Barbour was archdeacon of Aberdeen, Holland was a precentor of Moray Cathedral, and Douglas became bishop of Dunkeld. It is evident that some poets, such as Holland and Douglas, had aristocratic patrons. Others served in the royal household. James IV's servitors included not only Dunbar but several of his fellow poets—Stobo, Mersar, Walter Kennedy, and the notary Patrick Johnston, who devised dramatic entertainments for the palace at Linlithgow. Kings dispensed patronage in various ways, by bestowing fees, church benefices, and offices at court. Most of the poets whose names we know were associated with the eastern Lowlands; this was the richest and most fertile part of Scotland, the most exposed to continental influences, and also the area where Scots—as opposed to Gaelic—was predominantly spoken.

Lowland Scots was a northern descendant of Anglo-Saxon. In Barbour's time the language was not strikingly different from northern ME, but during the 15th century it diverged increasingly from English in phonology, spelling, and vocabulary. Until the end of the 15th century most vernacular writers called their tongue "Inglis"; Douglas was one of the first to distinguish his own language from English and to call it "Scottis." In literary Scots there existed considerable variety of usage, a variety largely determined not by regional dialect but by style and subject. The diction of narrative and comic verse thus tended to be densely Scottish; but poets who sought a refined and elegant style, and to emulate Chaucer, employed anglicized and often archaic words, spellings, and grammatical forms, along with more complex syntax and the "colours" of rhetoric. Late-medieval Scottish writers had available to them a remarkably wide range of linguistic options; the most confident and experimental among them, such as Dunbar and Douglas, gained much from this diversity.

Priscilla Bawcutt

Bibliography

PRIMARY

Bawcutt, Priscilla, and Felicity Riddy, eds. *Longer Scottish Poems.* Vol. 1: *1375–1650.* Edinburgh: Scottish Academic Press, 1987; Craigie, W.A., ed. *The Maitland Folio Manuscript.* STS n.s. 7, 20. Edinburgh: Blackwood, 1919–27; Craigie, W.A., ed. *The Asloan Manuscript.* STS n.s. 14, 16. Edinburgh: Blackwood, 1923–25; Hughes, Joan, and W.S. Ramson, eds. *Poetry of the Stewart Court.* Canberra: Australian National University Press, 1982; Ritchie, W.T., ed. *The Bannatyne Manuscript.* STS n.s. 22, 23, 26; 3d ser. 5. Edinburgh: Blackwood, 1928–34.

SECONDARY

New *CBEL* 1:651–64; *Manual* 4:961–1060, 1123–1284; Aitken, A.J. "The Language of Older Scots Poetry." In *Scotland and the Lowland Tongue: Studies . . . in Honour of David D. Murison,* ed. J. Derrick McClure. Aberdeen: Aberdeen University Press, 1983, pp. 18–49; Aitken, A.J., et al., eds. *Bards and Makars.* Glasgow: University of Glasgow Press, 1977; Fox, Denton. "The Scottish Chaucerians." In *Chaucer and Chaucerians,* ed. Derek S. Brewer. London: Nelson, 1966, pp. 164–200; Geddie, William. *A Bibliography of Middle Scots Poets.* STS o.s. 61. Edinburgh: Blackwood, 1912 [still valuable for authors other than James I, Henryson, Dunbar, Douglas]; Goldstein, R. James. *The Matter of Scotland.* Lincoln: University of Nebraska Press, 1993; Jack, R.D.S., ed. *The History of Scottish Literature.* Vol. 1: *Origins to 1660.* Aberdeen: Aberdeen University Press, 1988; Kratzmann, Gregory. *Anglo-Scottish Literary Relations 1430–1550.* Cambridge: Cambridge University Press, 1980; McClure, J. Derrick, and Michael R.G. Spiller, eds. *Bryght Lanternis: Essays on the Language and Literature of Mediaeval and Renaissance Scotland.* Aberdeen: Aberdeen University Press, 1989; Scheps, Walter, and J. Anna Looney. *Middle Scots Poets: A Reference Guide to James I of Scotland, Robert Henryson, William Dunbar, and Gavin Douglas.* Boston: Hall, 1986; Smith, Janet M. *The French Background of Middle Scots Literature.* Edinburgh: Oliver & Boyd, 1934; Wittig, Kurt. *The Scottish Tradition in Literature.* Edinburgh: Oliver & Boyd, 1958.

See also Alliterative Revival; Barbour; Chaucer; Chaucerian Apocrypha; Comic Tales; Douglas; Dunbar; Harry, "Blind"; Henryson; *Kingis Quair;* Language; Satire; Wyntoun

Fig. 122. Wells Cathedral, west facade. Courtesy of L. Hoey.

Screen Facades

A screen facade is one in which the lower roofs of the aisles in the basilican section typical of English medieval great churches are invisible behind masonry screens that extend the height of the central nave outward to the line of the aisle walls or beyond. In English architecture such screens are usually covered with horizontal layers of blind arcading and sometimes with statuary. The best-known examples are the facades of Wells (fig. 122) and Salisbury cathedrals, both of approximately the second quarter of the 13th century.

Wells and Salisbury differ in the details of their decoration, but a more substantive difference lies in their lateral terminations, which are true towers at Wells, set beyond the lines of the aisle walls, but at Salisbury are only stair turrets that project slightly. These two plans have separate genealogies that extend back into 12th-century English Romanesque architecture. The screen with stair turrets was used for the west facades of Malmesbury and Croyland abbeys, while the plan with towers can be found at St. Botolph's Priory in Colchester, at Earl's Colne Priory nearby, in an aborted west facade at St. Albans Abbey, and in the west front of St. Mary's Priory in Coventry, which was probably contemporary with Wells and Salisbury, if not later. While there are Romanesque predecessors for early Gothic screen facades, there are no late Gothic successors, for later churches tended toward simple sectional facades or the twin-tower facade most common in French Gothic.

Another screen facade of roughly contemporary date with Wells and Salisbury is that of Lincoln Cathedral. The difference is that the Lincoln facade is a composite of three periods, late 11th century, the 1140s, and the 1230s. The first campaign produced the beetling rectangular facade of a castle keep, the second added sculpture and west towers, and the third heightened and extended laterally the Romanesque facade, framing it with octagonal stair turrets. As in the two western cathedrals, the early Gothic portion was covered with blind arcading.

In contrast to these screen facades proper there were also a number of western transepts in English architecture with facades similar to those of the true screens, stretching horizontally across the church without acknowledgment of the section of nave and aisles behind them. Romanesque examples are found at Bury St. Edmunds, Ely, and Kelso, and early Gothic examples at Peterborough and Kilwinning. Ely and Kelso have central west towers and Peterborough its idiosyncratic portico of gargantuan size, but they share with each other and with the true screens discussed above a sense of free facade composition, similar to that found with different architectural forms in western France or Italy, untrammeled by any need or desire to reflect the shape of the building they preface.

Lawrence Hoey

Bibliography

McAleer, J. Philip. *The Romanesque Church Facade in Britain*. New York: Garland, 1984; McAleer, J. Philip. "Particularly English? Screen Facades of the Type of Wells and Salisbury Cathedrals." *JBAA* 141 (1988): 124–58; McAleer, J. Philip. "Le problème du transept occidental en Grande-Bretagne." *Cahiers de civilisation médiévale* 34 (1991): 349–56.

See also Lincoln Cathedral; St. Albans Abbey; Salisbury Cathedral; Wells Cathedral

Scrope, Stephen (ca. 1396?–1472)

Translator of didactic works. Scrope's life received its shape principally from his widowed mother's marriage to Sir John Fastolf (1409). Although he later blamed Fastolf for disinheriting him as well as allowing him to be disfigured in his youth by an illness, Scrope served Fastolf in France, apparently as his purchasing agent at Honfleur (before 1420). By the time Scrope appears in the Paston letters as a suitor of Elizabeth Paston (ca. 1449), he has fathered a married daughter. His marriage to Joan Bingham (ca. 1454) produced John, his heir. Fastolf's interests overshadowed Scrope's until Fastolf's death (1459); nor did Scrope prosper thereafter.

Notwithstanding the tensions between them Scrope translated at least two works of courtesy and moral instruction for Fastolf: Christine de Pizan's *Epistle of Othea* (ca. 1440) and the *Dicts and Sayings of the Philosophers* (ca. 1450). Couched as advice to a prince (Hector), the *Epistle* contains 100 verse texts, the last 95 of which are quatrains, each supported by a gloss and a prose allegorization. The prose *Dicts*, a translation of the French *Dits moraulx*, collects the words and actions of Greek philosophers. Some scholars also credit Scrope with translating the *Mirror of the World* from French and writing *The Book of Noblesse*. Scrope's translations are central to understanding the transition of English prose to its early-modern forms.

Elaine E. Whitaker

Bibliography

PRIMARY

Bühler, Curt F., ed. *The Dicts and Sayings of the Philosophers*. EETS o.s. 211. London: Humphrey Milford, 1941; Bühler, Curt F., ed. *The Epistle of Othea*. EETS o.s. 264. London: Oxford University Press, 1970.

SECONDARY

New *CBEL* 1:690–91; Hughes, Jonathan. "Stephen Scrope and the Circle of Sir John Fastolf: Moral and Intellectual Outlooks." In *The Ideals and Practice of Medieval Knighthood* 4. Woodbridge: Boydell, 1992, pp. 109–46.

See also Courtesy Literature; Family Letter Collections; Literary Influences: French; Moral and Religious Instruction; Patronage, Literary; Prose, ME; Translation; Wardship

Sculpture, Anglo-Saxon

Early Sculpture

Stone sculpture was an art form largely lost in England after the disintegration of Romano-British society during the 5th century. Although the production of carved stonework may have continued in the western parts of mainland Britain during the 5th to 7th centuries, and although some Anglo-Saxons may have been aware of its existence, stone carving does not seem to have been an art form practiced among the Anglo-Saxon population of England before the arrival of the Christian missions from the Mediterranean world at the end of the 6th century.

Because the art of stone carving was introduced through this (ecclesiastical) medium, most surviving early sculpture seems to have emerged within a religious context; it was a Christian art form, one deployed by the church, and so dependent on its establishment and well-being in England. Thus, before the late 9th century (and the redistribution of land and wealth, particularly in the areas of Scandinavian settlement), stone carving in Anglo-Saxon England was limited to monuments and functions that served primarily Christian purposes. It was used to decorate stone churches, it was used for funerary monuments (gravestones, tombs, and shrines), and it was used for the freestanding monumental crosses.

It is difficult to overestimate the initial impact of these monuments on the Anglo-Saxon landscape. Not only was the earliest stone carving an unusual phenomenon, it was also probably highly colored. Remains of gesso and paint have survived on a number of fragments, such as a Crucifixion plaque from Penrith (Cumbria) that retains traces of black, green, and red coloring. While this would have clarified greatly the carved detail, it would also have made monuments, such as the freestanding crosses, a remarkable sight, attracting attention to the existence of the church in Anglo-Saxon England and making more memorable the message of that church.

The exact chronology of a great deal of the material is uncertain, and in the absence of clear documentary evidence the dating of most individual monuments is dependent on stylistic, art-historical comparisons. As stone sculpture in its initial phases seems to have been produced in association with the earliest stone churches, comparison of the decorative motifs appearing on these early carvings has been used to develop chronologies for Anglo-Saxon sculpture as a whole. However, much debate surrounds the questions of chronological models based upon supposed stylistic degeneration or on the identification of Carolingian prototypes, especially within the context of the localized areas of influence of the workshops that produced the sculpture. As a result the dating of individual monuments can vary, but usually only within a 50- or 100-year time bracket.

The exact development and inspiration of the sculptured monument forms current in Anglo-Saxon England is also unclear, although it seems that most forms coexisted throughout the period. The earliest sculpture, that which formed part of the decoration of the new ecclesiastical stone buildings in the latter half of the 7th century, includes church furnishings, such as the stone abbot's or bishop's seat from Hexham (ca. 672), as well as architectural sculpture in the form of carved stringcourses, monumental low-relief figures, sundials, carved imposts, and ornamented door and window openings, used to decorate the outer fabric of buildings, as at Wearmouth (ca. 675–89); inside, friezes of animal, vinescroll, and geometric patterns were used to enhance the walls, as at Jarrow (ca. 685). Some of the later, 9th-century friezes and panels decorated with figural ornament, such as images of Christ, the Virgin, angels, and saints (e.g., Fletton, Northamptonshire), may have served additional purposes, perhaps functioning as sculptured icons, objects of veneration intended to inspire the viewer with awe and reverence.

Sculpture was also used from an early date for the production of funerary monuments. Initially, and almost exclusively at sites linked to the Celtic mission established at Lindisfarne in the 7th century, stone was employed for small, carefully cut grave markers (the so-called pillow stones), often decorated with no more than the name of the deceased and a central cross whose form was apparently inspired by the central crosses decorating the carpet pages of early insular manuscripts (e.g., the pillow stones from Lindisfarne). At Wearmouth and Jarrow, centers more closely associated with the Roman church, stone grave markers with central crosses were also produced, but these were larger monuments with more elaborate and deeply cut crosses, and the inscriptions were lengthier; these monuments are closer to the later Pictish cross slabs of Scotland in their general layout and appearance than the contemporary pillow stones of the Celtic foundations.

In the late 8th and 9th centuries sculpture was also used in funerary contexts for tombs and shrines in Northumbria and Mercia. The late-8th-century Hedda Stone at Peterborough is probably one of the earliest surviving Anglo-Saxon stone shrines, although its small size and apparently blocklike construction suggest that it is unlikely to have contained substantial human remains. However, the early-9th-century composite monuments at Hovingham in Yorkshire and Wirksworth in Derbyshire, of which only the front (at Hovingham) and the coped lid (at Wirksworth) remain, probably both contained the physical remains of a local saint; they functioned both as tombs and shrines, focal points of pilgrimage and worship. Both are carved with narrative figural scenes depicting events from the life of Christ and the Virgin Mary, scenes that refer the viewer to the Resurrection and consideration of the rewards of this life in heaven. Fragments of a similar coped monument exist at Bakewell (Derbyshire), and a number of the panels decorated with figural sculpture at Breedon in Leicestershire (fig. 136: see STONEWORK AS ECCLESIASTICAL ORNAMENT) are also assumed to have been part of a tomb or shrine.

At some point during the 8th century, and coexistent with the development of these various sculptured monument forms (architectural and funerary), it seems that freestanding decorated stone crosses were first introduced. The exact source of inspiration for these distinctive monuments is unclear, as, unlike architectural sculpture and stone funerary monuments, freestanding crosses were not a common feature of ecclesiastical art elsewhere in Europe. Archaeological evidence suggests freestanding totems were part of the Germanic Anglo-Saxon landscape (e.g., at Yeavering, Northumberland), and it appears that freestanding wooden crosses were part of the material culture of Celtic Christianity in the west of the British Isles. Adamnan's account of the life and death of St. Columba describes wooden crosses erected within the monastic complex of Iona, and in the 630s, when Oswald returned to Northumbria from exile among the monks of Iona, he is credited by Bede with raising just such a cross just before his battle at Heavenfield. It may be that the introduction of the art of stone carving by the Roman church fused with Celtic and local Germanic traditions in Anglo-Saxon England to produce the freestanding crosses, especially at a time when the cult of the True Cross was gaining popularity with the elevation of a fragment of this relic at Rome at the turn of the 8th century.

Whatever their inspiration, stone crosses were important ecclesiastical monuments in Anglo-Saxon England. Comparatively few have survived in situ, but from those that have, and

Fig. 123. Sandbach Crosses. Courtesy of A.J. Hawkes.

from documentary, archaeological, and art-historical evidence, it appears that they served a variety of purposes. Some were raised as boundary markers of estates and others as grave markers or commemorative monuments; some performed a complex liturgical role within ecclesiastical centers. The 8th-century cross at Bewcastle (fig. 74: see HIGH CROSSES) stands in situ and has a lengthy runic inscription that, although badly worn, implies it was raised as a commemorative monument; its figural ornament and sundial suggest that it also had a liturgical function on religious occasions. Other crosses, however, have been badly damaged in subsequent centuries, many being destroyed by iconoclasts in the 17th century.

The original function of these monuments has to be interpreted largely from their surviving decoration. The inscriptions and figural iconography of the Ruthwell Cross, which has been reconstructed within the village church, imply complex references to the eucharist and the rites of Easter week, suggesting a primarily liturgical role for the cross within a religious (monastic) community. The iconography of the two crosses (fig. 123) that have been reerected in the market square of Sandbach (Cheshire) suggests a more general appeal to a wider lay audience. It is concerned to proclaim the power and authority of the church as founded on Christ and his saints, while at the same time referring the viewer to the importance of the eucharist as the church's main sacrament. Although distinctions between monastic and episcopal churches were not clear in the early Anglo-Saxon period, it seems the Sandbach Crosses were more probably products of an episcopal center than a strictly monastic one, as was the Ruthwell Cross (figs. 111–14: see RUTHWELL CROSS).

The figural iconography of the sculpture can thus play an important role in our understanding of the earliest Anglo-Saxon stone carvings. But figural decoration was not a common feature of Anglo-Saxon sculpture; more usual were the plant scrolls and interlace patterns. The interlace of plait is the most common ornamental motif found on the sculpture, and although the large number of variations in its composition makes it difficult to categorize, identical patterns exist, and there seem to have been formal principles underlying its construction; recognition of this has led to various attempts at formal (and regional) grouping. The plant-scroll motifs, almost as common as interlace patterns in the decoration of Anglo-Saxon sculpture, were introduced into the artistic repertoire of Anglo-Saxon England together with the art of stone carving. Their theological significance was developed from the reference in St. John's Gospel (15:1–17) to Christ as the True Vine, but not being indigenous to the British Isles the insular carved representations of the vinescrolls vary considerably from the botanical plant; it is these variations that allow for regional and chronological analyses of the motifs and the monuments on which they appear.

The significance of early Anglo-Saxon sculpture lies in the fact that it was an art form alien to the Anglo-Saxon population of the British Isles and thus represents in its initial phases an essentially ecclesiastical medium. It appears to have performed functions over and above the decorative. Used to convey the developing institutional power and authority of the

Fig. 124. Langford, Oxfordshire. Rood, gable over south porch. Courtesy of A.J. Hawkes.

church, sculpture was also used for memorial purposes and as the focus for devotion and elucidation of the subtleties of Christian theology and dogma. Its decoration allows insight into the social context of the sculpture and into the possible developments of the medium.

Late Sculpture

Late Anglo-Saxon sculpture is generally understood to be that which was produced between the later 9th and 11th centuries in those areas of England lying beyond the traditional boundaries of the Danelaw, or in areas outside direct Scandinavian influence, such as Durham, where sculpture continued to be produced into the 11th century, using increasingly archaic (Anglian) decorative motifs and an old-fashioned iconography.

Most of the material that survives from this period, in geographical areas south of the Danelaw, indicates that there was a significant increase in sculptural activity in Anglo-Saxon Wessex and its satellite provinces and that much of the new carved stonework was produced to decorate renovated and rebuilt churches, probably as a result of the reforms to the church undertaken during the 10th and 11th centuries. Over five times as much sculpture survives from this later period as from the 7th to early 9th centuries, and approximately half of this later material represents architectural decoration, while less than a tenth represents the remains of monumental cross shafts; from the earlier period less than a third of the sculptural remains are architectural, while nearly half are cross-shaft fragments. This indicates a clear increase in sculptural production as well as changes in the function of carved stonework.

The surviving material also indicates that the number of centers producing the sculpture may also have increased. Whereas the earlier material seems to have emerged from a limited number of sites in restricted areas, such as modern-day Kent, Hampshire, and Gloucestershire, the later material is more widely dispersed geographically, and most is not obviously associated with those ecclesiastical centers thought to have been so influential in the 10th-century reform movement. The similarities between the carved decoration and that of other artifacts, such as ivories, metalwork, and manuscripts, nevertheless shows that there was contact between the major ecclesiastical centers and those producing the sculpture. These similarities also help date much of the late Anglo-Saxon sculpture that has not survived in situ.

The architectural stonework, which constitutes the largest body of surviving late Anglo-Saxon sculpture, is extremely varied. It consists of a number of baluster shafts (e.g., from St. Augustine's Abbey, Canterbury), cable-decorated window frames (Breamore, Hampshire), pilaster bases carved with foliate motifs (Corhampton, Hampshire), ornamented capitals (Langford, Oxfordshire), friezes and carved stringcourses (Sompting, Sussex), numerous sundials (Corhampton, Hampshire), and a number of large-scale figural carvings. Most of these latter are composite reliefs depicting the Crucifixion (Breamore, Headbourne Worthy, and Romsey in Hampshire [fig. 110: see ROMSEY ROODS]; Walkern, Hertfordshire; Langford, Oxfordshire [fig. 124]), but other figural scenes carved as single panels have also survived (such as the Harrowing of Hell at Bristol), as have panels carved with individual figures, such as those at Sompting (Sussex) and Daglingworth (Gloucestershire).

The mostly fragmentary remains of late Anglo-Saxon cross shafts indicate that round, as well as square- and rectangular-section, monuments were produced, while both free-armed and ringed cross heads were used. Most of the crosses seem to have been carved with foliate and interlace motifs, but a few, such as the fragments from All Hallows-by-the-Tower, London, did feature figural decoration.

Apart from the crosses and architectural sculpture, stone continued to be used for the production of funerary monuments in the late 9th to 11th centuries. This body of late Anglo-Saxon sculpture consists primarily of grave slabs, but the remains of some stone coffins and sarcophagi also survive (e.g., a coffin lid from Westminster Abbey). Most are decorated with panels of interlace set on either side of a median ridge, although gravestones decorated with figural ornament do survive, such as those from Newent (Gloucestershire) and Winchester Old Minster. It may well be that the limited decorative repertoire of these funerary monuments (and many of the cross shafts) represents the continuation of conservative traditions in these areas of sculptural activity, while the more varied architectural monument forms and their decoration reflect newer tastes.

The foliate ornament that decorates much of the late Anglo-Saxon sculpture indicates that some of these tastes were introduced from the Continent and reflect the influence of a classicizing movement that transformed the earlier insular features. The tree scroll, for instance (found on early-10th-century pieces from St. Oswald's Priory, Gloucester; Braunton in Devon; Wells, Somerset), based on a central axial stem with fleshy tendrils and extravagant flourishes, shows how earlier, 9th-century, Anglian scrollwork was transformed by the incorporation of the Carolingian acanthus-leaf motif. This process of transformation is found on a larger scale on the 10th-century column at Wolverhampton, where small animals, similar to those featured in 9th-century Anglian work, are set in registers of plant scroll that have their nearest parallels in Carolingian art; the monument probably represents a 10th-century antique revival in late Anglo-Saxon sculpture.

The figural decoration of this sculpture also reflects the influence of Carolingian art, but in the large-scale architectural reliefs there is little that recalls earlier Anglo-Saxon work; many of the figures are stone versions of the "Winchester style," more usually associated with manuscript art of the period, and characterized by lively figures and the acanthus plant scroll. The large-scale relief angels that have survived, probably from Crucifixion scenes, at such churches as Deerhurst (Gloucestershire), Bradford on Avon (Wiltshire), and Winterbourne Steepleton and Stinsford (Dorset) demonstrate the characteristics of the fashion with their contorted bodies and complicated layers of drapery with kicked-out hems.

The iconography of the Crucifixion scenes themselves also shows the influence of Carolingian innovations. The robed figures of Christ featured at Walkern and Langford, for instance, probably depend on a type that was rare in western Europe after the 9th century but that saw a brief revival in France and Germany in the late 10th and 11th centuries. Likewise images of Christ depicted as "dead" on the Cross, with his arms and legs hanging in a contorted manner, were rare before the late 10th century, when manuscript illustrations began to reflect contemporary theological interpretations of the Crucifixion. The appearance of this iconographic type at Breamore and Langford suggests the strong influence of such continental developments.

The sculpture that has survived from the latter part of the Anglo-Saxon period, particularly in southern England, thus demonstrates a change in function and an increase in production and variety of monument form. Stone carving was still used essentially for religious purposes, with the continuing production of funerary monuments and crosses, but the increased use of stone for architectural decoration marks a dramatic change. Apart from these architectural contexts the range of decorative motifs is relatively limited, particularly in the choice of figural subjects, but the strong influence of French and German developments resulted in a new complexity in the iconography of late Anglo-Saxon sculpture.

A. Jane Hawkes

Bibliography

EARLY SCULPTURE AND GENERAL

Collingwood, W.G. *Northumbrian Crosses of the Pre-Norman Age.* London: Faber & Gwyer, 1927; Cramp, Rosemary. *Early Northumbrian Sculpture.* Jarrow Lecture, 1966. Jarrow: St. Paul's Church, 1966; Cramp, Rosemary. *Corpus of Anglo-Saxon Stone Sculpture in England.* Vol. 1: *County Durham and Northumberland.* London: Oxford University Press, 1984; Cramp, Rosemary, and Richard N. Bailey. *Corpus of Anglo-Saxon Stone Sculpture.* Vol. 2: *Cumberland, Westmorland and Lancashire North-of-the-Sands.* London: Oxford University Press, 1988; Kendrick, T.D. *Anglo-Saxon Art to A.D. 900.* London: Methuen, 1938; Lang, James. *Anglo-Saxon Sculpture.* Aylesbury: Shire Archaeology, 1988; Lang, James. *Corpus of Anglo-Saxon Stone Sculpture.* Vol. 3: *York and Eastern Yorkshire.* London: Oxford University Press, 1991; Tweddle, Dominic, Martin Biddle, and Birthe Kjølbye-Biddle. *Corpus of Anglo-Saxon Stone Sculpture.* Vol. 4: *South-East England.* London: Oxford University Press, 1995; Wilson, David M. *Anglo-Saxon Art: From the Seventh Century to the Norman Conquest.* London: Thames & Hudson, 1984.

LATE SCULPTURE

Backhouse, Janet, Derek H. Turner, and Leslie Webster, eds. *The Golden Age of Anglo-Saxon Art 966–1066.* London: British Museum, 1984; Coatsworth, Elizabeth. "Late Pre-Conquest Sculptures with the Crucifixion South of the Humber." In *Bishop Æthelwold: His Career and Influence,* ed. Barbara Yorke. Woodbridge: Boydell, 1988, pp. 161–93; Cottril, F. "Some Pre-Conquest Stone Carvings in Wessex." *AntJ* 15 (1935): 144–51; Cramp, Rosemary. "Anglo-Saxon Sculpture of the Reform Period." In *Tenth-Century Studies: Essays in Commemoration of the Millennium of the Council of Winchester and Regularis concordia,* ed. David Parsons. London: Phillimore, 1975, pp. 184–99; Green, A.R., and P.M. Green. *Saxon Architecture and Sculpture in Hampshire.* Winchester: Wykeham Press, 1951; Wilson, David M. *Anglo-Saxon Art: From the Seventh Century to the Norman Conquest.* London: Thames & Hudson, 1984.

See also Architecture, Anglo-Saxon; Art, Anglo-Saxon; Art, Anglo-Saxon: Classical Influences; Art, Viking; Bradford; Bristol Harrowing of Hell; High Crosses; Ivory Carving, Anglo-Saxon; Lindisfarne Gospels; Romsey Roods; Ruthwell Cross; Sculpture, Gothic; Sculpture, Romanesque; Stonework As Ecclesiastical Ornament; Vikings; Winchester Old Minster; "Winchester School"; Yeavering

Sculpture, Gothic

Our understanding of Gothic sculpture will always be incomplete due to the enormous losses incurred largely during the 16th-century Dissolution of the monasteries. Sculpted roods and shrines, monuments that would have been included in the vast majority of churches, have all but completely disappeared. Wooden figural sculpture (with the exception of effigies) has also suffered enormously, although significant examples of this genre do survive in Scandinavia, where they were particularly popular in the later Middle Ages. Virtually all Gothic sculpture was originally brightly painted to a degree that we would consider gaudy today; the purity of the carved stone surfaces that we now associate with the material was never intended.

There is no sharp break between the end of the Romanesque style and the beginnings of Gothic sculpture. At the end of the 12th century Romanesque abstraction and expressionism gradually give way to the gentler, more naturalistic forms that characterize the Gothic. Perhaps most significantly draperies begin to reveal the form and movement of the figures they clothe, rather than simply defining contours and creating decorative patterns across the body's surfaces. There is also a growing interest in illusionism created through shade and highlighting and the play of refracted light. The transitional style is exemplified by the ca. 1200 polychrome oak Virgin and Child in the Victoria and Albert Museum, London (A.79–1925), from Langham Church, Essex. The seated wooden Madonna and Child is a Romanesque type of monument (the *sedes sapientiae*), and the Virgin retains the stiffness and frontality associated with the Romanesque; however, her facial features show a new softness and delicacy, and her body a new monumentality. Her robe falls in thick, soft folds, revealing the softly rounded forms of her arms and legs.

A true early Gothic style first emerges in England in the West Country in the early 13th century at such sites as Worcester and Wells. The capitals in the east end of Wells Cathedral are carved with "stiff-leaf" foliage, an English reworking of the purely French foliage style used for the capitals of the choir at Canterbury Cathedral (1174–79) and characterized by crisp outlines and regular rhythmical patterns. The retention of comical figures (a man with toothache, a peasant pulling a thorn from his foot) is also a reflection of English taste; such figures were not popular in contemporary France. Many of these images (e.g., the ca. 1250 corbel heads and labels stops—carved end of a moulding—from Westminster Abbey) achieve a psychological depth not seen in any but the best Gothic portraiture.

While the figural sculpture on the west facade of Wells also responds to the new style, the development of Gothic figural sculpture in England is best studied through the corpus of memorial effigies. Here, too, developments begin in the West Country, where in the late 12th century workshops at Corfe were turning out Purbeck "marble" (a type of dark limestone) slabs with incised or shallow relief images. Early in the 13th century the Purbeck marblers appear to have formed the first workshops for the large-scale production of sculpture. By ca. 1240 the West Country workshops, particularly at Wells, added depth and movement to their effigies, carving figures in a greater variety of recumbent poses; first the arms were brought up to lie on the chest, then the legs were crossed. By the 1250s figures were deeply undercut and lavish details, such as foliage or architectural elements, were added, particularly by the London workshops. The 13th century was dominated by the Purbeck-marble workshops of London and the West Country.

In the 14th century the desire for rich polychrome surfaces led to the use of cheaper stone that could be decorated with gems and painted. Around 1340 alabaster became a popular material, probably due to its translucence. Less costly but equally ornate wooden effigies were also produced. The oak effigy of Robert Curthose, duke of Normandy (Gloucester Cathedral), carved ca. 1250, depicts the duke with crossed legs, his right arm reaching for his sword, as if ready to spring to the defense of the realm. A drawing of 1569 indicates that it was originally richly painted.

The pivotal event in the development of Gothic sculpture was the rebuilding of Westminster Abbey by Henry III in the 1240s. While it is certain that Henry employed West Country sculptors on this project, it also marked the beginning of a recognizable "London School" of sculptors. The heart of the program was the tomb of Edward the Confessor created at a cost of £4,000–5,000. Over the 13th and 14th centuries the tombs of the royal family, the most magnificent collection of English Gothic tombs, were grouped around that of Edward, creating a monumental royal shrine.

In addition to Edward's shrine the rebuilding also necessitated a full range of architectural sculpture. The best known of these are probably the censing angels in the triforium spandrels at the north and south ends of the transepts. The softly rounded faces, gentle smiles, and fluttering draperies of the angels show an awareness of French works (e.g., the Reims angels), but the poses of the Westminster angels are much more dynamic than those of their French prototypes.

The mannered swaying poses of the Annunciation group (ca. 1253) from the chapter house doorway also show an awareness of French style, but their tense poses, particularly that of Gabriel, who stands with his legs crossed, hark back to the Romanesque. The drapery style, with its V-folds and long vertical pleats, is characteristic of the Westminster sculptors. Both the Virgin and the angel Gabriel have been attributed to the sculptor William Yxeworth, though they may not be the work of the same hand.

A painted oak St. Michael and the Dragon of ca. 1250–60 from Mosvik (Norway) old church (now UNIT-Vitenskapsmuseet Archaeological dep. Trondheim, T 2451) is carved in a similar style, with elongated body, crossed feet, and drapery that falls in a combination of V-folds and vertical pleats. It may be the product of a group of Westminster sculptors working in Norway, where 13th-century English wooden sculptures were popular.

The "Decorated style" (ca. 1290–1350), the first major English Gothic style, is characterized by a love of applied ornament and decorative detail and an increased use of secular subjects and presence of secular monuments within churches and abbeys. Scenes from romance become popular, as do depictions of aristocratic pastimes, heraldry, and "babewyns" (literally baboons, a term used to describe comical or grotesque subjects of all varieties). The introduction of the style is associated with Edward I and his emulation of monuments created under the patronage of Louis IX (St. Louis) and the kings of France. The twelve Eleanor crosses, the monuments traditionally associated with the introduction of the Decorated style, were erected under the influences of a series of crosses erected in Louis's memory by Philip III. Edward may also have been responding to Louis's creation of a royal shrine at St. Denis in his additions to the Westminster Abbey royal effigies. One of the earliest masterpieces of the style is the life-sized gilt-bronze effigy of Eleanor of Castile made for her tomb at Westminster by the goldsmith William Torel, ca. 1291–93. The idealized head of the queen rests on elaborately chased and gilded cushions, the whole embellished with enamel and paste jewels. The tomb on which the effigy rests is attributed to Alexander of Abingdon, who used Torel's effigy as the model for the statues of Eleanor he created for the Waltham Cross.

One of the characteristics of English Gothic art is its bringing together of different art forms in the creation of single monuments. This is exemplified by the Eleanor crosses, as well as by the tombs of Edward Crouchback and his wife, Aveline, added to Westminster ca. 1300. The effigies of Edward and his wife, angels at their heads, lie beneath elaborate tracery canopies filled with imitation stained-glass windows composed of colored glass on tinfoil backing. In the arches of the tomb bases stand weepers arranged in pairs, turning inward to each other as if in conversation while simultaneously stepping over the frames of the niches. This detail, along with the turned heads of the effigies, helps to unite sculptural space with the architectural space of the church.

Although not part of the Westminster group, the tomb of Edward II at Gloucester (ca. 1327–31) is one of the glories of the Decorated style, as well as one of the first tombs to use English alabaster. The idealized features and elegantly curled hair of the king may have been influenced by the beautiful lovers of contemporary romances; on the other hand they have also been linked to contemporary portrayals of God the Father and may have been used instead as a deliberate attempt to create a saintly image for the murdered king. The tomb is covered by a complex canopy of delicate tracery.

One of the characteristic monuments of the Decorated style is the Easter Sepulcher, a type of monument that appeared in England in the late 13th century and remained popular to the end of the Middle Ages. This elaborate, tomb-like structure was designed to hold the consecrated host from Good Friday to Easter Sunday. One of the earliest to survive

is the ca. 1290 sepulcher in Lincoln Cathedral, a flat tomb with relief carvings of the sleeping soldiers, surmounted by a simple canopy. Perhaps the finest example of this type of monument is the Percy Tomb in Beverley Minster (Yorkshire), erected ca. 1340. The tomb is a plain chest covered with ogee cuspings decorated with spreading foliage, lush ripe fruits, and the Percy arms. The deeply cut figural ornament includes images of the Virgin, Christ, St. Michael, and the Percys. The whole culminates in a serene image of God the Father receiving a naked soul.

Great shrines were one of the most common and most significant forms of Gothic sculpture, but few have survived. Documentary sources indicate that these, too, were decorated with gables, arcading, figural sculpture, and foliate motifs. The shrine of St. Albans Cathedral, carved ca. 1305–08, was made of painted and gilded Purbeck marble. During the 14th century it became popular to block the view of the shrine (located in the chancel) by placing a screen between it and the altar. Exactly why this occurred remains unclear, but it clearly did contribute to the mystery and drama of the mass. The 14th-century Neville Screen at Durham is an excellent example of this type of monument. The screen is carved in a miniaturist style (as if it were a monumental piece of goldwork), with faceted niches designed to hold small metalwork figures, a style typical of the London workshops. By the end of the 14th century shrines had become the focus for aristocratic burial (as at Westminster), burial in close proximity to the saints being one way to ensure salvation.

The late 14th century saw the rise of a new class of minor aristocrats and wealthy merchants and a consequent widening of the market for sculpture. Yet the overall quality of sculpture declined, probably due to a combination of mass production and loss of artists to the plague. The more costly effigies were produced by a small number of workshops in Chellaston, Nottingham, London, and York. On these effigies lineage and social status were often emphasized over personality and individual identity, a phenomenon also seen in funerary brasses. However, some of the finest effigies of this period are set apart by their realism. The 1386 gilt-copper effigy of Edward III at Westminster shows the king with a long, thin face and beard. It was probably produced under the influence of Jean de Liège's 1367 effigy for Edward's queen, Philippa of Hainault, for while the effigy appears quite realistic the accompanying weepers are stiff and impassive. The influence of Jean de Liège foreshadows the enormous influence Flemish-Burgundian art would have on English artists in the second half of the 15th century.

The same workshops that produced alabaster effigies also produced small figural panels for retables and altarpieces. The subjects depicted were often ones of great joy or sorrow, the Joys of the Virgin and the Passion of Christ being the two most popular subjects. A fine example of this type of subject is the late-14th-century altarpiece in the Victoria and Albert Museum (A.48–1946, A.50–1946, A.49–1946, A.51–1946, A.52–1946), which today consists of five panels depicting the Last Supper, Crucifixion, Deposition, Three Marys at the Tomb, and the Incredulity of Thomas; additional panels have been lost. The group is delicately carved and was originally embellished with paint and gilding, some of which survives in the background to the Crucifixion panel.

Scenes of the lives of popular saints were also depicted on devotional panels. An especially fine panel of ca. 1370 (private collection; see Alexander and Binski, 1987: no. 26) depicts the murder of Thomas Becket. Its style and the type of stone from which it is carved suggest that it may be a product of one of the Nottingham workshops. Much of the paint that currently covers the panel is postmedieval, but some of the details, particularly on the armor of the knights, may be original. The panel is unusual for the prominence given to the arms of the donors, Sir Godfrey Foljambe and his second wife, although the emphasis on heraldry is characteristic of the period.

The Flawford Alabasters (Nottingham Castle Museum 08–146, 147, 148) of ca. 1340–80 may also have been produced in Nottingham (figs. 125–27). The three figures of the Virgin and Child, St. Peter, and an unidentified bishop were

Fig. 126. Flawford Alabasters, St. Peter (Nottingham Castle Museum 08–147). Reproduced by permission of the City of Nottingham Museums; Castle Museum and Art Gallery.

Fig. 125. Flawford Alabasters, Virgin and Child (Nottingham Castle Museum 08–146). Reproduced by permission of City of Nottingham Museums; Castle Museum and Art Gallery.

originally part of an altarpiece, designed to stand against a flat surface (to which they were secured by wires), rather than to be freestanding, as they are exhibited today. The figures are carved in a style similar to that of the Percy Tomb. The drapery on all three figures is treated similarly: falling in long vertical folds over the arms and gathering in V-shaped folds across chest, stomach, and thigh. The bishop is shown in a stiff frontal pose, while the Virgin and St. Peter stand in gentle S-curve poses. Peter holds his keys in one hand and a church in the other; the small figure at his feet may be the donor. The Christ Child holds the Virgin's exposed breast, a motif common in contemporary manuscript illumination (e.g., the Cuerden

Fig. 127. Flawford Alabasters, Unidentified Bishop (Nottingham Castle Museum 08–148). Reproduced by permission of the City of Nottingham Museums; Castle Museum and Art Gallery.

the emotional content of art, is also evidenced by the introduction of emaciated cadavers and worm-eaten corpses in the 15th century (e.g., the stone cadaver of Sir John Golafre at Fyfield, Berkshire, ca. 1440–45). In fact the depiction of extremes of emotion, whether of sorrow or of joy, that began in the mid-14th century becomes far more pronounced in the 15th. At times the tension created by the depiction of gruesome subjects in a courtly style can be thought-provoking. A fragmentary chest front of ca. 1410 in the London Museum (75.2) is carved with scenes from (or related to) Chaucer's *Pardoner's Tale* (fig. 128). The figures are elegantly dressed and set in a lush landscape, but the narrative is one of greed, murder, and death.

The landscape background of the London chest has been compared with Flemish and Netherlandish textiles. Flemish influence is also apparent in the new delight in capturing realistic details, such as the thickness of woolen cloth or the pattern of veins on the back of the hand that can be observed on such monuments as the 1452–53 tomb of Richard earl of Warwick in St. Mary's, Warwick. This realism represents a shift in style that signals the end of the Gothic era and the beginning of the northern Renaissance.

Catherine E. Karkov

Bibliography

Alexander, Jonathan, and Paul Binski, eds. *Age of Chivalry: Art in Plantagenet England 1200–1400.* London: Royal Academy of Arts, 1987; Anderson, A. *Medieval Wooden Sculpture in Sweden.* 5 vols. Stockholm: Almqvist & Wiksell, 1964–80; Anderson, M.D. *The Medieval Carver.* Cambridge: Cambridge University Press, 1935; Carpenter, D. "Westminster Abbey: Some Characteristics of Its Sculpture: 1245–59: 'The Workshop of the Censing Angel in the South Transept.'" *JBAA,* 3d ser. 35 (1972): 1–14; Cheetham, F.W. *Medieval English Alabaster Carvings in the Castle Museum Nottingham.* Rev. ed. Nottingham: Castle Museum, 1973; Cheetham, F.W. *English Medieval Alabasters: With a Catalogue of the Collection in the Victoria and Albert Museum.* Oxford: Phaidon-Christies, 1984; Coldstream, Nicola. "Le Decorated Style." *Bulletin monumentale* 147 (1989): 55–80; Coldstream, Nicola. *The Decorated Style: Architecture and Ornament, 1290–1360.* Toronto: University of Toronto Press, 1994; Gardner, A. *English Medieval Sculpture.* Cambridge: Cambridge University Press, 1951; Phillips, J. *The Reformation of Images: Destruction of Art in England 1535–1660.* Berkeley: University of California Press, 1973; Prior, E.S., and J. Gardner. *An Account of Medieval Figure Sculpture in England.* Cambridge: Cambridge University Press, 1912; Sheingorn, Pamela. *The Easter Sepulchre in England.* Kalamazoo: Medieval Institute, 1987; Stone, Lawrence. *Sculpture in Britain: The Middle Ages.* 2d ed. Harmondsworth: Penguin, 1972; Tracy, Charles. *Catalogue of English Medieval Furniture and Woodwork.* London: Victoria and Albert Museum, 1987; Wilson, Christopher. *The Gothic Cathedral: The Architecture of the Great Church 1130–*

Psalter [New York, Pierpont Morgan Library M.756]) and probably linked to the increased interest in birth, death, and natural processes that characterized the late 14th and 15th centuries throughout Europe.

An interest in natural processes, as well as an increase in

1530. London: Thames & Hudson, 1990.

See also Angel Roofs; Architecture and Architectural Sculpture, Gothic; Art, Gothic; Eleanor Crosses; Metalwork, Gothic; Sculpture, Anglo-Saxon; Sculpture, Romanesque

Sculpture, Romanesque

A lack of confirmable dates and widespread damage confuses this difficult field. But the surviving works can be categorized into significant groups, formed by the geography and prestige of their location and defined by style, subject matter, and common motifs. Romanesque sculpture reflects the developing political situation in England.

The earliest group is found around Scandinavian settlements in London, East Anglia, and the Midlands, which had hoped for a Scandinavian king of England rather than the Norman, William I. These works have a perpendicular relief profile with flat upper surfaces, vertical incisions, and flat recesses. This accompanies derivatives of the Scandinavian Ringerike and Urnes styles, sometimes including elements of the 10th-century "Winchester style." Examples range from the pre-Conquest St. Paul's grave slab, with its Ringerike Great Beast (ca. 1030), to the tympanum from Southwell Minster (ca. 1120), with its Urnes and Ringerike beasts.

A group of related schools are found on rural churches inside a wide arc around Hereford, running from Shropshire to Somerset, an area frequently in revolt against the Norman crown. From the 1130s this area was associated with the empress Matilda until she rejoined her husband in Anjou in 1148. At the same time Arnulf de Montgomery, brother of the earl of Shrewsbury, married a Munster princess, thus fostering Irish contacts. As in the "Scandinavian" group there is a strong sense of folklore, the perpendicular relief profile, and a cumbersome rounded version of that profile also found on 11th-century Irish crosses and churches. Subjects are "savage": fighting beasts, St. Michael, St. George, tangled foliage, and geometric patterns in unframed panels, often set beneath

beakhead voussoirs. Biting or overlapping the torus, beakheads are an insular response to the masks on European Romanesque arches. Influences from this group are felt in Ireland, Anglo-Scandinavian areas, Matilda's Anjou, and places offended by King Stephen (1135–54). A "savage" tympanum reproducing motifs from a church in Oxfordshire appears in Ireland at Cormac's Chapel (1127–32); beakheads appear at Old Sarum at about the time that Bishop Roger of Salisbury (1102–39) was at loggerheads with King Stephen, and at Lincoln, ca. 1141 and the years following, under Bishop Alexander, Roger of Salisbury's nephew. At Reading they may be associated with Matilda rather than her father, Henry I, who founded the abbey in 1121. Foreign elements apparently entered the Hereford School after a local official, Oliver de Merlimond, went to Santiago ca. 1140. Evidently he took the westernmost route, as later Hereford School tympana at Brincop (ca. 1150) and Stretton Sugwas (ca. 1150) reproduce battle scenes from churches around that route, while inside Kilpeck (ca. 1150) are three-tiered column figures known from Santiago itself.

But for the large monasteries grander ideas were favored. By 1086 all but two foundations had been transferred to Norman control. Rebuilt or established with the ostensible help of Cluny, their churches were often designed after Cluny (III) itself and bore Cluny's long-distance sculptural stamp. In England, as in Europe, this was the distinctive "Plaque" style and its derivatives, recognized primarily by double-line drapery folds in parallel lines and curves, large hands and feet, and smooth flat faces with protruding eyes. This lasted ca. 1100 to ca. 1140, before mutating into a purely English style at Lincoln, Malmesbury, and Canterbury.

Possibly the earliest example, despite its presently attributed date, is a head from York that is remarkably similar to the Moissac Durandus of ca. 1100. At Wolvesey Palace in Winchester (head with human hairclip), Chichester (screen), and Norwich (head) are figures derived from the more refined and dynamic version of the Plaque style found at Silos and Souillac. Works at Norwich (capitals) and York (Virgin and Child) reflect the increasingly rigid banding on the capitals at Autun (ca. 1120–30), although the Virgin's heavy proportions show her roots in the original Plaque style. Ely's Prior's Door recalls the tympana of Moissac and Autun, and Rochester's tympanum reflects that of Cluny III. Finally at Lincoln (Majesty and St. Paul, ca. 1140–45), Canterbury (choir screen, 1180?), and Malmesbury (porch, ca. 1180?), we find a fluid derivation with no European parallels, possibly developed in England.

But Cluny did not itself use the Plaque style, and the Normans likewise rejected the style for their royal establishments. For these they employed the Canterbury School, which is recognized primarily by a lush winding foliage with raised beaded veins, borders, and other details. A richly decorative and attractive style, it has origins suggested in the Crucifixion leaf of the Anglo-Norman psalter BL Arundel 60, ca. 1070, where Winchester-style foliage has been elongated into winding tendrils with veins highlighted to suggest beading. This Norman adaptation of a royal Anglo-Saxon style may have been considered particularly appropriate for royal and archiepiscopal projects: Canterbury (crypt capitals, ca. 1120); Reading Abbey's cloister (ca. 1125); Hyde Abbey, Winchester (ca. 1125–30); Wolvesey Palace, Winchester (ca. 1140–50); Glastonbury Abbey (ca. 1150). The style is also well known in contemporary ivories and manuscripts attributed to the same Canterbury School, where it later acquired the damp-fold of the ca. 1135 Bury Bible.

Damp-fold appears on the rood screen from Durham, ca. 1155, which was made for Hugh le Puiset by a team of sculptors from Winchester. It is partly executed in a damp-fold style similar to the Bury Bible and partly in a plainer style found on some pages of the Winchester Psalter (ca. 1150). Hugh had been archdeacon of Winchester under Bishop Henry of Blois, who had been educated at Cluny, and it is interesting to find damp-fold tympana in Cluny's ambience at Charlieu (ca. 1140–50) and Jonzy (ca. 1140–50), where both display the cobweb effects found in the Winchester Psalter.

English Romanesque sculpture reflects England's history of invasion and settlement by Vikings and Normans, together with its Irish and Burgundian contacts. The English "Plaque" style parallels European developments, and it was similarly rejected for the most prestigious foundations. Charlieu and Jonzy suggest that artistic influence could travel in both directions, as do the beakheads in Anjou after Matilda's marriage to Count Geoffrey in 1128, and possibly also the similarities Zarnecki sees at Lincoln and St. Denis. Italian elements are found at Lincoln, whose facade friezes recall those of Modena in concept, and Durham, whose caryatids recall those of Parma.

Perette E. Michelli

Bibliography

Hearn, M.F. *Romanesque Sculpture: The Revival of Monumental Stone Sculpture in the Eleventh and Twelfth Centuries.* Ithaca: Cornell University Press, 1981; Henry, Françoise. *Irish Art in the Romanesque Period (1020–1170 A.D.).* Ithaca: Cornell University Press, 1970; Kahn, Deborah. *Canterbury Cathedral and Its Romanesque Sculpture.* London: Harvey Miller, 1991; Kahn, Deborah. *The Romanesque Frieze and Its Spectator: The Lincoln Symposium Papers.* London: Harvey Miller, 1992; Zarnecki, George. *Romanesque Art.* New York: Universe, 1971; Zarnecki, George. *Studies in Romanesque Sculpture, 1979.* London: Dorian Press, 1979 [collected essays]; Zarnecki, George, Janet Holt, and Tristram Holland, eds. *English Romanesque Art 1066–1200.* London: Weidenfeld & Nicolson, 1984.

See also Architecture and Architectural Sculpture, Romanesque; Durham Choir Screen Reliefs; Ivory Carving, Romanesque; Kilpeck; Malmesbury Abbey; Manuscript Illumination, Romanesque; Sculpture, Anglo-Saxon; Sculpture, Gothic; Winchester Psalter; York Virgin and Child

Scutage

A money payment made to the king by tenants-in-chief in lieu of military service, that is, quotas of knights owed in return for the lands held from the king.

Scutage was certainly levied by Henry I and probably by William I and William II. The king could demand it as a right and probably did so on each occasion he summoned an army, fixing the rate of payment at so many shillings for each knight or shield (*scuta*, hence "scutage") owed by his tenants-in-chief. It was up to each tenant to decide whether to send the due number of knights or pay scutage, in which case he was allowed to recoup the money from his own tenants. The king often preferred the money to the service, since he could then hire mercenaries. The rate at which scutage was levied varied. It was taken at 26*s.* 8*d.* per knight's fee in 1159 and 1161—precisely sufficient to hire a knight for the 40-day period of feudal service, assuming his wages were 8*d.* a day.

Later scutages under Henry II and Richard I, however, were levied at either 13*s.* 4*d.* or 20*s.*, while a knight's wages rose steadily, reaching 2*s.* a day in the 1200s. John attempted to do something about this situation. He levied scutage at rates rising to 40*s.* a shield and with greater frequency than before, sometimes without actually fighting a campaign. There were eleven scutages in his sixteen-year reign as opposed to seven in the 35 years of Henry II and three in the ten years of Richard I. Not surprisingly clauses 12 and 14 of Magna Carta laid down that scutages were to be levied only with the "common counsel of the kingdom." In the charter of 1217, however, as in all subsequent versions, these were replaced by the vague injunction that scutage was to be levied as in the reign of Henry II, which presumably meant less frequently and at lower rates than under John. In part, at least, this clause was obeyed. There were eleven scutages between 1218 and 1245, only two assessed as high as 40*s.* Thereafter 40*s.* became the standard rate; the tax was taken less and less frequently, only eight being levied between 1246 and 1306.

Scutage was difficult to collect and brought in only a few thousand pounds. Its yield was dwarfed by new taxes on movable property. Although still levied occasionally in the 14th century, it had become an anachronism.

D. A. Carpenter

Bibliography

Calendar of Various Chancery Rolls, 1277–1326. London: HMSO, 1912. Repr. Nendelm, Lichtenstein: Kraus, 1976 [the Scutage Rolls appear in this collection]; Keefe, Thomas K. *Feudal Assessments and the Political Community under Henry II and His Sons.* Berkeley: University of California Press, 1983.

See also Armies; Feudalism; Knight Service; Taxes

Seafarer, The

The Seafarer survives with other so-called OE elegies in one manuscript, the late-10th-century Exeter Book. Sometimes read as a poem about a literal or symbolic pilgrimage, or as an allegory of the soul's journey to God, or as a poem using a seafaring setting to develop its didactic message, *The Seafarer* has enjoyed little critical agreement except for near unanimity that it is one of the great English poems of the early Middle Ages. A disjunctive style making rich use of antithesis and parallelism adds to the usual textual and semantic problems faced by Anglo-Saxon scholars attempting to understand poetry from a distant past.

The Seafarer has two sections, a lyrically powerful description of both the miseries and attractions of seafaring (lines 1–64a), and a homiletic exhortation in the *contemptus mundi* ("contempt for the world") tradition (64b–124). Formerly critics distinguished between different speakers in the poem to explain the conflicting attitudes expressed toward seafaring and other attractions, such as worldly glory and comfort. Recent critics have seen a single speaker whose often antithetical statements are important to the larger didactic theme: the superiority of God's glory to any glory found in this transitory world.

Antithesis and parallelism, major rhetorical devices of Anglo-Saxon poetry, are here skillfully employed. The main contrast of the poem, between the instability of this transitory world and the eternal joy awaiting the Christian in heaven with God, was disparaged by early critics, and lines 64b to the end were often dismissed as a Christian addition. However, critics have long appreciated such contrasts as that in lines 8b–11a ("My feet were constricted with cold, bound by frost, with cold fetters, where those cares sighed hot around my heart") and the antithesis between several descriptions of comfortable living (especially the brief description of spring in lines 48–49) and the extended description of the winter storms and isolation the speaker experienced at sea.

Also appreciated as exemplary of Anglo-Saxon poetic style is the contrast of being locked in, denoted by *hreþerlocan* (58: "breast-locker, or body"), with the idea of flying or sailing out and away from the constraints of the body (58–61a: "my mind turns beyond the body, my spirit turns widely over the native land of the whale with the sea tide"). Use of contrasts extends to verbs like *hæbbe gebiden* (4b: "have experienced") and *gecunnade* (5a: "explored, ventured upon"), the first rather passive, the second notably active, but both denoting the speaker's involvement with sorrow. Similarly line 32a ("frost bound the earth") contrasts with 33b–34a ("thoughts now beat against the heart").

Particularly troubling to critics is the poem's repeated use of *forþon,* usually translated "therefore." Unwilling to articulate a causal relationship in lines 33 and 58, many critics resort to the less usual translation "indeed" when, after describing his misery contrasted with the fortune of other men, the speaker uses *forþon* to introduce clauses emphasizing his eagerness to depart on the sea voyage. In lines 64–66, however, the repetition of *forþon* ("*therefore* the joys of the Lord are hotter for me than this dead and transitory life on earth"), in the clause that closes the poem's first section, adds unity to the major and minor antitheses, uniting the contrast between seafaring and a more comfortable life in the first section and the contrast between worldly and spiritual joy in the second.

Phyllis R. Brown

Bibliography

PRIMARY

ASPR 3:143–47; Gordon, Ida L., ed. *The Seafarer.* New York: Appleton-Century-Crofts, 1966; Gordon, R.K., trans. *Anglo-Saxon Poetry.* Rev. ed. London: Dent, 1954, pp. 76–78.

SECONDARY

Calder, Daniel G. "Setting and Mode in *The Seafarer* and *The Wanderer.*" *NM* 72 (1971): 264–75; Greenfield, Stanley B. "Attitudes and Values in *The Seafarer.*" *SP* 51 (1954): 15–20. Repr. in *Hero and Exile: The Art of Old English Poetry,* ed. George H. Brown. London: Hambledon, 1989, pp. 155–60; Greenfield, Stanley B. "*Sylf,* Seasons, Structure and Genre in *The Seafarer.*" *ASE* 9 (1981): 199–211. Repr. in *Hero and Exile: The Art of Old English Poetry,* ed. George H. Brown. London: Hambledon, 1989, pp. 171–83; Jacobs, Nicolas. "Syntactical Connection and Logical Disconnection: The Case of *The Seafarer.*" *MÆ* 58 (1989): 105–13.

See also Exeter Book; Literary Influences: Irish; *Wanderer*

Seals

Marks of singular authority pressed in relief upon a plastic material by the impact of a matrix-engraved intaglio, medieval seals were not a medieval invention, though their medieval form and function were innovative. The history and modalities of medieval English seal usage display some unique features.

The kingdoms of the early period maintained the Roman use of seal rings to produce impressions that guaranteed the authenticity and closure of letters and functioned as tokens of credence or marks of office. This practice is evidenced in Anglo-Saxon England by the extant 9th-century signet rings of the kings Æthelwulf and Alfred the Great and of Queen Æthelswith; by the surviving matrices of Bishop Æthilwald (ca. 860), St. Edith of Wilton (757–94), Ælfric (ca. 980), Godwin and Godgytha (ca. 1000–ca. 1040), and Wulfric (ca. 1050); and by the seals of a few conventual houses (Durham, Exeter, Sherborne, Athelney, Glastonbury, and Christ Church, Canterbury).

On the Continent the Merovingian chancery attached wax seal impressions on its documents (diplomas) from the 6th century onward, a prerogative maintained by Carolingian kings and emperors and neighboring rulers. However, Anglo-Saxon diplomas remained unsealed. Sealed charters in the name of Offa of Mercia (790), of Æthelwulf of Wessex (857), and of Edgar (960) are forgeries.

Edward the Confessor's introduction of the sealed royal writ (ca. 1057) brought about a revolution in English seal usage and initiated a series of royal seals uninterrupted to the present day. Both the nature and form of the novel Edwardian seal established the characteristic features of English sealing practice, soon to expand within the context of Norman and Angevin rule.

English sigillography evolved from royal administrative requirements; sealed writs were royal written commands to local officials responsible for administrative matters. After the Conquest such writs expanded into a variety of royal sealed charters and letters—both patent, or left open with a seal attached, and close, or rolled up and sealed closed—by means of which the country was administered. The great seal was at first unique, traveling with the king and chancellor, in whose responsibility it was placed from the time of William I onward. As a sedentary bureaucracy developed, and with the extension of Anglo-Norman-Angevin dominions, a duplicate great seal, that of the exchequer, was kept at Westminster from the 12th century onward to ensure authentication in the absence of the mobile great seal. This is the most ancient of European departmental (or deputed) seals, and the first of a long series of deputed English great seals, including the great seals for Ireland, Gascony, France, Scotland, Wales, and the palatinates (Chester and Lancaster), as well as the judicial seals for the Queen's Bench and Common Pleas.

In the reign of Henry III the right to seal was delegated to various departments of the central administration, irrespective of the great seal's location, while the privy seal enabled the monarch to authenticate orders addressed to such departments. In the early 14th century the privy seal came to be reserved for a department and thus lost its personal association with the ruler. Signets, in the keeping of the king's secretary, developed for diplomatic correspondence and household purposes. The flexible system implicit in deputation of the great seal, and the use of numerous smaller official seals of central and local government, testify to a sigillographic process remarkably sensitive to, and reflective of, administrative structure.

Initially the act of sealing for documentary validation was a mark of sovereign authority. Its earliest diffusion throughout society was associated with the assertion of authority and, in the words of Henry II's justiciar Richard de Lucy, befitted exclusively kings and important people. Until 1100 only rulers and bishops possessed seals. By 1200 this privilege extended to barons and cities, by 1250 to knights and lesser clergy, and by 1300 to smallholders. Even "bondsmen" were expected to authenticate deeds with their seals, according to the Statute of Exeter (1285).

The seal derived a general authority from its early linkage to ruling power. In an evolution of fundamental importance such authority begot authenticity, as seals came to be necessary for the validation of written records and agents for imparting trust in their texts. This contribution to the growth of literate modes was enhanced by the material characteristics of seals.

A tangible object, like the physical symbols used for oral conveyances of property, the seal bore the name and title of its owner in the legend and thus enabled an illiterate person to sign his or her name. From the matrix—a personal object kept by its owner—identical wax impressions could be reproduced repeatedly and attached to charters. The writing on seals was associated with a pictorial device evocative of the sealer's social status. As visual symbols seals stood at the juncture of orality and textuality, with the pictorial component translating and certifying the textual component; as icons they articulated the organizing principles of medieval English society.

Brigitte Bedos-Rezak

Bibliography

Bedos-Rezak, Brigitte. "Seals and Sigillography: Western European." In *Dictionary of the Middle Ages,* ed. Joseph R. Strayer. Vol. 11. New York: Scribner, 1988; Bedos-Rezak, Brigitte. "The King Enthroned, a New Theme in Anglo-Saxon Royal Iconography: The Seal of Edward the Confessor and Its Political Implications." In *Form and Order in Medieval France: Studies in Social and Quantitative Sigillography.* Aldershot: Variorum, 1993, Item IV; Birch, Walter de Gray. *Catalogue of Seals in the Department of Manuscripts in the British Museum.* 6 vols. London: Clowes, 1887–1900; Ellis, Roger H. *Catalogue of Seals in the Public Record Office.* 3 vols. London: HMSO, 1978–86; Harvey, P.D.A., and Andrew McGuiness. *A Guide to British Medieval Seals.* Toronto: University of Toronto Press, 1996; Henderson, George. "Romance and Politics on Some Medieval English Seals." *Art History* 1 (1978): 26–42; Heslop, Timothy A. "Seals." In *English Romanesque Art 1066–1200,* ed. George Zarnecki, Janet Holt, and Tristram Holland. London: Weidenfeld & Nicolson, 1984, pp. 298–319; Heslop, Timothy A. "English Seals in the Thirteenth and Fourteenth Centuries." In *Age of Chivalry: Art in Plantagenet England 1200–1400,* ed. Jonathan Alexander and Paul Binski. London: Royal Academy of Arts, 1987, pp. 114–21; Jenkinson, Hilary. *A Guide to Seals in the Public Record Office.* 2d ed. London: HMSO, 1968.

See also Chancellor and Chancery; Great Seal; Literacy; Privy Seal; Signet

Sedulius (fl. ca. 425–50)

Sedulius, whose first name may have been Caelius or Coelius, wrote Christian works in Latin in the second quarter of the 5th century, probably while living in Greece. The introductory letters to his dual work, or *opus geminatum,* the *Carmen paschale,* written in hexameter verse, and the later *Opus paschale,* in prose, furnish some biographical information. Addressed to a priest named Macedonius, the letters reveal that Sedulius had turned from secular studies, perhaps in Italy, to write Christian poetry that combined the pleasures of profane verse with the knowledge of Christ. The first book of the *Carmen paschale* describes miracles of the Old Testament; the following four, based on the Gospels of Luke and Matthew, discuss New Testament miracles from the life of Christ. Sedulius later transposed this work into the prose *Opus paschale* at the request of Macedonius, thus adapting the classical Latin literary practice of *conversio* to Christian writing.

Many surviving manuscripts demonstrate the popularity of Sedulius's works, particularly the *Carmen paschale,* which frequently appears in "classbooks" for Latin students. One copy of the *Carmen paschale* is bound with the Parker Chronicle in Cambridge, Corpus Christi College 173. Following Sedulius's example, the Anglo-Latin writers Aldhelm, Bede, and Alcuin produced *opera gemina* of prose and poetry. As Bede notes in the *Ecclesiastical History,* Aldhelm's *Carmen de virginitate* is written in the style used by Sedulius.

Sedulius also composed biblical stories in elegiac couplets, known as the *Veteris et Novi Testamenti collatio,* and Latin hymns. The opening verse from his abecedarian hymn, *A solis ortus cardine,* has been adapted for the Feast of Christmas and the verse *Hostis Herodes impie* for the Epiphany. The Marian antiphon *O Virgo virginem* is based on the *Carmen paschale.*

Marjorie Brown

Bibliography

PRIMARY

Huemer, J., ed. *Sedvlii Opera Omnia.* CSEL 10. Vienna: Akademie der Wissenschaften, 1885. Repr. New York: Johnson Reprint, 1967.

SECONDARY

Godman, Peter. "The Anglo-Latin *Opus geminatum*: From Aldhelm to Alcuin." *MÆ* 50 (1981): 215–29; Springer, Carl P.E. *The Gospel as Epic in Late Antiquity: The Paschale Carmen of Sedulius.* Leiden: Brill, 1988.

See also Aldhelm; Anglo-Latin Literature to 1066; Literary Influences: Carolingian, Medieval Latin; Sedulius Scottus

Sedulius Scottus, or Scotus (fl. ca. 850)

Irish-born poet and scholar who traveled to Liège between 840 and 851, participating in the flowering of scholarship and the arts known as the "Carolingian renaissance." Little information exists about Sedulius in Ireland, but speculations about his birthplace suggest Kildare, Leinster province. Much of what is known about his later life comes from his own works, including a corpus of Latin poetry considered to be of a high standard.

Viking raids were taking a heavy toll on the Irish in Sedulius's lifetime, and monasteries were especially hard-hit. With these events in his homeland Sedulius took advantage of the Frankish kings' invitations to scholars from abroad. Upon their arrival in Liège Sedulius and his group received support from Bishop Hartgar, a patron of the arts who had important political connections. After Hartgar's death in 855

Bishop Franco continued to support the Irish circle until 881, when the Vikings overwhelmed Liège. It is not known what happened to Sedulius, when he died, or where he is buried. It has been suggested that Sedulius did not remain in Liège but also resided in Cologne, Metz, and Milan.

Sedulius and his fellow Irish scholars are known for preserving classical authors to a greater degree than most Christian scholars of this era. The Liège group was part of a larger community of Irish scholars on the Continent. Sedulius's own works include his poems, as well as grammatical commentaries on Eutyches and Priscian, commentaries on the epistles of Paul and Matthew, and a *Collectaneum* that demonstrates Sedulius's knowledge of Greek as well as Latin and that contains several works of Cicero preserved nowhere else. He also wrote the *De rectoribus christianis,* a "mirror for princes" thought to be composed for Lothar II, son of Lothar I, although recent claims suggest it may have been intended for Charles the Bald.

Mary E. Sokolowski

Bibliography

Doyle, Edward Gerard, trans. *On Christian Rulers and the Poems.* MRTS 17. Binghamton: MRTS, 1983; Simpson, Dean, ed. *Sedvlii Scotti Collectanevm Miscellanevm.* CCCM 67. Turnhout: Brepols, 1988.

See also Literary Influences: Carolingian, Classical, Irish; Sedulius

Sequence

A major genre of Latin liturgical chant, sung immediately following the Alleluia as an addition to the Proper of the mass. Sequence composition began around 850, and some 150 melodies and 400 texts were composed up to the end of the 10th century; over 5,000 existed by the end of the Middle Ages. A sequence is normally constructed as a long series of textual couplets or paired strophes, with each line of the couplet or strophe of the pair set to the same melody and a fresh melody composed for each new formal unit, resulting in a chain of double versicles. It may begin or end with a single, unpaired line or strophe. Although the term "sequence" is virtually synonymous with double-versicle structure, it should be stressed that this form was employed for other musical genres as well, including the French and Latin lai, the Latin planctus, rhymed offertories, Sanctus tropes, Matins proses, and the estampie (a type of medieval dance). Pieces not in this form were sometimes used as the sequence at mass—for example, the strophic devotional song *Angelus ad virginem,* specified as a sequence in the ordinal of St. Mary's, York (Cambridge, St. John's College D.27). And known liturgical sequences sometimes appear in different functional roles, as, for instance, hymn and offertory substitutes.

The development of the sequence is commonly described in terms of three epochs: the early or first epoch sequence of the later 9th and 10th centuries, the second or intermediate generation sequence of the later 10th to the earlier 12th centuries, and the standard or later rhymed ("Parisian" or "Victorine") sequence of the 12th through 16th centuries.

Early sequences, whose texts are in prose, display a wide variety of textual and musical styles and details of structure. The later sequence shows a gradual regularization of syllable count, accent, rhyme, and strophic pattern, culminating in the regular versification and uniform strophic structures of the third epoch, with corresponding musical developments in melodic idiom and tonality. The later sequence shares not only form but also musical language with contemporary, nonliturgical genres of Latin song, such as the planctus and lai.

The history of the sequence in England, the subject of significant current research, cannot yet be given authoritative treatment. Sequence collections tend to vary considerably with locale and to change over time. Despite pressures toward normalization emanating from diocese, religious order, and the authority of the prestigious Use of Salisbury, each surviving source preserves a chronologically multilayered and idiosyncratic selection of internationally well known works, nationally or regionally circulating pieces, and local products. Despite pioneering work, especially by Hesbert and Hiley, essential questions remain to be asked of most sources: How many sequences are local products? In these how much is locally contributed (text, music, or both)? Is there a local dialect or idiom of music or Latin evident in the local products? Do any of the more widely known pieces show signs of the local idioms in their melodic or textual variants?

A few broad observations about the evolution of the sequence in England can be made. There was a wholesale adoption of continental repertoire in the 10th century during the Benedictine Reform, represented by the mainly northern French repertoire of the Winchester tropers. This process of adoption was repeated in the 11th century at the time of the Norman Conquest, with its accompanying liturgical upheavals. In the last epoch no such dramatic turnover occurred, and a much lower proportion of earlier sequences was supplanted by the later rhymed sequences in England than on the Continent. From this era arise both Archbishop Stephen Langton's popular Pentecost sequence *Veni sancte spiritus* and an anonymous English Cistercian's strophic devotional poem *Dulcis Jesu memoria,* whose earliest musical setting (Bodl. Laud misc. 668, fol. 101–101v) is in varied double-versicle form. Beginning in the 13th century, polyphonic sequences began to supersede the monophonic sequence as the focus of insular compositional activity, with the demand for new sequences being driven primarily by the local expansion of the Marian liturgy (and to a lesser degree by new feasts). The polyphonic cantilena, whose principal function appears to have been that of sequence and offertory substitute, became a major insular genre in the 14th century.

Peter M. Lefferts

Bibliography

Crocker, Richard, and John Caldwell. "Sequence." *NGD* 17:141–56; Deusen, Nancy M. Van. "The Medieval Latin Sequence: A Complete Catalogue of the Sources and Edition of the Texts and Melodies." *Journal of the Plainsong and Mediaeval Music Society* 5 (1982): 56–60; Hesbert, René-Jean, ed. *Le tropaire-prosaire de Dublin.* Monumenta Musicae Sacrae 4. Rouen: Imprimerie Rouennaise, 1966 [facsimile]; Hiley, David. "The Norman Chant Traditions—Normandy, Britain, Sicily." *Proceedings of the Royal Musical Association* 107 (1980–81): 1–33; Hiley, David. "Further Observations on W1: The Ordinary of Mass Chants and the Sequences." *Journal of the Plainsong and Mediaeval Music Society* 4 (1981): 67–80; Hiley, David. "The Rhymed Sequence in England—A Preliminary Survey." In *Musicologie médiévale: Notations et séquences,* ed. Michel Huglo. Paris: Champion, 1987, pp. 227–46; Lefferts, Peter M. "Cantilena and Antiphon: Music for Marian Services in Late Medieval England." In *Studies in Medieval Music: Festschrift for Ernest H. Sanders,* ed. Peter M. Lefferts and Brian Seirup. *Current Musicology* 45–47 (1990): 247–82; Stevens, John. *Words and Music in the Middle Ages: Song, Narrative, Dance and Drama, 1050–1350.* Cambridge: Cambridge University Press, 1986.

See also Angelus ad virginem; Cantilena; Conductus; Hymns; Lai, Latin; Planctus; Songs; Trope

Serfs and Villeins

Persons who, while freer than slaves, still suffered particular legal restrictions and were bound to their landlords by ties not solely economic. Slavery, involving the public buying and selling of household or estate workers, disappeared in England early in the 12th century, but it is likely that tenants of small holdings—the nearly 200,000 *villani, bordarii,* and *cotarii* of Domesday Book (1086)—were by no means free to come and go, to take up or leave their holdings as they wished. It is likely, however, that the restrictions varied, perhaps a great deal, from place to place.

In the late 12th century, perhaps not until the 1190s, the royal courts began to recognize villeinage as a concept in common law. Certain tenants—often defined as those who owed unspecified labor services or who made a payment (merchet) on a daughter's marriage—were classed as villeins (Lat. *villani,* or neifs, Lat. *nativi*) and were held to be unable to bring a case in the royal courts in defense of their holdings; these lay exclusively in the jurisdiction of the lord of the manor.

By the mid-13th century a structure of detailed regulation, which owed something to the Roman law of slavery, emerged. The villein and his children were subject to the manorial lord. He could be evicted from his holding at any time, had no right of inheritance, and could own no personal property. All his money and goods belonged to his lord, who could thus exact whatever rents or other dues he pleased, plus any amount of labor services. Without the lord's permission the villein could not leave, exchange, or sell his holding; neither could he take holy orders nor go on pilgrimage, nor his daughter marry, nor his son go to school. So far did these ideas permeate legal thinking that the sale of villein holdings from one lord to another was expressed, in the charter of conveyance, as the sale of the villeins themselves and their families. The law distinguished in some respects between villeins by birth and villeins by tenure, the latter being free men who became tenants of villein holdings, and elaborated rules on the status of children born to parents of whom only one was a villein.

To those tenants who did not fall within it the royal courts' definition of villeinage probably gave increased freedom; they could appeal against locally imposed constraints. And in practice the villein's position was neither so complex nor so downtrodden as the letter of the law might suggest. His lord's jurisdiction was exercised in the manorial court, which administered not the common law of royal courts but the custom of the manor. This varied in detail from place to place but everywhere allowed the villein rights denied him by common law. It set carefully defined bounds to the "renders" he owed for his holding, whether in cash, produce, or labor, and assumed that his money and goods were his own property. Usually, however, the lord took a "heriot," the villein tenant's best beast (sometimes some other chattel or cash), when he died and required the villein to have his corn ground in the lord's mill, to the profit of the lord or his lessee.

Local custom usually allowed the villein's holding to be sublet or transferred, by gift or sale, and always to be inherited according to local custom, which might give it to the eldest son, the youngest, or to all the sons. The villein might even purchase manumission—freedom from villeinage—which was technically an absurdity, for the money paid already belonged in strict law to the lord. These were the rules by which the villein's day-to-day life was conducted, and though the lord of the manor could lawfully override them at any time, this seldom happened. When it did, the strenuous resistance that was often put up suggests that many villeins had little notion of the weakness of their position under common law. At the same time the depths of resentment are revealed by the extent of protest: corporately against the disabilities of villeinage, individually against the stigma of the name of villein.

These protests are most in evidence in the 14th century, but by then the distinctive features of villeinage were fast disappearing. Unspecified labor services (an inefficient form of rent from the lord's view) had mostly vanished by the 1340s and payment of merchet, together with other obligations peculiar to villeins, was in decay in the second half of the century. Declining population (particularly from the plagues of 1348–49, 1361–62, and 1369) forced lords to admit local tenants on easier terms, rather than leave holdings unoccupied, and protest was often against particular lords' insistence on obligations increasingly seen as archaic. Yet the law still maintained a distinction between free tenants, with access to the royal courts regarding their holdings, and customary tenants, whose holdings lay solely in the manorial lord's jurisdiction.

There was no formal abolition of villeinage. In the 15th century manorial lords continued to relax the disabilities and obligations of customary tenants. A significant change occurred in the 16th century, when courts, first of equity and then of common law, began (without overt change in the law) to hear cases brought by copyholders, customary tenants who held documents giving extracts ("copies") of the entries of their tenure on the manorial court rolls. This formalized and universalized what had been merely one of a number of kinds of customary tenure. However, isolated instances of the obliga-

tions characteristic of 13th-century villeinage—especially specified labor services, heriots, and particular customary rents—continued into the 16th century and later. Copyhold continued in existence as a distinctive form of tenure until the Law of Property Act of 1922.

P.D.A. Harvey

Bibliography

Gray, Charles M. *Copyhold, Equity, and the Common Law.* Cambridge: Harvard University Press, 1963 [sets out the now accepted chronology of the admission of copyhold cases to the royal courts]; Hatcher, John. "English Serfdom and Villeinage: Towards a Reassessment." *Past and Present* 90 (February 1981): 3–39; Hilton, Rodney H. *The English Peasantry in the Later Middle Ages.* Oxford: Clarendon, 1975 [villeinage and the tensions to which it gave rise, in the context of local rural society]; Hilton, Rodney H. *The Decline of Serfdom in Medieval England.* 2d ed. London: Macmillan, 1983 [succinct account of late-medieval changes in villeinage]; Hyams, Paul. *King, Lords and Peasants in Medieval England: The Common Law of Villeinage in the Twelfth and Thirteenth Centuries.* Oxford: Clarendon, 1980 [up-to-date treatment of material covered by Vinogradoff]; Vinogradoff, Paul. *Villeinage in England.* Oxford: Clarendon, 1892 [the classic expositions of a villein's legal disabilities].

See also Black Death; Labor Services; Manorial Courts; Manorialism; Peasant Rebellion; Population; Slavery

Sermons and Homilies

Strictly speaking, since preaching is an ephemeral art that vanishes into air with the preacher's words, it is impossible ever to know what medieval congregations actually heard in the sermons they attended, and we certainly cannot be sure that sermons preserved in manuscript were preached exactly as recorded. Many patently were not. Some sermons would never even have reached so finished a form; their written existence would have been no more permanent than as a set of notes. No doubt much has vanished. Yet despite the many reasons for the elusiveness of medieval preaching it is still possible to form some impression of its fortunes between the conversion of the Anglo-Saxons and the eve of the Reformation.

Old English Period

Old English homilies and sermons, along with all of OE prose, have begun in the last half-generation to take their proper and significant place in a total view of OE literature and culture. The major advances have come in the study of sources, the editing of texts, and to some degree the study of homilies and sermons as religious literature, but many major questions and problems remain. Perhaps the foremost difficulty is the need for a set of intellectual operations to eliminate preconceived notions and stock assumptions brought to the subject by a knowledge of later medieval sermons or even postmedieval religious literature. Unlike ME homilies and sermons OE works did not have a strong rhetorical or legislative impulse, but it is not true to say that neither rhetoric nor conciliar decrees existed. There is nothing in the earlier Middle Ages to match the rhetorical intricacy of Robert of Basevorn's *Forma praedicandi,* the exemplary medieval manual, but Augustine, Gregory the Great, and Martin of Braga had much to say about preaching and preachers. Augustine's *De doctrina christiana* gives advice, particularly in book 4, on how to preach, but Augustine's antipathy to classical rhetoric turned his would-be preacher away from style to truth-content. Gregory the Great is virtually obsessive in his concern, voiced in *Cura pastoralis* and *Moralia in Iob,* that above all the preacher must himself be a good man. Martin of Braga offers a rather more practical model for preaching in his brief *De correctione rusticorum.* Carolingian councils, such as the series of councils in 813, established the importance of preaching to the laity, while Carolingian writers and anthologists, notably Paul the Deacon and Smaragdus, assembled important collections useful as precedents and models.

It is now a virtual consensus that early-medieval preaching developed from the monastic night office, readings for which appear in anthologies known as homiliaries, such as Paul the Deacon's *Homiliary,* extant in later versions in Anglo-Saxon England. The discovery of the importance of homiliaries corrected the previous erroneous notion that the wide range of sources used in the OE homiletic tradition implied well-stocked libraries. Paul the Deacon's collection contains the homilies of Bede, Maximus of Turin, Leo the Great, and Gregory the Great, among others, while the Carolingian sermonary, represented by Cambridge, Pembroke College 25 (a form of the *Homiliary* of St. Père de Chartres, dated after 820), offers even the works of Alcuin (though unattributed to him).

The indebtedness of OE homiletics to Latin sources does not preclude original vernacular writing, but it is a rare sermon that, like Wulfstan's *Sermo Lupi,* responds to contemporary conditions. What remains as comparatively uncharted territory is the interactivity of vernacular and Latin or bilingualism, as in Ælfric, who composed in both languages. Parenetic writing (sermons that exhort the audience to do good) is particularly common, as are sermons urging penitential practices like fasting and almsgiving, but contemporary behavior is hard to see through the formulaic expression. It seems clear that the extant body of vernacular homiletic literature is the result of one of the impulses of the Benedictine Reform, but there is enough to indicate that before the late 10th century there may have been a flourishing tradition. Vercelli Homilies I and X (= Pseudo-Wulfstan 49) may in fact be witnesses to this earlier tradition.

The setting and audience for vernacular homilies and sermons are not all that clear. Were extant homilies and sermons delivered primarily in a liturgical setting like the mass, or were there other occasions, say before a council or a synod, where a given piece might have been delivered? Ælfric believed that there should be no preaching on *swigdagas,* "days of silence" (Holy Thursday, Good Friday, and Holy Saturday), but others clearly preached on those days, and their works fill the gap in collections that contain mainly Ælfric. Is there a line between the lay audience and the monastic audience that so far is hard to see? Ælfric had learned and literate lay patrons who appreciated his efforts at writing saints' lives, and the adaptation of monastic literature for them was certainly unstartling. What, finally, is the role of silent reading or private devotional use, if any? Whatever the answers to these many questions, it is clear that the work of Ælfric, Wulfstan, and anonymous figures had a major role in cultural life even into the 12th century, as the many manuscripts bear witness.

The matter of genre needs more work. It is customary for scholars to distinguish between *homilia,* an exposition on a passage from the Bible, and *sermo,* a more general exposition often featuring exhortation, but OE writers do not themselves observe such a hard distinction in practice. Ælfric's "homilies" often move easily within and beyond the two ideal forms, and the application of a biblical lesson to the moral life of the audience is easy and natural. The famous fourfold method of scriptural exegesis seems absent from most homilies where exegesis is prominent; at best there are explanations that are literal, broadly allegorical (i.e., nonliteral), and moral. There are no tight, comparatively rigid rhetorical structures imposed on the biblical text such as are often invoked in the analysis of Chaucer's *Pardoner's Tale* or explained in Robert of Basevorn.

One clear generic form is the running gloss. Vercelli Homily XVI is an exposition of Matthew 3:13–17, for the Epiphany, celebrating not the Magi but rather one of Christ's other manifestations, the Baptism in the Jordan. After a brief introduction the homilist goes line-by-line through the biblical text offering explanations and discussions, including an interesting discussion of the Trinity, which manifested itself at the Baptism, and of the miraculous flow of the Jordan. The homily ends with an exhortation to right Christian observance, but who, precisely, are the "men" urged to do good and avoid evil? Ælfric, who may be considered the master of the form, shows a somewhat differing practice in his *Catholic Homilies* I. BL Royal 7.C.xii, a version of the series that Ælfric clearly authorizes with his own annotations, offers translations of the pericopes, or biblical readings for the day, and the apparatus of the manuscript links the homilies more closely to the liturgical occasion. As yet no one has made the case for other homiletic genres or variations within the form.

The recent appearance of D.G. Scragg's edition of the Vercelli Homilies, M.R. Godden's edition of Ælfric's Second Series, the example of J.C. Pope's magisterial edition of the *Homilies of Ælfric: A Supplementary Collection,* the promised editions of Ælfric's *First Series* (by the late Peter Clemoes) and the Blickling Homilies (by Milton McC. Gatch and William Stoneman as successors to the late Rowland Collins), and the source work by *Fontes Anglo-Saxonici* and *Sources of Anglo-Saxon Literary Culture* will combine to offer a proper foundation for studies of the questions entertained here and new questions to arise. Even the movement to include theory in the discussion of OE literature welcomes the presence of prose as part of the cultural record.

Middle English Period

In the years following the Conquest that giant of Anglo-Saxon preaching, Ælfric, still commanded attention. His work was recycled in collections like the *Lambeth Homilies* (ca. 1200). The Augustinian canon Orm, who at about the same date wrote a versified set of ME sermons, the *Ormulum,* seems to have been in touch with an Ælfrician homiletic tradition, if not indeed with Ælfric's work firsthand. However, it would be wrong to conceive of the 12th century as merely a conservative transmitter of earlier preaching tradition. By the late 12th to early 13th century preaching was receiving a renewed seriousness of attention, witnessed, for example, in the attitude of a writer like Odo of Cheriton (ca. 1180–ca. 1246). Preaching for him was evidently almost sacramental in stature.

Attitudes like Odo's were a preview of the massive endorsement that preaching would receive a few years later. The Fourth Lateran Council of 1215 was concerned that preaching be as effective as possible. The tenth canon of the council reminded bishops that they were preachers ex officio but that they must recruit additional help from suitable deputies in order to carry out their duties adequately. Lateran IV linked preaching with confession, an association apparent in the many 13th-century manuscripts where material of interest to preachers and confessors alike is brought together.

One of the earliest steps taken to implement Lateran IV in England was at the Council of Oxford in 1222, held under Archbishop Stephen Langton, himself a notable preacher. The council enjoined on parish priests the instruction of the laity, and as the century progressed the content of this instruction was further specified. By 1281 the Council of Lambeth, held under Archbishop John Pecham, could require in its ninth canon, *Ignorancia sacerdotum,* that four times a year, straightforwardly and in English, priests must preach to their congregations the fourteen articles of faith, the Ten Commandments, the two evangelical precepts, the seven works of mercy, the seven deadly sins and their offspring, the seven principal virtues, and the seven sacraments. From Anglo-Saxon times catechetical material had always had its place in preaching to the laity, but the stress laid on it during the 13th century renewed its importance as a staple for sermons. In the 14th and 15th centuries preachers in English, mindful of the injunctions about the preaching of catechesis, would explore different ways of reconciling them with the traditional requirement to preach upon the pericope of the day.

The 13th century was one of exciting developments in several other respects: its earlier years saw the foundation of the Franciscans and Dominicans, orders that from their inception were charged explicitly with the task of preaching. The guides to sermon composition, the *artes praedicandi,* were now illustrating how sermons might be crafted according to the "modern" form, in which a theme was announced and divided into a number of principal parts, each of which was then discussed. "Modern" sermons were thus more structurally self-conscious and symmetrical than those in the "ancient" form (essentially a plainer procedure based on methodical exegesis of scripture). Although "ancient" sermons would tend to be eclipsed by enthusiasm for the "modern" until the later 14th

century, they were of too distinguished a pedigree ever to be entirely supplanted, having been used by no less than the Fathers of the Church themselves. Their comparative simplicity recommended itself to anyone contemplating preaching to the laity. Perhaps these were some of the reasons why, for example, the late-13th-century author of a substantial set of versified ME Gospel sermons known as the *Northern Homily Cycle* used a variety of "ancient" rather than "modern" form at a time when the "modern" was much in vogue.

It is not until the later 14th and early 15th centuries that sermons in ME start to appear in any bulk, no doubt partly as a result of the general upsurge of confidence in this period about writing in the vernacular. And their quantity is matched by a broadness in quality. In style the sermons of this period range from the sensational to the restrained to the austere (compare the *Festial* of John Mirk, the ME version of Robert of Gretham's *Miroir des évangiles,* and the Wycliffite sermon cycles, respectively, all of which were composed in these years). By 1400 sermon style and content were no neutral matter but had almost become politicized in the wake of the Lollard heresy. Lollards, for whom stringently Bible-based preaching was a point of principle, frequently accused the friars of adulterating "Godis lawe" with trivial exempla and fables when they preached, and though not all Lollards were similarly minded, Wyclif himself disliked the "modern" form, with which the preaching of the friars was often associated.

In an attempt to curb seditious Lollard preaching Pecham's *Ignorancia sacerdotum* would soon receive a powerful new sanction. It had remained in force throughout the 14th century—Archbishop John Thoresby reissued it in 1357 for his diocese of York—but now it was to be more controversially urged in the constitutions, or decrees, of Archbishop Thomas Arundel's Oxford Convocation of 1407. As part of the campaign to eradicate heresy preaching licenses were required of those to whom the constitutions were deemed to apply; henceforth unlicensed preachers must confine themselves to the catechesis of *Ignorancia sacerdotum.* But even if they helped to bridle heretics, Arundel's constitutions provoked the resentment of some orthodox preachers for the way they inhibited many for the sake of silencing a few. No doubt in some quarters the constitutions also led to a sense of first- and second-class preaching: a Passion Sunday sermon by the monk Hugo Legat, preached possibly sometime after the constitutions of 1407 had taken effect, puts indiscreet and untutored preachers firmly in their place by reminding them that "thei schulde not preche to hure pareschon, but onlich swiche thing as tei knowe skel upon, as te 5 wittis, the 7 dedly synnes, þe 10 comaundementis and swich oþur þat longen to here estat for to preche of." Anyone confining his sermons to catechesis would have been seen to proclaim himself as an unlicensed preacher.

ME sermon collections continued to be produced throughout the 15th century, but few were new compositions; texts that had already been written in the early 15th-century tended to be edited and adapted and so kept in circulation. Even originally heterodox material might be defused for orthodox preaching purposes. Consequently the content of many ME sermon manuscripts from about the 1450s on may give the impression that preaching was living off its capital. Yet this is not to imply that preaching on the eve of the Reformation was moribund. There is evidence that the laity showed considerable appetite for it, in some cases even leaving preaching endowments for its maintenance. The legacy that medieval preaching left to the Reformation was sizable. Many ME sermon manuscripts show clear signs of having been read and used well into the 16th century, and occasionally medieval sermons might still be preached, to the understandable displeasure of the reformed authorities.

Though most surviving ME sermons are dominical (based on Sunday Gospels), some no doubt for use at mass, a substantial number of the rest are for other occasions, like saints' days, weddings, or funerals. Many medieval men and women, then, would have had the opportunity to attend preaching not just at mass on Sunday. The other occasions were diverse: for example, the opening of parliament was normally marked with a sermon, sometimes in English; ecclesiastical synods might include vernacular preaching to the laity; and if the set of sermons known as *Jacob's Well* was ever preached, its congregation had the chance to hear a sermon every day for 95 days, probably from Ash Wednesday to the vigil of Pentecost.

The pervasiveness of preaching in medieval life has profound implications for our understanding of medieval English culture. If we wish to recover the dimensions of the spiritual, moral, and political ideologies to which the ordinary men and women of England were repeatedly exposed, sermons are an obvious place in which to look for them.

    Paul E. Szarmach
    Alan J. Fletcher

Bibliography

PRIMARY

Old English

Cross, J.E. *Cambridge, Pembroke College MS 25: A Carolingian Sermonary Used by Anglo-Saxon Preachers.* King's College London Medieval Studies 1. London: King's College, 1987; Eliason, Norman, and Peter Clemoes, eds. *Ælfric's First Series of Catholic Homilies.* EEMF 13. Copenhagen: Rosenkilde & Bagger, 1966; Godden, Malcolm R. *Ælfric's Catholic Homilies: The Second Series.* EETS s.s. 5. Oxford: Oxford University Press, 1979; Pope, John C., ed. *Homilies of Ælfric: A Supplementary Collection.* EETS o.s. 259–60. Oxford: Oxford University Press, 1967–68; Scragg, D.G., ed. *The Vercelli Homilies.* EETS o.s. 300. Oxford: Oxford University Press, 1992.

Middle English

Belfour, Algernon O., ed. and trans. *Twelfth Century Homilies in MS. Bodley 343.* EETS o.s. 137. London: Kegan Paul, Trench, Trübner, 1909; Charland, Th.-M., ed. *Artes praedicandi: Contribution à l'histoire de la rhétorique au moyen âge.* Publications de l'Institut d'Études Médiévales d'Ottawa 7. Paris: Vrin, 1936; Grisdale, D.M. *Three Middle English Sermons from the Worcester Chapter Manuscript F.10.* Kendal: Titus Wilson, 1939;

Hudson, Anne, and Pamela Gradon, eds. *English Wycliffite Sermons.* 5 vols. Oxford: Clarendon, 1983–96; Nevanlinna, Saara, ed. *The Northern Homily Cycle: The Expanded Version in MSS Harley 4196 and Cotton Tiberius E. VII.* Mémoires de la Société Néophilologique de Helsinki 38, 41, 43. Helsinki: Société Néophilologique, 1972–84; Powicke, Frederick M., and C.R. Cheney, eds. *Councils and Synods, with Other Documents Relating to the English* A.D. *1205–1313.* 2 vols. Oxford: Clarendon, 1964; Simmons, T.F., and H.E. Nolloth, eds. *The Lay Folk's Catechism.* EETS o.s. 118. London: Kegan Paul, Trench, Trübner, 1901.

SECONDARY

Old English

Clayton, Mary. "Homiliaries and Preaching in Anglo-Saxon England." *Peritia* 4 (1985): 207–42; Gatch, Milton McC. *Preaching and Theology in Anglo-Saxon England.* Toronto: University of Toronto Press, 1977; Hill, Joyce M. "Ælfric and Smaragdus." *ASE* 21 (1992): 203–37; Scragg, D.G. "The Corpus of Vernacular Homilies and Prose Saints' Lives before Ælfric." *ASE* 8 (1979): 223–77; Smetana, Cyril L. "Ælfric and the Early Medieval Homiliary." *Traditio* 15 (1959): 163–204; Smetana, Cyril L. "Ælfric and the Homiliary of Haymo of Halberstadt." *Traditio* 17 (1961): 457–69; Szarmach, Paul E. "The Earlier Homily: *De Parasceve.*" In *Studies in Earlier Old English Prose,* ed. Paul E. Szarmach. Albany: SUNY Press, 1986, pp. 381–99; Szarmach, Paul E., and Bernard F. Huppé, eds., *The Old English Homily and Its Background.* Albany: SUNY Press, 1978.

Middle English

D'Avray, D.L. *The Preaching of the Friars: Sermons Diffused from Paris before 1300.* Oxford: Clarendon, 1985; Heffernan, Thomas J. "Sermon Literature." In *Middle English Prose: A Critical Guide to Major Authors and Genres,* ed. A.S.G. Edwards. New Brunswick: Rutgers University Press, 1984, pp. 177–207; Owst, G.R. *Preaching in Medieval England: An Introduction to Sermon Manuscripts of the Period c. 1350–1450.* Cambridge: Cambridge University Press, 1926; Owst, G.R. *Literature and Pulpit in Medieval England.* 2d ed. Oxford: Blackwell, 1961; Pfander, Homer G. *The Popular Sermon of the Medieval Friar in England.* New York: New York University, 1937; Spenser, Helen Leith. *English Preaching in the Late Middle Ages.* Oxford: Clarendon, 1993; Wenzel, Siegfried. *Verses in Sermons: Fasciculus morum and Its Middle English Poems.* Cambridge: Medieval Academy of America, 1978.

See also Ælfric; Benedictine Reform; Blickling Homilies; Bozon; Caesarius; *Dives and Pauper;* Friars; Friars' Miscellanies; Grosseteste; *Jacob's Well;* Langton; Mirk; Moral and Religious Instruction; Orm; Paul the Deacon; Penitentials; Vercelli Homilies; Virtues and Vices, Books of; Wulfstan; Wyclif; Wycliffite Texts

Sheriff

In Anglo-Saxon England the king's reeves, officers of justice who ranked below the ealdormen, were among his principal agents in local government. By the late 10th and early 11th centuries reeves were being appointed to specific shires, responsible to the king for financial, judicial, military, and executive tasks.

The usefulness of the shire reeve (sheriff) was immediately recognized by the Norman conquerors. William I and William II enhanced the status of the post by repeatedly appointing leading barons. In the 12th century kings generally preferred men of lesser rank, familiar to the royal court and of proven administrative ability. From the 13th century most kings were content to leave the selection of local knights to their councillors or barons of the exchequer. A year's term of office became common in the 14th century and normal thereafter.

The typical early Norman sheriff, in person or through deputies, had numerous duties. He tried civil and criminal cases in shire and hundred courts; he policed his shire through the pursuit, arrest, and imprisonment of criminals and could summon a posse to help him; he commanded shire levies against rebels and invaders; he had custody of crown estates and sometimes held a royal castle; he was the king's chief executive, proclaiming warnings and commands in the shire court and responding to instructions in royal writs; he collected and paid to the treasury the king's revenues from the shire, chiefly from royal estates, profits of justice, and taxation.

In later centuries his power gradually diminished, as many of these duties were entrusted to specialists whom he was required to assist. In particular the introduction of the itinerant justices in eyre in the 12th century (alongside the acquisition of hundred jurisdiction by many feudal lords) deprived the sheriff of much of his importance as a trial judge. However, Henry II's procedural reforms gave him a crucial role in facilitating the justices' work; the sheriff received chancery writs to initiate pleading, heard preliminary presentments of suspects (often at the special twice-yearly sessions of the hundred courts, the sheriff's tourn), empaneled juries, ensured that defendants appeared for trial, and executed judicial decisions.

Sheriffs continued to service the new judicial commissions after the collapse of the eyre system in the late 13th century, finally losing significant jurisdiction of their own in 1461, when the preliminary hearing of presentments was transferred to the justices of the peace. Otherwise the 15th-century sheriff remained important for policing the shire, fulfilling administrative duties for king and justices, and supervising the return of knights of the shire to parliament.

G.J. White

Bibliography

Brown, Alfred L. *The Governance of Late Medieval England, 1272–1461.* London: Arnold, 1989; Green, Judith A. *English Sheriffs to 1154.* London: HMSO, 1990; Loyn, H.R. *The Governance of Anglo-Saxon England 500–1087.* London: Arnold, 1984; Morris, William A. *The Medieval English Sheriff to 1300.* Manchester: Manchester University Press, 1927; Palmer, Robert C. *The County Courts of Medieval England, 1150–1350.* Princeton: Princeton University Press, 1982; Stenton, Doris M. *English Justice between the Norman Conquest and the Great Charter, 1066–1215.* Philadelphia: American Philosophical Society, 1964; Storey, Robin L. *The End of the House of Lancaster.* 2d ed. Gloucester: Sutton, 1986.

See also Exchequer; Hundreds; Local Government; Parliamentary Elections; Shires

Ships and Shipbuilding

Seafaring in the British Isles has a long history predating the medieval era. Many vessels were oared, but some did have a mast and sail for propulsion. The large seagoing *curraugh,* of several thicknesses of hides stretched over a wooden frame, was capable of deep-water sailing. St. Brendan is said to have sailed such a vessel from Ireland to Greenland or America. The Romans also brought their vessels to Britain, large sailing craft common to the Mediterranean.

But the most important traditions of seafaring and shipbuilding were established by northern peoples. The Saxons and Angles crossed the North Sea regularly before the 5th century in clinker-built rowing barges, but they may have had mast and sail also. The Saxon burial ship of ca. 610–40 found at Sutton Hoo represents the oared-vessel type. Other finds, like the Kvalsund ship in Norway, are precursors of the oared sailing ship of the Viking era that influenced British ship construction. The hulk, a banana-shaped vessel with a sail, had no keel. The cog was similar, with a broader look and a flat bottom for more cargo. Keels were Viking-style vessels with true keels and a sail for propulsion.

The most dominant war vessel of the early-medieval era was the Viking longship, which gave the Scandinavians unmatched superiority at sea. Following their 9th-century invasion of Britain new elements of ship technology were developed and borrowed. The Anglo-Saxon Chronicle states that Alfred the Great built longships of 60 oars and more to challenge the Danish fleets. His victory allowed the Anglo-Saxons to recover much of Britain from the Danes.

Seafaring practices were influenced after 1066 by the Norman Conquest. The Normans were originally Danes who settled in France in the 10th century. Their successful conquest of Britain linked the island to the Continent. Viking-style vessels were used in the attack, shown on the visual record—the Bayeux Tapestry. Like other northern vessels they were clinker-built (the planks forming the hull overlapped one another), with stem and stern posts, and navigated by the use of a side steering oar. A single mast with a square sail propelled these vessels, some of which were large enough to carry horses for the knights.

In the succeeding two centuries the Norman or Viking-style vessel was modified and a larger sailing ship emerged without oars. A wider and deeper hull provided greater cargo capacity necessary for the bulk-carrying trades. Cargoes included salt, wool, wine, furs, timber, fish, and grain. A vessel's size was measured by its carrying capacity, usually in tuns of wine. Each wooden wine tun (a huge barrel) contained 252 gallons.

Vessels were constructed for trade with capacities of well over 100 tons. Such ships could not be rowed; for greater control and sailing power a second mast was added. This carried a lateen sail, triangular in shape and imported from the Mediterranean. The lateen sail on a mizzen mast greatly facilitated control of the ship and the ability to sail into the wind. Control was aided by the invention of the stern-post rudder, operated by a tiller. This was a much more efficient means of steering a vessel, provided greater stability, and enabled the construction of larger, taller vessels.

The principal cargo vessel of the late-medieval period was the cog, which evolved into a large, high-sided clinker-built vessel, flat-bottomed with a stern-post rudder and single mast with a square sail. Records from the 14th century contain lists of cogs up to 300 tuns transporting cargo, troops, and horses along the northern seas. Bulky and slow, the cog remained a mainstay of both commercial and naval fleets.

The principal changes in ship design after 1400 were the increase in size of vessels and their rigging. Ships grew to a capacity of hundreds of tuns, and multiple masts were added to support sails that propelled the large vessels. Combinations of square sails and lateen sails were employed. With the coming of the Tudors in 1485 ships were heavily utilized in war and trade. The carrack was a carvel-built ship, meaning that the planking on the hull was placed edge to edge, leaving a smooth surface. A square main and fore sail and a lateen sail on the mizzen mast propelled the ship. Vessels of this type were used by merchants, the king's navy, and explorers who sailed the Atlantic and Pacific oceans.

Timothy J. Runyan

Bibliography

Lewis, Archibald R., and Timothy J. Runyan. *European Naval and Maritime History, 300–1500.* Bloomington: Indiana University Press, 1985; Unger, R.W. *The Ship in the Medieval Economy, 600–1100.* London: Croom Helm, 1980.

See also Alfred; Bayeux Tapestry; Navy; Norman Conquest; Sutton Hoo; Trade; Vikings

Shires

The word "shire" (OE *scir,* originally meaning something separated off) was used of a variety of small governmental districts in the pre-Conquest period. Shires in the later sense of administrative counties apparently existed south of the Thames, in Wessex, by the end of the 8th century; here they were based closely on early tribal areas. Farther north most were created in the 10th century or early 11th, after the kings of Wessex had extended political control over England as a whole, often in succession to the Danes. These shires were deliberately imposed, many without reference to previous tribal groupings, and most (like Cambridgeshire and Oxfordshire) taking the name of the town that was the administrative and military focus. After the Conquest the Normans recognized the value of the shire and equated it with the term for the basic Frankish administrative unit: *comitatus,* or county. Cumberland, Westmorland, and Lancashire were the last to be organized as counties, in the mid-12th century.

The shire played a vital role in medieval government, particularly through its court, which (by the 13th century) met every four weeks and at which most tenants-in-chief were represented. The shire court was essential to the process of civil and criminal law, the sheriff dealing with lesser cases himself and preparing the way for the hearings of the justices in eyre (from the 12th century) and the justices of the peace (from the 14th). The court was also the place where announcements were made on behalf of the king, juries were empaneled, land transactions witnessed, outlawry proclaimed, and (from the mid-13th century) knights of the shire elected to parliament.

Central government found shires the most convenient unit for assessing, collecting, and recording financial dues, including the "shire farm" (covering income from royal estates and certain customary payments) and various sorts of taxation. It is significant that Domesday Book (1086), though a record of landholder's estates, is arranged by shires; without the administrative machinery provided by sheriff and shire court the survey would have been impossible.

G.J. White

Bibliography

Harding, Alan. *The Law Courts of Medieval England.* London: Allen & Unwin, 1973; Stenton, F.M. *Anglo-Saxon England.* Oxford History of England 2. 3d ed. Oxford: Clarendon, 1971 [chs. 9, 10, and 15 cover the topic]; Taylor, Charles S. "The Origin of the Mercian Shires." In *Gloucestershire Studies,* ed. H.P.R. Finberg. Leicester: Leicester University Press, 1957, pp. 17–51; Warren, W.L. *The Governance of Norman and Angevin England, 1086–1272.* London: Arnold, 1987.

See also Hundreds; Local Government; Parliament; Parliamentary Elections; Sheriff

Shirley, John (ca. 1366–1456)

An important copyist of the works of Chaucer and others, of particular significance for his copies of a number of Chaucer's works and for his ascriptions of some of those works to Chaucer. After service with Richard Beauchamp Shirley seems to have become involved with the London book trade. The terms of his involvement remain unclear. What is clear is that he copied a number of important collections of contemporary or near-contemporary literary works and that these and other collections copied by him (now lost) circulated extensively. His main surviving collections include Bodl. Ashmole 59; Cambridge, Trinity College R.3.20; BL Add. 16165; and Sion College Arc. L 40.2/E.44. These manuscripts include a number of Chaucer's shorter poems and his prose *Boece.* Some short poems, like "Adam Scriveyn" and "Gentilesse," are included in Chaucer's canon solely on Shirley's authority.

Shirley's manuscripts—and those derived from them—often have lengthy circumstantial rubrics that provide our only sense of the occasions of a number of works by Chaucer and Lydgate. How Shirley acquired his information and the purposes that led him to copy his manuscripts are uncertain. Although he evidently had connections with the London book trade, his activities may not have been commercial in impulse. But whatever his motivation, he played a major role in the consolidation of the reputations of Chaucer and Lydgate in the 15th century.

A.S.G. Edwards

Bibliography

New *CBEL* 1:693; *Manual* 4:1062–66, 1286–89; Boffey, Julia. *Manuscripts of English Courtly Love Lyrics in the Later Middle Ages.* Cambridge: Brewer, 1985; Brusendorff, Aage. *The Chaucer Tradition.* London: Humphrey Milford, 1925; Doyle, A.I. "More Light on John Shirley." *MÆ* 30 (1961): 93–101; Griffiths, Jeremy. "A Newly Identified Manuscript Inscribed by John Shirley." *The Library,* 6th ser. 14 (1992): 83–90; Lerer, Seth. *Chaucer and His Readers.* Princeton: Princeton University Press, 1993.

See also Chaucer; Chaucerian Apocrypha; Lydgate

Siege of Jerusalem, The

An unrhymed alliterative romance (ca. 1390) narrating in graphic detail the destruction of Jerusalem by Titus and Vespasian in the 1st century A.D. Its author is unknown, but the original dialect of the poem was probably Northwest Midland. The poem survives in eight manuscripts, all differing significantly in length and content. The widely varying dialects and dates of these manuscripts suggest broad dispersal across England throughout the 15th century.

The poem is approximately 1,300 lines long and is written in four-line units. It depicts in anachronistically chivalric terms the war fought by the Romans to avenge Christ's death. The poem begins with events preliminary to the war: Titus learns of the miracles of Christ, becomes a Christian, and is healed of cancer; he orders Veronica, who possesses a sacred veil bearing Christ's image, to be brought to Rome, where her veil cures Vespasian, Titus's father, of wasps in the nose. Titus and Vespasian vow revenge on the Jews who killed Christ, and the rest of the poem concerns the siege of Jerusalem, the Jews' terrible suffering from famine, and their defeat.

The primary source for the *Siege* is the Latin prose text *Vindicta salvatoris,* but the poet also borrows extensively from Higden's *Polychronicon,* the *Legenda aurea* of Jacobus de Voragine, and the French Bible of Roger d'Argenteuil. Related works include *Titus and Vespasian* (a longer but less effective couplet version of the story, written ca. 1400 and extant in eleven manuscripts), and a prose version (ca. 1470).

Deborah Everhart

Bibliography

PRIMARY

Kölbing, Eugen, and Mabel Day, eds. *The Siege of Jerusalem.* EETS o.s. 188. London: Humphrey Milford, 1932.

SECONDARY

New *CBEL* 1:452–53; *Manual* 1:160–62, 319–21.

See also Alliterative Revival; Bible in ME Literature; Chronicles; Hagiography; Romances

Signet

When the privy seal, its keeper, and associated paraphernalia passed out of the royal household to permanent headquarters at Westminster in the reign of Edward III—as had the great seal and chancery earlier—there arose a need for a seal immediately available for the king's use.

A small or secret royal seal was not a novelty, but in the latter part of Edward's reign a seal, gradually known officially as the signet, emerged as a regular cog in the administrative machine. It required time and experimentation before the signet seal, in the custody of the secretary (a recognized dependent of the king), was fully accepted in the administrative routine of the kingdom. The development was uneven but apparent from the reign of Richard II into the 15th century, and Edward IV used the signet extensively. Under Edward IV and Richard III it gained importance at the expense of the privy seal, although the glory days of the signet would come under the Tudor monarchs. No clear line was drawn between the competence of each seal; but more important matters, such as might come before the king's council or the exchequer, would more likely be set in motion by privy-seal letters, and less important matters or business more private to the king would be initiated by signet letters. The seal used would often even be a matter of mere convenience.

Signet letters were used for diplomatic letters, communicating instructions to individuals and local units of government, appeals for troops, setting the privy-seal office in motion, instructions related to chamber finance and royal revenue, the administration of crown lands, and the distribution of royal patronage or any other private business.

The duties of the secretary, beyond keeping the signet seal, were not clearly defined, though his work was necessarily confidential and he was a member of the king's household. The Black Book of the household, compiled in the early 1470s, indicated that the staff of the signet office, in addition to the secretary himself, included four senior clerks, three lesser or apprentice clerks, and servants. This entire staff would travel with the royal household. The signet records not regularly needed were initially stored in Windsor Castle and then at the Banqueting House at Whitehall, where they were destroyed when that building burned in 1619; thus no extensive signet archive survives.

A. Compton Reeves

Bibliography

Chrimes, Stanley B. *An Introduction to the Administrative History of Mediaeval England.* 3d ed. Oxford: Blackwell,

1966; Horrox, Rosemary, and Peter W. Hammond, eds. *British Library Harleian Manuscript 433.* 4 vols. Gloucester: Sutton, published for the Richard III Society, 1979–83; Kirby, John L., ed. *Calendar of Signet Letters of Henry IV and Henry V (1399–1422).* London: HMSO, 1978; Otway-Ruthven, A.J. *The King's Secretary and the Signet Office in the XV Century.* Cambridge: Cambridge University Press, 1939.

See also Chancellor and Chancery; Great Seal; Privy Seal; Seals

Simon de Montfort, Earl of Leicester (ca. 1208–1265)

A younger son of the Simon de Montfort who led the crusade against the Albigensian heretics in southern France, he first came to England in 1230 to pursue a family claim to the earldom of Leicester. Simon quickly won King Henry III's favor, secured the family inheritance, and married the king's sister in 1238. He thus aroused the resentment of established baronial families, who saw him as a self-seeking interloper. But his political career followed a path different from that of Henry's other favorites.

Simon was a proud, ambitious, and self-confident man who developed strong ecclesiastical friendships. Although he was at the center of affairs in the 1240s and 1250s, he came to despise Henry's military incapacity and to condemn his conduct of government. In 1258 he joined other magnates in imposing baronial government upon the king in the Provisions of Oxford. When Henry plotted to regain his power, Simon emerged as the chief advocate of the Provisions and Henry's implacable enemy. He rejected the arbitration of Louis IX of France and, though outnumbered, defeated Henry at the Battle of Lewes, 14 May 1264.

Simon now virtually ruled England, with the king as his prisoner, but he could not legitimize his authority. Faced with the hostility of the pope and most of the barons, he tried to strengthen his position by including representatives of the towns and counties in the parliament of January 1265, the first time they had been convened together. Simon's position weakened as some of his supporters deserted him, complaining of his arrogance and use of power to enrich his family; he was defeated and killed at the Battle of Evesham, 4 August 1265.

For some years he was popularly venerated as a saint who had died for the liberties of the realm. It was, in reality, the king's need for taxation that ensured the development of the medieval parliament, not Simon's novel expedient of convening all the interested parties, simultaneously, in 1265.

C.H. Knowles

Bibliography

Bemont, Charles. *Simon de Montfort, Earl of Leicester, 1208–1265.* New ed. Trans. Ernest F. Jacob. Oxford: Clarendon, 1930; Carpenter, D.A. "Simon de Montfort: The First Leader of a Political Movement in English History." *History* 76 (1991): 3–23; Knowles, C.H. *Simon de Montfort, 1265–1965.* London: Historical Association, 1965 [covers Simon's changing reputation]; Labarge, Margaret Wade. *Simon de Montfort.* London: Eyre & Spottiswoode, 1962; Maddicott, J.R. *Simon de Montfort.* Cambridge: Cambridge University Press, 1994 [the best account of his life].

See also Baronial Reform; Battles of Lewes and Evesham; Henry III; Parliament

Sir Orfeo

An anonymous narrative poem of about 600 lines in octosyllabic couplets, composed in the Westminster-Middlesex area, probably in the early 14th century. It survives in three manuscripts: Auchinleck (Edinburgh, National Library of Scotland Advocates' 19.2.1), ca. 1330–40; BL Harley 3810, early 15th century; and Bodl. Ashmole 61, late 15th century. The poem tells the story of Orfeo, king of Thrace, identified in the Auchinleck text as Winchester. Orfeo's queen, Heurodis, falls into the power of the fairies by sleeping under an orchard tree in the middle of the day and is carried off by them. Distraught, Orfeo leaves the kingdom in the hands of his steward and goes to live in the forest, where his only pleasure is in playing his harp to an enthusiastic audience of wild creatures. One day he sees the fairy ladies and Heurodis with them. He follows them through a cliff into fairyland, where he plays his harp so beautifully that the fairy king offers him anything he chooses as a reward, and in this way he wins Heurodis back. They return to their kingdom, to the joy of the faithful steward and the people.

A prologue identifying the poem as being based on a Breton lay occurs in the Harley and Ashmole texts and may once have existed in the Auchinleck copy. The poem seems to be more immediately derived, whether directly or not, from a French-language original, perhaps the *lai d'Orphey* referred to in three French works. The names indicate an indebtedness to the classical story of Orpheus and Eurydice, but the fairy apparatus is Celtic. Both Orfeo's kingship and Heurodis's safe return can be paralleled in Celtic folktales of stolen women. Both, however, can equally be accounted for by Christian developments of the Orpheus tradition: since Orpheus was used as a figure variously for Christ and for David, he could have been regarded as a king by a typological analogy with either, and success in saving his wife would have followed from the doctrinal imperative that Christ should succeed in saving his bride, the church. Either the Celtic or the christianized classical background may thus appear dominant. There is of course a general fondness in folktale and romance for royal protagonists and happy endings; and the fact that Orfeo is a king contextualizes the central story in an exemplary account of the relationship between a king and his subjects, an issue of great concern in medieval England. Other major themes explored, though without overt didacticism, include love, honor, and the impact of the irrational on the rational world. Various allegorical readings have been suggested. The basic appeal of the poem, however, probably continues to lie in the skillful handling of the plot, maximizing the inherent interest and suspense, and the imaginative depiction of psychologically credible characters in crisis.

The story of *Sir Orfeo* is also found in fragments of a Scots narrative poem, *King Orphius,* and in two versions of a Scots ballad, *King Orfeo.*

Diane Speed

Bibliography

PRIMARY

Bliss, A.J., ed. *Sir Orfeo.* 2d ed. Oxford: Clarendon, 1966.

SECONDARY

New *CBEL* 1:437–38; *Manual* 1:135–36, 293–94; Allen, Doreena. "Orpheus and Orfeo: The Dead and the Taken." *MÆ* 33 (1964): 102–11; Friedman, John B. *Orpheus in the Middle Ages.* Cambridge: Harvard University Press, 1970; Hynes-Berry, Mary. "Cohesion in *King Horn* and *Sir Orfeo.*" *Speculum* 50 (1975): 652–70; Rice, Joanne A. *Middle English Romance: An Annotated Bibliography, 1955–1985.* New York: Garland, 1987, pp. 481–501.

See also Allegory; Ballads; Breton Lay; Literary Influences: Classical, French; Romances; Scottish Literature, Early; Winchester

Skelton, John (ca. 1460–1529)

Tudor satirist and panegyrist. Born of a northern, possibly Yorkshire, family, Skelton was educated first at Cambridge and may be identified with the "Skelton" who was recorded as about to take his B.A. in 1480. Later he was at Oxford, where in about 1488 he was granted the title of "laureate," a degree or diploma in rhetoric. The universities of Louvain, in 1492, and Cambridge, in 1493, granted him the same title. He came to prominence in the royal service, where he was tutor to Prince Henry (later Henry VIII) ca. 1496–1501. He became a priest in 1498 and left court in about 1503 to become rector of Diss (Norfolk), a living he retained throughout his life. But he returned to court in 1512–13 and lived the rest of his life in or around Westminster.

His earliest known work is an English prose translation of Poggio's version of Diodorus Siculus's *Bibliotheca historia,* finished probably in 1488 and praised by Caxton in the Prologue to the *Eneydos.* Skelton's surviving works are mostly in verse, and since he was essentially a public poet he dealt in praise and blame, panegyric and satire, in both Latin and English. His earliest known poem, *Upon the Dolorous Death . . . of the . . . Earl of Northumberland,* laments in rime royal stanzas the murder of Henry Percy by a Yorkshire mob in 1489. From the 1490s come two collections of lyrics dealing mainly with the courtly and metropolitan underclass of aspiring courtiers, musicians, servants, soldiers, and prostitutes, and *The Bouge of Court,* an accomplished and devastating anticourtly satire in dream-vision form.

The poems written during Skelton's residence at Diss are again satiric, but in them he abandons rime royal for the more demotic "Skeltonic" form—leashes, or groups, of short rhyming lines, usually having two or three stresses. When he returned to court, he styled himself *orator regius* and, as the

title suggests, wrote mainly propaganda on Henry VIII's behalf—principally satires against the Scots and French. But from this period, from 1519–20, also comes his elaborate morality play *Magnificence,* an affectionate warning to the king to beware of flatterers and to control the expenditure of his household. From 1521–23 come three remarkable satires attacking the policies, style, and personality of Henry VIII's chief minister, Cardinal Thomas Wolsey: *Speak Parrot, Collyn Clout,* and *Why Come Ye Not to Court?*

In the autumn of 1523 Skelton returned to rime royal and the dream vision in *The Garland of Laurel,* where he reviews his poetic career and seeks to establish his claim to fame. Surprisingly the poem is dedicated to Wolsey, so there must have been a rapprochement, though in what circumstances is not known. And Skelton's last two poems—written on behalf of state and church, against a failed Scottish invasion in 1523 and against two Cambridge heretics in 1528—are again dedicated to Wolsey.

In a typical 15th- or early-16th-century manner Skelton invokes Gower, Chaucer, and Lydgate as his masters, but he sees himself in other roles, too—the English Juvenal or the divinely inspired *vates* (poet-prophet). His restlessness and capacity for bold innovation make Skelton one of the most original and interesting late-medieval poets.

V. J. Scattergood

Bibliography

PRIMARY

Scattergood, [V.] John, ed. *John Skelton: The Complete English Poems.* New Haven: Yale University Press, 1983.

SECONDARY

New *CBEL* 1:1015–19; Fish, Stanley Eugene. *John Skelton's Poetry.* New Haven: Yale University Press, 1965; Fox, Alistair, and Gregory Waite, eds. *A Concordance to the Complete English Poems of John Skelton.* Ithaca: Cornell University Press, 1987; Kinsman, Robert S. *John Skelton, Early Tudor Laureate: An Annotated Bibliography c. 1488–1977.* Boston: Hall, 1979; Walker, Greg. *John Skelton and the Politics of the 1520's.* Cambridge: Cambridge University Press, 1988.

See also Caxton; Drama, Vernacular; Dream Vision; Lydgate; Satire

Slavery and Slaves

Already known in Roman and Celtic Britain, slavery continued to exist in England from the coming of the Anglo-Saxons until the 12th century. Yet we know of no document written by a slave; only an imagined conversation with a plowman lamenting his lot in Ælfric's *Colloquy* permits us a brief moment of empathy.

Slavery under the Anglo-Saxons was essentially an agrarian phenomenon. Little is known about the living conditions of slaves in the early period, but by the 11th century they resided in their own dwellings. Alfred's laws permitted them to keep what they earned on certain holidays, and the

Rectitudines singularum personarum (ca. 1000–50?) reveals that they were entitled to food rations. Though slaves had thus acquired certain rights by the 11th century, theirs was the lowest rank in the social hierarchy. Instead of being permitted by law to make a monetary compensation for a wrong committed, they were usually punished by a lashing. This distinctive penalty shows that the law considered them "outsiders," devoid of many of the rights of the humblest free person. In legal terms they were largely chattels. There are reports of slaves being stolen.

The *Rectitudines* indicates that male slaves could be beekeepers and swineherds. Domesday Book implies that their most characteristic role was that of a plowman. Usually such plowmen worked in pairs on the lord's home farm or demesne. Female slaves performed domestic tasks and were dairymaids. These were mostly occupations with daily responsibilities.

People became slaves in several ways. Warfare was a fruitful source throughout the Anglo-Saxon period. Crime and debt led others into slavery. Sheer starvation caused by agrarian disaster or social upheaval must also have prompted some to enslave themselves to survive.

Slaves were freed or manumitted in various ways. Manumission at the altar was a common form. Slaves were also liberated symbolically at crossroads, a practice derived perhaps from Lombard Italy. Manumission documents exist from the 10th century on, and evidence from East Anglian wills shows that manumission was common in the early 11th century. By the time of Domesday Book (1086) slaves formed only 10 percent of the recorded population, though they were unevenly distributed, with the largest percentage being in the southwest, an area conquered rather late by the Anglo-Saxons.

Thereafter slavery disappeared rapidly. There are several probable reasons for this. Opposition from prominent clerics discouraged the slave trade. Norman control and subsequent domination of the surrounding seas inhibited enslavement through capture in raids. A rise in population perhaps encouraged Norman overlords to have their demesnes farmed by free labor in return for rents and services, rather than by slaves who had to be fed daily. Foreign landowners, furthermore, probably had little grasp of the outsider status of slaves and instead regarded those on their estates in terms of occupational function rather than legal status. The institution was almost extinct by the end of the reign of Henry I.

David A.E. Pelteret

Bibliography

Finberg, H.P.R. "Anglo-Saxon England to 1042." In *The Agrarian History of England and Wales.* Vol. I.ii: *A.D. 43–1042.* London: Cambridge University Press, 1972, pp. 383–525; Moore, John S. "Domesday Slavery." *Anglo-Norman Studies* 11 (1989): 191–220; Pelteret, David A.E. "Slave Raiding and Slave Trading in Early England." *ASE* 9 (1980): 99–114; Pelteret, David A.E. *Slavery in Early Mediaeval England: From the Reign of Alfred until the Twelfth Century.* Woodbridge: Boydell, 1995; Whitelock, Dorothy, ed. *English Historical Documents.* Vol. 1: *c. 500–1042.* 2d ed. London: Eyre Methuen, 1979 [contains translations of laws, wills, manumissions, and the *Rectitudines*].

See also Serfs and Villeins

Solomon and Saturn

Solomon and another wise man named Saturn figure in a number of so-called dialogues in OE literature. The two verse texts, *Solomon and Saturn I* and *II,* copied in a mid-10th-century hand in Cambridge, Corpus Christi College 422, are separated from each other by a fragmentary prose "dialogue." (The first 93 lines of *Solomon and Saturn I* also appear in Cambridge, Corpus Christi College 41.) Another text, the prose *Solomon and Saturn,* was copied in the mid-12th century in BL Cotton Vitellius A.xv, fols. 86v–93v. The single point of agreement among these works is the names of the participants in the "dialogues," but this agreement distinguishes the English works from analogues (in Latin, French, and German) on the Continent. Continental dialogues, considerably postdating those in OE, generally match Solomon with an opponent called Marcholfus or Marcol, and their subject matter is humorous or even ribald.

Solomon and Saturn I and its following prose fragment explore the powers of the Pater Noster (the Lord's Prayer or Our Father) in putting the Devil to flight. While both works conceptualize the Pater Noster as a material being, their emphases are significantly different. *Solomon and Saturn I* focuses on the Pater Noster as a written prayer, whose correct recitation will vanquish the Devil. The prayer's power resides in its individual letters, which the poem visualizes as attacking the Devil with various weapons. The prose fragment enumerates the shapes the Pater Noster will assume in its struggles with the Devil and ascribes to it a fantasized body of enormous proportions. *Solomon and Saturn II* is less clearly focused than the two "dialogues" that precede it in the manuscript. The encounter between the two wise men begins as a riddle contest but changes, in the latter part of the poem, into a dialogue where Saturn poses difficult questions for Solomon. The subjects of the exchange include the exotic (the whale-bodied bird called "Vasa Mortis"), the traditional (fate, old age, death), and what might loosely be termed "theological" (the fall of the angels and the origin of evil). The poem has been substantially affected by losses in the manuscript at three points.

The late OE text generally known as the prose *Solomon and Saturn* has no connection with the previously discussed dialogues other than the names of the participants, mentioned only in the opening sentence of the piece. This work is a collection of 59 questions and answers, generally cast in the form "Tell me. . . . I tell you. . . ." They demonstrate a broad, detailed knowledge of the Bible as well as of apocryphal material, and many questions are related to the *Joca monachorum,* a Latin collection of puzzling questions and answers. The prose *Solomon and Saturn* shares a number of questions with another late OE collection, the *Adrian and Ritheus,* but the different phrasings of the shared questions and answers indicate that the two texts did not have a common exemplar.

Katherine O'Brien O'Keeffe

Bibliography

PRIMARY

ASPR 6:31–48; Cross, James E., and Thomas D. Hill, eds. *The Prose Solomon and Saturn and Adrian and Ritheus.* Toronto: University of Toronto Press, 1982; Menner, Robert J., ed. *The Poetical Dialogues of Solomon and Saturn.* New York: MLA, 1941; Shippey, T.A., ed. and trans. *Poems of Wisdom and Learning in Old English.* Cambridge: Brewer, 1976, pp. 21–28, 86–103 [*Solomon and Saturn II*, with discussion].

SECONDARY

Nelson, Marie. "King Solomon's Magic: The Power of a Written Text." *Oral Tradition* 5 (1990): 20–36; O'Keeffe, Katherine O'Brien. "Source, Method, Theory, Practice—On Reading Two Old English Verse Texts." *BJRL* 76 (1994): 51–73.

See also Adrian and Ritheus; Debate Poems; Riddles; Wisdom Literature

Songs

Pre-Conquest

Anglo-Saxon musical life has left us little tangible evidence. There are no musical settings of OE texts and no genuine vernacular lyrics. The surviving OE poetry is a lettered and learned corpus, sober and bookish. Yet this poetry gives us several points of entry into the faintly heard world of song. It may itself contain traces of lost songs—words, phrases, verse types, rhetoric, or expressions that provide embedded glimpses of lost lyrical traditions.

Though some genres of OE poetry always may have been spoken aloud to—or read privately by—their aristocratic and monastic audiences, the public (often ceremonial) performance of epic narrative by gleoman or scop was musical. Here a pair of critical problems still vex modern scholars and remain open questions. If narrative poems were songs, then how were they performed (recited or fully sung, with metrical or free rhythms, with some kind of accompaniment on the harp)? And are epics like *Beowulf* likely to have been sung in their surviving forms, or are these monumental written formulations one or more steps removed from previous singable versions in an oral tradition (and indeed, to what degree does the use of formulas or oral-formulaic methods of composition necessarily imply musical delivery)?

Stepping back onto firmer ground, we can see that OE poetry, along with other vernacular and Latin literature of the period, documents the breadth and variety of musical practice in Anglo-Saxon England. The scop, teller of heroic deeds, sang songs of the ancient heroes, war songs and victory odes, laments at the death of kings and warriors, and praises for hosts, their present families, and their forebears. The gleoman had such eulogistic and narrative songs in his repertoire but added a wide range of convivial songs to be sung purely for entertainment (and remuneration) by the hearth in hall or tavern. And amateurs, from rustics to kings, sang their songs in court, town, and countryside, at work or play, including metrical charms and incantations, and the dance songs of women.

In later Anglo-Saxon England trained clerical singers entertained themselves with Latin songs drawn from an international tradition. A unique glimpse of this nonliturgical music is afforded us by the "Cambridge Songs," 49 lyrics plus a few other scattered additions copied into a schoolbook from a German exemplar at St. Augustine's, Canterbury, in the mid-11th century (CUL Gg.v.35). Only a few of the lyrics are provided with musical notation, and their neumes are imprecise as to pitch; however, four lyrics have a tune name attached, and the general impression is that all were intended to be sung. They show a variety of verse types, prominent among which is paired-versicle or sequence form, and from limited evidence it would seem that although some of the tunes were florid, the prevailing style was syllabic (one note to one syllable). Subject matter ranges from love songs, narrative fables, and celebratory or political songs, to hymns of Prudentius and settings of the meters from Boethius's *Consolation of Philosophy.* The overall impression is of a serious and learned Latin art song.

1066–1380

There are virtually no extant traces of secular song during the first 100 years of Norman rule, when the new aristocracy introduced its own familiar forms of domestic and public music making. The brilliant court and lavish patronage of Henry II and Eleanor of Aquitaine, however, attracted a stellar group of writers working in Anglo-Norman, Middle English, and Latin. Much of their output, both lyric and narrative, was intended in the first place for musical delivery. The notorious domestic and dynastic struggles of Henry, Eleanor, and their progeny became the subject of a substantial repertoire of songs by the leading troubadours and trouvères of the later 12th century, writing in Provençal, French, and even Italian. Richard I was himself an active poet-musician.

Over the next century and a half, despite copious documentation for the activities of Anglo-Norman trouvères and minstrels, some itinerant and some attached to households of the secular and ecclesiastical aristocracy, little Anglo-Norman courtly poetry survives with musical notation—just some twenty-odd Anglo-Norman lyrics with monophonic melodies found on flyleaves, binding strips, and isolated stray scraps of parchment. (These songs have yet to be collected, edited, and studied as a group.) In only a single instance (Bodl. Rawlinson G.22) does any of the fragments appear to have originated in a substantial chansonnier. Another leaf, now preserved at the Public Record Office in London (E163/22/1/2), records a prize-winning song crowned at a meeting of the London *puy,* a kind of middle-class guild active at the end of the 13th century that promoted the art of courtly love song. Like many medieval lyric genres, including the Latin conductus, the French motet, and continental trouvère song, collections of texts without music also survive, assembling Anglo-Norman lyrics (of widely varied subject matter and tone) along with English verse in well-known anthology manuscripts.

The survival rate for polyphonic settings of courtly Anglo-Norman lyrics in the 14th century is even worse than for the earlier monophonic songs—none at all was known until the discovery in the 1980s of a single fragmentary mid-century insular source (BL Add. 41340 [H]) containing two-voice settings of *forme fixe* poetry, apparently mainly rondeaux. Thus, though there may have been no figure at the English court comparable to the great French poet-musician Guillaume de Machaut, from whom Chaucer and Gower learned so much (as lyric poets, not musicians), we have tantalizing evidence that the lively court culture under Edward III and Richard II may not have been as barren of high-class courtly secular polyphony as it once appeared to be.

Songs with English words from before ca. 1400 are comparable in some respects to those in Anglo-Norman. The known repertoire is similar in size (some twenty-odd songs, only recently collected and edited by Dobson and Harrison), in circumstances of preservation (fugitive traces on scattered leaves), and in the existence of a larger body of lyrics not copied with music (secular, religious, devotional, historical, political) that are found systematically assembled in large anthologies—often in conjunction with Anglo-Norman verse. Strikingly at odds with the Anglo-Norman songs is the lack of refined poetry in the high style dealing with courtly love. The predominant tone of these ME settings is one of pious devotion, particularly to Mary, or a concern with Christ's suffering on the Cross (e.g., "Edi beo thu, heven quene" or "The milde Lomb, isprad o roode"). Only four songs (or five, counting the canon "Sumer is icumen in," which also has a sacred contrafact text in Latin) are on secular rather than sacred subjects. Two of these are monophonic ("Miri it is while sumer ilast" and "Brid one breere"), and two are in simple two-voice polyphony ("Fuweles in the frith" and "Lou, lou, lou! wer he goth!"). None adopts a courtly register or approaches the compositional sophistication of the Sumer Canon. Only at the end of the 14th century, in the Winchester Songbook, do we find songs in English related musically to an international tradition of courtly polyphonic song.

Songs of courtly love and religious devotion are most likely to have been committed to paper together with their melodies by clerks who possessed the necessary training to do so. Less apt to be preserved is the vast corpus of less refined popular song, about which our principal sources of knowledge are conventionalized literary descriptions and hostile clerical fulminations. Most frequently described and decried were the dance songs, the karoles in French and English, which constituted one of the principal forms of secular entertainment music in the later Middle Ages. These survive mainly as texts, though there are a fairly small number of notated refrains and refrain songs from this genre in continental sources. Other shorter popular lyrics, the staple of amateur and minstrel alike, are known only from scraps and snatches. Franciscan sermons are a rich source of lyric fragments. In the Red Book of Ossory Bishop Richard Ledrede of Ossory (d. 1360) provides text tags in English and Anglo-Norman for twelve of his 60 Latin hymns, thus preserving in Latin verse only the poetic form and accentual stress patterns of the vernacular original. Insular

motets of the later 13th and early 14th centuries often use a popular song as their tenor, sometimes providing the whole text though more often identifying the melody simply by a short tag (e.g., "Dou way Robin"; "Wynter"; "Va dorenlot"; "Mariounette douche").

Balancing the stock of refined and popular lyrics in the repertoire of the itinerant minstrel was narrative song. Minstrel versions may be mainly lost to us, but the vast hoard of lengthy metrical romances in Anglo-Norman and ME surviving from the later 13th century onward is testimony to the enduring popularity of narrative genres, and though this literature survives without melodies, some of it may originally have been sung rather than spoken. Even closer to the oral tradition are shorter narrative songs, the ME ballads, whose roots go back at least into the 13th century and which begin to emerge into the written record, stripped of their melodies, in the 15th century.

The last major repertoire to be mentioned here is nonliturgical Anglo-Latin song, a rich but understudied topic. Latin song flourished in England particularly from the later 12th century through the 14th; its poets deployed rhyme, accent, and syllable count to fashion complex verse in a wide variety of strophic, refrain, and sequence-type forms. Subject matter is of tremendous range, from contemporary politics and propaganda to religious devotions, philosophy, moral satire, love poetry, humorous stories, and drinking songs. As with the vernacular songs Latin lyrics survive in major insular sources of varied character and contents, some with, but most without, notation. This material still needs to be sorted out historically and geographically and studied in relation to the well-known continental anthologies with which it shares many concordances. Latin song was international in character, with wide circulation of conductus and cantio, Latin lai, planctus, and devotional song. This makes it difficult, and perhaps an issue of only limited interest or potential, to separate out the distinctively insular features of Anglo-Latin poets writing for a transnational, often university-educated, latinate readership. There were, however, two purely local genres setting Latin texts but not circulating abroad: the insular motet and the Latin carol.

1380–1485

Apart from the carol the vernacular song repertoire of these years is almost entirely of secular love lyrics, in or related to the fixed forms, with polyphonic music in two or three voices. The music belongs both in style and in function to a relatively unified repertoire reaching across Europe and numbering well over 2,000 pieces for these years. But the surviving insular sources are few. From the first quarter of the 15th century are four parchment leaves in the Bodleian (Douce 381, fols. 20–23), containing five English songs, two French songs, and one Latin piece, perhaps for keyboard; and a group of songs in Cambridge (CUL Add. 5943, fols. 161–169), with ten English songs, four French songs, and three Latin pieces. From the middle years of the century there are a further six leaves in the Bodleian (Ashmole 191, fols. 191–196), containing all or part of seven English songs, and eight songs assembled together within the Ritson Manuscript (BL Add. 5665, fols.

65v–73). A handful of songs were added later to the Ritson Manuscript, two added to the Selden Manuscript (Bodl. Selden arch, B.26, fols. 32v–33), and some in the Fayrfax Manuscript (BL Add. 5465) that could date from before 1485. The rest is a group of widely dispersed fragments or single leaves, adding perhaps a dozen more songs in varying states of completion. They make a scattered bunch.

But the picture can be expanded by cautious reference to continental sources in an age when English music circulated widely abroad. Some pieces appear with bits of garbled English text. Rather more have ascriptions to English composers (John Bedyngham, John Dunstable, Walter Frye, Robert Morton, Robertus de Anglia, Galfridus de Anglia, John Hothby), often with music for which the surviving Latin, Italian, or French text has obviously been grafted on. A few are concordant with material actually known from English manuscripts. And the context of this body of music often makes it possible to suggest English origin for other pieces. Caution is important here, but a few outlines can be suggested.

Virelai form, or something loosely resembling it, tends to predominate in the two early-15th-century insular sources. Continental concordances and their context, particularly in the Reina Manuscript (Paris, BN n. a. fr. 6771), suggest that the years around 1400 saw the cultivation of a relatively coherent genre with gently flowing lines over a formalized tenor. The music is considerably simpler than that of most continental virelais of the time, though it comes closer to the style of Machaut (d. 1377), whose influence on Chaucer is well attested. So far as the sources permit a judgment, it seems that this genre went out of favor in England around 1415, that is, at about the time when a different adaptation of the virelai form, the carol, began suddenly to appear.

Rondeau form dominated French song during the years 1420–50, and there seems a good case for thinking that it did so in England. French music was known and widely circulated in England. There is increasing evidence of contact with the Burgundian court composer Binchois (ca. 1400–1460), some of whose works were known in England or are found in English sources; a song by Grenon (d. 1456) has been found in an English manuscript. Rondeau music appears in several English fragments from the years 1415–40, though none of them now provides a complete piece of music. These were the years when Charles of Orléans was imprisoned in England and had a substantial influence on English culture: his own poetry from those years survives in both French and English versions, with musical evidence occasionally suggesting that the English may at least have had his authority. He shows a marked preference for the rondeau, apparently influencing William de la Pole, duke of Suffolk, to use the same form. The relatively few rondeaux in the surviving English poetry sources may well conceal a wider cultivation of the genre during those years.

But the ballade and rime royal seem to have dominated English song writing from ca. 1440. This is the form of all eight songs in the Ritson Manuscript and, more loosely, of most songs in the Fayrfax Manuscript. It is also the most common form among English secular lyrics of the later 15th century. The ballade seems to have fallen out of favor with continental composers after 1440, and current thought is that many later songs in ballade form in the continental sources are of English origin. Several are ascribed to English composers, and others are so similar in style as to make English origin all but certain. Using these and similar criteria, a volume of English song, 1400–85, in preparation for the series *Musica Britannica,* will include over 140 pieces.

A few examples of this continental transmission are worth specifying. *O rosa bella,* probably by John Bedingham (though it is also ascribed to John Dunstable), appears in over a dozen continental sources from the 1440s onward; but, more important, material from it was used as the basis for almost 30 further compositions over the next quarter-century. Its Italian text, by Leonardo Giustinian, had been set earlier and seems to have been misapplied to the English piece, which may therefore have had an English text that is now lost for lack of any insular source. The ballade "So ys emprentid in my remembrance," also probably by Bedyngham (but possibly by Walter Frye), does have a garbled version of its English text in the Neapolitan Mellon Chansonnier, but it also appears in a frenchification that opens "Soyez aprentis en amours," with another French text opening "Pour une suis desconfortee," and with the Latin text "Sancta Maria succurre." Walter Frye's *Ave regina celorum,* in ballade form and also perhaps originally composed for an English text, survives in over twenty continental sources (including the roof of a Loire château chapel), thus having more sources than any other piece of its generation. And one of the most stylistically puzzling songs of the century is the ballade-form work in one of the Trent codices with a text opening, apparently, "Agwillare habeth standiff."

Peter M. Lefferts
David Fallows

Bibliography

PRE-CONQUEST

Opland, Jeff. *Anglo-Saxon Oral Poetry: A Study of the Traditions.* New Haven: Yale University Press, 1980; Page, Christopher. "Music." *The Cambridge Guide to the Arts in Britain.* Vol. 1: *Prehistoric, Roman, and Early Medieval,* ed. Boris Ford. Cambridge: Cambridge University Press, 1988, pp. 247–53, 294–95 [includes bibliography]; Stevens, John. "The Cambridge Songs" and "The Old English Period." In *Words and Music in the Middle Ages: Song, Narrative, Dance and Drama 1050–1350.* Cambridge: Cambridge University Press, 1986, pp. 114–19, 204–12.

1066–1380

Dean, Ruth. *A Catalogue of Works in Anglo-Norman* (in preparation); Dobson, Eric J., and Frank Ll. Harrison, eds. and trans. *Medieval English Songs.* London: Faber & Faber, 1979; Page, Christopher. "A Catalogue and Bibliography of English Song from Its Beginnings to c. 1300." *Royal Musical Association Research Chronicle* 13 (1976): 67–83; Page, Christopher. "Secular Music." In *The Cambridge Guide to the Arts in Britain.* Vol. 2: *The Middle Ages,* ed. Boris Ford. Cambridge: Cambridge

University Press, 1988, pp. 235–50, 280–81 [includes bibliography and discography]; Stevens, John. *Words and Music in the Middle Ages: Song, Narrative, Dance and Drama, 1050–1350.* Cambridge: Cambridge University Press, 1986; Stevens, John. "Alphabetical Check-List of Anglo-Norman Songs *c.* 1150–*c.* 1350." *Plainsong and Medieval Music* 3 (1994): 1–22.

1380–1485

Boffey, Julia. *Manuscripts of English Courtly Love Lyrics in the Later Middle Ages.* Woodbridge: Brewer, 1985; Dobson, Eric J., and Frank Ll. Harrison, eds. and trans. *Medieval English Songs.* London: Faber & Faber, 1979; Fallows, David. "English Song Repertories of the Mid-Fifteenth Century." *Proceedings of the Royal Musical Association* 103 (1976–77): 61–79; Fallows, David. "Words and Music in Two English Songs of the Mid-15th Century: Charles d'Orléans and John Lydgate." *Early Music* 5 (1977): 38–43; Fallows, David. "Robertus de Anglia and the Oporto Song Collection." In *Source Materials and the Interpretation of Music: A Memorial Volume to Thurston Dart,* ed. Ian Bent. London: Stainer & Bell, 1981, pp. 99–128; Ficker, Rudolf. "*Agwillare:* A Piece of Late Gothic Minstrelsy." *Musical Quarterly* 22 (1936): 131–39; Stainer, John, et al., eds. *Early Bodleian Music: Sacred & Secular Songs . . . in the Bodleian Library.* 3 vols. London: Novello, 1901–13. Repr. Farnborough: Gregg, 1967; Stevens, John. *Music and Poetry in the Early Tudor Court.* 2d ed. Cambridge: Cambridge University Press, 1979.

See also Alanus; *Angelus ad virginem;* Ballads; Carol; Charles of Orléans; Conductus; Dunstable; Godric's Songs; Harley 978; Karole; Lai, Latin; Lyrics; Minstrels; Morton; Motet; Planctus; *Puy;* Sequence; *Sub arturo plebs;* Sumer Canon; Winchester Songbook

Soul and Body I and II

An important exemplar of the soul-and-body theme in medieval literature and one of the few OE poems to survive in two separate manuscript collections of poetry—in the Vercelli Book *(Soul and Body I)* and in the Exeter Book *(Soul and Body II).*

The poem recounts the address of a damned soul to its body, after death but before the Last Judgment. The damned soul berates the body for not thinking of the soul's fate and delighting only in worldly pleasures. The soul describes the body's corruption and looks ahead to the terrible judgment it will receive; the body cannot answer, being torn apart by worms. Finally the poet describes in grisly detail the worms' attack on the body. In *Soul and Body I,* there follows a briefer, corresponding address of a blessed soul to its body: the blessed soul praises the body for its self-denial and looks forward to their glorious reunion in heaven.

Soul and Body I dates from the second half of the 10th century and may be of West Saxon or Kentish provenance; *Soul and Body II* dates from the second half of the 10th or the first half of the 11th century and is also West Saxon. Both texts show signs of corruption; neither is the exemplar of the other. Scholars differ on how the separate versions came into being: some argue for oral transmission, others for written transmission. It has also been suggested that the address of the blessed soul is a later addition to an already finished poem.

No immediate source for either version is known, although parallels to other works have been noted, including homilies, vision literature, and Egyptian lore assimilated by early Christians. The poem did not have any direct influence on later poems, although the *Soul's Address to the Body* in the Worcester Fragment and later ME poems show continued use of the theme.

Criticism of *Soul and Body* is scarce and not always sympathetic. Scholars consider the poem primarily a didactic piece but frequently express distaste for its strident tone and gruesome details. However, some critics have praised the poem's construction or argued that the damned body's silence is logical and even eloquent testimony to the justice of the soul's complaint (see Frantzen, Ferguson). Anderson sees the poem as a part of a long triple riddle that includes *Deor* and *Wulf and Eadwacer.*

Michael R. Boudreau

Bibliography

PRIMARY

ASPR 2:54–59 *(SB I),* 3:174–78 *(SB II);* Moffat, Douglas, ed. and trans. *The Old English Soul and Body.* Wolfeboro: Brewer, 1990.

SECONDARY

Anderson, James E. "*Deor, Wulf and Eadwacer,* and *The Soul's Address:* How and Where the Old English Exeter Book Riddles Begin." In *The Old English Elegies: New Essays in Criticism and Research,* ed. Martin Green. Rutherford: Fairleigh Dickinson University Press, 1983, pp. 204–30; Ferguson, Mary Howard. "The Structure of the *Soul's Address to the Body* in Old English." *JEGP* 69 (1970): 72–80; Frantzen, Allen J. "The Body in *Soul and Body I.*" *ChauR* 17 (1982): 76–88.

See also Allegory; Debate Poems; Exeter Book; Sermons; Vercelli Book

Southampton

The Anglo-Saxon settlement of *Hamwih* was situated on the east side of a small peninsula at the head of Southampton Water, with its harbor on the River Itchen. By 1000 this site had been abandoned in favor of higher land to the west, with a harbor on the River Test. Southampton's sheltered roadsteads, its unique double tides, and its proximity to Winchester (the administrative capital of Wessex) guaranteed its early growth as a commercial center and headquarters for pre-Conquest kings.

Domesday Book records Southampton as a royal borough of 76 tenants-in-chief in 1066, plus 63 "Frenchmen" and 31 English-born burgesses who had settled there by 1086. The accession of the Angevins in 1154 drew Southampton into a trading partnership with southwestern France, one of the bases of the port's later prosperity. The Angevin kings regularly visited Southampton on their way to and from the Continent and were concerned to improve the royal castle (built in the mid-12th century) and its adjacent quay. In the 14th and 15th centuries Southampton was the natural embarkation point for military expeditions to France, the most famous being Henry V's fleet, which sailed on 11 August 1415 at the start of the victorious Agincourt campaign.

Lacking industries of its own and with competing market centers at Winchester and Salisbury, Southampton's prosperity depended largely on overseas trade, ranging from the Baltic to the Mediterranean. By the early 14th century the Gascon wine trade (in exchange for wool and cloth) formed a large part of the town's livelihood and made it the major port on the south coast. The arrival of Genoese vessels at the beginning of the 14th century and of Venetian galleys in 1319 placed the port, for the first time, on the direct trade route between Italy and northern Europe, so important to it over the next two centuries.

Southampton's trade was depressed by war and plague in the mid-14th century, but prosperity returned in the late 14th century with the resumption of regular visits by Italian carracks and galleys. The town became London's principal outport for cloth and wool exports to Italy. In return Mediterranean dyestuffs, spices, sweet wines, and other luxuries were sent by cart from Southampton to London and elsewhere.

Italian agents were resident in the town to handle the trade. In the 1480s the Florentine galleys and Genoese carracks ceased to visit Southampton, and only the Venetian galleys still appeared, albeit with decreasing frequency, until 1532. English ships established a new trade between England and Italy that was largely under English control, although Italian merchants had a major share in the boom in Southampton's cloth exports in the early 16th century. Thereafter overseas trade became increasingly centered on London, and Southampton stagnated until its 19th-century trade revival.

Henry S. Cobb

Bibliography

The Southampton Record Society (Southampton, 1905–41) and the Southampton Record Series (Southampton University, 1951–) have published many of the rich sources for Southampton's urban and economic history; Davies, J. Silvester. *A History of Southampton.* Southampton: Gilbert, 1883; Platt, Colin. *Medieval Southampton: The Port and Trading Community,* A.D. *1000–1600.* London: Routledge & Kegan Paul, 1973; Ruddock, Alwyn A. *Italian Merchants and Shipping in Southampton, 1270–1600.* Southampton: University College, 1951.

See also Towns; Trade

Speculum Vitae

A long, didactic ME verse treatise on the Lord's Prayer (16,396 lines in rhyming couplets), generally attributed to William of Nassington. The poem is of northern provenance and dates from the mid-14th century. Its popularity is evidenced by the survival of 40 manuscripts.

William of Nassington is named as the author in a colophon in two manuscripts. Another names Richard Rolle as the author. Modern scholars regard Nassington as the more likely candidate, not least because his position as an advocate in the archiepiscopal court at York would fit well with the interest in canon law demonstrated in the *Speculum Vitae.* If Nassington was the author, the poem must have been written before 1359, the year of his death.

The work was examined for heresy at Cambridge in 1384. No defects were found. This is a comparatively early date for examination, which suggests that the poem was already popular and widely circulated. The history of the extant manuscripts shows that the poem circulated in religious houses and among the nobility. It was intended for both private study and for reading aloud.

The poem has a complex, carefully organized structure. It begins with some 2,000 lines devoted to *Pater* ("Father"), *Noster* ("Our"), *Qui es* ("Who art"), and *In celis* ("In heaven"); the commentary includes discussion of the Ten Commandments, the twelve articles of the Creed, the sacraments, the seven gifts of the Holy Spirit, the theological virtues (faith, hope, charity), and the cardinal virtues (justice, fortitude, prudence, temperance). The main argument of the poem is then outlined, in a passage of about 1,000 lines explaining how each of the seven petitions of the Pater Noster (e.g., "Thy kingdom come") is related to one of the gifts of the Holy Spirit. The final and longest portion of the poem expands on this outline, showing how each gift combats one of the seven deadly sins and replaces it with one of seven additional virtues (e.g., humility, mercy). Each virtue brings one of the Beatitudes and its associated reward (e.g., "Blessed are the poor in spirit for theirs is the kingdom of heaven"; cf. Matt. 5:3–10).

Despite its didactic categorizing the poem is readable and often entertaining, with exempla that bring to life characters from all social stations. The language is always simple and direct, even when the subject matter concerns difficult theological or legal points. The meter, contrary to earlier opinion, is not quite the same as that of *The Prick of Conscience,* the *Speculum* being metrically much more regular. Lines are usually seven or eight syllables long, alternating stressed and unstressed syllables.

Attempts to identify a single source for the *Speculum Vitae* have proved unsuccessful, although parallels may be drawn between the 13th-century *Somme le roi* by Friar Laurent, the several English derivatives of the *Somme,* and Richard Rolle's *Form of Living.* The colophon mentioned above cites a Latin source by John de Waldeby, a contemporary of Nassington's at York, but his *Commentary on the Paternoster* is certainly not related to the *Speculum Vitae,* nor is any other of his surviving works. There is a prose version of the *Speculum Vitae,* the *Myrour to Lewde Men and Wymmen.* It is likely that the poem is the source of the prose version rather than vice versa. Authorship of the prose version is unknown.

Nassington may also have written *The Bande of Louynge*

and the *Stimulus Conscientiae Minor. The Prick of Conscience* has been attributed to Nassington, but differences in meter, in the distribution of some frequently occurring half-lines, and especially in tone between the vivacious, if didactic, *Speculum Vitae* and the unrelievedly solemn *Prick of Conscience* make common authorship unlikely.

Christine M. Robinson

Bibliography

PRIMARY

Nelson, Venetia, ed. *A Myrour to Lewde Men and Wymmen: A Prose Version of the Speculum Vitae.* Heidelberg: Winter, 1981.

SECONDARY

Manual 7:2261–62, 2479–80; 9:3087–88, 3447; Allen, Hope Emily. "The *Speculum Vitae:* Addendum." *PMLA* 32 (1917): 133–62; Nelson, Venetia. "An Introduction to the *Speculum Vitae." Essays in Literature* (Denver) 2.3 (August 1974): 75–102; Peterson, Ingrid J. *William of Nassyngton: Canon, Mystic, and Poet of the Speculum Vitae.* New York: Lang, 1986.

See also Moral and Religious Instruction; *Prick of Conscience;* Rolle; Virtues and Vices, Books of

Square

A musical term, current for about two centuries from the 1440s on, referring to short, mensural parts of tenor-bass range derived from the lowest voices of compositions of the mid-14th to the mid-15th century that originated in variously composed ways. Squares were extracted from discant settings of plainsongs, from free (cantilena-style) settings of sacred texts, from settings in faburden, and from secular, vernacular ballades; some collections of these monophonic mensural parts survive. Squares were used as the structural basis for new compositions, including pieces for mass and processions, and settings of the Magnificat at Vespers. Musically their later use in written polyphony is varied, and their impromptu use in a kind of extemporized partsong is justified by archival references, although possible techniques for this improvised practice are not documented. Compositions based on squares are often said to be "upon the square," and there are literary and archival references to the copying of squares, to books of squares, and to the teaching and singing of "squarenote" and "square song."

Peter M. Lefferts

Bibliography

Baillie, Hugh. "Squares." *Acta Musicologica* 32 (1960): 178–93; Bent, Margaret. "Square." *NGD* 18:29–30; Bergsagel, John. "An Introduction to Ludford." *Musica Disciplina* 14 (1960): 105–30; Harrison, Frank Ll. *Music in Medieval Britain.* 2d ed. London: Routledge & Kegan Paul, 1963.

See also Cantilena; Discant; Faburden; Magnificat

Stained Glass

The construction of decorative windows in a "mosaic" of colored, painted glass held together by strips of grooved lead (calmes or cames), is one of the medieval arts discussed at length by Theophilus in *De diversis artibus,* written in the first quarter of the 12th century.

Window glass, used extensively in the Roman world, was reintroduced into England only in the 7th century. The earliest documented references to its use in Anglo-Saxon churches concern the north of England; in about 670 Bishop Wilfrid beautified his church by replacing linen cloths and pierced slabs, or *transennae,* with glass. Bede describes how, in 675, Benedict Biscop imported Frankish glaziers to work at Wearmouth, for the craft of glazing had been lost to the Anglo-Saxons. Excavated fragments from the sites of Wearmouth and Biscop's second foundation, Jarrow, reveal these early windows to have consisted of colored, unpainted fragments. A surprisingly wide range of colors was available, probably arranged in decorative rather than figurative compositions. Fragments of similar date have been found at Escomb (County Durham), and all are characterized by their high soda content, typical of the highly durable glass of the Roman world. The earliest painted fragments have also been recovered by excavation: tendrils of foliage ornament at Winchester of late Saxon or early Norman date and three blue fragments from Archbishop Thomas of Bayeux's Minster in York (ca. 1080–1100).

Although the use of window glass thus has a long history in medieval England, it is only in the 12th century that extant evidence for glazing with painted glass becomes more plentiful. In York a number of figurative panels and decorative borders have survived from the Romanesque Minster, reused as "belles verrières" ("beautiful glass") in the 14th-century nave. These panels have been dated ca. 1180 and attributed to the patronage of Archbishop Roger of Pont l'Évêque. Although in a fragmentary condition, the figurative scenes and their foliage borders (approximately fifteen survive) are evidence of a sumptuous glazing scheme in the late-12th-century choir.

Of a slightly later date and representing a separate stylistic evolution is the glazing of the new choir of Canterbury Cathedral (fig. 129). The Canterbury scheme, begun as the York program drew to a close and executed from ca. 1180 to ca. 1220, with an interruption during the Interdict of 1208–13, provides a valuable insight into the evolution of English monumental painting in the period of transition from Romanesque to Gothic. The earliest figures, including those of the ancestors of Christ and the Jesse Tree, convey an almost classical monumentality particularly marked in the work of the Methusaleh Master. Features like the profile head of the prophet Semei and the nude idol in the first typological window even suggest a familiarity with late Roman antiquities, such as those collected by Henry of Blois at Winchester.

The later windows, especially those designed for the ambulatory of the Trinity Chapel dedicated to the life and miracles of Thomas Becket, display an elegance, small-scale delicacy, and liveliness characteristic of the Gothic idiom. The Canterbury artists were familiar with French stylistic trends exemplified by the work at Chartres, Bourges, and Sens, and

Fig. 129. Canterbury Cathedral, choir clerestory (now west window). RCHME, © Crown copyright. Reproduced by permission.

some may even have worked in France during the years of Stephen Langton's exile. Recent research has even suggested that the glass by the Petronella Master was the product of a workshop responsible for glass in Canterbury, St. Remi in Reims, and St. Yved in Braine.

Compared with the wealth of French 13th-century glazing, English survivals are disappointing. Apart from Canterbury no extensive scheme remains in reasonable condition, a loss particularly serious in a period that saw such a transformation of styles. From the first half of the century Lincoln preserves the fragmentary vestiges of a once impressive scheme that included the Last Judgment, Life of St. Hugh, Life of the Virgin, and the Old Testament, perhaps in a typological sequence, now confined to the north rose, east windows of the choir aisles, and north-transept lancets. The Lincoln glass, ca. 1200–ca. 1230, displays affinities with Canterbury but is unlikely to be by the same workshop.

Apart from the figurative glass Lincoln also preserves some grisaille panels, that is, panels executed in shades of grey, a type of glazing increasingly favored for the clear silvery illumination it provided. More impressive remains are to be found at Salisbury (glazed ca. 1200–58 and ca. 1270), where an appreciation of the surviving panels is enhanced by the wealth of antiquarian material. Salisbury preserves both types of grisaille favored in 13th-century England: the unpainted geometric or vegetal variety and the more costly type decorated with trails of painted foliage. In both types color is used sparingly. This type of glazing was not confined to cathedrals; parish churches preserve examples, as at Brabourne and

Hastingleigh (Kent) and Marston (Oxfordshire). All are characterized by a preference for regular rather than interlacing designs, as favored on the Continent.

The scant remains at Westminster Abbey suggest that a combination of figurative medallion and grisaille was also favored by Henry III's glaziers. The figurative panels now in the Jerusalem Chamber are all that survives of the glazing of the apsidal chapels of the choir (glazed ca. 1246–59); a single panel of foliage grisaille photographed before World War II has now disappeared. It is clear from documentary references that Henry III was an important patron to glass painters. His commission for the hall of Rochester Castle in 1247 is the earliest documented reference to heraldic display in stained glass, and a small quantity of heraldry survives in Westminster Abbey. The extensive use of heraldry in stained glass is one of the important new features to emerge in the 13th century. Another feature that owed much to the influence of Westminster is the use of naturalistic foliage forms, which appeared in Westminster sculpture ca. 1250. This only emerges in a fully developed form in English glass in the 1280s (Wells Cathedral Chapter House stair, York Chapter House, Merton College Chapel, Chartham [Kent]), although in tentative ways naturalism can already be seen in some of the grisaille in the Five Sisters Window at York and at Salisbury.

A further innovation was the abandonment of the earlier medallion-type frame exemplified by Canterbury and Lincoln and the introduction of architectural canopies. The canopied figures were positioned in a horizontal band that alternated with zones of lighter grisaille to create the so-called "band window," a balance of narrative decoration and illumination of the interior. An early experiment in the "band" effect is found in a single light in the York Chapter House (ca. 1285–90), but the most perfect 13th-century expression of this new aesthetic is the choir scheme of Merton College Chapel, Oxford, of ca. 1294. The gift of Henry de Mamesfeld, chancellor of Oxford University and subsequently dean of Lincoln, the windows contain stylized images of the donor, whose physical presence in stained glass is yet another innovative feature in glass from the end of the 13th century on.

The nave aisles of York Minster offer the best-preserved early-14th-century scheme to unite all these features. With their variety of donors, secular as well as clerical, the windows express a range of devotional tastes and reflect the careers and fortunes of their originators. The donor himself or herself is often prominently depicted, as in the window given by Peter de Dene, canon of the Minster (glazed ca. 1307–10), and the Bell Founders Window given by Richard Tunnoc, bell founder and goldsmith of York.

It is in Peter de Dene's Heraldic Window that the most important technical innovation of the 14th century makes probably its earliest appearance in English stained glass. Yellow stain is a liquid solution of silver nitrate or sulfide, which when painted onto the surface (usually the exterior) and fired will turn white glass yellow. This revolutionary new technique freed the glass painter of the need to cut and lead small fragments of pot-metal glass every time he wanted to give a figure a golden halo or silvery beard. This freedom is perfectly illustrated in the delicate decoration of the arms and arrow of a king of England in the canopy of the Heraldic Window.

The palette of the 14th century, which exploited the qualities of yellow stain to the full, was a rich one. The predominance of red and what Suger called the "sapphire blue," so noticeable at Chartres, was balanced by the frequent use of purple, a rich brown, and a warm green. Tracery lights, grisaille panels, and borders abound with motifs derived from the natural world, augmented by many creations of the imagination, the parallels of the grotesque and hybrid forms found in the margins of illuminated manuscripts (e.g., the Lucy and Latin chapels at Christ Church, Oxford).

In addition to the great cathedral and monastic schemes—York, Wells, Tewkesbury, Gloucester, Exeter, Ely, Bristol, Oxford—numerous windows of 14th-century date are to be found in parish churches throughout the country: Eaton Bishop (Herefordshire), Stanford on Avon (Northamptonshire), Kempsey (Worcestershire), Newark (Nottinghamshire), and Grappenhall (Cheshire), to name but a few, all attest to the vigor of English glass painting in the first half of the 14th century. When, in the 1350s, Edward III sought craftsmen to work on the now lost glazing of St. Stephen's Chapel, Westminster, writs were issued to 27 counties. The names of many of those employed reveal this to have been a successful trawl.

The loss of St. Stephen's Chapel has robbed us of what was undoubtedly the most important glazing commission of the 1350s. Without question the most significant surviving window of the mid-century is the east window of Gloucester Cathedral (formerly the church of the Benedictine monastery; fig. 130). Executed in sparkling white glass and heavily modeled with painterly washes, the figures are conceived with an

almost sculptural grandeur. The only substantial color is provided by the yellow stain and counter-changing red and blue backgrounds. In its palette, and its interest in painterly modeling and spatial effects, the Gloucester glass anticipates developments that are fully realized only in the 1380s. Gloucester stands in splendid isolation in the middle of the century, an experiment with no immediate imitators.

Stained glass of the third quarter of the 14th century is scarce and often of a disappointing quality. Squat figures with large heads and beady eyes survive at Wormshill (Kent), St. Thomas's Church in Salisbury, and Aston Rowant (Oxfordshire). In a style reminiscent of the slightly later Lytlington Missal, with broader faces and heavy-lidded eyes, are panels at Birts Morton (Worcestershire), West Horsley (Surrey), and the panel of William Cele and his wife in the Victoria and Albert Museum (said to have come from a church in Suffolk). A panel in identical style, and probably a companion to it, is in the Burrell Collection in Glasgow.

Some of the most important glass of the late 14th century was that commissioned by William of Wykeham, bishop of Winchester and chancellor of England. Wykeham's two educational foundations, New College in Oxford (founded 1372 and built 1380–86) and Winchester College (founded 1382, glazing in progress 1393), were glazed by the Oxford workshop of Thomas Glazier. In Thomas's work for New College an evolution away from a hard, linear style to a softer, more painterly and plastic International Gothic style can be discerned. The Jesse Tree executed in this soft style was removed from the college in the 18th century; vestiges are now preserved in the south choir aisle of York Minster. The later Winchester College glass is entirely in this International Gothic idiom. The Winchester Jesse has a sculptural quality and an interest in spatial effect only tentatively explored at New College. Thomas of Oxford's working life was a long one. He was active until 1421–22, and his workshop was probably responsible for the east window of Merton College Chapel, Oxford, and the choir clerestory glazing at Winchester Cathedral.

Recent research has added greatly to the corpus of stained glass conceived in the new "soft" style: the west window of Canterbury Cathedral (1396–1411), four figures in the east window of Exeter Cathedral by Robert Lyen (executed 1391), and the western choir clerestory of York Minster (perhaps by John Burgh) are all now recognized as evidence of an English response to International Gothic.

In many respects Thomas's stylistic heir was John Thornton of Coventry, employed in 1405 to glaze the east window of York Minster (fig. 131). Thornton, contracted on 10 December 1405, was in receipt of a salary of £46, with a bonus of £10 promised should the work be completed within three years. He was authorized to employ additional craftsmen and formed a special Minster workshop for this exceptional commission. By 1410, with the commission complete, he established an independent workshop and was admitted to the freedom of the city. Although no other documented work is recorded, many other windows in the Minster and city churches can be attributed on stylistic grounds to his workshop. The figures most confidently attributed to Thornton's

Fig. 130. Gloucester Cathedral, east window. RCHME, © Crown copyright. Reproduced by permission.

own hand display a masterly command of painting techniques, combined with a lively interest in the real world. Faces are almost coarse, with bulbous noses, shaggy brows and beards, and heavy limbs. They are remarkably expressive, displaying great realism.

The most expensive commission of the 15th century was undertaken for the king. In 1402 Henry IV paid William Burgh 3s. 4d. per foot for windows "diapered and worked with broom flower, eagles and scrolls inscribed *Souveraigne*" for his private apartments at Eltham Palace. These windows do not survive, but the description and their recorded price suggest their splendor. No royal commissions survive from this period, and the study of English medieval stained glass is hampered by the almost total loss of glazing schemes associated with royal patronage. The king was the most important patron other than the church, and the post of king's glazier the most prestigious. In the Beauchamp Chapel in St. Mary's Church, Warwick, is a glazing scheme executed in 1447 by the king's glazier, John Prudde, for the executors of Richard Beauchamp, earl of Warwick. The scheme is characterized by sumptuous color with white glass used relatively sparingly and the effect enhanced by the use of "jewels" leaded into hems and trimmings. The contract stipulated the use of only the finest imported colored glasses and reveals that the designs from which the craftsmen were to work were supplied as paper patterns by the patron.

The directing hand of the patron can also be discerned in the choir glazing of Holy Trinity, Tattershall (Lincolnshire), founded by Ralph Cromwell, lord treasurer of England, and executed 1466–80 under the direction of William Waynfleet, bishop of Winchester. This ambitious scheme has been shown to be indebted for its typological scenes to the 40-page block-book edition of the *Biblia pauperum* of 1464–65. Familiarity with this source so soon after its continental publication is more likely to reflect the reading habits of patrons than the literary sophistication of the glass painters, although one of the Tattershall glaziers, Richard Twygge, was later employed to glaze fourteen clerestory windows at Westminster Abbey.

By the 15th century most major towns in England supported a community of glass painters. London, York, Chester, Norwich, Canterbury, King's Lynn, Oxford, and Colchester were all important centers, and the Tattershall records reveal that the towns of Stamford, Peterborough, and Burton-on-Trent also had produced significant workshops. Recent research has challenged the traditional idea of "regional styles," although it is clear that certain prolific workshops exerted considerable influence on the character of a region.

The stylistic characteristics of International Gothic were long-lived in English stained glass; in the southwest they remained current into the third quarter of the 15th century. The harsher, mannered style typified in manuscript illumination by the work of William Abell can also be found in stained glass, particularly in East Anglia (fig. 132), although woodcut illustrations with strongly accentuated linear modeling were no doubt equally influential. In common with native illuminators native glass painters of the close of the 15th century were poorly equipped to counter the challenge of continental and particularly Netherlandish competition. The appointment in 1497 of a Fleming, Barnard Flower, to the post of king's glazier marked the formal recognition of the eclipse of the native craft. In 1474 the London guild had successfully petitioned the mayor and aldermen against foreign competitors settled outside the limits of guild jurisdiction. A quarter of a century later the battle against foreign incursion had been lost. The unregulated Southwark glass painters, among whom Flower was the leading figure, worked in styles that reflected the most avant garde developments in European painting of the day. The patronage of the king and the court circle secured the most lucrative commissions: for the foreigners and for Flower himself a string of royal work that culminated in 1515 with the contract for the greatest enterprise of all, the Chapel of King's College in Cambridge.

Sarah Brown

Bibliography

PRIMARY

Theophilus. *De diversis artibus.* Ed. and trans. C.R. Dodwell. London: Nelson, 1961.

SECONDARY

Brooke, Chris, and David Evans. *The Treat East Window of Exeter Cathedral.* Exeter: Exeter University Press, 1988; Brown, Sarah, and David O'Connor. *Medieval Craftsmen: Glass-Painters.* London: British Museum, 1991; Caviness, Madeline. *The Windows of Christ Church Cathedral, Canterbury.* Corpus Vitrearum Medii Aevi: Great Britain 2. London: Oxford University Press, 1981; Caviness, Madeline. "Stained Glass." In *English Romanesque Art 1066–1200,* ed. George Zarnecki, Janet Holt, and Tristram Holland. London: Weidenfeld & Nicolson, 1984, pp. 135–45; Caviness, Madeline. *Sumptuous Arts at the Royal Abbeys of Reims and Braine.* Princeton: Princeton University Press, 1990; Colvin, Howard M., ed. *The History of the King's Works.* Vols. 1–2: *The Middle Ages.* London: HMSO, 1963; Cramp, Rosemary. "Decorated Window-Glass and Millefiori from Monkwearmouth." *AntJ* 50 (1970): 327–35; Crewe, Sarah. *Stained Glass in England 1180–1540.* London: HMSO, 1987; Knowles, John A. *Essays in the History of the York School of Glass-Painting.* London: SPCK, 1936; Le Couteur, John D. *English Medieval Painted Glass.* London: SPCK, 1926; Marks, Richard. "The Medieval Stained Glass in Wells Cathedral." In *Wells Cathedral: A History,* ed. L.S. Colchester. Shepton Mallet: Open Books, 1982, pp. 132–47; Marks, Richard. *The Stained Glass of the Collegiate Church of the Holy Trinity, Tattershall (Lincs.).* New York: Garland, 1984; Marks, Richard. "Stained Glass c1200–1400." In *Age of Chivalry: Art in Plantagenet England 1200–1400,* ed. Jonathan Alexander and Paul Binski. London: Royal Academy of Arts, 1987, pp. 137–47; Marks, Richard. "Window Glass." In *English Medieval Industries,* eds. John Blair and Nigel Ramsey. London: Hambledon, 1991, pp. 265–94; Marks, Richard. *Stained Glass in England during the Middle Ages.* Toronto: University of Toronto Press, 1993; Morgan, Nigel. *The Medieval Painted Glass of Lincoln Cathedral.* Corpus Vitrearum Medii Aevi: Great Britain, Occasional Papers 3. London: Oxford University Press, 1983; Newton, Peter A. *The County of Oxford.* Corpus Vitrearum Medii Aevi: Great Britain 1. London: Oxford University Press, 1979; O'Connor, David E., and Jeremy Haselock. "The Stained and Painted Glass." In *A History of York Minster,* ed. G.E. Aylmer and Reginald Cant. Oxford: Clarendon, 1977, pp. 313–91; Rushforth, Gordon McN. "The Great East Window of Gloucester Cathedral." *Transactions of the Bristol and Gloucestershire Archaeological Society* 44 (1922): 293–304; Salzmann, Louis F. "The Glazing of St. Stephen's Chapel, Westminster, 1351–2." *Journal of the British Society of Master Glass-Painters* 1/4 (1926–27): 14–16, 31–35, 38–41; Wayment, Hilary G. *The Windows of King's College Cambridge.* Corpus Vitrearum Medii Aevi: Supplementary Vol. 1. London: Oxford University Press, 1972; Wayment, Hilary G. *The Stained Glass of the Church of St. Mary, Fairford, Gloucestershire.* London: Society of Antiquaries of London, 1984; Woodforde, Christopher. *Stained Glass in Somerset 1250–1830.* Oxford: Oxford University Press, 1946; Woodforde, Christopher. *The Norwich School of Glass-Painting in the Fifteenth Century.* Oxford: Oxford University Press, 1950; Woodforde, Christopher. *The Stained Glass of New College, Oxford.* Oxford: Oxford University Press, 1951.

See also Canterbury Cathedral; King's College, Cambridge; Wainfleet; Wells Cathedral; Westminster Abbey; William of Wykeham; Winchester Cathedral; York and Ripon Minsters

Staple

The term "Staple" denotes the monopolistic organization that in the later Middle Ages largely controlled the export of wool. Its members were known as merchants of the Fellowship of the Staple, or simply Staplers. It was the first of the English regulated trading companies whose heyday was the second half of the 16th century, though the exemplar itself was by then virtually defunct.

The Staple came of age in the last years of Edward III, but it grew up slowly and fitfully during the previous 100 years. The germ of the organization existed in the early 1270s, when merchants looked for ways to continue selling wool to Flemings, in defiance of a ban imposed by their government. Progress may have been checked over the next two decades but speeded up during the Anglo-French war (1294–97), when the wool trade played a major part in the crown's financial and diplomatic strategies.

By the beginning of the 14th century some merchants trading with the Low Countries had adopted a semicorporate structure and sought to focus their business on a staple town in that region. The first element of compulsion came in 1313. Because of hostility to Englishmen in Flanders a staple was set up in the neutral town of St. Omer, and it was decreed that all wool exported from England, whether by natives or aliens, must be taken there. Englishmen soon found that a compulsory staple guaranteed them a greater share of exports and they persisted with this policy. For a period the staple was at Antwerp, but in time of peace Bruges was found to be the most favorable location.

An alternative policy directed wool through specified towns in England (home staples) but allowed it to be exported to any place abroad. This was implemented briefly but unsuccessfully three times in the 14th century. Before the outbreak of the Hundred Years War the Staple was promoted chiefly by the wool merchants in their own interest. Thereafter its continued existence was ensured by royal interest, which also determined the choice of the staple town. At first Edward III favored Bruges, but in 1363 he had the staple removed to Calais, where it remained, except for two brief intervals, until the town was recaptured by the French in 1558.

The enforced routing of wool through Calais guaranteed a livelihood to the English inhabitants, while customs revenue, combined with loans from the Staple company, largely financed the garrison. It was now that the export of wool became virtually a monopoly of the English staplers. The only exceptions were exports by Italian merchants to the Mediterranean and, in the 15th century, of inferior north-country wool dispatched from Newcastle to the northern Low Countries. Most cloth manufacturers in the Low Countries, still wishing to use English wool, had to obtain it at Calais. The supply of wool to the Staple and the terms of sale there were controlled by the company, with the intention of upholding prices and supporting the bullionist policy of the government. The staplers traded individually or in small partnerships, taking their own profit or loss, but bound by the company regulations.

Latterly the chief raison d'être of the company was to provide support for English rule in Calais; this disappeared in 1558. The few surviving members tried for a time to maintain a staple at Bruges, but this did not survive long on account of friction with Spain. The company maintained a tenuous existence as long as Englishmen continued to export ever-declining quantities of wool. It was not formally wound up even when export was legally prohibited in 1614; in the end it simply atrophied.

T.H. Lloyd

Bibliography

Hanham, Alison. *The Celys and Their World: An English Merchant Family of the Fifteenth Century.* Cambridge: Cambridge University Press, 1985; Lloyd, T.H. *The English Wool Trade in the Middle Ages.* Cambridge: Cambridge University Press, 1977; Munro, John H.A. *Wool, Cloth, and Gold: The Struggle for Bullion in Anglo-Burgundian Trade, 1340–78.* Toronto: University of Toronto Press, 1972; Rich, E.E. *The Ordinance Book of the Merchants of the Staple.* Cambridge: Cambridge University Press, 1937.

See also Cloth; Hanseatic League; Trade

Statutes

The term used by modern historians to refer to instances of lawmaking, distinguishing the legislature's enactment of new law from the application of existing law, which is the province of the judiciary. The word "statute" *(statutum)* began to appear in something like the modern sense of the term during the later 13th century. Even then, however, the modern distinction between legislation, as lawmaking, and adjudication, as the application of law, was vague in the Middle Ages. The state's legislative and judicial functions both had their roots in a single institution, the king and his advisory council of barons and prelates.

During the 11th and 12th centuries there seems to have been little recognition of a difference between the power of the king and his council to decide a dispute between two litigants and the power to ordain a new remedy or otherwise change the law. J.H. Baker has summarized the issue: "What in later times were seen as two distinct features of the constitution—the king as head of the legislative assembly in parliament, and the king as head of the judicial system—had their origins in a less sophisticated notion of kingship in which legislation and adjudication were not distinguishable."

A functional separation emerged in the early 13th century, with the extensive though not total delegation of judicial authority to a corps of professional judges. The king and council retained lawmaking responsibility, though during succeeding centuries the nature of the legislative process changed, as did the composition of the lawmaking body.

While we can refer to many medieval mandates or ordinances of the king and council as statutes because of their innovative, general, and prospective character, it was some time before anyone thought that their lawfulness depended on popular assent. The king's legislative authority originated in his duty to receive the petitions of aggrieved subjects. Where appropriate, king and council might choose to formulate responses that not only addressed the specific request for relief but also sought to prevent, or to afford remedies for, similar injuries in the future.

These legislative proceedings did not conform to any set procedural routine. By the later 13th century some such meetings included representatives of the Commons, but this occurred for reasons of expediency rather than constitutional propriety. In Plucknett's words, "A statute in the reign of Edward I simply means something established by royal authority; whether it is established by the King in Council, or in a Parliament of nobles, or in a Parliament of nobles and commons as well, is completely immaterial."

During the 14th century "parliament" came to imply an assembly of king and council including the Commons, consisting of knights and burgesses as elected representatives. The Commons gradually assumed a greater role in the initiation of legislation and in its approval. Petitioners increasingly addressed their requests to the Commons rather than to the king directly. If approved by the Commons, the petition was then forwarded to the king and council. In this way the principal locus of legislative initiative gradually shifted from the king and council to the Commons, from above to below. Nevertheless, the assent of the Commons to particular legislative items probably was not considered indispensable until after 1400.

The modern bill-debate-amendment procedure did not become settled until a century or so after that. Only with the advent of the Tudors do we witness the careful attention to public-policy considerations and use of language that characterize modern statutes. Plucknett has observed that these statutes were "no longer the government's vague reply to vaguely worded complaints, but rather the deliberate adoption of specific proposals embodied in specific texts."

As sources of innovation in the law, statutes played a significantly more limited role than they do in modern legal systems. Some scholars have suggested that the medieval theory of legislation restricted statutory activity to the mere declaration of existing custom. Others have argued that medieval statutory practice differed little from judgments rendered in disputes between private parties. Under either view the central idea is that there was no inclination to change existing law in a deliberate, self-conscious way or, perhaps, no awareness of the power to do so. However, these interpretations are difficult to square with the many clear examples of medieval activity that is legislative in the modern sense of the term.

While Henry II's reign witnessed important remedial innovations that contributed to the development of the common law governing real property (i.e., real estate), it was Edward I who most boldly exercised the legislative prerogative. Plucknett described these initiatives as "the greatest outburst of legislation in England during the middle ages; it was only equalled in extent and importance by that of the first half of the 19th century." Important examples included the Statute of Mortmain (1279), restricting the right to alienate real property to religious corporations. The primary objective seems to have been to preserve the financial value to feudal lords of the customary incidents of tenure, though the crown soon indicated a willingness to license grants in mortmain upon payment of a fee.

Similarly motivated was the statute *Quia emptores terrarum* (1290), which required that grants of real property be by means of substitution rather than subinfeudation, or vassals enfeoffing subvassals. By prohibiting the grantor from creating a new tenancy by which the grantee would hold of him, the statute aimed to preserve the value of the feudal incidents to the grantor's lord. The statute known as *De donis conditionalibus* (1285) restricted the rights of certain owners (tenants in fee tail) to alienate real property to the prejudice of their heirs.

After Edward I there are several instances of legislation designed to address important social problems, like violence and the effects of the Black Death on labor markets, though the bulk of statutory activity related to relatively narrow and trivial matters. George Sayles stated the matter: "The statutes between Edward II and Henry VIII exhibit few great monuments of legislation."

David Millon

Bibliography

Arnold, Morris S. "Statutes as Judgments: The Natural Law Theory of Parliamentary Activity in Medieval England." *University of Pennsylvania Law Review* 126 (1977): 329–43 [surveys the medieval theory of legislation and the limits of earlier views]; Baker, John H. *An Introduction to English Legal History.* 3d ed. London: Butterworths, 1990; Evans, Michael, and R. Ian Jack, eds. *Sources of English Legal and Constitutional History.* Sydney: Butterworths, 1984 [translations of important medieval statutes]; Palmer, Robert C. *English Law in the Age of the Black Death, 1348–1381.* Chapel Hill: University of North Carolina Press, 1993; Plucknett, Theodore F.T. *Legislation of Edward I.* Oxford: Clarendon, 1949 [thorough assessment of the major burst of medieval statutory activity]; Richardson, H.G., and G.O. Sayles. "The Early Statutes." *Law Quarterly Review* 50 (1934): 201–23, 540–71 [discussion of 13th- and 14th-century statutes and an analysis of the character and content of legislative activity]; *Statutes of the Realm.* London: Eyre & Strahan, 1810–28. Repr. London: Dawsons, 1963 [editorial work not up to our current standards, but the only extensive collection of the statutes].

See also Law, Post-Conquest; Monarchy and Kingship; Parliament

Stephen (ca. 1096–1154; r. 1135–54)

The third surviving son of Stephen, count of Blois and Chartres, and Adela, daughter of William the Conqueror. It was his mother's family that was to shape his career. Nothing is known of his life before he was sent to the English court sometime between 1106 and 1113. There he became a magnate because of family ties rather than military or administrative service.

Between 1113 and 1125 his uncle Henry I made him count of Mortain, gave him extensive lands in England and Normandy, and married him to the heiress Matilda of Boulogne, making this younger noninheriting son one of the richest of the Anglo-Normans. In 1126 Stephen was joined at court by his younger brother Henry of Blois, a Cluniac monk elected abbot of Glastonbury and, in 1129, bishop of Winchester, the wealthiest English see and site of the royal treasury.

The major change in Stephen's career came when Henry I died, 1 December 1135. Henry's designated heir was his daughter, the empress Matilda, but she was handicapped by her gender, her education at the court of the Holy Roman Empire, and by her second husband, Geoffrey of Anjou, a traditional enemy of many of the Anglo-Norman barons. Stephen was in Boulogne; he hurried to England and was acclaimed king by the people of London and Winchester. He and his brother Henry convinced key men in the royal administration of his claim and took control of the treasury. Then Hugh Bigod, the future earl of Norfolk (1140/41–77), returned from Normandy, telling of a deathbed designation of Stephen by Henry I—neither supported nor contradicted by others present. Stephen was crowned on 22 December 1135. By April 1136 he had gained the support of most of the nobles and clergy in England.

Stephen's right to the throne continued to be disputed by Henry's daughter, who provided a rallying point for opposition. Between 1137 and 1141 many nobles—some having lost faith in Stephen's capability, others seeking particular gains—switched allegiance. The clergy also began to withdraw their support as they came to doubt the sincerity of his early Gregorian measures. He lost control of the kingdom in 1141, when he was captured at the Battle of Lincoln and held prisoner for nine months. He regained power as a result of Empress Matilda's alienation of her own supporters and of adroit negotiations by Stephen's wife, Queen Matilda. The queen's role was central, as she organized crucial military ventures and handled many negotiated truces.

Stephen's support among the barons continued to erode. In January 1153 the empress's son, Henry Plantagenet, invaded England, and Stephen agreed to a negotiated settlement, completed in November, three months after the death of Stephen's eldest son, Eustace. Henry, not Stephen's younger son William, was to be the next king (as Henry II). Stephen died on 25 October 1154.

In a time of personal rule Stephen's character is central to any discussion of the period. Many contemporary and modern historians have faulted him not because of cruel or dictatorial tendencies but because of perceived nonroyal weaknesses. The Anglo-Saxon Chronicle damns him as "a kindly man" of whom the nobles took advantage. Henry of Huntingdon wrote that his voice was too weak to deliver the battle speech before the Battle of Lincoln. Even Stephen's victories were credited to the merits of others, and no king who lost battles could be seen as a leader. Unable to win by military victory, he persistently refused to accept negotiated peace. He seems to have constantly misjudged individuals or situations, such as accepting advice from Waleran Beaumont over Henry of Blois on clerical appointments, or deciding to purge his administration by arresting unarmed bishops during court in 1138, thus breaking the king's peace. Acts like these lost Stephen his alliance with the church.

Stephen was also unable to check the building of unlicensed castles or to control subinfeudation, or vassals enfeoffing subvassals. Whether the alienated nobles were reacting to the previous reigns of strong kings or to disappointment that Stephen was not stronger, he could not hold their loyalty and instead relied on mercenary troops from Flanders, an act that triggered more alienation. He was the first Anglo-Norman king to give power away in any significant measure, in return for military support, when he created seventeen new earldoms to reward followers. In spite of this there was administrative continuity in record keeping and royal justice, though neither flourished without the peace or cooperation his predecessors enjoyed. It is in contrast to the successes of Henry I and Henry II that his reign palls. He lacked the innovation in administration and justice and the political tact that characterized both Henrys.

Charlotte Newman Goldy

Bibliography

Cronne, H.A., and R.H.C. Davis, eds. *Regesta Regum Anglo-Normannorum, 1066–1154.* Vol. 3: *Regesta Regis Stephani ac Mathildis Imperatricis ac Gaufridi et Henrici Ducum Normannorum, 1135–1154.* Oxford: Clarendon, 1968 [Stephen's charters in a scholarly edition]; Davis, A., and R.H.C. Davis, eds. *The Reign of Stephen, 1135–1154: Anarchy in England.* London: Weidenfeld & Nicolson, 1970; Davis, R.H.C. *King Stephen, 1135–1154.* 3d ed. London: Longman, 1990 [both these biographies are good, modern starting points for a study of the reign]; Potter, K.R., ed. and trans. *William of Malmesbury: Historia novella.* London: Nelson, 1955 [major source: pro-Matilda]; Potter, K.R., ed. and trans. *Gesta Stephani, regis Anglorum.* With new introduction and notes by R.H.C. Davis. Oxford: Clarendon, 1976 [a pro-Stephen contemporary source].

See also Anarchy; Henry I; Henry II; Matilda

Stockholm Gospels

An illuminated copy of the Gospels assigned to mid-8th-century Canterbury, also called the *Codex Aureus* (Stockholm, Royal Library A.135; fig. 133); it is a major example of southern Anglo-Saxon manuscript art.

The two surviving evangelist portraits, Matthew and John, display the romanizing art style of Southumbrian Christianity. The architectural settings with spatial references derived from late-antique art, the three-dimensional drapery and faces firmly modeled with carefully placed stripes

Fig. 133. Stockholm Gospels (Stockholm, Royal Library A.135), fol. 11. Christi Autem. Courtesy of the Royal Library, Stockholm.

of gradated values, and the luxurious but naturalistic colors appear in other 8th- and 9th-century examples. The evangelist figures, seated under tympana presenting symbols of winged man and eagle, possibly are based on those in the "Gospels of St. Augustine" (Cambridge, Corpus Christi College Cod. 286). Although additional Mediterranean models have been posited to account for the style, the portraits probably represent a later version of that found already in the Vespasian Psalter.

Alternating undyed and purple-stained leaves present the Gospel text. The purple folios are written in gold, white, and silver, the colors sometimes being varied on a single page to form a pattern, such as a cross or the Chi-Rho. The elegant, patterned pages emulate a specialized late-antique luxury page treatment, *carmina figurata*.

The beginnings of some sections of the text are given full-page decorative treatment, with multicolored display capitals set in panels of burnished gold or gold capitals in panels of plain vellum or of lacertine (interlaced) animal ornament, vinescroll, and Celtic trumpet spiral. The use of display capitals appears to escalate that seen in the Vespasian Psalter, and the lacertine animal ornament resembles that of later Southumbrian examples, such as the Barberini Gospels.

The massive use of gold probably had consequences for the manuscript's history, the book having been ransomed from Vikings, according to an inscription on fol. 11.

Carol A. Farr

Bibliography

Alexander, J.J.G. *Insular Manuscripts 6th–9th Century.* A Survey of Manuscripts Illuminated in the British Isles 1, ed. J.J.G. Alexander. London: Harvey Miller, 1978; Budny, Mildred. "The Visual Arts and Crafts (Early Medieval Britain)." In *The Cambridge Guide to the Arts in Britain.* Vol. 1: *Prehistoric, Roman, and Early Medieval,* ed. Boris Ford. Cambridge: Cambridge University Press, 1988, pp. 122–77; Webster, Leslie, and Janet Backhouse, eds. *The Making of England: Anglo-Saxon Art and Culture* A.D. *600–900.* London: British Museum, 1991.

See also Manuscript Illumination, Anglo-Saxon; Vespasian Psalter

Stonework as Ecclesiastical Ornament

Little ornamented stonework remains *in situ* in Anglo-Saxon ecclesiastical contexts, but numerous fragments of carved architectural decoration and church furnishings have survived, to provide some indication of the original appearance of the buildings.

From much of the material it is clear that carved stonework was often used to enhance entrances and doorways. The two-storied western entrance porch of Benedict Biscop's foundation at Wearmouth (added to the church by 689) provides us with a rare and early in situ instance, with its monumental low-relief figure set under the gable, its decorated stringcourse, and the western opening into the porch. This is flanked with lathe-turned baluster shafts and square soffits decorated with interlaced ribbon animals reminiscent of those found in earlier 7th-century metalwork, as well as insular manuscripts, such as the Book of Durrow (Dublin, Trinity College A.4.5[57]). Somewhat later in date, at Lastingham (North Yorkshire), vinescroll- and interlace-decorated door jambs survive from the 8th- or early-9th-century church, while the door between the nave and north porticus of the 9th-century church at Britford (Wiltshire) is set with carved panels of vinescroll; at Deerhurst (Gloucestershire) hood moldings framing entrance ways terminate in sculptured animal heads dated to the 9th century. In the 10th and 11th centuries carved stonework was also used to decorate the western towers that were added to many church buildings at that time. At Corhampton (Hampshire), for example, some of the pilaster strips are carved with an elaborate foliate motif (see also Barnack, Northamptonshire).

Apart from providing such decoration, stonework was also used to ornament the church walls. Sundials were set into the exterior fabric of some Anglo-Saxon churches, as at Escomb (County Durham), while (often extensive) friezes of figural, zoomorphic, vinescroll, and geometric ornament decorated interior walls (e.g., at Jarrow and Hexham in 7th-century Northumbria and, ca. 800, Breedon in Leicestershire [figs. 134–36]). In the 10th and 11th centuries the interior walls of several southern churches were further decorated with large-scale reliefs, often of the Crucifixion. The fragmentary remains of just such a rood survive in situ over the chancel arch at Bitton (Gloucestershire); more substantial remains occur (although not in their original settings), at such sites as Romsey (Hampshire; fig. 110: see ROMSEY ROODS) and Langford (Oxfordshire; fig. 124: see SCULPTURE, ANGLO-SAXON).

Fig. 134. Breedon-on-the-Hill, Leicestershire. Architectural animal frieze. Courtesy of A.J. Hawkes.

Fig. 135. Breedon-on-the-Hill, Leicestershire. Architectural frieze, plant scroll. Courtesy of A.J. Hawkes.

Fig. 136. Breedon-on-the-Hill, Leicestershire. Figural frieze (part of a shrine?). Courtesy of A.J. Hawkes.

Stone was also used for church furnishings. Stone altar tops, incised with a cross at each corner, were required in all churches, and in some cases stone fonts have survived (e.g., at Potterne [Wiltshire], and Deerhurst); ornamented stone altar screens may also once have existed. At Jarrow a number of lathe-turned baluster shafts were probably incorporated into just such a screen with narrow friezes of small-scale relief balusters in the late 7th or early 8th century; similar friezes of contemporary date survive elsewhere at Hexham and Simonburn (Northumberland). Other carved remains from Jarrow suggest stonework was also used for a lectern, and elsewhere stone was used for elaborate seats, as at Bamburgh (Northumberland); animal-decorated panels from Wearmouth may have functioned as bench ends. Complete bishop's or abbot's seats have survived from Hexham and Beverley (East Yorkshire).

Apart from providing some indication of the original appearance of Anglo-Saxon churches the decoration of ecclesiastical stonework has also been seen as significant by those attempting to establish the overall chronology for Anglo-Saxon sculpture. The carved motifs used in the decoration of the earliest stone churches are viewed as the starting point in the sculptural development of those motifs and so are crucial to the chronology of the material as a whole. So few pieces of ecclesiastical stonework have survived in clearly datable contexts that this body of material can provide only a general chronological basis on a local level.

A. Jane Hawkes

Bibliography

Colgrave, Bertram, trans. *The Life of Bishop Wilfrid by Eddius Stephanus*. Cambridge: Cambridge University Press, 1927; Colgrave, Bertram, and R.A.B. Mynors, eds. and trans. *Bede's Ecclesiastical History of the English People*. Oxford: Clarendon, 1969; Cramp, Rosemary. *Corpus of Anglo-Saxon Stone Sculpture in England*. Vol. 1: *County Durham and Northumberland*. London: Oxford University Press, 1984; Cramp, Rosemary. "The

Furnishings and Sculptural Decoration of Anglo-Saxon Churches." In *The Anglo-Saxon Church: Papers on History, Architecture and Archaeology in Honour of Dr H.M. Taylor,* ed. Lawrence A.S. Butler and Richard K. Morris. CBA Research Report 60. London: CBA, 1986, pp. 101–04; Cramp, Rosemary, and Richard N. Bailey. *Corpus of Anglo-Saxon Stone Sculpture.* Vol. 2: *Cumberland, Westmorland and Lancashire North-of-the-Sands.* London: Oxford University Press, 1988; Lang, James. *Corpus of Anglo-Saxon Stone Sculpture.* Vol. 3: *York and Eastern Yorkshire.* London: Oxford University Press, 1991; Taylor, Harold M. *Anglo-Saxon Architecture.* Vol. 3. Cambridge: Cambridge University Press, 1978; Taylor, Harold M., and Joan Taylor. *Anglo-Saxon Architecture.* Vols. 1–2. Cambridge: Cambridge University Press, 1965; Taylor, Harold M., and Joan Taylor. "Architectural Sculpture in Pre-Norman England." *JBAA,* 3d ser. 29 (1966): 4–51; Tweddle, Dominic, Martin Biddle, and Birthe Kjølbye-Biddle. *Corpus of Anglo-Saxon Stone Sculpture.* Vol. 4: *South-East England.* London: Oxford University Press, 1995; Webster, Leslie, and Janet Backhouse, eds. *The Making of England: Anglo-Saxon Art and Culture* A.D. *600–900.* London: British Museum, 1991.

See also Architecture, Anglo-Saxon; Ecclesiastical Architecture, Early Anglo-Saxon; Hexham and Ripon; Manuscript Illumination, Anglo-Saxon; Romsey Roods; Sculpture, Anglo-Saxon; Wearmouth-Jarrow: Architecture; York, Anglo-Saxon Churches in

Sub arturo plebs

The motet is one of the most complex and artful forms of medieval polyphony, and *Sub arturo plebs vallata / Fons citharizancium / In omnem terram* is one of the most ingenious motets to survive from the 14th century. It is noteworthy both for the complexity of its underlying construction, which makes it one of the most technically advanced motets of its day (it is a three-section isorhythmic motet with proportional diminution of the tenor in the ratio 9:6:4), and for its musical subject matter (it is perhaps the only fully secular motet in the English tradition).

Sub arturo plebs is one of an interlocking series of English and continental "musicians' motets." It appears to have been directly modeled on the first of the series, the anonymous continental motet *Apollinis eclipsatur / Zodiacum cum signis lustrantibus / In omnem terram.* The text of the duplum (the middle voice) gives a brief history of music, explains the proper rhythmic interpretation of the tenor, and names the composer (J. Alanus). Alanus can be identified as John Aleyn, who was a chaplain of Edward III's Chapel Royal from 1361 to 1373, the year of his death. In the text of the triplum (the top voice) Aleyn names fourteen English musicians with careers collectively spanning three successive generations between the 1340s and 1380s, either in service to Edward III or Richard II in the Chapel Royal, or in service to the Black Prince (Edward, Prince of Wales). Trowell proposed 1358 as the date of composition of

Sub arturo and suggested that it was written for a famous gathering of the Knights of the Garter at Windsor Castle that year. More recent scholarship now accepts a date in the very early 1370s to be more likely, in the years just prior to Aleyn's death. Another English motet of similar complexity and ingenuity, *O amicus / Precursoris,* survives adjacent to *Sub arturo* in the latter's only insular source (Ipswich, Suffolk Record Office HA30:50/22/13.5, *olim* Yoxford). Bent suggests this may be a companion piece to *Sub arturo* by the same composer.

Peter M. Lefferts

Bibliography

PRIMARY

Bent, Margaret, ed. *Two Fourteenth-Century Motets in Praise of Music[ians].* Newton Abbot: Antico Edition, 1977; Harrison, Frank Ll., ed. *Motets of French Provenance.* Polyphonic Music of the Fourteenth Century 5. Paris: L'Oiseau-Lyre, 1968.

SECONDARY

Bent, Margaret, with David Howlett. "*Subtiliter alternare:* The Yoxford Motet *O amicus / Precursoris.*" In *Studies in Medieval Music: Festschrift for Ernest H. Sanders,* ed. Peter M. Lefferts and Brian Seirup. *Current Musicology* 45–47 (1990): 43–84; Bowers, Roger. "Fixed Points in the Chronology of English Fourteenth-Century Polyphony." *Music and Letters* 71 (1990): 313–35; Lefferts, Peter M. *The Motet in England in the Fourteenth Century.* Ann Arbor: UMI Research Press, 1986; Trowell, Brian. "A Fourteenth-Century Ceremonial Motet and Its Composer." *Acta Musicologica* 29 (1957): 65–75; Wathey, Andrew. "The Peace of 1360–1369 and Anglo-French Musical Relations." *Early Music History* 9 (1990): 129–74.

See also Alanus; Motet; Songs

Sumer Canon

Also known as "Sumer is icumen in" after the beginning of its text, or as the Reading Rota after its probable place of origin, this composition of ca. 1250 is the most famous piece of medieval music. It is, further, one of a mere handful of secular ME lyrics with surviving musical settings from before ca. 1400. The Sumer Canon is uniquely structured as a *rota,* or round canon at the unison, over a *pes,* which in this case is an essential two-voice supporting substructure. The result is a hybrid, in some respects motetlike, form. By no means *sui generis* in respect to musical structure, the Sumer Canon has affinities with a rich literature of 13th-century English polyphony employing the techniques of voice exchange, rondellus, and rota. In its only source (BL Harley 978, fol. 11v) the Sumer Canon is written as a single upper voice, which yields the canonic parts, over the two voices of the *pes* in score. An elaborate accompanying rubric provides performance instructions—recommending, for instance, that two to four singers make the round over the *pes.* Two texts are written under the upper voice, the English ("Sumer is icumen in") in red and an alternative Latin text ("Perspice christicola") in black.

There is a large literature on the Sumer Canon. It has engendered controversies surrounding its date of origin, the original state of its notation in respect to both rhythm and melody, and the status of the vernacular text as original or contrafact.
Peter M. Lefferts

Bibliography

PRIMARY

Dobson, Eric J., and Frank Ll. Harrison, eds. and trans. *Medieval English Songs.* London: Faber & Faber, 1979; Sanders, Ernest H., ed. *English Music of the Thirteenth and Early Fourteenth Centuries.* Polyphonic Music of the Fourteenth Century 14. Paris: L'Oiseau-Lyre, 1979.

SECONDARY

Burstyn, Shai. "Gerald of Wales and the *Sumer Canon.*" *Journal of Musicology* 2 (1983): 135–50; Cooper, Barry. "A Thirteenth-Century Canon Reconstructed." *Music Review* 42 (1981): 85–90; Duffin, Ross W. "The *Sumer* Canon: A New Revision." *Speculum* 63 (1988): 1–21; Obst, Wolfgang. "'Sumer is icumen in'— A Contrafactum?" *Music and Letters* 64 (1983): 151–61; Sanders, Ernest H. "Sumer is icumen in." *NGD* 18:366–68.

See also Harley 978; Lyrics; Motet; Rondellus; Rota; Songs

Sutton Hoo

Basil Brown's 1939 excavation of the Mound 1 ship burial at Sutton Hoo, Suffolk, was a turning point in the study of early medieval art in England, as the richness of the find permanently changed the evaluation of the scope and quality of pre-Christian Anglo-Saxon art.

The clinker-built ship, traceable by the imprint of its timbers and by the placement of surviving iron rivets, was an open rowing boat approximately 90 feet in length, the longest vessel yet found from the early-medieval period. The burial chamber amidships contained a princely treasure, including both locally made and imported luxury objects, demonstrating both the quality and techniques of indigenous craftsmanship and the extent of the contacts of early East Anglia with other cultures of the British Isles and the Continent.

The hoard of jewelry found along the keel line was mostly produced in a local workshop, probably under the direction of a single master craftsman. The jewelry is made of gold, often inlaid with various materials. These include garnets, linking this workshop to others in Kent and on the Continent, such as the center that produced the treasure found in 1653 at Tournai in the tomb of the Merovingian king Childeric, and *millefiori,* a technique brought to England by the Romans and continued locally by Celtic craftsmen, including those who made the largest of the three hanging bowls found at the west end of the burial chamber at Sutton Hoo. The great gold buckle (fig. 137) is ornamented with interlacing snakes and small quadrupeds typical of contemporary Germanic art in England and on the Continent and has a hidden compartment possibly for an amulet or relic.

Fig. 137. Great Gold Buckle, Sutton Hoo (London, British Museum MLA 1939, 10–10,1). Courtesy of the Trustees of the British Museum, London.

A purse contained 37 continental gold coins, three blank slugs, and two plain ingots. Its hinged lid survives, showing *cloisonné* motifs set in white enamel, of which the outer pair closest to the clasp shows an upright man between two attacking animals. This closely parallels a stamp used for embossing bronze plates for decorating helmets found at Torslunda (Öland, Sweden), and on the helmet from boat grave VII at Valsgärde (Uppland), one of the many instances where the Sutton Hoo workshop had access to imported Scandinavian models.

Also along the keel line were a silver Byzantine salver with the stamps of Emperor Anastasius I (491–518); the remains of a banqueting assemblage, including two large drinking horns and six maplewood bottles; and a sword with gold and garnet fittings.

Across the west end of the burial chamber was an iron stand originally thought to be a portable flambeau but now widely considered to have been a standard. Nearby was a stone bar in the shape of a whetstone 2 feet in length, with carved human heads and metal fittings at either end, too large and unwieldy to have been used as a hone and so probably ceremonial, possibly functioning as a scepter. With these objects was an heirloom leather-covered wooden shield, repaired with metal zoomorphic mounts. Also here was an eastern Mediterranean footed bronze bowl containing the largest of the hanging bowls, which in turn held the remains of a lyre with silver-gilt bird-head mounts. Three feet from the west wall were eight eastern Mediterranean nested silver bowls with ornamental motifs in a cruciform layout, and two imported silver spoons inscribed in Greek with the names "Saulos" and "Paulos." On the north side of the keel and about a yard from the west wall was a shattered iron helmet originally covered with thin plates of bronze. Its design has been linked both to helmets from Vendel and Valsgärde in Sweden and to sub-Roman helmets from England and the Continent. A pattern of dancing warriors embossed on a surviving bronze plate shows definite links to Swedish workshops.

The richness of the burial and the possible symbolism of several objects ("standard," "scepter," and drinking horns) and of the animal motifs decorating these and other objects (helmet, purse lid, shield) have led to the hypothesis that Mound I honored one of the East Anglian kings who resided at nearby Rendlesham or Kingston, and with whom the extensive group of at least fifteen mounds at Sutton Hoo has been associated. As no human remains were preserved there, possibly owing to acidic soil conditions, it is uncertain whether Mound I was an inhumation, a cremation, a cenotaph, or a traditional burial ceremony for a convert buried elsewhere in a Christian context. Identification of the king remains hypothetical, as the coin dates are inconclusive; current scholarship suggests a date between about 610 and 640, a period including the reigns of the East Anglian kings Rædwald (d. 616/27), Earpwald (d. 627 or 628), and Sigeberht (death date uncertain).

The Sutton Hoo Research Project, under the direction of Martin Carver, undertook a new campaign of excavations from 1983 to 1992. The Project worked to a preset agenda that left the cemetery only partially excavated, thus conserving part of the site for exploration by future generations. The new campaign revealed an extensive cemetery consisting of twenty mounds (seven left unexcavated) and 44 burials without mounds. The latter group included both cremations and inhumation, as well as possible evidence of human sacrifice. The cemetery as a whole has been provisionally interpreted as a dynastic statement of "defiant pagan politics" (Carver, 1992: 365).

Carol Neuman de Vegvar

Bibliography

Bessinger, Jess B. "The Sutton Hoo Ship Burial: A Chronological Bibliography II." *Speculum* 33 (1958): 315–22; Bruce-Mitford, Rupert L.S. *The Sutton Hoo Ship Burial.* 3 vols. London: British Museum, 1975–83; Carver, Martin, ed. *The Age of Sutton Hoo.* Woodbridge: Boydell, 1992; Carver, Martin, ed. *Sutton Hoo Research Committee Bulletins 1983–1993.* Woodbridge: Boydell and the Sutton Hoo Research Trust, 1993; Evans, Angela Care. *The Sutton Hoo Ship Burial.* London: British Museum, 1986; Farrell, Robert T., and Carol L. Neuman de Vegvar, eds. *The Sutton Hoo Ship Burial: Fifty Years After.* Oxford, Ohio: American Early Medieval Studies, 1992; Hawkes, Christopher. "Sutton Hoo: Twenty-Five Years After." *Antiquity* 38 (1964): 252–56 [bibliography]; Magoun, Francis P., Jr. "The Sutton Hoo Ship Burial: A Chronological Bibliography." *Speculum* 29 (1954): 116–24; Werner, Martin. *Insular Art: An Annotated Bibliography.* Boston: Hall, 1984, entries E.15.1–24.

See also Archaeology; Art, Anglo-Saxon: Celtic Influences; Cemeteries; Metalwork, Anglo-Saxon

Swein (d. 1014; R. 1013–14)

Dubbed "Swein Forkbeard" in the 12th-century Roskilde Chronicle, he was king of Denmark and, for a few months, king of England from late in 1013 until his death on 3 February 1014. The son of Harald Bluetooth, he gained the Danish throne by rebelling against his father, probably in 987. An Anglo-Saxon charter implies that he made his first incursion into England in the early 980s, and the Anglo-Saxon Chronicle records that he was certainly there by 994.

Swein invaded England in 1003–04, possibly to avenge the death of his sister, killed with her husband in the St. Brice's Day massacre of Danes on 13 November 1002. In 1013, leaving his son Harald as his vicegerent in Denmark, he again invaded England with a second son, Cnut (later king), and an army. After landing at Sandwich in Kent he sailed to East Anglia and then up the River Trent to Gainsborough, where the Northumbrians submitted to him, as subsequently did those in the Danelaw north of Watling Street, the inhabitants of Oxford and Winchester, the western thegns, and, finally, the citizens of London.

The Chronicle says that the people then considered him to be "king in all respects," and King Æthelred II went into temporary exile after Christmas with his brother-in-law, Richard II, duke of Normandy. The German sources tend to be hostile to Swein, portraying him as an apostate who once or twice had to be ransomed by his supporters and who had been driven into exile for fourteen years. In fact he gained hegemony over Norway and may well have wielded some control over Sweden. The *Encomium Emmae reginae*, composed in Flanders in 1040–42, portrays him more favorably, declaring him to have been "the most fortunate of kings," a person of power who had the support of his army and his people.

David A.E. Pelteret

Bibliography

PRIMARY

Campbell, Alistair, ed. *Encomium Emmae reginae.* Camden Society, 3d ser. 72 (1949); Saxo Grammaticus. *Danorum regum heroumque historia: Books X–XVI.* Trans. Eric Christiansen. BAR Internat. Ser. 84/1. Oxford: BAR, 1980; Tschan, Francis J., ed. and trans. *History of the Archbishops of Hamburg-Bremen by Adam of Bremen.* New York: Columbia University Press, 1959;

Whitelock, Dorothy, ed., with David C. Douglas and Susie I. Tucker. *The Anglo-Saxon Chronicle: A Revised Translation*. London: Eyre & Spottiswoode, 1961.

SECONDARY

Lund, Niels. "The Armies of Swein Forkbeard and Cnut: *leding* or *lith*?" *ASE* 15 (1986): 105–18; Sawyer, Peter. "Swein Forkbeard and the Historians." In *Church and Chronicle in the Middle Ages: Essays Presented to John Taylor,* ed. Ian Wood and G.A. Loud. London: Hambledon, 1993, pp. 27–40.

See also Æthelred II; Cnut; Emma; Vikings

T

Tacitus (ca. 55–ca. 117)

Roman historian, of interest to medievalists mainly for his *Germania,* written in A.D. 98. From it is taken the term *comitatus,* commonly used by scholars to designate the aristocratic warrior bands of Germanic heroic poetry. The treatise has also often been juxtaposed with these poems as if it can be read as a straightforward historical witness to the sociological organization and ethical code that the literary tradition exemplifies. But the poems have their own rationale and in their present forms come from many hundreds of years later and from varied geographical and cultural backgrounds, while the *Germania* must itself be understood as a complex literary document that draws extensively upon older written models and sources.

The *Germania* is shaped, particularly in chapters 1–27, according to the conventions of the long-established genre of the ethnographic essay (chapters 28–46, which deal with individual tribes, have their own geographically determined arrangement). There are further complications in that Tacitus's understanding of Germanic social organization is influenced by Roman concepts and that he uses some of his material for moral and political purposes concerned chiefly with the Romans' supposed decadence and the topical (and perennial) issue of confrontation with and control of the Germanic tribes.

Joyce Hill

Bibliography

PRIMARY

Mattingly, H., trans. *The Agricola and The Germania.* Rev. S.A. Handford. Harmondsworth: Penguin, 1971; Winterbottom, M., and R.M. Ogilvie, eds. *Cornelii Taciti Opera Minora.* Oxford: Clarendon, 1975 [*Agricola, De Oratoribus, Germania*].

SECONDARY

Martin, Ronald. *Tacitus.* London: Batsford, 1981; Syme, Ronald. *Tacitus.* Oxford: Clarendon, 1958.

See also Anglo-Saxon Invasions; *Beowulf;* Literary Influences: Scandinavian; Paganism

Tatwine (d. 734)

The few known facts about Archbishop Tatwine of Canterbury (731–34) derive largely from Bede's brief account toward the end of his *Ecclesiastical History* (5.23). Tatwine's death is recorded in the Anglo-Saxon Chronicle as occurring within a year of Bede's, and it is remarked that these deaths were signaled by portentous events, as the moon appeared suffused with blood. Tatwine's 40 *Aenigmata* ("riddles" or "mysteries"—the number is fixed by a complicated acrostic) can be shown to be modeled closely on Aldhelm's in style and diction, although the range of subjects covered is rather different.

Tatwine may be credited with introducing the abstract into Anglo-Latin *aenigmata.* The opening three riddles deal with Philosophy; Hope, Faith, and Charity; and the Historical, Spiritual, Moral, and Allegorical Senses of Scripture. We also find riddles on Love, Evil, Humility, and Pride. The ecclesiastical background of the author is easily discerned in the riddles on Bell, Altar, Christ's Cross, Lectern, and Paten. In the same way Tatwine clearly celebrates his literary and grammatical interests in his riddles on Letters, Parchment, Pen, Lectern, and Prepositions with Two Cases. His *Ars Tatwini,* a detailed elementary grammar that seems to have been popular on the Continent in the late 8th and early 9th centuries, is extant.

A.P.M. Orchard

Bibliography

PRIMARY

Ars Tatvini, ed. Maria De Marco, and *Aenigmata Tatvini,* ed. F. Glorie and trans. Erika von Erhardt-Siebold. In *Tatvini Opera Omnia; Variae Collectiones Aenigmatvm Merovingicae Aetatis.* CCSL 133. Turnhout: Brepols, 1968, pp. 3–93, 167–208.

SECONDARY

Law, Vivien. "The Study of Latin Grammar in Eighth-Century

Southumbria." *ASE* 12 (1983): 43–71; Whitman, F.H. "Aenigmata Tatwini." *NM* 88 (1987): 8–17.

See also Aldhelm; Anglo-Latin Literature to 1066; Eusebius; Grammatical Treatises; Riddles

Taxes and Taxation

Medieval monarchy was dependent on taxation, but the form of tax levied was a matter of expediency. Methods of assessment were adopted, exploited, and then abandoned as they became ineffective. The picture is therefore a complex one of overlapping impositions, with innumerable variations and exemptions, and with an inevitable progression toward a series of set formulas or rates, as approved by parliament.

Two main levels of taxation may be distinguished: nationally raised taxes, payable to the king, and local taxes, paid to the lord or to the borough.

National Taxation

The Anglo-Saxon kings instituted the first land tax in medieval western Europe, the geld that continued in use until the reign of Henry II. Then the basis of assessment was changed, from land to the services due from a knight's fee, often rendered in cash terms: scutage, aids, and tallages. Overintensive exploitation of these feudal dues generated resentment under the Angevins. The revenue raised was completely inadequate to fund the growing cost of war. Hence the reign of Edward I saw the introduction of parliamentarily granted taxes on movables, an attempt to tap the resources of the realm more effectively. These taxes or subsidies were converted in 1334 into a fixed levy on each county, which in turn proved inadequate. Various unpopular expedients, such as the poll taxes of the late 14th century, were used to supplement the subsidies. During the 15th century resistance to the parliamentary granting of subsidies became so great that they were effectively abandoned between 1460 and 1513, when a new assessment was made on the basis of income.

The clergy were taxed separately from the laity. Initially the king was granted monies from papal revenues levied in England, but from the reign of Edward I the clergy began to be taxed in parallel with the laity, while papal taxation decreased in significance.

An alternative source of royal revenue was indirect taxes, particularly customs dues. The crown had ancient rights to levies, on wine and hides, for example, but from the late 13th century these were developed into a comprehensive national system. In 1275 a national custom on wool and hide exports was imposed to fund Edward I's wars; it was extended in 1303, and levies were placed on cloth exports in 1347. Tunnage was levied on wines, poundage on general merchandise. The Jews were taxed heavily until their expulsion in 1290.

Local Taxation

In rural areas a lord could demand a tallage, often an annual tax, from his unfree peasants in addition to their services and rents. Peasants also paid tolls on produce brought to market. Some townsmen benefited from exemption from tolls but made other forms of payment (renders) to the lord of the town. From the late 12th century towns began to compound with their lord to pay these as an annual lump sum known as the farm. Such revenues as the town needed for this and other purposes were raised in part from local taxes. A town could be granted the right to levy specific taxes, such as murage or pontage (for the maintenance of walls and bridges). The church also raised local taxes, the heaviest of which was the payment of a tithe on all produce.

Heather Swanson

Bibliography

Beresford, Maurice W. *The Lay Subsidies: The Poll Taxes of 1377, 1379, and 1381.* Canterbury: Phillimore, 1963; Glasscock, Robin E. *The Lay Subsidy of 1334.* London: Oxford University Press, for the British Academy, 1975; Gras, Norman S.B. *The Early English Customs System.* Cambridge: Harvard University Press, 1918; Harriss, G.L. *King, Parliament, and Public Finance in Medieval England to 1369.* Oxford: Clarendon, 1975; Heath, Peter. *Church and Realm, 1272–1461: Conflict and Collaboration in an Age of Crisis.* London: Fontana, 1988; Lander, J.R. *Government and Community: England, 1450–1509.* London: Arnold, 1980; Willard, James F. *Parliamentary Taxes on Personal Property, 1290 to 1334.* Cambridge: Mediaeval Academy of America, 1934.

See also Convocation; Customs Accounts; Knight Service; Parliament; Poll Tax; Scutage; Tunnage and Poundage

Technology

Medieval technology was more a matter of expansion and development than of invention; techniques and devices already known to antiquity or the Orient spread throughout western Europe, were improved and adapted to meet local requirements, and were often used more extensively than ever before. Improvements usually reached England later than other parts of Europe, and this sometimes had significant consequences, perhaps none more far-reaching than those of the simple foot stirrup.

Recorded in China by the 5th century, the stirrup was known in the West within 300 years. Germanic tribes on the Continent exploited its military advantage, and the superiority of mounted cavalry over infantry soldiers was demonstrated decisively at Hastings. Though many Anglo-Saxon troops rode horses equipped with stirrups, they dismounted for the battle and, in spite of numbers and position, proved no match for William's cavalry and crossbows. After this the military use of the stirrup was quickly introduced into Norman England.

The Middle Ages also witnessed two significant improvements in connection with the nonmilitary use of horses: the nailed iron shoe and the modern harness. Horseshoes had probably reached western Europe from Siberia by the end of the 9th century and were quite common by the 11th. They helped bring about the replacement of oxen by horses as draft animals in northern Europe, including England, where the damp climate made horses' hooves much more prone to damage than those of oxen.

The second improvement, the modern harness, was known to Germanic peoples by the 8th or 9th century. It represented a significant advance over the ancient yoke harness, which pressed against the horse's windpipe and jugular vein, restricting breathing and blood flow. Consisting of a stiff collar that pressed against the horse's shoulders instead, the modern harness allowed horses to pull heavier loads than with a yoke harness. As usual this innovation apparently spread throughout much of northern Europe before reaching England. Although horses were used in England by the 11th century—mainly for carting and hauling—they were not common as plow animals until the late 12th century, whereas some 300 years earlier Alfred the Great had expressed his surprise at their use for plowing in Scandinavia.

In addition to the introduction of horse power there were two other innovations in agriculture. A wheeled plow, much larger and heavier than that used in the south, was developed for the richer alluvial soils of the north. This plow eliminated the need for cross plowing, thus giving rise to the northern method of strip farming. A change from the older two-field system of crop rotation to the vastly superior three-field system began at the end of the 8th century, between the Seine and Rhine, but was apparently not used much in England until the 12th century. This new method increased the amount of land under cultivation at a given time, as well as its overall productivity, and led to a greater diversity of crops, including legumes, barley, and especially oats for the increasing number of horses.

A dramatic increase in the use of other kinds of power also took place in the Middle Ages, particularly mechanical power generated by water and wind. Watermills and windmills were known in the ancient and oriental worlds, but they were modified, improved, and used extensively in industrial processes throughout western Europe. Domesday Book (1086) lists 5,624 mills powered by water, up from fewer than 100 a century before. While its earliest use was probably for grinding corn, water power was applied to a great variety of industries and processes, from operating the bellows and hammers of forges to pulverizing ocher and other pigments for paints and dyes. In connection with textiles, for example, the fulling of cloth was one of the first processes to be mechanized during the 13th century, an important factor in the movement of the textile manufacturing industry from the southeast to the northwest in order to satisfy the increased need for water power.

Although there were windmills in Persia and Afghanistan possibly as early as the 7th century, their sails turned on a vertical axle and they do not appear to have any direct connection with the windmills of western Europe several centuries later. The European variety, perhaps patterned after watermills with vertical waterwheels—since their drive mechanisms were quite similar—had its sails on a horizontal axle, an arrangement that required the development of the post mill, on which the entire mill apparatus pivoted. This resulted in greater efficiency, as the sails always faced into the wind.

A subsequent improvement by the late 14th century was the tower mill; only the upper part of the structure bearing the sails turned. Although windmills undoubtedly existed in the West earlier, the first one to be documented stood in Yorkshire in 1185, and several others are known to have been in use prior to 1200. By the early 14th century mechanical power from both water and wind had become widespread and had relieved human beings from some of the drudgery associated with domestic and industrial processes.

In general the Middle Ages were much more familiar with mechanical devices than is usually thought. Nowhere is this more striking than with the mechanical clock. The unsuccessful attempts to construct a simple mechanical clock were described in detail in a treatise written by Robert the Englishman in 1271. These attempts possibly succeeded not long afterward, and the earliest mechanical clock may have been one made about 1286 by Bartholomew the Orologist of St. Paul's Cathedral and another in 1292 at Canterbury. Two of the first known mechanical clocks, probably already third- or even fourth-generation instruments, were Roger Stoke's tower clock with an astronomical dial, built in 1321–25 at Norwich Cathedral, and Richard of Wallingford's astronomical clock, begun about 1330 at St. Albans. Not only did the mechanical clock lead to the standardization of the length of the hour, which had previously varied between about 39 and 82 minutes at London, but it also gave rise to the metaphor of the mechanical universe, a cosmic clockwork set in motion by God, an idea already gaining currency by the end of the 14th century and providing the metaphysical basis for the impending Scientific Revolution.

Richard E. Rice

Bibliography

Gies, Frances, and Joseph Gies. *Cathedral, Forge, and Waterwheel: Technology and Invention in the Middle Ages.* New York: HarperCollins, 1994; Gille, Bertrand. *The History of Techniques.* Vol. 1: *Techniques and Civilizations.* Trans. P. Smithgate and T. Williamson. 2 vols. New York: Gordon & Breach, 1986; Gimpel, Jean. *The Medieval Machine: The Industrial Revolution of the Middle Ages.* 2d ed. Aldershot: Wildwood House, 1988; Klemm, Friedrich. *A History of Western Technology.* Trans. Dorothea W. Singer. New York: Scribner, 1959; Pacey, Arnold. *The Maze of Ingenuity: Ideas and Idealism in the Development of Technology.* New York: Holmes & Meier, 1975 [technical advances in the construction of cathedrals and mechanical clocks, and connections between them]; Singer, Charles, et al., eds. *A History of Technology.* Vol. 2: *The Mediterranean Civilizations and the Middle Ages, c. 700 B.C. to c. 1500 A.D.* Oxford: Clarendon, 1956 [significant articles on technology]; *Technology and Culture* [the journal of the Society for the History of Technology: publishes an annual "current bibliography" and carries a regular section on the Middle Ages]; White, Lynn, Jr. *Medieval Technology and Social Change.* Oxford: Clarendon, 1963 [important and controversial argument about the causative powers of technology in society); White, Lynn, Jr. *Medieval Religion and Technology: Collected Essays.* Berkeley: University of California Press, 1978.

See also Agriculture; Armies; Arms and Armor; Mills; Science; Utilitarian Writings

Tenures

We have only fragmentary information about the ways land was held before 1066. *Bocland* ("bookland") was land granted by the king or other magnate with a written document, probably with some restrictions on the grantee's right of alienation. *Folcland* ("folkland"), seldom mentioned, is more mysterious. It seems likely, however, that smaller properties were regarded in some sense as belonging to the family as a whole and on the death of the head of the family may have been divided among all his sons. That land might be leased for a determined period *(lænland)* is shown by surviving leases from the mid-10th century; whether military service was a specific rent for land has been long disputed, but service in war and the tenure of five hides of land were both seen as belonging to the dignity of a thegn.

After 1066 we are on surer ground, though it is disputed whether the changes that had occurred by the mid-12th century were made as a direct result of the Conquest itself or in the ensuing 50 years. All land was ultimately considered to be the king's. The royal estates were reserved for his direct financial profit; most other land was held of him in return for knight service. The magnates (tenants-in-chief) who owed this service secured it by subenfeoffment (or subinfeudation), granting portions to individual knights in return for their service.

Some lands were held, both of the king and of magnates, in sergeanty, that is, in return for nonmilitary personal service. Clergy and ecclesiastical institutions could hold land in free alms (frankalmoign) for spiritual services, mainly prayer. And a little land was held of the king, much more of other landlords, in socage, that is, simply for money or other rents, often more or less nominal. Besides these four kinds of free tenure—knight service, sergeanty, free alms, and socage—a fifth distinctive form had emerged by the 13th century: burgage tenure, characteristic of towns and the only form of tenure that permitted bequest to whomsoever the tenant wished.

The right of the eldest son to inherit lands held by military service was probably established only in the mid-12th century. Earlier the lord might regrant the land on the tenant's death as he wished. New procedures in the second half of the 12th century gave added legal protection to all tenures classed as free. In the course of the 13th century they became the subject of elaborate definition and precedent in common-law courts.

Over the same period tenures underwent other changes. Sergeanty virtually died out, and changes in military organization effectively replaced the actual service of knights with a money payment (scutage) that the king used for mercenaries. Military tenure was thus much more flexible; a knight's holding (i.e., a knight's fee) might now be divided into minute fractions, encouraging further levels of subenfeoffment.

This process ceased in 1290, when the statute *Quia emptores* forbade further subinfeudation. Other legislation (the Statute of Mortmain, 1279) restrained new tenure in free alms by forbidding grants of land to corporations (primarily monasteries), which, being eternal, would not produce the perquisites due to the superior lord on a tenant's death. This statute, however, was often evaded by special royal license. Thereafter the formal structure of free tenures scarcely changes until the Statute of Uses of 1535.

Serfs or villeins held by unfree customary tenure, also defined by the royal courts in the 12th century and elaborated in the 13th, the forerunner of copyhold. It should be remembered that all land held unfreely by villein tenants was at the same time held freely by their manorial lords, and local custom often, in practice, allowed these tenants to acquire free land besides their villein holdings. Unfree tenants could thus participate in the buying and selling of land, and this land market increasingly extended to their unfree holdings, technically unsellable.

Even more widely these unfree holdings might be sublet; leasing, for a fixed period or for the successive lives of one, two, or three tenants, was normal in all forms of free tenure. Domesday Book shows that by 1086 some tenants-in-chief were letting out portions of their estates to each other, and leasing out individual manors to local lessees (or farmers) for rent, in produce or money, as the method whereby large landholders normally drew profits from their estates. The exception was from the early 13th to the mid- or late 14th century, the period of so-called demesne farming, when lords mostly ran them through their own officials. In the mid-14th century portions of a manor were often leased to local tenants, foreshadowing the leasing out of the manor as a whole.

P.D.A. Harvey

Bibliography

John, Eric. *Land Tenure in Early England: A Discussion of Some Problems.* Leicester: Leicester University Press, 1960 [a general but controversial discussion]; Plucknett, T.N.T. *The Legislation of Edward I.* Oxford: Clarendon, 1949; Pollock, Frederick, and Frederic W. Maitland. *The History of English Law before the Time of Edward I.* 2d ed. 2 vols. Ed. S.F.C. Milsom. London: Cambridge University Press, 1968 [still of basic importance]; Poole, Austin Lane. *Obligations of Society in the XII and XIII Centuries.* Oxford: Clarendon, 1946; Simpson, A.W.B. *A History of the Land Law.* 2d ed. of *An Introduction to the History of the Land Law* (1961). Oxford: Clarendon, 1986 [a straightforward guide to tenure from 1066 on].

See also Feudalism; Knight Service; Labor Services; Mortmain; Quo Warranto Proceedings; Scutage; Serfs and Villeins; Statutes

Textiles and Embroideries, Anglo-Saxon

There is a significant amount of material and textual evidence for the production of a wide variety of textiles in Anglo-Saxon England. Textiles were produced primarily by women, and

Fig. 138. Anglo-Saxon regional fashions: Anglian (left), Kentish (center), Saxon (right). Drawing by Peter Dunn, in M. Welch (1992). Courtesy of B.T. Batsford, Ltd.

Anglo-Saxon women were renowned for their work. The number of objects associated with spinning, weaving, and embroidery that have come from the graves of Anglo-Saxon women suggests their identification with textile work from an early date. Fragments of the textiles themselves survive from 1,038 graves in nineteen counties. The most common types of cloth produced were varieties of tabby (plain weave) and twill. In the early period regional variations exist that are in accord with Bede's traditional division of the country into areas of Anglian, Saxon, and Jutish settlement (fig. 138). Fragments of woven gold braid from some pagan graves provide evidence of higher-quality dress. Fine silk was

imported from the Mediterranean and worn by both the secular and ecclesiastical elite. Aldhelm criticized the wearing of fine clothes by both men and women of the church, mentioning specifically linen shirts and blue tunics, embroidered sleeves and colored headdresses.

Embroidered wall hangings and furnishings were also produced. Portions of late-8th- or 9th-century embroidered vestments or altar cloths from the south of England are preserved in the Church of St. Catherine, Maaseik (Belgium). The decoration consists of interlace patterns, monograms, and animals and birds within arcades and roundels. The embroideries are worked on linen in surface-couched gold-wrapped threads and colored silks (red, cream, light blue, dark blue, green, and yellow). One, the "*velamen* of Harlindis," includes blue and green beads, pearls, and gilded sugar-loaf bosses.

Literary sources suggest that such luxurious items were often commissioned for presentation to the church. The stole, maniple, and girdle of St. Cuthbert were commissioned by Ælfflæd, wife of Edward the Elder, for Bishop Frithestan of Winchester between 909 and 916. The vestments are decorated with foliate ornament and figures of prophets, saints, and popes worked in colored silks and gold-wrapped thread on a ground of red silk. The style of both figures and acanthus ornament is related to the "Winchester style" of manuscript illumination, suggesting a degree of cross-fertilization between the media. They were presented to the shrine of St. Cuthbert by King Æthelstan in the second quarter of the 10th century. Æthelstan is also recorded as having donated three altar cloths to Chester-le-Street. Other donations include a golden cloak that King Edgar gave to Ely to be made into a chasuble in the third quarter of the 10th century and two gilded altar cloths given to Peterborough by Bishop Æthelwold.

In the late 10th century Edgar's daughter, St. Edith of Wilton, is said to have embroidered an alb with figures of Christ and the apostles that included an image of herself in a penitential pose, kissing the feet of Christ. The figures were worked in gold thread embellished with jewels, margarites, and pearls. Edith was herself rebuked by Bishop Æthelwold for her luxurious clothing.

Embroidered wall hangings also adorned the homes of the secular elite. The Bayeux Tapestry is the only such work to survive, though there are records of many others. Wall hangings adorned Hrothgar's hall, Heorot, in the poem *Beowulf.* The *Liber Eliensis* records that after Byrhtnoth's death in the Battle of Maldon (991) his widow, Ælfflæd, presented the monastery of Ely with a tapestry depicting his deeds. Ely may have been something of a needleworking center, as the *Liber Eliensis* also informs us that in the early 11th century Ethelswinth, a noblewoman, retired from the world in order to devote herself to making gold-embroidered vestments for the monastery with the help of her maidservant. Tapestries and wall hangings are also mentioned in the wills of women from the late Anglo-Saxon period, though they are not generally described in any detail.

While much, if not most, of the Anglo-Saxon textiles, wall hangings, and embroideries may have been made by women for domestic use, accounts like that of Ethelswinth suggest that by at least the 11th century many women may have been working professionally. This was clearly the case after the Conquest; both Domesday Book (1086) and the will of Queen Matilda mention professional Anglo-Saxon embroideresses in the employ of the new court. The tradition begun by these women would see its ultimate development in the Opus Anglicanum of the Gothic era.

Catherine E. Karkov

Bibliography

Budny, Mildred. "The Anglo-Saxon Embroideries at Maaseik: Their Historical and Art-Historical Context." *Medelingen van der Koniglijke Academie vor Wettenschappen, Lettern en Schone Kunsten von Belgie. Klasse der Schone Kunsten* 45/2 (1984): 57–133; Crowsfoot, Elizabeth, Francis Pritchard, and K. Staniland. *Textiles and Clothing ca. 1150–1450. Medieval Finds from Excavations in London 4.* London: HMSO, 1992; Dodwell, C.R. *Anglo-Saxon Art: A New Perspective.* Manchester: Manchester University Press, 1982; Dodwell, C.R. *The Pictorial Arts of the West 800–1200.* New Haven: Yale University Press, 1993; Fell, Christine with Cecilly Clark and Elizabeth Williams. *Women in Anglo-Saxon England and the Impact of 1066.* Bloomington: Indiana University Press, 1984; Jørgensen, Lise Bender. *North European Textiles until* A.D. *1000.* Aarhus: Aarhus University Press, 1992; Webster, Leslie, and Janet Backhouse, eds. *The Making of England: Anglo-Saxon Art and Culture* A.D. *600–900.* London: British Museum, 1991.

See also Art, Anglo-Saxon; *Battle of Maldon;* Bayeux Tapestry; Cloth; Opus Anglicanum; Textiles from St. Cuthbert's Tomb; Women and the Arts

Textiles from St. Cuthbert's Tomb

A number of silk textiles were recovered in 1827 from the tomb of St. Cuthbert (d. 687) in Durham Cathedral. None appears to date back to the 7th century, but as a group they confirm the importance of St. Cuthbert's shrine and cult. The embroidered stole and maniples and the tablet-woven bands are Anglo-Saxon and of high quality. In addition there are two full-width silks of ca. 800—the first, Byzantine with a design on the theme of Earth and Ocean, and the second, central Asian of uncertain decoration—and two textiles that are probably 11th- to 12th-century Spanish origin—a figured twill with a double-headed peacock and a twill with a stamped gold design of a mounted falconer.

The stole and its matching maniple were almost certainly among the gifts made in 934 to the shrine of St. Cuthbert at Chester-le-Street by Æthelstan, king of Wessex. Inscriptions show that they had been made in Winchester between 909 and 916. The fragmentary stole, measuring overall ca. 6.6 feet by 2.4 inches, is decorated with the standing figures of eleven prophets; the style is fluid and shows the influence of Byzantine manuscript illumination. The maniple, ca. 32.3 inches by 2.4 inches, with the figures of two popes and two deacons, is more robust and local in style. Figures, inscriptions, and foliage are in colored silk thread worked in split and stem stitch and the background is in surface-couched gold thread (in technique and organization the embroidery looks forward to later Opus Anglicanum). The borders are narrow tablet-woven bands.

A second, smaller maniple was originally a strip ca. 48.8 inches by 1 inch with wedge-shaped tabs, but at some point it was cut in half and sewn edge to edge. This may be another of Æthelstan's gifts, since its acanthus-leaf decoration resembles closely the lower borders of the frontispiece of the copy of Bede's *Lives of St. Cuthbert* donated by the king on the same occasion. Here the embroidery is two-sided with the same design either in couched gold thread against a split-stitch purple silk ground or with the colors reversed.

Three pieces of gold-brocaded silk tablet weaving must also date to the 10th century. One, ca. 24 inches by 0.8 inch, has been referred to as a "girdle" and the others, circles of 7.9 inches in circumference and 0.8 inch in width, as "wrist bands"; all were probably once sewn to a garment. The designs of acanthus leaves and so on again recall the borders of the Bede manuscript.

Among fragments possibly added to the relics while they were still on Lindisfarne are the remains of a garment, probably an ecclesiastical dalmatic, of the 8th to 9th century. This was made principally from two similar white silks edged with a brightly colored band, ca. 1.3 inches wide. The white silks, decorated with cross motifs, were perhaps imported from Italy. The design of the band, of repeating stylized palmettes and heart-shaped buds, relates closely to borders on contemporary Sogdian full-width silks. But the technique, tablet weaving with soumak brocading, shows it was locally made, at the time the garment was made up.

Hero Granger-Taylor

Bibliography

Battiscombe, C.F., ed. *The Relics of Saint Cuthbert.* Oxford: Oxford University Press, 1956; Bonner, Gerald, David Rollason, and Clare Stancliffe, eds. *St. Cuthbert, His Cult and His Community to A.D. 1200.* Woodbridge: Boydell, 1989; Granger-Taylor, Hero. "The Earth and Ocean Silk from the Tomb of St. Cuthbert at Durham." *Textile History* 20 (1989): 151–66.

See also Æthelstan; Coffin of St. Cuthbert; Cuthbert; Opus Anglicanum; Textiles, Anglo-Saxon

Textual Criticism
Old English

The traditional aim of OE textual criticism, in the words of S.O. Andrew, is "the 'making of a text,' that is, the restoration of the form presented by the MS. to that intended by the author" (145). Like all statements of first principles this one entails certain assumptions: first, that a given manuscript does not preserve exactly the text as authorized for circulation; second, that reliable methods are available for restoring the text of the author's intention from the surviving evidence; and third, that the text of the author's intention claims priority over all other versions.

When holographs survive in medieval literature, there is no need to assume anything about the accuracy of scribal transmission. Scholars can edit a work directly from the original document, and other copies (which still claim interest) can be compared directly with the original. But in the general absence of known authorial documents in OE it is reasonable to suppose that few surviving copies fully preserve authorial texts as originally recorded. Support for the assumption comes from the fact that any two copies of an OE work show differences or variants.

One class of variants, sometimes called "accidentals," consists of differences in format, morpheme division, capitalization, accentuation, punctuation, and spelling. Such variants are copious among the twenty-odd manuscript copies of Cædmon's Hymn—including the two earliest, Northumbrian versions—and seem inevitable in scribal transmission; most editors (rightly or wrongly) disregard all accidentals except spelling variants.

The more important class of variants consists of differences in the actual words, or "substantives." It is difficult to generalize about this category. In the case of Cædmon's Hymn the wording of the two 8th-century Northumbrian versions is virtually identical, and a 10th-century West Saxon version agrees with them apart from a single word. Other versions, however, show a freedom in copying substantives that suggests either the influence of oral tradition, in which wording is not regarded as final or fixed, or dictation from memory.

Prose works display similar variety. Some manuscripts of Alfred's translation of Gregory's *Pastoral Care* show what seems conservative copying, but others show deliberate lexical and syntactic modernization of the text. Hence, although no manuscript is likely to preserve the accidentals of the archetypal copy, some manuscripts may preserve, or come close to preserving, the original words. Each witness—including early-modern transcripts or early printed editions—must be judged on its own: on occasion the evidence is sufficient to permit drawing up a stemma, showing relations among witnesses; usually definitive judgments on particular witnesses are not possible.

Textual critics suspect that a reading is not authorial when it makes little or no sense or when it is somehow uncharacteristic of or inconsistent with the rest of the work (including, in the case of poetry, alliteration or meter). The underlying assumption is that poor readings are more likely to originate from copyists than from authors. To restore what they believe to be authorial readings textual critics employ collation (where possible), paleography, philology, history, source study, or stylistics—in short, whatever may illuminate a text. Scholars working with a text attested by more than one manuscript enjoy a decided advantage, as one copy may serve to correct another. (The advantage is rare in OE poetic texts, however; only about 7 percent of the extant 31,000 lines of OE verse survives in more than one copy.) But multiple copies may complicate matters when alternative readings make sense; even so—given the revising habits of many scribes—there is no guarantee that one of the readings is the author's.

In view of such uncertainty E.G. Stanley concludes, "We cannot get back to the author's original" (273). A less daunting formulation is that, in passages where we suspect there are nonauthorial readings, we have fairly plausible methods for attempting to return to the author's substantives but no certainty that we have actually restored them or even, in the case of emendations made for purely stylistic or aesthetic reasons, that the attempt is warranted.

Although recovering the text of the author's intention can be complicated by the fact that some authors (Ælfric most notably) issued different versions of their work, perhaps the majority of OE scholars would agree that an "authorial text" should in principle have priority over all other versions. The indeterminacy inherent in trying to establish the authorial ideal, however, has suggested to some critics a less speculative, more documentary approach. Those who provide a "scribal text" do not try to reconstruct the author's archetype but accept for practical purposes a given manuscript version, emending substantives only where they do not make sense. Reconstructing the author's archetype has also been challenged by "social text" theorists (e.g., McGann), who argue that a work is not created by an author alone but by all those contributing to the production of the text as we have it; in the field of OE such collaborators would include the scribes as well as any others whose editing, correcting, or glossing can be distinguished from that of the scribes.

In practice a social text may closely resemble a scribal text, but the underlying critical motives differ. In theory scribal and authorial texts are related, in that the editor of a scribal text typically selects a version believed closest to the author's. Authorial and social texts are at opposite ends of the spectrum, however, in both theory and practice: the authorial critic aims to restore an ideal text transcending any particular witness; the social critic selects and edits a particular witness on the basis of its historical importance or influence.

Middle English

Just as ME literature is different in subject, tone, and language from OE, so are the texts in which the two cultures are preserved. Like OE most ME occurs only in manuscript, but in the late 15th century some works (e.g., Malory's *Morte Darthur,* for which no manuscript was known until the 20th century) achieve wider distribution in print. ME manuscripts are written in a variety of scripts (unlike the single "pointed minuscule" of OE), and the linguistic range (by period and dialect) is similarly greater than OE. Although some important ME works resemble OE texts in that they survive in a single manuscript (e.g., the *oeuvre* of the *Pearl/Gawain*-poet), much ME literature appears in multiple manuscripts. Furthermore these manuscripts are often heavily reworked by their scribes, sometimes producing recognizably different "versions" (e.g., the three versions of *Piers Plowman*). Even works that have less internal variability (like the *Canterbury Tales*) are often multiform in intention, with each manuscript or group of manuscripts representing a different "state."

Unlike virtually all OE authors some ME authors are definitely not anonymous and in rare cases were scribes of their own works, which thus exist in holograph (e.g., Orm's *Ormulum,* possibly Chaucer's *Equatorie of the Planets,* many of Hoccleve's poems, and some of Capgrave's works). And finally ME encompasses a wider definition of "literature" than OE, with some genres (e.g., drama and extended prose fiction) that do not exist in the earlier period. Thus the multiplicity and complexity of ME literary documents mean that ME editors—like biblical, classical, and later vernacular scholars, but unlike OE editors—are typically confronted with problems of textual filiation, the attempt to discover the relations among documents.

The earliest editors of ME were the scribes themselves, who often practiced what Pearsall has called "creative engagement" with their authors (1985: 103). Some works, like *Piers Plowman,* seem to have been especially receptive to such treatment, but others, like Hoccleve's *Regement of Princes,* are comparatively stable. In some cases, even where only two manuscripts survive, there are essentially two scribal or possibly authorial versions, so comprehensive is the reworking (e.g., *The Owl and the Nightingale*). Following the scribes, the early printers "edited" the texts they printed, thereby both reflecting and helping to create the literary taste of their day. Caxton's dissatisfaction with the exemplar for his first edition of the *Canterbury Tales* and his decision to use another for his second, and Wynkyn de Worde's change of copy text for his edition of Trevisa's translation of Bartholomaeus Anglicus's *De proprietatibus rerum,* are well-known examples.

Early printers usually modernized and normalized their texts, and this practice, together with an impressionistic "improvement" of the language, was the norm until Madden's editions of romance and the Wycliffite Bible in the early 19th century. Even W.W. Skeat, the great philologist, had a "confidence that he knew what Chaucer meant even when the manuscripts did not" (Edwards, 1987: 47), a persuasion followed by Kane and Donaldson in the *Piers Plowman* B text. The opposite approach—documentary fidelity—is often associated with the Early English Text Society, begun by F.J. Furnivall to provide materials for the *Oxford English Dictionary* and hence disposed to preserving manuscript orthography. The EETS editions of the *Ancrene Riwle* (or *Ancrene Wisse*), where every scribal oddity is reproduced, leave the reader to create an edition out of the surviving copies.

There is thus a range of documentary fidelity available to the ME editor. At one extreme is the photographic facsimile, for a record of the bibliographical features of the work (e.g., its makeup or foliation) or as a register of taste, especially in anthology manuscripts. Next is the diplomatic transcript, where orthographic features are preserved, but in a modern typography. The next level of fidelity is the best-text edition, often described as being "in the form of" a specific manuscript witness, selected for its provenance or position in the descent of the text. Best-text editions will usually correct "obvious" errors but will otherwise remain conservative. Thereafter comes the "critical" edition created by recension, the comparison of errors in manuscripts and the arrangement of the manuscripts into a family tree, or stemma. And finally there is "deep editing" of the sort practiced by Kane and Donaldson, where recension will not yield a consistent descent and thus the editor attempts to construct a text impressionistically. "Eclectic" editing (conflated from various documents), "synoptic" or "genetic" editing (showing the growth of a work through its states), and "social" editing (charting the postauthorial states), associated with textual scholarship in later periods, have not yet had much effect on ME editing.

J.R. Hall
D.C. Greetham

Bibliography

OLD ENGLISH

Amos, Ashley Crandell. *Linguistic Means of Determining the Dates of Old English Literary Texts.* Cambridge: Medieval Academy of America, 1980; Andrew, S.O. "Scribal Error and Its Sources." *Postscript on Beowulf.* Cambridge: Cambridge University Press, 1948, pp. 133–52; Baker, Peter S. "A Little-Known Variant Text of the Old English Metrical Psalms." *Speculum* 59 (1984): 263–81; Hall, J.R. "Old English Literature." In *Scholarly Editing: A Guide to Research,* ed. D.C. Greetham. New York: MLA, 1995, pp. 149–83; Horgan, Dorothy M. "The Lexical and Syntactic Variants Shared by Two of the Later Manuscripts of King Alfred's Translation of Gregory's *Cura pastoralis.*" *ASE* 9 (1981): 213–21; Jabbour, Alan. "Memorial Transmission in Old English Poetry." *ChauR* 3 (1969): 174–90; Kiernan, Kevin S. *Beowulf and the Beowulf Manuscript.* New Brunswick: Rutgers University Press, 1981; Lapidge, Michael. "Textual Criticism and the Literature of Anglo-Saxon England." *BJRL* 73 (1991): 17–45; Liuzza, Roy Michael. "The Texts of the Old English *Riddle 30.*" *JEGP* 87 (1988): 1–15; McGann, Jerome J. *A Critique of Modern Textual Criticism.* Chicago: University of Chicago Press, 1983; O'Keeffe, Katherine O'Brien. *Visible Song: Transitional Literacy in Old English Verse.* Cambridge: Cambridge University Press, 1990; Robinson, Fred C. "Print Culture and the Birth of the Text." *Sewanee Review* 89 (1981): 423–30; Stanley, E.G. "Unideal Principles of Editing Old English Verse." *PBA* 70 (1984 [1985]): 231–73.

MIDDLE ENGLISH

Edwards, A.S.G. "Observations on the History of Middle English Editing." In *Manuscripts and Texts: Editorial Problems in Later Middle English Literature,* ed. Derek Pearsall. Cambridge: Brewer, 1987, pp. 34–48; Edwards, A.S.G. "Middle English Literature." In *Scholarly Editing: A Guide to Research,* ed. D.C. Greetham. New York: MLA, 1995, pp. 184–203; Kane, George. *Chaucer and Langland: Historical and Textual Approaches.* London: Athlone, 1989; Kleinhenz, Christopher, ed. *Medieval Manuscripts and Textual Criticism.* Chapel Hill: University of North Carolina Press, 1976; Machan, Tim William, ed. *Medieval Literature: Texts and Interpretation.* MRTS 79. Binghamton: MRTS, 1991; Machan, Tim William. *Textual Criticism and Middle English Texts.* Charlottesville: University Press of Virginia, 1994; Minnis, A.J., and Charlotte Brewer, eds. *Crux and Controversy in Middle English Textual Criticism.* Cambridge: Brewer, 1992; Moorman, Charles. *Editing the Middle English Manuscript.* Jackson: University Press of Mississippi, 1975; Pearsall, Derek. "Editing Medieval Texts: Some Developments and Some Problems." In *Textual Criticism and Literary Interpretation,* ed. Jerome J. McGann. Chicago: University of Chicago Press, 1985, pp. 92–106; Pearsall, Derek.

"Theory and Practice in Middle English Editing." *Text* 7 (1994): 107–26; Rigg, A.G., ed. *Editing Medieval Texts: English, French, and Latin Written in England.* New York: Garland, 1977; Ruggiers, Paul G., ed. *Editing Chaucer: The Great Tradition.* Norman: Pilgrim Books, 1984; *Textual Criticism.* Special Issue, *Romance Philology* 45 (August 1991).

See also Ælfric; Books; Cædmon; Capgrave; Caxton; Chaucer; Criticism, Modern, of Medieval Literature; Hoccleve; Literacy; Malory; Manuscripts of Polyphonic Music; *Owl and the Nightingale;* Paleography and Codicology; *Piers Plowman;* Wycliffite Texts

Thegns

The word *thegn* was part of everyday Anglo-Saxon vocabulary and only slowly came to acquire a specialized meaning. Connected with the verb *thegnian* ("to serve"), originally simply signifying a servant, it was used in that sense in poetry and prose late in the period.

Prestige was attached to royal service, and already in the laws of Ine (ca. 690) the heavy penalty of 60 shillings was exacted from anyone breaking into the fortified dwelling of a king's thegn, significantly more than the 35-shilling penalty if an ordinary nobleman were affected. The Alfredian translators used *thegn* to render a variety of Latin words, especially *miles* ("soldier, warrior") and *minister,* and to express a wide range of service, from members of the royal hearth troop to the lad who ran errands for an abbess.

The last phase of Anglo-Saxon England, however, from Alfred to the Conquest, saw a significant tightening of usage, reflecting substantial as well as terminological development. Thegns flourished, especially king's thegns, as the function of kingship itself became more sophisticated. By the end of the period a thegn was normally a landowner with precise military duties and special responsibility for keeping order within the shires. In the Danelaw, by the reign of Æthelred II, the twelve most prominent thegns in a *wapentake* (a subdivision of a shire) took solemn oaths to enforce justice; a thegn could lose his thegnship for bringing in a false verdict.

To be a thegn meant to enjoy a specific status. There are many indications of an evolution, as Anglo-Saxon thegnage became akin to manorial lordship and the county gentry of later times, as well as being close in many respects to the royal vassals of the rudimentary feudal order on the Continent. A man could be "thegn-born" or "ceorl-born." In the laws of Cnut (1020–23) thegns were distinguished by special heriots (the property returned to a lord on a tenant's death), and something of a hierarchy within the thegnage itself was suggested by the differentiation between the thegns in immediate relationship to the king and the others. A royal thegn was to have no other lord.

Mobility still existed within society. An 11th-century private compilation tells how a ceorl would be entitled to the rights of a thegn if he prospered to the point where he possessed fully "five hides of his own, a church and a kitchen, a bell and a castle gate, a seat and a special office in the king's hall." A merchant who made a trip overseas three times at his own expense was said to be worthy of thegn-right. In turn the thegn himself could flourish so that he became an earl. Some of the old generalized feeling of service was preserved in poetry and everyday speech, but by the end of the period the thegn with his rights and status was in many of his attributes the recognizable ancestor of the knight of the shire of the high Middle Ages.

H.R. Loyn

Bibliography

Loyn, H.R. *Anglo-Saxon England and the Norman Conquest.* 2d ed. London: Longmans, 1991.

See also Gentry; Knight Service

Theodore of Tarsus (602–690)

Archbishop Theodore of Canterbury (668–90) was one of the most learned men ever to hold that see. The outline of his career is known from Bede (*Ecclesiastical History* 4.1–2; 5.8) but can now be supplemented by incidental biographical details contained in recently published biblical commentaries composed in his school at Canterbury.

Born at Tarsus in the Greek-speaking province of Cilicia (now southern Turkey), Theodore probably received his early training at nearby Antioch and at Edessa in Syria; he subsequently went, as a young man, to Constantinople, which was then the center of learning in the Roman Empire. During these years Theodore acquired training in Roman civil law, philosophy, astronomy, medicine, rhetoric, and ecclesiastical computus. He later went to Rome, where he became involved in theological controversies and the Lateran Council of 649.

Appointed archbishop in 667, Theodore arrived in England in 668 and swiftly set about restructuring the English episcopal dioceses. He established a school at Canterbury, where, with his colleague Hadrian, he gave instruction in biblical exegesis and ecclesiastical computus, as well as astronomy, meter, and Roman law.

The results of this instruction are seen principally in the recently published biblical commentaries on the Pentateuch and Gospels, the record of Theodore's (and Hadrian's) oral teaching on the text of the Bible as written down by a group of English students. These commentaries, revealing an astonishing range of learning in Greek patristic exegesis, may represent the high point of Anglo-Saxon scholarship. Other texts from the Canterbury school of Theodore and Hadrian illustrate other aspects of their learning: a collection of glossaries known as the "Leiden Family"; some octosyllabic poems in a distinctive trochaic rhythm; a collection of *Iudicia,* or pronouncements, by Theodore on matters of penitence and canon law; and a chronographical-exegetical text known as the *Laterculus Malalianus,* translated in part from the Byzantine chronicle of John Malalas.

Michael Lapidge

Bibliography

Bischoff, Bernhard, and Michael Lapidge, eds. *Biblical Commentaries from the Canterbury School of Theodore and Hadrian.* Cambridge: Cambridge University Press, 1994; Brooks, Nicholas P. *The Early History of the Church of Canterbury.* Leicester: Leicester University Press, 1984; Lapidge, Michael. "The School of Theodore and Hadrian." *ASE* 15 (1986): 45–72; Lapidge, Michael, ed. *Archbishop Theodore.* Cambridge: Cambridge University Press, 1995; Stevenson, J. *The "Laterculus Malalianus" and the School of Archbishop Theodore.* Cambridge: Cambridge University Press, 1995.

See also Anglo-Latin Literature to 1066; Bishops; Canterbury, Ecclesiastical Province of; Conversion of the Anglo-Saxons

Theodulf of Orléans (ca. 760–821)

A Goth born in Spain, Theodulf was forced to flee his homeland, coming to the court of Charlemagne in 780. By 798 he was named bishop of Orléans by Charlemagne. In 801 Pope Leo III honored him with the title of archbishop. Theodulf enjoyed high visibility and favor in the courts of Charlemagne and his successor, Louis the Pious. His luck changed, however, in 817, when he was accused of conspiring against the emperor, whereupon he was removed from his bishopric and imprisoned. He died, thus disgraced, in 821.

Although Theodulf is best known today as one of the preeminent poets of the Carolingian renaissance, he was probably more valued among his contemporaries for his theological and pastoral works. Around 800 he composed his first *Capitula,* a manual for parish priests, in an attempt to institute a reform within his diocese, and a second somewhere between 800 and 813. Forty-one copies survive throughout Europe and England, written between the 9th and 12th centuries, attesting to the popularity of the work. At Charlemagne's request he wrote the *Libri Carolini* under the pretense that it was actually the emperor's work. He also wrote *De ordine baptismi* and supervised a revision of the Bible at his scriptorium.

Theodulf's *Capitula* was widely used during the Anglo-Saxon monastic reform and survives in four English manuscripts. In Latin and English it became a standard work for the clergy and a source for Anglo-Saxon prose. Vercelli Homily III and Assmann Homilies XI and XII draw from the *Capitula;* Ælfric seems to have used it in his pastoral letters; and Wulfstan used it in composing his homilies. The *De ordine baptismi* was also known to the Anglo-Saxons. The text, surviving in BL Royal 8.C.iii, was used by Wulfstan in Homily VIII.

Helene Scheck

Bibliography

PRIMARY

Napier, Arthur S., ed. *The Old English Version of the Enlarged Rule of Chrodegang . . . ; An Old English Version of the Capitula of Theodulf. . . .* EETS o.s. 150. London: Kegan Paul, Trench, Trübner, 1916; Theodulf. *Opera Omnia. PL* 105.

SECONDARY

Gatch, Milton McC. *Preaching and Theology in Anglo-Saxon England: Ælfric and Wulfstan.* Toronto: University of Toronto Press, 1977; Godman, Peter. *Poets and Emperors: Frankish Politics and Carolingian Poetry.* Oxford: Clarendon, 1987; McKitterick, Rosamond, ed. *Carolingian Culture: Emulation and Innovation.* Cambridge: Cambridge University Press, 1994.

See also Benedictine Reform; Literary Influences: Carolingian; Sermons; Wulfstan

Thomas of Canterbury, Office for

One of the first strictly rhymed offices written in England, and probably the most important, the *historia* for Thomas Becket was written between 1170 (the year of Thomas's martyrdom) and 1177 or 1193. Its original form was no doubt monastic, surely intended for use at St. Augustine's Abbey, Canterbury. The author of its texts and composer of its chants was Abbot Benedict of Peterborough, a former monk at Canterbury. But, adopted by the newly emerged Sarum Use, it is best known in its secular form. The high quality and distinctive features of the office have recently been described and may have been partly responsible for its wide distribution. Like the veneration of the saint, which quickly spread across the whole of Europe, the office itself was similarly distributed and used and formed the basis for dozens, perhaps hundreds, of later offices. Several of its chants were used as the tenors of polyphonic compositions, in the Notre Dame School, in the 14th century, and in the early-15th-century Old Hall Manuscript. One of its texts was set to polyphony by Palestrina. Interesting is its use of melisma for stressed and syllabic setting for unstressed syllables, what seems to be a motivic emphasis for important words, and two or three passages in which a subtle word painting may occur.

Some of the items in the office had different chants on the Continent, and, together with lesser variants in the sources, it is possible to isolate regional or local versions. Several other offices to the saint also exist, including two for his translation in 1220, and the complex relations between them have yet to be explored. In many English liturgical books the office has been torn out, blackened, or otherwise defaced, in an attempt by Henry VIII's commissioners to remove all traces of the saint.

Andrew Hughes

Bibliography

Hughes, Andrew. "Chants in the Offices of Thomas of Canterbury and Stanislaus of Poland." *Musica Antiqua* (Bydgoszoz) 6 (1982): 267–77; Hughes, Andrew. "Chants in the Rhymed Office of St Thomas of Canterbury." *Early Music* 16 (1988): 185–202; Hughes, Andrew. "British Rhymed Offices: A Catalogue and Commentary." In *Music in the Medieval English Liturgy: Plainsong and Mediaeval Music Society Centennial Essays,* ed. Susan Rankin and David Hiley. Oxford: Clarendon, 1993, pp. 239–84; Husmann, Heinrich. "Zur Überlieferung der Thomas-Officien." In *Organicae Voces: Festschrift Joseph Smits van Waesberghe.* Amsterdam: Instituut voor Middeleeuwse Muziekwetenschap, 1963, pp. 87–88; Stevens, Denis. "Music in Honor of St. Thomas of Canterbury." *Musical Quarterly* 56 (1970): 311–48.

See also Becket; Feasts, New Liturgical; Offices, New Liturgical

Tiberius Psalter

BL Cotton Tiberius C.vi is a Latin psalter in the Gallican version, complete only to Psalm 113. Each psalm has a continuous interlinear gloss in OE and is followed by a Latin collect. Prefatory text gatherings contain common psalter prefaces, instructions for the use of the psalter in private penitential devotions, a long confessional *ordo,* an OE homily on the seven gifts of the Holy Spirit, and extracts from a Pseudo-Jerome treatise on musical instruments, as well as computus tables. Its lavish illustration includes 24 full-page colored line drawings, two fully painted miniatures, five painted initial pages with "Winchester School" frames, and six smaller painted initials. Attribution to Winchester ca. 1060 is supported by paleographic, textual, stylistic, and iconographic evidence.

In accord with insular tradition Psalms 1, 51, 101, and 109 are marked with framed, painted initial pages, with the innovative addition of a similar initial page at the start of the prefatory texts. A clear hierarchy of images faces these pages. The two painted miniatures, an intercessory image of Christ the Judge and a portrait of the psalmist David with his musicians, form major visual stops in the manuscript at the opening pages of the two major textual segments, the prefatory matter and the psalter proper. Full-page line drawings of St. Jerome (?) and Christ trampling the beasts face initials to Psalms 51 and 101, and a half-page drawing of the Trinity faces Psalm 109. The initial psalms of the remaining liturgical divisions of the psalter are marked with smaller painted initials.

The manuscript is renowned as the first surviving psalter with a prefatory cycle of Old and New Testament miniatures. The cycle commences with illustrations associated with the computus: Christ/*Vita* triumphing over *Mors* (fig. 139), a horologium and paschal hand, and the Creation. Sixteen colored line drawings illustrate episodes from the lives of David and Christ and are chosen to emphasize the typological relationships between them. A drawing of St. Michael fighting the dragon concludes the cycle, echoing its major theme of the conquest of evil. Though Wormald speculated that the cycle might reflect a 10th-century model, recent research shows that it was assembled in the 11th century as a complement to the psalter's prefatory texts. Text choices and thematic emphases suggest compilation primarily for the private penitential devotions of an ecclesiastic, with occasional communal use a secondary function.

Following the St. Michael drawing are three pages of illustrations of musical instruments, annotated with extracts from the Pseudo-Jerome letter and accompanied by a full-page portrait of King David enthroned. Found in only a few early manuscripts, these arcane pictures closely reflect a Carolingian source.

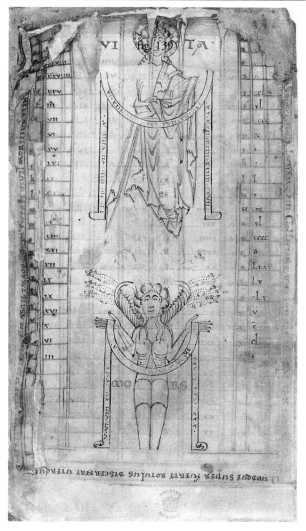

Bibliography

Backhouse, Janet, Derek H. Turner, and Leslie Webster, eds. *The Golden Age of Anglo-Saxon Art 966–1066.* London: British Museum, 1984, cat. no. 66; Campbell, Alastair P. *The Tiberius Psalter.* Ottawa Medieval Texts and Studies 2. Ottawa: University of Ottawa Press, 1974 [text edition]; Gameson, Richard. "English Manuscript Art in the Mid-Eleventh Century: The Decorative Tradition." *AntJ,* forthcoming; Heimann, Adelheid. "Three Illustrations from the Bury St. Edmunds Psalter and Their Prototypes." *JWCI* 29 (1966): 39–59; Heimann, Adelheid. "The Battle between Christ and Satan in the Tiberius Psalter." *JWCI* 52 (1989): 14–33; Openshaw, Kathleen M. "The Symbolic Illustration of the Psalter: An Insular Tradition." *Arte Medievale* 2, ser. 6 (1992): 41–60; Temple, Elżbieta. *Anglo-Saxon Manuscripts 900–1066.* A Survey of Manuscripts Illuminated in the British Isles 2, ed. J.J.G. Alexander. London: Harvey Miller, 1976; Wormald, Francis. *English Drawings of the Tenth and Eleventh Centuries.* London: Faber & Faber, 1952; Wormald, Francis. "An English Eleventh-Century Psalter with Pictures." *Walpole Society* 38 (1960–62): 1–13. Repr. in *Francis Wormald: Collected Writings,* ed. Jonathan J.G. Alexander, T. Julian Brown, and Joan Gibbs. Vol. 1. London: Harvey Miller, 1984, pp. 123–37; Zarnecki, George, Janet Holt, and Tristram Holland, eds. *English Romanesque Art 1066–1200.* London: Weidenfeld & Nicolson, 1984, cat. no. 1.

See also Galba Psalter; Psalters, Anglo-Saxon; "Winchester School"

The Tiberius Psalter compiler inventively synthesized a remarkable range of source materials and influences. The strong David-Christ typology is derived from the Irish world, and that milieu was the ultimate source of inspiration for the intercessory miniature of Christ the Judge. Three of the five narrative David scenes closely follow pre-Iconoclastic Byzantine sources, while one draws on contemporary Anglo-Saxon ruler imagery. The portrait of David with his co-psalmists combines Carolingian features with elements from an earlier Anglo-Saxon picture. The Christ cycle is assembled from a range of contemporary and earlier predominantly Anglo-Saxon pictorial sources, enriched with details reflecting monastic vernacular writing and Winchester iconographic traditions. This eclectic selection balances the equally eclectic prefatory texts. The function or purpose of this assemblage is reasonably clear, but the impetus for such a wide-ranging and comprehensive selection of contents remains a mystery. The numerous examples of rare or unique iconography combine with a forceful and accomplished, if somewhat static and eccentric, late "Winchester style." When executed in full body color, as in the miniature of David and his musicians, this style presages the Romanesque.

Kathleen M. Openshaw

Tiles

Ceramic tiles were used to make decorative floors for secular, monastic, and ecclesiastical buildings. Their use can be traced back to the 10th century, but the real development of tile floors begins in the 13th century under the patronage of Henry III and his half-brother Richard of Cornwall. Tiles, popular through to the 16th century, are an essential component of Gothic architecture.

Kiln sites have been located throughout England, and no doubt many remain to be discovered. The craft began as a luxury industry, providing tiles for a wealthy secular and ecclesiastical elite, but with the rise of a wealthy merchant class in the late 13th and 14th centuries demand grew and commercial workshops began to appear. Tilers produced roof tiles and floor tiles, using the same clay for each. By the late 13th century shaped tiles were created by scoring the design into square tiles and separating the pieces after the tile was fired. The variety of colors required for the more decorative floor tiles was achieved through the use of different lead-based glazes, inlay, and slips of different-colored clays. Decoration varied from simple geometrical or foliate forms (e.g., the ca. 1480–1515 pavement from Canynges House, Redcliffe Street, Bristol, now in the British Museum), to heraldic motifs (e.g., the royal arms included in the Westminster Chapter House pavement of ca.

Fig. 140. Chertsey Tiles, Richard and Saladin (London, British Museum MLA designs 467, 468, 602, 611, 614, 616–18, 648). Courtesy of the Trustees of the British Museum, London.

1250–80), and narrative subjects, exemplified by the famous tiles from Chertsey Abbey (fig. 140) produced 1250–80. The Chertsey tiles include scenes from the romance of Tristan and Isolde, the combat between Richard the Lionheart and Saladin, and the labors of the months. This range of subject matter suggests that they were originally designed for a palace rather than an abbey.

Tiles were made by pressing the clay over a square wooden frame or shaped template, trimming the pieces with a wire bow or knife, smoothing the tops, and drying in a shed. When dry the tiles were decorated and fired. Basic designs of individual tiles were commonly either stamped or molded. More elaborate designs could be individually cut. In the 14th century a *sgraffito* technique, in which lines were cut through the slip, revealing a second color beneath, was used to achieve fine details.

The design of a tile floor consisted of an overall pattern divided into panels, with the decorative design of each panel formed through the juxtaposition of the individually decorated tiles. Alternatively tiles could be cut into different shapes and combined to form a tile mosaic, a technique possibly developed in imitation of Italian floor mosaics. The technique could be used for the creation of elegant geometric patterns (e.g., the mosaics from Rievaulx Abbey, Yorkshire, some of which are in the British Museum), as well as more complex designs composed of panels incorporating figural or animal motifs *(opus sectile)*. The ca. 1324 Adam and Eve panel from Prior Cruden's Chapel, Ely, is a fine example of this technique. The subject is highly unusual in this medium and is no doubt based on similar scenes in manuscript illumination.

The most elaborate series of narrative tiles to survive are the ten Tring tiles now in the British Museum (eight) and the Victoria and Albert Museum (two). Decorated with scenes from the infancy of Christ, they have close parallels in manuscript illumination. Their excellent condition suggests that they may have been made for a wall rather than a floor.

While many tile floors were purely decorative, others had a didactic function. The positioning of the Adam and Eve panel in front of the altar in Prior Cruden's Chapel provides a lesson in fall and redemption. The pavement of the old refectory at Cleeve Abbey, Somerset, includes the arms of England, Clare, and Poitou and is likely to have been laid in celebration of the 1271/72 marriage of Margaret of Clare to Edmund, son of Richard of Cornwall (also count of Poitou) and nephew of Henry III. The depiction of Richard the Lionheart's defeat of Saladin on the Chertsey tiles carried an obvious political message whose meaning was made explicit by the accompanying Latin inscriptions.

Tile pavements remained a popular type of floor throughout the Middle Ages. They fell out of favor in the 16th century, when a taste for Italian-influenced architecture and black-and-white paneled floors developed.

Catherine E. Karkov

Bibliography

Austwick, J. *The Decorated Tile: An Illustrated History of English Tile-Making and Design.* New York: Scribner, 1981; Cherry, John. "Tiles" and related individual entries in *Age of Chivalry: Art in Plantagenet England 1200–1400,* ed. Jonathan Alexander and Paul Binski. London: Royal Academy of Arts, 1987, esp. pp. 181–82; Eames, Elizabeth. *Catalogue of Medieval Lead-Glazed Earthenware Tiles in the Department of Medieval and Later Antiquities, British Museum.* London: British

Museum, 1980; Eames, Elizabeth. *English Medieval Tiles*. London: British Museum, 1985; Eames, Elizabeth. *English Tilers*. London: British Museum, 1992; Stopford, J. "Modes of Production among Medieval Tilers." *Medieval Archaeology* 37 (1993): 93–108.

See also Architecture and Architectural Sculpture, Gothic; Art, Gothic

Tin Industry and Trade

English tin was the purest and most abundant in Europe. From the middle of the 3rd century (when production collapsed in northern Spain) until the middle of the 13th century (when deposits in Bohemia and Saxony began to be exploited) Devon and Cornwall possessed a virtual monopoly of European tin production. Even after the development of alternative sources England dominated the international markets of Europe and the Middle East until well into the 17th century.

Alluvial deposits, from which tin was extracted by "streaming," that is, washing away the accompanying stones and earth, were the richest source of English tin until the mid-16th century, although deeper mining occurred from the 14th century on. Many of the works were substantial, with up to 50 laborers (often employed by wealthy tin merchants), and the number of tinners in Cornwall and Devon must have reached 6,000 to 8,000 (including a large proportion of women and children) when production was booming. The industry was on a much larger scale in Cornwall than in Devon.

The tinners of Cornwall and Devon enjoyed extensive privileges, the most important of which was the right to search and dig freely for tin (granted in a royal charter of 1201) in return for giving a proportion of the tin to the lord of the soil. Civil and criminal jurisdiction over the tinners was in the hands of a warden of the "stannaries" (the districts comprising the tin works and smelting plants). In 1305 the tinners were granted exemption from most general taxation and freedom from tolls and market dues. In return they paid a heavy tax on production, called coinage duty.

Most tin went into the manufacture of pewter (an alloy of two or more metals, with tin predominant). The demand for pewter increased steadily, and by the late 15th century it was used by all but the poorer classes, for drinking pots, flagons, plates, spoons, and other tableware. Tin was used with copper for church bells and organs and for the casting of bronze cannon. Vast numbers of tin medallions and mementoes, especially of pilgrims' badges, were produced. There were pewterers' guilds in York, Bristol, Coventry, Norwich, and London, which was by far the largest center of production.

Tin was exported from England both unworked and manufactured into pewter; the greater part went overseas in large rectangular blocks weighing 100 to 300 pounds. From the 14th century Italian merchants (especially Venetians) exported large quantities of tin and pewter from London and Southampton directly, by sea, to the Mediterranean. This was to meet the enormous demand for tin in southern Europe and the East. English, Hanseatic, Dutch, and Zeeland merchants also engaged in the trade in tin and pewter with a peak (approximately 500 tons per annum) in the first decade of the 16th century. English merchants took over most of the trade as Italian vessels ceased to visit England later in the 16th century.

Henry S. Cobb

Bibliography

Hatcher, John. *English Tin Production and Trade before 1550*. Oxford: Clarendon, 1973; Hatcher, John, and T.C. Barker. *A History of British Pewter*. London: Longmans, 1974; Lewis, George R. *The Stannaries: A Study of the Medieval Tin Miners of Devon and Cornwall*. Harvard Economic Studies 3. Cambridge: Harvard University Press, 1907. Repr. Truro: Barton, 1965; Stannary Coinage Rolls (from 1300) and Stannary Court Rolls (beginning in 1333), Public Record Office, London [continuous figures can be found in these basic sources].

See also Metalwork, Gothic; Metalwork and Enamels, Romanesque; Trade

Towns and Urban Life

Perhaps the first thing to note about the condition of towns in medieval England is their small size in relation to towns in many other parts of western Europe. Even as late as 1500 London—by far the largest urban center in the realm—had but 50,000 to 65,000 inhabitants. Only a few others, including York, Norwich, Bristol, Exeter, and Newcastle, had as many as 5,000 to 10,000. Most of the 600 or 700 other towns in the realm had fewer than 1,500 inhabitants. Some straddled the functional divide between town and village, while most continued to exhibit characteristics of the countryside: livestock, pasture, orchards, and fields, both tilled and fallow, remained common in and immediately around most English towns.

The second striking point is that the condition and number of the towns changed dramatically during the medieval period, and not always toward the bigger, better, and more prosperous end of the scale. Determinants of such changes included seigneurial (including royal) policy, commercial prosperity, and the ebb and flow of population.

When William I surveyed his newly won domain, he found an urban network of sorts well in place. There is little to suggest that Roman towns continued to operate or to be inhabited continually after the departure of their founders in the 5th century. Yet the Saxons resettled some Roman towns between the 9th and 11th centuries and founded others in the same era. These pre-Conquest settlements emphasized fortifications and administration (ecclesiastical as well as civil) in addition to trade. Such centers as York, Canterbury, Carlisle, Coventry, Gloucester, Winchester, and London enjoyed particular strength, prosperity, and complexity by the 11th century. Though the Normans supported the urban growth already underway, it is difficult to see their role as innovative. In the century after the Conquest town growth seems more related to the general European revival of trade and population than to deliberate acts of royal policy.

Riding this wave of population growth and prosperity, English towns grew in number and size through the 12th and 13th centuries. Royal policy came to play an increasingly large role in these years. The need for administrative centers, military fortifications (especially in the underpopulated southern tier of the realm), and concentrations of taxable wealth led to royal support for the planting and settlement of new towns and the expansion of existing centers. Support by the nobility, anxious to establish towns on poorer parts of their lands in the hope of increased personal revenue and prestige, and by ecclesiastical authorities seeking revenues and support services, followed suit. Landlords of all types—royal, lay, and ecclesiastical—offered numerous privileges to induce settlement.

By around 1250 several hundred towns enjoyed considerable prosperity and growth. Many enjoyed substantial privileges as well, granted by charter, including burgage instead of feudal tenure, rights to elect some officials, rights to pay fees directly to the crown, and rights to administrative and economic self-regulation. A few towns gained recognition of their autonomy from feudal lordship on the basis of pre-Conquest precedents for self-rule.

Especially in economic terms the late 13th century may well represent the high point of medieval urban society. Shortly thereafter northern Europe experienced a climatic cooling, followed by widespread harvest failures and the beginning of population decline. Warfare, too, took its toll, as did shifts in foreign demand for raw wool. The *coup de grace* of this downturn came with the Black Death in 1348. This led to an astounding biological disaster. The population now fell by as much as a quarter or a third by 1350. With periodic recurrences of plague, as well as warfare and economic decline, it continued to stagnate for nearly two decades thereafter.

Despite patchy documentation it appears that increased rates of migration from the countryside offset the greater death rates characteristic of towns, allowing urban society to come through these times more successfully than agrarian society. As there was now a smaller net population to share the fruits of agriculture, trade, and handicraft manufacture, personal living standards may have risen. This seems to have sustained domestic demand and thus generated some continued level of prosperity in many towns through the first half of the 15th century. Port towns and towns with well-developed manufacture or trade in cloth seem often to have survived reasonably well. On the other hand many of the smaller market towns, especially those that had come into being in the prosperous period prior to the 14th century, proved marginal and fared poorly. A substantial minority ceased to function as towns altogether.

The condition of towns in the decades prior to the Reformation is the subject of a sustained debate. "Optimists" point chiefly to evidence of substantial building and economic prosperity in specific towns, to increases in cloth sales abroad and subsidy payments to the crown, and to a slight upturn in the population replacement rate by the end of the 15th century.

Against these claims we must balance the pessimistic reports of physical decay, from foreign visitors and townsmen themselves, the evidence of sympathetic government reaction to claims of inability to pay certain taxes, the widespread evasion of civic office because of high costs of officeholding, and the continued stagnation in rents. While this debate continues, few would argue that the economic condition, size, or number of English towns was as impressive in 1500 as in some earlier periods.

Robert Tittler

Bibliography

Beresford, Maurice W. *New Towns of the Middle Ages: Town Plantation in England, Wales, and Gascony.* London: Lutterworth, 1967; Bridbury, Anthony R. "English Provincial Towns in the Later Middle Ages." *EcHR,* 2d ser. 34 (1981): 1–25; Britnell, Richard H. *The Commercialisation of English Society, 1000–1500.* Cambridge: Cambridge University Press, 1993; Dobson, R.B. "Urban Decline in Later Medieval England." *TRHS,* 5th ser. 27 (1977): 1–22; Hatcher, John. *Plague, Population, and the English Economy, 1348–1530.* London: Macmillan, 1977; Lobel, Mary D., gen. ed., with W.H. Johns. *The British Atlas of Historic Towns.* 3 vols. London: Lovell Johns, 1969; London: Scolar, 1975; Oxford: Oxford University Press, 1989; Phythian-Adams, Charles. "Urban Decay in Late Medieval England." In *Towns in Societies: Essays in Economic History and Historical Sociology,* ed. Philip Abrams and E.A. Wrigley. Cambridge: Cambridge University Press, 1978, pp. 159–86; Phythian-Adams, Charles. *Desolation of a City: Coventry and the Urban Crisis of the Late Middle Ages.* Cambridge: Cambridge University Press, 1979; Platt, Colin. *The English Medieval Town.* London: Secker & Warburg, 1986; Reynolds, Susan. *An Introduction to the History of English Medieval Towns.* Oxford: Clarendon, 1977.

See also Black Death; Boroughs; Bristol; Cinque Ports; Coventry; Exeter; Guilds; Ipswich; Lincoln; London; Norwich; Population; *Puy;* Southampton; Tenures; Winchester; York, City of

Trade, Internal and External

Indications of English trade abound throughout the medieval period. Although none are as organized or as clear as one might hope, many observations can be made. One is that throughout the Middle Ages imports generally exceeded exports in variety, value, and perhaps even volume. Imports were largely luxury goods, manufactured or else obtainable only from other climates: silken and damask cloths from the Middle East and Italian producers; luxury woolen cloths from Flemish cities; glassware from the Rhineland and later from Italy; furs from the Baltic; wines from continental Europe, with an increasing emphasis on Gascony; spices from the East; dyestuffs and alum—used in the manufacture of cloth—from various places. Nearly all of this import trade was handled by alien merchants, although Englishmen, particularly Londoners, began to function as middlemen from the 11th century on.

Exports were mainly of raw materials. During the Anglo-Saxon period agricultural products seem to have predominated, although the volume of trade is unclear. In the 11th century grain appears as a major export, though it is rapidly overtaken by wool. English wool was the ideal basis for the high-quality cloths produced in such Flemish towns as Ypres, Arras, and Douai, and the heyday of the Flemish cloth industry—the 12th through the 14th century—coincided with the period of massive wool exports from England.

By 1275 wool was such a voluminous and lucrative export that it became the foundation of a whole new scheme of royal financing, in the form of the first regular customs duty: 6s. 8d. per sack of wool, each sack weighing 364 pounds. This "Great and Ancient" custom brought the king over £43,800 in its first four years of operation; it also has left excellent records for observing the volume, and even the location and personnel, of this trade. In the late 1270s around 26,750 sacks of wool were exported annually; by the mid-14th century (with some vicissitudes caused by sheep scab, murrain, or war) exports averaged 40,000 sacks. They decreased to about 8,500 sacks a year after 1439, partly because of disputes with Burgundy, which now controlled Flanders, but mainly because of the coming of age of the cloth industry in England.

The major ports for foreign trade were Boston and London, at least until the political wrangling over locations for collecting the tax began to disrupt export patterns. During the 12th century and certainly through the mid-13th wool exports were handled primarily by Flemish drapers, replaced in turn by Italians in the late 13th century and finally by Englishmen from about 1300, the result of wars with Flanders, of royal dependence on Italian bankers for deficit financing, and of the eventual shift to royal dependence on English commercial and industrial interests to support wars and other extraordinary enterprises.

The other major export was cloth. It would appear that this trade had begun by the 9th century, and by the early 13th century an indigenous industry in quality cloths, centering on eastern towns (Stamford, Lincoln, Beverley) was supplying exports found in Genoa and Sicily. This industry, at least as a source of exports, was squelched by the 1270s by the success of the Flemish cloth industry and the constraints imposed by urban guilds. However, early in the 14th century English cloth reappears, after the self-destructive internal and foreign wars of the Flemish cities and major reorganization of the industry within England. Now a range of medium- to lower-priced weaves, produced in localities both great and small, equaled wool in export value by the end of the 14th century and by 1470 exceeded wool even in volume of exports.

The increased value to internal trade and industry of this triumph of English cloth on the European market was enormous; internal trade, however, was still primarily agricultural in nature. There was some retailing of luxury imports, and marketing of the products of indigenous industry: salt, fish, and metal (iron, lead, coal, tin: the last two sufficiently developed and in demand to constitute major exports). Nonetheless, most of the crafts whose marketing constituted the bulk of trade in towns and fairs were closely related to rural pursuits:

baking, brewing, butchering, tanning and leatherworking generally, smithing, and working with wood. The marketing of produce and livestock constituted much of the rest of the activity in internal trade.

The greatest general trend in trade is its unmistakable increase. There was a proliferation of markets, turning many villages into small towns and small towns into larger centers. A temporary but significant innovation was the use of fairs for trade, both internal and external. Located in a half-dozen towns in eastern England, they constituted an annual cycle of two- to four-week marketing events in each location. They lost much of their importance, especially for international trade, by about 1320, the result of more sophisticated trading techniques and political developments.

The other general trend is the increased percentage of trade handled by Englishmen. Most of the internal trade was always in English hands, but imports and exports alike were handled by Frisians, Flemings, Brabanters, Italians, and the Hanse, more or less in succession, in varying degrees and lengths of time. Londoners were the first and always the most prominent but by no means the only denizens to take over internal retailing and then exporting of the products of international importance.

In England, as elsewhere, trade was encouraged by many developments: business companies, the law merchant, with special merchants' courts providing justice with great efficiency, and the promissory note (a double-edged sword). English kings were helpful in establishing a system of standard weights and measures and maintaining a stable currency: efforts in which they largely succeeded. On the other hand trade was hampered by royal purveyance, whereby the king could make purchases in such bulk that corruption was encouraged among his buyers, and many suppliers gained firsthand knowledge of the evils attendant upon abuses of payment by credit.

There are many sources for the study of medieval trade. Royal records are the most constant and reliable, since kings always claimed to regulate trade to some extent at least, and both royal wealth and royal needs operated on a scale far beyond that of any others. Royal accounts and chancery records, as well as many royal decrees, charters, and writs, constitute the core of our understanding of medieval trade. To those can be added, particularly from the 12th century on, the contents of municipal archives: market records, acknowledgments of debts, rolls of merchant and guild courts. The account records of abbeys, bishoprics, and other households are increasingly sought after and studied, with a view to understanding not only what was bought but also what marketing and transport facilities were involved.

Ellen Wedemeyer Moore

Bibliography

Bolton, J.L. *The Medieval English Economy, 1150–1500.* London: Dent, 1980; Carus-Wilson, E.M., and Olive Coleman. *England's Export Trade, 1275–1547.* Oxford: Clarendon, 1963; Dyer, Christopher. "The Consumer and the Market in the Later Middle Ages." *EcHR,* 2d ser. 42 (1989): 305–27; Hilton, Rodney H. "Medieval

Market Towns and Simple Commodity Production." *Past and Present* 109 (November 1985): 3–23; Lloyd, T.H. *The English Wool Trade in the Middle Ages.* Cambridge: Cambridge University Press, 1977; Miller, Edward, and John Hatcher. *Medieval England: Rural Society and Economic Change, 1086–1348.* London: Longman, 1978; Moore, Ellen Wedemeyer. *The Fairs of Medieval England: An Introductory Study.* Toronto: Pontifical Institute, 1985.

See also Aliens and Alien Merchants; Banks; Books; Cloth; Customs Accounts; Fairs and Markets; Food; Hanseatic League; Leather; Mills; Prices and Wages; Roads; Ships; Slavery; Southampton; Staple; Tin; Tunnage and Poundage

Translation and Paraphrase

Methods of text production that may account for more medieval English works than does original composition. Despite their importance, however, they elicited little direct theorizing, and the distinction between the two processes from a medieval perspective is not always clear either in theory or in practice.

In the Middle Ages the fountainhead of translation theory and indeed of translation itself was St. Jerome, who produced the Vulgate translation of the Bible in which most of the medieval period directly or indirectly knew the word of God. In a letter to Pammachius (Epistle 57) Jerome articulated the famous theory that underlay his work—that he translated not word for word but sense for sense. This phrase became axiomatic in medieval discussions of translations and is echoed by one of the earliest English translators, King Alfred, in the prefaces to his translations of the *Pastoral Care* and the *Consolation of Philosophy.* Because translation of the Bible involved recasting the word of God, Jerome's axiom was a way of avoiding heretical mistranslation. In the preface to his translation of Genesis the monk Ælfric observes that "the book is organized just as God himself dictated it to Moses, and we do not dare to write any more in English than the Latin has," but he also cautions translators to respect English idiom lest the translation prove misleading for those who do not know Latin idioms.

Ælfric's *Heptateuch* is actually a selective translation, and works like Ælfric's versions of Gregory the Great's homilies and the OE translations of the *Consolation* and Orosius's *History* also contain many interpolations and abridgments; the latter has a famous passage in which the travelers Ohthere and Wulfstan recount to King Alfred their voyages to the north and east. The OE translation of Bede's *History* is a close one—so close that parts of it are intelligible only through consultation of the Latin original. Also close are the later West Saxon Gospels and the prose version of the life of St. Guthlac, so it is clear the OE translators could in fact practice what they preached. But the preference seems to have been for a looser approach, perhaps on the grounds that some Christian concepts were so alien to Anglo-Saxon culture that they required a form of glossing.

Emblematic of this kind of translation is that practiced by the ignorant cowherd Cædmon, who, according to Bede, was able to ruminate on learned explanations of sacred history and transform them into vernacular poetry. A number of poetic biblical paraphrases survive, including ones of Genesis, Exodus, Daniel, Judith, and the apocryphal *Acts of Andrew and Matthew (Andreas).* These are decidedly Anglo-Saxon in orientation, however, and often the resemblance to scripture is minimal. In the poem *Judith* the heroine is portrayed as a warrior-queen whose victory over the army of Holofernes is accompanied by the conventional "beasts of battle," while in *Exodus* the Israelites descending into the Red Sea are described as Germanic retainers brandishing shields, helmets, and spears. *The Phoenix,* which generally speaking is a translation of a Latin work by Lactantius, opens with the characteristic "I have heard" formula of Germanic epic poetry and employs the martial vocabulary of that tradition. This sort of general reworking of a source received formal sanction from King Alfred, who, in the preface to his translation of Augustine's *Soliloquies,* portrays himself as a builder who has constructed his house from a variety of trees available in the forest of books. Indeed a patchwork pattern of translated texts, oral tradition, and poetic invention is apparent in works like *Guthlac B,* a poetic account of St. Guthlac's life, and *Christ and Satan,* which sketches Christian history from Creation to Judgment Day.

The absence of an extensive, explicit theory of translation in the Anglo-Saxon period may also account for the way translation and paraphrase overlap in it. In any case the transfer of texts from one language to another was an important activity, as the number of texts so produced indicates; in addition to those already noted a variety of riddles, homilies, and saints' lives can also be mentioned here. One of the lasting achievements of King Alfred (and Anglo-Saxon England in general) was the program of translation he introduced in the preface to his translation of the *Pastoral Care:* "It seems better to me . . . that we should also turn into the language that we all know [English] certain books that are most essential for all men to know." Numerous copies of these works—Gregory's *Dialogues* and *Pastoral Care,* Orosius's *History,* Bede's *History,* Boethius's *Consolation,* and Augustine's *Soliloquies*—survive, and the memory of what Alfred accomplished lasted into the time of William of Malmesbury (ca. 1095–ca. 1143), who in his *History of the English Kings* spoke highly of Alfred's love of learning and mentioned most of the Alfredian translations by name.

By William's time, however, French was becoming as important a source language as Latin. Moreover, during the course of the later Middle Ages, greater attention came to be paid to translation theory and practice themselves. This was perhaps inevitable, for by the time of the Wycliffites the very use of the vernacular was potentially controversial: it was the fact that the Wycliffites rendered theological arguments in English, rather than the arguments themselves, that was most troubling to their contemporaries. Throughout the ME period both paraphrases and translations continued to be produced in great numbers. Many romances, such as *King Horn, William of Palerne, Floris and Blancheflour,* and much of

Malory's *Morte Darthur,* are loosely based on French originals, while encyclopedic works like the *South English Legendary, Cursor Mundi,* and *Handlyng Synne* reflect the patchwork composition style observed in some OE texts. Works that would more strictly be considered translations include the first Wycliffite Bible, Chaucer's *Boece,* and some of Caxton's compositions. But a work like the *Boece* reflects the complexities involved in sorting ME translations from paraphrases, for though it is a close translation, its "source" is actually four texts that Chaucer selectively and uniquely combined: a version of the Latin text, a French translation, and commentaries by Nicholas Trevet and Remigius of Auxerre.

Certain aspects of medieval literary culture help to account for these complexities in the process of translation. For instance, in late-medieval rhetorical theory, translation was seen as an act of *inventio,* which originally meant the discovery of literary matter but came to mean interpretation. This interpretation was made possible through *dispositio,* or textual arrangement, and *elocutio,* the mastery of language. Translation, in other words, explicitly involved the interpretation of a source, perhaps through interpolations and glosses. Chaucer's insertion of Trevet's glosses in the *Boece* thus was entirely consistent with medieval translation theory, for he thereby delimited the meaning of the original as he understood it. Similarly the remarks on contemporary England that Trevisa incorporated in his translation of Higden's *Polychronicon* specified his interpretation. Though Nicholas Love is careful to mark his own insertions to the Pseudo-Bonaventure's *Mirror of the Blessed Life of Jesus Christ* with a marginal "N" and to use a marginal "B" where the original resumes, most ME translators provide no such way of distinguishing source from addition. While writers as diverse as Trevisa, Chaucer, and Gavin Douglas continued to echo Jerome's sense-for-sense dictum, translation into ME, far from being a mechanical exercise, had the potential to be itself a creative act.

Such potential assumed great importance in the context of medieval literary theory, which precluded vernacular writers from sharing in the authority of the ancient and patristic writers. Almost all of Chaucer's compositions could arguably be called translations by medieval standards, though his creative stamp is evident on each. Close translations like the *Boece* or the *Parson's Tale* may reflect sources that Chaucer compiled himself, while more original compositions, like the *Knight's Tale* and *The Book of the Duchess,* nonetheless derive from source texts. Works like Lydgate's *Fall of Princes* and Henryson's *Moral Fables* also exploit the creative potential inherent in translation. The distinction between this kind of theoretically sanctioned translation and entirely original composition could become tenuous, of course—a fact that was not lost on medieval writers. In *Troilus and Criseyde* Chaucer validates his imaginative reworking of Boccaccio's original by creating the fiction of an *auctor* named Lollius, whose text he claims to be translating.

If it is fair to say that works like the first Wycliffite Bible and some of Richard Rolle's translations are overly literal, perhaps even slavish, it is equally fair to say that for many ME writers translation was a useful opportunity for realizing their creativity. In light of this factor and of the gradual rise in prestige of the vernacular it is perhaps not surprising that the technicalities of translating vocabulary and syntax also received attention in the late ME period. In contrast to translated OE works late ME translations frequently contain prologues that indicate what is being translated and, quite often, how. In one of his prologues John Capgrave announces that he will translate the life of St. Gilbert as it appears before him, save for some additions that he has been directed to make.

Especially insightful in this regard are Trevisa's two prefaces on translation and the preface to the second Wycliffite Bible. In Trevisa's "Dialogue between a Lord and a Clerk on Translation" he argues at length for the validity of translation into English, while in his "Epistola" to Thomas, Lord Berkeley, he specifies his actual techniques: "In a certain place I shall set word for word, and active [voice] for active, and passive for passive in a row, just as it stands, without changing the order of the words." The Wycliffite Bible preface is similarly specific, indicating, for instance, how participial and absolute constructions will be expanded. This specificity was undoubtedly conditioned by the sacred nature of the text being translated and by the fact that the idiomatic style of the second version is a potentially heretical departure from the procedure of the first, where these constructions are in fact imitated in ME. But the syntactic expansions described in the preface to the second version, along with the similar expansion of a single source word into a doublet in ME, constitute a style that the preface indicates will make the meaning of the Bible "whole and open," a style through which most late ME translators rendered their sources.

In the Middle Ages translation and paraphrase overlapped much more than they do today. Most of the works that would be considered translations by medieval standards would be judged paraphrases by modern ones. The proliferation of translations, like the techniques used by the translators, reflect the distinctive but changing cultural contexts of the OE and ME periods. The final achievement of all the translations was at least threefold. First, translation introduced to English a number of texts, like Orosius's *History* or the Bible, that were part of the essence of medieval culture, and it thus helped to make England a part of that culture. Second, in the later Middle Ages, translation provided creative opportunities for writers like Chaucer who aspired to the authorial status culturally denied them. And third, the techniques of late-medieval translation introduced to English many of the words and structures that would subsequently become essential to literary style.

Tim William Machan

Bibliography

PRIMARY

Waldron, Ronald A., ed. "Trevisa's Original Prefaces on Translation: A Critical Edition." In *Medieval English Studies Presented to George Kane,* ed. Edward Donald Kennedy et al. Woodbridge: Brewer, 1988, pp. 285–99.

SECONDARY

Copeland, Rita A. "Rhetoric and Vernacular Translation in the Middle Ages." *SAC* 9 (1987): 41–75; Ellis, Roger. "The Choices of the Translator in the Later Middle English Period." In *The Medieval Mystical Tradition in England,* ed. Marion Glasscoe. Exeter: University of Exeter Press, 1982, pp. 18–46; Ellis, Roger, ed. *The Medieval Translator.* Cambridge: Boydell & Brewer, 1989; Kelly, L.G. *The True Interpreter: A History of Translation Theory and Practice in the West.* New York: St. Martin, 1979; Machan, Tim William. *Techniques of Translation: Chaucer's "Boece."* Norman: Pilgrim Books, 1985; Workman, Samuel K. *Fifteenth Century Translation as an Influence on English Prose.* Princeton: Princeton University Press, 1940.

See also Alfred; Boethius; Caxton; Hagiography; Literary Influences; Lollards; Orosius; Prose, ME; Romances; Trevisa

Treason

Both medieval and modern concepts of treason share the essential notion of betrayal. The modern concept is embedded in the system of international relations, where the nation or the state has the status of a (fictive) corporate person; a traitor betrays and thus endangers his country. Treason in the Middle Ages, however, only slowly and partially developed this level of abstraction; betrayal remained identified as conduct toward real, individual persons: one's feudal lord, especially the king. Medieval treason remained more an internal than an "international" concept and as much a private as a public offense. Precisely for these reasons it was viewed with as much repugnance as it is nowadays.

The English common law recognized and distinguished between "high" treason, betrayal of the king, and "petty" treason, betrayal of a feudal lord. Those convicted of either suffered forfeiture of property and gruesome capital punishment; both the law and actual example are much fuller for high treason. Both the personal inviolability of the king—stressed, for example, in Magna Carta—and the development of the public attributes of the royal office contributed to an elaborate body of law, culminating in the Statute of Treasons (1352). The statute groups treasonable offenses under three broad, interconnected headings.

The first of these is "personal," that is, planning or plotting the death of the king, the queen, or their heir or sexually violating women of the royal family. "Public" treason was counterfeiting the king's seal or coinage or killing certain classes of officials while engaged in governmental tasks. Then there was "political" treason, that is, waging war against the king in the kingdom or aiding and abetting his enemies.

It is clearly this last category that comes closest to, or prefigures, the modern doctrine. Those accused of high treason could not be protected by claims of sanctuary or benefit of clergy, nor could they obtain bail. Trial by battle remained on the books and was occasionally used, though jury trials were the norm. It has been calculated that the conviction rate in treason cases was much higher than in other, lesser categories

of criminal charges, such as felonies. Parliamentary legislation subsequent to the Statute of 1352 dealt with limits on, and exemptions from, property forfeiture, or procedures for pardons for traitors. Left unchanged, however, were the savage forms of corporal punishment, including drawing (dragging), live disembowelment, and quartering of limbs.

In the 15th century the process known as parliamentary attainder came to the fore as a swift and ruthless instrument of dealing with real (or fabricated) instances of treason. Attainder involved a summary charge and guilty verdict, normally without any sort of hearing, and besides sentencing the accused to death, it deprived his entire family and heirs of any and all property. Acts of attainders were frequently sought and employed in the dynastic struggles of Lancaster, York, and Tudor at the end of the Middle Ages.

Next to blasphemy or sacrilege treason was the gravest offense medieval society could imagine; that judgment remains largely unchanged today.

Michael Altschul

Bibliography
Bellamy, John G. *The Law of Treason in England in the Later Middle Ages.* Cambridge: Cambridge University Press, 1970 [the fullest modern treatment]; Bellamy, John G. *Crime and Public Order in England in the Later Middle Ages.* London: Routledge & Kegan Paul, 1973 [places treason in the broader context of law and English society]; Pollock, Frederick, and Frederic W. Maitland. *The History of English Law before the Time of Edward I.* 2d ed. Ed. S.F.C. Milsom. 2 vols. London: Cambridge University Press, 1968, pp. 500–08 [the classic brief account and starting point].

See also Attainder; Monarchy and Kingship

Trevet or Trivet, Nicholas (ca. 1258–after 1334)

Dominican commentator and historian. Educated at Oxford, where he later taught, Trevet was primarily concerned with providing literal explanation of classical and Christian texts. He wrote commentaries on the older and the younger Seneca, Livy, Augustine's *City of God,* the Pentateuch and the Psalter, Boethius's *Consolation of Philosophy,* and other works. The Boethius commentary, of which over 100 manuscripts survive, directly influenced Chaucer's *Boece* and *Troilus,* John Walton's verse translation of Boethius, and Robert Henryson's *Orpheus and Eurydice.*

Trevet's histories include the Latin *Annales* and *Historia* and the Anglo-Norman *Cronicles.* The *Cronicles* were used by Chaucer in the *Man of Law's Tale* and by Gower in the *Tale of Constance;* they were translated into ME in the mid-15th century.

Tim William Machan

Bibliography
Dean, Ruth J. "Nicholas Trevet, Historian." In *Medieval Learning and Literature,* ed. J.J.G. Alexander and Margaret T. Gibson. Oxford: Clarendon, 1976, pp. 328–52;

Smalley, Beryl. *English Friars and Antiquity in the Early Fourteenth Century.* Oxford: Blackwell, 1960.

See also Boethius; Chaucer; Chronicles; Gower; Henryson

Trevisa, John (early 1340s?–1402)

Translator of informational works. Born probably in Cornwall, Trevisa entered Exeter College, Oxford, in 1362 and remained there until 1365. In 1369 he entered Queen's College and subsequently became a fellow. He was ordained priest in 1370. Trevisa was expelled from Queen's in 1378 for alleged misuse of college property but appears to have returned there for lengthy periods in 1383–86 and 1394–96. It was possibly after his expulsion from Queen's that he became vicar of Berkeley in Gloucestershire and chaplain to Thomas, Lord Berkeley. He was also a nonresident canon of Westbury-on-Trym, near Bristol.

Trevisa's major undertakings were his translations of several lengthy Latin works. The first that can be securely dated is his translation of Ranulf Higden's *Polychronicon,* a universal history, which he completed in 1387. His translation of the *De proprietatibus rerum,* the medieval encyclopedia of Bartholomaeus Anglicus, was finished in 1398. He produced this translation, as well as one of Giles of Rome's *De regimine principum,* a treatise on kingship, under the patronage of Thomas, Lord Berkeley. Trevisa also translated several shorter works: the apocryphal *Gospel of Nicodemus,* Richard FitzRalph's antimendicant sermon *Defensio curatorum,* and William Ockham's *Dialogus inter militem et clericum.* His only original works seem to be two brief essays on translation that preface some manuscripts of his *Polychronicon* translation: the "Dialogue between a Lord and a Clerk on Translation" and the "Epistle. . . Unto Lord Thomas of Barkley upon the Translation of *Polychronicon.* . . ."

Trevisa's achievement as a translator has several important aspects. Most obviously, he made accessible to an English audience such widely popular Latin informational works as the *Polychronicon* and *De proprietatibus rerum.* The influence of these translations was considerable. Both appear to have circulated widely (given their massive sizes) in manuscript and were printed by Caxton and de Worde, respectively, in the late 15th century. The *Polychronicon* was reprinted in the 16th century, while the *De proprietatibus* achieved an extended influence through Thomas East's revised edition in 1582 of *Batman vppon Bartholome,* a commentary on the work by Stephen Batman. In the latter form it was still being read and used in the late 17th century.

Trevisa also had a valuable role as neologizer. His translations expanded the lexical range of English, particularly in his use of new scientific and technical terminology. His fluent and generally accurate renderings of Latin prose demonstrated the possibilities of English prose as an instructional medium, thereby extending his influence into form as well as content.

Trevisa has also been credited with a role in the translation of the Wycliffite Bible. He was certainly at Oxford at the same time as Wyclif and Nicholas Hereford. However, his involvement in the Wycliffite translation remains uncertain, although there is at least some circumstantial evidence for it. His authorship has also been urged for a translation of Vegetius's *De re militari* into ME, but this seems unlikely.

A.S.G. Edwards

Bibliography

PRIMARY

Babington, Churchill, and J.R. Lumby, eds. *Polychronicon Ranulphi Higden.* 9 vols. Rolls Series. London: Longmans, 1865–86; Perry, Aaron J., ed. *Dialogus inter Militem et Clericum; Richard FitzRalph's Sermon: "Defensio Curatorum"; and Methodius: "Þe Bygynnyng of þe World and þe Ende of Worldes."* EETS o.s. 167. London: Humphrey Milford, 1925; Seymour, M.C., gen. ed. *On the Properties of Things: John Trevisa's Translation of Bartholomaeus Anglicus De proprietatibus rerum.* 3 vols. Oxford: Clarendon, 1975–88; Waldron, Ronald A., ed. "Trevisa's Original Prefaces on Translation: A Critical Edition." In *Medieval English Studies Presented to George Kane,* ed. Edward Donald Kennedy et al. Woodbridge: Brewer, 1988, pp. 285–99.

SECONDARY

New *CBEL* 1:467–68, 806; *Manual* 8:2656–61, 2866–77; Edwards, A.S.G. "John Trevisa." In *Middle English Prose: A Critical Guide to Major Authors and Genres,* ed. A.S.G. Edwards. New Brunswick: Rutgers University Press, 1984, pp. 133–46; Fowler, David C. *John Trevisa.* Aldershot: Variorum, 1993.

See also Chronicles; Harrowing of Hell; Science; Scientific and Medical Writings; Technology; Translation; William of Ockham; Wyclif; Wycliffite Texts

Tribal Hidage

The earliest surviving English administrative document of substance; a list of 35 territories or peoples set out in OE, followed by an assessment measured in hides of their obligation in the way of tribute to an overlord.

Its origins are obscure. The most likely explanation for the present shape is as a document drawn up for the Northumbrian rulers of the third quarter of the 7th century, brought up to date by an 8th-century Mercian king, either Æthelbald (716–57) or Offa (757–96). Mercia appears first on the list, assessed at 30,000 hides, the entry referring to the central heartland of historic Mercia, the land of the Middle Trent, based on Lichfield, Tamworth, and Repton.

Then follow 29 entries relating to peoples, most of whom can be identified as constituent parts of Greater Mercia. They ranged from big groups—the *Hwicce* around Worcester, Lindsey with Hatfield Chase, and the settlers in the Wrekin, for whom an assessment at 7,000 hides was appropriate—to clusters of small folk assessed at a modest 300 hides (Hitchin or the dwellers around Whitlesey Mere in Huntingdonshire). There are some anomalies, such as the presence of the Isle of Wight and the district of Elmet around Leeds, both assessed at 600 hides. At least fourteen of the smaller groups, such as the North *Gyrwe,* the South *Gyrwe,* the *Spalda,* and the *Gifle,* can be identified with settlers who moved in from the Wash into and through the Fen country.

Unidentified peoples include the substantial *Noxgaga* and the *Ohtgaga* (7,000 hides between them), placed by scholarly inferences south of the Thames, mostly in Surrey. The document finishes with entries relating to five ancient kingdoms: East Anglia (30,000 hides), Essex with parts of Hertfordshire and Middlesex (7,000 hides), Kent (15,000 hides), Sussex (7,000 hides), and Wessex (100,000 hides). These assessments for East Anglia and Wessex appear to be truly penal.

The Tribal Hidage is important in all manner of ways. It shows that an elaborate system of assessment of tribute existed at an early stage in the development of Anglo-Saxon kingdoms. It also provides our only firm literary evidence, apart from what can be deduced from place-names, for the small political units of pagan times that preceded the historic kingdoms of England.

H.R. Loyn

Bibliography

Bassett, Steven, ed. *The Origins of Anglo-Saxon Kingdoms.* London: Leicester University Press, 1989; Davies, Wendy, and H. Vierck. "The Context of the Tribal Hidage: Social Aggregates and Settlement Patterns." *Frühmittelalterliche Studien* 8 (1974): 223–92; Hart, Cyril. "The Tribal Hidage." *TRHS,* 5th ser. 21 (1971): 133–57; Loyn, H.R. *The Governance of Anglo-Saxon England 500–1087.* London: Arnold, 1984.

See also Heptarchy; Hides; Offa

Trope

In the broadest sense tropes are all the later musical and textual accretions to the Franco-Roman nucleus of antiphonal and responsorial chants for mass and offices that we call Gregorian chant, a repertoire primarily fixed by the early 9th century. A trope might be a newly added textless melody (a melisma), text added to a preexistent melisma (a prosula), or newly composed text and melody added to an older item as an introduction or interpolation (a trope per se). The term is also applied to Ordinary chants of the mass, especially the Kyrie, that appear in early sources in two formats, either with just the words of the Ordinary (i.e., untroped) or with a lengthy Latin text (a Kyrie trope or prosula). The term is further extended by some to apply to polyphonic settings of chants and to some independent compositions that are liturgical additions (e.g., the sequence, viewed as an addition to the Alleluia) or substitutions (e.g., a polyphonic offertory or sequence substitute).

A major Anglo-Saxon repertoire of prosulae and tropes per se survives in three related pre-Conquest versions of the later 10th and early 11th centuries, two from Winchester (the Winchester tropers) and one from Canterbury (the Caligula troper). These contain tropes to Gregorian mass Propers (variable texts like the Introit, Offertory, Communion) and mass

Ordinaries (the constant texts of the Kyrie, Gloria, Sanctus, Agnus Dei), forming a little over a third of the contents of the Winchester volumes, for example. While the majority of the material is of French or Rhenish origin, about a third of the repertoire was composed in England, and many continental tropes have been reworked textually and musically. The insular tropes exhibit the distinctively ornate literary Latin of late-10th-century Anglo-Saxon authors; their plainsong melodies, unfortunately, are untranscribable.

From the 11th century on there is a sharp decline in the popularity of tropes for the Proper of the mass, but tropes for the Ordinary survive longer, especially in England. The rich 12th-century St. Albans repertoire in Bodl. Laud misc. 358 and BL Royal 2.B.iv is a case in point, as is the early-13th-century monophonic repertoire of troped ordinaries probably from London or Canterbury in Paris, Bibliothèque de l'Arsenal 135 (ArsA). Such collections have no such extensive plainsong counterparts after ca. 1250, but Kyrie prosulae, the *Spiritus et alme* and *Regnum tuum* tropes for the Gloria, and the *Marie filius* insertion for the Sanctus continue to appear in English service books down to the end of the Middle Ages.

In the later 13th and 14th centuries the troping impulse is sustained in England principally in the realm of polyphony. There are, in the first place, two- and three-voice polyphonic settings of troped mass Ordinary plainsongs, the richest source of which is the Marian music of the eleventh fascicle of the early-13th-century manuscript W1; these form a polyphonic counterpart to the monophonic troped chants in ArsA, for instance. In addition there is a distinctive English repertoire of three- and four-voice polyphonic settings of untroped plainsongs (including Kyries, Alleluias, and Marian Gradual verses, Introits, and Proses) in which the upper parts have been given new texts that trope the original chant text; these pieces are designated by musicologists as "troped chant settings." In the case of the Gloria this textual troping is applied to its tropes themselves, producing a small number of motetlike settings of the *Regnum tuum* prosula and a much larger number of paraphrases of the *Spiritus et alme* interpolations. Another manifestation of the troping impulse in the English polyphonic repertoire is the new composition of Latin-texted Kyries set in three-voice polyphony not constructed on any preexistent chant; a Durham piece, *Kyrie Cuthberte prece,* is perhaps the most striking example. Finally there is an isolated instance of a troped lesson for Christmas midnight mass (Harrison et al.: no. 82), in which the first and last sections are set in a simple two-voice style, framing plainsong delivery of the rest of the reading, a technique that adumbrates a wide range of extemporized practice for which no other traces remain.

Peter M. Lefferts

Bibliography

Harrison, Frank Ll., Ernest H. Sanders, and Peter M. Lefferts, eds. *English Music for Mass and Offices (I).* Polyphonic Music of the Fourteenth Century 16. Paris: L'Oiseau-Lyre, 1983; Hiley, David. "Further Observations on W1: The Ordinary of Mass Chants and the Sequences." *Journal of the Plainsong and Mediaeval Music Society* 4 (1981): 67–80; Planchart, Alejandro E. *The Repertory of Tropes at Winchester.* 2 vols. Princeton: Princeton University Press, 1977; Sanders, Ernest H., ed. *English Music of the Thirteenth and Early Fourteenth Centuries.* Polyphonic Music of the Fourteenth Century 14. Paris: L'Oiseau-Lyre, 1979; Steiner, Ruth. "Prosula." *NGD* 15:310–12; Steiner, Ruth. "Trope." *NGD* 19:172–86.

See also Caligula Troper; Discant; Liturgy and Church Music, History of; Mass, Polyphonic Music for; W1; Winchester Organa; Winchester Tropers

Truelove, The, or The Quatrefoil of Love

An alliterative poem (ca. 1390) written in 40 thirteen-line stanzas, one of a small group of related poems including *The Awntyrs of Arthur, Susannah, Summer Sunday,* and *De Tribus Regibus Mortuis. The Truelove* survives complete in two northern 15th-century manuscripts, one of which was copied by Robert Thornton (BL Add. 31042). Wynkyn de Worde printed it in London ca. 1510 under the title *The .iiii. Leues of the Trueloue*—the first known printing of an alliterative poem. Unaware of the early print, modern editors Gollancz and Weale edited the Thornton text, including some variants from the Oxford manuscript (Bodl. Add. A 106), and named the piece *The Quatrefoil of Love.*

The poem's dominant emblem is the four-leaf truelove plant (herb paris), whose cruciate form was popularly associated with the Cross and with the truelove knot signifying marriage. Drawing upon a contemporary tradition of allegorizing the plant for religious instruction, the poet expounds the meaning of divine love by likening the four leaves to the Trinity and Virgin. The poem's frame exploits the *chanson d'aventure* form of some medieval lyrics, in which a speaker wandering in the country encounters a woman; the *Truelove* narrator overhears a turtledove's counsel to a maiden seeking truelove—both the plant (a token of good luck in love) and a faithful lover. The bird's counsel is to seek truelove not in mortal companionship, which fades like the plant, but in God.

The Truelove's 40 stanzas may have a numerological meaning associated with the four leaves and the Cross. The central eight stanzas portray the Crucifixion and Resurrection, beginning with a depiction of Mary mourning Christ's death and ending with her Assumption and coronation as queen of heaven. The sixteen stanzas on either side explain this event from the different perspectives of the living and the dead: mercy versus judgment, the conditional promise of salvation and the inescapable effect of continuing in one's sins. Taken as a whole, the poem works as a diptych, divided by the bursting of hell's gates in stanzas 20–21. The first half recounts biblical history as a demonstration of God's love; the second half narrates the soul's lonely plight on the day of doom. The interplay of contrasting themes—friendship and loyalty versus disruptive acts of cruelty and treason, or the enactment of truth and love versus their perversion—creates an imagery of

union broken by disunion but ultimately reunited, suggestive of an interwoven knot.

The poem thus develops its religious themes through a skilled manipulation of the herbal conceit and its associations. The frame anticipates the Crucifixion imagery of the central section: the narrator watches the forlorn maiden behold the bird on the tree; later the reader pictures the sorrowful Mary behold Christ on the Cross. The poet also exploits a latent medicinal metaphor: the Trinity and the Virgin provide the "grace" (punning on "grass, herb") that actually cures the maiden's love-longing. The presence of the poem among herbals and medical recipes in the Oxford manuscript underscores this meaning. In its rich emblematic shaping of scriptural and popular traditions *The Truelove* stands as an elegant blend of pious didacticism and serious alliterative art.

Susanna Fein

Bibliography

PRIMARY

The .iiii. Leues of the Trueloue. London, 1510? (STC 15345); Gollancz, Israel, and Magdalene M. Weale, eds. *The Quatrefoil of Love.* EETS o.s. 195. London: Humphrey Milford, 1935.

SECONDARY

Manual 7:2334, 2541–42; Fein, Susanna Greer. "Why Did Absolon Put a 'Trewelove' under His Tongue? Herb Paris as a Healing 'Grace' in Middle English Literature." *ChauR* 25 (1991): 302–17; Fein, Susanna Greer. "Form and Continuity in the Alliterative Tradition: Cruciform Design and Double Birth in Two Stanzaic Poems." *MLQ* 53 (1992): 100–25; Lawton, David A. "The Diversity of Middle English Alliterative Poetry." *Leeds Studies in English* n.s. 20 (1989): 143–72 [see esp. 159–62]; Phillips, Helen. *"The Quatrefoil of Love."* In *Langland, the Mystics and the Medieval English Religious Tradition: Essays in Honour of S.S. Hussey,* ed. Helen Phillips. Cambridge: Brewer, 1990, pp. 243–58.

See also Allegory; Alliterative Revival; Lyrics; Moral and Religious Instruction; Popular Culture; Religious Allegories; Utilitarian Writings

Truth in Middle English Literature

Truth (spelled variously as *trouthe, treuthe, troth, trawthe*) is one of the major literary themes in late-14th-century England. "*Sir Gawain* is a poem about *truth,* in the medieval sense of the word" (Burrow, 1965: vii). *Piers Plowman* proclaims, "Whan alle tresors arn tried truþe is þe beste" (B.1.135). A Vernon lyric turns the words into a refrain, "treuþe is best." Chaucer's *Franklin's Tale* centers on the same proposition, "Trouthe is the hyeste thyng that man may kepe" (*FrankT* 1479); the *Clerk's Tale* celebrates the "trouthe and . . . obeisance" of patient Griselda (*ClT* 794); and inasmuch as the frame story depends upon the sworn agreement between the Host and the pilgrims, truth is arguably the theme of the

Canterbury Tales as a whole.

The word was popular in part because of the rich variety of meanings it had accumulated by the 14th century. Langland uses it "in at least a dozen distinct senses" (Kane, 1980: 9). From its primary meaning of "faith or loyalty" (particularly as pledged in a promise or agreement) the word expanded to include such concepts as "honesty," "integrity," "justice," and even, as in modern usage, "true statement or account, that which is in accordance with the fact."

The word came to embody certain social values. Truth was the chivalric virtue par excellence. Knights "sweren on hir swerd to seruen truþe euere, / That is þe profession apertli þat apendeþ to knyʒtes" (*Piers Plowman* B.1.99–100). Among Arthur's knights Gawain is the paragon of *trawthe*. Chaucer's knight "loved chivalrie, / Trouthe and honour, fredom and curtesie" (*Gen. Prol.* 45–46). In time this chivalric virtue was extended as an ideal for society as a whole. The word *truth* thus came to carry with it a specific worldview, at the center of which is that social system known to us as feudalism. Truth is not simply an abstract loyalty, such as any society in any age could embrace, but a loyalty manifested concretely in the obligations of status, in the duties of knighthood, in the subordination of one individual to another.

By the late 14th century, however, the breakup of this system had become obvious. Truth emerged as a battle cry at the very moment when the passing of the old order was felt most keenly. Writers of the period singled out "meed" (money, reward) and "will" (willfulness, ambition) as the two main causes for the decay of truth. Chaucer's complaint in *Lack of Steadfastness* is typical:

> Somtyme the world was so stedfast and stable
> That mannes word was obligacioun,
> And now it is so fals and deceivable
> That word and deed, as in conclusioun,
> Ben nothing lyk, for turned up-so-doun
> Is al this world for mede and wilfulnesse,
> That al is lost for lak of stedfastnesse.

Yunck's analysis of the situation can hardly be bettered: "The theme becomes . . . a vehicle of protest against a new world of nationalism, money, taxes, and collectors, in favor of a world long past and idealized, of feudal obligations and privileges, of settled class-distinctions, of personal mutual devotion between lord and vassal (such was the idealization) as the basis of social order" (1963: 219).

Even so, the protest might have been less vehement and widespread if the impetus had been only social. But the cry for truth was moral and religious as well. The church had taught for centuries that the "three estates" had been ordained by God. The doctrine is expounded as late as 1388 in Thomas Wimbledon's famous sermon at Paul's Cross, London: "In þe chirche beeþ nedeful þes þre offices: presthod, knyʒthod, and laboreris" (ed. Knight, 1967: 63). In *Piers* Holy Church herself presents the celestial hierarchy as a model for human society: God taught the angels "þe treuþe to knowe: / To be buxom at his biddyng" (B.1.109–10). Later in the poem Rea-son addresses a sermon to each estate in turn, in which he explicitly connects class obligations to the reward of salvation, concluding with the words:

> And ye þat seke Seynt Iames and Seyntes at Rome,
> Sekeþ Seynt Truþe, for he may saue yow alle. (B.5.56–57)

Truth is the virtue upon which both social and personal salvation rest. The two realms merge. The lesson for medieval readers was that to obey any rightful authority on earth was to obey God himself; to disobey was to risk his wrath and damnation. It is this premise that gives such urgency to the cries for truth in late-medieval English literature and such poignancy to complaints that it has fled England.

John A. Alford

Bibliography

PRIMARY

Kail, J., ed. *Twenty-Six Political and Other Poems*. EETS o.s. 124. London: Kegan Paul, Trench, Trübner, 1904 [a number of these lyrics lament the decline of truth]; Knight, Ione Kemp, ed. *Wimbledon's Sermon: Redde Rationem Villicationis Tue*. Pittsburgh: Duquesne University Press, 1967; "Truth Is Best." In *Religious Lyrics of the XIVth Century*, ed. Carleton Brown; 2d ed. rev. by G.V. Smithers. Oxford: Clarendon, 1957, pp. 168–70.

SECONDARY

Alford, John A. "The Design of the Poem." In *A Companion to Piers Plowman*, ed. John A. Alford. Berkeley: University of California Press, 1988, pp. 29–65; Burrow, J.A. *A Reading of Sir Gawain and the Green Knight*. London: Routledge & Kegan Paul, 1965; Kane, George. *The Liberating Truth: The Concept of Integrity in Chaucer's Writings*. John Coffin Memorial Lecture 1979. London: Athlone, 1980; Mohl, Ruth. *The Three Estates in Medieval and Renaissance Literature*. New York: Columbia University Press, 1933; White, Gertrude M. "The Franklin's Tale: Chaucer or the Critics." *PMLA* 89 (1974): 454–62; Yunck, John A. *The Lineage of Lady Meed: The Development of Mediaeval Venality Satire*. Notre Dame: University of Notre Dame Press, 1963.

See also Chaucer; *Pearl*-Poet; *Piers Plowman;* Satire

Tunnage and Poundage

Parliamentary subsidies, usually voted together, as customs duties levied on wine and the value of general merchandise, excluding wool, imported and exported. A specific rider was attached that the yield should be used for "the safekeeping of the seas." This rider shows that although both duties had earlier origins in the prise of wine (butlerage), in King John's levies on general merchandise, and in the petty custom of 3*d.* in the pound on alien merchandise, it was the needs of war, particularly the protection of Channel shipping, in 1346–47, that led to their imposition.

As with other subsidies a struggle ensued as to whether the king could levy them with the limited consent of the merchants or whether he had to seek general parliamentary approval. By 1359–60 the question had been settled. Thereafter they were granted by the Commons for specific terms (not always continuous, from year to year) and for life in 1415, 1453, and 1465, and then, from Richard III on, in the first year of each reign.

The general rates were 3s. a tun (252 gallons) on wine and 12d. in the pound on general merchandise, though both could be varied, as in 1431, when, as part of a search for money for the war in France, an extra 3s. a tun was imposed permanently on alien sweet wine and poundage was temporarily raised to 1s. 6d. The main problem was liability to poundage on general merchandise and the value of cloth exports. Aliens paid on both. Hansards claimed exemption on cloth exports and general merchandise—on the latter until at least 1425 and at times after that—while natives seem to have paid on both until 1422. When poundage was granted again, in 1425, native cloth was exempted, and the merchants thereafter strenuously resisted its reimposition, particularly in 1453–54. The payment of poundage on native cloth would not have offset declining yields from the wool subsidy, but it might have established a precedent for the levying of further duties on what was now England's chief export.

J.L. Bolton

Bibliography
Gras, Norman S.B. *The Early English Customs System.* Cambridge: Harvard University Press, 1918; Gray, H.L. "English Foreign Trade from 1446 to 1482" and "Tables of Enrolled Customs and Subsidy Accounts, 1399 to 1482: Introduction." In *Studies in English Trade in the Fifteenth Century,* ed. Eileen Power and M.M. Postan. London: Routledge & Kegan Paul, 1933, pp. 1–38, 321–29; Harriss, G.L. *King, Parliament, and Public Finance in Medieval England to 1369.* Oxford: Clarendon, 1975 [covers the critical years 1346–60 for the emergence of parliamentary subsidies]; Ormrod, W.M. "The Crown and the English Economy, 1290–1348." In *Before the Black Death: Studies in the Crisis of the Early Fourteenth Century.* Manchester: Manchester University Press, 1991, pp. 167–75.

See also Aliens and Alien Merchants; Cloth; Customs Accounts; Hanseatic League; Taxes; Trade

U

Universities: Oxford and Cambridge

Oxford and Cambridge, the only universities of medieval England, were not specifically founded. In common with the archetypal universities of Bologna and Paris they evolved; no precise dates can be ascribed to their origins. Oxford, which developed in a piecemeal fashion in the course of the 12th century, was regarded as a fully fledged *studium generale* (the medieval designation for a university) toward the close of that century, specializing in arts, civil and canon law, and theology. It thus belonged to Europe's primary group of universities, ranking alongside Bologna, Paris, and Montpellier.

The nascent university at Oxford was reinforced in the 1190s by the presence of a galaxy of prominent scholars, including Daniel of Morley, a student of Arabic science, and Alexander Neckham, the theologian and Aristotelian enthusiast. In the early 13th century Oxford's intellectual life was extended by the activities of scholars who are known to have taught at the university and who promoted in England the logical, metaphysical, and scientific works of Aristotle. The most important of these Aristotelian scholars were Robert Grosseteste, who was to become bishop of Lincoln, and Edmund of Abingdon, later archbishop of Canterbury. As a result of these intellectual developments Oxford was a European focus for those areas of Aristotelian science and philosophy that were suppressed at Paris in 1210 and 1215 and that were not taught openly there until the 1230s. It was thereby able to forge ahead in these invigorating spheres and was seen to be a university capable of participating in some of the most advanced realms of European scholarship.

Cambridge University had more modest beginnings. The evidence for the origins of Cambridge is of the most elusive kind. It does not appear to have been an outgrowth of either the town's grammar schools or the intellectual activities of the regional monastic houses. The university seems to have crystallized as a consequence of a migration of Oxford scholars in 1209, arising from the temporary closure of the Oxford schools following the hanging of several scholars by the mayor and burgesses in retaliation for the murder or manslaughter

of a woman by a scholar. The years immediately following the reopening of Oxford in 1214–15 saw the emergence of Cambridge as a *studium generale*. It may thus be accounted a member of the second wave of universities. A Cambridge chancellor is first recorded in 1225, only sixteen years after the Oxford exodus. Initially Cambridge specialized in arts, theology, and canon law, there being no faculty of civil law until the mid-13th century and no faculty of medicine until ca. 1270–80.

In organizational terms Oxford and Cambridge were broadly based upon the Parisian magisterial model, in which the faculty (masters, or *magistri*) governed the institution, as opposed to the student-controlled type of university exemplified by Bologna. The English universities, however, made notable constitutional adaptations to the Parisian archetype; and they exhibited important differences from each other. Cambridge was no mere derivative of Oxford, and in the course of the 13th century its degree of indigenous growth is striking. In 1318 Pope John XXII officially confirmed its legal status as a *studium generale*. Despite royal petitions to the papal curia Oxford never received a comparable official confirmation as a fully fledged university.

Oxford was by far the larger of the universities in the 13th and 14th centuries. In the late 14th century it has been reckoned that its academic population was around 1,500, while that of Cambridge may have ranged between 400 and 700. By the mid-15th century the number of scholars at Oxford may have settled in the region of 1,700, while Cambridge may have reached about 1,300. In the late 15th and 16th centuries Cambridge came close to rivaling Oxford in terms of size, and it probably achieved parity around 1600.

One reason for the increasing popularity of Cambridge in the later period was the differing stances of Oxford and Cambridge toward the heresies of Wyclif and the Lollards. Although every effort had been made to eradicate Wycliffite ideas and Lollardy from Oxford, traces of heresy persisted there throughout the 15th century. Cambridge remained largely orthodox and was regarded as a sound investment for patrons of learning and a safe harbor for undergraduates. The persistence of the heretical problem at Oxford may help explain why Cambridge obtained a complete exemption from ecclesiastical authority in 1433, some 46 years before Oxford acquired its comprehensive emancipation in 1479, although the struggle for autonomy from ecclesiastical dominion had been fought with a far greater intensity at Oxford than at Cambridge.

Secular colleges within the universities were later developments than at Paris. They first materialized in the form of Merton College, Oxford, and Peterhouse, Cambridge, founded in 1264 and 1284, respectively. Until the late 15th and early 16th centuries English colleges served primarily to accommodate graduate fellows, studying for advanced arts degrees or in one of the superior faculties. Exceptions were the royal College of the King's Hall, Cambridge, and New College, Oxford, which from the 14th century both admitted undergraduate members. The unendowed Oxford halls and Cambridge hostels provided the normal university environment for the majority of undergraduates and for many graduates until well into the 16th century.

At Oxford ten secular colleges were founded before 1500: three in the 13th century, four in the 14th, and three in the 15th. Cambridge harbored only one college in the 13th century but realized seven in the 14th and five in the 15th, making a total of thirteen secular colleges. Of these the most celebrated, unusual, and—until the mid-15th century—largest was the King's Hall, with origins in a detachment from Edward II's chapel royal set in the University of Cambridge. This settlement brought into being the first colony of royal clerks established in the English universities.

The Oxford colleges were more exposed to ecclesiastical influences than those of Cambridge. Of the ten secular colleges at Oxford by 1500 no fewer than nine had ecclesiastical founders. The thirteen Cambridge colleges had a preponderance of lay founders and were fiercely jealous of their independent status with regard to the university and ecclesiastical authorities. In addition to secular colleges Oxford maintained five monastic colleges, whereas Cambridge had only one. Both universities also contained houses of friars and regular canons.

The secular colleges of Oxford and Cambridge came to have a seminal impact on the evolution of the universities. In the later medieval period the colleges fell heir to the declining system of public instruction of the university schools. Through the growth of college lectureships and tutorial systems the colleges, from the late 15th century, could cater to basic undergraduate needs; the undergraduate populations began to infiltrate the colleges in some numbers. The attempts made by the universities to regenerate the ailing system of public instruction given by the regent masters met with limited success.

By the reign of Elizabeth the colleges had become the natural venues for undergraduate accommodation and teaching. With teaching largely decentralized in the colleges Oxford and Cambridge were transformed from universities of a centripetal nature to those of a centrifugal character. This decentralized structure has remained intact down to the 20th century.

The universities were insular; neither one recruited extensively from the Continent. Only about 2 percent of scholars at Oxford and 1 percent at Cambridge were drawn from abroad. Of those recruited from the Continent many were friars who came to study and take degrees in theology. In this regard the English universities had a peculiar attraction because, until 1359, only Paris, Oxford, and Cambridge had the right of promotion to the doctorate in theology. Within England Oxford recruited largely from the west and north, and Cambridge relied mainly upon the east and north. Cambridge drew only about 1 percent of its scholars from Wales, Scotland, and Ireland, compared with the 6 percent drawn by Oxford.

Although Cambridge was less prominent before the 16th century, several eminent scholars, including Thomas of York, Duns Scotus, John Bromyard, Robert Holcot, Roger Marston, and Thomas Cobham, as well as the mystical writer Walter Hilton, are known to have studied or taught there. In comparison with Oxford, however, the evidence for original speculative thought at Cambridge in the Middle Ages is limited.

The traditional curriculum was modified by the onset of humanist learning. The gradual humanist infiltration began piecemeal in the second half of the 15th century and became institutionalized in the course of the 16th. The impact was most extensive within the arts faculties. In general the universities incorporated those ingredients of humanism deemed to be compatible with the inherited corpus of learning. The humanist impact did not cause major reorientations from the traditional patterns of intellectual life. Oxford and Cambridge were not humanist centers compared, for example, with the universities of Germany, where curricula were radically reconstructed according to humanist criteria.

The tenor of life in the universities was less prone to disruption than in some of the more turbulent cosmopolitan continental universities, although the relative stability was occasionally punctuated by such events as Wycliffism at Oxford or the disturbances at Cambridge during the Peasant Rebellion of 1381. From the 13th to the 16th century they benefited from the sustained support of the monarchy and, intermittently, the papacy. They became highly privileged corporations and dominant forces within their towns and surrounding areas. The chancellors exercised a more extensive authority—spiritual, civil, criminal, and economic—than their continental counterparts, and their aggregate of powers made their office unique among Europe's university towns.

Alan B. Cobban

Bibliography

Catto, Jeremy, ed. *The History of the University of Oxford.* Vol. 1: *The Early Oxford Schools.* Oxford: Clarendon, 1984; Catto, Jeremy, and Ralph Evans, eds. *The History of the University of Oxford.* Vol. 2: *Late Medieval Oxford.* Oxford: Clarendon, 1992; Cobban, Alan B. *The King's Hall within the University of Cambridge in the Later Middle Ages.* London: Cambridge University Press, 1969; Cobban, Alan B. "Decentralized Teaching in the Medieval English Universities." *History of Education* 5 (1976): 193–206; Cobban, Alan B. *The Medieval*

English Universities: Oxford and Cambridge to c. 1500. Aldershot: Scolar, 1988; Cobban, Alan B. "John Arundel, the Tutorial System, and the Cost of Undergraduate Living in the Medieval English Universities." *BJRL* 77 (1995): 143–59; Gibson, Strickland, ed. *Statuta Antiqua Universitatis Oxoniensis.* Oxford: Clarendon, 1931; Hackett, Benedict. *The Original Statutes of Cambridge University: The Text and Its History.* Cambridge: Cambridge University Press, 1970; Hudson, Anne. "Wycliffism in Oxford, 1381–1411." In *Wyclif in His Times,* ed. Anthony Kenny. Oxford: Clarendon, 1986, pp. 67–84; Leader, Damien R. *A History of the University of Cambridge.* Vol. 1: *The University to 1546.* Cambridge: Cambridge University Press, 1989; Leff, Gordon. *Paris and Oxford Universities in the Thirteenth and Fourteenth Centuries.* New York: Wiley, 1968; McConica, James, ed. *The History of the University of Oxford.* Vol. 3: *The Collegiate University.* Oxford: Clarendon, 1986; Owen, Dorothy M. *Cambridge University Archives: A Classified List.* Cambridge: Cambridge University Press, 1988; Pantin, William A. *Oxford Life in Oxford Archives.* Oxford: Clarendon, 1972; Queen's Commissioners, eds. *Documents Relating to the University and Colleges of Cambridge.* 3 vols. London: HMSO, 1852; *Statutes of the Colleges of Oxford.* 3 vols. Oxford: Parker, 1853; Zutshi, Patrick, ed. *Medieval Cambridge: Essays on the Pre-Reformation University.* Woodbridge: Boydell, 1993.

See also Grosseteste; Learning; Schools; Science; Wainfleet; William of Wykeham; Wyclif

Usk, Thomas (d. 1388)

Author of *The Testament of Love,* a Boethian prose dialogue once attributed to Chaucer, in which the author's persona is instructed by Love about true happiness, free will, and predestination.

Born of a London family, Usk served as secretary to John of Northampton, mayor of London 1381–83. After the mayor's defeat in the election of 1383 Northampton and Usk were imprisoned by Northampton's successor, Sir Nicholas Brembre. Usk extricated himself by turning prosecutor against his former master (see *The Appeal of Thomas Usk*). He composed the *Testament* in the period 1384–87, partly as a way of clearing his name. In 1387 Usk was implicated in Brembre's arrest by the king, under pressure from the Appellants. On 4 March 1388 he was executed.

Usk's primary debt in the *Testament* is to Boethius's *Consolation of Philosophy* (or perhaps to Chaucer's translation) and to a work of Anselm on free will; he also draws on *The House of Fame* and *Troilus and Criseyde.* The work has been dismissed as totally derivative. But though its debts are obvious, this dismissal underrates the sophistication of the work in these respects: its awareness of literary theory, its philosophical vocabulary, and the paradox at the heart of the work, which seeks to reinstate its author's good name by professing Boethian detachment from worldly fame.

James Simpson

Bibliography

PRIMARY

Chambers, R.W., and Marjorie Daunt, eds. *The Appeal of Thomas Usk against John of Northampton.* In *A Book of London English 1384–1425.* Oxford: Clarendon, 1931, pp. 22–37; Skeat, Walter W., ed. *The Testament of Love.* In *The Complete Works of Geoffrey Chaucer.* Supplement (Vol. 7). Oxford: Clarendon, 1897, pp. 1–145.

SECONDARY

New *CBEL* 1:506–07; *DNB* 58:60–62; Strohm, Paul. "Politics and Poetics: Usk and Chaucer in the 1380s." In *Literary Practice and Social Change in Britain 1380–1530,* ed. Lee Patterson. Berkeley: University of California Press, 1990, pp. 83–112.

See also Appellants; Boethius; Chaucer; London

Utilitarian Writings

In the broadest sense utilitarian writings may be defined as those "useful" to the extent that they convey practical information. In the narrower sense employed here, however, utilitarian writings must be defined as only those works that apply information toward some tangible end, whether doing, using, or making. Obvious examples—and those to be discussed here—are writings on arithmetic, astronomy (especially as it concerns the calculation of liturgical feasts), judicial astrology (prognostics), professional skills like codicology (book making) and cooking, and various household activities. Other examples might include applied aspects of medicine (e.g., phlebotomy or surgery), sports, music, courtesy books, herbology, alchemy, grammar, charms, veterinary medicine, warfare, navigation, travel writing, weights and measures, or agriculture. Several of these topics are discussed under other entries in this volume.

An important category of utilitarian writings in OE is that related to the astronomical calculation of liturgical feasts (also called computus), not surprising in view of the church's interest in such calculations from at least 243, when the *De pascha computus,* once attributed to St. Cyprian, attempted to resolve the problem of calculating the date for Easter. The most important OE computus is Ælfric's *De temporibus anni* (ca. 993), which draws heavily on Bede's Latin work *De temporum ratione* (725). It explains how to calculate the movable feasts of Septuagesima, Lent, and Easter and discusses Egyptian days (days of ill omen) as well as such technical concepts as the concurrents and epacts. In turn, Ælfric's work provided the basis for Byrhtferth's *Manual* (1011). The number of manuscripts of these works attests to their consistent use, although monastic rather than lay. In addition OE notes and glosses throughout other ecclesiastical manuscripts calculate the position of the moon and its relation to the tides, days of fasting, names of the days of the week, the number of days and weeks in the year, and the length of days, nights, seasons, and shadows. The late-10th-century OE calendar poem, or *Menologium,* reflects this concern for time in its mnemonic presentation of the feasts and seasons of the year. The verse

"Seasons for Fasting" focuses upon a single aspect of the computus. A related category of material consists of the various OE prognosticary texts, which offer predictions of the future based on the phases of the moon, the weather (especially thunder) on New Year's Day, dreams, the alphabet, and so on.

Another important area of OE utilitarian works concerns cryptic writing. *The Rune Poem* (ca. 950–1000) mnemonically instructs its audience on the use of runes, giving first their names and phonetic values, then their various meanings, which illuminate their significance for OE riddles and other poems using runes. Other forms of cryptography also appear, as in the secret letters of Riddle 36 in the (*Exeter Book*) or the more theoretical text found in a Latin psalter of ca. 1050 in BL Cotton Vitellius E.xviii, fol. 16v.

In the ME period utilitarian writings grow in both number and variety. This becomes especially true toward the end of the 14th century, as more and more vernacular translations and adaptations were made from Latin works. By the time that printing was introduced in the late 15th century, such works had found widespread lay ownership and use.

In arithmetic ME examples belong largely to the area of computational mathematics known as algorism (from a corruption of al-Khwarizmi, author of an Arabic treatise on how to calculate with Hindu numerals, written ca. 825 and translated into Latin ca. 1140). *The Craft of Numbering* (ed. Steele) appears to be an early-15th-century translation of a gloss on Alexander of Villadien's *Carmen algorismo* (ca. 1220), while *The Art of Numbering* (ed. Steele) is a translation from the same period of John of Sacrobosco's *De arte numerandi* (ca. 1230). Many manuscripts contain variants and extracts of similar texts, as well as such brief notes as "On how to write up to 100,000" (BL Egerton 827, fol. 51v).

Astronomy is well represented in ME writings by a wide range of both theoretical and applied works. While the many versions of *De theorica planetarum* belong to the former category and should not be discussed here, the descriptive *Wise Book of Astronomy and Philosophy,* which circulated widely, is an important popular transition from astronomical data to judicial astrology (the application of astronomical data to human actions and decision making). It defines the nature of the heavens and the properties of the planets and signs and indicates their influence upon the microcosm. Two late-14th-century treatises on the astrolabe and equatorium, the first certainly and the second possibly by Chaucer, teach the construction and use of instruments for calculating the positions and movements of celestial bodies. Slightly later technical treatises include instructions for making a quadrant (Cambridge, Trinity College R.14.52, fols. 215–238v) and for making a sundial known as "the little ship of Venice," a geometrico-mechanical computing device, based upon spherical projection derived from Hellenistic theories described in Ptolemy's *Planisphaerium.* Although these two treatises do not appear to have been particularly popular or influential, they do indicate some of the variety of ME utilitarian writing.

In addition to such highly technical works are many popular works on the computus, representing—as in OE—a significant body of material, but now designed for the layman outside an ecclesiastical context. Calendars, tables, figures, volvelles (movable parchment or paper wheels), and verses containing astronomical or astrological and religious matter may all include computus matter. It is significant that the Dominican friar Henry Daniel includes in his *Dome of Urynes* or *Liber uricrisiarum* (based on Giles of Corbeil's uroscopy treatise, ca. 1350) a digression on how to calculate computistical date—the dominical letters, bissextile years, and concurrents—using mnemonic verses and a wheel with a pointer attached by a thread. Many other ME notes and verses, often added in the margins of books of hours or other private devotional works, offer mnemonic methods for calculating Easter or other feasts and defining the occupations and lengths of the months (e.g., "Thirti dayes hath nouembir").

Judicial astrology evaluates, or "judges," astronomical data, advises on proper action as a result of such data, and predicts or prognosticates on the future. Such works constitute a large part of ME utilitarian writing, and the majority were certainly not regarded—at least until the mid-16th century—as occult or pseudo-science. There are many categories. The most important is that dealing with the elections of times, that is, the relationship between such astronomical conditions as the position of the seven planets with regard to each other and to the twelve signs of the zodiac (aspect) and the times when certain events take place—birth, illness, travel, and so on. Treatises on elections aid their users in "electing" the most favorable times in which to perform a given activity. This was a popular topic among early Arabic writers, and it entered the Latin tradition by way of such influential works as John of Seville's translations of Haly Abenrudwan's *De electionibus* and Albumasar's *Flores astrologiae* and the various adaptations of and commentaries on Ptolemy's *Tetrabiblos.* These were in turn the main sources for John of Eschenden's (or Ashenden's) *De prognostica summula,* translated into ME ca. 1450 (Bodl. Ashmole 396, fols. 92–125v), and Richard of Wallingford's *Exafrenon pronosticationum temporis,* translated into English about the same time. The ME *Treatise on the Elections of Times* (found together with the *Exafrenon* in one manuscript; ed. Matheson and Shannon in Matheson, 1994) sets out the theoretical bases for this system, such as whether a sign is mobile, fixed, or mixed, whether masculine or feminine, and which planets are in which aspect within it.

In its applied forms the notion of election is most frequently represented by the many verse and prose variations of the lunary. Such texts, which may be called anything from *De cursione lune* to *The Dream of Daniel (Somnia Danielis),* are based upon the lunar month of 28.5 days and prognosticate on the nature of the moon's influence in each of its "mansions" or days for a wide variety of activities, such as birth, marriage, agriculture, travel, dreams, commerce, imprisonment, profession, illness, or phlebotomy. Another popular form of lunary election prognosticates on the basis of the moon's influence in each of the twelve signs, Aries to Pisces.

Related to the lunary are works on nativities, based on various versions of *De nativitatibus* attributed to Arabic originals by Alfraganus, Haly Abenragel, Messahala, and others.

One of the more popular is the *Book of the Destinary of the Twelve Signs,* predicting the physiognomy and destiny of both men and women according to the sign under which they were born and advising on health and choice of profession, which follows the *Wise Book of Philosophy and Astronomy* in twelve of its 27 known manuscripts.

Works on interrogations (ultimately derived from, among other sources, Latin translations of Dorotheus of Sidon's *De interrogationibus,* originally in Greek) ask questions and propose answers about such topics as illness, fortune, birth, journeys, the location of lost objects, and "urine not seen" (e.g., Bodl. Ashmole 210, pt. 2, fols. 22–23v). Important for the accuracy of the answer are both the hour when the question is asked (related to another prognosticary genre called the Horary) and the natural house within the horoscope governing the topic in question.

Geomancy texts also constitute a form of interrogations, based upon the practice of deriving sixteen figures from dot patterns and using these according to astrological principles to answer certain questions. The most complete ME treatise and handbook derives from Martin of Spain's *De geomancia* (ed. Means in Matheson, 1994) and appears in a mid-15th-century manuscript (Bodl. Ashmole 360, fols. 15–26v). Another form of applied prognostics is chiromancy or palmistry, a topic on which three major ME treatises have thus far been identified, including one by John Metham (ca. 1448). These are based upon Latin works in the Pseudo-Aristotelian tradition of physiognomy (the relation between bodily forms and character, summarized in such works as the *Secreta secretorum*), represented by the anonymous *De chiromantia.*

Prognosticary texts include weather predictions and dream books, a genre already represented in OE, although they descend through intermediate Latin sources. These include the *Erra Pater* or *Prophecies of Esdras,* with versions in both verse and prose, which predict the events of the coming year according to which day of the week Christmas (or New Year's) Day falls, or whether there is thunder on that day (Craig, 1916: 146–47, 157–58; Robbins, 1955: 63–67). While the outcome of dreams is also covered by lunaries, separate dream books, usually entitled *Somnia Danielis,* may be found, such as BL Lansdowne 388, which lists dreamed objects and their significance (ed. Bühler, 1962).

A number of utilitarian texts relate to crafts and professions. Among these are codicological texts, which describe how to make books: recipes are given for making parchment, ink, paint for illumination, glue, sizing for gold leaf, and leather for binding. For chefs culinary recipes abound in many manuscripts. Apart from many isolated recipes there appear to be at least four major collections, based ultimately upon popular Latin collections known as *De coquina.* One of the earliest in English, the *Diuersa servicia tam de carnibus quam de pissibus* (ca. 1381), contains 59 recipes for cooking meat and 33 for fish; the slightly later *Forme of Cury* (ca. 1390) contains over 200 recipes and was compiled for Richard II (ed. Hieatt and Butler).

The range of helps and recipes for stewards and other members of a household—such as "How to drive fleas out of a chamber"—is wide. Many of these are found in compendia, which may include agricultural, medical, culinary, or even religious matter and which were used—often until the early 17th century—as standard household reference works. The *Treatise on Lacemaking* may form part of a household reference book for a women's cloister. "How to Purchase Land" advises on legal aspects of land ownership and from its fourteen known manuscripts appears to have been one of the most popular pieces of utilitarian verse (Robbins, 1955: 70–71).

There are other related and important categories of ME utilitarian writing on aspects of household economy—for example, the widely circulating translations of works on horticulture by Gottfried of Franconia (ed. Cylkowski in Matheson, 1994) and Nicholas Bollard. Also important, especially for noble households, are the hunting and hawking treatises, the most popular of which was Edward duke of York's *Master of Game* (extant in 24 manuscripts).

Laurel Means

Bibliography
OLD ENGLISH

Primary
Halsall, Maureen, ed. *The OE "Rune Poem": A Critical Edition.* Toronto: University of Toronto Press, 1981; Henel, Heinrich, ed. *Ælfric's De Temporibus Anni.* EETS o.s. 213. London: Oxford University Press, 1942; Malone, Kemp, trans. "The OE Calendar Poem." In *Studies in Language, Literature, and Culture of the Middle Ages and Later,* ed. Elmer Bagby Atwood and Archibald A. Hill. Austin: University of Texas Press, 1969, pp. 193–99.

Secondary
New *CBEL* 1:300, 303, 317–21, 333–36; Greenfield, Stanley B., and Fred C. Robinson, *A Bibliography of Publications on Old English Literature to the End of 1972.* Toronto: University of Toronto Press, 1980, pp. 41–61, 246, 264, 270, 295–98, 344–45, 353, 355–56.

MIDDLE ENGLISH

Primary
Bühler, Curt F. "Two Middle English Texts of the *Somnia Danielis.*" *Anglia* 80 (1962): 264–73; Craig, Hardin, ed. *The Works of John Metham.* EETS o.s. 132. Oxford: Kegan Paul, Trench, Trübner, 1916; Hieatt, Constance B., and Sharon Butler, eds. *Curye on Inglysch.* EETS s.s. 8. London: Oxford University Press, 1985; Krochalis, Jeanne, and Edward Peters, eds. and trans. "The Wise Book of Philosophy and Astronomy." In *The World of Piers Plowman.* Philadelphia: University of Pennsylvania Press, 1975, pp. 3–17; Manzalaoui, M.A., ed. *Secreta Secretorum.* EETS o.s. 276. Oxford: Oxford University Press, 1977; Matheson, Lister M., ed. *Popular and Practical Science of Medieval England.* East Lansing: Colleagues, 1994; Means, Laurel. *Medieval*

Lunar Astrology: A Collection of Representative Middle English Texts. Lewiston: Mellen, 1993; North, J.D., ed. and trans. *Richard of Wallingford: An Edition of His Writings.* 3 vols. Oxford: Clarendon, 1976; Price, Derek J. [de Solla], ed. *The Equatorie of the Planetis.* Cambridge: Cambridge University Press, 1955; Price, Derek J. de Solla, ed. "The Little Ship of Venice—A Middle English Instrument Tract." *Journal of the History of Medicine and Allied Sciences* 15 (1960): 399–407; Robbins, Rossell Hope, ed. *Secular Lyrics of the XIVth and XVth Centuries.* 2d ed. Oxford: Clarendon, 1955; Stanley, Eric G., ed. "Directions for Making Many Sorts of Laces." In *Chaucer and Middle English Studies in Honour of Rossell Hope Robbins,* ed. Beryl Rowland. London: Allen & Unwin, 1974, pp. 89–103; Steele, Robert, ed. *The Earliest Arithmetics in English.* EETS e.s. 118. Oxford: Humphrey Milford, 1922.

SECONDARY

New *CBEL* 1:687, 695–98; Braswell [Means], Laurel. "Utilitarian and Scientific Prose." In *Middle English Prose: A Critical Guide to Major Authors and Genres,* ed. A.S.G. Edwards. New Brunswick: Rutgers University Press, 1984, pp. 337–87; Taavitsainen, Irma. *Middle English Lunaries: A Study of the Genre.* Helsinki: Société Néophilologique, 1988.

See also Ælfric; Alchemy; Astronomy; Bede; Berners, Juliana; Byrhtferth; Charms; Chaucer; Grammatical Treatises; Households, Royal and Baronial; *Mandeville's Travels;* Paleography and Codicology; Prose, ME; Runes; Science; Scientific and Medical Writings; Technology

V

Vainglory

An 84-line poem in the Exeter Book, appearing on folios 83r–84v of the manuscript, between *The Seafarer* and *Widsith.* The poem has been given various titles, all in some way reflecting upon a central concern with the need to avoid vainglorious pride. Because of its firmly didactic tone *Vainglory* is often termed "homiletic," and stylistically its nearest analogue within the corpus of Anglo-Saxon poetry is Hrothgar's "sermon" in *Beowulf.* Its main thrust is toward the fostering of wisdom, with argument conducted through the examination of contraries.

The narrator presents himself as having something of true value to impart, for he has learned how to distinguish God's own son from his weaker contrary (a contrast based on 1 John 3). His vivid presentation of dissension within this world, whether sparked by drunkenness or malice, is complemented by an account of how, long ago, paradise was lost to those angels among whom pride arose. The contents are tightly organized, with attention held by the simple device of addressing a listener directly. The poet's clear exposition of the distinction between good and evil leads neatly to the ironic half-line "if the prophet did not lie to me." The simple ending looks heavenward, its focus on the "best ruler of victories" following naturally from the constant comparisons set up throughout the poem.

Critics have emphasized the poet's use of rare words, but some forms identified as unique are attested elsewhere and the compounds generally would not seem out of place in many an OE homily. The *ic,* "I," of *Vainglory's* opening eight lines has put readers on profitless trails. Some, disappointed that it is not followed by further autobiographical musings, find the poem without overall unity. Others are eager to identify both the speaker's wise informant and that wise man's source of teaching. As a result the poem's contents have been variously blocked out, to accommodate putative sources that are supposed to reveal its structure. However, none of the proposed sources accounts for the whole content and ordering of the poem.

Jane Roberts

Bibliography

PRIMARY

ASPR 3:147–49; Pickford, T.E., ed. "An Edition of *Vainglory.*" *Parergon* 10 (1974): 1–40.

SECONDARY

Huppé, Bernard F. *The Web of Words: Structural Analyses of the Old English Poems Vainglory, The Wonder of Creation, The Dream of the Rood, and Judith.* Albany: SUNY Press, 1970, pp. 2–26; Regan, Catherine A. "Patristic Psychology in the Old English *Vainglory.*" *Traditio* 26 (1970): 324–35.

See also Beowulf; Exeter Book; Wisdom Literature

Vaulting

So far as we can tell, vaulted Anglo-Saxon buildings were nonexistent, and the story of English medieval vaulting begins with the Norman Conquest. Barrel, groin, and rib vaults all appear frequently in English Romanesque architecture, in a wide range of buildings and positions.

Barrel vaults were used less frequently than they were in many parts of the Continent, but they were popular in the West Country in the years around 1100 and probably covered originally the choirs, transepts, and possibly naves of Tewkesbury and Pershore abbeys and perhaps the choir of Gloucester Cathedral (formerly St. Peter's Abbey). The only high barrel vault that survives in England is that of St. John's Chapel in the Tower of London, of the late 11th century. Barrel vaults, usually pointed, were also used in some chapter houses; Gloucester preserves a good example, and there was originally another at Reading Abbey.

Groin vaults, almost always constructed of rubble, were the normal means of covering crypts and aisles in English Romanesque great churches. Good examples of the former still survive at Worcester and Canterbury cathedrals, and of the latter at Norwich and Ely cathedrals, or in the priory churches at Blyth and St. Bartholomew, London. High groin vaults seem to have been infrequent, although there is some evidence for their use in the choir of St. Albans Abbey and, although less certainly, Lincoln Cathedral. Groin vaults appear frequently outside of churches as well, particularly in the undercrofts or ground-floor ranges of dormitories (Canterbury, Lewes), refectories (Worcester, Durham), west ranges (Chester, Kirkstall), or even castle keeps (Castle Rising).

Durham Cathedral, begun 1093, contains the earliest examples of rib vaults in Europe. As completed in the 1130s, Durham was an entirely rib-vaulted building, but no other English great church preserves high rib vaults of the Romanesque period. Romanesque rib vaults are found frequently, however, in aisles (Winchester, Romsey, Peterborough), and chapter houses (Durham, Bristol, Forde). High rib vaults of French Gothic style appear at Canterbury in the rebuilding after the fire of 1174 and quickly become common in the south, appearing at Rochester and Chichester before 1200. In the west Gothic rib vaults were used at Wells and Glastonbury from the 1180s and quickly became the rule in large churches there as well. But in the north, in spite of completely vaulted churches like Beverley, many important buildings, including Whitby, Hexham, or Glasgow, continued to combine rib-vaulted aisles with wood-roofed main vessels. Even York Minster lacks high stone vaults, being covered instead by wooden facsimiles.

Canterbury introduced the French style of six-part vaulting to England, but although copied at Rochester and Lincoln, such vaults quickly disappeared from the English scene to be replaced by more elaborate types. Lincoln Cathedral, begun 1192, was the crucial catalyst in this change. The earliest surviving high vaults at Lincoln, in the east transepts, are six-part vaults over single bays, but in St. Hugh's Choir the master introduced an asymmetrical system with extra diagonal ribs meeting on a longitudinal ridge rib at two points of intersection, instead of the usual one point. These "crazy vaults," as Paul Frankl dubbed them, are the beginnings of an English fascination with the decorative possibilities of ribs that was to last until the Reformation and that represents an important break with the chaste French adherence to four- and six-part systems.

The Lincoln choir vaults could count no successors in their use of asymmetry but many in their use of extra diagonal and ridge ribs. The designer of the Lincoln nave kept both the latter features to create a vault with a regular pattern with two extra diagonal ribs per every one, reaching a boss on the longitudinal ridge rib and the other a boss on the transverse ridge rib. The visual effect of such cones of multiple ribs was to deny any emphasis to the bay defined by the normal four-part vault in favor of an emphasis on the point of bay division. The most extreme example of a tierceron vault can be found at Exeter Cathedral, begun ca. 1270.

At the end of the 13th century English masons began to connect diagonal ribs, tiercerons, and ridge ribs by shorter lengths of ribs known as liernes to create still more complex linear patterns. Early examples include the West Country choirs at Pershore and Bristol and the lower story of St. Stephen's Chapel in Westminster Palace, London. The visual results could be staggeringly complex, as in the choir vaults of Tewkesbury Abbey and Gloucester Cathedral, both of the mid-14th century. Structurally, however, these vaults are often simple pointed barrel vaults with interpenetrations for the windows; the ribs have simply become an applied surface pattern. The same is true for the so-called net vaults, such as the choir of Wells Cathedral, where diagonal ribs spanning double bays form a repetitive mesh texture.

The last English contribution to the history of medieval vaulting was the development of fan vaults. Although these develop formally out of the cones of tierceron ribs common from the 13th century, they embody new geometrical and constructional premises. A fan vault consists of multiple ribs springing from a single point that maintain equal spacing among themselves as they rise vertically. The ribs and webs between them form conoids that are generally concave in vertical section and convex in horizontal section. These fans were frequently constructed out of cut-stone masonry, where ribs and webs were fashioned from single blocks instead of the more traditional method of constructing them separately in a frame-and-panel technique, although this method was still used in some fan vaults, particularly those covering larger spans. The crown of a fan vault was a flat or slightly domed spandrel; these could be reduced in size or eliminated by intersecting the cones of ribs. Decorative pendant blocks might be combined with fan vaults, positioned in either the central spandrels or along the line of the transverse rib.

The earliest fan vaults surviving are those in the cloister of Gloucester Cathedral, built in the last twenty years of the 14th century. They long remained popular for smaller spaces, such as tomb canopies, chantries, porches, or towers, but their first use over large spans came only in the second half of the 15th century at Sherborne Abbey. The most spectacular examples of their use are in royal buildings of the late 15th and early 16th centuries, especially King's College Chapel in Cambridge and Henry VII's chapel at Westminster Abbey.

Lawrence Hoey

Bibliography

Bony, Jean. *The English Decorated Style: Gothic Architecture Transformed 1250–1350*. Oxford: Phaidon, 1979; Kidson, Peter. "St. Hugh's Choir." *BAACT* 8 (1986): 29–42; Leedy, Walter. *Fan Vaulting: A Study of Form, Technology, and Meaning*. London: Arts & Architecture Press, 1980; Willis, Robert. "On the Construction of the Vaults of the Middle Ages." *Transactions of the Royal Institute of British Architects of London* 1/2 (1842): 1–69. Repr. in Robert Willis, *Architectural History of Some English Cathedrals*. 2d ser. Chicheley: Minet, 1973; Wilson, Christopher. *The Gothic Cathedral: The Architecture of the Great Church 1130–1530*. London: Thames & Hudson, 1990.

See also Architecture and Architectural Sculpture, Gothic; Architecture and Architectural Sculpture, Romanesque; Canterbury Cathedral; Durham Cathedral; Ely Cathedral; Gloucester Cathedral; King's College, Cambridge; Lincoln

Cathedral; Norwich Cathedral; St. Albans Abbey; Wells Cathedral; Westminster Abbey; York and Ripon Minsters

Vercelli Book

A late-10th-century codex of 135 folios in a single, unpolished hand (Vercelli, Biblioteca Capitolare CXVII), containing 23 prose homilies and six passages of religious verse *(Andreas, The Fates of the Apostles, Soul and Body I,* a fragmentary poetic adaptation of Psalm 28:3 A.V., *The Dream of the Rood,* and *Elene).* The contents are all in English, although six homilies have Latin headings; the order of items appears to be random. The writing becomes smaller in the last third of the book, where the number of lines per page increases significantly.

Ker defines the script as Square Anglo-Saxon Minuscule of the second half of the 10th century. A case has been made for a later date on grounds of content, but some of the letter shapes used are archaic in the later 10th century, especially the very open form of *g,* used throughout the codex, the "double" form of *a,* and *f*-shaped *y,* both used occasionally. There is little ornament in the book: zoomorphic (animal-shaped) initials open two items, with a third part way through another item. Four items are rubricated. Loss of leaves shows that the book is an original compilation put together by the scribe, who drew upon a variety of exemplars.

On the basis of language and the analogy of contents with those of other books of known provenance it has been suggested recently that the Vercelli Book is of southeastern origin and specifically that it drew upon the resources of the library at St. Augustine's, Canterbury. There has been much speculation about how the book reached Vercelli, in northern Italy. Marginalia, including the pen trials of later copyists, show that the book was not taken abroad when first written, but a verse from a psalm in Latin was entered on a blank half-page in an Italian hand at the end of the 11th century. Vercelli was on the pilgrim route to Rome, and it seems likely that the book was taken as suitable reading matter for such a traveler, perhaps a member of the entourage of an 11th-century archbishop visiting Rome for his pallium.

A number of entries in later medieval and Renaissance catalogues of the cathedral books might refer to the Vercelli Book, but the manuscript was effectively lost to the sight of modern scholars until a German law professor published quotations of it in the 1820s. News of the book reached England only in 1832, after which a student, C. Maier, was sent from Tübingen to make a complete copy of it, now London, Lincoln's Inn Library Misc. 312. Maier is generally assumed to have been responsible for applying reagent to faded or erased passages of text, reagent that has since blackened the affected areas.

D.G. Scragg

Bibliography

PRIMARY

ASPR 2; Scragg, D.G., ed. *The Vercelli Homilies and Related Texts.* EETS o.s. 300. Oxford: Oxford University Press, 1992; Sisam, Celia, ed. *The Vercelli Book.* EEMF 19. Copenhagen: Rosenkilde & Bagger, 1976 [facsimile].

SECONDARY

Halsall, Maureen. "Vercelli and the Vercelli Book." *PMLA* 84 (1969): 1545–50; Ker, N.R. *Catalogue of Manuscripts Containing Anglo-Saxon.* Oxford: Clarendon, 1957, no. 394; Scragg, D.G. "The Compilation of the Vercelli Book." *ASE* 2 (1973): 189–207.

See also Andreas; Cynewulf; *Dream of the Rood;* Exeter Book; Junius Manuscript; Pilgrimages; *Soul and Body;* Vercelli Homilies

Vercelli Homilies

Twenty-three prose items in the Vercelli Book, forming the earliest surviving collection of homiletic prose in English. They are neither an ordered collection nor uniform in format. The items appear to have been put together piecemeal as the scribe or his master gathered material. Some were clearly copied in groups: Homilies VI–X form a numbered series, XI–XIV are rubricated in a distinctive way, and XIX–XXI are by a single author. They are probably of diverse dates and origin. Homilies XIX–XXI seem to have been composed only shortly before the Vercelli Book itself was made, while I, II and perhaps III are much older, possibly representing a vernacular homiletic tradition as old as the first half of the 10th century, or even earlier.

The content is also varied. Eschatological homilies predominate: Homilies II (in part in doggerel verse) and XV stress the terrors of the Last Days, IV and VII report dramatically the trial of the soul at Judgment, and III, VII, IX, X, XIV, and XXII are general exhortations to repentance because judgment is at hand. Two Rogation series, XI–XIII and XIX–XXI, also stress judgment. Each is a set of three intended for the days prior to Ascension Day, with the emphasis on the third day being on preparing now to meet God. By contrast there are few exegetical homilies: Homily I tells the Passion story from the synoptic Gospels, with little homiletic comment, but only V, VI, XVI, and XVII explain biblical texts, the first two set for Christmas, the latter two for Epiphany and Candlemas. And there are only two saints' lives, XVIII (Martin) and XXIII (Guthlac), the latter being no more than a few excerpts from the life by Felix of Crowland rounded off with a perfunctory homiletic ending.

Some of the pieces are based on earlier vernacular material and may well have been composed by the "scissors-and-paste" method so favored by 11th-century homilists. A large section of Homily XXI, for example, is a verbatim copy of an earlier version of Homily II, while II itself has awkward transitions that suggest that it, too, may have been compiled in the same way at an earlier stage. Most pieces are heavily dependent on Latin. Homilies III, XI, XV, VIII, XXII, and XXIII rarely depart from a literal rendering of known Latin sources. But there are also pieces that treat source material with great freedom. Homilies XIX–XXI are competently put together from a Latin anthology, while X, long known from the version printed from another manuscript by Arthur Napier as "Pseudo-Wulfstan homily XLIX," is a highly sophisticated creation. Although its ultimate sources are three brief paragraphs in Latin authors, its construction shows the application of a shrewd mind, one that can express ideas in highly wrought and often beautiful language. Vercelli Homily X thus marks one of the highest achievements of the anonymous homiletic tradition of the 10th century, paving the way for the work of Archbishop Wulfstan in the 11th.

D.G. Scragg

Bibliography

PRIMARY

Scragg, D.G., ed. *The Vercelli Homilies and Related Texts.* EETS o.s. 300. Oxford: Oxford University Press, 1992.

SECONDARY

Cross, J.E. "Portents and Events at Christ's Birth: Comments on Vercelli V and VI and the Old English Martyrology." *ASE* 2 (1973): 209–20; Szarmach, Paul E. "The Vercelli Homilies: Style and Structure." In *The Old English Homily and Its Backgrounds,* ed. Paul E. Szarmach and Bernard F. Huppé. Albany: SUNY Press, 1978, pp. 241–67; Szarmach, Paul E. "The Earlier Homily: *De Parasceve.*" In *Studies in Earlier Old English Prose,* ed. Paul E. Szarmach. Albany: SUNY Press, 1986; Wilcox, Jonathan. "Variant Texts of an Old English Homily: Vercelli X and Stylistic Effects." In *The Preservation and Transmission of Anglo-Saxon Culture,* ed. Szarmach, Paul E. and Joel T. Rosenthal. Kalamazoo: Medieval Institute, 1997.

See also Blickling Homilies; Felix of Crowland; Sermons; Vercelli Book; Wulfstan

Versification

From the point of view of the writer of verse, a great change overtook the literary language at the end of the OE period. OE poets had no choice of meters when embarking on poetry. After the Norman Conquest poets could choose between two kinds of meter: the traditional English *alliterative meter,* inherited from the Anglo-Saxons, and by them from their continental ancestors; or from a variety of meters, most of them with *rhyme,* borrowed from either medieval Latin verse or from the verse of Normandy and France. Alliterative meter continued to be used well into the 15th century, especially in the west Midlands and the north.

Old English Meter

The native alliterative tradition lacks the regular alternation of stress and unstress of meter derived from Latin or Norman or French models. Alliteration involves the commencement of at least two stressed syllables with the same sound in a verse line; one or two alliterating syllables occur in the first half of the line, and one only in the second half. In OE alliterative verse, rhyme, not always exact, is rare (other than in jingles of perhaps more popular origin than is attested in the largely monastic or formal manuscripts now extant); exceptions include the *Riming Poem* and Cynewulf's Epilogue to *Elene.* Stanzas are rarely used in OE; exceptions

include *Deor* and *The Seasons of Fasting.* In early ME rhyme is sometimes found in combination with meters that (like OE verse) lack regular alternation of stress and unstress; these meters are sometimes regarded as descended from OE.

No ancient treatise of how to scan OE verse is extant; all systems in use are derived by modern scholars by inspection of the verse. Some systems are thought applicable to all Germanic verse and are derived from the widest range of alliterative poetry in all the Germanic dialects. Some are derived from OE alliterative verse only, often with special reference to *Beowulf,* which is regular, or "strict." Many prosodists do not believe Germanic verse to be *isochronous,* that is, with every half-line taking the same amount of time in recitation. Others have held that isochronism is essential in reading verse.

Some OE poetic manuscripts mark off each *half-line* with a point. Such *metrical pointing* is found, for example, in the Junius Manuscript (Bodl. Junius 11). That teaches us to recognize these metrical units. Two half-lines, joined by alliteration, form a "long line." Verse is written continuously in the manuscripts, like prose.

The distribution of *stress* and *unstress* matters in OE verse. Stress is at two levels: full stress must fall on the stem syllable of nouns, adjectives, and adverbs preceding their verb and can fall on the stem syllable of all but function words; *half-stress* often falls on stressable words that are not given full stress in a particular line and that may include the stem syllable of the second element of nominal compounds. Half-stress also falls on the penult (second-to-last syllable) of trisyllabic words. Stress falls on long syllables (long either by virtue of vocalic length or because a short vowel is followed by a consonant in the same syllable). When a stressed syllable immediately follows a long stressed syllable, the second stressed syllable may be short. A stress may be *resolved*—that is, a short stressed syllable immediately followed by an unstressed syllable may, by *resolution,* be measured as if the two combined amounted to a long syllable. Function words, inflexional endings and other suffixes, and verbal prefixes and some nominal prefixes are unstressed. Finite verbs are often unstressed. At the end of a half-line only one unstressed syllable can occur, except when the first of two is used for resolution. Sense stress governs metrical stress, so that exceptional emphasis on a function word and exceptional positioning may lead to its taking metrical stress and alliteration.

Some lines of verse are distinctly longer than the norm; the purpose of these *hypermetric* lines is not understood, and there is no agreement on how to scan them. In one way of looking at them they might be regarded as similar to lines with a long initial nonalliterating element, except that they do alliterate. They often occur in groups. Some poems use hypermetric lines frequently, such as *Judith* (almost one line in five) and *The Dream of the Rood.*

Multisyllabic *dips* ("dip" means a position in the half-line to be filled by one or more unstressed syllables), hypermetric lines, oddities of alliteration, and rhymes are occasional features in OE. Some metrists have, unconvincingly, used linguistic changes to explain the metrical changes resulting in less "strict" verse. Reduction to zero of most inflexions, as a result of which English ceased to be—in a generalizing simplification—a language of disyllables and became a language of monosyllables, occurred in southern English verse no earlier than the 15th century. Perhaps an explanation might be sought in the syntactic changes of the *Transitional* period, as a result of which prepositions and articles were more often used, often in positions not permitted in "strict" OE meter. There is no known single explanation, certainly no simple linguistic explanation, for the changes that overtook English meter beginning before the Norman Conquest and continuing after the 12th century.

It is sometimes suggested that side by side with strict verse, of which *Beowulf* and most of the longer poems are examples and which may have been products of monastic scriptoria, there was a more popular form of less exact verse, of which the "Finnsburh Fragment" and some of the Chronicle poems are examples. It is thought that in the reforms of the later 10th century the monasteries ceased to be the nurseries of vernacular poetry so that popular, less exact forms prevailed. We have no evidence for such generalizations about the causes; all we have is the outcome, however caused: the metrically lax verse of the late period. The metrical psalms of the Paris Psalter of the 10th century, *Judgment Day II,* and the liturgical verse of the manuscripts Cambridge, Corpus Christi College 201, and Bodl. Junius 121 of the 11th century are less "strict" than *Beowulf*; yet they must be monastic.

Transitional and Middle English Verse in Native Meters

The Grave (in Bodleian Library, Bodley 343) and the alliterative verse in Worcester Cathedral F 174 belong to the Transitional period; the writing is dated as late 12th or early 13th centuries, and their composition is probably not much earlier. They represent a continuing alliterative tradition. Judged by the standards of "strict" OE verse, these Transitional poems illustrate various inexactnesses. Rhyme becomes common, especially in nonalliterative verse. In contravention of what in OE was a basic rule alliteration may fall on the second stress of the second half-line. Some lines comprise three half-lines alliterating on the same sound.

The Latin *Physiologus* (of about 1200) presents a range of metrical forms. The early ME translation of the 13th century traditionally called *The Bestiary* imitates the variety of meters by making use of the vernacular resources then available, including alliterative meter; but even when the alliteration is consistently maintained, the rules governing "strict" OE meter are not followed. The manuscript has metrical pointing and the lines are written continuously like prose. The text has rhyming verse with alliteration as well as other meters, including four-stress and three-stress *rhyming couplets, ballad stanzas* or *common meter* (consisting of four lines, the first and third having four stresses, the second and fourth lines rhyming and having three stresses), and the *septenarius* (a seven-stress line). The poet shows a prosodic freedom and delight in metrical variety not found elsewhere in early ME.

The *Proverbs of Alfred* are in rhyming alliterative verse, but the rhymes and the alliteration are used inconsistently.

One of the problems of ME prosody is that texts often survive in several manuscripts, none written by the poet, and in metrically different versions. There are four versions of the *Proverbs of Alfred,* the earliest (now fragmentary) of the early 13th century. With such textual variation it seems impossible to arrive at any precise conclusion about the meter of early ME alliterative rhyming verse. Scribes in general show little respect for the integrity of the texts they are copying; they leave out or add little words, and make other changes involving the count of syllables.

By the end of the 13th century the four-stress couplet without regular alternation of stress and unstress became a common metrical form. An example is *Havelok the Dane*; its poet tolerated two unstressed syllables where the meter requires one; omission of the initial unstress is not infrequent; alliteration is an occasional added feature. *Havelok* and *King Horn* (one copy of *Horn* is preserved in the same manuscript as *Havelok,* Bodl. Laud Misc. 108, and in two other manuscripts), differ substantially in meter. That of *Horn* is not to be readily reduced to a system, except that it is rhyming verse in short lines of two, three, and occasionally four stresses. Alliteration occasionally binds the two lines of a couplet. The three versions of *Horn* have many variants, and the poem is malleable in the hands of a textual critic or prosodic theorist. It seems unwarranted to see French influence (other than perhaps in the rhyming) and equally unwarranted to derive its meter from OE alliterative verse.

Lines of irregular length, but mainly with four stresses, rhyming in couplets, with occasional touches of ornamental alliteration, form the meter of *Kyng Alisaunder,* which survives in three widely differing manuscripts and one early print, the earliest of which (with only fragments of this poem) is the Auchinleck Manuscript (Edinburgh, National Library of Scotland Advocates' 19.2.1; ca. 1330–40). The manuscripts differ considerably. Other romances, too, are in loose, rhyming couplets. They are written out in verse lines in the manuscripts, as became usual for rhyming verse; the first letter of each line is a capital, in many manuscripts rubricated. The rhythms within the line are held to be the speech rhythms normal in the language, as is thought to be true of the rhythms of the native alliterative tradition (in OE and ME). The rhythms were not, however, sufficiently regular or insistent to guide the scribes when copying these texts, and in most lines there are syllabic differences among the extant versions.

ME alliterative verse exists both early and late. Our information is to some extent disjointed, and because there appears to be a gap between early and late ME alliterative verse, some scholars have spoken of an Alliterative Revival in the late ME period. In early ME Laʒamon's *Brut* is the foremost example of the continuance of an alliterative tradition going back to OE. The poem survives in two BL Cotton manuscripts, Caligula A.ix and Otho C.xiii, both of about the last quarter of the 13th century. Again the texts differ from each other; Otho has fewer of the poeticisms found in Caligula. The *Brut* uses alliteration frequently, as if to bind together the two half-lines into the long line as was done before the Conquest; but unlike OE poetry the *Brut* is not wholly and consistently alliterative. Instead of alliteration, and sometimes in addition to alliteration, it uses rhyme or near-rhyme. The length of the half-lines varies considerably. Laȝamon's *Brut,* especially in the Caligula version, often seems to echo the poetic effects of diction and rhythms of OE poetry at its most heroic. The rhythms, however, lack the precision of OE verse. The strict OE rules of alliteration cease to apply: the second as well as the first stressed syllable of the second half-line may share in the alliteration, and alliterative stress may fall on function words; alliteration on the last stress of the second half-line is not uncommon.

Alliterative verse without rhyme shows many varieties of line structure in late ME and Middle Scots. The form is not confined to romances; *Piers Plowman, Cleanness,* and "The Blacksmiths" (*Swarte smekyd smeþes. . .*) also use alliteration without rhyme in lines in which stress and unstress do not alternate regularly. The manuscripts are often late. It is not possible to establish a chronological order for the metrical varieties in use.

An obvious departure is the use of alliteration for ono-matopoeic effects, as in "The Blacksmiths," or the scene when the axe is ground in *Sir Gawain and the Green Knight* 2201–04. (Onomatopoeia is not demonstrable for OE or early ME, though critics have pointed to a few possible examples.) In some poems alliteration on the same letter over three lines was not avoided, as it had been in OE. Oddities (including occasional absence) of alliteration occur in many poems; in some cases editors have emended them away. It is not always clear if normally unstressed words can share in the alliteration. Most lines have two or more alliterative syllables in the first half-line and one or two alliterative stresses in the second half-line.

Because the alliterative poets of later ME inherited a system that had more alliteration in the first half-line than the second and because double alliteration supported heavier rhythmical structures in OE and later, the first half-line usually contains more syllables than the second. The ME first half-line, therefore, often looks as if it were descended from the OE hypermetric half-line; the second half-line is tighter.

Middle English Verse in Foreign Meters

ME verse in foreign meters is fundamentally different from verse in the native alliterative tradition and different from the short irregular lines in rhyming couplets of, for example, *Havelok, King Horn,* and *Kyng Alisaunder.* Foreign meters demand the regular alternation of stress and unstress. Most use rhyme; they may use alliteration as an added grace.

The earliest longer poem in a foreign meter is the *Ormulum.* Uniquely for poetry in OE or early ME, the manuscript, Bodl. Junius 1, of the late 12th century, is in the author's own hand. The verse is written continuously like prose, with metrical pointing. Orm, the poet, is aware that syllables matter for the meter he has chosen, the unrhymed *iambic septenarius.* The first half of Orm's line consists of eight syllables, the second of seven (x and / represent unstressed and stressed syllables, respectively):

x   / x /   x   / x   / | x /   x   / x /
Icc hafe sammnedd o þiss boc: þa goddspelless neh alle·

Orm admits some variety in his use of meter, but generally his meter is so exact and his manuscript so reliable that he provides firm linguistic and prosodic evidence of a kind we usually lack for early English. His system of scansion allows of no half-stress, so that it is significant that he usually stresses the middle syllable in a word of three syllables; usually *goddspelless* x / x , rarely / x / as in the line quoted, and always *goddspell* (/ x):

x   / x /   x   / x   / | x /   x   / x   / x
Icc hafe sett her o þiss boc: amang goddspelless wordess·

Iambic tetrameter rhyming in couplets is a common meter in ME. It is hardly ever used with rigorous regularity, so much so that it is sometimes more apt to refer to the meter as consisting of four-stress lines in rhyming couplets. The meter of *The Owl and the Nightingale* is a skillfully varied four-stress measure. Both Chaucer, in *The Book of the Duchess* and *The House of Fame,* and Gower, in *Confessio Amantis,* were accomplished poets in this meter. In *The House of Fame* 1094–98 Chaucer shows himself aware that, for easy, unpedantic verse, having one syllable less than the meter demands may not be disagreeable.

Later Chaucer chose for his nonstanzaic verse *iambic pentameter* in rhyming couplets, the English form of the heroic couplet, first in *The Legend of Good Women.* In the 15th and 16th centuries many poets use this meter, with varying degrees of exactness and skill. A particular feature of iambic pentameter in late ME is the clash of contiguous stresses in mid-line, characteristic of Lydgate's prosody, often combined with omission of the unstressed syllable at the beginning of the line. Such variation of the underlying, standard pattern often gives effective expression of movement beyond the confines of a single line: for example,

x   / x /   / x   x   / (x)
And in my hert quakyng for drede
(*The Title and Pedigree of Henry VI,* line 59)
/   x   / x   / x   / x   / (x)
Suffre hem boylle and taake of hem noon heede
(*A Mumming at Hertford,* line 103)

Stanzas go with rhyming foreign meters rather than with alliterative meter. Stanzas exist in many forms, various in the number of lines in each stanza, in the length of the lines, and in rhyming pattern. A basic problem in arranging ME stanzaic verse for the printer arises when the lines have a marked break at mid-line but rhyme only at the end, as in the *ballad stanza:*

Iudas, go þou on þe roc
heie upon þe ston,
Lei þin heued i my barm,
slep þou þe anon.

In many manuscripts of the 14th century and later the arrangement of lines on the page and bracketing of rhymes indicate rhyme schemes with great clarity. *Tail rhyme*—a stanza form in which selected lines are "tailed," or shorter than the rest—is common in ME, especially in verse romances. The rhyme scheme within a single poem may vary considerably, as does the number of lines, and there is flexibility within the line. Chaucer parodies tail-rhyme romances, including their metrics, in *Sir Thopas.*

Chaucer uses a variety of stanza forms, including a six-line stanza (rhyming ababcb, with five stresses to the line) at the end of the *Clerk's Tale,* an eight-line stanza (rhyming ababbcbc, with five stresses to the line) in the *Monk's Tale* and in "An ABC," and a nine-line stanza (with five stresses to the line) in much of the second half of *Anelida and Arcite.* "A Complaint to His Lady" has several metrical schemes, including a ten-line stanza (with five stresses to the line) in part IV; in parts II and III he uses Dante's *terza rima* (with five stresses to the line). In the first part of "A Complaint to His Lady," in the first half of *Anelida and Arcite,* and in *The Parliament of Fowls, Troilus and Criseyde,* the *Man of Law's Tale,* most of the *Clerk's Tale,* the *Prioress's Tale,* the *Second Nun's Tale,* and some of the minor poems Chaucer wrote in *rime royal,* the seven-line stanza (rhyming ababbcc, with five stresses to the line). No English poet seems to have used that stanza form before Chaucer; in Chaucer's use and throughout the late ME period after him it became one of the most important stanza forms among English and Scottish Chaucerians, including King James I of Scotland in *The Kingis Quair,* and it has been suggested that the king's use of the form may have given rise to its name.

Many other stanza forms were in use by English and Scottish Chaucerians; William Dunbar's practice exemplifies the range (usually with five stresses to the line, but sometimes with only four): a seven-line stanza rhyming aabbcbc; a stanza of nine lines, rhyming in various patterns, for example, aabaabbab; the *Monk's Tale* stanza of eight lines rhyming ababbcbc (occasionally ababbaba); a different eight-line stanza rhyming ababbcca; a five-line stanza rhyming aabba; a twelve-line stanza rhyming aabccbddbeeb like a tail rhyme stanza; and even a stanza of 24 lines rhyming aaabcccbddddbeeebfffbgggb. Among his many stanza forms, Dunbar uses refrains or similar repetitions of the end of stanzas, in a four-line stanza rhyming aabb; and an eight-line stanza rhyming ababbcbc like the *Monk's Tale.* Others repeat the same rhymes throughout. He uses also a *sestet* consisting of two triads rhyming aaabbb.

Dunbar occasionally uses alliteration ornamentally in stanzaic poems. That combination belongs to a widely diffused tradition of ME and Middle Scottish poetry. From the 13th century onward many ME lyrics in many stanza forms have ornamental alliteration with varying regularity. The lyrics of BL Harley 2253 include some of the most elaborate, among them "Blow Northern Wind," a carol, that is, a lyric with a *refrain* or *burden* following each stanza. *Pearl,* in BL Cotton Nero A.x, is written in stanzas of twelve four-stress lines rhyming abababababbcbc with concatenating repetitions.

In the *Pearl* manuscript *Sir Gawain and the Green Knight* combines in the body of the stanza a form of the native alliterative meter without rhyme, ending in a *bob line,* that is, a short line that introduces and rhymes with the antepenultimate (third-to-last) and the final line of the *wheel,* that is, four three-stress lines rhyming abab. *Bob and wheel* are nowhere else appended to nonrhyming alliterative verse. There are about 40 English and Scottish poems with bobs. The Towneley Plays have no fewer than sixteen varieties of stanzas, and the York Plays seven varieties, some of them with bobs. Chaucer uses bobs in five of the stanzas of *Sir Thopas.*

The meter of John Skelton's poetry in short lines (usually of two or three stresses), *Skeltonics,* is idiosyncratic. Couplets or triads or longer runs rhyming on the same sound follow each other in cascading succession, seemingly without order.

ME stanza forms are very varied, yet fourteen-line stanzas are exceptionally rare. The *sonnet* is not known as a metrical form before Sir Thomas Wyatt.

E.G. Stanley

Bibliography

Many scholarly editions of OE and ME poems and poets provide a section on the versification of the texts edited; for more general studies see Bliss, A.J. *The Metre of Beowulf.* Rev. ed. Oxford: Blackwell, 1967; Borroff, Marie. *Sir Gawain and the Green Knight: A Stylistic and Metrical Study.* New Haven: Yale University Press, 1962; Donaldson, E.T. "Chaucer's Final *-e.*" *PMLA* 43 (1948): 1101–24; Fulk, R.D. *A History of Old English Meter.* Philadelphia: University of Pennsylvania Press, 1992; Jefferson, J.A. "The Hoccleve Holograph and Hoccleve's Metrical Practice." In *Manuscripts and Texts: Editorial Problems in Later Middle English Literature,* ed. Derek Pearsall. Cambridge: Brewer, 1987, pp. 95–109; Kendall, Calvin B. *The Metrical Grammar of Beowulf.* Cambridge: Cambridge University Press, 1991; Le Page, R.B. "Alliterative Patterns As a Test of Style in Old English Poetry." *JEGP* 58 (1959): 434–41; Lewis, C.S. "The Alliterative Metre." In *Rehabilitations.* Oxford: Oxford University Press, 1939, pp. 119–32. Repr. in *Essential Articles for the Study of Old English Poetry,* ed. Jess B. Bessinger and Stanley J. Kahrl. Hamden: Archon, 1968, pp. 305–16; Mustanoja, Tauno. "Chaucer's Prosody." *Companion to Chaucer Studies,* ed. Beryl Rowland. Toronto: Oxford University Press, 1968, pp. 58–84; Norton-Smith, John. "On the Origins of Skeltonics." *Essays in Criticism* 23 (1973): 57–62; Oakden, J.P. *Alliterative Poetry in Middle English.* 2 vols. Manchester: Manchester University Press, 1930–35. Repr. 2 vols. in 1. Hamden: Archon, 1968; Orchard, Andy [P. M.]. "Artful Alliteration in Anglo-Saxon Song and Story." *Anglia* 113 (1995): 429–63; Pope, John C. *The Rhythm of Beowulf.* Rev. ed. New Haven: Yale University Press, 1966; Pyle, F. "The Origins of the Skeltonic." *N&Q* 171 (1936): 362–64; Pyle, F. "The Barbarous Metre of Barclay." *Modern Language Review* 32 (1937): 353–73; Pyle, F. "The Pedigree of Lydgate's Heroic Line." *Hermathena* 50 (1937): 26–59; Russom, Geoffrey. *Old English Meter and Linguistic Theory.* Cambridge: Cambridge University Press, 1987; Samuels, M.L. "Chaucerian Final *-e.*" *N&Q* n.s. 19 (1972): 445–48; Schipper, Jakob. *A History of English Versification.* Oxford: Clarendon, 1910; Sievers, Eduard. *Altgermanische Metrik.* Halle: Niemeyer, 1893; Spina, E. "Skeltonic Meter in *Elynour Rummyng.*" *SP* 64 (1967):

665–84; Stanley, E.G. "The Use of Bob-Lines in *Sir Thopas.*" *NM* 73 (1972): 417–26; Stanley, E.G. "Rhymes in English Medieval Verse: From Old English to Middle English." In *Medieval English Studies Presented to George Kane,* ed. Edward Donald Kennedy et al. Cambridge: Brewer, 1988, pp. 19–54; Stanley, E.G. "Chaucer's Metre after Chaucer." *N&Q* n.s. 36 (1989): 11–23, 151–62; ten Brink, Bernhard. *The Language and Metre of Chaucer.* 2d ed. Rev. Friedrich Kluge,

trans. M. Bentinck Smith. London: Macmillan, 1901; Tolkien, J.R.R. "On Metre." In *Beowulf and the Finnesburg Fragment: A Translation into Modern English Prose,* trans. J.R. Clark Hall, rev. C.L. Wrenn. London: Allen & Unwin, 1950, pp. xxviii–xliii.

See also Alliterative Revival; *Beowulf;* Chaucer; Dunbar; Formula; Language; Lydgate; Orality; Orm; *Pearl*-Poet; Scottish Literature, Early; Skelton

Fig. 141. Vespasian Psalter (BL Cotton Vespasian A.i), fol. 30v. David with musicians and dancers. Reproduced by permission of the British Library, London.

Vespasian Psalter

BL Vespasian A.i is a luxurious copy of the book of Psalms, made in southern England, most probably at Canterbury, during the second quarter of the 8th century. Usually considered the earliest of the "Tiberius" or "Canterbury" group of manuscripts from southern England, the Vespasian Psalter is important because of its decoration, script, and mid-9th-century gloss.

One full-page illustration survives, probably created as a frontispiece but now placed opposite the beginning of Psalm 26 (fig. 141). It depicts David enthroned as author of the Psalms, composing on his harp. He is aided by the accompaniment of musicians and clapping dancers and by the busy hands of scribes, who record his lyrics on tablet and scroll. The opulent, delicately painted picture combines Byzantine, Ravennate, East Mediterranean, Hiberno-Saxon, and perhaps Frankish elements, an expression of the romanizing Christian culture of Southumbria. The manuscript probably included at least two other full-page images: a carpet page and an incipit of Psalm 1, historiated with an image of Samuel.

The Vespasian Psalter may present the earliest surviving examples of historiated initials, letters with scenes placed within them. Historiated initials begin Psalm 26, showing David and Jonathan, and Psalm 52, David with a lion and a lamb. The historiated letters mark two of the eight liturgical divisions of the Psalter. The initials of the other divisions are decorated with animal and human figures independent of interlace, and the letters following are sometimes empaneled, both features of the Southumbrian "Tiberius" group. Historiated initials may be an insular invention, arising from a concern for integration of script, decoration, and illustration.

Other important features include the self-conscious, romanizing uncial script, especially appropriate to Canterbury, and the OE gloss, the oldest known English translation of any part of the Bible.

Carol A. Farr

Bibliography

Alexander, J.J.G. *Insular Manuscripts 6th–9th Century.* A Survey of Manuscripts Illuminated in the British Isles 1, ed. J.J.G. Alexander. London: Harvey Miller, 1978; Budny, Mildred. "The Visual Arts and Crafts (Early Medieval Britain)." In *The Cambridge Guide to the Arts in Britain.* Vol. 1: *Prehistoric, Roman, and Early Medieval,* ed. Boris Ford. Cambridge: Cambridge University Press, 1988, pp. 122–77; Sweet, Henry, ed. *The Oldest English Texts.* EETS o.s. 83. London: Trübner, 1885; Webster, Leslie, and Janet Backhouse, eds. *The Making of England: Anglo-Saxon Art and Culture A.D. 600–900.* London: British Museum, 1991; Wright, David. *The Vespasian Psalter.* EEMF 14. Copenhagen: Rosenkilde & Bagger, 1967.

See also Bible in OE Literature; Glosses; Manuscript Illumination, Anglo-Saxon; Psalters, Anglo-Saxon; Stockholm Gospels

Vikings in Britain

The Scandinavian impact on Britain did not begin with the first Viking raids in the 8th century, nor did it end with the death of the last Danish king of England in 1042. Invaders and settlers had come from Denmark and Norway in the 5th and 6th centuries, and the threat of Danish invasion was last felt as late as 1085.

Nevertheless, there were ten generations during which the history of Britain was particularly determined by Vikings. Norse (Norwegian) raids on England began not long before 800. Their tempo and seriousness increased with Danish involvement from about 835. The most critical phase began in 865, with the arrival of the Danish "Great Army." By 886, when Alfred of Wessex made peace with the Danish Guthrum, the political geography of England had been transformed. Of the four major kingdoms only Wessex had survived: East Anglia and most of Northumbria were under Danish rule, and Mercia had been divided between Alfred and Guthrum.

Between 911 and 919 Alfred's son Edward conquered all the lands the Danes held south of the Humber. These conquests were permanent (though temporarily lost, 940–44). The position north of the Humber was less stable, complicated by invasion and settlement by Norse from Ireland. An intermittent series of Viking rulers, often strongly connected with the Scandinavian colony of Dublin, ruled from York until 954, when Northumbria came permanently under English rule. A period of relative peace followed, but from 991 Viking raids on England began again. The Danish king Swein became involved. In 1016 his son Cnut became king of England, which thus became part of an Anglo-Scandinavian empire.

The most lasting effect of the Viking invasion was reactive; the ultimate union of England under the West Saxon dynasty was a consequence of the unique effectiveness of West Saxon resistance to the Danes. Hardly less important was the Scandinavian impact on the areas that they settled and, for a time, ruled. The distinctiveness that they brought about in the large part of northern and eastern England was recognized in the 11th and 12th centuries by the application to this area of the term "Danelaw."

The effect of Scandinavian settlement and influence in the Danelaw is controversial. Two points are agreed upon. First, its extent and nature must have varied from one area to another. Second, the influence of the Scandinavians upon the English language was strong. Some of the most basic words in modern English are of Norse origin—for example, "husband," "knife," and "their."

A maximum view of Scandinavian settlement in the Danelaw would stress the likelihood of extensive, though not precisely quantifiable, peasant settlement in wide areas, especially in Yorkshire and Lincolnshire. The evidence for this would be seen largely as follows. Within the areas concerned many places have names of Scandinavian origin (e.g., those ending in -*by*); and perhaps even more significantly names of Scandinavian origin for fields and minor features are common. A wide variety of Scandinavian personal names was in use even into the 12th century. In much of the Danelaw evidence from the 11th century and later shows a distinct social structure with many more freemen than elsewhere in England. The legal customs of the Danelaw are marked by distinct Scandinavian influence.

These views, argued forcefully by Frank Stenton, have been controverted. It is suggested that place-names may be indicative of lordship rather than of extensive settlement. Even field names may reflect the linguistic rather than the demographic circumstances. Social differences may be the product of Scandinavian rule rather than of settlement, while the legal integration of the Danelaw with the rest of England is much more conspicuous than are the admitted differences in legal custom.

Some of the elements in dispute have been settled. Attempts to argue that the Scandinavian invaders should be numbered in hundreds rather than in thousands have not been accepted. Nevertheless, the question of the scale of Scandinavian settlement remains unsettled. What is certain is that its influence was great. This is to be seen not only in important elements in the modern English language and in the abundant place-names but also, more tangibly, in the numerous pieces of stone sculpture from the north, showing strong Scandinavian influence. Occasional pagan elements in this body of sculpture are among our limited evidence for the religious history of the Danelaw; the conversion of the Scandinavians there, completed before the Norman Conquest, is a lost story.

One of the most important aspects of Scandinavian influence is urban. For Vikings trading went with raiding. There were major trading places in Scandinavia when the invasions began. The invaders founded others, most strikingly in Ireland, where they founded all the major towns: Dublin, Waterford, Wexford, Cork. In England York was both a Viking capital and a major trading place. Further south the Scandinavians were regarded as the "men of the Five Boroughs" (Lincoln, Stamford, Derby, Nottingham, and Leicester). Their urban influence extended beyond their area of control and was strong in London. The rise of Chester in the 10th century and of Bristol in the 11th has much to do with their relationship to Viking Dublin.

The understanding of Viking settlement in Britain should be set into a wider context. For example, there is a likely connection between Edward the Elder's successful campaign in the second decade of the 10th century and the simultaneous foundation of the Scandinavian colony in Normandy, as Viking enterprises and resources were directed elsewhere.

The Scandinavian influence on Wales and Scotland had effects that contrasted with those in England. In Wales the Vikings made coastal attacks and settlements. For a time it looked as if the Viking threat might drive Welsh rulers into a closer relationship with those of England than ever before. But when the dangers passed, it is remarkable, not how much, but how little Wales had been affected. In Scotland the northern and western lands and the far north of the mainland became largely absorbed into the Scandinavian world; a relationship that would endure for the Orkneys and Shetlands until they passed from Danish to Scottish control in 1468. Otherwise the most important effect of Scandinavian activity

on Scotland was indirect; by weakening the power of English rulers in northern Britain it helped to increase that of the kings of the Scots.

James Campbell

Bibliography

Crawford, Barbara, ed. *Scandinavian Settlement in Northern Britain: Thirteen Studies of Place-Names in Their Historical Context.* London: Leicester University Press, 1995; Fellows-Jensen, Gillian. "The Vikings in England: A Review." *ASE* 4 (1975): 181–206; Hines, John. *The Scandinavian Character of Anglian England in the Pre-Viking Period.* BAR Brit. Ser. 124. Oxford: BAR, 1984; Jones, Gwyn. *A History of the Vikings.* Rev. ed. Oxford: Oxford University Press, 1984; Lawson, M.K. *Cnut: The Danes in England in the Early Eleventh Century.* London: Longman, 1993; Loyn, H.R. *The Vikings in Britain.* London: Batsford, 1977; Lund, Niels. "The Settlers: Where Do We Get Them From, and Do We Need Them?" In *Proceedings of the Eighth Viking Congress,* ed. H. Bekker-Nielsen. *Medieval Scandinavia,* Supplement 2 (1981): 147–71; Marsden, John. *The Fury of the Northmen: Saints, Shrines, and Sea-Raiders in the Viking Age.* New York: St. Martin, 1995; Smyth, Alfred P. *Scandinavian Kings in the British Isles, 850–880.* Oxford: Oxford University Press, 1977.

See also Æthelflæd; Alfred; Cnut; Language; Literary Influences: Scandinavian; Names; Normandy; Swein

Virtues and Vices, Books of

Treatises of religious instruction popular in the Middle Ages, compiled primarily by listing basic elements of Christian belief and morality, often with considerable elaboration. Such works generally cover, among other things, the fourteen articles of faith, the Ten Commandments, the two evangelical precepts of charity, the seven deadly sins, the seven virtues, and the seven sacraments; they are frequently enlivened by a variety of exempla. English works of this type include *Handlyng Synne, Of Shrift and Penance,* and Peter Idley's *Instructions to His Son,* all deriving from the Anglo-Norman *Manuel des péchés;* and the *Ayenbite of Inwit* and *the Book of Vices and Virtues,* which translate Friar Laurent's *Somme le roi,* a handbook originally intended for Philip III of France. The *Speculum Vitae, Jacob's Well,* and *Mirror of the World* also depend, at least partly, on the *Somme,* while the *Lay Folk's Catechism, Manuale Credencium, Mirror of Holy Church,* and *Poor Caitiff* treatises spring from still other sources. Treatises on virtues and vices also occur as parts of other instructional, devotional, or even secular volumes.

The popularity of these treatises in the late Middle Ages can be explained in part by the desire of the bishops after the Fourth Lateran Council (1215) to educate both priests and laypeople. The council had determined that annual confession would henceforth be mandatory, and church officials feared that their flocks might lack the knowledge necessary to take full spiritual advantage of their confessions.

To assist with the enormous task of providing this knowledge 13th-century religious writers in England (and other countries) produced a substantial amount of educational literature pertaining to faith and morals. The first step was to enlighten the clergy, so that they might then illuminate their parishioners concerning basic points of Christian doctrine and behavior. Throughout the century diocesan and provincial statutes were enacted that required parish clergy to know—and teach their flocks—the commandments, the deadly sins, the sacraments, the Creed and other essential prayers, and so on. These mandates would become crucial for the sermon literature of the period and would contribute in an important way to the literature on virtues and vices.

Among the most influential sets of statutes were those of Richard Poore, bishop of Salisbury, issued shortly after Lateran IV (between 1217 and 1219); of Robert Grosseteste, bishop of Lincoln, issued ca. 1239; and of John Pecham, archbishop of Canterbury (1281), and Peter Quinel, bishop of Exeter (1287). Many statutes specify that such teaching take place "frequently" and "in the mother tongue" or "in the native language." By the time of Pecham's Lambeth Statues every pastor was being required, either by himself or with another's help, to teach his parishioners on mass days four times a year, in their own language, about "the fourteen articles of faith, the Ten Commandments, the two evangelical precepts of love, the seven works of mercy, the seven capital sins and their offspring, the seven principal virtues, and the seven sacraments," a set of lists that the statute goes on to define in some detail. As all of these topics could hardly be contained within a single sermon, it seems likely that more than four Sundays of the year would have had to be devoted to this instruction. This particular statute, also called the *Ignorantia sacerdotum (Ignorance of Priests)* from its opening words, was enormously influential. For the rest of the Middle Ages both clerical manuals and religious tracts for the English laity would be based on the archbishop's decree.

Despite their pedagogical utility many books of virtues and vices do not make for stimulating reading. No doubt influenced by the type of ethical listing often found in the Bible (see especially Col. 3:5–14 and Gal. 5:19–23 for enumerations of sins and contrasting virtues), some merely present *seriatim* the seven deadly sins—pride, envy, wrath, sloth, avarice, lechery, and gluttony, and their numerous progeny—or the four cardinal and three theological virtues—prudence, justice, temperance, fortitude, faith, hope, and charity—with little authorial comment. But anyone who has read Robert Manning's *Handlyng Synne,* one of the liveliest works of this genre, knows the quality of entertainment such treatises could provide. With the use of exempla (popularized by the preaching of the friars after the Fourth Lateran Council) Manning portrays lecherous priests, hypocritical monks, wicked lawyers, and false accounters—all destined straight for hell. And such books are important for more than their didactic content or their engaging storylines. Tales of ostentatiously dressed aristocracy or fastidious women ultimately "smyten with canker," for example, afford telling insights into the social history of the English Middle Ages.

Books of virtues and vices ultimately transcended their original audiences, leaving their mark on the major English poets of the day. John Gower's *Confessio Amantis,* for example, employs the device of a lover's confession to present tales of the sins and their corresponding virtues as they might be experienced in a lover's life. William Langland's *Piers Plowman* contains a confession scene in which each of the seven deadly sins is admonished to become its opposite trait—pride is thus to become humility; gluttony, abstinence; sloth, a pilgrim headed for Rome. And Chaucer's *Parson's Tale* includes a lengthy section on the sins and their "remedies," to "knytte up wel a greet mateere" of the *Canterbury Tales.* Pecham's decree and similar official mandates ultimately contributed to the art of the Middle Ages, and while those decrees lost none of their proper force as stimuli to religious instruction, their initial pedagogical purposes were expanded by later writers to accommodate poetic talents and address more sophisticated secular readers. After the Middle Ages elaborated catalogues of virtues and vices were often adopted by Renaissance humanists, helping to shape such works as Marlowe's *Doctor Faustus* and Spenser's *Faerie Queene.*

Mary Flowers Braswell

Bibliography

Manual 7:2255–78, 2467–2507; Bloomfield, Morton W. *The Seven Deadly Sins.* East Lansing: Michigan State College Press, 1952; Bloomfield, Morton W., et al., eds. *Incipits of Latin Works on the Virtues and Vices, 1100–1500 A.D.* Cambridge: Medieval Academy of America, 1979; Braekman, W.L. "The Seven Virtues As Opposed to the Seven Vices: A Fourteenth-Century Didactic Poem." *NM* 74 (1973): 247–68; Braswell, Mary Flowers. *The Medieval Sinner: Characterization and Confession in the Literature of the English Middle Ages.* London: Associated University Presses, 1983; Cheney, Christopher. *Medieval Texts and Studies.* Oxford: Clarendon, 1973, pp. 138–202 [three studies of later medieval English canon law]; Gibbs, Marion, and Jane Lang. *Bishops and Reform: 1215–1272.* London: Oxford University Press, 1934; Owst, G.R. *Literature and Pulpit in Medieval England.* 2d ed. Oxford: Blackwell, 1961; Pantin, W.A. *The English Church in the Fourteenth Century.* 1955. Repr. Toronto: University of Toronto Press, 1980; Pfander, H.G. "Some Medieval Manuals of Religious Instruction in England and Observations on Chaucer's *Parson's Tale.*" *JEGP* 35 (1936): 243–58; Robertson, D.W., Jr. "The Cultural Tradition of *Handlyng Synne.*" *Speculum* 22 (1947): 162–85.

See also Edmund of Abingdon; Grosseteste; Manning; Michel of Northgate; Moral and Religious Instruction; Penitentials; *Prick of Conscience;* Religious Allegories; Sermons; *Speculum Vitae*

Votive Observance

A term currently used widely by musicologists to signify certain categories of medieval devotion that are not directly related to the main pattern of daily liturgy laid down in the calendar. Some votive observances exist simply as appendages following items of the regular liturgy. Many take the form of additional antiphons or even complete hours modeled on the regular office. Others function as complete replacements for an office or mass and have a corresponding structure. Most votive observances are concerned with special intentions or are addressed to saints of particular local or devotional significance; the Blessed Virgin Mary was the subject of the greater proportion of the votive repertoire in England from the 12th century to the early 16th century. With the exception of the term *missa votiva* direct equivalents for the word "votive" are uncommon in medieval sources; the prevalence of the term in modern scholarship follows Frank Ll. Harrison's use of the word in *Music in Medieval Britain* (1958).

The adoption of additional devotions of a votive nature is first recorded in the 8th century, when the Carolingian monastic reformer Benedict of Aniane (ca. 750–821) promulgated a general expansion of liturgical observance. Many communities began to recite specially chosen groups of psalms (the seven penitential and fifteen gradual psalms are examples) before and after the daily offices, while contemporary sacramentaries testify to the multiplication of private masses for use in times of trouble and for other special intentions. Alcuin (ca. 730/35–804), an Englishman active in the Carolingian reforms, compiled a cycle of seven votive masses for weekly use, which achieved instant and enduring popularity. Each mass is offered for a particular intention, beginning with the Trinity on Sunday and concluding with the Virgin Mary on Saturday. Celebration of the Saturday *missa principalis* in honor of the Virgin was ubiquitous in England by the 12th century. There is also evidence that a daily Lady Mass (often celebrated privately) became a standard liturgical feature in many English establishments from the same period: Giraldus Cambrensis (Gerald of Wales) states that the Benedictine house of Rochester adopted a daily *Missa de Domina* during the reign of King Stephen (1135–54). From the early 13th century several English foundations provided an endowment for a small number of trained singers to attend the daily mass and hours in honor of the Virgin, usually in a separate Lady Chapel. Both archival evidence and surviving musical sources establish that such masses were often celebrated with vocal polyphony or the organ.

A parallel votive office, recited before or after the hours of the regular *cursus,* was adopted increasingly as a daily communal observance from the 12th century. The roots of this custom are of considerable antiquity, for a votive Office of the Dead (consisting only of Vigils, Lauds, and Vespers) is mentioned as a regular feature of some monastic liturgies in the early 9th century, while several 10th-century sources testify to the daily recitation of Vespers and Lauds of All Saints. But more prominent than either of these parallel observances was the Little Office of the Virgin, which began as a private devotion in the 11th century and ultimately achieved extensive popularity as the nucleus of the most widely owned of all medieval books, the book of hours. The exact origins of the Little Office are obscure, but examples appear as early as the

11th century, and there are references in 13th-century sources from the Benedictine establishments of Bury St. Edmunds, Worcester, Norwich, and Christ Church, Canterbury, and in the Sarum Customary (ca. 1270).

The commemorative office, unlike the daily votive office, was usually a weekly observance replacing the calendar liturgy. The earliest English examples appear in the Worcester Portiforium (ca. 1065), which contains an Office of the Holy Cross (Friday) and an Office of the Virgin (Saturday). Virtually all establishments seem to have adopted the Saturday commemorative office of the Virgin by the 13th century, and frequently at least one further day was set aside for another office, usually with particular local associations: Worcester celebrated a commemorative office of St. Oswald and St. Wulfstan (Thursday), and Christ Church, Canterbury, an office of St. Thomas of Canterbury. Like the daily Little Office of the Virgin most commemorative offices contained little genuinely new material but were compiled by rearranging existing texts for related feasts.

The form of votive observance of greatest interest and familiarity to the musicologist is perhaps the votive antiphon. This was normally sung after Compline as a short, self-contained ceremony, consisting of antiphon, versicle with response, and collect. It was almost invariably addressed to the Virgin Mary until the 16th century, when the decline in adoration of the saints (and in particular the Virgin) led to a shift of emphasis to a Jesus or Trinity antiphon. In some institutions the singers moved out of choir for its observance, gathering in front of an appropriate statue or altar: the votive antiphon was not always sung in church. Text and melody were usually elaborate; frequently the antiphon doubled as a processional antiphon or Magnificat antiphon for one of the major Marian feasts, and there are also instances of antiphons being borrowed from commemorative offices. The Roman Church standardized the use of four seasonal votive antiphons in 1350—*Alma redemptoris, Salve regina, Regina celi,* and *Ave regina. Salve regina* remained by far the most popular of the Marian antiphons and was set polyphonically on countless occasions by English and continental composers until well into the 16th century.

Sally E. Roper

Bibliography

Bishop, Edmund. *Liturgica Historica: Papers on the Liturgy and Religious Life of the Western Church.* Oxford: Clarendon, 1918; Harrison, Frank Ll. *Music in Medieval Britain.* 1958. 2d ed. London: Routledge & Kegan Paul, 1963; Hughes, Andrew. *Medieval Manuscripts for Mass and Office: A Guide to Their Organization and Terminology.* Toronto: University of Toronto Press, 1982; Leclercq, Jean. "Formes anciennes de l'office Marial." *Ephemerides Liturgicae* 74 (1960): 89–102; Roper, Sally E. *Medieval English Benedictine Liturgy: Studies in the Formation, Structure, and Content of the Monastic Votive Office c. 950–1540.* New York: Garland, 1993; Symons, Thomas. "Monastic Observance in the Tenth Century: The Offices of All Saints and of the Dead." *DownR* 50 (1932): 449–64 and 51 (1932): 137–52; Tolhurst, J.B.L. *Introduction to the English Monastic Breviaries (The Monastic Breviary of Hyde Abbey, Winchester,* 6). Henry Bradshaw Society 80. London: Harrison, 1942.

See also Antiphon; Feasts, New Liturgical; Lady Mass; Liturgy; Liturgy and Church Music, History of; Offices, New Liturgical; Processions; Salve Service

W

W1

The manuscript Wolfenbüttel, Herzog-August-Bibliothek 628 (hereafter W1), is the most significant single musical document that testifies to the cultivation of sacred polyphonic music in the British Isles between the Winchester tropers and the Old Hall Manuscript. It is one of the principal sources for the music of the so-called Notre Dame School, and it contains a version of the *Magnus liber organi* written by the Parisian composer of the late 12th century Leoninus. Its central position in the scholarship on late-12th- and early-13th-century sacred music is clear from the fact that it was selected as the source for the first edition of the *Magnus liber organi* (Waite, 1954).

The interrelated subjects of the manuscript's date and provenance have been matters of debate. Originally it was thought to have been copied in France and to be the earliest of the surviving copies of the *Magnus liber organi* (the other two copies are in Florence and in Wolfenbüttel also). It was Handschin (1933) who identified the manuscript's home as the Augustinian priory of St. Andrews, Scotland, and this has usually been accepted in subsequent inquiry. Estimations of W1's age range from the 1230s to the early 14th century; the most recent survey suggests the earliest of these dates, a fact that reinstates W1 as the earliest of the three "Notre Dame" manuscripts (the Florence manuscript has been dated to the period 1245–55). The curiosity of essentially Parisian music appearing in a manuscript copied in St. Andrews has been explained (Everist, 1990) by reference to the *familia,* or household, of the francophile bishop of St. Andrews Guillaume Mauvoisin (1202–38).

The music in W1 is divided, mostly according to genre, into eleven fascicles as follows: I: four-part organa; II: three-part organa and conducti; III: two-part organa for the office; IV: two-part organa for the mass; V: two-part clausulae; VI: two-part clausulae; VII: three-part organa; VIII-IX miscellaneous three- and two-part compositions; X: monophonic pieces; XI: two-part mass music. This, however, is to ignore the layered makeup of the volume and its contents. The nucleus of the manuscript consists of fascicles I–V and VIII–X, which represent two groups of works organized in terms of a decreasing number of voice parts (I–V: four-part, three-part, and three fascicles of two-part music; VIII–X: three-part, two-part, and monophonic works). To this nucleus were added three further layers: additions at the ends of gatherings in fascicles I–V and VIII–X as layer 2, fascicles VI and VII as layer 3, and the eleventh fascicle as layer 4. The layer 2 additions comprise tropes of the Ordinary of the mass in fascicles III and VIII and a group of three-part organa in fascicle III. This last group contains two responsories for the Feast of St. Andrew that have been at the center of discussions of the manuscript's provenance. Fascicles VI and VII can be seen as supplements to fascicles V (clausulae) and II and VIII (three-part organa), respectively. Fascicle XI, the final addition to the manuscript, is codicologically and repertorially discrete; there is a scribal colophon at the end of fascicle X.

The principal contents of W1 are French; the manuscript preserves a copy of the *Magnus liber organi* that exhibits notational and musical idiosyncrasies explained by its local compilation. Despite the fact that it may now be the earliest of the three sources of the *Magnus liber organi,* much of its interest lies in the music that falls outside the orbit of the Notre Dame School. This music falls into three categories: locally composed organa in two parts, conducti, and Ordinary tropes both in the eleventh fascicle and added to the third and eighth fascicles.

The organa appended to fascicle III include the two St. Andrew responsories: *Vir iste* and *Vir perfecte.* These do not form part of the main Notre Dame repertoire as found in other sources and must have been composed specifically for St. Andrews. Roesner believes all the layer 2 additions including these responsories to have been copied by the main text scribe but at a later time. Musically they bear comparison with other two-part organa preserved in fascicles III and IV and were written in imitation of French models.

Falck (1981) invited the consideration of a group of specifically English conducti in fascicle IX. Although the manuscript is key in discussions of the little-explored subject of the conductus in England, many of Falck's observations rest on dubious identifications of English pieces. The balance between French and insular material in the conductus collections in the manuscript is still uncertain.

The greatest importance of W1 to the history of music in the British Isles lies in the music of fascicle XI. Notre Dame or Parisian musical styles encompassed only the Gradual and Alleluia for the mass and responsories for the office, as well as settings of the Benedicamus Domino; by contrast the music in fascicle XI of W1 contains a wide variety of liturgical genres. There are only Alleluia settings in common between the two repertoires, and W1 also includes tropes to the Ordinary of the mass, a Tract, sequences, and Offertories troped and untroped. The stylistic division into organum, discantus, and copula that is the basis of the musical style of the *Magnus liber organi* is completely lacking in fascicle XI, where the music is organized in a neume-against-neume style, and sometimes note-against-note.

Mark Everist

Bibliography

PRIMARY

Baxter, James H., ed. *An Old St. Andrews Music Book (Cod. Helmst. 628) Published in Facsimile with an Introduction.* St. Andrews University Publications 30. Oxford: Oxford University Press, 1931; Gillingham, Bryan, ed. *The Polyphonic Sequences in Codex Wolfenbüttel 677.* Musicological Studies 35. Ottawa: Institute of Mediaeval Music, 1982; Lütolf, Max. *Die mehrstimmigen Ordinarium Missae-Sätze vom ausgehenden 11. bis zur Wende des 13. zum 14. Jahrhundert.* 2 vols. Bern: Haupt, 1970; Waite, William G. *The Rhythm of Twelfth-Century Polyphony: Its Theory and Practice.* New Haven: Yale University Press, 1954 [ed. of W1 version of *Magnus liber*].

SECONDARY

Brown, Julian, Sonia Patterson, and David Hiley. "Further Observations on W1." *Journal of the Plainsong and Mediaeval Music Society* 4 (1981): 53–80; Everist, Mark. "From Paris to St. Andrews: The Origins of W1." *Journal of the American Musicological Society* 43 (1990): 1–42; Falck, Robert. *The Notre Dame Conductus: A Study of the Repertory.* Musicological Studies 33. Henryville: Institute of Mediaeval Music, 1981; Handschin, Jacques. "A Monument of English Mediaeval Polyphony: The Manuscript Wolfenbüttel 677 (Helmst. 628)." *Musical Times* 73 (1932): 510–13 and 74 (1933): 697–704; Roesner, Edward H. "The Origins of W1." *Journal of the American Musicological Society* 29 (1976): 337–80; Roesner, Edward H. "The Problem of Chronology in the Transmission of Organum Duplum." In *Music in Medieval and Early Modern Europe: Patronage, Sources, and Texts,* ed. Iain Fenlon. Cambridge: Cambridge University Press, 1981, pp. 365–99.

See also Conductus; Lady Mass; Mass, Polyphonic Music for; Old Hall Manuscript; Trope; Winchester Tropers

Wace (after 1100–ca. 1175)

Norman verse chronicler who served Henry II; appointed canon of Bayeux by Henry by 1169. Wace's best-known work, the *Roman de Brut* (almost 15,000 octosyllabic lines in couplets), paraphrases and in places expands on Geoffrey of Monmouth's *Historia regum Britanniae (History of the Kings of Britain).* Written in Norman French and presented to Eleanor of Aquitaine in 1155, the *Brut* uses direct discourse, lively narration, and descriptive scenes and characters to tell the story of the British kings of England, and particularly of Arthur. Wace's work survives in over twenty manuscripts and inspired much later Arthurian literature, especially that of Laȝamon and Chrétien de Troyes.

Wace also wrote the unfinished *Roman de Rou* (the story of Rollo, ancestor of William the Conqueror) and several saints' lives.

Eileen Jankowski

Bibliography

PRIMARY.

Arnold, Ivor, ed. *Le Roman de Brut.* 2 vols. Paris: Société des Anciens Textes Français, 1938–40; Holden, A.J., ed. *Le Roman de Rou.* 3 vols. Paris: Picard, 1970–73; Mason, Eugene, trans. *Arthurian Chronicles: Wace and Layamon.* London: Dent, 1912. Repr. Toronto: University of Toronto Press, 1996.

SECONDARY

New *CBEL* 1:393–96; *Manual* 1:42, 232–33.

See also Anglo-Norman Literature; Chronicles; Eleanor of Aquitaine; Geoffrey of Monmouth; Henry II; Laȝamon; Matter of Britain

Wærferth of Worcester (d. 915)

Bishop of Worcester (872–915) and favored friend and scholar of King Alfred the Great, who invited Wærferth to court in the late 880s. Little documentation survives regarding Wærferth's personal life or activities as bishop of Worcester, though he issued a lease and witnessed several charters associated with the Worcester estates and is identified specifically in two of the king's most important documents; Alfred names Wærferth in his will and addresses the preface of his translation of Gregory's *Pastoral Care* to him.

In his *Life of King Alfred* Asser refers to Wærferth as the translator of Gregory the Great's *Dialogues,* saying that he made the translation at Alfred's request. Given the precise dating of Asser's work to 893, the translation of the *Dialogues* must have already been finished. Scholars suggest a completion date from the early 870s to the early 890s and conjecture that it was the first in a series of OE translations from Latin specifically done for Alfred, though not necessarily commenced after the invitation to Alfred's court. The translation survives completely in two 11th-century manuscripts: Cambridge, Corpus Christi College 322, and BL Cotton Otho C.i.

Wærferth's style is sophisticated even as it closely follows the Latin original, and his syntax, also found in his charters and leases, shares common components with the OE translation of Bede's *Ecclesiastical History.* While some attempts have been made to establish Wærferth as translator of this text, no conclusive proof exists save a close syntactical association that suggests only a connection to the Mercian scholars associated with Alfred's court. Florence of Worcester records Wærferth's death in 915. A revision of Wærferth's translation survives, probably completed at Worcester between 950 and 1050, though similarities in vocabulary to that of the Winchester group suggest an association with Æthelwold's school.

Virginia Blanton-Whetsell

Bibliography

PRIMARY

Hecht, Hans, ed. *Bischof Wærferths von Worcester Übersetzung der Dialoge Gregors des Grossen.* 2 vols. Bibliothek der angelsächsischen Prosa 5. Leipzig: Wigand, 1900–07. Repr. Darmstadt: Wissenschaftliche Buchgesellschaft, 1965.

SECONDARY

Bately, Janet M. "Old English Prose before and during the Reign of Alfred." *ASE* 17 (1988): 93–138; Yerkes, David. *Syntax and Style in Old English: A Comparison of the Two Versions of Wærferth's Translation of Gregory's Dialogues.* MRTS 5. Binghamton: MRTS, 1982.

See also Alfred; Fathers of the Church (Gregory); Translation

Wainfleet, William (ca. 1393–1486)

Bishop of Winchester. Born into a gentry family at Wainfleet, Lincolnshire, Wainfleet studied at Oxford and became headmaster of William of Wykeham's college at Winchester (1429–42). Henry VI noticed him while inspecting Winchester as a model for his own foundation, Eton College, and made him provost of Eton (1442–47) and bishop (1447–86). He was also chancellor (1456–60), playing a moderating role at a time of civil war, and remained in favor when Henry was overthrown by Edward IV in 1461.

Wainfleet was a notable educational patron himself, using his wealth to found Magdalen College, Oxford (1458), a large, well-endowed institution for 30 undergraduate scholars and 40 graduate fellows. It included a grammar school providing free education for all comers, and the bishop erected a similar school at Wainfleet. Magdalen was important in the evolution of colleges from small graduate societies into larger communities with undergraduates. Besides the 30 scholars Wainfleet allowed outsiders (commoners) to enter at their own expense, and this became a standard feature of colleges later on. Magdalen College School was also notable (ca. 1481–1500) in pioneering the teaching of humanist Latin grammar in England.

Nicholas Orme

Bibliography

Davis, Virginia. *William Waynflete: Bishop and Educationist.* Woodbridge: Boydell, 1993; Emden, Alfred B. *A Biographical Register of the University of Oxford to* A.D. *1500.* Vol. 3. Oxford: Clarendon, 1959, pp. 2001–03; Orme, Nicholas. *English Schools in the Middle Ages.* London: Methuen, 1973.

See also Bishops; Eton; Schools; Universities; William of Wykeham; Winchester College

Waits

"Wait" probably derives from the Old French *gait* or *guet,* a watchman. The word was used as early as the 13th century for the watchmen at the gates of cities and castles. Some English castles, like many French châteaux, had a watch tower from which the approaches to the gate could be surveyed. It is clear that the watchmen used the ox horn, the usual signaling instrument of huntsmen and soldiers, to warn of the approach of visitors to the gate.

Castle waits had a second function, to patrol the building at night, calling the time and monitoring fires. By the late 13th century these household waits, called *vigiles* in the royal household accounts, used a musical instrument as well as the horn, and the royal waits were sometimes rewarded for minstrelsy. It seems logical to suppose that their instrument was the "wait-pipe" (shortened to "wait"), which was probably the treble shawm. The royal waits, known as *vigilatores* from the mid-14th century, were rarely musical in the 15th. It is impossible to tell why they lost their status as supplementary minstrels. From the mid-15th century on the royal household waits—there is no evidence for other households—seem to have been watchmen only: Edward IV's *Black Book of the Exchequer,* ca. 1471–72, describes the wait's duties in detail, but no musical function is mentioned.

The use of "wait-(pipe)" to denote the wait's instrument meant that any player of that instrument might be called a "wait." The majority of waits in the 13th and 14th centuries were household watchmen, although the term "wait" could be applied to huntsmen and others: in what capacity these latter played the instrument it is impossible to say. The most important use of the term however was due to its transference, early in the 15th century, to the newly formed bands of civic minstrels.

The account books of English towns show that as early as the 14th century some towns made considerable use of minstrels for civic occasions. These seem to be local minstrels hired on an ad hoc basis. In the first decade of the 15th century, however, towns began to employ a band of minstrels on a full-time basis, apparently for the provision of loud ceremonial music at civic and mayoral events. These bands were roughly analogous to the loud minstrels of noble households, being given regular wages, liveries, and so on. Their precise functions were different, but only insofar as the mayor's public life differed from that of a noble.

Norwich probably employed town waits first, in 1408, but other towns and cities quickly followed suit. In a few cases the waits formed an occasional marching watch, but their duties were certainly analogous to those of the old household *vigilatores* rather than to the security patrols of the major cities, which were maintained by rosters of citizens. Where the information is available, we find that the town waits formed a shawm-and-trumpet band, the standard combination for loud music. Only in the 16th century did a considerable change take place, with the waits taking up many other kinds of instrument (including soft instruments, such as the lute) or earning money regularly as singers.

Richard Rastall

Bibliography

Rastall, Richard. "Wait." *NGD* 20:154–55; Woodfill, Walter L. *Musicians in English Society from Elizabeth to Charles I.* Princeton Studies in History 9. Princeton: Princeton University Press, 1953.

See also Households, Royal and Baronial; Minstrels; Musical Instruments; Towns

Waldere

The two single-leaf fragments of the OE heroic poem *Waldere*, now in the Royal Library, Copenhagen, are the only evidence for knowledge of the Walter legend in Anglo-Saxon England, although it was known throughout the Germanic world over a long period. Judging from the 10th-century continental Latin verse epic *Waltharius* (which evidently differed from the Anglo-Saxon version in some particulars), it seems that the OE poem, originally at least 1,000 lines long, described how two Germanic hostages, Waldere and Hildegyth, fled from Attila's court in order to preserve their betrothal, taking treasure with them. For the sake of this treasure they were pursued by Guthhere, king of the Burgundians, and his vassal Hagena, who had sworn brotherhood with Waldere when he was also a hostage. It is clear that the OE fragments preserve details of the ensuing confrontation. The order of the fragments is debatable: Hildegyth's address to Waldere is usually printed as "fragment I"; "fragment II" is part of a taunting exchange between the men. The manuscript is from ca. 1000, but the date of the poem's composition is unknown. Although brief, the fragments are rich in their expression of heroic values.

Joyce Hill

Bibliography

ASPR 6:4–6; Bradley, S.A.J., trans. *Anglo-Saxon Poetry.* London: Dent, 1982, pp. 510–12; Hill, Joyce, ed. *Old English Minor Heroic Poems.* 2d ed. Durham: Durham Medieval Texts, 1994, pp. 20–23, 36–38, 44–45; Zettersten, Arne, ed. *Waldere.* Manchester: Manchester University Press, 1979.

See also Literary Influences: Scandinavian

Wall Painting, Romanesque

Relatively few cycles of Romanesque wall paintings remain today; yet we can be certain that many, if not most, Romanesque churches originally received painted decoration. Original images have been lost through the ravages of time, rebuilding, changes in taste, and the wholesale destruction of the Reformation era, though a good number of paintings have managed to survive the centuries, and the corpus is growing with the recovery of Romanesque frescoes from beneath the plaster and paint of later generations.

The picture has been complicated by the discovery that Anglo-Saxon wall paintings were far more common than previously suspected. Anglo-Saxon paintings have been recovered from Winchester, Wearmouth-Jarrow, Colchester, St. Albans, and St. Oswald's, Gloucester, to name but a few of the better-known sites. Many of these works are attributable to the late Anglo-Saxon period and are often similar in style and iconography to Romanesque paintings. This has caused a re-evaluation of the extent to which Romanesque artists were indebted to their Anglo-Saxon predecessors, as well as heated debate over the proper attribution of a number of paintings (e.g., Clayton, Sussex).

In terms of technique most English Romanesque wall paintings are thought to be examples of true fresco, with the pigments applied directly to the fresh plaster. Further analysis has shown that the secco technique (pigments applied to dry plaster) was also used, particularly for the addition of detail. Technical studies currently underway promise to refine our knowledge of the processes and techniques employed by Romanesque mural artists.

The majority of the known Romanesque wall paintings are located in the south of England, with a significant cluster in Sussex. This early-12th-century group, traditionally known as the "Lewes Group," comprises the churches at Clayton, Hardham, Coombes, Plumbton, and Westmeston. In recent years it has come under increasing scrutiny. Originally linked together because of their proximity to Lewes Abbey, one of the primary Cluniac priories in England, the paintings in these churches were thought to reflect Cluniac emphasis on artistic patronage and possibly Cluniac iconography and promotion of the First Crusade. Yet iconographically the programs of the Sussex churches have only general parallels (apocalyptic imagery) with Cluniac houses elsewhere in England and on the Continent; crusader iconography (i.e., warrior saints), if present, is inconsistent at best; and only fragments of paintings survive from Lewes itself, so that there is little to suggest a direct participation of the priory in the decoration of the churches. There is still much debate as to whether these churches do form a group, their paintings possibly the products of a local workshop, or whether their differences outweigh their similarities and whether some of the group might indeed be transitional between the Anglo-Saxon and Romanesque eras and styles.

Most scholars agree that whatever the exact chronology of the churches, and whatever their relation, or lack of relation, to one another, English Romanesque wall paintings do reflect a variety of stylistic and iconographic sources. The influence of Byzantine art is evident in the damp-fold draperies, fully modeled faces, and dark outlines of the Canterbury figures (fig. 37: see CANTERBURY WALL PAINTINGS). Ottonian influence can be seen in the exaggerated poses of figures at Hardham and elsewhere. The red and white outlines used in the Clayton frescoes may reflect the influence of Anglo-Saxon "Winchester School" manuscripts, such as the Benedictional of Æthelwold (BL Add. 49598; fig. 26: see BENEDICTIONAL OF ÆTHELWOLD). We know that English artists traveled, and did so in increasing numbers during the Romanesque era, so that the influence of art from elsewhere in Europe is to be expected.

Perhaps the most interesting, and one of the least studied, aspects of these paintings is their inclusion of unusual iconographic details. At Coombes, for example, Joseph is included in the Annunciation, while at Hardham a dragon replaces the usual serpent in the Temptation, and Eve's postlapsarian labor is milking a cow rather than spinning.

While individual scenes may differ, by far the most popular overall iconographic program was the Last Judgment. Apocalyptic schemes are found at Hardham, Clayton, Coombes, and Westmeston (paintings destroyed in 1862); St. Mary's, Kempley (Gloucestershire); Swyncombe (Oxfordshire); and Canterbury, among other places. Their meaning and function would have been similar to the apocalyptic wall paintings of France (e.g., St. Savin sur Gartemps) or the portals of the pilgrimage churches (e.g., Moissac).

Many of the Romanesque wall paintings can also be linked directly to the liturgy. At St. Mary's, Kempley (1120–40), the episode of the Three Marys at the Sepulcher and other scenes have been linked to the influence of Easter sepulcher rites. The Easter liturgy also provides the key to understanding the wall paintings in the Chapel of the Holy Sepulcher at Winchester. The subjects of these paintings, the Deposition, Entombment, and Three Marys at the Sepulcher, provide visual narrative parallels for the rituals associated with Good Friday: the burial of a symbol of Christ, its return and elevation, and the story of the Three Marys.

English Romanesque wall painting is not confined to England. A gentler, more classicizing version of the Winchester mural style can be seen in the paintings on the choir vault of the chapel of the leper hospital at Le Petit-Quevilly, commissioned by Henry II in the later 12th century. Some of the finest English Romanesque paintings known were produced for the chapter house of the convent at Sigena, founded by Queen Sancha of Aragon in Huesca in the 1180s. The artists, also working in a style associated with Winchester, are thought to have arrived in Spain via Sicily, their travels again associated with the interests of Henry II. The Sigena paintings included Old and New Testament scenes from the Creation to the Harrowing of Hell, the ancestors of Christ, and a wealth of grotesque animals and other forms of marginal imagery. The frescoes were destroyed during the Spanish civil war. The restored fragments now housed in the Museum of Catalan Art, Barcelona, are all that survive of what many consider to be one of the finest masterpieces of English Romanesque art.

Catherine E. Karkov

Bibliography

Baker, Audrey. "Lewes Priory and the Early Group of Wall Paintings in Sussex." *Walpole Society* 31 (1942–43): 1–44; Cather, Sharon, David Park, and Paul Williamson. *Early Medieval Wall Painting and Painted Sculpture in England.* BAR Brit. Ser. 216. Oxford: BAR, 1990; Dodwell, C.R. *The Pictorial Arts of the West 800–1200.* New Haven: Yale University Press, 1993; Grabar, André. *Romanesque Painting.* New York: Skira, 1958; Oakeshott, Walter. *Sigena: Romanesque Paintings in Spain and the Winchester Bible Artists.* London: Harvey Miller & Medcalf, 1972; Park, David. "The 'Lewes Group' of Wall Paintings in Sussex." *Anglo-Norman Studies* 6 (1984): 201–37; Tristram, E.W. *English Medieval Wall Painting.* Vol. 1: *The Twelfth Century.* Oxford: Oxford University Press, 1944.

See also Art, Romanesque; Benedictional of Æthelwold; Canterbury Wall Paintings; Hardham Wall Paintings; Iconography

Wanderer, The

Sometimes called an elegy (though not in the classical sense), sometimes a wisdom poem, sometimes a *consolatio, The Wanderer* survives with similar poems (e.g., *The Seafarer, The Ruin*) in the Exeter Book. It is a 115-line poem about loss of community, the fall of human accomplishment into decay, and loneliness. Extensive scholarship and criticism on the poem have examined the integration of Christian and secular themes, the development of such themes as exile and the impermanence of worldly happiness, and the richness of the poem's diction and imagery.

The number of speakers in the poem is disputed. Some editions and translations present one long speech beginning in line 1 or 8 and continuing to line 110 or the end of the poem, with that speaker presenting a second point of view in lines 92–110, a famous *ubi sunt* ("where are they [now]?") passage. Others see the poem as a dramatic monologue with narrative interventions at lines 6–7, 88–91, and 111. Shifts between first-person and third-person points of view add to the controversy.

Nevertheless, the poem powerfully depicts the impermanence of worldly joy and accomplishment. Bereft of companions, lord, and homeland, the Wanderer invites the reader to see his plight as a clear instance of the stark reality of earthly existence. The poet employs vivid imagery to contrast the joy of the meadhall with the icy misery of a life of exile and the former joy of having his lord as a companion with the current misery of having grief as a companion. While some critics argue that the main contrast is between the instability and misery of worldly existence and the *faestnung,* "stability" or "place of security," of God's mercy, many see more nuanced contrasts: between former worldly joy and present misery, between former signs of secular security and present evidence of the transitoriness of all things mortal, between the harshness of fate and the mercy of God, as well as between the security offered by the secular lord and the heavenly Lord.

Drawing not only on the Anglo-Saxon poetic tradition but also on the classical Latin rhetorical devices that Christianity brought to England, the diction, imagery, and rhetoric of the poem are especially powerful. An important repeating image is that of locking or binding. The poet uses frequent metaphors of the heart and mind as places where thoughts must be locked up as though in treasure chests. Wintery waves are depicted as *gebind,* "bound." Grief and sleep together bind or enchain the solitary wanderer. At the same time binding on earth cannot prevent the loss and decay of earthly things. The end of the poem, however, offers a different binding in the *faestnung* of God, related etymologically to *faestnian,* "fasten, fix, secure, or bind." Throughout the poem appear classical rhetorical devices, such as *repetitio* and *interrogatio,* which, like the Latin-derived *ubi sunt* motif, are integrated beautifully with the Anglo-Saxon rhetorical devices, such as alliteration, variation, and the clustering of images, often formed through unusual compounding.

Phyllis R. Brown

Bibliography

PRIMARY

ASPR 3:134–37; Dunning, T.P., and A.J. Bliss, eds. *The Wanderer.* New York: Appleton-Century-Crofts, 1969; Kennedy, Charles W., trans. *An Anthology of Old English Poetry.* New York: Oxford University Press, 1960, pp. 5–8.

SECONDARY

Calder, Daniel G. "Setting and Mode in *The Seafarer* and *The Wanderer." NM* 72 (1971): 264–75; Clark, S.L., and Julian N. Wasserman. "The Imagery of *The Wanderer." Neophilologus* 63 (1979): 291–96; Cross, J.E. "On the Genre of *The Wanderer." Neophilologus* 45 (1961): 63–75. Repr. in *Essential Articles for the Study of Old English Poetry,* ed. Jess B. Bessinger, Jr., and Stanley J. Kahrl. Hamden: Archon, 1968, pp. 515–32; Greenfield, Stanley B. "*The Wanderer:* A Reconsideration of Theme and Structure." *JEGP* 50 (1951): 451–65. Repr. in *Hero and Exile: The Art of Old English Poetry,* ed. George H. Brown. London: Hambledon, 1989, pp. 133–47.

See also Exeter Book; *Seafarer*

Wardrobe

All branches of government ultimately derive from the royal household. Kings originally kept their treasure in their bedrooms (chamber); the royal robes were kept in the adjacent dressing room (wardrobe). The chamber therefore came to be the financial department of the household, though by the reign of Henry II the wardrobe had become the place where valuables (including money and royal records) were kept. Locations of other royal departments, such as the exchequer, became fixed, but the wardrobe continued to accompany the king on his travels.

At the beginning of the 13th century the wardrobe was still subordinate to the chamber. However, the wardrobe, which stored money, could also conveniently disburse it and so began its own record of expenditures. It was thus performing the same functions as the chamber, and for a time the two

departments overlapped. By the early years of Henry III, for reasons not now clear, the wardrobe became separate from the chamber and then superior to it. By the 1220s, as T.F. Tout wrote, "It is evident . . . that the wardrobe was responsible for the whole finance of the king's household, and therefore had . . . become the accounting and directive department of the palace."

Under Edward I the wardrobe's functions and staff were stabilized. When the king and household were far from the fixed branches of government, as during Edward's military campaigns, the wardrobe played a key role in the organization and execution of the war effort. The keeper of the wardrobe had overall responsibility for its activities; his subordinate, the controller, acted as the king's private secretary and kept the wardrobe, or privy, seal.

To keep the household running and to pay Edward's ongoing military expenses the wardrobe received regular, large payments from the exchequer, collected revenues in areas through which the king traveled, and negotiated loans with English and foreign merchants and bankers. By acting directly and bypassing the normal, slow process of tax collection the wardrobe enabled Edward to operate more flexibly and efficiently.

The growing size of both wardrobe operations and Edward's war effort caused sections of the wardrobe to set up permanent fixed treasuries. The great wardrobe, which bought cloth, furs, spices, wax, and other goods for the household, became first a subdepartment and later an independent one; a privy wardrobe, to store arms and armor, was established in the Tower of London. Expansion of the wardrobe made it less responsive to royal demands under Edward II, and personal royal finances were administered through the chamber.

In Edward II's time the wardrobe lost custody of the privy seal, and its main business came to be domestic accounting. A brief resurgence of wardrobe activity occurred in the early years of the Hundred Years War, but the war's financial demands were too great for the wardrobe and the exchequer took over financial administration. After the mid-14th century the wardrobe became a minor department whose main function was the day-to-day operation of the royal household.

Robin S. Oggins

Bibliography

Byerly, Benjamin F., and Catherine R. Byerly, eds. *Records of the Wardrobe and Household, 1285–1286.* London: HMSO, 1977; Johnson, J.H. "The King's Wardrobe and Household." In *The English Government at Work, 1327–1336.* Vol. 1: *Central and Prerogative Administration,* ed. James F. Willard and William A. Morris. Cambridge: Mediaeval Academy of America, 1940, pp. 206–49; Tout, T.F. *Chapters in the Administrative History of Mediaeval England: The Wardrobe, the Chamber and the Small Seals.* 6 vols. Manchester: Manchester University Press, 1920–33.

See also Exchequer; Households, Royal and Baronial; Privy Seal; Signet

Wardship

In the modern meaning a wardship exists when a young person is in the care of a guardian. In medieval England there were several kinds of wardship, most notably feudal and socage wardship, all of which governed a minor who was an heir to land or to an inheritance under a will. A permanent form of custody over the land and property of incompetents, termed idiots or lunatics, was exercised by the crown through appointed guardians.

The chief form of wardship was that enjoyed by a feudal lord during the minority of a vassal's heir. The lord, as guardian, received the profits of the estate and the right to arrange the heir's marriage. The prototype of modern wardship is that which governed minor heirs to socage lands—free tenures that owed nonmilitary service, now commuted to a money rent. This was in contrast to tenure by knight-service, which, while deemed more honorable, was more onerous. Socage tenure, including burgage or town tenure, and gavelkind (the customary form of tenure in Kent), was free from the feudal incidents of wardship and marriage.

Socage wardship was designed to benefit the ward, as the guardian was the closest relative who could not inherit the property; "the wolf would not have been left to guard the sheep" (an argument also used to justify the lord's guardianship as safer than that of possibly greedy relatives). The guardian of the socage ward was often the mother. The estate of the socage heir was to be managed for the heir's benefit; should the marriage be sold, the money accrued to the heir; an accounting was due upon majority.

Feudal guardianship arose as a necessary characteristic of the heritable fief. This type of guardianship compensated the lord for accepting a minor as the heir, since such an heir could not perform military service. And from the heir's view it was better to be a ward than deprived of an inheritance.

Control over marriage was justified by the personal nature of the feudal contract; the lord could not be expected to accept homage from a stranger or an enemy. This control was first seen in the crown's claim over the marriage of heiresses and widows of tenants-in-chief, but by 1185 rules of feudal marriage governed minor heirs of both sexes. Lesser lords exercised concomitant rights over the heirs of their vassals.

Feudal wardship was primarily a benefit to the lord and therefore nonfiduciary in modern terms. The guardian was to provide suitable maintenance for the ward and was not to disparage the heir by an unsuitable marriage. The ward had the right to refuse all offers, though this "forfeiture of marriage" had a monetary penalty. The guardian was to care for the estate and was forbidden to make capital depredations: cutting down the forest, selling off buildings, or driving away the manorial workers. Actions of waste were suable in common-law courts.

There were few complaints about the theory and practice of feudal wardship. Perhaps the self-interest of the lord often served to benefit the ward; if the lord or his assignee successfully sued to bring into wardship lands of a vassal taken by other claimants, they would belong to the heir at majority. In the long run a feudal lord and the heir had a similarity of interest in the inheritance.

The age of majority varied according to tenure. Male heirs to feudal property came of age at 21; females at fourteen if married, sixteen if unmarried. Socage heirs of both sexes came of age at fifteen or sixteen. As families often held both socage and feudal land, it was possible to have two kinds of guardian and different ages of majority. In regard to wardship of the body the rules of the superior tenure of knight-service would apply and the wardship and marriage would belong to the lord, together with the feudal land, while the socage tenure would be in familial custody. Should the same minor have been heir under a will, the ecclesiastical court might appoint yet another guardian, a tutor, in regard to the bequest.

Wardship law was complicated by the fact that freeholders held land by a variety of tenures and feudal land from several lords. Thus many disputes reached the royal courts. There were four actions protecting feudal wardship rights: *quod reddat custodiam* was the remedy for detention of ward or lands; ejectment, for ouster from a custody; ravishment, for abduction of the ward; the last plea, forfeiture, was sued against the ward for failure to pay for disobedience about marriage. Socage guardians could bring the first three actions, but not forfeiture, as the socage guardian had no pecuniary interest in the ward's marriage.

Wardship applied only to persons possessing property. Children who were not heirs to their father's property were probably left to the care of the widow on her dower lands. The true orphan or poor lunatic presumably was a case for charity. During the plague in the 14th century there were many children in need of guardians, and studies of manorial records reveal instances of ad hoc provisions for care made within individual estates.

Sue Sheridan Walker

Bibliography

Bean, J.M.W. *The Decline of English Feudalism, 1215–1540*. Manchester: Manchester University Press, 1968; Clark, Elaine. "The Custody of Children in English Manor Courts." *Law and History Review* 3 (1985): 333–48; Helmholz, R.H. "The Roman Law of Guardianship in England, 1300–1600." *Tulane Law Review* 52 (1978): 223–57; Holt, J.C. *Magna Carta*. 2d ed. Cambridge: Cambridge University Press, 1992 [clauses 2–6 and 37 of the Charter, pp. 450–53, 460–61]; Walker, Sue Sheridan. "The Feudal Family and the Common Law Courts: The Pleas Protecting Rights of Wardship and Marriage, c. 1225–1375." *JMH* 13 (1987): 13–31 [see also other articles cited in bibliography]; Walker, Sue Sheridan. "Wrongdoing and Compensation: The Pleas of Wardship in Thirteenth and Fourteenth Century England." *Journal of Legal History* 9 (1988): 267–307; Waugh, Scott L. *The Lordship of England: Royal Wardships and Marriages in English Society and Politics, 1217–1327*. Princeton: Princeton University Press, 1988.

See also Children; Marriage; Tenures; Widows

Wars of the Roses

The civil strife originating in the reign of Henry VI and ending with the establishment of the Tudor dynasty. Traditionally regarded as a struggle for the crown between rival branches of the royal family (see fig. 142A and 142B), the name is derived from their reputed emblems, the Red (Lancaster) and White (York) Roses. Though the term is a later invention, apparently first used by Sir Walter Scott in *Anne of Geierstein* (ch. 7), the thinking behind it can be traced back to at least 1485. It is misleading. That the rose emblems were little used in the wars is a point of detail. More seriously misleading is the implication that the wars were basically about rival claims to the crown.

At the outset the main issue was the ineptitude of Henry VI. By the late 1440s he had allowed a narrow faction, led by the duke of Suffolk, predominance in government. In 1450 dissatisfaction with corruption and mismanagement of the French wars led to Suffolk's indictment for treason and to a popular revolt that sought to rehabilitate the king's cousin and heir presumptive, Richard duke of York. On his return from Ireland York continued to find himself excluded from court, where the duke of Somerset now held sway.

In 1450 a move in parliament to have York acknowledged as heir to the throne backfired. In 1452, prompted as much by fear as by ambition, York raised an army but failed to dislodge Somerset from his position of influence. The king's

Fig. 142a. Houses of Lancaster and York. Simplified genealogy.

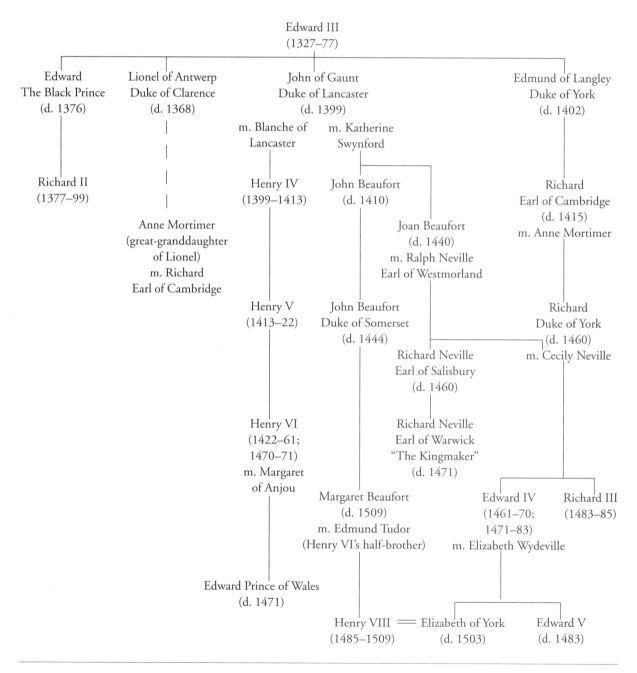

Houses of Lancaster and York

THE WARS OF
THE ROSES

Fig. 142b. Major battlefields. After W.P. Hall et al., A History of England and the Empire-Commonwealth, *5th edition (1971). Reprinted by permission of Xerox College Publishing.*

mental collapse in August 1453 made possible York's appointment as protector of the realm, but Henry's recovery at Christmas 1454 led to the return of Somerset. It was feared that York would be charged with treason at a parliament to be held at Leicester. York and his Neville allies (the earls of Salisbury and Warwick) intercepted the royal entourage at St. Albans (22 May 1455) and, in a bloody affray, captured the king and butchered Somerset and other lords.

Politically the Battle of St. Albans led nowhere. York did not claim the throne, and his resumption of the protectorate was short-term. Whatever his personal aims, the Yorkist coalition sought only to purge the government. Factionalism at court and rivalries in the country had fed off each other for some time; York had the support of the Nevilles because their North Country rivals, the Percys, had influence at court. From 1456 a broadly based royal council achieved a degree of harmony, but the real legacy of St. Albans was a blood feud.

Margaret of Anjou, Henry VI's queen, emerged as a steely champion of their son Edward (b. 1453), and a new generation of Lancastrian lords, some bent on vengeance, gathered around the court. In 1459 the queen and her party were clearly intent on the destruction of York and his allies, by legal means or otherwise. York marshaled his forces at Ludlow, while his allies recruited in the north. At Blore Heath (23 September 1459) the royal host mauled Salisbury's troops as they crossed the Midlands to join York at Ludlow, and in an encounter at Ludford Bridge it forced the Yorkist leaders to fly overseas.

The period from 1459 to 1464 was the time of most sustained conflict. From their base at Calais Edward earl of March, York's son, and the Nevilles invaded England in 1460, capturing the king at Northampton (10 July 1460). Returning from Ireland, York made a bid for the crown, but his allies conceded only that Henry should accept York as heir. The queen, raising a large army in the north, was not about to accept the disinheritance of her son. Lancastrian forces won a surprise victory at Wakefield (30 December), where York and Salisbury were slain.

The queen's advance on London early in 1461, however, was checked at the second Battle of St. Albans (17 February) by Warwick, while Lancastrian forces from Wales were defeated at Mortimer's Cross (2 or 3 February) by Edward, York's son, who on his return to London was hurriedly proclaimed as Edward IV. His position was strengthened by his destruction of the main Lancastrian army in a snowstorm at Towton on Palm Sunday (29 March 1461). The following years saw a gradual reduction of Lancastrian bases in the far north (1464–65) and in Wales (where Harlech held out until 1468) and the capture of Henry VI (1465).

Edward IV made progress in the restoration of order, but political stability proved elusive in the 1460s. While Henry VI remained alive, and while Margaret and Prince Edward were at large, the Yorkist regime was precarious. Edward IV made matters worse for himself; his secret marriage to Elizabeth Wydeville (1464) was political folly. With his influence waning Warwick "the Kingmaker" resorted to force to reassert his dominance in the king's council in 1468–69, and in 1470, after further intrigue, he fled overseas. With a cynicism remarkable even at the time the Kingmaker came to terms with Margaret in Paris, invaded England, drove Edward into exile, and restored the witless Henry VI. In his turn Edward, in a stunning series of moves, landed in Yorkshire, gathered an army, defeated and slew Warwick at Barnet (14 April), and then destroyed the Lancastrian army at Tewkesbury (4 May).

After 1471 Edward IV was undisputed master of his realm. The house of Lancaster was extinguished in the male line. Prince Edward was killed at Tewkesbury and Henry VI met his end in the Tower of London shortly afterward. A few diehard Lancastrians preferred exile, notably the earl of Oxford and the Tudors. Henry Tudor, nephew of Henry VI and heir of the Beauforts, survived as an improbable Lancastrian pretender. In England the Lancastrian cause was dead, the Wars of the Roses seemingly at an end. What led to a resumption of conflict was a crisis that split the Yorkist establishment in 1483.

The crisis, whose roots can be traced to the 1470s, surfaced with Edward IV's death. The regency council for the young Edward V was bitterly divided, not least between his maternal kinsmen (the Wydevilles) and his paternal uncle, Richard, duke of Gloucester, who usurped the throne as Richard III (26 June 1483). Generally held responsible for the murder of Edward V and his brother ("the Princes in the Tower"), Richard had to face a major rebellion in the south, suppressed only at great political cost. In promoting a marriage between Henry Tudor and Elizabeth, Edward IV's daughter, Richard's opponents set the stage for Henry's invasion of 1485 and the defeat and death of Richard III at the Battle of Bosworth (22 August). The accession of Henry VII, whose title was weak, was an incitement to other adventurers, and the Tudor regime was far from firmly established at the turn of the century. The defeat of the earl of Lincoln and the capture of the Yorkist imposter Lambert Simnel at the Battle of Stoke (16 June 1487) are usually taken to mark the end of the dynastic conflict.

Modern assessments of the Wars are at some variance with traditional views, especially as popularized by Shakespeare. The dynastic issue has certainly been overemphasized. It is not useful to talk about rival claims to the throne until 1460, and even then there were few diehards on either side. Modern scholarship has toned down the popular image of 30 years of bloody conflict, anarchy, and destruction. Warfare was far from continuous; there was serious campaigning in only ten of 30 years, and in all but a few years it was restricted to a few weeks.

While the civil strife, broadly defined to include feuding and lawlessness, had an adverse impact on English life in the 1450s and early 1460s, it is hard to sustain such a view with respect to the 1470s and 1480s, a time of increasing prosperity and cultural vitality. Another apparent "myth" is that the old nobility destroyed itself in the civil wars, clearing the way for a new political order characterized by a strong monarchy taking into partnership a newly independent gentry class.

Yet revisionism has perhaps gone too far. The traditional view has 15th-century roots. Tudor myth making after 1485 merely amplified and developed attitudes expressed in the 1460s and 1470s. The Yorkists, like the Tudors, had a clear interest in emphasizing the nation's tribulations prior to their restoration of order, and government propaganda must have accorded somewhat with popular perceptions. Balanced or not, perceptions play their part in history. Limited though its actual impact was by comparison with other civil wars, the Wars of the Roses clearly made a deep impression on English political culture and seem to have prepared the ground for the strengthening of central government and the virtual apotheosis of the monarchy in Tudor times.

Michael J. Bennett

Bibliography

Goodman, Anthony. *The Wars of the Roses: Military Activity and English Society, 1452–97*. London: Routledge & Kegan Paul, 1981; Pollard, Anthony J. *The Wars of the Roses*. Basingstoke: Macmillan Education, 1988.

See also Beaufort Family; Cade's Rebellion; Edward IV; Edward V; Henry VI; Henry VII; Malory; Neville Family; Richard III

Wearmouth-Jarrow and the Codex Amiatinus

A pandect (one-volume) manuscript of the Bible, the Codex Amiatinus (Florence, Biblioteca Medicea-Laurenziana Amiatinus 1) was the most splendid and important product of the scriptorium of the twin monasteries founded in 674 (Wearmouth) and 681 (Jarrow) by Benedict Biscop. Major sites for the cultivation of Mediterranean art forms introduced by the well-traveled founder, Wearmouth-Jarrow's scriptorium and library formed an important link with Rome for Anglo-Saxon monastics. Their house author, Bede, saw over his lifetime at Jarrow the familiarization of Mediterranean book art, wall painting, and stone architecture and sculpture.

The monastery's cultural achievements were shaped by the romanizing monastic forms set down by Benedict Biscop and also by the Bible-study program of Ceolfrid, who became abbot in 689. According to the two *Lives of the Abbots* Ceolfrid, like Biscop, brought many books from Rome, including an Old Latin pandect of the Bible. Although no longer extant, this pandect is usually believed to be identifiable as the Codex Grandior, a copy of the Vetus Latina translation described by Cassiodorus in his *Institutiones*. Cassiodorus tells of having

Fig. 143. Codex Amiatinus (Florence, Biblioteca Medicea Laurenziana Amiatinus 1), fols. 2v–3. Tabernacle in the Temple at Jerusalem. Reproduced by permission of the Biblioteca Medicea Laurenziana, Florence.

inserted into this manuscript plans of the Temple in Jerusalem and the Tabernacle and diagrams showing the divisions of scripture. These correspond to the plan of the Tabernacle (fig. 143) and three diagrams presented in the first quire of the Codex Amiatinus.

For this reason much modern scholarship considers the Codex Amiatinus a copy of Cassiodorus's pandect, updated with a Vulgate text, although it could as well represent a creative emulation or interpretation. Amiatinus is, however, clearly identical with one of three pandect Bibles produced by Ceolfrid's monks. Its original dedication inscription reproduces exactly the verses given in the anonymous *Lives of the Abbots* as those written in the third pandect, which was taken to Rome for presentation to the pope.

Besides being one of only a few early Anglo-Saxon manuscripts of documented origin, it is the earliest surviving complete Latin copy of the Bible, and its text, except for the Psalms and Epistles, is one of the best witnesses of the Vulgate. Formidable in scale, the manuscript is also visually impressive in its classicizing script styles and illusionistic full-page frontispiece depictions of Ezra copying the Bible and, preceding the New Testament, Christ in Majesty, both of which imitate late-antique art. Nevertheless, possibilities for selection and modification might have remained, allowing creation of an interpretation of Mediterranean forms, perhaps relating them to

Anglo-Saxon monasticism. For example, inclusion of the diagram of the Tabernacle seems to fit a general insular fascination with the structure of the Temple and Tabernacle, present in the writings of Bede and in manuscript illustrations in the books of Kells and Armagh. But to whatever degree its textual presentation and illustrations represent copy or creative interpretation, the Codex Amiatinus documents a close adherence to late-antique exemplars and speaks less eloquently of a cultural mix than of the authority of continental, especially Roman, forms of monasticism, learning, and manuscript production at Wearmouth-Jarrow.

Carol A. Farr

Bibliography

Alexander, J.J.G. *Insular Manuscripts 6th–9th Century.* A Survey of Manuscripts Illuminated in the British Isles 1, ed. J.J.G. Alexander. London: Harvey Miller, 1978; Bruce-Mitford, Rupert L.S. *The Art of the Codex Amiatinus.* Jarrow Lecture, 1967. Jarrow: St. Paul's Church, 1967. Repr. *JBAA,* 3d ser. 32 (1969): 1–25; Budny, Mildred. "The Visual Arts and Crafts (Early Medieval Britain)." In *The Cambridge Guide to the Arts in Britain.* Vol. 1: *Prehistoric, Roman, and Early Medieval,* ed. Boris Ford. Cambridge: Cambridge University Press, 1988, pp. 122–77; Corsano, Karen. "The First Quire of the Codex Amiatinus and the *Institutiones* of Cassiodorus." *Scriptorium* 41 (1987): 3–34; Henderson, George. *Bede and the Visual Arts.* Jarrow Lecture, 1980. Jarrow: St. Paul's Church, 1980; Kühnel, Bianca. *From the Earthly to the Heavenly Jerusalem: Representations of the Holy City in Christian Art of the First Millennium.* Römische Quartalschrift für christliche Altertumskunde und Kirchengeschichte. Supplementheft 42. Rome: Herder, 1987; Marsden, Richard. *The Text of the Old Testament in Anglo-Saxon England.* Cambridge: Cambridge University Press, 1995, pp. 76–201; Meyvaert, Paul. "Bede and the Church Paintings at Wearmouth-Jarrow." *ASE* 8 (1979): 63–77; Meyvaert, Paul. "Bede, Cassiodorus, and the Codex Amiatinus." Speculum 71 (1996): 827–83. Nordhagen, Per Jonas. *The Codex Amiatinus and the Byzantine Element in the Northumbrian Renaissance.* Jarrow Lecture, 1978. Jarrow: St. Paul's Church, 1978; Parkes, Malcolm B. *The Scriptorium of Monkwearmouth and Jarrow.* Jarrow Lecture, 1982. Jarrow: St. Paul's Church, 1982.

See also Bible in OE Literature; Ecclesiastical Architecture, Early Anglo-Saxon; Manuscript Illumination, Anglo-Saxon; Wearmouth-Jarrow: Architecture

Wearmouth-Jarrow: Architecture

St. Peter's Church at Wearmouth (now in Sunderland, County Durham) was built, according to Bede, within one year, between 674 and 675 (fig. 144). The Church of St. Paul's in the twinned monastery at Jarrow (fig. 145) was founded in 681 and dedicated in 685 (the dedication slab survives today although not in its original position). Both churches are then

Fig. 144. Plan of Wearmouth, Saxon Phase 3. After Cramp (1994). Courtesy of R.J. Cramp.

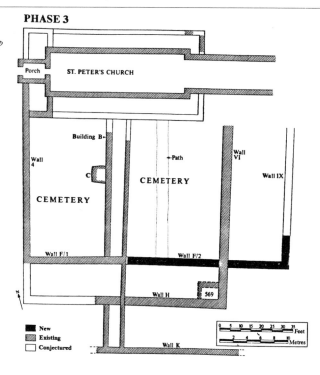

PHASE 3

Fig. 145. Plan of Anglo-Saxon Jarrow, excavated stone buildings. After Cramp (1994). Courtesy of R.J. Cramp.

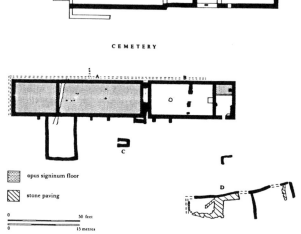

mouth's survives. This was flanked by two side chambers. Both churches apparently had a structure to the east that may have served as a funerary chapel.

Wearmouth's church and monastic buildings are constructed with limestone rubble blocks set in poured concrete; Jarrow's buildings are of sandstone ashlar, but at both sites the buildings have massive quoins laid in an alternate fashion, as in other Northumbrian churches, such as Escomb and Corbridge. Doors have roughly voussoired heads (using wedge-shaped pieces for the arch), but windows are formed with monolithic round heads and minimal upright and flat jambs. They are internally splayed, and at Jarrow the closure slabs to hold small areas of glass survive. Quantities of colored and plain window glass have been found in association with the excavated monastic buildings. The floors of the monastic buildings, and presumably of the churches, were of brick-faced concrete *(opus signinum)*. The buildings were decorated with external and internal stringcourses and friezes and internally with imposts, panels, and painted plaster. The motifs employed are balustrade ornament, interlace and animal ornament at Wearmouth, and at Jarrow also inhabited plant scrolls.

Rosemary J. Cramp

Bibliography

Cramp, Rosemary J. "Excavations at the Saxon Monastic Sites of Wearmouth and Jarrow, Co. Durham: An Interim Report." *Medieval Archaeology* 13 (1969): 21–66; Cramp, Rosemary J. "Jarrow Church." *ArchJ* 133 (1976): 220–28; Cramp, Rosemary J. "Monastic Sites." In *The Archaeology of Anglo-Saxon England*, ed. David M. Wilson. London: Methuen, 1976, pp. 229–41; Cramp, Rosemary J. "Monkwearmouth Church." *ArchJ* 133 (1976): 230–37; Cramp, Rosemary J. "Monkwearmouth and Jarrow in Their European Context." In *Churches Built in Ancient Times: Recent Studies in Early Christian Archaeology.* Occasional Papers of the Society of Antiquaries of London 16. Ed. Kenneth Painter. London: Society of Antiquaries, 1994, pp. 279–94; Fernie, Eric. *The Architecture of the Anglo-Saxons.* London: Batsford, 1983, pp. 47–59; Taylor, Harold M. *Anglo-Saxon Architecture.* Vol. 3. Cambridge: Cambridge University Press, 1978, pp. 740–41, 749, 752–53; Taylor, Harold M., and Joan Taylor. "Jarrow" and "Monkwearmouth." In *Anglo-Saxon Architecture.* Vol. 1. Cambridge: Cambridge University Press, 1965, pp. 338–49, 432–46.

See also Architecture, Anglo-Saxon; Art, Anglo-Saxon; Bede; Ecclesiastical Architecture, Early Anglo-Saxon; Stonework as Ecclesiastical Ornament; Wearmouth-Jarrow and the Codex Amiatinus

Wells Cathedral

Wells Cathedral contains work of essentially two periods. The western three bays of the choir arcade, the transepts, nave (fig. 146), and west front are part of an early Gothic

potentially very accurately dated structures. Unfortunately only the west wall and the porch survive of the early church at Wearmouth. At Jarrow, where there were two churches end to end, the small eastern church (now the chancel) survives, while the larger—the "basilica" mentioned in the dedication—is covered by the 19th-century nave. Excavation within the modern nave has revealed foundations of an independent church in the same technique as the excavated monastic buildings to the south.

The dimensions of both major churches are similar: Wearmouth nave 18.5 feet wide and 64 feet long; Jarrow, 18.5 feet wide, 65 feet long. Jarrow had in its first phase a square-ended chancel and a narrow north aisle. In a subsequent phase there is evidence for chambers flanking the nave. Each church probably had a western porch, although only Wear-

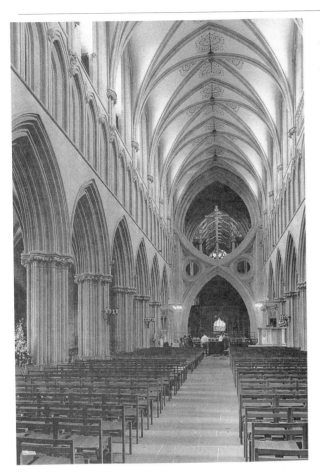

Fig. 146. Wells Cathedral, nave from west. Courtesy of L. Hoey.

campaign stretching from ca. 1180 to ca. 1245; the chapter house (fig. 39: see CHAPTER HOUSES), Lady Chapel, retrochoir, and presbytery represent the Decorated period of ca. 1280 to ca. 1340.

Wells is one of those rare English cathedrals built on an unencumbered site. The Anglo-Saxon and Norman churches lay south of the present cathedral and on a different axis. The lack of any major Anglo-Norman reconstruction at Wells can be explained by the historical circumstance of Wells losing its *cathedra* (status as episcopal seat) ca. 1090, when Bishop John de Villula moved the see to Bath. The chapter was reconstituted by Bishop Roger of Lewes in the mid-12th century, but Wells did not officially regain its cathedral status until the 1240s. Nevertheless, it is likely that the decision to rebuild on a fresh site and in the grand manner was predicated on the chapter's assumption that their church would regain its episcopal status, or was itself meant to be one of the arguments for regaining that status.

The new building was begun under Bishop Reginald ca. 1180 and was built continuously until the entire east arm, transepts, and five nave bays were completed. At this point there is evidence in the masonry of a break in construction, although there is no discernible change in the design. The break may be connected with the Interdict of 1208–12. It is not clear when work resumed, but the nave was probably complete by ca. 1225 and the west facade by 1239, when the church was dedicated, although some work was still underway in 1242.

The early Gothic work at Wells has long been recognized as one of the first and most distinctive statements of a particular style of English Gothic associated with the West Country. The massive piers with their eight groups of triple shafts and lavish foliate capitals, the broad and immensely complex arch moldings, the triforium with its continuously molded pointed arches, and the high-set vault shafts (at the triforium sill in the choir and transepts, in the triforium spandrels in the nave) are all characteristic features of the Wells design that combine to give it a strong horizontal impetus and a rich, sculptural texture. Wells retains the thick wall of the Anglo-Norman tradition, with wall passages at triforium and clerestory level. There are buttressing arches hidden under the triforium roof; these, with the thick wall, are sufficient to sustain the four-part high vaults with crowns 66 feet above floor level.

The west towers of the cathedral are set beyond the western aisle bays, and the whole west front formed a screen of uniform height before the addition of the Perpendicular towers. This screen facade (fig. 122: see SCREEN FACADES) is covered with gabled tabernacles supported by shafts of contrasting blue lias (a kind of stone) and filled with sculpted figures. The difference in style between the Wells west facade and the rest of the early Gothic church has led many to assume the arrival of a new master, but it may also be that the west facade was felt to demand a contrasting stylistic vocabulary from the interior and the exterior flanks of the church.

The original east end of the early Gothic cathedral terminated in a squared ambulatory with a Lady Chapel of undetermined form. This was all swept away in the Decorated rebuilding and extension of the early 14th century. The reasons behind this eastern extension may have had to do with a felt need for more processional space and a grander chapel for the Virgin Mary connected with the introduction of the Revised Use of Sarum in 1298, or they may have been connected with the chapter's hope that their recently deceased bishop, William of March, whose canonization they sought between 1324 and 1329, would need a suitable shrine in an appropriately elegant and modern architectural setting. The precise dating of the Decorated work at Wells has been controversial, with John Harvey arguing for a beginning in the first decade of the century and Peter Draper for a later beginning (ca. 1323). Given that the tower is documented as under construction from 1315, the latter dating is more likely, as it seems improbable that the sequence of Lady Chapel, retrochoir, and choir would have been interrupted to raise the central tower farther west. The new work seems to have been complete by ca. 1340.

The Decorated work at Wells has always been seen as the most sophisticated and complex example of an unusual interest in spatial manipulation evident among English builders in the early 14th century. Although constructed from east to west, the visitor experiences the spaces west to east. The three western arcade bays of the early Gothic choir were left intact but crowned with a new triforium of ogee-arched niches and a clerestory with Decorated window tracery. The three eastern bays of the choir were built *ex novo,* and although they continue the general proportions of those to the west, they alter the terms of the normal separation between arcade and upper stories by basing the pinnacles of the triforium niches on the extrados of the arcade arch itself. The whole choir is covered by what is structurally a pointed barrel vault with interpenetrations over the clerestory windows but that reads as a net vault with interlocking diagonal ribs broken by cusped lozenges.

From the choir aisles the visitor enters the retrochoir, arguably the most complex and disorienting space in Gothic architecture. Clustered Purbeck marble piers of varying shape are spaced in seemingly random fashion (they actually form an elongated hexagon) and support a bewildering vault of asymmetrical ridges and tierceron ribs. The lowness of the retrochoir adds to the feeling of spatial density and contrasts with the higher, more open spaces of choir and Lady Chapel to west and east. The latter is itself an unusually formed octagon, elongated toward the east and vaulted with a tierceron vault of daunting complexity. Five great reticulated windows light this easternmost part of the cathedral.

The chief Perpendicular work at Wells was the building of two west towers above the 13th-century screen facade by William Wynford in the late 14th century. The flat tops of these towers, perhaps inspired by the *ad quadratum* design of the earlier screen, twice as long as it is high, were extremely influential locally. The central tower was rebuilt after a fire in 1439. Earlier than this last alteration was the interior construction of the famous strainer arches in the crossing about 1350, which were designed to combat ominous deformation in the crossing piers.

Lawrence Hoey

Bibliography

Bilson, John. "Notes on the Earlier Architectural History of Wells Cathedral." *ArchJ* 85 (1928): 23–69; Colchester, Linzee, and John Harvey. "Wells Cathedral." *ArchJ* 131 (1974): 200–14; Draper, Peter. "The Sequence and Dating of the Decorated Work at Wells." *BAACT* 4 (1981): 18–29; Harvey, John. "Perpendicular at Wells." *BAACT* 4 (1981): 36–41; Harvey, John. "The Building of Wells Cathedral, I: 1175–1307" and "The Building of Wells Cathedral, II: 1307–1508." In *Wells Cathedral: A History,* ed. L.S. Colchester. West Compton House: Open Books, 1982, pp. 52–101; Rodwell, Warwick. "The Lady Chapel by the Cloister at Wells and the Site of the Anglo-Saxon Cathedral." *BAACT* 4 (1981): 1–9.

See also Architecture and Architectural Sculpture, Gothic; Art, Gothic; Chapter Houses; Misericords; Salisbury Cathedral; Screen Facades; Sculpture, Gothic; Stained Glass; Vaulting

Westminster Abbey

The coronation church of English monarchs and the frequent burial place of medieval kings; also the chief relic setting for the shrine of Edward the Confessor. The building itself was and remains perhaps the most magnificent

Fig. 147. Westminster Abbey, south choir and south transept, east elevations. Courtesy of L. Hoey.

constructed in medieval England (figs. 147–48). In the number and splendor of the tombs and effigies it is without parallel.

History

While a monastery was probably founded at Westminster by St. Dunstan in 959, it is with Edward the Confessor that its history really begins. He endowed the monks with extensive estates and built an entirely new church, in which he was buried. Both the church and the burial are graphically depicted on the Bayeux Tapestry. After his victory at Hastings William the Conqueror was crowned there on Christmas Day 1066, probably following Harold's precedent. Thereafter every English king and queen who has been crowned has been crowned at Westminster. The Confessor had also built a royal palace just by the abbey, thus beginning Westminster's history as a royal residence and seat of government.

From the 11th century onward the rolls and charters preserved in the abbey's muniment room illustrate its history as one of the kingdom's most prestigious and wealthiest Benedictine monasteries. In 1535, just before the Dissolution, the net income was at least £2,800, second only to Glastonbury Abbey. The administration of the estates has been analyzed by Barbara Harvey, and we know that the normal establishment of monks was just under 50.

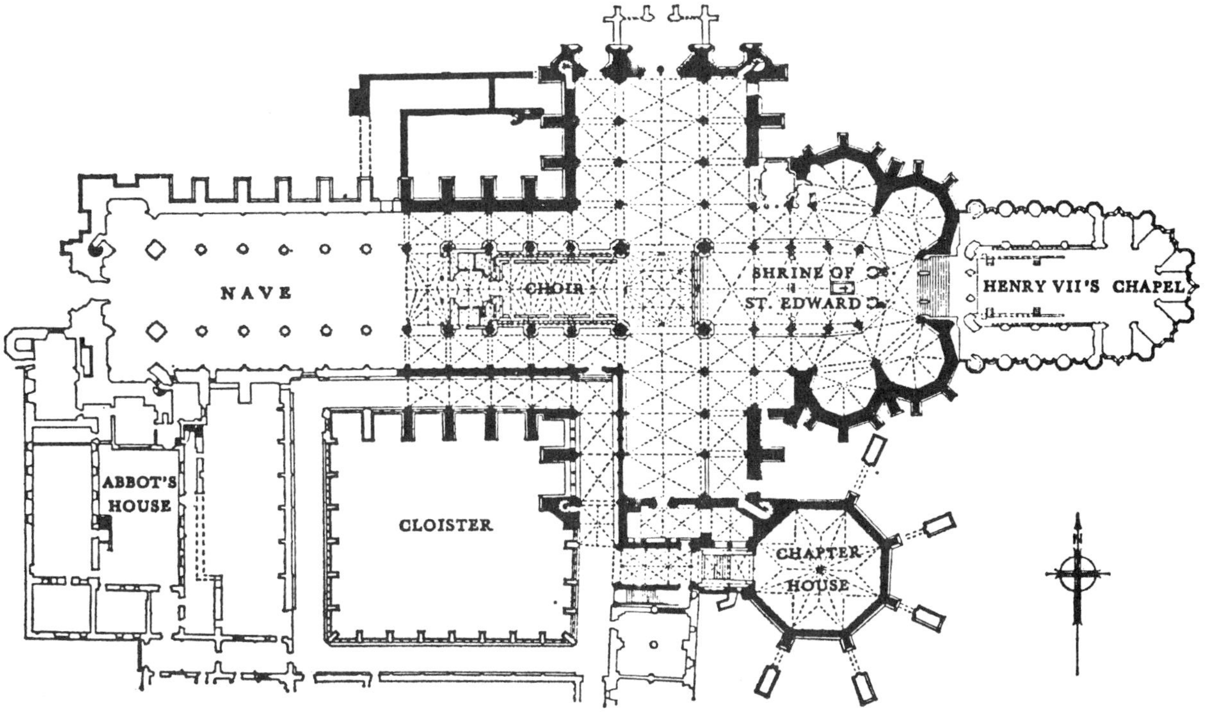

Fig. 148. Westminster Abbey. After G. Webb (1956). Reprinted by permission of Yale University Press.

The reign of Henry III marked a decisive new stage in the abbey's history. The loss of most of the Plantagenet dominions in France meant that Henry, unlike his predecessors, lived almost exclusively in England. The palace of Westminster, which he extensively rebuilt, became his favorite residence, largely because of the proximity to the abbey. In 1220, as a youth of thirteen, Henry laid the foundation stone of the new Lady Chapel; in the 1230s he developed an intense devotion to Edward the Confessor, canonized in 1161. In 1245 he decided to display his devotion by funding the complete rebuilding of the Confessor's church. All but the old nave was pulled down, and between 1245 and 1269 the present eastern chapels, presbytery, transepts, choir, and chapter house arose on the cleared site. His total expenditure was over £41,000, more than a year's royal income.

In its style the new abbey has been called "a great French thought expressed in excellent English." It showed extensive French influence in the plan of the eastern chapels, which came from Amiens, in the windows, modeled almost exactly on Reims, and the flying buttresses, which enabled the church to achieve its great height. At 103 feet to the crown of the vault it is the highest medieval church in England. But its decoration is overwhelmingly English. The desire to achieve an "all-over" decorative effect had long been a feature of English ecclesiastical architecture. At Westminster it reached a new degree of profusion and magnificence. At ground level ran a wall arcade, adorned with sculptures in the eastern chapels and with a series of heraldic shields in the choir. All the piers, columns, and shafts were in highly polished Purbeck marble, while the spandrels of the main arcade and triforium were adorned with diaper (cross-hatch, diamond-shaped decorations in different colors). Sculptures and the few plain surfaces were highly painted.

Henry III was no passive paymaster. He urged forward the work and exhibited a close interest in its design. He may well have taken major decisions, like that to have a stately galleried triforium, despite the huge extra expense. The various architectural possibilities were probably presented to him and the detailed plans drawn up by the master mason, Henry de Reyns, in charge of the works until his death in 1253. If he had worked at Reims, as his name and the abbey's design suggest, he clearly was also steeped in English taste and practice.

Alongside the work on the abbey itself Henry III constructed a new shrine for Edward the Confessor, to which the saint's body was translated in a splendid ceremony on 13 October 1269. Situated behind the high altar, the shrine was the focal point of the new church, and Henry was ultimately buried beside it. In the next 150 years his example was followed by his son and daughter-in-law, Edward I and Eleanor of Castile; by Edward III and his queen, Philippa of Hainault; by Richard II; and by Henry V in 1422, by which time all the places around the Confessor's shrine had been filled up. The tombs of these kings and queens, save that of Edward I, bore splendid effigies, although Henry V's is now virtually destroyed.

When Henry III died, his building had reached one bay west of the present choir screen, where it was tacked on, somewhat uneasily, to the nave of the Confessor's church. It was not until 1376 that the latter was thrown down and work begun on a new nave. It continued slowly, funded largely by the monks themselves, until the early 16th century, when everything was complete save for the western towers, not added until the 18th century. The design of the nave is that of the church of Henry III, without the decoration; the difference that immediately strikes the eye is the absence of diaper. The architect "original enough not to seek after originality in his work" was probably Henry Yevele. No higher tribute could have been paid to Henry III's church. Even a hundred years later it could not be bettered.

It was the first of the Tudors, Henry VII, who made the last great addition to the interior. In 1503 he began work on a new Lady Chapel to replace the one commenced in 1220. Henry VII's Chapel, as it is called, with its extraordinary fan and pendant vault, is perhaps the most remarkable example of late Perpendicular architecture. It is also, with the Tudor badges of rose and portcullis studded over its surface, a testimony to the pretensions of the new dynasty and a reaffirmation of the ties between the abbey and the royal house. It was such ties, forged above all by Edward the Confessor, Henry III, and Henry VII, that made the abbey what it remains to this day—a house of kings.

Architecture

The history of the fabric of the church is straightforward. A church of St. Peter at Westminster probably existed as early as the 7th century. The importance of this once-island site outside the walls of London begins, however, when Edward the Confessor became its patron after 1042 and commenced the building of a great church. It was his intention that it become a royal "private abbey," directly dependent upon the crown in the same way Caen and other Norman abbeys were dependent upon their ducal founders. Known through archaeological remains and literary descriptions, it was built before the Conquest in a Norman Romanesque style—a style the Confessor became familiar with during his exile in Normandy. It was a large church with western towers, a long nave, transepts, a central tower with stair turrets (as pictured in the Bayeux Tapestry), a short presbytery of two bays with solid side walls, and a circular eastern apse. The nave possibly had six square bays, divided by cruciform piers, which in turn were subdivided by square piers, creating an *abab* rhythm, as at Jumièges. The monastic buildings were also rebuilt. Edward did not attend its consecration in 1065, just days before his death. He was buried in the church, which eventually became his shrine. Although the western towers may not have been complete in time for the consecration, William the Conqueror was crowned at the abbey in 1066.

The Gothic church that we see today is largely the work of Henry III. Documentary evidence suggests that the idea to rebuild the abbey had appeared by 1220, when a new Lady Chapel—now replaced by Henry VII's Chapel—was begun by Henry III at the eastern end of the Confessor's church to accommodate the increasingly celebrated cult of the Virgin. This new Lady Chapel did not, however, set the style for the rebuilding of the whole abbey.

Ultimately the monastic hope to rebuild the entire abbey was connected to Henry III's offer to pay for it; the abbey must be understood as a royal enterprise, paid for and under the control of the crown. It was the most expensive and lavish English church of the 13th century. The ultimate cost per bay was two times that of Salisbury. More than the coronation church of his ancestors and personal piety motivated Henry to rebuild. Since he no longer ruled in Anjou, the ab-

bey was planned to take the place of Fontevrault Abbey as the royal burial place. It was to show that the House of Plantagenet had parity with the House of Capet. While reflecting Henry's extraordinary political ambitions, it also communicates the place of kingship in the divinely established order and the king's role as God's appointed vicar on earth. The massive building project coincides with the birth of parliament and the baronial movement to limit royal power. With royal funding ensured, the demolition of the old church took place in 1245 and construction started in 1246.

The initial financial organization of the work was under Edward of Westminster, and a "Master Henry" was the first master of the works. Little is known of his background, but after his death he was described as "Master Henry de Reyns, mason." Whether he was a Frenchman from Reims, or had just worked at Reims, or was from Raynes in Essex is not known. Since, however, the church has decidedly French characteristics, whoever designed it had firsthand knowledge of the important churches then rising in the Ile-de-France. Suggestions for some French details may have come from the king himself, who had visited Paris in 1254 and toured nearly all of the cathedrals in northern France.

French characteristics include an eastern chevet with polygonal apse and radiating chapels, north-transept facade with large portals and a rose window like Reims Cathedral, French bar tracery, trefoil-cusped lights in the tracery of the gallery that had appeared only a few years before in the Sainte-Chapelle, two-tier flying buttresses, and comparatively great internal height. By contrast many features of the design follow English models, such as the gallery—used to shout formal acclamations at coronations—conforming to the general scheme of Canterbury and Lincoln in its elevation toward the main vessels, standard high Gothic four-shaft piers close to those in the nave at Salisbury, and use of Purbeck marble. Technical details, such as the construction of vaulting ribs in sloping courses forming angled meetings at the ridges (as opposed to the French technique of horizontal coursing), greater thickness of shafts in the gallery, and the greater thickness of walls, are consistent with English practice. Based on the available evidence, scholars agree that the designer probably was English.

No doubt the Sainte-Chapelle, with its walls inlaid with glass and gilded to simulate enamels in imitation of the shrine of the relic of the Crown of Thorns, inspired the extraordinary ornamental feature of Westminster's internal elevation—a carved diaper pattern of stylized flowers originally brilliantly gilded and painted. Since this diaper pattern is also thought to have appeared on the now destroyed shrine of Edward the Confessor, the interior was to have a brilliant, polychromatic appearance based on the shrine that it enclosed. Since this diapering pattern is absent on the first part built, the original conception for the church changed over time.

The chapter house, with its vaulted crypt, was completed well before 1259. Octagonal in plan, it follows the precedent of centrally planned English chapter houses. Conceived like a "glass cage," its windows were filled with heraldic glass. The original vaulting, supported by a slender central pillar, was destroyed in the 18th century and was later restored.

The church was unfinished at Henry's death in 1272. The nave was not completed until the 15th century, and the west facade, partially designed by Sir Christopher Wren, was finished in 1734 by Nicholas Hawksmoor.

Numerous tombs and additions were made to the abbey, the most spectacular being the Chapel of Henry VII. Begun in 1503, it was conceived as a vast architectural display to buttress Henry VII's dubious claim to the throne and as the mausoleum for the new Tudor dynasty. Its main architectural feature is a pendant fan vault, which is one of the wonders of late Gothic architecture. Its stylistic features are connected to St. George's Chapel, Windsor.

> D.A. Carpenter
> Walter Leedy

Bibliography

HISTORY

Binski, Paul. *Westminster Abbey and the Plantagenets: Kingship and the Representation of Power 1200–1400*. New Haven: Yale University Press, 1995; Carpenter, D.A. *The Reign of Henry III*. London: Hambledon, 1996; Harvey, Barbara. *Westminster Abbey and Its Estates in the Middle Ages*. Oxford: Clarendon, 1977; Mason, Emma, ed. *Westminster Abbey Charters, 1066–c. 1214*. London Record Society 25. London: Record Society, 1988; Tanner, Lawrence. *The History and Treasures of Westminster Abbey*. London: Pitkin, 1953; Wormald, Francis. "Paintings in Westminster Abbey and Contemporary Painting." *PBA* 35 (1949): 161–77.

ARCHITECTURE

Branner, Robert. "Westminster Abbey and the French Court Style." *Journal of the Society of Architectural Historians* 23 (1964): 3–18; Brown, R. Allen, H.M. Colvin, and A.J. Taylor, eds. *The History of the King's Works*. Vols. 1–2: *The Middle Ages*. London: HMSO, 1963; Cocke, Thomas. *900 Years: The Restorations of Westminster Abbey*. London: Harvey Miller, 1995; Colvin, Howard M., ed. *Building Accounts of King Henry III*. Oxford: Clarendon, 1971; Flete, John. *The History of Westminster Abbey*. Ed. Joseph Armitage Robinson. Cambridge: Cambridge University Press, 1909; Great Britain, Royal Commission on Historical Monuments. *An Inventory of the Historical Monuments in London*. Vol. 1: *Westminster Abbey*. London: HMSO, 1924; Leedy, Walter. "The Design of the Vaulting of Henry VII's Chapel, Westminster: A Reappraisal." *Architectural History* 18 (1975): 5–11; Lethaby, William R. *Westminster Abbey and the King's Craftsmen*. London: Duckworth, 1906; Lethaby, William R. *Westminster Abbey Re-Examined*. London: Duckworth, 1925; Perkins, Jocelyn. *Westminster Abbey, Its Worship and Ornaments*. 3 vols. London: Oxford University Press, 1938–52; Wilson, Christopher. *The Gothic Cathedral: The Architecture of the Great Church 1130–1530*. London: Thames & Hudson, 1990; Wilson, Christopher, et al. *Westminster Abbey*. London: Bell & Hyman, 1986.

See also Architecture and Architectural Sculpture, Gothic; Architecture and Architectural Sculpture, Romanesque; Bayeux Tapestry; Chapter Houses; Coronation; Coronation Ceremony; Edward the Confessor; Henry III; Henry VII; Richard II; Vaulting; Westminster Chapter House Paintings; Westminster Retable; Windsor, St. George's Chapel

Westminster Chapter House Paintings

The Chapter House at Westminster Abbey (finished 1253) is an octagonal chamber with three different sets of paintings in the wall arcade on seven sides of the building and an entrance on the west side. Each arcade is composed of five trefoil-headed arches. The eastern arcade surrounds what remains of a fine Last Judgment, more accurately labeled a Majesty, since it lacks the separation of the blessed and the damned souls, as well as the heavenly host. This painting, which has Christ in the center, seated on an arc, his feet resting on a globe, and displaying his wounds, is executed in an English-italianate style. This is well demonstrated by the head of the seraph who stands on Christ's right, exquisitely painted in softly modeled forms. It relates broadly to Sienese work of ca. 1340–50, to that of Pietro Lorenzetti, and to the late work of Simone Martini, such as the sinopia, or fresco underdrawing, of Christ in Avignon Cathedral, which compares well with the seraph in question. Although now fragmentary, the Virgin can be made out on Christ's right; therefore it can be assumed that John the Baptist was once on Christ's left, thus forming the traditional iconographic type of the *deësis* (Christ flanked by Mary and John the Baptist). The scene is completed by a further seraph on Christ's left and angels, some of whom hold the instruments of the Passion.

This, and the Apocalypse cycle that originally occupied the arcades on the six other sides, were commissioned by John of Northampton, a monk at the abbey sometime between 1375/76 and 1404. The Majesty is generally considered to be earlier than the Apocalypse, but it is not possible to establish a precise date. There is little surviving monumental painting with which it can be compared. Both the tester over the tomb of the Black Prince in Canterbury Cathedral of 1394–97 and the wall painting in the Byward Tower of the Tower of London, which is undated, have been cited as possible, yet not wholly convincing, parallels; nor is the style found in illumination of the final quarter of the 14th century.

Whereas the Majesty is undoubtedly the work of an English painter under strong Italian influence, the Apocalypse stands in complete contrast and may have been carried out by foreign artists. The style, which is characterized by squat figures with rounded, vigorously highlighted draperies and large heads with long, round-ended noses, is remarkably similar on the one hand to that of the north German painter Master Bertram of Minden (German and other foreign artists are documented as working in London at this time), and on the other hand it relates to certain manuscripts produced at Westminster between the 1380s and the early 1400s, namely the *Liber regalis* (Westminster Abbey Library 38) and Rickert's Hand B of the Carmelite Missal (BL Add. 29704–05), both strongly Bohemian in character. This link with the manuscripts is reinforced by the fact that each of the Apocalypse scenes is accompanied by explanatory scrolls with the text of the Apocalypse written on vellum, affixed to the wall; in addition the Apocalypse cycle has been convincingly shown by Noppen to have been based on the version now Cambridge, Trinity College B.10.2. The artist of this work, whose style is unquestionably English, was one of the two principal hands of the Lytlington Missal (London, Westminster Abbey Library 37), illuminated for Westminster Abbey in 1383/84. The Trinity Apocalypse is datable to the 1390s, and the Chapter House Apocalypse could be of that decade or possibly of the early 15th century.

The Apocalypse originally occupied the entire wall arcade on the remaining six walls of the Chapter House, the cycle beginning in the northwest bay with scenes from the apocryphal life of St. John, continuing in a clockwise direction with the vision itself, bypassing the Majesty, to end in the southwest bay. It has been calculated that 96 scenes once occupied the 24 arches given over to the Apocalypse. The northwest, southeast, and southwest portions are the best preserved, the north and northeast are blank, and the south wall is almost destroyed. Where the paintings are intact each arch contains eight subjects, above which is a demiangel playing a musical instrument, the style of which stands midway between the English-italianate Majesty and the German/Bohemian-styled Apocalypse. The space below is divided into six compartments: the upper four accommodate the Apocalypse scenes, while the lower two contain what little survives of a bestiary cycle, thought to be early-16th-century.

A final, enigmatic painting on the east wall comprises a number of highly individualized heads that are looking in the direction of the adjacent Majesty. Perhaps the closest existing comparison for the distinctive facial types, with their elongated noses, is found in the style of Siferwas, the Dominican illuminator of the Sherborne Missal (on loan to the British Library [loan MS. 82] from the Trustees of the will of the 9th duke of Northumberland of Alnwick Castle). Their iconographic role is unclear; if they are to be seen in the context of the Majesty, then they were possibly added slightly later and, as Rigold has suggested, they could represent purgatory and be portraits of contemporary political figures.

Lynda Dennison

Bibliography

Alexander, Jonathan, and Paul Binski, eds. *Age of Chivalry: Art in Plantagenet England 1200–1400*. London: Royal Academy of Arts, 1987, p. 130 [catalogue 40 discusses the related Apocalypse in Trinity College, Cambridge]; Noppen, John George. "The Westminster Apocalypse and Its Source." *Burlington Magazine* 61 (1936): 146–59; Rickert, Margaret. *Painting in Britain: The Middle Ages*. 2d ed. Harmondsworth: Penguin, 1965; Rigold, Stewart E. *Chapter House and Pyx Chamber Westminster Abbey*. London: HMSO, 1976 [English Heritage, 1985], pp. 21–26; Simpson, Amanda. *The Connections between English and Bohemian Painting during the Second Half of the Fourteenth Century*. New York: Garland, 1984, pp. 169–74.

See also Chapter Houses; Manuscript Illumination, Gothic; Painting, Gothic; Westminster Abbey

Westminster Retable

The Westminster Retable (Westminster Abbey, ca. 1280), despite its poor condition and lack of documentation, is impressive for its singular beauty and sophistication and for the fact that it is the only major 13th-century panel painting to survive from France or England. It was presumably intended as an altarpiece at the back of an altar. Its size, subject matter, and detail all support the theory that it was made for the high altar of Westminster Abbey.

The Westminster Retable is a complex construction of oak, measuring 37.7 by 131.3 inches overall, gilded and decorated with cameos, gems, and enamels (all imitations made of glass, paint, and paste) to evoke the appearance of a golden reliquary. The elaborate frame divides the panel into five vertical compartments. For the center and ends Gothic architectural niches, complete with stained-glass windows, frame standing figures. In between, eight-pointed star medallions against a dark-blue glass background create the Islamic star-and-cross pattern.

To this structure an anonymous artist painted figures and scenes in the courtly Gothic style developed in France during the reign of King Louis IX. The technique incorporates oil, a medium especially suited for subtle modeling. Iconographically the artist was innovative as well. In the center Christ stands blessing and holding an orb on which is painted a miniature landscape. He is flanked by the Virgin Mary and St. John the Evangelist, each holding palm fronds, an arrangement alluding to the Crucifixion but unique. To either side biblical narratives fill the star medallions. The three to survive are rare scenes of Christ's miracles: the Raising of the Daughter of Jairus, the Healing of the Blind Man, and the Feeding of the Five Thousand. At the ends standing saints bracketed the composition: St. Peter on the left, patron saint of Westminster Abbey, was presumably paired with St. Paul on the right.

Compared most often with the Douce Apocalypse, the paintings in the south transept of Westminster Abbey, and other English works, the Westminster Retable also bears comparison with works in Paris and slightly later works by Duccio in Siena.

Pearson M. Macek

Bibliography

Alexander, Jonathan, and Paul Binski, eds. *Age of Chivalry: Art in Plantagenet England 1200–1400*. London: Royal Academy of Arts, 1987, cat. no. 329.

See also Painting, Gothic; Westminster Abbey

Widows and Widowhood

The widow was seen in medieval England as a person without normal familial supports, and many efforts were made to provide for that lack; kings and bishops were said to have a special obligation in her regard. The basic provision throughout the period—and this is true of different levels in society—was to ensure that she would control part of the property that had belonged to her husband and herself during their marriage.

Anglo-Saxon law, common law, and manorial custom all sought to bring this about. Anglo-Saxons of the landed class seem to have arranged for dower provisions and widows' rights in marriage settlements. After the Conquest widows of those who held by military service were provided with dower lands, either estates specified at the time of espousal *(dos nominata)* or a third of the properties held at that time *(dos rationabilis).* In the 13th century the reasonable dower was sometimes extended to mean a third of property that the husband had held during the marriage, thus providing for any increase of fortune that may have occurred in those years.

It was expected that dower be assigned to the deceased's wife within the first 40 days of widowhood. In addition property that she brought to the union and which had been controlled by her husband during the marriage, now returned to her use. Though there was much opposition to these arrangements, by the 13th century they were generally accepted and procedures were available to enforce them. Toward the end of the Middle Ages the marriage settlement came into more common use and removed some of the uncertainty attached to dower and its assignment. Where land was held in socage (free, nonmilitary tenure), the widow commonly received half of her late husband's holding. Among the peasants, much the largest part of the population, the widow was in a relatively better position than her free sisters; half, two-thirds, often all the family's property in land fell to her, at her disposition so long as she could provide the required services to the lord. She could also expect to receive a share of her husband's chattels.

By a custom that may have begun in Anglo-Saxon times and that was general for the first two centuries after the Conquest the widow's share, if there were a surviving child, was a third of his movable property. Where the couple was childless, she received half. Later, as testators obtained more control over their chattels, the custom weakened; sometimes she received more than the customary third, and on occasion she might receive much less. It is difficult to estimate what provision was made for widows at the poorest level of society, in the countryside and in towns. Rarely would there be rights in land, though she probably had a share in whatever chattels the couple possessed.

In the Anglo-Saxon and Norman periods the widow, especially if propertied, was subject to pressure not only to remarry but also to accept the spouse chosen for her. This was true at all levels of society. The king and other lords found control of widows' remarriage an important source of income; widows of the late 12th and early 13th centuries sometimes purchased permission to be free of these demands. In the laws of Cnut, before the Conquest, and later in Magna Carta efforts were made to allow her to remain unmarried or, should she choose otherwise, to select a spouse herself, though subject to approval by her lord. During the later Middle Ages the widow's right in these regards was accepted in principle, though she continued to be subject to pressure from family and lord as to her future state. Even in the late Middle Ages peasant widows, whose property usually required a male presence for its maintenance, were sometimes fined if they refused to remarry. On some manors spouses were chosen for them.

In the latter half of the Middle Ages the widow possessed many advantages. She enjoyed the income from property that had come to her from her family or other sources as well as the lands received in dower. Free from the legal control of a husband and male members of her family, she was in a good position to decide her future and, within the restrictions provided by that choice, to control her person, movements, and properties as she saw fit. Many widows preferred the society of a husband and remarried soon after their bereavement. Here, as in any marriage, there were varied motives; it is clear that some found the administration of estates too arduous and sought a solution to this difficulty.

Some widows entered convents as regular members of the community or with special arrangements for their support and care. Others dedicated themselves to a semireligious life in the world by private vows to the bishop. Still others, and their number has yet to be estimated, continued as heads of households, exercising the rights and obligations proper to the level of society to which they belonged. The widow was free to bequeath all her movable property as she saw fit.

Michael M. Sheehan

Bibliography

Bennett, Judith M. *Women in the Medieval English Countryside: Gender and Household in Brigstock before the Plague.* New York: Oxford University Press, 1987; Faith, Rosamund J. "Peasant Families and Inheritance Customs in Medieval England." *Agricultural History Review* 14 (1966): 77–95; Franklin, Peter. "Peasant Widows' 'Liberation' and Remarriage before the Black Death." *EcHR,* 2d ser. 39 (1986): 186–204; Holderness, B.A. "Widows in Pre-Industrial Society: An Essay upon Their Economic Functions." In *Land, Kinship and the Life Cycle,* ed. Richard M. Smith. Cambridge: Cambridge University Press, 1984, pp. 423–42; Labarge, Margaret Wade. "Three Medieval Widows and a Second Career." In *Aging and the Aged in Medieval Europe,* ed. Michael M. Sheehan. Toronto: Pontifical Institute, 1990, pp. 158–72; Mirrer, Louise, ed. *Upon My Husband's Death: Widows in the Literature and Histories of Medieval Europe.* Ann Arbor: University of Michigan Press, 1992; Razi, Zvi. *Life, Marriage and Death in the Medieval Parish: Economy, Society, and Demography in Halesowen, 1270–1400.* Cambridge: Cambridge University Press, 1980; Rosenthal, Joel T. "Aristocratic Widows in Fifteenth-Century England." In *Women and the Structure of Society,* ed. Barbara J. Harris and Jo Ann K. McNamara. Durham: Duke University Press, 1984, pp. 36–47; Stenton, Doris M. *The English Woman in History.* London: Allen & Unwin, 1957; Walker, Sue Sheridan, ed. *Wife and Widow in Medieval England.* Ann Arbor: University of Michigan Press, 1993.

See also Beaufort, Margaret; Hull; Marriage; Wardship; Wills; Women

Widsith

An OE poem found in the Exeter Book, cataloguing a variety of Germanic legends in 143 lines. *Widsith* has commonly been regarded as a 7th-century poem, but the linguistic evidence for this is not compelling and the dating has been influenced by the assumption that, since the poet seems to have known a wealth of Germanic legends and apparently assumes similar knowledge in his audience, the poem must be relatively close to the period when the legend cycles originated. Yet the only certainty is that it survives in a 10th-century manuscript; even if we suppose that a 7th-century text existed, it is not likely that the extant *Widsith* would have been identical with the original. For example, it is generally agreed that the references to biblical and oriental tribes (at a minimum lines 75 and 82–84) are accretions.

The poem is shaped as if it describes the personal experiences of a poet "Widsith," whose name means "far-traveler." He is introduced in the third person as the man who accompanies Ealhhild to be married to Eormanric, one of the great figures of heroic legend, but the first person is used thereafter as Widsith catalogues, and sometimes comments on, the kings, tribes, and heroes he claims to have known and visited. The poet is fictional, however, and so are his journeys, since the figures named lived at different times between the 4th and 6th centuries. In fact the poem is a kind of manifesto: the importance of the poet in establishing heroic reputation is emphasized and his ability to sing of legendary heroes is dramatically validated by being attributed to hard-won personal experience. An unspoken claim is thereby made for poets as men apart, who have special knowledge that comes from being able to "visit" the world of legend in their imaginations.

Yet the allusive nature of the text should not lead us to assume that the audience could have recognized all the names mentioned or that the poet could have related the adventures of each. Some may actually be common nouns passed off as tribal names in order to enhance the lists, and it is possible that, if *Widsith* originally functioned as a statement of repertoire, the poet was prepared to provide poems subsequently only on those figures to whom he draws attention by means of brief additional details: it may be no accident that these are the ones still known to us in history and legend. But this functional dimension relates more to the genesis of the poem than to its preservation in the Exeter Book, where it was presumably included because it catalogued "historical" knowledge in encyclopedic form. For the modern scholar it is precisely this encyclopedic quality that gives *Widsith* its preeminent position in the study of Germanic legend.

Joyce Hill

Bibliography

PRIMARY

ASPR 3:149–53; Bradley, S.A.J., trans. *Anglo-Saxon Poetry.* London: Dent, 1982, pp. 336–40; Hill, Joyce, ed. *Old English Minor Heroic Poems.* 2d ed. Durham: Durham Medieval Texts, 1994, pp. 12–14, 29–33, 41–42.

SECONDARY

Brown, Ray. "The Begging Scop and the Generous King in *Widsith.*" *Neophilologus* 73 (1989): 281–92; Hill, Joyce. "Widsið and the Tenth Century." *NM* 85 (1984): 305–15.

See also Deor; Exeter Book; Literary Influences: Scandinavian; Minstrels

Wife's Lament, The

A 53-line poem in the Exeter Book, usually classified as one of the elegies, sharing with these poems an intensely personal voice that speaks of the transitory nature of life and happiness from the pain of a stoically endured present. Some scholars would place it (along with *Wulf and Eadwacer*) in the broad category of *Frauenlieder,* a term originally applied to continental popular women's songs. The title *The Wife's Lament* is a 19th-century attribution, and the poem's enigmatic content has given rise to widely varying interpretations—among them that the speaker is a woman, a man, a revenant (someone returned from the dead), or a minor goddess. Grammatical endings in the first two lines, however, indicate strongly that the speaker is female. In recent years the strong woman's voice in *The Wife's Lament* has provided an important locus for feminist strategies of interpretation. Though varied in theoretical approach and subject of inquiry, feminist readings of *The Wife's Lament* aim to defamiliarize the poem and in essence re-present the speaking woman (and by extension woman in OE literature) as an active and effective agent rather than suffering object.

The general line of interpretation for the poem reads the speaker as a woman unwillingly parted from her husband. A variation on this approach sees two men involved, the woman's husband and a lover. The speaker does not provide a detailed narrative of her hardships, but the depth of grief in her separate life is painfully clear. She speaks of her misery in terms of exile or banishment *(wræcsið).* Most readers of the poem see the woman's misery in *The Wife's Lament* as a direct result of her enforced separation from her husband, to whom she refers in heroic terms as lord *(hlaford, frea).* Her husband leaves, possibly going into exile, and in her distress she attempts to follow, describing herself (also in heroic terms) as a lordless exile. Although the causal connection is unclear, at this point in the poem her husband's family plots to separate the couple, and her husband apparently sends her away to live alone.

The woman's solitary dwelling place is vividly detailed in the poem. A cave or tumulus beneath an oak tree shelters her, but her surroundings are wild and alien. Her longing finds no relief in gloomy valleys, high mountains, sharp hedges, and thick briars. While it is possible that this place is as much refuge as exile, she highlights her loneliness by contrasting the happy image of lovers in bed with her own lonely pacing inside her earthen shelter.

The final twelve lines of the poem have been construed variously, depending on whether the speaker's statements about the *geong mon* ("young man") are read as gnomic reflections, reference to an enemy, or reference to her husband. Part of the difficulty of interpretation lies in syntactic ambiguities in lines 45–47. Whatever interpretation one gives these lines, however, the speaker's bitter gnomic conclusion—that one who longs for a beloved will always be unhappy (52b–53)—locates the poem firmly in this world and sets *The Wife's Lament* apart from the consolatory religious closures of both *The Wanderer* and *The Seafarer*.

Katherine O'Brien O'Keeffe

Bibliography

PRIMARY

ASPR 3:210–11; Crossley-Holland, Kevin, trans. "Two Old English Elegies." *Listener* 70 (1973): 741–42 [*Wife's Lament and Husband's Message*]; Leslie, Roy F., ed. *Three Old English Elegies.* Rev. ed. Exeter: University of Exeter, 1988, pp. 47–48, 53–58.

SECONDARY

Belanoff, Patricia A. "Women's Songs, Women's Language: *Wulf and Eadwacer* and *The Wife's Lament.*" In *New Readings on Women in Old English Literature,* ed. Helen Damico and Alexandra Hennessey Olsen. Bloomington: Indiana University Press, 1990, pp. 193–203; Green, Martin. "Time, Memory, and Elegy in *The Wife's Lament.*" In *The Old English Elegies: New Essays in Criticism and Research,* ed. Martin Green. Rutherford: Fairleigh Dickinson University Press, 1983, pp. 123–32; Straus, Barrie Ruth. "Women's Words as Weapons: Speech as Action in 'The Wife's Lament.'" *Texas Studies in Literature and Language* 23 (1981): 268–85. Repr. in *Old English Shorter Poems,* ed. Katherine O'Brien O'Keeffe. New York: Garland, 1994, pp. 335–56; Wentersdorf, Karl P. "The Situation of the Narrator in the Old English 'Wife's Lament.'" *Speculum* 56 (1981): 492–516. Repr. in *Old English Shorter Poems,* ed. Katherine O'Brien O'Keeffe. New York: Garland, 1994, pp. 357–92.

See also Exeter Book; Women in OE Literature; *Wulf and Eadwacer*

Wilfrid of York (ca. 634–709)

Bishop and saint. The son of a Northumbrian thegn, Wilfrid entered Lindisfarne monastery when about fourteen. Between 653 and 659, while on a pilgrimage to Rome, he became acquainted with the Roman liturgy, the Easter question, and the Benedictine Rule. On his return to Northumbria King Oswiu's son Alchfrid, a convert to the Roman ecclesiastical usage, provided Wilfrid land for a monastery at Stanford and about 661, expelling the Celtic monks of Ripon, gave him that house as well.

In 664, to resolve the dispute between the Roman and Celtic factions in the English church, Oswiu called a conference at Whitby. Wilfrid, as Northumbria's main proponent of the Roman usage, was a leading spokesman. The victory at the Synod of Whitby went to Wilfrid and Rome.

About a year later Wilfrid was named bishop of York but,

going to Gaul for his consecration, returned to find that Cedda had been named in his place. Wilfrid's remaining years were filled with disputes that frequently saw him deprived of his offices and forced to flee Northumbria. These controversies centered on the efforts of ecclesiastical officials and rulers of Northumbria to reduce his extensive see and on his personal conflicts with the Northumbrian kings.

Wilfrid twice appealed to Rome for support of his case (680, 703–04), the first Englishman to make such an appeal; on both occasions he received papal approbation. During his absences from Northumbria he served at various times as bishop in Mercia, Wessex, and Sussex and was deeply involved in missionary work, in establishing monasteries, and in church construction. He briefly conducted missionary work among the heathen Frisians. In 705 Osred restored Wilfrid to the Abbey of Ripon and made him bishop of Hexham. He died in October 709, at Oundle, Northamptonshire, en route to visit King Ceolred of Mercia, and was buried at Ripon.

Wilfrid's renown stemmed from his significant role in eliminating the Celtic church discipline from England and setting a precedent of appeal to papal authority. He also contributed greatly to the firm establishment of the Benedictine Rule and the revitalization of church architecture in England.

Miles Campbell

Bibliography

Eddius Stephanus. *Life of Bishop Wilfrid.* Ed. and trans. Bertram Colgrave. Cambridge: Cambridge University Press, 1927; Mayr-Harting, Henry. *The Coming of Christianity to Anglo-Saxon England.* 3d ed. University Park: Pennsylvania State University Press, 1991.

See also Bede; Conversion of the Anglo-Saxons; Cuthbert

William I (1027/28–1087; r. 1066–87)

First Norman king of England; known as "the Conqueror." Born in 1027 or 1028 at Falaise in Normandy, William was the only, but illegitimate, son of Duke Robert of Normandy. His mother, Herleva, was the daughter of a tanner or, more probably, an undertaker of Falaise. Subsequently Robert married her off to a minor noble from the Seine Valley, Herluin de Conteville, by whom she had two further sons, Odo, later bishop of Bayeux (from 1050), and Robert, subsequently (from ca. 1060) count of Mortain.

William became duke of Normandy at the age of seven, when his father died in July 1035 while returning from a pilgrimage to Jerusalem. That he became duke at all, given his age and illegitimacy, was probably due to the lack of other candidates. Though Robert had taken the precaution to have him formally designated duke before departing for the Holy Land, William's rule in Normandy was to face serious challenges for more than twenty years. Law and order collapsed in the duchy during his minority, ducal power and property were usurped by contending nobles, and several members of his court, including some cousins, were murdered in factional disputes. This disorder culminated in a serious rebellion in western Normandy in 1047, led by Count Guy of Brienne, suppressed only with the help of the French king Henry I, who assisted William in defeating the rebels at the Battle of Val-es-Dunes near Caen.

In the years immediately after this success the domestic situation in Normandy was stable enough for William to start aggressive operations on his southern border, capturing the frontier fortresses of Domfront and Alençon in 1051/52. This in turn brought him into conflict with the overlord of Maine, Count Geoffrey Martel of Anjou, and with his erstwhile ally King Henry, and was also followed by renewed revolt in Normandy by a hitherto loyal supporter, his uncle Count William of Arques. The duke's position was saved by his own military prowess and activity, and smashing defeats were inflicted on French armies at Mortemer in 1054 and Varaville in 1057. The latter marked the end of the young duke's struggle for survival.

From 1062 onward William's chief concern seems to have been the acquisition of the county of Maine, after the death of the childless Count Herbert II. He was aided in this by the fact that the new king of France, Philip I, was a minor, while Anjou was weakened by a succession struggle between the sons of Geoffrey Martel. By 1065 William had placed a garrison in Le Mans, installed a Norman bishop, secured the fealty of the leading nobles of the county, and had his eldest son, Robert, recognized as count. But his hold over Maine was never fully consolidated and was to remain a problem for the rest of his life.

In 1051 the childless king of England, Edward the Confessor, had designated William, his cousin, as his successor. One source suggests that the duke visited England in 1051. This seems unlikely, given how difficult his position was in Normandy at that time; probably Archbishop Robert of Canterbury (a Norman) had acted as intermediary while on his way to Rome in that summer. Whether Edward persisted in his intention of having William as his heir also seems doubtful; he may have changed his mind several times. William's chance of securing the succession was much enhanced when his potential rival, Harold of Wessex, Edward's brother-in-law, visited Normandy in 1064 or 1065 and was persuaded or forced to swear fealty to the duke and to support his claim. Many details remain obscure; we cannot be certain why Harold went to Normandy, whether Edward sent him or not, or even the date of his visit.

Nor did it have any immediate effect on the English succession. When Edward died on 5 January 1066 Harold succeeded him. The designation of 1051 and Harold's oath had given William a *casus belli,* and he used them to orchestrate a propaganda campaign to secure recruits from all over France and to gain papal support. The invasion was launched, after some delays, at the end of September 1066, and on 14 October the Norman and English armies met a few miles north of Hastings. After a desperate struggle the English were defeated and Harold killed. Within two months the surviving English magnates and the church leaders had surrendered, and William was crowned king of England in Westminster Abbey on Christmas Day 1066.

This merely marked the start of the conquest of England.

To begin with William sought to emphasize the continuity of his rule with that of Edward, and to use Englishmen in his government. His first earl of Northumbria, Copsi, was an Englishman, and even Archbishop Stigand of Canterbury, whose appointment had been canonically dubious and who was regarded with disapproval by the papacy, was retained until 1070. But widespread rebellion, in the west and north in 1068, and more seriously in the north and in the fen country of East Anglia in 1069 and 1070—the latter with Danish support—led to a major change in policy and the widespread replacement of English landowners by Frenchmen. The king was under obvious pressure to satisfy what Orderic Vitalis called "his envious and greedy Norman followers." So serious was the revolt of 1069 that William resorted to the harshest of measures to quell it, devastating much of Yorkshire to prevent further rebellion and thereby condemning many of the inhabitants to death by starvation. Inured as they were to violence, contemporary chroniclers were shocked by the barbarity of his actions.

But this drastic treatment worked. The last bastion of English resistance, the Isle of Ely, surrendered in 1071. Thereafter William's rule in England was not seriously threatened. There was admittedly another rebellion in 1075, led by the Norman earl Roger of Hereford and the Breton earl Ralph of Norfolk, but this was crushed by William's subordinates, under the direction of Archbishop Lanfranc, while the king remained in Normandy. Indeed, in his later years, William was largely an absentee ruler, not visiting the country at all between 1076 and 1080 and spending eleven of his last fifteen years in Normandy. In his absence England was ruled largely by his half-brother Odo of Bayeux (until his disgrace and imprisonment in 1082) and Lanfranc. Queen Matilda played a similarly crucial role in Normandy until her death in 1083.

After 1070 renewed problems on the Norman frontiers helped to keep William in the duchy. The king suffered the only serious military setback of his life at Dol on the Breton border in September 1076. Relations with the king of France, Philip, deteriorated. Maine became restive under Norman rule. And worst of all, the king's son Robert Curthose rebelled, probably in the spring of 1078. There was an indecisive battle at Gerberoi in eastern Normandy in January 1079, in which William was slightly wounded. Although there was a temporary reconciliation early in 1080, relations remained difficult and Robert went into exile again in 1084. The root of the problem seems to have been Robert's wish to have an independent role in Normandy, of which he had been designated as duke before Hastings, and William's determination to keep his son firmly under supervision.

William's last visit to England came in 1085–86, to organize the defense of the kingdom against a threatened Danish invasion. But the most important result of this visit was the Domesday Book. Its purpose has been much debated. Probably it was a guide to both the resources of the country and the ownership of particular estates, made necessary by the large-scale redistribution of land caused by the Conquest.

The first draft of the Domesday survey was probably nearly completed when William held a court at Salisbury in

August 1086, where he exacted a comprehensive oath of loyalty from his magnates and the more important of their undertenants. Eleven months later, when campaigning at Mantes on the Norman border, he was taken seriously ill. He was carried to Rouen, where he died on 9 September 1087. On his deathbed he agreed to Robert's succession as duke of Normandy, his second surviving son, William Rufus, succeeding as king of England. He was buried at the monastery of St. Étienne at Caen, which he himself had founded a quarter of a century earlier.

Much of William's success came from a partnership with a small group of Norman nobles, such men as William Fitz Osbern, Roger de Montgomery, and his own half-brothers. It was not surprising that this group of seven or eight men were the chief beneficiaries of the Conquest. In ecclesiastical matters his chief adviser was Lanfranc, abbot of St. Étienne at Caen in 1063 and archbishop of Canterbury in 1070. Though favoring the moral reform of the clergy, William was always concerned to vindicate his own control of the church and to limit papal interference. He was not above appointing his half-brother Odo as bishop when the latter was well below the canonical age. After 1066 he was generally content to adopt existing English laws and institutions but to exploit them to the full; contemporaries agreed that his government was harsh and predatory. The Anglo-Saxon Chronicle called him "stern beyond all measure to people who resisted his will."

William was tall, strong, and of harsh voice and imposing appearance, tending to corpulence in later life. He married ca. 1050 Matilda, daughter of Baldwin V of Flanders, by whom he had four sons (one of whom, Richard, died young) and four or perhaps five daughters.

Graham A. Loud

Bibliography

PRIMARY

Chibnall, Marjorie, ed. and trans. *The Ecclesiastical History of Orderic Vitalis.* 6 vols. Oxford: Clarendon, 1969–80; Foreville, Raymonde, ed. and trans. (into French). *Histoire de Guillaume le Conquérant.* Paris: Les Belles Lettres, 1952 [the chronicle of William of Poitiers]; van Houts, Elisabeth M.C., ed. and trans. *The Gesta Normannorum Ducum of William of Jumièges, Orderic Vitalis and Robert of Torigni.* 2 vols. Oxford: Oxford University Press, 1992–95; Wilson, David M., ed. *The Bayeux Tapestry: The Complete Tapestry in Colour.* London: Thames & Hudson; New York: Knopf, 1985 [fascinating illustrated account of the campaign of 1066].

SECONDARY

Barlow, Frank. *Edward the Confessor.* Berkeley: University of California Press, 1970; Bates, David. *Normandy before 1066.* London: Longman, 1982; Bates, David. *William the Conqueror.* London: Philip, 1989 [excellent bibliography]; Douglas, David C. *William the Conqueror.* London: Eyre & Spottiswoode, 1964; John, Eric. "Edward the Confessor and the Norman Succession." *EHR* 94 (1979): 241–67; Le Patourel, John. *The Norman Empire.* Oxford: Clarendon, 1976; Loyn, H.R. *The Norman Conquest.* 3d ed. London: Hutchinson, 1982 [the best of several general books]; van Houts, Elisabeth M.C. "The Origins of Herleva, Mother of William the Conqueror." *EHR* 101 (1986): 399–404.

See also Battle of Hastings; Domesday Book; Edward the Confessor; Harold; Lanfranc; Norman Conquest; Normandy

William II (William Rufus; ca. 1060–1100; r. 1087–1100)

The third of the four sons of William the Conqueror, duke of Normandy, and Matilda of Flanders. Like his elder brothers, Robert Curthose and Richard, Rufus (the sobriquet means "the Red," for his ruddy complexion) was educated as a knight in his father's household. In 1087 the Conqueror, on his deathbed, bequeathed England to Rufus—and may have wanted him also to have Normandy and Maine—because Richard had died and the disloyal Robert was in exile, owing to his premature attempts to succeed to the French fiefs. These, however, Robert obtained while Rufus was negotiating his coronation (at Westminster Abbey, 26 September 1087). The youngest brother, Henry, possibly his mother's heir, got no land at his father's death but succeeded Rufus as king in 1100.

William Rufus was a successful ruler. His basic ambition, to restore and extend the Norman Empire, was helped by his steadiness of character, courage, and chivalry but hampered by his lack of natural dignity. A homosexual, he never married, although it is possible that in 1093 he became engaged to Edith (Matilda), daughter of Malcolm III, king of Scots, and simply deferred the obligation for too long. No skeptic or pagan, he was a considerable benefactor to several English churches. But, like many soldiers, he was irreligious and profane.

With the Norman dominions divided between them, the two brothers Robert and Rufus fought a sporadic war of succession, mainly by seducing each other's vassals and inciting rebellion. This ended in 1096, when Robert decided to go on the First Crusade and borrowed 10,000 marks of silver from Rufus on the security of the duchy. The king, without ever using French titles, effectively governed his disparate group of lands as a unit and began to rectify its damaged frontiers. In the British Isles he was unable to undo the great Welsh insurrection of 1094 but did tame Scotland. In 1092 he occupied Cumbria and Carlisle; after Malcolm's death while raiding England in 1093, he established Malcolm's son Edgar as a grateful client king (1097).

On the Continent Rufus aimed at recovering both his brother's and his father's losses. Campaigns in the Vexin in 1097–98 were inconclusive, but in 1098 he reconquered Maine. In 1099 he was toying with the idea of taking Poitou in pledge for a crusading loan to William IX of Aquitaine. His wars, fought mainly by mercenaries and subsidized allies, were expensive, and he had to exploit his financial and judicial rights extortionately.

A generous master, Rufus was exceptionally well served. His ablest and most trusted minister in England, whom he inherited from his father, was the chaplain Ranulf Flambard, who rose to become chief justiciar and bishop of Durham. In Rufus's reign, after years of innovation, the Anglo-Norman governmental system was consolidated and efficiently developed. The quest for money pressed heavily on all classes, especially on the farmers, the main producers of wealth, and on the church, which was both rich and relatively defenseless. The enlargement of the royal hunting preserves, the forest, was resented by the barons.

Like his father Rufus was determined to remain head of the English church and as free from papal interference as possible. His appointments to bishoprics and royal abbeys, although usually bought, were generally respectable. In 1093, when he thought he was dying, he forced Anselm, the saintly and learned abbot of Bec, to become archbishop of Canterbury. This appointment Rufus lived to regret, for Anselm castigated his immorality and ill-treatment of the church. When Anselm, in despair at his failures, went into exile (1097), Canterbury and the other bishoprics and abbeys that fell vacant were plundered by royal custodians. Rufus avoided papal reprisals by diplomacy and bribes.

In 1100, with Robert Curthose on his way back from the Holy Land with a Sicilian bride and her dowry, Rufus had to decide whether to let his brother redeem Normandy. But on 8 August, when he and his brother Henry were hunting in the New Forest, he was killed by an arrow, shot, it is believed, by Walter Tirel, count of Poix, one of his guests. Although conspiratorial theories have been proposed to explain William's death, such accidents, particularly when deer were driven past hunters stationed at butts, were common. Cut off in his prime, William Rufus's most lasting monument is the great hall in the Palace of Westminster, still an impressive building.

Frank Barlow

Bibliography

PRIMARY

Eadmer. *Historia novorum.* Trans. in *English Historical Documents.* Vol. 2: *1042–1189.* Ed. David C. Douglas and George W. Greenaway. 2d ed. London: Eyre Methuen, 1981 [the chronicle is document no. 107 in this vast collection]; Eadmer. *Vita Anselmi: The Life of St. Anselm, Archbishop of Canterbury.* Ed. and trans. R.W. Southern. London: Nelson, 1962; Whitelock, Dorothy, ed., with David C. Douglas and Susie I. Tucker. *The Anglo-Saxon Chronicle: A Revised Translation.* London: Eyre & Spottiswoode, 1961.

SECONDARY

Barlow, Frank. *William Rufus.* London: Methuen, 1983; Callahan, T., Jr. "The Making of a Monster: The Historical Image of William Rufus." *JMH* 7 (1981): 175–86; Hollister, C. Warren. "The Strange Death of William Rufus." *Speculum* 48 (1973): 637–53; Mason, Emma. "William Rufus: Myth and Reality." *JMH* 3 (1977): 1–20.

See also Anselm; Henry I; Investiture Controversy; William I

William Marshal (ca. 1145–1219)

William served five kings—Henry II, Henry the Young King (Henry II's eldest son), Richard I, John, and Henry III—and rose through their patronage from a landless younger son to earl of Pembroke. In youth he made his name for skill in tournaments; as a mature baron he was the leading authority on feudal custom and a byword for feudal loyalty.

Son of John FitzGilbert (also called John Marshal), the boy William barely escaped death as hostage for his father's allegiance to Stephen. He later came to the attention of Henry II and was appointed guardian for his eldest son. When his young lord died prematurely, William carried out his crusading vow. On returning he served Henry II. In Henry's last retreat before the pursuit of his rebellious son Richard, William saved the day by killing Richard's horse under him.

A few days later Richard became king at his father's death, but he recognized William's loyalty to his feudal lord and took him into his own service. The new king even carried out Henry's promise to marry William to Isabel de Clare, daughter of the earl of Pembroke. Under Richard I William was justice, sheriff, and military leader and marshal in the royal household at the death of his elder brother.

On Richard's death William favored John for the throne over John's nephew Arthur of Brittany. He continued to support John in the Barons' Wars and took part in the negotiations leading to Magna Carta. In 1216 he became regent for the boy king Henry III as his final service to the Angevin line. The description of the Marshal's deathbed in 1219 provides a vivid picture of the values of a feudal baron and his society. His tomb effigy is in the Temple Church, London.

The main source for William Marshal's life is a lengthy poem in Norman French, composed by a professional minstrel at the behest of William's son, William Marshal the Younger, and based on the testimony of John d'Erley, a close companion of the elder William.

Charles R. Young

Bibliography

Crouch, David. *William Marshal: Court, Career, and Chivalry in the Angevin Empire, 1147–1219.* London: Longman, 1990; Duby, Georges. *William Marshal, the Flower of Chivalry.* Trans. Richard Howard. New York: Pantheon, 1985 [emphasizes the ritual and chivalric customs]; Meyer, Paul, ed. *Histoire de Guillaume le Maréchal.* 3 vols. Paris: Société de l'Histoire, 1891–1901 [with a partial translation into modern French]; Painter, Sidney. *William Marshal: Knight-Errant, Baron, and Regent of England.* Baltimore: Johns Hopkins Press, 1933. Repr. Toronto: University of Toronto Press, 1982.

See also Baronial Reform; Chronicles; Court Culture; Eleanor of Aquitaine; Henry II; Henry III; John; Magna Carta; Richard I

William of Malmesbury (ca. 1095–ca. 1143)

Historian and Benedictine monk. William extended the English historical tradition begun by Bede to the first part of the Anarchy (1137–42), in his *Gesta regum Anglorum* (*History of the Kings of England), Historia novella (Recent History),* and *Gesta pontificum Anglorum (History of the Bishops of England).* He attributed the Norman Conquest to a decline in Anglo-Saxon morals and religion. Other works include *Polyhistor* (an anthology of selections from classical and patristic writers), lives of Sts. Wulfstan and Dunstan, a history of Glastonbury, and an account of the miracles of the Virgin. His histories had considerable influence on later historical writings in England and are of literary interest for their numerous biographical and legendary anecdotes.

Lara Ruffolo

Bibliography

PRIMARY

For editions to 1981 see Scott, below; Ouellette, Helen Testroet, ed. *Polyhistor: A Critical Edition.* Binghamton: CEMERS, 1982; Scott, John, ed. and trans. *The Early History of Glastonbury.* Woodbridge: Boydell, 1981 [bibliography, pp. vii–viii, 211–15].

SECONDARY

New *CBEL* 1:758–60; Thomson, Rodney. *William of Malmesbury.* Woodbridge: Boydell, 1987.

See also Anarchy; Bede; Chronicles; Dunstan

William of Ockham (ca. 1285–1347)

Philosopher and Franciscan theologian. William studied in London and Oxford. His writings include commentaries on the *Sentences* of Peter Lombard and lectures on Aristotle's logic and physics and reflect the influence of his fellow Franciscan John Duns Scotus (d. 1308).

Ockham was an outstanding dialectician and theologian, but his outspoken views were not without controversy. Although summoned in 1324 to the papal court at Avignon to justify his teaching on transubstantiation, there was no formal condemnation of his doctrines. His study of the papal constitutions on apostolic poverty led to his involvement in the debate over Franciscan poverty and the attack on John XXII (1316–34) as a heretic. Under the protection of Emperor Louis IV of Bavaria, the political opponent of the pope, Ockham wrote several political works, including the *Dialogue,* where he discussed his views on the errors of the papacy and its rights with respect to the Holy Roman Empire.

Ockham's doctrines marked a turning point in the history of philosophy and theology. He held that logic was separate from theology, that they are both true, and that they represent different kinds of truth. Thus theology cannot be proved by logic. This *via moderna* ("modern way") marked the separation between faith and reason and was a hallmark of late-medieval philosophy.

Ockham is usually associated with the rule of "Ockham's razor." Known also as the law of parsimony or economy, the dictum became a foundation stone of scientific method: the simpler a theory or explanation is, the less chance for error.

Ockham died 10 April 1347 in Munich and was buried in the Franciscan church. His nominalist philosophy, which emphasized the fundamental reality of individually existing things, and his political theory on the limitation of papal power, were to be highly influential in Reformation thought.

Phyllis B. Roberts

Bibliography

Courtenay, William J. "Nominalism and Late Medieval Thought: A Bibliographical Essay." *Theological Studies* 33 (1972): 716–34; Courtenay, William J. "Late Medieval Nominalism Revisited: 1972–1982." *Journal of the History of Ideas* 44 (1983): 159–64; Leff, Gordon. *William of Ockham: The Metamorphosis of Scholastic Discourse.* Manchester: Manchester University Press, 1975; William of Ockham. *Philosophical Writings: A Selection.* Ed. and trans. Philotheus Bohner. Edinburgh: Nelson, 1957.

See also Duns Scotus; Friars; Learning; Science; Universities

William of Palerne

An unrhymed alliterative poem of 5,540 lines, composed in the mid-14th century and thus one of the earliest datable poems of the Alliterative Revival. The author, who names himself William, declares he is writing for Humphrey de Bohun, earl of Hereford and Essex from 1336 to his death in 1361. The poem is a courtly romance of the most exotic sort, rich in fantastic adventure, involving a prince transformed into a werewolf; a wicked stepmother; multiple disguises; and at its center two young lovers, the foundling William and the princess Melior. Its source is the French poem *Guillaume de Palerne* (written ca. 1200), which the English translator treats with freedom and intelligence. About 200 lines are missing from the beginning of the English poem, but the story may be reconstructed from the French text.

William, young son of the king of Sicily, is rescued from his treacherous uncle by a werewolf, who is really the enchanted son of the king of Spain, and is brought up by a cowherd. The emperor of Rome discovers him, admires his grace, and brings him back to his palace, where William and the emperor's daughter Melior fall in love. Their secret idyll is shattered when the emperor betroths Melior to the Greek prince Partenedon. The young couple elope dressed in bearskins and are guided to Sicily by the werewolf, who provides them with deerskins as a change of outfit to elude their pursuers. Once in Sicily, William rescues his widowed mother the queen from the Spanish king, who is attempting to win William's sister Florence for his own son Braundinis, and forces the king to summon his wife to disenchant the werewolf, now revealed as the king's son Alphouns. Alphouns falls in love with Florence, and Braundinis falls for Melior's cousin. Everyone gets married, Alphouns becomes king of Spain, while William succeeds as king of Sicily and emperor of Rome; he rewards his foster father, the cowherd, with an earldom.

Many of the incidents are recognizably drawn from folktales, but, exceptionally among poems of the Alliterative Revival, the central theme is love, touchingly expressed in a soliloquy by Melior (lines 433–570) and in passionate scenes between the lovers (e.g., lines 850–1040). By contrast the battle scenes, at which alliterative poetry characteristically excels, are undistinguished. The writing is at times clumsy, though some of the slackness and ineptitudes are probably due not to the author but to the scribe of the single defective manuscript (Cambridge, King's College 13, part I), copied not long after the poem was composed. From an early date the manuscript was bound with another by a Gloucestershire scribe, and although there are some indications that the author of *William of Palerne* was from the same county, the dialect of the manuscript itself is mixed.

Thorlac Turville-Petre

Bibliography

PRIMARY

Bunt, G.H.V., ed. *William of Palerne: An Alliterative Romance.* Groningen: Bouma's Boekhuis, 1985; Skeat, Walter W., ed. *The Romance of William of Palerne.* EETS e.s. 1. London: Trübner, 1867.

SECONDARY

New *CBEL* 1:435–36; *Manual* 1:34–37, 223–24; Barron, W.R.J. "Alliterative Romance and the French Tradition." In *Middle English Alliterative Poetry and Its Literary Background: Seven Essays,* ed. David A. Lawton. Cambridge: Brewer, 1982, pp. 70–87.

See also Alliterative Revival; Literary Influences: French; Romances; Translation

William of Wykeham (ca. 1324–1404)

Bishop of Winchester. Wykeham came from a modest rural family at Wickham (Hampshire), attended school but not university, and entered the service of Edward III as a surveyor of buildings, rising to the top of the royal administration as chancellor in 1367. He also acquired numerous church benefices, culminating in his bishopric (1367–1404), and became rich. English defeats in France caused him to lose the chancellorship in 1371. He was tried for corruption and deprived of his possessions but returned to favor under Richard II in 1377 and served as chancellor again in 1389–91.

Wykeham used his wealth to endow Winchester College, a school for 70 pupils (founded 1382), and New College, Oxford (founded 1379), for 70 university students recruited from the Winchester pupils. His aim was to train skilled clergy to enhance the worship and learning of the church, and the colleges succeeded in doing so. In design his scheme was grand, original, and influential. It dwarfed all previous university colleges and school endowments, integrated a school and a college more closely than before, and was widely copied later on, notably at Eton College, King's College (Cambridge), Magdalen College (Oxford), and the new cathedral foundations of Henry VIII.

Nicholas Orme

Bibliography

Custance, Roger, ed. *Winchester College: Sixth-Centenary Essays.* Oxford: Oxford University Press, 1992; Moberly, G.H. *Life of William Wykeham, Sometime Bishop of Winchester.* Winchester: Warren, 1887; Orme, Nicholas. *English Schools in the Middle Ages.* London: Methuen, 1973.

See also Bishops; Eton; Schools; Universities; Wainfleet; Winchester College

Wills and Testaments

The practice of distributing property after death seems to have come to the Anglo-Saxons under the influence of Christian missionaries, who urged that individuals be allowed to dispose of some of their wealth by a post mortem gift of alms. By the 9th century many individuals, especially among the wealthier classes, exercised posthumous control over the devolution of at least part of their land and chattels. The element of "gift for the soul" is evident in virtually all testaments (*cwide* in OE) that survive. This religious motive was to remain strong throughout the Middle Ages.

With the coming of the Normans English usage came under greater influence from the testament as developed by canon law, and by the late 12th century the canonical testament, or last will, was becoming the norm. It involved simplified requirements for validity and the appointment of an executor to act for the deceased. As the use of the testament was extended to more and more of the population, the church court became the ordinary supervisor of implementation. It made a preliminary judgment as to the validity of the will, assigned administration of the deceased's property to the executor, received the final account, and dismissed the executor when the will had been implemented. Where there was dispute, the church court usually settled the matter. In cases touching land and in some pleas of debt the matter was settled by the civil courts.

If they were of legal age and capacity, all who had the right to own property had the right to dispose of at least part of it. Children and mentally incompetent adults who owned property were excluded. Under ordinary circumstances members of a religious order were denied ownership of property, though they sometimes made wills that were implemented. Married women, who by common law owned no chattels, had no right to make a will, though their husbands might permit it and often did. Similarly the unfree—the vast majority of the population—were deprived of this right; their lords claimed ultimate control of their chattels. On many manors, however, they were allowed to bequeath part of the movable property. All through the Middle Ages the church applied steady pressure to extend the right of bequest to all adults, and though common law never conceded the point, the teaching seems to have been of major practical importance.

Bequests of chattels were carefully distinguished from those of land. In the custom of the 11th century through the 13th the father of a family was usually allowed to control only one-third of his chattels. These could be given in alms or to other persons or purposes as the testator wished. Of the two remaining thirds one went to the widow, one to the children. Were there no children, the wife received one half and the husband could dispose of the remainder by will. Toward the end of the Middle Ages these restrictions were removed through much of England.

The bequest of land was forbidden by common law before the end of the 12th century. There were exceptions to this in some boroughs, on royal demesne, and on some manors where peasants were occasionally allowed to bequeath their holdings. Resistance to the common-law restriction by the landed classes was constant, and various expedients were developed to circumvent it. Of these the most important was the "use," an act whereby property was granted during the lifetime of an individual to persons of trust who, when the owner died, were expected to deliver it to beneficiaries identified by the donor before death or in his will.

The use could not be enforced by common law, but after attempts by church courts to do so, relief was given by chancery. Many of the cases that appeared before this court from the late 14th century onward involved post mortem distributions of land in this way. In many cases the beneficiary of the use was indicated in the testament of the deceased. This practice was made illegal by the Statute of Uses in 1532, but the reaction to the restriction was so strong that the Statute of Wills was introduced in 1540 to give relief; tenants in fee simple were allowed to dispose of all land in socage tenure and two-thirds of that held in knight service. With this statute the medieval restrictions on the bequest of land came virtually to an end.

Michael M. Sheehan

Bibliography

PRIMARY

Furnivall, Frederick J., ed. *The Fifty Earliest English Wills in the Court of Probate, London: A.D. 1387–1439.* EETS o.s. 78. London: Trübner, 1882; Whitelock, Dorothy, ed. and trans. *Anglo-Saxon Wills.* Cambridge: Cambridge University Press, 1930.

SECONDARY

Beauroy, Jacques. "Family Patterns and Relations of Bishop's Lynn Will-Makers in the Fourteenth Century." In *The World We Have Gained,* ed. Lloyd Bonfield et al. Oxford: Blackwell, 1986, pp. 23–42; Camp, Anthony J. *Wills and Their Whereabouts.* 4th ed. London: Phillimore, for the Society of Genealogists, 1974; Helmholz, R.H. "*Legitim* in English Legal History." *University of Illinois Law Review,* 1984, pp. 659–74; Jennings, John M. "The Distribution of Landed Wealth in the Wills of London Merchants, 1400–1450." *MS* 39 (1977): 261–80; Miskimin, H.A. "The Legacies of London, 1259–1330." In *The Medieval City: In Honor of Robert S. Lopez,* ed. H.A. Miskimin et al. New Haven: Yale University Press, 1977, pp. 209–27; Rosenthal, Joel T. *The Purchase of Paradise.* London: Routledge & Kegan Paul, 1972; Rosenthal, Joel T. "Aristocratic Cultural Patronage and Book Bequests, 1350–1500." *BJRL* 64 (1982): 522–48; Sheehan, Michael M. *The Will in Medieval England from the Conversion of the Anglo-Saxons to the End of the Thirteenth Century.* Toronto: Pontifical Institute, 1963; Sheehan, Michael M. "English Wills and the Records of the Ecclesiastical and Civil Jurisdictions." *JMH* 14 (1988): 3–12.

See also Alms; Chancellor and Chancery; Courts, Ecclesiastical; Law, Anglo-Saxon; Law, Post-Conquest; Mortmain; Widows

Wilton Diptych

The problematic Wilton Diptych (fig. 149), which belonged to Richard II and is now at the National Gallery in London, consists of two small panels (each wing measures 20.9 by 14.6 inches), hinged in the center, painted in egg tempera on oak. The righthand panel has the Virgin and Child surrounded by eleven angels, one of whom carries a small banner. In the lefthand panel Richard kneels toward them supported by two other English kings—St. Edmund and St. Edward the Confessor—as well as St. John the Baptist, his patron saints. This iconography clearly relates to that of the Epiphany (Richard was born at this season) and is seen as emphasizing Richard's divine right of kingship. A further reading of the iconography suggests that he is in the process of being received by the Virgin into heaven to join the company of angels.

The exterior of the diptych has a white hart with golden antlers, gorged with a crown and chained (Richard's livery from 1390), adjacent to the arms of Edward the Confessor impaling the quartered royal arms of France Ancient and England. These devices clearly indicate that the diptych was made for Richard himself. Indeed the use of heraldry is strong in the panels: Richard wears his personal badge of the white hart, as well as a collar of broomcods (the angels wear almost identical collars) and his robe is powdered with a pattern of broomcods encircling white harts. The presence of the broomcods (husks or pods of the broom plant) is puzzling. As a traditional emblem of France their appearance has been taken as a reference to Richard's second marriage. In 1396 he married Isabella, a daughter of Charles VI of France. However, her absence from the diptych has been cited as militating against this argument. Harvey has suggested that Richard deliberately chose this collar as a means of symbolically investing himself with the power and claims of the French king; Richard styled himself as Richard of Bordeaux. The broomcods (*planta genesta,* from which the word "Plantagenet" is derived) may be an allusion to Richard's ancestor, Geoffrey of Anjou.

The vexed question of dating hinges on these heraldic devices. Suggestions for its date range from Richard's succession in 1377 to the 1410s, several years after his death. Clarke and Harvey make a strong case for a date not earlier than ca. 1395/96 and before Richard's death in 1399. Although the emblem of the white hart had been used at the Smithfield tournament of 1390, there is no firm evidence that he assumed the arms of Edward the Confessor before ca. 1394/95–98. As stated, the broomcods could point to the

period of the Anglo-French *détente* of the mid-1390s. Although Richard's youthful appearance in the panel might tell against a date late in his comparatively short life, the painter could have been intentionally idealizing the king, as is often suggested. Further reinforcing this date, however, is a Parisian manuscript, "Un Epistre au Roy Richard" (BL Royal 20.B.vi), written by Philippe de Mézières concerning the Order of the Passion. Clarke has convincingly demonstrated that the banner held by one of the angels in the diptych (representing either redemption or the crusading flag of St. George) resembles that in one of the miniatures in this manuscript, which, in turn, illustrates Richard young and beardless. The manuscript dates to around 1395, when Mézières was founding the Order of the Passion and seeking Richard as one of its chief patrons. Harvey further narrows the date of the diptych to between summer 1394 and autumn 1395, before Richard grew a beard, and suggests that Richard's costume in the panel compares with that in the Mézières miniature.

The above evidence may marginally strengthen the argument in favor of a French origin for the diptych. Surviving English wall and panel paintings of the 1390s show nothing exactly comparable; nor does English illumination of this date offer any closer parallel. In comparison with the painted figures in the Byward Tower of the Tower of London, those in the diptych are well articulated and show greater naturalism. This again raises the question of a date for the diptych, Wormald having made some convincing parallels with English miniature painting of the first and second decades of the 15th century. He has compared the style of the right panel with the

Annunciation miniature in BL Royal 2.A.xviii of ca. 1403/04–10 and relates the faces to certain portrait heads of the Beaufort Hours (BL Add. 42131) of ca. 1414–20. Although this affinity cannot be denied, Wormald's theory—one supported by Panofsky—that the diptych was a memorial to Richard after his reburial at Westminster Abbey in 1413, is no longer widely accepted. Panofsky believed the work to be English, seeing it as an "Anglicisation of both the Flemish and French traditions."

If datable to the 1390s, it is with extant Parisian work that the closest stylistic correspondences exist. Not only does the often cited Brussels Hours (Brussels, Bibliothèque Royale 11060–61) have two adjacent miniatures that bear a striking formal parallel with the diptych, but like the diptych the faces have both the soft and more rugged types. This does not imply that the diptych is the work of more than one hand but suggests that these differences arose from iconographic factors. If a later date is thought tenable, then the extreme delicacy of the draperies and facial types so notable in the diptych compares with the work of the Limbourg brothers in the *Très riches heures* of Jean, duc de Berry, of 1413–16 (Chantilly, Musée Condé 65). The source of the style of the diptych might equally be sought in Burgundian painting of the 1390s of the circle of Jean Malouel. The sculptured facade of the Chartreuse de Champmol at Dijon by Claus Sluter, of the same decade, has two donors kneeling before the Virgin and Child, supported by their patron saints, and it is therefore reminiscent of both the Wilton Diptych and the Brussels Hours. Although the iconography of the Maestà is Italian, placing the Virgin and

Child in a direct relationship with the kneeling donor, supported by a patron saint (or saints), is an idea that was current in French courtly circles at that date. Perhaps the enigmatic diptych was produced in England by a Franco-Flemish painter.

Although both the date and country of origin of the diptych will remain controversial issues, there is no denying that it is a masterpiece of International Gothic painting, outstanding in quality and in the delicacy of its technique.

Scholars have further speculated as to the role of the diptych. Was it intended for private devotion in the context of a chapel, such as Westminster Abbey, or for Richard to take with him for this purpose on campaign, such as those to Ireland in 1394 and 1399?

Lynda Dennison

Bibliography

Alexander, Jonathan, and Paul Binski, eds. *Age of Chivalry: Art in Plantagenet England 1200–1400.* London: Royal Academy of Arts, 1987, pp. 134–35, 178, and fig. 104 [also mentioned under cat. nos. 448, 613, 659, 696, 713]; Clarke, Maude V. "The Wilton Diptych." In *Fourteenth Century Studies,* ed. L.S. Sutherland and M. McKisack. Oxford: Oxford University Press, 1937, pp. 272–92; Dunkerton, Jill, et al. *Giotto to Dürer: Early Renaissance Painting in the National Gallery.* New Haven: Yale University Press, 1991, pp. 236–39; Gordon, Dillian. *Making and Meaning: The Wilton Diptych.* London: National Gallery, 1993; Harvey, John H. "The Wilton Diptych—A Re-examination." *Archaeologia* 98 (1961): 1–28; Panofsky, Erwin. *Early Netherlandish Painting: Its Origin and Character.* Cambridge: Harvard University Press, 1953, pp. 118, 404–05; Rickert, Margaret. *Painting in Britain: The Middle Ages.* 2d ed. Harmondsworth: Penguin, 1965; Simpson, Amanda. *The Connections between English and Bohemian Painting during the Second Half of the Fourteenth Century.* New York: Garland, 1984, pp. 178–81; Wormald, Francis. "Wilton Diptych." *JWCI* 17 (1954): 191–203.

See also Iconography; Manuscript Illumination, Gothic; Painting, Gothic; Richard II

Winchester

The settlement of Winchester, where the east-west route across the Hampshire chalk downs crosses the River Itchen, has been traced to the 1st century B.C. and was already substantial by the time of the Roman invasion. The Romans built the walls that gave the city its shape throughout the Middle Ages and laid out a rectilinear street plan. Evidence suggests some structural continuity from the Romans into the 9th-century era of Alfred the Great, when the defenses were restored and the street plan redrawn. The river served as a source of water power for several mills, but its use as an artery of transport was always limited and did not extend into the central Middle Ages.

The administrative history of Winchester includes the development and interaction of three distinct authorities: the customs and institutions of the townsmen, of the bishop, and of the king. The townsmen enjoyed laws, customs, and physical boundaries even before the time of Alfred, and these seem always to have served as a strong force in the daily life of the community. By the late 12th century these indigenous elements of administration became embodied in the institutions of the merchant guild and came to be recognized by royal charter.

By 1200 the community came to have a mayor as its spokesman before the king, a common seal, and a governing structure including meetings of bailiffs and citizens, with the mayor and bailiffs remaining closely linked with the guild. At about the same time St. John's Hospital came to serve as both the center of local religious and charitable activities and the meeting place of the mayor and citizens. The city proper continued under the governance of the mayor and, by the 13th century, the familiar formulation of a council of 24 and a larger assembly representing the free citizenry, all under the authority of the king. This arrangement survived for the remainder of the medieval era.

The presence of several ecclesiastical institutions created a second locus of authority. The bishop held more city land than anyone save the king. His soke—the land directly under his control—included much of the area immediately surrounding the town and some land within it; by the mid-13th century this was already administratively distinct from the rest of the city. Hyde Abbey, St. Mary's Abbey, and Winchester College held important claims as well. Like many towns with an active ecclesiastical presence Winchester experienced frequent friction between its secular leaders and the bishop's officers throughout the period.

In addition to these two forces, and following from its close ties to the West Saxon kings, Winchester also constituted a royal borough from an early date. With London it served as the seat of royalty at the Norman Conquest and for a time thereafter. The king's reeves presided over various administrative functions in the 11th century, and by the 13th century the king's interests seem to have been represented by royal bailiffs. The royal palace and the king's castle both symbolized and invited the royal presence, just as the cathedral did the bishop's, and the guildhall the townsmen's.

The economic vitality of medieval Winchester depended more on its early role as a royal city and its rivalry with London than upon any other factors. When London nosed it out, both as an economic center and as the de facto capital city, both of which had been accomplished by the 14th century, Winchester declined to the level of most other provincial centers. Its religious institutions, commerce, and manufacturing remained in place, but especially the last two of these were subject to the usual vagaries of economic conditions.

Whether measured in assessed wealth, economic resources, or the vitality of industry and trade, Winchester's economic position underwent a gradual and relative but nevertheless long-term decline between the 12th and the 16th centuries. It ranked seventeenth among English towns in its tax quota, as calculated in 1334; 29th in tax-paying population, as assessed in 1377; 37th in the subsidy ranking of

1523–27. Though its clothing industry temporarily arrested this slide at the end of the 14th century, the Reformation found Winchester once again in physical decay, substantially smaller in population and area than in the 14th century, and its corporate government was plagued by frequent fiscal shortfalls.

Robert Tittler

Bibliography

Barlow, Frank, Martin Biddle, O. von Feilitzen, and Derek Keene. *Winchester in the Early Middle Ages.* Oxford: Oxford University Press, 1976; Furley, J.S. *City Government of Winchester from the Records of the XIV & XV Centuries.* Oxford: Clarendon, 1923; Keene, Derek. *Survey of Medieval Winchester.* 2 vols. Oxford: Oxford University Press, 1985.

See also Alfred; Towns; Winchester Cathedral; Winchester College; Winchester Old Minster

Winchester Cathedral

Winchester was the capital of later Anglo-Saxon England, and its Anglo-Saxon cathedral, the Old Minster (figs. 151–52: see WINCHESTER OLD MINSTER), is better known from archaeological excavation than any other. As with most important Anglo-Saxon churches the Old Minster grew outward from an early and modest core to become by the 10th century a building of several sections, with an extended eastern arm ending in a rectangular chapel and a large west block, several times rebuilt, that sheltered the tomb of St. Swithun. In spite of its size and antiquity this church was replaced by the first Norman bishop, Walkelin, by a much larger church set immediately to its south and east.

The Norman cathedral was begun in 1079 and may have been close to completion when Walkelin was buried in it in 1098. Walkelin's church, one of the largest in Romanesque Europe, seems to have incorporated features from diverse sources. The extended apse may be homage to the Old Minster, but most other features of the new cathedral's design were culled from the latest trends in European Romanesque. The three-storied elevation and most of its details are orthodox Norman Romanesque, although the alternating piers of the choir may have been chosen as a reference to the rival royal abbey church at Westminster. The aisled transepts, on the other hand, seem to be part of a general European fashion of the later 11th century, seen most famously in the "pilgrimage" churches of the Continent. The multiplicity of towers originally planned, including a crossing tower, a western tower or towers, and towers flanking the transept facades, suggests rivalry with the imperial cathedrals of the Rhineland. Even the dimensions of the building may make reference to another church, Old St. Peter's in Rome.

Except for the replacement of the original crossing tower, which collapsed in 1107, this prodigious building was not seriously altered before the addition of an early Gothic retrochoir (fig. 150) and Lady Chapel begun about 1202 by Bishop de Lucy. This eastern addition was probably inspired

Fig. 150. Winchester Cathedral retrochoir from the northwest, with Bishop William Wainfleet's chantry chapel. Courtesy of L. Hoey.

by the new eastern work at Canterbury, although its hall-church form has no parallel there. As at Canterbury its function may have been to provide a new and elegant setting for the house saint, in this case St. Swithun, although the evidence is ambiguous. The piers, with their detached Purbeck marble shafts, the complex arch and rib moldings they support, and the elegant outer walls with their dado arcades and double lancets are all characteristic of the mature Early English style.

The next major alterations to Winchester Cathedral were not made until the mid-14th century. The most important of these was the rebuilding of the Norman nave. Much of the Romanesque masonry seems to have been left in place, but recut to Perpendicular forms: the heavy compound piers, the unbroken vertical vault shafts of a fair diameter, and the thickness of wall illustrated by the arcade arches and the recessed clerestory windows. The elevation reads as two stories, with a prominent balustrade dividing the arcade and clerestory. Halfway up the latter springs a complex tierceron and lierne vault, anchored by an unbroken ridge rib and decorated with numerous foliate bosses. This vault is structurally a seemingly archaic pointed barrel with interpenetrations over the clerestory windows, an indication of how dominant visual pattern had become in English Gothic by that date. The nave rebuilding was begun by Bishop Edington before his death in 1366, but the bulk of the work was done under Bishop Wykeham by his mason, William Wynford, in the 1390s. The Norman choir was also rebuilt piecemeal in the later Middle Ages, the main elevation dating from the mid-14th century, while the aisles and wooden vault are early-16th-century.

Lawrence Hoey

Bibliography

Crook, John. "The Romanesque East Arm and Crypt of Winchester Cathedral." *JBAA* 142 (1989): 1–36; Crook, John, ed. *Winchester Cathedral, 900 Years: 1093–1993.* Chichester: Phillimore, 1993; Crook, John, and Yoshio Kusaba. "The Transepts of Winchester Cathedral: Archaeological Evidence, Problems of Design, and Sequence of Construction." *Journal of the Society of Architectural Historians* 50 (1991): 293–310; Draper, Peter. "The Retrochoir of Winchester Cathedral." *Architectural History* 21 (1978): 1–17; Draper, Peter. "The Retrochoir of Winchester Cathedral: Evidence and Interpretation." *JBAA* 139 (1986): 68–74; Gem, Richard. "The Romanesque Cathedral of Winchester: Patron and Design in the Eleventh Century." *BAACT* 6 (1983): 1–12; Willis, Robert. "The Architectural History of Winchester Cathedral." *Proceedings of the Archaeological Institute of Great Britain and Ireland, 1845.* London: Longman, Brown, Green, and Longmans, 1846. Repr. in Robert Willis, *Architectural History of Some English Cathedrals.* 1st ser. Chicheley: Minet, 1972; Woodman, Francis. "The Retrochoir of Winchester Cathedral: A New Interpretation." *JBAA* 136 (1983): 87–97.

See also Sculpture, Gothic; Sculpture, Romanesque; Winchester; Winchester Old Minster

Winchester College

The college of St. Mary Winchester was founded in 1382 by William of Wykeham, bishop of Winchester, providing for "seventy poor and needy scholars, clerks, living collegewise . . . studying and becoming proficient in grammaticals or the art and science of [Latin] grammar." Wykeham had already founded New College, Oxford; the two colleges were essentially complementary. The pattern was deliberately followed by Henry VI in the 1440s, when he founded Eton College and King's College, Cambridge, appointing the Winchester master, William Wainflete, as the first master at Eton.

Revised statutes of 1400, operative until 1857, provided for a warden, two fellows, three chaplains, three chapel clerks, sixteen choristers, 70 scholars, and a master and usher. In addition up to ten fee-paying boarding commoners could be admitted. Collegiate foundations were in essence religious institutions, but educational activities were given unusual prominence here; by the early 15th century the school's reputation was attracting pupils as commoners (many, probably, as day-boys) in large numbers.

The highly prized scholarships, meanwhile, were allocated by election to poor scholars aged between eight and twelve who had to be proficient in reading, plainsong, and Latin grammar. Preference was to be given first to the founder's kin, then to inhabitants of places where Wykeham's two colleges possessed estates, then to natives of Winchester diocese, then to inhabitants of a band of counties in southern England, and finally to any inhabitants of England.

For the remainder of the Middle Ages Winchester's pupils, from whom New College recruited exclusively, amply fulfilled the founder's intentions to educate men for the service of the church. There is little information about the curriculum or teaching methods before the Reformation, but the college archives contain a wealth of records relating to estates, administration, and buildings, among which the 1394 schoolroom is still in existence.

Helen M. Jewell

Bibliography

Custance, Roger, ed. *Winchester College: Sixth-Centenary Essays.* Oxford: Oxford University Press, 1982; Himsworth, Sheila, ed. *Winchester College Muniments.* 3 vols. Chichester: Phillimore, for the Warden and Fellows of Winchester College, 1976–84; Leach, Arthur Francis. *A History of Winchester College.* New York: Scribner, 1899.

See also Eton; Schools; Wainfleet; William of Wykeham; Winchester

Winchester Old Minster

Old Minster, the first cathedral of Winchester, was known only through documents until excavations between 1962 and 1969 uncovered the largely robbed foundations on a site just north of the present cathedral. From the archaeological evidence, which constitutes essentially a negative imprint of the plan, a complex structural sequence could be determined (figs. 151–52). Spanning four and a half centuries, two major building periods are evident with the early Saxon church incorporated into the late Saxon design.

The earliest structure is identified as the church built by Cenwealh, king of Wessex (642–72), and dedicated to Sts. Peter and Paul. It consists of an aisleless nave, rectangular porticus north and south, and a square east end. Of four circular foundations appearing at regular intervals along the interior nave the easternmost is identifiable as the main altar by four surrounding postholes, which probably held supports for a canopy. The cruciform layout of the plan based on a system of proportions suggests continental prototypes.

In the 8th century a detached tower dedicated to SS. Martin was built 65 feet from the west front. This was followed by the transformation of the east end into a semicircular apse, including new piers for a chancel arch. No further alterations were made to the original design until the early 10th century, when two massive wings were attached to the western end of the nave, thus forming a great facade.

Included in this phase of the structural sequence is a tomb-house built between the church and tower to mark the

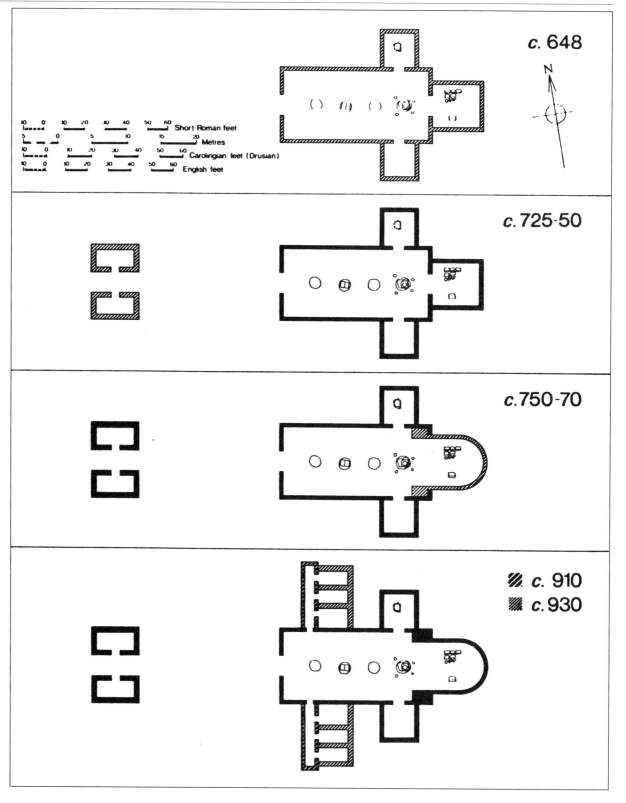

Fig. 151. Plan of Winchester Old Minster, ca. 648–ca. 930. Plan: M. Biddle, published in Butler and Morris (1986). Courtesy of the Council for British Archaeology.

burial site of St. Swithun, who was bishop of Winchester from 852 to 862 and became the central figure of worship in the 10th century. It was in his honor that Old Minster was reconstructed and greatly enlarged during the episcopates of bishops Æthelwold (963–84) and Alphege (984–1006). Commencing in 971 with the translation of Swithun's relics indoors, a large, double-apsidal structure was then built over his gravesite, linking the west front of the old church to St. Martin's Tower. A few years later massive additions north and south transformed this into a square westwork modeled on continental examples.

At this stage a tomb-chamber was built around Swithun's shrine, which, based on documentary evidence, probably con-

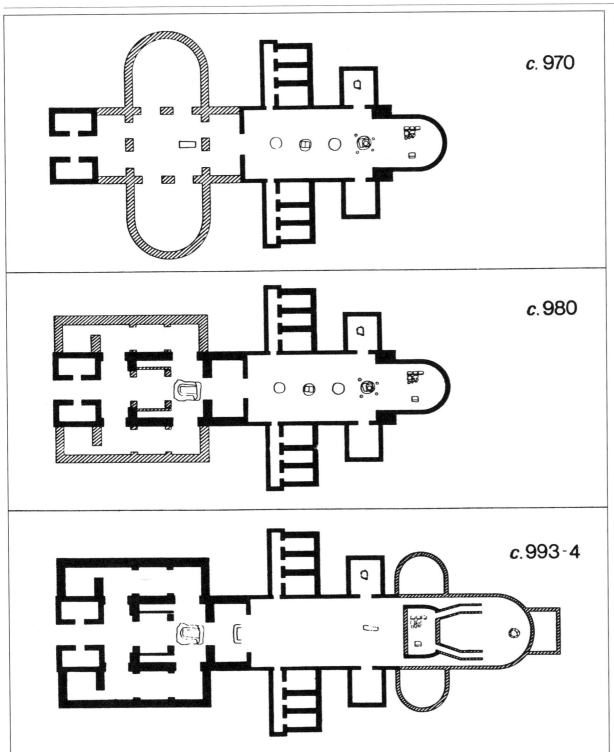

c. 970

c. 980

c. 993-4

Fig. 152. Plan of
Winchester Old
Minster, ca. 970–
ca. 993/94. Plan: M.
Biddle, published in
Butler and Morris
(1986). Courtesy of
the Council for British
Archaeology.

tained half of the saint's relics in a portable reliquary. The other half seems to have been connected to the high altar that was raised above a new, *confessio*-type crypt incorporating the old east end. The addition of smaller lateral apses, echoing those of the earlier link building, may further indicate the presence of Swithun's relics in these sections of the church. Beyond the altar the apse was greatly extended, ending in an exterior crypt at the eastern tip.

The 10th-century additions to the Old Minster reflect changes in the liturgy and the growing importance of pilgrimage and royal ceremony, which in turn relate to Winchester's position as the center of royal authority and monastic reform. The Anglo-Saxon cathedral received its final dedication ca. 993–94, only to be demolished a century later to make way and provide building material for its Norman successor.

Regina D'Innocenzi

Bibliography

Biddle, Martin. *The Old Minster: Excavations near Winchester Cathedral 1961–1969.* Winchester: Wykeham Press, 1970; Biddle, Martin, and Birthe Kjølbye Biddle. *The Anglo-Saxon Minsters at Winchester.* Winchester Studies 4(i), forthcoming; Butler, Lawrence A.S., and Richard K. Morris, eds. *The Anglo-Saxon Church: Papers on History, Architecture and Archaeology in Honour of Dr H.M. Taylor.* CBA Research Report 60. London: CBA, 1986; Fernie, Eric. *The Architecture of the Anglo-Saxons.* London: Batsford, 1983; Quirk, R.N. "Winchester Cathedral in the Tenth Century." *ArchJ* 114 (1957): 28–68; Taylor, Harold M. *Anglo-Saxon Architecture.* Vol. 3. Cambridge: Cambridge University Press, 1978; Yorke, Barbara A.E. "The Foundation of the Old Minster and the Status of Winchester in the Seventh and Eighth Centuries." *Proceedings of the Hampshire Field Club and Archaeological Society* 38 (1982): 75–83.

See also Architecture, Anglo-Saxon; Bishops; Monasticism; Winchester; Winchester Cathedral

Winchester Organa

The 173 organa notated in Cambridge, Corpus Christi College 473 (one of the Winchester tropers), constitute the only large repertoire of European polyphony written down before that associated with St. Martial-de-Limoges in the 12th century. A total of 157 of the 173 belong to a first layer notated ca. 1000; the major part of the rest were notated during the following 50 years. No organa appear in the other Winchester troper (Bodleian Library, Bodley 775), which is not in any case a sister manuscript.

The Winchester corpus includes settings for both the Ordinary and Proper of the mass (processional antiphons, Kyrie, Gloria, Alleluia, Sequence, Tract) and for the office (Invitatory, Responsory). Just over 100 organa (a proportion of two-thirds) relate to the mass; the rest relate to the office. Although parts of this large polyphonic repertoire suggest the intention to create cycles for the liturgical year (especially the 55 Alleluia settings) or substantial sets for specific feasts (the groups of Matins responsories for Trinity, St. Swithun, and an evangelist's feast), in no sense does the recorded material represent completion of such a project.

The arrangement of the organa in correct liturgical sequence, and by type in separate gatherings, however, argues against any sense in the planning of the manuscript that gaps remained to be filled. It is easier to appreciate the nature of this repertoire against a background of unwritten practice, the improvisation of accompanimental voice lines according to prescribed rules. What is notated in this Winchester book may then be understood as specific examples that were written down and thereby preserved because of their special qualities (the fact that they represent particularly successful organal accompaniments, for example). Although the organa are often repetitive, using the same accompanimental pattern to match common chant phrases and idioms, they also show a significant degree of deliberate variation in such situations.

This variation can often be explained as a response to structural qualities of the specific chant. There is thus a sense in which it can be argued that "the notated organa are to some extent composed music" (Fuller).

The organa are notated in semidiasematic insular neumes (i.e., they are only partially heighted in relation to pitch) and as single lines, without the chant voices on which they are based. Because of the difficulties of identifying the exact versions of chant melodies for which the organa were formulated, as well as those of interpretation of the notation, it is not possible to arrive at definitive reconstructions. Nevertheless, with knowledge of the main procedures employed—movement parallel to the chant at an interval of a fourth below, the holding of one tone against a moving chant voice, the observance of boundaries beyond which, in given situations, the organal voice does not move, and the arrival at a unison with the chant at points of cadence *(occursus)*—it is possible to make useful transcriptions and thus to understand something of the stylistic aesthetic of the organa.

While conforming in significant ways to the strategies spoken of by contemporary theorists, the organa represent an individual local repertoire, worked out according to its own conventions and rules. The name of Wulfstan, cantor at Winchester, poet, and author of a musical treatise (no longer extant) and of a long description of the magnificent Winchester organ, has been associated with both composition and notation of the organa. No identified example of his script survives, making this impossible to prove. In their unusually literary rubrics and their artful nature the Winchester organa can be set alongside the Winchester tropes as evidence of considerable interest in sophisticated musical techniques at Winchester in the years before and after the millennium.

Susan K. Rankin

Bibliography

Frere, Walter Howard. *The Winchester Troper: From Manuscripts of the Xth and XIth Centuries.* Henry Bradshaw Society 8. London: Harrison, 1894; Fuller, Sarah. "Early Polyphony." In *The Early Middle Ages to 1300.* The New Oxford History of Music 2. ed. Richard Crocker and David Hiley. Rev. ed. Oxford: Oxford University Press, 1990, pp. 485–556; Holschneider, Andreas. *Die Organa von Winchester: Studien zum ältesten Repertoire polyphoner Musik.* Hildesheim: Olms, 1968; Rankin, Susan. "Winchester Polyphony: The Early Theory and Practice of Organum." In *Music in the Medieval English Liturgy: Plainsong and Mediaeval Music Society Centennial Essays,* ed. Susan Rankin and David Hiley. Oxford: Clarendon, 1993, pp. 59–100; Reckow, Fritz. "Organum." *NGD* 13: 796–819.

See also Mass, Polyphonic Music for; Trope; Winchester Tropers

Winchester Psalter

BL Cotton Nero C.iv (fig. 153) contains the Psalms and Canticles in both Latin and Anglo-Norman French and 42 prayers in Latin, some with Anglo-Norman French versions. The text is preceded by a 38-page miniature cycle including scenes from the life of Christ, the life of the Virgin, and the Last Judgment, with inscriptions in Anglo-Norman French. Initials containing scenes from the life of David and floral ornament accompany the text.

The approximate date and provenance of the manuscript have been established on the basis of entries in the calendar and text. The absence of an entry for St. Edward the Confessor suggests that the manuscript was completed before his canonization in 1161. The association with Winchester was suggested on the basis of one of the private prayers following the psalms, which is addressed to St. Swithun and states that the petitioner offers his prayer in the house *(aula)* of the saint. This points to the Priory of Winchester Cathedral, since it was dedicated to St. Swithun.

The importance of the manuscript is due mainly to its extensive miniature cycle, which with 82 separate subjects is one of the most extensive cycles to survive from the mid-12th century. The choice of scenes, their iconography, and the juxtaposition of certain scenes are unusual and noteworthy. Equally significant is the way the artist enlivened the cycle with some of the most expressive caricatures in English art.

The style of 35 of the illuminated pages first appears in the Bury Bible (Cambridge, Corpus Christi College 2) in the 1130s. It is characterized by byzantinizing head and body types and by the use of wet or clinging drapery that falls over the figures in curvilinear folds. Another distinctive feature of the style is the use of large, luxuriant flowers with fine striations and hanging berries. Both the figural and floral compositions are more highly stylized and mannered than those in the Bury Bible, supporting a date around the middle of the century. They are also carried out primarily in a line-and-wash technique, with solid blue backgrounds, in contrast to the Bury Bible's rich body color. Two full-page miniatures depicting the Death of the Virgin and the Virgin Enthroned stand apart from the rest in their use of opaque body color and in their remarkably byzantinizing style, for which many direct parallels with contemporary Byzantine art have been suggested and which may have been intended to emphasize their similarity to eastern icons.

The iconography of the miniatures was derived from a wide range of sources. The illustrations from Genesis and Exodus incorporate a wealth of details that ultimately reflect an ancient tradition. Wormald detected Byzantine elements, while Haney emphasized western models having much in common with the early Christian Cotton and Vienna Genesis manuscripts. There are numerous indications, however, that this ancient source had already passed through the hands of Anglo-Saxon artisans, and it is generally agreed that Anglo-Saxon sources also influenced the David scenes. The New Testament illustrations incorporate not only Anglo-Saxon features but also others reflecting Ottonian art and models developed in 12th-century English and continental centers. One page, fol. 4, stands apart from the rest in that it illustrates Old Testament and apocryphal New Testament subjects. The exact identification of some subjects and reasons for their juxtaposition remain controversial. Wormald and Haney empha-

Fig. 153. Winchester Psalter (BL Cotton Nero C.iv), fol. 48. Angel locking the door to hell. Reproduced by permission of the British Library.

size themes related to the Virgin and her ancestors, while Cahn, Witzling, and Henderson stress the importance of Old Testament kingship.

Kristine E. Haney

Bibliography

Cahn, Walter. "The Tympanum of the Portal of Saint-Anne at Notre Dame de Paris and the Iconography of the Divisions of the Powers in the Early Middle Ages." *JWCI* 32 (1969): 55–72; Haney, Kristine Edmondson. *The Winchester Psalter: An Iconographic Study.* Leicester: University of Leicester Press, 1986; Henderson, George. "'Abraham Genuit Isaac': Transitions from the Old Testament to the New Testament in the Prefatory Illustrations of Some 12th-Century English Psalters." *Gesta* 26 (1987): 127–39; Kauffmann, C. Michael. *Romanesque Manuscripts 1066–1190.* A Survey of Manuscripts Illuminated in the British Isles 3, ed. J.J.G. Alexander. London: Harvey Miller, 1975; Witzling, Mara. "The Winchester Psalter: A Reordering of Its Prefatory Miniatures according to the Scriptural Sequence." *Gesta* 23 (1984): 17–25; Wormald, Francis. *The Winchester Psalter.* London: Harvey Miller, 1973.

See also Manuscript Illumination, Romanesque; Winchester

"Winchester School" of Illumination

In the century before the Norman Conquest southern England witnessed one of the great flowerings of medieval art.

From the time of Warner's 1910 publication of the Æthelwold Benedictional (BL Add. 49598; fig. 26: see BENEDICTIONAL OF ÆTHELWOLD) and Homburger's 1912 study of Winchester books works from this region and period have been attributed to the "Winchester School." The primary center was the ecclesiastical and royal city of Winchester, where the style originated, but it was not confined to that city, flourishing in other reformed Benedictine monasteries including Canterbury and Glastonbury. While a chronological development is discernible, many "Winchester School" manuscripts cannot be securely dated or located on the basis of painting style alone. This fact reflects considerable mobility among the monastic artists and also widespread English receptivity to the characteristics of the style.

Works of the Winchester School fuse a distinctive and expressive figural style with lush acanthus ornament entwined in golden frames. Figures, foliage, and frames interpenetrate, the forms of foliage and drapery in particular echoing each other and creating animated compositions with unrivaled decorative qualities. Deshman has emphasized the latent insular character of these highly ornamental pages, in many of which a *horror vacui* and lack of real space hark back to Hiberno-Saxon art.

The generally well articulated figures of the school are based on monumental and classicizing English figures of around 950, labeled by Wormald the "first style." The essentially sober figures are energized by numerous stylistic devices: fabric hems flare in multiple trumpet folds and flickering pleats, while amply folded draperies are enhanced with glittering and dynamic patterned lines that often hide the body completely. Both Wormald and Alexander have emphasized the Carolingian components of the style, though Wormald felt that it could not derive entirely from Carolingian art. Deshman identified the extra element as a strong Middle Byzantine contribution, pointing in particular to the characteristic use of linear double-line folds. The blend of disparate stylistic elements was subordinated to an insular taste for intricate linear decoration, resulting in the distinctive figures of the "school."

No less distinctive are the frames, and here again there was creative synthesis in response to indigenous taste. Fleshy and classicizing acanthus ornament from the Carolingian Metz School was married to paired, bossed frames of the Franco-Saxon School. The Winchester masterwork, Æthelwold's Benedictional, shows numerous variations on these frames. Early in the book the foliage is confined within the parallel boundaries; further on it bursts out and twines exuberantly through the bars, creating what is essentially 10th-century interlace. Later manuscripts have frames with more attenuated or straggly acanthus.

The "Winchester style" appeared in a developed form in the New Minster Charter of 964 (BL Cotton Vespasian A.viii; fig. 101: see NEW MINSTER CHARTER) and was almost immediately brought to a peak in the Æthelwold Benedictional. Its formula of luxuriantly framed initial pages facing framed miniatures was repeated in a closely related but slightly later pontifical now in Rouen (Bibliothèque Municipale Y.7), and

in the early-11th-century "Missal" of Robert of Jumièges (Rouen, Bibliothèque Municipale Y.6). Lush Winchester frames decorate many important Gospel books, including Cambridge, Trinity College B.10.4, and the Grimbald Gospels (BL Add. 34890); the latter incorporates unique iconography into roundels in the frames, and several other Gospel books have figural decorations at these points. Other manuscripts of the school also varied the synthesis. Particularly influential was the Ramsey Psalter, copied between 974 and 986 (BL Harley 2904), in which acanthus ornament married to a Franco-Saxon letter structure yielded the first of a long series of magnificent Beatus initials in English psalters. A monumental full-page Crucifixion in the same manuscript was executed in the expressive medium of colored line drawing that was really a reinterpretation of the linear Winchester figural style and was to become a prominent element in art of the Winchester School in the 11th century.

The restless, energetic tendencies of Winchester figural style increased toward the millennium, when they were complemented by the exposure of Anglo-Saxon artists to the Carolingian Utrecht Psalter. This 9th-century masterpiece of illusionistic drawing was copied at Canterbury in the 11th century, and elements of both its iconography and its style were absorbed into the southern English vocabulary. These were manifest in many 11th-century drawings, including those of the New Minster Liber Vitae and Ælfwine Prayerbook (BL Stowe 944 and Cotton Titus D.xxvi and xxvii), and a psalter of unknown origin, Paris, BN lat. 8824.

As the 11th century progressed, the English love of pattern reasserted itself in Winchester School depictions of figure and drapery. This can be seen particularly in the Tiberius Psalter of about 1060 (BL Cotton Tiberius C.vi; fig. 139: see TIBERIUS PSALTER), which in addition to several Winchester frames with attenuated and straggly acanthus has a cycle of colored line drawings. These are executed in a forceful and angular style that already presages the Romanesque at the very time that it marks the end of the Winchester School.

Kathleen M. Openshaw

Bibliography

Alexander, Jonathan J.G. "The Benedictional of St. Æthelwold and Anglo-Saxon Illumination of the Reform Period." In *Tenth-Century Studies: Essays in Commemoration of the Millennium of the Council of Winchester and Regularis concordia,* ed. David Parsons. London: Phillimore, 1975, pp. 169–83, 241–45; Backhouse, Janet, Derek H. Turner, and Leslie Webster, eds. *The Golden Age of Anglo-Saxon Art 966–1066.* London: British Museum, 1984; Brownrigg, Linda L. "Manuscripts Containing English Decoration 871–1066, Catalogued and Illustrated: A Review." *ASE* 7 (1978): 239–66; Deshman, Robert. "The Leofric Missal and Tenth-Century English Art." *ASE* 6 (1977): 145–73; Deshman, Robert. *The Benedictional of Æthelwold.* Princeton: Princeton University Press, 1995; Gameson, Richard. "English Manuscript Art in the Mid-Eleventh Century: The Decorative Tradition."

AntJ, forthcoming; Heslop, T.A. "The Production of *de luxe* Manuscripts and the Patronage of King Cnut and Queen Emma." *ASE* 19 (1990): 151–95; Homburger, Otto. *Die Anfänge der Malschule von Winchester im X. Jahrhundert.* Leipzig: Weicher, 1912; Rickert, Margaret. *Painting in Britain: The Middle Ages.* 2d ed. Harmondsworth: Penguin, 1965; Warner, George F., and Henry A. Wilson. *The Benedictional of St. Æthelwold.* Oxford: Roxburghe Club, 1910; Wormald, Francis. *English Drawings of the Tenth and Eleventh Centuries.* London: Faber & Faber, 1952; Wormald, Francis. *The Benedictional of St. Ethelwold.* London: Faber & Faber, 1959; Wormald, Francis. "L'Angleterre." In *Le siècle de l'an mil,* ed. L. Grodecki et al. Paris: Gallimard, 1973, pp. 227–54. Trans. and repr. as "Anglo-Saxon Painting" in *Francis Wormald: Collected Writings,* ed. Jonathan J.G. Alexander, T. Julian Brown, and Joan Gibbs. Vol. 1. London: Harvey Miller, 1984, pp. 111–22.

See also Benedictional of Æthelwold; Harley Psalter; New Minster Charter; Tiberius Psalter

Winchester Songbook

The most significant collection of polyphonic songs to survive from later medieval England is a group of eighteen—ten in English, four in French, and four in Latin—gathered in a separate quire ruled for music near the rear of a modest paper miscellany whose main contents are sermons (CUL Add. 5943, fols. 161–169). Analysis of scribal hands and watermarks, English dialect, and the evidence from entries on flyleaves, most recently and extensively reviewed by Dobson, establishes a fairly secure date and provenance for the music. It appears to have been copied by (or for) Thomas Turk at Winchester College between 1395 and 1401 (perhaps by 1398) and represents a collection put together for recreational use there by the scholars and fellows in hall on feast days during Christmastide. Turk, a fellow of Exeter College, Oxford, from 1385 to 1399, was also a fellow of William of Wykeham's new foundation at Winchester College from 1395 to 1398 and again briefly from 1400 to 1401 before a later career as vicar, rector, and eventually Carthusian monk. The songs are anonymous save for one, "Thys yol," whose lower part is inscribed "quod Edmundus." An Edmundus was a clerk of the chapel at Winchester College and *informator choristarum* (instructor of the boy choristers) in 1396–97; he may well have been the song's poet or composer. Provenance is reinforced by the presence of one song, definitely a local product, that sings the praises of the city of Winchester ("Me lykyth ever the lengere the bet / by Wyngestyr that ioly syte"), and the season of year in which they were enjoyed is suggested by songs for Yuletide ("Thys Yol" and the carol "Lolay lolay / As Y lay on Yoleis nyght").

The Winchester collection's mixture of songs in Latin, French, and English is typical of insular sources of lyrical verse. The English and French settings are similar in form and style, favoring six-eight rhythms, a two-voice texture of texted melody over a textless supporting tenor, and virelai form (ABB). The song repertoire of the manuscript Bodl. Douce 381, though smaller (five songs in English, two in French), is remarkably similar, and the two sources share one piece in common, the English song "I rede that thu be ioly and glad."

Peter M. Lefferts

Bibliography

Dobson, Eric J., and Frank Ll. Harrison, eds. and trans. *Medieval English Songs.* London: Faber & Faber, 1979; Rastall, Richard, ed. *Four French Songs from an English Song-Book.* Newton Abbot: Antico Edition, 1976; Rastall, Richard, ed. *Four Songs in Latin from an English Song-Book.* Newton Abbot: Antico Edition, 1979; Rastall, Richard, ed. *Two Fifteenth-Century Songbooks (Cambridge University Library: Add. MS 5943 and Oxford, Bodleian Library, Douce 381).* Musical Sources 27. Aberystwyth: Boethius Press, 1990 [facsimile]; Seaman, Ann-Marie, and Richard Rastall, eds. *Four 15th-Century Religious Songs in English.* Newton Abbot: Antico Edition, 1979; Seaman, Ann-Marie, and Richard Rastall, eds. *Six 15th-Century English Songs.* Newton Abbot: Antico Edition, 1979.

See also Songs

Winchester Tropers

Two 11th-century trope manuscripts from Winchester's Old Minster: Cambridge, Corpus Christi College 473, and Bodleian Library, Bodley 775. Together they form our most important source of information concerning liturgical music in Anglo-Saxon England. The main corpus of the Cambridge troper was probably copied early in the 11th century, and it has been plausibly conjectured that Wulfstan of Winchester, cantor at the Old Minster and author of the metrical *Life of St. Swithun,* may have been one of the scribes. Additions, some on new parchment, were made during the course of the century. Bodley 775 was written in the middle of the 11th century and is known to rely in part on a Winchester manuscript of the 970s. Additions were also made to this manuscript, and some of the original notation was modernized in the 12th century. It is preserved in its 12th-century binding.

As is the case with most tropers, the Winchester manuscripts contain not only tropes (musicotextual embellishments to the sung portions of the mass) but also other genres of chant. The Cambridge manuscript is famous for its repertoire of organa (new melodies sung as counterpoint to existing chant melodies). The Bodley manuscript, better termed a cantatorium (a cantor's book) than a troper, contains virtually all of the genres of chant customarily performed by the cantor rather than the choir at mass. Both manuscripts, in contrast to most continental tropers, have the character of prescriptive liturgical books, that is, they contain a limited repertoire explicitly organized for performance in the celebration of the mass. They are also extremely handsome manuscripts by comparison with their continental counterparts.

The repertoire of tropes contained in the Winchester

tropers includes both native English compositions and imported, mostly French, pieces. The continental tropes were probably learned through Winchester's contacts with Corbie and Fleury at the time of the 10th-century Benedictine monastic reform. The English tropes, which are all in quantitative verse (either hexameters or elegiac distichs), were probably composed at the Old Minster either during the episcopate of St. Æthelwold (963–84) or within a generation of his death. The English pieces, or a good number of them, may be the work of Wulfstan of Winchester, whom we know to have been knowledgeable about music and to have been composing verse in this period. The music in both manuscripts is written in typically Anglo-Saxon neumatic notation with a nearly perpendicular vertical axis. In principle this notation is adiastematic (i.e., it conveys only the shape and not the exact pitches of the melodies), but sometimes relative pitch is indicated through the use of significative letters.

Elizabeth C. Teviotdale

Bibliography

Frere, Walter Howard. *The Winchester Troper: From Manuscripts of the Xth and XIth Centuries.* Henry Bradshaw Society 8. London: Harrison, 1894; Holschneider, Andreas. *Die Organa von Winchester: Studien zum ältesten Repertoire polyphoner Musik.* Hildesheim: Olms, 1968; Planchart, Alejandro E. *The Repertory of Tropes at Winchester.* 2 vols. Princeton: Princeton University Press, 1977.

See also Benedictine Reform; Caligula Troper; Liturgy and Church Music, History of; Mass, Polyphonic Music for; Notation of Plainchant; Trope; Winchester Organa

Windsor, St. George's Chapel

Chapel connected to Windsor Castle, the primary English royal residence. The rebuilding of the chapel was the most important architectural undertaking of Edward IV (d. 1483). It functions as the seat of the Order of the Garter, the premier English chivalric order, and as a royal chantry chapel and mausoleum. It was given a vast, cathedrallike form and scale for these reasons but also for one more: in legends of Arthur, which had a firm hold on the imaginations of English royalty, Camelot was associated not only with the Round Table but with a wondrous church.

As originally conceived, the chapel was to have a choir with seven bays surrounded by a square ambulatory, a crossing with lantern tower, transepts with polygonal ends, and a nave and aisles of only six bays. This initial plan called for 26 freestanding piers, the same number as there were Knights of the Garter (the normal total of knights needed to form two tournament teams of thirteen each, based on Christ and the apostles). This symbolism was lost, however, ca. 1503, when funding patterns changed, and it was decided to extend the nave by one bay so that polygonal chantry chapels could be added.

Because of the restrictions of the site the bays are extremely narrow. By contrast the clear span of the central vessel is close to 36 feet. A frieze of angels, which both separate and link heaven and earth, encircles the nave and choir just below the clerestory windows.

The stylistic sources for the design evolved from the choir of Gloucester (paneling treatment) and the nave of Canterbury Cathedral (pier form and three-tier aisle windows).

The square aisle bays are covered with fan vaults, while the central vessels are covered with dazzling lierne vaults of amazing virtuosity, the bosses of which are carved with the heraldic devices mostly belonging to individual Knights of the Garter, who subscribed to the construction. Flat four-centered arches are employed throughout; and it is this astonishing flat pitch, which is even reflected in the vaulting of the central vessels, that gives distinctive character to the interior spatial conception.

Construction began in 1476–77, but planning went back to 1472–73; the surveyor of the work was Richard Beauchamp, bishop of Salisbury, while the first master mason, to whom the initial design is attributed, was Henry Janyns. Before 1483 the foundations were entirely laid, the choir and aisles were carried up first to their full height and roofed in but not vaulted, the transepts were partially built, and the nave was built in steps down, from bay to bay, until one bay east of the present front. In 1494 Henry VII started the rebuilding of the Lady Chapel, which he intended to be his future burial place and that of Henry VI. In 1498 Henry abandoned this location in favor of Westminster Abbey, and construction on the Lady Chapel came to a halt. The nave and west front, with its octagonal turret buttresses, were finished ca. 1503–06. Evidence in a 1506 contract with John Hylmer (or Aylmer) and William Vertue indicates that the nave vaulting was already complete. The choir vaulting was finished ca. 1511 and the Lady Chapel after 1512 (the vaulting is modern), when Henry VIII decided to be buried there. The idea for the lantern tower was abandoned, and, instead, the crossing was fan-vaulted in 1528. As a result the exterior has an unusual, uniform silhouette.

Walter Leedy

Bibliography

Cave, C.J.P., and H. Stanford London. "The Roof-Bosses in St. George's Chapel, Windsor." *Archaeologia* 95 (1953): 107–21; Colvin, Howard M., ed. *The History of the King's Works.* Vol. 2; Vol. 3, pt. 1. London: HMSO, 1963, 1975; Harvey, John H. "The Architects of St. George's Chapel." *Report of the Society of the Friends of St. George's Chapel, Windsor Castle* 4 (1961): 48–55 and 85–95; Hope, William Henry St. John. *Windsor Castle.* 2 vols. London: Office of Country Life, 1913; Kidson, Peter. "The Architecture of St. George's Chapel." In *The Saint George's Chapel Quincentenary Handbook,* ed. Maurice Bond. Windsor: Oxley, 1975; Wilson, Christopher. *The Gothic Cathedral: The Architecture of the Great Church 1130–1530.* London: Thames & Hudson, 1990.

See also Architecture and Architectural Sculpture, Gothic; Canterbury Cathedral; Gloucester Cathedral; Order of the Garter; Vaulting; Westminster Abbey

Winner and Waster

An allegorical dream-debate poem in 503 alliterative long lines, written between 1352 and ca. 1370. The poem is incomplete in the single manuscript (BL Add. 31042), but perhaps only a few lines are missing from the conclusion. Traditionally dated to the winter of 1352–53 on the basis of internal references, the poem is now less frequently read as a topical satire and the precision and accuracy of many of those references have been challenged. We know nothing certain about the poet, but he may have been a cleric trained in the west Midlands who later served Edward III or the Black Prince in London.

The poem sets up an elaborate series of allegorical and narrative frameworks before the debate proper begins. After an apocalyptic prologue lamenting the collapse of traditional values the narrator describes a beautiful meadow through which he wanders before falling asleep. He dreams of two armies marching to meet each other to fight before a king who will judge their dispute. A herald describes the armies, one of them in great detail, before summoning the two leaders, Winner and Waster, to the king. The king welcomes them as members of his household and invites them to debate their differences.

According to the Aristotelian conceptual model underpinning the poem Winner represents the extreme of avarice and Waster that of prodigality. Each, however, presents himself as a moderate, and his economic program as sufficient for the kingdom. Waster claims to preserve traditional class distinctions (if lords did not consume the produce of their estates, food would become too plentiful, and the rich could not attract servants) and accuses Winner of making personal profit out of scarcity by stockpiling grain in hopes of a bad harvest. Winner complains in turn that Waster neglects his estates and sells his inherited land to buy fashionable clothes, with no thought for the future. The poet uses various ethical, literary, and rhetorical traditions to characterize the two disputants, and the terms and central issues of the debate shift rapidly. A persistent strain, however, is to depict Winner as a middle-class merchant envious of Waster's more aristocratic lifestyle.

The king is unable to resolve the complexities of the dispute and arranges to keep his two servants separate. He sends Winner to the papal court, to enjoy luxury for which he does not have to pay, and directs Waster to London, to encourage consumption that will ultimately benefit the merchant class. Winner will be recalled when the king needs to finance his overseas wars.

There are many inconsistencies and ambiguities in the poem, but its metrical and rhetorical power is undeniable. Its closest affinities are with *Piers Plowman* and *The Parliament of the Three Ages*. Perhaps the greatest challenge is to identify the position from which the implied author speaks: the poet's willingness to use a variety of traditional voices and his mastery of rhetorical dispute leave the reader with a vivid sense of problems raised, rather than an authoritative solution.

Stephanie Trigg

Bibliography

PRIMARY

Gollancz, Israel, ed. and trans. *A Good Short Debate between Winner and Waster.* 2d ed. rev. Mabel Day. London: Humphrey Milford, 1930; Trigg, Stephanie, ed. *Wynnere and Wastoure.* EETS o.s. 297. Oxford: Oxford University Press, 1990.

SECONDARY

New *CBEL* 1:548; *Manual* 5:1500–01, 1702–03; Bestul, Thomas H. *Satire and Allegory in Wynnere and Wastoure.* Lincoln: University of Nebraska Press, 1974; Jacobs, Nicolas. "The Typology of Debate and the Interpretation of *Wynnere and Wastoure.*" *RES* n.s. 36 (1985): 481–500; Salter, Elizabeth. "The Timeliness of *Wynnere and Wastoure.*" *MÆ* 47 (1978): 40–65; Trigg, Stephanie. "The Rhetoric of Excess in *Winner and Waster.*" *YLS* 3 (1989): 91–108.

See also Alliterative Revival; Debate Poems; Edward III; Households, Royal and Baronial; Hundred Years War; *Parliament of the Three Ages; Piers Plowman*

Wisdom (Sapiential) Literature
Old English

The phrase "sapiential literature" is borrowed from biblical scholarship, where it refers to Old Testament books—e.g., Proverbs, Ecclesiastes, Ecclesiasticus—consisting largely of proverbs, maxims, and sentences, or "wise sayings." Medieval commentators included the Song of Songs and Job as part of the sapiential canon, but for present purposes we can simply accept the modern understanding of biblical sapiential texts as an appropriate model and define sapiential literature as those texts or portions of texts that are comparable to the biblical sapiential books. The related terms "proverb," "maxim," "gnome," and "sentence," or "sententia," are much disputed (cf. Whiting, 1968: x–xvii; Mieder, 1982, 1990, 1993), but in this article they will be used in a relatively unspecialized sense.

The amount of sapiential literature in OE prose is limited. There are no continuous translations of the biblical sapiential books into OE; portions of these texts, however, were translated and are conveniently available in Albert S. Cook's volumes of *Biblical Quotations in Old English Prose Writers.* A major collection of sapiential texts, Defensor's 7th-century *Liber scintillarum* (translated into OE ca. 1000), is almost entirely a collection of biblical and patristic sentences, and includes little secular and no "Germanic" wisdom literature. Two extensive proverb collections in OE prose do contain secular wisdom: the OE version of the *Disticha Catonis* and the *Durham Proverbs.* The *Disticha Catonis,* a late-antique collection of proverbs ascribed to Cato, was one of the first texts medieval students read as they learned Latin. The OE version of this text is more than a straightforward paraphrase of the Latin original and contains some apparently indigenous OE wisdom lore. The *Durham Proverbs* is a collection of vernacular proverbs that are not based on any known Latin source and that seem to be authentically vernacular. Some examples—"'It is far from well,' said he who heard wailing in hell" / "'Now it is up to the pig,' said the farmer on the boar's back"—have the kind of cogency and wit that one associates with saga prose and thus reflect an aspect of OE literature that is not well preserved in extant OE literary monuments.

There exists a much fuller corpus of OE wisdom literature in verse. Before describing these poems and discussing issues that they present it would be useful to consider in general terms some of the difficulties of interpretation peculiar to sapiential texts. The notion that proverbs are not straightforward, that they can be defined as the "aenigmata sapientium," "riddles of the wise" (Prov. 1:6), is part of the biblical definition of the genre. The obscurity of wisdom literature is based in part on the compressed, enigmatic, and often figurative language characteristic of proverbial texts. Unless one knows that the ant is associated with industriousness in biblical proverbial literature, the maxim "Go to the ant, O sluggard, and consider her ways and learn wisdom" (Prov. 6:6) is likely to be opaque.

A second problem related to proverbs and maxims is that these sayings often succinctly express cultural values and attitudes that an outsider can only laboriously reconstruct. If one does not already know something about the ethos of modern American businesses, the maxim "Business is business" is not likely to be informative. One often unrecognized problem is that authors of wisdom literature frequently embed controversial or problematic maxims in as banal a context as possible in order to lend as much conventional authority to the new truth as context can provide. "Reading" a given sentential statement can thus be problematic since such texts can either be dense and charged with meaning or straightforward and "empty"; it can be difficult for a modern literary historian or critic to discern the difference on first reading.

Given these reservations, we may note that a number of OE poems are entirely sapiential and thus directly comparable to Latin and biblical sapiential literature. The most famous are *Maxims I* and *Maxims II.* The former, a poem in three parts totaling about 200 lines, is preserved in the Exeter Book; the latter is found as a kind of prologue to a text of the Anglo-Saxon Chronicle. It is difficult to characterize these poems briefly. The poems are not unified; they fall into verse paragraphs of varying length dealing with a variety of topics. Their overall perspective is Christian, but they deal directly and explicitly with secular and at times even "pagan" topics, such as burial customs, dragons, and sexual love between a Frisian wife and her seafaring husband. Some passages are of high poetic value, and all this verse is interesting from the point of view of the literary or intellectual historian. Such lines as *Maxims II,* lines 26–27, "draca sceal on hlæwe / frod frætwum wlonc," "the dragon shall [live] on the barrow / old and proud [of his] treasure," have been cited innumerable times by *Beowulf* critics as an example of native OE dragon lore; one of the attractive features of the two *Maxim* poems is that they offer brief vignettes of animals and the natural world as well as of Anglo-Saxon society, parenthood, and

much else. Yet much remains obscure in these poems, and it is often difficult to be sure that we fully grasp the force of any given passage.

Perhaps the most attractive and interesting sapiential poem after *Maxims I* and *II* is *Solomon and Saturn II.* In this dialogue between a pagan "Saturn" and a Christian "Solomon" the protagonists discuss old age, good and evil, the necessary afflictions of sin and death, and other topics. Here again there is much excellent poetry, but also much that is difficult. There is also a good deal of Christian sapiential poetry in the Exeter Book and elsewhere. Such texts as *The Gifts of Men, Precepts, Vainglory, The Fortunes of Men, The Order of the World, Resignation A* and *B,* and the recently edited *Instructions for Christians* are for the most part a body of explicitly Christian wisdom literature. These texts are interesting in a number of ways. *The Fortunes of Men* and *The Gifts of Men* offer rare and precious insights concerning Anglo-Saxon assumptions about social life and the order of society. But these explicitly Christian wisdom texts are without the aesthetic appeal of *Maxims* or *Solomon and Saturn II.* They lack the nature imagery and the glimpses of secular and Germanic life and custom that make these poems so fascinating. It must be said, though, that on the whole they are a good deal easier to interpret than the more archaic or at least more secular sapiential texts.

Even if we limit our discussion of OE sapiential poetry to texts that consist entirely of sapiential material, there is a substantial corpus of such poetry preserved. Yet some of the most interesting sapiential poetry occurs in texts that are generically identified as elegiac, heroic, or epic. Both *The Wanderer* and *The Seafarer,* usually thought of as "elegiac" poems, have significant sapiential material concerning the definition of the wise man, the ages of the world, and the necessity for patience in adversity. Even in the heroic poem *The Battle of Maldon* the climax of the famous speech of Byrhtwold that concludes the poem as we have it is phrased as a heroic maxim that pertains to any men facing death in war. It is sapiential both in its content and in its phrasing, which echoes the *sceal/sculon* formulation that is such a striking feature of *Maxims I* and *II* and sapiential poetry elsewhere. One of the characteristics of the speeches of the main characters in *Beowulf* is a fondness for sapiential aphorisms appropriate to the context of their discourse. This is most true of Hrothgar, whose role as the wise old king of the Danes makes him an especially appropriate speaker of wisdom literature, but it is also true of other characters, such as the coast guard and Beowulf himself, both of whom utter wise generalizations at various occasions.

Though sapiential discourse is a common feature of different kinds of OE poetry, the scholarly community has consistently found it difficult to come to terms with this poetry. Further work on sapiential poetry and on the sapiential tradition generally is needed.

Middle English

Scholars face essentially the same methodological and conceptual problems in dealing with ME sapiential literature as they do with OE, but in addition they face the difficulty of having to deal with more, and more complexly entangled, kinds of discourse. Whereas in OE most texts are either "Christian" or "Germanic," or to one degree or another a mixture of the two, in ME there is courtly literature as well as Christian and traditional/folkloric literature, and there are greater or lesser degrees of foreign, for the most part French, influence. Again, in the ME period there are a number of distinct strands of Christian thought and culture, whereas in OE the essential distinction is between learned Latin Christianity as exemplified in the work of Alfred or Bede and "popular" Christianity as exemplified in the Vercelli Homilies and other even more folkloric texts. By contrast in the ME period there is, in addition to the distinction between popular and learned Christianity, the issue of antifraternalism, which looms large in the work of Chaucer and Langland, and in the late ME period the work of Wyclif and his followers represents yet another distinct current of Christian thought.

The size of the corpus of ME literature precludes the kind of survey offered above for OE literature. Indeed, if sapiential literature is pervasive in OE literature, it is almost as pervasive in "high" ME literature and in the huge corpus of religious and moral literature written in ME that is conventionally called didactic. The most immediate guide to ME sapiential literature is B.J. Whiting's *Proverbs, Sentences, and Proverbial Phrases from English Writings Mainly before 1500.* Despite its title this volume covers ME literature more fully than OE, reflecting Whiting's own interests; in his introduction and bibliography Whiting lists and discusses briefly such major sapiential texts as the *Proverbs of Alfred* and the *Poema Morale.* Whiting's work is an immensely useful gathering of material, and since there is no book-length study of ME sapiential literature as such, it is the best text for neophytes in this field, though it must be supplemented by consulting more recent scholarship.

Among the major ME authors Chaucer and Gower in particular wrote a number of sapiential poems. A good many of Chaucer's shorter poems, "Truth," "Gentilesse," and "Lak of Steadfastnesse" are explicitly sapiential, and a substantial number of Dunbar's works—the more than twenty poems that Dunbar's most recent editor, James Kinsley, gathers together and calls "Moralities"—are directly sapiential.

There is no question that sapiential literature is an important genre in ME literature, but in striking contrast to the various earlier literatures that directly or indirectly influenced ME, a number of poets seem to treat sapiential texts with some measure of irony. Two immediate examples from the corpus of major literary texts are *The Owl and the Nightingale,* in which some version of the *Proverbs of Alfred* is treated with considerable ironic detachment, and Chaucer's *Troilus,* where Pandarus's speeches are full of proverbs. The interpretation of the character of Pandarus, like much else in that enigmatic poem, is open to debate, but few critics would argue that Pandarus is simply speaking sapiential truths.

As with OE literature there is ample opportunity for original research and criticism on the ME sapiential corpus. An excellent recent example is Burrow's study of a "countercultural" medieval proverb and the responses that it engendered ("Young Saint, Old Devil").

Few forms of medieval literature are more alien to modern and postmodern readers than sapiential literature, in which "truths" about life and the ordering of society and the world are articulated directly and forcefully—without apparent concern for dissent or qualification. However, it is precisely those texts that are most alien that are most revealing. ME sapiential texts are a rich resource that requires much more attentive and sophisticated study.

Thomas D. Hill

Bibliography

PRIMARY

Arngart, Olof, ed. "The Durham Proverbs." *Speculum* 56 (1981): 288–300; Cook, Albert S. *Biblical Quotations in OE Prose Writers.* London: Macmillan, 1898; Cook, Albert S. *Biblical Quotations in OE Prose Writers.* 2d ser. New York: Scribner, 1903; Cox, Robert S., ed. "The OE *Dicts of Cato.*" *Anglia* 90 (1972): 1–42; Rhodes, E.W., ed. *Defensor's Liber Scintillarum.* EETS o.s. 93. London: Trübner, 1889; Shippey, T.A., ed. and trans. *Poems of Wisdom and Learning in Old English.* Cambridge: Brewer, 1976; Walther, Hans. *Proverbia Sententiaeque Latinitatis Medii Aevi.* 9 vols. Göttingen: Vandenhoeck & Ruprecht, 1963–86; Whiting, B.J. *Proverbs, Sentences, and Proverbial Phrases from English Writings Mainly before 1500.* Cambridge: Harvard University Press, 1968.

SECONDARY

Manual 3:669–745, 829–902 (Dialogues, Debates, and Catechisms), 7:2255–2378, 2467–2582 (Works of Religious and Philosophical Instruction); Burrow, J.A. "Young Saint, Old Devil: Reflections on a Medieval Proverb." In *Essays on Medieval Literature.* Oxford: Oxford University Press, 1984; Cross, J.E. "The Old English Poetic Theme of 'The Gifts of Men.'" *Neophilologus* 46 (1962): 66–70; Deskis, Susan E. *Beowulf and the Medieval Proverb Tradition.* Tempe: MRTS, 1996; Mieder, Wolfgang. *International Proverb Scholarship: An Annotated Bibliography.* With Supplements I (1980–1981) and II (1982–91). Garland Folklore Bibliographies 3, 15, 20. New York: Garland, 1982, 1990, 1993; Russom, Geoffrey R. "A Germanic Conception of Nobility in *The Gifts of Men* and *Beowulf.*" *Speculum* 53 (1978): 1–15; Taylor, Archer. *The Proverb.* Cambridge: Harvard University Press, 1931; Williams, Blanche Colton. *Gnomic Poetry in Anglo-Saxon.* New York: Columbia University Press, 1914.

See also Adrian and Ritheus; Judgment Day; Maxims; Orality; Popular Culture; Riddles; *Solomon and Saturn; Vainglory*

Women
Anglo-Saxon Period

Anglo-Saxon England is traditionally seen as a golden age for women, ending in 1066 with the Norman Conquest. Anglo-Saxon women are presented as exercising wide powers to hold and dispose of land, in contrast to their successors under common law. In the wills and legal disputes of the 10th and early 11th centuries women are seen bequeathing land, choosing heirs, even winning inheritance disputes against their sons. They appear in the courts, occasionally as active oath helpers, or compurgators, who swore together with defendants on behalf of their acquittal; that women could do this indicates that they had a public "word" of value.

In the church women are seen to have played a major part, epitomized by the great abbesses of 7th-century double monasteries. A woman like Hild, abbess of Whitby, was landholder, estate organizer, educator of bishops, ruler of her house, and an influence in the kingdom. The debatable imposition after 1066 of a feudal military society and its related emphasis on primogeniture is alleged to have reduced female landholding and general influence, a change in status compounded by the triumph of the male hierarchy in the church.

Though true in detail this picture requires revision. The situation in the 12th and 13th centuries can be caricatured to make the earlier period appear golden by contrast; the theory of the later common law requires tempering by, for example, the practical powers of many individual widows. A picture of extensive female landholding before 1066 is not borne out by Domesday Book (1086), a difficult source but the only comprehensive picture of Anglo-Saxon landholding. The proportion of female landholders on either side of 1066 is small. Women who did hold land in Anglo-Saxon England are not necessarily representative of all women. The majority were widows, who predominate in Domesday and in late Saxon wills. Widowhood was the period in life when a woman stood to control most land. Customary law already recognized a widow's right to a third, in some areas a half, of her husband's land. In practice Anglo-Saxon dower varied as much as it did later, already depending on the individual circumstances of families.

Women in Anglo-Saxon England were "legal persons." As such they were liable for their own crimes. They appear in court, though usually as defendants and often with men speaking for them. They offer legal proofs, but the only occasions on which they acted as oath helpers are when cases involve women, as in later common law. They never held lay offices.

Many women who received land grants or disposed of land were ecclesiastics or members of royal or great noble families. The handful of royal grants made directly to women were to one or other of these groups. Noble women did not enjoy parity with their brothers. The bulk of the inheritance went to men, and most female landholding was the temporary family provision of dower or dowry, or family patronage of churches to which their womenfolk belonged.

The role of women in the early church was significant, as abbesses and as missionaries to the Continent. There is a high proportion of female saints from the 7th and 8th centuries. However, this changes by the 10th century; in the monastic revival nunneries were less important. Former double houses like Ely, once ruled by an abbess, were refounded as male houses. The picture is distorted against the nunneries,

since we see it through later male Benedictine eyes. But the heyday had passed.

The 7th and 8th centuries were the period of conversion and the first interaction between Christian ideals and social structures. In such times ecclesiastical structures are often fluid, and all resources, including women, are drawn into this primary effort. Monasticism emerged as the perfect structure for the union of Christian ideals and the early-medieval family. Monasteries were noble family houses, and women fulfilled their family roles within them. A noble abbess ruled a monastic household. From the 9th century reform was aimed at ending this close involvement of lay family and monastery and at the related imposition of celibacy. Double monasteries and powerful abbesses were its casualties.

This was a Christian society that did not exclude women as nonpersons but that was dominated for women by roles within the family. Family and household need not always and everywhere be restrictive, and some restrictions applied to men, though men's lives were less circumscribed by such bonds. The mistress of a noble household was a powerful woman, but only one woman could be mistress at a time. We must be wary of generalizing from the lot of some to all women, while recognizing that the household and family models of early-medieval politics opened but limited opportunities for Anglo-Saxon queens to achieve importance.

Five centuries is too long a period for blanket generalizations. The fragmentary sources suggest changes within the period, affecting different groups of women. The first impact of Christianity brought changes in landholding to allow the endowment of the church out of family land. Noble women benefited as landholders from this loosening, and the enormous land acquisitions of the settlement era contributed to landed provision for women. More debatably, Christian views on marriage and divorce may also have benefited women.

There are hints of a tightening up during the 9th century, as the results of endowing women and churches became apparent. Great noble women did well in the 10th and 11th centuries, when the nobility as a whole were benefiting from the unification of England. Here a group of women profited with their class. "Anglo-Saxon women" is a simplification that must be resolved into periods, social groups, and the stages of the domestic cycle. The dependence of wives and daughters throughout the period should not be hidden behind the power of some widows.

Post-Conquest

Post-Conquest women were regarded less favorably by both the law and the church than their Anglo-Saxon predecessors, but in compensation the patterns of life in the later Middle Ages opened new avenues for women's activities, especially for townswomen and peasants.

The newly imposed code of Anglo-Norman feudal law and the development and codification of canon law both lessened women's legal rights. The legal status of a woman of any social class depended on whether she was single or married. Single or widowed, she could exercise the same private legal rights as a man; married, her rights were extinguished, and her person as well as her goods, lands, and chattels came under her husband's control. She regained her own estate and dowry only upon her husband's death, with the addition of a lifetime share in some portion of his estate. This share could be differently computed, depending on whether feudal or manorial law or civic customs applied, and might vary from place to place as well as from time to time.

The acceptance of primogeniture as the pattern for feudal inheritance tended to disqualify noble women from any share in the family wealth, except for their assigned dowry; although in default of sons, daughters could divide the total inheritance. Both townswomen and peasants were less tied by such inheritance patterns. In all classes, though most prominently among the nobility, the well-to-do widow often found herself with remarkable freedom of action. Despite their private rights women had no right to hold office or exercise public authority. Noble women holding fiefs with their own courts normally delegated their power to a male official.

Canon law, which dealt with both marriages and wills, reflected the clerical conviction of the inferiority of women and their need to be under male authority. But it also insisted on their right to free acceptance of their marriage partners and denied parents the right to force the marriage of children under the age of consent (twelve for girls, fourteen for boys). Canon law also consistently encouraged the making of wills, even by married women who technically had no power to do so without their husbands' consent, thus giving women more power over their own belongings.

Actual conditions frequently contradicted legal theory. Feudal lords were often absent on crusade, or on other military expeditions, or at court, and their wives found themselves in charge of large households with a full complement of officials, knights, and men-at-arms, fighting legal battles over rights to lands, and maintaining adequate military strength to protect their castles. Such women exercised considerable authority.

The rapid development of the towns and their fast-growing populations by the 12th century opened new doors for townswomen. They were allowed to join most craft guilds, though their ability to attain the rank of master, independently of their husband, is difficult to track. Apparently women did not hold office within the guilds, nor did they have any share in city government. Their right to conduct business on their own, even when married, was embodied in commercial law, where a female entrepreneur could elect to trade as a *fame sole* (the legal term for an independent woman, a "woman alone"). Since most trades and crafts were family businesses, women were naturally found in most of them but were most visible in such crafts as embroidery, silk spinning, and weaving. Rich merchants were always men, although their widows often continued to trade. Women were often retailers, tavern keepers, and brewers.

Women doctors, midwives, and schoolmistresses were few in number but still traceable. At the lowest level female servants and prostitutes abounded, and the two categories often overlapped. On the manors peasant women not only worked with their husbands and children in the fields but also might run small businesses—often brewing, occasionally baking.

The basic task of all married women was to bear and rear children. Noble women were married young and bore more children at younger ages, because of the importance of heirs; they had wetnurses and servants to assist them. Townswomen and peasants often delayed marriage for economic reasons and were likely to have smaller families. Whatever the social level, child mortality was high and the mother's death in childbirth frequent. Once past the crucial childbearing years, women's life expectancy seems to have been greater than men's. Although marriage was the norm for women, some girls remained single. Townswomen and peasants found it possible to support themselves by their own labor. For the upper class and well-to-do, however, religious life was the only alternative to marriage.

English nunneries were not as rich, as populous, or as numerous as religious houses for men, but they provided a respected alternative to marriage for the upper classes. Some houses, such as the priory of Amesbury, grew rich with royal patronage and attracted the relations of royalty, including the sister and niece of Edward I. Other houses were often founded by a particular family. The nuns' prime duty was to pray for the souls of patrons and for the family connection. It is not surprising that since noble birth and some wealth was required for entrance, nunneries were usually respectable but rarely fervent. Some nuns really had a religious vocation, some had intellectual interests most easily pursued in the cloister, some relished the positions of independent authority, such as abbess, prioress, or cellaress, that they could achieve. Other girls, unmarriageable because of physical or mental handicap, or the lack of dowry but with sufficient social status, became nuns as the only available alternative.

An unusual feature of English religious life was the considerable number of female recluses, or anchoresses, women who withdrew permanently to an individual cell for prayer and ascetic practice. Julian of Norwich was the most famous, and her mystical writings continue to have an audience. English women did not create major literary works or cultural monuments. Their achievements were overshadowed by the political and chivalric exploits interesting to male chroniclers. Nevertheless, many competent and some colorful English women can be uncovered and need to be remembered for their important share in creating the lively society of the later Middle Ages.

Pauline Stafford
Margaret Wade Labarge

Bibliography

ANGLO-SAXON PERIOD

Fell, Christine E., with Cecily Clark and Elizabeth Williams. *Women in Anglo-Saxon England and the Impact of 1066.* Bloomington: Indiana University Press, 1984; Klinck, Ann. "Anglo-Saxon Women and the Law." *JMH* 8 (1982): 107–21; Schulenberg, Jane T. "Sexism and the Celestial Gynaecaeum from 500 to 1200." *JMH* 4 (1978): 117–33; Stafford, Pauline. *Unification and*

Conquest: A Political and Social History of England in the Tenth and Eleventh Centuries. London: Arnold, 1989 [covers late Anglo-Saxon women in some detail]; Stafford, Pauline. "Women in Domesday." *Reading Medieval Studies* 15 (1989–90): 75–94; Stafford, Pauline. "Women and the Norman Conquest." *TRHS,* 6th ser. 4 (1994): 221–49; Stenton, Doris M. *The English Woman in History.* London: Allan & Unwin, 1957.

POST-CONQUEST

Baker, Derek, ed. *Medieval Women.* Oxford: Blackwell, 1978 [valuable articles in a *Festschrift* for Rosalind Hill]; Elkins, Sharon. *Holy Women of Twelfth-Century England.* Chapel Hill: University of North Carolina Press, 1988; Hanawalt, Barbara A. *The Ties That Bound: Peasant Families in Medieval England.* New York: Oxford University Press, 1986 [most complete and up-to-date study of the peasant family]; Labarge, Margaret Wade. *A Baronial Household of the Thirteenth Century.* New York: Barnes & Noble, 1965 [life of a noble woman and her responsibilities]; Labarge, Margaret Wade. *A Small Sound of the Trumpet: Women in Medieval Life.* Boston: Beacon, 1986 [English and continental women]; Nichols, John A., and Lillian T. Shank, eds. *Medieval Religious Women.* Vol. 1: *Distant Echoes.* Kalamazoo: Cistercian Publications, 1984 [essays on women in religious life]; Power, Eileen. *Medieval English Nunneries c. 1275 to 1535.* Cambridge: Cambridge University Press, 1922; Stenton, Doris M. *The English Woman in History.* London: Allen & Unwin, 1957; Thrupp, Sylvia L. *The Merchant Class of Medieval London, 1300–1500.* Ann Arbor: University of Michigan Press, 1948 [useful for townswomen].

See also Æthelflæd; Beaufort, Margaret; Brewing; Children; Eleanor of Aquitaine; Emma; Hild; Marriage; Matilda; Nuns; Queens; Wardship; Widows; Women and the Arts; Women in ME Literature; Women in OE Literature

Women and the Arts

Evidence for the participation of women in the production of art is extant from the earliest centuries of the Anglo-Saxon period. We are best informed about monastic women: site remains, even though most have yet to be fully excavated, and written sources, such as Boniface and Bede, provide glimpses of the materials produced for these houses. Carved architectural elements survive at Hackness and Hart; sculptural remains have been recovered from Hartlepool (including elaborate name-stones and metalworking equipment) and Hackness, where fragments of a large cross decorated with figures, interlace, and inscriptions were found. Whitby excavations have yielded objects like decorated combs, hanging bowls, rings, brooches, pins, and a glass bracelet, as well as imported glass cups and Frankish pottery.

Early Anglo-Saxon monastic women were apparently also involved with manuscript production: an ink horn and bronze styli were among the finds at Whitby, and Boniface's well-known letter of ca. 735 to Eadburga, abbess of Minster-in-Thanet, requested that she copy for him the Epistles of St. Peter in gold. Yet manuscripts, and especially illuminated manuscripts, that can now be linked to women's houses in this period are woefully rare. Only a few recorded references to deluxe manuscripts survive; the books themselves do not.

Graves, hoards, and wills furnish evidence of small-scale works of art owned by secular women that included rings, pendants, headbands, silver cups, and brooches, such as the inscribed silver disc brooch from Sutton, Isle of Ely, owned by the lady Aedwen. The wealthy Wynflæd even left books to her daughter in her will of about 950.

It seems likely that the major art form that engaged the majority of Anglo-Saxon women, both religious as well as secular, was textiles, an art rarely practiced by men. As early as 747 the ecclesiastical council at Clovesho decried the many hours spent in needlework at convents (and recommended that the nuns spend more time reading books and singing psalms). Textiles like bedclothes, table linens, seat covers, and wall hangings are often bequeathed in the wills of aristocratic women; it seems that textiles made by the women of the household were considered female property.

Textiles are quite perishable, especially in the damp British Isles, so losses have been vast; however, texts and manuscript illustrations attest to their ubiquitous presence throughout the Middle Ages. Of the few precious Anglo-Saxon textiles that survive the famous *casula* (chasuble) of St. Harlindis and St. Relindis and the *velamen* (veil) of St. Harlindis are the earliest, dating to the late 8th or early 9th century. The first extant examples of what came to be known as Opus Anglicanum (literally, "English work"), these embroideries worked in gold and colored silk on linen reveal a high level of skill. An even more exquisite group of Anglo-Saxon textiles, from the early 10th century, was preserved in the coffin of St. Cuthbert. These consist of a stole, maniple, and girdle, all embroidered in colored silks and gold thread, which were made at the command of Queen Ælfflæd for the bishop of Winchester, according to inscriptions on the stole and maniple.

The late Anglo-Saxon period continues to furnish evidence of women's involvement with the arts, most often in the capacity of patrons. Ealhswith, King Alfred's wife, was probably the founder of Nunnaminster at Winchester and apparently also gave the convent the small illuminated prayer book known as the Book of Nunnaminster (BL Harley 2965).

Two of the greatest female manuscript patrons of this time emerge during the second half of the 11th century from aristocratic lay society: Judith of Flanders and Margaret of Scotland. No less than four extant illuminated Gospel books can be connected to Judith's patronage (New York, Pierpont Morgan Library 708, 709; Monte Cassino, Archiv. Badia BB 437, 439; and Fulda, Landesbibliothek Aa21). Judith herself appears in the frontispiece of the Fulda Gospels and in Morgan 709 (fol. 1v) beneath the crucified Christ.

Margaret of Scotland, wife of Malcolm III, king of Scots, was praised as a great benefactor of Durham (which received many beautiful objects from her, including a cope, cross, and

Gospel book written in silver, according to Reginald of Durham) and a passionate lover of books who was especially fond of her own personal Gospel book. The St. Margaret Gospels (Bodl. lat. lit. F5) miraculously survives and is illuminated with four full-page evangelist portraits and gilt capitals. Other extant illuminated books linked to Margaret include a pocket psalter (Edinburgh, University Library 56), and the famous life of St. Cuthbert (Oxford, University College 165).

Little is known of late Anglo-Saxon women as artists themselves, aside from the textile medium, where needlework continued to be a skill cultivated by women. Such ladies as Æthelswitha, daughter of Queen Aelfgyva, retired to Ely to devote herself to gold embroidery, and the Domesday Survey includes at least two references to women who were apparently professional embroideresses. The most renowned of all English textiles, the 11th-century embroidery known as the Bayeux Tapestry, was almost certainly stitched by women (though a male "designer" is often posited).

Written sources tell us that the 12th-century religious woman Christina of Markyate gave three miters and a pair of sandals that she had embroidered by her own hand to Pope Adrian IV and also made a gift of traveling clothes to King Stephen. However, Christina is best known to art historians for the single extant object connected to her, the magnificent illuminated psalter often referred to as the St. Albans Psalter or the Psalter of Christina of Markyate (Hildesheim, St. Godehard). This psalter, which was probably made for Christina by the monks of nearby St. Albans, is a masterpiece of Romanesque illumination, containing 42 full-page miniatures, 211 historiated initials, and several line drawings. Christina herself appears in the initial beginning Psalm 105, where she is seen before Christ, interceding on behalf of the monks. The book in many ways reflects and echoes her personal experiences. Amazingly Christina's *Vita* has virtually nothing to say about her psalter (mentioning what may be it apparently only once, during a demon attack); this provides a useful example of the many lacunae encountered while tracing the role of medieval women and the arts.

The wealthiest female monastic house of the 12th century was Shaftesbury in southern England. Destroyed during the 16th-century Dissolution of the monasteries, it has been reduced to little more than its foundations. The abbey church had been rebuilt beginning ca. 1080 and was an enormous structure over 350 feet in length. We are left to imagine the splendor of the decoration the nuns ordered for their church; among the stone remnants salvaged from the partially excavated site were cable molding and palmettes, volute and leaf ornament, sculpted corbels, chevron, dog-tooth, and pellet decoration, leaf capitals, spiral and fluted shafts, as well as many figural fragments. Later Gothic embellishments to the church included decorated tiles and stained glass.

The nuns of Shaftesbury, like other female monastics, also utilized books. A 12th-century psalter from the abbey is extant. The Shaftesbury Psalter (BL Lansdowne 383) contained an illuminated prefatory cycle of full-page illuminations, of which only six survive, in addition to two others elsewhere in the manuscript. While the Shaftesbury Psalter

shares iconographic and stylistic similarities, as well as virtually the same date, with the Psalter of Christina of Markyate, the frontal, staring, iconic images of the Shaftesbury Psalter are not stressed in Christina's psalter. This suggests the images were designed to enhance subtle yet marked differences in the pieties of contemporary religious women, while perhaps also simultaneously reflecting variation in their aesthetic preferences.

It is unknown whether the nuns of Shaftesbury themselves were scribes or illuminators. Reliable evidence for women illuminators in England is notoriously elusive. However, in an early-12th-century manuscript (Bodleian Library, Bodley 451, fol. 119v) the earliest attestation of a female scribe in England is preserved. The *scriptrix* seems to have been a nun of the Nunnaminster at Winchester.

While Nunnaminster, Shaftesbury, Christina's priory, and nearly all other female monastic houses in England have been lost, one Romanesque abbey church survives in nearly perfect condition, although lacking its cloister: Romsey. The church, begun ca. 1120, incorporates a nearly life-sized stone rood (Crucifixion image) from the nuns' previous church. Romsey's architectural decor features grotesque-head corbels, elaborate acanthus scroll capitals, and two historiated capitals (one inscribed "Robert made me").

A large number of manuscripts commissioned by women patrons during the Gothic period have come down to us. Among the most deluxe of these is the Munich Psalter (Munich, Bayerische Staatsbibliothek Clm.835) of the early 13th century. It contains multiple picture cycles, including numerous illustrations of the lives of heroic women from the Old Testament. Additional manuscripts from the 13th century that have been identified include, from the monastic ambience, the Imola Psalter (Imola, Biblioteca Comunale 100), the Iona Psalter (Edinburgh, National Library of Scotland 10000), a psalter in Cambridge (Trinity College B.11.4), the Obituary Roll of Lucy (BL Egerton 2849), the Wilton Psalter (London, Royal Collection of Physicians 409), the Amesbury Psalter (Oxford, All Souls College 6), and the Carrow Psalter (Madrid, Biblioteca Nacional 6422). An Augustinian nun appears on fol. 148 of a psalter in the Bodleian Library (Laud lat. 114). This psalter probably belonged originally to Lacock Abbey, a prosperous convent, as corroborated by the elegant 15th-century cloister that remains on the site.

Secular female patrons also played a significant role in the production of deluxe 13th-century books. The Huntingfield Psalter (New York, Pierpont Morgan Library 43), the richly illuminated de Brailes Hours (BL Add. 49999), the Egerton Hours (BL Egerton 1151), and a psalter in Venice (Biblioteca Marciana lat. 1.77 [2379]) were all made for secular women. Secular women patrons were additionally responsible for at least two fine Apocalypse manuscripts. Eleanor of Provence, wife of Henry III, is the most likely patron of the Trinity Apocalypse (Cambridge, Trinity College R.16.2), the largest and most sumptuous of the 13th-century Apocalypses. Eleanor de Quincy, countess of Winchester, certainly commissioned the luxurious Lambeth Apocalypse (London, Lambeth Palace 209) and is shown in her devotions before the Virgin and Child on fol. 48 (fig. 154).

Fig. 154. Lambeth Apocalypse (London, Lambeth Palace 209), fol. 48. Virgin and Child with donor. Reproduced by permission of the Archbishop of Canterbury and the Trustees of Lambeth Palace Library.

Women's patronage is further hinted at in other media. At Worcester Cathedral a 13th-century spandrel in the Lady Chapel shows a laywoman giving orders to a master mason. Beatrix van Valkenburg (d. 1277) appears in a stained-glass panel probably from an Oxford church, the earliest surviving donor image in English glass. Isabella Marshall (d. 1240), countess of Clare, gave chalices, reliquaries, vestments, and books to Tewkesbury Abbey.

During the period 1250–1350 the art of embroidery by English women, Opus Anglicanum, rose to its greatest heights and was treasured throughout Europe. Mabel of Bury St. Edmunds, apparently one of the best 13th-century embroideresses, was frequently employed by Henry III. Only a few of the many outstanding examples of embroidery from the time can be mentioned here: the Pienza Cope (Pienza Cathedral), the Bologna Cope (Bologna, Museo Civico Medievale), and the red velvet chasuble owned by the Chichester-Constable family (New York, Metropolitan Museum). While much Opus Anglicanum was created by secular women, monastic women also continued the ancient tradition, as witnessed by the altar frontlet (London, Victoria and Albert Museum) signed by the nun Johanna Beverlai.

Numerous 14th-century illuminated manuscripts made for women survive. Among them are the Madresfield Hours (Madresfield Court M), the Vernon Psalter (San Marino, Huntington Library EL 9.H.17), the Hours of Alice de Reydon (CUL Dd.4.170), the Taymouth Hours (BL Yates Thompson 13), the Hours and Psalter of Elizabeth de Bohun (Ginge Manor), and the Fitzwarin Psalter (Paris, BN lat. 765).

Precious references to craftswomen during this century have been recovered. For example, in mid-14th-century London Dyonisia La Longe was a gilder, Matilda Weston a weaver, while Matilda Myms, widow of John, an "imaginour," owned her own materials for making pictures, which she later bequeathed to her apprentice, William. Katherine Lyghtefote was employed supplying the king's palace at Sheen in the 1380s along with her master-mason husband.

Fourteenth-century women continued to be important patrons. Eleanor de Clare was probably the patron responsible for rebuilding much of the east end of Tewkesbury Abbey during the 1320s and 1330s, while her contemporary Elizabeth de Burgh had in her hire at least four goldsmiths, endowed the Augustinian priory at Clare, Suffolk, and founded Clare College at Cambridge.

Judith Ellis

Bibliography

Backhouse, Janet. *The Madresfield Hours: A Fourteenth-Century Manuscript in the Library of Earl Beauchamp.* Oxford: Roxburghe Club, 1975; Bennett, Adelaide. "A Book Designed for a Noblewoman: An Illustrated *Manuel des péchés* of the Thirteenth Century." In *Medieval Book Production: Assessing the Evidence,* ed. Linda Brownrigg. Los Altos Hills: Anderson-Lovelace, 1990, pp. 163–81; Budny, Mildred, and Dominic Tweddle. "The Maaseik Embroideries." *ASE* 13 (1984): 65–96; Donovan, Claire. *The de Brailes Hours: Shaping the Book of Hours in Thirteenth-Century Oxford.* London: British Library, 1991; Farmer, D.H. "A Note on the Origin, Purpose and Date of University College, Oxford, MS 165." *JWCI* 41 (1978): 46–49; Fell, Christine E., with Cecily Clark and Elizabeth Williams. *Women in Anglo-Saxon England and the Impact of 1066.* Bloomington: Indiana University Press, 1984; Graham, Henry. "The Munich Psalter." In *The Year 1200: A Symposium.* New York: Metropolitan Museum of Art, 1975, pp. 301–12; Harrsen, Meta. "The Countess Judith of Flanders and the Library of Weingarten Abbey." *Papers of the Bibliographical Society of America* 24 (1930): 1–13; Havice, Christine. "Women and the Production of Art in the Middle Ages: The Significance of Context." In *Double Vision: Perspectives on Gender and the Visual Arts,* ed. Natalie Harris Bluestone. Madison: Fairleigh Dickinson University Press, 1995, pp. 67–94; Holdsworth, Christopher. "Christina of Markyate." In *Medieval Women,* ed. Derek Baker. Oxford: Blackwell, 1978, pp. 185–204; Kowaleski, Maryanne, and Judith Bennett. "Crafts, Gilds, and Women in the Middle Ages: Fifty Years after Marian K. Dale." In *Sisters and Workers in the Middle Ages,* ed. Judith Bennett et al. Chicago: University of Chicago Press, 1989, pp. 11–38; McNulty, J. Bard. "The Lady Aelfgyva in the Bayeux Tapestry." *Speculum* 55 (1980): 659–68; Neuman de Vegvar, Carol. "Saints and

Companions to Saints: Anglo-Saxon Royal Women Monastics in Context." In *Holy Men and Holy Women: Old English Prose Saints' Lives and Their Contents,* ed. Paul E. Szarmach. Albany: SUNY Press, 1996, 51–93; Peers, C., and Radford, C.R. "The Saxon Monastery at Whitby." *Archaeologia* 89 (1943): 27–88; Power, Eileen. *Medieval English Nunneries c. 1275 to 1535.* Cambridge: Cambridge University Press, 1922; Sandler, Lucy. *The Psalter of Robert de Lisle.* London: Harvey Miller, 1983 [a complex 14th-century book designed for a female audience]; Sekules, Veronica. "Women and Art in England in the Thirteenth and Fourteenth Centuries." In *Age of Chivalry: Art in Plantagenet England 1200–1400,* ed. Jonathan Alexander and Paul Binski. London: Royal Academy of Arts, 1987, pp. 41–48 [many of the objects mentioned in this entry are illustrated in this catalogue]; Sydenham, Laura. *Shaftesbury and Its Abbey.* Lingfield: Oakwood, 1959; Talbot, C.H., ed. *The Life of Christina of Markyate.* Oxford: Clarendon, 1959; Zarnecki, George. "A Twelfth-Century Column-Figure of the Standing Virgin from Minster-in-Sheppey." In *Studies in Romanesque Sculpture.* London: Dorian Press, 1979, article no. 14 (n.p.).

See also Amesbury Psalter; Apocalypses; Art, Romanesque; Bayeux Tapestry; Brailes, William de; Opus Anglicanum; Romsey Abbey; Romsey Roods; St. Albans Psalter; Textiles, Anglo-Saxon; Textiles from St. Cuthbert's Tomb; Women; Women in ME Literature; Women in OE Literature

Women in Middle English Literature

The study of women as writers and readers of ME literature, and as figures within that literature, has undergone sweeping changes in the last twenty years. Until the 1970s little critical attention was paid to female authors or audiences of medieval English literature, and studies of female characters in ME literary works tended to focus on such matters as anti-feminist satire, women as objects of courtly love, and the proper role or "place" of women in medieval literary debates on the nature of marriage. Following the rise of the women's movement and the subsequent development of various forms of feminist theory in the 1970s and 1980s new questions began to be asked about women in ME literature, and new answers to be suggested; although many of the questions remain open, the issues raised have made an unmistakable and irrevocable mark on ME literary studies as a whole.

The broad topic of women in ME literature can be examined under four relatively distinct subheadings: literature written by women, literature written for women, representations of women in the literature, and other theoretical issues related to women and gender in ME literature.

Literature by Women

Only a few women authors writing in ME are known by name, all from the end of the 14th century or later, and almost all are authors or translators of religious works. Among

these are the late-14th- and early-15th-century anchoress Julian of Norwich (author of the *Showings,* an account of her mystical visions); Margery Kempe (known for her spiritual autobiography, written down by a priest ca. 1438); Eleanor Hull (d. 1460; translator of a commentary on the penitential psalms and a series of devout meditations); Margaret Beaufort (translator, with William Atkinson, of Thomas à Kempis's *Imitation of Christ* [1504]); several 15th-century female letter writers; and, more tentatively, Dame Juliana Berners (sometimes credited with writing parts of *The Book of St. Albans,* a treatise on hunting and related sports printed in 1486).

There were doubtless other women writers in the period. The possibility of female authorship has been suggested for *The Owl and the Nightingale* (ca. 1200). The provincial compilation of lyrics and other poetry known as the Findern Manuscript (late 15th to early 16th century; CUL Ff.1.6) contains works possibly written and perhaps composed by women. The early-16th-century Devonshire Manuscript (BL Add. 17492), a collection of poetry probably done at court, may include lyrics by women. There also exist ME translations of works written by or attributed to women: for example, some of the lais of Marie de France (the only known Anglo-Norman woman author to be translated into ME), a variety of devotional and spiritual works by continental holy women like Birgitta (Bridget) of Sweden, a few of Christine de Pizan's works, and treatises on women's health attributed to Trotula of Salerno.

Literature for Women

The fact that a number of English women were book owners and patrons suggests that women were avid consumers, if not producers, of literature. Although work on medieval female literacy is only beginning, we do know generally that educational opportunities for women declined after the Norman Conquest and began to rise again only late in the ME period. In addition, while English literacy rates among women may have remained constant after the Conquest, pre-Conquest female Latin literacy appears, from the scant remaining evidence (e.g., the superb Latin of the nuns of Barking Abbey), to have been more advanced than that of nuns in later periods for whom no comparable works were written. Descriptions in 14th-century and later ME literature of women reading books or being read to by other women suggest that some women could and did read, especially in the vernacular. (Literacy in Anglo-Norman was relatively common among upper-class women from the 12th to the 14th century, but later in the period literary texts for aristocratic women came to be more commonly written in English than in Anglo-Norman.)

Women seem to have enjoyed a prominent role throughout the ME period as patrons and book owners. Women and those similarly untrained in Latin may have provided the primary audience for certain kinds of ME texts after the Conquest, since popular secular literature, such as romances, tended to be written in Anglo-Norman and much religious literature written for men was written in Latin. Works written for women in early ME tended to be religious in subject matter and included saints' lives (such as those of the Katherine

Group), religious lyrics (such as those of the Wooing Group—possibly written by women), religious guides for women (such as the *Ancrene Wisse*), and religious tracts (such as *Hali Meiðhad,* or *Holy Virginity*). This picture does not seem to have changed greatly in the later period, though more ME secular works may have been written for or read by women. Lydgate says that Chaucer wrote *The Legend of Good Women* at the request of Queen Anne, and in the 15th century writers like Capgrave, Bokenham, and Lydgate himself all wrote religious works for female patrons.

Representation

Representations of women in medieval English literature are affected by the period's prevailing attitudes toward them, attitudes that have their roots in Aristotelian medical theory. The Aristotelian model dichotomized men and women as being respectively analogous to such categories as active/passive; form/matter; completion/incompletion; possession/deprivation. These categories in turn informed Christian commentary, especially on Genesis, in which Eve was identified with the will and the body and Adam with intelligence and the mind. As daughters of Eve all women were believed to have inherited Eve's supposed dependence on the senses, inability to think abstractly, fundamental willfulness, and sexual guilt. The Middle Ages also inherited two opposing views of woman's spiritual nature, the Platonic view of the soul's neutrality with respect to gender and an Aristotelian view of the soul as differentiated by gender. Attitudes toward women were further conditioned by patristic discussions of virginity and marriage. Among those commentaries Jerome's vitriolic argument against marriage, the *Epistola adversus Jovinianum,* proved particularly influential; it contributed greatly to a Latin and vernacular tradition of antifeminist literature that influenced many major works, most notably Chaucer's *Wife of Bath's Prologue,* with its riposte to Jerome.

The genres in which women are represented in vernacular texts include sermons, saints' lives, legends of good or holy women, romances, fabliaux, allegories, and debate poems. Sermon literature usually draws on the traditional contrast between Mary and Eve as positive and negative female models, often with some reference to Old Testament figures, especially Judith and Esther. Saints' lives generally represent women of extraordinary power, although that power is almost always conditioned by the female saint's romantic dependence on Christ, who is usually presented as her lover and spouse. The spiritual power of these holy women is also offset in some ways by the brutal physical violence (often explicitly or implicitly sexual) done to many of them by their earthly antagonists, which the saints willingly suffer rather than renounce their faith. Like these female saints in virtuous steadfastness, but not officially canonized, are the various long-suffering "good women" found in a number of romances and romancelike narratives, such as *Octavian, Le Bone Florence of Rome,* the Breton lay *Emare,* or Chaucer's *Man of Law's Tale* and *Clerk's Tale.*

Complex representations of women occur in some ME romances: for example, Freine in *Lai le Freine,* Melior in *William of Palerne,* Chaucer's Criseyde, and Henryson's Cresseid. However, the focus of ME romances is more often on the fortunes and misfortunes of male protagonists, and many women in the romances are relatively one-dimensional; their characterization is often based on female stereotypes drawn from the conventions of courtly love or antifeminist satire. Also influenced by the antifeminist tradition is the fabliau, a genre most complexly developed in ME by Chaucer, which usually represents women as sensual, manipulative, cunning, and witty.

Female figures are commonly found in allegorical works, due largely to the feminine grammatical gender of most abstractions in Latin and French. Familiar examples include Langland's Holy Church, Lady Meed, and Dames Study and Scripture; Chaucer's goddess Nature and Lady Fame; the Maiden in *Pearl;* and the Boethian Lady Philosophy and Fortune. Although these allegorical figures are not primarily intended as mimetic representations, they can take on "character traits" related to the available medieval concepts of women's nature: courtly beauty, shrewishness, stern virtue, maternal nurture and correction, promiscuity, and various other features. Perhaps the most explicit discussions of how women should be described occur in debate poems on the nature of love and of women, including *The Owl and the Nightingale, The Thrush and the Nightingale,* and Clanvowe's *Book of Cupid.*

The class of the women represented in ME literature tends to be aristocratic, although Chaucer represented women of the middle classes as well. Langland presents the widest range of class and type of woman, although his allegorical mode tends to preclude the rich representation of character achieved by Chaucer and some of the romances and saints' lives. Margery Kempe's self-representation is particularly important as one of the first extended images of a middle-class woman in English.

Other Theoretical Issues

The subject of women in ME literature has drawn much attention recently from feminist critics, especially but not exclusively in connection with Chaucer. These critics are concerned, in their studies of works by both men and women, not only with representations of women but also with the interrelated social and literary questions concerning female and male gender roles, typical modes of discourse, and the origins of those roles and discourses. At present many feminist critics locate themselves at various points between two widely separated poles. The first, an ahistorical psychological essentialism, assumes that men and women's biological differences radically distinguish their perceptions and experiences of the world irrespective of the cultural conditions of the two sexes. The second, a position most often adopted by cultural materialists and new historicists, assumes that the phenomenon of differing gender roles is almost entirely sociopolitical (e.g., Judith Butler's analysis of gender as a performance). Some of the most fruitful recent feminist analyses of medieval literature seek a synthesis of these two extremes.

Representations of women in ME literature are clearly bound by both social and "natural" conditions (as defined by Aristotle and patristic writers) that limited women's literary roles to those of wife, virgin, mother, or lover. One of the first questions that might be asked in feminist analyses of ME works is whether the authors seek to promulgate or question these definitions. Some feminist critics assume that it is impossible for a male writer to represent women. For example, such critics would argue that Criseyde is only a projection of Chaucer's self, a construct that allows him to explore problems of masculinity, including his own problems as a writer. Others, however, see the possibility for some male writers to construct a genuine feminine voice, understood by them by virtue of their own marginalized position in society. From such a point of view Criseyde becomes a representation of difference, of what it means to be "other," that which cannot be subsumed or explained by traditional male logic or hierarchy.

Such variations of theoretical approach can complicate our understanding of representations of women. For example, at first glance, the conventions of *fin amour,* or courtly love, seem to invert the feudal subservience of woman by reversing her social role and placing her at the top of the hierarchy. This placement nonetheless does nothing to question the representation of women as passive objects of exchange, the prizes "won" by the service of their courtly suitors. On the other hand the association of woman with the human will and with the allegorical personification of Wisdom can allow her to become, like Dante's Beatrice, a stepping stone to God. The deity itself can be seen as "feminine" insofar as the Godhead stands for a force that calls worldly categories and assumptions into question. In mysticism, as Caroline Bynum has shown, a feminized Christ sometimes operates as a crucial center in works by both men and women.

Recent psychological theory distinguishing between a socially constructed "female" relational thinking and a socially constructed "male" hierarchical thinking has proved illuminating in some studies of medieval representations of women. For example, in the York Cycle Noah's secure place in the hierarchy is underscored by his privileged access to both God and God's knowledge and by his predominant desire to fulfill God's command no matter what the consequences are to others. Noah's wife, however, denied direct access to God or God's word, thinks relationally of the needs and concerns of her friends.

Finally we might consider stylistic questions, such as the relations between the style of a work, the sex and education of its author and its primary audience, its genre, and other aspects of its production. These and many other questions on women in ME literature cannot yet be answered fully due to the limited information presently available on medieval women writers and readers. As one critic says of the literary contributions of women throughout medieval Europe, "A comprehensive and authoritative treatment of the subject is not yet possible: . . . much certainly remains to be discovered and much to be charted for the first time" (Dronke, 1984: vii), especially in the large number of unedited religious works of the late Middle Ages. Feminist research and criticism have only begun to uncover the questions that can be asked about the subject of women in medieval English literature.

Elizabeth Robertson

Bibliography

PRIMARY

Barratt, Alexandra, ed. *Women's Writing in Middle English.* London: Longman, 1992; see also primary texts cited in entries on particular works by or addressed to women elsewhere in this volume.

SECONDARY

See also secondary bibliography cited in entries cross-referenced below and the *Medieval Feminist Newsletter* 1– (1986–) [interdisciplinary journal providing bibliography, reviews, reports of conference papers, and commentary and dialogue on theoretical issues]; Butler, Judith. *Gender Trouble: Feminism and the Subversion of Identity.* New York: Routledge, Chapman, & Hall, 1990; Butler, Judith. *Bodies That Matter: On the Discursive Limits of Sex.* New York: Routledge, 1993; Bynum, Caroline Walker. *Jesus as Mother: Studies in the Spirituality of the High Middle Ages.* Berkeley: University of California Press, 1982; Bynum, Caroline Walker. *Holy Feast and Holy Fast: The Religious Significance of Food to Medieval Women.* Berkeley: University of California Press, 1987; Coleman, Janet. *Medieval Readers and Writers, 1350–1400.* London: Hutchinson, 1981; Crane, Susan. *Gender and Romance in Chaucer's Canterbury Tales.* Princeton: Princeton University Press, 1994; Dinshaw, Carolyn. *Chaucer's Sexual Poetics.* Madison: University of Wisconsin Press, 1989; Dronke, Peter. *Women Writers of the Middle Ages.* Cambridge: Cambridge University Press, 1984; Erler, Mary, and Maryanne Kowaleski, eds. *Women and Power in the Middle Ages.* Athens: University of Georgia Press, 1988; Ferrante, Joan M. *Woman as Image in Medieval Literature: From the Twelfth Century to Dante.* New York: Columbia University Press, 1975; Fisher, Sheila, and Janet E. Halley, eds. *Seeking the Woman in Late Medieval and Renaissance Writings: Essays in Feminist Contextual Criticism.* Knoxville: University of Tennessee Press, 1989; Hansen, Elaine Tuttle. *Chaucer and the Fictions of Gender.* Berkeley: University of California Press, 1992; Maclean, Ian. *The Renaissance Notion of Woman: A Study in the Fortunes of Scholasticism and Medical Science in European Intellectual Life.* Cambridge: Cambridge University Press, 1980; Mann, Jill. *Geoffrey Chaucer.* Feminist Readings Series. London: Harvester Wheatsheaf, 1991; Meale, Carol M. *Women and Literature in Britain: 1150–1500.* Cambridge: Cambridge University Press, 1993; Moi, Toril. *Sexual/Textual Politics: Feminist Literary Theory.* London: Methuen, 1985; Power, Eileen. *Medieval Women,* ed. M.M. Postan. Cambridge: Cambridge University Press, 1975; Tavormina, M. Teresa. *Kindly Similitude: Marriage and Family in Piers Plowman.* Cambridge: Brewer, 1995; Utley, Francis Lee. *The Crooked Rib: An Analytical Index to the Argument about Women . . . to . . . 1568.* Columbus: Ohio State University Press, 1944; Warner, Marina. *Alone of All Her Sex: The Myth and the Cult of the Virgin Mary.* New York: Knopf, 1976.

See also Ancrene Wisse; Anglo-Norman Literature; Beaufort, Margaret; Berners, Juliana; Bokenham; Breton Lay; Chaucer; Courtesy Literature; Courtly Love; Debate Poems; Family Letter Collections; Hagiography; Hull; Julian of Norwich; Katherine Group; Kempe; Literacy; Lyrics; Marie de France; Nuns; *Owl and the Nightingale;* Queens; Romances; Widows; Women; Women and the Arts; Women in OE Literature

Women in Old English Literature

Women appear in the major extant manuscripts from the Anglo-Saxon period as characters in prose and poetry, as historical personages, and (using the term in its broadest sense) as authors. Excluded from the discussion below are the female figures represented in the illustrations along the borders or within the text of manuscripts.

Prose

Representations of women in prose are largely hagiographical, except for the secular belletristic *Apollonius of Tyre,* a translation into OE of a Greek romance. Featured therein are Arcestrate (Apollonius's wife), their daughter Thasia, and the unnamed daughter of Antiochus (with her nurse confidante), who is involved in an incestuous relationship with her father. But the major female characters are found in Ælfric of Eynsham's collection of saints' lives. Although Aldhelm had composed his *De virginitate* (dedicated to Abbess Hildelith and the nuns at Barking) and Bede his *Martyrology,* Ælfric's *Lives of the Saints* was the first collection of hagiographies in English. Ælfric's most prevalent female type is the virgin martyr; St. Agnes, St. Lucy, and the transvestite St. Eugenia are the most successfully rendered. Unlike Aldhelm's and Bede's works Ælfric's *Lives* are in alliterative prose and are characterized by clarity of style and simplicity of characterization. Among other prose hagiographic works are the fragmentary life of St. Mildrith (the granddaughter of King Penda of Mercia) in the *Lives of the Kentish Royal Saints* and the brief hagiographic narratives in the OE *Martyrology,* which include female saints like Perpetua and Felicitas and English women saints like Æthelthryth and Pega (the sister of St. Guthlac).

Historical and documentary prose is marked by portraits of strong, efficient, and intelligent women. In the OE translation of Bede's *Ecclesiastical History* the most remarkable is Abbess Hild of the double monastery of Whitby, who, among other acts, officiated over the Synod of Whitby in 664, encouraged the poet Cædmon to translate the Christian story into Germanic meter, and mentored five monks to bishoprics. Bede depicts other memorable women religious: Æthelburh of Barking and Æthelthryth of Ely, to whom he composes a praise song, are two of many.

In contrast the Anglo-Saxon Chronicle is reserved in its inclusion of women, although those it does refer to are women of strength and volition. It mentions the razing of Taunton by Queen Æthelburh (722), the rise to the throne of Queen Seaxburh (672), and the founding of Ely by Æthelthryth, though these are only noted in passing. It speaks more fully of Æthelred's and Cnut's queen, Emma, but again, were it not for the *Encomium Emmae* and later chronicles, the full

measure of her influence would be lost. In general the Chronicle steers away from emphasizing women's deeds: the West Saxon version, as an instance, avoids recording the deeds of the most prominent woman of the early 10th century, Æthelflæd, the Lady of the Mercians, King Alfred's daughter. In its treatment of women the Chronicle generally exemplifies the process of the editing out of women in history.

The extant legal writings place Anglo-Saxon women in a social context from which they emerge as serving maids, slaves, concubines, and adulteresses, as well as wives and widows. Anglo-Saxon legal codes attest to the basic rights of women (right to divorce; right of autonomy), although the evidence can only be partial since it may not reflect actual practice. In the 11th-century *Sermo Lupi ad Anglos,* for example, Archbishop Wulfstan points to the harassing and forcing of widows to remarry as a sign of social decay. Charters and wills refer to women as benefactresses of male and female monastic communities, as witnesses to numerous legal documents, and as generators of charters under their own names. A number of wills by women contain bequests that help to define more clearly the images of prosperous Anglo-Saxon women in the context of their society. Unfortunately such wills do not indicate whether the testatrix was literate or whether the will was dictated.

The literacy of OE women is clearly attested to, however, in the Anglo-Latin writings. Rudolf of Fulda's *Life of St. Leoba* and Otloh's *Life of St. Boniface* testify to the high level of learning attained by Anglo-Saxon nuns and serve as evidence for female authorship. The letters and poems of women like Berhtgyth, Bucge, Eadburh, Leoba, and a string of others reflect minds of active and creative intelligence. Even though the literature is in Latin, and not of primary concern here, the existence of these documents helps to place the women of vernacular literature in an appropriate context.

Poetry

Representations of women in the poetry present characters who range in type from sorceresses (in the charms) to Christian warrior saints (in the heroic poetry). Two of the charms ("For a Swarm of Bees"; "For a Sudden Stitch") make reference to women as victorious warriors with superior martial strength. Another ("For Unfruitful Land") represents woman as the center of the procreative and regenerative principles in the universe. Women's sexuality is treated with humorous double entendre in ten of the Riddles, and the collections known as *Maxims I* and *II* present sketches of women of various social classes, from a queen who gives "secret counsel" to a woman who must seek out her "friend" (lover) with "hidden skill" (magic)—qualities of prescience and intellectual acumen that are characteristic of the women in the heroic poetry as well.

Women's vulnerability and psychological isolation are strikingly depicted in a number of short lyrics. In the Advent Lyrics (also called *Christ I*) Mary suffers an adversarial relationship with the citizens of Salem and an estrangement from Joseph. In *Deor* Beadohild experiences the fury of Weland's revenge, and Mæthhild is ravaged by love. In the longer lyrics—*The Wife's Lament* and *Wulf and Eadwacer*—known as the OE *Frauenlieder* and linked to the Latin erotic women's songs of the mid-11th-century Cambridge Songbook, emotional and psychological disquietude is intensified, the effects of which determine and define the linguistic uniqueness in the poems. Because of the poems' situational and grammatical features arguments have been put forth not only to substantiate a female speaker but also to establish female authorship.

The range of the representation of women found in the minor, didactic poetry and in the lyrics narrows down to the depiction of three major figures in Christian and secular heroic poetry: the warrior woman, the counselor, and the peaceweaver—although, as a rule, the types overlap. The hybrid Old Testament–Christian Judith and Cynewulf's heroines Elene and Juliana are martial figures, a blend of the patristic *miles Christi* and the Germanic valkyrie— gold-adorned, quick and piercing of mind, assertive in speech, and intractable in action. In secular heroic poetry Hildegyth of the *Waldere* fragments is related to these, and Grendel's mother in *Beowulf* exemplifies the Germanic female warrior in her grim aspect. Complexity and strength of character define the OE warrior women: Elene and Judith emerge as political figures, counselors, and heads of state (a surrogate position in Elene's case), and Juliana wars against her adversaries with an oratorical and forensic skill that elevates her above the typical virgin martyr. In language and action these characters are the female equivalents to the Germanic hero.

In the Christian heroic poetry other than Cynewulf's the most prevalent female character is the counselor (whether failed, as is Eve in *Genesis B,* or successful, as is Sarah in *Exodus*). Women give counsel in the secular heroic poetry as well, Wealhtheow in *Beowulf* being the most prominent example. One of the most discussed, and perhaps the most equivocal, of the female character types is the *frēoðuwebbe,* "peaceweaver." In the past the term has had a domestic coloration, referring to a woman who had been given as a "peace token" by one tribe to another; however, L. John Sklute's recent word-field study cautions against such an interpretation and, on contextual analysis, suggests a more political and diplomatic function. Only Ealhhild in *Widsith,* Modthrytho in *Beowulf,* and the night messenger in *Elene* are thus characterized, although Wealhtheow is described by the related term *friðusibb.* The inclination of scholars to apply the attribute of a *frēoðuwebbe* to characters who are not referred to as such (e.g., Eve and Sarah) only tends to obscure our understanding of the female functions of peaceweaving and counseling in the OE canon.

Although the first discussions of women in OE literature date to the 19th century, it is only within the last twenty years that concerted studies of them have been undertaken. For the most part the early commentaries and surveys, following the 19th-century attitudes about women, concluded that, in and out of the literature, women were socially inferior. There were exceptions, of course, that did present the Anglo-Saxon woman as socially responsible: for example, Sharon Turner in his *History of the Anglo Saxons* at the beginning of the century, Lina Eckenstein in *Woman under Monasticism* at the end. In the 20th century the ground-breaking arguments that systematically established Anglo-Saxon wom-

en's autonomous position were those by Frank and Doris Stenton and, later, by Dorothy Whitelock and Christine Fell.

In literary criticism women characters, as a rule, were not chosen as subjects of inquiry but rather were part of excursuses into genre, sources, or the lexicon. Except for Damico's study of Wealhtheow, on those occasions when a woman character was singled out for analysis the approach was (and in some instances continues to be) allegorical. Feminist literary approaches to the characters in OE prose and poetry have been less intense and numerous than those in ME literature, a situation caused, in part by the conservative nature of scholarship in OE, in part by the language barrier, and in part by the lesser number of primary materials scholars have had available to them. Nonetheless, there has been a slow but steady advance. Questions relating to women's personal autonomy, for example, have brought into the foreground portraits of aristocratic women with social and political strength, and religious women with independent status (Fell; Stafford). Questions of voice and style have gone toward pinpointing the distinct differences in impulse and expression between women's talk and men's (Belanoff), and questions related to feminine imagery and structure have offered alternative readings to traditionally male-oriented texts (Heffernan). In general current feminist approaches lean more toward realistic interpretations, placing the characters in literary, social, or historical contexts.

Helen Damico
Alexandra Hennessey Olsen

Bibliography

PRIMARY

For primary texts see entries elsewhere in this volume on particular works and authors cited above.

SECONDARY

Bandell, Betty. "The English Chroniclers' Attitude toward Women." *Journal of the History of Ideas* 16 (1955): 113–18; Chance, Jane. *Woman As Hero in Anglo-Saxon Literature.* Syracuse: Syracuse University Press, 1986; Damico, Helen. *Beowulf's Wealhtheow and the Valkyrie Tradition.* Madison: University of Wisconsin Press, 1984; Damico, Helen, and Alexandra Hennessey Olsen, eds. *New Readings on Women in Old English Literature.* Bloomington: Indiana University Press, 1990 [many relevant essays; see esp. Patricia A. Belanoff, "Women's Songs, Women's Language: *Wulf and Eadwacer* and *The Wife's Lament,*" pp. 193–203; L. John Sklute, "*Freoðuwebbe* in Old English Poetry," pp. 204–10; Frank M. Stenton, "The Historical Bearing on Place-Name Studies: The Place of Women in Anglo-Saxon Society," pp. 79–88]; Davidson, Clifford. "Erotic 'Women's Songs' in Anglo-Saxon England." *Neophilologus* 59 (1975): 451–62; Fell, Christine E., with Cecily Clark and Elizabeth Williams. *Women in Anglo-Saxon England and the Impact of 1066.* Bloomington: Indiana University Press, 1984; Heffernan, Carol Falvo. *The Phoenix at the Fountain: Images of Women and Eternity in Lactantius's "Carmen de Ave Phoenice" and the Old English "Phoenix."* Newark: University of Delaware Press, 1988; Klinck, Anne Lingard. "Anglo-Saxon Women and the Law." *Journal of Medieval History* 8 (1982): 107–21; Luecke, Janemarie. "The Unique Experience of Anglo-Saxon Nuns." In *Medieval Religious Women II: Peaceweavers,* ed. John A. Nichols and Lillian Thomas Shank. Kalamazoo: Cistercian Publications, 1987, pp. 55–65; Meyer, Marc A. "Women and the Tenth Century English Monastic Reform." *Revue bénédictine* 87 (1977): 34–61; Stafford, Pauline. *Queens, Concubines, and Dowagers: The King's Wife in Wessex in the Early Middle Ages.* Athens: University of Georgia Press, 1984; Stenton, Doris M. *The English Woman in History.* London: Allen & Unwin, 1957.

See also Apollonius of Tyre; Beowulf; Cynewulf; Emma; Exeter Book; Hagiography; Hild; *Judith;* Nuns; Queens; *Wife's Lament;* Wills; Women; Women and the Arts; Women in ME Literature; *Wulf and Eadwacer*

Worcester Fragments

A group of fragments of medieval English polyphonic music, 62 leaves in all, removed from the bindings of manuscripts originally belonging to the Dean and Chapter Library, Worcester, that represent the incomplete remains of perhaps as many as a half-dozen music volumes. Forty-three leaves are in Worcester Cathedral Library, while the remainder are in the Bodleian Library and the British Library. The reclamation of most of these pages took place during the years 1906–26, when the library was being renovated and the manuscripts were catalogued by Floyer. The discovery in 1990 of a partial bifolio of music in another Worcester manuscript in this library suggests that there may be additional fragments remaining to be recovered from the covers and spines of other Worcester manuscripts that remain in their medieval bindings, not only in the Cathedral Library but also in those books dispersed to other collections in England. The 43 leaves in the Chapter Library are catalogued together under a single shelf number, Add. 68. The 27 leaves in the Bodleian Library have been assembled into a composite manuscript, Latin liturgical d. 20, which is made up of actual manuscript pages and rotographic copies of pages from Worcester and the British Library. The British Library manuscript (Add. 25013) comprises two leaves and two fragments in London.

Worcester Cathedral Chapter Library, originally one of the largest in medieval Britain, is today one of only two medieval monastic libraries that have remained in place and relatively intact following the suppression of the monasteries in the 16th century. Because of this good fortune we have access to a body of English polyphonic music unprecedented in its size and scope that was produced over a timespan of more than a century. Most of the manuscript pages appear to have been produced in the 13th century, perhaps at Worcester Cathedral, though there is no conclusive evidence to support this often repeated supposition regarding provenance. Additions of new polyphonic works to a number of the leaves

by a number of scribes seem to have taken place throughout the 14th century. These additions suggest that the original music books may have remained in use and intact until shortly before their dismemberment in the late 14th or early 15th century. The survival of the fragments to our own time is utterly fortuitous, as it appears that they were consigned to the binder's waste bin at the very time that the Cathedral Library was undertaking a rebinding campaign for many of its manuscripts. The incorporation of leaves from these dismembered music books into manuscripts whose contents were unrelated to music or the mass and divine office no doubt saved them from the destruction accorded virtually every medieval Catholic service book during the reign of Henry VIII and the Protectorate of Oliver Cromwell.

The fragments vary not only in size, format, content, and date but also in their state of preservation. At least two different groups of leaves preserve polyphonic music on pages that appear to have come originally from manuscripts devoted to plainsong. Two other groups were part of large anthologies of polyphony. One of the latter contained at least 131 folios, the largest manuscript from 13th-century England to have a significant amount of its contents extant. A second preserves medieval foliation up to sixteen. The remaining fragments may have come from at least another four separate music manuscripts. Three of these are small pieces of pages from one or more fine music books. Any attempt to reconstruct the originals from the evidence of these fragments is virtually impossible. The leaves in the Bodleian Library are clearly related to the two larger manuscript books, as are the fragments in the British Library. Paleographical connections between these two groups of leaves from the two anthologies, even though they differ in size and format, strongly suggest that both parent manuscripts were produced in the same scriptorium.

Over 110 anonymous individual musical compositions are contained in this body of fragments. More than 80 percent are for three voices; the remainder are for two or four. They set a wide variety of sacred texts including those from the mass, both Proper and Ordinary (with and without tropes), the divine office, and extraliturgical devotional texts. In this latter group the bulk of the settings are in praise of the Virgin Mary. The genres represented include organal settings, motets (of three different types: whole-chant settings, motets on a *pes,* and motets based on a portion of a *cantus firmus*), conducti, troped chant settings, English discant, and English cantilena. Because the manuscripts vary in age they contain compositions in varying styles. Some of the earliest do not have a determinable rhythmic pattern, while others employ the most up-to-date notational devices of the late 13th century, which often display the English penchant for trochaic rhythms. Some of the later additions to certain leaves are notationally advanced as well. Notable compositional devices include the use of rota, rondellus, and voice exchange. Also of note is an apparent increase in the use of four voices in the later-13th-century compositions, a pattern not retained after the early 14th century. The musical, liturgical, and compositional richness and diversity of the works found in this large group of fragments suggests that vibrant centers of musical activity existed in 13th-century England, one of which was perhaps at Worcester Cathedral itself.

William J. Summers

Bibliography

PRIMARY

Dittmer, Luther, ed. *The Worcester Fragments.* Rome: American Institute of Musicology, 1957; Dittmer, Luther, ed. *Worcester Add. 68; Westminster Abbey 33327; Madrid, Bibl. Nac. 192.* Brooklyn: Institute of Mediaeval Music, 1959 [facsimile]; Dittmer, Luther, ed. *Oxford, Latin Liturgical D 20; London, Add. MS. 25031; Chicago, MS. 654 App.* Brooklyn: Institute of Mediaeval Music, 1960 [facsimile]; Hughes, Anselm, ed. *Worcester Mediaeval Harmony of the Thirteenth and Fourteenth Centuries.* Burnham: Plainsong & Mediaeval Music Society, 1928 [partial ed. and facsimile]; Sanders, Ernest H., ed. *English Music of the Thirteenth and Early Fourteenth Centuries.* Polyphonic Music of the Fourteenth Century 14. Paris: L'Oiseau-Lyre, 1979.

SECONDARY

Floyer, J.K., and S.G. Hamilton. *Catalogue of Manuscripts Preserved in the Chapter Library of Worcester Cathedral.* Oxford: Parker, 1906; Sanders, Ernest H. "Sources, MS, V, VI." *NGD* 17:655–61; Sanders, Ernest H. "Worcester Polyphony." *NGD* 20:524–28; Summers, William J. "Unknown and Unidentified English Polyphonic Music from the Fourteenth Century." *Research Chronicle* 19 (1983–85): 57–67.

See also Manuscripts of Polyphonic Music

Writs

The Anglo-Saxon writ, or *breve* in Latin, dates at least back to the time of Alfred the Great. It was a short letter, written in English, sent by the king and authenticated by his seal, ordering someone—usually the sheriff—to carry out a royal command. These terse and direct communications, so different from the cumbersome diplomas of continental monarchs, provided easy and efficient contact between the court and outlying regions. Because William I and his successors recognized its usefulness, the writ was one of the Anglo-Saxon instruments of government to survive, although the language became Latin.

Henry II took these Anglo-Norman administrative writs and "judicialized" them. Instead of occasional royal interventions in local or feudal courts they became instruments for regular and routine extension of the king's jurisdiction over nonroyal courts. Under Henry II writs *de cursu* could be purchased from the chancery, enabling the purchaser to initiate suits in the royal court or to secure transfer from a local court or from his lord's feudal court. Certain writs initiated possessory assizes, directing the sheriff to summon a jury to settle a question of landholding. Other writs, such as the writ of right or the *praecipe,* still commanded someone to do something, such as to do justice to the purchaser or restore a landholding to him.

Disobedience to the writ would place the addressee in contempt of a royal command and cause him to be summoned to the king's court to answer the charge, in effect transferring the case there. By the end of the 13th century new writs were no longer readily available. Litigants for whom no appropriate writ existed could find no remedy under common law, and they had to petition the chancellor, opening the way for chancery jurisdiction.

The late-12th-century legal treatise known as *Glanville* consists in large part of a collection of writs with commentaries on how the proceeding should progress following issue of the original writ. It gives nineteen writs initiating actions and about 30 dealing with subsequent steps in the proceedings. The treatise we attribute to Bracton, the successor to *Glanville,* also follows to some extent a writ-based scheme of organization. Registers of writs, useful to royal clerks and to litigants or their representatives, date from the early 13th century.

Ralph V. Turner

Bibliography

Barraclough, Geoffrey. "The Anglo-Saxon Writ." *History* 39 (1954): 193–215; de Haas, Elsa, and G.D.G. Hall, eds. *Early Registers of Writs.* Selden Society 87. London: Quaritch, 1970; Harmer, Florence E. *Anglo-Saxon Writs.* 2d ed. Stamford: Watkins, 1989; van Caenegem, R.C., ed. *Royal Writs in England from the Conquest to Glanvill.* Selden Society 77. London: Quaritch, 1959.

See also Bracton; Glanville; Henry II; Law, Anglo-Saxon; Law, Post-Conquest

Wulf and Eadwacer

The nineteen-line *Wulf and Eadwacer* is one of the few OE poems generally agreed to have a female narrator, but it is also one of the most obscure of all OE poems. The exasperated comment of Benjamin Thorpe, the poem's 19th-century editor, "of this I can make no sense," fairly typifies the reaction of many readers to this day. Critics agree that the poem is an expression of suffering, but there is little agreement on the narrative context of that suffering, and a remarkable diversity of readings has been proposed. Because the only extant copy of the poem, in the Exeter Book miscellany of OE poetry, is separated from a series of riddles by no clear paleographical demarcation, early commentary regarded the poem as a riddle, the proposed solutions of which included an ingenious but now discredited theory that it is an autobiographical riddle by the poet Cynewulf. Other proposed interpretations have associated the poem with Germanic legends, especially the Odoacer legends, a connection most recently and convincingly argued by Joseph Harris. It has also been read as a dog's lustful dream of a wolf, a charm against disease, and a complaint about bad copying.

The most widely accepted reading today is that the poem is a *Frauenlied* ("woman's song") whose unnamed speaker is a woman lamenting separation from her lover. She is on one island; her lover, Wulf, is on another. They are kept apart by some hostile figure, apparently a man named Eadwacer, who may be the woman's husband; however, it has also been suggested that Wulf is her husband—or son—and that Eadwacer is not a name but merely a noun meaning "property watcher."

Janet Schrunk Ericksen

Bibliography

PRIMARY

ASPR 3:179–80; Baker, Peter S., ed. "A Classroom Edition of Wulf and Eadwacer." *OEN* 16/2 (Spring 1983): Appendix.

SECONDARY

Desmond, Marilynn. "The Voice of Exile: Feminist Literary History and the Anonymous Anglo-Saxon Elegy." *Critical Inquiry* 16 (1990): 572–90; Harris, Joseph. "Elegy in Old English and Old Norse: A Problem in Literary History." In *The Old English Elegies,* ed. Martin Green. Rutherford: Fairleigh Dickinson University Press, 1983, pp. 46–56.

See also Exeter Book; *Wife's Lament;* Women; Women in OE Literature

Wulfstan of York (d. 1023)

Bishop of London 996–1002, bishop of Worcester 1002–16, and archbishop of York 1002–23, who served two kings (Æthelred II and Cnut) as adviser and author of legislation while addressing the pressing moral and ecclesiastical issues of his time. One of two great stylists in the history of OE prose (with Ælfric), Wulfstan had a distinguished career as a homilist and statesman. Although educated as a Benedictine, he was very much a public figure who began signing himself "Lupus" ("Wolf") early in his career, as he developed a reputation for spoken and written eloquence and for moral reform. The 12th-century *Liber Eliensis* (*Book of Ely*) provides the only medieval information, much of that questionable, about his life.

When he assumed the sees of Worcester and York in plurality (holding both simultaneously) upon the death in 1002 of Archbishop Eadulf, Wulfstan had experienced the worst ravages of the Danes and the largely ineffectual responses of Æthelred's army. With its rich library and scriptorium removed from the worst of the fighting Worcester provided him an opportunity to study important patristic and canonical texts and thus to develop as a writer and reformer. Much of his work was also done at York, where he performed the functions of a leader of the church. Extant manuscripts from both centers show Wulfstan's hand in the annotations. In addition several versions of his "commonplace book" survive, containing collections of materials intended for use in his own work. Either at Worcester or York he wrote versified entries for 957 and 975 in the D version of the Anglo-Saxon Chronicle.

Wulfstan's reputation grows from his sermons. These include a series of eschatological works, impassioned calls for repentance in response to signs of the coming of Doomsday. Another series on the elements of Christian faith treats the subjects of baptism, the Creed, the gifts of the Holy Spirit, and the duties of a Christian. In both series he draws on a variety of Latin sources largely from the Carolingian period and shapes his work to specific audiences. Only two of his sermons are proper to the church year, and those address the matter of penance during Lent. Wulfstan's sermons are topical, hortative, and utilitarian messages rather than explications of the Gospels or hagiographic narratives.

The best-known sermon also seems to have been the most popular in its time: *Sermo Lupi ad Anglos* (*The Sermon of Wolf to the English*), so called from the opening words of its rubric. Surviving in five manuscript versions, this work probably was composed in 1014, the year in which Æthelred was exiled. The *Sermo Lupi* is noteworthy for drawing on themes and materials that engaged Wulfstan throughout his career, here brought together and presented urgently when it seemed that God was punishing the English at the hands of the Danes. In particular Wulfstan uses phrases from his eschatological sermons in depicting the present evils that presage the end of the world. He ends with a typical exhortation to return to the faith of baptism, where there is protection from the fires of hell.

As trusted counselor to Æthelred, and to his Danish successor Cnut, Wulfstan wrote a variety of legislation intended to reassert the laws of earlier Anglo-Saxon kings and bring order to a country that had been unsettled by war and the influx of Scandinavians. Although he put into writing edicts that had been decreed by the ruling witan, or council, Wulfstan echoed there the concerns about present conditions and the urgency for change expressed in his homiletic writings. The laws are of three distinct types: short codes addressing such specific issues as the need to christianize the Danelaw, protect the clergy and the church, and reinforce a hierarchical social order consistent with the past; drafts of legislation for Æthelred and Cnut; and a comprehensive, formal code for Cnut. Through these legal writings Wulfstan used his influence to press for social, moral, religious, and political reforms extending even to the obligations of the king.

Beginning about 1005 a remarkable interchange occurred between Wulfstan and his talented contemporary Abbot Ælfric of Eynsham. Wulfstan requested from Ælfric two pastoral letters in Latin treating duties of the secular clergy. Shortly thereafter he asked Ælfric to translate the letters into OE. Although the versions that survive today bear evidence of Wulfstan's revisions, they are important because they strongly influenced his own prescriptions for the secular clergy, the *Canons of Edgar,* as well as the code he drafted for Æthelred at Enham in 1008. These and other letters by Ælfric formed part of a group of canonistic materials including Frankish capitularies and Wulfstan's translation of Amalarius's *De regula canonicorum,* materials that underlie one of Wulfstan's sermons on baptism, his *Institutes of Polity,* and certain legal codes, in addition to the *Canons of Edgar.*

Because they provide yet another strong example of his reforming philosophy, Wulfstan's own canonistic works command interest. The *Canons of Edgar,* so-called because they hark back to better times during the reign of Edgar, provide instruction on proper conduct and training for the secular clergy and detailed instructions on their duties, including how to conduct the mass. The *Institutes of Polity* form a treatise on the organization of society, an early example of estates literature that attempts to define the duties of each class. His lengthy discussion of the bishop's role provides insight into the career Wulfstan fashioned for himself. Wulfstan also translated prose portions of the Benedictine office into OE, presumably to help the secular clergy with their devotions.

The effectiveness of Wulfstan's writing owes much to his rhythmic style, distinctive vocabulary, and use of rhetorical figures. He usually wrote with two-stress, alliterating, sometimes rhyming phrases syntactically independent of one another, which he could use to build toward a powerful climax. His stylistic touches include a large stock of intensifying words, repeated phrases, and forceful compounds. Figures of sound as taught by medieval manuals of rhetoric appear prominently in his work. All of these tools Wulfstan used in his attempts to restore England to the order and piety it had enjoyed before the Viking depredations.

Mary P. Richards

Bibliography

PRIMARY

Bethurum, Dorothy, ed. *The Homilies of Wulfstan.* Oxford: Clarendon, 1957; Fowler, Roger, ed. *Wulfstan's Canons of Edgar.* EETS o.s. 266. London: Oxford University Press, 1972; Jost, Karl, ed. *Die "Institutes of Polity, Civil and Ecclesiastical": Ein Werk Erzbischof Wulfstans von York.* Schweitzer anglistische Arbeiten 47. Bern: Francke, 1959; Ure, James M., ed. *The Benedictine Office: An Old English Text.* Edinburgh University Publications in Language and Literature 11. Edinburgh: Edinburgh University Press, 1957; Whitelock, Dorothy, ed. *Sermo Lupi ad Anglos.* 3d ed. New York: Methuen, 1966.

SECONDARY

Bethurum, Dorothy. "Archbishop Wulfstan's Commonplace Book." *PMLA* 57 (1942): 916–29; Bethurum, Dorothy. "Wulfstan." In *Continuations and Beginnings: Studies in Old English Literature,* ed. Eric G. Stanley. London: Nelson, 1966, pp. 210–46; Gatch, Milton McC. *Preaching and Theology in Anglo-Saxon England: Ælfric and Wulfstan.* Toronto: University of Toronto Press, 1977; Ker, N.R. "The Handwriting of Archbishop Wulfstan." In *England before the Conquest: Studies in Primary Sources Presented to Dorothy Whitelock,* ed. Peter Clemoes and Kathleen Hughes. Cambridge: Cambridge University Press, 1971, pp. 315–31; Richards, Mary P. "The Manuscript Contexts of the Old English Laws: Tradition and Innovation." In *Studies in Earlier Old English Prose,* ed. Paul E. Szarmach. Albany: SUNY Press, 1986, pp. 171–92; Stafford, Pauline. "The Laws of Cnut and the History of Anglo-Saxon Royal Promises." *ASE* 10 (1981): 173–90; Whitelock, Dorothy. "Wulfstan's Authorship of Cnut's Laws." *EHR* 70 (1955): 72–85; Wormald, Patrick. "Æthelred the Lawmaker." In *Ethelred the Unready,* ed. David Hill. BAR Brit. Ser. 59. Oxford: BAR, 1978, pp. 47–80.

See also Ælfric; Æthelred; Bishops; Cnut; Law, Anglo-Saxon; Monasticism; Sermons; Swein; Vikings; York, Ecclesiastical Province of

Wyclif, John (ca. 1330–1384)

The most distinguished English philosopher and theologian of the later 14th century and a significant influence on the emergence of the heretical Lollard movement. His popular fame as a church reformer, however, is largely unjustified and only dates from the Reformation period.

Wyclif was probably born in Yorkshire. For most of his adult life he was a scholar and teacher at Oxford, and only in his last decade did he make any impression on a wider stage, first as a royal servant and then as the inspiration of heresy. He first appears in the records as a fellow of Merton College in 1356, as master of Balliol College in 1360, and later as warden of Canterbury Hall, an appointment that involved him in a struggle with the regular clergy. He proceeded from Arts to Theology in the late 1360s and became a doctor of theology about 1372–73. He was, it appears, a conventional academic and like most of his contemporaries was supported, as an absentee, by the revenues of various benefices, none of great value. He was granted a canonry at Lincoln in 1371, though the promise of a prebend there with substantial resources was never fulfilled. In 1374 he was granted the Leicestershire benefice of Lutterworth, which was in the gift of the crown.

This undoubtedly was a reward for services as a polemicist and a diplomat. He defended the crown's right to tax the clergy and even its violation of sanctuary in order to arrest crown debtors, and in 1374 he took part in a diplomatic mission to Bruges. By 1378 he was compelled to withdraw from politics, although his lay patrons continued to protect him from the assaults of church authorities who had secured papal condemnation of his views on the subject of civil and divine lordship. In 1381 he was forced to leave Oxford, retiring to Lutterworth, where he died of a stroke at the end of 1384. Although his enemies alleged that he had inspired the Peasant Rebellion of 1381, this view cannot be substantiated and his earlier strong royalism makes it inherently unlikely.

Increasing knowledge of the development of scholastic philosophy has enhanced Wyclif's reputation as a thinker. A man of great learning and incisive mind, he was a vigorous defender of realist metaphysics against the nominalism of William of Ockham. In this he followed the tradition active during his formative years in Oxford, but he went beyond his teachers as an independent thinker. As a philosopher his views remained acceptable, but when he began teaching theology he clashed with the authorities.

His early theological concern with questions of dominion and grace probably arose more from his activities as a royal servant than from philosophical principles. Concurrently with his royal service, however, he became involved in biblical studies, writing a commentary on the whole Bible, something none of his contemporaries did. His reverence for scripture led to a fundamentalist view of the Bible as eternally present in God and probably influenced his denial of transubstantiation in the eucharist, an opinion in accord with his metaphysical views. There has been recent debate on whether metaphysics or biblicism gave the first impetus to this opinion, the issue that led to his final breach with orthodoxy. Even by the end of his life Wyclif had probably not worked out his precise belief in the nature of the eucharist, but it may have come close to the later Lutheran doctrine of consubstantiation.

His influence survived his death, and his eucharistic views were, in a simplified form, one of the hallmarks of later Lollardy. More important perhaps was the production by his followers, under the influence of his biblicism, of two English versions of the Bible, the staple reading for heretical groups and material for works of orthodox devotion. His philosophical views were taught for a time in Oxford and spread also to Bohemia, where they influenced the thought of religious reformers. Later his theological teachings also reached Bohemia and probably contributed to the more radical wing of Hussite thought. A substantial number of Wycliffite manuscripts have survived in libraries there.

By this time the church authorities were taking steps against his writings. Forty-five articles from his works were condemned at Prague in 1403, 267 articles were condemned after Archbishop Arundel's purge at Oxford in 1409, and the attacks continued at the councils of Rome (1413) and Constance (1415). At the last a command was issued for the exhumation and burning of his body, though this part of the sentence was not carried out until 1428.

J.A.F. Thomson

Bibliography

Kenny, Anthony. *Wyclif.* Oxford: Oxford University Press, 1985 [best introduction]; Kenny, Anthony, ed. *Wyclif in His Times.* Oxford: Clarendon, 1986 [valuable essays on many aspects of the man and his influence]; Leff, Gordon. *Heresy in the Later Middle Ages: The Relation of Heterodoxy to Dissent, c. 1250–c. 1450.* Manchester: Manchester University Press, 1967 [a good summary of Wyclif's teachings]; McFarlane, K.B. *John Wycliffe and the Beginnings of English Nonconformity.* London: English Universities Press, 1952 [illuminating and good for biography; unfair to Wyclif as a thinker]; Thomson, Williell R. *The Latin Writings of John Wyclyf: An Annotated Catalog.* Toronto: Pontifical Institute, 1983 [the best bibliographical treatment of Wyclif's writings]; Workman, Herbert B. *John Wyclif: A Study of the English Medieval Church.* 2 vols. Oxford: Clarendon, 1926 [the fullest life, though the interpretation is colored by Reformation apologetics].

See also Lollards; Pecock; Universities; William of Ockham; Wycliffite Texts

Wycliffite Texts

Works associated with the heretic John Wyclif (d. 1384) and his English followers, the Wycliffites or Lollards (terms we should probably use synonymously). Although we know Wyclif sometimes wrote in English, we now have only Latin texts we can confidently assign to him. All the English texts that have reached us are probably the work of his followers. These texts develop the vernacular as a vehicle for expressing theological and political ideas; some are also fine pieces of writing in their own right. Most Wycliffite texts are in prose; many remain unedited.

Scholars long tried to assign particular texts to particular persons. If we set aside the Latin texts we know to be by Wyclif, however, we are increasingly having to accept that with few exceptions these texts remain anonymous. We cannot date most of them any more precisely than after ca. 1380 (a date determined by their occasional topical allusions) and before ca. 1420 (a date determined by the handwriting in their manuscripts). For some we cannot even do this, usually because they have reached us only in late, even postmedieval, copies.

A large body of these texts survives, for the Wycliffites were exceptional among medieval heretics in the importance they gave the written word. Wyclif evolved the views that finally carried him into heterodoxy during a distinguished career as a philosopher and theologian at Oxford. His was undoubtedly a charismatic presence, and he successfully spread his views in lecture hall and from pulpit. But he also prepared the many texts that allowed these views to be influential far beyond England and well after he had died. The able young scholars he inspired quickly realized how well the written word could serve their purposes. Besides attempting to spread the Wycliffite message around the country in person, therefore, they systematically set about the large-scale production and distribution of texts. The preachers and teachers they inspired did likewise, though on a smaller scale. And texts remained the valued possession of the tightly knit communities that kept the Wycliffite message alive until the English Reformation.

Nevertheless, because the Wycliffites came to be persecuted as heretics, many of their texts must be lost to us. Wyclif's own views were condemned three times during his lifetime. They had caused him to challenge the authority of members of the established church with increasing virulence, and they provided his followers with a justification in theory for dismissing that church's authority in fact. When these followers showed some success in providing the laity with the spiritual learning they claimed the church was maliciously withholding, the church's hostility was ensured. From 1401 on the penalty for a relapse into heresy could be death by burning, and burnings took place from that year until Lollard merged with Reformer in the 16th century. Books, too, were burned, sometimes along with their owners. We would more than halve our present knowledge of both Wyclif's and the Wycliffites' Latin texts if they had not survived outside England (especially in Bohemia, home of the reformer and heretic Jan Hus). That we know as much as we do of the vernacular texts, whose only chance of survival lay at home, testifies to how well-organized and influential the Wycliffite movement must initially have been.

Wyclif's own writings range from the philosophical and political to the theological, exegetical, and homiletic: those that seem most directly to have influenced his English followers include sermons, a commentary on the Ten Commandments, and the *Opus evangelicum,* a stridently polemical commentary on Matthew 5–7 and 23–25 and John 13–17. These are less central to the Wycliffite textual corpus, however, than the texts designed by Wyclif's immediate followers. The latter texts almost certainly stem from team endeavor, for they bear witness to elaborate processes of correction and revision. They also seem to have come from some well-endowed center or centers when the concern for secrecy was not yet pressing, for they often survive in multiple copies and in good-quality manuscripts. Most prominently they include two major versions of a translation of the whole Bible into English; they also include an extensive vernacular sermon cycle, part of a similar cycle in Latin, two major versions of a preacher's handbook in Latin, and three versions of a vernacular commentary on the Gospels.

There are also other, more peripheral texts. These often reach us in unique, sometimes incomplete, copies in manuscripts of relatively poor quality. Their number and variety speaks to how voracious the Wycliffite appetite for the written word must have been. So do their sources, for their writers often seem simply to have taken over and adapted almost anything that came to hand—texts by Wyclif, texts by other Wycliffites, texts by all sorts of orthodox writers. They include further texts appropriate to an evangelical program—sermons and sermon notes, a concordance and summaries to facilitate use of the Bible translation, preachers' proof texts. They also include didactic treatises—several on the Pater Noster, for example, as well as versions of such well-known orthodox works as Rolle's *Psalter Commentary,* the *Ancrene Wisse,* and *The Poor Caitiff.* More open confrontations with authority appear in polemical tracts, political manifestos, even satirical poems; still other works were molded by the judicial response to the Wycliffites—model answers to help suspects on trial for heresy, two firsthand accounts of their trials by such suspects, and a Latin Apocalypse commentary written by a suspect while in prison.

We may have assigned some of these texts wrongly to the movement. We have tended to rely on ideological criteria alone when trying to decide on a text's Wycliffite affiliations. But the Wycliffites drew their ideas from well-established sources, and their discussion then caused them to become widely pervasive. These ideas were never entirely distinctive. It does seem, however, that for ideological reasons the Wycliffites tried to speak and write distinctively. If we turn our attention to the rhetorical and stylistic features of known Wycliffite texts, we may be able to refine our criteria for assigning other texts to the movement. At the very least we would enhance our understanding of the Wycliffites' literary achievement.

Christina von Nolcken

Bibliography

PRIMARY

In addition to editions listed in the bibliographies below note: Hudson, Anne, ed. *Selections from English Wycliffite Writings.* Cambridge: Cambridge University Press, 1978; Hudson, Anne, and Pamela Gradon, eds. *English Wycliffite Sermons.* 5 vols. Oxford: Clarendon, 1983–96; Mueller, Ivan J., ed., with Anthony Kenny, trans., and Paul Vincent Spade, intro. *John Wyclif: Tractatus de universalibus.* 2 vols. Oxford: Clarendon, 1985.

SECONDARY

New *CBEL* 1:487–88, 491–96, 789–93; *Manual* 2:354–80, 517–33; Hudson, Anne. "Contributions to a History of Wycliffite Writings." Repr. in *Lollards and Their Books.* London: Hambledon, 1985, pp. 1–12, 249–52; Hudson, Anne. *The Premature Reformation: Wycliffite Texts and Lollard History.* Oxford: Clarendon, 1988; Kenny, Anthony. *Wyclif.* Oxford: Oxford University Press, 1985; McFarlane, K.B. *John Wycliffe and the Beginnings of English Nonconformity.* London: English Universities Press, 1952; Thomson, Williell R. *The Latin Writings of John Wyclyf: An Annotated Catalog.* Toronto: Pontifical Institute, 1983; Workman, Herbert B. *John Wyclif: A Study of the English Medieval Church.* 2 vols. Oxford: Clarendon, 1926.

See also Clanvowe; *Jack Upland;* Literacy; Lollards; Pecock; *Pierce the Plowman's Creed;* Popular Religion; Prose, ME; Satire; Sermons; Translation; Trevisa; Wyclif

Wyntoun, Andrew (ca. 1350–ca. 1422)

A canon regular at St. Andrews who became prior of St. Serf's Inch, Lochleven, by the early 1390s; author of the *Orygynale Cronykil of Scotland,* a universal history in four-stress couplets, beginning with the creation of the angels and running (in its later forms) to 1408. The *Cronykil* survives in three versions, the last completed ca. 1420; it incorporates some material from Barbour's *Bruce* as well as drawing on a wide range of other historical sources, both English and Scottish.

Lister M. Matheson

Bibliography

PRIMARY

Amours, F.J., ed. *The Original Chronicle of Andrew of Wyntoun.* 6 vols. STS 50, 53, 54, 56, 57, 63. Edinburgh: Blackwood, 1903–14.

SECONDARY

Manual 8:2686–90, 2905–13.

See also Barbour; Chronicles; Scottish Literature, Early

Year Books

Of all the materials available to the historian of medieval English law the year books are preeminent. It is through their pages that we experience, almost at first hand, the cut and thrust of skilled advocacy that refined the common law. They may also claim (in Maitland's words) a "unique position . . . in the history of civilization, in the history of mankind," being the earliest systematic reports of oral debate from anywhere in Europe.

Though more concerned with pretrial procedure and oral pleading than with the process of trial and judgment, they are the lineal ancestors of the law reports published throughout the common-law world today. Indeed there is no meaningful break between the year books and the "reports" of later times; the tradition of reporting was more or less continuous. All English law reports before 1500 are generally reckoned as "year books"; the name refers simply to the custom of citing them by regnal year. For reports after 1500, however, the term is reserved for those texts that were *printed* as year books in the 16th century, the last of which are dated to the 27th year of Henry VIII's reign (1535).

The reports preserve in Anglo-French (or law French) the arguments of counsel and judges in the central royal courts in Westminster Hall, especially the Common Pleas, and (until 1330) on the traveling circuits known as the eyre. A few have also been found from local courts. French was the language of the courts when they began, but not when they ended; the style, however, is throughout one of précis rather than a verbatim record. The earliest reports date from the 1250s or 1260s, and by the 1290s they were being regularly produced and circulated, though the annual format was not established as the norm before the end of the century. How and why they began is a matter of doubt; they may well have originated from a case method of instruction in the shadowy law school that preceded the Inns of Court. An old legend that the reporters were once crown officials was demolished by Maitland. If the continuity and growing regularity suggest some kind of organization, no evidence of such organization has yet come to light.

The identity of the reporters is unknown before the 15th century. The earliest so far identified, John Bryt (fl. 1410), was an obscure apprentice of the law who attended and reported cases at Wiltshire assizes as well as in Westminster Hall in termtime. Several reporters later in the century are known to have continued reporting throughout their careers, a characteristic of the better reporters of later times; the earliest example is Roger Townshend (d. 1493), who began in the 1450s as a student of Lincoln's Inn and was still reporting as a judge in the 1480s.

The precious heritage of the year books still languishes in a state of some neglect. The old printed texts are often inadequate and cannot safely be used without recourse to manuscripts. They are poorly indexed, if at all, and use has still to be made of alphabetical reference books printed in the 16th and 17th centuries. Valiant work has been done on the earlier year-book manuscripts by modern editors, beginning with the Rolls Series (1866–1911) and followed in the present century by the Selden Society and Ames Foundation. For most years, however, there are no modern editions; no small number of wholly unprinted texts await attention.

Most of the year books have still to be approached through the ten-volume "vulgate" reprint of 1679–80, itself recently reprinted in facsimile (Abingdon: Professional Books, 1981); and the only printed text of the later years of Edward II is the inaccurate "Maynard" edition of 1678. A full bibliography of the pre-1678 printed editions is found in the second edition of the *Short Title Catalogue of Books Printed in England . . . before 1640.* Some modern editions, mostly of years missing from the vulgate, have been published in the Rolls Series (part of Edward I and 11–20 Edward III), by the Selden Society (Edward I before 1290, most of 1–14 Edward II, and some later examples), and by the Ames Foundation (much of Richard II). These editions give variant readings, relevant material from the plea rolls, parallel translations, and indexes. There is a preliminary list of manuscripts by Jennifer Nicolson, *Register of Manuscripts of Year Books Extant* (London: Historical Manuscripts Commission, for the Selden Society, 1956).

John H. Baker

Fig. 155. Plan of
Yeavering,
Northumberland:
Phase III A/B (top left),
Phase III C (top right),
Phase IV (bottom left),
Phase V (bottom right).
After M. Welch Anglo-
Saxon England. Lon-
don: Batsford, 1992.
Courtesy of B.T.
Batsford.

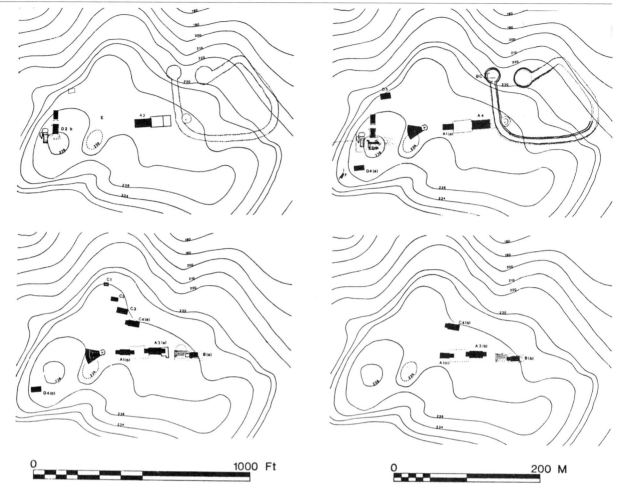

Fig. 155. Plan of Yeavering, Northumberland: Phase III A/B (top left), Phase III C (top right), Phase IV (bottom left), Phase V (bottom right). After M. Welch Anglo-Saxon England. London: Batsford, 1992. Courtesy of B.T. Batsford.

Bibliography

Baker, John H. "The Last Year Books." In *The Reports of Sir John Spelman*. Vol. 2. Selden Society 94. London: Selden Society, 1978 (for 1977), pp. 164–70; Baker, John H. "John Bryt's Reports (1410–1411) and the Year Books of Henry IV." *Cambridge Law Journal* 48 (1989): 98–114; Baker, John H. "Records, Reports and the Origins of Case-Law in England." In *Judicial Records, Law Reports and the Growth of Case-Law*, ed. John H. Baker. Comparative Studies in Continental and Anglo-American Legal History 5. Berlin: Dunckler & Humblot, 1989, pp. 15–46; Ives, Eric W. "The Purpose and Making of the Later Year Books." *Law Quarterly Review* 89 (1972): 64–86; Maitland, Frederic W. "Of the Year Books in General." In *Year Books of Edward II*. Vol. 1: *1 and 2 Edward II, A.D. 1307–1309*. Selden Society 17. London: Quaritch, 1903, pp. ix–xx; Simpson, A.W.B. "The Circulation of Yearbooks in the Fifteenth Century." *Law Quarterly Review* 73 (1957): 492–505.

See also Courts and the Court System; Law, Post-Conquest; Lawyers

Yeavering

Bede's mention of "Ad Gefrin" ("Hill of the Goats"), the royal palace of the Northumbrian king Edwin, visited by the missionary Paulinus, has always been taken to refer to Yeavering, a hill in Northumberland. The probable site of the palace was identified from aerial photographs in 1949 and excavated in the 1950s (fig. 155).

The site was already important to the local Celtic Britons of Bernicia. Although there is a twelve-acre Iron Age hill fort on the summit, the focus of Celtic activity was on a lower slope overlooking the River Glenn and was defined by cremation burials concentrated near a western ring ditch with a central standing stone, encircled by stone uprights, and a ditched barrow to the east. A fortlike Great Enclosure was built nearby and cremation gave way to inhumation between A.D. 300 and 500, when a wooden structure with a central post replaced the western stone complex, while the eastern round barrow received its own central wooden post. The Celtic ritual function of the site was adapted after the mid-6th century by the Anglian invaders, who retained the Celtic place-names and continued to erect wooden posts. Celtic freestanding posts at Yeavering had cognates in the Germanic world.

The absence of Romano-British objects shows that the first structures belonged to the 5th century or later, but only two objects from the site can be dated with any certainty: a gold coin and a silver-inlaid iron buckle, both 7th century. Differing interpretations identify the earliest buildings as

Anglian or British. The more important are accepted as Anglian, including a probable pagan temple, with associated freestanding posts and inhumation burials, and a wooden outdoor theater, whose formal antecedents are clearly Roman.

The largest of the excavated structures, the "great hall," was aligned with the central post of the eastern round barrow and had a burial under a post at its eastern entrance. (A wooden stave with an iron tip and copper-alloy mount from this burial has been compared with objects from burials at Benty Grange, Derbyshire, and Sutton Hoo, Suffolk.) A partially excavated palisaded enclosure has been interpreted as a "corral" into which animals owed as tribute to the king were herded. Ox skulls associated with another structure could be evidence of ritual slaughter.

King Edwin of Northumbria introduced Christianity to the area ca. 627, when Paulinus, the first archbishop of York, taught and baptized at Yeavering. The burning of the complex may be linked to Edwin's overthrow by Penda of Mercia and Cadwallon of Gwynedd ca. 632–33. Christianity survived, and a wooden church with a fenced graveyard, possibly reflecting the architectural tradition of Iona, was built over the southwestern corner of the destroyed fort. The wooden church was rebuilt later in the 7th century with an annex, which Douglas Mac Lean suggests may be a porticus, recalling the late-7th-century stone churches known from Wearmouth and Jarrow.

Because of the long occupation of the site, the numerous alterations of destruction and rebuilding, and the merging of cultures and styles Yeavering poses many questions about patterns of settlement and assimilation, about the transition from paganism to Christianity, and about the emergence of a dominant royal authority in the north.

David A. Hinton
Douglas Mac Lean

Bibliography

Alcock, Leslie. *Bede, Eddius and the Forts of the North Britons.* Jarrow Lecture, 1988. Jarrow: St. Paul's Church, 1988; Fernie, Eric. *The Architecture of the Anglo-Saxons.* London: Batsford, 1983; Hope-Taylor, Brian. *Yeavering: An Anglo-British Centre of Early Northumbria.* Department of Environment Archaeological Reports 7. London: HMSO, 1977; Scull, C. "Post-Roman Phase I at Yeavering: A Reconsideration." *Medieval Archaeology* 35 (1991): 51–63.

See also Archaeology; Conversion of the Anglo-Saxons; Heptarchy; Paganism; Sutton Hoo; Wearmouth-Jarrow: Architecture

York, Anglo-Saxon Churches in

Architecturally the ecclesiastical history of York begins in 627, when King Edwin erected a wooden church dedicated to St. Peter for his own baptism. The plan of Edwin's church does not survive. The fact that it was used for baptism suggests that it may be a central-plan structure, but this is far from certain. The wooden church was later enclosed in stone, a process begun by Edwin shortly before his death and completed by his successor Oswald. When St. Wilfrid became bishop of York in 669, he whitewashed the walls of the church, added glass to the windows, and covered the roof with sheets of lead.

No trace of the plan or fabric of the Anglo-Saxon Church of St. Peter survives, although its presence is noted in documentary sources. Alcuin writes that Archbishop Ælberht (767–80) raised an altar to St. Paul in the church, and Simeon of Durham records the crowning of King Eardwulf at Ælberht's altar in 796. Fragments of Anglo-Saxon sculpture from beneath the present minster provide material evidence for pre-Conquest use of the site.

According to the Anglo-Saxon Chronicle St. Peter's was burned and looted by the Danes in 1069 and 1075, respectively. The earliest surviving structural remains are the foundation of the Norman Cathedral built by Archbishop Thomas of Bayeux (1069–1100).

A church dedicated to the *alma sophia* (Holy Wisdom) was also built by Archbishop Ælberht and dedicated in October 780. Alcuin describes the church as having 30 altars, rounded arches, porticus, and upper chambers, details that call to mind Wilfrid's church at Hexham. The accuracy of Alcuin's description has been questioned. No trace of the church has ever been discovered, and its precise location remains uncertain.

Richard Morris has suggested that the *alma sophia* was most likely a monastic church, hence the need for 30 altars, located in the Bishophill district of York across the Ouse from St. Peter's. Prior to Danish settlement York would then have had two ecclesiastical centers, serving different but related functions, and perhaps also reflecting the multifocal settlement of the area. Moreover, if Christ can be identified as Divine Wisdom, the dedication of York's two major churches may have been patterned after those of 8th-century Rome and Canterbury.

Catherine E. Karkov

Bibliography

Harrison, K. "The Saxon Cathedral at York." *Yorkshire Journal of Archaeology* 39 (1958): 436–44; Harrison, K. "The Pre-Conquest Churches of York." *Yorkshire Journal of Archaeology* 40 (1959–61): 232–49; Lang, James. *Corpus of Anglo-Saxon Stone Sculpture.* Vol. 3: *York and Eastern Yorkshire.* London: Oxford University Press, 1991; Morris, Richard K. "Alcuin, York and the *alma sophia.*" In *The Anglo-Saxon Church: Papers on History, Architecture and Archaeology in Honour of Dr H.M. Taylor,* ed. Lawrence A.S. Butler and Richard K. Morris. CBA Research Report 60. London: CBA, 1986, pp. 80–89; Taylor, Harold M., and Joan Taylor. "York." In *Anglo-Saxon Architecture.* Vol. 2. Cambridge: Cambridge University Press, 1965, pp. 697–709.

See also Alcuin; Architecture, Anglo-Saxon; York, City of; York, Ecclesiastical Province of; York and Ripon Minsters

Fig. 156. Plan of
medieval York. After
York Archaeological
Trust, in Schofield and
Vince, Medieval Towns
(1994). Reprinted by
permission of
Associated University
Presses.

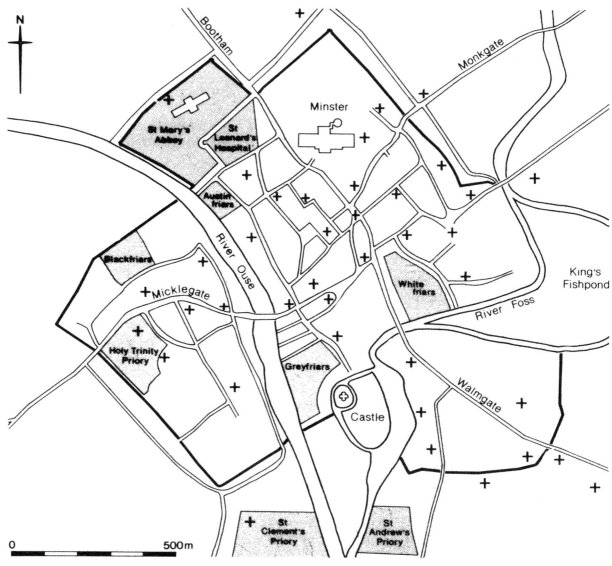

York, City of

Unlike the great majority of medieval English cities York was founded as an act of deliberate will. In A.D. 71 the Roman commander Q. Petilius Cerialis chose a previously obscure site at a river crossing on the Ouse as headquarters for the Ninth Legion when it advanced from Lincoln to invade the territory of the Brigantes. Within a few years Eboracum was the most important military center and most substantial civilian settlement, or *colonia,* in the north. Despite the many vicissitudes ahead, for at least the next 1,500 years York was usually the most important provincial city in the country (fig. 156). All in all the aldermen of York during the 1390s were still justified in describing themselves as the rulers of the "secounde citee du Roialme."

Of the many phases in the complex history of medieval York the most mysterious by far was the two centuries, ca. 400–ca. 600, during which groups of Anglians gradually infiltrated the southern part of what came to be the kingdom of Northumbria. By the early 7th century York had reemerged as a major power base of Edwin (616–32), a monarch whose authority was recognized—in however vague a fashion—

throughout the whole of Anglo-Saxon England. More significantly he was the first king of Northumbria to be baptized a Christian, at York on Easter Day 627. From that date on there was never any doubt that the church of York, raised to metropolitan status in 735, would enjoy primacy in the ecclesiastical organization of northern England. By the late 8th century, when Alcuin, its greatest scholar, was summoned to Charlemagne's court to serve as one of his intellectual elite, York Minster was the most active center of higher learning in England.

Alcuin himself lived long enough to lament the destruction caused by the first Viking attacks on the holy places of Northumbria, but it was only in 866–67 that a great Danish army, led by Ivar the Boneless, ejected the last Anglian rulers from York itself. The two centuries (866–1066) of Viking York (Jorvik) are poorly recorded. However, during the 1970s and 1980s the lack of written documentation has been redeemed by perhaps the most intensive excavations hitherto conducted in any medieval English town. The York Archaeological Trust's recreation of an urban street at the Jorvik Viking Centre provides modern tourists with a unique opportunity to experience the bustling if squalid quality of life in what was one of the great entrepots of the Scandinavian world. According to one contemporary, writing about the year 1000, York was then a city "crammed with the goods of traders who come from all parts of the world, especially those of the Danish people."

Much of that commercial activity, and much of York's economic prosperity, was temporarily reversed after the battles of Stamford Bridge and Hastings in 1066. Indeed the most obvious surviving memorial to the Norman regime in York are the remains (misleadingly known as Clifford's Tower) of the most important royal castle in the north. It was here that the king himself, as well as his officials, usually stayed during their frequent visits; it was here that the sheriff of Yorkshire administered the largest county on behalf of his monarch; and it was here, less happily, that the Jews of York were massacred in March 1190, when they vainly sought royal protection.

More impressive still were the successive ecclesiastical building campaigns that transformed the physical appearance of York during the two centuries after the Conquest. Both York Minster itself and the Benedictine Abbey of St. Mary's, the richest monastery in the north, were built—first in large-scale Romanesque and then in even more spectacular Gothic—and during the course of the 13th century mendicant convents of the Franciscans, Dominicans, Carmelites, and Austin friars were gradually added to the city's many existing smaller religious houses and hospitals.

Equally revealing in a different sphere was the constant building and rebuilding of the parish churches. That there were at least 40 of these by the 13th century (of which half survive, from a total greater than in any English town except London and Winchester) testifies to the economic growth of a city that probably had a total population of over 15,000 by the eve of the Black Death.

It is something of a paradox that the citizens of York have left us the greatest evidence of their personal attitudes and priorities at exactly the period when they were forced to wrestle with the strains of acute demographic and economic recession. From the 1370s on the archives of the city, minster, and archbishop (above all perhaps the latter's probate registers) survive in considerable quantity; as a result recent research has made the canons, merchants, and artisans of 15th-century York better known than their counterparts anywhere in England. It is, for instance, now quite clear that despite the onslaught of plague York still enjoyed a considerable degree of economic and artistic efflorescence until at least the middle of the 15th century.

The reputation of the city's stained glass and of its famous Corpus Christi plays was at its height in the years around 1400. It was exactly then that the merchant oligarchy that ruled York was not only at its most individually wealthy but had also recently acquired (18 May 1396) a charter from Richard II elevating the city to county status, an urban privilege previously only secured by London and Bristol.

A century later the high self-confidence of the citizens was rapidly evaporating, under the evils of inadequate recruitment from the countryside and successful economic competition from London's merchants and the new textile centers of West Yorkshire. For us the consolation for the townsmen's impoverished years is that the post-Reformation inhabitants of York nearly always lacked the resources to destroy the medieval monuments that now make the city one of the most-visited medieval towns of the world.

R.B. Dobson

Bibliography

PRIMARY

Collins, Francis, ed. *Register of the Freemen of the City of York*. 2 vols. Surtees Society 96, 102. Durham: Andrews, 1897–1900; Dobson, R.B., ed. *York City Chamberlains' Account Rolls, 1396–1500*. Surtees Society 192. Durham: Surtees Society, 1980; Farrer, William, and Charles T. Clay, eds. *Early Yorkshire Charters*. 12 vols. Vols. 4–12 as Yorkshire Archaeological Society Record Series. Extra Series 1–3, 5–12. Edinburgh: Ballantyne, Hanson, 1914–65; Raine, Angelo, ed. *York Civic Records*. Yorkshire Archaeological Society. Record Series 98, 103, 106, 108, 110, 112, 115, 119, 138. Wakefield and Leeds: For the Society, 1939–78; Raine, James, et al., eds. *Testamenta Eboracensia*. Surtees Society 4, 30, 45, 53, 79, 106. London: Nichols, 1832; Durham: Andrews, 1855–1902; Sellers, Maud, ed. *York Memorandum Book*. Surtees Society 120, 125. Durham: Andrews, 1912–15.

SECONDARY

Addyman, Peter V., and Valerie Black, eds. *Archaeological Papers from York Presented to M.W. Barley*. York: York Archaeological Trust, 1984; Bartlett, I. Neville. "The Expansion and Decline of York in the Later Middle Ages." *EcHR*, 2d ser. 12 (1959): 17–33; Dobson, R.B. "Admissions to the Freedom of the City of York in the Later Middle Ages." *EcHR*, 2d ser. 26 (1973): 1–22; Dobson, R.B. *The Jews of Medieval York and the Massacre of March 1190*. York: St. Anthony's, 1974; Great Britain, Royal Commission on Historical Monuments. *An Inventory of the Historical Monuments in the City of York*. 5 vols. London: HMSO, 1962–81; Heaton, Herbert A. *The Yorkshire Woollen and Worsted Industries*. 2d ed. Oxford: Clarendon, 1965; Hutchinson, John, and David Palliser. *York: Bartholomew City Guide*. London: Bartholomew, 1980; Miller, E. "Medieval York." In *A History of Yorkshire: The City of York*, ed. P.M. Tillott. London: Oxford University Press, for the Institute of Historical Research, 1961, pp. 25–116; Palliser, David. *Tudor York*. Oxford: Oxford University Press, 1979; Raine, Angelo. *Mediaeval York: A Topographical Survey Based on the Original Sources*. London: Murray, 1955; Swanson, Heather. *Building Craftsmen in Late Medieval York*. Borthwick Paper 63. York: University of York, 1983.

See also Drama, Vernacular; Towns; Vikings; York, Anglo-Saxon Churches in; York, Ecclesiastical Province of; York and Ripon Minsters

York, Ecclesiastical Province of

The city of York, where Constantine the Great was probably proclaimed Roman emperor in A.D. 306, is almost as old as Christianity itself, and as early as 314 there existed a bishop of York, probably named Eburius, known to have attended the Council of Arles.

More significantly it seems to have been memories in faraway Italy of the long years during which Eboracum, or York, had been the capital of the Romano-British province of *Britannia inferiora* that influenced Pope Gregory I's famous and fateful letter of 601 to Augustine of Canterbury. In what is the single most important document for the history of the church of York the pope recommended that after the Anglo-Saxon peoples had been converted, they should be spiritually subject to many bishops but to only two archbishops, one at London (later Canterbury) and one at Eboracum.

After the initial missionary successes in Yorkshire of one of Augustine's disciples, Paulinus, consecrated as first post-Roman bishop of York in 625, the new see proved vulnerable to pagan revivals and confrontations between warring Christian factions. The controversial Wilfrid (archbishop, 664–78) was, however, able to impose Roman usages in his cathedral see, and in 735 York was raised to the archiepiscopal dignity and the metropolitan primacy in northern England it has never lost.

The history of the province and archdiocese of York in the later Anglo-Saxon period is nevertheless mysterious. Not one of the several churches known to have served at various times as York Minster has yet been discovered by archaeological excavation, and it seems certain that much of the pastoral work involved in supervising so vast a diocese was delegated to subordinate "minsters," notably the famous churches of Ripon, Beverley, and Southwell in Nottinghamshire, all well-endowed pilgrimage centers long before the Conquest.

York Minster itself harbored a famous library and a distinguished reputation for scholarship during the 50 years or so before the death of Alcuin in 804. Thereafter neither learning at the cathedral nor the spiritual nor political authority of the archbishop altogether recovered from the dislocation of the Viking invasion—until the Normans restored order and discipline to the northern ecclesiastical scene after 1066.

During the first 50 years after William the Conqueror's "harrying of the north" in 1069–70 a series of gifted Norman and French archbishops placed the affairs of the archdiocese on a new and more secure footing. Admittedly it took longer to regularize York's supremacy over the two other sees, Carlisle and Durham, in the northern province. In addition the dispute for primacy between Canterbury and York remained potentially explosive until the end of the Middle Ages. Meanwhile the archbishop's own cathedral, York Minster, was built and rebuilt, more or less continuously, during the 400 years preceding its final service of consecration and dedication in July 1472. By then—indeed long before then—it was the largest cathedral in England.

Even more essential to the welfare of the diocese and province of York was the establishment of a large complement of cathedral canons (36 after 1294), together with their vicars-choral and an increasingly numerous group of chantry priests. The great majority of these secular canons were always absent from their cathedral, for not the least important function of the churches of York, Beverley, Ripon, and Southwell was to divert wealth to the hands of ecclesiastical administrators in the service of the national government. However, the copious evidence of York's splendid series of archiepiscopal registers from the pontificate of Walter de Gray (1215–55) onward leaves no doubt of the central role played by the residentiary canons in supervising a vast disciplinary and pastoral machine with, or even without, the archbishop himself.

A proper assessment of the religious life of the archdiocese in the later Middle Ages is by no means easy. Despite the popular cult of Richard Scrope after his execution, on orders of Henry IV, for his role in the Percy rebellion of 1405, the archbishops rarely emerge as vivid figures from their administrative records. Nevertheless, and whether under archiepiscopal sponsorship or not, recent research has done much to suggest that a diocese that produced both the most influential heretic (John Wyclif) and the most influential mystical writer (Richard Rolle) of late-medieval England can hardly be found guilty of religious torpor.

R.B. Dobson

Bibliography

PRIMARY

Brown, William, and A. Hamilton Thompson, eds. *Register of William Greenfield, Lord Archbishop of York, 1306–1315.* 5 vols. Surtees Society 145, 149, 151–53. Durham: Andrews, 1931–40; Burton, Janet E., ed. *English Episcopal Acta, 1070–1154.* Oxford: Oxford University Press, for the British Academy, 1988; Johnson, Charles, ed. and trans. *Hugh the Chanter: The History of the Church of York, 1066–1127.* Rev. ed. Ed. M. Brett et al. Oxford: Clarendon, 1990; Raine, James, ed. *Register or Rolls of Walter Gray, Lord Archbishop of York.* Surtees Society 56. Durham: Andrews, 1872; Raine, James, ed. *Historians of the Church of York and Its Archbishops.* 3 vols. Rolls Series 71. London: Longman, 1879–94.

SECONDARY

Aston, Margaret. *Thomas Arundel: A Study of Church Life in the Reign of Richard II.* Oxford: Clarendon, 1967; Aylmer, G.E., and Reginald Cant, eds. *A History of York Minster.* Oxford: Clarendon, 1977; Dobson, R.B. "The Residentiary Canons of York in the Fifteenth Century." *Journal of Ecclesiastical History* 30 (1979): 145–74; Grassi, John. "Royal Clerks from the Archdiocese of York in the Fourteenth Century." *Northern History* 5 (1970): 12–33; Hughes, Jonathan. *Pastors and Visionaries: Religion and Secular Life in Late Medieval Yorkshire.* Woodbridge: Boydell, 1988; Moran, Jo Ann Hoeppner. "Clerical Recruitment in the Diocese of York." *Journal of Ecclesiastical History* 34 (1983): 19–54; Nicholl, Donald. *Thurstan, Archbishop of York, 1114–1140.* York: Stonegate, 1964.

See also Alcuin; Bede; Canterbury, Ecclesiastical Province of; Wilfrid; Wulfstan; York, Anglo-Saxon Churches in; York, City of; York and Ripon Minsters

York and Ripon Minsters

In 1154 the archdeacon of Canterbury, Roger of Pont l'Évêque (d. 1181), was elected archbishop of York, and shortly thereafter the rebuilding of the east end of St. Peter's Cathedral, damaged in a fire of 1137, began. The new choir was to become one of the great monuments of Transitional English Gothic architecture. It combined elements of traditional English Romanesque architecture with new Gothic features introduced to the north of England, from France, via Cistercian architecture. This combination of traditional English forms with specific elements of French contemporary style would become a hallmark of English Gothic architecture.

Roger's choir was built outside of rather than on the walls of its Norman predecessor; nevertheless, its flat eastern wall and elevation, consisting of a tall nave arcade, single-arched false gallery, and clerestory with triple arcades and wall passage, preserved characteristic features of Anglo-Norman design. The choir was eight bays deep with aisles, an ambulatory, and an eastern transept (each arm consisting of a single bay), the latter a Cluniac innovation that appealed to English tastes. A pier with four detached shafts stood at the center of the opening of each arm of the transept from the choir wall. Elsewhere the choir was supported by clustered piers and clustered wall shafts that helped to unite the different parts of the structure visually. The choir was most likely designed to rival that of Canterbury; not only were the two churches traditional rivals, but there was animosity between Roger and Canterbury's archbishop, Thomas Becket.

Due to remodeling in 1391 the Transitional choir at York no longer survives. However, much of its original flavor is preserved in the choir at Ripon.

Rebuilding of the western transept of St. Peter's, York, commenced in the early 13th century. Under the influence of Cistercian architecture three square chapels were built on the eastern side of each arm, though they disappeared in the later rebuildings of the 13th and 14th centuries. Both arms of the transept are three bays deep, with an elevation consisting of arcade, false gallery decorated with plate tracery, and a low clerestory. The wooden high vault has been described as one of the finest examples of Early English wooden vaulting (Wilson, 1990: 170). The combination of lancets and rose window that crowns the south transept is a typically French detail added ca. 1250.

French influence continues in the nave (begun ca. 1291), the finest example of the 13th-century Rayonnant style in England. Here the clerestory is enlarged, flat, and decorated with bar tracery that extends down into the triforium level, visually uniting the two upper levels of the elevation. The narrow pointed arches of the nave arcade rise to triforium level, while slender wallshafts rise uninterrupted to the springing of the vaults, now level with the base of the clerestory. A French-style quadripartite vault was also planned; however, in 1345 the nave

was covered with a wooden lierne vault decorated with gold stars on a blue field. The present vault is a 19th-century reproduction.

The increased French influence in the York nave may be due to the new French archbishop, John le Romeyn. The contributions of the local nobility are commemorated by statues in the openings of the triforium (one per bay) and by heraldic motifs in both the stonework and the stained-glass windows. The western window was inserted in 1338.

Possibly as a concession to local taste some traditionally English elements are maintained; the nave is wide and supported by thick walls, and the profiles of piers and moldings are more complex than their French counterparts. While the design of the York nave did not have much of an impact on architecture beyond the diocese, the Rayonnant extension of tracery from window to wall surface would be developed to become an important feature of the English Perpendicular style.

Remodeling of the choir, begun in 1361 under the direction of local architect William Holton, was intended to continue the style of the nave into the east end of the church. However, the addition of Perpendicular tracery to both the windows and wall surfaces of the new choir makes the cathedral an example in microcosm of the development of 14th-century English architectural style.

Ripon was one of four minsters in the archdiocese of York, and it is therefore appropriate that the architecture of this subsidiary cathedral reflect that of the central minster. An Anglo-Saxon monastery dedicated to St. Peter, Ripon gained minster status in the 11th century. Its Gothic rebuilding began ca. 1160 when work commenced on a new choir, again under the patronage of the archbishop of York, Roger of Pont l'Évêque. The church was also rededicated at this time to Sts. Peter and Wilfrid (Hearn, 1983: 95). The choir at Ripon is only six bays deep and has no eastern transept, but its flat eastern wall and elevation, consisting of a tall nave arcade, low false gallery (glazed ca. 1300), and triple-arcaded clerestory with wall passage, mirrors that of York. As at York the clustered piers, recalling the compound piers of the Romanesque, are typically English. French influence is evident in the slender nave piers, narrow arches of the nave arcade, and pointed ribbed-groin vaults covering the aisles. Originally intended to be roofed with a quadripartite vault, the choir was ultimately covered by a flat wooden ceiling, which was replaced by a vault ca. 1300. The present vault is a 19th-century reproduction.

Hearn has suggested four phases for construction of the minster: 1) 1160s–1181: the choir, transepts, and chapter house were begun but left incomplete at Bishop Roger's death, which necessitated a scaling back in the plans; 2) 1180s: the choir transepts and chapter house were completed; 3) 1180s–1210: the nave and crossing tower were completed and the west front begun; 4) ca. 1217–ca. 1224: the west front was completed.

The transepts are three bays deep, half as long as the new choir but of equal width; two chapels built into the eastern side of each transept may reflect the early-13th-century design of the western transepts at York. Analysis of the elevation of the transept indicates that, as in the choir, a Gothic high vault was intended but that plans were changed at the clerestory level, possibly due to lack of funds.

Little of the 12th-century nave survives, though evidence suggests that it was modeled on the late-11th-century nave at York. The Ripon nave was aisleless, with a tall triforium, composed of alternating blind double bays with narrow arches and lighted single bays with wide arches, and a low clerestory displaying similar alternations. There is no indication that a high vault was planned, the architects seemingly preferring a flat wooden ceiling.

Although they had little influence outside of their immediate locality, both Ripon and York minsters are important examples of the birth and development of the Gothic style in the north of England. Beyond that they are important examples of the way in which architectural innovation might be used to political ends, expressing rivalry with Canterbury at York and dependence on York at Ripon.

Catherine E. Karkov

Bibliography

Aylmer, G.E., and Reginald Cant, eds. *A History of York Minster.* Oxford: Clarendon, 1977; Bony, Jean. "French Influences on the Origins of English Gothic Architecture." *JWCI* 12 (1949): 1–15; Draper, Peter. "Recherches récentes sur l'architecture dans les Iles Britanniques à la fin de l'époque romane et au début du Gothique." *Bulletin monumentale* 144 (1986): 305–28; Hearn, M.F. "On the Original Nave of Ripon Cathedral." *JBAA,* 3d ser. 35 (1972): 39–45; Hearn, M.F. "Postscript on the Nave of Ripon Cathedral." *JBAA* 139 (1976): 93–94; Hearn, M.F. *Ripon Minster: The Beginning of the Gothic Style in Northern England.* Transactions of the American Philosophical Society 73.6 (1983); Kidson, Peter, Peter Murray, and Paul Thompson. *A History of English Architecture.* 2d ed. Harmondsworth: Penguin, 1979; Wilson, Christopher. "The Cistercians as 'Missionaries of Gothic' in Northern England." In *Cistercian Art and Architecture in the British Isles,* ed. C. Norton and D. Park. Cambridge: Cambridge University Press, 1986, pp. 86–116; Wilson, Christopher. *The Gothic Cathedral: The Architecture of the Great Church 1130–1530.* London: Thames & Hudson, 1990.

See also Architecture and Architectural Sculpture, Gothic; Cistercian Architecture; York, Ecclesiastical Province of; York Virgin and Child

York Virgin and Child

A stone block carved in relief presently in the east wall of York Minster's choir and measuring approximately 33 inches high by 15 inches wide. It is thought to have originally come from the Lady Altar of the Norman choir (ca. 1080), which apparently survived until 1361.

The Virgin holds the Child in both hands as in a Presentation or Adoration. This iconography has only one English parallel: a 12th-century ivory Virgin and Child (London, Victoria and Albert Museum A.25–1933), which may have been part of an Adoration group, since an ivory magus in the same style and scale and dyed the same greyish purple also survives. That this ivory Virgin came from a Yorkshire collection connects it more closely with the York relief.

The iconography may be Byzantine. The large Child raised above the Virgin's lap, his head almost level with hers, is paralleled in the mid-12th-century Mellon Madonna. But MacLagan finds similar parallels in combined Adoration and Nativity reliefs in Italy, southern France, and Spain (e.g., St. Gilles du Garde, ca. 1150–75; Parma Baptistery, ca. 1196), and this subject matter may be more closely connected with the York relief. MacLagan's stylistic parallels include the ambulatory sculptures at Toulouse, which head a well-established group of southern French and Spanish sculptures dating from the late 11th to mid-12th century, and the York relief probably finds its origin in this ambience. But the closest stylistic parallels are the relief figures at Lincoln, ca. 1145, and those made for Malmesbury Abbey between 1145 and 1169.

Zarnecki has suggested that the York relief was produced in the ambience of William, archbishop of York 1142, deposed 1147. After arguing his case in Rome William stayed with Roger of Sicily before being reinstated in 1153. William's travels could account for the stylistic and iconographic parallels of the relief and coincide with its date, which must be around the middle of the 12th century.

Perette E. Michelli

Bibliography

MacLagan, Eric. "A Romanesque Relief in York Minster." *PBA* 11 (1923): 1–7; Williamson, Paul. *An Introduction to Medieval Ivory Carvings.* London: HMSO, 1982, no. 38; Zarnecki, George, Janet Holt, and Tristram Holland, eds. *English Romanesque Art 1066–1200.* London: Weidenfeld & Nicolson, 1984 [see Zarnecki, George. "Virgin and Child Relief," p.188, cat. nos. 153 and 143; Stratford, Neil. "Virgin and Child," p. 226, cat. nos. 209 and 210].

See also Sculpture, Romanesque; York and Ripon Minsters

Index

Full entry page numbers are in bold print; illustration page numbers in italic.